COLLECTABLES
HANDBOOK

rouge rosé
Biscuits

COLLECTABLES HANDBOOK

Judith Miller
and Mark Hill

MILLER'S

Miller's Collectables Handbook

First published in Great Britain in 2010 by Miller's, a division of Mitchell Beazley, imprints of Octopus Publishing Group Ltd., Endeavour House, 189 Shaftesbury Avenue, London, WC2H 8JY.
www.hachette.co.uk

Miller's is a registered trademark of Octopus Publishing Group Ltd.
www.millersguides.com

Reprinted 2011
This edition published in association with WHSmith.

ISBN 978 1 84533 664 6

A CIP catalogue record for this book is available from the British Library
Set in Frutiger

Colour reproduction by United Graphics, Singapore
Printed and bound in China by C&C Offset Printing Co., Ltd.

Authors Judith Miller & Mark Hill

Publishing Manager Julie Brooke
Editors Davida Saunders, Carolyn Madden
Digital Asset Co-ordinator Katy Armstrong
Editorial Assistants Laura Hill, Danielle Shaw
Advertising Sales Christine Havers

Photography Graham Rae, Jeremy Martin, Robin Saker

Design Tim & Ali Scrivens, TJ Graphics
Indexer Diana LeCore
Production Lucy Carter
Jacket Design Pene Parker

Photographs of Judith Miller and Mark Hill by Simon Upton and Graham Rae

CONTENTS

HARRY POTTER

"MATCHBOX"
SERIES

LIST OF CONSULTANTS

AUTOMOBILIA

Geoffrey Weiner
carsofbrighton.co.uk

BEADS

Victor Caplin
Alfie's Antiques Market, London

BOOKS

Roddy Newlands
Bloomsbury Auctions, London

CERAMICS

Beth & Beverley Adams
Alfie's Antiques Market, London

Dr Graham Cooley
Private Collector

William Farmer
Fielding's Auctioneers, Stourbridge

Kevin Graham
potteryandglass.forumandco.com

Patrick & Petra Folkersma
outernational.info

FASHION & ACCESSORIES

Dawn Crawford
candysays.co.uk

Kerry Taylor
Kerry Taylor Auctions, London

Sparkle Moore & Cad van Swankster
thegirlcanthelpit.com

GLASS

Dr Graham Cooley
Private Collector

William Farmer
Fielding's Auctioneers, Stourbridge

Nic Wilson
zeitgeist-i.com

INUIT ART

Duncan McLean
Waddingtons, Toronto, Canada

PENS & WRITING EQUIPMENT

Simon Gray
penhome.co.uk

POSTERS

Patrick Bogue
onslows.co.uk

RADIOS

Steve Harris
vintageradio.co.uk

TOYS, TEDDY BEARS & DOLLS

Susan Brewer
britishdollshowcase.co.uk

Colin Lewis
The Magic Toybox, Hampshire

Leanda Harwood
leandaharwood.co.uk

SPORTING

Graham Budd
Graham Budd Auctions, London

We are also grateful to all our friends and experts who gave us so much help and support – Nigel Benson of 20thcentury-glass.com, Ian Broughton of Alfie's Antique Market, Mark Block, Simon Cooper of Rosebery's, David Encill, Julie D'Arcy Evans, Jeanette Hayhurst, Kevin Harris of undercurrents.biz, Michael Jeffrey of Woolley & Wallis, Mark Laino of Mark of Time, Peter Layton, Kathy Martin, Lesley McNamee of retropolitan.co.uk, Marcus Newhall of sklounion.com, Steven Moore of Anderson & Garland, Wesley Payne of Alfie's Antiques Market, Thomas Plant of Special Auction Services, Geoffrey Robinson of Alfie's Antiques Market, Alison Snelgrove of thestudioglassmerchant.co.uk, Ron & Ann Wheeler of artiusglass.co.uk, and Nigel Wiggin of The Old Hall Club.

HOW TO USE THIS BOOK

Subcategory heading Indicates the sub-category of the main heading.

Page tab This appears on every page and identifies the main category heading as identified in the Contents List on pages 5-6.

Caption The description of the item illustrated, including when relevant, the period, the maker or factory, medium, the year it was made, dimensions and condition. Many captions have **footnotes** which explain terminology or give identification or valuation information.

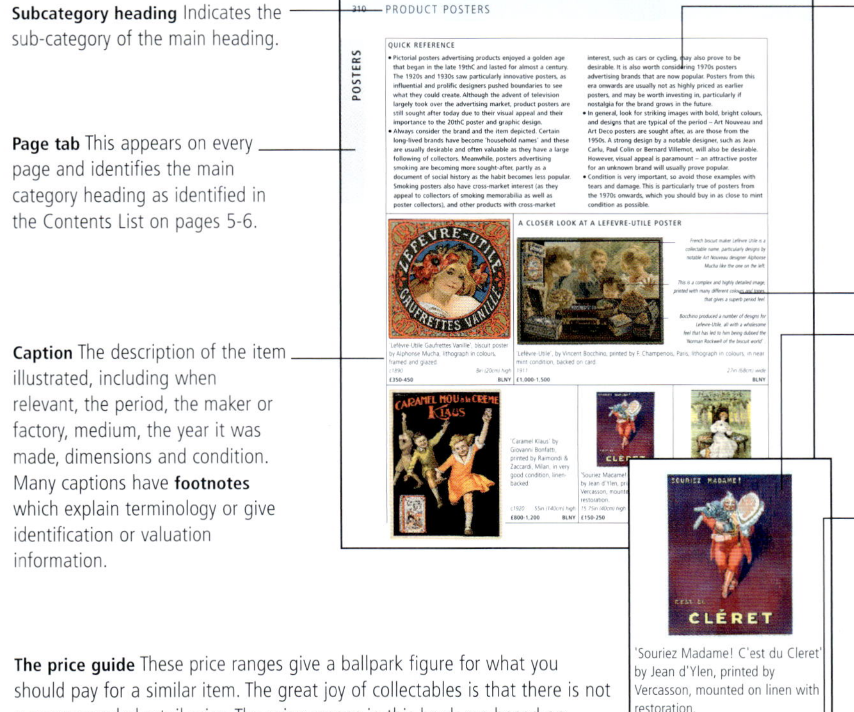

The price guide These price ranges give a ballpark figure for what you should pay for a similar item. The great joy of collectables is that there is not a recommended retail price. The price ranges in this book are based on actual prices, either what a dealer will take or the full auction price.

Quick reference Gives key facts about the factory, maker or style, along with stylistic identification points, value tips and advice on fakes.

Quick reference and **closer look** These are where we show identifying aspects of a factory or maker, point out rare colours or shapes, and explain why a particular piece is so desirable.

The object The collectables are shown in full colour. This is a vital aid to identification and valuation. With many objects, a slight colour variation can signify a large price differential.

Source code Every item has been specially photographed at an auction house, a dealer, an antiques market or a private collection. These are credited by code at the end of the caption, and can be checked against the Key to Illustrations on pages 408-410.

Welcome to the new edition of Miller's Collectables Handbook. As ever, you will find a selection of thousands of items from across the world, all illustrated in colour and accompanied by a descriptive caption and price guide. Additional information and insiders' tips are included in the 'Quick Reference' sections and footnotes, while our 'Closer Look' features help you to understand more. The result is the best full-colour, fully illustrated collectables price guide in the world.

This year is an important one for Miller's. As well as continuing to publish a range of exciting books, we are developing our new website at www.millersonline.com. We are delighted that many of you have already explored the site. For those of you who have not visited it yet, the site is packed with useful tips and information including what we believe is the most comprehensive fully illustrated A-Z of terms available. You can also search a catalogue containing tens of thousands of antiques and collectables, each with a description and price guide, and browse the innovative Dealers & Auctioneers listings. All of this is available at no cost. And we are not stopping there. Keep checking back, as there are plenty of exciting developments in store.

Of course, the past year has been a notable one. With the collapse of an international bank and the 'credit crunch' it's not surprising that the market for antiques and collectables has been dramatically affected. However, a couple of months after the recession began, an unexpected development occurred: rather than saving their money, many people began to buy antiques and collectables. Perhaps they saw it as a way to invest their cash in tangible goods that had the potential to hold their value. Attendance at fairs rocketed, and auctions reported strong sales, particularly for scarcer, finer pieces.

Although this has subsided, many dealers and auction houses continue to report strong sales. This follows the advice of an analyst at the firm of accountants, Deloitte, who reported that he believed the credit crunch had encouraged people 'to put their money into a range of assets' and that antiques 'generally avoid the big price swings seen in financial markets'. It's certainly true that vintage, retro and antique items hold more value than most of their contemporary counterparts. Not only that but you can cherish and enjoy them in your home – they are far more attractive than money or shares in a bank.

A Czechoslovakian Chlum u Trebone glassworks vase worth £100-150

Another exciting development is the new initiative Antiques are Green, which aims to promote antiques as an alternative form of recycling and means of conserving natural resources. By encouraging new and existing antiques and collectables buyers to see their collections as the ultimate in recycled goods, it hopes to make a tangible difference and be part of an environmental conscience which will eventually permeate all areas of daily life.

A De La Rue 'Onoto The Pen' worth £120-180

While prices for low- and mid-range items have remained largely static, or have perhaps even fallen slightly, prices for the very best have risen. Fashion also plays an important role. Even though the 'Ikea-style' modern look is still popular, a strong trend for creating unique interiors filled with antique and vintage statement pieces is developing. If the style of an item appeals, it will be desirable. Although many traditional areas such as blue and white ceramics are still in the doldrums, it seems we are not the only ones who have noticed that low prices mean now is the time to buy, and a revival in these areas seems likely.

On more specific fronts, costume jewellery continues to be hotly soughtafter, particularly pieces by major designers and makers. Twentieth century glass, especially examples from Murano and Czechoslovakia, is also receiving the attention it deserves, at long last. As demand from an increasing number of collectors grows against a limited supply, prices have risen. Now that fountain pens dating from before WWII have become both valuable and scarce, models from the 1960-90s have risen in price. You will find comprehensive sections covering all these areas in this edition.

We have also included some new sections this year, including ceramics by Pablo Picasso, paperweights, and ceramics by Wade. You will also notice that we have included areas from other countries, such as the work of a few American potteries. This reflects the truly global nature of collecting today, and also gives you the edge over everyone else. Often ignored in this country, values can be high. We feel that our new, larger format combined with this variety and depth of information and coverage makes this edition the best yet. We hope you agree.

Judith Miller.

Mark Hill

QUICK REFERENCE

- Vintage advertising is a good way to track changing styles, social trends and aspirations. Although 19thC advertising and packaging can be found, most items available today date from the early 20thC, when advertising began to diversify rapidly. Collectors typically focus on one subject area, such as tobacco, or one type of object (tins or signs are the most popular), or a brand. Items from popular brands, such as Kellogg's, attract the most collectors and therefore tend to fetch the highest prices. Items with cross-market interest, such as railway advertising, will appeal to a greater number of collectors.
- Tins holding biscuits, tobacco and sweets were common between 1860-1950. From the 1890s, the shapes of these became more inventive, as companies tried to outdo each other to appeal to customers. Many tins from this period were designed to be kept and used as storage containers or toys. Examples by major manufacturers, such as Huntley & Palmers, and those with moving parts, are often the most valuable.
- Do not ignore packaging that would have been thrown away. Even if many examples were produced, few may have survived. If both rare and desirable, the item's value can be surprisingly high. Vintage packaging in mint condition is particularly rare and consequently sought after. If the original contents are included this will not necessarily increase value, unless the package is also sealed.
- Look for visually appealing advertising in good condition, which represents the brand effectively, subject area or period. The colour, style of lettering and logo will help with dating. Art Nouveau, Art Deco and 1950s-style pieces will usually find favour with collectors, as will eye-catching, designs featuring bright colours, recognisable logos and popular characters.

A very rare W.K. Kellogg 'Drinket' tin, with dated paper label.

Kellogg' s sold two soft drinks, the coffee-like 'Drinket' from 1914-21 and 'Fizz-Aide' from 1956-58. The early date makes this one of the first tins of ' Drinket' produced.

1915. 4.25in (10.5cm) high

£40-60 BH

An American 'Postmaster Smokers' printed tinplate tobacco tin.

Although dented, the graphics and bright colour are appealing, and tobacco advertising and packaging is sought after.

5.5in (13.5cm) high

£15-20 BH

A 1960s Huntley & Palmers 'Butlinland' biscuit tin, with printed photographic decoration, and printer's code '61/2649'.

8.75in (22cm) wide

£5-8 SAS

A Co-operative Wholesale Society lithographed tinplate 'Crumpsall Cracker' travelling trunk biscuit tin, in good condition.

4.75in (12cm) wide

£20-30 SAS

A Wade Bell's Scotch Whisky commemorative advertising ceramic bell-shaped bottle, with applied gilt label with wording 'A MEMENTO OF YOUR VISIT TO BELL'S HEAD OFFICE'.

6.25in (16cm) high

£15-20 DSC

A 1950s full-length male painted advertising figure, possibly for 'Aertex' underwear, modelled standing, on a plinth base.

Male and female underwear advertising figures have become sought after in recent years. The eye-appeal of the figure is important to value. Modelling, facial features and hair style that are typical of their time add to desirability. Always examine a piece closely, as many have become worn.

19.75in (50cm) high

£550-750 **SAS**

A CLOSER LOOK AT A STORE DISPLAY

These would have been used as dramatic store displays, or even parade figures, at a time when exotic animals such as tigers were fashionable.

Rare surivors: a pair is extremely unusual, and these are in excellent condition, and complete with their packing cases which bear amusing wording.

With their crouching poses and bared, snarling teeth, the tigers are full of drama and would make superb display pieces today.

Learbury Clothes was based in Syrcacuse, New York, and produced fine quality menswear which often bore the labels of other brands. As it was a lesser known brand, few of these expensive displays would have been produced.

A pair of crated papier mâché advertising tigers, on moulded naturalistic bases, marked 'Learbury Tiger', with original packing crates marked 'Handle With Care This Box Contains Learbury Fashion Display', in excellent condition.

c1910-20

£10,000-15,000 **JDJ**

A 1930s possibly French male mannequin head, naturalistically painted with applied hair.

12.5in (32cm) high

£200-300 **SAS**

An Art Deco Harley Sport plaster male display bust, with painted features in composition plaster, the bust inscribed 'Harley Sport' in painted blue, on a rectangular plinth and square base.

23.5in (60cm) high

£400-600 **SAS**

An Art Deco French jewellery display bust, the cut-out bust modelled as a glamorous young woman, on a square wooden plinth, with an Art Deco green and white beadwork fringe necklace.

£300-500 **SAS**

A 1950s-60s French Lalique moulded glass shop display sign, with moulded and gilded lettering.

£70-100 **CARS**

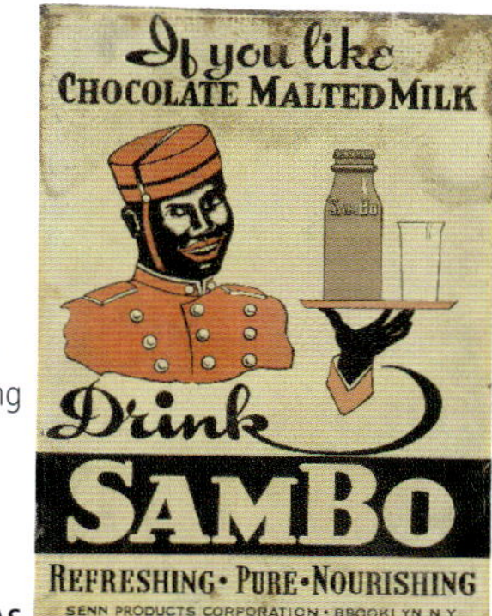

A 1940s 'Drink SamBo Chocolate Malted Milk' printed tin advertising sign.

£250-350 **MAS**

A 1950s Pepsi Cola transfer-printed tinplate shop large sign.

49in (124cm) high

£300-500 **QU**

A Coca Cola printed tinplate advertising tray, made by The H.D. Beech Co., of Coshocton, Ohio.

Coca Cola trays are highly sought after, particularly if made before 1930 or bearing artwork by Hamilton King. This very early example is known as 'The Exhibition Girl' as the 1909 World's Fair in Seattle can be seen behind her.

1909 *13.25in (33.5cm) high*

£600-900 **SOTT**

A very rare 1940s 12-sized aluminium Coca Cola bottle carrier.

This is very rare as most bottle carriers were made for 6-packs. Aluminium was a typical material used during this period as large supplies were produced for the war effort and were turned over for civilian use after the end of World War II.

16.25in (41cm) wide

£70-100 **SOTT**

A CLOSER LOOK AT AN ADVERTISING CALENDAR

This is a very early and very rare advertising calendar, but the truly superb condition makes it even rarer and more desirable.

The Daisy BB gun subject matter also contributes to the value – in the US, where this was sold, vintage guns and related memorabilia are highly collectable.

The printing is very fine, with a good level of detail and several colours – note how one of the daisies has been drawn over the inset of the boys in a skiff to add perspective.

The first Daisy BB gun was given away by the Plymouth Iron Windmill Co. as a promotion to farmers who bought a windmill. In 1895 the nearly bankrupt company changed its name to Daisy and limited itself to manufacturing guns.

A very rare Daisy Manufacturing Co. 'Model 96' air rifle calendar, lithographed in colours by Calvert Lith. Co., with illustration of two boys in a skiff with a gun, and complete with 12 date sheets and brass ring grommet, in excellent condition with only a few scuffs.

1896

£4,000-6,000 **JDJ**

A 1950s-60s Royal Alma circular Double Diamond Advertising Dish, the back with black printed mark.

5in (12.5cm) diam

£12-18 **RET**

A Hamleys 'The Finest Toy Shop In the World' catalogue, illustrated with sepia overprinted primary colours showing toys, games, activities including Meccano, FROG, Schuco and Trix products.

1938

£30-50 **SAS**

A Hires Munimaker marble, nickel, and glass syrup dispenser, the square marble base with brass Hires plaques on four sides and topped with a flared white milk glass globe.

c1900-10 *35in (89cm) high*

£1,500-2,500 **JDJ**

A chrome plated steel Schneider Trophy commemorative ashtray, the plane based on the Rolls Royce powered Supermarine S6B Schneider Trophy seaplane, with rotating propeller.

4.5in (11.5cm) high

£100-150 **CARS**

A De Havilland DH 106 Comet silver plated presentation model, mounted on an onyx ashtray base, with a good level of detailing.

Factors that influence values of airplane ashtrays include the model of plane, the size, materials used, and the level of detail. If the piece is connected to a famous event or aviator, the price can rise.

10in (25.5cm) wide

£200-250 **GROB**

A World War II onyx and metal airplane ashtray, with a Supermarine Spitfire mounted on top of a chome plated sphere.

8.25in (21cm) long

£80-120 **CW**

A World War II aluminium 'Trench Art' airplane ashtray with Supermarine Spitfire model with moving propellor, mounted on a machine component, possibly a cylinder head.

c1945 *6.5in (16cm) high*

£70-90 **GCHI**

A 1930s chrome plated airplane ashtray, with seaplane model, the base with with 'SP' within a shield mark.

6in (15cm) high

£60-90 **CW**

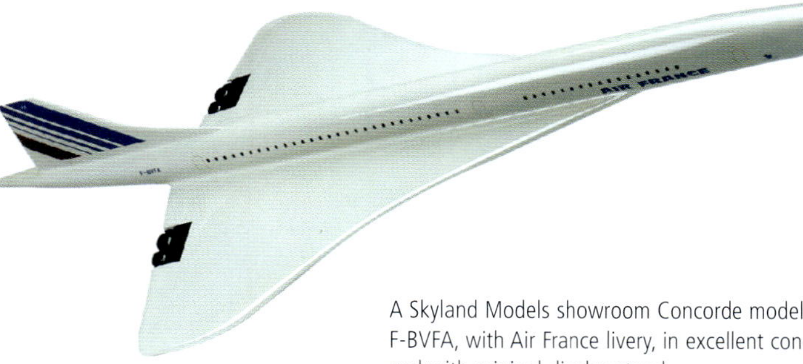

A Skyland Models showroom Concorde model, F-BVFA, with Air France livery, in excellent condition and with original display stand.

Concorde made its maiden flight in 1975, and was retired in 2003. It can now be seen at Dulles Airport, Washington DC. In 1998 it completed a round-the-world trip in 41 hours and 27 minutes.

48in (122cm) long

£400-600 **TCA**

A B&M Ceramics United States Navy 'Tactical Support Center' transfer-printed souvenir mug, with 'Tobias' transfer.

3.5in (9cm) high

£3-4 **AEM**

A rare 1920-30s South Coast Flying Club member's car badge, decorated with four colours of enamel, with some repairs, the back stamped with 'COLLINS LONDON' makers mark.

If the enamel was undamaged, the value might rise to £500.

4.25in (10cm) high

£350-450 **CARS**

An unusual Schneider Trophy commemorative vase, probably made by Bough, with panels of anthropomorphic birds in blue, between Scottish rose and foliate borders on a yellow ground, the base painted 'EJMJ Mifflin, SOUTHAMPTON SEPTEMBER 1929, Schneider Trophy won by G Brit Waghorn'.

The origins of this cup or trophy are unclear. The name Mifflin cannot be found connected with this event, which was held over the Solent some distance away from the city of Southampton. Waghorn did, however, win the event. The Art & Crafts styling is unusual for this date.

10in (25.5cm) high

£300-400 **W&W**

A Brooklands Aero Club octagonal enamelled metal member badge for 1937, numbered '255', with original cord, the back moulded 'NOT TRANSFERABLE' and with ' W.O. LEWIS B'HAM' maker's mark.

1.5in (3.5cm) high

£200-250 **CARS**

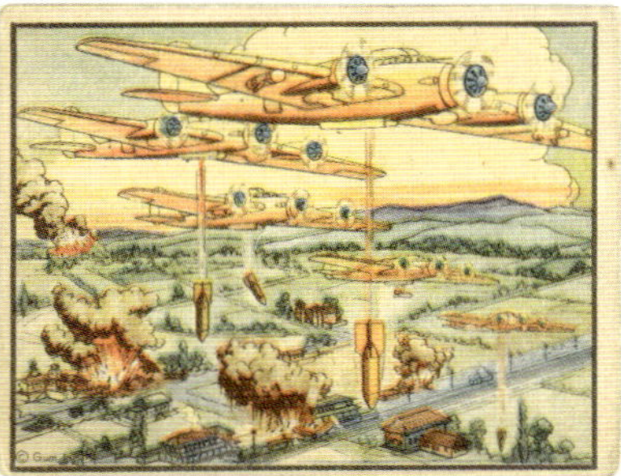

Two American Gum Inc 'Horrors of War' colour printed cards, comprising no.24 'Italian Squadrons Flying Low Slaughter Ethiopians' and no.20 'Spanish Insurgents Bomb Government Territory', from a series of 240 cards.

1936 *3.25in (8cm) wide*

£5-8 EACH **SOTT**

A Bishops & Stonier ceramic child's bowl with a transfer-printed scene of Blériot's plane.

9.25in (23.5cm) diam.

£150-200 **PC**

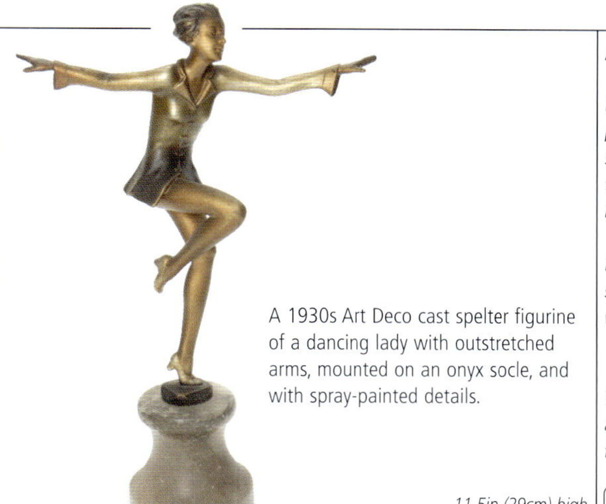

A 1930s Art Deco cast spelter figurine of a dancing lady with outstretched arms, mounted on an onyx socle, and with spray-painted details.

11.5in (29cm) high

£100-150 **CARS**

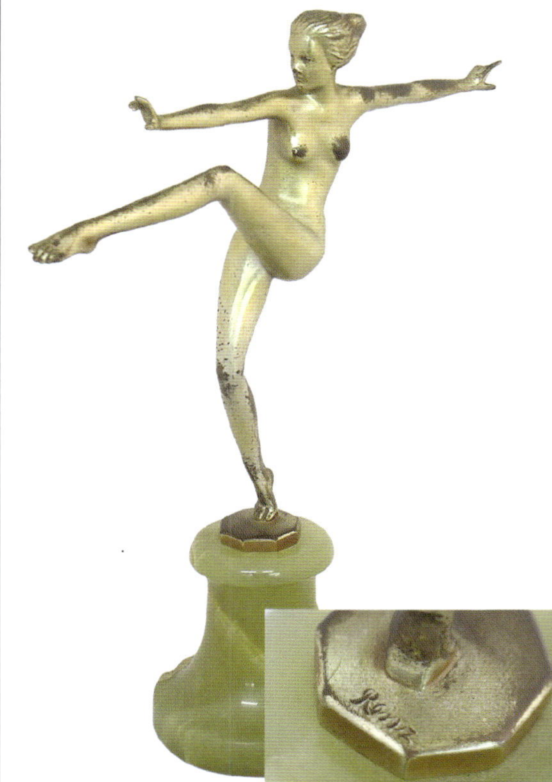

An Art Deco gilt bronze figure, modelled as a naked female dancer upon a circular green onyx socle, signed 'Renz', gilding badly damaged.

Although little is known about the designer, this figurine is gilt bronze suggesting a quality figure and the pose is desirable.

10in (25.5cm) high

£500-600 **GHOU**

A CLOSER LOOK AT AN ART DECO STATUE

Inexpensive statuettes made from moulded plastic and a lightweight metal alloy called spelter were produced during the 1920s and 30s to imitate more expensive carved ivory and cast bronze statues by Ferdinand Preiss, Demêtre Chiparus and others.

Pieces can be found for around £30-150 depending on the quality, size and pose, and offer the look of more expensive figurines, without the high prices

This is one of the better examples, with a lively pose, a sense of movement to the dress, a necklace, and fashionably bobbed hair.

The detail is not as fine as the pieces it was designed to imitate, and examples are frequently damaged or stained.

A 1930s Art Deco spelter statuette of a lady leaning backwards in a dance, with spray painted details and cream moulded plastic head and hands, mounted on an onyx socle.

9in (23cm) high

£100-150 **CARS**

A 1930s Art Deco spelter statuette, with draped shawl under her arms and spray painted details, the onyx base with a striker cigarette or cigar lighter, with some wear to the spray paint.

10in (25.5cm) high

£50-70 **CARS**

A 1930s Art Deco spelter statuette, of a standing girl, with flower-like skirt, fan, and disc-shaped hat, mounted on a marble base.

10in (25.5cm) high

£80-120 **CARS**

A 1930s Art Deco spelter statuette of a kneeling girl with an onyx ball, mounted on an oval onyx base.

This may have been one of a pair of bookends.

7in (17.5cm) high

£150-200 **CARS**

QUICK REFERENCE

- Automobilia is a diverse global collecting area, surrounding the lively vintage car market and encompassing everything from car parts to advertising to works of art. In general, appealing pieces that look good on display from the major marques are at the higher end of the market. These marques include Bentley, Rolls Royce, Jaguar, Buick, Ferrari and Chevrolet. Collectors tend to focus on one marque, or on a particular type of item.
- Apart from the cars themselves, car mascots usually fetch the largest sums of money. These were mounted on the front of the bonnet of a car, and can be found in many different shapes. Types include 'manufacturer mascots', made by the company that made the car, 'advertising mascots' made by a company such as Michelin to advertise its products, and 'accessory mascots' which include animals, figures and characters.
- Look for examples that conjure up feelings of the excitement and speed of motoring. Novelty forms can also be popular. Names to look for include Lalique, Red Ashay, Sabino and A & E Lejeune. Condition counts, and reproductions are known, so try to view and handle as many authentic examples as possible.
- Car badges, which adorned car grilles, are also popular and often more affordable. Most showed membership of an association such as an enthusiasts club. They are usually made from nickel- or chrome-plated cast brass, which may then be enamelled with a colourful design. Appealing pieces from major marques, or smaller but well-known clubs from the 1900s-30s, tend to be the most desirable.
- Many associations also produced badges for their members, and these have been rising in value recently. As before, appeal and marque are key factors to desirability and value. Also look out for lamps and advertising pieces, such as enamel signs. Items related to famous drivers, such as Stirling Moss, or events, such as Grand Prix, are also desirable due to their association.

A 1920s French A.E. Lejeune Bentley 'Flying B' chrome plated brass car mascot, stamped 'AEL' and mounted on a mottled brown Bakelite stand, made for a Pacific Open Tourer.

3.5in (9cm) high

£250-300 **CARS**

A large 1920s Joseph Fray chrome plated brass Bentley 'Flying B' car mascot, stamped 'JOS. FRAY B'HAM' and mounted on a Bakelite stand.

This mascot is smaller than similar examples. It may have been designed for an opening bonnet.

2.75in (7cm) high

£350-450 **CARS**

A 1920s Joseph Fray chrome plated brass Bentley 'Flying B' car mascot, mounted on a brown Bakelite stand, stamped 'JOS. FRAY B'HAM'.

Made for, and generally seen on, a Bentley Open Tourer. This example would have been worth more had it not been over-polished, leading to its plating being polished away and becoming 'brassed'.

Mascot 2in (5cm) high

£250-300 **CARS**

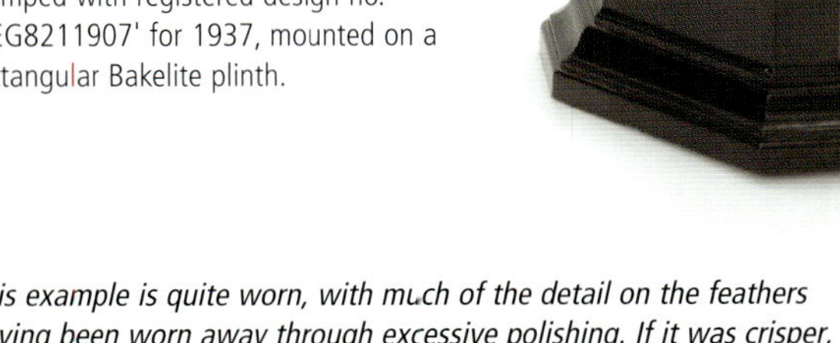

A late 1930s Bentley 'Flying B' car mascot, with the 'B' leaning back and stamped with registered design no. 'REG8211907' for 1937, mounted on a rectangular Bakelite plinth.

This example is quite worn, with much of the detail on the feathers having been worn away through excessive polishing. If it was crisper, the value would be around £250-300.

5.25in (13cm) long

£200-250 **CARS**

A 1930s Bentley chrome plated brass 'Flying B' car mascot, with long wings, mounted on a brown Bakelite stand.

This was not used for a long period as it was deemed too large, particularly the wings. Look out for examples with only one wing behind, as these are very rare.

5.25in (13cm) long

£550-600 **CARS**

A CLOSER LOOK AT A BENTLEY CAR MASCOT

This is a rare prototype design that did not go into production and was never used on a car – very few examples exist.

The style reflects the Art Deco tastes of the period, but lacks the elegance and sense of speed of other designs.

It may have been designed by Frederick Gordon Crosby, who designed the logo for the first car in 1921.

It was probably made by Joseph Fray, who made most of Bentley's mascots.

A rare 1930s chrome plated brass prototype Bentley 'Flying B' car mascot, possibly designed by Frederick Gordon Crosby and made by Joseph Fray, unmarked and mounted on a metal stand.

3.5in (9cm) high

£550-600 **CARS**

A late 1920s French Lalique 'Cinque Chevaux' (Five Horses) moulded glass car mascot, no.1122, moulded 'R.LALIQUE FRANCE' mark, mounted on a period display base.

This design was introduced on 26th August 1925, and was originally mounted on an illuminated radiator fitting made by Brèves Galleries of Knightsbridge. This example has a couple of internal air bubbles, which may deter some collectors. Without bubbles the value could increase by around £500.

5.5in (14cm) long

£6,000-6,500 **CARS**

A CLOSER LOOK AT A LALIQUE CAR MASCOT

Beaks were often damaged, as the mascot is top heavy. If the beak is not damaged the value can rise to £2,500-3,500.

This dramatic and evocative mascot was model no.1124, and was introduced on the 5th August 1925.

Very few Lalique car mascots were produced in coloured glass, with tinted glass being slightly more common.

Beware of modern fakes, where a colourless mascot has been treated with radiation to add a tint – these are usually darker: lilac examples are more purple in tone.

A late 1920s French Lalique 'Faucon' (Falcon) moulded glass car mascot, with a faint lilac tint, moulded 'R.LALIQUE' and etched 'FRANCE' marks.

6in (15cm) high

£2,000-2,500 **CARS**

A 1930s French Lalique 'Sirene' (Mermaid) opalescent moulded glass car mascot, moulded 'R.LALIQUE' mark.

This example has a chipped base, a common problem with vintage car mascots, but luckily the damage does not affect the figure itself. In perfect condition, it might fetch up to £1,500. Sirene was numbered 831 as a statuette in 1920. It was turned into a car mascot in 1925.

4in (10cm) high

£900-1,200 **CARS**

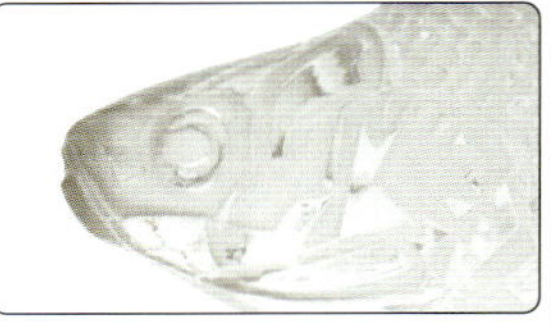

A 1950s-60s French Lalique colourless glass 'Perche Poisson' (Perch) moulded glass car mascot, no.1158, introduced on the 20th April 1929, the base with 'LALIQUE FRANCE' acid stamp.

Note that the glass on mascots from this period is slighty darker in tone than more modern examples, such as the one to the right, which are brighter and cleaner. This shape was discontinued in 2006.

3.75in (9.5cm) high

£550-650 **CARS**

A 1980s-90s French Lalique colourless glass 'Perche Poisson' (Perch) moulded glass car mascot, no.1158, introduced on the 20th April 1929, the base with diamond point engraved 'LALIQUE FRANCE' inscription and factory labels.

3.75in (9.5cm) high

£550-650 **CARS**

A 1980s-90s French Lalique clear and frosted moulded glass 'Sanglier' (Wild Boar) car mascot, no.1157 introduced on the 3rd October 1929, the base with diamond point engraved 'Lalique France' script mark.

2.75in (6.5cm) high

£350-450 **CARS**

A CLOSER LOOK AT A GORDON CROSBY JAGUAR CAR MASCOT

Known as the 'mottled cat', this was designed by Gordon Crosby, who designed the famous 'Leaping Cat' mascot for Jaguar in 1937.

It was used for one year from 1935-36 only on a Jaguar car, before being relaced by the more familiar design as Jaguar founder Sir William Lyons did not like it.

It was re-used on the Panther J72 built by Jankel during the late 1970s and early 1980s, which itself was loosely based on a Jaguar SS100 from the late 1930s.

The value given is for the mascot only, the cap itself is worth around £50.

A large Panther chrome plated car mascot, for a Jaguar model J72, designed by Gordon Crosby, on a radiator cap with an applied black enamel Panther winged logo.

7.25in (8cm) high

£350-450 **CARS**

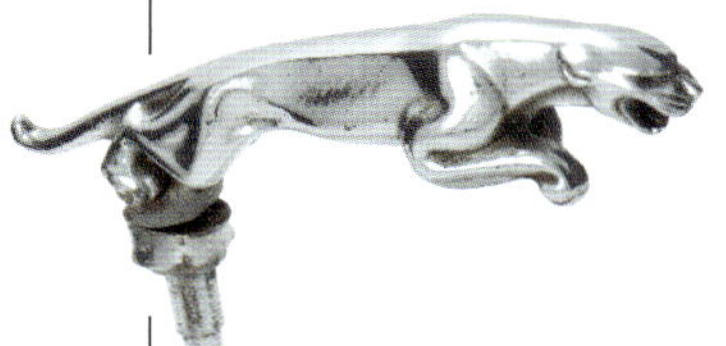

A 1950s Jaguar chrome plated brass 'Leaping Cat' car mascot, with longer tail, designed by Gordon Crosby, for an Mk6, on a cylindrical mount stamped 7/2645/0, the base of the mascot ground down.

If the base had not been ground down, the value might have been £450-550. If the shaft is missing, the value falls by around £50.

8in (20.5cm) long

£300-350 **CARS**

A 1960s Jaguar chome plated brass 'Leaping Cat' car mascot, designed by Gordon Crosby, for S-Type models, on a long mount with two fixing screws.

7.75in (19.5cm) long

£100-150 **CARS**

A Singer Gazelle chrome plated car mascot, mounted on a wooden plinth.

Mascot 6in (15cm) long

£100-150 **CHT**

A modern reproduction chrome plated flying stork car mascot, in the style of Frederick Bazin, mounted on a radiator cap.

5.5in (14cm) high

£70-100 **CHT**

A Rolls Royce nickel-plated brass large 'Spirit of Ecstasy' car mascot, for a Phantom II, stamped with copyright marks and 'Charles Sykes', mounted on a wooden base.

1919-25 *6in (15cm) high*

£900-1,200 **CARS**

An Automobile Association type 1B nickel plated brass full member's badge, impressed 'Stenson Cooke Secretary', numbered '4410'.

6in (15cm) high

£100-150 **CHT**

A late 1950s-60s Automobile Association (AA) enamelled and chromed car grille badge, in original condition with double screw fitting for a grille, numbered '38774Z'.

3.5in (9cm) high

£25-30 **CARS**

A Royal Automobile Club (RAC) Centenary commemorative chrome plated and enamelled car grille badge.

Only available in the centenary year of 1997, members were allowed to buy two examples, at a cost of £29.95 each.

1997 *4.75in (12cm) high*

£65-75 **CARS**

A 1950s-60s Company of Veteran Motorists member's grille badge, awarded to a member of 49 years standing, the back marked 'THE PROPERTY OF C.V.M.'.

THE CVM was founded in 1932 and promoted safe driving. In 1983 it became GEM, and then GEM Motoring Assist.

3.75in (9.5cm) high

£7-10 **CARS**

An Royal Automobile Club of Italy type 3B badge, enamelled in blue, white, red and black, with some enamel losses.

4.5in (11.5cm) wide

£35-45 **CHT**

A 1960s Aston Martin Owner's Club enamelled chromed brass car grille badge.

The original owner has removed his name under the enamelled area with a drill, revealing the brassy metal. If this had not been done, the value may have risen to £40-50. Also look out for more decorative vitreous enamelled examples, as these can fetch £70-100.

6in (15cm) high

£30-40 **CARS**

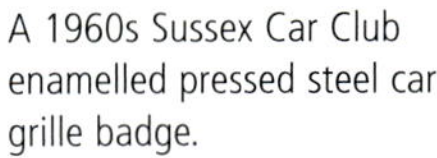

A 1960s Sussex Car Club enamelled pressed steel car grille badge.

As this was a smaller regional club, fewer badges would have been made, meaning they are harder to find today even though demand for them is limited.

4.5in (11.5cm) high

£40-50 **CARS**

A Brooklands Automobile Racing Club member's enamel badge set, comprising member's badge on cord and two guest badges, each numbered '404'.

1926 *1.25in (3cm) high*

£280-320 **CHT**

A Brooklands Automobile Racing Club blue enamelled gold-metal member's badge for 1929, together with a bow-shaped guest pin, each numbered 189, the back moulded 'W.O. LEWIS B'HAM'.

Introduced in 1907, these sets have become highly sought after. A full set comprises one member's badge and two guest pins. If this set had been complete, it could have been worth up to £100 more.

1928 *1.5in (3.5cm) high*

£200-250 **CARS**

A CLOSER LOOK AT A MEMBER'S BADGE SET

The brightly coloured geometric Art Deco style, and the design shaped like the front of a car, makes this set highly desirable.

The design was changed every year, so that current members could be quickly and easily identified.

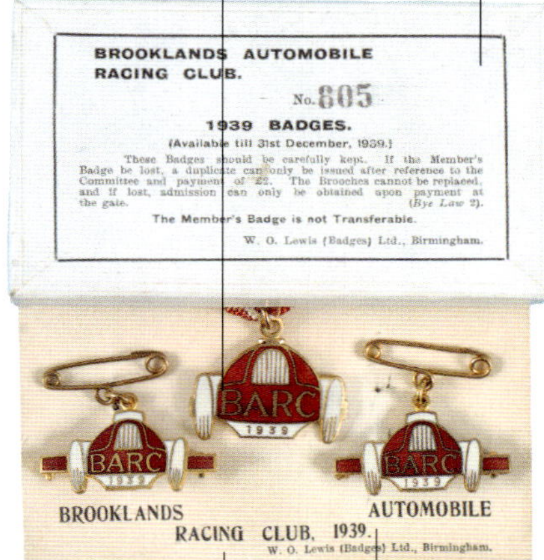

This is a complete set. Always look for matching numbers on each piece – the original box adds up to 50% of the value of the pins.

1939 was the last year these sets of badges were made. Members' badges were produced from 1941-42, before they too were phased out.

Look out for sets of 1916 badges made in cream Bakelite as a complete set can fetch up to £2,000.

A Brooklands Automobile Racing Club member's enamel badge set, comprising member's badge on cord and two guest badges, each numbered 805, in original box, with printed membership number and rules to lid.

1939 *1.25in (3cm) high*

£500-700 **CHT**

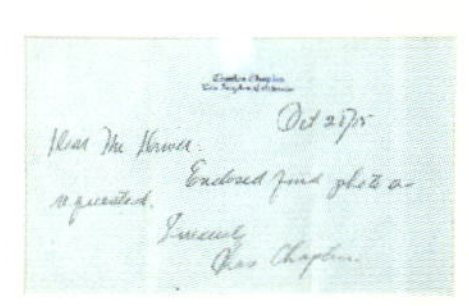

A Charlie Chaplin signed manuscript letter and photograph, the letter addressed from Los Angeles, California, with stamped hand written envelope, mounted in composite frame.

£450-540 **AH**

A Pete Best signed photograph of the Beatles.

Best was the original drummer for the Beatles, from 1960-1962. He was replaced by Ringo Starr.

10in (25.5cm) wide

£30-40 **ACOG**

A Maria Teresa de Filippis signed Silverstone motor racing programme

9in (23cm) high.

£25-35 **COC**

A Gerald Ford signed presidential portrait.

£450-550 **MAS**

A Harrison Ford as Han Solo signed photograph.

The signature isn' t his best as it runs across a dark area of the photograph and appears lost.

c1980

£150-250 **PC**

A Stephen Fry signed postcard.

Dedications are less desirable.

6in (15cm) high

£10-15 **PC**

A Whoopi Goldberg signed photograph.

£35-45 **ACOG**

An Audrey Hepburn signature, mounted with a photograph from the film 'Breakfast at Tiffany's'.

16in (40.5cm) wide

£180-200 **PC**

AUTOGRAPHS

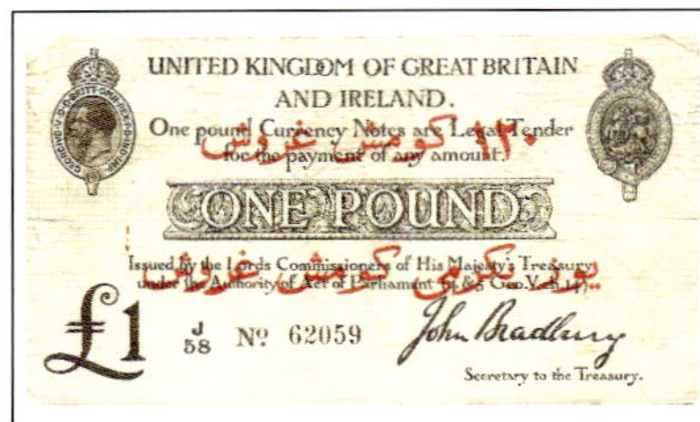

A British one pound note for use by the British Military Expeditionary Forces in the Mediterranean and the Naval Expeditionary Forces in 1915, signed by John Bradbury, Secretary to the Treasury, overprinted in Arabic.

£1,800-2,400 **PAMW**

A Bank of England five pound note, signed by E.M.Harvey, issued in Hull.

1918

£700-800 **PAMW**

An British Treasury ten shilling note, signed by John Bradbury.

Treasury notes signed with Bradbury's name are known as 'Bradburys'.

£100-150 **CWD**

A Bank of England Britannia series ten shilling note, signed by L.K. O'Brien.

This note has a million serial number.

1955

£40-60 **PAMW**

A first issue Bank of England fifty pound note, A01 prefix.

1981

£100-150 **CWD**

A French Revolutionary assignat five livres note, year 2.

£5-10 **CWD**

A German fifty million mark note, from the Hyper Inflation period.

£2-3 **CWD**

A French one hundred new francs note, with Napoleon portrait.

£20-25 **CWD**

A Munster & Leinster five pound Ploughman note, signed by J.L. Gubbins, dated.

1929

£700-900 **PAMW**

A Japanese occupation of Malaya one thousand dollar note.

£1-2 **CWD**

A USA Confederate States fifty dollar note, with Lincoln portrait.

1864

£40-60 **CWD**

A USA five dollar Pioneer Family series note,.

1907

£100-150 **CWD**

QUICK REFERENCE

- Beads were one of the earliest types of personal adornment. The very earliest beads were made from natural materials, such as shells, pebbles, bone fragments, seeds and feathers. The oldest examples known are shells dating from approximately 100,000 years ago. Many cultures attached social or cultural importance to beads, and status to those who made and wore them.
- As human societies developed, so did the forms, designs and materials used for beads. Glass beads were introduced around 30,000 years ago, with perhaps the oldest being Egyptian. Glass bead-making grew during the Phoenician and Roman periods.
- The value of a bead depends on a number of factors including its age, material, size, quality of decoration, rarity and desirability to collectors. Due to this wide variation, beads make an ideal collecting field to suit a wide range of budgets and tastes.
- A necklace does not always have to have its original stringing as most of the value is often in the beads themselves. However, if the original stringing was metal, or unique in some way, then it will be important to value.
- Examine beads for wear or damage, although a degree of wear is acceptable in older examples.
- Beads have been made in nearly every country at some point, and many are being reproduced today, so consulting a reliable dealer and buying a comprehensive reference book is highly recommended to help differentitate originals and copies.

Two early Venetian glass elongated barrel-shaped beads, with applied combed red and white striped trails on opaque dark bodies.

largest 0.75in (2cm) long

£15-25 EACH VC

An early Venetian glass bead, with spiralling pink, white and green striped trail over a 'coiled' opaque dark body.

0.5in (1.5cm) long

£25-35 VC

Two early Venetian glass spherical beads, with applied white and multicoloured spots on opaque dark bodies.

0.5in (1cm) long

£15-25 EACH VC

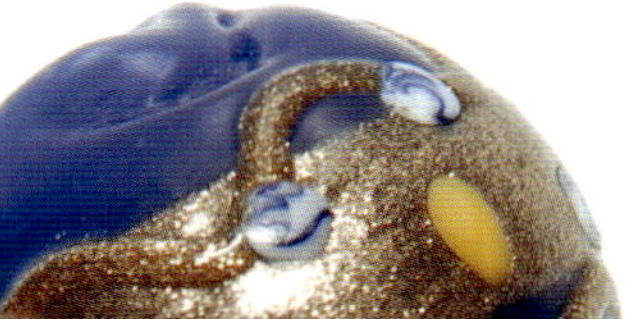

A 1930s Venetian lamp-wound 'Wedding Cake' blue spherical glass bead.

0.5in (1.5cm) long

£3-5 VC

Three 1950s Murano glass beads, teardrop-shaped with multicoloured millefiori.

0.75in (2cm) long

£2-3 EACH VC

A 1930s necklace with Venetian lamp-wound 'Wedding Cake' green spherical glass beads.

Necklace 15in (38cm) long

£50-70 **VC**

A CLOSER LOOK AT A VENETIAN BEAD NECKLACE

The beads are complex, with more details than on other examples.

These are known as 'Wedding Cake' beads as the details are built up individually, using molten glass, much like the icing on a wedding cake.

This necklace has more beads, and so is more valuable than an example with fewer beads.

Each bead in handmade, with flowers, curling and swirling lines and spots being typical decoration – check that there is no damage and look for signs of age as they are being reproduced.

A 1930s necklace with Venetian lamp-wound 'Wedding Cake' green spherical glass beads.

Necklace 15in (38cm) long

£70-90 **VC**

A 1930s necklace with Venetian lamp-wound 'Wedding Cake' green, red and blue spherical glass beads.

Necklace 15in (38cm) long

£60-80 **VC**

Four Parthian period shaped 'etched' carnelian spherical beads, from Ur.

c2,500 BC largest 0.5in (1.5cm) long

£35-45 EACH **VC**

Four Parthian period shaped 'etched' carnelian beads, from Ur.

Despite being known as 'etched', the pattern was not carved at all, but was instead painted on using an alkaline solution. Each bead was then baked to set and fix the pattern.

c2,500 BC largest 0.75in (2cm) long

£35-45 EACH **VC**

QUICK REFERENCE

- A true first edition will be from the first print run (impression) of the first published hardback edition. First editions can then have subsequent impressions, in which errors are corrected, but these are less desirable. A small first edition print run is likely to make a book more desirable. Consequently, although famous, iconic titles will always be prized, first edition books written at the height of an author's power may be worth less than early/less-well received books, as fewer were published. Those with an eye for the future may choose to buy (preferably) signed first editions of up-and-coming authors nominated for major prizes, such as the Man Booker, before the winner is announced.
- Learn how to recognise the different styles of numbering. This often takes the form of a '1' in the series of numbers on the inside copyright page that indicates the edition of the book. Other publishers state that a book is the first edition or use a sequence of letters. Check that the publishing date and copyright date match, and that these match the original publishing date and publisher for the title in a reference book.
- Though there are consistently popular classic authors, such as Ian Fleming and Agatha Christie, fashion can dictate which authors are most desirable. The popular rediscovery of a classic or a successful film or TV series adaptation will usually increase value of first editions.
- The author's signature adds value, particularly if on a limited special edition. Dedications are typically less desirable, unless the recipient is famous or connected to the author. Book signings are becoming more common, so this may become less of a factor in future.
- Condition is extremely important: mint condition commands a premium. Dust jackets should be clean, un-faded and un-damaged, though many can be restored. If the jacket is missing, value can fall by over 50 per cent. You should also check that the book is complete and has not been defaced or damaged.

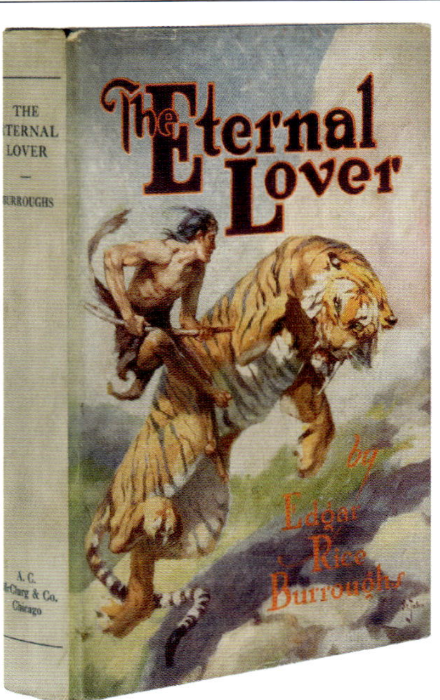

Edgar Rice Burroughs, 'The Eternal Lover', first American edition, published by A.C. McClurg and Co. of Chicago, with illustrations by St John, original black-stamped blue cloth boards with faded spine and dust jacket with light wear.

1925

£1,000-1,500 BLNY

Pearl S. Buck, 'The Good Earth', first American edition, first issue, with pictorial endpapers, modern full brown morocco and gilt binding by Bayntun-Riviere.

The misspelling of 'fleas' as 'flees' on p.100 identifies this as the first issue of the first edition. This novel won a Pulitzer prize in 1932, and returned to the bestseller list after being included on Oprah Winfrey's Book Club in 2004.

1931

£350-450 BLO

Edgar Rice Burroughs, 'Tarzan and the Jewels of Opar', first edition, published by A.C. McClurg and Co. of Chicago, with frontispiece and illustrations by St John, dark green gilt-stamped cloth and dust jacket with minor losses, and corners clipped.

1918

£1,000-1,500 BLNY

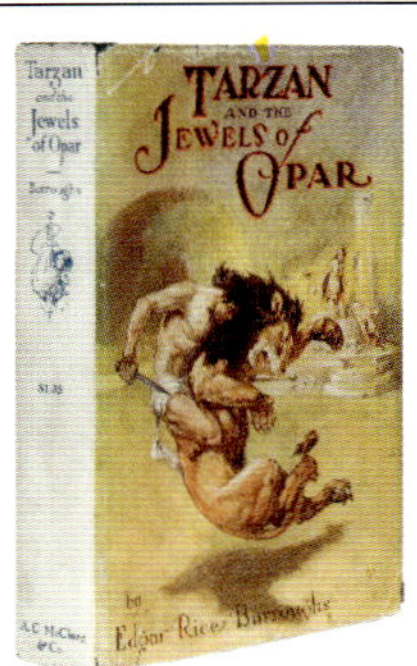

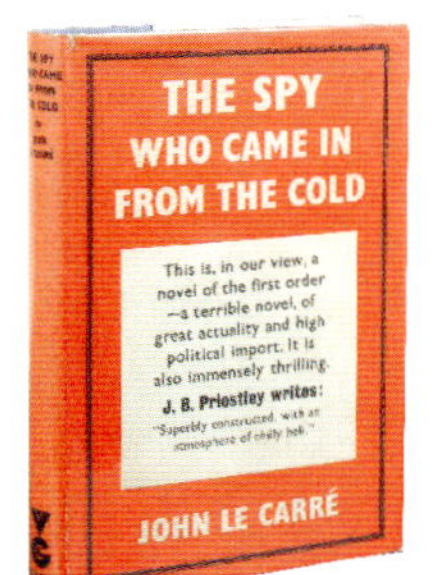

John Le Carré, 'The Spy Who Came in from the Cold', first edition, first impression, published by Gollancz, London, signed presentation copy, dust jacket, with small chips.

1963

£1,800-2,200 BLO

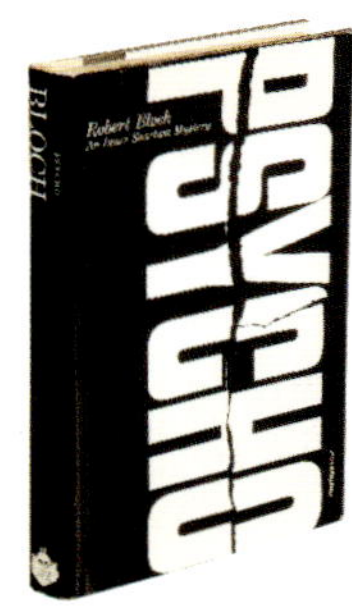

Robert Bloch, 'Psycho', first American edition, published by Simon and Schuster, New York, with original half cloth in dust jacket.

1959

£600-900 BLNY

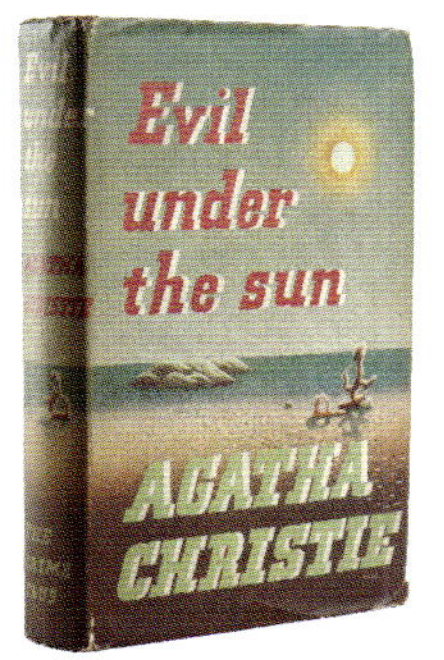

Agatha Christie, 'Evil Under The Sun', first edition, published by Collins, London, with original orange cloth, pictorial dust wrapper, price '7s 6d.', backstrip slightly faded and with small chips to head and tail.

1941

£400-600 **L&T**

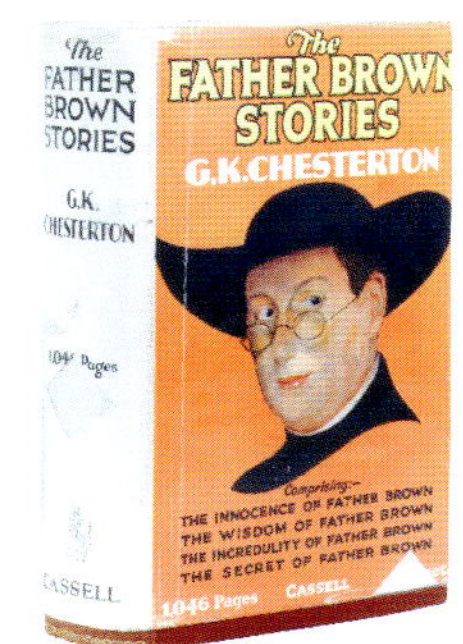

G.K. Chesterton, 'The Father Brown Stories', first edition, published by Cassell & Co., London, with inked name on front free endpaper, original cloth, dust jacket, price clipped, and with rubbed corners.

1929

£250-300 **BLO**

Colin Dexter, 'Last Seen Wearing', first edition, first impression publisher's sample copy, published by Macmillan, signed by the author on the title page, with publisher's stamp on front endpaper, with original boards and dust jacket.

This is Dexter's second novel in the popular Inspector Morse series. It is also the scarcest first edition in the series.

1976

£1,000-1,500 **BLO**

A CLOSER LOOK AT A BURROUGHS FIRST EDITION

Burroughs' seminal work was first published by Olympia Press in Paris in 1959, titled 'The Naked Lunch'.

The first American edition was published three years later as it had been deemed pornographic. 'The' was dropped from the title, as the author never intended it to be there.

This American edition is also different from the Olympia Press edition as it was based on an earlier manuscript from 1958 owned by Burroughs' friend, the poet Allen Ginsberg.

Time magazine included the book in its list of '100 Best English-language Novels from 1923 to 2005'. It was made into a film by David Cronenberg in 1991, reigniting interest in it.

William Burroughs, 'Naked Lunch', first American edition, third printing, published by Grove Press, with black cloth over grey boards, dust jacket with very light rubbing to top and head of spine.

1962

£150-250 **BLNY**

Arthur Conan Doyle, 'The Hound of the Baskervilles', first edition, first issue, published by George Newnes, London, with 16 plates by Sidney Paget, cut signature of the author mounted on title page, original pictorial cloth, spine slightly dulled, in modern custom-made drop-back box replicating the book cover design.

1902

£1,800–2,200 **BLO**

Arthur Conan Doyle, 'The Hound of the Baskervilles, Another Adventure of Sherlock Holmes', first edition, published by George Newnes, London, illustrated with frontispiece and 15 plates, one plate detached but present, endpapers foxed and page edges lightly browned, cloth with few small stains.

1902

£1,000-1,500 **BLNY**

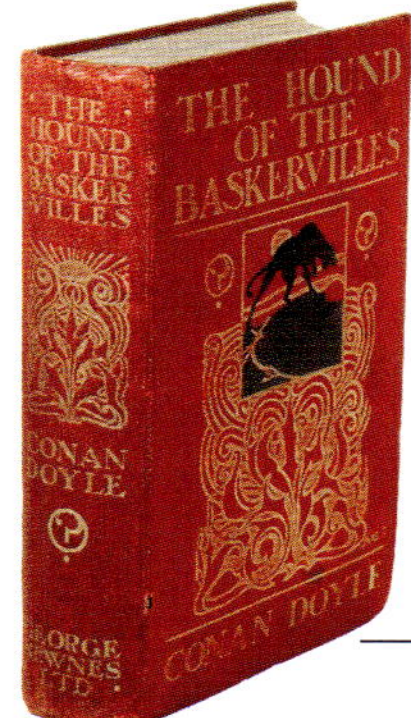

Oliver La Farge, 'Laughing Boy', first American edition, published by Houghton Mifflin Company, Cambridge, with publisher's thickly woven yellow cloth, maroon lettering to spine and upper cover, in slightly rubbed dust jacket, with slightly faded spine.

This novel won a Pulitzer Prize in 1930.

1929

£300-400 **BLNY**

Mervyn Peake, 'The Gormenghast trilogy', comprising three first editions, published by Eyre & Spottiswoode, London, comprising 'Titus Groan', 'Gormenghast', and 'Titus Alone', original red cloth, dust wrappers, some slight offsetting to endpapers.

1946-59

£900-1,200 **L&T**

A CLOSER LOOK AT A T. PRATCHETT FIRST EDITION

This is the scarce first edition of the first book of the internationally popular Discworld series.

This copy was bought direct from the publisher at the time of publication – reputedly only 506 copies were printed.

This true first impression of the first edition has no price, but bears a sticker reading ' Publisher' s Price £7.95' .

Later issues had overlays, or stickers, with book reviews on the flaps, this copy does not.

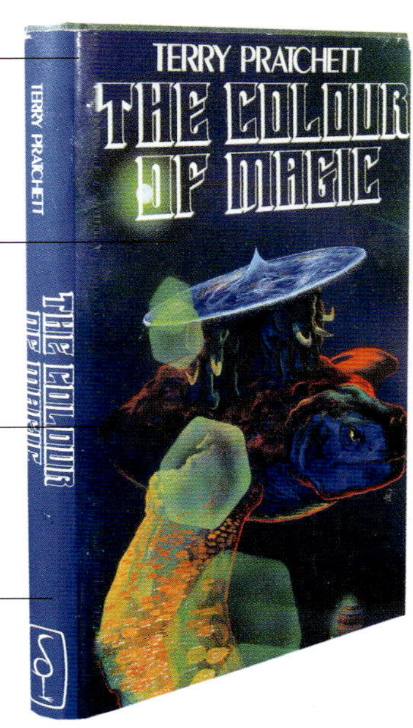

Terry Pratchett, 'The Colour of Magic', first edition, first impression, published by Colin Smythe, Gerrards Cross, original boards, dust jacket, with price sticker on inside front flap slight rubbing to fore edges and corners.

1983

£4,000-6,000 **BLO**

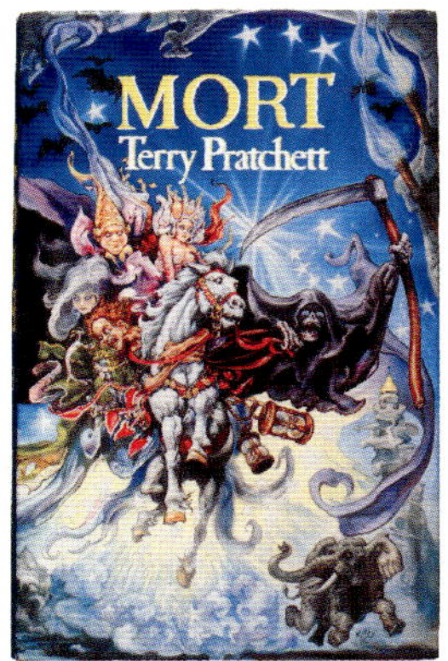

Terry Pratchett, 'Mort', first edition, published by Gollancz, London, with original boards and dust jacket, in excellent condition.

The fourth book of the Discworld series and many readers' favourite, ensuring a strong following.

1987

£300-500 **BLO**

Philip Pullman, 'The Subtle Knife', first edition, published by Scholastic Press, London, with full number line, original green cloth and gilt stamp of dagger, dust jacket, and bookplate of The Children's Book Award on front free endpaper.

1997

£300-500 **L&T**

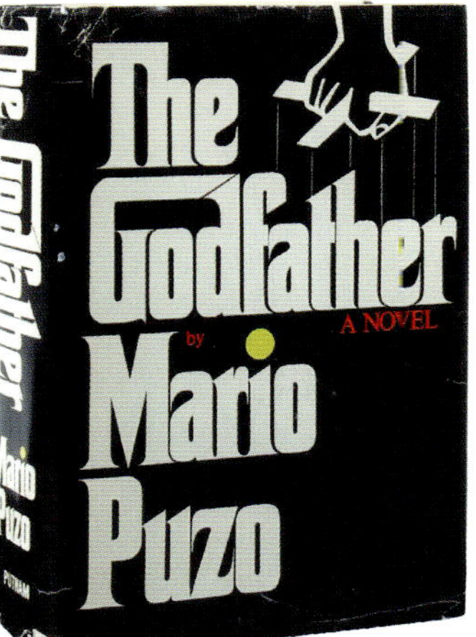

Mario Puzo, 'The Godfather', first edition, first impression, published by Putnam, New York, with red endpapers, original black and off-white cloth lettered in gilt, dust jacket, slight staining and creasing to jacket.

As the jacket is priced '$6.95' and bears the code numbering '6903', it is a first edition jacket. This copy is made more desirable as it is signed by Puzo. This was his first 'commercial' fiction book, following two moderately successful titles – it went on to outsell every other book during the 1970s.

1969

£1,200-1,800 **BLO**

QUICK REFERENCE – HARRY POTTER

J. K. Rowling's Harry Potter titles are among the most widely prized first editions on today's market. The first title in the series, 'Harry Potter and the Philosopher's Stone' has gained an almost legendary status. According to the publisher Bloomsbury, only 500 copies of the first print run of the first edition were produced, most of which were sold to British libraries or schools. This copy is one of those, and shows the level of wear and damage that can be expected from use in a school, as well as bearing the school library's stamp. Had it been in mint condition, the price could have risen to over £10,000. The true first editions have a full line of numbers on the imprint page, leading down to a '1', and do not have a dust jacket. Even the first British paperback issue of this title, also published in 1997, is sought after – copies have fetched over £1,500, as reputedly only 200 were printed.

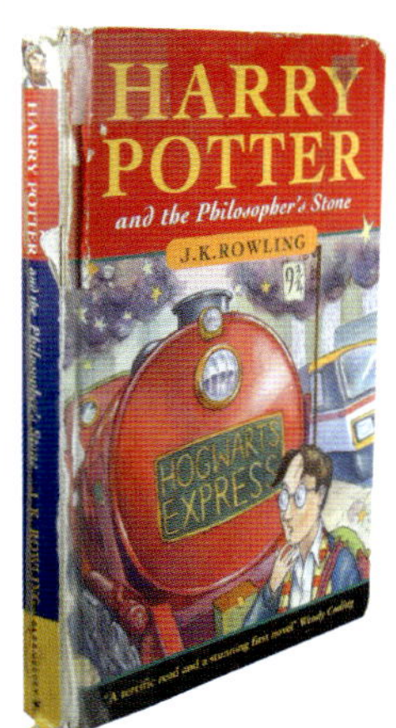

J.K. Rowling, 'Harry Potter and the Philosopher's Stone', first edition, first impression, published by Bloomsbury, London, with unusual slight browning, ex-library copy with stamp and small sticker to verso of title, new endpapers, original pictorial boards, worn at edges and corners, loss and tape repairs around spine.

1997

£1,500-2,000 **BLO**

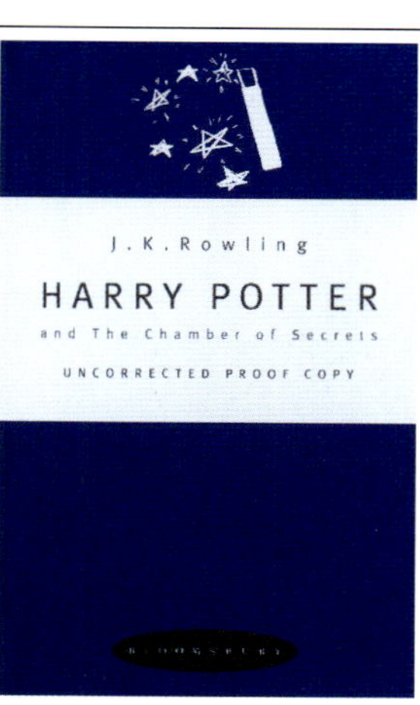

J.K. Rowling, 'Harry Potter and the Chamber of Secrets', uncorrected proof copy, original blue and white printed wrappers.

A 'proof copy' is sent out by a publisher to people including major booksellers, literary editors, and reviewers. The purpose is to promote the book before the final version is printed, and to give the author and publisher the chance to make final corrections or revisions. However, by this stage, the text is usually the closest version to the final product.

1998

£800–1,200 **BLO**

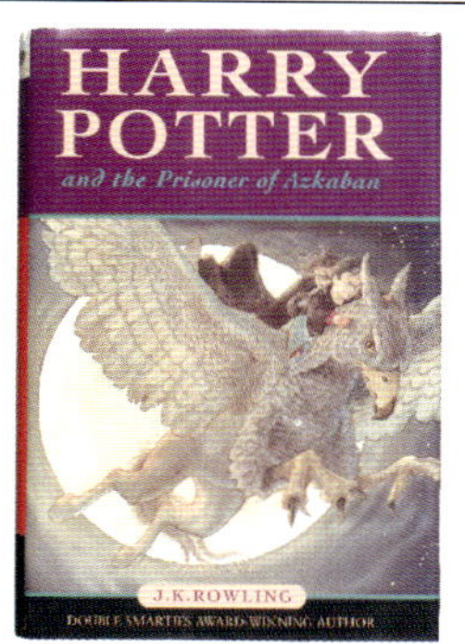

J.K. Rowling, 'Harry Potter and the Prisoner of Azkaban', first edition, first issue, published by Bloomsbury, London, with original pictorial boards and dust jacket.

This can be identified as the first issue due to the copyright wording reading 'Joanne Rowling' rather than 'J.K. Rowling', and the dropped text on p.7.

1999

£500-700 **BLO**

Siegfried Sassoon, 'Memoirs of a Fox-Hunting Man', Faber & Faber, London, first English illustrated edition, published by Faber & Faber, London, no.224 from a limited edition of 300 signed by the author and illustrator, illustrations by William Nicholson, original vellum lettered in black with designs in red and black.

1929

£700-1,000 **L&T**

CHALLENGE

BY

V. SACKVILLE-WEST

Author of "Heritage," "The Heir and Other Stories," "The Dragon in Shallow Waters," etc.

This story of Julian Davenant, of the girl, Eve, and of the woman, Kato, belongs to that character of novels in English of which Joseph Conrad's superb "Nostromo" has for nearly twenty years been the finest example.

In her imaginary (but true) picture of the Greek islands V. Sackville-West might so easily have sacrificed, for the color and exoticism of that setting, the simplicity and inner drama of Julian, Kato and Eve. She has not made this mistake.

The picture is one of youth in the idealism of an early morning, before the white noon has killed its ardor, before the long afternoon of life has lengthened shadows, before the silent cruelty of night has fallen.

"Her small portraits are clear, cold, flashing. Then again she lets herself swing into rhythms of almost poetic passion. Artistry that is amazing . . . I only know that I have been thoroughly taken in by the magic of an astonishing book!"

John Farrar, the Editor of THE BOOKMAN

GEORGE H. DORAN COMPANY : *Publishers* : New York

Victoria (Vita) Sackville-West, 'Challenge', first edition, second American issue, published by Doran, New York, with original titled red cloth, dust jacket with light surface marking, and spine slightly dulled, with some tears.

This book was scheduled to be published by Collins in the UK, but Sackville-West withdrew it after pressure from her mother and her husband, Harold Nicolson. Doran used Collins' sheets, insert a new title page, to produce 2,000 copies. Supposedly written with Vita's female lover Violet Trefusis, the lead character is called Julian, which was the name used by Vita when she dressed as a man while travelling with Trefusis. Due to this connection, Vita's mother banned the British version, which was not published until 1974, 12 years after Vita's death.

1923

£350-450 **BLO**

Mickey Spillane, 'I, the Jury', first edition, published by E. P. Dutton & Co., New York, with original black cloth and slightly creased and rubbed dust jacket, with some tape residue.

1947

£800-1,200 **BLNY**

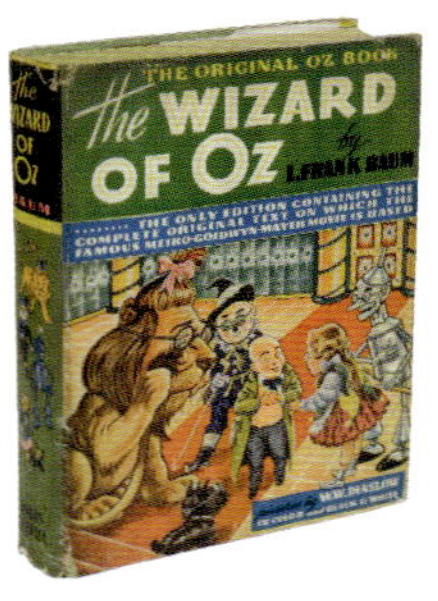

L. Frank Baum, 'The New Wizard of Oz', first edition with pictorial endpapers of stills from the 1939 MGM film, published by Bobbs Merrill, illustrated by W. W. Denslow, including eight coloured plates, pictorial endpapers, spine lightly faded, bookplate on front pastedown, damp stained dust jacket, price clipped.

From the Fred. M. Meyer collection.

£300-500 **BLNY**

A CLOSER LOOK AT AN OZMA OF OZ FIRST EDITION

The dust jacket, missing on this copy, is extremely rare and can double the value.

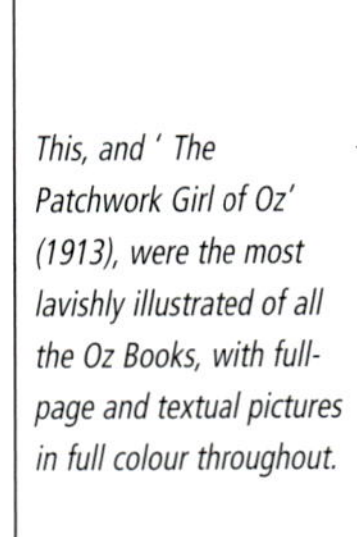

This, and ' The Patchwork Girl of Oz' (1913), were the most lavishly illustrated of all the Oz Books, with full-page and textual pictures in full colour throughout.

The 'O' in the word 'Ozma' on the fifth line of the Author's Note on p.11 is present, indicating this is an early example of the first issue, as it 'fell out' during the print run.

Pages 135-6 and 221-2 are integral to the rest of the book – during the print run, these pages smudged in many copies, so were taken out and replaced.

L. Frank Baum, 'Ozma of Oz', first edition, published by Reilly & Britton Co. Chicago, illustrated by John R. Neil, with colour stamped tan cloth, pictorial endpapers, housed in a lettered clamshell case, spine lightly faded with tips gently rubbed.

1907

£600-900 **BLNY**

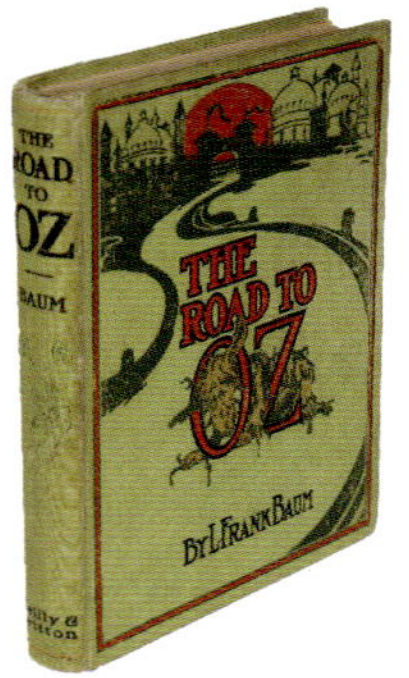

L. Frank Baum, 'The Road to Oz', first edition, published by Reilly & Britton Co., illustrated by John R. Neill, printed on paper of several different colours, colour stamped green cloth with some fading and rubbing, owner's signatures on ownership leaf and half-title.

This copy can be identified as a first edition as it has the publisher' s name at the foot of the spine in upper and lowercase, ' Toto on' in line four of p.34 and the numeral on p.121 in perfect type and other features. From the Fred M. Meyer collection.

1909

£400-600 **BLNY**

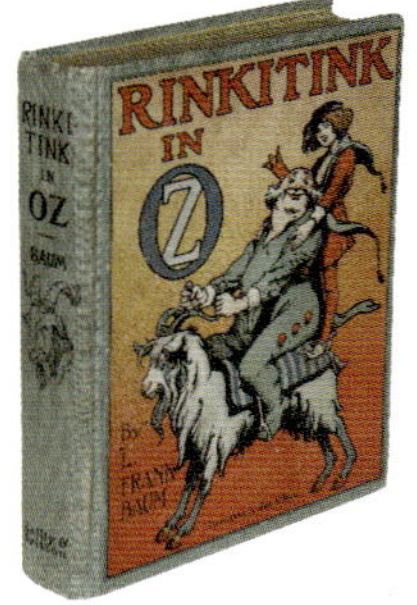

L. Frank Baum, 'Rinkitink in Oz', first edition, published by Reilly & Britton Co., Chicago, illustrated by John R. Neill, 12 colour plates tipped in, stamped pictorial light blue cloth and pictorial endpapers, covers rubbed and soiled, name and address rubberstamped on ownership page.

1916

£400-600 **BLNY**

Dorothy Craigie, (Graham Greene), 'The Little Train', first edition, published by Eyre & Spottiswood, London, with cloth boards, dust jacket with losses and rubbing, and very clean interior.

A rare copy of Graham Greene' s first book for children, written anonymously while working as a director for the publisher Eyre & Spottiswoode.

1946

£500-700 **L&T**

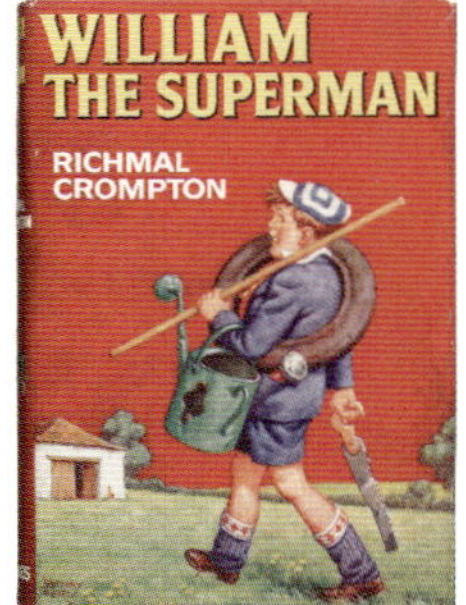

Richmal Crompton, 'William the Superman', first edition, original boards, dust jacket in very good to excellent condition.

1968

£200-300 **BLO**

Captain W.E. Johns, 'Sergeant Bigglesworth C.I.D.', first edition paperback, published by Hodder & Stoughton.

1954

£4-6 ZDB

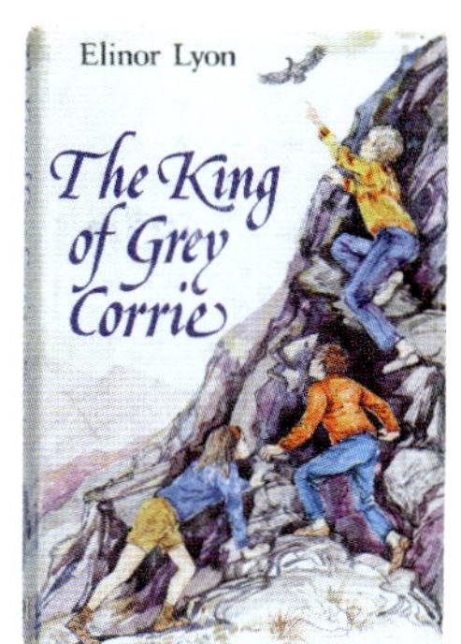

Elinor Lyon, 'The King of Grey Corrie', first edition, published by the Brockhampton Press, signed by the author on the title page, rubbed and creased dust jacket.

1975

£150-250 BLO

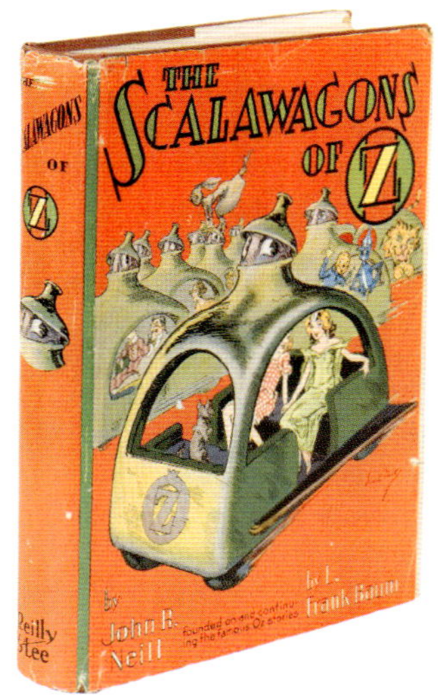

John R. Neill, 'The Scalawagons of Oz', first edition, published by Reilly & Lee Co., Chicago, illustrated by the author, red cloth, pictorial label and endpapers, jacket slightly faded with a few small nicks.

1941

£300-500 BLNY

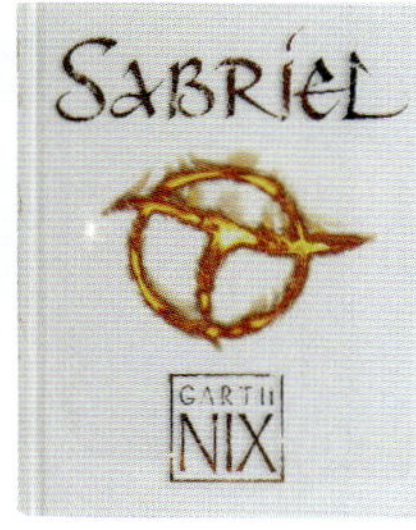

Garth Nix, 'Sabriel', first edition, published by Harper Collins.

1995

£15-25 BIB

Dr. Seuss (Theodor Seuss Geisel), 'The Cat in the Hat Comes Back', first edition, published by Random House, New York, illustrated, with original boards and slightly rubbed dust jacket, interior very clean.

1958

£400-600 L&T

J.R. Pepper, 'A Trip To The Moon' moveable picture book, published by the L.W. Walter Company of Chicago, with moving parts inside operated by pulling down on the sliding tab at the bottom of each page.

This was possibly released in conjunction with, or inspired by, a silent animation film of the same name released in the same year. Written and directed by Vincent Whitman, all copies of the film have been lost meaning this may be the only record of the story. It may have been based on Frenchman Georges Melies' earlier film of 1902, which is widely said to be the first successful science fiction film.

1914

£200-300 PC

QUICK REFERENCE

- The first photography dates from 1839, when Louis Daguerre launched the daguerreotype: the first commercially viable photographic process. However, these early cameras were bulky, expensive and difficult to use. By the 1880s, with the ready availability of prepared 'dry' photographic plates and advances in camera design, the market was opened to many more people. A large number of these wood- and brass- bodied, dry-plate cameras survive and they are often desirable (though less than the earlier wet-plate cameras). Collectors should look for names including Sanderson, Watson and Lancaster.
- The world's most collectable camera is perhaps the Leica, made by Leitz, in Wetzlar, Germany. Developed in 1913, the Leica used 35mm film and was small, light and easy to use. It had a fixed lens until 1930, when interchangeable screw-fit lenses were introduced. This system only changed in 1954, with the bayonet lens mounts of the 'M' series. Many are still usable, or can be repaired due to Leitz's fine quality engineering
- Each Leica has a unique serial number on its top plate, which you can use to identify the model and year of manufacture. Prices range from around £100 for more common models, such as the Model IIIa, to tens of thousands. Variations and unusual engravings add value, as will accessories such as lenses. Scratches, dents, and damaged mechanisms will seriously affect value, with most Leica collectors looking to buy in mint condition.
- With other mass-produced cameras, look for fine quality construction and well known brand names, such as Nikon Voigtlander, Canon and Zeiss Ikon. Condition is important, but usually not as much as for Leicas. Variation in colour and features, such as lenses, adds value.

A Canon S-II camera, no.15326, chrome, engraved 'Seiki-Kogaku, Tokyo', with shutter speeds 20–500, slow speeds dial, with a 'Nippon Kogaku' Nikkor-Q.C. f/3.5 5cm lens no. 570999, body covering replaced.

This can be dated to 1946, as in 1947 the company name changed to 'Canon Camera Company Ltd', replacing the 'Seiki Kogaku' wording.

1946

£300-400 SK

A Franke & Heidecke Wide-Angle Rolleiflex Reflex twin lens reflex camera, no.W2490135, with Zeiss Distagon 1:4 f=55mm lens.

£600-900 ROS

A Franke & Heidecke Tele Rolleiflex twin lens reflex camera, no.S2302261, with Zeiss Sonnar 1:4 f=135mm lens.

£120-180 ROS

A Hasselblad 1000F camera, with a Tessar 1:2.8 f=80mm lens.

Of fine and functional quality, the 1000F, and its predecessor the 1600F, can be hard to find in working order.

1953-57

£250-300 ROS

A Kodak no.5 Cirkut revolving back cycle view 360 degree panoramic roll film camera, no.46969, patented by William Folmer.

c1915-1917

£200-300 ROS

A Kodak 3A Panoram panoramic roll film camera.

c1926-1928

£60-80 **ROS**

A Leica IIIC camera, no.502557, chrome, with Leitz f3.5 Elmar lens and cap, with leather case, some faults.

1950

£150-250 **TOV**

A Leica MI camera, no.967287, chrome, with Leitz 50mm Elmar lens, and leather case.

1959

£200-300 **TOV**

A CLOSER LOOK AT A LEICA CAMERA

Leica cameras are hotly sought after by many collectors across the world. Those produced in strictly limited numbers are among the most desirable and valuable.

As well as model and age, condition is key – those in truly mint condition will always fetch more than used examples, particularly when they have their paperwork and box, as here.

This example is from a limited edition of 150 cameras, but only 30 had this lens type, commemorating the 150th anniversary of the Wetzlar Optisches Institut.

This is no ordinary M6 with a commemorative engraving – each one is platinum plated, covered with karung leather, and has a unique, special serial number relating to a year from 1849-1999.

A Leica M6 platinum 150th anniversary camera, no. 2490145, commemorative no.1994, the top-plate engraved '150 Jahre Optik 1849–1999 Summilux-M f/1.4 35 ASPH', with diced green-grey leather body covering, with a commemorative Leitz Summilux-M f/1.4 35mm lens, in silk-lined polished walnut root case, with warranty, manual, commemorative booklet, receipt, hood, caps, and strap.

1999

£3,500-5,000 **SK**

A Leica M4 50th anniversary camera, no.1412936, black, the front with commemorative '50 Jahre' laurel leaf motif, the back numbered '136-E', complete with manual, registration certificate and card box.

According to Leitz records, 1,730 units of this model were made, 350 each with the letters L, E, I and C, and 330 with the letter A.

1974

£2,200-2,800 **SK**

A rare Japanese chrome Muley Leica-type camera, no.102, the base plate engraved 'Made in Occupied Japan', leather-covered body, speed-housing engraved in script 'Muley' and in capitals 'G.T.S.'

A rare Japanese copy of a Lecia Standard by an unknown (and presumably small) Japanese workshop.

c1946-52

£2,000-3,000 **SK**

A Nikon F2, with chrome body, and Nikkor 50mm F.1.4 lens.

c1971

£100-150 **ROS**

A Zeiss Ikon Kolibri 523/18 compact camera, with rimset Compur shutter, and Tessar f=3.5 lens.

1930-35

£50-80 **ROS**

A CLOSER LOOK AT A NIKON CAMERA

Like Leica, Nikon has a large following of collectors around the world, which means demand is high for rare models.

This first civilian Nikon camera is the 'holy grail' for many collectors, and only around 700 examples are thought to have been produced.

Its serial number, 609117, dates from early on in the production, dating from before some 200 additional Nikon Is were converted into Nikon Ms by changing the focal plane, top and base plates and adding a sprocket wheel.

Examples in such excellent condition are rare and this affects value.

A Nikon I camera, no.609117, chrome with leather-covered body, with back numbered internally '609117', base-plate engraved 'Made in Occupied Japan', with a Nippon Kogaku W-Nikkor C f/3.5 3.5cm lens no.9101079.

1948

£6,000-9,000 **SK**

A rare black Nikon S 'Life Magazine' camera, no.6101424, black with leather-covered body, the top plate engraved 'Nippon Kogaku, Tokyo', enlarged wind and rewind knobs for field use, chrome lens and tripod mounts and a Nippon Kogaku Nikkor-H.C. f/2 5cm lens no.625463.

This Nikon S was produced for 'Life' magazine photographers and is extremely rare. Only 20 examples were commissioned by the magazine after they were impressed by photographs of the Korean war taken by war photographers such as David Douglas Duncan and Carl Mydams – this is one of only two surviving cameras known.

£15,000-20,000 **SK**

A Zeiss Ikon, Contarex Special camera, no meter, interchangeable reflex or prism view hood, with a Planar 1:2 f=50mm lens.

c1966

£300-400 **ROS**

A Zeiss Ikon Contarex Super Second 35mm camera, chrome, with a Zeiss 1:4 f=35mm lens.

c1970

£180-220 **ROS**

A late 19thC Sanderson mahogany and brass quarter plate field folding camera, with black leather bellows, spare plates, tripod, and other accessories.

£280-320 **FLD**

A Paillard Bolex H8 Reflex cine camera, the C mount fitted with 1:1.3 f=12.5mm, 1:1.4 f=36mm and Cine-Tele-Xenar 1:2.8/75 lenses in fitted leather maker's case, with accessories and instruction leaflets.

£60-80 **ROS**

A CLOSER LOOK AT A ZEISS CAMERA

Introduced in 1935, many consider this to be one of the most technically impressive cameras ever built, but it was heavy and tricky to use.

It was the first camera to have a built-in light meter, and was extremely expensive in its day, costing £233 including a Sonnar lens in 1939.

This camera is in excellent, working condition – if it is worn through use, or the shutter or light meter do not work, the value will be reduced by over a half as it is complex to repair.

This example has its original Sonnar lens plus a Tessar lens, manual, case, and a collection of accessories, many of which can be hard to find today and add value.

A Zeiss Contaflex twin lens reflex camera, no.A46226, chrome with leather-covered body, with a Zeiss f/2.8 8cm viewing lens no.1724131 and a Zeiss Tessar f/2.8 5cm taking lens no.1514331, in maker's case, together with a Zeiss Sonnar f/2 8.5cm taking lens no.2401465 in leather pouch and maker's box, manual, leather hood and accessories.

£1,200-1,800 **SK**

A Houghton-Butcher 'Ensign Special' Reflex Tropical model camera with brass-bound teak body.

'Tropical' cameras were made using teak and the fabric bellows were treated so they repelled insects when used in tropical climes.

£200-300 **ROS**

A Paillard Bolex H-16 cine camera, the C mount fitted with a Yvar 1:2.8 f=75mm, a Trioplan 1:2.8 Foc 3in, and a Ross 1in F 1.9 cine lens.

£50-70 **ROS**

A 1960s-70s Kodak shop display over-sized model of an Instamatic camera, with attached 'flash bulb' fitting.

£60-80 **ROS**

A carved walking cane, by 'Schtockschnitzler' Simmons, with bird whistle grip.

29in (73.5cm) high

£600-900 **POOK**

A carved cane, by 'Schtockschnitzler' Simmons, with bird grip.

£500-800 **POOK**

A carved cane with bird grip, by 'Schtockschnitzler' Simmons.

£800-1,200 **POOK**

A Bally carver cane, with painted bird grip.

33in (84cm) high

£2,500-3,500 **POOK**

QUICK REFERENCE – FOLK ART CANES

'Folk Art' is the term given to unique works by untrained or self-trained, usually country-based, artisans. This varied area has become immensely popular with collectors over the past few years, after being largely ignored for decades. Although folk art is now collected all over the world, the US market is the strongest and generally sees the highest prices. Prices paid for folk art walking canes have now even exceeded those paid for gadget canes containing functional items. Although the level of detail, condition, subject and date count, the primary consideration is the artist. 'Schtockschnitzler' Simmons was an itinerant German, whose nickname means 'cane carver'. He paid for his bed and board around Pennsylvania from c1895-1910 by selling his carvings, which also included decorative trees with seated birds. This rare and desirable example (below) retains its original paint, which is also unusually bright and unworn; for a functional item this is very rare. Birds are his hallmark design and are highly sought after, and this is a particularly desirable 'bird in hand' design.

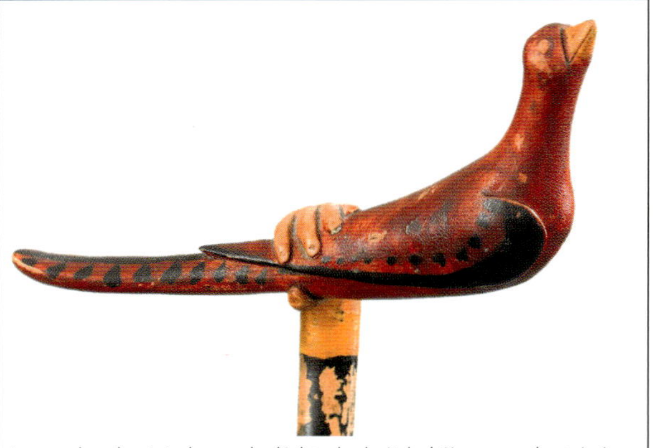

A carved and painted cane, by 'Schtockschnitzler' Simmons, the grip in the form of a hand clasping a bird.

38.25in (97cm) high

£4,000-6,000 **POOK**

A carved and painted cane, by 'Schtockschnitzler' Simmons, the grip in the form of a hand supporting a bird on a basket.

38.25in (97cm) high

£6,000-9,000 **POOK**

A Bally carver cane, the handle carved as a bird and leaves.

33in (84cm) high

£400-600 **POOK**

A folk art carved cane, with grip in the form of a dog with a turtle in its mouth, the stock carved with various animal heads, and silver band and tip.

c1900 *33.25in (84.5cm) high*

£300-400 **POOK**

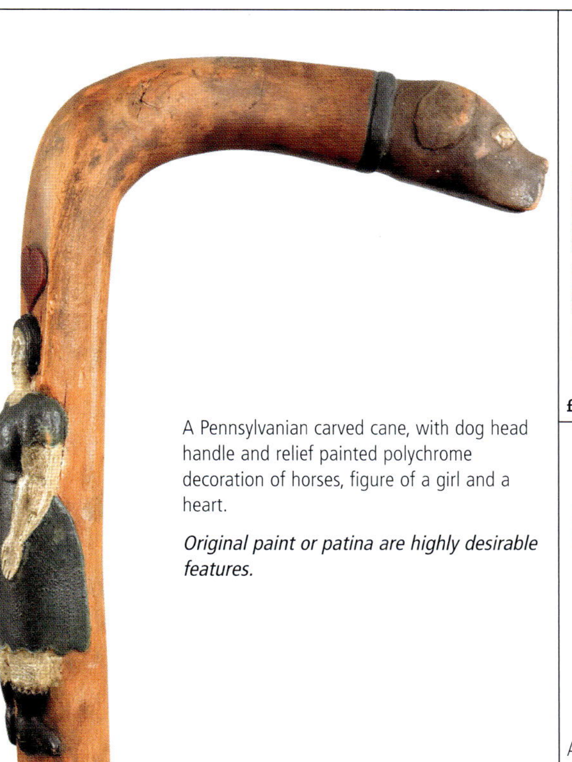

A Pennsylvanian carved cane, with dog head handle and relief painted polychrome decoration of horses, figure of a girl and a heart.

Original paint or patina are highly desirable features.

40in (101.5cm) high

£600-900 **POOK**

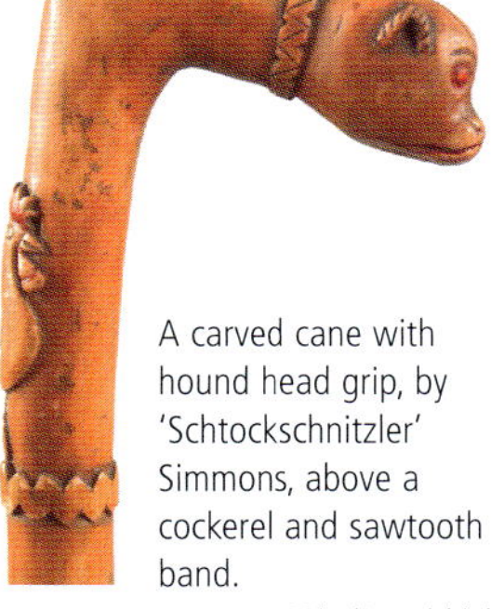

A carved cane with hound head grip, by 'Schtockschnitzler' Simmons, above a cockerel and sawtooth band.

33in (84cm) high

£600-900 **POOK**

A folk art carved cane, the handle carved as a seated dog on its haunches, wearing a long hat.

37in (94cm) high

£250-350 **POOK**

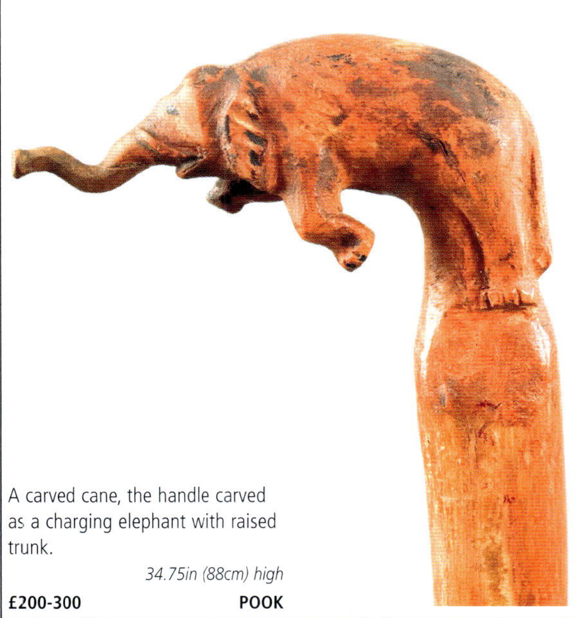

A carved cane, the handle carved as a charging elephant with raised trunk.

34.75in (88cm) high

£200-300 **POOK**

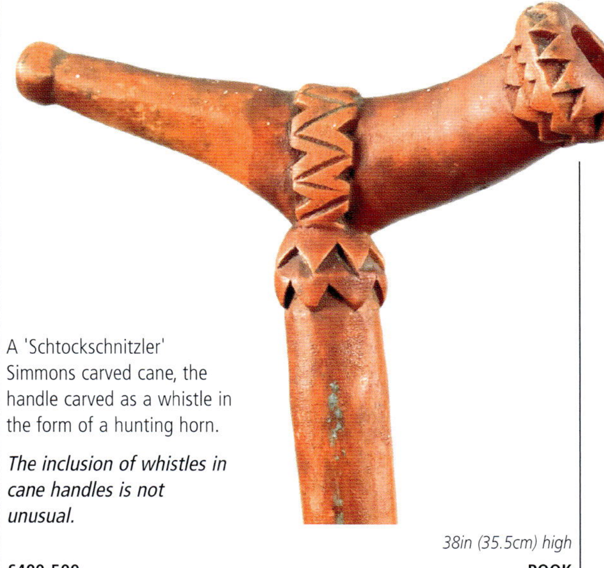

A 'Schtockschnitzler' Simmons carved cane, the handle carved as a whistle in the form of a hunting horn.

The inclusion of whistles in cane handles is not unusual.

38in (35.5cm) high

£400-500 **POOK**

QUICK REFERENCE

- The Beswick Pottery was founded in Loughton, Staffordshire in 1894. The animal figurines for which Beswick is now best known began to appear as early as 1900. By 1930, they had become a major part of production. The company was sold to Royal Doulton in 1969, but the Beswick name was in use until 1989, when the production of Beswick and Doulton animal figurines was merged under the Royal Doulton name. The Beswick name was used again from 1999 until the factory closed in 2002. Prices rose after the closure and remain strong.
- Collectors tend to focus on one type of animal, with cattle currently one of the most popular. Other popular figurines include the series of Beatrix Potter characters launched in 1946 and the subsequent range of Disney figurines.
- The work of Arthur Gredington, who joined in 1939, is desirable. Other notable modellers include Colin Melbourne, Graham Tongue, Albert Hallam and Alan Maslankowski.
- Look for variation in colour, glaze, form (i.e. differently positioned legs), as these will affect value. 'Roan' and 'Rocking horse grey' are typically valuable. Similarly, matt glazes can be more valuable than glossy. Early pieces are generally the most desirable, but can be hard to identify as the Beswick backstamp and shape numbers were only used from 1934. Limited editions from as late as 1990 can be valuable if the edition was small. Condition is important. Examine protruding horns, thin legs and tails for breakages.

A Beswick 'Green Woodpecker' bird figure, model 1218, designed by Arthur Gredington, with gloss finish, the base with impressed marks and applied paper label.

The original version, produced from 1961-67, had high relief flowers applied to the base, and can be worth up to twice the value of this example.

1967-89 *8.75in (22cm) high*

£150-200 **WW**

A Beswick 'Songthrush' bird figure, model 2308, designed by Albert Hallam, with gloss finish, the base with impressed mark.

1970-89 *5.75in (14.5cm) high*

£100-150 **WW**

A Beswick 'Leghorn Cockerel' figurine, model 1892, designed by Arthur Gredington, the base with impressed mark.

1963-83 *9.75in (25cm) high*

£150-200 **LOC**

A Beswick 'Grouse (pair)' figure, model 2063, designed by Albert Hallam, impressed factory marks.

1966-75 *6in (15cm) high*

£350-450 **WW**

A Beswick 'Fan-tailed Dove' figure, model 1614, designed by Arthur Gredington, the base with impressed and printed mark.

1959-69 *6in (15.5cm) high*

£180-220 **WW**

A set of three Beswick 'Mallard' graduated wall plaques, model 596, designed by Mr Watkin, with gloss finish, the backs with impressed and printed marks.

1938-73 Largest 11.75in (30cm) wide

£100-150 WW

A Beswick 'Bird' figurine, model 1415, designed by Colin Melbourne, from the CM series, the base with factory marks.

1956-1962 5.25in (13.5cm) high

£150-200 W&W

A rare Beswick 'Huntsman Standing' figurine, model 1501, designed by Arthur Gredington, with a gloss glaze, on a Skewbald horse and wearing a red jacket.

The horse in this model is an exceptionally rare colour, and is not listed in any standard reference books on Beswick. Nevertheless, this very high price shows what can happen when a small number of collectors in a specialist market compete to own a rare piece.

8.25in (21cm) high

£5,000-6,000 TEN

A rare Beswick 'Huntsman Standing' figurine, model 1501, designed by Arthur Gredington, with a gloss glaze, sitting on a Palomino horse and wearing a red jacket.

1965-71 8.25in (21cm) high

£4,000-5,000 TEN

A Beswick 'Huntswoman' figurine, model 982, designed by Arthur Gredington, with gloss finish and factory marks to base.

1942-67 10.25in (26cm) high

£200-250 LOC

A Beswick 'Huntsman on Rearing Horse', model 868, designed by Arthur Gredington, with a dark chestnut horse, red jacket and factory marks to base.

1940-52 9.5in (24cm) high

£180-220 LOC

A Beswick 'King Charles Spaniel Josephine of Blagreaves' figurine, model 2107B, designed by Arthur Gredington, with gloss finish.

1967-94 *7.5in (19cm) long*

£20-30 **SAS**

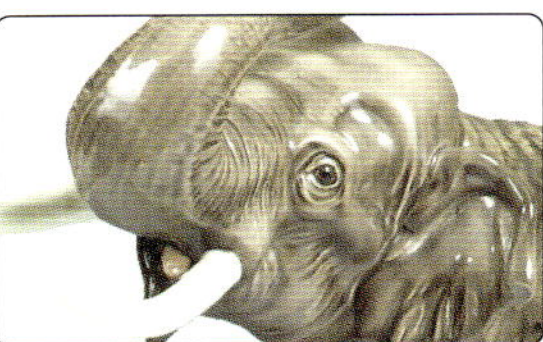

A Beswick 'Elephant And Tiger' figurine, model 1720, designed by Arthur Gredington, with a gloss finish, and circular printed mark.

1960-75 *11.75in (30cm) high*

£200-300 **SWO**

A CLOSER LOOK AT A BEATRIX POTTER CHARACTER FIGURINE

This is the rare, first model of Duchess, the second has her holding a pie rather than flowers and was produced from 1979-82.

When released, she was not popular with collectors or the buying public, so very few examples were sold at the time, making her hard to find today.

The value of this model varies widely depending on the location and demand at the time of sale – prices have ranged from £500 to over £2,000 during the past five to seven years.

The base has an oval shaped printed 'Beswick England' mark – those with circular marks are even rarer and were the earliest of this model ever produced.

A Beswick Beatrix Potter 'Duchess' figurine, model 1355, designed by Graham Orwell, with gloss finish and printed gold oval factory mark.

1955-67 *3.75in (9.5cm) high*

£1,000-1,500 **FLD**

A Beswick Beatrix Potter 'Benjamin Bunny' figurine, model 1105/3, third version with brown shoes, and ears and shoes tucked in, the base with printed factory mark.

Earlier models had arms extended with shoes held out and protruding ears, but as these parts were often broken the design was changed on later models.

c1980-2000 *4in (10cm) high*

£20-30 **SAS**

A Beswick Beatrix Potter 'Anna Maria' figurine, model 1851, designed by Albert Hallam, the base with printed brown five line mark.

1974-83

£50-70 **PC**

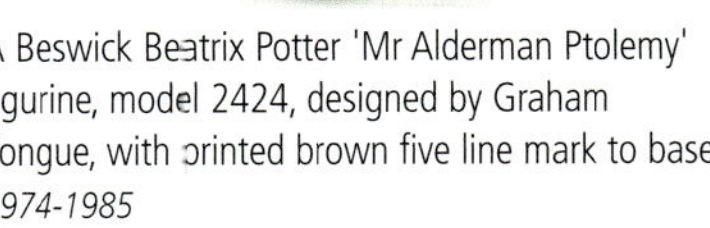

A Beswick Beatrix Potter 'Mr Alderman Ptolemy' figurine, model 2424, designed by Graham Tongue, with printed brown five line mark to base.

1974-1985

£25-35 **PC**

QUICK REFERENCE – BRIGLIN POTTERY

The Briglin Pottery was founded in central London in 1948 by Brigitte Appleby and Eileen Lewenstein. Each piece was potted and decorated by hand, with sgraffito and wax-resist techniques being used, often with a manganese oxide glaze. Colours tend towards earthy browns, beiges and creams, sometimes with a light blue, or greeny-blue. Patterns focus on the natural world, with stylisation being common and desirable to collectors. A white clay gave way to a more common red clay in the late 1950s. Pieces are generally marked with a 'BRIGLIN' impressed mark. Despite being highly successful in the 1960s and 70s, the pottery closed in 1990.

A 1970s Briglin cylinder vase, with wax-resist design of a seeding flower in cream and blue glazes, the base impressed 'BRIGLIN'.

7.25in (18.5cm) high

£50-70 **GC**

A 1970s Briglin vase, with wax-resist and manganese oxide black flowers with incised detail, the base impressed 'BRIGLIN'.

7.75in (19.5cm) high

£30-40 **GC**

A Briglin waisted cylindrical vase with wax-resist leaf design, the base with impressed 'BRIGLIN' mark.

9.75in (24.5cm) high

£60-80 **GC**

A Briglin baluster vase, with design of green leaves on a cream ground, the base impressed 'BRIGLIN'.

7.75in (19.5cm) high

£40-60 **GC**

A very large Briglin bowl, with wax-resist design of seeding country flowers, and covered with a transparent glaze, the base impressed 'BRIGLIN'.

12.75in (32cm) diam

£200-250 **GC**

A very large Briglin bowl, with wax-resist design of country flowers with a brushed brown glaze, and covered with a transparent glaze, the base inscribed 'BRIGLIN POTTERY AP'.

The 'AP' may stand for Alan Pett, a thrower at the London pottery. These bowls must have been among the largest pieces made at the pottery.

12.75in (32cm) diam

£200-250 **GC**

QUICK REFERENCE

- The Carlton Works were established in Stoke-on-Trent in 1890 by Wiltshaw & Robinson. Pieces were produced under the name 'Carlton Ware' from 1894 and this became the company's name in 1958, although most production before this is generally known as Carlton Ware.
- In the 1920s and 1930s, Carlton Ware became known for its rich Art-Deco-styled lustre pieces, created in response to Wedgwood's more expensive Fairyland Lustre range.
- The factory also introduced a completely different style of ceramic in the 1930s, which became a mainstay of Carlton Ware for nearly two decades. This pastel-coloured, moulded range used flowers, leaves and fruit either as decorative motifs or as the main shape of the piece. Certain motifs, such as 'Cherries', and colours are rare, as are some combinations. For example, 'Buttercup' is easy to find in yellow, but relatively rare in pink and consequently more desirable. As a large number of pieces were produced, condition is very important – inspect lids, rims and bases as these are often damaged. Look for boxed gift sets, and even empty boxes, as these add value.
- Carlton Ware went bankrupt in 1989, but the name and some moulds were bought by Francis Joseph in 1997, who continues to sell ceramics under the brand. There are Carlton Ware fakes on the market, so you should examine pieces closely and ensure the back stamp is appropriate for the item and period of manufacture.

A Carlton Ware embossed yellow and pink 'Waterlily' mug, the base impressed '1787'.

4.25in (11cm) high

£60-80 BEV

A Carlton Ware embossed yellow and green 'Waterlily' mug, the base with printed factory mark and impressed '1783'.

4.25in (11cm) high

£60-80 BEV

A Carlton Ware embossed pink 'Buttercup' mug, the base with printed marks and impressed '1585'.

This is a more desirable colour.

4.25in (11cm) high

£80-100 BEV

A Carlton Ware embossed yellow cabbage leaf milk jug, with printed factory mark and impressed '1524'.

4.25in (11cm) high

£80-120 BAD

A 1930s Carlton Ware embossed green and yellow 'Lily' teapot, the base with printed factory mark and impressed '1786'.

5.25in (13.5cm) high

£80-120 BAD

A 1930s Carlton Ware large embossed yellow 'Apple Blossom' jug, the base with printed factory mark and impressed '1700/1'.

This the largest of three sizes.

14.5in (37cm) high

£200-300 **BAD**

A CLOSER LOOK AT A CARLTON WARE BISCUIT BARREL

This is one of the rarest and most desirable items from the fruit and floral embossed ranges.

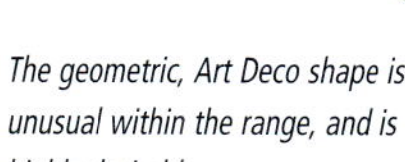

The geometric, Art Deco shape is unusual within the range, and is highly desirable.

This shape was only used for this biscuit jar and a small jam pot, and in Raspberry and Blackberry only.

Always check the corners, handles and lid for damage – note how the foot and knob on the lid are modelled as a raspberries.

A 1930s Carlton Ware Art Deco pink fruit embossed Raspberry biscuit jar, the base with factory marks and impressed '1565'.

5.5in (14cm) high

£200-250 **BEV**

A Carlton Ware Salad Ware embossed pink 'Buttercup' dish, the base with printed mark and impressed '1395'.

4.5in (11.5cm) long

£35-45 **BAD**

A Carlton Ware Salad Ware yellow embossed 'Buttercup' crescent dish, the base with printed factory mark and impressed '1529/3'.

7.5in (19cm) long

£35-45 **BAD**

A Carlton Ware embossed green 'Foxglove' handled basket, with printed and impressed marks to base.

10.25in (26cm) long

£80-120 **BEV**

A Carlton Ware yellow embossed 'Lily' Salad Ware toast rack, the base with printed marks and impressed '1861'.

4in (10cm) long

£80-120 **BEV**

A 1930s Carlton Ware 'Handcraft' plate, hand painted with a longboat, the back with printed and painted marks.

Introduced in 1928 and produced until the late 1930s, this entirely hand painted range is usually found with a matte finish. Colours tend to be bright, and the more Art Deco the pattern is, the more valuable it is likely to be.

10.5in (27cm) diam

£350-450 **WW**

A 1930s Carlton Ware 'Hollyhocks' bowl, pattern no.3973, printed and painted in colours and gilt on a green lustre ground, printed and painted marks.

10.75in (27cm) wide

£100-150 **WW**

A 1930s Carlton Ware 'Secretary Bird' twin-handled oval dish, pattern 4017, decorated on an orange lustre ground with gilded highlights.

The Japanese-inspired Secretary Bird pattern is scarce and sought after.

12in (30.5cm) wide

£200-300 **GHOU**

A 1930s Carlton Ware hand painted novelty 'Humpty Dumpty' toby jug.

These can also be found with musical mechanisms, but these are even rarer and can fetch up to £500-800.

7.5in (19cm) high

£300-500 **BAD**

A scarce 1930s Carlton Ware hand painted mushroom-shaped cruet set, with printed marks to base, lacking spoon.

Always examine all parts carefully as cracks or chips are common.

5in (12.5cm) diam

£150-200 **BEV**

A 1970s Carlton Ware orange owl money box, the base printed 'Carltonware made in England' and with trademark.

5in (12.5cm) high

£30-40 **CANS**

A 1970s Carlton Ware yellow-lime green lidded butter dish, with black printed mark to base.

5.75in (14.5cm) long

£18-22 **RET**

QUICK REFERENCE

- Clarice Cliff is one of the most desirable names in Art Deco ceramics. Prices can start as low as £50, but can rise into many thousands for rare and sought-after designs. Born in 1899 in Tunstall in the heart of the Staffordshire Potteries, Cliff began her career as an apprentice decorator at Linguard Webster & Co. in 1912, before joining A.J. Wilkinson in 1916.
- Her talents became obvious at Wilkinson, and the company's owner, Colley Shorter, gave Cliff her own studio in 1920 at the recently acquired Newport Pottery. There, she hand-painted defective blank wares with striking geometric or stylised floral patterns in bright colours, which covered the flaws. These developed into the now legendary 'Bizarre' series, launched in 1928.
- Neither 'Bizarre' (used until 1935) nor 'Fantasque' (used 1928-34) are range names, but are instead general titles, with patterns usually having their own names. Cliff trained a team of women, known as the 'Bizarre Girls' to produce these designs, which were applied to modern shapes.
- When evaluating desirability and value, consider the shape and size of the piece, the pattern and the colours used. Some patterns, and colourways within these patterns, are rarer than others. Orange tends to be more commonly found, while blue and purple are often rarer. Muted colours and more traditional floral designs are less sought after.
- In general, Cliff's brightly coloured, highly stylised Art Deco designs from 1928-c1934 are the most sought-after. If the shape is modern and Art Deco too, so much the better. Always look at the mark, and ensure that it is under the glaze. Beware as fakes do exist – experience of handling authentic pieces will help you to spot them.

A Clarice Cliff Bizarre 'Autumn Crocus' pattern Stamford shape milk jug and sugar bowl, with printed marks to base.

2.75in (7cm) high

£280-320 **WW**

A Clarice Cliff Bizarre 'Autumn Crocus' pattern Perth shape jug, printed mark to base and some wear to glaze.

5in (13cm) high

£80-120 **WW**

A Clarice Cliff Bizarre 'Blue Crocus' pattern ribbed beer tankard, with printed mark to base, minor scuffs to banding.

c1935 *6.25in (16cm) high*

£200-300 **FLD**

A pair of Clarice Cliff Bizarre 'Autumn Crocus' pattern square-section candlesticks, with 'Bizarre' and 'CROCUS' printed marks.

Candlesticks are comparatively scarce, and the corners are often chipped through use.

c1930 *7.75in (20cm) high*

£350-450 **FLD**

A Clarice Cliff Bizarre 'Autumn Crocus' pattern Isis shape vase, with large script printed mark.

c1929 *9.75in (25cm) high*

£750-950 **FLD**

A Clarice Cliff Fantasque Bizarre 'Pastel Melon' pattern Athens shape jug, with combined printed 'FANTASQUE' and 'Bizarre' mark.

c1930 *7in (18cm) high*

£350-450 **FLD**

A Clarice Cliff Fantasque 'Melon' pattern vase, shape 376.

7in (18cm) high

£800-1,200 **GHOU**

A CLOSER LOOK AT A CLARICE CLIFF MELON JUG

Melon was produced from 1930-32 in orange, green, red and pastel colourways – orange is the most common with pastel being rarer.

The pattern of stylised fruit may have been inspired by Cubist paintings, as well as the geometric Art Deco style of the time.

The Lotus jug (the handle is not seen here) is a very popular form and displays the pattern well. It tends to be hard to find.

Note how the shapes are outlined in yellow rather than black to give more emphasis to the coloured forms rather than the outlines.

A Clarice Cliff 'Pastel Melon' single-handled Lotus jug, with combined printed 'FANTASQUE' and 'Bizarre' mark, with a few minor paint scuffs.

c1931 *11.5in (29cm) high*

£800-1,200 **FLD**

A Clarice Cliff Fantasque 'Melon' pattern circular plate, with printed 'Fantasque' mark, few minor scuffs.

c1930 *10in (25.5cm) diam*

£120-180 **FLD**

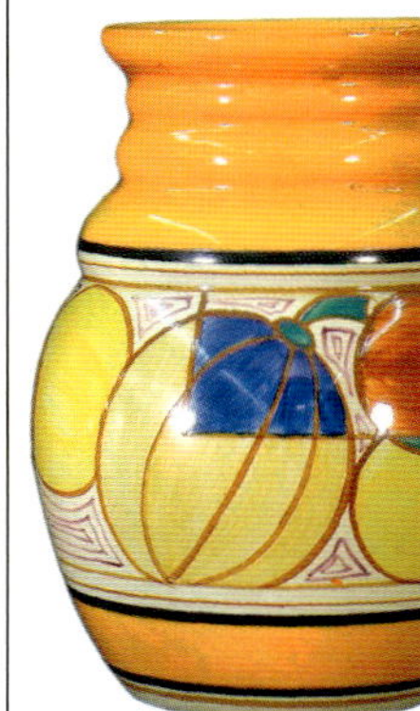

A Clarice Cliff Fantasque 'Melon' pattern vase, shape no.358.

8in (20cm) high

£650-850 **GHOU**

A Clarice Cliff 'Green Melon' pattern octagonal plate, with printed 'Fantasque' mark and 'Lawleys' gold back stamp, with broken body and chips to rim.

Lawleys were a specialist retailer of ceramics who dealt with many leading ceramics factories.

c1930 *8in (20.5cm) high*

£60-90 **FLD**

A Clarice Cliff Bizarre 'Rhodanthe' pattern Tyrol shape bowl, with printed 'Bizarre' mark, and a few minor scuffs to decoration.

c1934 *4in (10cm) wide*

£480-520 **FLD**

QUICK REFERENCE – RHODANTHE PATTERN

Rhodanthe was introduced in 1934 and shows stylised trees with flower-like foliage and sinuous trunks and branches. It became very popular and took over from Crocus as Cliff's best-selling pattern. As this design was still produced after World War II, it is comparatively common today. It shows a move away from the typical Bizarre style – the pattern is not banded, geometric or heavily outlined. Also, the hand-painted colours were blended into each other in a process known as 'etching'. The most common colourway is shown here, with dominant orange tones. Variations in colour have different names – the pink Viscaria and the blue Aurea. Both are less common, Viscaria particularly so.

A Clarice Cliff Bizarre 'Rhodanthe' pattern Conical sugar sifter, with printed 'Bizarre' mark, restored chips.

c1934 *4in (10cm) wide*

£480-520 **FLD**

A Clarice Cliff Bizarre 'Aurea' Mei Ping vase, shape 14, with printed 'Bizarre' mark.

c1936 *8.75in (22.5cm) high*

£450-550 **FLD**

A Clarice Cliff Bizarre 'Rhodanthe' vase, shape 212, with Delecia glazed interior, and plain 'Claire Cliff' script printed mark.

c1935-6 *5.5in (14cm) high*

£350-450 **FLD**

A large Clarice Cliff Bizarre 'Aurea' pattern conical footed bowl, shape 383, with Delecia streaked glazed exterior, and painted green 'Clarice Cliff' and 'Bizarre' mark, chip to foot and some scratching.

9in (23cm) wide

£180-220 **FLD**

A Clarice Cliff Bizarre 'Viscaria' pattern Leda plate, with printed mark to underside.

9in (23cm) wide

£100-150 **GORL**

A Clarice Cliff Fantasque Bizarre 'Pastel Autumn' pattern vase, shape 362, painted with a stylized tree and cottage landscape, with printed marks and light crazing to the glaze.

c1932 *8.25in (21cm) high*

£1,200-1,500 **FLD**

A CLOSER LOOK AT AN ORANGE AUTUMN WALL PLAQUE

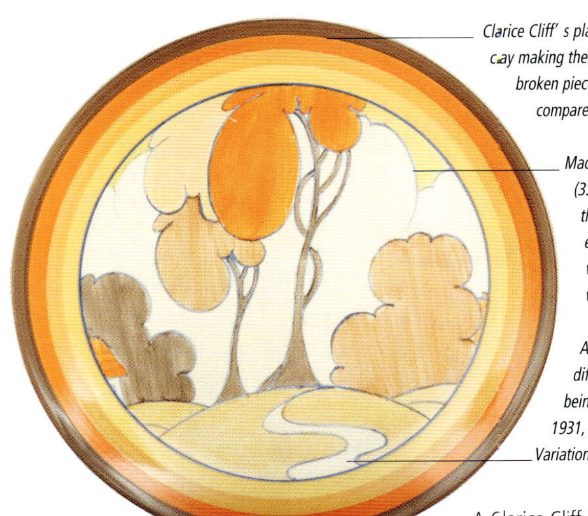

Clarice Cliff' s plaques were pressed from solid clay making them one of the most easily broken pieces – few have survived compared to the number made.

Made in 10.5in (25.5cm), 13in (33cm) and 18in (46cm) sizes, they display the pattern extremely well and are popular with collectors. The footrim was drilled for hanging.

Autumn was produced in many different colourways, with Red being the earliest and first made in 1931, and Pastel being scarcer. Variations abound.

A Clarice Cliff Bizarre 'Orange Autumn' large wall plaque, with printed 'Bizarre' mark.

c1932 *13in (33cm) diam*

£1,800-2,200 **FLD**

A Clarice Cliff 'Pastel Autumn' small pedestal nut bowl, shape 260, with combined 'FANTASQUE' and 'Bizarre' printed marks.

c1931 *2.25in (6cm) high*

£350-450 **FLD**

A Clarice Cliff Fantasque Bizarre 'Blue Autumn' large cauldron, with printed 'FANTASQUE' and 'Bizarre' marks, with a few minor scuffs.

c1931 *4.25in (11cm) high*

£350-450 **FLD**

A Clarice Cliff Bizarre 'Green Autumn' pattern flying swan flower block, shape 423, with a brightly coloured relief moulded bird, and printed 'Bizarre' mark.

c1931 *6.25in (16cm) high*

£400-600 **FLD**

A Clarice Cliff Bizarre 'Broth' globe vase, shape 370, with printed 'Bizarre' mark, with a few minor scuffs and light crazing to glaze.

c1930 *5.5in (14cm) high*

£1,200-1,800 **FLD**

A Clarice Cliff 'Cloud Flowers' vase, shape 896, the base with relief moulded script signature mark.

The cloud-like design recalls Chinese textiles, showing the breadth of Cliff's sources of inspiration. It is also sometimes known as Nemesia and can be found in other colours.

c1935 *8.75in (22.5cm) high*

£350-450 **FLD**

A Clarice Cliff Fantasque 'Comets' sandwich tray, shape 334, with printed 'Fantasque' mark, with minor scuffs.

This is a desirable and early abstract pattern.

c1929

£550-650 **FLD**

A Clarice Cliff Bizarre 'Delecia' range shape no.451 vase, with dripped glazes and printed marks.

8in (20.5cm) high

£180-220 **WW**

A Clarice Cliff 'Orange Erin' pattern rectangular Biarritz shape plate, with Royal Staffordshire 'Biarritz' mark, a few minor scuffs.

c1933 *9in (23cm) wide*

£300-400 **FLD**

A Clarice Cliff 'Green Erin' pattern circular plate, with printed 'Bizarre' mark.

c1933 *9in (23cm) diam*

£300-400 **FLD**

A Clarice Cliff Fantasque Bizarre 'Red Gardenia' pattern Coronet shape jug, with some fading.

7in (18cm) high

£150-200 **GHOU**

A Clarice Cliff 'Latona Dahlia' pattern fruit bowl, with 'Bizarre' and 'LATONA' printed marks.

c1931 *7in (18cm) wide*

£280-320 **FLD**

A Clarice Cliff oval lily bowl, shape no.973, with printed marks to base.

Designed to hold flower bulbs, this shape was introduced in 1938 and produced until the late 1950s. Reputedly over 250,000 were sold.

9in (23cm) wide

£50-70 **GHOU**

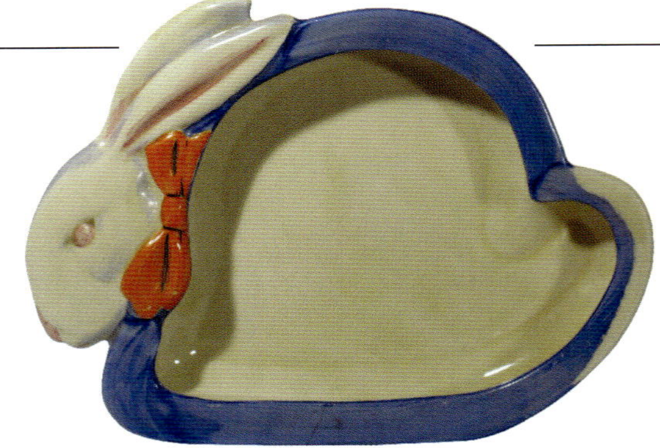

A Clarice Cliff Bizarre nursery ware bowl, the rim modelled as a rabbit, with printed factory mark and wear to blue band.

8.5in (21.5cm) wide

£250-300 **WW**

A Clarice Cliff pipe holder, modelled as a small bird, with printed 'Clarice Cliff' script mark.

3in (7.5cm) high

£50-70 **FLD**

A Clarice Cliff tree stump planter, with two moulded budgerigars, and brown printed script signature, and small hairline crack to bowl.

10.75in (27.5cm) long

£45-55 **FLD**

A Clarice Cliff 'Circus' breakfast cup and saucer, with transfer-printed clown pattern designed by Laura Knight, and pink printed 'Laura Knight' signature and 'Bizarre' marks.

c1935

£200-250 **FLD**

A Clarice Cliff 'Circus' circular side plate, with transfer-printed clown pattern designed by Laura Knight, and pink printed 'Laura Knight' signature and 'Bizarre' marks, with two scuffs to banding.

c1935 *6in (15cm) diam*

£250-350 **FLD**

FIND OUT MORE...

Greg Slater and Jonathan Brough ' Comprehensively Clarice Cliff' . London: Thames & Hudson, 2005.

Sevi Guatelli, ' The Best of Clarice Cliff' . Edinburgh: Best 50 Limited, 2008; www.thebestofclaricecliff.com

ESSENTIAL REFERENCE - ART IN INDUSTRY

The influential 'Modern Art for the Table' exhibition held at Harrods department store, London in late 1934 aimed to showcase the work of leading artists in ceramic and glass. Dame Laura Knight's 'Circus' pattern was a central display and other contributors included Frank Brangwyn and Duncan Grant. All the earthenware was produced by Wilkinson's and unusually included Clarice's name alongside the artist's. Although many designs were shown again at the prominent Royal Academy 'Art In Industry' exhibition in 1935, they were not successful commercially and were withdrawn from sale.

A first edition Clarice Cliff 'Circus' circular side plate, with transfer-printed horse pattern designed by Laura Knight, and pink printed 'Laura Knight' signature and 'Bizarre' marks.

1934 *6.75in (17cm) diam*

£250-350 **FLD**

QUICK REFERENCE – CUPS & SAUCERS

- **Cups and saucers dating from the 1860s to the 1930s have risen in desirability again. Their popularity as part of 19thC tableware sets fell sharply for a few years as fashions moved away from a chintzy, floral look. As such, even fine quality sets could often be found at auction for under £100. Today the story is different, with people mixing patterns and shapes to create 'harlequin' sets to use at tea parties, causing a renewal in collecting interest.**
- **Look out first for major makers by checking marks on the base, as this will usually indicate fine quality. Pieces by factories such as Royal Doulton, Coalport, Royal Worcester, Hammersley, Paragon and Shelley will typically be priced at the higher end of the market. Many of these names have large and loyal bands of collectors, ensuring prices remain high. Popular designer names such as Susie Cooper, Clarice Cliff and others will also command higher prices.**
- **Always look for signs of quality in the decoration. Many pieces have hand-painted details, often highlighted in gilt – a fact that surprises many considering the time and skill required to decorate by hand. Sets with finely detailed and well-executed patterns will be more desirable and valuable, as will those that have shapes or patterns that exemplify the style of the day – for example, the Art Deco style of the 1920s and 30s.**
- **Many of the most decorative examples with gilt interiors were intended for display rather than use. These 'cabinet' cups are also rising in desirability again, although not as sharply as examples that can be used. Always examine the pieces closely – items that were in regular use may have been damaged over time. Worn patterns or gilding, and particularly cracks and chips, will reduce desirability and value.**

An Aynsley cup and saucer, with gilt rim.

Saucer 4.5in (11cm) diam

£30-50 **MA**

A 1920s Aynsley transfer and hand-painted teacup and saucer, decorated with orange flowers and cobalt and orange panels.

Saucer 5.25in (13.5cm) diam

£20-25 **W&L**

An Aynsley bone china transfer-printed tea cup and saucer, with blue cornflower or love-in-a-mist flowers, and lavender scalloped rim, with yellow butterfly handle, the back with reg no.765788 for 1931.

Saucer 5.25in (13.5cm) diam

£120-160 **BEV**

An Aynsley teacup and saucer, with pink transfer-printed flowers and yellow hand-painted butterfly handle, the back with printed marks.

Saucer 5.25in (13.5cm) diam

£100-150 **BEV**

An Aynsley teacup and saucer, with yellow exterior, gilt rim and hand-painted butterfly handle, the back with printed marks and registered no.705789 for 1924.

Saucer 5in (13cm) diam

£120-180 **BEV**

A CLOSER LOOK AT AN AYNSLEY CUP & SAUCER

Note that the butterfly motif has been repeated on the inside of the cup as well – this is a rare and sought-after feature.

The butterfly handle is very well painted and detailed, with its legs and antennae painted onto the bowl.

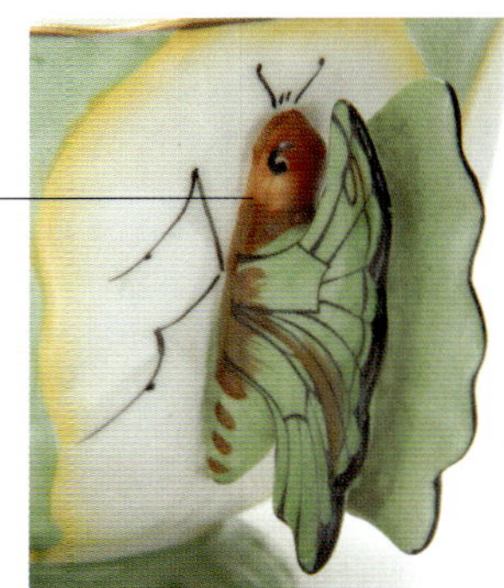

Known as the 'Tulip' shape, the cup and saucer are moulded to represent petals or leaves.

Three colour examples, such as this with green, yellow and white, are more decorative, desirable and valuable.

An Aynsley 'Tulip' shape teacup and saucer, moulded and painted in white, yellow and green, and with hand-painted butterfly handle, the base with printed marks and registered no.765788 for 1931.

Saucer 5.25in (13.5cm) diam

£180-220 **BEV**

A 1920s Royal Bayreuth teacup and saucer, with transfer-printed sprays of flowers in panels, and green ground with gilt floral, scrolling and hatched pattern.

Saucer 5in (12.5cm) diam

£50-70 **BAD**

A Brown Westhead Moore & Co. Cauldon Ware cup and saucer, with a yellow scalloped border with scrolling birds and flower garlands.

Saucer 4.75in (12cm) diam

£70-90 **BEV**

A 1930s Burleigh 'Belvedere' shape teacup and saucer, with hand-painted green band and sprays of multicoloured flowers on a cream background, marked 'no.309992 MADE IN ENGLAND BELVEDERE REGD'.

Saucer 5.75in (14.5cm) diam

£30-50 **BEV**

A 1930s Burleigh Zenith shape teacup and saucer, with hand-painted 'Lemon Tree' pattern with blue border, the cup with angular and shaped handle, the base with printed marks and registered no.769495, for 1931.

This is a rare and desirable pattern, on a quintessential Art Deco shape.

5.75in (14.5cm) diam

£55-65 **BEV**

A 1930s Burleigh Ware Imperial shape teacup and saucer, with hand-painted floral and foliate design and shaped handle.

5.75in (14.5cm) diam

£30-40 **BEV**

QUICK REFERENCE – BURGESS & LEIGH

Founded in 1851 as Hulme & Booth, the company became Burgess & Leigh (later shortened to Burleigh) in 1877. It was known for toilet sets and tablewares until the 1920s, when the focus moved to tea sets and tablewares. During the 1920s and 1930s, it became associated with brightly hand-painted tea sets and jugs, which often had shaped or figural handles as on this teacup. Many shapes were designed by Ernest Bailey, with patterns by Harold Bennett. Charlotte Rhead also produced designs from 1926-31. The company remained in the family of the co-founding Leigh family until 1999, when it was rescued from bankruptcy by the Dorling family, and was renamed Burgess, Dorling & Leigh.

A 1930s Burleigh Ware Imperial shape teacup and saucer, designed by Ernest Bailey, with hand-painted garden scene with balustrade, the back painted with no.11516 and with printed factory and Australian registration marks.

5.75in (14.5cm) diam

£30-40 **BEV**

A W&L teacup and saucer, with transfer-printed foliate and floral pattern on a mottled blue band, with scrolling and panels, the back with factory mark and registered no.152134 for 1890.

5.5in (14cm) diam

£18-22 **W&L**

A Carltonware Rita shape teacup and saucer, decorated with green raised dots on a cream ground, and with gilt interior.

This pattern, no.4225, can be found in a number of different colour combinations including white on Rouge Royale.

Saucer 4.5in (11.5cm) diam

£80-120 **BEV**

A 1930s Carltonware blue 'Barge' pattern Rita shape cabinet cup and saucer, with gilt interior.

Exotic hand-painted patterns on lustre grounds were first introduced in the 1920s.

Saucer 4.5in (11.5cm) diam

£100-150 **BEV**

A 1920s Carltonware yellow 'Mikado' pattern coffee can and saucer, with gilt interior, with 'W&R' printed mark.

The presence of the Wiltshaw & Robinson mark indicates that this is an early piece from the 1920s.

Saucer 4.25in (10.5cm) diam

£80-120 **BEV**

A Coalport quatrefoil-shaped cabinet teacup and saucer, with gilt interior, with panels of red with raised applied gilt with turquoise glazed dots, and hand-painted landscapes, with some wear.

Saucer 4.75in (12cm) wide

£80-120 **BAD**

A Copeland Spode cup and saucer, of scalloped form, with hand-painted and transfer-printed flowers inside and out, gilt scallop edged rim and reeded bodies, with printed mark and painted mark '571'.

Saucer 4.75in (12cm) diam

£40-60 **BEV**

A Davenport Imari-style hand-painted and transfer-printed teacup and saucer, with gilt highlights.

Imari is the name given to a type of porcelain made at Arita in Japan, and exported via the port of Imari. Cobalt blue, red and gilt are characteristic colours, often arranged in panels containing stylised natural motifs.

c1880s *Saucer 5.5in (14cm) diam*

£60-80 **BEV**

A 1920s Crown Staffordshire teacup and saucer, with hand-painted and transfer-printed green mottled rim and pagoda on a cliff design, and with black handle.

Saucer 5.5in (14cm) diam

£30-35 **W&L**

A 1930s Royal Doulton hand-painted 'Aspen' pattern teacup and saucer.

The style of this tree, cliff and sea landscape was clearly inspired by Clarice Cliff's landscape patterns. However, note that the shape was not, being much more traditional.

5.25in (13.5cm) diam

£25-35 **BEV**

A 1930s Royal Doulton Art Deco 'Deluxe' pattern teacup and saucer, with hand-painted green and black geometric design with silver details.

This set is typically Art Deco in style, from the conical shape of the cup, to the angular handle and geometric pattern in light green and black and picked out in silver.

Saucer 5.5in (14cm) diam

£70-100 **BAD**

An Art Deco Fielding's Crown Devon fully hand-painted cup and saucer, decorated with arrows and sun design on a beige ground, the back with printed mark and painted 'A195'.

Saucer 4.5in (11.5cm) diam

£75-85 **BEV**

A Foley cup and saucer, with transfer-printed chintz pattern on a green ground, the base painted 'V1770' and printed 'English Bone China FB7 '.

c1932 *5.5in (14cm) diam*

£30-40 **BEV**

A Foley China octagonal cup and saucer, with blue transfer-printed pattern of urns and scrolling vines, the back with printed factory mark, painted '10024' and with registered no.447136 for December 1904.

c1895-97 *5.25in (13.5cm) diam*

£55-65 **W&L**

A Foley Bone China 'Montrose' pattern teacup and saucer, with blue panels with pheasant and gold scrolling pattern, and sprays of pink roses, with shaped and gilded handle.

Saucer 5.75in (14.5cm) diam

£15-20 **W&L**

A Grafton China teacup and saucer, with hand-painted orange four-leaf clovers and clumps of primroses amid trees, the back with printed marks and painted '5432' pattern number.

5.5in (14cm) diam

£20-25 **W&L**

A CLOSER LOOK AT A ROYAL WINTON TEACUP AND SAUCER

A 1930s Grimwades Royal Winton chintzware teacup and saucer, with transfer-printed 'Hazel' pattern and printed marks to reverse.

5.75in (14.5cm) diam

£55-65 **W&L**

An A.B. Jones & Sons Ltd Royal Grafton Bone China light blue transfer-printed cup and saucer, with scrolling rim, decorated with beige/gold diagonal leaf shapes containing sprays of pink and purple roses.

Saucer 5.5in (14cm) diam

£20-25 **W&L**

A Hammersley scalloped edge teacup and saucer, with ornate handle and transfer-printed and hand-painted scene of flowers in front of trellis, with printed marks to base.

6in (15cm) diam

£25-35 **W&L**

A Hammersley & Co. cylindrical coffee can and saucer, with floral gilt border and large pink roses.

1900-18 *Saucer 4.5in (11.5cm) diam*

£45-55 **BEV**

A Haviland & Co. Limoges teacup and saucer, with moulded panels and transfer-printed blue cornflowers and corn ears.
1876-79 *Saucer 4.75in (12cm) diam*
£20-30 **BEV**

A George Jones & Sons 'Abbey 1790' blue and white transfer-printed teacup and saucer, with printed marks to reverse.
Saucer 5.75in (14.5cm) diam
£30-40 **BEV**

A C.T. Maling cup and saucer, with pink fringed gilt scrolls, transfer-printed pink roses, with printed tower mark and painted 'A3122/4'. c1895 Saucer *5.5in (14cm) diam*
£30-50 **BAD**

A Midwinter Fashion shape cup and saucer, with transfer-printed 'Bali H'ai' pattern on saucer, designed by John Russell in 1960.
Saucer 4.75in (12cm) wide
£15-18 **RET**

A Noritake Imari-style teacup and saucer, decorated with orange chrysanthemums and foliage in panels, with gilt detailing, the back with printed leaf marks.

This is both an early mark and an early pattern based on traditional Japanese ceramics, but modified for Western tastes.
c1908 *Saucer 5.25in (13.5cm) diam*
£30-40 **W&L**

A Minton Haddon Hall pattern ribbed teacup and saucer, designed by John Wadworth, pattern B4451, with green vines with pink and blue flowers, with printed mark to back.

The double 'S' mark through the factory mark on the back indicates that this was a factory second. Other factories, such as Royal Doulton, score marks through with lines. Be aware of how factories identify seconds, as they will never be as desirable or valuable as first quality pieces in the same condition.
Saucer 4.5in (11.5cm) diam
£18-22 **W&L**

A 1980s Paragon teacup and saucer, with the transfer-printed and hand-painted 'Rockingham' pattern of floral sprays surrounded by a burgundy border with gold scrolling patterns.
6in (15cm) diam
£22-28 **W&L**

A Paragon double-handled teacup and saucer, with transfer-printed sprays of flowers in panels surrounded by gold flowers on a burgundy background, with scrolling patterns around, the back with printed marks.

c1939 *5.75in (14cm) diam*

£20-25 **W&L**

A CLOSER LOOK AT A SHELLEY CUP AND SAUCER

Produced from 1930-33 only, Shelley's Vogue shape is one of the most desirable and valuable Art Deco teacup forms.

The solid handle caused some problems for buyers as it was difficult to hold, leading to the similar Eve shape, with an open handle, being introduced in 1932.

The geometric, footed conical shape with a triangular handle is quintessentially Art Deco.

The bright 'Sunray' pattern makes this example even more desirable – Art Deco patterns on Art Deco shapes are highly sought after.

A 1930s Shelley Art Deco Vogue shape teacup and saucer, with the hand-painted 'Sunray' pattern, no.11742, the base with printed factory mark and registered design no.756538 for 1930.

5.5in (14cm) diam

£80-120 **BEV**

A 1930s Paragon Art Deco hand-painted china cup and saucer, decorated with yellow crocuses, the base with registration no.766514 for 1931.

Saucer 5.25in (13.5cm) diam

£30-40 **BEV**

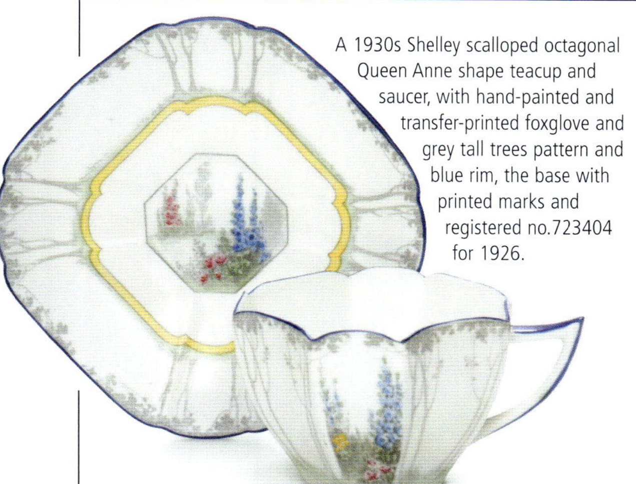

A 1930s Shelley scalloped octagonal Queen Anne shape teacup and saucer, with hand-painted and transfer-printed foxglove and grey tall trees pattern and blue rim, the base with printed marks and registered no.723404 for 1926.

This popular shape was produced from 1926-33, and again in the 1950s, and can be found with over 170 different patterns.

Saucer 5.25in (13.5cm) wide

£40-60 **BAD**

A 1920s-30s Rosenthal teacup and saucer, with the transfer-printed 'Donatello' pattern of flowers and a gilt scrolling border.

4.25in (11cm) diam

£55-65 **BEV**

An R.H. & S.L. Plant 'Tuscan China' teacup and saucer, with hand-painted and transfer-printed pattern of foxgloves, flowers and a garden wall.

5.5in (14cm) diam

£20-25 **W&L**

An R.H. & S.L. Plant Ltd 'Tuscan China' trio set, decorated with a transfer-printed and hand-painted pattern of garlands and plums, with a black edged rim.

Saucer 6.75in (17cm) diam

£22-28 **W&L**

A late 1930s R.H. & S.L. Plant 'Tuscan China' teacup and saucer, with transfer-printed and hand-painted flowers and blue rim, the base with printed marks and registered no.771590 for 1932.

5.75in (14.5cm) diam

£20-25 **W&L**

A 1930s Sampson Smith Ltd 'Wetley China' cup and saucer, with hand-painted pattern of irises and blue rim, the back with printed marks and registered no.731211 for 1927.

Saucer 4.25in (11cm) diam

£30-50 **BEV**

A late 19thC H.M. Williamson & Sons 'Kaiser' pattern teacup and saucer, with hand-painted and transfer-printed scrolling and mottled pattern with blue, yellow and pink flowers, with 'W & Sons' printed marks.

Saucer 5.25in (13.5cm) diam

£18-22 **W&L**

A Royal Worcester armorial cup and saucer, decorated with gilded panels containing a coat of arms, a monogram, butterflies and flower sprays, printed marks and date codes, the saucer with a restored stress crack.

1895 Saucer 6.25in (16cm) diam

£55-65 **WW**

A 1920s Royal Worcester cabinet teacup and saucer, with hand-painted flowers and transfer-printed green bows and flowers, with gilt interior, with printed factory mark.

Saucer 3.75in (9.5cm) diam

£80-120 **BEV**

A Royal Worcester teacup and saucer, pattern no.333, decorated with blue Classical panels and laurel rim.

Saucer 5in (13cm) diam

£30-40 **W&L**

QUICK REFERENCE

- Founded in 1815 by John Doulton, Martha Jones and John Watts in Lambeth, south London, Doulton initially produced utilitarian ceramics, such as chimney pots and pipes. The company began producing decorative wares from around 1871. Many of these pieces were designed and decorated by students from the nearby Lambeth School of Art. Look for the typical motifs and artists' monograms of notable artists, including Lambeth-trained sisters Florence and Hannah Barlow, and brothers Arthur and George Tinworth. These 'Doulton Lambeth' pieces included stoneware, which was often made in the Art Nouveau style, a 'faience' range, which featured naturalistic hand painting, and a 'Silicon' ware range.
- In 1877, Doulton took over the Pinder, Bourne & Co. factory in Burslem, Staffordshire, which produced earthenware and bone china. Its name was changed to Doulton and Company Ltd in 1882, and the company soon became known for fine porcelain. The title 'royal' was granted in 1901 by Edward VII and 'Royal Doulton' marks appeared in 1902. The Lambeth factory closed in 1956, but production continues at Burslem.
- The production of figures, for which Royal Doulton is now well known, took off in 1913, under the direction of modeller Charles Noke. These figures were all given an individual 'HN' number, after Harry Nixon, then manager of the painting department. More than 4,000 of these numbers have subsequently been assigned to different models and colourways, many of which were designed by Leslie Harradine. In general, the most desirable figures are those produced for a short time only, usually before WWII, particularly if finely modelled and in a rare colourway.
- Vases are often worth more than bowls or jardinières. Pairs are more desirable than singles or matched pairs. Those in a High Victorian style typical of the factory and period, like the piece shown bottom right, may be worth investing in as prices are lower than 10 years ago and quality is high.
- Condition is important, particularly with figures, as damage reduces value considerably, so check all over for chips, scratches and cracks. Over the past decade, value and demand for Doulton pieces have declined, though the finest pieces, particularly stoneware and very rare figurines, are still sought after. Now may, therefore, be a good time to buy, as a potential revival in the future would cause prices to rise.

A Doulton Lambeth stoneware ovoid vase, by Hannah Barlow, sgraffito-decorated with ponies and sheep in a landscape with oxide tint between repeat carved foliate borders in tan and tonal blue, impressed and incised marks.

10.5in (27cm) high

£600-900 **FLD**

A Doulton Lambeth stoneware ovoid vase, by Hannah Barlow, sgraffito-decorated with ponies and sheep in a landscape setting, between carved foliate borders, with impressed and incised marks, restored neck.

10.5in (27cm) high

£200-300 **FLD**

A pair of Doulton Lambeth stoneware pedestal vases, by Louisa Edwards, carved with a stylised Classical-inspired stiff leaf design within repeat borders, the base with impressed and incised marks.

11in (27.5cm) high

£500-700 **FLD**

A Doulton Lambeth vase, by Hannah Barlow, sgraffito-decorated with a deep band of ponies and cattle with oxide glaze between carved borders with a repeat palmette design, impressed and incised marks.

11in (28cm) high

£600-900 **FLD**

A Doulton Lambeth stoneware vase, by Elisa Simmance, incised and applied with scrolling flowers and foliage with beadwork decoration, the base with impressed mark, incised monogram, damaged.

18.5in (47cm) high

£150-200 **WW**

A pair of Doulton Lambeth stoneware vases, by Hannah Barlow, incised with a continuous band of horses between stiff and scrolling leaf collars, the bases with incised marks.

9.25in (23.5cm) high

£700-1,000 **FLD**

A pair of Doulton Lambeth waisted and footed vases, bearing monograms for Frank Butler, Ernest Bishop and Elizabeth Atkins, and incised '524' and '523', decorated with stylised, entwined foliage and flower heads.

1879 *10.25in (26cm) high*

£300-500 **HALL**

A CLOSER LOOK AT A DOULTON VASE

The vase was decorated by Hannah Barlow (1851-1916), who is celebrated for her lively and life-like animal designs.

Barlow used the sgrafitto technique, where a sharp point scratches a design into the wet clay – the body is then wiped with an oxide stain, which settles in the lines to highlight them.

It is an unusually large size, and would have cost a considerable sum in its day, making it rare today.

The price would have more than doubled if it was part of an original, matching pair.

A Doulton Lambeth stoneware floor vase, by Hannah Barlow, decorated with a deep sgraffito band of sheep in a highland setting with oxide tint between carved and tube-line foliate borders, the base with incised and impressed marks.

18in (46cm) high

£800-1,200 **FLD**

A pair of Doulton Lambeth stoneware vases, by Hannah Barlow, each incised with a continuous band of cows in pasture between stiff and scrolling leaf collars, the bases with incised marks.

9.25in (23.5cm) high

£700-1,000 **FLD**

A pair of Doutlon Lambeth vases, by George Tinworth, incised with scrolling and raised beads, on a shaded brown glaze, signed with initials on the body, one with a firing crack.

11.75in (30cm) diam

£600-800 **SWO**

A Victorian Doulton Lambeth stoneware vase, by Emily Stormer, decorated overall with raised rosettes, beading and stylised leaves, impressed marks and signature to base.

6in (15cm) high

£400-600 **DUK**

A Royal Doulton 'Brangwyn Ware' slender ovoid vase, designed by Frank Brangwyn, numbered 'D5081', incised with stylised leaves and buds, the base with printed mark, moulded '7936'.

Sir Frank William Brangwyn (1867-1956) was a progressive artist, illustrator, and designer, who was a member of the Royal Academy and the Royal Watercolour Society.

11.5in (29.5cm) high

£200-300 **DN**

A CLOSER LOOK AT A ROYAL DOULTON VASE

The Titanian range used titanium oxide to give a green or blue glaze ranging from light grey-blue to a deep royal blue – it is typically speckled, cloudy or streaked.

Birds are typical motifs, as are Oriental figures, and the treatment was used by Harry Tittensor, Harry Allen and other notable decorators.

This range was produced from 1915-c1930. Look out for Egyptian motifs inspired by the discovery of Tutankhamun's tomb in 1922 as these fetch higher sums than birds.

Bases are generally marked with the factory mark and also the name of the range.

A Royal Doulton blue 'Titanian' cylindrical vase, decorated and gilded with a perched peacock and peahen, with printed mark to base.

10.25in (26cm) high

£400-600 **DA&H**

A Royal Doulton Veined Flambé vase, the ovoid body decorated with cobalt over red glazes, numbered '1622'.

15.75in (40cm) high

£150-250 **FLD**

A Royal Doulton porcelain twin-handled ovoid vase, with transfer-printed scene titled 'Ophelia', and printed factory mark to base.

8.25in (21cm) high

£70-100 **SAS**

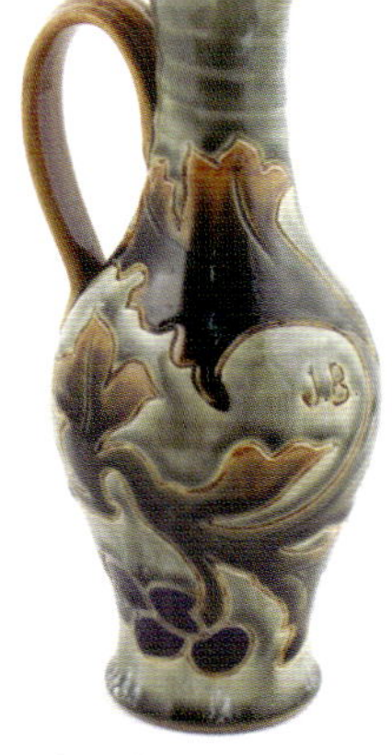

A Royal Doulton bottle neck bulbous jug, of green ground with incised leaf decoration in brown and incised initials 'JB', with impressed mark to base with decorator's initials 'MVM'.

9in (23cm) high

£250-300 **LOC**

A Royal Doulton 'Titanian' vase, painted with a young coal tit on a green ground, signed 'H. Allen' for Harry Allen.

Although this example is hand-painted, not all Titanian wares were – many were transfer-printed and highlighted in gilt.

3.5in (9cm) high

£200-300 **LT**

A Royal Doulton 'Titanian' large bowl, the mottled grey-green ground decorated with gilt exotic birds on branches of chrysanthemums, with jewelled rim with additional floral sprays.

14.5in (37cm) diam

£450-550 **LT**

A Royal Doulton plate, decorated with a portrait of an Art Nouveau maiden, the back with impressed and printed marks.

9.25in (23.5cm) diam

£70-100 **WW**

A Royal Doulton 'John Peel' loving cup, with fox and whip handles, numbered 293 from a limited edition of 500, moulded on one side with figures, on the other with hounds.

1923 *9in (23cm) high*

£400-600 **BE**

A Royal Doulton Robin Hood loving cup, designed by Charles Noke and Harry Fenton, numbered 393 from a limited edition of 600, relief decorated with scenes in Sherwood Forest, with printed marks to base.

Introduced in 1938, this was part of a range of limited edition jugs or cups produced from 1930-38.

8.5in (21.5cm) high

£650-750 **LT**

A Royal Doulton large 'Bacchus' character jug, D6499, designed by Max Henk, with rare City of Stoke-on-Trent Jubilee Year backstamp.

1959 *7in (18cm) high*

£700-1,000 **TOV**

A CLOSER LOOK AT A DOULTON CHARACTER JUG

This example can be identified as a prototype rather than a variation as the base is printed ' Design Original Sample and Decorating Sample 1' .

The handle on this prototype is modelled slightly differently to the production piece, and has the Flag of St. George to the reverse of the Union Jack.

The production model had a beige, not green, balaclava, the coat was brown not buff, and the face was painted differently.

Prices for trials and unique pieces have remained strong, despite the general downturn in the Doulton market.

A Royal Doulton prototype 'Captain Scott of the Antarctic' large character jug, similar to D7116, wearing olive green balaclava and buff coat, with printing to base.

7in (18cm) high

£3,000-5,000 **LT**

A Royal Doulton 'King Charles' figure, HN404, designed by Charles Noke and Harry Tittensor, with an unusual buff base, the base with printed green mark and initialled 'PS'.

Note the large size of this desirable figurine, which is valuable in all three of its variations.

1920-51 *16.75in (42.5cm) high*

£750-950 **TEN**

A Royal Doulton 'Sir Walter Raleigh' figure, HN1751, designed by Leslie Harradine, with printed marks to base.

1936-49 *12.25in (31cm) high*

£400-500 **A&G**

A Royal Doulton 'Vice Admiral Lord Nelson' figure, HN3489, designed by Alan Maslankowski, numbered 351 from a limited edition of 950, with certificate.

1993 *12.5in (31.5cm) high*

£500-700 **LT**

A Royal Doulton 'The Moor' large figurine, HN3642, with a flambé glaze, designed by Charles Noke in 1929.

1994-95 *17.25in (44cm) high*

£800-1,200 **FLD**

A Royal Doulton 'In the Stocks' figure, HN1474, designed by Leslie Harradine, some restoration.

1931-38 *5in (12.5cm) high*

£600-800 **LT**

A CLOSER LOOK AT A ROYAL DOULTON FIGURINE

Figures produced for long periods of time are usually the most affordable and have also have fallen in value recently, as so many exist.

This example has a grey skirt, violet blouse and green and purple tartan shawl, all of which are different to the standard production model.

The biggest difference between this and the standard model is the fact that she is meant to be a balloon seller, but here she has no balloons.

She has a hairline crack to her skirt, but this does not deter collectors who are keen to collect as many rare variations as possible.

A Royal Doulton 'Biddy Penny Farthing' figure, HN1843 without balloons, designed by Leslie Harradine (1938-present).

9in (23cm) high

£2,000-3,000 **LT**

A Royal Doulton 'Pierette' figure, HN1749, designed by Leslie Harradine.

Although she can also be found with a red skirt, (HN1391), values are roughly the same.

1936-49 *9.5in (24cm) high*

£600-800 **LT**

A Royal Doulton protoype 'Charity' figure, HN3087, designed by Eric Griffiths, with a different purple blanket and yellow dress, Lawley's in a limited edition of 9,500 for the NSPCC.

1987 *8.5in (21.5cm) high*

£80-120 **SAS**

A Royal Doulton protoype 'Faith' figure, HN3082, designed by Eric Griffiths, with a different coloured pink and red coat, commissioned by Lawley's in a limited edition of 9,500 for the NSPCC.

8.5in (21.5cm) high

£80-120 **SAS**

A Royal Doulton 'Lambing Time' figure, HN1890, designed by W.M. Chance, with printed marks to base.

1938-81 *9.25in (23.5cm) high*

£35-45 **SAS**

A Royal Doulton 'Gandalf' figurine, HN2911, with blue cloak, designed by D. Lyttleton, from the Middle Earth series.

1980-84 *7in (18cm) high*

£40-60 **PC**

A Royal Doulton 'The Homecoming' figure, HN3295, and a 'Welcome Home' figure, HN3299, designed by A. Hughes from the Children of the Blitz series, both numbered 1944 from a limited edition of 9,500.

1990-91 *Tallest 8.5in (21.5cm) high*

£150-200 **HT**

A Royal Doulton 'The Boy Evacuee' figure, HN3202, and a 'The Girl Evacuee' figure, HN3203, designed by A. Hughes from the Children of the Blitz series, both numbered 7809 from a limited edition of 9,500.

1989 *Tallest 8.25in (21cm) high*

£250-350 **HT**

A Royal Doulton Archives Collection 'T'ang Horse' figurine, BA25, with flambé glaze, designed by Alan Maslankowski from a limited edition of 250 from the Burslem Artwares series.

2001 *10.5in (27cm) high*

£250-300 **FLD**

A Royal Doulton Archives Collection 'Hebei Goat', BA36, in a flambé glaze, designed by Alan Maslankowski from a limited edition of 250 from the Burslem Artwares Collection.

2002 *10.5in (26.5cm) high*

£200-250 **FLD**

QUICK REFERENCE - DOULTON FLAMBÉ GLAZE

The ancient Chinese 'sang-de-boeuf' glaze was much admired by John Slater and Charles Noke, who attempted to copy it in the 1890s. Cuthbert Bailey joined Doulton in 1901 and Bernard Moore, in 1902. Together they made a breakthrough and their results won prizes when first exhibited at the St Louis World's Fair in 1904, and the glaze is still popular and desirable today. Animals are highly sought after, particularly those designed by Noke. This is the largest elephant from a series of three, and also the most valuable.

A Royal Doulton frog, with a flambé Sung glaze, mottled crimson, green, yellow glazes, impressed '1162'.

The Sung glaze is highly sought after, particularly in combination with the flambé glaze. This shape is different from the standard frog numbered HN1162, more closely resembling HN905. This combination also suggests an early date.

4.5in (11.5cm) wide

£3,200-3,800 **LT**

A Royal Doulton large elephant, HN1121, with flambé glaze and trunk down, designed by Charles Noke.

c1938-57 *13in (33cm) wide*

£2,000-3,000 **LT**

A Royal Doulton 'Lop Eared Rabbit', HN1165B, with flambé and Sung glazes, the base impressed '1165B' and dated.

1923 *4in (10cm) long*

£3,000-4,000 **LT**

A Royal Doulton 'Lion on rock' figurine, HN2641, designed by Charles Noke from the Prestige series.

1952-92 *10.25in (26cm) wide*

£150-250 **FLD**

A Royal Doulton 'Bulldog with Tam O'Shanter & Haversack', HN153, designed by an unknown modeller, and with khaki glaze and printed registered no.663408 for 1918, one fore paw re-glued and chipped.

The values for these wartime commemoratives have fallen, and continue to do so, as highly accurate, very good quality reproductions are being made. Look out for the examples in the Titanian glaze, as values for these are holding strong.

1918-c1925

£250-300 **DN**

QUICK REFERENCE

- The Fulper Pottery Co. was founded in 1814 in Flemington, New Jersey by Samuel Hill. It operated until 1935, when it was acquired by Stangl. It initially produced utilitarian wares, introducing art pottery in 1909. Wares were slip-moulded and Fulper became renowned for its varied range of rich glazes.
- Their first art pottery line, produced from 1909 until WWI, was known as 'Vasecraft'. Many forms were Germanic in their solid and architectural feel, and glazes were of a particularly high quality. Production from this early period is usually the most sought-after and valuable.
- After c1914, shapes became more curved, with inspiration drawn from Oriental forms. Glaze quality began to deteriorate gradually, particularly during the late 1920s. From the late 1920s until the factory closed, the Art Deco movement influenced forms, and glazes were of considerably poorer quality.
- Bodies also became lighter in weight over time, and although heavy examples are not always better quality, light examples are almost always lower quality. Always consider the glaze as every piece was glazed by a skilled decorator, making each unique. The more complex and interesting the glaze and shape, the better the piece is likely to be.

A Fulper corseted two-handled vase, with frothy Copperdust Crystalline glaze over Flemington Green flambé, with vertical mark.

9.5in (24cm) high

£250-350 **DRA**

A Fulper two-handled vase, covered in Copperdust Crystalline and Mirrored Black flambé glaze, with paper label over vertical mark.

9.75in (25cm) high

£350-450 **DRA**

A Fulper baluster vase, covered in a fine frothy Cucumber Matt glaze, with vertical mark.

12in (30.5cm) high

£700-900 **DRA**

A Fulper two-handled urn, of hammered texture covered in frothy Chinese Blue and Amber flambé glaze, with horizontal mark and '490'.

12.5in (32cm) high

£500-700 **DRA**

A large Fulper bullet vase, covered with a dripped Cat's Eye flambé glaze, the base with factory mark.

10in (25.5cm) high

£250-350 **DRA**

A Fulper melon-shaped vase, covered in a Cat's Eye flambé glaze, with vertical mark.

7in (18cm) high

£300-400 **DRA**

A CLOSER LOOK AT A FULPER VASE

At 16in (40.5cm) high, this is a large piece, with superb visual impact.

The form was inspired by Chinese ceramics, and can be dated to a period from the late 1910s to the mid-1920s.

Fulper is known for its complex, specially produced glazes that vary from being 'mirrored' to mottled to micro-crystalline – the former and the latter effects are particularly desirable.

Although some examples from this period do not bear the highest quality glazes, this example is very well-glazed.

A tall Fulper ovoid vase, covered in Cucumber Crystalline glaze, the base with raised racetrack mark.

16in (40.5cm) high

£1,500-2,500 **DRA**

An early Fulper lamp base, covered in Mouse Grey to blue flambé glaze, the base with '17' ink stamp.

Fulper lamps were only made for a short period from c1910-15, making them scarce today. They were produced under the strictest production standards, meaning quality was high. Lamps with their original shades with glass inserts are particularly prized, even more so if they have geometric or natural motifs.

17.25in (44cm) high

£800-1,200 **DRA**

A large Fulper squat vessel, covered in brown crystalline glaze dripping over Mustard Matt, small chip to foot ring, with vertical mark.

10in (25.5cm) wide

£800-1,200 **DRA**

A rare Fulper factory lamp base, in Cat's Eye flambé glaze, with vertical mark and numbered '107'.

11.25in (28.5cm) high

£300-400 **DRA**

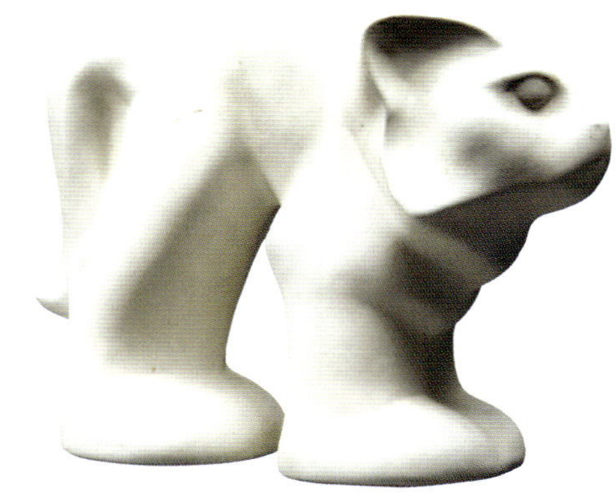

A Fulper cat figure, in White Matt glaze, with horizontal mark.

8.5in (21.5cm) high

£500-700 **DRA**

QUICK REFERENCE – HORNSEA

Hornsea Pottery was founded by Colin and Desmond Rawson in a large house in East Riding, Yorkshire in 1949. In 1954, the successful pottery moved into an old brick factory. Around this time, they also began to employ designers, including John Clappison, the son of an investor in the company. Hornsea's success grew into the 1960s with ranges such as 'Home Decor' (introduced 1960-62), 'Slipware' (introduced 1963), 'Heirloom' (1967-87), and others, all designed by Clappison, who was appointed chief designer in 1958 and continued to be so until the company closed in 1984. Some ranges, such as 'Heirloom', were so successful that the many examples on the market mean that prices are low. Rarer ranges and unusual colourways or shapes tend to fetch higher prices.

A mid-late 1960s Hornsea grey glazed 'Slipware' jardiniere, designed by John Clappison in 1963, the base with printed mark.

10in (25.5cm) wide

£70-100 **GC**

A mid-late 1960s Hornsea Mustard glazed 'Slipware' jardiniere, designed by John Clappison in 1963, the base with printed mark.

10in (25.5cm) wide

£70-100 **GC**

A mid-late 1960s Hornsea mauve glazed 'Slipware' baluster vase, designed by John Clappison in 1963, the base with printed mark.

Always examine these appealing period pieces all over as the glaze can craze easily, and small chips or glaze flakes are often found on the rim or base. Both factors devalue a piece considerably.

9.25in (23.5cm) high

£60-80 **GC**

A mid-late 1960s Hornsea light green glazed 'Slipware' baluster vase, designed by John Clappison in 1963, the base with printed mark.

7.5in (19cm) high

£40-60 **GC**

A mid-late 1960s Hornsea light blue glazed 'Slipware' squat baluster vase, designed by John Clappison in 1963, the base with printed mark.

4in (10cm) high

£20-30 **GC**

A small Hornsea pottery 'White Bud' jardinière, from the Home Decor range designed by John Clappison c1951, with moulded spot design.

9.5in (24cm) wide

£35-45 **SAS**

A Hornsea Pottery dish, in the form of a Viking longboat, from the Home Decor range designed by John Clappison c1961, with a cream glaze and printed Studiocraft marks.

c1965 *11in (28cm) wide*

£50-70 **MHT**

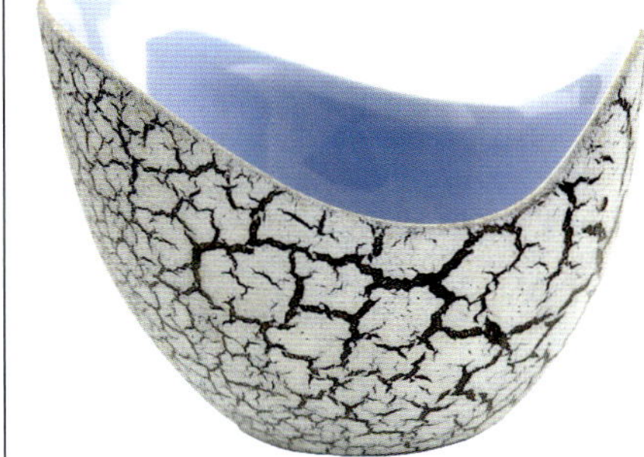

A Hornsea Pottery 'Coastline' pattern sugar bowl, with white crackle glaze on a black ground.

The curving asymmetric form is typical of the 1950s, and the pattern is very similar to the 'Cortina' range released in 1955 by West German factory Jasba.

c1957 *3.35 in (8.5cm) high*

£18-22 **PC**

A Hornsea Pottery cruet set on tray, comprising a salt and pepper shaker, mustard pot and oil bottle, lacking mustard-spoon, the base with black printed factory marks.

9in (23cm) long

£40-50 **RET**

A Hornsea black and white cruet set, on a black dish, designed by John Clappison.

c1962 *5.25in (13.5cm) high*

£10-15 **TCM**

A Hornsea Pottery tapering vase with moulded stylised foliate design on a grey ground, with printed Hornsea mark, and impressed '422'.

6.75in (17cm) high

£28-32 **RET**

A late 1960s Hornsea Pottery 'Springtime' pattern white square box with beige impressed flower design and turquoise lid, designed by John Clappison in 1964, the base impressed '280', and with printed factory and 'SPRINGTIME' marks.

3.25in (8cm) high

£18-22 **RET**

A rare 1960s Hornsea Pottery 'Studiocraft' waisted vase, designed by John Clappison in 1966, with screen-printed stylised leaves and printed marks to base.

This is a very rare range and is not connected with the earlier Studio Craft range of 1960-62.

7.75in (19.5cm) high

£40-60 **RET**

QUICK REFERENCE

- Addis Emmett Hull founded the A.E. Hull Pottery in Crooksville, Ohio in 1905. Initially he produced utilitarian stonewares, and from 1907, dinnerwares, following the purchase of the Acme Pottery Co. Although some decorative vases were produced in the 1920s, it is the colourful matte glazed art pottery introduced in the 1930s that is collected today.
- Using moulds, wares were mass-produced with floral patterns. Although gloss glazes were produced, glazes are typically soft and matte, and were sprayed on to give a graduated effect. Colours are typically light and pastel-based, although a vibrant pink is commonly found.
- In 1950, the pottery burnt down and was rebuilt, opening again in 1952. The new machinery could not replicate the matte glazes, so the company was forced to concentrate on gloss glazes. By the late 1970s, the focus of production had moved to dinnerware, which was made until the company closed in 1986.
- Look out for well-moulded forms with even, graduated effects to the glazes. Glazes should be free of crazing. Inspect pieces all-over for any damage such as cracks or chips as this reduces value considerably. Pieces produced before 1950 tend to be the most desirable, with sought-after ranges including 'Calla Lily', 'Woodland' and 'Tokay'.

A Hull 'Water Lily' pattern double-handled vase, in pink and green, marked 'Hull Art USA L-4-6 1/2'.

6.75in (17cm) high

£30-40 **BEL**

A Hull 'Magnolia' pattern matte graduated pink and blue double handled urn vase, the base molded 'Hull Art U.S.A. 46 1/4'.

6.5in (16.5cm) high

£30-40 **AEM**

A Hull 'Calla Lily' pattern graduated light green and cream glazed vase, the base marked '340/33-6'.

6.25in (16cm) high

£70-90 **BEL**

A Hull pink 'Magnolia' pattern vase, with blue flowers, the base impressed 'H-13-10 1/2'.

11in (28cm) high

£30-40 **TSIS**

A Hull 'Magnolia' pattern matte glazed cornucopia, the base marked 'Hull Art USA 19-8 1/2"'.

8.75in (22cm) high

£20-30 **BEL**

A pair of Hull 'Tokay' pattern gloss glazed cornucopia vases, the bases impressed 'Tokay U.S.A.'.

The 'Tokay' range, with its grapes and moulded vine-like handles, was introduced in 1958.

6.25in (16cm) high

£50-70 **AEM**

A CLOSER LOOK AT A HULL LITTLE RED RIDING HOOD BUTTER DISH

A range of Little Red Riding Hood items was produced during the 1940s and early 50s, including a lamp, salt and pepper shakers and the famous cookie jar.

This range is very popular and fakes are known – these are often made from a brighter white ceramic, and have larger flower transfers and more heavily applied gilt, than originals.

The butter dish, with Little Red Riding Hood appearing to curtsey, is among the rarest items in the range.

Look out for different transfers on this range as the value can be affected – poinsettia transfers are particularly desirable and valuable.

A very rare Hull Little Red Riding Hood butterdish, the base marked 'Pat. Des. No. 135889'.

Most pieces from this range were made by Hull and decorated by Royal China (part of Regal China), before being sent back to Hull for sale, but Regal also produced examples themselves.

7in (17.5cm) long

£300-400 **BB**

A Hull double handled urn vase, with green dripped glaze, the base unmarked.

This is a typical Arts & Crafts form and glaze.

4.75in (12cm) high

£50-70 **TSIS**

A rare Hull 'Little Red Riding Hood' teapot, with transfer-printed daisy and poppy pattern and gilt and hand-painted detailing, the base moulded 'U.S.A.'.

1943-57 *8in (20cm) long*

£200-250 **BB**

A Hull 'Water Lily' pattern flower pot with attached saucer, the base marked 'Hull Art USA L-25-5 3/4"', in mint condition.

5.75in (14.5cm) high

£30-50 **BEL**

A Hull 'Tokay' pattern pink and green glazed fruit bowl, the base marked '7 Tokay USA', with restored rim.

9.75in (24.5cm) wide

£30-50 **BEL**

QUICK REFERENCE

- Italian ceramics of the 1950s and 1960s have risen in popularity in recent years, and are colourful and relatively affordable. They can be found anywhere from car boot sales to specialist auctions, and prices range from a few pounds to over £2,000. The highest prices tend to be paid for pieces by notable designers such as Guide Gambone (1909-1969) and Marcello Fantoni (b.1915).
- After WWII Italy enjoyed an influx of money and a renewal of confidence that caused a boom in many industries. A large number of potteries produced affordable decorative ceramics for export. Forms were moulded, but decorated by hand. Colours are typically bright with abstract, stylised designs, and the influence of contemporary modern art can be seen in geometric and figurative patterns.
- Shapes included vases, lampbases, dishes and bowls and, depending on the quality and price, were sold in a range of shops from discount outlets to high end department stores such as Macy's or Heal's. Distributors included Raymor in the US and Hutcheson & Son Ltd in the UK. Many distributors applied their own labels to pieces.
- Look out for well-formed, well-decorated examples that show skill in execution and detail in design. Colours and patterns should be representative of the period and style. Larger pieces are usually worth more, particularly if they are well made, and damage reduces value dramatically.
- Currently, very little is known about the majority of designers or factories. Bases are marked only 'Italy' followed by a number, possibly indicating the pattern, shape, or order number. Many names indicate towns, with these pieces being sold as tourist souvenirs. Bitossi's 'Rimini Blue' range, designed by Aldo Londi in 1953, is currently popular with collectors, particularly animal forms.

A 1950s-60s Italian vase with hand-painted multi-coloured squares and random white streaks on a textured pink ground, the base painted 'ITALY 6801'

8in (20.5cm) high

£40-60 **GC**

A 1950s-60s Italian vase with hand-painted multi-coloured squares and random white streaks on a textured light blue ground, the base painted 'ITALY 6514'

9in (23cm) high

£60-80 **GC**

A 1950s-60s Italian floor vase, hand-painted with lozenges in different colours, the base painted 'ITALY 40/200 56'.

16.25in (41cm) high

£60-80 **M20C**

A 1950s-60s Italian large bottle vase, the body decorated with a sgraffito design of stylised people, the top and base covered with a beige lava-like glaze, the base inscribed 'Sestri Levante'.

16.25in (41.5cm) high

£150-200 **GC**

A 1950s-60s Italian large conical vase, the body decorated with a panel of a sgraffito design of a stylised musician, the top and base covered with a beige lava-like glaze, the base inscribed 'Sestri Levante'.

Sestri Levante is a seaside resort and fishing port on the Italian Riviera. It is likely that these bottles were tourist souvenirs.

15.75in (40cm) high

£150-200 **GC**

A 1960s Italian vase, with hand-painted stylised flowers or peacock feather eyes, and trefoil rim, the base painted 'ITALY 5Z'.

9.75in (24.5cm) high

£60-80 **GC**

A CLOSER LOOK AT A FANTONI VASE

Marcello Fantoni (b.1915) is an important Italian ceramicist whose work during the 1950s-70s was particularly influential on European ceramic design.

The shape is clean-lined and modern, and although it can be used as a vase, it is primarily intended as a display piece.

The angular figural design is typical of Fantoni's work and Italian pottery of the period, with its inscribed sgraffito outlines and brightly glazed geometric shapes.

It is signed on the base, but is unlikely to have been made by Fantoni himself – the company produced a large number of ceramics that were exported widely, including to the US via Raymor.

An Italian Fantoni bottle vase, with a sgraffito and glazed gossiping women design on a glossy red glazed background, with turquoise glazed interior, the base painted 'Fantoni Italy', with hairline crack to rim.

6.75in (17cm) high

£300-500 **W&W**

A 1950s Italian vase, hand-painted and sgraffito image of two women, the base painted 'ITALY 692'.

The asymmetric shape is typically 1950s. The figures are very similar to those used by Marcello Fantoni, as seen on the vase above.

12in (30.5cm) high

£60-100 **GROB**

A 1960s-70s Italian Bitossi green glazed footed cylindrical vase, impressed with geometric and runic symbols, the base painted '711 ITALY'

10in (25cm) high

£40-60 **RET**

A 1950s-70s Italian blue glazed torpedo vase, impressed with geometric symbols, probably by Bitossi.

10in (25cm) high

£40-60 **RET**

A 1960s-70s Italian Bitossi dark blue glazed low vase, impressed with geomtric and runic symbols, the base painted 'H-67/72 ITALY'.

£20-30 **RET**

A 1950s Italian jug, with diagonally ribbed body, applied angled handle, textured white glaze and hand-painted yellow and brown design of umbrellas, leaping stags and baskets of flowers amid sprigs of leaves and star shapes, the base painted '6057 ITALY'.

9.25in (23cm) high

£30-40 **PC**

A CLOSER LOOK AT A CANTAGALLI DISH

Cantagalli was founded by Ulisse Cantagalli (1839-1901) in Florence in 1877 and is renowned for its reproductions of 16thC maiolica and other historic ceramics.

The curving, asymmetric shape, which is made more asymmetric with the addition of two small feet, is typical of 1950s forms.

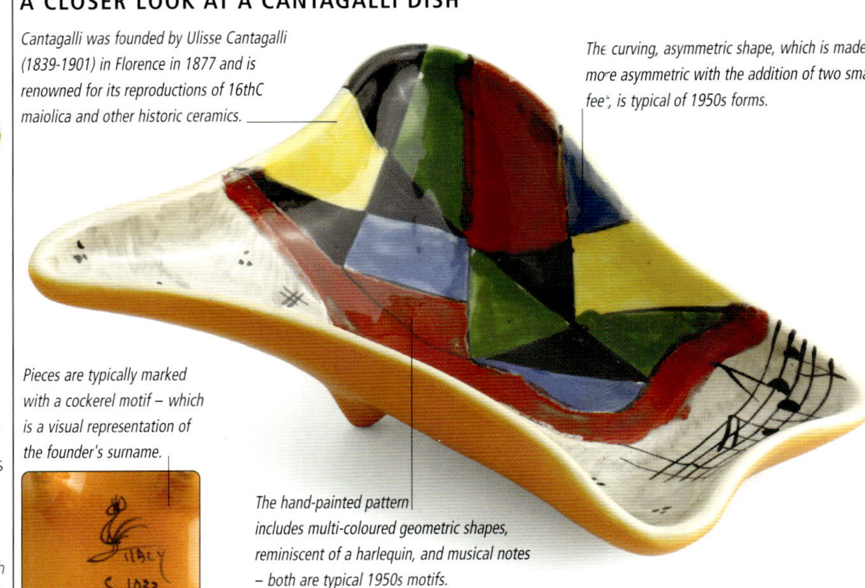

Pieces are typically marked with a cockerel motif – which is a visual representation of the founder's surname.

The hand-painted pattern includes multi-coloured geometric shapes, reminiscent of a harlequin, and musical notes – both are typical 1950s motifs.

A 1950s Italian Cantagalli dish, with hand-painted harlequin and musical notes pattern, the back with painted cockerel mark.

6.25in (16cm) longest

£30-40 **PC**

A 1950s-60s Italian clown jug, with applied handle and strap, the base painted '14708/162/1' and stamped 'MADE IN ITALY'.

Cheerful novelty designs such as this are popular with collectors.

3.5in (9cm) high

£20-30 **MA**

A pair of Italian Fantoni for Raymor figural abstract vases, modelled as a man and woman with hand-modelled features picked out in bright polychrome glazes, the base with hand-painted marks.

11.5in (29.5cm) high

£800-1,200 **FLD**

A 1950s-60s Italian jug, with multi-coloured spots, applied white knobbles, blue glazed interior and gilt details, the base painted '14794/27E ITALY'.

This is probably from a factory in or around Deruta.

8in (20.5cm) high

£18-22 **RET**

A 1950s-60s Italian Bitossi 'Rimini Blu' bull, designed by Aldo Londi in 1953, impressed with runic and geometric motifs and covered with a blue-green glaze.

This form is not part of the animal range still being made by Bitossi today.

12in (30.5cm) long

£180-200 **GC**

QUICK REFERENCE – LLADRO

Lladro was founded in Spain in 1953, and has since produced over 4,000 different designs. Elongated figurines, decorated in pastel colours with a high gloss glaze are typical. 'Gres' is similar to the earthy tones of stoneware, and comprises a sub-range of its own. Until 1971, when the blue printed mark was introduced, impressed or incised marks were used. Beware of fakes, with one key indicator being that Lladro never uses black for eyes. Look out for small limited editions, or models that were only produced for a short period of time. Similarly, retired models are likely to fetch higher values.

A Lladro 'Woman with dog' porcelain figure, no.4761, designed by Vincente Martínez, in excellent condition.

1971-94 *13.75in (35cm) high*

£120-180 **SAS**

A Lladro 'Nurse' porcelain figure, no.4603, designed by Salvador Furío, in excellent condition.

1970-90 *15.75in (40cm) high*

£60-80 **SAS**

A Lladro 'Nuns' porcelain figure, no.4611, designed by Fulgencia García, in excellent condition.

1970-2005 *13in (33cm) high*

£35-45 **SAS**

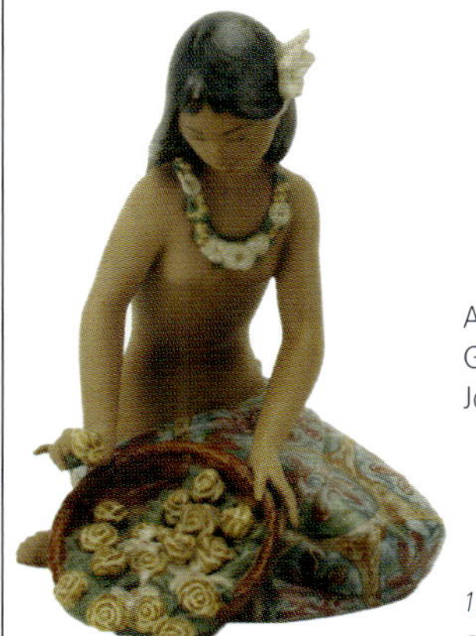

A Lladro 'Hawaiian Flower Vendor' Gres figure, no.2154, designed by Jose Puché, in excellent condition.

1985-2001 *11in (28cm) high*

£100-150 **SAS**

A Lladro 'Monks at Prayer' Gres figure, no.5155, designed by Salvador Debón, in excellent condition.

1982-2003 *14.5in (37cm) high*

£60-80 **SAS**

A Lladro 'Couple From The Arctic' Gres figure, no.2038, designed by Juan Herta, in excellent condition.

1971-2000 *13in (33cm) high*

£100-150 **SAS**

A Lladro 'Typical Peddler' porcelain figure, no.4859, designed by Salvador Furío, in excellent condition.

1974-85 *10.25in (26cm) high*

£150-200 **SAS**

QUICK REFERENCE

- The Lotus Pottery was founded in Devon by Michael and Elizabeth Skipwith in 1958 after they met at the Leeds College of Art. Initially known as Loversal Pottery, after Michael's birthplace in Doncaster, the couple changed the name when they moved to Old Stoke Farm in Stoke Gabriel in Devon. Although some decorative wares were made, the mainstay of production was kitchen and tablewares.
- By 1968, a number of glazes were in use, the most popular of which was the then-fashionable olive green shown here. Patterns differed widely and were based on natural themes, with the stylised daisy being the most popular, and the most common today. Other glazes included 'Dartside Green', white on red, and the blue on white 'Loire' range introduced in 1974. Look out for unusual glazes and patterns, as these tend to be popular.
- Bulls and larger decorative wares tend to fetch the highest prices, with tableware being generally affordable – few items fetch over £80 and most are under £30. Look out for the 'Alpine' range, decorated in sage green at the top and white at the bottom and inside. Introduced in 1966, it was accepted for the Design Council's Index of British Design.
- Most examples are marked around the base with the impressed 'LP' pottery monogram, although this is rarely found on the smallest pieces. The company prospered in the early 1970s, but suffered from increased competition from other potteries later in the decade. The Lotus Pottery closed in 1982, but Michael and Elizabeth Skipwith continued to pot individually.

A Lotus Pottery medium sized bull, designed by Elizabeth Skipwith, with a pattern of repeated g's or circles with curves on an olive green glaze, and with moulded hair to head.

Note the moulded hair on this example – not all Lotus bulls have this feature.

9in (22.5cm) long

£30-40 **M20C**

A Lotus Pottery small bull, designed by Elizabeth Skipwith, with mottled cream circle design on an olive green glaze.

6in (15cm) long

£20-30 **DSC**

A Lotus Pottery small bull, designed by Elizabeth Skipwith, with a hand-painted foliate seaweed-like design on an olive green glaze.

3in (7.5cm) high

£10-15 **M20C**

A Lotus Pottery small bull, designed by Elizabeth Skipwith, with a cream flower on an olive green glossy glaze.

5in (12.5cm) long

£20-25 **M20C**

A Lotus Pottery large bull, designed by Elizabeth Skipwith, with star-like stylised flower on an olive green glaze.

12.75in (32.5cm) long

£50-70 **M20C**

QUICK REFERENCE – LOTUS POTTERY BULLS

The bull is the most collectable and best-loved form produced by the pottery. It was made from the late 1960s to the mid-1970s in four different sizes from 5in (12.5cm) long to 13in (32.5cm) long. Stylised bulls in general from this period have become highly desirable. Lotus bulls can be differentiated from those produced by Bitossi, Beswick (see p41) and other makers by their glazes and bulky form, even though they are typically unmarked. This is a very unusual and scarce glaze that recalls patterns used by Briglin (see p43). If it was in a more common glaze, such as the typical flower on an olive ground, the value would be around £20-30.

A Lotus Pottery medium sized bull, designed by Elizabeth Skipwith, with wax-resist spirals and a cream glaze.

6.25in (16cm) long

£30-40 **M20C**

A Lotus Pottery bird figurine, with mottled cream flower on an olive green glaze.

This is a rare shape, and very similar to 'folk art' pottery whistles produced in US states such as Pennsylvania by early settlers.

6.25in (16cm) high

£30-40 **DSC**

A Lotus Pottery vase, with a mottled cream flower on an olive green glaze, the side with impressed marks.

8in (20cm) high

£25-35 **DSC**

A Lotus Pottery triangular dish, with stylised flower motif on a glossy olive glaze.

4.5in (11.5cm) wide

£7-10 **RET**

A Lotus Pottery salt shaker, with mottled cream flower on an olive green glaze.

3.25in (8cm) high

£3-5 **DSC**

A Lotus Pottery pebble-shaped sugar sifter, with mottled cream flower on an olive green glaze, the centre with holes.

3.5in (8cm) diam

£8-12 **DSC**

QUICK REFERENCE

- The eccentric Martin Brothers are best known for their pottery bird-shaped jars, which can fetch anything from around £10,000 upwards at auction today. As well as these, they also produced salt-glazed stoneware pottery, including vases, jugs and dishes, which can be more affordable. Damage and restoration reduces values considerably, with pieces often being available for under £1,000.
- Robert Wallace Martin founded his first pottery in the 1860s, making terracotta sculpture. In 1873, he opened a new pottery in Fulham, London with his brothers Charles, Walter and Edwin. In 1877, they moved to Southall where most of their work was produced. The pottery prospered producing Gothic Revival style wares until the 1910s when deaths in the family left it foundering, until it closed in 1915.
- Look for the complex, unusual and sometimes 'grotesque' patterns and forms based on natural and mythological themes for which the brothers are best known. Robert Wallace was responsible for most of the grotesque figural jars and face jugs, Charles managed the business, Walter brought technical expertise, particularly with glazes, and Edwin was the thrower and decorator, having previously worked at Doulton.
- The brothers often signed the pieces they were responsible for, and most pieces are also dated. Marks can also help date pieces. From 1873-74 marks included the Fulham address, from 1874-78 the mark was simply 'London', from 1878-79 it was 'Southall', and from 1879-1915 it included 'London' and 'Southall'. The word 'Bros' or 'Brothers' was used after 1882.

A Martin Brothers stoneware miniature vase, incised and painted with blossom in white and brown on a buff ground, the base incised 'Martin London'.

2.25in (6cm) high

£350-450 **WW**

A Martin Brothers stoneware vase, by Robert Wallace Martin, with flowering plants, the base incised 'R W Martin & Bros., London & Southall 2.1886', extensive cracking.

Undamaged this vase may have fetched over three times as much.

1886 *9.5in (24cm) high*

£280-320 **DN**

A Martin Brothers stoneware vase, incised with scrolling foliage, painted in shades of brown and ochre, incised '9-1890, Martin Bros, London & Southall', cracked.

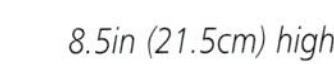

8.5in (21.5cm) high

£500-700 **WW**

A pair of early Martin Brothers stoneware vases, by Robert Wallace Martin, incised with simple foliage and berries on a banded design, incised 'R W Martin Southall, 1878', hairline crack to one, repair to rim of other.

1878 *10in (25.5cm) high*

£600-900 **WW**

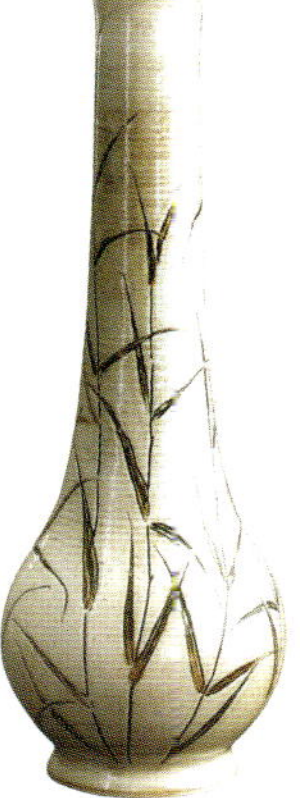

A tall Martin Brothers stoneware vase, of slender form, incised and painted with simple grasses, the base incised 'Martin Bros, London & Southall, 10-1903', hairline crack to top rim.

1903 *9.25in (23.5cm) high*

£300-500 **WW**

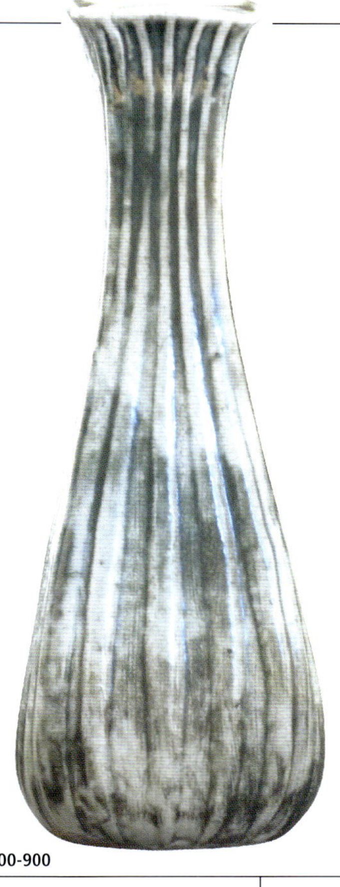

A Martin Brothers ribbed stoneware gourd vase, with mottled green glazes, the base incised 'Martinware Southall', minor restoration to exterior of top rim.

9in (23cm) high

£600-900 **WW**

A CLOSER LOOK AT A MARTIN BROTHERS JUG

The decoration is typical in terms of its concern with the Medieval 'grotesque', as well as the Far and Middle Eastern influences seen in the curling arabesques.

As well as being well-potted, the inscribed and painted design is extremely well-executed.

Although jugs are less popular than vases, particularly birds and figural forms, they are becoming more sought after as prices for the best pieces continue to rise.

It dates from 1895, which can be considered a highpoint of the brothers' output.

A Martin Brothers square section stoneware dragon jug, each side incised and painted with a ferocious dragon on an ochre ground, the base incised 'Martin Brothers London & Southall, 4-1895', professional restoration to the top rim.

1895 *9.75in (24.5cm) high*

£2,000-3,000 **WW**

A large Martin Brothers footed vase, with a tall collar neck incised with humming birds and lilies over a tonal blue ground, incised mark and date to base, restored.

1898 *12.5in (32cm) high*

£300-500 **FLD**

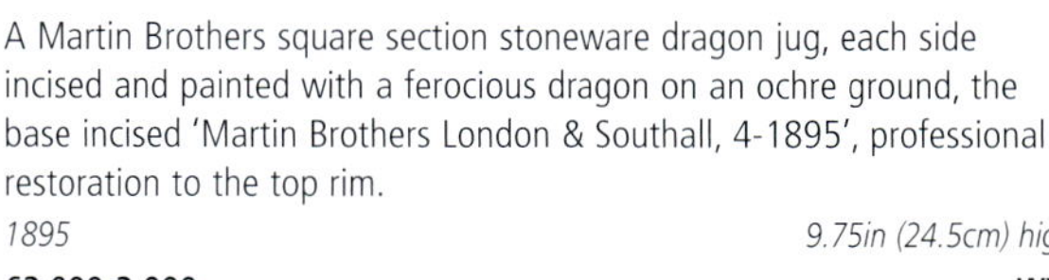

A small Martin Brothers stoneware bottle vase, incised with a ruffle shoulder band in green with a blue neck and brown body, the base incised 'Martin London'.

5in (12.5cm) high

£300-500 **DN**

A Martin Brothers stoneware vase, by Robert Wallace Martin, of lobed form with four cylindrical necks, incised with weave decoration, the base incised 'R W Martin D38', chips.

6in (15cm) high

£400-600 **WW**

A Martin Brothers stoneware jug, incised with finches flying and resting in boughs, incised 'R W Martin & Bros, London & Southall, 1-1887', restored base rim.

1887 *8.75in (22cm) high*

£400-600 **WW**

QUICK REFERENCE

- William Moorcroft (1872–1945) began working as a designer at James MacIntyre & Company, Burslem in 1897, and was promoted to Manager of Ornamental Ware in 1898. His first designs were the 'Florian' and 'Aurelian' ranges, typified by their complex Moorish-inspired symmetrical patterns of natural themes including leaves and flowers. Highly stylised, they are typical of the Art Nouveau style prevalent at the time.
- Moorcroft's hand-thrown shapes were decorated with a tube-lining process, where an outline of liquid clay was piped onto the surface and then filled with liquid glaze. After great success, Moorcroft left MacIntyre in 1912 in order to found his own company with backing from London retailer Liberty. His success continued and, in 1929, Moorcroft was awarded the Royal Warrant.
- Colours are typically rich and deep, and patterns continued to be inspired by the natural world, although as the Art Nouveau style went out of fashion new ranges were created. After William's death, his son Walter took over and continued many of his father's designs, as well as introducing some of his own.
- The most desirable and valuable ranges tend to be early, from 1900–20s, and include 'Florian', 'Aurelian' and any of the landscape or mushroom patterns. However, more modern ranges produced by designers including Sally Tuffin (at Moorcroft from 1986–92) and Rachel Bishop (joined 1993) are also growing in value on the 'secondary market', particularly if they are from a limited edition or in an unusual colour or pattern variation.
- Patterns produced for long periods tend to be the most affordable, particularly if the piece is small. The pattern, shape, size and type of marks on the base can help to date a piece, and always examine the entire body for signs of damage.

A MacIntyre & Co. 'Aurelian' pattern part tea service, designed by William Moorcroft, comprising a hot water jug, two plates, three saucers and five cups, the bases with registration no.314901 for 1898, and 308931 for 1897.
c1899 *Jug 5.75in (14.5cm) high*
£250-350 **DN**

A Moorcroft 'Flamminian' pattern small baluster vase, for Liberty & Co., designed by William Moorcroft, the red ground with foliate roundels, with incised signature and printed marks.
1906-1913 *4.75in (14.5cm) high*
£200-300 **DN**

A MacIntyre & Co. twin-handled jar, with blue Forget-me-not flower pattern, designed by William Moorcroft, printed mark, missing lid.
c1903 *4.25in (11cm) high*
£70-100 **SAS**

A MacIntyre & Co. miniature vase, with the 'Poppy' design, designed by William Moorcroft, the base impressed '28', and brown printed 'MacIntyre' mark and 'WM' in green.

Probably produced from c1910-20 as salesman's samples, miniatures are very rare and desirable. The idea was revived in the 1970s, but backstamps and patterns differ. These later pieces are worth from around a tenth of this value.

2.25in (6cm) high
£1,000-1,500 **SWO**

An MacIntyre & Co. Florian ware 'Seaweed' pattern biscuit barrel and cover, designed by William Moorcroft, the base with script 'WM' mark.
c1902 *6.25in (16cm) high*
£300-500 **SWO**

QUICK REFERENCE – POMEGRANATE

'Pomegranate' was designed by William Moorcroft and introduced in 1910. Along with 'Pansy', introduced a year later, it marked a sea-change in Moorcroft's designs. Background colours were mottled and merged together, and motifs were limited to one area of the piece, usually arranged in a band around the body – often the shoulder. First retailed by Liberty & Co., it became Moorcroft's most successful design by the 1920s, sold around the world. Examples made from 1910-c1919 had yellow or green backgrounds, while later examples had deeper blue and purple backgrounds.

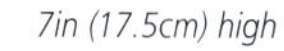

A Moorcroft 'Pomegranate' pattern baluster vase, designed by William Moorcroft, on a dark blue and green ground, with signed and printed marks to base.

7in (17.5cm) high

£50-80 **SAS**

A Moorcroft 'Celadon Pomegranate' pattern large bowl, designed by William Moorcroft, with a pale green glazed ground, the base with painted signature.

10.25in (26cm) diam

£1,800-2,200 **FLD**

A Moorcroft 'Pomegranate' pattern spherical vase, designed by William Moorcroft, on a blue ground, with impressed signature and 'Potter to H M The Queen', with blue painted initials.

5.25in (13.5cm) high

£400-600 **DN**

A Moorcroft 'Pomegranate' pattern slender ovoid tall vase, designed by William Moorcroft, on a shaded blue ground, with impressed mark, cracked.

12.5in (31.5cm) high

£200-300 **DN**

A Moorcroft 'Pomegranate' pattern trumpet-shaped vase, designed by William Moorcroft, the base impressed 'Moorcroft Made in England' and with painted signature.

c1937 *7.25in (18.5cm) high*

£400-600 **SWO**

A miniature William Moorcroft pomegranate and berry pattern vase, with a dark blue ground, green initials and impressed marks.

3.5in (9cm) high

£150-200 **SWO**

A Moorcroft 'Amazon Twilight' pattern ovoid vase, designed by Nicola Slaney, with impressed mark, artist signed and dated '17.9.98'.

This was Slaney's first design for Moorcroft; it was enormously successful.

1998 *8.25in (21cm) high*

£300-500 **DN**

A Moorcroft 'Anna Lily' pattern double-handled vase, designed by Nicola Slaney, the base with printed and script marks.

1998 *10.25in (26cm) high*

£300-500 **SWO**

A Moorcroft 'Coneflower' pattern vase, designed by Anji Davenport, the base with factory and artist's marks, paw stamp, and mushroom stamp.

2001 *7.5in (19cm) tall*

£80-100 **BEL**

A Moorcroft 'Cotton Top' pattern baluster vase, designed by Sian Leeper, with impressed and painted marks, numbered 111 from a limited edition of 150.

2002 *8.75in (22.5cm) high*

£150-250 **DN**

A Moorcroft 'Kyoto' pattern vase, designed by Rachel Bishop, numbered 70 from a limited edition of 100, the base with printed and painted marks, and with certificate.

The design is based on that found on the gate to the Imperial Palace in the ancient Japanese capital of Kyoto. Along with Sally Tuffin, Bishop is one of Moorcroft's most sought-after contemporary designers.

c1994/95 *24in (61cm) high*

£1,200-1,800 **LT**

A Moorcroft trial 'D'Larch' pattern ginger jar and cover, with stylised trees in yellow and green, on a graduated navy blue ground, initialled to reverse, dated '3.10.2000'.

2000

£350-450 **LT**

A Moorcroft 'Finches' pattern baluster vase, designed by Sally Tuffin, on a blue ground, with painted initials and date code.

1993 *7.25in (18.5cm) high*

£200-300 **DN**

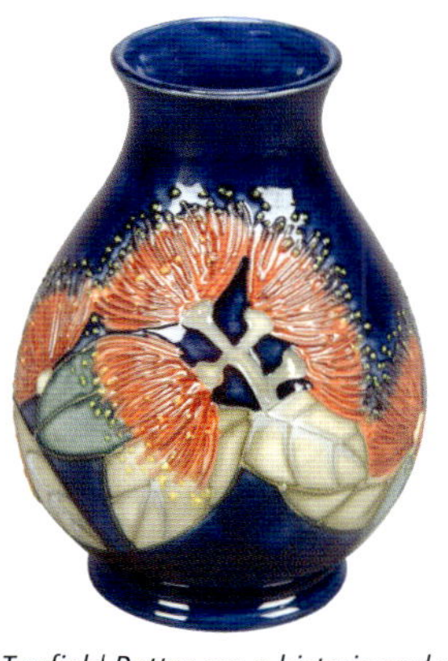

A Moorcroft 'Pohutukawa' pattern baluster vase, designed by Sally Tuffin, from a limited edition of 100 for Tanfield Potter, with impressed mark and date code, with Tanfield Potter retailer's label.

Tanfield Potter are a historic and respected ceramics and glass retailer in Auckland, New Zealand. They commissioned this design, which was also produced on a charger made in 1992 in a limited edition of 220. Related to the myrtle, the evergreen flowering Pohutukawa is also called the 'New Zealand Christmas Tree'.

1900 *13in (33cm) high*

£150-200 **DN**

QUICK REFERENCE – SALLY TUFFIN

Sally Tuffin (b.1938) studied at the Royal College of Art's fashion school before co-founding the fashion and textile design company 'Tuffin & Foale' that became synonymous with fashion during the Swinging Sixties. In 1986, after bringing up two children, she returned to design as Moorcroft's third ever designer – and the first from outside the Moorcroft family. She remained there until 1993, when she founded the Dennis Chinaworks with her husband Richard Dennis, a thriving company that she still runs today. From 1995-98, she also designed for Poole Pottery. Her work is hotly sought after by collectors, with five figure prices being paid for unique items and scarce, desirable ranges.

A Moorcroft 'Siberian Iris' pattern vase, designed by Sian Leeper, numbered 208 from a limited edition of 250, the base with impressed and painted marks.

2003 *8.75in (22cm) high*

£250-350 **DN**

A Moorcroft 'Torridon' pattern ovoid vase, designed by Philip Gibson, with impressed and painted marks.

2004 *8in (20.5cm) high*

£250-350 **DN**

A Moorcroft 'Raincloud' pattern vase, designed by Sally Tuffin, numbered 147 from a limited edition of 150, initialled and dated 'Sally Tuffin' and signed 'J. Moorcroft' 1993'.

1993 *16.75in (45.5cm) high*

£1,000-1,500 **LT**

A Moorcroft 'H.M.S. Sirius' pattern charger, designed by Sally Tuffin, numbered 9 from a limited edition of 150, together with original box.

This pattern was originally made to commemorate the Australian Bicentenary in 1988, but opened up to a wider audience later. The edition size was 250, with 100 being made specially for the Australian market.

1988 *14in (35.5cm) diam*

£350-450 **WW**

A Moorcroft 'Underwood' pattern ovoid vase, designed and decorated by Debbie Hancock, numbered 235 from a limited edition of 350 produced for MacIntyre of Leeds, with impressed and printed marks, and painted initials.

7in (18cm) high

£200-300 **DN**

FIND OUT MORE...

Paul Atterbury ' Moorcroft' , *published by Richard Dennis, 1996*

QUICK REFERENCE

- Nursery ware ceramics, such as plates, mugs and other tableware, was made for children. The first examples appeared in the early 19thC, when surfaces were decorated with colour transfers, depicting moral and educational images and mottos. The idea was that, as the child ate, they could be educated or instructed on their moral code.
- By the early 20thC, nursery ware moved away from these serious themes and became more playful. Scenes from nature, animals, children's stories and nursery rhymes were all used. Related figurines were also produced.
- Many charming designs were produced by Grimwades Ltd (sometimes known under their brand name, Royal Winton). These are decorated with characters, such as Pip the Panda.
- In general, look out for popular images, such as the 'Man in the Moon'. Be aware that wear to transfers, as well as chips or cracks, will reduce the value of any piece. These pieces were made to be used by children, so pieces in mint condition will command a premium.
- Fakes have been produced. Be wary of any examples with transfers over the glaze, rather than under it.

A 1930s Grimwades 'The Circus' child's oval bowl, with printed 'Baby's Plate' mark, with some wear to transfers and chip to base.

Without the wear and damage, this dish could have fetched up to twice this value.

8in (20.5cm) diam

£30-40 **BAD**

A 1930s Grimwades 'Old Country Nursery Rhymes' child's dish, with a transfer-printed design of an elf and a sheep, the back with printed globe factory mark.

7in (17.5cm) diam

£40-60 **BAD**

A 1920s-30s Grimwades 'Baa Baa Black Sheep' oval child's dish, the back with printed marks and registered no.554903 or 557903 for 1910.

8in (20.5cm) wide

£30-40 **BAD**

A Royal Winton child's mug, with a transfer-printed rabbit drummer, a pig playing trumpet and a panda conducting.

3.75in (9.5cm) high

£30-50 **BAD**

A 1950s Royal Winton child's mug, with a transfer-printed scene of a panda teaching a rabbit and pig, the base with printed mark.

3.75in (9.5cm) high

£35-45 **BAD**

A large Royal Winton 'Bunny's Playtime' circular bowl, with a transfer-printed design of a rabbit watering plants.

6.75in (17cm) diam

£30-40 **BAD**

A Royal Winton 'Bunny's Playtime' transfer-printed child's dinner or pudding bowl.

6.25in (16cm) diam

£25-35 **BAD**

A Royal Winton 'Bunny's Playtime' transfer-printed double-handled nursery mug, with a rabbit painting a chick's portrait.

3.25in (8.5cm) high

£30-50 **BAD**

A Royal Winton 'Bunny's Playtime' transfer-printed nursery wall clock, with six vignettes of rabbits at play.

This was made by drilling a standard plate and fitting it with a clock mechanism. Note how an 'adult' sized and more ornate dinner plate has been used. Always examine the mechanism and particularly the hands to ensure they are original. Wall clocks are much harder to find than cups, bowls and dishes.

8.75in (22.5cm) wide

£60-90 **BAD**

A Royal Winton 'Pip The Panda' transfer-printed cup and saucer, the back and base with printed mark.

6in (15cm) diam

£30-50 **BAD**

QUICK REFERENCE – MABEL LUCIE ATTWELL

Artist and illustrator Mabel Lucie Attwell (1879-1964) rose to prominence in the early years of the 20thC with drawings of fairies and children. After designing posters and producing book illustrations, she turned to ceramic design, registering her first designs for children's ware for Shelley in 1926. These usually incorporated her hallmark chubby children, reputedly inspired by her daughter Peggy, and her 'Boo Boo' elf characters. Produced into the 1930s, they are highly popular with collectors today. Nearly all pieces are 'signed' with her printed name, and bear a green shield Shelley mark on the bases or backs. Beware of fakes made from original Shelley pieces, which are either all hand-painted or bear transfer-printed designs over the glaze. Also look at the Shelley marks carefully, as entirely faked ceramics and designs are known. Attwell did not design for Susie Cooper, despite the rise in supposedly 'rare' Cooper ceramics bearing designs like Attwell's.

A Shelley 'Boo Boo' teaset, designed by Mabel Lucie Attwell, comprising a milk jug in the form of a saluting elf, a teapot in the form of a toadstool house, and a toadstool-shaped sugar bowl, each with facsimile name printing, and factory printed marks to base.

Milk jug 6.5in (16.5cm) high

£400-600 HT

A Shelley 'Boo Boo' Nursery ware teapot and cover, designed by Mabel Lucie Attwell, printed and enamelled in colours, printed factory mark.

4.5in (11.5cm) high

£120-180 WW

A 1930s Shelley nursery ware saluting 'Boo Boo' elf-shaped milk jug, designed by Mabel Lucie Attwell, the base with printed marks and registered no.724421 for 1926.

6in (15.5cm) high

£100-150 BAD

A 1930s Shelley nurseyware child's mug, with transfer-printed scene of a baby with elves seated on a crescent moon, designed by Mabel Lucie Attwell, the back with printed factory marks.

2.75in (7cm) high

£120-180 PC

A 1930s Shelley nurseryware child's mug, with transfer-printed design of a child with a bunny seated on a caravan, with animals and elves around him, designed by Mabel Lucie Attwell, with printed marks to back.

2.75in (7cm) high

£120-180 PC

A Shelley nurseryware child's plate, designed by Mabel Lucie Attwell, with a transfer-printed scene of a little girl pushing animals in a wheelbarrow, with light blue rim, and printed factory marks to back.

6in (15cm) diam

£80-120 BAD

A 1930s Shelley child's dish, with a transfer-printed and hand-painted pattern of elves in a plane and parachuting elves, the back with printed factory marks.

6in (15cm) diam

£120-180 PC

A 1940s-50s Simpsons Pottery Ambassador Ware bowl, designed by Mabel Lucie Attwell, with transfer-printed cart, pixie, donkey and little girl pattern and pink rim, the back with printed marks.

Despite being an authentic Attwell design, as it is not Shelley this is less desirable to collectors. Ambassador ware was a higher quality range from Stafforshire's Soho Pottery, which was known as Simpson's from 1944.

5.25in (13.5cm) diam

£30-50 BAD

QUICK REFERENCE

- In summer 1946, Pablo Picasso (1881–1973) went to the annual Vallauris pottery festival during a holiday in the South of France. While he was there he met Suzanne and George Ramié, owners of the Madoura pottery. Later he visited their pottery and created three of his own pieces.
- Upon his return to the town a year later, he revisited the pottery and was given an area to produce his own designs. Between then and 1971, he created over 3,500 designs in the stylised, abstract and avant garde style of his paintings. Although many unique items were created, the vast majority of examples that can be found today will be from the limited edition ranges produced from his originals by a team of potters at Madoura.
- The limited editions were produced either by directly copying Picasso's form and design, or by using a plaster mould that had been carved or decorated by Picasso himself. Each example from a limited edition was then stamped with a mark in French meaning 'Original Print of Picasso', often together with other information such as the size of the edition.
- Designs focus on the subjects typically found in his paintings such as mythology, Classical subjects, animals, faces and bull-fighting. Picasso also worked the clay surface, creating texture and raised, moulded motifs.
- When buying it is best to learn about the marks used as these will help you identify the best pieces, and spot fakes. All pieces are marked in some way, but always look for the official pottery mark. The appeal of the design, the size of the edition and the condition will all affect value. Values range from as little as £400 to over £20,000.

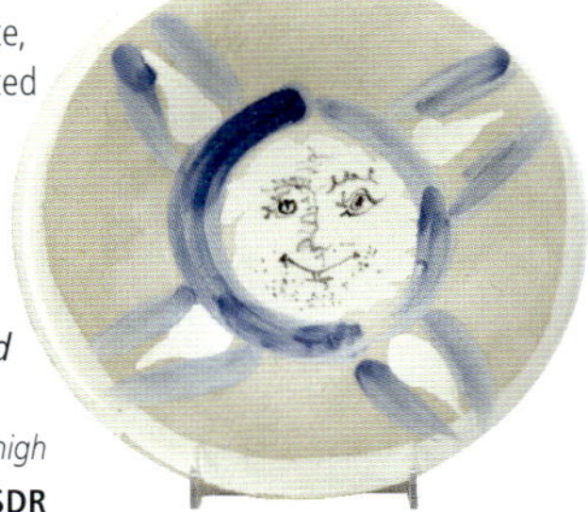

A Madoura glazed faience earthenware 'Visage No.72' plate, designed by Pablo Picasso, painted with abstract face, marked 'No. 72 EDITION PICASSO 120/150 MADOURA'.

This design was conceived in 1963 and produced in a limited edition of 150.

10.25in (26cm) high

£1,800-2,200 SDR

A Madoura faience plate, designed by Pablo Picasso on 10th March 1953, hand-painted with face and sunray motif and 'Vallauris 10 3 53', stamped 'Plein Feu Empreinte Originale De Picasso'.

8in (20.5cm) diam

£1,500-2,000 DRA

A Madoura faience plate, from the 'Service Visage Noir', designed by Pablo Picasso, with abstract face on black ground, signed 'EDITION PICASSO', stamped 'EDITION PICASSO MADOURA PLEIN FEU'.

This design, from the 'Black Face Service', was conceived in 1948.

9.25in (23.5cm) diam

£2,000-3,000 DRA

A glazed Madoura faience plate, designed by Pablo Picasso, depicting a goat, stamped 'Madoura Plein Feu Empreinte Originale De Picasso'.

10in (25.5cm) wide

£2,000-3,000 DRA

A Madoura faience wall plaque, designed by Pablo Picasso, moulded with four dancing figures in black on a white ground, the back with impressed 'Madoura/ Plein Feu/ Empreinte/ Originale De/ Picasso' marks.

9.75in (25cm) diam

£1,200-1,800 L&T

A glazed Madoura faience plate, designed by Pablo Picasso, with still-life, stamped 'Madoura'.

This example is valuable because the design is close to Picasso's stylised, abstract painting. It is truly a 'painting on clay'.

1956 *9.5in (24cm) wide*

£3,000-4,000 **DRA**

A Madoura faience pitcher, designed by Pablo Picasso, with design of abstract faces, spots and a stylised branch, signed and stamped 'EDITION PICASSO MADOURA'.

6.25in (16cm) wide

£2,000-3,000 **DRA**

A Madoura faience pitcher, designed by Pablo Picasso, with abstract masks, signed 'EDITION PICASSO MADOURA'.

6in (15cm) wide

£1,500-2,500 **DRA**

A CLOSER LOOK AT A PICASSO PITCHER

Picasso's animal and anthropomorphic pottery forms are particularly sought after by collectors, and tend to be valuable.

Pitchers are typically modelled as stylised birds, usually known as a 'chouette', the French word for 'owl', and were produced in many variations from the 1950s onwards.

The hand-painted design on this example is comparatively simple – had it been more decorative, it could have been worth more.

Its three-dimensional form was entirely handmade, rather than being moulded from a carved plaster cast, and is more appealing than a dish.

A Madoura faience pitcher, designed by Pablo Picasso, with abstract bird design, signed 'EDITION PICASSO MADOURA'.

11.5in (29cm) high

£4,000-5,000 **DRA**

A Madoura faience pitcher, designed by Pablo Picasso, with wax-resist image of Don Quixote and bull, the back with impressed edition mark.

5in (12.5cm) wide

£450-650 **GORL**

A Madoura ceramic water pitcher, designed by Pablo Picasso, no. 276 from an edition of 300, of abstract bird form, signed 'Edition Picasso 276/300 Madoura Plein Feu'.

9.5in (24cm) high

£3,000-4,000 **SDR**

A 1930s Poole Pottery bowl, shape no.434, decorated in a stylised floral and foliate pattern designed by Truda Carter, with decorator's monogram 'UA'.

9.5in (24cm) diam

£150-200 **BAD**

A 1930s Poole Pottery vase, of shouldered ovoid form decorated in the VY 'Blue bell' pattern designed by Truda Carter, the base with impressed and painted marks.

8in (20.5cm) high

£70-100 **FLD**

A Carter Stabler & Adams Poole Pottery 'Mary Mary, Quite Contrary' hand painted plate, from the Nursery Rhymes range, designed by Dora Batty, the back with impressed and painted marks.

8in (20.5cm) diam

£30-40 **W&W**

QUICK REFERENCE – POOLE POTTERY

The world famous Poole Pottery began as a subsidiary acquired in 1921 by the Carter, Stabler & Adams pottery. The pottery's fame grew during the 1920s with the introduction of a range of hand painted Art Deco stylised floral and foliate patterns designed by Truda Carter, which dominated production into the 1950s. During the 1950s, the 'Contemporary' and 'Freefrom' ranges were introduced, designed by Alfred Read and Ruth Pavely. The employment of Robert Jefferson as designer in 1958 led to the introduction of the experimental Poole Studio, whose work led to the 'Delphis' range. The 1960s and 70s were dominated by 'Delphis', and by the 'Aegean', 'Ionian' and 'Atlantis' ranges that were developed within the innovative new Craft Section. The fashionable oranges, reds and greens of the period were typical. This important vase bears a label showing it was exhibited at the Royal Academy Exhibition of British Art & Industry. Being such an important piece, it is likely that Carter painted, as well as designed, the pattern.

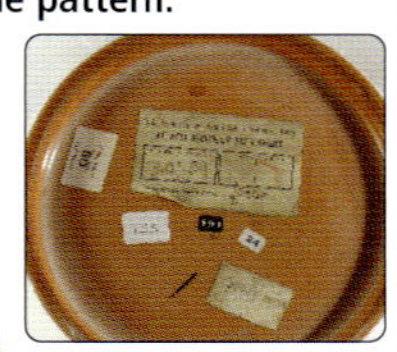

A Carter, Stabler & Adams (Poole Pottery) vase, shape no.946, designed and probably painted by Truda Carter, the base with impressed factory marks, applied exhibition and auction paper labels, firing fault to top rim.

c1934 15.75in (40cm) high

£1,000-1,500 **WW**

A 1950s Poole Pottery 'Contemporary' range vase, shape 722 designed by Alfred Read, with PV pattern designed by Ruth Pavely, the base with printed and painted marks.

9.5in (24cm) high

£180-220 **WW**

A 1950s Poole Pottery 'Contemporary' range vase, pattern PKC, designed by Alfred Read, the base with printed and painted marks.

6in (15cm) high

£180-220 **WW**

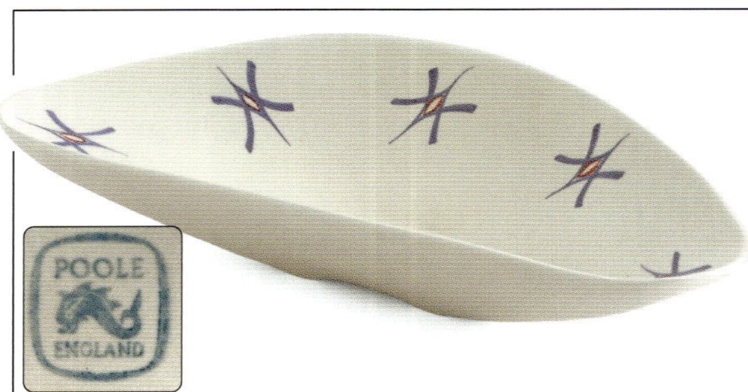

A 1950s Poole Pottery 'Contemporary' range bowl, shape 338 designed by Alfred Read, decorated with the FSU pattern designed by Ruth Pavely, the base with printed mark.

This mark was used from 1955-59. A more rectangular version was used 1959-67.

17.5in (44cm) wide

£60-90 **WW**

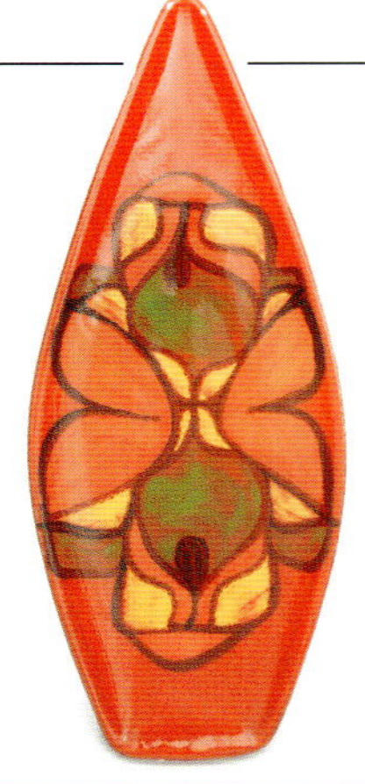

A Poole Pottery orange, green and yellow 'Delphis' large spear dish, with printed black POOLE dolphin mark, stamped '82', and with painted 'iY or CY' monogram.

17.5in (44cm) long

£40-50 **M20C**

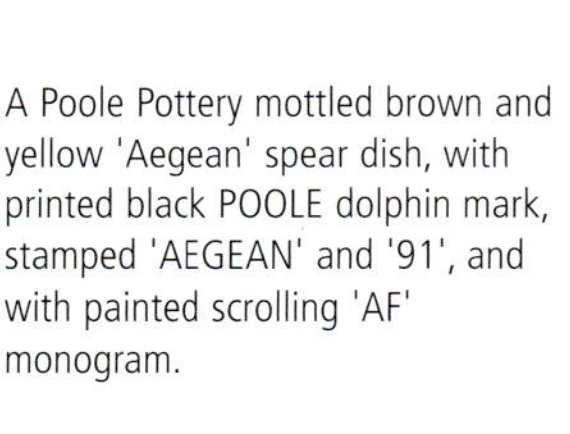

A Poole Pottery mottled brown and yellow 'Aegean' large spear dish, with printed black POOLE dolphin mark, stamped 'AEGEAN' and '82', and with painted 'iY or CY' monogram.

17.5in (44cm) long

£40-50 **M20C**

A Poole Pottery mottled brown and yellow 'Aegean' spear dish, with printed black POOLE dolphin mark, stamped 'AEGEAN' and '91', and with painted scrolling 'AF' monogram.

12in (30.5cm) long

£30-40 **M20C**

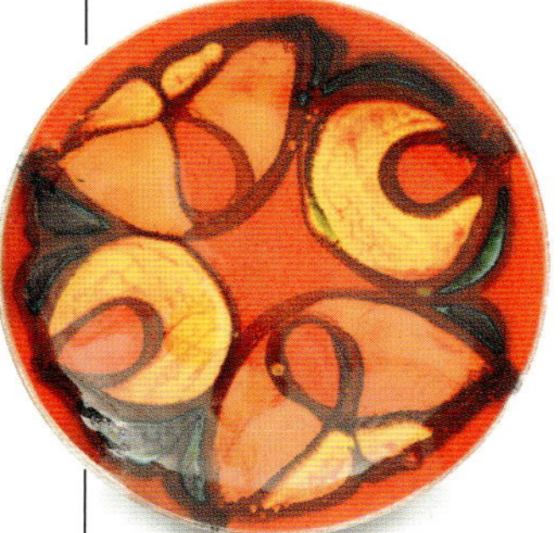

A Poole Pottery 'Delphis' bowl, with printed factory mark, stamped '3', and with painted 'MA' monogram for Mary Albon.

1972-74 *8in (20.5cm) diam*

£30-40 **M20C**

A Poole Pottery white glazed vase with wax resist band of a spiralling pattern, covered all over with a glossy transparent glaze, the base with black printed 'POOLE ENGLAND' mark, with painted ABC monogram and painted JM monogram for Jacqueline MacKenzie.

1972-77 *12in (30.5cm) high*

£30-40 **M20C**

A Poole Pottery stoneware 'Grouse' group figurine, designed by Barbara Linley Adams, together with a bird on a pinecone figurine, each with impressed and printed marks.

These figurines are believed to have been produced as test samples, and are in addition to the limited edtion of 1,000 pieces. From the collection of Roy Holland, Managing Director of Poole Pottery.

13in (33cm) wide

£150-250 **W&W**

QUICK REFERENCE

- Rookwood was founded in Cincinnati, Ohio in 1880 by Maria Longworth Nichols, a wealthy heiress who decorated ceramics as a hobby. Initially, the pottery lost money, until Nichols invited William Watts Tyler to run the company in 1883. Tyler set about organising the structure of the company and standardising lines. When Nichols moved abroad in 1890, Tyler took over the now profitable pottery.
- Well-proportioned and balanced shapes were thrown and decorated by hand. These shapes were then glazed with one of the many different glazes developed by Rookwood from the mid-1880s onwards. Tyler encouraged experimentation: glaze technicians were employed to reproduce ancient techniques and glazes, and develop new ones. The first to be produced is known as Standard, which is typified by a graduated brown background, usually painted with flowers. Portraits are rare and desirable.
- Much of the interest for collectors lies in Rookwood's glazes, many of which were inspired by Japanese ceramics. Following the success of Standard, the clear, glossy Iris glaze and the green-tinted Sea Green glaze were introduced in 1894. Vellum, which creates an Impressionistic appearance by diffusing the painted decoration (usually plants or landscapes) it covers, was launched in 1900. Matte glazes followed in 1901. As the glaze is so important, crazing (a fine network of lines) will reduce value, as will damage that detracts from the glaze or design.
- Rookwood employed many highly skilled decorators, such as Matthew Daly, Sara Sax and Maria Storer, and their work can be highly desirable. Pieces tend to be signed, so look out for marks.

A rare tall Rookwood Standard glaze vase, decorated by Sallie Toohey, with poppies on a graduated brown and beige ground, the base with flame mark, '856B' and artist's cipher.

1899 *15.5in (39.5cm) high*

£2,500-3,500 **DRA**

A Rookwood Iris Glaze vase, by Lenore Asbury, with white clematis, the base with flame mark and 'VI/951C/W./L.A'.

Rookwood's 'Iris' glaze was introduced in 1894, and was exhibited at the 1900 Paris Exposition.

1906 *9.5in (24cm) high*

£2,000-3,000 **DRA**

A Rookwood Standard glaze vase, decorated by Edith Felten with floral decoration, marked with Rookwood logo, 'IV', shape no.914F and the artist's initials, restored top rim.

1904 *4.25in (11cm) high*

£100-150 **BEL**

A Rookwood vase, decorated by Carl Schmidt with white roses, the base with the Rookwood flame mark, dated 'IV', impressed '612EZ', and artist's initials 'CS'.

7.75in (19.5cm) high

£800-1,200 **JDJ**

A Rookwood Iris glaze bulbous vase, decorated by Clara Lindeman with a branch of pink apple blossoms on shaded ground, the base with flame mark and 'VIII/654C/C.C.L.'

1908 *5in (12.5cm) high*

£800-1,200 **DRA**

A Rookwood Scenic Vellum vase, painted by E.T. Hurley, with a misty forest landscape, with flame mark and 'VIII/904D/V/E.T.H'.

1908 *8.5in (21.5cm) high*

£1,500-2,500 **DRA**

A Rookwood Scenic Vellum vase, painted by M.G. Denzler, with a bucolic landscape, with flame mark and 'XVI/9232E/V/MGD', some pitting around shoulder.

1916 *8in (20.5cm) high*

£1,000-1,500 **DRA**

QUICK REFERENCE – VELLUM GLAZE

The 'Vellum' glaze range was introduced at the St Louis exposition in 1904, and grew to become highly successful. It was developed by Stanley Burt, Rookwood's chemist and superintendant, who joined Rookwood in 1892. The matt outer glaze diffused the painted design beneath, giving a pleasing hazy effect. Most pieces were produced before 1915 – many have a fine network of cracks (crazing) today, which reduces the value. After 1915, Rookwood changed its clay composition so crazing is not found on these later Vellum pieces – however, they are rare. Flowers are the most common design, followed by landscapes. Look out for pastel tones and greens, as these are scarcer. Large sizes over 10in (20.5cm) in height, like this, are also rare. The vase shown below is also considerably more valuable because it was decorated by Rookwood's best and most famous decorator, Kataro Shirayamadani (1865-1948).

A Rookwood Scenic Vellum vase, decorated by Kataro Shirayamadani, with a scene of a wooded pond, marked with the Rookwood logo, 'XII', shape no.1369B, the letter 'V' for vellum and the artist's incised Japanese signature, minor nick to the glaze.

1912 *15in (38cm) high*

£8,000-12,000 **BEL**

A Rookwood Scenic Vellum ovoid vase, decorated by Ed Diers with tall trees, the base with flame mark 'XVII/30D/ED', restored chip at rim.

1917 *10in (25.5cm) high*

£800-1,200 **DRA**

A Rookwood Scenic Vellum vase, decorated by Lenore Asbury with a lake scene, the base with Rookwood flame logo, shape no.1661, and 'L.A.' artist initials.

8.75in (22.25cm) high

£1,000-1,500 **POOK**

A Rookwood Vellum vase, decorated by Fred Rothenbusch with white petunias on a graduated blue and white ground, with flame mark and 'XXV/2262E/FR'.

1925 *5.5in (14cm) high*

£800-1,200 **DRA**

QUICK REFERENCE

- The Roseville Pottery company was founded in the 'pottery state' of Ohio in 1890, and began by producing utilitarian stoneware. Its output included flowerpots, cuspidors (spittoons) and umbrella stands. The company's success allowed it to buy other potteries and, by 1910, production had been relocated to Zanesville, Ohio.
- Jumping on the art pottery 'bandwagon' in 1900, Roseville released 'Rozane', a range that mimicked the highly successful 'Standard Glaze' series by Rookwood (see p93). By 1908, the demand for expensive, hand-decorated art pottery had ebbed, and all but one range was discontinued at Roseville in favour of mass-produced moulded wares, which the company produced until it closed in 1954.
- Moulded designs were typically based on natural motifs, such as flowers and leaves. Although the coloured glazes were still applied by hand, the designs were much quicker and easier to decorate. Notable designers at Roseville include Frederick Rhead from 1904-08, Frank Ferrell from 1917-54, and George Krause, who worked on glazes from 1915-54. Ferrell in particular was responsible for the most successful mass-produced art pottery ranges.
- Value is determined by a combination of range, shape, colour, size and quality of decoration. More common and less desirable ranges from the 1940s, such as 'Bittersweet', tend to be less valuable. However, the similarly common ranges of 'Dahlrose' and 'Pine Cone' are widely collected and tend to be more valuable.
- Look out for large sizes or shapes that were easily damaged but in excellent condition. Always look closely at protruding parts such as handles and examine the glaze all over the piece. Chips, restoration, glaze skips and other factory flaws reduce value considerably.
- Consider how well the decoration is applied. As moulds wore down through use, look for well-detailed, sharply moulded patterns, with glazes correctly applied. Carelessly applied glazes reduce the value.

A Roseville brown 'Fuchsia' pattern vase, marked '901-10' and with a silver foil factory label to base.

10.25in (26cm) high

£150-250 **BEL**

A Roseville green and brown Fuchsia pattern vase, with two handles, marked '891-6'.

6.25in (16cm) high

£120-180 **BEL**

A Roseville brown 'Fuchsia' pattern ovoid vase, marked '347-6', with a small glaze skip to the white of one flower.

8.5in (21.5cm) wide

£120-180 **BEL**

A Roseville blue 'Fuchsia' vase, with impressed '904-15' mark, and restoration to rim.

15in (38cm) high

£250-350 **DRA**

A Roseville 'Fuchsia' pattern floor vase, with two handles, the base impressed '905-18'.

The large size, full range of vibrant colours, and excellent moulded detail make this piece particularly desirable. Fuchsia was introduced in 1938 in a variety of tones based on brown, blue and green.

18.25in (46.5cm) high

£2,000-3,000 **BEL**

A Roseville 'Futura' range Bamboo Leaf Ball vase, no.387-7", with professional restoration between base and body, unmarked.

7.25in (18.5cm) high

£250-350 **BEL**

A Roseville 'Futura' Twist vase, 398-6 1/2", with a small area of professional restoration to the rim.

6.75in (17cm) high

£200-300 **BEL**

A CLOSER LOOK AT A ROSEVILLE FUTURA VASE

Introdcued in 1928, Futura is one of the most popular of Roseville's ranges as it appeals to modern design and Art Deco collectors, as well as Roseville.

The geometric form is typical of both the Art Deco movement, and the unique shapes Frank Ferrell designed for the range.

Note how the damage and restoration on the example shown top left has affected the price – this example is in excellent condition

The unusually angled base recalls the Roseville 'Tank' vase, which is very rare and can fetch over £6,000.

A Roseville 'Futura' range Bamboo Leaf Ball vase, 387-7", in blue with dark blue and green stylised leaves.

7.5in (19cm) high

£700-1,000 **BEL**

A Roseville 'Futura' range four-footed four-sided vase, with stylised floral pattern on a burgundy ground, with small glazed-over chip to inner foot.

9in (23cm) high

£800-1,200 **DRA**

A Roseville 'Futura' range handled urn vase, no.382-7", in excellent condition.

7.25in (18.5cm) high

£250-350 **BEL**

A Roseville blue 'Futura' range hibachi footed dish, no.198-5", repairs to two areas of the rim and two darkened lines at the rim among the crazing.

A hibachi is a traditional Japanese heating or cooking bowl filled with hot charcoal.

5.25in (13.5cm) wide

£250-350 **BEL**

A large Roseville brown 'Pine Cone' urn, no.912-15", the base with impressed mark.

With its origins in Classical architecture, this is a rare shape.

15.25in (39cm) high

£1,000-1,500 **DRA**

A Roseville blue 'Pine Cone' ovoid vase, with two small branch-like handles, no.856-12", the base with impressed mark.

12in (30.5cm) high

£800-1,200 **DRA**

A Roseville green 'Pine Cone' footed bowl, 261-6", with original foil label to base.

6.5in (16.5cm) high

£150-250 **BEL**

A pair of Roseville brown 'Pine Cone' triple candleholders, no.1106, the bases marked '1106-5 1/2"', each with a number of small chips.

5.5in (14cm) high

£100-150 **BEL**

A Roseville blue 'Pine Cone' wall pocket, 1273-8", with restoration to tip of branch, and raised mark to back.

Wallpockets are a popular theme for many Roseville collectors, so are often comparatively highly priced.

8in (20.5cm) high

£300-400 **DRA**

A Roseville blue 'Pine Cone' candy dish, no.497, the base marked 'Roseville USA 497"'

7in (18cm) high

£60-80 **BEL**

QUICK REFERENCE – ROSEVILLE PINE CONE

'Pine Cone' was introduced in 1935 and went on to become one of the company's best-selling ranges. Designed by Frank Ferrell, it probably saved the company during the Depression. More than 150 shapes were produced. It was made in green, blue, brown and pink colourways, with blue usually being the most desirable and pink extremely rare. This particular piece displays well-placed colouring as well as crisp moulding. Complete and undamaged jardinières are hard to find, and are usually valuable in any range.

A Roseville blue 'Pine Cone' jardinière and pedestal, the jardinière marked 'Roseville USA 403-10"' and the pedestal marked 'Roseville USA 406-10", with one chip to the inside of the foot and slight wear to the top surface.

28.5in (72cm) high

£1,000-1,500 **BEL**

QUICK REFERENCE – ROSEVILLE MARKS

Roseville used many different marks over time, but many pieces were left unmarked. The word 'USA' was only used on raised, moulded marks. Beware of faintly moulded examples, as these may be fakes. Also consider the style of the wording and individual letters, as this can help identify fakes made primarily in the Far East. If in doubt, compare to a piece you are sure is original, also taking the colours and form of the body into account.

Early Rozane Ware 'wafer' mark with 'Woodland' range name.

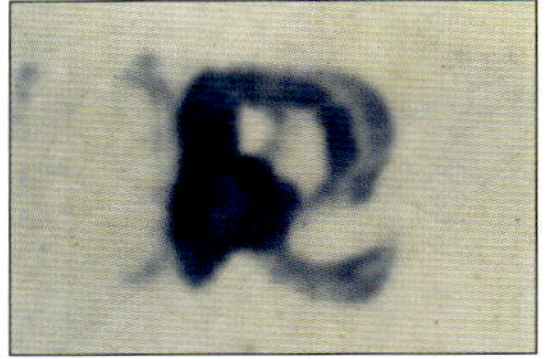

Stamped 'RV' ink mark, c1923-c1927.

Foil or paper label and handwritten shape number, c1927-35.

Impressed Roseville mark and shape number, 1936-40.

Moulded Roseville USA mark, shape number and size, 1940 onwards.

A 1940s-Roseville pink 'Apple Blossom' basket, 309-8", marked 'Roseville USA 309-8"'.

8.5in (20.5cm) high

£150-250 **BEL**

A Roseville blue 'Bleeding Heart' vase, 961-4", marked 'Roseville USA 961-4"'.

4.75in (12cm) wide.

£100-150 **BEL**

A Roseville 'Blackberry' vase, 567-4", with glaze flake and an area of branch handle repaired.

4in (10cm) high

£200-300 **BEL**

A Roseville blue 'Bushberry' vase, marked 'USA 32-7'.

7.25in (18.5cm) high

£180-220 **BEL**

QUICK REFERENCE – ROYAL COPENHAGEN

Royal Copenhagen was founded under Danish Royal patronage in 1775. Although it is well known for its fine tableware (such as 'Flora Danica'), it is 20thC decorative wares that attract the most interest from collectors today. Important designers include Axel Salto, Knud Kyhn, Arnold Krog, Johanne Gerber, and the long-serving Nils Thorsson. Forms tend to be simple, with much inspiration for the pattern taken from nature. The pieces are subject to strongly modern stylisation. The base of the popular 'Baca' and similar ranges of the 1950s-70s bear monograms for each designer, which are known as 'chop' marks. The one shown here is for Johanne Gerber.

A Royal Copenhagen Baca Fajance bottle vase, with a handpainted pattern of leaves and branches, no.780/3259, designed by Johanne Gerber, the base with printed and painted marks.

7.75in (19.5cm) high

£50-80 GC

A Danish Royal Copenhagen Fajance vase, no. 711/3755, designed by Nils Thorsson, with painted and printed factory marks to base.

7.5in (19cm) high

£40-60 RET

A Royal Copenhagen Fajance pottery vase, no.726/3259, designed by Nils Thorsson, with painted and printed factory marks to base.

8.75in (22.5cm) high

£60-80 SAS

A Danish Royal Copenhagen Baca Fajance chimney vase, no. 635/3121, designed by Ellen Malmer, with printed and painted marks to base.

7.75in (19.5cm) high

£50-60 M20C

A Danish Royal Copenhagen Baca Fajance dish, no.730/2883, designed by Nils Thorsson, the base with printed factory marks.

6.75in (17cm) wide

£30-40 RET

A Royal Copenhagen Fajance square dish, no.704/2883, designed by Nils Thorsson, with painted and printed factory marks to base.

6.5in (16.5cm) wide

£50-70 SAS

CERAMICS

A Royal Copenhagen celadon lidded fluted bowl, no.457/2939, the finial modelled as a seated figure and with crackle glaze, with gilt highlights, the base with printed and painted marks.

6in (15.5cm) high

£80-120 **W&W**

A Royal Copenhagen spherical stoneware vase, designed by Axel Salto, embossed with a tree pattern under black and mahogany glaze, the base incised 'Salto 1243 'with factory mark.

7.75in (19.5cm) high

£2,000-2,500 **DRA**

An Art Deco Royal Copenhagan celadon glaze free standing mask, 'Medusa', designed by Hans Henrik Hansen in 1927, model no. 1/2950, the base with impressed and painted marks.

1927 *10.5in (27cm) high*

£500-700 **WW**

A Royal Copenhagen bear cub, no. 21434, designed by Knud Kyhn.

Earlier glazes are lighter in tone, being more creamy in colour, sometimes with green tones.

3.25in (8cm) high

£50-80 **WW**

A 1950s-60s Royal Copenhagen bowl, designed by Gerd Bogelund, the interior decorated with a fine brown haresfur glaze, the exterior with impressed and sgrafitto stylised motifs of ears of wheat, the base with printed three wave mark and painted 'GB'.

4.75in (12cm) high

£120-180 **UCT**

A CLOSER LOOK AT AN AXEL SALTO ROYAL COPENHAGEN VASE

Axel Salto (1889-1961) is regarded by many as most influential Danish ceramics designer. He worked for the company from 1933 onwards.

Beginning to pot in the mid-1920s, he won numerous awards including the Grand Prix at the Milan Triennale 1951.

Salto' s powerfully modelled 'budding', 'sprouting' or 'living' themed stonewares were inspired by organic forms such as buds and tree cones. They cross the boundary between functional vase and decorative sculpture.

His dark and rich glazes match the natural form perfectly, and were inspired by ancient Chinese examples such as Sung period wares.

A Royal Copenhagen stoneware 'budding' vase, designed by Axel Salto, covered in mottled brown glaze, the base incised 'SALTO', with factory marks, and numbered '20559'.

10in (25.5cm) wide

£6,000-8,000 **DRA**

QUICK REFERENCE

- The Worcester porcelain factory (established in 1751) first began operating under the name Worcester Royal Porcelain Company in 1862. George III had granted the first of several royal warrants in Worcester's illustrious history in 1789.
- The late Victorian period was very successful for Royal Worcester. The company became known for the colour of its porcelain: soft ivory and pink tints, which echoed art glass. Key designers include George Owen and James Hadley.
- The early years of 20thC saw a simplification of forms and decorative styles. There was a greater output of everyday ware, but hand-painted porcelain was still produced and contributed to the company's success. Vases, plates and other forms were decorated by well-known painters, including Harry Davies and the Stinton family (the best known are Harry Stinton, his father John Stinton Jnr., and uncle James Stinton). By this time all major Royal Worcester artists were signing their work, so look for marks, as a well-known artist may add value.
- Naturalistically painted, modelled ceramic sculptures were introduced in the 1930s. Dorothy Doughty's bird and flower models (produced from 1935) are popular with collectors, as are Doris Lindner's animal figures. Look for small limited editions, as these may be rare and desirable.
- Royal Worcester became a public company in 1954 and merged with Spode in 1978. From this period, Royal Worcester stopped their decorative pieces, focusing on high-quality tableware and figure modelling. In 2009, having gone into administration, Royal Worcester was bought by rival company, Portmeirion Pottery.
- Pieces are marked 'Royal Worcester', with a dot added to this mark for every year between 1892 and 1916. After this, an asterisk was added to the dots.

A Royal Worcester miniature vase, painted by James Stinton with a pheasant in a landscape, with gilt scrolling handles, puce mark to the base and no.'287'.

5.5in (14cm) high

£250-350 **DUK**

A Royal Worcester 'blush' double-handled vase, with pierced collar and painted with flowers and a butterfly, on gilt-painted and moulded base.

13.5in (38.5cm) high

£180-220 **A&G**

A Royal Worcester porcelain two-handled pedestal ovoid vase, shape no.2277, painted by Ernest Philips with two panels of summer flowers and a pink ribbon bow, within blue and gilt striped bands, signed, printed mark in puce, date cipher.

1912

£350-450 **TEN**

A Royal Worcester prismatic enamel pedestal urn, decorated with trailing gilt blossom and enamelled flowers on pink-blush-tinted ivory ground below mask head handles strung with 'silk' swags below short pierced neck, restored.

11.75in (30cm) high

£300-400 **FLD**

A Royal Worcester two-handled pedestal vase, shape 998/G, painted by G.H. Cole with lilies within green and gilt stiff-leaf band borders, with green printed marks, dated.

£300-500 **DN**

A Royal Worcester pedestal vase, the globular body decorated with brightly coloured clover, buttercups and forget-me-nots, the base with printed mark and date code.

1903 *9.75in (25cm) high*

£180-220 **WW**

A Royal Worcester trumpet vase, painted with roses and buds by Millie Hunt, signed 'M Hunt', within sponged gold borders, dated.

1931

£220-280 **FLD**

A CLOSER LOOK AT A PAIR OF ROYAL WORCESTER VASES

Miniature vases are scarce and desirable. The fact that they are an original pair adds to the value.

They required great skill to decorate due to their size. This traditional shape shows off the pattern very well.

They were decorated by Harry Stinton (1883-1968), who is considered to be the best of the famed Stinton family of decorators at Worc ester.

Stinton is particularly celebrated for his Highland cattle scenes, which were similar to those produced by his father John, but use a more purple palette.

A pair of Royal Worcester baluster vases, shape no.461, painted with Highland cattle in a mountainous setting by Harry Stinton, signed 'H. Stinton', green mark, bearing retailer's stamp of John Ford & Co., 39 Princes Street, Edinburgh.

4in (10cm) high

£800-1,000 **A&G**

A pair of Royal Worcester trumpet vases, each painted with pink and claret roses by Millie Hunt, signed 'M Hunt', within gilt sponged collars, dated, 1934 and 1937

7.5in (19cm) high

£500-600 **FLD**

A pair of Royal Worcester small baluster vases, painted with fruit by Albert J. Shuck, shape no.2491, one with two apples and blackberries with reverse blackberries vignette, the other with two apples and cherries, the reverse with fruiting strawberry vignette, both signed, one with indistinct date code.

c1937 *4in (10cm) high*

£600-700 **TEN**

An early 20thC Royal Worcester footed vase, painted by James Stinton with a cock pheasant and flying hen bird in a landscape setting, with pierced collar, signed, green printed mark, pattern '42/G'.

5.75in (14.5cm) high

£250-350 **L&T**

A Royal Worcester porcelain 'Warwick Vase', shape 2130, painted with landscape scenes and signed 'H. Davies' within raised gilt pendant husk and floral swag borders on a white and apple green ground, dated, restored.

9.75in (25cm) diam

£400-500 **FLD**

A Royal Worcester tyg, painted with pink and claret rose sprays below a moulded border reading 'Auld Lang Syne', restored.

9.5in (24cm) high

£300-400 **FLD**

A Royal Worcester jug, with hand-painted floral pattern and gilded dragon-shaped handle, the base with printed factory marks, also printed '11048' and with registered no.21627 for 1893.

6in (15.5cm) high

£100-150 **BAD**

A late 20thC Royal Worcester teapot, painted by Terence Nutt on one side with two apples and blackberries, on the other with a peach, blackberries and green grapes, with gilded and gadrooned rim, spout, handle and circular foot, printed crown and wheel mark in black, initialled 'RB/BB', signed.

6in (15cm) high

£1,000-1,500 **TEN**

A late 19thC Royal Worcester Persian-style ewer, painted with a study of an owl on a branch and moonlit clouds by Charles Baldwyn, restored.

10.25in (26cm) high

£100-150 **FLD**

A late 19thC Royal Worcester sugar bowl and sparrow beak milk jug, hand-decorated with bamboo and geometric Oriental motifs in floral blue and gilt.

3.5in (9cm) high

£120-180 **LOC**

A Royal Worcester bonbon dish, in the form of a conch shell, with coral and weed stem with a circular base, in gilt, bronze and ivory effect, puce printed mark to the base, with impressed mark and 'no. 94'.

8.75in (22cm) high

£250-300 **DUK**

A Royal Worcester 'British Friesian bull', RW3746, modelled by Doris Lindner, numbered 268 from a limited edition of 500, with black printed marks, wood stand and certificate.

Issued 1962

£450-550 **DN**

A Royal Worcester 'Dairy Shorthorn bull', RW3781, modelled by Doris Lindner, numbered 106 from a limited edition of 500, with black printed marks, wood stand and certificate.

Issued 1965

£450-550 **DN**

A Royal Worcester 'Jersey bull', RW3776, modelled by Doris Lindner, numbered 167 from an edition of 500, with black printed marks, wood stand and certificate.

£450-550 **DN**

A Royal Worcester 'Jersey Cow', modelled by Doris Lindner, numbered 357 from a limited edition of 500, with stand and certificate.

7in (18cm) high

£400-600 **LOC**

A Royal Worcester 'Dairy Shorthorn Bull', modelled by Doris Lindner, numbered 250 from a limited edition of 500, with stand and certificate.

8.75in (22cm) high

£350-450 **LOC**

QUICK REFERENCE – DORIS LINDNER

Sculptor Doris Lindner (1896-1979) became one of Royal Worcester's most notable modellers after she was asked to contribute to an exhibition in London in 1931. Her first model was of a polar bear, followed by dogs and other animals such as foxes, some in the Art Deco style of the day. In 1935, she began modelling horses and produced her first limited edition, of 'Princess Elizabeth on Tommy', in 1948. The 1960s were her heyday, and she produced more than 20 limited edition figurines, modelled from life. Most edition sizes were 500, with a few smaller (and scarcer) editions of 100 or 150. Today, her work is sought after by a dedicated group of collectors, meaning prices have remained strong, even during the economic downturn. The model should retain its wooden plinth and certificate.

A Royal Worcester 'Aberdeen Angus' bull, RW3697, modelled by Doris Lindner, numbered '286' from a limited edition of 500, with wooden stand and certificate. Issued *1959*

7.5in (19cm) high

£700-900 **LOC**

A Royal Worcester model 'Laurieston & Richard Meade OBE', modelled by Doris Lindner, numbered 13 from a limited edition of 500, on a wooden plinth and in a glass case with certificate.

14.25in (36cm) wide

£600-800 **LOC**

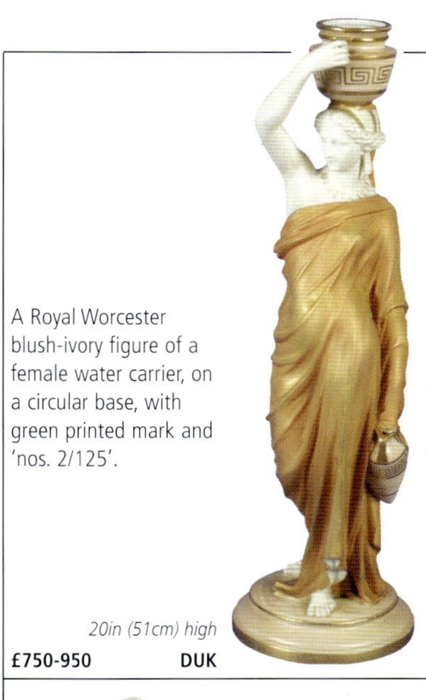

A Royal Worcester blush-ivory figure of a female water carrier, on a circular base, with green printed mark and 'nos. 2/125'.

20in (51cm) high

£750-950 **DUK**

A Royal Worcester 'The Tea Party' figure group, RW3700, modelled by Ruth Esther van Ruyckevelt, from a limited edition of 250, from the Victorian Figures series, in colours and gilt, black printed crown and wheel mark, title and facsimile signature, impressed '42', in original box with certificate.

1960 *8in (20cm) high*

£700-1,000 **TEN**

A Royal Worcester candle snuffer, modelled as a nun, with printed mark and date code.

1924 *4in (10cm) high*

£70-100 **WW**

A Royal Worcester blush-ivory figure of a rustic girl at a spring, model no.1810, partially coloured and gilt, with green marks.

1900 *6.75in (17cm) high*

£200-300 **DN**

A Royal Worcester 'Mephistopheles' Toby jug, shape 2850, the base with printed marks.

3.25in (8.5cm) high

£50-60 **FLD**

A Royal Worcester 'Spitfire' figure group, RW3352, designed by Eileen Soper from the Wartime series, dated, minor restoration.

This is the rare coloured version, which is worth considerably more than plain white. During the war, when this was produced, raw materials were strictly limited and could not generally be used on decorative pieces.

1941

£1,000-1,500 **FLD**

A pair of late 19thC Royal Worcester 'Irish Navvy and Wife' figures, by James Hadley, shape no.1810, typically modelled, in shades of green and pink, printed and impressed marked.

Tallest 7in (18cm) high

£300-400 **HT**

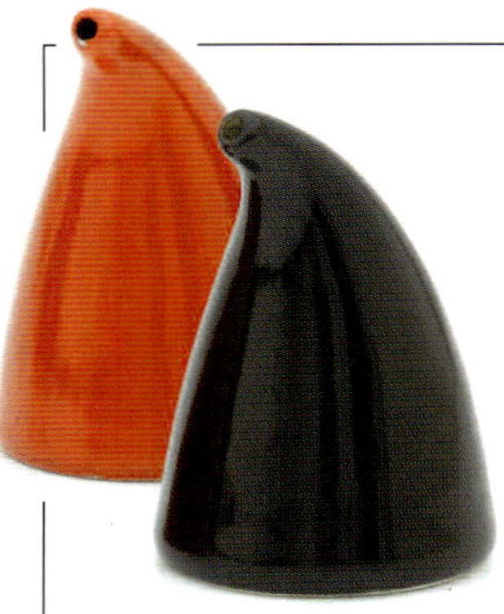

A pair of Finnish Arabia salt and pepper shakers, designed by Kaj Franck in 1955, glazed in glossy black or red.

2.75in (7cm) high

£40-60 **QU**

A Danish Soholm Stentoj rectangular wall plaque, with stylised floral design, designed by Joseph Simmonds, with impressed mark on back, numbered '3540', and with painted 'LE' monogram.

17.5in (44.5cm) long

£100-150 **RET**

A 1970s Swedish Elbogen Pottery 'Marg' figure, the base with painted marks.

This was part of a range of different handmade female figures, each with its own name.

13.5in (34cm) high

£80-120 **M20C**

A CLOSER LOOK AT BJORN WIINBLAD CANDELABRA

Bjorn Wiinblad (1918-2006) was a Danish artist, illustrator, designer and ceramicist whose work has attracted a worldwide reputation and group of collectors.

Bjørn Wiinblad was born in Copenhagen and was educated at the Royal Academy of Arts in Copenhagen. He first started working with ceramics at Lars Syberg's studio, and set up his own studio in 1952.

From 1946, he worked at (and subsequently owned) the Danish factory Nymolle, and also worked with Germany's Rosenthal from 1956 onwards. He designed mass-produced transfer printed ceramics for both companies. He also ran his own pottery studio, from 1952, and it was there that these handmade, hand-painted candelabra were made.

His work is inspired by traditional Danish myths, music and nature, and often features whimsical characters in his individual and eccentric style.

Two Danish studio earthenware candelabra, by Bjorn Winblad, each of conical form, modelled as figures beneath a bowl and sconces, dated. 1972

Tallest 15.75in (40cm) high

£500-700 **SWO**

A Norwegian Figgjo Flint Turi Design 'Lotte' pattern transfer-printed and painted beaker, with printed marks to base.

3in (7.5cm) high

£12-18 **RET**

A Swedish Gustavsberg stoneware poodle, from the 'Kennel' series designed by Lisa Larson in 1972, with painted and impressed marks to base.

3.5in (9cm) high

£50-70 **SAS**

QUICK REFERENCE

- The Shelley brand was devised c1910 by the Wileman & Co. pottery in Staffordshire, England, but was not used officially until 1925. The company was founded c1892 and became known for its art pottery. However, it became world famous for its tea and tablewares during the 1920s and '30s. The pottery closed in 1966.
- Notable designers who produced important ranges which are sought after by collectors today, include Frederick Alfred Rhead, Walter Slater and his son Eric; and illustrators Hilda Cowham and Mabel Lucie Attwell, who are known for their desirable nursery ware (see p86-88).
- Among the most collectable and valuable Shelley designs are the two Art Deco geometric teaware ranges, 'Mode' and 'Vogue' designed by Eric Slater, and produced from 1930-33. The teacups had solid handles, which made them difficult to hold, and this led to the development of the hollow-handled 'Eve' shape in 1932. Also look out for the 'Queen Anne' shape, which was decorated with over 170 different patterns, and the popular 'Dainty' shape, which was designed in 1896.
- The most desirable and valuable patterns are Art Deco in style, typically executed in the bright colours typical of the era. Values vary depending on the pattern. Desirability is maximised when these are found on a strongly Art Deco shape, such as 'Vogue' or 'Mode'. Transfer-printed floral 'chintz' wares are also sought after, but values for them have fallen over the past five years. More attention is being paid to Eric Slater's banded and dripped 'Harmony' ranges.
- Look out for complete teasets as these tend to fetch the largest sums. Teapots and individual teacups are also desirable, and are always worth considering when undamaged. Rhead's late 19thC art pottery ranges are also well worth looking out for as prices tend to be high due to their scarcity and his increased popularity among collectors in the UK and the US.

A Shelley blue lustre vase, designed by Walter Slater, printed and painted with a Chinese dragon, highlighted in gilt, with printed mark and facsimile signature to base.

Walter Slater replaced F. A. Rhead as Art Director, working there from 1905-37.

15in (38cm) high

£1,200-1,800 **WW**

A very rare Shelley Intarsio range 'Pomegranate' pattern vase, with printed marks to base.

Shelley were forced to withdraw this pattern by Moorcroft as it was similar to their Pomegranate pattern. A ginger jar in the same pattern can fetch up to £1,800.

8in (20.5cm) high

£700-1,000 **GOL**

A Wileman & Co. Intarsio range temple jar, with the 'Rabbits' pattern, designed by Frederick Alfred Rhead.

Notable ceramics designer Frederick Alfred Rhead (1856-1933) was Art Director at Wileman & Co. from 1896-1905. He produced a number of innovative ranges, the most desirable of which was Intarsio. This is a very scarce pattern on a rare and highly desirable form.

c1900

£2,000-2,500 **GOL**

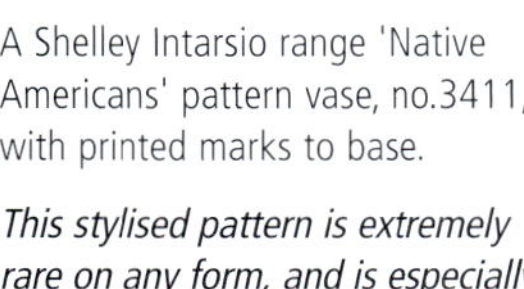

A Shelley Intarsio range 'Native Americans' pattern vase, no.3411, with printed marks to base.

This stylised pattern is extremely rare on any form, and is especially desirable on large impressive vase forms such as this.

11in (28cm) high

£2,800-3,300 **GOL**

A 1930s Shelley cake stand with handpainted circle design and shaped chrome stand, the base with green printed factory mark.

10in (25.5cm) high

£50-60 **RET**

A 1930s Shelley Vogue shape part coffee set, comprising coffee pot, four cups and saucers and milk jug, handpainted with the very rare 'Coral Martian' pattern, no.11867, with printed marks to bases.

The pattern name has been applied by collectors, and was not the original name. The pattern was also available in green, which is worth around the same amount.

1931-33 *7in (18cm) high*

£2,000-2,500 **GOL**

A very scarce Shelley lemonade set, with jug and six beakers, decorated with the 'Apples' pattern, with printed marks to the base.

The jug is very similar to Clarice Cliff's iconic Art Deco 'Conical' shape, showing how popular styles were reproduced by different makers.

8in (23cm) high

£800-1,200 **GOL**

A 1930s Shelley Mode shape teaset for two, hand-painted with the yellow butterfly wing pattern, no.11758, with printed marks to base.

Teapot 5in (12.5cm) high

£2,000-2,500 **GOL**

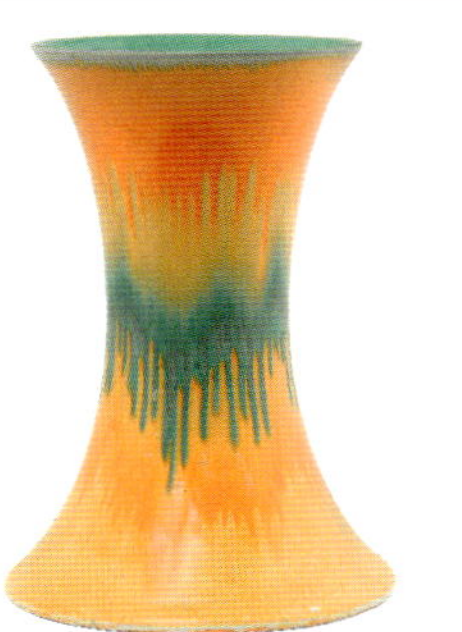

A Shelley Harmony waisted vase, with dripping bands of orange and green.

c1930 *21cm high*

£130-160 **BEV**

FIND OUT MORE...

' Shelley Potteries' , by Chris Watkins, William Harvey and Robert Senft, published by Barrie & Jenkins, 1980.

The Shelley Group, www.shelley.co.uk or The National Shelley Club, www.nationalshelleychinaclub.com

A CLOSER LOOK AT A SHELLEY TEA SERVICE

The Harmony range of Dripware was discovered 'by accident' when Eric Slater mixed too much turpentine in glazes, which dripped in an attractive manner.

Evenly distributed banding is highly desirable, particularly on the desirable Art Deco 'Eve' shape.

Purple Harmony is very rare – yellows, blues and greens are more common.

Slater accentuated the effects and widened it into a range of decorative wares – tablewares are harder to find, particularly in sets.

A 1930s Shelley 'Harmony' range Eve shape teaset, designed by Eric Slater, comprising teapot, six cups and saucers, milk jug and sugar bowl, decorated with the purple Harmony patte n no.12084.

Teapot 7in (18cm) high

£2,500-3,000 **GOL**

A Stangl Pottery 'Bluebird', no.3276, with 'STANGL' brown oval mark, incised '3276' and with artist's initials 'ES'.

5.25in (13.5cm) high

£50-70 **BEL**

A Stangl Pottery 'Western Bluebird' figurine, no.3815, with printed factory marks and decorator's initials.

7in (17.5cm) high

£75-95 **BH**

A Stangl Pottery 'Key West Quail Dove', no.3454, marked 'STANGL 3454' in blue ink and artist signed 'RV' initials.

9.25in (23.5cm) high

£150-200 **BEL**

A Stangl Pottery 'Cardinal' in matte finish, no.3444, with small brown oval 'STANGL' mark, incised '3444' and with artist's initials, a small glaze flaw at the tip of the tail.

6.75in (17cm) high

£100-150 **BEL**

QUICK REFERENCE – STANGL BIRDS

Partly inspired by Audubon's famous 'Birds of America', Stangl's birds were originally produced from 1940-72. Values are based on the size and complexity of the figurine, and how well it has been decorated. Decorators, whose numbers were swelled with homeworkers at busy times, were able to choose their own colours, and their level of skill varied widely. Even though artists often signed their work with initials, the work of individual artists does not really affect value, so this information is only of use for dating. In 1972, some models were re-released, and these are often signed and dated. As with 'vintage' Stangl, they can still be desirable and valuable if they are well decorated. This pair of woodpeckers is an excellent example of a good design that has been well decorated.

A Stangl Pottery 'Gray Cardinal', no.3596, marked with partial small black 'STANGL POTTERY BIRDS' mark, incised '3596' and with 'BM' artist's initials.

4.75in (12cm) high

£45-55 **BEL**

A Stangl Pottery large 'Cockatoo', no.3584, with large black oval 'STANGL POTTERY BIRDS' mark and '3584' in black.

12.25in (31cm) high

£150-200 **BEL**

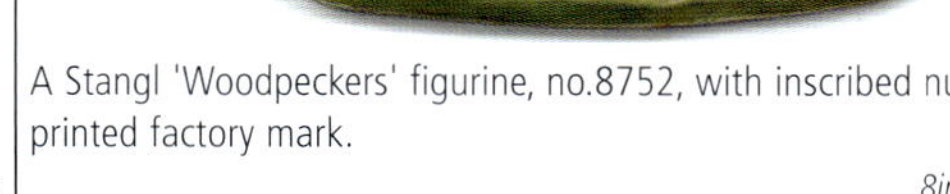

A Stangl 'Woodpeckers' figurine, no.8752, with inscribed number and printed factory mark.

8in (20.5cm) high

£300-400 **BH**

QUICK REFERENCE

- The term 'studio pottery' is used to describe pottery made by the owner of an independent pottery, or under their supervision. Quantities are typically limited, and each piece is, in effect, unique as it was handmade or hand-decorated. Although some studio pottery was made in the 19thC, it developed into a movement of its own after World War II.
- Key figures include forerunners Bernard Leach, his colleague Shoji Hamada, Lucie Rie, and Hans Coper. Later names, many of whom studied with or were inspired by one of these influential potters, include Alan Caiger-Smith, David Leach, Marianne de Trey and John Maltby. In the US, leading potters such as the Natzlers, Peter Voulkos, Maija Grotell, Beatrice Wood and others were also highly influential.
- Although the work of these important potters is usually very expensive, look out for the work of their students, as this is often more affordable and just as important when put in context. Similarly, the work of many potters is yet to be 'discovered'. Learn how to recognise styles of certain potters and find out a little about their backgrounds.
- Always consider the form, glaze and size. Look for pieces that are well made, and of good quality. Collecting by theme, such as glaze, is often rewarding as there are many variations to be found. Consider a potter's work in context of his time – those that innovated or led a new style, or exemplified the 'look' of the day, are often worth considering. Invest in a book of marks (often called 'seals') to help you learn how to identify particular potters.

An Aldermaston Pottery bowl, by Alan Caiger-Smith, with green, blue and black curving lines and painted monogram.

10.75in (27.5cm) diam

£500-700 **WW**

An Aldermaston Pottery bowl, by Alan Caiger-Smith, the interior with stylised panels in blue and ochre, the exterior with a simple blue band, the base with painted marks.

11.75in (30cm) diam

£300-500 **WW**

An Aldermaston Pottery waisted cylindrical vase, by Alan Caiger-Smith, with red lustre panels and printed and painted marks to base.

Caiger-Smith founded the Aldermaston Pottery in 1955. Considered a key training ground for a new generation of potters, it closed in 2006 when he retired. He is known for his tin and lustre glazes, which are often combined with Hispano-Moresque patterns and styles.

9.25in (23.5cm) high

£350-450 **WW**

An 1960s Ambleside footed vase, designed and possibly made by George Cook, with sgrafitto geometric pattern, the base inscribed 'Ambleside'.

4.75in (12cm) high

£30-50 **GC**

A Richard Batterham stoneware jar, in a pale celadon glaze over impressed dot and line decoration.

9.75in (25cm) high

£150-200 **WW**

A Seth Cardew stoneware jug, with a tenmoku gaze and inscribed with bands and wavy lines, with impressed 'SC' seal mark.

6.25in (16cm) high

£30-50 **W&W**

A Carn Pottery asymmetric vase, with moulded low relief stylised designs, the base with black printed factory mark.

5.25in (13cm) high

£15-25 **UCT**

A Carn Pottery fan vase, with low relief moulded curving and circular design to one side and stylised flower design to the other, the base with factory black printed mark.

Along with cats, fan vases are the most desirable shapes.

6in (15cm) high

£20-30 **UCT**

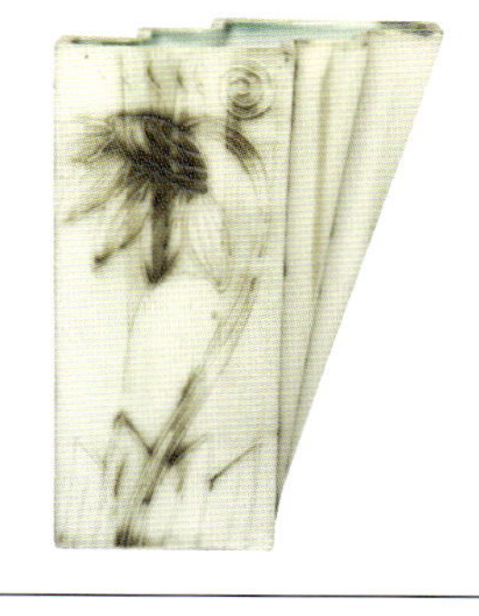

A Michael Casson basket, with a mottled brown salt glaze, the base with impressed seal.

13.25in (33.5cm) high

£120-180 **W&W**

A Deichman Pottery jardinière bowl, decorated with fish in a green glaze on a cream ground, the base painted with 'EKD' and 'NB' monograms.

Danish-born Kjeld and Erica Deichmann founded a pottery in New Brunswick, Canada in 1935. Inspired by Scandinavian pottery they had grown up around, they pioneered studio pottery and the craft tradition in Canada. Erica was responsible for the glazes, whilst Kjeld produced the forms. The pottery closed in 1963, when Kjeld died. This pattern is unusual, most pieces are plain.

6in (15cm) high CAD

£700-1,000 **TAC**

A Coldrum Pottery baluster vase, by Reginald Wells, covered with a mottled blue and lavender glaze, the base stamped 'Coldrum'.

9.25in (23.5cm) high

£100-150 **W&W**

A Canadian Deichmann mug, with green dripped glaze, the base inscribed 'Deichmann 45' and with 'NB' monogram, damaged handle.

5.25in (13cm) high CAD

£80-120 **TAC**

A Farnham Pottery owl money bank, with incised and applied decoration and green glaze, minor chips.

Founded in Surrey in 1872, the company produced art pottery from 1880 onwards. Typically covered in a green glaze, wares were sold by Liberty and Heal's among others. Owls are typical motifs, but jugs are more common and were produced into the 1950s.

2.25in (6cm) high

£300-400 **WW**

An earthenware animal-shaped shower caddy, by Deborah Halpern, with painted 'Deborah D Halpern' signature.

Australian artist and ceramicist Halpern (b.1957) is known for her quirky and colourful animals inspired by Picasso.

14.25in (36cm) high

£300-500 **JA**

A large David Leach Lowerdown Pottery cut-sided vase, covered in a dolomite glaze, with impressed seal marks.

7.5in (19cm) high

£450-550 **WW**

An early St Ives stoneware bowl, by Bernard Leach, incised to interior and exterior with cloud motif under an ash glaze, impressed 'St Ives' and 'BL' script seal marks.

5.5in (14cm) diam

£300-500 **WW**

A CLOSER LOOK AT A STUDIO POTTERY SCULPTURE

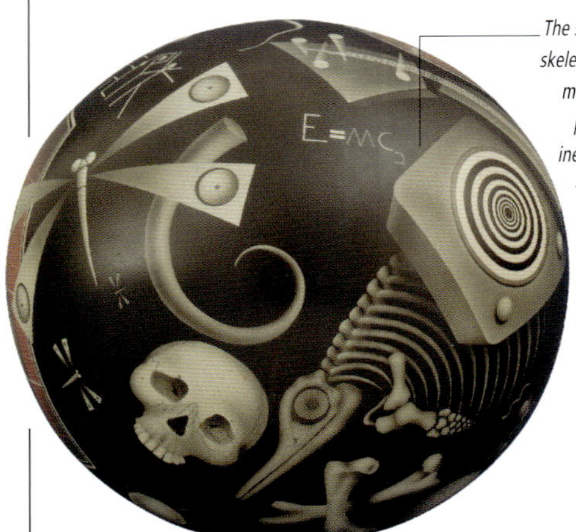

The skull and dinosaur skeleton are 'momento mori', hinting at the passing of life and inevitability of death – a theme used in art since the Renaissance.

A Steven Gunderson ceramic sphere, decorated with geometric biological forms in black, white and red, with ball inside.

19in (48cm) diam

£800-1,200 **SK**

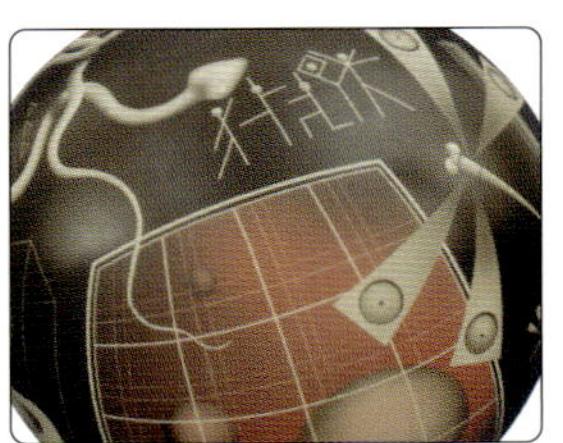

The spherical form suggests the world, with objects in it showing developments across time, such as bacteria under a microscope, and a television.

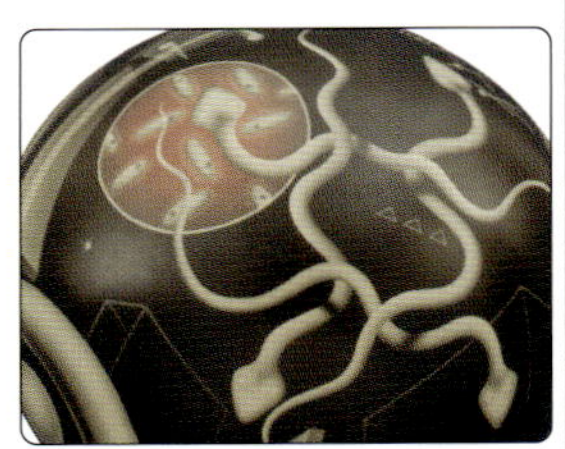

It is well-designed and finely painted, being an excellent example of ceramics used as an art form to convey a message.

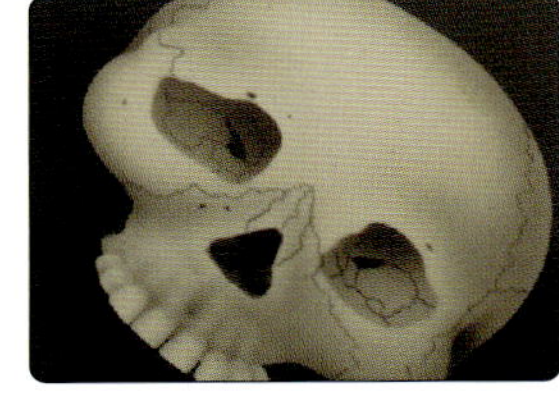

A Bernard Leach stoneware tea bowl, with tenmoku glaze outside and khaki glaze inside, and impressed 'BL' and 'St Ives' seals.

Pieces by Leach (1887-1979) are highly sought after. Generally considered to be the 'father' of studio ceramics, he founded the influential St Ives pottery with Shoji Hamada in 1910, from where he trained many of the great names in studio pottery.

4.75in (12cm) diam

£700-1,000 **TEN**

A Bernard Leach stoneware tea bowl, blue glaze with khaki on one side, with impressed 'BL' and 'St Ives' seals.

c1960 *3.25in (8.5cm) high*

£500-600 **TEN**

A John Maltby stoneware unomi, octagonal with painted panels, impressed seal.

Born in 1936, Maltby is one of the UK's most celebrated living studio potters. He trained in sculpture under David Leach and founded his own pottery in 1964. He is known today for his unique sculptural forms, simple geometric motifs and creating contrasts between light and dark. A unomi is a traditional Japanese tea bowl.

3.75in (9.5cm) high

£250-300 **WW**

A Bernard Leach earthenware mug, inscribed 'S.S. White Heather 1921' and decorated with a view of the boat with an 'X4' brown glaze, incised 'BL' and 'St Ives'.

The S.S. White Heather was a herring boat. This mug was made by Leach as part of a set.

4.25in (10.5cm) high

£200–300 **TEN**

One of a pair of Lorenzen salt and pepper shakers, decorated with abstract fish and waves on a mottled grey ground, the bases inscribed 'Lorenzen's Lanz Nova Scotia'.

c1960 *2.25in (5.5cm) high*

£20-30 PAIR **MHC**

A John Maltby stoneware elliptical vase, decorated with diamond motifs, with impressed seal mark.

5in (12.5cm) high

£80-120 **WW**

A Paul Metcalfe early figural bottle vase, decorated with a stylised figure of a robed lady in green and white oxide glazes, the base with painted monogram and date.

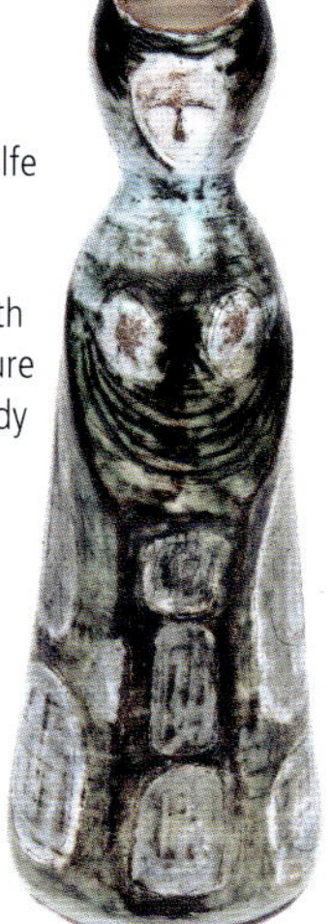

1962 *17in (44.5cm) high*

£100-150 **FLD**

QUICK REFERENCE – NATZLER

Viennese born Otto (b.1908) and Gertrud (1908-71) Natzler founded their pottery in Los Angeles upon their arrival in the US in 1938. Forms, produced by Gertrud, were typically simple with bowls being the first shapes produced. Otto devised the glazes, and it is primarily for these that the couple have become celebrated. The most desirable (and valuable) glazes resemble bubbled and cratered lava, but complex crystalline glazes, as seen on this bowl, are also sought after. The Natzler name is typically inscribed into the base.

A Natzler earthenware footed bowl, in a blue crystalline glaze, signed 'Natzler'.

6.25in (16cm) diam

£7,000-10,000 **SDR**

A Natzler beaker-shaped earthenware vase, with indented lip, covered in grey sea glaze, signed 'Natzler'.

5.5in (14cm) high

£3,500-4,500 **SDR**

A Natzler earthenware footed small bowl, in a blue and brown glaze, signed on the base.

4.5in (11.5cm) diam

£2,000-3,000 **DRA**

A Natzler footed bowl, in olive-green, turquoise and brown mottled semi-matte glaze, the base signed 'NATZLER'.

8.5in (21.5cm) diam

£1,200-1,800 **DRA**

A Natzler free-form earthenware bowl, covered in matte stone grey glaze, signed 'Natzler'.

This mottled and striated glaze, and the one on the blue bowl above, bear many similarities to the 'hare' s-fur' glazes used by Scandinavian ceramics companies such as Palshus and Gustavsberg.

6.25in (16cm) high

£3,000-4,000 **SDR**

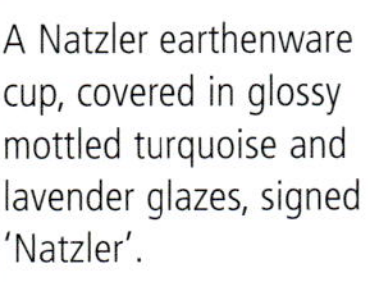

A Natzler earthenware cup, covered in glossy mottled turquoise and lavender glazes, signed 'Natzler'.

c1962 3.75in (9.5cm) high

£2,500-3,500 **SDR**

A William Newland earthenware bull, slip-trailed with geometric motifs in cream on an ochre ground, with painted signature and dated '58', repaired horn.

Newland (1919-98), along with Margaret Hine and Nicola Vergette, was part of a group known as the 'Picassoettes' since they took their inspiration from Picasso. Bulls and other animal forms, decorated with exotic motifs, are typical.

1958 *12.25in (31cm) wide*

£700-900 **WW**

A CLOSER LOOK AT A PARKINSON SCULPTURE

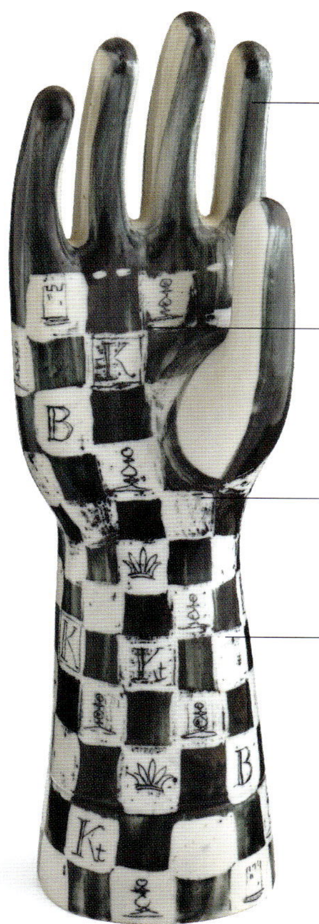

Parkinson pottery, which is hard to find, has become highly sought-after since a book and exhibition in 2004.

It has a surreal appearance, recalling glove display hands in department stores, and accentuated by the chess board design.

Black and white painted slip-cast domestic and sculptural animals and figures are typical – this is an extremely rare design.

Susan studied at the Royal College of Art. The pottery was active for only eleven years from 1952-63.

A Richard Parkinson Ltd 'Hand in Glove' sculpture, designed by Susan Parkinson, painted with geometric panels of chess pieces, minor restoration on base rim.

13.75in (35cm) high

£1,000-1,500 **WW**

A Richard Parkinson Ltd slip cast porcelain bust of schoolboy, designed by Susan Parkinson, with black enamel decoration, the base with impressed marks.

6in (15cm) high

£550-650 **FLD**

A Richard Parkinson Ltd heraldic lion, designed by Susan Parkinson, painted in dark grey-blue on a white ground, with impressed mark.

9.5in (24cm) wide

£380-420 **WW**

A Katharine Pleydell-Bouverie stoneware cut-sided vase, covered in a green glaze, impressed seal mark, painted 'BX'.

2.25in (5.5cm) high

£100-150 **WW**

A tin-glazed earthenware jug, decorated by Alfred Powell with a lakeside landscape scene in blue, the reverse with a similar scene of a country house, the base with painted monogram.

Athough better known for his work with Wedgwood, Powell and his wife Louise also decorated a series of blanks.

5.25in (13.5cm) high

£150-200 **W&W**

A CLOSER LOOK AT A SUSIE COOPER VASE

This spherical shape is typical of the geometricity of the Art Deco movement. This shape was hard to make and is rare today.

The right angles and straight lines of the hand-painted pattern contrast against the curving shape, but are also typical of the Art Deco movement.

This is typical of Cooper's most desirable Art Deco designs from c1928-30. Had it been in brighter colours and not cracked, it would have fetched more

The mark on the base shows a galleon amidst waves with yellow sails – this style of mark was used from 1921-31.

A Gray's Pottery ball vase, designed by Susie Cooper, pattern no.8215, painted with geometric design in shades of yellow, black and grey, printed factory mark, painted number, hairline crack to base.

c1929 *7in (18cm) high*

£450-650 **WW**

A late 1930s Susie Cooper Kestrel shape coffee set for six, decorated in the 'Crescents' pattern, no.1543, comprising coffee pot, milk jug, sugar bowl, ten cups, saucers and side plates and others, the bases with printed and painted marks, minor damages.

Coffee Pot 7.5in (19cm) high

£100-150 **WW**

A late 1930s Susie Cooper 'Panel Spray' part service, pattern no.1690, comprising milk jug and sugar bowl, six cups, saucers and side plates and a sandwich plate, the bases with printed marks.

This is a very rare pattern, probably as production was interrupted by the onset of war in 1939. Each of the six ' trio' sets, which comprise a cup and saucer and side plate, are commercial and collectable. The scarcer milk jug and sugar bowl are an additional bonus.

£1,000-1,500 **WW**

A late 1930s Susie Cooper 'Blue Crescent' Kestrel bachelor set, comprising teapot, two hot-water pots, milk jug and sugar basin, cup, saucer and side plate, a muffin dish and cover, cruet and a toast rack, the bases with printed factory marks, minor damages.

Teapot 5in (12.5cm) high

£200-300 **WW**

A Grays Pottery hand painted circular plate, designed by Susie Cooper, with an abstract geometric pattern in yellow, black and red with overlapping geometric forms.

c1929 *10in (25.5cm) diam*

£80-120 **FLD**

A Susie Cooper 'Endon' pattern 'Spiral' shape dinner service, comprising six dinner plates, six dessert plates, six side plates, two meat plates, five side plates, five dessert plates, six fruit bowls, six saucers and two tureens, one lidded.

The 'Spiral' shape was introduced in 1938, and the 'Endon' pattern dates from a similar time.

£120-180 **SWO**

QUICK REFERENCE

- **Joseph Szeiler (1924–1986) was born in Hungary and studied to become a veterinary surgeon before emigrating to England, via Austria, in 1948. He first worked for J&G Meakin as a mould runner, later gaining more experience at Wade Heath & Co. In 1951, he took the decision to found his own company, renting a room in Hanley, Staffordshire. His first production included animals and figures: Szeiler created the designs and moulds, then made and glazed the figurines.**
- **In 1955, his business had expanded enough to allow him to buy larger premises in Burslem, where his company remained until his death and its closure in 1986.**
- **Animal figurines are the most common and most desirable designs, with many being highly stylised and elongated. Fawn and cream, sometimes with a light blue, are typical colours. Prices have begun to rise, as more collectors are drawn to Szeiler's work, but rarely fetch over £50.**

A Szeiler elongated dog figurine, with printed mark to base.

3in (7.5cm) high

£7-10 **DSC**

A Szeiler sleeping dog in a basket.

Animals in woven baskets are a hallmark range for Szeiler, and can be found in many different variations.

Basket 1.5in (4cm) high

£5-8 **DSC**

A Szeiler long-eared small donkey figurine in repose, with printed mark to base.

The long ears are a typical feature of many Szeiler animals. The mark is earlier in date, although no precise date ranges are yet known.

3.25in (8cm) long

£8-10 **DSC**

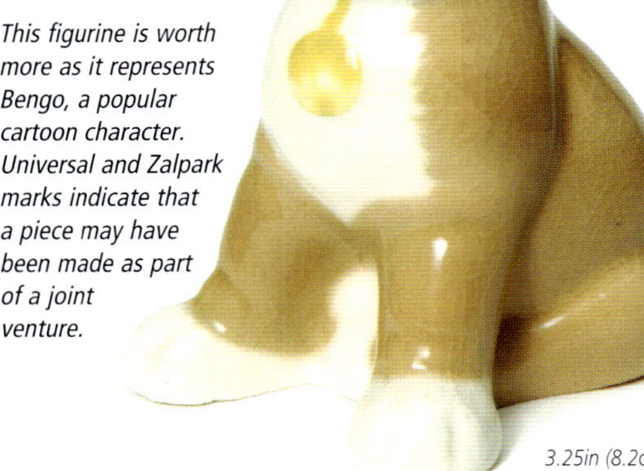

A Szeiler-type 'Bengo' figurine, with blue collar and tag, the base with 'UNIVERSAL MADE IN ENGLAND' printed mark.

This figurine is worth more as it represents Bengo, a popular cartoon character. Universal and Zalpark marks indicate that a piece may have been made as part of a joint venture.

3.25in (8.2cm) high

£20-25 **DSC**

A Szeiler blue and white donkey figurine, with elongated ears, the base with printed mark.

4.75in (12cm) high

£25-30 **DSC**

A Szeiler donkey and cart figurine, with printed mark to base.

6in (15cm) long

£15-20 **DSC**

A Szeiler koala and cub figurine, with printed mark to base.

3.5in (9cm) high

£15-20 **DSC**

A Copeland Spode blue and white transfer printed 'Italian' pattern teapot.

9.75in (24.5cm) long

£60-80 **BAD**

QUICK REFERENCE – SADLER CAR TEAPOTS

Sadler's car teapots were first released in 1937 and produced again after WWII. Green, cream or yellow are the most commonly found single colours. Produced in the 1930s only, black, grey, maroon, blue or pink are scarcer colours. They have platinum luste details. The rarest variation from the 1930s has transfer-printed patterns of pixies and animals in the style of (but not by) Mabel Lucie Attwell, along with orange detailing, and can fetch over £500. When present, the numberplate is 'OKT42' indicating 'Okay, tea for two', but this was generally only applied to pre-war examples. After the war, single colour and mottled examples were produced, and impressed marks included the Sadler name. Prices have remained stable, due to their appeal to collectors of teapots and automobilia.

A 1920s-30s handpainted 'cottage ware' teapot, unmarked but possibly by Price Bros., with two chips to the corner of the lid and knob.

c1930s *8.5in (21.5cm) wide*

£7-10 **PC**

A 1930s Royal Doulton handpainted 'Aspen' pattern teapot, with gilded foot, handle, rim and spout.

5.25in (13.5cm) diam

£50-60 **BEV**

A 1930s-50s Sadler novelty motor car teapot, with a green glaze, the base with impressed marks and registered number 820236 for 1937.

8.75in (22.5cm) wide

£30-50 **WW**

A 1930s Royal Doulton teapot, with handpainted arabesque pattern in green yellow, black and gold, the base marked 'V.1289'.

c1934 *5in (12.5cm) high*

£80-100 **BEV**

A Shelley 'Mode' shape teapot and cover, pattern number 11754, in green and gold, the base with printed and painted marks.

Designed by Eric Slater and produced from 1930-33, Mode is one of Shelley's two strongest Art Deco forms. This popular pattern was also available in yellow, red, black, blue or pink – all with similar gold handles and details.

5in (13cm) high

£300-400 **WW**

A Shelley fine bone china transfer printed 'Anemone' pattern 35oz teapot.

7in (17.5cm) high

£70-100 **W&L**

A Royal Grafton Fine Bone China teapot, handpainted with large brown flower and blue leaves.

7in (17.5cm) high

£20-30 **W&L**

A CLOSER LOOK AT A TEAPOT

Crossed legs from the 'Walking Ware' range are scarcer than others.

Pay attention to the colours and patterns of the shoes and, if applicable, the socks – some colours or colour combinations can be very rare.

Teapots, particularly in smaller sizes like this, are typically more valuable than cups or eggcups, unless the pattern is rare.

The bodies are usually white, those with transfer printed patterns, such as tropical islands, are rarer.

A Carltonware 'crossed legs' teapot with yellow shoes and green and brown socks, designed by Roger Michell of the Lustre Pottery, with printed marks to base.

1978 *8.25in (21cm) high*

£100-150 **BEV**

A Grindley small teapot, transfer printed with sprays of colourful flowers, with black detail and rims.

3.5in (9cm) high

£25-35 **W&L**

A 1950s Sadler teapot, with sprial ribbed body and transfer printed with roses, with impressed marks to base.

4.75in (12cm) high

£18-22 **W&L**

A Midwinter 'Fashion' shape coffee pot, with the transfer-printed 'Bali H'ai' design, designed by John Russell, with printed marks to base.

7.5in (19cm) high

£40-60 **RET**

A Midwinter 'HMS Mary' novelty teapot and cover, the base with impressed and printed marks.

c1940 *9.5in (24cm) wide*

£250-350 **WW**

A Grueby tile, decorated in cuenca with a yellow tulip and green leaves on a green ground, marked 'KY', with two corner chips.

6in (15cm) wide

£1,000-1,500 **DRA**

A W.B. Simpson tile panel of a knight, painted in colours, the back with impressed marks and paper label, cracked into twopieces.

24.5in (62cm) high

£280-320 **WW**

A Batchelder horizontal tile, depicting a Dutch boy and girl with dog-drawn carriage in typical Dutch landscape, the back covered with grout, hiding probable mark.

17.75in (45cm) wide

£450-550 **DRA**

A CLOSER LOOK AT A SET OF EAST GERMAN TILES

This set, and the others on this page, were part of a series produced for an East German holiday home as part of a series showing the power and modernity of the Communist block.

Communist bloc.
The angular, brightly coloured design is appealing and typical of the period – the shapes of the tiles themselves echo and creatre the lines of the design.

The design includes a TV tower, which were considered important statement buildings – examples were built in Moscow, Stuttgart, Riga and Berlin amongst other cities.

The sputnik satellite
can also be seen amid the dots that represent stars in outer space – furthermore, the sun shines on the

A set of East German enamelled copper wall tiles, showing the Alexander TV tower in Berlin, the Sputnik satellite, and a radiating sun, framed in metal.

c1975 *28in (71cm) high*

£700-900 **VZ**

A set of East German enamelled copper wall tiles, showing an idyllic countryside landscape in the background with a dam, power station and a crane, framed in metal.

c1975 *30.5in (76.5cm) wide*

£650-750 **VZ**

A set of East German enamelled copper wall tiles, showing an industrial landscape with factory chimneys, a chemical plant, a modern high speed train and a flowery meadow with trees, framed in metal.

c1975 *40in (101cm) wide*

£650-750 **VZ**

QUICK REFERENCE

- The Troika Pottery was founded in 1963, at the Wells Pottery in Wheal Dream, St Ives, Cornwall, by potter Benny Sirota, painter Leslie Illsley and architect Jan Thompson (who left in 1965). Early pieces were smooth and glossy, often in white. Shapes were slip-moulded using liquid clay poured into moulds to ensure uniformity and ease of production.
- New shapes were introduced 1965. Illsley was influenced by Scandinavian ceramics as well as the work of Paul Klee and Constantin Brancusi, therefore circle and geometric designs in earthy muted colours were common. Success followed, due in part to the tourist industry, and in part because several high-profile London stores began stocking Troika wares.
- In 1970 the pottery expanded and moved to Newlyn. The characteristic matte, textured glaze became the main glaze around 1974.
- Consider the form, size, colours and the style of decoration. Practical, rectangular vases were produced in large numbers and are more common today. Meanwhile, scarcer hallmark shapes, such as 'wheel', 'anvil' and 'chimney' vases, remain popular with collectors. Well-executed, complex geometric patterns are desirable. Figural and pictorial images are extremely rare. Damage will reduce value considerably.
- From 1963 to 1967, pieces were usually marked 'St Ives' with a stylised trident in a square. The trident was phased out after 1967, and when the pottery moved to Newlyn, the 'St Ives' was also dropped.

A rare early Troika St Ives rectangular wall plaque, with abstract geometric decoration of squares and raised circles within a black border, with printed Trident mark.

7.5in (19cm) high

£200-300 **GORL**

A Troika St Ives 'Thames' wall plaque, modelled with a stylised curve of the river with two dimensional buildings surrounding, with Trident mark.

9.75in (25cm) high

£800-1,200 **GORL**

A Troika 'Chimney' vase, relief decorated to each side with abstract carved motifs, and with white tin-glazed sides, painted mark and initialled for Avril Bennett.

1973-79 *8in (20.5cm) high*

£250-350 **FLD**

A Troika St Ives 'Chimney' vase, decorated with a gingerbread man in black oxide over a blue ground with an abstract pattern, with a black oxide glazed shoulder, hand painted St Ives mark.

7.75in (20cm) high

£300-500 **FLD**

A Troika Pottery 'Chimney' vase, incised with sun and keypad motif, with a panel of 'Studio St Ives' stamped decoration, glazed in purple, blue and bronze, the base with painted marks and unidentified decorator's monogram.

7.75in (20cm) high

£350-450 **WW**

A Troika Pottery 'Rectangle' vase, decorated by Avril Bennett in relief and washed with oxide glazes in a palette of green and brown, the base with painted marks.

1973-79 *12.75in (33cm) high*

£280-320 **FLD**

A CLOSER LOOK AT A TROIKA MASK

Troika's masks are rare because they were complex to make and took up space in the kiln, making them expensive to buy and so comparatively few were sold.

Always inspect the corners and the base, which are often cracked or chipped. Prices have fallen slightly over the past few years, even for those in mint condition.

They were inspired by the work of artist Paul Klee, Aztec designs and also sometimes African or Oceanic tribal art and masks.

The backs of these masks are also decorated, but any decoration is usually much simpler than on the front.

A rare Troika pottery mask, doubled sided with typical geometric moulded decoration, with a brown ground, the base with painted mark and indistinct decorator's initials.

10in (25.5cm) high

£600-900 **GORL**

A Troika Pottery square jardinière, decorated by Louise Jinks, the base with painted factory marks, and with hairline crack to the rim.

Jinks was a senior decorator from 1979-81.

1976-81 *7.5in (19cm) high*

£180-220 **GHOU**

ESSENTIAL REFERENCE

- Wade was founded by Henry Hallam in 1810, and produced industrial ceramic fittings. In 1867, it moved to Burslem, Staffordshire, becoming known as Wade & Colcough. By the mid-1940s, the three Wade brothers each owned a factory in England; a fourth was founded in Ireland in the 1950s. In 1958, the three factories were combined into Wade Potteries Ltd by Sir George Wade. The company still exists, although the Irish factory closed in the 1990s.
- Wade is perhaps best known for its ranges of miniature, moulded porcelain figurines known as 'Whimsies'. The company had produced miniature figurines since the 1930s, and Whimsies were introduced in 1954. Sold in boxed sets, they were available until 1959, when they were given away as free gifts with products such as Red Rose tea or Christmas crackers. They were offered as premiums in Canada from 1967, and the US from 1983.
- In 1971, they were re-introduced for sale, but were sold individually in boxes. This continued until 1984, when they were withdrawn once again, to be re-introduced recently. Although millions have been made, they have become highly sought-after, with higher prices paid for scarcer, earlier examples, or unusual variations in glaze or form. Excepting the most recent release, earlier examples are considered as being more finely modelled and decorated.
- The company also produced other ranges of figurines, trays and small ceramic items from the mid-1950s into the 1980s, which are also collectable. These include 'Minikins', 'Whoppas', and the two very popular 'Hat Box' ranges of cartoon film characters, licensed by Disney. Available from 1956-65 and again from 1981-85, the ranges also attract interest from Disney collectors.
- Always consider condition, as this is important to value, as so many examples exist. Run your fingers all over a Whimsie to check for chips and examine them closely to look for repair – either can reduce value by as much as 70 per cent or more. Excellent condition original boxes can double the value.
- In the selection shown here, range names and numbers have been taken from the Charlton Standard Catalogue and, unless otherwise indicated, precise date ranges given refer to the range, or a combination between a figure's introduction date and the production dates of the range.

A Wade 'St Bernard' Whimsie, from Set Seven, the Pedigree Dogs range.

Many early Whimsies have separate legs – these were abandoned on later examples, presumably as they were too fragile and easily broken.

1957-61 *1.75in (4.5cm) long*

£25-30 **DSC**

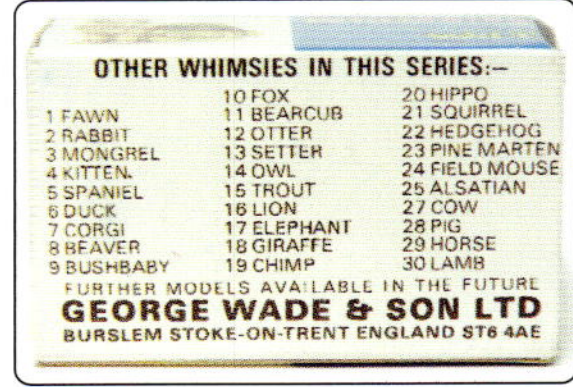

A Wade 'Collie' Whimsie, from the English Whimsies range, complete with original box.

The figure on its own is usually worth around £3-4.

1975-84 *1.5in (3.5cm) high*

£5-8 **DSC**

A Wade 'Alsatian' Whimsie, from Set Seven, the Pedigree Dogs range.

1957-61 *1.5in (4cm) long*

£20-25 **DSC**

A Wade 'Spaniel With Ball' Whimsie, finished in white, from Set One, the English Animals range.

A rarer variation has a beige glazed rump. Perhaps made as protoypes, examples can fetch twice this value or more.

1954-58 *2in (5cm) long*

£15-20 **DSC**

A Wade 'Jock' figurine, with no tartan coat, from Set One of the original Disney 'Lady and the Tramp' Hat Box range.

This is the rarest and most valuable variation of the three Jocks from the first issue of this range.

1956-65 *1.75in (4.5cm) high*

£30-35 **DSC**

A Wade 'Jock' figurine, with green tartan coat, from Set One of the original Disney 'Lady and the Tramp' Hat Box range.

1956-65 *1.75in (4.5cm) high*

£15-20 **DSC**

A Wade 'Jock' figurine, with blue tartan coat, from Set One of the original Disney 'Lady and the Tramp' Hat Box range.

1956-65 *1.75in (4.5cm) high*

£15-20 **DSC**

A Wade 'Scamp' figurine, from the re-issued Disney 'Lady and the Tramp' Hat Box range, with original plastic 'hat box' with paper labels.

1981-85 *1.75in (4cm) long*

£20-25 **DSC**

A Wade 'Lady' figurine from the re-issued Disney 'Lady and the Tramp' Hat Box series, with gilt label to stomach and plastic 'hat box' with paper labels.

Original moulds were used for many figurines in the second series, and it can be hard to tell which period they were made in without the box. However, as some moulds were worn through use, details on re-issues can be flatter. Painted details may also differ e.g. later versions of Lady (like this one) lack a blue collar.

1981-85 *1.75in (4cm) long*

£20-25 **DSC**

MILLERS COMPARES

This is the first version of Tramp. In the second version he is seated, as the legs on the earlier version proved fragile and easily broken.

Like many Whimsies, the modelling and painting on this earlier version are better.

This simpler second version was introduced in 1985 to complete the re-issued set in the last year of its production.

The base is ridged, which is a hallmark of authentic Whimsies, and this style of label was used 1981-1985.

A Wade 'Tramp' figurine, from Set One of the original Disney 'Lady and the Tramp' Hat Box range.

1956-6 *52.25in (5.5cm) high*

£20-25 **DSC**

A Wade 'Tramp' figurine, from the re-issued Disney 'Lady and the Tramp' Hat Box range, the base with gilt label.

1985 *2in (5cm) high*

£15-20 **DSC**

CERAMICS

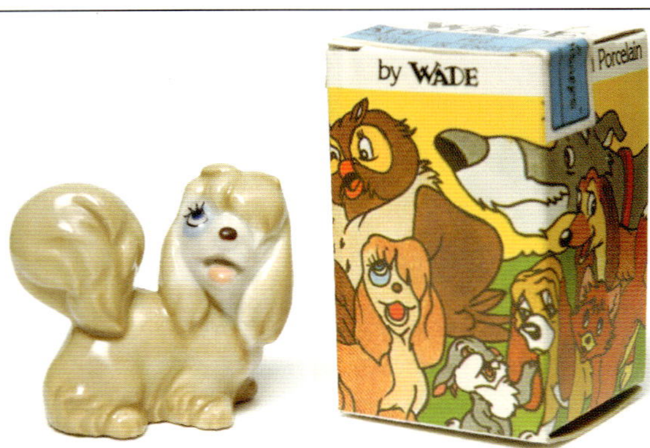

A Wade 'Peg' figurine, from the re-issued Disney 'Lady and the Tramp' Hat Box range, with original printed card box.

Card boxes replaced plastic 'hat boxes' towards the end of the production period, with Peg only being sold in a card box.

1985 *1.75in (4cm) long*

£20-25 **DSC**

A Wade 'Si' figurine from Set Two of the Disney 'Lady and the Tramp' Hat Box range.

1956-65 *2in (5cm) high*

£30-35 **DSC**

A Wade 'Am' figurine from Set Two of the Disney 'Lady and the Tramp' Hat Box range.

1956-65 *2in (5cm) high*

£30-35 **DSC**

A rare Wade 'Tod' figurine from the re-issued Disney 'Fox & The Hound' Hat Box range.

Tod was not as popular as other characters with buyers at the time, making him rare today.

1982-85 *2in (5cm) high*

£40-50 **DSC**

A Wade 'Dumbo' figurine, from Set Two of the the Disney Hat Box range.

As well as being a desirable character, undamaged examples of ' Dumbo' are scarce.

1956-65 *1.5in (4cm) high*

£30-35 **DSC**

A Wade 'Bambi' figurine from the first issue of Set Two of the Disney 'Bambi' Hat Box range, with original printed card 'hat box'.

This is the original card 'hat box' packaging from the 1950s and 60s.

1956-65 *1.75in (4cm) high*

£30-35 **DSC**

A Wade 'Pegasus' figurine, from Set Two of the Disney Hat Box range.

Always examine the wings carefully as they are often damaged. Pegasus is from Dinsey's 'Fantasia'.

1956-65 *2in (5cm) high*

£40-50 **DSC**

ESSENTIAL REFERENCE – MINIKINS

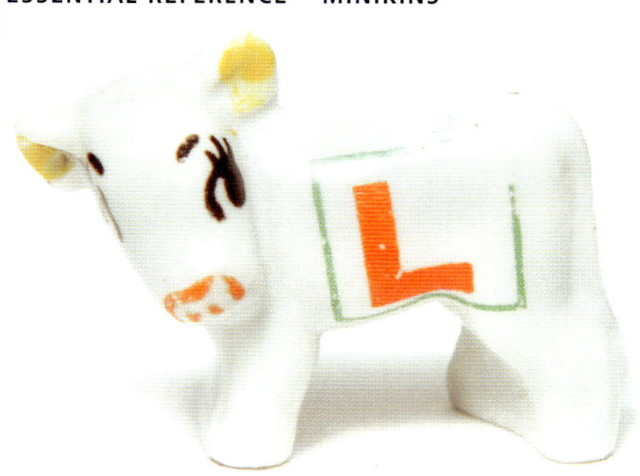

A Wade 'Cow' Minikin, from Series Two, with 'L-plate' motif to front and musical notes to back.

Minikins were issued from 1955-58 in three different series, each comprising differently shaped figurines modelled by William Harper. All are unmarked and covered in a glossy white glaze, but bear different combinations of motifs and coloured facial features. In all, these differences created 48 variations per set. At an original cost of 1/- each, they were sold to retailers in boxes of 48. With its 'L' plate and musical notes on a cow, this model is a scarce combination.

1956-58 *1.25in 93cm) long*

£20-25 **DSC**

A Wade 'Cat Walking' Minikin, from Series One, with blue tail and ears.

1955-58 *1.5in (4cm) long*

£10-15 **DSC**

A Wade 'Cat Standing' Minikin, from Series One, with green star and yellow ears.

1955-58 *1.25in (3cm) high*

£10-15 **DSC**

A Wade 'Dog' Minikin, from Series Three, with red collar and yellow ears.

1957-58 *1.25in 93cm) high*

£20-25 **DSC**

A Wade 'Mouse' Minikin, from Series Two, with blue spot.

1956-58 *1in (2.5cm) high*

£10-15 **DSC**

A Wade 'Rabbit' Minikin, from Series Two, with musical note decoration.

1956-58 *1.25in (3cm) long*

£10-15 **DSC**

A Wade 'Fawn' Minikin, from Series Three, with flower to chest and pink ears.

This model is quite rare as it was only produced for one year. Note the oversized head, which is typically 1950s in style and also hinted at Disney's 'Bambi'.

1957-58 *1.25in (3cm) high*

£25-30 **DSC**

A very rare Wade 'Pelican' Minikin, from Series Three, with anchor decoration.

This is rare as it was produced for only one year before the Minikin range was discontinued. The Pelican was also less popular than other more 'cuddly' and collected animals such as dogs and cats.

1957-58 *1.25in (3cm) high*

£30-35 **DSC**

A CLOSER LOOK AT A NATWEST PIGGY BANK

Many believe these unmarked Woody versions are fakes – all Wade banks are marked 'WADE ENGLAND' on the base.

The deeper pink skin colour and the unmarked base indicate that this example was made by Sunshine Ceramics.

Sunshine Ceramics received the initial commission to manufacture the piggy banks, but could not keep up with demand and consquently it lost the commission to Wade in 1983.

Although they are rarer than Wade's version, over 100,000 Woodies were reputed to have been made, but only 400 full sets of the family were made.

A Sunshine Ceramics 'Woody' piggy bank, modelled by Paul Cardew, and produced for the National Westminster Bank, the base unmarked.

1982 *5.25in (13cm) high*

£5-8 **DSC**

A Wade 'Woody' piggy bank, modelled by Paul Cardew, produced for the National Westminster Bank, the base moulded 'WADE ENGLAND'.

1983-88 *5.25in (13cm) high*

£10-15 **DSC**

A Wade 'Annabel' piggy bank, modelled by Paul Cardew, produced for the National Westminster Bank, the base moulded 'WADE ENGLAND'.

1983-88 *6in (15cm) high*

£15-20 **DSC**

A Wade 'Maxwell' piggy bank, modelled by Paul Cardew, produced for the National Westminster Bank, the base moulded 'WADE ENGLAND'.

1983-88 *6.5in (16cm) high*

£25-30 **DSC**

A Wade 'Lady Hilary' piggy bank, modelled by Paul Cardew, produced for the National Westminster Bank, the base moulded 'WADE ENGLAND'.

1983-88 *6.75in (17cm) high*

£35-40 **DSC**

ESSENTIAL REFERENCE: NATWEST PIGGY BANKS

A Wade 'Sir Nathaniel' piggy bank, modelled by Paul Cardew, produced for the National Westminster Bank, the base moulded 'WADE ENGLAND'.

The National Westminster bank offered these piggy banks from 1982-88 as an incentive for children to save. Woody was given when a child opened an account, with Annabel being given when the balance had reached £25, Maxwell when the balance reached £50, Lady Hilary when it reached £75, and Sir Nathaniel when it reached £100. As £100 was a large sum of money for a child in the 1980s, far fewer examples of Sir Nathaniel were given away compared to Woody. 'Cousin Wesley', modelled by Ken Holmes, was given away in 1998, expanding the family to six. Only 5,000 examples were made and he can fetch £300 or more today with box and slip. Also look out for the 'Gold Woody', decorated with 22 carat gold leaf, of which only only around 30 examples were made, each accompanied by a certificate of authenticty. Fakes are known. These include the 'Gold Woody', and a 'Gold Annabel' which was never made by Wade. Sir Nathaniel banks in white coats are also fakes. In 2007, Paul Cardew's Rame Pottery re-released the pig family with silver detailing to celebrate its 25th anniversary. A new full set costs £200.

1983-88 *7in (17.5cm) high*

£50-60 **DSC**

A 1950s Wade set of four transfer printed ballet dancer dishes, complete with original box.

Dishes 4.75in (10.5cm) wide

£30-40 **DSC**

A Wade 'Alsation Puppy Lying' pup in a basket dish, with an Alsatian Puppy Lying Whimsy figurine, from the Cat and Puppy Dishes range. 1974-8

1 3.25in (8cm) wide

£10-15 **DSC**

A 1950s-60s Wade Viking longboat dish, with green and beige glazes and moulded marks to base.

7.5in (19cm) long

£10-15 **DSC**

A 1950s Wade Mermaid vase, with moulded mermaids on two sides.

The shape and design was perhaps inspired by similar 1930s Art Deco pressed glass vases from Czechoslovakia, Germany and England.

4.25in (10.5cm) wide

£20-25 **DSC**

A 1950s-60s posy vase, with a Koala on a branch.

2.5in (6.5cm) high

£20-25 **DSC**

An Irish Wade trinket box, with moulded shamrocks and transfer printed horse racing scene, with moulded marks and grey-blue glaze to base.

The grey glaze, often with greeny-blue tones, is typical of Wade's Irish production.

5in (12.5cm) wide

£15-20 **DSC**

A 1930s Wade jug vase, in the form of a budgerigar perched on a branch curling up a column, the base printed 'WADE ENGLAND'.

10.25in (26cm) high

£25-30 **DSC**

FIND OUT MORE...

www.wade.co.uk – *the official company website*

Pat Murray, Wade Whimsical Collectable, *The Charlton Press, 2004*

QUICK REFERENCE

- Wedgwood was founded by Josiah Wedgwood (1730-1796) in Burslem, Staffordshire in 1759. Success came quickly, and he expanded in 1764, and again in 1768. After meeting the businessman Thomas Bentley, who became his partner in 1769, Wedgwood became fascinated by Classical Greek and Roman designs, and these influenced the company's designs from then on. Although all types of pottery were made, the company is famous for its matte Jasper ware developed c1774-75 and produced in blue, black or green with applied white friezes of Classical scenes.
- The company continued to be an important and innovative pottery during the 20th century, and employed a number of notable designers from the 1930s onwards. Perhaps the most important of these was New Zealand architect and Modernist designer Keith Murray (1892-1981). His geometric Art Deco designs in cool, Classical matte glazes have become highly sought after today. Forms are simple, with moulded ribs, or plain bands cut into the bodies with a lathe. They were produced in a range of colours including 'Moonstone' white, 'Straw Yellow' and green.
- Other notable designers included Daisy Makeig-Jones (1881-1945) who is known for her complex 'Fairyland Lustre' range of the late 1910s and 1920s, and illustrator Eric Ravilious (1903-42) who designed nursery and table ware from c1936 to 1940. Norman Wilson (1902-85), John Skeaping (1901-80) and Millicent Taplin (1902-80) are other notable names whose various designs from the 1920-60s are worth looking out for.
- Wedgwood has attracted a huge following of collectors, and prices are strong, particularly for 20thC designs. It will be interesting to see how the company's recent insolvency affects values over the coming years.

A Wedgwood matte green ball vase, shape 4197, designed by Keith Murray, the base with printed full signature mark.

6in (15.5cm) high

£350-400 **BEV**

A Wedgwood Straw yellow tapering cylindrical vase, shape 4315, designed by Keith Murray, the base with printed 'KM' mark.

7.5in (19cm) high

£450-550 **BEV**

A Wedgwood Straw yellow ball vase, shape 4197, designed by Keith Murray, the base with printed full signature mark.

This mark was introduced 1932.

6in (15cm) high

£350-450 **BEV**

A 1930s Wedgwood matte green horizontally fluted globe vase, shape 4324, designed by Keith Murray, the base with impressed 'KM' mark.

This is an extremely rare design. This mark was introduced in 1934. It is more commonly seen printed, rather than impressed.

7in (17.5cm) high

£500-700 **PC**

A Wedgwood bowl, designed by Norman Wilson, of fluted form, glazed black and white, impressed marks, printed 'NW'.

Here, a Black Basalt slip has been applied to a Moonstone white glazed body, which has then been cut back on a lathe to reveal the underlying colour.

10.75in (27cm) diam

£280-380 WW

A Wedgwood Black Basalt bowl, by Norman Wilson, of fluted form, glazed black, impressed marks, minor chips to top rim.

10in (25.5cm) diam

£380-480 WW

A rare Wedgwood earthenware bowl, by Norman Wilson, sky blue cut back to black, the interior black, impressed marks, 'NW' monogram.

6.25in (16cm) diam

£420-480 WW

QUICK REFERENCE – NORMAN WILSON

Norman Wilson (1902-1985) was invited to join Wedgwood as Works Manager in 1926. Part of a young, dynamic team, he became Production Director in 1946, having introduced new production processes including the installation of a tunnel kiln. Among collectors, he is best known for his glaze experiments, and matte glazes that were used by Keith Murray. After studying ancient Chinese Sung glazes, Wilson developed a range of unique experimental glazes that were applied to production and specially commissioned forms. Known as 'Norman Wilson Unique Ware', these were produced erratically from 1928-63, with no two pieces being exactly the same.

A Wedgwood earthenware bowl, designed by Norman Wilson, the exterior salmon pink, the interior mottled pink, the base with impressed marks and 'NM' monogram.

8in (20.5cm) diam

£400-500 WW

A Wedgwood Dragon Lustre dish, designed by Daisy Makeig-Jones, with mythical beast printed in gilt on a pearl lustre ground, the base with printed and painted marks.

3.5in (9cm) diam

£100-150 WW

A Wedgwood Fairyland Lustre 'Candlemas' pattern vase, designed by Daisy Makeig-Jones, shape 2410, printed and painted in colours and gilt on a black ground, the base with printed factory mark, and 'NJW Baker' retailer's paper label.

'Candlemas' was introduced in 1918, and was based on the ritual ceremony of the blessing of candles, which would then be carried in a procession. Produced in four different colour variations, it was made until 1929.

7.5in (19.5cm) high

£800-1,200 WW

A Wedgwood part tea set, retailed by Thomas Goode & Co., painted with a trailing fruiting vine, pattern no. A5061, comprising eight cups, eight saucers, eleven tea plates, two bread and butter plates, a sugar bowl and a milk jug.

£150-200 **DA&H**

A Wedgwood 'Persephone' pattern oval meat dish, designed by Eric Ravilious with chip and some wear to glaze and pattern.

c1938 *16.75in (42.5cm) wide*

£70-100 **SWO**

A CLOSER LOOK AT A WEDGWOOD FAIRYLAND LUSTRE BOWL

Bowls are particularly popular with collectors – as they are decorated both inside and out, you get a lot of 'pattern for your pound'.

Wedgwood's Fairyland Lustre range has risen in price over the past few years, primarily due to interest from American collectors. However, prices may be peaking.

The 'Dana – Castle on a Road' pattern was designed in 1917 and released in the same year – it was popular and soon became a bestseller.

Makeig-Jones' innovative and complex designs were highly influential and expensive in their day. Carltonware and Crown Devon produced similar, more affordable ranges, but none matched the quality of Fairyland Lustre.

A Wedgwood Fairyland Lustre 'Dana - Castle on a Road' pattern octagonal punch bowl, designed by Daisy Makeig Jones, printed and painted in gilt and enamels, the base with printed and painted marks to base including the 'Z5125' pattern number.

9in (23cm) wide

£1,000-1,500 **L&T**

A Wedgwood 'Persephone' pattern six place dinner service, designed by Eric Ravilious, comprising six each of four sizes of plates, six handled bowls, two lidded tureens, an oval bowls and a gravy boat and stand, each with transfer-printed design.

c1938 *Plates 9in (23cm) diam*

£400-600 **SWO**

A rare Wedgwood 'Garden Implements' pattern Liverpool-shape lemonade jug and four beakers, designed by Eric Ravilious in c1938, printed in black and pink lustre, the bases with printed factory marks.

Jug 7.75in (20cm) high

£1,200-1,800 (SET) **WW**

FIND OUT MORE...

Maureen Batkin ' Wedgwood Ceramics 1846-1959' . *Ilminster: Richard Dennis Publications, 1982.*

Robin Reilly and George Savage ' Wedgwood – The New Illustrated Dictionary' . *London: The Antique Collectors' Club, 1999.*

QUICK REFERENCE

- Samuel Weller (1851-1925) founded Weller in Fultonham, Ohio in 1872, and moved the company to Zanesville in 1888. Like local rival Roseville, it initially produced utilitarian wares, before moving into the art pottery market.
- Weller bought W. A. Long's Lonhuda Pottery in 1894. Within a year, he had learned Long's special glazing techniques, which had been developed by ex-Rookwood decorator Laura Fry, and the partnership between Long and Weller was dissolved. The Lonhuda range, which featured hand-painted natural motifs on brown glossy background, much like Rookwood's Standard Glazed pieces, was re-launched by Weller as Louwelsa. Although competition was strong, Weller prospered and by 1904 had become the largest art pottery in the world.
- Weller continued to produce high-quality hand-decorated ranges at affordable prices. These included Aurelian (c1897), Eocean (1898), Dickensware (1900) and Sicardo (1902). Designers included Charles Upjohn (working 1895-1904), Jacques Sicard (1902-07) and Frederick Rhead (1903-04).
- Many factories stopped producing hand-decorated ranges as the 1920s approached, turning to faster and less expensive moulded wares. Weller reacted against this by releasing the hand-painted Hudson range in 1917, but the Great Depression after 1929 forced even Weller to move to entirely moulded wares by 1935. Much was designed by Rudolph Lorber and his assistant, Dorothy England Laughead. These pieces were of good quality and new glazes, such as 'Burnt Wood' and 'Graystone', were still being developed.
- Hand-decorated lines, such as Louwelsa, Eocean and Hudson, usually command the highest prices, particularly large examples with all-over surface decoration. Look for artists' signature as this will usually add value. Later moulded forms are generally not as valuable, though the most complex or rarest ranges by notable designers can be desirable. Be sure to look for damage on all examples, as this always reduces value, especially on the moulded ranges.

A Weller 'Louwelsa' large baluster vase, decorated by Sarah McLaughlin, the base with a partial Louwelsa stamp and numbered, with glaze flake to base and hairline to rim.

11in (28cm) high

£150-200 BEL

A Weller 'Hudson' vase, painted by Ruth Axline, with a branch of yellow, blue and pink dogwood blossoms around the upper body, and with kiln stamp/artist's cipher.

9in (23cm) high

£300-400 DRA

A Weller 'Hudson' vase, painted by Sarah McLaughlin with irises, with circular factory ink stamp and artist's mark to base.

9.25in (23.5cm) high

£600-800 DRA

A Weller 'Hudson Light' tapered vase, painted with pink and yellow columbine, the base stamped 'WELLER'.

13.75in (35cm) high

£300-400 DRA

A Weller 'Hudson' vase, painted by Mae Timberlake, with nasturtium blossoms, stamped kiln mark and signed 'Timberlake'.

12.75in (33.5cm) high

£600-800 DRA

A Weller scenic 'Hudson' vase, painted by Hester Pillsbury with a cabin in the woods, against a mountainous landscape, repair to two cracks through body, kiln stamp.

Scenic Hudson vases are scarcer than floral patterns. Had this vase not been cracked it might have been worth double this price.

9in (23cm) high

£600-800 **CRA**

A CLOSER LOOK AT A WELLER VASE

The Sicard range was designed by Frenchman Jacques Sicard, who had previously worked for notable French potter Clement Massier.

One of Weller's most sought-after ranges among collectors, this example is enhanced by a decorative shape typical of the period.

Developed under great secrecy with the aim of putting Weller back among the top pottery companies in the US, the range was sold from 1902-12.

The range is typified by iridescent glazes and motifs derived from nature.

This example displays a superb range of colours and a complex and detailed pattern.

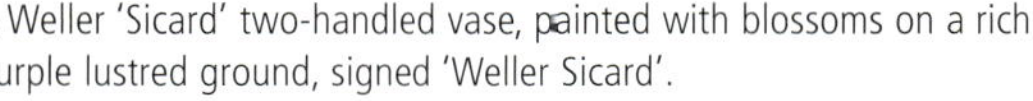

A Weller 'Sicard' two-handled vase, painted with blossoms on a rich purple lustred ground, signed 'Weller Sicard'.

9in (23cm) high

£1,500-2,500 **DRA**

A Weller 'Etna' vase, moulded with pink daisies against a shaded dark grey ground, the base stamped 'WELLER WARE ETNA'.

10.75in (27.5cm) high

£250-350 **DRA**

A Weller 'Sicard' vase with scrolling leaf and daisy pattern, the base with script factory mark, glaze chip to bottom, possibly from grinding.

5.5in (14cm) high

£450-550 **DRA**

A Weller 'Turada' bowl, with heavy slip decoration and black glaze, the base marked 'Weller Turada 44'.

Turada was designed by Samuel Weller.

c1898 *4.5in (11.4cm) diam*

£60-80 **BEL**

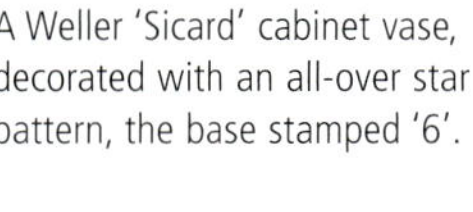

A Weller 'Sicard' cabinet vase, decorated with an all-over star pattern, the base stamped '6'.

4in (10cm) high

£350-450 **DRA**

A rare Weller 'Fru Russett' tapering vase, with pierced rim, large applied yellow flowers and green leaves on a pale purple ground, restored rim, the base with impressed mark.

The Arts and Crafts style Fru Russett range was introduced in 1905 and is very rare today. Typical colours include matte green, brown, or blue and motifs are usually floral.

10.5in (26.5cm) high

£1,200-1,800 **CRA**

A Weller 'Knifewood' vase, with owls, squirrels and birds on oak branches, the base stamped 'Weller'.

7in (18cm) high

£450-550 **DRA**

A rare Weller Matt Green-glazed basket vase, on a 'Silvertone' blank, crisply decorated, unmarked, and with restoration to handle.

Such green glazes were typical of Arts and Crafts potteries, and are desirable among collectors today.

9in (23cm) high

£200-300 **DRA**

A very rare Weller 'Muskota' wall hanging 'Tree Squirrel', with restored paws.

The Muskota line of animals was produced from 1915-28 and is very popular with collectors today. The range also included butterflies, birds and fish, with this form being very scarce.

13.75in (35cm) long

£450-550 **BH**

A Weller 'Tutone' chalice vase, with green highlights, the base with Weller Pottery full kiln stamp, and three tight lines at the rim.

5.5in (14cm) high

£15-25 **BEL**

A Weller 'Velva' vase, in brown with floral panel, the base with script Weller Pottery mark.

7.5in (19cm) high

£60-80 **BEL**

A Weller 'Woodcraft' tree-shaped vase, with climbing squirrel and owl, with tight crack to rim, and second restored crack.

18in (45.5cm) high

£600-800 **DRA**

A rare Weller Art Deco owl figurine, in a semi-matte blue glaze, the Greek letters 'Kappa Kappa Gamma' on the base.

9.75in (25cm) high

£400-600 **BEL**

QUICK REFERENCE

- Wemyss ware was produced by the Fife Pottery in Kirkaldy Scotland from 1882, after the owner's son, Robert Methven Heron, invited Bohemian decorators to join the pottery. The pottery had its origins in the 18thC producing objects in muted colours, but when Karel Nekola, one of the new staff, decorated pieces with flowers and leaves inspired by his love of nature, production changed direction and Wemyss ware was born.
- Popularity grew rapidly, and pieces were sold by top London retailer Thomas Goode & Son, whose marks can often be found on pieces.
- Following Nekola's death in 1915. Edwin Sandland took over decoration. After his death in 1928 he was in turn succeeded by Nekola's son Joe. A loss in popularity due to changing public tastes forced the pottery to close in 1930. Joe Nekola moved to the Bovey Tracey pottery in Devon, taking the Wemyss moulds with him. After his death in 1952, Esther Weeks took over until 1957. She is still decorating Wemyss today at the Griselda Pottery, Fife (established 1985).
- The colourful, cheery and quirky style of Wemyss ware has attracted a legion of loyal collectors, including personalities such as Elton John, the late HM Queen Elizabeth the Queen Mother, and HRH Prince Charles. Most collectors collect Wemyss ware by pattern and some patterns and shapes are more desirable than others. The work of Karel Nekola is particularly sought after.
- Examine pieces all over for signs of damage, as this reduces value dramatically. Wares made in Fife are particularly prone to crazing and chipping. Devon-produced pieces have a cleaner white 'glassy' glaze, and are lighter in weight than examples from Fife. They are also generally less valuable, giving a more affordable entry point to the market.

An early 20thC Wemyss dog bowl, decorated with cabbage roses and inscription 'Plus je connais les hommes/Plus j'admire les chiens', with painted and impressed marks 'Wemyss', restoration to rim, cracks.

The charming inscription means "The more I know [about] men, the more I admire dogs." Dog bowls are scarce and valuable.

4.25in (11cm) diam

£300-500 **L&T**

A Wemyss basket jardinière, decorated with cabbage roses, the base with impressed 'Wemyss' mark.

c1900 *11.5in (29.5cm) diam*

£280-320 **L&T**

A small Wemyss loving cup, decorated with dog roses, with impressed 'Wemyss Ware R. H. & S.' mark, and 'T. Goode & Co.' retailer's mark, glaze losses on rim.

c1900 *4.25in (10.5cm) high*

£280-320 **L&T**

A small Wemyss basket, decorated with cabbage roses, with impressed 'Wemyss Ware R. H. & S.' mark, and 'T Goode & Co.' retailer's mark.

c1900 *8in (20.5cm) long*

£250-300 **L&T**

An early 20thC Wemyss low pomade and cover, with dog roses, possibly by Karel Nekola, with impressed and painted 'Wemyss' mark, chip to rim.

3.75in (9.5cm) diam

£350-400 **L&T**

A 1920s Wemyss biscuit barrel and cover, decorated in the 'Jazzy' pattern with cabbage roses, the cover inscribed 'Biscuits', with painted 'Wemyss 213' mark.

'Jazzy' is the name given to the multi-coloured, brushed background, which replaces the standard white on other pieces.

4.75in (12cm) diam

£250-350 **L&T**

A Wemyss 'Cabbage Rose' biscuit box and cover, painted in colours, impressed and painted 'Wemyss' painted and printed marks.

5in (12.5cm) diam

£220-280 **WW**

A large early 20thC Wemyss mug, decorated with cabbage roses, with impressed mark 'Wemyss'.

5.5in (14cm) high

£280-320 **L&T**

A Wemyss 'Cabbage Rose' jug and a basin, painted in colours, the bases with various marks, damaged.

Had this not been damaged, it may have fetched over £800.

Jug 6.25in (16cm) high

£150-200 **WW**

An early 20thC Wemyss pin tray, decorated by Karel Nekola with dog roses and bearing the inscription "Sois satisfait des fruits, des fleurs, même des feuilles/ Si c'est dans ton jardin à toi que tu les cueilles", impressed and painted mark "Wemyss", hairline crack.

The wording reads, 'Be satisfied with the fruits, flowers, and same with the leaves/If it is in your garden that you picked them'. Plaques are scarce and desirable.

5.75in (14.5cm) wide

£500-700 **L&T**

A CLOSER LOOK AT A WEMYSS GOBLET

The rose, shamrock and thistle motifs are typical of decoration on Wemyss, but are rarely found together on one piece.

The rose can be read as indicating England, the thistle Scotland, and the shamrock Ireland.

The goblet bears the VR monogram for 'Victoria Regina' – royal commemoratives are widely collected, which widens the market.

The goblet shape is appealing, and the decoration is very detailed.

A small Wemyss Victoria goblet, with decoration of roses, thistles and shamrock, and bearing crown and cipher, impressed mark 'Wemyss Ware R. H. & S.', 'T. Goode & Co.' retailer's mark.

c1900

5.5in (14cm) high

£200-300 **L&T**

A small early 20thC Wemyss pig, covered in a green glaze.

6.25in (16cm) long

£350-450 L&T

A Wemyss pottery pig, covered in a pink glaze, with impressed mark.

6.25in (16cm) high

£320-380 WW

A small Wemyss pig figure, covered in a white glaze, with impressed 'Wemyss' mark.

c1900 *6.25in (16cm) long*

£350-450 L&T

A Wemyss pig, painted in shades of black and white, its snout and toes painted pink, painted 'Wemyss', and printed 'Made in England'.

6.5in (16.5cm) wide

£350-450 WW

A Wemyss goose flower holder, naturalistically painted in typical colours, on an oval foot, impressed 'Wemyss Ware R.H. & S.' and a pink stamped mark for T. Goode & Co.

c1900 *8in (20.5cm) high*

£320-380 DN

A CLOSER LOOK AT A WEMYSS PIG

Pigs can be found in a number of different patterns and plain glazes, but beware of fakes which have glossier glazes in different tones when compared to authentic examples.

Plump seated pigs are perhaps the most celebrated and recognisable of Wemyss' shapes and are highly sought after.

Smaller Plichta pigs dating from after 1930, such as this one, tend to be more affordable than earlier examples.

In 2004, Sotheby's sold a rare sleeping piglet painted with roses for a record price of £34,800.

A small post-1930 Wemyss pig figure, decorated by Joe Nekola with shamrocks, printed marks 'Plichta London England', painted marks 'Nekola/pinx'.

6.25in (16cm) long

£320-380 L&T

QUICK REFERENCE

- West German ceramics from the 1950s-1970s have recently become highly collectable. Interest in this field is understandable, as this period enjoyed an explosion of innovation and design in West German pottery, which changed dramatically from decade to decade. Established companies, such as Bay Keramik, Dümler & Breiden, Emons & Söhne and Ruscha, underwent a revival, as new companies, such as Scheurich and Otto Keramik, opened.
- The ceramics of the 1950s are typified by curving, organic or geometric forms, and painted in bright, primary colours, often outlined in black. Patterns comprised ovals, circles, lines and stylised, curving, natural motifs. Angled or asymmetric curving handles or rims were common. Largely ornamental, jug vases with handles were particularly popular. These handles were often strongly angled in the 1950s, taking on ring forms in the 1960s.
- There was a complete change of style in the 1960s-70s. Colour and texture became extremely important. Rather than forming planned patterns, glazes were trailed, dripped or daubed over the body of the piece. Many of these glazes were thick 'lava' glazes, arranged in bands or stripes of bright colours, such as orange or red.
- Look for wilder, thick glazes, known by collectors as 'Fat Lava', as these tend to be more desirable, particularly in unusual forms. Many 'Fat Lava' pieces were produced in limited numbers, as opposed to tamer designs in less exuberant colours, which are more common.
- Makers can be identified by considering shape, colour, type of glaze and style of moulded marks on the base. Some pieces were inscribed or had impressed marks: some even have labels. Handle as many identified pieces, ideally those with labels, as possible.

A 1950s Marzi & Remi 'sugarglaze' vase, with inscribed curving lines through a brick coloured glaze, the base marked '2015-50'.

19.75in (50cm) high

£80-120 **OUT**

A 1950s West German Bay Keramik torpedo vase, with white textured glaze and hand-decorated multicoloured crescent and curving line decoration, the base moulded '529 38'.

15.25in (38.5cm) high

£20-30 **RET**

A 1960s Bay Keramik floor vase, with hand-painted cell-like design, introduced in 1961, the base with moulded numbers.

Many have attributed this design to Bodo Mans due to the abstract nature and bright colours of the design, but this has not been confirmed.

£100-150 **OUT**

A 1950s West German Conradt Gebrüder vase, with hand-painted round and curving line design, the base marked "100/5".

10in (25cm) high

£40-60 **OUT**

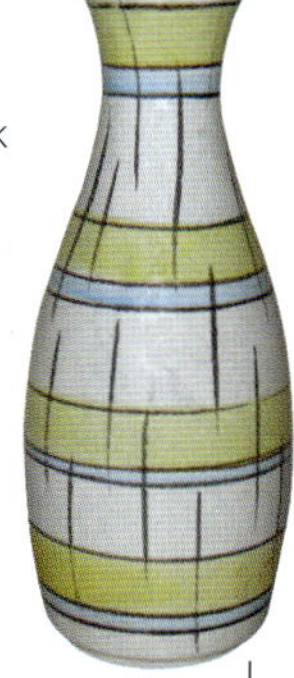

A 1950s West German Bay Keramik baluster vase, with hand-painted yellow and blue bands and black dashes, designed by Bodo Mans, the base moulded '584-25'.

10in (25cm) high

£30-50 **OUT**

A 1950s West German Fürstenberg porcelain bull, with black glaze, the base marked 'F'.

6in (15cm) high

£40-60 **OUT**

A 1950s Keto 'Komposition' vase, with hand-painted multicoloured triangles and inscribed lines, the base printed 'Keto Keramik Handarbeit Komposition 1004'.

9in (23cm) high

£40-60 **OUT**

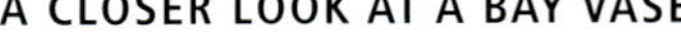

A CLOSER LOOK AT A BAY VASE

Defined areas of bright, saturated colour combined with inscribed 'sgrafitto' or painted lines are typical of 1950s designs.

Patterns were often named after romantic, foreign places as the 1950s was the age of the jet plane and an increase in foreign travel.

Bodo Mans was one of the most notable designers during the 1950s, and produced many similar designs inspired by modern art.

Despite the pattern being modern, the shape is more traditional – had that been more modern as well, the value would have been higher.

A West German Bay Keramik 'Paris' pattern urn vase, designed by Bodo Mans in 1960, the base moulded '1014-25 WEST-GERMANY'.

10in (25cm) high

£30-40 **MA**

A 1960s West German Marzi & Remy blue and white arabesque patterned jug vase, with impressed 'MR' monogram used from 1960-67, numbered '2027/32A'.

Marzi & Remy (1879-1994) are best known for their beer steins, which were mostly decorated with the design protruding through the coloured glaze, as in this example. This moulded pattern recalls tiles of the Arts and Crafts movement of the late 19thC and early 20thC.

1960-67 *12.5in (32cm) high*

£20-30 **M20C**

A 1970s Ruscha wall plate, decorated with a sgraffito and glazed design of grazing fawns on a mottled cream ground, the back printed 'RUSCHA HANDARBEIT' and moulded '717/1'.

1969-78 *7.25in (18.5cm) diam*

£22-28 **RET**

A 1950s West German Schramberg Majolika Fabrik hand-painted 'Cuba' pattern dish, the base marked '4370 Cuba'.

5in (12cm) wide

£15-20 **OUT**

A West German Scheurich floor vase, the grey bubbly 'lava' glaze cut through to reveal the red underglaze in the form of horses, the base with moulded marks.

18in (46cm) high

£100-150 **WW**

A West German Scheurich 'Lora' pattern floor vase, with a copper-coloured micro-crystalline glaze over a glossy red glaze, the base moulded '517 45 W.GERMANY'.

This type of coppery micro-crystalline glaze was developed by Oswald Kleudgen and became a signature glaze of his.

17in (43cm) high

£80-100 **M20C**

A CLOSER LOOK AT A SCHEURICH VASE

Known to collectors as the 'Flame' pattern, the range was actually called 'Lora'.

This is a comparatively large size, had it been a floor vase, the value could have been doubled.

This particular colour combination is very unusual, particularly the green.

Before firing, layers of glaze are cut away by hand to reveal underlying colours, making the pattern on each unique.

A West German Scheurich 'Lora' pattern floor vase with three layers of glaze, comprising a beige lava glaze over glossy orange over glossy green, the base with indistinct numbering.

15in (38cm) high

£70-100 **M20C**

A 1970s West German Scheurich torpedo vase, with thin grey lava glaze and glossy white and dripped blue bands, the base moulded '522-20'.

8in (20cm) high

£40-60 **OUT**

A West German Scheurich floor vase, with banded orange and green design and tube-lined curlicue designs in a lava glaze.

20in (51cm) high

£30-50 **SAS**

A 1970s Scheurich cylinder vase with orange band and tube-lined grey 'lava' glaze design, with beige and grey 'lava' glaze top and base, the base moulded '231 15 W GERMANY'.

This form number was used on three different shapes by Scheurich, showing how shape numbers were reused at different times.

6in (15cm) high

£15-20 **RET**

A 1970s Scheurich 'Wien' series bulb vase, designed by A. Seide, with lava glazed ribbed top and dripped glazed body designed by Oswald Kleudgen, the base with indistinct moulded marks.

7in (17.5cm) high

£20-30 **RET**

A 1970s West-German Scheurich 'Wien' series jug vase, designed by A. Seide, covered with a dripped orangey red glaze over a bronze-brown ground, the base numbered '269-27'.

10.5in (27cm) high

£40-60 **OUT**

A mid-late 1970s West German Scheurich jug vase, with glossy orange and brown glazes, the base moulded 400-22 W.GERMANY.

8.75in (22cm) high

£15-20 **M20C**

A West German Scheurich jug vase, with glossy mottled red central band and cream foamy glaze over a brown ground, the base moulded 400-22 W.GERMANY.

8.75in (22cm) high

£20-25 **M20C**

QUICK REFERENCE - GLAZES AND SHAPES

Ruscha were one of the many companies to produce one shape and then apply a myriad of different glaze treatments, known as the 'decor' to collectors, with the famed 313 jug designed by Kurt Tschörner in 1954. The practice was taken up by many other companies, with Scheurich being a the most prolific practitioner. Given the vast choice available in the marketplace, many collectors choose to focus on one shape by one maker and then aim to collect as many different variations on the decor as possible. This particular example is more valuable than the other two on this page as it has the most appealing lava glaze. In many cases, shapes can fetch more if they have been focused on by a large number of collectors.

A West German Scheurich jug vase, with heavy cream and brown lava glaze over a matte cobalt blue ground, the base moulded '400-22 W.GERMANY'.

8.75in (22cm) high

£25-30 **M20C**

A 1970s West German Scheurich 'Montignac' pattern, Linie 72 series bottle vase, with bull outlined in a lava glaze, the base moulded 281-19.

By the 1950s, ceramic design began to show the influence of the prehistoric cave paintings found in the Lascaux caves, France, 1940. Montignac is the nearest town to the caves. The decoration is rare.

7.5 (19cm) high

£40-60 **OUT**

A 1970s Bay cylindrical footed vase, moulded decoration, blue glaze, base moulded '604-11 BAY W.-GERMANY', with silver foil manufacturer's label.

This design imitates Aldo Londi's popular 1953 'Rimini Blue' design for Bitossi, although the pattern is moulded, not impressed.

7in (17.5cm) high

£20-25 **RET**

A 1970s West German Bay Keramik jug vase, with white speckled glaze and orange and brown 'lava' glazed band, the base moulded 'W.-GERMANY 2 20'.

8in (20.5cm) high

£25-30 **RET**

A 1970s Carstens Luxus series vase, with green, orange and red glazes and stylised floral design, designed by Dieter Peter, the base with moulded factory logo and numbered '7692-45 W.-GERMANY'.

17.75in (45cm) high

£100-150 **RET**

A Carstens glossy lime green footed cylinder vase, with grey salt glaze swirls, the base moulded '147-28' and with printed white semi-circular 'WEST-GERMANY' mark.

11.5in (29cm) high

£30-40 **RET**

A 1970s Austrian Carstens small handled jug vase, with orange, beige and green glazes and stylised floral design, designed by Dieter Peter, the base moulded '3967-18 AUSTRIA'.

7.25in (18.5cm) high

£35-45 **RET**

A West German Carstens waisted vase, with alternating bands of a brown glaze with copper inclusions and orange salt-glaze, with factory silver foil label, the base moulded '3643-30 W.-GERMANY'.

12in (30.5cm) high

£30-35 **RET**

A 1960s West German Carstens 'Ankara' pattern vase, designed by Scholtis, the base with moulded Carstens mark, numbered '1236-23'.

Although prices for many West German ceramics of this period can vary widely, this design seems to fetch consistently good prices when offered at modern design auctions.

9in (23cm) high

£40-60 **OUT**

A 1970s West German Roth Keramik double-handled disc vase, shape no.314, with glossy red and black lava glazes, base unmarked.

This is also found in a smaller size.

15.5in (39cm) high

£300-350 **GC**

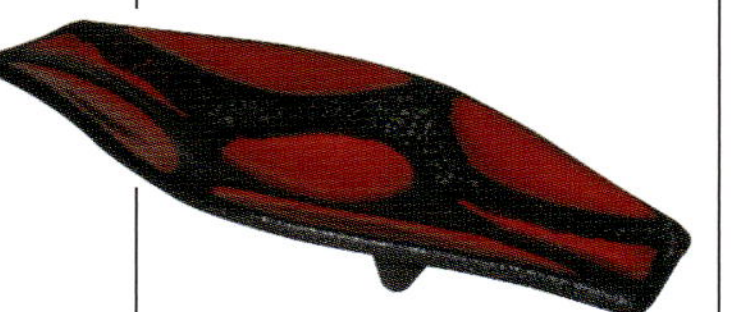

An extremely rare 1970s Roth Keramik red dish, with red glossy curving shapes between black 'lava' glazes, unmarked.

8in (20cm) long

£300-500 **OUT**

A CLOSER LOOK AT A ROTH VASE

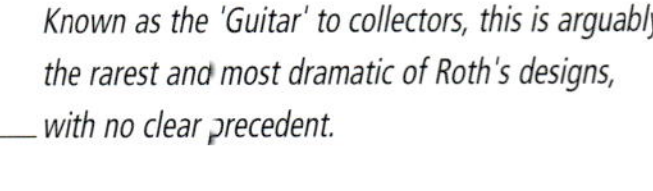

Known as the 'Guitar' to collectors, this is arguably the rarest and most dramatic of Roth's designs, with no clear precedent.

It can be found in a number of different colours, including red, purple, yellow, blue, and different green tones – values rise in that order to as much as £600.

An extremely rare 'reverse' variation is also known, with glossy red glazed lines between 'lava' glazed shapes.

Roth's pieces are not marked with the company name on the base, but are sometimes labelled.

A 1970s West German Roth Keramik orange and black lava glaze 'guitar' vase, shape no.312, by an unknown designer, the base unmarked.

12.25in (31cm) high

£250-300 **GC**

A 1970s West German Ruscha no.717 dish, with red stylised flower pattern, crystalline copper glaze and tubelined lava glaze, the base moulded '717/2'.

11in (27.5cm) diam

£40-50 **M20C**

A late 1970s-early 1980s West German Ruscha no.717 dish, with orange stylised flower and leaf pattern and tube-lined lava glaze, the base moulded '717/2'.

11in (27.5cm) diam

£35-45 **M20C**

A 1970s Ruscha wall charger with applied discs and rectangles and mottled and cloudy brown, beige and orange glazes, inscribed on back '717/2'.

The 717 dish is one of the most common dish shapes found today, and was produced from the 1950s onwards in a variety of decor types. This design is not too hard to find. The discs are often raised, almost resembling mushrooms.

11in (28cm) diam

£50-70 **RET**

An extremely rare Ruscha vase, shape 816/1, with tube-lined gun-metal grey lava glaze in a grid pattern, and a glossy turquoise glaze, the base unmarked.

Both the glaze and the shape are very hard to find – this combination is extremely rare.

8.5in (21.5cm) high

£120-180 **MHC**

A 1960s West German Ruscha 'Vulkano' glaze vase, the shape designed by Kurt Tscörner, the glaze by Otto Gerharz Snr, the base marked 320/2.

7in (18cm) high

£30-50 **OUT**

A 1970s West German Ruscha 'Antique' vase with a moulded pattern of charioteers, and red glaze over a brown background, the base marked '508-18'.

7in (18cm) high

£40-60 **OUT**

A 1970s East German Strehla waisted, footed vase with tube-lined lava glaze on a red ground, unmarked.

East German companies were keen to cash in on the success of West German ceramics, and produced their own, very similar, versions.

8.25in (21cm) high

£22-28 **RET**

QUICK REFERENCE - RUSCHA'S VULKANO GLAZE

The 'Vulkano' glaze marks the turning point in West German ceramics design between the linear, abstract designs in primary colours of the 1950s, and the freely applied, dripping and 'volcanic' lava glazes of the 1960s and 70s. Designed for leading factory Ruscha by talented glaze technician Otto Gerharz Snr in 1959, the focus became the glaze itself, rather than the patterns that could be created with it. Look out for a good variety of strong colours including green, as shown here, as these tend to be popular with collectors.

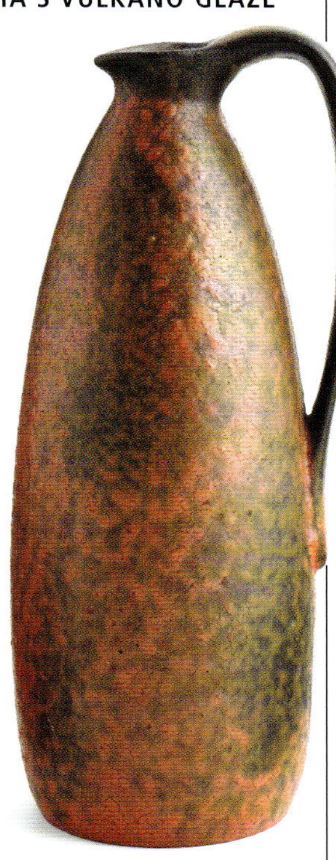

A 1960s Ruscha 'Vulkano' glaze jug, the form designed by Kurt Tschörner, the glaze by Otto Gerharz Snr, the base moulded '314/2'.

10.75in (27cm) high

£80-100 **GC**

A 1960s West German Übelacker Keramik jug vase, with mottled blue glaze and red and green band, the base impressed with an Ü motif and numberec 1628/30, and with silver manufacturer's label.

12ir. (30.5cm) high

£35-45 **RET**

FIND OUT MORE...

Fat Lava: West German Pottery From the 1960s & 70s, *by Mark Hill, published by www.markhillpublishing.com*

From Spritzdekor to Fat Lava and West & East German Pottery: Makers' Marks & Form Numbers, *by Kevin Graham, published privately, kj_graham@gmx.de*

QUICK REFERENCE

- This section is arranged alphabetically by manufacturer, with the final page comprising ceramics by as yet unidentified factories. Unlike glass, most ceramics are marked on the base. Marks may include the factory name, and possibly the designer's name as well, although this generally only appears on 20thC ceramics. Other marks may include an impressed number identifying the shape, and a painted or printed number or name to indicate the pattern or range.
- In 1890, the American McKinley Tariff Act required the name of the country of orgin to be marked on goods, including ceramics. This lead to the appearance of marks such as 'England', 'Bavaria' and 'Nippon' (Japan). In 1921 the act was amended, requiring the words 'Made in' to appear before the country. There are some exceptions, including Wedgwood, who used 'Made in England' from 1898.
- Other marks can help identify a country of origin. For example, 'Déposé would indicate manufacture in France and 'Gesetzlich Geschütz' (Ges.Gesch) in Germany. Look out for 'Reg'd' (registered) design numbers and diamond marks as these can both supply further information when researched in reference books. 'Trademark' and 'Limited' or 'Ltd' were not used before c1861-62, and are often much later.
- Be aware that the styles and shapes of marks often changed over time, which can help with dating. If a piece is unmarked, consider the way it was made: was it hand-potted or moulded, or decorated by hand? Compare the style of the form and the decoration with examples in reference books or on websites, but always cross-reference any possible identifications with other sources, particularly if found online.

An Arequipa ovoid vase, finely carved with an iris under a matte green glaze, the base with stamped mark, restoration to a small area at rim.

7.75in (19.5cm) high

£800-1,200 **DRA**

A Canadian Beauce Pottery wine carafe, shape G-121, and four goblets, shape G-119, with ribbed cog-like decoration and green glaze, designed by Jacques Garnier in 1964, the base with 'arrow heads' factory mark.

This is typical of the geometric, almost Modernist, solid forms produced by Garnier.

9in (23cm) high

£50-80 **TWF**

A 1960s-70s Canadian Blue Mountain Pottery jug, with a dripped and mottled cobalt and light blue glaze, the base with moulded three tree mark.

10.25in (26.5cm) high

£30-50 **TWF**

An early 1970s Canadian Blue Mountain Pottery tall bottle vase with flared neck and rim, with 'Flame' glaze with some orange dripping/mottling, the base with moulded 'three tree' mark.

8.25in (21cm) high

£20-40 **TWF**

A 1970s Canadian Blue Mountain Pottery 'Spitoon' vase, shape 32A, with scarce brown glaze overlaid with randomly trailed foam-effect white glaze.

5.25in (13cm) high

£20-40 **TWF**

A modern Burleigh Ware 'Guardsmen' jug, modelled in low relief with marching guardsmen and a sentry box, the base with printed factory marks.

This stunning jug was designed and first released in the early 1930s. Very few original examples survive today, and these can fetch over £1,000 in undamaged condition. Beware, as reproductions have been made since the late 1970s, and are considerably less valuable. Authentic Burleigh reprodutions like this, which are better painted and moulded than copies by other factories, are more desirable.

7.75in (20cm) high

£120-180 **WW**

A Bursley Ware rectangular tray, designed by Charlotte Rhead, pattern TL43, painted with flower designs in pastel shades.

13in (33cm) wide

£150-200 **GHOU**

A C. & Co. Ltd slip decorated planter, painted with white 'Glasgow Rose' motif, on a green ground, printed mark.

7.5in (19cm) diam

£80-120 **WW**

A 19thC Capo di Monte oval box and cover, with gilt-metal mounts, decorated with moulded cherubs at play.

5in (13cm) wide

£80-120 **L&T**

A Cauldon 'Chariots' pattern blue and white transfer-printed octagonal vase.

5in (12.5cm) high

£75-85 **BAD**

QUICK REFERENCE - CANDY WARE

Candy & Co. Ltd was founded in 1875 in Newton Abbott in Devon, England and began by producing bricks and tiles. In 1922, it launched its 'Wescontree Ware' range of art pottery, changing the name to 'Candy Ware' in 1936. Comprising vases, jugs, bowls, lamp bases, chargers, ashtrays and others, a hand-thrown and hand-decorated range was introduced in 1936. Primarily filling the kiln around the core production of utilitarian products, the art pottery range was discontinued in the 1950s when a new kiln was installed. The company itself closed in 1998.

A Clermont Fine China limited edition model of the Cleveland Bay stallion 'Mulgrave Supreme', modelled by Robert Donaldson, numbered 17/100, contained in a mahogany and glazed display case, together with certificate.

12in (30.5cm) high

£700-900 **A&G**

A late 1930s Candy Ware ribbed vase, with light blue and beige dripped glaze, silver embossed Candy Ware label and indistinct circular pr nted mark to the base.

7.5in (19cm) high

£20-30 **M20C**

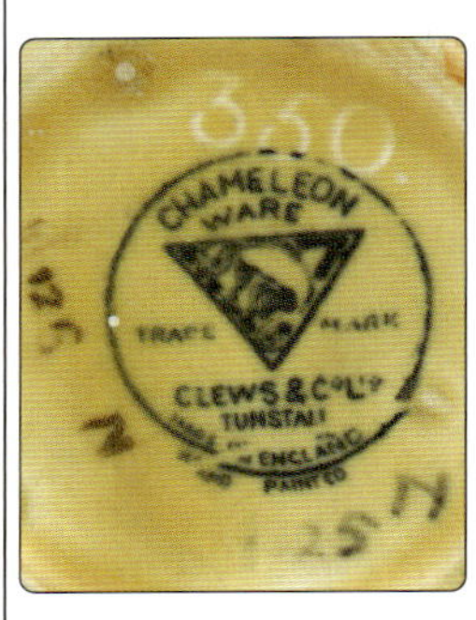

A 1920s Clews & Co. Ltd 'Chameleon Ware' vase with hand-painted stylised leaf design.

Chameleon ware was designed by David Capper, Works Manager at Clews. Introduced from 1913-14, Capper developed experimental semi-matte glazes to imitate the popular Ruskin art pottery glazes, and applied them to Oriental inspired forms. The affordable range won a gold medal at the Philadelphia Exposition in 1926, and grew to make up 80 per cent of the factory's output. Look out for Egyptian, Middle Eastern and Oriental patterns, inspired by archaeological finds at the time.

6.25in (15.5cm) high

£40-60 **P&I**

A 1930s Clews & Co. 'Chameleon Ware' squat vase with mottled blue and green glaze, with tripod firing mark to base.

4in (10cm) diam

£20-30 **P&I**

A 1960s Crown Devon ovoid jardinière, handpainted with a geometric design possibly designed by Colin Melbourne, the base impressed '1508'.

9in (23cm) long

£8-10 **M20C**

A Crown Devon 'Delph' vase, pattern no. 2055, painted in colours with factory marks to base.

8.75in (22cm) high

£30-40 **WW**

A CLOSER LOOK AT A COWAN PLATE

Viktor Schreckengost (1906-2008) was an important American artist, industrial designer and ceramics designer who worked through the Art Deco and mid-century modern styles.

His best known work is the 'Jazz Bowl' created in 1930 for Eleanor Roosevelt which is now considered an Art Deco masterpiece, and an example is in the Cleveland Museum of Art.

This hand-painted charger is also recognisably Art Deco, and was part of a series of similar designs showing sporting activities that also includes 'Polo'.

Large, visually impressive and typical of his style, they are sought-after and hard to find.

A Cowan 'The Hunt' wall plate, with low-relief moulded and hand-painted pattern, designed by Viktor Schreckengost.

1930-31 *11.5in (28.5cm) diam*

£700-1,000 **ANT**

QUICK REFERENCE - COLIN MELBOURNE

Colin Melbourne is arguably one of the most ignored British modernist ceramic designers. A graduate of the Royal College of Art, he produced highly modern, stylised animal figurines for Beswick from 1955. Known as the 'CM' range, produced from 1956-66, their avant garde style was unpopular at the time, and they are comparatively rare today. In 1954, he formed a design consultancy with David Queensberry called Drumlanrig Melbourne, and also worked for Crown Devon, where he continued to produce highly modern designs. His work is still underrated today, and represents an excellent opportunity for collectors with an eye for the future.

A Crown Ducal 'Rhodian' pattern shape 150 ovoid vase, pattern no. 3272, designed by Charlotte Rhead, the base with printed and painted marks.

c1933 *4.5in (11.5cm) high*

£80-120 **GHOU**

A pair of Crown Ducal vases, of bulbous cylindrical form, with red glazed interior, cream ground with piped panels containing red and brown leaves, with printed mark.

6in (15cm) high

£60-80 **LOC**

A Crown Devon 'Memphis' range vase, designed by Colin Melbourne, with a gilt chevron transfer pattern over a black glazed ground, the base with printed and impressed marks.

7.75in (20cm) high

£80-120 **FLD**

A Crown Devon 'Memphis' range vase, designed by Colin Melbourne, with a gilt chevron transfer pattern over a black glazed ground, printed marks.

10.25in (26cm) high

£80-120 **FLD**

A Crown Lynn vase, by Frank Carpay, the vase thrown by Daniel Steenstra, decorated with bands of forest green, orange, black and teal, with stylised celestial spheres representing the Sputnik, and silver lustre glaze at the rim.

Crown Lynn was founded near Auckland, New Zealand, in 1854. Tableware production began in 1941, and the company produced wares for the war effort and for New Zealand railways. The company still produces table and decorative wares today. Dutchman Frank Carpay (1917-1985) studied under Picasso at Madoura in France, and also Roger Capron at Vallauris. He worked for Crown Lynn's 'Specials Department' from 1953-56, producing designs such as this, which was commissioned by the vendor during a visit to the pottery.

c1955 *9.75in (25cm) high*

£700-900 **WEB**

A late 1950s Denby Pottery 'Crystalline' range two-handled vase, designed by Glynn Colledge, hand-painted with a stylised floral sprig and bands to the base, the base with printed mark.

7.25in (18.5cm) high

£40-60 **GC**

A Hammersley scalloped and gilded milk jug and sugar bowl, with hand-painted flowers.

The teacups are in the same shape as the sugar bowl.

c1900-14 *Milk jug 3in (7.5cm) high*

£40-60 **BAD**

A Haviland porcelain cake plate, decorated by Anna B. Leonard, with gourds and leaves in orange and green, stamped 'Haviland France' and painted 'Anna B. Leonard'.

14in (35.5cm) diam

£300-500 **DRA**

A 1970s Honiton Pottery rectangular dish with a hand-painted fish design, the base impressed 'HONITON ENGLAND' and painted 'DC'.

11.25in (27cm) long

£15-20 **M20C**

A 1960s-70s Dutch Jema bull, impressed with runic and geometric symbols and covered with a blue-green glaze, the stomach impressed 'JEMA HOLLAND 79'.

14.5in (36.5cm) long

£50-70 **M20C**

A tall Kenton Hills vase, with pink blossoms on pearl grey ground, the base drilled probably at the factory, with leaf stamp and '176'.

12.5in (32cm) high

£300-500 **DRA**

A Kenton Hills 'Unica' vase, by Alza Stratton, in brown butterfat on white ground, signed 'Alza Stratton Unica', stamped mark, restoration.

8.25in (21cm) high

£200-300 **DRA**

A large Katshutte Pottery figure of a Spanish dancer, painted in colours, printed factory mark, paper label, repaired fan.

20in (51cm) high

£400-600 **WW**

A Robert Lallemant elliptical pottery vase, blue and black painted marks, with damage.

Lallemant (1902-1954) studied at the Ecole des Beaux-Arts in Dijon and at Lachenal c1921, founding a pottery in Paris in 1923 producing modern and stylised patterns on clean-lined angular forms. If it had not been damaged, it may have fetched over three times this value.

6.75in (17cm) high

£100-150 **WW**

A Langley Pottery vase, designed by Glynn Colledge and hand-painted with a stylised foliate design, the base with printed windmill mark.

8in (20.5cm) high

£30-40 **M20C**

A 1960s-70s Langley Pottery bulbous vase hand-painted with a stylised natural motif in green, brown and orange glazes, designed by Glynn Colledge, the base with printed windmill factory mark and painted 'J.M.'.

Staffordshire based firm Lovatt & Lovatt, who made Langley pottery, was acquired by Denby in 1959, which explains how Denby designer Glynn Colledge came to design for them. This is a scarce shape and a desirable pattern.

7.75in (19.5cm) high

£80-120 **GC**

A 1960s-70s Langley Pottery footed cylindrical vase, hand-painted with a stylised natural motif, designed by Glynn Colledge, printed windmill factory mark.

7.75in (19.5cm) high

£50-70 **GC**

A Canadian Laurentian Pottery sculptural jug vase, with integral handle, organic curving rim and orange and brown dripped glaze.

11.75in (29.5cm) high

£20-40 **TWF**

A McCoy 'Loy-Nel-Art' vase, with loop handles and floral decoration, marked '02' on the base, glaze slightly scratched and flaked at base.

12.25in (31cm) high

£100-150 **BEL**

A French Longwy vase, the base painted 'F=3024-D:56907', with printed green factory mark.

4.5in (11cm) high

£80-120 **BEV**

A 19thC Meissen box and cover, painted with flowers, the cover formed as a shell with a cartouche of figures standing on the docks to the interior, cancelled crossed swords mark, damage and restoration.

4.75in (12cm) wide

£80-120 **WW**

A 20thC Meissen group of two songbirds, modelled perched on a stump, with blue crossed swords mark, incised '3071'.

£180-220 **DN**

A 1960s Midwinter Fashion shape transfer-printed 'Petite Rose' cake stand, with chrome plated fittings, designed by John Russell.

9in (23cm) high

£20-30 **RET**

A Minton cabinet plate, with pierced Greek key gilt border and pâte-sur-pâte style border of dolphins and shells on a pale blue ground, with printed mark.

1891-1902 *9.5in (24cm) diam*

£30-40 **LOC**

A pair of Minton models of cockatoos, each perched on a branch.

£320-380 **L&T**

A Myott & Sons hand-painted 'Diamond' vase, with original flower frog, the base with gold printed factory mark and painted '9185' pattern mark.

6in (15cm) high

£120-180 **BAD**

A 1930s Myott 'Squareneck' jug, painted in beige, yellow, orange green and brown tones with a fruiting pattern, the base with gold printed mark, painted 9104 pattern mark and registered no. 739316 for 1928.

8.75in (22.5cm) high

£80-120 **BAD**

A CLOSER LOOK AT A MYOTT JUG

Myott was founded in 1898 but is best known for its colorful Art Deco ceramics produced in the 1930s. Records were destroyed in a fire in 1949, making it hard for collectors to find out more.

Autumnal oranges and browns are typical of Myott - red, blue and green are rarer - but watch out for flaking to the orange. Printed gold marks were used from 1930-42.

Prices are currently considerably lower than those for other Art Deco ceramics by Susie Cooper and Clarice Cliff – this is an area to watch as their appeal is obvious.

Pieces bearing the 'B.A.G.' mark were made for export by British American Glass. The quality of the design and painting is usually higher on such pieces, and the patterns may have been exclusive to them.

A 1930s Myott baluster shaped jug, with a hand-painted green and orange floral and geometric design, the base with gold printed 'BAG Co Ltd, HAND PAINTED' mark and stamped 'B.G 76'.

7.75in (19.5cm) high

£100-150 **BAD**

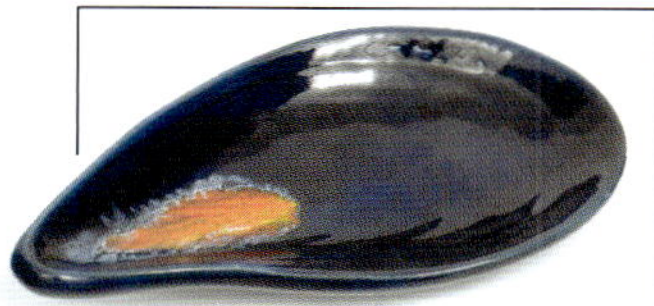

A 1960s-70s French Vallauris blue glazed mussel-shaped dish, with orange glazed spot.

13in (33cm) long

£15-25 **M20C**

A Volkmar three-handled vase, covered in mottled indigo matte glaze, incised 'V'.

7in (18cm) high

£600-900 **DRA**

A CLOSER LOOK AT A VALLAURIS VASE

The town of Vallauris is well-known for its many potteries which have attracted notable artists and designers, including Pablo Picasso who worked at the Madoura pottery from 1948-55.

Other designers include Roger Capron and Charles Voltz – the designer of this piece is not yet known, but the glaze type and colours link it to a Vallauris pottery.

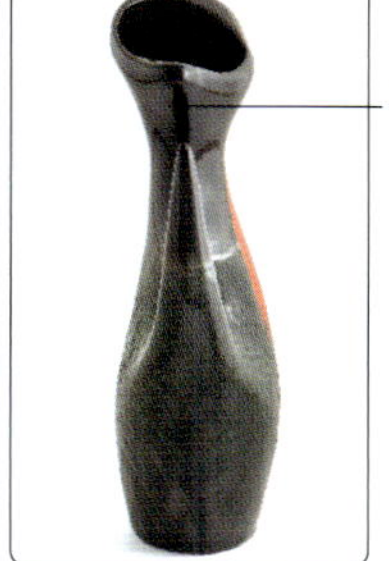

The curving, asymmetric form, that even extends to the the shape of the rim and the body, which curves backwards, is typical of the period.

The base is unmarked but the light weight and clay type indicate that it was made by pouring liquid clay, known as slip, into a mould rather than being hand potted.

A late 1950s/early 1960s French Vallauris large floor vase, with curving asymmetric form, handle and rim.

15 5in (40cm) high

£40-60 **MHC**

A 1930s Wade Heath waisted cylindrical jug, handpainted with orange flowers, green leaves and grey and yellow patches, the base with printed lion mark, and impressed '127'.

7.75in (19.5cm) high

£30-50 **BAD**

A Watcombe Pottery terracotta jug, designed by Dr Christopher Dresser, of angular form with three serrated bands, printed "Watcombe Torquay" with registered diamond for 3rd June 1872.

8in (20.5cm) high

£120-180 **WW**

A Watcombe pottery model of a winking cat with long neck, covered in an ochre glaze and with one glass eye, the base with inscribed marks.

12in (30.5cm, high

£180-220 **BE**

A Wheatley vase, with four buttressed feet, the top embossed with leaves and buds, covered in matte green glaze, marked 'WP' and 'C102'.

10in (25.5cm) high

£1,000-1,500 **DRA**

A Wheatley tall tapering cylindrical vase, covered in a fine feathered matte green glaze, and with 'WP' mark.

10in (25.5cm) high

£800-1,200 **DRA**

A CLOSER LOOK AT A WALLEY VASE

William J. Walley (1852-1919) was born the son of a potter in Ohio. He travelled to England to study at Minton in the 1860s before founding his first pottery in Maine in 1873.

Hand-sculpted motifs are also typical and range from leaves in the manner of Grueby, to this famous and highly sought-after devil's head.

Following an important aspect of the Arts and Crafts movement, he believed that every pot should be made and decorated by hand rather than being moulded and produced on a factory production line.

Simple but strong greens and blue matte glazes are typical, gloss glazes are more unusual – particularly with this amount of colour variation.

A W.J. Walley vase with devil mask, losses and crude repair to glaze flaking, the base stamped 'WJW'.

12in (30.5cm) high

£1,700-2,000 **DRA**

A T.J. Wheatley 'Albertine' vase, modelled with applied hibiscus on a barbotine painted ground, stamped 'WHEATLEY' and artist signed 'KW', a few minor losses and touch-ups.

The three-dimensional underglaze slip decoration, called 'Barbotine', was derived from Limoges faience, and became extremely popular in the US, and particularly in Cincinnati. Thomas Jerome Wheatley was involved in several Cincinnati pottery businesses between 1879 and 1882. The Cincinnati Art Pottery was incorporated in Ohio at the end of 1880 with Wheatley as a partner, and operated under the name T. J. Wheatley & Company until he left the business in 1882. This particular example, from the range often known as 'Albertine', was exhibited in "From Our Native Clay," held by the American Ceramic Arts Society in New York in 1987.

c1880 *19in (28cm) high*

£600-900 **CRA**

A T.J. Wheatley vase with applied thistle, under matte green glaze, no visible mark, several flecks and nicks.

11.5in (29cm) high

£500-800 **DRA**

A late 19thC Hungarian Zsolnay Pecs earthenware vase, decorated with hand-painted red, green and blue Moorish or Turkish style flowers on a mustard ground.

10.25in (26cm) tall

£50-80 **LOC**

A Hungarian Zsolnay Pecs heart-shaped dish, painted with a central bird within Persian style foliage, in geometric borders, the back with printed spire mark.

10in (25.5cm) diam

£280-320 **GORL**

An Arts and Crafts earthenware charger, painted with a bird in a landscape in shades of blue and yellow, painted marks, dated, hairline crack to rim.

1881 *12in (30.5cm) diam*

£150-200 **WW**

A Continental tin-glazed earthenware Gallé-style seated cat figurine, probably Mosanic, painted with honey-coloured fur patches and green eyes, and pseudo 'De Roos' mark to base.

The shape is also very similar to figures by Wemyss.

c1900 *11.75in (30cm) high*

£500-800 **TOV**

An early 20thC Continental porcelain tazza, applied with flowers, the base mounted with a maiden.

Despite the large amount of skill and time that went into creating such a detailed piece, fashions and tastes have moved away from ornate, floral designs such as this. Tazzas are also largely impractical today. Considering its size and obvious decorative appeal, its price seems very reasonable.

13.25in (34cm) high

£50-80 **WW**

A 19thC majolica figure, possibly Vesta, wearing a laurel wreath and carrying an eternal flame.

10.25in (26cm) high

£120-180 **FLD**

A late 19thC Staffordshire copper lustre jug with moulded and hand-painted flowers, unmarked.

7.75in (19.5cm) high

£20-30 **BAD**

An early 20thC French beeware basket, with bee on handle, handpainted with people in a row holding hands in landscape, with an 'X' on the base, the side signed 'I Berty Nice'.

6in (15cm) high

£50-70 **BAD**

QUICK REFERENCE

- Collectors look for characters associated with happy times in their own childhood or those that are widely popular. Pieces associated with comic books, TV programmes and films, or those by major brands, are usually popular. Official, licensed products are usually more desirable and more accurately modelled.
- Famous characters will usually have enthusiastic collecting bases and therefore will often fetch the largest sums. Look for typical clothes, poses, accessories or phrases associated with that character. Pieces produced before a character became well known are typically rare and desirable, as they would have been made in smaller numbers. Do not ignore minor characters as these can be rarer than more popular characters, and collectors will often want to complete a set.
- Many character items were intended for promotional use. Most were not made to last and few pieces are likely to have survived in good condition, making a truly mint example highly desirable.
- Limited editions may become valuable if the demand exceeds supply. For this reason, it is preferable to invest in pieces from small production runs (for example, under 1,000). The maker and quality of moulding and decoration will add desirability, as will an accurate depiction of the character. Limited editions should ideally come with mint condition boxes and paperwork.
- With the nostalgic nature of the market, demand ebbs and flows as generations mature. It is therefore a good idea to hunt for new collectable characters. For example, Buzz Lightyear is likely to be popular in the future.

A 1960s large soft vinyl jointed Mickey Mouse figure, unmarked.

13.75in (35cm) high

£15-20 EWA

A 1960s Walt Disney Productions soft vinyl Mickey Mouse figure, with tail, marked 'C WALT DISNEY PRODUCTION MADE IN ITALY'.

9.75in (25cm) high

£20-25 EWA

A 1970s Walt Disney Productions Mickey Mouse poseable vinyl advertising figurine, in yellow shirt and red and white polka dot shorts, marked 'C WALT DISNEY PRODUCTIONS MADE IN HONG KONG', with woven tag.

7.5in (19cm) high

£10-15 EWA

A Mattel Walt Disney Productions speaking Mickey Mouse figure, with oversized head containing the mechanism, marked 'C 1971 MATTEL Inc WALT DISNEY PRODUCTIONS BURBANK TOYS INC'.

c1971 5in (13cm) high

£15-20 EWA

A Playcraft 'Squeeze 'N Squeak' Mickey Mouse figure, marked 'C WALT DISNEY PRODUCTION 1979'.

5in (12.5cm) high

£10-15 EWA

A Kohner plastic 'Mickey Mouse' Peppy Puppet, marked 'Walt Disney Productions', mint and unopened with original bubble packaging.

1970 *11in (28cm) high*

£25-35 **MTB**

A 1930s Britains 'Minnie Mouse' and 'Clarabelle', each with detachable heads, paintwork in fair condition, one head pin replaced by matchstick.

Britains' lead figures of Disney characters are hard to find. Minnie is scarcer than Mickey, and Clarabelle is even rarer. Although she was created in 1928, the same year Mickey Mouse made his debut in 'Steamboat Willie', she only appeared as a bit-character on screen afterwards. She was originally paired with Horace Horsecollar, Mickey's friend, but was later seen stepping out with Goofy. After 1942, she almost faded into obscurity, appearing in only four films. However, she appeared more frequently in Disney's comics.

£300-500 **SAS**

A Walt Disney Productions Goofy vinyl figure, marked 'C WALT DISNEY PRODUCTIONS MADE IN HONG KONG' and 'MADE FOR INGERSOLL MARKETING LTD'.

Ingersoll (now part of Timex) made its first Disney watch, featuring Mickey Mouse, in 1933. Since then it has been in continuous production, being made by a number of different watchmakers. This figurine is likely to have been made as part of a promotional countertop display. Well made, licenced and relatively detailed with his clothing, he seems likely to be a great bet for the future.

8.75in (22cm) high

£20-30 **EWA**

A Walt Disney Productions Pinocchio vinyl figure, marked 'WALT DISNEY PRODUCTIONS' on shoes and impressed on back of hat, with woven Ingersoll Marketing tag.

8in (20.5cm) high

£20-30 **EWA**

A scarce 1930s Wadeheath 'Donald Duck' child's teapot and cover, hand-painted in characteristic yellow, blue and black.

5in (12.5cm) long

£400-600 **LT**

A Snow White and the Seven Dwarfs ceramic musician band, of unidentified manufacture, each individually modelled, Doc has repaired left foot, otherwise minor chips and scratches.

Snow White 8in (20cm) high

£70-100 THE SET **VEC**

CHARACTER COLLECTABLES

A 1930s W.Goebel decanter, probably depicting Andy Capp, with hand-painted details and removeable head stopper, the base with impressed Crown mark and 'K.L. 904'.

10in (25cm) high

£180-220 **BAD**

A Hanna-Barbera 'The Banana Splits Annual'.

10.5in (27cm) high

£10-15 **MTS**

A Wade 'Batman' figurine, produced for Out Of The Blue Ceramics (Collectables Magazine) in an un-numbered limited edition of 1,939 examples, the base printed 'WADE Produced for Out Of The Blue Ceramics C DC Comics 1999 Limited Edition 1,939'.

7.25in (19cm) high

£35-45 **DSC**

A Wade 'Betty Boop' figurine, produced for C&S Collectables in a limited edition of 1,500 pieces, the base with 'C King Features Syndicate INC Fleischer Studios INC Wade Limited Edition' printed mark.

1996 *3.75in (9cm) high*

£50-80 **DSC**

'The Bonzooloo Book', by G.E. Studdy, printed in London, with colour pictorial bands, 12 colour plates, and other illustrations.

Illustrator George Ernest Studdy (1878-1848) developed his small dog character in the late 1910s, and he first appeared in a comic strip in The Sketch as 'Studdy Dog' in 1918. In 1922, he was renamed 'Bonzo' and a legend was born.

c1928

£200-300 **FRE**

A 1970s Nayytex child's Charlie Brown printed t-shirt,with Charlie Brown on the Apollo rocket.

c1970 *16.5in (42cm) high*

£15-20 **CANS**

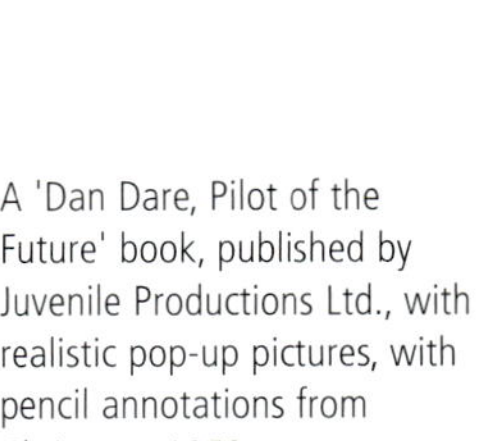

A 'Dan Dare, Pilot of the Future' book, published by Juvenile Productions Ltd., with realistic pop-up pictures, with pencil annotations from Christmas 1953.

1953 *10.5in (21cm) wide*

£50-80 **GAZE**

A 1950s Marx TV-Tinykins 'Huckleberry Hound' miniature figurine, made and hand-painted in Hong Kong, mint and boxed.

2.5 (6.5cm) high

£8-12 **MTB**

A Marx Fairykins 'Jack Be Nimble' miniature figurine, mint and boxed.

2.25in (5.5cm) high

£8-12 **MTB**

A CLOSER LOOK AT A POPEYE DOORSTOP

Painted cast iron doorstops are highly sought after in the US, and in 2006 a very rare Littco doorstop of a girl dressed as a 'ghost' and holding a pumpkin made over $70,000 at auction.

Hubley is a prolific and collectable maker, and are also known for its cast iron cars and other toys.

Bunches or pots of flowers are more common forms – this is a rare and desirable cartoon character, so would appeal to both Popeye and character collectors.

It is in unusually excellent condition for a doorstop, with nearly all of its original paint intact and in bright condition, and as a result has fetched a high price.

A rare Hubley cast iron 'Popeye' doorstop, full figure, with vibrant colours, in near mint condition.

9in (23cm) high

£10,000-15,000 **BER**

A 1960s Combex soft vinyl Noddy advertising doll, marked 'COMBEX MADE IN ENGLAND NSRCL 1960 4563'.

8.75in (22cm) high

£20-25 **EWA**

A complete set of five Einson-Freeman Co. colour lithographed paper 'Par-T-Masks' of the major characters from 'The Wizard of Oz' (Dorothy shown here), with minor creases but with intact original rubber bands.

These MGM licensed character masks are rare. They were issued in September 1939 in time for Hallowe' en, and given away by department stores as free premiums during the holiday season.

1939

£200-280 **BLNY**

A rare colour lithographed 'The Tin Woodman of the Magical Land of Oz announces Jean Gros' French Marionettes' die-cut bookmark, with advertisement for American Seating Co. to back, published by Schroeder & Gunther, Inc.

This advertised a play by Ruth Plumly Thompson. The picture of the Tin Woodman was reprinted from the endpaper in ' The Patchwork Girl of Oz' (1913). A list of the Oz Books through ' The Giant Horse of Oz' (1928) appears on the verso of this bookmark.

1932

£400-600 **BLNY**

Three American Colourtype Co. MGM 'Wizard of Oz' colour lithograph valentine cards.

1940

£100-150 **BLNY**

An A.A. Burnstein Sales Organisation MGM rubber 'Tin Man' toy, the back marked 'JACK HALEY/WIZARD OF OZ', nose chipped and body partially compressed with some flaking of colour.

It is suspected that most of these figures were destroyed when children donated them to World War scrap drives.

1939 *6.5in (16.5cm) high*

£280-330 **BLNY**

A rare unused free gift from Pow! comic of an iron-on Spiderman transfer sheet, with ink stamp for '28th January 1957'.

As a transfer, the image is obviously viewed in reverse before application.

1957 *8.75in (22cm) high*

£10-20 **SAS**

A CLOSER LOOK AT A SUPERMAN FIGURINE

The production of this figurine was beset with problems, such as the 'S' transfer bubbling after application.

A number of these licensed figurines were also stolen from the pottery and the actual release date was 2001, not 1999 as printed.

Due to these problems, the official edition size was reduced to only 250 examples, rather than the originally planned 1,938.

Of these, 61 examples came in a special presentation box, with a certificate and special backstamp – these can fetch over 25 per cent more.

A Wade 'Superman' figurine, produced for Out Of The Blue Ceramics (Collectables Magazine) in a limited edition of 250, the base printed 'WADE Produced for Out Of The Blue Ceramics C DC Comics 1999', and numbered '066/189'.

7.25in (19cm) high

£120-180 **DSC**

A Wade 'Tom' figurine, the base moulded 'WADE ENGLAND C M.G.M.'

1973-79 *3.5in (9cm) high*

£20-25 **DSC**

A Wade 'Jerry' figurine, the base moulded 'WADE ENGLAND C M.G.M.'

1973-79 *2in (5cm) high*

£20-25 **DSC**

A late 1960s Western Germany Westra red and white plastic pedestal alarm clock, with black snooze button.

8in (20.5cm) high

£40-50 **M20C**

A 1970s Japense Tokyo Takei chromed plastic pedestal alarm clock, the blue face marked '2 JEWELS JAPAN'.

8in (20.5cm) high

£30-40 **M20C**

A 1960s-70s Coral chrome plated plastic pedestal 2 jewel alarm clock, with silver face and chrome plated metal ring-shaped stand.

6.25in (16cm) high

£30-40 **M20C**

A late 1960s West German Kaiser chrome plated plastic alarm clock with blue face.

Note the 'space age' disc-shaped design of the alarm indicator on the left of the face.

4in (10cm) high

£20-30 **M20C**

A 1970s Japanese model no.51113 alarm clock, with blue dial and silver hands with luminous lines, and red and silver markers.

5.5in (14cm) high

£40-50 **M20C**

A 1970s Japanese red and white plastic rounded cube-shaped Rhythm transistor alarm clock, model no.7RA032.

5.5in (14cm) high

£40-50 **M20C**

A 1970s-80s AP plastic clock and barometer.

9.25in (23cm) high

£50-60 **MTS**

A 1960s-70s Western German Uwestra red plastic triangular alarm clock.

3.5in (9cm) high

£20-30 **M20C**

QUICK REFERENCE

- Although royal commemorative ware was made before Queen Victoria's reign, it was not until then that production boomed. Ceramics (the first and most common kind of royal memorabilia) could be produced and distributed economically due to the advent of transfer printing, canals and the railways. Popularity grew during the late 19thC and the early 20thC, and memorabilia is still produced today.
- As so much memorabilia was produced, collectors tend to focus on one monarch, or one event. Queen Victoria and the current Queen are among the most popular subjects, partly because of the number and variety of pieces produced during their long reigns. Some events commemorated within these reigns are scarcer than others. For example, many more pieces commemorating Queen Victoria's Golden Jubilee were produced than for her marriage. Interest in items celebrating the lives of younger members of current royal family is also growing.
- Value typically depends on the quality and maker of the piece. Well-known, high quality manufacturers, such as Royal Worcester, Royal Crown Derby, Minton and Copeland are consistently popular. You should also look out for the work of popular 20th century designers such as Eric Ravilious, Charlotte Rhead and Richard Guyatt. However, well decorated pieces that are not by major makers or designers are also often desirable. Brightly coloured and detailed pieces appeal are likely to appeal to a wide range of collectors.
- Look for limited editions, particularly pieces from editions of less than 250. Keep all paperwork and boxes as these are essential to value.
- Condition is very important. Many 19thC pieces were not made to last, so some wear is acceptable. However cracks and chips will reduce desirability. Damage on recent pieces reduces value considerably.

A Copeland & Garrett '1837/38 Victoria' miniature pottery plate, printed with a named portrait surmounted by flowers of the Union within a scrolling border, the reverse with impressed and printed marks.

4.25in (11cm) diam

£580-680 **SAS**

A Wedgwood & Co. earthenware tea bowl and saucer, printed in black and enamelled in colours, the reverse named 'Victoria', with impressed and printed marks.

c1838

£180-220 **SAS**

An '1840 Victoria & Albert Wedding' blue printed pottery jug, with named portraits, the reverse with a crown centred by the date.

4.5in (11.5cm) high

£100-150 **SAS**

An '1838 Victoria' commemorative octagonal nursery plate.

The portrait on this desirable plate was developed after a portrait painted by Sir George Hayter.

c1838

£200-300 **SAS**

A Hines Bros '1887 Victoria's Jubilee' octagonal pottery plate, printed in black, with gilt lined rim.

c1887 *9.75in (24.5cm) wide*

£50-70 **SAS**

A Doulton Lambeth '1897 Diamond Jubilee' blue glazed stoneware jug, moulded with green young and old oval portraits of Queen Victoria.

8.75in (22cm) high

£120-180 **SAS**

An Adderley '1937 George VI Coronation' loving cup, printed in colours with St. George slaying the dragon.

1936 *4.75in (12cm) high*

£200-250 **SAS**

A CLOSER LOOK AT A TILE

Founded in 1877, Sherwin & Cotton of Staffordshire was a well-known tile producer until its take-over by Johnsons in 1911, which continued to use the name for some time.

This was designed by George Cartlidge, and was part of a series of 'photographic' tiles he produced. Cartlidge also designed some Morrisware for S.Hancock & Sons.

Showing Victoria as most imagine her to have appeared, this was made to commemorate the Diamond Jubilee.

This series of tiles was renowned at the time for its translucent glazes and three-dimensional appearance.

A Sherwin & Cotton relief and intaglio moulded photographic dust-pressed tile panel, depicting Queen Victoria in sepia glaze, framed.

c1897 *9in (23cm) high*

£100-150 **FLD**

A Paragon '1937 Edward VIII Coronation' loving cup, with twin gilt lion handles, numbered 562 from an edition of 1,000.

Memorabilia for Edward VIII's (better known as the Duke of Windsor) proposed coronation is not as rare as many think. Although he abdicated in December 1936, manufacturers had nearly a year, from George V's death in January 1936, to produce commemorative wares.

1936 *4.5in (11.5cm) high*

£70-100 **GHOU**

A Copeland for Goode '1937 George VI Coronation' pottery tyg, printed with sepia portraits and decorated in colours, small hairline crack.

£200-300 **SAS**

A small Shelley George VI and Queen Elizabeth '1939 Visit to America' loving cup, decorated in colours and gilt, with printed marks to the base.

1939 *3.5in (8.5cm) high*

£120-180 **SAS**

A Crown Devon '1937 George VI Coronation' musical tankard, moulded with superimposed portraits oval flags and flowers in colours, playing 'Here's a Health unto His Majesty'.

c1937 *6in (15.5cm) high*

£80-120 **SAS**

An Aynsley '1953 Elizabeth II Coronation' plate, with central printed portrait flanked by flags and flowers and inscribed border.

c1953 *9in (23cm) diam*

£200-300 **SAS**

A Paragon '1953 Elizabeth II Coronation' limited edition loving cup, set with twin gilt lion handles, numbered 555 from an edition of 1,000.

4.75in (12cm) high

£120-180 **SAS**

A Spode '1981 Price Charles & Lady Diana Wedding' limited edition loving cup, with sepia portrait ovals decorated in colors with flowers on a gilded cobalt blue ground, numbered 229 from an edition of 250, with certificate.

6.25in (16cm) high

£60-90 **SAS**

A transfer printed 'George VI Coronation' mug designed by Dame Laura Knight, the base with printed mark reading 'R.R. No.814375/6 DESIGNED & MODELLED BY DAME LAURA KNIGHT D.B.E. R.A.' and with GR cypher and facsimile Laura Knight signature, the inside of the rim printed 'PRESENTED ON CORONATION DAY BY SIR ARTHUR STANLEY TREASURER OF ST THOMAS HOSPITAL'.

1937 *3.25in (8cm) high*

£35-40 **CARS**

An Aynsley '1953 Elizabeth II Coronation' plate, with printed colour portrait and profuse gilt decoration.

c1953 *9in (23cm) diam*

£100-150 **SAS**

A Wedgwood '1953 Elizabeth II Coronation' mug, with printed design designed by Eric Ravilious, the base with printed factory mark.

c1953 *4.25in (10.5cm) high*

£180-220 **WW**

A 'Nelson in Memoriam' commemorative reverse handpainted glass picture, depicting Britannia with an oval portrait of Nelson beneath his battle honours with dates, framed.

c1805 *16.25in (41cm) high*

£2,500-3,500 **SAS**

An '1805 Nelson' death of Nelson pearlware jug, printed in brown and highlighted in colours with an inscribed portrait oval and on the reverse HMS Victory centred by an oval cartouche inscribed with honours, restored.

6.75in (17cm) high

£350-450 **SAS**

An unusual '1812 Constitution and Russian Campaign' silver lustre decorated pearlware jug, printed with loyal cartouche flanked by a lion and unicorn and on the reverse 'A. Cossack of the Oural Mountains'.

1812 *5.25in (13.5cm) high*

£250-350 **SAS**

A Copeland for Goode 'Transvaal Tyg', subscriber's copy, decorated in colours and gilt, cracked.

c1900 *5.5in (14cm) high*

£150-200 **SAS**

An Elliot pottery jug, commemorating the relief of 'Mafeking' on May 17th 1900, applied with monograms of Queen Victoria and Baden-Powell, hound handle.

1900 *6.75in (17.5cm) high*

£120-180 **FLD**

A Booth '1914 Great War' cylindrical mug, printed in grey and decorated in colours with servicemen from the allied forces.

£80-120 SAS

A Paragon '1938 Munich Peace Conference' plate, printed with a named portrait of Chamberlain and inscribed on the reverse.

1938 *9in (21cm) diam*

£100-150 SAS

A Wilkinson Ltd Marechal Foch toby jug, designed by Sir Francis Carruthers Gould, seated with a glass of champagne, the bottle inscribed 'Au Diable Le Kaiser' (The Kaiser to the devil), the plinth with animals, the base with black printed marks and Carruthers Gould's facsimile signature.

This jug was produced for and distributed by Soane & Smith as a limited edition along with ten others to celebrate the allied leaders of World War I. The rarest is of General Louis Botha, as only 150 examples were produced. An example fetched over £1,500 at auction in 2005, and a complete set fetched £9,000 at auction in 2009.

1918 *11.75in (30cm) high*

£400-600 DN

A Wilkinson Ltd. 'Admiral Beatty - Dread Nought' character jug, designed by Sir Francis Carruthers Gould, decorated in underglaze colours, enamelled and gilded, the underside with printed manufacturer's and retailer's mark and facsimile signature of Carruthers Gould.

Issued by Soane & Smith Ltd during World War I.

10.75in (27cm) high

£250-350 SAS

A CLOSER LOOK AT A WINSTON CHURCHILL TOBY JUG

Churchill is an iconic British figure and commemorative pieces are still highly sought after by specialist collectors, especially items produced in his lifetime.

This is made more appealing due to the well-modelled, characterful face and his fingers which are posed in his famous 'V' for victory sign.

It is modelled and glazed in the manner of Ralph Wood, and is considered one of the best traditional toby jugs made in the 20thC, so it appeals to toby jug collectors too.

Examples are known decorated in more colours. In 2008 an undamaged, more finely decorated, example sold for over £1,800 at auction.

A 'The Rt Hon Winston S Churchill OM CH FRS MP' pottery toby jug, by Leonard Jarvis, modelled in relief and painted in colours, incised marks, chips to paint brushes.

c1946 *7in (18cm) high*

£350-450 WW

An Annalee Gulf War commemorative 'Desert Storm' mouse, in mint condition with card tag, clothing and flag.

1991 *8.25in (21cm) high*

£20-30 BH

SPRING
SUMMER
WINTER
Antiques for Everyone
THE NEC BIRMINGHAM
HALLS 17-19
Free Car Parking • Vetted for Authenticity
For ticket bookings call: 0844 581 0827
or Book Online
www.antiquesforeveryone.co.uk
All bookings are subject to a single transaction fee
Rights of admission reserved. Security searches in operation. Visitors are not permitted to bring antiques into the fair.
CLARION ARTS
HOMES & ANTIQUES

QUICK REFERENCE

- Costume jewellery has risen dramatically in popularity over the last ten years, and values have risen accordingly. However, while iconic pieces by well-known designers are now commanding prices close to those paid for precious jewellery, much costume jewellery is still comparatively affordable. With a great variety of pieces available, there is a look for every taste and occasion.
- Desirable makers include Trifari, Chanel, Christian Dior, Stanley Hagler, Schiaparelli, Miriam Haskell and Joseff of Hollywood, and their names are usually marked on the back of their pieces. Copies are becoming more common, particularly at the upper end of the market, so learn to recognise marks and the quality of materials.
- Style and eye-appeal are also very important to value. As many buy costume jewellery to wear, a great design with the 'sparkle' factor will generally be desirable and valuable, even without a renowned maker's name.
- During the 1930s and 1940s, many pieces were made from solid silver, sometimes plated with gold, and these are usually marked 'Sterling' to the reverse.
- The quality, colour and size of the stones are important to value: look out for chunky 'baroque' faux pearls, and Murano or Czech glass beads. The way the stones are set also helps indicate a piece's quality. The best examples are held in place with metal prongs, with work done by hand. Much costume jewellery has three-dimensional effects that may be hand-wired onto frame, and these pieces are particularly desirable.
- Missing stones will reduce value. Although they can be replaced, it is often hard to find an exact match of size or colour. The beads and faux pearls, used by designers like Miriam Haskell are even more difficult to find as they were exclusive designs and are no longer made to the same quality.

A mid-1950s Art wreath pin, gold tone metal set with pastel Lucite flowers and aurora borealis highlights, marked "Art".

1.75in (4.5cm) diam

£40-60 **PC**

A pair of Boucher holly wreath Christmas earrings, set with green and gold glass spheres.

1in (2.5cm) diam

£6-8 PAIR **AEM**

A very rare 1980s Butler & Wilson Amy Johnson pin, plastic and chrome, the back with white painted "Butler & Wilson" mark.

2.75in (7cm) wide

£100-150 **TDG**

A Robert DeMario gilt metal flower and leaf pin, set with faux anthracite and pearls, some stones missing, the back marked "DeMario N.Y".

2.5in (6.5cm) wide

£10-15 **PC**

A pair of Kramer clip-on earrings, with red, colourless and purple rhinestones, and faux pearls, the clip impressed KRAMER.

1in (2.5cm) high

£15-20 **PC**

A 1980s Christian Lacroix 'Rococo' gold-plated heart shaped pin, set with shocking pink glass and with Lacroix's entwined CL logo, marked "CL Paris Christian Lacroix".

2.75in (7cm) wide

£30-50 **TDG**

A 1950s pair of earrings, attributed to Rousselet, comprised of multicoloured glass drops set on gold tone chains.

2.75in (7cm) long

£50-80 **PC**

A 1960s pair of Schreiner faux aquamarine earrings, the large central stones surrounded by circular and teardrop shaped rhinestones.

1.25in (3cm) high

£50-70 PAIR **CRIS**

A Lea Stein Rhodoid small scottie dog pin, with applied black bow and eye and nose details, the clip marked 'LEA STEIN PARIS'

1.5in (3.5cm) high

£25-35 **PC**

A CLOSER LOOK AT A ROBERT NECKLACE AND EARRINGS

There are a number of different types of cut rhinestones, including the rectangular 'baguette', which also have many facets – both are signs of quality.

Blue is a very desirable colour, and the different, complimentary tones of blue add visual appeal.

The lighter blue stones are 'aurora borealis' stones, which have an applied iridescence that changes and sparkles as they move in the light.

The rhinestones are 'prong set', rather than being glued into a moulded setting – this is another sign of quality and also allows more light to enter the rhinestones.

A Robert necklace and pair of earrings, set with aquamarine and cobalt blue cut fax stones.

Earrings 1.25in (3cm) wide

£100-150 **PC**

A late 1950s Trifari gold plated pin in the form of three fish, the eyes with inset ruby red cabouchon rhinestones.

2.25in (6.5cm) high

£70-100 **ROX**

A 1950s Trifari gold-plated butterfly pin, the wings inset with 'plique à jour' style coloured glass ovoid beads.

2in (5cm) wide

£50-80 **PC**

A mid-1950s Trifari gold-plated pin in the form of a basket of flowers, the flowers inset with coloured rhinestones.

1.75in (4.5cm) high

£40-60 **PC**

A 1940s Trifari vermeil bow-shaped pin, with red ruby baguette and colourless pavé-set rhinestones.

3.5in (9cm) wide

£300-500 **PC**

A 1990s Vivienne Westwood silver tone metal bow and orb pin, pavé set with clear rhinestones.

1.5in (3.5cm) long

£50-80 **PC**

A Vivienne Westwood gold-tone metal heart-shaped perfume holder pin, surmounted by a trademark orb and ribbon, with red enamel, and ring fitting to transform into necklace/choker, containing Boudoir perfume.

c2000 *2in (5cm) high*

£40-60 **TDG**

QUICK REFERENCE – TRIFARI

Trifari's origins lay in a company founded by Italian emigré Gustavo Trifari in New York around 1910. Success first came when sales manager Leo Krussman joined in 1917, and grew when salesman Carl Fishel joined in 1923, and 'Trifari, Krussman & Fishel (TKF) was founded in 1925. Designer Alfred Philippe joined in 1930, and his designs are amongst the most sought-after today. During the 1930s, the company designed pieces for a number of Broadway musicals, as well as for film and theatre stars, which cemented its success. Quality was always high, even after World War II, with only the best rhinestones being used in good quality settings. During the 1940s, a number of gold-plated sterling silver (vermeil) pieces were made, which are usually valuable. The company continues to produce innovative and sought-after designs today. This brightly coloured set has further appeal due to the patriotic colours used, as well as the all-important 'sparkle' factor, enhanced by the differently cut rhinestones.

A 1950s Trifari pin and earrings, set with colourless and blue baguette cut rhinestones and light blue rectangular rhinestones, the backs stamped 'TRIFARI PAT PEND'.

Pin 2.25 (5.5cm) high

£150-200 **PC**

A pair of unmarked clip earrings, set with cut faux aquamarines and teardrop shaped brown glass stones, in a gold tone mount.

1.25in (3cm) high

£20-25 **PC**

A pair of unmarked earrings, the gold tone mounts set with faceted aurora borealis stones and large faux amber teardrops.

1.25in (3cm) high

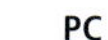

£30-40 **PC**

A pair of unmarked earrings and matching leaf shaped pin, the gold tone metal mounts with prong set striped 'tiger's eye' rhinestones.

Pin 2.75in (7cm) high

£70-90 **PC**

A pair of unmarked earrings, with vintage stones prong-set in a modern matte gold-tone metal mount.

1.5in (4cm) high

£20-30 **PC**

A 1920s unmarked cold enamelled orchid-shaped pin, set with faceted diamanté.

2in (5cm) high

£20-30 **PC**

A 1950s unmarked vintage gold plated patriotic US flag pin, prong-set with red, colourless and blue rhinestones.

1.5in (3.5cm) high

£5-8 **AEM**

A 1930s Art Deco Continental silver clip, with red plastic bar and inset diamanté, the back with Continental control marks, and stamped 'MD'.

1.5in (3.5cm) high

£50-80 **PC**

QUICK REFERENCE – SINDY

- Sindy was launched by Pedigree in 1963 as a competitor to Mattel's Barbie fashion doll. Rather than produce Barbie under license, Sindy was modelled on another American doll, Ideal's Tammy. Her 'girl next door' look made her instantly more popular than Barbie in Britain, and she became a bestseller in 1968 and 1970. Initially, Pedigree also produced a wider range of clothing and accessories than Mattel.
- In 1978 Sindy was launched in the US by Marx Toys, but as the company went into receivership in 1980, was discontinued. Fashions were updated in the 1980s, and in 1989 she was redesigned to look more like Barbie, who dominated the market during the late 1980s and '90s. In 1997, Sindy was removed from major retailers after a law suit from Mattel, until her successful relaunch in 1999.
- Look out for early dolls and outfits from the late 1960s and early 1970s. Some accessories were lost, making them rare today, and some outfits and dolls are more desirable than others. As with most plastic fashion and similar dolls, items must be in as close to shop-bought condition as possible. Stains, fading and cut or messy hair, reduce value. Although 'the doll you love to dress' is usually the most valuable item, values for some outfits can match those paid for the dolls.

A Pedigree Sindy doll, first issue with original 'Weekenders' outfit, with original original box.

First issue Sindy dolls are becoming increasingly hard to find, particularly with their original boxes and clothes. On this example, the original pink card band adds value as it is usually missing. This outfit was designed by Foale & Tuffin. Sally Tuffin went on to produce ceramic desgns for Poole and, ultimately, her own company.

c1964 *12in (30.5cm) high*

£120-180 **MTB**

A 1970s Pedigree 'Funtime' blonde Sindy doll, with original clothing, in mint, unopened condition in original window box.

12in (30.48cm) high

£100-150 **MTB**

A Pedigree 'Sweet Dreams' Sindy doll, with sleeping eyes, twist neck, twist body, bending knees, and original 'Good Morning' clothes, in mint condition in unopened card window box.

1978 *12in (30.48cm) high*

£100-150 **MTB**

A Marx Toys Sindy doll, with original clothes, in mint condition in unopened, worn card window box.

1978 *13in (33cm) high*

£50-80 **MTB**

A 1980s Pedigree 'Ballerina' Sindy doll, with original clothes, in mint condition, in unopened card window box.

13in (33cm) high

£50-70 **MTB**

A Pedigree Sindy 'Party Time' doll, with original blue dress and shoes and 'We're Havin' a Party' 45rpm record, in mint condition in unopened card window box.

'Party Time' Sindy was only sold with blonde hair and a choice of three coloured outfits in royal blue, yellow and pink.

1981 *12in (30.5cm) high*

£120-180 **MTB**

A CLOSER LOOK AT A PAUL SINDY DOLL

The first issue Paul from 1965 had moulded hair. This second issue, with rooted hair, was introduced in 1966.

He was named after Paul McCartney, since The Beatles were the most popular band at the time, and even his hair mimics the famous 'mop top'.

Even though he was also dubbed 'the well-dressed young man', Paul didn't sell well and was withdrawn shortly after his introduction.

Paul's white sneakers are rare as they were usually lost, as was his plastic stand.

A Pedigree Paul doll, in mint condition with original 'Casuals' clothing, plastic stand and box.

1966 *12in (30.5cm) high*

£100-150 **MTB**

A Hasbro 'Rainbow Sindy' doll, with multicoloured hair, original clothes and hair styling guide, in mint condition in unopened, original card window box.

1992

£20-25 **MTB**

A Pedigree 'Patch' doll, with original schoolgirl outfit with plastic satchel, complete and in mint condition.

Patch is Sindy's little sister.

1966 *9in (23cm) high*

£50-60 **DSC**

A Pedigree Sindy 'Seaside Sweetheart' outfit, complete in unopened box.

1964 *12.5in (31.5cm) wide*

£100-150 **MTB**

A Pedigree Sindy 'Country Walk' outfit, complete in unopened box.

This early set, which originally retailed for £19/11d, is sought after because it still has the original bone and dog bowl. A similar set was issued by Mattel for Barbie, but the dog was a terrier rather than a poodle.

1963 *12.5in (31.5cm) high*

£120-180 **MTB**

QUICK REFERENCE – DAISY DOLLS

The Daisy doll range was produced from 1973-83 in Hong Kong and distributed and marketed by Flair Toys in the UK, the US and Europe. Her unique selling point was that her clothes were designed by top fashion designer Mary Quant, with her name being taken from Quant's orange and white daisy company logo. Her outfits were themed around a world trip, and many were given names of activities associated with cities or named after the cities themselves. There are several variations: a budget 'Dizzy Daisy' without bendable legs or a twisting waist; a version with both features; and 'Dashing Daisy' with bendable waist and curved hands enabling her to hold things. From 1979, Daisy had centre-parted hair and rooted eyelashes. The small-headed version is preferred by collectors to the later large head, and this coloured leotard is a hard-to-find variant on the standard one.

A 1970s Flair Toys Ltd 'Dizzy Daisy' doll, with small head, blonde hair and original clothing, in complete and mint condition in unopened card window box.

9.5in (24cm) high

£100-150 **MTB**

A 1970s Flair Toys Ltd 'Daisy Long Legs' doll, complete with original clothes, stand, booklet and badge, and in mint condition in original card window box.

Daisy Long Legs was released in 1978, and at 15in (38cm) high, is taller than the standard 9in (23cm) high Daisy. As she was taller, a special range of clothes was produced to fit her.

1978-83 *17in (43cm) high*

£80-120 **MTB**

A 1970s American Gabriel Industries Inc. 'Dotty' Daisy doll, with large head, blonde hair, and original clothing, in complete and mint condition, in unopened original box.

10.5in (26.5cm) high

£65-75 **MTB**

An American Gabriel Industries Inc. 'St. Tropez' Daisy doll, with medium-sized head and original clothes, in complete and mint condition, in original unopened card window box.

10.5in (26.5cm) high

£120-180 **MTB**

A late 1970s Flair Toys Ltd 'Dashing Daisy' 'Skidoo' doll, complete with original clothes and skateboard, in mint condition in slightly damaged original card window box.

The back of the box shows a number of the accessories and different outfits designed by Mary Quant to accompany Daisy. As would be expected from such a fashion designer, she really was 'on trend' for her time!

12in (30.5cm) high

£150-200 **MTB**

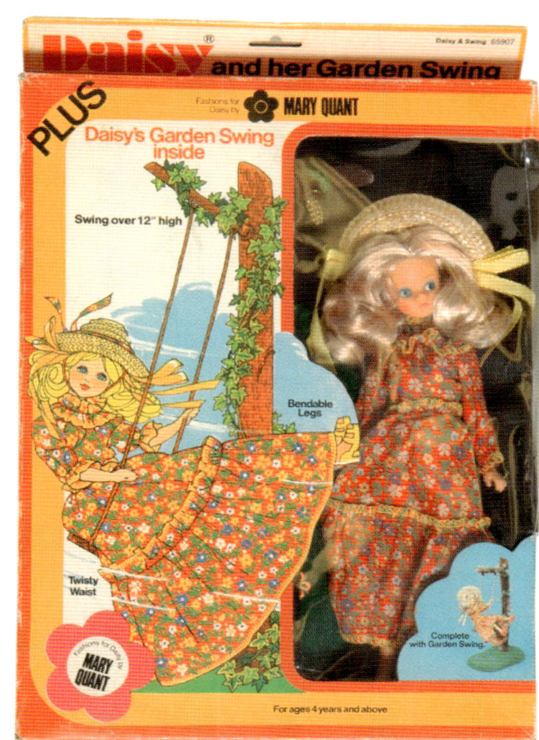

A 1970s Flair Toys Ltd 'Daisy & Swing' doll playset, complete with Daisy doll with bendable legs, clothes, and plastic garden swing, in mint condition in original card window box.

This set is hard to find, particularly complete and in its original box.

12in (30.5cm) high

£120-180 **MTB**

A 1970s Flair Toys Ltd Daisy 'Fandango' outfit, designed by Mary Quant, complete and in mint condition with original packaging.

8in (20cm) high

£35-45 **MTB**

A 1970s Flair Toys Ltd Daisy 'Bee-Bop' outfit, designed by Mary Quant, complete and in mint condition with original packaging.

8in (20cm) high

£30-40 **MTB**

A 1970s Flair Toys Ltd Daisy 'Hoedown' outfit, designed by Mary Quant, complete and in mint condition with original packaging.

11.5in (29cm) high

£32-38 **MTB**

A 1970s Flair Toys Ltd Daisy 'Guinevere' outfit, designed by Mary Quant, complete and in mint condition with original packaging.

12in (30.5cm) high

£32-38 **MTB**

A 1970s Flair Toys Ltd Daisy 'Showbiz' outfit, designed by Mary Quant, complete and in mint condition with original packaging.

12.5in (31.75cm) high

£20-30 **MTB**

A 1970s Flair Toys Ltd Daisy 'St. Moritz' outfit, designed by Mary Quant, complete and in mint condition with original packaging.

12in (30.5cm) high

£25-35 **MTB**

QUICK REFERENCE - PIPPA

Pippa, 'the pocket sized fashion doll' was produced by Palitoy from 1972-80. At only 7in (18cm) in height, she was smaller than her more famous competitors Barbie or Sindy, allowing little girls to carry her around in their pockets or bags. A couple of hundred different, colourful outfits were produced and these have become collectable today, particularly if complete, as many small pieces were lost. Pippa's condition is important to collectors. As she was carried around, she is often worn, and her honey blonde hair tended to yellow unappealingly with age. In 1979, this fourth issue was released and had much fairier hair. As with other variations, these can be of more interest to collectors looking to complete a collection. This particular dress (right) is also hard to find. Mint and boxed examples will fetch the higher values.

A Palitoy Pippa doll, fourth issue in multicoloured daisy print yellow dress, in mint condition in original card window box.

1979 *7in (18cm) high*

£150-200 **MTB**

A Palitoy Princess Pippa doll, in mint condition, in unopened card window box.

c1974 *7in (18cm) high*

£200-250 **MTB**

A Palitoy Pippa's friend 'Tammie' doll, third issue in gingham dress, in complete and mint condition, in original card window box.

Tammie's first issue outfit (1972) of blue trousers and a top printed with vines and leaves in blue tones is very hard to find.

1975 *7in (18cm) high*

£100-150 **MTB**

A late 1970s Palitoy Princess Pippa doll, complete and in mint condition, in original card window box.

With long hair down to her feet, Princess Pippa was introduced in 1974, with this dancing version arriving in 1975. Look out for the almost 'Arctic blonde' fair-haired variation, which is very rare.

c1976 *7in (18cm) h*

£200-300 **MTB**

A rare Palitoy Pippa's friend 'Penny' doll, first issue with dungarees, in mint condition, in original card window box.

1976 *7in (18cm) high*

£200-300 **MTB**

A Palitoy Pippa's friend 'Mandy' doll, first issue with red pocket on dress, in complete and mint condition, in original card window box.

1976 *7in (18cm) high*

£100-150 **MTB**

A Palitoy Pippa's friend 'Pete' doll, with original clothes, in mint and complete condition, in original card window box.

Pete is virtually identical to Topper's 'Gary' doll.

c1977 *7in (18cm) high*

£70-90 **MTB**

A Palitoy Pippa 'In the Pink' outfit from the Vienna Collection, in complete and mint condition in original box.

1974 *8in (20cm) wide*

£45-50 **MTB**

A Palitoy Pippa 'Monaco Collection' outfit, complete and in mint condition with original box.

The white, wide-brimmed hat is the rarest part as it was usually lost.

1976 *8in (20cm) wide*

£20-25 **MTB**

A Palitoy Pippa 'Riviera Collection' outfit, in complete and mint condition, in unopened original card box.

c1976 *8in (20cm) wide*

£45-50 **MTB**

A Palitoy Pippa 'Holiday Girl' clothing set, comprising three outfits, in complete and mint condition with original box.

The 'Disco Fan' set released in the same year also contained three outfits.

1975 *9in (23cm) high*

£100-150 **MTB**

A Palitoy Pippa 'Oriental Collection' outfit, with fan, in complete and mint condition in original, unopened box.

c1977 *7in (18cm) wide*

£45-50 **MTB**

A Meccano Pippa 'Holiday Collection' outfit, for the French market, complete and in mint condition with unopened box.

1978 *8in (20cm) wide*

£40-50 **MTB**

A Mattel 'Midge' doll, with 'brownette' hair, 'bendable' legs and original clothing, complete and unopened in original card box.

This was the most expensive Midge doll produced, and is scarce today as she was also not as popular as Barbie herself. Midge is Barbie's best friend.

1964 12in (30.5cm) high

£400-500 MTB

A Mattel 'bubble-cut' Barbie doll, with blond hair, model 850, with original red swimsuit, stand and leaflet, in very good condition with original box.

Released in 1959, the ever youthful Barbie celebrated her 50th birthday last year. Vintage, pre-1973, dolls are as sought after today as they were by the little girls who played with Barbie originally.

'962-67 12in (30.5cm) high

£150-200 MTB

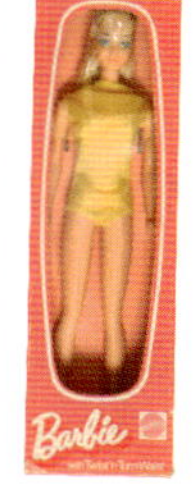

A Mattel Barbie doll, with 'Twist 'n Turn' waist, produced for the European market, in mint condition, in unopened slightly worn box.

These inexpensive versions of Barbie were bagged inside the box, but sold in the US without the box, leading to them being called 'baggies' by collectors.

1973 12in (30.5cm)

£40-60 MTB

A Mattel black 'Tropical Barbie', model 1022, with long hair and original clothes, in mint condition in unopened, original box.

Sold 'with the longest hair ever', she cost $6.99, and was a variant of the white Tropical Barbie released in the same year.

1985 12in (30.5cm) high

£20-30 MTB

A Mattel Barbie 'Solo in the Spotlight' special edition reproduction doll, model 13534, with brunette hair, in mint condition in unopened mint condition box.

This doll was also retailed in Hallmark card stores.

1994 13in (33cm) high

£40-60 MTB

A Mattel 'Skipper' doll, model 950, blonde hair, original swimsuit and shoes, card box with taped ends.

Although the doll is in very good condition overall, the box has been repaired, which reduces the overall value, which may have topped £150 in mint condition.

1964-66 10in (25.4cm) high

£80-120 MTB

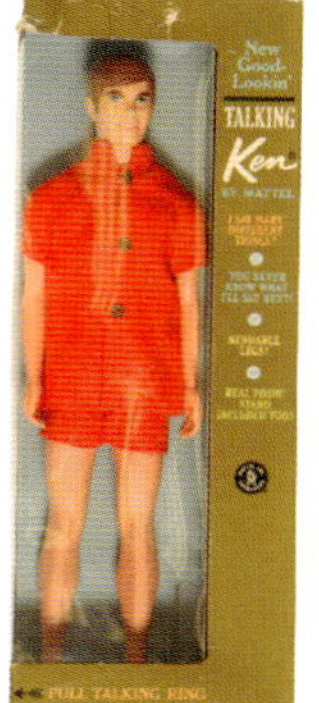

A Mattel 'Talking Ken' doll, model 1111, with original red outfit, and sealed in original card window box.

1968 13in (33cm) high

£70-100 MTB

A scarce Mattel 'Barbie Ponytail' printed vinyl carrying case.

1961 10.75in (27cm) wide

£30-50 BH

QUICK REFERENCE - TRESSY

Released in 1964, Tressy's unique feature was her 'growing' hair, operated by pushing a button on her stomach, and wound back in using a key in a slot in her back. She was made by Palitoy in the UK, American Character in the US and Bella in France. Her sister was Toots (Cricket in the US), her friend was Mary Make-Up, and her clothing line was 'Budget Fashions'. This first issue had sideways glancing eyes and was boxed in a fragile, and now very rare, triangular box.

A Palitoy Tressy, first issue, with brown hair, and knickers, together with an original triangular cardboard box.

c1965 *15in (38cm) high*

£60-90 MTB

A Palitoy Tressy doll, fourth issue, with original clothing, in mint condition in unopened card window box.

Released in the mid-1970s, this version had gripping hands and a built-in key in her back to wind her hair. She was also available in an identical blue outfit.

15in (38cm) high

£100-150 MTB

A French Bella Tressy doll, with original clothing, in mint condition in unopened card window box.

c1966 *14in (35.5cm) high*

£55-65 MTB

A Palitoy 'Toots' doll, complete with ballet dress, style book and hairgrips, with rare red triangular box.

c1966 *10.5in (26.5cm) high*

£80-120 MTB

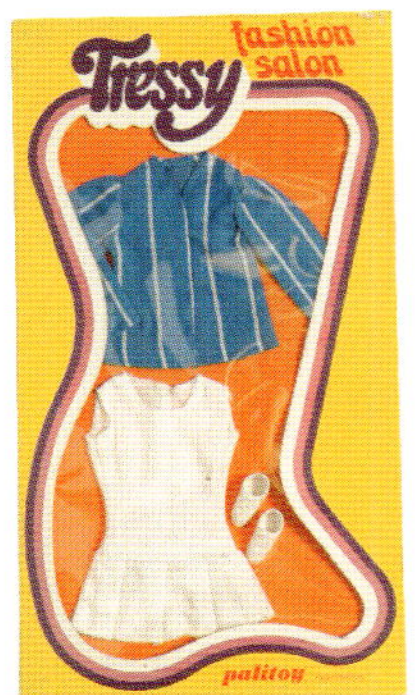

A late 1960s-70s Palitoy Tressy tennis or sports outfit, in complete and mint condition in original packaging.

12in (30.5cm) high

£10-15 MTB

A late 1960s Tressy 'Emerald Princess' outfit, in complete and mint condition in original packaging.

10.5in (26.5cm) high

£50-80 MTB

A 1960s Palitoy Tressy 'Mix n' Match' outfit, complete and in mint condition in original packaging.

9.5in (24cm) high

£15-20 MTB

An Ideal Tammy doll, first issue, with original skiing outfit and skis, complete with original card box.

Tammy was produced from 1962-66. This is and example of the first issue, with a first issue box. Intended as a competitor to the wildly successful Barbie, she also had an extensive wardrobe, and a set of friends and accessories, but was more wholesome than Barbie.

1962 *13in (33cm) high*

£100-150 **MTB**

An Ideal Tammy doll, with original blue jumpsuit and stand, in original card box.

c1964 *13in (33cm) high*

£100-150 **MTB**

An Ideal Dad doll, complete with original clothes, rare shoes and stand, and original card box.

Tammy's Mom is much harder to find than her Dad.

c1964 *13in (33cm) high*

£70-100 **MTB**

An Ideal Ted doll, complete with original clothes and stand, and original card box.

Ted was Tammy's brother, and is very similar to Tammy's boyfriend Bud. However, Bud has darker eyebrows and is the hardest doll of Tammy's friends and family to find.

c1964 *13in (33cm) high*

£70-100 **MTB**

An American Mattel Rock Flowers 'Rosemary' doll, complete with original clothes, record and card window box.

8in (20.5cm)

£60-80 **MTB**

An American Mattel Rock Flowers 'Heather' doll, complete with original clothes, record and card window box.

Produced from 1971-74, Mattel's Rock Flowers series were similar to Dawn dolls and had bendy bodies, rooted hair and painted faces. In total, five dolls, including Doug, were produced. The record played two songs that were typical of the period.

8in (20.5cm) high

£50-70 **MTB**

An American Mattel Rock Flowers 'Lilac' doll, complete with original clothes, record and card window box.

8in (20.5cm) high

£50-80 **MTB**

A Palitoy 'Dancing Tammie' pocket-sized doll, complete with original clothing, in mint condition in unopened original card window box.

7in (18cm) high

£50-80 **MTB**

A Palitoy 'Dancing Marie' pocket-sized doll, complete with original clothing, in mint condition in unopened original card window box.

Marie was one of Palitoy' s miniature fashion dolls, like Pippa. Her novelty lies in her ability to dance – if her arms were moved, her body twisted.

7in (18cm) high

£160-180 **MTB**

A Dutch Otto Simon Fleur 'Showjumper' doll, with riding outfit, in complete and mint condition, in original card window box.

Fleur was a European 'clone' of Sindy, released in 1978 after Pedigree ceased sales of Sindy in the Netherlands. She proved to be highly successful in her home country and, although she met with some success internationally from 1983, sales were highest in the Netherlands. Fleur was redesigned in the late 1980s, and discontinued in 1988. This doll was one of the less expensive in the range, and packaged in a box to mimic Sindy.

14in (35.5cm) high

£20-30 **MTB**

An American Mattel 'Twiggy' doll, with twisting waist, and original clothes and plastic boots.

The boots in particular are scarce. Without the original clothing, the doll alone is usually worth up to £30.

1966-67 11in (28cm) high

£40-50 **DSC**

A Dutch Otto Simon & B.T. Toys International Fleur 'Mount Everest' doll, with mountain climbing outfit, in complete and mint condition, in original card window box.

14in (35.5cm) high

£20-30 **MTB**

An Ideal Dorothy Hamill doll, with original clothes and medal, in mint condition in original card window box.

Dorothy Hamill was the US Olympic figure skating champion who won a gold medal in the 1976 Innsbruck Winter Olympics.

1977 13in (33cm) high

£40-60 **MTB**

An Armand Marseille AM 996 doll, with sleeping blue eyes, painted eyebrows and eyelashes, open mouth with two teeth, and jointed composition body.

20in (51cm) high

£100-150 **SAS**

An Armand Marseille AM 996 doll, with sleeping blue eyes, painted eyebrows, hair eyelashes, open mouth with flicking tongue, two teeth, brown wig, and jointed composition body.

20in (51cm) high

£100-150 **SAS**

An Armand Marseille AM 351 'Dream Baby', with sleeping blue eyes, painted eyelashes, open mouth with two teeth, and composition body.

9.75in (25cm) high

£50-80 **SAS**

A Simon & Halbig 1078 doll, with sleeping blue eyes, painted eyebrows and eyelashes, open mouth with four teeth, pierced ear-lobes, and jointed composition body.

18in (46cm) high

£180-220 **SAS**

A Robert Carl 25 doll, with sleeping brown eyes, painted eyebrows and eyelashes, open mouth with four teeth, jointed composition body, dressed as a nurse.

16.25in (41cm) high

£80-120 **SAS**

A Simon & Halbig 949 doll, with fixed blue eyes, painted eyebrows and eyelashes, closed mouth, pierced ear lobes, kid body with porcelain lower arms, four fingers incomplete, in original box.

18.5in (47cm) high

£250-350 **SAS**

A Bruno Schmidt 2097.2 baby doll, with sleeping blue eyes, painted eyebrows and eyelashes, open mouth with two teeth, joined composition body.

14.25in (36cm) high

£100-150 **SAS**

A 1930s American sprayed composition 'Topsy' doll, with cotton dress and woven socks, unmarked.

Composition is a hard material made up of glue, resin and wood particles. More resistant to damage and cheaper to produce than bisque, surfaces are often spray painted. Topsy dolls, with their hallmark top knots of hair, were popular in the US during the 1930s. The value depends on the maker, expression on the face, size and condition.

11in (28cm) high

£40-50 **DSC**

A 1930s American sprayed composition 'Topsy' doll, with floral printed red clothing, unmarked.

9in (23cm) high

£30-40 **DSC**

A 1930s Canadian Reliable sprayed composition black doll, with later blue knitted cardigan, nappy and socks.

Many of Reliable's dolls were exported, including to the UK.

11in (28cm) high

£25-30 **DSC**

A Norah Wellings 'Welsh Girl' fabric doll, with original clothing, in mint condition with card tag.

As well as being desirable to Norah Wellings collectors, these are also sought after by costume doll collectors.

9in (23cm) high

£50-60 **DSC**

A 1920s-30s Norah Wellings 'Island Girl' fabric doll, with original clothes, in good condition, with some wear.

14.25in (36cm) high

£20-30 **DSC**

A 1930s Chad Valley 'Greek Boy' fabric doll, in original clothes, with red embroidered label to sole of left foot, very slight discoloration, otherwise in excellent condition.

17in (33cm) high

£100-150 **VEC**

A German Steiff 'Musician' brown felt 1911 replica doll, from a limited edition 1,200, with white tag numbered '411915', tags and certificate, in mint condition, with original box.

1997-98 *17in (43cm) high*

£50-80 **VEC**

A 1950s Linda hard plastic doll, with red corduroy dress and bonnet, the back moulded 'MADE IN HONG KONG', in original and excellent condition.

These dolls were copies of the popular, but comparatively expensive, Miss Rosebud dolls. They were sold in cornershops at prices which were more affordable to children saving pocket money. The style of bonnet and dress is a typical feature.

8in (20.5cm) high

£15-20 **DSC**

A 1950s Amanda Jane 'Jinx' hard plastic doll, dressed as a sailor, in complete condition.

7.5in (19cm) high

£40-50 **DSC**

A 1950s Rosebud 'Miss Rosebud' hard plastic doll, with polka dot printed dress, the back moulded 'Miss Rosebud MADE IN ENGLAND'.

As well as considering condition, look at the clothes, as these make a difference to value. For example, the complete fairy outfit can mean the same doll may fetch around £150.

7.5in (19cm) high

£40-50 **DSC**

A 1950s Palitoy hard plastic 'Marcher' doll, in complete original condition with printed floral skirt, socks and plastic shoes.

This doll gained its name due to her unusual walking movement, which looks almost like marching.

19.25in (49cm) high

£40-50 **DSC**

A 1950s Welsh Tudor Rose hard plastic 'Island Girl' Topsy-style black doll, with grass skirt and ribbons tied in her three hair knots.

Tudor Rose dolls have been increasing in value over the past few years.

8in (20.5cm) high

£25-30 **DSC**

A 1950-53 Vogue hard plastic Ginny, with factory purple ribbon trimmed dress and painted lashes.

7.5in (19cm) high

£120-180 **BH**

A 1950s hard plastic Roberta Walker, wearing a pink dress with grey trim.

8in (20cm) high

£20-30 **BH**

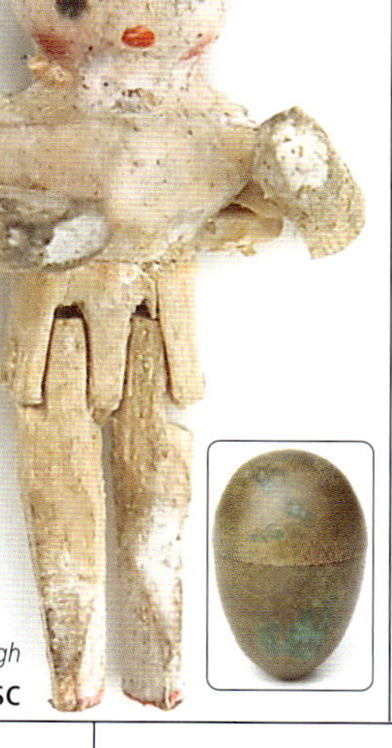

A late 19thC to early 20thC 'Smallest Doll In The World', the fully jointed, carved wooden miniature doll contained inside a wooden egg.

Despite its tiny size, the doll's feet are painted, as are her facial features and her hair.

Doll 0.5in (1.5cm) high

£80-120 **DSC**

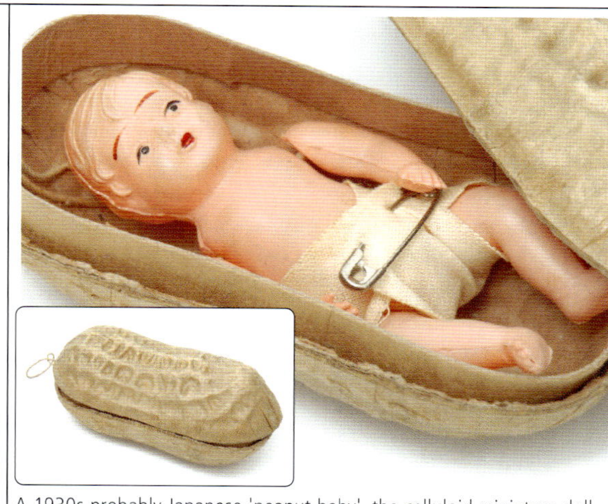

A 1930s probably Japanese 'peanut baby', the celluloid miniature doll with fabric nappy contained inside a pressed pulp peanut shell.

Peanut 4in (10cm) high

£20-25 **DSC**

A 1920s Japanese painted moulded solid bisque 'My Little Pet' miniature doll, with felt clothes, mounted on original printed sales card.

Card 4.5in (11.5cm) high

£20-30 **DSC**

A 1930s Japanese 'Bathing Set' celluloid miniature doll, with celluloid bath, oversized dummy, and section of fabric, contained in a matchbox with original printed label.

Bath 1.5in (3.5cm) long

£25-30 **DSC**

A 1950s 'Smallest Baby In The World' plastic miniature doll, with red plastic bath and original box.

Bath 1.25in (3cm) long

£10-15 **DSC**

A 1950s Rodnoid hard plastic miniature doll, with jointed arms and legs.

The Rodnoid name could only be used for one year, as the company found that it was already in use by another company for one of its products.

2.75in (7cm) high

£10-15 **DSC**

A CLOSER LOOK AT MINIATURE DOLLS

The box is rare as most would have been thrown away as these were inexpensive dolls at the time.

These were often used in doll houses, due to their small size.

Note the wild statements about the dolls printed on the box

On its own, each doll is worth around £5.

A 1950s boxed set of three Japanese moulded rubber 'Three Little Sisters' miniature dolls, imported by CODEG, complete with original box.

Dolls 2.25in (5.5cm) high

£25-30 **DSC**

QUICK REFERENCE

- Shallowpool Handicrafts were produced by Peggy Pryce, Joan Rickarby and Muriel Fogarty in Devon, England. After World War II, the three women bought a rural cottage and set up a business in fabric homewares, producing items such as rugs and lampshades. They began making dolls during the mid-1950s. Rickarby designed the painted plaster heads and hands, former hairdresser Pryce produced the wigs, and Fogarty assembled the dolls on wire armatures, and handled business matters.
- Dolls were based on Cornish or historical characters, painstakingly researched to ensure that costumes were as accurate and detailed as possible. They were sold in local shops, and gift and souvenir shops in Cornwall for tourists.
- The company grew to be very successful, employing 16 doll makers and exporting to shops in the US as well as around the UK. In the late 1970s, Pryce married and left the business, with Rickarby and Fogarty carrying on with production until the mid-1980s, when they both retired and Shallowpool Handicrafts was closed.
- To ensure you are buying a complete doll, it is helpful to familiarise yourself with the dolls produced, including their clothes and accessories. There may be variations, particularly in fabrics used for clothing, but this does not usually affect value. Avoid staining, fading, tears, or damage to the paint, especially on the faces, as these will reduce the desirability.

A Shallowpool 'Cornish Pasty Seller' doll, with painted plaster Cornish pasties on a plate and printed poem about pasties in her apron pocket.

This is one of the most commonly found dolls, undoubtedly due to the popularity of Cornish pasties.

8in (20.5cm) high

£15-20 **DSC**

A Shallowpool 'Bal Maiden' doll, with cane and plaster long-handled hammer stick and knitting in her apron pocket.

This Cornish character broke up rocks dug out of copper or tin mines, an activity known as 'spalling', to earn a living.

7.5in (19cm) high

£25-30 **DSC**

A Shallowpool 'Old Mother Hubbard' doll, with white painted plaster dog on a fabric ribbon.

9in (23cm) high

£40-50 **DSC**

A Shallowpool 'Fanny Wheeler' doll, holding a painted plaster lantern.

Fanny Wheeler assisted her father in his smuggling activities, taking a boat to France with him to bring back kegs of illicit spirits.

7.75in (19.5cm) high

£40-50 **DSC**

A Shallowpool 'Cornish Lady' dressed in early 17thC riding costume, with a feathered hat.

This figure was inspired by Lady Howard of Fitzford from Daphne du Maurier's 1964 novel 'The King's General'.

8in (20.5cm) high

£20-25 **DSC**

QUICK REFERENCE

- Although there are still collectors who buy vintage eyewear as a record of optical developments and changing styles, most of today's buyers are looking to wear their new purchases. The most popular frames are colourful and date from the 1950s onwards. Value depends on style, condition, the name of the maker or designer, and materials used.
- Frames that effectively represent their period are particularly desirable, with the 'cat's eye' style of the 1950s and oversized rounded frames of the 1960s being widely sought after. Rare 'wild' styles in bright or clashing colours and shapes that might have been unpopular or expensive at time are often the most valuable.
- Consider the material and work that has gone into making the frames. Hand-crafted elements, such as enamelling, painting or complex laminating or cutting, will generally add value.
- Look for the names or monograms of famous designers, as these will generally add value. Notable eyewear designers include Alain Mikli and Emmanuelle Khanh; frames were also designed for or by Christian Dior, Emilio Pucci and Pierre Cardin. Some designers' monograms changed over time, which can help with dating.
- Always examine frames for burn marks, cracks or splits, which cannot be repaired easily and will make the frames less attractive to prospective buyers. Warped or bent plastic can sometimes be corrected by professionals and is therefore often less problematic. Look for 'dead' unused shop stock, which is usually unworn.
- Scratched, cracked, or even missing lenses do not typically affect value, as buyers often intend to fit their own lenses. Unusual original lenses, such as those with a graduated tint in matching or contrasting colour, may add value, however, and should be kept even if they are replaced.

A pair of 1930s-40s clear pink tinged plastic half-hexagonal frames, unmarked.

5in (12.5cm) wide

£40-60 **VE**

A pair of 1940s-60s small tortoiseshell plastic frames, with half hexagonal rims and curved arms.

Retro styles such as this, particularly in tortoiseshell, have recently become fashionable again, after years of modern styles being popular.

5in (12.5cm) wide

£70-100 **VE**

A pair of 1960s French black plastic sunglasses with half hexagonal-shaped top rims, curved arms and "VERGO FILTRANT FRANCE" oval sticker on the original lenses.

5in (12.5cm) wide

£70-100 **VE**

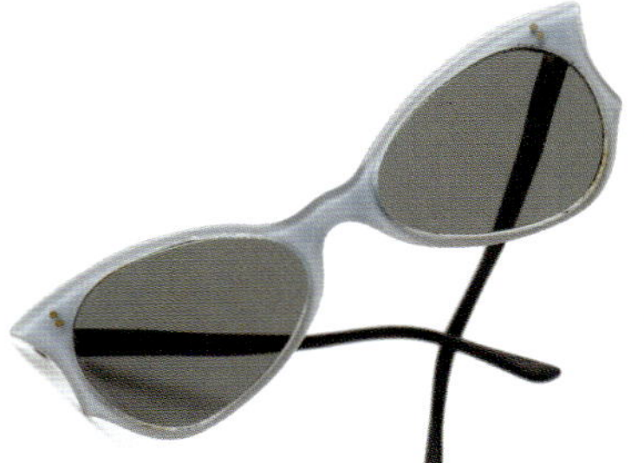

A pair of 1950s plastic sunglasses, the frames of transparent light blue over opaque white.

5in (13cm) wide

£30-40 **CANS**

A pair of 1950s brown and white laminated plastic sunglasses.

5in (13cm) wide

£30-50 **CANS**

A 1960s pair of American Renauld metal-framed angular rectangular sunglasses, with white enamel detailing.

During the early and mid 1960s, Renauld advertised a wide range of avant garde, futuristically shaped sunglasses.

6in (15.5cm) wide

£120-180 **VE**

A 1960s pair of red and white over clear laminated plastic frames, with inset diamond pattern, unmarked.

5.75in (14.5cm) wide

£70-100 **VE**

A pair of 1960s French grey pearlescent and white laminated plastic frames, the upper layer cut through with dots, lines and curls, marked "France WOC".

5.25in (13.5cm) wide

£120-180 **VE**

A 1960s pair of carved red pearlescent plastic frames, marked "AM 26".

6in (15.5cm) wide

£120-180 **VE**

A pair of 1960s-70s brown and white moulded plastic imitation bamboo frames, marked "Frame France Made in France".

Bamboo-style frames became highly fashionable during the 1970s. The classic frame shape, typical of the late 1940s-50s, is given extra life by the shaped arms.

5.5in (14cm) wide

£120-180 **VE**

A 1960s-70s pair of French black and white laminated plastic 'swirl' frames, marked "Frame France".

6in (15cm) wide

£100-150 **VE**

A pair of late 1960s-70s Italian transparent pink plastic frames, marked "FRAME ITALY 820".

5.75in (14.5cm) wide

£25-35 **BB**

A pair of 1960s brown amber and clear laminated plastic sunglasses, the arms cut with lines through the brown layer, the frames pierced with geometric and curving shapes, unmarked.

5in (13cm) wide

£80-120 **VE**

A pair of 1960s-70s Italian brown tortoiseshell plastic frames, marked "FRAME ITALY".

Large, visually 'heavier' frames such as these have become fashionable for men over the past few years, particularly with the 'geek chic' trend.

5.75in (14.5cm) wide

£25-35 **BB**

A pair of 1960s American laminated purple and light blue plastic frames, marked "Graceline USA

5in (12.5cm) wide

£20-25 **BB**

A pair of 1980s French blue and black back laminated plastic frames, marked "FRAME FRANCE STEPPE".

Popularised by films in the 1980s, such as 'Top Gun' starring Tom Cruise, the 'aviator' frame shape championed by RayBan has become popular again recently.

5.25in (13.5cm) wide

£15-20 **BB**

A pair of 1980s 'Les Halles Espace' blue aluminium frames.

5.75in (14.5cm) wide

£40-60 **VE**

A CLOSER LOOK AT A PAIR OF GLASSES

These frames clearly look back to the large, oval 'bug eye' styles of the 1960s; eyewear designers often look to the past for inspiration.

The award-winning 'Boz' brand was led by Jean Francois Rey from 1991. He was inspired by African and Asian cultures, which can be seen here in the snakeskin effect.

The son of eyewear designers, Rey is considered by many to be one of the best avant garde eyewear designers today.

The eclectic choice of colours and patterns is typical of his creativity. He also draws inspiration from Japan and its culture.

A pair of 1990s French Boz 'Frames And Fun' snakeskin effect and red laminated plastic frames, marked "Made in France Lana SA/274", with lens sticker.

5.25in (13.5cm) wide

£80-120 **VE**

QUICK REFERENCE

- Vintage fashion is still a hot collecting area. Examples are not only sought after by collectors, but also by fashionistas who follow the trend for wearing vintage set by celebrities such as Kate Moss and Sarah Jessica Parker. Although this rise in popularity has meant prices have risen too, there's plenty still available to suit every budget. Pieces can be found at auctions, vintage fashion dealers and even in charity shops.
- The top end of the market is dominated by the work of leading 20thC designers such as Christian Dior, Gianni Versace and Coco Chanel. These pieces can be divided into two categories: couture, made in limited quantities after pieces from seasonal collections, and 'diffusion' ranges that can be bought 'off the peg'. Couture examples are usually more desirable, particularly if they are from notable collections, and fetch higher sums. Learn to recognise the difference by researching the different labels used.
- Although the top end of the market may be the most stable area in terms of value, the middle and lower ends have seen similar rises, and can be more fun to collect. Clothes often cost the same as, or even less than, something from the high street. Currently, the 1950s, 60s and 70s are the most popular decades. Always check the label as some makers may have been 'cult' names. Look out for prestigious locations which can indicate good quality makers or retailers.
- Look for pieces that are well cut, made from high grade materials, well finished and which have good stitching. Avoid pieces that are torn or stained – unless this is intentional. Examine vintage photographs and fashion books to learn more about the styles of the period you are interested in. After the work of leading designers, pieces that epitomise the fashion of the age are the most sought after by collectors.

An early 20thC American cotton and lace day dress, with tapework and lace panels and trim, and embroidered flowers and leaves, with elasticated waist.

Dresses from this period are scarcer than most, due to their age and fragile material. The style came back into fashion in the 1970s, with names such as Gunne Saxe. More common in the US than the UK, if the condition is as good as this, it should make an excellent buy.

c1915 *41.5in (105cm) high*

£100-150 **CANS**

A 1920s brown corduroy coat, with a a detachable fox fur collar or stole, lined in cotton, and with ruched sleeves, unlabelled.

45.75in (116cm) high

£200-250 **CANS**

A 1930s-40s black crepe dress, with red and white beaded pockets with stylized flower within a shield design, in excellent condition.

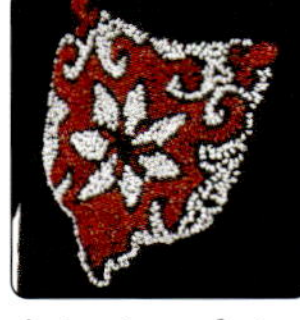

As well as the dress fabric being in perfect condition, there is, surprisingly, no damage to the beaded pockets. Damage to beaded designs like these is almost impossible to repair satisfactorily and can reduce value by over 75 per cent.

39.5in (100cm) long

£80-120 **CANS**

A 1930s yellow chiffon or georgette tea dress, printed with red and yellow flowers and green leaves, with ruffled neck.

42.25in (107cm) long

£100-150 **CANS**

A 1940s green cotton dress, printed with black and white flowers, with bow to front, and matching jacket with cream lapels, unlabelled.

58in (147cm) long

£100-150 **CANS**

A late 1940s burgundy crushed velvet belted dress, with ruched shoulders and glass buttons, unlabelled.

£80-120 **CANS**

A late 1940s-50s Canadian Sty-Val silver-grey acetate dress, woven with roses in silver and gold coloured thread, labelled.

38.25in (97cm) high

£80-100 **CANS**

A 1940s black crepe dress, with pleated fan effect to front, scooped neck line, and high split skirt.

47in (119cm) high

£60-80 **CANS**

A 1940s American Brookmar day dress, printed with red berries, purple leaves and green flowers, with torn label.

42.25in (107cm) long

£60-80 **CANS**

A 1940s Utility houndstooth coat with attached hood, original Bakelite buttons, matching belt, and deep cuffs.

41in (104cm) high

£180-220 **CANS**

A 1950s 'London Town MADE IN MAYFAIR LONDON ENGLAND' purple, orange, brown and green floral printed halterneck dress, with boned and structured inside mesh petticoat underneath, and trail to the scoop back.

37in (94cm) long

£80-100 **CANS**

A CLOSER LOOK AT A 1950S DRESS

The bright colours reflect the change from the austerity of wartime and post-war 1940s utility-wear.

The stylised pink rose and polka dot motifs are also typical of the period and add a whimsical touch.

The condition is excellent, making it very wearable today – an important factor in its valuation.

The cut of the dress with its full skirt and bolero jacket, is typical of the 1950s.

A 1950s American sleeveless halterneck cotton dress and matching bolero jacket, printed with pink roses in white wavy bands, and white polka dots on blue, with label reading 'LO ROCO MODEL in Marchington'.

45in (114cm) long

£80-100 **CANS**

A 1950s cotton belted dress, printed with roses and polka dots, the pockets with black trim, unlabelled.

34.75in (88cm) long

£70-90 **CANS**

A 1950s green cotton belted maxi-dress, printed with white flowers and with 'angel' or 'flutter' sleeves.

51.75in (131cm) long

£40-50 **CANS**

A 1950s white cotton shirtwaister dress, printed with polka dots and with spherical buttons inset with rhinestones, unlabelled.

40.5in (103cm) long

£60-80 **CANS**

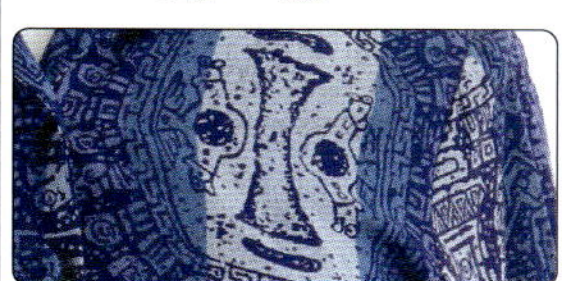

A 1950s American Kabro of Houston tonal blue, grey and purple cotton shirtwaister dress, with Tiki style print.

As American GIs returned to the US from overseas, Hawaiian inspired Tiki prints underwent a style revival in the 1950s and 60s, affecting everything from barware to fashion.

43.75in (111cm) long

£60-80 **CANS**

A mid-1950s Jeanne Lanvin black Chantilly lace cocktail dress, with boned strapless bodice, bouffant tiered skirt, large silk rose, horse-hair stiffened petticoat, bearing large woven label.

£420-480 **KT**

QUICK REFERENCE - CHRISTIAN DIOR

On February 12th 1947, a 42 year old Christian Dior (1905-57) exploded onto the international fashion scene with his first collection. Named 'Corolle', it brought elegance back to fashion with wasp-like waists, longer fuller skirts, a high bust and rounded shoulders. Within months the curvaceous style had become known as the 'New Look', and it went on to be copied across the world. Although the waist on this example is more relaxed, it still bears many of the hallmarks of Dior's original designs.

A Christian Dior Export slubbed silk cocktail dress, no.25713, with curving shoulders, boat neckline, large fringed bow to one hip, labelled 'Christian Dior Europe, manufacturé par Christian Dior Export'.

c1956–7 *Bust 34in (86cm)*

£380-420 **KT**

A 1950s ball gown, the cream ground embroidered with a floral pattern in green tones, with two green pleats and small bow to chest, unlabelled.

45.25in (115cm) long

£100-150 **CANS**

A 1950s jade green halterneck ball gown, woven with a vein-like design and bow to chest, with stiffened calico petticoat and and hooped layer underneath.

Ball gowns of this period make superb buys, as they are generally not hard to find, often of very good quality and are considerably less expensive than modern dresses. They also add a certain vintage style to an occasion. The pattern on this vibrantly coloured example is unusual.

47.75in (121cm) long

£150-200 **CANS**

A 1950s Liberty of London waisted Astrakhan collar wool coat, with 'Liberty of London' label to inside.

The waisted shape, buttons and Astrakhan collar give this a Victorian or Edwardian feel. Asktrakhan is the tightly curled fur from Persian or kerakul lambs.

39.5in (100cm) long

£150-200 **CANS**

An Ossie Clark printed velvet coat, with Russian-style button closure down one side, printed with multicoloured flowers designed by Celia Birtwell, with black on white printed label.

c1970 *Bust 34in (86cm)*

£450-550 **KT**

A CLOSER LOOK AT A DOLLYROCKERS DRESS

DollyRockers was designed by Samuel Sherman, also known as 'Sambo' and was active from c1963-75.

They were promoted in conjunction with Dolcis shoes by Smith's Crisps model Pattie Boyd (b.1944), who married Beatle George Harrison and Eric Clapton.

Look out for dresses that are made from Liberty print, a fact indicated on the label, as these can fetch over £100.

Labels reading 'Dollyrockers London' are different, being new clothes made from vintage fabric, and sold today through London retailers.

A 1960s DollyRockers cotton dress, printed with brown, yellow and orange repeated flowers and foliage on a bright blue ground, with frill under bust, labelled.

32.75in (83cm) long

£60-80 **CANS**

A late 1960s Pucci printed silk jersey evening gown, printed in shades of blue and green over a turquoise skirt, labelled.

Bust 36in (92cm)

£280-320 **KT**

A 1970s Emilio Pucci Kelly green cotton poplin skirt and blouse, printed with violet and blue floral pattern, with twill A-line skirt with welt pockets, with 'Emilio Pucci' label.

Now owned by luxury goods group LVMH, the Pucci name has never been out of fashion for long. Always look for the 'Emilio' name in the print as the company's classic 1960s and ' 70s look was widely copied. The colour and pattern of this suit are typical of Pucci's look.

size 6-8

£280-320 **FRE**

An early 1960s HF Couture of London pink cotton dress, printed with a green, black and white curving abstract pattern.

Despite dating from the 1960s, the shape is very 1950s and the pattern recalls the Art Deco period of the 1930s.

36in (91cm) long

£50-60 **CANS**

A 1960s Shifts International of Miami cotton dress, printed with blue fish and lime green seahorses on a white background, trimmed with lace.

The colours, pattern and shape are similar to dresses by Lily Pulitzer, which were also popular.

35in (89cm) long

£50-60 **CANS**

A 1950s Kittiwake swimsuit, with purple-brown and white wicker-like pattern, unworn.

22.75in (57.5cm) long

£30-40 **CANS**

An early 1960s Slix navy blue swimsuit, with diagonal red and white stripes, unworn.

18.5in (47cm) long

£40-50 **CANS**

ESSENTIAL REFERENCE - 1940S UTILITY CLOTHING

Utility clothing is the term used to describe clothes produced in Britain during the war, when materials were rationed and skilled labour was limited. The range was introduced in 1941, and bore the 'CC41' label shown here, which stood for Civilian Clothing 1941'. The government regulated the import, distribution and use of cloth, limiting the 'austere' styles and the range itself. They also controlled the price to ensure people could afford clothing of suitable quality. Much was worn out or altered, making surviving intact examples rare. Initial dislike turned into apathy, and the range was withdrawn in 1952.

A 1940s Capstan utility-wear woven pink cotton swimsuit, printed with seashells and fish, size 36, with Capstan and Utility labels.

18.5in (47cm) long

£60-80 **CANS**

An early 1960s Slix brown and white swimsuit, with diagonal stripe of alternating coloured leaves.

18.5in (47cm) long

£40-60 **CANS**

A mid 1960s Slix light blue swimsuit, with horizontal red stripe with woven white flowers, unworn.

18.5in (47cm) long

£35-45 **CANS**

A 1950s British Kittiwake swimsuit, with folded 'V' shape to front, unworn, size 34.

The label indicates that the elasticated material was tested by Courtaulds.

22.75in (57.5cm) high

£40-60 **CANS**

A 1960s-70s Jon Wood polyester and acrylic long-sleeved men's shirt, printed with motifs of a lady and a spinning wheel and a man and a pipe organ.

£25-35 **CANS**

A 1970s Jaytex blue cotton long-sleeved men's shirt printed with light blue horses and jockeys.

£25-30 **CANS**

A 1970s Marshall Lester cotton t-shirt, printed with multi-coloured advertising style designs.

24in (61cm) long

£25-30 **CANS**

Two 1960s-70s Nayytex 100% acrylic ladies' sweaters, printed with flower motifs, unworn and with original card tags.

19.75in (50cm) high

£22-28 EACH **CANS**

A 1960s psychedelic printed nylon slip, with black piping and straps.

Although it looks like a floral design, on closer inspection it is made up of faces. Spot the Twiggy-like face with the side parting.

23.25in (59cm) long

£15-20 **CANS**

A 1960s Japanese printed and PVC-coated cotton rainmac with stylised floral pattern, unworn, with matching hat.

This fetches as much as this due to the fact that it is complete and entirely unworn.

34.75in (88cm) high

£65-75 **CANS**

A 1960s yellow elasticated roll-on girdle, with suspenders.

1950s examples usually have metal clips.

12.5in (31.5cm) high

£15-20 **CANS**

QUICK REFERENCE

- Along with handbags, vintage shoes have become hotly sought after over the past few years. Although some collect for historical reasons, most buy to wear. As a result, shoes from before the Second World War tend to be less desirable due to their fragility and, often, their small sizes. Shoes from before the 20thC, and particularly those from before the 19thC, are scarce and typically very valuable.
- The most popular period is currently the 1950s-60s, when shoe designs became fun and elegant after wartime restrictions. While 1940s shoes can also be sought after, they are too austere for many. Shoes and boots from the 1970s and 80s are growing in popularity, particularly examples that are evocative of the 'disco' period. In general, look for bright colours, and shapes and materials that are typical of any given period.
- Famous designer names, such as Salvatore Ferragamo, will add value. Also look for notable store locations, such as London's Bond Street or New York's Fifth Avenue, as these usually indicate a good retailer and therefore high quality. The quality of the decoration also adds to value.
- Condition is all-important, particularly to collectors who buy to wear. Examine the soles and uppers carefully looking for wear, splits or missing decoration. While some shoes can be resoled and repaired, this may reduce their resale value.

A pair of 1940s black mesh and black and white leather shoes, marked 'Carmellites Shoes for the Lovely Nahm's Shoe Store 205 West Fox Street Carlsbad New Mexico'.

£150-200 LDY

A pair of 1940s 'Styleez Selby Shoe Flare Fit' black suede shoes with pierced sides and curl detail to upper.

£30-50 CANS

A pair of 1940s brown nubuck wedges, with peep-toe, cut decoration and diamond-shaped panels lined with mesh.

£80-120 CANS

A pair of 1940s Palter de Liso navy leather platform shoes, with peep-toe and cut decoration, styled by Wexee.

£120-180 GCHI

A pair of 1940s white nubuck and brown leather brogue-style shoes.

£35-45 CANS

A pair of 1940s cork wedges with leopardskin fabric uppers, marked 'La Rose Jacksonville Florida'.

£150-200 **GCHI**

A 1950s blue leather shoe by Rayne, with leather tassel decoration, marked 'Rayne by Appointment'.

£20-30 **LDY**

One of a pair of 1950s brown suede peep-toe court shoes, with brown leather strapped decoration.

£20-30 **LDY**

A 1940s pair of mules, with burgundy suede uppers with embroidered flowers, and carved-wood platform soles, made in the Philippines.

Sometimes known as 'sweetheart souvenirs', these were sent or taken home to wives and girlfriends by American GIs stationed in the Philippines during and after WWII. Houses, foliage and flowers painted in bright colours are typical motifs. The use of coloured woven raffia is another common feature.

£150-200 **GCHI**

QUICK REFERENCE – SALVATORE FERRAGAMO

Salvatore Ferragamo (1898-1960) was one of the greatest innovators in shoe design. After an apprenticeship in Italy, he moved to Southern California in 1914, where he studied anatomy to ensure his shoes were comfortable. His handmade, innovative designs combined function with ornamental forms, and he rapidly gained a celebrity following including Rudolph Valentino and Mary Pickford. In 1927, he returned to Italy, where he continued his innovative work, introducing new materials such as the cork wedge, which was patented in 1937. He continued to attract celebrity clients, including Eva Peron and Marilyn Monroe, after the war. His reputation as a visionary designer of elegant and innovative shoes continued until his death.

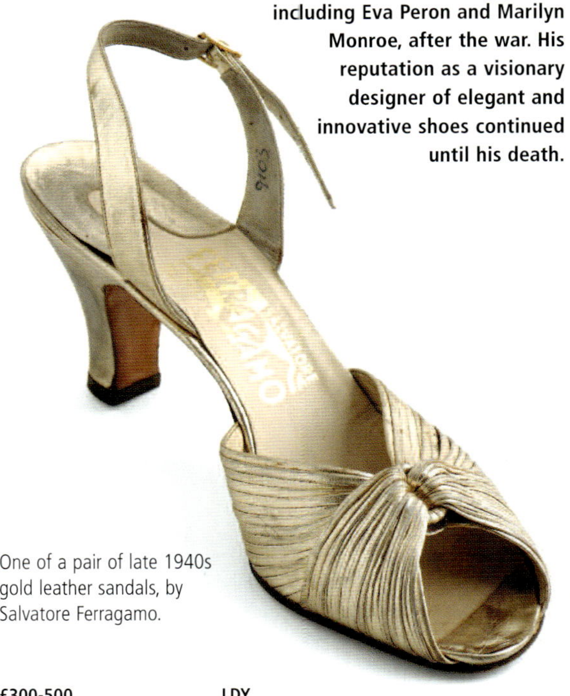

One of a pair of late 1940s gold leather sandals, by Salvatore Ferragamo.

£300-500 **LDY**

A CLOSER LOOK AT A PAIR OF 1950S SHOES

The uppers and strap are made from clear flexible Perspex – plastics such as this were new and fashionable in the 1950s.

The choice of pink and the added sparkle from the diamanté complemented the fashions of the day.

The glamorous design contrasts with the austere fashions of the 1940s, which saw restrictions and rationing.

The stiletto is said to have been developed by French designer Charles Jordan in 1952 – two years later a more cost-effective plastic and metal version was developed, which began the trend.

A pair of 1950s Perspex and metallic pink 'Countess' last slingbacks, with diamanté detail on the toes and clear and diamanté-decorated heels, marked 'Mackay Starr New York'.

£120-180 **GCHI**

A pair of 1950s black suede court shoes, the toes decorated with red velvet ribbon bows, marked 'Michelé Fifth Avenue Paris custom made'.

£150-200 **GCHI**

A pair of 1950s Danbarale blue leather stilettos, with diamanté and fan detail.

£150-200 **IVD**

A pair of 1950s unworn American peep-toe slingbacks, with knot detail, marked 'The Guarantee Shoe Store'.

£35-45 **CANS**

A pair of 1950s flexible Perspex slingbacks, with Perspex 'bows', the painted heels decorated with diamanté, the shoes marked 'Jacqueline designed by Wohl'.

£70-100 **GCHI**

A pair of 1950s mink and black velvet slippers, marked 'Mandel's fascinating slippers' and 'Genuine Mink'.

£120-180 **GCHI**

A pair of 1950s Nina Original gold-coloured wood paltform mules, with black lace-effect plastic uppers.

£100-150 **GCHI**

A pair of 1950s faux-leopard skin fabric mules, with wing-shaped uppers.

£150-200 **GCHI**

A pair of 1950s Nylonette waterproof shoe protectors/galoshes, with black suedette flaps and a fastening button.

The hollow heels allowed the wearer to slip these over their shoes for protection.

£40-60 **CANS**

A pair of 1950s straw mules with wooden soles and Perspex heels, the heels inset with raffia flowers.

Always examine raffia closely, as it can be damaged very easily.

£200-250 **GCHI**

A pair of 1950s black suede zipped boots, with fur trim, marked 'Kickerino Alaskans', in excellent condition.

£100-150 **GCHI**

A pair of 1980s French Cassis, Cote d'Azur, black suede and gold leather court shoes, with chain detail at heel.

£70-100 LDY

QUICK REFERENCE - 1980S SHOES

The bold style of these shoes matches the dominant style of the period – power dressing. As more women entered executive jobs and strived for ever-increasing success in the working world, their clothes began to reflect their determination and power. Shoulder pads and suits in bold colours and patterns were typical. Examples include Signourney Weaver's character Katharine Parker in the 1988 film 'Working Girl', Prime Minister Margaret Thatcher, and Alexis Colby from the TV series 'Dynasty'. As many of today's designers are already beginning to look back to 1980s fashions, it will be interesting to see how this affects the value and desirability of original shoes and clothes.

A pair of 1980s R.P. Ellen green, white and navy blue slingbacks.

£20-30 CANS

A pair of 1980s 'Wild Pair' black sequin stilettos.

£45-55 IVD

A pair of 1980s Corsina grey leather peep-toe shoes, with applied cream leather butterfly detail.

£45-55 IVD

A pair of 1980s black and white swirl leather heels, by Gina.

£30-50 CANS

A 1980s Yves Saint Laurent suede and leather laced court shoe.

Saint Laurent updated the classic, clumpy brogue of the 1970s and devised a shoe that looks back to the early 20thC, reflects period fashions and is supremely elegant, with great proportions. With the Yves Saint Laurent label and high quality materials, these shoes are desirable and valuable.

£150-200 LDY

QUICK REFERENCE

- It's not just collectors who are snapping up vintage handbags. With the surge of interest in vintage clothing seen over the past decade, fashionable people of all ages are buying handbags to give an individual touch.
- Prices range from as little as £20 to over £5,000 for a highly desirable Hermès 'Kelly' bag. However, most bags can be found for under £100 at vintage clothing stores, auctions, car boot sales and charity shops. When buying always look inside for designer labels, and examine a bag all over to assess its condition.
- Value depends on a number of factors including desirability, the maker, the quality of construction and the materials used, age and condition. Bags made from leather and the rarer animal skins are usually the most valuable, although bags made of other materials that exemplify the style of the day or have novelty appeal can be equally valuable.
- Away from the best names such as Chanel, Hermès and Gucci, look out for labels of makers in desirable locations, such as Fifth Avenue, New York or Bond Street, London, as this usually indicates a high quality bag.
- Condition is very important. A bag in truly mint, shop-bought, condition will fetch a considerable premium over one that shows signs of use. Look inside as torn or stained interiors reduce desirability and value. Although bags from the 1950s and 60s are currently the most popular, iconic bags from the 1980s are beginning to see a surge of interest, so could be a good investment.

A 1920s Whiting & Davis chain mesh bag with embroidered pink fabric lining, metal frame, stamped inside.

Whiting & Davis, founded in 1876 in Massachusetts, is synonymous with high quality mesh bags. It made bags printed with brightly coloured Art Deco patterns. Although the company fell out of fashion in the mid20thC, it returned briefly during the 'disco' age in the 1970s. The companys's bags remain popular with collectors.

5in (12.5cm) wide

£70-100 CANS

A 1930s brown silk Art Deco bag, the clasp set with cut steel rhinestones, cream silk lined interior, metal frame, marked 'Made in England'.

6in (15cm) high

£30-40 CANS

A 1930s brown ruffled silk bag, pink satin lining, with original mirror, rhinestone clasp, marked 'Made in England'.

The quality and condition of the bag contribute to its value.

8.5in (22cm) wide

£40-60 CANS

A 1930s Art Deco woven Corde handbag, with brass fittings and frame covered with cream bakelite panels, marked 'Made in England'.

8.25in (21cm) high

£50-80 CANS

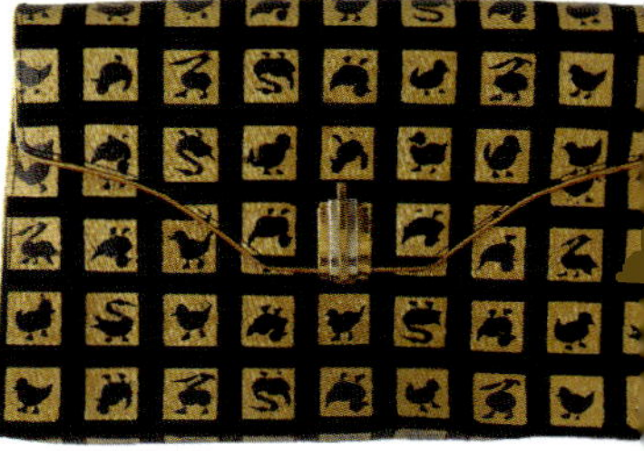

A 1930s woven silk clutch bag, the silk hand-printed with ducks and birds, with black silk lining and gold piping in and out, bevelled hand mirror and an Art Deco clasp.

7.5in (19.5cm) wide

£40-60 CANS

A 1930s Art Deco iridescent beaded bag, with black Lucite and chromed metal frame.

7in (18cm) wide

£120-180 **GCHI**

A 1940s bag, with a hand-painted and beaded garden and floral design, the padded handle with small floral motifs.

9in (23cm) wide

£150-200 **AHL**

A 1940s brown leather bag with crocodile skin panel decoration, with expandable front pocket and arrow-shaped catch.

10.5in (26.5cm) high

£60-90 **CANS**

A 1940s-50s British faux-snakeskin bag with wrist handle and purse.

6.75in (17cm) high

£30-50 **CANS**

A 1940s blue felt bag, with applied posy of felt flowers and hearts.

15in (38cm) wide

£60-80 **GCHI**

A CLOSER LOOK AT A 1940S HANDBAG

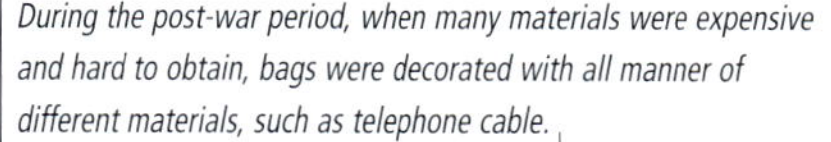

During the post-war period, when many materials were expensive and hard to obtain, bags were decorated with all manner of different materials, such as telephone cable.

Box bags are also typical of the period. The bright, jaunty colours and pattern of the telephone cables added colour and cheer at a time of great austerity.

Avoid dirty or stained examples as they are hard to clean. Breaks in the cord also reduce value.

These bags were made in a variety of patterns and colour combinations – generally the more complex the pattern and the more colours are present, the better.

A 1940s telephone cable covered box bag, lined with red woven fabric on a frame.

7.25in (18.5cm) wide

£60-80 **CANS**

A 1950s-60s woven box bag, white plastic and yellow and black straw, metal clasp, unmarked.

11in (28cm) wide

£30-50 **CANS**

A CLOSER LOOK AT AN ENID COLLINS HANDBAG

Enid Collins founded her company in 1959 in Texas and quickly became a popular name with fashionable young women into the 1970s.

The most collectable and desirable bags are sturdy wooden box bags decorated with painted designs highlighted with rhinestones, faux jewels, sequins and other materials.

Authentic bags made before Collins sold the company in 1970 are stamped 'ec' on the outside, together with the name of the design, and also bear a stamp on the interior.

The more detailed and amusing the design, and the more materials and colours used, the more the bag is likely to be worth – but check carefully for missing parts.

A 1960s Enid Collins 'Night Owl' box bag, decorated with rhinestones, marked inside, with plastic handle.

8.5in (22cm) wide

£50-70 **CANS**

A 1950s-60s Souré Bag of New York, of plastic-covered printed cotton, decorated with embroidered multicoloured gloves, applied rhinestones and faux pearls.

15.25in (38.5cm) long

£220-280 **GCHI**

A 1960s basketwork box handbag, with applied plastic fruit and woven wool leaves and faux-leather handles, in excellent condition.

10.25in (26cm) high

£100-150 **GCHI**

A 1950s Hovland Swanson woven raffia drawstring bag, with applied raffia covered fruits and raffia 'grass', with original price and shop tickets.

8in (20cm) high

£50-70 **GCHI**

A set of 1950/60s Manderin Jiffy Juvenile Product elasticated permanently knotted ties for boys, in original shop display box.

Box 12.5in (32cm) wide

£40-60 CANS

A 1980s enamelled 'kissing fish' belt buckle, with grey woven belt.

5in (12.5cm) wide

£15-20 CANS

A 1980s embossed metal buckle in the shape of a large fish eating a small fish, on a red elasticated belt.

5in (13cm) wide

£20-30 CANS

A 1980s Valentino red and black chequered dyed fox stole, fully articulated with rhinestone eyes, labelled "Valentino Night/Made in Italy".

£75-95 FRE

A pair of 1930s Plaza silk stockings, in original, unopened packaging with dog shaped card, marked 'Made in England'.

The scarcity of an unopened pack, the dog motif and Art Deco font that make these appealing – some collectors even specialise in stockings.

6.75in (17cm) wide

£20-25 CANS

A set of six 1950s handpainted plastic Bobby Pins hairpins, on original shop display card.

Card 4.75in (12cm) high

£10-15 CANS

A set of six 1950s handpainted plastic Bobby Pins hairpins, on original shop display card.

Card 4.75in (12cm) high

£10-15 CANS

A 1950s handpainted solid plaster girl wall mask, with ponytail and inset rhinestones, in mint condition.

9.5in (24cm) high

£40-50 **MA**

A 1950s-60s Japanese moulded and handpainted miniature lady head vase, for cacti or hairpins.

This small size is unusual.

3.25in (8cm) high

£20-30 **MA**

A 1950s handpainted solid plaster Chinese girl wall mask, in mint condition.

Always examine these very closely. Any paint loss, even if 'touched up' reduces value dramatically. Only those in truly mint condition will fetch such high sums.

11in (28cm) high

£50-60 **MA**

A 1950s slip-moulded cat figurine, with handpainted leaf designs, unmarked.

12in (30.5cm) high

£25-35 **RET**

A 1950s printed vinyl portable record case.

10.5in (27cm) high

£20-30 **CANS**

An early 1950s 'Crinoline Lady' fabric, netting and painted plaster dressing table lamp, with wire frame to support her dress.

Considered 'kitsch' by many, always look at the doll, as good quality 19thC bisque 'half dolls' can fetch over £100. Complete examples, such as this, are scarce.

15in (38cm) high

£20-30 **MA**

An early 1950s guitar-shaped wall mirror, with handpainted floral decoration, mounted on wood.

Ignoring the chintzy floral decoration, this shows the beginning of the rock 'n roll movement. These are hard to find in such good condition.

17in (43cm) high

£50-70 **MA**

ESSENTIAL REFERENCE – SHATTALINE PRODUCTS

Shattaline Products produced a range of resin lampbases, paperweights, pen deskbases and small tables from the mid-1960s until the mid-1970s. The crackle effect was gained by using a catalyst in the resin which caused random internal cracks. Colours included orange, yellow, green, blue and red, but tones can vary as the colourant was applied to batches by hand. Pieces were then sanded and polished by hand. The range was sold by Selfridges, Liberty and other major department stores in the UK, with candleholders being sold through Price's candles. Contrary to popular belief, British Home Stores did not sell this product, but rather a similar, competitive product. The production process was designed by retired army Major turned sculptor Lewen Tugwell during the mid 1960s and pieces were first made in Surrey, with production moving to Scotland in the early 1970s.

A 1960s-70s Shattaline green resin small cylindrical lampbase, with original textured cream fibreglass shade.

Base 5.5in (13.5cm) high

£30-40 **M20C**

A 1960s-70s Shattaline red resin square section lampbase, with original textured amber fibreglass shade.

Base 11.5in (29cm) high

£60-70 **M20C**

A pair of 1970s American Burwood Products Company silver painted plastic wall candleholders, the back with moulded company name.

The textured, almost space age, design was also reflected in jewellery from the period – particularly that made in Scandinavia.

15.5in (39.5cm) high

£80-100 **M20C**

A 1960s-70s orange and red resin cylindrical lampbase, with original textured cream fibreglass shade.

The different colours used, and the fact that the inside of the base appears to be made up of chunks of resin, rather than a single block of internally cracked resin, indicates that this was made to imitate Shattaline products. A number of imitators existed at the time, one based in Germany (Solarstein) and another using the name 'Scatterlite'.

Base 11.5in (29cm) high

£60-70 **M20C**

A 1950s-60s teak framed table lamp, with brass fitments and textured pink shade.

Pink shades are rare, they are usually orange or off-white in colour. This is the smallest of three sizes of this lamp.

10in (25.5cm) high

£30-40 **M20C**

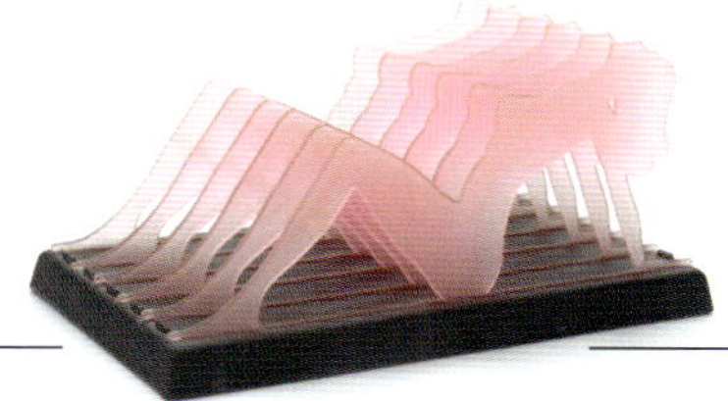

A 1970s plastic reclining nude pink and black plastic letter rack.

6in (15.5cm) long

£15-20 **MA**

QUICK REFERENCE

- Caithness glass was founded near John O'Groats in Scotland in June 1961, primarily to create employment for local people. Talented Irish designer Domnhall O'Broin co-founded the company, and became its technical director and designer from 1961-1966, being responsible for many of their most successful designs. The company is now owned by Dartington Glass.
- O'Broin is arguably one of the over-looked names in 20th century glass design. He trained under Helen Monroe Turner at the Edinburgh College of Art and was one of the first apprentices at Waterford Crystal from 1950, where he worked under Miroslav Havel, and designed patterns such as 'Colleen'. O'Broin left Caithness in 1966, moving to the US where he worked for Pilgrim and Fenton before setting up on his own.
- His designs are typified by modern, yet elegant, shapes with clean lines. Scandinavian glass, being imported into Britain at the time in large numbers, was a strong inspiration. Rims were machine cut and the bases heavily cased in clear glass which 'lifted' and contrasted with the colour. Pieces were spun at high speed in moulds, giving an even, rounded base with a smooth central depression.
- The jewel-like colours used were inspired by the Scottish landscape, gaining patriotic and evocative names such as 'Loch Blue', 'moss' (green), 'Peat' and 'Heather' (purple). Pieces are generally unmarked, although 'CG' paper, or later 'Caithness Glass' labels may have survived.
- Avoid examples that are chipped or scuffed or have internal bubbles or limescale from water, as these factors detract from the purity of the colour and form. After O'Broin left, other designers worked for the company, including Charles Orr from 1967-72 and, notably, Colin Terris from 1972 onwards. Along with O'Broin's, their designs are becoming increasingly sought-after.

A 1960s-90s Caithness Glass footed fruit bowl, designed by Domhnall O'Broin in 1961.

7in (17.5cm) high

£20-30 GC

A 1960s-70s Caithness Glass Heather purple 'Cased' vase, no.4010/M, designed by Domhnall O'Broin in 1961.

7in (17.5cm) high

£30-50 GC

A 1960s-80s Caithness Glass small Loch blue 'Barrel' vase, no.4019/115, designed by Domhnall O'Broin in 1961.

5in (12.5cm) high

£15-20 GC

A Caithness Glass cased 'Moss Green' posy vase, by Domhnall O'Broin, factory and 'Design Centre London' paper labels.

4in (10cm) high

£10-15 MHC

A Caithness Glass Loch Blue 'Stroma' rose bowl, designed by Domhnall O'Broin in 1961.

The colour variation is brought about by the thickness of the glass – near the rim it is extremely thin.

XXin (XXcm) high

£20-30 GC

A 1960s Caithness Glass Loch Blue tall cylindrical mould blown vase, designed by Domhnall O'Broin in 1963, with paper label.

10.5in (26.5cm) high

£80-120 GC

A 1960s-70s Caithness Glass Peat brown 'Barrel' vase, no.4019/235, designed by Domhnall O'Broin in 1961.

9in (23cm) high

£50-70 GC

A 1960s-70s Caithness Glass Moss green lamp base, designed by Domhnall O'Broin in 1961, with original 'CG' paper label.

This was featured in the influential book 'Modern Glass' by Geoffrey Beard, as an example of a very modern design for the period. Larger pieces such as this are harder to find than smaller vases.

7.25in (18.5cm) high

£80-120 GC

A 1960s-70s Caithness Glass Heather lamp base, no.4010/LL, designed by Domhnall O'Broin in 1961.

10in (25.5cm) high

£70-100 GC

A 1960s-70s Caithness Glass Peat brown decanter with hollow blown stopper, designed by Domhnall O'Broin in 1961.

11.25in (28.5cm) high

£40-60 GC

A 1960s-70s Caithness Glass Heather cased purple decanter, with hollow stopper, designed by Domhnall O'Broin.

Colour tones can vary widely, and it can be hard to tell which colour a piece was intended to be. Clearly identifiable colours such as this are the most desirable.

11.25in (28.5cm) high

£60-80 GC

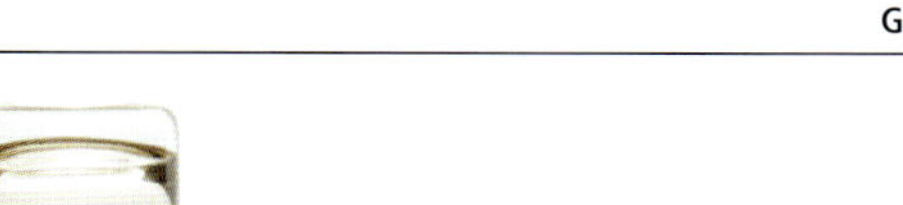

A Caithness Glass Peat brown Morven decanter, shape no.4025/D, designed by Domhnall O'Broin in 1961, with hollow stopper.

This starkly modern, squared off form is typical of O'Broin's forms. Unusually for a decanter, the inside of the rim is not ground, with the seal coming only from the weight of the well-fitted blown stopper.

9.75in (24cm) high

£30-40 M20C

A Caithness Glass Heather purple 'Morven' decanter, shape no.4025/D, designed by Domhnall O'Broin in 1961.

9.75in (25cm) high

£40-50 **GAZE**

A 1990s Caithness Glass cased mottled jade green 'Concerto' rose vase, with ribbed base and cellophane label.

Concerto was available in three colourways: Blue, Jade and Pink.

7in (17.5cm) high

£20-25 **GC**

A Caithness Glass 'Xanadu' range ovoid vase, designed by Colin Terris in 1996, with layers of pulverised coloured enamel over an opaque white core and an applied blue trail.

7.25in (18.5cm) high

£70-100 **GC**

A Caithness Glass graduated purple vase, engraved with a bird perched on a thorny branch.

A cutting and engraving department was founded at Caithness by Colin Terris in 1968, meaning all cut or engraved ranges date from after this year. Natural or animal motifs, and commemorative designs, are typical. Designs commemorating personal events, such as a wedding, usually devalue a piece.

9in (23cm) high

£10-15 **GC**

A Caithness Glass colourless cylindrical 'Oban' vase, designed by Charles Orr, with applied green and blue ribbon trails.

7in (17.5cm) high

£20-30 **GC**

A CLOSER LOOK AT A CAITHNESS GLASS VASE

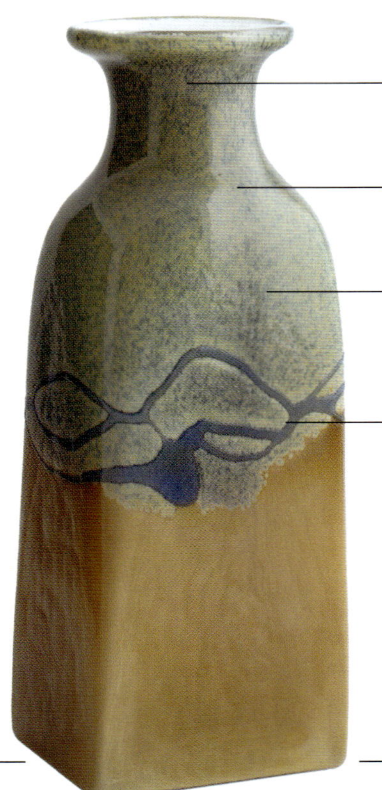

Xanadu uses many layers of glass over an opaque white base to create a mottled, stone-like effect, and can be found in triangular, ovoid, rectangular and hexagonal forms.

The pattern was created by hand in a time-consuming process using coloured enamel frit and randomly applied hot glass trails, making each piece unique.

This range was expensive and comparatively unpopular at the time, so was withdrawn from sale only a few years after being introduced, meaning that it is comparatively scarce today.

It can be found in a range of colours including orange and red, green and blue, and purple and grey.

A Caithness Glass 'Xanadu' range bottle vase, designed by Colin Terris in 1996, with layers of pulverised coloured enamel over an opaque white core and an applied blue trail.

10in (25.5cm) high

£100-150 **GC**

QUICK REFERENCE

- Wines from the Champagne region have been prized since Roman times, and were often used at royal ceremonies. In 1662, English scientist Christopher Merret developed the first intentionally sparkling wine, although French Benedictine monk Dom Perignon is usually credited with this achievement. However, his version was developed some 40 years after Merret's.
- From the 17thC to the 20thC, champagne was sweet, often being served as a dessert. Dry 'brut' champagne only became popular in the late 19thC.
- Two types of glass are used to serve champagne: a tall flute with a rim that may curve slightly inwards, and a low, saucer-shaped dish. Both are mounted on stems to keep the hand from touching the bowl and warming the wine. The taller version is preferred by connoisseurs.
- The saucer, known as a 'coupe', was reputedly developed in 1663, although facts are scarce. Legend has it that its form was based on the shape of the breasts of Madame de Pompadour or Queen Marie Antoinette. This is almost certainly false, as examples exist that predate both women. The style saw peaks in popularity during the mid-19thC and during the 1920s and 30s, when it was also used for cocktails.
- Value depends on the maker, glass, and the style and quality of any decoration. Prices for vintage examples can be lower than those for brand new glasses. Although unusual motifs can make a glass desirable, simple and almost 'modern', geometric cuts are often the most popular with collectors.
- Edwardian acid-etched examples are currently very affordable, and are typically made from a delicate, thin glass. Look for simpler classical or geometric patterns, as these may rise in value over time. Owning vintage glasses can add a stylish dash of originality to entertaining.

A 1930s-50s coupe champagne glass, cut with a pattern of stylised leaves and flowers.

Patterns like this tend to be less popular and desirable. The stem is also not cut.

4.5in (11.5cm) high

£10-12 **GROB**

A 19thC coupe champagne glass, the bowl copper wheel-cut with a pattern of leaves and ferns, with plain, waisted cylindrical stem.

4.5in (11.5cm) high

£12-15 **GROB**

A 19thC or early 20thC coupe champagne glass, the bowl cut with thistles and leaves, with straight faceted stem.

This is possibly by notable company Edinburgh & Leith.

4.75in (12cm) high

£20-25 **GROB**

A late 19thC or early 20thC coupe champagne glass, the bowl with acid-etched stylised floral swag and scrolling motif, with hatched band with stylised roses.

4.5in (11.5cm) high

£10-12 **GROB**

A mid 20thC coupe champagne glass, the bowl cut with trailing strawberry plants and strawberries, with conical baluster stem.

Strawberries are popular motifs – probably because of the luxurious association of strawberries and champagne.

4.5in (11.5cm) high

£10-12 **GROB**

A late 19thC or early 20thC coupe champagne glass, with acid-etched bands of loops and interlaced circles, and tapering cylindrical stem.

4.75in (12cm) high

£8-12 **GROB**

A mid-20thC Continental coupe champagne glass, the bowl cut with a curving pattern of 'thumbprint' ovals, with conical baluster stem.

4.75in (12cm) high

£10-15 **GROB**

An early 20thC Continental coupe champagne glass, the bowl cut with a curving pattern of 'thumbprint' ovals, with conical baluster stem.

4.75in (12cm) high

£10-15 **GROB**

A late 19thC cut crystal coupe champagne glass, cut with diamonds and fans, and faceted, slightly waisted stem.

5in (12.5cm) high

£25-35 **W&L**

A 20thC Continental coupe champagne glass, the bowl cut with 'thumbprint' ovals and trefoil cuts, the conical baluster stem with annulated knop above.

Although this stem is comparatively complex compared with some examples, buyers often prefer the simpler, less ornate examples.

4.75in (12cm) high

£12-15 **GROB**

A 1920s-30s coupe champagne glass, the bowl with criss-cross diamond and star patterns, with facet-cut stem.

4.75in (12cm) high

£10-12 **GROB**

A 19thC coupe champagne glass, with heavy, hollow baluster stem, and bowl cut with large facets.

4.5in (11.5cm) high

£15-18 **GROB**

A 19thC coupe champagne glass, the hollow stem and base of the bowl cut with facets.

The hollow stem is a desirable feature for collectors.

5in (12.5cm) high

£25-30 **GROB**

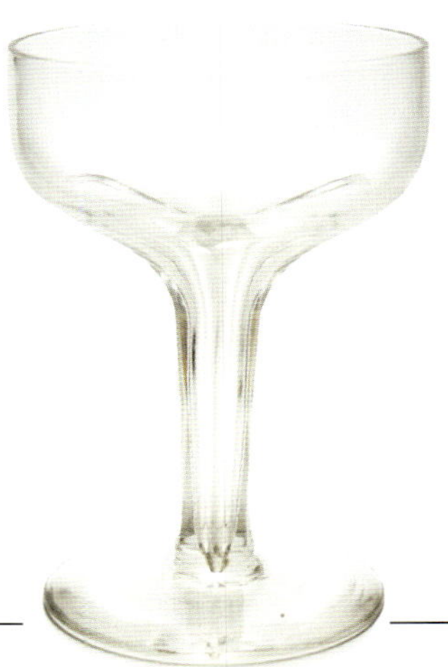

QUICK REFERENCE - CHANCE GLASS

Chance Brothers, founded in 1824 outside Birmingham, produced its first tableware in the 1930s. Its varied Fiesta range was introduced in 1951, and became immensely popular. Plate glass was heated until it 'slumped' into a mould, or over an object, to take its form. The 'handkerchief' vase was one of their most prolific and popular ranges. Look out for the rare reversed version of the pattern below, with red dots on a white background, as this can fetch over three times the value of this one. As with Gingham, the pattern continued to be produced by Fiesta Glass (successor to Chance Glass) from 1981.

A Chance Glass small red 'Polka Dot' transfer-printed handkerchief vase.

1974-81 *4in (10cm) high*

£10-15 **GC**

A 1970s Chance Glass light blue 'Bandel II' pattern screen-printed small handkerchief vase.

4in (10cm) high

£7-10 **RET**

A Chance Glass 'Large Flemish' handkerchief vase.

The lightly textured 'Large Flemish' pattern had been used for window glass at Chance since the late 19thC. It was allegedly inspired by the rippling effect of canals that ran through the factory.

7in (18cm) high

£15-25 **GC**

A 1980s Chance Glass small green and white 'Gingham' pattern transfer-printed handkerchief vase.

1978-81 *4in (10cm) high*

£15-20 **GC**

A 1970s Chance Glass screen-printed gold 'Calytpo' pattern ovoid tray, the pattern designed by Michael Harris in 1959.

The popularity of Calypto was long-lived as it was produced until at least 2000. Usually found in white, the gold colourway was introduced after 1970.

13.5in (34cm) long

£10-15 **RET**

QUICK REFERENCE

- The areas that make up much of today's Czech Republic have been renowned for glass design and production for centuries. The late 19thC and early 20thC saw much glass in the dominant Art Nouveau style being produced. Most pieces are commonly attributed to the company Loetz, but recent research has revealed that companies such as Kralik and Rindskopf also had a large output.
- As the country was 'behind the Iron Curtain' from 1945 until 1989, the major revolution in design has been largely ignored. As glass collectors and researchers have found more, prices have begun to rise.
- Complexity and rarity are currently the main indicators to value. The designer is also important, but as the market is so new many names are yet to become widely known. Hot-worked, enamelled and cut and engraved pieces that are unique and influential tend to fetch the highest sums. However, such pieces often inspired ranges that were mass-produced, and are more affordable.
- Many of these are hot-worked or pressed glass designs, and the modern, avant garde style developed from the late 1950s to the early 1970s are the most desirable. Leading designers, whose work is sought after by collectors, include Adolf Matura, Frantisek Vizner, and Frantisek Zemek, as well as the influential names known for producing more unique works such as Stanislav Libensky, Pavel Hlava, René Roubícek and Jirí Harcuba.
- As much glass is unmarked, it is best to consult a reference book to learn how to recognise designs. Many pieces are currently mistaken for the work of factories on Murano or in Scandinavia. A considerable amount of research is yet to be undertaken, and the area looks set to grow in importance over the next few years.

A Czechoslovakian Kralik gold and amber 'Silberband' vase, with melted-in light green trails and heavy iridescent surface.

Both 'Silberband' and 'Silveria' (see right) are terms given by a collector, rather than the official range names. There are two variations: those with a combination of either cranberry and amber, or of green and amber, spots.

c1905 *6in (15cm) diam*

£350-450 **MDM**

A Kralik 'Silveria' vase, the textured, mould blown lobed body with applied pink enamel to the base and randomly applied green trails, with a light iridescent surface.

c1900

£280-320 **MDM**

A Kralik red 'Banded' near-spherical vase, with pulled rim, reddish-pink enamel spots, and applied and melted in white trail and heavily iridised surface.

c1905

£350-450 **MDM**

A pair of tiny Kralik salts, in the 'Wavy' pattern, with silver rims.

1905

£140-160 **MDM**

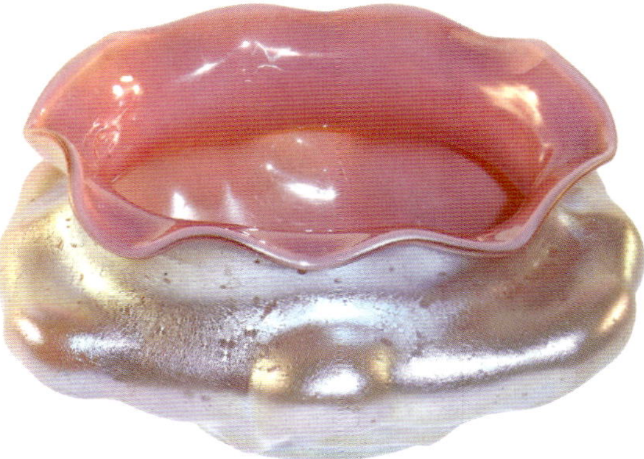

A Kralik rare opalescent pink lobed bowl, of organic form, the exterior with heavy silvery iridescence.

c1905 *6.5in (16.5cm) diam*

£350-450 **MDM**

A Kralik 'Corrugated' tapered vase, with wavy rim, pulled pattern and heavy iridescent surface.

c1905

£350-450 **MDM**

A Kralik 'King Tut' vase, with green mottles and applied and pulled dark blue trails melted into the body.

c1905

£300-400 **MDM**

A Rindskopf waisted vase, applied pulled, 'feathered' trails over opaque body, iridescent surface.

c1900

£350-450 **MDM**

A Rindskopf floriform vase, applied, melted-in pulled and feathered white trails, and an iridised surface.

c1900

£450-550 **MDM**

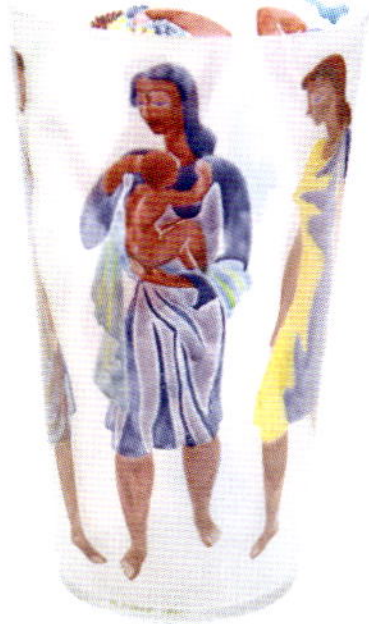

A large tumbler vase, designed by Karel Poner, with hand-enamelled with Classically dressed female figures over a white cloudy ground, with engraved and enamelled signature with date.

Little is known about Poner, apart from that he studied under Professor Kysela at the School of Applied Arts in Prague. During the late 1930s and early 1940s he produced enamelled vessels in a modern, painterly style, featuring Classically dressed characters, or people going about their lives. Examples can be found in the Museum of Decorative Arts in Prague.

1941 *11.75in (30cm) high*

£350-450 **FLD**

A CLOSER LOOK AT A LOETZ VASE

The organic form and colour are typical of the Art Nouveau movement, and much of the glass produced by Loetz.

The iridescent, mottled green finish identifies it as being part of the successful 'Papillon' range, which was produced in quantity and was more affordable than other ranges.

It is further embellished with silver overlay, which was complex to apply. The overlay is also in the Art Nouveau style and is itself embellished with engravings.

This particular piece is visually stunning and would have been expensive and highly fashionable in its day.

A Loetz Creta 'Papillion' glass vase, swollen with a trefoil neck, the floral silver overlay with engraving.

c1900 *8.25in (21cm) high*

£1,000-1,500 **DN**

A 1960s-70s Czechoslovakian Zelezny Brod Citrine tapered vase, with applied brown trails, designed by Frantisek Zemek.

This form was designed by Zemek in 1957 and was shown in the landmark publication 'Modern Bohemian Glass' by Josef Raban. The design, whilst typical of the 1950s obsession with curving organic forms, also hints at machinery, reminiscent of a screw or propeller.

8.25in (21cm) high

£50-70 **MHC**

A 1960s Czechoslovakian Msistov glassworks 'Rhapsody' range large vase, designed by Frantisek Zemek in 1960.

15.25in (38.5cm) high

£120-180 **TCF**

A Czechoslovakian Novy Bor mould blown ball vase, with optic moulded columns and iridescent surface effect, machine cut rim.

8.25in (22cm) high

£70-90 **GC**

A Czechoslovakian Moser vase, no.54303, designed by Jiri Suhajek in 1976, with applied light green side casing and stylised red and green flower to centre.

8.5in (21.5cm) high

£300-400 **VZ**

A Czechoslovakian Skrdlovice glassworks teardrop shaped vase, designed by Vladimìr Jelìnek or Zdenka Strobachovà, with graduated blue bands fading to rose pink, and 'kicked up' conical base.

c1960 *11.5in (29cm) high*

£1,200-1,800 **QU**

A CLOSER LOOK AT A CHLUM U TREBONE GLASS VASE

The colour variation is created by heating this heat-sensitive glass for different periods of time.

This type of glass was a speciality of the factory, with and orange-red 'Garnet' colourway being much more commonly found.

The UFO form is typical of its time, and the protrusion in the base recalls studio glass by fellow Czech designer Pavel Hlava.

The glass is blown into a ribbed mould before being blown to shape, which gives the linear optical effect.

A Czechoslovakian Chlum u Trebone glassworks optic mould blown 'Garnet & Blue' glass vase, designed by Jan Gabrhel in 1962, with protrusion in base.

4.5in (11.5cm) high

£100-150 **PC**

A 1970s Czechoslovakian Prachen glassworks amber glass cylindrical vase, applied blue prunts stamped with stylised floral motifs, designed by Josef Hospodka in 1969.

Although blue, the prunts appear green due to the transmitted light through the yellow-amber body.

9.75in (25cm) high

£80-120 SAS

A CLOSER LOOK AT A VÌZNER VASE

Frantisek Vì zner (b.1936) is one of Czechoslovakia's most influential and famous glass designers, with a global reputation.

Vì zner' s forms tend to be solid, with a monumental and almost industrial or architectural feel. They also hint at his later, simpler cut and polished studio works.

It was made using the challenging 'gathering on the post' technique, where the partially blown body is used to gather a second mass of differently coloured glass.

The 'peg' cased in a heavy base is recurring form in Vì zner' s work for Skrdlovice at the time – after 1977 he produced his own studio works.

A late 1970s Skrdlovice glassworks vase, no.7410 designed by Frantisek Vìzner in 1974, the ribbed colourless body cased with a heavy green base, unmarked.

This design was produced in at least three sizes, being roughly 25cm, 19cm or 15cm in height, although sizes do vary as each piece was handmade.

£200-300 PC

A 1960s Borské Sklo colourless cased pink torpedo vase, with polished pontil to base.

9in (23cm) high

£22-28 RET

A 1960s-70s Czechoslovakian Skrdlovice glassworks cased bottle vase, with internal air bubbles, designed by Jaroslav Svoboda.

12in (30.5cm) high

£300-400 GC

A 1970s Czechoslovakian Berànek or Chribskà glassworks 'Niagara' range amber and blue bowl, with pulled rim and lobes.

9in (23cm) long

£25-30 RET

A late 1960s-70s Czechoslovakian Borské Sklo green vase, designed by Pavel Hlava in 1967, with colourless casing.

Pavel Hlava (1924-2003) was one of the most notable Czech post-war glass designers. It is likely that this design was produced by blowing the molten glass into a modified wire cage, creating the undulating and warped bulges. It shows how his studio glass techniques were translated into glass produced in a factory.

10.25in (26cm) high

£70-100 M20C

A 1990s-2000s Czechoslovakian Bohemia Glass cased pink bowl, with pulled rim, polished base and blue foil factory label.

Although hot-worked bowls such as these have been produced since the late 1950s, this example can be dated to after 1990 as the label reads 'Czech Republic', not 'Czechoslovakia'.

7in (17.5cm) diam

£10-15 **M20C**

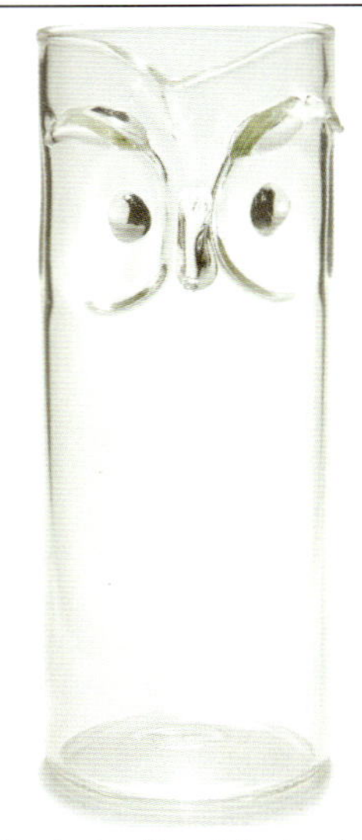

A Czechoslovakian stylised owl lampworked cylindrical jug, designed by Vera Liskova, with some applied features.

5.25in (13.5cm) high

£15-20 **GC**

A Czechoslovakian blown and lampworked glass bird pourer, with applied eyes and legs, designed by Vera Liskova.

3.75in (9.5cm) high

£25-30 **GC**

A Czechoslovakian Zelezny Brod Alexandrite glass vase, designed by Miroslav Klinger, engraved with a stylised, geometric heron standing amidst grasses, possibly by J. Maresova, signed 'JM 64'.

Alexandrite (or Neodymium) glass changes colour from a pale ice blue under flourescent lighting to this colour under incandescent lighting. The presence and style of any engraved design affects value considerably. Modern, stylised designs like this are much more desirable than simple, naturalistic renderings of flowers.

1964 *6.75in (17cm) high*

£100-150 **PC**

A Czechoslovakian blown and lampworked glass bird, designed by Vera Liskova.

Vera Liskova (1924-1985) is renowned for her lampworked abstract forms and animals formed from borosilicate glass. Each fragile piece is finely blown and formed by hand over a gas burner. Liskova elevated Lampworking to an art form in her larger abstract works, which can fetch many thousands of pounds.

3.75in (9.5cm) high

£20-25 **GC**

A 1970s Czechoslovakian Podebrady glassworks paperweight, with internal trapped rings of air, designed by Josef Svarc in 1968.

2.5in (6.5cm) high

£70-100 **PC**

A Rudolfova glassworks green pressed glass vase, no.13157, designed by Rudolf Jurnikl and produced from 1963.

8in (23cm) high

£70-100 **GC**

A Rudolfova glassworks blue pressed glass vase, no.12992, designed by Vaclav Hanus and produced from 1957.

This is often incorrectly attributed to the Art Deco period.

10in (25cm) high

£40-60 **GC**

A late 1950s-80s Czechoslovakian Rosice glassworks large blue 'Lens' vase, no.914, designed by Rudolf Schrötter in 1955.

8in (20.5cm) high

£30-40 **RET**

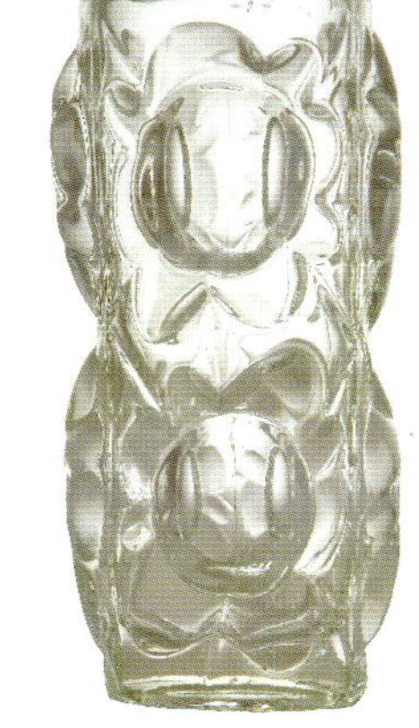

A Hermanova glassworks colourless pressed glass vase, no.20307, designed by Frantisek Peceny and produced from 1979.

6in (15.5cm) high

£15-25 **GC**

A Libochovice glassworks colourless pressed glass vase, no.3236, designed by Frantisek Vìzner and produced from 1965.

In 1965 the numerous factories producing pressed glass in Czechoslovakia were amaglamated under the umbrella name 'Sklo Union' – it is by this name that the glass is known to collectors today. This is typical of Vì zner's pressed glass designs, with its heavy moulded motifs on a simple cylinder. Lenses were a motif commonly used in Czech cut and pressed glass.

11in (28cm) high

£80-120 **GC**

A Hermanova glassworks large colourless 'Dragon's Head' colourless pressed glass large vase, no.20235, designed by Frantisek Peceny and produced from 1972.

Note how the form resembles the head of a dragon costume that may be seen at Chinese street celebrations. Unusually, this gives the vase a definitive 'front', which is shown here.

9.75in (25cm) high

£60-80 **GC**

A Rosice glassworks blue pressed glass ashtray, from the 'Praha' range of kitchen and tablewares designed by Adolf Matura from 1968-71.

5.25in (13cm) diam

£22-28 **RET**

QUICK REFERENCE

- Dartington Glass was founded in 1966 in Torrington, Devon by the Dartington Hall Trust, who aimed to bring work and prosperity to area by introducing a new industry. The chief designer was Frank Thrower, who had worked alongside Ronald Stennett-Willson (who was later to found King's Lynn Glass) at British importers, Wuidart from 1953 to 1960. Thrower had also designed for Portmeirion, and his work at both these companies had taught him about Scandinavian designs, which greatly influenced his work. Dartington also employed Scandinavian blowers, including master glassmaker and factory manager, Eskil Vilhelmsson.
- Thrower was responsible for over 500 designs, most of which have concave and convex moulded decoration. The output was dominated by tablewares and Dartington decanters attract interest from dedicated group of collectors. In general, however, decorative pieces, such as vases, are more popular with collectors. Shape, colour and size are all important. The textured range is especially popular, and collectors often aim to own an example of every shape in every colour.
- Smokey grey 'Midnight' and clear glass are the most common colours. Rarer colours, such as 'Flame' red and 'Kingfisher' blue are more desirable. Look out for liming from water, as this detracts from the colour, and other damage as this will decrease value.
- Until an exhibition book in 2007, Thrower's work was largely ignored by collectors, but it is becoming sought after, particularly his hallmark late 1960s and early 1970s designs. Wedgwood acquired 50 per cent of Dartington in 1982 and Thrower continued to design ranges for them, until he died in 1987. These later designs are currently less popular, so it may be a good time to buy them.

A 1970s Dartington Glass Clear FT60 candleholder or vase, designed by Frank Thrower in 1968.

4.75in (12cm) high

£15-25 **RET**

A Dartington Glass Kingfisher blue FT60 candleholder or vase, designed by Frank Thrower in 1968, with red cellophane label.

Kingfisher was discontinued c1973. The red label indicates this was a 'first' quality piece.

1968-c1973 *4.75in (12cm) high*

£25-30 **RET**

A Dartington Glass Kingfisher blue FT66 vase with abstract moulded designs and flared rim, designed by Frank Thrower in 1968.

5in (12.5cm) high

£25-35 **GC**

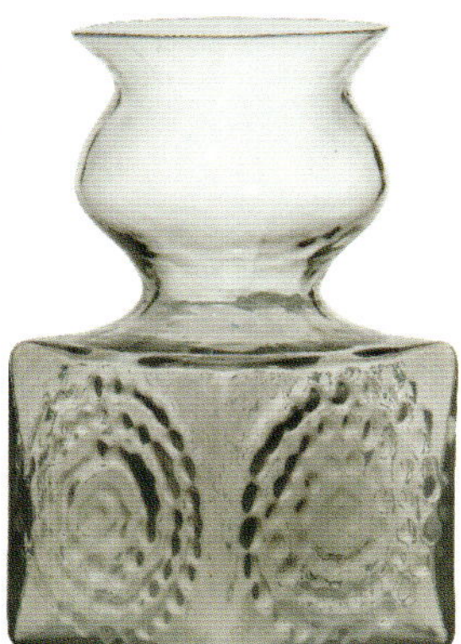

A 1970s Dartington Glass Midnight grey FT62 'hyacinth vase', designed by Frank Thrower in 1968.

6in (15cm) high

£20-30 **GC**

A Dartington Glass Kingfisher blue FT2 posy vase, designed by Frank Thrower in 1967.

This shape went out of production after a few years and the number was re-used for small circular paperweights.

c1970 *3.25in (8.5cm) high*

£20-25 **RET**

A Dartington Glass cobalt blue FT58 'Greek Key' small vase, designed by Frank Thrower in 1968.

This popular shape was produced in cobalt blue glass for only six months in 1994.

5.5in (14cm) high

£80-120 **GC**

A very rare Dartington Glass mould blown Smokey 'Candy Jar', no.FT223 designed by Frank Thrower in 1979.

This vase was part of a range manufactured at Woods Brothers near Barnsley for Dartington Glass. The range was only available for six months, with only a single shipment being delivered. Colours included Amber, Green, Smokey and Jet. Smokey and Jet are the rarest colours.

11in (28cm) high

£50-70 **PC**

A CLOSER LOOK AT A DARTINGTON GLASS VASE

These are known by collectors as 'Stig' vases as they were developed by Thrower with Dartington's master glassmaker Stig Peterssen.

Peterssen was also reputedly one of the few glassmakers skilled enough to roll the lip tightly over.

These are rare as they were only made for two years. They were also produced in a lower, wider shape numbered FT75.

Produced in Kingfisher blue, Midnight grey and colourless, the rarest colour of all is Flame red – an example may fetch over £500.

A Dartington Glass Kingfisher blue large FT76 'Polo Neck' vase, with hand-rolled rim.

1968-70 *9in (23cm) high*

£250-350 **GC**

An extremely rare Dartington Glass Kingfisher blue FT85 decanter, designed by Frank Thrower in 1968.

The Kingfisher blue colour is the rarest colour for this shape – most are found in colourless or the scarcer Midnight grey glass.

1968-70 *10.25in (26cm) high*

£180-220 **GC**

A Wedgwood Crystal Midnight grey FJT15 'Marcel' decanter, by Frank Thrower in 1982.

1982-87 *13.5in (34cm) high*

£40-60 **RET**

A pair of Dartington Glass pressed glass FT137 avocado dishes in a later box, designed by Frank Thrower in 1971.

These were promoted as 'Avocado Pair', showing Thrower and his team's gentle sense of humour. They also demonstrated Thrower's skill at creating products that mirrored fashions of the day – avocados were an exotic dinner party favourite of the 1970s.

5.5in (14cm) wide

£15-25 **RET**

QUICK REFERENCE - GALLÉ

Emile Gallé founded a glass decorating workshop in Nancy, France, in 1873. In 1874, he took over his father's glass and ceramics business and began producing his own designs, which won gold medals when exhibited at the International Exposition in Paris in 1878. His love of nature can be seen in his high quality floral and foliate designs which became the epitomy of the Art Nouveau style. The popularity of his work expanded, leading him to produce commercial cameo designs from 1899, which were made using acid-etched techniques. Gallé died in 1904, and from then a star was added next to his signature until 1914. The factory closed in 1936.

A tall Gallé cameo glass vase, with amber nasturtium over a graduated yellow to amber and clear ground, signed 'Gallé' on body.

18in (46cm) high

£1,200-1,800 DRA

A Gallé cameo glass solifleur vase, purple overlay with wisteria flowers, cameo signature.

8.75in (22cm) high

£600-800 WW

A Gallé carved crystal Jack-in-the-Pulpit vase, etched 'Modèle et Decor Deposés Cristallerie Emile Gallé Nancy'.

13.25in (33.5cm) high

£1,200-1,500 DRA

An Emile Gallé vase, of colourless glass, with all-round opaque yellow and pink overlay decoration, etched five times, showing wisteria in bloom, relief-engraved 'Gallé' with three dots on side.

1904 *13.5in (34.5cm) high*

£3,500-4,500 WKA

A Gallé cameo glass vase, with blue and purple dogwood blossoms on a frosted blue and yellow mottled ground, minor burst to rim.

10.75in (27.5cm) high

£1,200-1,800 DRA

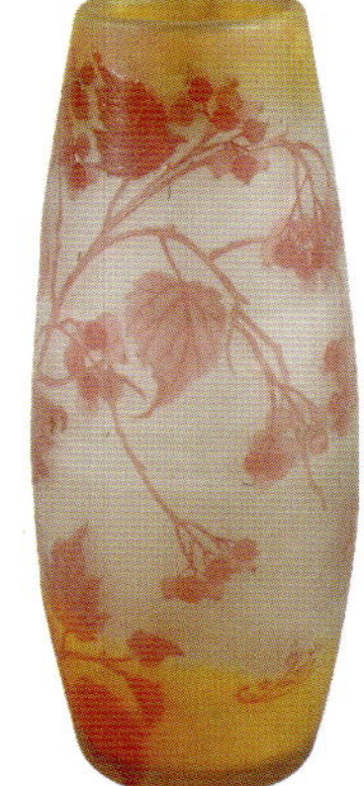

A tall post-1904 Gallé cameo glass barrel vase, yellow tinted with pink berried branches, signed 'Gallé' and with a star, small chip to foot.

12.25in (31cm) high

£500-700 DN

QUICK REFERENCE

- Founded in Zealand, Denmark in 1825, Holmegaard initially produced bottles and other functional pieces. Early designers included Oluf Jensen and Orla Juul Nielsen, whose designs for tableware were exhibited at the 1925 Paris Exposition. However, it was the work of three designers who changed the company's fortunes.
- The first, Jacob Bang (1899-1965) joined Holmegaard in 1927, and was partly inspired by Nielsen's designs. His designs were predominantly period Modernist and austere in style with minimal surface decoration. Bang left Holmegaard in 1941 to design ceramics, but returned to glass in 1957 when he joined Kastrup, Holmegaard's sister company.
- The second was Per Lütken (1916-98), whose designs are the focus of many collectors today. Recruited from art school in 1942, Lütken is known for his asymmetric, organic and flowing designs from the 1950s. Curving bud-like or teardrop forms with heavy walls in grey or blue are typical of his work. Many of his designs are signed with a PL monogram, and dates were included up until 1962.
- In contrast to these, Lütken also designed the Carnaby range, which has a strong 'Pop Art' plastic appearance. This is similar to the 'Palet' range designed by the third key designer, Michael Bang (b1944), son of Jacob. Also popular are the 'Gulvvase' bottles, designed by Otto Brauer.
- The Kastrup factory was founded in 1847 to augment production at Holmegaard, and had a sister factory at Odense. In 1873, Kastrup was sold, but was merged with Holmegaard again in 1965. Generically, all pieces are known to collectors as 'Holmegaard'. Demand and prices for smaller and more common pieces have remained static, but unique pieces by the Bangs and designers other than Lütken may rise as more information is uncovered.

A Danish Kastrup Holmegaard 'Gulvvase', no. 540021, with transparent red cased opaque white body, designed by Otto Brauer in 1962.

Cased examples with opaque white interiors are the most desirable and valuable versions – red in particular. Transparent colours include cobalt blue, brown and olive green.

1965-80 *17in (43cm) high*

£180-220 QU

A 1970s English Cascade Glass kingfisher blue bottle, after Otto Brauer's 1962 Gulvvase.

This design was produced during the late 1970s. Cascade Glass can be identified by colour – this blue, colourless, pewter grey and smokey topaz.

10in (25.5cm) high

£10-15 M20C

A Danish Kastrup cobalt blue mid-size Gulvvase no.40230, designed by Otto Brauer in 1962.

12in (30.5cm) high

£50-70 M20C

A 1960s Danish Kastrup Glas blue bottle vase, from the Capri series designed by Jacob Bang in 1961, with original label.

6in (15cm) high

£30-50 ZI

A Danish Kastrup 'Capri' blue bottle vase, with applied prunt impressed 'JB', designed by Jacob Bang in 1961, catalogue number 32652.

8.75in (22cm) high

£50-70 ZI

A Danish Kastrup vase from the 'Antik Grøn' series, with applied prunt with impressed head, design no.32708 by Jacob Bang in 1964.

1964-70 *6in (15cm) high*

£50-70 **ZI**

A Danish Kastrup-Holmegaard candleholder from the 'Napoli' series, designed by Michael Bang in 1969.

1969-71 *4in (10cm) high*

£40-60 **ZI**

A 1960s Danish Holmegaard Majgron (May-Green) vase, no.46022, designed by Per Lütken, the base with inscribed factory marks.

11.5in (29cm) high

£40-60 **GC**

QUICK REFERENCE – KASTRUP

This design is often incorrectly attributed to Per Lütken and described as a 'Duckling' or 'Naebvase' (Beak vase). The designer of this piece is not known and, like the vase to the right, it is typical of a number of 'generic' vases produced by the company in response to popular tastes. This particular design can be found with this model number in the 1960 Kastrup catalogue, and was discontinued in 1965 after the company's merger with Holmegaard.

A Danish Holmegaard torpedo-shaped mould blown vase from the Grønland series, catalogue no.17706, designed by Per Lütken in 1960, the base signed 'Holmegaard 1961 PL'.

1961-64 *9.75in (24.5cm) high*

£70-90 **ZI**

A Danish Kastrup cased blue large 'Orchidevase', shape no.32003, with internal controlled spiral of bubbles, designed by an unknown designer.

c1954-65 *12.5in (32cm) high*

£50-80 **M20C**

A Danish Kastrup small double cased swung-out vase, with opaque opal glass sandwiched between two layers of transparent sapphire blue, by an unknown designer.

c1960 *9in (23cm) high*

£50-80 **ZI**

A Danish Holmegaard light green 'Duckling' vase, cat. no. 14405, by Per Lütken in 1952, base signed 'Holmegaard 1954 PL'.

Produced from 1950 into the 1970s, these are wrongly called 'Naebvase' (Beak vases), which was a Danish nickname. Available in a range of sizes, colours include colourless, smoke grey and light green.

1954 *8in (20cm) high*

£30-50 **ZI**

A CLOSER LOOK AT A HOLMEGAARD VASE

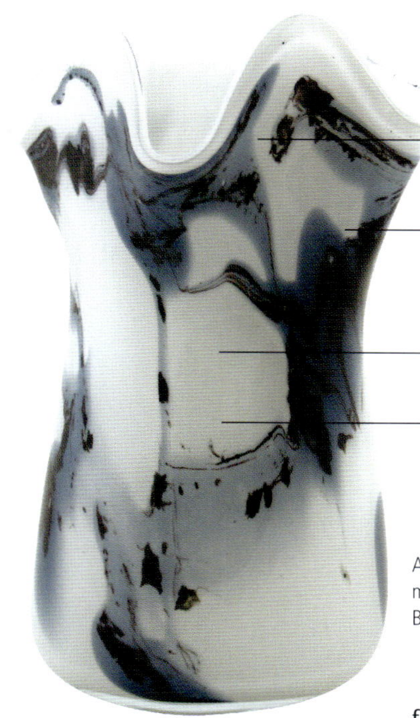

This is a protype piece produced during the development of the 'Atlantis' range.

It was produced when the designer Michael Bang was discussing his ideas for the range with master glassblower Emanuel Anderson.

As it is freeblown with random patterning, it is unique – such early protoype examples are higly desirable.

These colours went on to be included in the 'Atlantis' factory production range.

A Danish Holmegaard free-blown test-piece vase made by Emanuel Andersen, designed by Michael Bang and Emanuel Andersen c1981.

8.25in (21cm) high

£300-350 **ZI**

A Danish Kastrup Holmegaard unique, free-blown abstract vase or sculpture, form no.2386, designed by Per Lütken for an exhibition in November 1970, the foot signed 'Holmegaard 2386 PL'.

1970 *18.75in (47.5cm) high*

£800-1,200 **ZI**

A Danish Holmegaard colourless cased green orchid vase, from the 'Flamingo' series, catalogue no.16028, designed by Per Lütken in 1956, the base inscribed 'Holmegaard 1958 PL'.

1958 *6.25in (16cm) high*

£80-£120 **ZI**

A 1960s Danish Kastrup Natblå (Night Blue) mould blown vase, catalogue no.32315, designed by Jacob Bang in 1959.

9in (23cm) high

£50-80 **ZI**

A Danish Holmegaard Sapphire blue large folded vase, designed by Per Lütken in 1955, the base signed 'Holmegaard 1955 PL'.

1955 8.25in (21cm) high

£150-200 **ZI**

QUICK REFERENCE - CARNABY & PALET

There is much confusion over which brightly coloured opaque cased glass forms are from the 'Carnaby' and 'Palet' ranges, and which are by Holmegaard. Many examples attributed to Holmegaard are in fact by German factories such as Hirschberg or Friedrich. The 'Carnaby' range comprises only 16 shapes, which are vases, except for one pitcher (shown on this page), whilst the 'Palet' range is an extensive set of tablewares. Rims on 'Carnaby' pieces are not machine-cut, but are rounded. Values for 'Palet' vary widely, and depend on condition. As it was made to be used, it is often damaged or stained, meaning value is reduced.

A 1970s Kastrup-Holmegaard Coral Opal vase from the Carnaby series, designed by Per Lütken in 1969, catalogue no.341 10 94.

1969-76 *4in (10cm) high*

£50-80 **ZI**

A 1970s Kastrup-Holmegaard Coral Opal ball vase from the Carnaby series, catalogue no.56 03 16, designed by Per Lütken in 1969.

1969-76 *5.25in (13.5cm) high*

£80-120 **ZI**

A 1970s Danish Kastrup-Holmegaard Yellow Opal vase from the Carnaby series, catalogue no.341 10 67, designed by Per Lütken in 1969.

1969-76 *5in (12.5cm) high*

£50-80 **ZI**

A 1970s Danish Kastrup-Holmegaard Yellow Opal 120cl pitcher from the Palet series, catalogue no. 331 24 02, designed by Michael Bang in 1970.

The yellow colourway was introduced to the series in 1971.

8in (20.5cm) high

£50-70 **ZI**

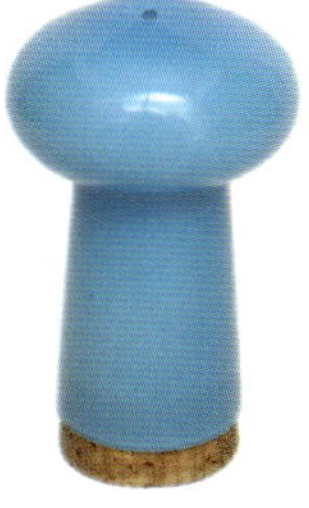

A 1970s Kastrup-Holmegaard Opal Blue sugar shaker, no. 392183, with cork stopper, designed by Michael Bang in 1970.

The use of a large cork stops the contents from falling out and also acts as a cushioned base for the thin glass body.

1970-75 *5.5in (14cm) high*

£40-60 **UCT**

A 1970s Kastrup-Holmegaard Jade Grøn 2.2ltr Cheese Jar from the Palet series, catalogue no.351 26 32, with applied prunt impressed 'OST', designed by Michael Bang in 1970.

6in (15cm) high

£150-200 **ZI**

A 1970s Kastrup-Holmegaard Blue Opal pitcher, from the Carnaby series, designed by Per Lütken in 1969, catalogue no.39 13 00.

8in (20.5cm) high

£80-120 **ZI**

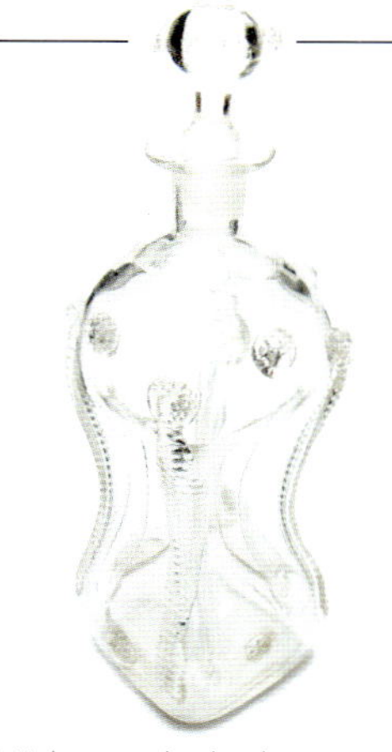

A Holmegaard colourless 'Klukflaske' or 'Kuttrolf' decanter, with applied vines and rosettes, catalogue no.186, designed by an unknown designer.

c1900 *11in (28cm) high*

£80-120 **ZI**

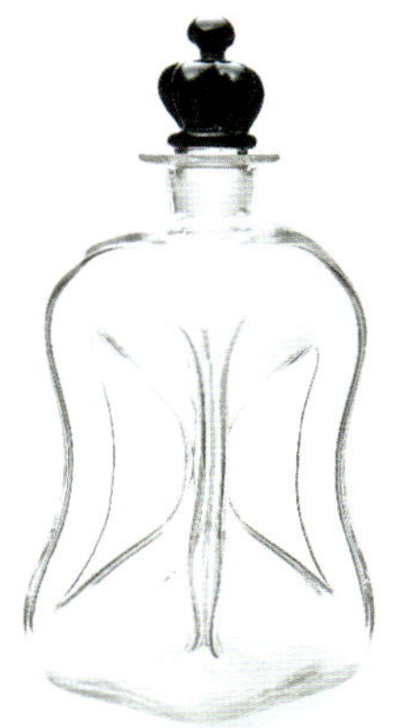

A Danish Holmegaard colourless 'Klukflaske' or 'Kuttrolf' decanter from the Viol series, with black crown-shaped stopper, designed by Jacob Bang in 1938.

10in (25cm) high

£50-80 **ZI**

A CLOSER LOOK AT A HOLMEGAARD DECANTER

The crown-shaped stopper indicates that this was from the 'Viol' series.

It is based on the traditional German 'kluk kluk' decanter made for centuries and so-named due to the glugging noise it makes when pouring.

With its crimped form, it is very practical to grip and handle. It can also be found with blue or colourless bodies.

Legend has it that the leaning 'drunken' form and crown hinted at an alcoholic Swedish king.

A 1950s-70s Danish Holmegaard Smoke grey 'tired' Klukflaske decanter from the Viol series, with crown-shaped knop, based on a design by Jacob Bang from 1928.

10in (25cm) high

£30-40 **ZI**

A 1990s Danish Holmegaard decanter, designed by Michael Bang, from the 'Amateur Schnappsmaker' series, with screen-printed 'Prunus spinosa L' sloe berry decoration designed by Finn Clausen in 1989, catalogue no.4 240 005.

1989-2005 *6.5in (16.5cm) high*

£20-30 **ZI**

A Holmegaard 'Skaal' decanter and matching shot glasses, with handpainted sailor motif and 'Skaal' wording, catalogue no.M256, designed by Jacob Bang in 1937.

'Skaal!' is Danish for 'Cheers!' This schnapps set was also available with other hand-painted designs and finishes, including sandblasting.

1937-57 *7.75in (19.5cm) high*

£100-150 **ZI**

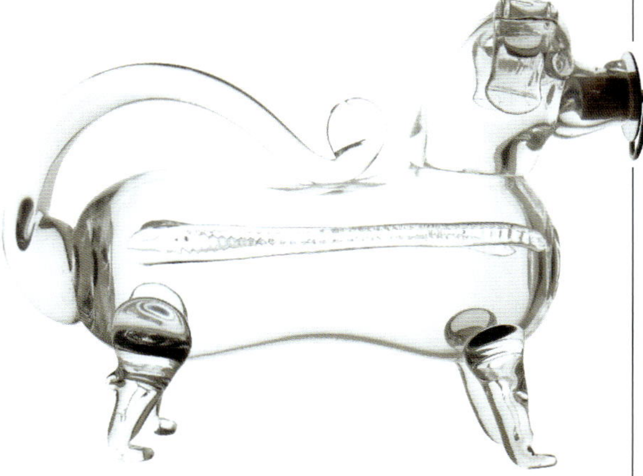

A Danish Holmegaard 'Fyldehund' or 'Snapsehund' decanter, in the form of a dog, with stoppered nose and tail handle, marked 'HG7'.

With its origins in the late 19thC, Holmegaard produced this form during the 1920s, reviving it again in the mid-1970s.

1977 *9in (23cm) long*

£60-90 **ZI**

A Danish Kastrup pitcher from the Grøn Series, designed by Jacob Bang in 1960, catalogue no.7178.

This form was also available with a bamboo wrapping (cat. no. 7278). These examples are harder to find intact as the bamboo often becomes loose and damaged. When intact, these usually fetch a little more.

9.75in (24.5cm) high

£40-60 **ZI**

A CLOSER LOOK AT A HOLMEGAARD DECANTER

The impressed viking's head seal indicates this was made for Danish wine company Torben Anton. Other seals can be found; a CE under a crown for Cherry Elsinore, and with the logo of British wine merchants Stowells of Chelsea.

A taller blue version was also produced in 1955 – both have a hand-finished rim giving the effect that each is hand-blown.

The glasses are harder to find than the decanter.

A 1960s Danish Holmegaard 'Viking' mould blown decanter with hand-finished rim, and four matching glasses, designed by Ole Winther.

1962-70 *9in (23cm) high*

£25-35 **M20C**

One of a set of six Holmegaard 'Labrador' grey sherry glasses, 'Atlantic' range, by Per Lütken, 1962.

'Labrador' was a favourite colour of of Lütken's from the 1950s.

4.25in (11cm) high

£30-50 SET **ZI**

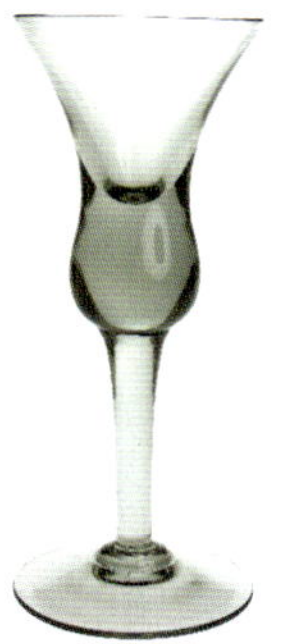

One of a set of six Holmegaard Smoke grey Dutch Cordial glasses.

Available in delgrun (Dark Green), Smoke (grey), clear and violet. Frequently found with klukflaskes on the secondary market, but they were not originally sold combined as sets.

c1958 *5.75in (14.5cm) high*

£30-50 SET **ZI**

A 1950s Danish Holmegaard cordial or schnapps glass from the Mercur series, designed by Per Lütken in 1948.

2in (5cm) high

£50-80 FOR A SET OF SIX **ZI**

A Danish Holmegaard blue-green sugar bowl and creamer from the 'Baltica' series, catalogue no.s 19765 and 19764 respectively.

The Mocca creamer set is available in blue-green, cobalt blue, ruby and clear glass.

Largest 2.75in (7cm) high

£30-50 PAIR **ZI**

A Danish Holmegaard Sapphire blue mould-blown goblet-shaped vase, from the Saphir series, catalogue no.18163, designed by Per Lütken c1960, the base marked 'Holmegaard 18163 PL'.

3.5in (9cm) high

£40-60 **ZI**

A Danish Holmegaard Smoke grey ashtray, with pulled rim, catalogue no.16517, designed by Per Lütken c1960, the base inscribed 'Holmegaard 1962 PL'.

1962 *6in (15cm) long*

£30-50 **ZI**

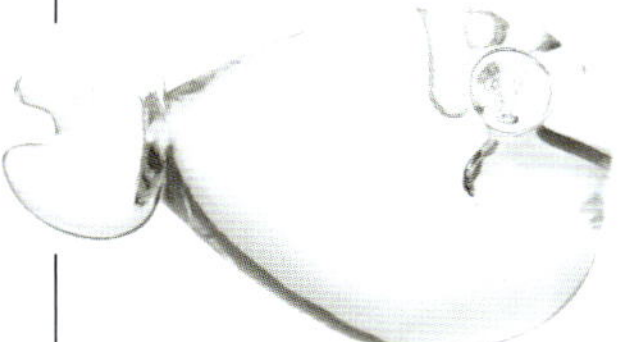

A Danish Kastrup-Holmegaard 24% lead crystal fish sculpture, catalogue no.341 45 06, designed by Michael Bang c1974, marked 'HG5 MB'.

1975 *3.5in (9cm) long*

£30-50 **ZI**

A Danish Kastrup-Holmegaard furnace-worked bowl with random scalloped rim and knobbles, catalogue no.620719, from the Rosalin series, designed by Christer Holmgren in 1968, the base inscribed 'Holmegaard C. 620719'.

5.75in (14.5cm) diam

£40-60 **ZI**

An early 1970s Danish Kastrup-Holmegaard novelty bird figurine.

Sold as novelties through the shop in large quantities, these can be identified as Holmegaard by the colours used.

2.5in (6cm) high

£30-50 **ZI**

A Danish Kastrup-Holmegaard Smoke grey suncatcher with probably unique impressed abstract patterns, created using tools and objects in the factory.

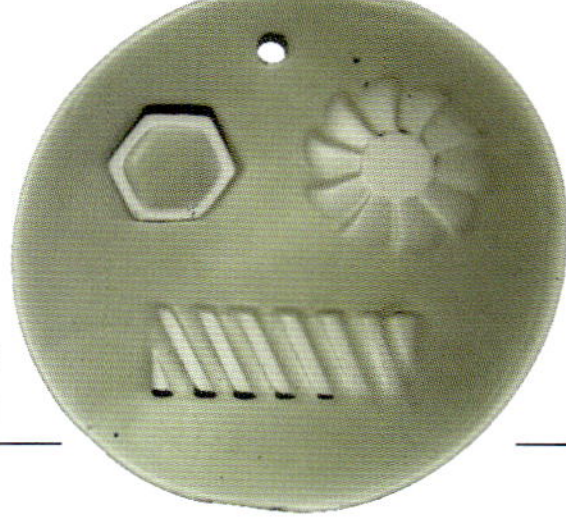

c1970 *4.75in (12cm) diam*

£20-30 **ZI**

A Holmegaard bottle or decanter from the 'Apotekerflasker' series, with transfer printed design, marked 'HG80'.

Each year from 1975-99, Holmegaard produced a limited production copy of an late 18thC apothecary bottle from the Thisted Apotek (now Svane Apoteket) in Denmark. Each piece is marked 'HG for Holmegaard, followed by two digits for the year. As commissioned objects, they were not sold through Holmegaard's distributors.

1980 *6.5in (16.5cm) high*

£50-70 **ZI**

FIND OUT MORE...

www.holmegaardresource.com - *an independent online resource to vintage designs.*

www.glashistoriskselskab.dk - *Danish site providing a useful visual resource.*

QUICK REFERENCE - LALIQUE

René Lalique (1860-1945) began his career designing and making jewellery in the 1880s, turning to glass through perfume bottles he designed for Coty around 1906. By 1918, success led him to buy and to move into larger premises, where he designed quintessentially Art Deco style vases, bowls, lamps and perfume bottles using the mass-production techniques of pressing and moulding. Despite using these techniques, quality was high and Lalique's products were expensive. Over 150 designs were produced from 1920-30, with motifs focusing on stylised natural forms, animals and nudes. Lalique died in 1945, and from then all marks comprised his surname only, without the 'R' initial. The company still produces many of his original designs today.

A René Lalique 'Dentelle' clear and frosted vase, no.943, moulded 'R. LALIQUE', with chip to one rib.

c1912 *7.5in (19cm) high*

£400-600 DRA

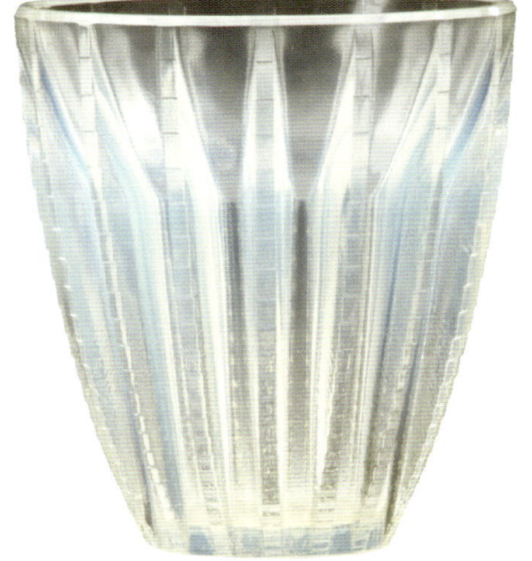

A René Lalique 'Chamonix' opalescent vase, no.1090, stencilled 'R. LALIQUE FRANCE', with small nicks to buttresses.

c1933 *6in (15cm) high*

£500-800 DRA

A René Lalique 'Domremy' green vase, no. 979, moulded with thistles, etched mark 'R Lalique France No. 979', minor rim fault.

Green is a rarer colour than the much more common opalescent.

8.5in (21.5cm) high

£1,200-1,800 TEN

A Lalique 'Domremy' opalescent glass vase, no. 979, designed by René Lalique, stencil 'R Lalique', etched 'France'.

8.75in (22cm) high

£700-1,000 WW

A René Lalique 'Grenade' dark amber vase, no.1045, the base engraved 'R. Lalique France'.

4.5in (11.5cm) high

£1,500-2,000 DRA

A Lalique 'Nymphale' deep blue glass vase, the base engraved 'Lalique France'.

8.5in (21.5cm) high

£350-550 DN

A Lalique 'Rampillon' clear, frosted and blue-stained vase, no.991, the base with stencilled 'R Lalique' signature.

5in (13cm) high

£700-1,000 **WW**

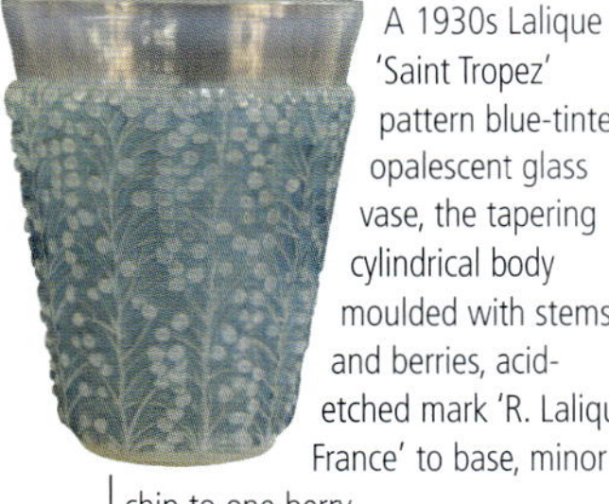

A 1930s Lalique 'Saint Tropez' pattern blue-tinted opalescent glass vase, the tapering cylindrical body moulded with stems and berries, acid-etched mark 'R. Lalique, France' to base, minor chip to one berry.

7.5in (19cm) high

£1,500-2,000 **TOV**

A CLOSER LOOK AT A LALIQUE VASE

This is a comparatively scarce design, perhaps as it was less popular at the time meaning fewer were sold.

It retains some of its white patina, which helps to highlight the moulded pattern of peppercorns.

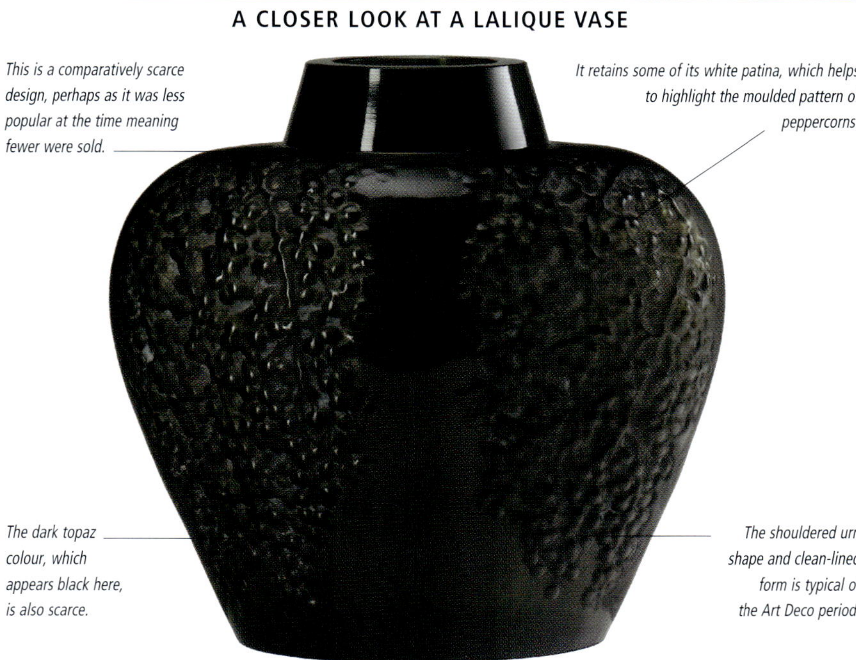

The dark topaz colour, which appears black here, is also scarce.

The shouldered urn shape and clean-lined form is typical of the Art Deco period.

A René Lalique deep topaz 'Poivre' vase, no.901, with whitish patina, the base moulded 'R. Lalique'.

c1921 *9.5in (24cm) high*

£2,000-3,000 **DRA**

A René Lalique 'Sauge' vase, no.1014, of clear and frosted glass with green patina, the base engraved 'R. Lalique'.

c1927 *9in (23cm) high*

£1,200-1,800 **DRA**

A René Lalique 'Sirenes' opalescent and blue stained glass perfume atomiser, no.660, the base marked 'R Lalique', metal fittings missing.

5.5in (14cm) high

£800-1,200 **WW**

A Lalique blue glass decanter, the reeded body with a blue glass stopper, marked 'Lalique made in France'.

11.25in (28.5cm) high

£150-250 **SWO**

A René Lalique 'Danseuses Egyptiennes no. 1' perfume burner, for Marcas et Bardel, with orange enamel and original chromium cap, moulded 'R. Lalique FRANCE'.

c1926 *5.25in (13.5cm) high*

£800-1,200 **DRA**

Two René Lalique 'Perles' clear and frosted glass perfume bottles, no.602, with brown patina, and moulded marks.

c1926 *5.75in (14.5cm) high*

£400-600 **DRA**

QUICK REFERENCE

- Mdina Glass was founded on Malta in 1968 by Michael Harris, an ex-Royal College of Art glass tutor. At Mdina Harris adapted new studio glass techniques acquired in the USA in 1966 to commercial production of art glass. His designs, often shallow dishes and bottle shaped vases, were made from thick glass and in colours that evoked the sea and the beach: turquoise, tan, aqua, greens and blues. Each piece is unique, as it was handmade.
- Production was aimed at the tourist and international gift market. Typical pieces were inexpensive and small, as these were easier to transport. Although much of Mdina's success was due to the tourist industry, it was helped by export sales to the UK, USA and Germany.
- Harris left Malta in 1972 and set up a glass factory on the Isle of Wight. Early pieces were similar to Mdina, but more finely blown. In 1978, saw the introduction of the Azurene range, designed by Harris and William Walker. It featured 22ct gold and silver leaf on coloured glass bodies. It was successful and continues to be desirable. Other popular ranges are Meadow Garden, Kyoto and Golden Peacock.
- Mdina pieces have 'Mdina' inscribed on their bases. Some may have their original stickers: paper stickers were earlier than plastic ones. Isle of Wight pieces can also be identified by a signature on the base or a sticker.
- Prices are rising, though affordable. Large, unusual designs and those signed by Michael Harris are the most desirable.

A Mdina Glass large stoppered bottle, designed by Michael Harris, of cylindrical form with swollen neck and spherical stopper with internal blue green and sandy ochre swirl, the base inscribed 'Mdina'.

Note the large size of this piece. These are considerably rarer than smaller examples, and seem only to have been produced until the mid-1970s.

16.25in (41cm) high

£350-450 FLD

A 1980s Mdina Glass bottle, the mottled ochre body with randomly applied green trails, the base inscribed 'Mdina'.

8in (20cm) high

£30-40 M20C

A 1980s Mdina Glass large bottle, with ochre mottling and applied colourless trails, the base inscribed 'Mdina'.

13.5in (34cm) high

£40-60 M20C

A Mdina Glass 'Tiger' ovoid vase with flared neck, the base inscribed 'Mdina 1987'.

1987 6in (15.5cm) high

£50-70 VZ

A Mdina Glass vase, with flared rim and horizontal green trails outlined in sand brown over a colourless base with a fine network of ochre crackle lines, the base inscribed 'Mdina 1987'.

6in (15cm) high

£50-70 VZ

A 1970s Mdina Glass disc-shaped vase, with elongated neck and blue and green striated band, the base inscribed 'Mdina'.

6in (15.5cm) high

£50-70 GC

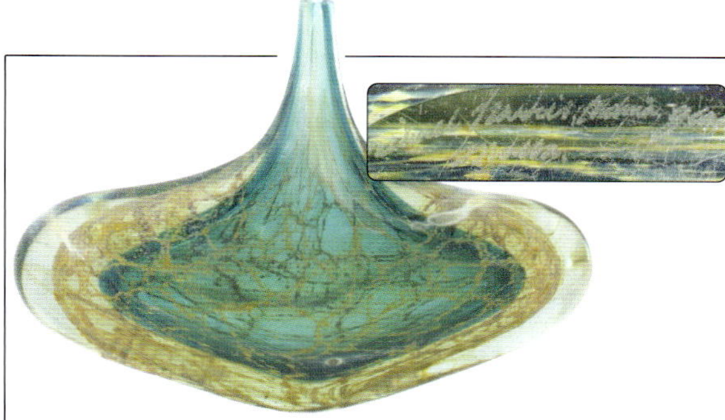

An extremely rare Mdina Glass 'Crizzle Stone', designed, made and signed by Michael Harris, with iridescent streak of silver chloride around the body, the base signed 'Michael Harris Mdina Glass Malta'.

Derived from his iconic 'Fish' vases, these are the rarest and most complex forms produced by Michael Harris at Mdina. See p.233 ' Miller's Collectables Price Guide 2009' for an example valued at £1,200-1,800 but unsigned by Harris – only two other signed examples are known.

7.5in (19cm) high

£2,800-3,400 **ART**

A large Mdina 'Cut Ice' Fish vase, designed by Michael Harris, the randomly strapped interior cased in colourless glass with two polished facets to one side.

c1971 *9in (23cm) high*

£250-350 **FLD**

A 1970s Mdina Glass 'Lollipop' vase, designed by Michael Harris, with green and blue curving forms with silver chloride colouring, cased in colourless glass, the base inscribed 'Mdina 1985', and with studio paper label.

1985 *6.75in (17cm) high*

£70-100 **VZ**

A mid-1970s Mdina 'Fish' vase, designed by Michael Harris, the purple and ochre core with silver chloride, cased in colourless glass with straps.

8.75in (22cm) high

£150-250 **FLD**

A 1980s Mdina Glass 'Fish' vase, with squared transparent blue wings over a mottled pink core, the base inscribed 'Mdina'.

7in (17.5cm) high

£40-60 **VZ**

A Mdina Glass object, comprising a 'Side Stripe' bottle vase embedded in a 'Sculpture' with green and ochre trails, the base signed 'Michael Harris Mdina Glass Malta', with annealing crack.

It is difficult to work out why this unusual and experimental piece was produced, and even more difficult to work out why it was signed by Michael Harris!

c1970 *11in (28cm) long*

£250-350 **SAS**

A Mdina Glass 'Tricorn' vase, designed by Michael Harris, with a mottled green and ochre body with silver chloride colouring, the base inscribed 'Mdina'.

c1970-74 *10.5in (27cm) diam*

£250-350 **FLD**

A Mdina Glass goblet, with blue straps applied over a mottled orange and yellow bowl, the foot engraved 'Mdina 1980'.

1980 *6.5in (16.5cm) high*

£40-50 **M20C**

A late 1970s-80s Mdina Glass random sculpture, with colourless and blue trails, the base inscribed 'Mdina'.

8.5in (21.5cm) high

£30-50 **M20C**

A CLOSER LOOK AT A MDINA GLASS BOTTLE

These are often mistaken for a Geoffrey Baxter design for Whitefriars due to the bark texture – Harris knew Baxter and had discussed the idea of a bark textured range with him around 1964.

It was made using the 'gathering on the post' technique, where the part blown neck was used to gather more glass, which was then blown into a mould to form the body.

These bottles are usually tall and thin, this wide form is very rare.

These bark textured bottles were only made from c1970, when metal moulds made in England had arrived in Malta, until c1972, when Harris left Mdina Glass.

A Mdina Glass mould blown bark textured bottle vase, designed by Michael Harris, the base with concave polished pontil mark.

c1971 *8.75in (22.5cm) high*

£150-200 **GC**

An Isle of Wight Studio Glass 'Tortoiseshell' low bottle vase, designed, made and signed by Michael Harris, the base with 'coachbolt' pontil mark and engraved 'Michael Harris Isle of Wight England'.

Although the Tortoiseshell range was produced from 1973-c82, the presence of a plain, concave 'coachbolt' pontil mark identifies this as coming from 1973.

1973 *6in (15cm) diam*

£180-220 **FLD**

An Isle of Wight Studio Glass 'Tortoiseshell' bell vase, designed by Michael Harris, with impressed 'flame' pontil mark to base and black triangular studio sticker.

c1978-80 *8in (20.5cm) high*

£120-180 **VZ**

An Isle of Wight Studio Glass 'Pink Azurene' cylinder vase, the mottled pink body overlaid with silver and 22ct gold leaf, the base engraved 'Michael Harris ENGLAND 11/500'.

This 'limited edition' style of signature shows that it was made for export to US department stores, such as JC Penney.

11.5in (29cm) high

£300-400 **FLD**

QUICK REFERENCE

- Glass has made on Murano since the 13thC, when glassmakers moved from Venice to protect the wealthy city from furnace fires. For centuries, traditional glass-making techniques were handed down through families and though design underwent a radical transformation in the 1950s, these historic techniques were simply used in new, innovative ways. Colours became brighter and exuberant, while forms became more abstract and sculptural. New designers were invited to the island and by the end of the decade the new movement was in full swing.
- The most desirable and valuable pieces are the work of influential designers, such as Paolo Venini, Fulvio Bianconi, Flavio Poli, Ercole Barovier and Dino Martens. As well as the designer, the factory is important. Notable factories include Venini (founded 1921), Seguso Vetri D'Arte (1933-92), Barovier & Toso (founded 1942) and A.V.E.M (founded 1932). Landmark designs include Dino Martens's 'Oriente', Flavio Poli's Sommerso, and Venini's 'fazzoletto' vases.
- Many pieces are not signed, so check reference books to help you identify the work of these factories and designers. Original labels will also help with identification, though these have usually been removed. Successful designs were widely copied or imitated by other designers and glass factories, so it is also advisable to study as many identified examples as you can, to get a feel for authentic pieces.
- Consider the technique used – the more visually appealing and complex it is, the more desirable your piece is likely to be. For example, with sommerso designs, brightly coloured, well-balanced forms with clearly demarcated layers are usually desirable. Bear in mind that the market is wider and often more affordable away from major designers, with some pieces available for £20.

A Seguso Vetri d'Arte sommerso glass vase, designed by Flavio Poli, with graduated pink/red core, covered with layer of green and yellow glass and an outer layer of colourless glass.

c1965 *14in (35.5cm) high*

£1,800-2,200 DOR

A Seguso Vetri D'Arte sommerso torpedo shaped vase, designed by Flavio Poli, the light green core overlaid with an ice blue layer also forming the base, with factory label to base.

c1960 *17.5in (44.5cm) high*

£800-1,200 VZ

A Seguso Vetri D'Arte sommerso glass vase, no.12024, with a brown core covered with a heavily ribbed honey yellow casing.

c1970 *12.75in (32cm) high*

£400-600 VZ

A Seguso Vetri D'Arte sommerso glass vase, designed by Flavio Poli, the tapering cylindrical green core cased in bright yellow, with heavy base.

c1960 *11.25in (28.5cm) high*

£300-500 GC

A Seguso Vetri D'Arte sommerso bottle vase with cylindrical neck, designed by Flavio Poli, the purple core covered with a light violet layer.

c1960 *10in (25.5cm) high*

£800-1,200 VZ

A Seguso Vetri D'Arte sommerso vase, designed by Flavio Poli, the ovoid form triple cased in green, blue, red and colourless glass.

c1955 *7in (18cm) high*

£600-800 **QU**

A Seguso Vetri D'Arte sommerso vase, designed by Flavio Poli, of flattened conical form, the base of the blue core cased in a layer or pinky-red and with an outer layer of colourless glass.

c1958 *10.75in (27.5cm) high*

£800-1,200 **VZ**

A CLOSER LOOK AT A SEGUSO VASE

Appointed design director at Seguso in 1934, Poli went on to revolutionise the company's designs and became a key designer on post-war Murano.

The purity of the curving form and vivid colour is typical of his work at this time, and became enormously influential.

The elliptical form and slit opening that is almost like a mussel, indicates this was from Poli's celebrated 'Valva' (valve) range.

This range won grand prizes at the 1950 Biennale and the 1951 Triennale, and his sommerso designs won a Golden Compass award in 1954.

A Seguso Vetri D'Arte 'Valva' vase, designed by Flavio Poli, the light turquoise-blue core overlaid with two layers of different tones of violet glass, with outer colourless layer.

c1952 *9.75in (24.5cm) high*

£3,500-4,500 **VZ**

A Seguso Vetri D'Arte sommerso bowl, the pink core cased with a layer of yellow and with a thick colourless outer layer, with pulled rim.

c1950 *13.75in (35cm) high*

£300-500 **DOR**

A Seguso Vetri D'Arte sommerso bowl, the green core with yellow and orange casing, and a colourless outer layer, with asymmetrically pulled and curled rim.

c1950 *11.5in (29cm) high*

£1,200-1,800 **DOR**

A Seguso Vetri D'Arte textured light blue glass cubic paperweight, in the form of an ice block, with manufacturer's model number label reading '54461'.

c1978 *3.5in (9cm) high*

£250-300 **VZ**

A Barovier & Tcso 'Crepuscolo' lampbase, the shaped clear glass body with iron wool inclusions, the applied foot and rings with gold foil inclusions, designed by Ercole Barovier.

c1950 *13.5in (34cm) high*

£400-600 **QU**

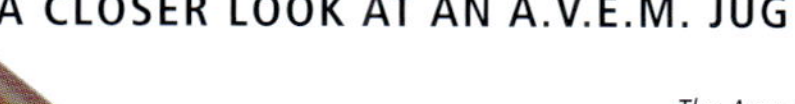

A CLOSER LOOK AT AN A.V.E.M. JUG

The Ansa Volante range of jugs was exhibited at the 1952 Biennale exhibition in Venice, and the asymmetric form is a typical feature.

The term means 'flying handle', referring to the integral handle and dynamic form wih its sweeping lines – some have two handles.

The range was produced in red or green glass, both with an iridescent surface created by 'fuming' the piece in metallic salts.

A scarcer variation also included randomly placed aventurine filament inclusions.

An A.V.E.M. 'Ansa Volante' jug vase, designed by Giorgio Ferro in 1952, the organic, pulled deep red glass with a heavily iridised surface.

Ferro worked for A.V.E.M. from 1951-55 before leaving for Ferro Galliano.

13in (33cm) high

£800-1,200 **VZ**

A Barovier & Toso 'Neolitico' bowl, bands of trapped air bubbles and dark brown trails combed into columns, designed by Ercole Barovier.

The pattern is created by applying trails which are melted into the body and then 'combed' with tools in a similar way to Art Nouveau glass designs by Louis Comfort Tiffany.

1954 *10.5in (26.5cm) diam*

£800-1,200 **QU**

A Cenedese sommerso glass vase, the graduated blue and yellow core with layers of yellow, light blue and colourless glass.

c1950 *23in (60cm) h*

£1,000-1,500 **DOR**

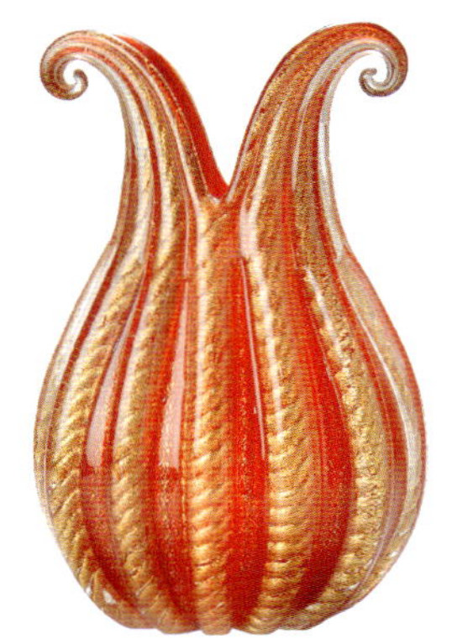

A Barovier & Toso 'Cordonato Oro' ovoid vase with pulled and curled rim, designed by Ercole Barovier, the red core with gold foil inclusions, covered with a colourless layer of ribbed glass, the ribs containing rope-twist effect gold foil inclusions, the base with factory label.

This range was shown by Barovier & Toso in the 1950 Biennale in Venice, and is a fusion between modern and traditional techniques and styles.

1950 *11.25in (28cm) high*

£450-550 **VZ**

A Cenedese sommerso vase, designed by Antonia da Ros, with cylindrical and flared neck and yellow casing over a blue core, the base inscribed 'Cenedese'.

c1968 *8.75in (22cm) high*

£700-1,000 **VZ**

QUICK REFERENCE - MURRINES

A murrine is the term given to a small glass tile cut from a rod containing a pattern, typically in the form of a flower (for example a millefiori, or 'a thousand flowers'), lines, or other motifs. These are arranged in a pattern like a mosaic on a glassblower's table, and the part-blown hot glass body is rolled over them, picking them up. The whole is then inserted in the furnace, all the parts are melted together and the body finally blown into shape. The technique dates back to the Roman era, but in the post-war period it was revised and updated. Vittorio Ferro (b.1932) is one of the leading modern exponents of the style, and was the maestro at Fratelli Toso until the 1980s. Following his 'retirement', he continued to design and produce his individual style of murrines at the De Majo and Fratelli Pagnin factories. The brightly coloured, black-lined murrines and almost iridescent effect are hallmarks of his style, which is increasingly popular with collectors and looks to be a good bet for the future.

A De Majo 'Estate' baluster vase, designed and made by Vittorio Ferro, with grey and green murrines with internal black iridised veins, and red 'rose' murrines, the base inscribed 'Vittorio Ferro 1998'.

10.75in (27cm) high

£800-1,200 **VZ**

A Cenedese sommerso cylindrical vase, designed by Antonia da Ros, with cylindrical and flared neck and yellow casing over a green core, the base inscribed 'Cenedese'.

c1968 *12.5in (32cm) high*

£1,200-1,800 **VZ**

An Alberto Donà vase, of flattened ovoid form with pulled, curving neck, with yellow and turquoise green vertical stripes covered with a layer of colourless glass, the surface cut with shallow slices, the base signed 'Alberto Donà Murano 1993'.

1993 *19.5in (49.5cm) high*

£1,200-1,800 **VZ**

A Carlo Moretti ruby red glass vase, of double conical form, with applied rectangular shards of colourless glass with white stripes.

c1970 *6.5in (16.5cm) high*

£550-650 **DOR**

A 1950s Pustetto Zanetti 'Arte Nuova' sommerso glass vase, probably designed by Aldo Fuga, with green, yellow and colourless layers, with factory foil label.

The Arte Nuova glassworks was founded in 1954 by Itamo Pustetto and Mario Fuga and known for its sommerso designs, many by Pustetto and Nino D' Este. Designs by Aldo Fuga were acclaimed at the Brussels Exposition 1958. It closed in the mid-1960s. Works are often misattributed to Seguso.

11.75in (30cm) high

£400-600 **DOR**

A Fratelli Toso vase, the colourless glass body covered with stylised flower murrines with white metals and orange centres, designed by Ermanno Toso, with applied orange rim.

c1960 *6.75in (17cm) high*

£1,000-1,500 **VZ**

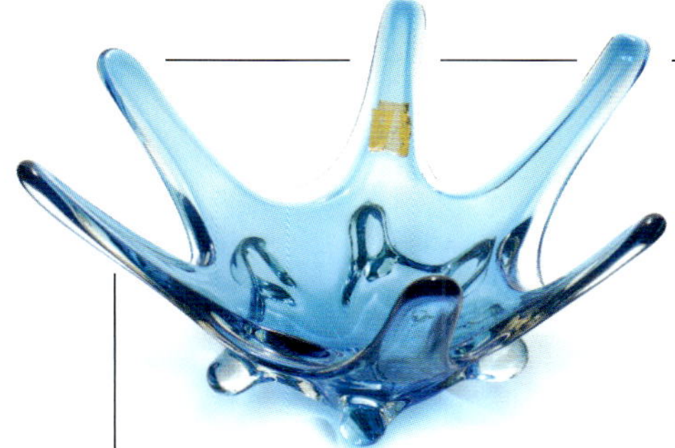

A 1950s-60s Fratelli Toso large cased blue 'splash' vase, with pulled arms and nodules, with 'MURANO CHAMBORD' gold foil label.

Chambord was a trade name used by Fratelli Toso, whose name appears at the bottom of the (usually) shield-shaped label, which is damaged on this example.

17in (43cm) diam

£120-180 GC

A Venini & C. 'Corroso' amber glass vase, in the form of a double-handled urn, with acid-etched textured surface, the base with three line 'venini murano italia' acid stamp.

The surface of this vase is treated with acid to give a mottled, lightly textured surface.

c1940 *9.75in (24.5cm) h*

£800-1,200 VZ

A scarce Venini & C. 'Foglia' leaf-shaped bowl, designed by Tyra Lundgren, the colourless glass with blue stripes, and iridescent surface, the base with 'venini murano MADE IN ITALY' three line mark.

Swedish glass designer Lundgren produced a number of prize-winning designs for Venini shortly before the war, which were exhibited in both Murano and Sweden.

c1938 *8.8in (22cm) long*

£1,200-1,800 VZ

A Venini & C. 'corroso' bowl, designed by Carlo Scarpa, of clear and turquoise-blue cased glass, with frosted exterior.

Corroso indicates a lightly textured matt exterior treated with acid.

c1940 *7.8in (19.5cm) wide*

£200-250 VZ

A Venini & C 'Tuuli' bottle, designed by Timo Sarpaneva, with opaque yellow and black bands, and black stopper, the base inscribed 'venini 90 Sarpaneva'.

This 'Tuuli' range was created using the complex and challenging 'incalmo' technique, where separate gathers of different glass were blown to precise sizes and joined together while hot. The austerity of design is typical of Sarpaneva's Finnish aesthetic.

1990 *12.25in (31cm) high*

£1,000-1,500 VZ

A Venini & C. 'Tuuli' bowl, designed by Timo Sarpaneva in 1988, the cylindrical form with applied opaque red and dark violet bands, with light violet tinted central band, the base inscribed 'venini 91 Sarpaneva'.

1991 *5.25in (13.cm) high*

£800-1,200 VZ

A Vittorio Zuffi & C. murrine vase, the urn-shaped colourless body with applied green handles and alternating columns of green star murrines and colourless glass with heavy aventurine inclusions.

c1895 *5.25in (13cm) high*

£400-500 QU

QUICK REFERENCE - MEMPHIS AND MURANO

Eccentric and geometric forms in bright colours are typical of the Postmodern style promoted by the Memphis group in the 1980s. Although other designers and artists contributed to the group, Ettore Sottsass is considered their notional leader. Complex to make, and as much a piece of decorative sulpture as a functional form, each component of this bowl was separately blown before being joined together. Compagnia Vetreria Muranese produced Memphis glass designs from 1982 until c1992, becoming known as Toso Vetri D'Arte from 1982-90. Examples can be quite scarce as these were never mass-produced or inexpensive, and may be a good tip for the future if the style is re-appraised by more design collectors.

A Compagnia Vetreria Muranese 'Sol' bowl, designed by Ettore Sottsass for Memphis in 1982, comprised of transparent red, blue and green components, with an opaque lining, the base inscribed 'E. SOTTSASS PER MEMPHIS by COMPAGNIA VETRERIA MURANESE'.

8.5in (21.5cm) high

£1,000-1,500 **VZ**

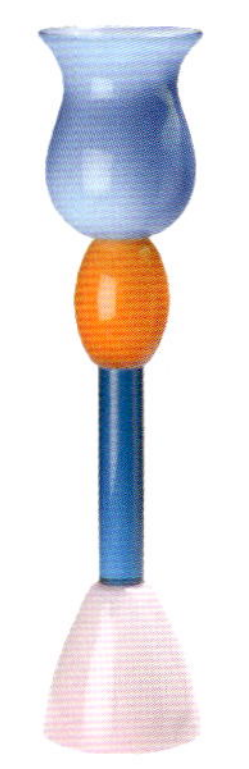

A Compagnia Vetreria Murano for Memphis 'Erinna' vase, designed by Ettore Sottsass, with pink, blue and orange components, the base inscribed 'E. SOTTSASS PER MEMPHIS'.

1986 *19in (48cm) high*

£1,000-1,500 **VZ**

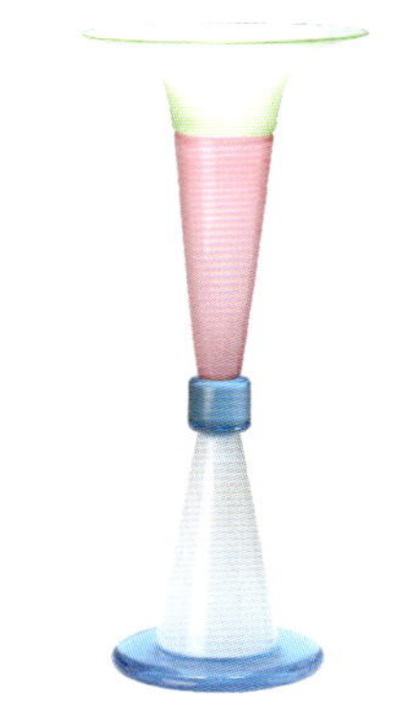

A Compagnia Vetreria Muranese 'Pasifila' glass vase, designed by Ettore Sottsass in 1986, comprised of cone forms in blue, translucent white, pink and opal green, the base inscribed 'E.SOTTSASS PER MEMPHIS'.

18.25in (46cm) high

£1,000-1,500 **VZ**

A Vistosi limited edition 'Pink Cigar' table centrepiece, designed by Peter Shire, the asymmetric form comprised of blue, black (dark violet), pink and yellow geometric forms, the base inscribed 'PETER SHIRE X VISTOSI 2/4'.

c1985 *16.5in (42cm) high*

£1,000-1,500 **VZ**

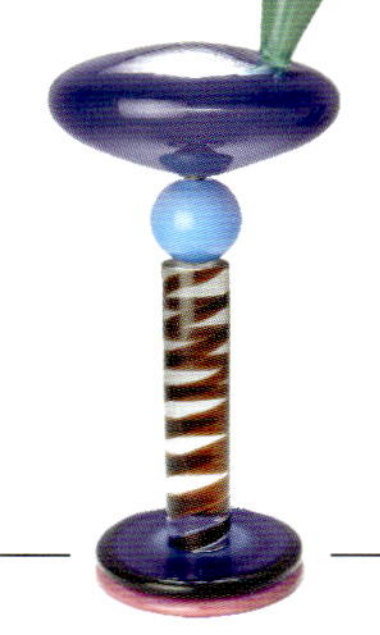

A Vistosi limited edition table centrepiece, designed by Peter Shire, with green conical and light and dark blue disc and spherical forms on a colourless column with a brown spiralling trail, the base inscirbed 'PETER SHIRE X VISTOSI 4/6'.

c1985 *24in (61cm) high*

£800-1,200 **VZ**

A Vistosi 'Faleria' limited edition lidded jar, designed by Ettore Sottsass in 1980, the yellow body with green hemispherical lid and lined in black, the base engraved 'E.SOTTSASS 150-250 VISTOSI'.

c1981 10.75in (27cm) high

£2,500-3,500 **QU**

A 1950s-60s Murano glass yellow cased red 'sommerso' bottle, with attenuated neck and remains of foil label to neck.

The elongated neck of this bottle, shouldered body and vibrant colours suggest Seguso as a maker. However, this cannot be confirmed by the label despite the quality being suitably high. The interior of the neck has also not been ground to hold a stopper.

14.25in (36cm) high

£80-120 **RET**

A 1960s Murano glass yellow cased brown vase with colourless outer layer, elongated neck and winged body.

7.25in (18.5cm) high

£22-28 **RET**

A 1960s Murano 'sommerso' glass green cased red vase, with elongated neck and colourless outer casing.

17in (43cm) high

£60-80 **RET**

A 1960s Murano glass yellow cased green 'sommerso' vase with outer colourless casing, pulled rim and winged body.

These forms are often misattributed to Flavio Poli. A company called 'Turca' produced similar forms, and their link with Poli has not been confirmed.

11in (27.5cm) high

£65-75 **RET**

A 1960s Murano glass red and yellow cased bowl with curved and pulled rim.

13.5in (34cm) high

£45-55 **RET**

A 1960s Murano 'sommerso' glass yellow cased red bowl, with cut and pulled rim and 'MURANO MADE IN ITALY' red and silver foil label.

Similarly coloured circular foil labels with the same wording and scalloped edging can be attributed to Seguso during the 1950s.

11.25in (27cm) high

£45-55 **RET**

A 1950s-60s Murano sommerso glass yellow cased green bowl, with wavy and pulled rim.

12.5in (31.5cm) wide

£20-30 **RET**

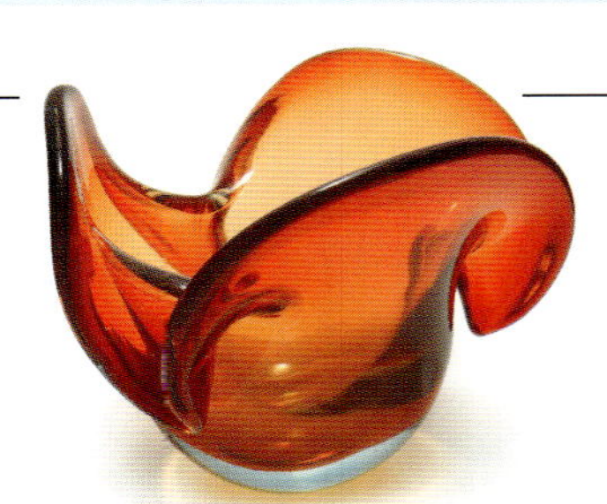

A 1960s-70s Murano glass colourless cased orange-red heat sensitive glass bowl with pulled rim.

Here, a special chemical has been added to the glass so that it changes colour from orange to deep red when reheated in the furnace. The blue casing is unusual, as it would usually be colourless.

6in (15cm) diam

£30-40 **RET**

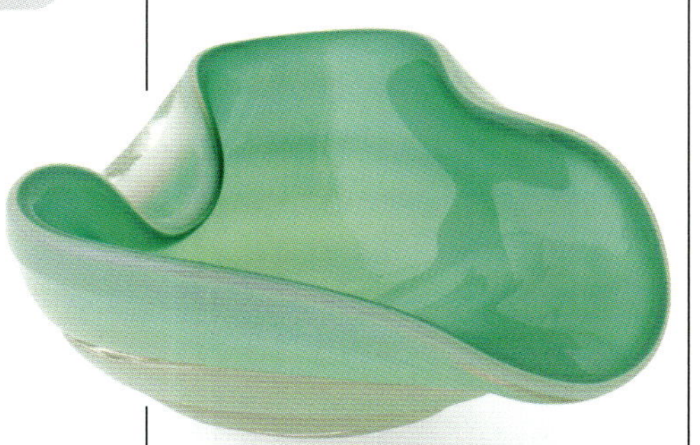

A 1950s-60s Murano glass green 'Opaline' ashtray, with pulled and folded rim.

7.25in (18cm) high

£30-50 **MHT**

A 1960s Murano sommerso glass yellow cased green oval bow , with pinched thick rim.

These heavily rendered, vibrantly coloured bowls are sometimes known as 'geode' bowls after the geological rock forms containing crystal-lined cavities.

7.25in (18.5cm) high

£30-40 **RET**

A 1960s Murano glass sommerso bowl with a red core, a layer of controlled bubbles and aventurine inclusions, cased with green tinged clear glass with pulled wings.

4.5in (11.5cm) diam

£30-40 **RET**

A 1960s Murano glass aqua green ashtray with colourless casing and pulled lobes.

9in (23cm) diam

£20-25 **RET**

A 1950s-70s Murano glass cased green and yellow ashtray, with pulled rim and network of controlled internal bubbles.

6.75in (17cm) diam

£10-15 **M20C**

A Murano glass dish, the graduated violet and colourless glass with applied cobalt blue abstract splash motif, and heavy colourless base.

The designer and maker of this bowl remain unknown. Some collectors have attributed it to Czechoslovakia, although this has not been confirmed and a Muranese origin is more likely. Regardless, it would have been very complex and hard to make.

c1960 *6.75in (17cm) diam*

£120-180 **QU**

A 1960s Murano glass yellow tinted cased red 'sommerso' bowl, cut with facets, the base cut with a hobnail pattern.

5.25in (13cm) wide

£35-45 **RET**

A 1960s-70s Murano 'sommerso' glass green and blue faceted ashtray, the outer layer tinged with violet.

5.25in (13cm) wide

£30-50 **TGM**

A 1970s Murano glass cylinder vase, the gracuated blue to colourless body overlaid with multicoloured star murrines, unmarked.

9.25in (23.5cm) high

£300-500 **QU**

A Murano glass cylinder vase, the colourless body with graduated violet, yellow and purple bands.

c1965 *9.5in (24cm) high*

£300-500 **QU**

A Murano glass footed vase, the conical form with cylindrical neck and flared rim overlaid with multicoloured millefiori murrines.

c1910 *5.5in (14cm) high*

£300-400 **QU**

A small Murano glass teardrop shaped vase, the colourless glass overlaid with columns of zanfirico canes and multicoloured ribbon twist canes, unmarked.

5.5in (14cm) high

£100-150 **QU**

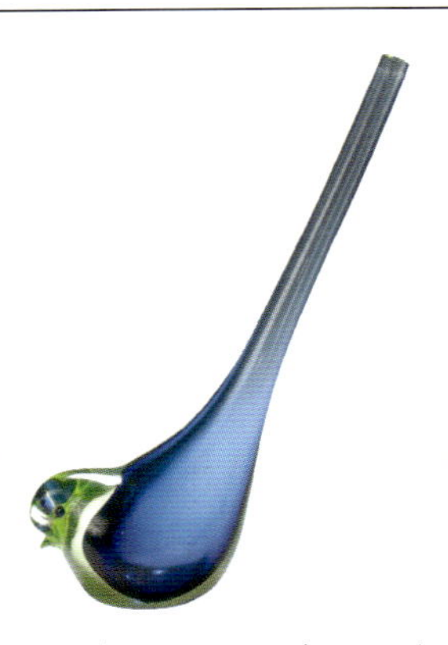

A Cenedese sommerso glass vase in the form of a bird, the tail forming the vase, designed by Antonia da Ros, the blue core covered with a layer of colourless glass and an outer layer of green glass.

c1961 *10.75in (27cm) high*

£80-120 **VZ**

A 1960s Murano glass bird with applied and hot-worked features, on a spiralling base containing aventurine inclusions.

17.25in (44cm) high

£40-60 **RET**

A 1950s-60s Murano glass sommerso bird, the red core cased with uranium glass, unsigned.

Although unsigned, the way the tail and beak are handled is indicative of Seguso.

6in (15cm) long

£20-30 **TGM**

A Seguso Vetri d'Arte yellow glass cockerel, designed by Flavio Poli.

7in (18cm) wide

£1,000-1,500 **DOR**

QUICK REFERENCE - MURANO GLASS ANIMALS

An entire zoo of glass animals has been produced on Murano since the 1950s. Although leading designers and factories produced examples, the many smaller factories produced their own versions copied from, or inspired by, the works of the masters. There is an enormous gap in values, with most copies or pieces by smaller factories being worth under £150, and usually under £80. The work of a master can fetch many thousands. The key is to study original factory catalogues and books, and identify items by their shape and colour. The work of leading factories is also very well executed, sometimes using complex techniques that require skill, experience and time. Size can also indicate a finer quality piece. This fish is a good example. Antonio da Ros joined Cenedese in 1958, where he was encouraged to experiment by Gino Cenedese. His early works were thickly blown, with simple forms. He explored colour by using one or two colours in different tones, usually in different internal layers.

A Cenedese sommerso glass fish, designed by by Antonio Da Ros, with cobalt blue core overlaid with dark violet and light blue layers.

1962 *6in (15cm) wide*

£600-800 **DOR**

A Cenedese sommerso glass fish, designed by Antonio Da Ros, the multi-layered deep rose pink core overlaid with light blue glass, with a rose pink tail and a matching light blue cube pedestal.

1965-66 *10.5in (27cm) high*

£1,800-2,200 **DOR**

QUICK REFERENCE

- Post WWII Scandinavian glass has increased in popularity and value, as glass collectors re-evaluate its importance to 20thC glass design, due to a widening knowledge base.
- 1950s pieces were predominantly asymmetric, with curving forms and cool colours. Designers took their inspiration from natural forms. By the 1960s, this became a clean-lined, geometric, brightly coloured Modern style. Textured forms became popular and continued to be so into the 1970s.
- Both the factory and the designer are important in determining value and desirability. Factories include Orrefors, Kosta Boda and Iittala, with stylish pieces by Riihimäen Lasi Oy and Orrefors currently proving popular. Look for the work of leading designers, who influenced others and helped define the movement, such as Vicke Lindstrand, Simon Gate, Tapio Wirkkala, Sven Palmqvist, Tamara Aladin and Nanny Still. This can seem confusing, because some designers, such as Lindstrand, moved between factories, or the factories merged. Examination of the engraved marks on its base may identify the designer or, if unmarked, the designer and maker may be identified from the style, colour and way it was made.
- Investigate the secondary factories, designers or ranges that are still being researched. These include John Orwar Lake for Ekenas, Strömbergshyttan, and Erik Höglund for Boda. Now may be the time to buy, as these designers may become more collectable and valuable later.
- Consider how a piece was made and its colour, as some techniques and colours are rare. Unique vases are usually worth more than mould-blown pieces. Condition and 'eye appeal' are a major factors in determining desirability. Examine pieces for damage which detracts from the purity of colour and form that is typical of Scandinavian glass.

A mid-late 1970s Finnish Riihimäen Lasi Oy green footed waisted cylindrical vase, by an unknown designer and produced from 1976 as part of the 'Export Collection'.

10in (25cm) high

£20-30 **M20C**

A 1960s-70s Finnish Riihimaki Lasi Oy mould blown cased green tapered 'Stromboli' vase, designed by Aimo Okkolin in 1963.

7in (18cm) high

£20-30 **NPC**

A 1960s Finnish Riihimäen Lasi Oy green 'Chimney' vase, designed by Aimo Okkolin in 1960.

10in (25cm) high

£20-30 **M20C**

A mid 1960s-70s Finnish Riihimäen Lasi Oy green footed vase, with trumpet neck, by an unknown designer.

10in (25cm) high

£20-30 **M20C**

A Finnish Riihimäen Lasi Oy cased green vase, with solid, heavy foot, by an unknown designer.

4.5in (11.5cm) high

£20-30 **M20C**

A 1960s-70s Finnish Riihimäen Lasi Oy mould blown cased green vase, designed by Helena Tynell.

7in (18cm) high

£80-120 **GC**

A Finnish Riihimäen Lasi Oy cased blue large vase, with disc centre and waisted neck and base, by an unidentified designer.

10.5in (26.5cm) high

£30-50 **M20C**

A Finnish Riihimäen Lasi Oy green mould blown vase from the 'Fossil' range, designed by Helena Tynell.

8.75in (22.5cm) high

£100-150 **GC**

A Finnish Riihimäen Lasi Oy blue mould blown vase from the 'Fossil' range, designed by Helena Tynell.

In taking its inspiration from natural history rather than the drawing board and geometry set, the Fossil range is very rare.

6.25in (16cm) high

£100-150 **GC**

A Finnish Riihimäen Lasi Oy blue 'Safari' textured vase, no.1495, designed by Tamara Aladin in 1970.

Unusually for Riihimaki, this was machine blown into a mould, rather than being spun to create the textured finish. As such, a mould line appears down each side of the vase. It was produced in three sizes, of which this is the medium. Colours include green, dark blue, this blue and colourless.

10in (25cm) high

£40-50 **M20C**

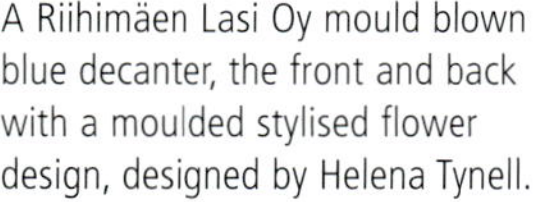

A Riihimäen Lasi Oy mould blown blue decanter, the front and back with a moulded stylised flower design, designed by Helena Tynell.

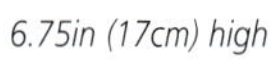

6.75in (17cm) high

£60-90 **UCT**

A Riihimäen Lasi Oy, blue mould blown 'Pala' vase, with textured surface, designed by Helena Tynell in 1964.

1964-76 *2.75in (7cm) high*

£15-18 **UCT**

A 1960s Finnish Riihimäen Lasi Oy cased yellow vase, no.1379, the design attributed to Tamara Aladin, the base with acid etched mark and engraved '1379'.

The presence of the mark indicates this was produced for the mainland European market: examples intended for the UK market are generally unmarked.

8in (20cm) high

£30-40 **M20C**

A CLOSER LOOK AT A RIIHIMAKI VASE

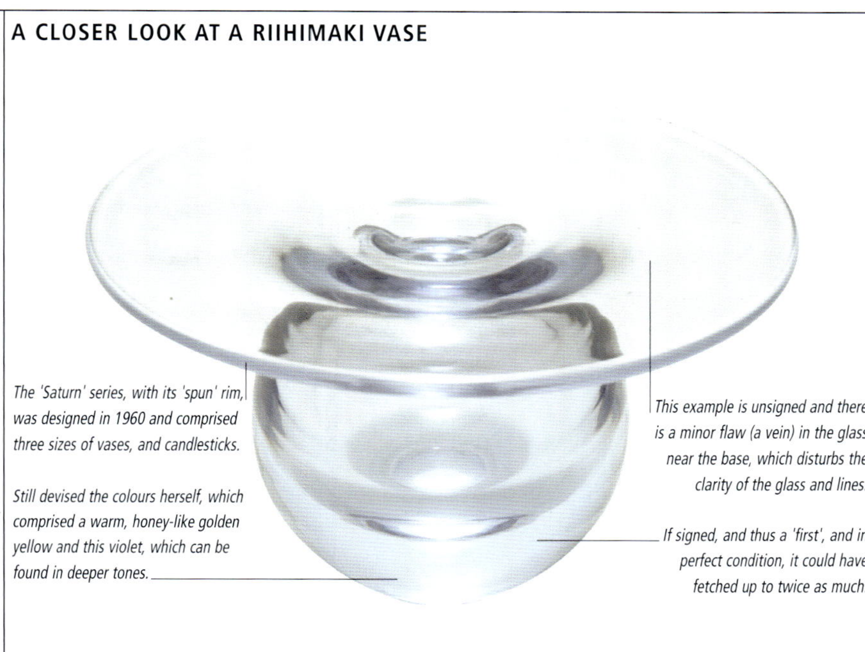

The 'Saturn' series, with its 'spun' rim, was designed in 1960 and comprised three sizes of vases, and candlesticks.

Still devised the colours herself, which comprised a warm, honey-like golden yellow and this violet, which can be found in deeper tones.

This example is unsigned and there is a minor flaw (a vein) in the glass near the base, which disturbs the clarity of the glass and lines.

If signed, and thus a 'first', and in perfect condition, it could have fetched up to twice as much.

A Finnish Riihimäen Lasi Oy 'Saturn' light violet vase, designed by Nanny Still in 1960.

3.25in (8cm) high

£50-80 **UCT**

A Finnish Riihimäen Lasi Oy yellow vase, the design attributed to Tamara Aladin.

1965-1971 *11in (28cm) high*

£40-50 **M20C**

A 1980s Finnish Riihimäen Lasi Oy red waisted and tapered vase, shape no.6012, designed by Aimo Okkolin in 1982.

10in (25cm) high

£20-30 **M20C**

A Finnish Riihimäen Lasi Oy 'Tuulikki' range red vase, designed by Tamara Aladin in 1972.

1972-76 *8in (20cm) high*

£20-25 **M20C**

GLASS

A Swedish Orrefors cut and fire-polished vase, by an unknown designer, the base inscribed 'Orrefors'.

After being cut, the body was reheated and the edges of the facets were smoothed off and rounded using a fire torch, or by inserting the piece back into the glory hole for a short time.

9in (23cm high

£80-120 **GC**

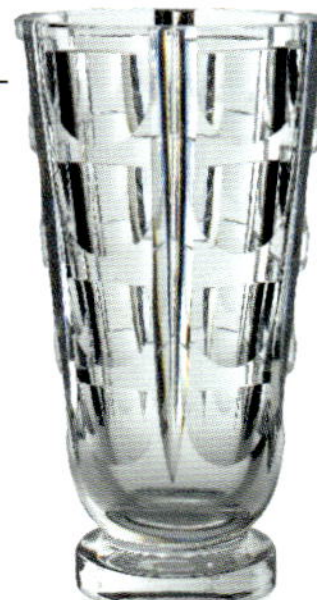

An Orrefors '1000 Windows' series glass vase, cut with semi-circular lenses, by Simon Gate, the base inscribed 'Orrefors 90895/211'.

Gate designed this Regency style pattern in 1934. Sales remained strong and this vase, modified from earlier vase shapes, was still sold by Orrefors in 2003.

7.75in (19.5cm) high

£20-30 **AEM**

A Swedish Orrefors 'Selina' opalescent bowl, designed by Sven Palmqvist from 1954, the base engraved 'Orrefors Pu XXXX'.

8in (20.5cm) diam

£80-120 **PC**

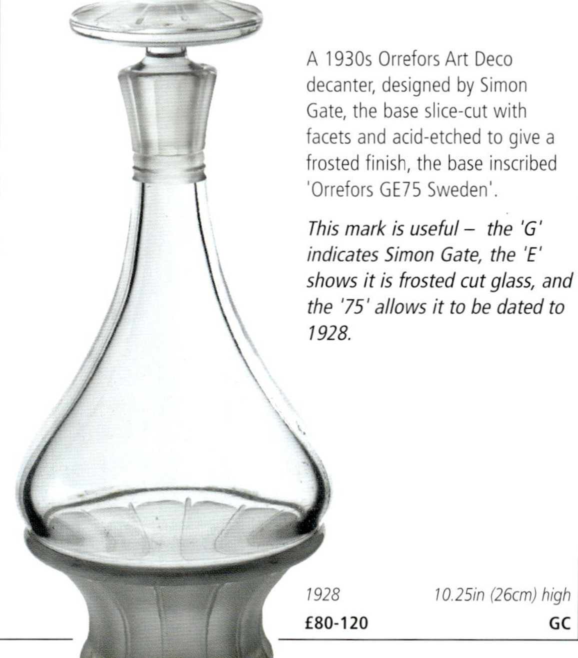

A 1930s Orrefors Art Deco decanter, designed by Simon Gate, the base slice-cut with facets and acid-etched to give a frosted finish, the base inscribed 'Orrefors GE75 Sweden'.

This mark is useful – the 'G' indicates Simon Gate, the 'E' shows it is frosted cut glass, and the '75' allows it to be dated to 1928.

1928 *10.25in (26cm) high*

£80-120 **GC**

A CLOSER LOOK AT AN ORREFORS GOBLET

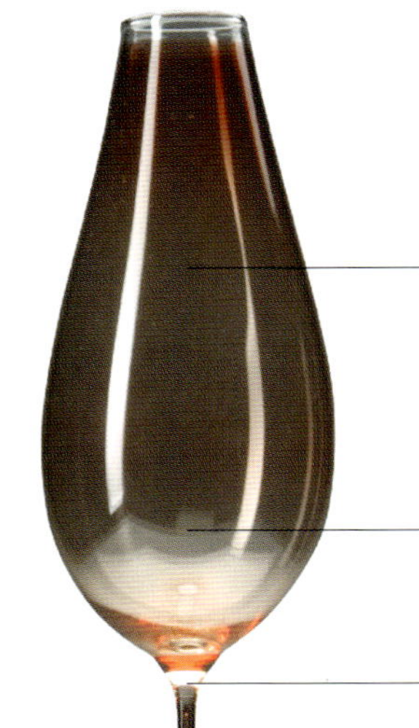

Designed in 1957, the Tulpan series won a gold medal at the important Milan Triennale exhibition in 1957, the year this piece was made. It has become an icon of Scandinavian glass design.

Tulpan is Swedish for 'tulip', the form of the flower being echoed in the gently curving bowl.

At 17in (27cm) high, the size is important – larger examples do exist, but are very rare.

This required great skill to create, particularly the regularity of the form and the hollow conical foot. Landberg is known for his elegant, classical shapes at this time.

An Orrefors ruby red 'Tulpanglass' vase, designed by Nils Landberg in 1954, the base engraved 'Orrefors Expo Nu 312-57'.

1957 *17in (43cm) high*

£1,200-1,800 **DRA**

An Orrefors colourless glass seated polar bear, the base inscribed 'Orrefors CB4354 - 1/1'.

3.75in (9cm) high

£35-40 **TGM**

A 1930s Kosta colourless optic tapering cylindrical vase, designed by Elis Bergh, with an applied black foot.

10in (25.5cm) high

£120-180 **UCT**

A 1990s Kosta Boda vase, designed by Göran Wärff, with cut panel to front, and low-relief, moulded star shape surrounded by applied powdered enamels to the reverse, the base engraved 'KOSTA 47317 WARFF', and with cellophane label.

4.5in (11.5cm) high

£70-90 **TGM**

A Kosta Boda 'October' bowl with applied enamelled trees and birds and multicoloured chips to form the flowery meadow, designed by Kjell Engmann in 1983, the base signed 'Bow 68628 K. Engmann'.

6.25in (15.5cm) high

£50-70 **TGM**

A Swedish Kosta bottle vase, with randomly applied coloured trails and chips, designed by Bertil Vallien, the base with broken pontil mark, unsigned.

9in (23cm) high

£80-100 **GC**

A 1970s-80s Kosta Boda bowl, designed by Göran Wärff in 1973, the exterior with applied purple and black enamels over a colourless base, with star and irregular shaped exclusions, the rim signed 'KOSTA 56773 WARFF'.

Five digit numbers have been used for designs from the 1970s onwards, with the last two numbers indicating the year of design rather than production of that piece. Wärff joined Orrefors from Pukeberg in 1964, before leaving to travel and teach in 1974. He returned in 1984 and still produces organic, earthy inspired designs, that accentuate the qualities of glass.

6in (15cm) diam

£70-100 **TGM**

A Kosta solifleur vase, designed by Vicke Lindstrand, of tapered cylindrical form, cased in clear over a graduated colour ground, with a single tear-shaped bubble to the base, the base with full engraved signature.

11in (28cm) high

£100-150 **FLD**

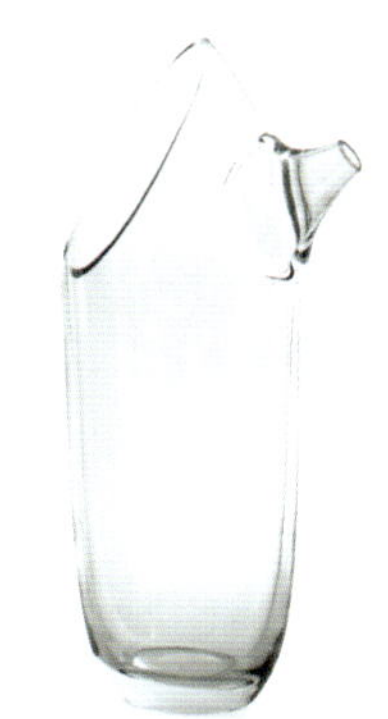

A Swedish Kosta carafe or decanter, with applied spout, designed by Vicke Lindstrand in 1959, the base inscribed 'Kosta LH1463'.

11.5in (29cm) high

£60-80 **GC**

A Swedish Flygsfors cased vase, with angled cut rim, designed by Paul Kedelv, the base inscribed 'Flygsfors 63'.

11in (28cm) high

£50-70 **RET**

A 1960s Boda orange goblet, designed by Eric Hoglund, with random internal bubbles.

6.75in (17cm) high

£30-50 **GC**

A 1960s Swedish Gullaskruf mould blown teal blue bottle vase, designed by Arthur Percy.

Percy (1886-1976) worked for Gullaskruf from 1951-70.

9.75in (24.5cm) high

£8-12 **M20C**

A Norwegian Hadeland cased olive green tapering vase, possibly designed by Willy Johansson.

6.5in (15cm) high

£20-30 **M20C**

A 1970s Hadeland ovoid vase with acid etched and sandblasted design of a little girl seated and hugging a doll, with factory foil labels, unsigned.

7.5in (19cm) high

£60-80 **GC**

A 1970s Norwegian Hadeland troll, with applied ears, nose and eyes, the base acid stamped 'Hadeland'.

3in (7.5cm) high

£22-28 **RET**

A Finnish Iittala blue 'Bird' bottle vase, shape no. i-401, from the i-line range, designed by Timo Sarpaneva in 1956.

1957-68 *6.75in (17cm) high*

£80-120 **QU**

A Finnish Nuutajarvi Nostjo cased blue footed vase, with heavy colourless foot and machine-cut rim, designed by Kaj Franck in 1962, the base inscribed 'KF Nuutajarvi Nostjo-62'.

The restrained, sombre colour and austere form with its clean lines are typical of Franck's Modernist designs.

6.25in (16cm) high

£280-320 **UCT**

A CLOSER LOOK AT A RUDA VASE

Ruda Glasbruk was based near other Swedish glass factories Orrefors and Kosta from 1910-72 - their decorative glass was always secondary to their industrial glass.

Augustsson was designer from 1947-72 and most of his designs are textured, having been blown into a mould, before being finished by hand.

This was from a range that also included tankards, jugs and other vase shapes.

'Kobolt' Blue is the most common colour found, with green (known as 'Turkos') and an amber-brown (known as 'Orient') being harder to find.

A 1960s Swedish Ruda Glasbruk mould-blown textured blue 'Kobalt' vase, designed by Göte Augustsson, with factory label, the base with polished concave pontil mark.

6.5in (16.5cm) high

£30-50 **M20C**

A 1970s Swedish Reijmyre colourless cased purple vase, with tapering neck, machine-cut rim and base moulded with concentric circles.

10in (25.5cm) high

£40-50 **UCT**

A 1960s Swedish Ruda Glasbruk mould blown textured blue 'Kobalt' bottle vase, designed by Göte Augustssen, the base with polished concave pontil mark.

8.75in (22cm) high

£30-50 **M20C**

A Swedish Skruf tapering cylindrical glass vase, by Bengt Edenfalk, cased in colourless glass with applied ribbon trail decoration, the base etched 'Edenfalk Skruf'.

This range can be found in a number of shapes and colours, including grey, brown and sage green. A vase from this range was included in an exhibition of modern glass at the Corning Glass Museum in 1959. Edenfalk (b.1924) worked for Skruf from 1953-78, leaving to produce designs for Kosta.

13in (33cm) high

£120-180 **WW**

A 1930s Strömbergshyttan brown vase with scalloped rim, the base with polished pontil mark.

These were imported into the UK by Elfverson & Co., run by H.J. Dunne Cooke. This shape, available in 6in, 8in, 10in and 12in sizes, was numbered 3055A.

8.25in (21cm) high

£60-90 **GC**

QUICK REFERENCE

- Peter Layton was born in Prague in 1937, and brought up in England. He studied ceramics at the Central School of Art and Design in London, before discovering glassblowing while teaching at the University of Iowa in the 1970s.
- Largely self-taught, he established his own glass studio at his pottery at Morar in the Highlands of Scotland, before moving to Rotherhithe in London. He went on to establish a glass department at Hornsey College of Art (Middlesex University), and founded the influential London Glassblowing Workshop in 1976.
- Layton has since played a major role in the development of studio glass in Britain. As well as mentoring many new glassmakers and designers, helping them mould their style, identity and confidence, he has offered facilities enabling them to work.
- His designs are inspired by the fluidity of molten glass, vivid colour and controlled yet asymmetric form. Nature and landscape are also influences. Pieces are typically built up using a number of layers of glass, with patterns being created with applied coloured swirls, speckles and trails.
- Smooth, rounded forms inspired by pebbles are typical, and the 'dropper bottle', with its thin, elongated neck, is a hallmark form that can be found in many of his ranges. As each piece is handmade and freeblown, each one is unique in terms of its precise form and patterning. Values depend on the size, range, colour and complexity of the design, and range from as little as £150 to over £5,000.
- Layton has also produced a number of unique, individual works for exhibitions that explore themes such as the human body, life and death. These usually incorporate other materials such a metal piping and even medical equipment. He is also known for his architectural commissions in association with Simon Moss. Layton's designs can be found in many private and public collections across the world.

A Peter Layton 'Turquoise Paradiso' stone form vase, the graduated sky blue, yellow, green and cream core with a diagonal black striped orange zig-zag, the base signed 'Peter Layton'.

2007 *6.75in (17cm) high*

£800-1,200 **GC**

A Peter Layton 'Aeriel' stone form vase, the blue core overlaid with ochre and cream swirls, and cased in colourless glass, the base signed 'Peter Layton'.

2006 *7in (18cm) high*

£300-400 **GC**

A Peter Layton 'Spirale' stone form, the spiralling burgundy and blue and yellow striped core overlaid with a colourless layer, the base signed 'Peter Layton'.

8in (20.5cm) high

£700-1,000 **GC**

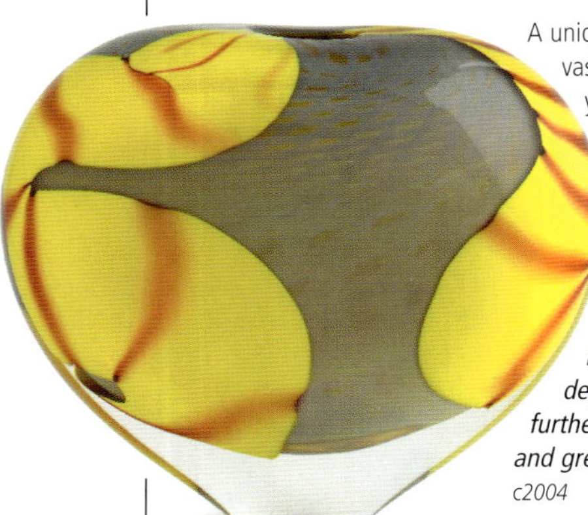

A unique Peter Layton stone form vase, the buff-grey core with a yellow grid-like pattern and applied large yellow stylised floral murrines with orange stripes, the base signed 'Peter Layton'.

The murrines have been applied to a colourless layer over the core, giving depth to the design, which is further highlighted by the yellow and grey grid pattern of the core.

c2004 *7.5in (19cm) high*

£1,000-1,500 **GC**

A Peter Layton 'Forest Floor' stone form vase, the core with applied multi-coloured chips, and cased in colourless glass, the base signed 'Peter Layton'.

2006 *7in (18cm) high*

£300-400 **GC**

A Peter Layton 'Yellow Paradiso' large flattened bottle, the base signed 'Peter Layton'.

2006 *11.25in (28.5cm) high*

£1,000-1,500 **GC**

A Peter Layton 'Turquoise Paradiso' ovoid vase, the base signed 'Peter Layton'.

c2007 *6.5in (17.5cm) high*

£800-1,000 GC

A Peter Layton 'Aurora' ovoid vase, the base signed 'Peter Layton'.

c2005 *9.5in (24cm) high*

£300-500 GC

A Peter Layton 'Kimono' ovoid vase, with matte finish, the base signed 'Peter Layton'.

1989 *8in (20.5cm) high*

£400-600 GC

A Peter Layton 'Landscape' dropper bottle, the base signed 'Peter Layton'.

1995 *9in (23cm) high*

£250-350 GC

A Peter Layton 'Ice Basket', the colourless glass cage form with acid-etched surface, the base signed 'Peter Layton'.

2003 *9in (23cm) high*

£600-800 GC

A CLOSER LOOK AT A PETER LAYTON BLOWN BASKET

This unique bowl is related to the 'Ice Basket' range, like the vase shown on the left, but colours were not used in the 'Ice Basket' range.

The random rim and trails on the body give a sense of great movement, and suggests water, or glass in a molten state.

This bowl was created by blowing a purple bubble of molten glass into a colourless 'Ice Basket' form, causing it to open up in a random manner.

Although the 'Ice Basket' range was put into production, these 'blown out' pieces were not – to date only three pieces are known.

A Peter Layton 'Blown Basket', the purple core overlaid with colourless random trails, the base signed 'Peter Layton'.

2006 *7in (17.5cm) high*

£800-1,200 GC

QUICK REFERENCE

- Studio glass is glass produced by individual glass artists working outside a factory environment. This became possible after Americans, Harvey Littleton and Dominick Labino developed a process in the early 1960s by which individuals could melt, form and blow glass. Artists could work alone, although many still chose to work in teams. The movement spread to Europe in the late 1960s-70s.
- As artists developed and shared skills, pieces became more complex and appealing. Glass began to be considered an art form and has developed into a vibrant movement, with major museums exhibiting studio glass by the 1980s.
- Be aware that with studio glass, date is not always a good indicator of value. Some early examples of styles are crude, although they do represent notable developments. Learning about key makers and styles helps with identification.
- Pieces by major names, such as Dale Chihuly and Marvin Lipofsky, already make high sums. However, works by those they taught, or those by lesser-known makers, are usually more affordable and may appreciate in value, as more people become aware of these artists and start collecting their work. Learn about your chosen artist's background, whom they studied with, and their style, to help you identify their work. Many pieces are signed but are often hard to read; others may be unsigned.
- Study how glass is made, so you can spot complex pieces, that would have been time-consuming to make and therefore expensive at the time. Such pieces may be rare today as fewer were made. Large pieces, and pieces by well-known makers may make good investments as more collectors are drawn to the area and demand rises.

A 1980s Iestyn Davies cased cylindrical vase, cut with windows containing Japanese symbols and with mottled black and white surface, applied gold and silver leaf and red trailed band, the base signed.

This heavy vase was complex to produce, and incorporates a number of hot and cold working steps including cutting and The application of gold and silver foil and hot red trails. The Japanese symbols are typical of 1980s and early 1990s fashions.

13.5in (34cm) high

£600-800 **GC**

A Glasform bowl, designed by John Ditchfield, no.1917, of compressed spherical form with a swirled tonal green to blue body, engraved to the base and with foil label.

5in (13cm) high

£150-250 **FLD**

A Glasform 'Lily pad' pebble shaped vase, designed by John Ditchfield, with applied trails and waterlily leaves and iridescent surface, the base signed 'Glasform1=8/L'.

4.25in (11cm) high

£70-100 **GAZE**

A Julia Donnelly flattened oval vase, with mottled surface of coloured chips, signed 'Julia Donnelly 1990'.

Julia Donnelly worked for Siddy Langley from 1987-2002 - pieces produced during this period are signed with her initials only.

1990 *6in (15cm) high*

£30-40 **TGM**

A Carin von Druhle tall ovoid vase, the exterior with applied random trails and strong iridescence, the base signed 'Carin von Druhle 1990'.

1990 *7in (17.5cm) high*

£80-120 **TGM**

A Robert Eickholdt studio glass vase, the cobalt blue body overlaid with fragmented silver foil, cased in clear glass and then with a layer of fragmented gold foil and a final layer of colourless glass, the base signed 'Eickholdt 1996'.

1996 *10.25in (26cm) high*

£120-180 **TGM**

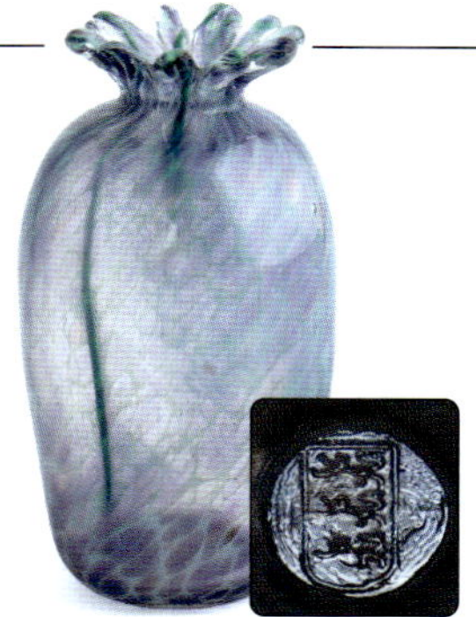

An Island Glass vase, with mottled blue and violet decoration, green trail and lobed rim, the base with impressed three lion pontil mark.

Island Glass was co-founded by Michael Harris in the early 1980s on the island of Guernsey in the Channel Islands. The mottled effects, and particularly the lobed rim, are style hallmarks.

6.75in (17cm) high

£25-30 **GC**

A CLOSER LOOK AT A SAM HERMAN VASE

Sam Herman (b.1936) is considered by many to be the father of the British studio glass movement, introducing studio glass techniques to the UK in 1966.

This is a very early piece and was made at either the Royal College of Art in London, where Herman was tutor in glass, or at the newly founded Glasshouse.

This style of applied trailing is very similar to designs produced for Herman's exhibition at the Victoria & Albert Museum, London in 1971.

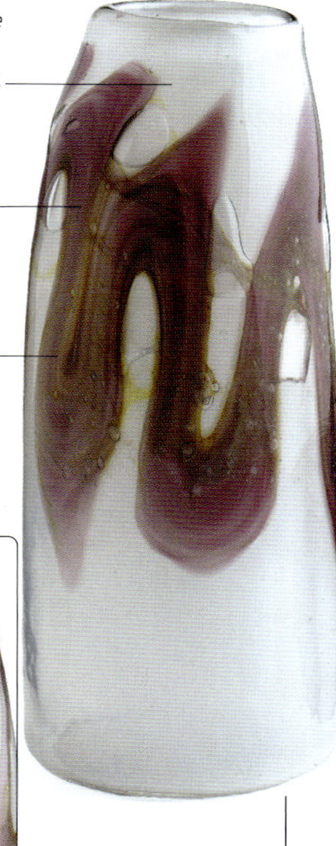

One side appears cracked, but this contains silver chloride and is completely fused, leaving just a line – it is likely that the piece cooled slightly when being made.

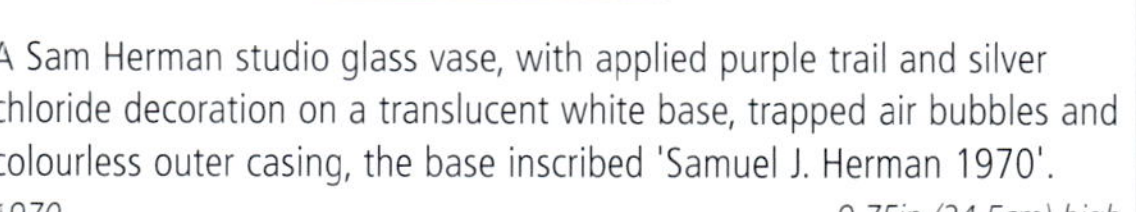

A Sam Herman studio glass vase, with applied purple trail and silver chloride decoration on a translucent white base, trapped air bubbles and colourless outer casing, the base inscribed 'Samuel J. Herman 1970'.

1970 *9.75in (24.5cm) high*

£300-400 **PC**

A Sam Herman for Val St. Lambert studio glass sculpture, with heavily cased wings, the base inscribed 'Val 212 Samuel Herman 1979'.

Herman worked at Val St Lambert over a number of years, becoming a consultant in 1990. Although he produced the designs, not all the pieces were produced by him.

1979 *15.75in (40cm) high*

£1,500-2,000 **GC**

A Sam Herman for Val St Lambert glass vase, of swollen cylindrical form with tapering shoulder, signed in script 'Samuel Herman 1979 VAL 88'.

1979 *12.25in (31cm) high*

£650-850 **L&T**

A 1970s Scottish Kirkhill Glass blue vase with random applied trails, designed and made by John Airlie, the base with broken pontil mark, unsigned.

5.5in (14cm) high

£40-60 **GC**

An Isgard Moje glass arm ring, with diagonal light blue stripes and painted with horizontal coloured bands, the rims gilded.

c1975 *2in (5cm) deep*

£300-500 **QU**

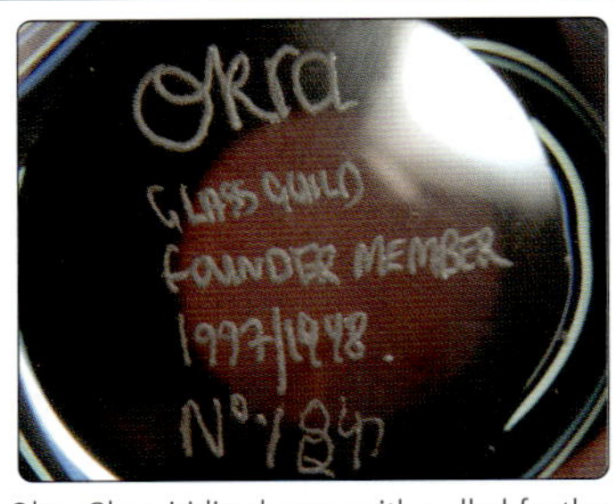

An Okra Glass iridised vase, with pulled feather pattern, the base inscribed 'Okra GLASS GUILD FOUNDER MEMBER 1997/1998 No.847'.

These vases were given by Okra Glass to founder members of the Guild collectors' club in 1997 and '98.

1997 *4.5in (11.5cm) high*

£70-100 **TGM**

A Pauline Solven glass vase, with mottled pink and green pattern, signed and dated.

Pauline Solven was part of the first wave of studio glassmakers, studying at the Royal College of Art under Michael Harris and Sam Herman. She continues to blow glass today.

1980 *6in (15cm) high*

£100-150 **SAS**

An Anthony Stern ovoid vase, the red body with an applied white stripe cased in colourless glass, the base signed 'Anthony Stern'.

c2000 *7.25in (18.5cm) high*

£70-100 **TGM**

An Anthony Stern studio glass bowl, the colourless bowl with an iridised exterior, the applied black foot signed 'Anthony Stern'.

3in (7.5cm) high

£20-30 **TGM**

An Anthony Stern studio glass bowl, the mottled translucent blue body with wide, then tight reversed spiralling design, the base signed 'Anthony Stern'.

6in (15cm) high

£50-70 **TGM**

QUICK REFERENCE - WEBB'S FLAIR RANGE

Long established Stourbridge glassmakers such as Webb (est.1802) approached post-war modern design cautiously, preferring to stick with trusted cut designs. During the late 1950s, works manager Sven Fogelburg encouraged designers to travel to the innovative Scandinavian factories, whose work was becoming increasingly popular. Following a visit in 1959, designer David Hammond and technician Stanley Eveson began to produce sculptural forms by shaping molten glass with wet pads and piercing them with a metal spike to create an aperture. Pieces were also swung and spun while molten to give dramatic winged and lobed forms. Bubbles were added using a mould, and colours cased in colourless glass. The progressive resultant 'Flair' range was produced in limited numbers and can be hard to find today, particularly in large sizes.

A 1960s Thomas Webb large 'Flair' vase, designed by David Hammond and Stan Eveson in 1961, with yellow rim and amber base with controlled internal air bubbles.

13in (33cm) high

£120-150 GC

A Thomas Webb 'Flair' cased blue tall vase, with swungout rim, the base with internal controlled air bubbles, designed by David Hammond and Stanley Eveson in 1961.

6in (15cm) high

£80-100 GC

A 1960s Thomas Webb 'Flair' small vase, designed by David Hammond and Stanley Eveson in 1961, with swung rim and green base with internal bubbles.

8in (20.5cm) high

£60-80 GC

A Thomas Webb 'Flair' cased blue oval bowl with swungout rim, the base with internal controlled air bubbles, designed by David Hammond and Stanley Eveson in 1961.

13in (33cm) wide

£80-120 GC

A 1930s Webb vase, with moulded lobes, internal green swirls and air bubbles, the base with broken pontil mark.

8in (20.5cm) high

£50-70 GC

A Thomas Webb Domino pattern cut glass vase, with alternating acid-etched frosted and clear panels, designed by David Hammond, the base with acid stamp.

10in (25.5cm) high

£200-250 GC

QUICK REFERENCE

- **Whitefriars glass has become a sought-after name in 20th century glass design on both sides of the Atlantic over the past few years. The most popular and desirable range is currently the 'Textured' range, designed by Geoffrey Baxter in 1966 and produced into the 1970s. Royal College of Art graduate Baxter, who joined the company in 1954 as designer, also contributed many other designs, many of which were inspired by Scandinavian designs.**
- **The company was founded in 1680, in London. It was originally called Powell & Sons, but as it was founded on the site of a monastery, it was more commonly known as Whitefriars. In 1923, the company moved to Wealdstone, Harrow, in North-west London, and in 1962, it took on the Whitefriars name officially. The company closed in 1980 due to competition from abroad.**
- **During the late 19thC, it produced glass in the Art Nouveau style, and glass inspired by Venetian designs. Although collected, these finely crafted designs are not currently as popular with collectors. During the 1920s and '30s, it produced fashionable art glass, some in the Art Deco style. Interest in this area has remained stable, although bargains may be found as many overlook this period.**
- **Consider the form, colour and size of pieces, as these factors affect value considerably. Some colours and shapes, and combinations of them, are rare. For example, the value of an iconic 'Drunken Bricklayer' can nearly double for a large example in an unusual colour such as Meadow Green or Kingfisher.**
- **With the textured range, look for crisp moulded details as moulds wore down over time, leaving lower levels of texture. As demand and prices have risen, fakes have begun to appear. Three of these, along with guidance on how to identify them are shown on page 260. Whitefriars enjoys a lively and stable market, particularly on the internet, and looks set to remain a collector's favourite in years to come as research uncovers more information.**

A Whitefriars cased green 'Teardrop' vase, no.9572, designed by Geoffrey Baxter in 1966.

5.5in (14cm) high

£20-30 **RET**

A Whitefriars tall cased green 'Teardrop' vase, no.9571, designed by Geoffrey Baxter in 1966.

8in (20.5cm) high

£30-40 **RET**

A Whitefriars cased Ruby red 'Teardrop' vase, no.9572, designed by Geoffrey Baxter in 1966.

5.5in (14cm) high

£20-30 **RET**

A Whitefriars Willow cased glass vase, designed by Geoffrey Baxter. in 1965.

9.75in (25cm) high

£150-250 **WW**

A Whitefriars Cinnamon cased vase, no.9651, designed by Geoffrey Baxter in 1965.

An elongated version of this form, produced at the same time, and seen on the next page, was created by swinging the molten glass and using gravity to elongate it. In this colourway, it is no. 9650.

1965-69 *9.5in 24.5cm) high*

£200-250 **GC**

A Whitefriars Willow 'Swungout' vase, no.9650, designed by Geoffrey Baxter in 1965.

This is the elongated version of the shape shown in Cinnamon on the previous page.

c1966 *15.75in (40cm) high*

£500-600 **GC**

A CLOSER LOOK AT A WHITEFRIARS VASE

Look closely at the base – this vase is made from two contrasting colours of glass, rather than the usual single colour.

The green and blue glasses used were not compatible in the furnace, meaning examples tended to crack into pieces after manufacture.

Only around five successful examples are currently known to collectors.

Another variation was the blue and pink cased 'Evening Sky', which is similarly very rare.

A very rare Whitefriars Aquamarine double colour cased vase, designed by Geoffrey Baxter in 1957.

3.75in (9.5cm) high

£700-800 **GC**

A Whitefriars Arctic Blue glass vase with cut and polished rim, no.9557, the design attributed to Geoffrey Baxter c1956.

c1957-60 *6in (15.5cm) high*

£25-35 **GC**

A Whitefriars cased Indigo blue tapering oval section ovoid vase, designed by Geoffrey Baxter in 1961.

9.75in (24.5cm) high

£50-60 **GC**

A very rare Whitefriars 'Lichen' cased vase, designed by Geoffrey Baxter.

Lichen is a rare combination of pewter and green, and was only available in 1970.

c1970 *6.75in (17cm) high*

£200-300 **GC**

A Whitefriars Arctic Blue ovoid vase, no.9495, by Geoffrey Baxter in 1957, cut rim, polished pontil.

The design features in the 1957 catalogue but Arctic Blue was introduced in 1959.

8in (20.5cm) high

£30-50 **M20C**

QUICK REFERENCE - FAKES

Over the past few years, as prices for Whitefriars' Textured range have risen, a number of fakes, produced in the Far East or Eastern Europe, have appeared. The iconic 'Drunken Bricklayer' was the first, but others from the range are now being made. These fakes can be identified from a number of features that differ from those on authentic examples. These features comprise colour, texture, the pontil mark, and the general feel and appearance. The glass used for most fakes has an almost waxy feel, and the colourless casing is different, not being as well balanced or executed as on authentic examples. The next page features authentic examples of the 'Drunken Bricklayer' and 'Hoop' vases.

The colours are wrong – colours of fakes currently comprise red, green, cobalt blue and a strong amber. In cases where Whitefriars used these colours, the fakes are the wrong tone.

There is a moulded long, shallow trench on the top of the bottom brick – this does not appear on originals.

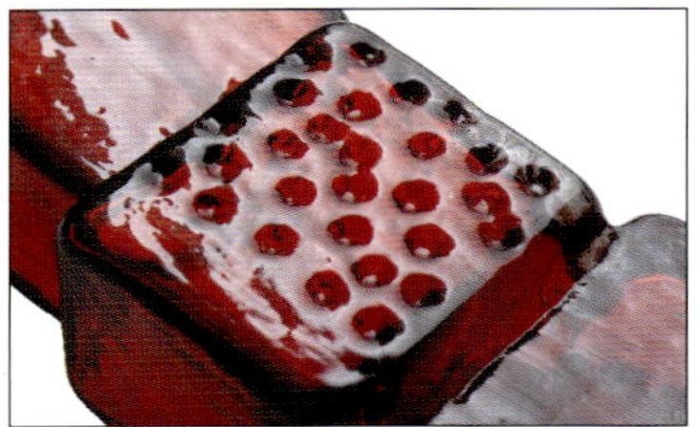

The middle brick has more dimples (28) than authentic examples, and they are also in a different formation.

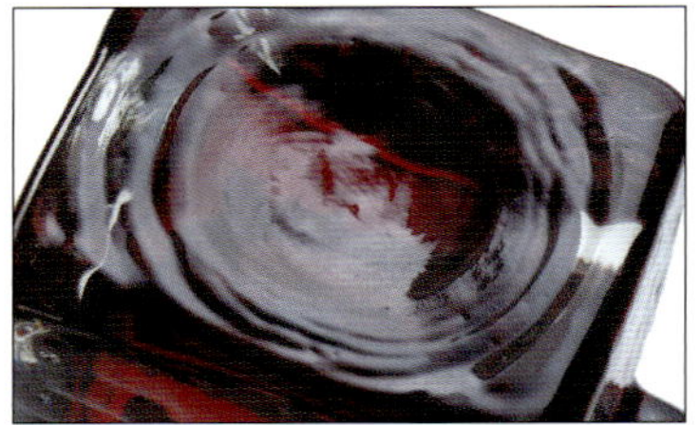

The concave pontil mark is a part of the moulded design, rather than being polished out by a machine as with authentic examples.

A modern fake Whitefriars cased Ruby red 'Drunken Bricklayer' vase, copied from pattern no.9673 designed by Geoffrey Baxter in 1966.

c2008 *8.25in (21cm) high*

£15-20 **GC**

A fake Whitefriars cased red 'Onion' vase, copied from pattern no.9758 designed by Geoffrey Baxter in 1972.

This vase was not originally produced in this colour, the polished pontil mark is a part of the moulded design, and the textured design is smoother and less detailed than on originals.

c2008 *5.5in (14cm) high*

£8-12 **GC**

A fake Whitefriars cased Ruby red 'Hoop' vase, copied from pattern no.9680, designed by Geoffrey Baxter in 1966.

Of all the identified Whitefriars fakes, this is the perhaps the easiest to spot as the textured pattern is completely different to the original. The red tone is also wrong, and this shape was never made in red.

12in (30.5cm) high

£20-30 **GC**

A Whitefriars Willow 'Totem' vase, no.9671 from the 'Textured' range designed by Geoffrey Baxter in 1966.

1967-72 *10.25in (26cm) high*

£120-180 **FLD**

A Whitefriars Willow 'Cucumber' vase, no.9679 from the 'Textured' range designed by Geoffrey Baxter in 1967.

1967-73 *12in (30.5cm) high*

£120-180 **RET**

A Whitefriars Tangerine 'Hoop' vase, no.9680 from the 'Textured' range designed by Geoffrey Baxter in 1966.

1967-73 11.5in (29.5cm) high

£200-250 **WW**

A Whitefriars Tangerine 'Drunken Bricklayer' vase, no.9672 from the 'Textured' range designed by Geoffrey Baxter in 1966.

1967-74 *8.25in (21cm) high*

£200-300 **WW**

A Whitefriars cased Cinnamon brown 'Bark' vase, pattern no.9691 from the 'Textured' range designed by Geoffrey Baxter in 1966.

1966-69 *7.75in (18.5cm) high*

£60-80 **M20C**

A Whitefriars cased Kingfisher blue 'Bottle' vase, pattern no. 9730 from the 'Textured' range, designed by Geoffrey Baxter in 1969.

1969-72 *8in (20.5cm) high*

£50-70 **M20C**

A Whitefriars Aubergine 'Stitched Square' vase, no.9811, from the 'Late Textured' range, designed by Geoffrey Baxter in 1972.

6in (15cm) high

£120-160 **GC**

A Whitefriars Sea Green vase with applied band of swags, pattern no.9004, designed by William Wilson in 1938, the base with broken pontil mark.

7.25in (18.5cm) high

£60-80 GC

A late 1920s-30s Whitefriars green and blue 'Cloudy' glass vase, no.8608, with white and air bubble inclusions, cased in clear glass.

9in (23cm) high

£280-320 WW

A 1930s Whitefriars vase, the Sea Green body overlaid with blue applied threads, no.8894, designed by Barnaby Powell in 1938.

9in (23cm) high

£200-300 GC

An extremely rare Whitefriars Ruby red eight-lobed 'Tricorn' vase, no.9570 designed by Geoffrey Baxter in 1961.

As its name suggests, these vases usually have three lobes. Only one or two examples with more than three lobes have been found, and were probably prototypes.

1962-78 8in (20.5cm) high

£80-100 GC

A Whitefriars Ruby red three-cornered bowl, no.9588 designed by Geoffrey Baxter.

1964-70 9.5in (24cm) widest

£35-50 RET

A Whitefriars flared vase, with a Tangerine swirl applied on a Pewter grey body, no.9708 designed by Geoffrey Baxter in 1969.

1969-71 8in (20.5cm) high

£50-70 MHC

A Whitefriars 'Antique' baluster vase, with blue, brown and purple random streaks, no.9784, designed by Geoffrey Baxter.

c1972 7in (18cm) high

£80-120 GC

FIND OUT MORE...

Lesley Jackson, Whitefriars Glass: Art of James Powell & Sons *Richard Dennis, 1996*

Wendy Evan, Catherine Ross and Alex Werner, Whitefriars Glass: *James Powell & Sons of London, Art Books International, 1996*

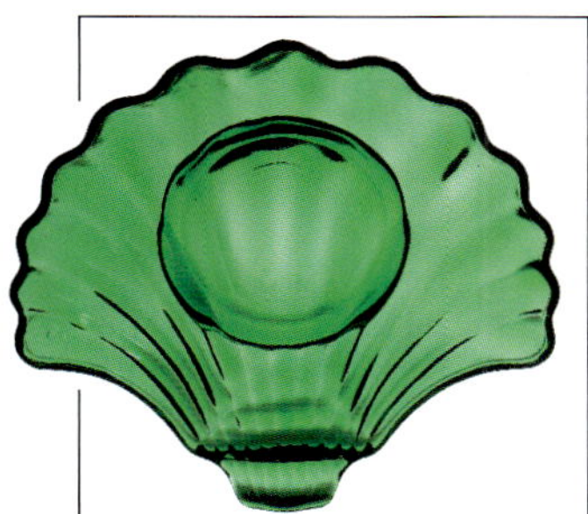

An Anchor Hocking Forest Green 'Shell' Depression glass dish.

7in (17.5cm) wide

£3-5 **AEM**

An Imperial 'Heavy Grape' pattern purple or amethyst Carnival glass bowl.

4.5in (11.5cm) diam

£12-18 **AEM**

A Dugan-Diamond 'Grapevine Lattice' purple Carnival glass dish.

7in (17.5cm) diam

£60-100 **BH**

A Northwood 'Singing Birds' pattern marigold Carnival glass mug.

3.75in (9.5cm) high

£20-40 **AEM**

A set of six amorphous glass bottles, screen-printed with Surrealist designs after Salvador Dali, each with facsimile 'Dali' signature.

Tallest 13.5in (34cm) high

£100-150 **WW**

A rare Davidson orange cloud glass powder jar.

Red is even rarer and more valuable.

1933-35 *5.5in (14cm) high*

£80-120 **BAD**

An unusual Davidson brown cloud glass ovoid vase, pattern no.34 SVG.

This shape is comparatively hard to find.

1934-41 *7.5in (19cm) h*

£70-100 **BAD**

A Duncan Miller 'Sandwich' pattern Crystal Depression glass 9oz (255g) goblet.

Note the difference in the design to Anchor Hocking's version. Coloured examples by Duncan Miller are harder to find than colourless 'Crystal'.

1924-55 *6in (15cm) high*

£7-12 **AEM**

A CLOSER LOOK AT A HARTLEY WOOD VASE

Hartley Wood was founded in 1837 in Sunderland, and produced 'crown' window and other similar types of glass. It produced limited quantities of decorative wares from the 1930s onwards.

The bright colours that had been used for the company's stained glass windows were emulated. The larger or more colours a piece has, the more desirable it will be.

Known as 'Antique Glass', each piece is unique as it was handmade, charming, slightly off-centre and uneven forms are typical.

Earlier pieces from the 1930s have an oily feel to the thickly blown glass, later pieces are thinner and lighter in weight, and were often blown into moulds so are more regular in form.

A 1930s Hartley Wood hollow-footed 'Antique Glass' vase with flared rim, and random green, yellow, blue, purple and red swirling pattern, the base with broken pontil mark.

8in (20cm) high

£80-120 **GC**

A Fenton hand painted pink graduated vase, the base with a square Fenton label and signed 'handpainted by A Findlay' and 'W.C. Fenton'.

5.75in (14.5cm) high

£50-80 **TSIS**

A Fenton Topaz 'Coin Dot' ruffled vase, shape no.1441.

Made for only a short period of time, Topaz Coin Dot is hotly sought after.

1959-61 *7in (17.5cm) high*

£50-80 **TSIS**

A 1990s Gozo Glass 'Sea Collection' perfume bottle, with deep internal pulled swirls, inscribed "Gozo Glass" on the base.

5.25in (13cm) high

£28-32 **TGM**

A 1930s Hartley Wood 'Antique Glass' vase, with random green, yellow and orange swirling pattern, the base with broken pontil mark.

9.5in (24cm) high

£100-150 **GC**

A very rare Stevens & Williams (Royal Brierley) two colour, lens-cut 'Rainbow' vase, pattern no.68307.

This scarce range was only produced for a few years from 1938 due to the onset of war. Most examples bear cut features, with the lenses here adding an interesting optical effect.

c1939 *10in (25.5cm) high*

£800-1,200 **GC**

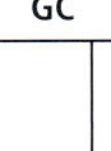

A 1930s Stevens & Williams (Royal Brierley) pink glass vase with random internal bubbles, designed by Keith Murray, on an applied colourless pad foot.

Known as 'Cased Bubbly', pink and blue were the first colours to be produced in this scarce range, and were followed by amethyst and green. Some pieces bear acid etched marks with Murray's name.

c1938-39 *8.5in (22cm) high*

£300-400 **GC**

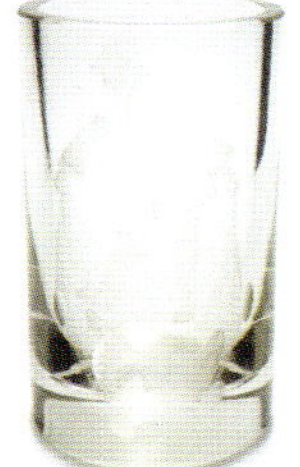

A Strathearn cylindrical vase sand-blasted and vibropen etched with a fisherman and net, the base signed in vibropen 'STRATHEARN 1978'.

1978 *7.75in (19.5cm) high*

£70-100 **GC**

A 1980s Stuart 'Dark Crystal' rectangular vase, designed by Iestyn Davis, with mottled red textured surface and machine-cut rim.

3.75in (9.5cm) high

£20-30 **MHC**

A CLOSER LOOK AT A STEVENS & WILLIAMS VASE

The bubbly, mottled design follows the 1930s fashion for bubbly glass, such as that produced by Monart, Graystan and Walsh Walsh.

The surface is rough to the touch, and may have been treated with chemicals or coloured enamels to further the 'ancient' feel.

The surface is also treated with metal oxides to give it an iridescent finish, which was inspired by ancient Roman glass.

This is a pleasing classic form, more valuable forms have applied prunts or handles with impressed patterns inspired by Ancient designs.

A 1930s Stevens & Williams 'Caerleon' range baluster vase, with random internal air bubbles, blue and yellow powdered enamel mottled design and iridescent surface, the base with broken pontil mark.

8in (20.5cm) high

£200-250 **GC**

A 1980s Stuart 'Dark Crystal' baluster vase, designed by Iestyn Davis, with mottled red textured surface and machine-cut rim.

Introduced in 1982 along with 'Ebony & Gold', Dark Crystal is much harder to find today. Both ranges were only produced for a few years, and Dark Crystal appears to have sold in much lower quantities at the time.

5.25in (13.5cm) high

£40-60 **GC**

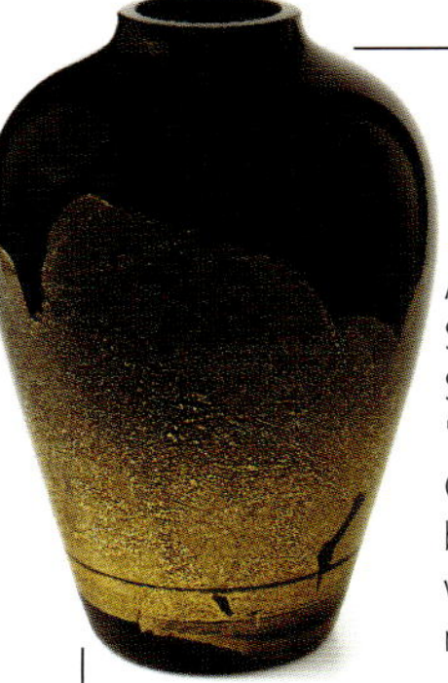

A 1980s Stuart Strathearn 'Ebony & Gold' baluster vase, shape no.SS001.

The horizontal scratch in the gold leaf was probably created when the gold leaf was being applied and smoothed onto the surface. Note the similarity between Michael Harris' Azurene and this short-lived range by Iestyn Davies. These are entirely mould blown, so light in weight. Such large sizes are hard to find.

9.25in (23.5cm) high

£70-100 **PC**

A 1970s Wedgwood Glass purple 'Sheringham' glass candleholder, with three discs, shape no.RSW13 designed by Ronald Stennett-Willson in 1967 for King's Lynn Glass.

6.25in (16cm) high

£35-40 **SAS**

A CLOSER LOOK AT A BUBBLY GLASS VASE

Bubbly glass was fashionable during the 1930s, with many makers producing it, often with a 'waxy feel' and an unfinished pontil mark. As there were several producers, identification can be hard.

The shape and colour hint at Walsh Walsh's 'Pompeiian' range, released in 1929 as an inexpensive art glass range – if so, its value would be around £80-120.

Under ultraviolet light, the yellow glass glows bright green, showing that it is 'uranium' glass – this is unusual for Walsh Walsh.

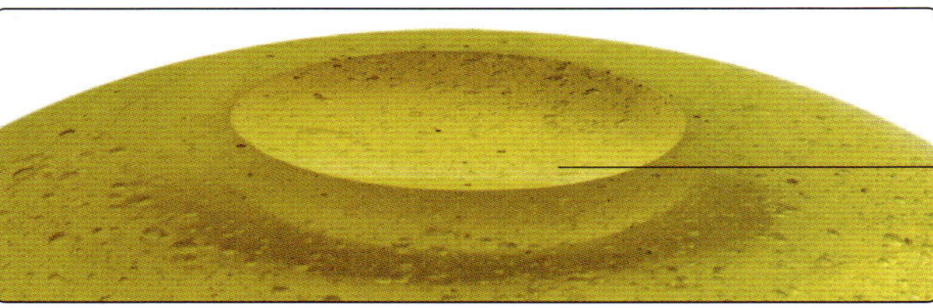

The pontil mark on the base is polished and finished off well, which is typical of Walsh Walsh's high quality production, but it does not bear their acid etched mark.

A 1930s uranium glass spherical vase, probably by Walsh Walsh, with random pattern of integral bubbles of different sizes, the base with polished concave pontil mark.

6in (15cm) high

£40-60 **PC**

A German Vereinigte Lausitzer Glaswerke grey-blue ovoid footed vase, designed by Wilhelm Wagenfeld, with oval cut lenses designed by Erich Jachmann.

Jachmann (b.1925) also later produced cut and optic-blown designs for WMF. Bauhaus designer Wagenfeld worked as Art Director for VLG from 1935-47.

c1950 *6.25in (16cm) high*

£300-400 **VZ**

A late 1970s Wedgwood Glass purple moulded textured bowl, no.RSW267, designed by Ronald Stennett-Willson in 1975.

6.75in (17cm) diam

£50-60 **RET**

A Wedgwood Glass colourless glass squirrel, shape no.SG410, the base with factory acid stamp.

4in (10cm) high

£22-28 **TGM**

An American pressed and flashed ruby souvenir glass creamer, etched 'Gettysburg 1863'.

4in (10cm) high

£20-30 **BH**

An American pressed and flashed ruby souvenir glass small mug or handled toothpick holder, etched 'Atlantic City Edna Heck'.

2.5in (6cm) high

£20-40 **BH**

A 19thC Bohemian ruby flashed tankard, with a slice cut body, loop handle and thumb lift cover, cut and engraved with deer in a wooded landscape.

7in (18cm) high

£100-150 **FLD**

A 19thC Stourbridge crystal oil lamp, with a wide fluted ruby base rising to a wrythen fluted column with applied crystal trim below a ruby cased and flash cut paraffin reservoir fitted with a 'Messengers Patent' fitment.

16.25in (41cm) high

£180-220 **FLD**

A late 19thC Stourbridge crystal water jug, of footed ovoid form, collar neck, loop handle decorated with a cranberry threading over clear crystal ground, with a matched wine goblet.

£180-220 **FLD**

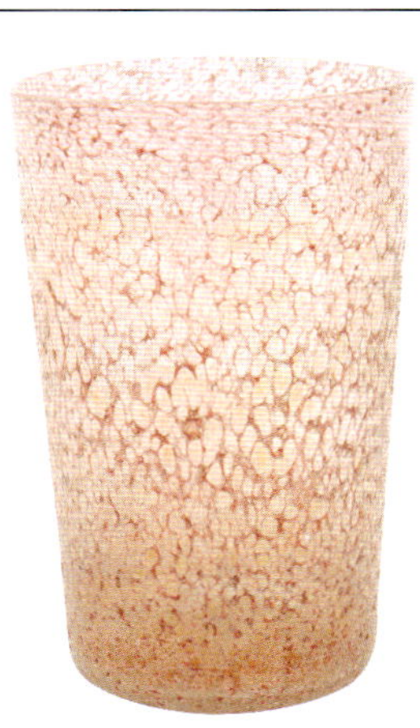

A mid-20thC art glass vase, of tumbler form with a mottled and fissured air bubble ground, in tonal pink over clear.

9.5in (24cm) high

£50-80 **FLD**

A green beeer bottle, Brown & Plummer, Swindon.

8in (20.5cm) high.

£2-5 BS

A green half pint beer bottle, Marchants, Reading.

8in (20.5cm) high.

£2-5 BS

A late Georgian blue spirit bottle, Bristol, with wheel engraving 'Speed of the Plough', dedicated to M. Dickson Aug 1832.

11in (28cm) high

£200-250 AG

A Ye Olde Fulham Pottery stoneware bottle, with original top.

9in (23cm) high.

£50-60 BS

QUICK REFERENCE

- Though the Inuit art heritage goes back to the Athabascan and Thule cultures of 10thC Alaska and Northern Canada, most collectable Inuit art dates from the 1950s onwards. It first came to prominence in 1949 after James Houston, a young Canadian artist, visited the Canadian Arctic with the intention of finding out whether the native art was appealing and could be sold. Creation and trade became increasingly organised in the 1950s and 1960s. Interest has subsequently grown across the world, with the market seeing rapid development in the last 25 years.
- Most works are sculptural and created from the native soft yet durable soapstone. Soapstone ranges in colour from deep grey through to green and can be polished to a high shine, earning it a reputation as 'Canadian jade'. Drawings, textiles and prints are also collected. Subjects include scenes from Inuit daily life as well as myths, Shamanism and abstract ideas. Well-executed, stylised or even abstract designs, particularly those displaying wit or humour, find the most favour with collectors. Polar bears, real and mythical creatures and 'transformation' sculptures are also desirable.
- Influential artists such as John Pangnark, Osuitok Ipeelee, Pauta Saila, Jessie Oonark and Judas Ullulaq are the most collectable. A large proportion of the most valuable pieces were made by these artists, many of whom are now dead. The growing popularity of Inuit art has resulted in many pieces of average or poor quality coming onto the market. Of the many contemporary artists working today, only a few will come to be considered masters of the form. Research artists and market trends in reference books, or visit dealers and auction to inspect desirable examples yourself.
- Many pieces are signed on the bottom with syllabics (the Inuit form of verbal lettering), or with a disc number beginning with an E or W, which can be used to identify the artist by consulting an online reference guide. Look out for the Canadian government sticker on more contemporary Inuit pieces.

A stone 'Embracing Mother, Child and Bird' figure, by Kenojuak Ashevak, E7-1035, from Cape Dorset.

9.75in (25cm) high

£4,500-5,500 **WAD**

A stone 'Mother Holding Children' group, by Miaiji Uitangi Usaitaijuk (1911-1965), E9-1174, from Salluit, signed in syllabics with disc number.

c1950 *6in (15cm) wide*

£2,200-2,800 **WAD**

A stone 'Mother and Child' figure, by Mannumi Shaqu, E7-824, from Cape Dorset.

Shaqu (1917-2000) is considered an early master of Cape Dorset sculpture. An example of his work is owned by HM The Queen, and has appeared on a postage stamp. His work has also been included in a large number of exhibitions in Canada, the UK and the US.

c1970 *12in (30.5cm) high*

£5,000-7,000 **WAD**

A stone 'Mother and Child' figure, by an unidentified artist, from Cape Dorset.

This early sculpture was acquired by Sir Norman Hartnell, the Queen' s dressmaker, during one of his visits to Canada in the 1950s.

c1955 *9.5in (24cm) high*

£5,000-7,000 **WAD**

A stone figure of a drummer, by Adamie Alariaq, (1930-1990), E7-1090, from Cape Dorset, signed in Roman.

16in (40.5cm) high

£450-550 **WAD**

QUICK REFERENCE – WHALEBONE

As well as various forms of soapstone, Inuit artists used materials found in the environment, such as this section of whale vertebra which has been cleverly used to form a body and arms. Bone is usually found in distressed condition, having been exposed to the weather and elements. It has been used for centuries by Inuit and pre-Inuit communities such as the Thule. Apart from considering the style and subject matter, dating a piece such as this is usually impossible. Also most are not signed by the sculptor. Collectors should find out about the import and export regulations that apply to this material before buying or selling.

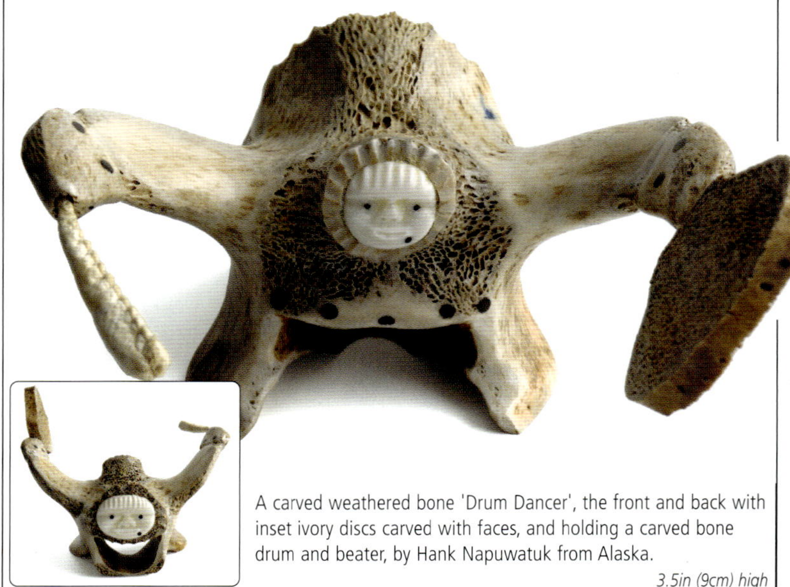

A carved weathered bone 'Drum Dancer', the front and back with inset ivory discs carved with faces, and holding a carved bone drum and beater, by Hank Napuwatuk from Alaska.

3.5in (9cm) high

£300-400 **THG**

A carved whalebone bone 'Drum Dancer' figure, by an unidentified artist.

c1970 *20in (51cm) high*

£3,000-4,000 **WAD**

A stone and ivory 'Articulated Fisherman' figure, by Charlie Ugyuk, E4-341, from Spence Bay, signed in Roman.

Charlie Ugyuk (1931-1998) was the uncle of top-rated Inuit sculptor Karoo Ashevak. Typical of the Taloyoak (Spence Bay) style, this particular work is detailed and highly expressive, particularly the face. Ugyuk's work can be found in many private and public collections across the world.

18in (45.5cm) high

£15,000-25,000 **WAD**

A dark soapstone figure, by Annie Okalik (b.1927), E1350, from Arviat, with a multicoloured beaded coat.

4in (11cm) high

£400-500 **WAD**

A stone, sinew, antler and ivory figure of a shaman, by Judas Ullulaq, (1937-1998), E4-342, from Gjoa Haven.

The depiction of a mystical figure, the grotesque appearance and the use of inset bone or ivory teeth and eyes are all typical of Ullulaq, whose work is highly sought after.

c1980 *7in (18cm) high*

£3,000-5,000 **WAD**

A stone and antler 'Shaman' figure, by Josiah Nuilaalik (1928-2005), E2-385, from Baker Lake, signed in syllabics.

15in (38cm) high

£4,500-5,500 **WAD**

A stone 'Shaman Posing' figure, by Davie Atchealak (1947-2006), E7-1182, from Iqaluit, signed in Roman.

12.5in (32cm) high

£4,000-5,000 **WAD**

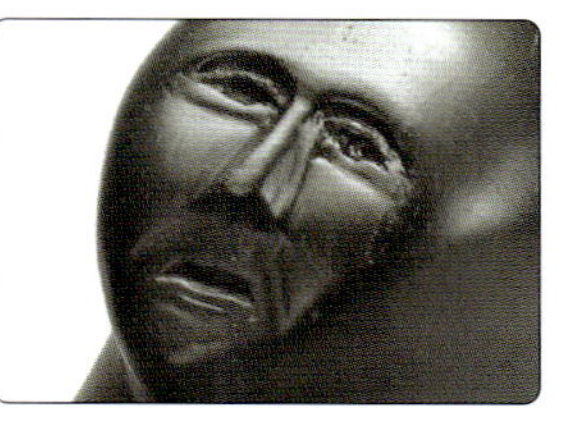

A soapstone 'Shaman/Bird' figure, by Elizabeth Tunnuq (b.1928), E-2133, from Baker Lake.

c1968 *7in (18cm) high*

£1,500-2,500 **WAD**

A stone figure of Tupilak, from Cape Dan, unsigned and by an unknown artist.

A Tupilak is a mystical and gruesome 'doll' made from materials such as human hair, animal parts, and even parts of a dead child's body. Once carved, magic spells were chanted and the figure was imbued with power from its creator's sexual organs. The Tupilak was then cast into the sea to seek and destroy an enemy. However, if the enemy had greater powers than those of the person who created it, the Tupilak was reversed and could destroy its creator. As original Tupilaks were destroyed or lost, reproductions made for sale were carved in bone, horn or stone.

c1971 *6.5in (16.5cm) high*

£1,500-2,000 **WAD**

A CLOSER LOOK AT A JOHN PANGNARK FIGURE

Pangnark is known for his highly abstract forms that resemble hills or rocky outcrops, and have a monumental feel despite their small size.

Most are inscribed or carved with simple lines to form basic facial features.

The subject matter of a shaman transformation figure is very unusual for Pangnark, which adds value to this piece.

The Inuit believed that shamen gained many of their mystical powers from an animal 'familiar' (here it is a seal), which they could transform into at will.

A stone seal/shaman transformation figure, by John Pangnark, (1920-1980), E1-104, from Arviat.

7.5in (19cm) high

£12,000-15,000 **WAD**

An untitled coloured pencil drawing, by Luke Anguhadluq (1895-1982), signed in syllabics.

30in (75cm) wide

£400-500 **WAD**

A 'Sentient Owl' stonecut by Kenojuak Ashevak, (b.1927), E7-1035, from Cape Dorset.

1970 *33.5in (85cm) wide*

£1,000-1,500 **WAD**

A 'Loon Protects The Owl', limited edition stonecut, by Kenoujak Ashevak (b.1927), E7-1035, numbered 6 from an edition of 100, from Cape Dorset.

2002 *31in (78.5cm) wide*

£1,000-1,500 **WAD**

An untitled coloured pencil drawing by Luke Anguhadluq (1895-1982), signed in syllabics.

26in (66cm) high

£1,000-1,500 **WAD**

A limited edition 'Eskimo Boat in Ice' woodcut print, by James Houston (1921-2005), from Baffin Island, from an edition of 30, framed.

Artist James Houston 'discovered' Inuit art, and brought it to the world' s attention during the 1950s.

14.5in (37cm) wide

£700-1,000 **WAD**

An 'Angagok Conjuring Birds' stencil print, by Jessie Oonark (1906-1985), E2-384, from Baker Lake, from a limited edition of 45.

30in (76cm) high

£1,500-2,000 **WAD**

A graphite drawing, by Parr (1893-1969), E7-1022, from Cape Dorset, marked 'June 1961'.

1961 *24in (61cm) high*

£5,000-7,000 **WAD**

QUICK REFERENCE

- 'Casino Royale', the first novel to feature Ian Fleming's super spy James Bond, was first published in 1953. Fewer than 5,000 'true first editions' (first print run of the first edition) of the novel were printed and many went to libraries, leaving them in poor condition. This means good condition copies of this book are rare and sought after.
- In general, true firsts are most desirable, however, the first batch of Fleming's fifth Bond novel, 'From Russia, With Love' was sent to a book club due to their poor quality. The effective second printing (marked Cape) is therefore considered the true first edition. 'From Russia, With Love' is widely considered not only Fleming's best book but also the best film adaptation, and good condition copies are extremely sought after and valuable. A copy signed by Fleming, especially one dedicated to a close friend or colleague, will be particularly desirable. Other Bond authors, such as John Gardner who revived the Bond series in 1981, are also collectable.
- EON Productions were granted the film adaptation rights for all the Bond novels in the 1950s (except 'Casino Royale', which was only granted in the 1990s). The first adaptation, 'Dr. No', was released in 1962 and featured Sean Connery as Bond. The film launched Bond as a global phenomenon. Connery was followed in the role by George Lazenby (1969), Roger Moore (1973-1985), Timothy Dalton (1987-1989), Pierce Brosnan (1995-2000) and Daniel Craig (2006-). In general, merchandise from the immensely popular Sean Connery era is most desirable.
- James Bond's many cars and gadgets have been made into toys by a wide variety of manufacturers. Iconic cars, such as the Aston Martin, are likely to be most desirable. Condition is important, with mint condition examples usually commanding the highest prices. Models should also ideally be accompanied by their original boxes, which should also be in good condition. Always look for licensed products by known makers, although some unlicensed toys can be rare.

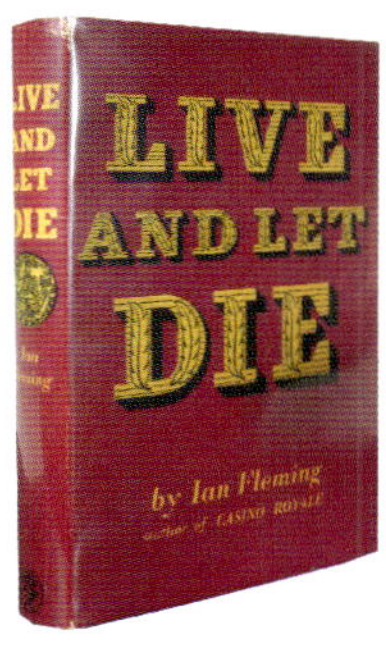

Ian Fleming, 'Live and Let Die', first edition of 7,500 copies, first impression, with original boards, first state dust jacket, price-clipped and slightly rubbed at corners.

1954

£5,000-7,000 **BLO**

Ian Fleming, 'From Russia, With Love', first edition of 15,000 copies, with original boards, dust jacket with small tear to head of spine, otherwise a very good copy.

1957

£1,200-1,800 **BLO**

Ian Fleming, 'Goldfinger', first edition of 24,000 copies, signed by the author on front free endpaper, with original boards and creased and rubbed dust jacket with tears at spine ends.

1959

£3,500-4,500 **BLO**

Ian Fleming, 'Moonraker', first edition, first impression, with original boards and price-clipped dust jacket, with some browning, rubbed at edges, and spine slightly dulled.

The first print run comprised 9,900 copies. The word 'shoot' on p.10 is sometimes misspelt 'shoo' in the first edition. In general, the correct spelling (in this example) is preferred.

1955

£1,500-2,000 **BLO**

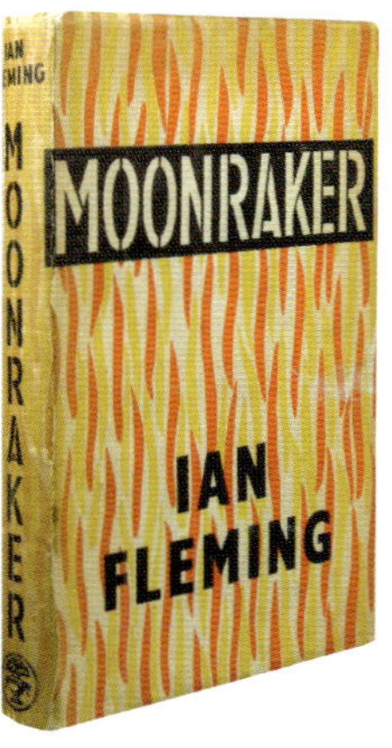

Ian Fleming, 'Dr No', first edition of 20,000 copies, first impression, with small contemporary ink name on front free endpaper, original plain first state boards, dust jacket, rubbed at corner tips and spine ends.

1958

£800-1,200 **BLO**

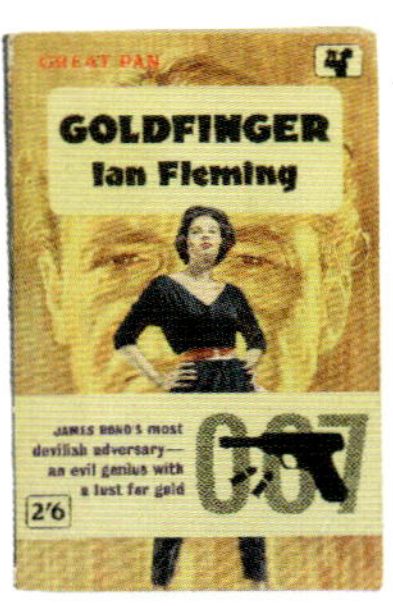

Ian Fleming, 'Goldfinger' paperback, published by Pan Books Ltd., a reprint with the same cover as the first paperback edition.

1962

£7-10 **PC**

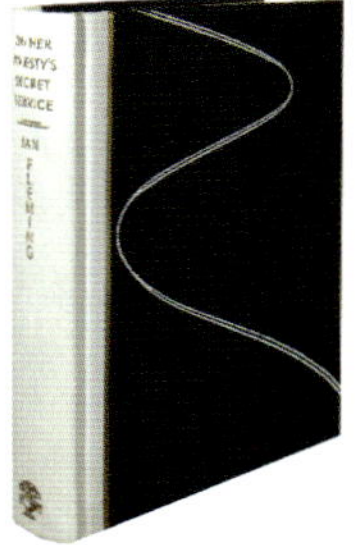

Ian Fleming, 'On Her Majesty's Secret Service', first edition, numbered 151 from a limited edition of 250 copies signed by the author, with colour portrait by Amherst Villiers, original vellum-backed black buckram boards and original glassine plastic jacket.

1963

£3,800-4,800 **BLO**

A CLOSER LOOK AT A JAMES BOND FIRST EDITION

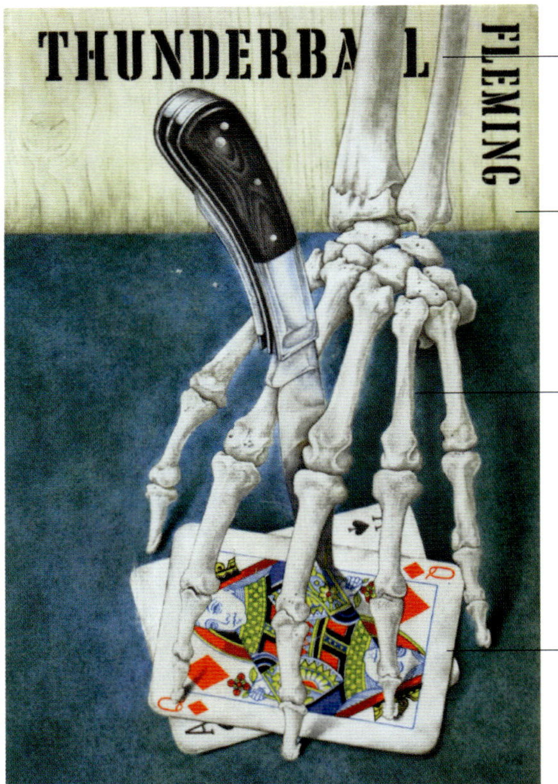

Thunderball was the ninth Bond book, and was written with the intention of being turned into a film, making it the first novelisation of a Bond screenplay.

The cover design was by illustrator and artist Richard Chopping (1917-2008) who produced a number of cover designs for Bond books, typically in a trompe l'oeil style.

Fleming's signature automatically adds value, but the witty and Secret Intelligence Service (MI6) related inscription adds even more interest and value.

More importantly, 'Jack' may be Jack Whittingham, who worked with Fleming on the initial screenplay for the film, before a legal case erupted, making this an important dedication.

Ian Fleming, 'Thunderball', first edition of 50,398 copies, near full-page inscription from the author on front free endpaper that reads 'To Jack, By appointment, M.O. to the SIS!, Ian', original boards, dust jacket, slightly rubbed at tips of corners.

1961

£8,000-12,000 **BLO**

Ian Fleming, 'You Only Live Twice', first edition, signed and dedicated 'To Julie...' on the front free endpaper, minor spotting to extreme edges, with original boards and dust jacket, in excellent condition.

Julie was the lady who hand-rolled Fleming's cigarettes – dedications connected with Fleming's life or work are sought after. Although Bond smokes rarely on screen, the character in the novels was a heavy smoker, puffing his way through some 60 cigarettes a day.

1964

£3,500-4,500 **BLO**

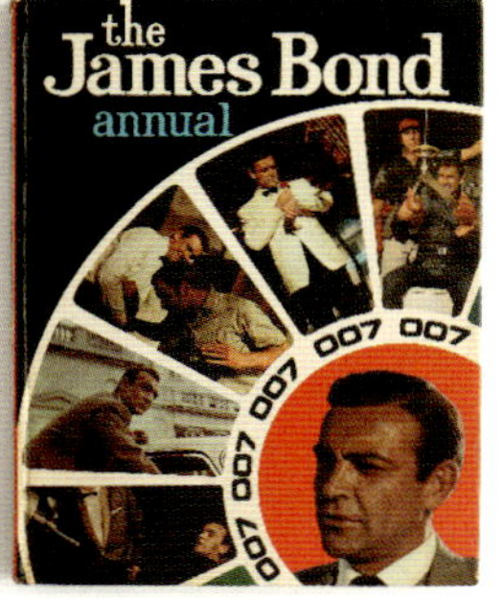

A 'The James Bond Annual', including pictures from 'Goldfinger' and 'You Only Live Twice', and with Sean Connery cover.

1968 *10.75in (27cm) high*

£20-30 **PC**

Peter Haining, 'James Bond: A Celebration', published by Planet, page 187 with a dedication and Desmond Llewelyn (Q) signature.

1987 *10.75in (27cm) high*

£70-100 **SAS**

An American 'Dr. No' one sheet poster, linen-backed.

1962 41in (102cm) high

£1,200-1,800 **ATM**

An American 'From Russia with Love', one sheet poster, linen-backed.

This was chosen as the second 007 film after President John F. Kennedy listed the book among his top ten favourite novels.

1964 40in (101.5cm) high

£600-900 **ATM**

An Italian 'Dalla Russia Con Amore' ('From Russia With Love') locandino poster, linen-backed.

1964 26.75in (68cm) wide

£200-300 **ON**

An American 'Goldfinger' one sheet poster, linen-backed.

1965 41in (104cm) high

£1,200-1,500 **P**

An American 'Diamonds Are Forever' three sheet poster produced for the foreign market, with blue ink Dutch stamp, with folds and minor holes, dated.

1971 74.75in (190cm) high

£120-180 **SAS**

A CLOSER LOOK AT A JAMES BOND POSTER

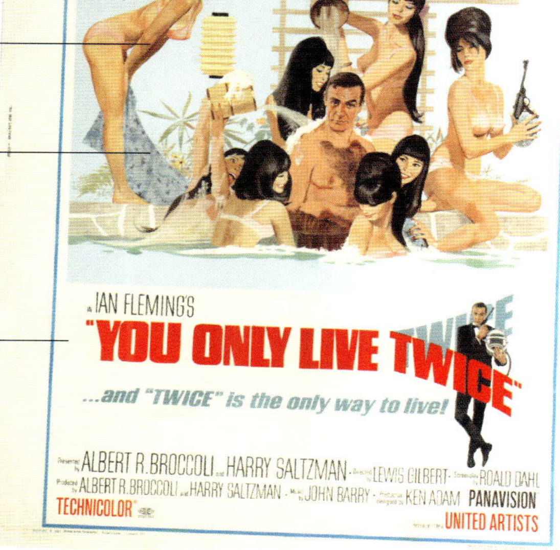

It was designed by notable poster artists Robert McGinnis (b.1926) and Frank McCarthy (1924-2002), who designed a number of Bond posters, with McGinnis also designing the famous 'Breakfast At Tiffany's' poster.

This scene, with Bond taking a bath with exotic women, is the desirable style C version of the poster.

Style A shows Blofeld's volcano lair from the film, and Style B featured Bond's 'Little Nellie' mini-helicopter in a mid-air fight.

International versions of this poster usually used the Little Nellie image, with only a few exceptions.

A British 'You Only Live Twice', style 'C' one sheet poster, linen-backed.

1967 40in (101.5cm) high

£1,000-1,500 **ATM**

A Corgi James Bond silver Aston Martin, no.270, with gold bumpers, revolving number plates and tyre slashers, in excellent condition, with unopened packet, in good condition original window box.

This type of box is particularly scarce, and the envelope of accessories is unopened – both contribute to the price.

1968-73

£300-500 SAS

A CLOSER LOOK AT A CORGI ASTON MARTIN

This model is complete with all its accessories, including the spare assassin and the sticky lapel badge, which was usually used and lost.

It is important that the model, box, and accessories are all in the best condition possible.

This was released to coincide with the release of 'Goldfinger' in 1964 and dominated Christmas sales in December 1965.

It also includes the catalogue, which indicates an early example from the four year production run.

A Corgi James Bond gold Aston Martin DB5, no.261, with two assassins, lapel badge, instructions, packets, with 'Car Makers To James Bond' catalogue, in very good condition with original box in very good condition.

1965-69

£180-220 SAS

A Corgi James Bond silver Aston Martin, no.270, with lapel badge, unused number plate labels, instructions and spare assassin, in excellent condition, in excellent condition original striped window box.

1973-76

£250-300 SAS

A Corgi James Bond Lotus Esprit, no.269, with nine rockets on sprue, in excellent condition, in very good condition original box.

1977-83

£40-60 SAS

A Corgi James Bond CC07505 'Die Another Day' Aston Martin Vanquish, in original box, signed by Barbara Broccoli and Michael G. Wilson.

c2003

£1,000-1,500 SAS

A Corgi Rockets D928 James Bond 'On Her Majesty's Secret Service' Spectre Mercedes-Benz 280 SL, in unopened vacuform packaging.

1970-72

£250-300 SAS

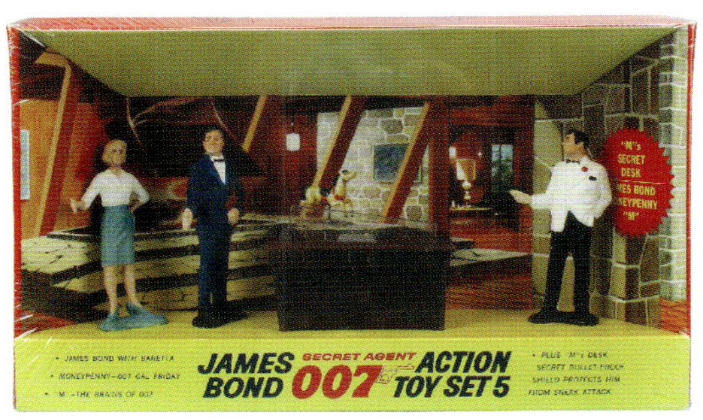

An A.C. Gilbert James Bond 'Action Toy Set 5', no.16565, in excellent condition, in original box.

£70-100 SAS

QUICK REFERENCE - A.C. GILBERT & JAMES BOND

The A.C. Gilbert Co. was founded in 1909 and grew to be one of the largest American toys companies. It is best known for its Erector Set, similar to Britain's Meccano, and also produced model trains. After the death of founder Alfred Gilbert in 1961, the company struggled financially but won the license to produce James Bond toys in 1965. A large number of figures and toys were produced, and are hotly sought after by collectors today. In 1966, the company's fortunes took a turn for the worst when large numbers of their hastily produced 'James Bond Road Race Set' were returned to retailer Sears due to poor quality. In 1967, they went out of business, and lost the license, with companies such as Mego stepping in to create licensed Bond toys. This desirable set contains all ten small figurines produced by Gilbert and is complete with the speargun, rifle and breathing tank accessories, which are often lost.

An A.C. Gilbert James Bond 'Action Toy Set 4', no.16564, in original box, lacking cellophane, one ankle fractured.

£35-45 SAS

An A.C. Gilbert James Bond 'Ten Movie Characters' set, no.16525, in excellent condition, in original box.

£120-180 SAS

An A.C. Gilbert James Bond figurine.

This figurine is from the boxed sets also shown on this page. When the Gilbert company went bankrupt, all remaining stocks were sold off by Sears individually or in sets, usually without the original boxes.

3.5in (9cm) high

£7-11 KNK

A late 1960s A.C. Gilbert James Bond Auric Goldfinger figurine.

3.25in (8.5cm) high

£6-9 KNK

A Triang TG4 James Bond 'Thunderball' '007 Underwater Battle Game', with frogmen figures, strip catalogue, in excellent condition in fair condition original box.

£350-450 SAS

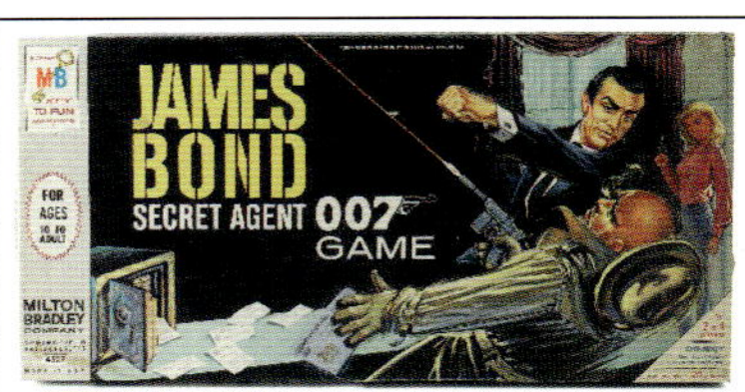

An American MB Games 'James Bond 007 Secret Agent' game, with original box in very good condition.

c1964 *19in (48cm) wide*

£70-100 **NOR**

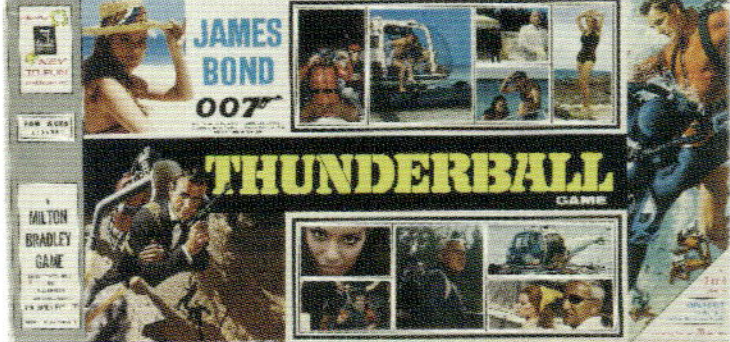

An Australian Milton Bradley 'James Bond 007 Thunderball' game.

c1966 *19in (48cm) wide*

£40-60 **GAZE**

A Spears 'James Bond 007 Secret Service Game' board game, in excellent condition, in very good condition box.

1966 *19in (48cm) wide*

£15-25 **SAS**

A late 1960s Jumbo Games 'James Bond 007' game, with instructions in Dutch, in original 'snakeskin' look attaché case box, some graffiti.

£25-35 **SAS**

A 1980s Coibel 186 'Official James Bond 007 Secret Agent Set', in original box.

£180-220 **SAS**

An Arrows 'James Bond Thunderball' jigsaw, in near mint to mint complete condition, in good condition picture boxes.

c1966

£70-100 **VEC**

A Lone Star James Bond 'Super Action Set', no.1210, in excellent condition in original window box.

1973

£300-500 **SAS**

A Multiple Toymakers James Bond 'Bond-X Automatic Shooting Camera', no.3021, in worn original box.

Multiple Toymakers made a number of James Bond toys and were a major producer of toys in the 1970s.

1966

£350-450 **SAS**

QUICK REFERENCE

- Interest in marbles is increasing as yesterday's children become today's collectors. Collectable marbles can be divided into three groups: handmade, machine-made and artist marbles.
- The earliest marbles were handmade, primarily in Germany from the 1860s to the 1920s. M. F. Christensen developed a marble-making machine in 1905, and companies in the USA began to produce machine-made marbles. Production of this sort of marble peaked in the 1920s and 1930s.
- Handmade marbles can be identified by the presence of rough pontil marks, where they were broken away from the glass rod to form a sphere. Rarer marbles such as the opaque Indians and 'sulphides' (which have internal white porcelain-like forms) are the most sought after, as are large marbles and those in truly mint condition. Handmade marbles are typically the most desirable, but they have become so hard to find and valuable that many collectors' interest has shifted to the best machine-made marbles.
- By the 1950s and 1960s, poorer quality machine-made marbles, such as 'cat's eyes', were being produced in large numbers. These are generally of little interest to collectors.
- Machine-made marbles have no pontil mark. Makers to look out for are Christensen Agate (1905-1917) and the largest USA producer, Akro Agate, which produced marbles from 1910 until 1951, when the factory closed.
- Several artists, including Mark Matthews, still produce contemporary pieces, which are often collectable. Many are made from dichroic glass, which contains micro-layers of metal oxide, creating an iridescent effect. When viewed from different angles and under different lighting conditions, the marble's colours appear to shift and change.
- The type of marble affects value: pattern, colour and size are important, with symmetry in design, and unusual or very bright colours typically popular with collectors. 'Eye appeal' will also determine value, as what may appeal to one collector may not appeal to another. Mint condition marbles can often be worth twice as much as a damaged version. Chips, scuffs, marks and wear will reduce value, particularly of machine-made marbles. Chips are less important on handmade-marbles, unless the pattern is affected. Packaging can also be desirable, as so much was thrown away.

A German handmade 'Mist' marble, with translucent and transparent blue and yellow strands over a transparent core.

Note the rough top area of the marble, which shows where it was broken off the rod before being formed and finished.

c1860-c1920 *0.5in (1.5cm) diam*

£30-40 **AB**

A German handmade solid core 'lobed swirl' marble.

c1860-c1920 *0.75in (2cm) diam*

£30-40 **AB**

An American Akro Agate Company 'Popeye Corkscrew' machine-made marble.

c1927-35 *0.5in (1.5cm) diam*

£15-25 **AB**

An American Peltier Glass Company National Line Rainbo 'Burnt Christmas Tree' machine-made marble.

c1925-32 *0.5in (1.5cm) diam*

£60-100 **AB**

An American Champion Agate Company Furnace 'Scraping Swirl' machine-made marble.

c1980-1990 *0.5in (1.5cm) diam*

£15-25 **AB**

An American Christensen Agate Company 'Bloodie' machine-made marble.

c1927-28 *0.5in (1.5cm) diam*

£25-35 **AB**

An Eddie Seese six-panel swirl marble, with alternating bands of dichroic glass and multicoloured swirling bands over a cobalt blue ground, signed.

1.5in (4cm) diam

£40-60 **BGL**

A Shane Caswell dichroic blue and green 'vortex' marble, the back with torchwork 'rake pull' decoration, signed.

1.75in (4.5cm) diam

£30-40 **BGL**

A Francis Coupal limited edition floral marble, with stretched and pulled murrine canes, signed.

2in (5cm) diam

£200-300 **BGL**

A Bobbie Seese multicoloured Onionskin marble, with pulled multicoloured caned and dichroic glass over an opaque white base, signed.

1.75in (4.5cm) diam

£40-60 **BGL**

A CLOSER LOOK AT A JOSH SIMPSON MARBLE

Simpson's immensely popular 'Planet' range began in 1976 when he was demonstrating glassmaking to school children, who reacted better to stories about imaginary planets than to goblets and vases.

Traditional techniques associated with Murano glass, such as ' millefiori' and sections of twisted 'filigrana' canes, are combined with more modern innovations such as dichroic glass.

Each element is hand-applied, making every planet unique and creating complex patterns mimicking land masses, deep seas and even cities that draw the eye in.

The presence of an 'orbiting spaceship', here a section of ' filigrana' cane, show that this planet is 'inhabited'.

A Josh Simpson 'Inhabited Planet' marble, containing canes, murrines, dichroic 'gold glass' and a 'spaceship' on a blue ground, signed.

1.75in (4.5cm)

£120-180 **BGL**

A Julie Powell translucent purple marble, with a hand-painted overlay of a hummingbird, flowers and leaves, signed.

Powell designed Fenton glass before she began producing these unique works.

1.5in (4cm) diam

£60-80 **BGL**

A Milon Townsend studio glass sphere or marble, with lampworked three-dimensional horse and paddock enclosed within colourless glass.

Townsend is a key American studio glass artist, who specialises in lampworked designs. This piece crosses the boundary between studio glass and contemporary marble making. His marbles containing human figural forms are particularly sought after.

1.5in (4cm) diam

£100-120 **BGL**

QUICK REFERENCE – CONRAH

The Conrah range was designed by Ronald Hughes in 1967, and produced in south Wales during the 1970s. The range of vases, bowls and candlesticks was made from anodised aluminium in bright colours, which were cut through by machine, leaving reflective sparkling geometric patterns arranged in wide bands around the bodies. Fine lines may also be found in addition to the main pattern. Often misread as 'Conran', marks were tooled or printed on to a plastic disc set into the base. The range was also known as 'Cristillium'. Currently, prices and understanding of the area are low, but this may change as the vases are both visually appealing and typical of the time they were produced. Avoid scratched, and especially dented, examples as damage is impossible to restore.

A Conrah green anodised aluminium large cylinder vase, cut with faceted lozenge motifs, the base with inset black plastic Conrah mark.

10in (25.5cm) high

£60-80 GC

A Conrah pink anodised aluminium large cylinder vase, cut with a faceted lattice design, the base with inscribed Conrah mark.

10in (25.5cm) high

£60-80 GC

A Conrah gold-finish anodised aluminium small cylinder vase, cut with a faceted lattice design, the base with inset black plastic Conrah mark.

8in (20.5cm) high

£30-40 GC

A 1970s Conrah anodised aluminium medium cylinder vase, finely cut with horizontal lines and cut with faceted lozenge shapes, the base with inset plastic disc.

9in (23cm) high

£60-80 GC

A Conrah black anodised aluminium candlestick, cut with a faceted lattice design, the base with inset black plastic Cristillium mark.

6.75in (17cm) high

£20-25 GC

A Conrah blue anodised aluminium flower pot, cut with a faceted lattice design, the base with inset black plastic Conrah mark.

3.75in (9.5cm) high

£15-20 GC

A Conrah black anodised aluminium bowl, cut with a faceted lattice design, the base with inset black plastic Conrah mark.

5.25in (13cm) diam

£20-25 GC

QUICK REFERENCE – VINERS & STUART DEVLIN

Stuart Devlin (b.1931) is one of the most innovative British silversmiths and metalworkers of the late 20thC, and was awarded a Royal Warrant in 1982. He is best known for his silver and gold designs, which contrast shiny silver with textured gold areas. Viners commissioned Devlin to produce a range of stainless steel tableware in the early 1970s, following the success of, among others, Robert Welch's stainless steel designs for Old Hall. Nine shapes were produced, including the iconic spherical 'rose bowl' below, which was said to have been inspired by the 1969 moon landing. A limited number of pieces were produced in solid silver, but are very rare today. The range was phased out in 1979, and prices are much more affordable than for his solid silver and gold designs, allowing collectors to buy into the classic Devlin look at a much lower price.

A 1970s Viners 'Devlin Collection' stainless steel and gold-plated metal small wine or water goblet, designed by Stuart Devlin, the base with inset plastic disc.

5.25in (13.5cm) high

£25-35 **GC**

A 1970s Viners 'Devlin Collection' stainless steel and gold plated metal tall wine goblet, designed by Stuart Devlin, the base with inset plastic disc.

7in (18cm) high

£25-35 **GC**

A 1970s Viners 'Devlin Collection' stainless steel and gold plated metal champagne goblet, designed by Stuart Devlin, the base with inset plastic disc.

4.5in (11.5cm) high

£15-20 **GC**

A 1970s Viners stainless steel and gold-plated metal candleholder, designed by Stuart Devlin, the base with inset plastic disc.

£20-30 **GC**

A 1970s Viners 'Devlin Collection' stainless steel and gold-plated metal nut dishes or candleholders, designed by Stuart Devlin.

5in (13cm) diam

£20-30 **GC**

A 1970s Viners 'Devlin Collection' stainless steel and gold-plated metal 'Violet Bowl', designed by Stuart Devlin, with pull-off, friction fit textured, domed top.

3.25in (8cm) high

£40-50 **GC**

QUICK REFERENCE – OLD HALL

Old Hall stainless steel tablewares were produced by J. & J. Wiggin Ltd from 1934-84, and have become highly collectable. The mark can help to date a piece: 'Staybrite' marks date from before WWII, 'Olde Hall' was used from 1928-59, 'Ye Olde Hall' in 1934-35 only, with 'Old Hall' being used from 1959-84. Pieces designed by Robert Welch after 1955 are perhaps the most desirable today due to their fashionable modern styling, but look out for pre-war designs such as those by Dr Harold Stabler. Quality was very high and ranges to look out for include 'Cottage', 'Avon', 'Alveston' and 'Campden'.

An Olde Hall 'Cottage' range stainless steel one-pint teapot, with 'Staycool' handle, designed by Nellie Wiggin, the base with registered design no.828398 for 1938.

1938-59 *6in (15cm) high*

£25-30 **GC**

A 1950s Olde Hall honey or conserve pot, with lid attached to the geometric handle, the base with registered design no.627169 for 1949.

3.5in (9cm) high

£15-20 **GC**

An Old Hall 'Avon' range stainless steel teapot, designed by Robert Welch in 1966, the base with registered no.928252 for 1966.

5.75in (14.5cm) high

£45-50 **GC**

An Old Hall 'Avon' range stainless steel milk jug, designed by Robert Welch in 1966, the base with registered no.928252 for 1966.

4in (10cm) high

£10-15 **GC**

An Old Hall 'Oriana' range stainless steel milk jug, with angled handle, designed by Robert Welch in 1958.

3.5in (9cm) high

£8-12 **GC**

An Old Hall 'Avon' range stainless steel coffee pot, designed by Robert Welch in 1966, the base with registered no.928252 for 1966.

7in (17.5cm) high

£45-50 **GC**

An Old Hall 'Oriana' range stainless steel teapot, with angled handle and 180 degree flip lid, designed by Robert Welch in 1958.

This range was designed for the P&O cruise liner 'Oriana', although examples were also sold commercially. Those produced for use on the ship were marked 'P&O Line' or 'ShipCo' on the base.

5.75in (14.5cm) high

£35-40 **GC**

QUICK REFERENCE – OKIMONO

An okimono is the Japanese term given to small or medium sized ornamental objects placed near altars or in the traditional 'tokonoma' display alcove.The name means 'object for placement on display', and okimono are larger than netsuke, which saw their origins as functional toggles in traditional Japanese dress. They are carved in ivory, but may also be found in wood, bronze or stone. The late 19thC until the 1920s saw a boom in the production of okimono, with many being exported to the West. Human figures or animals are the most commonly found subjects, and they may show scenes from Japanese life or mythology. Value is determined by the carver, the skill of the carver, and the subject, size, date and complexity of the piece itself. Those that are well-detailed, with realistic, expressive features are usually the most desirable and valuable.

A Japanese Meiji period ivory okimono of a basket maker, carrying various baskets in both hands and on his back, his clothing decorated with red, green and mother-of-pearl inset roundels, with red seal mark.

5.75in (14.5cm) high

£800-1,200 L&T

A Japanese Meiji period carved ivory figure of a father, feeding grapes to his two small boys, cracks and chips.

10in (25.5cm) high

£280-320 WW

A Japanese late Meiji period one piece carved ivory figure of a hunter, standing with one foot on a cut tree stump, holding a matchlock gun, wearing straw hood and outer jacket and stockings, game birds hanging from his belt, with three character engraved mark on the base.

8in (20.5cm) high

£550-750 TEN

A Japanese one piece carved ivory figure of a poultryman, standing full length and smiling, holding a chick in his upheld right hand, a hen beneath his left arm, a cockerel at his feet, incised two character mark on inset red kakihan.

c1900 6.75in (17.5cm) high

£500-700 TEN

A Japanese one piece carved ivory figure group, with bijin standing wearing a kimono and elaborate chignon, the base with inset rectangular kakihan with incised two character mark, and with rustically carved shaped oval wood base.

c1920 7.25in (18.5cm) high

£300-500 TEN

A Japanese Meiji period one piece carved ivory mythological scroll painter figurine, a figure of Hotei on horseback appears magically from mist issuing from the scroll, the base with inset red kakihan with incised two character mask.

A kakihan is an artist' s mark.

9.25in (23.5cm) high

£250-350 TEN

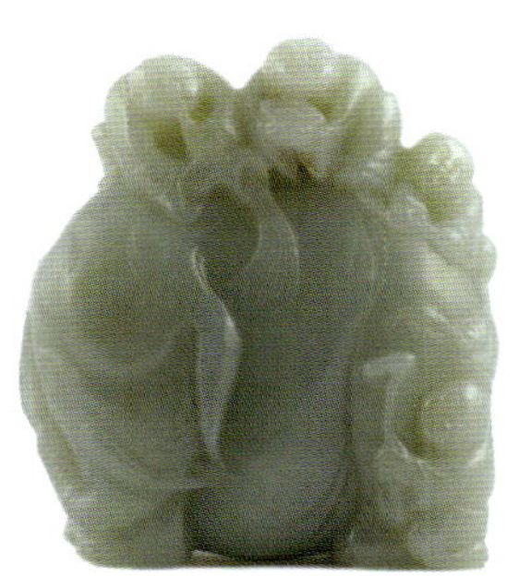

A Chinese jade carving of an elephant, with three boys scrambling on its back, two holding onto a string of cash, one pouring water out of a cornucopia, a figure to the reverse holding up a tall lingzhi fungus.

3in (7.5cm) high

£120-180 **WW**

A Chinese pale celadon jade carving of a recumbent hound, its neck twisted and looking back, raised on a wood stand.

In 2009, an 18thC spinach green jade water buffalo made for a Qing dynasty Japanese emperor, and with an all-important impeccable noble provenance, sold for £3.4 million at the same salerooms as this later piece. The quality and expressive nature of a piece of carved jade, together with a cast-iron provenance allowing it to be dated and identified, are key factors for value.

5.5in (14cm) wide

£180-220 **WW**

A Chinese pale celadon jade carving of a boy, dancing and wearing flowing robes.

2.5in (6.5cm) high

£120-180 **WW**

A 19thC/20thC Chinese jade Buddhistic lion, with areas of rust coloured stone.

4.25in (11cm) wide

£120-180 **WW**

A 19thC Chinese bronze censer, cast in relief with scaly dragons highlighted in gold, the base with a Qianlong mark.

6.75in (17cm) wide

£150-250 **WW**

A 19thC Japanese Meiji period bronze figure of a rat, the crouching animal holding a nut between its front feet, signed to base.

2.75in (6.75cm) high

£400-600 **JA**

A 17th or 18thC Chinese bronze model of a crouching horned lion dog, baring its teeth.

5.5in (14cm) high

£450-550 **WW**

A Baccarat pansy paperweight, with a millefiori garland and a star cut base.

c1850 *2.5in (6.5cm) diam*

£1,000-1,500 **DCP**

A Baccarat butterfly paperweight, with millefiori wings, surrounded by a millefiori garland, and with a star cut base.

c1850 *3in (7.5cm) diam*

£1,300-1,600 **DCP**

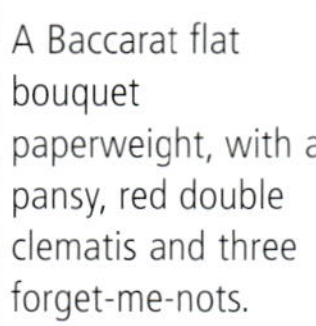

A Baccarat flat bouquet paperweight, with a pansy, red double clematis and three forget-me-nots.

This contains a larger number of different flowers, hence the higher value. Each element of the flowers was made when the glass was hot, using a 'lampworking' technique. The bunch was encased in colourless glass when finished. The glassmaker had to be skilled enough to ensure no air bubbles are trapped under this layer.

c1850 *2.5in (6.5cm) diam*

£4,000-5,000 **DCP**

A Baccarat red 'thousand petalled; rose paperweight, with a star cut base.

c1850 *3in (7.5cm) diam*

£2,500-3,000 **DCP**

A Clichy concentric millefiori paperweight, the petalled design set on an opaque turquoise ground.

c1850 *3in (7.5cm) diam*

£1,000-1,500 **DCP**

A Clichy swirl paperweight, with an opaque light blue and white swirl emanating from a single large millefioricentral cane.

c1850 *3in (7.5cm) diam*

£1,300-1,600 **DCP**

A CLOSER LOOK AT A CLICHY PAPERWEIGHT

This is known as a 'barber pole' design due to the blue and white spiral pattern canes, which resemble barber's poles – some collectors call them 'candy cane'.

The design, with its sectioned-off millefiori, is also known as a 'chequer' pattern, and is time-consuming to make.

Clichy is famous for its trademark rose millefiori, of which there are three different examples in this weight.

This example is regular, colourful and well organised, and would have been made by a skilled glassmaker.

A Clichy 'barber pole' chequer paperweight, with three different roses.

c1850 *2.75in (7cm) diam*

£2,000-3,000 **DCP**

A mid-19thC Clichy 'scramble' paperweight, the jumble of canes including pink, yellow and white roses, some scratching.

'Scramble' designs include many different types and colours of millefiori and canes, arranged and melted together in a random pattern. They tend not to be as valuable as complex set-ups.

2.25in (6cm) diam

£250-350 **WW**

A St. Louis mixed fruit paperweight, with two pears and two cherries, on an opaque white double swirl ground.

c1850 *2.75in (7cm) diam*

£600-800 **DCP**

A Pantin paperweight with a bunch of grapes and vine leaves on a plain white ground.

c1878 *3in (7.5cm) diam*

£4,000-5,000 **DCP**

QUICK REFERENCE – ST LOUIS

St Louis was founded in French Alsace-Lorraine in 1767 and, like other French makers, produced paperweights from the mid 19thC. Single flower or fruit designs are typical of its weights, which also often have higher domes than those of its competitors. Swirling white or pink grounds are another hallmark feature. Some weights have been found with date canes, these usually read 1848, with dates of 1845 and 1849 being much rarer.

A 1930s Scottish paper weight, in the style of Paul Ysart for Monart, with a radial star formation of ruffle and cog millefiori canes on a turquoise powder ground, the base with rough pontil.

3in (7.5cm) diam

£180-220 **FLD**

A St. Louis purple dahlia paperweight, with striped petals, a millefiori centre, and green leaves.

c1850 *2.25in (6cm) diam*

£1,300-1,600 **DCP**

A Liskeard Glass paperweight, with blue internal swirls over a trappped air bubble, designed by John Randle, the base with impressed stamp and dated 1976.

3.25in (8cm) diam

£20-25 **GC**

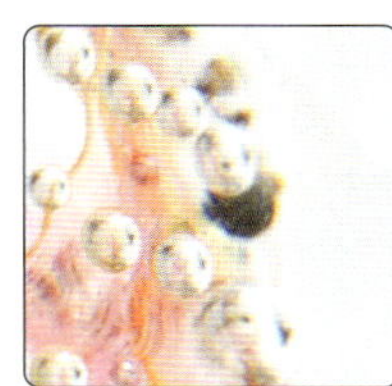

A Caithness Glass paperweight with opaque multi-coloured internal swirl core under a curtain of trapped air bubbles, the base with acid mark.

The mark on the base is 'CIIG', with the 'II' mark indicating this is a second. Looking closely, there is a piece of grit or other material from the manufacturing process trapped inside.

3.25in (8cm) diam.

£10-15 **GC**

QUICK REFERENCE

- The collector's market for vintage fountain pens began in the late 1970s, and grew throughout the 1980s and 1990s. The most sought after pens are still those produced by the three big brands: Parker, Waterman and Montblanc. Dunhill Namiki maki-e lacquer models from the 1930s are also extremely desirable and usually command the highest prices.
- While collectors have traditionally been interested in pens from their own countries, this has changed. The Internet allows collectors a wider choice than ever before, and pens (unlike larger objects) can be shipped quickly and easily. Consequently, formerly less widely appreciated brands, such as England's Conway Stewart, are now proving popular across the world.
- As well as the brand, size, rarity and quality count. Many pen collectors are men and therefore favour larger pens that fit their hands. Also desirable are those pens with high immediate visual impact, and those with gold-plated overlays, lacquerwork designs or unusual, brightly coloured celluloids.
- Pens should be in working order, as many collectors intend to use them for writing. Condition is also extremely important. Avoid cracked or chipped examples and ensure that replaceable parts, such as nibs and clips, are correct for that model.
- Fountain pens were mass-produced before the ballpoint took over in the 1960s and, with so many on the market, standard pens are often worth under £50, even with original gold nibs. However, these pens can often make useful and interesting writing instruments.
- Modern limited editions are often produced in large numbers and are only of value if kept in unused condition, with boxes and paperwork. Used examples are usually much less desirable, unless extremely rare. Look for early editions, such as Montblanc's 'Lorenzo de Medici', or those pens from small editions (ideally under 1,000).

An 'S. Mordan & Co.' silver pencil, with rare large foliate, agate set terminal revealing lead storage, engraved with presentation engraving 'H.T. Lister' in script, with 'SM' hallmarks for London 1859.

1859 *4in (10cm) long*

£120-180 **PC**

A very rare Sampson Mordan and Gabriel Riddle silver pencil, with crown-like terminal, with 'SM*GR' hallmarks for London 1825, and marked 'S.MORDAN & CO'S PATENT'.

The propelling pencil was patented by Hawkins and Mordan in 1822, and so this is an early and very scarce example. It was produced under the partnership of Mordan and the wealthy stationer Riddle.

4in (10cm) long

£250-300 **PC**

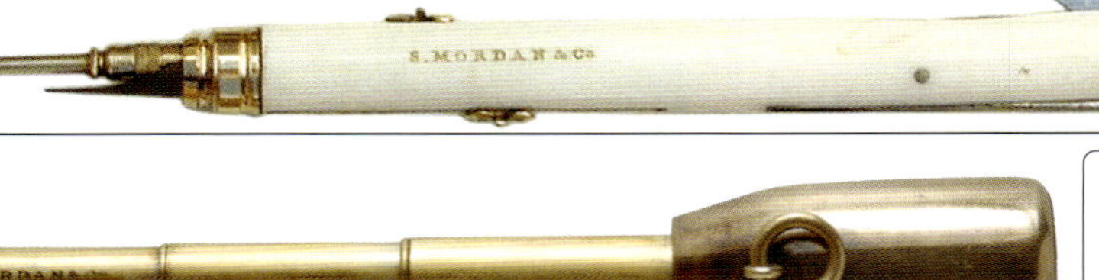

A Sampson Mordan ivory cased pen, pencil and folding knife combination, with two gold butterfly collars sliding down to operate the pen holder and pencil, marked 'S.MORDAN & CO.'.

c1880

£180-220 **BLO**

An S. Mordan & Co. silver telescopic propelling pencil in the form of a champagne bottle.

During the late 19thC, Mordan & Co. produced a wide range of novelty shaped pencils, many of which are detailed in the only surviving Mordan catalogue, dating from 1897. Shapes include a cross, a pistol and an owl, all of which are popular with collectors.

c1890

£250-350 **AMER**

QUICK REFERENCE – THE DUOFOLD

Designed in 1919 by Parker employee Lewis Tebbel, the Duofold was launched in late 1921 amid scepticism about its high price of $7. It met with great success, and has since become the company's 'flagship' model. Many collectors know the original Duofold as the 'Big Red', due to its bright orangey red colour, which was a novelty at a time when nearly all pens were black. From 1922 onwards, the Duofold was almost constantly modified in some way, meaning collectors can usually date pens to within a few years. A number of different colours and sizes can be found, including the large 'Senior', the smaller 'Junior' and 'Lady', the slimmer 'Special' and the tiny 'Vest Pocket'. During the 1930s, both ends of the pen became slightly tapered, or 'streamlined'. When it was reintroduced after WWII, it was largely mass-produced as a more affordable pen, only becoming a top-of-the-range model again when it was reintroduced again in 1988 to celebrate Parker's centenary.

An American Parker Lucky Curve Duofold Senior, with a fine P. Duofold Pen USA nib.

c1927

£120-180 **HSR**

A 1920s Parker Mandarin Yellow Lucky Curve Duofold Senior button-filler, with Duofold USA nib.

'Mandarin Yellow' is the rarest and most valuable colour for a 1920s-30s Duofold. Always examine the barrel and cap closely, as they are prone to cracking, with cracks showing up as grey.

£500-700 **BPH**

A 1990s Parker Duofold Centennial Mark I blue marbled convertor/cartridge-filler, with gold-filled trim, with 18k Parker Duofold two colour nib.

£150-200 **BPH**

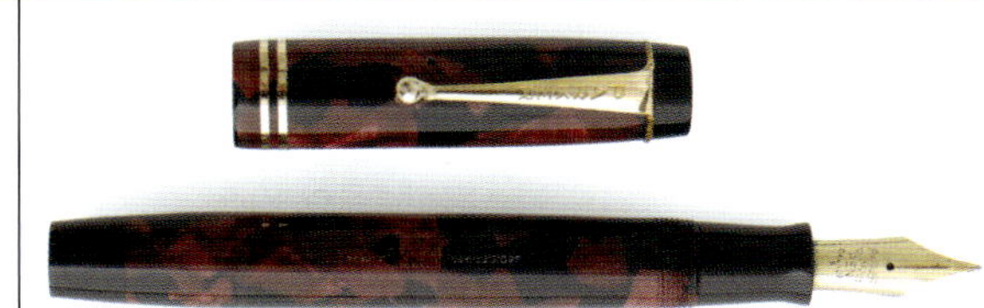

A 1940s English Parker red and black marbled Duofold Senior, with Canadian Duofold Pen nib.

These high quality 1930s-style English Duofolds are hard to find.

c1945

£200-300 **PC**

A 1930s Parker Lapis 'Blue on Blue' Duofold Junior Streamline, with Duofold nib.

£300-350 **BPH**

A 1930s Parker 'Pearl & Black' Duofold Senior Streamline, with Canadian Parker Duofold nib.

The discolouring of the barrel is the result of sulphur leaching out from the internal rubber ink sac, which causes the plastic to darken or take on amber tones.

£150-200 **BPH**

A 1950s English Parker Duofold burgundy aerometric-filler, with Duofold Parker 14ct nib, in excellent condition.

£20-30 **PC**

An English Parker 61 'Presidential' 9ct solid gold trio set, comprising capillary-filling pen, twist-action pencil and push action ball-pen, with fine barley pattern, with London hallmark for 1974, in original presentation box, with instructions and two pouches, with original clip labels in place.

Introduced in 1956, the 61 used a special spongey material in a tube to absorb and hold the ink. If clogged with dry ink, they are almost impossible to repair. The solid gold 'Presidential' was the most expensive model in the line.

£1,000-1,500 HSR

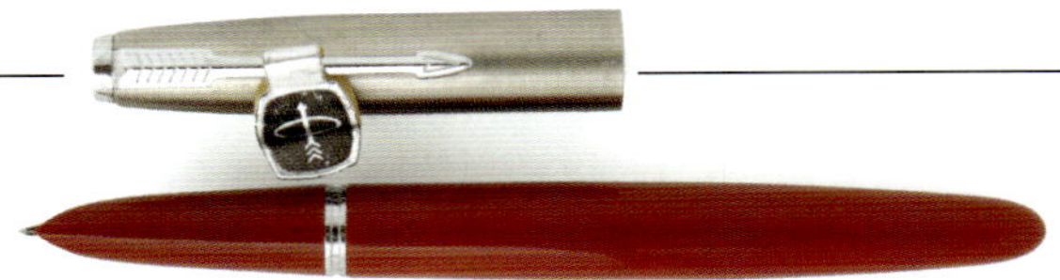

An American Parker red Super 21 aerometric-filler, with Lustraloy cap, fine octanium nib, and original nib grade label.

1956

£35-45 HSR

A 1950s-1970s English Parker Teal blue 51 Classic aerometric-filler, with medium nib and Lustraloy cap.

£30-50 PC

A Parker 61 'Heirloom' green pencil, with two-colour 'Heirloom' cap.

This is a very rare cap finish, as it tended to wear away with use and polishing.

£60-80 BPH

A 1950s American Parker 51 'Signet' aerometric-filler and Clutch pencil, with gold-plated barrels and caps.

c1952

£150-200 BPH

A CLOSER LOOK AT A PARKER 51 DEMONSTRATOR

Introduced in 1941, Parker's modern, rocket-shaped 51 was revolutionary – its hooded nib allowed the use of a special, quick drying ink known as 'Quink'.

This example shows Parker's 'Vacumatic' system, which was introduced in 1932 and uses a plunger and diaphragm to create a vacuum in the body, sucking in the ink.

The plastic plunger on this example dates it to after 1941. Examples made from 1948 onwards used Parker's 'Aerometric' squeezable tube system.

Transparent 'Demonstrator' pens were used by pen salesmen to show retailers how the mechanism worked, with shop owners also often using them to show customers.

A Parker 51 Vacumatic Lucite 'Demonstrator' pen, with medium nib and Lustraloy cap.

1945

£150-200 PC

A Parker Lucky Curve Pastel Green Moiré ring-top button-filler, with a Lucky Curve nib and engraved barrel.

c1927

£40-60 **AMER**

A Parker Gold Pearl Vacumatic Standard, with later English Parker nib.

c1942

£120-180 **AMER**

A Parker Lucky Curve 'True Blue' ring-top button-filler, with Canadian Lucky Curve nib.

This example has a very good colour, the white often goes yellow due to the internal rubber ink sac degrading.

1928

£150-200 **BPH**

A Parker Silver Pearl Vacumatic Maxima, with matching cap and barrel end 'jewels', and two-colour Parker Arrow fine nib.

The Maxima was the largest and most expensive model in the Vacumatic series. The partly transparent hallmark ' Vacumatic' striped plastic barrel allowed the ink level to be seen.

c1936

£220-280 **HSR**

A 1980s French Parker 75 gold plated 'Cisele' convertor/cartridge-filler, in mint condition.

£70-100 **BPH**

A 1980s Parker 45 'Grey Shield' Harlequin convertor/cartridge-filler, with medium nib.

£30-40 **PC**

A Parker limited edition 'RMS Queen Elizabeth' convertor/cartridge-filler, numbered 1558 from an edition of 5,000, with fine nib, wooden presentation box, card outer, certificate, instructions, guarantee card, nib adjuster, two cartridges and convertor.

These pens were made from brass taken from the propeller of this luxury liner, which sank in Hong Kong harbour in 1972. Each pen is numbered. Ensure that the accessories are complete and the packaging and certificate bear matching numbers.

1977

£650-750 **HSR**

A Parker 180 'Bark-finish' silver-plate convertor/cartridge-filler, with two sided gold medium nib, with shop tag, boxed.

£50-80 **HSR**

A rare early Waterman's chased black hard rubber No.22 'Taper Cap' eyedropper pen, with glass and rubber eyedropper.

c1904

£60-80 **PC**

A 1910s-20s Waterman's chased black hard rubber no.12 eyedropper, with crisp barrel imprint and Waterman's Ideal no.2 nib, and box, in near mint condition.

£30-50 **PC**

A Waterman's chased black hard rubber no.12P pump-filler, with Waterman's Ideal Reg US Pat Off 2 nib and added accommodation clip.

Introduced in 1903, this used a piston mechanism to fill the pen. It was not very successful, so was discontinued soon after.

c1904

£100-150 **AMER**

A 1920s Waterman's chased black hard rubber 42 1/2 V safety pen, with two 9ct gold bands with London hallmarks for 1929 and marked 'F.D.W.', with Watermans Ideal no.2 nib, in excellent condition.

£40-60 **PC**

A Waterman's red and black 'Woodgrain' mottled hard rubber No. 16 eydropper, with Waterman's Ideal New York no.6 nib.

The final number in a Waterman's model number indicates the size of the nib, and so the size of the pen. A 6 is larger than a 2.

c1915

£180-220 **AMER**

A CLOSER LOOK AT THE SMALLEST PEN IN THE WORLD

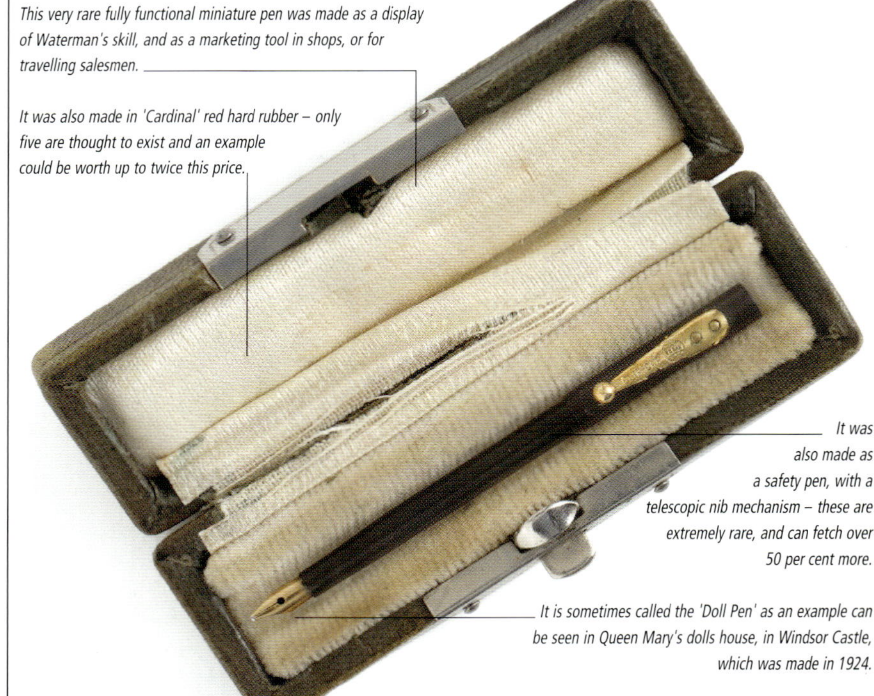

This very rare fully functional miniature pen was made as a display of Waterman's skill, and as a marketing tool in shops, or for travelling salesmen.

It was also made in 'Cardinal' red hard rubber – only five are thought to exist and an example could be worth up to twice this price.

It was also made as a safety pen, with a telescopic nib mechanism – these are extremely rare, and can fetch over 50 per cent more.

It is sometimes called the 'Doll Pen' as an example can be seen in Queen Mary's dolls house, in Windsor Castle, which was made in 1924.

A Waterman's 'Smallest Pen in the World' black hard rubber eyedropper pen, with plain gold nib with circular vent, slit and iridium point, in an original plush and satin lined case, with metal clasp.

c1914 *Pen 1.5in (4cm) long*

£2,000-2,500 **AMER**

A 1920s Italian Waterman's rolled gold overlaid no.42 safety pen, with alternating engine turned, wavy line and plain panels, ivy motif barrel and cap band, marked 'Waterman's Ideal 18KR' with a Waterman's No.2 nib, initialled and dated by turning screw.

Most Waterman safety pens with fancy rolled gold overlays marked as this example were made in Italy.

£300-400 **AMER**

A 1920s American Waterman's red and black Ripple no.42 safety pen, with Italian scrolling hexagonal gold-plated overlay, and Waterman's no.2 nib.

£200-300 **PC**

An American Waterman's no.0552 lever-filler, with gold filled 'Pansy Panel' overlay and Waterman's Canada no.2 Ideal nib.

c1925

£200-250 **HSR**

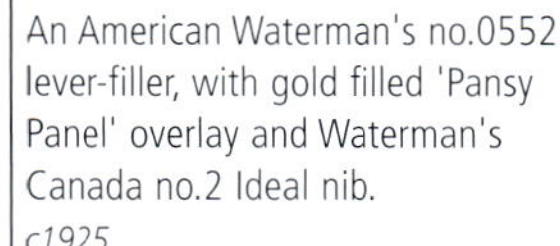

A Waterman's black hard rubber 552 lever-filler, with 9ct gold 'Gothic' overlay with London halllmarks for 1923 and marked F.D.W., with Waterman's no.2 Ideal nib, the barrel with engraved name.

Engraved names and initials usually reduce desirability, unless the name is famous, or the initials are exceptionally beautiful.

1923

£120-180 **AMER**

A 1920s Waterman's red and black 'Ripple' hard rubber no.52V lever-filler, with ring-top cap, and fine Waterman's Ideal no.2 nib.

£200-250 **PENF**

A Waterman's 'Turquoise' Lady Patricia lever-filler, with gold plated trim, initialled and dated, with Canadian Waterman's no.2 nib.

This is a scarce colour in excellent condition.

c1932

£100-150 **AMER**

QUICK REFERENCE – WATERMAN'S RIPPLE SERIES

With its bright orange colour, the 1921 Parker Duofold revolutionised pen design at a time when most pens were black. In answer to this, Waterman's released its 'Ripple' range in 1923. The pattern on each pen is unique due to the way the plastics were mixed. Resistant to staining, colours comprised orangey red and black, green and blue, and red and tan. Produced until the 1930s, they are popular with collectors today. Look out for the scarce no.5 and no.7 series, which were fitted with special nibs for specific tasks such as 'stiff fine' for accountants. The different nib grades were indicated by coloured cap bands.

A Canadian Waterman's no.56 red and black Ripple hard rubber lever-filler, with matching Ripple feed and Waterman's New York no.6 nib, with replaced lever.

c1923

£220-280 **HSR**

A 1920s Conway Stewart black hard rubber 'The Duro' lever-filler, with early lever and clip, and medium Conway Stewart 14ct nib.

The large size of this pen adds to its desirability.

£220-280 BPH

A 1920s Conway Stewart red and black mottled hard rubber Lady-sized lever-filler, with Conway Stewart 14ct nib.

£60-80 BPH

A Conway Stewart no.388 light and dark pink pearl and black marbled lever-filler, with a medium 14ct Conway Stewart nib.

c1939

£50-80 HSR

A Conway Stewart no.15 black veined light and dark green pearl lever-filler, with a medium 14ct Conway Stewart nib.

c1953

£40-60 HSR

A Conway Stewart No. 22 'Floral' lever-filler, with Conway Stewart no.5 nib.

The pattern is printed on paper, sandwiched between two layers of celluloid. Over time, the paper discolours from cream to yellow, reducing the value. It was generally believed that this pen had a limited production run of 200 examples, but this is not true, although it is hard to find.

£120-180 PC

QUICK REFERENCE – THE 'CRACKED ICE' SERIES

The 1930s and the 1950s saw Conway Stewart using a wide variety of different types of coloured plastic for their pens. Marbled plastics are the most common, and alternatives sometimes very scarce. Perhaps the most desirable is this black plastic shot through with silver veins, which has been dubbed the 'Cracked Ice' by collectors. Larger-sized examples with evenly distributed, bright silver veins will be more desirable than those with duller, uneven veins. Version from the 1950s, recognised by their tapered ends, are often brighter and more visually appealing. Also look out for the rare 'Reverse Cracked Ice' plastic, with silver marbling shot through with black veins, as these can fetch around 25 per cent more.

A 1930s Conway Stewart No.475 'Cracked Ice' celluloid lever-filler, with a medium Conway Stewart 14ct nib.

£120-180 BPH

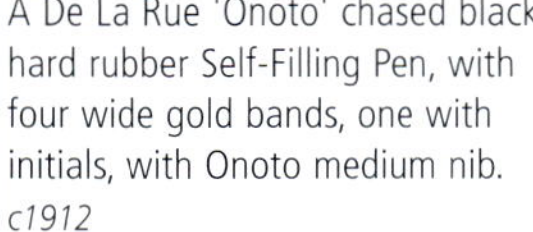

A De La Rue 'Onoto' chased black hard rubber Self-Filling Pen, with four wide gold bands, one with initials, with Onoto medium nib.

c1912

£50-80 **AMER**

A De La Rue 'Onoto The Pen' Regina blue plunger-filler, with wide oblique Onoto no.3 nib.

c1935

£80-120 **AMER**

An De La Rue 'Onoto The Pen' No.3234 burgundy pearl and black marbled plunger-filler, with Onoto medium no.5 two tone nib.

These handsome and elegant marbled pens, dating from the 1940s and early 1950s, are of high quality and have become very desirable over the past few years.

c1948

£120-180 **HSR**

A De La Rue Onoto 'Magna' No.1873 piston-filler, with engine-turned wavy line decoration and Onoto two-tone no.7 nib, in excellent condition.

As its name suggests, the 'Magna' was De La Rue's largest standard production pen, and is sought after today. The hallmark plunger mechanism and 'Onoto' brand name were developed in 1905. The name Onoto was chosen because it had no meaning and the pronunciation was similar in all languages.

c1947

£250-350 **PC**

A De La Rue 'Onoto' green pearl and black marble lever-filler, with Onoto fine no.3ST nib.

c1950

£60-90 **HSR**

A 1920s Sheaffer 'Secretary' bright red flat top lever-filler, stamped 'C' on the barrel end, with a Sheaffer Secretary nib.

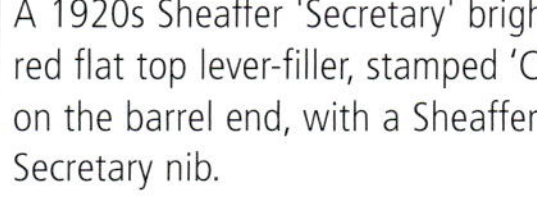

£80-120 **AMER**

A 1950s Sheaffer green Sentinel snorkel-filler, with silver tone cap, and Sheaffer two-colour 14k nib.

£40-60 **BPH**

A Sheaffer Balance pearl and black lever-filler, with ring-top cap, and Sheaffer two-tone 15k nib.

c1930

£80-120 **BPH**

QUICK REFERENCE – SHEAFFER'S PFM

PFM stands for 'Pen For Men', and is often said to have been the last great design of the golden age of the fountain pen. Introduced in 1959, it came in five different models, ranging from the PFM I, with a plastic barrel, stainless steel clip and palladium silver nib, upwards. All were set with Sheaffer's new 'inlaid' nib that has since become a hallmark of the company. Despite being popular with collectors today, it was not successful at the time. By 1963, the range was cut down to the III and V, and the model was phased out in 1968. This PFM V fountain pen retailed at £15 in 1959, and was marketed as having a 'man-sized barrel' with 'the only inlaid point in the world...built to take man-sized pressure'.

An American Sheaffer PFM V blue snorkel-filler and ballpen set, with gold-filled caps, and with Sheaffer fine 14ct inlaid nib.

1959-68

£200-250 **HSR**

An American Sheaffer PFM V snorkel-filler, with gold-filled cap and burgundy barrel, and medium Sheaffer 14K inlaid nib.

1955

£60-90 **HSR**

A 1980s Sheaffer Targa convertor/cartridge-filler, with 18k Sheaffer inset nib.

£100-150 **BPH**

A Sheaffer limited edition Lifetime Balance lever-filler, from an edition of 6,000.

This is a faithful copy of Sheaffer's 1929 Balance pen.

1997

£500-700 **PC**

An English Mabie Todd & Co. Swan chased black hard rubber eyedropper 'Chatelaine' pen, with scroll embossed gold-plated cap and barrel ends and chain.

c1905

£80-120 **PC**

A Mabie, Todd & Co. Swan black hard rubber eyedropper pen, with gold-filled scrolling filigree overlay, metal overfeed and a medium flexible Mabie, Todd & Co. nib, the barrel engraved 'H.H.S'.

It is rare to find Swan pens with gold-plated filigree overlays from this period in such excellent condition.

c1910

£320-380 **HSR**

A late 1920s Mabie, Todd & Co. Swan Eternal no.644B/61 red and black mottled hard rubber lever-filling pen, with Swan no.8 nib.

This is a scarce large no.8 size pen, and is highly desirable.

£200-300 **PC**

Two Mabie Todd & Co 'Blackbird' lever-filling pens one in green, the other in blue, in mint condition, with original price bands.

c1948

£50-80 **BPH**

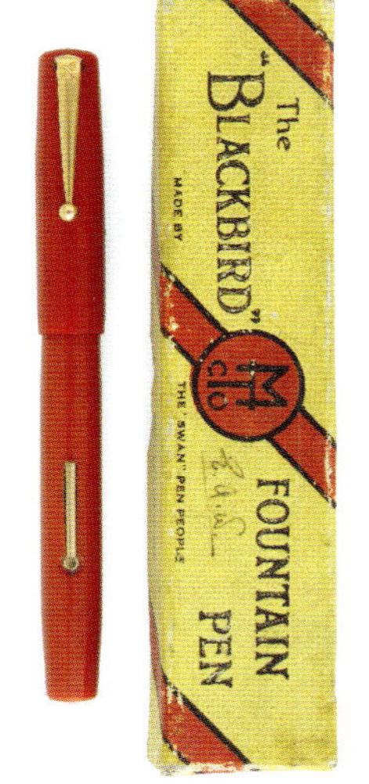

A Mabie Todd & Co 'Blackbird' red lever-filler, with Blackbird nib and period box.

The Blackbird range was the company's mid-range brand, and was sold at more affordable prices. This bright, pillar box red is the rarest colour in the series.

c1948

£50-70 **BPH**

A CLOSER LOOK AT A SWAN PEN SET

Swan's Leverless pens were introduced in 1932 and were filled by twisting the bottom part of the barrel, which moved an internal metal bar to compress the ink sack and draw in ink when released.

This model is rare, and it is even harder to find a pen and pencil set in such excellent condition.

The Art Deco styling with its flat-top, which is typical of the period, and repeated gold plated band design, is appealing.

The pen became even more desirable after it was featured on the cover of the landmark book 'Fountain Pens Vintage & Modern' by Andreas Lambrou.

A Mabie Todd Swan no.275/60 Leverless pen and Fyne Poynt pencil set, with rolled gold overlay and bands to cap and barrel, with broad Swan no.2 nib.

c1934

£400-500 **HSR**

A 1920s Montblanc smooth black hard rubber 4B safety pen, with Montblanc 14ct no.4 nib.

The barrel is marked Simplo, which was the original brand name used by the company founded in Hamburg, Germany in 1908 that became Montblanc. Many early Montblanc, and all Simplo 'Rouge et Noir' pens were safety pens.

£300-400 **AMER**

A 1930s Montblanc 333 1/2 EF black celluloid piston-filler, with plain ink window and Montblanc 3 1/2 14ct nib, in excellent condition.

£200-300 **AMER**

A 1950s Montblanc Meisterstück 144G-F black celluloid piston-filler, with striped ink window and two-colour Montblanc 14ct fine nib.

£150-200 **AMER**

A Montblanc 254 black celluloid piston-filling pen, with gold plated trim, clear ink window and Montblanc medium 14ct nib.

c1955

£70-100 **PC**

A Montblanc 'Peter I The Great' fountain pen, numbered 412 from a limited edition of 888, in dark green resin with white gold overlay, the cap top set with emeralds, with a Montblanc 18k medium nib, in presentation box, with paperwork and card outer box.

Montblanc has become known for its limited-edition pens, which must be in unused, mint condition and complete with their boxes and paperwork to fetch high values. This was the sixth pen in the 'Patrons of Art' series. A version with a gold-plated overlay was made in an edition size of 4810, which corresponds with the height of Mont Blanc in metres.

1997

£2,000-2,500 **AMER**

A CLOSER LOOK AT A MONTBLANC PEN

This rare and unusual model is not recorded in any Montblanc reference book. The steel nib and brass trim indicate that this was a budget 3-series pen.

Montblanc often sold branded components, such as nibs, to factories in countries such as Spain, Denmark and Italy, where they would be assembled.

Spanish and Italian examples are often marked with the country of manufacture, but this simply bears the Montblanc cap star and the Montblanc name and mountain logo.

It is likely that this was made in France, as the size, clip style, and torpedo shape bear similarities to pens made in France at the time.

A 1940s probably French Montblanc black celluloid button-filler, with brass trim and a medium-oblique Montblanc no.3 steel nib.

£100-150 **PC**

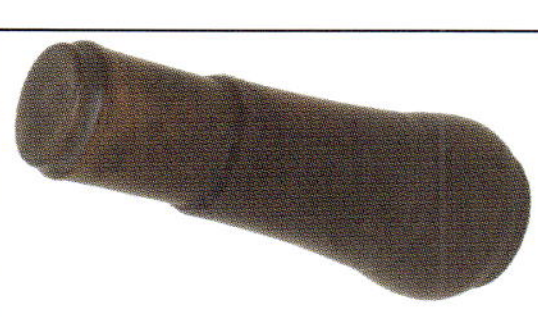

A rare 18thC rootwood inkhorn, with screw-off cover over the inkwell, and screw-off base with pierced wooden plate for pounce, in excellent condition.

Pounce was a powder sprinkled over a newly written document to dry the ink. Once it was dry, the pounce was poured back into its container.

3.5in (9cm) high

£100-150 BLO

An unusual late 19thC spelter inkwell, probably Scandinavian, the hinged cover with mask of a Green Man, the body decorated with female heads at each corner, lion maks and floral garlands, the legs decorated with lion masks and pad feet, with ceramic liner.

4in (10cm) wide

£70-90 BLO

A German Soennecken black hard rubber füllflacshe (inkflask) Nr 902, in original card box, together with a Montblanc-style black hard rubber inkbottle with cracked cap and oxidation.

c1920

£70-100 BLO

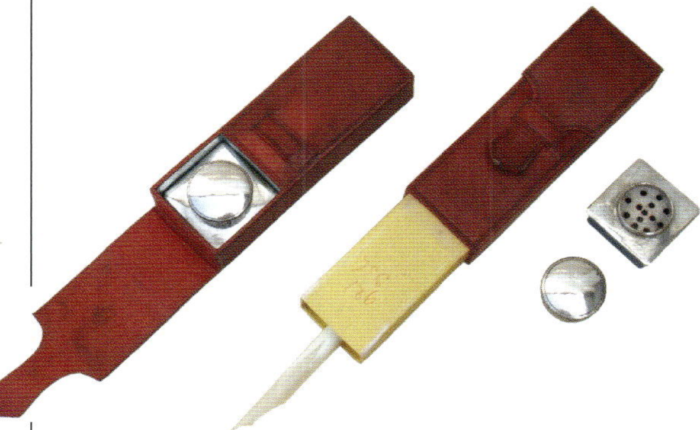

A rare English travelling writing compendium, the rectangular red morocco leather case in two parts to hold quill pens, with a Sheffield Plate inkwell with screw-off cover, and a similar pounce pot, in excellent condition.

c1810-20 *7.25in (18.5cm) long closed*

£350-450 BLO

A 'Parker Quink Ink' ceramic jar, designed by Hobbs Welch, with printed mark and Design Centre paper label.

Modelled on the famous Quink bottle, these were typically used as countertop displays and storage jars in shops. This is a particularly strong price for one of these, as they often fetch around half this price or under. Always look out for cracks, as they were easily damaged.

c1982 *7.75in (20cm) high*

£70-100 WW

A 1920-1930s Stephens' travelling ink bottle case, the top embossed 'Stephens', with an empty bottle of Stephens red ink.

£20-30 PC

A 1980s English Parker Duofold-style ceramic oversized display pen, with lift-off lid.

These were also used as counter top displays in shop.

£20-30 PC

QUICK REFERENCE – BAKELITE

- In 1907 Belgian chemist Dr Leo Baekeland developed the first entirely synthetic plastic, known as Bakelite. Cheap to produce and extremely versatile, it became known as 'the material of 1,000 uses' and was used both in industry and for decorative and functional purposes in the home.
- Bakelite was produced in a range of different colours with black and brown being the most common. Rarer colours were red, green and blue.
- The development of Bakelite prompted a boom in the plastics industry that led to many variants being produced. Although these are slightly different materials, the name 'bakelite' is commonly used to refer to many early plastics.

A 1930s brown Bakelite inkwell and pen box, marked 'INSURE WITH THE BRITISH GENERAL INSURANCE COMPANY'.

The well proportioned, rounded form is particularly well made.

6in (15.5cm) long

£50-60 **P&I**

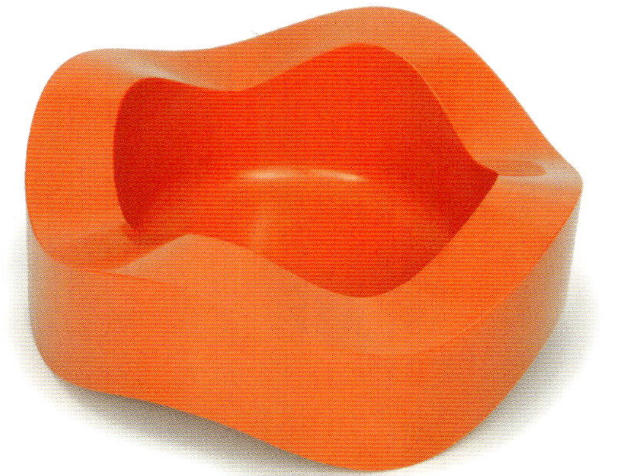

A 1960s-70s German Helit '11 Sinus' orange Melamine stacking ashtray, designed by Walter Zeischegg in 1966, the base moulded 'HELIT 84005 MADE IN GERMANY'.

This famous ashtray can be found in a range of colours, and the form was also produced in Bakelite by Kartro in Brazil. Walter Zeischegg (1917-1983) studied sculpture in Vienna, and was one of the founders and lecturers of the Ulm School of Design. Devoting himself to design from 1950 onwards, he followed the work of Max Bill and worked with Carl Aubock, before designing primarily for Helit.

5.25in (13cm) diam

£10-15 **M20C**

A 1920s Linsden multicoloured mottled Bakelite box, with revolving compartmentalised tray, the base moulded 'Linsden'.

These can also be found in mottled brown Bakelite, which is less desirable. This example is unfaded, with even the outside retaining its variety of strong colours. The Bakelite around the metal pins that allows the panel to revolve, and between the top and sides, is also not damaged. Although it is often mistaken for a stationery box, this was actually a smoker's companion.

3.75in (9.5cm) high

£30-50 **P&I**

A rare 1930s Bonbons Martougin mottled brown Bakelite box, the top with moulded head of Minerva.

6.25in (15.5cm) diam

£70-100 **P&I**

Four 1970s Pentagram stacking and interlocking plastic dishes or ashtrays, the bases moulded 'DO REG.NO.954,589 PENTAGRAM'.

The design registration number dates from late 1971.

4.25in (10.5cm) diam

£20-25 EACH **M20C**

A rare brown Bakelite miniature quaitch, marked 'MADE IN SCOTLAND'.

Scottish-made Bakelite is scarce.

4.25in (11cm) long

£8-12 **P&I**

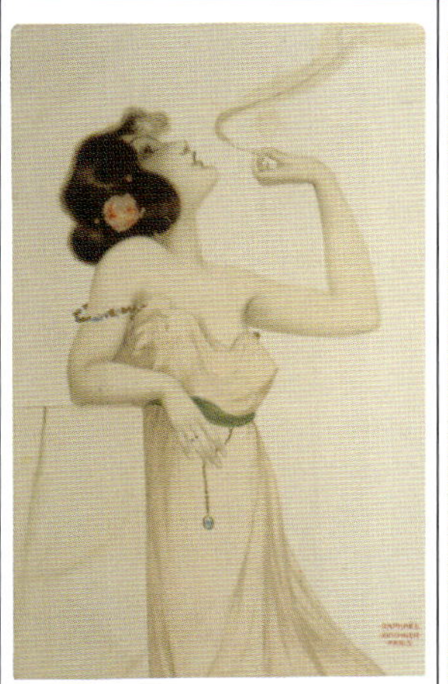

A French Art Nouveau glamour postcard, by Raphael Kirchner.

£40-60 MCS

A comic postcard, by Donald McGill.

£4-5 MCS

A 'The Bully' cat postcard, by Louis Wain.

Louis Wain (1860-1939) was an English artist, known for his illustrations of cats with personality. In 1917, he began to suffer from schizophrenia and was admitted to a mental hospital in 1924.

5in (12.5cm) high.

£25-35 M&C

A hand embroidered silk postcard, of the kind made by Second World War troops.

£5-7 MCS

A black and white photographic postcard, depicting the Cairngorm Mountains, from The Best of All Series, published by J. B. White, Dundee.

50P-£1 SOR

QUICK REFERENCE

- Promotional film posters come in many shapes and sizes, ranging from small glossy stills for display inside cinemas to 24-sheet billposters. The most popular of these are the more easily displayed US one-sheet 27in (68.5cm) by 41in (104cm) size and the UK quad 30in (76cm) by 40in (84cm) size.
- Posters for popular films, classic and cult favourites are usually desirable, particularly those with an appealing image or style. Little-known films are generally less sought after, unless the poster was created by a famous artist, such as Robert Peal, Giuliano Nistri or Saul Bass.
- Different promotional posters are produced for each country the film is released in. Apart from being in a foreign language, they can also have different artwork and vary from the original in other ways. For example, Belgian posters tend to be smaller but often have visually stunning artwork, while Australian posters are larger but sometimes have weaker artwork. In general, you should look out for original posters produced for the film's country of origin, as these are usually most popular.
- Posters may be re-issued if a film is re-released or has won an award, or following its release on video or DVD. These re-releases should not be confused with the originals, which are usually more valuable. Reproductions (photographic images of the original, printed on shiny poster paper) are also common, as are fakes. In forged or reproduced posters, the image may be pixelated or in different tones of colour. The best way to avoid buying a fake is to gain familiarity with originals from reputable dealers or auction houses.
- Condition is important, with folding, tears and stains reducing value, particularly if the surface of the image is affected. However, mint condition examples can be hard to find, and some damage can be restored. Posters can also be professionally backed onto linen or other materials. This does not reduce value and can enhance desirability.

'Batman', American one sheet, framed and glazed, in very good condition.

1966 *40in (101.5cm) high*

£500-750 **MAS**

'A Bigger Splash', by David Hockney (b.1937), printed by Nonsdale & Bartholomew, Nottingham, original UK quad, in near mint condition, linen-backed.

1974 *40in (102cm) wide*

£200-300 **BLNY**

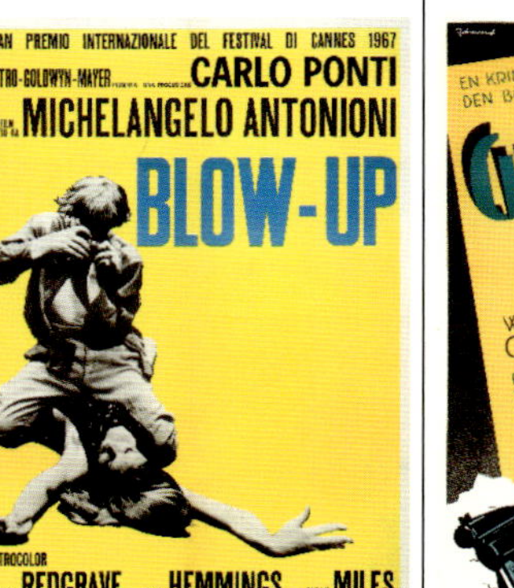

'Blow-Up', printed by Rotolito, original Italian due-foglio (two-sheet), linen-backed.

1967 *55in (140cm) high*

£550-750 **BLNY**

'Charlie Chan I London', Swedish film poster by Rohman, lithograph in colours printed by J. Olsens, linen-backed.

1934 *39in (99cm) high*

£300-500 **BLNY**

'A Clockwork Orange', designed by Philip Castle, printed by W.E. Barry, Ltd., Bradford, original UK quad, linen-backed.

1971 *40in (102cm)*

£300-450 **BLNY**

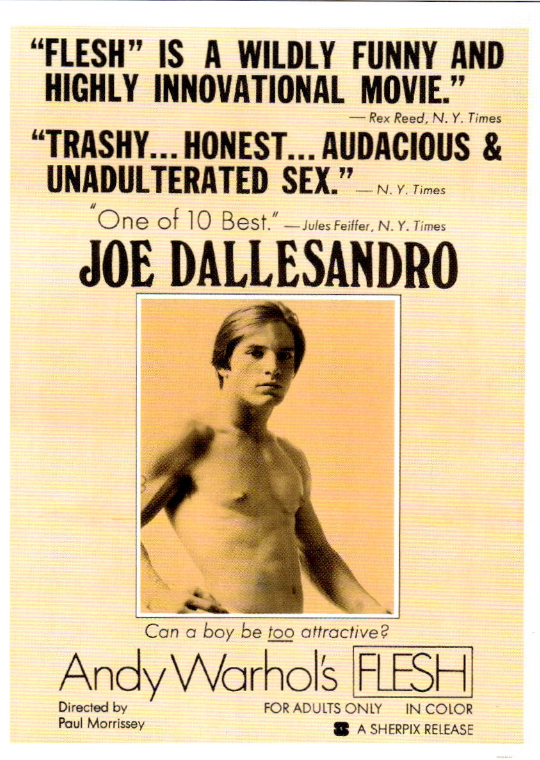

'Andy Warhol's Flesh', American one sheet, in near mint condition, linen-backed.

Directed by Joe Morrissey, the controversial 'Flesh' was one of the first general release films to objectify the naked male body, in this case that of the New York hustler, Joe Dallesandro.

1970 *41in (104cm)*

£300-450 **BLNY**

'Jour de Fête', by Rene Péron, French issue for the 16mm release, lithograph in colours, linen-backed.

1948 *47in (119cm) high*

£450-550 **BLNY**

'The Godfather', American one sheet, offset lithograph in black and white, in near mint condition, linen-backed.

1972 *41in (104cm)*

£150-250 **BLNY**

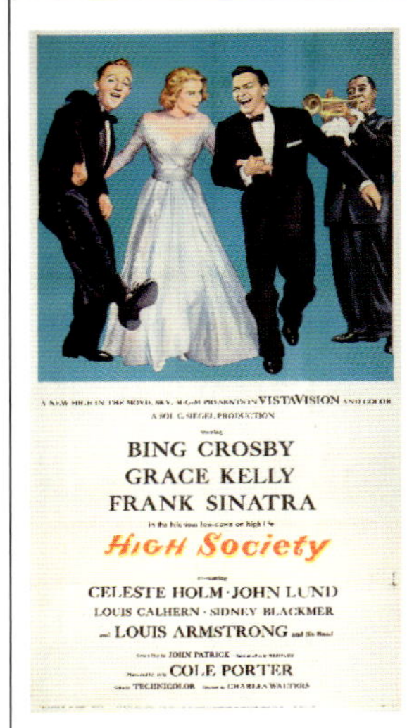

'High Society', by an unknown designer, American one sheet, linen-backed.

1956 *81in (206cm)*

£500-750 **BLNY**

'The Lord of the Rings', British one sheet artists' poster, printed by Berry Ltd, folded.

The first film produced from Tolkien's famous series is best known for its use of 'Rotoscope' animation, where live-action film images are traced over into animation. Although a financial success, it was panned by many critics and the second half was never made.

1978 *40in (101.5cm) wide*

£80-120 **GORL**

'Manhattan', American one sheet, Style B, in near mint condition, linen-backed.

This Style B version is considered scarcer and more desirable than others.

1979 *41in (104cm) high*

£150-200 **BLNY**

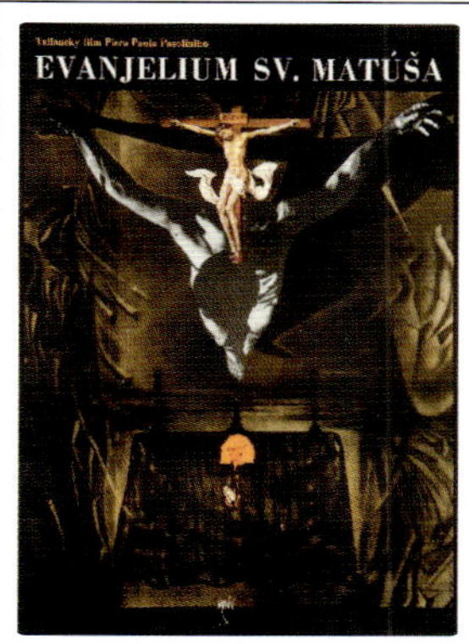

'Evanjelium Sv. Matusa' Czech one sheet, by Josef Vyletal, lithograph in colours, linen-backed.

Vyletal is considered a leading and innovative designer, working from the 1960s onwards.

1967 *33in (84cm) high*

£200-300 **BLNY**

'Wakacje Pana Hulot' (Mr Hulot's Holiday), by Zbigniew Lengren (1919-2003), original Polish issue, offset lithograph in colours, linen-backed.

1953 *33in (84cm)*

£350-450 **BLNY**

QUICK REFERENCE – EASTERN EUROPEAN POSTERS

Poster design from the former Eastern Block, particularly the Czech Republic and Poland, has become highly desirable over the past decade. Innovative artists produced startling designs that often incorporated unusual visual elements, such as photomontage, collage and a dynamic use of composition, colour, perspective and typography. This Russian poster, by the noted Stenberg brothers, is typical. The Stenbergs, who created most of their work in Moscow from 1924-33 following the principles of Russian avant garde art, are considered forerunners of this diverse and increasingly popular style.

'Mabul', by Vladimir & Georgii Stenberg, Russian lithograph in colours, linen backed.

1927 *28in (71.5cm) high*

£2,000-3,000 **BLNY**

'Moulin Rouge', by Rosie, East German lithograph poster in colours, linen-backed.

This design clearly uses Toulouse Lautrec as inspiration, a theme that marries up with the title of the film perfectly.

1952 *33in (84cm) high*

£1,000-1,500 **BLNY**

'Vecírek' (The Party), Czechoslovakian poster, by an unknown designer, linen-backed.

1970 *33in (84cm) high*

£150-200 **BLNY**

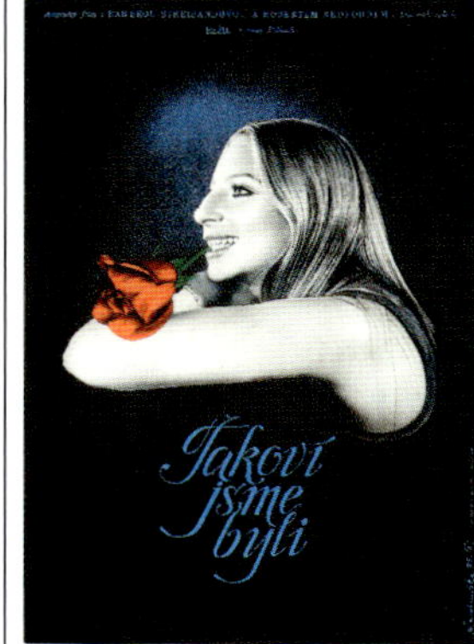

'Takoví Jsme Byli' (The Way We Were), by an unknown designer, Czechoslovakian poster, in near mint condition, linen-backed.

1973 *33in (84cm)*

£150-200 **BLNY**

QUICK REFERENCE

- By the mid20thC, travel was available and cheap enough to be a viable option for more people than ever before. As more people took holidays, travel posters began to rapidly increase in popularity. The earliest and most prolific of these were ocean-liner and railway company posters, and these continue to be the most popular with collectors. Airlines began to compete commercially with cruise liners from the 1950s onwards and, despite the arrival of television advertising, many appealing and collectable posters were produced during this period.
- Many railway posters did not feature images of trains or railways. Instead, most aimed at luring people away from their everyday lives by displaying brightly-coloured, exotic scenes, unlike any to be seen in the busting city. These included ships, golfing scenes or hotels, and town, seaside an countryside views. Images of green, rolling hills in England tend to be particularly popular with collectors.
- Artwork by popular designers, such as Cassandre (Adolphe Mouron), Frank Brangwyn and Tom Purvis, will usually be desirable, as will major names in travel, such as White Star, BOAC, Air France and Canadian Pacific. However, the 'eye appeal' of the image is often the primary indicator to value, because many buyers will wish to display these posters in their homes. Striking, brightly coloured designs that display the excitement and glamour of travel are desirable, particularly those in popular styles, such as Art Deco or 1950s.
- As aesthetic appeal is paramount, condition is important. Many posters were folded in storage before they became popular collectables, so folds are acceptable and can often easily be removed by a professional restorer. However, tears that extend into the image and any damage that seriously mars the surface of the image will reduce a poster's value and desirability considerably.

'Helensburgh', by Frank H Mason, railway poster printed for LNER by McCorquodale & Co Ltd.

1941 *40in (102cm)*

£350-450 ON

'North East England Warksworth Castle', railway poster printed for the North Eastern Railways by Albery & Co., with small losses to margins.

40in (102cm) high

£150-200 ON

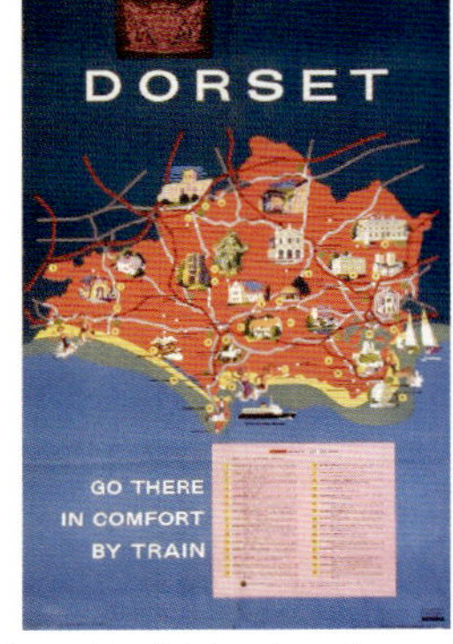

'Dorset' by Eric Lander, railway poster printed for the Southern Railway (British Rail) by Leonard Ripley & Co Ltd.

40in (102cm) high

£120-180 ON

'Great Western Railway, Sunny South Wales', by an anonymous designer, with vignettes showing golf, tennis, yachting and a map of the system, printed by Felix J Pole.

40in (102cm) high

£250-350 ON

A Longman Facts and Figures 1 Passenger Services poster, printed for BR(WR) by Stafford & Co Ltd.

40in (102cm) high

£150-200 ON

'Brides les Bains', by Leon Benigni, for PLM railways, lithograph in colours, linen-backed.

1929 *39in (99cm) high*

£1,200-1,500 **BLNY**

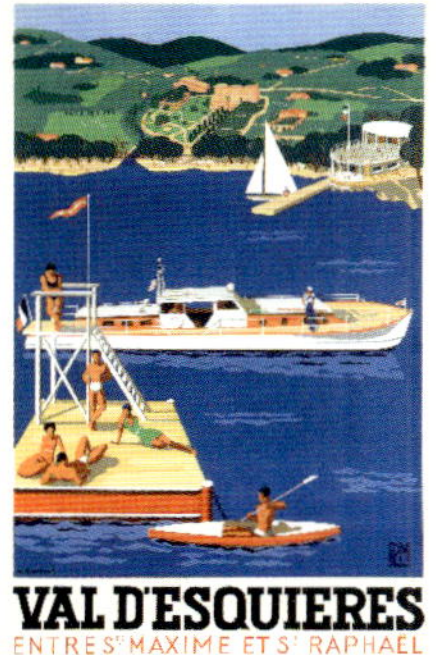

'Val D'Esquières', by Michel Bouchaud, printed by Lucien Serre & Cie for PLM railways, linen-backed.

c1930 *39in (99cm)*

£1,000-1,500 **BLNY**

A CLOSER LOOK AT A FRENCH RAILWAY POSTER

The flat planes of colour and limited palette recall the work of the famous French Art Deco poster designer Adolphe Mouron, known as 'Cassandre', whose work can fetch thousands of pounds.

The use of the railway, and the sharp angle and sense of perspective it gives, are also hallmarks of Cassandre, and many of the best Art Deco travel posters.

PLM was the Paris to Lyon and the Mediterranean railway. Its appealing posters for desirable holiday spots along its routes are highly sought after.

This poster can be found in three different colourways, this purple, green, and white and light blue – there is little difference in the price.

'Vers le Mont Blanc', by George Dorival, printed by Lucien Serre & Cie for PLM railways, linen-backed.

1928 *41in (104cm) high*

£1,500-2,000 **BLNY**

'Saint Raphaël', by J. Munier, lithograph in colours printed by Moullot for SNCF, linen backed.

As well as railway collectors, this colourful and attractive French poster would also appeal to tennis memorabilia collectors, and posters with this theme are hard to find.

c1925 *39in (100cm) high*

£600-950 **BLNY**

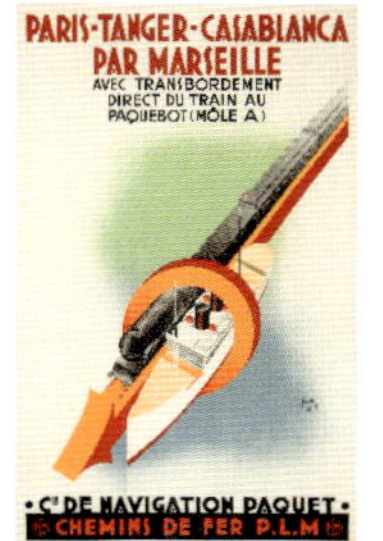

'Paris Tanger Casablanca Par Marseille, Cie de Navigation Paquet', by Hardy, lithograph in co ours printed by M. Dechaux for PLM railways, linen-backed.

1933 *39.5in (100cm) high*

£600-950 **BLNY**

'The Ancient Theatre at Arles' by Leopold Lelée, printed by Lucien Serre & cie for PLM railways, with folds.

39.5in (100cm) high

£40-60 **ON**

'Pan American World Airways to Australia and New Zealand', by an anonymous designer, lithograph in colours, linen-backed.

c1950 *39.5in (101cm) high*

£450-550 **BLNY**

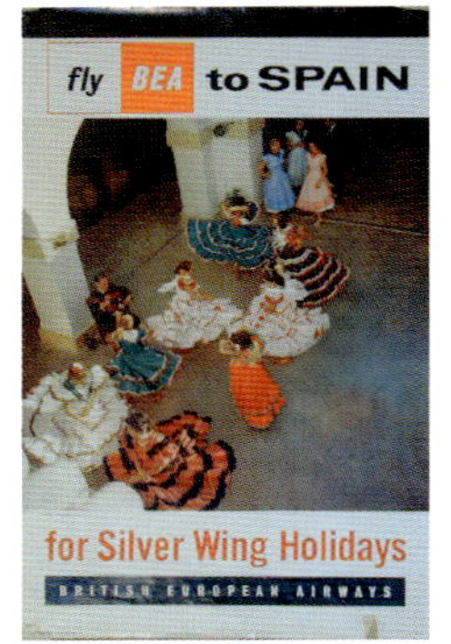

'Fly BEA to Spain for Silver Wing Holidays', colour photographic poster by an anonymous designer.

c1965 *40in (102cm) high*

£30-40 **ON**

A CLOSER LOOK AT AN AIRLINE POSTER

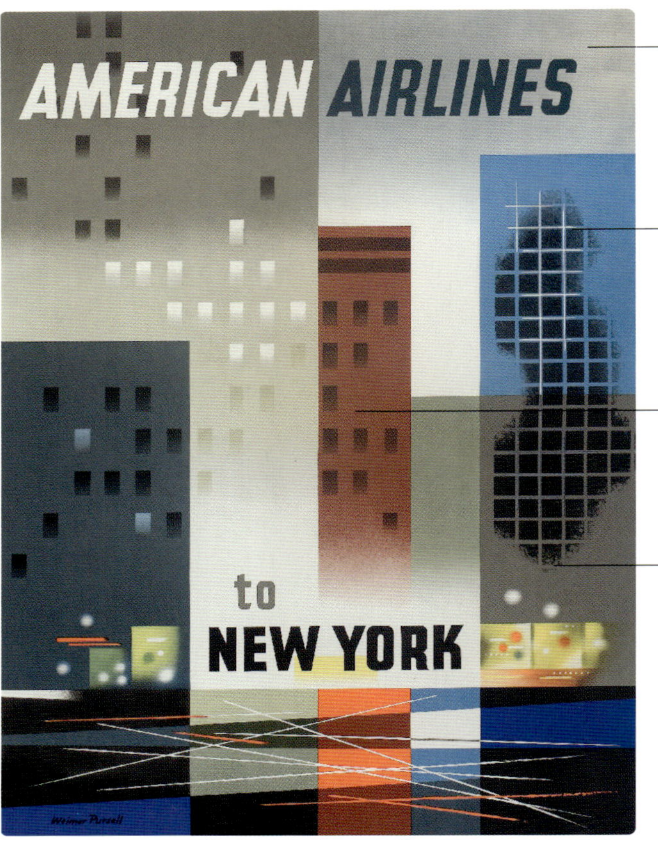

Award-winning artist Weimer Pursell (1906-1974) produced poster designs for major companies including Coca Cola, Standard Oil and American Airlines.

The use of geometric forms and lines in bright colours contrasted against black is typical of Pursell's work, and reflect his interest in modern abstract art.

The abstract forms are buildings in Manhattan, with the lines on the 'pavement' hinting at people going places, or even the subway system.

He is also known for his Art Deco poster designs for the 1933 Chicago World's Fair. His work is sought after and can be hard to find.

'American Airlines to New York', designed by Weimer Pursell, with minor wrinkles.

c1956 *39.75in (101cm) high*

£3,000-5,000 **SWA**

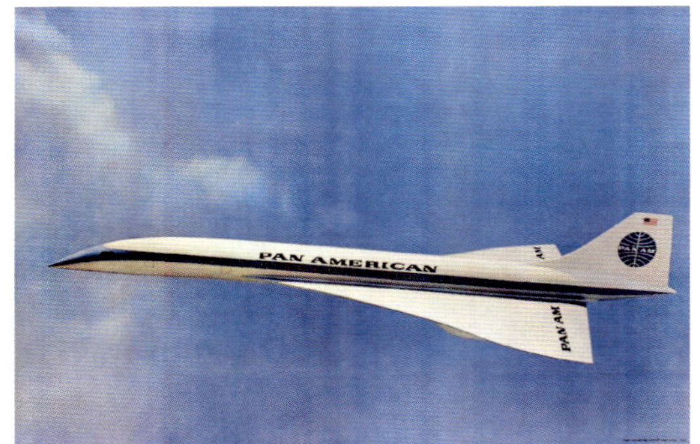

'Pan Am's Supersonic Clipper' photographic poster featuring Concorde, printed in America.

c1965 *111.5in (283cm) wide*

£120-180 **VSA**

'Blue Star Line to South America', by Norman Wilson, lithograph in colours, printed by McCorquodale & Co., London, linen-backed.

c1930 *40in (102cm) high*

£600-950 **BLNY**

'Blue Star Line A Europa', by an anonymous designer, lithograph in colours printed by John Waddington, London, linen-backed.

c1925 *40in (102cm) high*

£1,500-2,000 **BLNY**

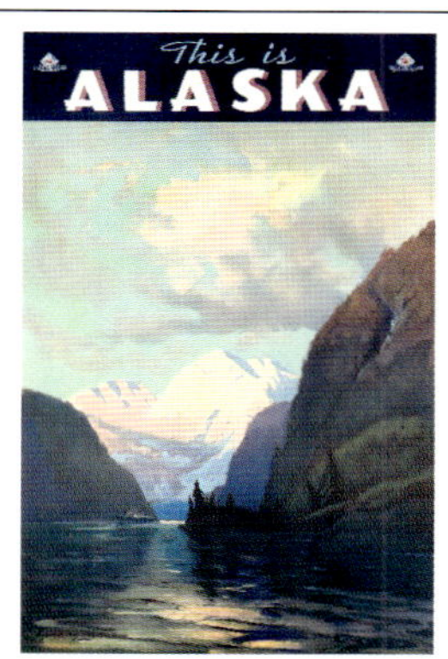

'This Is Alaska', by an anonymous designer, lithograph in colours printed for the Alaska Steamship Line, backed on linen.

c1950 *34in (86cm) high*

£300-400 **BLNY**

'Spiez', by Otto Baumberger, lithograph in colours, printed by Fretz & Frères, Zurich, backed on Japan paper.

1938 *40in (102cm) high*

£400-500 **BLNY**

'Route des Pyrènnées, Services d'autocar de la Cie du Midi', by Roger Soubie, printed by Baudelot, with tears, folds and losses.

40.5in (103cm)

£300-400 **ON**

'Roman & Mediaeval France', coaching poster by Lajos Marton, printed by McCorquodale for PLM Autocars.

1935 *39.5in (100cm) high*

£40-60 **ON**

'Avranches Baie de Mont St Michel', by Albert Bergevin for the Avranches Syndicat D'Initiative, lithograph in colours, linen-backed.

Bergevin (1887-1974) lived in Avranches, a hillside town that overlooks the bay of Mont St Michel. The colourful Art Nouveau style, very much inspired by Henri de Toulouse Lautrec, is appealing.

c1920 *42in (107cm) high*

£1,200-1,500 **BLNY**

'Play Golf in Germany', by Osswald, lithograph in colours, printed by Oscar Consee, Munich, linen-backed.

As with the tennis-themed poster on a previous page, the golfing theme adds value to this poster.

1930 *39in (99cm) high*

£800-1,000 **BLNY**

'Coq Sur Mer', tourism poster by Martin Melsen, printed by Henri Melsen, Brussels, linen-backed.

1923 *39in (99cm) high*

£500-700 **BLNY**

QUICK REFERENCE

- Pictorial posters advertising products enjoyed a golden age that began in the late 19thC and lasted for almost a century. The 1920s and 1930s saw particularly innovative posters, as influential and prolific designers pushed boundaries to see what they could create. Although the advent of television largely took over the advertising market, product posters are still sought after today due to their visual appeal and their importance to the 20thC poster and graphic design.
- Always consider the brand and the item depicted. Certain long-lived brands have become 'household names' and these are usually desirable and often valuable as they have a large following of collectors. Meanwhile, posters advertising smoking are becoming more sought-after, partly as a document of social history as the habit becomes less popular. Smoking posters also have cross-market interest (as they appeal to collectors of smoking memorabilia as well as poster collectors), and other products with cross-market interest, such as cars or cycling, may also prove to be desirable. It is also worth considering 1970s posters advertising brands that are now popular. Posters from this era onwards are usually not as highly priced as earlier posters, and may be worth investing in, particularly if nostalgia for the brand grows in the future.
- In general, look for striking images with bold, bright colours, and designs that are typical of the period – Art Nouveau and Art Deco posters are sought after, as are those from the 1950s. A strong design by a notable designer, such as Jean Carlu, Paul Colin or Bernard Villemot, will also be desirable. However, visual appeal is paramount – an attractive poster for an unknown brand will usually prove popular.
- Condition is very important, so avoid those examples with tears and damage. This is particularly true of posters from the 1970s onwards, which you should buy in as close to mint condition as possible.

'Lefèvre-Utile Gaufrettes Vanille', biscuit poster by Alphonse Mucha, lithograph in colours, framed and glazed.

c1890 *8in (20cm) high*

£350-450 **BLNY**

A CLOSER LOOK AT A LEFEVRE-UTILE POSTER

French biscuit maker Lefèvre Utile is a collectable name, particularly designs by notable Art Nouveau designer Alphonse Mucha like the one on the left.

This is a complex and highly detailed image, printed with many different colours and tones, that gives a superb period feel.

Bocchino produced a number of designs for Lefevre-Utile, all with a wholesome feel that has led to him being dubbed the 'Norman Rockwell of the biscuit world'.

'Lefèvre-Utile', by Vincent Bocchino, printed by F. Champenois, Paris, lithograph in colours, in near mint condition, backed on card.

1911 *27in (68cm) wide*

£1,000-1,500 **BLNY**

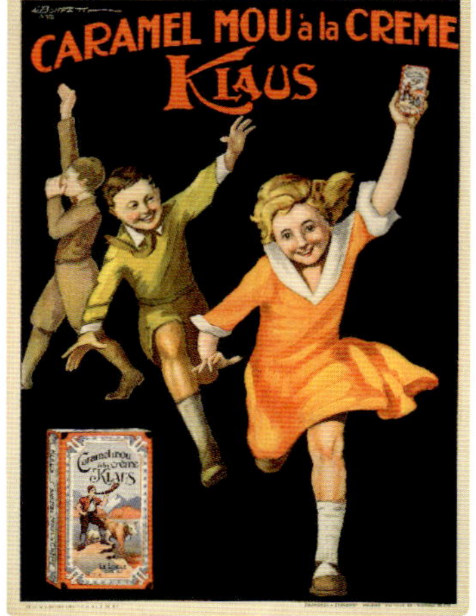

'Caramel Klaus' by Giovanni Bonfatti, printed by Raimondi & Zaccardi, Milan, in very good condition, linen-backed.

c1920 *55in (140cm) high*

£800-1,200 **BLNY**

'Souriez Madame! C'est du Cleret' by Jean d'Ylen, printed by Vercasson, mounted on linen with restoration.

15.75in (40cm) high

£150-250 **ON**

'Mazawatte Tea', by an unknown designer, printed by Stafford & Co., two sheet poster, lithograph in colours, mint condition, linen-backed.

c1920 *40in (102cm)*

£600-900 **BLNY**

'Monet Goyon', by P.D., printed by Affiches Gaillard, Paris, lithograph in colours, linen-backed.

c1930 *43.5in (110cm) high*

£1,000-1,500 **BLNY**

'Monet Goyon', by P.D., printed by Affiches Gaillard, Paris, lithograph in colours, in near mint condition, linen-backed.

Art Deco and later posters that hint at the speed of cars or motorcycles, as here, are usually highly sought after.

c1930 *44in (112cm)*

£1,200-1,600 **BLNY**

A CLOSER LOOK AT A SHELL POSTER

This is executed in the typical muted colour palette found on many Shell posters of the 1930s-50s, and is titled in the same way as much of the rest of the series.

Mann is not considered one of the most sought after designers in the series, but the angular, abstract and modern style is appealing.

The campaign, aimed at making people drive more, included designs by leading and innovative modern artists including Edward McKnight Kauffer and Hans Schleger.

Cathleen Mann (1896-1959) studied at the notable Slade School of Fine Art and produced a number of designs for Shell, British Petroleum and the London Underground.

'Film Stars use Shell', by Cathleen Mann, printed by The Baynard Press, lithograph in colours, in near mint condition, linen-backed.

1938 *45in (114cm) wide*

£800-1,200 **BLNY**

'Roval Voiture Pratique & Economique' by an anonymous designer, printed by Wall, Paris,, mounted on linen.

40in (102cm) wide

£500-700 **ON**

'Eco-Pneus', by an anonymous designer, lithograph in colours printed by Havas, Caen, linen-backed.

c1930 *46in (117cm) high*

£300-400 **BLNY**

'Pneu-Velo Continental', by an anonymous designer, printed by Editions & Publicité, Paris, linen-backed.

c1910 *30.5in (77cm) high*

£800-1,200 **BLNY**

'Starlight Savon', by Henri Meunier, lithograph in colours, printed by O. de Rycker, Brussels, linen-backed.

1899 *34in (87cm) high*

£1,000-1,500 BLNY

'Ripolin' paint advertising poster, by Jean d'Ylen, printed by Vercasson, mounted on linen with restoration.

29.5in (75cm) high

£400-600 ON

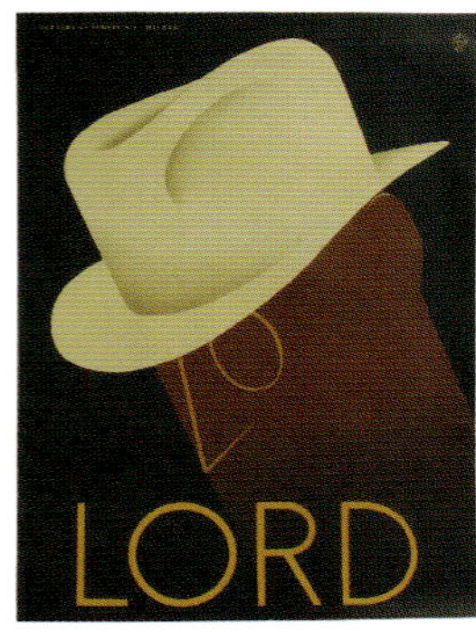

'Lord' hat advertising poster, by Paolo Federico Garretto, Alfieri & Lacroix S.A.-Milano, in excellent condition, linen-backed.

1930 *36in (91.5cm) high*

£150-250 SAS

'Splendid' cigar advertising poster, by Fred Neukomm (1905-1988), printed by Kummerly & Frey, Berne, lithograph in colours, linen-backed.

c1930 *50in (127cm) high*

£800-1,200 BLNY

QUICK REFERENCE - BERNARD VILLEMOT

French artist, illustrator and poster designer Bernard Villemot (1911-89) is considered one of the most important French post-war poster designers. He created his first poster for Bally in 1967 and worked with them for 22 years until his death. His first poster, known as 'Legs', won the Martini Prize Gold Medal, and subsequent designs went on to win the Grand Prix for poster design more than five times. This design, released during the peak of his skills, is known as 'Bally Kick'. He also worked for Air France, Orangina, and other companies. Influenced by the Bauhaus, his hallmark style uses flat planes of bold, contrasted colours, thin outlines and stylised abstracted forms. The result is a simple, yet highly feminine image that promotes Bally shoes as being glamourous and modern, and having great flair.

'Bally' shoe advertising poster, by Bernard Villemot, offset lithograph in colours, printed by A. Kacher, Paris, linen-backed.

1972 *65in (166cm) high*

£300-400 BLNY

'Vichy', by Bernard Villemot, lithograph in colours, printed by S.A. Courbet, Paris, linen-backed.

1953 *39.5in (100cm) high*

£500-600 BLNY

QUICK REFERENCE

- One of the first kinds of attractive packaging, these ceramic lids were used to cover pots containing products such as food, bear's grease (a hair product), or toothpaste. They were manufactured in Staffordshire, by companies including F. & R. Pratt, who were granted a related patent in 1848, T. J. & J. Mayer and J. Ridgway.
- The first pot lids were produced in the 1820s, and were transfer printed in blue and white, or black and white. By the 1830s they were being produced in bulk. Coloured lids appeared in the early 1840s. Over 350 images are known, some of which featured bears, which indicated bear's grease in the pot below. Some collectors choose to collect by image type, with bears and scenes of Pegwell Bay most popular.
- Before 1860, lids were flat and lightweight, and had a screw thread. The quality of these early pieces was high, and so they are usually the most desirable. The lids became heavier and convex between 1860 and 1875, and heavier still with flat tops after 1875. It is a good idea to handle as many lids as you can to get a feel for these weights.
- It is not possible to narrow down the date of most pot lids beyond these periods, as most are not dated and many images were produced for long periods. Examples that commemorate specific event, such as the Great Exhibition in 1851, can be dated c1851 as it is unlikely they were produced for long afterwards. Changes to design and some maker's marks can also help with dating.
- Collectors look for examples in excellent condition or those with unusual variations in design or borders. Always examine a scene carefully to identify any variations. Chips to flange and rim do not seriously affect value, but chips to design can cause a drop of 50-75 per cent. Be aware of reproductions – run your finger over a lid. If you feel the transfer, the piece is likely to be a later reproduction.
- The numbers given are used in K. V. Mortimer's 'Pot Lids Reference & Price Guide', the current standard reference guide for pot lids.

A Staffordshire 'The Volunteers' pot lid, no.217, probably produced by the Bates, Brown-Westhead, Moore & Co. factory from 1859.

£120-180 **SAS**

A Staffordshire 'The Wolf And The Lamb' pot lid, no.343, produced by the Pratt factory.

4.25in (10.5cm) diam

£25-35 **SAS**

A Staffordshire 'Our Pets' pot lid, no.330, with glaze flaking, produced by the Pratt factory, with registration diamond for March 1852 near the horse's tail.

4in (10cm) diam

£120-180 **SAS**

A Staffordshire 'On Guard' pot lid, no.334, with dog under the bench, produced by the Pratt factory.

On some lids, the dog is replaced by a bucket, but this does not usually affect the value.

4.25in (10.5cm) diam

£40-60 **SAS**

A Staffordshire 'The Snow-drift' pot lid, no.267, with a line and dot border.

The scene was based on Sir Edwin Landseer's oil painting 'Highland Shepherd's Dog In The Snow'.

4.25in (10.5cm) diam

£30-40 **SAS**

A Staffordshire 'New Houses of Parliament, Westminster' later issue pot lid, no.232, produced by the Pratt factory.

5.25in (13cm) diam

£100-150 **SAS**

A Staffordshire 'Albert Memorial' pot lid, no.241, produced by the Pratt factory.

This variation with the carriage is slightly less valuable than the one without. Earlier examples have green, rather than brown, trees.

4.25in (10.5cm) diam

£70-90 **SAS**

A large Staffordshire 'Drayton Manor' pot lid, no.102, with gilt-lined border, produced by the Mayer factory.

Showing the residence of politician and Prime Minister Sir Robert Peel, this lid was reproduced up to the 1960s by Mayer and Kirkhams, explaining its low value.

£50-70 **SAS**

A Staffordshire 'Great Exhibition 1851' pot lid, no.142, produced by the Mayer factory, restored.

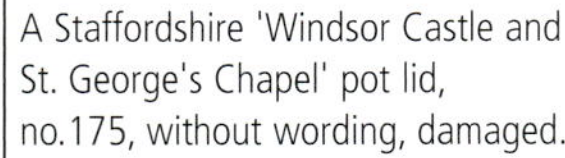

4.25in (10.5cm) diam

£40-60 **SAS**

A Staffordshire 'Windsor Castle and St. George's Chapel' pot lid, no.175, without wording, damaged.

A variation with advertising wording for Royal Windsor Toilet Cream can fetch over five times the price of this damaged example.

3.5in (9.5cm) diam

£60-80 **SAS**

A very rare Staffordshire 'Holy Trinity Church' pot lid, no. 229, with leaf and scroll border, produced by the William Pratt factory, restored.

This is the rarest of the series of lids showing buildings associated with Shakespeare.

5in (13cm) diam

£650-750 **SAS**

A Staffordshire 'The Administration Building World's Fair, Chicago 1893' pot lid, no.156, with a grey print.

Look out for other colours such as buff or a yellowy brown as these are extremely rare and may fetch over five times this sum.

4.25in (10.5cm) diam

£350-450 **SAS**

A Staffordshire 'Paris Exhibition 1878' pot lid, no.153, produced by the Pratt factory, with a dotted border and hairline crack.

4.5in (11cm) diam

£40-60 **SAS**

A Staffordshire 'The Ins' pot lid, no.15.

Produced as a pair with 'The Outs' shown below, examples with fancy borders fetch more. For an example, see 'Miller's Collectables Price Guide 2009', p.371.

3.5in (8cm) diam

£250-300 **SAS**

A Staffordshire 'The Village Wakes' pot lid, no.321, with fancy border, produced by the Pratt factory.

A very rare variation lacking the title, two children and the monkey can fetch over four times the value of this standard scene.

4in (10cm) diam

£450-550 **SAS**

A Staffordshire 'Bears on Rock' pot lid, no.10, with brown bears and gold banded border and flange, produced by the Mayer factory.

Brown bears on this early and small lid are very rare – black is more common.

3.25in (8cm) diam

£700-1,000 **SAS**

A Staffordshire 'The Outs' pot lid, no.16, by the Pratt or Ridgway factory.

3.5in (9cm) diam

£150-250 **SAS**

A Staffordshire 'The Bear Pit' pot lid, no.6, with wavy line border and without the dome on the left, produced by the Pratt factory.

3in (7.5cm) diam

£120-180 **SAS**

A CLOSER LOOK AT A POT LID

This is part of a popular trio of lids which includes 'The Village Wakes'.

Bear subjects are sought after, and this has a green printed base, as well as an unusual and fancy border which adds value.

'The Village Wakes' was taken from a watercolour by Jesse Austin. This was taken from a painting by the notable painter David Wilkie RA (1785-1845).

This lid bears a diamond registration mark near the roof of the house, showing it was registered in July 1852.

A Staffordshire 'The Parish Beadle' pot lid, no.322, complete with green printed Punch base.

4in (10cm) diam

£1,000-1,500 **SAS**

A Staffordshire 'Balaklava, Inkerman, Alma' pot lid, no.204, depicting the Earl of Cardigan, Lord Raglan, General Simpson and the Duke of Cambridge, produced by the Mayer factory, restored.

Later issues have poorer colours and are worth less than strongly coloured early examples, which can fetch around £600 or more.

5in (12.5cm) diam

£250-350 SAS

A Staffordshire 'Wellington with Cocked Hat' late issue pot lid, no.182, without lettering on the border, produced by the Mayer factory.

5.25in (13.5cm) diam

£400-600 SAS

A medium Staffordshire 'Tria Juncta in Uno' pot lid, no.202, depicting Queen Victoria, Napoleon II and Sultan Abd-ul-Majid, produced by the Mayer factory.

5in (13cm) diam

£350-450 SAS

A Staffordshire 'Napoleon III and Empress Eugenie' pot lid, no.181, with double line, laurel and berry border.

5.25in (13cm) diam

£200-300 SAS

A Staffordshire 'Queen Victoria and the Prince Consort' pot lid, no.167, almost certainly by the Pratt factory.

Look out for the extremely rare variation where Queen Victoria has no earring in her left ear.

5in (13cm) diam

£280-320 SAS

A CLOSER LOOK AT A POT LID

This rare lid was made by Bates, Walker & Co. around 1876 to commemorate the centenary of the War of Independence.

Hand-coloured examples are much rarer than monochrome lids and can fetch around twice this amount.

Exhibition lids are a collectable subject area, and the American War of Independence theme is also highly desirable.

It was probably produced for sale at H.P. & W.C. Taylor's stand at the Philadelphia Exhibition – look out for larger sizes as these are even rarer.

A Staffordshire 'Washington Crossing the Delaware' pot lid, no.157, smaller size, monochrome version, with base.

3.5in (9cm) diam

£1,500-2,500 SAS

A rare Staffordshire 'The Matador' pot lid, no.78, probably produced by the Mayer factory.

This very rare lid was also produced in an even smaller size.

3.5in (8.5cm) diam

£700-900 **SAS**

A Staffordshire 'Lady Brushing Hair' pot lid, no.111, with purple bodice and yellow skirt, produced by the Pratt factory.

Look out for a differently coloured variation with a bare breast – deemed too risqué for Victorian tastes it was withdrawn and is rare today. However, the rarest variation features the lady wearing a yellow bodice and short sleeves – this can fetch over three times the value of this example.

3in (7.5cm) diam

£200-300 **SAS**

A very rare Staffordshire 'The Kingfisher' pot lid, no.286, with gold line border, produced by the Mayer factory, restored.

5.25in (13cm) diam

£650-850 **SAS**

A Staffordshire 'The Swallow' pot lid, no.129, produced by the Bates, Elliott & Co. factory, restored.

3.75in (9.5cm) diam

£100-150 **SAS**

A Staffordshire 'Shells' pot lid, no.73, restored.

3.25in (8cm) diam

£50-80 **SAS**

A Staffordshire 'Rose & Convulvulus' pot lid, no.401, with gold line border, produced by the Pratt factory.

4in (10cm) diam

£180-220 **SAS**

A Staffordshire 'Royal Coat of Arms' pot lid, no.173, with blank blue panel beneath, restored.

Look out for the name 'J.N. Osborn' in the panel, as this can increase value by at least half.

4in (10cm) diam

£300-400 **SAS**

QUICK REFERENCE

- Surprisingly, the most important factor to consider is the case, as to most collectors the style and colour matter more than the internal radio mechanism. The golden age of radio design lasted from the 1930s until the late 1950s, with pre-war radios generally the most valuable.
- Most examples from the 1930s are in the Art Deco style. Look for strong geometric or stepped forms and designs influenced by architecture such as skyscrapers. Grilles were the first feature to change in the early 1930s, and examples with decorative grilles are worth looking out for. During the 1950s, shapes generally became more streamlined and curved.
- As well as the form consider the material. The first radios were housed in simple wooden cases, but during the late 1920s inlays and other materials were used, with plastics such as Bakelite and Catalin beginning to appear in the 1930s. Although most Bakelite examples are found in brown, plastics freed radios from the dull monotony of woods.
- Bright colours such as red, green and blue are therefore highly desirable, but the classic Art Deco combination of black and chrome is also sought after. Coloured British radios are particularly scarce. Brand names are another important factor, with desirable names including FADA, EKCO, Philco and Emerson.
- The highest prices paid today are for classic Art Deco radios in brightly coloured Catalin by American makers. In 2007, a very rare baby blue 'Air King' fetched $51,000 at auction.
- However, as few can afford to buy at this level, and examples in good condition are limited, many collectors look elsewhere. Appealing radios in wooden cases that represent the style of the 1930s represent the largest part of the market, and prices look set to remain strong.

A Philips model 2531 radio and separate hexagonal speaker, with brown Bakelite cases and stylised floral grille.

c1930 *19in (48cm) high*

£150-250 **OTA**

A German Mende radio, with black Bakelite case and original grille cloth.

German sets from this period are not common.

c1933

£400-600 **OTA**

An E.K. Cole Ltd Ekco SH25 radio, designed by J.K. White, with brown Bakelite case, anodised copper grille, and original grille cloth.

This classic design incorporates some of the Egyptian references found in the Art Deco style of the period.

1932 *18in (45.5cm) high*

£450-650 **OTA**

A rare Zetavox model ST radio, with stepped and geometric brown Bakelite case and geometric speaker panel.

1933

£400-600 **OTA**

A Co-operative Wholesale Society 'Defiant' radio, model M900, with brown bakelite case and printed factory label.

This is the most desirable Co-operative Society Defiant radio, due to the shaped case, as well as the rarest model. The 'Defiant' name was used as the company was defying industry rules concerning the minimum cost of a radio at the time.

1935 *13.25in (34cm) high*

£1,000-1,500 **WW**

A Philco 'People's Set' radio, model no. 444, with mottled dark brown Bakelite case, applied factory labels.

This was designed purely for the UK market and was sold at a very low price, hence the 'People's Set'.

1936 *16.5in (42cm) high*

£320-380 **WW**

A German model VE301 DYN radio, from the 'Volksempfänger' (People's Radios) range commissioned by the National Socialist government, with brown Bakelite case.

1936

£100-200 **OTA**

A CLOSER LOOK AT AN EKCO RADIO

Originally released as an economy radio, this was available in black and chrome or brown Bakelite versions.

Although the black and chrome version was only slightly more expensive, it is usually worth up to double the value of the brown today!

Wells Coates (1895-1958) was an important Modernist designer, best known for his architecture, which included London's Isokon Building.

There were five models of round EKCO radio, each with different front designs – this is one of the most popular.

An E.K. Cole Ltd Ekco AD36 black Bakelite radio, designed by Wells Coates, with chrome detailing.

1935 *14.5in (37cm) high*

£450-650 **OTA**

An E.K. Cole Ltd Ekco AC97 black Bakelite radio, with chrome and ivory Bakelite detailing and original grille cloth.

The striking Modernist design of this radio was also available in brown, which is less desirable to collectors today.

1937 *21in (53cm) high*

£700-1,000 **OTA**

A Murphy Radio Ltd model AD94 radio, with black Bakelite cabinet.

This was Murphy's first bakelite cabinet, and was produced to meet wartime conditions.

1940 *13.5in (34cm) high*

£80-150 **OTA**

A Fada Streamliner Model 1000 'Bullet' radio, with Butterscotch Catalin case and knobs.

1940 *10.25in (26cm) wide*

£300-400 **OTA**

A Raymond 'Minit' radio, with red bakelite case and grille.

1949 *10in (25cm) long*

£70-150 **OTA**

A scarce 1950s French Marquett type 63 radio receiver, with brown and cream bakelite case, and applied factory label to base.

8.25in (21cm) wide

£120-180 **WW**

A Murphy Model A3A radio, with walnut veneered wooden case designed by R.D. Russell, and original stand and grille cloth.

The stand is rare and worth £50-80 alone. At the time, detractors called the radio the 'Pentonville Special', as the grille bars resemble those of a prison cell.

1932 *18.5in (47cm) high*

£150-250 **OTA**

A CLOSER LOOK AT A PYE RADIO

A newer type of valve developed during the war enabled small battery powered radios to be made for 'personal' portable use.

Also available in black and cream Perspex, this model was unsuccessful, largely due to poor construction.

The Pye 'Sunrise' trademark (used since 1929) was similar to the Japanese flag – as news came in of prisoners of war being ill-treated in Japanese camps it fell in popularity.

This model is made of flimsy Perspex, and examples in perfect condition are rare, particularly with an original instruction booklet.

A Pye model M78F battery powered portable radio, with light green and pinky-cream Perspex case, and original instruction leaflet.

1948 *7.25in (18.5cm) high*

£300-850 **OTA**

A late 1950s Czechoslovakian Tesla Talisman, no.308U, with streamlined brown bakelite case, designed in 1956.

This stylish design was made under licence in Czechoslovakia. Once considered vary rare, after the fall of the Berlin wall many examples were suddenly found on street markets, severely reducing the value.

12.5in (32cm) long

£50-150 **OTA**

A rare Pye Model K radio, with a solid walnut case and 'Sunrise' design speaker grille.

1932 *15.5in (39cm) high*

£100-200 **OTA**

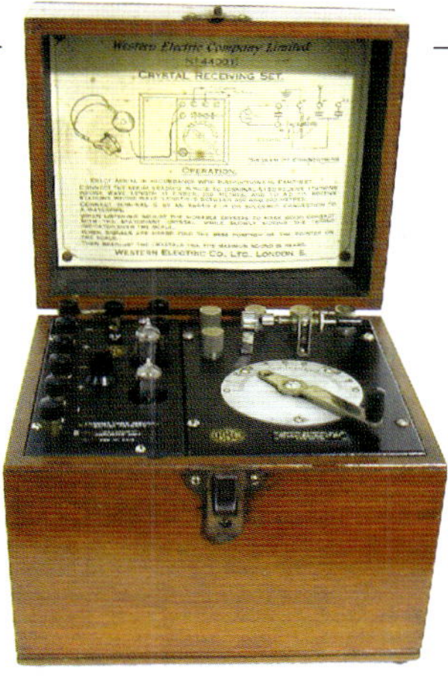

A Western Electric Co. Model 44001 crystal radio set with built-in 2-valve amplifier.

Most crystal sets were intended for headphone use and did not use any power source. This set had an optional amplifier to enable more headphones or a horn speaker to be used for family listening. This was an expensive extra for a cheap set, and few have survived.

1924 *5in (12.5cm) high*

£200-400 **OTA**

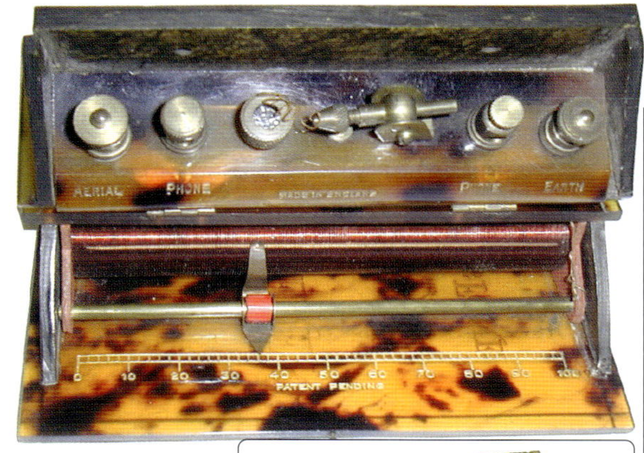

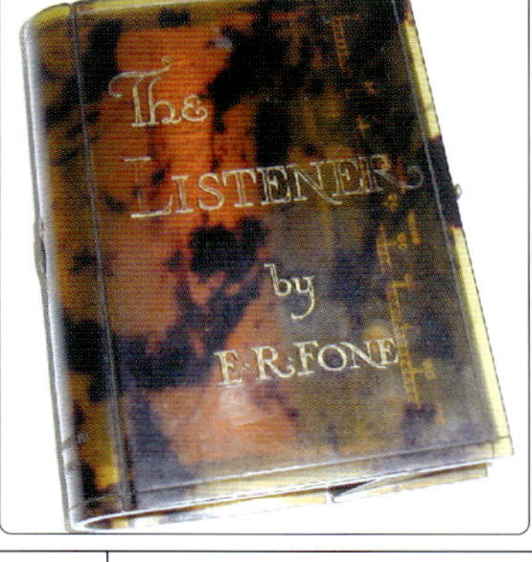

A Kenmac 'The Listener' crystal set, contained in a tortoiseshell effect celluloid case in the form of a book.

c1924 *4.75in (12cm) high*

£400-600 **OTA**

A Japanese Matsushita Electrical Industries Panasonic red plastic model R-70 Panapet transistor radio.

Examine the case as damage reduces the value considerably. The rarest colour is purple, which often fetches up to twice the value of more common colours such as red. The Panapet radio was made only for the Western market.

4in (10cm) high

£30-40 **M20C**

An S.G. Brown Ltd model H2 black metal horn-shaped radio speaker.

As early radios had no built in speakers, many types of speaker were made, often using a horn to amplification. Value depends mainly on the appearance.

c1924

£60-80 **OTA**

FIND OUT MORE...

Jonathan Hill ' Radio! Radio!' . *Exeter: Sunrise Press, 1996*

Tony Thompson ' Collecting Vintage Radios' . *Marlborough: The Crowood Press Ltd, 2007*

A C/I 'Chelford No. 2' rectangular plate, face restored.

12in (30.5cm) wide

£50-60 **GWRA**

A Henschel & Sohn worksplate, kassel number "28977", dated.

Ex Malawi Railways G Class 2-8-2 Locomotive number 64.

1954

£400-500 **GWRA**

A Beyer Peacock & Co. 'Manchester' brass worksplate, dated.

Ex Bengal & Assam Railway 4-6-0 'RS' class in the range 31863 - 31870.

1914 *9.75in (25cm) wide*

£150-200 **GWRA**

A Hudswell Clark & Co Ltd Railway Foundry Leeds brass worksplate, number "D1254", in ex loco condition, "D10" stencilled onto reverse, dated.

Ex Manchester Ship Canal 204hp 0-6-0DM which was sold to Hunslet January 1976 where it was rebuilt under order HE 8522.

1962

£60-80 **GWRA**

A 'The Thames-Clyde Express' cast aluminium locomotive name plate, with letters in relief on red background.

40in (101.5cm) wide

£2,500-3,000 **HT**

A 'Melton Mowbray' enamelled totem station sign.

36.5in (92.5cm) wide

£500-700 **HT**

A British Railways E. R. 'Fairlop' enamelled station name board, in good condition, with two chips and some fading to background.

58in (147.5cm) wide

£80-100 **W&W**

A 'Road Narrows' alloy sign, fitted with reflective beads, all beads intact, stress cracks at the top of sign, one fixing bracket remains.

£50-70 **GWRA**

A brass plaque, with belt-shaped rim and raised lettering 'Great North Eastern Railway', two lion crests and Scottish Thistle and English Rose decoration.

23in (58.5cm) diam

£450-550 A&G

A Letterkenny railway gate crossing lamp, the interior stamped with the company initials 'L.R.', with brass plate marked 'SAXBY FARMER LTD SIGNALLING ENGINEERS LONDON'.

£80-120 GWRA

A Beatles metal lunchbox, by Aladdin Industries, with embossed 3-D portraits and signatures, with thermos flask.

This was the first metal box to feature pop music performers

Lunchbox 8in (20.5cm) wide

£200-250 **HER**

A Beatles unused diary, by Beat Productions, Glasgow, Scotland, the pages printed with 'fun Fab four facts'.

1965

£60-80 **KA**

The Beatles 'New Beat Guitar', by Selcol Ltd., of orange and burgundy plastic with four strings, in original box with applied sticker of the band and facsimile signatures, with instructions and song chart.

£250-300 **GORL**

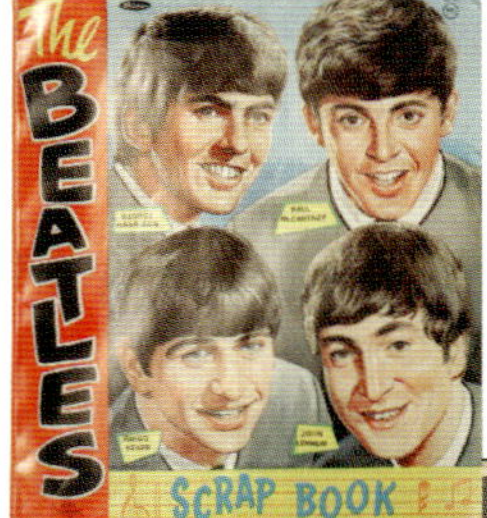

An American Beatles 1964 scrap book, published by Whitman (linked with NEMS Enterprises).

Originally sold for 29cents, filled with American newspaper clippings from August 1964 when "A Hard Day' s Night" premiered at the Salem Paramount movie theatre (13 August 1964).

£70-80 **KA**

A Washington Pottery 'Beatles' plate, transfer printed with an image of the Beatles and their script signatures.

£40-50 **KA**

A set of four coloured plastic figures of The Beatles, made by Emirober.

£45-50 **KA**

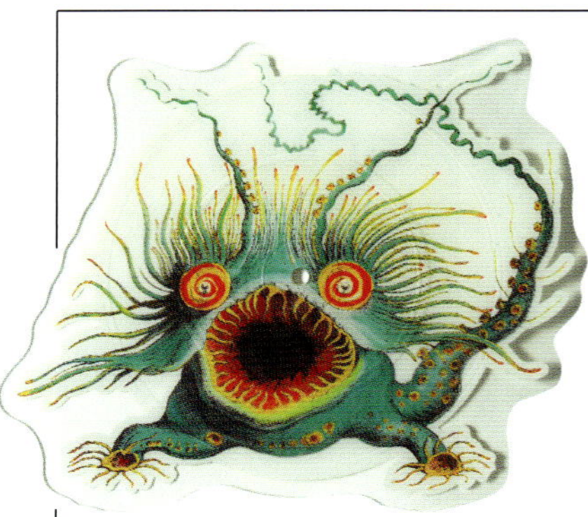

Queen, I'm Going Slightly Mad, EMI, shaped single picture disc.

SINGLE £25-30 PC

A CLOSER LOOK AT A PICTURE DISC

The value of picture discs is dependant on the recording artist, with popular artists, such as Madonna and Queen, commanding higher values.

Look for examples with high quality and appealing artwork that is typical of the artist or album. Some images are rare and, if desirable, may be valuable.

The sound quality produced by picture discs is typically poor, so visual appeal is perhaps the most important factor to value.

Picture discs were produced from the early 1930s, when they were made from a sheet of thin vinyl film placed over a thick paper print and pressed with grooves. Coloured vinyl picture discs were introduced in the 1970s by Metronome Records.

Queen, Innuendo, 12"single picture disc, EMI.

SINGLE £25-30 PC

A Bob Dylan 'The Freewheelin' Bob Dylan' US stereo LP, by CBS label, serial no BPG-62193.

£25-30 PC

A Manic Street Preachers 'You Love Us' UK stereo LP, by Heavenly, serial no. HVN 10.

£20-25 PC

An Oi Polloi 'Unite and Win!' UK LP, by Oi! records, serial no OIR-011.

£20-25 PC

A Pink Floyd 'The Best of Pink Floyd' stereo LP record, by Colombia.

£100-120 PC

A Michael Jackson vinyl doll, by Ljn, NY under licence from MJJ Productions Inc, in the `Beat It' outfit .

This is one of a series of four dolls, originally retailed for $14.99.

14in (35.56cm)

£70-90 **MTB**

A Fuller calculator, by Stanley, London, with bakelite mounts, in a fitted bow with brass mounting arm, with copies of instructions.

£250-300 WW

A pair of 19thC apothecary's balance, by S. Mawson & Sons, with brass beam and pans, standing on stained wood base with two underlying drawers, with various weights.

Balances are a very specialised market, with few dedicated collectors. Value depends on the maker and the use: coin or cabinet scales can be more desirable.

£100-150 A&G

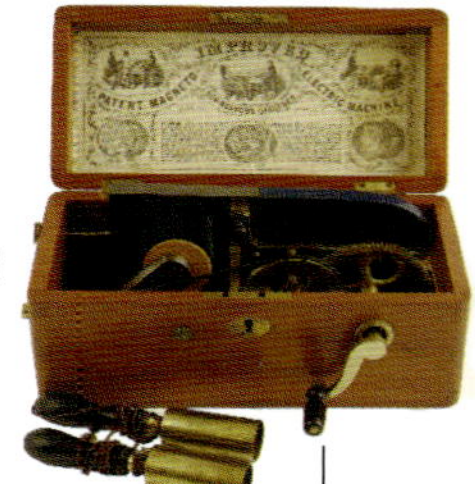

An 'Improved Patent Magneto-Electric Machine for Nervous Diseases', with a brass and steel frame and ebonised handled grips, with a printed label to the interior of the mahogany case, with winding handle.

10.25in (26cm) wide

£100-150 WW

An 18thC brass gunner's sector, divided in eight horizontal scales, including 'Paces Pynt Blanck, Bredth of the Ladell Waight of the Shot'.

8in (20.5cm) long

£350-400 WW

A silver pincushion shaped as a swimming duck, by Crisford & Norris of Birmingham, with textured plumage.

1908 *2in (5.5cm) long*

£150-200 **WW**

A silver plated pincushion, modelled as a pig, unmarked.

2in (5cm) long

£30-40 **SAS**

A pair of silver novelty pincushions, by Adie & Lovekin of Birmingham, in the form of a swimming swans.

Pairs of novelty pincushions by the same maker are rare, as most people only needed one pincushion.

1907 *Larger 2.75in (7cm) wide*

£300-400 **WW**

A silver pincushion shaped as a seated chick emerging from an egg, by S. Mordan & Co., with Chester hallmarks.

Sampson Mordan & Co. was a well known maker of fine silver and gold objects, as well as propelling pencils, whose work is sought after. The Chester assay office closed in 1962.

1906 *1.75in (4.5cm) high*

£120-180 **WW**

A silver pincushion in the shape of a small standing pig, by Henry Matthews of Birmingham.

1906 *2in (5cm) long*

£120-180 **WW**

An Edwardian silver novelty pin cushion, Saunders & Shepherd, Birmingham, in the form of a standing elephant.

1905 *2in (5cm) wide*

£100-150 **WW**

A CLOSER LOOK AT A NOVELTY PIN CUSHION

Rollerskating themed items are scarce, particularly of this early date.

The first recorded use of roller skates was in 1743, with the four wheeled version we know today being invented in the US in 1863 by James Leonard Plimpton.

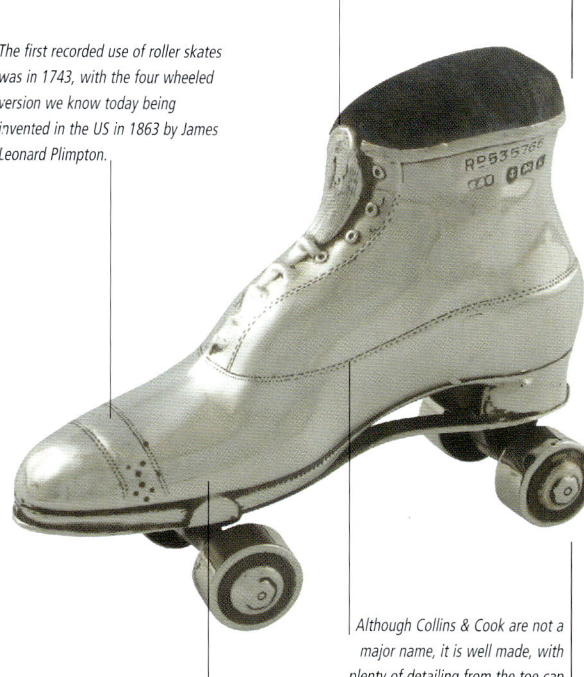

Although Collins & Cook are not a major name, it is well made, with plenty of detailing from the toe cap to the serrated sole welt and wheel axles.

The shape and style of the boot is consistent with Edwardian fashions

An Edwardian silver novelty roller skate pin cushion, by Collins & Cook of Birmingham, with registered design number '535766' for 1909.

1909 *2.75in (7cm) long*

£180-220 **WW**

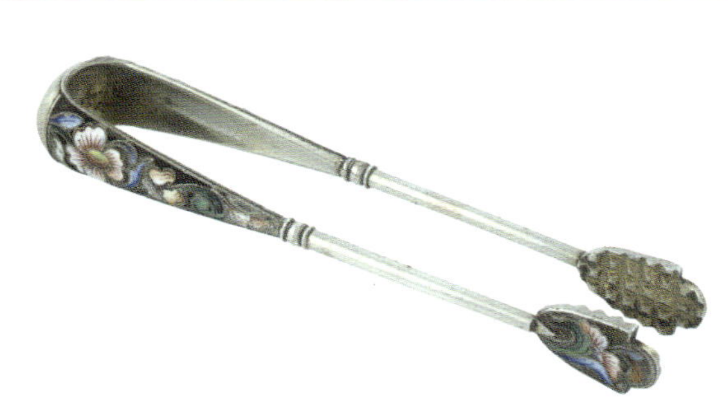

A pair of Russian silver multi-coloured, cloisonné enamel sugar tongs, by Mari Serrenova, with shaded floral designs.

1908-1917

£220-280 **WW**

A pair of late 19thC to early 20thC Russian silver gilt and cloisonné enamelled sugar tongs, initialled, with Russian state marks.

1896-1908

£250-350 **WW**

A late Victorian silver cigar cutter, by H. Matthews of Birmingham, in the form of a pair of scissor snuffers.

1894 *4.5in (11.5cm) long*

£150-200 **WW**

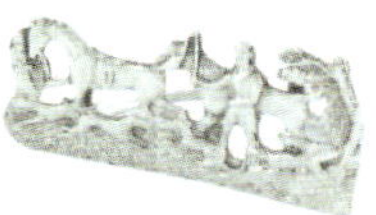

A set of four late Victorian silver menu holders, by S. Clifford of London, on a fox hunting theme.

Despite the recent ban in the UK, pieces related to fox hunting and country pursuits are sought after. Even though their use is now outdated, menu holders are strongly collectable.

1899

£250-350 **WW**

A Victorian silver heraldic menu holder, by Henry William Dee of London, in the form of a squirrel eating a nut, on a curved base.

Certain animals are more collectable than others, especially dogs and cats. Squirrels are comparatively rare, however, hence the higher price. This is also well made, with plenty of detail.

1877 *2in (5cm) high*

£320-380 **WW**

A silver commemorative model of a pile driving engine, by Sunard & Co., inscribed 'Rowden Barter & Co. presented to Sir George LE Hunt, as a memento of the ceremony of driving the first pile – outer Harbour S.A. 20/7/04'.

c1904 *8.75in (22cm) high*

£380-420 **WW**

A pair of Edwardian silver mounted boar tusk pepperettes, by Atkin Brothers of Sheffield, mounted on oval bases.

1902 *2.5in (6.5cm) high*

£400-600 **WW**

QUICK REFERENCE – DUNHILL LIGHTERS

Dunhill are often called the 'Rolls Royce' of cigarette lighters, having produced some of the most luxurious models ever made. The 'Unique' lighter was developed by scientific instrument makers Wise & Greenwood in 1919. With its snuffer arm and a mechanism that allowed it to be operated with one hand, it became a bestseller. Look out for examples in precious metals, those with lacquered designs by Japanese company Namiki, or ones that contain hidden features, such as watches or compacts. Prices range from under £100 for a plated 'Unique', to over £10,000 for a rare watch lighter in a precious metal.

A Dunhill 9ct gold 'Unique' lighter, with engine turned design, and control marks.

2.25in (5.5cm) high

£350-450 **SAS**

An Elisorm Auto-Tank 9ct gold lighter, with engine turned decoration to the body, marked '9ct' and with 'JP' owner's initials.

£35-45 **SAS**

A late 1930s Dunhill silver plated 'Unique' pipe lighter, with extending wick and slider, engine turned design.

The slider moves a tube containing the wick up and down, allowing tobacco in a pipe bowl to be lit.

2.25in (5.5cm) high

£100-150 **SAS**

A 1970s Dunhill 70 gold plated 'Rollagas' rolled gold cigarette lighter, with engine turned pattern, impressed 'DUNHILL 70' and numbered 'BR889', with some wear from use.

2.25in (6cm) high

£30-40 **CARS**

A 1950s Dunhill 'Aquarium' table lighter, with reverse-cut and painted underwater scene of tropical fish, and metal fittings.

Look out for the half-size 'Miniature', as this is rarer. If birds or other animals or motifs replace the fish, the price will also rise, as these can be very rare.

4in (10cm) high

£600-900 **SWO**

An Art Deco 9ct gold vesta case, with hinged lid, engine turned centre and Greek key border, and with London hallmarks for 1923.

1923

£200-300 **SAS**

A silver circular vesta case, decorated in low relief with figures playing bowls on the lawn, maker's mark worn, with Birmingham hallmarks for 1907.

As well as appealing to vesta case collectors, the bowls theme is very rare and would appeal to collectors of sporting memorabilia, which is why this example has a high price.

1907 *1.5in (4cm) diam*

£500-700 **WW**

A Victorian silver novelty vesta and slow match holder, in the form of a carriage lamp with clear convex lens, with London hallmarks for H.W. Dee, 1870.

Railwayana attracts a greater number of buyers than bowls, the subject of the vesta shown above. This is also an appealing shape and of an early date.

1870 *1.75in (4.5cm) high*

£800-1,200 **WW**

An Art Deco silver cigarette box, with engine turned decoration, an ivory thumbpiece and an applied enamel plaque, with Birmingham hallmarks for Hassett & Harper Ltd, 1935.

1935 *6.5in (17cm) long*

£100-150 **WW**

A CLOSER LOOK AT A NAMIKI CIGARETTE CASE

Maki-e lacquer is a historic technique that takes many years to learn and designs can take weeks of painstaking work to create, layer by layer.

The right hand column of the mark reads 'Namiki kan', showing this to have been made in the 1930s. The left hand column is the artist's name and red 'kao' symbol, revealing that it was decorated by Maizawa Shobi.

Cigarette cases are scarce, but the value of this example is reduced by more than half because it is worn, bears a presentation engraving and the design is comparatively simple.

The goldfish design is one of the most commonly found on Namiki products, with the fish representing good fortune and luck.

A 1930s Japanese Namiki maki-e lacquer metal cigarette case, decorated with a goldfish and pondweed design by Maizawa Shobi, the gold washed interior inscribed 'Jose Pablo Costa 8-12-41'.

Shobi was a pupil of Shiroyama in 1899, on the staff of the Iwate Prefecture Technical High School in 1905, and worked as an independent lacquer artist after 1907. He was also one of the six committee members at the time of the establishment of the school of lacquer artists known as the Kokkokai. The year of the inscription is interesting as this was the year Japan bombed Pearl Harbor.

4in (10cm) high

£150-200 **MHC**

An oak Zebrano effect smoker's cabinet, with doors backed with pipe racks, the fitted interior with square cut crystal decanter to the right, blue and white tobacco jar to the centre, with three drawers, the base moulded to edge.

15.75in (40cm) wide

£180-220 **DA&H**

An Art Deco bronze penguin floor smoker's ashtray, with circular top fitted with a well and verdigris finish.

23.5in (59.5cm) high

£400-500 **SK**

QUICK REFERENCE

- Football's continued popularity creates a strong demand for memorabilia, particularly for items connected to famous teams, popular players or important matches.
- Memorabilia relating to Manchester United is among the most widely collected. Other popular teams include Liverpool, Chelsea and Arsenal. Well-known Arsenal players of the past include Charlie George, Frank McLintock and Peter Storey; modern players include Thierry Henry, Ian Wright and Patrick Vieira. Memorabilia connected to Arsenal's 'Double' win (premier league and FA Cup) in 1970-71 is desirable, as is that connected to the "Invincibles", who won the Premiership (2003-04) unbeaten.
- Shirts, boots and other equipment are all sought-after and can be extremely valuable, particularly if they were used during an important match or signed by the player and their team mates. Items connected with footballing legends, such as Pelé, George Best, Bobby Charlton and Bobby Moore, are still in high demand, but today's football players and teams can attract equally significant sums.
- Medals, representing a team's success, are sought after with collectors, as are team caps.
- Programmes are another popular area of collecting. A large variety is available and values vary greatly. Programmes for FA and European Cup finals, international games and early, pre-WW1 games are typically the most desirable and valuable, but be aware that some matches (e.g. the 1966 World Cup) were are so obviously significant at the time that many programmes were stored in good condition keeping values low. Modern programmes are printed in large numbers and many fans keep them, meaning this is an affordable entry into collecting. Look for examples in clean condition.

A squad-signed red and white short-sleeved Tony Adams Arsenal no. 6 jersey, with Premier League flashes, 21 signatures in black marker pen, sold with a copy of Tony Adams' Testimonial programme.

£600-800 **GBA**

A long-sleeved yellow Arsenal no. 11 jersey from the 1969 League Cup final jersey worn by George Armstrong, embroidered club crest and inscribed 'WEMBLEY, 1969'.

Swindon Town defeated Arsenal 3-1 at Wembley. George Armstrong made 621 first-team appearances in a 15-year playing career.

c1969

£1,800-2,800 **GBA**

A signed short-sleeved white England no. 8 international jersey 1995 worn by Peter Beardsley, with a letter of authenticity signed by Peter Beardsley.

In his letter of authenticity Peter Beardsley states that he wore this jersey in a 1995 Umbro Cup match against Brazil.

£150-250 **GBA**

A white long-sleeved Real Madrid No.23 jersey worn by David Beckham in the Champions League match v Bayern Munich on the 10th March 2004, with UEFA Champions League flashes, dirt and blood stains; sold together with a certificate of authenticity issued by Star Chamber.

c2004

£800-1,200 **GBA**

An orange Holland no. 10 short-sleeved jersey worn by Dennis Bergkamp in the match v France at Euro 2000, embroidered with Dutch and French national flags and inscribed '21 JUNI 2000, Euro 2000 and Fair Play flashes.

In this group D match Holland beat France 3-2.

2000

£600-900 **GBA**

A short-sleeved red and white Arsenal no. 12 jersey worn by Martin Hayes in the 1988 Football League Cup final, inscribed '1988, WEMBLEY'.

Martin Hayes replaced Perry Groves and scored in the 74th minute. However, two late goals gave victory to Luton Town 3-2.

£1,000-1,500 GBA

A long-sleeved green Arsenal 1980 F.A. Cup final goalkeeping jersey worn by Pat Jennings, inscribed 'F.A. CUP FINAL, WEMBLEY 1980'.

1980

£1,500-2,000 GBA

A white short-sleeved Chelsea No.8 jersey worn by Frank Lampard during the season 2006-07 season , with Premier League flashes, the reverse lettered LAMPARD.

This jersey was gained as a swap by a West Ham United player after the match at Upton Park on 18th April 2007.

c2006

£300-400 GBA

A CLOSER LOOK AT AN ENGLAND FOOTBALL JERSEY

The Umbro diamond first appeared on England jerseys in the Greece match on 21st April 1971, with Banks wearing the yellow jersey in this and other 1971 matches.

Arguably the greatest goalkeeper England has ever produced, Banks is best remembered for saving Pele's header during the 1970 World Cup. He retired in 1973.

The jersey was purchased at a charity auction in 1971, an event which Gordon Banks attended.

As well as being worn by Banks, it is signed by him in a good, easily displayed position.

A signed long-sleeved yellow England international goalkeeping jersey worn by Gordon Banks, with Umbro diamond, three lions badge, the reverse with a red no. 1, signed by Gordon Banks in fine marker pen.

1971

£1,800-2,800 GBA

A short sleeved yellow and blue Arsenal no. 12 jersey worn by Paul Merson in the match v Manchester United 2nd April 1989.

In Arsenal' s 1988-89 Championship winning season, this was the match when the famous Tony Adams ' donkey chant' was first heard.

c1989

£400-600 GBA

A short-sleeved white England no. 19 World Youth Championship jersey 1993, inscribed 'WORLD YOUTH CHAMPIONSHIPS, AUSTRALIA 1993'.

Although Brazil won the 1993 tournament. England attained their best finishing position in the competition' s history.

£60-90 GBA

A Liverpool v Woolwich Arsenal 9th programme for February 1907, a combined-issue also covering Everton Reserves v Barrow, in very good condition.

1907

£700-1,000 **GBA**

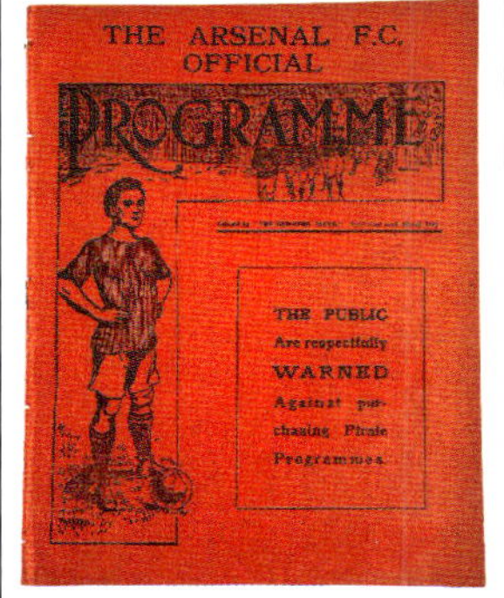

An Arsenal v Tufnell Park programme for 19th September 1914, first-team fixture in the London F.A. Challenge Cup, a combined issue also featuring the reserves fixtures v Swindon Town.

£600-800 **GBA**

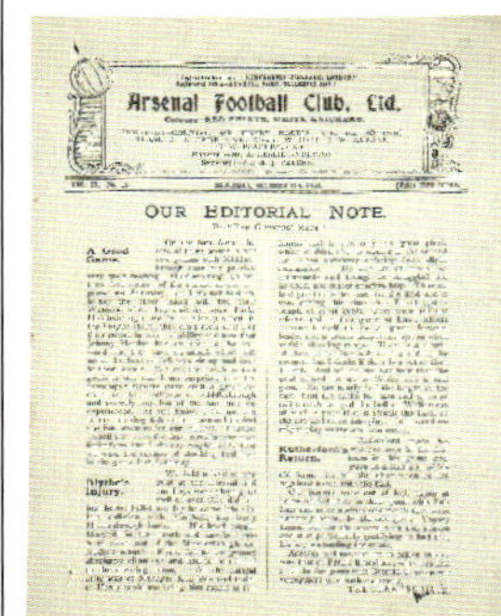

An Arsenal v Bolton Wanderers four-page programme for 9th October 1920.

1920

£250-350 **GBA**

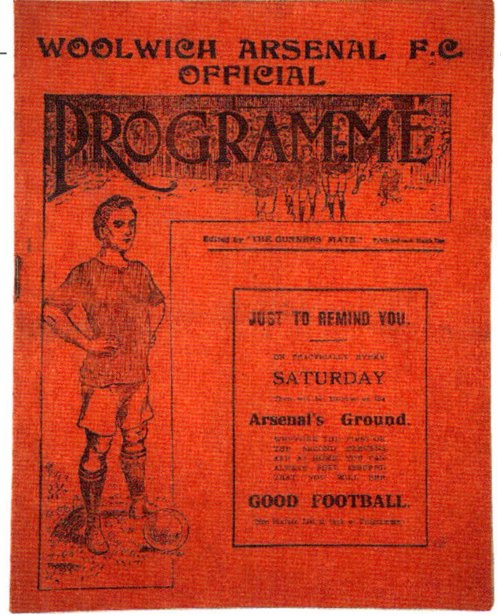

A Woolwich Arsenal v Birmingham programme from the first season at Highbury 1913-14, played on the 22nd November.

1913

£1,000-1,500 **GBA**

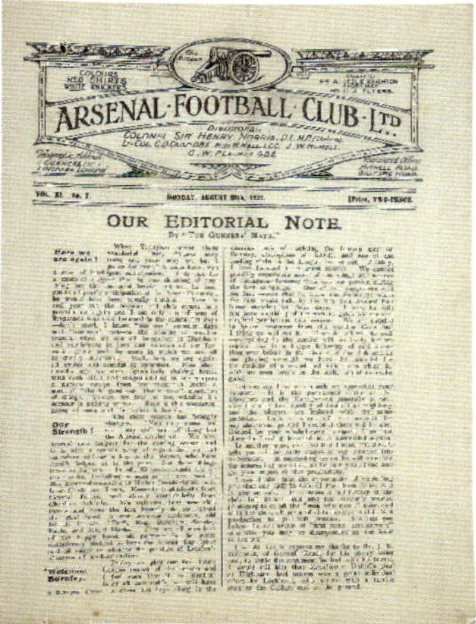

An Arsenal v Burnley four-page programme for 28th August 1922.

£250-350 **GBA**

A copy of the official programme for Arsenal v Tottenham Hotspur played at Higbury 29th August 1925, including an article titled 'Permit me to introduce Mr Herbert Chapman'.

£550-650 **GBA**

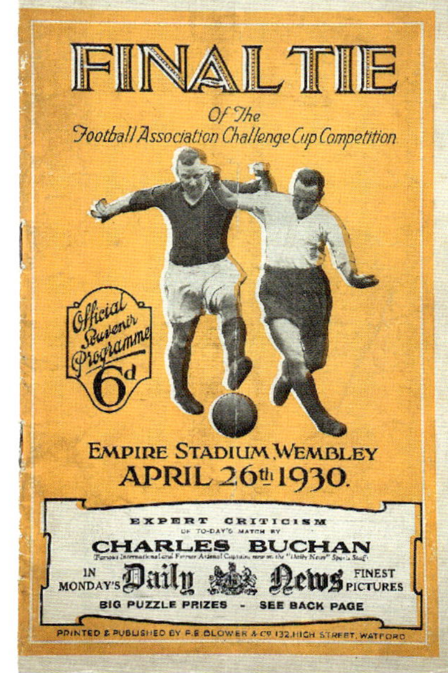

An F.A. Cup final programme for Arsenal v Huddersfield Town, on 26th April 1930.

The 1930 F.A. Cup Final was won by Arsenal who beat Huddersfield Town 2-0. This was the first cup final in which both teams entered the pitch side-by-side, and was in honour of Arsenal manager Herbert Chapman who had managed Huddersfield very successfully in the 1920s. The 1930 F.A. Cup Final is also remembered for the sinister image of the Graf Zeppelin looming over Wembley Stadium during the first half.

1930

£800-1,200 **GBA**

An F.A. Cup semi-final programme Arsenal v Manchester City played at Villa Park 12th March 1932, with Sellotaped repairs to centre pages.

1932

£300-500 GBA

An F.A. Cup final programme for Huddersfield Town v Preston North End on 30th April 1938.

1938

£300-400 GBA

A European Cup final programme for Real Madrid v Stade Reims, played in Stuttgart on 3rd June 1959.

1959

£250-350 GBA

An F.A. Cup final programme for Arsenal v Sheffield United, on 25th April 1936.

Although there is some staining through age, the blue and red are comparatively unfaded, and the inclusion of one of Wembley's famous 'twin towers' in an Art Deco-style design is appealing.

1936

£400-600 GBA

A Belgium v England international programme, played at the Heysel Stadium on 21st September 1947.

1947

£300-500 GBA

A souvenir tournament programme from the Campeonato Mundial de Futbol in 1962 in Chile, the Spanish text by Bernard Joy and David Bravo, printed in Chile.

1962

£220-280 GBA

A 15ct gold London Football Combination winner's medal presented to Arsenal's R. Robinson, for the 1927-28 season, inscribed 'LONDON FOOTBALL COMBINATION, ARSENAL F.C., WINNERS, R. ROBINSON, 1927-28', in original fitted case.

£450-550 **GBA**

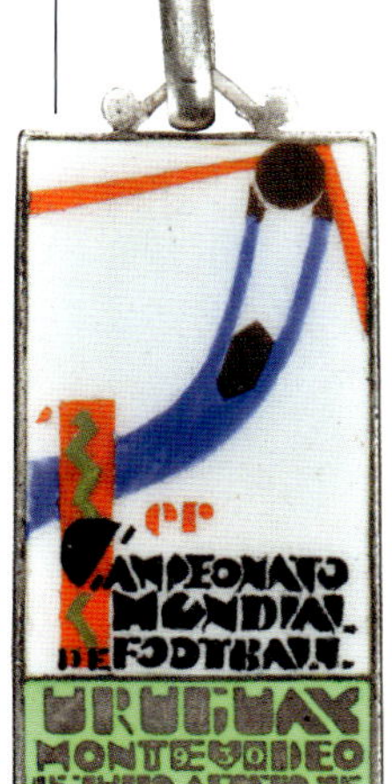

A silver and enamel medal for the 1930 World Cup finals, by Stefano Johnson of Milan, with enamelled obverse, the reverse inscribed '1ER CAMPEONATO MUNDIAL DE FOOTBALL, URUGUAY, MONTEVIDEO, 15 JULIO AGOSTO 15'.

The enamelled design is after Guillermo Laborde' s official poster design for the 1930 World Cup.

£550-750 **GBA**

A 15ct gold F.A. Charity Shield medal presented to Arsenal's George Male in 1931, inscribed 'FOOTBALL ASSOCIATION CHARITY SHIELD', in replacement case.

Arsenal beat West Bromwich Albion 1-0.

£1,000-1,500 **GBA**

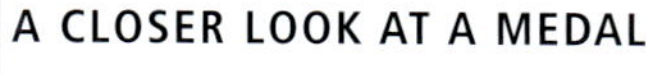

A CLOSER LOOK AT A MEDAL

Herbert 'Herbie' Roberts (1905-1944) was a serving police officer and played amateur football for his local side Oswestry Town.

In 1926, he was signed to Arsenal by Herbert Chapman for £200, and turned professional.

He was the team's first choice centre-half from 1930-37, and went on to win F.A. Cup runners-up and winner' s medals in 1932 and 1936.

He retired after breaking his leg in 1938. He then trained the reserves team until war broke out. He died in 1944 while serving with the Royal Fusiliers.

A 9ct gold F.A. Cup runners-up medal for the 1931-32 season, awarded to Arsenal's Herbie Roberts, inscribed 'THE FOOTBALL ASSOCIATION CHALLENGE CUP, RUNNERS-UP', in original fitted case inscribed 'THE FOOTBALL ASSOCIATION CHALLENGE CUP, 1931-32'.

£2,000-3,000 **GBA**

A 14ct gold F.A. Cup winner's medal presented to Arsenal's goalkeeper Alex Wilson in 1936, inscribed 'THE FOOTBALL ASSOCIATION, WINNERS, ARSENAL F.C. 1935-36, A. WILSON', in fitted case.

Alexander Wilson (1908-1971) was signed by Arsenal in 1933.

£7,000-10,000 **GBA**

A 9ct gold and enamel Football League Division Three Championship medal awarded to Neil Webb, the obverse inscribed 'FOOTBALL LEAGUE CHAMPIONSHIP, DIVISION 3, WINNERS', the reverse inscribed 'SEASON 1982-83, N WEBB', in original fitted case.

Neil Web won this medal during his first season at Portsmouth. They finished the season with 91 points, five clear of their nearest rivals Cardiff City.

£1,000-1,500 **GBA**

A pair of Ashley Cole football boots, white, black and red Adidas Predators, the right tongue inscribed 'COLEY 3'.

£150-250 **GBA**

A pair of Saloman Kalou football boots, white and blue Adidas F50 boots, the tongue bearing the national flag of the Ivory Coast and inscribed 'KALOU' and 'JUNIOR'.

£150-250 **GBA**

A pair of Adidas football boots worn by Steven Gerrard in an England training session prior to the World Cup qualifier vs. Greece. Embroidered 'SG', signed by Gerrard, Nick Barmby and Sammy Lee, together with a letter of authenticity signed by Gerrard and a colour photograph of Gerrard wearing the boots and with Barmby and Lee.

2001

£350-450 **GBA**

A panelled leather football signed by the Celtic 1967 European Cup final team, with printed inscription, and eleven faded autographs in ink.

£150-200 **GBA**

A white Slazenger 25 Challenge leather football signed by the England 1966 World Cup winners, signed in pen by Sir Alf Ramsey, the 11 England finalists and additionally by squad members Greaves and Bonetti, with a programme for the final and a souvenir magazine.

£1,200-1,800 **GBA**

Jack Kelsey's last Wales international cap for season 1961-62, the red cap inscribed '1961-62, E, S, I, B, B'.

Kelsey is regarded as one of Wales' greatest goalkeepers. In the 1961-62 season, he played in the internationals v England, Scotland and Northern Ireland, and in the two friendlies against Brazil. He injured his back while trying to save at the feet of the Brazilian Vavà and, despite extensive attempts to rectify the problem, he was forced to retire a year later.

£1,500-2,000 **GBA**

An old Highbury red and white corner flag, lettered 'A.F.C.'

£650-750 **GBA**

A full-size silver plated replica of the Football Association Challenge Cup Trophy, the two-handled cup and cover realistically modelled and inscribed, fitted to ebonised plinths, with F. A. Cup ribbons, with a custom-built portable and lockable wooden cabinet.

27.25in (69cm) high

£5,000-7,000 **GBA**

A German stoneware half-litre stein with football decoration, inscribed "Hipp Hipp Hurrah".

7.25in (18.5cm) high

£80-120 **GBA**

Jimmy Dugdale's electroplated winner's tankard from the first Football League Cup final in 1961, engraved with the crest of the Football League and inscribed 'THE FOOTBALL LEAGUE CUP, 1960-61, WINNERS'.

5in (13cm) high

£1,000-1,500 **GBA**

A large Bohemian porcelain figure, decorated as a Uruguayan Olympic footballer in sky blue and white, in commemoration of their gold medal winning team at Amsterdam, the base inscribed 'OLYMPICOS', factory marks to underside of base, restored.

c1928

£450-650 **GBA**

An extremely rare Marx "World Cup Willie' Rollakin miniature figure, the base with ball-bearing to allow him to roll along.

With its original box, the value can rise to over £100.

1.5in (4cm) high

£60-70 **MTB**

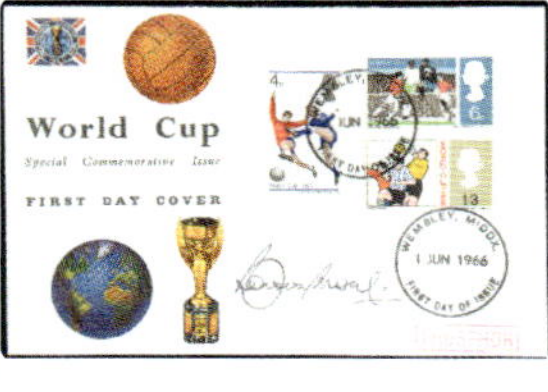

A 1966 World Cup first day cover signed by Bobby Moore, postmarked Wembley 1st June 1966, signed in black biro.

1966

£300-500 **GBA**

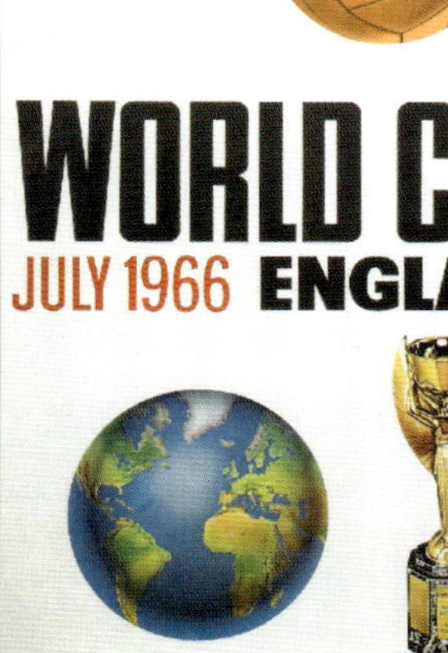

An official poster for the England 1966 World Cup July 1966, after Carvosso, published by McCorquodale & Co. Ltd, framed and glazed.

26in (66cm) high

£600-800 **GBA**

QUICK REFERENCE

- Baseball cards were introduced in 1933 by the Goudey Gum Company to encourage children to buy more gum. This idea was copied from cigarette cards, which had been produced from the 19thC.
- By 1951 other companies, including Bowman Gum and Topps Chewing Gum, began producing collectable baseball cards. When Topps acquired Bowman in 1956, they became the world's largest sports card manufacturer.
- Collecting cards was largely a pastime for children until the early 1970s. Once adults began collecting too, prices for rare and desirable cards leapt in value. Only a few hundred examples of the legendary 1909-1911 T206 Honus Wagner card were produced and only 57 examples are known today, one of which sold for £1.5 million in 2007. Backs and colours of backgrounds can differ.
- Aside from rarity, one of the most important indicators to value is 'centring'. The printed image should ideally be surrounded by an even amount of white space.
- Condition is also important. Creases, abrasions, folds, tears and other damage will lessen value.
- Fakes are common, but these can often be identified by a blurred or pixellated image and the thickness of the card.

An American Tobacco Co. Piedmont Cigarettes Albert (Chief) Bender baseball card, with trees in the background.

1909 *2.75in (6.8cm) high*

£100-150 AEM

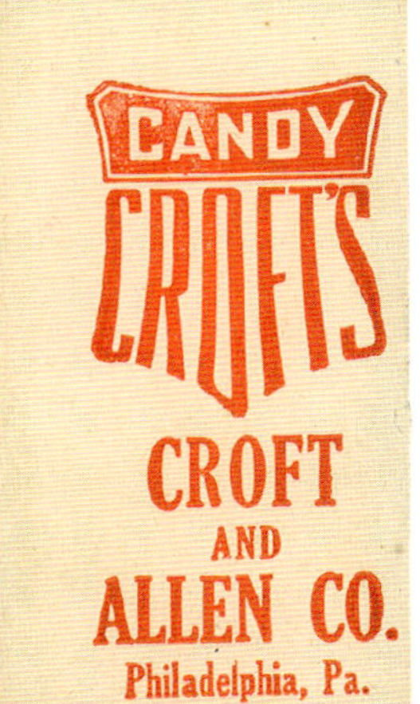

A Crofts Candy 'Dots Miller Fielding' baseball card, E92, with rare red-printed back.

1909

£1,200-1,500 MAS

A Bowman Richie Ashburn rookie baseball card.

This very rare card is not in the best condition and is not well centred, hence its lower value. If in better condition, it could fetch well over twice this value.

1949 *2.5in (6.5cm) high*

£150-250 BH

A Topps 'Connie Mack's All-Stars Eddie Collins' baseball card, sealed in box with SGC rating of 40 (VG3).

1951

£100-150 MAS

A Topps 'Connie Mack's All-Stars, Jimmy Collins' baseball card, sealed in box with SGC rating of 60 (Ex5).

1951

£150-250 MAS

A Topps Rocco Colavito rookie baseball card.

1957 *3.5in (9cm) high*

£30-50 **BH**

A Sport Magazine Willie Mays baseball card.

1959 *3.5in (9cm) high*

£20-30 **AEM**

A CLOSER LOOK AT A BASEBALL CARD

Mickey Mantle and Hank Aaron are two of baseball's greatest names. They are both depicted on this card.

The card is also signed by them. Had it not been signed, its value would have been around $200-400, depending on condition.

Showing switch-hitting Mantle, who was pitted against fight-handed slugger Aaron in front of the Yankee stadium, this style was used again in 2006 with opponents Pujols and Ordonez.

The signatures have been certified as authentic by the official PSA/DNA authentication service, and the card has been sealed in a protective wallet.

A Topps 'World Series Batting Foes Mickey Mantle and Hank Aaron' baseball card, number 418, dual signed, PSA/DNA authenticated.

1958

£1,000-1,500 **MAS**

A Topps Jim Palmer rookie card, priced according to condition.

1966 *3.5in (9cm) high*

£25-35 **BH**

A Topps Bob Clemente baseball card.

1964 *3.5in (9cm) high*

£50-70 **BH**

A Topps Hank Aaron baseball card.

1968 *3.5in (9cm) high*

£25-35 **AEM**

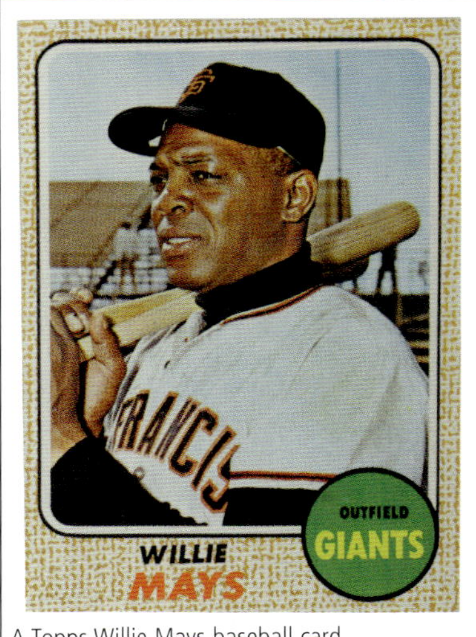

A Topps Willie Mays baseball card.

1968 *3.5in (9cm) high*

£25-35 **AEM**

A 1968 Rookie Stars baseball card featuring Jerry Koosman and Nolan Ryan.

This card, featuring Hall of Famer Nolan Ryan, is one of the iconic cards of the period. Koosman's appearance is considered less important by many and, although Ryan was not the greatest pitcher in baseball, he was considered dominant in his prime. Neverthless, Koosman also made a number of high achievements, making this a superb example of a dual rookie card. Prices have fallen over the past few years, with this card once fetching around £1,000 in the 1990s.

1968 *3.5in (9cm) wide*

£250-350 **AEM**

A Score Joe DiMaggio signed baseball card, numbered 'JD18' from 56 examples from a limited edition of 2,500, with certificate of authenticity, from the DiMaggio estate.

1992 was the first year that baseball card companies began inserting signed cards into their packs. This was from a series of five, which is considered highly desirable as it features the legendary DiMaggio, has his signature on a card, and was one of the first signed series sold in this way.

1992 *3.5in (9cm) wide*

£200-300 **BH**

A Topps Cal Ripken, Bob Bonner and Jeff Schneider baseball card.

This was Ripken's rookie card, with Ripken entering the Hall of Fame in 2007.

1982 *3.5in (9cm) high*

£20-40 **BH**

A Nabisco All Star Autographs Ernie Banks baseball card, signed by Banks, together with a certificate of authenticity.

1993 *3.5in (9cm) high*

£20-30 **BH**

An Upper Deck Brooks Robinson baseball card, signed in blue marker by Robinson.

1998 *3.5in (9cm) high*

£15-25 **BH**

A Hillerich & Bradsby & Co. 'The Famous Slugger Year Book', with Mize and Di Maggio '1939 Batting Champions' cover.

1940 *6.5in (16.5cm) high*

£40-60 **BH**

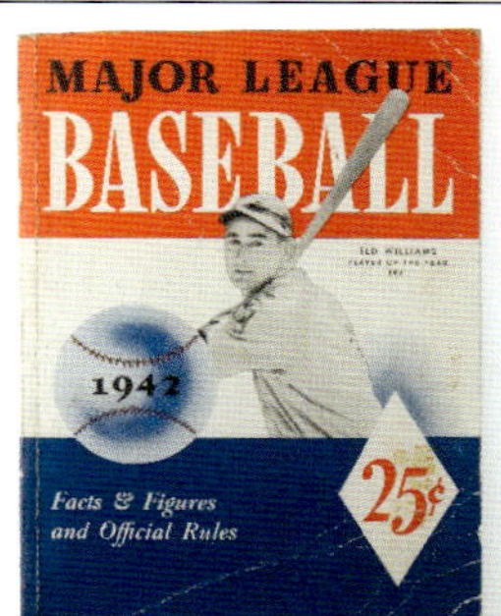

'Major League Baseball Facts & Figures', featuring Ted Williams on the cover, published by Whitman Publishing Company.

Williams was Player of the Year in 1941.

1942 *6.75in (17cm) high*

£10-15 **BH**

A 'The Official Encyclopedia of Baseball' book, first edition, published by A.S Barnes & Company.

1951 *10in (25.5cm) high*

£30-50 **BH**

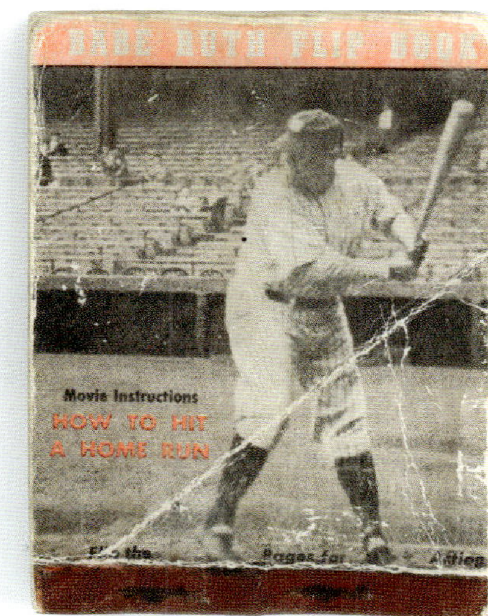

A very rare early 1950s Babe Ruth photographic miniature Flip Book, with pictorial cover, with wear and damage.

4in (10cm) high

£100-150 **BH**

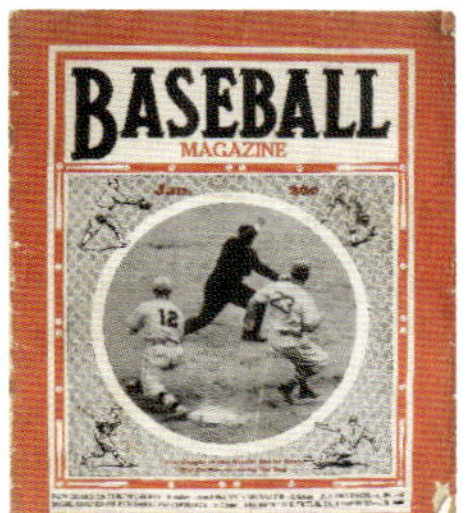

Baseball magazine, January 1937, with wear and damage.

1937 *11.5in (29cm) high*

£7-10 **BH**

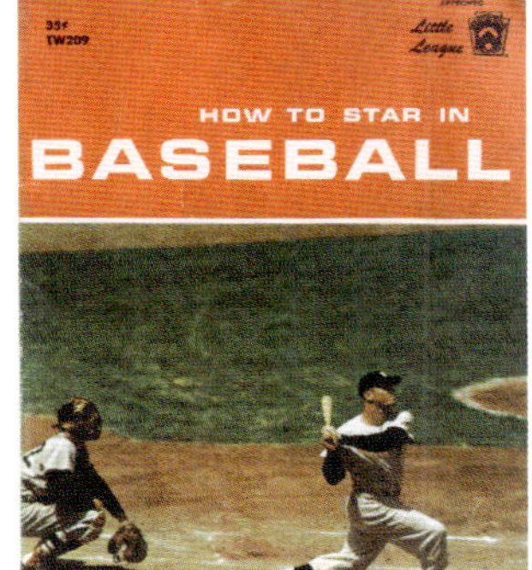

A Little League 'How To Star in Baseball' book, with Mickey Mantle photographic cover.

1961 *8in (20.5cm) high*

£5-7 **BH**

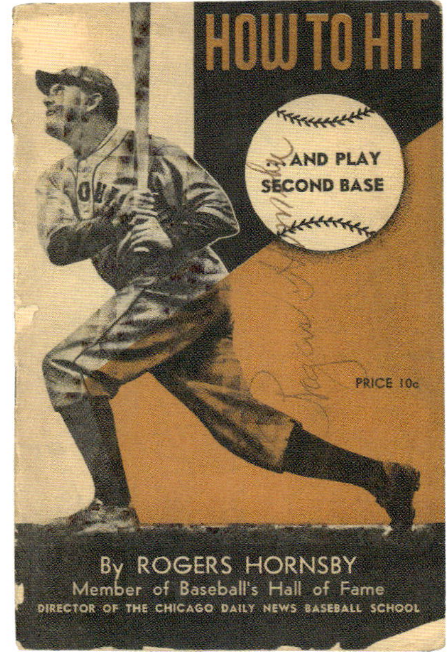

A Rogers Hornby 'How to Hit…And Play Second Base' signed booklet.

1945

£600-800 **MAS**

A very rare Babe Ruth Memorial Mission tract (and 1927 Yankee), published by Faith, Prayer & Tract League of Grand Rapids, Mich.

1948 *5.75in (14cm) high*

£20-30 **BH**

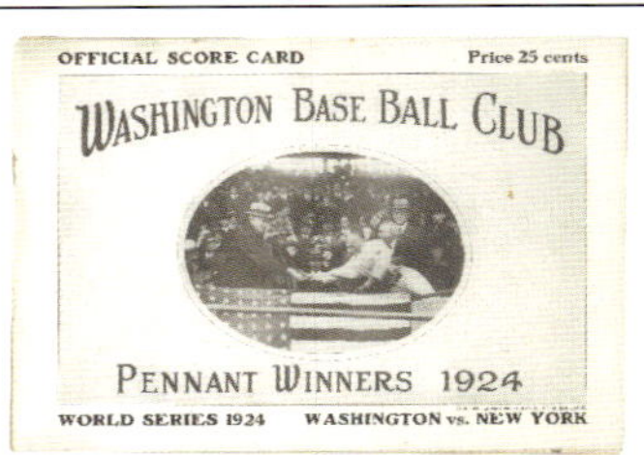

A 1924 World Series Washington Base Ball Club Pennant Winners program and score card.

1924

£200-300 **MAS**

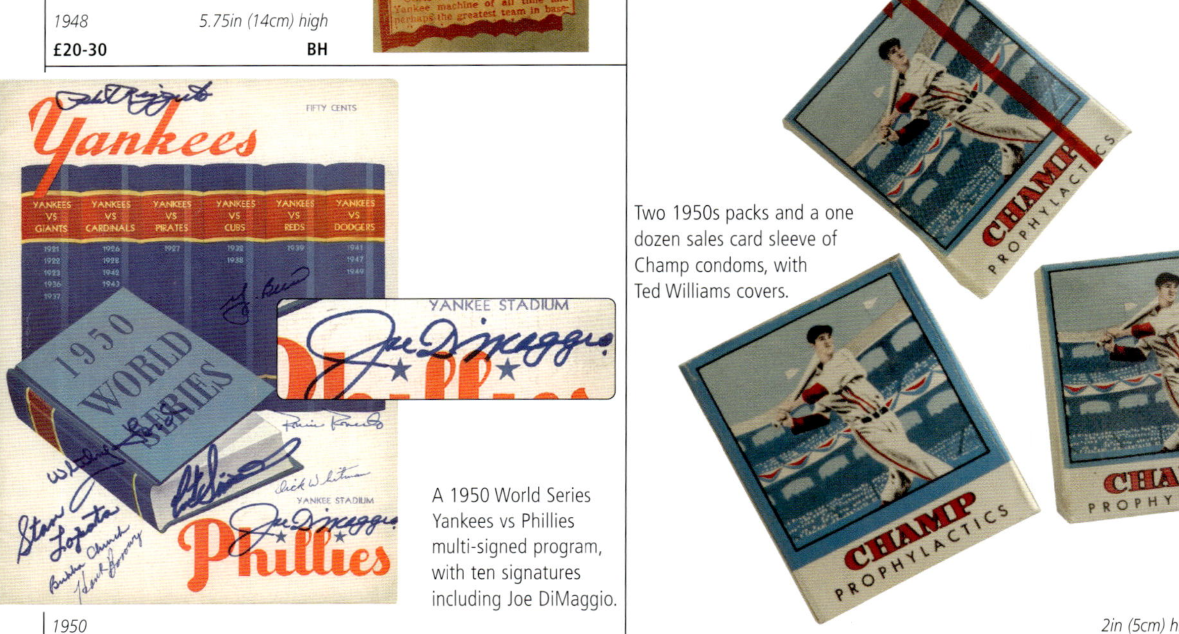

A 1950 World Series Yankees vs Phillies multi-signed program, with ten signatures including Joe DiMaggio.

1950

£600-800 **MAS**

Two 1950s packs and a one dozen sales card sleeve of Champ condoms, with Ted Williams covers.

2in (5cm) high

£200-300 FOR THREE **BH**

A Post Toasties corn flakes cereal box, complete and in mint condition with baseball cards back, framed and glazed.

1962

£450-550 **MAS**

A 1950s Dizzy Dean endorsed 'Falstaff Beer' advertising sign.

£250-350 **MAS**

A Ty Cobb Detriot American League printed felt B18 baseball blanket, issued as a cigarette premium.

This is in slightly poor condition, and has its top left margin cut off. In better and brighter condition, it can fetch up to £300 due to Cobb's popularity.

1914 *5.25in (13cm) wide*

£100-150 **BH**

Two New Hall Pottery Staffordshire water jugs, both featuring an oval portrait of Don Bradman with printed oval signature, one white glazed, the other blue glazed, the reverse with a vignette of crossed bats, balls and stumps, chips and staining.

6.75in (17cm) high

£350-450 GBA

A sterling silver mounted cricket ball, with presentation inscription,

£300-400 GORL

A Bussey cricketers' tape measure.

4.5in (11.5cm) diam.

£80-120 MSA

A Victorian silver and enamel 'Cricket' fob, Robinson Brothers, Birmingham.

1889

£250-300 BEX

A silver snuff box, Edward Smith, with engine-turned decoration, the cover with cartouche engraved with the inscription 'Presented to John Sherman by Members of the Manchester Cricket Club, 1848'.

It was noted in Lillywhite's Cricketing Almanack of 1850, that John Sherman's 'slow bowling proved very effective against the Eleven of England in 1848', this at the age of 60.

7.75in (19.5cm) wide 3.31oz

£550-650 BEA

A silver 'S.B.S.' (Special Boat Service) inter-port cricket game medal, Phillips, Aldershot.

£50-80 FOF

QUICK REFERENCE – CRICKET

Apart from a move to straight bats from curved in the mid-18thC, cricket equipment has changed very little since the invention of the game in the 17thC. Collectors' interest is therefore largely focused on memorabilia connected to famous matches, events or players. Items connected or signed by players such as Dr. W. G. Grace (1848-1915), Gary Sobers (b1936), and Don Bradman (1908-2001) are usually extremely desirable, although firm provenance must be established. Items associated with popular modern players, such as Andrew Flintoff, also attract interest. A great deal of other memorabilia has been produced from the mid-19thC, including ceramics, programmes, tickets, photographs and accessories and, in good condition, these are all popular with collectors.

A Boy's Own Paper 'Famous English Cricketers' supplement print, mounted.

1880 *15in (38cm) wide*

£150-250 GBA

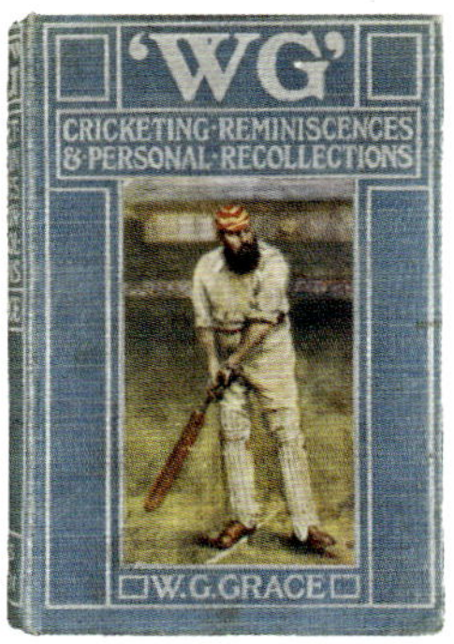

Grace, W. G., 'W G, Cricketing Reminiscences & Personal Recollections', published by James Bowden.

1899

£25-35 GBA

A Jack Hobs Press Club dinner menu profusely signed by guests, signatures in ink to the reverse.

£250-300 GBA

An autographed display for the 1957 West Indians to England, including the signatures of the touring squad on Surrey CCC headed paper, a tour brochure, dinner menu and squad photograph, mounted, framed and glazed.

34in (86.5cm) high

£300-400 GBA

An antique dark green satinised cotton jockey's jacket and cap, Merry & Co. of St James's, cap and sleeves light green sleeves, in good condition.

c1900

£150-200 GBA

A set of Stavros Niarchos racing colours signed by Cash Asmussen in 1993, Gibson (Saddlers) of Newmarket, the white cap signed in blue biro.

The most successful horse to carry Mr Niarchos' s familiar colours was the filly Miesque who won the English and French 1,000 Guineas, the Breeders' Cup Mile and many other important races. Mr Niarchos (1909-1996) was the leading owner in France on two occasions, and topped the breeders' list three times.

£450-550 GBA

A silver picture frame containing locks of mane hair from the 1989 Derby winner Nashwan and his half-brother Unfuwain, the hair mounted alongside colour portrait photographs of the two stallions.

The photos and mane hair were obtained at a Shadwell Stud open day in 2001.

8.5in (19cm) high

£150-200 GBA

An enamel stickpin, picturing the racehorse 'Spearmint'.

' Spearmint' won the 1906 Grand Prix de Paris - one of the most important horse races in France outside the Classics. ' Spearmint' also won the prestigious Derby in 1906. He was owned by Major Edmund Loder and trained by Peter Gilpin.

0.75in (2cm) diam.

£15-20 WORA

QUICK REFERENCE

- Golf probably originated in Scotland around the 12thC, with shepherds knocking stones into rabbit holes. The sport had grown in popularity by the 15thC, when the Scottish Parliament created two acts prohibiting "gowf," which was taking time away from the archery practice considered necessary for national defence.
- Golf memorabilia dating from the 15thC to the early 19thC is extremely rare and can be valuable. Late 19thC/early 20thC pieces are more plentiful and often more affordable. Golf clubs and balls are consistently sought after, with the most valuable pieces being early, rare or high-quality examples by renowned manufactures, such as Thomas Dunn, Douglas McEwan, Tom Morris and Robert Forgan. As most equipment is worn after being used, good condition pieces will typically be the most desirable. While golf is one of the oldest sports still played today, women did not generally participate until the early 20thC. Memorabilia featuring female players is therefore rare and sought after.
- The Victorian enthusiasm for the sport resulted in the production of a vast quantity of golfing themed metalware, glass, artwork and books, as well as ceramics, by factories such as Doulton, Shelley and Spode. Ephemera relating to games and tournaments, such as programs and tickets is also popular and can be affordable.
- Specialist golfing auctions are relatively common, with several in July around the time of the Open Championship.

A B.G.I. Co. one piece wood, with leather insert to face, ebony sole plate, and lead counterweight.

£800-1,200 **L&T**

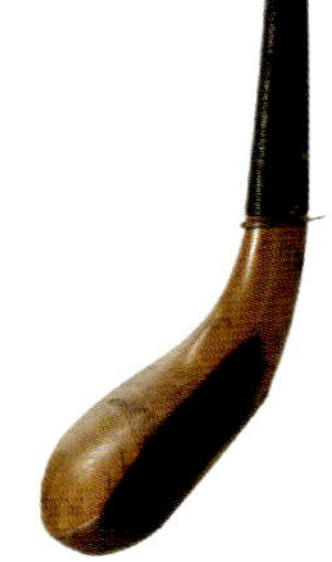

A McEwan long nosed driver, in golden beech, hickory shaft, in good condition, with listing but lacking original grip.

c1885

£700-1,000 **GBA**

QUICK REFERENCE – THE RYDER CUP

Held biannually, the first Ryder Cup competition was in 1927. Since then the US has won over 25 times, against Britain's three wins and Europe's seven wins. Memorabilia related to the event has risen in popularity over the past few years. Programmes are highly desirable, with 1959 being arguably the rarest, although a copy of the first, from 1927, would be the most valuable – if any exist. Values depend on the year, and the signatures that appear on the piece. Entire teams and key players are the most desirable. Won by the US in 1971, the value of this competition menu would have risen had it also been signed by British and American team captains Eric Brown and Jay Hebert. However, star players Arnold Palmer's and J.C. Snead's signatures are desirable.

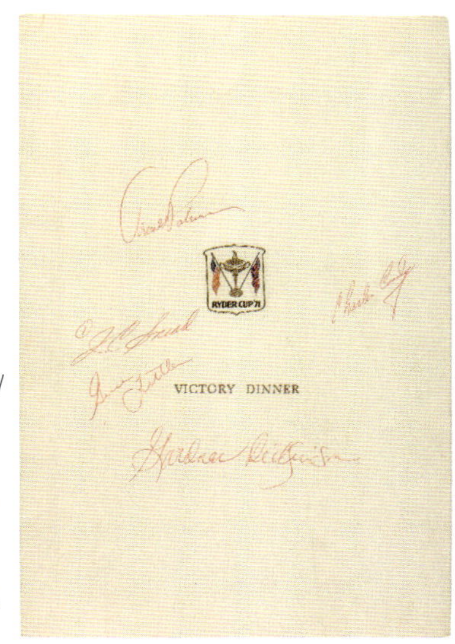

A Ryder Cup Victorian dinner menu, held at the Old Warson Country Club, Saint Louis, Missouri, on 18th September 1971, the cover signed by Arnold Palmer, Gene Littler, Gardner Dickinson, Charles Coody, and J.C. Snead.

£400-600 L&T

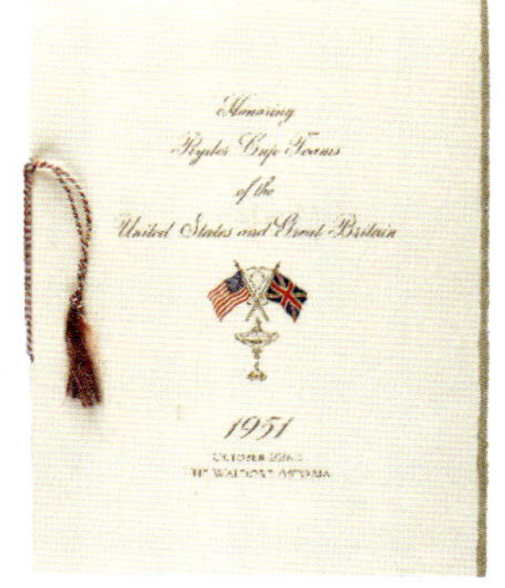

A dinner menu, "Honouring the Ryder Cup Teams of the United States and Great Britain", held at the Waldorf Astoria on October 22nd, 1951.

1951

£400-500 L&T

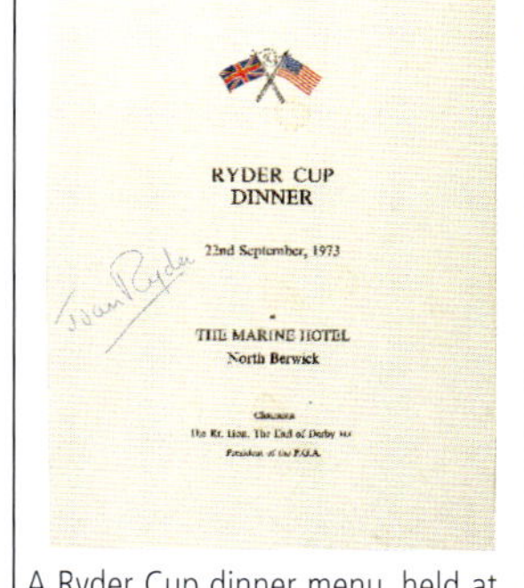

A Ryder Cup dinner menu, held at the Marine Hotel, North Berwick, on 22nd September 1973, the cover signed by Joan Ryder.

£400-600 L&T

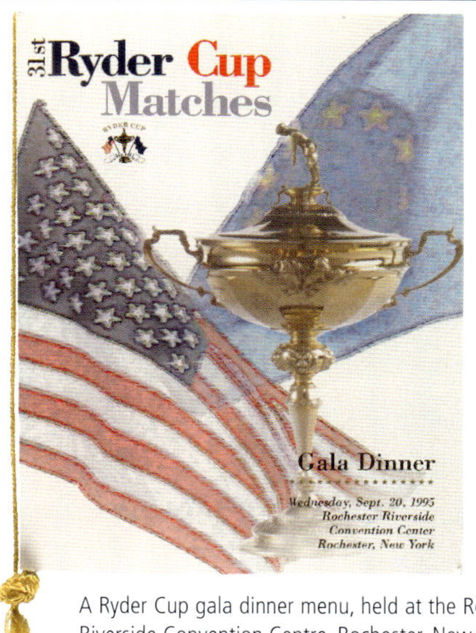

A Ryder Cup gala dinner menu, held at the Rochester Riverside Convention Centre, Rochester, New York, on Wednesday 20th September 1995.

1995

£150-250 L&T

A Ryder Cup welcoming dinner menu, held at The Greenbrier, White Sulphur Springs, West Virginia, on September 13th 1979.

1979

£200-300 L&T

A Ryder Cup gala dinner menu, held at The Omni Hotel, Charleston, South Carolina, on Wednesday 25th September 1991.

1991

£120-180 L&T

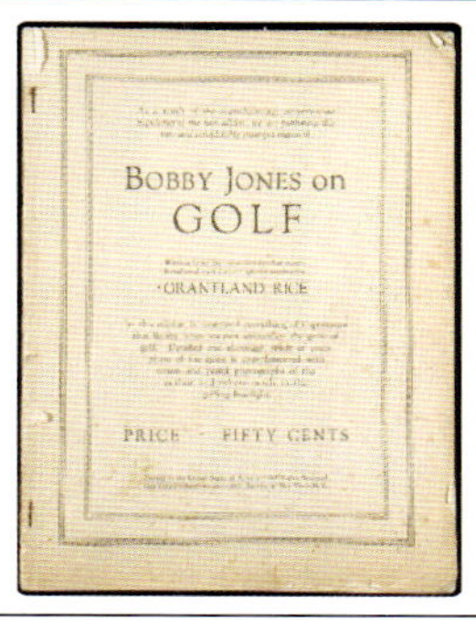

Jones, Bobby, 'Bobby Jones on Golf', with an introduction from Grantland Rice, published by One Time Publications, New York, numerous studies of the game by Jones, plus the rules of gold, lacking back wrapper.

c1930

£150-200 GBA

Walter Hagen, "The Walter Hagen Story" as told to Margaret Seaton Heck, published by Simon and Schuster, first edition, with dustwrapper, and a presentation inscription from Hagen.

1956

£300-400 L&T

A 1950s Walter Hagen black and white photograph, showing Hagen seated on a golf course with a club.

£80-120 MAS

After Michael Brown, 'Life Association of Scotland Calendar 1903', 'First International Golf Match – England v Scotland – Hoylake, 1902, framed.

21.75in (55cm) wide

£700-1,000 L&T

A silver-plated three-piece mesh pattern ball bachelor's tea set, comprising teapot, cream jug and sugar basin.

Had the golfing shape and theme not been here, a standard silver plated teaset would usually be worth under £100.

c1900

£2,000-2,500 L&T

A late Victorian electroplated inkstand, decorated with foliage engraving, crossed clubs and a mesh pattern ball, with hinged cover enclosing a glass liner, on four volute supports, bearing trade label for John Macfarlane, Alloa.

6.75in (17cm) long

£200-300 L&T

A silver golfing medal, one side with a scene of a golfer and inscribed Amateur Golf Championship, the other with a ribbon tied laurel wreath in relief, with ring suspension, no inscription, with Birmingham hallmarks for 1954.

1954 *1.75in (4.5cm)*

£800-1,200 L&T

An American Amateur Championship gilt metal and enamel contestant's badge, reading "September 1-6. 1913", centrally with the initials of "USGA", by The Whitehead & Hoag Company, lacks pin .

1.25in (3cm) wide

£800-1,200 L&T

A Michael Jordan North Carolina signed replica basketball jersey.

£300-400 MAS

An official Spalding basketball, signed by Wilt Chamberlain.

Wilton Norman Chamberlain, also known as 'Wilt The Stilt', was inducted into the Basketball Hall of Fame in 1978. Considered one of, if not the, best player in basketball to date, he had a good rapport with this fans. The fact that this is on a baseball is a nice touch.

£1,200-1,800 MAS

A Hawthorne Milk 'Jerry Sloan, Chicago Bulls' basketball card.

1970-1

£400-500 MAS

A bronze figure of an American footballer, with pale brown patina, mounted on a wooden plinth.

10.5in (27cm) high

£80-120 GBA

A rare Moyer football player ceramic money bank, with orange, black and white uniform, marked '© Moyer' on side of base, with some wear to the painting.

Mr. Moyer reportedly used his own face to model this player.

7.5in (19cm) high

£70-100 BEL

A 1970s Wilson OJ Simpson signature series plastic football and original box.

11.5in (29cm) high

£50-70 BH

A Mitre '5' white rugby ball signed by the England squad from the inaugural Rugby World Cup in 1987, stamped 'OFFICIAL MATCH BALL, RUGBY WORLD CUP 1987', signed by the team manager Geoff Cooke, the coach, and a total of 21 players including Rendall, Moore, Probyn, Dooley, Skinner, and others, mounted in a wooden display case.

c1987

£500-600 GBA

An limited edition 1997 New Zealand 'All Blacks' rugby shirt display, numbered 59 from an edition of 300, the shirt with two columns of signatures, framed with certificate of authenticity taped to the backboard.

The signatures are of all the All Blacks who played in the undefeated run of eight test matches during 1997 season.

1997 *42.5in (108cm) wide*

£450-650 **GBA**

A Pennsylvania Resident Citizen's Fishing License pin, numbered 57318.

1941 *1.75in diam*

£20-25 **BH**

A Victorian brass paper holder, with spring-loaded crossed racquets and balls clip, on a shaped wooden base.

5in (13cm) wide

£120-180 **GBA**

A bronze figure of a boxer, with rich brown patina, mounted on a marble base.

8.5in (21.5cm) high

£120-180 **GBA**

Two Kinsella ceramic figures of boy cricketers, one titled 'The Hope of his Side', the other based on the Kinsella print 'Out First Ball', with the two Kinsella cricket prints that the figures were based on.

Largest 5in (13cm) high

£400-500 **GBA**

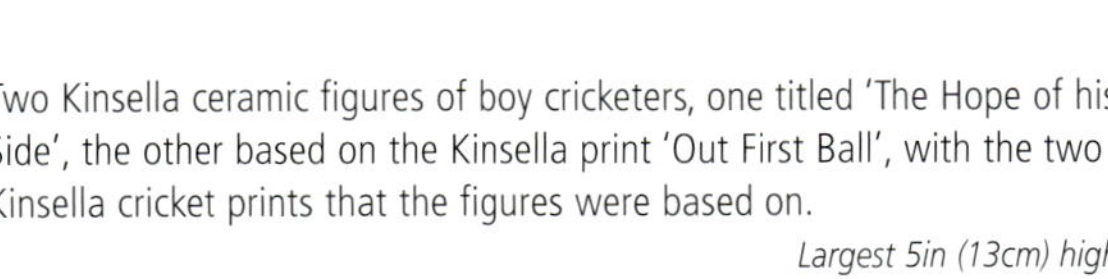

A silvered metal figurine of a stylised fencer, mounted on a black striated marble base.

13in (33cm) wide

£120-180 **WW**

A 1939 World Student Games poster, designed by Franz Kralicek, the colour lithograph printed by Christoph Reisser Sohne, Vienna.

Note the strong Fascist version of the Art Deco style.

1936 *38.5in (98cm) high*

£100-150 **GBA**

QUICK REFERENCE

- Teddy bears are named after American president, Theodore (Teddy) Roosevelt, who refused to shoot a bear-cub on a hunting trip in 1902. Morris Michtom (who later founded the Ideal Novelty and Toy Company) produced a soft toy 'teddy bear' to sell at his Brooklyn store. The bear was so popular that it started a craze, which is still with us today.
- Despite the teddy's American origin, German company, Steiff (founded 1886) are considered the best maker. Other collectable German makers include Gebrüder Hermann. Bing and Schreyer & Co. (Schuco). British companies to look out for include Farnell, Merrythought and Chad Valley. The American companies Ideal, Gund and Knickerbocker have also produced collectable bears.
- Bears can be identified and dated from labels, if they are still attached, or from their materials, colour and form. Before WWII, bears tended to have long limbs with large, upturned paw pads, pronounced snouts and humped backs. They were usually made from mohair and feel solid, as they were stuffed with wood shavings or kapok. Post-war bears usually have shorter limbs and plumper bodies, less pronounced snouts, and rounder heads. Synthetic materials were used from the 1960s. Try to handle as many bears as possible to get a feel for the different styles
- Large bears in unusual colours are often more desirable to collectors, as are those with 'eye appeal' – an appealing expression will always capture a collector's heart. A lot of damage can be restored, but tears, stains, replaced pads and worn fur will often reduce value.
- Bears by contemporary bear artists and modern limited edition bears, from notable makers such as Steiff, are beginning to fetch good prices on the secondary market. Always keep limited edition bears in mint condition, and retain the box and paperwork. Some limited editions, particularly those of Steiff, are replicas of older bears, and these should not be confused with the originals, which are usually worth more. If in doubt, smell a bear, as the scent of an old bear cannot be faked.

A Steiff blonde mohair bear, with boot button eyes, original pads and ear button.

This bear displays all of the features associated with pre-war bears, particularly those by Steiff, such as a hump and long limbs.

c1908 *9.5in (24cm) high*

£700-900 **PC**

A 1930s Steiff small blond 'Teddy Baby', with velvet fur, internal wire frame and large feet allowing him to stand, and ear button.

3in (7.5cm)

£300-400 **PC**

A 1930s-40s Steiff golden mohair small bear, with glass eyes and ear button, in very good condition.

5.25in (13.5cm) high

£350-400 **PC**

A late 1940s Steiff blond mohair bear, with glass eyes, original pads and stitching and ear button, lacking tag.

13.5in (34cm) high

£300-400 **PC**

A 1950s Steiff white mohair miniature bear, with original features, in excellent condition.

3.5in (9cm)

£60-80 **PC**

A 1950s Steiff bear, from the 'Original Teddy' range, bright golden mohair and original red ribbon, no button.

5.25in

£80-100 **PC**

A Steiff red and blue mohair 'Harlequin' teddy bear, from a limited edition of 6,850, with ceramic medallion, certificate, and white ear tag numbered '420214', in mint condition with box.

2000-2001 *14in (35.5cm) high*

£100-150 **VEC**

A Steiff 'Schwarzbar' black mohair bear, from a limited edition of 1,500 exclusive to the UK market, with certificate, in mint condition with box.

2001 *13.75in (35cm) high*

£100-150 **VEC**

A CLOSER LOOK AT A STEIFF ZOTTY BEAR

'Zotty' bears were introduced by Steiff in 1951, and are named after 'zottig', the German word for shaggy, due to their fur. They are currently less popular meaning prices have fallen – it is therefore a good time to buy,

As well as the distinctive fur, they typically have open felt-lined mouths, and they were copied by many makers including Hermann.

Steiff was the only company to use plain 'bibs' on their bears' chests, which helps with identification.

The fur is often tipped with a different tone – do not confuse these with the similar but rarer Steiff 'Petsy' bears from c1929, which have reddy-brown tipped blond mohair and closed mouths.

A 1950s-60s Steiff 'Zotty' bear, with tipped fur, original felt pads and mouth and original eyes and stitching, in excellent condition.

£100-150 **PC**

A Steiff '1908 Rosé Replica' bear, from a limited edition of 3,000, with felt paws, black glass eyes and growler, in presentation box with certificate.

In 1908 Steiff produced samples in black, pink, green or yellow mohair for the English market. No more were then produced. This is a replica of the pink sample bear.

2008 *13.75in (35cm)*

£120-160 **TBW**

A Steiff 'Henderson' bear, from a limited edition of 2,000, with long curled mohair and growler, together with a presentation box and certificate.

This bear was named after pioneer teddy bear collector and researcher Lt Col Bob Henderson, whose collection was sold at aution in 1994. The highest price was £110,000, paid for his life-long companion, a 1904 cinnamon mohair Steiff known as 'Teddy Girl'.

1997 *21.5in (55cm)*

£220-280 **TBW**

A late 1920s Schuco brown mohair 'Piccolo' bear, with original foot pads, boot button eyes and stitching, with worn fur.

At a tiny 2.5in (6.5cm) high, this was the smallest bear produced by Schuco.

2.5in (6.5cm) high

£200-250 **PC**

A 1930s Schuco gold mohair miniature bear, with a metal internal body and original eyes and stitching.

3.5in (9cm) high

£180-220 **BEJ**

A 1920s-30s Schuco orange mohair miniature bear, with original stitching, the head removing to reveal a glass perfume bottle, in excellent condition.

3.5in (9cm) high

£200-250 **PC**

QUICK REFERENCE – SCHUCO MINIATURES

Along with Steiff, Schuco are well-known for their miniature bears, which were produced in large numbers during the 1920-70s. The most commonly found are in gold mohair, but look out for a number of unusual variations, as these can fetch higher values. The rarest colour is purple, but examples were also produced in other colours including red, orange, peach, green, grey and pink. Some also hide a secret, having removable heads, or opening to reveal accessories such as perfume bottles, or compacts. These are particularly sought after, and can fetch over £500 in complete and excellent condition.

A 1920s-30s Schuco gold mohair miniature bear, with removeable head, which conceals a glass perfume bottle, in excellent condition.

5in (12.5cm) high

£500-700 **PC**

Three miniature Schuco bears, in red, green and pink mohair, each wearing knitted tunics, possibly given them by their original owner.

3.5in (9cm) high

£450-550 EACH **PC**

A Schuco brown mohair miniature bear, with metal crown, and a green and yellow cord with 'BP' embossed tinplate button.

This bear was given away as a promotional present at BP petrol station from 1958-60. Complete examples are rare today.

1958-1960 *5in (12.5cm) high*

£100-150 **PC**

A 1920s-30s Schuco gold mohair tumbling miniature bear, with working clockwork mechanism that moves his long arms.

5in (12.5cm) high

£650-750 **PC**

A 1950s Schuco gold mohair small 'Yes/No' bear, with working tail mechanism to nod and shake head.

5in (13cm)

£250-350 **PC**

A CLOSER LOOK AT A SCHUCO YES/NO BEAR

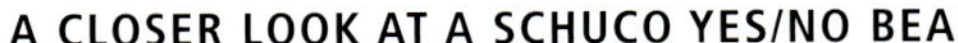

This bear is known as a 'Yes/No' bear as he has an internal mechanism that makes him nod or shake his head, depending on how his tail is moved.

Many collectors prefer post-war examples as they have appealing and charming round faces – but look out for rare pre-war bears, especially in different colours, as they are valuable.

Schuco were better known for producing a large range of clockwork metal toys, enabling them to make such mechanisms. This type of bear was introduced in 1921.

Post-war bears also have downturned paws on longer limbs, and flat feet, allowing them to stand.

A 1950s Schuco gold mohair 'Yes/No' bear, with original stitching, pads and glass eyes, and later neckerchief, with internal mechanical.

9in (29cm) high

£400-600 **TED**

A 1960s-70s Schuco 'footballer' bear, with golden mohair head and 'pipe cleaner' body and limbs, in original woven football kit with plastic boots.

3.75in (9.5cm)

£150-200 **PC**

An early Schuco gold mohair plush bear, with a home-knitted dress, with re-covered felt pads and wear to fur.

10in (25.5cm) high

£250-300 **BEJ**

A 1930s Merrythought bear, with long golden mohair and kapok and excelsior stuffing, felt paw pads, stitched nose, amber and black glass eyes, celluloid button in the ear and fabric label to foot.

This bear can be identified from the the foot label and ear button. Had these not been present, the characteristic paw stitching combined with the shape of the body and his head would have helped indicate the maker. Only Farnell and Merrythought used this style of stitching, but their bears are different in form.

19in (45.5cm) high

£600-800 **PC**

A Merrythought 'Cheeky' gold mohair bear, the large ears with bells sewn inside them, one foot with 'Regd. Design' Merrythought fabric label.

1960

£300-400 **PC**

A rare Merrythought gold mohair and fabric 'Mr Twisty Cheeky' bear, with internal wire frame.

Look out for rare Mrs Cheeky.

1966-68 *11in (28cm)*

£200-250 **TBW**

A late 1960s-70s Merrythought 'Cheeky' rare blue plush bear, in very good condition, with original stitching, eyes and label to foot pad.

18.25in (46cm) high seated

£380-420 **LHT**

A CLOSER LOOK AT A MERRYTHOUGHT BEAR

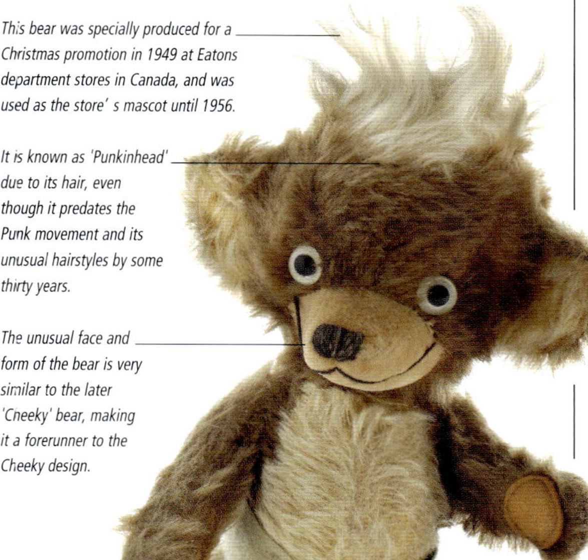

This bear was specially produced for a Christmas promotion in 1949 at Eatons department stores in Canada, and was used as the store' s mascot until 1956.

It is known as 'Punkinhead' due to its hair, even though it predates the Punk movement and its unusual hairstyles by some thirty years.

The unusual face and form of the bear is very similar to the later 'Cheeky' bear, making it a forerunner to the Cheeky design.

It was dressed in velvet shorts, which are typically faded or even lost – these can be found in green, yellow, red or blue.

A Merrythought 'Punkinhead' bear, with brown mohair body and pale chest and ear linings, sewn-on velvet shorts, fully jointed, in good condition.

c1950 *16in (40.5cm) high*

£800-1,000 **TBW**

A 1960s Merrythought gold mohair 'Cheeky' bear, with bells in his ears, and original pads and stitching in excellent condition, with 'Reg'd Design' Merrythought label to foot.

The instantly recognisable 'Cheeky' bear with bells in its ears was released in 1957. Labels typically carry 'registered design' wording as this popular design was distinctive enough to be registered, and therefore protected.

10in (25.5cm) high

£150-200 **PC**

A 1970s Merrythought gold mohair bear, with original stitching and plastic eyes, and label on the right foot.

10in (25.5cm) high

£30-40 **PC**

A Merrythought 'Little Patchwork Punkie' limited edition pellet-filled mohair bear, from a limited edition of 150, with 23 patches in different colours, felt paws, glass eyes, and certificate.

8in (20cm) high

£65-85 **TBW**

A Merrythought brown tipped cream mohair 'Happy Cheeky' bear, from a limited edition of 50.

2009 *25.25in (38cm)*

£150-180 **TBW**

QUICK REFERENCE - DATING MERRYTHOUGHT

Before 1945, Merrythought usually marked its bears with a metal button. Often missing, other hallmarks such as claw style can help with identification. Also look out for remains of labels or stitching or a lack of fading or wear in a label-sized area, as the position and size of this are also useful. After WWII, Merrythought bears were labelled, and the style of the label will help with dating.

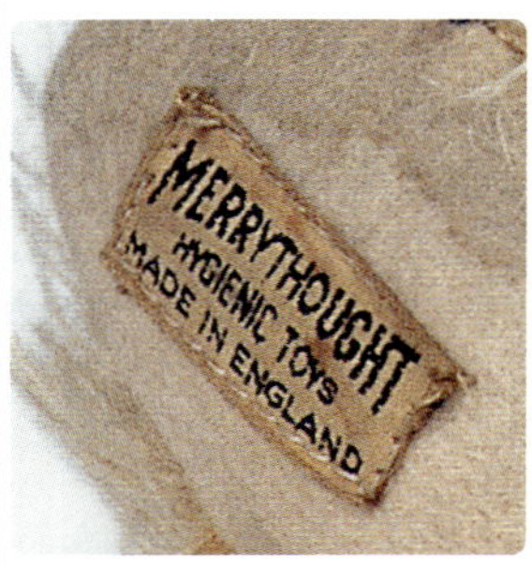

From 1945-56, an embroidered fabric label with the company name and 'Hygenic Toys' wording was used.

From 1957 until 1991, a printed fabric label was used, including the wording 'Ironbridge Shropshire'.

From 1991 onwards, the label included a 'wishbone' motif as well as wording.

A 1990s Merrythought golden mohair bear, with leather paw pads and original labels, in mint condition.

£200-300 **BEJ**

A limited edition Merrythought 'Cheeky Toggles' bear, in felt duffel coat.

2009 *11.5in (29cm) high*

£100-150 **TBW**

A limited edition Merrythought bear, 'Sleepy Cheeky', in matching nightshirt and cap.

2009 *25.25in (38cm)*

£80-120 **TBW**

A scarce Farnell white or blond mohair 'Alpha' bear, with pale brown rectangular vertically stitched nose, webbed paw stitching and flat foot pads.

c1925

£1,000-1,500 **TBW**

A 1930s Farnell rare blue mohair bear, with original glass eyes, pale brown facial stitching and pads, with some wear to his fur.

9.25in (23.5cm) high

£1,800-2,200 **PC**

A 1930s Farnell bear, with wool plush fur and replaced pads, wearing a later leather collar, with patches of wear to his fur.

20in (50.5cm) high

£200-300 **PC**

A 1930s Farnell bear, with blond mohair head and paws and blue and red plush integral clothing, with original blue eyes and stitching.

10in (25.5cm) high

£100-120 **PC**

A Farnell red mohair 'soldier' miniature bear, with original eyes.

These were often sold as gifts for sweethearts to take with them during WWI, their upturned faces allowing them to peek out of the breast pocket of a soldier' s uniform. They were made in patriotic colours of red, white and blue, as well as the traditional gold colour.

1915 *3.75in (9.5cm)*

£300-400 **TBW**

A CLOSER LOOK AT A FARNELL BEAR

This bear is large and of very high quality – this has led to Farnell being dubbed the 'English Steiff'.

Gold mohair is the most common colour, with blond, blue or red being much scarcer. Blond bears should have light brown nose and mouth stitching.

The long limbs, shaved protruding snout, large flat foot pads, rounded face and humped back are typical features of pre-war Farnell bears.

The paw stitching is a characteristic feature of Farnell bears made before 1930 – it was also used by Merrythought, which hired one of Farnell's directors in 1920.

A late 1920s Farnell gold mohair large bear, with original stitching and eyes and webbed claws, with broken growler.

25in (63.5cm) high

£1,500-2,000 **PC**

A 1930s-40s Chiltern pale gold mohair 'Hugmee' bear, with original velvet paw pads, stitching and amber and black glass eyes.

Chiltern released the 'Hugmee' bear in 1923, and it became extremely popular. Note the shape of the head, and the size and length of the arms and legs – these are all typical of features of Hugmee bears from the 1930s onwards.

15in (38cm) high

£350-450 **BEJ**

A late 1940s/50s Chiltern gold mohair bear, with original paw pads, stitching, woven nose and glass eyes, in excellent condition.

The thick-thighed 'drumstick' legs are characteristic of Chiltern bears from the 1930s onwards.

£200-250 **TBW**

A Chiltern gold mohair 'Hugmee' teddy bear, with original foot pads, woven nose, glass eyes and original tag.

1930s-40s *13in (33cm) high*

£400-500 **LHT**

A late 1940s-early 1950s Chiltern small gold mohair 'Hugmee' bear, with card-lined paws, velvet pads and original stitching and eyes.

8in (20cm) high

£200-300 **PC**

A late 1950s Chiltern large blond mohair 'Hugmee' bear, with original stitching, eyes and paw pads, lacking label.

This was the largest standard production size in the Hugmee range.

26in (66cm) high

£400-600 **PC**

A 1950s Chiltern golden moahir 'Ting-a-Ling Bruin' musical bear, with Rexine pads and original pads, stitching and eyes.

The Ting-a-Ling Bruin bear was introduced by Chiltern after WWII, and contained a mechanism that produced a musical tinkling sound when moved.

12in (30.5cm) high

£250-350 **PC**

A 1960s Chiltern 'Ting-a-Ling' musical bear, with gold, light blue and pink plush, and original stitching, plastic label and card label, in mint condition.

7in (17.5cm) high

£200-250 **PC**

QUICK REFERENCE – AMERICAN TEDDY BEARS

Many US bears were not labelled and so identification is difficult for today's collectors. A great many factories sprang up during the teddy bear 'fever' of the 1910s and 20s, including Ideal, Knickerbocker, Bruin, Aetna and Gund. However, many were short-lived and most did not mark or label their bears. Typical features of pre-war American bears include a wide, triangular head, large ears at the corners, arms slung lower down on the body and the bodily shape of German bears. This example, by market leader Ideal, is typical.

A 1920s American Ideal cinnamon mohair bear, with large flat feet, felt paw pads, small amber coloured glass eyes and a long snout.

15in (38cm) high

£700-800 **BEJ**

An early American gold mohair bear, with replaced foot pads, original stitching and boot button eyes, with some wear to the fur.

1905-06 *18in*

£300-400 **PC**

An American gold mohair 'sleepy eye' bear, with original stitching and celluloid spherical eyes, one paw pad recovered, with wear to his fur.

Rather than the standard boot button or two-colour glass eyes, these eyes are made from celluloid balls fixed in a metal mounting. The balls are weighted so that when the bear is laid down on its back, they roll down showing a plain side, thus appearing 'closed'.

1910-12

£800-1,000 **PC**

A 1950s American gold mohair 'mascot' bear, made for the University of California, with matching blue felt paw pads, sewn-on 'C' and 'California' badge, with original light blue eyes and stitching.

£40-50 **TBW**

An American bear-on-wheels, with fixed head position, original tail and metal frame and wheels.

American bears-on-wheels are more unusual than German.

1900-10

£300-500 **PC**

An early American pale gold plush bear, with original nose stitching, boot button eyes, and 'pinched' ears, paw pads re-covered in chamois.

c1910 *20in (51cm) high*

£700-800 **BEJ**

A Chad Valley blond alpaca fur 'Cubby' bear, with original stitching, eyes and original label to foot pad.

c1954 *9.5in (24cm) high*

£150-250 **PC**

A 1950s Chad Valley golden mohair 'Bear Brand' shop display large bear, with original paw pads, stitching and glass eyes, with panel where a label was once sewn on.

This enormous bear was originally part of a display selling women's stockings.

45in (114cm) high

£450-550 **PC**

A CLOSER LOOK AT A CHAD VALLEY BEAR

Chad Valley, founded in 1820, produced its first bears in 1915 and became very successful. Many British children of the 1940s-60s grew up with a Chad Valley bear.

This is characteristic of post-war Chad Valley bears, with ears placed flat on its head, a vertically stitched bulbous nose and long, curving arms.

Its fur and stitching is in excellent condition, if it had enjoyed years of love and wear, value would plummet to around £30 or less.

It still bears the company label on its foot pad. The label wording can help to date the bear, as it refers to Elizabeth Queen Consort of King George VI as 'Her Majesty the Queen', and can therefore be dated to before the 1953 Coronation of Queen Elizabeth II, when wording changed to 'Queen Mother'.

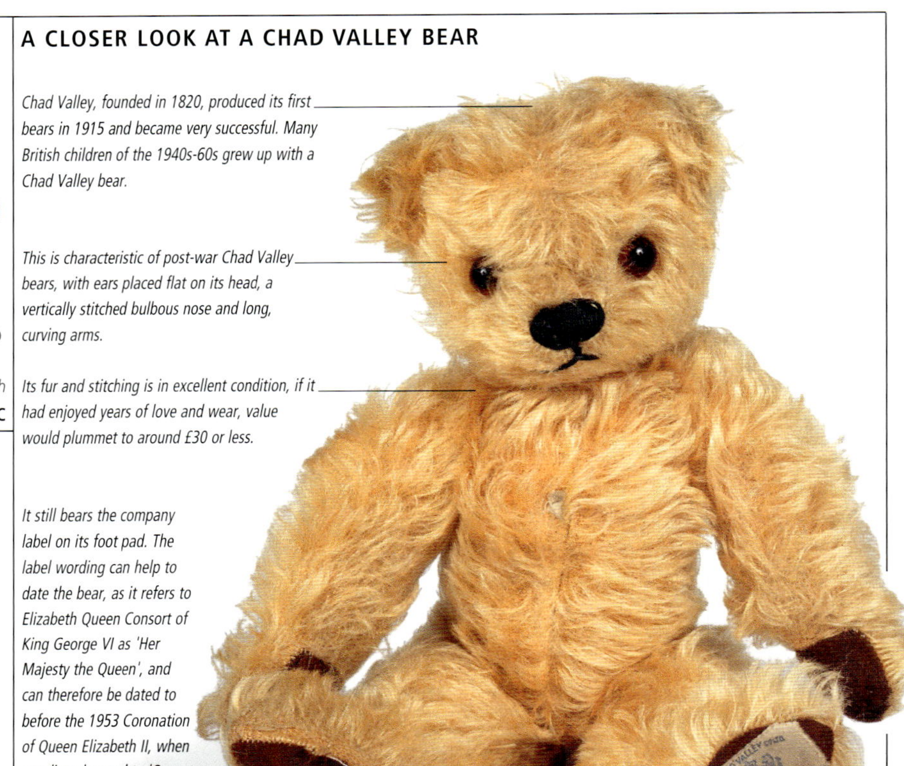

A late 1940s-early 1950s Chad Valley golden mohair small bear, with original paw pads, stitching and eyes, with label to right-hand paw pad.

£500-700 **TED**

A 1930s Chad Valley white mohair polar bear, with down-turned paws, original stitching and eyes, and Chad Valley label on left foot pad.

Polar bears were popular from the 1930s onwards, but grew again in popularity in the 1950s after the birth of a polar bear cub named Brumas in London Zoo in 1949.

£600-800 **PC**

A rare German Eduard Crämer musical bear, with internal mechanism operated by moving the neck up and down, with original stitched woollen nose and claws.

c1930 *18in (45.5cm) high*

£2,200-2,800 **TCT**

A 1930s Dean's Rag Book Co. rare blue mohair bear, with original paw pads, shaved snout and original stitching and eyes, and cupped ears.

c1926

£400-500 **TBW**

A rare Einco white mohair bear, with side-glancing 'googly' type eyes, and original paw pads, in good condition.

Einco was the trade name used by Eisenmann & Co., a toy import company based in London. Founded in the late 19thC by brothers Josef and Gabriel Eisenmann, the company had an office in Germany and distributed bisque dolls, teddies and other toys. In 1908, Josef and Leon Rees founded the Chiltern Toy Works in Buckinghamshire, producing their first bear (Master Teddy) in 1915. This 'mousey' look is unusual, and is even more rodent-like than Deans' bears.

1915-20

£400-600 **TBW**

A 1950s German Diem yellow mohair bear, with short plush mohair on snout and paws, with internal growler.

£200-250 **PC**

A 1930s French Faye gold silk plush teddy, with original eyes and stitching, in excellent condition.

6.5in (16.5cm) high

£120-180 **BEJ**

A 1960s German Grisly Spielwaren blond bear, with synthetic plush fur, open mouth, original eyes, and manufacturer's button to chest.

Grisly Spielwaren was founded In Germany in 1954, and saw a peak in sales during the 1960s and 70s. The company is still active today.

£80-120 **PC**

A 1930s German Hermann pin-jointed blond mohair bear, in period South German style woven wool outfit, with original stitching, eyes and paw pads.

6.75in (17cm) high

£200-300 **PC**

A 1930s German Hermann 'Helvetic' pale gold plush bear, with Rexine pads and original eyes, stitching and paw pads.

The term 'Helvetic' is used to describe a mechanical music box, usually Swiss, inside the bear.

18in (46cm) high

£700-900 **BEJ**

A 1950s Australian Joy Toys bright gold mohair plush bear, with original paw pads and eyes.

£200-300 **TBW**

A British Gabrielle Designs 'Paddington' bear, designed by Shirley Clarkson in 1972, with hat, duffel coat, Wellingtons and luggage tag.

The earliest versions from around 1973 have no hint of a foot inside their child's Dunlop wellington boots.

£40-60 **PC**

A Gabrielle Designs 'Aunt Lucy' bear, complete with clothing and accessories, including Peruvian coins in a pocket in her petticoat.

As she was not as popular as Paddington, Aunt Lucy is much harder to find today.

£150-200 **PC**

An American R. John Wright alpaca plush Paddington Bear, with 'Please look after this bear' label to neck, leather suitcase complete with marmalade, from a limited edition 2,500, in mint condition and with box in excellent condition.

R. John Wright is a noted American bear and doll artist whose work, often produced under license from Disney and others, is highly sought after by collectors.

2001 *13.5in (34cm) high*

£380-420 **VEC**

A Steiff 'Rupert Bear', with white alpaca fur, wearing traditional outfit, with stitch-sculpted fingers and thumb, from a limited edition.

2008 *11in (28cm) high*

£100-150 **TBW**

An unusual cotton plush 'Rupert Bear' style bear, with pale gold mohair head and paws, with wooden mechanism that opens the mouth when the tummy is squeezed.

c1930

£300-400 **BEJ**

A 1960s Chad Valley plush 'Sooty' teddy bear, wearing red dungarees, with original paw pads.

£15-20 **PC**

A Steiff 'Karl Lagerfeld' white alpaca fur bear, designed by Karl Lagerfeld, with Italian wool jacket over striped denims, a black silk cravat set with a Swarovski crystal, miniature Lagerfeld Eyewear Collection glasses, and exclusive white gold ear button, from a limited edition of 2,500, with box and certificate.

2008 *15.5cm (40cm)*

£600-800 **TBW**

A British 'Brennus' (King) artist bear, by Jean and Bill Ashburner, jointed at the wrists and with two joints to the neck, with a needle sculpted nose and realistic three-dimensional polymer pads on unltrasuede paws, numbered five from a limited edition of eight.

18in (46cm)

£320-370

A German Freche Früchte Bären 'pumpkin' bear, by Kerstin Jeske, with label at the back in seam.

4in (10cm) high seated

£90-110 PC

A German 'Freche Früchte Bären' 'cake' bear, by Kerstin Jeske, with label at the back in seam.

5in (12cm) high seated

£80-90 PC

A British 'Gabriel Oak' artist bear, by June Kendall, with gold mohair and ultrasuede paws, glass eyes, and green-checked scarf, part filled with steel shot for weight, numbered six from a limited edition of twelve.

June Kendall is based in Hampshire, England, and was inspired to make bears at a time when she was involved in events in Dorset celebrating the 150th anniversary of Thomas Hardy. As a result she named her creations ' Hardy Bears' . This bear is themed on a character from ' Far From the Madding Crowd' .

2008 *4.25in (11cm) high*

£40-60 **TBW**

An American 'Stella' artist bear, by Sue Lain, made with dusky pink mohair, and wearing a vintage broderie anglaise dress, numbered four from a limited edition of eight.

2008 *12in (30cm)*

£120-180 **TBW**

A British 'Miranda' artist bear, by Elizabeth Leggat, made from antique short pile plush mohair, and wearing a 1920s-style silk dress trimmed with vintage ribbon, with silver purse made from vintage material, weighted with steel shot, from a limited edition of six.

The purse is made from pieces of an original Edwardian purse.

2008 *4in (10cm)*

£450-500 **TBW**

An English miniature 'Mikey' artist bear, by Elisabeth Marsden, with knitted wool golly doll and yellow cardigan, and split pin joints and glass eyes.

2.75in (7cm) high

£45-50 **PC**

An American 'Algernon' artist bear, by Jeanette Warner, made of sparse cinnamon mohair with black glass bead eyes and aged felt paws.

2008/09 *13in (33cm) high*

£100-140 **TBW**

A Dany-Bären Riualdo artist bear, by Danielo-Rebecca Melse, in red aged mohair, with tags, black glass eyes, black vertically stitched nose, felt pads, and black claw stitching, numbered one from a limited edition of two, in near mint condition.

16in (41cm) high

£300-500 **VEC**

A Japanese 'Puu' artist bear, by Yuki Yamanaka, made of aged viscose, with a gingham patch and 'replaced' footpad, numbered four from a limited edition of ten.

Yuki Yamanaka, from Chiba, Japan, designed clothes after leaving university. She was inspired to start making bears in 1997 by an antique teddy that she particularly loved. The large head and tiny eyes are typical of contemporary Japanese animated and cartoon characters.

2007 *8in (20cm)*

£80-120 **TBW**

A Swedish L. M. Ericsson telephone, the black tinplate body with gilt transfer decoration, nickel-plated cradle, and original cable.

c1910 *13.25in (33cm) high*

£100-150 **WDL**

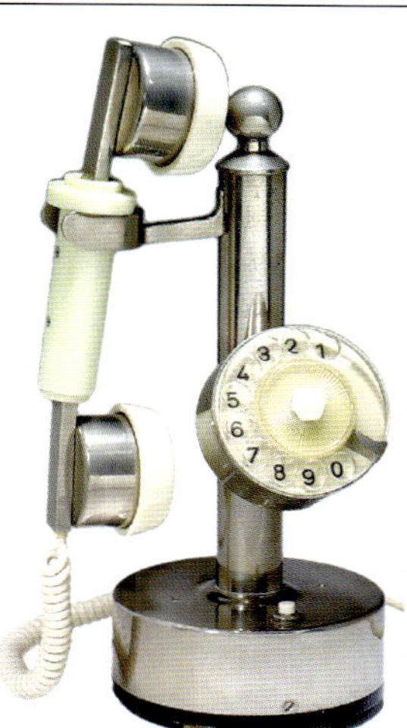

A 1960s replica of the famous 'candlestick' telephone, originally manufactured by GEFA A.G. of Vienna in the 1920s.

c1965

£250-350 **ATK**

A 1930s black bakelite 200 series telephone.

8in (20cm) wide

£180-220 **L**

A 1950s black bakelite 300 series telephone, with original lead.

6in (15cm) wide

£100-150 **L**

A 1960s red plastic telephone, by the Reliance Telephone Co.

5in (12.5cm) wide

£40-60 **L**

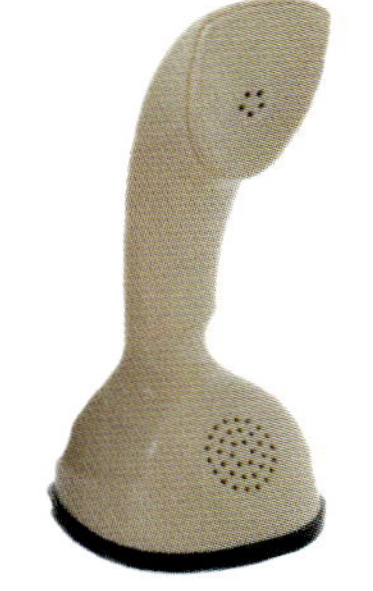

A 1970s cream plastic Ericofon telephone, by Ericsson.

8.25in (21cm) high

£70-100 **L**

TELEPHONES

An American candlestick telephone, with 'Stars & Stripes' decoration.

c1974 *11in (28.5cm) high*

£70-100 **NOR**

A Northern Telecom moulded plastic airplane telephone, in two tones of orange, with rotary dial and large Lucite 'propeller', embossed mark and foil label.

9in (23cm) wide

£50-80 **CRA**

A blue plastic 'Ola' T1000GD telephone, by Thomson, designed by Phillipe Starck.

11in (28cm) long

£50-60 **L**

A Swatch Twinphone transparent green plastic telephone, Deluxe model.

9.5in (24cm) long

£30-50 **MHT**

A wooden Trub telephone, by gfeller, designed in the 1970s.

c1994 *8.25in (21cm) wide*

£70-90 **L**

A 1980s red plastic 'Hot Lips' telephone.

8.5in (21.5cm) wide

£35-45 **L**

QUICK REFERENCE

- Corgi toys were first produced in 1956 by Welsh toy company Mettoy, founded in 1933 by Phillip Ullman of the German toymaker Tipp & Co. Corgi toys were released to compete with Dinky's successful range of diecast toys, including the new Supertoys range. However, Corgi's vehicles featured exciting additions, such as plastic windows, and doors and boots that opened.
- Suspension, marketed as 'Glidamatic' was introduced in 1959. Clockwork, self-propelled versions were also introduced and are generally worth more than 'free-wheeling' models today. Innovations continued during the 1960s, including steering and jewelled head lights. Faceted ruby rear lights were introduced on a Bentley Continental released in 1961. 'Trans-o-lite' headlamps that transmitted daylight to give the appearance of illumination were introduced in 1963.
- The 1960s and 70s also saw a range of models tied in with popular TV programmes and films. These included Batman's Batmobile, James Bond's Aston Martin and Chitty Chitty Bang Bang. These models were enormously popular at the time, and remain so with collectors today. Other popular ranges include Chipperfields Circus, and boxed gift sets which have seen an enormous rise in popularity over the past few years.
- As with other diecast toys, look out for variations by considering the colour, decals or stickers and other features such as the interior or wheels. To fetch the best prices, models should be accompanied by their boxes and any accessories they were sold with. The inclusion of the inner packaging is also a desirable feature. Always look for models in mint condition, and avoid pieces with repainting.

A Corgi No.351 Land Rover 'RAF' Vehicle, greyish blue, spun hubs, tow hook, in near mint condition, with good condition carded box.

The version of this model with suspension is worth roughly 25 per cent more.

1958-62

£100-150 VEC

A Corgi No.472 Land Rover public address vehicle 'Vote for Corgi', with spun hubs and two figures, in near mint condition, with good condition carded box.

1964-66

£100-150 VEC

A Corgi No.438 Land Rover 'Lepra', metallic green, cream plastic canopy, lemon interior, cast hubs, silver plastic tow hook, in mint condition, with mint condition window box.

This is a scarce variation with different coloured canopy. It is usually found with a green canopy and no decal, which would usually be worth under £100 in excellent, boxed condition.

1963-77

£650-850 VEC

A Corgi No.417 Land Rover 'Breakdown Service', red, yellow tin canopy, spun hubs, in mint condition, with mint condition, inner carded packing Collectors Club leaflet, in good condition box.

1960-62

£120-180 VEC

A Corgi No.487 Land Rover 'Chipperfield Circus' parade vehicle, red, blue, lemon interior, spun hubs, clown and monkey figures, in excellent condition, with good condition carded box.

1965-69

£80-120 VEC

A Corgi No.348 Ford Mustang Fastback, in lilac with a pale green interior, cast hubs, psychedelic 'flower power' decals with racing number 20 to doors, in near mint condition, with near mint carded box, with Collectors Club leaflet.

Produced for only a short period of time, this a very rare model in mint condition. The 'Pop Art' decoration is also obviously of its time and, along with that on a Mini Cooper, has become sought after in recent years.

1968-69

£1,000-1,500 **VEC**

A Corgi No.233 Heinkel Trojan Economy Car, red body, lemon interior, flat spun hubs, in mint condition, with mint condition carded box complete with Collectors Club folded leaflet.

1962-72

£70-100 **VEC**

A Corgi No.341 Mini Marcos GT850, maroon body, grey chassis, cream interior, golden jack take-off wheels, in mint condition, with near mint condition box, with Collectors Club folded leaflet.

1968-70

£50-70 **VEC**

A Corgi No.437 Cadillac Superior 'Ambulance', with battery operated red roof-light and cast hubs, in mint condition, with inner packing card and Collectors Club leaflet, with excellent condition carded box.

1965-68

£120-180 **VEC**

A Corgi No.474 Ford Thames 'Walls Ice-cream' Van, with musical chimes and spun hubs, in excellent condition, with good condition carded box.

1965-68

£150-200 **VEC**

A Corgi No.431 VW Pick-up, with plastic canopy and spun hubs, in mint condition, with mint condition Collectors Club leaflet and carded box.

The variation with a metallic gold body and red VW emblem can be worth around 50 per cent more.

1964-66

£100-150 **VEC**

A Corgi No.490 VW Breakdown Truck, with tan body, spun hubs, in mint condition, with good condition carded box with Collectors Club leaflet.

1967-69

£100-150 **VEC**

A Corgi No.1121 'Chipperfield Circus' six-wheel Crane Truck, with chrome jib, lacking hook and string but otherwise in excellent condition, with good condition carded picture box.

1963-69

£70-100 VEC

A Corgi No.1142 Ford Holmes Wrecker Truck, with unpainted booms, in excellent condition with two figures and instruction sheet, with excellent condition inner tray, and good condition outer window box.

1967-74

£150-200 VEC

A Corgi No.1120 Midland Red Motorway Express Coach, with yellow interior and flat spun hubs, in mint condition, with near mint condition box with Collectors Club leaflet.

£120-180 VEC

A Corgi No.50 Massey Ferguson 65 Tractor, with excellent condition carded box with inner packing card.

1959-66

£100-150 VEC

A Corgi Major Toys gift set no. 28, 'Car Transporter with four cars', comprising a Bedford TK cab transporter in red with mid and light blue trailer, Fiat 2100 (232), Renault Floride (222), Ford Consul Classic (234) and a Mercedes Benz 220 SE couple (230), vehicles in mint condition, with Corgi dog dummy boxes, box complete with internal packaging and instructions, minor wear to lid.

This is a very rare and desirable set and is in superb condition. Corgi gift sets in similar condition have been rising rapidly in value over the past few years.

1963-65

£600-800 W&W

A CLOSER LOOK AT A CORGI TANKER

The dark blue colour and decals on this model were produced as a special promotion for Shell Chemicallen of Holland c1963-64 only.

The variation of the lighter blue 1129 'Milk' Bedford tanker with an S-Type cab produced from 1962-65 is more common and worth around £150-200.

They were sold in special boxes with leaflets promoting Shell's various products – a mint and boxed example may sell for over £1,000 if found.

Reputedly only around 500 examples were ever made, making them very rare today and explaining the high price for this example in poor condition.

A Corgi 1129 blue and white Bedford S-Type 'Shell Petrol' Tanker, in poor condition.

c1963-64

£250-350 SAS

A Corgi 'Batman' 107 Batboat, in excellent condition, in excellent condition original striped window box.

1974-81

£70-100 SAS

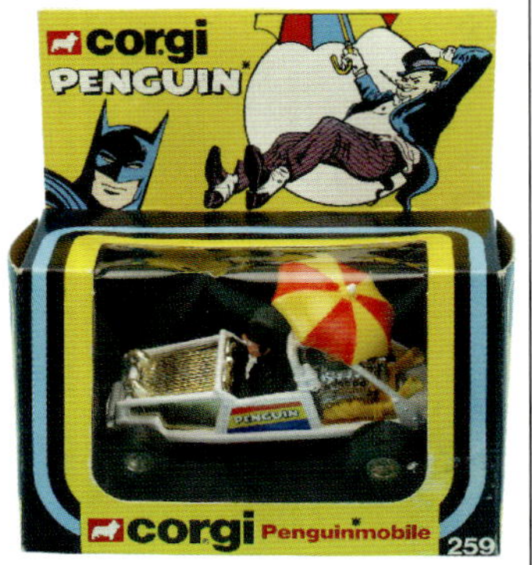

A Corgi 259 Penguinmobile, in excellent condition, in excellent condition original striped window box.

1979-80

£50-70 SAS

A CLOSER LOOK AT A BATMOBILE

Corgi released the Batmobile for Christmas 1966, having dominated the Christmas market in 1965 with James Bond's Aston Martin – the Batmobile proved just as popular.

It was produced in different variations until 1979, but the rarest examples are the first issues from 1966-67, of which this is one.

This example is rarer still as it has a matte, not gloss, black body and is in excellent condition.

Although it retains its appealing pictorial box, it is not in great condition, and some of the many accessories are missing, which reduces the value by as much as a third.

A Corgi matte black 267 Batmobile, with three rockets and Club Slip, in excellent condition, in fair condition original box, inner plinth slightly torn.

1966-67

£600-800 SAS

A Corgi 647 'Buck Rogers' Starfighter, with Wilma and Tweaky plastic figurines, in excellent condition, in very good condition original striped window box.

1980-83

£50-70 SAS

A Corgi 434 'Charlie's Angels' Van, in excellent condition, in very good condition original pictorial window box.

1978-80

£30-40 SAS

A Corgi 342 'The Professionals' Ford Capri, in excellent condition, in very good condition original box.

1980-82

£80-120 SAS

A Corgi 320 'The Saint' Jaguar XJS, in excellent condition, in excellent condition original striped pictorial window box.

1978-81

£20-30 SAS

A Corgi 436 Spidervan, in excellent condition, in excellent condition original striped pictorial window box.

1979-80

£25-35 SAS

A CLOSER LOOK AT NODDY'S CAR

This model is hard to find, particularly in such excellent condition, as it was produced for only one year.

Always look closely at the Golly's face – the value can nearly double if Golly has a tan face, and can triple if he has a black face.

At the time, Noddy's popularity was waning, meaning fewer were sold and the model was discontinued relatively quickly.

If Golly has been replaced by a brown Master Tubby, the value falls to around half this price.

A Corgi 801 Noddy's Car, with Noddy, Big Ears, and a grey-faced Golly, in excellent condition, in excellent condition original box.

1969

£300-400 SAS

A Corgi 292 'Starsky & Hutch' Ford Torino, in excellent condition, in very good condition original box.

Unusually, an export model (produced in 1986) is worth around a tenth of this value – mainly as it was made in a run of 20,000 and was generally kept in mint condition by many collectors.

1977-82

£80-120 SAS

A Corgi 348 Vegas Ford Thunderbird, with Dan Tanner as driver, in excellent condition, in excellent condition original striped pictoral box.

1980-81

£30-40 SAS

A Corgi 497 'The Man From U.N.C.L.E.' Thrush-Buster, with purplish-blue body, Waverly Ring, Club Slip, packing disc, packing ring and corrugated packing piece, in excellent condition, in very good condition original box.

To fetch this price, the model must have the ring and both internal card packing components. Look out for the white finished body, which was produced in the first year only (1966) and can fetch over twice this price.

1966-69

£300-400 SAS

QUICK REFERENCE

- Dinky toys were first produced in 1933 by Meccano Ltd as accessories to their popular range of Hornby model railways. They originated in a range known as 'Model Miniatures' introduced in 1931, which comprised 22 sets including one of model vehicles. In 1934, this set became the first set of 'Meccano Dinky Toys', intended to compete with America's Tootsie Toys, which were being imported into the UK and proving very popular with children.
- Dinky toys were made in Liverpool until 1979, and also at Bobigny in France from 1937–72. Following the closure of the Liverpool factory in 1979 the name was acquired by Matchbox in 1987, and then Mattel, who have not used it since 2001.
- Collectors consider the 'golden age' of Dinky to be the 1930s. By 1935, over 200 models were made, and examples are usually highly sought after. Survivors are rare as many pre-war models were made from a metallic alloy that tends to crumble over time.
- In 1947 the smaller scale 'Supertoys' range was released, followed by the 'Speedwheels' range in 1969. These are easier to find, and often less expensive to collect. Supertoys are particularly sought after by collectors.
- When buying, look for models in good condition, and beware of any repainting, even in small areas, as this reduces desirability considerably. If the original box is present and in good condition it can add over 40 per cent to the value.
- Look out for variations in paint colour, details such as cab stripes and hubs, and even plastic interiors. Some variations may indicate special models that were exported to certain countries in limited numbers, and can fetch high prices today.

A Dinky No.167 A.C. Aceca Coupé, grey body, red roof, shaped spun hubs, in excellent condition, with excellent condition incorrect colour spot card picture box.

The colour of the car on the box does not match the colour of the model. For some collectors, this makes this example less desirable. This is more valuable than the example with matching red hubs.

1958-63

£100-150 **VEC**

A Dinky No.110 Aston Martin DB3S, mid-green, red seats, ridged hubs, white driver, racing number 22, in excellent condition, with good condition correct colour spot card picture box.

1956-59

£180-220 **VEC**

A Dinky No.176 Austin A105 Saloon, grey body, red side flash and ridged hubs, in near mint condition, with near mint condition correct colour spot card picture box.

1958-59

£100-150 **VEC**

A Dinky No.112 Austin Healey Sprite MkII, red body, cream interior, spun hubs, in near mint condition, with good condition card picture box.

Look out for the South African export variation with a turquoise, pink, light blue or dark blue body, as this can fetch around four times as much as this.

1961-66

£80-120 **VEC**

A Dinky No.38A Frazer Nash BMW Car, grey, red seats and ridged hubs, in excellent condition, needs cleaning.

Frazer Nash were a British car manufacturer who were active from 1922-c1957. From 1934-39, they were the offical importer and assembler for BMW in the UK.

1947-50

£220-280 **VEC**

A French Dinky No.500 Citroen 2CV, orange body, plastic open-top, cream interior, shaped spun hubs, near mint condition, with near mint condition colour card picture box.

£100-150 VEC

A Dinky No.515 Ferrari 250GT 2 + 2, red body, white interior, concave spun hubs, in near mint condition, with near mint condition full colour card picture box.

£100-150 VEC

A Dinky No.1408 Honda S800, yellow body, red interior, concave spun hubs, in excellent condition, with near mint condition card picture box.

£80-120 C

A Dinky No.57/005 Ford Thunderbird, mid blue body, white roof, shaped cast wheels, plated bumpers, red interior, in near mint condition, with excellent condition card picture box.

This number indicates this model was made in Hong Kong, and is one of the more desirable and valuable of the small range made there from 1965-80. Yellow 'see-through' window boxes for Hong Kong models are scarce.

1965-67

£150-200 VEC

A Dinky No.165 Humber Hawk, maroon roof, lower body, cream middle, shaped spun hubs, slight spotting to roof, otherwise excellent condition, with excellent condition correct colour spot card picture box.

1959-60

£100-150 VEC

A CLOSER LOOK AT A DINKY CAR

This model was also produced from 1950-54 numbered 139b.

Many colour variations of this model number are sought after. Cream bodies with dark maroon roofs are more affordable at around half this value.

This colour variation with a 'lowline' long-slung configuration and blue hubs was only available from 1958-59, making it rarer than other variations.

As this is an American car, it has appeal to diecast collectors on both sides of the Atlantic, widening demand.

A Dinky No.171 Hudson Commodore Sedan, lowline, light grey body, mid blue upper and ridged hubs, factory paint touch-in to bonnet, in excellent condition, with near mint condition correct colour spot card picture box.

1958-59

£200-300 VEC

A Dinky no.157 Jaguar XK120, turquoise lower body, cerise upper body, red ridged hubs, in excellent condition.

1957-59

£100-150 **VEC**

A Dinky No.22A Maserati Sport 2000, dark red, plated convex hubs, white driver, in excellent condition, with good condition yellow card picture box.

£70-100 **VEC**

A Dinky No.108 MG Midget Sports Car, red body and ridged hubs, tan interior, racing number 24, white driver, in excellent condition, with excellent condition white colour spot card picture box.

This is a desirable car and is in red, rather than the plainer white.

1955-59

£200-300 **VEC**

A French Dinky Simca 8 Sport, pale duck egg green, red interior, chromed convex hubs, white tyres, in near mint condition.

£300-500 **VEC**

A Dinky pre-war No.22G Streamlined Tourer, dark blue body and smooth hubs, white tyres, upper windscreen missing, steering wheel complete, some light play wear but in overall good condition.

1935-41

£120-180 **VEC**

A rare Dinky no.105 Triumph TR2 touring with spun hubs, in light grey, with red interior, spun hubs with black knobbly tyres, includes driver, in excellent condition.

This variation, with its spun hubs, is usually worth up to twice the amount of the more common version with red cast hubs.

1957-60

£180-220 **VEC**

A Dinky No.254 Austin Taxi, green lower body, yellow upper and ridged hubs, black interior and baseplate, in near mint condition, with excellent condition correct colour spot card picture box.

Look out for the rarer blue variation, with matching blue hubs, as this can be worth over three times the value of this two-tone variation.

1956-59

£100-150 **VEC**

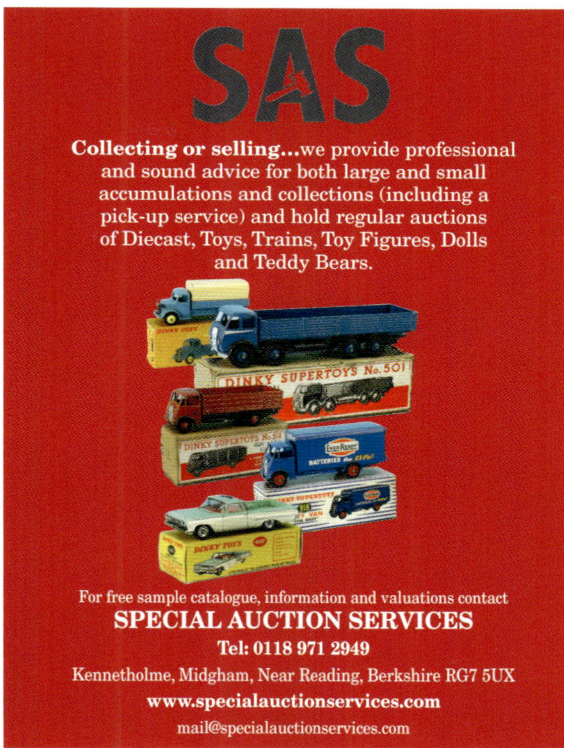

A Dinky No.273 Mini Van 'RAC Road Service', blue, white roof, red interior, in near mint condition, with good condition carded box.

1965-70

£100-150 **VEC**

A Dinky No.987 Mobile Control Room 'ABC Television', blue, grey, red, plastic hubs, in excellent condition, complete with cameraman and camera, with good condition lift-off-lid box.

1962-69

£150-200 **VEC**

A Dinky No.491 'Jobs Dairy' Van, cream, red chassis and ridged hubs, black knobbly tyres, in excellent condition, with excellent condition correct colour spot yellow card box.

This model was made for promotional purposes, and is rare today. Always check the transfers, as wear reduces value. Job's Dairy was founded in 1819 in Middlesex, London and is still selling milk today.

£150-200 **VEC**

A Dinky No.923 Big Bedford Van 'Heinz', red cab, chassis, yellow back, hubs, replacement decals.

The Heinz transfers on this rare model have been replaced. Had they been original and the model in mint condition and complete with its box in similar condition, the value could have been £2,000.

1958-59

£80-120 **VEC**

A CLOSER LOOK AT A DINKY VAN

Dinky's ranges of delivery vans are one of the most collectable Dinky areas, with the '28' series being highly popular.

Pre-war models are harder to find, particularly in excellent or mint condition, and most were only produced for short time periods of a few years or less.

Values depend on the 'decal' transfers. Other desirable examples include 'Pickfords', 'Wakefield's Castrol' and 'Hornby Trains'.

Learn the differences between the three different shapes, or 'types', as this affects value. Early 'type one' shapes are usually the most valuable.

A Dinky No.28L 'Crawfords' Delivery Van, type one, red body, metal wheels, solid casting, some traces of original green lacquer, slightly distorted, some restoration to paint and decals on rear section, otherwise in good condition.

1934-35

£300-500 **VEC**

A Dinky No.25B Covered Wagon, type four, black chassis, cream cab, back, red tin tilt, ridged hubs, chrome loss to grille assembly, otherwise in excellent condition.

1947-50

£180-220 **VEC**

A Dinky No.575 Panhard SNCF Semi Trailer, dark blue cab, trailer, concave metal hubs, tin tilt with printing to both sides, in near mint condition, with fair condition complete card picture box.

£150-200 **VEC**

A Dinky No.502 Foden Flat Truck, green cab, flatbed, ridged hubs, black chassis, silver flash, black herringbone tyres, overall in good condition.

Foden flatbed trucks are popular with collectors, with rare export models in mint condition sometimes fetching over £10,000.

1947-48

£80-120 **VEC**

A Dinky No.434 Bedford TK Crash Truck 'Auto Services', metallic red cab, deep red interior and plastic hubs, grey back, in excellent condition, with good condition carded picture box.

The 'Auto Services' transfer is rarer than the 'Top Rank Motorway Services', although values do not differ too much.

1966-70

£80-120 **VEC**

A Dinky No.430 Breakdown Lorry, dark tan cab and chassis, green back, red ridged hubs, 'Dinky Service' in black to sides, in excellent condition, with excellent condition blue and white striped lidded box.

The most valuable variation has a red, glazed cab and a pale grey back, and can fetch over double the value of this colourway.

1954-64

£180-220 **VEC**

QUICK REFERENCE

- A nostalgic name from many childhoods, Matchbox toys were produced by Lesney Products. Founded in London in 1947, the company produced its first toys in 1949. Aiming to produce pocket-sized toys for pocket money prices, its first major success was a coronation coach, produced from 1952 for the coronation of Queen Elizabeth II. The 'Matchbox' name was registered in 1954, and was used on base plates from 1955.
- Although no consistent scale was used, the most common was the 1-75 range, launched in 1953. This forms the core of most collections, along with the 'Models of Yesteryear' range launched in 1967. From 1953–69, Lesney's toys were distributed by Moko, whose name appeared on packaging, with Lesney acquiring the company in 1959. Metal wheels were discontinued in 1958 and were replaced with plastic.
- The 1960s were a 'golden age' for Matchbox, and by 1966 the company was producing 100 million models per year. In 1969, the 'Superfast' range, with suspension, was launched to compete with 'faster' cars such as those made by Corgi, or Mattel's 'Hot Wheels'. 'Superfast' cars were made until 1983.
- Later ranges, from c1971 onwards, include 'Super-Kings' and 'Speed Kings', although these are not currently as popular with collectors, they may prove to be an area to watch for the future. Lesney closed in 1982, with the brand being acquired by Tyco in 1992. Modern limited editions 'collectors' models may turn out to be a very long term investment, as so many have been kept mint and boxed.
- The majority of examples to be found cost under £30 and allow a collection to be built up affordably. However, look out for rare variations, considering features such as colours, decals, wheels, base plates and the interior, which can fetch hundreds of pounds. Always aim to buy in mint condition, as this is most likely to ensure an item holds or increases its value.

A Matchbox 'Regular Wheels' No.65b Jaguar 3.8 Saloon, in red, with a silver base and black plastic wheels, in near mint condition, with box in excellent condition.

Check the wheels, as the same model and colour with silver plastic wheels can be worth over twice the value of this version.

Introduced in 1962

£120-180 VEC

A Matchbox 8e Ford Mustang, in orange with red interior and solid chrome hubs, in very good condition, with good condition original box.

The orange body is the most valuable variation, white bodies are usually worth roughly a tenth of this value if they are in similar condition.

Introduced in 1966

£280-320 SAS

A Matchbox 31b Ford Station Wagon, in yellow with maroon baseplate, with windows and silver plastic wheels, in excellent condition, in good condition original box.

Introduced in 1960

£150-200 SAS

A Matchbox 'Models of Yesteryear' No.Y5-2 1929 Bentley 4.5 litre, metallic apple green, red seats and tonneau, racing number 5, Union Jack decals to both side doors, in excellent condition, unboxed.

1963

£70-100 VEC

A Matchbox Superfast No.57f Range Rover Carmichael Rescue Vehicle, finished in yellow with black base and trim.

The yellow body and lack of decals indicate that this is a very rare pre-production model – production models were in red or white and had 'Police Rescue' or 'Fire' decals.

c1982

£200-300 VEC

A Matchbox 'Models of Yesteryear' No.Y11 Aveling and Porter Road Roller, green, red, gold trim and maker's plate, in near mint condition, unboxed.

The gold maker's plate on this example makes it around twice as valuable as those without.

1958

£100-150 **VEC**

A Matchbox 'Models of Yesteryear' No.Y9 Fowler Showman's Engine in bright red with 'Lesney Modern Amusements' decal, with white roof, yellow wheels, in excellent condition, with box in near mint condition.

1965

£40-60 **VEC**

A Matchbox 'Regular Wheels' No.G3 'Farm' gift set, containing No.4 Dodge Stake Truck, No.12 Land Rover Safari, No.37 Dodge Cattle Truck, No.39 Ford Tractor, No.40 Hay Trailer, No.43 Pony Trailer, No.65 Claas Combine Harvester and No.72 Standard Jeep, all in mint condition, with near mint blue and yellow window box with detailed picture, still shrink-wrapped.

1968

£200-300 **VEC**

A Matchbox No.G1 'Auto Transporter' gift set, comprising five cars and car transporter, overall conditions are generally near mint, with good condition presentation window box, inner plastic tray is in near mint condition.

£25-35 **VEC**

A Matchbox 'Kingsize' No.G8 gift set, containing No.K1 Foden 'Hoveringham' Tipper, No.K11 Fordson Super Major Tractor with Farm Tipping Trailer, No.K12 Foden Wreck Truck and No.K15 Merryweather Turntable Fire Engine, in mint condition, with inner plastic tray, near mint condition outer blue and yellow window box, still shrink-wrapped, with original Sellotape marks to window.

The addition of the K1 Foden tipper is unusual.

c1965

£280-320 **VEC**

A Matchbox 'Kingsize' No.G8 'Construction' gift set, containing No.K1 Foden 'Hoveringham' Tipper, No.K7 'Curtiss' Rear Dumper, No.K10 'Aveling Barford' Tractor Shovel, No.K13 ERF Concrete Mixer and No.K14 'Taylor' Jumbo Crane, in mint condition, with excellent condition box.

The inner plastic tray is both rare and in excellent condition. The pictorial sleeve is also in unusually excellent condition. This example shows how the combination of models and a box in mint condition can push up the price for desirable gift sets.

£750-850 **VEC**

A Matchbox 'Leslie Smith OBE' poseable figure, no.186 of only up to 500 produced, dressed in grey suit and holding Matchbox book, in mint condition, with carded box.

Smith (1918-2005) was the co-founder of Lesney in 1947. This model was produced in 1990 to commemorate the Matchbox MICA UK Convention on the 24th March 1990.

1990

£70-100 **VEC**

QUICK REFERENCE

- Tinplate toys are made from sheets of steel plated with tin. These sheets were painted by hand, or decorated with lithographic transfers, and cut into shapes, bent, embossed and fixed together to form toys. Tinplate became popular in the mid-19thC and replaced wood and cast iron as it was more economical and provided wider scope for manufacture.
- Germany was the 'home' of the tin toy, with factories exporting toys around the world. Notable makers include Märklin (founded 1856), Gebrüder Bing (1863-1933), and Schreyer & Co (1912-78), whose Schuco name is still used for toys today. Toys by these companies are particularly popular. The US became a secondary centre from the 1880s onwards, with names such as Marx (1896-c1982) and Ferdinand Strauss (c1914-42) being sought after.
- From the late 19thC-1930s, production focused on cars, trucks, zeppelin airships and aircraft. The earliest examples from the mid-late19thC were hand-painted. Look closely to see brush marks, especially on details.
- After WWII, the centre of production moved to Japan and names such as Horikawa (SH), Nomura (TN Toys) and Yonizawa are sought after. The development of the battery allowed for novelty features such as flashing lights and sounds; the more numerous and bizarre the 'actions' the more a toy is likely to be worth. Robots and spacecraft also became popular reflecting the excitement of the 'Space Race' to the moon in the 1950s and 60s.
- Value is dependent on the type of toy, the maker, the size, the date and the condition. Scratched transfers are almost impossible to restore, although shallow dents can sometimes be fixed. Early hand-painted pieces are highly sought after, but the desirability of humorous features in later toys should not be underestimated. Large, early ships or zeppelins by Märklin can fetch over £20,000, while a simple 1960s Japanese spacecraft can be found for under £50.

A 1920s-30s Bing black lithographed tinplate clockwork 19872 Model T Ford, with driver.

6.25in (16cm) long

£300-500 **SAS**

A late 20thC reproduction JB Carette-style navy blue non-powered painted tinplate Limousine, with bisque driver and passenger, in excellent condition.

If this were an original Carette limousine, it could have fetched over £3,000.

12.5in (32cm) long

£30-50 **SAS**

A 1920s German Gebrüder Bing red lithographed tinplate clockwork tourer, with driver, in good condition, but lacking rear seat.

5.5in (14cm) long

£120-180 **SAS**

A US Zone German Schuco Kommando Anno 2000, red, plated radiator, opening bonnet to reveal engine, paint finish crazed overall, otherwise in excellent condition, with good condition box and instructions.

c1946-c1949 *6in (15cm) long*

£80-120 **VEC**

A US Zone German Schuco Varianto-Limo 3041, red tinplate clockwork car, complete with control wire, very minor wear to edges, otherwise in excellent condition, with fair condition box and instructions.

The 'US Zone' wording refers to the period from 1945-49, when Western Germany was divided into administrative zones by the Allies, following WWII.

c1946-c1949

£100-150 **VEC**

A US Zone German Schuco Fex 1111, green bodywork with plated radiator and windscreen, red wheel hubs, very minor chips, wear to edges, otherwise in good condition, boxed.

c1946-c1949 *6in (15cm) long*

£80-120 **VEC**

A rare French CIJ clockwork tinplate Renault Fregate, finished in greyish-green, with electric head lights, opening driver's door, steerable front wheels, plated bumpers and grille, lacking rear seat assembly, otherwise in good condition.

CIJ is a sought-after name, and this is very good quality car.

12.5in (32cm) long

£350-450 **VEC**

A 1950s German Tipp & Co. US Navy Staff Car, tinplate friction drive car in dark green, with US Navy 63 transfers, plastic hubs and tyres, plated parts, in near mint condition.

7.5in (19cm) long

£60-90 **VEC**

A Japanese TN Toys tinplate 'Sonic Dodge Charger', battery operated, with passenger detail to interior, rubber tyres, whistle and aerial accessory, in generally excellent condition, with good condition card box.

16in (41cm) long

£80-120 **VEC**

A rare Japanese Modern Toys large tinplate American Car, finished in red, battery-operated, with steerable front wheels, rubber tyres, some discolouration to plated parts, lacks aerial, in good condition, with some wear.

14in (36cm) long

£70-100 **VEC**

A rare French CIJ two tone friction drive Renault Dauphine, with detailed printing, rubber wheels, and registration number '5-56', light scratching on roof, otherwise in excellent condition.

8.75in (22cm) long

£250-350 **VEC**

A late 1960s Japanese Ichiko friction-powered lithographed tinplate pop-art Jaguar Saloon, in good condition, headlamps replaced.

It's the fabulous graphics that make this car so desirable and valuable, as well as the fact that it is a Jaguar.

7.75in (20cm) long

£150-200 **SAS**

QUICK REFERENCE - FIRE ENGINES

Fire engines and vehicles are as popular with today's grown-up collectors as they were with the young boys who played with them originally. Nostalgia plays a key part, perhaps as so many wanted to be firemen when they were young. Fire engines also form an easily definable collecting area, yet still give a challenge to collect as many different types as possible from the 1900s-70s. Key makers' names, such as Märklin, Bing or Arnold, are important, but also look out for examples with an excellent level of detail to the transfer printing. Other desirable features include separately modelled firemen, such as on the example below, and extra actions such as an extending and elevating ladder. The more complex and large an engine is, the more valuable it is likely to be.

A rare French Unis tinplate clockwork Fire Engine, red, with detailed tin-printing, two tinplate firemen, elevating ladder, with permanent key and grey tinplate wheels, revolving turntable, in generally excellent condition.

8.25in (21cm) long

£120-£180 **VEC**

A rare Wells or similar tinplate clockwork Fire Engine, red, with extending and elevating cream tinplate ladder, revolving turntable, permanent key, with three seated firemen figures, tinplate balloon wheels, slight creasing to ladder, otherwise in excellent condition.

12in (30cm) long

£100-150 **VEC**

A rare early Spanish Paya tinplate miniature Fire Engine, in red with detailed printing including fireman, with ladder and black wheels, in good condition.

Paya were founded near Alicante in 1902, and have been making toys ever since. During the mid-1980s they began to re-release many of their earlier classic toys in limited editions. These are accompanied by certificates and appealingly colourful boxes.

4.25in (11cm) long

£40-60 **VEC**

A French tinplate clockwork Fire Engine, red, with plated ladder and wheels, and elevating single section ladder with revolving turntable, in good condition.

10in (25cm)

£50-70 **VEC**

A German tinplate clockwork Fire Engine, red, with silver rear platform, wheels and single elevating ladder, permanent key, in excellent condition.

6in (15cm) long

£40-60 **VEC**

A German Goso tinplate Turntable Fire Escape, red, with silver ladder and grille, plated hub caps, rubber tyres, single section ladder, some wear to top of cab, otherwise in good condition.

10.25in (26cm) long

£80-120 **VEC**

A rare German Wimmer articulated Aerial Fire Truck, brick red bakelite cab, with clockwork motor, tinplate trailer with single elevating ladder, and rubber wheels, in good condition.

9in (23cm) long

£50-80 **VEC**

An unusual 1960s European tinplate large Fire Truck, with friction drive and ladder, with beige roof and fittings, some plated parts and two firemen figures in rear, in good condition.

13.5in (34cm) long

£50-80 **VEC**

A Märklin late edition 1991 clockwork tinplate Fire Engine, with certificate, in excellent condition, in excellent condition original box.

1991

£100-150 **SAS**

A CLOSER LOOK AT AN ARNOLD FIRE ENGINE

Arnold was founded in Nürnberg, Germany by Karl Arnold in 1906. Arnold tinplate toys are sought after, especially if they date from before WWII like this one.

The box is original, rather than reproduction, and in very good condition, which adds to the desirability, particularly as it has such charming artwork.

As the clockwork motor drives the car along, a mechanism in the 'boiler' causes sparks to fly out – actions like this are desirable.

The transfers are detailed and in largely excellent condition.

A German Arnold No.640 clockwork Steam Fire Engine, in red, with detailed printing, with driver figure and boiler to rear, with key, in excellent condition, with good condition box.

4.75in (12cm) long

£200-300 **VEC**

A 1930s French RL Toys tinplate clockwork Fire Car, with detailed printing, green tinplate wheels, with '1946' registration number, some wear otherwise in good condition.

5.5in (14cm) long

£50-80 **VEC**

A German KD tinplate Fire Engine, with friction drive and opening rear door, detailed tinprinting including firemen, aerial and beacon to roof, in excellent condition, with excellent condition red card box.

6.25in (16cm) long

£60-90 **VEC**

A German Gama large tinplate Tipper, with orange tipping body and lower cab, hub caps, beige cab roof, black trim, opening rear tailgate and steerable front wheels, in good condition but some wear to edges.

14in (36cm) long

£120-180 **VEC**

A German Gama Articulated Transport Truck, with detailed interior, steerable front wheels, silver trailer with 'International Transport' to sides, detailed tin-printing, drop-down rear door, rubber tyres, in overall good condition, but lacking spare wheel.

19in (48cm) long

£150-250 **VEC**

A CLOSER LOOK AT A RICH TOYS VAN

The Rich Manufacturing Company was founded in Illinois in 1915 and produced toys until 1962, being known as 'Rich Toys Inc' from 1935 when the company moved to Clinton, Iowa.

This example retains many of its original accessories, including wooden and glass milk bottles and carriers, and has a driver and opening doors – all are desirable features.

Their pre-war toys are prized and comparatively scarce. Most were pull-along and made of wood, or where tinplate was used, they were usually horse-drawn.

Advertising toys can be scarce and also appeal to collectors of advertising memorabilia, a factor which often drives prices up.

A rare Rich Toys lithographed tin 'Bordens' delivery van, with yellow wooden roof and wooden bonnet, stencilled 'Bordens', with seated driver and two cases of milk bottles, one with four glass bottles, the other two wooden bottles, rear doors open, in good condition.

13.5in (34cm) long

£4,500-6,000 **BER**

A German Arnold large tinplate Tipper Truck, with friction drive, orange chassis and hub caps, detailed tin-printed interior and steering wheel, yellow tipping body with opening tailgate, in good condition but lacking driver.

11in (28cm) long

£250-350 **VEC**

A rare German Gama No.291/1 'International Express' Van, with opening rear door, friction drive, detailed cab interior, lacking one rear door handle, head light lenses and front hub caps, otherwise in good condition.

13.75in (35cm) long

£100-150 **VEC**

A rare German Goso miniature clockwork Breakdown Truck, with blue cab, silver chassis, brick red jib and rubber wheels, in excellent condition.

5.25in (13cm) long

£40-60 **VEC**

A 1950s German Tipp & Co. transfer-printed tinplate motorcycle and rider, the rider wearing a red jacket and plus fours, marked 'MADE IN U.S. ZONE GERMANY' and with 'TCO' maker's monogram.

Known for their motorbikes, Tipp & Co. (1912-71) are a sought-after name. The Ullman Brothers, who owned Tipp & Co., fled Germany during WWII after the government seized their company, and founded Mettoy in Britain. After the war, both companies ran concurrently.

7.5in (19cm) long

£250-350 **QU**

A Spanish Rico clockwork Touring Motorcyclist, with brown and red rider with white helmet on blue bike, plain brown tinplate wheels and stabilisers, clockwork inoperable, otherwise in good condition.

£120-180 **VEC**

A US Zone German Huki clockwork red and white motorbike with sidecar, with brown and grey rider, registration 'K-1021', sidecar with number '21', in excellent condition.

c1946-c1949 *6.25in (16cm) long*

£250-350 **VEC**

A German Günthermann tinplate Crawler Tractor, with driver, orange wheels, working motor, lacking tracks, otherwise in excellent condition.

7in (18cm) long

£60-£80 **VEC**

A 1960s Japanese Marusan friction-powered lithographed 'Silver Pigeon' Motorcycle, in good condition, part of base-plate overpainted.

5.25in (13.5cm) long

£200-300 **SAS**

A CLOSER LOOK AT A FISCHER MOTORCYCLE

This toy's small size indicates that it is a penny toy, an inexpensive toy sold for a penny in stores and by street vendors.

Despite so many having been made and sold, few have survived the ravages of a child's attention as they are so small and fragile, making them scarce today.

Fischer is a notable German maker and their unusual, amusing toys, such as this example, are sought after.

Value also depends on the level of detail and the condition. Although this piece is well-detailed, it is worn; had it been in mint condition it may have fetched up to twice as much.

A Fischer penny toy red and gold motorcycle, with rider and passenger in front chair, in fair condition, slight varnishing to wheels.

3.5in (8.5cm) long

£400-600 **SAS**

A Gama lithographed tinplate clockwork tractor and trailer, with plastic driver, lacks clockwork motor.

1937 *12in (30.5cm) long*

£50-80 **VEC**

A Marx clockwork crawler tractor, finished in orange with yellow detailing, with silver metal wheels and black rubber tracks, lacking seat and chimney stack, otherwise in good condition.

£25-35 **VEC**

A 1920s German Lehmann 651 EPL 1 Zeppelin, lacking celluloid blades and in poor condition, bent at back, scratched surface and rusting.

This very worn example is worth as much as this due to the notable maker and the subject matter. Zeppelins are highly sought after.

£120-180 **SAS**

A clockwork painted tinplate airship, finished in grey and red.

By an unknown maker, the form of this example is not as realistic or detailed as the one above.

7.75in (20cm) long

£60-80 **SAS**

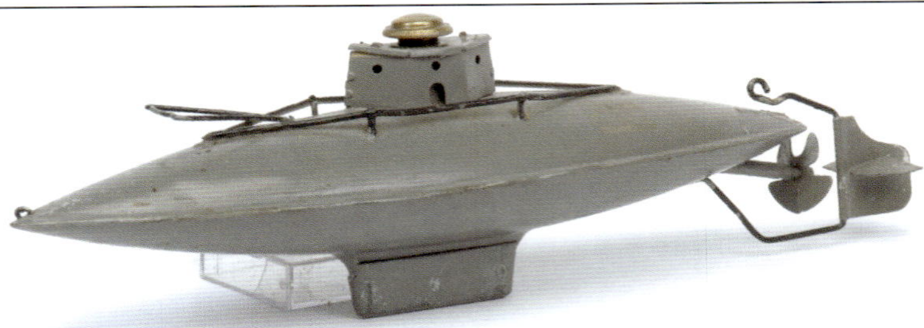

A tinplate clockwork submarine, possibly by Bing, finished in grey, with black hand-rails, brass screw on cap, propeller and rudder, in good condition.

10in (25cm)

£150-200 **VEC**

A 1920s German Fischer yellow and blue speedboat penny toy, numbered '5', lacking rear flag, wheels overpainted, otherwise in good condition.

The overpainting and missing part reduce the value of this whimsical wheeled boat.

6.25in (16cm) long

£180-220 **SAS**

A rare 1930s German Günthermann acrobatic aircraft, in dark blue and grey, with clockwork motor and flip-over acrobatic action, lacks tailfin and rear jockey wheel but includes pilot, permanent key, in fair condition.

7.75in (20cm) wingspan

£80-120 **VEC**

A French JRD novelty character driving a clockwork eccentric action tinplate car, with logo to bonnet and boot '1949 RF', the driver with moustache and bowler hat, blue jacket, yellow waistocat and red bow tie, in good condition with some wear to finish.

7in (18cm) long

£80-£120 **VEC**

A Greppert & Kelch 552 clockwork lithographed tinplate red, white and blue three-wheel trolley car, with lady driver, dog and boy.

6in (15cm) high

£100-150 **SAS**

A CLOSER LOOK AT A LEHMANN TOY

Lehmann were founded in Nuremberg in 1881 and produced often complexly constructed lightweight tinplate toys that were exported across the world.

Along with Günthermann, their toys are loved for their fun and inventive forms, often with a bizarre sense of humour – the Balky Mule is typical.

The clown is well dressed and the mule has a textured finish. When wound the clown rocks back and forth as the mule bucks.

The theme and unusual action were popular with children and this toy was made for decades from the early 1900s, making it one of the more common and affordable of Lehmann's toys.

A Lehmann transfer-printed tinplate EPL 245 Balky Mule, in good condition.

7.5in (19cm) long

£280-320 **SAS**

A 1950s American Marx 'Milton Berle' lithographed tinplate 'Crazy Car', with vivid and colourful illustrations and catchphrases, revolving head and 'eccentric' movements, in fair condition with some wear and damage.

Milton Berle (1908-2002) was a famous 1950s US radio and television star known to millions as 'Uncle Miltie'. The damage and lack of a box has reduced the value, although he does retain his plastic hat, which is often missing.

7in (18cm) long

£60-90 **VEC**

A 1960s Japanese Masutoku Toy Factory M-T Co Hand Car, no.3296, battery operated, three actions, in near mint condition, with good condition illustrated box.

£70-£100 **VEC**

A Lehmann transfer-printed tinplate Sea Lion, with key, in very good condition.

Lehmann's animal toys are highly collectable. Including a climbing monkey and a walking crocodile, they were often inspired by German colonial activities in Africa.

7.25in (18.5cm) long

£250-350 **SAS**

A Schuco clockwork pig violinist, complete with sailor's uniform, cap, violin and bow, in good condition.

5.5in (14cm) high

£80-120 **SAS**

QUICK REFERENCE - SCHUCO FIGURES

Schuco was the tradename used by Schreyer & Co., founded in Nuremberg, Germany in 1912, until 1921 when the company was renamed Schuco. Their mechanical toys were loved before and after the war, and included bears (such as the famous Yes-No teddy bear) and cars. These small clockwork figures form a collecting area of their own – many are animals that play instruments or perform acrobatics. Look out for unusual figures that may not have appealed at the time so would have sold in fewer numbers making them rarer today. One example is a monk with a beer tankard, or 'Mr Atom' who can fetch over £500. Unless very rare, to be of interest the clockwork mechanism must work, accessories should be complete and the clothes must not be faded.

A Schuco clockwork Pig drummer, complete with drum, sticks, hat and clothes, in good condition.

5.5in (14cm) high

£80-120 **SAS**

A Schuco 882 clockwork acrobatic 'Turn Clown', in fair condition with original clothes by wear to his face, in poor condition original box.

£60-80 **SAS**

A British lithographed tinplate lever-action red, blue and yellow minstrel dancer, in good condition.

£40-60 **SAS**

A Schuco 986 'Solisto' clockwork monkey drummer, complete with drum, sticks, hat and clothes, in good condition.

5.5in (14cm) high

£60-80 **SAS**

A Japanese 1950s-60s Nomura 'TN Toys' transfer-printed tinplate, fabric and soft vinyl bartender clockwork toy in mint condition.

11.5in (29cm) high

£50-80 **MA**

A 1950s Japanese grey transfer-printed tinplate clockwork robot.

5in (12cm) high

£150-180 **QU**

A 1960s Japanese Yonezawa transfer-printed tinplate and plastic robot, marked 'MADE IN JAPAN'.

8in (20cm) high

£500-700 **QU**

A Mainland battery operated 99/30 dark metallic grey painted and lithographed tinplate 'Moon Explorer', in good condition, in good original box.

£70-100 **SAS**

A 1950s-60s Japanese TM Modern Toys tinplate and plastic 'Mischief Monkey' clockwork toy, in mint condition.

The scarce box refers to this toy as 'Mischievous Monkey' and can add more than 50 per cent to the value.

8in (20cm) long

£20-30 **MA**

A Zeppelin tinplate carousel, probably German, crank handle operates musical roundabout, in generally excellent condition, with original plain card box.

8in (20cm) high

£120-180 **VEC**

A 1950s Czechoslovakian transfer-printed tinplate clockwork train scene, unmarked, in mint condition with original card box.

9.5in (24cm) long

£18-22 **MTB**

A 1950s Louis Marx 'G Man Automatic' tinplate child's pistol, with rare original box and decals.

This is in excellent condition and retains its box, hence the high value. However, look for signs of age and wear as the box is being reproduced today for a collectors' market.

3.25in (8cm) high

£100-150 **BB**

QUICK REFERENCE

- The first model trains, produced in the 1850s, were stylised, bulky and unrealistic. By the 1890s, more realistic tinplate models, with clockwork- or steam mechanisms, were being produced by German manufacturers such as Märklin (est 1759) and Gebrüder Bing (1863-1933). Many of these were exported to the US and Europe, although production and exports ceased during the two World Wars.
- Gauge sizes were introduced by Märklin in 1891. Their larger gauges (II and III) were quickly replaced by smaller gauges (I and 0) in 1910 as demand for smaller trains sets grew. By 1938, gauge I had also been discontinued, and in 1935 even gauge 0 had been replaced by the smaller 00-gauge. Märklin's HO gauge, which was even smaller, was used from 1948.
- The well-known British company Hornby began making trains in 1920 and their pre-WWII gauge 0 trains are now widely collected. Post War examples were of comparatively poor quality, and the range was discontinued in 1969. Hornby's Dublo range, designed to compete with small gauge sets by Märklin and Trix, was introduced in 1938 and is also highly collectable today. Nationalised livery trains (produced 1953-1957) are less desirable. Hornby was taken over by Tri-ang in 1964, with the name Tri-ang Hornby being used from 1965.
- As many trains were played with and have become worn or damaged, good condition examples will command the highest prices. The precise model, date and livery also affects value, with rare models being more desirable.

An early Hornby O gauge No. 2 4-4-4 clockwork Tank locomotive, LMS maroon No. 4-4-4, with nickel couplings and brass buffers, in excellent condition.

This was the only 4-4-4 gauge model made by Hornby, with the earliest models being in LMS and LNER liveries.

1923-29

£420-480 **VEC**

A Hornby 0 gauge EM120 0-4-0 tank loco, LNER green No.2900 20v electric, in very good condition, with reproduction box.

£150-200 **VEC**

A Hornby O gauge No. 2 Special 4-4-0 Loco and Tender 'COUNTY OF BEDFORD' GWR green No. 3821, 20v electric, repainted, lined and transferred.

With the crest on the tender and a black running plate used from 1930-36, this scarce 20v electric version is usually worth up to twice the value of the clockwork version.

1936-41

£700-1,000 **VEC**

A Hornby Dublo three-rail pre-war EDL1 4-6-2 LNER blue A4 Class Loco No. 4498 'Sir Nigel Gresley', in good condition with some wear to paint, in fair condition box, dated '9/38'.

Made from 1938-41, prewar models have full wheel valances and a push rod gear, instead of valve gear.

1938

£600-800 **VEC**

A Hornby Dublo three-rail EDG7 0-6-2 GWR green Tank Loco No. 6699, with gold decal to bunker rear, with horseshoe-type motor and instruction booklet dated '8/49', in excellent condition, and good condition pale blue box with 'GW' sticker to one end and dated '6/48'.

c1948

£700-1,000 **VEC**

A CLOSER LOOK AT A HORNBY DUBLO TRAIN

This is a rare version of this model with smoke deflectors on each side of the front of the boiler.

The deflectors indicate models that were repaired at the Binns Road factory using new 'Duchess of Montrose' bodies painted in 'Duchess of Atholl' livery.

A standard 'Duchess of Atholl' model, made from 1947-53, is usually worth under £200.

Also look out for the version with a cream nameplate, as this can fetch up to twice the price of the standard model.

A Hornby Dublo three-rail EDL2/D2 4-6-2 LMS maroon Princess Coronation class locomotive and tender No.6231 'Duchess of Atholl', in excellent condition, with repair box with end packing pieces and repair No.34064 to both ends, with tender box in good condition and dated "2/50".
1950
£700-1,000 **VEC**

A Hornby Dublo three-rail EDL7 0-6-2 LNER green N2 Class Tank No. 9596, with horseshoe type motor and gold decal to bumper rear, in excellent condition with faded pale blue box, the lid dated '5/49'.
1949
£220-280 **VEC**

A Hornby Dublo three-rail 3232 Co-Co green Diesel Loco, complete with instruction booklet dated '8/60', in excellent condition, in excellent condition box.
1960
£180-220 **VEC**

A rare Hornby Dublo three-rail EDL7 LNER Tank Goods set, containing 0-6-2 black N2 Class Tank No. 9596, with gold decal to bunker rear and horseshoe type motor, with three NE Goods Vehicles in green/grey Open, brown Vent Van and Brake Van, and with track, controller with wires, instruction flyer, oil bottle, instruction booklet dated '9/47', purple guarantee slip, pre-war printed and tested/guarantee slip dated 30th January 1947, in excellent condition, in complete excellent condition box.

This first post-war set is very rare as most were exported when it was issued in Autumn 1947.
c1947
£1,200-1,800 **VEC**

A Hornby Dublo two-rail 2220 4-6-0 BR green Castle class locomotive No.7032 'Denbigh Castle', with instructions dated "8/59", in excellent condition with excellent condition plain red box.
1959
£200-300 **VEC**

A Hornby Dublo Suburban Electric train set, comprising SR Electric Motor Coach RN 265326, SR Electric unpowered Driving Trailer RN S77511, both in BR SR green livery, with track, in very good condition with box and instructions.
£280-320 **W&W**

QUICK REFERENCE - BASSETT-LOWKE

Founded in Northampton in 1901, Bassett-Lowke was primarily a sales organisation that marketed and distributed model trains, ships and other toys made by other manufacturers. These included Wintringham of Northampton, and German companies Gebrüder Bing (from 1902), Carette, and Trix (from 1935). However, it also produced its own models, the first locomotive being made in 1903. As can be expected from such notable German makers quality was high. Many trains were designed by the company's designer Henry Greenly. It began to decline in the 1950s as children moved away from mechanical trains, and less expensive models were produced by competitors. In 1964, it sold its shops and closed a year later. The brand was acquired by a number of different people, and is owned today by Hornby, which produces new ranges under this historic name.

A Bing for Bassett-Lowke gauge I locomotive and tender 'SINGLE', GNR green No. 266, three-rail Electric, finished in green and black, with running number '266', with a modern mechanism with a Skate Pick-up, tender with 'GNR' lettering and 'Bassett-Lowke' transfer to back, in very good condition.

£800-1,200 **VEC**

A Bing for Bassett-Lowke gauge 1 4-4-0 clockwork locomotive and tender, LNWR black 'PRECURSOR' No. 513, finished in black, lined in red and white with 'Precursor' over front splasher and running number '513', in good condition.

£800-1,200 **VEC**

A Basset-Lowke Gauge 1 4-4-0 live steam locomotive and tender, Midland maroon 'COMPOUND' No. 1000, with 'LOWKE' transfer to tender, and running number '1000' sides, in fair condition.

Despite its poor condition, this is a mechanically and structurally sound model train. Some restoration will improve its visual appeal and increase its value.

£800-1,200 **VEC**

A Carette for Basett-Lowke gauge 1 4-4-2 three rail electric locomotive and tender, 'ATLANTIC' GNR green No. 1442, finished in green and black, lined in yellow and orange, with running number '1442', and tender with 'GNR' lettering, in good condition.

£800-1,200 **VEC**

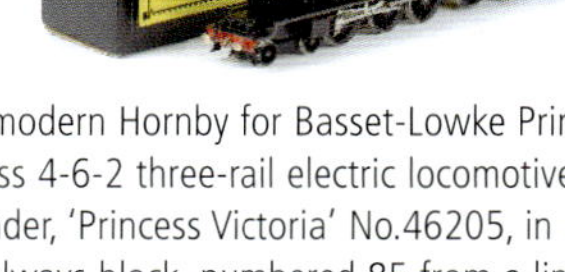

A modern Hornby for Basset-Lowke Princess class 4-6-2 three-rail electric locomotive and tender, 'Princess Victoria' No.46205, in British Railways black, numbered 85 from a limited production range, in mint condition, with guarantee slip, instructions and Basset-Lowke cloth, with box in excellent condition and with outer mailer.

£550-750 **VEC**

A Carette for Bassett-Lowke Gauge 1 LNWR 12-wheel Dining Saloon No. 13210, the sides in good condition, roof in fair condition.

£250-350 **VEC**

A Tri-ang R56 4-6-4 maroon Baltic Tank locomotive No. 4830, with Tri-ang Railway decals, fitted with closed couplings but missing rear lamp, in excellent condition, in good condition box.

£80-120 **VEC**

A unique Australian Tri-ang R52 0-6-0 maroon plastic Jinty Tank locomotive, with head-lamp and no buffers, in excellent condition.

£250-350 **VEC**

A Tri-ang R155 Bo-Bo yellow Diesel switcher No. 5007, the early style body moulding with 'Tri-ang Railways' to sides and maroon stripe to running board, with open couplings, in excellent condition, in good condition box.

£60-90 **VEC**

A Tri-ang R155 Bo-Bo green Diesel switcher No. 5007, with Tri-ang Railways to sides, open couplings, fading to numbers and Tri-ang Railways transfer, in good condition with some rusting, in good condition box with lower insert.

£60-90 **VEC**

A rare Tri-ang TT unboxed gold-plated 4-6-2 Streamlined Merchant Navy Class Loco 'Clan Line' and three Mk. 1 Coaches, slide bar detached from connecting rod to loco left side, tender right side has glue repair to rear, in good condition, the coaches in excellent condition, but Brake Coach has rear coupling missing.

This very rare set is one of only 500 made in the mid-1960s for the Kays Mail Order Catalogue Co.

£400-600 **VEC**

A rare Australian Tri-ang R450A plastic New South Wales (NSWR) Suburban Overhead Electric Motor Car, in dark brown, rusting and slight damage to pantograph, in production box.

£250-350 **VEC**

A Tri-ang Hornby R644A Inter City passenger train set, comprising Bo-Bo BR blue class AL1 overhead electric loco No.E3001 single pantograph, two blue/grey Mk.2 second class coaches with lights and one blue/grey Mk.2 brake/first class, with instruction booklet dated "15/9/69" and instruction flyer for overhead power supply system, in excellent condition with good condition complete box with fair condition lid.

Models marked with the Tri-ang Hornby brand date from after 1964, as Tri-ang acquired the troubled Meccano Group, which owned Hornby, in that year.

1969

£80-120 **VEC**

A Marklin Gauge 1 clockwork tinplate 4-4-0 locomotive and tender 'Precursor' LNWR black No. 513, finished in black red and white with 'Precursor' to front splasher and running number '513' to cab side, with a modern 3-rail four coupled mechanism fitted, the tender with the Marklin stamp under the tender, both couplings refixed, in excellent condition.

£800-1,200 **VEC**

A Wrenn W2213 4-6-2 NE Wartime black A4 Class locomotive No. 4903 'Peregrine', with larger driving wheels fitted to Mk 1 chassis, in near mint condition, in mint condition box with base stamped '91 729'.

£800-1,200 **VEC**

QUICK REFERENCE

- Lead figures became the favourite toys of young boys in the late 18thC and early 19thC, and are now collected by grown-ups for their nostalgic value.
- Made as early as the 18th century, the first mass-produced lead figures were flat. As their popularity increased, solid figures ('rounde-bosse') were introduced. However, lead figures did not become ubiquitous until 1893, when William Britain Jr., founder of Britains (established in 1845), introduced the 'hollow-casting' method, which released the molten lead from the centre of a figure: halving the cost of a box of soldiers. This began the 'golden age' of the lead soldier, which ran until to the late 1950s, when lead was replaced by cheaper, safer plastics.
- William Britain became the largest maker of lead soldiers in the world, producing more than 100 different British Army regiments sets, and setting the standard size (2in/5.5cm) for toy soldiers. Other well-known and collectable makers include Charbens, C.B.G. Mignot, Taylor & Barrett, and John Hill Co.
- Though soldiers were the most popular form of figure, domestic and pastoral scenes, such as farms and zoos, were also produced. These were most popular after World War I, when interest in military subjects waned after the horrors of the war.
- Look for fine detailing and original paint. Completely opaque, overly bright paint or unusual colour tones may indicate a repainted figure. These should be avoided, as should figures that have had parts replaced, re-attached or customised. If you are buying a set, ensure that it is complete, and that the figures match: paintwork can vary subtly from batch to batch. Original boxes will typically add value, particularly if they are in excellent condition, as these were often thrown away or damaged, and examples are therefore scarce.

A Britains Regiments Of All Nations series Indian Army Services Corps set no. 1893, comprising officer, mule, handler and four soldiers with rifles at the trail, in mint condition, tied into box.

£100-150 **W&W**

A rare Britains Regiments of All Nations Australian Army Infantry set no. 2030, comprising officer and seven soldiers, all unusually in black ceremonial dress.

£150-200 **W&W**

A rare Britains Zoological series set no. 4Z, including rhinoceros, hippopotamus, elephant, giraffe, crocodile, camel, lion, tiger llama, penguins, three palm trees, all in good condition, in original box with good reproduction inserts, orange box with applied label, some wear.

£700-1,000 **WW**

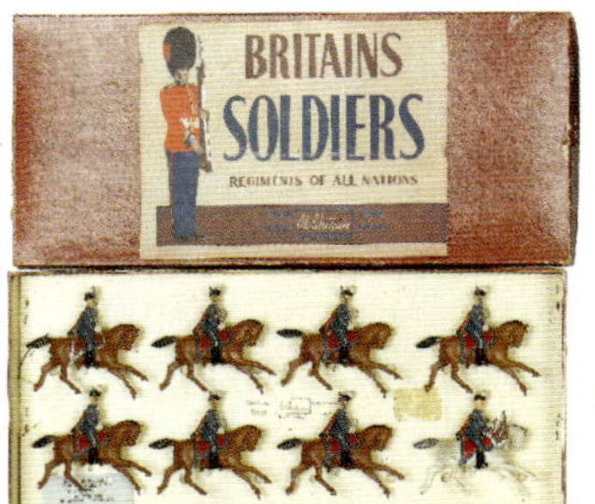

A Britains Regiments Of All Nations Danish Army soldiers set no. 2018, comprising eight mounted Gardehusarregimete, a trumpter and six Hussars and officer, in very good condition, in original box with insert, pieces not tied in, minor wear to lid.

£150-250 **WW**

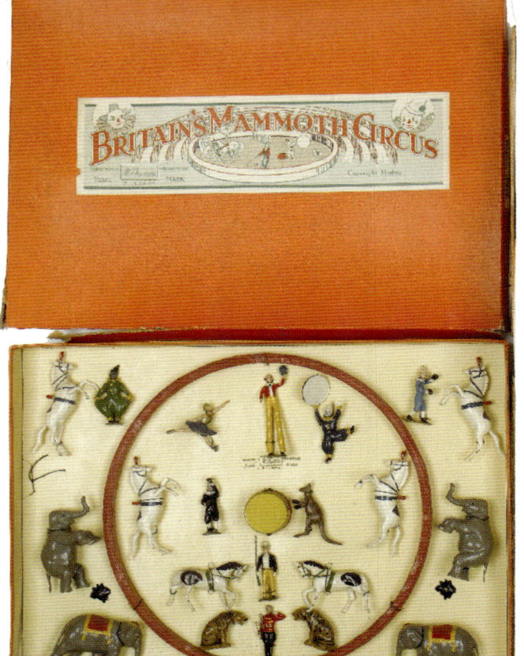

A rare mid-1950s Britains Mammoth circus set no. 1539, comprising circus ring, ring master, four horses, lion tamer and two lions, boxing clown and kangaroo, four elephants, three additional clowns, one with long stilted legs, equestrienne and clown with hoop, both with horses, red painted wooden ring with central raised dias, two small black painted, leaf shaped metal bases, in very good condition, orange paper covered box with applied label, contents tied in.

£800-1,200 **WW**

An early 1950s Britains Rodeo set no. 2043, including stockade bars, posts and feet, three mounted cowboys (two with lassoos), a cowboy with lasso, a cowboy with rifle, four sitting cowboys, one additional horse, one steer and one bench, in very good condition, in original box with applied paper label andinstruction sheet to inside of lid, tied into original insert, some age wear to box.

£380-480 WW

A Britains set 178 Austro Hungarian Foot Guards, comprising eight figures, in overall good condition.

£400-600 SAS

A Britains set 225 The Kings African Rifles, with matt black face paint, in fair condition.

£15-25 SAS

A Britains Spanish Cavalry Review Order, comprising four mounted soldiers, in fair condition, two swords missing.

£150-250 SAS

A Johillco Union Confederates Set no.359, in good condition, figures lack two swords and one head, incomplete, in fair condition box with end-label.

£80-120 SAS

A Schoenhut reduced size jointed wood buffalo, painted in deep brown, with leather horns and rope tail.

Introduced in 1906, around six versions are known. The earliest versions had fabric manes.

6in (15cm) long

£120-180 **BER**

A Schoenhut Bactrian hand-painted, jointed wood camel, two hump moulded and textured head and body, rope tail, painted eyes.

Introduced in 1908, this is the later version with a moulded, rather than carved, body and head.

£120-180 **BER**

A Schoenhut reduced size hippo jointed wood figure, with painted eyes, leather ears, red painted mouth and white teeth, brown painted overall.

The reduced size hippo did not have tusks.

6.5in (16.5cm) long

£150-250 **BER**

A Schoenhut jointed wood elephant, with glass eyes, leather ears, tusks, original trunk, brightly coloured woven original blanket and headdress.

Of the three versions of this popular and long-lived figure, those with howdah blankets are the most sought after.

1903-1930s *9.75in (25cm) long*

£250-350 **BER**

QUICK REFERENCE – SCHOENHUT FIGURES

German immigrant Albert Schoenhut founded his toy company in Philadelphia, Pennsylvania in 1872. His clown toy, introduced in 1903, became a bestseller in its day and was soon followed by the 'Humpty Dumpty' circus. Over the next few years, the range was expanded to include all manner of animals and characters and it became immensely successful. There are many variations in terms of size, shape and materials used – values vary accordingly. A smaller-sized range was introduced in the 1920s, with a very rare miniature series being sold in 1929 only. Unusually, this kangaroo was produced in one size only. Another notable variation is the type of eye. Glass eyes were used until c1918, when Schoenhut lost its supply of German-produced glass eyes due to WWI. Eyes were then painted, and many animals were also redesigned at this point. During the 1930s, handpainting proved to be too expensive and variable in terms of quality, so transfer printed (decal) eyes with black borders were used instead. Today these unique and often amusing toys are popular with folk art and toy collectors.

A Schoenhut white horse with circus platform jointed wood figure, with glass eyes, bride and platform saddle.

Introduced 1905 *10.25in (26cm) long*

£150-250 **BER**

A Schoenhut kangaroo jointed wood figure, with painted eyes, wooden tail, leather ears, open carved mouth.

Introduced 1907 *7.25in (18.5cm) highest*

£450-550 **BER**

A 1920s Schoenhut reduced size lion jointed wood figure, with carved mane and rope tail.

There are over seven different types of lion. The first was produced for the circus range in 1906 and has a fabric mane. This all-wood, smaller size was sold separately in a box during the 1920s and came with either an open or closed mouth.

5.5in (14cm) long

£100-150 **BER**

A Schoenhut jointed wood monkey figure, with white face, two-part head, red felt outfit with yellow fringe, rope tail.

Produced from 1906-1930s, this two tone faced monkey is the earliest version. Values are reduced by over a third if the clothing is missing or damaged.

8in (20.5cm) high

£300-400 **BER**

A Schoenhut reduced size painted eye ostrich wood jointed figure, with closed mouth.

9.5in (24cm) long

£250-350 **BER**

A Schoenhut reindeer jointed wood figure in greenish-tan with white undercoat and white spots, with glass eyes, closed mouth, with leather ears, antler and tail.

This was part of the Teddy Roosevelt series – few were sold and examples are scarce today.

Introduced 1909 7in (18cm) long

£300-400 **BER**

A rare Schoenhut wolf wooden jointed figure, with painted eyes, brown hues, long wood tail, open mouth.

Introduced in 1908 as a farm animal as well as a circus animal, early versions of this scarce figure have fabric tails and felt tongues.

8.5in (21.5cm) long

£400-500 **BER**

A Schoenhut hand-painted, wooden jointed African Chief (Dude) figure, with two part face, leather ears, purple jacket, checked trousers, yellow waistcoat and tall white top hat.

The leather ears indicate that this figure was made after the Teddy Roosevelt safari sets had been discontinued. When a number of African Chief heads were discovered, leather ears were added to turn them into a different 'African Dude' character. The Arab Chief is the rarest character from the set.

c1915

£600-800 **BER**

QUICK REFERENCE – THE MAN FROM U.N.C.L.E.

The Man From U.N.C.L.E. was a popular American spy series comprising 105 episodes in four series originally broadcast on NBC from September 1964 to January 1968. Ian Fleming contributed to the series, which originally featured a girl teamed with Napoleon Solo: Russian agent Illya Kuryakin replaced her after a popular walk-on role in the pilot. The United Network Command for Law and Enforcement agents battled agents from Technological Hierarchy for the Removal of Undesirables and the Subjugation of Humanity (T.H.R.U.S.H.) and captured the minds of a generation. Nostalgia drives most collectors, who were young at the time the series was aired. Memorabilia is harder to find than than for most other cult TV series, particularly in good and complete condition like this action doll.

An A.C. Gilbert The Man From U.N.C.L.E. 'Napoleon Solo' doll, no.16120, with raising arm, pistol with clip, agent card, folding badge and instructions, in very good condition, in very good condition original box.

c1965 *12.5in (31.5cm) high*

£200-300 SAS

An A.C. Gilbert The Man from U.N.C.L.E. 'Illya Kuryakin' doll, no.16125, with raising arm, pistol with clip, agent card, folding badge and instructions, in excellent condition, in very good condition box.

c1965 *12.5in (31.5cm) high*

£180-220 SAS

A rare 'Made in Hong Kong' The Man From U.N.C.L.E. HC1/1718 'Illya Kuryakin' doll, in very good condition, in fair condition original box.

£280-320 SAS

An A.C. Gilbert The Man from U.N.C.L.E. 'Spy Magic Secret Agent Tricks' set, no.15330, comprising Mystery Gun, Magic Money Converter, Jewel Trick, X-Ray Scope, Lie Detector, Spy Tag, Double Agent Card Trick and Vanishing Key, in very good condition, in good condition box.

c1965

£150-250 SAS

A The Man From Uncle 'The Getaway' jigsaw puzzle, complete with box in fair condition.

c1967

£12-18 SAS

A Lone Star 'The Girl From U.N.C.L.E. Spy Kit', no.1337, complete and in original box in excellent condition.

The Girl from U.N.C.L.E. was a spin-off TV series that aired on NBC for one season from September 1966 to April 1967. Although the 'girl' was first played by Mary Ann Mobley in 'The Moonglow Affair' episode of The Man from U.N.C.L.E. in February 1966, Stefanie Powers played 'April Dancer' in the spin-off series. Merchandise is unsurprisingly scarce, particularly in good condition, although it tends to be less popular than that produced for the main series.

£300-500 SAS

A 1960s base metal ring, with 'winking' image of Illya Kuryakin and Napoleon Solo.

0.75in (2cm) high

£9-12 GCHI

A Marx black battery-operated black plastic Dalek, with flashing light, in excellent condition, in good condition original box.

This first toy Dalek, with its 'bump 'n go' movement is complete and in excellent condition. Look out for the examples made in the UK as they are more desirable than the majority of toys that were made in Hong Kong. The Daleks were created by famed Dr Who writer Terry Nation, designed by BBC designer Raymond Cusick, and first shown on screen in December 1963 in the second Dr Who serial.

c1964

£100-150 **SAS**

A Denys Fisher 'Muhammad Ali' action figure, with punching action, complete, mint and boxed.

The yellow and white attachment fits around his waist and gives him the punch action. The clips that hold it on his body were frequently broken – if this piece is broken or missing, the value plummets to under 50% of a complete example.

1976 *Box 12in (30.5cm) high*

£120-180 **MTB**

A very rare Pedigree "Candy" soft vinyl doll, with original clothes.

This example lacks a couple of the fingers, but a truly mint condition example could fetch over £100.

c1967 *6.5in (16.5cm) high*

£60-80 **MTB**

A PPC Mork & Mindy 'Mork' poseable action figure, with original space suit and silver plastic boots.

c1979 *9.5in (24.5cm) high*

£15-20 **NOR**

A Thermos 'Knight Rider' metal lunchbox, with K.I.T.T., Michael Knight, Devon Miles and Bonnie Barstow artwork, lacks Thermos flask, but in excellent condition.

c1983 *8.5in (21.5cm) wide*

£10-15 **BH**

A CLOSER LOOK AT STAR TREK FIGURE

This second series of Star Trek action figures was released to coincide with the first movie in 1979 and was an attempt to cash in on the success of the Star Wars figures released in 1977.

They were produced by Mego Corp. and distributed in the UK by Pedigree – sales were not as high as expected, perhaps due to the film being slow and disappointing compared to Star Wars.

They are in mint, unopened condition which helps their value – but the discovery of a cache of mint and carded Star Trek figures in a Canadian warehouse in the late 1980s held values down.

The Kirk figure was produced for sale in Germany and bears Mego affailites Lion Rock and Airfix branding.

The Decker character only appeared in the film.

Three American Mego Corp. Star Trek action figures, comprising Captain Kirk, Spock and Willard Decker, in unopened, carded condition.

c1979 *Card 9in (23cm) high*

£80-120 **W&W**

QUICK REFERENCE

- The wristwatch is a 20thC phenomenon, although examples were produced for the German navy in the late 19thC, and in 1904 Brazilian aviator Alberto Santos-Dumont ordered a wristwatch from Cartier. They became popular with the general public after WWI.
- In the last five years, vintage wristwatches have become popular as a smarter look returns to fashion. Men's magazines have promoted this look, and vintage wristwatches are now widely sought after by those wishing to own an unusual yet elegant watch. Rolex and Longines watches from the mid-20thC are sometimes more affordable than modern examples.
- Value depends on the maker, complexity of movement, style, and materials used. High-end, high quality brands such as Patek Philippe and Rolex are sought-after, with iconic models, such as Rolex's Submariner, being the most desirable. The more complex a watch is the more valuable it is likely to be. Chronographs and watches with extra features, such as moon phases, alarms or perpetual calendars are highly desirable.
- The style of a watch can help date it. Small round faces (almost like pocket watches) date from the early 20thC, with rectangular watches taking over in the 1930s. Watch cases became more stylised and innovative from the late 1940s, as well as taking on period jewellery styles. Simple, circular faces and rectangular watches were again popular during the 1950s, though this had changed by the late 1960s and 70s when many watches were made with large sculptural cases in futuristic styles. The simple, classic styles of the 1930s and 1950s are particularly popular today.

An Audemars Piguet 'Royal Oak' gentleman's brushed grey stainless steel and gilt wristwatch, no.056D34567, with a 33 jewel automatic movement adjusted to heat/cold and five positions, and original bracelet, dial and movement signed.

c1990

£2,500-3,000 **DN**

A 1950s Swiss Audemars Piguet gentleman's wristwatch, with 18ct solid gold case with two tone white and yellow gold bezel, ultra-thin 17 jewel movement with four adjustments, and signed on the dial, case and movement.

£1,500-2,000 **ML**

A 1950s-60s Ernest Borel gentleman's 'Cocktail' watch, with display skeleton back, and 17 jewel movement.

The dial on this sought-after watch is made up of moving discs with arrowheads to indicate the time. As the discs revolve, the printed 'starburst' pattern changes, creating an interesting optical effect.

£150-200 **ML**

A 1920s-30s Bulova doctor's watch, with gold-filled rectangular case, three dials, and 12-jewel movement.

This watch, used for timing in medical examinations, is rare with three dials.

£500-800 **ML**

A 1940s LeCoultre gentleman's wristwatch, triple signed on the case, dial and movement, with stainless steel case, two tone military-style 24 hour dial with luminous hands and numbers, and LeCoultre 17-jewel movement.

£250-300 **ML**

A Longines 'Flagship' automatic gentleman's wristwatch, with 18ct gold case, silvered dial, and date aperture.

c1970 *1.5in (3.5cm) diam*

£300-500 **GHOU**

An Omega Seamaster De Ville gold-plated gentleman's wristwatch, with matching bracelet, with baton numerals and date.

£150-200 **SAS**

A CLOSER LOOK AT A WRISTWATCH

Designed in the late 1960s by André Le Marquand as a tribute to man landing on the moon, the watch was inspired by the astronauts' space helmets and visors.

It was released at the Basel Watch fair in 1972 and was followed by the rectangular and more valuable Spaceman 'Audacieuse' a few years later.

It was produced until 1977 in a range of colours, with the brighter ones being more popular. It was also produced under a variety of brands, including Fortis and Jules Jürgensen.

If the strap has been replaced with a different type, the value falls by over a third. Correct replacement straps can be found for around £20-30.

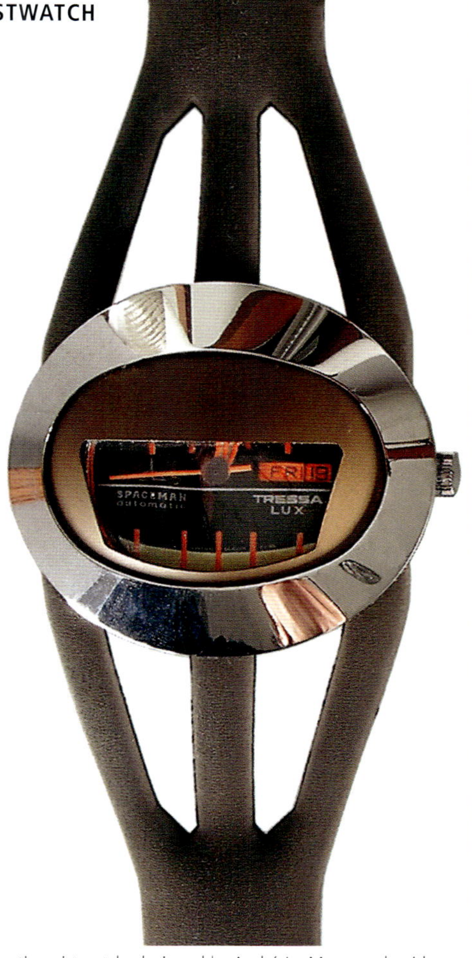

A 1970s Tressa Lux 'Spaceman' automatic wristwatch, designed by André Le Marquand, with shiny stainless steel case, copper and black face, and Corfam strap.

£80-120 **RSS**

An Omega 'Constellation' Chronometer automatic gold plated and steel gentlemen's wristwatch, the brown dial with baton markers, with a calibrated 751 jewel movement.

1.5in (3.5cm) diam

£200-300 **GHOU**

A 1930s Rolex Art Deco wristwatch, the square dial with Roman numerals and silver square case, marked 'Rolex' to movement.

£150-200 **SAS**

An Edwardian Goldsmiths and Silversmiths ladies silver wristwatch, with white enamel face with Roman numerals, and plain silver case with Birmingham hallmarks.

1905

£40-60 **SAS**

QUICK REFERENCE - SWATCH

The first Swatches were released in 1983, and were plain by comparison to the colourful, design or designer led, models the brand is known for today. With only 51 components, and plastic cases and straps, the watches could be easily mass-produced. By 1984, over one million had been made. A number of designers have produced designs for the company including Keith Haring, Vivienne Westwood and Christian Lacroix, and these are among the most valuable today. Also look out for the famed 'Jellyfish' transparent watches, commemorative Olympic watches, and limited editions. To be of interest to a collector, the watch must be in excellent condition with its original strap. Being in mint condition, with its box and paperwork makes a watch even more desirable. Although Swatch collecting has declined since the glory days of the 1990s, there is still a healthy trade over the internet, with most fetching under £200. The watch below was the first special edition produced. It is a US Special, and commemorates the First Breakdance World Championship held at the Roxy in New York City. Designed by the artists Marlyse Schmid and Bernard Muller, variations of the hands, dial and colour of the case are known and are worth roughly the same.

A limited edition Swatch 'Breakdance' wristwatch, GO 0001, from an edition of 9,999.

£500-600 **ML**

A Swatch 'Stormy Weather' wristwatch, GV 100, from the Dream Waves series, with multi-coloured strap.

Look for rare variation without the Swatch logo at '12 o'clock', which is worth about twice the normal version.

1989

£30-40 **ML**

A Swatch 'Needles' wristwatch, GB 408, from the Signal Corps series, with original perforated red strap.

1988

£30-50 **ML**

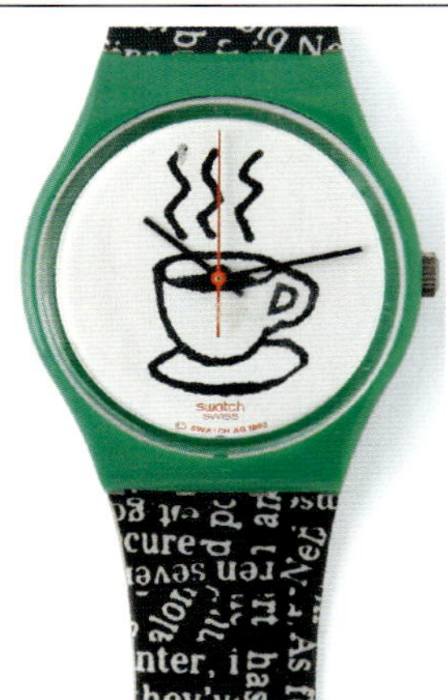

A Swatch 'World Record' wristwatch, GB 721, from the Sprint series, with original ribbed yellow and green straps.

1990

£30-40 **ML**

A Swatch 'Cappuccino' wristwatch, GG 121, from the Sunday Brunch series, designed by Jennifer Morla.

1992

£30-40 **ML**

A Swatch 'Silver Patch' wristwatch, GN 132, from the Nespolo series, with original multicoloured strap.

1993

£30-40 **ML**

A Hamilton gold-filled pocket watch, the dial and movement signed "Motor Barrel 952", with 19-jewel movement, adjusted to five positions.

2in (5cm) diam

£250-350 **GHOU**

A Tiffany & Co 18ct gold hunter pocket watch, the engraved scroll body with sprung cover, white enamel face with painted centre, Roman numerals and subsidiary seconds dial, the case marked 'Tiffany & Co New York No. 38676', cover marked 'T&Co 0.750'.

£450-650 **SAS**

A CLOSER LOOK AT A POCKET WATCH

The psychedelic design and 'Flower Power' wording are typical of the late 1960s when this watch was designed and made.

Loftus designed a range of watches for The Beatles' 'Apple' boutique store which opened on London's King's Road in 1967 and closed 8 months later due to financial problems. It is possible that this watch was designed for sale there.

The 'Old England' brand was used by Accurist, which made this watch. Its designer, Richard Loftus, was one of three sons of Accurist founders Asher and Rebecca Loftus.

Accurist watches were highly successful, and were worn and endorsed by celebrities including The Beatles, Twiggy and The Princess Royal.

An Old England 'Flower Power' medallion watch, probably designed for the Beatles' Apple store, by Richard Loftus, the square pendant on a gilt metal chain.

Chain 27.5in (70cm) long

£150-200 **DN**

A Waltham 10ct gold pocket watch, with Roman numerals, the engraved case marked '10ct'.

£60-90 **SAS**

A 1920s-30s Continental silver pocket watch, the gold circular face with Arabic numerals, and second subsidiary seconds dial, European control marks to interior.

£20-30 **SAS**

An unmarked silver pocket watch, with white enamel dial, Roman numerals and seconds subsidiary dial, engraved monogram to reverse.

£30-40 **SAS**

Every item illustrated in the Miller's Collectables by Judith Miller and Mark Hill has a letter code that identifies the dealer, auction house or private collector that owns or sold it. In this way the source of the item can be identified. The list below is a key to these codes. In the list, auction houses are shown by the letter A, dealers by the letter D, and private collectors by the letter P. Inclusion in this book in no way constitutes or implies a contract or a binding offer on the part of any of our contributors to supply or sell the goods illustrated, or similar items, at the prices stated.

A&G Ⓐ
ANDERSON & GARLAND
Anderson House, Crispin Court, Newbiggin Lane, Westerhope, Newcastle upon Tyne, NE5 1BF
www.andersonandgarland.com

AAC Ⓐ
ALDERFER AUCTION COMPANY
501 Fairground Road, Hatfield, PA 19440 USA
Tel: 001 215 393 3000
www.alderferauction.com

AB Ⓟ
AUCTION BLOCKS
blockschip@aol.com

ACOG Ⓓ
THE AUTOGRAPH COLLECTORS GALLERY
7 Jessops Lane, Gedling, Nottingham, NG4 4BQ.
www.autograph-gallery.co.uk

AEM Ⓓ
ANTIQUES EMPORIUM
29 Division Street, Somerville NJ 08876, USA
Tel: 001 908 218 1234
bkr63@patmedia.net

AG Ⓓ
ANTIQUE GLASS @ FRANK DUX ANTIQUES
33 Belvedere, Lansdowne Road, Bath, BA1 5HR
Tel: 01225 312 367
www.antique-glass.co.uk

AH Ⓐ
ANDREW HARTLEY
Victoria Hall Salerooms, Little Lane, Ilkley, West Yorkshire LS29 8EA
Tel: 01943 816 363
www.andrewhartleyfinearts.co.uk

AHL Ⓓ
ANDREA HALL LEVY
PO Box 1243, Riverdale, NY 10471
Tel: 001 646 441 1726
barangrill@aol.com

AMER Ⓐ
AMERSHAM AUCTION ROOMS
125 Station Rd, Amersham, Buckinghamshire, HP7 0AH
Tel: 08700 460606
www.amershamauctionrooms.co.uk

ANT Ⓓ
THE ANTIQUE GALLERY
8523 Germantown Avenue, Philadelphia PA 19118, USA
Tel: 001 215 248 1700
www.antiquegal.com

ART Ⓓ
ARTIUS GLASS
Tel: 01458 443694
Mob: 07860 822666
www.artiusglass.co.uk

ATK Ⓐ
AUCTION TEAM KÖLN
Otto-Hahn-Str. 10
50997 Köln (Godorf), Germany
Tel: (0049) 2236 38 4340
www.breker.com

ATM Ⓓ
AT THE MOVIES
Tel: 07770 777 411
www.atthemovies.co.uk

BAD Ⓓ
BETH ADAMS
Unit GO23-25 Alfie's Antique Market, 13 Church Street, Marylebone, London NW8 8DT
Mob: 07776 136 003
www.alfiesantiques.com

BB Ⓓ
BARBARA BLAU
South Street Antiques Market
615 South 6th Street, Philadelphia, PA 19147-2128 USA
Tel: (001) 215 592 0256
bbjools@msn.com

BE Ⓐ
BEARNE'S, HAMPTON & LITTLEWOOD
St Edmund's Court, Okehampton St, Exeter, Devon, EX41LX.
Tel: 01392 413 100
info@bhandl.co.uk
www.bearnes.co.uk

BEJ Ⓓ
BÉBÉS ET JOUETS
c/o Lochend Post Office, 165 Restalrig Road, Edinburgh EH7 6HW
Tel: 0131 332 5650
bebesetjouets@tiscali.co.uk

BEL Ⓐ
BELHORN AUCTION SERVICES
PO Box 20211, Columbus, OH 43220 USA
Tel: 001 614 921 9441
www.belhorn.com

BER Ⓐ
BERTOIA AUCTIONS
2141 De Marco Drive
Vineland, NJ 08360 USA
Tel: 001 856 692 1881
www.bertoiaauctions.com

BEV Ⓓ
BEVERLEY ADAMS
Stand G028-30, Alfie's Antiques Market, 13-25 Church Street, Marylebone, London NW8 8DT
Mob: 07776 136 003
www.alfiesantiques.com

BEX Ⓓ
DANIEL BEXFIELD ANTIQUES
26 Burlington Arcade, Mayfair, London. W1J 0PU
Tel: 020 7491 1720
www.bexfield.co.uk

BGL Ⓟ
BLOCK GLASS LTD
blockglss@aol.com
www.blockglass.com

BH Ⓓ
BLACK HORSE ANTIQUES SHOWCASE
2180 North Reading Road
Denver, PA 17517, USA
Tel: 001 717 335 3300
www.blackhorselodge.com/Antiques.asp

BIB Ⓓ
BIBLION
1/7 Davies Mews, London W1K 5AB
Tel: 020 7629 1374
www.biblion.com

BLNY Ⓐ
BLOOMSBURY AUCTIONS NEW YORK
6 West 48th Street, New York NY 10036-1902, USA
Tel: 001 212 719 1000
www.bloomsburyauctions.com

BLO Ⓐ
BLOOMSBURY AUCTIONS
Bloomsbury House,
24 Maddox St, London W1S 1PP
Tel: 020 7495 9494
www.bloomsburyauctions.com

BPH Ⓓ
BATTERSEA PEN HOME
PO Box 6128, Epping, CM16 4CG
Tel: 01992 578 885
www.penhome.com

C Ⓐ
COTTEES
The Market, East Street, Wareham, Dorset BH20 4NR
Tel: 01929 552 826
www.auctionsatcottees.co.uk

CANS Ⓓ
CANDY SAYS
39 Elm Road, Leigh-on-Sea, Essex, SS9 1SW
Tel: 01277 212134
www.candysays.co.uk

CARS Ⓓ
CLASSIC AUTOMOBILIA & REGALIA SPECIALISTS (C.A.R.S.)
4-4a Chapel Terrace Mews, Kemp Town, Brighton, BN2 1HU.
Tel: 01273 622 722
carsofbrighton@aol.com
www.carsofbrighton.co.uk
www.laliquemascots.co.uk

CHT Ⓐ
CHARTERHOUSE
The Long Street Salerooms, Sherborne, Dorset DT9 3BS
Tel: 01935 812 277
www.charterhouse-auctions.co.uk

COC Ⓓ
COMIC CONNECTIONS
4a Parsons Street, Banbury, Oxfordshire, OX16 5LW
Tel: 01295268989
comicman@freenetname.co.uk

CRIS Ⓓ
CRISTOBAL
26 Church Street, Marylebone, London NW8 8EP
Tel: 020 7724 7230
www.cristobal.co.uk

CW Ⓟ
CHRISTINE WILDMAN
wild123@allstream.net

CWD Ⓓ
COLLECTORS WORLD
118 Wollaton Road, Wollaton, Nottingham, NG8 1HJ.
Tel: 01159280347
www.collectorsworld-nottingham.com

DCP Ⓓ
THE DUNLOP COLLECTION
PO Box 6269, Statesville, NC 28687 USA
Tel: 001 871 2626
dunloppaperweights@mac.com

DODA Ⓓ
DODA ANTIQUES
434 Richards Street Vancouver, BC, Canada
Tel: 001 604 602-0559
www.dodaantiques.com

DOR Ⓐ
DOROTHEUM
Palais Dorotheum, Dorotheergasse 17, 1010 Vienna, Austria
Tel: 0043 1 515 600
www.dorotheum.com

DN Ⓐ
DREWEATTS
Donnington Priory Salerooms, Donnington, Newbury, Berkshire RG14 2JE
Tel: 01635 553 553
www.dnfa.com/donnington

DRA Ⓐ
DAVID RAGO AUCTIONS
333 North Main Street, Lambertville, NJ 08530 USA
Tel: 001 609 397 9374
www.ragoarts.com

DSC Ⓟ
DOLL SHOWCASE
squibbit@ukonline.co.uk
www.britishdollshowcase.co.uk

DUK Ⓐ
HY DUKE AND SON
The Dorchester Fine Art Salerooms, Weymouth Avenue, Dorchester, Dorset DT1 1QS
Tel: 01305 265 080
www.dukes-auctions.com

EWA Ⓓ
EAST WEST ANTIQUES
Stand S054-56
Alfies Antiques Market,
13 Church Street, London,
NW8 8DT
Tel: 020 7723 0564
ewa_thomson@hotmail.com
www.alfiesantiques.com

FLD Ⓐ
FIELDING'S AUCTIONEERS
Mill Race Lane, Stourbridge,
West Midlands DY8 1JN
Tel: 01384 444140
www.fieldingsauctioneers.co.uk

FOF Ⓓ
FOSSACK & FURKLE
P.O. Box 733, Abington,
Cambridgeshire, CB1 6BF
Tel: 01223 894296
fossack@btopenworld.com

FRE Ⓐ
FREEMAN'S
1808 Chestnut Street,
Philadelphia, PA 19103 USA
Tel: 001 215 563 9275
www.freemansauction.com

GAZE Ⓐ
THOS. WM. GAZE & SON
Diss Auction Rooms,
Roydon Rd, Diss,
Norfolk IP22 4LN
Tel: 01379 650 306
www.twgaze.com

GOL Ⓓ
GAZELLES OF LYNDHURST
The Old Cinema, 160 Chiswick High
Road, London, W1 4PR
Tel: 02380 811610
www.gazelles.co.uk

GBA Ⓐ
GRAHAM BUDD AUCTIONS
P.O. Box 47519,
London N14 6XD
Tel: 020 8366 2525
www.grahambuddauctions.co.uk

GC Ⓟ
GRAHAM COOLEY COLLECTION
Mob: 07968 722 269
gc@itm-power.com

GCHI Ⓓ
THE GIRL CAN'T HELP IT!
Grand Central Window,
Ground Floor,
Alfie's Antiques Market,
13-25 Church Street,
London NW8 8DT
Tel: 0207 724 8984
Mob: 07958 515 614
www.thegirlcanthelpit.com

GHOU Ⓐ
GARDINER HOULGATE
Bath Auction Rooms,
9 Leafield Way, Corsham,
Nr Bath SN13 9SW
Tel: 01225 812 912
www.gardinerhoulgate.co.uk

GORL Ⓐ
GORRINGES
15 North Street, Lewes,
East Sussex BN7 2PD
Tel: 01273 472 503
www.gorringes.co.uk

GROB Ⓓ
GEOFFREY ROBINSON
Stand GO77-78 & GO91-92
Alfies Antiques Market,
13-25 Church Street,
London NW8 8DT
Tel: 07955 085 723
www.robinsonantiques.co.uk

GWRA Ⓐ
GLOUCESTERSHIRE WORCESTERSHIRE RAILWAY AUCTIONS
Tel: 01684 773 487 /
01386 760 109
www.gwra.co.uk

HALL Ⓐ
HALLS FINE ART
Welsh Bridge, Shrewsbury, SY3 8LA
Tel : 01743 284 777
www.hallsgb.com

HER Ⓐ
HERITAGE AUCTION GALLERIES
3500 Maple Avenue, 17th Floor,
Dallas, Texas 75219-3941, USA
Tel: (214) 528-3500
www.ha.com

HSR Ⓓ
HANS VINTAGE FOUNTAIN PENS
www.hanspens.com

HT Ⓐ
HARTLEY'S
Victoria Hall, Little Lane, Ilkley,
LS29 8EA
Tel: 01943 816363
www.andrewhartleyfinearts.co.uk

IVD Ⓓ
IT'S VINTAGE DARLING
Tel: 01778 344949
www.itsvintagedarling.com

JA Ⓐ
JOEL AUSTRALIA
333 Malvern Road, South Yarra,
3141, Victoria, Melbourne, Australia
www.leonardjoel.com.au

JDJ Ⓐ
JAMES D JULIA INC
PO Box 830, Fairfield,
Maine 04937 USA
Tel: 001 207 453 7125
www.juliaauctions.com

JTB Ⓓ
JIM CALL
bottles@3gsmilkbottles.com
www.3gsmilkbottles.com

KA Ⓓ
KINGSTON ANTIQUES CENTRE
29 Old London Road, Kingston-
Upon-Thames, Surrey, KT2 6ND
Tel: 020 8549 2004
johncobbold1@yahoo.co.uk
www.kingstonantiquesmarket.co.uk

KNK Ⓓ
KITSCH-N-KABOODLE
South Street Antiques Market,
615 South 6th Street, Philadelphia,
PA 19147-2128 USA
Tel: 001 215 382 1354
kitschnkaboodle@yahoo.com

KT Ⓐ
KERRY TAYLOR AUCTIONS
Unit C25,
Parkhall Road Trading Estate
40 Martell Road, London SE21 8EN
Tel: 0208 676 4600
www.kerrytaylorauctions.com

L Ⓓ
LUNA
139 Lower Parliament Street,
Nottingham, NG1 1EE
Tel: 0115 924 3267
www.luna-online.co.uk

L&T Ⓐ
LYON AND TURNBULL LTD.
33 Broughton Place,
Edinburgh EH1 3RR
Tel: 0131 557 8844
www.lyonandturnbull.com

LDY Ⓓ
LADY DOUBLE YOU
info@ladydoubleyou.com
www.ladydoubleyou.com

LHT Ⓓ
LEANDA HARWOOD
Tel: 01529 300 737
leanda.harwood@virgin.net
www.leandaharwood.co.uk

LOC Ⓐ
LOCKE & ENGLAND
18 Guy Street, Leamington Spa,
CV32 4RT
Tel: 01926 889100
www.leauction.co.uk

LT Ⓐ
LOUIS TAYLOR
Britannia House, 10 Town Road,
Hanley, Stoke on Trent ST1 2QG
Tel: 01782 214111
www.louistaylorfineart.co.uk

M&C Ⓓ
M&C CARDS
Shop 30, Antique Centre, Severn
Road, Gloucester, GL1 2LE
Tel: 01452 506 361
www.mandccards.co.uk

M20C Ⓓ
MID20THC
Tel: 07760 218 749
info@mid20c.co.uk
www.mid20c.co.uk

MA Ⓓ
MANIC ATTIC
Alfies Antiques Market, Stand
S48/49, 13-25 Church Street,
London NW8 8DT
Tel: 020 7723 6066
ianbroughton@hotmail.com

MAS Ⓐ
MASTRO AUCTIONS
Now trading as
Legendary Auctions, LLC
17542 Chicago Avenue
Lansing, IL 60438 USA
Tel: 001 708 889-9380
www.legendaryauctions.com

MCS Ⓓ
MEMORIES COLLECTORS SHOP
130/132 Brent Street, Hendon,
London, NW4 2DR
Tel: 020 8203 1500
www.memoriespostcards.co.uk

MDM Ⓓ
M&D MOIR
manddmoir@aol.com
www.manddmoir.co.uk

MHC Ⓟ
MARK HILL COLLECTION
books@markhillpublishing.com
www.markhillpublishing.com

MHT Ⓓ
MUM HAD THAT
info@mumhadthat.com
www.mumhadthat.com

ML Ⓓ
MARK LAINO
Mark of Time, 132 South 8th Street,
Philadelphia, PA 19107 USA
Tel: 001 215 922 1551
lecoultre@verizon.net
eBay ID: lecoultre

MSA Ⓓ
MANFRED SCHOTTEN ANTIQUES
109 Burford High Street, Burford,
Oxfordshire OX18 4RH
Tel: 01993 822 302
www.schotten.com

MTB Ⓓ
THE MAGIC TOYBOX
210 Havant Road, Drayton,
Portsmouth, Hampshire PO6 2EH
Tel: 02392 221 307
www.magictoybox.co.uk

MTS Ⓓ
THE MULTICOLOURED TIMESLIP
dave_a_cameron@hotmail.com
eBay ID: dave65330

NPC Ⓓ
MICHELLE GUZY
Tel: 07966 017 914
signedanddesigned@aol.com

NOR Ⓓ
NEET-O-RAMA
6 Division Street, Somerville,
NJ 08876 USA
Tel: 001 908 722 4600
koehnhome@mindspring.com
www.neetstuff.com

ON Ⓐ
ONSLOWS
The Coach House, Manor Road,
Stourpaine, Dorset DT11 8TQ
Tel: 01258 488 838
www.onslows.co.uk

OTA Ⓓ
ON THE AIR LTD
The Vintage Technology Centre,
Hawarden, Deeside, CH5 3DN
Tel: 01244 530 300
www.vintageradio.co.uk

OUT Ⓓ
OUTERNATIONAL
Tel: 0049 221 1793914
info@outernational.info
www.outernational.eu

P Ⓓ
POSTERITATI
239 Centre Street, New York, NY
10013 USA
Tel: 001 212 2226 2207
www.posteritati.com

P&I Ⓓ
PAOLA & IAIA
Unit S057-058, Alfie's Antiques Market, 13-25 Church Street, London NW8 8DT
Tel: 07751 084 135
paola_iaia_london@yahoo.co.uk
www.alfiesantiques.com

PAMW Ⓓ
PAM WEST BRITISH NOTES
PO Box 257, Sutton, Surrey, SM3 9WW.
Tel: 0208 641 3224
pamwestbritnotes@aol.com
www.britishnotes.co.uk

PC Ⓟ
PRIVATE COLLECTION

QU Ⓐ
QUITTENBAUM KUNSTAUKTIONEN
Theresienstrasse 60, D-80333 Munich, Germany
Tel: 00 49 89 2737021-25
www.quittenbaum.de

RCC Ⓓ
ROYAL COMMEMORATIVE CHINA
Paul Wynton & Joe Spiteri
Tel: 020 8863 0625
Mob: 07930 303 358
royalcommemoratives @hotmail.com

RET Ⓓ
RETROPOLITAN
Tel: 07772 280 565
enquiries@retropolitan.co.uk
www.retropolitan.co.uk

ROS Ⓐ
ROSEBERY'S
74-76 Knight's Hill, West Norwood, London SE27 0JD
Tel: 020 8761 2522
www.roseberys.co.uk

RSS Ⓐ
ROSSINI SVV
7 Rue Drouot, Paris 75009, France
0033 1 53 34 55 00
www.rossini.fr

RTC Ⓐ
RITCHIES
No longer trading

SAE Ⓓ
ANTIQUES EMPORIUM
29 Division Street, Somerville NJ 08876, USA
Tel: 001 908 218 1234
bkr63@patmedia.net

SAS Ⓐ
SPECIAL AUCTION SERVICES
Kennetholme, Midgham, Nr. Reading, Berkshire RG7 5UX
Tel: 0118 971 2949
www.specialauctionservices.com

SDR Ⓐ
SOLLO:RAGO MODERN AUCTIONS
333 North Main Street, Lambertville, NJ 08530 USA
Tel: 001 609 397 9374
www.ragoarts.com

SK Ⓐ
SLOANS & KENYON
7034 Wisconsin Avenue, Chevy Chase, Maryland 20815 USA
Tel: 001 301 634 2330
www.sloansandkenyon.com

SOR Ⓓ
SOLDIERS OF RYE
Mint Arcade, 71 The Mint, Rye, East Sussex, TN31 7EW
Tel: 01797 225952

SOTT Ⓓ
SIGN OF THE TYMES
Mill Antiques Center, 12 Morris Farm Road, Lafayette, NJ 07848 USA
Tel: 001 973 383 6028
jhap@nac.net
www.millantiques.com

SWA Ⓐ
SWANN GALLERIES IMAGE LIBRARY
104 East 25th Street, New York, NY 10010 USA
Tel: 001 212 254 4710
www.swanngalleries.com

SWO Ⓐ
SWORDERS
14 Cambridge Road, Stansted Mountfitchet, Essex CM24 8BZ
Tel: 01279 817 778
www.sworder.co.uk

TAC Ⓓ
TORONTO ANTIQUES CENTER
284 King Street West, 1st Floor, Toronto, Ontario M5V 1J2. Canada
Tel: 001 416 260-9057
askcynthia@cynthiafindlay.com
www.torontoantiquesonking.com

TBW Ⓓ
TEDDY BEARS OF WITNEY
99 High Street, Witney, Oxfordshire, OX28 6HY
Tel: 01993 706616
www.teddybears.co.uk

TCA Ⓐ
TRANSPORT CAR AUCTIONS
14 The Green, Richmond, Surrey TW9 1PX
Tel: 020 8940 2022
www.tc-auctions.com

TCM Ⓓ
TWENTIETH CENTURY MARKS
Whitegates, Rectory Road, Little Burstead, Nr Billericay, Essex, CM12 9TR
Tel: 01474 872 460
www.20thcenturymarks.co.uk

TCT Ⓓ
THE CALICO TEDDY
Tel: 001 410 433 9202
calicteddy@aol.com
www.calicoteddy.com

TEN Ⓐ
TENNANTS
The Auction Centre, Leyburn, North Yorkshire, DL8 5SG
Tel: 01969 623 780
www.tennants.co.uk

TGM Ⓓ
THE STUDIO GLASS MERCHANT
Tel: 07775 683 961
Tel: 0208 668 2701
www.thestudioglassmerchant.co.uk

THG Ⓓ
HERITAGE
Toronto Antiques on King
284 King Street West, Toronto, Ontario M5V 1J2 Canada
Tel: 001 416 260 9057
www.torontoantiquesonking.com

TOV Ⓐ
RUPERT TOOVEY
Spring Gardens, Washington, West Sussex, RH20 3BS
Tel: 01903 891955
www.rupert-toovey.com

TSIS Ⓓ
THREE SISTERS
South Street Antiques Market, 615 South 6th Street, Philadelphia, PA 19147-2128 USA
Tel: 001 215 592 0256

TWF Ⓓ
TWICE FOUND
608 Markham Street, Mirvish Village, Toronto, Ontario M6G 2L8, Canada
Tel: 001 416 534 3904
www.twicefound.com

UCT Ⓓ
UNDERCURRENTS
28 Cowper Street, London, EC2A 4AS
Tel: 0207 251 1537
www.undercurrents.biz

VC Ⓓ
VICTOR CAPLIN
Stand G075-76, Alfie's Antiques Market, 13-25 Church Street, London NW8 8DT
Mob: 07947571592
victorcaplin@aol.com
www.alfiesantiques.com

VE Ⓓ
VINTAGE EYEWEAR OF NEW YORK CITY INC.
1A The Fantastic Umbrella Factory
4820 Old Post Road, Charlestown Rhode Island, USA
Tel: 001 917 721 6546
vintageyes60@yahoo.com

VEC Ⓐ
VECTIS AUCTIONS LTD
Fleck Way, Thornaby, Stockton on Tees TS17 9JZ
Tel: 01642 750 616
www.vectis.co.uk

VSA Ⓐ
VAN SABBEN AUCTIONS
Appelsteeg 1-B, NL-1621 BD, Hoorn, Netherlands
0031 229 268 203
www.vansabbenauctions.nl

VZ Ⓐ
VON ZEZSCHWITZ KUNST UND DESIGN GMBH & CO KG
Friedrichstrasse 1a, 80801 Munich, Germany
Tel: 00 49 89 38 98 930
www.von-zezschwitz.de

W&L Ⓓ
W&L ANTIQUES
Stand G060, Alfie's Antiques Market, 13-25 Church Street, London NW8 8DT
Tel: 0207 723 6066
Mob: 07788 486 297
teddylove@blueyonder.co.uk

W&W Ⓐ
WALLIS & WALLIS
West Steet Auction Galleries, Lewes, East Sussex BN7 2NJ
Tel: 01273 480 208
www.wallisandwallis.co.uk

WAD Ⓐ
WADDINGTON'S AUCTIONEERS
111 Bathurst Street, Toronto, Ontario, Canada M5V 2R1
Tel: 001 416 504 9100
www.waddingtons.ca

WEB Ⓐ
WEBBS
18 Manukau Road, PO Box 99 251, Newmarket, Auckland 1000, New Zealand
Tel: 09 524 6804
www.webbs.co.nz

WDL Ⓐ
KUNST-AUKTIONSHAUS MARTIN WENDL
August-Bebel-Straße 4, 07407 Rudolstadt, Germany
Tel: 0049 3672 424 350
www.auktionshaus-wendl.de

WKA Ⓐ
WIENER KUNST AUKTIONEN - PALAIS KINSKY
Freyung 4, 1010 Vienna, Austria
Tel: 00 43 15 32 42 00
www.palais-kinsky.com

WORA Ⓓ
WORCESTER ANTIQUES CENTRE
Reindeer Court, Mealcheapen Street, Worcester, WR1 4DF
Tel: 01905 610 680
worcantiques@aol.com

WW Ⓐ
WOOLLEY & WALLIS
51-61 Castle Street, Salisbury, Wiltshire SP1 3SU
Tel: 01722 424 500
www.woolleyandwallis.co.uk

ZI Ⓓ
ZEITGEIST INTERIORS
Tel: 07522 680 827
info@zeitgeist-i.com
www.zeitgeist-i.com

If you wish to have any item valued, it is advisable to contact the dealer or specialist in advance to check that they will carry out this service and whether there is a charge. While most dealers will be happy to help you with an enquiry, do remember that they are busy people with businesses to run. Telephone valuations are not possible. Please mention the Miller's Collectables by Judith Miller and Mark Hill when making an enquiry.

ADVERTISING

Dan Tinman
Lipka Arcade (Portobello Road), Unit 13-14 Lower Ground, 282 Westbourne Grove, London W11
Tel: 01761 462 477 or 07768 166 808
dan@dantinman.com
www.dantinman.com

Huxtins
Saturdays at: Portobello Road, Basement Stall 11/12, 288 Westbourne Grove, London W11
Tel: 07710 132 200
david@huxtins.com
www.huxtins.com

Junktion
The Old Railway Station, New Bolingbroke, Boston, Lincolnshire
Tel: 01205 480068 or 07836 345 491
junktionantiques@hotmail.com

The Tin Shop
Market Vaults, Scarborough, North Yorkshire YO11 1EU
Tel: 01723 351 089
www.tinshop.co.uk

ANIMATION ART

Animation Art Gallery
13-14 Great Castle Street, London W1W 8LS
Tel: 020 7255 1456
Fax: 0207 436 1256
gallery@animaart.com
www.animaart.com

ART DECO

Art Deco Etc
73 Gloucester Road, Brighton, Sussex, BN1 3LQ
Tel: 01273 329 268
johnclark@artdecoetc.co.uk

AUTOGRAPHS

Lights, Camera Action
6 Western Gardens, Western Boulevard, Aspley, Nottingham, HG8 5GP
Tel: 0115 913 1116
Mob: 07970 342 363
www.lca-autographs.co.uk

Special Signings
Tel: 01438 714 728
sales@specialsignings.com
www.specialsignings.com

The Autograph Collectors Gallery
7 Jessops Lane, Gedling, Nottingham
Tel: 0115 961 2956
graham@autograph-gallery.co.uk
www.autograph-gallery.co.uk

AUTOMOBILIA

Automobilia Planet
P.O. Box 321, Hartlepool TS24 4EL
Tel: 01429 286 146
info@automobiliaplanet.com
www.automobiliaplanet.com

C.A.R.S. of Brighton
The White Lion Garage Clarendon Place, Kemp Town, Brighton Sussex
Tel: 01273 622 722
Fax: 01273 622 722
whiteliongarage@fsmail.net
www.carsofbrighton.co.uk

Finesse Fine Art
Tel: 07973 886 937
tony@finesse-fine-art.com
www.finesse-fine-art.com

Junktion
The Old Railway Station, New Bolingbroke, Boston, Lincolnshire
Tel: 01205 480068 or 07836 345 491
junktionantiques@hotmail.com

BOOKS

Biblion
1-7 Davies Mews, London W1K 5AB
Tel: 020 7629 1374
info@biblion.com
www.biblion.co.uk

Zardoz Books
20 Whitecroft, Dilton Marsh, Westbury, Somerset BA13 4DJ
Tel: 01373 865 371
www.zardozbooks.co.uk

Banknotes, Bonds & Shares
Colin Narbeth & Sons Ltd
20 Cecil Court, Leicester Square, London WC2N 4HE
Tel: 0207 379 6975
colin.narbeth@btinternet.com
www.colin-narbeth.com

Intercol
43 Templar's Crescent, Finchley, London N3 3QR
Tel: 020 8349 2207
sales@intercol.co.uk
www.intercol.co.uk

BREWERIANA

Junktion
The Old Railway Station, New Bolingbroke, Boston, Lincolnshire
Tel: 01205 480068 or 07836 345 491
junktionantiques@hotmail.com

Gordon Litherland
25 Stapenhill Road, Burton on Trent, Staffordshire
Tel: 01283 567 213 or 07952 118 987
gordon@jmp2000.com

CERAMICS

A1 Collectables
Bohemia, 46 High Street, Hampton Wick, Surrey
Tel: 0208 977 7230
denise.woods@blueyonder.co.uk
www.a1-collectables.co.uk

Beth Adams
Stand G023-25, Alfies Antique Market, 13-25 Church Street, Marylebone, London NW8 8DT
Mob: 07776 136 003
www.alfiesantiques.com

The Ceramic Studio
2 Potters Hill Farm Cottages, Langley, Witney, Oxfordshire
Tel: 01993 878 833
info@theceramicstudio.co.uk
wwww.theceramicstudio.co.uk

China Search
4 Princes Drive, Kenilworth, Warwickshire CV8 2FD
Tel: 01926 512 402
Fax: 01926 859 311
info@chinasearch.uk.com
www.chinasearch.uk.com

Collectables
134B High Street, Honiton, Devon EX14 1JP
Tel: 01404 470 024
chris@collectableshoniton.co.uk
www.collectableshoniton.co.uk

Cornishware.biz
Vintage-Kitsch, 1 Crown & Anchor Cottages, Horsley, Newcastle, Tyne & Wear
Tel: 07979 857 599
info@cornishware.biz
www.cornishware.biz

Adrian Grater
25-26 Admiral Vernon Antiques Centre, 141-149 Portobello Road, London W11 2DY
Tel: 0208 579 0357
adriangrater@tiscali.co.uk

Gallery 1930
18 Church St, London NW8 8EP
Tel: 020 7723 1555
Fax: 020 7735 8309
gallery1930@aol.com
www.susiecooperceramics.com

Gillian Neale Antiques
P.O. Box 247, Aylesbury HP20 1JZ
Tel: 01296 423754
Fax: 01296-334601
gillianneale@aol.com
www.gilliannealeantiques.co.uk

Tony Horsley
P.O. Box 3127, Brighton, East Sussex
Tel: 01273 550 770
enquiries@tonyhorsley.co.uk
www.tonyhorsley.co.uk

KCS Ceramics
Tel: 0208 384 8981
www.kcsceramics.co.uk

Louis O'Brien
Tel: 01276 32907

Past Caring
76 Essex Road, Islington, N1 8LT

Nick Ainge
Tel: 01832 731 063
Mob: 07745 902 343
nick@ainge1930.fastnet.co.uk
decoseek.decoware.co.uk

ReMemories Antiques
74 High Street, Tenterden, Kent
Tel: 01580 763 416

Retroselect
info@retroselect.com
www.retroselect.com

Rick Hubbard Art Deco
Tel: 01794 513133
www.rickhubbard-artdeco.co.uk

Geoffrey Robinson
Stand GO77-78 & GO91-92, Alfies Antiques Market, 13-25 Church Street, London, NW8 8DT
Tel: 020 7723 0449
www.robinsonantiques.co.uk

Rogers de Rin
76 Royal Hospital Rd, Paradise Walk, London SW3 4HN
Tel: 020 7352 9007
Fax: 020 7351 9407
www.rogersderin.co.uk

Sue Norman
Antiquarius, Stand L4, 135 King's Rd, London SW3 4PW
Tel: 020 7352 7217
www.sue-norman.demon.co.uk

Undercurrents
28 Cowper Street, London, EC2A 4AS
Tel: 0207 251 1537
shop@undercurrents.biz
www.undercurrents.biz

Richard Wallis Antiks
Tel: 0208 529 1749
info@richardwallisantiks.co.uk
www.richardwallisantiks.com

CIGARETTE CARDS

Carlton Antiques
Rear No.12, Worcester Road, Malvern, Worcestershire WR14 4QU
Tel: 01684 573 092
www.carlton-antiques.com

COINS & MONEY

British Notes
P.O. Box 257, Sutton, Surrey SM3 9WW
Tel: 0208 641 3224
pamwestbritnotes@aol.com
www.britishnotes.co.uk

Coincraft
44-45 Great Russell Street, London WC1B 3LU
Tel: 0207 636 1188
info@coincraft.com
www.coincraft.com

Colin Narbeth
20 Cecil Court, Leicester Square, London WC2N 4HE
Tel: 0207 379 6975
colin.narbeth@btinternet.com
www.colin-narbeth.com

Intercol
43 Templar's Crescent, Finchley, London N3 3QR
Tel: 020 8349 2207
sales@intercol.co.uk
www.intercol.co.uk

COMICS

Phil's Comics
P.O. Box 3433, Brighton Sussex BN50 9JA
Tel: 01273 673 462
phil@phil-comics.com
www.phil-comics.com

The Book Palace
Bedwardine Road, Crystal Palace, London SE19 3AP
Tel: 020 8768 0022
www.bookpalace.com

COMMEMORATIVE WARE

Hope & Glory
131a Kensington Church Street, London W8 7LP
Tel: 020 7727 8424

Commemorabilia
15 Haroldsleigh Avenue, Crownhill, Plymouth
Tel: 01752 700 795
ron_smith@commemorabilia.co.uk
www.commemorabilia.co.uk

Recollections
5 Royal Arcade, Boscombe, Bournemouth, Dorset BH1 4BT
Tel: 01202 304 441

Royal Commemorative China
Paul Wynton & Joe Spiteri
Tel: 020 8863 0625
Mob: 07930 303 358
royalcommemoratives@hotmail.com

COSTUME & ACCESSORIES

Beyond Retro
110-112 Cheshire Street, London E2 6EJ
Tel: 020 7613 3636
www.beyondretro.com

Cad van Swankster at The Girl Can't Help It
Alfies Antiques Market, Grand Centre Window, Ground Floor, 13-25 Church Street, London NW8 8DT
Tel: 020 7724 8984
Mob: 07958 515 614
sparkle@sparklemoore.com
www.thegirlcanthelpit.com

Decades
20 Lord Street West, Blackburn BB2 1JX
Tel: 01254 693320

Echoes
650a Halifax Road, Eastwood, Todmorden
info@echoes-vintage.co.uk
www.echoes-vintage.co.uk
Tel: 01706 817 505

Fantiques
Tel: 020 8840 4761
paula.raven@ntlworld.com

Kerry Taylor
Unit C25, Parkhall Road Trading Estate, 40 Martell Road, London, SE21 8EN
Tel: 0208 676 4600
www.kerrytaylorauctions.com

Linda Bee
Grays Antiques Market, 1-7 & 58 Davies Street, London W1Y 2LP
Tel/Fax: 020 7629 7034
info@graysantiques.com
www.graysantiques.com

Old Hat
66 Fulham High Street, London SW6 3LQ
Tel: 020 7610 6558

RetroBizarre
25 St Mary's Row, Moseley, Birmingham, B13 8HW
Tel: 0121 442 6389
info@retrobizarre.biz

Rokit
101 Brick Lane, London E1 6SE (and other London locations)
Tel: 0207 375 3864
www.rokit.co.uk

Sparkle Moore at The Girl Can't Help It
Alfies Antiques Market, Grand Centre Window, Ground Floor, 13-25 Church Street, Marylebone, London NW8 8DT
Tel: 020 7724 8984 or 07958 515 614
sparkle@sparklemoore.com
www.thegirlcanthelpit.com

Steptoe's Dog Antique & Vintage Online Store
Tel: 01132 748 494
www.steptoesantiques.co.uk

Vintage Modes
Grays Antiques Market, 1-7 Davies Mews, London W1Y 5AB
Tel: 020 7409 0400
www.vintagemodes.co.uk

Vintage to Vogue
28 Milsom Street, Bath, Avon BA1 1DG
info@vintagetovoguebath.co.uk
www.vintagetovoguebath.co.uk
Tel: 01225 337 323

Wardrobe
51 Upper North Street, Brighton, East Sussex
Tel: 01273 202 201

COSTUME JEWELLERY

Cristobal
26 Church St, London NW8 8EP
Tel: 020 7724 7230
sminers@aol.com
www.cristobal.co.uk

Eclectica
Tel/Fax: 020 7226 5625
liz@eclectica.biz
www.eclectica.biz

Richard Gibbon
neljeweluk@aol.com

Ritzy
7 The Mall Antiques Arcade, 359 Upper Street, London N1 0PD
Tel: 020 7704 0127

William Wain at Antiquarius
Stand J6, Antiquarius, 135 King's Road, London SW3 4PW
Tel: 020 7351 4905
w.wain@btopenworld.com

Crested China
The Crested China Company Highfield, Windmill Hill, Driffield, East Riding of Yorkshire YO25 5YP
Tel: 01377 257042
dt@thecrestedchinacompany.com
www.thecrestedchinacompany.com

DOLLS

Bébés & Jouets
c/o Lochend Post Office, 165 Restalrig Road, Edinburgh EH7 6HW
Tel: 0131 332 5650
bebesjouets@tiscali.co.uk

British Doll Showcase
squibbit@ukonline.co.uk
www.britishdollshowcase.co.uk

Lolli Dollies
8 Athol Terrace, Dover, Kent

Pollyanna
34 High Street, Arundel,
West Sussex
Tel: 01902 885 198 or
07499 903 457

Sandra Fellner
A18-A19 and MB026,
Grays Antique Market
Tel: 020 8946 5613
sandrafellner@blueyonder.co.uk
www.graysantiques.com

Victoriana Dolls
101 Portobello Road,
London W11 2BQ
Tel: 01737 249 525
Fax: 01737 226 254
heather.bond@homecall.co.uk

FIFTIES, SIXTIES & SEVENTIES

Twentieth Century Marks
Whitegates, Rectory Road,
Little Burstead, Near Billericay,
Essex CM12 9TR
Tel: 01474 872 460
info@20thcenturymarks.co.uk
www.20thcenturymarks.co.uk

Design20c
Tel: 01276 512329 /
0794 609 2138
sales@design20c.co.uk

Fragile Design
14-15 The Custard Factory,
Digbeth, Birmingham B9 4AA
Tel: 0121 224 7378
info@fragiledesign.com
www.fragiledesign.com

High Street Retro
39 High Street, Old Town,
Hastings, East Sussex TN34 3ER
Tel: 01424 460 068

InRetrospect
37 Upper St James Street,
Kemptown, Brighton,
East Sussex BN2 1JN
Tel: 01273 609 374

Luna
139 Lower Parliament Street,
Nottingham NG1 1EE
Tel: 0115 924 3267
info@luna-online.co.uk
www.luna-online.co.uk

Manic Attic
Alfie's Antiques Market,
Stand S48-49,
13-25 Church St,
London NW8 8DT
Tel: 020 7723 6105
ianbroughton@hotmail.com
www.alfiesantiques.com

Modern Warehouse
243b Victoria Park Road,
London E9 7HD
Tel: 0208 986 0740 or
07747 758 852
info@themodernwarehouse.com
www.themodernwarehouse.com

Multicoloured Timeslip
eBay Store: multicoloured timeslip
eBay ID: dave65330
Mob: 07971 410 563
dave_a_cameron@hotmail.com

Planet Bazaar
Unit 87, The Stables Market,
Chalk Farm Road,
London NW1 8AH
Tel: 020 7485 6000
info@planetbazaar.co.uk
www.planetbazaar.co.uk

Retrocentre
Tel: 01189 507 224
al@retro-centre.co.uk
www.retro-centre.co.uk

Retropolitan
24 Wells House,
London NW10 6EE
Tel: 07772 280 565
enquiries@retropolitan.co.uk
www.retropolitan.co.uk

FILM & TV

The Prop Store of London
Great House Farm, Chenies,
Rickmansworth, Herts WD3 6EP
Tel: 01494 766 485
steve.lane@propstore.co.uk
www.propstore.co.uk

GLASS

Andrew Lineham Fine Glass
Tel/Fax: 01243 576 241
Mob: 07767 702 722
andrew@antiquecolouredglass.com
www.antiquecolouredglass.com

Antique Glass at Frank Dux Antiques
33 Belvedere, Lansdown Road,
Bath, Avon BA1 5HR
Tel/Fax: 01225 312 367
m.hopkins@antique-glass.co.uk
www.antique-glass.co.uk

Artius Glass
Tel: 07860 822 666
wheeler.ron@talktalk.net
www.artiusglass.co.uk

Cloud Glass
info@cloudglass.com
www.cloudglass.com

Francesca Martire
Stand F131-137, First Floor, 13-25 Alfies Antiques Market, 13
Church St, London NW8 0RH
Tel: 020 7724 4802
www.francescamartire.com

Glass etc
18-22 Rope Walk, Rye,
East Sussex TN31 7NA
Tel: 01797 226 600
andy@decanterman.com
www.decanterman.com

Grimes House Antiques
High Street, Moreton in Marsh,
Gloucestershire GL56 0AT
Tel: 01608 651 029
grimes_house@cix.co.uk
www.cranberryglass.co.uk

Jeanette Hayhurst Fine Glass
32A Kensington Church Street,
London W8 4HA
Tel: 020 7938 1539
www.antiqueglass-london.com

Mum Had That
info@mumhadthat.com
www.mumhadthat.com

Nigel Benson 20th Century Glass
Mob: 07971 859 848
nigelbenson@20thcentury-glass.com
www.20thcentury-glass.com

No Pink Carpet
Tel: 01785 249 802
www.nopinkcarpet.com

Past Caring
76 Essex Road, Islington,
N1 8LT

Pip's Trip
13 Pyne Road, Surbiton,
Surrey KT6 7BN
Tel: 08451 650 274
sales@pips-trip.co.uk
www.pips-trip.co.uk

The Studio Glass Merchant
Tel: 07775 683 961
Tel: 0208 668 2701
info@thestudioglassmerchant.co.uk
www.thestudioglassmerchant.co.uk

KITCHENALIA

Appleby Antiques
Geoffrey Vans' Arcade,
Stand 18, 105-107 Portobello
Road, London W11
Tel/Fax: 01453 753 126
mike@applebyantiques.net
www.applebyantiques.net

Below Stairs of Hungerford
103 High Street, Hungerford,
Berkshire RG17 0NB
Tel: 01488 682 317
Fax: 01488 684294
hofgartner@belowstairs.co.uk
www.belowstairs.co.uk

Jane Wicks Kitchenalia
Country Ways,
Strand Quay, Rye,
East Sussex TN31 7AY
Tel: 01424 713 635
janes_kitchen@hotmail.com

Mechanical Music
Terry & Daphne France
Tel: 01243 265 946
Fax: 01243 779 582

The Talking Machine
30 Watford Way,
London NW4 3AL
Tel: 020 8202 3473
Mob: 07774 103 139
talkingmachine@gramophones.ndirect.co.uk
www.gramophones.ndirect.co.uk

MILITARIA & MEDALS

Jim Bullock Militaria
P.O. Box 217, Romsey,
Hampshire SO51 5XL
Tel: 01794 516 455
jim@jimbullockmilitaria.com
www.jimbullockmilitaria.com

The Old Brigade
10a Harborough Road,
Kingsthorpe,
Northampton NN2 7AZ
Tel: 01604 719 389
mail@theoldbrigade.co.uk
www.theoldbrigade.co.uk

West Street Antiques
63 West Street,
Dorking, Surrey RH4 1BS
Tel: 01306 883 487
weststant@aol.com
www.antiquearmsandarmour.com

MODERN TECHNOLOGY

Junktion
The Old Railway Station,
New Bolingbroke,
Boston, Lincolnshire
Tel: 01205 480068 or
07836 345 491
junktionantiques@hotmail.com

Pepe Tozzo
contact@tozo.co.uk
www.tozzo.co.uk

PAPERWEIGHTS

Sweetbriar Gallery Ltd
56 Watergate Street
Chester, Cheshire, CH1 2LA
Tel: 01244 329249
sales@sweetbriar.co.uk
www.sweetbriar.co.uk

PENS & WRITING

Battersea Pen Home
PO Box 6128,
Epping CM16 4CG
Tel: 01992 578 885
Fax: 01992 578 485
orders@penhome.co.uk
www.penhome.co.uk

Hans' Vintage Pens
Tel: 01323 765 398 or
07850 771 183
hseiringer@aol.com
www.hanspens.com

Henry The Pen Man
Admiral Vernon Antiques
Market, 141-149 Portobello Rd,
London W11
Tel: 020 8530 3277
Saturdays only
www.henrysimpole.com

PLASTICS & BAKELITE

Paola & Iaia
Unit S057, Alfies Antiques
Market, 13-25 Church Street,
London NW8 8DT
Tel: 07751 084 135
paola_iaia_london@yahoo.com
www.alfiesantiques.com

POSTERS

At The Movies
info@atthemovies.co.uk
www.atthemovies.co.uk

Barclay Samson
By appointment only
Tel: 020 7731 8012
richard@barclaysamson.com
www.barclaysamson.com**DOD
O**
Alfies Antiques Market,
Stand F071,13-25 Church
Street, Marylebone, London
NW8 8DT
Tel: 020 7706 1545
www.dodoposters.com

Limelight Movie Art
135 King's Road, London
Tel: 0207 751 5584
sales@limelightmovieart.com
www.limelightmovieart.com

The Reelposter Gallery
72 Westbourne Grove,
London W2 5SH
Tel: 020 7727 4488
info@reelposter.com
www.reelposter.com

Rennies
47 The Old High Street,
Folkestone, Kent CT20 2RN
Tel: 01303 242427
info@rennart.co.uk
www.rennart.co.uk

POWDER COMPACTS

Sara Hughes Vintage Compacts, Antiques & Collectables
Mob: 0775 9697 108
sara@sneak.freeserve.co.uk

Mary & Geoff Turvil
Vintage Compacts, Small
Antiques & Collectables
Tel: 01730 260 730
mary.turvil@virgin.net
www.glitzguru.com

Wildewear
Tel: 01395 577 966

RADIOS

On the Air Ltd
The Vintage Technology Centre,
Hawarden, Deeside CH5 3DN
Tel/Fax: 01244 530 300
info@vintageradio.co.uk
www.vintageradio.co.uk

Junktion
The Old Railway Station,
New Bolingbroke,
Boston, Lincolnshire
Tel: 01205 480068 or
07836 345 491
junktionantiques@hotmail.com

Philip Knighton
1c South Street, Wellington,
Somerset TA21 8NS
Tel: 01823 661 618
philip.knighton@btconnect.com

ROCK & POP

Beanos
Middle Street, Croydon,
Surrey CR0 1RE
Tel: 0208 680 1202
shop@beanos.co.uk
www.beanos.co.uk

Briggs Rock & Pop Memorabilia
Loudwater House, London
Road, Loudwater, High
Wycombe, Buckinghamshire
Tel: 01494 436 644
music@usebriggs.com
www.usebriggs.com

Collectors Corner
P.O. Box 8, Congleton, Cheshire,
CW12 4GD
Tel: 01260 270 429
dave.popcorner@ukonline.co.uk

More Than Music
PO Box 2809, Eastbourne,
East Sussex BN21 2EA
Tel: 01323 649 778
morethnmus@aol.com
www.mtmglobal.com

Spinna Disc Records
2b Union Street, Aldershot,
Hampshire GU11 1EG
Tel: 01252 327 261
www.spinnadiscrecords.com

Sweet Memories Vinyl Records
101 Fratton Road, Portsmouth,
Hampshire, PO1 5AH
Tel: 02392 837730
www.vinylrecords.co.uk

Tracks
PO Box 117, Chorley,
Lancashire PR6 0UU
Tel: 01257 269726
sales@tracks.co.uk
www.tracks.co.uk

SCIENTIFIC, TECHNICAL, OPTICAL & PRECISION INSTRUMENTS

Arthur Middleton Antiques
Tel: 020 7281 8445
Mob: 07887 481 102
arthur@antique-globes.com
www.antique-globes.com

Branksome Antiques
370 Poole Rd, Branksome,
Dorset BH12 1AW
Tel: 01202 763 324

Charles Tomlinson
Tel: 01244 318 395
charlestomlinson@tiscali.co.uk

SMOKING MEMORABILIA

Richard Ball
collector@lighter.co.uk
www.lighter.co.uk

Tom Clarke
Admiral Vernon Antiques
Centre, Unit 36, Portobello Rd,
London W11
Tel: 020 8802 8936

SPORTING MEMORABILIA

Manfred Schotten
109 High Street, Burford,
Oxfordshire OX18 4RH
Tel: 01993 822 302
www.schotten.com

Old Troon Sporting Antiques
49 Ayr St, Troon, Ayrshire,
Scotland KA106EB
Tel: 01292 311 822
www.golf-art.co.uk

Rhod McEwan
Glengarden, Ballater,
Aberdeenshire AB35 5UB
Tel: 01339 755 429
teeoff@rhodmcewan.com
www.rhodmcewan.com

Simon Brett
Creswyke House,
Moreton-in-Marsh GL56 0LH
Tel: 01608 650 751

Warboys Antiques
St. Ives, Cambridgeshire
Tel: 01480 463891
Mob: 07831 274774
johnlambden@
sportingantiques.co.uk
www.sportingantiques.co.uk

Graham Budd
P.O. Box 47519,
London N14 6XD
Tel: 020 8366 2525
gb@grahambuddauctions.co.uk
www.grahambuddauctions.co.uk

TELEPHONES

Candlestick & Bakelite
P.O. Box 308, Orpington,
Kent BR5 1TB
Tel: 0208 467 3743
candlestick.bakelite@mac.com
www.candlestickandbakelite
.co.uk

Retrobrick (Mobile Phones)
www.retrobrick.co.uk

Telephone Lines
304 High Street, Cheltenham,
Gloucestershire GL50 3JF
Tel: 01242 583 699
www.telephonelines.net

TOYS & GAMES

Automatomania
414 The Field of Dreams,
Findhorn, Forres, Moray IV36
3TA, Scotland
Tel: 01309 691 692
Mob: 07790 71 90 97
www.automatomania.com

Collectors Old Toy Shop & Antiques
89 Northgate, Halifax,
West Yorkshire HX11XF
Tel: 01422 360 434
collectorsoldtoy@aol.com

Colin Baddiel
B24-B25, Grays Antique Market, 1-7 Davies Mews, London W1K 5AB
Tel: 020 7408 1239
toychemcol@hotmail.com

Andrew Clark Models
Unit 113, Baildon Mills, Northgate, Baildon, Shipley BD17 6JX
Tel: 01274 594 552
www.andrewclarkmodels.com

Dave's Classic Toys
Antiques Centre Gloucester, 1 Severn Road, The Historic Docks, Gloucester
Tel: 01452 529 716

Donay Games
Tel: 01444 416 412
info@donaygames.co.uk
www.donaygames.com

Garrick Coleman
75 Portobello Rd, London W11 2QB
Tel: 020 7937 5524
www.antiquechess.co.uk

Gerard Haley
Hippins Farm, Black Shawhead, nr Hebden Bridge, Yorkshire
Tel: 01422 842 484
gedhaley@yahoo.co.uk

Hugo Lee-Jones
Tel: 01227 375 375
Mob: 07941 187 2027
electroniccollectables@hotmail.com

Intercol (Playing Cards)
43 Templars Crescent, Finchley, London N3 3QR
Tel: 020 8349 2207
Mob: 077 68 292 066
www.intercol.co.uk

John & Simon Haley
89 Northgate, North Bridge, Halifax, Yorkshire
Tel: 01422 360 434
collectorsoldtoys@aol.com
www.collectorsoldtoyshop.com

Karl Flaherty Collectables
Tel: 02476 445 627
kfcollectables@aol.com

The Magic Toybox
210 Havant Road, Drayton, Portsmouth
Tel: 02392 221 307
www.magictoybox.co.uk

Metropolis Toys
31 Derby Street, Burton on Trent, Staffordshire
Tel: 01283 740 400
chris@metropolistoys.co.uk
www.metropolistoys.co.uk

Mike Delaney
Tel: 01993 840 064 or 07979 910 760
mail@vintagehornby.co.uk
www.vintagehornby.co.uk

Mimififi
27 Pembridge Road, Notting Hill Gate, London W11
Tel: 0207 243 3154
www.mimififi.com

Sue Pearson Dolls & Teddy Bears
147 High Street, Lewes, East Sussex BN7 1XT
Tel: 01273 472677
www.suepearson.co.uk

Teddy Bears of Witney
99 High Street, Witney, Oxfordshire OX28 6HY
Tel: 01993 706616
www.teddybears.co.uk

Toydreams
sales@toydreams.co.uk
www.toydreams.co.uk

The Vintage Toy & Train Shop
Sidmouth Antiques & Collectors' Centre, All Saints' Road, Sidmouth EX10 8ES
Tel: 01395 512 588

Vintage Toy Box
contact@vintagetoybox.co.uk
www.vintagetoybox.co.uk

Wheels of Steel (Trains)
Gray's Mews Antiques Market, B10-B11, 58 Davies Street, London W1K 5LP
Tel: 020 7629 2813
wheelsofsteel@grays.clara.net
www.graysantiques.com

WATCHES

Kleanthous Antiques
144 Portobello Road, London W11 2DZ
Tel: 020 7727 3649
antiques@kleanthous.com
www.kleanthous.com

70s Watches
graham@70s-watches.com
Tel: 01603 741222
www.70s-watches.com

The Watch Gallery
1129 Fulham Road, London SW3 6RT
Tel: 020 7581 3239
www.thewatchgallery.co.uk

INDEX TO ADVERTISERS

The following list of general antiques and collectables centres, shops and markets has been organised by region. Any owner who would like to be listed in our next edition, space permitting, or who wishes to update their contact information, should email info@millers.uk.com.

LONDON

Alfie's Antiques Market
13-25 Church St, NW8 8DT
Tel: 020 7723 6066
www.alfiesantiques.com
(Closed Monday)

Antiquarius
131-141 King's Road, SW3 5EB
Tel: 020 7823 3900
www.antiquarius.co.uk

Bermondsey Market
Crossing of Long Lane & Bermondsey St, London SE1
Tel: 020 7351 5353
Every Friday morning from 5am

Camden Passage Antiques Market
Camden Passage, Angel, Islington N1
(Wednesday & Saturday mornings)
www.camdenpassageislington.co.uk

Covent Garden Antiques Market
Jubilee Hall, Southampton Street, Covent Garden WC2
Tel: 0207 240 7405
(Mondays from 6am)

Gray's Antiques Market
58 Davies Streets & 1-7 Davies Mews, London W1K 5AB
Tel: 0207 629 7034
www.graysantiques.com

Kensington Antiques Centre
58-60 Kensington Church Street W8 4DB
Tel: 0207 376 0425

Northcote Road Antiques Market
155a Northcote Road, Battersea SW11 6QB
Tel: 0207 228 6850
www.spectrumsoft.net/nam.htm

Palmers Green Antiques Centre
472 Green Lanes, Palmers Green N13 5PA
Tel: 0208 350 0878

Past Caring
76 Essex Road, N1 8LT
(Opens 12pm)

Portobello Rd Market
Portobello Rd, W11
Every Saturday from 6am
www.portobelloroad.co.uk

Spitalfields Antiques Market
Lamb Street, Commercial Street, E1
Tel: 0207 240 7405
(Thursdays from 7am)

BEDFORDSHIRE

Ampthill Antiques Emporium
6 Bedford Street, Ampthill, Bedfordshire MK45 2NB
Tel: 01525 402131
www.ampthillantiquesemporium.com

Woburn Abbey Antiques Centre
Woburn Abbey, Woburn, WK17 9WA
Tel: 01525 292 118
www.woburnantiques.co.uk

BERKSHIRE

Great Grooms at Hungerford
Riverside House, Charnham St, Hungerford, RG17 0EP
Tel: 01488 682 314
www.greatgrooms.co.uk

Stables Antiques Centre
1a Merchant Place (off Friar Street), Reading, RG1 1DT
Tel: 01189 590 290

BUCKINGHAMSHIRE

Jackdaw Antiques Centre
25 West Street, Marlow SL7 2LS
Tel: 01628 898 285

Marlow Antiques Centre
35 Station Road, Marlow SL7 1NW
Tel: 01628 473 223

CAMBRIDGESHIRE

Cambridge Antiques Centre
206 Mill Road, Cambridge CB1 3NF
Tel: 01223 247 324

Waterside Antiques Centre
The Wharf, Ely CB7 4AU
Tel: 01353 667 066
www.ely.org.uk/waterside.html

DERBYSHIRE

Alfreton Antique Centre
11 King Street, Alfreton DE55 7AF
Tel: 01773 520 781
www.alfretonantiquescentre.com

Bakewell Antiques & Works of Art
King Street, Bakewell DE45 1DZ
Tel: 01629 812 496

Heanor Antiques Centre
1-3 Ilkeston Rd, Heanor, Derbyshire
Tel: 01773 531 181
www.heanorantiquescentre.co.uk

Matlock Antiques & Collectables
7 Dale Road, Matlock DE4 3LT
Tel: 01629 760 808

DEVON

Quay Centre
Topsham, Nr Exeter EX3 0JA
Tel: 01392 874 006
www.quayantiques.com

ESSEX

Debden Antiques
Elder Street, Debden, Saffron Walden CB11 3JY
Tel: 01799 543 007
www.debden-antiques.co.uk

GLOUCESTERSHIRE

Gloucester Antiques Centre
1 Severn Road, The Historic Docks, Gloucester GL1 2LE
Tel: 01452 529 716
www.gacl.co.uk

Church Street Antiques Centre
3-4 Church Street, Stow-on-the-Wold, GL54 1BB
Tel: 01451 870 186

Durham House Antiques
Sheep Street, Stow-on-the-Wold GL54 1AA
Tel: 01451 870 404
www.durhamhousegb.com

Top Banana Antiques Mall
1 New Church Street, Tetbury GL8 8DS
Tel: 0871 288 1102
www.topbananaantiques.com

HAMPSHIRE

Dolphin Quay Antique Centre
Queen Street, Emsworth PO10 7BU
Tel: 01243 379 994

Lymington Antiques Centre
76 High Street, Lymngton SO41 9AL
Tel: 01590 670 934

Squirrel Collectors Centre
9 New Street, Basingstoke RG21 1DE
Tel: 01256 464 885
antiques@onmail.co.uk

HEREFORDSHIRE

Hereford Antique Centre
128 Widemarsh Street, Hereford HR4 9HN
Tel: 01432 266242

HERTFORDSHIRE

By George Antique Centre
23 George Street, St Albans AL3 4ES
Tel: 01727 853 032

Riverside Antiques Centre
The Maltings, Station Road, Sawbridgeworth CM21 9JX
Tel: 01279 600 985

IRELAND

Archives Antiques Centre
88 Donegall Pass, Belfast, County Antrim BT7 1BX
Tel: 02890 232383

Powerscourt Centre
59 South William Street Dublin 2
Tel: (+353) (0)1 6717000

KENT

Burgate Antiques Centre
23A Palace Street,
Canterbury CT1 2DZ
Tel: 01227 456 600

Castle Antiques
1 London Road,
Westerham TN16 1BB
Tel: 01959 562 492

Copperfields Antiques & Crafts Centre
Spital Street, Dartford DA9 2DE
Tel: 01322 281 445

Nightingales
89-91 High Street, West
Wickham BR4 0LS
Tel: 0208 777 0335

Otford Antiques and Collectors Centre
26-28 High St,
Otford TN15 9DF
Tel: 01959 522 025
www.otfordantiques.co.uk

Tenterden Antiques Centre
66-66A High Street,
Tenterden TN30 6AU
Tel: 01580 765 655

LANCASHIRE

The Antiques & Decorative Design Centre
56 Garstang Road,
Preston PR1 1NA
Tel: 01772 882 078

GB Antiques Centre
Leisure Park, Wyresdale Road,
Lancaster LA1 3LA
Tel: 01524 844 734
www.gbantiquescentre.com

Heskin Hall Antiques
Heskin Hall, Wood Lane, Heskin,
Chorley PR7 5PA
Tel: 01257 452 044
www.heskinhallantiques.co.uk

Kingsmill Antiques Centre
Queen Street, Harle Syke,
Burnley BB10 2HX
Tel: 01282 431 953
www.kingsmill.demon.co.uk

LINCOLNSHIRE

Hemswell Antiques Centre
Caenby Corner Estate,
Hemswell Cliff,
Gainsborough DN21 5TJ
Tel: 01427 668 389
www.hemswell-antiques.com

St Martins Antiques Centre
23a High Street, St Martins,
Stamford PE9 2LF
Tel: 01780 481 158
www.st-martins-antiques.co.uk

NORFOLK

Tombland Antiques Centre
AugustineSteward House, 14
Tombland, Norwich NR3 1HF
Tel: 01603 761 906

Old Granary Antiques Centre
King Staithe Lane,
King's Lynn PE30 1LZ
Tel: 01553 775509

NORTHAMPTONSHIRE

Brackley Antique Cellar
Drayman's Walk,
Brackley NN13 6BE
Tel: 01280 841 841

Magpies Antiques & Collectables Centre
1 East Grove,
Rushden NN10 0AP
Tel: 01933 411 404

NOTTINGHAMSHIRE

Castlegate Antiques Centre
55 Castlegate,
Newark NG24 1BE
Tel: 01933 411 404

Newark Antiques Centre
Regent House, Lombard Street,
Newark NG24 1XP
Tel: 01636 605 504

Occleshaw Antiques Centre
11 Mansfield Road, Edwinstowe
NG21 9NL
Tel: 01623 825 370

Top Hat Antiques Centre
70-72 Derby Road,
Nottingham NG1 5FD
Tel: 0115 941 9143

OXFORDSHIRE

Deddington Antiques Centre
Laurel House, Market Place,
Bull Ring, Deddington,
Nr Banbury OX15 0TT
Tel: 01869 338 968

Lamb Arcade Antique Centre
High Street,
Wallingford OX10 0BX
Tel: 01491 835 166
www.thelambarcade.co.uk

The Quiet Woman Antiques Centre
Southcombe,
Chipping Norton OX7 5QH
Tel: 01608 646 262

The Swan Antiques Centre
High Street Tetsworth, Nr Thame
OX9 7AB
Tel: 01844 281777
www.theswan.co.uk

SCOTLAND

Now and Then
9 West Crosscauseway,
Edinburgh EH8 9JW
Tel: 0131 668 2927
www.oldtoysandantiques.co.uk

Rait Village Antiques Centre
Rait, Perthshire PH2 7RT

Scottish Antiques & Arts Centre
Abernyte, Perthshire PH14 9SJ
Tel: 01828 686 401
www.scottish-antiques.com

The Peebles Antiques Centre
Innerleithen Road,
Peebles EH45 8BA
Tel: 01721 724666

SHROPSHIRE

Shrewsbury Antiques Market
Frankwell Quay Warehouse,
Shrewsbury SY3 8LG
Tel: 01743 350 916

Stretton Antiques Market
Sandford Avenue, Church
Stretton SY6 6BH
Tel: 01694 723 718

SOMERSET

Assembly Antiques
6 Saville Row, Bath BA1 2QP
Tel: 01225 448 488

Bath Antiques Market
Guinea Lane (off Landsdown
Road), Bath BA1 5NB
Tel: 07787 527 527

Bartlett St Antiques Centre
5-10 Bartlett St, Bath BA1 2QZ
Tel: 01225 466689
Monday to Saturday (excluding
Wednesday)

Old Bank Antiques Centre
14-17 & 20 Walcot Buildings,
London Rd, Bath BA1 6AD.
Tel: 01225 469282 / 338818

STAFFORDSHIRE

Compton Mill Antique Emporium
Compton Mill, Compton, Leek
Tel: 01538 373396

Curborough Hall Antiques
Watery Lane, Lichfield
Tel: 01543 417100

Lion Antiques Centre
8 Market Place, Uttoxeter (opp.
War Memorial)
Tel: 01889 567717

Potteries Antique Centre
271 Waterloo Rd, Cobridge,
Stoke-on-Trent ST6 3HR
Tel: 01782 201 455
www.potteriesantiquecentre.com

Rugeley Antique Centre
161 Main Road, Brereton,
Nr Rugeley WS15 1DX
Tel: 01889 577 166

SUFFOLK

Badgers Den Antique & Collectables Centre
6 Sun Lane, off High Street,
Newmarket
Tel: 01638 666 676

Meltord Antiques Warehouse
Hall Street, Long Melford
Tel: 01787 379 638

Snape Maltings Antiques & Collectors Centre
Saxmundham IP17 1SR
Tel: 01728 688038

SURREY

Kingston Antiques Centre
29 London Road, Kingston-
upon-Thames KT2 6ND
Tel: 0208 549 2004
www.kingstonantiquescentre
.co.uk

Pilgrims Antiques Centre
7 West Street,
Dorking, RH4 1BL
Tel: 01306 875028

Serendipity Antiques Centre
7 Petworth Road,
Haslemere GU27 2JB
Tel: 01428 642 682

SUSSEX (EAST)

The Brighton Lanes Antiques Centre
12 Meeting House Lane,
Brighton BN1 1HB
Tel: 01273 823 121

Brighton Flea Market
31a Upper St. James's Street,
Brighton BN2 1JN
Tel: 01273 624 006
www.brightonlanesantiques.co.uk

Church Hill Antiques Centre
6 Station Street,
Lewes BN7 2DA
Tel: 01273 474 842

The Emporium Antiques Centre Too
24 High Street, Lewes BN7 2LU
Tel: 01273 477 979

Lewes Antiques Centre
20 Cliffe High Street,
Lewes BN7 2AH
Tel: 01273 476 148

Snooper's Paradise
7-8 Kensington Gardens,
Brighton BN1 4AL
Tel: 01273 602558
www.northlaine.co.uk/snooperparadise/snoopers.html

SUSSEX (WEST)

Antique & Collectors Market
Old Orchard Building, Old House, Adversane,
Nr Billingshurst RH14 9JJ
Tel: 01403 782 186

Arundel Antiques Centre
6 High Street,
Arundel BN18 9AB
Tel: 01903 884 164
www.arundelantiques.co.uk

WALES

Afonwen Antiques
Afonwen,
nr Caerwys, nr Mold,
Flintshire CH7 5UB
Tel: 01352 720 965

Offa's Dyke Antiques Centre
4 High Street, Knighton,
Powys LD7 1AT
Tel: 01547 528 635

Second Chance Antiques & Collectables Centre
Ala Road, Pwlheli,
Gwynedd LL53 5BL
Tel: 01758 612 210

WARWICKSHIRE

Stratford-upon-Avon Antique Centre
59-60 Ely St,
Stratford-upon-Avon CV37 6LN
Tel: 01789 204180

WEST MIDLANDS

Birmingham Antiques Centre
1407 Pershore Road,
Stirchley,
Birmingham B30 2JR
Tel: 0121 459 4587

WORCESTERSHIRE

Worcester Antiques Centre
Reindeer Court, Mealcheapen Street, Worcester WR1 4DF
Tel: 01905 610 680

YORKSHIRE

The Antiques Centre York
Allenby House, 41 Stonegate,
York YO1 8AW
Tel: 01904 635 888
www.theantiquescentreyork.com

Cavendish Antique & Collectors Centre
44 Stonegate, York YO1 8AS
Tel: 01904 621 666

The Collectors' Centre
35 St Nicholas Cliff,
Scarborough YO11 2ES
Tel: 01723 365 221
www.collectors.demon.co.uk

The Ginnel Antiques Centre
Off Parliament St, Harrogate,
North Yorkshire HG1 2RB
Tel: 01423 508 857
www.theginnel.co.uk

Stonegate Antiques Centre
41 Stonegate, York YO1 8AW
Tel: 01904 613 888
www.antiquescentreyorkeshop.co.uk

DIRECTORY OF AUCTIONEERS

The following list of auctioneers who conduct regular sales by auction is organised by region. Any auctioneer who would like to be listed in the our next edition, space permitting, or to update their contact information, should email info@millers.uk.com.

LONDON

Bloomsbury Auctions
Bloomsbury House,
24 Maddox Street W1 S1PP
Tel: 020 7495 9494
www.bloomsburyauctions.com

Bonhams
101 New Bond Street,
W1S 1SR
Tel: 020 7629 6602
www.bonhams.com

Christies (South Kensington)
85 Old Brompton Road,
SW7 3LD
Tel: 020 7581 7611
www.christies.com

Chiswick Auctions
1 Colville Road,
Chiswick W3 8BL
Tel: 0208 992 4442
www.chiswickauctions.co.uk

Criterion Auctioneers
53 Essex Road,
Islington N1 2SF
Tel: 0207 359 5707
41-47 Chatfield Road,
Wandsworth, SW11 3SE
Tel: 0207 228 5563
www.criterionauctions.co.uk

Graham Budd Auctions
P.O. Box 47519, N14 6XD
Tel: 0208 366 2525
www.grahambuddauctions.co.uk

Lots Road Auctions
71 Lots Road,
Chelsea SW10 0RN
Tel: 0207 376 6800
www.lotsroad.com

Rosebery's
74-76 Knights Hill,
West Norwood, SE27 0JD
Tel: 020 8761 2522
www.roseberys.co.uk

Sotheby's
34-35 New Bond Street,
W1A 2AA
Tel: 0207 293 5000
www.sothebys.com

BEDFORDSHIRE

W. & H. Peacock
The Auction Centre,
26 Newnham St,
Bedford MK40 3JR
Tel: 01234 266366
Fax: 01234 269082
www.peacockauction.co.uk

BERKSHIRE

Dreweatts
Donnington Priory, Donnington,
Nr. Newbury RG142JE
Tel: 01635 553553
donnington@dnfa.com
www.dnfa.com

Special Auction Services
First Floor, Kennetholme, Bath Road, Midgham,
Nr Reading RG7 5UX
Tel: 0118 971 2949
www.specialauctionservices.com

BUCKINGHAMSHIRE

Amersham Auction Rooms
125 Station Road,
Amersham HP7 0AH
Tel: 08700 460606
www.amershamauctionrooms.co.uk

CAMBRIDGESHIRE

Cheffins
Clifton House, 1&2 Clifton Road, Cambridge CB1 7EA
Tel: 01223 213 343
www.cheffins.co.uk

CHANNEL ISLANDS

Martel Maides Ltd.
The Old Bank,
29 High Street GY1 2JX
Tel: 01481 713463
www.martelmaides.co.uk

CHESHIRE

Bonhams (Chester)
New House, 150 Christleton Road, Chester CH3 5TD
Tel: 01244 313 936
www.bonhams.com

Bob Gowland International Golf Auctions
The Stables, Claim Farm, Manley Rd Frodsham, WA6 6HT
Tel: 01928 740668
bob@internationalgolfauctions.com

CLEVELAND

Vectis Auctioneers (Toys & Dolls)
Fleck Way Thornaby,
Stockton-on-Tees TS17 9JZ
Tel: 01642 750616
www.vectis.co.uk

CORNWALL

W. H. Lane & Son
Jubilee House, Queen Street,
Penzance TR18 4DF
Tel: 01736 361447
www.whlaneauctioneersandvaluers.co.uk

David Lay FRICS
The Penzance Auction House,
Alverton, Penzance TR18 4RE
Tel: 01736 361414
www.davidlay.co.uk

CUMBRIA

Mitchells Fine Art Auctioneers
Station Road, Cockermouth
CA13 9PZ
Tel: 01900 827800
www.mitchellsfineart.com

Penrith Farmers' & Kidds
Skirsgill Saleroom, Skirsgill,
Penrith CA11 0DN
Tel: 01768 890781
www.pfandk.co.uk

DERBYSHIRE

Bamfords Ltd
The Old Picture Palace,
133 Dale Road,
Matlock DE4 3LT
Tel: 01629 574460
bamfords-www.bamfords-auctions.co.uk

DEVON

Bearne's
St Edmund's Court,
Okehampton Street,
Exeter EX41LX
Tel: 01392 207000
www.bearnes.co.uk

Bonhams
Dowell St, Honiton,
Devon EX14 1LX
Tel: 01404 41872
www.bonhams.com

DORSET

Charterhouse
The Long Street Salerooms,
Sherborne, Dorset DT9 3BS
Tel: 01935 812277
www.charterhouse-auctions.co.uk

HY Duke & Sons
Weymouth Avenue, Dorchester,
Dorset DT1 1QS
Tel: 01305 265080
www.dukes-auctions.com

Onslows
The Coach House, Manor Road,
Stourpaine DT11 8TQ
Tel: 01258 488 838
www.onslows.co.uk

Semley Auctioneers
Station Rd, Semley,
Nr Shaftesbury SP7 9AN
Tel: 01747 855122
www.semleyauctioneers.com

ESSEX

Sworder & Sons
14 Cambridge Road,
Stansted Mountfitchet
CM24 8DE
Tel: 01279 817778
www.sworder.co.uk

GLOUCESTERSHIRE

Simon Chorley
Prinknash Abbey Park GL4 8EX
Tel: 01452 344499
www.simonchorley.com

Dreweatt's
St. John's Place,
Apsley Road, Clifton,
Bristol BS8 2ST
Tel: 0117 973 7201
www.dnfa.com/bristol

Cotswold Auction Co.
Chapel Walk, Cheltenham,
Gloucestershire GL50 3DS
Tel: 01242 256363
www.cotswoldauction.co.uk

Mallams Fine Art Auctioneers & Valuers
26 Grosvenor Street,
Cheltenham GL52 2SG
Tel: 01242 235712
www.mallams.co.uk

Moore, Allen & Innocent
The Norcote Salerooms,
Burford Road, Norcote,
Nr Cirencester, GL7 5RH
Tel: 01285 646 050
www.mooreallen.co.uk

HAMPSHIRE

Andrew Smith & Son
The Auction Rooms,
Manor Farm, Itchen Stoke,
Nr Winchester SO24 0QT
Tel: 01962 735988
www.andrewsmithandson.com

Jacobs & Hunt Fine Art Auctioneers
Lavant Street,
Petersfield GU32 3EF
Tel: 01730 233 933
www.jacobsandhunt.com

HEREFORDSHIRE

Brightwells
The Fine Art Saleroom,
Easters Court,
Leominster HR6 0DE
Tel: 01568 611122
www.brightwells.com

HERTFORDSHIRE

Tring Market Auctions
Brook Street,
Tring HP23 5EF
Tel: 01442 826 446
www.tringmarketauctions.co.uk

ISLE OF WIGHT

Shanklin Auction Rooms
79 Regent Street,
Shanklin, PO37 7AP
Tel: 01983 863441
www.shanklinauctionrooms.co.uk

KENT

Dreweatts (Office)
10 Mount Ephraim,
Tunbridge Wells TN4 8AS
Tel: 01892 544500
www.dnfa.com/tunbridgewells

Gorringes (Office)
85 Mount Pleasant Road,
Tunbridge Wells TN2 5TD
Tel: 01892 619 670
www.gorringes.co.uk

Humberts Fine Art
The Estate Office,
Stone Street,
Cranbrook TN17 3HD
Tel: 01580 713828

Lambert & Foster
102 High Street,
Tenterden TN30 6HT
Tel: 01580 762083
www.lambertandfoster.co.uk

LANCASHIRE

Capes Dunn & Co.
38 Charles St,
Manchester M17DB
Tel: 0161 273 1911
Fax: 0161 273 3474
www.capesdunn.com

LEICESTERSHIRE

Gilding's
64 Roman Way, Market
Harborough, LE16 7PQ
Tel: 01858 410414
www.gildings.co.uk

Tennants Co.
The Auction Centre, Leyburn,
North Yorkshire, DL8 5SG
Tel: 01969 623 780
www.tennants.co.uk

LINCOLNSHIRE

Golding Young & Co.
Old Wharf Rd, Grantham,
Lincolnshire NG31 7AA
Tel: 01476 565118
www.goldingyoung.com

MERSEYSIDE

Cato, Crane & Co
6 Stanhope St, Liverpool L8 5RE
Tel: 0151 709 5559
www.cato-crane.co.uk

NORFOLK

T. W. Gaze & Son
Diss Auction Rooms, Roydon
Road, Diss IP22 4LN
Tel: 01379 650306
www.twgaze.com

Keys Auctioneers & Valuers
Aylsham Salerooms, Palmers
Lane,Aylsham, NR11 6JA
Tel: 01263 733195

Knights Sporting Auctions
Cuckoo Cottage, Town Green,
Alby, Norwich NR11 7PR
Tel: 01263 768488
www.knights.co.uk

NOTTINGHAMSHIRE

Mellors & Kirk
Gregory Street,
Nottingham NG7 2NL
Tel: 0115 9790 000
www.mellorsandkirk.com

Neales of Nottingham
192 Mansfield Road,
Nottingham NG1 3HU
Tel: 0115 962 4141
www.dnfa.com/nottingham

Vennett-Smith Auctioneers and Valuers
11 Nottingham Road, Gotham,
Nottingham NG11 0HE
Tel: 0115 9830541
www.vennett-smith.com

OXFORDSHIRE

Mallams
Dunmore Court, Wootton Road,
Abingdon, OX13 6BH
Tel: 01235 462840
www.mallams.co.uk

Mallams
Bocardo House,
24a St. Michaels Street,
Oxford OX1 2EB
Tel: 01865 241358
www.mallams.co.uk

Soames Country Auctions
Pinnocks Farm Estate,
Northmoor, Witney OX8 1AY
Tel: 01865 300626
www.soamesauctioneers.co.uk

SHROPSHIRE

Halls Fine Art
Welsh Bridge,
Shrewsbury SY3 8LA
Tel: 01743 284 777
www.hallsestateagents.co.uk

Walker Barnett & Hill
Cosford Auction Rooms,
Long Lane, Cosford, TF11 8PJ
Tel: 01902 375555
wbhauctions@lineone.net

Mullock Madeley
The Old Shippon,
Wall-under-Heywood,
Nr Church Stretton SY6 7DS
Tel: 01694 771771
www.mullocksauctions.co.uk

SOMERSET

Clevedon Salerooms
The Auction Centre,
Kenn Road, Kenn, Clevedon,
North Somerset BS21 6TT
Tel: 01934 830111
www.clevedon-salerooms.com

Gardiner Houlgate
9 Leafield Way, Corsham,
Bath SN13 9SW
Tel: 01225 812912
www.gardinerhoulgate.co.uk

Lawrence's Fine Art Auctioneers Ltd
South Street,
Crewkerne, TA18 8AB
Tel: 01460 73041
www.lawrences.co.uk

STAFFORDSHIRE

Potteries Specialist Auctions
271 Waterloo Road,
Cobridge,
Stoke-on-Trent, ST6 3HR
Tel: 01782 286622
www.potteriesauctions.com

Richard Winterton
Lichfield Auction Centre
Fradley, Lichfield, WS13 8NF
Tel: 01543 263256

Wintertons
Uttoxeter Auction Centre, Short
Street, Uttoxeter,
Staffordshire ST14 7LH
www.wintertons.co.uk

SUFFOLK

Diamond Mills
117 Hamilton Road,
Felixstowe IP11 7BL
Tel:01394 671 791
www.diamondmills.co.uk

Neal Sons & Fletcher
26 Church St,
Woodbridge IP12 1DP
Tel: 01394 382263
www.nsf.co.uk

SURREY

Barbers
The Mayford Centre,
Smarts Heath Road,
Woking GU22 0PP
Tel: 01483 728939

Clarke Gammon
4 Quarry Street,
Guildford GU1 3TY
Tel: 01483 880900
www.clarkegammon.co.uk

Ewbank Auctioneers
The Burnt Common Auction
Rooms,
London Rd, Send,
Woking GU23 7LN
Tel: 01483 223101
www.ewbankauctions.co.uk

Dreweatt Neate (Formerly Hamptons)
Baverstock House,
93 High Street,
Godalming GU7 1AL
Tel: 01483 423 567
www.dnfa.com/godalming

SUSSEX (EAST)

Burstow & Hewett
Lower Lake, Battle TN33 0AT
Tel: 01424 772 374
www.burstowandhewett.co.uk

Dreweatt Neate (Eastbourne)
46-50 South St,
Eastbourn BN21 4XB,
Tel: 01323 410419
www.dnfa.com

Gorringes
Terminus Road,
Bexhill-on-Sea TN39 3LR
Tel: 01424 212994
www.gorringes.co.uk

Gorringes
15 North Street,
Lewes BN7 2PD
Tel: 01273 472503
www.gorringes.co.uk

Raymond P. Inman
The Auction Galleries,
98A Coleridge Street,
Hove BN3 5AA
Tel: 01273 774777
www.invaluable.com/
raymondinman

Wallis & Wallis
West St Auction Galleries,
Lewes BN7 2NJ
Tel: 01273 480208
www.wallisandwallis.co.uk

TYNE & WEAR

Anderson and Garland
Anderson House, Crispin Court,
Newbiggin Lane, Westerhope,
Newcastle upon Tyne NE5 1BF
Tel: 0191 430 3000
www.andersonandgarland.com

Corbitts
5 Mosley St,
Newcastle-upon-Tyne NE1 1YE
Tel: 0191 232 7268
www.corbitts.com

WARWICKSHIRE

Locke & England
18 Guy Street,
Leamington Spa CV32 4RT
Tel: 01926 889100
www.leauction.co.uk

WEST MIDLANDS

Bonhams
Knowle, The Old House,
Station Road, Knowle,
Solihull B93 0HT
Tel: 01564 776151
www.bonhams.com

Fellows & Sons
Augusta House,
19 Augusta St, Hockley,
Birmingham B18 6JA
Tel: 0121 212 2131
www.fellows.co.uk

WEST SUSSEX

John Bellman
New Pound Wisborough Green,
Billingshurst RH14 0AZ
Tel: 01403 700858
www.bellmans.co.uk

Denhams
The Auction Galleries,
Dorking Road,
Warnham,
Nr Horsham RH12 3RZ
Tel: 01403 255699
www.denhams.com

Rupert Toovey
Spring Gardens,
Washington RH20 3BS,
Tel: 01903 891955
www.rupert-toovey.com

WILTSHIRE

Finan & Co
The Square, Mere,
Wiltshire BA126DJ
Tel: 01747 861411
www.finanandco.co.uk

Henry Aldridge & Sons
The Devizes Auctioneers,
Unit 1,
Bath Rd Business Centre,
Devizes SN10 1XA
Tel: 01380 729199
www.henry-aldridge.co.uk

Woolley & Wallis
51-61 Castle St,
Salisbury SP1 3SU
Tel: 01722 424500
www.woolleyandwallis.co.uk

WORCESTERSHIRE

Andrew Grant
Tel: 01905 357547
www.andrew-grant.co.uk

Gloucestershire Worcestershire Railwayana Auctions
'The Willows',
Badsey Road,
Evesham WR117PA
Tel: 01386 760109
www.gwra.co.uk

Phillip Serrell
The Malvern Saleroom,
Barnards Green Road,
Malvern WR143LW
Tel: 01684 892314
www.serrell.com

EAST YORKSHIRE

Dee, Atkinson & Harrison
The Exchange Saleroom,
Driffield YO25 6LD
Tel: 01377 253151
www.dee-atkinson-harrison.co.uk

NORTH YORKSHIRE

David Duggleby
The Vine St Salerooms,
Scarborough YO11 1XN
Tel: 01723 507111
www.davidduggleby.com

Tennants
The Auction Centre,
Leyburn DL8 5SG
Tel: 01969 623780
www.tennants.co.uk

SOUTH YORKSHIRE

A. E. Dowse & Sons
Cornwall Galleries,
Scotland Street,
Sheffield S3 7DE
Tel: 0114 2725858
www.aedowseandson.com

BBR Auctions
Elsecar Heritage Centre,
5 Ironworks Row,
Wath Rd, Elsecar,
Barnsley S74 8HJ
Tel: 01226 745156
www.onlinebbr.com

Sheffield Railwayana
4 The Glebe, Clapham,
Bedford MK41 6GA
Tel: 01234 325 341
www.sheffieldrailwayana.co.uk

WEST YORKSHIRE

Andrew Hartley Fine Arts
Victoria Hall Salerooms,
Little Lane, Ikle LS29 8EA
Tel: 01943 816363
www.andrewhartleyfinearts.co.uk

SCOTLAND

Bonhams Edinburgh
22 Queen St,
Edinburgh EH2 1JX
Tel: 0131 225 2266
www.bonhams.com

Loves Auction Rooms
52-54 Canal St, Perth,
Perthshire PH2 8LF
Tel: 01738 633337

Lyon & Turnbull
33 Broughton Place,
Edinburgh EH1 3RR
Tel: 0131 557 8844
www.lyonandturnbull.com

Lyon & Turnbull
182 Bath St,
Glasgow G2 4HG
Tel: 0141 333 1992
Fax: 0141 332 8240
www.lyonandturnbull.com

Thomson, Roddick & Medcalf Ltd.
Coleridge House, Shaddongate,
Carlisle, Cumbria CA2 5TU
Tel: 01228 528 939
www.thomsonroddick.com

WALES

Bonhams Cardiff
7-8 Park Place, Cardiff,
Glamorgan CF10 3DP
Tel: 02920 727 980
www.bonhams.com

Peter Francis
Curiosity Salerooms,
19 King St, Carmarthen,
South Wales
Tel: 01267 233456
www.peterfrancis.co.uk

Welsh Country Auctions
2 Carmarthen Road,
Cross Hands, Llanelli,
Carmarthenshire SA14 6SP
Tel: 01269 844428
www.welshcountryauctions.co.uk

IRELAND

HOK Fine Art
4 Main St, Blackrock,
Co Dublin, Ireland
Tel: 00 353 1 2881000
fineart@hok.ie

Mealy's
The Square, Castlecomer,
County Kilkenny, Ireland
Tel: 00 353 56 41229
/41413
www.mealys.com

MAJOR FAIR & SHOW ORGANISERS

IACF (International Antique & Collectors Fair)
Newark (Nottinghamshire),
Ardingly (Sussex), Detling
(Kent), Swinderley (Nr. Lincoln)
and Shepton Mallet (Somerset)
www.iacf.co.uk

Clarion Events
Antiques for Everyone,
Birmingham
www.antiquesforeveryone.co.uk
Olympia Antiques Fairs, London
www.olympia-antiques.co.uk

Nelson Fairs
Alexandra Palace, London
www.nelsonfairs.com

Arthur Swallow Fairs
Swinderby Airfield, Lincolnshire
www.arthurswallowfairs.co.uk

The following list is organized by the type of collectable. If you would like your club, society or organisation to appear in our next edition, or would like to update details, please contact us at email info@millers.uk.com.

ADVERTISING

Antique Advertising Signs
The Street Jewellery Society, 11 Bowsden Ter, South Gosford, Newcastle-Upon-Tyne NE3 1RX

AUTOGRAPHS

A.C.O.G.B. (Autograph Club of Great Britain)
info@autographcouncil.co.uk
www.acogb.co.uk

AUTOMOBILIA

Brooklands Automobilia & Regalia Collectors' Club,
P.O. Box No 4,
Chapel Terrace Mews,
Kemp Town, Brighton,
East Sussex BN2 1HU
Tel: 01273 622 722
www.barcc.co.uk

BAXTER PRINTS

The New Baxter Society
c/o Reading Museum & Art Gallery, Blagrave Street, Reading, Berkshire RG1 1QH
www.rpsfamily.demon.co.uk

BANK NOTES

International Bank Note Society
43 Templars Crescent,
London N3 3QR
www.theibns.org

BOOKS

The Enid Blyton Society
93 Milford Hill, Salisbury,
Wiltshire SP1 2QL
Tel: 01722 331937
www.enidblytonsociety.co.uk

The Followers of Rupert
www.rupertthebear.org.uk

BOTTLES

Old Bottle Club of Great Britain
2 Strafford Avenue,
Elsecar, Nr Barnsley,
South Yorkshire S74 18AA
Tel: 01226 745 156
www.onlinebbr.com/home/

BREWERIANA

The British Beermats Collectors' Society
69 Dunnington Avenue,
Kidderminster DY10 2YT
www.britishbeermats.org.uk

CERAMICS

Beswick Collectors Club,
PO Box 310, Richmond,
Surrey TW10 7FU
www.collectingdoulton.com

Carlton Ware Collectors' International
The Carlton Factory Shop,
Copeland St, Stoke-upon-Trent,
Staffordshire ST4 1PU
Tel: 01782 410 504
www.lattimore.co.uk/deco/carlton.htm

Clarice Cliff Collectors Club
PO Box 2706,Eccleshall,
Stafford ST21 6WY
www.claricecliff.com

Fieldings Crown Devon Collectors Club
P.O. Box 462, Manvers,
Rotherham S63 7WT
Tel: 01709 874 433
www.fieldingscrowndevclub.com

Friends of Blue Ceramics Society
PO Box 122, Didcot D.O.,
Oxford OX11 0YN
www.fob.org.uk

Goss Collectors' Club
Tel: 01159 300 441
www.gosschina.com

Hornsea Pottery Collectors' & Research Society
128 Devonshire St, Keighley,
West Yorkshire BD21 2QJ
www.easyontheeye.net/hornsea/society.htm

M.I. Hummel Club (Goebel)
Porzellanfabrik, GmbH & Co. KG, Coburger Str.7, D-96472 Rodental, Germany
Tel: +49 (0) 95 63 72 18 03
www.mihummel.com

Keith Murray Collectors' Club
Fantasque House, Tennis Drive,
The Park, Nottingham NG7 1AE

Lorna Bailey Collectors' Club
The Old Post Office, 12
Wedwood, Burslem,
Stoke-on-Trent ST6 4JH
Tel: 01782 837 341
www.lorna-bailey.co.uk

Mabel Lucie Attwell
Abbey Antiques,
63 Great Whyte, Ramsey,
Huntingdon PE26 1HL
Tel: 01487 814753
www.mabellucieattwellclub.com

Moorcroft Collectors' Club
Sandbach Rd, Burslem,
Stoke-on-Trent, ST6 2DQ
Tel: 01782 820500
www.moorcroft.com

Myott Collectors Club
P.O. Box 110,Sutton SM3 9YQ
www.myottcollectorsclub.com

Pendelfin Family Circle
Cameron Mill,
Howsin St, Burnley,
Lancashire BB10 1PP
Tel: 01282 432 301
www.pendelfin.co.uk

Poole Pottery Collectors' Club
The Quay, Poole,
Dorset BH15 1RF
Tel: 01202 666200
www.poolepottery.collectorsclub.co.uk

Potteries of Rye Collectors' Society
22 Redyear Cottages,
Kennington Rd, Ashford,
Kent TN24 0TF
www.potteries-of-rye-society.co.uk

Royal Doulton International Collectors' Club
Minton House, London Road,
Stoke-on-Trent, ST4 7QD
Tel: 01782 292292
www.royaldoulton.com/collectables

Royal Winton International Collectors' Club
Dancers End, Northall,
Bedfordshire LU6 2EU
Tel: 01525 220 272

The Shelley Group
7 Raglan Close, Frimley,
Surrey GU16 8YL
Tel: 01483 764097
www.shelley.co.uk

Susie Cooper Collectors' Group
Panorama House,
18 Oaklea Mews,
Aycliffe Village,
County Durham DL5 6JP
www.susiecooper.net

The Sylvac Collectors' Circle
174 Portsmouth Rd, Horndean,
Waterlooville, Hampshire
www.sylvacclub.com

Novelty Teapot Collectors' Club
Tel: 01257 450 366
vince@totallyteapots.com

Official International Wade Collectors' Club
Royal Works, Westport Rd,
Stoke-on-Trent, Staffs ST6 4AP
Tel: 01782 255255
www.wade.co.uk

Wade Collectors Club
PO Box 3012
Stoke-on-Trent ST3 9DD
Tel: 0845 246 2525
www.wadecollectorsclub.co.uk

Royal Worcester Collectors' Society
Severn Street,
Worcester, WR1 2NE
Tel: 01905 746 000
www.royal-worcester.co.uk

CIGARETTE CARDS

Cartopulic Society of GB
7 Alderham Avenue, Radlett,
Herts WD7 8HL

COINS, BANKNOTES & PAPER MONEY

British Numismatic Society
c/o The Warburg Institute,
Woburn Square,
London WC1H 0AB
www.fitzmuseum.cam.ac.uk/coins/britnumsoc/

Royal Numismatic Society
c/o The British Museum,
Great Russell Street,
London WC1B 3DG
Tel: 020 7636 1555
www.numismatics.org.uk

International Bank Note Society
www.theibns.or

International Bond and Share Society
www.scripophily.org

COMMEMORATIVE WARE

Commemorative Collectors Society & Commemoratives Museum
Lumless House, 77 Gainsborough Road, Winthorpe, Newark,
Nottinghamshire NG24 2NR
http://commemoratives collecting.co.uk

COMICS

Association of Comic Enthusiasts
L'Hopiteau, St Martin du Fouilloux 79420, France
Tel: 00 33 549 702 114

Comic Enthusiasts Society
80 Silverdale, Sydenham,
London SE26 4SJ

The Beano & Dandy Collectors' Club,
PO Box 3433,
Brighton BN50 9JA
www.phil-comics.com/collectors_club.html

COSTUME & ACCESSORIES

The British Compact Collectors' Society
P.O. BOX 64, Langford,
Biggleswade SG18 9BF
www.compactcollectors.co.uk

The Costume Society
28 Eburne Road,
London N7 6AU
www.costumesociety.org.uk

Hat Pin Society of GB
PO Box 089, Maidstone,
ME14 9BA
www.hatpinsociety.org.uk

DISNEYANA

Walt Disney Collectors' Society
c/o Enesco, Brunthill Road,
Kingstown Industrial Estate,
Carlisle CA3 0EN
Tel: 01228 404 062
www.wdccduckman.com

DOLLS

Barbie Collectors' Club of GB
117 Rosemount Avenue,
Acton, London W3 9LU
wdl@nipcus.co.uk'

British Doll Collectors Club
'The Anchorage', Wrotham Rd,
Culverstone Green,
Meopham, Kent DA13 0QW

Doll Club of Great Britain
PO Box 154, Cobham,
Surrey KT11 2YE

The Fashion Doll Collectors' Club of GB
PO Box 133, Lowestoft,
Suffolk NR32 1WA
Tel: 07940 248127
voden@supanet.com

EPHEMERA

The Ephemera Society
PO Box 112, Northwood,
Middlesex HA6 2WT
Tel: 01923 829079
www.ephemera-society.org.uk

FILM & TV

James Bond 007 Fan Club
PO Box 007, Surrey KT15 1DY
Tel: 01483 756007

Fanderson – The Official Gerry Anderson Appreciation Society
www.fanderson.org.uk

GLASS

The Carnival Glass Society
P.O. Box 14, Hayes,
Middlesex UB3 5NU
www.carnivalglasssociety.co.uk

The Glass Association
150 Braemar Road,
Sutton Coldfield B73 6LZ
www.glassassociation.org.uk

Isle of Wight Studio Glass Collectors' Club
Old Park, St Lawrence,
Isle of Wight, PO38 1XR
www.isleofwightstudioglass.co.uk

Jonathan Harris Studio Glass Collectors Club
Woodland House, 24 Peregrine Way, Apley Castle, Telford
TF1 6TH
www.jhstudioglass.com

Pressed Glass Collectors' Club
4 Bowshot Close,
Castle Bromwich B36 9UH
Tel: 0121 681 4872
www.webspawner.com/users/pressedglass

KITCHENALIA

National Horse Brass Society
2 Blue Barn Cottage,
Blue Barn Lane,
Weybridge,
Surrey KT13 0NH
Tel: 01932 354 193

The Old Hall Stainless Steel Tableware Collectors Club,
Sandford House, Levedale,
Stafford ST18 9AH
www.oldhallclub.co.uk

The British Novelty Salt & Pepper Collectors Club
Coleshill,
Clayton Road,
Mold,
Flintshire CH7 15X

MARBLES

Marble Collectors Unlimited
P.O. Box 206
Northborough,
MA 01532-0206 USA
marblesbev@aol.com

MECHANICAL MUSIC

Musical Box Society of Great Britain
www.onbsgb.org.uk

The City of London Phonograph & Gramophone Society
www.clpgs.org.uk

METALWARE

Antique Metalware Society
PO Box 63, Honiton,
Devon EX14 1HP
amsmemsec@yahoo.co.uk

MILITARIA

Military – Crown Imperial
37 Wolsey Close, Southall,
Middlesex UB2 4NQ

Military Historical Society
National Army Museum,
Royal Hospital Rd,
London SW3 4HT

Orders & Medals Research Society
123 Turnpike Link,
Croydon CR0 5NU

PAPERWEIGHTS

Paperweight Collectors Circle
P.O. Box 941, Comberton,
Cambridgeshire CB3 7GQ
Tel: 02476 386 172

Caithness Glass Paperweight Collectors' Society
Caithness Glass
Perth PH1 3TZ Scotland
www.caithnessglass.co.uk/collectors

PENS & WRITING

The Writing Equipment Society
www.wesonline.org.uk

PERFUME BOTTLES

International Perfume Bottle Association
www.ipba-uk.co.uk

PLASTICS

Plastics Historical Society
31a Maylands Drive,
Sidcup, Kent DA14 4SB
www.plastiquarian.com

POSTCARDS

Postcard Club of Great Britain
Drene Brennan,
34 Harper House,
St.James Crescent,
London SW9 7LW
Tel: 0207 771 9404
www.postcards.co.uk

POTLIDS

The Pot Lid Circle
Collins House,
32/38 Station Road,
Gerrards Cross,
Buckinghamshire SL9 8EL
Tel: 01753 279 001
www.thepotlidcircle.co.uk

QUILTS

The Quilters' Guild of the British Isles
St Anthony's Hall,
York YO1 7PW
Tel: 01422 347 669
www.quiltersguild.org.uk

RADIOS

The British Vintage Wireless Society
59 Dunsford Close,
Swindon,
Wiltshire SN1 4PW
Tel: 01793 541 634
www.bvws.org.uk

RAILWAYANA

Railwayana Collectors Journal
7 Ascot Rd,
Moseley,
Birmingham B13 9EN

SCIENTIFIC & OPTICAL INSTRUMENTS

Scientific Instrument Society
90 The Fairway,
South Ruislip,
Middlesex HA4 0SQ
www.sis.org.uk

SEWING

International Sewing Machine Collectors' Society
www.ismacs.net

The Thimble Society
147 Portobello Road,
London W11 2DY
www.thimblesociety.com

SMOKING

Lighter Club of Great Britain
richard-ball@email.msn.com
www.lighterclub.co.uk

SPORTING

International Football Hall of Fame
info@ifhof.com,
www.ifhof.com

UK Football Programme Collectors Club,
PO Box 3236,
Norwich NR7 7BE
Tel: 01603 449 237
www.pmfc.co.uk

British Golf Collectors Society
secretary@golfcollectors.co.uk
www.britgolfcollectors.wyenet.co.uk

Rugby Memorabilia Society
PO Box 57, Hereford HR1 9DR
www.rugby-memorabilia.co.uk

STAMPS

Postal History Society
PO Box 999, Cheltenham,
GL50 9GA
www.postalhistory.org.uk

Royal Mail Collectors' Club
Freepost, NEA1431,
Sunderland SR9 9XN

STANHOPES

The Stanhope Collectors' Club
jean@stanhopes.info
www.stanhopes.info

STAINLESS STEEEL

The Old Hall Club
Sandford House,
Levedale,
Stafford ST18 9AH
Tel: 01785 780 376
www.oldhallclub.co.uk

TEDDY BEARS & SOFT TOYS

British Teddy Bear Association
PO Box 290
Brighton, Sussex
Tel: 01273 697 974

The Dean's Collectors Club
PO Box 217,
Hereford HR1 9AB
Tel: 01981 240 966
www.deansbears.com

Merrythought International Collectors' Club
Ironbridge, Telford,
Shropshire TF8 7NJ
Tel: 01952 433 116

Steiff Club Office
Margaret Steiff GmbH,
Alleen Strasse 2,
D-89537 Giengen/Brenz,
Germany

TOYS

Action Man Club
PO Box 142,
Horsham, RH13 5FJ

The British Model Soldier Society
www.btinternet.com/~model.soldiers

Corgi Collectors' Club
PO Box 323, Swansea,
Wales SA1 1BJ

Hornby Collectors Club
www.hornby.co.uk

The Matchbox Toys International Collectors' Association
P.O. Box 120, Deeside,
Flintshire CH5 3HE
www.matchboxclub.com

International Society of Meccanomen
72a Old High Street,
Headington, Oxford OX3 9HW
www.meccanotec.com

The Historical Model Railway Society
Tel: 01773 745 959
www.hmrs.org.uk

The English Playing Card Society
11 Pierrepont St, Bath,
Somerset BA1 1LA
Tel: 01225 465 218
www.wopc.co.uk/epcs/

The Hornby Railway Collectors Association
PO Box 3443, Yeovil,
Somerset, BA21 4XR
www.hrca.net

Train Collectors' Society
P.O. Box 20340,
London NW11 6ZE
Tel: 020 8209 1589
www.traincollectors.org.uk

William Britain Collectors Club
P.O. Box 32,
Wokingham RG40 4XZ
Tel: 01189 737080
ales@wbritaincollectorsclub.com

The British Smurf Collectors Club
www.kittyscavern.com

WATCHES

British Watch & Clock Collectors' Association
5 Cathedral Lane, Truro,
Cornwall TR1 2QS
Tel: 01872 264010
Fax: 01872 241953
tonybwcca@cs.com

Collectables are particularly suited to online trading. When compared with many antiques, most collectables are easily defined, described and photographed, whilst shipping is relatively easy, due to average sizes and weights. Collectables are also generally more affordable and accessible, and the internet has provided a cost effective way of buying and selling without the overheads of shops and auction rooms. A huge number of collectables are offered for sale and traded daily over the internet, with websites varying from global online marketplaces, such as eBay, to specialist dealers' sites.

• There are a number of things to be aware of when searching for collectables online. Some items being sold may not be described accurately, meaning that general category searches, and even purposefully misspelling a name, can yield results. If something looks, or sounds, too good to be true, it probably is. Using this book should give you a head start in getting to know your market, and also enable you to tell the difference between a real bargain, and something that sounds like one. Good colour photography is absolutely vital – try to find online listings that include as many images as possible, including detail shots, and check them carefully. Be aware that colours can appear differently between websites, and even between computer screens.

• Always ask the vendor questions about the object, particularly regarding condition. If no image is supplied, or you want to see another aspect of the object, ask for more information. A good seller should be happy to cooperate if approached politely and sensibly.

• As well as the 'e-hammer' price, you will very likely have to pay additional transactional fees such as packing, shipping and possibly regional or national taxes. Ask the seller for an estimate of these additional costs before leaving a bid, as this will give you a better idea of the overall amount you will end-up paying.

• In addition to large online auction sites, such as eBay, there are a host of other online resources for buying and selling. The internet can also be an invaluable research tool for collectors, with many sites devoted to providing detailed information on a number of different collectables.

INTERNET RESOURCES

Miller's Antiques & Collectables
www.millersonline.com
Miller's new website is the ultimate one-stop destination for collectors, dealers, or anyone interested in antiques and collectables. Join the Miller's Club to search through a catalogue containing many thousands of authenticated antiques and collectables, each illustrated in full colour and accompanied by a full descriptive caption and price range. Browse through practical articles written by Judith Miller, Mark Hill, and a team of experts to learn tips and tricks of the trade, as well as learning more about important companies, designs, and the designers behind them. Read Judith's daily blog, and order the full range of Millers books direct. You can also search the best fully illustrated A-Z of specialist terms on the internet; a dealer, appraiser and auctioneer database; a guide to silver hallmarks; and learn about care and repair of your antiques and collectables. The site is continually updated, so check back regularly to see what's new.

Live Auctioneers
www.liveauctioneers.com
A free online service which allows users to search catalogues from selected auction houses in Europe, the USA and the United Kingdom. Visitors to the site can bid live via the Internet into salerooms as auctions happen. Registered users can also search through an archive of past catalogues and receive a free e-mail newsletter.

The Saleroom.com
www.the-saleroom.com
A free online service that allows users to search catalogues from selected auction houses in Europe, the USA and the United Kingdom. Visitors to the site can bid live via the internet into salerooms as auctions happen. Registered users can also search through an archive of past catalogues and receive a free e-mail newsletter.

eBay
www.ebay.com
Undoubtedly the largest and most diverse of the online auction sites, allowing users to buy and sell in an online marketplace with over 52 million registered users from across the world.

ArtFact
www.artfact.com
Provides a comprehensive database of worldwide auction listings from over 2,000 art, antiques and collectables auction houses. User can search details of both upcoming and past sales and also find information on a number of collectors' fields. Basic information is available for free, access to more in depth information requires a subscription. Online bidding live into auctions as they happen is also offered.

The Antiques Trade Gazette
www.antiquestradegazette.com
The online edition of the UK trade newspaper, including British auction and fair listings, news and events.

Maine Antique Digest
www.maineantiquedigest.com
Online version of America's trade newspaper including news, articles, fair and auction listings and more.

La Gazette du Drouot
www.drouot.com
The online home of the magazine listing all auctions to be held in France at the Hotel de Drouot in Paris. An online subscription enables you to download the magazine online.

Auction.fr
www.auction.fr
An online database of auctions at French auction houses. A subscription allows users to search past catalogues and prices realised.

Go Antiques/Antiqnet
www.goantiques.com
www.antiqnet.com
An online global aggregator for art, antiques and collectables dealers. Dealers' stock is showcased online, with users able to browse and buy.

CAMPERS...

EUROPE

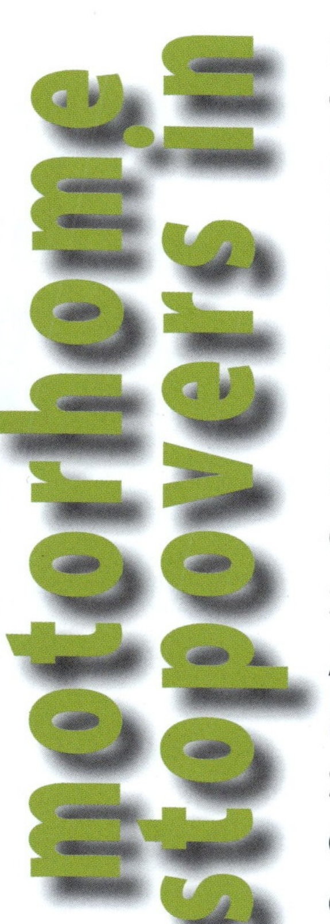

United Kingdom
The Netherlands
Belgium
Luxemburg
France
Spain
Portugal
Denmark
Germany
Switzerland
Austria
Italy
Slovenia
Croatia
Greece

2014

Publisher - Herausgeber - Éditeur - Editore

COLOPHON

A publication of:

Facile Media, Berghem
Hoessenboslaan 40
NL-5351 PD Berghem
Postbus 555
NL-5340 AN Oss
tel: +31 412 65 68 85

Chief editor
Anne van den Dobbelsteen

The draft of this version is saved in October 2013

Comments or suggestions can be sent to the publisher:

Facile Media
Postbus 555, NL-5340 AN Oss
Tel.: +31 412 65 68 85
E-mail: info@camperstop.com
Internet: www.camperstop.com

ISBN 978-90-76080-37-6

Preface

Since 1996, Facile Media has been publisher of European motorhome guides. As of 2005, the information about motorhome stopovers in Europe is available in a multilingual version.

In 2013, due to the great interest of the English motorhome enthusiasts, we decided to release a full English version of the guide: Camperstop Europe.

Our guides contain indispensable information about motorhome stopovers, service facilities and tourist information in the main European motorhome countries.

Traveling with "Camperstop Europe " will be a pleasant experience and a relaxed vacation in your motor home. We therefore wish you happy motorhome season, with many pleasant and surprising travels in 2014.

Anne van den Dobbelsteen
Chief editor

Reliable information

Every summer, 50 teams of Facile Media drive all across Europe to inspect the motorhome stopovers. The inspections take place according to predefined guidelines. The inspections by these specially trained motorhome enthusiasts have made it possible to make the information in the guide as up-to-date as possible. Almost 7900 motorhome stopovers and more than 5700 illustrative photos are the result.

Unique way to find the motorhome sites

The motorhome stopovers can be easily located on the 40 maps. Next to each map, you'll find a location name index with map referral and a page number where the location can be found in the guide. In addition, the type of motorhome stopover is indicated. In a glance, you'll be able to see whether it is the type of stopover you had in mind. In order to provide you with additional information, the location is described extensively on the relevant page, usually with a picture.

GPS-data sets on your navigation system

In addition to this guide, you can order datasets online, which you can download. The sets can be uploaded to the most common navigation systems. This allows you to drive to the motorhome stopovers listed in this guide without any effort. More information about this is available on page 8.

Table of contents

Table of contents

How to use the guide

Searching in a region

In the table of contents, at the beginning of the guide, one can search a region in preferred country. On the page of the region a map indicates the different departments/provinces with a reference to the pages.

Maps

On pages 10-11 the countries are divided into sections. The number in each box is the number of the map. On the map the red dots indicate the location of the town. Next to each map an index is published with the places on maps. The index shows the name, type of stopover, map code and page number of each location. This way the description of the motorhome stopover can be found quickly and easy.

Searching for a town

Places identified in this guide can be found under the name of the local town in the alphabetical index at the back. Use the index like a dictionary to look for specific towns, the facilities offered, map references and relevant page numbers.

Country specific rules

When travelling you have to take into account that each country has its own rules and regulations. These rules are written on the first page of each countries section.

Advise

It is recommended not to wait to long to look for an overnight stop. It could be that chosen motorhome stopover is already full and you have to go looking for an alternative.

How to use the guide

Description motorhome stopover

The information per motorhome stopover always begins with a colored block containing the type of stopover, town name and reference to the map. Directly below the name, address, GPS coordinates mostly followed by a picture. Beneath the picture you find the following information: number of pitches, rate, facilities and opening period. After that, if known, distances to city centre, shop, restaurant etc. Specific information of the motorhome stopover and a brief route description.

Motorhome facilities

 **MOTORHOME PARK**
This symbol indicates a motorhome park, a park designed for motorhomes with a range of facilities.

 **OFFICIAL MOTORHOME STOPOVER**
This symbol indicates an area suitable for overnight parking

 **OVERNIGHT PARKING TOLERATED**
In some countries tolerated places are mentioned. This means that it is officially prohibited but is being tolerated by local authorities. Therefore the local or national situation may change at any time. Nevertheless these places are listed because they were frequently being used by motorhomes at the time of writing.

 **OVERNIGHT STAY AT FARM/VINEYARD**
Farms and vineyards that welcome motorhomes, you may be encouraged to sample and buy their fare.

 **OVERNIGHT STAY AT RESTAURANT**
Motorhomes are allowed to stopover on the car park of a hotel, restaurant or bar. You should expect to dine or drink in the bar. Some restaurants insist on you having dinner. Sometimes a nominal charge is asked for the overnight stay

 **OVERNIGHT STAY AT SPA**
A growing number of spas and thermal baths offer stopovers to motorhomes.

 **OVERNIGHT STAY AT ZOO/MUSEUM/ AMUSEMENT PARK**
Motorhomes are allowed to stopover on the car park of a zoo, museum or amusement park. Entrance is not always obligated.

 **OVERNIGHT STAY AT COMPANY/ ENTERPRISE**
Overnight stay, mostly inside the gates, at companies/ enterprises.

 **OVERNIGHT STAY OUTSIDE THE CAMPSITE**
Motorhomes are allowed to stopover on the parking place outside the gate of a campsite.

 **CAMPSITE**
Overnight stay on a campsite.

 **CAR-PARK**
Motorhome parking bays, suitable for daytime use only. Often in large cities and/or tourist towns, charges may apply.

Other symbols

- Motorhome stopover, number of pitches and rate
- Signposted on the spot
- Signposted in town
- No signs to indicate the motorhome stopover

Payment

- Collector parking fee
- Parking meter
- Payment only with a credit/debit card
- Payment with cash and credit/debit card

S Service facilities
This symbol indicates that there are service facilities available.

- drinking water
- grey water dump
- Ch chemical toilet disposal point
- charging battery
- electricity available
- WC toilets
- showers
- washing machine/ dryer on the spot
- wifi access point

GPS - convenience

Downloading GPS-coordinates

Downloads of the gps-coordinates for the motorhome stopovers listed in this guide are available from www.camperstop.com. The files are suitable for most navigation systems. The data that appears on the screen gives the town name and page number in this guide so you can look up the details of the facilities very easily.

The downloadable files list the stopovers and most of the other facilities mentioned in the guide. Therefore it could be a stopover with or without service facilities, a place with service facilities only, but also a tourist information office or a campsite.

You can easily check for your nearest stopover, the navigation system will list the stopovers by distance. Use the guide to see what facilities are available. Once a choice has been made you can navigate to there without a problem.

The costs for downloading are € 3.00 per country/dataset. The Netherlands/Belgium/Luxembourg are sold as one country, also Austria/Switzerland and Spain/Portugal are treated the same.

Full downloading instructions are found on at www.camperstop.com. There are different downloads of several navigation systems.

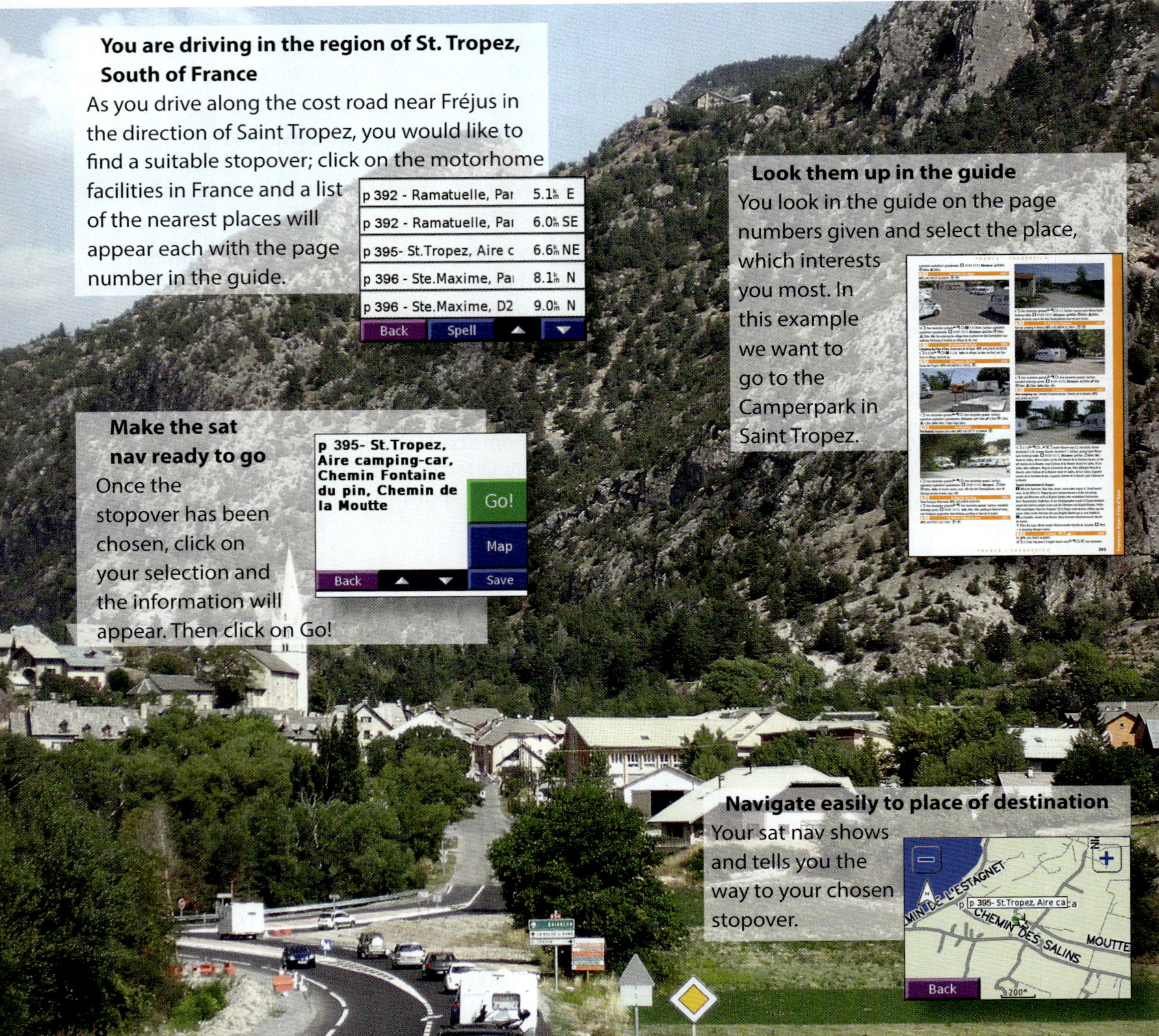

Driving regulations in Europe

Each country has different driving rules. For motorhomes sometimes there are different regulations. Here below an overview with maximum speed limits for motorhomes.

Per country there are also different rules as for warning triangles, security vests or driving with daily lights. Here below this information at a glance.

	within towns	single carriageway	expressway	motorway	compulsory in your vehicle:
GB Great Britain	30 48km	50 80km	70 112km	70 112km	Speed limits in mph.
NL The Netherlands	50	80	100 <3,5T / 80 >3,5T	130 <3,5T / 80 >3,5T	>3,5 ton = motorhome on truck basis.
B Belgium	50	90		120 <3,5T / 90 >3,5T	
L Luxemburg	50	90 <3,5T / 75 >3,5T		130 <3,5T / 90 >3,5T	Speed limits on a dry road.
F France	50	90	110 <3,5T / 100 >3,5T	130 <3,5T / 110 >3,5T	Speed limits on a dry road. Safety vest also for bicycles.
ES Spain	50	80	90	110	Set of spare bulbs.
P Portugal	50	100 <3,5T / 90 >3,5T		120 <3,5T / 110 >3,5T	
DK Denmark	50	80 <3,5T / 70 >3,5T	110 <3,5T / 80 >3,5T	130 <3,5T / 80 >3,5T	
D Germany	50	100 <3,5T / 80 >3,5T	130 <3,5T / 100 >3,5T	130 <3,5T / 100 >3,5T	130km/h is a recommended speed limit.
CH Switzerland	50	80	100	120 <3,5T / 100 >3,5T	
A Austria	50	100 <3,5T / 70 >3,5T		130 <3,5T / 80 >3,5T	A10-A12-A13-en A14 : 22-05h max. 110km/h.
I Italy	50	90 <3,5T / 80 >3,5T	110 <3,5T / 80 >3,5T	130 <3,5T / 100 >3,5T	Speed limits on a dry road.
SLO Slovenia	50	90 <3,5T / 80 >3,5T	100 <3,5T / 80 >3,5T	130 <3,5T / 80 >3,5T	Set of spare bulbs.
HR Croatia	50	110 <3,5T / 80 >3,5T	110 <3,5T / 90 >3,5T	130 <3,5T / 90 >3,5T	Set of spare bulbs.
GR Greece	50	90	110 <3,5T / 80 >3,5T	120	

warning triangle · security vest · fire extinguisher · first aid kit · daily lights · recommended

Information is based on information available in September 2013.

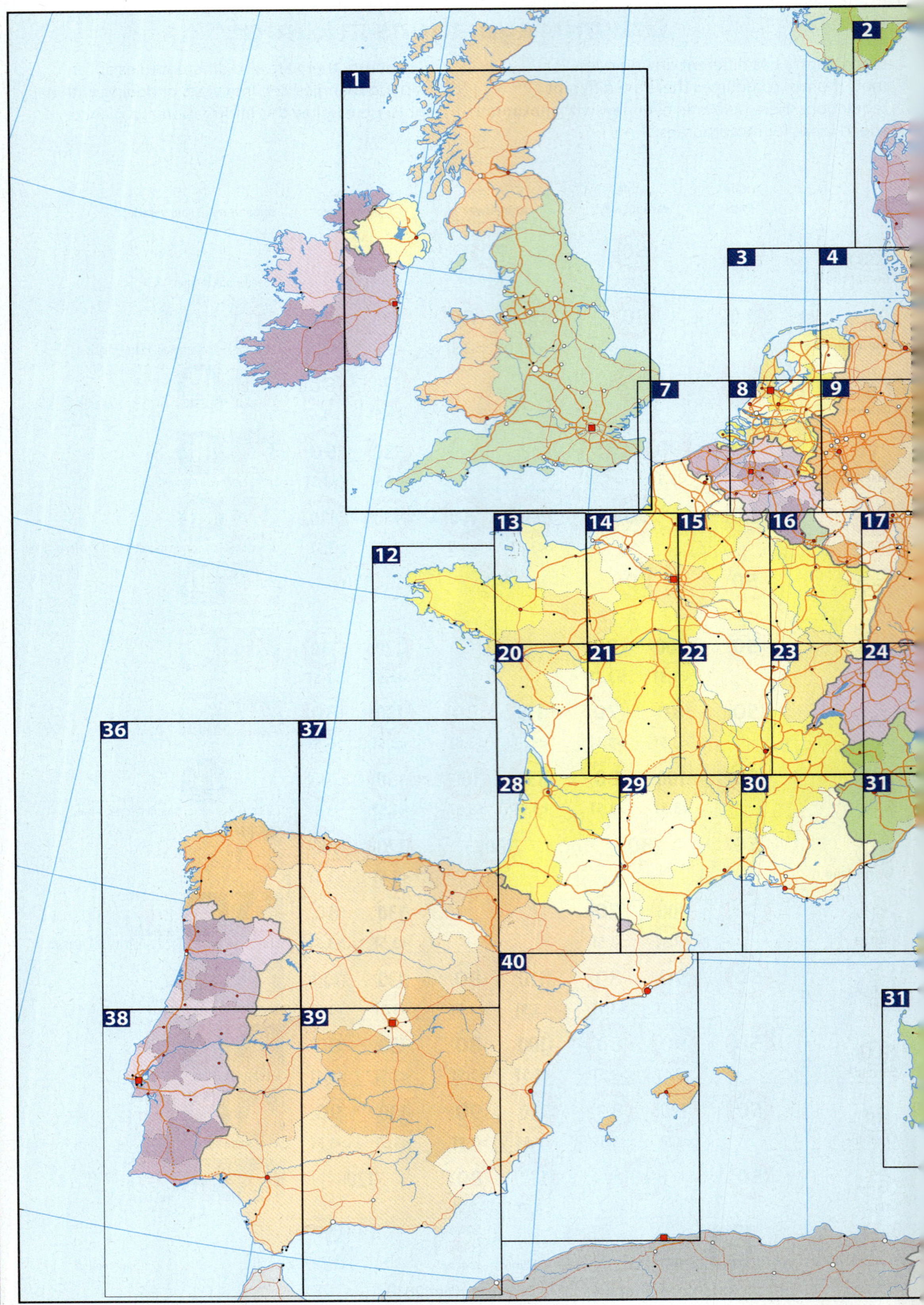
1
2
3
4
7
8
9
12
13
14
15
16
17
20
21
22
23
24
28
29
30
31
36
37
38
39
40
31

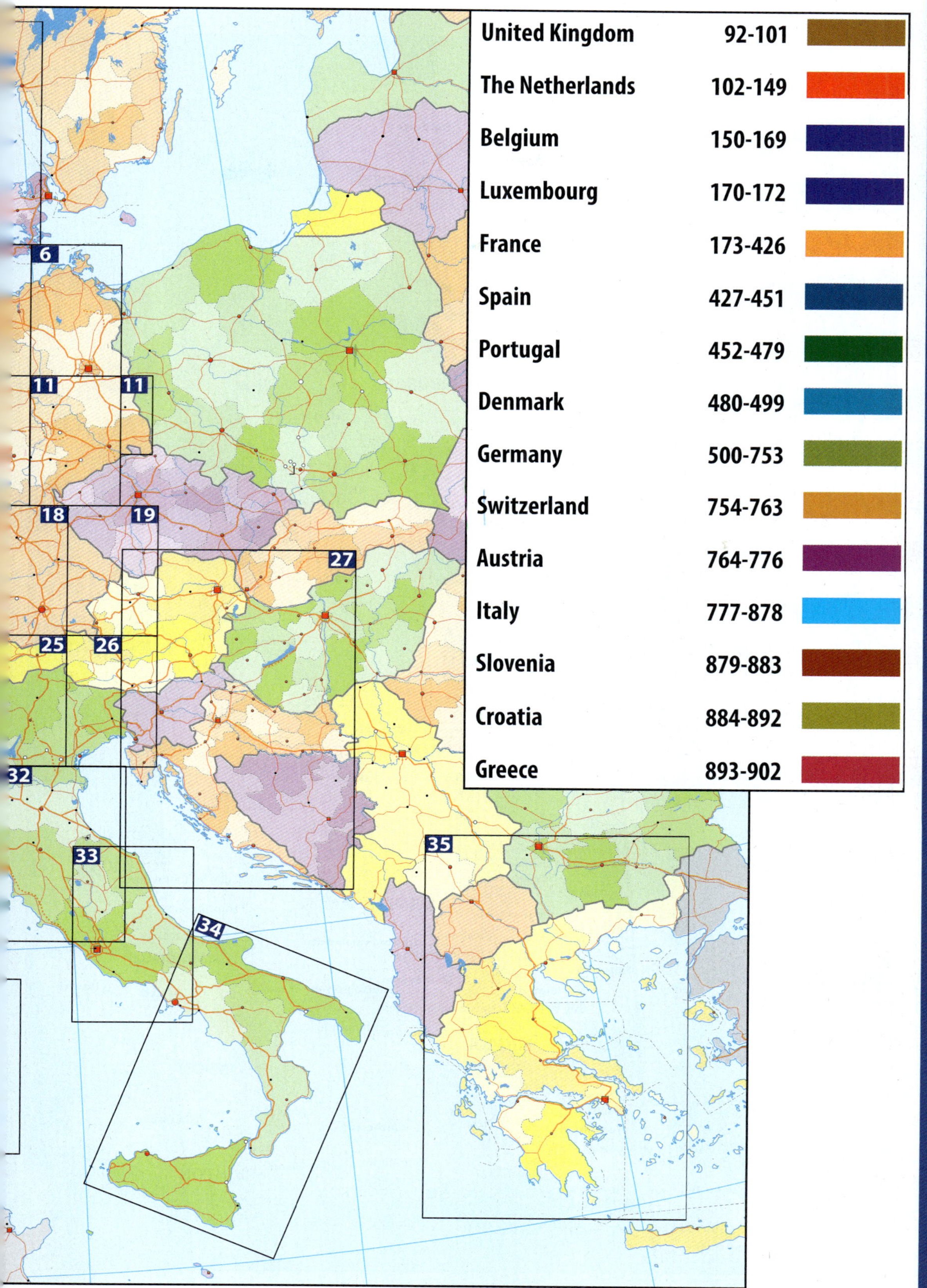

United Kingdom 92-101
The Netherlands 102-149
Belgium 150-169
Luxembourg 170-172
France 173-426
Spain 427-451
Portugal 452-479
Denmark 480-499
Germany 500-753
Switzerland 754-763
Austria 764-776
Italy 777-878
Slovenia 879-883
Croatia 884-892
Greece 893-902
6
11
11
18
19
27
25
26
32
33
34
35

A
B
C
D
1
2
3
4
5
6
Dunthulm
Dufftown
Aberdeen
ABERDEEN
Fettercairn
Ballachulish
Rhugarbh
Oban
Easdale
GLASGOW
EDINBURGH
Holy Island
Eglinton
Givran
Aghadowey
Ballymoney
Broughshane
Antrim
Whitehead
Dumfries
New Abbey
BELFAST
Carrickfergus
Ballinamallard
Newtownards
Killyleagh
M6
Ambleside
Darlington
Scarborough
Pickering
Sewerby
LEEDS
HULL
M4
Oldham
DUBLIN
Moelfre
LIVERPOOL
MANCHESTER
M9
Chester
Bakewell
Salthouse
Abergynolwyn
Welshpool
Newton
NORWICH
Whaplode St. Catherines
Llanidloes
BIRMINGHAM
M1
Knighton
Huntingdon
Llandrindod Wells
Presteigne
St. Ives
Builth Wells
Stratford-upon-Avon
Hay-on-Wye
Tarrington
Bury St.Edmunds
CAMBRIDGE
Nantgaredig
Brecon
Cheltenham
Tenby
Crickhowell
Bourton-on-the-Water
Thaxted
Ipswich
M11
NEWPORT
Newnham on Severn
M40
Abingdon
Cirencester
BRISTOL
M4
LONDON
CARDIFF
Westward Ho!
Appledore
Bideford
Canterbury
Aldershot
Torrington
Maidstone
Yeovil
Winchester
Tintagel
Holsworthy
M5
New Milton
Hayling Island
BRIGHTON
St.Austell
Newton Abbot
SOUTHAMPTON
Ivybridge
Marazion
Mevagissey
Praa Sands
PLYMOUTH
40km

A
B
C
D
1
2
3
4
5
6
N
SE
DK
E18
E6
E45
E39
E20
E47
E55
GÖTEBORG
Skagen
Hjørring
Aalbæk
Hirtshals
Strandby
Sindal
Kvissel
Tårs (Hjørring)
Frederikshavn
Løkken
Brønderslev
Saltum
Flauenskjold
Sæby
Pandrup
Hjallerup
Voersâ
Aabybro
Asâ
Hanstholm
Fjerritslev
Brovst
Aalborg
Vesløs
AALBORG
Hals
Nibe
Thisted
Storvorde
Ejerslev
Løgstør
Gistrup
Bælum
Snedsted
Erslev
Hadsund
Vestervig
Nykøbing Mors
Nørager
Roslev
Mariager
Hurup
Skals
Havndal
Thyholm
Harboøre
Hobro
Højslev
Spøttrup
Bønnerup
Lemvig
Allingâbro
Glesborg
Grenaa
Randers
Struer
Vinderup
Langå
Thorsager
Karup
Fårvang
Ulfborg
Sunds
AARHUS
Egå
Ebeltoft
Tim
Jutland
Aarhus
Vejby
Ikast
Silkeborg
Ry
Engesvan
Hundested
Ringkøbing
Malling
Nykøbing
Østbirk
Hvide Sande
Skjern
Brædstrup
Odder
KØBENHAVN
Horsens
Hemmet
Tarm
Hoven
Hørve
Føllenslev
Sdr. Omme
Taastrup
Copenhagen
Nørre Nebel
Stouby
Juelsminde
Vandel
VEJLE
Vipperød
Vallensbæk
Børkop
Martofte
Jyderup
Seeland
Varde
Egtved
Vejers Strand
Fredericia
Otterup
Esbjerg
Strøby
Hvidbjerg
Holsted
Asperup
Ringsted
Kolding
Middelfart
ODENSE
ESBJERG
Brørup
Nr. Aby
Odense
Nyborg
Korsør
Rødvig
Bjert
Sjølund
Fanø
Rødding
Hejls
Boeslunde
Ribe
Funen
Rude
Fakse
Gram
Haderslev
Assens
Hesselager
Karrebæksminde
Haarby
Toftlund
Tranekær
Skærbæk
Ebberup
Faaborg
Stenstrup
Stege
Rømø
Rødekro
Nordborg
Skårup
Svendborg
Faro
Bredebro
Åbenrå
Rudkøbing
Lolland
Torrig
Augustenborg
Guldborg
Bylderup-Bov
Tinglev
Søby, ærø
Tårs (Harpelunde)
20km
5

A
B
C
D
1
2
3
4
5
6
Lauwersoog
Groningen
Eenrum
Onderdendam
Brantgum
Zoutkamp
Leens
Hogebeintum
Dokkum
Winsum
Sint Jacobiparochie
Burdaard
Kollum
Garnwerd
Zwaagwesteinde
Lutjegast
Den Horn
Groningen
Ried
Doezum
Harkstede
Sexbierum
Leeuwarden
Sumar
Matsloot
Harlingen
Bergum
Eelderwolde
Friesland
Wartena
Surhuisterveen
Texel/De Cocksdorp
Haren
Earnewâld
Oudega
Roden
Wommels
Zurich
Drachten
Bolsward
Tersoal
Oudeschoot
Makkum
Akkrum
Nes
Sneek
Assen
IJlst
Joure
Workum
Appelscha
Den Helder
Woudsend
Langweer
Heerenveen
Den Oever
Ypecolsga
Molkwerum
Koudum
Rohel
Westerbork
Balk
Sloten
Drenthe
Stavoren
Nijetrijne
Oldemarkt
Dwingeloo
Oudemirdum
Lemmer
Middenmeer
Steenwijk
Wijster
Schagen
Luttelgeest
Ufelte
Medemblik
Overijssel
Hoogeveen
Noord-Holland
Opperdoes
Flevoland
Giethoorn
Meppel
Vollenhove
Nieuwlande
Enkhuizen
Urk
Nagele
Belt Schutsloot
Elim
Zwartsluis
A31
A7
A32
A6
A28
E22
E232
E233
12km
8

A
B
2
C
D
1
2
3
4
5
6
3
5
DK
Süderlügum
Aventoft
Ladelund
Flensburg
Harrislee
Niebüll
FLENSBURG
D
Dagebüll
Großsolt
Oeversee
Ockholm
Bredstedt
Reußenköge
Drelsdorf
Schleswig-Holstein
Nordstrand
Husum
Simonsberg
Osterhever
Tönning
St.Peter Ording
Pahlen
Heide
Albersdorf
Büsum
Hanerau-Hademarschen
Meldorf
Friedrichskoog
Quickborn bei Burg
Schleswig-Holstein
Wilster
Brunsbüttel
Brokdorf
Cuxhaven
Krummendeich
Freiburg/Elbe
Balje
Otterndorf
Glückstadt
Cadenberge
Wischhafen
Spieka-Neufeld
Oberndorf/Oste
Dorum
Nordholz
Drochtersen
Osten
Neuharlingersiel
Niedersachsen/Bremen
Wangerland
Dornum
Esens
Butjadingen
BREMERHAVEN
Norddeich
Westerholt
Jever
Norden
Wittmund
WILHELMSHAVEN
Bremerhaven
Blomberg
Bremervörde
Grossheide
Schortens
Sande
Wilhelmshaven
Nordenham
Krummhörn
Friedeburg
Aurich
Gnarrenburg
D
Wiesmoor
Zetel
EMDEN
Stadland
Sandstedt
Bockhorn
Losdorp
Emden
Grossefehn
Jade
Hambergen
Zeven
Delfzijl
Ovelgönne
Hesel
Remels
Brake
Appingedam
Ditzum
Moormerland
Wiefelstede
Osterholz-Scharmbeck
Schwanewede
Tarmstedt
Groningen
Dollart
Rastede
Leer
Detern
Apen
Elsfleth
Eggestedt
Grasberg
Westover-ledingen
Bad Zwischenahn
Berne
Slochteren
Bunde
Barßel
Westerstede
Lemwerder
Ottersberg
Weener
Ostrhauderfehn
BREMEN
Zuidbroek
Winschoten
Hude
Rhauderfehn
Edewecht
Oldenburg
Bremen
Veendam
Oyten
Saterland
Rhede/Ems
Papenburg
Wardenburg
Delmenhorst
Wildervank
Surwold
Kirchlinteln
Eext
Stadskanaal
Esterwegen
Thedinghausen
Großenkneten
NL
Sellingen
Dörpen
Walchum
Wildeshausen
Borger
Musselkanaal
Bruchhausen-Vilsen
Werlte
Cloppenburg
Hoya/Weser
Drenthe
Niedersachsen/Bremen
Eystrup
Emmen
Haren/Ems
D
Balge
Vechta
Barger Compascuum
Sulingen
Oosterhesselen
Meppen
Herzlake
Nienburg
Twist
Haselünne
Berge
Diepholz
Steyerberg
A7
E45
A23
A27
E234
A29
A28
A31
E22
A1
E233
E37
A37
E233
A
12km
B
9
C
D

A
B
2
C
D
1
2
3
4
5
6
DK
D
Sydals
Humble
Nakskov
Maribo
Horbelev
Nykøbing F.
Langballig
Bagenkop
Lolland
Westerholz
Norgaardholz
Dannemare
Rødby
Pommerby
Gelting
Hasselberg
Maasholm
Sörup
Kappeln
Grödersby
Damp
Brodersby
Puttgarden
Schleswig
Fehmarn
Eckernförde
Schönberg/Ostsee
Altenhof
Kiel
Jagel
Laboe
Hohenfelde
Heiligenhafen
Großenbrode
Bistensee
Behrensdorf
Kropp
Hohwacht
Graal-Müritz
Sehestedt
KIEL
Büdelsdorf
Blekendorf
Rendsburg
Schacht-Audorf
Rostock
Fockbek
Molfsee
Lensahn
Kühlungsborn
Wittenbeck
Heiligendamm
Kägsdorf
Preetz
Langwedel
Bad Malente
Bargeshagen
Sievers-
hagen
Rerik
Grömitz
Plön
Eutin
Bordesholm
Schashagen
ROSTOCK
Schleswig-Holstein
Bösdorf
Neustadt in Holstein
Pepelow
Bosau
Boiensdorf
Neumünster
Sierksdorf
Aukrug
Timmendorf
Scharbeutz
Niendorf
NEUMÜNSTER
Timmendorfer Strand
Boltenhagen
Dassow
Passin
Beckerwitz
Hornstorf
Mistorf
Travemünde
LÜBECK
Grossenaspe
Bad Segeberg
Wismar
Krassow
Kellinghusen
Lübeck
Neukloster
Itzehoe
Bad Bramstedt
Reinfeld
Bobitz
Kremperheide
Mecklenburg-Vorpommern
Kaltenkirchen
Krempe
Bad Oldesloe
Sternberg
Seehof
Barmstedt
Elmshorn
Ratzeburg
Roggendorf
SCHWERIN
Dobbertin
Seestermühe
Schwerin
Langen Brütz
Möllin
Lassahn
Uetersen
Muess
Hollern
Banzkow
Wedel
Stade
Brook
Wittenburg
HAMBURG
Jork
Parchim
Hamburg
Buxtehude
Brenz
Harsefeld
Drage/Elbe
Selsingen
Artlenburg
Lauenburg/Elbe
Ludwigslust
Hohnstorf/Elbe
Winsen/Luhe
Ahlerstedt
Brietlingen
Grabow
Adendorf
Fresenbrügge
Bleckede
Karenz
Vielank
Scharnebeck
Eldena
Buchholz/Nordheide
Lüneburg
Neu Kaliss
Westergellersen
Sittensen
Rüterberg
Brandenburg
Salzhausen
Hitzacker
Dömitz
Egestorf
Undeloh
Bienenbüttel
Bispingen
Schneverdingen
Gorleben
Weisen
Amelinghausen
Bad Bevensen
Gartow
Wahrenberg
Rotenburg (Wümme)
Bad Wilsnack
Lüchow
Soltau
Abbendorf
Niedersachsen
Clenze
Uelzen
Visselhövede
Arendsee
Seehausen
Wietzendorf
Salzwedel
Walsrode
Fassberg
Bomlitz
Hermannsburg
Bergen
Sachsen-Anhalt
Hankensbüttel
Ahlum
Essel
Stendal
Rodewald
Celle
Tangermünde
Hohne
CELLE
12km
10
A1
A7
A14
A20
A21
A23
A24
A26
A27
A39
A215
E22
E26
E45
E47
E55
E234

A
B
C
D
1
2
3
4
5
6
Putgarten
Dranske/Bakenberg
Lohme
Binz
Bergen/Rügen
Ostseebad Sellin/Rügen
Sehlen
Lauterbach
Zingst
Ahrenshoop
Barth
Dabitz
Neuendorf
Stralsund
Poseritz
Ostseebad-
Wustrow
STRALSUND
Greifswald
GREIFSWALD
Lütow
Ückeritz
Bansin
Neuhof
Heringsdorf
Ahlbeck
Mecklenburg-Vorpommern
Gützkow
Dalwitz
Anklam
Karnin
Usedom
Kamminke
Mönkebude
Altwarp
Ueckermünde
Sommersdorf
Malchin
Güstrow
PL
D
Neubrandenburg
NEUBRANDENBURG
SZCZECIN
Nossentin
Waren
Kargow
Alt Schwerin
Malchow
Lenz über
Malchow
Sembzin
Petersdorf
Neustrelitz
Carpin
Röbel
Wesenberg
Buchholz
Lychen
Priepert
Fürstenberg (Havel)
Templin
Schwedt-Oder
Angermünde
Brandenburg
Stolzenhagen
Baumgarten
Nackel
Havelberg
Dreetz
Kienitz
Tiefensee
Berlin
BERLIN
BRANDENBURG
AN DER HAVEL
Alt-Zeschdorf
FRANKFURT
(ODER)
Potsdam
POTSDAM
Schmergow
Sachsen-Anhalt
E22
E251
E65
A20
A19
E28
A11
E55
A24
E26
A10
E51
A12
E30
12km
5
11

GB
NL
B
F
Zuid-Holland
Ouddorp
Zierikzee
Kamperland
Oostkapelle
Wolphaartsdijk
Middelburg
Zeeland
Hansweert
Breskens
Groede
Kloosterzande
Knokke-Heist
Terneuzen
Hengstdijk
Vogelwaarde
Zaamslag
St.Laureins
Axel
Assenede
Westdorpe
Sas van Gent
Bredene
BRUGGE
Brugge
Maldegem
Eeklo
Westende
Oudenburg
Gistel
Nieuwpoort
Aartrijke
Beernem
Lokeren
Aalter
Veurne
Diksmuide
Wingene
GENT
DUNKERQUE
Kortemark
Gentbrugge
Berlare
Oye-plage
Calais
Gravelines
Bergues
Vlaanderen
CALAIS
Hondschoote
Roeselare
Zulte
Wissant
Gavere
Tardinghen
Poperinge
Zonnebeke
Kortrijk
Ambleteuse
Harelbeke
Cassel
Geraardsbergen
Comines
Boulogne-sur-Mer
Arques
Bailleul
Mesen
Mouscron
Le Portel
Equihen-Plage
Dottignies
Exeter
Lessines
Longfossé
Wallonie
LILLE
Lahamaide
Hardelot
Nord-Pas-de-Calais
Tournai/Doornik
Leuze-en-Hainaut
Brugelette
Le Touquet-Paris Plage
Richebourg
Aubechies
Antoing
Beloeil
Basecles
Stella-plage
Embry
Quevaucamps
Blaton
Merlimont
Bernissart
Harchies
Nimy
Berck-sur-Mer
Quaregnon
Hornu
Mons/Bergen
Fort Mahon Plage
Quend
Roisin
Quend-plage-les-Pins
Nunq-Hautecôte
Bavay
Arras
Le Crotoy
Picardie
E312
E34
E40
E403
E17
A25
E402
A16
E15
A26
E42
E429
A23
E17
A1
12km

A
B
3
C
D
1
2
3
4
5
6
7
6
15
16
12km
Stompetoren
Oudendijk
Oosthuizen
De Rijp
E22
Purmerend
Katwoude
Volendam
Monnickendam
Noord-Holland
A9
Amsterdam
AMSTERDAM
Almere
Almere-Haven
Naarden
Huizen
Bunschoten
Spakenburg
Laren (NH)
A4
Abbenes
Sassenheim
Mijdrecht
E35
Leiden
Zevenhoven
Baarn
Utrecht
Amersfoort
Terschuur
DEN HAAG
UTRECHT
Bunnik
IJsselstein
A12
Leusden
Overberg
A30
Veenendaal
Leersum
Rhenen
Vianen
Culemborg
Delft
Bleiswijk
Gouda
Oudewater
ROTTERDAM
Zuid-Holland
Schiedam
Vlaardingen
Hoogblokland
A27
Nieuwland
Leerdam
Geldermalsen
Tiel
Meteren
Alblasserdam
Goudriaan
Giessenburg
Oud Beijerland
Dordrecht
A15
Gorinchem
Kerkwijk
Maasbommel
Maasdam
A29
E19
Wijk en Aalburg
Heusden
A16
Strijensas
Numansdorp
Geertruidenberg
Raamsdonksveer
Heeswijk-Dinther
Oosterland
Oosteind
Noord-Brabant
De Heen
Etten-Leur
Boxtel
Zeeland
Roosendaal
Breda
Hulten
Tholen
A58
E312
NL
Best
Bergen op Zoom
Zundert
Essen
EINDHOVEN
Kruiningen
Hoogerheide
Vessem
E312
A4
Kalmthout
Paal
Brecht
Turnhout
Reusel
Arendonk
Graauw
St.Job-in-'t-Goor
E34
Hulst
Antwerpen
Brasschaat
B
E34
ANTWERPEN
Antwerpen
Grobbendonk
Kasterlee
Lommel
Neerpelt
E17
Herentals
Temse
Bazel
Lier
Hamme
Bornem
Boom
Puurs
Koningshooikt
St.Amands
Willebroek
Putte
Herselt
Vlaanderen
Mechelen
Merchtem
E19
Aalst
Grimbergen
Diest
E313
E314
Leopoldsburg
Hechtel
Eksel
Helchteren
Herk-de-Stad
Limburg(B)
E40
Bruxelles/Brussel
Bruxelles/BRUSSEL
St.Truiden
Hoepertingen
E429
E40
E411
Soignies
Ronquières
Ecaussinnes
E420
Le Roeulx
La Louvière
Houdeng
Aimeries
Morlanwelz
Mariemont
Binche
Trazegnies
Courcelles
Fleurus
Charleroi
Marchienne-au-Pont
Bouffioulx
Thuin
Solre-Sur-Sambre
CHARLEROI
Wallonie
Profondeville
E42
Huy
Hamoir
E46
Durbuy
Hotton
Lelystad
Kampen
Hasselt
Rouveen
Dedemsvaart
Hardenberg
Nieuwleusen
Zwolle
Overijssel
Zalk
Hattem
Dalfsen
Ommen
Flevoland
A6
Elburg
E232
A50
Straelen
Hellendoorn
Wijhe
Heerde
Nunspeet
Heeten
Nijverdal
Wierden
Harderwijk
A28
Epe
Schoonheten
Ermelo
Emst
Enter
Vaassen
Deventer
Bathmen
Putten
Zeewolde
Garderen
Twello
Gorssel
Diepenheim
Nijkerk
Apeldoorn
Laren (GE)
A1
Voorthuizen
Voorst
Almen
Neede
Gelderland
Zutphen
Borculo
Ruurlo
Otterlo
Hengelo
Groenlo
E35
Zelhem
Lichtenvoorde
Bredevoort
Lathum
Varsseveld
Aalten
Heteren
Westendorp
Huissen
Braamt
Silvolde
De Heurne
Beek
Sinderen
E31
Doornenburg
Aerdt
Stokkum
Breedenbroek
Ressen
Bemmel
Gendringen
Appeltern
Nijmegen
Millingen
Tolkamer
Bocholt
Emmerich
Isselburg
Oijen
Groesbeek
Kleve
Kranenburg
Grave
Bedburg-Hau
Rees
Oss
A50
Linden
Milsbeek
D
Kalkar
A3
Escharen
Beers
Plasmolen
Gennep
Goch
Uedem
Ottersum
Xanten
A57
Weeze
Well
Gemert
Alpen
E31
Nieuw Bergen
Kevelaer
Bakel
NL
Geldern
Kamp-Lintfort
Issum-Sevelen
A73
Rheurdt
Lottum
Mierlo
Grubbenvorst
Kerken
Moers
Venlo
A67
Wachtendonk
Asten
Kempen
Nettetal
Meijel
Maasbree
Grefrath
Oedt
Limburg(NL)
Neer
KREFELD
Viersen
Brüggen
Hamont
A2
Weert
E25
Overhetfeld
Mönchengladbach
A52
Bocholt
Ittervoort
Heel
Thorn
Peer
Wegberg
Tongerlo
Bree
Maaseik
Wassenberg
Waldfeucht
Brüggelchen
Meeuwen-Gruitrode
A46
Neeroeteren
Heinsberg
A61
Dilsen-Stokkem
Hückelhoven
Houthalen
Nordrhein-Westfalen
Bolderberg
Sittard
Gangelt
Genk
Brunssum
Hasselt
D
Jülich
Diepenbeek
Rekem
Landgraaf
Bilzen
Kortessem
A4
Veldwezelt
Valkenburg
Schalkhoven
NL
AACHEN
Düren
Gronsveld
Aachen
Blégny-Mine
Hürtgenwald
Roetgen
Nideggen
LIÈGE
Eupen
Heimbach
B
Simmerath
Schleiden
Monschau
Kall
Sourbrodt
E25
E42
Malmedy
Hellenthal
Waimes
Dahlem
St.Vith
D
E29

A
B
4
C
D
1
2
3
4
5
6
8
10
16
17
12km
NL
D
Niedersachsen
Overijssel
Nordrhein-Westfalen
Hessen
Rheinland-Pfalz
Geeste
Bippen
Eggermühlen
Holdorf
Steinfeld
Lembruch
Stolzenau
Mardorf
Lingen/Ems
Fürstenau
Ankum
Damme
Hüde
Stemwede
Uchte
Leese
Rehburg-Loccum
Uelsen
Emsbüren
Diepenau
Bramsche
Nordhorn
Geesteren
Tubbergen
Hopsten
Bohmte
Petershagen
Lüdersfeld
Hille
Stadthagen
Almelo
Recke
Mettingen
Bad Essen
Lübbecke
Minden
Hertme
De Lutte
Schüttorf
Osnabrück
Bückeburg
Saasveld
Rheine
Ibbenbüren
Lotte
OSNABRÜCK
Bad Oeynhausen
Borne
Bad Bentheim
Hörstel
Bissendorf
Melle
Bünde
Löhne
Rinteln
Losser
Gronau
Tecklenburg
Großenwieden
Hessisch Oldendorf
Enschede
Lienen
Haaksbergen
Steinfurt
Saerbeck
Herford
Bad Salzuflen
Aerzen
Ladbergen
Rekken
Ahaus
Schöppingen
Altenberge
Greven
Ostbevern
BIELEFELD
Barntrup
Eibergen
Rosendahl
Sassenberg
Bielefeld
Bad Pyrmont
Vreden
Havixbeck
MÜNSTER
Telgte
Steinhagen
Detmold
Stadtlohn
Münster
Warendorf
Harsewinkel
Horn
Schieder
Winterswijk
Billerbeck
Everswinkel
Schloss Holte/Stukenbrock
Velen
Coesfeld
Nottuln
Rheda-Wiedenbrück
Senden
Sendenhorst
Ennigerloh
Hövelhof
Brakel/
Bellersen
Rhede
Borken
Reken
Dülmen
Ascheberg
Oelde
Rietberg
Bad Lippspringe
Altenbeken
Drensteinfurt
Lüdinghausen
Ahlen
Beckum
Delbrück
Paderborn
Bad Driburg
Raesfeld
Haltern am See
Nordkirchen
Wadersloh
Bad Waldliesborn
Lippstadt
Dorsten
Werne
Bad Westernkotten
Bottrop
Waltrop
Bergkamen
Bad Sassendorf
Soest
Büren
Dinslaken
Gladbeck
DORTMUND
Rüthen
Bad Wünnenberg
Warburg
Gelsenkirchen
Dortmund
Möhnesee
Oberhausen
Marsberg
Duisburg
ESSEN
Hüsten
Warstein
Bad Arolsen
DUISBURG
Witten
Iserlohn
Arnsberg
Bestwig
Diemelsee
Mülheim/Ruhr
Hattingen
Hemer
Wolfhagen
Heiligenhaus
Altena
Balve
Meschede
Willingen
Velbert
Ennepetal
Wülfrath
WUPPERTAL
Plettenberg
Waldeck
Düsseldorf
Lüdenscheid
Winterberg
Edertal
DÜSSELDORF
Solingen
Herscheid
Schmallenberg
Vöhl
Remscheid
Bad Wildungen
Bad Berleburg
Neuss
Meinerzhagen
Lennestadt
Dormagen
Attendorn
Kirchhundem
Frankenberg/Eder
Bad Zwesten
Kürten
Olpe
Erndtebrück
Battenberg
Leverkusen
Lindlar
Eckenhagen
Hilchenbach
Biedenkopf
Köln
Kreuztal
Bad Laasphe
Gilserberg
Bergheim
Wiehl
Netphen
KÖLN
Hessen
Waldbröl
Freudenberg
Siegen
Erftstadt
Windeck
Wilnsdorf
Marburg
Gladenbach
Brühl
Dillenburg
Bad Endbach
BONN
Burbach
Bonn
Königswinter
Zülpich
Hachenburg
Bad Marienberg
GIESSEN
Grünberg
Rheinbach
Rheinbreitbach
Mechernich
Wetzlar
Unkel
Remagen
Linz am Rhein
Braunfels
Bad Neuenahr
Sinzig
Bad Hönningen
Bad Münstereifel
Mayschoss
Weilburg
KOBLENZ
Nettersheim
Andernach
Neuwied
Weilmünster
Villmar
Blankenheim
Urmitz/Rhein
Vallendar
Bad Nauheim
Neuhäusel
Mendig
Altendiez
Bad Ems
Weilrod
Friedberg
Birgel
Mayen
Kobern
Polch
Becheln
Hillesheim
Alken
Braubach
Aarbergen
Dohm
Löf
A1
A30
A31
A33
A43
A3
A2
A44
A4
A1
A565
A61
A48
A3
A45
A5
E30
E34
E331
E31
E37
E40
E29
E31
E35
E40
E44
E41

A
B
5
C
D
Gifhorn
Wolfsburg
WOLFSBURG
Bertingen
Burg bei Magdeburg
Steinhude
HANNOVER
Bad Nenndorf
Barsinghausen
BRAUNSCHWEIG
Braunschweig
Haldensleben
Helmstedt
MAGDEBURG
Magdeburg
Königslutter am Elm
Niedersachsen
Büddenstedt
Bad Münder
Salzgitter
Schöppenstedt
HILDESHEIM
Coppenbrügge
Salzhemmendorf
Hameln
Gronau
Emmerthal
Bockenem
Alfeld/Leine
Berssel
Bodenwerder
Lamspringe
Eschershausen
Stadtoldendorf
Bad Gandersheim
Lautenthal
Ilsenburg
Darlingerode
Quedlinburg
Schulenberg
Wernigerode
Bevern
Einbeck
Altenau
Blankenburg
Weddersleben
Holzminden
Ballenstedt
Elend
Altenbrak
Höxter
Osterode
Braunlage
Allrode
Northeim
St.Andreasberg
Harzgerode
Bruchhausen
Uslar
Hardegsen
Bad Lauterberg
Ilfeld
Beverungen
Bad Karlshafen
Bad Sachsa
Wahlsburg
GÖTTINGEN
Nordhausen
Sangerhausen
Duderstadt
Göttingen
Hofgeismar
Reinhardshagen
Kelbra
Hannoversch Münden
Sondershausen
Calden
Ziegenhagen
Bad Frankenhausen/Kyffhäuser
Habichtswald
KASSEL
Witzenhausen
Kassel
Asbach/Sickenberg
Kaufungen
Bad Sooden-Allendorf
Baunatal
Thüringen
Helsa
Berkatal
Bad Emstal
Eschwege
Wanfried
Bad Kösen
Edermünde
Hessisch Lichtenau
Bad Langensalza
Treffurt
Waldkappel
Fritzlar
Ringgau
ERFURT
Sontra
JENA
Eisenach
Homberg/Efze
Rotenburg a/d Fulda
Erfurt
Weimar
Frielendorf
Hessen
Bebra
Dankmarshausen
Ruhla
Bad Berka
Ichtershausen
Schwalmstadt
Friedrichroda
Bad Hersfeld
Oberaula
Tiefenort
Bad Liebenstein
Tambach-Dietharz
Neukirchen
Kirchheim
Ottrau
Stadtlengsfeld
Bad Salzungen
Nimritz
Rudolstadt
Geschwenda
Alsfeld
Breitungen
Oberhof
Ilmenau
Rasdorf
Sitzendorf
Saalfeld
Burghaun
Schlitz
Hünfeld
Tann/Rhön
Zella-Mehlis
Schwalmtal
Bad Salzschlirf
Lauterbach
Meiningen
Ulrichstein
Fulda
Lauscha
Bad Lobenstein
Herbstein
Themar
FULDA
Poppenhausen
Grebenhain
Ostheim
Eisfeld
Oberelsbach
Mellrichstadt
Rothenkirchen
Bad Steben
Bischofsheim an der Rhön
Hirzenhain
Bad Rodach
Bad Neustadt
Bad Colberg/Heldburg
Steinau a/d Strasse
Bad Brückenau
Bad Königshofen
Kronach
Bad Bocklet
Coburg
Bad Soden-Salmünster
Ahorn
Münnerstadt
Bad Orb
Bad Kissingen
Bayern
Burgkunstadt
Kulmbach
Gelnhausen
Oberthulba
Hofheim in Unterfranken
A352
A39
E30
A2
A14
A395
E49
A38
A7
A44
E331
A71
A49
A4
E40
A5
A73
E45
A66
1
2
3
4
5
6
9
11
17
18
12km

Brandenburg
Werder-Havel
Bad Saarow
Belzig
Luckenwalde
Sachsen-Anhalt
Brandenburg
Lübbenau
Burg/Spreewald
COTTBUS
Kolkwitz
Klein-Ossnig
Aken/Elbe
Wörlitz
Altdöbern
Bitterfeld
Prettin
Dollenchen
Geierswalde
Bad Düben
Brieske
Elsterheide
Brachwitz
Halle/Saale
HALLE (SAALE)
Leipzig
LEIPZIG
Rothersdorf
Diesbar-Seusslitz
DRESDEN
Dresden
Weissenfels
Selb
Bad Lausick
Naumburg(Saale)
Königsfeld-Stollsdorf
Heidenau
Sebnitz
Sachsen
Königstein
Freiberg
DECIN
CZ
Bad Klosterlausnitz
Reichenbach
CHEMNITZ
Thüringen
Oberschindmaas
Amtsberg
Hermsdorf
Neustadt/Orla
ZWICKAU
Marienberg
KAART 11A
Linda
Zeulenroda
Grünhain
Bad Muskau
Schleiz
Crottendorf
PLAUEN
D
Breitenbrunn
Oberwiesental
Sachsen
PL
Biehain
Eichigt
Zwota
Thräna
Naila
Hof/Saale
Adorf
CZ
GÖRLITZ
Selbitz
Bad Elster
Bayern
Ebersbach/Sachsen
Kirchenlamitz
Marktleuthen
Thierstein
Zittau
Hohenberg an der Eger
Röslau
Arzberg
12km

A B C D

1 2 3 4 5 6

Trégastel
Pleubian
Pleumeur-Bodou
Trébeurden
Ploubazlanec
Tréguier
Lézardrieux
Kerlouan
Santec
Roscoff
Plougasnou
Paimpol
Guissény
Plouguerneau
Plouescat
St.Pol-de-Léon
Carantec
La Roche-Derrien
Plestin-les-Grèves
Plouézec
Goulven
Portsall
Le Folgoët
Penzé
Plouha
Lannilis
St.Derrien
Morlaix
Plévenon
Plouvorn
E50
Belle-Isle-en-Terre
Erquy
Binic
Bourg-Blanc
Plabennec
Landivisiau
Pléneuf-Val-André
Fréhel
Lampaul-Plouarzel
St.Servais
St.Thégonnec
Guingamp
Plouarzel
St.Renan
Landerneau
Guimiliau
Plérin
St.Cast-le-Guildo
Ploumoguer
Brest
BREST
La Martyre
Trémuson
Le Conquet
Locmaria-Plouzané
Commana
Hillion
Planguenoual
Plougonvelin
Plougastel-Daoulas
Callac
Huelgoat
Quintin
Meslin
Saint-Rivoal
St.Carreuc
E401
Camaret-sur-Mer
Crozon
Carhaix-Plouguer
Lanfains
Maël-Carhaix
Moncontour
Rostrenen
Plonévez-Porzay
Saint-Gelven
Plessala
Glomel
Cléden-Cap-Sizun
Bretagne
Loudéac
Plogoff
Pont-Croix
St.Aignan
Plémet
Primelin
Locronan
Neulliac
St.Barnabé
Audierne
Le Croisty
La Chèze
Landudec
QUIMPER
Scaër
Gueltas
Priziac
Pontivy
Mauron
Plomelin
Rohan
Combrit
Paimpont
Pont-l Abbé
Concarneau
Le Trévoux
Les Forges
Trégunc
Campénéac
Penmarch
Fouesnant
Quimperlé
Josselin
Pont-Aven
LORIENT
Loctudy
Névez
Clohars-Carnoët
Baud
Locminé
Guidel
Languidic
Moëlan-sur-Mer
Larmor-Plage
Sérent
Locmiquelic
Ploemeur
Locqueltas
Malestroit
Riantec
E60
Brech
Port-Louis
Elven
St.Guyomard
Gâvres
Plouhinec
Auray
VANNES
Rochefort-en-Terre
Étel
Belz
Sulniac
Erdeven
Vannes
Theix
Malansac
Crach
Arradon
Carnac
Berric
Locmariaquer
Larmor-Baden
Arzon
St.Gildas-de Rhuys
Saint-Pierre-Quiberon
Marzan
Quiberon
La Roche-Bernard
Damgan
Sarzeau
Arzal
Pénestin
Asserac
St.Lyphard
Piriac-sur-Mer
Guérande
La Turballe
SAINT-NAZAIRE
Le Croisic
La Baule
Batz-sur-Mer
Saint-Nazaire
St.Michel-Chef-Chef
Préfailles
La Plaine-sur-Mer
Pornic
La Bernerie-en-Retz
Noirmoutier-en-l Ile
Bouin
Beauvoir-sur-Mer
Notre-Dame-de-Monts
St.Jean-de-Monts
St.Hilaire de Riez

13

16km

A B C D

A
B
C
D
1
2
3
4
5
6
12
14
20
12km
Goury
Jobourg
Gréville-Hague
Equeurdreville
Tourlaville
St.Pierre-Eglise
Barfleur
Cherbourg
Réville
Sideville-Lorimier
Siouville-Hague
Tréauville
St.Vaast-la-Hougue
Les Pieux
Rauville-la-Bigot
Valognes
Le Rozel
Surtainville
Montebourg
Bricquebec
Ste.Marie-du-Mont
Barneville-Carteret
Englesqueville-la-Percée
Ste.Mère-Eglise
St.Sauveur-le-Vicomte
Ste.Honorine-des-Pertes
Portbail
Grandcamp-Maisy
Arromanches-les-Bains
Formigny
Port-en-Bessin-Huppain
Courseulles-sur-M.
Langrune-sur-M.
Isigny-sur-Mer
Saint-Vigor-le-Grand
Luc-sur-Mer
Lion-sur-M.
Bayeux
Hermanville-sur-M.
Ouistreham
Colleville-Montgomery
Merville F.
Dives-sur-Mer
Villers-sur-Mer
Cabourg
Sallenelles
Deauville
Le Havre
LE HAVRE
St.Fromond
Pirou-Plage
Cerisy-la-Forêt
Montfiquet
Rots
Bréville-les-Monts
Hérouvillette
Gouville-sur-Mer
Marigny
St.Lô
Bretteville-sur-Odon
CAEN
Beuvron-en-Auge
Agon-Coutainville
Caumont-l Éventé
Cambremer
Villers-Bocage
Montmartin-sur-Mer
Guilberville
Grainville-Langannerie
Saint-Pierre-sur-Dives
Bréhal
Gavray
Gouvets
Soumont-Saint-Quentin
Le Billot
Coudeville-Plage
Granville
St.Pair-sur-Mer
Villedieu-les-Poêles
Saint-Sever-Calvados
Clecy
Vire
Pont-d Ouilly
La Lucerne-d Outremer
SAINT-MALO
Carolles
Sourdeval
Normandie
Cancale
St.Malo
Avranches
St.Jacut-de-la-Mer
St.Benoit-des-Ondes
Hirel
Le Mont-Saint-Michel
Mortain
La Ferrière-aux-Etangs
Ploubalay
Beauvoir
Ducey
Pleslin-Trigavou
Le Vivier-sur-Mer
Sains
Ardevon
St.Hilaire-du-Harcouët
La Ferté-Macé
Dol-de-Bretagne
Dinan
Taden
Bagnoles-de-l Orne
Léhon
Lanvallay
Antrain
Mellé
Couterne
Tremblay
St.Brice-en-Coglès
Lassay-les-Châteaux
Tinténiac
Hédé-Bazouges
Romagné
Fougères
Saint-Loup-du-Gast
Caulnes
St.Aubin d Aubigné
Ernée
Averton
Mayenne
Liffré
Châtillon-en-Vendelais
Fresnay-sur-Sarthe
Bédée
Chailland
Juvigné
Deux-Evailles
Rennes
La Baconnière
Sillé-le-Guillaume
RENNES
Cesson-Sévigné
St.Jean-sur-Mayenne
Changé
LAVAL
Laval
Piré-sur-Seiche
Guichen
Vaiges
Pays de la Loire
Janzé
LE MANS
Le Mans
Villiers-Charlemagne
Arnage
Grez-en-Bouère
La Suze-sur-Sarthe
Château-Gontier
Pouancé
Mezeray
E3
E401
E50
A84
A88
E402
A28
A81
A11
E501

A
B
7
C
D
1
2
3
4
5
6
13
Cayeux-sur-Mer
St.Valery-sur-Somme
Doullens
Ault
Bourseville
Le Tréport
Mers-les-Bains
Criel-sur-Mer
Dieppe
Picquigny
AMIENS
St.Valery-en-Caux
Veules-les-Roses
St.Nicolas d Aliermont
Veulettes-sur-Mer
Angiens
St.Pierre-le-Vieux
Fécamp
Etretat
Doudeville
Auffay
Conty
La Poterie-Cap-d'Antifer
St.Jouin-Bruneval
Sainte-Saire
Grigneuseville
Clères
Forges-les-Eaux
Buchy
Picardie
St.Nicolas-de-Bliquetuit
Montville
La Mailleraye-sur-Seine
Honfleur
Heurteauville
ROUEN
Gournay-en-Bray
La-Rivière-Saint-Sauveur
Jumièges
Le Mesnil-Jumièges
Lyons-la-Forêt
Oissel
Pont-L'Eveque
Campigny
Normandie
Cormeilles
Lisieux
La Vespière
Notre-Dame-de-Courson
Le Noyer-en-Ouche
ÉVREUX
Broglie
Vimoutiers
Gisay-la-Coudre
Saint-André-de-l'Eure
Le Sap
Rugles
PARIS
Gacé
Nonancourt
Brézolles
Normandie
Nogent-le-Roi
Île-de-France
La Fresnaye-sur-Chédouet
Courville-sur-Eure
Mamers
Milly-la-Forêt
Thiron-Gardais
Centre
Brou
Marboué
Saint-Denis-les-Ponts
Châteaudun
Montfort-le-Gesnois
Pays de la Loire
St.Calais
Saran
Vitry-aux-Loges
ORLÉANS
Azé
Saint-Jean-le-Blanc
La Chapelle-Saint-Mesmin
Châteauneuf-sur-Loire
A28
A29
E402
A29
E44
A151
E5
A131
E46
A13
E46
E46
E401
A16
E46
E46
A28
E5
A1
E19
E15
E402
E15
A6
E5
A10
E50
A11
E60
A19
E502
E60
A77
A
12km
B
21
C
D

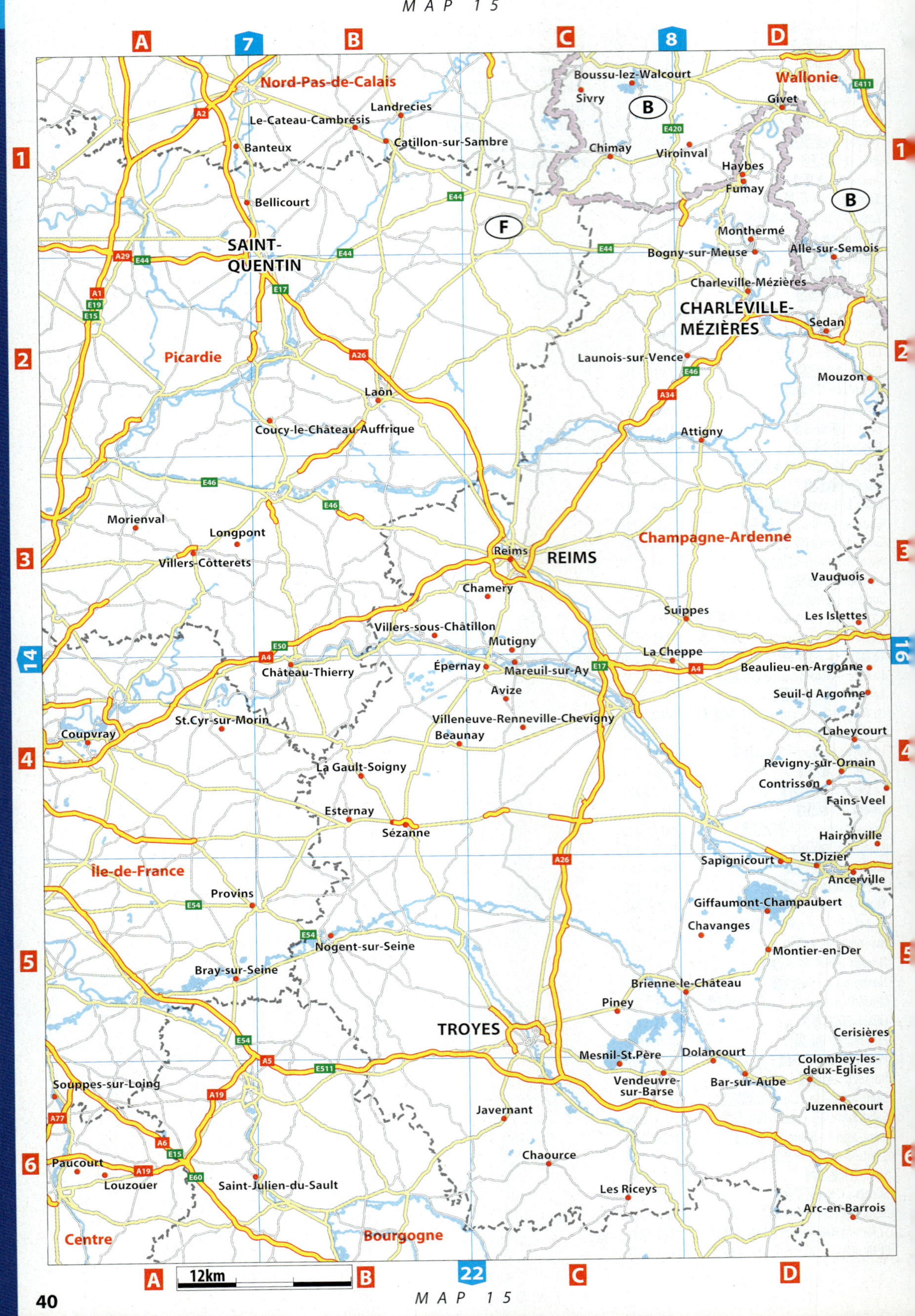
A
7
B
C
8
D
1
2
3
4
5
6
14
16
Nord-Pas-de-Calais
Landrecies
Le-Cateau-Cambrésis
Banteux
Catillon-sur-Sambre
Bellicourt
SAINT-QUENTIN
Boussu-lez-Walcourt
Sivry
Chimay
Viroinval
Wallonie
Givet
Haybes
Fumay
Monthermé
Bogny-sur-Meuse
Alle-sur-Semois
Charleville-Mézières
CHARLEVILLE-MÉZIÈRES
Sedan
F
B
Picardie
Laon
Coucy-le-Château-Auffrique
Launois-sur-Vence
Mouzon
Attigny
Morienval
Longpont
Villers-Cotterets
Reims
REIMS
Champagne-Ardenne
Chamery
Vauquois
Suippes
Les Islettes
Villers-sous-Châtillon
Mutigny
La Cheppe
Château-Thierry
Épernay
Mareuil-sur-Ay
Beaulieu-en-Argonne
Avize
Seuil-d Argonne
St.Cyr-sur-Morin
Villeneuve-Renneville-Chevigny
Coupvray
Beaunay
Laheycourt
La Gault-Soigny
Revigny-sur-Ornain
Contrisson
Fains-Veel
Esternay
Sézanne
Haironville
Sapignicourt
St.Dizier
Ancerville
Île-de-France
Provins
Giffaumont-Champaubert
Chavanges
Nogent-sur-Seine
Montier-en-Der
Bray-sur-Seine
Brienne-le-Château
Piney
TROYES
Cerisières
Mesnil-St.Père
Dolancourt
Colombey-les-deux-Eglises
Vendeuvre-sur-Barse
Bar-sur-Aube
Souppes-sur-Loing
Javernant
Juzennecourt
Chaource
Paucourt
Louzouer
Saint-Julien-du-Sault
Les Riceys
Arc-en-Barrois
Centre
Bourgogne
A2
A29
E44
A1
E19
E15
E17
A26
E46
E420
E411
A34
E50
A4
A5
E54
E511
A19
A77
A6
E60
12km
22

A
8
B
C
9
D
1
2
3
4
5
6
15
23
La Roche
Rochefort
Nisramont
Han-Sur-Lesse
Ave-et-Auffe
Saint-Hubert
Bastogne
Redu
Wallonie
Herbeumont
Redange/Attert
Arlon
Luxembourg
LUXEMBOURG
Maulusmühle
Obereisenbach
Hoscheid
Vianden
Heiderscheid
Bleesbrück
Diekirch
Ermsdorf
Larochette
Echternach
Mersch
Pronsfeld
Waxweiler
Gerolstein
Manderscheid
Eisenschmitt
Wittlich
Gillenfeld
Lutzerath
Cochem
Valwig
Ernst
Briedern
Bremm
Neef
Ellenz/Poltersdorf
Sankt Aldegund
Ediger/Eller
Alf
Pünderich
Reil/Mosel
Zell/Mosel
Lösnich
Enkirch
Ürzig
Kinheim
Nonnweiler
Traben-Trarbach
Bernkastel
Graach/Mosel
Brauneberg
Mülheim/Mosel
Kesten
Veldenz
Piesport
Wintrich
Neumagen-Dhron
Minheim
Klüsserath
Köwerich
Ensch
Leiwen
Trittenheim
Schweich/Mosel bei Trier
Longuich/Mosel
Schleich
Mehring
Klingenberg
Herrstein
Morbach
Kempfeld
Fischbach
Thalfang
Idar/Oberstein
Trier
TRIER
Oberbrombach
Rheinland-Pfalz
Lauterecken
Burgen
Kamp-Bornhofen
Simmern/Hunsrück
Baumholder
Sankt Julian
Thallichtenberg
Elzweiler
Nohfelden
Eckersweiler
Altenglan
Wadern
Kusel
Jettenbach
Tholey
Föckelberg
Glan-Münchweiler
Sankt Wendel
Landstuhl
Ottweiler
Bexbach
Neunkirchen/Saar
Sankt Ingbert
Zweibrücken
Blieskastel
Pirmasens
Hornbach
Eppenbrunn
Saarburg
Palzem
Weiskirchen
Losheim am See
Schwebsange
Perl
Mettlach
Merzig
Beckingen
Saarlouis
Völklingen
Saarbrücken
SAARBRÜCKEN
Dudelange
Stenay
Longuyon
Dun-sur-Meuse
Damvillers
Loison
Avocourt
Thierville-sur-Meuse
Etain
Verdun
Dieue-sur-Meuse
Metz
METZ
Lachaussée
Souilly
Nubécourt
La Croix-sur-Meuse
Issoncourt
Heudicourt sous les Côtes
Nonsard Lamarche
St.Mihiel
Pont-à-Mousson
Marbotte
Millery
Lorraine
Harskirchen
Fénétrange
Phalsbourg
Rhodes
Saverne
Niderviller
Breisach/Rhein
Bar-le-Duc
Longeville-en-Barrois
Commercy
Tannois
Bruley
Velaines
NANCY
Montplonne
Void-Vacon
Toul
Nancy
Ligny-en-Barrois
Nant-le-Grand
Saint-Nicolas-de-Port
Lunéville
Alsace
Morley
Montigny-lès-Vaucouleurs
Vaucouleurs
Richardménil
Champougny
Gondrecourt-le-Château
Maxey-sur-Vaise
Pierre-Percée
Obernai
Joinville
Maxey-sur-Meuse
Favières
Baccarat
Heiligenstein
Souslosse sous St.Elophe
Mittelbergheim
Charmes
Donjeux
Rollainville
Etival-Clairefontaine
Rebeuville
Certilleux
Froncles
Tilleux
Ste.Marie-aux-Mines
Pompierre
Thaon-les-Vosges
Viéville
Goncourt
Ribeauvillé
Bulgnéville
Fraize
Épinal
Le Bonhomme
Riquewihr
Champagne-Ardenne
Orbey
Kaysersberg
Trois Epis
Chaumont
Gérardmer
Turckheim
Colmar
Eguisheim
St.Nabord
La Bresse
Munster
Monthureux-sur Saône
Pfaffenheim
Westhalten
Plombières-les-Bains
Lautenbach
Fessenheim
Ventron
Orschwir
Murbach
Guebwiller
Corre
Franche-Comté
Rupt-sur-Moselle
Soultz
Champigny-lès-Langres
St.Loup-sur-Semouse
Ungersheim
12km
E46
E411
E421
E29
A60
E42
E44
E25
E29
A64
A1
E422
A6
A30
E50
A8
A4
E52
A33
A35
E23
A31
E21
E512
E17
E31

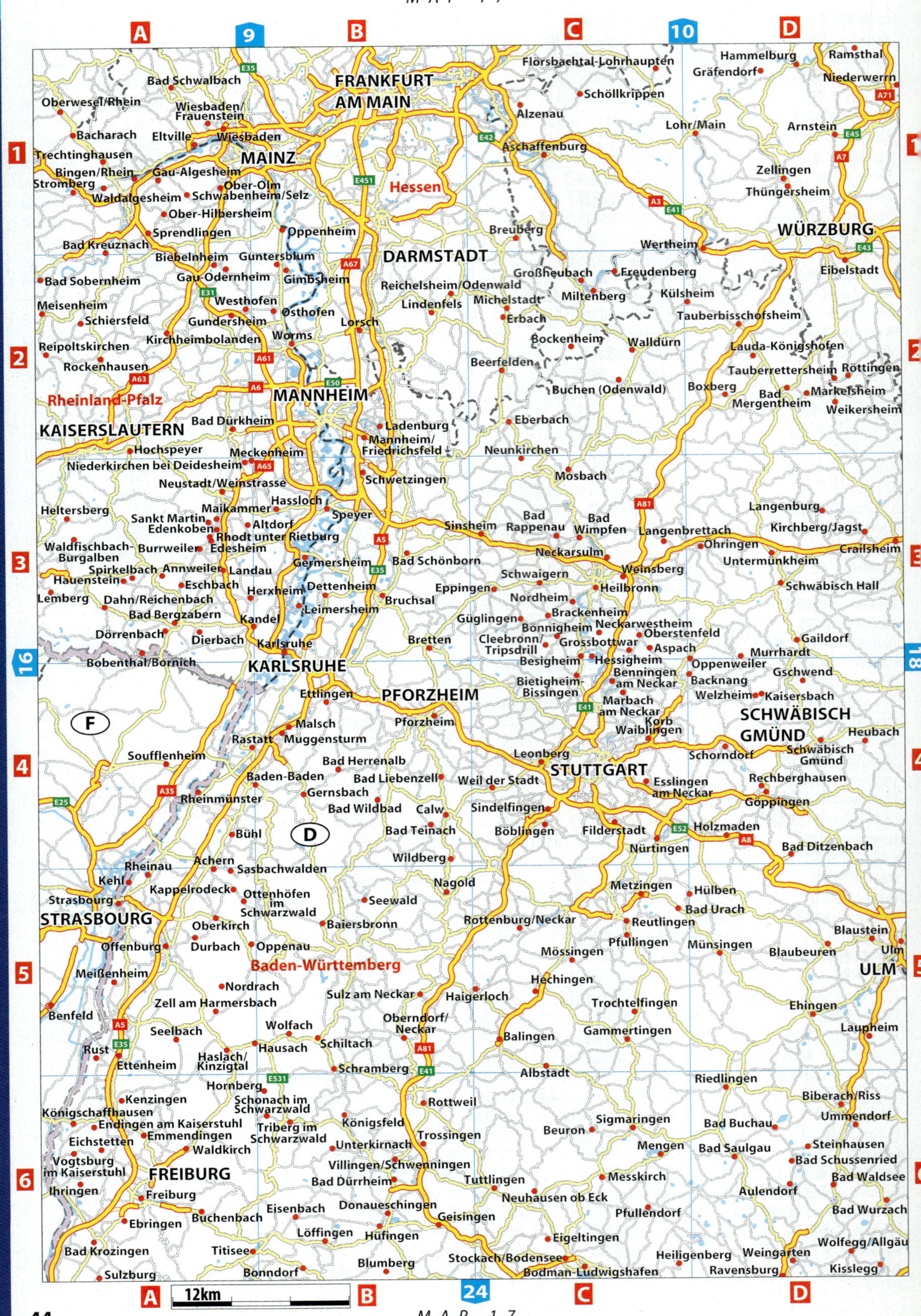
A
9
B
C
10
D
1
2
3
4
5
6
16
18
24
12km
FRANKFURT AM MAIN
Bad Schwalbach
Oberwesel/Rhein
Wiesbaden/Frauenstein
Bacharach
Eltville
Wiesbaden
MAINZ
Trechtinghausen
Bingen/Rhein
Stromberg
Gau-Algesheim
Ober-Olm
Waldalgesheim
Schwabenheim/Selz
Ober-Hilbersheim
Sprendlingen
Bad Kreuznach
Biebelnheim
Guntersblum
Oppenheim
Bad Sobernheim
Gau-Odernheim
Gimbsheim
Meisenheim
Westhofen
Osthofen
Schiersfeld
Gundersheim
Worms
Lorsch
Reipoltskirchen
Kirchheimbolanden
Rockenhausen
Rheinland-Pfalz
MANNHEIM
KAISERSLAUTERN
Bad Dürkheim
Hochspeyer
Meckenheim
Niederkirchen bei Deidesheim
Neustadt/Weinstrasse
Hassloch
Maikammer
Heltersberg
Sankt Martin
Edenkoben
Altdorf
Speyer
Rhodt unter Rietburg
Waldfischbach-Burgalben
Burrweiler
Edesheim
Germersheim
Spirkelbach
Annweiler
Landau
Hauenstein
Eschbach
Herxheim
Dettenheim
Lemberg
Dahn/Reichenbach
Leimersheim
Bad Bergzabern
Kandel
Dörrenbach
Dierbach
Karlsruhe
Bobenthal/Bornich
KARLSRUHE
Ettlingen
PFORZHEIM
Pforzheim
Malsch
Rastatt
Muggensturm
F
Soufflenheim
Bad Herrenalb
Baden-Baden
Bad Liebenzell
Gernsbach
Rheinmünster
Bad Wildbad
Calw
Bad Teinach
Bühl
D
Wildberg
Rheinau
Achern
Sasbachwalden
Kehl
Nagold
Strasbourg
Kappelrodeck
Ottenhöfen im Schwarzwald
Seewald
STRASBOURG
Oberkirch
Baiersbronn
Offenburg
Durbach
Oppenau
Baden-Württemberg
Meißenheim
Nordrach
Zell am Harmersbach
Sulz am Neckar
Benfeld
Wolfach
Oberndorf/Neckar
Seelbach
Hausach
Schiltach
Rust
Haslach/Kinzigtal
Ettenheim
Schramberg
Hornberg
Kenzingen
Schonach im Schwarzwald
Königschaffhausen
Triberg im Schwarzwald
Königsfeld
Endingen am Kaiserstuhl
Eichstetten
Emmendingen
Unterkirnach
Vogtsburg im Kaiserstuhl
Waldkirch
Villingen/Schwenningen
FREIBURG
Bad Dürrheim
Ihringen
Freiburg
Eisenbach
Donaueschingen
Ebringen
Buchenbach
Löffingen
Hüfingen
Bad Krozingen
Titisee
Blumberg
Sulzburg
Bonndorf
Flörsbachtal-Lohrhaupten
Schöllkrippen
Alzenau
Aschaffenburg
Hessen
Darmstadt
DARMSTADT
Breuberg
Reichelsheim/Odenwald
Lindenfels
Michelstadt
Erbach
Großheubach
Miltenberg
Beerfelden
Ladenburg
Mannheim/Friedrichsfeld
Schwetzingen
Neunkirchen
Eberbach
Mosbach
Sinsheim
Bad Rappenau
Bad Wimpfen
Neckarsulm
Bad Schönborn
Schwaigern
Eppingen
Bruchsal
Nordheim
Heilbronn
Brackenheim
Güglingen
Bönnigheim
Neckarwestheim
Bretten
Cleebronn/Tripsdrill
Grossbottwar
Oberstenfeld
Besigheim
Hessigheim
Aspach
Bietigheim-Bissingen
Benningen am Neckar
Marbach am Neckar
Korb
Waiblingen
Leonberg
STUTTGART
Weil der Stadt
Sindelfingen
Böblingen
Filderstadt
Esslingen am Neckar
Nürtingen
Metzingen
Rottenburg/Neckar
Reutlingen
Pfullingen
Mössingen
Hechingen
Haigerloch
Balingen
Trochtelfingen
Gammertingen
Albstadt
Rottweil
Trossingen
Tuttlingen
Sigmaringen
Beuron
Mengen
Messkirch
Neuhausen ob Eck
Pfullendorf
Geisingen
Eigeltingen
Stockach/Bodensee
Bodman-Ludwigshafen
Hammelburg
Ramsthal
Gräfendorf
Niederwerrn
Lohr/Main
Arnstein
Zellingen
Thüngersheim
WÜRZBURG
Wertheim
Freudenberg
Eibelstadt
Külsheim
Tauberbischofsheim
Bockenheim
Walldürn
Lauda-Königshofen
Tauberrettersheim
Röttingen
Buchen (Odenwald)
Boxberg
Bad Mergentheim
Markelsheim
Weikersheim
Langenburg
Kirchberg/Jagst
Langenbrettach
Öhringen
Crailsheim
Untermünkheim
Weinsberg
Schwäbisch Hall
Gaildorf
Murrhardt
Oppenweiler
Gschwend
Backnang
Welzheim
Kaisersbach
SCHWÄBISCH GMÜND
Heubach
Schorndorf
Schwäbisch Gmünd
Rechberghausen
Göppingen
Holzmaden
Bad Ditzenbach
Hülben
Bad Urach
Blaustein
Münsingen
Blaubeuren
Ulm
ULM
Ehingen
Laupheim
Riedlingen
Biberach/Riss
Bad Buchau
Ummendorf
Bad Saulgau
Steinhausen
Bad Schussenried
Bad Waldsee
Aulendorf
Bad Wurzach
Wolfegg/Allgäu
Heiligenberg
Weingarten
Ravensburg
Kisslegg
E35
E42
E451
A67
A61
A63
A6
E50
A65
A5
E31
A35
E25
A81
E41
E52
A8
A3
A7
A71
E45
E43
E531

A
10
B
C
11
D
1
2
3
4
5
6
17
CZ
D
Dittelbrunn
Königsberg
Ebern
Weismain
Bischofsgrün
Wunsiedel
Marktredwitz
Waldsassen
Neualbenreuth
Schonungen
Goldkronach
Fichtelberg
Pechbrunn
Zeil am Main
Hassfurt
Baunach
Mehlmeisel
Mitterteich
Bayreuth
Ebelsbach
Mistelgau
Weidenberg
Friedenfels
Eltmann am Main
Kemnath
Aufseß
Erbendorf
Eisenheim
Gerolzhofen
Bamberg
Bärnau
Escherndorf
Volkach
Wiesenttal
Ebrach
Parkstein
Nordheim am M.
Prichsenstadt
Ebermannstadt
Pottenstein
Dettelbach
Schlüsselfeld
Albertshofen
Forchheim
Pleystein
Mainstockheim
Kitzingen
Burghaslach
Adelsdorf
Vohenstrauss
Plech
Mainbernheim
Moosbach
Betzenstein
Iphofen
Scheinfeld
Segnitz
Marktbreit
Herzogenaurach
Sulzbach-Rosenberg
Hersbruck
Oberviechtach
Poppenricht
Ippesheim
Neustadt/Aisch
Amberg
Bad Windsheim
Nürnberg
Kümmersbruck
Cadolzburg
NÜRNBERG
Kastl/Oberpfalz
Schwandorf
Zirndorf
Burgbernheim
Reichelshofen
Feucht
Bodenwöhr
Rothenburg ob der Tauber
Hohenburg
Steinberg am See
Neumarkt/Oberpfalz
Geslau
Ansbach
Herrieden
Hilpoltstein
Enderndorf
Berching
Schnelldorf
Beratzhausen
Absberg
REGENSBURG
Gunzenhausen
Greding
Dinkelsbühl
Beilngries
Wassertrüdingen
Weissenburg
Riedenburg
Bad Abbach
Kelheim
Treuchtlingen
Denkendorf
Oettingen
Altmannstein
Ellwangen
Eichstätt
Mörnsheim
Bad Gögging
Deiningen
Monheim
INGOLSTADT
Aalen
Bopfingen
Nördlingen
Huisheim
Ingolstadt
Baden-Württemberg
Neuburg/Donau
Neresheim
Manching
Donauwörth
Rain/Lech
Nattheim
Bayern
Heidenheim
Wolnzach
LANDSHUT
Herbrechtingen
Schrobenhausen
Wertingen
Giengen
Öllingen
Aichach
Langenau
Günzburg
AUGSBURG
Neusäß
Erding
Ettenbeuren
Augsburg
Friedberg
Sulzemoos
Königsbrunn
München
Asschheim
MÜNCHEN
Markt Wald
Landsberg am Lech
Bad Wörishofen
Prien am Chiemsee
Memmingen
Dießen
Bad Aibling
Mühlberg
Frasdorf
Ottobeuren
Kaufbeuren
Weilheim in Oberbayern
ROSENHEIM
Bad Feilnbach
Schongau
Bad Tölz
Leutkirch im Allgäu
Biesenhofen
Peiting
Wackersberg
Bad Wiessee
Oberaudorf
Altusried
Benediktbeuern
Schliersee
Bayrischzell
Walchsee
A70
E48
A73
E51
E50
A6
A3
E56
A93
E45
A9
E53
A92
A8
E52
E552
A94
E43
A7
E533
A95
E54
A96
E45
A8
E60
E532
A93
12km
25

A
B
C
D
1
2
3
4
5
6
18
27
26
PLZEN
CZ
D
A
Bayern
CESKE BUDEJOVICE
PASSAU
LINZ
WELS
STEYR
SALZBURG
Chammünster
Bad Kötzting
Arnbruck
Viechtach
Bodenmais
Steinach/Straubing
Bernried
Bogen
Deggendorf
Lalling
Grafenau
Freyung
Waldkirchen
Plattling
Eging am See
Landau/Isar
Vilshofen
Passau
Dingolfing
Neuhaus/Inn
Bad Birnbach
Bad Griesbach
Suben
Bayerbach
Bad Füssing
Kirchham
Massing
Eggenfelden
Ranshofen
Altötting
Burghausen
Burgkirchen
Haslach
Bad Großpertholz
Langschlag-Mitterschlag
Kefermarkt
Königswiesen
Gallneukirchen
Eferding
Naarn
Marchtrenk
Aschbach Markt
Weistrach
Geboltskirchen
Kremsmünster
Gmünden
Scharnstein
Nußdorf am Attersee
Mondsee
St.Pankraz
Hollenstein/Ybbs
Ebensee
Unterach am Attersee
Wonneberg
Petting
Traunstein
Freilassing
Übersee/Chiemsee
Siegsdorf
Bergen/Chiemgau
Inzell
Ruhpolding
Bad Reichenhall
St.Wolfgang
Liezen
Reit im Winkl
Berchtesgaden
Kössen
Bischofswiesen
Gosau
12km

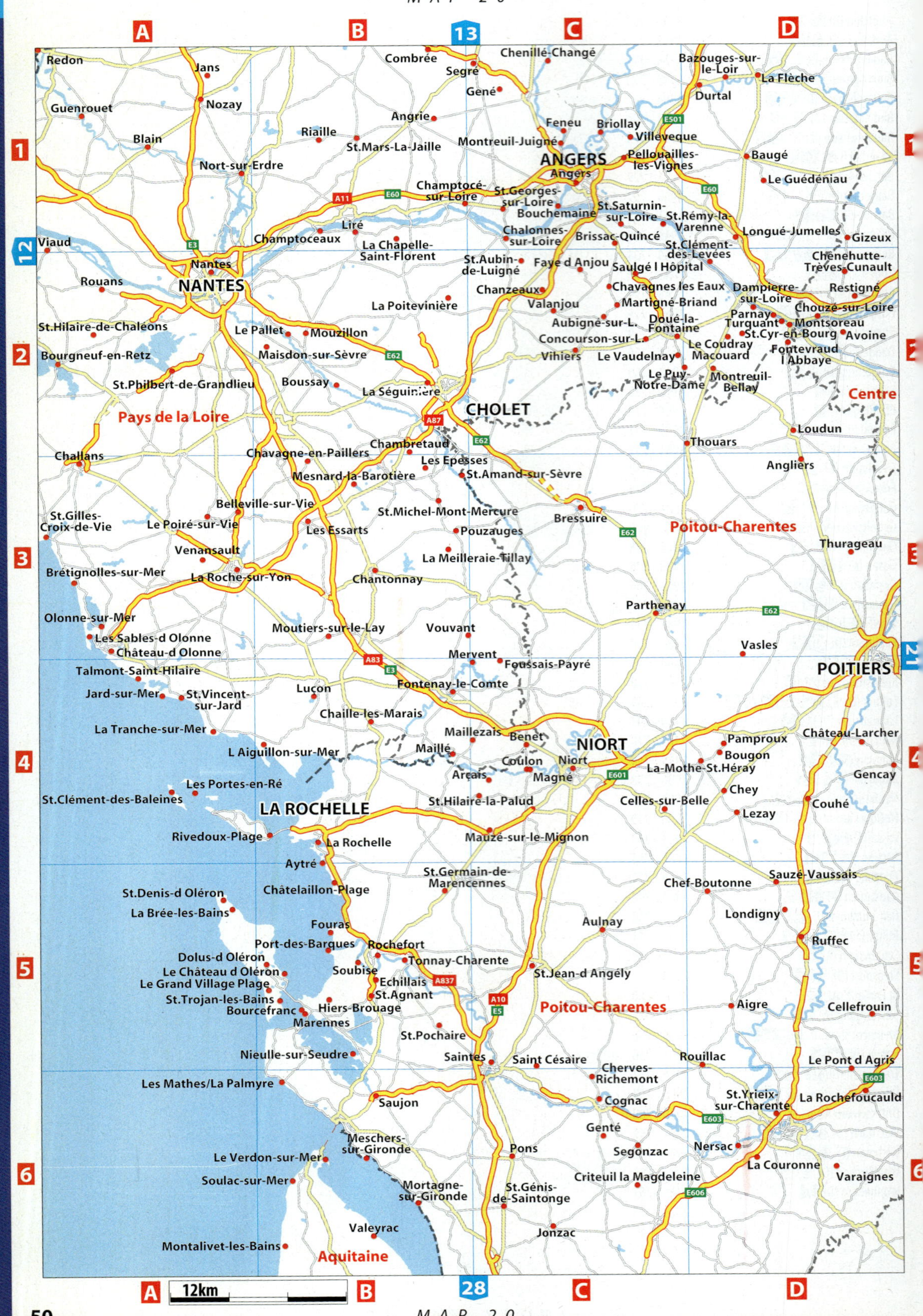
A
B
13
C
D
Redon
Jans
Combrée
Segré
Chenillé-Changé
Bazouges-sur-le-Loir
La Flèche
Durtal
Nozay
Gené
Guenrouet
Angrie
Feneu
Briollay
E501
Villevêque
Blain
Riaille
St.Mars-La-Jaille
Montreuil-Juigné
1
ANGERS
Angers
Pellouailles-les-Vignes
Baugé
Nort-sur-Erdre
Le Guédéniau
Champtocé-sur-Loire
St.Georges-sur-Loire
E60
A11
E60
Bouchemaine
St.Saturnin-sur-Loire
St.Rémy-la-Varenne
Liré
Chalonnes-sur-Loire
Brissac-Quincé
Longué-Jumelles
Gizeux
E3
Champtoceaux
La Chapelle-Saint-Florent
12
Viaud
St.Clément-des-Levées
St.Aubin-de-Luigné
Faye d Anjou
Saulgé l Hôpital
Chenehutte-Trèves-Cunault
Nantes
Rouans
NANTES
Chanzeaux
Chavagnes les Eaux
Dampierre-sur-Loire
Restigné
La Poitevinière
Valanjou
Martigné-Briand
Chouzé-sur-Loire
Parnay
St.Hilaire-de-Chaléons
Aubigné-sur-L.
Doué-la-Fontaine
Turquant
Montsoreau
Le Pallet
Mouzillon
St.Cyr-en-Bourg
Avoine
Concourson-sur-L.
Le Coudray Macouard
Fontevraud l Abbaye
2
Bourgneuf-en-Retz
Maisdon-sur-Sèvre
E62
Vihiers
Le Vaudelnay
Le Puy-Notre-Dame
Montreuil-Bellay
Boussay
St.Philbert-de-Grandlieu
La Séguinière
Centre
CHOLET
Pays de la Loire
A87
Loudun
E62
Chambretaud
Thouars
Challans
Chavagne-en-Paillers
Les Epesses
Angliers
Mesnard-la-Barotière
St.Amand-sur-Sèvre
Belleville-sur-Vie
St.Michel-Mont-Mercure
St.Gilles-Croix-de-Vie
Le Poiré-sur-Vie
Bressuire
Poitou-Charentes
Les Essarts
Pouzauges
E62
Venansault
Thurageau
3
La Meilleraie-Tillay
Brétignolles-sur-Mer
La Roche-sur-Yon
Chantonnay
Parthenay
E62
Olonne-sur-Mer
Moutiers-sur-le-Lay
Vouvant
Les Sables-d Olonne
Vasles
Château-d Olonne
Mervent
21
POITIERS
Foussais-Payré
A83
Talmont-Saint-Hilaire
E3
Jard-sur-Mer
St.Vincent-sur-Jard
Luçon
Fontenay-le-Comte
La Tranche-sur-Mer
Chaille-les-Marais
Château-Larcher
Maillezais
Benet
Pamproux
NIORT
L Aiguillon-sur-Mer
Maillé
4
Bougon
Coulon
Niort
Gencay
La-Mothe-St.Héray
Arçais
Magné
E601
Les Portes-en-Ré
Chey
St.Clément-des-Baleines
St.Hilaire-la-Palud
Celles-sur-Belle
Couhé
LA ROCHELLE
Lezay
Rivedoux-Plage
Mauzé-sur-le-Mignon
La Rochelle
Aytré
St.Germain-de-Marencennes
Sauzé-Vaussais
St.Denis-d Oléron
Châtelaillon-Plage
Chef-Boutonne
La Brée-les-Bains
Londigny
Aulnay
Fouras
Port-des-Barques
Rochefort
Ruffec
Dolus-d Oléron
Tonnay-Charente
Soubise
5
Le Château d Oléron
St.Jean-d Angély
Le Grand Village Plage
Echillais
A837
St.Agnant
St.Trojan-les-Bains
A10
Bourcefranc
Hiers-Brouage
Poitou-Charentes
Aigre
Cellefrouin
E5
Marennes
St.Pochaire
Nieulle-sur-Seudre
Saintes
Saint Césaire
Rouillac
Le Pont d Agris
Cherves-Richemont
Les Mathes/La Palmyre
E603
St.Yrieix-sur-Charente
La Rochefoucauld
Saujon
Cognac
E603
Genté
Meschers-sur-Gironde
Pons
Nersac
Segonzac
Le Verdon-sur-Mer
6
La Couronne
Varaignes
Criteuil la Magdeleine
Soulac-sur-Mer
Mortagne-sur-Gironde
St.Génis-de-Saintonge
E606
Jonzac
Valeyrac
Montalivet-les-Bains
Aquitaine
A
12km
B
28
C
D

A
B
14
C
D
Pays de la Loire
Vendôme
La Chapelle-Saint-Mesmin
Dry
Beaugency
Lailly-en-Val
Marcilly-en-Villette
Sully-sur-Loire
Ternay
Montoire-sur-le-Loir
St.Gondon
Gien
Grez-Neuville
BLOIS
Chambord
Blois
Lamotte-Beuvron
Chaon
St.Brisson-sur-Loire
Neuillé-Pont-Pierre
Villedômer
Tour-en-Sologne
La Ferte-Beauharnais
Argent-sur-Sauldre
Chaumont-sur-Loire
Nouan-le-Fuzelier
La Daguenière
TOURS
Cheverny
Barlieu
Amboise
Aubigny-sur-Nère
Blaison-Gohier
Vouvray
Vailly-sur-Sauldre
Villandry
Chenonceaux
Angé
Veigné
Athée-sur-Cher
Theillay
Azay-le-Rideau
Esvres-sur-Indre
Selles-sur-Cher
Langon
Villaines les Rochers
Mennetou-sur-Cher
Chabris
Humbligny
Reignac-sur-Indre
Genillé
Méry-sur-Cher
Allogny
Menetou-Salon
Loches
Sainte-Maure-de-Touraine
Montrésor
Valençay
BOURGES
Guilly
Bourges
Centre
St.Georges-sur-Arnon
Levet
Neuvy-Pailloux
Martizay
La Roche-Posay
Châteauroux
Neuillay-les-Bois
CHÂTEAUROUX
Luant
Vicq-sur-Gartempe
St.Amand-Montrond
La Pérouille
Coëx
Pouligny-Saint-Pierre
Thenay
Le Châtelet
Le Blanc
Oulches
St.Bonnet-Tronçais
Argenton-sur-Creuse
La Châtre
Culan
Nieuil-l'Espoir
Sainte-Sévère-sur-Indre
Cuzion
Montmorillon
Lussac-les-Châteaux
Estivareilles
Moulismes
Montluçon
Poitou-Charentes
Néris-les-Bains
St.Laurent
Jarnages
Gouzon
Chambon-sur-Voueize
Bessines-sur-Gartempe
Cressat
Chénérailles
Confolens
Limousin
Châtelus-le-Marcheix
Javerdat
Oradour-sur-Glane
Roumazières-Loubert
Montboucher
Bourganeuf
Aubusson
Nieul
Chabanais
St.Junien-la-Bregère
Felletin
LIMOGES
Peyrat-le-Château
Auvergne
St.Laurent-sur-Gorre
Bujaleuf
Auphelle
Beaumont du Lac
Les Salles-Lavaugyon
Pageas
Saint Estèphe
St.Merd-les-Oussines
St.Sauves d'Auvergne
St.Saud-Lacoussière
Messeix
Nontron
Meuzac
Murat-le-Quaire
Aquitaine
La Coquille
Treignac
Meymac
Ussel
La Bourboule
St.Yrieix-la-Perche
La Tour-d'Auvergne
St.Front-la-Rivière
Chastreix
St.Jean-de-Côle
28
12km
29
1
2
3
4
5
6
20
77

A
B
15
C
D
1
2
3
4
5
6
21
23
29
30
12km
Nogent-sur-Vernisson
Gurgy
Auxerre
Chablis
Laignes
Ouzouer-sur-Trézée
Briare-le-Canal
Châtillon-sur-Loire
Saint-Fargeau
Bonny-sur-Loire
Léré
Boulleret
Clamecy
Semur-en-Auxois
Rouvray
Savigny-le-Sec
E15
Dijon
DIJON
Marsannay-la-Côte
A77
Centre
E60
A6
A31
E21
E17
Bourgogne
La Charité-sur-Loire
Villequiers
Pougues-les-Eaux
Anost
Nuits-Saint-Georges
Châtillon-en-Bazois
Château-Chinon
A36
Beaune
Nolay
Autun
Neuvy-Le-Barrois
St.Honoré-les-Bains
Chiddes
Sancoins
Décize
Fours
Étang-sur-Arroux
Chalon-sur-Saône
Givry
Luzy
Lurcy-Lévis
Ecuisses
E607
CHALON-SUR-SAÔNE
Bessais-le-Fromental
Beaulon
Moulins
St.Gengoux-le-National
Génelard
Buxières-les-Mines
E62
Digoin
Charolles
Villefranche-d'Allier
Jaligny-sur-Besbre
Treteau
St.Marcel-en-Murat
Montoldre
Le Donjon
St.Pourçain-sur-Sioule
Varennes-sur-Allier
Prissé
Vinzelles
A40
Lapalisse
Pruzilly
Pont-de-Veyle
A71
Auvergne
Billy
La Chapelle-de-Guinchay
Illiat
St.Eloy-les-Mines
Pouilly-sous-Charlieu
Charlieu
Belmont-de-la-Loire
Ebreuil
Bellerive-sur-Allier
St.Jean d Ardières
Ambierle
Cours-la-Ville
Saint-Étienne-la-Varenne
St.Rémy-de-Blot
Saint-Germain-Lespinasse
Belleville
Saint-Haon-le-Châtel
Aigueperse
Renaison
Les Noës
Roanne
Lamure-sur-Azergues
Sauret-Besserve
Villars-les-Dombes
Saint-André-d'Apchon
Randan
Arcon
Villefranche-sur-Saône
Manzat
Amplepuis
E70
Villerest
Le Cheix-sur-Morge
Châtel-Guyon
E11
Trévoux
St.Just-en-Chevalet
Riom
Les Sauvages
Thiers
Charbonnières-les-Varennes
Joux
Pontcharra-sur-Turdine
A432
A89
Lezoux
Violay
Saint-Forgeux
Clermont Ferrand
Noirétable
CLERMONT-FERRAND
Orcines
Panissières
Bibost
Boën
Aubusson-d'Auvergne
LYON
La Roche-Blanche
Chalmazel
Rhône-Alpes
A72
Aydat
Montpeyroux
Saint-Martin-en-Haut
Murol
Champeix
Saint-Symphorien-sur-Coise
A46
Chambon-sur-Lac
Tourzel-Ronzières
St.Georges d'Espéranche
A7
Super Besse
Solignat
St Anthème
Fontanes
Vienne

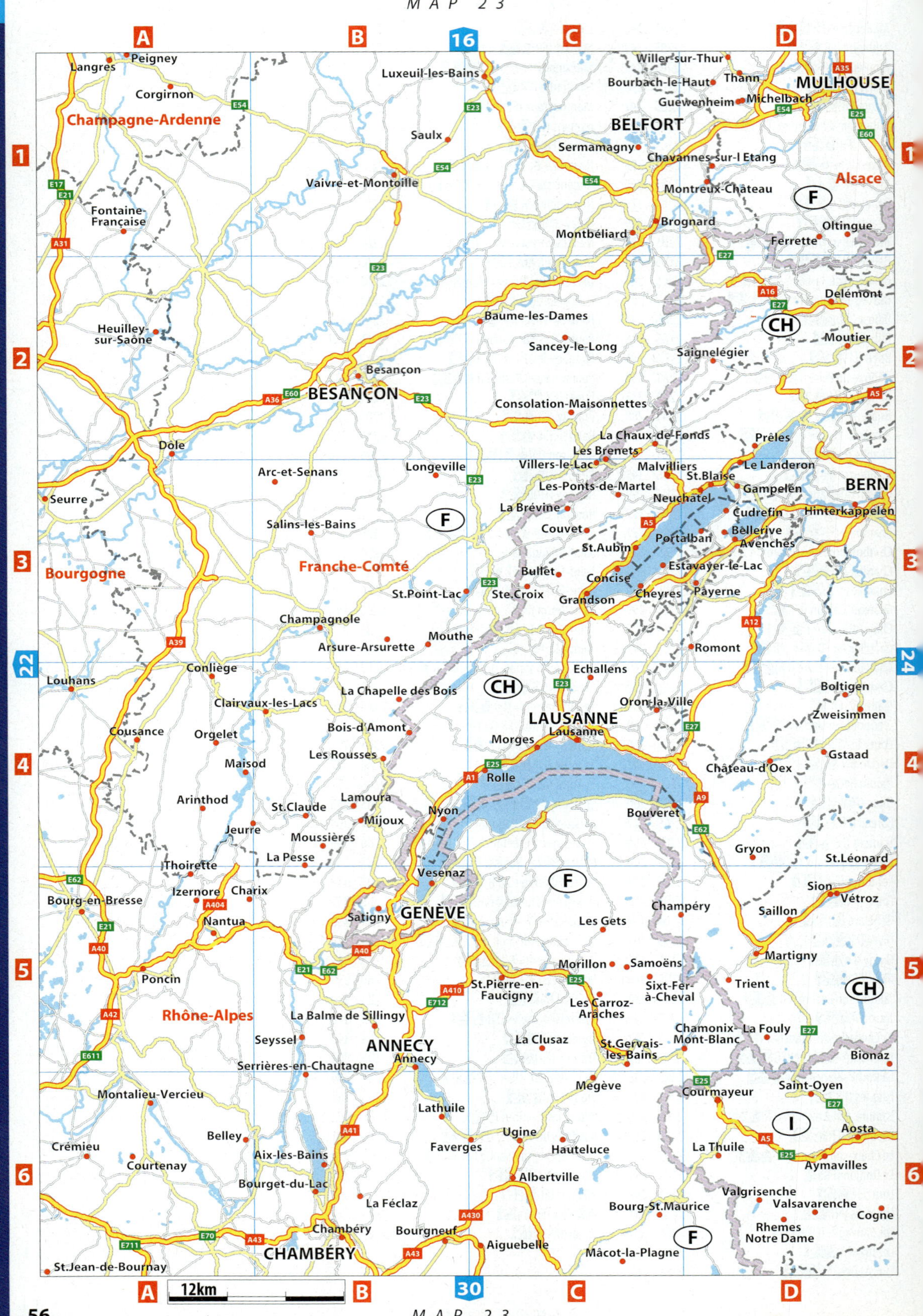
A
B
16
C
D
1
2
3
4
5
6
22
24
30
12km
Langres
Peigney
Corgirnon
Champagne-Ardenne
Fontaine-Française
Heuilley-sur-Saône
Luxeuil-les-Bains
Saulx
Vaivre-et-Montoille
Willer-sur-Thur
Thann
Bourbach-le-Haut
MULHOUSE
Guewenheim
Michelbach
BELFORT
Sermamagny
Chavannes-sur-l Etang
Montreux-Château
Alsace
F
Brognard
Montbéliard
Oltingue
Ferrette
Delémont
CH
Moutier
Baume-les-Dames
Sancey-le-Long
Saignelégier
Besançon
BESANÇON
Consolation-Maisonnettes
Dole
La Chaux-de-Fonds
Les Brenets
Villers-le-Lac
Prêles
Malvilliers
St.Blaise
Le Landeron
Arc-et-Senans
Longeville
Les-Ponts-de-Martel
Neuchâtel
Gampelen
BERN
Seurre
La Brévine
Cudrefin
Hinterkappelen
Salins-les-Bains
Couvet
Portalban
Bellerive
St.Aubin
Avenches
Bourgogne
Franche-Comté
Bullet
Concise
Estavayer-le-Lac
St.Point-Lac
Ste.Croix
Grandson
Cheyres
Payerne
Champagnole
Mouthe
Arsure-Arsurette
Romont
Conliège
Echallens
Louhans
La Chapelle des Bois
Boltigen
Clairvaux-les-Lacs
Oron-la-Ville
LAUSANNE
Lausanne
Zweisimmen
Cousance
Bois-d'Amont
Orgelet
Morges
Les Rousses
Gstaad
Maisod
Château-d'Oex
Rolle
Arinthod
Lamoura
St.Claude
Nyon
Mijoux
Bouveret
Jeurre
Moussières
Gryon
La Pesse
Thoirette
Vesenaz
St.Léonard
Charix
Izernore
Sion
Vétroz
Bourg-en-Bresse
Champéry
Satigny
GENÈVE
Saillon
Nantua
Les Gets
Martigny
Morillon
Samoëns
Poncin
St.Pierre-en-Faucigny
Sixt-Fer-à-Cheval
Trient
Les Carroz-Arâches
Rhône-Alpes
La Balme de Sillingy
Chamonix-Mont-Blanc
La Fouly
Seyssel
ANNECY
Annecy
La Clusaz
St.Gervais-les-Bains
Bionaz
Serrières-en-Chautagne
Megève
Saint-Oyen
Montalieu-Vercieu
Courmayeur
Lathuile
I
Belley
Ugine
Aosta
Crémieu
Faverges
Hauteluce
La Thuile
Aix-les-Bains
Courtenay
Aymavilles
Albertville
Bourget-du-Lac
Valgrisenche
Valsavarenche
La Féclaz
Bourg-St.Maurice
Cogne
Chambéry
Rhemes Notre Dame
Bourgneuf
CHAMBÉRY
Aiguebelle
Mâcot-la-Plagne
St.Jean-de-Bournay
A35
E54
E25
E60
E23
E17
E21
A31
E27
A16
A5
A36
E60
A39
A12
A9
E62
A1
A404
A40
E21
E62
A410
E712
A42
E611
A41
E711
E70
A43
A430

A
B
17
C
D
Müllheim
Sankt Blasien
Schluchsee
Bernau im Schwarzwald
Höchenschwand
Todtmoos
Bad Bellingen
Wutöschingen
Lauchringen
Wehr
BASEL
Waldshut-Tiengen
Murg
Laufenburg
Bad Säckingen
Frick
Reinach
Singen
Neuhausen
Überlingen
Allensbach
Radolfzell
Öhningen/Schienen
Reichenau
Eschenz
Steckborn
Konstanz
Kreuzlingen
Uhldingen-Mühlhofen
Meersburg
Stetten
Oberteuringen
Meckenbeuren
Amtzell
Wangen im Allgäu
Friedrichshafen
Tettnang
Kressbronn
Scheidegg
Lindau
Bregenz
WINTERTHUR
SANKT GALLEN
ZÜRICH
Zürich
Appenzell
Ennetbühl
FELDKIRCH
Nüziders
Nenzing
Vaduz/Liechtenstein
VADUZ
Langenthal
Huttwil
Sempach
Willisau
Dürrenroth
Burgdorf
LUZERN
Zug
Luzern
Weggis
Horw
Brunnen
Engelberg
Breil/Brigels
Churwalden
Davos
Brienz
Meiringen
Gwatt-Thun
Interlaken
Böningen
Aeschi
Gündlischwand
Grindelwald
Frutigen
Lauterbrunnen
Grimselpas
Vals
Andeer
Savognin
Splügen
Sankt Moritz
Bivio
Reckingen
Leukerbad
Chiavenna
Brig
Raron
Sierre
Simplon
Gordevio
Avegno
Tenero
Locarno
Bellinzona
Novate Mezzola
Sorico
Colico
Morbegno
Grimentz
Evolene
Les Haudères
Saas Fee
Santa Maria Maggiore
Cannobio
LUGANO
Germignaga
Agno
Muzzano-Lugano
Oggebbio
Luino
Molinazzo di Montegio
Mandello del Lario
Macugnaga
Piemonte
Verbania
Cervinia/Breuil
Carcoforo
Baveno
Meride
Lecco
Valle D'Aosta
Rimasco
Omegna
Gavirate
Olginate
Gressoney
Cravagliana
Antey-Saint-André
Torgnon
Riva Valdobbia
Varallo
Orta San Giulio
Ternate
Monte Marenzo
Alzano Lombardo
Madonna del Sasso
Lombardia
Merate
Saint-Denis
Brusson
Chatillon
Borgosesia
Seriate
Stezzano
Verrès
Bielmonte
Pombia
Saronno
Biassono
BERGAMO
Champorcher
Pont-Saint-Martin
Oropa
Valle Mosso
Nova Milanese
Hône
Pollone
Piatto
Treviglio
Biella
Ponderano
Candelo
Donato
Mongrando
Montalto Dora
Zubiena
Ivrea
NOVARA
MILANO
D
CH
I
1
2
3
4
5
6
23
25
31
12km

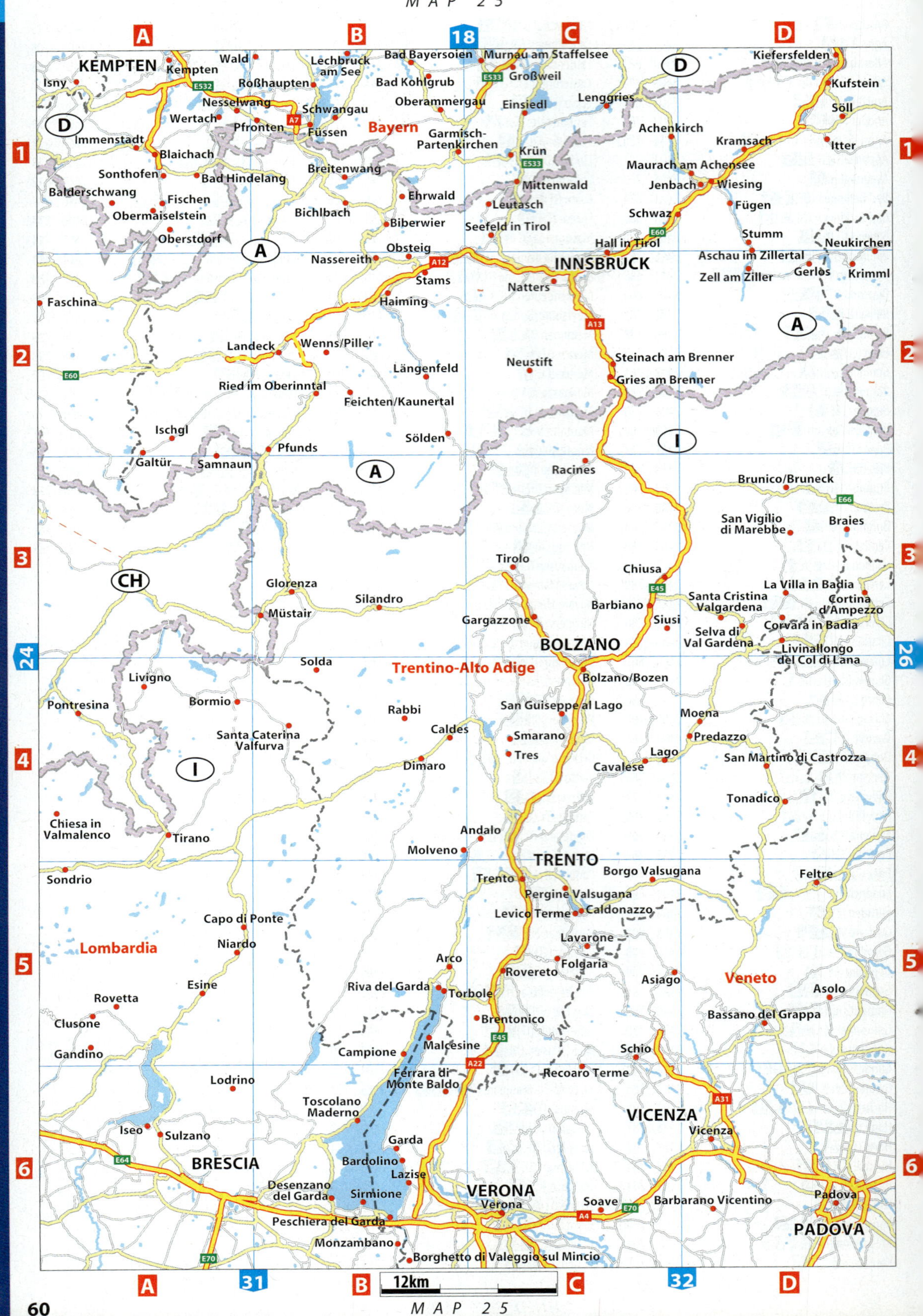
A
B
18
C
D
1
2
3
4
5
6
24
26
31
32
12km
KEMPTEN
Kempten
Isny
Wald
Lechbruck am See
Bad Bayersoien
Murnau am Staffelsee
Großweil
Kiefersfelden
Kufstein
Söll
Roßhaupten
Bad Kohlgrub
Nesselwang
Schwangau
Oberammergau
Einsiedl
Lenggries
Wertach
Pfronten
Füssen
Bayern
Garmisch-Partenkirchen
Immenstadt
Blaichach
Achenkirch
Kramsach
Itter
Krün
Sonthofen
Bad Hindelang
Breitenwang
Maurach am Achensee
Jenbach
Wiesing
Mittenwald
Balderschwang
Fischen
Ehrwald
Leutasch
Fügen
Obermaiselstein
Bichlbach
Schwaz
Biberwier
Seefeld in Tirol
Stumm
Neukirchen
Oberstdorf
Hall in Tirol
Aschau im Zillertal
Obsteig
Nassereith
INNSBRUCK
Gerlos
Krimml
Zell am Ziller
Stams
Natters
Faschina
Haiming
Landeck
Wenns/Piller
Steinach am Brenner
Neustift
Längenfeld
Gries am Brenner
Ried im Oberinntal
Feichten/Kaunertal
Ischgl
Sölden
Pfunds
Galtür
Samnaun
Racines
Brunico/Bruneck
San Vigilio di Marebbe
Braies
Tirolo
Chiusa
CH
Glorenza
La Villa in Badia
Santa Cristina Valgardena
Cortina d'Ampezzo
Silandro
Barbiano
Müstair
Siusi
Gargazzone
Selva di Val Gardena
Corvara in Badia
BOLZANO
Livinallongo del Col di Lana
Solda
Trentino-Alto Adige
Livigno
Bolzano/Bozen
Pontresina
Bormio
Rabbi
San Guiseppe al Lago
Moena
Santa Caterina Valfurva
Caldes
Smarano
Predazzo
Tres
Lago
San Martino di Castrozza
Dimaro
Cavalese
Tonadico
Chiesa in Valmalenco
Tirano
Andalo
Molveno
TRENTO
Borgo Valsugana
Sondrio
Trento
Feltre
Pergine Valsugana
Levico Terme
Caldonazzo
Capo di Ponte
Lavarone
Lombardia
Niardo
Arco
Folgaria
Rovereto
Asiago
Veneto
Esine
Riva del Garda
Torbole
Asolo
Rovetta
Brentonico
Bassano del Grappa
Clusone
Malcesine
Campione
Schio
Gandino
Ferrara di Monte Baldo
Recoaro Terme
Lodrino
Toscolano Maderno
VICENZA
Iseo
Sulzano
Vicenza
Garda
BRESCIA
Bardolino
Lazise
Desenzano del Garda
Sirmione
VERONA
Verona
Soave
Barbarano Vicentino
Padova
Peschiera del Garda
PADOVA
Monzambano
Borghetto di Valeggio sul Mincio
E532
A7
E533
E60
A12
A13
E66
E45
A22
A31
E64
E70
A4

A
B
19
C
D
1
2
3
4
5
6
25
27
32
D
A
I
SLO
HR
St.Martin bei Lofer
Waidring
St.Johann im Tirol
Fieberbrunn
Hochfilzen
Oberndorf in Tirol
Kitzbühel
Hütten
Maria Alm
Werfen
Schladming
Radstadt
Altenmarkt im Pongau
St.Johann im Pongau
Zell am See
Bruck an der Großglocknerstraße
Tweng
Oberwölz
Judenburg
Hüttschlag
Mühlen
Matrei
Malta
Obervellach
Mörtschach
Döbriach
Lienz
Ossiach
Villach
Annenheim
Kötschach Mauthen
San Candido
Hermagor
VILLACH
Drobollach
Schiefling am See
St.Primus
Sesto/Sexten
Faak/See
Ledenitzen
Ferlach
Santo Stefano di Cadore
Misurina
Sappada
Auronzo di Cadore
Tarvisio
DovjeMojstrana
Jerzersko
Sauris
Domegge di Cadore Belluno
Forni di Sopra
Bled
Bovec
Bohinjsko jezero
KRANJ
Kobarid
Gemona del Friuli
Smlednik
Tarcento
Tolmin
Friuli-Venezia Giulia
Andreis
Barcis
San Daniele del Friuli
UDINE
Montereale Valcellina
Belluno
NOVA GORICA
Dolegna del Collio
Corno di Rosazzo
Gorizia
Locatec
Pordenone
Zoppola
Zalosce
Gradisca d'Isonzo
San Vito al Tagliamento
Postojna
Conegliano
Sernaglia della Battaglia
Veneto
Grado
TRIESTE
Trieste
Treviso
Torre di Mosto
Bibione
Caorle
Izola
Portoroz
KOPER
Savudrija
Bašanija
Lido di Jesolo
VENEZIA
Umag
Rijeka
Mirano
Marghera
Cavallino-Treporti
Motovun
Icici
Venezia
Punta Sabbioni
Novigrad
Mošcenicka Draga
Baderna
Porec
E651
E55
A10
E66
A2
E652
A23
E61
E70
A27
A28
A4
E751
12km

A
B
C
D
1
2
3
4
5
6
19
26
33
Schremms
Retz
Pulkau
Bernhardsthal
Hohenau/March
Wilfersdorf
Bad Großpertholz
Zwettl
Eggenburg
Gars am Kamp
Schönberg
Langschlag-Mitterschlag
Armschlag
Stockerau
Pillichsdorf
Klosterneuburg
Arbesbach
Ottenschlag
Rossatzbach
Kefermarkt
Königswiesen
Tulln an der Donau
Wien
Hainburg/Donau
Laimbach am O.
Aggsbach Markt
Gallneukirchen
Waldhausen im S.
Altlengbach
WIEN
Orth/Donau
Naarn
St.Martin am Ybbsfelde
Erlauf
Alland
Traisen
Gumpoldskirchen
Deutsch Jahrndorf
Marchtrenk
Aschbach Markt
Purgstall an der Erlauf
Altenmarkt a/d T.
St.Andrä
Weistrach
Wiener Neustadt
Rust
Andau
Kremsmünster
Gaming
Mörbisch/Neusiedlersee
Reichenau/Rax
Hollenstein/Ybbs
St.Pankraz
Horitschon
Veitsch
Liezen
Vordernberg
GRAZ
Oberwölz
Judenburg
Unterlamm
Jennersdorf
Mühlen
St Stefan im Rosental
Stainz
Bad Sankt Leonhard
Bad Gams
Jagerberg
Deutschlandsberg
Oberrakitsch
Schwanberg
Gleinstätten
Moravske Toplice
Pölfing-Brunn
Murfeld
Gamlitz
Lendava
Villach
Ossiach
Annenheim
Eberndorf
Soboth
Ljutomer
Schiefling
Bleiburg
Kamnica
Drobollach
St.Primus
Ivanjkovci
Faak/See
Ferlach
Rogla
Ptuj
Ledenitzen
Zrece
Solcava
Tepanje
Dovje-Mojstrana
Recica ob Savinji
Jerzersko
Luce
Celje
Bled
Kamniska Bistrica
Prebold
Podcetrtek
Bohinjsko jezero
Smlednik
Lukovica
Laško
Ljubljana
Tolmin
LJUBLJANA
Obrezje Jug
Podsmreka
Visnja Gora
ZAGREB
Zalošce
Locatec
Dolenjske Toplice
Postojna
SLO
KARLOVAC
Trieste
Izola
Portoroz
Rijeka
Icici
Motovun
Kraljevica
Mošcenicka Draga
Omišalj
Crikvenica
Baderna
Njivice
Selce
Klimno
Ilo
Klenovica
Porec
Malinska
Novi Vinodolski
Plitvica
Vrsar
Rabac
Krk/
Krk
Punat
Racovica
Rovinj
Labin
Baška
Senj
Cres
Pinezici
Fažana
Koromacno
Valun
Rab
Pula
Cres/
Martinšcica
Korenica
Medulin
Osor
Nerezine
Kolan
Lošinj/Mali Lošinj
Pag
Tribanj
Povijana
Ražanac
Starigrad/Paklenica
Privlaka
Vir
Vinjerac
Nin
Zaton
Vrsi
Rovanjska
Petrcane
Posedarje
Zadar
Bibinje
Novigrad
Lukoran
Sukošan
Ždrelac
Sv. Filip I Jakov
Biograd na Moru
Vransko Jezero
Pako tane
Tkon
Kornati/Murter
Sibenik
Kaštel Kambelovac
Vodice
Zaboric
Kaštel
Grebaštica
Kaštel Stari
Stafilic
Split
Podstrana
Primošten
Trogir
Slatine
Dugi Rat
Omiš
Lokva Rogoznica
Sutivan
Supetar
Baška Voda
Podgora
Bol
Živogošce
Zaostrog
Opuzen
Pelješac
Kucište
Lovište
Viganj
Peljesac/Orebic
Mokalo
Drace-Pelješac
Vela Luka
Korcula
Zuljana
Žrnovo
Slano
Mljet
Ston
Orašac
Babino Polje
Mlini
Dubrovnik
DUBROVNIK
ANCONA
I
A
H
HR
NITRA
BRATISLAVA
SK
BUDAPEST
PECS
OSIJEK
SLAVONSKI BROD
Lipovac
BIH
SARAJEVO
E49
E65
E75
E571
E58
E77
E71
E60
E75
E59
A9
E57
A2
E66
E73
E661
E-662
E61
E70
E-70
E-661
E71
E-73
E-761
E-661
E-761
E-762
E55
A14
31km

A
B
20
C
D
1
2
3
4
5
6
37
29
Vertheuil
St.Caprais de Blaye
Saint-Estèphe
Orioles
Poitou-Charentes
Aubeterre-sur-Dronne
Brantôme
La Chapelle-Faucher
Bourdeilles
Sorges
Lanouaille
Excideuil
Celles
Hourtin
Montguyon
St.Antoine Cumond
Douchapt
Ribérac
Mensignac
Château-l'Evêque
Hautefort
Nailhac
Carcans
Blaye
St.Savin
Clérac
La Roche-Chalais
St.Vincent-Jalmoutiers
St.Leon-sur-l'Isle
Périgueux
Azerat
Lacanau
Bourg-sur-Gironde
Montpon-Ménestérol
Sourzac
Montignac
Macau
Le Porge
St.Léon-sur-Vézère
Ste.Alvére
Les Eyzies
Sainte-Nathalène
Le Bugue
Sarlat-la-C.
BORDEAUX
Saint-Emilion
Branne
Montcaret
Bergerac
St.Sauveur
Badefols-sur-D.
St.Cyprien
Beynac-et-C
La Roque
Lège-Cap-Ferret
Andernos-les-Bains
Lanton
Créon
Frontenac
Pellegrue
St.Vincent-de-Cosse
Vitrac
Veyrines-de-D.
Domme
Monbazillac
Capian
Ladaux
Sauveterre de Guyenne
Beaumont du Périgord
Arcachon
Cadillac
Monségur
Monpazier
Preignac
La Réole
Monteton
Biron
Fontet
Sanguinet
Biscarrosse
Hostens
Monbahus
Fourques-sur-Garonne
Marmande
Cancon
Monflanquin
Puy l'Eveque
Luzech
Fumel
Parentis-en-Born
Bazas
Caumont-sur-Garonne
Casseneuil
Prayssac
Gastes
St.Sylvestre-sur-Lot
Alblas
Ste.Livrade-sur-Lot
Tournon-d'Agenais
Ste.Eulalie-en-Born
Bernos-Beaulac
Bouglon
Villeton
Le Temple-sur-Lot
Roquecor
Mimizan
Casteljaloux
Damazan
Montcuq
Buzet-sur-Baïse
Aquitaine
Contis-Plage
Houeillès
Lavardac
Sainte-Colombe-en-Bruilhois
Lauzerte
Castelculier
Lit-et-Mixe
Nérac
Layrac
Morcenx
Donzac
Valence
Moissac
Vielle St.Girons
Labastide-d'Armagnac
St.Nicolas-de-la-Grave
Barbotan-les-Thermes
Condom
Saint-Antoine
Bardigues
Castelsarrasin
Léon
Montréal (Gers)
Messanges
Moliets-et-Maa
Montauban
Vieux-Boucau-les-Bains
Valence-sur-Baïse
St.Puy
St.Clar
Grenade-sur-l Adour
Soustons
St.Paul-les-Dax
Mugron
Fleurance
Seignosse
Le Houga
Grenade-sur-Garonne
Dax
Sarrant
Capbreton
Aire-sur-l Adour
Preignan
Labenne
Cadours
Ondres
Amou
Auch
Peyrehorade
Gimont
Anglet
Arzacq-Arraziguet
Midi-Pyrénées
Salies-de-Béarn
BAYONNE
Samatan
St.Thomas
Lombez
Miélan
St.Pée-de-Nivelle
St.Palais
Sauvagnon
Vic-en-Bigorre
Pau
Espés Undurein
L'Hôpital-St.Blaise
PAU
St.Sulpice-sur-Lèze
Tarbes
St.Jean-Pied-de-Port
Oloron-Sainte-Marie
F
Auzas
St.Martory
Le Fossat
Sévignacq Meracq
Lourdes
Bagnères-de-Bigorre
Mazères-sur-Salat
Ste.Croix-Volvestre
Roncesvalles
La Pierre-Saint-Martin
Pierrefitte-Nestalas
Valcabrère
Laruns
Soulom
Arrens-Marsous
Eaux-Bonnes
St.Girons
Lhers
Castelnau-Durban
ES
Marbre
Arreau
Cauterets
Aoiz
Bonac Irazein
St.Lary Soulan
Ansó
Oust
Gavarnie
Aragnouet
Loudenvielle
Bagnères-de-Luchon
Jaca
Torla
Bielsa
Botaya
Aínsa
La Seu dÚrgell
A10
E606
A89
E70
E72
A63
E5
E7
A65
E80
E07
A64
A-21
A-136
E-7
A-138
E9
16km
40

A
21
B
C
22
D
Uzerche
Concèze
Vigeois
Egletons
Liginiac
Bort-les-Orgues
Condat
Limousin
Objat
Sadroc
Allassac
Ayen
Donzenac
Riom-es-Montagnes
Valette
Mauriac
Salins
Ségur-les-Villas
Allanche
Blesle
Massiac
Brioude
Lavaudieu
Chomelix
Auvergne
Le Breuil-sur-Couze
Viverols
Arlanc
St.Victor-sur-Loire
St.Bonnet-le-Château
Craponne-sur-Arzon
Tiranges
St.Romain-Lachalm
Retournac
Raucoules
Vorey-sur-Arzon
Beaulieu
Dampniat
Servières-le-Château
BRIVE-LA-GAILLARDE
Drugeac
Pleaux
Salers
Neussargues-Moissac
La Chapelle-Laurent
Turenne
Collonges-la-Rouge
Arnac
Mandailles-Saint-Julien
Super Lioran
Murat
Talizat
Coltines
Valuéjols
Chaspuzac
Le Vernet
Puy-en-Velay
Gignac
Salignac-Eyvigues
St.Paul-des-Landes
Crandelles
Velzic
Thiézac
St.Flour
St.Georges
Ruynes-en-Margeride
St.Christophe-sur-Dolaison
Souillac
Martel
Lacapelle-Viescamp
Ytrac
Naucelles
Aurillac
Vic-sur-Cère
Pierrefort
Faverolles
Saugues
Le Monastier-sur-Gazeille
Les Estables
Pinsac
Calès
Rocamadour
Alvignac
Gramat
Sousceyrac
St.Céré
Latronquière
St.Mamet-la-Salvetat
Sansac-de-Marmiesse
Vézac
Therondels
Mur de Barrez
Chaudes-Aigues
St.Just
Le Malzieu-Ville
Chanaleilles
Le Lac d'Issarlès
Coucouron
Gourdon
Thémines
St.Maurice-en-Q.
Lacapelle Marival
Cardaillac
Montet-et-Bouxal
Cayrols
Marcolès
Prunet
Lacroix-Barrez
Ste.Geneviève-sur-Argence
St.Chély-d'Apcher
Lachamp-Raphaël
Pradelles
Langogne
Meyras
Thueyts
Calvinet
Montsalvy
Maurs
Montézic
Labastide-Murat
Bagnac-sur-Célé
Cassaniouze
Montmurat
Entraygues-sur-Truyère
Laguiole
Rieutort-de-Randon
Rhône-Alpes
Figeac
Vieillevie
Boisse Penchot
Senergues
Aubrac
Bouillac
Campuac
Marvéjols
Douelle
Vers
Cajarc
Naussac
Cransac
Le Monastir
Mende
Cahors
St.Cirque-Lapopie
Villeneuve
Peyrusse le Roc
St.Geniez-d Olt
Lablachère
Saint-Genest-de-Beauzon
St.Alban-Auriolles
Berrias-et-Casteljau
Lanuéjouls
Rignac
Campagnac
La Canourgue
Ispagnac
Laissac
Rodez
Génolhac
Banne
Villefranche-de-Rouergue
Pont-de-Salars
Saint-Paul-le-Jeune
Florac
Barjac
Monteils
Baraqueville
Caylus
Castanet
Ségur
Najac
Sauveterre-de-Rouergue
Naucelle
Les Mages
Caussade
Laguepie
Arvieu
Mirandol-Bourgnounce
St.Just-sur-Viaur
St.Jean-du-Gard
Alès
St.Antonin Noble Val
Cordes-sur-Ciel
Le Ségur
Millau
Requista
Le Garric
Valderiés
Castelnau-de-Montmiral
Cahuzac-sur-Vère
ALBI
Broquies
Roquefort-sur-Soulzon
Anduze
Arre
Avèze
Gaillac
Coupiac
Sauve
Rivières
Albi
Vabres-l'Abbaye
St.Jean et St.Paul
La Couvertoirade
Lisle sur Tarn
Frejairolles
Le Caylar
St.Mamert-du-Gard
Nimes
Belmont sur Rance
Mont Roc
Camares
St.Mathieu-de-Tréviers
Sommières
NÎMES
Midi-Pyrénées
Lacaune
Lunas
Le Bosc
Aniane
MONTPELLIER
Castres
Nages
Octon
Clermont-l'Hérault
TOULOUSE
Puylaurens
Brassac
Fraïsse-sur-Agout
Bédarieux
Mourèze
Montpellier
La Grande Motte
Montcalm
Labruguiere
Vailhan
Palavas-les-Flots
Carnon
Aigues-Mortes
Mazamet
Montagnac
Vénerque
St.Felix-Lauragais
Revel
Arfons
Murviel-lès-Béziers
Pézenas
Villeneuve-lès-Maguelone
Mèze
Le Grau du Roi
Languedoc-Roussillon
Saint-Thibéry
Balaruc-les-Bains
Auterive
Montferrand
Servian
Le Ségala
Sète
Villeneuve-Minervois
BÉZIERS
Salles-sur-l Herbs
Ouveillan
Agde
Marseillan-Plage
Alzonne
Pezens
CARCASSONNE
Valras-Plage
Le Cap d Agde
Sérignan-Plage
Portiragnes
Belpech
Carcassonne
Fanjeaux
Narbonne
Fleury-d'Aude
Gruissan
Routier
Lagrasse
Mirepoix
Limoux
Tournissan
Peyriac-de-Mer
Bargnac
Félines-Termenès
Port-la-Nouvelle
Serres-sur-Arget
Quillan
Duilhac-sous-Peyrepertuse
Fitou
Leucate
F
Les Cabannes
Lapradelle Puilaurens
Vicdessos
Bélesta
Ax-les-Thermes
PERPIGNAN
L Hospitalet-près-l Andorre
Rigarda
F
Saint-Cyprien
Matemale
Latour-Bas-Elne
Pas de la Casa
Les Angles
Thues-entre-Valls
St.Marsal
St.Andre
ANDORRA
Casteil
Collioure
Mont-Louis
Le Boulou
Port Vendres
Sant-Julia-de-Lòria
Latour-de-Carol
Saillagousse
Amélie-les-Bains-Palalda
ES
ES
A
16km
B
40
C
D
1
2
3
4
5
6
28
30
A89
E70
E9
A20
A68
A66
A61
E9
A75
E11
A9
E15
E-15

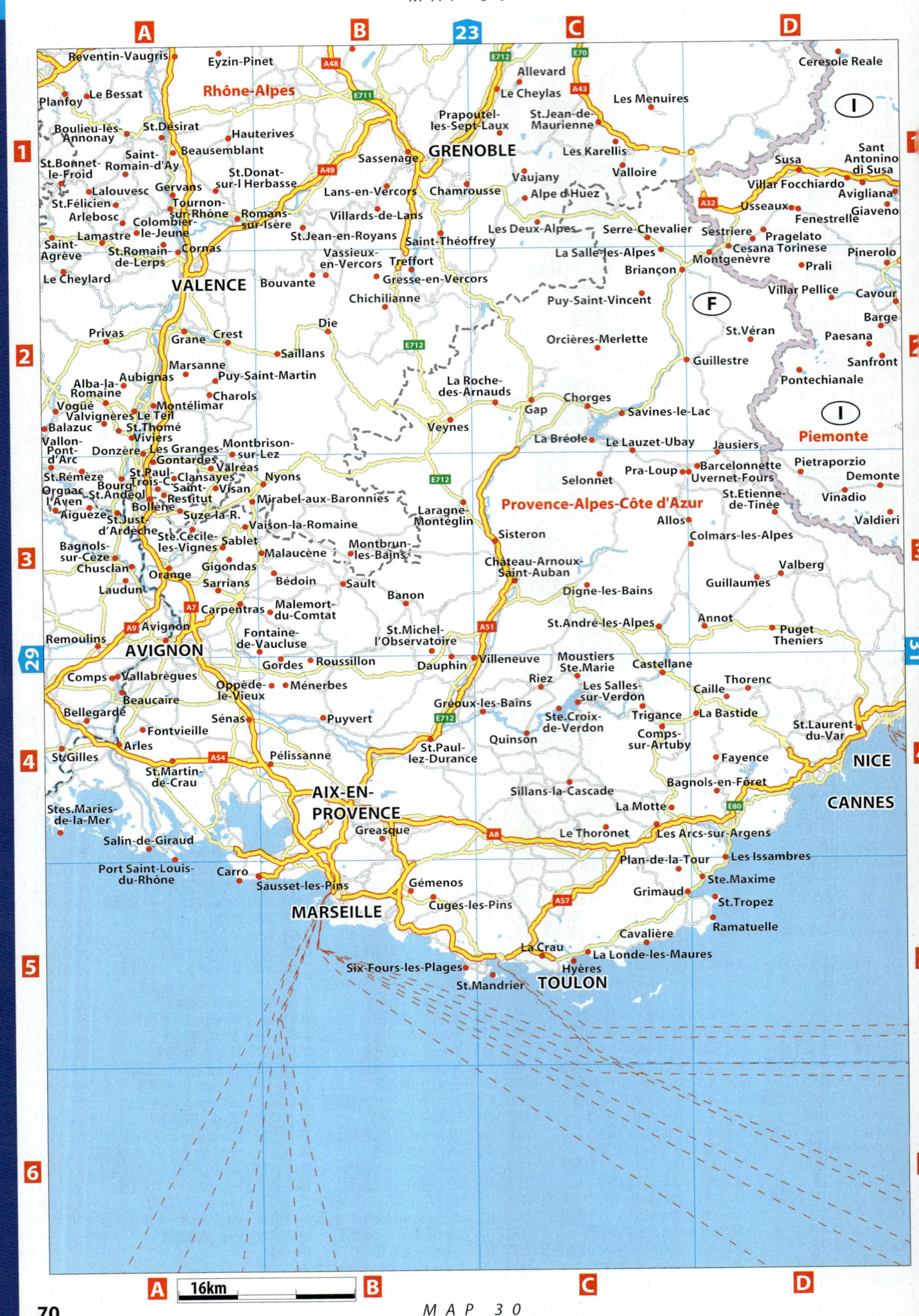
A
B
23
C
D
Reventin-Vaugris
Eyzin-Pinet
Ceresole Reale
Allevard
Le Cheylas
Planfoy
Le Bessat
Rhône-Alpes
Les Menuires
Prapoutel-
les-Sept-Laux
St.Jean-de-
Maurienne
I
Boulieu-lès-
Annonay
St.Désirat
Hauterives
1
Beausemblant
GRENOBLE
Les Karellis
Susa
Sant
Antonino
di Susa
St.Bonnet-
le-Froid
Saint-
Romain-d'Ay
Sassenage
St.Donat-
sur-l Herbasse
Vaujany
Valloire
Villar Focchiardo
Lalouvesc
Gervans
Lans-en-Vercors
Chamrousse
Alpe d'Huez
Avigliana
St.Félicien
Arlebosc
Tournon-
sur-Rhône
Colombier-
le-Jeune
Romans-
sur-Isère
Villards-de-Lans
Usseaux
Giaveno
Fenestrelle
Lamastre
St.Jean-en-Royans
Les Deux-Alpes
Serre-Chevalier
Sestriere
Pragelato
Saint-
Agrève
St.Romain-
de-Lerps
Cornas
Vassieux-
en-Vercors
Saint-Théoffrey
La Salle-les-Alpes
Cesana Torinese
Pinerolo
Treffort
Montgenèvre
Prali
Le Cheylard
VALENCE
Bouvante
Gresse-en-Vercors
Briançon
Villar Pellice
Chichilianne
Puy-Saint-Vincent
F
Cavour
Die
Barge
Privas
Grane
Crest
St.Véran
2
Orcières-Merlette
Paesana
Saillans
Guillestre
Sanfront
Marsanne
Aubignas
Puy-Saint-Martin
La Roche-
des-Arnauds
Pontechianale
Alba-la-
Romaine
Charols
Chorges
Montélimar
Gap
Savines-le-Lac
I
Vogüé
Valvignères
Le Teil
St.Thomé
Veynes
Balazuc
Viviers
La Bréole
Le Lauzet-Ubay
Piemonte
Vallon-
Pont-
d'Arc
Donzère
Les Granges-
Gontardes
Montbrison-
sur-Lez
Jausiers
Valréas
Pra-Loup
Barcelonnette
Pietraporzio
St.Rémèze
St.Paul-
Trois-C.
Clansayes
Selonnet
Uvernet-Fours
Demonte
Bourg-
St.Andéol
Saint-
Restitut
Visan
Nyons
Orgnac-
l'Aven
Mirabel-aux-Baronnies
Provence-Alpes-Côte d'Azur
St.Etienne-
de-Tinée
Vinadio
Bollène
Laragne-
Montéglin
Aiguèze
St.Just-
d'Ardèche
Suze-la-R.
Allos
Valdieri
Vaison-la-Romaine
Ste.Cécile-
les-Vignes
Sisteron
Colmars-les-Alpes
Bagnols-
sur-Cèze
Sablet
Montbrun-
les-Bains
3
Malaucène
Chusclan
Gigondas
Château-Arnoux-
Saint-Auban
Valberg
Orange
Bédoin
Laudun
Sarrians
Sault
Guillaumes
Banon
Digne-les-Bains
A7
Carpentras
Malemort-
du-Comtat
Annot
A9
Avignon
A51
St.André-les-Alpes
Puget
Theniers
Remoulins
Fontaine-
de-Vaucluse
St.Michel-
l'Observatoire
29
AVIGNON
31
Moustiers
Ste.Marie
Villeneuve
Gordes
Roussillon
Dauphin
Castellane
Comps
Vallabrègues
Riez
Thorenc
Oppède-
le-Vieux
Ménerbes
Les Salles-
sur-Verdon
Caille
Beaucaire
Gréoux-les-Bains
Bellegarde
Sénas
Trigance
La Bastide
Ste.Croix-
de-Verdon
Puyvert
St.Laurent-
du-Var
Fontvieille
Comps-
sur-Artuby
Arles
Quinson
St.Paul-
lez-Durance
4
St.Gilles
A54
Pélissanne
Fayence
NICE
St.Martin-
de-Crau
Sillans-la-Cascade
AIX-EN-
PROVENCE
Bagnols-en-Forêt
CANNES
Stes.Maries-
de-la-Mer
La Motte
Greasque
A8
Le Thoronet
Les Arcs-sur-Argens
Salin-de-Giraud
Plan-de-la-Tour
Les Issambres
Port Saint-Louis-
du-Rhône
Carro
Gémenos
Ste.Maxime
Sausset-les-Pins
Grimaud
A57
St.Tropez
MARSEILLE
Cuges-les-Pins
Ramatuelle
Cavalière
La Crau
La Londe-les-Maures
5
Six-Fours-les-Plages
Hyères
St.Mandrier
TOULON
6
A
16km
B
C
D

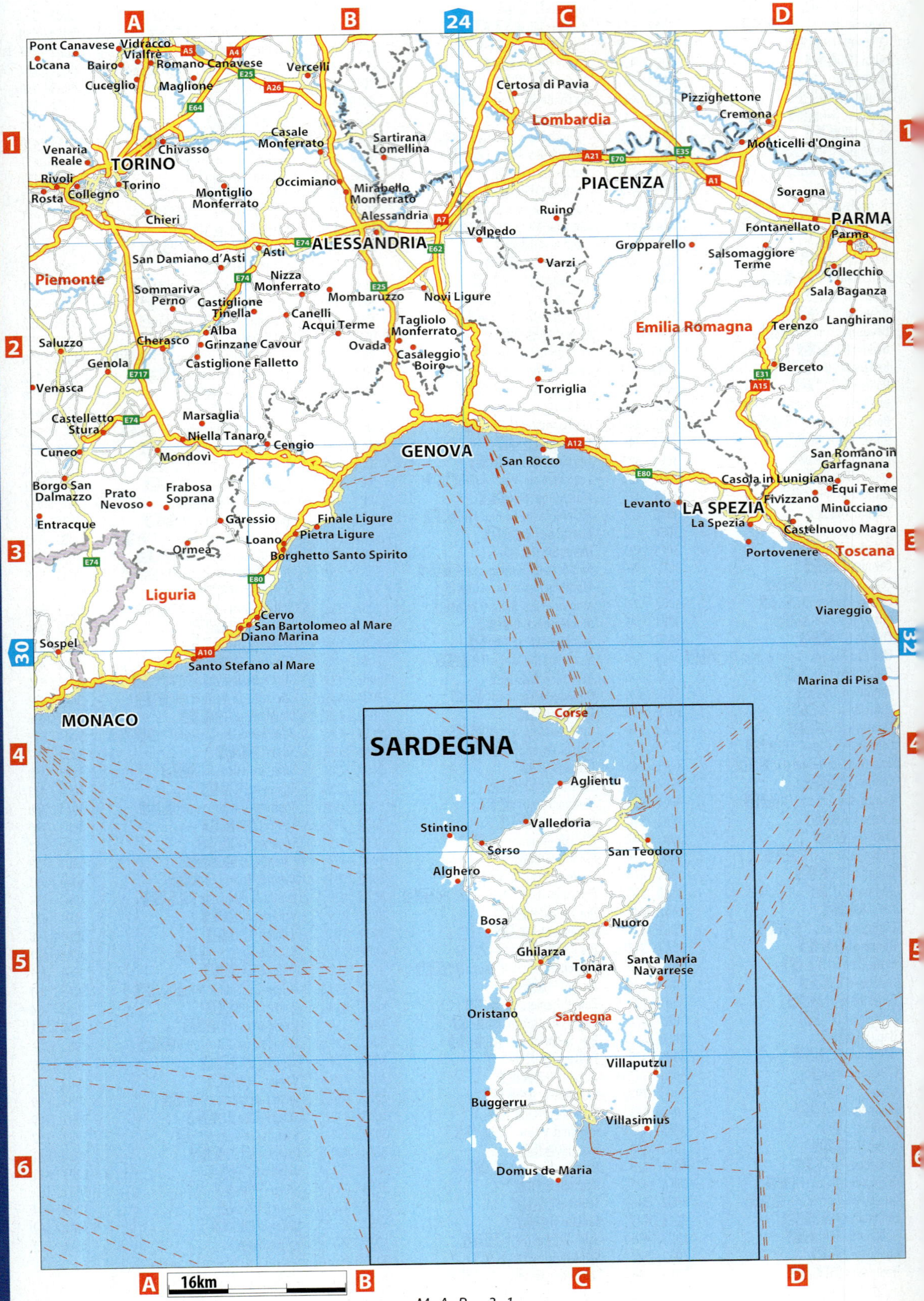

A B 24 C D

Pont Canavese
Vidracco
Vialfrè
Locana
Bairo
Romano Canavese
Vercelli
Cuceglio
Maglione
Certosa di Pavia
Pizzighettone
Cremona
Lombardia
Casale Monferrato
Sartirana Lomellina
Monticelli d'Ongina
Venaria Reale
TORINO
Chivasso
Rivoli
Collegno
Torino
Rosta
Montiglio Monferrato
Occimiano
Mirabello Monferrato
PIACENZA
Soragna
Alessandria
Ruino
Chieri
Volpedo
Fontanellato
PARMA
Parma
Asti
ALESSANDRIA
Gropparello
Salsomaggiore Terme
San Damiano d'Asti
Varzi
Collecchio
Piemonte
Nizza Monferrato
Sala Baganza
Sommariva Perno
Mombaruzzo
Novi Ligure
Castiglione Tinella
Canelli
Acqui Terme
Tagliolo Monferrato
Emilia Romagna
Terenzo
Langhirano
Saluzzo
Cherasco
Alba
Grinzane Cavour
Ovada
Casaleggio Boiro
Genola
Castiglione Falletto
Berceto
Venasca
Torriglia
Marsaglia
Castelletto Stura
Niella Tanaro
Cengio
GENOVA
Cuneo
Mondovì
San Rocco
San Romano in Garfagnana
Borgo San Dalmazzo
Prato Nevoso
Frabosa Soprana
Casola in Lunigiana
Equi Terme
Levanto
LA SPEZIA
Fivizzano
Minucciano
Entracque
Garessio
Finale Ligure
La Spezia
Castelnuovo Magra
Loano
Pietra Ligure
Ormea
Portovenere
Toscana
Borghetto Santo Spirito
Liguria
Viareggio
Cervo
San Bartolomeo al Mare
Diano Marina
Sospel
Santo Stefano al Mare
Marina di Pisa
MONACO
Corse

SARDEGNA

Aglientu
Stintino
Valledoria
Sorso
San Teodoro
Alghero
Bosa
Nuoro
Ghilarza
Tonara
Santa Maria Navarrese
Oristano
Sardegna
Villaputzu
Buggerru
Villasimius
Domus de Maria

1 2 3 4 5 6

30 32

A 16km B C D

Lombardia
Veneto
Emilia Romagna
Toscana
Umbria
Marche
Lazio
MODENA
FERRARA
BOLOGNA
RAVENNA
FORLÌ
RIMINI
SAN MARINO
FIRENZE
LIVORNO
AREZZO
PERUGIA
GROSSETO
TERNI
Mantova
Chioggia
Montagnana
Borgofranco sul Po
Arquà Polesine
Sabbioneta
Magnacavallo
Moglia
Ro
Mesola
Porto Tolle
Guastalla
Mirandola
Ferrara
Tresigallo
Lagosanto
Carpi
Bomporto
Portomaggiore
Comacchio
Reggio nell Emilia
Argenta
Rubiera
Marzaglia
Modena
Conselice
Anita
Casal Borsetti
Porto Corsini
Castellarano
Maranello
Bagnacavallo
Ravenna
Castelnovo ne Monti
Serramazzoni
Castel San Pietro Terme
Imola
Faenza
Castel Bolognese
Cervia
Cesenatico
Pavullo nel Frignano
Vergato
Brisighella
Forlimpopoli
Bellaria-Igea Marina
Casola Valsenio
Bertinoro
Rimini
Palazzuolo sul Senio
Cesena
Riccione
Castelnuovo di Garfagnana
Suviana
Barberino di Mugello
Firenzuola
Tredozio
Rocca San Casciano
Borello
Misano Adriatico
Marradi
Cusercoli
Civitella di Romagna
Gradara
Barga
Cutigliano
Scarperia
San Marino
Pesaro
Gallicano
San Piero a Sieve
Premilcuore
Santa Sofia
Borgo a Mozzano
Pistoia
Abbadia di Fiastra
San Piero in Bagno
Sant Agata Feltria
San Leo
Fano
Montecatini Terme
Dicomano
Bagno di Romagna
Macerata Feltria
Marotta
Pietrarubbia
Sassocorvaro
Senigallia
Sesto Fiorentino
Stia
Carpegna
Urbino
Lucca
Larciano
Firenze
Pontassieve
Pratovecchio
Riandimeleto
Fossombrone
Bibbiena
Sestino
Mondavio
Corinaldo
Vinci
Urbania
Capraia e Limite
Montemignaio
Poppi
Borgo Pace
Acqualagna
Morro d'Alba
Pisa
Calci
San Miniato Basso
Pieve Santo Stefano
Mercatello sul Metauro
Jesi
Montespertoli
San Casciano in Val di Pesa
Apecchio
Montopoli in Val d Arno
Greve in Chianti
Anghiari
Sansepolcro
Mergo
Castelfiorentino
Montevarchi
Sassoferrato
Cupramontana
Certaldo
Castellina in Chianti
Radda in Chianti
Arezzo
Città di Castello
Scheggia e Pascelupo
Genga
Peccioli
Fabriano
Livorno
Gaiole in Chianti
Cerreto D'Esi
San Gimignano
Poggibonsi
Castiglion Fiorentino
Montone
Gubbio
Rosignano Marittimo
Matelica
Volterra
Monteriggioni
Monte San Savino
Gualdo Tadino
Siena
San Severino Marche
Marina di Cecina
Lucignano
Foiano della Chiana
Pioraco
Radicondoli
Rapolano Terme
Passignano sul Trasimeno
Camerino
Monteroni d Arbia
Torrita di Siena
Borghetto
Castelnuovo di Val de Cecina
Perugia
Castagneto Carducci
Buonconvento
Castiglione del Lago
Assisi
Pievebovigliana
Montepulciano
Torgiano
Chiusdino
Cannara
Spello
San Quirico d Orcia
Pienza
Visso
San Vincenzo
Suvereto
Chiusi
Panicale
Bevagna
Montalcino
Venturina
Campiglia Marittima
Massa Marittima
Castiglione d Orcia
Montefalco
Trevi
San Casciano dei Bagni
Monte Castello di Vibio
Piombino
Castel del Piano
Radicofani
Follonica
Ficulle
Cascia
Arcidosso
Santa Fiora
Todi
Spoleto
Acquapendente
Orvieto
Castiglione della Pescaia
Ferentillo
Bolsena
San Gemini
Leonessa
Isola dElba
Marina di Grosseto
Saturnia
Lubriano
Terni
Alberese
Gradoli
Amelia
Capodimonte
Montefiascone
Vitorchiano
Rieti
Viterbo
Tuscania
Orbetello
Civita Castellana
Porto Ercole
Pescia Romana
Farfa in Sabina
Castel di Tora
Villa San Giovanni in Tuscia
Montalto di Castro
Colle di Tora
Tarquinia
Oriolo Romano
Bracciano
A22
E45
A13
E55
A14DIR
A14
A11
E76
E78
E35
A12
E80
A1
16km
A
B
C
D
1
2
3
4
5
6
25
31
33

A
32
B
C
D
1
2
3
4
5
6
ANCONA
PERUGIA
TERNI
L'AQUILA
PESCARA
CITTÀ DEL VATICANO
ROMA
LATINA
NAPOLI
Marche
Umbria
Lazio
Abruzzo
Molise
Campania
Carpegna
Piandimeleto
Urbino
Fossombrone
Senigallia
Marina di Montemarciano
Mondavio
Corinaldo
Sestino
Urbania
Pieve Santo Stefano
Borgo Pace
Mercatello sul Metauro
Acqualagna
Morro d'Alba
Ancona
Jesi
Castelfidardo
Sansepolcro
Apecchio
Mergo
Loreto
Porto Recanati
Anghiari
Sassoferrato
Cupramontana
Recanati
Potenza Picena
Città di Castello
Scheggia e Pascelupo
Genga
Fabriano
Macerata
Montelupone
Montone
Gubbio
Cerreto D'Esi
Matelica
Pollenza
Monte San Giusto
Porto San Giorgio
Fermo
Gualdo Tadino
San Severino Marche
Tolentino
Urbisaglia
Colmurano
Monte Vidon Corrado
Pioraco
Falerone
Pedaso
Borghetto
Passignano sul Trasimeno
Camerino
Petritoli
Montefiore dell'Aso
Assisi
Pievebovigliana
Sarnano
Grottammare
Castiglione del Lago
Perugia
Montalto delle Marche
Cossignano
San Benedetto del Tronto
Torgiano
Spello
Amandola
Offida
Panicale
Cannara
Chiusi
Visso
Ascoli Piceno
Bevagna
Trevi
Sant Egidio alla Vibrata
Tortoreto Lido
Montefalco
Castelluccio di Norcia
Monte Castello di Vibio
Acquasanta Terme
Roseto degli Abruzzi
Ficulle
Todi
Spoleto
Cascia
Notaresco
Pineto
Orvieto
Amatrice
Ferentillo
Lubriano
San Gemini
Campotosto
Bolsena
Terni
Isola del Gran Sasso
Penne
Amelia
Leonessa
Capodimonte
Montefiascone
Santo Stefano di Sessanio
Vitorchiano
Rieti
Fossacesia
L'Aquila
Lanciano
Torino di Sangro
Tuscania
Viterbo
San Demetrio ne' Vestini
Casalbordino
Civita Castellana
Colle di Tora
Castel di Tora
Villa San Giovanni in Tuscia
Farfa in Sabina
Oriolo Romano
Cansano
Anversa degli Abruzzi
Bracciano
Villalago
Tivoli
Roccaraso
Lunghezza
Pescasseroli
Ladispoli
Roma
Castel Gandolfo
Colleferro
Albano Laziale
Monteroduni
Cassino
Castro dei Volsci
San Gregorio Matese
Nettuno
Latina
Sperlonga
Gaeta
San Felice Circeo
Napoli
Pozzuoli
Bacoli
Pompei
E45
E35
E55
A14
A1
A24
E80
A25
A12
E842
16km

A
B
C
D
1
2
3
4
5
6
33
Peschici
Vico del Gargano
Vieste
Rodi Garganico
Mattinata
San Giovanni Rotondo
Petacciato Marina
Lesina
San Salvo Marina
Termoli
Zapponeta
Margherita di Savoia
BARI
Bari
Monopoli
Torre Canne di Fasano
Brindisi
Castellana Grotte
Putignano
Alberobello
Lecce
Melendugno
Otranto
Molise
Lucera
FOGGIA
Troia
Puglia
Massafra
TARANTO
Santa Maria al Bagno
Uggiano la Chiesa
Sannicola
Gallipoli
Campobasso
Casalbore
San Gregorio Matese
Metaponto
Benevento
Basilicata
Campania
Contursi Terme
Sala Consilina
Grumento Nova
NAPOLI
Napoli
Pompei
Cava de' Tirreni
Tramonti
Bacoli
SALERNO
Paestum
Morano Calabro
Praia a Mare
Corigliano Calabro
Palinuro
Marina di Camerota
Scalea
Cirella
Crotone
Calabria
Cropani Marina
Amantea
Catanzaro Marina
Rossano
Palmi
MESSINA
Bova Marina
Condofuri Marina
Terme Vigliatore
Furnari
Oliveri
REGGIO DI CALABRIA
Roccalumera
Francavilla di Sicilia
Motta Camastra
Giardini Naxos
Taormina
Reitano
Sicilia
San Giovanni La Punta
PALERMO
CATANIA
Palermo
Augusta
Enna
Siracusa
San Vito Lo Capo
Castelluzzo
Scopello
Castellammare del Golfo
Mussomeli
Caltanissetta
Piazza Armerina
Caltagirone
Sutera
Trapani
Noto
Montevago
Portopalo di Capo Passero
Marsala
Gela
Pachino
Sciacca
Ribera
Porto Empedocle
Pozzallo
Ispica
Montallegro
Realmonte
Licata
Marina di Ragusa
Scicli
E55
E90
E842
E45
E846
27km

A
B
C
D
1
2
3
4
5
6
PLOVDIV
BG
SKOPJE
MK
GR
THESSALONIKI
AL
KAVALA
Porto Lagos
Alexandroupoli
Moustheni
Ouranoupoli
Metamorphosi
Gerakani
Nikiti Akti Koytloumousi
Akt Armenistis Sithonia
Ag.Mamas
Moudania
Sithonia
Neos Marmaras
Kastoriá
Lithóchoro
LARISA
VOLOS
Pilion
Métsovo
Ioánnina
IOANNINA
Corfu
Igoumenitsa
Plataria
Gliki
Parga
Ammoudia
Préveza
Vonitsa
Boukka
Levkas
Paralia Agias Annas
Stilada
Erétria
Metéora
Delphi
Arahova
Itea
Vagia
Kifisia
Marathon
Nea Makri
Rafina
Agios Nikolaos
Hiliadou
Nafpaktos
Eratini
Krioneri
Mesolóngi
Lambiri
Diakofto
Paralia Platanou
Eleonas
Diakofto Achaia
Paralia Rizomilos
Elefsina
Athens
ATHINA
Perahóra
Korinthos
Sounion
Legrena
Kato Alissos
Kalogria
Pátra
Alepochori
Korfos
Mycenae
Epidaurus
Galatas
Killini
Kastro
Glifa Kyllini
Savalia
Nafplio
Assini
Salandi
Tolo
Ermioni
Kilada Ermionidos
Dimitsána
Olympia
Paralia Astros
Agios Andreas
Tyrchu
Zacharo
Kakovatos
Plaka
Kyparissia
Agios Kiriaki
Petalidi
Gialova Pylou
Pylos
Koroni
Mayroyouni/ Gythion
Gythion
Kameras Irion
Kamares
Skoutari
Neo Itylo
Kotronas
Agia Kyriaki
Monemvasia
Agios Fokas
Gerolimenas
Porto Kagio
E-80
E79
E80
E773
E85
E-851
E-65
E-75
E90
E75
E65
E86
E853
E92
E55
E952
E961
35km

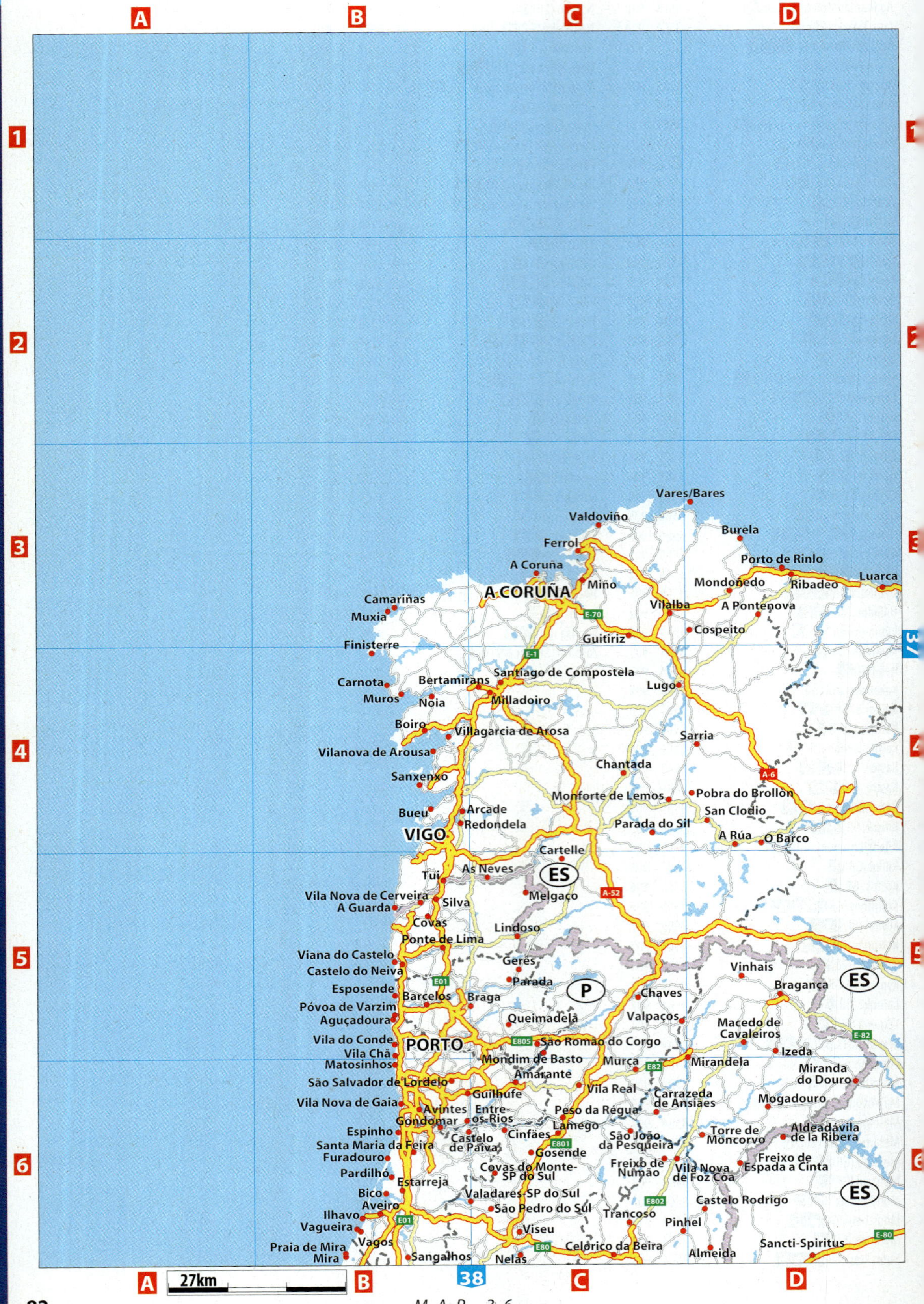

A B C D

1 2 3 4 5 6

Vares/Bares
Valdoviño
Burela
Ferrol
Porto de Rinlo
A Coruña
Luarca
Mondoñedo
Ribadeo
Miño
A CORUÑA
Camariñas
Vilalba
A Pontenova
Muxia
E-70
Cospeito
Guitiriz
Finisterre
E-1
Santiago de Compostela
Carnota
Bertamirans
Lugo
Muros
Noia
Milladoiro
Boiro
Villagarcia de Arosa
Sarria
Vilanova de Arousa
Chantada
Sanxenxo
A-6
Monforte de Lemos
Pobra do Brollon
Bueu
Arcade
Redondela
San Clodio
Parada do Sil
VIGO
A Rúa
O Barco
Cartelle
Tui
As Neves
ES
Vila Nova de Cerveira
Melgaço
A-52
A Guarda
Silva
Covas
Lindoso
Ponte de Lima
Viana do Castelo
Geres
Vinhais
Castelo do Neiva
E01
Parada
P
Bragança
ES
Esposende
Barcelos
Braga
Chaves
Póvoa de Varzim
Valpaços
Aguçadoura
Queimadela
Macedo de Cavaleiros
Vila do Conde
PORTO
E805
São Romão do Corgo
E-82
Vila Chã
Izeda
Matosinhos
Mondim de Basto
Murça
E82
Mirandela
Miranda do Douro
Amarante
São Salvador de Lordelo
Vila Real
Guilhufe
Carrazeda de Ansiães
Vila Nova de Gaia
Mogadouro
Avintes
Entre-os-Rios
Peso da Régua
Gondomar
Lamego
Espinho
Castelo de Paiva
Cinfães
São João da Pesqueira
Torre de Moncorvo
Aldeadávila de la Ribera
Santa Maria da Feira
E801
Furadouro
Gosende
Freixo de Espada a Cinta
Covas do Monte-SP do Sul
Freixo de Numão
Vila Nova de Foz Coa
Pardilhó
Estarreja
Bico
Valadares-SP do Sul
Castelo Rodrigo
ES
Aveiro
E802
Ilhavo
São Pedro do Sul
Trancoso
Vagueira
E01
Pinhel
Viseu
Vagos
E-80
Praia de Mira
E80
Celorico da Beira
Almeida
Sancti-Spiritus
Mira
Sangalhos
Nelas

37

A 27km B 38 C D

A B C D

1
2
3
4
5
6

Cudillero
Gozon
Carreno
Avilés
Gijón
OVIEDO
GIJÓN
La Vega
Cangas de Onís
San Martín del Rey Aurelio
Teverga
San Vicente de la Barquera
Comillas
Suances
Santillana del Mar
Cabárceno
SANTANDER
Ribamontán al Monte
Laredo
Liérganes
Castro Urdiales
Gorliz
Bakio
Bermeo
BILBAO
Bilbao
Lekeitio
Saturrarán
Zumaia
Guetaria
Hondaribbia
Hendaye
San Sebastián
SAN SEBASTIÁN
Biarritz
St.Jean de-Luz
Behobia
Sare
Renteria
Arrigorriaga
Fuente Dé
Potes
Hermandad De Campoo De Suso
Piedrasluengas
Espinosa de los Monteros
Legazpi
Cervera de Pisuerga
Aguilar de Campoo
Vitoria Gasteiz
VITORIA
LEÓN
León
Astorga
Saldaña
Miranda de Ebro
Pamplona
PAMPLONA
Estelle
Haro
Osorno
LOGROÑO
Logroño
Torremontalbo
Villada
Carrión de los Condes
Frómista
Burgos
BURGOS
Navarrete
Bretocino
Palencia
Villalpando
VALLADOLID
Valladolid
Pesquera de Duero
Aranda de Duero
Soria
Zamora
Peñafiel
Pollos
Foncastín
Cuellar
Burgo de Osma
Olmedo
Almazán
Coca
Sepúlveda
Ariza
SALAMANCA
Cabrerizos
Salamanca
Turégano

A-231 A-67 A-66 A-6 A-52 E-5 A-132 E-80 E-82 E-803 A-66 E-80 A-50 A-15 A-121

27km

36 28 39

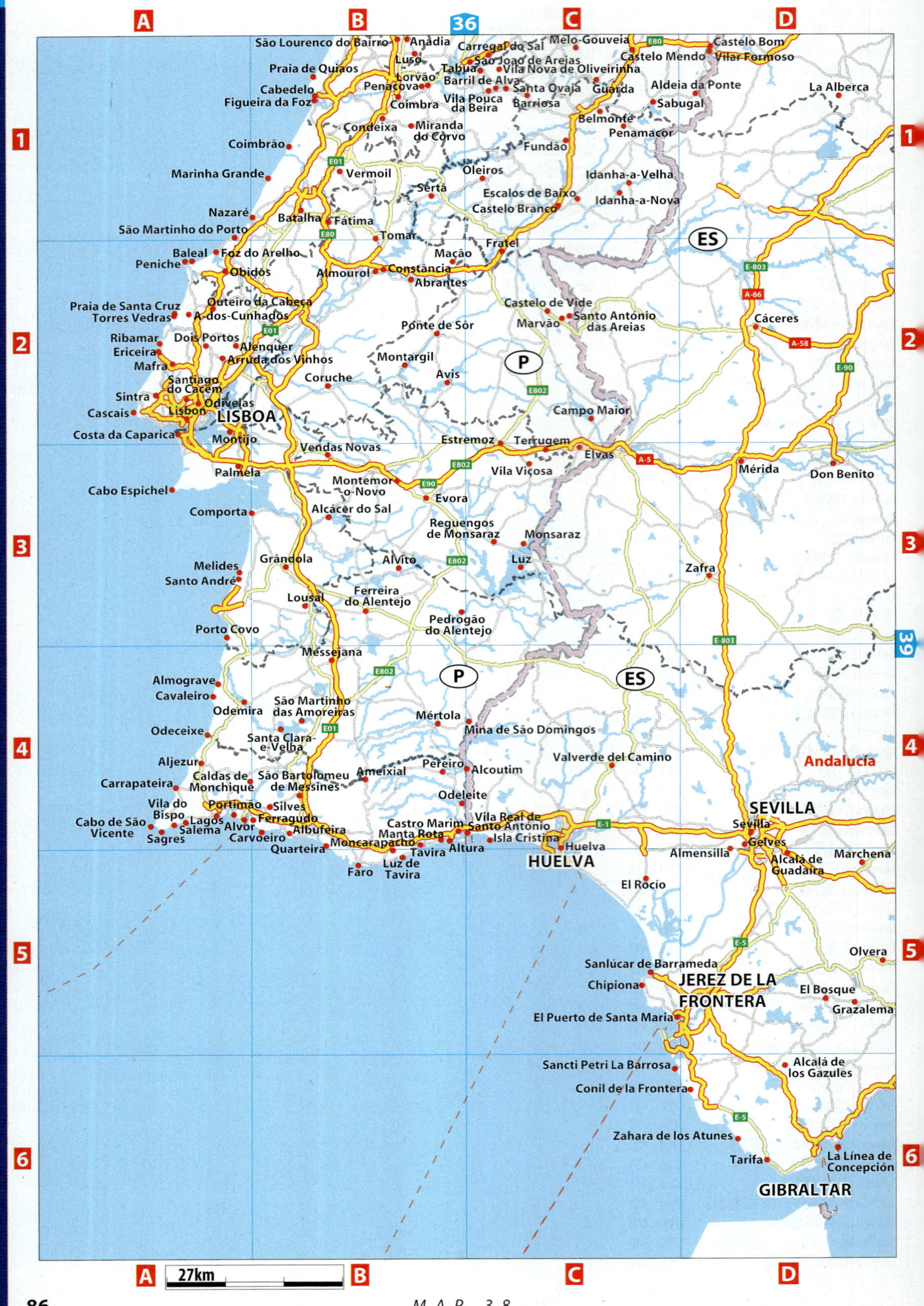
A
B
36
C
D
1
2
3
4
5
6
39
São Lourenco do Bairro
Anadia
Carregal do Sal
Melo-Gouveia
Castelo Bom
Praia de Quiaos
Luso
São João de Areias
Castelo Mendo
Vilar Formoso
Tabua
Vila Nova de Oliveirinha
Lorvão
Barril de Alva
Cabedelo
Penacova
Santa Ovaia
Guarda
Aldeia da Ponte
Figueira da Foz
Coimbra
Vila Pouca da Beira
Barriosa
Sabugal
La Alberca
Condeixa
Miranda do Corvo
Belmonte
Penamacor
Coimbrão
Fundão
Vermoil
Oleiros
Marinha Grande
Sertã
Idanha-a-Velha
Escalos de Baixo
Idanha-a-Nova
Nazaré
Castelo Branco
Batalha
Fátima
São Martinho do Porto
Tomar
Fratel
ES
Baleal
Foz do Arelho
Mação
Peniche
Óbidos
Almourol
Constância
Abrantes
Outeiro da Cabeça
Castelo de Vide
Praia de Santa Cruz
Marvão
Santo António das Areias
Torres Vedras
A-dos-Cunhados
Cáceres
Ponte de Sôr
Ribamar
Dois Portos
Ericeira
Alenquer
Mafra
Arruda dos Vinhos
Montargil
P
Santiago do Cacém
Coruche
Avis
Sintra
Odivelas
Cascais
Lisbon
Campo Maior
LISBOA
Costa da Caparica
Montijo
Vendas Novas
Estremoz
Terrugem
Elvas
Palmela
Vila Viçosa
Mérida
Don Benito
Montemor-o-Novo
Cabo Espichel
Évora
Comporta
Alcácer do Sal
Reguengos de Monsaraz
Monsaraz
Grândola
Alvito
Luz
Zafra
Melides
Santo André
Ferreira do Alentejo
Lousal
Pedrogão do Alentejo
Porto Covo
Messejana
P
ES
Almograve
Cavaleiro
São Martinho das Amoreiras
Odemira
Mértola
Mina de São Domingos
Odeceixe
Santa Clara-e-Velha
Aljezur
Valverde del Camino
Andalucía
Caldas de Monchique
São Bartolomeu de Messines
Ameixial
Pereiro
Alcoutim
Carrapateira
Vila do Bispo
Portimão
Silves
Odeleite
SEVILLA
Cabo de São Vicente
Lagos
Ferragudo
Castro Marim
Vila Real de Santo António
Sevilla
Salema
Alvor
Albufeira
Manta Rota
Isla Cristina
Gelves
Sagres
Carvoeiro
Moncarapacho
Huelva
Almensilla
Alcalá de Guadaira
Marchena
Quarteira
Tavira
Altura
HUELVA
Faro
Luz de Tavira
El Rocío
Olvera
Sanlúcar de Barrameda
JEREZ DE LA FRONTERA
Chipiona
El Bosque
Grazalema
El Puerto de Santa Maria
Sancti Petri La Barrosa
Alcalá de los Gazules
Conil de la Frontera
Zahara de los Atunes
Tarifa
La Línea de Concepción
GIBRALTAR
E80
E01
E802
E90
E-803
A-66
A-58
E-90
A-5
E-1
E-5
27km

A
B
37
C
D
1
2
3
4
5
6
38
40
E-803
A-50
Palazuelos de Eresma
Avila
MADRID
A-23
Lagartera
Toledo
Logrosán
Consuegra
E-901
A-3
A-31
A-43
ALBACETE
Peñarroya-Pueblonuevo
A-423
Yelca
El Pinos
CÓRDOBA
Córdoba
MURCIA
Mula
Murcia
A-44
Santaella
Alcaudete
A-351
Cabra
Priego de Córdoba
Vélez-Rubio
A-45
Rute
E-902
Alicún de las Torres
Cullar
Cañada de Callego
Cartagena
Cuevas de San Marcos
Taberno
Ramonete
La Azohia
Villanueva de Algaidas
GRANADA
A-334
E-15
Calnegre
A-384
Granada
Güejar Sierra
Archidona
San Juan de los Terreros
Sierra Nevada
A-349
Vera
A-338
A-356
A-348
E-15
MÁLAGA
Orgiva
ALMERÍA
Agua Amarga
A-397
Alhaurin del la Torr
Almayate
La Garrofa
Almeria
La Isleta
Cabo de Gata
Marbella
Almerimar
27km

A
B
28
C
D
1
2
3
4
5
6
39
Alquézar
Tremp
Ripoll
Figueres
Cadaqués
Navata
Garrigàs
Vic
Sant Hilari Sacalm
Quart
E-804
La Joyosa
Peñaflor
Zaragoza
ZARAGOZA
LLEIDA
Calaf
Navarcles
Viladrau
Santa Cristina d'Aro
Platja d'Aro
San Feliu de Guixols
Montseny
E-90
Lleida
BARCELONA
Mataro
Avinyonet del Penedès
Barcelona
E-7
A-222
L Arboç
TARRAGONA
Ascó
Sitges
Altafulla
Tortosa
Amposta
Els Muntells
Morella
San Raphael del Río
La Salzadella
Peñíscola
E-15
A-23
Benicasim
Jérica
Segorbe
Canet d En Berenguer
VALENCIA
Olimar
Valencia
Turis
PALMA DE MALLORCA
Jalance
Ayora
Carcaixent
Alqueria de la Comtessa
Oliva
Dénia
E-15
Jávea
Ibi
Calpe
L'Alfàs del Pi
A-7
Altea
El Campello
Romana
E-15
ALICANTE
Elche
Sta.Pola
ELX
La Marina
San Fulgencio
A
27km
B
C
D

UNITED KINGDOM

Scotland
pages: 93-94
Aberdeen
Glasgow
Edinburgh
prime meridian
Northern Ireland
pages: 93
Dublin
Leeds
Hull
Liverpool
Manchester
Wales
pages: 94-96
England
pages: 96-101
Cardiff
London
Plymouth
Portsmouth

GB

Capital: London
Government: Constitutional monarchy
Official Language: English
Population: 61,400,000 (2012)
Area: 244,820 km^2

General information
Dialing code: 0044
General emergency: 112
Currency: Pound sterling (GBP),
£1 = € 1,18, € 1 = £0.85 (October 2013)

Regulations for overnight stays
Wild camping is forbidden in the UK. Motorway service stations allow overnight parking.

Additional public holidays 2014
March 17 St. Patricksday (Northern Ireland)
April 18 Good Friday
April 21 Easter monday
May 1 Labour Day
May 5 Early May Bank Holiday
May 26 Spring Bank Holiday
June 12-14 Orangemen’s Day (Northern Ireland)
August 25 Summer Bank Holiday
October 31 Halloween
November 51 Guy Fawkes Day
December 26 Boxing Day

Great Britain

Northern Ireland

Aghadowey 1A3

Golf Car Park, Brown Trout Golf and Country Inn, 209 Agivey Road, A54. **GPS**: n55,02413 w6,59985.
free.
Remarks: Max. 2 nights.

Antrim 1A3

The Ramble Inn, 236 Lisnevenagh Road. **GPS**: n54,77412 w6,24533.
free.
Distance: Antrim 7km.

Ballinamallard 1A3

Ballinamallard Football Club, Ferney Park. **GPS**: n54,41340 w7,6006.

free.
Distance: 1,5km.
Tourist information Ballinamallard:
Ballinamallard River, Kilgortnaleague Bridge, A35 Enniskillen > Irvinestown. Wild Salmon and Trout River.

Ballymoney 1A3

Anglers' Rest, 139 Vow Road. **GPS**: n54,99597 w6,56997.
free.
Tourist information Ballymoney:
Tourist Information Office, Ballymoney Townhall, 1 Townhead Street.
Leslie Hill Open Farm, 9, Macfin Road.Living history on the farm, picnic area, playground, Tea-room etc. Easter-31/05: Su-Bank Holidays 14-18h, 01/06-30/06: Sa-Su 14-18h, 01/07-31/08: Mo-Sa 11-18h, Su 14-18h.
Old Bushmills Distillery, Main Street, Bushmills.World's oldest licensed whiskey distillery. Mo-Sa 9.30-17h, Su 12-17h Good Friday, 12/07, 25-26/12, 31/12-01/01.

Broughshane 1A3

Houston Mills, Buckna road. **GPS**: n54,89307 w6,20107.

free , 1 Ch.

Carrickfergus 1A3

Carrickfergus Harbour Car Park, Rodgers Quay. **GPS**: n54,71177 w5,8119.
Ch.

Eglinton 1A2

Decks Bar & Restaurant, McLean Road, Campsie Industrial Estate. **GPS**: n55,04060 w7,2006.
free.

Killyleagh 1A3

Ringdufferin Country Club, Ringdufferin Road. **GPS**: n54,43210 w5,6528.
free.
Distance: Killyleagh 4km.
Tourist information Killyleagh:
Castle Ward, Strangford, Downpatrick.18th-century mansion.
01/01-31/12.
Sea Treks of Strangford, 11 Shore Road.Water taxi service on Strangford Lough. 01/01-31/12. £10/h.

Newtownards 1A3

Daft Eddys, Sketrick Island. **GPS**: n54,48812 w5,64807.

free.
Distance: Newtownards 17km.
Tourist information Newtownards:
Somme Heritage Centre, 233 Bangor Road, Conlig, A21.The centre examines Ireland's role in the 1st World War.
Castle Espie Wildfowl And Wetlands Centre, 78 Ballydrain Road, Comber.
01/01-31/12 23-25/12.

Whitehead 1A3

Car Park. **GPS**: n54,76391 w5,71238.
Ch.

Scotland

Aberdeen 1C1

Hazlehead Park, Hazledene Road. **GPS**: n57,13987 w2,17956.

free. **Surface:** asphalted.
Distance: 200m 400m 400m.

Ballachulish 1B1

Glencoe, A82 Ballachulish > Achallader. **GPS**: n56,63295 w4,82744.

free.
Remarks: Parking ski-lifts.

Dufftown 1C1

Castle Road. **GPS**: n57,45325 w3,12912.

+20 free. **Surface:** asphalted.
Distance: 400m 400m 400m.

Dumfries 1B3

P Long Stay, White Sands. **GPS:** n55,06722 w3,6125.

10 free. **Surface:** asphalted. 01/01-31/12
Distance: 100m on the spot on the spot 100m.

Dunthulm 1A1

Isle of Skye. **GPS:** n57,65020 w6,40459.
12 £12 Ch WC. **Surface:** metalled.
Distance: on the spot.
Remarks: Neaby Dunthulm Castle.

Easdale 1B2

Souvenir shop, Ellenabeich, Isle of Seil. **GPS:** n56,29540 w5,6462.

10 £10 Ch WC. **Surface:** metalled.
Distance: on the spot on the spot on the spot on the spot.

Fettercairn 1C1

Car Park Bowling Club, Fettercairn, Laurencekirk. **GPS:** n56,84971 w2,57306.

Tourist information Fettercairn:
Fettercairn Distillery Visitor Centre Information, Distillery Road.One of Scotland's oldest malt whiskey distilleries. 01/05-30/09, Mon-Sa 10-14.30h.
T free.

Givran 1B2

Harbour street- Henriettastreet. **GPS:** n55,24324 w4,85869.

50 free. **Surface:** asphalted. 01/01-31/12
Distance: 100m sandy beach 50m 50m.

New Abbey 1B3

Parking Sweetheart Abbey, A710, Main Street. **GPS:** n54,98070 w3,61966.

6 free. **Surface:** metalled.

Oban 1B2

Longsdale Car park, Longsdale Road. **GPS:** n56,41997 w5,46846.
± 10 free. **Location:** Simple, central. **Surface:** asphalted.
01/01-31/12
Distance: 400m 300m 50m 400m.

Rhugarbh 1B2

Parking Scottish Sea Life Sanctuary, A828 Rhugharb - Barcaldine. **GPS:** n56,51731 w5,34679.

10 free. **Surface:** metalled.

Wales

Abergynolwyn 1B4

Riverside Guest House, Llanegryn Street. **GPS:** n52,64584 w3,95856.

5 £10/night Ch included 6/night. **Location:** Rural, comfortable, central, quiet. **Surface:** grassy/metalled.
01/01-31/12
Remarks: Arrival <18h, narrow entrance (2,6m), Snowdonia National Park.

Brecon 1B5

The Watton Car Park, Heol Gouesnou. **GPS:** n51,94609 w3,38531.

25 £0.50/h, max. £2.50 8-18h, overnight stay free WC free,150m.
Location: Urban, simple, quiet. **Surface:** asphalted. 01/01-31/12
Distance: on the spot on the spot.
Remarks: Max. 1 night per 7 nights.

GB

Brecon 1B5

Canal Road Car/Coach-Lorry Park, Canal Road. **GPS**: n51,94486 w3,38993.

10 8-18h parking rate, overnight stay free. **Location:** Urban, simple, central, quiet. **Surface:** asphalted. 01/01-31/12

Distance: 100m 100m.

Remarks: Max. 1 night per 7 nights.

Brecon 1B5

The Promenade Car Park, Fenni-Fach Rd. **GPS**: n51,95089 w3,4036.

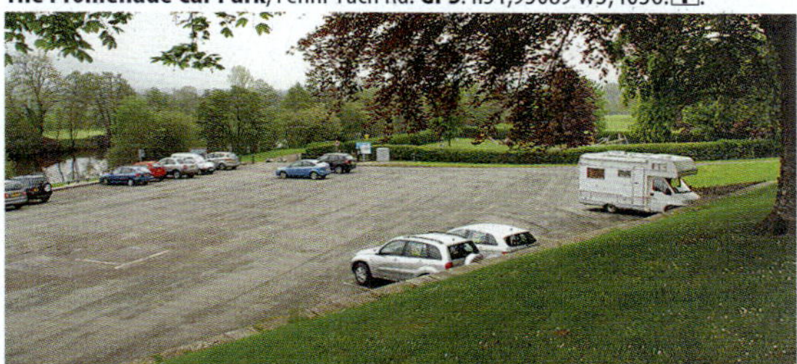

25 8-18h parking rate, overnight stay free. **Location:** Urban, simple, isolated, quiet. **Surface:** asphalted. 01/01-31/12

Distance: 600m on the spot 700m.

Remarks: Max. 1 night per 7 nights.

S Builth Wells 1B5

The Groe Car Park, The Strand. **GPS**: n52,14969 w3,40252.

20 8-18h parking rate, overnight stay free WC. **Location:** Urban, simple, quiet. **Surface:** asphalted. 01/01-31/12

Distance: on the spot on the spot on the spot.

Remarks: Max. 1 night per 7 nights.

Builth Wells 1B5

Smithfield Car Park, Brecon Rd. **GPS**: n52,14714 w3,40261.

50 8-18h parking rate, overnight stay free. **Location:** Urban, simple, central. **Surface:** asphalted. 01/01-31/12

Distance: 200m.

Remarks: Max. 1 night per 7 nights.

Crickhowell 1B5

Beaufort Street Car Park, Greenhill Way. **GPS**: n51,85838 w3,13557.

8 8-18h parking rate, overnight stay free. **Location:** Urban, simple, central, quiet. **Surface:** asphalted. 01/01-31/12

Distance: 50m.

Remarks: Max. 1 night per 7 nights.

S Hay-on-Wye 1B5

Oxford Road Car Park, Oxford Road. **GPS**: n52,07316 w3,12592.

25 £0.50/h, max. £2.50 8-18h, overnight stay free WC free. **Location:** Urban, simple, central, quiet. **Surface:** asphalted.
01/01-31/12

Distance: 150m 150m 150m on the spot.

Remarks: Max. 1 night per 7 nights.

S Knighton 1B5

Bowling Green Lane Car Park, Bowling Green Lane. **GPS**: n52,34324 w3,04553.

30 £0.50/h, max. £2.50 8-18h, overnight stay free WC free. **Location:** Rural, simple, central, quiet. **Surface:** asphalted.
01/01-31/12

Distance: 200m 300m on the spot.

Remarks: Max. 1 night per 7 nights.

Llandrindod Wells 1B5

High Street Car Park, High Street. **GPS**: n52,24151 w3,38042.

30 8-18h parking rate, overnight stay free. **Location:** Urban, simple, central. **Surface:** asphalted. 01/01-31/12

GB

Distance: 150m on the spot.
Remarks: Max. 6m, 1 night per 7 nights.

Llanidloes 1B5

Mount Street Car Park, Mount Lane. **GPS**: n52,44750 w3,53938.

12 8-18h parking rate, overnight stay £5. **Location:** Urban, simple, central, quiet. **Surface:** asphalted. 01/01-31/12
Distance: on the spot 100m 100m 100m.
Remarks: Max. 1 night per 7 nights.

Moelfre 1B4

Lligwy Bay. **GPS**: n53,35910 w4,26132.
£10/night.
Remarks: Beach parking.

Nantgaredig 1B5

Railway Hotel, B4310. **GPS**: n51,86533 w4,18976.
5 £5 WC. 01/01-31/12

Newton 1B5

Back Lane Car Park, Back Lane. **GPS**: n52,51534 w3,31735.

40 8-18h parking rate, overnight stay £5 WC free. **Location:** Urban, simple, central, quiet. **Surface:** asphalted. 01/01-31/12
Distance: 150m on the spot on the spot.
Remarks: Max. 1 night per 7 nights.

Newton 1B5

The Gravel Car Park, Heol Les Herbiers. **GPS**: n52,51421 w3,31167.

25 8-18h parking rate, overnight stay £5. **Location:** Urban, simple, central. **Surface:** asphalted. 01/01-31/12
Distance: 250m 50m 250m.
Remarks: Max. 1 night per 7 nights.

Presteigne 1B5

Hereford Street Car Park, Hereford Street. **GPS**: n52,27245 w3,00488.

10 8-18h parking rate, overnight stay free WC free. **Location:** Urban, simple, central, quiet. **Surface:** asphalted. 01/01-31/12
Distance: 100m on the spot.
Remarks: Max. 6m, 1 night per 7 nights.

Welshpool 1B5

Berriew Street Car Park, Berriew Rd. **GPS**: n52,65875 w3,14806.

30 8-18h parking rate, overnight stay £5 WC free. **Location:** Urban, simple, central, quiet. **Surface:** asphalted. 01/01-31/12
Distance: 200m 500m.
Remarks: Max. 1 night per 7 nights.

Welshpool 1B5

Church Street Car Park, Church Street. **GPS**: n52,66031 w3,1438.

25 8-18h parking rate, overnight stay £5 WC free. **Location:** Urban, simple, central, quiet. **Surface:** asphalted. 01/01-31/12
Distance: 150m 300m.
Remarks: Max. 1 night per 7 nights.

England

Abingdon 1C5

Rye Farm Pay & Display car park, Bridge Street, A415. **GPS**: n51,66746 w1,27799.

8 £7.30/24h WC. **Location:** Urban, simple.
Surface: asphalted.
01/01-31/12
Distance: 500m 500m 800m.

GB

Remarks: Max. 24h, first call or mail, carparks@southandvale.gov.uk, 01235 547665. A415 going south, on the left hand side just across the bridge.

Tourist information Abingdon:

Tourist Information Centre, 25 Bridge Street.

Aldershot 1C6

Parsons Barracks Car park, Ordnance Road. **GPS**: n51,24979 w0,75731.
£1. **Surface:** asphalted. 01/01-31/12

S Ambleside 1C3

Miller Field Motorhome Camping, Rothay Rd. **GPS**: n54,42898 w2,96586.
50 £10 Ch. **Location:** Rural, comfortable, quiet.
Surface: grassy.
Distance: 200m Lake Windmere 800m on the spot on the spot.
Remarks: At Lake District National Park.

S Appledore 1B6

Churchfields Car Park, The Quay. **GPS**: n51,05464 w4,19135.

25 £5 18-10h, £3 day WC free. **Location:** Urban, simple, quiet.
Surface: asphalted. 01/01-31/12
Distance: 150m 50m 200m.
Remarks: Max. 2 nights, min. 6m space between motorhomes.

Bakewell 1C4

Car Park, Asford Lane, Monsal Head. **GPS**: n53,24015 w1,72325.
£10.
Distance: on the spot.

Tourist information Bakewell:

Bakewell tourist information office, Old Market Hall, Bridge Street, www.visitpeakdistrict.com.

Bideford 1B6

Riverbank (long stay) Car Park, Kingsley road. **GPS**: n51,02086 w4,20386.

20 £5 18-10h, £3 day. **Location:** Urban, simple, quiet.
Surface: asphalted. 01/01-31/12
Distance: 1,5km 50m 500m 1km 500m.
Remarks: Max. 2 nights, min. 6m space between motorhomes.

S Bourton-on-the-Water 1C5

Bourton Rovers, Rissington Road. **GPS**: n51,87995 w1,7513.

5 £10 Ch WC free,Password at the bar. **Location:** Rural, simple, central, quiet. **Surface:** grassy. 01/01-31/12

Distance: 500m 500m 500m.

S Bourton-on-the-Water 1C5

Bourton Vale Car & Coach Park, Station Rd. **GPS**: n51,88512 w1,75471.

10 9-18h parking rate, overnight stay £8 WC free. **Location:** Urban, simple, central, quiet. **Surface:** asphalted. 01/01-31/12
Distance: 200m on the spot on the spot.

S Bury St.Edmunds 1D5

Ram Meadow Carpark Annexe, Cotton Lane. **GPS**: n52,24775 e0,71893.

5 £2.20 8-18h, overnight stay free WC free. **Location:** Urban, simple, central, quiet. **Surface:** asphalted. 01/01-31/12
Distance: 300m 300m 300m.
Remarks: Max. 1 night.

S Canterbury 1D6

Canterbury Coach Park, Kingsmead Road. **GPS**: n51,28554 e1,08492.

12 £10/12h WC free. **Location:** Urban. **Surface:** asphalted.
01/01-31/12
Distance: 650m 650m.

S Canterbury 1D6

New Dover Road Park&Ride, New Dover Road. **GPS**: n51,26199 e1,10258.

24 £3 Chincluded WC free. **Location:** Rural, simple, isolated, quiet. **Surface:** asphalted.
Acces Mo-Sa 6.30-20.30h, exit 24/24
Distance: Vintage Inn on the spot.
Remarks: Max. 24h, bus to city centre incl.

Tourist information Canterbury:

GB

Canterbury Tourist Information Centre, The Buttermarket, 34 St Margret's Street, www.canterbury.co.uk.

Cheltenham 1C5

The Gloucester Old Spot, Tewkesbury Road, A4109. **GPS**: n51,93325 w2,14881.

5 free, use of a meal obligated WC included,during opening hours. **Location:** Rural, simple, isolated. **Surface:** gravel/sand. 01/01-31/12

Distance: 500m on the spot.

Chester 1B4

Car Park, Little Roodee, Castle Road. **GPS**: n53,18447 w2,89245.

£5/18-09h, gates closed 22.30-7.00h WC.

Distance: 3,5km.

Remarks: A483 Grosvenor Road > Castle Road, by river Dee.

Tourist information Chester:

Tourist Information Centre, Town Hall, Northgate Street, www.chestertourism.com.Tourist town with historical centre.

Cirencester 1C5

Old Cricklade Road lorry park, Cricklade Road. **GPS**: n51,70760 w1,955.

20 £6.40 WC free. **Location:** Urban, simple. **Surface:** asphalted. 01/01-31/12

Distance: 1,5km 50m 150m.

Remarks: Near McDonalds.

Cirencester 1C5

The Crown Inn, High Street, Cerny Wick. **GPS**: n51,66264 w1,88933.

5 £10 Ch WC during opening hours. **Location:** Rural, simple. **Surface:** grassy/metalled. 01/01-31/12

Distance: on the spot.

Darlington 1C3

Car Park, Chesnut Street. **GPS**: n54,52993 w1,54758.

£4/day £2/night. **Surface:** metalled.

Distance: 700m 4,7km.

Exeter 7C5

Huntisbeare, Oak Road, Aylesbeare. **GPS**: n50,72816 e3,33599.

5 £12/night Ch WC included. **Location:** Rural, simple, isolated, quiet. **Surface:** metalled. 01/01-31/12

Distance: 1,5km 1,5km.

Remarks: Arrival <18h.

Hayling Island 1C6

West Beach Car Park, Sea Front. **GPS**: n50,78530 w1,0007.

40 8-22h parking rate, max. £6, overnight stay £10, 01/03-01/10 £20 free Ch WC At TI, 7 Sea-Front (600m). **Location:** Rural, simple, quiet. **Surface:** grassy/gravel. 01/01-31/12

Distance: on the spot on the spot 600m.

Remarks: Max. 72h.

Holsworthy 1B6

The Manor Car Park, Western Road. **GPS**: n50,81133 w4,35282.

12 £5 18-10h, £3 day. **Location:** Urban, simple, quiet. **Surface:** asphalted. 01/01-31/12

Distance: on the spot 150m 150m.

Remarks: Max. 2 nights.

Holy Island 1C2

Lindisfarne Causeway. **GPS**: n55,67815 w1,87552.

5 . **Surface:** metalled.

Huntingdon 1D5

Wellsbridge Motorhomes Sales, Ramsey Forty Foot, Ramsey. **GPS**: n52,47540 w0,08834.

5 £5 WC. **Location:** Rural, simple, isolated, quiet. **Surface:** asphalted. 02/01-23/12

Distance: on the spot.

Ipswich 1D5

Burnt House Farm, Wash Lane, Witnesham. **GPS**: n52,11418 e1,20094.

5 £8 Ch WC included. **Location:** Rural, comfortable, isolated, quiet. **Surface:** grassy/metalled. 01/01-31/12

Distance: 2km 2km.

Ipswich 1D5

Orwell Crossing Lorry Park, A14 Eastbound, Nacton. **GPS**: n52,02473 e1,22678.

20 £12. **Location:** Highway, simple, noisy. **Surface:** asphalted. 01/01-31/12

Distance: on the spot.

Ivybridge 1B6

Lee Mill Services, A38. **GPS**: n50,38493 w3,97041.

10 £8/night. **Location:** Simple, noisy. **Surface:** asphalted. 01/01-31/12

Distance: on the spot 500m.

Maidstone 1D6

Maidstone Services, M20. **GPS**: n51,26568 e0,61588.

8 £20 WC against payment. **Location:** Highway, simple, noisy. **Surface:** asphalted. 01/01-31/12

Distance: 200m on the spot.

Tourist information Maidstone:

Maidstone Tourist Information Centre, The Gatehouse, Palace Gardens, Mill Street.

Museum of Kent Life, Lock Lane, Sandling.History and traditions of Kent. 14/02-05/11, 10-17h.

Marazion 1A6

Car Park, Kings Road. **GPS**: n50,12415 w5,47587.

12 £10. **Location:** Simple, quiet. **Surface:** metalled. 17-09h 9-17h.

Distance: 50m on the spot 100m 100m.

Remarks: Parking at sea, nearby Saint Michael's Mount, not suitable for big motorhomes. Follow Marazion Car Parkings.

Tourist information Marazion:

Tourist Information Centre, Station Road, Penzance.

Saint Michael's Mount.Rocky island with medieval castle and church. 01/04-31/10.

Mevagissey 1A6

Willow Car & Coach Park, Valley Road. **GPS**: n50,27155 w4,79044.

10 10-18h parking rate, overnight stay £7.50 On demand. **Location:** Urban, simple, central. **Surface:** metalled. 01/01-31/12

Distance: 150m 1km 300m.

New Milton 1C6

New Lane Orchard, New Lane, Bashley. **GPS**: n50,77182 w1,6645.

5 £13 Ch included. **Location:** Rural, comfortable, isolated, quiet. **Surface:** grassy/metalled. 01/01-31/12

Distance: 400m 6,5km on the spot New Forest.

Remarks: Arrival <18h.

Newnham on Severn 1C5

Elton Farm, Littledean Road, A4151. **GPS**: n51,82355 w2,44753.

5 £5 Ch. **Location:** Rural, simple, isolated. **Surface:** grassy. 01/01-31/12

Distance: on the spot on the spot.

Newton Abbot 1B6

Sunnyside, Yvonne Bassett, Totnes Road, A381, Ipplepen. **GPS**: n50,48591 w3,63376.

5 £6/night Ch WC included. **Location:** Rural, simple, quiet. **Surface:** grassy/metalled. 01/01-31/12

Distance: 100m.

Remarks: Arrival <18h.

Oldham 1C4

The Hawthorn, Roundthorn Road. **GPS**: n53,53352 w2,08637.

5 £9 , 2,50/night.

Distance: 3km.

Pickering 1C3

Antiques Centre, Southgate. **GPS**: n54,24413 w0,78026.

5 £10 Ch. **Location:** Simple. **Surface:** asphalted. 01/01-31/12

Distance: 500m.

Praa Sands 1A6

Car Park, Castle Drive. **GPS**: n50,10375 w5,38888.

against payment.

GB

Salthouse 1D6

GPS: n52,95525 e1,10136.
free.
Remarks: Beach parking.

Scarborough 1D3

South Moor Farm, Dalby Forest Drive. **GPS**: n54,30049 w0,61169.
5 £10 Ch. **Location:** Rural, simple. **Surface:** grassy.
01/01-31/12

Sewerby 1D6

The Ship Inn, Cliff Road. **GPS**: n54,10167 w0,16411.
5 £15 Ch. **Surface:** unpaved.
Distance: on the spot.

St. Ives 1D5

The Seven Wives, Ramsey road. **GPS**: n52,33193 w0,07634.

5 £5 Ch 6/night WC. **Location:** Urban, simple, central.
Surface: metalled. 01/01-31/12
Distance: 1,4km on the spot.

St.Austell 1A6

Edgemoor, Enniscaven, St.Dennis. **GPS**: n50,39636 w4,8676.

5 £5/night Ch WC included. **Location:** Comfortable, quiet.
Surface: grassy/metalled.
01/01-31/12
Distance: St.Austell 14,5km on the spot on the spot.
Remarks: Arrival <18h. Between Roche and St.Dennis, nearby Gothers Road.

Stratford-upon-Avon 1C5

Stratford Marina Car Park, Bridgeway. **GPS**: n52,19280 w1,70154.

10 9-18h £8, overnight stay £15. **Location:** Urban, simple, central.
Surface: asphalted. 01/01-31/12
Distance: 200m 200m 200m.

Stratford-upon-Avon 1C5

The New Inn Hotel, Clifford Chambers. **GPS**: n52,16929 w1,7168.

5 £8 4,80. **Location:** Rural, simple. **Surface:** grassy.
01/01-31/12
Distance: on the spot on the spot.

Tourist information Stratford-upon-Avon:
Birthplace of William Shakespeare.

Tarrington 1C5

The Tarrington Arms, Ledbury road. **GPS**: n52,06473 w2,5604.

5 free WC free. **Location:** Rural, simple. **Surface:** metalled.
Distance: 200m on the spot.

Tenby 1A5

Carew Airfield & Pavilion, Sageston. **GPS**: n51,69362 w4,80973.

5 £15-20/night Ch WC included. **Location:** Comfortable, quiet. **Surface:** concrete. 01/01-31/12
Distance: 150m 8km 500m 1,5km 1,5km.

Thaxted 1D5

Margaret Street Car Park, Margaret Street. **GPS**: n51,95530 e0,34328.

2 free WC free. **Location:** Urban, simple, central, quiet. **Surface:** concrete.
01/01-31/12
Distance: 150m 150m.
Remarks: Max. 48h in fortnight.

Tintagel 1A6

King Arthur's Car Park, Fore Street. **GPS**: n50,66356 w4,75129.
50 £3 10.00-16h, £3 16-10h WC. **Location:** Simple. **Surface:** asphalted.
16-10h
Distance: on the spot on the spot 100m.

GB

Remarks: Opposite Tintagel Old Post Office.

Tintagel 1A6

Mayfair Car Park, Fore Street. **GPS:** n50,66329 w4,75103.
50 £2 8.00-20h, £3.50 20-08h. **Location:** Urban, simple, central. **Surface:** asphalted/grassy. 01/01-31/12
Distance: on the spot 100m.
Remarks: Next to King Arthur's Car Park.

Tintagel 1A6

Sword in Stone Car Park, Bossine Rd. **GPS:** n50,66257 w4,74763.
20 £2 10.00-20h, £3.50 20-10h. **Location:** Urban, simple. **Surface:** asphalted. 01/01-31/12
Distance: 150m 250m.

Tourist information Tintagel:
Tourist Information Centre, Bossiney Road, www.visitboscastleandtintagel.com.
Tintagel Old Post Office, Fore Street.600 year-old traditional Cornish Longhouse.
King Arthur's Castle, Castle Road. 10-17/18h 24-26/12, 01/01.

Torrington 1B6

Sydney House Car Park, South Street. **GPS:** n50,95121 w4,14438.

20 £5 18-10h, £3 day. **Location:** Urban, simple, quiet. **Surface:** asphalted. 01/01-31/12
Distance: 300m 250m 250m.
Remarks: Max. 2 nights, min. 6m space between motorhomes.

Westward Ho! 1B6

Main Car Park, Golf Links Rd. **GPS:** n51,04069 w4,23728.

8 £5 18-10h, £7 day. **Location:** Urban, simple, central, quiet. **Surface:** asphalted. 01/01-31/12
Distance: on the spot 200m 200m 150m.
Remarks: Max. 5000kg, min. 6m space between motorhomes.

Whaplode St. Catherines 1D5

The Bleu Bell Inn, Cranesgate S. **GPS:** n52,75956 w0,0155.
5 £5 Ch (2x), 2,50/night. **Location:** Simple. **Surface:** .
01/01-31/12 Mo.
Distance: on the spot.
Remarks: Free with a meal.

Winchester 1C6

Car Park, Worthy Lane, B3044. **GPS:** n51,06396 w1,31632.
£4.
Remarks: Max. 24h.

Tourist information Winchester:
Tourist Information Centre, Winchester Guildhall, High Street, www.visitwinchester.co.uk.

Yeovil 1B6

Cartgate Truckstop and Picnic Area, A303/A3088 roundabout. **GPS:** n50,96926 w2,74087.

20 free WC Password at the restaurant. **Location:** Highway, simple, noisy. **Surface:** asphalted/metalled. 01/01-31/12
Distance: 15km on the spot.

GB

THE NETHERLANDS

Groningen
pages: 112-116
Friesland
pages: 105-112
Drenthe
pages: 116-118
North Holland
pages: 103-105
Flevoland
pages: 123-125
Overijssel
pages: 118-123
Amsterdam
South Holland
pages: 136-139
Utrecht
pages: 134-136
Gelderland
pages: 125-134
Rotterdam
Zealand
pages: 139-143
North Brabant
pages: 143-146
Limburg
pages: 146-149
Maastricht

NL

Capital: Amsterdam
Government: Constitutional monarchy
Official Language: Dutch
Population: 16,805,000 (2013))
Area: 41, 526 km^2.

General information
Country dial code: 0031
General emergency: 112
Currency: Euro
Credit cards are not accepted everywhere.

Regulations for overnight stays
Wild camping is forbidden in the Netherlands. Several motorhome-friendly municipalities have regulated facilities where overnight parking is allowed.

Additional public holidays 2014
April 26 Kingsday
May 5 Liberationday
June 9 Pentecost Monday
December 26 Boxing day

North Holland

Abbenes 8A2

Hoeve 't Groene Hart, Kaagweg 50. **GPS**: n52,22630 e4,61911.

15 € 10, 2 pers.incl Chincluded (6x)€ 2/24h. **Location:** Rural, comfortable, quiet. **Surface:** grassy/gravel. 15/03-01/11
Distance: 4km 900m 1,5km 1,5km 1,5km 4km Leiden <> Amsterdam on the spot on the spot.
Remarks: Bicycle rental € 11/day.

Amsterdam 8B1

Amsterdam City Camp, Papaverweg 55. **GPS**: n52,39847 e4,90010.

60 € 15, Jul/Aug € 20, 2 pers. Incl € 2/100liter Ch (30x)€ 3,10Amp included. **Location:** Urban, comfortable.
Surface: metalled. 01/01-31/12
Distance: 2km 20m 100m 1km 1,5km 500m.
Remarks: Video surveillance, free ferry to city centre.

Amsterdam 8B1

Het Amsterdamse Bos, Kleine Noorddijk 1, Amsterdam-zuid. **GPS**: n52,29271 e4,82171.
100 € 9 + € 5/pp Ch € 4,50WC. 15/03-01/12
Distance: 1km on the spot on the spot on the spot 100m.
Remarks: A9 exit 6, N231 dir Aalsmeer, after 500m turn right: Bosrandweg, campsite on the left after 2 km.

Amsterdam 8B1

Fam. Ackermann, Lutkemeerweg 149, Amsterdam-Osdorp. **GPS**: n52,36358 e4,77240.

16 € 10 2 pers.incl, >7m: +€ 1 m € 2,50 Ch € 4,50/day.
Surface: metalled.
01/01-31/12
Distance: 10km city centre 2km 1km.
Remarks: Via Osdorperweg, special license.

Tourist information Amsterdam:
VVV, Stationsplein 10 en Leidseplein 1, www.visitamsterdam.nl.Amsterdam Pass: Card gives entrance to museums, public transport, boattrip on the canals etc., 24h/€ 39, 48h/€ 49, 72h/€ 59, available at VVV.
Canalbus.Boat trip on the canals. € 13.
Joods Historisch Museum, Jonas Daniel Meijerplein 2/4.Jewish historical museum. 11-17h.
Nemo, Oosterdok 2.Science and technology. Tue-Su 10-17h, holidays Mo-Su. € 11.
Stelling van Amsterdam.Forts built to protect Amsterdam.
Albert Cuyp, Albert Cuyp.Arts and antiques market. daily Su.
Antiek, Noordermarkt. 01/05-30/09 last Sa of the month.
Artis.City-zoo. 9-17/18h.
Villa Arena, Naast Arena.Furniture mall, 80 shops. Tue-Sa 10-18h, Mo 13-18h.

De Rijp 8B1

Bloembolbedrijf Stoop, Zuiddijk 34. **GPS**: n52,54813 e4,83416.

€ 7 € 1. **Surface:** concrete. 01/01-31/12
Remarks: Between Alkmaar and Purmerend, exit De Rijp.

Den Helder 3B6

Willemsoord, Willemsoord 47. **GPS**: n52,96134 e4,76856.

15 € 10 € 0,50/80liter Ch € 0,50 € 3. **Surface:** metalled.
01/01-31/12
Distance: 400m.
Remarks: Max. 48h, ferry boat to Texel 500m, caution sanitary € 15.

Tourist information Den Helder:
VVV, Bernhardplein 18, www.vvvkopvannoordholland.nl.Country's main naval base.
Toeristische juttersmarkt.
summer Tue 10-17h.

Den Oever 3B6

Haventerrein Oostkade, Oostkade 3. **GPS**: n52,93395 e5,03974.

15 € 11 € 0,50/100liter € 0,50Ch WC included. **Surface:** metalled.
01/01-31/12
Distance: 500m 1,4km 200m offshore fishing 500m 500m on the spot.
Remarks: Max. 3 days, Sa-morning fishmarket. At old harbour.

Enkhuizen 3B6

Dirck Chinaplein. **GPS**: n52,69806 e5,29005.

6 € 10/12-12h WC.
Surface: asphalted.
Distance: on the spot.
Remarks: Max. 48h.

Tourist information Enkhuizen:
Zuiderzeemuseum.Historical little town.
Apr-autumn holiday 10-17/18h.

S Hoorn 8B1

Jachthaven Hoorn, Visserseiland 221. **GPS**: n52,63467 e5,05676.

15 € 12,50 Ch WC € 0,50. **Surface:** metalled.
01/04-31/10
Distance: 500m 2,8km 50m 100m on the spot.
Remarks: Check in at harbourmaster.

Huizen 8B1

Recreatieterrein Wolskamer, IJsselmeerstraat. **GPS**: n52,30860 e5,24046.

8 free. **Location:** Simple. **Surface:** grassy.
Distance: on the spot.
Remarks: Max. 48h.

Tourist information Huizen:
Weekmarkt. Sa.

Katwoude 8B1

De Simonehoeve, Wagenweg 2. **GPS**: n52,48620 e5,03196.

10 free. 18(20)-8h
Remarks: Cheese farm, nearby Hotel Volendam. Nearby hotel Volendam.

S Laren (NH) 8B1

Sportcomplex De Biezem, Schapendrift 64. **GPS**: n52,25717 e5,23884.

2 free Ch WC. **Surface:** metalled.
Distance: 1km.
Remarks: Max. 1 night. Nearby sports complex 'De Biezem'.

S Medemblik 3B6

Haven Medemblik, Pekelharinghaven 50. **GPS**: n52,77139 e5,11361.

3 € 8 + € 0,70/pp tourist tax Ch € 1,75.
Surface: metalled.
Distance: 1km 1km 1km.
Remarks: Max. 48h.

Tourist information Medemblik:
Museum Stoomtram.Steam tram museum: Hoorn-Medemblik.
Kasteel Radbout.Medieval citadel.
Easter-Oct Mo-Sa 10-17, Su 12-17h, winter Su.

S Middenmeer 3B6

Jachthaven Middenmeer, Havenstraat. **GPS**: n52,81236 e4,99112.

6 € 5 + € 1/pp tourist tax Ch € 1 WC € 0,50.
Surface: metalled. 01/01-31/12
Distance: 500m 1,7km 500m.
Remarks: Max 48h, check in at harbourmaster.

S Monnickendam 8B1

Jachthaven Waterland, Galgeriet 5a. **GPS**: n52,45920 e5,04059.

5 € 18,50 € 0,50/100liter Ch € 0,50/2kWh WC. 30/04-15/10
Distance: 500-800m on the spot.

NL

Remarks: Check in at harbourmaster.

S Naarden 8B1

Jachthaven Naarden, Onderwal 4. **GPS:** n52,30874 e5,14703.

10 € 12.50 + € 2/pp tourist tax Ch WC € 5,dryer € 3 included. **Location:** Rural, comfortable, quiet.
Surface: grassy/metalled. 01/01-31/12
Distance: Naarden-vesting (fortress) 2,3km 600m 500m lake Gooi on the spot on the spot on the spot.

Tourist information Naarden:
Fortified city with city walls.
Vestingmuseum.Fortress museum. 01/03-31/10 Tue-Fri 10.30-17h, weekend 12-17h, summer Mo-Fri, 01/11-28/02 Su 12-17h.

Oosthuizen 8B1

Recreatieknooppunt Oosthuizen, Hoornse Jaagweg. **GPS:** n52,57609 e4,99719.

2 free. **Location:** Quiet. **Surface:** . 01/01-31/12
Distance: 200m 500m 100m > Volendam on the spot on the spot.
Remarks: Max. 48h.

S Opperdoes 3B6

Imkerij de Bijenstal, Zwarte pad. **GPS:** n52,76367 e5,08253.

3 € 10,50, 2 pers.incl € 1/100liter € 2. **Surface:** gravel.
Remarks: Boat rental.

Tourist information Opperdoes:
Museum stoomtram, Medemblik.Steam tram museum: Hoorn-Medemblik. € 12.

Oudendijk 8B1

Bruin Eetcafé Les Deux Ponts, Slimdijk 2. **GPS:** n52,60462 e4,95983.

Remarks: Between Hoorn and Purmerend, exit Averhorn.

Purmerend 8B1

Neckerstraat/West. **GPS:** n52,50972 e4,93944.

5 free. **Surface:** metalled. 01/01-31/12
Distance: 450m 400m.
Remarks: Max. 72h.

Tourist information Purmerend:
Centrum. Tue.

S Schagen 3B6

Jachthaven, Lagedijkerweg 2B. **GPS:** n52,79088 e4,78746.

15 € 5,10 + € 0,80/pp tourist tax € 0,50/100liter Ch € 1,50 WC € 0,50 washing machine/dryer € 4 € 2. **Surface:** metalled.
01/01-31/12
Distance: 500m on the spot 400m 500m.
Remarks: Check in at harbourmaster, caution key sanitary building € 15.

Tourist information Schagen:
VVV, Loet 10.
West Friese Folkloremarkt.Folkore market. Jun-Jul-Aug: Thu.

Stompetoren 8B1

Het Schermer Wapen, Oterlekerweg 3. **GPS:** n52,61420 e4,82115.
4 .

Texel/De Cocksdorp 3B5

De Krim, Roggeslootweg 6. **GPS:** n53,15110 e4,85996.
8 € 15-€ 25. **Surface:** metalled. 01/01-31/12

S Volendam 8B1

Marinapark Volendam, De Pieterman 1. **GPS:** n52,48944 e5,05972.

36 € 6 10-17h, € 14 17-10h Ch included .
Surface: grasstiles/metalled.
01/01-31/12
Distance: 1,5km 50m 50m 300m 300m 300m.

Tourist information Volendam:
VVV, Zeestraat 37, www.vvv-volendam.nl.Old fishermen's village.
Volendams Museum, Zeestraat 41.
Life and Work in Volendam, 1800-1900. Easter-autumn holiday 10-17h.

Friesland

S Akkrum 3C5

Tusken de Marren, Ulbe Twijnstrawei 31. **GPS:** n53,04853 e5,82577.

NL

20 € 12,50 € 0,50/100liter Ch € 2/night WC € 0,50 free.
Surface: grassy/metalled. 15/03-01/11
Distance: 200m on the spot on the spot 700m 500m.
Remarks: Information at harbourmaster, boat rental.

S Appelscha 3D6

De Compagnonshoeve, Vaart Noordzijde 104. **GPS**: n52,95222 e6,36278.

10 € 7 Ch € 1. **Surface:** grassy. 01/01-31/12
Distance: on the spot 3km on the spot 200m 400m 400m 50m.

Tourist information Appelscha:
Speelpark Duinenzathe, Noorder Es 1.Playground.
01/04-30/09 + autumn holiday + weekend Oct 9.30-17h. >3: € 11.

NL

S Balk 3C6

Jachthaven Lutsmond, Sleatemar 1a. **GPS**: n52,90389 e5,59694.

10 € 10 excl. tourist tax Ch € 2 WC. **Surface:** grassy.
01/01-31/12
Distance: 1km on the spot on the spot nearby 1km.

S Bergum 3C5

Camperterrein Prinses Margriet Kanaal, Opperdijk van Veenweg 22. **GPS**: n53,18643 e6,00176.

25 € 10/night Chincluded € 2/night 1h free, 1 day € 7,50.
Location: Urban, comfortable, quiet. **Surface:** grassy/metalled.
01/01-31/12
Distance: 2km 2km on the spot 2km 2km on the spot on the spot on the spot.

S Bergum 3C5

Jachthaven Burgumerdaam, Bergumerdaam 51. **GPS**: n53,18705 e5,99299.

10 € 10 € 0,50/100liter Ch € 0,50/kWh WC € 0,50/5minutes € 3,50,dryer € 3,50 included. **Location:** Urban, comfortable, central, quiet. **Surface:** metalled. 15/03-01/11
Distance: 500m 500m 5km on the spot 500m 500m 500m on the spot on the spot.
Remarks: Max. 72h.

S Bolsward 3C5

Camperplaats Half-Hichtum, Hichtumerweg 14. **GPS**: n53,07365 e5,52253.

6 € 14 Ch WC included € 3,50. **Location:** Rural, comfortable, quiet. **Surface:** grassy/metalled. 01/04-01/11
Distance: 1km 1,3km 6km 500m 1km 1km 200m on the spot on the spot.

S Brantgum 3C5

Camperplaats Veldzicht, Veldbuurtsterweg 9. **GPS**: n53,35556 e5,93632.

15 € 10 Ch included. **Location:** Rural, comfortable, isolated, quiet. **Surface:** grassy/metalled. 01/01-31/12
Distance: Dokkum 7km 2km 3km 3km on the spot on the spot.
Remarks: Ferry boat to Ameland 3km.

S Burdaard 3C5

Jachthaven Mouneheim, Mounewei 17. **GPS**: n53,29711 e5,88261.

12 € 8 Ch € 1/night,10Amp WC € 0,50/5minutes € 4,50,dryer € 2,50 included. **Location:** Rural, comfortable, quiet.

Surface: grassy/gravel. 01/01-31/12
Distance: on the spot 2km on the spot on the spot 100m 500m 2km on the spot on the spot.
Remarks: Passerby € 1/100l.

Dokkum 3C5

Kalkhuisplein, Kalkhuisplein. **GPS:** n53,32650 e6,00936.

3 € 5. **Location:** Urban, simple, quiet.
Surface: metalled.
15/03-31/12
Distance: 500m 1km 20m 20m 1km 1km 1km on the spot on the spot.
Remarks: Only overnight stays 18-9h, max. 1 night.

Tourist information Dokkum:
Het Admiraliteitshuis, Diepwal 27.Regional museum. Tue-Sa 13-17h.
Natuurmuseum, Kleine Oosterstraat.Natural museum. Mo-Fri 10-12h, 13-17h.

Drachten 3D5

VV Drachten, Gauke Boelensstraat. **GPS:** n53,10289 e6,08832.

5 free. **Surface:** asphalted.
Distance: 500m 500m.

Earnewâld 3C5

Eilansgrien. **GPS:** n53,12958 e5,93630.

5 € 5,20 + € 0,80/pp tourist tax € 0,50 Ch € 0,50/kWh WC € 0,50 washing machine/dryer € 3,50. **Surface:** asphalted.
01/01-31/12
Distance: 200m 500m 200m.
Remarks: Sanitary/washing machine at tourist office (Summer season), max. 72h.

Harlingen 3C5

Tsjerk Hiddesluizen, Nieuwe Vissershaven 17. **GPS:** n53,17938 e5,41731.

10 € 5 Ch (16x) WC.
Surface: asphalted.
Distance: 500m 500m 500m 100m.
Remarks: Max. 72, laundromat/toilets/shower 500m.

Tourist information Harlingen:
VVV, Voorstraat 34, www.friesekust.nl.Historical city and port.

Heerenveen 3C6

Thialf, Pim Mulierlaan 1. **GPS:** n52,93843 e5,94495.

4 free. **Surface:** metalled.
01/01-31/12 during event.
Distance: 2km 2km 2km.
Remarks: Max. 72h, on parking ground of skating rink.

Heerenveen 3C6

De Koningshof, Prinsenweg 1. **GPS:** n52,94759 e5,94438.

4 free. **Surface:** asphalted. 01/01-31/12
Distance: 1km on the spot 4km 500m.
Remarks: Large parking near A32, max. 72h.

Heerenveen 3C6

Gemeentewerf, Venus 4. **GPS:** n52,96663 e5,93502.
free. Mon-Fri 9-15u

Hogebeintum 3C5

Bezoekerscentrum Terp Hegebeintum, Pijpkedijk 4. **GPS:** n53,33609 e5,85244.

4 free. **Surface:** asphalted.
Distance: 4km.
Remarks: Parking information centre/VVV, highest mound in the Netherlands,

NL

max. 2 days.

IJlst 3C6

De Tsjalk, De Tsjalk. **GPS**: n53,00846 e5,62741.

4 free ,6 Amp WC free € 0,50/5minutes. **Location:** Urban, simple, central, quiet. **Surface:** metalled. 01/01-31/12

Distance: 200m on the spot 200m 200m 200m on the spot on the spot.

Joure 3C6

Jachthaven, Grienedyk. **GPS**: n52,97210 e5,78836.

4 € 12,50 € 0,50/70liter € 1,50 € 1. **Surface:** metalled.
01/03-01/11

Distance: 500m 50m.

Remarks: Max. 72h.

NL

Joure 3C6

Sauna de Woudfennen, Woudfennen 10, Boornzwaag. **GPS**: n52,96383 e5,76627.

use of sauna obligatory. **Surface:** asphalted.

Remarks: A7 exit 23, Joure west.

Tourist information Joure:

In de Witte Os, Midstraat 97.Nostalgic store. mo 13.30-17h, thue-sa 10-17h.

Museum Joure, Geelgietersstraat 1-11.Frisian handicraft. sa-mo 14-17h, thue-fri 10-17h holiday.

Kollum 3D5

Jachthaven de Rijd, Cantecleer 2. **GPS**: n53,28727 e6,15139.

12 € 9 Ch € 1,50/night,10Amp WC € 1 included.

Location: Urban, simple, central, quiet. **Surface:** metalled.
01/05-01/10

Distance: on the spot on the spot 500m 500m 500m on the spot on the spot.

Remarks: Max. 72h.

Koudum 3C6

De Kuilart, De Kuilart 1. **GPS**: n52,90305 e5,46706.

10 + 2 € 10, Quick-Stop € 8 Ch included € 1/night,6 Amp WC € 0,35/5minutes € 4,40,dryer € 2,35 . **Location:** Rural, luxurious, noisy.

Surface: grassy/metalled.
01/01-07/05, 22/05-05/07, 25/08-31/12 holidays.

Distance: 1,5km on the spot on the spot on the spot 1km 1km on the spot on the spot.

Langweer 3C6

Passantenhaven Langweer, Buorren 5. **GPS**: n52,96091 e5,72240.

3 € 12,50 € 0,20 Ch WC included € 0,50 washing machine/dryer € 3,50 . **Surface:** grassy.
01/04-31/10

Distance: 500m on the spot on the spot 500m 500m 500m.

Langweer 3C6

Brandweerkazerne, Pontdyk. **GPS**: n52,96000 e5,71972.

4 free. **Surface:** metalled. 01/01-31/12

Distance: 500m 500m 500m 500m.

Remarks: Max. 72h.

Leeuwarden 3C5

Leeuwarder Jachthaven, Jachthavenlaan 3. **GPS**: n53,19886 e5,83019.

6 € 12,50 Ch WC € 1/5minutes included. **Location:** Urban, comfortable, isolated, quiet. **Surface:** grassy/gravel.
01/01-31/12
Distance: 2,5km 1km on the spot on the spot 500m 500m 300m on the spot on the spot.
Remarks: Check in at harbourmaster.

S Leeuwarden 3C5

Prinsentuin, Wissesdwinger 1. **GPS**: n53,20528 e5,79659.

4 € 9,08 Ch € 0,34/kWh,6 Amp WC € 4,31,dryer € 3 included. **Location:** Urban, comfortable, central, quiet. **Surface:** metalled. 01/01-31/12 sanitary building: 1/11-1/4.
Distance: on the spot 2km on the spot on the spot on the spot on the spot on the spot on the spot on the spot.

S Leeuwarden 3C5

Taniaburg, Vierhuisterweg 72. **GPS**: n53,21955 e5,79286.

8 € 11,10 Ch € 2,40/night,6 Amp WC € 2,50,dryer € 3 included. **Location:** Rural, comfortable, quiet. **Surface:** grassy/gravel.
01/04-01/11
Distance: 3km 1km on the spot on the spot 500m 500m on the spot on the spot.
Remarks: Canoe and bicycle rental.

S Lemmer 3C6

Jachthaven, Plattedijk 6. **GPS**: n52,84708 e5,69696.

8 € 10 Ch WC against payment. **Surface:** metalled.
01/04-01/10
Distance: 1km on the spot 1km.

Tourist information Lemmer:
Ir. D.F. Woudagemaal.The biggest steam pumpingstation of Europe.
M Oudheidkamer.History of the Lemster barges.
Mo-Fri 9.30-16h.

S Makkum 3C5

Gemeentehaven Makkum, Workumerdijk 2. **GPS**: n53,05329 e5,40317.

2 € 10 Ch WC included € 2,dryer € 2.
Location: Urban, simple, central, noisy.
Surface: metalled.
01/04-31/10 service: 01/11-01/04.
Distance: 100m on the spot 400m 950m 950m on the spot on the spot.
Remarks: Max. 72h. At marina.

Tourist information Makkum:
Koninklijke Tichelaar, Turfmarkt 65.Manufacture of pottery covered with tin.
guided tour Mo-Thu 11h, 13.30h, 15h, Fri 11h, 13.30h, shop Mo-Fri 9-17h.30, Sa 10-17h.
M Aldfaers Erf.Museum route, the life and working in 1900.
01/04-31/10 10-17h.

Molkwerum 3C6

Camperplaats 't Seleantsje, 't Seleantsje 2. **GPS**: n52,90419 e5,39493.

18 € 10 Ch WC included € 0,50/6minutes € 4,dryer € 2,50 € 5/day. **Location:** Rural, comfortable, quiet. **Surface:** grasstiles.
15/03-01/11
Distance: 300m on the spot on the spot on the spot 4km 1km on the spot on the spot.

S Nes 3C5

Manege Nes, Burdineweg 2. **GPS**: n53,05468 e5,85558.

10 € 3 Ch € 2/night,16 Amp WC included. **Location:** Rural, simple, quiet. **Surface:** grassy/metalled. 01/01-31/12
Distance: 700m 1km 10km 50m 700m 700m 700m on the spot on the spot.
Remarks: At manege.

Nijetrijne 3C6

Paviljoen Driewegsluis, Lindedijk 2a. **GPS**: n52,83261 e5,92467.

NL

customers free.
Distance: on the spot on the spot.

S Oudega 3C5

Jachthaven Oudega, Roundeel. **GPS:** n53,12315 e5,99961.

2 € 7 € 1/100liter € 2,50 € 0,50. **Surface:** grassy. 01/04-01/11
Distance: 200m 200m 200m.
Remarks: Max. 48h.

S Oudemirdum 3C6

Landgoed de Syme, Jan Schotanuswei 106a, via Oude Balksterweg. **GPS:** n52,85746 e5,51115.

2 € 5 included € 2,50/night. **Location:** Rural, simple, isolated, quiet. **Surface:** grassy/metalled. 01/01-31/12
Distance: 4km 6km 6km 4km 4km on the spot on the spot.
Remarks: Entrance Oude Balksterweg.

Oudeschoot 3D5

Woutersbergje, Van Bienemalaan 15-17. **GPS:** n53,07347 e6,23986.

15 € 10,40 Ch € 2/night,6 Amp WC € 3,dryer € 1 included.
Location: Rural, comfortable, central, quiet.
Surface: grassy/metalled. 01/01-31/12
Distance: 3,5km 300m on the spot on the spot.

Ried 3C5

Jachthaven it Kattegat, Berlikumerweg 13. **GPS:** n53,22416 e5,59330.

3 + 4 € 9,50. **Location:** Rural, simple, quiet. **Surface:** grassy/metalled. 01/04-01/10
Distance: on the spot 500m on the spot on the spot 500m on the spot on the spot.

S Rohel 3C6

Aktiviteitenboerderij, Vierhuisterweg 29. **GPS:** n52,90337 e5,84540.

5 € 15 Ch WC included. **Location:** Quiet. **Surface:** metalled. 01/01-31/12
Distance: on the spot on the spot on the spot on the spot.

Sexbierum 3C5

Restaurant Liauckama State, Liauckamaleane 2. **GPS:** n53,22028 e5,47656.

5 € 10, free for clients. 01/01-31/12
Distance: 1km 1km 1km.

Sint Jacobiparochie 3C5

Zeedijk, Zwarte Haan. **GPS:** n53,30915 e5,63051.

free. **Surface:** grassy. 01/01-31/12
Distance: Sint Jacobiparochie 8km Wadden Sea 100m on the spot on the spot.

Sloten 3C6

Jachthaven Lemsterpoort, Jachthaven 7. **GPS:** n52,89265 e5,64486.

NL

8 € 11 € 0,50/100liter Ch € 2,50/24h,6 Amp WC € 1/5minutes included. **Location:** Urban, comfortable, quiet. **Surface:** grassy/metalled. 01/01-31/12

Distance: 100m 2km on the spot on the spot 100m 100m 500m on the spot on the spot.

S Sneek 3C6

Jachthaven Holiday Boatin, Eeltjebaasweg 3. **GPS**: n53,02184 e5,56702.

4 € 10 Ch € 1/night,10Amp WC included. **Location:** Urban, comfortable, quiet. **Surface:** concrete. 01/01-31/12

Distance: 3,6km 2km on the spot on the spot 4km 2km, bakery 300m 300m on the spot on the spot.

Tourist information Sneek:

M Fries scheepvaartmuseum en Sneker Oudheidkamer, Kleinzand 14.
Mo-Sa 10-17h, Su 12-17h. T € 1.

S Stavoren 3C6

Marina Stavoren, Suderstrand. **GPS**: n52,87398 e5,36762.

20 € 20 Ch WC included. **Surface:** metalled.
01/04-31/10

Distance: 1km on the spot on the spot on the spot on the spot.

S Stavoren 3C6

Camperplaats Stavoren Bolwerk - Stavoren

camperplaats@stavorenbolwerk.nl - http://www.stavorenbolwerk.nl/

Beautiful view
Sanitary facilities
Located directely at Lake IJsel

Camperplaats Stavoren Bolwerk, Bolwerk. **GPS**: n52,88543 e5,35662.

8 € 15, discount with a meal in restaurant Ch WC .

Location: Comfortable. **Surface:** metalled. 01/01-31/12

Distance: on the spot on the spot on the spot on the spot on the spot.

Remarks: Check in at restaurant, beautiful view.

S Sumar 3D5

Recreatiecentrum Bergumermeer, Solcamastraat 30. **GPS**: n53,19044 e6,02316.

10 € 18 Ch WC included. **Location:** Rural, luxurious, quiet. **Surface:** grassy/metalled. 01/04-31/10

Distance: 5km.

Sumar 3D5

Recreatiecentrum Bergumermeer, Solcamastraat-30. **GPS**: n53,19044 e6,02316.

1 € 8 17-10h. 01/04-31/10

S Surhuisterveen 3D5

Zwembad Wettervlecke, Badlaan 3. **GPS**: n53,17987 e6,16124.

5 € 5 WC . **Surface:** grassy.

Distance: on the spot.

S Tersoal 3C5

Watersportbedrijf Lege Geaen, Buorren 2. **GPS**: n53,07729 e5,74360.

6 € 10 Ch € 2,50/night WC included. **Location:** Rural, comfortable, quiet. **Surface:** grassy/gravel. 01/01-31/12

Distance: 8km 1,5km on the spot on the spot 1,5km 8km on the spot on the spot.

S Wartena 3C5

Jachthaven Wartena, Bûtenstreek 3. **GPS**: n53,15044 e5,90398.

NL

10 € 10 + € 1/pp Ch WC € 1 € 6.
Surface: grassy/metalled. 01/01-31/11
Distance: 200m on the spot on the spot 500m 500m on the spot.

Wommels 3C5

Jachthaven Wommels, Terp 14. **GPS:** n53,10957 e5,58765.

5 € 10 Ch WC included € 0,50. **Surface:** grassy/metalled.
01/04-01/10
Distance: 300m on the spot 100m.
Remarks: Market 100m, museum 200m.

Tourist information Wommels:
Museum It Tsiispakhûs, Keatsebaen 1.Dairy museum. 01/04-31/10 Tue-Su 13.30-16.30.
Weekmarkt. Tue-morning.

Workum 3C6

Jachthaven Bouwsma, Moleburren 11. **GPS:** n52,98230 e5,45518.

6 € 10 Ch € 2,50/night,6 Amp WC € 1/7minutes € 8,dryer incl. included. **Location:** Urban, central, quiet.
Surface: grassy/metalled. 01/04-31/10
Distance: 750m 1,5km on the spot 500m 500m 200m on the spot on the spot.

Workum 3C6

Abma's pôle, Nijhuizumerdijk 3. **GPS:** n52,98363 e5,47049.

10 free Ch voluntary contribution. **Location:** Rural, simple, quiet.
Surface: concrete.

01/01-31/12
Distance: 2,5km 1km on the spot on the spot 2,5km 2,5km 2,5km on the spot on the spot.

Tourist information Workum:
Jopie Huisman Museum, Noard 6.Autodidact, paintings and drawings.
01/04-31/10 10-17h, 01/03-30/11 + Su 13-17h.

Woudsend 3C6

Recreatiecentrum De Rakken, Lynbaen 10. **GPS:** n52,94649 e5,62732.

5 € 16,50 + € 0,65 tourist tax Ch WC included € 4,40,dryer € 2,25 € 6. **Surface:** grassy/metalled. 15/03-15/10
Distance: 1km 100m 100m 1km 1km.

Ypecolsga 3C6

Camperplaats Waterloo, Nr. 19. **GPS:** n52,92758 e5,59549.

10 € 8, 2 pers.incl, tourist tax € 1/pp Ch included WC Use sanitary € 1,50/pp € 4,50,dryer € 2. **Surface:** grasstiles. 01/01-31/12
Distance: 3km 1km 1km 3,5km 3,5km nearby.

Zurich 3C5

Camperplaats Zurich, Caspar di Roblesdijk 3. **GPS:** n53,11235 e5,39335.
3 € 10. **Location:** Urban, simple, central, noisy. **Surface:** metalled.
01/01-31/12
Distance: on the spot 1,5km on the spot on the spot on the spot on the spot on the spot on the spot on the spot.
Remarks: Max. 72h.

Zwaagwesteinde 3D5

Camperpark Kuikhorne, Kuikhornsterweg 31. **GPS:** n53,24124 e6,01875.

25 € 8, 2 pers.incl € 0,50 Ch € 1 WC € 0,50 € 4,dryer € 3.
Surface: grassy. 15/03-01/11
Distance: 2km on the spot 2km, pizzeria within walking distance 2km. **Remarks:** Max. 72h.

Groningen

Appingedam 4A5

Camperplaats Appingedam, Farmsumerweg 21. **GPS:** n53,32062 e6,86689.

NL

10 free free € 1/1kWh,10Amp. **Location:** Urban, simple, central, noisy. **Surface:** metalled. 01/01-31/12
Distance: 750m Damsterdiep 500m 500m on the spot on the spot on the spot.
Remarks: Max. 72h.

Delfzijl 4A5

Zeebadweg, Zeebadweg. **GPS**: n53,33582 e6,92650.

4 free.
Distance: 500m on the spot on the spot 100m 300m.

S Den Horn 3D5

Tempelboerderij, Nieuwbrugsterweg 4. **GPS**: n53,23814 e6,47053.

3 €7 Ch €1 WC €0,50 €2,50.
Surface: metalled.
01/01-31/12
Distance: 2km 600m.

Tourist information Den Horn:
Schansenroute.Route along defensive works from the 80-year's War.

S Doezum 3D5

Landgoed Jonker, Provincialeweg 133a. **GPS**: n53,20411 e6,26018.

60 € 8,50, 2 pers.incl €0,50 €0,50 Ch (20x)€ 2/night WC included. **Surface:** grassy.
01/01-31/12 facilities 01/10-31/03.
Distance: 1km on the spot.

Tourist information Doezum:
Abel Tasman Kabinet, Kompasstraat 1, Grootegast.Local archaeological museum seafarer Abel Tasman. Mo-Fri 13-17h, Sa 9-12h, 13-16h.

S Eenrum 3D5

Jachthaven De Dobbe, Dobbepad. **GPS**: n53,36311 e6,45151.

4 € 13,50 Ch WC €0,50. **Surface:** grassy/metalled.
Distance: 500m on the spot 500m 500m.
Remarks: Check in at harbourmaster.

Tourist information Eenrum:
Abrahams Mosterdmakerij, Molenstraat 5.Groninger mustard factory, restaurant.
Wed-Su >11h. € 2.

S Garnwerd 3D5

Restaurant Ad Nooren, Hunzeweg 38a. **GPS**: n53,30503 e6,49427.

6 € 10 Ch € 2 WC € 1 € 6 € 5/h. **Surface:** grassy.
Distance: 500m on the spot on the spot on the spot.
Remarks: Bread-service.

Groningen 3D5

Sportcentrum Kardinge, Bieskemaar. **GPS**: n53,23946 e6,59680.

15 free. **Surface:** metalled.
01/01-31/12
Distance: 3km 1km on the spot.
Remarks: Max. 72h.

Tourist information Groningen:
VVV, Grote Markt 25, www.vvvgroningen.nl.Former residence of the prefects Maurits and Willem.
Prinsenhof en prinsenhoftuin. 15/03-15/10.
Noordelijk Scheepvaartmuseum/ Niemeyer Tabaksmuseum, Brugstraat 24.
Tue-Sa 10-17h, Su 13-17h.

Haren 3D5

Jachthaven Zuidwesthoek, Meerweg 247. **GPS**: n53,15855 e6,56619.

NL

10 € 7. **Location:** Rural, simple, quiet. **Surface:** metalled.
01/01-31/12
Distance: 2km on the spot on the spot on the spot 2km 500m on the spot on the spot.
Remarks: Temporary stopover.

S Harkstede 3D5
Grunopark, Hoofdweg 163. **GPS**: n53,21135 e6,66161.

10 € 5 On demand WC . **Surface:** metalled.
01/01-31/12
Distance: 3km 100m.
Tourist information Harkstede:
Hortus in Haren.Garden, exposition, restaurant. 9-17/18h.

S Lauwersoog 3D5
Havenkantoor Lauwersoog, Haven 2. **GPS**: n53,40819 e6,19768.

NL

2 € 1,50/m Ch WC included. **Location:** Urban, simple, quiet.
Surface: metalled. 01/01-31/12
Distance: on the spot on the spot on the spot on the spot on the spot.

S Lauwersoog 3D5
Lauwersmeerplezier, Kustweg 30. **GPS**: n53,40625 e6,20044.

14 € 15, 2 pers.incl WC included € 3. **Surface:** grassy/metalled.
01/01-31/12
Distance: 500m on the spot on the spot 500m 500m.

Lauwersoog 3D5
Jachthaven Noordergat, Noordergat 1. **GPS**: n53,40493 e6,20311.

30 € 14 Ch included € 2,10/24h € 0,50/5minutes € 3,dryer € 2,50. **Location:** Rural, simple, quiet. **Surface:** concrete.
01/01-31/12
Distance: on the spot on the spot on the spot on the spot.
Tourist information Lauwersoog:
Lauwersmeergebied.Breeding area for birds and recreation area. 01/04-31/10 Tue-Su 11-17h.

S Leens 3D5
Leenstertillen. **GPS**: n53,34992 e6,36913.
15 € 5/pp WC. **Location:** Rural, quiet. **Surface:** grassy.
01/01-31/12
Distance: 1,5km 50m 50m 1,5km 1,6km.

S Losdorp 4A5
Restaurant Eemshaven, Schafferweg 29. **GPS**: n53,37214 e6,84411.

4 consuming is appreciated WC . 01/01-31/12 Mo.
Distance: 2km 2km.
Remarks: Delfzijl-Eemshaven.

Lutjegast 3D5
't Kompas, Kompasstraat 1. **GPS**: n53,23498 e6,25972.

5 free. **Surface:** metalled. 01/01-31/12
Distance: on the spot on the spot 200m on the spot.
Remarks: Behind the club-building.

S Musselkanaal 4A6
Jachthaven Spoordok, Havenkade 1. **GPS**: n52,92694 e7,01389.

25 € 7,50 € 0,50/100liter Ch (25x) WC included.

Surface: grassy/metalled. 01/05-01/10
Distance: 500m on the spot on the spot on the spot nearby on the spot.
Remarks: Max. 72h.

Tourist information Musselkanaal:
Former peat colony.
Plattelandsklooster, Boslaan 3-5, Ter Apel.Ecclesiastical art and history. Tue-Sa 10-17h, Su 13-17h.

S Onderdendam 3D5

Watersportvereniging Onderdendam, Warffumerweg 12. **GPS**: n53,33652 e6,58600.

6 € 6 + € 1/pp Ch (6x) WC € 0,50. **Surface:** grassy/metalled.
Distance: 500m on the spot on the spot 500m 500m.

S Sellingen 4A6

De Bronzen Eik, Zevenmeersveenweg 1. **GPS**: n52,95482 e7,13848.
10 € 9, € 0,80/pppd tourist tax Ch WC . **Surface:** gravel. 01/01-31/12
Distance: 1km on the spot 1km.
Remarks: Arrival after 7pm.

S Slochteren 4A5

Duurswoldje, Edserweg. **GPS**: n53,19412 e6,80556.

7 € 5 Ch included. **Surface:** grassy. 01/01-31/12
Distance: 500m on the spot on the spot 1km on the spot.
Remarks: Covered picnic area, small stock accommodation.

S Stadskanaal 4A6

Pagedal, Dwarsweg. **GPS**: n52,98973 e6,98499.

5 free Ch. **Surface:** metalled.
01/04-15/10
Distance: 3km on the spot on the spot on the spot 3km 3km.
Remarks: Sa market. Recreation area.

Tourist information Stadskanaal:
Pagedal, www.stadskanaal.nl.Daytime recreation.
Musica, Scheepswerfkade 34-35.Collection antique musical instruments.
01/04-31/10: Sa/Su 14-17, 01/07-31/08 Tue-Su 14-17.

S Veendam 4A5

Borgerswold, Flora 2. **GPS**: n53,10637 e6,84826.

60 € 9/night Ch WC included.
Location: Rural.
Surface: grassy.
01/01-31/12
Distance: 2km beach 50m on the spot 2km 1km.

Tourist information Veendam:
Museumspoorlijn STAR, Parallelweg 4, Veendam.Museum railway line, tickets available at railwaystation.
01/04-31/10, 27/12-03/01. round trip € 9,50.
Veenkoloniaalmuseum, Museumplein 5.History of the peat, shipping and industry.
Tue-Fri 11-17h, Sa-Su 13-17h 01/09-30/06 Mo.

S Wildervank 4A5

J. Geerling, Wildervanksterdallen 69. **GPS**: n53,04316 e6,89637.

5 € 5 . **Surface:** grassy. 01/01-31/12
Distance: 500m 7km.
Remarks: Max. 72h.

S Wildervank 4A5

Sauna 't Dalhuus, Wildervanksterdallen 59. **GPS**: n53,05479 e6,88384.
4 customers free € 1. **Surface:** metalled. 01/01-31/12
Distance: 5km.
Remarks: Max. 24h. Some kilometres south-east of Wildervank.

S Winschoten 4A5

Hotel Café Restaurant Bowling In den Stallen, Oostereinde 10. **GPS**: n53,15371 e7,06528.

10 consuming is appreciated On demand .
Surface: asphalted/metalled.
Distance: 1km 600m 600m on the spot 1km 600m.
Remarks: A7 Groningen-Nieuweschans, exit Winschoten, then dir Beerta.

Tourist information Winschoten:
Stoomgemaal, Winschoter Oostereinde.Steam-engine 1895.

NL

Winsum 3D5

Jachthaven/Camping Marenland, Winsumerstraatweg. **GPS**: n53,33177 e6,51015.

10 € 15 Ch € 3/night,4 Amp WC € 6,50, included,at restaurant. **Location:** Urban, comfortable, quiet. **Surface:** grassy/metalled. 01/04-01/11

Distance: 300m 200m on the spot on the spot 500m 200m on the spot Pieterpad.

Zoutkamp 3D5

Jachthaven Hunzegat, Strandweg 17. **GPS**: n53,34083 e6,29000.

10 € 10 excl. tourist tax Ch dump chem.toilet only with biodegradable liquid (10x) WC washing machine/dryer € 7,40 .

Surface: grassy/metalled. 01/01-31/12

Distance: 500m 500m 300m. **Remarks:** Bread-service.

Tourist information Zoutkamp:

Waddencentrum, Hoofdstraat 83, Pieterburen.Wadden en Wadlope, Exhibition mud-flats and wading in the mudflats. 01/04-30/11 Tue-Su 13-17h, 01/11-31/03 Sa-Su 13-17h. free.

Zeehondencrèche, Hoofdstraat 94a, Pieterburen.Sanctory to cure sick seals. 9-18h. € 4,50.

Zuidbroek 4A5

De Broeckhof, W.A. Scholtenweg 18. **GPS**: n53,16103 e6,86235.

3 free WC . **Surface:** metalled. 01/04-30/09

Distance: 500m 1km.

Remarks: Max. 72h. Parking community centre.

Drenthe

Assen 3D6

Van Hobokenstraat 5. **GPS**: n53,00030 e6,57123.

5 free € 0,50 € 1. **Surface:** metalled. 01/01-31/12

Distance: 1km 50m 500m.

Remarks: Max. 72h.

Tourist information Assen:

VVV, Marktstraat 8-10.

Barger Compascuum 4A6

Nationale Veenpark, Berkenrode 4. **GPS**: n52,75504 e7,02546.

50 € 5 included. **Surface:** grassy. 01/01-31/12, 01/11-31/03 weekend, Mo-Fri by request

Distance: 100m.

Remarks: Max. 3x24h.

Tourist information Barger Compascuum:

Veenpark-Wereld van Veen, Berkenrode 4.Life and Work in peat area, 160 acres of nature, peat and villages. 01/04-31/10 10-17h, 01/07-31/08 10-18h. >5: € 12,75.

Borger 4A6

Nuuverstee, Rolderstraat 4. **GPS**: n52,92630 e6,77459.

5 € 15 Ch WC included. **Location:** Comfortable.

Surface: .

Distance: 1km on the spot on the spot.

Dwingeloo 3D6

Torentjeshoek, Leeuweriksveldweg 1. **GPS**: n52,81927 e6,36077.

6 € 12 € 1/100liter Ch € 1/night,10Amp WC included,on camp site. **Location:** Rural, luxurious, quiet. **Surface:** grassy/metalled. 01/01-31/12

Distance: 2km 2km 200m 200m 2km 2km 1km on the spot on the spot.

Tourist information Dwingeloo:

VVV, Brink 1.

Eelderwolde 3D5

Scandinavisch Dorp, Oude Badweg 1. **GPS**: n53,16984 e6,55391.

NL

5 free. **Location:** Rural, simple, quiet. **Surface:** asphalted/grassy.
01/01-31/12 Restaurant: Tue, 01/10-01/04 Mo-Tue.
Distance: 2km 5km 500m on the spot on the spot 2km 200m on the spot on the spot.

S Eext 4A6

Schaopvolte, Stationsstraat 60a. **GPS:** n53,00007 e6,72862.

6 €7 €1 Ch (6x)€1 WC €0,50 €4,50 €2/day.
Surface: grassy/gravel. 01/04-01/11
Distance: 2km.

S Elim 3D6

De Barswieke, Barsweg 9. **GPS:** n52,67144 e6,57821.

10 €6 Ch included €1,50 WC . **Surface:** grassy.
01/01-31/12
Distance: 1km 1km.

Emmen 4A6

Kerkhoflaan- van Schaikweg. **GPS:** n52,78091 e6,90330.

5 free. 01/04-31/10
Distance: 1km Albert Heijn 600m.
Remarks: Behind hotel Eden, ,ax. 72h, Zoo Emmen 900m.

Tourist information Emmen:
VVV, Hoofdstraat 22, www.vvvemmen.nl.
Noorder Dierenpark, Hoofdstraat 18.Zoo.
from 10h.

Hoogeveen 3D6

Terpweg 3. **GPS:** n52,72639 e6,50040.

3 free. **Surface:** metalled. 01/01-31/12
Distance: 2km 2,2km 100m 1km 1km.
Remarks: At sports park, max. 72h.

Tourist information Hoogeveen:
M Museum de 5000 Morgen, Hoofdstraat 9.Town history. Tue-Su 13-17h.
T €2.

S Matsloot 3D5

Camping Pool, Matsloot 1a. **GPS:** n53,19354 e6,44980.

10 €5,50 Ch WC included €5. **Surface:** grassy.
01/04-15/10
Distance: 5km 200m.
Remarks: On Leekster lake.

S Meppel 3D6

Jachthaven, Westeinde 32. **GPS:** n52,69615 e6,18096.

5 €3,50/pp Ch €3,dryer €3. **Surface:** grassy.
Distance: 500m on the spot on the spot on the spot 400m.

S Nieuwlande 3D6

Bonenstee, Brugstraat 87. **GPS:** n52,67889 e6,61194.

20 €6 Ch (6x)€1,50 WC included. **Location:** Rural.
Surface: grassy/metalled. 01/04-31/10
Distance: 2km 4km 4km 2km 2km 100m bike junction on the spot.
Remarks: Max. 72h.

NL

Oosterhesselen 4A6

Sauna Hesselerbrug, Verlengde Hoogeveensevaart 32. **GPS**: n52,73535 e6,72029.

10 use of sauna obligatory. **Surface:** metalled. 01/01-31/12
Distance: 4km on the spot on the spot on the spot 4km.

Roden 3D5

Restaurant de Pompstee, Brink 25. **GPS**: n53,13577 e6,43312.
2.

Rouveen 8D1

De Roustap, Dedemsvaartseweg 35, N377. **GPS**: n52,58620 e6,21180.

Ufelte 3D6

De Blauwe Haan, Weg achter de es 11. **GPS**: n52,80220 e6,27264.

6 € 12 Ch € 2,50/night,10Amp WC included.
Location: Rural, luxurious, quiet. **Surface:** grassy/metalled. 01/04-31/10
Distance: 5km 2km 3km 3km 2,5km 5km 2km on the spot on the spot.

Westerbork 3D6

Landgoed het Timmerholt, Gagelmaat 4. **GPS**: n52,86850 e6,61748.

4 € 10, 19/07-02/08 € 12,50 Ch included WC € 1,50/pppd € 1,50/pppd € 3,90,dryer € 2,75 h. **Location:** Rural, luxurious, quiet.
Surface: grassy/metalled. 01/01-31/12
Distance: 2km 4km on the spot on the spot on the spot 2km 2km on the spot on the spot.

Tourist information Westerbork:

Herinneringscentrum Kamp Westerbork, Oosthalen 8, Hooghalen. Mo-Fri 10-17h, Sa-Su 13-17h, 01/07-31/08 11-17h.

Wijster 3D6

Grondsels, Grondselweg 7. **GPS**: n52,80227 e6,48975.

6 € 5 Ch € 2 WC. **Surface:** grassy/metalled. 15/03-31/10
Distance: 3km on the spot 3km 5km.

Overijssel

Almelo 9A1

De Grenzen, Havenkade. **GPS**: n52,36000 e6,65694.

3 € 4,50 Ch WC included washing machine/dryer € 2,25.
Surface: metalled. 01/01-31/12
Distance: 300m on the spot 200m 200m 100m.
Remarks: Parking marina (in centre) north side, max. 72h, check in at harbourmaster.

Tourist information Almelo:

VVV, Rosa Luxemburgstraat 8, www.vvvalmelo.nl.
De Meelzolder/Bolletjewinkel, Grotestraat Zuid 182.Baker's shop and bakery museum. Tue-Fri 10-17.30h, Sa 10-17h.
Weekmarkt, Centrumplein. Thu 8-16h, Sa 8-17h.

Bathmen 8D1

De Uutvolg, Prinses Margrietlaan 14. **GPS**: n52,25066 e6,30004.

2 free. **Surface:** metalled. 01/01-31/12
Distance: 1km 2,5km.
Remarks: Parking gymnasium.

Belt Schutsloot 3D6

Café-Restaurant de Belt, Havezatheweg 4. **GPS**: n52,66774 e6,05189.

10 free for clients WC. **Surface:** asphalted. 01/01-31/12
Distance: 3km 1km 1km on the spot 3km.

NL

Remarks: North of Zwartsluis, at Belter- and Beulakerwijde.

Borne 9A1

Parking de Koem, De Koem. **GPS:** n52,29957 e6,75800.

1 € 5/24h. **Surface:** metalled. 01/01-31/12
Distance: on the spot 50m on the spot.
Remarks: Max. 72h.

Dalfsen 8D1

Stationsweg 4. **GPS:** n52,49882 e6,25977.
3 free. **Location:** Simple. **Surface:** grasstiles. 01/01-31/12
Distance: on the spot.

Dalfsen 8D1

Starnbosch, Sterrebosweg 4. **GPS:** n52,47522 e6,26346.
7 € 10 + € 0,85/pp Ch WC included against payment.
Location: Rural, comfortable. **Surface:** grassy/sand. 01/01-31/12
Distance: 5km on the spot.

De Lutte 9A1

Erve Velpen, Beuningerstraat 25. **GPS:** n52,33224 e7,01197.

9 € 6 + tourist tax € 0,90/pp € 1 Ch € 2 included. **Location:** Rural, comfortable, isolated, quiet. **Surface:** grassy.
01/01-31/12
Distance: 4km 300m bike junction on the spot.

Dedemsvaart 8D1

Camperplaats Dedemsvaart, Langewijk 112. **GPS:** n52,60435 e6,45108.

20 € 5 € 2,50 € 2,50. **Surface:** metalled.
01/01-31/12
Distance: 700m 300m 200m.
Remarks: Max. 48h.

Deventer 8D1

Zeil- en Motorbootvereniging Deventer, Rembrandtkade. **GPS:** n52,26660 e6,12828.

4 € 10 € 0,50 Ch WC € 0,50 included. **Surface:** metalled.
Distance: on the spot.
Remarks: Check in at harbourmaster, park right after turning into road (end of the road too small to turn).

Tourist information Deventer:
VVV/Historisch museum, Brink 56, www.vvvdeventer.nl.Hanseatic city with historical centre.

Diepenheim 8D2

't Holt, Hengevelderweg 1A. **GPS:** n52,19500 e6,59186.

3 € 5, free for clients Ch free. **Surface:** metalled.
01/01-31/12
Distance: 3km on the spot 3km.
Remarks: Golf court (pitch+putt).

Diepenheim 8D2

In de Kokkerieje, Grotestraat 94. **GPS:** n52,19923 e6,55452.

free with a meal.
Distance: on the spot 1km 500m.
Remarks: Parking behind restaurant.

Enschede 9A2

Diekmanterrein, Weggelhorstweg. **GPS:** n52,20543 e6,90096.

5 free. **Location:** Urban, simple, simple, isolated, quiet. **Surface:** asphalted.
01/01-31/12
Distance: 2km 1,4km on the spot.

Enschede 9A2

De Loeks, Moorvenweg 2a. **GPS:** n52,17757 e6,86599.

NL

15 € 7, 01/04-31/10 € 15 Ch WC included. **Location:** Rural, isolated, quiet. **Surface:** grassy/metalled.
01/01-31/12 sanitary 01/11-31/03.
Distance: 3km 1km on the spot on the spot.

Enter 8D1

Werfstraat. **GPS:** n52,29812 e6,58310.
3 free. **Location:** Simple. **Surface:** metalled/sand. 01/01-31/12
Distance: 600m 600m 700m on the spot on the spot.

S Geesteren 9A1

Zalencentrum Spalink, Koelenbeekweg 10. **GPS:** n52,44060 e6,69555.

15 guests free Ch WC. **Surface:** grassy/gravel.
01/01-31/12
Distance: 3,5km on the spot 3,5km on the spot on the spot.

S Giethoorn 3D6

Passantenhaven Zuidercluft, Vosjacht 1G. **GPS:** n52,72134 e6,07449.

30 € 10, 2 pers.incl., 1/11-1/4 € 5 € 0,50/100liter Ch € 1/2kWh WC € 0,50. **Surface:** grassy. 01/01-31/12
Distance: 1km on the spot on the spot.
Remarks: Water closed during wintertime, check in at harbourmaster.

S Giethoorn 3D6

Camperplaats Haamstede, Kanaaldijk 17. **GPS:** n52,72828 e6,07570.

35 € 11, 2 pers.incl € 0,50 Ch € 2 WC € 0,50. **Location:** Rural, comfortable, central, quiet. **Surface:** grassy. 01/04-31/10
Distance: 2km 1km 20m 1km 1km on the spot on the spot.

Tourist information Giethoorn:
VVV, Eendrachtsplein 1, www.kopvanoverijssel.nl.
Village in nature reserve De Weerribben, Dutch Venice, boat trips possible.

S Haaksbergen 9A2

Henk Pen Caravans en Kampeerauto's, Westsingel 2. **GPS:** n52,14917 e6,71167.

2 free . **Surface:** asphalted. 01/01-31/12
Distance: 1km on the spot on the spot 1km.
Remarks: Motorhome dealer.

S Hardenberg 8D1

De Kuserbrink, Parkweg. **GPS:** n52,57746 e6,62927.

4 € 10 € 0,50/100liter Ch (4x)€ 1/kWh. **Location:** Rural, comfortable, central, quiet. **Surface:** grasstiles. 01/01-31/12
Distance: centre 500m on the spot on the spot.
Remarks: Max. 72h.

S Hardenberg 8D1

Fam. Pullen, Allemansweg 1a, Collendoorn. **GPS:** n52,58845 e6,59146.

20 € 8,50 Ch included. **Location:** Rural, comfortable, isolated, quiet. **Surface:** grassy. 01/01-31/12
Distance: 3km 3km bike junction on the spot.
Remarks: Dog on leads.

S Hasselt 8D1

Jachthaven de Molenwaard, Van Nahuysweg 151. **GPS:** n52,59309 e6,08706.

NL

5 € 8, tourist tax excl Ch € 1,50 WC € 0,50.
Surface: metalled.
01/01-31/12
Distance: 500m on the spot on the spot 500m 500m 500m.
Remarks: Check in at harbourmaster.

S Heeten 8D1

De Baanbreker, Speelmansweg 8. **GPS**: n52,36026 e6,31190.

10 € 3,50 € 1 € 0,50 Ch € 0,50 € 1,50. **Surface:** metalled.
01/01-31/12
Distance: 2km 2km 2km.

S Hellendoorn 8D1

Camperplaats Hancate, Ommerweg 150/a. **GPS**: n52,43420 e6,44072.

10 € 8 Ch included. **Surface:** grassy. 01/01-31/12
Distance: Hellendoorn 5km 100m 200m.

S Hertme 9A1

Camperpark Rabo Scheele, Hertmerweg 37. **GPS**: n52,32663 e6,74698.

25 € 12, 2 pers.incl Ch WC included.
Surface: grassy/metalled. 01/01-31/12
Distance: Hertme 500m, Borne 2km 100m 500m 2km.

S Kampen 8C1

Burgemeester Berghuisplein 1. **GPS**: n52,55274 e5,91306.

25 free free Ch WC € 0,50. **Surface:** metalled.
01/01-31/12
Distance: historical centre 500m on the spot on the spot.
Remarks: Max. 72h, entrance code sanitary building at town hall.

Tourist information Kampen:

VVV, Oudestraat 151, www.vvvkampen.nl.Former Hanseatic town on the IJssel.

Losser 9A1

Brilmansdennen, Bookholtlaan. **GPS**: n52,26917 e7,01361.

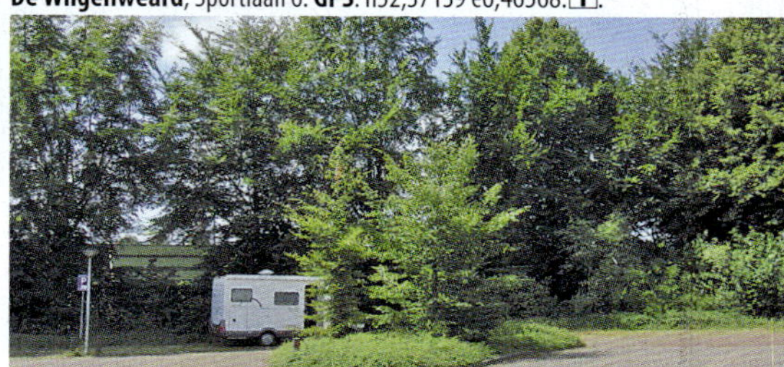

3 free. **Surface:** metalled. 01/01-31/12
Distance: 1km.
Remarks: At sports park, max. 72h.

Nieuwleusen 8D1

Koninging Julianalaan. **GPS**: n52,58144 e6,28380.
3 free. **Location:** Simple. **Surface:** metalled. 01/01-31/12
Distance: 300m.

S Nijverdal 8D1

De Wilgenweard, Sportlaan 6. **GPS**: n52,37139 e6,46568.

3 € 5 + € 0,50/pp tourist tax Ch WC included. **Surface:** grasstiles/metalled. 01/01-31/12, service 01/05-31/10
Distance: 500m on the spot on the spot on the spot 500m.

Tourist information Nijverdal:

M Amerikaans Motorfiets Museum, Zwolsestraat 63C, Raalte.Collection of motorcycles, Harley Davidson and curiosa. Fr-Sa 11-17, Su 13-17, 01/05-31/10: Mo-Sa 11-17, Su 13-17.

Oldemarkt 3C6

Vaartjes partycentrum, Kruisstraat 86-88. **GPS**: n52,82095 e5,96698.

NL

10 free for clients. **Surface:** asphalted. 01/01-31/12

Distance: 200m on the spot on the spot on the spot 200m.

Remarks: A32, exit 7, north of Weerribben.

S Ommen 8D1

Landgoed De Stekkenkamp, Beerzerweg 3. **GPS:** n52,50722 e6,49806.

8 € 7,50/night, € 0,80pp tourist tax included.

Distance: 1,2km.

Remarks: Max. 72h, at historical farmhouse.

S Ommen 8D1

De Lindenberg, Balkerweg 17a. **GPS:** n52,53527 e6,40993.

10 free for clients. **Surface:** metalled.

01/01-31/12 Mon, Tue.

Distance: on the spot 80m.

Tourist information Ommen:

VVV, Kruisstraat 6.

Oudheidkamer, Den Oordt 7.Historical costumes, jewellery, school interior.

Tue-Fri 10-17h, Sa 12.30-16h.

Tinnen Figuren Museum, Markt 1.Tinware. Apr-Oct Tu-Sa 11-17h, Su/holidays 13-17h.

Saasveld 9A1

Café-Restaurant Het Molenven, Bornsestraat 60. **GPS:** n52,32814 e6,78360.

Remarks: At road Borne-Weerselo.

S Schoonheten 8D1

Boerderij fam. Berenpas, Speelmansweg 8. **GPS:** n52,36071 e6,31197.

10 € 4 € 1 Ch € 0,50 € 1,50/24h. **Location:** Rural, isolated.

Surface: metalled. on the spot on the spot.

S Steenwijk 3D6

Jachthaven, Houthaven. **GPS:** n52,78627 e6,10006.

20 € 10 € 1. **Surface:** grassy. 01/01-31/12

Distance: 1km on the spot on the spot 300m.

Remarks: Check in at harbourmaster.

Tourist information Steenwijk:

Kermis- en Circusmuseum, Onnastraat 3. Tue-Fri 10-12h, 14-16.30h, 01/07-31/08 Mo-Fri 11-16.30h.

Tubbergen 9A1

De Vlaskoel, Sportlaan 3. **GPS:** n52,41043 e6,78316.

2 free. **Location:** Simple, simple. **Surface:** metalled.

01/01-31/12

Distance: 500m 600m 600m on the spot on the spot.

Remarks: At swimming pool.

S Vollenhove 3C6

De Haven. **GPS:** n52,68277 e5,94862.

6 € 10 Ch € 1 WC € 0,50. **Surface:** metalled.

01/01-31/12

Distance: 100m 100m 1km.

Remarks: Check in at harbourmaster.

S Vollenhove 3C6

Recreatiecentrum 't Akkertien, Op de Voorst, Noordwal 3. **GPS:** n52,67609 e5,93914.

20 € 8 Ch included.
01/01-31/12
Distance: 900m on the spot on the spot 400m peak season.

Wierden 8D1

De Huurne, Zandinksweg 22. **GPS**: n52,34899 e6,57191.

10 € 10 Ch included. 15/02-15/12 during wet period.
Distance: 2km 3km 2km 700m.
Remarks: Max. 3 nights, max 3,5t.

Wierden 8D1

Wijngaard Baan, Kloosterhoekweg 15, Rectum. **GPS**: n52,32172 e6,56709.

6 € 6 € 1 Ch € 2.
Remarks: Vineyard.

Wijhe 8D1

Passantenhaven, Loswal. **GPS**: n52,38611 e6,12750.

5 € 5 Ch WC € 0,50. **Surface:** metalled.
01/05-01/10
Distance: 500m on the spot 500m.
Remarks: Max. 72h. At the dike from Zwolle to Deventer, marina at IJssel, N337.

Tourist information Wijhe:
Village on the river IJssel, signposted cycle and hiking routes.
Weekmarkt, Marktplein. Tue-morning.

Zalk 8C1

Wegrestaurant Hotel Zalkerbroek, Rijksweg 3. **GPS**: n52,50619 e5,97004.

Zwartsluis 3D6

Voetbalvereniging DESZ, Clingellanden. **GPS**: n52,64437 e6,07810.

15 € 5 Ch. **Surface:** gravel. **Remarks:** Service at marina.

Tourist information Zwartsluis:
VVV, Stationsweg 32.
Stoomgemaal Mastenbroek, Kamperzeedijk 5, Genemuiden.Pumping-engine, 1856.

Zwolle 8D1

Jachthaven de Hanze, Holtenbroekerdijk. **GPS**: n52,53012 e6,07410.

10 € 8 Ch € 1/kWh WC . **Location:** Comfortable, isolated, quiet. **Surface:** grassy. 01/05-01/11
Distance: 2,5km 2km 1km bike junction 500m.
Remarks: Max. 72h.

Zwolle 8D1

Turfmarkt. **GPS**: n52,51333 e6,10369.

3 mo-sa 8-18h € 5/day, free overnight stay.
Surface: metalled.
Distance: 650m.

Tourist information Zwolle:
VVV, Grote Markt 20, www.vvvzwolle.nl.Former Hanseatic town on the IJssel.
Sassenpoort, Koestraat 46.Medieval gate building.
Wed-Fri 14-17h, Sa-Su 12-17h.
Ecodrome, Willemsvaart 19.Theme park, history of nature, geology.
01/04-31/10 10-17, 01/11-31/03 Wed, Sa, Su 10-17h.

Flevoland

Almere 8B1

Marina Muiderzand, IJmeerdijk 4. **GPS**: n52,34302 e5,13521.

NL

10 € 12,50 Ch WC included € 5,dryer € 3 .
Surface: asphalted. 01/05-30/09
Distance: 8km on the spot on the spot on the spot on the spot 1km.
Remarks: Check in at harbourmaster.

S Almere-Haven 8B1

Haven, Sluis. **GPS**: n52,33366 e5,22170.

2 € 1,05/m per night Ch WC € 0,50. **Surface:** metalled.
02/05-04/09
Distance: on the spot 1km on the spot on the spot 1km.
Remarks: Max 72h, check in at harbourmaster.

S Almere-Haven 8B1

WSV Almere, Sluiskade 11. **GPS**: n52,33257 e5,21715.

40 € 11, 2 pers.incl Ch (12x)€ 0,50/2kWh WC € 5 included.
Location: Urban, simple. **Surface:** grassy. 01/01-31/12
Distance: on the spot on the spot 200m on the spot.

Tourist information Almere-Haven:
Weekmarkt, De Brink. Fri 9-16h.

Lelystad 8C1

P Houtribhoek, Houtribslag. **GPS**: n52,54630 e5,45750.

4 free. **Surface:** metalled. 01/01-31/12
Distance: 2km on the spot on the spot on the spot 2km.
Remarks: Max. 48h.

Tourist information Lelystad:
Bataviawerf, Oostvaardersdijk 01-09.Ship-historical museum, reconstruction VOC-ships, historical dutch trading ships.
Mo-Su 10-17h.
Nieuw Land Erfgoedcentrum.Reclamation of land of the former Zuiderzee.
Oostvaardersplassen.6000 acres of lakes, mud fields, reed swamps, hiking route 5km and cycle route 35 km.
Batavia Stad, Bataviaplein 60.Outlet-shopping.
daily 10-18h.
free, parking € 2,50/4h.

Luttelgeest 3C6

Recreatie en Horeca bedrijf Craneburcht, Kuinderweg 52. **GPS**: n52,78304 e5,84331.

10 € 10. **Surface:** metalled. 01/03-30/11 winter: Mo-Tue.
Distance: 200m on the spot 7km.
Remarks: >17h <10h.

S Nagele 3C6

Afslag Nagele, Han Stijkelweg 11. **GPS**: n52,65278 e5,68417.

10 € 11 Ch € 2 WC included. **Location:** Comfortable, isolated, quiet. **Surface:** grassy/metalled. 01/01-31/12
Distance: 3km.
Remarks: Max. 72h.

S Urk 3C6

Haven, Burgemeester Schipperkade. **GPS**: n52,66040 e5,59975.

24 € 15 Ch (18x) WC included.
Surface: metalled.
01/01-31/12
Distance: 200m 100m 100m, bakery 300m.

Tourist information Urk:
VVV, Wijk 3 2, www.vvvflevoland.nl.
Old fishermen's village, former island.
Het Oude Raadhuis, Wijk 2 2.Regional museum.
01/04-31/10 Mo-Fr 10-17h, Sa 10-16h, 01/03-30/11 Mo-Sa 10-16h.
Weekmarkt, Urkerhard. Sa 8.30-13h.
Stegentocht/Ginkiestocht.Guided walk, reservation at Touristinfo Urk.
€ 4.

NL

Zeewolde 8C1

Camperpark De Wielewaal, Wielseweg 9. **GPS**: n52,25981 e5,43727.

50 € 11 Ch WC against payment. **Surface:** metalled.
01/01-31/12
Distance: 7km on the spot on the spot 7km.

Gelderland

Aalten 8D2

't Noorden, Lichtenvoordsestraatweg 44. **GPS**: n51,93326 e6,58221.

4 € 10 € 1/80liter Ch included WC free. **Location:** Rural.
Surface: gravel.
01/01-31/12
Distance: 700m on the spot.

Tourist information Aalten:

VVV, Landstraat 24, www.vvvaalten.nl.
Wijngoed De Hennepe, Romienendiek 3.Guided tour and tastery.
shop Tue-Fr 13.30h-sunset, Sa 10h, guided tour/tasting Jul/Aug We 15h.
Weekmarkt, Hoge Blik. Thu 8-12h.

Aerdt 8D2

De Aerdtse Wacht, Heuvelakkersestraat 18. **GPS**: n51,88634 e6,08861.

4 € 10 € 1/80liter Ch . **Location:** Rural. **Surface:** metalled.
01/01-31/12
Distance: on the spot on the spot on the spot on the spot.

Almen 8D2

De Nieuwe Aanleg, Scheggertdijk 10. **GPS**: n52,16639 e6,29750.

10 € 10 € 0,75/100liter WC € 0,75. **Surface:** metalled.
01/01-31/12
Distance: 3km on the spot on the spot on the spot on the spot.
Remarks: Behind restaurant, at the Twentekanaal.

Tourist information Almen:

Mosterdmakerij Boesveld, Dorpsstraat 39. Tue-Fri 13.30-17h, Sa 9-16h.

Apeldoorn 8C2

Malkander, Dubbelbeek 38. **GPS**: n52,18305 e5,96673.

4 free. **Location:** Simple, isolated. **Surface:** metalled.
01/01-31/12, 15-09h
Distance: 2km 150m 1km.

Appeltern 8C3

Herberg 't Mun, Molenstraat 10, Blauwe Sluis. **GPS**: n51,84048 e5,56360.

6 free (2x)On demand. **Location:** Rural, simple, isolated, quiet.
Surface: metalled. 02/01-23/12
Distance: 2km 2,3km Gouden Ham Trout farm on the spot 2km on the spot.
Remarks: Show-garden Appeltern 3km, max. 24h.

Beek 8D2

De Sprokkelaar, Sint Jansgildestraat 77. **GPS**: n51,90440 e6,19073.
3 .
Remarks: N335, Didam-Zeddam.

Beek 8D2

Hotel-Café-Restaurant 't Heuveltje, Sint Jansgildestraat 27. **GPS**: n51,91413 e6,19423.
Remarks: N335, Didam-Zeddam.

Bemmel 8C2

Dijkstraat/Wardstraat. **GPS**: n51,88972 e5,90972.

3 free. **Surface:** metalled. 01/01-31/12
Distance: 400m.
Remarks: Max. 72h.

Bemmel 8C2

Het wapen van Bemmel, Dorpsstraat 52. **GPS**: n51,89116 e5,89791.

NL

Borculo 8D2

Hambroekplas, Hambroekweg 10. **GPS**: n52,11573 e6,53758.

4 € 10 € 1/80liter Ch included. **Location:** Rural, comfortable, quiet. **Surface:** gravel. 01/03-31/10
Distance: 500m 150m 50m on the spot on the spot.

Borculo 8D2

Bruggink Campers, Kamerlingh Onnestraat 19. **GPS**: n52,12281 e6,52682.

6 free On demand. **Surface:** metalled. 01/01-31/12, 18-9h
Distance: 1,5km 2km 500m 1,5km 1,5km.

Braamt 8D2

De Blonde Hoeve, Braamweg 2. **GPS**: n51,92789 e6,26084.

4 € 10 € 1/80liter Ch included. **Location:** Rural, quiet. **Surface:** grassy. 01/01-31/12 bike junction on the spot.

Bredevoort 8D2

P2, recreatieplaats Slingeplas, Kruittorenstraat 10b. **GPS**: n51,94749 e6,62346.

8 € 10 € 1/80liter Ch (8x)included. **Location:** Rural, comfortable, quiet. **Surface:** metalled. 01/01-31/12
Distance: 200m 100m 400m 500m.
Remarks: Max. 72h.

Tourist information Bredevoort:
City with half-timbered houses.
Book market. 3rd Sa of the month 10-17.

Breedenbroek 8D2

Café-Restaurant Koenders, Terborgseweg 61. **GPS**: n51,87324 e6,47406.
01/01-31/12
Remarks: North of Dinxperlo.

Culemborg 8B2

Jachthaven de Helling, Helling. **GPS**: n51,96117 e5,22148.

6 € 10 € 0,50/100liter Ch € 3 WC washing machine/dryer € 4.
Surface: grassy/sand. 01/04-01/11
Distance: 500m on the spot on the spot on the spot 500m 1,5km.
Remarks: Check in at harbourmaster.

De Heurne 8D2

De Haar, Caspersstraat 14. **GPS**: n51,89802 e6,50035.

± 10 € 10 € 1/80liter Ch included. **Location:** Rural, quiet.
Surface: grassy. 01/01-31/12
Distance: 1km 8km.
Remarks: Filling station gas bottles 300m.

Doornenburg 8D2

Kerkstraat. **GPS**: n51,89416 e6,00129.

3 free. **Location:** Rural, quiet. **Surface:** metalled. 01/01-31/12
Distance: 400m 200m cafetaria 200m 400m on the spot.
Remarks: Max. 3 days, view on castle Doornenburg.

Eibergen 9A2

Café-Restaurant Grenszicht, Vredenseweg 2, Holterhoek. **GPS**: n52,05381 e6,68445.
5 .
Remarks: Dir Zwillbrock.

Elburg 8C1

Havenkade 1. **GPS**: n52,45081 e5,82972.

NL

5 € 7,50 + € 0,90/pp tourist tax Ch € 0,50/kWh WC included € 0,50. **Surface:** metalled. 01/01-31/12
Distance: 250m on the spot on the spot 300m.
Remarks: Max. 3 days.

S Emst 8C1
De Kievit, Zwarteweg 20. **GPS**: n52,30344 e5,99320.

15 € 10, 2 pers.incl, extra pers € 1,50 Ch € 2/night,6 Amp included. **Location:** Rural, simple, quiet. **Surface:** grassy/metalled.
01/01-31/12
Distance: 3km 1km 1km on the spot on the spot.

S Emst 8C1
Recreatiepark 't Smallert, Smallertsweg 8. **GPS**: n52,30910 e5,98126.

20 € 5 free. **Surface:** metalled. 01/01-31/12
Distance: 2km on the spot.

Epe 8C1
Pastoor Somstraat. **GPS**: n52,34965 e5,98331.

3 free. **Location:** Urban, simple. **Surface:** metalled.
01/01-31/12
Distance: on the spot 3km on the spot on the spot.

S Ermelo 8C1
Surfcamping Horst, Buitenbrinkweg 82. **GPS**: n52,31222 e5,56611.

40 € 7 € 3 Ch WC € 0,50 free. **Surface:** grassy.
01/03-31/10
Distance: 4km 200m 200m 500m 4km.

Garderen 8C2
Hotel Restaurant Overbosch, Hooiweg 23. **GPS**: n52,22483 e5,70702.

10 € 5 € 5. **Surface:** gravel.
Remarks: Use of a meal appreciated, not obliged.

Garderen 8C2
Gasterij Zondag, Apeldoornsestraat 163-165. **GPS**: n52,21443 e5,70696.

10 free. **Location:** Rural.
Surface: gravel.
01/01-31/12 Restaurant: Tue.
Distance: 2km 3,5km on the spot on the spot on the spot.
Remarks: Max. 1 night, restaurant visit appreciated.

Geldermalsen 8B2
Kostverlorenkade. **GPS**: n51,88421 e5,28985.

1 free. **Surface:** metalled.
Distance: 100m 3,6km on the spot on the spot on the spot.
Remarks: Parking at departure excursion boat.

Gendringen 8D2
Willem Alexanderplein. **GPS**: n51,86999 e6,37948.

NL

3 free. **Location:** Simple. **Surface:** asphalted. 01/01-31/12
Distance: 200m 100m 500m.
Remarks: Max. 72h.

S Gendringen 8D2

Diekshuus, Ulftseweg 4a. **GPS**: n51,87397 e6,38489.

4 € 10 included. **Location:** Rural, simple. **Surface:** gravel.
01/01-31/12
Distance: 600m 600m.
Remarks: At manege.

S Gorssel 8D2

De Vlinderhoeve, Bathmenseweg 7. **GPS**: n52,21825 e6,26255.

5 € 14 Ch WC € 5,dryer € 1,50 included. **Location:** Rural, luxurious, quiet. **Surface:** forest soil. 01/04-31/10
Distance: 8km on the spot on the spot on the spot on the spot on the spot.

S Groenlo 8D2

Camping Marveld, Elshofweg. **GPS**: n52,03698 e6,63187.

4 € 10 € 1/80liter Ch . **Surface:** metalled. 01/01-31/12

S Groesbeek 8C3

Hotel-Restaurant Rozenhof, Nijmeegsebaan 114, Heilig Landstichting. **GPS**: n51,81659 e5,88220.

2 € 5, free with a meal € 5/night .
05/01-27/12

Tourist information Groesbeek:

Afrikamuseum, Postweg 6, Berg en Dal.Africa museum.
Mo-Fri 10-17h, Sa-Su 11-17h 01/11-31/03 Mo.
Bevrijdingsmuseum 1944, Wylerbaan 4.Liberation museum.
10-17h, Su 12-17h.
Amusementspark Tivoli, Oude Kleefsebaan 116, Berg en Dal.Amusement park.
01/04-31/10 10-17.30h, 01/04-30/04, 01/09-31/10 Wed, Fri-Su. € 11.

Harderwijk 8C1

P Parkweg, Parkweg. **GPS**: n52,34088 e5,62977.

3 free. **Location:** Urban, simple. **Surface:** metalled.
01/01-31/12
Distance: 1,2km 3km 1,3km 800m.

S Hattem 8D1

Jachthaven Hattem, Geldersedijk 20. **GPS**: n52,47750 e6,06981.

10 € 10 + € 0,85 tourist tax Ch WC included.
Surface: grassy/metalled. 01/01-31/12
Distance: 200m on the spot on the spot 200m 200m 50m.
Remarks: Max. 72h, check in at harbourmaster.

Tourist information Hattem:

Bakkerijmuseum 'Het Warme Land', Kerkhofstraat 13. Tue-Sa 10-17.

S Heerde 8D1

Restaurant De Keet Van Heerde, Eperweg 55. **GPS**: n52,37084 e6,02079.

10 free, use of a meal desired (2x)included WC.
Surface: grassy/gravel.
Distance: 3km 1,5km 1,5km on the spot 2km 100m.
Remarks: A50, exit 28, Heerde south, then after ±200m.

Hengelo 8D2

Sportvelden/zwembad, Elderinkweg 1-9. **GPS**: n52,04457 e6,30377.

2 free. **Surface:** asphalted. 01/01-31/12
Distance: 500m 100m.
Remarks: Max. 24h.

Hengelo 8D2

Camperplaats Eulerhook, Vöckersweg 19. **GPS**: n52,24652 e6,75365.

15 € 8 Ch WC included. **Location:** Rural, luxurious, noisy. **Surface:** grassy/metalled. 01/01-31/12
Distance: 4km 2km 500m 4km 3km 1km on the spot on the spot.
Remarks: Nearby motorway.

Heteren 8C2

Boterhoeksestraat/Nijburgsestraat. **GPS**: n51,95450 e5,73072.

3 free. **Surface:** metalled.
Distance: 2km.
Remarks: Max. 72h. Metalled motorhome parking nearby former castle.

Huissen 8C2

Looveer. **GPS**: n51,93674 e5,94505.

3 free. **Surface:** metalled.
Distance: 200m Bathing 200m 200m 200m 200m.
Remarks: Max. 72h.

Kerkwijk 8B3

Hippisch Centrum Bommelerwaard, Jan Stuversdreef 1-3. **GPS**: n51,78876 e5,19929.

4 € 10 WC included. **Surface:** metalled. 01/01-31/12 Su.

Laren (GE) 8D2

Hotel-Café-Restaurant Stegeman, Dorpsstraat 1. **GPS**: n52,19222 e6,36614.
2.
Remarks: Between Lochem and Deventer.

Lathum 8D2

Jachthaven 't Eiland, De Muggenwaard 16. **GPS**: n51,98890 e6,04921.
6 € 8,50 Ch included (6x)€ 1,50/day WC € 0,50/4minutes € 3/day. **Location:** Rural, comfortable, quiet. **Surface:** metalled.
01/01-31/12
Distance: 5km on the spot on the spot on the spot 2km on the spot.
Remarks: At marina, max. 48h.

Lichtenvoorde 8D2

't Meekenesch, Kerkhoflaan 5. **GPS**: n51,99305 e6,56831.

3 free. **Surface:** metalled. 01/01-31/12
Distance: 1km 100m.
Remarks: Parking swimming pool, max. 72h.

Tourist information Lichtenvoorde:

Museum Erve Kots, Eimersweg 4, Lievelde.Open air museum.
10-17, inn 10-19.30/20.

Maasbommel 8C3

Saletmeubelen, Kapelstraat 30. **GPS**: n51,82459 e5,53193.

NL

5 € 10 Ch included. 01/01-31/12
Distance: 300m 1km 1km 1km 300m.

Meteren 8B2

Restaurant den Tol, Rijksstraatweg 80. **GPS**: n51,85759 e5,28009.

5 free.
Remarks: A15 Rotterdam-Nijmegen, exit Meteren.

Millingen a/d Rijn 8D2

't Crumpse Hoekje, Crumpsestraat 28. **GPS**: n51,85624 e6,03145.

6 € 6,50 + tourist tax € 0,75/pp € 1/90liter Ch (6x)€ 2/day WC free € 1. **Location:** Rural, luxurious, quiet. **Surface:** gravel.
01/01-31/12
Distance: 1,4km 2km 1,4km 1,4km.

Neede 8D2

Den Blanken, Diepneheimseweg 44. **GPS**: n52,18013 e6,58603.

4 € 10 € 1/80liter Ch included. **Location:** Quiet.
Surface: grassy. 01/01-31/12 on the spot on the spot.

Neede 8D2

Café restaurant De Olde Mölle, Diepenheimseweg 21. **GPS**: n52,14153 e6,61035.

8 € 10 € 1/80liter Ch . **Surface:** metalled. 01/01-31/12
Distance: on the spot.

Neede 8D2

Partycentrum 't Haantje, Borculoseweg 111. **GPS**: n52,13437 e6,59886.

5 € 5, free with a meal WC included. **Surface:** gravel.
Distance: 600m on the spot 500m on the spot.
Remarks: Rental of electric scooters and bicycles.

Nijkerk 8C2

Camperplaats Nijkerk, Watergoorweg 31. **GPS**: n52,22641 e5,47711.

2 free. **Location:** Urban, simple, noisy. **Surface:** metalled.
01/01-31/12
Distance: 500m 2km 2km 500m 500m 500m 200m
on the spot on the spot.

Nijmegen 8C2

Lindenberghaven, Waalkade. **GPS**: n51,84889 e5,86936.

6 € 20 (6x)€ 0,50/kWh. **Location:** Urban, simple, central, noisy. **Surface:** metalled.
01/05-01/09 during the Four Days Marche.
Distance: on the spot on the spot on the spot.
Remarks: Along the river Waal, max. 72h.

Nunspeet 8C1

Camperplaats De Zwaan, Hardenbrinkweg 46. **GPS**: n52,37901 e5,75363.

25 € 12 Ch 4Amp WC included. **Surface:** grasstiles.
01/01-31/12
Distance: 1,5km 1km 1,5km.
Remarks: No arrival on Sunday.

S Nunspeet 8C1

Routiers Nunspeet, Rijksweg A28. **GPS**: n52,36199 e5,77061.

free WC. **Surface:** asphalted.
Remarks: Use of sanitary free with a meal.

S Otterlo 8C2

De Wije Werelt, Arnhemseweg 100-102. **GPS**: n52,08592 e5,77319.

16 € 18 Ch included WC. **Location:** Rural, simple.
Surface: grassy. 01/04-01/11
Distance: 2km on the spot campsite supermarket on the spot on the spot.
Remarks: Max. 2 nights.

Tourist information Otterlo:
Kröller Möller Museum.Collection.
De Hoge Veluwe.Nature reserve, signposted cycle and hiking routes.
01/04-31/08 8h-sunset, 01/09-31/03 9h.

Putten 8C1

Brinkstraat. **GPS**: n52,26254 e5,60758.

2 free. **Surface:** metalled. 01/01-31/12
Distance: 200m 300m 300m 250m.
Remarks: Max. 48h.

Rekken 9A2

Grensovergang, Oldenkotseweg. **GPS**: n52,09783 e6,75568.

5 € 5. **Surface:** metalled. 01/01-31/12
Distance: on the spot on the spot on the spot.
Remarks: Max. 72h, cycle and hiking routes.

S Ressen 8C2

De Woerdt, Woerdsestraat 4. **GPS**: n51,88867 e5,87215.

15 € 7,50 + € 1/pp tourist tax (10x)included. **Location:** Rural.
Surface: grassy/metalled.
01/01-31/12
Distance: 2km 3,6km 2km.
Remarks: Regional products, pitches in the orchard.

S Ruurlo 8D2

Camping Tamaring, Wildpad 3. **GPS**: n52,10239 e6,44257.

2 € 10 € 1/80liter Ch included. **Location:** Simple, isolated.
Surface: forest soil. 01/01-31/12
Distance: 3km.
Remarks: Max. 8m.

Silvolde 8D2

Parking de Paasberg, Terborgseveld. **GPS**: n51,91633 e6,37194.

4 free. **Location:** Urban. **Surface:** metalled. 01/01-31/12
Distance: city centre 1km 300m.
Remarks: Parking at swimming pool, max. 72h.

S Sinderen 8D2

Biezenhof, Kapelweg 42a. **GPS**: n51,90370 e6,45285.

NL

4 € 10 € 1/80liter Ch included. **Location:** Rural, simple. **Surface:** gravel. 01/01-31/12

Sinderen 8D2

Natuurlijkbuiten, Toldijk 11. **GPS**: n51,91297 e6,42384.

2 € 12, 01/05-30/09 € 15 € 1/80liter WC included € 2.
Location: Rural. **Surface:** gravel. 01/01-31/12
Distance: 3km 3km on the spot 3km 3km on the spot on the spot.
Remarks: Bread-service.

Stokkum 8D2

Camping Brockhausen, Eltenseweg 20. **GPS**: n51,87778 e6,21167.

4 € 10 € 1/80liter Ch included € 4/day. **Location:** Rural.
Surface: gravel. 01/01-31/12
Distance: 800m 500m 2,5km 2km on the spot on the spot.
Remarks: Max. 2 nights, bread-service.

Terschuur 8C2

Camperplaats Groot Westerveld, Leemweg 2. **GPS**: n52,16819 e5,53239.

4 € 7,50 Ch € 2,50/night, 10Amp WC included.
Location: Rural, simple, quiet. **Surface:** grassy/metalled. 01/03-30/09
Distance: 1,5km 4km 2km 3km 2km 1km on the spot on the spot.

Tiel 8C2

Parking Waalkade, Waalkade. **GPS**: n51,88518 e5,44079.

4 € 5,10. **Surface:** asphalted. 01/01-31/12
Distance: 500m on the spot on the spot on the spot 500m on the spot.
Remarks: Max. 2 nights, cash payment.

Tolkamer 8D2

Europakade, Europakade. **GPS**: n51,85130 e6,09927.

10 € 7,40. **Surface:** metalled. 01/01-31/12
Distance: 150m 200m.
Remarks: Max. 48h.

Tolkamer 8D2

De Swaenebloem, Bijland 3. **GPS**: n51,86268 e6,07800.

free with a meal. 01/01-31/12
Distance: Lobith 3,5km 100m on the spot on the spot.
Remarks: Max. 2 nights, charging point for electric bicycles. Along rivier, follow recreation area Bijland.

Twello 8D2

Jachtlustplein 7. **GPS**: n52,23424 e6,09810.

2 free. **Surface:** metalled.
Distance: within walking distance within walking distance.
Remarks: Max. 24h.

Vaassen 8C1

Julianalaan. **GPS**: n52,29040 e5,96550.

NL

4 free. **Location:** Simple. **Surface:** asphalted.
Distance: on the spot 100m.
Remarks: Max. 48h.

S Varsseveld 8D2

Pallandtbad, Pallandtstraat 4. **GPS:** n51,94444 e6,46639.

4 free. **Surface:** metalled. 01/01-31/12
Distance: 200m 200m 200m 200m.
Remarks: Max. 24h.

S Voorst 8D2

De Adelaar, Rijksstraatweg 49. **GPS:** n52,17760 e6,14150.

10 € 12,50 Ch (10x)€ 2 WC € 0,50 € 4,dryer € 4 . **Location:** Rural. **Surface:** grassy/metalled. 01/01-31/12
Distance: 500m 7km on the spot on the spot 150m 1km.
Remarks: Use camp-site facilities incl.

S Voorst 8D2

Boerderij de Kolke, Klarenbeekseweg 30. **GPS:** n52,17355 e6,13318.

16 € 6 Chincluded € 1. **Surface:** grassy/metalled.
Remarks: Regional products.

S Voorthuizen 8C2

Ackersate, Harremaatweg 26. **GPS:** n52,18683 e5,62547.

5 € 14, 2 pers.incl Ch WC included € 1 € 5,50,on camp site . **Location:** Rural, simple. **Surface:** metalled. 01/04-27/10
Distance: 1,3km 4,2km on the spot on the spot on the spot on the spot.

S Westendorp 8D2

Recreatieoord Hippique, Doetinchemseweg 141. **GPS:** n51,94964 e6,42084.

4 € 10 € 1/80liter Ch included WC € 2 washing machine/dryer € 5 . **Surface:** grasstiles. 01/01-31/12
Distance: 500m 500m 3km 600m on the spot.
Remarks: Arrival 9><20h.

S Winterswijk 9A2

Landgoed Kreil, Heenkamppieperweg 1. **GPS:** n51,93573 e6,67907.

2 € 10 € 1/80liter Ch included against payment.
Location: Rural, isolated. **Surface:** metalled. 01/03-31/10
Distance: Breedevoort 4,5km Located on estate.

S Winterswijk 9A2

Camping Ten Hagen, Waliënsestraat 139A. **GPS:** n51,99131 e6,71898.

4 € 10 € 1/80liter Ch included. **Location:** Rural, simple, isolated, quiet. **Surface:** grassy. 01/01-31/12
Distance: city centre 3km lake.
Remarks: Max. 24h, Manufacturer of wooden clogs.

S Winterswijk 9A2

Vreehorst, Vreehorstweg 43. **GPS:** n51,95028 e6,69251.

NL

4 € 10 € 1/80liter Ch included. **Location:** Rural, comfortable.
Surface: gravel. 01/01-31/12
Distance: 3,6km.

Zelhem 8D2

Carpoolplaats, Stikkenweg/N330. **GPS**: n51,99893 e6,34541.

2 free. **Surface:** asphalted. 01/01-31/12
Distance: 1km.
Remarks: Max. 24h.

Zutphen 8D2

Houtwal. **GPS**: n52,13565 e6,19866.

8 € 10 € 1/80liter Ch included. **Surface:** metalled.
01/01-31/12
Distance: 1km.
Remarks: Nearby police station, beautiful view, max. 48h.

Zutphen 8D2

IJsselkade. **GPS**: n52,14037 e6,19119.

2 € 7,80. **Surface:** metalled. 01/01-31/12
Distance: 1km.
Remarks: Max. 48h, motorhome max. 6m.

Tourist information Zutphen:

VVV, Stationsplein 39, www.vvvzutphen.nl.Tour past art and antique stores.
Biologische boerenmarkt, Lange Hofstraat. Thu 8-13h.
Weekmarkt, Groenmarkt-Houtmarkt-Zaadmarkt. Thu 8-12h, Sa 8-17h.

Utrecht

Amersfoort 8C2

Aan de Eem, Klein Koppel. **GPS**: n52,16210 e5,37829.

3 € 1,10/meter WC included. **Location:** Urban, noisy. **Surface:** metalled. 01/01-31/12
Distance: 600m 500m 500m on the spot.
Remarks: At fire-station, max. 24h.

Baarn 8B2

De Zeven Linden, Zevenlindenweg 4. **GPS**: n52,19721 e5,24838.

3 € 10 € 2,50 Ch € 5 . **Location:** Simple. **Surface:** metalled.
01/04-01/11
Distance: 2km 1km 2km 300m on the spot on the spot.

Tourist information Baarn:

VVV, Brinkstraat 12.The most famous house the Palace Soestdijk, former home of princess Juliana.

Bunnik 8B2

Camping de Boomgaard, Parallelweg 9. **GPS**: n52,06065 e5,19943.

6 € 7,50 Ch WC € 2. **Surface:** metalled.
01/04/31/10
Distance: 3km 800m.
Remarks: Use camp-site facilities allowed, >17h <10h check in at reception next morning.

Tourist information Bunnik:

Natuurgebied De Brakel.Nature reserve, information VVV Zeist (52,08271 5,24013). guided tour 01/04-30/09 Wed 10.30h, Sa 13.30h, Su 10.30h, 13.30h.

Bunschoten-Spakenburg 8C1

Jachthaven Nieuwboer, Westdijk 36. **GPS**: n52,26070 e5,37238.

NL

8 € 15, 2 pers.incl Ch WC € 3,50 included. **Location:** Rural, simple, quiet. **Surface:** grassy. 01/01-31/12
Distance: 800m 6km 100m 700m 700m 700m on the spot on the spot.

S IJsselstein 8B2

Jachthaven Marnemoende, Noord IJsseldijk 107b. **GPS**: n52,04583 e5,01861.

3 € 15 Ch WC € 4,dryer € 2 included. **Surface:** gravel.
01/01-31/12
Distance: 2km on the spot on the spot on the spot 2km 2km.

Leersum 8C2

Touché, Rijksstraatweg 54. **GPS**: n52,00974 e5,43507.

5 free. **Location:** Urban, simple. **Surface:** gravel.
01/01-31/12 Mo.
Distance: 200m on the spot 200m on the spot on the spot.
Remarks: N225, milestone 27.

Leusden 8C2

De Mof, Arnhemseweg 95. **GPS**: n52,10654 e5,41445.

5 free, use of a meal desired. **Location:** Rural, simple. **Surface:** gravel.
01/01-31/12 Mon, Tue.
Distance: 4km 4km on the spot on the spot on the spot.
Remarks: First check in at restaurant.

Mijdrecht 8B2

Rondweg. **GPS**: n52,20804 e4,86879.

4 free. **Surface:** metalled. 01/01-31/12
Distance: 500m 500m 500m 500m.
Remarks: Max. 48h.

S Oudewater 8B2

Trekkerscamping Statenland, Statenland 1. **GPS**: n52,01778 e4,87306.

6 € 10 € 2 WC 5x€ 0,50.
Surface: grassy.
01/05-15/09
Distance: 3km on the spot 3km 3km 500m.
Remarks: Check in at swimming pool (<17h), max. 3 nights.

Tourist information Oudewater:
VVV, Leeuweringerstraat 10, www.vvvgroenehart.nl.Historical small town.
01/04-31/10 Tue-Sa 10-17h, Su 12-17h.

Overberg 8C2

De Holle Boom, Dwarsweg 63. **GPS**: n52,02914 e5,50061.

5 free with a meal. **Location:** Rural, simple, quiet.
Surface: gravel.
Distance: on the spot on the spot on the spot on the spot.

Rhenen 8C2

Restaurant 3 Zussen, Kerkewijk-zuid 115. **GPS**: n52,00682 e5,54006.

5 free. **Location:** Rural, simple. **Surface:** asphalted.
01/01-31/12
Distance: 1km Veenendaal on the spot 1km on the spot on the spot on the spot.

NL

Remarks: Free, use of a meal desired. N233, Veenendaal-Ochten, milestone 49.

Veenendaal 8C2

Sauna de Heuvelrug, Dijkstraat-West 189. **GPS**: n52,02496 e5,51990.

free. **Surface:** gravel. 01/01-31/12
Distance: 2km.
Remarks: Use of sauna obligatory. On ring-road N233 exit Overberg and campsite, entrance sauna after ±2km.

Vianen 8B2

Kanaalweg, P1. **GPS**: n51,99549 e5,09620.

4 free. **Surface:** metalled.
01/01-31/12
Distance: 500m.
Remarks: Max. 48h, during events: Hazelaarplein.

Tourist information Vianen:
VVV, Voorstraat 97, www.vvv-vianen.nl.Historical centre.
Voorstraat (zuid). Wed 10-16h.

South Holland

Alblasserdam 8A2

Haven 4. **GPS**: n51,86106 e4,65799.

10 € 10 € 0,50 Ch WC . **Surface:** asphalted. 01/01-31/12
Distance: 500m 1,3km on the spot 500m.
Remarks: At cultural centre 'Landvast', Kinderdijk ± 4,5km, sanitary in harbour building against payment.

Tourist information Alblasserdam:
VVV, Cortgene 2, www.alblasserdam.nl.
Molens, Nederwaard 1, Kinderdijk.World famous mill-area.
01/07-31/08 Sa, 1st Sa of the month.
Weekmarkt, Wilgenplein.
Mo-afternoon.

Bleiswijk 8A2

Jan van de Heidenstraat. **GPS**: n52,01415 e4,53411.

2 free. **Location:** Urban. **Surface:** metalled. 01/01-31/12
Distance: 300m 5km 500m Jumbo 400m.
Remarks: Next to fire station, dir Quimper.

Delft 8A2

Delftse Hout, Korftlaan 5. **GPS**: n52,01772 e4,37945.
20 € 20-28 Ch (20x) € 6,50 included.
Location: Urban, comfortable, central.
Surface: grasstiles. 01/04-01/11
Distance: 1,5km 1,2km 500m on the spot on the spot on the spot summer > centre on the spot on the spot.
Remarks: Check in at reception.

Tourist information Delft:
VVV, Hippolytusbuurt 4, www.delft.nl.Historical centre with canals and merchant houses. church 01/03-31/10 Mo-Sa 9-18h, 01/11-28/02 Mo-Sa 11-16h.

Dordrecht 8A3

Weeskinderendijk 5. **GPS**: n51,80861 e4,65611.

2 free. **Surface:** metalled. 01/01-31/12
Distance: 500m 500m 500m 100m.
Remarks: Max. 72h.

Giessenburg 8B2

Boerenterras De Groot, A.M.A. Langeraadweg 9. **GPS**: n51,85327 e4,92205.

8 € 10 WC included. **Location:** Rural, simple, isolated, quiet. **Surface:** concrete.
01/01-31/12
Distance: 1,5km 3km on the spot 1,5km 3,5km on the spot.

Giessenburg 8B2

Halfomhoeve, Bovenkerkseweg 76/78. **GPS**: n51,84632 e4,87610.

NL

3 € 10 included WC . **Location:** Rural, simple, isolated, quiet. **Surface:** concrete. 01/01-31/12
Distance: 2km 3km on the spot 1,5km 1,5km on the spot on the spot.

S Giessenburg 8B2

Landscheiding Giessenburg, Landscheiding 1. **GPS**: n51,47370 e4,92320.
10 € 10 Ch included. **Surface:** grassy/metalled. 01/01-31/12

S Gorinchem 8B3

WSV Merwede, Buiten de Waterpoort 8. **GPS**: n51,82697 e4,96477.

8 € 7,50 Ch € 2,50 € 0,70. **Surface:** gravel/metalled.
01/01-31/12
Distance: 500m on the spot on the spot 300m.
Remarks: Max. 72h, check in at harbourmaster.

Tourist information Gorinchem:
VVV, Grote Markt 17, www.gorinchem.nl.Historical centre with city walls.
Slot Loevestein, Loevestein 1, Poederoijen.Castle, 14th century.
01/05-30/09 Tue-Fri 11-17h Sa-Su-Mo-holidays 13-17h, 01/10-30/04 Sa-Su 13-17h.
Weekmarkt, Grote Markt.
Mo 8.30-12.30h.

S Gouda 8B2

Parking Klein Amerika, Fluwelensingel. **GPS**: n52,01185 e4,71576.

25 € 7,50 Ch WC included. **Surface:** metalled. 01/01-31/12
Distance: 1km.
Remarks: Max. 3 days.

Tourist information Gouda:
VVV, Markt 27, www.vvvgouda.nl.Historical centre with 300 monuments, famous for its Gouda-cheese.
Kaaswaag, Markt.History of the Gouda cheese.
01/04-30/09 13-17h, Thu 10-17h.
Montmartre, Markt.Antiques and flea market.
01/05-30/09 We 9-17h.
Weekmarkt, Markt. Thu 8.30-13h, Sa 8.30-17h.

S Goudriaan 8B2

Boerderij de Verwondering, De Hoogt 14. **GPS**: n51,89150 e4,90741.

3 € 7,50 € 2,50 Ch € 2,50. **Surface:** concrete.

S Hoogblokland 8B2

Landwinkel De Bikkerhoeve, Bazeldijk 66. **GPS**: n51,89716 e4,99563.

6 € 10 Ch WC included. **Location:** Rural, simple, isolated, quiet. **Surface:** concrete. 01/03-31/10
Distance: 2km 1,4km 2km 2km on the spot on the spot.

S Leerdam 8B2

De Galgenwaard, Lingedijk 8a, Oosterwijk. **GPS**: n51,87451 e5,07311.

3 € 8 WC. **Location:** Rural, simple, quiet. **Surface:** metalled.
01/04-01/10
Distance: Leerdam 2km on the spot on the spot 300m Along the river Linge.
Remarks: Opening hours 7-22h, passenger ferry across the Linge.

Leerdam 8B2

Groenzoom, Lingedijk. **GPS**: n51,88296 e5,08671.

2 free. **Location:** Rural, simple. **Surface:** asphalted.
01/01-31/12
Distance: 1km on the spot 1km on the spot.

Leerdam 8B2

Jachthaven Oude Horn, Sundsvall 1. **GPS**: n51,88984 e5,09532.

3 free. **Location:** Urban, simple. **Surface:** gravel.
01/01-31/12
Distance: 300m 300m 300m.
Remarks: Max. 72h.

Leerdam 8B2

Parking, Lingedijk. **GPS:** n51,88288 e5,08670.

2 free. **Location:** Urban, simple. **Surface:** metalled.
01/01-31/12
Distance: 2,5km 2,5km 2,5km on the spot.
Remarks: In front of Lingedijk 27, small pitches.

Leiden 8A2

P Haagweg, Haagweg 6. **GPS:** n52,15963 e4,47852.

15 € 10/24h. **Surface:** metalled.
Distance: 800m 800m 800m Free bus to centre.
Remarks: Video surveillance, free shuttle (till 2am).

Maasdam 8A3

De Fruitgaarde, Polderdijk 47. **GPS:** n51,79814 e4,53125.

20 € 14 Ch € 2 WC. **Location:** Rural, comfortable, quiet.
Surface: grassy/metalled. 01/04-01/11
Distance: 1km 2km 2km on the spot 2km on the spot on the spot.
Remarks: Teahouse, sheep breeding, small shop with farm products.

Nieuwland 8B2

De Grienduil, Geer 25. **GPS:** n51,90106 e5,02622.

4 € 10 Ch WC included. **Location:** Simple, quiet.
Surface: gravel. 01/01-31/12
Distance: on the spot 2km 4km on the spot on the spot.
Remarks: In winter limited services.

Numansdorp 8A3

Fort Buitensluis, Fortlaan 10. **GPS:** n51,71727 e4,43866.
5 € 15 Ch included. **Surface:** unpaved.
01/04-01/10
Distance: 1,5km 5km on the spot on the spot 1,5km on the spot on the spot.
Remarks: At Hollands Diep, golf court 3km.

Oud Beijerland 8A3

De Oude Tol, Randweg 31a. **GPS:** n51,82933 e4,39585.

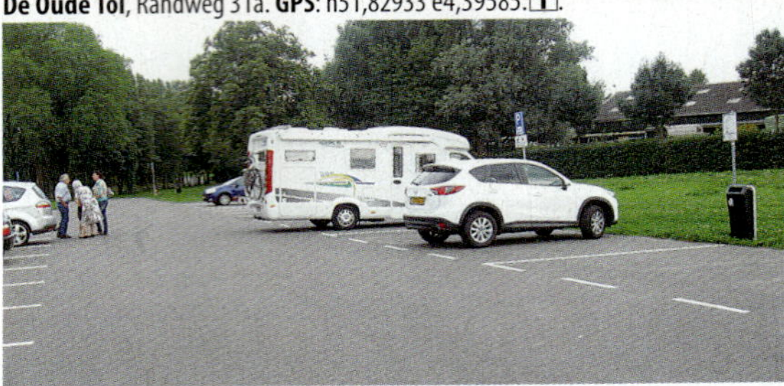

4 free. **Location:** Rural, simple, isolated, quiet. **Surface:** asphalted.
01/01-31/12
Distance: 2km on the spot 100m on the spot on the spot.
Remarks: Max. 24h, arrival >16h.

Ouddorp 7D3

Drive-in Camperpark Klepperduinen, Vrijheidsweg 1. **GPS:** n51,81724 e3,89850.

51 € 8-10/12h, € 14,50-18/24h + tourist tax € 0,81/pp, dog € 3,50/day
€ 3,50/100liter Ch (51x)€ 3/24h WC included
Location: Rural, luxurious, isolated, quiet. **Surface:** grassy/metalled.
01/01-31/12
Distance: 500m 1km on the spot on the spot on the spot.

Sassenheim 8A2

Jachthaven Jonkman, Jonkman 1. **GPS:** n52,22074 e4,54476.

NL

6 € 15 € 0,50 Ch WC € 0,50 € 5 included.
Location: Comfortable. **Surface:** grassy/gravel. 15/03-01/11
Distance: 2km 1km on the spot on the spot on the spot 2km on the spot.
Remarks: Check in at harbourmaster.

S Schiedam 8A2

Nieuwe Haven 97. **GPS**: n51,91135 e4,40050.

2 free . **Surface:** metalled. 01/01-31/12
Distance: 5 min 1,8km 50m.
Remarks: Max. 72h. A20 exit 11 centrum, end of the road to the right at roundabout to the left, in front of restaurant Le Pêcheur.

Schiedam 8A2

Doelenplein. **GPS**: n51,91972 e4,40111.

2 € 5,50. **Surface:** metalled. 01/01-31/12
Distance: 500m 1,5km on the spot on the spot 500m 500m 500m.
Remarks: Max. 72h.

Tourist information Schiedam:
VVV, Buitenhavenweg 9, www.ontdekschiedam.nu.
Het Jenever Museum, Lange Haven 74-76.Making distilled spirits.
Tue-Sa 12-17h, Su 13-17h.
Weekmarkt, Lange Kerkstraat. Fri 9-16h.

S Strijensas 8A3

Jachthaven Strijensas, Sassendijk 6. **GPS**: n51,71472 e4,58735.

6 € 7,50 € 0,50/100liter Ch € 2,50 WC € 1. **Surface:** asphalted.
01/01-31/12
Distance: 500m on the spot on the spot on the spot.
Remarks: Max. 72h.

Vlaardingen 8A2

Parking Deltabrug, Oosthavenkade 81. **GPS**: n51,90364 e4,34769.

4 free. **Surface:** metalled. 01/01-31/12
Distance: 1km on the spot 50m 100m 500m.
Remarks: Max. 48h. Nearby sluices, along railwayline.

S Zevenhoven 8B2

Camperplaats Zevenhoven, Noordeinde 36. **GPS**: n52,19475 e4,77305.

5 € 10 Ch included. **Location:** Rural, comfortable. **Surface:** grassy/metalled. 01/01-31/12
Distance: 1km 1km on the spot on the spot.

Zealand

Axel 7D4

P Watertoren, Kinderdijk 4. **GPS**: n51,25972 e3,91028.

2 free. **Location:** Urban, simple, noisy. **Surface:** metalled.
01/01-31/12
Distance: 500m on the spot on the spot 500m on the spot on the spot.
Remarks: Max. 24h.

Tourist information Axel:
Weekmarkt, Noordstraat. Sa 8-16h.

S Breskens 7D4

Roompot Recreatie, Nieuwe Sluisweg. **GPS**: n51,40193 e3,54420.

NL

10 € 14 Ch included WC . **Location:** Rural, comfortable, quiet. **Surface:** metalled. 01/01-31/12
Distance: 500m 400m 100m 100m on the spot on the spot.
Remarks: Servicepoint at camping Zeebad, ferry to Vlissingen 500m (pedestrian/bicycles).

Tourist information Breskens:
VVV, Kaai 1, www.vvvzvl.nl.Fishing-port and marina.
Vismijn, Kaai 1. Mo-Fri 8-17h, auction Mo-Thu 15h, Fri 8h.

Graauw 8A4

Zandbergsestraat. **GPS**: n51,32519 e4,10420.

7 free. **Location:** Rural, simple, quiet. **Surface:** gravel/sand.
01/01-31/12
Distance: 400m 400m on the spot.
Remarks: Max. 72h.

Groede 7D4

De Ploeg, Parking Zuid, Voorstraat 47. **GPS**: n51,38232 e3,51268.

40 € 5 17-10h, € 12,50/24h Ch (35x)€ 2,50/night WC .
Location: Comfortable, central, quiet. **Surface:** grasstiles/metalled.
01/04-01/10 22-7h.
Distance: 100m 3km 100m 100m 100m > Terneuzen on the spot on the spot.
Remarks: Sanitary/washing machine at campsite, caution € 10.

Groede 7D4

Strandcamping Groede, Zeeweg 1. **GPS**: n51,39632 e3,48719.

50 € 0,80/h. **Location:** Rural, simple, quiet. **Surface:** gravel.
01/01-31/12
Distance: Groede 3km sandy beach 200m 60m on the spot on the spot on the spot.

Tourist information Groede:
Museumstraatje van het Vlaemsche Erfgoed, Slijkstraat 1.
summer Mo-Sa 10-17h.

Hansweert 7D3

Westhavendijk. **GPS**: n51,44483 e4,00629.

5 free. **Location:** Rural, simple, isolated, quiet. **Surface:** asphalted.
01/01-31/12
Distance: 250m 4km on the spot on the spot on the spot.

Hengstdijk 7D4

De Zeeuwse Adelaar, Heernisse kerkpad 2. **GPS**: n51,32597 e4,01383.

4 € 7,50 Ch . **Surface:** metalled.
Remarks: Max. 72h.

Hulst 8A4

Parkeerterrein Havenfort, Havenfort. **GPS**: n51,27700 e4,04912.

15 € 0,80/h, mo-sa 9-17h, su 12-18h. **Surface:** metalled.
01/01-31/12
Distance: on the spot 25m 150m 150m 200m.
Remarks: Max. 72h, shops open on Sunday.

Tourist information Hulst:
VVV, Grote Markt 19, www.bezoekhulst.nl.Fortified city with city walls, shops open on Sunday.
Streekmuseum "De vier Ambachten", Steenstraat 28.
Easter-autumn holiday 14-17h, winter changing visiting hours.

S Kamperland 7D3

Camperpark Zeeland, Campensweg 5. **GPS**: n51,57495 e3,65236.
102 € 10-15,50, 2 pers.incl, extra pers € 7, € 1,05/pp tourist tax , dog € 3 € 0,20/min Ch (75x)€ 4/24h,16Amp WC € 0,25/min € 6,dryer € 3 included. **Location:** Rural, comfortable, luxurious, quiet.
Surface: grassy/metalled. 01/01-31/12
Distance: 3km 2km 100m 100m 100m 3km on the spot on the spot.

S Kamperland 7D3

Roompot Beach Resort, Mariapolderseweg 1. **GPS**: n51,58972 e3,71666.

20 € 6 10-17h, € 14 17-10h Ch WC € 4,50,dryer € 1,20 . **Surface:** asphalted. 01/01-31/12
Distance: 3km 500m 500m 500m 500m 1km.

Kloosterzande 7D4

Hulsterweg. **GPS**: n51,36555 e4,02121.

2 free. **Location:** Rural, simple, central, quiet. **Surface:** metalled.
01/01-31/12
Distance: 500m 80m 700m on the spot on the spot.

S Kruiningen 8A4

Den Inkel, Polderweg 12. **GPS**: n51,43485 e4,04448.
6 € 16-22 Ch WC included. 01/01-31/12

S Middelburg 7D3

Hof van Tange, Hof van Tange. **GPS**: n51,49688 e3,60474.

6 € 9,50, Su/holidays free WC € 0,50. **Location:** Simple, central, quiet.
Surface: gravel/sand.
01/01-31/12 1st week Aug.
Distance: on the spot 5km 500m 300m on the spot on the spot on the spot.
Remarks: Max. 48h, motorhomes <6m.

S Middelburg 7D3

Oude Veerseweg. **GPS**: n51,50071 e3,62842.

5 free € 1 (4x)€ 1. **Location:** Comfortable, central, quiet.
Surface: metalled. 01/01-31/12
Distance: 1km 100m 500m 1km on the spot.

Middelburg 7D3

Kanaalweg. **GPS**: n51,49432 e3,61519.

3 € 9,50. **Location:** Urban, simple, central, noisy. **Surface:** concrete.
01/01-31/12
Distance: 500m on the spot on the spot 500m on the spot.
Remarks: Max. 48h.

Oosterland 8A3

Wok van Zeeland, Rijksweg 6. **GPS**: n51,65767 e4,05336.

3 free. **Location:** Simple, isolated, noisy. **Surface:** asphalted.
01/01-31/12
Distance: 2km on the spot.
Remarks: Only overnight stays.

S Oostkapelle 7D3

De Pekelinge, Landmetersweg 1. **GPS**: n51,55725 e3,55139.

NL

20 € 18,50-27,50 Ch included.
Location: Simple, isolated, quiet.
Surface: gravel/sand.
27/03-01/11
Distance: nearby nearby on the spot on the spot.
Remarks: Max. 1 night >20h <10h.

Tourist information Oostkapelle:
VVV Domburg, Schuitvlotstraat 32, www.vvvwnb.nl.Family seaside resort.
01/03-30/11 Tue-Su 13-17h.
Kasteel Westhove.Medieval castle.
01/11-31/03 Tue-Su 12-17h, summer 10-18h.

Paal 8A4

Jachthaven, Zeedijk van de van Alsteinpolder. **GPS**: n51,35331 e4,10937.

1 free. **Location:** Rural. **Surface:** asphalted/metalled. 01/01-31/12
Distance: 100m on the spot on the spot on the spot on the spot on the spot.
Remarks: Max. 72h.

Sas van Gent 7D4

Kanaaleiland, Oostkade. **GPS**: n51,22527 e3,80246.

2 free. **Surface:** metalled.
Distance: 100m 100m 100m.
Remarks: Max. 24h.

Tourist information Sas van Gent:
Weekmarkt, Keizer Karelplein. Tue 9-16h.

Terneuzen 7D4

Oostsluis, Binnenvaartweg. **GPS**: n51,33555 e3,82117.

4 free. **Location:** Rural, simple, isolated, quiet. **Surface:** grassy/metalled.
01/01-31/12
Distance: 500m on the spot 500m 200m on the spot on the spot.
Remarks: Max. 24h.

Tourist information Terneuzen:
Portaal van Vlaanderen, Zeevaartweg 11.Interactive Visitors Centre at the Terneuzen Locks, guided tour and boat excursions. Apr-Jun We, July-Aug Tue-We-Thu, guided tour 13.30h.
Weekmarkt, Markt. Sa 9-16h.

Tholen 8A3

Jachthaven, Contre Escarpe 4. **GPS**: n51,53112 e4,22390.

4 € 7,50, service incl. € 10 Ch WC . **Surface:** metalled.
01/03-01/10
Distance: 100m 100m 100m.

Vogelwaarde 7D4

Populierenstraat. **GPS**: n51,32562 e3,97758.

2 free. **Location:** Urban, simple, quiet. **Surface:** metalled.
01/01-31/12
Distance: on the spot on the spot on the spot on the spot.

Westdorpe 7D4

De Baeckermat, Bernhardstraat. **GPS**: n51,22917 e3,82167.

2 free. **Location:** Rural, simple, quiet. **Surface:** metalled.
01/01-31/12
Distance: 500m on the spot 100m 500m on the spot on the spot on the spot.
Remarks: Max. 24h.

Wolphaartsdijk 7D3

Camping 't Veerse Meer, Veerweg. **GPS**: n51,54325 e3,81253.

7 € 15/22 Ch (5x) WC on camp site on camp site included.
Location: Rural, comfortable, isolated, quiet. **Surface:** .
01/01-31/12 15/11-15/12.
Distance: 1,5km 100m 100m 100m on the spot on the spot on the spot.

NL

Tourist information Wolphaartsdijk:
VVV, Singelstraat 13, Goes, www.vvvzuidbevelandentholen.nl.Historical centre.

Zaamslag 7D4

Kraaghof, Terneuzensestraat 89. **GPS**: n51,31284 e3,90869.
. 12-21h Mon, Tue.

Zierikzee 7D3

De Zandweg - Zierikzee

zandweg30@zeelandnet.nl - www.camperplaatszierikzee.nl
Paved and flat motorhome pitches
Free wifi access
Excellent location for city visit

De Zandweg, Zandweg 30. **GPS**: n51,65691 e3,91210.
12 € 12,50 Ch (12x),10Amp included. **Location:** Rural, comfortable, central, noisy. **Surface:** asphalted. 01/01-31/12
Distance: 800m on the spot on the spot 350m 1km 350m on the spot.

North Brabant

Asten 8C4

Camperpark Wetland - Asten

info@wetland.nl - www.wetland.nl
Beautiful view
Paved and flat motorhome pitches
Located in a quit location

Camperpark Wetland, Tureluurweg 7. **GPS**: n51,36687 e5,84214.
50 € 8,30, 2 pers.incl Ch (37x)€ 1,50 WC € 2,dryer € 2 included. **Location:** Rural. **Surface:** grassy/metalled. 01/01-31/12
Distance: 2km 4km 9km 5km 2km 1,5km on the spot on the spot.
Remarks: Located in nature reserve De Groote Peel.

Tourist information Asten:
Nationaal Beiaardmuseum, Ostaderstr 23.Collection bells and bell-founding.
Tue -Fri 9.30-17h, Sa-Mo 13-17h.

Bakel 8C3

De Beekakker. **GPS**: n51,50061 e5,74377.
2 free. **Location:** Simple. **Surface:** metalled. 01/01-31/12
Distance: 500m on the spot on the spot.
Remarks: At gymnasium.

Beers 8C3

Kerkeveld 10. **GPS**: n51,73302 e5,82955.

10 € 6 Ch WC included. **Surface:** metalled.
01/01-31/12

Bergen op Zoom 8A3

De Boulevard Noord. **GPS**: n51,48735 e4,27708.

5 free. **Surface:** metalled. 01/01-31/12
Distance: 1km 3,8km on the spot on the spot.
Remarks: Max. 72h. On the level of restaurant 'La Playa'.

Tourist information Bergen op Zoom:
VVV, Kortemeestraat 19, www.bergenopzoom.nl.Historical centre with 700 monuments.
De Markiezenhof, Steenbergsestraat 8.Medieval city palace.
Tue-Su 11-17h.

Best 8C3

Carpoolplaats De Wilg. **GPS**: n51,52106 e5,39423.
3 free. **Location:** Isolated. **Surface:** metalled. 01/01-31/12
Distance: 150 m.
Remarks: Max. 24h.

Boxtel 8B3

Dennenoord, Dennendreef 5. **GPS**: n51,59770 e5,28661.

4 € 12,50, 2 pers.incl Ch WC € 4 included.
Location: Rural, simple, isolated. **Surface:** metalled. 01/01-31/12
Distance: 4km 4km.
Remarks: Max. 3 nights.

Breda 8B3

Citycamp Liesbos, Liesdreef 40. **GPS**: n51,56504 e4,69618.
6 from € 17,95 Ch WC included € 0,15/1minutes against payment. **Surface:** grassy. 01/04-01/10
Distance: 3,5km 8km 6km on the spot 3,5km 700m.
Remarks: Tel:+31(0)76-5143514.

Tourist information Breda:
VVV, Willemstraat 17-19, www.vvvbreda.nl.Many historical bldg. And castles.

Akkermans leisure&golf, Heensemolenweg 23. **GPS**: n51,60654 e4,24547.

De Heen 8A3

NL

10 € 12,50 Ch (16x) WC included. **Location:** Rural, comfortable, isolated, quiet. **Surface:** asphalted/metalled. 01/01-31/12
Distance: on the spot on the spot on the spot.

Escharen 8C3

Bar Bistro De Brouwketel, Hoogeweg 9. **GPS:** n51,74152 e5,73376.

free. **Surface:** grassy. 01/01-31/12

S Etten-Leur 8A3

Jachthaven Turfhout, Westerpolderpad 6. **GPS:** n51,59556 e4,65444.

18 € 10 Ch WC included € 1 free. **Surface:** grassy. 01/01-31/12
Distance: 1,5km on the spot 500m.
Remarks: Max. 72h.

Tourist information Etten-Leur:
Mo-morning.

S Geertruidenberg 8B3

Statenlaan 2. **GPS:** n51,70333 e4,86333.

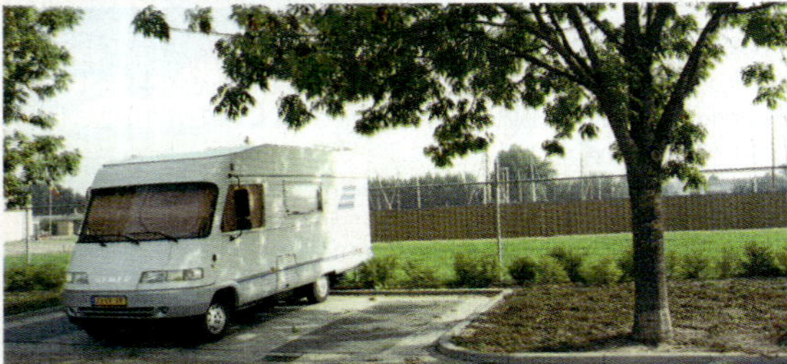

2 free. **Surface:** metalled. 15/03-31/10
Distance: 500m 500m.
Remarks: Max. 24h. Parking in front of marina, nearby centre.

S Geertruidenberg 8B3

WSV Geertruidenberg, Statenlaan 15. **GPS:** n51,70362 e4,86311.

8 € 10 Ch WC included. **Location:** Comfortable, quiet. **Surface:** gravel. 01/05-31/10
Distance: 500m 3km on the spot on the spot 500m.
Remarks: Max. 9m, max. 3 days, only cash payment.

Tourist information Geertruidenberg:
VVV, Markt 46, www.geertruidenbergdigitaal.nl.Fortified city with historical centre.

Gemert 8C3

Koksehoeve, Koksedijk 25. **GPS:** n51,57380 e5,65846.

10 free, use of a meal obligated. **Location:** Rural, simple, isolated, quiet. **Surface:** metalled. 01/01-31/12 Wed.
Distance: 2km.

Grave 8C3

Pater van den Elsenstraat. **GPS:** n51,76143 e5,73695.

free. **Location:** Simple, central, quiet. **Surface:** gravel. 01/01-31/12
Distance: 100m 100m 150m 150m.
Remarks: Max. 72h.

S Heeswijk-Dinther 8C3

De Leygraaf, Meerstraat 45A. **GPS:** n51,66445 e5,47511.
4 € 11,20 Ch included WC € 2,50. **Location:** Rural, comfortable. **Surface:** grassy. 01/01-31/12
Distance: 1,5km 6km on the spot on the spot on the spot.

Heusden 8B3

Wijkse poort, 't Ravellijn. **GPS:** n51,73472 e5,13417.

2 free. **Surface:** metalled.
01/01-31/12
Distance: 200m on the spot on the spot on the spot 200m.
Remarks: Max. ^3m. Parking within the fortifications, at the Wijksepoort, in village follow signs centre, not P-vesting.

Tourist information Heusden:
VVV, Pelsestraat 17, www.heusden.nl.Fortified city.
Vismarkt. Thu 13-18h.

Hoogerheide 8A4

METO parking, Huijbergseweg. **GPS**: n51,42318 e4,33452.
5 free. **Location:** Simple. **Surface:** metalled. 01/01-31/12
Distance: 800m 800m 800m.

Hoogerheide 8A4

Fa. Broos, Buitendreef 4. **GPS**: n51,42522 e4,34656.

5 free (3x)free. **Location:** Rural, simple, isolated.
Surface: metalled. 01/01-31/12
Distance: 3km 3km 3km 3km on the spot on the spot.
Remarks: Industrial area 'de Kooi'.

Hulten 8B3

Restaurant Stad Parijs, Rijksweg 6. **GPS**: n51,56996 e4,96446.

15 free € 0,75. **Location:** Rural, simple, quiet. **Surface:** asphalted.
01/01-31/12
Distance: on the spot.
Remarks: Free, use of a meal obligated. N282 provincial route Tilburg-Breda.

Linden 8C3

Jachthaven Brasker, Hardweg 15. **GPS**: n51,75182 e5,82740.

11 € 10, 2 pers.incl, tourist tax € 0,70/pp Ch € 1,50/day WC € 1 € 2/day. **Surface:** grassy. 15/04-15/10
Distance: on the spot on the spot on the spot on the spot.
Remarks: Check in at harbourmaster 9-12h, 15-18h, caution key sanitary building € 20.

Mierlo 8C4

Boscamping 't Wolfsven, Patrijslaan 4. **GPS**: n51,43888 e5,59000.
6 from € 16 WC € 4,50,dryer € 1,20 .
Surface: asphalted. 26/03-21/10
Distance: 3km 150m 150m 1km on the spot 1km.

Oijen 8C3

Speciaalbierbrouwerij Oijen, Oijensebovendijk. **GPS**: n51,81049 e5,53126.
3 € 10, free with a meal included. **Location:** Rural, simple, quiet.
Surface: grassy/gravel. 01/01-31/12
Distance: on the spot on the spot on the spot on the spot on the spot.

Oosteind 8B3

Camperplaats Oosteind, Ter Horst 19. **GPS**: n51,64705 e4,88326.

4 € 8 Ch included. **Location:** Rural, comfortable, isolated.
Surface: grassy. 01/01-31/12
Distance: 2km 1km 500m.

Oss 8C3

Van Venrooy Motorhomes, Galliërsweg 39. **GPS**: n51,75981 e5,55642.

2 free . **Surface:** metalled. 01/01-31/12

Raamsdonksveer 8B3

De Uilendonck, Lageweg 8, Raamsdonk. **GPS**: n51,68540 e4,91380.

3 free. **Location:** Rural, simple, isolated, quiet. **Surface:** metalled.
01/01-31/12
Distance: 1km on the spot.

Raamsdonksveer 8B3

Kloosterweg 1. **GPS**: n51,68908 e4,87582.

4 free. **Surface:** metalled.
Distance: 800m on the spot 800m.
Remarks: Parking at sports park.

NL

Reusel 8B4

Café-Restaurant de Klok, Turnhoutseweg 32. **GPS**: n51,35564 e5,14272.

3 free WC free. **Location:** Simple. **Surface:** metalled.
01/01-31/12
Distance: 2km.
Remarks: Free, use of a meal desired.

Reusel 8B4

De Wekker, Wilhelminalaan 97. **GPS**: n51,36187 e5,17339.

5 free, use of a meal obligated. **Location:** Simple, quiet. **Surface:** sand.
01/01-31/12 Wed.
Distance: on the spot.

Roosendaal 8A3

Mobildrôme, Argon 31-33. **GPS**: n51,56333 e4,46278.

8 free € 0,50 Ch € 0,50. **Surface:** metalled.
Distance: 2km 1,1km 2km.

Tourist information Roosendaal:
VVV, Markt 71, www.vvvroosendaal.nl.
Rosada, A17, afrit 19.Factory outlet.

Vessem 8B4

Eurocamping Vessem, Zwembadweg 1. **GPS**: n51,41197 e5,27490.
40 € 6/€ 9 € 1/80liter Ch € 0,60/kWh € 0,50 € 5/day.
Location: Rural. **Surface:** grassy. 01/01-31/12
Distance: 1,5km 7km 5km on the spot 1,5km on the spot 300m on the spot on the spot.

Wijk en Aalburg 8B3

Bakkerij Hardeman, Torenstraat 4. **GPS**: n51,75976 e5,13123.

3 € 5 Ch WC included. 01/01-31/12
Distance: on the spot on the spot.
Remarks: Parking bakery, next to church of Wijk.

Zundert 8A3

Museum de Scooter, Heischoorstraat 4. **GPS**: n51,49025 e4,64532.

10 € 10 Ch WC included. 01/01-31/12
Distance: 2,8km A1 7km on the spot on the spot.
Remarks: Reservation during flower parade: museum@lambretta-nl.net.

Limburg

Brunssum 8D5

Schutterspark P1, Heidestraat 20. **GPS**: n50,94582 e5,98385.

12 free free. **Surface:** metalled. 01/01-31/12
Distance: 1,5km 100m Schuttershuuske.
Remarks: Max. 72h, barefoot path.

Gennep 8C3

Martinusplein. **GPS**: n51,69985 e5,97206.

5 free. **Location:** Urban, simple, quiet. **Surface:** metalled.
01/01-31/12
Distance: 100m 4,6km 200m 150m bakery 100m, supermarket 250m on the spot on the spot.
Remarks: Max. 72h.

Gronsveld 8C5

A2 Campeercentrum, Veilingweg 13. **GPS**: n50,80632 e5,72201.
4 .
Distance: 500m.
Remarks: Max. 24h. Near A2, industrial area.

Grubbenvorst 8D4

Het Kompas, Meerlosebaan 7. **GPS**: n51,42861 e6,12889.

40 € 10 € 2 Ch included . **Location:** Rural.
Surface: grasstiles/grassy. 01/03-30/11
Distance: 2km 500m 2km 2km.

Heel 8C4

Koffieterras De Tump, Heelderweg 13. **GPS**: n51,17698 e5,88315.

5 € 7. **Surface:** grassy. 01/05-31/10 Mo.
Distance: 1km on the spot.
Remarks: Max. 48h.

Ittervoort 8C4

Camperplaats Ittervoort, Brigittastraat 31. **GPS**: n51,17565 e5,82228.

15 € 9,10, 2 pers.incl included € 2,50 € 1/day.
Location: Rural, simple. **Surface:** grassy. 01/01-31/12
Distance: Ittervoort 500m, Thorn 2km 2,6km Jan Linders 750m.
Remarks: Vineyard Thorn 600m.

Landgraaf 8D5

De Watertoren, Kerkveldweg 1. **GPS**: n50,91016 e6,07300.

6 € 10, peak season € 15 + € 0,90/pp tourist tax € 1/90liter Ch included . **Location:** Simple, isolated, quiet. **Surface:** grassy/gravel.
01/01-31/12

Lottum 8D3

Camperplek IndeVerte, Horsterdijk 97. **GPS**: n51,45130 e6,13144.

50 € 12 € 1/100liter Ch (50x) € 1 € 4 included.
Location: Comfortable, isolated, quiet. **Surface:** grassy. 01/01-31/12
Distance: 3km.

Maasbree 8D4

Restaurant Boszicht, Provincialeweg 2. **GPS**: n51,36395 e6,07980.

3 free, use of a meal obligated. **Location:** Simple, noisy. **Surface:** gravel.
Distance: 2km 2km on the spot.

Meijel 8C4

Nieuwehof, Vieruitersten 25. **GPS**: n51,35410 e5,89717.
29 € 10 + € 1/pp Ch WC included On demand.
Location: Rural, comfortable, quiet. **Surface:** grassy/sand. 01/01-31/12
Distance: 1,8km 14km on the spot on the spot.

NL

Milsbeek 8C3

Toeristisch knooppunt de Diepen, Zwarteweg 60. **GPS**: n51,73788 e5,95510.

free. **Surface:** sand.
Remarks: Next to Eethuis de Diepen.

S Neer 8D4

Jachthaven Hanssum, Hanssum 40b. **GPS**: n51,25778 e6,00361.

5 € 7,50 Ch WC. **Surface:** grassy/metalled.
Distance: 3km on the spot 200m.
Remarks: Max. 48h, service near marina. At the edge of village.

Neer 8D4

Café Restaurant Boothuis de Troost, Hanssum 47. **GPS**: n51,25964 e6,00380.

4 € 7,50, guests free. **Surface:** metalled.

S Nieuw Bergen 8D3

Camperplaats Bos&Heide, Op de Paal 4. **GPS**: n51,59008 e6,07269.

25 € 6,50 + € 0,93/pp tourist tax € 1/100liter Ch (15x)€ 1,50 WC.
Surface: grassy. 01/03-31/10
Distance: 1,5km 2km 1,5km 1,5km.
Remarks: Located in nature reserve Maasduinen.

Ottersum 8D3

Bier-Café Restaurant Old Inn, Siebengewaldseweg 13. **GPS**: n51,68935 e6,00728.

20 free. **Surface:** metalled. 01/01-31/12
Remarks: Near Maria Roepaan.

S Plasmolen 8C3

Eldorado, Witteweg 18. **GPS**: n51,73284 e5,91639.

13 € 15,50 2 pers.incl, dog € 2 € 1/100liter Ch (13x)€ 0,50/kWh WC included € 1 € 3 € 5/24h. **Location:** Rural, comfortable, quiet.
Surface: grassy.
01/01-31/12 Service: winter.
Distance: 200m 8km on the spot on the spot 200m 200m on the spot on the spot.
Remarks: Check in at Eldorado Boatshop Witteweg 9, max. 72 h.

S Sittard 8C5

De Nieuwe Hateboer, Sportcentrumlaan. **GPS**: n51,00794 e5,88150.

10 free Ch WC use sanitary facilities at swimming pool.
Surface: asphalted. 01/01-31/12
Distance: 2km 6,2km 2km 2km 100m on the spot.
Remarks: At swimming pool, max. 48h, check in with SMS (licence plate number) +31 6 27 82 55 82.

Thorn 8C4

Waterstraat. **GPS**: n51,15860 e5,84403.

3 € 2,50/9-18h. **Surface:** gravel. 01/01-31/12
Distance: 150m 150m.
Remarks: Max. 24h. Special part for motor homes.

Tourist information Thorn:

VVV, Wijngaard 14, www.lekker-genieten.nl.The white village, with historical

NL

centre and Gothic collegiate church.

S **Valkenburg** 8C5

Camperplaats Valkenburg aan de Geul, Heunsbergerweg 1. **GPS**: n50,86037 e5,83148.
30 € 15-21 € 1/100liter Ch (30x)€ 0,60/kWh,10Amp WC included € 0,70 € 4,75,dryer € 2,25 € 5/24h.
Location: Rural, comfortable, quiet. **Surface:** grassy/metalled.
01/01-31/12
Distance: 500m 1km 1km on the spot on the spot on the spot on the spot on the spot.
Remarks: Maastricht 15km.

P **Valkenburg** 8C5

Burgemeester Henssingel. **GPS**: n50,86361 e5,83725.

6 € 1,60/h 10-20h. **Surface:** metalled.
01/01-31/12
Distance: 300m.

Tourist information Valkenburg:
VVV, Th.Dorrenplein 5, www.vvvzuidlimburg.nl.
Popular holiday resort.
Gemeentegrot, Cauberg 4.Marl caves.
Steenkolenmijn, Daalhemerweg 31.
Visiting a gallery of a mine.
01/04-30/11 10-17, 01/11-07/01 + weekend, guided tour 12h, 13.30h, 15h, remaining 14h.

S **Venlo** 8D4

De Boswesels, Weselseweg 43. **GPS**: n51,39279 e6,20032.

16 € 10 Ch (16x) included. **Location:** Simple.
Surface: metalled. 01/04-01/11
Distance: 3km 2,8km 1,8km.

S **Venlo** 8D4

Jachthaven, Jachthavenweg 50. **GPS**: n51,39245 e6,14854.

20 € 12,50 10Amp WC included € 3,dryer € 2.
Surface: metalled. 01/04-30/10
Distance: Venlo centre 4km 3,5km 500m.
Remarks: Max 48h, check in at harbourmaster.

S **Weert** 8C4

Suffolkweg Zuid 30. **GPS**: n51,25435 e5,69283.

20 € 8, 2 pers incl., 1 pers + € 2 Ch included€ 2.
Remarks: Max. 72h.

S **Well** 8D3

Camperplaats De Wellsche Hut, Wezerweg 13. **GPS**: n51,58687 e6,12344.

18 € 10 Ch WC included. **Surface:** metalled.
01/01-31/12
Distance: 4km 6km on the spot.
Remarks: Dog on leads, at mountainbike trail, nature reserve Maasduinen. Near German border at road from Well to Weeze.

S **Well** 8D3

Jachthaven 't Leuken, De Kamp 7a. **GPS**: n51,56361 e6,06360.

30 € 10 Ch WC included. **Location:** Simple, quiet.
Surface: grassy. 01/04-01/11
Distance: Well 2km 11km on the spot on the spot on the spot.
Remarks: Acquatic sports area.

NL

BELGIUM

Antwerp
pages: 155-158
Antwerp
East Flanders
pages: 153-155
West Flanders
pages: 151-153
Limburg
pages: 159-163
Flemish Brabant
pages:158-159
Brussels
pages: 163-164
Brussels
Hainaut
pages: 165-167
Liège
pages: 164-165
Namur
pages: 167-168
Luxembourg
pages: 168-169

Capital: Brussels
Government: Constitutional monarchy
Official Language: Dutch/Flemish, French and German
Population: 11,082,000 (2013)
Area: 30,518 km^2.

General information
Dialling code: 0032
General emergency: 112
Currency: Euro

Regulations for overnight stays
Wild camping is forbidden.

Additional Public Holidays 2014
May 1 Labour Day
July 11 Feast Flemish Community
July 21 National Day
August 15 Assumption Day
September 27 Feast of the Walloon Region
November 1 All Saints' Day
November 11 Armistice Day 1918

Belgium

West Flanders

Aartrijke 7C4

Sint-Aarnoutstraat. **GPS**: n51,11341 e3,08983.
3 free. **Surface:** asphalted. 01/01-31/12
Distance: 400m 50m.

Beernem 7C4

Kanaaloever Beernem, Oude Vaartstraat. **GPS**: n51,13482 e3,33427.

6 € 10/24h Ch WC included,sanitary at harbour building.
Surface: metalled. 01/01-31/12
Distance: 1,9km.
Remarks: Max. 72h.

Bredene 7C4

Sportcentrum Ter Polder, Spuikomlaan 21. **GPS**: n51,23074 e2,96340.

4 free. **Surface:** metalled. 01/01-31/12
Remarks: Small pitches, max. 24h.

Brugge 7C4

Ringlaan/Bargeweg. **GPS**: n51,19654 e3,22664.

60 € 15, € 22,50 01/04-30/09 Ch included **Location:** Urban, simple, central.
Surface: metalled.
01/01-31/12
Distance: within walking distance on the spot.
Remarks: Monitored parking, <3,5T parking allowed on all parkings.

Tourist information Brugge:
Toerisme Brugge, 't Zand 34, www.brugge.be.City with medieval character, hiking itinerary available at Tourist office.
Boat excursion from Bruges to Damme with the `Lamme Goedzak', departure Noorweegse Kaai.
Brugs Brouwerij-Mouterijmuseum, ingang Verbrand Nieuwland 10.Brewery museum. 01/04-30/09 Wed-Su 14-18h. € 3.
Huisbrouwerij Brugse Bierkaai, Nieuwstraat 9.Brewery museum. restaurant/bar 11-23h, guided tour Tue-Fri 15.30h, 16.30h, Sa 15.30h, 16.30h, 19.30h, Su 12.30h, 15.30h. € 6.
Diamantmuseum, Katelijnestraat 43.Diamond museum. 10.30-17.30h. € 9.
Boudewijnpark, Alfons De Baeckerstraat 12, Sint-Michiels.Attractions park with dolphinarium, seal island etc., in winter large skating rink covered.

Diksmuide 7C4

Nesthof, Zijdelingstraat 2a. **GPS**: n51,07178 e2,86422.

5 € 5. **Location:** Rural, isolated, quiet. **Surface:** grassy.
01/01-31/12
Distance: 5km.
Remarks: Bread-service.

Gistel 7C4

Sportstraat. **GPS**: n51,16112 e2,96495.

2 free Ch free. **Surface:** metalled.
Distance: 3,3km.
Remarks: Parking behind swimming pool, key service at swimming pool, many walking and bicycle area.

Harelbeke 7C5

Kampeerautoterrein de Mol, Stasegemsesteenweg 21. **GPS**: n50,84396 e3,31057.

8 € 5 Ch included WC € 1,25.
Surface: metalled.
01/01-31/12
Distance: 4,5km.
Remarks: Parking next to midget golf, service during opening hours: 8-20h.

Tourist information Harelbeke:
Dienst Toerisme Harelbeke, Marktstraat 98, www.harelbeke.be. Historical city.

Knokke-Heist 7C4

Holiday, Natiënlaan 72. **GPS**: n51,33612 e3,28866.
10 € 17 01/10-31/03 € 19 01/04-30/09 Ch WC included.
Surface: metalled.

Kortemark 7C5

Sporthal Kortemark, Ichtegemstraat 2a. **GPS**: n51,03166 e3,04194.

BE

2 free € 2 Ch € 2. **Surface:** metalled. 01/01-31/12
Distance: 500m on the spot.
Remarks: Max. 48h.

S Kortrijk 7C5

Lagaeplein, Heule. **GPS:** n50,84473 e3,23569.

1 free .
Remarks: Next to swimming pool.

Tourist information Kortrijk:
Dienst Toerisme, Sint-Michielsplein 5, www.kortrijk.be.Historical little town with Beguine convent.
Nationaal Vlasmuseum, E. Sabbelaan 4.Flax-growing and working demonstration. 01/03-30/11 9.30-12.30h, 13.30-18h, Sa-Su 14-18h Mo, holiday.

Mesen 7C5

Kerkstraat. **GPS:** n50,76391 e2,89825.

3 free. **Surface:** metalled. 01/01-31/12
Distance: on the spot frituur 200m 100m.
Remarks: In opposite of church, max. 24h.

S Nieuwpoort 7C4

De Zwerver, Brugsesteenweg 29, N367. **GPS:** n51,12931 e2,76576.

28 € 6 € 0,50 Ch WC . **Surface:** grassy. 01/01-31/12
Distance: within walking distance 3,3km.

Tourist information Nieuwpoort:
Dienst Toerisme, Marktplein 7.

S Oudenburg 7C4

Carpool, Stationsstraat. **GPS:** n51,19527 e3,00632.

free 2x € 0,50 Ch.
Distance: 800m.
Remarks: P service max. 30 min.

Tourist information Oudenburg:
Wed-afternoon.

Poperinge 7B5

Oudstrijdersplein. **GPS:** n50,85300 e2,72300.

.
Distance: 50m.

Tourist information Poperinge:
Dienst Toerisme, Grote Markt 1, ww.poperinge.be.Centre of hop, beer and lace.

Roeselare 7C5

O.L. Vrouwenmarkt. **GPS:** n50,94786 e3,13450.

1 free. **Surface:** metalled.
18-9h, 01/01-31/12h
Distance: on the spot.
Remarks: Max. 1 night, temporary 2 pitches: Trakelweg n50,94504 o3,13245.

S Veurne 7B4

Kaaiplaats/Lindendreef. **GPS:** n51,07052 e2,66484.

6 free WC € 0,50 € 1,50,sanitary at harbour building. **Surface:** metalled.
Distance: on the spot 2km.

BE

Remarks: Motorhome max. 6,50m.

S Westende 7C4

Kompas kampeerautoterrein, Strandjuttersdreef. **GPS**: n51,15594 e2,76019.

35 20h € 9,50-14,50, 44h € 17,50-27,50 Ch included.
Surface: grasstiles/metalled. 01/01-31/12
Distance: Taverne, Frituur on the spot.

Westende 7C4

Sint Laureinsstrand, Koning Ridderdijk. **GPS**: n51,16655 e2,76447.

€ 5/day. **Surface:** asphalted. 01/01-31/12
Distance: Westende 1,4km on the spot on the spot Coast Tram.
Remarks: Beach parking.

S Wingene 7C4

Smart - ijs BVBA, Noordakkerstraat 1a.

6 € 6, guests Bistro free Ch free.
Location: Rural.
Distance: 2km bike junction.

Zonnebeke 7C5

Café De Dreve, Lange Dreef 16. **GPS**: n50,85410 e2,97924.

free. **Surface:** gravel. 01/01-31/12
Distance: Zonnebeke 2,7km 3,5km A19 snacks.
Remarks: Passendalemuseum-Zonnebeke.

East Flanders

S Aalst 8A5

Zwembadlaan 2. **GPS**: n50,93825 e4,05829.

2 free 100liter Ch included 1h.
Surface: metalled.
Distance: city centre ± 1km 3,8km.

Tourist information Aalst:

Dienst Toerisme, Grote Markt.
Oud-Hospitaal, Oude Vismarkt 13.
Tue-Fri 10-12h, 13-17h, Sa-Su 14-18h.
Thu-morning.

Aalter 7D4

Vaart-Zuid, Bellem. **GPS**: n51,09864 e3,49300.

25 free. **Surface:** asphalted.
Distance: Canal.

Aalter 7D4

Vaart-Noord, Bellem. **GPS**: n51,09875 e3,49468.
25 free.

Aalter 7D4

Bellemdorpweg. **GPS**: n51,09323 e3,48308.

2 free. **Surface:** metalled.
Remarks: At football ground.

Tourist information Aalter:

Kasteel Poeke, Kasteelstraat 26, Poeke. weekend, holidays, 01/04-31/10 Su 14-17h.
Wed-morning.

S Assenede 7D4

Kapelledreef. **GPS**: n51,23067 e3,74891.

BE

5 € 5/72h € 1/60 Ch WC free € 1/1. **Location:** Urban, comfortable, quiet. **Surface:** grassy.
01/01-31/12 Service: winter.
Distance: 500m 600m on the spot on the spot.
Remarks: Max. 72h, behind gymnasium, sanitary during opening hours.

Bazel 8A4

Sporthal De Dulpop. GPS: n51,14778 e4,30583.

free. **Surface:** asphalted.
Distance: 200m.
Remarks: Barn-museum 200m.

Tourist information Bazel:
Dienst Toerisme, Kasteel Wissekerke, Koningin Astridplein 17.Castle can be visited. Mo-Fri.

BE

Berlare 7D5

Donklaan, Berlare-Overmere. **GPS:** n51,04258 e3,98293.

4 free. **Surface:** grasstiles. 01/01-31/12
Distance: Donkmeer on the spot.

Eeklo 7D4

Jachthaven Eeklo, Nijverheidskaai. **GPS:** n51,17884 e3,54959.

12 € 7 € 0,50 Ch € 3,10Amp WC .
01/01-31/12
Distance: 1,5km 1,5km 800m.
Remarks: Use of showers only during the weekend, check in at harbourmaster.

Tourist information Eeklo:

Provinciaal Domein "Het Leen", Gentsesteenweg 80.Nature reserve.
9-12h, 13-17h Mo.
Heemkundig museum, Gentsesteenweg 80.Regional museum.
Tue-Fr 10-17h, 01/09-30/05 Su 14-17h, 01/06-31/08 Sa/Su 14-17h.

Gavere 7D5

Sportdreef. **GPS:** n50,92823 e3,65810.

12 free. **Surface:** asphalted. 01/01-31/12
Distance: on the spot.
Remarks: Behind sports complex.

Tourist information Gavere:
VVV 't Gaverland, Markt 1.

Gentbrugge 7D5

Sportcentrum Driebeek, Driebeekstraat 22. **GPS:** n51,03762 e3,76628.

5 free. **Surface:** asphalted. 01/01-31/12
Distance: 900m, Gent 4,5km 1,5km Tram Ghent-centre.
Remarks: Ghent Festival the week of July 21.

Tourist information Gentbrugge:
Ledebergplein, Ledeberg. Su 7.30-13h.
Schooldreef. Mo 7.30-13h.
Lazy River, Arsenaal.Jazz festival and village fair. Whitsuntide.

Geraardsbergen 7D5

Jeugherberg 't Schipken, Kampstraat 59, N460, dir Ninove. **GPS:** n50,79500 e3,90412.

4 free. **Surface:** grassy. 01/01-31/12
Distance: Geraardsbergen 3,7km on the spot.
Remarks: Max. 1 night.

Tourist information Geraardsbergen:
Dienst Toerisme, Markt, www.geraardsbergen.be.
Manneke Pis museum, StadhuisMarkt. free.
Provinciaal Domein "de Gavers", Onkelzelestraat 280.Recreation area; swimming, watersports, fishing, boat trips and tennis.Free entrance, payment per attraction.

Hamme 8A4

Camperplaats Hamme, Mirabrug, Hamveer. **GPS:** n51,10418 e4,14246.

3 free. **Surface:** metalled.
Distance: 400m.
Remarks: Max. 48h.

Lokeren 7D4

Veerstraat. **GPS**: n51,11013 e3,97163.
5 free. **Surface:** asphalted. 01/01-31/12
Remarks: Max. 48h, parking in front of church.

Lokeren 7D4

Verloren Bos, Aardeken. **GPS**: n51,10981 e3,99525.
2 free. **Location:** Rural. **Surface:** unpaved.
01/01-31/12
Distance: 500m.

Tourist information Lokeren:
Dienst Toerisme, Markt 2, www.lokeren.be.Town with medieval buildings.
Rommelmarkt, Stationsplein. Su 7-12h.
Molsbroek.Protected European Nature Reserve, 80ha marsh area with many birds, asphalted hiking trail.
Su 14-17h, 01/07-31/08 Wed-Su 14-17h.

S Maldegem 7D4

Zwembad St.Anna, Gidsenlaan. **GPS**: n51,21160 e3,44172.

free . **Surface:** asphalted/metalled.
Remarks: Check in at swimming pool.

Maldegem 7D4

't Brigandje, Urselweg 100. **GPS**: n51,16907 e3,47099.

customers free. **Surface:** gravel.

Tourist information Maldegem:
Dienst Toerisme, Oud Schepenhuis, Marktstraat 38, www.maldegem.be.
M Stoomcentrum, Station.Steam museum.
01/07-31/08 10-18h, 01/09-30/06 Su.

St.Laureins 7D4

Taverne 't Oud Gemeentehuis, Sint Margrietestraat 44, Sint-Margriete. **GPS**: n51,28065 e3,54677.

4 free. **Surface:** grassy.

Temse 8A4

De Zaat. **GPS**: n51,12466 e4,21007.
free. **Surface:** asphalted.
Distance: 400m.
Remarks: Temporary stopover, behind police station.

S Temse 8A4

Camperbedrijf Alpha Motorhomes, Kapelanielaan 13a, N16. **GPS**: n51,13699 e4,18017.

free Ch free. **Surface:** metalled.
Distance: city centre 3km.

Tourist information Temse:
Informatiekantoor 'De Watermolen', Wilfordkaai 23, www.temse.be.
M Gemeentemuseum, Kasteelstraat 16.Regional museum. Sa-Su 14-18h.
T free.
Warenmarkt, Grote Markt. Fri-morning.

S Zulte 7D5

Leihoekstraat, Machelen. **GPS**: n50,96095 e3,48305.

8 €8 €1 Ch included. **Surface:** metalled. 01/01-31/12
Distance: 150m 50m 150m.
Remarks: Max. 72h.

Antwerp

S Antwerpen 8A4

Vogelzang, Vogelzanglaan 7-9, Antwerp (Antwerpen). **GPS**: n51,18983 e4,40074.

BE

140 € 8, July-Aug € 10 € 0,50 Ch € 1. **Surface:** grassy/metalled.
01/01-31/12 24/10-31/11, 07/01-28/02.
Distance: city centre 3km 1km 3km 500m 1km 3km 200m.

Tourist information Antwerp (Antwerpen):
Toerisme Antwerpen, Grote Markt, 13, www.visitantwerpen.be.Large port city, worth seeing is the city centre.
Rubenshuis, Wapper 9-11.Living and work place of P. Rubens. Tue-Su 10-17h holiday.
Diamantmuseum, Koningin Astridplein.Diamond museum. 01/05-31/10 10-18h, 01/11-30/04 10-17h.
Nationaal Scheepvaartmuseum "Steen", Steenplein.Shipping history. Tue-Su 10-17h.
Provinciaal museum Sterckshof-zilvercentrum, Groendomein Rivierenhof Cornelissenlaan.Regional museum. Tue-Su 10-17h. free.
Antiekmarkt, Lijnwaadmarkt. Easter-Oct Sa 9-17h.
Brocantemarkt, St. Jansvliet. Su 9-17h.
Exotische markt, Theaterplein. Sa.
Vogelenmarkt, Theaterplein.Famous flea market. Su-morning.
Warenmarkt, Dageraadsplaats. Thu 8-13h.
Warenmarkt, St. Andriesplaats. Tue 8-13h.
Warenmarkt, St. Jansplein. Wed, Fri 8-13h.
Antwerpse Zoo.City-zoo. 10h-sunset.

S Arendonk 8B4

De Vloed. **GPS**: n51,32253 e5,08610.

free .
Distance: 400m on the spot 100m.
Remarks: Parking in front of swimming pool, water during openinghours swimming pool, max. 24h.

S Boom 8A4

Recreatiedomein De Schorre. **GPS**: n51,08836 e4,37706.

4 free € 1 Ch . **Surface:** metalled.
Distance: De Schorre.
Remarks: Follow 'De Schorre'.

Bornem 8A4

Kasteel d'Ursel, Koningin Astridlaan. **GPS**: n51,10294 e4,27261.
free. **Location:** Rural. **Surface:** unpaved. 01/01-31/12
Remarks: Next to castle.

S Brasschaat 8A4

P5b, Elshoutbaan 17. **GPS**: n51,28555 e4,50325.

15 free € 1/100liter Chfree € 0,50/kWh. **Surface:** metalled.
01/01-31/12
Distance: 1,7km 6km 500m 500m on the spot on the spot.
Remarks: Parking sports and recreation centre, max. 72h.

Tourist information Brasschaat:
Armand Reusensplein. Mo 8-13h.

Brecht 8A4

Mudeausstraat. **GPS**: n51,34814 e4,64123.

2 free.
Surface: metalled.
Distance: on the spot 1,2km 150m 150m.
Remarks: Max. 48h.

Tourist information Brecht:
Dienst Toerisme, Mudaeusstraat 2.Walking and bicycle area.
Kempisch museum, Museumstraat. 01/04-30/09 3rd Su 14-17h.

S Essen 8A3

Kerkeneind, N133. **GPS**: n51,47086 e4,46401.

2 free Chfree. **Location:** Urban, simple, central, quiet.
Surface: metalled. 01/01-31/12
Distance: on the spot 150m on the spot on the spot.
Remarks: Max. 24h.

S Grobbendonk 8B4

Vaartkom. **GPS**: n51,18954 e4,73638.

6 free € 1/5minutes free Ch€ 1 (6x)€ 1. **Surface:** asphalted.

BE

Distance: 200m 3,6km frituur 200m.

Tourist information Grobbendonk:

Infokantoor Toerisme, Kabienstraat 2a.

S Herentals 8B4

Herenhoutseweg. **GPS**: n51,16586 e4,82664.

Surface: asphalted.

Distance: 1,5km 2,8km bakery 200m.

Remarks: Parking multipurpose area, next to footballstadium VC Herentals.

Tourist information Herentals:

Dienst Toerisme, Grote Markt 41.Historical little town.

Augustijnenlaan. Su-morning.

Grote Markt. Fri-morning.

S Herselt 8B4

Taverne Herberg Mie Maan, Diestsebaan 28. **GPS**: n51,06025 e4,92897.

6 free . **Surface:** gravel.

01/01-31/12

Distance: 3km on the spot 3km.

Remarks: Restaurant visit appreciated, intersection hiking and biking trails.

Kalmthout 8A4

Kalmthoutse Heide, Heibloemlaan. **GPS**: n51,37688 e4,44911.

free. **Location:** Rural, simple, isolated, quiet. **Surface:** grasstiles.

01/01-31/12

Distance: city centre 2km 50m on the spot on the spot.

Remarks: Max. 24h, parking nature reserve.

S Kasterlee 8B4

Sint Hubertushoeve, Vinkendreef. **GPS**: n51,20560 e4,89714.

10 free Chfree. **Location:** Rural, simple, quiet. **Surface:** grassy.

01/01-31/12

Distance: Kasterlee 6km, Herentals 6km on the spot.

Remarks: Caution key service € 5.

Koningshooikt 8A4

Donderheide. **GPS**: n51,08439 e4,56541.

free. **Surface:** unpaved.

Distance: on the spot.

Remarks: In front of 'Het Fort'.

Koningshooikt 8A4

Motorhomes Konings, Sander de Vosstraat 141. **GPS**: n51,08774 e4,62816.

€ 2,50 € 2 € 2,50. **Surface:** asphalted.

Remarks: Apply during openinghours.

S Lier 8A4

Parking Mol Poort, Aarschotsesteenweg. **GPS**: n51,12525 e4,57332.

3 € 1 Ch. 01/01-31/12

Lier 8A4

Zaat, Leuvense Poort. **GPS**: n51,13013 e4,58232.

BE

2 free. **Surface:** metalled.
01/01-31/12

Tourist information Lier:
Dienst Toerisme, Grote Markt 57.City with old centre worth a visit.
City walls, prison tower and Zimmertoren. 10-12h, 14-17/18h.
Grote Markt/Eikelstraat. Sa 6-13h.
Duivenmarkt, Grote Markt. Su 6-12h, Easter, Whitsuntide, Christmas.
Kerststallentocht. Dec.

Mechelen 8A5

De Nekker, Nekkerspoel-Spuibeekstraat. **GPS:** n51,02667 e4,50367.

free. **Surface:** unpaved.
01/01-31/12
Distance: city centre 1,5km.
Remarks: Parking at sports and recreation centre 'de Nekker', max. 1 night.

Tourist information Mechelen:
Dienst Toerisme Stad Mechelen, Hallestraat 2-4, www.mechelen.be/.
Historical city, city of carillons.
Brouwerijmuseum Het Anker.Old brewery, 1369.
01/04-30/09 14-18h, guided tour 15h. € 3,30.
De Nekker.Sports and recreation area with ponds, sports grounds etc.
Dierenpark Planckendael.Zoo. 10-18h.
Technopolis.Interactively "discover" museum.
Caroluswandeling.City walk along historical bldg. And breweries, information Dienst Toerisme.

Putte 8A5

Ixenheuvel, Heuvel. **GPS:** n51,04678 e4,62564.

2 free Chfree. **Location:** Simple. **Surface:** asphalted.
01/01-31/12
Distance: 1,5km.
Remarks: Max. 48h.

Puurs 8A4

Eeuwfeeststraat/ Kerkhofstraat. **GPS:** n51,07476 e4,28337.

2 free Chfree. **Surface:** metalled. 01/01-31/12
Distance: 5,3km.
Remarks: Max. 48h, intersection hiking and biking trails.

St.Amands 8A4

Parking Noord, Emile Verhaerenstraat. **GPS:** n51,05906 e4,20206.

2 free Chfree. **Surface:** metalled. 01/01-31/12

St.Job-in-'t-Goor 8A4

Vaartlaan. **GPS:** n51,30151 e4,56888.
2 free. 01/01-31/12
Distance: on the spot 50m 50m.

Turnhout 8B4

Baalse Hei, Roodhuisstraat. **GPS:** n51,35385 e4,95591.
7 € 19 - € 25 Ch WC 15/01-15/12
Distance: 3km on the spot on the spot on the spot.

Tourist information Turnhout:
Toerisme Turnhout, Grote Markt 44, www.turnhout.be.City of the playing cards with historical centre.
Begijnhof.Beguine convent. Tue-Sa 14-17h, Su 11-17h Christmas.
Nationaal museum van de speelkaart, Druivenstraat 18. Tue-Sa 14-17h, Su 11-17h. € 3,50.

Willebroek 8A4

Dijlelaan. **GPS:** n51,06028 e4,34472.

3 free € 1 Ch. **Surface:** metalled. 01/01-31/12
Distance: 300m.
Remarks: Max. 2 nights. A12, exit 7, first road to the left.

Flemish Brabant

Diest 8B5

De Halve Maan, Omer Vanaudenhovelaan. **GPS:** n50,98607 e5,06373.

BE

4 € 15 Ch (4x)included. **Location:** Comfortable, quiet.
Surface: grassy/gravel.
Distance: 1,2km, beguine convent 350m 20m 200m 100m 100m. **Remarks:** Max. 72h, check in at pay desk recreation centre.

Tourist information Diest:
Socio-Culturele dienst, Stadhuis, Koning Albertstraat 16a, www.diest.be.Old fortress city.
Begijnhof.Beguine convent. Art studios open: sa/so afternoon and in july/aug each afternoon. Beguine convent daily, Angel convent Sa/Su 14.30-17h, church Easter-Oct Su 14-17h.
Stadsmuseum De Hofstadt, Grote Markt 1. 10-12h, 13.30-17h holiday.

Grimbergen 8A5

K.S.C. Grimbergen, Brusselsesteenweg. **GPS**: n50,92787 e4,36610.
10 free. **Location:** Simple. **Surface:** asphalted. 01/01-31/12
Distance: 1km.

Tourist information Grimbergen:
Gemeentelijke Dienst voor Toerisme, Prinsenstraat 22.Well-known for the Abbey beer, info at the beer museum.
Abdijkerk.Abbey-church. 10-12h, 13-17h.
Abdijbiermuseum, Abdijstraat 8.The start and evolution of the Abbey beer.
Jaarmarkt.Village festival with among other things fair, cattle market.
1st weekend Sep.

Merchtem 8A5

Brusselsesteenweg. **GPS**: n50,95553 e4,24011.

3 free free.
Surface: metalled.
Distance: Good bus connection for Brussels.
Remarks: Next to cemetery and sports fields, no camping activity.

Limburg

Bilzen 8C5

Parking Lanakerdij, Lanakerdij. **GPS**: n50,86985 e5,52215.

7 free € 2 Ch . **Surface:** asphalted. 01/01-31/12
Distance: 300m 300m 300m on the spot on the spot.
Remarks: Max. 24h.

Tourist information Bilzen:
Toerisme Bilzen, Markt, toerisme.bilzen.be.
Landcommanderij Alden Biesen, Rijkhoven. 10-18h, Nov-Easter 11-18h Mo.
Zuivelhoeve 't Wanthof.Dairy farm. Tue-Fri 10-22h, Sa-Su 9-23h.
Apostelhuis, Bosselaar 11, Rijkhoven.Nature centre. 10-18h, Nov-Easter 11-18h Wed.
Weekmarkt. Wed.

Bocholt 8C4

Heuvelzicht, Schipperstraat 1. **GPS**: n51,17722 e5,58500.

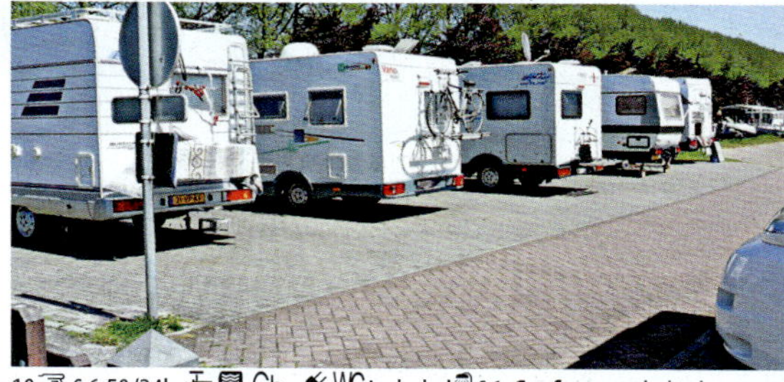

10 € 6,50/24h Ch WC included € 1. **Surface:** asphalted.
01/01-31/12
Distance: on the spot 50m 100m 50m 50m.
Remarks: Parking marina at Zuidwillemsvaart, max. 48h.

Tourist information Bocholt:
Toerisme Bocholt, Dorpsstraat 16, www.bocholt.be/toerisme/.
opening hours library.
Brouwerijmuseum, Dorpsstraat 53.Large brewery. Individual visits only in july and august. 01/07-31/08 13-17h. € 5.

Bolderberg 8B5

Domein Bovy, Galgeneinde. **GPS**: n50,98690 e5,27048.

3 free € 2 Ch € 2/1h. **Location:** Rural.
Surface: metalled.
Distance: 500m 150m bike junction on the spot.
Remarks: Estate with i.e. restaurant, bar, brasserie, marked hiking trails, herb garden, petting zoo, old tools.

Bree 8C4

N721, Opitter. **GPS**: n51,11844 e5,64358.

5 free. 01/01-31/12
Remarks: Parking next to church, in front of petrol station, max. 48h.

Tourist information Bree:
Toerisme Bree, Markt, www.bree.be.Small historical city.
De Gulden Tas, Ter Rivierenwal 18.Coffee-roasting factory.
Tue-Fri 9-12h, 13-17h. € 2,50.
Vrijthof. Fri.
Sint-Antoniuskapel, Opitter.

BE

S Diepenbeek 8C5

Demerstrand, Stationsstraat. **GPS**: n50,91392 e5,42209.

4 free € 2/100liter Ch € 2/8h. **Surface:** asphalted.
01/01-31/12
Distance: 500m 250m 1km.
Remarks: At gymnasium, video surveillance.

Dilsen-Stokkem 8C5

De Wissen, Burg. Prevotlaan. **GPS**: n51,02451 e5,74950.

4 free. **Surface:** metalled.
01/01-31/12
Distance: 500m on the spot on the spot Taverne Maascentrum 500m on the spot.
Remarks: Parking at tourist office De Wissen, starting point of cycle routes.

BE

S Genk 8C5

Parking Kattevennen, Planetariumweg 19. **GPS**: n50,95728 e5,53337.

8 free Ch .
Surface: asphalted.
Distance: 3km taverne on the spot.
Remarks: National park Hoge Kempen, mountainbike and hiking trails.

Tourist information Genk:
Uit in Genk, Europalaan 34, www.uitingenk.be.Tourist information.
Mo-Fri 9.30-16.30h, Sa 9-12h, 13-16h.
Zondagsmarkten.Flea market.
01/06-31/08 9-13h.

Hamont 8C4

Kerkplein. **GPS**: n51,25152 e5,54612.

5 free. **Surface:** metalled. 01/01-31/12
Distance: on the spot 50m 50m 50m.
Remarks: Behind church, max. 24h.

Hamont 8C4

Michielsplein, Achel. **GPS**: n51,25423 e5,47985.

free.
Remarks: Behind church of Achel, max. 24h, at bicycle trail Limburgse Kempen.

Hamont 8C4

Stadpark. GPS: n51,25085 e5,55200.

free.
Surface: unpaved.
Remarks: Large parking in the centre behind tennis-courts, max. 24h.

Tourist information Hamont:
VVV, Generaal Dempseylaan 1, www.hamontachel.com.Historical little town.
Mo-Fri 9-12h, 13-16h, Sa 9-12h.

S Hasselt 8C5

Sporthal Alverberg, Herkenrodesingel. **GPS**: n50,93998 e5,32072.

>5 free € 2 Ch. **Surface:** metalled. 01/01-31/12
Distance: city centre 3km Carrefour Free bus to centre.

Hasselt 8C5

Restaurant Myosotis, Overdemerstraat 20, Kuringen. **GPS**: n50,94663 e5,30877.

8 guests free.
Distance: on the spot bakery 50m.

Hechtel/Eksel 8C4

Kamertstraat. **GPS**: n51,13273 e5,35641.

free.
Surface: sand.
Distance: 1,5km.
Remarks: N73 dir Leopoldsburg, nature reserve 'In de Brand'.

Hechtel/Eksel 8C4

Parking CC De Schans, Rode Kruisplein 10, Hechtel. **GPS**: n51,12391 e5,36271.

free. **Surface:** asphalted.

Hechtel/Eksel 8C4

Pijnven, Bosmuseum, Kiefhoekstraat. **GPS**: n51,16133 e5,31091.

free. **Surface:** asphalted.
Remarks: Parking in the forest.

Tourist information Hechtel/Eksel:
Dienst Toerisme, Don Boscostraat 5, www.hechtel-eksel.be. Mo-Fri 9-12.

Helchteren 8C4

Parking de Dool, Sportstraat. **GPS**: n51,06087 e5,38650.

10 free. **Surface:** asphalted. 01/01-31/12
Distance: 1km 500m 500m.
Remarks: Next to castle.

Herk-de-Stad 8B5

Park Olmenhof, Pikkeleerstraat. **GPS**: n50,93361 e5,16654.

7 free € 1/100liter Ch € 0,60/kWh WC. **Location:** Rural, simple.
Surface: asphalted. 01/01-31/12
Distance: 400m 7km 50m 300m.
Remarks: Max. 48h.

Hoepertingen 8B5

De Verborgen Parel, Hoenshovenstraat 5. **GPS**: n50,80170 e5,28944.
6 € 7 Ch . **Surface:** metalled. 01/01-31/12
Distance: 1,5km 1,5km 1,5km.

Houthalen 8C5

De Dool, Sportstraat. **GPS**: n51,06143 e5,38670.

5 free. **Surface:** asphalted. 01/01-31/12
Distance: Helchteren 800m 5,6km 800m.

Houthalen 8C5

Parking Kelchterhoef, Kelchterhoefstraat. **GPS**: n51,03015 e5,44063.

6 free. **Surface:** metalled. 01/01-31/12
Distance: 6km on the spot.
Remarks: In front of abbey farm.

Kortessem 8C5

Kapittelstraat. **GPS**: n50,85724 e5,39126.

BE

5 free. **Surface:** asphalted. 01/01-31/12
Distance: 200m 200m bakery 200m.
Remarks: At gymnasium, max. 2 nights.

Tourist information Kortessem:
Toerisme Kortessem, Kerkplein, 12, www.kortessem.be.
't Rood Kasteel, Guigoven.Former medieval water castle.

S Leopoldsburg 8B4
Jachthaven, Antwerpsesteenweg 129. **GPS:** n51,12765 e5,25113.

20 € 8 € 2 WC € 1. **Surface:** asphalted. 01/01-31/12
Distance: 2km on the spot on the spot 2km.
Remarks: Check in at harbourmaster.

S Leopoldsburg 8B4
De Lido, Lidostraat 171. **GPS:** n51,13633 e5,24179.

35 € 7 Ch € 0,30/kWh included. **Location:** Rural, comfortable, isolated, quiet. **Surface:** gravel. 01/01-31/12
Distance: 3km fish pond on the spot.

Tourist information Leopoldsburg:
Dienst Toerisme, Hechtelsesteenweg 7. Mo-Fri 9-12.30h, 14-17h.

S Lommel 8C4
Taverne Haven de Meerpaal, Boskantstraat 60. **GPS:** n51,24266 e5,36891.

15 € 10 € 0,50 Ch (6x)€ 1 WC € 1. **Surface:** asphalted.
Distance: on the spot.
Remarks: At marina.

Maaseik 8C4
Sportlaan P4. **GPS:** n51,10108 e5,78964.

20 free. **Surface:** asphalted. 01/01-31/12
Distance: historical centre 200m.

Tourist information Maaseik:
Toerisme Maaseik, Markt 1, www.maaseik.be.
Catharinakerk. Tue-Su 10-17h, 01/07-31/08 Mo-Su, 01/10-31/03 Sa-Su. € 5.
Marktplein. Wed 9-12h.

Meeuwen-Gruitrode 8C4
CC Gruitrode, Royerplein 1, Gruitrode. **GPS:** n51,08939 e5,58949.

free. **Surface:** metalled. 01/01-31/12
Distance: 200m on the spot 200m 200m.
Remarks: Max. 24h.

Neeroeteren 8C4
Cultureel Centrum, Borglaan. **GPS:** n51,08745 e5,69977.

20 free. **Surface:** asphalted. 01/01-31/12
Distance: 800m on the spot on the spot on the spot.
Remarks: Parking cultural centre, max. 24h.

S Neerpelt 8C4
De Welvaart, Jaak Tassetstraat. **GPS:** n51,23290 e5,43206.

10 free Ch free. **Surface:** metalled. 01/01-31/12
Distance: 500m.
Remarks: Parking marina, on the canal, max. 48h, coin waste dump € 1.

BE

Tourist information Neerpelt:
Dienst Toerisme, Kerkstraat 7, www.neerpelt.be.

Peer 8C4
P1 Aan den Boogaard. **GPS**: n51,13193 e5,45741.
free.
Distance: 100m.
Remarks: Max. 24h.

Peer 8C4
P2 Noordervest. **GPS**: n51,13422 e5,45511.
free.
Distance: 150m.

Rekem 8C5
Kanaalstraat. **GPS**: n50,92297 e5,70622.

free. **Surface:** unpaved.
Distance: 1km on the spot on the spot 500m 1km 100m.
Remarks: Walking and bicycle area, max. 48h. N78, exit Rekem-centrum, follow Oud Rekem, along canal.

Tourist information Rekem:
Oud-Rekem with museum-church, city walls and castle, marked walking route 2km.

Schalkhoven 8C5
Nollekes Winning, Schalkhovenstraat 79. **GPS**: n50,84531 e5,44687.

4 WC. **Surface:** gravel. 01/01-31/12
Distance: 200m on the spot.

St.Truiden 8B5
Kampeerautoterrein Sint Truiden, Speelhoflaan. **GPS**: n50,82118 e5,18935.

20 free € 0,50/100liter Ch (20x)€ 0,50/kWh. **Surface:** metalled.
01/01-31/12
Distance: 750m 100m 500m 100m.
Remarks: Max. 72h.

Tourist information St.Truiden:
Toerisme Sint-Truiden, Stadhuis, Grote Markt, www.sint-truiden.be.Abbey-town.
Grote Markt, Groenmarkt, Trudoplein, Minderbroedersplein. Sa 7.30-13h.
Veemarkt, Speelhoflaan.Antiques and flea market. Sa 6-12h.

Tongerlo 8C4
De Kieper, Keyartstraat. **GPS**: n51,12397 e5,65449.

5 free. **Surface:** metalled.
Distance: 10 min walking.

Veldwezelt 8C5
Omstraat 20. **GPS**: n50,86195 e5,62696.

2 free. **Surface:** metalled. 01/01-31/12
Distance: 800m 200m 500m.
Remarks: Parking gymnasium.

Bruxelles

Bruxelles/Brussel 8A5
Bruparck, Wemmel/Heizel, Brussels (Bruxelles/Brussel). **GPS**: n50,89745 e4,33826.

Remarks: Overnight stays with a motorhome are not possible in Brussels, not even on the campsite (only tents). Ring road Brussels exit 8.

Bruxelles/Brussel 8A5
GPS: n50,84052 e4,36165.

Remarks: In front of royal palace.

Bruxelles/Brussel 8A5
Heizel/Heysel Metro, Brussels (Bruxelles/Brussel) . **GPS**: n50,89736 e4,33827.

Remarks: Nearby Bruparck.

Tourist information Brussels (Bruxelles/Brussel):
Bureau van Toerisme, Office de Tourisme, Grote Markt 1, Grand Place, www.brucity.be.Capital of Belgium, with a history of more than 1000 years. A lot of buildings worth seeing and historical places.
Koninklijke Serres van Laken, Les serres royales à Laeken.Park, garden, nature area.
Autoworld, Jubelpark, Parc du Cinquantenaire.Motorcar history from 1886 up to 1970s. 01/04-30/09 10-18h, 01/10-31/03 10-17h.
Koninklijk Legermuseum, Musée royal de l'armée et d'histoire militaire, Jubelpark, Parc du Cinquantenaire.Army museum. Tue-Su 9-12h, 13-16.45h.
Museum van de stad Brussel Broodhuis, Musée de la ville Bruxelles, Grote Markt 44, Grand Place.History of the city. Tue-Su 10-17h.
Basiliek van Koekelberg, basilique de Koekelberg.The fifth largest church of the world. 01/10-18/10 Su 14-17.45h, 01/07-31/08 Sa-Su. € 2,50.
Grote Markt, Grand place.Flowers and plant market. 8-18h.
Grote Zavel, Place du Grand Sablon.Antiques and book market. Sa 9-17h, Su 9-13h.
Vossenplein. 7-14h.
Kunstmarkt, marché d'art, Boterstraat, rue au Beurre.Painters and portraitists. 11-18h.
Atomium, Bruparck, Boulevard du Centenaire, Laeken.Built for the occasion of the 1958 Brussels World Fair, symbolising a crystallised iron molecule to the scale of its atoms enlarged 160 thousand million times. 10-18h, 01/04-31/08 9-20h. € 5.

BE

Bruparck, Boulevard du Centenaire 20, Laeken.Family park with among other things Mini-Europe, paradise pool and The Village with restaurants, cafés and shops. 01/01-31/12.

Mini-Europe, Bruparck, Boulevard du Centenaire, Laeken.Europe in miniature, 300 monuments. 30/03-03/01.

Oceade, Bruparck, Boulevard du Centenaire, Laeken.Subtropical leisure pool park. holidays, Sa-Su 10-22h.

Liège

S Blégny-Mine 8C5

Domaine de Blégny-Mine, Rue Lambert Marlet. **GPS**: n50,68617 e5,72367.

8 free Chfree (8x)€ 2/12h. **Location:** Rural, comfortable, isolated, quiet. **Surface:** gravel. 01/01-31/12

Distance: 4,6km on the spot on the spot on the spot.

Remarks: At former coalmine, UNESCO World Heritage, access € 9,30, 1 day all inclusive € 29,50, coins electricity at reception park.

Eupen 8D6

Langesthal 164. **GPS**: n50,62180 e6,09148.

free. **Surface:** asphalted.

Distance: Eupen 4km 150m Taverne.

Remarks: At weir, isolated.

Tourist information Eupen:

M Chocolademuseum, Rue de l'Industrie 16. Mo-Fri 9-17h.

M Stadtmuseum, Gospert 52.Regional museum.

Tue-Fri 10-12h, 13-16h, Sa 14-17h, Su 10-12h, 14-17h.

Rommelmarkt, Eupen/Keltenis. Su 7-16h.

Weekmarkt, Benedenstad. Wed 7-12.30h.

S Hamoir 8C6

Complexe Sportif, Quai du Batty. **GPS**: n50,42463 e5,53522.

10 free Chfree. **Surface:** grassy/gravel. 01/01-31/12

Remarks: Parking at the Ourthe River.

Tourist information Hamoir:

i Office du Tourisme, Place del Cour 1.

Huy 8B6

Avenue Godin Pamajon. **GPS**: n50,52379 e5,24310.

2 free. **Surface:** asphalted. 01/01-31/12

Distance: 500m on the spot 500m.

Remarks: Parking in front of restaurant Quick.

Huy 8B6

Quai de Namur. **GPS**: n50,51895 e5,23759.

2 free. **Surface:** asphalted. 01/01-31/12

Distance: 500m on the spot on the spot 500m.

Remarks: Under the citadel, along the Meuse River, in front of Hôtel du Fort to the right to the quay.

Tourist information Huy:

i Office du Tourisme, Quai de Namur,1, www.huy.be.Tourist town, citadel above the city.

M Fort en museum. Easter-Sep 10-17/18/19h.

S Malmedy 8D6

Avenue de la Gare, N62. **GPS**: n50,42282 e6,03080.

30 € 5/24h Ch (8x)included. **Surface:** gravel/metalled.

01/01-31/12

Distance: 300m 300m bakery 100m, supermarket 800m Waimes 5km.

Remarks: At cycle route (former railroad).

Tourist information Malmedy:

i Maison du Tourisme, Place Albert I, 29 A, www.malmedy.be.Small tourist town at the south edge of nature reserve Hautes Fagnes, high fens.

M Musée National du Papier et musée du carnaval, Maison Cavens, Place de Rome 11.Museum of paper and the carnival museum. 14-17h Mo.

Weekmarkt, Place St. Géréon. Fri 7-13h.

Hautes Fagnes.Nature reserve Hautes Fagnes.

Sourbrodt 8D6

Signal de Botrange, Rue de Botrange. **GPS**: n50,50148 e6,09312.

BE

20 free. **Surface:** gravel. 01/01-31/12
Distance: on the spot on the spot.

St.Vith 8D6

An den Weyern, Rodter Strasse 9a. **GPS**: n50,28091 e6,12240.
20 free Ch against payment. **Surface:** asphalted. 01/01-31/12
Distance: on the spot.
Remarks: At sports centre.

Waimes 8D6

La Faitafondue, Rue de Merkem 4. **GPS**: n50,39532 e6,07024.
€ 9, free with a meal WC . **Location:** Rural. **Surface:** gravel.
01/01-31/12
Distance: 4km 6km on the spot on the spot 200m.

Hainaut

Antoing 7D6

Parking, Place Bara. **GPS**: n50,56550 e3,44838.
free.
Remarks: Max. 24h.

Antoing 7D6

Parking, Place de Péronnes. **GPS**: n50,56413 e3,45093.
free.
Remarks: Max. 24h.

Antoing 7D6

Parking, Rue de la Pêcherie. **GPS**: n50,56728 e3,44505.
free.
Remarks: Max. 24h.

Tourist information Antoing:
Office de Tourisme, Place Bara 18, www.antoing.net.

Aubechies 7D6

Parking Archéosite, Rue de l'Abbaye 1Y. **GPS**: n50,57419 e3,67546.
.

Tourist information Aubechies:
Archéosite d'Aubechies.Archeological open air museum. Easter-01/11 Mo-Fri 9-17h, Sa, Su 14-18h.

Basècles 7D6

Place de Basécles. **GPS**: n50,52580 e3,64885.
free.

Beloeil 7D6

Château Beloeil. **GPS**: n50,55000 e3,73242.
free. 01/01-31/12
Remarks: Parking castle.

Beloeil 7D6

Camping à la Ferme, Rue de la Hunelle 16. **GPS**: n50,55165 e3,73275.
12 € 6 + € 2/pp Ch € 1WC . 15/03-15/11
Remarks: Minicamping.

Tourist information Beloeil:
Château de Beloeil, www.beloeil.be/. 01/06-30/09 10-19h, 01/04-31/05 Sa,Su 10-19h.

Bernissart 7D6

Musée de l'Iguanodon, Ruelle des Médecins. **GPS**: n50,47530 e3,64958.

free.
Remarks: Parking 100m of dinosaur museum.

Tourist information Bernissart:
Musée de l'Iguanodon, Ruelle des Médecins, www.bernissart.be/.Prehistoric museum. 10-17h.

Binche 8A6

Pastures, Rue des Pastures. **GPS**: n50,41557 e4,16810.
free. **Surface:** asphalted. 01/01-31/12
Remarks: Parking just outside centre.

Tourist information Binche:
Office du Tourisme, Parc communal, rue des Promenades, 2, www.binche.be.Medieval city with ramparts.
Musée International du Carnaval et du Masque, Rue Saint Moustier 10.Carnivals and maskmuseum. 9.30-12.30h, 13.30-18h Fri + Sa morning-, Ash Wednesday, 01/11, Christmas.

Blaton 7D6

Place de Feignies. **GPS**: n50,50179 e3,66135.

free.
Remarks: Nearby Romanesque church.

Bouffioulx 8A6

Rue du Général Jacques. **GPS**: n50,39075 e4,51456.
Ch against payment. **Surface:** metalled.
Remarks: Next to Centre d'Interprétation de la Poterie.

Boussu-lez-Walcourt 15C1

Route de la Plate Taille. **GPS**: n50,19265 e4,37958. .

20 free Chfree. **Surface:** asphalted. 01/01-31/12
Distance: on the spot on the spot on the spot on the spot.

Brugelette 7D6

Parc Paradisio, Domaine de Cambron. **GPS**: n50,58892 e3,88670.

BE

€ 4.

Tourist information Brugelette:

Parc Paradisio, Domaine de Cambron,.Park with bird paradise and monkey island. Easter-Oct 10-18h.

Charleroi — 8A6

Quai de la Gare Sud. **GPS**: n50,40537 e4,44199.

10 free.

Remarks: Parking behind station south.

Charleroi — 8A6

Rue des Rivages. **GPS**: n50,40867 e4,43673.

free. **Surface:** metalled.

Remarks: Parking for tram-cars, next to the ministery of finance.

Charleroi — 8A6

Rue Montignies. **GPS**: n50,40900 e4,44405.

2 free.

Remarks: Parking in front of swimming pool.

Tourist information Charleroi:

Office du Tourisme, 100 avenue Mascaux, Marcinelle, www.charleroi.be.Former centre of the coal mines.

Chimay — 15C1

Place Froissart. **GPS**: n50,04728 e4,31307.

Chimay — 15C1

Place Léopold. **GPS**: n50,04747 e4,31784.

Comines — 7C5

Parking Pont-Neuf. **GPS**: n50,76580 e3,00371.

free. **Surface:** metalled.

Distance: 100m.

Comines — 7C5

Place Sainte Anne. **GPS**: n50,76855 e2,99914.

free. **Surface:** metalled.

Distance: 150m.

Comines — 7C5

Musée de la Rubanerie, Rue du Fort 50. **GPS**: n50,76576 e3,00471.

4 free. **Surface:** metalled.

Distance: 100m.

Tourist information Comines:

Office du Tourisme, Chemin du Moulin Soete 21.

Courcelles — 8A6

Rue du château d'eau, Place Franklin Roosevelt. **GPS**: n50,46250 e4,37654.

Remarks: Behind Centre Culturel de la Posterie.

Dottignies — 7C5

Rue des Écoles 75b. **GPS**: n50,72821 e3,30011.

free. 01/01-31/12

Distance: 1,3km.

Remarks: Square behind fire-station.

Ecaussines — 8A6

Fort Château, La Grand-Place, Place des Comtes, Rue de Seneffe. **GPS**: n50,56868 e4,17676.

free Ch.

Ecaussines — 8A6

Château de la Folie, Rue de la Folie. **GPS**: n50,57443 e4,17851.

free.

Ecaussines — 8A6

Eglise Sainte Aldegonde, Rue Jacquemart Boulle 28, Ecaussines-Lalaing. **GPS**: n50,57085 e4,18107.

free.

Fleurus — 8A6

Parking Gare, Avenue de la Gare. **GPS**: n50,48215 e4,54433.

Fleurus — 8A6

Stade Communal, Rue de Fleurjoux. **GPS**: n50,47852 e4,55237.

free.

Harchies — 7D6

Place du Rivage. **GPS**: n50,47106 e3,69619.

Hornu — 7D6

Le Site du Grand Hornu, Rue Sainte-Louise 82. **GPS**: n50,43488 e3,83707.

free.

Tourist information Hornu:

Grand-Hornu.Old industrial mining complex, a remarkable reminder of the Industrial Revolution. Tue-Fri 10-18h. € 6.

Houdeng Aimeries — 8A6

Musée de la Mine de Bois-du-Luc, Rue Saint-Patrice. **GPS**: n50,47081 e4,14952.

free.

La Louvière — 8A6

Boulevard de Roi Baudouin. **GPS**: n50,46619 e4,19055.

free.

Remarks: P Station Sud.

Tourist information La Louvière:

Ascenseur Funiculaire de Strépy-Thieu, Strépy-Bracquegnies.Drawworks, 19th century. 01/02-27/11 9.30-18.30.

Site ouvrière et musée de la mine, Rue Saint-Patrice 5bis.Coal town and mining museum. Easter-Oct Tue-Fri 9-17h, Sa-Su 10-18h.

Weekmarkt, Rue du Marché. Sa 8-13h.

Lahamaide — 7D5

Place Plada. **GPS**: n50,69521 e3,72709.

Remarks: At Ecomuseum.

Le Roeulx — 8A6

Grand Place. **GPS**: n50,50019 e4,10919.

Le Roeulx — 8A6

Place de la Chapelle. **GPS**: n50,50294 e4,10874.

Le Roeulx — 8A6

Place de la Tannée. **GPS**: n50,50339 e4,10819.

Le Roeulx — 8A6

Place du Château. **GPS**: n50,50406 e4,11024.

Remarks: Parking at castle.

Lessines — 7D5

Rue des 4 fils Aymon. **GPS**: n50,71280 e3,83403.

free.

Leuze-en-Hainaut — 7D6

Rue du Pont de la Cure. **GPS**: n50,59924 e3,61347.

free.

Marchienne-au-Pont — 8A6

Musée d'Histoire et d'Archéologie Industrielle, 134 rue de la Providence. **GPS**: n50,41301 e4,40450.

free.

Remarks: In front of museum.

Mons/Bergen 7D6

Maison Van Gogh, Rue de Pavillon 3, Cuesmes, Mons (Mons/Bergen). **GPS**: n50,44174 e3,92630.
free.
Remarks: In case of city-visit use parking nearby station or bypass.

Tourist information Mons (Mons/Bergen):
Maison du Tourisme, Grand-Place, 22, www.mons.be.Old university city with many art treasures.
Chapelle Saint Calixte, Square du Château.Museum of the Count's Castle with archeological discoveries, medieval iconography etc.
12-18h Mo.
Maison Van Gogh, Rue du Pavillon 3, Cuesmes.Former place of residence of painter Van Gogh 1879/80, exhibition of reproductions.
10-18h Mo.
Musée des Arts Décoratifs François Duesberg, Square Franklin Roosevelt 12.Decorative arts museum. Tue-Su 13.30-18h.
Musée des Beau-Arts.Museum of Fine Arts.
Château Havré, Havré.Castle, 12-13th century.

Morlanwelz-Mariemont 8A6

Musée Alex Louis Martin, Place de Carnières, 52, Carnières. **GPS**: n50,44402 e4,25416.
10 free.

Mouscron 7C5

Musée du Folklore, Rue des Brasseurs, 3. **GPS**: n50,74217 e3,21795.
free.
Remarks: Possibility make a reservation tel 02.56.33.23.36.

Nimy 7D6

Musée de la Pipe et du Vieux Nimy, Rue Mouzin. **GPS**: n50,47499 e3,95853.
free. **Surface:** metalled.
Remarks: Museum closed: Nov-Mar.

Quaregnon 7D6

La Grand Place. **GPS**: n50,44369 e3,86428.
2 .

Quevaucamps 7D6

Musée de la Bonneterie, Rue Paul Pastur. **GPS**: n50,52671 e3,68776.

free. 01/01-31/12
Remarks: Parking in front of museum, via N527.

Roisin 7D6

Musée Verhaeren, Rue Emile Verhaeren, 23, Honnelles. **GPS**: n50,34285 e3,71044.
free.
Remarks: Parking nearby museum.

Ronquières 8A6

Grande tour et promenade en Bateau Mouche, Route de Baccara. **GPS**: n50,59121 e4,22115.
free.

Tourist information Ronquières:
Site de Ronquières.Inclined plane of Ronquières. follow the barge in its daily life, boat-trip. 01/04-31/10 10-19h.

Sivry 15C1

Observatoire de Sivry, Route de Mons 52. **GPS**: n50,17897 e4,22646.
2 .
Remarks: Centre for nature studies.

Soignies 8A6

Collégiale et vieux cimentière, La Grand Place, la Place Vert, la Place Van Zeeland. **GPS**: n50,57832 e4,06869.
free. **Surface:** gravel/sand.
Distance: on the spot.
Remarks: Thu closed because of market.

Solre-Sur-Sambre 8A6

Château-Fort, Rue du Chateau Fort. **GPS**: n50,30918 e4,15585.
free.
Remarks: At castle.

Thuin 8A6

Drève des Alliés. **GPS**: n50,33951 e4,29860.
.
Remarks: Max. 24h.

Thuin 8A6

L'Abbaye d'Aulnes, Rue Vandervelde. **GPS**: n50,36592 e4,33324.
free.
Remarks: Near abbey, max. 24h.

Thuin 8A6

Place du Chapitre. **GPS**: n50,33980 e4,28724.
.
Remarks: Max. 24h.

Tournai/Doornik 7C6

Maison de la Culture, Boulevard Frère Rimbaud, Tournai (Tournai/Doornik). **GPS**: n50,60432 e3,38199.
15-20 free Ch free. **Surface:** metalled. 01/01-31/12
Distance: 5 min walking 5 min walking 5 min walking.

Tourist information Tournai (Tournai/Doornik):
Dienst Toerisme, Vieux Marché aux Poteries, 14, www.tournai.be.One of the oldest cities of Belgium.
Musée Royal d'armes et d'histoire militaire, Rue Roc Saint-Nicaise 59-61. Military museum. 10-12h, 14-17.30h Tue.

Trazegnies 8A6

Place Albert I 32. **GPS**: n50,46248 e4,33025.
.
Distance: 1,5km.
Remarks: Parking at castle.

Namur

Alle-sur-Semois 15D2

Recreatiecentrum Recrealle, restaurant les Pierres du Diable, Rue Léon Henrard 16. **GPS**: n49,84648 e4,97579.

10 free. **Surface:** unpaved. Apr-Oct daily, Febr-Mar, Oct-Nov fr-su
01/01-31/01.
Distance: on the spot fishing permit obligatory on the spot.
Remarks: Max. 1 night. E411 exit Wellin, dir Gedinne, Bièvre then follow Recrealle.

Tourist information Alle-sur-Semois:
Region with slate mines.
Ardoisalle, Rue de Reposseau 12.Slate mine with museum. 01/05-30/06, 01/09-31/10 Wed-Su 10-12h, 14-17h, 01/07-31/08 daily.
Recrealle.Canoe rent; departures for canoe and kayaks, fishing and swimming possibilities, bowling, tennis, play ground, restaurant.

Ave-et-Auffe 16A1

Le Roptai, Rue du Roptai 34. **GPS**: n50,11101 e5,14084.
10 € 16 01/02-06/07, 20/08-31/12 Ch (10x)€ 3/24h WC included € 1 € 4 € 3,50/24h. **Location:** Rural, comfortable, quiet. **Surface:** grassy/ gravel. 08/01-31/12
Distance: 4km 2km 1km 5km 1km.
Remarks: Han 5km.

Han-Sur-Lesse 16A1

Rue de la Lesse. **GPS**: n50,12730 e5,18660.

BE

30 € 7,50, Jul/Aug € 10 Ch WC included. **Surface:** asphalted.
01/01-31/12
Remarks: Parking nearby caves and centre.

Tourist information Han-Sur-Lesse:

Tourist centre around the caves.

Belgacom, rue de l'Antenne 63 Lessive (Rochefort).Ground station telecommunication by means of satellites. Easter-Oct 9.30-17h.

Grottes de Han.Caves, son-et-lumière and boat trip on underground river. 01/04-31/10 10-16/18h, 01/11-31/03 11.30-16h.

Musée du Monde Sousterrain, Place Theo Lannoy 3.Exposition of archeological findings. 01/04-15/11 11-17h, 01/07-31/08 11-19h.

Réserve d'Animaux.European animals alive today and those which lived previously in this area. 01/03-31/12 10-17h, 01/07-31/08 9.30-18h.

Profondeville 8B6

Chaussée de Namur. **GPS**: n50,37644 e4,87106.

4 free. **Surface:** asphalted. 01/01-31/12
Distance: 50m 150m 50m.
Remarks: Max. 24h.

Rochefort 16A1

Route de Marche. **GPS**: n50,15742 e5,22562.

free. **Surface:** metalled.
Remarks: From Marche N86 on entering the city, at roundabout follow 'toutes directions', 1st small street to the right, nearby centre.

Saint-Hubert 16A1

Chemin des Etangs/ Rue de Lavaux. **GPS**: n50,02689 e5,38088.

3 Ch free. **Location:** Comfortable.
Surface: gravel.
01/01-31/12
Distance: 500m 500m 500m on the spot on the spot.
Remarks: 10 parking places tolerated, european campital of hunting, events: 1st weekend September and November 1st Saint Hubert.

Viroinval 15D1

Rue Longue. **GPS**: n50,07075 e4,54879.

free € 1,50 Ch. **Surface:** asphalted.
Distance: Nismes 600m.
Remarks: Coins at Tourist Info.

Luxembourg

Arlon 16B2

Casserne Callemeyn, Rue de Redange, N882. **GPS**: n49,68990 e5,81929.

4 free free. **Surface:** asphalted. 01/01-31/12
Distance: 600m 5,8km.
Remarks: At fire-station, max. 48h.

Tourist information Arlon:

Maison du Tourisme du Pays d'Arlon, rue des Faubourgs, 2.The historical capital of the province, founded by the Romans.

Musée Luxembourgeois, Rue des Martyrs.Exposition of Gallo-Roman findings. Mo-Sa 9-12, 14-17h.

Parc Archéologique, Rue des Thermes.Archeological site. 9-12h, 14-17h.

Antiekmarkt. 01/03-31/10 1st Su of the month 7-19h.

Bastogne 16A1

Avenue Albert I. **GPS**: n49,99825 e5,71526.

± 10 free free. **Location:** Simple, central.
Surface: asphalted.
Distance: 300m 3km 300m 300m.

Durbuy 8C6

P Mobilhome Le Vedeur, Rue Fond de Vedeur. **GPS**: n50,35320 e5,45543.

20 € 15, 2 pers.incl Ch WC included. **Surface:** gravel. Easter-31/10

Distance: 750m on the spot fishing permit obligatory 750m.

Tourist information Durbuy:

Tourisme Durbuy, Place aux Foires, 25.Small tourist town with old centre.

Confiturerie Saint Amour, Rue St Amour 13.Production of traditional products. 10-18h 01/10-31/03 Mo. free.

Diamour, Rue de la Prevoté.Centre of diamonds and goldsmithing. 10.30-19.30h Tue-Wed. free.

Parc des Topiaires, Rue Haie Himbe.Model garden. 10-18h 01/01-31/01. € 4,50.

Antiques and flea market. 01/03-30/09, 9-17h, 2nd Sa of the month.

S Herbeumont 16A2

Avenue de Combattants. **GPS:** n49,77800 e5,23600. .

50 free Ch free.

Distance: 500m 500m.

Remarks: Parking of old station.

Tourist information Herbeumont:

Royal Syndicat d'Initiative, Avenue des Combattants, 7, www.herbeumont.be.Beautiful position in the Ardennes landscape. Ruins of medieval castle, free entry.

Grottes, 7 km di Bertrix.Caves. 01/04-30/09 daily, 01/11-31/03 Sa-Su. € 7.

Hotton 8C6

Rue des Vergers. **GPS:** n50,26853 e5,44759.

free.

Distance: on the spot 100m.

Remarks: Parking places in front of 'hall omnisports'.

Tourist information Hotton:

Office du Tourisme, Rue Haute 4.Small tourist town.

Grottes de Hotton.Caves.

01/04-31/10 10-17h, 01/07-31/08 10-18h.

La Roche 16A1

Rue du Harzé. **GPS:** n50,19075 e5,57432.

5 free. **Surface:** asphalted. 01/01-31/12

Distance: 300m.

Remarks: Parking at sports park.

Tourist information La Roche:

Syndicat d'Initiative, Place du Marché, 15, www.la-roche-tourisme.com.Small town totally destroyed during the battle of the Ardennes, 1944/45.

Musée de la Roche, Rue Châmont 5.War museum, Battle of the Ardennes.

Medieval citadel. 10-12h, 14-17h, 01/07-31/08 10-19h, winter Sa-Su frost.

Nisramont 16A1

Barrage de Nisramont, Rue de barrage. **GPS:** n50,14089 e5,67118.

10 free. **Location:** Simple, isolated, quiet. **Surface:** metalled. 01/01-31/12

Distance: 3,7km 15km on the spot on the spot on the spot on the spot.

Remarks: At artificial lake.

Redu 16A1

Place de l'Esro. **GPS:** n50,00733 e5,16000.

free. **Surface:** gravel.

Distance: on the spot.

Remarks: Parking in front of church.

Redu 16A1

Rue de Saint Hubert. **GPS:** n50,00877 e5,16348.

free.

Distance: on the spot.

Remarks: Parking before entering the village.

BE

LUXEMBOURG

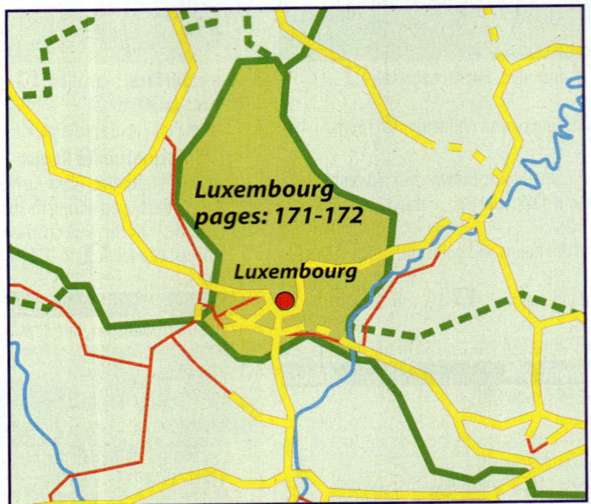

LU

Capital: Luxembourg
Government: Grand duchy
Offi cial Language: French, German, Luxembourgish
Population: 514,000 (2013)
Area: 2,586 km^2.

General information

Calling code: 00352
General emergency: 112
Currency: Euro

Regulations for overnight stays

Parking overnight and camping by public road is forbidden. Motorhome-service only on campsites.

Additional public holidays 2014

May 1 Labor day
June 6 National Holiday
August 15 Assumption of the Virgin Mary
November 1 All Saints' Day

Luxemburg

Luxembourg

Bleesbrück 16B1

Camping Bleesbrück, 1, Bleesbreck. **GPS**: n49,87270 e6,18940.
2+2 from € 9 Ch.

Diekirch 16B1

Camping de la Sûre, Route de Gilsdorf. **GPS**: n49,86597 e6,16489.

8 € 12 Ch WC included, sanitary only summer € 3 free.
Surface: grasstiles.
01/01-31/12
Distance: 100m 100m 100m (permit € 4/month) 100m 100m.

Tourist information Diekirch:
Syndicat d'intitiative et de Tourisme, place de la Libération, www.diekirch.lu/fr/index.htm.Itinerary biking and hiking cards available.
Mo-Fri 9-12h, 14-17h, Sa 14-16h.
Conservatoire National de véhicules historique, 20-22, rue de Stavelot. Exhibition of historical vehicles. 10-18h Mo.
Musée National de l'histoire militaire, 10, Bamertal.War museum.
01/04-31/10 10-18h, 01/11-31/03 14-18h.
Weekmarkt, Rue St.Antoine. Tue 8-12h.
Al Dikkirch.Folk festival. 2nd week Jul.

Dudelange 16B2

Parking Gare-Usines. **GPS**: n49,47176 e6,07772.

6 free Chfree. **Surface:** asphalted.
01/01-31/12
Distance: 1km 4,1km near train station.
Remarks: Max. 3 nights, Luxemburg city 20min with train.

Tourist information Dudelange:
Musée National des Mines de Fer, carreau de la Mine, Rumelange.History of the mines. 14-17h. € 7,50.

Echternach 16C2

Villa Romaine, Route de Luxembourg. **GPS**: n49,80500 e6,40750.

free. **Surface:** asphalted/metalled. 01/01-31/12
Distance: 1,5km 500m on the spot.

Tourist information Echternach:
Syndicat d'intitiative et de Tourisme, 9-10, Parvis de la Basilique, www.mullerthal.lu.
Sprangprossessioun.Dancing procession. Tue after Whitsuntide.

Ermsdorf 16B2

Neumühle. **GPS**: n49,83917 e6,22503.
2 . 01/01-31/12

Heiderscheid 16B1

Quickstop, Fuusekaul 4. **GPS**: n49,87806 e5,99278.

34 € 10, Jul/Aug € 15 Chincluded 6Amp.
Surface: gravel.
01/01-31/12
Distance: 8km on the spot 8km on the spot on the spot on the spot.
Remarks: Max. 1 night, >16h <11h.

Tourist information Heiderscheid:
Heischter Mart.Traditional market. end Jul.

Hoscheid 16B1

Hotel-Restaurant Des Ardennes, Haaptstrooss. **GPS**: n49,94676 e6,08036.

4 free with a meal WC included. **Surface:** asphalted.
01/02-15/12
Distance: on the spot on the spot.
Remarks: Parking behind hotel.

Larochette 16B2

Camping Birkelt, Um Birkelt 1. **GPS**: n49,78483 e6,21068.

8 € 15,25 Ch WC included € 5. **Surface:** grasstiles.
01/03-31/10
Distance: 1km on the spot on the spot 1km.
Remarks: Quick-Stop: >17-9h, max. 1 night.

Larochette 16B2

Camping Auf Kengert. **GPS**: n49,80021 e6,19788.
6 from € 18,50 Ch. carnival 31/10
Remarks: Quick-Stop: >19-09h.

Tourist information Larochette:
Syndicat d'intitiative et de Tourisme, 4, rue de Medernach, www.luarochette.lu. Mo-Fri 10-12h, 13.30-16h.
Schiessentümpel.Waterfall with three cascades.
Château. Easter-Oct, 10-18h, daily.

LU

Maulusmühle 16B1
Woltzdal. **GPS**: n50,09266 e6,02869.
2. 01/04-31/10

Mersch 16B2
Um Krounebierg. **GPS**: n49,74403 e6,09075.
5 € 15-19,80. 15/03-31/10

Obereisenbach 16B1
Kohnenhof. **GPS**: n50,01630 e6,13682.
. 31/03-01/11

Redange/Attert 16B2
Rue de la Piscine 24. **GPS**: n49,76918 e5,89459.

12 free Ch free. **Surface:** asphalted. 01/01-31/12
Distance: 800m on the spot.
Remarks: Max. 72h.

Schwebsange 16B2
Camport, Rue du Port. **GPS**: n49,51163 e6,36249.

18 € 9 Ch included € 1,50 WC € 2,50 at restaurant.
Surface: grasstiles. 01/04-15/10
Distance: 500m fishing permit obligatory on the spot on the spot 500m.
Remarks: At marina.

Tourist information Schwebsange:
A Possen, 1 rue Aloyse Sandt, Bech-Kleinmacher.Folkore and wine museum. 01/05-31/10 14-19h, 01/03-30/04, 01/11-31/12 Fri-Su 14-19h Mo.

Vianden 16B1
39, rue du Sanatorium. **GPS**: n49,93717 e6,20556.

free. **Surface:** asphalted. 01/01-31/12
Distance: 500m 500m.
Remarks: At the chair-lifts (télesiege).

Tourist information Vianden:
Syndicat d'intitiative et de Tourisme, 1,a rue du vieux Marché, www.tourist-info-vianden.lu. Mo-Fri 8-12h, 13-17h, summer daily.
SEO.Large hydro-electric power-station. Easter-Sep 10-20h. free.
Bakkerij museum, Grand rue 96-98. Easter-Oct 11-17h Mo.
Château de Vianden. 01/04-30/09 10-18h, 01/10-31/03 10-16h 02/11, 25/12, 01/01.
Nessmoort.Nuts market. 2nd Su Oct.
Télesiège.Chair-lift. Easter-Oct.

FRANCE

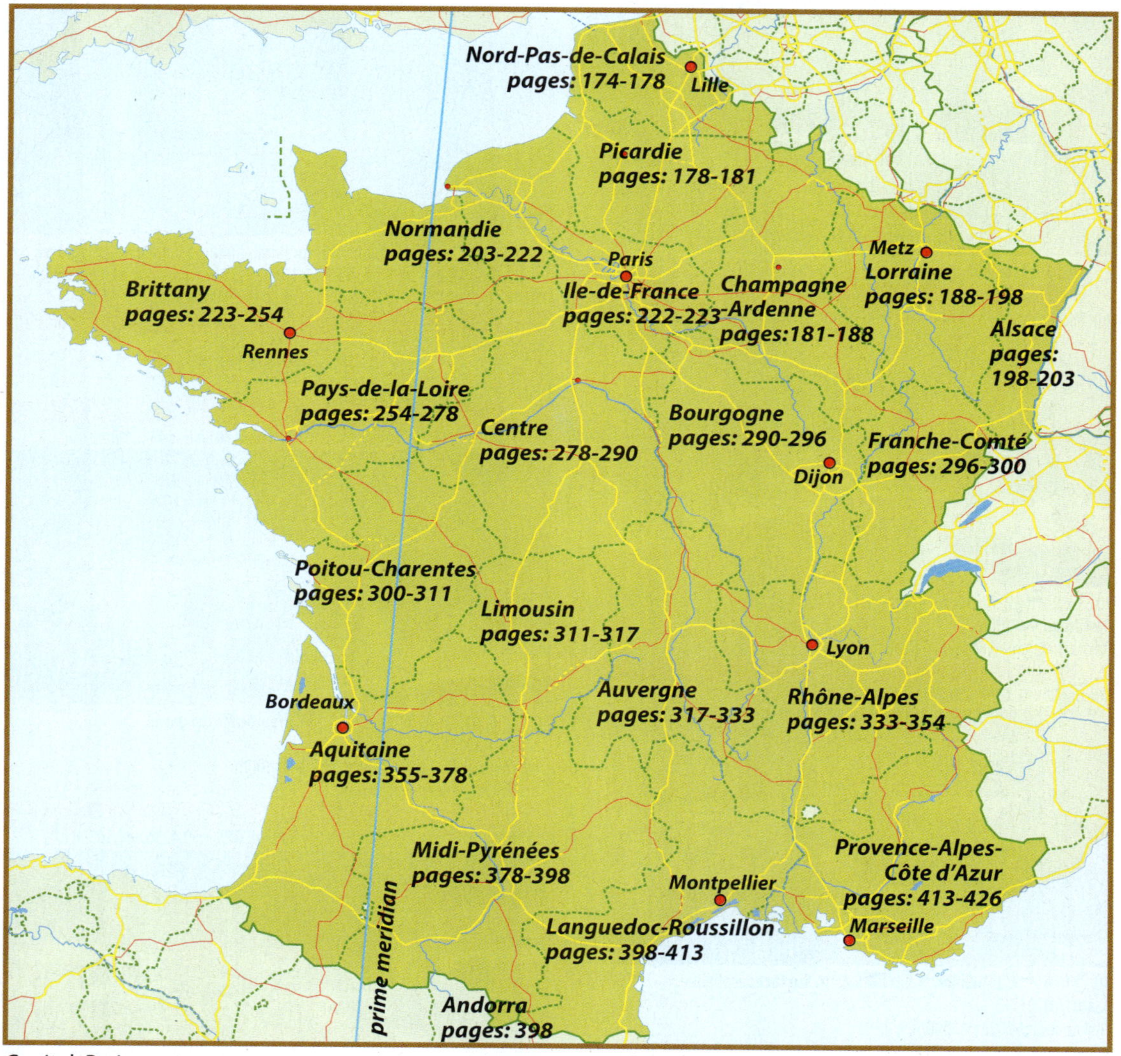

Capital: Paris
Government: Unitary republic
Official Language: French
Population: 65.800.000 (2013)
Area: 543,965 km^2.

General information

Dialling code: 0033
General emergency: 112
Currency: Euro
Payments by credit card are accepted almost everywhere, however chip and pin systems are non-compatible with British cards and fuel for example can only be bought at supermarkets during opening hours.

Regulations for overnight stays

Wild camping is accepted almost everywhere throughout inland France. Special regulations for motor homes you can find on signs by entering the town. It is permitted to stopover at motorway services, be aware that toll roads often issue time-constrained tickets.

Additional public holidays 2014

April 18 Good Friday
May 1 Labor Day
May 8 Liberation Day
July14 National Holiday
August15 Assumption of the Virgin Mary
November 1 All Saints Day
November 11 Armistice Day 1918

France

FR

Nord-Pas de Calais

Ambleteuse 7A5

D940 > Wimereux. **GPS**: n50,80638 e1,61484.

7 € 3. **Surface:** grassy.

Arques 7B5

Rue Michelet. **GPS**: n50,74551 e2,30459.

20 € 2 € 2,50. **Surface:** gravel. 01/04-31/10

Distance: 100m.

Remarks: Behind camp site Beauséjour.

Arras 7C6

Rue des Rosati. **GPS**: n50,29463 e2,78812.

10 free € 2/100liter Ch € 2/1h. **Surface:** asphalted.

01/01-31/12

Distance: 700m 500m.

Tourist information Arras:

Office de Tourisme, Hôtel de Ville, Place des Héros, www.ot-arras.fr.City, fortified by Vauban, became French territory in 1659.

Hôtel de Ville.Town hall in Gothic style. Also guided tours of the subterranean passages of Arras.

Wed, Sa.

Bailleul 7B5

Rue du collège. **GPS**: n50,74010 e2,73170.

20 free. **Surface:** asphalted. 01/01-31/12

Distance: 700m 2,8km.

Remarks: At commemorative monument.

Banteux 15A1

GPS: n50,06259 e3,20106.

5 € 5 Chfree. **Location:** Rural, simple. **Surface:** grassy/gravel.

01/01-31/12 service 01/11-31/03.

Distance: 500m 2,5km on the spot on the spot.

Bavay 7D6

Chemin de Ronde. **GPS**: n50,30004 e3,79551.

10 free Chfree. **Surface:** gravel. 01/01-31/12

Distance: 200m 200m.

Berck-sur-Mer 7A6

Baie d'Authie, Chemin aux Raisins. **GPS**: n50,39701 e1,56431.

80 € 6, 01/10-01/04 free Chfree. **Surface:** gravel.

01/01-31/12

Distance: 1,5km 100m frituur 100m.

Remarks: Baker every morning.

Berck-sur-Mer 7A6

Parking Terminus, Rue Dr. Calot, Berck-Nord. **GPS**: n50,42361 e1,56750.

40 € 5,50/24h Chincluded. **Location:** Simple. **Surface:** gravel.

01/01-31/12

Distance: beach 200m.

Tourist information Berck-sur-Mer:

Bagatelle, CD 940.Amusement park. Easter-Sep 10-18.30h.

Bergues 7B5

Rue Maurice Cornette. **GPS**: n50,96543 e2,43596.

FR

50 free. **Surface:** gravel. 01/01-31/12
Distance: 500m 2,2km.
Remarks: Behind football ground, max. 48h.

S Boulogne-sur-Mer 7A5

Parking Moulin Wibert, Boulevard Sainte Beuve, D940. **GPS:** n50,74308 e1,59688.

40 € 5,10/24h € 3/10minutes Ch . **Surface:** metalled.
Distance: centre 2,5km 5,5km on the spot.
Remarks: Max. 48h, at sports grounds.

Boulogne-sur-Mer 7A5

Boulevard Chanzy. **GPS:** n50,72194 e1,60027.

free. **Surface:** asphalted.
Distance: 500m 4,5km.
Remarks: Nearby casino.

Tourist information Boulogne-sur-Mer:
Office de Tourisme, 24, quai Gambetta, www.coteo.com.Lively city with large fishing port and historical city centre.
Boulevard Clocheville. Wed-morning.
place Dalton, centre. Wed + Sa morning.
place Vignon. Su-morning.

S Calais 7A5

Digue Gaston Berthe. **GPS:** n50,96688 e1,84406.

60 free, 01/04-31/10 € 7/24h Ch WC included. **Surface:** asphalted.
Distance: 500m 100m 100m 100m.
Remarks: At the end of beach in front of the ferry terminal.

S Calais 7A5

Quai Edmond Pagniez. **GPS:** n50,96050 e1,84466.

100 free, 01/04-31/10 € 7/24h Ch included. **Surface:** asphalted.
01/01-31/12
Distance: 300m 350m.
Remarks: Service: Digue Gaston Berthe.

Tourist information Calais:
Office de Tourisme, 12, boulevard Clemenceau, www.coteo.com.Port city.
Fort Nieulay.Fortress, 13th century, war museum.
Centre d'Information Eurotunnel.Exhibition about the Channel tunnel.
Wed, Thu, Sa.

S Cassel 7B5

Route d'Oxelaere, C301. **GPS:** n50,79328 e2,48852.

5 free € 2 Ch € 2. **Surface:** gravel.
01/01-31/12
Remarks: At sports park, a little isolated, coins at Office de tourisme.

S Catillon-sur-Sambre 15B1

N43. **GPS:** n50,07624 e3,64615.

5 € 5 Ch free. **Surface:** asphalted. 01/01-31/12
Distance: 200m on the spot.
Remarks: At the canal, max. 72h.

Catillon-sur-Sambre 15B1

Rue de la Gare. **GPS:** n50,07699 e3,64404.

20 free. **Surface:** gravel. 01/01-31/12

FR

Distance: on the spot.

Embry 7A6

Les Salons de l'Embryenne, D108. **GPS**: n50,49534 e1,96610.

8 € 6 € 2,50 Ch € 2,50/4h WC € 2,50 . **Surface:** gravel.
01/01-31/12

Equihen-Plage 7A5

Plage de la Crevasse, Rue du Beurre Fondu. **GPS**: n50,67910 e1,56884.

20 € 5 € 3/10minutes Ch (6x)€ 3/12h. **Surface:** grassy/gravel.
01/01-31/12
Distance: 100m 100m 100m.

Tourist information Equihen-Plage:
Office de Tourisme, Place Albert Bécard.

Gravelines 7B5

Parking des Miaules, Rue des Islandais/Rue du Port. **GPS**: n50,98766 e2,12232.

20 € 3, 01/04-01/10 € 6. **Location:** Rural, simple, quiet.
Surface: gravel.
Distance: 500m nearby 300m.
Remarks: From Dunkerque at entry straight on to small harbour, behind fort, parking at marina.

Gravelines 7B5

Rue de la Gendarmerie. **GPS**: n50,99342 e2,13177.
€ 2 Ch .

Tourist information Gravelines:
Office de Tourisme, 11, rue de la République, www.tourisme.fr/gravelines. Bathing resort and water sports centre.
L'Arsenal.Arsenal.

Hardelot 7A5

Place R.L. Peeters. **GPS**: n50,63500 e1,59888.

free. **Surface:** asphalted. 01/01-31/12
Distance: 1,7km.

Hondschoote 7B5

Impasse Spinnewyn. **GPS**: n50,97628 e2,58033.

8 free € 2/100liter Ch € 2/1h. **Surface:** asphalted.
Distance: 800m nearby.
Remarks: Behind Moulin de la Victoire, coins available, addresses indicated on the spot.

Landrecies 15B1

Avenue Dumey. **GPS**: n50,12715 e3,69007.
4 . 01/01-31/12

Le Portel 7A5

Rue des Champs. **GPS**: n50,71188 e1,57485.

30 € 3, 01/06-30/09 € 4 € 2/100liter Ch € 2/4h .
Surface: metalled. 01/01-31/12
Distance: 200m 300m 300m 300m.
Remarks: Next to sports fields, 300m from beach (stairs).

Le Touquet-Paris Plage 7A6

Centre Nautique du Touquet Base Nord, Avenue Jean Ruet. **GPS**: n50,53588 e1,59285.

60 € 9 € 2/100liter Ch € 2/55minutes. **Surface:** asphalted.
01/01-31/12
Distance: 10 min walking on the spot on the spot on the spot on the spot.
Remarks: Next to marina, at beach, follow signs.

FR

Le Touquet-Paris Plage 7A6

Parc International de la Canoke, Boulevard de la Canche. **GPS**: n50,52648 e1,59869.

100 € 7,50 € 2/100liter Ch € 2/1h. **Surface:** grassy/gravel.
01/01-31/12
Distance: 10 min walking on the spot on the spot on the spot on the spot.

Tourist information Le Touquet-Paris Plage:
Office de Tourisme, Palais de l'Europe, Place de l'Hermitage, www.letouquet.com/.Popular bathing resort.
Aqualud.Leisure pool park. 15/02-30/11 10-18h.

Le-Cateau-Cambrésis 15B1

Avenue du Maréchal Leclerc, N43. **GPS**: n50,10256 e3,55429.

5 free Ch free. **Surface:** asphalted. 01/01-31/12
Distance: 1km.

Longfossé 7A5

Ferme du Louvet, 5, Route de Wierre, D52 Desvres > Samer. **GPS**: n50,64667 e1,79062.

8 € 6 € 3 Ch included. **Surface:** gravel.
Remarks: Narrow entrance.

Merlimont 7A6

Place de la Gare. **GPS**: n50,46026 e1,58053.

12 free. **Surface:** gravel. 01/01-31/12

Nunq-Hautecôte 7B6

La Pommeraie, 13, route nationale. **GPS**: n50,30516 e2,29375.

5 € 5 € 2 Ch € 5 free. **Surface:** gravel. 01/01-31/12
Distance: 50m.
Remarks: Covered pool € 3.

Oye-plage 7A5

Les Huttes d'Oye Plage. **GPS**: n50,99703 e2,04228.

10 free Ch. **Surface:** gravel.
01/01-31/12
Distance: on the spot 100m.
Remarks: Beach parking, service Oye-Plage: 50,97713 2,03966.

Richebourg 7B6

Rue de la Briqueterie. **GPS**: n50,58028 e2,74639.

6 free € 2/100liter € 2/55minutes. **Location:** Rural, comfortable.
Surface: grasstiles. 01/01-31/12
Distance: 500m on the spot on the spot.
Remarks: Max. 48h.

Stella-plage 7A6

Cours des Champs Elysées. **GPS**: n50,47470 e1,57726.

30 free. **Surface:** asphalted.

Tardinghen 7A5

Le site des 2 caps, La Ferme d'Horloge, 1615 Route d'Ausques, D249. **GPS**: n50,86250 e1,64890.

FR

30 € 5/24h € 3 Ch included. **Surface:** metalled.
01/01-31/12
Distance: 1,6km.
Remarks: Swin-golf € 5.

Tardinghen 7A5

Le site des 2 caps, La Fleur des Champs. **GPS**: n50,85639 e1,65139.

50 € 5/24h. **Surface:** grassy. 01/01-31/12
Distance: 2km 2km.

Tardinghen 7A5

Le site des 2 caps, Le Fond de Sombre, Hervelinghen > Wissant. **GPS**: n50,89361 e1,68972.

10 € 5/24h. **Surface:** grassy. 01/01-31/12
Distance: 1km.

Wissant 7A5

Parking Wissant, Avenue Georges Clémenceau. **GPS**: n50,88684 e1,67064.

30 free Chfree. **Surface:** metalled. 01/01-31/12
Distance: 700m 1,1km.

Picardie

Ault 14C1

Rue Gest. **GPS**: n50,10333 e1,45083.

10 free € 2 Ch € 2. **Surface:** asphalted. 01/01-31/12
Distance: within walking distance 5 min walking 200m 200m.

Bellicourt 15A1

Hameau de Riqueval, D1044. **GPS**: n49,95156 e3,23519.

2 free Ch Service € 4. **Surface:** asphalted.
01/01-31/12 service: 01/10-31/03.
Distance: 300m on the spot on the spot.
Remarks: Coins at Tourist Info.

Bourseville 14C1

Lotissement le Village. **GPS**: n50,10350 e1,52702.

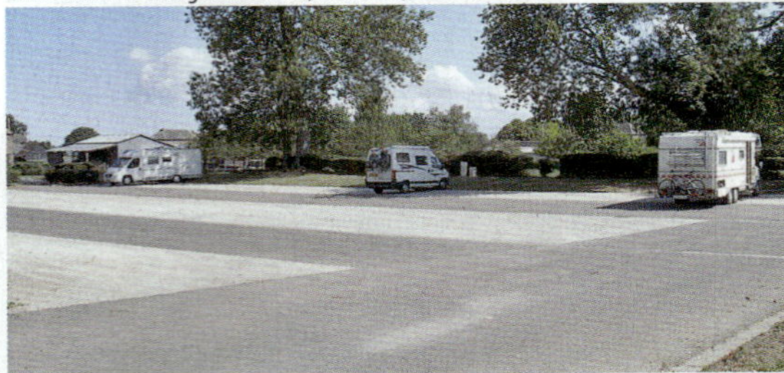

35 free € 2 Ch € 2. **Surface:** asphalted. 01/01-31/12
Distance: 500m 3km 500m 500m.

Cayeux-sur-Mer 14C1

Rue Faidherbe. **GPS**: n50,20300 e1,52612.

30 € 5 € 3 Ch. **Surface:** gravel. 01/01-31/12
Distance: 2km At the sea, no beach 2km 2km.
Remarks: In front of campsite.

Cayeux-sur-Mer 14C1

Route blanche, Le Hourdel, D102. **GPS**: n50,21448 e1,55208.

FR

30 free. **Location:** Simple, isolated, quiet. **Surface:** gravel. 01/01-31/12

Distance: 500m, Cayeux 6km sea 50m 500m 3km.

S Château-Thierry 15B4

Aire de Château. **GPS**: n49,03657 e3,38365.

13 € 6,50 Ch € 1,50/12h WC included. **Location:** Urban, comfortable. **Surface:** asphalted. 01/01-31/12

Distance: centre 1,8km on the spot on the spot on the spot on the spot on the spot on the spot.

Remarks: Along the Marne river.

S Conty 14D2

Rue du Marais. **GPS**: n49,74333 e2,15583.

30 free € 2/100liter Ch WC. **Surface:** grassy. 01/01-31/12

Distance: 200m 6,5km 300m 300m 300m.

Remarks: Coins at Tourist Info, town hall and bakery.

S Coucy-le-Château-Auffrique 15B2

Chemin du Val Serain. **GPS**: n49,52037 e3,31150.

6 € 5 Ch included. **Location:** Rural, comfortable. **Surface:** gravel. 01/01-31/12

Distance: 500m on the spot 500m.

Remarks: Castle 1km.

S Doullens 14D1

Rue du Pont à l'Avoine, N25-Arras-Amiens. **GPS**: n50,15390 e2,34260.

4 free free. **Surface:** asphalted.

S Fort Mahon Plage 7A6

Plage Parking de la Dune, Rue de la Bistouille. **GPS**: n50,33833 e1,55611.

60 € 8 Ch WC free. **Surface:** gravel. 01/01-31/12

Distance: 200m 5 min walking.

S La Pérouille 21B3

Étang de la Roche, Le Champ Perrot. **GPS**: n46,70507 e1,52259.

free € 2 Ch WC. **Location:** Rural, isolated, quiet. **Surface:** grassy/gravel.

Distance: 750m 5km A20 750m.

Remarks: Coins at town hall and restaurant (750m), al small lake.

Laôn 15B2

Promenade de la Couloire. **GPS**: n49,56313 e3,62967.

6 free. **Surface:** metalled.

Distance: 300m 500m.

Remarks: Near city wall.

S Le Crotoy 7A6

Aire Camping-car, Bassin des Chasses. **GPS**: n50,21800 e1,63300.

50 € 5/24h € 2/100liter Ch € 2/1h. **Surface:** sand. 01/01-31/12

Distance: 5 min walking 15 min walking Laverie Crotelloise, 20, avenue du Gal de Gaulle.

Remarks: In harbour.

S Le Crotoy 7A6

Aire Camping-car, Chemin du Marais. **GPS**: n50,22886 e1,61253.

FR

35 € 5/24h € 2/10minutes Ch € 2/1h. **Surface:** sand.
01/01-31/12

Distance: 10 min walking on the spot Laverie Crotelloise, 20, avenue du Gal de Gaulle.

Tourist information Le Crotoy:
Office de Tourisme, 1, rue Carnot, www.tourisme-crotoy.com.Seaside resort at the mouth of the river Somme.

S Longpont 15A3

Rue Saint-Louis, D17. **GPS**: n49,27395 e3,22129.

4 free Chagainst payment. **Location:** Rural. **Surface:** gravel.
01/01-31/12

Distance: 100m.

Remarks: Abbey 150m.

S Mers-les-Bains 14C1

Chemin de la Petite Allée. **GPS**: n50,06175 e1,40150.

50 € 5,50 € 2 Ch. **Location:** Comfortable. **Surface:** gravel.
01/01-31/12

Distance: 1,3km sandy beach 1,5km Auchan 600m.

S Morienval 15A3

Route de Pierrefonds 32. **GPS**: n49,30352 e2,92309.

21+9 € 8 € 2/100liter Ch stay (21x)€ 2/day. **Location:** Rural, comfortable, quiet. **Surface:** grassy/gravel. 22/03-16/11

Distance: 500m 500m 500m.

Remarks: In case of absence, money in an envelope in mail box.

S Picquigny 14D1

Rue de la Cavée d'Airaines. **GPS**: n49,94388 e2,13496.

8 € 5 Chincluded € 2. **Location:** Rural. **Surface:** grassy.

Distance: 500m 500m.

S Quend 7A6

Ferme de la Grande Retz. **GPS**: n50,32893 e1,61811.

10 € 5 Ch € 3. **Surface:** grassy. 01/01-31/12

Distance: 3km 9km 9km 2km.

S Quend-plage-les-Pins 7A6

Plage des Pins. **GPS**: n50,32410 e1,55545.

100 € 7/24h € 2/10minutes Ch € 2/1h. **Surface:** gravel.
01/01-31/12

Distance: 800m beach 900m.

S St.Valery-sur-Somme 14C1

Rue de la Croix l'Abbé. **GPS**: n50,18220 e1,62881.

180 € 9/24h Chincluded. **Location:** Rural. **Surface:** gravel.
01/01-31/12

Distance: 1km nearby nearby.

Remarks: Su market.

Tourist information St.Valery-sur-Somme:
Office de Tourisme, place Guillaume le Conquérant.Fishing town and family bathing resort in the bay of the Somme river.

S Villers-Côtterets 15A3

Avenue De Compiègne. **GPS**: n49,26052 e3,08713.

6 free € 3/10minutes Chfree € 3/1h . **Location:** Urban, comfortable, quiet. **Surface:** gravel/metalled. 01/01-31/12
Distance: on the spot 600m 600m.
Remarks: Service 50m.

Villers-Côtterets 15A3
Grand Bosquet Parc du Château, Place Aristide Briand. **GPS**: n49,25483 e3,09400.

6 free. **Location:** Urban, simple, central, noisy. **Surface:** grassy/metalled. 01/01-31/12
Distance: on the spot 20km 200m 500m 100m.

Champagne Ardenne

Arc-en-Barrois 15D6
Camping municipal, D3/D159. **GPS**: n47,95056 e5,00528.

25 € 5 Ch WC included,on camp site. **Location:** Simple.
Surface: gravel. 01/01-31/12 Whitsuntide.
Distance: 500m 500m 500m.

Attigny 15D2
D987. **GPS**: n49,48583 e4,58077.

4 free Chfree. **Location:** Rural, simple.
Distance: 800m 800m 900m.

Avize 15C4
Place du Bourg Joli. **GPS**: n48,97175 e4,00999.

5 free Chfree. **Location:** Urban, simple, central, quiet.
Surface: asphalted. 01/01-31/12
Distance: on the spot 200m bakery 50m.
Remarks: Next to town hall.

Bar-sur-Aube 15D6
7, Rue des Varennes. **GPS**: n48,23491 e4,70065.

1 free € 3,50/100liter Ch € 3,50/1h. **Location:** Simple.
Surface: asphalted. 01/01-31/12
Distance: on the spot on the spot on the spot.

Beaunay 15B4
Ferme Du Bel Air, Rue Principale. **GPS**: n48,88177 e3,87475.

12 € 6 Ch (6x)included . **Location:** Rural, simple, isolated, quiet. **Surface:** gravel. 01/01-31/12
Distance: 2km 2km 2km.

Bogny-sur-Meuse 15D2
Rue de la Meuse. **GPS**: n49,85780 e4,74225.

6 free € 2/100liter Ch € 2/2h,only 2-euro coins. **Location:** Rural, simple, quiet. **Surface:** asphalted. 01/01-31/12
Distance: on the spot on the spot 250m 400m 500m.
Remarks: Along the Meuse river, service 75m.

Brienne-le-Château 15D5
Rue de la Gare. **GPS**: n48,39617 e4,53130.

FR

10 free € 3/10minutes Ch € 3/55minutes. **Location:** Simple, noisy. **Surface:** asphalted.
01/01-31/12 water disconnected in winter.
Distance: 300m 400m 300m.
Remarks: At former station, coins at Office du Tourisme, supermarket Champion.

S Cerisières 15D5

D186, Froideau. **GPS**: n48,29921 e5,06339.

20 free Ch free. **Location:** Rural, simple, isolated, quiet.
Surface: gravel. 01/01-31/12
Distance: 2km.

S Chamery 15C3

Salle Polyvalente, Rue du Château Rouge. **GPS**: n49,17475 e3,95446.

5 free € 2/100liter Ch € 2/2h. **Location:** Rural, simple, quiet.
Surface: gravel. 01/01-31/12
Distance: 300m 400m.
Remarks: In front of community centre.

S Champigny-lès-Langres 16A6

Rue du Port, D74. **GPS**: n47,88167 e5,33861.

6 free WC. **Location:** Simple, noisy. **Surface:** gravel.
01/01-31/12
Distance: 400m 800m.

S Chaource 15C6

Chemin de Ronde/Rue des Roises. **GPS**: n48,05944 e4,13861.

10 free € 2/100liter Ch € 2/1h.
Location: Comfortable, quiet.
Surface: grassy.
Distance: 100m on the spot on the spot on the spot on the spot.
Remarks: Coins at Tourist Info, 2, Grande rue, mo.morning market.

S Charleville-Mézières 15D2

Rue des Pâquis. **GPS**: n49,78056 e4,72056.

8 free € 2/100liter Ch € 2/55minutes € 5,40,ask at camp site.
Surface: asphalted.
01/01-31/12 electricity: 01/11-31/03.
Distance: 800m on the spot 500m 2km 600m Nearby campsite Nearby campsite.
Remarks: Service only with 2-euro coins, ask for electricity at campsite.

Tourist information Charleville-Mézières:

- Office de Tourisme, 4, place Ducale.Big city with historical centre.
- Musée Ardennes.Regional museum.
- Sa 21.15h all 12 scenes Mo.
- Nôtre Dame de l'Espérance.Gothic basilica.
- place Ducale.Regional products. Tue, Thu, Sa.

S Chaumont 16A6

Port de la Maladière, RN74 Neufchâteau > Chaumont. **GPS**: n48,11815 e5,15437.

12 € 6,50, € 0,20/pp tourist tax Ch included WC € 2,40 € 2,20,dryer € 3,20 free. **Location:** Quiet. **Surface:** metalled.
01/04-31/10
Distance: 4km Canal de la Marne 100m nearby.
Remarks: Baker at 8am.

Tourist information Chaumont:

- Office de Tourisme, Place du Général de Gaulle.

S Chavanges 15D5

Ruelle du Fief Berthaux. **GPS**: n48,50691 e4,57627.

8 free € 3 Ch . **Location:** Simple, quiet. **Surface:** asphalted/gravel.
01/01-31/12
Distance: 300m 400m.
Remarks: Coins available at the shops.

S Colombey-les-deux-Eglises 15D6

Rue de Général de Gaulle. **GPS**: n48,22316 e4,88619.

10 free Ch WC free. **Location:** Simple, quiet.
Surface: asphalted/gravel. 01/04-30/11
Distance: on the spot 50m 50m.
Remarks: Museum and Memorial Général De Gaulle 800m.

S Corgirnon 23A1

Allée du Parc. **GPS**: n47,80681 e5,50308.

8 € 4 Ch included. **Location:** Rural, comfortable, isolated, quiet. **Surface:** gravel. 01/01-31/12 water disconnected in winter.
Distance: 500m 10km 500m, baker on site (Tue-Su).
Remarks: Bread-service.

S Dolancourt 15D6

Nigloland, RN19. **GPS**: n48,26086 e4,60945.

28 € 6/24h, free with a meal Ch included. **Location:** Simple, isolated. **Surface:** asphalted. 03/04-03/11
Distance: on the spot.
Remarks: Parking amusement park, max. 24h.

S Donjeux 16A5

Halte Nautique, D67a. **GPS**: n48,36586 e5,14891.

4 free Ch (4x)free. **Location:** Comfortable, quiet.
Surface: gravel/metalled. 01/01-31/12
Distance: 1km Canal de la Marne on the spot 1km 800m on the spot.
Remarks: Baker every morning.

S Épernay 15C4

Rue Dom Pérignon. **GPS**: n49,03602 e3,95130.

3 free € 2/100liter Ch € 2/1h WC € 0,50/time. **Location:** Urban, simple, central, noisy.
Surface: asphalted.
Distance: within walking distance Avenue Jean Jaurès.
Remarks: Behind church St.Pierre-St.Paul,coins at Tourist Info.

Tourist information Épernay:
Office de Tourisme, 7, avenue de Champagne. 01/10-30/04 Mo-Fr 9.30-12.30h 13.30-17.30h, 01/05-30/09 Mo-Sa 9.30-12.30h 13.30-19h.
Cave de Catellane, 154, avenue de Verdun.
Coöperative des Premiers crus de la Marne, 5, rue de la Brèche.
Tue-Fri 8.30-11.30h, 13.30-17h, Aug closed.
Mercier, 70, avenue de Champagne.
Mo-Sa 9.30-11.30h, 14-16.30h, Su/holidays 9.30-11.30h, 14-17.30h.
Musée de la Préhistoire d'Archéologie Régionale et du Vin de Champagne.
01-03-31/11.

S Esternay 15B4

Place des Tilleuls, D48, Rue de la Paix. **GPS**: n48,73196 e3,55719.

8 free free. **Location:** Urban, simple, central, quiet. **Surface:** gravel.
water: 15/03-15/11
Distance: within walking distance 200m 400m.
Remarks: Behind church.

S Froncles 16A5

Halte Nautique. **GPS**: n48,29954 e5,15246.

FR

10 € 1,50 € 1,50/day Ch (8x)€ 1,50/1day € 2/2time € 3,dryer € 3. **Location:** Comfortable. **Surface:** gravel.
01/01-31/12
Distance: 500m river-beach on the spot on the spot 1km on the spot.
Remarks: Baker on site (Tue-Su).

Fumay 15D1

Rue des Carmélites. **GPS**: n49,99736 e4,70986.
+10 free. **Surface:** unpaved.
Distance: on the spot.
Remarks: Along the Meuse river.

S Giffaumont-Champaubert 15D5

Site de Chantecoq, Rue du grand Der. **GPS**: n48,56880 e4,70294.

50 free € 3,80/80liter Ch € 3,80/45minutes WC. **Location:** Rural, simple. **Surface:** metalled.
01/01-31/12
Distance: on the spot 900m.
Remarks: At lake Der de Chantecoq, coins at Tourist Info.

S Giffaumont-Champaubert 15D5

Station Nautique, Rue du Port. **GPS**: n48,55354 e4,76715.

50 € 7,50 20-8h, parking free Ch included .
Location: Rural. 01/01-31/12
Distance: on the spot 200m 8km Montier-en-Der on the spot on the spot.

Givet 15D1

Rue Jean Jaurès. **GPS**: n50,13593 e4,82138.

12 free. **Location:** Urban, simple, central, quiet. **Surface:** asphalted.
01/01-31/12

S Givet 15D1

Camping Municipal, Rue Berthelot. **GPS**: n50,14291 e4,82611.

5 free € 3/100liter Ch € 3/h. **Location:** Rural, simple.
Surface: asphalted. 01/01-31/12
Distance: 750m 750m 1km.
Remarks: Coins available at campsite.

S Goncourt 16A6

Rue des Lottes, D74. **GPS**: n48,23685 e5,60998.

30 € 2 € 2 Ch. **Location:** Rural, comfortable.
Surface: asphalted/gravel. 01/01-31/12
Distance: 100m on the spot 100m 100m.
Remarks: Max. 48h, baker every morning, along the Meuse river.

Haybes 15D1

Halte Fluviale, Quai du Docteur Adolphe Hamai. **GPS**: n50,01100 e4,70693.
free. **Surface:** metalled.
Distance: on the spot 200m.
Remarks: Along the Meuse river, service at camping municipal.

S Javernant 15C6

Le Cheminot, N77. **GPS**: n48,14789 e4,01046.

5 free Chfree. **Location:** Simple. **Surface:** asphalted.
01/01-31/12
Remarks: 2013: during inspection service out of order.

FR

S Joinville 16A5

Halte Nautique, Rue des Jardins. **GPS**: n48,44583 e5,15000.

12 free € 2 Ch € 2 . **Location:** Simple, quiet. **Surface:** gravel/metalled. 01/01-31/12

Distance: 500m on the spot on the spot 800m 100m on the spot.

S Juzennecourt 15D6

Place de la Mairie. **GPS**: n48,18429 e4,97890.

4 free Ch WC. **Location:** Simple, quiet. **Surface:** metalled. 01/01-31/12

Distance: on the spot bakery in the village on the spot.

Remarks: Parking townhall.

S La Cheppe 15C4

Champ d'Attila, Rue de Champo d'Attila. **GPS**: n49,04892 e4,49377.

5 free € 2/100liter Ch € 2/2h WC . **Location:** Rural, simple, quiet. **Surface:** asphalted. 01/01-31/12

Distance: 500m.

S La Gault-Soigny 15B4

Rue de la Liberté, D373. **GPS**: n48,81758 e3,59072.

8 free Chfree. **Location:** Rural, simple, quiet. **Surface:** asphalted. 01/01-31/12

Distance: on the spot.

Remarks: Near Salle des Fêtes, service 50m.

S Langres 23A1

Ruelle de la Poterne. **GPS**: n47,85795 e5,32989.

15 free Chfree. **Location:** Simple, quiet. **Surface:** asphalted. 01/01-31/12

Distance: 800m.

Langres 23A1

Parking Panorama, Allée des Marronniers. **GPS**: n47,86104 e5,33674.

free. **Location:** Simple, quiet. **Surface:** asphalted. 01/01-31/12

Distance: on the spot on the spot.

Remarks: Free elevator to old town, inclining pitches.

Langres 23A1

Place de Bel Air. **GPS**: n47,85885 e5,33225.

free WC. **Location:** Urban, simple, noisy. **Surface:** asphalted. 01/01-31/12

Distance: on the spot on the spot.

Tourist information Langres:

Office de Tourisme, Square Olivier Lahalle-place Bel'Air, www.tourisme-langres.com.City worth a visit, the city centre surrounded by a wall of 4 kilometres.

Cathédrale St Mammes.

Fri.

Launois-sur-Vence 15D2

Avenue Louis Jolly. **GPS**: n49,65467 e4,54005.

10 free. **Location:** Rural, simple, quiet. **Surface:** unpaved. 01/01-31/12

Distance: on the spot 50m.

Remarks: In front of tourist office, max. 48h.

FR

S Launois-sur-Vence 15D2

Rue du Thin. **GPS**: n49,65810 e4,53987.
€ 2/100liter Ch € 2/1h.
Remarks: Coins at Office de Tourisme.

Tourist information Launois-sur-Vence:
Relais de Poste.Monthly antiques and flea market. 3rd Su of the month 9-18h.

S Les Riceys 15C6

D452. **GPS**: n47,99222 e4,36458.

40 free € 2 Ch € 2. **Location:** Simple, isolated, quiet. **Surface:** asphalted. 01/01-31/12
Distance: 500m 500m 500m.

S Mareuil-sur-Ay 15C4

Relais nautique, Place Charles de Gaulle. **GPS**: n49,04522 e4,03490.

8 free Ch € 5/3h. **Location:** Urban, comfortable, central, quiet. **Surface:** asphalted. 01/01-31/12 water disconnected in winter.
Distance: on the spot on the spot on the spot on the spot on the spot.
Remarks: On the canal, coins at supermarket.

Mesnil-St.Père 15C6

Rue du Lac. **GPS**: n48,25524 e4,34090.

50 free. **Location:** Simple. **Surface:** asphalted. 01/01-31/12
Distance: beach 400m.
Remarks: Nearby lake Orient.

S Monthermé 15D1

Rue du Général de Gaulle, D989. **GPS**: n49,88278 e4,73000.

6 free € 3,80 Ch . **Location:** Rural, simple, quiet. **Surface:** grassy. 01/01-31/12
Distance: 100m on the spot 400m.
Remarks: Coins at town hall, office du tourisme, 2013: during inspection service out of order. On edge from village, dir D1 Rocroi follow.

S Montier-en-Der 15D5

Rue de l'Isle. **GPS**: n48,47861 e4,76861.

6 free € 2,60/8minutes Ch € 2,60/55minutes WC. **Location:** Simple. **Surface:** gravel.
Distance: on the spot 500m 500m.
Remarks: Coins at Tourist Info.

S Mouzon 15D2

Halte fluviale. **GPS**: n49,60687 e5,07710.
8 € 7,80, 01/11-31/03 free Ch WC included.
Surface: asphalted.
01/01-31/12 Service: winter.
Distance: 100m.
Remarks: Along the Meuse river, sanitary and wifi code at harbour master.

S Mutigny 15C3

Aire de l'étang, Route de Montflambert. **GPS**: n49,06894 e4,02669.

8 free € 5/100liter € 5/3h . **Location:** Rural, simple, isolated, quiet. **Surface:** asphalted. 01/01-31/12
Distance: 1km 3km 3km.

S Nogent-sur-Seine 15B5

Parking camping/piscine, Rue du camping. **GPS**: n48,50388 e3,50888.

FR

5 € 6,58/night, € 2,99/3h Chfree (2x)included3h. **Location:** Urban, simple, quiet. **Surface:** asphalted. 01/01-31/12
Distance: 1,5km 2km 1,5km 1,5km 2km.
Remarks: Max. 48h.

S Peigney 23A1

Lac de la Liez, D284, rue Côté de Recey. **GPS**: n47,87272 e5,38077.

8 € 10,50 Ch € 2. **Location:** Simple.
Surface: asphalted.
01/01-31/12
Distance: 500m on the spot on the spot on the spot on the spot.

S Piney 15C5

Place des Anciens Combattants, Rue du Général de Gaulle. **GPS**: n48,35878 e4,33442.

3 free € 3/10minutes Ch € 3/1h. **Location:** Simple.
Surface: metalled.
01/01-31/12 water: frost.
Distance: 500m 500m 500m.
Remarks: Coins at Office de Tourisme Mesnil-Plage and restaurant le Tadorne.

S Reims 15C3

Parc du CIS de la Comédie, Esplanade André Malraux, chaussée Bocquaine. **GPS**: n49,24881 e4,02110.

7 free Chfree. **Location:** Urban, simple, central, noisy.
Surface: metalled.
Distance: 15 min walking 1,4km 350m 100m.
Remarks: Max. 48h, noisy place, call for entrance code. A4, exit Reims-centre.

S Sapignicourt 15D5

Rue Deperthes à Larzicourt. **GPS**: n48,65111 e4,80583.

4 € 2,50/10minutes Ch € 2,50/55minutes. **Location:** Rural, simple, isolated, quiet. **Surface:** grassy.
Distance: 500m.
Remarks: Coins at mairie and Mr. Bauer, 14, grande rue.

Sedan 15D2

Rue Hue Tanton. **GPS**: n49,70145 e4,95092.
free. 01/01-31/12
Remarks: Parking places around the castle of Sedan.

S Sézanne 15B4

Place du Champ Benoist. **GPS**: n48,72222 e3,72125.

7 free € 2/100liter Ch € 2/1h WC free. **Location:** Urban, simple, central, noisy. **Surface:** asphalted.
01/01-31/12 Sa market.
Distance: on the spot 50m 300m 50m.

S St.Dizier 15D5

Centre Loisirs Caravanning, Route de Villiers en lieu. **GPS**: n48,64255 e4,91035.

6 free Ch WC free. **Location:** Simple. **Surface:** asphalted.
01/01-31/12
Distance: 1,5km 400m.
Remarks: Motorhome dealer, coins available during opening hours.

S Suippes 15D3

Rue de l'Abreuvoir. **GPS**: n49,13074 e4,53419.

10 free € 2/liter Ch € 2/1h . **Location:** Urban, simple.
Surface: asphalted. 01/01-31/12

FR

Distance: on the spot 200m 200m.

S Vendeuvre-sur-Barse 15C6

Place du 8 mai 1945, Rue du Pont Chevalier. **GPS**: n48,23727 e4,46646.

5 free €3 Ch €3. **Location:** Urban, simple, simple. **Surface:** asphalted.
Distance: 100m on the spot ATAC on the spot.

S Viéville 16A6

Halte Nautique La Licorne. **GPS**: n48,23825 e5,12988.

6 € 1,50 € 1,50/day (6x)€ 1,50/day. **Location:** Rural, simple, quiet.
Surface: gravel.
Distance: on the spot 3km 500m on the spot on the spot.

S Villeneuve-Renneville-Chevigny 15C4

Champagne Leclère-Massard, 12, rue du Plessis. **GPS**: n48,91488 e4,05959.

6 €5 Ch included € 2/day. **Location:** Comfortable.
Surface: asphalted.
Distance: 3km 2km 3km 3km on the spot.
Remarks: Champagne tastery, Tu-Su fresh bread.

S Villers-sous-Châtillon 15B3

Halte camping-cars, Rue du Parc. **GPS**: n49,09642 e3,80078.

5 free € 3/100liter Ch € 3/1h. **Location:** Rural, simple, quiet.
Surface: asphalted. 01/01-31/12
Distance: 1,2km 50m 1,2km 2km.
Remarks: Coins at town hall and restaurant du Commerce.

Lorraine

Ancerville 15D5

Impasse des Pransons. **GPS**: n48,63641 e5,01582.

2 free. **Location:** Urban, simple, quiet. **Surface:** metalled.
01/01-31/12
Distance: 400m 400m.

Avocourt 16A3

Restaurant La Terrasse, Rue du Moulin. **GPS**: n49,20417 e5,14227.
4 free. **Location:** Rural, simple. **Surface:** unpaved.
01/01-31/12

S Baccarat 16C5

Place du General Le'Clerc. **GPS**: n48,44667 e6,74000.

15 € 4/night € 2/100liter Ch € 2/3minutes WC. **Surface:** asphalted.
01/01-31/12 Fri-morning market.
Distance: 300m on the spot on the spot 300m 300m.
Remarks: Along river, max. 24h.

Tourist information Baccarat:

Office de Tourisme, 2, rue Adrien Michaut, www.ville-baccarat.fr.Important French crystal manufacture (not to visit). Many shops with crystal.

Musée du Cristal.Crystal museum. Mo-Sa 10-18h. € 2,50.

S Bar-le-Duc 16A4

Halte du port fluvial, Rue du débarcadère. **GPS**: n48,77536 e5,16654.

8 free € 2/100liter Ch € 2/55minutes.
Location: Urban, simple, noisy. **Surface:** asphalted.
01/01-31/12
Distance: on the spot on the spot 150m 150m 150m on the spot.
Remarks: On the canal, coins available at office de tourisme, 7 rue Jeanne d'Arc.

Beaulieu-en-Argonne 15D4

Parking Mairie, Grande Rue, D2B. **GPS**: n49,03183 e5,06665.

FR

6 free. **Location:** Urban, simple, central, quiet. **Surface:** asphalted.
01/01-31/12
Distance: on the spot 50m on the spot on the spot.
Remarks: In opposite of police station.

Beaulieu-en-Argonne 15D4

Parking St. Rouin, D2. **GPS**: n49,03554 e5,02975.

4 free. **Location:** Isolated. **Surface:** gravel.
Distance: Beaulieu 6km.
Remarks: Isolated parking.

Bruley 16B4

D118, rue Saint-Martin. **GPS**: n48,70640 e5,85554.

10 free € 3/10minutes Ch (2x)€ 3/8h. **Surface:** gravel.
01/01-31/12
Distance: 200m 300m 300m.

Bulgnéville 16B6

Étang des Récollets, Rue des Récollets. **GPS**: n48,20733 e5,83899.

10 € 3/24h Ch WC included. **Location:** Rural, luxurious, quiet.
Surface: asphalted.
15/04-31/12
Distance: 700m 1,8km on the spot on the spot 100m 700m.

Certilleux 16A5

Rue de l'Église. **GPS**: n48,31193 e5,72679.

8 free free. **Location:** Urban, simple. **Surface:** asphalted.
01/01-31/12
Distance: on the spot.
Remarks: Beautiful view.

Champougny 16A5

D145f. **GPS**: n48,54410 e5,69277.

3 free. **Location:** Rural, simple, quiet. **Surface:** grassy.
01/01-31/12
Distance: 200m 25m.

Charmes 16B5

Port de plaisance. **GPS**: n48,37334 e6,29542.

100 € 6 included Ch (80x)€ 2 WC € 1,50 € 3/day. **Surface:** gravel/metalled. 01/01-31/12. **Distance:** 1km 1,5km on the spot on the spot within walking distance.

Tourist information Charmes:

Motorhome friendly village on the Mosel river.
Fri-morning.

Commercy 16A4

Rue du Docteur Boyer. **GPS**: n48,76374 e5,59616.

4 free € 3/15minutes Ch (4x)€ 3/4h free.
Location: Comfortable. **Surface:** asphalted. 01/01-31/12
Distance: 800m on the spot on the spot 600m 100m.
Remarks: On the canal.

Contrisson 15D4

Ballastière. **GPS**: n48,80530 e4,94714.

FR

10 free WC. **Location:** Rural, simple, isolated, quiet. **Surface:** unpaved.
01/01-31/12
Distance: 800m 1km 1km.
Remarks: At small lake.

Damvillers 16A3

Rue de L'Ile d'Envie, D905. **GPS:** n49,33790 e5,39752.

4 free € 2/100liter Ch € 2. **Location:** Urban, simple, central.
Surface: asphalted. 01/01-31/12
Distance: on the spot on the spot on the spot.

Damvillers 16A3

Etang, D905. **GPS:** n49,34978 e5,39970.
10 free. **Location:** Isolated. **Surface:** grassy. 01/01-31/12
Distance: Damvillers 1km.

Dieue-sur-Meuse 16A3

Port de plaisance, Route des Dames. **GPS:** n49,07110 e5,42634.

15 free Ch free. **Location:** Rural, simple, quiet. **Surface:** gravel.
01/01-31/12
Distance: 200m on the spot on the spot 200m 200m.
Remarks: On the canal.

Dun-sur-Meuse 16A3

Rue du Vieux Port. **GPS:** n49,38919 e5,17787.

16 € 7 Ch (8x) WC included . **Location:** Rural, comfortable, central, quiet. **Surface:** gravel.
01/01-31/12 sanitary building: 1/11-1/4.
Distance: 600m on the spot on the spot 400m 600m.

Épinal 16C6

Port d'Épinal, Quai de Dogneville, D12. **GPS:** n48,18671 e6,44493.

5 summer € 5, winter € 8 Ch Service € 3/15min .
Surface: asphalted.
Distance: 1km 3,5km.
Remarks: Max. 48h.

Etain 16A3

Allée du champ de foire, D631. **GPS:** n49,20942 e5,63755.
6 free. **Location:** Simple, noisy. **Surface:** metalled.
01/01-31/12
Distance: on the spot 500m 500m.

Etival-Clairefontaine 16C5

Rue du Vivier. **GPS:** n48,36355 e6,86504.

20 free Ch free. **Surface:** asphalted.
01/01-31/12 water disconnected in winter.

Fains-Veel 15D4

Halte Fluviale, Rue du Stade. **GPS:** n48,79298 e5,12503.

2 free. **Location:** Simple, quiet. **Surface:** metalled.
01/01-31/12
Distance: 450m on the spot on the spot on the spot on the spot.

Favières 16B5

Base de Loisirs. GPS: n48,46660 e5,96124.

8 free € 2 Ch € 2 WC . **Location:** Rural, comfortable, central, quiet. **Surface:** gravel/metalled.

FR

Distance: 200m 13km on the spot on the spot on the spot bakery 300m on the spot on the spot.

S Fénétrange 16D4

Wally Services, Route de Sarre Union. **GPS**: n48,85365 e7,02723.
5 free € 2 Ch € 2. **Surface:** grassy/metalled.
Remarks: Max. 48h.

S Fraize 16D6

Impasse de la Gare/ Place Jean Sonrel. **GPS**: n48,18188 e7,00360.

6 free € 2 Ch € 2 WC. **Surface:** asphalted. 01/01-31/12
Distance: 100m 100m 100m.
Remarks: Behind Tourist Office.

S Gérardmer 16C6

Parking de la Prairie, Boulevard d' Alsace. **GPS**: n48,07173 e6,87296.

100 € 4 Ch WC free . **Surface:** asphalted/gravel. 01/01-31/12
Distance: on the spot.

Gérardmer 16C6

Chemin de la Rayée, La Mauselaine. **GPS**: n48,05846 e6,88862.

€ 4/24h. **Surface:** asphalted. 01/01-31/12
Distance: Gérardmer 1,7km.
Remarks: Parking at skipistes.

Tourist information Gérardmer:

Office de Tourisme, 4, Place des Déportés, www.gerardmer.net.Lively holiday destination on lake of same name, watersports in the summer several wintersports during winter, 20 ski runs.
Thu, Sa.

Gondrecourt-le-Château 16A5

Parking Musée du Cheval, Rue Saint Blaise. **GPS**: n48,51390 e5,50975.
2 free. **Surface:** metalled.
Distance: 50m 50m.

Gondrecourt-le-Château 16A5

Rue du Général Leclerc. **GPS**: n48,51373 e5,50386.
3 free. **Location:** Urban. **Surface:** unpaved. 01/01-31/12
Distance: on the spot.

S Haironville 15D4

GPS: n48,68438 e5,08586.

5 free € 2/10minutes Ch € 2/50minutes. **Location:** Rural, simple, central, quiet. **Surface:** gravel. 01/01-31/12
Distance: 200m 200m.
Remarks: Coins available at the shops.

S Heudicourt sous les Côtes 16A4

Ste Nautique de Madine. **GPS**: n48,93549 e5,71548.

50 first night € 10, € 7 each additional night Ch WC . **Location:** Rural, comfortable, quiet. **Surface:** grassy/gravel. 01/04-31/10
Distance: 3km on the spot on the spot on the spot.
Remarks: View on Lac de Madine.

Heudicourt sous les Côtes 16A4

Entrée 2, D133. **GPS**: n48,94035 e5,71741.

50 € 7. **Location:** Rural, simple, quiet. **Surface:** grassy.
01/04-31/10
Distance: 3km 100m 100m.
Remarks: Next to campsite.

Issoncourt 16A4

Parking Relais de la Voie Sacrée. **GPS**: n48,97070 e5,28776.

4 free. **Location:** Rural, simple, quiet. **Surface:** gravel.
Distance: 50m.

La Bresse 16D6

Route de Lispach. **GPS**: n48,04354 e6,93348.
free. **Surface:** unpaved. 01/01-31/12
Remarks: At cross-country skiing circuit.

FR

La Bresse 16D6

Camping Belle Hutte. GPS: n48,03500 e6,96268.

20 € 12,50-22,50 Ch WC against payment. **Surface:** grassy/gravel. 01/01-31/12

Distance: 9km 100m 500m.

Remarks: Summertime on campsite, wintertime in front of campsite.

La Bresse 16D6

Camping du Haut Des Bluches, 5, route des Planches. **GPS:** n48,00005 e6,91718.

18 € 5 12.00-12.00h Ch WC included.
01/01-31/12 05/11-14/12.

Remarks: Zone camping-car.

La Bresse 16D6

Route de Niachamp. **GPS:** n47,99430 e6,85431.
€ 2/100liter Ch. 01/01-31/12

La Croix-sur-Meuse 16A4

Auberge de la Truite, Route de Seuzey. **GPS:** n48,98267 e5,53393.

4 free (4x)€ 3/24h WC . **Location:** Rural, comfortable, quiet. **Surface:** grassy. 01/01-31/12

Distance: 2km on the spot on the spot.

Lachaussée 16B4

Domaine du Vieux Moulin, Grande Rue. **GPS:** n49,03507 e5,81735.
4 . **Location:** Rural, simple. **Surface:** gravel.

Distance: 100m 50m on the spot.

Remarks: Along Étang de Lachaussée.

Laheycourt 15D4

Rue de la Gare. **GPS:** n48,88903 e5,02165.

3 free. **Location:** Rural, simple, quiet. **Surface:** grassy/gravel.
01/01-31/12

Distance: on the spot 50m 50m.

Remarks: Along the Chée river.

Les Islettes 15D3

Route du Lochères. **GPS:** n49,12122 e5,03684.

16 € 5/24h € 1 Ch € 1 WC . **Location:** Rural, comfortable. **Surface:** gravel. 01/01-31/12

Distance: 3km 10,5km 3km 3km.

Ligny-en-Barrois 16A4

Relais Nautique, Rue Jean Willemert. **GPS:** n48,68787 e5,31943.

10 free € 2/80liter Ch € 2/50minutes. **Location:** Comfortable, central, quiet. **Surface:** asphalted.

Distance: on the spot on the spot 50m 50m on the spot on the spot.

Remarks: Along Canal de la Marne au Rhin.

Loison 16A3

Parking Camp Marguerre. GPS: n49,28962 e5,56737.

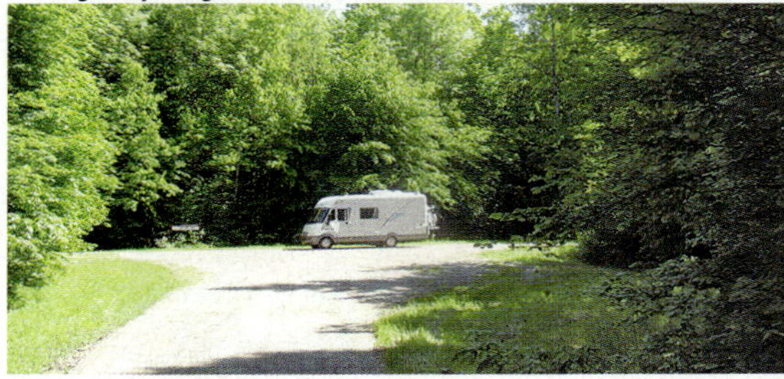

6 free. **Location:** Rural, simple, isolated.

Remarks: Isolated parking, Camp Marguerre: militair erfgoed '14-18.

Longeville-en-Barrois 16A4

Gr Grande Rue. **GPS:** n48,74201 e5,20645.

FR

10 free. **Location:** Urban, simple, quiet. **Surface:** gravel.
Distance: on the spot 100m 100m on the spot on the spot.
Remarks: Along the Ornain river.

S Longuyon 16A3

Parking Salvador Allende, N18. **GPS**: n49,44802 e5,59973.

2 free Ch WC.
Location: Urban, simple, central, noisy.
Surface: asphalted.
Distance: on the spot on the spot 100m.
Remarks: Parking next to Office du Tourisme, not suitable for big motorhomes.

S Lunéville 16C5

Les Bosquets, Chemin de la Ménagerie. **GPS**: n48,59652 e6,49865.
13 € 5 Ch included.

Tourist information Lunéville:
Château Petit Versailles.Castle, 18th century and museum.
10-12h, 14-18h Tue.

Marbotte 16A4

Parking de la Mairie, Rue Principale, D12. **GPS**: n48,83445 e5,58142.

2 free. **Location:** Simple, quiet. **Surface:** unpaved.
Distance: on the spot.

S Maxey-sur-Meuse 16A5

GPS: n48,44861 e5,69500.

4 free (4x)free. **Location:** Simple. **Surface:** gravel. 14/05-31/12
Distance: 2km 2km 500m.

Maxey-sur-Vaise 16A5

Gr Grande Rue. **GPS**: n48,53836 e5,66705.

6 free. **Location:** Simple, central, quiet.
01/01-31/12
Distance: on the spot.

S Metz 16B3

Allée Metz Plage. **GPS**: n49,12371 e6,16887.

8 free Chfree. **Surface:** asphalted.
Distance: 350m 1,5km 300m.
Remarks: At entrance campsite, max. 48h, inclining pitches.

Tourist information Metz:
Office de Tourisme, 2, place d'Armes, tourisme.mairie-metz.fr.Industrial city with old interesting centre.
Église St Pierre-aux-Nonnains.One of the oldest French churches.
Place St Louis.Square surrounded by houses from the 14th century.
Musée de la Cour d'Or.Collection of ceramics.
10-17h, Sa-Su 11-17h Tue, holiday. € 4,60.
Cathédrale St Etienne.Cathedral.
Fonds Saint Martin, Rombas.Climbing wall.
Zoo, Amnéville.Zoo. 01/04-30/09 9.30-19.30h, 01/10-31/03 10h-sunset.

S Millery 16B4

Avenue de la Moselle, D40. **GPS**: n48,81507 e6,12716.

20 free Chfree. **Surface:** asphalted.
01/04-31/10 water: 01/11-31/03.
Distance: on the spot 3,5km.
Remarks: Along Mosel.

S Monthureux-sur Saône 16B6

D460. **GPS**: n48,03199 e5,97390.

FR

8 free Ch WC free € 3/48h, WiÒ-Stop. **Location:** Comfortable, quiet.
01/01-31/12
Distance: on the spot on the spot 200m 75m.
Remarks: At football ground.

Montigny-lès-Vaucouleurs 16A5

Rue de la Côte. **GPS**: n48,58875 e5,63007.

10 free. **Location:** Rural, simple, quiet. **Surface:** gravel.
01/01-31/12
Distance: 700m.

Montplonne 16A4

Rue du Four. **GPS**: n48,68630 e5,16934.

4 free. **Location:** Rural, simple. **Surface:** gravel.

Morley 16A5

Parking Lavoir, D5A. **GPS**: n48,57848 e5,24878.

5 free.
Location: Rural, simple, central, quiet.

Nancy 16B4

Port Saint Georges, N57, boulevard du 21ème Régiment d'Aviation. **GPS**: n48,69221 e6,19318.

6 € 10/night Ch WC included. **Surface:** asphalted.
01/05-01/11
Distance: 500m on the spot on the spot 100m 100m 100m.
Remarks: Max. 5 nights, check in at harbourmaster.

Nancy 16B4

Parking Faubourg les III Maisons, Rue Charles Keller. **GPS**: n48,70403 e6,17598.

€ 0,50-3,50. **Surface:** asphalted. 01/01-31/12
Distance: city centre ± 1km.

Tourist information Nancy:

Office de Tourisme, Place Stanislas, www.ot-nancy.fr.Art city, old capital of the Dukes of Lorraine.
Musée Historique Lorraine, Palais Ducal.Regional museum.
15/06-15/09 Tue.
Muséum Aquarium de Nancy, 34 rue Sainte-Catherine.Museum with a tropical aquarium.
Zoo Haye, Velaine-en-Haye.Zoo with centre for wild birds.

Nant-le-Grand 16A4

Grand Rue, D169A. **GPS**: n48,67530 e5,22382.

4 free. **Location:** Rural, simple, central, quiet.
Surface: gravel.
Distance: on the spot.

Niderviller 16D4

Marina Niderviller, Avenue de Lorraine. **GPS**: n48,71748 e7,09901.
12 € 10 € 1/100liter Ch € 0,50/kWh.

Nonsard Lamarche 16B4

Base de Loisirs, Base de Loisirs de Madine. **GPS**: n48,93064 e5,74873.

FR

30 € 7 € 3 Ch. **Location:** Rural, simple, isolated, quiet.
Surface: grassy/metalled. 01/04-31/10
Distance: 700m on the spot on the spot on the spot.
Remarks: At lake Madine, coins at campsite.

Nubécourt 16A4

D151, Rue Raymond Poincaré. **GPS:** n48,99704 e5,17256.

10 free. **Location:** Rural, simple, central, quiet. **Surface:** metalled.
01/01-31/12
Distance: on the spot 200m on the spot on the spot.

S Phalsbourg 16D4

Avia, ZAC Louvois, Route du Luxembourg. **GPS:** n48,77047 e7,24198.
free € 2 Ch € 2. **Surface:** asphalted. 01/01-31/12
Distance: on the spot.

Pierre-Percée 16C5

D182A. **GPS:** n48,46723 e6,92911.

± 8 free. **Surface:** asphalted.
Distance: on the spot on the spot.
Remarks: Picnic area at artificial lake.

S Plombières-les-Bains 16C6

Avenue des Etats-Unis. **GPS:** n47,96208 e6,45411.

6 € 4/24h (5x)included. **Surface:** asphalted. 01/04-15/10

S Pompierre 16A6

Chemin de la Corvée. **GPS:** n48,25691 e5,67188.

3 free free. **Location:** Urban, simple, noisy. **Surface:** asphalted.
01/01-31/12
Distance: 1km 500m 500m.

S Pont-à-Mousson 16B4

Port de plaisance, Avenue des Etas Unis, D910. **GPS:** n48,90296 e6,06088.

42 € 8 Ch WC included. **Location:** Luxurious.
Surface: asphalted. 01/04-31/10
Distance: 400m 3,4km on the spot 400m 400m
on the spot.
Remarks: Check in at reception.

S Rebeuville 16A5

Rue du Cougnot. **GPS:** n48,33530 e5,70128.

3 free Ch free. **Location:** Rural, comfortable, isolated.
Surface: asphalted. 01/01-31/12
Distance: 5km on the spot 5km 5km 500m.

S Revigny-sur-Ornain 15D4

Stade/Office de Tourisme, Rue de l'Abattoir. **GPS:** n48,82642 e4,98330.

2 free € 3 Ch € 3. **Location:** Urban, simple, central, quiet.
Surface: asphalted. 01/01-31/12
Distance: on the spot 100m on the spot on the spot
on the spot.

S Rhodes 16C4

Port Municipal, Rue Principale. **GPS:** n48,75784 e6,90053.
30 € 15/24h Ch WC included. **Surface:** grassy.
Easter-01/10

FR

Distance: on the spot on the spot.
Remarks: Along Etang du Stock.

Richardmenil 16B5

Rue de Lac. **GPS**: n48,59457 e6,16078.

5 free Ch (4x)free. **Surface:** asphalted. 01/01-31/12
Distance: 1km on the spot on the spot 500m 1km 1km.

Rollainville 16B5

Rue de la Cure. **GPS**: n48,36185 e5,73842.

1 free free. **Location:** Urban, simple, central. **Surface:** asphalted.
01/01-31/12
Distance: on the spot.
Remarks: Baker every morning at 8am.

FR

Rupt-sur-Moselle 16C6

Quai de la Parelle. **GPS**: n47,92061 e6,66194.

6 free € 3/10minutes Ch (4x)€ 3/3h WC. **Surface:** asphalted.
Distance: 350m on the spot Voie Verte.
Remarks: Coins available at the shops and town hall.

Saint-Nicolas-de-Port 16B5

Rue du jeu de Paune. **GPS**: n48,63515 e6,30048.

10 free € 1 Ch € 1/1h (2x). **Location:** Urban, simple, central, quiet. **Surface:** gravel. 01/01-31/12
Distance: on the spot 150m 200m 100m.

Seuil-d'Argonne 15D4

Rue du Commandant Laflotte, D2/D20. **GPS**: n48,98294 e5,06215.

5 free. **Location:** Urban, simple, quiet. **Surface:** gravel.
01/01-31/12
Distance: 650m 650m 650m 650m.
Remarks: In fron of sports fields.

Souilly 16A4

Route de St.André-en-Barrois, D159. **GPS**: n49,02730 e5,27985.
6 free. **Surface:** gravel. 01/01-31/12
Distance: 600m.

Souslosse sous St.Elophe 16B5

Square Guy Bellamy. **GPS**: n48,40953 e5,73886.

3 free Chfree. **Location:** Rural, simple. **Surface:** gravel.
01/01-31/12
Distance: 500m.

St.Mihiel 16A4

Chemin Gué Rapeau. **GPS**: n48,90227 e5,53960.

4 € 3 Chfree € 3/24h. **Location:** Rural, simple, isolated, quiet.
Surface: asphalted. 01/01-31/12
Distance: 1,5km 1km 1,5km.
Remarks: Directly beside river, nearby sluices, next to campsite municipal, max. 24h.

Tourist information St.Mihiel:
Office de Tourisme, Rue du Palais de Justice.

St.Nabord 16C6

Rue de la Croix Saint Jacques. **GPS**: n48,04527 e6,58175.

3 free € 3/80liter Ch € 3. **Surface:** gravel. 01/01-31/12

Distance: 300m 200m 50m.

S Stenay 16A2

Aire Camping-car, D947. **GPS**: n49,48979 e5,18323.

47 €8 Ch WC €4,dryer €4 included. **Location:** Rural, comfortable, quiet. **Surface:** metalled. 01/01-31/12
Distance: 150m 150m 800m, bakery 300m.
Remarks: Pay and entrance code at harbourmaster, Musée Européen de la Bière, beer museum.

S Stenay 16A2

Port de plaisance, Rue du Port. **GPS**: n49,49096 e5,18312.

6 €8 Ch WC €4,dryer €4 included. **Location:** Comfortable, quiet. **Surface:** asphalted. 01/01-31/12
Distance: on the spot 200m 500m.
Remarks: Pay at harbourmaster.

Tourist information Stenay:
Office de Tourisme, Place Raymond Poincaré 5.
Musée de la Bière.Beer museum.
Château, Louppy-sur-Loison.Renaissance castle, 17th century.

Tannois 16A4

Parking du Belvédère, D169. **GPS**: n48,71977 e5,22967.

10 free. **Location:** Rural, simple, isolated, quiet. **Surface:** gravel.
01/01-31/12
Distance: 1,3km 1,5km on the spot on the spot.
Remarks: Isolated parking.

S Thaon-les-Vosges 16C6

Aire du Coignot, Rue du Coignot. **GPS**: n48,24889 e6,42611.

20 free Ch free. **Surface:** asphalted/gravel. 01/03-01/10
Distance: 1,5km 400m.
Remarks: Next to port fluvial.

Thierville-sur-Meuse 16A3

Thierville sur-meuse, Avenue de l,etangbleu. **GPS**: n49,17499 e5,36357.

20 free. **Location:** Rural, simple, central.
01/01-31/12
Distance: 100m 50m 50m.
Remarks: Along the Meuse river.

S Tilleux 16A5

Grande Rue. **GPS**: n48,29300 e5,72250.

8 free free. **Location:** Simple. **Surface:** gravel.
01/01-31/12
Distance: 100m.
Remarks: Entrance road max. 3,5t, inclining pitches.

S Toul 16B4

Avenue du Colonel Péchot. **GPS**: n48,67939 e5,88806.

9 €7 Ch (8x)included. **Surface:** asphalted. 01/01-31/12
Distance: 4km.
Remarks: In opposite of police station.

Tourist information Toul:
Office de Tourisme, Parvis de la Cathédrale, www.toul.fr.8-angular fortress city.
Salle Lapidaire du musée d'art et d'histoire de Toul, Chapelle de l'ancienne Maison-Dieu XIIIe siècle.Medieval ceramics and earthenware.

FR

Basilique Saint-Nicolas-de Port.Basilica, 16th century, place of pilgrimage for Saint Nicolas.
Cathédrale Saint Etienne.Cathedral, 13-16th century.

S Vaucouleurs 16A5

Rue du Cardinal Lépicier. **GPS**: n48,60179 e5,66737.

3 €5 €2/100liter Ch €2 WC. **Location:** Urban, simple, central. **Surface:** asphalted. 01/01-31/12
Distance: on the spot 500m 500m.

Vauquois 15D3

Parking municipal, D212. **GPS**: n49,20405 e5,07398.

8 free. **Location:** Rural, simple. **Surface:** gravel.
Distance: on the spot.

Velaines 16A4

D120A. **GPS**: n48,70589 e5,29804.

4 free. **Location:** Simple, central. **Surface:** gravel.
Distance: on the spot.

Ventron 16C6

Route de Frère Joseph. **GPS**: n47,92495 e6,86364.
free. **Surface:** asphalted. 01/01-31/12
Distance: Ventron 3,2km on the spot.
Remarks: Parking at skipistes.

Verdun 16A3

Dragées Braquir, Rue du Fort de Vaux, D112. **GPS**: n49,15955 e5,39989.

10 free. **Location:** Urban, simple, central.
Surface: metalled.

Remarks: Max. 1 night.

S Void-Vacon 16A4

Rue de la Gare. **GPS**: n48,68240 e5,61960.

20 free €2/100liter Ch €2. **Location:** Rural, simple, isolated, quiet.
Surface: grassy/gravel. 01/01-31/12
Distance: 700m 10m 10m.
Remarks: Coins at shop/town hall.

Alsace

S Benfeld 17A5

Concessionnaire CLC Alsace, 9, Rue de Hollande, RN83 dir Strasbourg-Colmar.
GPS: n48,37772 e7,59778.
5 free Ch free. **Surface:** gravel/metalled. 01/01-31/12
Distance: 2km 2km 2km.
Remarks: Motorhome dealer.

S Bourbach-le-Haut 23D1

Route Joffre. **GPS**: n47,79463 e7,02868.

5 €5 Ch included. **Surface:** asphalted. 15/03-15/11
Distance: 50m 100m 100m 5km.
Remarks: Nearby kindergarten.

S Chavannes-sur-l'Etang 23D1

Aire pique-nique La Porte d'Alsace, RD419, Rue d'Alsace. **GPS**: n47,63325 e7,01858.

15 €5 (19.00-09.00) Ch WC free. **Surface:** asphalted.
01/01-31/12
Distance: 900m 1km.
Remarks: Parking picnic area, information: 16-19h.

Colmar 16D6

Rue de la Cavalerie/Rue des Brasseries. **GPS**: n48,08218 e7,35990.

FR

20 € 2,40/4h, overnight stay free. **Surface:** asphalted.
Distance: 200m on the spot on the spot on the spot.

Tourist information Colmar:
Office de Tourisme, 4, rue des Unterlinden, www.ot-colmar.fr.Old city with historical centre.

Eguisheim 16D6

Bannwarth, Rue de Bruxelles 3. **GPS**: n48,04434 e7,30539.

6 free Ch free.
Surface: metalled.
Distance: 100m.
Remarks: On entering the village follow 'Poids Lourds', 3rd road on the right.

Ferrette 23D1

Route de Lucelle. **GPS**: n47,48882 e7,31118.

4 free € 2/10minutes Ch € 2/55minutes. **Surface:** asphalted.
Distance: 700m 2km 2km.

Fessenheim 16D6

Allée de la Guyane. **GPS**: n47,91833 e7,53139.

30 free € 2 Ch € 2. **Surface:** asphalted. 01/01-31/12
Distance: 700m 700m 200m.
Remarks: Coins available at swimming pool, supermarket.

Guebwiller 16D6

Avenue Maréchal Foch. **GPS**: n47,90554 e7,21869.

free. **Surface:** gravel/metalled. 01/01-31/12
Distance: 300m on the spot 300m 300m 300m 5km.

Tourist information Guebwiller:
Office de Tourisme, Hôtel de Ville, 73, rue de la République, www.ville-guebwiller.fr.Industrial city with textile industry.

Guewenheim 23D1

Le Doller. **GPS**: n47,75612 e7,09855.

10 free € 3,50 Ch WC . **Surface:** gravel.
01/01-31/12
Distance: 2km 1km 2km 2km.

Harskirchen 16D4

Port de Plaisance, Rue de Bissert. **GPS**: n48,93930 e7,02759.
2 € 6 Ch included. **Surface:** gravel. 15/03-15/11
Remarks: At canal Houillères de la Sarre.

Heiligenstein 16D5

Lieu-dit Lindel, D35. **GPS**: n48,42234 e7,45147.

3 free. **Surface:** gravel. 01/01-31/12
Distance: 800m 300m 500m.
Remarks: Hiking trails and wine tasting.

Tourist information Heiligenstein:
Village in wine-growing region.

Kaysersberg 16D6

Aire Camping-car P1, Rue du 18 Décembre 1944. **GPS**: n48,13565 e7,26325.

FR

80 € 2/day, € 4/night Ch WC free. **Surface:** asphalted. 01/01-31/12
Distance: 300m 300m 300m.
Remarks: Wifi at Office de Tourisme.

Tourist information Kaysersberg:
Office de Tourisme, 39 rue du Gal de Gaulle, www.kaysersberg.com.City with half-timbered houses in a wine region.
Musée Albert Schweitzer.The life of Albert Schweitzer.

Lautenbach 16D6

Parking Vivarium, Rue du Moulin, Lautenbachzell. **GPS**: n47,94167 e7,14972.

10 free. **Surface:** grassy/metalled. 01/01-31/12
Distance: 1km on the spot on the spot 1km 1km on the spot 5km 5km.

Le Bonhomme 16D6

Col du Bonhomme, D148, route des Crêtes. **GPS**: n48,16495 e7,07971.

free. **Surface:** gravel.
Distance: on the spot.

Michelbach 23D1

Salle des polyvalente, Rue Principale. **GPS**: n47,75800 e7,11000.

5 free. **Surface:** metalled. 01/01-31/12
Distance: 250m 2km 2km 1km 1km.
Remarks: Behind community centre.

Mittelbergheim 16D5

Parking Zotzenberg. **GPS**: n48,39869 e7,44194.

4 free. **Surface:** asphalted.

Distance: 300m 3,1km 300m 300m.
Remarks: Hiking trails and wine tasting.

Munster 16D6

Place de la salle des Fêtes. **GPS**: n48,03944 e7,13944.

8 free. **Surface:** asphalted.
01/01-31/12
Distance: 300m 300m 300m on the spot.

Murbach 16D6

Abbaye de Murbach, Rue de Guebwiller. **GPS**: n47,92321 e7,16059.

20 free Ch . **Surface:** gravel/metalled. 01/01-31/12
Distance: 350m on the spot on the spot 500m 5km.

Obernai 16D5

Parking des Remparts, Rue Poincaré. **GPS**: n48,45972 e7,48667.

12 free. **Surface:** gravel. 01/01-31/12
Distance: 300m 2,7km 300m 300m 200m.
Remarks: Large parking in centre.

Obernai 16D5

Camping municipal Le Vallon de l'Ehn, 1, rue de Berlin. **GPS**: n48,46471 e7,46757.
€ 2 Ch. 01/01-31/12

Tourist information Obernai:
Office de Tourisme, Place du Beffroi, www.obernai.fr.

Oltingue 23D1

Place Saint Martin. **GPS**: n47,49158 e7,39068.

3 free € 2/10minutes Ch € 2/55minutes. **Surface:** asphalted.
01/01-31/12
Distance: 100m 200m.

Orbey 16D6

Hôtel Restaurant Les Terrasses du Lac Blanc. GPS: n48,13540 e7,08957.

8 € 5 included Ch (8x)€ 2,50. **Surface:** grassy/gravel.
Distance: 500m 500m on the spot.
Remarks: Customers free.

Tourist information Orbey:
Pisciculture, La Blanc et Noir.Information centre about fish/trout.
01/03-31/10 10-12h, 14-18h.

Orschwir 16D6

Rue de la Source. **GPS:** n47,93722 e7,23083.

4 free Ch € 4,10. **Surface:** asphalted. 01/01-31/12
Distance: 200m 200m 500m.

Pfaffenheim 16D6

Aire du Winzerhof, Rue de la Tuilerie. **GPS:** n47,98639 e7,29167.

5 free € 3 Ch (5x)€ 2 WC. **Surface:** gravel/metalled.
01/01-31/12
Distance: 400m 400m 500m.

Ribeauvillé 16D6

Route de Guémar. **GPS:** n48,19231 e7,32867.

15 € 1,50/5h, € 1,50/night € 2 Ch. **Surface:** gravel.
01/01-31/12
Distance: 400m on the spot on the spot.

Remarks: Next to Cave de Ribeauvillé.

Tourist information Ribeauvillé:
Office de Tourisme, 1 Grand' Rue.Town on the Alsace wine road.
Sa.

Riquewihr 16D6

Avenue Jacques Présis. **GPS:** n48,16608 e7,30175.

6 € 2/3h, € 4/night € 2 Ch € 2. **Surface:** asphalted.
01/01-31/12
Distance: 200m 200m 200m.
Remarks: Parking on entering the village, <7m.

Tourist information Riquewihr:
Office de Tourisme, Rue de 1ère Armée.Picturesque street with houses of the 16th century.

Saverne 16D4

Rue des Emouleurs. **GPS:** n48,74512 e7,36854.
free. 01/01-31/12
Distance: centre 650m.

Saverne 16D4

Rue du Père Liebermann. **GPS:** n48,73131 e7,35504.
Chfree. 01/04-30/09
Remarks: In front of campsite.

Tourist information Saverne:
Office de Tourisme, 37 Grand' Rue, voetgangerzône, www.ot-saverne.fr.Small touristic town with half-timbered houses on the border of nature reserve Vosges du Nord.
Château de Rohan.Museum, former summer residence of the bishops of Strasbourg.

Soufflenheim 17A4

Rue des Menuisiers. **GPS:** n48,82940 e7,95395.

3 free € 2 Ch € 2. **Surface:** asphalted. 01/01-31/12
Distance: 300m 200m 300m 200m.

Soultz 16D6

Rue de la Marne. **GPS:** n47,88806 e7,23139.

30 free Ch. **Surface:** asphalted. 01/01-31/12
Distance: 500m 500m 500m 500m 500m.
Remarks: Payment only by bank card.

FR

Ste.Marie-aux-Mines 16D6

Place des Tisserands. **GPS**: n48,24700 e7,18322.

4 free. **Surface:** asphalted. 01/01-31/12
Distance: 300m 300m 300m.
Remarks: Max. 24h.

Tourist information Ste.Marie-aux-Mines:
Office de Tourisme, 86, rue Wilson, www.tourisme.fr/office-de-tourisme/sainte-marie-aux-mines-68.htm.Mineral city with silvermine, Mine d'Argent Sainte-Barthélemy.

S Strasbourg 17A5

Parking Auberge de Jeunesse des Deux Rives (Parc du Rhin), Rue des Cavaliers. **GPS**: n48,56659 e7,79975.

20 free € 2,50/100liter Ch € 2,50/1h. **Surface:** gravel.
01/01-31/12
Distance: Strasbourg centre 5km bus 21 + tram.

Tourist information Strasbourg:
Office de Tourisme, 17, Place de la Cathédrale, www.ot-strasbourg.fr.City with a rich history and worth seeing centre.
Maison Kammerzell.Restaurant, 1467-1589, one of the most beautyfull half-timbered houses in the Alsace region.
Musée Alsacien.Folk art and handycrafts.
Cathédrale de Nôtre-Dame.

S Thann 23D1

Place du Bungert, Rue des Pélerins. **GPS**: n47,81159 e7,10450.

10 free Ch free. **Surface:** asphalted.
01/01-31/12 Sa-morning market.
Distance: 600m on the spot 500m 500m 500m.

S Thann 23D1

Rue du Général de Gaulle. N66. **GPS**: n47,80889 e7,10460.
30 free Ch Service € 4. **Location:** Noisy. **Surface:** asphalted.
01/01-31/12
Distance: 250m 50m 50m.

S Trois Épis 16D6

Place des Antonins. **GPS**: n48,10101 e7,22948.

25 free € 2 Ch WC € 1. **Surface:** asphalted. 01/01-31/12
Distance: 150m 150m 150m.

Turckheim 16D6

Quai de la gare. **GPS**: n48,08555 e7,27739.

6 free. **Location:** Noisy. **Surface:** metalled. 01/01-31/12
Distance: historical centre 250m 250m 300m on the spot.

S Turckheim 16D6

Camping municipal Les Cigognes, 4, quai de la Gare. **GPS**: n48,08539 e7,27535.
€ 5,40 Ch. 15/03-31/10

S Ungersheim 16D6

Ecomusée. **GPS**: n47,85200 e7,28400.

20 € 5,50 included. **Surface:** gravel/metalled. 01/01-31/12
Distance: 6km.

Tourist information Ungersheim:
Ecomusée d'Alsace.Largest open air museum of France.
01/03-31/12 10-17/18h.

S Villefranche-sur-Saône 22D5

Camping-car Park, 2788 Route de Riottier. **GPS**: n45,97278 e4,75135.
128 € 12 Ch included. **Location:** Urban, luxurious.
15/05-15/09
Distance: A6 1,3km Station > Lyon 3,4km.
Remarks: Wifi code: 692712.

S Westhalten 16D6

Rue St Blaise, D18, Vallée Noble, dir Soultzmatt.. **GPS**: n47,95189 e7,26389.

6 free € 2 Ch € 2. **Surface:** asphalted. 01/03-30/11
Distance: nearby nearby on the spot.
Remarks: Max. 48h.

Willer-sur-Thur 23D1

Place de l'Eglise. **GPS**: n47,84315 e7,07292.

3 free Chfree. **Surface:** asphalted. 01/01-31/12
Distance: 250m 500m 500m, bakery 50m 500m 500m.

Normandie

Agon-Coutainville 13B3

Flot Bleu Park, Boulevard Louis Lebel-Jéhenne. **GPS**: n49,05176 w1,59123.

25 € 6/24h Ch included . **Surface:** grassy.
01/01-31/12
Distance: 800m.
Remarks: Service only € 2,50.

Angiens 14B1

Aire de Château d'Iclon, Impasse des Roseaux. **GPS**: n49,84390 e0,81945.

10 € 5 + € 1/pp Chincluded € 3. **Surface:** grassy/gravel.
01/01-31/12
Distance: 3km.

Ardevon 13B4

La Bidonnière, Route de la Rive 5. **GPS**: n48,60352 w1,47612.

66 € 10/24h Ch € 2/6h WC € 2/4minutes .
Surface: metalled. 01/01-31/12
Distance: 4km 3km.

Remarks: View on Mont-Saint-Michel.

Arromanches-les-Bains 13C2

Rue François Carpentier. **GPS**: n49,33904 w0,62553.

14 free € 2/10minutes Ch € 2/1h free15minutes.
Surface: asphalted. 01/01-31/12
Distance: 150m 100m 100m 250m.
Remarks: Next to campsite municipal.

Arromanches-les-Bains 13C2

Arromanches 360, Cinéma Circulaire, Chemin du Calvaire / D514. **GPS**: n49,33924 w0,61419.

20 € 6. **Location:** Rural, comfortable.
01/01-31/12
Distance: 400m 300m.
Remarks: Beautiful view.

Auffay 14B2

Place de Bleckede. **GPS**: n49,71755 e1,10055.

6 free € 3/100liter Ch. **Surface:** asphalted. 01/01-31/12
Distance: on the spot 100m 100m.

Avranches 13B4

Centre Culturel, Boulevard Jozeau Marigné. **GPS**: n48,68585 w1,367.

8 free € 2 Ch. **Surface:** metalled. 01/01-31/12
Distance: 200m 1,9km 200m 200m.
Remarks: Behind community centre, max. 1 night.

Tourist information Avranches:

Office de Tourisme, 2, rue Général de Gaulle, www.ville-avranches.fr.

FR

Jardins des Plantes.Garden with exotic plants.
Musée Bibliothèque.Manuscripts from the files of Mont Saint Michel.
Basilique St Germain. 9-12h, 14-16h.
place des Halles. Sa + Tue-morning.

Bagnoles-de-l'Orne 13C4

D235. **GPS**: n48,55821 w0,4129.

6 free. **Surface:** gravel. 01/01-31/12
Distance: on the spot.
Remarks: Behind Office de Tourisme, Place du Marché.
Tourist information Bagnoles-de-l'Orne:
Office de Tourisme, Place du Marché, www.bagnoles-de-lorne.com.Thermal centre.

Barfleur (50) 13B2

Route Alfred Rossel, D1. **GPS**: n49,66998 w1,26355.

8 free Ch WC. **Surface:** metalled.
Distance: 200m.

Barneville-Carteret 13A2

Quai Émile Valmy, rue du port. **GPS**: n49,37300 w1,789.

free. **Surface:** asphalted.
Remarks: In front of the Gare Maritime.

Barneville-Carteret 13A2

Carrefour, Route du Pont Rose. **GPS**: n49,38553 w1,75239.

180 free € 2 Ch € 2. 01/01-31/12
Distance: 300m on the spot centre.

Bayeux 13C3

Place Gauquelin-Despallières. **GPS**: n49,28044 w0,70775.

5 free Ch WC free. **Location:** Urban. **Surface:** asphalted. 01/01-31/12
Distance: on the spot 100m 100m on the spot.
Remarks: Max. 12h.
Tourist information Bayeux:
Office de Tourisme, Pont Saint Jean, www.bayeux-tourism.com.Medival city with half-timbered houses and small inner courts.
Centre Guillaume-le-Conquerant.Tapisserie de la Reine Mathilde, tapestry of 70m long.
Musée Memorial 1944.Battle of Normandy, June 6 till August 22, 1944.
9.30-17h, 01/05-30/09 9-19h.
Cathédrale Nôtre Dame.Gothic cathedral.

Beauvoir 13B4

Aire de camping-car du mont St Michel, Route de Mont St Michel. **GPS**: n48,59326 w1,51335.

122 € 12,50 Ch (122x)included free. **Location:** Rural, comfortable, luxurious, quiet. **Surface:** gravel. 01/01-31/12
Distance: 500m 500m.
Remarks: Le Mont Saint Michel 5km.

Beauvoir 13B4

La Ferme Saint Michel, Route du Mont Saint Michel, D976. **GPS**: n48,61112 w1,50978.

35 guests free Ch at restaurant. **Surface:** gravel. 01/01-31/12
Mo.
Distance: 600m on the spot 600m.

Beuvron-en-Auge 13D3

Parking de la Gare, Avenue de la Gare. **GPS**: n49,18560 w0,0495.

FR

16 € 6 Ch included. **Location:** Rural, comfortable, quiet.
Surface: gravel. 01/01-31/12
Distance: 200m on the spot on the spot.
Remarks: Pay and coins at Tabac-Presse 200m.

S Bréhal 13B3

Rue des Pierres Foucard. **GPS**: n48,89818 w1,56626.

25 € 3/24h Ch WC free. **Surface:** asphalted. 01/01-31/12
Distance: 300m beach 150m 400m 400m.

S Bretteville-sur-Odon 13D3

Camping-car service, 4-6 Avenue des Carrières. **GPS**: n49,18449 w0,41465.

6 free Ch free. **Location:** Urban, simple. **Surface:** metalled.
01/01-31/12
Distance: 1km 500m.

S Bréville-les-Monts 13D3

Rue des Dentellières. **GPS**: n49,24167 w0,228.

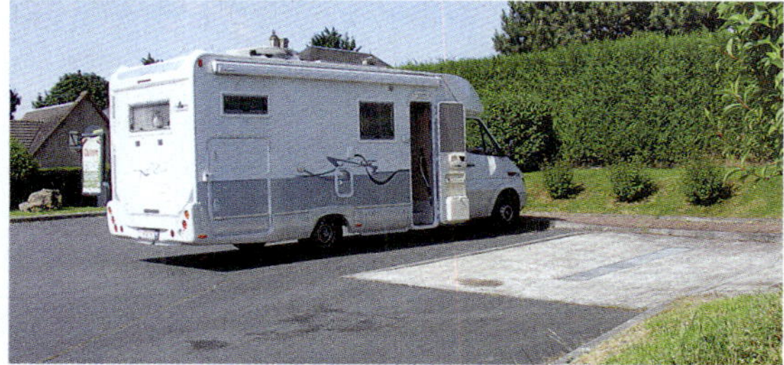

4 free € 2/10minutes Ch. **Location:** Simple, comfortable.
Surface: asphalted. 01/03-15/11
Distance: on the spot.
Remarks: Max. 72h, (may-july-aug) 48h, Coins at Office du Tourisme Merville and harbour.

S Bricquebec 13B2

Bas de Cattigny, D900, route de Cherbourg. **GPS**: n49,47402 w1,64674.

6 free Ch free. **Surface:** gravel.

S Broglie 14A3

Parc de la bibliothèque. **GPS**: n49,00563 e0,52948.

8 € 5/night € 2,50/100liter Ch € 2,50/1h.
Surface: grassy/metalled. 01/03-31/10 7-22h, 01/11-28/02 7.30-19h
Distance: 200m 200m 200m, 7.30-19h.

Tourist information Broglie:
Fri 7-13h.

S Buchy 14B2

D919, Route de Forges. **GPS**: n49,58538 e1,36417.

6 free € 2 Ch € 2. **Surface:** asphalted. 01/01-31/12
Distance: 500m 500m 500m.

S Cabourg 13D3

Avenue Michel d'Ornano. **GPS**: n49,28225 w0,11994.

6 free € 2/10minutes Ch . **Location:** Rural, comfortable, quiet.
Surface: asphalted. 01/01-31/12
Distance: centre 900m 7,5km 1,6km on the spot.
Remarks: Nearby Hippodrome.

S Cambremer 13D3

Place de l'Europe/Avenue des Tilleuls. **GPS**: n49,14991 e0,04729.

FR

7 free € 2/100liter Ch € 2/1h. **Location:** Rural, simple, central, quiet. **Surface:** gravel. 01/01-31/12
Distance: 50m 100m bakery 100m.
Remarks: Coins available at the shops and town hall. D50, exit 'poids lourds', nearby police station.

S Campigny 14A3

Chemin de la Motte. **GPS**: n49,31139 e0,55223.

3 free Chfree. **Surface:** grassy. 01/01-31/12
Remarks: On inner court of old presbytery, max. 24h.

S Carolles 13B4

Rue du Mont Dol. **GPS**: n48,75931 w1,57062.

15 € 7 € 3/100liter Ch € 3/55minutes. **Surface:** grassy/sand.
01/01-31/12
Distance: 150m on the spot on the spot.
Remarks: Check in at restaurant O Gal'eau.

S Carolles 13B4

La Guériniére, Residence les Jaunets. **GPS**: n48,74989 w1,55695.
5 free € 2 Ch € 2. **Surface:** asphalted. 01/01-31/12
Distance: on the spot 2km.
Remarks: Parking in front of town hall.

S Caumont-l'Éventé 13C3

Souterroscope des Ardoisières, Route de Saint Lô, D71. **GPS**: n49,08868 w0,81645.

free € 2 Ch € 2 WC. **Surface:** asphalted.

S Cerisy-la-Forêt 13C3

GPS: n49,19806 w0,93389.

10 free € 2 Ch € 2. 01/01-31/12
Distance: on the spot.
Remarks: Next to the abbey.

Cherbourg 13B2

Musée Cité de la Mer, Llée du President Menut. **GPS**: n49,64740 w1,61782.

40 free. **Location:** Simple. **Surface:** asphalted.
Distance: 1km on the spot 1km on the spot.
Remarks: Max. 1 night.

Tourist information Cherbourg:

- Maison de Tourisme, 2, Quai Alexandre III, www.ot-cherbourg-cotentin.fr.Port city.
- Musée Fort du Roule.War museum. 9.30-12h, 14-17.30h.
- Basilique Sainte Trinité.Basilica in gothic style.

S Clecy 13C4

Rue du Stade. **GPS**: n48,91886 w0,48114.
5 free € 2 Ch € 2. 01/01-31/12
Distance: 300m 300m 300m.
Remarks: Coins available at the shops.

S Clères 14B2

Rue Edmond Spalikowski, Côte du Mont Blanc. **GPS**: n49,60228 e1,11667.

10 free € 4 Ch . **Surface:** gravel.
01/01-31/12 service: 01/11-28/02.
Distance: 500m 500m 500m.
Remarks: Nearby football ground, max. 72h, coins available at bakery, butcher and Bar-Tabac.

Tourist information Clères:

- Zoo Clères.Zoo.

S Colleville-Montgomery 13D3

Rue de Saint-Aubin/Rue les Petites Rues. **GPS**: n49,27166 w0,29891.

9 free Chfree. **Location:** Rural, simple, quiet. **Surface:** grassy.
01/01-31/12
Distance: 200m 450m.

Tourist information Colleville-Montgomery:
Office de Tourisme, Av. de Bruxelles, www.colleville-montgomery.fr/.
Musée Omaha Beach, St.Laurent-sur-Mer.Collection of military vehicles, weapons and costumes.

S Cormeilles 14A3
Avenue de Chepstow, D810. **GPS:** n49,24830 e0,37446.

8 free Chfree. **Surface:** asphalted. 01/01-31/12
Distance: 400m river 400m.

S Coudeville-Plage 13B3
Avenue de la Mer D351. **GPS:** n48,88707 w1,56607.

10 € 5/24h Ch included . **Surface:** grassy/gravel.
01/01-31/12
Distance: 500m 200m 200m 500m 500m.

S Courseulles-sur-Mer 13D3
Avenue de la Libération. **GPS:** n49,33440 w0,44551.

13 € 6,20 Chincluded. **Location:** Urban, comfortable, central.
Surface: asphalted. 01/01-31/12
Distance: 50m 200m pizzeria 50m.
Remarks: Nearby entrance campsite, max. 24h.

Courseulles-sur-Mer 13D3
Juno Beach, Voie des Français Libres. **GPS:** n49,33694 w0,46502.

25 free. **Location:** Central, quiet. **Surface:** metalled.
01/01-31/12
Distance: 100m 50m.

S Couterne 13C5
Place de la Mairie. **GPS:** n48,51223 w0,41417.

10 free Ch WC free. **Surface:** asphalted. 01/01-31/12
Distance: on the spot nearby nearby.
Remarks: Max. 1 night, closed when frosty.

Criel-sur-Mer 14B1
Rue de la Plage, D222. **GPS:** n50,03296 e1,31150.

75 free. **Surface:** grassy/gravel. 01/01-31/12
Distance: 500m on the spot on the spot 500m 1km.

S Deauville 13D3
Boulevard des Sports. **GPS:** n49,35727 e0,08417.

8 free Ch (6x)free. **Location:** Urban, simple, quiet.
Surface: gravel. 01/01-31/12
Distance: on the spot 800m 500m.
Remarks: Behind stadium, max. 24h.

Tourist information Deauville:
Office de Tourisme, Place de la Mairie, www.deauville.org.Bathing resort.

S Dieppe 14B1
Quai de la Marne. **GPS:** n49,93139 e1,08667.

FR

45 € 7/24h Ch free. **Surface:** metalled. 01/01-31/12
Distance: 500m on the spot on the spot 500m 500m.
Remarks: Motorhome parking right side of harbour, max. 48h, wifi card available at harbour master.

Tourist information Dieppe:
Office de Tourisme, Quai du Carenage, www.dieppetourisme.com.Seaside resort with fishing port.
Porte des Tourelles.City gate, 15th century.
Château Dieppe.Castle, 15th century, with maritime museum.
10-12h, 14-18h 01/10-31/05 Tue.
Église Saint Jacques.
Tue, Thu 8-14h.
Normandic market. Sa 8-14h.

S Dives-sur-Mer 13D3

Rue de l'avenir. **GPS**: n49,29028 w0,10345.

10 free € 2/10minutes Ch . **Location:** Rural, comfortable, quiet.
Surface: asphalted. 01/01-31/12
Distance: 500m 900m.
Remarks: Nearby Port Guillaume.

S Doudeville 14B2

Place du Mont Criquet, centre-ville. **GPS**: n49,72000 e0,78750.

25 free Ch. **Surface:** asphalted. 01/01-31/12
Distance: 100m 100m 100m.

S Ducey 13B4

Rue St Quentin. **GPS**: n48,62513 w1,294.

30 free € 2 Ch € 2 WC. **Surface:** metalled. 01/01-31/12
Distance: 500m 500m 500m.

S Englesqueville-la-Percée 13C2

Ferme de la Rouge Fossé, D514. **GPS**: n49,38781 w0,94829.
6 € 5 Ch € 3 included. **Surface:** grassy/gravel. 01/01-31/12
Distance: 500m.

Equeurdreville 13B2

Rue Jean Bart. **GPS**: n49,65465 w1,65044.

6 free. **Surface:** gravel.

S Etretat 14A2

Aire de stationnement Maupassant, Rue Guy de Maupassant. **GPS**: n49,70009 e0,21579.

30 € 8/24h € 3/100liter Ch € 3/55minutes. **Surface:** gravel/metalled. 01/10-31/12
Distance: 1km 1,2km 1km 1km.
Remarks: Max. 24h, next to campsite municipal.

Tourist information Etretat:
Office de Tourisme, Place Maurice Guillard, www.etretat.net.The cliffs which have the shape of an arch are a well-known tourist attraction.
Château des Aygues, Rue offenbach.Castle, 1866, former summer residence of Spanish kings. 01/07-20/09 14-18 Tue.

S Fécamp 14A2

Parking de la Mâture, Chaussée Gayant. **GPS**: n49,76024 e0,37412.
+10 free € 3 Ch. **Location:** Urban. **Surface:** asphalted.
Distance: on the spot.

Fécamp 14A2

Quai Sadi Carnot. **GPS**: n49,76087 e0,37157.

10 free. **Surface:** asphalted. 01/01-31/12
Distance: 200m on the spot on the spot 200m 500m.
Remarks: Between pier and marina.

Tourist information Fécamp:
Office de Tourisme, 113, rue Alexandre le Grand, www.fecamptourisme.com. City against the chalk-cliff of the Côte d'Albâtre, fishing-port is now mainly a marina.
Palais Bénédictine.Museum with Bénédictine distillery and tasting-pub.
01/07-31/08 10-18h, 01/09-30/06 10.30-11.30h, 14-17h.

M Musée des Terres Neuvas, boulevard Clocheville.Fishery as from the Viking period. 10-12h, 14-17.30h, 01/07-31/08 10-19h.

S Forges-les-Eaux 14C2

Boulevard Nicolas Thiessé. **GPS**: n49,60569 e1,54288.

35 € 6,12, 01/11-15/03 free Ch included. **Surface:** asphalted. 01/01-31/12 service in winter.

Distance: 2km.

Remarks: Max. 15 days. Cross roads D919-D915.

S Formigny 13C2

La Ferme du Lavoir, D517. **GPS**: n49,34041 w0,89654.

6 € 10/night Ch WC included. **Location:** Rural, comfortable, quiet. **Surface:** asphalted/grassy.

Distance: 300m 3km.

Remarks: Organic orchards, cider production.

S Gacé 14A4

Rue du Marché aux Bestiaux. **GPS**: n48,79500 e0,29583.

30 free € 2 Ch € 2. **Surface:** asphalted. 01/01-31/12

Distance: on the spot 2,6km 50m.

Remarks: In front of tourist office, max. 24h.

S Gavray 13B3

D7. **GPS**: n48,91085 w1,35162.

8 free free. **Surface:** grassy/gravel. 01/01-31/12

Distance: 100m 100m 100m.

S Gisay-la-Coudre 14A4

D35. **GPS**: n48,95001 e0,62670.

6 free € 2/100liter Ch 16Amp. **Surface:** asphalted. 01/01-31/12

Distance: on the spot 300m.

Remarks: Coins available at restaurant La Tortue. Follow signs from La Barre and Ouche, D49.

S Gournay-en-Bray 14C2

Avenue Sadi Carnot. **GPS**: n49,48055 e1,72640.

10 free Ch free. **Surface:** asphalted. 01/01-31/12 Thu-morning closed because of market + 2nd weekend Sep.

Distance: on the spot on the spot on the spot on the spot.

Remarks: Max. 48h.

Goury 13A1

GPS: n49,71616 w1,94324.

20 free. **Surface:** grassy/sand. 01/01-31/12

Distance: nearby.

S Gouvets 13B3

Le Bourg D454. **GPS**: n48,93133 w1,09492.

20 WC free. **Location:** Rural, simple, isolated, quiet. **Surface:** grassy/metalled. 01/01-31/12

Distance: on the spot 6km on the spot.

S Gouville-sur-Mer 13B3

Chemin du Beau Rivage. **GPS**: n49,09970 w1,60896.

40 € 4/19-10h € 4/100liter Ch € 4/55minutes WC. **Surface:** gravel. 01/01-31/12

Distance: on the spot on the spot.

FR

S Grainville-Langannerie 13D3

Rue de Lapford. **GPS**: n49,01438 w0,26805.

6 free € 2/10minutes Ch € 2/55minutes. **Location:** Rural, comfortable. **Surface:** metalled. 01/01-31/12
Distance: 100m.
Remarks: Near Salle des Fêtes.

S Grandcamp-Maisy 13C2

Rue du Moulin Odo. **GPS**: n49,38620 w1,03782.

14 free € 2 Ch. **Surface:** asphalted/gravel.
Distance: 500m 500m.
Remarks: Coins at Tourist Info, rue Aristide Briand.

S Granville 13B4

Haute Ville, Rue du Roc. **GPS**: n48,83530 w1,6095.

20-25 € 6 € 2,80/10minutes Ch € 2,50/55minutes.
Surface: gravel.
01/01-31/12
Distance: 500m 500m 500m.
Remarks: Motorhome parking behind sea aquarium, upper city, max. 24h, Atlantic Wall 50m.

Tourist information Granville:
Office de Tourisme, 4, Cours Jonville, www.ville-granville.fr.The old centre, Haute-Ville, is surrounded by ramparts. The lower city is a bathing resort.
Musée Vieux Granville, Grand Porte.Regional museum. 10-12h, 14-18h.
Wed, Sa.

S Gréville-Hague 13A1

D402. **GPS**: n49,67509 w1,80127.

10 free € 2 Ch € 2 WC. **Surface:** metalled.
Distance: 100m.
Remarks: Next to sports fields.

S Grigneuseville 14B2

La Plaine d'Hermesnil, 7 rue de la Plaine. **GPS**: n49,64427 e1,19900.

7 € 6 Ch included. **Surface:** gravel.
Distance: 2,5km 2,5km 2,5km.

S Guilberville 13C3

D159. **GPS**: n48,98871 w0,94844.

20 free € 2/100liter Ch € 2/1h. **Surface:** gravel. 01/01-31/12
service: 01/11-01/03.
Distance: 300m 1,5km 300m 300m.
Remarks: Coins at Tourist Info, Bistro and bakery.

S Hermanville-sur-Mer 13D3

Rue Verte. **GPS**: n49,28592 w0,31243.

6 free Chfree. **Location:** Simple, central, quiet. **Surface:** asphalted.
01/01-31/12
Distance: on the spot 200m.
Remarks: Tue market.

Tourist information Hermanville-sur-Mer:
Tue morning.

Hérouvilette 13D3

Place l'Aiguillon, Avenue de Caen, D 513A. **GPS**: n49,21983 w0,24497.

FR

8 free Chfree. **Location:** Rural, comfortable. **Surface:** asphalted.
01/01-31/12
Distance: 250m 200m.

S Heurteauville 14B2

Les Cerisiers, Rue de Village. **GPS**: n49,44777 e0,81333.

12 € 5 € 3 Ch € 2. **Surface:** gravel. 01/04-31/10
Distance: 3km 20m 20m 3km 3km.
Remarks: Along the Seine river.

S Honfleur 14A2

Bassin de l'Est, Quai de la cale. **GPS**: n49,41916 e0,24166.

120 € 10 Ch (60x)included.
Location: Urban, simple, central.
Surface: gravel.
01/01-31/12 service in winter.
Distance: 500m 2,7km 300m 500m.
Remarks: Parking east of city, on entering from dir Pont de Normandie.

Tourist information Honfleur:

Office de Tourisme, Quai lepaulmier, www.ot-honfleur.fr.Smal port city with many tourists and artists.

Greniers à Sel.Former salt warehouses, exhibitions of Honfleur painters.
01/03-31/10.

Musée de la Marine.History of navigation of Honfleur.
01/02-30/11, 01/12-31/01 Sa-Su.

S Isigny-sur-Mer 13B2

Quai Neuf. **GPS**: n49,32221 w1,10649.

6 free € 2 Ch. **Surface:** asphalted.
Distance: 300m 200m.

S Jobourg 13A1

Nez de Jobourg, D202. **GPS**: n49,67722 w1,93806.

10 free WC free. **Surface:** metalled. 01/01-31/12
Distance: within walking distance.

S Jumièges 14B2

Rue Alphonse Callais. **GPS**: n49,43106 e0,81452.

20 free € 3 Ch. **Surface:** gravel. 01/03-30/11
Distance: 1km 500m 200m 200m.
Remarks: Coins at Tourist Info and bakery.

S La Ferrière-aux-Etangs 13C4

Camping du Lac, Rue de l'Etang. **GPS**: n48,65931 w0,51706.

7 free € 2 Ch (3x)€ 2,16Amp. **Surface:** metalled.
01/01-31/12
Distance: 400m 400m 400m.
Remarks: At lake, near tennis-court.

S La Ferté-Macé 13D4

Ruelle des Fournelles, D916. **GPS**: n48,59018 w0,35528.

15 free Chfree. **Surface:** asphalted. 01/01-31/12
Distance: on the spot on the spot on the spot.
Remarks: Via D916.

S La Lucerne-d'Outremer 13B4

D35. **GPS**: n48,78437 w1,42727.

FR

6 free Ch WC free. **Surface:** asphalted. 01/01-31/12
Distance: on the spot 100m 100m.
Remarks: Max. 2 days, next to castle.

S La Mailleraye-sur-Seine 14B2

Quai Paul Girardeau. **GPS**: n49,48444 e0,77333.

34 € 5, 1/11-31/3 free € 3/10minutes Ch . **Surface:** grassy.
01/01-31/12
Distance: 200m on the spot on the spot on the spot 200m.
Remarks: Coins at shops/town hall, along the Seine river.

La Poterie-Cap-d'Antifer 14A2

GPS: n49,68317 e0,16480.

4 free. **Location:** Simple, quiet. **Surface:** grassy/gravel.
01/01-31/12
Distance: 2km.

S La Vespière 14A3

Chemin de la Grand Mare/Campaugé. **GPS**: n49,02763 e0,42221.

2 free € 2/100liter Ch € 2/1h. **Location:** Simple, comfortable.
Surface: asphalted. 01/01-31/12
Distance: 300m A28 2,2km Carrefour 200m.

S La-Rivière-Saint-Sauveur 14A2

Parking de l'Orange - Place Albert Harel, Chemin des Bancs, D580. **GPS**: n49,40856 e0,26926.

20 free € 5/100liter Ch € 5/30minutes. **Location:** Rural, simple, central, quiet. **Surface:** asphalted. 01/01-31/12
Distance: on the spot 700m supermarket + bakery 100m.
Remarks: Coins at the shops in the village. 4km from Honfleur.

Langrune-sur-Mer 13D3

Rue du Colonel Pierre Harivel. **GPS**: n49,32474 w0,36814.

3 free. **Location:** Comfortable, central. **Surface:** asphalted/metalled.
01/01-31/12
Distance: on the spot beach 50m 50m.

S Le Billot 13D3

D39. **GPS**: n48,96948 e0,07217.

4 free € 2,50 Ch € 2,50 WC. **Location:** Rural, simple.
Surface: gravel/metalled. 01/01-31/12
Distance: 200m.
Remarks: Coins at Relais du Billot 200m, beautiful view.

S Le Havre 13D2

Chaussée John Kennedy. **GPS**: n49,48499 e0,10673.

19 free Ch € 5 . **Location:** Simple, central. **Surface:** asphalted.
01/01-31/12
Distance: 5 min walking on the spot on the spot 200m 200m.
Remarks: Max. 48h.

Tourist information Le Havre:

Office de Tourisme, 186 Boulevard Clémenceau, www.ville-lehavre.fr.Big port and industrial town.

FR

Musée de l'Ancienne Havre, rue Jerome Bellarmato.History of the city.
Wed-Su 14-18h.
Musée Maritime, Dock Vaubanquai Frissard.Maritime museum.
10-12h, 14-18h.
Canyon Parc, CD34, Epretot.Family park in western style.

S Le Mesnil-Jumièges 14B2

Base de loisirs UCPA, Route de Mesnil. **GPS**: n49,41172 e0,84494.

10 free, July-Aug € 10 Ch. **Surface:** asphalted. 01/01-31/12
Distance: 1km 200m 200m 1km 1km.

S Le Mont-Saint-Michel 13B4

Aire Camping-car du Mont-Saint-Michel. **GPS**: n48,61381 w1,50576.

€ 8,70/24h Ch. **Surface:** grassy.
Distance: La Rotisserie on the spot.
Remarks: Cross roads D976-D275.

Le Mont-Saint-Michel 13B4

Parking Mont-Saint-Michel no.8. **GPS**: n48,62910 w1,50729.

50 € 12,50/14-14h. **Location:** Simple. **Surface:** metalled.
01/01-31/12
Distance: on the spot 100m on the spot.
Remarks: Overnight stay allowed, free shuttle to Le Mont-Saint-Michel.

Tourist information Le Mont-Saint-Michel:

Office de Tourisme, Corps de Garde des Bourgeois, www.mont-saint-michel.net.
Town with abbey on a cliff in the sea.

S Le Noyer-en-Ouche 14A3

Ferme Lesur, La Godinière, D140. **GPS**: n49,01017 e0,72444.

5 € 7,50 € 3 € 3. **Surface:** grassy. 01/01-31/12

S Le Rozel 13A2

Camping Le Ranch. **GPS**: n49,48034 w1,84219.

8 Ch. **Surface:** metalled.

S Le Sap 14A4

Les Terriers, Rue Nicolas Lesieur, D12. **GPS**: n48,89525 e0,33249.

4 free Ch free. **Surface:** gravel. 01/01-31/12
Distance: 500m on the spot 500m 500m.
Remarks: Next to fire station, dir Quimper.

S Le Tréport 14C1

Du Funiculaire, Route Touristique, D126E. **GPS**: n50,05777 e1,36222.

25 € 5,80 € 2,10/100liter Ch € 2,10/55minutes .
Location: Comfortable, isolated, quiet.
Surface: grasstiles.
Distance: Le Tréport centre 2km 2km 100m.
Remarks: Max. 48h, free transport to city centre. Le Tréport > Criel Plage.

S Le Tréport 14C1

Parc Sainte Croix, Rue Pierre Mendès France. **GPS**: n50,05954 e1,38919.

FR

61 € 9,30, tourist tax incl Ch (61x)included. **Location:** Comfortable, isolated, quiet. **Surface:** asphalted. 01/01-31/12
Distance: 700m 700m 500m Mr.Ed.
Remarks: Max. 48h, industrial area, near campsite.

Tourist information Le Tréport:
Office de Tourisme, Quai Sadi Carnot, www.ville-le-treport.fr.Bathing resort and fishing town on the mouth of the Bresle river.
Château d'Eu, Eu.Royal castle, 19th century. 15/03-01/11 Sa.

Les Pieux 13A2

Plage Sciotot. GPS: n49,50722 w1,84731.
free. **Surface:** metalled. 01/01-31/12
Remarks: Large parking, 50m from beach.

S Les Pieux 13A2

Intermarché, Route de Cherbourg. **GPS:** n49,51736 w1,79797.

6 free € 2 Ch. **Surface:** asphalted.
Distance: on the spot.

Tourist information Les Pieux:
Château, Bircquebec.Castle, 13th century and museum.
summer 10-12h, 14-18.30h Wed.

Lion-sur-Mer 13D3

Rue du General Gallieni. **GPS:** n49,30174 w0,31316.

4 free. **Location:** Urban, central, noisy. **Surface:** asphalted.
01/01-31/12
Distance: on the spot on the spot 100m.
Remarks: Parking townhall, at sea, only overnight stay allowed.

S Lisieux 14A3

Parking du Carmel, Rue d'Alençon. **GPS:** n49,14413 e0,22788.

free € 3/100liter Ch € 3/1h WC. **Surface:** asphalted.
01/01-31/12
Distance: on the spot river on the spot on the spot.

Luc-sur-Mer 13D3

Route de Lion-sur-Mer. **GPS:** n49,31430 w0,34346.

4 free. **Location:** Rural, simple. **Surface:** asphalted.
01/01-31/12
Distance: 200m.

Lyons-la-Fôret 14C2

La Cuette. **GPS:** n49,39908 e1,47912.
free.
Distance: 100m 100m 100m.

S Lyons-la-Fôret 14C2

Les Grandes Molaises, Les Hogues. **GPS:** n49,41312 e1,42562.

20 € 8 + € 0,20/pp tourist tax included. **Location:** Rural, isolated.
Surface: grassy.

S Marigny 13B3

Rue Auguste Eudeline, D53. **GPS:** n49,09911 w1,24776.

10 free Ch € 2. **Surface:** metalled. 01/01-31/12
Distance: 700m 700m 700m.

S Merville Franceville 13D3

Boulevard Wattier. **GPS:** n49,28483 w0,21071.

FR

6 free € 2/10minutes Ch. **Location:** Comfortable, quiet.
Surface: asphalted. 01/03-15/11
Distance: 75m.

S Montebourg 13B2

Parking Louis Lecacheux. **GPS**: n49,48486 w1,37449.

10 free Chfree. 01/01-31/12

S Montfiquet 13C3

Hotel-Restaurant Relais de la Fôret, L'Embranchement, D572. **GPS**: n49,19400 w0,863.

60 € 14 Chincluded WC Use sanitary € 2. **Surface:** asphalted.
01/01-31/12
Remarks: Picnic tables available. Bayeux dir Mont Saint Michel.

S Montmartin-sur-Mer 13B3

Rue du Clos d'Auguet. **GPS**: n48,98573 w1,51602.

5 free € 2/100liter Ch € 2,16Amp. **Surface:** asphalted.
01/01-31/12
Distance: 1km 1km 1km.
Remarks: Parking at garage, car washing place.

S Montville 14B2

Place de l'Abbé Kerebel. **GPS**: n49,54780 e1,07388.

15 free € 3 Ch free,(8-22.30). **Surface:** gravel.
01/01-31/12
Distance: 400m 400m.
Remarks: Coins at mairie, restauration Hexagone, museum.

Tourist information Montville:
Mo-morning.

S Mortain 13C4

Place du Château. **GPS**: n48,64887 w0,94489.

6 free Ch free. **Surface:** asphalted. 01/01-31/12
Distance: on the spot on the spot on the spot.
Remarks: Max. 48h.

Tourist information Mortain:
Office de Tourisme, Rue du Bourglopin, www.ville-mortain.fr.Hiking trail to the Grande and Petite Cascade, waterfalls.

S Nonancourt 14B4

D53, Rue Hippolyte Lozier. **GPS**: n48,77269 e1,19261.
4 free Chfree . **Surface:** asphalted.
Distance: 200m.

S Notre-Dame-de-Courson 14A3

D4. **GPS**: n48,99021 e0,25922.

9 free € 2/20minutes Ch € 2/20minutes. **Location:** Rural, comfortable, quiet. **Surface:** gravel. 01/01-31/12
Distance: 200m Le Tournebroche 200m.
Remarks: Service only with 1-euro coins.

S Oissel 14B3

Rue du Bras St.Martin. **GPS**: n49,33783 e1,09183.

FR

2 free € 2/100liter Ch € 2/55minutes.
Surface: gravel.
01/01-31/12
Distance: 200m on the spot on the spot 200m 200m.
Remarks: <7m, Coins at the bakery: 1, Rue du Maréchal Foch.

S Ouistreham 13D3

Rue des Dunes/Boulevard Maritime. **GPS**: n49,28716 w0,24968.

45 € 8 Ch included. **Location:** Urban, comfortable, noisy.
Surface: asphalted/gravel. 01/01-31/12
Distance: 650m 150m 2km.
Remarks: Near car ferry.

S Pirou-Plage 13B3

Rue des Hublots. **GPS**: n49,16522 w1,58937.

6 free € 2/10minutes Ch € 2/1h. **Surface:** asphalted.
01/01-31/12
Distance: 500m.
Remarks: Coins available at campsite Le Clos Marin and restaurant La Marée.

S Pont-d'Ouilly 13D4

Rue de la Libération. **GPS**: n48,87794 w0,41304.

43 € 10/24h € 2 Ch (43x)included. **Location:** Rural.
Surface: gravel. 01/01-31/12
Distance: 550m on the spot 550m 550m.
Remarks: Along the Orne river.

Pont-l'Évêque 14A3

Les Mouettes, Avenue de Verdun. **GPS**: n49,28563 e0,18769.

6 free. **Location:** Urban, simple, central.
01/01-31/12
Distance: on the spot 6km 100m 150m.

Port-en-Bessin-Huppain 13C2

Rue du 11 Novembre. **GPS**: n49,34583 w0,75861.

17 € 3,50/night. **Location:** Rural, simple. **Surface:** sand.
01/01-31/12
Distance: 300m 400m 400m 500m.

Port-en-Bessin-Huppain 13C2

Super U, Avenue du Général de Gaulle. **GPS**: n49,34307 w0,75212.

12 free € 3 Ch € 3. **Location:** Simple. **Surface:** gravel.
01/01-31/12
Distance: 200m 400m 400m on the spot.

S Portbail 13B2

Rue Gilles Poerier. **GPS**: n49,33776 w1,69273.

4 free € 2 Ch € 2. **Surface:** asphalted.

S Rauville-la-Bigot 13B2

D900. **GPS**: n49,51723 w1,68368.

FR

10 free Chfree. **Surface:** asphalted.

Réville 13B2

Ferme de la Froide Rue, 165, Rue des Monts. **GPS:** n49,62583 w1,25278.

first night € 7, € 4 each additional night Ch.
Surface: grassy/gravel. 01/01-31/12
Distance: 1km.

Rots 13C3

Centre Commercial Cora, Chemin de la Croix Vautier, RN13. **GPS:** n49,19985 w0,46027.

free Chfree. **Location:** Noisy. **Surface:** asphalted.
01/01-31/12
Distance: 1km on the spot on the spot.
Remarks: Terrain with video surveillance.

Rugles 14A4

Place de la Liberté. **GPS:** n48,82230 e0,70846.

4 free Ch free. **Surface:** metalled. 01/01-31/12
Distance: on the spot 200m 200m.
Remarks: Max. 48h.

Saint-André-de-l'Eure 14B4

Boulevard Verdun. **GPS:** n48,90644 e1,26927.

10 free WC. **Location:** Urban, comfortable, noisy. **Surface:** metalled.
01/01-31/12
Distance: 1km on the spot 1km on the spot.
Remarks: Along railwayline.

Saint-Pierre-sur-Dives 13D3

Aire Camping-Cars de la Halle Médiévale, Place du Marché. **GPS:** n49,01713 w0,03047.

12 € 5/24h Ch. **Location:** Urban, simple, central.
Surface: gravel. 01/01-31/12 Mo-morning market.
Distance: on the spot 50m 150m.
Remarks: Passerby € 3.

Saint-Sever-Calvados 13B4

Place de la Mairie. **GPS:** n48,84169 w1,04842.

15 free Chfree. **Surface:** gravel. 01/01-31/12
Distance: 100m 15km 100m.

Saint-Vigor-le-Grand 13C3

Les Peupliers, Rue de Magny. **GPS:** n49,29949 w0,67436.

7 € 6, € 9 service incl Ch included. **Location:** Rural, comfortable, isolated, quiet. **Surface:** gravel. 01/01-31/12
Distance: 2km.
Remarks: Baker every morning, Bayeux centre 3,5km, Arromanches beaches 6,5km, passerby € 2,50.

Sainte-Saire 14C2

Rue de la Gare, D7. **GPS:** n49,69677 e1,49476.
free Ch. **Location:** Rural, comfortable, quiet.

FR

Surface: asphalted/grassy. 01/01-31/12
Distance: 300m Avenue Verte.

S Sallenelles 13D3

Boulevard Maritime D514. **GPS**: n49,26474 w0,22694.

2 free € 2/10minutes Ch. **Location:** Rural, simple, quiet. **Surface:** asphalted. 01/01-31/12
Distance: 100m on the spot 300m.
Remarks: Max. 48h.

S Sideville-Lorimier 13B2

Camping-car l'Orimier, Route du Pont Roger, D152. **GPS**: n49,58722 w1,69222.

6 € 6/night Ch included. **Surface:** asphalted/grassy.

S Siouville-Hague 13A2

Avenue des Peupliers. **GPS**: n49,56356 w1,8442.

30 free € 2 Ch. **Surface:** grassy.
Distance: 200m.

S Soumont-Saint-Quentin 13D3

Rue de la Mine. **GPS**: n48,97840 w0,25.

20 € 6 + € 0,20/pp tourist tax Ch included. **Location:** Simple. **Surface:** grassy. 01/01-31/12
Distance: 1km.
Remarks: Former iron mine.

S Sourdeval 13C4

Parc Saint-Lys, Rue Jean Baptiste Janin. **GPS**: n48,72603 w0,92308.

10 free Ch free. **Surface:** gravel/metalled.
01/01-31/12
Distance: 100m 400m 400m.

S St.Fromond 13B3

Place des Gabariers, D8. **GPS**: n49,22202 w1,08956.

50 free € 2 Ch € 2. **Surface:** asphalted/gravel. 01/01-31/12
Distance: 50m.
Remarks: Centre.

Tourist information St.Fromond:
Office de Tourisme, Bd de Verdun, Carentan, www.ot-carentan.fr.Old bishop city with Gothic cathedral.

S St.Hilaire-du-Harcouët 13B4

Place de la Motte. **GPS**: n48,57602 w1,09086.

free € 2 Ch € 2. **Surface:** metalled. 01/01-31/12
Distance: on the spot on the spot on the spot.
Remarks: Behind church.

St.Jouin-Bruneval 14A2

Plage de Bruneval. **GPS**: n49,64970 e0,15349.

10 free. **Surface:** gravel. 01/01-31/12
Distance: 4km pebbled beach on the spot nearby 4km.

S St.Lô 13B3

Place de la Vaucelle. **GPS**: n49,11351 w1,10309.

FR

10 free € 2 Ch € 2 . **Surface:** asphalted. 01/01-31/12
Distance: 100m 100m 100m on the spot.
Remarks: Along the river.

Tourist information St.Lô:
Office de Tourisme, Place Général de Gaulle, www.saint-lo.fr.Modern city built on the ruins of the bombardments 1944.
Haras National, Rue du Maréchal Juin.National Stud farm established by Napoleon in 1806. 01/06-30/09 14-18.
Musée de la Libération, place du Champ de Mars.Invasion in 1944. 10-19h, winter 14-19h Tue. free.
Nôtre Dame.Renovated church 13th century.

S St.Nicolas d'Aliermont 14B1
Place du 19 Mars 1962, Rue d'Arques. **GPS:** n49,88026 e1,22160.

2 free € 2 Ch € 2. **Surface:** asphalted.
01/01-31/12
Distance: 200m 12km 200m 200m.
Remarks: Behind town hall, coins available at town hall and library, max. 48h.

S St.Nicolas-de-Bliquetuit 14A2
Route du Bac. **GPS:** n49,52083 e0,72777.

12 free € 2 Ch € 2. **Surface:** asphalted. 01/01-31/12
Distance: 1,4km on the spot on the spot 2km 2km.
Remarks: Coins at town hall, along river, hiking routes along the river Seine.

S St.Pair-sur-Mer 13B4
Avenue Léon Jozeau-Marigné. **GPS:** n48,81711 w1,56988.

30 € 5 € 2/10minutes Ch € 2/55minutes.

Surface: asphalted/gravel. 01/01-31/12
Distance: 500m beach 500m 500m on the spot.
Remarks: Parking at tennis-court, max. 48h.

S St.Pierre-Eglise 13B2
Parking du 8 Mai 1945. **GPS:** n49,66897 w1,40387.

free € 1,50 Ch. **Surface:** metalled. 01/01-31/12

S St.Pierre-le-Vieux 14B1
Ferme du Moulin, D237. **GPS:** n49,85816 e0,88000.

5 € 5 + € 1/pp Ch € 3. **Surface:** grassy/gravel. 01/01-31/12
Distance: 1km 1km 1km.

S St.Sauveur-le-Vicomte 13B2
Place Auguste Cousin. **GPS:** n49,38678 w1,52947.

free Chfree. **Surface:** asphalted.
Remarks: Next to town hall, max. 48h.

S St.Vaast-la-Hougue 13B2
Aire de la Gallouette, Rue Galouette. **GPS:** n49,58400 w1,267.

27 € 7 € 2/10minutes Ch € 2/1h. **Surface:** metalled.
01/01-31/12
Distance: 300m 300m.
Remarks: Near campsite Gallouette.

St.Vaast-la-Hougue 13B2
Quai du Commandant Albert Paris. **GPS:** n49,58972 w1,26583.

FR

free. **Surface:** metalled.
Distance: on the spot.

Tourist information St.Vaast-la-Hougue:
Office de Tourisme, 1, place Gen. de Gaulle, www.saint-vaast-reville.com. Important port for allied forces in 1944. Now large marina.
Île de Tatihou, Port.Island in front of the coast, maritime museum and bird hide. 01/04-30/09 10-18h.

S St.Valery-en-Caux 14A1

Quai d'Aval. **GPS**: n49,87220 e0,70898.

40 free, peak season € 5/day + € 0,20/pp € 3 Ch.
Surface: asphalted.
01/01-31/12
Distance: 600m on the spot on the spot 500m bakery 600m.
Remarks: Max. 48h, coins available at office de tourisme.

Tourist information St.Valery-en-Caux:
Office de Tourisme, Maison Henri IV, www.cauxmaritime.com. Popular seaside resort with pleasant marina.

S Ste.Honorine-des-Pertes 13C2

Garage Vally, Route d'Omaha Beach, D514, dir Colleville-sur-Mer. **GPS**: n49,34868 w0,81635.

32 € 6 € 1,50/100liter Ch (32x)included. **Location:** Rural, comfortable, quiet. **Surface:** grassy. 01/01-31/12
Distance: 200m 500m on the spot.
Remarks: Passerby € 2,50, automatic bread distributor.

S Ste.Marie-du-Mont 13B2

Camping-car Park, La Madeleine, D913. **GPS**: n49,41417 w1,17917.

49 € 12 Ch € 4,dryer € 3,50 included. **Location:** Simple, quiet. **Surface:** grassy/gravel. 01/01-31/12
Distance: 500m.
Remarks: Code wifi: f2d1941a5c.

Tourist information Ste.Marie-du-Mont:
Musée du Débarquement, Utah-Beach.Landing museum.

Ste.Mère-Eglise 13B2

Rue du Général Koenig. **GPS**: n49,40830 w1,3159.

25 free, € 5/night. **Surface:** asphalted.
01/01-31/12
Remarks: Parking behind church, max. 24h, bell-ringing every 15min.

S Ste.Mère-Eglise 13B2

Super U, ZA les Crutelles. **GPS**: n49,40461 w1,32223.
€ 2 Ch.
Distance: on the spot.
Remarks: Motorhome washing place max. ^3.80m.

Tourist information Ste.Mère-Eglise:
Borne 0 de la voie de la Liberté.Marker 0, start of the Libery Road.
Office de Tourisme, 2, Rue Eisenhower, www.sainte-mere-eglise.info.
Village well-known for the paratrooper who landed on the church-tower.
Musée Airborne.Exhibition about the invasion at St.-Mère-Eglise.
10-12h, 14-18h.

S Surtainville 13A2

Rue des mielles. **GPS**: n49,46373 w1,82871.

10 free € 3 Ch . **Surface:** metalled.
Distance: 100m.

S Tourlaville 13B2

Espace Loisirs Colignon, piscine-camping municipal, Rue des Algues. **GPS**: n49,65398 w1,56606.

FR

free € 2 Ch. **Surface:** asphalted.
Remarks: Coins at campsite or swimming pool.

Tourlaville 13B2

Quai Amiral Kniskern/Boulevard Maritime. **GPS:** n49,64549 w1,59976.

.
Remarks: Parking at ferry-boat.

Tréauville 13A2

1, La Chaussee, D65. **GPS:** n49,54444 w1,83472.

10 € 6,50 Ch included. **Surface:** grassy/metalled.
Distance: 2,5km.

Valognes 13B2

Place Félix Buhot. **GPS:** n49,51159 w1,47813.

7 free € 2 Ch € 2. **Surface:** asphalted.
Distance: on the spot.
Remarks: Next to supermarket Champion.

Valognes 13B2

Zone Artisanale d'Armanville, Chemin de la Brique. **GPS:** n49,51433 w1,50004.

€ 5/24h € 2 Ch € 2WC. **Surface:** asphalted.
Remarks: Station de lavage Eléphant Bleu.

Veules-les-Roses 14B1

Parking des Falaises. **GPS:** n49,87555 e0,79269.

free. **Surface:** grassy. 01/01-31/12
Distance: 500m on the spot on the spot 500m 500m.

Veules-les-Roses 14B1

Camping des Mouettes, Avenue Jean Moulin. **GPS:** n49,87596 e0,80289.

15 € 5/24h € 3 Ch. **Surface:** metalled. 01/01-31/12
Distance: 300m 500m 500m 300m 300m on the spot.
Remarks: Parking next to campsite des Mouettes, max. 48h, coins available at campsite, 12-14h closed.

Tourist information Veules-les-Roses:
Office de Tourisme, 12, rue du Marché, www.veules-les-roses.fr.

Veulettes-sur-Mer 14A1

Chemin des Courses. **GPS:** n49,85233 e0,60165.

15 € 4,50 € 3,50/100liter Ch (16x). **Surface:** asphalted.
01/01-31/12
Distance: 200m 200m 200m 200m 200m.
Remarks: Side-street D10, behind Syndicat d'Initiative.

Veulettes-sur-Mer 14A1

Parking de la Plage, D10. **GPS:** n49,85488 e0,60702.

FR

50 € 4,50 € 3,50/10minutes € 3,50/1h. **Surface:** grassy.
01/01-31/12
Distance: 200m 50m 50m.
Remarks: Beach parking, max. 24h.

Villedieu-les-Poêles 13B4

Parc de la Commanderie, Rue Taillemarche. **GPS**: n48,83682 w1,22436.

5 free. **Surface:** asphalted. 01/01-31/12
Distance: on the spot 2,4km 100m 100m.

Villers-Bocage 13C3

Rue du Canada. **GPS**: n49,07973 w0,6609.

5 free € 2 Ch € 2. **Surface:** asphalted. 01/01-31/12
Distance: 1,5km 400m.

Villers-sur-Mer 13D3

Paleospace l'Odyssee, Rue des Martois. **GPS**: n49,32910 e0,01273.
14 € 10 € 4 Ch included € 1 . **Location:** Urban, comfortable, quiet. **Surface:** metalled. 01/01-31/12
Distance: 1km beach 250m bakery 1,5km.
Remarks: Max. 48h.

Vimoutiers 14A4

D916, Avenue du Dr. Dentu. **GPS**: n48,93152 e0,19604.

6 free Ch (2x) WC free. **Location:** Urban, simple, central. **Surface:** asphalted. 01/01-31/12
Distance: 400m 500m Carrefour 200m.
Remarks: Major centre in the Camembert-region, Camembert museum.

Vire 13C4

Place du champ de foire. **GPS**: n48,84084 w0,88862.

50 free Ch free. **Surface:** asphalted. 01/01-31/12 Fri-Sa.
Distance: on the spot on the spot on the spot.
Remarks: Fri-Sa market, no water during winter time.

Ile-de-France

Bray-sur-Seine 15A5

Quai de l'Ile. **GPS**: n48,41713 e3,23745.

20 free Ch free. **Surface:** asphalted.
Distance: 100m 100m.
Remarks: Max. 72h.

Tourist information Bray-sur-Seine:
Fri 8-13h.

Coupvray 15A4

Parking Disneyland Paris, Boulevard du Parc. **GPS**: n48,87500 e2,79700.

€ 30/day Ch WC included. **Surface:** asphalted.
01/01-31/12
Remarks: Motorhome area at amusement park, note: tariffs will be charged per day, even if you arrive in the evening.

Tourist information Coupvray:
Crescend'O, Marne-la-Vallée.Water show in circus ambiance.
Mo, Tue, Wed, Fri 19.30, Sa 18, 21, Su 15, 18.
Disneyland Paris, Marne-la-Vallée.Attractions and themepark.

Milly-la-Forêt 14D5

Route de Nemours. **GPS**: n48,39798 e2,48021.
6 free Ch free. **Location:** Rural. **Surface:** asphalted.
01/01-31/12
Distance: 1km 9,4km A6.
Remarks: Gate opens automatically, in front of Conservatoire Nationale des Plantes.

Milly-la-Forêt 14D5

Total, 49-51 Avenue de Ganay. **GPS**: n48,40720 e2,46782.

FR

€ 3,50 Ch. **Surface:** grassy. 01/01-31/12
Distance: centre 500m 7,7km A6.
Remarks: Behind petrol station, gate open 6-21h.

S Provins 15A5

Parking Office de Tourisme, Chemin de Villecran. **GPS**: n48,56090 e3,28112.

30 € 4 € 2,50 Ch € 2,50 . **Surface:** asphalted.
01/01-31/12 service: frost.
Distance: 500m 500m.

Tourist information Provins:
Sa 8-14h.

S Souppes-sur-Loing 15A6

GPS: n48,18083 e2,72343.

5 € 5 Ch included. **Surface:** asphalted.
Remarks: Max. 72h.

S St.Cyr-sur-Morin 15A4

Avenue Daniel Simon. **GPS**: n48,90641 e3,18463.
4 free Chfree. **Surface:** grassy. 01/01-31/12
Distance: nearby.
Remarks: Behind church.

Britanny

S Antrain 13B5

Route de Pontorson. **GPS**: n48,46307 w1,47938.

2 free Ch WCfree. **Surface:** asphalted.

S Arradon 12D4

Camping municipal, Rue de la Mairie. **GPS**: n47,62245 w2,82495.

12 free, 15/6/15/9 € 15 € 2 Ch € 2. **Surface:** asphalted.
01/01-31/12
Remarks: ± 12 pitches free on campsite if campsite is closed.

Tourist information Arradon:
Syndicat d'Initiative Municipal, 2, place de l'Eglise.Seaside resort in the Gulf of Morbihan.

Arzal 12D4

Barrage d'Arzal, D139. **GPS**: n47,50089 w2,38074.

15 free. **Surface:** asphalted. 01/01-31/12
Distance: 1,5km 50m 50m 50m 50m.

S Arzon 12D4

Aire d'accueil des Camping-cars de Kermor, Avenue de Kerlun, Kerjouanno. **GPS**: n47,53886 w2,88028.

49 € 6,70/24h Ch (16x)included. **Surface:** asphalted.
Remarks: Nearby Plage du Fageo, max. 72h.

S Audierne 12B3

Rue Lamartine. **GPS**: n48,02733 w4,53721.

10 free € 2/10liter Ch . **Location:** Simple. **Surface:** unpaved.
01/01-31/12
Distance: 1,5km 500m.

S Auray 12C4

Chemin de Bellevue. **GPS**: n47,66365 w2,97393.

FR

free € 3/20minutes Ch . **Surface:** asphalted.
Distance: 200m.

S Auray 12C4

Place du Golhéres. **GPS:** n47,66524 w2,99036.

3 free Chfree. **Surface:** asphalted.
Distance: 500m on the spot.
Remarks: Follow Culturel Athena and Piscine.

Tourist information Auray:
Mo.

Baud 12C3

Rue du Champ de Foire. **GPS:** n47,87375 w3,02008.

20 free. **Surface:** metalled.

S Baud 12C3

Route de Locminé. **GPS:** n47,88112 w2,97465.
Ch free. 01/01-31/12

S Bédée 13A5

Rue de Dinan. **GPS:** n48,18099 w1,94416.

6 free Chfree. **Surface:** asphalted.
Distance: 200m 50m.
Remarks: Nearby cemetery.

S Belle-Isle-en-Terre 12C2

Rue Guerveur, D33. **GPS:** n48,54332 w3,39417.

10 free Ch free. **Surface:** gravel. 01/01-31/12
Distance: 100m 10m.

Belz 12C4

Rue des Sports. **GPS:** n47,66940 w3,17744.

10 free. **Surface:** gravel/metalled. 01/01-31/12

S Berric 12D4

Chemin de l'Étang. **GPS:** n47,63365 w2,52806.

6 € 5 € 2/10minutes Ch € 2/55minutes. **Surface:** asphalted.
Distance: 500m on the spot on the spot 500m 500m.
Remarks: Access via Rue du Grand Pont, parking fee being collected, coins at the shops in the village.

S Binic 12D2

Aire camping-car de l'Ic, Rue de l'Ic. **GPS:** n48,60059 w2,83573.

50 free Chfree. **Location:** Urban, simple, central, quiet. **Surface:** gravel. 01/01-31/12
Distance: 500m 700m 500m 500m.

Tourist information Binic:
Office de Tourisme, Avenue du Général de Gaulle, www.ville-binic.fr.Seaside resort with marina.
Thu.

S Bourg-Blanc 12B2

Rue de Brest. **GPS:** n48,49194 w4,50256.

FR

6 free Chfree. **Surface:** grassy. 01/01-31/12
Distance: fish pond 100m.

S Brech 12C4

Rue de Pont Douar/Avenue des Pins, D768. **GPS**: n47,71917 w3,00111.

6 free € 1,50 Ch. **Surface:** grassy. 01/01-31/12
Distance: 100m Small lake 200m 200m.
Remarks: Parking nearby small lake, plan d'eau.

Brest 12B2

Parking Océanopolis, Rue du Cormoran. **GPS**: n48,38893 w4,43535.

24 free. **Surface:** asphalted. 01/01-31/12
Distance: on the spot on the spot 300m.
Remarks: Busy parking during the day, gate closes at 18h.

S Brest 12B2

Port du Moulin Blanc, Rue Eugène Berest. **GPS**: n48,39202 w4,43553.

Ch free. 01/01-31/12

Tourist information Brest:

Office de Tourisme, Place de la Liberté, www.mairie-brest.fr/.Modern city with natural harbour, important naval harbour.

Tour Tanguy.Diorama old Brest. daily, 01/10-31/05 Wed, Su afternoon.

M Musée de la Marine, Château de Brest.Navy museum. 01/02-31/03, 01/09-15/12 10-12h, 14-18h, 01/04-31/08 10-18.30h Tue.

Océanopolis.Sea-centre, penguin and seals. 01/04-31/08 9-18h, 01/09-31/03 10-17h Mo.

S Callac (22) 12C2

Av Ernest Renan. **GPS**: n48,40200 w3,43737.

8 free € 2 Ch € 2. **Surface:** gravel. 01/01-31/12
Distance: 200m 200m.
Remarks: Lac Verte Vallée.

S Camaret-sur-Mer 12B2

Rue Georges Ancey. **GPS**: n48,27513 w4,60793.

75 01/04-31/10 € 6 € 2/100liter Ch € 2/55minutes. **Location:** Rural, comfortable, quiet. **Surface:** gravel.
01/01-31/12
Distance: 1km 500m 500m 500m on the spot on the spot.
Remarks: Max. 72h.

S Campénéac 12D3

Rue de l'Étang. **GPS**: n47,95736 w2,29039.

30 free € 2 WC. **Surface:** grassy. 01/01-31/12
Distance: 250m.
Remarks: Coins available at Fauchoux, rue nationale 32.

S Campénéac 12D3

Rue de la Fontaine. **GPS**: n47,95667 w2,29332.
Chfree.

S Cancale 13A4

Aire camping-car Ville Ballet, Rue des Français Libres. **GPS**: n48,67004 w1,86583.

100 free, 15/03-15/11 € 6/24h 10minutes Ch 55minutes,€ 3.
Surface: grassy. 01/01-31/12

FR

Distance: on the spot 1km 800m 100m.
Remarks: Bread-service.

Tourist information Cancale:
Office de Tourisme, 44, rue du Port, www.ville-cancale.fr.Centre of the oyster culture.
La Ferme Marine.Guided tour oyster farm. summer 11h,15h,17h Français, 14h English, 16h Deutsch.
St Meloir des Ondes, l'Atelier du Verre.Glass studio with demonstrations. 10.30-12.30h, 14.30-18.30h, 01/07-31/08 10-13h, 14-19h. free.

S Carantec 12B2

Aire du Meneyer, Rue Castel an Dour. **GPS**: n48,65967 w3,9138.

20 free €3/15minutes Ch €3/55minutes. **Surface:** gravel/metalled. 01/01-31/12
Distance: 500m.
Remarks: Max. 48h.

Carantec 12B2

Chemin du Roch Glaz. **GPS**: n48,65235 w3,90308.

10 free. **Surface:** asphalted. 01/01-31/12
Distance: beach 300m on the spot.
Remarks: Seaview.

Carantec 12B2

Rue Pen Al Lann. **GPS**: n48,66861 w3,895.

15 free. **Surface:** asphalted. 01/01-31/12
Distance: 500m 150m 150m 1km 1km.
Remarks: At tennis-courts, max. 48h.

Carantec 12B2

Square du Grand Sacconex, Rue du Kélenn. **GPS**: n48,66980 w3,91335.

10 free. **Surface:** unpaved.
Distance: 300m on the spot on the spot on the spot 300m on the spot.
Remarks: At gymnasium.

Tourist information Carantec:
Office de Tourisme, 4, rue Pasteur, www.ville-carantec.com/.Seaside resort with marina.
Musée Maritime.Navigation museum.

S Carhaix-Plouguer 12C3

Rue de Bazeilles/Rue des Augustins. **GPS**: n48,27829 w3,57257.

10 free Ch free. **Surface:** metalled. 01/01-31/12
Distance: 200m 200m 200m.

S Carnac 12C4

Square d'illertissen. **GPS**: n47,58505 w3,08242.

±30 free €2. **Surface:** asphalted. 01/01-31/12
Distance: 50m 50m 50m.
Remarks: Max. 1 night.

Tourist information Carnac:
Office de Tourisme, 74, avenue des Druides, www.carnac.fr.Seaside resort and important place of finding of 30.000 prehistoric menhirs.
Musée de la Préhistoire.Prehistoric museum. 12-18h, Sa-Su 10-12.30h, 14-18h. € 5.

S Caulnes 13A5

Lavoir Fontaine, Rue de Dinan. **GPS**: n48,28655 w2,15517.

FR

10 free € 2/10minutes Ch € 2/1h WC. **Surface:** gravel.
15/03-15/11
Distance: 500m 100m 100m 200m.
Remarks: Max. 24h.

S Cesson-Sévigné 13A5

Route de La Valette. **GPS:** n48,11802 w1,59121.

8 free € 2/10minutes Ch € 2/55minutes. **Surface:** metalled.
01/01-31/12

S Châtillon-en-Vendelais 13B5

D108. **GPS:** n48,23112 w1,17959.

10 free Ch free. **Surface:** asphalted.
Distance: lake.
Remarks: At the lake, next to campsite.

S Cléden-Cap-Sizun 12A3

Place du 19 mars 1962, Rue de la ville d'ys. **GPS:** n48,04803 w4,65008.

20 free € 1/10minutes Ch WC. **Location:** Rural, simple, quiet.
Surface: asphalted/metalled. 01/01-31/12
Distance: on the spot.

S Cléden-Cap-Sizun 12A3

Pointe du Van, D7. **GPS:** n48,05936 w4,70727.

20 free WC. **Surface:** gravel. 01/01-31/12
Distance: Cléden-Cap-Sizun ± 5km on the spot.

Cléden-Cap-Sizun 12A3

Route de Kastel Koz, Beuzec-Cap-Sizun. **GPS:** n48,08473 w4,51844.

10 free. **Location:** Rural, simple, isolated. **Surface:** grassy/gravel.
01/01-31/12
Distance: on the spot on the spot.

S Clohars-Carnoët 12C3

D16, Rue de Quimperlé. **GPS:** n47,79810 w3,58516.
4 free € 2 Ch € 2. **Surface:** asphalted. 01/01-31/12
Distance: 200m 10km beach 4,5km bakery 200m.

S Clohars-Carnoët 12C3

Place de NAVA, Rue de Quimperlé. **GPS:** n47,79790 w3,585.

3 free € 2 Ch € 2. **Surface:** asphalted. 01/01-31/12

S Combrit 12B3

Place du 19 mars 1962, Hent Ty Plouz. **GPS:** n47,88755 w4,1546.

10 free € 2/10minutes Ch € 2. **Location:** Simple, quiet.
Surface: metalled. 01/01-31/12
Distance: on the spot.
Remarks: Coins available at the shops.

S Commana 12B2

Place du salles de Sports, D11. **GPS:** n48,41611 w3,96139.

5 free free. **Location:** Rural, simple, isolated, quiet. **Surface:** grassy.
01/01-31/12
Distance: 200m 300m bakery 300m on the spot on the spot.

S Concarneau 12B3

Le Porzou, Allée Jean Bouin. **GPS:** n47,86320 w3,9051.

FR

20 € 2 Ch WC. **Surface:** asphalted. 01/01-31/12
Distance: on the spot.
Remarks: Foot ferry to centre.

S Concarneau 12B3

Parking de la Gare, Avenue de la Gare. **GPS**: n47,87864 w3,9202.

47 € 2/20-08h € 4 Ch € 4. **Surface:** metalled.
01/01-31/12
Distance: 500m beach 1,4km.
Remarks: Parking station.

Tourist information Concarneau:
Office de Tourisme, Quai d'Aiguillon, www.ville-concarneau.fr.Important fishing-port, old city with city walls.
Ville-Close.History and techniques of the international offshore fishing.
10-12h, 14.30-18.30h, summer 9.30-20h.
Mo, Fri.

S Crac'h 12C4

Intermarché, AC Les Alizés. **GPS**: n47,60421 w2,99669.

8 free € 2/10minutes Ch. **Surface:** asphalted. 01/01-31/12
Distance: on the spot on the spot.

S Crozon 12B2

Parking du Loc'h, Rue de l'Atlantique, Morgat. **GPS**: n48,22523 w4,50851.

30 € 4,08 € 3,20/10minutes Ch € 3,20/55minutes. **Location:** Simple. **Surface:** asphalted. 01/01-31/12
Distance: 300m on the spot on the spot 100m.
Remarks: Market on We.

S Crozon 12B2

Le Fret, Le Sillon, D55. **GPS**: n48,28457 w4,50934.

6 free € 2,08/10minutes Ch. **Location:** Rural, simple, quiet.
Surface: unpaved. 01/01-31/12
Distance: on the spot Resto 250m.

S Crozon 12B2

Parking office de tourisme, Boulevard de Pralognan, D887. **GPS**: n48,24770 w4,4934.

20 free € 2 € 2. **Location:** Urban, simple. **Surface:** asphalted.
01/01-31/12
Distance: on the spot.
Remarks: Nearby Office de Tourisme.

S Damgan 12D4

Parking de Kervoyal, Boulevard de l'atalante. **GPS**: n47,51465 w2,56038.

76 € 6 Ch included. **Surface:** metalled/sand. 01/01-31/12
Distance: 600m sandy beach.
Remarks: Parking at the beach, max. 48h.

Dinan 13A4

Rue du Port, D12. **GPS**: n48,45450 w2,0389.

30 € 0,30/30min 9-19h, overnight stay free. **Surface:** asphalted.
01/01-31/12
Distance: 800m 500m.

S Dol-de-Bretagne 13A4

Place Jean Hamelin. **GPS**: n48,54736 w1,75442.

FR

16 € 2 € 2 Ch € 2. **Surface:** asphalted.
Distance: nearby 100m 100m 150m.

Elven 12D4

Avenue des Martyrs de la Résistance, Le Guého. **GPS:** n47,73278 w2,58972.

7+25 € 1 + € 1,50/pp € 3 Ch € 2/20minutes (12x)€ 2,50.
Surface: grassy/gravel. parking 01/01-31/12 service 01/07-31/08
Distance: nearby nearby nearby.

Erdeven 12C4

Boulevard d'Atlantique. **GPS:** n47,61429 w3,15958.

20 € 6,50/24h € 2,50/4minutes Ch € 2,50/4minutes .
Surface: grassy.
Distance: 500m 200m 200m.

Erdeven 12C4

Place de St Margen. **GPS:** n47,64200 w3,157.

10 free. **Surface:** metalled. 01/01-31/12
Distance: 50m 50m 50m.
Remarks: Parking in centre.

Erdeven 12C4

Rue des Menhirs. **GPS:** n47,63750 w3,15156.

10 € 5 € 3 Ch . **Surface:** grassy/metalled.
Distance: 500m on the spot Lidl 300m.

Erquy 12D2

Caroual Plage, Rue des Hirondelles. **GPS:** n48,62120 w2,4724.

47 € 6/24h € 2 Ch € 2. **Surface:** metalled. 01/04-15/11
Remarks: Beach parking, max. 48h.

Tourist information Erquy:

Office de Tourisme, Boulevard de la Mer, "Le Rial",, www.erquy-tourisme.com. Fishing-port.

Étel 12C4

Camping municipal, Rue de la Barre. **GPS:** n47,65100 w3,202.

25 € 6,50/night € 2 Ch. **Surface:** grassy. 01/04-30/09
Remarks: Baker every morning (Jul/Aug).

Fouesnant 12B3

Chemin de Kerlosquen. **GPS:** n47,85444 w3,99255.

10 free. **Location:** Simple. **Surface:** grassy/sand. 01/01-31/12
Distance: beach 50m.
Remarks: Beach parking.

Fouesnant 12B3

Plage Mousterlin, Chemin de Kerneuc. **GPS:** n47,85144 w4,04662.

FR

15 free. **Surface:** grassy/sand.
Distance: beach 50m.
Remarks: Beach parking, max. 48h.

S **Fouesnant** 12B3

Leclerc, D45, Route de Quimper. **GPS**: n47,90234 w4,02938.

12free € 2/10minutes Ch € 2/55minutes. **Surface:** asphalted. 01/01-31/12
Distance: on the spot.

S **Fougères** 13B5

Allée des Fêtes. **GPS**: n48,35660 w1,20242.

free Ch WC free. **Surface:** asphalted. 01/01-31/12
Distance: 500m 200m 200m.

S **Fougères** 13B5

Parking de la Poterne, Ruelle des Anglais. **GPS**: n48,35524 w1,2113.

16 free Ch free. 01/01-31/12
Distance: on the spot 250m.
Remarks: Castle of Fougères 500m.

S **Fréhel** 12D2

La Ville Oie, Rue des Sports, D117, Pléhérel-plage. **GPS**: n48,65032 w2,35241.

40 free € 2,50/100liter Ch € 2,50/30minutes .
Surface: unpaved. 01/01-31/12
Distance: 1,1km beach 1,2km.

S **Gâvres** 12C4

Aire de la presqu'île de Gâvres, Boulevard de l'Océan, D158. **GPS**: n47,69583 w3,34778.

25 free € 2 Ch. 01/01-31/12
Distance: 100m.

S **Glomel** 12C3

Etang du Coronc, Rue du Lac. **GPS**: n48,22052 w3,38972.

12 free € 2/100liter Ch € 2/1h . **Surface:** asphalted. 01/01-31/12
Distance: 150m.
Remarks: At lake.

S **Goulven** 12B2

Aire Naturelle Ty Poas. **GPS**: n48,63109 w4,30833.

15 € 5 + tourist tax € 2 Ch € 2 WC . **Location:** Comfortable, quiet. **Surface:** grassy/metalled. 15/06-30/09
Distance: 500m beach 200m 500m.

S **Gueltas** 12D3

Cité des Écureuils, D125. **GPS**: n48,09667 w2,80111.

FR

10 free Ch free. **Surface:** gravel.
Distance: 200m.
Remarks: Nearby sports park.

S Guichen 13A6

Le Boel, Pont Réan. **GPS**: n48,00221 w1,77336.

5 free Ch WC free. **Surface:** metalled. 01/01-31/12
Distance: on the spot on the spot bakery 150m.

S Guidel 12C4

Guidel plage. **GPS**: n47,76640 w3,5258.

22 free Ch free. **Location:** Simple. **Surface:** metalled.
01/01-31/12
Remarks: Behind yachting school, max. 24h.

Guidel 12C4

Plage du Loc'h, D152, Guidel-Plage > Fort-Bloqué. **GPS**: n47,75052 w3,50654.

20 free. **Surface:** sand.
Distance: on the spot.
Remarks: Behind Résidence Maéva.

S Guidel 12C4

Arc-en-Ciel, ZA de Pen Mané. **GPS**: n47,80980 w3,4633.

service € 2, during opening hours Ch WC. 01/01-31/12

S Guimiliau 12B2

Parking Salle Polyvalente, Rue des Bruyeres. **GPS**: n48,48676 w3,99665.

15 free free. **Location:** Simple, central, noisy. **Surface:** metalled.
01/01-31/12
Distance: on the spot 400m 400m on the spot on the spot.
Remarks: Max. 2 nights.

S Guingamp 12C2

Place du Vally. **GPS**: n48,56024 w3,1489.

free Ch free. **Surface:** asphalted.
Distance: on the spot.
Remarks: Max. 24h.

S Guissény 12B2

Rue de Plouguerneau. **GPS**: n48,63299 w4,41127.

free € 2 Ch. **Location:** Comfortable. **Surface:** gravel.
01/01-31/12
Distance: on the spot beach 550m 250m bakery.
Remarks: Coins available at the shops and town hall.

Hédé-Bazouges 13A5

La Magdelaine. **GPS**: n48,30592 w1,79218.

FR

50 free. **Location:** Simple. **Surface:** grassy/gravel. 01/01-31/12
Distance: 1km 50m on the spot on the spot.

S Hillion 12D2

Le Tertre Piquet, Lermot-plage. **GPS**: n48,53098 w2,66387.

20 free Ch WC free. **Surface:** grassy. 01/01-31/12
Distance: sandy beach 100m.
Remarks: Beach parking.

S Hillion 12D2

Rue Olivier Provost. **GPS**: n48,51743 w2,66772.

7 free Ch free. **Surface:** gravel. 01/01-31/12
Distance: 500m 100m.

S Hirel 13A4

D155. **GPS**: n48,60841 w1,82032.

100 € 6 € 2/100liter Ch € 2/55minutes. **Surface:** grassy.
Distance: 700m 200m.

S Huelgoat 12C2

Place du Camping-cars, Route du Fao, D769a. **GPS**: n48,36115 w3,75612.

30 free € 5/10minutes Ch 1h. **Location:** Rural, simple, quiet.
Surface: metalled. 01/01-31/12
Distance: 500m on the spot on the spot 500m 500m 500m 500m 500m.
Remarks: In front of campsite municipal, service 100m.

S Janzé 13A6

Aire du Hardier, D41. **GPS**: n47,97258 w1,53825.

5 free € 2 Ch. **Surface:** asphalted.

S Josselin 12D3

Josselin, Place St.Martin. **GPS**: n47,95639 w2,55056.

50 free € 2,50 Ch WC. **Surface:** metalled. 01/01-31/12
Distance: 300m N24 900m 300m bakery 300m.
Remarks: Castle of Josselin 400m.

Tourist information Josselin:

Office de Tourisme, Place de la Congregation, www.paysdejosselin.com.City is dominated by the castle of Rohan.

Musée de Poupées, Château de Rohan.Private collection of antique dolls.
01/04-31/05, 01/10-31/10 Wed,Sa,Su 14-18h, 01/06-30/09 daily.

S Kerlouan 12B2

GPS: n48,66952 w4,36161.

free € 2 Ch. **Surface:** grassy. 01/01-31/12
Remarks: Former campsite.

Kerlouan 12B2

La Digue, La Digue. **GPS**: n48,66195 w4,37879.

4 free. **Location:** Isolated. **Surface:** gravel. 01/01-31/12
Distance: 100m on the spot on the spot.

S La Chèze 12D3

Chemin d'Aliénor, Allée du 19 Mars 1962. **GPS**: n48,13419 w2,65787.

10 free Ch (6x) WC free. **Surface:** asphalted. 01/01-31/12
Distance: 200m 200m.
Remarks: Parking at small lake.

S La Martyre 12B2

Route de Ploudiry, D35. **GPS**: n48,44861 w4,15694.

10 free Ch WC free. **Surface:** gravel. 01/01-31/12
Distance: 100m 100m 100m.
Remarks: Nearby Maison du Plateau.

La Roche-Bernard 12D4

Place du Dôme. **GPS**: n47,51753 w2,29733.

>20 free. **Surface:** asphalted. 01/01-31/12
Distance: 50m 100m 50m.

S La Roche-Bernard 12D4

Halte Camping-car, Rue du Patis. **GPS**: n47,52012 w2,30466.

15 € 9,30, 01/07-25/08 € 10,90 Ch € 4 WC . **Surface:** grassy.
02/04-16/09
Distance: 100m 50m 50m 100m 100m.
Remarks: Next to campsite du Patis.

Tourist information La Roche-Bernard:

Small town especially known for the beautiful hanging bridge over the Vilaine river, 50m high and over 400m long.

S La Roche-Derrien 12C2

Rue du Jouet. **GPS**: n48,74696 w3,25976.

12 € 2 € 2 Ch (6x). **Location:** Rural, simple, central, quiet.
Surface: gravel. 01/01-31/12
Distance: 100m 100m 100m.
Remarks: In centre, next to bank Crédit Agricole.

S Lampaul-Plouarzel 12A2

Aire de Porspaul, Dir Beg ar Vir. **GPS**: n48,44667 w4,77722.

50 free, 01/04-15/10 € 3,50, Jul/Aug + € 0,40/pp € 2/20minutes Ch € 2/55minutes WC € 1,60 € 3,dryer € 3,50. **Location:** Comfortable.
Surface: grassy. 01/01-31/12
Distance: 150m 100m 200m 500m on the spot on the spot.
Remarks: Shower and washing machine Jul/Aug.

S Landerneau 12B2

Rue du Calvaire. **GPS**: n48,44694 w4,25667.

25 € 5, incl. electricity € 2 Ch included . **Location:** Comfortable. **Surface:** grassy/gravel. 01/01-31/12
Distance: 500m river 500m 500m on the spot.

Landivisiau 12B2

P de Keravel, Rue du Manoir. **GPS**: n48,51015 w4,0758.

3 free Chfree. **Surface:** asphalted. 01/01-31/12
Distance: on the spot on the spot 100m centre.

Landudec 12B3

Super U, Rue des Écoles. **GPS**: n48,00143 w4,34088.

5 free € 2/10minutes Ch € 2. **Location:** Rural, simple. **Surface:** asphalted. 01/01-31/12
Distance: 1km on the spot on the spot.
Remarks: Motorhome washing place.

Lanfains 12D3

Étang du Pas, Le Pas, D7. **GPS**: n48,34982 w2,90116.

6 free Ch WC free. **Surface:** asphalted/grassy. 01/04-31/10
Distance: on the spot on the spot.
Remarks: Parking at small lake.

Languidic 12C3

Zone Lanveur, Place du Bouilleur de Cru. **GPS**: n47,83722 w3,16188.

20 free Chfree. **Surface:** metalled. 01/01-31/12
Distance: 700m N24 300m.

Lannilis 12B2

Aire Fontaine Rouge. **GPS**: n48,55667 w4,50528.

12 free Ch WC. **Surface:** metalled.
01/01-31/12
Distance: 1km 1,5km 1,5km.
Remarks: D13/D11, from church dir Brest straight on, till end of dead end street.

Lannilis 12B2

Rue Haie Blanche. **GPS**: n48,57125 w4,52151.

free Chfree. **Surface:** asphalted. 01/01-31/12
Distance: 100m bakery 150m.
Remarks: In front of cemetery.

Lanvallay 13A4

Rue du terrain des sports. **GPS**: n48,45420 w2,03028.

5 free € 2 Ch € 2. **Surface:** asphalted. 01/01-31/12
Distance: 50m.

Larmor-Baden 12C4

Route d'Auray. **GPS**: n47,58816 w2,89868.

3 free. **Surface:** asphalted. 01/01-31/12
Distance: 50m 100m 100m.

Larmor-Plage 12C4

Parking les Pins, Rue des Pins. **GPS**: n47,70970 w3,3791.

FR

4 free Ch WC free. **Surface:** asphalted. 01/01-31/12
Distance: 50m 100m 100m.
Remarks: Nearby plage de Toulhars, max. 72h.

S Le Conquet 12A2

Parking Parklec'H, Rue Général Leclerc. **GPS**: n48,36055 w4,7701.

+10 free € 2/100liter Ch € 2/1h. **Surface:** gravel.
01/01-31/12
Distance: 200m beach 800m 400m bakery 300m
on the spot.

S Le Croisty 12C3

Aire de pique-nique, D132, Kergoff. **GPS**: n48,06510 w3,38144.

8 free € 2 Ch € 2/55minutes WC . **Location:** Comfortable, isolated, quiet. **Surface:** asphalted. 01/01-31/12
Distance: 1,5km on the spot.

S Le Folgoët 12B2

Parking Frepel, Route de Gorrékear. **GPS**: n48,56002 w4,33507.

30 free Ch free. **Surface:** gravel/metalled.
01/01-31/12
Distance: on the spot 100m 100m.
Remarks: Nearby basilica.

S Le Trévoux 12C3

Rue des Sports. **GPS**: n47,89683 w3,64228.

free Ch free. **Location:** Simple. **Surface:** gravel.
01/01-31/12
Distance: on the spot.
Remarks: Max. 48h, nearby tennis-court.

S Le Vivier-sur-Mer 13A4

Rue de la Grève, D155. **GPS**: n48,60383 w1,7799.

10 € 5 € 2/100liter Ch € 2/1h. **Surface:** metalled.
01/01-31/12
Distance: 200m on the spot on the spot on the spot.

S Léhon 13A5

Parking Club de Tennis. **GPS**: n48,44177 w2,04233.

6 free Ch free. **Surface:** asphalted. 01/01-31/12
Distance: on the spot bakery 100m.

S Les Forges 12D3

Place de l'Église, D117. **GPS**: n48,01820 w2,6482.

5 free WC free. **Surface:** metalled. 01/01-31/12
Distance: 100m 100m.

Lézardrieux 12C2

Rue de l'Île à Bois. **GPS**: n48,83002 w3,08165.

FR

5 free. **Location:** Simple, isolated, quiet. **Surface:** gravel/sand.
01/01-31/12
Distance: Lézardrieux 6km 50m on the spot.
Remarks: Max. 24h.

S Lézardrieux 12C2

Camping Municipal. **GPS**: n48,78021 w3,1147.

4 € 3 € 3,20 Ch WC € 1,26. **Surface:** asphalted.
01/01-31/12
Distance: 500m 200m 300m 300m on the spot.

S Liffré 13B5

Intermarché. **GPS**: n48,22459 w1,50165.

free Ch free. **Surface:** asphalted. 01/01-31/12
Distance: 300m on the spot.

S Locmaria-Plouzané 12B2

Plage de Portez, Rue de Portez, Porsmilin. **GPS**: n48,35501 w4,67269.

8 € 4,40 Ch included. **Surface:** gravel. 01/01-31/12
Distance: 3,5km beach 50m on the spot on the spot.
Remarks: To be paid at campsite.

S Locmaria-Plouzané 12B2

Zône détente Ty Izella, Rue de la Fontaine. **GPS**: n48,37306 w4,64306.

12 free € 2 Ch € 2. **Location:** Quiet. **Surface:** gravel.
01/01-31/12
Distance: 100m 250m 250m.
Remarks: Coins at town hall.

Locmariaquer 12C4

Aire de Pierres Plates, > Route des Plages. **GPS**: n47,55720 w2,9486.

±30 free. **Surface:** metalled. 01/01-31/12
Distance: beach 500m on the spot.
Remarks: 500m from 'Les Pierres Plates', max. 24h.

S Locmariaquer 12C4

Camping La Falaise. **GPS**: n47,55639 w2,94139.
€ 2 Ch.
Remarks: 6/6/11 during inspection service point out of order.

Tourist information Locmariaquer:
Office de Tourisme, Rue de la Victoire, www.ot-locmariaquer.com.
Port city with many megalithics, signed dolmen.

S Locminé 12D3

Fue Laennec / rue du Pont Person. **GPS**: n47,88788 w2,83174.

free Ch free.
Distance: N24 1,4km.
Remarks: Max. 48h.

Locmiquelic 12C4

Port de Ste. Catherine, Quai Rallier du Baty. **GPS**: n47,72364 w3,34958.

free. **Surface:** asphalted.

FR

Distance: on the spot.
Remarks: Max. 1 night.

S Locqueltas 12D4

Rue de la Fontaine. **GPS**: n47,75841 w2,76901.

6 free Chfree (4x)€ 3,05. **Surface:** grassy.
01/01-31/12
Distance: 100m 600m 100m 100m.
Remarks: Max. 24h, coins at Bar-Tabac, 18 Place de la Mairie, town hall.

S Locronan 12B3

Rue du Prieuré. **GPS**: n48,09811 w4,21245.

10 free, 01/06-15/10 € 5/24h € 2 Ch € 2 WC.
Surface: grassy/sand.
01/01-31/12
Distance: 50m.

Tourist information Locronan:
Office de Tourisme, Place de la Mairie.Historical town.

Loctudy 12B3

Plage des Sables Blancs, Rue du Beau Rivage. **GPS**: n47,79883 w4,19739.

3 free. **Location:** Rural, simple. **Surface:** asphalted.
01/01-31/12
Distance: 4km beach 80m.
Remarks: Beach parking.

S Loudéac 12D3

Parking de la Gare, Boulevard de la Gare. **GPS**: n48,18058 w2,76277.

3 free Chfree. **Surface:** metalled. 01/01-31/12

Distance: 600m 50m 200m 200m.

S Maël-Carhaix 12C3

Place de l'école, Route de Rostrenen. **GPS**: n48,28344 w3,42148.

5 free € 2 Ch WC. **Surface:** asphalted. 01/01-31/12
Distance: 100m 100m 100m.
Remarks: Coins at town hall.

S Malansac 12D4

Rue Saint Fiacre. **GPS**: n47,67820 w2,29942.

5 free Chfree. **Surface:** grassy.
Distance: 100m 100m 100m.

S Malestroit 12D4

Chemin des Tanneurs. **GPS**: n47,80772 w2,37885.

12 free Chfree. **Surface:** gravel/metalled. 01/01-31/12
Distance: 500m on the spot 350m.

S Malestroit 12D4

Rue de Narvik. **GPS**: n47,80896 w2,37591.

free Chfree. **Surface:** asphalted.
Distance: 1,5km 600m 600m 2km 1km.

Malestroit 12D4

Chemin de l'Écluse. **GPS**: n47,81250 w2,38197.

FR

12 free. **Surface:** metalled/sand. 01/01-31/12
Distance: 100m on the spot on the spot 100m 100m.
Remarks: Max. 48h.

Marzan 12D4

Rue de la Source. **GPS**: n47,54023 w2,32383.

+20 free Ch WC free. **Surface:** asphalted.
Distance: 50m 20m.

Mauron 12D3

Rue de la Libération. **GPS**: n48,08472 w2,2833.

free Ch free. **Surface:** asphalted.
Distance: 150m 150m.

Mellé 13B5

Rue Rouviel. **GPS**: n48,48919 w1,18814.

6 free Ch WC free. **Surface:** metalled.
Distance: 200m 200m.
Remarks: Nearby football ground, max. 48h.

Meslin 12D2

Allée des Loisirs, D28. **GPS**: n48,44363 w2,56994.

10 free Ch free. **Surface:** metalled.
Distance: bar/crêperie 50m 50m.

Moëlan-sur-Mer 12C3

Rue de Beg Tal Gward. **GPS**: n47,77749 w3,64404.

4 free. **Location:** Isolated, quiet. **Surface:** asphalted. 01/01-31/12
Distance: Moëlan 5km sea 50m.

Moncontour 12D3

Camping la Tourelle, Rue François Lorant. **GPS**: n48,35271 w2,63719.

4 € 2 € 2 Ch € 2/55minutes. **Surface:** gravel.
01/01-31/12
Distance: 1,5km 1,5km 1,5km.
Remarks: Max. 48h.

Morlaix 12C2

Rue de Brest. **GPS**: n48,57422 w3,8316.

5 free Ch free. **Location:** Urban, simple, central, noisy. **Surface:** asphalted. 01/01-31/12
Distance: on the spot on the spot 200m 100m 200m on the spot on the spot.

Neulliac 12C3

Rue des Deux Croix, D767. **GPS**: n48,12812 w2,98552.

FR

3 free € 2 Ch € 2. **Surface:** asphalted.
Distance: 300m 300m.

S Névez 12B3

Rue de Port Manech, Impasse du Stade. **GPS**: n47,81560 w3,7894.

20 free € 2 Ch € 2. **Surface:** asphalted. 01/01-31/12
Remarks: Parking next to stadium, max. 24h.

Névez 12B3

Plage de Dourveil, Rue de Dourveil, D1. **GPS**: n47,79407 w3,8101.
4 free. **Surface:** sand.
Remarks: No camping activity.

Névez 12B3

Plage de Tahiti, Kerstalen. **GPS**: n47,79287 w3,79011.

± 11 free. **Surface:** grassy/sand. 01/01-31/12
Distance: beach 150m.
Remarks: Beach parking, max. 24h.

Névez 12B3

Route de la Plage. **GPS**: n47,80499 w3,74261.
5 free. **Surface:** asphalted. 01/01-31/12
Distance: 50m.
Remarks: Max. 24h.

Névez 12B3

Rue des Iles, Raguénez. **GPS**: n47,78908 w3,80174.
10 free. **Surface:** asphalted. 01/01-31/12
Distance: sea 10m, beach 150m.
Remarks: Max. 24h.

S Paimpol 12D2

Parking Pierre Loti, Rue Pierre Loti. **GPS**: n48,78404 w3,0463.

15 free, summer € 5 € 3,30/100liter Ch € 3,30/55minutes.
Surface: gravel/sand. 01/01-31/12
Distance: on the spot 1km 400m 100m on the spot on the spot.
Remarks: Service 100m.

S Paimpol 12D2

Rue Pierre Loti/ D7. **GPS**: n48,78278 w3,0475.

15 free € 3,30/100liter Ch € 3,30/55minutes.
Location: Urban, simple, central, noisy.
Surface: gravel.
01/01-31/12
Distance: on the spot 1km 300m 300m 300m 300m 300m.
Remarks: Max. 48h. Access via roundabout Champ de Foire, 250m of harbour.

Paimpol 12D2

Parking de Goas Plat, Rue de Goas Plat. **GPS**: n48,77535 w3,04009.

6 free. **Location:** Urban, simple, central, quiet.
Surface: asphalted.
Distance: centre 500m 2km 500m 500m.
Remarks: Max. 24h.

S Paimpont 12D3

Rue de l'Enchanteur Merlin. **GPS**: n48,02286 w2,17128.

10 free € 2/10minutes Ch. **Surface:** gravel.

S Pénestin 12D4

Allée du Grand Pré. **GPS**: n47,48111 w2,47361.

FR

20 free, € 5,30/night + € 0,20/pp € 2/100liter Ch € 2/1h.
Surface: asphalted.
Distance: 500m 1,5km 500m.
Remarks: Max. 48h, coins at Office de Tourisme, check in all aires in Pénestin: Office de tourisme; Bar-PMU Le Narval, Rue Calvaire; Café 0 20 100 0, Port de Tréhiguier.

Pénestin 12D4

Allée de la Poudrantais. **GPS**: n47,46681 w2,48716.

4 free, € 5,30/night + € 0,20/pp. **Surface:** gravel/metalled.
Distance: 50m.
Remarks: Max. 48h.

Pénestin 12D4

Allée de Camaret. **GPS**: n47,49010 w2,49078.

FR

4 free, € 5,30/night + € 0,20/pp. **Surface:** gravel.
Distance: 100m.
Remarks: Max. 48h.

Pénestin 12D4

Allée du Palandrin. **GPS**: n47,44955 w2,46351.

6 free, € 5,30/night + € 0,20/pp. **Surface:** grassy/sand.
Distance: 50m.
Remarks: Max. 48h.

Pénestin 12D4

Plage de la Source, Allée du Maro. **GPS**: n47,48158 w2,49005.

10 free, € 5,30/night + € 0,20/pp. **Surface:** grassy/metalled.
Distance: 300m.
Remarks: Max. 48h.

Pénestin 12D4

Plage du Palandrin, L'Isle du Clos Parc, Kerséguin. **GPS**: n47,45000 w2,46417.

6 € 5,30 + € 0,20/pp tourist tax. **Location:** Simple, isolated. **Surface:** grassy.
01/01-31/12
Distance: sandy beach 1km.
Remarks: Pay at tourist office.

Pénestin 12D4

Route du Loguy. **GPS**: n47,49050 w2,49667.

20 free, € 5,30/night + € 0,20/pp. **Surface:** grassy/metalled.
Distance: 150m.
Remarks: Max. 48h.

Penmarch 12B3

Aire de Port du Bouc, Route du Ster Kérity. **GPS**: n47,79981 w4,34794.

10 € 4/19-9h. **Location:** Rural. **Surface:** grassy.
01/01-31/12
Distance: 1,5km 50m 1km 5km.

Penmarch 12B3

Aire du Viben, Rue de la Plage. **GPS**: n47,82390 w4,3708.

30 9-19h free, 19-9h € 4. **Location:** Rural, simple, quiet.
Surface: metalled. 01/01-31/12
Distance: bakery 1km 900m on the spot on the spot.

S Penmarch 12B3

Aire de Keramеil, Rue du Pont Nevez. **GPS**: n47,81369 w4,36077.

€ 2/10minutes Ch. **Location:** Rural, simple.
01/01-31/12
Distance: 3km.
Remarks: Only overnight stays 19-9h.

S Penzé 12B2

Rue du Dossen. **GPS**: n48,59811 w3,93439.

5 free € 2 Ch € 2 WC. **Location:** Simple, quiet. **Surface:** asphalted.
01/01-31/12
Distance: 100m on the spot on the spot 50m 250m on the spot on the spot.
Remarks: Nearby port.

S Piré-sur-Seiche 13B6

Rue de Boistrudan. **GPS**: n48,00719 w1,42871.

15 free Chfree. **Surface:** metalled.
Distance: 300m 300m.
Remarks: At fish lake.

S Plabennec 12B2

Rue de l'Aber. **GPS**: n48,50155 w4,43374.

5 free Chfree. **Location:** Simple. **Surface:** metalled.
01/01-31/12 on the spot.
Remarks: Parking at small lake.

S Planguenoual 12D2

Bien y Vient. **GPS**: n48,53447 w2,54506.
6 € 5 € 2. **Surface:** grassy. 01/01-31/12

S Planguenoual 12D2

Ferme Gesbert, D786. **GPS**: n48,54883 w2,5556.

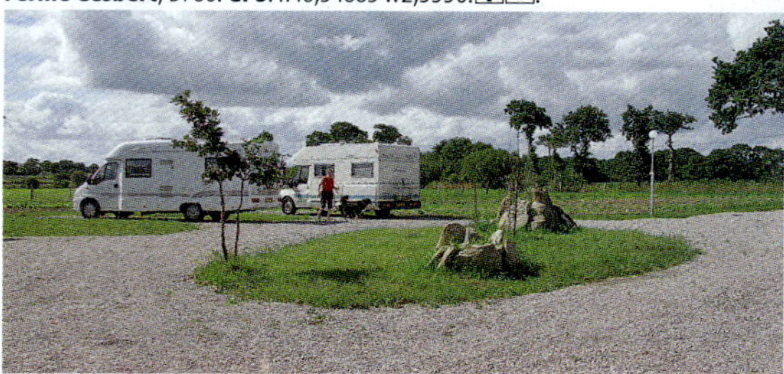

6 free Chfree. **Surface:** grassy/gravel. 01/01-31/12
Distance: 1km 1km 1km.

S Plémet 12D3

Rue de l'Étang, D16. **GPS**: n48,17897 w2,58918.

15 free Ch free. **Surface:** gravel. 01/01-31/12
Remarks: Parking at small lake.

S Pléneuf-Val-André 12D2

Port de Plaisance de Dahouët, Bassin des Salines, Chemin du Bignon. **GPS**: n48,57528 w2,56639.

45 € 3,60/24h, tourist tax € 0,20/pp € 2 Ch € 2 WC € 2 € 4/h.
Surface: gravel. 01/01-31/12
Distance: 300m.

S Plérin 12D2

Sous la Tour, Rue de la Tour, D24. **GPS**: n48,53146 w2,72483.

FR

20 free Ch free. **Surface:** gravel. 01/01-31/12
Distance: on the spot 300m 1km.

Pleslin-Trigavou 13A4

D28. **GPS:** n48,53631 w2,05009.

20 free Ch free. **Surface:** asphalted.
Distance: on the spot.
Remarks: Cycle and hiking routes: voie verte, Circuit des Mégalithes.

Plessala 12D3

Rue de l'Étang. **GPS:** n48,27394 w2,62427.

12 free Ch free. **Surface:** gravel. 01/01-31/12
Distance: 200m on the spot.
Remarks: At fish lake, fishing permit available.

Plestin-les-Grèves 12C2

Voie Communale de l'Armorique. **GPS:** n48,68157 w3,63411.

6 free. **Surface:** unpaved. 01/01-31/12
Distance: 3km 50m 2km on the spot.
Remarks: Beach parking.

Plestin-les-Grèves 12C2

Route de la Corniche. **GPS:** n48,67235 w3,63602.

6 free. **Location:** Rural, simple, quiet. **Surface:** grassy/sand.
01/01-31/12
Distance: 1km on the spot 300m Lidl 2km.
Remarks: Max. 24h.

Plestin-les-Grèves 12C2

Rue de Guergay. **GPS:** n48,66232 w3,62562.
€ 2/10minutes Ch € 2/1h.
Remarks: Motorhome washing place.

Pleubian 12C2

Port Béni. **GPS:** n48,84834 w3,17053.

4 free. **Location:** Rural, simple, isolated, quiet. **Surface:** asphalted.
01/01-31/12
Distance: Pleubian 2,5km on the spot 2,5km on the spot.
Remarks: Max. 24h.

Pleubian 12C2

Rue de Kermagen, Kermagen. **GPS:** n48,85667 w3,14194.

4 free. **Surface:** grassy. 01/01-31/12
Distance: Pleubian 1,6km beach 100m on the spot.
Remarks: Max. 24h.

Pleubian 12C2

Rue de Pen Lan, Lanéros. **GPS:** n48,85760 w3,07883.

4 free. **Surface:** asphalted.
Distance: Pleubian 5,5km on the spot on the spot.
Remarks: Max. 24h.

FR

S Pleumeur-Bodou 12C2

Parking de Toul ar Stang, Rue de Toul ar Stang, Ile Grande. **GPS**: n48,79868 w3,58342.

6 € 5/night € 2/10minutes Ch € 2/1h.
Location: Rural, simple, quiet. **Surface:** grassy.
01/01-31/12
Distance: Plemeur-Bodu 6km sandy beach 150m 150m on the spot.

S Pleumeur-Bodou 12C2

Cosmopolis-Parc Scientifique, Route du Radome. **GPS**: n48,78472 w3,52694.

20 free Ch WC . **Surface:** gravel/sand. 01/01-31/12
Distance: 1km 1km on the spot on the spot.

P Plévenon 12D2

Parking Cap Fréhel. **GPS**: n48,68174 w2,31811.

40 free, 01/06-30/09 € 4. **Surface:** metalled.
Distance: 50m.

S Ploemeur 12C4

Rue Louis Lessart. **GPS**: n47,73790 w3,4314.

7 free Chfree. **Surface:** asphalted. 01/01-31/12
Remarks: Parking in the centre, max. 24h.

Ploemeur 12C4

Aire du Courégant, D152, Boulevard de l'Atlantique. **GPS**: n47,71111 w3,47138.
7 free. **Surface:** asphalted. Easter-01/11
Distance: 200m on the spot.
Remarks: Only overnight stays 20-10h.

Ploemeur 12C4

Golf Ploemeur, D152, Boulevard de l'Atlantique. **GPS**: n47,72316 w3,48156.

10 free. **Surface:** gravel. 01/01-31/12
Distance: Ploemeur 5km N165 10km beach 300m 1,8km.

S Plogoff 12A3

Aire Naturelle Kerguidy Izella, Rue Guillaume Pennamen. **GPS**: n48,03694 w4,68139.

30 € 12 Ch WC included. **Location:** Comfortable. **Surface:** grassy. 01/01-31/12
Distance: 2km.
Remarks: 9><20h.

S Plogoff 12A3

Parking de l'Eglise, Rue Cleder cap Sizum. **GPS**: n48,03752 w4,6657.

4 free € 2/10minutes Ch. **Location:** Rural, comfortable.
Surface: asphalted. 01/01-31/12
Distance: centre.

Plogoff 12A3

Aire de la Pointe du Raz, Route des Langoustiers. **GPS**: n48,03651 w4,7173.

40 € 15-20. **Location:** Rural, simple. **Surface:** metalled.
01/01-31/12
Distance: 3km 50m.

Plogoff 12A3

Parking du Stade, Rue du 19 Mars 1962. **GPS**: n48,03245 w4,66316.

15 free. **Location:** Rural, simple. **Surface:** grassy/metalled.

FR

01/01-31/12
Distance: on the spot 450m 450m bakery.

Plomelin 12B3

Plomelin, Rue Hent Keramer. **GPS**: n47,93410 w4,1515.

5 free € 2/10minutes Ch . **Location:** Rural, simple, quiet. **Surface:** asphalted. 01/01-31/12
Remarks: Parking sports park, max. 24h.

Plonévez-Porzay 12B3

Plonévez-Porzay, Rue des Eglantines. **GPS**: n48,12469 w4,22414.

15 free € 2/10minutes Ch . **Location:** Rural, comfortable. **Surface:** grassy. 01/01-31/12
Distance: 600m 450m bakery + Spar.

Plonévez-Porzay 12B3

Kervel Izella. **GPS**: n48,11570 w4,28065.

10 free. **Location:** Rural, simple, simple. **Surface:** grassy/sand. 01/01-31/12
Distance: 5,5km 50m on the spot.
Remarks: Max 48h, beautiful view, beach parking.

Plouarzel 12A2

Aire de camping-car de Ruscumunoc, Route de Ruscumunoc. **GPS**: n48,42232 w4,78486.

free, 15/5-15/9 € 3,60 € 2,20/10minutes Ch € 2,20/50minutes . **Location:** Comfortable, quiet. **Surface:** grassy. 01/01-31/12
Distance: 3km 100m.

Ploubalay 13A4

Rue des Ormelets. **GPS**: n48,58057 w2,14524.

3 free Ch free. **Surface:** asphalted. 01/01-31/12
Distance: 100m 500m. **Remarks:** D768 Dinard-Lamballe, at roundabout dir D768 Dinard-Lamballe, after 30m left.

Ploubazlanec 12D2

Pointe l'Arcouest, Route de l'Embarcadère. **GPS**: n48,82102 w3,01948.

20 free, 30/06-30/09 € 6/24h. **Location:** Simple, isolated, quiet. **Surface:** grassy. 01/01-31/12
Distance: 2km 50m on the spot.

Plouescat 12B2

Rue de Pen an Théven. **GPS**: n48,65902 w4,21863.

6 free. **Surface:** metalled. 01/01-31/12
Distance: 3,5km 100m.

Plouescat 12B2

Intermarché, La Rocade-Kerchapalain. **GPS**: n48,65083 w4,18444.

4 free € 2 Ch € 2. **Location:** Comfortable. **Surface:** asphalted. 01/01-31/12
Distance: 500m 600m on the spot on the spot.
Remarks: Parking supermarket.

Plouézec 12D2

Place du 19 mars 1962. **GPS**: n48,74788 w2,9853.

FR

6 free. **Surface:** asphalted. 01/01-31/12
Remarks: Servicepoint at camping municipal.

S Plougasnou 12C2

Parking de la Métairie, Rue Charles de Gaulle. **GPS:** n48,69404 w3,79209.

7 free € 2/10minutes Ch € 2/1h WC. **Location:** Rural.
Surface: gravel. 01/01-31/12
Distance: on the spot sandy beach 1,4km 200m 250m bakery on the spot on the spot.
Remarks: Tue-morning market.

S Plougasnou 12C2

Rue des Grands Viviers, Le Diben. **GPS:** n48,70811 w3,82731.

7 free € 2 Ch . **Location:** Rural, simple, isolated, quiet.
Surface: asphalted. 01/01-31/12
Distance: 300m on the spot on the spot 300m on the spot.
Remarks: Coins available at town hall.

Plougasnou 12C2

Parking de la Baie, Rue du Grand Large, Primel-Trégastel. **GPS:** n48,71201 w3,81621.

7 free. **Location:** Rural, simple, central, quiet. **Surface:** gravel.
01/01-31/12
Distance: 50m.
Remarks: Max. 48h.

S Plougastel-Daoulas 12B2

Rue de la Fontaine Blanche. **GPS:** n48,37111 w4,36428.

15 free Ch free. **Surface:** asphalted. 15/05-15/10
Distance: 450m 450m 450m.
Remarks: Parking at sports grounds.

S Plougonvelin 12A2

Rue de Bertheaume. **GPS:** n48,33792 w4,70742.

100 € 6 Ch WC included. **Location:** Comfortable, quiet.
Surface: grassy/sand. 01/01-31/12
Distance: 1km beach 650m.

S Plougonvelin 12A2

Intermarché, Rue du Stade. **GPS:** n48,34245 w4,72248.

€ 6 € 2/100liter Ch € 1/1h € 5. **Surface:** asphalted.
Distance: on the spot.

S Plouguerneau 12B2

Lilia. GPS: n48,61891 w4,55341.

10 free € 4/10minutes Ch € 4/55minutes. **Location:** Comfortable.
Surface: asphalted. 01/01-31/12
Distance: 400m 850m 450m.

S Plouha 12D2

Plage de Palus, Route du Palus. **GPS:** n48,67667 w2,88556.

FR

20 free € 2/10minutes Ch € 2/1h WC. **Location:** Rural, simple, isolated, quiet. **Surface:** grassy. 01/03-31/10
Distance: 3km sandy/pebbled beach 100m 50m on the spot.
Remarks: Max. 3 days, baker every morning.

Plouhinec 12C4

Kervelue. **GPS**: n47,68116 w3,23633.

45 € 8 Ch (16x) WC. **Surface:** metalled.
01/01-31/12
Distance: Plouhinec 2,5km.

Ploumoguer 12A2

Rue Huon de Kermadec, D28. **GPS**: n48,40507 w4,72492.

30 free, July-Aug € 3 € 2/80liter Ch € 2/45minutes WC € 2 € 4,dryer € 2,30. **Surface:** metalled. 01/04-30/11
Distance: 200m 200m 200m.
Remarks: Next to stadium, max. 48h, coins at town hall, supermarket, baker and Tabac.

Plouvorn 12B2

Plan d'Eau de Lanorgant. **GPS**: n48,57722 w4,03056.

15 free € 2 Ch € 2 WC. **Location:** Simple, quiet. **Surface:** metalled.
01/01-31/12
Distance: 500m 100m 100m 500m 500m.
Remarks: Parking at small lake.

Pont-Aven 12C3

Rue Louis Lomenech. **GPS**: n47,85401 w3,74333.

20 free € 2,45 Ch € 2,45. **Surface:** asphalted.
01/01-31/12
Distance: 450m 450m.
Remarks: Parking near stadium Sinquin, coins at Office de Tourisme (D783).

Pont-Aven 12C3

Rue des Abbès Tanguy. **GPS**: n47,85646 w3,75203.
free. **Surface:** asphalted. 01/01-31/12
Distance: 400m.

Pont-Croix 12B3

Place de la Métairie. **GPS**: n48,04207 w4,48549.

40 free € 2/10minutes Ch. **Location:** Urban, simple.
Surface: metalled. 01/01-31/12
Distance: 10min on the spot.
Remarks: Thu (market).

Tourist information Pont-Croix:

Office de Tourisme, Rue Laënnec, www.chez.com/pontcroix/.Built as an anfiteatro. A number well-known artists stayed there.
Thu.

Pont-l'Abbé 12B3

Parking de la Gare, Rue de la Gare. **GPS**: n47,87070 w4,22506.

5 free Ch free. **Location:** Urban. **Surface:** asphalted.
01/01-31/12
Distance: on the spot.

Pont-l'Abbé 12B3

Leclerc, Route de Saint Jean Trolimont. **GPS**: n47,86390 w4,2367.

13 free € 2 Ch € 2. **Location:** Urban, simple. **Surface:** asphalted. 01/01-31/12
Distance: on the spot on the spot.
Remarks: At supermarket, centre.

S Pontivy 12C3

Rue de la Fontaine. **GPS**: n48,06758 w2,96941.
6 free free. **Location:** Urban, simple. **Surface:** metalled. 01/01-31/12

S Port-Louis 12C4

Aire de la Côte Rouge, D781 Port-Louis > Riantec. **GPS**: n47,70873 w3,34295.

18 € 5/24h, 01/06-15/09 € 10/24h Ch included.
Surface: asphalted. 01/01-31/12
Distance: on the spot on the spot.

S Port-Louis 12C4

Aire des Remparts, Promenade Henri François Buffet. **GPS**: n47,70496 w3,35602.

20 € 5/24h, 01/06-15/09 € 10/24h Chincluded. 01/01-31/12
Remarks: In front of campsite.

S Portsall 12A2

Aire camping-cars Kerros, Rue de Porsguen. **GPS**: n48,56583 w4,69944.

35 free € 2,10 Ch € 2,10. **Location:** Comfortable, quiet.
Surface: grassy. 01/01-31/12
Distance: on the spot 350m 200m 200m.
Remarks: Max. 3 days.

S Primelin 12A3

Camping Municipal de Kermaléro, Route de l'Océan. **GPS**: n48,02550 w4,61821.

15 free € 2 Ch € 2. **Location:** Simple. **Surface:** metalled. 01/01-31/12

S Priziac 12C3

Base de Loisirs du Lac du Bel Air, Etang du Bel Air. **GPS**: n48,06183 w3,41132.

€ 5,50 Ch included.
Distance: 300m.

S Quiberon 12C4

Rue de Port Kerné. **GPS**: n47,49165 w3,13941.

140 € 6/24h € 1/30liter Ch. **Surface:** asphalted. 01/01-31/12 service: 15/10-01/04.
Distance: 2km sea 250m.
Remarks: Next to campsite municipal, max. 72h, seaview.

Tourist information Quiberon:

Office de Tourisme, 14, rue de Verdun, www.quiberon.com.Lively bathing resort with boulevard and sandy beaches.

S Quimperlé 12C3

Aire Saint Nicolas, Rue du Viaduc. **GPS**: n47,86640 w3,54334.

3 free Chfree. **Surface:** metalled. 01/01-31/12

S Quintin 12D2

Place du Champ de Foire. **GPS**: n48,40056 w2,90222.

FR

free Chfree. **Surface:** asphalted. 01/01-31/12
Distance: on the spot on the spot.
Remarks: Near the lake.

Tourist information Quintin:
Tue-morning.

S Redon 20A1

Quai Robert Surcouf. **GPS:** n47,64510 w2,0897.

10 free Chfree. **Surface:** asphalted. 01/01-31/12
Distance: 500m on the spot 100m 200m 200m.
Remarks: In front of Bureau du Port de Plaisance.

Tourist information Redon:
Manoir de l'Automobile de Loheac.Car collection: Ferrari, Lamborghini, Porsche, Maserati.

S Rennes 13A5

Rue du Professeur Maurice Audin. **GPS:** n48,13531 w1,64542.

5 free € 2/100liter Ch € 2/1h € 1/30minutes.
Surface: asphalted. 01/01-31/12
Remarks: In park, near entrance of campsite, max. 48h.

Tourist information Rennes:
Office de Tourisme, 11, rue Saint Yves, www.tourisme-rennes.com/.University town with a historical centre.
Musée de Bretagne.Regional museum.
Tue-Sa.

S Riantec 12C4

Route de Plouhinec. **GPS:** n47,71111 w3,29889.

€ 4 . 01/01-31/12
Remarks: Parking lake.

Rochefort-en-Terre 12D4

Parking des Grées. **GPS:** n47,69975 w2,33384.

>100 € 2/24h. **Surface:** gravel. 01/01-31/12
Distance: 200m.

Rohan 12D3

Port de Plaisance, Rue Saint-Gouvry. **GPS:** n48,07139 w2,755.

6 free. **Surface:** asphalted. 01/01-31/12
Distance: 500m on the spot 500m.
Remarks: At the Nantes-Brest Canal.

S Romagné 13B5

Allée des Prunus, D812. **GPS:** n48,34409 w1,27415.

5 free Ch WC free. **Surface:** metalled. 01/01-31/12
Distance: 100m 1,7km 200m 50m.

S Roscoff 12B2

Route du Laber. **GPS:** n48,71215 w3,99918.

FR

30 free Ch free. **Location:** Isolated. **Surface:** asphalted.
01/01-31/12
Distance: 2km.
Remarks: Service 200m.

Tourist information Roscoff:
Office de Tourisme, 46, rue Gambetta, www.roscoff-tourisme.com.Seaside resort and former pirates town.
Wed.

Rostrenen 12C3

Rue Rosa l'Hénaff, D23. **GPS**: n48,23318 w3,32019.

6 free € 2/100liter Ch € 2/1h. **Surface:** asphalted.
01/01-31/12
Distance: 100m.
Remarks: Coins at office de tourisme, town hall, maison de presse, tabac.

Sains 13B4

Rue du puits Rimoult. **GPS**: n48,55305 w1,58603.

10 € 5 Ch free. **Surface:** grassy/metalled. 01/01-31/12
Distance: 100m 150m 150m.
Remarks: Via RN176.

Saint-Gelven 12C3

Rue de l'Ecole, D95. **GPS**: n48,22513 w3,09535.

10 free Ch free. **Surface:** concrete. 01/01-31/12

Saint-Pierre-Quiberon 12C4

Rue du Stade. **GPS**: n47,51160 w3,13903.

43 € 5/24h € 2/10minutes Ch € 2/55minutes .
Surface: asphalted. 01/01-31/12
Distance: 1km 1,5km.
Remarks: Max. 48h.

Saint-Rivoal 12B2

D42. **GPS**: n48,34930 w3,99782.

6 free Ch free 1h. **Surface:** grassy/metalled.
01/01-31/12
Distance: 200m.

Santec 12B2

Bistrot à Crèpes, Rue de Méchouroux. **GPS**: n48,70102 w4,03868.

15 € 3 € 2 Ch included WC . **Location:** Quiet. **Surface:** grassy.
01/01-31/12
Distance: Beach Staol 50m on the spot 800m.

Sarzeau 12D4

Banastère, Rue du Palud Bihan. **GPS**: n47,51444 w2,66778.

10 € 5/18-8h € 2 Ch € 2. **Surface:** metalled.
01/01-31/12
Distance: on the spot.

Sarzeau 12D4

Rue de Brénudel. **GPS**: n47,52969 w2,7598.

FR

20 € 5/24h € 2 Ch € 2. **Surface:** asphalted.
01/01-31/12 school hours (8-16h).

Sarzeau 12D4

Rue du Port St.Jacques, Kerbodo. **GPS**: n47,48906 w2,79297.

10 € 5/18-8h Ch free WC € 2. **Surface:** asphalted.
01/01-31/12
Distance: 500m 100m 200m.
Remarks: Nearby port, max. 48h.

Sarzeau 12D4

Rue du Raker/Rue du Pont Neui, Plage du Rohaliguen. **GPS**: n47,49769 w2,76748.

10 € 5/18-8h Ch WC free. **Surface:** metalled.
01/01-31/12
Distance: on the spot.

Sarzeau 12D4

Rue du Stang, St.Colombier. **GPS**: n47,54665 w2,72151.

5 € 5/18-8h Ch free. **Surface:** asphalted.
Distance: St.Colombier 100m 50m 50m.

Sarzeau 12D4

Pointe de Penvins, Route de la Chapelle. **GPS**: n47,49472 w2,68139.

15 € 5. **Surface:** asphalted. 01/01-31/12
Distance: on the spot.
Remarks: Follow Pointe de Penvins.

Scaër 12C3

Rue Louis Pasteur. **GPS**: n48,02774 w3,6951.
free € 2/10minutes Ch € 2/55minutes. **Surface:** gravel.
Distance: 500m.
Remarks: Max. 72h, shady, coins at camping municipal.

Sérent 12D4

Du Pont Salmon, Rue du Général De Gaule,. **GPS**: n47,82445 w2,50194.

10 free. **Surface:** asphalted. 01/01-31/12
Distance: 400m 400m 400m.

St.Aignan (Morbihan) 12C3

Place de l'Église. **GPS**: n48,18306 w3,01361.

6 free Ch WC free. **Surface:** metalled. 01/01-31/12
Remarks: Square behind the church.

St.Aubin d'Aubigné 13A5

Rue de Rennes. **GPS**: n48,26147 w1,60621.

5 free Ch WC free. **Surface:** asphalted. 01/01-31/12
Distance: on the spot 100m on the spot on the spot.

St.Barnabé 12D3

Place du Vieux Chêne, Rue Pierre Loti. **GPS**: n48,13672 w2,70146.

FR

10 free Chfree. **Surface:** gravel. 01/01-31/12
Distance: 200m bakery 50m.

St.Benoit-des-Ondes 13A4

Rue Bord de Mer. **GPS:** n48,61681 w1,84714.

10 free € 3/80liter Ch € 3/15minutes. **Surface:** asphalted.

St.Brice-en-Coglès 13B5

Rue de Normandie, D102. **GPS:** n48,41150 w1,36283.

8 free € 2/100liter Ch € 2/55minutes WC.
Surface: asphalted/metalled. 01/01-31/12
Distance: 300m 500m 400m 300m.

St.Carreuc 12D2

Rue de la Lande, D27. **GPS:** n48,40300 w2,73923.

12 free € 2/10minutes Ch € 2/55minutes.
Surface: grassy/gravel. 01/01-31/12
Distance: 300m on the spot.
Remarks: At Etang-du-Plessis, max. 24h.

St.Cast-le-Guildo 12D2

Bois Bras. GPS: n48,61083 w2,26806.

free. **Location:** Simple, isolated. 01/01-31/12
Distance: 2,5km 2,5km Intermarché 500m.

St.Derrien 12B2

GPS: n48,54760 w4,18114.

20 free € 3 Ch € 3 WC. **Location:** Quiet. **Surface:** gravel/metalled.
01/05-31/10
Distance: 100m on the spot on the spot 300m 300m.
Remarks: Nearby recreation area.

St.Gildas-de Rhuys 12D4

Route de la Baie d'Abraham. **GPS:** n47,51359 w2,84627.

20 free. **Surface:** unpaved.
Distance: 1,5km beach 50m.
Remarks: Nearby beach des Goh-Velins, max. 48h.

St.Gildas-de Rhuys 12D4

Camping municipal de Kervert, Route du Rohu. **GPS:** n47,52238 w2,85803.

20 € 6/24h € 2 Ch. **Surface:** grassy/metalled.
01/01-31/12
Distance: 4km 50m 400m 4km.

St.Guyomard 12D4

Route de Bohal, D112. **GPS:** n47,78166 w2,51188.

FR

20 € 5/night € 3 Ch € 3. **Surface:** asphalted.
Distance: 300m 100m.
Remarks: Behind church, check in at town hall.

St.Jacut-de-la-Mer 13A4

Rue de la Manchette. **GPS:** n48,58969 w2,18947.

26 € 5. **Surface:** grassy/gravel.
Distance: 1km 500m.
Remarks: Baker at 8am.

S St.Jacut-de-la-Mer 13A4

Rue de Dinan. **GPS:** n48,58727 w2,19027.
€ 2 Ch € 2.

S St.Malo 13A4

Les Iltots, Avenue de la Guimorais, Rothéneuf. **GPS:** n48,68109 w1,96348.

50 € 5, 01/07-31/08 € 10,30 Ch included. **Surface:** grassy.
15/04-30/09
Distance: sandy beach 100m 200m.

S St.Malo 13A4

Parking Paul Féval, Rue Paul Féval. **GPS:** n48,64341 w1,99385.

200 € 7,40, 19.00-09.00h free € 2 Ch. **Surface:** gravel.
holidays + 01/07-07/09
Distance: 800m Free bus to centre.
Remarks: 01/07-03/09 free shuttle bus to centre, 9am-12pm.

Tourist information St.Malo:
Office de Tourisme, Esplanade St-Vincent, www.saint-malo-tourisme.com. City with restored centre.

M Château.Castle, 14/15th century, historical museum.
10-12h, 14-18h. T € 4,50.
Fort National.Fort designed by Vauban. At ebb accessible by foot.
T € 5.

S St.Pol-de-Léon 12B2

Quai de Pempoul. **GPS:** n48,68361 w3,97083.

30 free € 2 Ch € 2 WC. **Surface:** metalled. 01/01-31/12
Distance: 800m on the spot on the spot 800m 800m.
Remarks: At the sea.

S St.Pol-de-Léon 12B2

Rue Hervé Mesguen. **GPS:** n48,67919 w3,99749.

8 free € 2/10minutes Ch € 2/55minutes. **Location:** Comfortable.
Surface: asphalted. 01/01-31/12
Distance: on the spot.
Remarks: In front of supermarket Leclerc.

S St.Rénan 12B2

Route de l'Aber. **GPS:** n48,43878 w4,63063.

10 free € 2 Ch € 2. **Surface:** gravel. 01/01-31/12
Remarks: Jul/Aug max. 48h.

S St.Servais 12B2

Cité Yan d'Argent. **GPS:** n48,50984 w4,15434.

10 free Ch free WC. **Location:** Simple, quiet.
Surface: gravel/metalled. 01/01-31/12
Distance: 200m 200m 200m.

FR

St.Thégonnec 12B2

Park an Iliz, D118. **GPS**: n48,52215 w3,94637.

25 free Ch free. **Location:** Urban, comfortable, central, quiet. **Surface:** gravel. 01/01-31/12
Distance: on the spot 150m 150m on the spot on the spot.
Remarks: Coins available at the shops.

Tourist information St.Thégonnec:
Fri.
Crêperie Steredenn, Rue de la Gare 6.

Sulniac 12D4

Salle des Fêtes, Rue des Écoles. **GPS**: n47,67756 w2,56642.

15 free Chfree. **Surface:** grassy/sand. 01/01-31/12
Distance: 400m bakery 500m.

Taden 13A4

Salle Neuville, Rue de la Robardais. **GPS**: n48,47251 w2,02203.

20 free € 2 Ch € 2. **Surface:** gravel. 01/01-31/12
Distance: 700m 100m 100m 500m.

Theix 12D4

Allée de Noyalo. **GPS**: n47,62726 w2,66183.

4 free Chfree. **Surface:** asphalted.
Distance: 500m 500m 500m.

Tinténiac 13A5

Quai de la Donac. **GPS**: n48,33168 w1,83202.

10 free Chfree. **Surface:** grassy/gravel. 01/01-31/12
Distance: 500m Along river 100m 550m.

Trébeurden 12C2

Route de Lannion, D65. **GPS**: n48,76711 w3,5514.

5 free € 2,05 Ch € 2,05 . **Location:** Rural, comfortable, central, quiet. **Surface:** asphalted.
Distance: on the spot 1,4km 1,5km 1km bakery, Intermarché 1,5km.

Trébeurden 12C2

Plage Goas-Treiz, Chemin de Crec'h Hellen. **GPS**: n48,78231 w3,57714.

35 € 5, Jul/Oct € 10. **Location:** Rural, simple, isolated. **Surface:** unpaved. 01/01-31/12
Distance: Trébeurden 2km sandy beach 80m 2km on the spot.
Remarks: Beach parking.

Tourist information Trébeurden:
Office de Tourisme, Place de Crec'h Hery, www.ville-trebeurden.fr.st.Bathing resort.

Trégastel 12C2

Rue de Poul-Palud. **GPS**: n48,82437 w3,49874.

56 € 4, 01/03-15/11 € 7,50 Chfree. **Location:** Rural, comfortable, isolated, quiet. **Surface:** asphalted. 01/01-31/12
Distance: 1km 1km Super U on the spot.
Remarks: Max. 5 nights, Aug max. 3 nights.

Tréguier 12C2

Boulevard Anatole le Braz. **GPS**: n48,78932 w3,23144.

FR

20 free Chfree. **Surface:** asphalted. 01/01-31/12
Distance: 100m 20m 20m 100m 100m.

S Tréguier 12C2

Super U, Boulevard Jean Guehenno. **GPS:** n48,77892 w3,23346.
€ 1/10minutes Ch. 01/01-31/12
Distance: 200m on the spot.

S Trégunc 12B3

Parking Quentel, Place de la Mairie, Rue de Pont-Aven. **GPS:** n47,85472 w3,85139.

6 free € 3 Ch € 3 . **Surface:** metalled. 01/01-31/12
Remarks: Parking behind town hall, max. 24h.

Trégunc 12B3

Parking de Pouldohan. **GPS:** n47,84435 w3,88832.
5 free. **Surface:** grassy.

Trégunc 12B3

Plage Ster Greich. **GPS:** n47,84918 w3,88656.
6 free. **Surface:** sand. 01/01-31/12
Remarks: Max. 24h.

Trégunc 12B3

Route de Kerlaëron. **GPS:** n47,82964 w3,8872.
5 free. **Surface:** sand. 01/01-31/12
Remarks: Max. 24h.

Trégunc 12B3

Rue de Porzh Breign. **GPS:** n47,84079 w3,89736.
6 free. **Surface:** asphalted. 01/01-31/12
Remarks: Max. 24h.

S Trégunc 12B3

Supermarché Casino, Route de Concarneau, D783. **GPS:** n47,85633 w3,86343.
4 free € 2 Ch € 2 . **Surface:** asphalted.

Tremblay 13B5

Route de Fougères. **GPS:** n48,42328 w1,47095.

free € 2/10minutes € 2/55minutes. **Surface:** asphalted.
01/01-31/12
Distance: 400m 200m.

S Trémuson 12D2

Aire du Buchon, Rue de Brest, D712. **GPS:** n48,52250 w2,85278.

5 free Chfree. **Surface:** asphalted. 01/01-31/12
Distance: 50m 500m.
Remarks: Max. 48h. RN12 exit La Barricade (from dir Brest) or exit Aéroport (from dir Rennes).

S Vannes 12D4

Camping-car Parc, Avenue du Maréchal Juin. **GPS:** n47,63283 w2,77996.

33 € 12/24h Chincluded € 4 .
Surface: asphalted.
01/01-31/12
Remarks: In front of campsite Conleau, Note: access only after buying entrance (3 formulas) via www.campingcarpark.com
(wifi available).

Tourist information Vannes:

Office de Tourisme, 1, rue Thiers, www.tourisme-vannes.com.The old district is surrounded by ramparts with gates and parks with historical wash places.
Château Gaillard.Archeological regional museum.
Cathédrale St Pierre.

Pays de la Loire

S Angers 20C1

Boulevard Olivier-Couffon. **GPS:** n47,46616 w0,56549.

20 € 4/4h, € 7/10h Chfree. **Location:** Urban, noisy. **Surface:** asphalted. 01/01-31/12
Distance: centre 950m 3km.
Remarks: Max. 36h, château d'Angers 600m.

Tourist information Angers:

Office de Tourisme, 7, Place Kennedy, www.angers-tourisme.com.City with historical centre, former capital of Anjou.
Haras National du Lion d'Angers.National stud-farm.
15/04-11/09 daily, 12/09-14/04 Sa-Su 10.30h, 14.30h, 16h.
Château d' Angers.Fortified castle, museum for contemporary art.
10-17.30h. € 6.

S Angrie 20B1

Route du Vieux Bourg. **GPS:** n47,57176 w0,97312.

FR

10 free Chfree. **Location:** Rural. **Surface:** gravel/metalled.
01/01-31/12
Distance: 400m on the spot.
Remarks: Max. 48h.

S Arnage 13D6
GPS: n47,93035 e0,18418.

2 free € 2 Ch . **Location:** Urban, simple, quiet. **Surface:** asphalted.
01/01-31/12
Distance: 250m on the spot 500m on the spot.

S Assérac 12D4
Camping-Car Park de la Baie, Ker Avelo. **GPS**: n47,42446 w2,44688.
10 € 12 Ch WC included. **Location:** Rural, comfortable, quiet. **Surface:** metalled. 01/01-31/12
Distance: Assérac 5km sandy beach 350m.

Assérac 12D4
Chemin de la Baie des Mulets. **GPS**: n47,42556 w2,45528.

5 free WC. **Location:** Simple. **Surface:** grassy. 01/01-31/12
Distance: 50m 100m 100m 200m 200m.

Assérac 12D4
Route de la Grande Isle. **GPS**: n47,43111 w2,45194.

free WC. **Surface:** metalled.
Distance: 1km 300m 300m 2km 2km.

S Aubigné-sur-Layon 20C2
Rue de 17 mars 1962. **GPS**: n47,21167 w0,46383.

3 free Chfree. **Surface:** metalled. 01/01-31/12
Distance: 100m.

S Averton 13D5
Étang des Perles. **GPS**: n48,34744 w0,24468.

10 free € 2 Ch WC. **Location:** Rural. **Surface:** gravel.
01/01-31/12
Distance: lake on the spot on the spot on the spot.

S Batz-sur-Mer 12D5
Route de la Govelle. **GPS**: n47,26747 w2,4537.

8 free € 2 Ch € 2 WC. **Location:** Simple. **Surface:** metalled.
01/01-31/12
Distance: 1,5km 100m 100m 1,5km 50m.
Remarks: Max. 48h.

Batz-sur-Mer 12D5
Baie du Manéric, Route du Dervin. **GPS**: n47,27028 w2,46139.
± 10 free. **Surface:** grassy. summer
Distance: 50m.

S Baugé 20D1
Chemin du Pont des Fées. **GPS**: n47,53886 w0,09637.

10 free € 3/15minutes Ch € 3/15minutes. **Location:** Rural.
Surface: gravel.
Distance: 2km 400m.

S Baugé 20D1
Rue de la Croix de Mission, Le Vieil Baugé. **GPS**: n47,53066 e0,11899.

FR

8 free Chfree. **Location:** Rural. **Surface:** gravel.
01/01-31/12
Distance: on the spot bakery 100m.
Remarks: Service 50m.

Bazouges-sur-le-Loir 20D1

Voie de la Liberté. **GPS:** n47,68994 w0,16952.

free. **Location:** Rural, quiet. **Surface:** gravel. 01/01-31/12
Distance: 200m 200m.

Beauvoir-sur-Mer 12D5

Rue de Nantes. **GPS:** n46,91685 w2,0465.

24 free, overnight stay € 5 € 2,50/3minutes Ch € 2,50/15minutes WC . **Location:** Urban, simple. **Surface:** asphalted.
01/01-31/12
Distance: 400m 800m 800m.
Remarks: Max. 48h.

Belleville-sur-Vie 20A3

Rue des Écoliers. **GPS:** n46,78160 w1,42875.

15 free. **Surface:** gravel. 01/01-31/12
Distance: 500m 500m 200m.
Remarks: Near Salle des Fêtes.

Benet 20C4

Rue de la Gare. **GPS:** n46,36896 w0,59482.

10 free Ch WC free. **Surface:** asphalted.
Distance: 300m 300m on the spot 50m.

Blain 20A1

Place Jollan de Clerville, Rue Victor Schoelcher. **GPS:** n47,47444 w1,76139.

30 free Chfree. **Surface:** gravel. 01/01-31/12
Distance: 100m 100m.

Blaison-Gohier 21A1

Rue de Thibaut de Blaison. **GPS:** n47,39923 e0,37515.

5 free Chfree. **Surface:** asphalted. 01/01-31/12
Distance: on the spot 200m 200m.

Bouchemaine 20C1

Rue Chevrière. **GPS:** n47,41913 w0,61117.

40 free, 01/03-30/11 € 10 € 0,50/50liter Ch WC € 1 included.
Surface: grassy/gravel.
01/01-31/12 service: 01/12-28/02.
Distance: 50m.
Remarks: Former campsite, along the river Maine, baker every morning (Jul/Aug).

Bouin 12D5

GPS: n47,00918 w2,02782.

FR

10 free. **Location:** Rural, simple. **Surface:** grassy/gravel.
01/01-31/12
Distance: on the spot.

Bouin 12D5

GPS: n46,99821 w2,03314.

10 free. **Location:** Simple. **Surface:** metalled. 01/01-31/12
Distance: on the spot on the spot.

Bouin 12D5

Port du Bec, Rue du Port du Bec. **GPS**: n46,93696 w2,07182.

free. **Surface:** gravel. 01/01-31/12

Bourgneuf-en-Retz 20A2

D758. **GPS**: n47,04028 w1,95704.

10 free Ch WC free. **Location:** Simple. **Surface:** asphalted.
01/01-31/12 Service: winter.
Distance: 300m 200m 300m 300m.
Remarks: Parking office de tourisme, max. 48h.

Boussay 20B2

Place des Marronniers. **GPS**: n47,04240 w1,18648.

4 free € 2 Ch € 2. **Surface:** asphalted. 01/01-31/12
Distance: 200m 200m 200m.
Remarks: Max. 48h, coins at mairie/poste.

Brétignolles-sur-Mer 20A3

Parking de la Normandelière, Rue de la Source. **GPS**: n46,61664 w1,85974.

25 free. **Location:** Simple. **Surface:** metalled. 01/01-31/12
Distance: 1,5km sandy beach 500m 1,5km on the spot on the spot.
Remarks: Service: Super U D38, GPS 46,62537 -1,85787.

Tourist information Brétignolles-sur-Mer:
Thu, Su.

Briollay 20C1

Plage de Briollay. **GPS**: n47,56766 w0,50733.
10 free Ch free. **Surface:** grassy/gravel. 01/01-31/12
Remarks: Along Sarthe River, closed when frosty and high water.

Tourist information Briollay:
Syndicat d'Initiative, 6 rue de la Mairie.Small historical place in the Loire-valley.

Brissac-Quincé 20C1

Rue de l'Aubance. **GPS**: n47,35465 w0,4463.

2 free Ch. **Surface:** asphalted. 01/01-31/12
Distance: 300m 300m 300m.

Chailland 13C5

Coccimarket. **GPS**: n48,22139 w0,86583.

FR

4 free Chfree. **Location:** Rural, simple. **Surface:** asphalted.
01/01-31/12
Distance: 300m 300m on the spot.
Remarks: Max. 24h.

S Chaille-les-Marais 20B4

Rue du 8 Mai 1945. **GPS**: n46,39228 w1,02127.

20 free € 3 Ch. **Surface:** grassy.
01/01-31/12 Thu-morning.
Distance: 100m 300m 50m.
Remarks: At fire-station and sports park.

S Challans 20A3

Parking du Viaud Marais. **GPS**: n46,85027 w1,8742.

15 free Chfree. **Surface:** asphalted. 01/01-31/12
Distance: 1km 500m 500m 100m.
Remarks: Max. 3 days.

S Chalonnes-sur-Loire 20C1

Avenue de la gare. **GPS**: n47,34961 w0,74847.

15 free Chfree. **Surface:** forest soil. 01/01-31/12
Distance: 1km 1km on the spot.
Remarks: Parking nearby caveau the dégustation and swimming pool.

S Chambretaud 20B2

Aire des Diamants, Rue Notre Dame. **GPS**: n46,92300 w0,9717.

5 free € 2 Ch WC. **Surface:** asphalted. 01/01-31/12
Distance: 1km 5km on the spot 1km.

S Champtocé-sur-Loire 20B1

Rue de la Hutte. **GPS**: n47,41143 w0,86958.

8 free Chfree. **Location:** Rural, simple. **Surface:** asphalted.
01/01-31/12
Distance: 300m 5,7km 400m 400m.
Remarks: At stadium.

S Champtoceaux 20B1

Parking Champalud, Place de Niederheimbach. **GPS**: n47,33816 w1,2649.

5 free Ch € 3/24h WC. **Surface:** asphalted. 01/01-31/12
Distance: 150m 23km.
Remarks: Square behind the church, max. 48h.

S Champtoceaux 20B1

Le Port du Moulin, Le Cul du Moulin, D751. **GPS**: n47,33913 w1,27445.

3 free WC free. **Surface:** metalled. 01/01-31/12
Distance: 1,5km on the spot on the spot on the spot 1,5km.
Remarks: Along Dordogne river, max. 48h.

S Changé 13C6

Parking du plan d'eau du Port, Rue du Bac. **GPS**: n48,10083 w0,78556.

10 free Chfree. **Location:** Urban, simple. **Surface:** gravel/sand.
01/01-31/12
Distance: 5km 800m.
Remarks: Along the Mayenne river.

S Chantonnay 20B3

Rue de l'Arc en Ciel. **GPS**: n46,68754 w1,04104.

FR

5 free € 2 Ch € 2. **Surface:** asphalted. 01/01-31/12
Distance: 1km 500m 1km.
Remarks: Next to sports fields.

Chanzeaux 20C2

Aire de Ploizeau, D121. **GPS**: n47,25548 w0,63848.

6 free € 2/100liter Ch. **Surface:** metalled. 01/01-31/12
Distance: 1km on the spot 1km 1km.

Château-d'Olonne 20A3

Rue des Plesses. **GPS**: n46,49132 w1,74293.

20 € 6,10/night, € 10,20/2 nights € 2/6minutes Ch € 3/10minutes.
Location: Simple. **Surface:** asphalted.
01/01-31/12
Distance: 500m.

Château-Gontier 13C6

Quai-du-Docteur Lefevre. **GPS**: n47,82450 w0,70206.

30 free. **Location:** Urban, simple, central. **Surface:** asphalted.
01/01-31/12
Distance: 200m on the spot 50m.
Remarks: Along the Mayenne river.

Tourist information Château-Gontier:
Office de Tourisme, Péniche l'Elan, Quai d'Alsace, www.sud-mayenne.com. City on the Mayenne river, place for watersports.

Chavagne-en-Paillers 20B3

Place des Arcades. **GPS**: n46,89083 w1,24917.

3 free € 2/100liter Ch € 2/55minutes. **Surface:** asphalted.
01/01-31/12
Distance: 300m 50m 100m 300m.
Remarks: Coins at Office de Tourisme.

Chavagnes les Eaux 20C2

Place de la Mairie. **GPS**: n47,27024 w0,45437.

3 free Chfree. **Surface:** metalled. 01/01-31/12
Distance: on the spot 150m.
Remarks: Behind church.

Chênehutte-Trèves-Cunault 20D2

Rue Beauregard, D751, Cunault. **GPS**: n47,32685 e0,19459.

40 free € 3/100liter Ch € 3/6h. **Surface:** grassy.
01/01-31/12
Distance: 500m 500m 500m.

Chenillé-Changé 20C1

Le Pin, D78. **GPS**: n47,69919 w0,66693.

8 € 2,80-4 € 2,80 Ch. **Location:** Simple. **Surface:** gravel.
01/01-31/12
Distance: on the spot 100m.
Remarks: Along the Mayenne river, coins at cafe.

Coëx 21C3

Rue des Goélettes. **GPS**: n46,69717 e1,76410.

FR

4 free € 2/10minutes Ch € 2/55minutes. **Location:** Rural. **Surface:** asphalted. 01/01-31/12
Distance: 200m 500m 500m.
Remarks: Max. 48h, coins at town hall.

S Combrée 20B1

Rue de Bretagne, Bel-Air. **GPS**: n47,71281 w0,9989.

3 free Ch WC free. **Location:** Rural. **Surface:** unpaved. 01/01-31/12
Distance: 100m.

Combrée 20B1

D203. **GPS**: n47,70321 w1,02755.

3 free. **Location:** Rural, quiet. **Surface:** asphalted. 01/01-31/12
Distance: 200m 50m.
Remarks: Behind tennis-court.

S Concourson-sur-Layon 20C2

Aire de Repos, D960. **GPS**: n47,17405 w0,34317.

10 free € 2 Ch WC. **Surface:** asphalted. 01/01-31/12
Distance: 400m 400m 400m.

S Dampierre-sur-Loire 20D2

L'Aigrette, Route de Montsoreau. **GPS**: n47,24157 w0,0232.

40 free Ch WC. **Surface:** forest soil. 01/04-02/11
Distance: on the spot on the spot on the spot.
Remarks: On the river Loire.

S Deux-Evailles 13C5

Site de la Fenderie, Champ de Vigne, D129. **GPS**: n48,20203 w0,52018.

20 free € 2 Ch € 2 WC. **Location:** Rural, comfortable, quiet. **Surface:** grassy/gravel. 01/01-31/12
Distance: 1km 20m 20m 20m 5km Montsurs on the spot.
Remarks: Coins at Auberge.

S Doué-la-Fontaine 20C2

Rue Jean Gaschet. **GPS**: n47,18280 w0,25742.
3 free Ch free.

Durtal 20D1

Rue du Petit Port. **GPS**: n47,66842 w0,24172.

5 free. **Location:** Rural, quiet. **Surface:** asphalted.
Distance: 300m 2,4km.

S Durtal 20D1

Rue Beausite. **GPS**: n47,67139 w0,2406.

2 free € 2/10minutes Ch € 2/60minutes. **Location:** Simple. **Surface:** asphalted. 01/01-31/12
Distance: 300m 2,4km.
Remarks: Inclining pitches.

S Ernée 13C5

Plan d'eau d'Ernée, Plan d'eau d'Ernée. **GPS**: n48,29670 w0,93997.

FR

2 free WC free. **Location:** Urban, simple, quiet. **Surface:** asphalted.
01/01-31/12
Distance: 500m on the spot 500m 500m.
Remarks: Parking at small lake.

S Faye d'Anjou 20C2

Chateau du Fresne, D55, Rue des Monts. **GPS**: n47,29923 w0,53806.

10 free Chfree. **Surface:** gravel. 01/01-31/12
Distance: 2km 3km.

S Feneu 20C1

Port Albert. **GPS**: n47,56560 w0,60994.

6 free € 2 Ch. **Location:** Rural, quiet. **Surface:** gravel.
01/01-31/12
Distance: 1,5km.
Remarks: Along the Mayenne river.

S Fontenay-le-Comte 20B4

Avenue du Général de Gaulle. **GPS**: n46,46203 w0,80544.

10 free € 3 Ch. **Surface:** metalled.
01/01-31/12
Distance: 500m 500m 500m.
Remarks: Max. 24h, centre, in front of police station.

Tourist information Fontenay-le-Comte:
Office de Tourisme, 8, rue du Grimouard, www.tourisme-sudvendee.com.
Old city, capital of the Southern Vendée, city walk 'mille ans d'histoire'.

S Fontevraud l'Abbaye 20D2

Allée des Bruyères. **GPS**: n47,18444 e0,04917.

9 free Ch WC free. **Surface:** asphalted.
Distance: 400m 400m 400m.

Tourist information Fontevraud l'Abbaye:
Abbaye Royale de Fontevraud.
daily 9-18.30h, 01/10-30/05 10-18h 01/01, 01/05, 01/11, 11/11, 25/12.

S Foussais-Payré 20C4

Place du Prieuré. **GPS**: n46,53000 w0,68275.

20 free Chfree. **Surface:** gravel. 01/01-31/12
Distance: 500m 500m 200m.

S Fresnay-sur-Sarthe 13D5

Rue de la Gare. **GPS**: n48,28171 e0,02978.

8 free Chfree. **Location:** Simple. **Surface:** gravel.
01/01-31/12
Distance: 600m 600m 50m.

S Gené 20C1

Escale du Haut Anjou, La Petite Fenouillère. **GPS**: n47,63770 w0,79641.

7 € 12 Ch included. **Location:** Rural, simple. **Surface:** gravel.
01/01-31/12
Distance: 1,2km fish pond.
Remarks: Cheese farm.

S Grez-en-Bouère 13C6

Place A. Peigné. **GPS**: n47,87306 w0,52306.

FR

6 free Ch free WC. **Location:** Rural, simple. **Surface:** asphalted.
01/01-31/12, service: 01/04-30/11
Distance: 50m 50m 100m.
Remarks: Max. 48h.

S Grez-Neuville 21A1

Rue du Port, D291. **GPS:** n47,60119 e0,68504.

8 free Ch free. **Location:** Rural, simple. **Surface:** grassy.
01/01-31/12
Remarks: Former campsite.

S Guenrouet 20A1

GPS: n47,52376 w1,95177.

2 free € 2 Ch € 2. **Surface:** asphalted.
01/04-31/10
Distance: 200m 50m 200m 200m.
Remarks: Next to campsite Saint Clair, along canal of Nantes/Brest, max. 24h.

S Guérande 12D4

Geen naam, Rue du Parc Savary, D99E. **GPS:** n47,33389 w2,42083.

20 free € 5/100liter Ch € 5/1h . **Location:** Simple, noisy.
Surface: asphalted/grassy. 01/01-31/12
Distance: 1km.

Tourist information Guérande:

Office de Tourisme, 1, place du Marché au Bois, www.ot-guerande.fr.Fortified city.

Office de Tourisme, 8, Place de la Victoire, La Baule, www.labaule.fr.Mundane bathing resort to the Côte d'Armour.

S Jans 20A1

Route Tréffieux. **GPS:** n47,62222 w1,61222.

6 free Ch WC free. **Surface:** gravel. 01/01-31/12
Remarks: Behind town hall.

S Jard-sur-Mer 20A4

Route des Goffineaux. **GPS:** n46,41074 w1,59358.

16 € 6,20/24h, € 10,40/48h € 2,10/10minutes Ch .
Location: Rural, simple. **Surface:** asphalted. 01/01-31/12
Distance: 1km 50m 1,5km 1,5km.

S Juvigné 13B5

Plan d'Eau de Saint Martin, Rue de lCroixille, D29. **GPS:** n48,22806 w1,03806.

20 free Ch WC free. **Location:** Urban, simple. **Surface:** gravel.
01/01-31/12
Distance: 200m 20m 200m 100m on the spot.
Remarks: Max. 24h.

S La Baconnière 13C5

Place de l'Eglise. **GPS:** n48,18361 w0,89139.

5 free Ch free. **Location:** Urban, simple. **Surface:** asphalted.
01/01-31/12
Distance: on the spot 100m.
Remarks: Behind church, service (winter) on demand.

FR

S La Baule 12D5

Boulevard Guy de Champsavin, La Baule-Escoublac. **GPS**: n47,28196 w2,42509.

20 free € 3 Ch (20x)€ 3/55minutes. **Location:** Urban, comfortable, quiet. **Surface:** metalled.
Distance: beach 700m.

S La Bernerie-en-Retz 12D5

Parking Wilson, Avenue de Jean d Arc. **GPS**: n47,07871 w2,03399.

37 € 5,33-6,56 € 3,30 Ch € 3,30 WC.
Surface: asphalted. 01/01-31/12
Distance: 300m 100m 300m 300m on the spot.
Remarks: Max. 48h.

S La Chapelle-Saint-Florent 20B1

Aire du Stade, Rue de l'Evre. **GPS**: n47,33411 w1,05178.

6 free Ch. **Surface:** gravel. 01/01-31/12
Distance: 300m 300m 50m.

S La Daguenière 21A1

Chemin de Beausse, Rue de Stade. **GPS**: n47,42222 e0,43936.

12 free Chfree. **Location:** Rural. **Surface:** asphalted.
01/01-31/12
Distance: 200m 300m 300m.
Remarks: Next to sports fields.

La Daguenière 21A1

Port Maillard. **GPS**: n47,41743 e0,43781.

6 free WC. **Location:** Rural. **Surface:** unpaved. 01/01-31/12
Remarks: Along the Loire river.

S La Flèche 20D1

Promenade du Maréchal Foch. **GPS**: n47,69767 w0,07875.

10 free free. **Location:** Urban. **Surface:** asphalted.
01/01-31/12 Wed, market.
Distance: 100m 100m 100m.

S La Fresnaye-sur-Chédouet 14A5

La forêt de Perseigne, Les Ventes du Four, D236. **GPS**: n48,43469 e0,25972.

20 free Chfree. **Location:** Rural, quiet. **Surface:** gravel.
01/01-31/12
Distance: La Fresnaye 1,5km on the spot.

S La Meilleraie-Tillay 20B3

Rue des Ombrages. **GPS**: n46,73923 w0,84578.

6 free € 2 Ch WC € 1. **Surface:** asphalted. 01/04-31/10
Distance: 700m 700m 700m.

S La Plaine-sur-Mer 12D5

Chemin de la gare. **GPS**: n47,13944 w2,19139.

FR

8 free Chfree. **Location:** Simple, isolated. **Surface:** asphalted. 01/01-31/12
Distance: 300m 800m 500m.
Remarks: Max. 24h.

La Poitevinière 20B2

Place de la Fontaine, D15. **GPS**: n47,22723 w0,897.

4 free Ch WC free. **Surface:** asphalted. 01/01-31/12
Distance: 50m on the spot 50m.
Remarks: Coins available at bar.

La Roche-sur-Yon 20A3

Boulevard Italie. **GPS**: n46,66833 w1,41861.

20 free Ch free.
Distance: 500m 500m 500m.
Remarks: Max. 36h.

La Séguinière 20B2

Avenue de Nantes. **GPS**: n47,06005 w0,93668.

10 free €2/100liter Ch €2/1h WC. **Surface:** asphalted.
Distance: 100m on the spot 50m.

La Suze-sur-Sarthe 13D6

Rue du Camping. **GPS**: n47,88917 e0,03040.

10 €3 Ch free WC. **Location:** Urban, simple. **Surface:** grassy/gravel. 01/01-31/12
Distance: 300m 300m on the spot on the spot.
Remarks: Along Sarthe River.

La Tranche-sur-Mer 20A4

Boulevard de la Petite Hollande. **GPS**: n46,34965 w1,44769.

20 free €2,50 Ch . 01/01-31/12
Remarks: Max. 24h.

La Tranche-sur-Mer 20A4

Parking de la Baleine, Place des Baleines. **GPS**: n46,34340 w1,46222.

10 free. **Surface:** gravel. 01/01-31/12
Distance: 200m on the spot on the spot.
Remarks: Max. 24h. Follow 'Le Phare'.

Tourist information La Tranche-sur-Mer:
Office de Tourisme, Place de la Liberté, www.ot-latranchesurmer.fr.Bathing resort.

La Turballe 12D4

Boulevard de la Grande Falaise. **GPS**: n47,33106 w2,49919.
6 €3 Ch included. **Location:** Simple. **Surface:** gravel. 01/01-31/12
Distance: 2km.

La Turballe 12D4

Rue Alphonse Daudet. **GPS**: n47,34870 w2,50804.

22 €3 Chfree. **Location:** Simple, quiet. **Surface:** gravel. 01/01-31/12
Distance: 200m 500m 100m 100m.

FR

Remarks: Max. 5 days.

S Lassay-les-Châteaux 13C5

Allée du Haut Perrin. **GPS**: n48,43777 w0,49822.

free €2 Ch. **Location:** Urban, simple, central. **Surface:** asphalted.
01/01-31/12
Distance: 100m.
Remarks: Coins at the bakery.

S Laval 13C6

Parking de la Halte Fluviale, Rue du Vieux Saint-Louis. **GPS**: n48,07589 w0,77142.

10 free Chfree. **Location:** Urban, simple. **Surface:** asphalted.
01/01-31/12
Distance: 300m on the spot on the spot on the spot.
Remarks: Parking nearby viaduct.

Tourist information Laval:

Office de Tourisme, 1, Allée du Vieux St-Louis, www.laval-tourisme.com. Historical art city with old centre, on the Mayenne river.

Vieux Château.Medieval castle, museum with collection of naive art.
10-12h, 14-18h.

S Le Coudray Macouard 20D2

Route de Bron. **GPS**: n47,18806 w0,11722.

5 free . **Surface:** grassy. 01/01-31/12
Distance: 800m 800m.

S Le Croisic 12D5

Le Lin Gorzé, Rue du Lin Gorzé. **GPS**: n47,29917 w2,52194.

9 € 5,20 € 2 Ch . **Location:** Simple, quiet. **Surface:** asphalted.
01/01-31/12
Distance: 500m 500m 500m 800m.
Remarks: Max. 48h.

S Le Croisic 12D5

Les Courlis, Rue des Courlis. **GPS**: n47,29000 w2,505.

15 € 5,30 € 2 Ch . **Location:** Simple. **Surface:** gravel. 01/04-31/10
Distance: 500m 500m 500m 500m.
Remarks: Max. 48h.

Le Croisic 12D5

La Vigie, Avenue de Pierre Longue, D45. **GPS**: n47,28917 w2,53667.

9 € 5,30. **Location:** Simple. **Surface:** asphalted. 01/01-31/12
Distance: 3km 50m 3km 3km.
Remarks: Max. 48h.

Le Croisic 12D5

Les Bassins, Rue du Bassin. **GPS**: n47,29194 w2,50741.

9 € 5,30. **Location:** Urban, simple, quiet. **Surface:** asphalted.
01/01-31/12
Distance: 200m 20m 200m 200m.
Remarks: Max. 48h.

Le Croisic 12D5

P1 Kerdavid, Rue Kerclavid 1. **GPS**: n47,29835 w2,51995.

8 € 5,30. . **Location:** Urban, simple, quiet. **Surface:** asphalted.
01/01-31/12

FR

Distance: 500m 500m 500m 800m.

Tourist information Le Croisic:

Office de Tourisme, Place du 18 Juin 1940, www.ot-lecroisic.com.Seaside resort and fishing-port with old quay, coast line with cliffs and small beaches.

Océarium du Croisic.Sea aquarium. 01/06-31/08 10-19h, 01/05-31/05, 01/09-30/09 10-12h, 14-18h, 01/10-30/04 14-18h.

S Le Guédéniau 20D1

Rue du Lavoir. **GPS**: n47,49405 w0,04488.

15 free Chfree. **Location:** Rural. **Surface:** metalled.
01/01-31/12

Distance: on the spot.

Remarks: Recreation area at lake.

S Le Mans 13D6

Quai de l'Amiral Lalande. **GPS**: n48,00233 e0,18915.

7 free Chfree. **Location:** Urban, simple. **Surface:** asphalted.
01/01-31/12

Distance: centre 1km 8km.

Remarks: Along the river Sarthe.

Le Mans 13D6

Quai Louis Blanc. **GPS**: n48,01111 e0,19750.

50 free. **Location:** Urban, simple, noisy. **Surface:** asphalted.
01/01-31/12

Distance: 500m 500m 500m.

Remarks: Max. 24h, Sunday morning market.

Tourist information Le Mans:

Office de Tourisme, Hotel des Ursulines, Rue de l'Etoile, www.ville-lemans.fr.Historical centre.

Circuit Le Mans.Motorcar museum.

Place des Jacobins. Wed + Su-morning, Fri.

S Le Pallet 20B2

Rue Pierre Abelard. **GPS**: n47,13494 w1,3305.

20 free € 1 Ch. **Surface:** asphalted. 01/01-31/12

Distance: 500m 500m 500m.

Remarks: Wine museum, coins service at the shops in the village.

S Le Poiré-sur-Vie 20A3

Rue de Roc. **GPS**: n46,76773 w1,51162.

5 free Ch free. **Surface:** gravel. 01/01-31/12

Distance: 500m 500m 500m.

S Le Puy-Notre-Dame 20D2

Place du Gâte Argent. **GPS**: n47,12390 w0,23155.

free Chfree. **Surface:** metalled. 01/01-31/12

Distance: 100m 200m 200m.

Remarks: Next to cemetery.

S Le Puy-Notre-Dame 20D2

Cave-Champignonnière St.Maur, 1, Rue du Chateau, Sanziers. **GPS**: n47,11755 w0,20526.

8 free WCfree. **Surface:** metalled. 01/03-30/10

Distance: 2km.

Remarks: At mushroom grower.

S Le Puy-Notre-Dame 20D2

Domaine de la Renière, Les Caves. **GPS**: n47,13429 w0,24256.

5 € 5 included. **Surface:** metalled. 01/03-01/11

Distance: 700m.

Remarks: At wine-grower.

S Le Puy-Notre-Dame 20D2

Domaine du Vieux Tuffeau, Les Caves. **GPS**: n47,13498 w0,24704.

FR

6 free . **Surface:** metalled. 01/01-31/12
Distance: 1km.
Remarks: At wine-grower.

Le Puy-Notre-Dame 20D2

Domaine de la Girardrie, Rue Fontaine de Cix. **GPS:** n47,11616 w0,24127.

5 free. **Surface:** gravel. 01/01-31/12
Distance: 1km 1km 1km.

Tourist information Le Puy-Notre-Dame:
Champignonnière.Mushroom farm in cellar of the 16th century. 01/03-31/10.

Le Vaudelnay 20C2

Domaine du Vieux Pressoir, 235, Rue Château d'Oiré. **GPS:** n47,14669 w0,25239.

4 free. **Surface:** metalled. 01/01-31/12
Distance: 3km 3km 3km.
Remarks: At wine-grower.

Les Epesses 20B3

Le Puy du Fou, D27. **GPS:** n46,89425 w0,92506.
€ 5 € 2 Ch. **Surface:** grassy.
Remarks: Baker every morning, free shuttle to Puy du Fou.

Les Essarts 20B3

Rue de la piscine. **GPS:** n46,77380 w1,23499.

10 free € 2 Ch. **Surface:** asphalted. 01/01-31/12
Distance: 600m 5,6km 600m 600m.
Remarks: At swimmingpool and campsite.

Les Sables-d'Olonne 20A3

Les Salines, 120 route de l'Aubraie. **GPS:** n46,51635 w1,80533.

20 € 5 Ch included € 4 free. **Location:** Rural.
Surface: sand.
01/04-30/09
Distance: 600m on the spot.
Remarks: July/Aug only overnight stays (18-11h), baker every morning.

Les Sables-d'Olonne 20A3

Parking Vinci Parc, Rue Printanière. **GPS:** n46,49646 w1,77493.

150 € 12, winter free Ch WC included. **Location:** Simple.
Surface: metalled. 01/01-31/12 service 06/11-31/03.
Distance: beach 400m.

Les Sables-d'Olonne 20A3

Parking de la Sablière. **GPS:** n46,50585 w1,78796.
free. **Surface:** asphalted.

Tourist information Les Sables-d'Olonne:
Office de Tourisme, Centre de Congrès les Atlantes 1, Promenade Joffre, www.lessablesdolonne-tourisme.com.Important bathing resort in the Vendee.
Cours Dupont. Wed + Sa morning.
Zoo d'Olonne.Zoo.

Liré 20B1

Le Haut Fief, Square Espéranto. **GPS:** n47,34130 w1,16751.

5 free Ch WC free. **Surface:** asphalted. 01/01-31/12
Distance: 500m 250m 50m.
Remarks: Max. 48h.

Longué-Jumelles 20D1

Boulevard Victor Hugo. **GPS:** n47,38119 w0,11254.

FR

10 free Ch WC free. **Location:** Simple, quiet. **Surface:** gravel.
01/01-31/12
Distance: 100m 3,3km on the spot on the spot.
Remarks: Attention: follow the signs, service 300m: N 47,38046 W -0,11488.

S Luçon 20B4

Domaine des Guifettes. GPS: n46,43339 w1,18189.
€ 10,50, dog € 2,60 Ch included.
Remarks: Free entrance swimming pool, jacuzzi, sauna, midget golf.

Tourist information Luçon:
Office de Tourisme, Square Edouard Herriot, www.ville-lucon.fr.
Centre Ville. Wed + Sa morning.

S L'Aiguillon-sur-Mer 20B4

Aire des Dunes, Point d'Aiguillon. **GPS**: n46,27673 w1,22399.
30 € 5 € 2 Ch.
Remarks: Beach parking.

S L'Aiguillon-sur-Mer 20B4

Centre de Voile, Avenue Amiral Coubert. **GPS**: n46,33238 w1,30726.

30 € 5 € 2 Ch. **Surface:** asphalted. 01/01-31/12
Distance: 300m on the spot on the spot 300m 300m.
Remarks: At lake, ecole de voile.

S Maillé 20B4

La Petite Cabane. **GPS**: n46,34082 w0,79349.
€ 8 Ch included.
Remarks: Check in at harbourmaster, service only € 3.

S Maillezais 20C4

Rue de l'Ecole. **GPS**: n46,37081 w0,74123.

20 free € 2 Ch. **Surface:** asphalted. 01/01-31/12
Distance: 500m 500m 200m.

S Maisdon-sur-Sèvre 20B2

Domaine des Croix, Les Croix. **GPS**: n47,10710 w1,38757.
12 free Ch € 4/24h WC € 1. **Location:** Rural. **Surface:** gravel.
01/01-31/12
Distance: 1km.
Remarks: Max. 72h, wine tasting.

S Mamers 14A5

Complexe de loisirs La grille, Rue de la Piscine. **GPS**: n48,35834 e0,37139.

9 € 5/night, € 12/3 nights Ch included. **Location:** Rural, comfortable. **Surface:** grassy/gravel. 01/01-31/12
Distance: 1km 500m 500m 1km 1km.
Remarks: Entrance code available at campsite.

S Martigné-Briand 20C2

Jardin des Vieux Pressoirs, Rue d'Anjou. **GPS**: n47,23584 w0,42851.

4 free Ch free. **Surface:** metalled. 01/01-31/12
Distance: 200m 200m 100m.
Remarks: Closed when frosty.

S Mayenne 13C5

Quai Carnot. **GPS**: n48,30000 w0,62.

4 free € 1,50 Ch. **Location:** Urban, simple, noisy. **Surface:** asphalted.
01/01-31/12
Distance: 1km 10m.
Remarks: Max. 24h, coins at Office de Tourisme.

S Mervent 20C4

Chemin du Chêne Tord. **GPS**: n46,52304 w0,75737.

free € 2 Ch.
Remarks: At cemetery, coins available at Office du Tourisme.

S Mesnard-la-Barotière 20B3

Base de Loisirs de la Tricherie. **GPS**: n46,85280 w1,11764.
free € 3 Ch. **Surface:** grassy.

FR

Distance: beach on the spot.
Remarks: At lake of Tricherie.

S Mezeray 13D6

Parking, Rue de la Vezanne. **GPS**: n47,82300 w0,01485.

8 free € 2 Ch € 2. **Location:** Rural, simple. **Surface:** gravel.
01/01-31/12
Distance: 300m.

S Montfort-le-Gesnois 14A6

Parc des Sittelles, Parc des Sittelles. **GPS**: n48,03763 e0,41375.

16 € 10 Ch included. **Location:** Rural, simple, quiet. **Surface:** forest soil. 01/01-31/12
Distance: 50m.

S Montreuil-Bellay 20D2

Rue Georges Girouy. **GPS**: n47,13272 w0,15835.

20 free € 2 Ch. **Surface:** gravel/metalled.
15/06-15/09 19-10h
Distance: 150m 150m 150m.
Remarks: Nearby campisite Les Nobis, along the river.

S Montreuil-Bellay 20D2

Caveau de la Prévoté, Rue du Cohu 55, Méron. **GPS**: n47,13522 w0,11121.

3 free Ch free. **Surface:** metalled. 01/01-31/12
Distance: 50m 3km 3km.
Remarks: At wine-grower.

Tourist information Montreuil-Bellay:
Office de Tourisme, Place du Concorde, www.ville-montreuil-bellay.fr.City with a fortress from 1025.

S Montreuil-Juigné 20C1

Rue Saint Jean Baptiste. **GPS**: n47,54132 w0,61526.

8 free Ch free. **Location:** Rural, simple. **Surface:** gravel/metalled.
01/01-31/12
Distance: 1km 50m 800m.
Remarks: Along the Mayenne river.

Montsoreau 20D2

Domaine de la Perruche, 29, Rue de la Maumenière. **GPS**: n47,21828 e0,05079.

Distance: 500m 500m.
Remarks: At wine-grower, 10.30><18.30h.

S Moutiers-sur-le-Lay 20B3

Palias. **GPS**: n46,55375 w1,15483.

6 free Ch WC free. **Surface:** grassy. 01/01-31/12
Distance: 400m 400m 400m.
Remarks: At gymnasium.

S Mouzillon 20B2

Route de la Vendée. **GPS**: n47,13944 w1,28194.

12 free € 2 Ch. **Surface:** asphalted.
Distance: 200m 200m 200m.

S Nantes 20A2

Camping-car park du Petit Port, Boulevard du Petit Port. **GPS**: n47,24252 w1,5568.

FR

15 € 12/24h Ch included. **Location:** Urban, simple, central.
Surface: grassy/metalled. 01/01-31/12
Distance: on the spot 3,5km on the spot 300m tram 150m.
Remarks: Wifi code: 44-2207, entrance code 2207A.

Tourist information Nantes:
Office de Tourisme, Le souffle Atlantique, 7, rue de Valmy, www.nantes-tourisme.com.City with beautiful squares and broad shopping streets.
Musée des Salorges.Navigation museum.
Musée Jules Verne.

S Noirmoutier-en-l'Ile 12D5
Place des Ormeaux, L'Epine. **GPS**: n46,98060 w2,26404.

40 € 7/24h, € 13/48h, € 19/72h 100liter Ch included50minutes WC. **Surface:** metalled. 01/01-31/12
Distance: 100m 1,3km on the spot 200m 3km.
Remarks: Max. 72h.

S Noirmoutier-en-l'Ile 12D5
Place Florent Caillaud, Noirmoutierr-en-l'Ile. **GPS**: n47,00139 w2,25167.

182 € 5, 01/04-30/09 € 8, parking free € 2/100liter Ch € 2/2h free. **Surface:** asphalted. 01/01-31/12
Distance: 750m sandy beach 2,5km 750m.
Remarks: Max. 7 days.

S Noirmoutier-en-l'Ile 12D5
Place R. Ganachaud, l'Herbaudière. **GPS**: n46,83058 w2,12996.

18 € 5, 01/04-30/09 € 8, parking free € 2/100liter Ch € 2/1h.
Surface: asphalted. 01/01-31/12
Distance: on the spot 350m.
Remarks: Parking behind town hall.

S Noirmoutier-en-l'Ile 12D5
Rue de la Tresson, La Guérinière. **GPS**: n46,96588 w2,21451.

20 € 5, 01/04-30/09 € 8, parking free Ch free 4.
Surface: gravel. 01/01-31/12
Distance: sandy beach 450m 200m 100m.
Remarks: Max. 48h.

Tourist information Noirmoutier-en-l'Ile:
Office de Tourisme, Route du Pont, Barbatre, www.ile-noirmoutier.com.Island now accessed via a bridge.
Château Noirmoutier.Regional museum. daily.
Musée de la Construction Navale.Naval architectural museum.
Musée de la Guériniere.Traditional folk art.
Place de la République. Fri.
Sealand Aquarium, Le Vieux Port.

S Nort-sur-Erdre 20A1
13 Place du Bassin. **GPS**: n47,43746 w1,49546.

15 free € 2 Ch WC free. **Location:** Simple, quiet.
Surface: asphalted. 01/01-31/12
Distance: 300m 100m 300m 300m.
Remarks: Max. 24h.

S Notre-Dame-de-Monts 12D5
Aire de la Clairière, Rue de la Clairière. **GPS**: n46,83460 w2,14282.

35 € 5/20-8h Ch free. **Location:** Rural, simple.
Surface: gravel. 01/01-31/12
Distance: 800m 200m 200m 800m 800m.
Remarks: Motorhome parking at the beach.

S Notre-Dame-de-Monts 12D5
Aire Place de Gaulle, Rue des Maraichins. **GPS**: n46,83058 w2,12994.

FR

20 € 5/20-8h Ch WC free. **Surface:** asphalted.
01/01-31/12
Distance: 300m 500m 300m.

S Nozay 20A1

Étang de Nozay. **GPS**: n47,57500 w1,62528.

16 € 5 Ch (16x) WC included. **Surface:** gravel.
01/01-31/12 service: frost.
Distance: 200m 2km 10m 200m 200m.

S Olonne-sur-Mer 20A3

Aire de Camping-car Olonne Escale, Rue des Anciens Combattants d'Afrique du Nord. **GPS**: n46,53814 w1,77517.

21 € 8/24h Ch included.
Location: Simple.
Distance: 300m 600m.
Remarks: Max. 72h, Jul/Aug max. 48h.

S Parnay 20D2

D947. **GPS**: n47,23146 e0,01098.

5 free € 1,50 Ch. **Surface:** asphalted. 01/01-31/12
Distance: 200m.
Remarks: Parking in the centre.

S Pellouailles-les-Vignes 20C1

Rue Nationale, D323. **GPS**: n47,52141 w0,43698.

3 free Ch free. **Location:** Rural. **Surface:** asphalted.
01/01-31/12
Distance: on the spot 1,4km 100m bakery 50m.

S Piriac-sur-Mer 12D4

Parking de Brambel, Avenue du Général de Gaulle, D452. **GPS**: n47,39680 w2,51245.

12 € 5 Ch free WC. **Location:** Comfortable. **Surface:** metalled.
01/01-31/12
Distance: 2km 50m 2km 2km.
Remarks: Parking to sea.

S Piriac-sur-Mer 12D4

Parking de Lérat, Route de Mesquêne, D99, Lieu-dit Lérat. **GPS**: n47,36770 w2,53196.

50 € 5 Ch free. **Location:** Simple. **Surface:** metalled.
01/01-31/12
Distance: 200m 600m 600m 500m 500m.
Remarks: Max. 48h.

Tourist information Piriac-sur-Mer:

Office de Tourisme, 7, rue des Cap-Horniers.Marina and seaside resort.
01/06-30/09 Mo + Wed + Sa-morning, 01/10-30/05 Tue.
Arts market. 01/07-31/08 Thu-evening.

S Pornic 12D5

Le Val Saint-Martin. **GPS**: n47,12053 w2,09162.

7 free € 2/100liter Ch. **Location:** Comfortable, isolated.
Surface: asphalted. 01/01-31/12

FR

Distance: city centre 1,5km.
Remarks: Next to swimming pool.

S Pouancé 13B6

Rue de l'hippodrôme, Aubin. **GPS**: n47,75223 w1,18007.

10 € 2,75 Ch (4x) WC free. **Location:** Rural, simple, quiet.
Surface: grassy. 01/01-31/12
Distance: 500m small beach 20m 20m 1km 1km.
Remarks: Along étang de Saint-Aubin.

S Pouzauges 20B3

Parking de la Vallée, D49/D203. **GPS**: n46,77639 w0,82861.

10 free Ch free. **Surface:** asphalted. 01/01-31/12
Distance: 1km 1km 1km.

FR

S Préfailles 12D5

Camping-Car Park de La Pointe, Chemin du Port aux Anes. **GPS**: n47,13872 w2,22213.

49 € 12/24h Ch included. **Location:** Comfortable.
Surface: grassy/gravel. 01/01-31/12

S Préfailles 12D5

Rue de la Prée. **GPS**: n47,13388 w2,21221.
4 free € 2,50/100liter Ch. **Location:** Simple.
01/01-31/12
Distance: 500m.
Remarks: Coins at Tourist Info.

Préfailles 12D5

Chemin de Biochon, Pointe de Saint Gildas. **GPS**: n47,13078 w2,18963.

75 free, 15/4-15-10 € 3. **Location:** Rural, simple, quiet.
Surface: gravel/sand. 01/01-31/12
Distance: 3km 500m 500m 3km 3km.
Remarks: Max. 48h, baker every morning.

Préfailles 12D5

D313, chemin des Pinettes. **GPS**: n47,13663 w2,23843.

45 free, 01/05-30/09 € 3. **Location:** Rural, simple, quiet.
Surface: grassy/gravel. 01/01-31/12
Distance: 3km 50m 200m 3km.
Remarks: Max. 48h, baker every morning.

S Riaille 20B1

Rue de la Benate. **GPS**: n47,51412 w1,28803.

5 free Ch WC free. **Location:** Rural, simple, quiet. **Surface:** gravel.
01/01-31/12
Distance: 700m 700m 700m.
Remarks: Max. 48h.

S Rouans 20A2

Aire naturelle de Messan, Route des Marais. **GPS**: n47,19272 w1,85419.

8 € 3 Ch WC free. **Location:** Rural, simple. **Surface:** grassy/metalled.
01/01-31/12
Distance: 1km on the spot on the spot 1km.
Remarks: To be paid at town hall.

S Saint-Loup-du-Gast 13C5

Zone d'Activité du Creusot. **GPS**: n48,38750 w0,58548.

6 free Ch free. **Location:** Rural, simple. **Surface:** asphalted/grassy.

01/01-31/12
Distance: 350m.
Remarks: Departure Vélorail, € 15 per bike for 4 pers.

S Saint-Nazaire 12D5
Route de l'Océan, D292, Saint-Marc-sur-Mer. **GPS**: n47,23700 w2,30033.

15 free € 3/100liter Ch € 3/1h. **Location:** Rural, simple, quiet.
Surface: gravel. 01/01-31/12
Distance: 2km 100m 100m.

Saint-Nazaire 12D5
Bois-Joalland, Route de Quelmer. **GPS**: n47,27669 w2,25771.
3 free. **Location:** Rural, simple, quiet. **Surface:** unpaved.
01/01-31/12
Distance: 1km 5m on the spot on the spot.
Remarks: Nearby base nautique.

Saint-Nazaire 12D5
Boulevard Paul Leferme. **GPS**: n47,27760 w2,20362.

50 free. **Location:** Urban, simple, isolated. **Surface:** asphalted.
01/01-31/12
Distance: on the spot 500m 50m.

Saint-Nazaire 12D5
Route du Bois Joalland. **GPS**: n47,27954 w2,26229.

5 free. **Location:** Simple, central. **Surface:** gravel.
01/01-31/12
Distance: 500m 10m 10m on the spot on the spot.

S Saulgé l'Hôpital 20C2
Terrain de Loisirs, Chemin de la Planche. **GPS**: n47,29853 w0,38344.

15 free Ch free. **Surface:** gravel. 01/01-31/12
Distance: 100m 100m 100m.

S Segré 20C1
Aire de l'Europe, D775. **GPS**: n47,68497 w0,85719.

free Ch WC free. **Location:** Rural. **Surface:** asphalted.
01/01-31/12
Distance: 1km.

S Segré 20C1
Place du Moulin sous la Tour, Rue Emile Zola. **GPS**: n47,68409 w0,87436.

10 free Ch free. **Location:** Rural, simple. **Surface:** gravel.
01/01-31/12 Service: winter.
Distance: 300m on the spot 100m on the spot.

S Sillé-le-Guillaume 13D5
2, Place de la Gare. **GPS**: n48,18167 w0,13111.

8 free € 2 Ch € 2. **Location:** Urban, simple. **Surface:** asphalted.
01/01-31/12
Distance: 300m 300m 400m train 50m.
Remarks: May 2012 during inspection service out of order.

S St.Aubin-de-Luigné 20C2
Domaine La Biquerie, D17. **GPS**: n47,30843 w0,70211.

FR

30 free Ch free. **Surface:** grassy. 01/01-31/12
Distance: 5km.
Remarks: At wine-grower.

S St.Calais 14A6

Boulevard du Docteur Gigon. **GPS**: n47,92416 e0,74459.

4 free Ch WC free. **Location:** Rural, simple. **Surface:** asphalted.
01/01-31/12
Distance: 400m on the spot.

S St.Calais 14A6

Le Champ Long, D249. **GPS**: n47,93375 e0,74568.

5 free WC. **Location:** Rural. **Surface:** asphalted. 01/01-31/12
Distance: 1,6km lake on the spot on the spot.

S St.Clément-des-Levées 20D2

Rue de la Laiterie. **GPS**: n47,33064 w0,18042.

10 free € 2 Ch. **Surface:** metalled. 01/01-31/12
Distance: 300m.
Remarks: Coins at the shops in the village and town hall.

S St.Cyr-en-Bourg 20D2

Cave de Saumur, Route du Mureau. **GPS**: n47,19642 w0,07266.

15 free Ch WC free. **Surface:** asphalted.
15/03-15/09
Distance: 3km.
Remarks: Max. 48h, wine tasting 300m. Follow signs Cave de Saumur.

S St.Georges-sur-Loire 20C1

Rue de la Villette. **GPS**: n47,40610 w0,76301.

20 free Ch free. **Location:** Rural, simple. **Surface:** asphalted.
01/01-31/12
Distance: 300m 100m 300m 300m.
Remarks: Next to the old abbey, max. 24h.

S St.Gilles-Croix-de-Vie 20A3

La Rabalette, Rue de la Rabalette. **GPS**: n46,70302 w1,94728.

35 15/03-15/11 € 5/night € 2,60/10minutes Ch. **Location:** Urban, simple. **Surface:** asphalted.
01/01-31/12
Distance: 500m 1km 500m 500m.
Remarks: Nearby lake Soudinière, coins at Tourist Info.

S St.Gilles-Croix-de-Vie 20A3

Stade de la Chapelle, Rue du Bois. **GPS**: n46,69449 w1,92716.
€ 5 € 2,60 Ch.
Surface: asphalted.
01/04-30/09 weekend and school holidays
Distance: centre 500m.
Remarks: Coins at Tourist Info, 2013: during inspection service out of order.

Tourist information St.Gilles-Croix-de-Vie:
Office de Tourisme, Boulevard de l'Egalité, www.stgillescroixdevie.com. Seaside resort with fishing port.
St.Gilles: Tue, Thu, Su; Croix de Vie; Wed, Sa.

S St.Hilaire de Riez 12D6

Base des vallées, Chemin des Vallées. **GPS**: n46,73154 w1,91132.

FR

10 free € 2,60/10minutes Ch. **Location:** Rural, simple.
Surface: asphalted. 01/01-31/12
Distance: St.Hilaire 3,7km 7km.

S St.Hilaire de Riez 12D6

Parking des Becs, Avenue des Becs. **GPS:** n46,76040 w2,02656.
20 € 5/24h € 2,60/10minutes Ch. **Location:** Rural.
Surface: asphalted. 01/01-31/12
Distance: sandy beach 750m 200m.
Remarks: Max. 3 nights.

St.Hilaire de Riez 12D6

Allée de la Plage de la Parée Préneau. **GPS:** n46,72865 w1,99167.

48 free, night € 5. **Location:** Rural. **Surface:** metalled.
01/01-31/12
Distance: on the spot.
Remarks: Beach parking.

St.Hilaire de Riez 12D6

Champ Gaillard, Avenue de Baisse. **GPS:** n46,76903 w2,03337.

28 free. **Location:** Rural, isolated. **Surface:** gravel.
01/01-31/12
Distance: sandy beach 1km.

S St.Hilaire-de-Chaléons 20A2

Rue Eloi Guitteny, D61. **GPS:** n47,10389 w1,86639.

2 free Ch WC free. **Surface:** asphalted. 01/01-31/12
Distance: 100m 500m 100m.
Remarks: Next to campsite de l'Etoile, max. 24h.

S St.Jean-de-Monts 12D6

Le Repos des Tortues, Route de Notre Dame de Monts 38. **GPS:** n46,79879 w2,07344.

98 € 8, 01/07-31/08 € 12 Ch (49x),4Amp WC € 5/stay € 4 included. **Location:** Rural, luxurious. **Surface:** grassy/gravel.
01/01-31/12
Distance: 800m 1,5km 50m 2km.
Remarks: Terrain with video surveillance.

S St.Jean-de-Monts 12D6

Aire de stationnement des Pimprenelles, Rue des Pimprenelles. **GPS:** n46,78882 w2,07939.
20 € 8 Ch included. **Location:** Comfortable.
01/01-31/12
Distance: sandy beach 200m.

Tourist information St.Jean-de-Monts:
Wed, Sa.

S St.Jean-sur-Mayenne 13C5

Les Marchanderies. **GPS:** n48,12793 w0,75244.

25 € 6,20 Ch WC included. **Location:** Rural, luxurious, quiet.
Surface: grassy/gravel. 01/01-31/12
Distance: 500m on the spot 300m 400m bakery.
Remarks: Along the Mayenne river.

S St.Lyphard 12D4

Route Herbignac, D47. **GPS:** n47,39900 w2,30091.

6 free € 2 Ch. **Surface:** grassy/metalled. 01/01-31/12
Distance: 500m 200m 500m.
Remarks: At small lake, max. 1 night.

S St.Mars-La-Jaille 20B1

Rue Neuve. **GPS:** n47,52327 w1,18357.

FR

12 free Ch WC free. **Location:** Rural. **Surface:** asphalted. 01/01-31/12

Distance: 200m on the spot.

Remarks: Parking at small lake.

S St.Michel-Chef-Chef 12D5

Camping-Car Park Le Thar-Cor La Plaine sur Mer, Avenue Cormier. **GPS:** n47,16017 w2,16881.

22 € 12/24h Ch included. **Location:** Simple, isolated, quiet. 01/01-31/12

Distance: sandy beach 400m 400m 400m.

S St.Michel-Chef-Chef 12D5

Chemin du Puits Martin. **GPS:** n47,18209 w2,14664.

30 free, 20-8h € 5 € 2,80/100liter Ch. **Location:** Simple. **Surface:** asphalted. 01/01-31/12

Distance: 300m 300m 300m.

Remarks: Parking townhall, oins at town hall, office du tourisme.

S St.Michel-Chef-Chef 12D5

Camping Clos Mer et Nature, Route de Tharon. **GPS:** n47,17309 w2,15779.

€ 5 € 2/100liter Ch € 2. **Location:** Simple, quiet. **Surface:** grassy. 01/01-31/12

Distance: 500m sandy beach 400m 300m.

Remarks: Check in at reception.

S St.Michel-Mont-Mercure 20B3

Place du Sommet. **GPS:** n46,83222 w0,88222.

20 free € 2/150liter Ch. **Surface:** gravel/sand.

Remarks: Near church.

S St.Philbert-de-Grandlieu 20A2

Chemin de la Plage. **GPS:** n47,04500 w1,64172.

10 free Ch free. **Surface:** gravel. 01/01-31/12

Distance: 1km on the spot on the spot 550m 1km.

Remarks: From Nantes first exit after Grande Surface, at roundabout dir city, first road to the right.

S St.Rémy-la-Varenne 20C1

Rue St Aubin-D132. **GPS:** n47,39805 w0,31612.

3 free Ch WC free. **Surface:** asphalted. 01/01-31/12

Distance: on the spot 100m 100m.

S St.Saturnin-sur-Loire 20C1

Route de Saumur, D751. **GPS:** n47,39267 w0,43285.

3 free Ch free. **Surface:** metalled. 01/01-31/12

Distance: on the spot 100m 100m.

S St.Viaud 20A1

Rue du parc des sports. **GPS:** n47,25917 w2,015.

10 free Ch (2x)free. **Location:** Rural, comfortable, quiet. **Surface:** metalled. 01/01-31/12

Distance: 500m 100m 500m 500m.

Remarks: At recreational lake, max. 8 days.

S St.Vincent-sur-Jard 20A4

Chemin des Roulettes, Le Goulet. **GPS:** n46,41038 w1,5413.

FR

43 € 0,35/h € 2/10minutes Ch € 2/55minutes . Location: Rural, simple. Surface: metalled. 01/01-31/12 Service: winter.
Distance: 1km 100m 400m.

Talmont-Saint-Hilaire 20A4

Parking des Gâtines, Rue des Gâtines. **GPS**: n46,46761 w1,61718.

16 € 5/24h € 3/100liter Ch € 3/50minutes. **Location:** Rural, simple. **Surface:** asphalted. 01/01-31/12
Distance: 500m Small lake (100m) 100m.

Talmont-Saint-Hilaire 20A4

Parking du Château Guibert, Avenue de la Plage. **GPS**: n46,44098 w1,66351.

16 € 5/24h € 3 Ch WC . **Location:** Rural, simple.
Surface: metalled. 01/04-31/10
Distance: 1km.
Remarks: Max. 48h.

Turquant 20D2

Rue des Ducs d'Anjou. **GPS**: n47,22393 e0,02858.

10 free € 2,50 Ch. **Surface:** metalled. 01/01-31/12
Distance: 100m 50m 50m on the spot.
Remarks: Behind church, coins at the shops in the village.

Vaiges 13C6

Rue Robert Gletron, D57. **GPS**: n48,04189 w0,48285.

5 free € 2 Ch. **Location:** Urban, simple. **Surface:** gravel. 01/01-31/12
Distance: 500m 1,7km 20m 700m bakery.

Valanjou 20C2

Aire de Plaisance, Rue de la Mairie. **GPS**: n47,21658 w0,60326.

6 free Ch WC free. **Surface:** metalled. 01/01-31/12
Distance: 200m.
Remarks: Nearby town hall.

Venansault 20A3

Rue Pierre Nicolas Loué. **GPS**: n46,68250 w1,51472.

5 free. **Surface:** sand. 01/01-31/12
Distance: 500m 100m 300m 500m.

Vihiers 20C2

Rue Champ de Foire des Champs. **GPS**: n47,14355 w0,5358.

5 free Ch WC. **Surface:** asphalted. 01/01-31/12
Distance: 50m 100m 100m.

Villeveque 20C1

Rue du Port. **GPS**: n47,56222 w0,42257.
6 free € 1 Ch WC. 01/01-31/12
Distance: 100m 50m bakery 200m.

Villiers-Charlemagne 13C6

Village Vacances et Pêche, Rue des Haies. **GPS**: n47,92083 w0,68167.

FR

25 free Ch free. **Location:** Rural, comfortable, quiet. **Surface:** grassy.
01/01-31/12
Distance: on the spot day pass available 500m on the spot.
Remarks: Max. 24h.

S Vouvant 20B3

Rue de Château Neuf. **GPS**: n46,57462 w0,77462.

20 free Ch free. **Surface:** gravel. 01/01-31/12
Distance: 500m 500m 500m.

Centre

S Allogny 21D2

D944. **GPS**: n47,21913 e2,32329.

10 free free. **Surface:** asphalted. 01/01-31/12
Distance: 800m 50m 50m.

S Amboise 21B1

Vinci Park, Allée de la Chapelle Saint-Jean. **GPS**: n47,41761 e0,98742.

20 € 10/24h Ch included (20x)€ 2 . **Location:** Rural, comfortable, central, quiet. **Surface:** asphalted/grassy.
01/01-31/12
Distance: 200m 200m 200m 200m on the spot on the spot.
Remarks: Next to campsite, castle 500m.

Amboise 21B1

Parking St. Jean, Avenue Leonardo da Vinci 43 , D61. **GPS**: n47,40814 e0,98986.

11 free. **Location:** Urban, simple, isolated, quiet. **Surface:** asphalted.
01/01-31/12
Distance: on the spot 1,5km 1,5km on the spot.

S Angé 21B2

Place de la Mairie. **GPS**: n47,33250 e1,24389.

20 free Ch free. **Surface:** metalled. 01/01-31/12

S Argent-sur-Sauldre 21D1

Super U, D940. **GPS**: n47,54916 e2,44797.

2 free € 2 Ch. **Surface:** asphalted. 01/01-31/12
Distance: 1,1km.

Argenton-sur-Creuse 21B4

Rue de la Grenouille. **GPS**: n46,58715 e1,52497.

50 free. **Surface:** gravel. 01/01-31/12
Distance: 50m 3,4km 50m 50m.

S Argenton-sur-Creuse 21B4

Alleé du Champ de Foire. **GPS**: n46,58556 e1,52222.
Ch WC free. 01/01-31/12
Distance: on the spot.

Tourist information Argenton-sur-Creuse:

Office de Tourisme, 13, place de la République, www.ot-argenton-sur-creuse.fr.

Musée de Chemiserie, Rue Charles Brillaud.Textile museum.
01/03-31/12 9.30-12h, 14-18h Mo. € 4.

Musée Gallo Romain, Les Mersans, St. Marcel.Roman findings.
9.30-12h, 14-18h. € 4.

Athée-sur-Cher 21A2

Aire d'Athée-sur-Cher, D83, Rue de Cigogné. **GPS**: n47,31439 e0,91756.

3 free Chfree. **Location:** Rural, simple, isolated, quiet.
Surface: metalled. 01/01-31/12
Distance: 800m 11km 1,5km 1km on the spot.
Remarks: Max. 24h.

Aubigny-sur-Nère 21D1

Parc des Sports, D7. **GPS**: n47,48201 e2,44995.

12 free Chfree. **Surface:** asphalted. 01/01-31/12
Distance: 1km 1km 2km.

Aubigny-sur-Nère 21D1

Parking du Pré qui Danse, Mail Guichard. **GPS**: n47,49140 e2,43830.

40 free Ch WCfree. **Surface:** asphalted. 01/01-31/12
Distance: 200m 200m 200m.

Avoine 20D2

Avenue de la République. **GPS**: n47,21287 e0,17706.

11 € 4 € 2/10liter Ch (11x)€ 2/24h . **Location:** Rural, comfortable, luxurious, isolated, quiet. **Surface:** asphalted/metalled. 01/01-31/12
Distance: 1km Lac Mousseau 300m 300m.
Remarks: Max. 3 nights.

Azay-le-Rideau 21A2

Camping municipal Le Sabot, Rue du Stade. **GPS**: n47,25925 e0,46992.

12 free € 3/100liter Ch € 1,70. **Location:** Urban, comfortable, central, quiet. **Surface:** asphalted. 01/04-01/10
Distance: 200m 300m on the spot on the spot.
Remarks: Max. 48h, coins at camping (9/16h), shower on campsite € 1,70, castle 300m.

Azé 14B6

M et Mme Hersant, Les Places, D957 Épuisay-Galette. **GPS**: n47,86451 e0,97659.

6 € 10 Ch included. **Location:** Rural, comfortable, isolated, quiet. **Surface:** grassy. 01/01-31/12
Distance: 7km on the spot.

Barlieu 21D1

Base de loisirs de Badineau. **GPS**: n47,47918 e2,63168.

15 € 2, first night € 3,50 Ch WC free. **Surface:** grassy/gravel. Easter-01/11
Distance: 1km nearby.

Beaugency 21C1

Quai Dunois. **GPS**: n47,77949 e1,63646.

20 free € 2/10minutes Ch € 2/55minutes WC .
Surface: metalled. 01/01-31/12
Distance: 100m 8,8km 100m 50m 100m 100m.
Remarks: Quay along the Loire river, special place in front of motorhomes, max. 24h.

Tourist information Beaugency:
Office de Tourisme, 3, Place Dr Hyvernaud.Medieval city on the river Loire.

FR

Bessais-le-Fromental 22A3

Base de loisirs de l'Étang de Goule, Champ de la Croix. **GPS**: n46,73402 e2,80034.

50 free € 2 Ch. **Surface:** asphalted/grassy.
Distance: 4km on the spot on the spot on camp site on camp site.

Blois 21B1

P2, Rue Jean Moulin. **GPS**: n47,58677 e1,32615.

20 € 5/24h Ch free. **Surface:** asphalted. 01/05-30/09
Distance: on the spot 6,9km 100m 100m on the spot.

Tourist information Blois:

Office de Tourisme, 23 place du Château.
Quartier juif.Rue Pierre de Blois leads to this medieval Jewish district.
Château de Blois.
Cathédrale St Louis.
Quatier Coty. Wed 7-13h.

Bonny-sur-Loire 22A1

Chemin de la Cheuille. **GPS**: n47,55925 e2,83967.
6 free Ch free. **Location:** Rural. **Surface:** gravel.
Distance: 150m 50m on the spot on the spot on the spot.
Remarks: Along La Cheuille river.

Boulleret 22A2

Place des Charmes. **GPS**: n47,42304 e2,87244.

5 free € 2/100liter Ch (2x)€ 2/6h WC. **Surface:** asphalted.
01/01-31/12
Distance: nearby nearby nearby.
Remarks: Coins available at post office, restaurant, shops.

Bourges 21D2

Boulevard de l'Industrie. **GPS**: n47,07224 e2,39337.

5 free Ch free. **Surface:** metalled. 01/01-31/12
Distance: 500m 500m 500m.
Remarks: 100m from campsite.

Bourges 21D2

Rue Jean Bouin. **GPS**: n47,07597 e2,39897.

50 free Ch free. **Surface:** asphalted. 01/01-31/12
Distance: 50m 500m 500m.
Remarks: Max. 48h.

Tourist information Bourges:

Office de Tourisme, 21, rue Victor Hugo, www.bourges-tourisme.com.Large historic city, centre of the armaments industry for centuries.
Hôtel Lallemant Musée des Arts Décoratifs, rue Bournonnoux.Collection of moquettes, porcelain and pieces of furniture.
Musée de Bery.Regional museum.
Palais Jaques Coeur.Gothic palace named after the arms dealer Coeur.
Ballades de Bourges.Festivities and market in the city centre. 01/07-31/08.

Brézolles 14B4

Rue de Verneuil, D939. **GPS**: n48,69083 e1,06972.

10 free Ch free. **Surface:** metalled. 01/01-31/12
Distance: 200m 200m.

Briare-le-Canal 22A1

Camping-Car Park. **GPS**: n47,64304 e2,72270.

12 € 7/24h Ch included. **Surface:** grassy.
01/01-31/12

FR

Distance: on the spot on the spot on the spot 800m 800m.
Remarks: Max. 72h.

S Briare-le-Canal 22A1

Rue des Vignes. **GPS**: n47,63215 e2,73981.

40 free € 2 Ch . **Surface:** gravel. 01/01-31/12
Distance: 300m 50m on the spot.

S Briare-le-Canal 22A1

Port du Commerce, Quai de Mazoyer. **GPS**: n47,63470 e2,74030. .

10 free WC free. **Surface:** asphalted. 01/01-31/12
Distance: 200m 4,5km on the spot on the spot.

S Brou 14B5

Madison Cars 28. **GPS**: n48,21379 e1,14681.

15 € 5 € 1/100liter € 1 Ch € 1 (4x)€ 3/24h € 1. **Location:** Rural, comfortable, isolated, quiet. **Surface:** gravel. 01/01-31/12
Distance: 1km 1km on the spot.
Remarks: Bread-service.

S Chabris 21C2

Place du Champ de Foire. **GPS**: n47,25317 e1,65211.
free € 2 Ch € 2.
Location: Rural.
Distance: on the spot 250m 250m.
Remarks: Coins at Tourist Info and Maison de la Presse (250m).

Chambord 21B1

Château de Chambord, Place St.Louis. **GPS**: n47,61608 e1,51057.

100 <7.90m € 6/day + € 20/night, >7.90m € 30/day + € 30/night.

Surface: asphalted.
Distance: 100m 100m.
Remarks: Parking castle, max. 1 night.

S Chaon 21D1

D129. **GPS**: n47,60942 e2,16611.

10 free Ch free. **Surface:** grassy/metalled. 01/01-31/12
Distance: 200m.

S Châteaudun 14B6

Aire de Châteaudun, Rue des Fouleries. **GPS**: n48,07172 e1,32421.

15 free € 2/100liter Ch € 2/20minutes WC. **Location:** Urban, comfortable, central, quiet. **Surface:** asphalted. 01/01-31/12
Distance: 400m Canoe rental on the spot on the spot.
Remarks: Along Loir river, castel of Châteaudun 300m.

S Châteauneuf-sur-Loire 14D6

Camping municipal La Maltournée, Route de la Plage, Sigloy D11. **GPS**: n47,85671 e2,22963.
€ 7,10 Ch € 3,90 WC included. **Surface:** grassy/metalled. 01/04-31/10
Distance: 800m on the spot on the spot 800m 800m.

S Châteauroux 21C3

17, Avenue de Parc des Loisirs. **GPS**: n46,82278 e1,69507.

5 free € 2,50 Ch € 2,50/1h. **Surface:** asphalted. 01/05-31/10
Distance: 3,6km 2km 2km.
Remarks: Parking at wave pool.

Tourist information Châteauroux:
Office de Tourisme, 1, Place de la Gare, www.ville-chateauroux.fr.

S Châtillon-sur-Loire 22A1

Rue du Port. **GPS**: n47,59128 e2,76044.
± 6 free Ch. **Location:** Rural, comfortable, quiet.
Surface: asphalted/gravel.
Distance: 800m 9km A77 400m bakery 500m.
Remarks: On the canal.

S Chaumont-sur-Loire 21B1

Promendae de Trouillas. **GPS**: n47,48347 e1,19127.

FR

20 free € 2 Ch € 2. **Surface:** grassy/metalled.

Chenonceaux 21B2

Aire de Chenonceaux, Chemin de la Varenne. **GPS**: n47,33053 e1,06824.

10 free. **Location:** Rural, simple, isolated, noisy. **Surface:** grassy.
01/01-31/12
Distance: 500m 500m on the spot on the spot.
Remarks: Along railwayline.

P **Chenonceaux** 21B2

Rue du Château. **GPS**: n47,33020 e1,06648.

20 free. **Location:** Rural, simple, isolated. **Surface:** metalled.
01/01-31/12
Distance: 500m 500m on the spot.
Remarks: Parking at castle of Chenonceaux.

Tourist information Chenonceaux:
Castle.

Cheverny 21B1

Château Cheverny. GPS: n47,49762 e1,46097.

20 free. **Surface:** metalled.
9.30-12h, 14.15-17h, Apr-Sep 9.30-18.15h
Distance: 100m 100m.

Tourist information Cheverny:
Château Cheverny.Castle. 9.30-12h, 14.15-17h, Apr-Sep 9.30-18.15h.

S **Chouzé-sur-Loire** 20D2

Aire de Chouzé-sur-Loire, Rue de l'Église. **GPS**: n47,23809 e0,12649.

6 free € 2 Ch. **Location:** Rural, comfortable, central, quiet.
Surface: gravel. 01/01-31/12
Distance: on the spot 250m on the spot on the spot on the spot.
Remarks: Coins available at the shops and town hall.

S **Courville-sur-Eure** 14B5

Avenue Thiers. **GPS**: n48,44600 e1,24166.
6 free € 2/100liter Ch € 2/55minutes. **Surface:** asphalted.
01/01-31/12
Remarks: Coins at campsite and shops.

S **Culan** 21D4

Place du Champ de Foire. **GPS**: n46,54714 e2,34521.

20 free € 1,50 Ch € 1,50 WC. **Surface:** asphalted.
01/01-31/12
Distance: 50m 50m 50m.
Remarks: Near office de tourisme.

Cuzion 21C4

Base de Loisirs Pont des Piles. GPS: n46,45639 e1,61167.

6 free. **Surface:** grassy/metalled. 01/01-31/12
Remarks: Max. 1 night.

S **Dry** 21C1

Rue de Meung. **GPS**: n47,79824 e1,71419.

10 free € 1/10minutes Ch € 1/55minutes. **Location:** Simple.
Surface: metalled. 01/01-31/12
Distance: on the spot 1km 50m.
Remarks: Coins at town hall.

FR

S Esvres-sur-Indre 21A2

Impasse Auguste Noyant. **GPS**: n47,28267 e0,78526.

7 free free. **Location:** Urban, simple, central, quiet. **Surface:** gravel. 01/01-31/12 water disconnected in winter.
Distance: on the spot 100m 250m on the spot on the spot on the spot.

S Genillé 21B2

Ferme Jouvin, La Galerie, D 764 Loches> Montrichard. **GPS**: n47,21409 e1,10871.

€ 2 service € 3 Ch included. **Location:** Rural, simple, isolated, quiet. **Surface:** grassy. 01/01-31/12
Distance: 2,7km on the spot.

S Gien 21D1

Route de Briare. **GPS**: n47,67985 e2,64308.

8 free € 2 Ch € 2. **Surface:** asphalted. 01/01-31/12
Distance: 2km on the spot.
Remarks: Max. 48h, coins available at swimming pool.

S Gizeux 20D1

Aire de Gizeux, Route du Lavoir. **GPS**: n47,39275 e0,19689.

20 free € 3/100liter Ch € 3/1h. **Location:** Rural, comfortable, central, quiet. **Surface:** gravel.
Distance: 200m 500m In village on the spot on the spot.
Remarks: Château de Gizeux 400m, coins available at the shops and town hall.

S Guilly 21C2

Le Prieuré Chambres d'Hôtes, Rue du Prieuré. **GPS**: n47,07920 e1,72100.

10 € 5 € 3 Ch . **Surface:** grassy/metalled.
Distance: 150m 10m 150m.

S Humbligny 21D2

D44. **GPS**: n47,25451 e2,65850.

10 free € 2/100liter Ch € 2/10minutes. **Surface:** gravel.
01/01-31/12
Distance: on the spot.
Remarks: Coins at town hall (10m).

S La Chapelle-Saint-Mesmin 14C6

Aire camping-cars, Chemin de Fourneaux. **GPS**: n47,88550 e1,83990.

23 € 5/24h, € 9/48h, € 12/72h Ch included. **Location:** Urban, comfortable, quiet. **Surface:** grassy. 01/04-31/12
Distance: 500m, Orléans 5km 2,7km 50m 50m 500m 500m on the spot on the spot.
Remarks: Along the Loire river.

La Châtre 21C4

Rue du Champ de Foire. **GPS**: n46,58250 e1,98250.

10 € 2. **Surface:** asphalted.
Distance: 50m 50m 50m.

S La Châtre 21C4

Supermarché Super U, Avenue d'Auvergne, D943. **GPS**: n46,58278 e2,00139.
10 free € 2/10minutes Ch € 2/1h. **Surface:** asphalted.
01/01-31/12
Distance: 800m 50m.

FR

La Ferte-Beauharnais 21C1

D922. **GPS**: n47,54455 e1,84882.

12 free € 2/10minutes Ch € 2/55minutes WC.
Surface: grassy/metalled. 01/01-31/12
Distance: 300m on the spot on the spot 250m 100m.

Lailly-en-Val 21C1

GPS: n47,77023 e1,68544.

50 free Ch WC free. **Surface:** gravel.
Distance: 100m 50m 300m 200m.

Lamotte-Beuvron 21C1

Avenue de la Republique. **GPS**: n47,59795 e2,02524.

5 free Ch WC free. **Surface:** metalled.
01/01-31/12 Fri-morning, water disconnected in winter.
Distance: 200m 4,5km on the spot on the spot 300m 300m.

Tourist information Lamotte-Beuvron:
Avenue de la Republique.Market. Fri-morning.

Langon (Loir-et-Cher) 21C2

Parking Canal du Berry, D976. **GPS**: n47,28194 e1,82722.

7 free € 2/10minutes Ch € 2/1h. **Surface:** asphalted.
01/01-31/12 Service: winter.
Distance: 50m 20m 100m 100m.
Remarks: Coins at shops/town hall.

Le Blanc 21B3

Place du Général de Gaulle. **GPS**: n46,63154 e1,06164.

free € 2/100liter Ch € 2/1h. **Location:** Central, noisy.
Surface: asphalted. 01/01-31/12 service: 01/11-01/04.
Distance: on the spot 250m.

Le Châtelet 21D4

Le Tivoli, Avenue de la Gare. **GPS**: n46,64502 e2,27863.

5 free € 2 Ch. **Surface:** asphalted. 01/01-31/12
Distance: 50m 50m 300m.

Léré 22A1

Le Port, Rue du Champ des Noyers. **GPS**: n47,47485 e2,87477.
4 free Ch. **Location:** Rural. **Surface:** asphalted.
01/01-31/12
Remarks: On the canal.

Levet 21D3

Chemin du Crot A Thibault. **GPS**: n46,92306 e2,40639.

3 free Ch free (3x). **Surface:** gravel. 01/03-31/10
Distance: 250m 250m 250m.
Remarks: Max. 24h.

Loches 21B2

Rue Amiral des Pointis. **GPS**: n47,13315 e1,00023.
8 free. **Surface:** gravel. 01/01-31/12
Distance: centre 250m.
Remarks: Max. 24h.

Loches 21B2

Rue Aristide Briand. **GPS**: n47,12240 e1,00164.

Ch free. 01/01-31/12

Louzouer 15A6

Cidre Chivet, 323 Les Mussereaux. **GPS**: n48,02833 e2,87062.

FR

5 €5 €3 Ch. **Location:** Comfortable. **Surface:** asphalted/metalled. 15/03-31/12
Distance: 1,5km.
Remarks: Max. 24h.

S Luant 21B3

L'Étang Duris. **GPS**: n46,72222 e1,57338.
10 free €2 Ch €2. **Location:** Isolated, quiet. **Surface:** gravel. 01/01-31/12
Distance: 3km 3,3km A20 lake bar/brasserie on the spot.

S Marboué 14B6

Aire de Marboué, Lieu-dit les 3 Fontaines. **GPS**: n48,11240 e1,32870.

8+5 free €2/100liter Ch €2/1h. **Location:** Rural, comfortable, central, quiet. **Surface:** grassy/gravel. 01/01-31/12
Distance: on the spot 500m 150m on the spot on the spot.
Remarks: N10 dir Châteaudun, before bridge to the right.

S Marcilly-en-Villette 21C1

Rue du Lavoir. **GPS**: n47,76197 e2,02448.
6 free Chfree. **Location:** Rural, quiet. **Surface:** gravel.
Distance: 200m 400m on the spot.

S Martizay 21B3

Aire de Loisirs. **GPS**: n46,80528 e1,03806.

9 free Ch WC free. **Surface:** metalled/sand. 01/01-31/12
Distance: on the spot bakery 500m.

S Menetou-Salon 21D2

Rue de la Mairie. **GPS**: n47,23162 e2,49002.

6 free Chfree. **Surface:** gravel/metalled. 01/01-31/12
Distance: on the spot 50m 100m.

S Mennetou-sur-Cher 21C2

Place du 11 Novembre, N76. **GPS**: n47,26861 e1,86472.

8 free €2/10minutes Ch €2/1h. **Surface:** sand. 01/01-31/12
Distance: 150m 100m 150m 150m.
Remarks: Small fortified town, coins at shops and tourist office.

S Méry-sur-Cher 21C2

Chemin Lucien Bonneau/N76. **GPS**: n47,24586 e1,98989.

6 €5/24h, parking fee being collected Ch WC included.
Surface: metalled. 01/01-31/12
Distance: 150m 100m.

S Meung-sur-Loire 21C1

Chemin des Grèves. **GPS**: n47,82327 e1,69814.
8 free €2 Ch. **Location:** Rural. **Surface:** gravel. 01/01-31/12
Distance: 250m 300m 250m bakery.
Remarks: At swimming pool.

S Montoire-sur-le-Loir 21A1

Avenue de la République. **GPS**: n47,75750 e0,86928.

9 free Chfree €1. **Location:** Urban, comfortable, quiet.
Surface: asphalted. 01/01-31/12
Distance: on the spot 500m 500m on the spot.
Remarks: At former station.

FR

Montoire-sur-le-Loir 21A1

Aire de Montoire-sur-le-Loir, Boulevard des Alliés, Quartier Marescot. **GPS**: n47,74990 e0,86317.

8 free. **Location:** Urban, simple, central, quiet. **Surface:** asphalted.
01/01-31/12
Distance: 50m on the spot on the spot 500m 500m on the spot on the spot.

Montrésor 21B2

Rue du 8 Mai. **GPS**: n47,15750 e1,20169.
10 free Ch free. **Surface:** asphalted. 01/01-31/12
Distance: 200m.

Neuillay-les-Bois 21B3

Route de Buzançais, D1. **GPS**: n46,76917 e1,47333.

5 free Ch WC free. **Surface:** metalled. 01/05-31/10
Distance: 50m 50m 50m 50m.
Remarks: Max. 24h.

Neuillé-Pont-Pierre 21A1

Parc Chauvin, Rue De Gaulle, D766. **GPS**: n47,54803 e0,55278.

10 free Ch (12x)free WC. **Location:** Urban, simple, noisy.
Surface: asphalted. 01/01-31/12
Distance: on the spot 3,5km on the spot on the spot.

Neuvy-Le-Barrois 22A3

Monsieur Thévenin, Le Pénisson, D45. **GPS**: n46,86159 e3,03930.

6 € 6 Ch € 4 € 2. **Surface:** gravel/metalled. 01/04-31/10
Distance: 200m 200m.

Neuvy-Pailloux 21C3

Les Gloux, RN151. **GPS**: n46,88278 e1,83682.
15 free Ch WC free. **Surface:** asphalted. 01/01-31/12
Remarks: Isolated parking.

Tourist information Neuvy-Pailloux:
Small town.

Nogent-le-Roi 14C4

Rue du Pont des Demoiselles. **GPS**: n48,65059 e1,52894.
Ch .

Nogent-sur-Vernisson 22A1

GPS: n47,84055 e2,73996.

6 free. **Location:** Simple, quiet. **Surface:** gravel. 01/01-31/12
Distance: 1km on the spot on the spot 1km.

Nogent-sur-Vernisson 22A1

Rue Georges Bannery. **GPS**: n47,85363 e2,74014.
€ 2,50 Ch € 2,50.
Remarks: Coins at office de tourisme, PMU Rue Bannery or bar in Rue A. Briand.

Nouan-le-Fuzelier 21C1

Rue Gauchoix. **GPS**: n47,53324 e2,03437.

6 free. **Surface:** grasstiles/metalled. 01/01-31/12
Distance: 300m 300m 300m.

Oulches 21B4

Impasse de l'Étang. **GPS**: n46,61339 e1,29547.
free € 2 Ch € 2. **Location:** Rural. **Surface:** gravel.
Distance: on the spot 100m.

Ouzouer-sur-Trézée 22A1

Parking halte nautique, Rue Saint-Roche/ Canal de Briare. **GPS**: n47,67000 e2,80888.

5 free . **Surface:** asphalted. 01/04-31/10
Distance: 500m on the spot 500m.
Remarks: At canal 'de Briare', max. 48h.

Ouzouer-sur-Trézée 22A1

Camping municipal, Chemin du Rochoir. **GPS**: n47,66819 e2,80611.

FR

6 € 4,50 Ch € 2,60 WC included. **Surface:** gravel.
01/04-31/10

Paucourt 15A6

Rue de l'Église. **GPS:** n48,03441 e2,79179.

free Chfree. **Location:** Rural. **Surface:** asphalted.
01/01-31/12
Distance: on the spot 4,5km.

Pouligny-Saint-Pierre 21B3

Route du Blanc, D950, Bénavent. **GPS:** n46,65591 e1,02054.
10 free € 2 € 2Ch€ 2 € 2. **Location:** Rural, quiet.
Surface: gravel.
Distance: bakery 50m.
Remarks: Coins at the bakery.

Reignac-sur-Indre 21A2

Rue Louis de Barberin, D58. **GPS:** n47,22922 e0,91585.

5 free € 2/100liter Ch. **Location:** Rural, simple, central, noisy.
Surface: asphalted/metalled. 01/01-31/12
Distance: 300m 20km on the spot on the spot on the spot.
Remarks: Max. 24h, coins at the shops in the village.

Restigné 20D2

Rue Basse. **GPS:** n47,28041 e0,22614.

10 free € 2/100liter Ch. **Location:** Rural, simple, central, quiet.
Surface: gravel. 01/01-31/12
Distance: on the spot on the spot on the spot on the spot.
Remarks: Coins at town hall.

Saint-Denis-les-Ponts 14B6

Aire de Saint Denis-les-Ponts, Rue Jean Moulin. **GPS:** n48,06643 e1,28950.

+10 free € 2/100liter Ch. **Location:** Urban, comfortable, central, quiet. **Surface:** gravel.
01/01-31/12 Service: winter.
Distance: Châteaudun 3km on the spot on the spot 100m on the spot on the spot.
Remarks: Coins available at the shops, Châteaudun (city and castle) 4km.

Saint-Jean-le-Blanc 14C6

Base de loisirs de l'Ile Charlemagne, Levée de la Chevauchée. **GPS:** n47,89437 e1,93870.
free € 2 Ch. **Surface:** sand.
Distance: Orléans 3km.

Sainte-Maure-de-Touraine 21A2

Aire du Bois Chaudron, D910, Le Bois Caudron. **GPS:** n47,09315 e0,61275.

40 € 2,50, 2 pers.incl € 1 € 2Ch€ 3 (4x)€ 2/12h WC € 4 € 2.
Location: Rural, comfortable, isolated, quiet. **Surface:** grassy.
01/01-31/12
Distance: 1,5km 4,4km 1,5km 1,5km on the spot.
Remarks: Bread-service.

Sainte-Maure-de-Touraine 21A2

Parking Ronsard, Avenue Ronsard. **GPS:** n47,11056 e0,61750.

15 free Chfree WC. **Location:** Urban, simple, central, quiet.
Surface: asphalted. 01/01-31/12
Distance: 200m 3km 200m 200m on the spot.

Sainte-Sévère-sur-Indre 21C4

Place du Champ de Foire, rue de Verdun. **GPS:** n46,48724 e2,07167.
free € 2 Ch. **Location:** Rural. **Surface:** gravel/sand.
Distance: 100m 180m.

Sancoins 22A3

Quai du Canal. **GPS:** n46,83356 e2,91568.

FR

20 free Ch WC free. **Surface:** gravel/metalled. 01/01-31/12
Distance: 200m on the spot on the spot 200m.

S Saran 14C6

Allée Claude Bernard. **GPS:** n47,95106 e1,87315.
10 free Ch free. **Surface:** gravel. 01/01-31/12
Distance: on the spot on the spot on the spot.

S Selles-sur-Cher 21C2

Avenue Kleber-Loustau. **GPS:** n47,27639 e1,55889.

15 €5 Ch. **Surface:** asphalted/grassy. 01/01-31/12
Distance: 500m 200m 500m 500m.
Remarks: Coins at camping, office de tourisme, town hall.

S St.Amand-Montrond 21D3

Base de Loisirs Virlay. **GPS:** n46,73362 e2,48851.

20 free Ch free. **Location:** Rural. **Surface:** asphalted/grassy.
01/01-31/12
Distance: 1km 5km 500m 500m.

S St.Amand-Montrond 21D3

Quai Lutin, via Avenue Maréchal Foch. **GPS:** n46,71818 e2,50480.

12 free Ch WC free. **Surface:** asphalted/gravel. 01/01-31/12
Distance: nearby on the spot on the spot 300m 300m.

S St.Brisson-sur-Loire 21D1

Rue des Ruets, route d'Autry, D52. **GPS:** n47,64680 e2,68028.

6 free Ch free. **Surface:** asphalted. 01/01-31/12
Distance: 100m 100m 100m 50m.
Remarks: Parking nearby town hall.

S St.Georges-sur-Arnon 21C3

N151. **GPS:** n46,97740 e2,06908.

10 free Ch WC free. **Surface:** asphalted.

S St.Gondon 21D1

Rue de Sully. **GPS:** n47,69808 e2,53876.

3 free Ch free. **Surface:** asphalted. 01/01-31/12
Distance: 300m on the spot 300m.
Remarks: Max. 48h.

S St.Gondon 21D1

Rue du Petit Clou. **GPS:** n47,69995 e2,54356.
10 free Ch free. **Location:** Rural. **Surface:** metalled.
01/01-31/12
Remarks: In front of cemetery.

S Sully-sur-Loire 21D1

Chemin de la Salle Verte. **GPS:** n47,77139 e2,38451.

16 free Ch free. **Surface:** gravel/metalled. 01/01-31/12
Distance: 800m on the spot on the spot 800m 800m.
Remarks: Narrow entrance, nearby castle of Sully.

S Ternay 21A1

Plan d'eau, Rue Saint Père. **GPS:** n47,73114 e0,77617.

FR

10 free Chfree WC. **Location:** Rural, simple, central, quiet.
Surface: gravel. 01/01-31/12
Distance: on the spot on the spot on the spot.

S Theillay 21C2

Chemin du Ronaire. **GPS**: n47,31849 e2,03775.

10 free Chfree. **Surface:** gravel/metalled. 01/01-31/12
Distance: 250m 250m.

S Thenay 21B3

Rue de la Paix, D48. **GPS**: n46,63199 e1,43096.
free € 2 Ch € 2. **Surface:** metalled.
Distance: 200m.
Remarks: Coins available at the shops and town hall.

S Thiron-Gardais 14B5

Aire de Thiron-Gardais, Avenue de la Gare. **GPS**: n48,31194 e0,99583.

10 free Chfree. **Location:** Urban, simple.
Surface: asphalted.
Distance: 100m 300m 300m 300m on the spot 100m.

S Tour-en-Sologne 21B1

Rue de la Mairie. **GPS**: n47,53786 e1,49973.

10 free € 2 Ch WC. **Surface:** metalled.
Distance: 50m 200m bakery 100m.

S Vailly-sur-Sauldre 21D1

Rue du Pont. **GPS**: n47,45727 e2,64665.

8 € 3,50 Chfree € 2,50 WC € 0,80. **Surface:** gravel/metalled.
01/04-31/10
Distance: 300m on the spot nearby nearby.
Remarks: At D923 on entering the village from Aubigny, along river.

Tourist information Vailly-sur-Sauldre:
Fri.

S Valençay 21C2

Avenue de la Résistance. **GPS**: n47,16080 e1,56163.

10 free € 2 Ch . **Surface:** metalled. 01/01-31/12
Distance: 100m 100m 100m.
Remarks: Nearby entrance castle.

Tourist information Valençay:
Office de Tourisme, 2, Avenue de la Résistance, www.pays-de-valencay.com.
Château.Castle, 15th-18th century. 01/03-30/11.

S Veigné 21A2

Camping de la Plage, 'D50. **GPS**: n47,28921 e0,73436.
3 free € 2/100liter Ch € 2/10minutes. **Location:** Comfortable, noisy. **Surface:** metalled.
Distance: on the spot on the spot on the spot 100m 100m.

Vendôme 21B1

Aie de Vendôme, Rue Geoffroy Martel. **GPS**: n47,79111 e1,07528.

5 free. **Location:** Urban, simple, central. **Surface:** asphalted.
01/01-31/12
Distance: 500m.

S Villaines les Rochers 21A2

Aire de Villaines-les-Rochers, Place de la Mairie/ Rue des Ecoles. **GPS**: n47,22083 e0,49583.

FR

6 free Ch WC free. **Location:** Urban, comfortable, central, quiet. **Surface:** asphalted. 01/01-31/12
Distance: on the spot 100m 100m on the spot on the spot.
Remarks: Max. 24h.

S Villandry 21A2

Aire de Villandry, Rue Principale. **GPS**: n47,34100 e0,51127.

25 free € 2/100liter Ch WC. **Location:** Rural, comfortable, central, quiet. **Surface:** grasstiles.
01/01-31/12
Distance: 50m 3,1km 300m 90m 90m on the spot on the spot on the spot.
Remarks: Coins at Office de Tourisme(100m), Château de Villandry 200m.

S Villedômer 21A1

Aire de Villedômer, Rue du Lavoir. **GPS**: n47,54465 e0,88727.

5 free, 15/06-15/09 € 5 € 2/100liter Ch € 2/1h. **Location:** Rural, simple, central, quiet. **Surface:** metalled.
01/01-31/12
Distance: 100m 8,1km 100m 200m 200m on the spot on the spot.
Remarks: Max. 24h, coins at town hall (200m), bakery (200m) and supermarket (50m).

S Villequiers 22A2

L'Étappe Berrichonne, Le Petit Azillon. **GPS**: n47,08828 e2,77429.

6 € 6 € 3 Ch. **Surface:** gravel/metalled. 01/01-31/12
Distance: 3km.

S Vitry-aux-Loges 14D6

Rue des Érables. **GPS**: n47,93915 e2,27078.
free Ch free. **Location:** Rural. **Surface:** asphalted.
01/01-31/12
Distance: 100m 100m on the spot on the spot.
Remarks: At canal of Orléans.

S Vouvray 21A1

Parking Bec de Cisse, Rue Bec de Cisse. **GPS**: n47,40929 e0,79735.

8 free € 2/100liter Ch € 2/1h WC. **Location:** Rural, comfortable, central, quiet. **Surface:** asphalted.
01/01-31/12 Service: winter.
Distance: on the spot 8,5km 500m 150m 150m on the spot on the spot.
Remarks: Coins at campsite (100m) and tourist office.

Bourgogne

S Anost 22C2

Place Centrale. **GPS**: n47,07778 e4,09869.

10 free Ch free. **Location:** Rural, simple, quiet. **Surface:** metalled.
01/01-31/12
Distance: on the spot.

S Autun 22C3

Route de Chalon. **GPS**: n46,95548 e4,31667.

18 free € 3,50 Ch. **Location:** Urban, simple.
Surface: asphalted.
01/01-31/12
Distance: city centre 2km 100m 100m supermarket 900m on the spot on the spot.
Remarks: Parking at small lake Le Vallon at N80, in front of McDonalds.

Tourist information Autun:
Office de Tourisme, 2, Avenue Charles de Gaulle, www.autun.com.
Musée Rolin.Roman and Medieval excavations.
Wed, Fri, Su.

S Auxerre 22B1

Quai de la République. **GPS**: n47,79636 e3,57633.

FR

free free. **Surface:** asphalted.
Distance: on the spot 100m on the spot.
Remarks: Along the Yonne river.

Tourist information Auxerre:
Office de Tourisme, 1-2, Quai de la République, www.ot-auxerre.fr.
Tue, Fri.

S Beaune 22D3

Parking Charles de Gaulle. **GPS**: n47,01731 e4,83628.

5 free € 3,50 Ch € 3,50/2h . **Location:** Urban, simple, central.
Surface: asphalted.
Distance: 500m 2,6km 200m centre commercial 300m.
Remarks: 5 special pitches, all parking places permitted.

Tourist information Beaune:
Office de Tourisme, 1, Rue de l'Hôtel-Dieu, www.ot-beaune.fr.Tourist place worth seeing, old centre with ramparts.
M Hôtel Dieu et Musée.Former hospital, 15th century, museum.
Château de Meursault, Meursault.Castle with vineyard and wine tastery.

S Chablis 22B1

Route d'Auxerre, D235. **GPS**: n47,81711 e3,78425.

5 free free. **Location:** Simple. **Surface:** asphalted.
Distance: centre 500m on the spot.

S Chalon-sur-Saône 22D3

P Ville Historique, Promenade Sainte Marie. **GPS**: n46,78365 e4,86046.

2 free Ch free. **Location:** Simple. **Surface:** asphalted.
Distance: 500m 50m.
Remarks: Free shuttle to centre.

Tourist information Chalon-sur-Saône:
Office de Tourisme, Square Chabas - 29, Boulevard de la République, www.chalon-sur-saone.net.
M Musée Nicéphore Niepce.Photography museum. 9.30-11.30h, 14.30-17.30h, 01/07-31/08 10-18h Tue, holiday.

S Charolles 22C4

Route de Viry. **GPS**: n46,43956 e4,28203.

5 € 3 Ch € 3. **Location:** Simple. **Surface:** gravel.
01/04-01/10
Distance: 300m.
Remarks: Max. 48h.

S Château-Chinon 22C3

Rue Jean Sallonnyer. **GPS**: n47,06304 e3,93627.

10 free Ch free WC. **Location:** Simple. **Surface:** metalled.
01/01-31/12
Distance: 200m 250m 250m.
Remarks: Max. 24h.

Châtillon-en-Bazois 22B3

Place Pierre Saury. **GPS**: n47,05310 e3,65511.

5 free. **Surface:** metalled. 01/04-31/10
Distance: 50m.

S Chiddes 22C3

Le Bourg. **GPS**: n46,86108 e3,94091.

FR

4 free Ch free WC. **Location:** Simple. **Surface:** gravel. 01/01-31/12
Distance: on the spot on the spot.
Remarks: Max. 48h, free coins available at restaurant.

Clamecy 22B2

Rue de l'Abattoir. **GPS**: n47,46222 e3,52250.

6 free. **Location:** Simple. **Surface:** gravel. 01/01-31/12
Distance: 350m 150m.

Décize 22B3

Esplanade des Halles, Allée Marcel Merle. **GPS**: n46,83223 e3,46133.

± 15 free € 3 Ch. **Location:** Simple. **Surface:** metalled.
01/01-31/12
Distance: 200m on the spot on the spot.
Remarks: On the river Loire.

Tourist information Décize:
Musée de la Mine, La Machine.Life of the coalminer. summer 10-12h, 15-19h Tue. € 1,60.

Digoin 22C4

Place de la Grève, Route de Vichy. **GPS**: n46,48102 e3,97288.

± 15 free Ch (4x)free. **Location:** Simple, central. **Surface:** asphalted. 01/01-31/12
Distance: on the spot on the spot on the spot on the spot.
Remarks: Next to Office du Tourisme.

Tourist information Digoin:
Office de Tourisme, 8, rue Guilleminot, perso.wanadoo.fr/office-de-tourisme-de-digoin.

Dijon 22D2

Aire de Dijon, 3, Boulevard Chainoine Kir. **GPS**: n47,32125 e5,01090.

16 € 10/24h Ch (17x)included. **Location:** Urban, comfortable, noisy. **Surface:** asphalted.
01/01-31/12 water: frost.
Distance: centre Dijon 1,5km 10km 300m 300m 500m 500m >Dijon 150m 10m.
Remarks: Attention: motorhomes ^3m take access road from southerly direction.

Tourist information Dijon:
Office de Tourisme, Place Darcy, www.dijon-tourism.com.City worth a visit with a number of large mansions and streets with half-timbered houses.
Musée de Moutarde Amora, 48, quai Nicolas-Rolin.History of mustard and the Amora factory. free.
Tour Filippe le Bon-Mairie.Tower, 15th century, overlooking the city.
01/07-31/08 daily, 01/09-30/06 Sa, Su.
Nôtre Dame.

Ecuisses 22C3

Place Marcel Pagnol, Route du Bourg. **GPS**: n46,76019 e4,52283.

20 free free. **Location:** Simple. **Surface:** metalled.
01/01-31/12
Remarks: Max. 48h.

Étang-sur-Arroux 22C3

Place du Mousseau. **GPS**: n46,86631 e4,18946.

free Ch free. **Location:** Simple. **Surface:** asphalted.
01/01-31/12
Distance: 100m 100m.

Fontaine-Française 23A1

Rue Berthault. **GPS**: n47,52487 e5,36768.

FR

5 free € 3 Ch. **Location:** Rural, simple. **Surface:** asphalted/grassy.
01/01-31/12

Distance: 100m 16km on the spot 250m bakery.

Remarks: Coins available at the shops, at river nd betwee 2 lakes. Parking at river.

S Fours 22B3

Rue des Saules, D981. **GPS**: n46,81720 e3,71806.

10 free Ch free. **Location:** Simple. **Surface:** gravel.
01/01-31/12

Distance: 200m 200m 200m.

S Génelard 22C4

Place du Bassin, D974. **GPS**: n46,57750 e4,23500.

2 free Ch free. **Location:** Simple. **Surface:** asphalted.
01/01-31/12

Distance: on the spot.

S Givry 22D3

Relais camping-car, Rue de la Gare. **GPS**: n46,78000 e4,74830.

15 free € 2/100liter Ch € 2/10minutes. **Location:** Comfortable.
Surface: asphalted. 01/01-31/12

Distance: on the spot.

Remarks: Coins available at restaurant.

Tourist information Givry:

Marché.Market. Thu.

La Voie Verte de Givry à Cluny.Cycle route on former railway,.

S Gurgy 22B1

Quai des Fontaines. **GPS**: n47,86348 e3,55376.

20 free € 4/10minutes Ch € 4/1h. **Surface:** grassy/gravel.
01/04-31/10

Distance: 50m 7km on the spot 500m 300m.

Remarks: Along the Yonne river, coints at supermarket.

S Heuilley-sur-Saône 23A2

Rue Condé. **GPS**: n47,32800 e5,45471.

20 free € 3 Ch WC. **Location:** Rural, quiet. **Surface:** gravel/sand.
01/01-31/12

Distance: on the spot 100m 100m.

Remarks: Coins at town hall.

S La Chapelle-de-Guinchay 22D5

Le Clos Meziat. **GPS**: n46,21017 e4,76720.

± 10 free Ch WC free. **Location:** Rural, comfortable, quiet.
Surface: gravel/metalled. 01/01-31/12

Distance: centre 1,2km A6 10km 1,2km 1,2km.

S La Charité-sur-Loire 22A2

Quai Romain Mollot. **GPS**: n47,17483 e3,01123.

5 free € 4 Ch . **Surface:** asphalted. 01/01-31/12

Distance: 250m on the spot on the spot on the spot on the spot on the spot.

Remarks: Parking at river.

La Charité-sur-Loire 22A2

Quai de la Tête de l'Ourth. **GPS**: n47,17577 e3,01254.

FR

3 free. **Surface:** asphalted. 01/01-31/12
Remarks: Parking at river.

Laignes 22C1

Chemin du Moulin Neuf, D965. **GPS:** n47,84850 e4,36132.

6 free. **Location:** Simple, quiet. **Surface:** grassy. 01/01-31/12
Distance: 1km on the spot.
Remarks: Parking at river, max. 24h.

Louhans 23A4

Halte nautique, Rue du Port. **GPS:** n46,62952 e5,21302.

15 free, 01/05-30/09 € 5 + € 0,20/pp tourist tax Ch WC included.
Location: Comfortable, quiet. **Surface:** gravel.
Distance: 400m.
Remarks: Sanitary building: 1/5-30/9, to be paid at Halte Nautique.

Louhans 23A4

Boivin Claude, Rue de la Griffonnière. **GPS:** n46,63070 e5,24857.
12 € 5 Ch included € 5. **Surface:** gravel. 01/01-31/12

Luzy 22C3

Place du champ De Foire. **GPS:** n46,79028 e3,96840.

4 free Ch WC free. **Location:** Simple. **Surface:** metalled.
01/01-31/12
Distance: centre 300m 100m 200m 500m.
Remarks: Max. 48h, coins at the shops and restaurant.

Marsannay-la-Côte 22D2

Espace du Rocher, Rue du Rocher. **GPS:** n47,27099 e4,99224.

5 free Ch free. **Location:** Urban, simple, quiet. **Surface:** asphalted.
01/01-31/12
Distance: 500m 3,5km 750m.
Remarks: Via N74/D974.

Marsannay-la-Côte 22D2

Rue de Mazy, D122. **GPS:** n47,27027 e4,98761.
free. **Surface:** asphalted. 01/01-31/12
Distance: on the spot 5km.
Remarks: Parking next to Office du Tourisme.

Nolay 22D3

Avenue de la Liberté. **GPS:** n46,95016 e4,62828.

± 10 free Ch service € 2. **Location:** Urban, simp e.
Surface: gravel. 01/01-31/12
Distance: 100m 300m 300m.
Remarks: Coins at town hall.

Tourist information Nolay:
Site Champetre du Bout du Monde, Vauchignon.Water falls.

Nuits-Saint-Georges 22D2

Rue de Cussigny. **GPS:** n47,13178 e4,95189.

10 free Ch free. **Location:** Urban, simple. **Surface:** asphalted.
01/01-31/12
Distance: 400m 2,1km 500m Intermarché 300m.

Tourist information Nuits-Saint-Georges:
Office de Tourisme, 3, Rue Sonoys, www.ot-nuits-st-georges.fr.Small city the famous Burgundian vineyards, signposted wine routes.
Fri.

Pougues-les-Eaux 22A2

D907. **GPS:** n47,08315 e3,09382.

5 free € 2/10minutes Ch € 2/10minutes . **Surface:** asphalted.
01/01-31/12
Distance: 250m 1,4km 100m.

Prissé 22D4

Cave de Prissé. **GPS:** n46,32226 e4,75257.

FR

5 free Ch WC free. **Location:** Rural, simple. **Surface:** asphalted.
01/01-31/12
Distance: 500m 3km.
Remarks: Max. 24h.

S Pruzilly 22D5

La Croix Blanche, salle des Fêtes. GPS: n46,25708 e4,69792.

6 free Ch WC free. **Location:** Rural, simple, quiet. **Surface:** asphalted.
01/01-31/12
Distance: on the spot on the spot.
Remarks: Max. 48h, vins de Côte de Beaujolais.

S Rouvray 22C2

Place du Champs de foire, D906. **GPS:** n47,42271 e4,10412.

4 free Ch free. **Surface:** metalled.
Distance: on the spot.
Remarks: Max. 48h.

S Saint-Fargeau 22A1

Rue de Laveau, D18. **GPS:** n47,63968 e3,06999.

10 free Ch WC free. 01/01-31/12
Distance: 50m 50m.

S Saint-Julien-du-Sault 15A6

Stade Jean Sax, Rue du Stade. **GPS:** n48,02906 e3,30116.
13 free Ch free. 01/01-31/12

S Savigny-le-Sec 22D2

Rue de la Mare. **GPS:** n47,43365 e5,04607.

10 € 3,50 € 2 Ch WC. **Location:** Rural, simple, isolated, quiet.
Surface: asphalted/gravel. 01/01-31/12
Distance: 1,3km bakery 1,3km.

S Semur-en-Auxois 22C1

Avenue Pasteur. **GPS:** n47,49529 e4,38810.

30 free Ch free. **Location:** Simple, quiet.
Surface: asphalted.
01/01-31/12 water: Nov-March.
Distance: historical centre 1,3km 10km 800m 800m.
Remarks: Behind stadium, near police station.

Tourist information Semur-en-Auxois:
Alise-Ste-Reine.Findings of Gallo-Roman city. 01/04-31/10 daily.

S Seurre 23A3

FR

Rue de la Perche à l'Oiseau. **GPS:** n47,00405 e5,14318.

15 free Ch Service € 4/20min. **Location:** Rural, simple, quiet.
Surface: asphalted. 01/01-31/12
Distance: 800m 100m 100m 700m 700m.

S St.Gengoux-le-National 22D4

GPS: n46,60624 e4,66844.

16 free € 3/15minutes Ch € 3/50minutes WC. **Location:** Simple, quiet. **Surface:** metalled. 01/01-31/12
Distance: 500m.
Remarks: At former station.

Tourist information St.Gengoux-le-National:

La Voie Verte.Cycle route on former railway,.

S St.Honoré-les-Bains 22B3

Allée de la Cressonnière. **GPS**: n46,90471 e3,84059.

4 free € 2 Ch € 2. **Location:** Simple. **Surface:** gravel. 01/01-31/12

Distance: 300m 300m 50m.

Remarks: Max. 48h, coins at town hall and supermarket.

S Vinzelles 22D5

Clos Bonin. **GPS**: n46,27145 e4,77008.

10 free Chfree. **Location:** Rural, simple. **Surface:** asphalted. 01/01-31/12

Distance: 200m A6 2,8km on the spot on the spot on the spot.

Franche Comté

S Arc-et-Senans 23B3

Grande rue. **GPS**: n47,03343 e5,78120.

free € 1 Ch. **Surface:** gravel. 01/01-31/12

Remarks: Coints at mairie, supermarket, campsite.

S Arinthod 23A4

Rue de la Prélette. **GPS**: n46,39654 e5,57013.

6 € 6 Ch included. **Surface:** gravel. 01/01-31/12

S Arsure-Arsurette 23B3

Châlet des Arches. **GPS**: n46,72168 e6,08402.

10 free € 2 WC . **Surface:** asphalted. 01/01-31/12

S Baume-les-Dames 23C2

Quai du Canal. **GPS**: n47,34000 e6,35806.

32 € 6,50 Ch WC included € 1,50. **Surface:** asphalted/grassy. 01/01-31/12

Distance: on the spot 5,3km on the spot.

Remarks: Max. 24h.

Tourist information Baume-les-Dames:

Office de Tourisme, 6, rue de Provence.Small tourist town in the heart of Doubs valley.

Abbaye Nôtre Dame.Historical monument, 18th century.

S Besançon 23B2

Parking du Crous, Cité Carnot, Quai Veil Picard. **GPS**: n47,23702 e6,01644.

12 free Ch. **Surface:** asphalted. 01/01-31/12

Distance: on the spot.

Tourist information Besançon:

Office de Tourisme, 2, place de la 1re Armée Française, www.besancon-tourisme.com.City worth a visit along the Doubs river. Victor Hugo was born in the house at Grande Rue number 40.

Jardin Botanique, avenue de la Paix.Botanical gardens.

Citadelle; Musée de la Résistance et de déportation.War museum.

Musée Populaire Comtois, Citadelle.Folkore museum. 9-18/19h, winter 10-17h.

Muséum d'Histoire Naturelle comprenant le jardin zoologique, l'aquarium, l'insectarium et le noctarium, Citadelle.Natural museum.

Château, Vaire-le-Grand. 15/08-18/09, 19/09-14/08 by agreement.

Cathédrale St Jean.

Tue, Fri, Su.

Parc Zoologique de la Citadelle, Citadelle.Zoo. 10-17/19h. € 7.

S Bois-d'Amont 23B4

Musée de la Boisellerie, Impasse de l'Eglantine. **GPS**: n46,53771 e6,13934.

FR

10 free € 2 Ch € 2. **Surface:** asphalted.
Distance: on the spot on the spot on the spot.
Remarks: Service at town hall 300m.

Brognard 23C1

Base de Loisirs de la Savoureuse, Rue de Paquis. **GPS**: n47,52834 e6,85652.

3 free Ch free. **Surface:** asphalted. 01/01-31/12
Distance: 50m 1,3km.
Remarks: Max. 48h.

Champagnole 23B3

20, Rue Georges Vallerey. **GPS**: n46,74633 e5,89918.

5 free, 1/6-15/9 € 5 Ch € 5. **Surface:** gravel.
01/01-31/12
Distance: 500m 250m.
Remarks: Max. 1 night, coins at campsite.

Clairvaux-les-Lacs 23B4

Route de Lons-le-Saunier, D678. **GPS**: n46,58246 e5,74660.

6 free Ch free. 01/01-31/12
Distance: nearby.
Remarks: On entering village, nearby police station.

Conliège 23A4

Rue du Saugeois. **GPS**: n46,65270 e5,59981.

2 free Ch WC free. **Surface:** asphalted.
Distance: 100m.

Consolation-Maisonnettes 23C2

Parc du Seminaire du Cirque de Consolation.. **GPS**: n47,15848 e6,60600.

10 € 5/24h Ch WC included. **Surface:** asphalted.

Corre 16B6

Fluvial Loisirs, Pré le Saônier. **GPS**: n47,91402 e5,99308.

32 € 6 01/11-31/03, € 8 01/04-31/10 Ch included € 1,50
€ 4 € 3/2day. **Location:** Rural, comfortable, quiet.
Surface: gravel. 01/01-31/12
Distance: 200m 50m 50m bakery 300m, supermarket 500m
100m.

Cousance 23A4

Grande rue, Champs de foire. **GPS**: n46,52929 e5,39154.

4 free Ch WC free. **Surface:** asphalted. 01/01-31/12
Distance: 100m 6,6km 100m.

Dôle 23A2

Parking de Lahr, Avenue de Lahr. **GPS**: n47,08983 e5,49641.
20 free. **Location:** Simple, central, noisy. **Surface:** asphalted.
Distance: on the spot on the spot.

Tourist information Dôle:

Office de Tourisme, Place Grevy, www.dole.org.City on the Doubs river with many monuments.

Maison natale de Louis Pasteur, 43 de la rue Pasteur.Birth house Pasteur, museum.

FR

1/4-31/10 10-12h, 14-18h, 01/11-31/03 Sa-Su 14-18h Su-morning.
free.
Musée des Beaux-Arts, 85, rue des Arènes.Museum of Fine Arts.

Jeurre 23A4

35, Rue Principale. **GPS**: n46,36662 e5,70769.

40 € 4 € 2 Ch € 2. **Surface:** grassy. 01/05-31/10
Remarks: From Lons le Saunier dir Saint Claude.

La Chapelle des Bois 23B4

Station de ski, Chemin du Marais Blanc. **GPS**: n46,60307 e6,11317.
free € 3 Ch. **Surface:** unpaved.
Distance: on the spot.

La Pesse 23B4

GPS: n46,28400 e5,84764.

free € 2 Ch WC. **Surface:** unpaved. 01/01-31/12
Distance: on the spot.
Remarks: At start of langlauf circuit.

La Pesse 23B4

Ferme Auberge de La Combe aux Bisons, Lieu-dit Pré Reverchon. **GPS**: n46,29278 e5,86011.
3 guests free . 01/01-31/12
Distance: on the spot.

Lamoura 23B4

Route de Prémanon, D25. **GPS**: n46,39810 e5,98300.

20 free Ch free. **Surface:** asphalted.
Distance: on the spot on the spot.

Les Rousses 23B4

Parking l'Aube, Route du Lac. **GPS**: n46,48779 e6,06690.

30 free, € 4/Winter € 3,60/100liter Ch € 3,60/1h . **Surface:** asphalted. 01/01-31/12
Distance: 200m.

Les Rousses 23B4

Porte du Balanciers, Route Blanche, N5. **GPS**: n46,44852 e6,07591.

30 free, € 4/Winter € 3,50 Ch WC. **Surface:** asphalted.
01/01-31/12
Distance: Restaurant 5km.
Remarks: Ski station, ski rental, ski school, coins at Tourist Info.

Tourist information Les Rousses:

Jura community in an attractive green environment, also winter sports possibilities.
Musée de la Lunetterie, 5, rue Lamartine, Morez.Optical museum.

Longeville 23B3

Coulet, Grande Rue. **GPS**: n47,04148 e6,22678.

10 € 5 + € 1/pp Ch WC included. **Surface:** gravel/sand.
01/04-31/10

Luxeuil-les-Bains 23C1

Place de l'Etang de la Poche, Rue Gambetta. **GPS**: n47,81679 e6,38659.

20 free € 2/100liter Ch € 2/1h. **Location:** Simple, quiet.
Surface: gravel. 01/01-31/12
Distance: 1km 100m 1km Auchan/Aldi 500m 1km.

Tourist information Luxeuil-les-Bains:

Fougerolles.Since the 16th century the small town is the centre of distilleries

FR

(Kirsch and cherry brandy).

Musée de la Tour des Echevins, 36, rue Victor Genoux.Art from 19th-20th the century.

S Maisod 23A4

La Mercantine. **GPS**: n46,46500 e5,68864.

40 €9 €2 Ch. **Location:** Rural. **Surface:** gravel.
Distance: 100m 200m.
Remarks: At lake Vouglans.

S Montbéliard 23C1

Parking du Champ de Foire. **GPS**: n47,50663 e6,79128.

4 free € 1,60 Ch € 1,60. **Surface:** asphalted.
Remarks: Max. 48h.

S Montreux-Château 23D1

D11. **GPS**: n47,60283 e7,00252.

8 €5/24h Ch (8x) WC. **Surface:** gravel.

S Moussières 23B4

GPS: n46,32111 e5,89778.

6 free €2 Ch € 2. **Surface:** gravel. 01/01-31/12
Remarks: Cheese farm.

S Mouthe 23B3

Place de l'Eglise. **GPS**: n46,71042 e6,19570.

20 free €3 Ch . **Surface:** asphalted.
Remarks: Coins at the bakery, supermarket, tourist office.

S Orgelet 23A4

Place Ancien Champ de Foire, Rue du Faubourg de l'Orme. **GPS**: n46,52232 e5,60860.
10 free Ch WC free. **Surface:** gravel. 01/01-31/12
Remarks: Closed when frosty.

Tourist information Orgelet:

Old village in French Jura in natural environment.

S Salins-les-Bains 23B3

Rue de la République, D472. **GPS**: n46,93254 e5,87899.

8 free Ch free. **Surface:** asphalted.
Distance: 50m.
Remarks: Permitted to park/stay overnight on all parkings.

S Sancey-le-Long 23C2

D31/D464. **GPS**: n47,30513 e6,59477.

2 free €2 Ch € 2. **Surface:** gravel.
Remarks: Coins at supermarket, cafe, centre commercial.

S Saulx 23B1

Place de l'Eglise. **GPS**: n47,69620 e6,28030.

4 free € 2/100liter € 2/2h WC free. **Location:** Simple, quiet.
Surface: metalled.
Distance: on the spot baker on site.

FR

Sermamagny 23C1

Rue Alfred Lallemand. **GPS**: n47,67348 e6,81418.

30 free. **Surface:** grassy.

St.Claude 23B4

Avenue de la Libération, D436. **GPS**: n46,38049 e5,85209.
3 free Ch free. **Surface:** asphalted. 01/01-31/12

Tourist information St.Claude:
Tourist town, production of pipes.
Musée du Pipe et Diamant.Pipes and diamond exhibition. 01/06-30/09 9.30-12h, 14-18.30h, 01/10-31/05 14-18h Su.

St.Loup-sur-Semouse 16B6

Rue de Champ de Tir. **GPS**: n47,88303 e6,26048.

4 free € 3 Ch . **Surface:** asphalted.
01/03-30/11
Distance: on the spot 500m on the spot on the spot on the spot.
Remarks: Behind church, max. 24h.

Tourist information St.Loup-sur-Semouse:
Office de Tourisme, 14, place Léon Jacquez, regionsaintloup.free.fr.

St.Point-Lac 23B3

Aire d'acceuil pour camping-cars, Rue du lac. **GPS**: n46,81268 e6,30375.

40 € 6 Ch WC free. **Surface:** gravel/sand. 01/03-30/11
Distance: on the spot.
Remarks: Max. 1 night, no camping activity. Follow rive gauche.

Thoirette 23A5

Grande Rue. **GPS**: n46,26924 e5,53529.

7 € 6 Ch included. **Surface:** gravel.
Distance: 50m 25m.

Vaivre-et-Montoille 23B1

Avenue des Rives du Lac. **GPS**: n47,62938 e6,12701.

7 free € 2,50 Ch. **Location:** Rural, simple, quiet. **Surface:** sand.
01/01-31/12
Distance: 1,5km beach 100m 100m 25m on the spot on the spot.
Remarks: Swimming pool complex, lake.

Vaivre-et-Montoille 23B1

Avenue du Lac. **GPS**: n47,63718 e6,10752.
5 free. **Location:** Rural. **Surface:** asphalted. 01/01-31/12
Distance: on the spot on the spot on the spot.
Remarks: Directly at the lake.

Villers-le-Lac 23C3

Rue du Clos Rondot. **GPS**: n47,05948 e6,67195.

8 free € 2 Ch . **Surface:** concrete.

Villers-le-Lac 23C3

Bateaux du Saut du Doubs. GPS: n47,05500 e6,67000.

free for clients . **Surface:** asphalted.
Remarks: Max. 1 night.

Poitou Charentes

Aigre 20D5

Parc Les Charmilles, Rue des Charrières. **GPS**: n45,89341 e0,00578.

FR

10 €5 Ch (4x)included WC. **Surface:** metalled.
01/04-31/10
Distance: on the spot on the spot on the spot.
Remarks: 4th night free.

S Angliers 20D3

Aire de repos de la Briande, D347. **GPS**: n46,95861 e0,10472.

8 free €2 Ch free WC. **Surface:** asphalted. 01/01-31/12
Distance: Angliers 1km 50m.
Remarks: 5km south of Loudon.

S Arçais 20C4

Aire camping-cars du Coursault, Rue de Coursault. **GPS**: n46,29583 w0,69.

20 free, 1/4-30/9 €6 Ch WC free. **Surface:** grassy.
01/01-31/12
Distance: 400m on the spot nearby nearby.

S Aubeterre-sur-Dronne 28C1

D2, Route de Ribérac. **GPS**: n45,26980 e0,17570.

10 free Ch. **Surface:** metalled. 01/01-31/12
Distance: 500m on the spot 300m 500m.
Remarks: At tennis-courts, to be paid at Berthon, superette SAP.

Tourist information Aubeterre-sur-Dronne:
Office de Tourisme, Place du Château, aubeterresurdronne.free.fr.
Musée Papillon.Butterflies and African art. Easter-Sep 9-20h, Oct-Easter Sa-Su 14-20h.
Place de Village. Thu, Su.

S Aulnay 20C5

Rue de Salles. **GPS**: n46,02239 w0,34528.

10 free Ch free. **Surface:** gravel.
Distance: 200m 200m 200m.
Remarks: Max. 24h.

Aulnay 20C5

Place Charles de Gaulle, Rue Haute de l'Eglise. **GPS**: n46,02306 w0,35444.

10 free. **Surface:** metalled. 01/01-31/12
Distance: 200m 200m 200m.
Remarks: Follow Église St.Pierre.

S Aytré 20B5

Route de la Plage. **GPS**: n46,11311 w1,12331.
10 free Ch free. **Surface:** asphalted.
Distance: on the spot.

S Bougon 20D4

Musée des Tumulus, La Chapelle. **GPS**: n46,37845 w0,06825.

10 free Ch free. **Surface:** asphalted. 01/01-31/12
Distance: 3km.
Remarks: Parking museum.

Tourist information Bougon:
Tumulus de Bougon.Archeological site.

S Bourcefranc 20B5

Port du Chapus, La Pointe du Chapus. **GPS**: n45,85511 w1,16905.
10 €4 Ch . 01/01-31/12
Remarks: Coins at town hall, office du tourisme.

Bourcefranc 20B5

Bois de Pin. **GPS**: n45,82611 w1,14278.

FR

20 € 5. **Surface:** asphalted/metalled. 01/05-31/10

Bourcefranc 20B5

Parking de la Plage. **GPS**: n45,82917 w1,14889.

8 € 5. **Surface:** asphalted. 01/05-31/10

Bressuire 20C3

Place de la Libération, Boulevard Joffre. **GPS**: n46,83811 w0,4918.

10 free Ch free. 01/01-31/12

Distance: 50m 150m.

Remarks: Max. 24h.

Cellefrouin 20D5

D739. **GPS**: n45,89361 e0,38639.

50 free Ch WC free. **Surface:** gravel. 01/01-31/12

Distance: 300m.

Celles-sur-Belle 20C4

Rue du Bouchaud. **GPS**: n46,26278 w0,20806.

10 free Ch free. **Surface:** metalled. 01/01-31/12

Distance: 100m nearby nearby nearby.

Chabanais 21A5

Chemin des Tanneries, N141. **GPS**: n45,87447 e0,72008.

4 free. **Location:** Rural, simple. **Surface:** asphalted.

01/01-31/12 Thu.

Distance: on the spot 100m 100m.

Remarks: Along the river Vienne.

Château-Larcher 20D4

Val de Clouère. **GPS**: n46,41444 e0,31556.

10 € 3 € 3 Ch WC. **Surface:** grassy/metalled. 01/03-31/11

Distance: 1km.

Châtelaillon-Plage 20B5

Allée du Stade. **GPS**: n46,07741 w1,08715.

free. **Surface:** metalled. 01/01-31/12

Chef-Boutonne 20D5

Aire camping-cars, Chemin du Parc. **GPS**: n46,10972 w0,07694.

20 free WC free. **Surface:** grassy/metalled. 01/04-31/10

Distance: on the spot on the spot on the spot on the spot on the spot.

Cherves-Richemont 20C6

Allee des Coquelicots. **GPS**: n45,74030 w0,35607.

FR

6 free Chfree. **Surface:** asphalted.
01/01-31/12 service 01/11-15/04.
Distance: 500m 100m 500m.

S Chey 20D4

Place de la Liberté. **GPS**: n46,30500 w0,04972.

3 free Ch WC free. **Surface:** gravel. 01/01-31/12
Distance: on the spot on the spot on the spot.

S Clérac 28C1

D261e. **GPS**: n45,17998 w0,22728.

free Chfree. **Surface:** gravel.
Distance: 200m on the spot 100m 100m.
Remarks: Behind bakery, at small lake.

S Cognac 20C6

Place de la Levade, Quartier Saint-Jacques. **GPS**: n45,69847 w0,33265.

10 free Chfree. **Surface:** asphalted. 01/01-31/12
Distance: on the spot on the spot on the spot 500m on the spot.

Tourist information Cognac:

Office de Tourisme, 16, rue du 14 juillet, www.ville-cognac.fr.Old place worth seeing which gave her name to the well-known spirits.
Otard.Cognac distillery in 16th century castle. Guided tour and tasting.
daily 01/10-31/03 weekend.
Cognac-musée.Culture around the Cognac. 01/10-31/05 14-17.30h, 01/06-30/09 10-12h, 14-18h.

S Confolens 21A5

Camping les Ribières, Avenue de Sainte-Germain. **GPS**: n46,01894 e0,67570.

€ 5/night Ch WC included. **Surface:** metalled.
01/01-31/12

Tourist information Confolens:

Office de Tourisme, Place des Marronniers, www.tourisme-confolens.com.Old city on the Vienne river.
Wed, Sa.
Festival international de Danses et Musiques du Monde.Internationally folk festival. Aug.

S Couhé 20D4

Place du Marché. **GPS**: n46,29906 e0,17882.
free WCfree. **Location:** Simple, central, quiet. **Surface:** asphalted.
01/01-31/12
Distance: 50m 50m 100m.

S Coulon 20C4

Parking d'Autremont, Rue de l'Autremont. **GPS**: n46,32131 w0,58918.

30 € 6/night Ch WC free. **Surface:** grassy. 01/04-30/11
Distance: 200m nearby 200m.

S Criteuil la Magdeleine 20C6

GPS: n45,53778 w0,21556.

5 free Ch WC free. **Surface:** asphalted. 01/01-31/12
Distance: on the spot.
Remarks: In the village.

S Dolus-d'Oléron 20B5

Route du Stade. **GPS**: n45,91137 w1,25255.
free € 4/100liter € 4/1h. **Surface:** grassy.
Distance: 1,2km Hypermarché.

S Echillais 20B5

Place de la Carrière. **GPS**: n45,89753 w0,95545.
€ 4 € 3 Ch. **Surface:** asphalted.
Remarks: Access via rue de l'église.

S Fouras 20B5

Place Jean Moulin. **GPS**: n45,98139 w1,0875.

FR

15 € 6 € 1/50liter Ch. **Surface:** asphalted. 01/01-31/12
Distance: on the spot 350m on the spot on the spot.
Remarks: Nearby Plages Sud and Espérance, max. 48h, coins available at campsite and office de tourisme, wastewater disposal: attention mark!.

S Fouras 20B5

Plage Nord, Avenue du Cadoret. **GPS**: n45,99194 w1,08694.

15 € 6 € 1/50liter. **Surface:** metalled. 01/01-31/12
Distance: on the spot on the spot on the spot.
Remarks: In front of campsite Cadoret, Fun golf, max. 48h, coins available at campsite and office de tourisme.

S Fouras 20B5

Prairie du Casino, Dir pointe de la Fumée. **GPS**: n45,99583 w1,10611.

FR

20 € 6 € 1/50liter. **Surface:** metalled. 01/01-31/12
Distance: on the spot on the spot on the spot.
Remarks: Max. 48h. Parking on peninsula beyond Office du Tourisme.

Tourist information Fouras:
Bathing resort.

S Gencay 20D4

Place du Champs de Foire. **GPS**: n46,37315 e0,40638.

10 free € 2 Ch € 2 WC. **Surface:** metalled. 01/01-31/12
Distance: on the spot on the spot on the spot.
Remarks: Coins available at the shops.

S Genté 20C6

Rue de l'eglise. **GPS**: n45,62861 w0,315.

6 free Ch (6x) WC free. **Surface:** asphalted. 01/01-31/12
Distance: on the spot on the spot on the spot.

Hiers-Brouage 20B5

D3. **GPS**: n45,86250 w1,07667.

20 free. **Surface:** grassy/gravel. 01/01-31/12
Distance: 250m 250m 250m.
Remarks: Arrival 20h, departure 09h.

S Hiers-Brouage 20B5

Rue Palissy, D3. **GPS**: n45,85284 w1,07745.
€ 4 Ch . **Surface:** unpaved. 01/01-31/12

P S Jonzac 20C6

Place du 8 Mai 1945. **GPS**: n45,44800 w0,433.

8 free € 1/100liter Ch € 1/1h. **Surface:** asphalted.
01/01-31/12
Distance: on the spot on the spot on the spot on the spot.
Remarks: Behind police station, ± 200m from D2.

S La Brée-les-Bains 20A5

Rue de la Baudette. **GPS**: n46,01083 w1,35694.

50 free Ch. **Surface:** asphalted. 01/01-31/12
Remarks: Coins at Office de Tourisme.

S La Couronne 20D6

Rue du Champs de Foire. **GPS**: n45,60619 e0,10015.

free Ch WC free. **Surface:** asphalted.
01/01-31/12 Wed-morning, Sa-morning market.
Distance: on the spot on the spot.

La Roche-Posay 21A3

Super U, ZA Les Chaumettes. **GPS:** n46,79361 e0,79750.

free Ch free. **Surface:** asphalted. 01/01-31/12
Distance: 1,5km.

La Rochefoucauld 20D6

Aire camping-car, Rue des Flots, Rivières. **GPS:** n45,74505 e0,38085.

+20 Ch WC 01/01-31/12
Distance: 1km.
Remarks: Next to campsite, beside river Tardoire, Château de La Rochefoucauld 1,3km.

La Rochelle 20B4

Vieux Port, Avenue Jean Moulin. **GPS:** n46,15250 w1,13944.

50 € 10/24h Ch. **Surface:** asphalted. 01/01-31/12
Distance: 1,5km free.
Remarks: Shuttle to centre.

La Rochelle 20B4

Esplanade des Parc, Chemin des Remparts. **GPS:** n46,16620 w1,1544.
24 free. **Surface:** asphalted. 01/01-31/12
Distance: 250m 100m 250m 50m.

La Rochelle 20B4

Lycée hotelier, Les Minimes, Avenue des Minimes. **GPS:** n46,14417 w1,16083.

20 free. **Surface:** asphalted. 01/01-31/12
Distance: on the spot.
Remarks: Max. 48h.

Tourist information La Rochelle:

Office de Tourisme, Place de la Petite Sirène, Le Gabut, www.larochelle-tourisme.com.Old port city with marina.

Grosse Horloge, Centre ville.Old city gate, 13th century.

Tour de Lanterne, Centre ville.Monumental tower,15th century.
16/09-14/05 10-12.30h, 14-17.30h, 15/05-30/06, 01/09-15/09 10-12.45h 14-18.30h, 01/07-31/08 10-19h 16/9-14/5 Mo.

La Maison Henri II, Rue de Augustins.Archeological museum.
15/5-30/9 Sa-Fr 10-19h Sa-Su 14-19h.

Musée Maritime de la Rochelle, Bassin des Chautiers.Shipping museum.
daily 10-19.30h.

Aquarium, Port des Minimes.Sea aquarium. 01/07-31/08 9-23h, 01/09-30/06 10-19/20h.

La-Mothe-St.Héray 20D4

Rue du Pont l'Abbé. **GPS:** n46,35971 w0,11775.

4 free € 1/50liter Ch WC. **Surface:** metalled. 01/01-31/12
Distance: 500m 200m 200m.

Le Château d'Oléron 20B5

Boulevard Philippe Daste. **GPS:** n45,89641 w1,20236.
90 € 9,50 Ch WC **Location:** Comfortable. **Surface:** grassy.
Remarks: Former campsite.

Le Grand Village Plage 20B5

Allée des Pins. **GPS:** n45,86222 w1,24111.
15 € 6 Ch € 4. **Location:** Rural.
Surface: unpaved.
01/01-31/12
Remarks: Coins at office de tourisme, town hall or camping les Pins.

Le Pont d'Agris 20D6

D6, Rue de Mansle. **GPS:** n45,78619 e0,33944.

6 free € 2 Ch € 2. **Surface:** asphalted. 01/01-31/12
Distance: 10m 10m 10m.

FR

Les Mathes/La Palmyre 20B6

Parking du Corsaire, Avenue de l'Atlantique. **GPS**: n45,68783 w1,187.

90 € 6/24h € 4 Ch . **Surface:** asphalted. 01/01-31/12

Distance: 200m 200m.

Remarks: Next to Office du Tourisme.

Les Mathes/La Palmyre 20B6

Rue de la Garenne, Les Mathes. **GPS**: n45,71444 w1,1475.

€ 8 € 2 Ch € 2 WC. **Surface:** metalled.

01/01-31/12

Remarks: Near centre, large flat parking, coins available at town hall Mo-Fri 9-18h and office de tourisme La Palmyre daily 9-19h in July/Aug.

Les Mathes/La Palmyre 20B6

Boulevard de la Plage, La Palmyre. **GPS**: n45,68287 w1,17942.

€ 8. **Surface:** gravel.

Distance: 100m.

Tourist information Les Mathes/La Palmyre:

Office de Tourisme, Av. de Royan, Les Mathes, www.la-palmyre-les-mathes.com.Seaside resort, signposted cycle routes.

Parking de la Plage.

Syndicat d'Initiative, Rond-Point de la Poste, Royan, www.royan-tourisme.com.Modern bathing resort with 5 large beaches.

Zoo de la Palmyre.Zoo, 1600 animals, 14Ha. 01/04-30/09 9-20.30h, 01/10-31/03 9-12h, 14-18h.

Les Portes-en-Ré 20A4

Parking de la Patache, Route du Fier. **GPS**: n46,22925 w1,48315.

10 € 10/24h Ch. **Surface:** metalled.

Distance: on the spot on the spot.

Remarks: Max. 24h.

Lezay 20D4

Rue de Gâte Bourse. **GPS**: n46,26500 w0,01139.

15 free Chfree. **Surface:** asphalted. 01/01-31/12

Remarks: Next to Office du Tourisme.

Londigny 20D5

Place de l'eglise. **GPS**: n46,08333 e0,13472.

5 free Ch WCfree. **Surface:** gravel. 01/01-31/12

Remarks: Max. 48h.

Loudun 20D2

Place de la Porte Saint Nicolas. **GPS**: n47,01357 e0,07833.

Ch.

Lussac-les-Châteaux 21A4

Place l' Amitié entre les Peuples. **GPS**: n46,40250 e0,72583.

20 free Ch WCfree. **Surface:** metalled.

01/01-31/12 Fri.

Distance: on the spot nearby nearby.

Magné 20C4

Embarcadére Cardinaud, Avenue de la Repentie. **GPS**: n46,32130 w0,5803.

30 free. **Surface:** grassy. 01/01-31/12

Distance: 900m on the spot on the spot.

Magné 20C4

Super U, Avenue du Marais Poitevin. **GPS**: n46,31632 w0,55656.

€ 1,50 Ch € 1,50. 01/01-31/12

Marennes 20B5

1 Avenue William Bertrand. **GPS**: n45,82218 w1,13885.

€ 5,50 Ch.

Distance: on the spot.

Remarks: Near campsite Domaine des Pins.

Mauzé-sur-le-Mignon 20C4

Le Port, Rue du Port. **GPS**: n46,20000 w0,67778.

10 free € 3 Ch WC. **Surface:** metalled. 01/01-31/12

Distance: 1km on the spot.
Remarks: Coins at campsite and shops.

Meschers-sur-Gironde 20B6

Capitainerie, 80, Avenue du Port. **GPS**: n45,55387 w0,94467.

10 € 6 Ch free. **Surface:** asphalted. 01/01-31/12
Remarks: Marina.

Montguyon 28C1

Rue de Vassiac. **GPS**: n45,21796 w0,18368.

15 free Ch WC free. **Surface:** gravel. 01/01-31/12
Distance: 500m 500m 500m.

Montmorillon 21A4

Leclerc, 2, Avenue de Provence. **GPS**: n46,41903 e0,85358.
10 free Ch free. **Surface:** asphalted. 01/01-31/12
Remarks: Parking supermarket.

Mortagne-sur-Gironde 20B6

Rue de l'Europe. **GPS**: n45,47472 w0,79778.

€ 6 Ch WC free. **Surface:** grassy.
01/01-31/12
Remarks: In harbour, in front of Capitainerie.

Moulismes 21A4

RN147. **GPS**: n46,33306 e0,81000.

50 free € 3 Ch WC. **Surface:** metalled. 01/01-31/12
Distance: on the spot on the spot.
Remarks: At small lake (plan d'eau).

Nersac 20D6

Rue d'Epagnac. **GPS**: n45,62578 e0,04776.

7 free Ch (4x)free. **Surface:** asphalted. 01/01-31/12
Distance: on the spot 100m 100m 100m.
Remarks: Max. 48h.

Nieuil-l'Espoir 21A4

Allée du champ de foire. **GPS**: n46,48505 e0,45417.

10 free € 2 Ch € 2. **Surface:** grassy/metalled. 01/01-31/12
Distance: 200m 150m.
Remarks: At Base de Loisirs, oins at the shops.

Nieulle-sur-Seudre 20B5

Place de la Mairie. **GPS**: n45,75185 w1,00204.

4 free Ch . 01/01-31/12

Niort 20C4

Aire des camping-cars du Pré Leroy, Rue de Bessac. **GPS**: n46,32917 w0,46444.

16 € 7 Ch included. **Surface:** metalled. 01/01-31/12
Distance: 1,2km 150m 300m.

Tourist information Niort:
Office de Tourisme, 16, rue du Petit Saint-Jean, www.niortourisme.com.
Tue, Sa.
Marais Poitevin.Swamp area, possibility of making boat trips.

Oriolles 28C1

Ferme Auberge chez Baron, D131. **GPS**: n45,36180 w0,11784.

FR

8 € 9,10, guests free Ch included € 1,50 € 3.
01/07-31/08

Pamproux 20D4

Rue de la Cueille. **GPS**: n46,39625 w0,05874.

3 free € 2/20minutes Ch € 2/20minutes. **Surface:** asphalted.
01/01-31/12
Distance: 100m 5,2km 100m.

Parthenay 20C3

Aire base de loisirs Bois Vert, Rue de Boisseau 14. **GPS**: n46,64088 w0,26689.

10 € 6, Jul/Aug € 8 Ch included € 3 € 4,dryer € 1,50
€ 7/day. **Surface:** grassy/metalled. 22/03-31/10
Distance: 2,5km on the spot nearby 2km 100m.
Remarks: Along the Sioule river, car rental € 5/day + € 0,19/km.

Tourist information Parthenay:

Service Tourisme-Accueil, 8, rue de la Vau St Jacques, www.cc-parthenay.fr.City with Medieval centre worth a visit.
Les Halles.Important cattle market. Wed.

Pons 20C6

Avenue du Poitou. **GPS**: n45,57765 w0,55536.
4 free Ch € 6. **Surface:** asphalted.

Port-des-Barques 20B5

Pré des Mays, Avenue des Sports. **GPS**: n45,94722 w1,09.

€ 6 free. **Surface:** metalled. 15/03-15/11
Remarks: In front of stadium, parking fee being collected.

Rivedoux-Plage 20B4

125, Av Gustave Perreau. **GPS**: n46,15889 w1,27139.

10 € 8,60 € 4 Ch. **Surface:** asphalted. 01/01-31/12
Distance: 100m.
Remarks: Next to campsite Le Platin.

Rochefort 20B5

Port de Plaisance, Quai Lemoigne de Sérigny. **GPS**: n45,94444 w0,95556.

15 free Chfree. **Surface:** metalled.
01/01-31/12
Remarks: In marina, nearby Capitainerie, max. 24h.

Tourist information Rochefort:

Office de Tourisme, Avenue Sadi-Carnot, Porte de l'Arsenal, www.ville-rochefort.fr.Old city with seaport and river harbour.
Corderie Royale.Old royal rope-walk.
Maison de Pierre Loti.House of the writer Pierre Loti.
daily guided tour Tue-Su morning.
Musée de la Marine, place de la Galissonniere.Model boats and frigates.
daily 10-12h, 14-18h.
Tue, Thu, Sa.

Rouillac 20D5

Super U, Rue de Genac. **GPS**: n45,77650 w0,06133.

8 € 3 € 3 Ch . **Surface:** asphalted. 01/01-31/12
Distance: 500m 500m 50m.
Remarks: Coins available at supermarket.

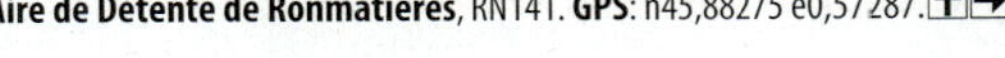

Roumazières-Loubert 21A5

Aire de Détente de Ronmatiéres, RN141. **GPS**: n45,88275 e0,57287.

FR

3 free Ch WC free. **Surface:** asphalted. 01/01-31/12
Distance: 500m 100m 300m.

S Ruffec 20D5

SARL Remy Frères Camping-Cars, D26. **GPS:** n46,03316 e0,18366.

10 free Ch free. **Surface:** asphalted.
Distance: 1km.
Remarks: Motorhome dealer.

Tourist information Ruffec:
Office de Tourisme, 18, place des Martyrs de l'Occupation.Old city.

S Saint Césaire 20C5

Parking Paléosite, Rue de Groies. **GPS:** n45,75370 w0,50744.
20 free Ch free. **Surface:** asphalted/metalled. 01/01-31/12
Distance: on the spot 500m 100m.

Tourist information Saint Césaire:
Paléosite, Route de la Montée Verte.Interactive park, in the footsteps of the Neanderthals. 10.30-18.30, Jul-Aug 10-20 January.

S Saintes 20C5

Aire camping-cars, Rue de Courbiac. **GPS:** n45,75483 w0,62905.

12 free € 5/10minutes Ch € 5/50minutes. **Surface:** asphalted.
01/01-31/12
Distance: 900m 4,4km.

P Saintes 20C5

Rue Geoffroy Martel. **GPS:** n45,74738 w0,63617.
10 free. **Surface:** asphalted. 01/01-31/12
Distance: on the spot 300m.
Remarks: Follow abbay au Dames.

Tourist information Saintes:
Office de Tourisme, Villa Musso, 62 cours National, www.ot-saintes.fr.Historical city with Roman vestiges.
Les Arènes.Roman anfiteatro.
Place 11 November. Tue + Fri morning.
Grande Foire.Large regional market. 1st Mon of the month.

S Saujon 20B6

Route de Ecluses. **GPS:** n45,67503 w0,932.

10 free Ch free. **Surface:** concrete. 01/01-31/12
Distance: 900m.

S Sauzé-Vaussais 20D5

Place des Halles. **GPS:** n46,13540 e0,10660.

free Ch WC free. **Surface:** asphalted.
01/01-31/12 water: Nov-March.
Distance: on the spot on the spot on the spot.

S Segonzac 20C6

Place Blanche. **GPS:** n45,61456 w0,22113.

4 free Ch (4x) WC free. **Surface:** gravel.
01/01-31/12
Distance: 500m 500m 500m.
Remarks: Cognac 8km. Dir d'Archaic, RD736 next to the Jeu de Boules area.

S Soubise 20B5

Aire camping-car, Le Port/rue Colbert. **GPS:** n45,92833 w1,00666.

17 € 6,50 Ch WC included. **Surface:** grassy/metalled.
01/01-31/12
Distance: on the spot 50m.
Remarks: Along river, max. 24h, incl. showers and warm water.

S St.Agnant 20B5

Place de Verdun. **GPS:** n45,86635 w0,9641.

FR

10 free Chfree. **Surface:** asphalted. 01/01-31/12
Remarks: Next to town hall.

St.Amand-sur-Sèvre 20B3

Le Moulin Chaligny. **GPS**: n46,88493 w0,82342.
7 gift Ch € 3. 01/01-31/12

St.Clément-des-Baleines 20A4

Rue de la Forêt. **GPS**: n46,22756 w1,54644.

30 € 7, 2 nights € 12 € 4/100liter Ch € 4/1h.
Distance: 250m 500m.
Remarks: Next to campsite.

St.Denis-d'Oléron 20A5

Aire du Moulin, Route des Huttes. **GPS**: n46,02750 w1,38306.

150 € 9 Ch WC included . **Surface:** grassy.
01/01-31/12
Distance: 1km.
Remarks: Max. 4 nights.

St.Génis-de-Saintonge 20C6

Place Alcide Beauvais, N137. **GPS**: n45,47985 w0,56844.

6 free Ch (3x) WC free. **Surface:** asphalted.
01/01-31/12
Distance: 200m 300m 300m.
Remarks: Max. 48h.

St.Germain-de-Marencennes 20B5

Place Saint-André. **GPS**: n46,07719 w0,78747.

4 free Ch WCfree. **Surface:** metalled. 01/01-31/12
Remarks: 15/11-15/03 water disconnected.

St.Hilaire-la-Palud 20C4

Place de la Marie. **GPS**: n46,26444 w0,71306. .

10 free. **Surface:** asphalted. 01/01-31/12
Distance: on the spot on the spot on the spot.
Remarks: Parking in front of town hall, max. 2 nights.

St.Jean-d'Angély 20C5

Base de Plein Air, Avenue de Marennes, D18. **GPS**: n45,94537 w0,53735. .

10 free Chfree. **Surface:** gravel. 01/01-31/12
Distance: 1km 100m 100m 200m 1km.
Remarks: Max. 2 nights.

St.Pochaire 20B5

Place du Champ de Foire. **GPS**: n45,81883 w0,7765.

10 free ChWCfree. **Surface:** gravel.
01/01-31/12
Remarks: Max. 48h, play garden and picnic area present.

St.Trojan-les-Bains 20B5

Parking de la Liberté, Rue Marie Curie. **GPS**: n45,84371 w1,20899. .

FR

20 free €4 Ch . **Surface:** asphalted. 01/01-31/12
Distance: on the spot.

St.Trojan-les-Bains 20B5

Parking Patoizeau, Boulevard de la plage. **GPS:** n45,84100 w1,20491.
10 free. **Surface:** asphalted. **Remarks:** In front of fire-station.

Tourist information St.Trojan-les-Bains:
Bureau Municipal de Tourisme, Carrefour du Port, www.st-trojan-les-bains.fr.Seaside resort on the island of Oléron, well-known for the mimosa and oyster culture.
place de Filles de la Sagesse.Food and drugs market. Thu + Sa-morning, summer daily.
Marche Nocturne, rue de la République.Evening market. Thu from 17h.

St.Yrieix-sur-Charente 20D6

Rue du Plan d'Eau, Impasse des Ooyères. **GPS:** n45,69176 e0,14517.

10 €6,80/8,60 Ch free. **Surface:** asphalted. 01/04-31/10
Distance: 2km 1km 1km 1km 3km 1km.
Remarks: Max. 24h.

Thouars 20D2

Rue Felix Gellusseau. **GPS:** n46,97614 w0,21151.

free Ch WC free. **Surface:** metalled. 01/01-31/12
Distance: 100m 100m 100m.

Tourist information Thouars:
Office de Tourisme, 3, bis Bd Pierre Curie, www.ville-thouars.fr/tourisme.City with half-timbered houses.
Château d'Oiron.Contemporary art.
Tue, Fri.

Thurageau 20D3

Fam. Turpeau, Agressais. **GPS:** n46,78388 e0,25644.

5 free Ch free. **Surface:** gravel. 01/01-31/12
Distance: 2,5km.
Remarks: Goat farm, farm products.

Tonnay-Charente 20B5

Quai des Capucins. **GPS:** n45,93921 w0,88171.
15 free Ch free. **Surface:** gravel.

Vasles 20D3

Mouton Village, Rue de la Cité. **GPS:** n46,57317 w0,02266.

10 free Ch WC free. **Surface:** gravel. 01/01-31/12
Distance: 400m 400m.

Vicq-sur-Gartempe 21A3

25, Route de la Roche Posay. **GPS:** n46,72414 e0,86189.

10 free Ch WC free. **Surface:** gravel. 01/01-31/12
Distance: 500m.

Limousin

Allassac 29A1

Avenue du Saillant. **GPS:** n45,25897 e1,47358.

4 free Ch (2x)free. **Surface:** gravel/sand. 01/01-31/12
Distance: 500m 5km 500m 500m.
Remarks: Parking station.

Aubusson 21C5

Parking Champ de Foire, Rue des Fusilles, D988. **GPS:** n45,95694 e2,17528.

FR

10 free Ch free WC. **Surface:** asphalted. 01/01-31/12
Distance: 500m 500m 500m.

Auphelle 21C6

GPS: n45,80750 e1,84111.

80 free. **Surface:** grassy.
Distance: Lac de Vassivière 300m.

Ayen 29A1

Route de la Noix, Ayen Bas. **GPS:** n45,24964 e1,32343.

10 free Chfree. **Surface:** gravel. 01/01-31/12
Distance: 300m.
Remarks: Nearby D39, campsite and sports grounds.

Beaumont du Lac 21C6

GPS: n45,78640 e1,87077.

20 free € 2/100liter Ch € 4/1h. **Surface:** gravel.
01/01-31/12
Distance: 5km on the spot on the spot 100m.
Remarks: At lake Vassivière.

Bessines-sur-Gartempe 21B5

Rue d'Ingolsheim. **GPS:** n46,10979 e1,37008.

10 free € 2 Ch € 2. **Surface:** asphalted. 01/01-31/12
Distance: 900m 100m.

Bort-les-Orgues 29B1

Rue Fort Grande/rue Prémontal. **GPS:** n45,39913 e2,49710.

10 free Chfree. **Surface:** asphalted. 01/01-31/12
Distance: 200m river 200m 200m.

Bourganeuf 21C5

Place de l'Etang, Avenue du Dr Butaud. **GPS:** n45,95444 e1,75750.

5 free Chfree. **Surface:** gravel.
01/01-31/12 tue-evening, wed-morning (market).
Distance: on the spot on the spot on the spot.

Tourist information Bourganeuf:
Tour de Zizim. 01/07-15/09.

Bujaleuf 21B6

Route du Champ de Foire. **GPS:** n45,79747 e1,63141.

10 free Chfree. **Surface:** gravel. 01/01-31/12
Distance: 500m 500m.
Remarks: Max. 24h.

Chambon-sur-Voueize 21D5

Rue du Stade. **GPS:** n46,18579 e2,43426.

FR

4 free € 2 Ch € 2. **Surface:** asphalted. 01/01-31/12
Distance: 500m 500m 200m.
Remarks: Near camping municipal.

S Châtelus-le-Marcheix 21B5

Rue du Tursaud. **GPS**: n45,99894 e1,60339.

8 free € 2 Ch € 2. **Surface:** asphalted. 01/01-31/12
Distance: 300m 300m 300m.
Remarks: Next to campsite municipal.

S Chénérailles 21C5

Route d'Aubusson, lotissement Marlaud, D990. **GPS**: n46,11058 e2,17753.

5 free € 2 Ch € 2. **Surface:** asphalted. 01/01-31/12
Distance: 200m 50m.
Remarks: Coins available at restaurant le Coq d'Or (50m).

S Collonges-la-Rouge 29A1

Parking le Marchadial. **GPS**: n45,05833 e1,65889.

20 € 5/24h Ch WC included. **Surface:** gravel.
01/01-31/12
Distance: 500m 500m 500m.

S Concèze 29A1

D56e. **GPS**: n45,35472 e1,34583.

3 free Ch free. **Surface:** gravel. 01/01-31/12
Distance: on the spot.

S Cressat 21C5

D990, rue de Laprade. **GPS**: n46,13956 e2,11015.

5 free € 2 Ch € 2. **Surface:** asphalted.
01/01-31/12
Distance: 100m 500m.
Remarks: At fish lake, coins available at superette 'la Montagne' (500m).

S Dampniat 29A1

Stade, Le Mas. **GPS**: n45,16262 e1,63728.
free € 2/10minutes Ch € 2/55minutes. **Location:** Rural, simple.
Surface: gravel.
Distance: 850m.

S Donzenac 29A1

Village de Vacance La Rivière, Rue du 19 Mars 1962. **GPS**: n45,21897 e1,51829.

10 € 3, 1/6-30/9 € 9 Ch € 3,10/night, peak season WC free.
Surface: gravel. 01/01-31/12
Distance: 4km 1,3km 4m 4km.
Remarks: Max. 48h.

S Egletons 29A1

Parking Espace Ventadour, Rue Henri Dignac. **GPS**: n45,40406 e2,04791.

20 free Ch free. **Surface:** gravel. 01/01-31/12 Service: winter.
Distance: 300m 3,5km 300m 300m.

FR

S Felletin 21C5

Parking Lagrange, Avenue Joffre. **GPS**: n45,88308 e2,17667.

20 free Chfree. **Surface:** gravel. 01/01-31/12
Distance: on the spot.

S Gouzon 21D5

Place du champ de foire, Rue d'Alcantera. **GPS**: n46,19139 e2,24028.

6 free Chfree. **Surface:** sand. 01/01-31/12
Distance: 300m 300m 300m.

S Jarnages 21C5

Route des Promenctes, D65. **GPS**: n46,18417 e2,08098.

6 free € 2 Ch € 2. **Surface:** asphalted. 01/01-31/12
Distance: 500m 500m 500m.
Remarks: At tennis-courts.

S Javerdat 21A5

GPS: n45,95323 e0,98600.

4 free Ch . **Surface:** gravel. 01/01-31/12
Distance: 100m.
Remarks: Coins at Auberge Limousine (100m).

S Les Salles-Lavaugyon 21A6

Le Tilleul, Route de St Mathieu. **GPS**: n45,73972 e0,70278.

4 € 4 included. **Surface:** gravel. 01/01-31/12

S Liginiac 29B1

Le Maury-Liginiac. **GPS**: n45,39158 e2,30387.

free Ch free. **Surface:** gravel.
Distance: Liginiac 4,5km sandy beach on the spot.
Remarks: At lake Neuvic. Follow restaurant Le Maury.

S Meuzac 21B6

Étang de la Roche, D243. **GPS**: n45,54933 e1,43869.

15 free Chfree. **Surface:** gravel. 01/01-31/12
Distance: 100m 5km on the spot on the spot 100m.

S Meymac 21C6

Parking Lac de Sechemailles. **GPS**: n45,52500 e2,12761.

20 free € 2,60 Ch € 2,60. **Surface:** gravel. 01/01-31/12
Distance: 2km 500m 500m.
Remarks: Coins available at Office du Tourisme and bar.

S Montboucher 21C5

GPS: n45,95056 e1,68083.

FR

5 free Ch WC free. **Surface:** grassy/gravel. 01/01-31/12

S Nieul 21B5

Rue de la Gare, D28. **GPS**: n45,92564 e1,17236.

5 free Ch WC free. **Surface:** asphalted. 01/01-31/12

Distance: 400m 400m 400m.

S Objat 29A1

Parc Aquatique Espace Loisirs, Avenue Jules Ferry. **GPS**: n45,27110 e1,41147.

20 € 5 € 2/50liter Ch included WC € 2 .

Surface: grassy/metalled.

01/01-31/12

Distance: 500m 500m.

Remarks: Entrance code available at office de tourisme, max. 7 days, baker Tue-Sa.

S Oradour-sur-Glane 21A5

Aire camping-car, Rue du Stade. **GPS**: n45,93570 e1,02471.

20 free € 2 Ch € 2 WC. 01/01-31/12

Distance: nearby.

Remarks: Metalled pitches, play ground.

Tourist information Oradour-sur-Glane:

Office de Tourisme, Place du Champ de Foire.Martyre town, was attacked by 200 SS-soldiers on 10 June 1944. They assassinated the population. Afterwards the village was burned down. In commemoration a wall was built round the the city after the war. free.

S Pageas 21A6

GPS: n45,67758 e1,00224.

10 free € 3 Ch WC. **Surface:** grassy. 01/01-31/12

Distance: 100m on the spot on the spot on the spot.

Remarks: Near N21.

S Peyrat-le-Château 21C6

Parking Pré de l'Age. GPS: n45,81468 e1,77085.

20 free € 2 Ch. **Surface:** gravel. 01/01-31/12

Distance: on the spot on the spot.

Remarks: Coins at town hall, office du tourisme.

Tourist information Peyrat-le-Château:

Office de Tourisme, 1, Rue du Lac, www.peyrat-tourisme.com.Tourist town close water sports lake, Lac de Vassivière, marked cycle and hiking routes.

Sa-Su 15-17h. free.

S Sadroc 29A1

Place du Château. **GPS**: n45,28362 e1,54806.

6 free Ch free. **Surface:** asphalted. 01/01-31/12

Distance: on the spot 5,2km 50m.

Remarks: Max. 24h.

S Servières-le-Château 29A1

Centre touristique du lac de Feyt. GPS: n45,14415 e2,03665.

15 free € 2/100liter Ch € 2/1h. **Surface:** asphalted.

01/01-31/12

Distance: sandy beach on the spot.

FR

S St.Junien-la-Bregère 21C5

Rue du Chevalier de Châteauneuf. **GPS**: n45,88056 e1,75028.

3 free Chfree. **Surface:** asphalted. 01/01-31/12

S St.Laurent 21C5

Rue des Cerisiers. **GPS**: n46,16639 e1,96167.

4 free Ch free. **Surface:** metalled. 01/01-31/12

Distance: on the spot.

S St.Laurent-sur-Gorre 21A6

Les Chênes, Allée des Primevères. **GPS**: n45,76528 e0,95639.

20 € 6 Ch WC included. **Surface:** grassy.

01/01-31/12

Distance: 300m 20m 20m 300m 300m.

Remarks: Special motorhome washing place.

S St.Merd-les-Oussines 21C6

D109 > Tarnac. **GPS**: n45,63500 e2,03719.

6 free € 2 Ch. **Surface:** gravel. 01/01-31/12

Distance: 400m.

Remarks: Coins at Auberge du Mont-Chauvet.

S St.Yrieix-la-Perche 21B6

Avenue de Lattre de Tassigny, D901. **GPS**: n45,51222 e1,20556.

5 free € 3,50 Ch. **Surface:** asphalted.

01/01-31/12

Distance: 300m 300m 300m.

Remarks: Coins available at Office du Tourisme, bar and maison de la presse.

S St.Yrieix-la-Perche 21B6

Ferme du Poumier, Lieu-dit Poumier, Marcognac. **GPS**: n45,52065 e1,26853.

4 € 3 € 4 Ch . **Surface:** gravel. 01/01-31/12

Distance: St.Yrieix 5km.

Remarks: Near D901 dir Coussac-Bonneval.

S Treignac 21C6

Les Rivières, D940. **GPS**: n45,54341 e1,79950.

25 free Ch WC free. **Surface:** grassy/gravel.

01/01-31/12 service: frost.

Distance: 2km on the spot.

Remarks: Along the river.

Tourist information Treignac:

Office de Tourisme, 1, Place de la République.Free itinerary city tour along all curiosities, available at OT.

S Turenne 29A1

Aire camping-cars, Avenue du Sénateur Labrousse, D8. **GPS**: n45,05391 e1,57988.

10 free € 2 Ch € 2 WC. **Surface:** gravel. 01/01-31/12

Distance: on the spot 100m 100m.

Remarks: Narrow road, not suitable for motorhomes +7m, behind office de tourisme, coins at Office de Tourisme, supermarket.

FR

Tourist information Turenne:

Office de Tourisme, Le Bourg, www.brive-tourisme.com.Small medieval town. Tour de Cesar. Easter-Oct daily, winter Su.

S Ussel 21D6

Aire du lac de Ponty. **GPS**: n45,54762 e2,28330.

15 free €2 Ch €2 WC. **Surface:** asphalted. 01/01-31/12

Distance: Ussel 3km 8,5km.

Remarks: At lake, in front of entrance campsite.

S Uzerche 29A1

Place de la Petite Gare, Rue Paul Langevin. **GPS**: n45,42477 e1,56696.

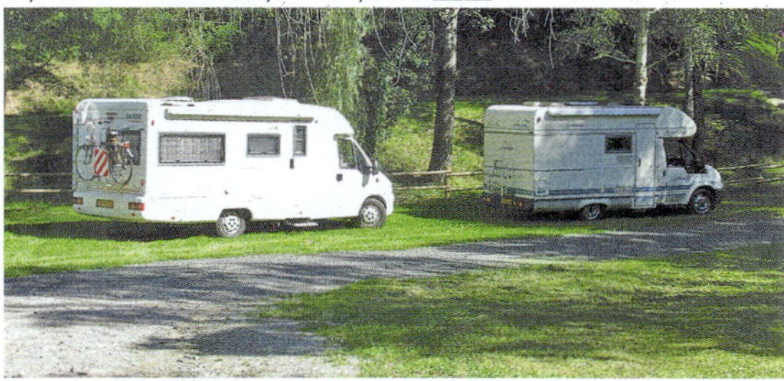

20 free Ch WC free. **Surface:** asphalted. 01/01-31/12

Distance: 300m 4,4km little stream.

Tourist information Uzerche:

Office de Tourisme, Place de la Libération, www.uzerche.fr.Little town on the Vézère river with ruins of the abbey of Saint Peter.

S Vigeois 29A1

D7, route de Brive. **GPS**: n45,36717 e1,53392.

12 free €2 Ch €2. **Surface:** grassy. 01/01-31/12

Distance: 2km 7,2km beach 150m.

Remarks: Coins at bars in the village.

Auvergne

S Aigueperse 22A5

Place du Foirail, Rue de la Porte aux Boeufs. **GPS**: n46,02634 e3,20313.

15 free €2/10minutes Ch €2/1h. **Location:** Urban, simple, central, quiet. **Surface:** asphalted.

Distance: on the spot nearby nearby.

Remarks: Market square.

S Allanche 29C1

Aire de la Gare, Chemin de la Roche Marchal. **GPS**: n45,23000 e2,93139.

25 free €2 Ch. **Location:** Rural, simple, quiet.

Surface: gravel/sand.

01/05-01/11, parking 01/01-31/12

Distance: 300m 300m 300m.

Remarks: Altitude ±1000m. Follow 'vélo gare du Cezalier'.

S Arlanc 29D1

Loumans. **GPS**: n45,41233 e3,71782.

+10 free Ch free. **Location:** Rural, simple, quiet.

Surface: asphalted/grassy. 01/01-31/12

Distance: 500m on the spot on the spot 100m 1km on the spot.

Remarks: At swimming pool and small lake.

S Arnac (Cantal) 29B1

Aire camping-cars, RD61. **GPS**: n45,06056 e2,23389.

2 free €2/100liter Ch €2/1h. **Location:** Rural, simple, quiet.

Surface: grassy/gravel. 01/01-31/12

Distance: 50m 150m 150m.

S Aubusson-d'Auvergne 22B6

Base de Loisirs-lac d'Aubusson. **GPS**: n45,75377 e3,61079.

50 €6 Ch WC free. **Location:** Rural, simple, isolated, quiet.

FR

Surface: metalled. 01/01-31/12
Distance: on the spot on the spot 200m 8km on the spot.

S Aurillac 29B2

Place du Champ de Foire, Cours d'Angoulême. **GPS**: n44,92944 e2,44963.

10 free € 3,50 Ch € 3,50. **Location:** Urban, simple, noisy. **Surface:** asphalted. 01/01-31/12 service: 31/10-01/05.
Distance: on the spot 100m 100m.
Remarks: Max. 24h, coins at Office de Tourisme.

Tourist information Aurillac:
Office de Tourisme, Rue de Carmes, www.iaurillac.com.Old city centre with alleys and half-timbered houses.
European street theatre and festival. 3rd week Aug.

S Aydat 22A6

Aire camping-cars. **GPS**: n45,66025 e2,97778.

41 € 9/24h Ch (28x) WC included. **Location:** Rural, comfortable, quiet. **Surface:** grassy. 01/01-31/12
Distance: 200m on the spot on the spot on the spot 250m.
Remarks: Former campsite, max. 8,20m.

S Beaulieu 29D1

Zone d'Activité la Gerle. **GPS**: n45,12597 e3,94608.

15 free Ch (2x)free. **Location:** Rural, simple, quiet.
Surface: gravel. 01/04-31/10
Distance: 400m.

S Beaulon 22B4

Écluse de Beaulon, La Curesse. **GPS**: n46,60443 e3,65840.

+10 free Ch (4x)free. **Location:** Rural, simple, isolated, quiet.
Surface: gravel. 01/01-31/12
Distance: 1,2km Canal on the spot 1,2km 1,2km on the spot on the spot.

S Bellerive-sur-Allier 22B5

Riv'Air Camp, Rue Claude Decloitre. **GPS**: n46,11514 e3,43114.

50 € 10 Ch (50x) WC included. **Location:** Urban, comfortable, isolated, quiet. **Surface:** metalled. 01/01-31/12
Distance: 2,5km 17km on the spot on the spot on the spot 800m.
Remarks: Along the Allier river.

S Billy 22B5

Rue de la Fontaine. **GPS**: n46,23586 e3,43044.

free Chfree. **Surface:** asphalted. 01/01-31/12
Distance: on the spot.
Remarks: Max. 48h.

S Blesle 29C1

Hôtel-Restaurant Le Scorpion, D909. **GPS**: n45,31219 e3,18677.

25 € 15 Ch (8x) WC included. **Location:** Rural, comfortable, quiet. **Surface:** grassy. 01/01-31/12
Distance: 5,8km on the spot.
Remarks: A75 exit 19, 22 or 23 from southern dir exit 20, 22 or 24.

Tourist information Blesle:
Office de Tourisme, Place de l'Eglise, www.tourismeblesle.fr.Ancient little town, 9th century, built around Benedictine monastery.

S Brioude 29C1

Parking des Remparts, Avenue de Lamothe, D588. **GPS**: n45,29444 e3,38778.

FR

30 free € 2 Ch € 2. **Location:** Urban, simple, central, quiet. **Surface:** asphalted. 01/01-31/12
Distance: 100m 100m 100m.
Remarks: Coins at Office du Tourisme (100m).

Tourist information Brioude:
Office de Tourisme, Place Lafayette, www.ot-brioude.fr.Old fortress city.
L'aquarium-la Maison du Saumon et de la Rivière, Place de la Résistance. Museum about the salmon. 01/04-30/11.

S Buxières-les-Mines 22A4

Le Boucher. **GPS**: n46,45464 e2,96791.
6 € 12,50 Ch (6x),12Amp WC € 5,dryer € 3,50 included. **Location:** Rural, comfortable, isolated. **Surface:** grassy.
01/01-31/12
Distance: 2km 12km 5km 2km 5km 2km.

S Calvinet 29B2

Aire de Calvinet, Terrain de sport. **GPS**: n44,71023 e2,35914.

6 free € 2 Ch € 2. **Location:** Rural, simple, quiet. **Surface:** gravel.
01/01-31/12 service 01/11-31/03.
Distance: 1,5km 1,5km 1,5km.
Remarks: Nearby sports ground.

S Cassaniouze 29B2

Aire camping-cars, Le Bourg. **GPS**: n44,69347 e2,38233.

6 free € 2/80liter Ch € 2/1h € 1. **Location:** Rural, simple, quiet. **Surface:** gravel.
01/01-31/12 service 01/11-31/03.
Distance: 600m 600m 600m.

S Cayrols 29B2

Aire camping-cars, La Devèze, D51. **GPS**: n44,83000 e2,23278.

10 free € 3,80 Ch € 3,80 WC. **Location:** Rural, comfortable, quiet. **Surface:** metalled. 01/01-31/12 service 01/11-31/03.
Distance: 100m 200m.
Remarks: Max. 1 week, coins at the shops in the village.

S Chambon-sur-Lac 22A6

Camping Les Bombes, La Vergne. **GPS**: n45,56991 e2,90176.

30 € 6 € 3 Ch. **Location:** Rural, simple, quiet.
Surface: grassy/gravel. 01/01-31/12 service: 15/09-01/05.
Distance: 500m 200m 1km 500m 500m bakery on the spot on the spot.
Remarks: Pay and coins at campsite.

S Champeix 22A6

Champeix, Route de Montaigut, D996. **GPS**: n45,58845 e3,11568.

+10 free € 2 Ch. **Location:** Rural, simple, isolated, quiet.
Surface: grassy/gravel. 01/01-31/12
Distance: 1,3km 1,3km 500m.

S Chanaleilles 29C2

Le Bourg. **GPS**: n44,85971 e3,49083.

FR

5 free Ch. **Location:** Rural, comfortable, isolated, quiet.
Surface: grassy/gravel.
Distance: 500m 375m.

S Charbonnières-les-Varennes 22A5

Route de Saint-Georges, Paugnat. **GPS**: n45,88457 e2,97993.

10 free € 2/10minutes Ch € 2/55minutes. **Location:** Rural, comfortable, quiet. **Surface:** grassy. 01/01-31/12
Distance: 500m bakery 500m on the spot.
Remarks: Coins available at the shops, trail to volcano crater.

S Chaspuzac 29D1

Rue du Vol à Voile. **GPS**: n45,07491 e3,76131.

6 free € 2 Ch. **Location:** Rural, simple, quiet.
Surface: asphalted.
Distance: 50m.
Remarks: View on airport.

S Chastreix 21D6

Parking Station de Ski, Chastreix Sancy. **GPS**: n45,53507 e2,77695.

14 free Ch € 9,(winter) WC € 2,(winter). **Location:** Rural, simple, quiet. **Surface:** metalled. 01/01-31/12
Distance: Chastreix 6km on the spot.
Remarks: Check in between 9-17h.

S Châtel-Guyon 22A5

Place de la Musique Nationale. **GPS**: n45,92324 e3,06590.

7 € 5/day € 2 Ch WC. **Location:** Urban, comfortable, central, quiet.
Surface: asphalted. 01/01-31/12
Distance: nearby 400m 400m.
Remarks: Check in at police station, coins at Tourist Info.

Châtel-Guyon 22A5

Parking des Roches, Chemin de Bussane. **GPS**: n45,91789 e3,06545.

10 free. **Location:** Urban, simple, quiet. **Surface:** asphalted.
01/01-31/12
Distance: 500m 600m 600m.

S Chaudes-Aigues 29C2

Parking Beauredon, Avenue Georges Pompidou, D921. **GPS**: n44,84972 e3,00306.

10 free € 2 Ch € 2/55minutes. **Location:** Urban, simple.
Surface: gravel. 15/04-15/10
Distance: 100m 300m 300m.

Tourist information Chaudes-Aigues:
Office de Tourisme, 1, avenue Georges Pompidou, www.chaudesaigues.com. Small town with warm thermal sources (82ºC).

S Chomelix 29D1

Centre Multi Activités Les Marches d'Auvergne, Route d'Estables, D135. **GPS**: n45,26219 e3,82573.

6 free € 4 Ch. **Location:** Rural, simple, quiet. **Surface:** gravel.
01/01-31/12
Distance: on the spot on the spot mountainbike trail on the spot.

FR

Clermont Ferrand 22A6

P&R Les Pistes, Rue de la Fontaine de la Ratte. **GPS**: n45,79810 e3,11222.

6 €5 Chfree. **Location:** Urban. **Surface:** asphalted.
01/01-31/12
Distance: historical centre 3km 50m.
Remarks: Nearby Michelin museum, check in at parking attendant.

Coltines 29C1

D40. **GPS**: n45,09612 e2,98555.

5 free €2/100liter Ch €2. **Location:** Rural, simple.
Surface: gravel.
Distance: 400m 400m 400m.
Remarks: Coins at Epicerie-Presse, Centre Chantarisaen de Maire.

Condat 29B1

Parking au Pont, D678. **GPS**: n45,33889 e2,76250.

4 free Service €2,50 Ch . **Location:** Simple. **Surface:** asphalted.
01/01-31/12 service: 01/10-01/05.
Distance: 50m 10m 50m.
Remarks: Coins at campsite La Borie Basse (500m).

Coubon 29D1

Route du Plan d'Eau. **GPS**: n44,99735 e3,91742.

5 free ChWC. **Surface:** metalled. 01/01-31/12
Remarks: Along river.

Crandelles 29B1

Aire camping-cars, Lac des Genevrières. **GPS**: n44,95877 e2,34289.

10 free €3,50 Ch. **Location:** Comfortable, central, quiet. **Surface:** gravel. 01/01-31/12 service: 01/11-01/04.
Distance: 300m 50m 50m 50m 300m.

Craponne-sur-Arzon 29D1

Avenue de la Gare. **GPS**: n45,33360 e3,85057.

+20 free €2 Ch €2/1h. **Location:** Urban, simple, quiet.
Surface: asphalted/gravel. 01/01-31/12
Distance: 150m 150m on the spot.

Drugeac 29B1

Aire de campingcars, La Gare SNCF. **GPS**: n45,16694 e2,38667.

4 free €2/100liter Ch €2/1h. **Location:** Rural, simple, quiet.
Surface: asphalted. 01/01-31/12 service: 01/11-01/05.
Distance: 100m 100m 100m.
Remarks: At former station, now start Vélorail.

Tourist information Drugeac:

Office de Tourisme, Place Tyssandier d'Escous, Salers.Small town built from grey lava stones with ramparts from the 15th century.

Ebreuil 22A5

Parking du Stade, D915. **GPS**: n46,10954 e3,07606.

10 free. **Location:** Simple. **Surface:** gravel. 01/01-31/12
Distance: 6,5km.
Remarks: Service 500m, in front of campsite municipal.

Ebreuil 22A5

Chemin des Nières. **GPS**: n46,11083 e3,08111.
Chfree. 01/01-31/12

FR

Remarks: Next to campsite municipal, overnight stay on Parking du Stade.

S Estivareilles 21D4

Salle Polyvalente, Via: rue de la République. **GPS**: n46,42471 e2,61529.

20 free free. **Location:** Urban, simple. **Surface:** gravel.
01/01-31/12
Distance: on the spot 9km 200m bakery 200m.

S Faverolles 29C2

D248 Centre village. **GPS**: n44,93917 e3,14750.

6 free € 2/100liter Ch € 2/55minutes WC. **Location:** Rural, simple.
Surface: gravel. 01/01-31/12
Distance: on the spot 100m 200m.

S Jaligny-sur-Besbre 22B4

Rue de la Chaume. **GPS**: n46,38155 e3,59147.

5 free Ch (5x)free. **Location:** Rural, simple, quiet.
Surface: gravel. 01/01-31/12
Distance: 200m on the spot on the spot 250m 250m.
Remarks: Along the Besbre river.

La Bourboule 21D6

Plateau de Charlannes. **GPS**: n45,57811 e2,73513.

10 free. **Location:** Rural, simple, quiet. **Surface:** asphalted.
01/01-31/12
Distance: 6,5km Snackbar on the spot on the spot.
Remarks: Parking at funicular railway.

La Bourboule 21D6

Rue Fernand Forest, D130. **GPS**: n45,58984 e2,74953.

10 free. **Location:** Urban, simple. **Surface:** asphalted.
01/01-31/12
Distance: 500m 500m 500m.

S La Chapelle-Laurent 29C1

Aire camping-cars, D10. **GPS**: n45,18028 e3,24389.

5 free Ch free. **Location:** Rural, simple. **Surface:** grassy.
parking 01/01-31/12, service 01/04-15/11
Distance: 50m nearby 100m 100m.

S La Roche-Blanche 22A6

Madame BLAZANIN, La Pigné Sud, Route des Fours à Chaux. **GPS**: n45,71567 e3,14790.

100 € 6 € 2/100liter Ch (4x)€ 6/6h. **Location:** Rural, simple, isolated, quiet. **Surface:** grassy. 01/03-30/11
Distance: 1,1km.

S La Tour-d'Auvergne 21D6

Route de Bagnols. **GPS**: n45,53290 e2,68213.

25 free Ch free. **Location:** Simple, quiet. **Surface:** metalled.
01/01-31/12
Distance: on the spot 650m 650m bakery.

S Lacapelle-Viescamp 29B2

Aire camping-cars, D18. **GPS**: n44,92167 e2,26361.

FR

5 free € 3/100liter Ch € 3/1h. **Location:** Rural, simple.
Surface: metalled. 01/01-31/12
Distance: 100m 100m on the spot.
Remarks: Coins available at the shop.

S Lapalisse 22B5

Place Jean Moulin, RN7 dir Roanne. **GPS:** n46,25000 e3,63500.

50 free € 2 Ch € 2 WC. **Location:** Urban, simple, central, quiet.
Surface: asphalted. 01/01-31/12
Distance: 300m on the spot on the spot on the spot.

Lavaudieu 29C1

Le Bourg. **GPS:** n45,26297 e3,45606.

+10 free. **Location:** Simple, isolated, quiet. **Surface:** grassy/gravel.
01/01-31/12
Distance: 200m on the spot.

S Le Breuil-sur-Couze 29C1

Allée de Treize Vents. **GPS:** n45,46867 e3,26121.

8 free Ch free. **Location:** Urban, simple. **Surface:** gravel.
01/01-31/12
Distance: 900m 700m bakery, supermarket.
Remarks: Along railwayline.

S Le Cheix-sur-Morge 22A5

D425. **GPS:** n45,95096 e3,17884.

6 free Ch free. **Location:** Rural, simple, isolated, quiet.
Surface: gravel. 01/01-31/12
Distance: 500m.
Remarks: Max. 48h.

Le Donjon 22B4

Place du Champ de Foire, Rue Georges Gallay. **GPS:** n46,34940 e3,79473.

free. **Location:** Simple, central, quiet. **Surface:** gravel.
01/01-31/12
Distance: 100m 50m.
Remarks: Tue market.

Le Monastier-sur-Gazeille 29D2

Rue Augustin Ollier. **GPS:** n44,93720 e3,99250.

10 free. **Location:** Rural, simple. **Surface:** grassy.
01/03-31/10
Distance: 300m 300m 300m.

S Le Monastier-sur-Gazeille 29D2

Le Moulin de Savin. **GPS:** n44,93680 e3,98600.
Ch.
Remarks: Next to campsite.

Le Puy-en-Velay 29D1

Avenue Charles Dupuy. **GPS:** n45,04358 e3,89240.

12 € 8, € 2/3h. **Location:** Urban, simple, central, noisy.
Surface: asphalted. 01/01-31/12
Distance: 500m.
Remarks: Max. 24h, behind bus terminal.

FR

S Le Puy-en-Velay 29D1

Boulevard de Cluny. **GPS**: n45,04963 e3,88976.

€ 2 Ch.

S Le Vernet 29D1

Le Bourg. **GPS**: n45,03560 e3,66952.

10 € 2 € 2/80liter Ch € 2/10minutes. **Location:** Rural, simple, isolated, quiet. **Surface:** grassy/sand. 01/01-31/12

Distance: 50m on the spot.

S Les Estables 29D2

Le Bourg. **GPS**: n44,90231 e4,15679.

8 free Ch free. **Location:** Rural, simple. **Surface:** asphalted. 01/01-31/12

Distance: 50m 50m on the spot.

Remarks: Free wifi, code at office de tourisme.

S Lezoux 22B6

Parking Musée départemental de la Céramique, Rue de la République. **GPS**: n45,82686 e3,38459.

30 free Ch WC free. **Location:** Comfortable, central, quiet. **Surface:** gravel. 01/01-31/12 water: 01/11-31/03.

Distance: 500m 3,5km 500m 500m.

S Lurcy-Lévis 22A3

Plan d'eau des Sézeaux, Rue de Fontgroix. **GPS**: n46,73797 e2,93863.

6 free € 3/100liter Ch € 3/55minutes WC. **Location:** Rural, comfortable, quiet. **Surface:** grassy/gravel. 01/01-31/12

Distance: 800m Small lake on the spot 800m 800m.

Remarks: Coins at cafe, in front of the church.

S Mandailles-Saint-Julien 29B1

Aire de camping-cars, Le Mas, D17. **GPS**: n45,06916 e2,65611.

5 free € 3,50 Ch. **Location:** Rural, simple, quiet. **Surface:** metalled. 01/01-31/12 service: 30/09-01/05.

Distance: 200m 200m 200m on the spot.

Remarks: Max. 24h, coins at restaurants.

S Manzat 22A5

Place du 14 Juillet. **GPS**: n45,96180 e2,93883.

20 free Ch free. **Location:** Rural, simple, quiet. **Surface:** unpaved. 01/01-31/12

Distance: on the spot 5,6km 250m 200m.

Remarks: In opposite of police station.

S Marcolès 29B2

Aire camping-cars, Terrain de sport. **GPS**: n44,78028 e2,35?89.

5 free Ch free. **Location:** Rural, simple, quiet. **Surface:** gravel. 01/01-31/12 service 01/11-31/03.

Distance: 100m 100m 100m.

Remarks: Artists village.

Massiac 29C1

Rue Jacques Chaban Delmas. **GPS**: n45,25278 e3,19667.

9 free. **Location:** Rural, simple. **Surface:** grassy. 01/01-31/12

Distance: 200m 1,3km 200m 200m.

FR

S Mauriac 29B1

Aire de campingcars, Rue du Val Saint Jean. **GPS**: n45,21863 e2,32183.

10 free € 2/100liter Ch € 2/1h. **Location:** Rural, simple, quiet. **Surface:** metalled. 01/01-31/12
Distance: 1km beach 300m 1,2km 1,2km.

S Maurs 29B2

Maurs La Jolie, Route de Quezac. **GPS**: n44,71442 e2,19615.

5 free € 2/100liter Ch € 2/1h. **Location:** Urban, simple, central, quiet. **Surface:** asphalted. 01/01-31/12
Distance: 300m 300m 300m 300m.
Remarks: Coins at Papetterie and tourist office.

S Messeix 21D6

Place des Pins. **GPS**: n45,61576 e2,55621.

6 free € 2/10minutes Ch € 2/55minutes. **Location:** Urban, simple, quiet. **Surface:** asphalted. 01/01-31/12
Distance: 500m 18km 1,7km on the spot.
Remarks: Coins available at the shops.

S Montluçon 21D4

Route de l'Etang de Sault, Prémilhat. **GPS**: n46,33469 e2,55855.

8 free € 6/150liter Ch (6x)€ 2,50/10h. **Location:** Rural, comfortable. **Surface:** gravel. 01/01-31/12
Distance: 5km Montluçon 2,6km 150m 150m 500m.
Remarks: Max. 72h.

S Montluçon 21D4

Place de la Fraternité, Rue des Marais. **GPS**: n46,35535 e2,58686.

15 free € 5/150liter Ch € 2,50/10minutes WC. **Location:** Urban, simple, noisy. **Surface:** asphalted.
01/01-31/12 water: Nov-March.
Distance: on the spot A71 16km on the spot on the spot on the spot.
Remarks: Thu-morning closed because of market (6-15h). From Châteauroux, on entering the town.

Tourist information Montluçon:
Office de Tourisme, Boulevard du Courtais, www.montlucontourisme.com.

S Montmurat 29B2

Aire camping-cars, Le Bourg, D345. **GPS**: n44,62811 e2,19804.

10 free € 1 Ch. **Location:** Rural, simple, isolated, quiet. **Surface:** gravel. 01/01-31/12
Distance: on the spot.

S Montoldre 22B4

D21. **GPS**: n46,33272 e3,44727.

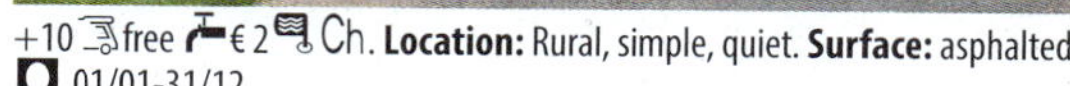

+10 free € 2 Ch. **Location:** Rural, simple, quiet. **Surface:** asphalted. 01/01-31/12
Distance: centre on the spot.
Remarks: Parking in front of town hall.

S Montpeyroux 22A6

D797C, Rue De l'Hume. **GPS**: n45,62373 e3,19911.

+10 free € 2,50 Ch € 2,50/1h. **Location:** Rural, simple, quiet. **Surface:** gravel. 01/01-31/12
Distance: 100m 200m 200m.

FR

Remarks: Coins available at the shops.

Tourist information Montpeyroux:
Small town with wine-cellar Cave de Montpeyroux. Mo/Sa 8.30-12.30h, 14-18/19h, Su 10.30-12h, 16-19h.

S Montsalvy 29B2

Aire camping-cars, Route de Junhac. **GPS**: n44,70778 e2,49667.

21 free € 2 Ch € 2 WC € 1. **Location:** Rural, comfortable, quiet. **Surface:** asphalted. 01/01-31/12
Distance: 400m 400m 400m.

S Moulins 22A4

Flot Bleu Park, Chemin de Halage. **GPS**: n46,55852 e3,32491.

92 € 0,10/h € 2 Ch € 2 € 2/20minutes (12x) € 2/4h .
Location: Urban, comfortable, central, quiet. **Surface:** grassy/metalled. 01/01-31/12
Distance: city centre 1km 100m 300m on the spot.

S Murat 29C1

Place du 19 mars. **GPS**: n45,10917 e2,86917.

8 free € 2 Ch € 2 WC. **Surface:** asphalted. 01/05-31/10

Murat 29C1

Avenue d'Olonne-sur-mer. **GPS**: n45,10757 e2,85975.

free. **Location:** Urban, simple. **Surface:** concrete. 01/01-31/12
Remarks: At sports park.

Murat 29C1

Parking du Stade, Rue du Stade. **GPS**: n45,10861 e2,87027.

free. **Surface:** asphalted. 01/01-31/12

Tourist information Murat:
Office de Tourisme, Place de l'Hôtel de Ville.Medieval city, city tour available at OT.
Fri-morning.

S Murat-le-Quaire 21D6

Les Rives du Lac, Route de la Banne d'Ordanche. **GPS**: n45,60274 e2,73797.

37 € 8/24h Ch (8x) WC included € 1. **Location:** Rural, comfortable, quiet. **Surface:** grassy/metalled. 01/01-31/12
Distance: 1,2km 12km 100m 100m day pass available on the spot on the spot 100m 5km.
Remarks: Bread-service.

S Murol 22A6

Rue du Tartaret, D5. **GPS**: n45,57288 e2,94101.

20 free service € 2 Ch . **Location:** Urban, simple. **Surface:** asphalted.
Distance: 450m 300m.
Remarks: Service 100m, pay at tourist office.

Tourist information Murol:
Bureau de Tourisme Grande Vallée, Rue de Jassaguet, www.grandevallee.com.Holiday resort, dominated by the Château de Murol, 13th century.

S Naucelles 29B1

Aire camping-cars, Rue du Terrou. **GPS**: n44,95694 e2,41757.

FR

5 free € 3,50/100liter Ch € 3,50/1h. **Location:** Urban, simple, quiet. **Surface:** asphalted. 01/01-31/12
Distance: Spar 300m.
Remarks: Coins at supermarket in the village.

S Néris-les-Bains 21D4

Camping du Lac, Avenue Marrx Dormoy, D155. **GPS:** n46,28673 e2,65235.

6 €7 Ch (6x) WC included. **Location:** Urban, comfortable. **Surface:** gravel. 01/03-31/10
Distance: 500m 12km bakery 500m.
Remarks: Max. 3 nights, to be paid at campsite.

S Neussargues-Moissac 29C1

Allée des Peupliers. **GPS:** n45,13438 e2,98130.

5 free € 2/100liter Ch € 2/2h. **Location:** Rural, comfortable, quiet. **Surface:** gravel. 01/01-31/12 water disconnected in winter.
Distance: 300m 50m 300m.

S Orcines 22A6

Route du Puy de Dôme, D68. **GPS:** n45,76958 e2,98624.
free Ch free. **Location:** Rural, isolated. **Surface:** asphalted. 01/01-31/12 Service: winter.

Orcines 22A6

D941. **GPS:** n45,80394 e2,98726.

10 free. **Location:** Simple, noisy. **Surface:** metalled. 01/01-31/12
on the spot.

S Orcines 22A6

D941B dir Orcines Vulcania. **GPS:** n45,78765 e3,00947.

€ 2/100liter Ch € 2/1h. **Location:** Simple, noisy.
01/01-31/12

S Pierrefort 29C2

Côte de Chabridet. **GPS:** n44,92172 e2,84199.

20 free € 2/100liter Ch € 2. **Location:** Simple. **Surface:** gravel.
01/01-31/12
Distance: 100m 200m 200m.

S Pleaux 29B1

Parc des Auzerals, Place d'Empeyssine. **GPS:** n45,13556 e2,22833.

30 free Ch WC free. **Location:** Urban, simple, central, quiet. **Surface:** asphalted/gravel. 01/01-31/12
Distance: on the spot 100m 100m.

S Pradelles 29D2

Aire de la Salaison, N88. **GPS:** n44,77540 e3,88752.

20 free Ch free (8x)€ 2. **Location:** Rural, comfortable, noisy. **Surface:** grassy. 01/01-31/12
Distance: 1km on the spot.
Remarks: Regional products and bread.

S Prunet 29B2

Aire camping-cars, Le Bourg. **GPS:** n44,82049 e2,46398.

FR

3 free Ch free. **Location:** Rural, simple, quiet. **Surface:** gravel. 01/01-31/12 service 01/11-31/03.
Distance: 300m 300m.

S Randan 22A5

Rue du Puy de Dôme. **GPS**: n46,01630 e3,35075.

5 free € 2/15minutes Ch € 2/15minutes. **Location:** Urban, simple, quiet. **Surface:** gravel. 01/01-31/12
Distance: 500m 500m 200m.
Remarks: Coins at Maison de la Presse, Rue de Commerce.

S Raucoules 29D1

Raucoules, Le Bourg. **GPS**: n45,18640 e4,29750.

4 free € 2 Ch (4x)€ 2. **Location:** Rural, comfortable, central, quiet.
Surface: asphalted. 01/01-31/12
Distance: 200m 300m.
Remarks: Coins available in village.

S Retournac 29D1

Rue de la Loire. **GPS**: n45,20328 e4,04501.

20 free Ch free. **Location:** Rural, simple, isolated, quiet.
Surface: gravel. 01/01-31/12 Service: winter.
Distance: city centre 1km on the spot on the spot 650m on the spot.
Remarks: Along the Loire river.

S Riom 22A5

-, Route d'Ennezat, D224. **GPS**: n45,89455 e3,12477.

4 free € 2/15minutes Ch € 2/15minutes. **Location:** Urban, simple, central, noisy. **Surface:** gravel. 01/01-31/12
Distance: 700m 2,5km nearby nearby.

S Riom-es-Montagnes 29B1

Rue du Champ de Foire. **GPS**: n45,28444 e2,65389.

€ 2/100liter Ch € 2/1h. **Location:** Simple.
Surface: metalled.
01/01-31/12
Distance: on the spot 100m 100m.
Remarks: Overnight stay on Parking de la Piscine, GPS N 45,27902 E 2,66403.

S Ruynes-en-Margeride 29C1

GPS: n45,00111 e3,22389.

6 free € 2/10minutes Ch € 2/55minutes. **Surface:** asphalted.
01/01-31/12
Distance: 50m 50m 50m.

S Salers 29B1

Le Mouriol, Route du Puy Mary. **GPS**: n45,14718 e2,49900.

15 € 3,70 + € 0,50 tourist tax € 2,10 Ch € 1,50,on camp site.
Location: Rural. **Surface:** gravel.
Distance: 1,2km 50m.
Remarks: Next to camping municipal, coins at campsite and tourist office.

Salers 29B1

D680. **GPS**: n45,14010 e2,49478.
12 € 3. **Location:** Rural. **Surface:** asphalted/metalled.

FR

Distance: 500m.
Remarks: Max. 24h, no camping activities.

Salers 29B1

Rue Notre-Dame. **GPS:** n45,13898 e2,49583.
6 € 3. **Surface:** asphalted. 01/01-31/12
Distance: 250m.
Remarks: Max. 24h, no camping activities.

S Salins 29B1

Aire de campingcars, D722. **GPS:** n45,19167 e2,39361.

3 free free. **Surface:** gravel. 01/01-31/12
Distance: 50m.

S Sansac-de-Marmiesse 29B2

Aire camping-cars, Rue de la Vidalie. **GPS:** n44,88389 e2,34639.

3 free € 3,50 Ch € 3,50. **Location:** Urban, simple, central.
Surface: asphalted. 01/01-31/12 service: 01/10-30/04.
Distance: on the spot 200m on the spot.
Remarks: Coins at the bakery.

S Saugues 29C1

Place du Brieul. **GPS:** n44,95940 e3,54395.

10 free Chfree. **Location:** Simple. **Surface:** asphalted.
Distance: on the spot.

S Sauret-Besserve 22A5

D523. **GPS:** n45,99389 e2,81001.

4 free € 2 Ch€ 2. **Location:** Rural, simple, isolated.
01/01-31/12

Remarks: Near church, June 2012 during inspection service out of order.

S Ségur-les-Villas 29B1

Aire de camping-cars, Le Bourg. **GPS:** n45,22311 e2,81818.

10 free € 2/100liter Ch € 2/1h. **Location:** Rural, simple, quiet.
Surface: grassy. 01/05-31/10
Distance: 200m 300m 200m.
Remarks: Nearby football ground, coins available at shops.

S Solignat 22A6

Route des Dauphins d'Auvergne, D32. **GPS:** n45,51701 e3,17074.

+50 free € 2/100liter Ch € 2/1h. **Location:** Rural, simple, quiet.
Surface: grassy. 01/01-31/12
Distance: 100m.

S St Anthème 22B6

Rambaud. **GPS:** n45,52354 e3,91464.

30 € 2 Chincluded. **Location:** Rural, simple, central, quiet.
Surface: grassy/gravel. 01/01-31/12 Water when frosty.
Distance: 200m beach 250m 200m on the spot.
Remarks: Next to campsite Rambaud, water disconnected.

S St.Bonnet-le-Froid 30A1

Chemin de Brard. **GPS:** n45,14136 e4,43454.
6 € 4 Ch included. **Surface:** gravel. 01/03-01/11
Distance: 150m 150m 150m.
Remarks: Access via D105.

S St.Bonnet-Tronçais 21D3

Parking du Stade, Route de Tronçais, D39. **GPS:** n46,66096 e2,69442.
free € 3/50liter . **Surface:** gravel.
01/01-31/12 water disconnected in winter.
Remarks: Coins at the bakery.

St.Bonnet-Tronçais 21D3

Rue de l'Étang. **GPS:** n46,65896 e2,69228.
10 free. **Location:** Simple, central. **Surface:** gravel.
01/01-31/12
Distance: on the spot 27km Lake 450m bakery 200m.

S St.Christophe-sur-Dolaison 29D1

Le Bourg. **GPS:** n44,99811 e3,82147.

FR

6 free € 2 Ch € 2. **Location:** Rural, simple.
Surface: asphalted.
Distance: 100m 150m.

St.Eloy-les-Mines 22A5

Rue du Puy-de-Dôme, RN144. **GPS:** n46,15559 e2,83615.

30 free € 2 Ch € 2. **Location:** Rural, simple. **Surface:** metalled.
01/01-31/12
Distance: on the spot 700m 400m Carrefour Market.
Remarks: Max. 48h.

St.Flour 29C1

Place de l'Ander, ville basse. **GPS:** n45,03556 e3,09750.

8 free € 2 Ch € 4. **Location:** Urban, simple. **Surface:** asphalted.
01/01-31/12
Distance: 300m 4km 300m 300m.
Remarks: Lower part of the city, nearby campsite.

St.Flour 29C1

Cours Chazerat. **GPS:** n45,03389 e3,08750.

20 free. **Location:** Urban, simple. **Surface:** metalled. 01/01-31/12
Distance: on the spot 4,6km 50m 50m.
Remarks: Higher part of the city.

Tourist information St.Flour:

Office de Tourisme, 17bis, place d'Armes, www.saint-flour.com.City with car-free historical centre, Vieux Saint Flour.

Musée de la Haute Auvergne, Place d'Armens.Regional museum.

01/05-30/09. € 3,50.

St.Georges 29C1

GPS: n45,03167 e3,13500.

20 free € 2 Ch € 2 WC. **Location:** Highway. **Surface:** asphalted.
01/01-31/12
Distance: 3km 1km 200m on the spot.
Remarks: At petrol station Esso.

St.Just 29C2

GPS: n44,88972 e3,20889.

10 € 8 € 2/100liter Ch € 2/55minutes WC. **Location:** Comfortable, quiet. **Surface:** grassy. 01/01-31/12
Distance: 50m 6,2km 100m 100m.
Remarks: Use camp-site facilities incl.

St.Mamet-la-Salvetat 29B2

Aire camping-cars, D20. **GPS:** n44,85714 e2,30981.

3 free € 2/100liter Ch € 2/1h WC. **Location:** Rural, simple, quiet.
Surface: asphalted. 01/01-31/12
Distance: 500m 350m.
Remarks: Coins available at the shops and town hall.

St.Marcel-en-Murat 22A4

D243. **GPS:** n46,32184 e3,00837.

10 free € 2/100liter Ch € 2/1h. **Location:** Rural, simple.
Surface: gravel. 01/01-31/12
Distance: 3,5km exit 11 A71 nearby.
Remarks: Coins at town hall and restaurant.

St.Paul-des-Landes 29B1

Aire camping-cars, Rue du Moinac. **GPS**: n44,94250 e2,31694.

3 free € 3,50 Ch € 3,50. **Location:** Rural, simple, central, quiet.
Surface: asphalted. 01/01-31/12
Distance: 50m 200m 50m.
Remarks: Coins at petrol station.

St.Pourçain-sur-Sioule 22A4

Aire Camping-car de la Moutte, Rue de la Moutte. **GPS**: n46,31262 e3,29656.

60 free € 2 Ch€ 2 (8x)€ 2/4h. **Location:** Urban, comfortable, central, quiet. **Surface:** grassy. 01/01-31/12
Distance: 800m on the spot on the spot on the spot.
Remarks: Along the Sioule river.

St.Rémy-de-Blot 22A5

Place du Bourg. **GPS**: n46,07722 e2,93139.

7 free WC. **Location:** Rural, simple, isolated, quiet. **Surface:** grasstiles.
01/01-31/12
Distance: on the spot.

St.Romain-Lachalm 29D1

Rulière. **GPS**: n45,26399 e4,33576.
4 free Ch (4x)€ 2/4h. **Surface:** asphalted.
Distance: 100m bakery 200m.
Remarks: Coins available at the shops and town hall.

St.Sauves d'Auvergne 21D6

Domaine de Lavaux, D82. **GPS**: n45,61688 e2,68975.

50 € 8 Ch (10x)€ 4/day WC included € 1,25 € 5. **Location:** Rural, comfortable, isolated, quiet. **Surface:** grassy. 15/05-30/09
Distance: 1km on the spot.

Super Besse 22A6

Ronde de Vassivière. **GPS**: n45,50644 e2,85342.

172 € 5,10/24h-€ 36,20/8 days € 1/20minutes Ch (100x)€ 1/4h. **Location:** Comfortable, quiet.
Surface: asphalted.
01/01-31/12
Distance: 300m 300m on the spot 300m.
Remarks: No camping activities.

Super Lioran 29B1

Aire de Laveissière, Parking Font d'Alagnon. **GPS**: n45,08856 e2,73819.

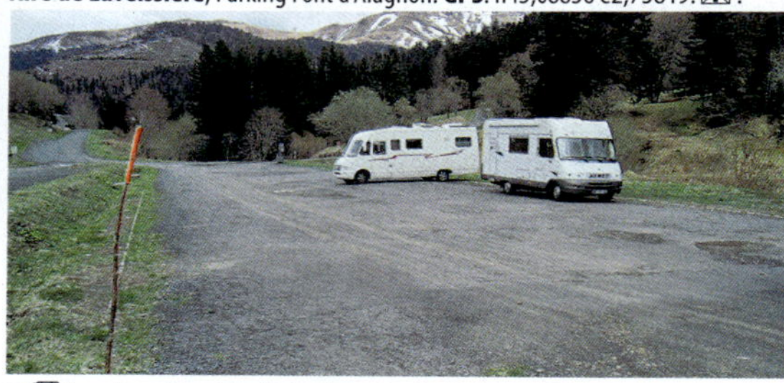

25 free. **Location:** Rural, simple, quiet. **Surface:** asphalted.
01/01-31/12
Distance: 200m 200m 50m 30m 30m.

Talizat 29C1

Place du 19 mars 1962. **GPS**: n45,11417 e3,04583.

3 free € 2 Ch € 2. **Location:** Rural, simple, quiet.
Surface: asphalted. 01/01-31/12
Distance: on the spot 100m 100m.
Remarks: Behind town hall.

Thiers 22B6

Base de loisirs Iloa, D44 > Dorat. **GPS**: n45,87070 e3,48311.

50 free free. **Location:** Rural, simple, isolated, quiet.

FR

Surface: metalled. 01/01-31/12
Distance: 2,6km.
Remarks: D 44 dir Dorat.

S **Thiézac** 29B1

Aire de camping-cars, D59. **GPS**: n45,01583 e2,66278.

8 free €2 Ch €2. **Location:** Rural, simple, quiet. **Surface:** asphalted. 01/01-31/12
Distance: 50m 100m 100m.
Remarks: Max. 24h, coins at Office de Tourisme and petro station.

S **Tiranges** 29D1

Accueil Camping Car, La Nerceyre. **GPS**: n45,30702 e3,99107.

10 free €2 Ch. **Location:** Rural, simple, quiet. **Surface:** asphalted. 01/01-31/12
Distance: 400m.

S **Tourzel-Ronzières** 22A6

Aire camping-car, Chemin du Clos, D23. **GPS**: n45,52888 e3,13611.

15 free Ch WC free. **Location:** Rural, simple, isolated, quiet. **Surface:** grassy/gravel. 01/01-31/12
Distance: 500m 500m.

S **Treteau** 22B4

Rue du Rosier, D21. **GPS**: n46,36800 e3,51758.

+10 €3/night €2 Ch €2 WC. **Location:** Rural, simple, quiet. **Surface:** grassy/metalled. 01/03-31/10
Distance: 500m on the spot day pass available 100m.
Remarks: At small lake.

S **Valette** 29B1

Aire camping-cars, D678. **GPS**: n45,27000 e2,60222.

5 free €2 Ch €2. **Location:** Rural, comfortable, quiet. **Surface:** gravel. 01/01-31/12 service: 01/11-01/05.
Distance: 50m 100m 150m.
Remarks: Quiet place.

S **Valuéjols** 29C1

Place de 19 Mars 1962, D34. **GPS**: n45,05333 e2,92944.

12 free €3 Ch WC . **Location:** Rural, simple. **Surface:** asphalted. 01/01-31/12
Distance: 400m 400m 400m on the spot.

S **Varennes-sur-Allier** 22B4

Place Hôtel de Ville, Rue de Beaupuy. **GPS**: n46,31288 e3,40476.

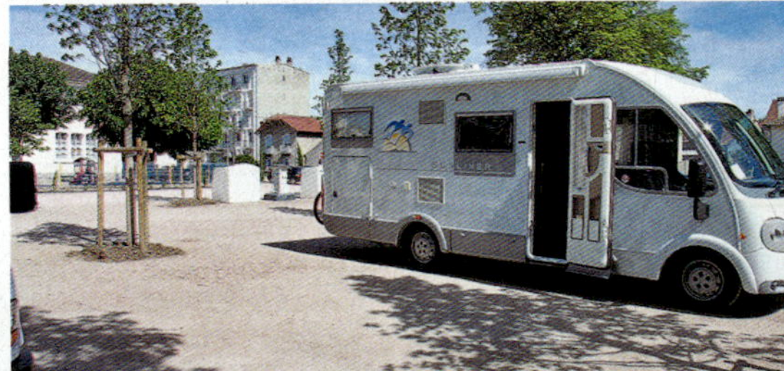

30 free €2 Ch WC. **Location:** Urban, simple, central, noisy. **Surface:** metalled. 01/01-31/12
Distance: on the spot on the spot on the spot.
Remarks: Coins at town hall.

S **Velzic** 29B1

Lavernière, Rue de Fracort. **GPS**: n45,00166 e2,54638.

4 free €3,50 Ch. **Location:** Rural, simple, isolated. **Surface:** asphalted. 01/01-31/12 service: 30/09-01/05.
Distance: 1km 1km 1km on the spot.
Remarks: Coins at épicerie Pas de Peyrols.

S **Vézac** 29B2

Aire de camping-cars, Route de Cavanière. **GPS**: n44,89028 e2,51806.

FR

2 € 3,50 Ch. **Location:** Rural, simple. **Surface:** asphalted.
01/01-31/12
Distance: 100m 50m 700m.
Remarks: At golf court, coins at bar/tabac.

S Vic-sur-Cère 29B1

Aire de camping-cars, Avenue des Tilleuls. **GPS**: n44,98194 e2,63111.

10 free € 2 Ch € 2. **Location:** Rural, comfortable, quiet.
Surface: asphalted. 01/01-31/12
Distance: 200m 200m 150m.
Remarks: Coins at Office de Tourisme, Avenue Mercier.

S Vieillevie 29B2

Aire de Vieillevie, Le Bourg. **GPS**: n44,64432 e2,41773.

5 free € 2 Ch € 2. **Location:** Rural, comfortable, quiet.
Surface: gravel. 01/01-31/12
Distance: 50m 100m 50m 50m.

S Villefranche-d'Allier 22A4

Avenue du 8 Mai 1945. **GPS**: n46,39565 e2,85672.

4 free € 2/10minutes Ch (4x)€ 2/2h. **Surface:** asphalted.
01/01-31/12
Distance: 150m 12km 150m 150m.
Remarks: Coins available at the shops.

S Viverols 29D1

Camping Le Pradoux, Le Ruisseau. **GPS**: n45,43257 e3,89299.

6 free € 2 Ch € 2. **Surface:** gravel. 01/04-31/10

S Vorey-sur-Arzon 29D1

Chemin de Félines. **GPS**: n45,18640 e3,90648.

5 € 2 € 3 Ch. **Surface:** gravel. service: 01/04-31/10
Distance: 200m on the spot 200m 200m on the spot on the spot.
Remarks: Next to camping Les Moulettes, at river, coins and code wifi available at campsite.

S Ytrac 29B2

Aire camping-cars, Impasse Jean de la Fontaine. **GPS**: n44,91417 e2,36389.

3 free € 3,50 Ch € 3,50. **Location:** Rural, simple, central.
Surface: asphalted. 01/01-31/12
Distance: 150m 100m 150m.
Remarks: Coins at the shops in the village and tourist office.

Rhône Alpes

S Aiguebelle 23C6

Place du Souvenir Français, N6. **GPS**: n45,54289 e6,30635.

30 free Ch free. **Surface:** asphalted/grassy.
01/01-31/12 Thu-morning closed because of market.
Distance: on the spot 6,1km.
Tourist information Aiguebelle:
Tue-morning.

FR

S Aix-les-Bains 23B6

Avenue du Grand Port. **GPS**: n45,70504 e5,88810.

16 free free WC. **Location:** Urban, simple, noisy. **Surface:** gravel.
01/01-31/12
Distance: city centre 2km 2km Lake 100m 150m bread service 500m on the spot.
Remarks: Max. 48h, market We and Sa.

S Alba-la-Romaine 30A2

Bragigous. **GPS**: n44,55329 e4,59741.

free € 2 Ch. **Location:** Rural, quiet. **Surface:** grassy/gravel.
01/01-31/12
Distance: on the spot 200m 200m.
Remarks: Service to be paid at retirement home.

FR

S Albertville 23C6

Montée Adolphe Hugues, Conflans. **GPS**: n45,67389 e6,39694.
6 free € 3,50 Ch. **Surface:** asphalted.
Distance: 10 min walking.

Tourist information Albertville:
Office de Tourisme, Place de l'Europe, www.albertville.com.
Quai des Allobroges. Thu 6-18h.

S Allevard 30C1

Place du David. **GPS**: n45,38838 e6,07110.
+10 € 4 Ch WC free. **Location:** Rural. **Surface:** unpaved.
01/01-31/12
Distance: 500m 300m.
Remarks: Max. 48h.

S Alpe d'Huez 30C1

Parking de Brandes. **GPS**: n45,08654 e6,07916.
65 € 10/day + € 0,40/pp tourist tax Ch WC.
Surface: asphalted.
Distance: on the spot.
Remarks: First buy a parking ticket at Palais des Sports et des Congrès.

S Alpe d'Huez 30C1

Parking l'Eclose, Rue du 93me Ram. **GPS**: n45,08709 e6,07983.

25 € 10/day + € 0,20/pp tourist tax Ch WC included.
Surface: asphalted. 01/12-01/04, 11/07-31/08
Distance: 200m 200m 200m on the spot.
Remarks: First buy a parking ticket at Palais des Sports et des Congrès.

S Ambierle 22B5

Complexe sportif, Rue Sainte Claude. **GPS**: n46,10663 e3,89334.

3 free Ch free. **Location:** Rural, simple, quiet.
Surface: asphalted.
Distance: on the spot 200m 300m.
Remarks: At sports park.

S Amplepuis 22C5

Rue Paul de la Goutte. **GPS**: n45,97027 e4,33085.
free Ch free. **Surface:** asphalted.
Distance: on the spot 50m 100m on the spot.
Remarks: Behind gymnasium.

S Annecy 23B5

Parking de Colmyr, Rue des Marquisats, N1508. **GPS**: n45,89070 e6,13915.

14 free Ch free. **Location:** Urban, simple, central, quiet.
Surface: asphalted. 01/01-31/12
Distance: 700m 100m on the spot 700m 700m.
Remarks: Max. 24h, market days Tue, Fr, Su.

Tourist information Annecy:
Office de Tourisme, Bonlieu, 1 rue Jean Jaurès, www.lac-annecy.com.Located on lake of the same name and surrounded by mountain peaks. The old city centre exists of covered lanes, canals and bridges.
M Musée du Palais de L'Isle.Regional museum.
Place de Romains. Tue.

S Arçon 22B5

Le Bourg. **GPS**: n46,00977 e3,88793.

3 free Ch free. **Location:** Rural, simple, quiet.
01/01-31/12
Distance: on the spot 50m.

S Arlebosc 30A1

Place du Marché aux Fruits. **GPS**: n45,03683 e4,65238.

10 free Ch free. **Location:** Rural, simple. **Surface:** gravel.
01/01-31/12
Distance: on the spot bakery 150m on the spot.

Aubignas 30A2

Aire camping-cars. GPS: n44,58732 e4,63177.

10 voluntary contribution € 2 € 2/100liter Ch WC. **Surface:** gravel.
Distance: 300m.
Remarks: Beautiful view. On entering the village from RN 102.

Balazuc 30A2

Parking Champsgelly, La Croisette. **GPS:** n44,50601 e4,37366.

free. **Location:** Rural. **Surface:** gravel. 01/01-31/12
Distance: 1km.

Banne 29D3

Quartier l'Eglise, D251. **GPS:** n44,36539 e4,15691.

25 free € 2/60liter Ch € 2/1h 2. **Surface:** gravel/metalled.
01/01-31/12
Distance: 500m.
Remarks: Behind church, beautiful view.

Barjac 29D3

Rue Pierre Andre Benoit. **GPS:** n44,30589 e4,34343.

20 free Ch € 3,water 10 min + electricity 55min. **Location:** Simple. 01/01-31/12
Distance: 100m 100m on the spot.
Remarks: Coins at town hall, office du tourisme, Fr market.

Beausemblant 30A1

Aire camping-cars, D122. **GPS:** n45,21826 e4,83282.

6 free Ch free. **Location:** Simple. **Surface:** gravel.
Distance: 100m 100m on the spot.
Remarks: Max. 48h. Via D122.

Belleville 22D5

Ancienne Avenue du Port. **GPS:** n46,10626 e4,75470.

8 free Ch free. **Surface:** asphalted. 01/01-31/12
Distance: centre 500m A6 900m 500m 500m.

Belley 23A6

Route de Saint-Germain, D41. **GPS:** n45,75535 e5,67790.

20 free € 2 Ch € 2. **Location:** Urban, simple, central, quiet.
Surface: asphalted. 01/01-31/12
Distance: city centre 1km 1km 1km 1km.
Remarks: Near sports park, service only with 1-euro coins.

Belmont-de-la-Loire 22C5

Place de l'Église. **GPS:** n46,16543 e4,34634.

FR

2 free Ch 2 WC free. **Location:** Rural, simple, quiet.
Surface: metalled. 03/03-19/07, 01/08-31/10
Distance: 50m 100m 100m on the spot.

S Berrias-et-Casteljau 29D3

Place du 7 juillet, Les Borels. **GPS**: n44,39956 e4,21332.

free Ch € 3. **Surface:** gravel. 01/01-31/12
Distance: Berias-et-Casteljau 3,5km.

S Bibost 22D6

D91. **GPS**: n45,79500 e4,55144.
free Ch free. **Location:** Rural, quiet. **Surface:** gravel. 01/01-31/12
Remarks: Beautiful view.

S Boën 22C6

Boulevard Moizieux. **GPS**: n45,74401 e4,00263.

free Ch free. **Surface:** gravel. 01/01-31/12
Distance: 200m 200m 300m.

S Boulieu-lès-Annonay 30A1

Chemin du Lavoir. **GPS**: n45,26928 e4,66963.

6 free Ch WC free. **Location:** Rural, comfortable, quiet.
Surface: gravel.
Distance: 400m 400m 400m.
Remarks: Voluntary contribution, market on Su.

S Bourg-en-Bresse 23A5

Parking V.L./Bus, Boulevard de Brou. **GPS**: n46,19854 e5,23766.

10 free WC 100m. **Location:** Urban, simple, central, noisy. **Surface:** asphalted.
Distance: on the spot 6km 100m 200m on the spot on the spot.
Remarks: Follow signs monastère/musée.

S Bourg-St.Andéol 30A3

Chemin de la Barrière. **GPS**: n44,37520 e4,64327.

30 free Ch free. **Surface:** asphalted. 01/01-31/12
Distance: 750m 50m Lidl.
Remarks: Max. 48h, along railwayline.

S Bourg-St.Maurice 23C6

Arc1600. **GPS**: n45,59523 e6,78951.
20 € 2 Ch € 2. 01/01-31/12
Distance: Bourg St.Maurice 15km.

Tourist information Bourg-St.Maurice:
Mountain city, centre of winter sports.
Musée du Costume.Costumes of the region.

S Bourget-du-Lac 23B6

International au l'Ile de Cygnes. **GPS**: n45,65250 e5,86378.

32 € 5,90-10,65 Ch WC included. **Location:** Rural, comfortable, quiet. **Surface:** metalled.
01/01-31/12 service: 01/12-01/03.
Distance: 500m 500m beach 300m 100m on the spot on the spot 100m on the spot on the spot.

S Bourgneuf 23B6

Aire camping-cars, D925. **GPS**: n45,55257 e6.21091.

FR

30 free € 1,50 € 1,50 Ch € 1,50. 01/01-31/12
Distance: 5km Brasserie/Pizzeria bakery.
Remarks: Coins available at Pizzeria/Tabac.

S **Bouvante** 30B2

Font d'Urle, Font d'Urle. **GPS**: n44,89789 e5,32195.

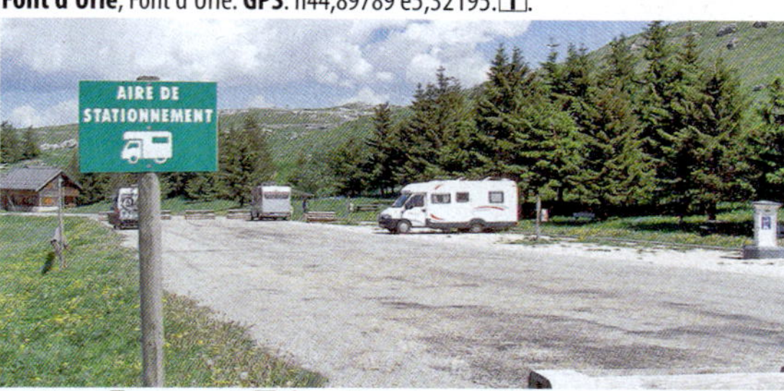

10 free € 2/100liter Ch (5x)€ 7/24h WC € 2/time. **Location:** Simple, quiet. **Surface:** gravel. 01/01-31/12, service: 01/06-31/08
Distance: on the spot nordic walking on the spot.
Remarks: Coins at riding school, altitude 1550m.

S **Chalmazel** 22B6

Le Bourg Le Pont d'Ouest. **GPS**: n45,70149 e3,85459.

8 free € 2 Ch € 2/4h. **Location:** Comfortable. **Surface:** metalled.
01/01-31/12
Distance: 50m on the spot 50m 50m on the spot on the spot 2km.
Remarks: At little stream.

S **Chambéry** 23B6

Rue de la Cardinière. **GPS**: n45,56289 e5,93302.
6 free Ch free. **Surface:** asphalted.
Distance: 500m 1,2km 500m 500m.
Remarks: Service closed during wintertime.

Tourist information Chambéry:

Office de Tourisme, 24, Boulevard de la Colonne, www.chambery-tourisme.com.City with Italian influences.
Les Charmettes.Rousseau museum.
Vieux Cité.Historical centre with old mansions.
Château des Ducs de Savoie.Complex of buildings, 13-14th century.

S **Chamonix-Mont-Blanc** 23D5

Parking Grépon, Aiguille du Midi, D1506. **GPS**: n45,91578 e6,86970.

50 € 12/24h € 2 Ch WC. **Surface:** asphalted. 01/01-31/12, service only during summer period
Distance: 5 min.

Tourist information Chamonix-Mont-Blanc:

Office de Tourisme, 85, Place du Triangle de l'Amitié, www.chamonix.com. Tourist town, summer and winter.
Musée Alpin.Museum of the Alps, the history of the winter sports.
Aiguille du Midi.Telpher carrier from Chamonix (1036 m.) To Aiguille de Midi (3842m).
Montenvers et mer de Glace.Tramline from Montenvers to the ice lake, a glacier of 7 km long and 1.2 km broad.

S **Chamrousse** 30B1

Place des Niverolles, Rue de la Cembraie. **GPS**: n45,12666 e5,87356.
12 € 8 Ch included. **Surface:** asphalted. 01/01-31/12
Remarks: Max. 24h.

S **Charix** 23A5

Auberge du Lac Genin. **GPS**: n46,21981 e5,69556.

20 € 5 + € 0,20/pp tourist tax, guests free Ch free. **Location:** Rural, simple, isolated, quiet. **Surface:** gravel.
Distance: 4,7km lake on the spot on the spot on the spot on the spot.

S **Charlieu** 22C5

Place d'Eningen. **GPS**: n46,16031 e4,17813.

5 free Ch WC free. **Location:** Rural. **Surface:** gravel/metalled.
01/01-31/12
Distance: historical centre 500m 500m 500m.
Remarks: In opposite of police station.

Tourist information Charlieu:

Office de Tourisme, Place St Philibert, www.leroannais.com.Historical centre with old trade houses.

S **Charols** 30A2

Aire municipale, D9. **GPS**: n44,59160 e4,95441.

FR

10 free free. **Surface:** asphalted. 01/01-31/12
Distance: 200m 200m 50m.

S Chichilianne 30B2

Passière. **GPS**: n44,81226 e5,57532.

free € 3 Ch. **Surface:** grassy. 01/01-31/12 water disconnected in winter. **Distance:** on the spot on the spot.
Remarks: Coins at town hall or Maison du Parc.

S Clansayes 30A3

Aire de Toronne, Quartier Toronne RD133. **GPS**: n44,36975 e4,79901.

25 € 10, Jul/Aug € 13 Ch € 4/day WC € 4/time.
Location: Rural, comfortable, luxurious, isolated, quiet. **Surface:** grassy/gravel.
01/01-31/12
Distance: 2km 10km buvette-menu rapide-restauration 3km.
Remarks: Bread-service.

S Colombier-le-Jeune 30A1

Place de la Marie, Le Bourg. **GPS**: n45,01106 e4,70132.

free Chfree. **Location:** Rural. **Surface:** metalled.
01/01-31/12 water disconnected in winter.
Distance: on the spot on the spot on the spot on the spot.

S Cornas 30A2

Impasse de Iris, Grande Rue, D86. **GPS**: n44,96024 e4,84722.

5 free Chfree. **Location:** Simple. **Surface:** gravel.
01/01-31/12
Distance: 200m 200m bakery 200m.
Remarks: Max. 48h, several 'Caves' with wine tasting.

S Coucouron 29D2

Les Eygades. **GPS**: n44,80168 e3,96148.

30 01/05-30/09 € 7/day Ch included. **Location:** Rural, simple.
Surface: gravel. 01/01-31/12
Distance: 1km on the spot on the spot 1km on the spot.
Remarks: At Lac de Coucouron, max. 7 days, outside season free stay on campsite municipal (no facilities).

S Cours-la-Ville 22C5

La Rivière. **GPS**: n46,10399 e4,32315.

10 free Chfree. **Location:** Rural, simple. **Surface:** grassy/gravel.
01/01-31/12
Distance: 300m on the spot on the spot on the spot.
Remarks: Along the river Trambouze, to be reached from northern direction , Boulevard Pierre de Coubertin.

Courtenay 23A6

Etang de Salette. **GPS**: n45,72417 e5,37124.

7 free. **Location:** Rural, isolated, quiet. **Surface:** gravel.
Distance: 1km Pizzeria bread service 1,2km on the spot.

S Crémieu 23A6

Rue du 19 mars 1962. **GPS**: n45,72549 e5,24670.

FR

12 free Ch free. **Location:** Urban, simple, central. **Surface:** asphalted.
01/01-31/12
Distance: 300m 250m 300m 100m.

S Crest 30A2

Place du Champ de Mars, Avenue Agirond. **GPS**: n44,72600 e5,02100.

17 free Ch € 5,10 min. water + 1h electricity free. **Location:** Urban, simple. **Surface:** asphalted.
01/01-31/12
Distance: 200m pizzeria bakery 50m.

Tourist information Crest:

Office de Tourisme, Place du Docteur Rozier, www.vallee-drome.com/ot-crest.
Naturodrôme.Minerals and fossils.
Tour de Crest.Exhibitions. 01/05-30/09 10-19h, 30/09-01/05 14-18h.

S Die 30B2

Aire de Meyrosse, Avenue du Maréchal Leclerc, D238. **GPS**: n44,75103 e5,37385.

30 € 5/24h Ch WC free. **Surface:** grassy/gravel.
01/01-31/12
Distance: 300m 300m 1km.
Remarks: Max. 1 night, pay at Police Municpale.

Tourist information Die:

Fête de la Transhumance.On Saturday gathering and crossing of the herd in the town, the final ascent on Sunday. 21st-22nd June 2014.

S Donzère 30A2

Aire de respos. **GPS**: n44,44060 e4,71899.

free Ch WC free. **Surface:** asphalted. 01/01-31/12
Distance: 500m 7km.
Remarks: Near RN7.

S Eyzin-Pinet 30A1

Rue du Stade. **GPS**: n45,47463 e4,99965.

6 free Ch free. **Location:** Rural, simple, central, quiet. **Surface:** gravel.
01/01-31/12
Distance: 50m 50m 20m on the spot on the spot.

S Faverges 23C6

Route d'Annecy, D2508. **GPS**: n45,74943 e6,28626.

20 free Ch free. **Location:** Rural, simple, noisy. **Surface:** gravel.
01/01-31/12 Service: winter.
Distance: 800m 800m on the spot 100m 100m.
Remarks: Max. 48h, market We.

S Fontanes 22C6

Hameau Chantemerle. **GPS**: n45,54681 e4,44027.

3 free Ch free. **Location:** Rural, simple, quiet. **Surface:** asphalted.
01/01-31/12
Distance: 500m 13km 400m.
Remarks: At tennis-courts, inclining pitches.

S Gervans 30A1

Place des Amandiers, Rue de l'école. **GPS**: n45,10932 e4,83031.

FR

4 free Ch free. **Location:** Simple. **Surface:** gravel.
Distance: on the spot on the spot on the spot.
Remarks: Max. 24h, no camping activities.

S Grane 30A2

Domaine Distaise, D104. **GPS:** n44,75564 e4,86768.

15 € 2/pp . **Surface:** grassy. 01/01-31/12

S Gresse-en-Vercors 30B2

D8D, La Ville. **GPS:** n44,89184 e5,54766.

free Ch. **Surface:** gravel.
Distance: on the spot.
Remarks: Max. 24h, service on campsite.

S Hauteluce 23C6

Parking de la Fôret, Tetras, D123. **GPS:** n45,74633 e6,53441.

5 free € 2 Ch € 2. **Surface:** gravel. 01/01-31/12
Distance: 3km 3km 3km.

S Hauteluce 23C6

Parking Du Col des Saisies, D218b. **GPS:** n45,76297 e6,53382.

40 € 7 € 2 Ch € 2. **Surface:** asphalted. 01/01-31/12
Distance: 500m on the spot 500m 200m 200m.

Tourist information Hauteluce:
Office de Tourisme, 316, Avenue des Jeux Olympiques, www.Lessaisies.com. Mountain village. Both in summer and winter an attractive touristic destination.

S Hauterives 30A1

D538. **GPS:** n45,25497 e5,03022.

free, 01/04-31/10 € 5/24h € 2/50liter Ch included WC free. **Location:** Rural, simple. **Surface:** gravel.
Distance: 250m 250m.

Tourist information Hauterives:
Palais Idéal du Facteur Cheval.

S Illiat 22D5

GPS: n46,18495 e4,88802.

4 free Ch WC free. **Location:** Rural, simple, quiet. **Surface:** gravel.
01/01-31/12
Distance: 650m on the spot on the spot 650m on the spot on the spot.
Remarks: At small lake.

S Izernore 23A5

Rue de l'Oignin. **GPS:** n46,21847 e5,55041.

15 free Ch free. **Location:** Rural, simple, central, quiet. 01/01-31/12
Distance: on the spot 6km 500m 500m 500m 500m.

FR

Remarks: On the foot of the Monts Berthiand.

S Joux 22C5

Salle des Fêtes, La Noirie, D79. **GPS**: n45,88869 e4,37587.

10 free Chfree. **Location:** Rural. **Surface:** asphalted.
01/01-31/12 water disconnected in winter.
Distance: 200m 3,2km 200m 200m.
Remarks: Nearby castle garden.

S La Balme de Sillingy 23B5

Aire de Camping-cars Domaine du Tornet, D508. **GPS**: n45,97124 e6,03135.

30 € 5 Chfree. **Location:** Rural, simple, central, quiet.
Surface: gravel. 01/04-31/10
Distance: 100m (fishing permit available) 100m on the spot.
Remarks: Max. 48h, recreation park.

La Clusaz 23C5

Route des Confins. **GPS**: n45,92298 e6,48380.
free. **Surface:** asphalted. 01/01-31/12
Remarks: Parking at pistes.

S La Féclaz 23B6

Aire Camping-cars de la Féclaz, D206a. **GPS**: n45,64210 e5,98411.

40 € 4 € 1,50 Ch € 1,50 . **Surface:** asphalted. 01/01-31/12
Distance: on the spot on the spot on the spot 300m.

S Lablachère 29D2

La Ferme Théâtre, D104, Notre Dame. **GPS**: n44,45481 e4,22004.

20 € 5/24h, guests free € 2 € 3/12h. **Location:** Rural.
Surface: gravel.
01/01-31/12
Distance: 1km 150m.
Remarks: Max. 24h, theater, regional products.

S Lachamp-Raphaël 29D2

D122, Le Village. **GPS**: n44,81133 e4,28860.

5 free € 2 Ch. **Location:** Rural, simple, quiet. **Surface:** gravel.
01/01-31/12
Distance: 300m 300m Bread 300m departure "Nordic.
Remarks: Beautiful view, altitude 1330m, coins at bar/hotel, 2013: during inspection service out of order.

S Lalouvesc 30A1

Vallon d'Or, Sainte Agathe. **GPS**: n45,11947 e4,53384.

3 free WC. **Location:** Simple, central. **Surface:** asphalted.
01/01-31/12
Distance: on the spot 100m 100m.

S Lalouvesc 30A1

La Fontaine. **GPS**: n45,12149 e4,53393.

€ 2/15minutes Ch € 2. 15/05-15/10
Remarks: Coins at petrol station and camping municipal.

S Lamastre 30A1

Parking Pont de Tain, Place Pradon. **GPS**: n44,98672 e4,58001.

20 free € 4,40/100liter Ch € 2,20/1h . **Location:** Simple.
Surface: asphalted. 01/01-31/12
Distance: on the spot on the spot on the spot.

FR

Lamure-sur-Azergues 22C5

Place de la gare. **GPS**: n46,06120 e4,49185.

10 free € 2 Ch € 2 WC. **Location:** Rural, simple. **Surface:** asphalted. 01/01-31/12
Distance: on the spot 100m 100m train/bus on the spot.
Remarks: Near train station.

Lans-en-Vercors 30B1

Route de l'Aigle. **GPS**: n45,12570 e5,59002.

30 free Ch WC free. **Location:** Rural, simple. **Surface:** gravel. 01/01-31/12
Distance: 500m on the spot.
Remarks: Large parking, Tue and Sa market.

Lathuile 23B6

190 route de la Porte, Bout du lac, N 508. **GPS**: n45,79480 e6,20796.

24 € 8 Ch included (24x)€ 2. **Location:** Rural, simple.
Surface: grassy. 01/06-31/08
Distance: Lake of Annecy 750m.
Remarks: Max. 24h.

Le Bessat 30A1

Croix de Chaubouret. **GPS**: n45,36812 e4,52768.

4 free € 2,50/20minutes Ch (4x)€ 2,50/6h. **Location:** Rural.
Surface: asphalted.
01/01-31/12
Distance: 1km 100m mountainbike trail on the spot on the spot.
Remarks: Coins available at Chalet des Alpes and the shops, altitude 1200m.

Le Cheylard 30A2

Super U, Chemin du pre-jalla, ZI la Palisse. **GPS**: n44,91143 e4,44162.

20 free € 2 Ch € 2. **Location:** Simple, noisy. **Surface:** asphalted.
01/01-31/12
Distance: on the spot on the spot.
Remarks: Max. 24h.

Le Cheylas 30C1

Avenue de la Libération. **GPS**: n45,37170 e5,99014.
free Ch WC free. **Surface:** asphalted/metalled.
Distance: on the spot nearby.

Le Lac d'Issarlès 29D2

D16. **GPS**: n44,81948 e4,06156.

16 € 8,50 + € 0,25/pp tourist tax Ch WC included.
Location: Central. **Surface:** metalled. 01/05-31/10
Distance: 100m 100m 100m.
Remarks: Attention: this town is not Issarlès!.

Le Teil 30A2

Alleé Paul Avon. **GPS**: n44,55138 e4,68972.

6 free Ch free. **Location:** Noisy. **Surface:** grassy/metalled.
Distance: on the spot on the spot 500m.
Remarks: Nearby D86.

Tourist information Le Teil:
Thu morning.

Les Carroz-Arâches 23C5

Télécabine Les Cluses. **GPS**: n46,02500 e6,64361.

FR

free Ch free. 01/06-30/11
Remarks: Parking funicular railway.

S Les Deux-Alpes 30C1

Avenue de la Muzelle, D213. **GPS:** n45,02394 e6,12120.
€ 7 Ch included. **Surface:** asphalted.
Remarks: Beautiful view.

S Les Gets 23C5

Route des Grandes Alpes. **GPS:** n46,14992 e6,65673.

€ 14/1 night, € 20/2 nights, € 0,90pp tourist tax Ch .
Surface: gravel. 01/01-31/12
Distance: 1km on the spot. **Remarks:** Bus to centre every 30 minutes.

Tourist information Les Gets:

Office de Tourisme, Place de la Mairie, www.lesgets.com.Winter sports resort.

Musée de la Musique Mécanique.Collection of mechanical musical instruments.

Musée du Ski, Restaurant Belvedère.Exhibition of the history of the ski. Can only be reached by means of telpher carrier of Mont Chéry.

Week market. Thu-morning.

S Les Granges-Gontardes 30A3

Domaine de la Tour d'Elyssas, Quartier Combe d'Elissas. **GPS:** n44,41811 e4,75465.

15 free Ch free. **Surface:** gravel. 01/01-31/12
Distance: 9km.
Remarks: At wine-grower. Follow Dôme d'Elyssas.

Les Karellis 30C1

GPS: n45,22778 e6,40639.
free. 01/01-31/12
Remarks: Mountain station nearby St.Jean-de-Maurienne.

S Les Menuires 30C1

Les Bruyères, Dir Val Thorens. **GPS:** n45,31410 e6,53750.
40 € 5<12h, € 10/24h, tourist tax € 0,20/pp Ch (7x)€ 2/4h .
Surface: asphalted. 01/01-31/12
Distance: on the spot on the spot on the spot.
Remarks: Near the pistes.

Tourist information Les Menuires:

Office de Tourisme, Imm. Belledonne, www.lesmenuires.com.Winter sports resort.

S Les Noës 22B5

Le Bourg, D47. **GPS:** n46,04083 e3,85206.

3 free Ch free. **Location:** Rural, simple, quiet. **Surface:** gravel. 01/01-31/12
Distance: on the spot 50m.

S Les Sauvages 22C5

D121. **GPS:** n45,92083 e4,37711.

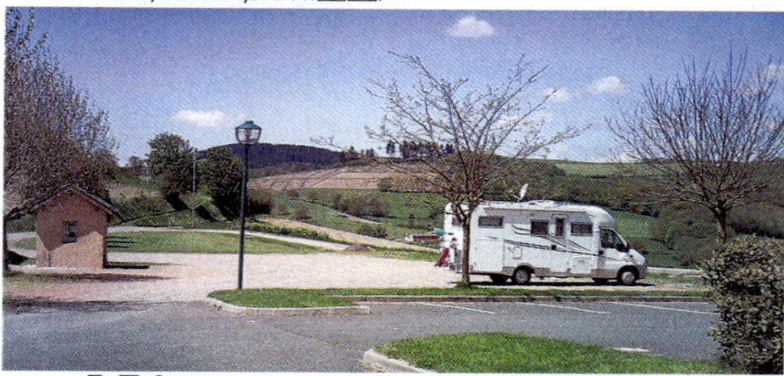

free Ch free. **Location:** Rural, simple, quiet. **Surface:** gravel. 01/01-31/12
Distance: on the spot 100m 100m on the spot.

S Mâcot-la-Plagne 23C6

GPS: n45,50677 e6,68652.
46 free, Winter € 10 € 2 Ch € 4/8h. **Surface:** asphalted.
01/01-31/12
Distance: on the spot.

S Marsanne 30A2

Avenue de Bailliencourt, D57. **GPS:** n44,64568 e4,87175.

10 free Ch free. **Location:** Rural, quiet. **Surface:** grassy.
Distance: 300m 300m nearby.
Remarks: Max. 48h, medieval village.

Megève 23C6

Chemin des Ânes. **GPS:** n45,86401 e6,62010.
free. 01/01-31/12
Remarks: In front of parking Télécabine du Jaillet.

S Meyras 29D2

Aire camping-cars, Grande rue, D26. **GPS:** n44,67939 e4,26847.

FR

15 € 4 € 3 Ch € 3. **Surface:** asphalted. 01/04-31/10
Distance: 200m 200m nearby.
Remarks: Coins available at shops in the village, max. 48h.

Tourist information Meyras:
Office de Tourisme, Place du Champ de Mars, www.meyras-tourisme.com.

S Mijoux 23B4
D50, Route de la Combe-en-Haut. **GPS:** n46,36963 e6,00247.

20 free € 2 Ch € 2. **Surface:** gravel.
Distance: 500m 500m 500m on the spot on the spot.

S Mirabel-aux-Baronnies 30A3
Aire camping-cars, Chemin des Grottes. **GPS:** n44,31260 e5,09968.

6+10 voluntary contribution Ch free. **Location:** Rural.
Surface: grassy/metalled. 01/01-31/12
Distance: 200m.

S Montalieu-Vercieu 23A6
Chamboud. **GPS:** n45,82776 e5,42100.

6 free Ch WC campsite. **Location:** Rural, simple, isolated, quiet.
Surface: asphalted.
Distance: 2km 2km 2km 1,5km.
Remarks: Next to campsite /Bade de Loisirs de la Vallée Bleue, max. 2 nights.

S Montbrison-sur-Lez 30A2
Place Publique. **GPS:** n44,43663 e5,01779.

6 free free. **Surface:** metalled. 01/01-31/12
Distance: 100m 100m 100m.

S Montbrison-sur-Lez 30A2
GPS: n44,42751 e5,02438.

€ 2/60liter Ch € 2. **Location:** Isolated.
Remarks: Coins at bar and garage.

S Montbrun-les-Bains 30B3
Toscan. **GPS:** n44,17247 e5,43881.
free . **Location:** Rural. **Surface:** grassy.
Distance: 500m.
Remarks: Free wifi at office de tourisme.

S Montbrun-les-Bains 30B3
Condamine. **GPS:** n44,17413 e5,44071.
€ 2 Ch € 2.

S Montélimar 30A2
Domaine du Bois de Laud, Chemin du Bois de Laud. **GPS:** n44,56522 e4,75691.

17 € 4,30 Ch included. **Location:** Urban.
Surface: grassy/metalled. 01/01-31/12
Distance: 500m 100m.
Remarks: Max. 48h, near Centre Commercial Leclerc.

S Morillon 23C5
GPS: n46,08289 e6,67968.
10 free Ch WC free. **Surface:** asphalted.
Distance: 200m 100m 300m 100m.

S Nantua 23A5
D74. **GPS:** n46,15497 e5,59656.

FR

13 € 7 + € 0,20/pp tourist tax Ch free WC. **Location:** Urban, comfortable, central. **Surface:** gravel. 01/04-30/09
Distance: 700m 7km on the spot on the spot 150m 150m on the spot on the spot.
Remarks: At Nantua lake.

Tourist information Nantua:
Office de Tourisme, Place de la Déportation, www.nantua-tourisme.com. Tourist town with historical centre.
Musée de la Résistance, Montée de l'Abbaye. War museum.

S Noirétable 22B6

Aire d'accueil de camping-cars, Lieu-dit La Roche. **GPS**: n45,80674 e3,77133.

7 free € 3 Ch € 1/2h. **Location:** Simple, quiet. **Surface:** metalled. 01/01-31/12
Distance: 800m 100m 100m 100m 800m on the spot on the spot on the spot.
Remarks: Next to campsite (50m), coins at campsite.

S Nyons 30B3

Promenade la Digue. **GPS**: n44,35778 e5,13861.

20 € 9/24h Ch WC included. **Surface:** gravel. 01/01-31/12
Distance: 250m 250m 250m 250m.
Remarks: Max. 48h, next to Parc loisirs aquatique.

S Nyons 30B3

Domaine Rocheville, D 538. **GPS**: n44,36850 e5,11775.

6 € 6, 2 pers.incl € 4/100liter Ch € 3,50 WC included, summer free. **Surface:** grassy.

Tourist information Nyons:
Pavillon du Tourisme, Place de la Libération. Important Olive-city in the Provence.
Musée de l'Olivier. Museum about the olive-tree and production of olive oil. daily 01/11-28/02 Su.
Centre-ville. Regional market. Thu-morning.

S Orgnac l'Aven 30A3

Le Fez, D217. **GPS**: n44,30419 e4,43240.

5 free Ch free. **Location:** Rural. **Surface:** gravel. 01/01-31/12
Distance: 200m 10m 300m.
Remarks: Caves of Aven d'Orgnac 2km.

S Panissières 22C6

Aire camping-cars, Allée des Acacias. **GPS**: n45,78835 e4,34355.

4 € 6,50 Ch included 4 WC Use sanitary € 3,30/pp. **Location:** Rural, simple, quiet. **Surface:** metalled. 01/01-31/12 Service: winter.
Distance: 300m 300m 300m.
Remarks: Use sanitary € 2,40/pp per day. Dir 'gîte La Ferme Seigne'.

S Planfoy 30A1

Chemin du Vignolet. **GPS**: n45,37445 e4,44910.

10 free € 2,50/15minutes Ch (8x)€ 2,50/6h. **Location:** Rural, comfortable, quiet. **Surface:** asphalted. 01/01-31/12
Distance: 1,3km 7km 1,3km on the spot.
Remarks: Coins available at the shops.

S Poncin 23A5

Rue de la Verchère. **GPS**: n46,08710 e5,40396.

FR

5 free Chfree. **Location:** Urban, simple, central, quiet.
Surface: gravel/metalled.
Distance: on the spot 1km 200m on the spot on the spot.
Remarks: Nearby Stade Guy Drut.

Pont-de-Veyle 22D5

D933, Rue de la Poste. **GPS:** n46,26437 e4,88697.

20 free . **Location:** Urban, simple, central, noisy.
Surface: gravel.
Distance: on the spot 3,5km on the spot on the spot 50m 150m.

S Pontcharra-sur-Turdine 22C6

Place A. Schweitzer. **GPS:** n45,87405 e4,49133.

4 free Ch WC free. **Location:** Urban.
01/01-31/12
Distance: 50m on the spot 50m 50m on the spot.

S Pouilly-sous-Charlieu 22C5

Place du Marché, Rue de la République. **GPS:** n46,14335 e4,10832.
free Ch WC free. **Surface:** asphalted.
Distance: on the spot.

Pouilly-sous-Charlieu 22C5

Rue de la Berge. **GPS:** n46,14699 e4,10075.
4 free. **Surface:** gravel. 01/01-31/12
Remarks: Parking at the Loire river.

S Prapoutel-les-Sept-Laux 30C1

D281. **GPS:** n45,25775 e5,99551.

free WC. **Surface:** metalled. 01/01-31/12
Distance: 50m.
Remarks: Parking at pistes.

S Privas 30A2

Avenue de la gare. **GPS:** n44,73134 e4,59309.

10 free Ch. **Location:** Urban. **Surface:** gravel/metalled.
01/01-31/12
Distance: centre 750m.

S Puy-Saint-Martin 30A2

Aire de camping-car. **GPS:** n44,62753 e4,97492.

13 free Ch. **Location:** Rural, comfortable. **Surface:** grassy.
Distance: on the spot.
Remarks: Max. 48h, former campsite.

S Renaison 22B5

GPS: n46,04757 e3,92124.

5 free Chfree. **Location:** Rural, simple, quiet. **Surface:** grassy/gravel.
01/01-31/12
Distance: 400m on the spot 700m.
Remarks: At little stream.

S Renaison 22B5

Auberge du Barrage, La Tâche, D41 dir les Barrages. **GPS:** n46,04519 e3,87272.

12 € 4, free with a meal Ch € 4,guests free . **Surface:** grassy.
15/03-01/11 Mon, Tue (except Jul/Aug).
Distance: Renaison ± 4km 100m on the spot 4km.
Remarks: Construction work during inspection June 2013.

FR

Reventin-Vaugris 30A1

Rue Mouret. **GPS**: n45,46821 e4,84239.

10 free WC. **Location:** Rural, simple, central, quiet. **Surface:** gravel/metalled. 01/01-31/12
Distance: on the spot 6km 20m bakery 10m.

Roanne 22C5

Port de Plaisance, Allée Amiral Vermeilleux du Vignaux. **GPS**: n46,03750 e4,08306.

10 € 6 € 2/15minutes € 2 Ch € 2 € 2,10 € 2/8kWh WC
Location: Urban, comfortable, quiet. **Surface:** metalled.
01/01-31/12
Distance: 500m on the spot 500m 2km 2km on the spot on the spot on the spot.
Remarks: Max. 72h.

Romans-sur-Isère 30A1

Avenue Gambetta. **GPS**: n45,04521 e5,05879.

4 free. **Location:** Urban, simple. **Surface:** metalled.
01/01-31/12
Distance: centre 700m.
Remarks: Max. 48h, parking in front of Marques Avenue.

Tourist information Romans-sur-Isère:
Office de Tourisme, Le Neuilly Place Jean Jaurès, www.ville-romans.com/. Medium city in the Drôme, shoe city, shoe museum.

Saillans 30B2

Parking Gite Rural, Montmartel. **GPS**: n44,69549 e5,19350.

20 free € 2 Ch. **Location:** Rural, simple. **Surface:** gravel.
Distance: 300m.
Remarks: Along the Drôme river, closed when high water.

Saint-Agrève 30A1

Coussac. **GPS**: n45,01042 e4,39339.

free € 3 Ch € 3,water 10 min + electricity 50min WC. **Location:** Simple. **Surface:** asphalted. 01/01-31/12
Distance: 500m 500m 500m.
Remarks: Coins at Tourist Info.

Saint-Agrève 30A1

Le Lac de Véron, Pré de Gardy, D120. **GPS**: n44,99981 e4,40164.

5 € 5/24h On demand free. **Location:** Rural, comfortable, quiet.
Surface: unpaved. 01/04-31/10
Distance: Village 1km on the spot on the spot on the spot on the spot.
Remarks: At fish lake.

Saint-André-d'Apchon 22B5

La Prébande. **GPS**: n46,03385 e3,92705.

3 free Ch free. **Location:** Rural, simple, quiet. **Surface:** gravel.
01/01-31/12
Distance: 300m 100m.

Saint-Étienne-la-Varenne 22D5

Le Bourg. **GPS**: n46,07731 e4,63024.

4 free Ch free. **Location:** Rural, simple, quiet.
Surface: gravel/metalled. 01/01-31/12

FR

Distance: on the spot 50m on the spot on the spot.
Remarks: Next to church.

Saint-Forgeux 22C6

Le Tram. **GPS**: n45,85733 e4,47566.

free Ch free WC. **Location:** Rural, simple, quiet.
Surface: metalled. 01/01-31/12
Distance: 300m 300m 300m on the spot.

Saint-Genest-de-Beauzon 29D2

Domaine la Pize, La Pize. **GPS**: n44,43759 e4,19431.

€ 10 Ch WC included . **Location:** Rural, isolated, quiet.
Surface: unpaved. 01/01-31/12
Distance: 1,6km.

Saint-Germain-Lespinasse 22C5

Place du 8 mai 1945. **GPS**: n46,10510 e3,96229.

2 free Ch free. **Location:** Rural, simple, quiet.
Surface: gravel.
Distance: 200m 50m 50m.

Saint-Haon-le-Châtel 22B5

Fondanges, Route de la Croix du Sud, D39. **GPS**: n46,06362 e3,91313.

3 free Ch free. **Location:** Rural, quiet. **Surface:** metalled.
01/01-31/12
Distance: 400m 400m 400m 400m.

Saint-Martin-en-Haut 22C6

Etang du Kaiser, Lieu-dit-Jeangouttière. **GPS**: n45,64206 e4,53511.

4 free Ch WC. **Location:** Rural, comfortable, quiet. **Surface:** gravel.
01/01-31/12
Distance: St.Martin 4km on the spot on the spot on the spot.
Remarks: Max. 72h, at small lake.

Saint-Paul-le-Jeune 29D3

Rue Louis Roux, D901. **GPS**: n44,33999 e4,15322.

free € 2 Ch € 2. **Location:** Rural. **Surface:** grassy.
01/01-31/12
Distance: on the spot 100m.
Remarks: Coins available at the shops.

Saint-Restitut 30A3

Le Village. **GPS**: n44,33144 e4,79093.

free Ch free. **Surface:** asphalted. 01/01-31/12
Distance: on the spot.

Saint-Romain-d'Ay 30A1

Praperier, D6. **GPS**: n45,16430 e4,66339.

4 free € 2/20minutes Ch (4x)€ 2/4h WC. **Location:** S mple.
Surface: asphalted. 01/01-31/12
Distance: 550m 100m.
Remarks: Coins at town hall and superette.

Saint-Symphorien-sur-Coise 22C6

Bois des Pinasses. **GPS**: n45,62578 e4,45837.

FR

free. **Location:** Rural, simple. **Surface:** gravel.
01/01-31/12
Distance: 1km 50m.
Remarks: Next to sports fields.

S Saint-Symphorien-sur-Coise 22C6

Rue des Rameaux. **GPS**: n45,63378 e4,45883.

Chfree. **Location:** Simple. 01/01-31/12
Remarks: Free coins at Bar-Tabac and town hall.

S Saint-Théoffrey 30B1

Camping Ser-Sirant, Chemin du Lavoir. **GPS**: n45,00034 e5,77819.
4 € 8-9,50 € 1,50 Ch. **Location:** Rural. **Surface:** grassy.
Distance: beach Saint Théoffrey.
Remarks: Pay at reception campsite, at lake Laffrey.

S Samoëns 23C5

Le Fayet-Samoëns. **GPS**: n46,07278 e6,69895.

10 free Ch € 5. **Surface:** metalled.
01/01-31/12 Service: winter.
Distance: 2km 100m 2km.

S Samoëns 23C5

Parking du Giffre. **GPS**: n46,07666 e6,71899.

5 free Ch . **Surface:** asphalted.
01/01-31/12 Service: winter.
Distance: 100m 100m 100m Skibus to Samoëns 1600 100m on the spot.
Remarks: Near campsite du Giffre, parking 150m.

S Sassenage 30B1

Rue Pierre de Coubertin. **GPS**: n45,21346 e5,66858.
2+3 free Chfree. **Surface:** asphalted. 01/01-31/12 on the spot on the spot.
Remarks: Next to sports fields.

S Serrières-en-Chautagne 23B6

GPS: n45,87964 e5,84230.

15 free Ch WCfree. **Location:** Rural, central, quiet.
Surface: metalled. 01/01-31/12 Service: winter.
Distance: on the spot 1km beach 50m on the spot 200m 100m 100m.
Remarks: At little mountain stream.

S Seyssel 23B5

Parking Base de Loisirs, Quai du Rhône. **GPS**: n45,95146 e5,83343.

4 free Chfree. **Location:** Rural, simple, central, quiet.
Surface: gravel. 01/01-31/12
Distance: 800m on the spot on the spot 500m 800m on the spot.
Remarks: At recreational lake and Rhone river.

Seyssel 23B5

Quai du Rhône. **GPS**: n45,95001 e5,83406.

12 free. **Location:** Rural, simple, central, quiet. **Surface:** gravel.
01/10-01/06
Distance: 400m on the spot on the spot 400m 400m 400m on the spot.

S Sixt-Fer-à-Cheval 23C5

Route du Cirque du Fer à Cheval. **GPS**: n46,05698 e6,78048.

FR

30 free Ch € 4/12h. **Surface:** asphalted. 01/01-31/12
Distance: 500m on the spot 500m.

S St.Alban-Auriolles 29D3

Rue Marius Perbost. **GPS:** n44,42693 e4,30096.

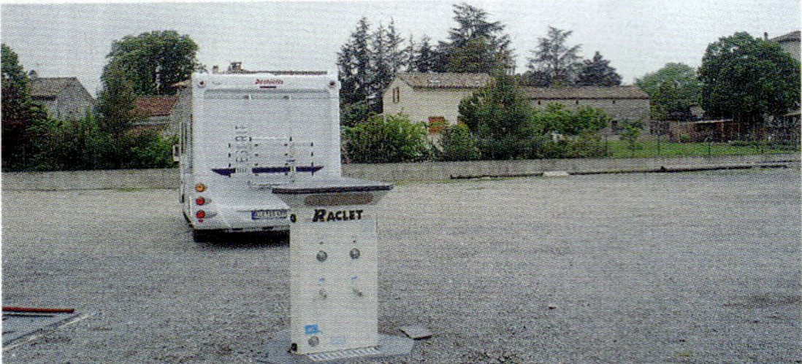

free € 3 Ch € 3. **Surface:** gravel.
Distance: 300m 200m.

S St.Bonnet-le-Château 29D1

Esplanade de la Boule. **GPS:** n45,42514 e4,06436.

50 free Ch WC free. **Location:** Simple. **Surface:** metalled.
Distance: 200m 1km 200m 200m.

Tourist information St.Bonnet-le-Château:
M Musée de la Pétanque et des Boules, Esplanade de la Boule.All about the beloved French national sport. 01/04-31/10.
M Musée International Pétanque et Boules, Boulevard des Chauchères. Fri.

S St.Désirat 30A1

Musée de l'Alambic ,Distillerie Jean Gauthier, D291. **GPS:** n45,25856 e4,79261.

free WC free. **Location:** Simple. **Surface:** asphalted.
Distance: 300m 300m.
Remarks: Max. 1 night.

Tourist information St.Désirat:
M Musée de l'Alambic, D291.Museum with distillery, tasting and sales.
10-12h, 14-18.30h. T free.

S St.Donat-sur-l'Herbasse 30A1

Route de St.Bardoux. **GPS:** n45,11902 e4,98284.

free Ch free. **Location:** Simple.
01/01-31/12
Distance: 400m 400m 1km.
Remarks: In front of gymnasium, max. 1 night.

S St.Félicien 30A1

Place du Pré Lacour. **GPS:** n45,08453 e4,62848.

6 free € 2 Ch. **Location:** Urban, simple. **Surface:** asphalted/gravel.
01/01-31/12
Distance: on the spot on the spot on the spot.
Remarks: Max. 24h.

S St.Georges d'Espéranche 22D6

Chemin des Platières. **GPS:** n45,55560 e5,07478.

14 free Ch free. **Location:** Rural, simple, central, quiet.
Surface: metalled. 01/01-31/12
Distance: on the spot 100m 500m.
Remarks: Max. 48h.

S St.Gervais-les-Bains 23C5

77, impasse Cascade. **GPS:** n45,88864 e6,71287.

20 free € 2 Ch € 2. **Surface:** asphalted.
Distance: 200m 200m 200m 300m.
Remarks: Parking skating rink.

S St.Jean d'Ardières 22D5

Domaine de Grande Ferrière, 831 route des Rochons. **GPS:** n46,12954 e4,71581.

5 free Ch free € 5/4night WC. **Location:** Rural, simple, quiet.
Surface: gravel.
Distance: 3km 6km 5km 500m 3km 3km.

S St.Jean-de-Bournay 23A6

Place du Marche. **GPS**: n45,50130 e5,13845.

10 free free Ch. **Location:** Rural, simple, central, quiet.
Surface: asphalted. 01/01-31/12
Distance: on the spot 100m 100m.

S St.Jean-de-Maurienne 30C1

Rue Louis Sibue. **GPS**: n45,27995 e6,34776.
10 free € 2 Ch € 2 WC. **Surface:** asphalted. 01/01-31/12
Distance: 2,5km 100m.

Tourist information St.Jean-de-Maurienne:
Office de Tourisme, Ancien Evêché, Place de la Cathédrale, www.saintjeandemaurienne.com.Mountain village.
Musée de l'Opinel.The history of the knife. Mo/Sa 9-12h, 14-18h. free.

S St.Jean-en-Royans 30B1

Rue de la Gare. **GPS**: n45,02028 e5,29032.

3 free Ch free. **Location:** Simple. **Surface:** gravel.
Distance: 200m 200m 200m.

S St.Just-d'Ardèche 30A3

Domaine La Favette, D86, route des Gorges d'Ardèche. **GPS**: n44,30134 e4,60649.

6 € 5 € 2 Ch € 2. 01/01-31/12
Remarks: At wine-grower, max. 24h.

Tourist information St.Just-d'Ardèche:
Good starting point to discover the Ardèche gorges.
Thu.

S St.Just-en-Chevalet 22B5

Boulevard de l'Astrée. **GPS**: n45,91411 e3,84727.

5 free Ch free. **Location:** Rural, simple.
01/01-31/12 Thu-morning.
Distance: on the spot on the spot on the spot on the spot.

S St.Paul-Trois-Châteaux 30A3

Parking Office de Tourisme, Le Courreau, Place Chausy. **GPS**: n44,34786 e4,76995.

free Ch free WC. **Location:** Urban. **Surface:** asphalted.
Distance: 50m 50m.
Remarks: Max. 24h.

Tourist information St.Paul-Trois-Châteaux:
Office de Tourisme, Place Chaussy, www.office-tourisme-tricastin.com.
Marché. Tue-morning.
Marché aux truffes du Tricastin. Dec-Mar Su-morning.

S St.Pierre-en-Faucigny 23C5

Avenue de la Gare. **GPS**: n46,06096 e6,37874.

4 free Ch free. **Surface:** asphalted.
Distance: on the spot 60m nearby on the spot.
Remarks: Nearby railway station.

S St.Rémèze 30A3

Les Chais du Vivarais, D362. **GPS**: n44,39536 e4,50576.

FR

free Chfree. **Surface:** asphalted. 01/03-15/11
Distance: 500m 200m.
Remarks: Max. 48h.

Tourist information St.Rémèze:
Grotte de la Madelaine.Caves. Apr-Oct 10-18h.
Grotte de Marzal.Caves. Sa/Su/Holidays, 01/04-30/09 10.30-18h.
M Musée de la lavande.Museum and distillery with lavender fields.
01/05-30/09 10-17h, Apr + Oct Sa-Su-holiday 10-17h.

S St.Romain-de-Lerps 30A1

Le Village, D287. **GPS:** n44,98029 e4,79596.

10 free Ch € 4,100 liter water + 1h electricity WC. **Location:** Rural, simple, quiet. **Surface:** gravel. 01/01-31/12 01/10 en 01/04.
Distance: 100m 100m bakery 100m.
Remarks: Panoramic view over the Rhône-valley 200m, less suitable for motorhomes >6,5m, coins at bakery, bar/resto 3duPic and town hall.

N107, Les Crottes. **GPS:** n44,50059 e4,63445.

S St.Thomé 30A2

1 free Chfree. **Surface:** asphalted.

Base Nautique du lac de Grangent. GPS: n45,44787 e4,25626.

S St.Victor-sur-Loire 29D1

10 free Chfree (4x)€ [illegible]0/4h WC **Location:** Rural, comfortable.
Surface: asphalted. 01/01-31/12
Distance: on the spot on the spot on the spot.
Remarks: Max. 72h, coins available in village.

Route de Bollène, D94. **GPS:** n44,28598 e4,83185.

S Suze-la-Rousse 30A3

gratis free. **Surface:** grassy/gravel. 01/01-31/12
Distance: 850m on the spot on the spot.
Remarks: Next to sports fields.

S Suze-la-Rousse 30A3

50 Impasse de la Zone Artisanale. **GPS:** n44,28965 e4,84783.

Chfree. 01/01-31/12
Distance: 1,5km.

S Thueyts 29D2

Chemin d'Echelle du Roi, via N102. **GPS:** n44,67274 e4,21917.

10 free € 2 Ch € 2/10minutes. **Location:** Rural, simple, quiet.
Surface: grassy/gravel. 01/01-31/12
Distance: 200m 200m on the spot.
Remarks: Max. 24h, near the Ardèche river and Pont du Diable.

S Tournon-sur-Rhône 30A1

Chemin de la Beaume/D86. **GPS:** n45,07337 e4,82150.

25 € 5 Chfree. **Location:** Urban, simple. **Surface:** asphalted.
01/01-31/12
Distance: 1km 5km 1km 1km.

Tourist information Tournon-sur-Rhône:
Office de Tourisme, Hôtel de la Tourette, www.ville-tournon.com.
Wed, Sa.
Route Panoramique, place Jean Jaurès.Starting point touristic route.

S Treffort 30B2

Plage de la Salette, D110b. **GPS:** n44,90732 e5,67208.

FR

12 € 9,50 € 2 Ch € 2 WC. **Surface:** gravel.
01/05-31/10
Distance: 3km lake lake on the spot on the spot on the spot.
Remarks: At lake Monteynard.

S Trévoux 22D5

Chemin du Camping. **GPS**: n45,94017 e4,76694.

4 € 5 € 2 Ch. **Location:** Urban, simple, central, quiet.
Surface: grassy/metalled.
01/01-31/12
Distance: on the spot 7km 100m 1km 1km 1km.
Remarks: At entrance campsite, along the river, pay at campsite or town hall.

S Ugine 23C6

Place du 8 Mai 1945. **GPS**: n45,74634 e6,41774.
free € 2 € 2. **Surface:** asphalted. 01/01-31/12
Distance: 50m 50m 50m.

Tourist information Ugine:
Syndicat d'Initiative, 15 Place du Val d'Arly, www.ugine.com.
Wed, Sa-morning.

Valloire 30C1

Rue de la Bonne Eau. **GPS**: n45,16824 e6,42893.
free. **Surface:** gravel. 01/01-31/12

S Valloire 30C1

Route des Villards. **GPS**: n45,16566 e6,42978.
Ch . 01/01-31/12
Distance: ± 800m.
Remarks: Nearby camping-municipal.

S Vallon-Pont-d'Arc 30A3

Chemin du Chastelas. **GPS**: n44,40537 e4,39683.

20 € 6/24h € 2 Ch € 2 WC. 01/01-31/12
Distance: 100m 100m 100m.
Remarks: Free shuttle to the Pont d'Arc, 2x per hour.

S Vallon-Pont-d'Arc 30A3

Domaine de l'Esquiras, Chemin du Fez. **GPS**: n44,41583 e4,37738.

5 € 8, peak season € 10 + € 0,60/pp tourist tax Ch € 3 WC
free. **Surface:** gravel. 12/04-21/09
Distance: 800m.
Remarks: Use sanitary facilities + swimming pool € 4/pp.

Tourist information Vallon-Pont-d'Arc:
Office de Tourisme, 1, place de l'ancienne gare, www.vallon-pont-darc.com. Small tourist town with the well-known Pont d'Arc, a natural arc over the Ardèche river.
Grotte des Huguenots.Former shelter of the Huguenots.
15/06-31/08.
Ma Magnanerie, Lagorce.Silkworm farm.
Easter -15/09 Mo/Sa 10-12h, 14-18h.
Thu-morning.

S Valvignères 30A2

Le Colombier. **GPS**: n44,49904 e4,57672.

€ 7,70, 2 pers.incl. Chfree. 27/03-30/09 Service: winter.

S Vassieux-en-Vercors 30B2

Avenue du Mémorial, D76. **GPS**: n44,89703 e5,36927.

30 free Chfree. **Location:** Rural, simple.
Surface: metalled.
Distance: 200m 200m 200m on the spot 7km Font D'Urle on the spot.
Remarks: Next to football ground.

S Vaujany 30C1

Télécabine. **GPS**: n45,15694 e6,08011.

FR

15 free Chfree € 5. **Surface:** gravel. 01/01-31/12
Distance: 300m 300m 300m 300m.
Remarks: Max. 24h, coins at Office de Tourisme (electricity).

S Vienne 22D6

Place Joseph Muray et Jean Tardy, N7. **GPS**: n45,53860 e4,87271.

10 free Chfree. **Location:** Urban, simple, central, noisy.
Surface: asphalted.
Distance: 50m 2km 50m 50m 50m.

Villards-de-Lans 30B1

Chemin des Bartavelles. **GPS**: n45,06681 e5,55584.

15 free. **Surface:** asphalted.
Remarks: Max. 48h.

Villars-les-Dombes 22D5

Parc des Oiseaux, RN83. **GPS**: n45,99126 e5,02582.

100 free. **Location:** Simple, quiet. **Surface:** asphalted/grassy.
01/01-31/12 sundays, holidays, winter.
Distance: 2km 1km 1km 2km 2km on the spot.
Remarks: Parking bird park, max. 1 night, gate closed from 21-8h.

Tourist information Villars-les-Dombes:
Parc des Oiseaux.Bird park, 23ha. 8.30-19h, winter 8.30-17.30h. € 10.

S Villerest 22C5

Aire camping-car du Grezelon, D18, Route de Seigne. **GPS**: n45,98610 e4,04300.

15 € 5 € 4 Ch. **Surface:** gravel.
01/01-31/12 service: 01/10-30/04.
Distance: on the spot 1km on the spot.
Remarks: Max. 48h, at Lac du Villerest and barrage.

S Violay 22C6

Place Giroud. **GPS**: n45,85268 e4,35564.

2 free free Ch. **Location:** Rural, simple, quiet. **Surface:** metalled.
01/01-31/12
Distance: 100m A89 9km 200m 150m.
Remarks: Beautiful view.

S Virieu 30B1

Rue du May, D17. **GPS**: n45,48166 e5,47746.

4 free Ch WC free. **Location:** Rural, simple, central, quiet.
Surface: gravel.
Distance: on the spot 200m 200m on the spot.
Remarks: Picnic area at edge of the village.

S Viviers 30A2

Rue Valpeyrousse. **GPS**: n44,48225 e4,67999.

26 € 6,50 Ch WC included. **Location:** Rural, luxurious, quiet. **Surface:** metalled. 15/04-29/09
Distance: 1km 1km.
Remarks: Former campsite.

Tourist information Viviers:
Office de Tourisme, 5, Place Riquet.
Tue.

Vogüé 30A2

Chemin de Setras. **GPS**: n44,55163 e4,41308.

20 free. **Surface:** asphalted. 01/01-31/12

FR

Distance: 50m Ardèche 200m.
Remarks: At cemetery.

Aquitaine

S Aire-sur-l'Adour 28B4

Rue des Graviers. **GPS**: n43,70333 w0,25535.

50 €3 €1 Ch. **Location:** Simple, quiet. **Surface:** gravel. 01/01-31/12 3rd week Jun.
Distance: 200m on the spot on the spot.
Remarks: Max. 72h, near campsite.

S Amou 28B4

Stade de Sport, Promenade pour Piétons. **GPS**: n43,58917 w0,74083.

10 free Ch free. **Surface:** asphalted. 01/01-31/12
Distance: 1km on the spot on the spot 1km 1km.

S Andernos-les-Bains 28A2

Port Ostréicole, Avenue du Commandant Allègre. **GPS**: n44,74400 w1,10823.

60 €7,70 €2,15/10liter Ch . **Surface:** grassy. 01/01-31/12
Distance: 50m.
Remarks: In harbour, max. 48h.

S Anglet 28A4

Parking des Corsaires, Boulevard des Plages. **GPS**: n43,50696 w1,53373.

72 free, July-Aug €7 Ch included. **Surface:** asphalted.
Distance: 500m 500m 500m 500m.
Remarks: Baker every morning, max. 24h, Biarritz 2km. D5, Boulevard des Plages.

S Anglet 28A4

Terroirs d'Aventures, Avenue de l'Adour, D405. **GPS**: n43,52608 w1,51488.

10 €6 €3 Ch. **Surface:** sand. 01/07-31/08
Distance: 1km 300m 50m 500m 500m 100m.
Remarks: Private property.

S Arcachon 28A2

Boulevard Mestrézat, D650. **GPS**: n44,65094 w1,15002.

20 free Chfree. **Location:** Urban, simple, noisy. **Surface:** gravel. 01/01-31/12
Distance: 1km 50m.
Remarks: Max. 24h.

Tourist information Arcachon:
Office de Tourisme, Esplanade G. Pompidou, www.arcachon.com.Bathing resort.
place du XI Novembre.Covered market. 01/06-31/08 daily 7-13h.

S Arzacq-Arraziguet 28B4

Aire de camping cars, Place du Marcadieu. **GPS**: n43,53481 w0,41035.

10 free Ch free. **Surface:** asphalted. 01/01-31/12
Distance: on the spot 500m 500m 100m 100m.
Remarks: In village.

S Azerat 28D1

Le Bourg. **GPS**: n45,14954 e1,12496.

6 €2 €3 Ch. **Location:** Simple, quiet. **Surface:** gravel.

FR

01/01-31/12
Distance: 50m.
Remarks: Pay at town hall.

S Badefols-sur-Dordogne 28D2

Le Bourg. **GPS:** n44,84254 e0,79160.

10 free € 2 Ch. **Surface:** asphalted.
01/01-31/12 Sa market.
Distance: on the spot bakery 50m.
Remarks: Coins at town hall.

S Bazas 28B2

Cours Gambetta/Allée des Tilleuls. **GPS:** n44,43389 w0,21509.

free Ch WC free. **Location:** Simple, noisy. **Surface:** asphalted.
01/01-31/12
Distance: 200m 3,1km 350m 300m.

S Beaumont du Périgord 28D2

Avenue Rhinau, D660. **GPS:** n44,77469 e0,76559.

40 free Ch free. **Surface:** asphalted. 01/01-31/12
Distance: 800m.
Remarks: Behind community centre.

S Bergerac 28C1

Parc Public de Pombonne, Route de Podestat. **GPS:** n44,87296 e0,49720.
6 free € 2/100liter . **Surface:** metalled.
Remarks: Max. 24h.

Tourist information Bergerac:

Office de Tourisme, 97, rue Neuve d'Argenson, www.bergerac-tourisme.com. Small port city, worth seeing is the old city centre.
Musée du Tabac, Maison Peyrarède, Place du Feu.History of tobacco.
Mo-Fri 10-12h, 14-18, Sa 10-12h, 14-17h, Su 14.30-17.30h, Nov-Mar Mo-Fr.
Église Notre Dame, Rue Saint Esprit.
Wed, Sa 7-13h.

S Bernos-Beaulac 28B2

La Grande Route, N524. **GPS:** n44,36946 w0,24355.

10 free € 2 Ch. **Location:** Simple, quiet. **Surface:** metalled.
01/01-31/12 water: frost.
Distance: river on the spot bakery 100m.
Remarks: Coins at petrol station.

Beynac-et-Cazenac 28D2

Le Parc, D703. **GPS:** n44,84466 e1,14560.

free. **Surface:** gravel. 01/01-31/12
Distance: 100m, ville historique 500m.

S Biarritz 37D4

Parking Milady, Avenue de la Milady, Biarritz-sud, D911dir Bidart. **GPS:** n43,46520 w1,57194.

40 € 10 Ch included. **Surface:** asphalted. 15/05-15/10
Distance: 500m 300m 500m 500m.

Tourist information Biarritz:

Office de Tourisme, Square d'Ixelles, www.biarritz.fr.Glamorous bathing resort with old centre. Important surf centre.
Rue des Halles. daily.

Biron 28D2

Route de Vergt de Biron. **GPS:** n44,63080 e0,87055.

10 free. **Surface:** grassy/metalled. 01/01-31/12
Distance: 250m.
Remarks: From Monpazier, dir Villéral then exit Biron, from Villérial dir Monpazier exit Biron.

FR

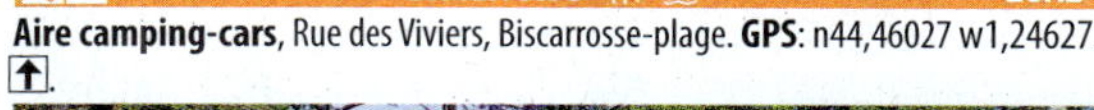

Biscarrosse 28A2

Aire camping-cars, Rue des Viviers, Biscarrosse-plage. **GPS**: n44,46027 w1,24627.

100 free, € 12 (May-Sept) Ch WC. **Location:** Simple, quiet. **Surface:** forest soil.
01/05-31/10
Distance: 400m Superette 100m 50m.
Remarks: No camping activities, guarded (jul/aug), shady.

Biscarrosse 28A2

Biscarrosse Plage Sud, Chemin de Navarosse. **GPS**: n44,43223 w1,16566.

30 1/7-31/8 € 8 Chfree. **Location:** Simple. **Surface:** metalled.
01/05-31/10
Distance: 50m 100m 50m.
Remarks: No camping activities, guarded (jul/aug).

Biscarrosse 28A2

Centre Leclerc, Avenue Laouadie. **GPS**: n44,41063 w1,16803.
free Chfree WC. **Location:** Simple.
Surface: asphalted.
Distance: on the spot on the spot on the spot.

Tourist information Biscarrosse:
Office de Tourisme, 55, place G. Dufau, Biscarrosse-plage, www.biscarrosse.com.Bathing resort between lakes. Many beaches and water sports.

Blaye 28B1

Parking de la Citadelle. **GPS**: n45,12521 w0,66623.
free. **Surface:** metalled. 01/01-31/12
Distance: 250m 300m.

Bouglon 28C2

Le Clavier. **GPS**: n44,38599 e0,10271.

4 free WC. **Location:** Simple, quiet. **Surface:** asphalted.
01/01-31/12
Distance: 500m 500m 500m.
Remarks: Picnic area.

Bourdeilles 28D1

Plaine de loisirs. **GPS**: n45,32270 e0,58260.

20+ € 3 € 2 Ch. **Location:** Comfortable, quiet. **Surface:** grassy.
01/01-31/12
Distance: on the spot on the spot 200m 200m.
Remarks: Coins at town hall.

Tourist information Bourdeilles:
Syndicat d'Initiative, Place des Tilleuls, www.bourdeilles.com.Historical small town around Château de Bourdeilles. Wed-Mo, 01/07-31/08 daily.

Bourg-sur-Gironde 28B1

Quai Jean Bart. **GPS**: n45,03794 w0,55762.
free. **Surface:** asphalted. 01/01-31/12
Distance: on the spot On the river Gironde.

Brantôme 28D1

Chemin de Vert Galant. **GPS**: n45,36134 e0,64842.

80 € 4 € 2 Ch. **Location:** Simple, quiet. **Surface:** grassy.
01/01-31/12
Distance: 200m 100m 300m.

Brantôme 28D1

Aire Camping-cars Font Vendôme, Route de Nontron. **GPS**: n45,37924 e0,64588.

4 € 5 Ch included. **Surface:** asphalted. 01/01-31/12
Distance: on the spot on the spot on the spot.

Tourist information Brantôme:
Office de Tourisme, Abbaye - Boulevard Charlemagne, www.ville-brantome.fr.
Fri-morning.

Buzet-sur-Baïse 28C3

Port de Buzet-Val d'Albret. **GPS**: n44,25799 e0,30569.

FR

20 free € 2 Ch € 2 WC € 2/24h. **Surface:** grassy.
Distance: 6,5km.

S Cadillac 28B2

Allée du Parc. **GPS:** n44,63871 w0,31721.

10 free Chfree € 2/3h. **Surface:** asphalted.
01/01-31/12
Distance: on the spot on the spot on the spot on the spot.
Remarks: Max. 3 nights, closed when frosty.

S Cancon 28D2

GPS: n44,53638 e0,62562.

10 free Ch WC free. **Surface:** metalled. 01/01-31/12
Distance: 100m 100m 100m.
Remarks: Via N21.

S Capbreton 28A4

Plage l'Océanide, Parking des Ortolans, Allée des Ortolans. **GPS:** n43,63578 w1,44681.

120 € 9 Ch (120x)included. **Surface:** asphalted.
Distance: 1,5km on the spot on the spot 1,5km 1,5km.
Remarks: Beach parking.

Capian 28B2

D13/Chemin de Lavergne. **GPS:** n44,71177 w0,33093.

25 . **Surface:** gravel.

S Carcans 28A1

Route de Bombannes, Maubuisson. **GPS:** n45,08545 w1,14866.

20 € 5,80/20-9h Ch free. **Surface:** asphalted/metalled.
01/06-31/09
Distance: on the spot.
Remarks: No parking, only overnight stays.

Tourist information Carcans:

Office de Tourisme, Maison de la Station, www.carcans-maubuisson.com. Touristic town between the ocean and a wine region, 120km signposted cycle routes.

S Casseneuil 28D2

Rue Grande, D225. **GPS:** n44,44667 e0,61861.

20 free Chfree. **Surface:** gravel. 01/01-31/12
Distance: 100m on the spot on the spot 100m 800m.

S Castelculier 28D3

GPS: n44,17475 e0,69452.

5 free € 2 Ch. **Surface:** metalled. 01/01-31/12
Distance: 200m.

S Casteljaloux 28C3

Ste Castel Chalets, D933. **GPS:** n44,29230 e0,07361.

FR

20 € 10 Ch WC included. **Location:** Comfortable, quiet. **Surface:** gravel/sand. 01/10-31/10
Distance: 2km Lac de Clarens.

S Casteljaloux 28C3

Impasse de la Fôret. **GPS**: n44,31056 e0,07861.

4 free Ch free. **Location:** Simple, quiet. **Surface:** asphalted. 01/01-31/12
Distance: 250m 250m.
Remarks: Parking at swimming pool.

S Caumont-sur-Garonne 28C2

Bourg de Caumont. **GPS**: n44,44202 e0,17887.

9 free € 1 Ch € 1/2h. **Surface:** gravel. 01/01-31/12
Distance: 8km.

Celles 28C1

Le Bourg. **GPS**: n45,29364 e0,41065.
free. **Surface:** unpaved.
Distance: Small lake.

S Château-l'Evêque 28D1

Place de la Fontaine. **GPS**: n45,24472 e0,68743.

8 free € 2 Ch € 2. **Surface:** gravel. 01/03-31/10 summer: Su (flea market).
Distance: 50m 100m on the spot.
Remarks: Max. 12h, coins at shops in the village 08-21h.

S Contis-Plage 28A3

Avenue du Phare. **GPS**: n44,09333 w1,31861.

76 € 7, 01/06-01/09 € 11/24h, 01/12-28/02 free € 2 Ch WC. **Location:** Simple. **Surface:** gravel. 01/01-31/12
Distance: 200m on the spot.
Remarks: Max. 72h.

S Créon 28B2

Vélo-centre, Boulevard Victor Hugo, D20. **GPS**: n44,77663 w0,34815.

5 free € 2 Ch € 2. **Surface:** asphalted. 01/01-31/12 tue-evening, wed-morning (market).

S Damazan 28C3

Chambre D'Hôtes Constantine, Route Cap de Bosc. **GPS**: n44,28130 e0,26285.
6 € 5 Ch € 7 WC . 01/01-31/12
Distance: 500m 1km.

S Dax 28A4

Parking du Pont des Arènes, Boulevard des Sports. **GPS**: n43,71427 w1,04931.

8 free free. **Location:** Simple, noisy. **Surface:** asphalted. 01/01-31/12
Distance: on the spot.
Remarks: Max. 72h, sa market in the halls.

Tourist information Dax:
Office de Tourisme, 11, cours Foch, www.dax.fr.Health resort with warm water sources and medicinal mud.

S Domme 28D2

Le Pradal. **GPS**: n44,80053 e1,22156.

20 € 5 € 2/10minutes Ch € 2/1h. **Location:** Simple, quiet.

FR

Surface: asphalted. 01/01-31/12 Service: winter.
Distance: 500m 500m.
Remarks: Note: follow the signs, no gps-coordinates.

Tourist information Domme:
Office de Tourisme, Place de la Halle, www.ot-domme.com.Fortified city worth seeing, parking for motorhomes outside of the town, being indicated.

S Douchapt 28C1

Beauclair. **GPS**: n45,25145 e0,44335.
free € 2 Ch € 2. **Surface:** metalled. 01/01-31/12
Distance: 1,5km Dronne river.
Remarks: Coins at Village Vacances Beauclair.

Eaux-Bonnes 28C5

Parking du Ley. **GPS**: n42,96304 e0,33933.

20 free. **Surface:** asphalted. 01/01-31/12
Distance: 1,4km 1,4km 1,4km 1,4km.

S Espés Undurein 28A4

Etche Gochoki, D11. **GPS**: n43,26388 w0,88083.

6 € 8 € 2 Ch € 2. **Surface:** grassy/metalled. 01/01-31/12
Distance: 500m 500m 400m.

S Excideuil 28D1

rue Léon Barreau. **GPS**: n45,33605 e1,05239.

4 € 3 € 3 Ch . **Surface:** asphalted.

S Fontet 28C2

Base de Loisirs Fontet. **GPS**: n44,56118 w0,02282.

25 € 8 Ch WC included € 1. **Surface:** grassy/gravel. 01/01-31/12
Distance: on the spot bakery 500m, supermarket 4km.
Remarks: At lake.

Tourist information Fontet:
Musée d'Artisanat et Monuments d'Allumettes, 2, Couture.Exhibitions, monuments of matches and maquettes. 01/02-30/09 14-18h, 01/10-30/11 Su 14-18h.

S Fourques-sur-Garonne 28C2

Halte Nautique d Pont des Sables, Pont des Sables, D933. **GPS**: n44,46081 e0,13932.
4 free Ch . **Surface:** metalled. 01/03-31/10
Distance: Fourques 2,5km 3km.

S Frontenac 28C2

D236. **GPS**: n44,73781 w0,16308.

100 € 2,50 free. **Surface:** grassy. 01/01-31/12
Distance: 200m 200m bakery 200m.
Remarks: Max. 48h, behind town hall.

S Fumel 28D2

Place Du Saulou, rue Massenet, D911. **GPS**: n44,49809 e0,97165.

10 free Chfree. **Surface:** asphalted. 01/01-31/12
Distance: 200m 200m.
Remarks: Château de Bonaguil 7km.

Tourist information Fumel:
Office de Tourisme, Place Georges Escande, www.tourisme-fumelois.fr.
Château-fort de Bonaguil.Very well kept castle/fortress. 01/02-30/11, 10.30-12.30, 14-17.30h, 01/07-31/08 10-19h.

S Gastes 28A2

Port de Gastes, Avenue du lac. **GPS**: n44,32880 w1,15068.

100 € 2-4,50, 15/3-15/11 € 7 Ch WC included.
Location: Comfortable. **Surface:** grassy. 01/01-31/12 service in winter.
Distance: Parentis-en-Born 7km on the spot on the spot 800m 800m.
Remarks: Along lake, baker every morning.

FR

Gastes 28A2

Camping Les Echasses, 193 rue de Bernadon. **GPS**: n44,31871 w1,13879.

10 € 5-8 € 3 Ch included. **Location:** Simple. **Surface:** grassy. 01/01-31/12

Distance: Gastes Lac 2km on the spot.

Remarks: Max. 1 night, no camping activity.

Grenade-sur-l'Adour 28B3

Place du 19 mars 1962. **GPS**: n43,77500 w0,43472.

40 free Ch WC free. **Location:** Simple. **Surface:** asphalted/gravel.

Distance: 100m 100m 100m.

Remarks: Next to cemetery, max. 24h.

Hautefort 28D1

Route de Boisseuil. **GPS**: n45,25945 e1,14889.

5 free € 2 Ch € 2 WC. **Surface:** asphalted. 01/01-31/12

Distance: 50m 100m Intermarché 1km.

Tourist information Hautefort:

Office de Tourisme, Place du Marquis J. F. de Hautefort.

Château Hautefort.Classified castle. 01/04-30/09 daily, 01/10-31/03 afternoons.

Wed-morning.

Hendaye 37D4

Gare des deux Jumeaux, Rue d'Ansoenia. **GPS**: n43,37019 w1,7648.

12 free Ch free. **Surface:** asphalted. 01/01-31/12

Distance: on the spot 800m 450m 450m on the spot.

Remarks: Railway-station Hendaye-plage.

Hostens 28B2

Rue Chantegrue. **GPS**: n44,49321 w0,62898.

4 free service € 3 Ch . **Location:** Simple, quiet. 01/01-31/12

Distance: 1km on the spot on the spot on camp site on camp site.

Remarks: Next to campsite Ariales, June 2012 during inspection service out of order.

Houeillès 28C3

Aire de Repos, Rue du 19 Mars 1962. **GPS**: n44,19611 e0,03250.

free WC. **Location:** Simple, quiet. **Surface:** grassy/gravel. 01/01-31/12

Distance: 100m 250m.

Remarks: Max. 24h.

Hourtin 28A1

Mombet, Hourtin-Port. **GPS**: n45,18083 w1,08056.

90 € 5, 01/04-30/09 € 8,15 € 2 Ch WC. **Surface:** forest soil. 01/01-31/12

Distance: 50m 50m 50m.

Remarks: Parking in harbour.

La Chapelle-Faucher 28D1

Champignonnière de Rochevideau, D78. **GPS**: n45,36195 e0,74112.

6 € 3 Ch free. **Location:** Simple, quiet. **Surface:** concrete. 01/01-31/12

FR

Distance: 4km 4km.

La Coquille 21A6

N21, Place de l'église. **GPS**: n45,54250 e0,97778.

5 free Ch WC free. **Location:** Simple, central. **Surface:** asphalted.
01/01-31/12
Distance: 100m 200m 200m.

La Pierre-Saint-Martin 28B5

Aire de campingcar de la Pierre-Saint-Martin, Braça de Guilhers. **GPS**: n42,97918 w0,7487.

40 free Ch € 10/2kWh,(winter).
Surface: asphalted.
01/01-31/12
Distance: 300m 300m 150m.

La Réole 28C2

Les Justices, Avenue Gabriel-Chaigne. **GPS**: n44,58057 w0,03018.
10 € 4 Chfree. **Surface:** grassy. 15/04-01/10
Remarks: Centre ville, D1113 diri Marmande Agen, nearby Musée Automobile et Militaire.

La Roche-Chalais 28C1

Parking Intermarché, d'Avenue d'Aquitaine. **GPS**: n45,15043 e0,01245.
Ch. **Surface:** asphalted. 01/01-31/12

La Roque-Gageac 28D2

D703. **GPS**: n44,82428 e1,18376.

20 € 7 € 2/10minutes Ch € 2/1h.
Surface: metalled.
01/01-31/12
Distance: on the spot on the spot on the spot 200m 200m.
Remarks: Along the Dordogne river.

Tourist information La Roque-Gageac:
www.cc-perigord-noir.fr.Small town worth seeing, in the Dordogne valley.

Labastide-d'Armagnac 28B3

Les Embarrats. **GPS**: n43,97205 w0,18602.

20 free Chfree. **Location:** Rural, simple, quiet.
Surface: grassy.
Distance: 300m.

Labenne 28A4

Route Océane. **GPS**: n43,59616 w1,45492.

50 € 7,50 Ch included. **Surface:** metalled. 10/04-02/10
Distance: 1km 2km 2km 1km 1km.
Remarks: Max. 48h, camping forbidden.

Lacanau 28A1

Le Huga, Rue des Sauviels. **GPS**: n45,00583 w1,16528.

125 € 13/24h Ch included. 01/01-31/12
Remarks: In front of heliport, max. 48h.

Ladaux 28B2

Vignobles Lobre & Fils, Le Bos. **GPS**: n44,69677 w0,24393.

5 free WC. **Surface:** grassy/metalled. 01/01-31/12
Distance: 300m.

Lanouaille 28D1

Rue du Chemin Neuf. **GPS**: n45,39248 e1,14002.

FR

6 free Ch WC free. **Location:** Comfortable, central, quiet. **Surface:** asphalted. 01/01-31/12
Distance: 50m 100m 100m.
Remarks: Max. 48h.

S Lanton 28A2

Allée Albert Pitres, Taussat. **GPS:** n44,71710 w1,06991.

10 free Ch free. **Surface:** asphalted. 01/01-31/12
Distance: sandy beach 100m.

S Laruns 28B5

Artouste Fabrèges. **GPS:** n42,87914 w0,39693.

20 free € 4/100liter Ch € 4/1h WC. **Surface:** asphalted. 01/01-31/12
Distance: 200m on the spot on the spot on the spot on the spot 1km.
Remarks: Coins at Office de Tourisme. Parking in centre, 20km from Laruns, follow signs hamlet Artouste Fabrèges, along lake.

S Laruns 28B5

Avenue de la Gare. **GPS:** n42,98819 w0,42458.

25 free € 3,10 Ch WC. **Surface:** asphalted. 01/01-31/12
Distance: 450m 450m 450m 400m.
Remarks: Max. 24h, coins at Office de Tourisme.

S Laruns 28B5

Parking Eaux-Chaudes. **GPS:** n42,95444 w0,43833.

5 € 3 Ch WC. **Surface:** asphalted. 01/01-31/12
Distance: on the spot on the spot on the spot on the spot 100m 100m 100m. **Remarks:** Coins at Office de Tourisme.

Tourist information Laruns:

Office de Tourisme, Maison de la Vallée d'Ossau, www.tourisme64.com, www.station-artouste.com.Summer and winter destination, thermal centre. Route to the Col d'Aubisque (Tour de France).

Le Petit Train d' Artouste, Artouste Fabrèges.This sightseeing electric train, which connects Fabrèges lake with Artouste lake, 2,000 meters in altitude, enables you to discover the highest and most beautiful summits of the Atlantic Pyrenees. 01/05-30/09.

La Falaise aux Vautours, Aste Béon.Vultures being watched by camera and visible on a huge screen. 01/04-31/10 14-17/18, 01/06-31/08 10.30-12.30 14/17/18.

S Lavardac 28C3

Rue de la Victoire - Place du Foirail. **GPS:** n44,17883 e0,29928.

3 free Ch free. **Location:** Simple. **Surface:** asphalted.
Distance: on the spot 22km bakery 150m.

S Layrac 28D3

Aire de Layrac, Rue du 19 Mars 1962. **GPS:** n44,13233 e0,65946.
6 free Ch WC free. **Surface:** asphalted.

S Layrac 28D3

Le Moulin, D129. **GPS:** n44,13675 e0,66533.

max. 4 € 10/24h Ch . **Surface:** grassy. 01/01-31/12
Distance: on the spot.
Remarks: Call if no one is present.

S Le Bugue 28D1

Place Léopold Salme. **GPS:** n44,91679 e0,92775.

FR

+50 free Ch free. **Location:** Simple. **Surface:** metalled.
01/01-31/12 Service: winter.
Distance: 200m 20m 100m Intermarché 100m.
Remarks: Along the river Vézère.

Le Bugue 28D1

Aux Etangs du Bos, Audrix, St Chamassy. **GPS:** n44,86820 e0,96920.
Distance: Etang de Bos.
Remarks: Recreation park, not accessible with heavy rainfall.

Le Porge 28A1

Avenue de l'Océan. **GPS:** n44,89437 w1,2131.

free. **Surface:** forest soil. 01/01-31/12
Distance: Le Porge 10km.
Remarks: Max. 24h.

Le Porge 28A1

Intermarché. **GPS:** n44,87574 w1,07883.
€ 2 Ch.

Le Temple-sur-Lot 28C2

Avenue de Verdun. **GPS:** n44,38000 e0,52639.

4 free Ch WC free. **Surface:** asphalted. 01/01-31/12
Distance: 50m 100m.

Le Verdon-sur-Mer 20B6

Plage fluviale, Allée des Baïnes. **GPS:** n45,54582 w1,05433.

30+20 € 5/24h, 01/06-30/09 € 8/24h € 2 Ch. **Surface:** gravel.
01/01-31/12

Distance: 50m 500m 2km on the spot.
Remarks: Coins available at town hall, office de Tourisme and the shops at the beach.

Lège-Cap-Ferret 28A2

Route des Pastourelles, Avenue Charles de Gaulle, D106, Claouey. **GPS:** n44,75127 w1,18033.

± 15 free Ch Service € 3,30/15min. **Surface:** forest soil.
01/01-31/12
Remarks: Coins at camping municipal, day parking also allowed, overnight stay on motorhome stopovers.

Lège-Cap-Ferret 28A2

Avenue Edouard Branly. **GPS:** n44,75203 w1,18809.

15 free. **Surface:** forest soil.
Remarks: Near campsite Les Embruns.

Lège-Cap-Ferret 28A2

D106, Avenue de Bordeaux, L'Herbe. **GPS:** n44,68655 w1,2451.

15 free. **Surface:** unpaved.

Léon 28A3

Aire camping-cars, Route de Puntaou. **GPS:** n43,88444 w1,31861.

150 € 10 Ch included. **Location:** Simple. **Surface:** grassy/gravel. 01/04-31/10
Distance: 1km 250m 50m 50m 50m.
Remarks: Nearby lake.

Les Eyzies 28D1

Parking de la Vézère, Promenade de la Vézère. **GPS:** n44,93863 e1,00907.

FR

25 € 4/night € 2/100liter Ch. **Location:** Comfortable, quiet. **Surface:** grassy. 01/01-31/12
Distance: 100m 100m 100m.
Remarks: Along the river Vézère, summer max. 48h, parking fee being collected at 9AM.

Tourist information Les Eyzies:
Office de Tourisme, 19, rue de la Préhistoire.Also called the prehistoric capital.
Le Village Troglodytique de la Madeleine, Turzac.Troglodyte-village.
Le Village du Bournat, Le Bugue.Open air museum. 01/04-31/10 10-17/18h.
Musée Préhistorique National, 1, rue du musée.Collection of flint and other objects. 01/10-31/03. € 5.

S Lhers 28B5

La Nabe. **GPS**: n42,91028 w0,61939.

20-25 € 7 Ch WC included. **Location:** Rural, comfortable, isolated, quiet. **Surface:** gravel.
Distance: 7km 100m on the spot.

S Lit-et-Mixe 28A3

Cap de l'Homy, 600, avenue Océan. **GPS**: n44,03846 w1,33764.

36 € 8-15 Ch WC. **Location:** Simple, quiet. **Surface:** forest soil. 01/01-31/12
Distance: on the spot 200m 200m on the spot.
Remarks: Next to campsite municipal.

S L'Hôpital-St.Blaise 28B4

Parking l'Église. **GPS**: n43,25088 w0,76925.

5 free WC. **Surface:** asphalted. 01/01-31/12
Distance: on the spot on the spot on the spot on the spot.

Macau 28B1

Domaine du Prat, 51, Avenue de la Coste. **GPS**: n45,00380 w0,60508.

5 free. **Location:** Simple. 01/01-31/12
Distance: on the spot.

S Macau 28B1

Chemin du Mahoura. **GPS**: n45,00722 w0,61278.

Ch free. 01/01-31/12

S Marmande 28C2

La Filhole, Rue de la Filhole. **GPS**: n44,49667 e0,16412.

50 € 5 Ch. **Surface:** grassy. 03/06-05/09

S Marmande 28C2

Place du Moulin. **GPS**: n44,49833 e0,16028.

FR

2 free Ch free. **Surface:** asphalted. 15/09-15/05
Distance: 150m on the spot.
Remarks: Max. 48h.

Mensignac 28D1

Combecouyere-Sud. **GPS**: n45,22309 e0,56553.
3 free € 2 Ch. **Surface:** gravel. 01/03-31/10

Messanges 28A3

Plage principale, Avenue de la Plage. **GPS**: n43,81549 w1,40088.

10 free. **Location:** Simple. **Surface:** metalled/sand.
Distance: 1,5km 750m.
Remarks: Max. 48h.

Mimizan 28A3

Hélistation Plage Sud, Rue des Lacs, Mimizan-Plage. **GPS**: n44,20517 w1,29675.

85 € 8, 01/06-30/09 € 12 Ch included. **Location:** Comfortable. **Surface:** asphalted. 01/01-31/12
Distance: 500m on the spot 500m 200m.
Remarks: Parking at dune, no trailers allowed.

Mimizan 28A3

Route du C.E.L.. **GPS**: n44,21375 w1,28239.

100 € 6 € 3 Ch. **Location:** Simple. **Surface:** grassy/gravel.
summer
Distance: beach 1,5km on the spot.

Mimizan 28A3

Camping du Lac, Avenue de Woolsack, Mimizan-lac. **GPS**: n44,21956 w1,22972.

21 € 10-15, 2 pers.incl, tourist tax excl., dog € 1,05-1,82 € 2 Ch.
Location: Comfortable. **Surface:** gravel. 01/04-30/09

Moliets-et-Maa 28A3

Avenue de l'Océan, Moliets-Plage. **GPS**: n43,85091 w1,38188.

50 € 5, 1/6-50/11 € 11 Ch WC. **Location:** Comfortable, noisy. **Surface:** grassy/gravel.
Distance: 200m 750m 200m 200m.
Remarks: Shady.

Monbahus 28C2

Le Bourg, D124. **GPS**: n44,54738 e0,53517.
3 free Ch free. **Surface:** asphalted.
01/01-31/12 Service: winter.
Remarks: Steep entrance road, beautiful view.

Monbazillac 28C2

Château du Haut Pezaud, Les Pezauds. **GPS**: n44,78471 e0,48687.

10 free free € 1 WC € 1. **Surface:** grassy.
01/01-31/12
Distance: table d'hôtes.
Remarks: Tasting of regional products.

Monbazillac 28C2

Domaine La Lande, Route de Ribagnac, D13. **GPS**: n44,78822 e0,49587.

10 free Ch WC free. **Surface:** grassy. 01/01-31/12

FR

Remarks: Sale of wine on the spot.

Monflanquin 28D2

Zone commercial, D124. **GPS:** n44,52477 e0,75642.

5 free Chfree. **Surface:** gravel. 01/01-31/12
Distance: 1,3km 100m.

Tourist information Monflanquin:
Office de Tourisme, Place des Arcades, www.monflanquin-tourisme.com. Medieval town.

Monpazier 28D2

La Duelle-nord. **GPS:** n44,68499 e0,89362.

10 free Chfree. **Surface:** gravel. 01/01-31/12
Distance: 200m.
Remarks: Square behind fire-station.

Monségur 28C2

Place du 8 mai. **GPS:** n44,65060 e0,08363.

5 free Ch WC free. **Surface:** asphalted. 01/01-31/12
Distance: nearby.
Remarks: Max. 48h. No access via La Bastide.

Montalivet-les-Bains 20B6

Avenue de l'Europe. **GPS:** n45,37349 w1,1442.

30 € 8 Ch included. **Location:** Quiet. **Surface:** forest soil.
01/05-30/09
Distance: 800m nearby nearby.
Remarks: Max. 48h.

Montalivet-les-Bains 20B6

Boulevard de Lattre de Tassigny, Montalivet-sud. **GPS:** n45,37611 w1,15667.

30 € 5 € 1 Ch. **Surface:** grassy/metalled. 01/05-30/09
Distance: on the spot.
Remarks: Parking at sea, max. 48h.

Tourist information Montalivet-les-Bains:
Fri.

Montcaret 28C1

Le Chalet du Gourmet, D936. **GPS:** n44,85349 e0,03964.

16 € 6,50 Ch € 2 WC € 2 € 3.
Surface: grassy.
01/01-31/12
Distance: Resto Rapid.
Remarks: Bread-service, fruit-vegetables-wine-regional products for sale.

Monteton 28C2

D423. **GPS:** n44,62226 e0,25635.

25 free Chfree. **Surface:** grassy. 01/01-31/12
Distance: on the spot.
Remarks: Beautiful view.

Montignac 28D1

Avenue Aristide Briand, D65. **GPS:** n45,06083 e1,15888.

20 free Ch WC free. **Location:** Simple. **Surface:** asphalted.
01/01-31/12
Distance: on the spot 300m 500m.
Remarks: Along the river Vézère, next to sports fields, sometimes forbidden.

FR

Montignac 28D1

Avenue Alsace-Loraine. **GPS**: n45,06800 e1,16547.

20 free. **Location:** Simple, central. **Surface:** gravel.
01/01-31/12
Distance: 200m 200m 200m.

Montignac 28D1

P Vieux Quartiers. **GPS**: n45,06781 e1,16486.
free. 01/01-31/12
Distance: centre 500m 250m.

Montignac 28D1

Ferme du Bois Bareirou, Les Baraques, Montignac-Lascaux. **GPS**: n45,09053 e1,11143.

20 free € 3 Ch € 3. **Surface:** grassy. 01/01-31/12
Distance: 5km.
Remarks: Max. 3 days.

Montpon-Ménestérol 28C1

Chez Lou Cantou, 46 rue Gustave Eiffel, D730. **GPS**: n45,02101 e0,15997.
4 € 10/24h € 3/100liter Ch € 3.
01/04-31/10 frost.

Morcenx 28A3

Chemin des Abattoirs. **GPS**: n44,03811 w0,90914.

free Chfree. **Location:** Simple.
Distance: 500m 8,8km.
Remarks: Along railwayline.

Mugron 28B4

Avenue des Martyrs de la Résistance, D32e. **GPS**: n43,74846 w0,75063.

4 free Ch (4x)free. **Location:** Rural, simple.
Surface: gravel.
Distance: 300m on the spot.
Remarks: Max. 24h.

Nailhac 28D1

Ferme de la Jalovie. **GPS**: n45,23640 e1,13569.

6 free Ch free. **Surface:** metalled. 01/01-31/12

Nérac 28C3

Place du Foirail. **GPS**: n44,13435 e0,33655.

10 free WC. **Location:** Simple. **Surface:** asphalted.
01/01-31/12
Distance: 50m on the spot on the spot.

Nontron 21A6

Super U, 26, Avenue Jules Ferry. **GPS**: n45,53670 e0,66660.

3 free € 2 Ch € 2. **Location:** Noisy. **Surface:** asphalted.
01/03-31/10
Distance: 1km 1km on the spot.
Remarks: Parking supermarket, max. 24h.

Oloron-Sainte-Marie 28B5

Parking Trivoli, Rue Adour Oloron. **GPS**: n43,18371 w0,60845.

FR

7 free € 4/55minutes Ch € 4/55minutes. **Surface:** asphalted.
01/01-31/12
Distance: 100m on the spot on the spot 400m 400m.
Remarks: Max. 48h.

S Ondres 28A4

P3, Avenue de la Plage, Ondres-Plage. **GPS**: n43,57611 w1,48611.

41 € 7, 01/07-31/08 € 9 Ch WC free. **Surface:** asphalted.
01/06-30/09
Distance: 3km on the spot on the spot on the spot on the spot.
Remarks: Service also in winter available, 01/07-31/08 max. 48h. Third beach parking on the right.

S Parentis-en-Born 28A2

Site du Lac, Route des Campings. **GPS**: n44,34432 w1,09879.

30 € 7 Ch (4x)included. **Location:** Comfortable. **Surface:** gravel.
01/01-31/12 service in winter.
Distance: 3km 50m 50m.

Pau 28B4

Place de Verdun, Rue Ambroise Bordelongue. **GPS**: n43,29876 w0,37589.

20 free. **Surface:** asphalted. 01/01-31/12
Distance: on the spot on the spot 200m.

S Pellegrue 28C2

Le Touran, Rue du Lavoir. **GPS**: n44,74498 e0,07528.

4 free Ch free. **Surface:** metalled.
01/01-31/12
Distance: 100m.
Remarks: To edge of town.

S Périgueux 28D1

Espace des Prés, Rue des Prés. **GPS**: n45,18770 e0,73081.

40 € 5 Ch included. **Location:** Comfortable, central.
Surface: asphalted. 01/01-31/12 water disconnected in winter.
Distance: 800m on the spot.
Remarks: Max. 2 nights.

Tourist information Périgueux:

Office de Tourisme, 26, place Francheville, Tour Mataguerre, www.tourisme-perigueux.fr.Old city, la Cité, the old Vesunna, with remainders, excavation of the old Roman city, many antique stores.

Le Musée d'art et d'archéologie du Périgord, 22 cours Tourny.Collection of prehistoric findings.

S Peyrehorade 28A4

Des Gaves, Route de la Pêcherie. **GPS**: n43,54300 w1,1071.
16 € 8 Ch € 2,50 WC. **Surface:** grassy.
01/06-30/09
Distance: 150m on the spot on the spot 150m 150m 200m.

S Peyrehorade 28A4

Place Jean Bridart, Route de Sorde l'Abbaye D817. **GPS**: n43,54300 w1,09994.

10 free Ch free. **Surface:** metalled. 01/01-31/12
Distance: 50m on the spot on the spot 100m on the spot.
Remarks: In front of supermarket Carrefour.

S Preignac 28B2

Parking de la Mairie, D1113. **GPS**: n44,58551 w0,29597.

FR

10 free Chfree. **Surface:** asphalted. 01/01-31/12
Distance: on the spot 6,8km 250m.

S Ribérac 28C1

Place Pradeau. **GPS:** n45,24931 e0,33771.

4 free Chfree. **Surface:** asphalted.
01/01-31/12 Fri-morning.

S Ribérac 28C1

Aux Deux Ponts Ouest, D708. **GPS:** n45,25704 e0,34255.

10 free, 01/06-15/09 € 5 Chfree. **Surface:** gravel. 01/01-31/12
Water when frosty.
Distance: 50m Leclerc 900m.

S Saint Estèphe 21A6

Etang de Saint Estèphe. **GPS:** n45,59008 e0,67396.

10 free Chfree. **Location:** Comfortable. **Surface:** gravel.
01/01-31/12
Distance: 700m lake on the spot 3km, baker/ 800m.
Remarks: Summer: beach, bar, restaurant.

S Saint-Emilion 28C1

Château Gerbaud, St.Pey-d'Armens. **GPS:** n44,85310 w0,10699.

50 € 5 Ch (8x)€ 4. **Surface:** grassy. 01/01-31/12
Distance: 200m bakery 200m, supermarket 2km.
Remarks: Max. 48h.

S Saint-Estèphe 28B1

Rue des Pêcheurs. **GPS:** n45,26460 w0,75784.

5 free Ch Service € 5. **Surface:** metalled.
Remarks: Free, coins available at restaurant.

S Sainte-Colombe-en-Bruilhois 28C3

Lieu-dit Bécade. **GPS:** n44,17889 e0,51692.

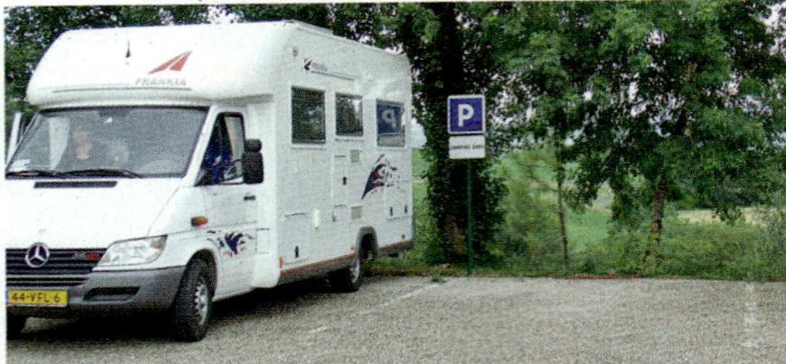

4 free Ch WC free. **Surface:** gravel. 01/01-31/12
Distance: on the spot.

S Sainte-Nathalène 28D1

Les Ch'tis, Le Bourg, D47. **GPS:** n44,90409 e1,28765.

6 € 10 Ch included. **Surface:** gravel. 01/01-31/12
Distance: Sarlat 7km 50m bread service 50m.

S Salies-de-Béarn 28A4

Aire Campincar du Herre, Quartiér du Herre. **GPS:** n43,47270 w0,9339.

24 € 6 Ch included. **Surface:** metalled. 01/01-31/12
Distance: 300m on the spot on the spot 300m 300m 300m.

S Salignac-Eyvigues 29A1

Rue des Ecoles. **GPS:** n44,97257 e1,32061.

10 free Ch free. **Location:** Comfortable, quiet. **Surface:** grassy.
01/01-31/12
Distance: 300m 300m 250m.

S Sanguinet 28A2

Aire du camping-car Les Bardets, 1131, Avenue de Losa. **GPS:** n44,48416 w1,09114.

15 free, € 7 (15/6-15/9) Ch free. **Location:** Simple, quiet.
Surface: metalled. 01/01-31/12
Distance: 800m on the spot on the spot 50m on the spot.
Remarks: At lake, max. 48h.

S Sanguinet 28A2

Parking du Pavillon, 459, Avenue de Losa. **GPS:** n44,48579 w1,08479.

30 free, € 8 (15/6-15/9) WC. **Location:** Simple, quiet. **Surface:** forest soil.
01/01-31/12
Distance: on the spot Le Pavillon.
Remarks: Max. 48h.

S Sare 37D4

Place de Campingcars de Sare. **GPS:** n43,31307 w1,57679.

10 € 6 Ch included. **Surface:** metalled. 01/01-31/12
Distance: 300m 300m 300m. **Remarks:** Max. 48h.

Tourist information Sare:

Office de Tourisme, Bourg, www.sare.fr.Typical Basque village in Labourd-region.

Le petit train de la Rhune, Col de Saint Ignace.The little train runs through the mountains in the Basque Country on the Franco-Spanish border.
15/03-15/11 from 9h.

Les Grottes de Sare.Caves, prehistoric park and museum. 01/02-31/12.

S Sarlat-la-Canéda 28D2

Place Flandres Dunkerque. **GPS:** n44,89530 e1,21266.

50 € 5/24h, € 12/48h € 2 Ch € 2 . **Location:** Noisy.
Surface: asphalted. 01/01-31/12. **Distance:** 300m 100m bakery 50m.

Tourist information Sarlat-la-Canéda:

Office de Tourisme, Ancien Evêché - Rue Tourny, www.sarlat-tourisme.com. Small tourist and historical town. The streetscape is predominated by Lauzes, the soft yellow flat stones of which the houses have been built.

Centre ville.Centre of the French trade in foie grass. Sa-morning.

S Sauvagnon 28B4

Champ de Foire, Rue du Béarn. **GPS:** n43,40361 w0,38635.

6 free Ch WC free. **Surface:** asphalted. 01/01-31/12
Distance: on the spot on the spot on the spot on the spot.

S Sauveterre de Guyenne 28C2

Boulevard de 11 Novembre. **GPS:** n44,69051 w0,0867.

FR

4 free € 0,50 Ch € 1,50/90minutes. **Surface:** metalled.
01/01-31/12
Remarks: Coins at Office du Tourisme, supermarket.

S Seignosse 28A4

Aire camping-cars, D79. **GPS**: n43,69089 w1,42539.

75 € 8 Ch WC included. **Surface:** grassy/gravel. 01/01-31/12
Distance: 500m 500m 500m 500m 500m.
Remarks: Next to campsite municipal Hourn-Nao.

S Sévignacq Méracq 28B5

Aire du gave d'Ossau, Quartier Raguette. **GPS**: n43,10712 w0,419.

20 € 7 Ch WC. **Surface:** grassy/gravel. 01/01-31/12
Distance: 1km on the spot on the spot 1km 1km.

S Sorges 28D1

Le Bourg. **GPS**: n45,30403 e0,87255.
Ch free.

Sorges 28D1

Aire de repos Grangearias, RN21. **GPS**: n45,30486 e0,87273.

4 free. **Surface:** metalled. 01/01-31/12

S Soulac-sur-Mer 20B6

Boulevard de L'Amélie. **GPS**: n45,49938 w1,1373.

50 € 8 € 2 Ch. 01/01-31/12
Distance: 50m 2,5km 2,5km on the spot on the spot.

S Sourzac 28C1

D6089. **GPS**: n45,05147 e0,39518.

8 free Ch free. **Location:** Comfortable, central.
01/01-31/12 water disconnected in winter.
Distance: 100m 100m 100m.
Remarks: Along the Isle river.

S Soustons 28A3

Parking du Lac Marin, Avenue de la Pêtre, Soustons Plage. **GPS**: n43,77560 w1,41167.

82 01/10-31/04 € 6, 01/05-30/09 € 12 Ch WC included.
Location: Simple. **Surface:** gravel/metalled. 01/01-31/12
Distance: city centre 3km lake 50m, ocean 300m 50m 50m on the spot.
Remarks: Max. 72h.

S St.Antoine-Cumond 28C1

Le Bourg, D43. **GPS**: n45,25553 e0,19963.
5 free Ch WC free. **Surface:** gravel. 01/01-31/12
Distance: 300m 300m.
Remarks: Max. 48h.

S St.Caprais de Blaye 28B1

Route de Saintes, RN137, Ferchaud. **GPS**: n45,29120 w0,5692.

8 free Ch WC free, cold shower. **Surface:** asphalted.
01/01-31/12
Distance: 6,4km on the spot on the spot.
Remarks: Tourist information and picnic tables available.

S St.Cyprien (Dordogne) 28D2

Place Mackenheim, Rue du Priolat. **GPS**: n44,86828 e1,04435.

8 free € 3,50 Ch (8x)€ 3,50/12h. **Surface:** asphalted.
01/01-31/12
Distance: 50m bakery 50m, supermarket 100m.
Remarks: Max. 48h, coins at supermarket, tourist office.

Tourist information St.Cyprien (Dordogne):
Office de Tourisme, Place Charles de Gaulle.
Marché repas gourmand. summer Thu-evening.

S St.Front-la-Rivière 21A6

Place Louis Moreau, D83. **GPS**: n45,47450 e0,72430.

10 free Ch WC free. **Location:** Isolated. **Surface:** asphalted.
01/01-31/12
Distance: 500m.
Remarks: Picnic area.

S St.Jean-de-Côle 21A6

Le Bourg. **GPS**: n45,41984 e0,84048.

6 free € 2 Ch. **Location:** Comfortable, quiet. **Surface:** metalled.
01/01-31/12
Distance: 100m 300m 200m.
Remarks: At tennis-court, coins at tourist office.

S St.Jean-de-Luz 37D4

Pont Charles de Gaulle, N10. **GPS**: n43,38527 w1,6629.

18 free Ch free. **Surface:** asphalted.
Distance: 200m 2,2km 300m 300m 100m 100m.
Remarks: Max. 48h. Parking at station, via RN10.

Tourist information St.Jean-de-Luz:
Office de Tourisme, Place du Maréchal Foch, www.saint-jean-de-luz.com. Tourist town with beautiful shops. The local speciality is chipirones, octopus cooked in its own ink.
Halles, Bd Victor Hugo. morning.

S St.Jean-Pied-de-Port 28A5

Parking du Lai Alai. **GPS**: n43,16540 w1,23323.

70 € 5,50/24h Ch free. **Surface:** metalled. 01/01-31/12
Distance: 350m 350m 350m 350m 350m.
Remarks: Nearby stadium, max. 48h.

Tourist information St.Jean-Pied-de-Port:
Office de Tourisme, 14, Place Charles de Gaulle, www.pyrenees-basques.com.Fortified city on the foot of the Roncesvallespass on the road to Santiago de Compostela.
Forêt d'Iraty.Nature reserve, hiking trails available at OT.

S St.Leon-sur-l'Isle 28C1

Avenue de la République. **GPS**: n45,11515 e0,50034.

4 free Ch free. **Location:** Simple. **Surface:** asphalted.
01/01-31/12
Distance: 200m 5,3km 200m.

S St.Léon-sur-Vézère 28D1

Le Bourg, C201. **GPS**: n45,01230 e1,08978.

free € 2 Ch WC. **Location:** Simple, quiet. **Surface:** grassy/gravel.
01/01-31/12
Distance: 100m 200m 150m.
Remarks: Sanitary building 100m, shower € 0,50, coins available at tourist office.

S St.Palais 28A4

Parking Place Ste. Elisabeth. **GPS**: n43,32944 w1,0325.

10 free Ch WC free. **Surface:** asphalted. 01/01-31/12
Distance: 200m 250m 250m.

FR

S St.Paul-les-Dax 28A3

Allée Salvador Allende. **GPS**: n43,73460 w1,07865.

8 free Ch free. **Location:** Simple. **Surface:** gravel/sand.
01/01-31/12
Distance: 500m 500m.
Remarks: Max. 72h, shady.

S St.Pée-de-Nivelle 28A4

Flot bleu park St. Pée sur Nivelle. **GPS**: n43,34945 w1,5215.

30 € 8,50/24h € 2/120liter Ch € 2/4h. **Surface:** asphalted.
01/01-31/12
Distance: 3km on the spot 500m Restaurant Aintzira Le Lac.
Remarks: Parking at lake, max. 48h.

S St.Saud-Lacoussière 21A6

Domaine Sous Chardonnièras, 4, Impasse Sous Chardonnièras. **GPS**: n45,54053 e0,81909.

4 € 12 WC included. **Surface:** unpaved. 01/01-31/12
Distance: 500m 2km 2km 500m 500m.

S St.Sauveur 28D2

Le Bourg, D21. **GPS**: n44,86850 e0,58834.

3 free Ch WC free. **Surface:** asphalted. 01/01-31/12
Distance: 100m 100m 100m.

S St.Savin 28B1

Aire de Civrac-de-Blaye, Parc de la Mairie, D36, Civrac-de-Blaye. **GPS**: n45,11222 w0,44444.

1 free WC free. **Surface:** grassy. 01/01-31/12
Distance: 50m 100m.

S St.Savin 28B1

Aire de St.Girons d'Aiguevives, St.Girons d'Aiguevives. **GPS**: n45,13972 w0,5425.

2 free . **Surface:** grassy/gravel. 01/01-31/12
Distance: on the spot 4km 10km.
Remarks: In front of the church.

S St.Savin 28B1

Aire des Lacs du Moulin Blanc, St.Christoly-de-Blaye. **GPS**: n45,15167 w0,47583.

2 free WC free. **Surface:** gravel. 01/01-31/12
Distance: 800m 50m on the spot on the spot 3km.
Remarks: Parking to lake.

S St.Savin 28B1

Aire des Lagunes, St.Mariens. **GPS**: n45,11000 w0,39.

2 free WC free. **Surface:** asphalted. 01/01-31/12
Distance: on the spot 6km 6km 2km 3km.

S St.Savin 28B1

Parking Centre Culturel. **GPS**: n45,13800 w0,4465.

2 free WC. **Surface:** gravel. 01/01-31/12
Distance: on the spot 3km 3km 150m 800m.

St.Savin **28B1**

Parking Maison des Jeunes, Cubnezais. **GPS**: n45,07500 w0,40861.

12 free free. **Surface:** asphalted. 01/01-31/12
Distance: 50m 3km 3km.

St.Savin **28B1**

Aire de l'Église, Générac. **GPS**: n45,18000 w0,54.
2 free. 01/01-31/12
Distance: on the spot 6km 10km.
Remarks: Church square.

St.Savin **28B1**

Aire de Marcenais, Marcenais. **GPS**: n45,05000 w0,33.

2 free. 01/01-31/12
Distance: on the spot 6km 6km.
Remarks: Next to community centre.

St.Savin **28B1**

Aire de Saugon, Saugon. **GPS**: n45,17795 w0,50243.
2 free. 01/01-31/12
Distance: on the spot 6km 6km 3km 6km.
Remarks: Behind town hall.

St.Savin **28B1**

Aire de St. Vivien, RN137, St.Vivien-de-Blay. **GPS**: n45,09000 w0,51.

2 free. 01/01-31/12
Distance: on the spot 3km 3km 3km 3km.

Remarks: Parking at church.

St.Savin **28B1**

Aire du Dojo, Cézac. **GPS**: n45,09000 w0,41.

1 free. 01/01-31/12
Distance: on the spot 6km 6km 3km 3km.
Remarks: Nearby town hall.

St.Savin **28B1**

Aire du Lac des Vergnes, Laruscade. **GPS**: n45,10000 w0,34.
2 free. 01/01-31/12
Distance: 200m on the spot 500m 2km.
Remarks: Parking to lake.

St.Savin **28B1**

Aire Maison de la Forêt, Donnezac. **GPS**: n45,24000 w0,44.

2 free. 01/01-31/12
Distance: on the spot 6km 6km.
Remarks: Next to community centre.

St.Savin **28B1**

Parking communal Aire de Cavignac, Rue de Paix, Cavignac. **GPS**: n45,09976 w0,39048.

2 free. 01/01-31/12
Distance: on the spot 8km 50m 300m.

St.Savin **28B1**

Parking communal Aire de Saint Yzan, Parking de la Gare, St.Yzan-de-Soudiac. **GPS**: n45,13000 w0,39.
2 free. 01/01-31/12
Distance: on the spot 12km 800m 3km 3km on the spot.

St.Savin **28B1**

Parking de Marsas, Rue Chaignaud, Marsas. **GPS**: n45,06770 w0,3849.
2 free. 01/01-31/12
Distance: on the spot 4km 4km.

S **St.Savin** **28B1**

St.Christoly-de-Blaye. **GPS**: n45,15000 w0,47.

FR

Chfree. 01/01-31/12
Distance: on the spot.
Remarks: Parking in front of town hall.

S St.Sylvestre-sur-Lot 28D2
Place du Lot, Avenue Jean Moulin. **GPS**: n44,39621 e0,80499.

12 free. **Surface:** asphalted. 01/01-31/12
Distance: 150m, Penne d'Agenais centre 1,8km 100m 50m.

S St.Sylvestre-sur-Lot 28D2
GPS: n44,39566 e0,80568.
Chfree.

S St.Vincent-de-Cosse 28D2
Ferme d'Enveaux. GPS: n44,82669 e1,09822.

50 guests free Chfree.
Surface: unpaved.
01/01-31/12
Distance: pebbled beach 50m on the spot on the spot.
Remarks: Max. 48h, along the Dordogne river, key service at canoe rental.

Tourist information St.Vincent-de-Cosse:
Château de Milandes, Les Milandes.Former dwellinghouse of Josephine Baker, nowadays exhibition concerning her.

S St.Vincent-Jalmoutiers 28C1
Le Bourg. **GPS**: n45,20055 e0,19091.
free Ch WC free. **Surface:** grassy/gravel. 01/01-31/12
Distance: 350m 350m.

S Ste.Alvére 28D1
Rue de la Fontaine Saint Jean. **GPS**: n44,94500 e0,80499.

10 free € 2,50/100liter Ch € 2,50/1h. **Location:** Simple, isolated.
Surface: metalled. 01/01-31/12
Distance: 500m 500m 500m.
Remarks: At sports centre, coins at town hall.

S Ste.Eulalie-en-Born 28A2
Route du Port, D652. **GPS**: n44,30634 w1,18206.

40 € 6,50, 01/04-31/10 € 4 Ch WC included € 3. **Location:** Comfortable, quiet. **Surface:** grassy.
01/04-31/10 service 01/11-01/03.
Distance: 50m 50m on the spot on the spot.
Remarks: At marina, to be paid at campsite.

S Ste.Livrade-sur-Lot 28C2
Avenue René Bouchon. **GPS**: n44,39588 e0,59179.

8 free Chfree. **Surface:** asphalted. 01/01-31/12
Distance: 850m.
Remarks: At fire-station.

S Tournon-d'Agenais 28D2
Base de Loisirs Camp Beau, Pont Roumio, Route de Libos, D102. **GPS**: n44,40444 e0,99833.

15 free Chfree. **Surface:** metalled. 01/01-31/12

Valeyrac 20B6
Port de Goulée, Route Castillonaise. **GPS**: n45,40500 w0,91028.

FR

free. **Surface:** asphalted/grassy.
Distance: 50m on the spot 20m.
Remarks: At harbour.

S Varaignes 20D6

Place du Château. **GPS**: n45,59784 e0,31450.

4 free Ch WC free. **Location:** Simple, central. **Surface:** gravel.
01/01-31/12
Distance: on the spot 100m bakery 50m.

S Vertheuil 28B1

Château Ferré, 3 rue des Aubépines. **GPS**: n45,26225 w0,82798.

5 free Ch WC. **Surface:** gravel. 01/01-31/12

S Veyrines-de-Domme 28D2

Boutique des Bois d'Envaux, Route des Milandes, 6-102 Le Falgueyrat. **GPS**: n44,82090 e1,10394.

30 free free. **Location:** Simple. **Surface:** grassy.
Distance: on the spot.
Remarks: Sale of foie gras and wine.

S Vielle St.Girons 28A3

Lac de Léon, plage de Vielle. **GPS**: n43,90279 w1,30944.

30 € 9-12, dog € 4,70 Ch (30x)€ 4,50/night WC. **Location:** Simple. **Surface:** gravel/metalled. 01/04-30/09
Distance: 100m 300m 50m 100m.
Remarks: Max. 48h.

S Vielle St.Girons 28A3

Les Tourterelles, Saint Girons-Plage. **GPS**: n43,95278 w1,35778.

40 € 8,90, July-Aug € 12,50 € 2,70/10liter Ch 55minutes WC.
Location: Comfortable. **Surface:** gravel/metalled. 01/01-31/12 Service 01/10-26/04.
Distance: 300m 500m 500m.

S Vieux-Boucau-les-Bains 28A3

Aire camping-cars Village, Avenue des Pêcheurs. **GPS**: n43,77971 w1,40041.

120 € 6, 01/05-30/09 € 12 Ch included. **Location:** Comfortable. **Surface:** gravel/sand. 01/01-31/12
Distance: 500m 200m 500m 500m on the spot.
Remarks: >3,5t not allowed.

S Vieux-Boucau-les-Bains 28A3

Aire du Marensin Plage, Boulevard du Marensin. **GPS**: n43,79485 w1,4051.

35 € 6, 01/05-30/09 € 12 Ch. **Location:** Simple, quiet.
Surface: gravel. 01/01-31/12
Distance: 1,5km Ocean 500m 1,5km 1,5km on the spot.
Remarks: Max. 48h, >3,5t not allowed.

S Villeton 28C2

D120. **GPS**: n44,36386 e0,27279.

FR

4 free €2 Ch €2. **Surface:** gravel. 01/01-31/12
Distance: 10,5km on the spot on the spot on the spot.

S Vitrac 28D2

Montfort, D703. **GPS:** n44,83558 e1,24852.

10 free €3 Ch WC. **Surface:** grassy/gravel. 01/01-31/12
Distance: 50m 2km beach at Dordogne river 200m.
Remarks: Coins available at restaurant Le Point Vue (200m).

Midi Pyrénées

Albi 29B3

Parking Cathédrale. GPS: n43,92750 e2,14111.

9 free. **Surface:** asphalted.
Distance: 50m 50m 100m.
Remarks: Parking nearby cathedral Sainte Cécile, max. 48h.

S Albi 29B3

Rue Michelet. **GPS:** n43,94583 e2,15111.
Chfree. 01/01-31/12

Tourist information Albi:
Office de Tourisme, Palais de la Berbie, place Sainte-Cécile, www.mairie-albi.fr.Old city with narrow streets round the cathedral, birth town of Toulouse Lautrec. Musée de Toulouse-Lautrec, Palais de la Berbie, is a complete collection of the painter.

S Alblas 28D2

Pech del Gal. **GPS:** n44,47480 e1,23275.

10 free free. **Surface:** gravel.

Remarks: Near campsite.

S Alvignac 29A2

Route de Padirac. **GPS:** n44,82504 e1,69711.

10 free Ch. **Surface:** asphalted.
Distance: 100m 200m 200m.

S Aragnouet 28C5

P5, Piau Engaly. **GPS:** n42,78599 e0,15800.
100 €6 Ch (100x)€6 WC. **Surface:** asphalted. 01/12-31/08
Distance: 300m 300m 300m.
Remarks: A64 exit Tarbes, dir Spain (RD929).

S Arfons 29B4

Pierron-Les Escudiés. **GPS:** n43,43972 e2,19472.

4 €5 Ch WC. **Surface:** grassy. 01/01-31/12
Distance: 4km 1km 4km 4km.

S Arreau 28C5

Chemin de Fregel, Avenue de la gare. **GPS:** n42,90708 e0,35912.

27 €2 Chfree. **Surface:** asphalted. 01/01-31/12
Distance: 100m 100m 300m 300m 200m.

S Arrens-Marsous 28B5

GPS: n42,95806 w0,20722.

10 free Chfree. **Surface:** asphalted. 01/01-31/12
Distance: 1,5km 1,5km 1,5km.
Remarks: Behind 'services techniques'.

S Arvieu 29B3

GPS: n44,19205 e2,65938.

11 € 2/80liter Ch WC. **Surface:** gravel. 01/04-30/11
Distance: 100m on the spot on the spot on the spot.

S Aubrac 29C2

D533. **GPS**: n44,62026 e2,98705.
10 Ch WC free. **Surface:** gravel. 01/01-31/12
Distance: 50m on the spot on the spot on the spot on the spot.

S Auch 28C4

Camping municipal, Rue des Cormorans. **GPS**: n43,63654 e0,58854.

3 € 4 Ch free € 1,50. **Surface:** asphalted. 01/01-31/12
Distance: 15min 15min 15min.

S Auterive 29A4

Grande Allée du Ramier. **GPS**: n43,35025 e1,47730.

6 free free. **Surface:** asphalted. 01/01-31/12
Remarks: At fire-station.

S Auzas 28D5

GPS: n43,17060 e0,88690.

5 € 3 Ch included. **Surface:** asphalted.
Distance: on the spot.
Remarks: At lake.

Ax-les-Thermes 29A6

Parc d'Espagne. **GPS**: n42,71504 e1,84142.

35 free. **Surface:** metalled. 01/01-31/12
Distance: 500m 500m 500m.

S Bagnac-sur-Célé 29B2

Parking de la Planquette. **GPS**: n44,66806 e2,15861.

6 free Ch free. **Surface:** asphalted. 01/01-31/12
Distance: on the spot 100m 100m 200m.

S Bagnères-de-Bigorre 28C5

Rue René Cassin. **GPS**: n43,07319 e0,15256.

10 free Ch WC free. **Surface:** gravel. 01/01-31/12
Distance: 500m 1km 1km.

Bagnères-de-Bigorre 28C5

Place de la Gare. **GPS**: n43,06917 e0,14889.

10 free. **Surface:** asphalted.
Distance: 200m 200m 200m.
Remarks: At station.

S Bagnères-de-Luchon 28C5

Allée du Corp Franc Pommiès. **GPS**: n42,79540 e0,59875.

30 € 4/24h Ch € 6. **Surface:** asphalted.
01/01-31/12 service: 01/12-01/04.

S Baraqueville 29B3

Rue du Val de l'Enne. **GPS**: n44,27850 e2,43407.

10 free € 3 Ch WC. **Surface:** asphalted. 01/01-31/12
Distance: on the spot 50m on the spot on the spot.
Remarks: Inclining pitches, coins at the shops in the village.

Barbotan-les-Thermes 28C3

Avenue des Thermes. **GPS**: n43,94884 w0,04344.

6 free, overnight stay against payment. **Surface:** asphalted. 01/01-31/12
Distance: 500m 50m 500m.

S Bardigues 28D3

GPS: n44,03869 e0,89271.

4 free € 2 Ch. **Surface:** gravel. 01/01-31/12
Distance: 150m 8,6km 150m 150m.
Remarks: Dir cemetery, A62 exit Valence d'Agen, dir Aurillac then Bardigues.

S Bargnac 29A5

La Bastide-de-Sérou. **GPS**: n43,00194 e1,44556.

15 € 13,60 Ch WC included. **Surface:** asphalted/gravel.
06/03-13/11
Remarks: Next to campsite.

S Belmont sur Rance 29B4

Parking de la Mairie, Place de la Maririe RD 32. **GPS**: n43,81630 e2,75269.

3 free Ch free. **Surface:** asphalted. 01/01-31/12
Distance: on the spot.

S Boisse Penchot 29B2

Rue du Chateau Bas. **GPS**: n44,59208 e2,20616.

8 free € 3/100liter Ch € 3/1h.
Surface: asphalted.
01/01-31/12
Distance: 100m on the spot on the spot on the spot on the spot.

S Bonac Irazein 28D5

Lac Bonac. **GPS**: n42,87541 e0,97565.

10 € 5/night Ch included. **Surface:** grassy/gravel.
Distance: on the spot.
Remarks: At artificial lake of Bonac.

S Bouillac 29B2

Aire pique-nique, D840. **GPS**: n44,57333 e2,15750.

FR

6 free € 3 Ch. **Surface:** metalled. 01/03-30/11
Distance: on the spot on the spot on the spot 600m.
Remarks: Max. 24h, coins at the shops.

S Branne 28C2

Route de Cabara. **GPS**: n44,83191 w0,18448.
free € 2/100liter Ch € 2/1h.
Distance: on the spot.

S Brassac 29B4

Place Belfortès. **GPS**: n43,62968 e2,49434.
6 free Ch WC. **Surface:** asphalted. 01/01-31/12
Distance: on the spot.
Remarks: Access via RD622.

S Broquies 29B3

Rue du Lavoir. **GPS**: n44,00498 e2,69371.

30 free Ch WC free. **Surface:** gravel. 01/04-30/11
Distance: 50m on the spot on the spot.

S Cadours 28D4

Rue Malakoff. **GPS**: n43,72280 e1,04880.

5 free Chfree. **Surface:** grassy.
01/01-31/12 tue-evening, wed-morning.
Distance: 1km 1km.
Remarks: At football ground.

S Cahors 29A2

Parking Chartreux, Rue de la Chartreuse. **GPS**: n44,44062 e1,44170.

3 free Chfree. **Surface:** gravel. 01/01-31/12
Distance: 500m on the spot 250m 50m on the spot.
Remarks: Along river.

Cahors 29A2

Parking Saint George, Rue Saint George. **GPS**: n44,43875 e1,44111.
20 free. **Surface:** asphalted. 01/01-31/12
Distance: 1,2km 15km 100m on the spot.
Remarks: Shuttle to centre.

Tourist information Cahors:
Maison de Tourisme, Place François Mitterrand, www.quercy.net.The city is famous because of the wine. Moreover it has a rich architecture heritage.
Wed, Sa.

S Cahuzac-sur-Vère 29A3

Place du Mercadial. **GPS**: n43,98194 e1,91111.

5 free Ch WC. **Surface:** gravel.
Distance: 200m 200m 200m.

S Cajarc 29A2

Place de la Gare. **GPS**: n44,48458 e1,84573.

8 free € 1 Ch. **Surface:** grassy. 01/01-31/12
Distance: 100m 200m 200m.

S Calès 29A2

D673. **GPS**: n44,81298 e1,53780.

4 free Chagainst payment.
Distance: on the spot.

S Camares 29C4

Base de loisirs des Zizines. **GPS**: n43,81654 e2,87988.

FR

10 free Ch WC free. **Surface:** gravel. 01/04-31/10
Distance: 100m on the spot on the spot.

S Campagnac 29C2

GPS: n44,41903 e3,08210.

5 € 3 Ch. **Surface:** metalled. 01/04-31/10
Distance: 50m on the spot on the spot.

S Campuac 29B2

GPS: n44,57027 e2,59162.
10 free Ch WC free. **Surface:** gravel. 01/01-31/12
Distance: 100m on the spot.

S Cardaillac 29A2

Le Pré del Prie. GPS: n44,67868 e1,99805.

12 free Ch free. **Surface:** metalled. 01/01-31/12
Distance: 100m 100m.
Remarks: Behind church.

S Castanet 29B3

GPS: n44,27889 e2,28944.

4 € 3 Ch included. **Surface:** gravel. 01/01-31/12
Distance: on the spot on the spot.

S Castelnau-de-Montmiral 29A3

Les Miquels. GPS: n43,96667 e1,80278.

6 € 9,50, 2 pers.incl Ch . **Surface:** grassy. 01/01-31/12
Distance: 2,5km on the spot 2,5km.

S Castelnau-Durban 28D5

D117. **GPS:** n42,99994 e1,33976.

10 free € 2 Ch WC. **Surface:** metalled.
Remarks: In front of church.

S Castelsarrasin 28D3

Allée de la Source. **GPS:** n44,03861 e1,10221.

40 € 3/24h € 2,50/100liter Ch € 2,50/24h. **Surface:** gravel.
01/01-31/12
Distance: 500m 500m 500m.

S Castelsarrasin 28D3

Rue Louis Braille. **GPS:** n44,03833 e1,11473.

15 free Ch free. **Surface:** asphalted. 01/01-31/12
Distance: 200m 3km 250m.
Remarks: Along Canal des 2 Mers.

Castres 29B4

Parc de Gourjade, Avenue de Roquecourbe, D89. **GPS:** n43,62049 e2,25357.

FR

5 free. **Surface:** metalled.
Distance: 2km.
Remarks: Max. 24h.

Castres 29B4

Place Gerard Philipe. **GPS:** n43,60168 e2,24939.

free. **Surface:** asphalted. 01/01-31/12
Distance: 2km 2km 2km.
Remarks: Free shuttle to centre.

S Castres 29B4

Route de l'Industrie Z.I. de Melou. **GPS:** n43,59069 e2,20648.
Ch free. 01/01-31/12

Tourist information Castres:
Office de Tourisme, 3, rue Milhau-Ducommun, www.ville-castres.fr.Centre of the textile industry.
Palais Episcopal.Episcopal palace.
Tue, Thu-Su.

Caussade 29A3

Place de la Halle, Boulevard Léonce Granier. **GPS:** n44,16111 e1,53583.

10 free. **Surface:** asphalted.
Distance: on the spot on the spot on the spot on the spot.

S Cauterets 28B5

Place de la Patinoire, D920. **GPS:** n42,89361 w0,11256.

80 € 8/24h Ch free. **Surface:** asphalted. 01/01-31/12
Distance: 300m 300m 300m.
Remarks: Max. 21 nights.

Tourist information Cauterets:
Office de Tourisme, Place Foch.Mountaineering village with thermal sources.

S Caylus 29A3

Base de loisirs Labarthe. **GPS:** n44,23363 e1,77225.

6 free Ch free. **Surface:** grassy/gravel. 01/01-31/12
Distance: 200m 200m 200m.
Remarks: D19 dir St.Antonin, along lake.

Tourist information Caylus:
St.Antonin.Small town with the oldest town hall of France.

S Condom 28C3

Ferme de Parette, Route de Nérac, RN930. **GPS:** n43,99944 e0,35639.

8 € 8 Ch included against payment. **Surface:** grassy.
01/01-31/12
Distance: 2km 2km 2km. **Remarks:** 800m from hamlet Parette.

Tourist information Condom:
Larressingle.Small fortified town, surrounded by ramparts and tower of defence.
Office de Tourisme, Place Bossuet, www.tourisme-tenareze.com.Historical place and centre of the Armagnac.
Musée de l'Armagnac.All about Armagnac.

S Cordes-sur-Ciel 29A3

Parking les Tuileries. **GPS:** n44,06453 e1,95802.

40 € 3,50 Ch included. 01/01-31/12
Distance: 250m.

Tourist information Cordes-sur-Ciel:
Office de Tourisme, Maison Fonpeyrouse, www.cordes-sur-ciel.org.Medieval city with renovated city walls and archways.

S Coupiac 29B3

Route de Martin. **GPS:** n43,95174 e2,58464.
10 free Ch free. **Surface:** grassy. 01/01-31/12
Distance: 500m.
Remarks: Nearby petrol station at D60.

S Cransac 29B2

Aire de Camping-car Cransac, Avenue de la Gare. **GPS:** n44,52278 e2,27444.

FR

6 € 5 Chfree. **Surface:** gravel. 01/01-31/12
Distance: 500m 500m 500m.
Remarks: In front of campsite.

S Donzac 28D3

Lac de Sources, D30. **GPS:** n44,11308 e0,82044.

10 free Chfree. **Surface:** gravel.
Remarks: Max. 48h.

S Douelle 29A2

Domaine Marcilhac, D8. **GPS:** n44,47927 e1,34947.

10 free € 2 Ch. **Surface:** gravel. 01/01-31/12
Distance: 1km 1km 1km 1km.

Entraygues-sur-Truyère 29B2

GPS: n44,64417 e2,56278.

5 free. **Surface:** gravel. 01/01-31/12
Distance: 50m 150m 150m.

Entraygues-sur-Truyère 29B2

Route de Villecomtal, D904. **GPS:** n44,64020 e2,56925.

free. **Surface:** grassy. 01/04-31/12
Distance: 50m on the spot on the spot 50m 50m.

S Entraygues-sur-Truyère 29B2

Rue du 16 Août 1944. **GPS:** n44,64167 e2,56611.

Ch .

S Figeac 29A2

Parking le Foirail, Boulevard Colonel Teulié. **GPS:** n44,60833 e2,03806.

5 free € 2 Ch. **Surface:** asphalted. 01/01-31/12
Distance: 100m 400m 100m 100m.

Tourist information Figeac:

Office de Tourisme, Hôtel de la Monnaie, Place Vival, figeac.quercy-tourisme.com/.

Musée Champollion.Collection of old Egyptian art. Tue-Su 10-12h, 14.30-18.30h.

Marché régional.Regional market. Sa-morning.

S Fleurance 28D3

Boulevard de Metz. **GPS:** n43,85164 e0,66184.

20 free € 2 Ch € 2. **Surface:** gravel.
Distance: 200m on the spot on the spot.

S Frejairolles 29B4

Le Grand Chêne, D81. **GPS:** n43,86043 e2,24799.
5 € 5, free for clients Ch included.

S Gaillac 29A3

Parking des Rives Thomas. GPS: n43,89951 e1,89494.

free Ch free. **Surface:** asphalted. 01/01-31/12
Distance: 200m 200m 200m.

S Gavarnie 28B5

Parking Holle, D923. **GPS**: n42,73857 w0,01959.

20 € 4 Ch included. 01/01-31/12
Distance: 800m 100m 100m 800m 800m 600m 1,5km 1,5km.

Gavarnie 28B5

Parking du Cirque, Chemin du cirque. **GPS**: n42,73694 w0,01278.

20 free. **Surface:** asphalted. 01/01-31/12
Distance: 200m 200m 200m 200m.

Tourist information Gavarnie:

Office de Tourisme, www.gavarnie.com.Village, World Heritage Site of UNESCO. Summer and winter destination.

Cirque de Gavarnie.Can be reached with a donkey, a horse or by foot. A giant waterfalll, snow pillars and mountain slopes.

S Gignac 29A1

Le Moulin, Place des Troubadours. **GPS**: n45,00624 e1,45687.

10 free Ch. **Surface:** metalled. 01/01-31/12
Distance: 50m 150m 150m.

S Gimont 28D4

Avenue de Cahuzac, RN124. **GPS**: n43,62987 e0,87009.

12 free Ch free.
01/01-31/12
Distance: 100m on the spot on the spot 300m 300m 300m.
Remarks: At lake, max. 48h.

S Gourdon 29A2

Esplanade du foirail. **GPS**: n44,73423 e1,38523.

8 € 6 Ch included. **Surface:** gravel.
Distance: 200m 100m 200m on the spot.

S Gramat 29A2

La Garenne, Avenue Paul Mezet. **GPS**: n44,77972 e1,72833.

10 free Ch . **Surface:** metalled. 01/01-31/12
Distance: 400m 400m 400m.
Remarks: Max. 24h.

S Grenade-sur-Garonne 28D4

Quai de Garonne. **GPS**: n43,77201 e1,29673.

4 free Ch. **Surface:** gravel.
Distance: 100m 100m 100m 100m.
Remarks: Service: Allées Alsace Lorraine (100m).

La Couvertoirade 29C3

GPS: n43,91171 e3,31478.

FR

10 € 3 € 3/100liter WC. **Location:** Rural, isolated, quiet. **Surface:** gravel.
01/01-31/12
Distance: 50m 50m.
Remarks: Large parking on edge from village.

Tourist information La Couvertoirade:
Citadelle de l'Ordre de Tempeliers.Fortified city in original state. Now many old craft industries are exercised. There is a toll-house at the entrance of the village, entrance fee is charged.

S Labastide-Murat 29A2
Route de Gramat. **GPS**: n44,64944 e1,57061.
free Ch. **Location:** Rural, simple. **Surface:** asphalted.
Distance: 300m on the spot.
Remarks: At supermarket Carrefour.

S Labruguiere 29B4
Domaine d'en Laure, Rue du Parc du Montimont. **GPS**: n43,53139 e2,25528.

10 free € 2/10minutes Ch € 2/minutes. **Surface:** grassy.
01/01-31/12
Distance: 1km on the spot on the spot 1,3km 1,3km.

S Lacapelle Marival 29A2
Place de la Roque. **GPS**: n44,72806 e1,92944.

50 free Ch free. **Surface:** asphalted. service 15/05-30/09
Distance: 100m 50m.
Remarks: Follow dir Aurillac, in centre, between PTT and castle.

Lacaune 29B4
Rue de la Balme. **GPS**: n43,70795 e2,69010.

20 free. **Surface:** gravel. 01/01-31/12
Distance: on the spot on the spot.

Tourist information Lacaune:
Office de Tourisme, Place du Général De Gaulle, www.lacaune.com.

S Lacroix-Barrez 29B2
GPS: n44,77793 e2,63086.
10 € 2,50 + € 0,30 tourist tax Ch free. **Surface:** grassy.
01/01-31/12 service: 01/11-17/04.
Distance: 400m.

S Laguepie 29A3
Quai de l'Aveyron. **GPS**: n44,14485 e1,97226.

6 free Ch free. **Surface:** asphalted. 01/01-31/12
Distance: 200m 200m on the spot.

S Laguiole 29C2
Rue de Lavernhe. **GPS**: n44,68408 e2,85048.

10 free Ch free. **Surface:** gravel.
01/01-31/12, service: 17/04-15/10
Distance: on the spot.

S Laissac 29B3
Place du Foirail des Ovins, RN88. **GPS**: n44,38584 e2,28215.

6 free Ch free. **Surface:** asphalted. 01/03-30/11
Distance: 500m 500m 500m.
Remarks: Max. 24h.

FR

Lanuéjouls 29B2

Aire Campingcar Lanuéjouls. **GPS**: n44,42528 e2,16139.

14 € 5 Ch WC included. **Surface:** gravel. 01/01-31/12

Distance: 100m 100m 100m.

Remarks: Via D1.

Latronquière 29A2

Place du 19 mars 1962. **GPS**: n44,79917 e2,07917.

4 free Ch WC free. **Surface:** asphalted. 01/01-31/12

Distance: 300m 3km 3km 300m 300m.

Lauzerte 28D3

1, Place du Foirail. **GPS**: n44,25471 e1,13762.

10 free Ch WC free. **Surface:** asphalted.

01/01-31/12 tue-evening, wed-morning.

Distance: 500m on the spot on the spot.

Lauzerte 28D3

D2, Vignals. **GPS**: n44,26750 e1,14083.

20 free Ch WC free. **Surface:** grassy/gravel.

01/01-31/12

Distance: Lauzerte 2km on the spot 2km.

Tourist information Lauzerte:

Office de Tourisme, Place des Cornières.Medieval town.

Wed-morning.

Le Fossat 28D5

Aire des Lallières, Place de la Mairie. **GPS**: n43,17201 e1,41170.

20 € 6,50 Ch WC included. **Surface:** gravel.

Le Garric 29B3

Cap Découverte. **GPS**: n44,01361 e2,13778.

18 € 8 Ch included. **Surface:** asphalted. 01/01-31/12

Distance: 300m.

Le Houga 28C4

Ferme aux Cerfs, Route de Mont de Marsan, D6. **GPS**: n43,78430 e0,20997.

15 free Ch free. **Surface:** grassy. 01/01-31/12

Distance: 2,5km on the spot.

Le Ségur 29A3

Place de Marie. **GPS**: n44,10889 e2,05861.

3 free Ch WC free. **Surface:** metalled. 01/01-31/12

Distance: 50m 100m 100m.

Les Cabannes 29A6

Quartier la Bexane. **GPS**: n42,78493 e1,68301.

FR

30 € 4/24h € 2/100liter Ch WC. **Surface:** asphalted.

S Lisle sur Tarn 29A3

Aire de Bellevue. **GPS**: n43,86167 e1,81833.

12 free Ch. **Surface:** gravel. 01/01-31/12

Distance: 1,5km on the spot on the spot 1,5km 1,5km.

S Lombez 28D4

Route de Toulouse, D632. **GPS**: n43,47417 e0,91592.

20 free WC free. **Surface:** gravel.

Distance: 200m 150m 200m.

S Loudenvielle 28C5

GPS: n42,79633 e0,40743.

200 free, € 3/ski season + Jul/Aug € 2 Ch € 2.

Surface: asphalted/grassy.

S Lourdes 28B5

Le Vieux Berger, Route de Julos. **GPS**: n43,10444 w0,03311.

27 € 13 Ch WC included. **Location:** Rural.

Surface: grassy/gravel. 01/01-31/12

Remarks: Next to campsite.

S Lourdes 28B5

Parking Arrouza, Esplanade du Paradis. **GPS**: n43,08831 w0,05273.

€ 10 € 5 Ch. **Surface:** asphalted.

Distance: city centre 1km.

Tourist information Lourdes:

Office de Tourisme, Place Peyramale, www.lourdes-infotourisme.com.Lively place of pilgrimage.

Basilique St.Pius X.Underground basilica, of the largest sanctuaries in the world, there is place for 25,000 people.

S Luzech 28D2

Les Berges de Caïx, D9. **GPS**: n44,49121 e1,29348.

50 €7,50 Ch WC included. 01/01-31/12

Distance: 2km.

Remarks: Along Lot river, opening hours 9-21h.

L'Hospitalet-près-l'Andorre 29A6

N22. **GPS**: n42,58823 e1,79833.

5 free. **Surface:** asphalted.

Distance: 100m.

Marbre 28C5

Lac de Payolle, D918, Campan > Col de Aspin. **GPS**: n42,93528 e0,29222.

FR

free. **Surface:** grassy/gravel.
Distance: 40m 40m.

S Martel 29A1

La Fontanel, Avenue de Nassogne. **GPS**: n44,93505 e1,60656.

12 free Ch. **Surface:** gravel. 01/01-31/12
Distance: 250m 250m 250m.

S Mazamet 29B4

Rue du Champ de la Ville. **GPS**: n43,49083 e2,37944.

free Chfree. **Surface:** asphalted. 01/01-31/12
Distance: 300m 500m 300m.

S Mazamet 29B4

Soulever la Grille, Rue Galibert-Ferret, Champ de la Ville. **GPS**: n43,49089 e2,37918.
10 free Chfree. **Surface:** asphalted.
01/01-31/12 Fri-Sa market.
Distance: on the spot on the spot.
Remarks: At townhall, max. 24h.

S Mazères-sur-Salat 28D5

Rue de Vieux Ruisseau. **GPS**: n43,13457 e0,97633.

15 free Ch free. **Surface:** metalled. 01/01-31/12
Distance: 4,5km river.

S Miélan 28C4

Chemin du Cubet. **GPS**: n43,43319 e0,30900.
6 free Chfree. 01/01-31/12

S Millau 29C3

Rue de la Saunerie 19. **GPS**: n44,09610 e3,08577.

44 € 9,60, 01/07-31/08 € 12 Ch included.
Location: Comfortable. **Surface:** gravel.
01/01-31/12
Distance: 500m.
Remarks: Motorhomes <7.5m, video surveillance, entrance code night: parknight.

Tourist information Millau:
Office de Tourisme, 1, Place du Beffroi, www.ot-millau.fr.City tourist in the Valley of the Tarn and the Dourbie. Important for the leather trade.
Grands Causses.Limestone plateaus with ravines.
La Graufesenque.Archeological findings, 1st century.
Vieux Millau.Historical hiking route, info at Office de Tourisme.

S Mirandol-Bourgnounce 29B3

Place de Foirail. **GPS**: n44,14167 e2,16667.

8 free Ch WCfree. **Surface:** asphalted. 01/01-31/12
Distance: on the spot on the spot 50m.

S Mirepoix 29A5

Parking des Capitouls, Alée des Soupirs. **GPS**: n43,08500 e1,87444.

20 free Ch WCfree. 01/01-31/12
Remarks: Next to community centre.

Tourist information Mirepoix:
Office de Tourisme, Hôtel-de-Ville, Place Maréchal Leclerc, www.ot-mirepoix.fr.Village with half-timbered houses and square with arcades.
Cattle market. winter 2nd, 4th Mo of the month.
Thu, Sa.

S Moissac 28D3

Promenade Sancert. **GPS**: n44,10011 e1,08540.

FR

4 free € 2/4h. **Location:** Urban, simple. **Surface:** metalled.
01/01-31/12
Distance: 100m 100m.
Remarks: Coins at Office de Tourisme.

S Mont Roc 29B4
Salle de Fêtes. **GPS**: n43,80330 e2,37192.

8 free € 2 Ch € 2 WC. **Surface:** metalled. 01/01-31/12
Distance: 50m on the spot on the spot.

S Montauban 28D3
Mr. Lacaze, aire camping-car, 225, route de Corbarieu, D21. **GPS**: n43,99188 e1,35196.

15 € 6 € 2 Ch WC € 1. **Surface:** gravel.
01/01-31/12
Distance: Montauban 3km 1km.
Remarks: Motorhomes < 3,5t.

Tourist information Montauban:
Office de Tourisme, 2, rue du Collège, officetourisme.montauban.com.City of roses.
Sa.

S Montcuq 28D3
Route de Cahors, D653. **GPS**: n44,34082 e1,20242.

15 free € 2 Ch . **Surface:** gravel. 01/01-31/12
Distance: 250m 250m 250m.
Remarks: Coins at Tourist Info and petrol station.

S Monteils 29A3
D47. **GPS**: n44,26694 e1,99667.

4 free Chfree. **Surface:** gravel. 01/01-31/12
Distance: 100m 100m 50m.

S Montet-et-Bouxal 29A2
D653, La Vittarelle. **GPS**: n44,74111 e2,01944.

5 free Ch WCfree. **Surface:** asphalted. 01/01-31/12
Remarks: In village behind petrol station.

S Montézic 29B2
Les Prades Sud. **GPS**: n44,71054 e2,64413.

4 free Chfree. **Surface:** asphalted. 01/03-31/10
Distance: 500m on the spot on the spot.

S Montréal (Gers) 28C3
Stade André Daubin, D29. **GPS**: n43,95375 e0,19730.

free Chfree. **Surface:** gravel. 01/01-31/12
Distance: 200m 500m 500m.
Remarks: Parking at rugby ground.

Tourist information Montréal (Gers):
Office de Tourisme, place de l'Hôtel de Ville, www.montrealdugers.com/. Fortified city with ramparts, square with arcades and picturesque alleys.

S Mur de Barrez 29B2
Parc de la Caurette, Place du Foirail. **GPS**: n44,84842 e2,65980.

FR

free Chfree. **Surface:** asphalted. 01/01-31/12
Distance: 100m on the spot 50m.

S Nages 29B4

Rieu Montagné, Lac du Laouzas, D162. **GPS:** n43,64694 e2,78194.

15 € 6,10 Ch included. 01/01-31/12
Remarks: Nearby base nautique, quiet place with view at the lake.

S Najac 29A3

GPS: n44,22167 e1,96778.

10 free € 2 Ch. **Surface:** asphalted. 01/01-31/12
Distance: 1,8km on the spot 1,8km.

S Naucelle 29B3

Place du Ségala. **GPS:** n44,19723 e2,34175.

4 free Chfree. **Surface:** asphalted. 01/01-31/12
Distance: on the spot 500m 500m.

S Naussac 29A2

Aire de Loisirs de Peyrelevade. **GPS:** n44,52167 e2,07944.

10 € 4 Ch WCincluded. **Surface:** gravel. 01/01-31/12
Remarks: Recreation area, follow aire de loisirs.

S Oust 28D5

Aire camping-car, Foute d'Aulus les Bains. **GPS:** n42,87167 e1,21833.

10 € 10,50/night Ch € 5,60WC. **Surface:** grassy.
01/04-30/09
Remarks: Next to campsite Les 4 Saisons.

S Peyrusse le Roc 29B2

D87. **GPS:** n44,49500 e2,13972.

8 free Chfree. **Surface:** sand. 01/01-31/12
Distance: 500m 500m 500m.

S Pierrefitte-Nestalas 28B5

Place Lamartine. **GPS:** n42,96037 w0,07743.

10 free Chfree. **Surface:** asphalted. 01/01-31/12
Distance: 200m 200m 200m.
Remarks: Max. 1 night.

S Pinsac 29A2

Parking Salle des Fêtes, D43. **GPS:** n44,85500 e1,51222.

FR

5 free € 2 Ch € 2. **Surface:** gravel. 01/01-31/12
Distance: on the spot 9,5km 700m.

S Pont-de-Salars 29B3

Place de la Rivière. **GPS:** n44,27822 e2,72853.

5 free € 2 Ch WC. **Surface:** asphalted. 01/05-31/10
Distance: 100m 1km 1km on the spot nearby.
Remarks: Along river, max. 3 days.

S Prayssac 28D2

Avenue des Acacias. **GPS:** n44,50352 e1,19197.

10 free Ch WC. **Surface:** grassy/gravel.

S Preignan 28C4

Rue Emile Zola. **GPS:** n43,71243 e0,63378.

30 free Ch free. **Surface:** gravel.
Distance: 1km.
Remarks: At sports park.

S Puy l'Eveque 28D2

Place de la Gendarmerie. **GPS:** n44,50536 e1,13808.

4 free Ch WC free. **Surface:** gravel.
01/01-31/12 05/08-14/08.
Distance: 250m 300m 300m.
Remarks: In front of town hall, upper city, max. 24h.

S Puylaurens 29A4

Rue Albert Thorel. **GPS:** n43,56861 e2,01194.

10 free Ch WC. **Surface:** gravel. 01/01-31/12
Distance: 700m 700m 400m.
Remarks: Wifi at supermarket.

S Requista 29B3

Place François Fablé. **GPS:** n44,03465 e2,53599.

6 free free. **Surface:** gravel. 01/01-31/12
Distance: 200m.

S Revel 29A4

Chemin de la Pergue. **GPS:** n43,45444 e2,01528.

€ 7,60, 2 pers.incl. € 3 Ch € 3. **Surface:** grassy.
01/01-31/12
Distance: 1km 1km 1km.

S Rignac 29B2

Hameau du Lac, La Peyrade. **GPS:** n44,40456 e2,28958.

12 free Ch. **Surface:** grassy. 01/01-31/12
Distance: 600m 600m 600m.

S Rivières 29A3

Aire de Salta, La Courtade Haute. **GPS**: n43,91072 e1,98889.
6 € 9,50, € 15 service incl Ch . **Location:** Rural, luxurious.
Surface: grassy/gravel. 01/06-30/09
Distance: 200m.
Remarks: Along the Tarn river.

Rocamadour 29A2

D673. **GPS**: n44,80000 e1,61528.

30 free. **Surface:** gravel.
Distance: 100m.

S Rodez 29B3

Z.I. Cantaranne, Rue de Salelles. **GPS**: n44,35731 e2,59374.

6 free Chfree. **Surface:** asphalted. 01/01-31/12
Distance: 1km.
Remarks: Max. 72h.

Rodez 29B3

Parking du Foirail, Avenue Victor Hugo. **GPS**: n44,35143 e2,56822.
4 . 01/01-31/12
Distance: on the spot.
Remarks: In front of Avenue Victor-Hugo.

Tourist information Rodez:
Office de Tourisme, Place Foch, www.ot-rodez.fr.Medieval city.

S Roquecor 28D3

GPS: n44,32346 e0,94496.

6 free Chfree. **Surface:** asphalted. 01/01-31/12
Distance: 250m 250m.
Remarks: Max. 48h.

S Roquefort-sur-Soulzon 29C3

D23. **GPS**: n43,98120 e2,98163.

free Ch WCfree. **Surface:** asphalted. 01/01-31/12
Distance: 100m.
Remarks: Parking behind Office du Tourisme, no water during winter time.

S Saint-Antoine 28D3

GPS: n44,03587 e0,84209.

10 free Chfree. **Location:** Rural, simple, quiet.
Surface: asphalted.
Distance: 200m 4,3km.

S Samatan 28D4

Base de Loisirs, Avenue de Lombez et Barave, D39. **GPS**: n43,48791 e0,92616.

10 € 3,80/24h Ch WCincluded. **Surface:** asphalted.
01/01-31/12
Distance: 500m on the spot on the spot 250m 250m
250m.

S Sarrant 28D4

Route de Solomiac. **GPS**: n43,77532 e0,92822.

FR

100 free Ch free. **Surface:** grassy/gravel. 01/01-31/12
Distance: 150m 150m.
Remarks: In front of football stadium.

S Sauveterre-de-Rouergue 29B3

Le Sardou. **GPS**: n44,21613 e2,31700.
10 free Ch € 1,50 WC € 1,50. **Surface:** grassy. 01/01-31/12
Distance: on the spot on the spot on the spot.
Remarks: Parking at D997.

S Ségur 29B3

GPS: n44,29087 e2,83503.
5 free Ch WC € 2. **Surface:** asphalted. 01/01-31/12
Distance: 500m on the spot.
Remarks: Covered picnic area with electricity. Parking at D29.

S Senergues 29B2

La Ferme des Autruches, La Besse. **GPS**: n44,58861 e2,48361.
5 free Ch free. **Surface:** grassy/gravel. 01/03-30/11
Distance: 2km.

S Serres-sur-Arget 29A5

GPS: n42,96990 e1,51972.

€ 4 Ch included. **Surface:** metalled. 01/01-31/12
Remarks: Next to community centre.

S Souillac 29A2

Parking de Baillot, Chemin de Baillot. **GPS**: n44,89139 e1,47667.

20 free € 3 Ch € 3. **Surface:** asphalted. 01/01-31/12
Distance: 400m 4,5km 400m 500m.

Tourist information Souillac:
Bd Louis-Jean Malvy.Monastery-city, 12th century, between the regions Périgord and Quercy.

S Soulom 28B5

Place des Fêtes, D921. **GPS**: n42,95611 w0,0725.

10 free free. **Surface:** asphalted. 01/01-31/12
Distance: 200m 500m 200m 200m.

S Sousceyrac 29A2

Place des Condamines. **GPS**: n44,87255 e2,03649.

10 free Ch WC free. **Surface:** asphalted. 01/01-31/12
Distance: 100m.
Remarks: Parking in front of town hall, max. 1 night.

S St.Antonin Noble Val 29A3

Chemin de Roumégous. **GPS**: n44,15222 e1,75139.

15 free Ch free. **Surface:** asphalted. 01/01-31/12
Distance: 200m 300m 100m.

S St.Céré 29A2

D940. **GPS**: n44,86139 e1,88583.

3 free Ch free. **Surface:** asphalted. 01/01-31/12
Distance: 200m 200m 150m.
Remarks: Behind stadium, nearby cemetery.

S St.Cirque-Lapopie 29A2

Porte Roques, halte nautique-plage, D662. **GPS**: n44,47055 e1,68050.

FR

40 € 8 € 2/100liter Ch € 2 WC € 2. **Surface:** grassy/gravel. 01/01-31/12
Distance: 1,5km on the spot 50m.
Remarks: Along Lot River, nearby campsite de la Plage.

Tourist information St.Cirque-Lapopie:
Village, entirely under preservation order, has been built on a rock above the river Lot.
Cajarc.Village worth seeing with medieval houses.
Grotte de Pech-Merle, Cabrerets.Temple cave, monument from the Paleolithicum with images of mammoth, horses and bizons.

S St.Clar 28D3

Aire de repos, Route de Valence. **GPS**: n43,89111 e0,77250.

10 free Ch WC free. **Surface:** gravel. 01/01-31/12
Distance: 500m 250m.

S St.Felix-Lauragais 29A4

Lac de Lenclas, D622. **GPS**: n43,42667 e1,89806.

10 free Ch WC. **Surface:** gravel. 01/01-31/12
Distance: nearby nearby.
Remarks: Max. 24h.

Tourist information St.Felix-Lauragais:
Office de Tourisme, Le Beffroi, place Philippe VI de Valois, Revel, www.revel-lauragais.com.
Musée Spéleologique du Grand Sud-Ouest, Revel.Speleology, the underground world. Tue-Sa 14-18h.

S St.Geniez-d'Olt 29C2

Avenue de la gare. **GPS**: n44,46305 e2,97563.

10 free Ch WC free. **Surface:** gravel. 01/01-31/12
Distance: on the spot on the spot on the spot on the spot on the spot.
Remarks: Max. 24h.

Tourist information St.Geniez-d'Olt:
The river Lot seperates the old and new city.

S St.Girons 28D5

Rue Aristide Berges. **GPS**: n42,98865 e1,13852.

7 free € 3 Ch. **Surface:** asphalted.
Distance: 100m.

S St.Jean et St.Paul 29C3

Saint Jean d'Alcas. **GPS**: n43,92646 e3,00887.
free Ch WC free. **Surface:** gravel. 01/01-31/12
Distance: on the spot.

S St.Just-sur-Viaur 29B3

Parking La Fabrie, D532. **GPS**: n44,12402 e2,37588.
5 free Ch WC free. **Surface:** gravel. 01/04-30/11
Distance: 100m on the spot.

S St.Lary Soulan 28C5

Route de Vieille Aure. **GPS**: n42,82248 e0,32329.

10 € 6/night € 2 Ch € 2. **Surface:** asphalted. 01/01-31/12
Distance: 300m 300m.
Remarks: Parking behind stadium.

Tourist information St.Lary Soulan:
Office de Tourisme, 37, rue Vincent Mir, www.saintlary.com.Mountain village in the Pyrenees with information centre of the Parc National des Pyrénées. Winter sports area with 100 km of skiruns.

S St.Martory 28D5

Place Nationale, D52E, D117. **GPS**: n43,14141 e0,93033.

FR

7 free Ch WC free. **Surface:** asphalted.
Distance: 3km.
Remarks: Along the river, max. 1 night.

St.Maurice-en-Quercy 29A2

Place de l'église. **GPS:** n44,74306 e1,94722.

10 free. **Surface:** gravel. 01/01-31/12

S St.Nicolas-de-la-Grave 28D3

Rue de la Calle. **GPS:** n44,06379 e1,02471.

free Ch free. **Surface:** asphalted/gravel. 01/01-31/12
Distance: 100m 50m 100m.

S St.Puy 28C3

Grande Rue, D654. **GPS:** n43,87611 e0,46250.

3 free Ch WC free. **Surface:** gravel. 01/01-31/12
Distance: 20m 50m 20m.

S St.Sulpice-sur-Lèze 28D4

Stade Municipal. **GPS:** n43,32924 e1,32944.

5 free € 2 Ch. **Surface:** gravel.

S St.Thomas 28D4

Ferme Le Gros, D58. **GPS:** n43,50190 e1,07451.
10 € 3 Ch included. **Surface:** grassy/gravel.
Distance: 2km.

S Ste.Croix-Volvestre 28D5

GPS: n43,12673 e1,17094.

free Ch free. **Surface:** grassy/gravel. 01/01-31/12
Remarks: Sports park, parking village square nearby lake.

S Ste.Geneviève-sur-Argence 29B2

Rue de l'Argence. **GPS:** n44,80194 e2,76222.

20 free € 1 Ch . **Surface:** gravel. 01/01-31/12
Distance: 300m 500m 500m 300m 300m.
Remarks: On entering the village.

S Tarbes 28C5

Avenue de la Libération. **GPS:** n43,24316 e0,06785.

38 € 10 € 2 Ch included. **Surface:** asphalted. 01/01-31/12
Distance: 500m 500m 500m.
Remarks: Service only € 2, water + electricity € 5.

S Thémines 29A2

Place de L'église. **GPS:** n44,74083 e1,82972.

FR

3 free. **Surface:** asphalted. 01/01-31/12
Distance: on the spot 100m 100m.
Remarks: Nearby church.

S Therondels 29B2

GPS: n44,89474 e2,75807.
20 free Ch free. **Surface:** grassy. 01/04-15/11
Distance: on the spot 100m 100m.

S Vabres-l'Abbaye 29B3

Le Coustel, D999. **GPS:** n43,94575 e2,83779.
free Ch free. **Surface:** gravel. 01/04-30/10
Distance: 50m on the spot.
Remarks: 4Km from S. Affrique, near bridge.

Valcabrère 28C5

Parc de la Basilique Saint Just. GPS: n43,02812 e0,58370.
free. **Surface:** asphalted. 01/01-31/12
Remarks: Nearby Saint Bertrand de Comminges.

S Valderiés 29B3

Place de Mairie, D91. **GPS:** n44,01167 e2,23333.

5 free Ch WC. **Surface:** asphalted. 01/01-31/12
Distance: on the spot on the spot on the spot.
Remarks: Weighbridge.

S Valence (Tarn-et-Garonne) 28D3

M. Cadot, aire privée, 341, Route des Charretiers, Valence-sud. **GPS:** n44,09907 e0,89013.
8 € 8 Ch free. **Surface:** gravel. 01/01-31/12
Remarks: Max. 24h. Dir campsite municipal, 500m before campsite.

S Valence-sur-Baïse 28C3

Route d'Auch, D930. **GPS:** n43,87220 e0,38807.

7 free Ch WC free. **Surface:** gravel. 01/01-31/12
Distance: 500m 500m 500m on the spot.
Remarks: On entering village from dir Auch, nearby police station.

Tourist information Valence-sur-Baïse:
Syndicat d'Initiative, Rue Jules Ferry.Fortified city, 13th centrury, with cistercian abbey of Flaran.

S Vénerque 29A4

Allée du Duc de Ventadour. **GPS:** n43,43356 e1,44021.

10 free Ch free. **Surface:** metalled.
Distance: on the spot.

S Vers 29A2

Halte Nautique. GPS: n44,48551 e1,55503.

20 € 5 Ch WC free. **Surface:** grassy. 01/05-30/09
Distance: 100m 100m 200m 100m.

S Vic-en-Bigorre 28C4

Rue du Stade, Avenue de Pau D6. **GPS:** n43,38472 e0,04917.

4 free Ch free. **Surface:** grassy. 01/01-31/12
Distance: 500m 1km 1km.

S Vicdessos 29A6

GPS: n42,76891 e1,50257.

20 € 6 Ch included. **Surface:** metalled. 01/01-31/12
Distance: on the spot.

Villefranche-de-Rouergue 29A3

Parking des Ruelles, Boulevard de Gaulle. **GPS:** n44,35111 e2,03333.

FR

3 free. **Surface:** asphalted. 01/01-31/12
Distance: 100m 100m 100m.

Villefranche-de-Rouergue 29A3

Quai du Temple. **GPS**: n44,34937 e2,03917.

2 free. **Surface:** asphalted. 01/01-31/12
Distance: 300m 200m 300m.
Remarks: At quay in front of the old bridge.

Tourist information Villefranche-de-Rouergue:
Maison de Tourisme, Promenade du Guiraudet, www.villefranche.com.
place Notre Dame. Thu.

Villeneuve (Aveyron) 29A2

Place du sol de la Dime. **GPS**: n44,43855 e2,03269.

13 free Ch WC free. **Surface:** asphalted. 01/01-31/12
Distance: 100m 100m 100m.

Andorra

Pas de la Casa 29A6

GPS: n42,54468 e1,73525.
20-9h € 1. **Surface:** metalled.

Sant-Julia-de-Lòria 29A6

Carretera de la Rabassa. **GPS**: n42,46573 e1,49462.

4 € 0,50/h, 20.00-08.00 free Ch (4x)included. **Surface:** asphalted. 01/01-31/12
Distance: 1km.

Languedoc Roussillon

Agde 29C5

Les Peupliers. **GPS**: n43,29846 e3,45194.

30 € 8, Jul/Aug € 10 Ch (30x)€ 2. **Surface:** gravel/metalled.
03/04-14/11
Distance: 2km 1,7km on the spot.

Tourist information Agde:
Office de Tourisme, Cap d'Agde.Modern lively seaside resort with marina and recreation island.
Office de Tourisme, Espace Molière, 1, place Molière.Pleasant tourist city with medieval centre, Vieux Cité.
Cathédrale Ste Étienne.Romanesque fortified cathedral, 12th century.

Aigues-Mortes 29D4

Les Poissons d'Argent, CD62. **GPS**: n43,56476 e4,16289.
80 € 9/24h, € 12 all included Ch.
Surface: gravel. 01/03-31/10
Distance: 2,5km 3km on the spot on the spot 1,5km Lidl on the spot.
Remarks: At fish lake, fishing permit incl., bread-service.

Aigues-Mortes 29D4

Rue du Port. **GPS**: n43,56631 e4,18575.

50 € 16 Chfree. **Location:** Simple. **Surface:** metalled.
01/01-31/12
Distance: 600m.
Remarks: Max. 24h.

Tourist information Aigues-Mortes:
Office de Tourisme, Place Saint Louis, www.ot-aiguesmortes.fr.Medieval

fortress, 13th century, in the swamp of the Camargue, tourist attraction. T free.
La Tour Carbonnière, Place Saint Louis.Tower, guard-post for the defence of the city.

Aiguèze 30A3

GPS: n44,30530 e4,55250.

+20 free. **Location:** Rural. **Surface:** grassy. 01/01-31/12
Distance: 300m 300m.

Alès 29D3

Place du camping-car, Avenue Jules Guesde. **GPS**: n44,12013 e4,08207.

6 free Ch free. **Location:** Urban, comfortable, central, noisy.
Surface: asphalted. 01/01-31/12
Distance: on the spot on the spot on the spot 400m 600m on the spot routes available at tourist office.

Alzonne 29B5

La Pujade, Route de Montolieu. **GPS**: n43,25412 e2,17745.

8 € 8/24h Ch € 3 WC Use sanitary € 3/pp per day.
Surface: grassy. 01/01-31/12
Distance: 1,5km 1,5km 1,5km.

Amélie-les-Bains-Palalda 29B6

GPS: n42,48063 e2,67951.
40 free € 3 Ch. **Surface:** gravel. 01/01-31/12
Remarks: Behind hotel du Lion D'Or.

Amélie-les-Bains-Palalda 29B6

Camping municipal, Avenue Beau Soleil, D115. **GPS**: n42,48035 e2,67847.

5 free € 3 Ch. **Surface:** grassy/gravel. 01/01-31/12

Distance: on the spot.
Remarks: Max. 48h.

Anduze 29D3

Place de la Gare. **GPS**: n44,05000 e3,98444.

20 free Ch. **Location:** Urban, simple, central, quiet. **Surface:** asphalted. 01/01-31/12
Distance: on the spot 300m 400m on the spot on the spot.
Remarks: Max. 48h.

Anduze 29D3

Camping l'Arche. **GPS**: n44,06889 e3,97282.

5 € 12/night Ch WC included,sanitary at campsite.
Location: Rural, simple, isolated, quiet. **Surface:** asphalted.
01/04-30/09
Distance: 3km on the spot on the spot 100m on the spot on the spot.

Tourist information Anduze:
Office de Tourisme, Plan de Brie, www.ot-anduze.fr.Historical city, gate to the Cévennes.
Bambousserie de Prafrance.Bamboo garden laid out in 1835, with a large variety of bamboo species. 01/03-15/11.
Train Touristique.Tourist train from Anduze to St. Jean-du-Gard. T € 6,50.

Aniane 29C4

Le Pont du Diable. **GPS**: n43,70270 e3,55988.

€ 4/day, € 14/24h € 3 Ch . **Location:** Rural, isolated.
Surface: gravel. 01/01-31/12
Distance: 9km.
Remarks: Max. 48h, Pont du Diable 600m, St.Guilhem-le-Désert 4km, free shuttlebus Mai-Sept: weekend (11-19h), July-Aug daily (10-23h).

Aniane 29C4

Boulevard Saint-Jean. **GPS**: n43,68550 e3,58500.

FR

+10 free. **Surface:** gravel. 01/01-31/12
Distance: 300m nearby 300m 300m.

S Arre 29C3
D999. **GPS:** n43,96771 e3,52139.

6 free € 2/100liter Ch € 2/1h WC. **Location:** Rural, simple, central, quiet. **Surface:** metalled. 01/01-31/12
Distance: on the spot on the spot on the spot on the spot bakery 200m on the spot.

S Avèze 29C3
Aire du pont vieux, D999. **GPS:** n43,97517 e3,59899.

4 free stay Ch free € 2/1h. **Surface:** metalled.
01/01-31/12
Distance: 500m 500m 500m 500m 500m on the spot.
Remarks: Next to campsite municipal.

S Bagnols-sur-Cèze 30A3
Av. de l Europe, D8086. **GPS:** n44,16820 e4,61958.

20 free Ch against payment. **Surface:** gravel.
Distance: 200m 200m 200m.
Remarks: Max. 24h.

S Balaruc-les-Bains 29D4
Avenue des Hespérides 335. **GPS:** n43,44499 e3,67564.

12 € 8,50 Ch. **Location:** Rural, quiet. **Surface:** unpaved.
01/01-31/12
Distance: on the spot.

S Balaruc-les-Bains 29D4
Thermes Hespérides, Avenue des Hespérides. **GPS:** n43,44574 e3,67770.

6 € 7 Ch 55minutes WC included . **Location:** Simple, quiet.
Surface: asphalted. 01/01-31/12
Distance: 1km.
Remarks: Free bus to centre.

S Beaucaire 30A4
Les Marguilliers, Chemin des Marguilliers. **GPS:** n43,81667 e4,64107.

9 € 12/24h Ch included. **Surface:** gravel. 01/01-31/12
Distance: 500m 500m 500m 500m.

S Beaucaire 30A4
Quai de la Paix. **GPS:** n43,80615 e4,63739.

10 free € 2/100liter Ch € 2/1h. **Location:** Urban, simple.
Surface: asphalted. 01/01-31/12 water disconnected in winter.
Distance: 300m 300m bakery 300m.
Remarks: Coins at Tourist Info.

S Bédarieux 29C4
Avenue Jean Moulin. **GPS:** n43,61071 e3,15329.

FR

10 free Ch free. **Location:** Urban, simple, central, quiet. **Surface:** grassy. 01/01-31/12
Distance: on the spot on the spot on the spot 800m.
Remarks: Along the Orb river.

S Bélesta 29B6

Rue des Loisirs. **GPS**: n42,71545 e2,60918.

10 free € 2 Ch € 1. **Surface:** grassy/gravel. 01/04-31/10
Distance: 100m.

S Bellegarde 30A4

Port de plaisance, Las Courrejos Est. **GPS**: n43,74422 e4,51890.

free € 2 Ch € 2/1h. **Location:** Rural, simple. **Surface:** gravel/sand. 01/01-31/12
Distance: city centre 1,5km.
Remarks: At marina, max. 48h, coins service at harbourmaster.

S Belpech 29A5

Stade municipal, Rue du Stade. **GPS**: n43,19717 e1,75278.

15 free Ch free WC. **Surface:** grassy. 01/01-31/12
Distance: 1km 1km 1km.

Carcassonne 29B5

Parking Cité, P2. **GPS**: n43,20534 e2,37189.

free from 20-08h. **Surface:** asphalted.
Distance: 5km.

P Carcassonne 29B5

Place Gaston-Jourdanne. **GPS**: n43,21000 e2,36028.

20 free. **Surface:** asphalted/metalled.
Distance: 900m.

Tourist information Carcassonne:

Office de Tourisme, 15, Boulevard Camille Pelletan, www.carcassonne-tourisme.com.Medieval fortified city, museum city with many curiosities.

The new city has a modern shopping centre.

S Carnon 29D4

Avenue Grassion Cibrand, Carnon-plage. **GPS**: n43,55097 e3,99417.

15 € 11,50, 01/07-31/08 € 13 Ch WC included,on camp site € 5. **Location:** Rural. **Surface:** asphalted. 01/04-15/10
Distance: 1km 80m 50m.
Remarks: Next to campsite Les Saladelles.

Casteil 29B6

D116. **GPS**: n42,53324 e2,39230.

5 free. **Surface:** grassy/gravel. 01/04-31/10
Distance: 1km.

S Chusclan 30A3

Cave Chusclan, Route d'Orsan, D138. **GPS**: n44,14552 e4,67762.

FR

6 free Ch free. 01/01-31/12
Distance: 500m 500m.
Remarks: Max. 48h.

S Clermont-l'Hérault 29C4

Aire de stationnement camping-car, Lac du Salagou. **GPS**: n43,64677 e3,38915.

8 € 5-7 € 2/100liter Ch (6x). **Location:** Rural, simple, isolated, quiet. **Surface:** gravel. 01/01-31/12
Distance: 7km on the spot on the spot on the spot 7km on the spot on the spot.
Remarks: Coins at campsite.

Tourist information Clermont-l'Hérault:
Office de Tourisme, 9, Rue René Gosse.Medieval city on artificially lake, Lac de Salagou, 750ha.

S Collioure 29C6

Route de Madeloc. **GPS**: n42,52566 e3,06861.

12 + 80 € 15/24h Ch (12x) WC included.
Location: Comfortable, quiet. **Surface:** asphalted. 01/05-31/10
Distance: 2km 2,3km 2km 2km.
Remarks: Guarded parking, May-Sep free shuttle to Collioure.

Tourist information Collioure:
Office de Tourisme, Place du 18 Juin, www.collioure.com.Seaside resort and Catalonian harbour, source of inspiration for many famous painters: Picasso, Juan Gris, Derain and Duffy.
Quartier de Moure.District with small blank paved alleys.
Château Royal.Castle of the Templars, 12th century.

S Comps 30A4

Place des Arènes. **GPS**: n43,85402 e4,60724.

50 € 3 € 2/10minutes Ch € 2/55minutes WC .
Location: Rural. **Surface:** unpaved. 01/01-31/12
Distance: 100m.

Comps 30A4

GPS: n43,85390 e4,60912.

30 € 3. **Location:** Rural. **Surface:** unpaved. 01/01-31/12
Remarks: Along the river.

S Duilhac-sous-Peyrepertuse 29B5

GPS: n42,86160 e2,56527.

25 free € 2 Ch € 2 WC. **Surface:** asphalted. 01/04-31/10
Distance: 200m 200m.

S Fanjeaux 29A5

Chemin des Fontanelles. **GPS**: n43,18611 e2,03222.

15 free Ch free. **Surface:** grassy/gravel. 01/01-31/12
Distance: 100m.
Remarks: Next to maison de retraite (home for the elderly), max. 48h.

S Félines-Termenès 29B5

Av. de Termenes, dir Mouthoumet. **GPS**: n42,98691 e2,61285.

FR

3 free Ch free. **Surface:** gravel. 01/01-31/12

Distance: 50m.

Remarks: Closed when frosty.

Tourist information Félines-Termenès:

Cité Médiéval, Villerouge Termenes.Medieval village and castle from 12-14th century. 01/07-30/09.

Fitou 29C5

Aragon, Route Nationale 9, Les Cabanes de Fitou. **GPS**: n42,89275 e2,99672.

15 € 5/12h, € 7/24h Ch € 2,50 included. **Location:** Rural.

Surface: gravel. 01/01-31/12

Distance: A9 6,5km on the spot 500m.

Remarks: Terrain with video surveillance.

Fleury-d'Aude 29C5

Base de Loisirs Étang de Pissevache, Saint-Pierre-la-Mer. **GPS**: n43,18972 e3,19694.

100 € 6,50 € 2 Ch € 2/4h . **Surface:** unpaved.

01/01-31/12

Distance: sandy beach 300m.

Remarks: Parking directly behind the beach, next to tennis park and small surf lake, follow Base de Loisirs.

Fleury-d'Aude 29C5

Les-Cabanes-de-Fleury. **GPS**: n43,21529 e3,23315.

100 € 6,50 € 2 Ch. **Surface:** metalled/sand.

01/01-31/12

Distance: on the spot on the spot 200m.

Remarks: Next to camping Rive d'Aude, coins at capitainerie.

Florac 29C3

D16. **GPS**: n44,32582 e3,59032.

23 free € 2/100liter Ch € 2/1h WC free. **Location:** Rural, comfortable, central, quiet. **Surface:** asphalted. 01/01-31/12

Distance: 150m 300m 300m 150m 150m mountainbike trail on the spot.

Remarks: Nearby cemetery.

Tourist information Florac:

Office de Tourisme, Av J. Monestier, www.mescevennes.com.Old town in the National Park of the Cévennes.

Château de Florac. 01/01-31/12.

Fraïsse-sur-Agout 29B4

Allée des Tilleuls. **GPS**: n43,60583 e2,79778.

15 € 6 Ch (1x)included. **Surface:** asphalted/grassy.

01/01-31/12

Distance: 400m 20m 20m 400m.

Remarks: At the edge of village, on the Agout river.

Génolhac 29D3

Les Taillades, Place du 19 Mars 1962, D906. **GPS**: n44,35388 e3,94844.

10 free Ch free. **Location:** Rural, simple, isolated, quiet.

Surface: metalled. 01/01-31/12

Distance: 200m 800m on the spot.

Gruissan 29C5

Aire des 4 Vents, Avenue des quatre vents. **GPS**: n43,10444 e3,09944.

FR

80 free, 01/03-30/11 € 8,50 Ch WC included. **Surface:** gravel. 01/01-31/12
Distance: on the spot on the spot on the spot on the spot on the spot.

S Gruissan 29C5

Aire des Châlets, Avenue de la Jetée, Gruissan-plage. **GPS**: n43,09583 e3,11111.

80 free, 01/03-30/11 € 8,50 Ch included. **Surface:** gravel.
01/03-30/11
Distance: 2km on the spot on the spot 2km 2km.

S Gruissan 29C5

Étang de Mateille, Gruissan dir Narbonne-Plage, base de voile, D332. **GPS**: n43,12083 e3,11417.

150 € 8,50-10 Ch (24x)€ 1 WC .
Surface: grassy/metalled.
01/07-31/08
Distance: 4km on the spot on the spot 800m Lidl 2km.

Tourist information Gruissan:

Office de Tourisme, 1, boulevard du Pech-Maynaud, www.ville-gruissan.fr.Bathing resort and old town on the hillside of the Clape.

L'Hospitalet.Probably the largest wine-cellar of the world.

Vieux Port.Old fishing-port.

S Ispagnac 29C3

Le Pavillon, D907. **GPS**: n44,37077 e3,53687.

6 free Ch € 2 WC free. **Location:** Rural, simple, central, quiet.
Surface: asphalted/gravel. 01/04-31/10
Distance: 100m river 200m 100m 100m on the spot.

S La Canourgue 29C2

Avenue du Lot, D998. **GPS**: n44,43325 e3,20775.

10 free Ch free. **Location:** Rural, simple, isolated, quiet.
Surface: metalled. 01/01-31/12 Jul/Aug: tue.
Distance: 500m 1,3km 600m 600m 600m.
Remarks: Max. 24h.

S La Grande Motte 29D4

Aire camping-car Les Cigales, Avenue de la Petite Motte. **GPS**: n43,56789 e4,07404.

50 € 11, May-Sep € 16 Ch WC . **Location:** Rural.
Surface: gravel. 01/01-31/12
Distance: 2km 1,2km 2km 2km.

S Lagrasse 29B5

Parking de la Promenade, D3. **GPS**: n43,09273 e2,62004.

40 free Ch free. **Surface:** gravel.
01/01-31/12 Market day.
Distance: on the spot on the spot on the spot on the spot on the spot.

S Langogne 29D2

Base Nautique l'Espace Bleu. **GPS**: n44,73598 e3,83489.

50 € 12 Ch included. **Location:** Rural, simple, quiet.
Surface: unpaved. 01/01-31/12
Distance: 2km beach 1km on the spot 2km 2km.
Remarks: At lake Naussac, max. 48h.

S Langogne 29D2

Centre Polyvalente. **GPS**: n44,72281 e3,85419.

FR

10 free € 2/100liter Ch. **Location:** Central, quiet. **Surface:** asphalted. 01/01-31/12
Distance: on the spot 300m 300m on the spot.
Remarks: Coins at Tourist Info.

Tourist information Langogne:
Office de Tourisme, 15, Bd des Capucins, www.langogne.com.

S Lapradelle Puilaurens 29B6
D117. **GPS**: n42,81003 e2,30854.

6 free Chfree. **Surface:** gravel.
Distance: on the spot on the spot on the spot.
Remarks: At fire-station.

S Latour-Bas-Elne 29C6
Aire de Latour Bas Elne, Route de la Mer. **GPS**: n42,60017 e3,00667.

40 € 10, € 14 Jun-Aug, trailer € 4 Ch included € 3/2day.
Location: Comfortable. **Surface:** grassy. 01/01-31/12
Distance: 3km.
Remarks: Guarded parking, baker at 8am.

S Latour-de-Carol 29A6
Village Club Yravals, 2 Rue de Saneja. **GPS**: n42,45829 e1,89460.

5 € 5 Ch WC included € 2/day. **Surface:** grassy.
01/04-31/10
Distance: 2km.

S Laudun 30A3
Place des Arènes. **GPS**: n44,10791 e4,65556.

3 free € 4 Ch. **Surface:** asphalted. 01/01-31/12
Distance: 300m 300m 300m.

S Le Bosc 29C4
Parc Activités Méridienne. **GPS**: n43,68932 e3,35328.

10 free € 2/100liter Ch € 2/1h. **Location:** Highway, simple, isolated. **Surface:** asphalted. 01/01-31/12
Distance: 400m on the spot Intermarché 50m.

S Le Boulou 29B6
Chemin du Moulin Nou. **GPS**: n42,52719 e2,83704.

21 free ChWCfree. **Surface:** asphalted. 01/01-31/12
Remarks: In front of cemetery, max. 24h.

S Le Cap d'Agde 29C5
Rue du Gouverneur. **GPS**: n43,28600 e3,51739.

30 € 5 02/11-26/03, € 10 27/03-02/11 € 2/25 Ch included.
Location: Rural, comfortable, central. **Surface:** asphalted/metalled.
01/01-31/12
Distance: on the spot 500m 500m 500m.
Remarks: Nearby Camping La Clape, video surveillance.

S Le Caylar 29C4
Domaine des Templiers, Route de la Couvertoirade, D609. **GPS**: n43,86944 e3,31466.

FR

30 € 3 € 2,10/100liter Ch € 2,10/15minutes (9x)€ 2,10/4h.
Location: Comfortable, isolated, quiet. **Surface:** gravel. 01/04-31/10
Distance: 600m 500m on the spot.

Le Grau du Roi 29D4

Parking de la plage, Rue du Commandant Marceau. **GPS**: n43,54061 e4,13349.

40 € 8,80, June-Aug € 12,50 € 2/100liter Ch € 2/55minutes.
Surface: asphalted.
01/01-31/12
Distance: centre 550m sandy beach 20m on the spot on the spot.
Remarks: Beach parking with video surveillance.

Le Malzieu-Ville 29C2

Place Foirail. **GPS**: n44,85506 e3,33385.

6 free Ch WC free. **Location:** Rural, simple, comfortable, central, quiet. **Surface:** asphalted. 01/01-31/12
Distance: on the spot 10km on the spot 200m 200m
on the spot.

Le Monastir 29C2

Place de la Gare. **GPS**: n44,50896 e3,25162.

4 free Ch WC free. **Location:** Rural, simple, isolated, quiet.
Surface: asphalted. 01/01-31/12
Distance: 1km 1,5km 1km.
Remarks: Coins at petrol station, picnic area present, 2013: during inspection service out of order. Motorhome parking, A75 Clermont Ferrand-Millau exit 39, 10km south of Marvejols.

Le Ségala 29A4

Esplanade du Canal. **GPS**: n43,34089 e1,83544.

10 free € 1 Ch € 2 WC. **Surface:** gravel. 01/01-31/12
Distance: on the spot on the spot on the spot on the spot.

Les Angles 29A6

Pla del Mir. GPS: n42,56365 e2,06599.

100 free Ch WC free. **Surface:** asphalted. 01/01-31/12
Distance: 2,6km.

Les Mages 29D3

Serre Marine, D904, St. Ambroix/Alés. **GPS**: n44,23442 e4,16967.

7 free Ch free. **Location:** Rural, simple, isolated, noisy.
Surface: metalled. 01/01-31/12
Distance: 700m 700m 800m.
Remarks: Picnic area.

Leucate 29C5

Aire camping-car, Chemin du Mouret, Leucate Plage. **GPS**: n42,90022 e3,05272.

100 € 7,20/24h € 2 Ch. **Location:** Rural, simple.
Surface: asphalted/gravel. 01/01-31/12
Distance: 300m on the spot on the spot.
Remarks: Beach parking, baker on site (20/03-31/10).

Leucate 29C5

Chemin des Coussoules, La Franqui. **GPS**: n42,94329 e3,02917.

FR

70 € 6 Ch on camp site € 5. **Surface:** unpaved. 01/02-30/11
Distance: 2km on the spot on the spot 2km 2km.
Remarks: Next to campsite Coussoules, check in at reception.

S Leucate 29C5

Le Goulet, D627. **GPS:** n42,91145 e3,01946.

150 free, 15/02-15/11 € 7,20/24h € 2 Ch € 2.
Location: Rural, simple. **Surface:** unpaved.
01/01-31/12
Distance: centre Leucate 850m on the spot on the spot.
Remarks: Terraces, at lake of Leucate, baker on site (20/03-31/10).

Tourist information Leucate:
Office de Tourisme, Espace Culturel, www.leucate.net.

S Limoux 29B5

Parking, Rue Louis Braille. **GPS:** n43,05741 e2,21490.
10 free Ch free. **Surface:** metalled. 01/01-31/12

S Lunas 29C4

Base de Loisirs Prade, D35. **GPS:** n43,70555 e3,18555.

75 free Ch free. **Location:** Urban, simple, isolated, quiet.
Surface: grassy. 01/01-31/12
Distance: 900m on the spot on the spot 200m 700m 200m.

S Marseillan-Plage 29C5

Rue des Goélands. **GPS:** n43,31902 e3,54864.

122 € 4-6-10/24h € 2/10minutes Ch
Location: Comfortable, quiet. **Surface:** gravel. 01/01-31/12
Distance: on the spot sandy beach 600m on the spot on the spot.

S Marvéjols 29C2

Boulevard Aurelle de Paladines, Le Pré de Suzon. **GPS:** n44,55406 e3,28753.

10 free Ch WC free. **Location:** Central.
Surface: asphalted.
Distance: on the spot 7,5km on the spot on the spot.

Tourist information Marvéjols:
Maison de Tourisme, Porte du Soubeyran, www.ville-marvejols.fr.Old fortress city, gates with battlements and towers.

Matemale 29A6

Rue de la Truite. **GPS:** n42,57106 e2,10984.

10 free. **Location:** Rural. **Surface:** gravel. 01/01-31/12
Distance: 500m 20m 20m 500m 500m.
Remarks: Parking at lake.

S Matemale 29A6

Camping du Lac, Route des Cariolettes. **GPS:** n42,58197 e2,10584.
€ 12 € 3 Ch WC . **Surface:** grassy. 01/01-31/12
Distance: 1km.

S Mende 29C2

Rue du Faubourg Montbel. **GPS:** n44,52063 e3,49660.

23 free € 2/10minutes Ch free € 2/55minutes. **Location:** Urban, comfortable, central, quiet. **Surface:** asphalted.
01/01-31/12
Distance: on the spot on the spot 200m 400m on the spot on the spot.
Remarks: Max. 4 days, along the Lot river.

S Mèze 29C4

Complexe sportif des Sesquiers, Route de Villeveyrac. **GPS:** n43,44135 e3,59436.

FR

6 free Ch free. **Location:** Noisy. **Surface:** gravel.
Distance: 2,5km 10km.

Tourist information Mèze:

Lagunage.Sea-farm for preservation of natural beauty and aquarium.

Le Mourre Blanc, Bassin de Thau.Oyster culture houses.

S Mont-Louis 29A6

Parking des Remparts. GPS: n42,50765 e2,12273.

20 €3 included. **Surface:** asphalted.
Distance: 200m 200m 200m.
Remarks: Parking at city wall.

Tourist information Mont-Louis:

Fortified city, 17th century.

FR

S Montagnac 29C4

D613. **GPS:** n43,47520 e3,49129.

3 free Ch free. **Surface:** gravel.
Distance: 1km 1km 1km.

Montcalm 29D4

Le Caveau du Chêne, Route d'Aigues Mortes, D58. **GPS:** n43,57322 e4,30505.

40 free for clients. **Location:** Rural, isolated, quiet. **Surface:** grassy.
01/01-31/12

S Montferrand 29A4

Col de Naurouze, Route du Ségala, N113> D218. **GPS:** n43,35238 e1,82390.

20 free . **Surface:** gravel. 01/01-31/12
Distance: 2km on the spot 2km.

P Montpellier 29D4

Parking Joffre, Rue D'Argencour. **GPS:** n43,61316 e3,88608.
€ 1/h. **Surface:** asphalted. 01/01-31/12
Distance: 4km.
Remarks: Overnight stay possible. Via avenue Jean Mermoz.

Tourist information Montpellier:

Office de Tourisme, 30, Allée Jean de Lattre de Tassigny, Esplanade Comédie, www.ot-montpellier.fr.

Corum.Opera-complex.

Place de la Comédie.Square with many cafés.

S Mourèze 29C4

D8. **GPS:** n43,61728 e3,36111.

6 €6 Ch WC included. **Location:** Simple, isolated, quiet.
Surface: gravel. 01/01-31/12
Distance: on the spot 300m on the spot.

S Murviel-lès-Béziers 29C4

Route de Réals, D36. **GPS:** n43,43953 e3,13420.

12 €3 Ch (6x) WC included. **Location:** Rural, comfortable, isolated, quiet. **Surface:** unpaved. 15/04-15/10
Distance: 700m 10km 700m on the spot.
Remarks: Max. 7 nights.

S Narbonne 29C5

Parking du Parc des Sports, Avenue de la Mer. **GPS:** n43,18017 e3,02294.

36 € 9/day € 2 Ch € 2 .
Surface: asphalted.
01/01-31/12
Distance: on the spot 2,3km Carrefour.
Remarks: Free bus to centre every 30 minutes.

Tourist information Narbonne:
Office de Tourisme, Place Roger Salengro.Old Roman port city.
Autorail Touristique du Minervois.Train tourist from Narbonne to Bize.
01/07-17/09.
Musée d'Archéologie et de Préhistoire.Archeological findings.
Palais des Archevêques.Palace, 11th century, with cathedral.
Thu, Su.
Réserve Africain, Sigean.Safaripark, 200 ha.
daily from 9h.

S Nîmes 29D4

Domaine de Fontbespierre, 3359, route d'Anduze. **GPS**: n43,87142 e4,27746.

50 € 8 € 2 Ch € 2/day WC. **Surface:** grassy. 01/01-31/12
Distance: 6km 6km 6km.
Remarks: Terrain with video surveillance.

Octon 29C4

Avenue de la Molière. **GPS**: n43,65390 e3,30378.

free. **Surface:** gravel.
Distance: 50m 50m 50m.
Remarks: Parking behind 'Clamery', walking and bicycle area, Lac du Salagou.

S Ouveillan 29C5

Place Cave Coopératieve. **GPS**: n43,29204 e2,97080.

7 free Ch free. **Surface:** gravel/metalled. 01/01-31/12
Distance: 2km 2km 2km.

S Palavas-les-Flots 29D4

D62E2. **GPS**: n43,53281 e3,92654.

23 € 11-19 Ch included. **Surface:** asphalted. 01/01-31/12
Distance: centre 600m sandy beach 800m.

S Palavas-les-Flots 29D4

Port Fluvial, Base Paul Riquet, Avenue de Lattre Tassigny. **GPS**: n43,53091 e3,92316.

200 € 11, Jul-Aug € 19 + € 0,22/pp tourist tax, extra charge >8m and trailer
€ 3 Ch € 2 WC included . **Surface:** asphalted.
01/01-31/12
Distance: 1km 1km 1km.

Tourist information Palavas-les-Flots:
Office de Tourisme, Place de la Méditerranée, www.palavaslesflots.com. Bathing resort and fishermans village, separated by a canal and linked by a telpher carrier, Transcanal.

S Peyriac-de-Mer 29C5

Rue des Étangs. **GPS**: n43,09372 e2,96205.

20 € 5 Ch WC . **Location:** Rural, simple, simple.
Surface: grassy/metalled. 01/01-31/12
Distance: 1km on the spot 1km 1km on the spot on the spot.
Remarks: Next to rugby ground.

Pézenas 29C4

Promenade du Pré St.Jean, Avenue du Maréchal Leclerc. **GPS**: n43,46054 e3,42622.

free. **Surface:** metalled. 01/01-31/12
Distance: on the spot 1km.
Remarks: Parking in the centre.

FR

Tourist information Pézenas:

Office de Tourisme, Place Gambetta, www.paysdepezenas.net.Artists village with historical centre.

Barbier Gely.Barbers' boutique.

Musée Vulliode St German.Collection of tapestry.

Sa.

Pezens 29B5

Place de la Liberté, D6113. **GPS**: n43,25528 e2,26361.

5 free free. **Surface:** gravel. 01/01-31/12

Distance: 50m 50m 50m.

Port Vendres 29C6

Plage des Tamarins, Route de la Jetée. **GPS**: n42,51778 e3,11375.

30 € 5,50, Jul/Aug € 9 € 2/100liter Chincluded WC. **Location:** Rural, simple. **Surface:** gravel. 01/01-31/12

Distance: 1,3km 100m on the spot.

Tourist information Port Vendres:

Port Venus.Old fishing-port, quay for cruise ships.

Port-la-Nouvelle 29C5

Chemin des Vignes. **GPS**: n43,01366 e3,04077.

30 free, May-Jun, Sep € 4, Jul/Aug € 7 € 2/15minutes Ch € 2/15minutes included,on camp site. **Location:** Rural, simple.

Surface: grassy/gravel.

Distance: 2km 8,6km 2km 2km 1km Huit-à-huit, Passage de l'Abbé Gavanon.

Portiragnes 29C5

Avenue de la Grande Maïre. **GPS**: n43,27558 e3,35156.

± 15 free. **Location:** Rural, simple, quiet. **Surface:** unpaved.

01/01-31/12

Distance: sandy beach 200m.

Remarks: Max. 2 days.

Quillan 29B5

Parking Joseph Courjétaire, D117. **GPS**: n42,87366 e2,18266.

10 free € 2 Ch WC. **Surface:** asphalted. 01/01-31/12

Distance: on the spot on the spot on the spot on the spot on the spot.

Remarks: Nearby railwayline.

Remoulins 30A3

N86. **GPS**: n43,93789 e4,55851.

10 free € 5/20minutes Ch. **Location:** Urban. **Surface:** asphalted.

Distance: 100m 100m 100m.

Remarks: Parking nearby river, service on the other side of the bridge: Route du Pont du Gare.

Tourist information Remoulins:

Pont du Gard.Roman aqueduct.

Rieutort-de-Randon 29C2

Lac de Charpal. **GPS**: n44,62491 e3,56046.

10 free. **Location:** Rural, isolated, quiet. **Surface:** unpaved. 01/01-31/12

Distance: 8km 18km on the spot on the spot on the spot on the spot.

Remarks: At lake Charpal.

FR

S Rigarda 29B6

Aire 66, Route de Finestret. **GPS**: n42,62585 e2,52898.

30 € 5 Ch included. **Location:** Rural, simple, isolated, quiet. **Surface:** grassy/gravel. 01/01-31/12
Distance: Vinça 2,7km 2,7km 2,7km.

S Routier 29A5

Place Malèbre. **GPS**: n43,10737 e2,12738.

± 7 free free. **Surface:** gravel/metalled. 01/01-31/12
Distance: on the spot.

Tourist information Routier:

Corbières.Region is known for its wines and the Cathar citadels, the castle of Queribus in Cucugan is one of the last bastions of the Cathars.

S Saillagousse 29A6

Rue des Sports. **GPS**: n42,45764 e2,03766.

7 free € 3 Ch WC. **Surface:** asphalted.
01/01-31/12
Distance: on the spot on the spot on the spot.
Remarks: Coins at Mairie, office de tourisme. N116, behind Hotel Christiannia.

S Saint-Cyprien 29C6

Aire du Théâtre de la Mer, Quai Arthur Rimbaud. **GPS**: n42,61776 e3,03512.

49 € 12,50/24h15/10-31/03 € 10,15/24h Ch included.
Location: Comfortable. **Surface:** asphalted.
01/01-31/12 service 15/10-31/03.
Distance: 450m marina 300m.

S Saint-Thibéry 29C4

Domaine de la Vière, Chemin de la Vière. **GPS**: n43,38301 e3,40137.
€ 10 Ch WC included. **Surface:** unpaved.
01/01-31/12
Distance: 2km A9 3km 14km.
Remarks: During the weekend possible inconvenience of motocross.

S Salles-sur-l'Herbs 29A5

Allée des Platanes. **GPS**: n43,29194 e1,78844.

10 free Ch free. **Surface:** gravel. 01/01-31/12
Distance: on the spot 100m 100m.

S Sauve 29D3

D999. **GPS**: n43,94017 e3,95218.

5 free Chfree. **Location:** Urban, simple, central, noisy.
Surface: metalled. 01/01-31/12
Distance: 50m 50m on the spot.

S Sérignan-Plage 29C5

Parking Mini-Golf, Avenue de la Plage. **GPS**: n43,26892 e3,33629.

20 € 13, Jul/Aug € 17 Ch WC included € 4. **Location:** Rural, comfortable, quiet. **Surface:** unpaved. 01/01-31/12
Distance: 150m on the spot 150m.
Remarks: Behind restaurant, swimming pool, bread-service.

S Servian 29C4

Servian Camping-cars, Zone d'Activité de la Baume, D18E5. **GPS**: n43,38994 e3,31368.
€ 8 € 2 Ch € 2. **Surface:** asphalted. 01/01-31/12
Distance: 2km.
Remarks: Motorhome dealer, on industrial area.

S Sète 29C5

Parking Les 3 Digues. **GPS**: n43,36663 e3,61523.

FR

30 free € 2/10 Ch. **Location:** Rural, simple. **Surface:** gravel. 01/01-31/12
Distance: 50m on the spot on the spot.
Remarks: Beach parking, 01/06-30/09 no dogs allowed on the beach.

S Sommières 29D4

Chemin de la Princesse. **GPS:** n43,78701 e4,08717.

25 free € 3 Ch. **Surface:** gravel.
Distance: 500m.
Remarks: In front of campsite municipal.

S St.André 29C6

Parking de Taxo. GPS: n42,55248 e2,97303.

6 € 2,30 € 2 Ch € 2. **Surface:** asphalted. 01/01-31/12
Distance: on the spot.
Remarks: Max. 3 nights, coins at Office de Tourisme.

S St.Chély-d'Apcher 29C2

Parking du Péchaud, Boulevard G. d'Apcher, N9. **GPS:** n44,80084 e3,27296.

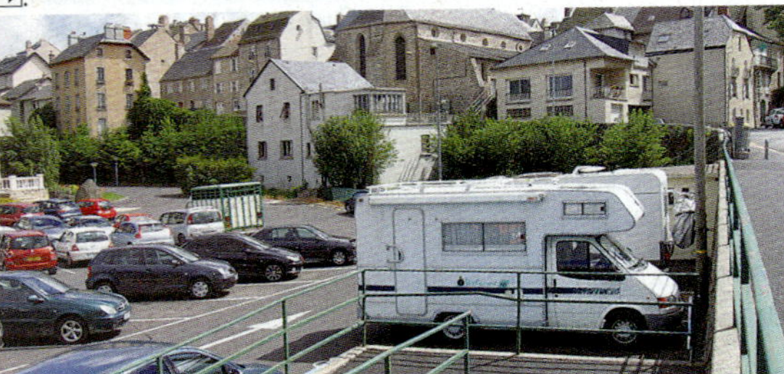

2 free € 2/100liter Ch € 2/10minutes. **Location:** Simple, central, quiet. **Surface:** asphalted. 01/01-31/12
Distance: 200m 2,5km 200m 200m on the spot.
Remarks: Coins at Tourist Info.

St.Gilles 30A4

Quai du Canal. **GPS:** n43,67154 e4,43281.

free. **Location:** Rural. **Surface:** asphalted. 01/01-31/12
Distance: 500m 200m 500m.
Tourist information St.Gilles:
Abbay St.Gilles.Abbey with underground church.

S St.Jean-du-Gard 29D3

Av. de la Resistance. **GPS:** n44,10210 e3,88347.

20 free Ch WC free. **Location:** Urban, simple. **Surface:** metalled. 01/01-31/12
Distance: on the spot 100m 100m 50m 300m on the spot.
Remarks: 2013: during inspection service out of order.

S St.Mamert-du-Gard 29D4

Route du Stade. **GPS:** n43,88479 e4,19057.

6 free Ch free. **Surface:** metalled. 01/01-31/12
Distance: 200m.
Remarks: Between Uzès and Sommières.

S St.Marsal 29B6

GPS: n42,53755 e2,62242.
25 € 2,50 Ch WC free. **Surface:** asphalted. 01/01-31/12
Distance: on the spot nearby nearby.

S St.Mathieu-de-Tréviers 29D4

D17. **GPS:** n43,76206 e3,86016.

8 € 5 Ch included. **Surface:** gravel. 01/01-31/12
Distance: 1km.
Remarks: Check in at gymnasium.

FR

S Thues-entre-Valls 29B6

Gorges de la Carança. GPS: n42,52320 e2,22203.

25 € 4 Ch included. **Surface:** gravel.
01/01-31/12 frost.
Distance: 2km.

S Tournissan 29B5

M. Bailly, Route de Saint Laurent B452, Lieu-dit la Paulette. **GPS:** n43,08068 e2,67280.

3 free Ch free. **Surface:** gravel. 01/04-31/10
Distance: 500m.

S Vailhan 29C4

Parking de l'Eglise. GPS: n43,55527 e3,29882.

6 free Ch free. **Surface:** gravel. 01/01-31/12
Distance: 1km 200m 50m.

S Vallabrègues 30A4

Route d'Aramon, D183A. **GPS:** n43,85763 e4,62639.

5 free € 2 Ch € 2. **Location:** Rural. **Surface:** gravel.
01/01-31/12 high water.
Distance: 500m.
Remarks: At lake and along the Rhone river.

S Valras-Plage 29C5

Avenue du Casino. **GPS:** n43,28162 e3,24230.

30 free € 2 Ch.
Surface: asphalted/metalled.
01/10-30/06 summer.
Distance: on the spot 200m on the spot on the spot on the spot.
Remarks: Behind casino/disco, no camping activity, service: Boulevard Pierre Giraud 200m.

S Villeneuve-lès-Maguelone 29D4

Avenue René Poitevin. **GPS:** n43,52980 e3,86584.

26 € 9, 26/04-30/09 € 14/24h Ch included.
Location: Rural. **Surface:** asphalted.
01/01-31/12
Distance: 500m 8km 2,5km 500m 250m 50m on the spot.
Remarks: 26/04-30/09: also cash payment at office de tourisme (200m).

S Villeneuve-Minervois 29B5

Avenue du Jeu de Mail. **GPS:** n43,31516 e2,46432.

20 free Ch WC. **Surface:** asphalted/metalled. 01/01-31/12
Distance: on the spot on the spot on the spot.
Remarks: Max. 48h, parking in front of town hall.

Provence-Alpes-Côte d'Azur

S Allos 30D3

GPS: n44,24289 e6,62220.

30 € 5 Ch (9x)included WC. **Surface:** asphalted.
01/01-31/12

FR

Distance: 500m 200m 500m 500m 200m 200m.
Remarks: Driving out of village dir Base de Loisirs.

Allos 30D3

Parking de la Cluite. **GPS**: n44,24677 e6,66918.

6 free. **Surface:** gravel.
Distance: Allos 6,5km.
Remarks: Isolated parking, Jul/Aug shuttle bus to Lac d'Allos.

Allos 30D3

La Foux d'Allos. **GPS**: n44,29583 e6,56944.

5 free Ch WC free. **Surface:** asphalted.
Distance: 1km 100m 100m Skibus 50m 50m.
Remarks: Follow Col d'Allos.

Annot 30D3

Chemin de la Colle Basse. **GPS**: n43,96351 e6,66386.

20 free Ch free. **Surface:** grassy/gravel. 01/01-31/12
Distance: 400m 400m 400m.

Arles 30A4

Place Lamartine. **GPS**: n43,68151 e4,63046.

6 free Ch free. **Surface:** asphalted.
Distance: 50m on the spot on the spot 50m 100m.

Tourist information Arles:

Office de Tourisme, Boulevard des Lices, www.tourisme.ville-arles.fr.City on the border of the nature reserve Camargue with Roman ruin. The painter Van Gogh lived in Arles, 1888-89.

Église St.Trophine.Romanesque and Gothic construction.

Palais Constantin.Large Roman imperial palace of which only the baths are left.

Avignon 30A3

Chemin de l'Ile Piot. **GPS**: n43,95167 e4,79361.

20 free. **Surface:** asphalted. 01/01-31/12
Distance: 800m 800m 800m on the spot.
Remarks: Free bus to centre every ten minutes.

Tourist information Avignon:

Office de Tourisme, 41, cours Jean Jaurès, www.ot-avignon.fr.Roman city dominated by the Palais du Papes. 01/04-31/08, 01/10-31/10 9-17h, 01/09-30/09 9-20h, 01/11-31/03 9-12.45h, 14-18h.

Place d'Horloge.Cosy square in the old centre of the city.

Pont Saint Bénézet.Known as the Pont d'Avignon, bridge over the river Rhône.

Petit Palais.Former residence of the archbishop.

Bagnols-en-Fôret 30D4

Parc de Notre-Dame Les Merles, 1 chemin des Meules, D47. **GPS**: n43,53590 e6,68893.

€ 5 € 4. **Location:** Rural. **Surface:** grassy. 01/01-31/12
Distance: 1km 1km 1km.

Banon 30B3

Rue de la Grande Fontaine. **GPS**: n44,03982 e5,63006.

± 15 € 3/24h Ch free WC. **Location:** Rural, simple.
Surface: metalled.
Distance: 250m 250m 100m.
Remarks: Tue-morning market.

Barcelonnette 30D3

Parking du Bouguet, Chemin des Alpages. **GPS**: n44,38222 e6,65778.

15 € 6 € 2/100liter Ch € 2/1h. **Surface:** grassy.
01/01-31/12
Distance: 500m 200m 500m 500m.

S Bédoin 30B3

Chemin des Sablières. **GPS**: n44,12472 e5,17167.

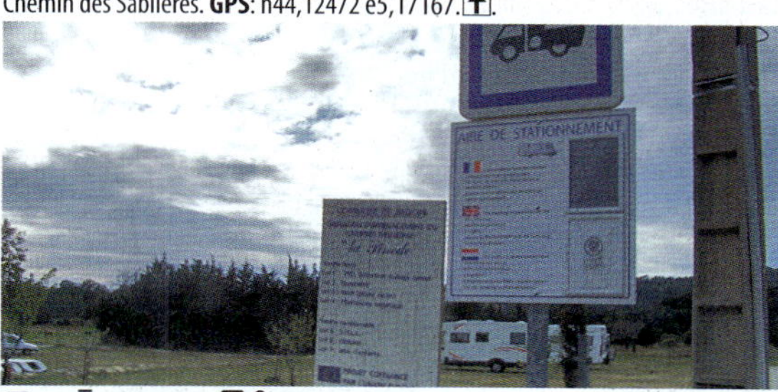

€ 3 € 2/100liter Ch. **Surface:** grassy.
Remarks: Max. 3 nights.

S Bollène 30A3

Centre Leclerc, Route de Saint Paul Trois Châteaux, D26. **GPS**: n44,32222 e4,74306.

free Chfree. 01/01-31/12
Distance: 4,3km.
Remarks: Service only during opening hours shop.

Tourist information Bollène:
Office de Tourisme, Place Reynaud de la Gardette, www.bollenetourisme.com.
Village Troglodyte.Cave dwelling village. 01/04-31/10 9.30-19h, 01/11-31/03 Sa-Su, holidays 14-18h 01/12-31/01.

S Briançon 30C2

Parc des Sports, Rue Jean Moulin. **GPS**: n44,89010 e6,62824.
free Ch.
Remarks: At sports park.

Tourist information Briançon:
Office de Tourisme, 1, place du Temple, www.ot-briancon.fr.Highest city of Europe, fortress is now a tourist centre, in winter as winter sports resort and in summer parapente, rafting and biking.
Parc des Écrins.Nature reserve.

S Caille 30D4

Aire de Caille, Chemin de la Plaine. **GPS**: n43,77893 e6,73331.

3 free € 2/15minutes Ch € 2/15minutes. 01/01-31/12
Distance: 50m 50m 100m.

S Carpentras 30A3

Chemin de la Roque-sur-Pernes. **GPS**: n44,04398 e5,05372.
8 free Chfree. **Surface:** asphalted.
Distance: 1,5km.
Remarks: Max. 24h.

Tourist information Carpentras:
Office de Tourisme, Place Aristide Briand, www.ville-carpentras.fr.Old city with historical centre. Mo-Fri Jewish holiday.
Hôtel Dieu.Former hospital, 18th century.
Centre-ville. Fri-morning.

S Carro 30A5

Quai Jean Verandy. **GPS**: n43,32931 e5,04076.

70 € 6, 01/04-30/06 € 8, 01/07-31/08 € 10 Ch included.
Surface: metalled. 01/01-31/12
Distance: on the spot on the spot 200m 200m.
Remarks: Max. 72h, fish sales from 08h.

S Castellane 30C4

GPS: n43,84667 e6,51406.

28 € 5 Ch included. **Surface:** asphalted.
Distance: 100m on the spot.
Remarks: Directly at the river, near Pont du Roc.

Tourist information Castellane:
Office de Tourisme, Rue Nationale, www.castellane.org.Holiday resort and good starting point for a visit to the Gorges du Verdon.
Sa-morning.

S Cavalière 30C5

GPS: n43,15242 e6,43221.

FR

30 € 15. **Surface:** sand.
Distance: 50m Plage-Restaurant-Bar Le Cannier 200m.
Remarks: Parking at beach, at coast road D559.

S Château-Arnoux-Saint-Auban 30C3

Avenue Gén. de Gaulle, N85. **GPS:** n44,09543 e6,01022.
+10 free Chfree. **Location:** Central, noisy.
Surface: asphalted.
Distance: on the spot.

S Chorges 30C2

Place du champ de foire. **GPS:** n44,54600 e6,28008.

10 free free. 01/01-31/12
Remarks: Max. 12h.

Tourist information Chorges:

Lac de Serre Ponçon, Serre Ponçon.Clear blue artificial lake, many water sports.

Office de Tourisme, Place Centrale, www.otchorges.com.

S Colmars-les-Alpes 30D3

GPS: n44,17943 e6,62695.

10 free € 2 Ch. **Surface:** asphalted. 01/01-31/12
Distance: 300m 50m 50m 300m 300m.
Remarks: Tue market.

S Comps-sur-Artuby 30C4

D955. **GPS:** n43,70652 e6,50678.

free € 3 Ch WC. **Surface:** gravel. 01/01-31/12
Distance: 350m pizzeria/crêperie.

Remarks: Max. 12h.

S Cuges-les-Pins 30B5

Le Jardin de la Ville. GPS: n43,28114 e5,70592.

10 € 3/12-12h Ch included. 01/01-31/12
Distance: 500m 500m 500m.
Remarks: Monitored parking.

Tourist information Cuges-les-Pins:

M Musée Légion Etrangères, Aubagne.Museum about the French Foreign Legion.

S Dauphin 30B4

Route de la Rencontre. **GPS:** n43,90028 e5,78417.

free Chfree. **Surface:** metalled.
Remarks: Near Salle des Fêtes.

S Digne-les-Bains 30C3

Le Vallon des Sources, Avenue des Thermes. **GPS:** n44,07998 e6,26091.

25 free € 2 Ch. 01/01-31/12
Distance: 2,5km 750m 2km 100m.
Remarks: Coins available at pay-desk of theTherme. Follow Therme.

S Fayence 30D4

Allée des Jardins. **GPS:** n43,62308 e6,68982.
5 free € 4 Ch.
Remarks: Max. 48h, at tennis-court and swimming pool.

Fontvieille 30A4

Parking du Moulin de Daudet, Allée des Plns. **GPS:** n43,72000 e4,71200.

€ 3. **Surface:** gravel.
Distance: 800m.

S Gap 30C2

Parking Dumont, Avenue Commandant Dumont, N85. **GPS**: n44,56544 e6,08447. →.

3 free € 3 Ch € 3. **Surface:** asphalted.
Distance: 500m on the spot on the spot.
Remarks: Stay overnight allowed at other pitches.

Tourist information Gap:
Office de Tourisme, 2a, Cours Frédéric Mistral, www.ville-gap.fr.

S Gémenos 30B5

Cours Sudre. **GPS**: n43,29772 e5,62953.

3 free Ch free. **Surface:** metalled.
Distance: 100m 100m 100m.
Remarks: Max. 24h.

S Gigondas 30A3

Domaine des Florets, Route des Dentelles, D80. **GPS**: n44,16220 e5,01725. ↑.

3 free free. **Surface:** gravel.
Distance: 1,7km 500m.
Remarks: Check in at tasting room.

Gordes 30B4

D2. **GPS**: n43,90056 e5,19306. ↑.

20 free. **Surface:** gravel. 01/01-31/12
Distance: 2km 2km 2km.

S Greasque 30B4

Musée de la Mine, Route de Puits Hely d'Oissel. **GPS**: n43,43281 e5,53439.

15 free Ch free. **Surface:** gravel. 16/01-20/12
Distance: 600m.

S Gréoux-les-Bains 30C4

Aire Camping-car, Chemin de la Barque. **GPS**: n43,75562 e5,88862. ↑→.

80 € 7 Ch WC included. **Surface:** grassy.
01/01-31/12
Distance: 150m 150m 150m.
Remarks: Max. 3,5t.

S Grimaud 30C5

Saint Pons Les Mûres, D98. **GPS**: n43,28000 e6,57806. ↑.

12 € 13 € 2,50 Ch € 2,50. **Location:** Simple.
Surface: asphalted. 01/01-31/12
Distance: 800m 200m 500m.
Remarks: Max. 72h.

Grimaud 30C5

Plage du Gros Pin, N98. **GPS**: n43,28450 e6,59498. ↑.
10. **Surface:** asphalted.
Distance: 5km on the spot.

S Guillaumes 30D3

D2202. **GPS**: n44,08861 e6,85285. ↑→.

10 free € 2/100liter Ch € 2/1h. 01/01-31/12
Distance: 50m on the spot on the spot 50m 50m.
Remarks: Coins at Bar-Tabac, office de tourisme, town hall.

FR

S Guillestre 30D2

Quartier Saint James. **GPS**: n44,65731 e6,63306.
Ch € 5. 01/01-31/12, 8-20h
Remarks: Nearby campsite Saint James les Pins.

Tourist information Guillestre:
Maison de Tourisme, Place Salva, www.pays-du-guillestrois.com.
Mo.

S Hyères 30C5

Le Mérou, D42, L'Ayguade. **GPS**: n43,10897 e6,18117.

6 € 3/15minutes Ch .

S Hyères 30C5

Les Etangs de Sauvebonne, 566 Route de Pierrefeu. **GPS**: n43,16120 e6,12133.

20 € 10 Chincluded € 3/day. **Location:** Rural, quiet.
Surface: grassy. 01/01-31/12
Distance: on the spot on the spot.

S Jausiers 30D3

Route de Jausiers-Barcelonette, D900. **GPS**: n44,41266 e6,72936.

3 free € 3 Ch . **Surface:** metalled. 01/01-31/12
Distance: 600m 50m 100m 400m.

Jausiers 30D3

Lotissement des Neiges. **GPS**: n44,41278 e6,72472.

15 free. **Surface:** unpaved. 01/01-31/12
Distance: 600m on the spot 100m 400m.
Remarks: Service 200m.

S La Bastide 30D4

GPS: n43,73806 e6,62583.

4 free Ch. **Surface:** asphalted. 01/01-31/12
Distance: 200m 100m 100m.

S La Bréole 30C2

Bourg La Bréole. **GPS**: n44,45777 e6,29194.

6 free Ch WC free. **Surface:** asphalted. 01/01-31/12
Distance: on the spot 2km 2km Lac de Serre Ponçon 100m 100m.

S La Crau 30C5

Espace Lavage Auto Grand Bleu, La Moutonne. **GPS**: n43,12417 e6,07444.

3 € 4/night Ch WCincluded. **Surface:** concrete.
01/01-31/12
Remarks: Free after washing the motor home (€ 10).

S La Londe-les-Maures 30C5

Rond-point Ducourneau, chemin du Pansard. **GPS**: n43,13185 e6,23053.

4 free € 3 Ch .
Distance: 800m.
Remarks: Max. 24h.

S La Motte 30C4

Moulin de Vallongues, Avenue Fréderique Mistral, D47. **GPS**: n43,49630 e6,53134.

FR

10 free Ch € 6 **Surface:** gravel. 01/01-31/12
Distance: 600m 600m 4km.
Remarks: Max. 24h.

La Roche-des-Arnauds 30C2

D994, Chemin des Digues. **GPS:** n44,56134 e5,95637.

5 free. **Surface:** asphalted. 01/01-31/12
Distance: 100m on the spot on the spot 100m.
Remarks: Max. 24h.

La Salle-les-Alpes 30C2

Chemin de l'Oratoire, Villeneuve. **GPS:** n44,94417 e6,55583.

16 € 6, winter € 17 Ch included. **Surface:** gravel.
01/01-31/12
Distance: 200m 50m.
Remarks: Parking at skipistes.

Laragne-Montéglin 30B3

Avenue de Provence, D1075. **GPS:** n44,31212 e5,82543.

15 free Ch free. **Surface:** asphalted.
Distance: 300m 300m 300m.

Laragne-Montéglin 30B3

Intermarché, D1075. **GPS:** n44,30300 e5,83700.

30 free € 2 Ch. 01/01-31/12
Distance: 2km.

Le Lauzet-Ubay 30C2

D900. **GPS:** n44,42833 e6,43389.

6 free WC free. **Surface:** gravel. 01/01-31/12
Distance: 50m 50m 50m 100m.

Le Thoronet 30C4

D17, boulevard du 17 aout 1944. **GPS:** n43,45097 e6,30411.

3 free € 3 Ch. **Location:** Rural. **Surface:** asphalted.
01/01-31/12
Distance: on the spot 50m.
Remarks: Coins available at Tourist Info.

Les Arcs-sur-Argens 30C4

Cellier des Archers. **GPS:** n43,45509 e6,47750.

10 free Ch free. **Surface:** gravel/sand. 01/01-31/12
Distance: 1km 8km 100m Super U 1km 1km 200m.
Tourist information Les Arcs-sur-Argens:
Thu morning.

Les Issambres 30D4

Chez Marcel, Plage La Gaillarde, N98. **GPS:** n43,36559 e6,71202.

FR

50 € 12/night, peak season € 15,50/night Chincluded € 3/day € 0,50 € 5. **Location:** Simple, comfortable. **Surface:** gravel/sand.
01/01-31/12
Distance: 50m 200m 200m.

Les Salles-sur-Verdon 30C4

L'Ermitage, D957. **GPS:** n43,77434 e6,21773.

€ 6 € 5 included. **Surface:** gravel/sand.
Distance: 700m Lac de Ste Croix 1km on the spot.
Remarks: Swimming pool incl.

Malaucène 30B3

Avenue Charles de Gaulle. **GPS:** n44,17792 e5,12970.

15 free Chfree. **Surface:** asphalted/metalled. 01/01-31/12
Distance: 150m 150m 150m.
Remarks: Between sports fields and gendarmerie.

Tourist information Malaucène:
Marché Provencal. Wed-morning.

Malemort-du-Comtat 30B3

Avenue Docteur Tondut, D5. **GPS:** n44,02175 e5,15714.
free Chfree. **Location:** Rural. **Surface:** gravel.
Distance: 200m on the spot.

Ménerbes 30B4

GPS: n43,83193 e5,20828.

free.
Distance: 250m 100m.

Montgenèvre 30D2

Parking le Collet. GPS: n44,93324 e6,72547.

250 € 10 Ch (80x)included. **Surface:** metalled.
01/01-31/12
Remarks: Driving ou village dir Italy.

Tourist information Montgenèvre:
Office de Tourisme, Route d'Italie, www.montgenevre.com.Ski station on the border with Italy. In the summer canyoning.

Moustiers Ste.Marie 30C4

P5, D952. **GPS:** n43,84361 e6,21874.

€ 6/night € 2 Ch € 2. **Surface:** gravel.
Distance: 10 min walking.

Tourist information Moustiers Ste.Marie:
Office de Tourisme, Place de l'église, ville-moustiers-sainte-marie.fr.City of faïence.
Musée de la Faïence, Mairie. summer: 09-12h,14-19h.

Oppède-le-Vieux 30B4

GPS: n43,83107 e5,15911.

€ 5/day free.
Distance: 500m 500m.
Remarks: Parking on entering the village.

Tourist information Oppède-le-Vieux:
Hiking route through medieval top-hill village.

Orange 30A3

Parking Sully. GPS: n44,14100 e4,80800.
10 free. **Surface:** asphalted.
Distance: 1km 2km.
Remarks: Via Avenue A.Artaud.

Tourist information Orange:
Office de Tourisme, 5, cours Aristide Briand, www.provence-orange.com. Roman city between the vineyards of the Côtes du Rhône.
Amfithéâtre.Open-air theater built under emperor August.
Arc d'Orange.Roman triumphal arch 20 after Christ.
Ruine de Château des Princes Oranges.Ruins of the castle of the Princes of Orange.
Thu.

FR

Orcières-Merlette 30C2

Camping-car Casse Blanche, Station d'Orcières, P3. **GPS**: n44,69465 e6,32098.

30 € 12/24h Ch included. **Surface:** asphalted.
01/01-31/12
Distance: on the spot on the spot.

Pélissanne 30B4

Chemin de la Prouvenque. **GPS**: n43,62805 e5,15307.

6 free Ch free.
Distance: 500m 8km.
Remarks: Parking stadium.

Plan-de-la-Tour 30C5

Parking Boulodrôme, D74. **GPS**: n43,33827 e6,54902.

free. **Surface:** asphalted. 01/01-31/12 Thu.
Distance: 100m 100m 100m.
Remarks: At tennis-courts.

Tourist information Plan-de-la-Tour:
Office de Tourisme, Place du 19 Mars.
Thu morning 6-12h.

Port Saint-Louis-du-Rhône 30A4

GPS: n43,38464 e4,82165.

50 € 6 Ch included. **Surface:** asphalted/gravel. 01/01-31/12
Distance: 2km 50m 2km 2km.
Remarks: Baker every morning.

Pra-Loup 30C3

Parking des Choupettes. **GPS**: n44,36806 e6,60611.

50 free Ch consumption,€ 0,50-2 WC. **Surface:** asphalted.
01/01-31/12
Distance: 400m 400m 400m 50m.
Remarks: Parking skiruns.

Puget Theniers 30D3

Aire de la Condamine, Avenue Bisschofsheim. **GPS**: n43,95306 e6,89944.

10 € 3,50 Ch included. **Surface:** asphalted. 01/01-31/12
Distance: 300m 20m 300m 300m.

Puy-Saint-Vincent 30C2

GPS: n44,83245 e6,48331.
20 € 6 Ch included. 18/12-25/04
Remarks: Max. 15 days, information at funicular railway. Follow signs Station 1600m, first parking on the right next to funicular railway.

Tourist information Puy-Saint-Vincent:
Office de Tourisme, Chapelle St-Jacques, Les Alberts, www.puysaintvincent.com.

Puyvert 30B4

Super U, D118. **GPS**: n43,74689 e5,33644.

5 free Ch (4x)free € 4. **Surface:** asphalted.
01/01-31/12
Distance: 1,5km on the spot.

Quinson 30C4

Les Prés du Verdon. **GPS**: n43,69801 e6,03911.

9 free Ch free. **Surface:** gravel/sand. 01/01-31/12
Distance: 100m 100m 300m 500m.

FR

Ramatuelle 30D5

Parking de Tamaris, Plage de Pamplonne, Route des Tamaris. **GPS**: n43,23893 e6,66149.

60 € 5/day, € 5/night, 1/7-31/8 € 9day, € 9/night, dog € 1 Ch (20x)€ 7/day. **Location:** Rural. **Surface:** gravel.
Distance: on the spot on the spot on the spot.
Remarks: Beach parking.

Ramatuelle 30D5

Parking Municipal, Plage de Pamplonne, Route de Bonne-Terrasse. **GPS**: n43,21126 e6,66217.

90 € 7,70 Ch WC . **Location:** Rural. **Surface:** gravel.
01/04-31/10
Distance: 200m 200m 2km.
Remarks: Beach parking, bread service.

Tourist information Ramatuelle:
Office de Tourisme, Place de l'Ormeau, www.ramatuelle-tourisme.com.
La place de l'Ormeau.Provencal Market. Thu, Su.

Riez 30C4

Place Maxime Javelly. **GPS**: n43,81650 e6,09188.

7 free Ch free. **Surface:** asphalted/grassy.
Distance: 50m 100m 100m.

Roussillon 30B4

Parking Saint Joseph, D149. **GPS**: n43,89660 e5,29593.

10 € 2/day, € 5/night.
Distance: 800m 800m.

Tourist information Roussillon:
Office de Tourisme, Place de la Poste, www.roussillon-provence.com.
Sentier des Ocres.Hiking trail, 45 min.

Sablet 30A3

Domaine du Parandou, D977. **GPS**: n44,19325 e4,99522.
5 € 3 Ch included. **Surface:** unpaved.

Salin-de-Giraud 30A4

Rue de la Bouvine. **GPS**: n43,41222 e4,73056.

20 € 2 Ch € 0,80. 01/04-31/10

Sarrians 30A3

GPS: n44,07943 e4,97788.

10 free € 2 Ch € 2. **Surface:** metalled. 01/01-31/12
Distance: 800m.

Sault 30B3

P3, Route de Saint-Trinit. **GPS**: n44,09434 e5,41308.

15 free € 2/10minutes Ch € 2/1h. **Surface:** gravel. 01/01-31/12
Distance: 500m 500m.

Sausset-les-Pins 30A5

Avenue Pierre Matraja. **GPS**: n43,33890 e5,10916.

15 free € 2/100liter Ch € 2/1h. **Surface:** asphalted.
01/01-31/12
Distance: 1,2km 1,2km 1,2km 5m.
Remarks: At stadium.

FR

Savines-le-Lac 30C2

Parking du Barnafret, Av. du Faubourg, D954. **GPS**: n44,52495 e6,40090.

30 € 7 € 2/120liter Ch (20x). **Surface:** asphalted.
Distance: 300m 100m.

Selonnet 30C3

Quartier de Boulangère. **GPS**: n44,36862 e6,31525.

7 free € 2/10minutes Ch € 2/55minutes. **Surface:** gravel.
01/01-31/12
Distance: 300m 300m 300m.
Remarks: Coins available at town hall/bakery/supermarket/bar-tabac, free wifi at town hall.

Sénas 30A4

Avenue des Jardins. **GPS**: n43,74403 e5,08020.

6 free € 3 Ch. 01/01-31/12
Distance: 200m 1,5km 200m 200m.

Serre-Chevalier 30C1

Parking des Charmettes, Serre Chevalier 1500, D1091, Le Monêtier-les-Bains. **GPS**: n44,97602 e6,50933.
40 € 4,80/day + tourist tax Ch free. **Surface:** metalled.
01/01-31/12
Distance: on the spot.
Remarks: Parking at skipistes.

Serre-Chevalier 30C1

Parking de Pontillas, Hameau de Bez. **GPS**: n44,94805 e6,55564.
20 € 8, tourist tax excl Ch included. **Surface:** metalled.
Distance: 20m.

Sillans-la-Cascade 30C4

GPS: n43,56837 e6,18196.

free . 01/01-31/12
Distance: on the spot 50m.
Remarks: Park along river, water falls 800m. D560 Dir Salernes.

Sisteron 30C3

Aire de Saint Jaume, D951. **GPS**: n44,20028 e5,94389.

€ 2 Ch € 2. 01/01-31/12
Distance: 4,5km.
Remarks: On entering city from dir Gap, before tunnel.

Tourist information Sisteron:
Office de Tourisme, Place de la République, www.sisteron.fr.Small fortress town.

Six-Fours-les-Plages 30B5

Port de la Coudoulière. **GPS**: n43,09750 e5,81194.

8 € 8 WC included. **Surface:** asphalted. 01/10-30/04
Distance: 100m 100m 100m.

Six-Fours-les-Plages 30B5

Promenade Gén. Charles de Gaulle. **GPS**: n43,10750 e5,81750.
€ 3 Ch. 01/01-31/12
Remarks: Behind Office du Tourisme, 8-12, 14-19h.

Sospel 31A3

Stade E. Donato, D2566. **GPS**: n43,87876 e7,44213.

4 free Ch free. **Surface:** asphalted. 01/01-31/12
Distance: 300m 300m 300m.

FR

S St.André-les-Alpes 30C3

GPS: n43,96535 e6,50639.

30 free € 3/10minutes Ch . **Surface:** asphalted.
01/01-31/12
Distance: 250m 100m 250m.
Remarks: On entering the village from southern dir.

S St.Etienne-de-Tinée 30D3

Camping du Plan d'Eau, Boulevard de la Digue. **GPS**: n44,25620 e6,92350.
6 € 8,50 € 2,50 Ch € 2,50.
Remarks: In village, by lake.

S St.Laurent-du-Var 30D4

Route des Pugets. **GPS**: n43,68584 e7,18459.

7 free Ch free. **Surface:** asphalted.
Distance: 1,2km 4,5km 1,2km 1,2km.
Remarks: Max. 7 days.

St.Laurent-du-Var 30D4

Avenue Francis Teisseire. **GPS**: n43,66628 e7,19595.
5 free. **Location:** Central, noisy. **Surface:** asphalted.
01/01-31/12
Distance: city centre 2km 200m 500m.
Remarks: Max. 8m.

S St.Mandrier 30C5

Pin Roland, Impasse de la Mer. **GPS**: n43,07771 e5,90444.

6 free Ch free. **Surface:** asphalted. 01/01-31/12
Distance: 500m 500m.
Remarks: Max. 48h.

S St.Martin-de-Crau 30A4

Place François Miterrand. **GPS**: n43,63859 e4,81454.
3 free free. **Surface:** metalled. 01/01-31/12
Remarks: Max. 48h, parking in front of town hall.

S St.Michel-l'Observatoire 30B3

GPS: n43,91611 e5,71667.

6 free € 2 Ch. **Surface:** grassy/sand. 01/03-15/11
Distance: 800m 800m 800m.
Remarks: At tennis-courts.

S St.Paul-lez-Durance 30B4

Rue du Camping le Retour. **GPS**: n43,68694 e5,70611.

6 free Ch free. **Surface:** metalled. 01/01-31/12
Distance: 300m 4km 500m 700m.
Remarks: Max. 48h.

S St.Tropez 30D5

Aire camping-car, Chemin Fontaine du pin, Chemin de la Moutte. **GPS**: n43,26468 e6,67227.

15 € 11 € 2 Ch € 2,50 WC € 1. **Location:** Comfortable, isolated, quiet. **Surface:** grassy/sand. 01/01-31/12.
Distance: 3km 800m.
Remarks: Route les Salins, dir Les Salins, to the left chemin de la Fontaine du pin, to the left chemin de la Moutte, near Château de la Moutte.

Tourist information St.Tropez:
Office de Tourisme, Quai Jean Jaurès, www.saint-tropez.st.Small tourist town.
La Citadelle, musée de la Marine.Navy museum.
Place des Lices.Week market. Wed + Sa morning.

S St.Véran 30D2

D5. **GPS**: n44,70447 e6,86091.
20 € 2/day, € 5/night Ch WC free. **Surface:** metalled.
01/01-31/12
Distance: 100m 100m 200m on the spot 200m.

S Ste.Cécile-les-Vignes 30A3

Cave des Vignerons Reunis, D976. **GPS**: n44,25099 e4,89020.

FR

free Chfree. **Surface:** asphalted. 01/01-31/12

S Ste.Croix-de-Verdon 30C4

Route du Lac. **GPS**: n43,75944 e6,15194.

20 € 6 Ch WCincluded.
Remarks: Max. 3 nights, service closed during wintertime.

S Ste.Maxime 30D5

D25, le Muy dir Ste.Maxime. **GPS**: n43,31730 e6,62999.

50 € 10/24h Chfree. **Surface:** metalled. 01/01-31/12
Distance: city centre 1km 1,2km McDonalds 50m Lidl 200m.
Remarks: Max. 48h. Parking at roundabout, near McDonalds.

Tourist information Ste.Maxime:
Thu-morning.
Les Greniers du Golfe, Aire des Magnoti.Bric-a-brac. Wed 08-18h.

S Stes.Maries-de-la-Mer 30A4

Avenue d'Arles, D570. **GPS**: n43,45535 e4,42750.

60 € 10, > 7,5m € 20 Ch WCincluded. **Surface:** asphalted. 01/01-31/12
Distance: 200m beach 400m 100m 50m 100m.
Remarks: Max. 48h, srevice: 8.30-11.30, 16-19.30.

S Stes.Maries-de-la-Mer 30A4

Plage Ouest, Route d'Aigues-Mortes, D38. **GPS**: n43,44991 e4,40407.
50 € 10, >7.50m € 20 Chincluded. **Surface:** asphalted/gravel.
01/01-31/12
Distance: 1,5km 50m.

S Stes.Maries-de-la-Mer 30A4

Valée des Lys, Parking Plage Est, Avenue Cousteau. **GPS**: n43,45364 e4,43695.

150 € 10 Chfree WC. **Surface:** metalled. 01/01-31/12
Distance: 250m beach 50m 100m 250m.

S Stes.Maries-de-la-Mer 30A4

Camping de la Brise. GPS: n43,45572 e4,43620.
50 € 16 + tourist tax Ch WC. 16/12-11/11
Distance: 850m direct access to sandy beach on the spot on the spot.

S Thorenc 30D4

Lac de Thorenc, D2. **GPS**: n43,79930 e6,80838.

10 free Chfree. 01/01-31/12
Distance: 750m 100m épicerie 750m.

S Trigance 30C4

Quartier Saint Roch. **GPS**: n43,76018 e6,44159.

10 € 5 Ch free. **Surface:** asphalted. 01/01-31/12
Remarks: Max. 2 days.

S Uvernet-Fours 30D3

Losissement Le Bachelard, D902. **GPS**: n44,36816 e6,62783.

6 free € 2 Ch € 2. **Surface:** gravel/sand. 01/01-31/12

S Vaison-la-Romaine 30A3

Aire camping-car, Avenue André Coudray. **GPS**: n44,24650 e5,07392.

FR

25 €6 Ch free. 01/01-31/12 Tue-morning.
Distance: 800m.

Tourist information Vaison-la-Romaine:
Office de Tourisme, Place du Chanoine-Sautel, www.vaison-la-romaine.com. City from the Roman time, archaeological findings.
city daily.
Le Pont Romain. Bridge from the Roman Empire.
Le Château. Ruins of the castle of the Counts of Toulouse.
Tue.

S Valberg 30D3

Le Lagopède, Route de Rouya. **GPS**: n44,09615 e6,93675.

21 € 10 + € 0,20/pp tourist tax Ch (21x)included WC.
Surface: asphalted. 01/01-31/12
Distance: 500m on the spot on the spot on the spot 600m.

Tourist information Valberg:
Office de Tourisme, Centre Administratif, www.valberg.com. Ski station, alpine and cross country skiing. In the summer large open-air swimming pool.

S Valréas 30A3

Domaine du Lumian, Route de Montélimar, D941. **GPS**: n44,39028 e4,96421.

6 free Ch free. **Surface:** gravel. 01/01-31/12
Distance: 2,5km.

S Veynes 30B2

Base de Loisirs Les Iscles, Les Graviers, D994. **GPS**: n44,51830 e5,79860.
€ 5 . **Surface:** gravel.
Distance: on the spot on the spot.
Remarks: Wifi at restaurant.

S Villeneuve 30B4

GPS: n43,89611 e5,86167.

8 free Ch free. **Surface:** unpaved.
01/01-31/12, service: 01/03-30/11
Distance: 200m 5,5km.

S Visan 30A3

Domaine des Lauribert, D976. **GPS**: n44,34833 e4,97276.

20 free Ch (8x)€ 2 WC. **Surface:** unpaved. 01/01-31/12
Remarks: At wine-grower, max. 72h.

FR

SPAIN

Capital: Madrid
Government: Constitutional monarchy
Official Language: Spanish
Population: 47,265,000 (2013)
Area: 505,782 km^2.

General information

Dialling code: 0034
General emergency: 112
Currency: Euro

Regulations for overnight stays

Wild camping is allowed having gained permission from the municipality, olice or property owner. Along the Mediterranean coast wild camping is almost always forbidden. Parking places (P) mentioned here can be considered as tolerated places to stay overnight.

Additional public holidays 2014

January 6 Epiphany
April 18 Good Friday
May 1 Labor Day
June 19 Corpus Christi
August 15 Assumption of the Virgin Mary
October 22 National Holiday
November 1 All Saints' Day
December 6 Constitution Day
December 8 Immaculate Conception

Spain

Green Spain

A Coruña 36C3

Puerto de San Pedro de Visma, Zona de O Portiño. **GPS**: n43,37167 w8,44472.

12 free Chfree. **Surface:** metalled.
Distance: 3km on the spot 50m 1km Carrefour 1km.
Remarks: Max. 48h.

A Coruña 36C3

Tore de Hercules. **GPS**: n43,38378 w8,40228.
free. **Surface:** asphalted.
Distance: on the spot 50m 50m.

A Guarda 36B5

GPS: n41,89892 w8,87825.
Remarks: Parking in harbour.

A Pontenova 36D3

Rua de la Estación. **GPS**: n43,34739 w7,19171.

8 free Chfree. **Surface:** asphalted.
Distance: 200m 100m.
Remarks: Max. 48h.

A Rúa 36D4

Área Recreativa O Aguillón. **GPS**: n42,38800 w7,11459.
10 free Chfree. **Surface:** asphalted/grassy. 01/01-31/12
Distance: 500m on the spot 500m 500m.
Remarks: Next to football ground.

Arcade 36B4

Rúa do Peirao. **GPS**: n42,33946 w8,61329.
5 free Ch. **Surface:** metalled. 01/01-31/12
Distance: nearby nearby.

Arrigorriaga 37C4

Carretera Buia Etorbidea. **GPS**: n43,23772 w2,91938.
8.

As Neves 36C5

Camino del Emenjeric. **GPS**: n42,08726 w8,41374.
8 free Chfree. 01/01-31/12
Distance: 200m 200m.
Remarks: Max. 48h.

Avilés 37A3

Restaurante Rias Baixas, Camino Heros, 3. **GPS**: n43,55120 w5,93451.
7 € 6/24h Ch.
Distance: on the spot 500m.

Bakio 37C4

Parking, BI 3101. **GPS**: n43,42783 w2,80442.
free. **Surface:** asphalted.

Behobia 37D4

N10, Calle de Aria Juncal. **GPS**: n43,34310 w1,7598.

6 day time € 2,25, overnight stay free. **Surface:** asphalted.
Distance: 500m.

Bermeo 37D4

Área de la Pérgola, Itsasoan Galdurakoen Lamera. **GPS**: n43,42306 w2,72556.

10 free Chfree. **Surface:** asphalted.
Remarks: Nearby football ground, max. 48h.

Bertamirans 36C4

Paseo Fluvial. **GPS**: n42,86009 w8,64838.

15 free Chfree. **Surface:** asphalted. 01/01-31/12
Distance: 100m 50m Carrefour dir. Santiago every 30 min.
Remarks: Max. 48h.

Bilbao 37C4

Kobetamendi, Monte Kobeta, 31. **GPS**: n43,25961 w2,96355.
72 € 15/day Ch. **Surface:** asphalted.
Distance: centre 4,5km 2,8km Bilbao-bus 58. **Remarks:** Max. 72h.

Tourist information Bilbao:

Bilbao.Capital of the Basque Country and previously centre of the iron industry.
Museo Guggenheim, Avenida Abandoibarra, 2, Bilbao.Collection of modern art. Tue-Su 10-20h, 01/07-31/08 10-21h.
Basilica de Begoña, Virgen de Begoña, 38, Bilbao-Vizcaya.Basilica.

Boiro 36B4

Playa Jardín de Barraña. **GPS**: n42,64183 w8,89481.

10 € 3-6 Chfree. **Surface:** asphalted. 01/01-31/12
Distance: 500m 20m 200m Bistro Prima 400m.

ES

Remarks: Max. 48h.

Boiro 36B4

Playa Mañons, S/n 15930 Chancelas–Abanqueiro. **GPS**: n42,63138 w8,85311.

10 € 3-6 Ch.

Distance: on the spot.

Bueu 36B4

PO315 dir Cabo Udra. **GPS**: n42,33460 w8,8248.

free. **Surface:** sand.

Remarks: Max. 48h.

Bueu 36B4

Puerto, Avda. de Montero Rios. **GPS**: n42,32732 w8,7838.

Burela 36D3

Area de Burela, Parque de O Campón, parking Hospital de Burela. **GPS**: n43,65216 w7,35891.

5 free Chfree. **Surface:** asphalted.

Distance: 200m ⊗300m 200m.

Remarks: Max. 48h.

Cabárceno 37C4

Área Lago del Acebo, N634> dir Parque de la naturaleze de Cabárceno. **GPS**: n43,35802 w3,81959.

30 free Chfree. **Surface:** asphalted.

Distance: 100m 50m 50m ⊗on the spot.

Remarks: Max. 48h.

Camariñas 36B3

Jachthaven. **GPS**: n43,12694 w9,18333.

5 free. **Surface:** asphalted.

Cangas de Onís 37B4

Parking Lanzadera Picos de Europa, Calle del Llreau. **GPS**: n43,35211 w5,12536.

15 free Chfree. **Surface:** asphalted.

Distance: ⊗100m.

Remarks: Max. 48h.

Carnota 36B4

Portocubelo. **GPS**: n42,80145 w9,14492.

4 free. **Surface:** asphalted.

Distance: Carnota 5km 10m.

Remarks: Parking next to hatchery.

Carreno 37A3

Puerto Perlora. **GPS**: n43,58342 w5,75713.

5.

Remarks: Tolerated place.

Cartelle 36C5

Camperpark O Mundil, Antigua Carretera OU-659. **GPS**: n42,21444 w8,03306.

24 € 10 Ch WC free.

Surface: gravel. 01/01-31/12

Distance: 1km zona fluvial Río Arnoia ⊗10m.

Castro Urdiales 37C4

Parking Parco Cotolino. **GPS**: n43,37364 w3,20899.

€ 2/3h (10.00-20.00). **Surface:** asphalted.

Chantada 36C4

Champ de Sangoñedo. **GPS**: n42,60598 w7,77989.

3 free Chfree.

Remarks: At footballstadium.

Comillas 37B4

Parking, Calle de Manuel Noriega. **GPS**: n43,38821 w4,28319.

free. **Surface:** asphalted.

Cospeito 36D3

Camino de la Laguna. **GPS**: n43,23984 w7,55579.

5 free Ch free. **Surface:** asphalted. 01/01-31/12

Distance: ⊗300m.

Cudillero 37A3

Puerto. **GPS**: n43,56568 w6,1517.

5.

Remarks: Parking in harbour.

Ferrol 36C3

Ctra. de la Malata. **GPS**: n43,49333 w8,23972.

15 free Chfree. **Surface:** asphalted.

Distance: 700m ⊗300m.

Finisterre 36B4

Praia de Langosteira. **GPS**: n42,92320 w9,26149.

ES

5 free.
Distance: on the spot 1km 1km.
Remarks: Parking on beach, max. 48h.

Finisterre 36B4
Cabo de Finisterre. **GPS**: n42,88651 w9,2724.
10 free.

Fuente Dé 37B4
Picos de Europa, C621. **GPS**: n43,14433 w4,81274.
free. **Surface:** sand.
Remarks: Parking funicular railway.

Gijón 37A3
Camino de las Mimosas, El Rinconin. **GPS**: n43,54708 w5,63648.
20 free. **Surface:** asphalted.
Distance: 300m.
Remarks: In front of instituto de Salut Mental Pérez-Espinez Oria.

Gorliz 37C4
Paseo de Astondo. **GPS**: n43,41220 w2,94194.
free. **Location:** Simple. **Surface:** asphalted.
Distance: 500m 50m 20m.
Remarks: Parking on beach.

Gozon 37A3
Parking El Penoso. **GPS**: n43,60341 w5,77325.
3. **Distance:** 150m.

Guetaria 37D4
N634. **GPS**: n43,30388 w2,2075.
free. **Surface:** asphalted.
Remarks: Parking on beach.

Guitiriz 36C3
Rua do Voluntariado. **GPS**: n43,17727 w7,88062.
5 free Ch free. **Surface:** gravel. 01/01-31/12
Distance: 800m 100m.

Hermandad De Campoo De Suso 37B4
Estación Invernal Alto Campoo, C 628 Reinosa - Espinilla, dir: Alto Campoo. **GPS**: n43,03839 w4,37036.
20 Ch.
Distance: on the spot.

Hondaribbia 37D4
Ramón Iribarren Pasalekua. **GPS**: n43,37929 w1,79768.

20 € 1,24/h. **Surface:** asphalted. 01/03-31/12
Remarks: Parking on beach.

La Vega 37B3
GPS: n43,48009 w5,13416.
10 € 7.
Remarks: Parking on beach.

Laredo 37C4
Avda. de la Victoria. **GPS**: n43,43227 w3,45024.
5.

Remarks: Tolerated place.

Legazpi 37D4
Parque Mirandaola de Legazpi, Carretera Legazpia, GI 2630. **GPS**: n43,03678 w2,33758.
8 free Ch free. **Surface:** asphalted.
Distance: on the spot.
Remarks: Max. 48h.

Liérganes 37C4
Calle de Puente Romano. **GPS**: n43,34479 w3,74183.
10 free Ch free.
Remarks: Parking nearby station, max. 48h.

Luarca 36D3
Avda. de la Argentina, AS219. **GPS**: n43,53658 w6,53255.
10.
Remarks: At sports park.

Lugo 36C4
Pabellón Municipal de Deportes, Avda. de Santiago. **GPS**: n43,00452 w7,56144.

10 free Ch free. **Surface:** asphalted.
Distance: 10min 5,2km.
Remarks: Parking gymnasium, max. 48h.

Lugo 36C4
Plaza de Asturias, Rúa Ánxel Fole. **GPS**: n43,00972 w7,55805.
15 € 12/24h free. **Surface:** asphalted.

Milladoiro 36C4
Traversia do Porto. **GPS**: n42,84512 w8,58079.

20 free Ch free. **Surface:** asphalted.
Distance: 200m 200m dir. Santiago every 15 min.
Remarks: Max. 48h. A9 exit Santiago de Compostello zouth, N550 dir Pontevedre, near swimming pool.

Miño 36C3
AP-9 Coruña-Ferrol ><, km 15,5. **GPS**: n43,37404 w8,18736.
12 free Ch WC free. **Surface:** asphalted.
Distance: on the spot on the spot.
Remarks: Parking nearby motorway.

Miranda de Ebro 37C5
Calle de Burgos. **GPS**: n42,68880 w2,95403.

ES

10 free Chfree. **Surface:** metalled. 01/01-31/12
Distance: 3km.
Remarks: Max. 48h.

Tourist information Miranda de Ebro:
Oficina de Turismo, Parque Antonio Machado, 4.
Medieval annual fair. around May 1.
Week market. Sa.

S Mondoñedo 36D3
Calle de Vicedo. **GPS**: n43,42778 w7,37028.
10 free Chfree. **Surface:** metalled.

S Monforte de Lemos 36C4
Auditorio Multiusos de Monforte, Calle de la Circuvalación / Calle de Santa Clara.
GPS: n42,52750 w7,5119.

30 free Chfree. **Surface:** asphalted.
Distance: 500m 550m 300m.
Remarks: Max. 48h.

Muros 36B4
C 550. **GPS**: n42,77516 w9,0573.
free. **Surface:** asphalted.
Remarks: Parking harbour.

S Muxia 36B3
Calle de la Rua Marina. **GPS**: n43,10593 w9,21682.
10 free . **Surface:** asphalted.
Distance: on the spot on the spot on the spot on the spot 50m.
Remarks: Parking in harbour.

Noia 36B4
Rúa de Pedra Marques. **GPS**: n42,78783 w8,8906.

free. **Surface:** asphalted.
Distance: on the spot 50m 50m Bus 20m.

Tourist information Noia:
El Pendo, 5km S. Santander.Cave with petroglyphs.

S O Barco 36D4
Malecón Campiño. **GPS**: n42,41063 w6,97493.

12 free Chfree. **Surface:** unpaved. 01/01-31/12
Distance: 400m 250m 250m.

S Parada do Sil 36C4
Rural Pepe, Campo da Feira 17. **GPS**: n42,38287 w7,57106.
4 guests free Ch. 01/01-31/12
Distance: on the spot on the spot.

S Pobra do Brollòn 36D4
Campo Municipal de Fut. **GPS**: n42,56944 w7,39417.
8 free Chfree. **Surface:** metalled.

Porto de Rinlo 36D3
GPS: n43,55703 w7,10352.
Remarks: Several parking along the coast till Cabo Burela.

S Potes 37B4
Santo Toribio de Liébana, CA885. **GPS**: n43,15028 w4,65389.

free free. **Location:** Isolated, quiet.
Surface: asphalted.
Distance: Potes 3km on the spot.
Remarks: Parking monastery.

Tourist information Potes:
Local products. Mo.
Historical cattle market, since 1379. 01/08-15/08.

S Redondela 36B4
Avda. de Mendiño. **GPS**: n42,28972 w8,61055.
15 free Ch.
Distance: 600m 500m 600m 600m.

S Rentería 37D4
Área Rural de Listorreta-Barrengoloia. **GPS**: n43,26800 w1,90135.

5 free Chfree. **Surface:** asphalted. 01/01-31/12
Distance: Renteria 7km.
Remarks: Max. 48h. A8 exit Renteria, GI 2132 dir Zamalbide > 5km left then follow this road for 3km.

Ribadeo 36D3
Rua Daniel Cortezón. **GPS**: n43,53553 w7,04614.
7 free. **Surface:** asphalted. 01/01-31/12
Distance: 300m 2km.

ES

S Ribamontán al Monte 37C4
A8 Bilbao > Santander. **GPS**: n43,40282 w3,62877.
10 free Chfree.

S Ribamontán al Monte 37C4
A8 Santander > Bilbao. **GPS**: n43,40446 w3,62476.
10 free Chfree. **Location:** Highway. **Surface:** asphalted.

S San Clodio 36D4
Parque de Pena da Mula, Calle del Troque. **GPS**: n42,46750 w7,28583.

3 free Chfree. **Surface:** asphalted. 01/01-31/12
Distance: 200m Playa Fluvial 25m cafetaria.

S San Martín del Rey Aurelio 37A4
Área del Pozo Entrego, Avda. de la Vega, AS17. **GPS**: n43,28639 w5,63889.
3 free Chfree. **Surface:** asphalted.
Distance: on the spot Alcampo 1km.
Remarks: Max. 48h.

S San Sebastian 37D4
Paseo de Berio nº 2. **GPS**: n43,30797 w2,01426.

44 € 6,25 Ch. **Location:** Urban.
Surface: grasstiles.
01/01-31/12
Distance: 2km 50m 100m.
Remarks: Max. 48h, marked pitches, registration with licence plate number.

Tourist information San Sebastian:
Centro de Atracción y Turismo (CAT), Reina Regente, www.donostia.org.Old city with,
Parte Vieja, historical city centre with numerous cafés, restaurants and tapa bars.
Museo de San Telmo.Basque collections.
Palacio del Mar.Museum for oceanografics.
10-19h, Sa-Su 10-21h, 15/06-15/09 10-21h.
Castillo de la Mota.War museum.
Su-morning.

San Vicente de la Barquera 37B4
Barrio Rupuente, C6316. **GPS**: n43,39372 w4,36166.

free.
Remarks: Not suitable for big motorhomes. Along coast road, next to Playa Merón.

Tourist information San Vicente de la Barquera:
Oficina de Turismo, Avenida del Generalísimo, nº 20.
Old fortress city.

P S Santiago de Compostela 36C4
Rúa Manuel María. **GPS**: n42,89560 w8,5317.
100 8-20h € 3 € 3 Ch.
Surface: asphalted.
01/01-31/12
Distance: centre 2,5km 3km 50m line 1 > centre.
Remarks: Ticket for overnight stay € 12.

Tourist information Santiago de Compostela:
Oficina de Turismo, Rúa del Villar, 43, www.santiagoturismo.com.
City known for the termination of the pilgrime route.
Plaza de la Quintana.Impressive square.
Fiesta del Apóstol Santiago.Most important festival of Galicia.
15/07-31/07.

Santillana del Mar 37B4
Ctra. C6316. **GPS**: n43,38845 w4,10803.

€ 2/24h. **Surface:** asphalted.

Tourist information Santillana del Mar:
Small medieval town.

S Sanxenxo 36B4
Área de Cachadelos, PO-308. **GPS**: n42,41652 w8,86833.
65 € 6 Ch . **Surface:** grassy.
Distance: 200m 2km on the spot.

S Sarria 36D4
Calle de Castelo. **GPS**: n42,77194 w7,41028.

12 free Chfree. **Surface:** asphalted.
Distance: 800m on the spot 800m.

S Saturrarán 37D4
GPS: n43,31968 w2,41165.
5 free free.
Remarks: Parking on beach.

Suances 37B4
Playa de los Locos. **GPS**: n43,44300 w4,0465.
free.
Remarks: Parking at lighthouse.

S Teverga 37A4
Parking Senda del Oso, Entrago. **GPS**: n43,17178 w6,09562.
20 free Chfree. **Surface:** asphalted.
Distance: on the spot.
Remarks: Max. 48h.

ES

Tui 36B5

Puente Tripes, Avenida de Portual. **GPS**: n42,04333 w8,64656.
6 free Chfree. **Surface:** asphalted.
Distance: 1,3km 500m Lidl 150m.
Remarks: Max. 48h.

Tui 36B5

Parking Rio Mino. **GPS**: n42,04751 w8,64388.
free.
Distance: 1,5km.

Valdoviño 36C3

Playa da Frouxeira, Estrada da Lagoa. **GPS**: n43,61389 w8,1515.
5 free free.
Distance: on the spot on the spot.
Remarks: Parking on beach, max. 48h.

Vares/Bares 36D3

Porto de Bares. **GPS**: n43,77142 w7,66811.
25 against payment . **Surface:** asphalted.

Vilalba 36C3

Rua da Feira. **GPS**: n43,29556 w7,67694.
15 free Chfree. **Surface:** asphalted.
Distance: 300m 300m.

Vilanova de Arousa 36B4

Avda. Mola. **GPS**: n42,56293 w8,82833.

Villagarcia de Arosa 36B4

Area Camping Rio Ulla, Bamio , Campanario Nº 65. **GPS**: n42,63417 w8,76028.

6 € 15 Ch included. **Surface:** grassy.
Distance: 10m.
Remarks: >20h <10h.

Vitoria Gasteiz 37D4

Área de Lakua, Portal de Foronde. **GPS**: n42,86684 w2,68539.
10 free Chfree. **Location:** Urban, comfortable, central, quiet.
Surface: asphalted. 01/01-31/12
Distance: 2km 5km 100m bakery 50m 50m.
Remarks: Wed, market.

Zumaia 37D4

Calle de la Estación. **GPS**: n43,29302 w2,24701.

25 free Chfree. **Surface:** asphalted.
Distance: 4,4km.

Navarre and Rioja

Aínsa 28C6

Plaza del Castillo. **GPS**: n42,41916 e0,13515.
free. **Surface:** sand.

Tourist information Aínsa:
The capital of a medieval kingdom by surrounded fortress walls.
Castillo de Aínsa.Castle, 11-13th century, with Eco museum.
Tue.

Alquézar 40B1

Alquézar, Ctra.Barbastro,. **GPS**: n42,17097 e0,02382.
. 01/01-31/12

Tourist information Alquézar:
Historical city.

Ansó 28A5

Ctra. de Ansó a Fago. **GPS**: n42,75648 w0,83102.
2 .

Aoiz 28A5

Hotel Ekai. **GPS**: n42,77624 w1,38536.
10 free .

Ariza 37D6

Area de Servicios La Cadiera, A2 Madrid > Zaragoza. **GPS**: n41,31210 w2,00329.
5 .

Bielsa 28C6

Calle Mayor. **GPS**: n42,63437 e0,21893.
3 .

Botaya 28B6

Parking Monasterio de San Juan la Peña. **GPS**: n42,50699 w0,66414.

3 free.

Estelle 37D5

Calle St. Barbara Calea. **GPS**: n42,67306 w2,03972.

3 free. **Surface:** asphalted. 01/01-31/12

Tourist information Estelle:
Puebte la Reine. Sa.

Haro 37C5

LR111. **GPS**: n42,57296 w2,86423.

4 free free. 01/01-31/12

Haro 37C5

Parking centro deportivo, Av de los Ingenieros del Ministerio Obras Públicas, LR-111. **GPS**: n42,57677 w2,85222.

ES

4 free free. 01/01-31/12
Remarks: At sports park.

Tourist information Haro:
Capital of Rioja wine.

Jaca 28B6
Calle de Archén. **GPS**: n42,57113 w0,54421.
4 free.
Remarks: Tolerated place.

Logroño 37D5
Avenue de la Sonsierra, LR132. **GPS**: n42,47916 w2,4571.

3 free Ch free. **Location:** Quiet.
Surface: metalled. 01/01-31/12
Distance: 700m 100m 400m 300m 20m.
Remarks: Max. 48h.

Navarrete 37D5
Calle de la Carretera. **GPS**: n42,42458 w2,55584.

4 free. **Surface:** asphalted. 01/01-31/12
Remarks: Parking at swimming pool.

Pamplona 37D5
Parque de la Tejería, Calle Playa de Capparoso. **GPS**: n42,81908 w1,63766.

4 <6m. **Surface:** asphalted.

Pamplona 37D5
Plaza Errotozar, Calle del Rio Arga. **GPS**: n42,82057 w1,64932.

10 free. **Surface:** metalled.

Roncesvalles 28A5
Paseo Ibaneta. **GPS**: n43,02018 w1,32401.
5 .

Torla 28B6
Torla, Ordesa National Park, A135. **GPS**: n42,62582 w0,11196.
. **Surface:** asphalted.
Remarks: Large parking.

Torremontalbo 37C5
LR318. **GPS**: n42,51079 w2,6915.

2 free. **Surface:** grassy/gravel. 01/01-31/12
Remarks: Picnic area.

Zaragoza 40A1
Parque de Atracciones de Zaragoza. **GPS**: n41,61994 w0,90122.
10 .
Distance: 4,5km.

Mediterranean Sea Communities

Alqueria de la Comtessa 40B4
Camperpark Km zero, Metge Panella nº 1. **GPS**: n38,93878 w0,15276.
35 € 8-12 Ch (35x),6Amp WC € 3,dryer € 3 included.
Surface: asphalted. 01/01-31/12
Distance: 100m 1,5km 4km 200m 200m 150m 300m 500m.

Altafulla 40C2
Área de Servicio Mèdol, AP-7 km 237, Barcelona > Taragona. **GPS**: n41,14157 e1,34590.
2 free Ch free. **Surface:** asphalted. 01/01-31/12
Distance: on the spot on the spot.

Altafulla 40C2
Área de Servicio Mèdol, AP-7 km 237, Taragona > Barcelona.
GPS: n41,14054 e1,34746.
2 free Ch free. **Surface:** asphalted. 01/01-31/12
Distance: on the spot on the spot.

Altea 40A5
San Antonio Camperpark, Ctra. del Albir 5/6, CV7651.
GPS: n38,58544 w0,05989.
50 € 15 Ch € 0,50/kWh WC € 3 included. **Location:** Comfortable. **Surface:** . 01/01-31/12
Distance: Altea > 1km < Albir 100m 300m 200m, tram 1km.
Remarks: Bread-service, discount longer stays.

Tourist information Altea:
Oficina de Turismo, C/Sant Pere, 9.Fisherman's village, 10km from Benidorm.

ES

Amposta 40B2

Masia Vora Riu, Calle Zamora, 8. **GPS**: n40,75006 e0,56069.
5 € 10 Ch included. **Surface:** sand. 01/01-31/12

Amposta 40B2

Casa de Fusta, Partida L'Encanyissada. **GPS**: n40,65851 e0,67475.

15 free € 3 Ch. **Location:** Rural, comfortable.
Surface: unpaved.
Distance: on the spot on the spot.

Ascó 40B2

C/ Alcalde Tomas Biarnes Radua. **GPS**: n41,18673 e0,56802.

25 free Chfree. **Surface:** asphalted.

Avinyonet del Penedès 40C2

Area Cellar Can Battle - Artcava, Masia Can Batlle s/n, BV2411.
GPS: n41,36790 e1,77306.

free Chfree. **Location:** Rural, isolated, quiet. **Surface:** grassy/gravel.
01/01-31/12
Distance: 1km 6km.
Remarks: Wine tastery.

Ayora 40A4

Ayora, N330. **GPS**: n39,04382 w1,04126.

5 € 10 € 1 Ch € 2 WC included € 5 . **Surface:** gravel.
01/01-31/12
Distance: 2,5km.

Barcelona 40D2

Park & Ride del Besòs, Carrer del Taulat, B10 > salida 24 / 25, Sant Adrià del Besos. **GPS**: n41,41333 e2,22222.

20 € 30/24h, € 3/h Ch WC included . **Location:** Urban.
Surface: metalled. 01/01-31/12
Distance: 1km 300m 300m Tram 100m, metro 500m.
Remarks: Max. 72h, guarded parking.

Benicasim 40B3

Calle de Ausias March. **GPS**: n40,05527 e0,05916.
Chfree.

Cadaqués 40D1

Parking, Riera de Sant Vicenç. **GPS**: n42,28964 e3,27260.

€ 20,20/24h WC. **Surface:** asphalted.
Distance: 100m 1km 1,5km 100m 100m.

Tourist information Cadaqués:
La Riera.Week market. Mo 8-14h.

Calaf 40C1

Calle de Leida-Girona. **GPS**: n41,73306 e1,52667.

5 free Chfree. **Location:** Comfortable. **Surface:** asphalted.
Remarks: At petrol station.

Calaf 40C1

Carrer Berlin. **GPS**: n41,73500 e1,51389.

4 free Chfree. **Surface:** gravel/metalled.
Remarks: Max. 24h, Saturday market.

ES

S Calnegre 39D5

Camperpark Taray, RM-D21, Puntas Calnegre. **GPS**: n37,51515 w1,39845.

50 € 6 € 1/100liter Ch € 4. **Surface:** sand. winter

Distance: 100m 500m 500m.

S Calnegre 39D5

Puntas Calnegre, Ctra. Puntas de Calnegre, nº 42. **GPS**: n37,51179 w1,41198.

17 € 10,50 Ch included. **Surface:** metalled. 15/09-01/04

Distance: 600m.

S Calpe 40A5

Odissea Camper Area Calpe, Avda. Bulgaria. **GPS**: n38,64893 e0,06665.

58 € 12 (discount longer stay), 01/07-31/08 € 15 Ch WC included € 2/day. **Location:** Comfortable, central.

Surface: gravel. 01/01-31/12

Distance: on the spot 1km 100m.

S Calpe 40A5

Euro Nautica, Ctra. N233. **GPS**: n38,65578 e0,03660.

10 € 10 Ch. **Surface:** metalled. 01/01-31/12 Sa-Su.

Remarks: Motorhome dealer, arrival during opening hours.

Cañada de Callego 39D5

Loma de St.Antonio, Camino de Perchèles. **GPS**: n37,53542 w1,37226.

free. **Surface:** sand.

Remarks: Parking to sea.

Canet d'En Berenguer 40A3

Puerto Canet, Paseo Maritimo 9 de Octobre. **GPS**: n39,67443 w0,20338.

5.

Remarks: At marina.

S Carcaixent 40A4

Hort de Soriano. **GPS**: n39,07045 w0,40918.

15 € 15 Ch free. **Surface:** sand.

Distance: 7km on the spot.

Remarks: Max. 48h, picnic area present.

At recreation area, first drive into Carrer Julián Ribera (39°7'19'N 00°27'04'W) ± 5km, than follow Hort de Soriano.

S Cartagena 39D5

Area Autocaravanas Cartagena. **GPS**: n37,65373 w1,00345.

30 € 7, € 10 service incl Ch WC € 2 € 4. **Surface:** gravel.

01/01-31/12

Distance: centre 5km, port 8km 400m 400m 400m on the spot on the spot.

Remarks: Bread-service, Su market Bohio 500m, Thu market Dolores 1km.

S Cartagena 39D5

Área Belmonte Plus, Ctra. de Tentegorra, 1. **GPS**: n37,61500 w1,00555.

5 € 10 Ch included. **Surface:** asphalted.

Distance: 500m.

S Dénia 40A4

Odissea Camper Area, Ctra. Marines km11.6/Riu de Vernissa.

GPS: n38,87027 w0,015.

63 € 12 (discount longer stay), 01/07-31/08 € 15 Ch WC included € 1 € 3 € 2/day.

Surface: sand.

01/01-31/12

Distance: 2km 100m 50m 1km 20m.

Tourist information Dénia:

Oficina de Turismo, Plaza Oculista Buigues, 9.Seaside resort with fishing port.

S El Campello 40A5

Bar-Restaurant, N332 km124. **GPS**: n38,45746 w0,36129.

ES

2-3 free WC included. **Surface:** sand.
Distance: on the spot.
Remarks: 3 days free.

El Pinós **39D4**

Bonnie's Bar. **GPS**: n38,40917 w1,08639.

5 € 10-12 Ch WC included.
Surface: metalled. 01/01-31/12

Elche **40A5**

MH VICKY, Partida de Pusol 153, Deramador. **GPS**: n38,19711 w0,7314.

10 € 8 Ch € 2/day WC € 1 € 2 € 2/day.
Surface: gravel. 01/01-31/12
Distance: Elche 6km 2km 4km 1,5km.
Remarks: 2 bicylcles available, bread-service, jacuzzi € 1.

Els Muntells **40B2**

Carrer Major. **GPS**: n40,66869 e0,75929.

10 € 6 Ch WC included. **Location:** Rural, isolated.
Surface: asphalted/gravel.
Distance: 1,2km.

Figueres **40D1**

Parking Supermercado Esclat, Avda. de los Paisos Catalans, N260. **GPS**: n42,26042 e2,95096.

5 free. **Surface:** asphalted.
Distance: on the spot 500m on the spot 50m.
Remarks: Max. 48h.

Tourist information Figueres:
Rambla.Antiques market. 3rd Sa of the month.
Plaza Catalunya en Plaza del Gra. Tue, Thu, Sa.

Garrigàs **40D1**

Área del Empordà Norte, A7 km-35. **GPS**: n42,17333 e2,93194.
10 free WC free. **Surface:** metalled. 01/01-31/12

Garrigàs **40D1**

Área del Empordà Sur, A7 km-35. **GPS**: n42,17456 e2,93074.

10 free WC free. **Surface:** metalled. 01/01-31/12

Ibi **40A5**

Área Chambit, Calle Pedro Valdivia. **GPS**: n38,62222 w0,56694.
25 free Ch free. **Surface:** sand. 01/01-31/12
Distance: 2,3km.

Jalance **40A4**

N330. **GPS**: n39,18740 w1,0761.

10 free Ch free. **Surface:** asphalted.
Remarks: Parking next to swimming pool, max. 48h.

Jávea **40B5**

Avda.de Tamarits. **GPS**: n38,76982 e0,19097.
5 . **Surface:** unpaved.

Jérica **40A3**

Carre del Rio. **GPS**: n39,91116 w0,57385.

ES

5. 01/01-31/12
Distance: 2,2km on the spot.
Remarks: Along river, max. 7m.

La Azohia 39D5
Carretera a La Azohía. **GPS**: n37,56332 w1,17393.

free. **Surface:** unpaved.
Distance: 50m 100m 100m.

La Marina 40A5
Finca La Escuera, Escuera 300. **GPS**: n38,14360 w0,66939.

6 € 10 Ch € 0,20/kWh WC.
Surface: sand. 01/01-31/12
Distance: 300m 3km 300m 300m 300m on the spot.

La Marina 40A5
La Marina Elche, Cami del Molar o Pinet. **GPS**: n38,15628 w0,63791.

20 € 8 Ch included € 0,50/kWh,16Amp. winter

La Marina 40A5
Camino del Pinet, La Marina nord. **GPS**: n38,15087 w0,63276.

40 free. **Surface:** asphalted.

La Romana 40A5
Camperpark EuroPeCa, Cuevas de San Anton 2. **GPS**: n38,35662 w0,90378.

7 € 7,50 Ch € 2 WC € 1 included. **Location:** Rural, comfortable. **Surface:** gravel. 01/01-31/12
Distance: 1,5km 1,5km 1,5km on the spot.
Remarks: Possibility for reservation: 0034638278693.

La Salzadella 40B3
Av. Tomas Molins. **GPS**: n40,41611 e0,17305.

5 free Ch free. **Surface:** asphalted.
Distance: 250m.
Remarks: Village of cherries: cherry soap, cherry jam.

La Seu dÚrgell 28D6
Portal de cerdanya. **GPS**: n42,35888 e1,46447.
8.

Lleida 40B1
AP-2 Zaragoze > Barcelona km 143. **GPS**: n41,54111 e0,63917.
10 Ch.
Distance: on the spot.

ES

S L'Alfàs del Pi 40A5

Camper Park Costa Blanca, Cami des Alguers, 79.
GPS: n38,58389 w0,08139.
42 € 12, 01/05-30/09 € 10 Ch (42x)€ 2 WC € 0,50 € 4,dryer € 4 included. **Location:** Rural, comfortable, quiet.
Surface: metalled. 01/01-31/12
Distance: L'Alfas del Pi 1km, Playa Albir 1km 5km sandy beach 2km 2km 500m 1km Tram 600m.

S L'Alfàs del Pi 40A5

Camper Park Orange Grove, Cami d`Alguers 65. **GPS**: n38,58526 w0,08405.
30 € 12 Ch € 3 WC . **Surface:** gravel. 01/01-31/12

S L'Arboç 40C2

Área del Penedés Norte, AP7 dir Barcelona. **GPS**: n41,28794 e1,59117.
10 Chfree. **Surface:** metalled. 01/01-31/12
Distance: on the spot on the spot.

S L'Arboç 40C2

Área del Penedés Sur, AP7 dir Taragona. **GPS**: n41,29029 e1,59235.

10 Chfree. **Surface:** asphalted. 01/01-31/12
Distance: on the spot on the spot.

S Mataro 40D1

Autocaravanas del Sol, Calle de Torrent de Madá, El Cros. **GPS**: n41,53564 e2,41790.

4 € 10 Ch WC included. 01/01-31/12
Distance: 300m > Barcelona 100m.
Remarks: Motorhome dealer, max. 7 nights.

S Montseny 40D1

Área de Montseny, AP7-Nord km-117 > Francia. **GPS**: n41,64700 e2,42586.

20 free free. **Surface:** metalled. 01/01-31/12
Distance: on the spot on the spot.

S Montseny 40D1

Área de Montseny, AP7-Sur>Barcelona. **GPS**: n41,65000 e2,44222.

20 free free. **Surface:** metalled. 01/01-31/12
Distance: on the spot on the spot.

S Morella 40A2

N232. **GPS**: n40,62398 w0,09141.

30 free Chfree. **Surface:** metalled. 01/01-31/12
Distance: 2km 2km.
Remarks: Max. 72h.

S Mula 39D4

Camino de las Curtis. **GPS**: n38,03972 w1,48139.
5 free Chfree. **Surface:** asphalted. 01/01-31/12
Distance: 500m 500m.

S Murcia 39D4

Camperpark Huerta de Murcia, Carril los Cánovas, Rincón de Almodóvar, Los Ramos. **GPS**: n38,00722 w1,04361.

32 € 12 Ch WC included € 3 free. **Surface:** gravel. 01/01-31/12
Distance: Alquerías 1,7km 500m 500m on the spot.
Remarks: Bread-service.

S Navarcles 40C1

Calle de la Font de la Cura. **GPS**: n41,75661 e1,90833.

ES

5 free Ch free. **Location:** Isolated, quiet.
Surface: gravel.
Distance: 500m on the spot.

S Navata 40D1

Restaurante Can Janot, Ctra. de Olot nº 2. **GPS**: n42,22600 e2,86325.

40 € 4 € 2 . **Location:** Quiet. **Surface:** grassy.
Distance: on the spot 100m.
Remarks: Free with a meal.

S Olimar 40A4

Area de Ocio Nostrum Caravaning. **GPS**: n39,47051 w0,64056.
100 € 15 Ch included. **Surface:** metalled/sand.
Distance: 300m.
Remarks: 100m from camper/caravan Ocio Nostrum.

ES

Oliva 40A4

GPS: n38,91448 w0,07703.

free. **Surface:** gravel/sand.
Distance: 150m.
Remarks: Parking on beach.

S Peñíscola 40B3

Area camper Vizmar, Cami de la Volta. **GPS**: n40,39357 e0,40778.
25 € 6 Ch WC . **Surface:** grassy. 01/01-31/12
Distance: 500m.

S Peñíscola 40B3

Stop&Go La Volta, Camino de la Volta. **GPS**: n40,39793 e0,40316.
70 € 6, 01/07-31/08 € 12, 2 pers incl., 1 pers + € 1-2 Ch €
3 WC € 3,dryer € 4-5 . **Location:** Rural.
Surface: grassy/gravel. 01/01-31/12

S Platja d'Aro 40D1

Calle Roma. **GPS**: n41,81028 e3,05767.

30 € 8 Ch included. **Location:** Comfortable, quiet.
Surface: asphalted.
Distance: 750m.
Remarks: Max. 2 days.

S Quart 40D1

Avinguda de la Bóbila. **GPS**: n41,93944 e2,83917.

4 free Ch free. **Surface:** metalled. 01/01-31/12
Distance: on the spot 6,5km on the spot on the spot.
Remarks: Max. 48h, motorhome max. 8m.

S Ramonete 39D5

Wo-Mo Puerto Villa Brisa, Los Curas, D21, Puntas de Calnegre. **GPS**: n37,52589 w1,4336.

50 € 6 € 0,10/10liter Ch € 0,50 € 2 washing machine/dryer € 4 . **Surface:** gravel. 19/09-30/05
Distance: 5km 5km 5km 5km.
Remarks: Bread-service. At D21, Ramonete dir Puntas de Calnegre.

Ripoll 40D1

Raval de Barcelona. **GPS**: n42,20008 e2,18695.

5 free. **Surface:** asphalted.
Distance: 300m 500m 500m.
Remarks: Max. 24h, no camping activities.

Tourist information Ripoll:
Centrum.Week market. Sa-morning.

S San Feliu de Guixols 40D1

Parking Narcis Massanas, Ronda Narcis Massanas. **GPS**: n41,78020 e3,02303.

15 free Chfree. **Location:** Simple, quiet.
Surface: unpaved.

S San Fulgencio 40A5

Camper Park San Fulgencio, Mar Cartabrico 7, Centro Comercial las Dunas. **GPS:** n38,12080 w0,66005.

38 first day € 14, then € 12 Ch WC € 3 included.
Location: Comfortable. **Surface:** gravel. 01/01-31/12
Distance: 1,5km 200m 150m 150m.

S San Fulgencio 40A5

Oasis, Caminal del Convenio. **GPS:** n38,11972 w0,66194.

14 € 14, from 15th night € 12 Ch WC € 3,dryer € 2 included.
Surface: gravel. 01/09-30/04
Distance: San Fulgencio 7km beach 1,5km 200m 200m 300m.

S San Raphael del Río 40B2

Restaurante Spätzle-Fritz, Planes del Reine, San Jorge, CV-11. **GPS:** n40,57507 e0,39333.

50 free with a meal, € 6 Ch WC . **Location:** Quiet. **Surface:** gravel. 01/01-31/12
Distance: 3,5km 9km on the spot.

S Sant Hilari Sacalm 40D1

Carretera de la Font Picant. **GPS:** n41,88417 e2,50778.

10 free Chfree . **Location:** Rural.
Surface: gravel/sand. 01/01-31/12
Distance: 200m 200m 200m.
Remarks: Max. 48h.

S Santa Cristina d'Aro 40D1

Costa Brava Park, Carretera Platje d'Aro. **GPS:** n41,81306 e3,01119.

46 € 15 € 3 Ch included € 6. **Surface:** metalled/sand.
Distance: 6km 100m.

S Segorbe 40A3

Area de Segorbe, Escalera de la Estación. **GPS:** n39,84805 w0,48166.
12 free Chfree. **Surface:** asphalted/metalled.
Remarks: Max. 48h.

S Sitges 40C2

Avda. del Cami Pla. **GPS:** n41,25083 e1,81838.

10 € 5 1/11-31/3, € 8 1/4-31/10 . **Location:** Simple. **Surface:** asphalted. 01/01-31/12
Distance: Boulevard/beach Sitges 2,5km 50m.
Remarks: Max. 7 days, industrial area, Barcelona 40km.

S Sta.Pola 40A5

Europa-Area, Carrer dels Electricistas. **GPS:** n38,20805 w0,57416.

33 € 8 Ch € 3 .
Surface: gravel/metalled. 01/01-31/12
Distance: 1,7km 1,8km 1,7km.

S Tortosa 40B2

Área de Tortosa, Cami de la Toia. **GPS:** n40,80277 e0,51388.

ES

30 € 5/24h € 1 Ch. **Surface:** asphalted. 01/01-31/12
Distance: 1,1km 10km 900m 1km.

S Tremp 40B1
Passeig de Conca de Tremp. **GPS:** n42,16312 e0,89043.

5 free free € 1/2h. **Surface:** asphalted.
Remarks: Max. 48h.

S Turis 40A4
Carretera de Silla Tunis. **GPS:** n39,38944 w0,69777.
10 free Chfree. **Surface:** unpaved. 01/01-31/12

S Valencia 40A4
Area Camping-car La Marina, Carrer del Rio 556B, El Saler. **GPS:** n39,38727 w0,33213.
70 € 11 Ch WC. **Surface:** gravel.
Distance: Valencia 10km beach 150m 600m on the spot.
Remarks: Discount longer stays.

S Valencia 40A4
Valencia Camper Park, Diseminado Providencia 467, Bétera. **GPS:** n39,56126 w0,43213.

78 € 12 Ch € 3 WC included. **Location:** Luxurious.
Surface: gravel. 01/01-31/12
Distance: Valencia 12km train 300m.

S Valencia 40A4
Parking Valencia, Avda. Peris y Valero, 27. **GPS:** n39,45627 w0,37806.

8-10 € 25 Ch WC included. **Location:** Urban, central, noisy.
Surface: asphalted/gravel.
Distance: city centre 1,7km 2,5km 200m.
Remarks: Monitored parking.

S Vic 40D1
Carrer de la Fura. **GPS:** n41,93444 e2,24000.

10 free € 2/100liter Ch € 6/3h. **Surface:** grassy.
Distance: 1,8km 400m.
Remarks: Max. 48h.

S Viladrau 40D1
Carrer Montseny s/n. **GPS:** n41,84544 e2,38732.

16 free Ch free. **Location:** Rural. **Surface:** gravel/sand. 01/01-31/12
Distance: 500m 500m 500m.
Remarks: Max. 48h, nature reserve.

S Yelca 39D4
Portichuelo, Paraje el Portichuelo. **GPS:** n38,52833 w1,03944.

3 € 10 Ch included. **Surface:** grassy. 01/01-31/12
Distance: Yelca 10km on the spot.
Remarks: Check in at B&B <22h.

Spanish interior

S Aguilar de Campoo 37B4
N611, Ctra Palencia-Aguillar de Campoo. **GPS:** n42,78631 w4,25757.

10 free Chfree. **Surface:** asphalted.
Distance: on the spot 3,1km 200m 200m.
Remarks: Max. 48h.

ES

Aldeadávila de la Ribera 36D6

GPS: n41,22028 w6,61333.

4 free Chfree. **Surface:** asphalted. 01/01-31/12
Distance: on the spot 200m.
Remarks: Max. 48h.

Almazán 37C6

Camino Viejo del Cubo de la Solana. **GPS**: n41,49259 w2,53385.

Remarks: Parking at swimming pool.

Aranda de Duero 37B6

Dª Ruperta Baraya/Manzane M1. **GPS**: n41,66833 w3,69583.

10 free Chfree. **Surface:** asphalted. 01/01-31/12
Distance: 150m on the spot.
Remarks: Max. 48h.

Astorga 37A5

Parking plaza de Toros. GPS: n42,45138 w6,06593.

15 free Chfree. **Surface:** metalled.
Distance: 500m 1,4km 500m 500m.
Remarks: Max. 48h.

Avila 39A1

Parking del Palacio de Congresos, Calle Molino dell Carril. **GPS**: n40,66111 w4,70472.

10 free. **Surface:** asphalted.
Distance: 2,2km.

Tourist information Avila:
Small medieval town surround by ramparts.
The San Vicenta basilica is a Roman building.

Bretocino 37A5

Area para Autocaravanes, Cuesta de los Nogales. **GPS**: n41,88654 w5,75517.
€7 Chincluded € 3. 01/01-31/12

Burgo de Osma 37C6

Calle de Santos Iruela. **GPS**: n41,58662 w3,07338.

10 free . **Location:** Rural, simple.
Surface: metalled. 01/01-31/12
Distance: 500m 200m 500m.

Burgos 37C5

N120, Calle de Cartuja de Miraflores. **GPS**: n42,34037 w3,69361.

5 € 0,60/h, max. € 2,50, 20.00-10.00 free. **Surface:** asphalted.
Distance: 2,6km.
Remarks: Parking beside river.

Tourist information Burgos:
City, 8th century, with a lot of curiosities such as the cathedral, the castle and Monasterio de las Huelgas.

Cabrerizos 37A6

Don Quijote, Ctra. Aldealengua km 4. **GPS**: n40,97500 w5,60306.
€ 16 Ch. 01/03-31/10
Remarks: Formula camper.

Cáceres 38D2

Avda. Lope de Vega. **GPS**: n39,48041 w6,36649.

15 free Ch free. **Surface:** asphalted.
Distance: 600m 6,7km.
Remarks: Monitored parking.

Tourist information Cáceres:
Oficina de Turismo, Plaza Mayor, nº 3, www.inedito.com/caceres/.City with historical centre.
Museo Arquelogico Provincial, Casa de las Veletas.
PeroPalo.Traditional celebration. 21/02-24/02.

ES

Carrión de los Condes — 37B5

C/ Las Huertas. **GPS**: n42,33875 w4,60808.

10 free Chfree. **Surface:** metalled.
Distance: 200m 200m 200m.
Remarks: Max. 48h.

Cervera de Pisuerga — 37B4

C/ El Maderao. **GPS**: n42,87139 w4,49972.
10 free Chfree. **Surface:** sand.
Distance: 200m 200m 200m.
Remarks: Along the river, max. 48h.

Coca — 37B6

GPS: n41,21348 w4,52733.

5 free. **Surface:** metalled.
Remarks: Parking castle.

Consuegra — 39B2

GPS: n39,45339 w3,6106.
free. **Surface:** sand.
Remarks: Isolated parking at foot of hill with windmills.

Cuellar — 37B6

Área El Castillo, Calle del Alamillo, 40. **GPS**: n41,40083 w4,32028.
15 free free.
Distance: 2km.
Remarks: At castle.

Don Benito — 38D3

Avda. de los Deportes. **GPS**: n38,96250 w5,86305.
3 free Chfree. **Surface:** metalled. 01/01-31/12
Distance: on the spot on the spot on the spot.

Espinosa de los Monteros — 37C4

Parking Las Cocinas, BU-570 > Bárcenas. **GPS**: n43,08556 w3,5575.
10 free Chfree. **Surface:** asphalted.
Remarks: Max. 48h.

Foncastín — 37A6

A6, salida 175. **GPS**: n41,44131 w4,97957.
10 free Chfree. **Surface:** asphalted. 01/01-31/12
Distance: 250m on the spot.

Frómista — 37B5

Paseo de Julio Senador, P-980. **GPS**: n42,26494 w4,41198.
10 free Chfree. **Surface:** metalled. 01/01-31/12
Distance: 600m 200m.
Remarks: Max. 48h, at sports grounds, weigh bridge nearby € 0,50.

La Alberca — 38D1

Casa del Parque. **GPS**: n40,48833 w6,11583.
10 free Chfree. **Surface:** metalled.
Distance: 300m.
Remarks: Max. 48h.

La Joyosa — 40A1

Área de Marlofa, Calle Sobradiel. **GPS**: n41,73744 w1,06664.
21 free Ch € 3 WC . **Surface:** asphalted/grassy.
Distance: 9km.

Lagartera — 39A2

Camino de la Estacion. **GPS**: n39,91151 w5,19978.

3 free free. **Surface:** asphalted. 01/01-31/12
Distance: on the spot 1,4km 100m.
Remarks: Max. 48h.

León — 37A4

Avda. De los Peregrinos, 5. **GPS**: n42,60471 w5,58525.

10 free Chfree. **Surface:** metalled.
Distance: 300m.
Remarks: Max. 48h.

Logrosán — 39A2

El Palomar, Calle Palomar. **GPS**: n39,33188 w5,48044.
10 free free. 01/01-31/12
Remarks: Max. 48h.

Mérida — 38D3

P Hernan Cortez, Calle Cabo Verde. **GPS**: n38,91861 w6,33611.
20 € 13,25/24h Ch.
Surface: metalled.
Distance: 4km.

Tourist information Mérida:
Oficina de Turismo, Calle Santa Eulalia, 64.Also called Spanish Rome. Former stopover on the old silver trail.
Museo Arquelogio, Santa Clara.Roman findings.

Olmedo — 37B6

Parque del Mudejar, N601, km 148,1. **GPS**: n41,29167 w4,68194.

10 free Chfree. **Surface:** metalled. 01/01-31/12
Distance: 100m 200m.
Remarks: Max. 48h.

Osorno — 37B5

Los Chopos, N611 Osorno > Herrera de Pisuerga. **GPS**: n42,41694 w4,35111.

ES

30 free Ch free. **Surface:** asphalted.
Distance: 700m 2,2km on the spot.
Remarks: Max. 48h, guarded parking.

Palazuelos de Eresma 39B1

Calle Cordel. **GPS:** n40,92848 w4,05529.
30 free. **Surface:** metalled. 01/01-31/12
Distance: 4km.

Palencia 37B5

Parque Isla Dos Aguas, Avda. Ponce de León, 12. **GPS:** n42,00389 w4,53333.

10 free Ch free. **Surface:** asphalted.
Distance: on the spot 4km on the spot El Arbol 50m 100m.
Remarks: Max. 48h.

Tourist information Palencia:
Oficina de Turismo, Plaza San Pablo s/n.

Peñafiel 37B6

GPS: n41,59440 w4,11582.

5 free. **Surface:** asphalted. 01/01-31/12
Remarks: Parking castle.

Peñaflor 40A1

Parking Surrecreo, Urbanizacion Los Rosales Peñaflor. **GPS:** n41,72777 w0,79194.
150 € 15 Ch WC included.
Distance: 8 km.

Pesquera de Duero 37B6

Parking Ermita. GPS: n41,64571 w4,16636.

2 free. **Surface:** grassy.
Distance: Pesquera de Duero 3km.
Remarks: Near church.

Piedrasluengas 37B4

C627. **GPS:** n43,03674 w4,45705.
Remarks: Flat parking on the col Piedrasluengas.

Pollos 37A6

Estación de Servicios La Loba 2000, A62, salida 169. **GPS:** n41,41004 w5,13396.

10 free Ch free. **Surface:** asphalted.
Distance: 200m on the spot on the spot.
Remarks: Petrol station.

Salamanca 37A6

Parking Turismus, Avenida del Padre Ignacio Ellacuria. **GPS:** n40,95758 w5,67646.

50 free. **Location:** Urban. **Surface:** asphalted.
Distance: city centre 1,5km 50m Lidl/Mercadona on the spot.

Saldaña 37B5

Calle Polideportivo. **GPS:** n42,51750 w4,74139.
6 free Ch. **Surface:** metalled. 01/01-31/12
Remarks: Max. 48h.

Sancti-Spiritus 36D6

Hostal-Restaurante La Ponderosa, Carretera nacional 620 km303. **GPS:** n40,73481 w6,36093.

customers free .

ES

Distance: 3km.
Remarks: Daily menu € 8.

Sepúlveda 37B6

Calle de el Postiguillo. **GPS:** n41,29897 w3,74479.

10 free. **Surface:** asphalted.
Distance: 300m 12km 100m.

Soria 37D6

Monte de las Animas. **GPS:** n41,76769 w2,45391.

free. **Surface:** gravel.

Toledo 39B2

Parking de la Estación, Avda. de Castilla la Mancha.
GPS: n39,86472 w4,01944.
50 free.
Surface: asphalted.
Distance: 1,3km.

Tourist information Toledo:

Oficina de Turismo, Puerta de Bisagra, s/n.Old city with historical centre, World Heritage Site.

Iglesia del Christo de la Vega.Medieval citadel, built for protection of the Puente de Alcantara, the bridge.

Catedral.Cathedral known for its richness.

Iglesia del Christo de la Vega,.Former mosque, catholic church since 12th century.

El Alcázar.Roman castle ruins, 16th century.

Turégano 37B6

CL603. **GPS:** n41,15194 w4,00806.
10 free Ch free. **Surface:** asphalted. 01/01-31/12
Distance: 200m.
Remarks: Max. 48h.

Valladolid 37B6

San Lorenzo, Avda. Ramon Pradera, 6. **GPS:** n41,65583 w4,73722.

10 € 2,50/24h included. **Location:** Urban.
Surface: asphalted.
Distance: city centre 1km 3,2km 400m.
Remarks: Max. 48h.

Villada 37B5

C/ San Fructuoso, Calle del Ferial Nuevo. **GPS:** n42,25389 w4,96667.

6 free Ch WC free. **Surface:** gravel.
Distance: 200m 200m 200m.
Remarks: Max. 48h.

Villalpando 37A5

Area de Servicios Villalpando, A6, salida 236. **GPS:** n41,85906 w5,41993.
10 free Ch free. **Surface:** asphalted.
Distance: 200m on the spot on the spot.
Remarks: Petrol station.

Zafra 38D3

Ctra. de los Santos de Maimona, Ex101. **GPS:** n38,42527 w6,41083.

30 free Ch free. **Surface:** asphalted. 01/01-31/12

Zafra 38D3

Restaurante La Cabaña, N435. **GPS:** n38,42580 w6,41008.
50 Ch.

Zamora 37A6

Estadio Barrio 3 Arboles, Calle de los Pisones. **GPS:** n41,50337 w5,75585.

30 free. **Surface:** asphalted.

Andalusia

Agua Amarga 39D5

GPS: n36,93883 w1,93657.

20 free. **Surface:** gravel/sand. 01/01-31/12
Distance: on the spot 100m 50m 500m 2km.

ES

Remarks: Riverbed.

S Alcalá de Guadaíra 38D5

Autocaravanas Hidalgo, A92 Sevilla><Malaga km 7. **GPS**: n37,32856 w5,8056.

18 € 0,50 Ch .
Distance: 170m exit 15.
Remarks: Motorhome dealer, max. 2 nights.

S Alcalá de los Gazules 38D6

Los Gazules, Ctra. Patrite, km.4.
GPS: n36,46392 w5,66479.
7 € 13 Ch. 01/01-31/12
Remarks: Formula Camper € 16, 01/10-28/02, >18h <10h.

S Alcaudete 39B4

Plaza del Castillo de Alcaudete, Calle de Paco del Arriero.
GPS: n37,58972 w4,08916.
6 free Ch free. **Surface:** sand. 01/01-31/12
Distance: 300m 300m.

S Alhaurín del la Torr 39A5

Área de Autocaravanas Sol, Camino de las Curtis. **GPS**: n36,68083 w4,53611.
150 € 10 Ch included.
Distance: 9 km 100m.
Remarks: Guarded parking.

Alicún de las Torres 39B5

GR6104. **GPS**: n37,50836 w3,10802.

3 free. **Surface:** metalled. 01/01-31/12
Distance: 100m 100m.
Remarks: Next to the spa resort.

S Almayate 39A5

Area AMB, Carretera Nacional 340, km 266,5. **GPS**: n36,72372 w4,13999.
€ 6 Ch included € 3. **Surface:** metalled.
Distance: 100m 100m 4km.
Remarks: Motorhome dealer.

S Almensilla 38D5

San Diego, A-8054.
GPS: n37,31361 w6,09333.
15 free Ch free.
Remarks: At petrol station BP, restaurant visit appreciated.

S Almería 39C6

Area Autocaravanas Playa de Almería, Av. Cabo de Gata 280.
GPS: n36,81602 w2,43228.
40 € 10 Ch included € 2 WC € 1 € 1. **Surface:** asphalted.
Distance: 200m on the spot.
Remarks: Behind petrol station, max. 72h.

S Almerimar 39C6

Area del Puerto Deportivo Almerimar, Torre del puerto. **GPS**: n36,69612 w2,79425.

20 € 7,95 Ch € 3,50 WC included € 3,50. **Surface:** asphalted.
01/01-31/12
Distance: on the spot 150m 100m 100m.
Remarks: Check in at harbourmaster 9-14h, 16-21h.

S Archidona 39A5

A7200. **GPS**: n37,09097 w4,38879.

12 free Ch free. **Surface:** concrete. 01/01-31/12
Distance: 250m 1km 500m 1km.

S Cabo de Gata 39C6

Cabo de Gata, Ctra. Cabo de Gata s/n, Cortijo Ferrón. **GPS**: n36,80083 w2,24611.
40 € 16 Ch. 01/01-31/12
Remarks: Formula Camper, summertime > 20h < 10h, wintertime >18h, period excluded: 15/07-31/08.

S Cabra 39A5

Auditorio Municipal Alcalde Juan Muños, Juanita la Larga.
GPS: n37,46608 w4,42361.

10 free Ch free. **Surface:** asphalted. 01/01-31/12
Distance: 300m 300m 300m.
Remarks: Max. 48h.

Chipiona 38C5

Carretera de la Playa. **GPS**: n36,70442 w6,42915.

8 free. **Surface:** asphalted. 01/01-31/12
Distance: 4km on the spot on the spot 1,5km.

S Conil de la Frontera 38D6

La Rosaleda, Ctra. del Pradillo, km 1,3. **GPS**: n36,29305 w6,09555.

ES

20 € 15. 01/01-31/12
Remarks: Formula Camper, summertime > 20h < 10h, wintertime >18h, July/August € 30.

S Conil de la Frontera 38D6

Roche, Carril de Pilahito.
GPS: n36,31138 w6,11333.
30 € 15. 01/01-31/12
Remarks: Formula Camper, summertime > 20h < 10h, wintertime >18h.

P Conil de la Frontera 38D6

Avda. del Rio. **GPS**: n36,27282 w6,08994.

20 free. **Surface:** asphalted. 01/01-31/12
Distance: on the spot 500m 500m.
Remarks: Parking along coast road.

Córdoba 39A4

Avda. de los Custodios. **GPS**: n37,87528 w4,78778.
30 against payment. **Surface:** asphalted. 01/01-31/12
Distance: historical centre 300m 2,3km.
Remarks: In opposite of police station.

P Córdoba 39A4

Avda. del Campo de la Verdad/Calle del Compositor Rafael Castro.
GPS: n37,87515 w4,76626.
free. **Surface:** asphalted.
01/01-31/12
Distance: 1km.

Tourist information Córdoba:

- Puerta de Almodovar.Entrance gate to the old Jewish district, Barrio de la Juderia.
- M Museo Municipal Taurino, Plaza de las Bulas.Museum about bull-fighting.
- M Torre de la Calahorra.Urban museum.
- Oficina de Turismo, Torrijos, 10 (Palacio de Congresos), www.ayuncordoba.es.Historical and culturally rich city, city of the flamenco and bull-fighting.
- Palacio del Marqués de Viana.Palace with collections of leather, silverware, porcelain etc.
- Mezquita.World-famous Moorish mosque.

S Cuevas de San Marcos 39A5

GPS: n37,26059 w4,40237.

10 free Chfree. **Surface:** asphalted.
Distance: 1km 500m 1km.
Remarks: Parking at swimming pool.

S Cullar 39C5

Venta de Peral2, A-92. **GPS**: n37,55336 w2,6144.

20 free WC free. **Surface:** asphalted. 01/01-31/12
Distance: 3km 10m 10m.

S El Bosque 38D5

Calle de Juan Ramón Jiménez. **GPS**: n36,75670 w5,51056.

5 free Chfree. **Surface:** metalled. 01/01-31/12
Distance: on the spot 100m 300m.

S El Puerto de Santa Maria 38C5

Playa Dunas de San Anton, Paseo Maritimo Puntilla. **GPS**: n36,58722 w6,2405.
10 €15 Ch. 01/01-31/12
Remarks: Formula Camper, summertime > 20h < 10h, wintertime >18h, period 01/10-31/05.

P El Puerto de Santa Maria 38C5

Plaza de Toros. **GPS**: n36,59692 w6,23191.

5 free. **Surface:** asphalted. 01/01-31/12
Distance: on the spot 100m 300m.
Remarks: Parking arena for bullfighting.

S El Rocío 38C5

La Aldea, Ctra.El Rocío Km.25. **GPS**: n37,14141 w6,49093.
10 € 15 Ch. 01/01-31/12
Remarks: Formula Camper, summertime > 20h < 10h, wintertime >18h, period excluded: pilgrimage.

S Gelves 38D4

Puerto Gelves, Calle de Puerto Gelves. **GPS**: n37,33934 w6,02405.

20 € 11,80 Ch € 2,73 WC.

ES

Surface: asphalted. 01/01-31/12
Distance: on the spot 4,3km on the spot on the spot on the spot.
Remarks: Sevilla 10km, Good bus connection.

S **Granada** 39B5

Área de Geysepark-Cármenes, Torre de Comares. **GPS**: n37,15136 w3,59533.

30 € 16/day Ch included. **Surface:** asphalted. 01/01-31/12
Distance: 200m 2km 200m 200m 200m.
Remarks: Parking, entrance motorhomes 2nd ramp.

P **Granada** 39B5

Alhambra, P5. **GPS**: n37,17168 w3,57974.

50 € 46,65/24h, 01/10-31/05 € 26,60/24h.
Surface: gravel. 01/01-31/12
Distance: 1,5km 200m 200m 100m.

Tourist information Granada:
Oficina de Turismo, C/Mariana Pineda, s/n
.Former capital of Moorish Andalusia at the foot of the Sierra Nevada.
Alhambra.Most important curiosity of the city, the best kept Arab palace.
9-20h, winter, Sa 20-22h, Su 9-18h, summer Tue,Thu, Sa 22-24h.
Cuevas del Sacromonte.Caves in Sacromonte mountain, gypsies previously lived here.
Now important tourist attraction and stage of flamenco shows.
El Albaicín.Moorish district facing the Alhambra.

Grazalema 38D5

Calle Juan de la Rosa. **GPS**: n36,75807 w5,36365.

4 free. **Surface:** asphalted. 01/01-31/12
Distance: 300m 200m 500m.

S **Güejar Sierra** 39B5

Las Lomas, Ctra. de Güejar Sierra, Km. 6.
GPS: n37,15972 w3,45388.
5 € 16 Ch. 01/01-31/12
Remarks: Formula Camper, summertime > 20h < 10h, wintertime >18h.

Huelva 38C4

Monumento a Colón, Avenida Francesco Montenegro. **GPS**: n37,21333 w6,93972.

15 free. **Surface:** asphalted. 01/01-31/12
Distance: 6km 50m on the spot 6km 500m.
Remarks: Parking at monument of Columbus, dir Al Rocio.

S **Isla Cristina** 38C4

Giralda, Ctra. Provincial 4117, km 1,5. **GPS**: n37,20000 w7,301.
10 € 16 Ch. 01/01-31/12
Remarks: Formula Camper, summertime > 20h < 10h, wintertime >18h, period excluded: 15/07-31/08.

S **La Garrofa** 39C5

La Garrofa, Ctra.N-340, km 435,5. **GPS**: n36,82638 w2,51722.
40 € 15 Ch. 01/01-31/12
Remarks: Formula Camper, summertime > 20h < 10h, wintertime >18h, period excluded: 15/07-31/08.

La Isleta 39C6

Playa del Pénom blanca, Carreta Noria. **GPS**: n36,81670 w2,05146.

15 free. **Surface:** gravel.
Distance: 100m sandy beach 20m 150m 300m.
Remarks: Parking to sea.

La Línea de Concepción 38D6

Avda. Principe de Asturias. **GPS**: n36,15583 w5,34553.

50 € 1/h, € 15/24h. **Surface:** metalled. 01/01-31/12
Distance: 500m 1km 200m 1km.
Remarks: Wed, market.

S **Lekeitio** 37D4

Iñigo Artieta Etorbidea. **GPS**: n43,35849 w2,50743.

ES

14 free € 1/100liter Ch. **Surface:** asphalted. 01/01-31/12
Distance: 500m 500m 500m 300m.

Marbella 39A6

Cabopino, Ctra. N340 km 194,7. **GPS**: n36,48861 w4,74277.
50 € 15 Ch. 01/01-31/12
Remarks: Formula Camper, summertime > 20h < 10h, wintertime >18h, periods excluded: Easter, July/August.

Tourist information Marbella:
Oficina de Turismo, Glorieta de la Fontanilla, s/n, www.andalucia.org.
Conmemoración de la Conquista de los Cristianos.Traditional celebration. 11/06.

Marchena 38D5

Ctra. de las Paradas. **GPS**: n37,33083 w5,42416.
20 free Chfree. **Surface:** metalled.

Olvera 38D5

Vía Verde de la Sierra. **GPS**: n36,94138 w5,25305.
48 € 5 Ch included. 01/01-31/12
Distance: 1km.

Orgiva 39B5

Orgiva, Carretera A-348.
GPS: n36,88708 w3,41754.
7 € 15,50 Ch. 01/01-31/12
Remarks: Formula Camper € 16, 01/10-28/02, >18h <10h.

Peñarroya-Pueblonuevo 39A3

El Pantano. **GPS**: n38,27694 w5,27722.

20 € 5-7 ChService € 1,50 € 2 included. **Location:** Comfortable, isolated, quiet. **Surface:**. 01/01-31/12
Distance: 4km lake on the spot on the spot on the spot.
Remarks: Direct access to the beach, motorhome washing place € 1, swimming pool.

Priego de Córdoba 39A5

Avda. Niceto Alcalá Zamora. **GPS**: n37,44194 w4,21194.

9 free Ch WC free. **Surface:** concrete. 01/01-31/12
Distance: 500m 500m 500m.

Tourist information Priego de Córdoba:
Iglesia de la Aurora.

Rute 39A5

Calle de Jésus Obrero. **GPS**: n37,33113 w4,37323.

6 free Chfree. **Surface:** asphalted.
Distance: 500m 500m 300m.
Remarks: Parking next to police station, max. 48h.

San Juan de los Terreros 39D5

Playa de Entrevista, A332. **GPS**: n37,35083 w1,67972.

>20 free . **Surface:** gravel/sand. 01/01-31/12
Distance: 500m 100m 2km 2,5km.
Remarks: Parking on beach.

Sancti Petri La Barrosa 38C6

Carretera de la Barossa. **GPS**: n36,38612 w6,2053.

20 free. **Surface:** metalled. 01/01-31/12
Distance: 2km 200m 1km 5km.
Remarks: Parking on beach.

Sanlúcar de Barrameda 38C5

Sanlúcar AC Parking, Camino de lReyerta, s/n. **GPS**: n36,76195 w6,39617.

50 € 12 Ch WC . 01/01-31/12
Distance: 100m 50m 50m.

Santaella 39A4

La Campiña, Ctra. Aldea de Quintana. **GPS**: n37,62277 w4,85944.
3 . 01/01-31/12
Remarks: Formula Camper € 14, 01/10-01/04, >18h <10h.

Sevilla 38D4

Area Ac Sevilla Centro, Avenida De Garcia Morato S/N, Seville (Sevilla). **GPS**: n37,36239 w5,99452.
50 € 12 Ch (20x)€ 3 WC included.
Surface: asphalted. 01/01-31/12
Distance: on the spot 200m 500m on the spot 200m on the spot on the spot.

Sevilla 38D4

Parking PublicoTorneo, Calle Marqués de Paradas, Seville (Sevilla). **GPS**: n37,39180 w6,00172.
€ 15/night. **Surface:** asphalted. 01/01-31/12
Distance: 150m. **Remarks:** Parking nearby station.

Sevilla 38D4

Parking Kansas City, Avda. de Kansas City, Seville (Sevilla). **GPS**: n37,39194 w5,97333.
€ 18/24h.
Surface: asphalted.

Tourist information Seville (Sevilla):
Oficina de Turismo, Avda. de la Constitución, 21B, www.andalucia.org.Capital of Andalusia with a lot of curiosities.
Barrio de Santa Cruz.Former Moorish and Jewish district in the city centre.
Casa Pilatos.Copy of the house of Pilate in Jerusalem. 9-18h.
Almeda de Hercules. Su-morning.
Calle de las Sierpes.Famous shopping street.

Sierra Nevada 39B5

Los Peñones de San Francisco. GPS: n37,09859 w3,39059.

60 € 15/day Ch included. **Surface:** asphalted.
Distance: 3km 1km 300m.
Remarks: Free shuttle to centre. Ring-road Granada, Ronda Sur, exit 5b, carretera de Sierra Nevada.

Tourist information Sierra Nevada:
Parc Natural de Sierra Nevada.Large nature park with Europe's most southern ski resort.

Taberno 39C5

Área El Rancho, Los Llanos (La Carrasquilla), Santopetar. **GPS**: n37,46028 w2,03833.
8 € 8 Ch (4x)included. **Surface:** gravel.
Distance: 600m A7 13km.
Remarks: Swimming pool.

Tarifa 38D6

GPS: n36,06804 w5,6856.

20 free. **Surface:** sand. 01/01-31/12
Distance: 10km on the spot 50m 100m.
Remarks: Parking on beach.

Tourist information Tarifa:
Tourist Office, Duke of Kent House, Cathedral Square, Gibraltar, www.gibraltar.gi.British colony at the northwest end of the Rock of Gibraltar.
Siege Tunnels, Gibraltar.Labyrinth of tunnels, ingenious defence system.

Valverde del Camino 38C4

Ctra. de Zalamea. **GPS**: n37,58111 w6,75138.

10 free Chfree. **Surface:** asphalted/sand. 01/01-31/12
Distance: 500m.

Vélez-Rubio 39C5

Área Puerta Oriental de Andalucía, Calle Granada. **GPS**: n37,65194 w2,07555.

10 free Chfree. **Surface:** metalled. 01/01-31/12 1st week Aug. **Distance:** 500m 2,2km 500m 500m.

Vera 39D5

Acvera Motorhome Park & Aire. GPS: n37,26030 w1,85347.
150 € 7-9 Ch included. **Location:** Rural, comfortable. **Surface:** metalled.
Distance: Vera 2km 4,7km beach 7km on the spot.
Remarks: Tennis & padel lessons, 11 tennis courts.

Vera 39D5

Oasis al Mar, Av del Salar. **GPS**: n37,22731 w1,82819.
50 € 7-9, trailer € 1 Ch € 3/day € 3 included. **Location:** Rural, comfortable. **Surface:** gravel. 01/10-01/05
Distance: centre Vera 4,4km 2km.
Remarks: Motorhome washing place € 4.

Villanueva de Algaidas 39A5

Calle de la Archidona, A-7201. **GPS**: n37,17824 w4,44858.
20 free Chfree. **Surface:** asphalted. **Remarks:** Max. 48h.

Zahara de los Atunes 38D6

GPS: n36,13720 w5,84363.
. **Distance:** 100m 1km 100m 100m 100m.
Remarks: Parking beside river.

ES

PORTUGAL

Braga
Portugal North
pages: 453-458
Porto
Beira
pages: 458-465
Coimbra
Portugal Central
and Lisbon
pages: 465-470
Lisbon
Alentejo
pages: 470-475
Algarve
pages: 475-479
Faro

PT

Capital: Lisbon
Government: Parliamentary democracy
Official Language: Portuguese
Population: 10,800,00 (2012)
Area: 91,642 km^2.

General information

Dialling code: 00351
General emergency: 112
Currency: Euro
Payments by credit card are accepted almost everywhere.

Regulations for overnight stays

Wild camping is not officially allowed. Overnight parking places mentioned here are not official motorhome stopovers but tolerated areas. You will not find an official motorhome sign.

Additional public holidays 2014

January 6 Epiphany
April 18 Good Friday
April 25 Liberationday
May 1 Labor Day
June 10 National Holiday
June 19 Corpus Christi
August 15 Assumption of the Virgin Mary
October 5 Republic day
November 1 All Saints' Day
December 8 Immaculate Conception

Portugal

Portugal North

Aguçadoura 36B5

Aguaçadoura Futebol Clube. GPS: n41,44389 w8,77722.

free. **Surface:** sand. 01/01-31/12
Distance: 500m 50m 500m 500m.
Remarks: At the beach, dir Estela.

Amarante 36C6

Av. Alexandre Herculano. **GPS**: n41,27286 w8,07178.

. **Surface:** metalled.
Distance: 800m on the spot on the spot 50m.
Remarks: Parking at sports complex.

Amarante 36C6

GPS: n41,27863 w8,06768.
.
Distance: 200m 200m.
Remarks: Parking swimming pool.

Amarante 36C6

GPS: n41,27020 w8,07708.

. **Surface:** metalled.
Distance: on the spot on the spot.
Remarks: Market square along the river.

Amarante 36C6

Penedo da Rainha, São Gonçalo. **GPS**: n41,28031 w8,06925.
Ch . 01/02-30/11
Distance: 1km on the spot on the spot 1km.

Tourist information Amarante:
Museu Municipal Amadeu de Souza Cardoso, Alameda Teixeira Pascoaes. Modern art.

Avintes 36B6

Parque Biológico de Gaia, Rue da Cunha. **GPS**: n41,09730 w8,55414.

9 € 4 + € 4 /pp, entrance park incl Ch included WC free,at reception. **Location:** Luxurious, quiet. **Surface:** grasstiles. 01/01-31/12
Distance: 10km 800m 100m.
Remarks: Check in at reception.

Barcelos 36B5

R.Rosa Ramalho. **GPS**: n41,52829 w8,61547.
12 free. **Surface:** metalled. 01/01-31/12
Distance: centre 800m 3,5km.
Remarks: Parking swimming pool.

Tourist information Barcelos:
Posto de Turismo, Largo da Porta Nova (Torre de Menagem).
Museu de Olaria de Barcelos, R. Cónego Joaquim Gaiolas.Ceramics and archeology. Tue-Su 10-12.30h, 14-18h, Thu 10-18h.

Bico 36B6

R. Vasco da Gama. **GPS**: n40,73016 w8,64747.

30 free free. **Location:** Rural, simple, isolated, quiet. **Surface:** metalled. 01/01-31/12
Distance: 300m on the spot on the spot on the spot.
Remarks: In fishing port. In fishing port, north of Aveiro N109 dir Estarreja, then Murtosa-Bico.

Braga 36C5

Bom Jesus do Monte. **GPS**: n41,55278 w8,38137.

free. **Surface:** gravel/sand. 01/01-31/12
Distance: 6km 20m on the spot.
Remarks: Parking at funicular railway.

Braga 36C5

Sameiro. **GPS**: n41,53928 w8,36743.

PT

free. **Surface:** gravel/sand.
Remarks: Parking at place of pilgrimage.

Tourist information Braga:
Old city centre.
Semana Santa.Procession.
week before Easter.
Parque Nacional da Peneda-Gerês.Hiking routes.

S Bragança 36D5
Parque de Merendas, Rue Miguel Torga. **GPS:** n41,80417 w6,74611.

30 free Ch free. **Location:** Rural, comfortable, quiet.
Surface: metalled.
01/01-31/12
Distance: 200m 200m 200m.
Remarks: P below the castle, between 01/07-15/09 max. 24h, beautiful viex.
Tourist information Bragança:
Medival upper city and castle.
M Museu Militar. 9-11.45h, 14-18.15h.
Parque Natural de Montesinho.Nature reserve.

Cabedelo 38B1
R.do Cabedelo. **GPS:** n40,14403 w8,86395.

10 . **Location:** Simple. **Surface:** sand. 01/01-31/12
Distance: on the spot on the spot.
Remarks: Beach parking.

S Carrazeda de Ansiães 36C6
GPS: n41,24498 w7,30386.
Ch. 01/01-31/12
Remarks: Parking swimming pool.

Carregal do Sal 38C1
Quinta de Cabriz. GPS: n40,42465 w8,01856.
free. **Surface:** unpaved.
Distance: on the spot.
Remarks: Portugal Tradicional, max. 24h.

S Carregal do Sal 38C1
Luzio, Arruamento Urbano a Sul da Vila. **GPS:** n40,43116 w7,99471.

3 free Ch free. **Location:** Simple. **Surface:** grassy.
01/01-31/12
Distance: 1km.
Remarks: Behind petrol station.

Castelo do Neiva 36B5
Av, de Santoinho. **GPS:** n41,67501 w8,78243.
.
Remarks: At N13, 8km south of Viana do Castelo.

Chaves 36C5
Alameda do Trajano. **GPS:** n41,73694 w7,46917.

free. **Surface:** metalled. 01/01-31/12
Distance: historical centre 300m 8,6km 100m 100m.
Remarks: Along the Tâmega river.

S Chaves 36C5
Quinta do Rebentão, Vila Nova de Veiga. **GPS:** n41,70127 w7,50013.
Ch . 01/01-30/11
Distance: 4km 400m 1km 800m.
Tourist information Chaves:
M Torre de Mengem.Military museum.

S Covas 36B5
Parque Campismo de Covas, Lugar de Pereiras. **GPS:** n41,88758 w8,69497.
Ch . 01/01-31/12

S Entre-os-Rios 36B6
GPS: n41,08357 w8,29322.

4 WC Lunchroom & co. **Location:** Simple, central, noisy.
01/01-31/12
Distance: 100m on the spot on the spot 100m 100m.
Remarks: South-east of Porto, N108, parking along the Douro river.

S Espinho 36B6
GPS: n40,98889 w8,64306.

40 free free,beach. **Location:** Rural, simple, isolated, quiet. **Surface:** gravel/sand. 01/01-31/12

Distance: 1km 25m 1km 1km.

Remarks: Beach parking.

Espinho 36B6

Municipal de Espinho, Zona da Ribeira dos Mochos. **GPS**: n41,01402 w8,63743. 01/01-31/12

Tourist information Espinho:

Posto de Turismo, Rua 23, nº 271, www.cm-espinho.pt.Bathing resort.

Esposende 36B5

Forte de S.João Baptiste, Rue do Farol. **GPS**: n41,54222 w8,79111.

free free. **Surface:** asphalted.

01/01-31/12

Distance: 1,5km on the spot on the spot 1,5km.

Remarks: Free wifi for clients restaurant. Parking next to lighthouse.

Esposende 36B5

Parque de Campismo de Fão, Lírios - Fão. **GPS**: n41,50778 w8,77833.

Ch . 01/01-31/12

Distance: 500m 500m on the spot 500m.

Tourist information Esposende:

Posto de Turismo, Avenida Marginal.Seaside resort at the mouth of the river Rio Cavado.

Freixo de Espada a Cinta 36D6

Espaço Multiusos, R. do Samiteiro de Cima. **GPS**: n41,08826 w6,81751.

12 free Ch (12x)free. **Surface:** metalled. 01/01-31/12

Distance: 900m 900m.

Remarks: Arrival <18h.

Freixo de Numão 36C6

Area de autocaravanas Jean Pierre Rossi, Sebarigos. **GPS**: n41,06000 w7,22111.

30 € 5/night Ch WC included. **Surface:** metalled.

Distance: 900m 500m 500m.

Gerês 36C5

Vila do Gerês. GPS: n41,73538 w8,15969.

. **Surface:** asphalted.

Distance: on the spot.

Gondomar 36B6

Medas, Gavinho - Medas. **GPS**: n41,03917 w8,42694.

Ch. 01/01-31/12

Gosende 36C6

Cooperativa Capuchinhas CRL, Campo Benfeito. **GPS**: n40,99799 w7,9269.

free. **Surface:** unpaved.

01/01-31/12

Distance: 5,1km.

Remarks: Portugal Tradicional.

Guilhufe 36B6

EM594. **GPS**: n41,19541 w8,31605.

8 free Chfree. **Location:** Simple, noisy. **Surface:** metalled.

01/01-31/12

Distance: 1km 1,6km 1km 1km.

Izeda 36D5

Largo do Toural. **GPS**: n41,56750 w6,72333.

30 free Chfree. **Location:** Rural, simple, central, quiet.

Surface: metalled. 01/01-31/12

Distance: centre 200m 200m.

Lamego 36C6

Parque Lamego, N2, Lugar da Raposeira. **GPS**: n41,09016 w7,82214.

40 € 5 + € 3/pp Ch € 4/day WC . **Location:** Luxurious, isolated, quiet. **Surface:** unpaved. 01/01-31/12

Distance: 1,2km 4,5km 500m 2km on the spot.

Remarks: Near Caves da Raposeira, beautiful view, baker every morning, sale of wines.

Lamego 36C6

GPS: n41,09501 w7,80372.

PT

free. **Surface:** metalled. 01/01-31/12
Distance: on the spot on the spot on the spot.
Remarks: At the foot of monumental stairs of the Santuari.

Tourist information Lamego:
www.cm-lamego.pt.Known for its Raposeira white wine.
Bodega Raposeira. free.
Nossa Senhora dos Remédios.Pilgrimage in Portugal, most important festivity of the country. end Aug-beginning Sep.

Lindoso 36C5
GPS: n41,86834 w8,19851.

Remarks: At the edge of village.

S Macedo de Cavaleiros 36D5
Rua das Piscinas. **GPS**: n41,53756 w6,95715.

8 free € 2/100liter Ch € 2/1h. **Location:** Urban, simple, central, quiet. **Surface:** asphalted. 01/01-31/12
Distance: 200m 200m 300m on the spot.

Macedo de Cavaleiros 36D5
Barragem do Azibo, Frada da Pegada. **GPS**: n41,58333 w6,89944.

10 free. **Location:** Rural, simple, quiet. **Surface:** metalled.
01/01-31/12
Distance: 2km sandy beach on the spot (peak season).
Remarks: At barrage, guarded during summer period.

Matosinhos 36B6
Av. de Praia. **GPS**: n41,26044 w8,72434.

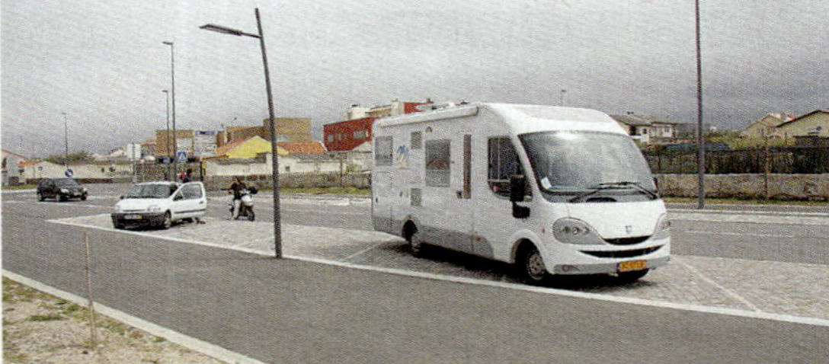

10 free. **Location:** Simple, noisy. **Surface:** metalled.
01/01-13/12
Distance: 200m 200m 600m on the spot.
Remarks: Beach parking. Parking to beach.

S Matosinhos 36B6
Municipal de Angeiras. **GPS**: n41,26722 w8,71972.
Ch. 01/01-31/12

Melgaço 36C5
Porta de Lamas de Mouro, Lamas de Mouro. **GPS**: n42,05202 w8,19413.
free. **Surface:** metalled.

Miranda do Douro 36D6
Av. Eduardo Quero. **GPS**: n41,49167 w6,27333.

free. **Surface:** metalled.
Distance: 25m 200m.
Remarks: Parking at city wall, south-east.

Miranda do Douro 36D6
Largo do Cestelo. **GPS**: n41,49611 w6,275.

free. **Surface:** metalled.
Distance: on the spot 50m 50m.
Remarks: Parking near ruins of castle.

S Mirandela 36D5
GPS: n41,48685 w7,18391.

free Fon. **Location:** Rural, simple, central, noisy.
Surface: metalled.
Distance: centre on the spot on the spot on the spot.
Remarks: Large parking along the river.

S Mirandela 36D5
Três Rios-Maravilha. **GPS**: n41,50683 w7,19716.
Ch.
15/05-31/09

Tourist information Mirandela:
www.mirandela-online.net.Old city.
Museu municipal.Modern Portuguese painting art. free.
Villa Flôr.Village museum. free.

S Mogadouro 36D6
Mogadouro, Complexo Desportivo Municipal. **GPS**: n41,33528 w6,71861.

Ch. 01/04-30/09
Distance: 500m on the spot 500m.

Mondim de Basto 36C5

Area Mondim de Basto. GPS: n41,41199 w7,95137.

30 free Chfree. **Location:** Urban, simple, central. **Surface:** metalled.
01/01-31/12
Distance: 300m 300m 300m.
Remarks: Fri market.

Montalegre 36C5

Rua João Rodrigues Cabrilho. **GPS:** n41,82280 e7,78684.
free Chfree. **Surface:** metalled. 01/01-31/12
Distance: 500m.

Murça 36C6

Murça-Estádio, Variante à N15. **GPS:** n41,40421 w7,44994.

free. **Surface:** asphalted. 01/01-31/12
Distance: 500m 300m.
Remarks: At footballstadium.

Nelas 36C6

Paço dos Cunhas de Santar, Largo do Paço, Santar. **GPS:** n40,57229 w7,89154.
free.
Remarks: Portugal Tradicional, vineyard/restaurant, max. 24h.

Parada 36C5

Santuàrio. GPS: n41,68806 w8,20167.

Peso da Régua 36C6

Parque Ovar, Av. de Ovar. **GPS:** n41,16278 w7,79222.

4 free (4x) WC free,150m. **Location:** Urban, simple, central, noisy.
Surface: asphalted. 01/01-31/12
Distance: on the spot 4km on the spot on the spot on the spot.

Ponte de Lima 36B5

Alameda de São João. **GPS:** n41,77052 w8,5847.

Remarks: Parking beside river.

Póvoa de Varzim 36B5

Rio Alto, Estela. **GPS:** n41,46277 w8,77369.
Ch. 01/01-31/12

Queimadela 36C5

Parque de Campismo do Baragem. GPS: n41,50379 w8,16216.
€ 5 Ch. **Surface:** grassy/metalled.
Distance: 100m 100m on the spot.

Santa Maria da Feira 36B6

GPS: n40,91972 w8,54306.

5 free. **Location:** Rural, simple, quiet. **Surface:** gravel/sand.
01/01-13/12
Distance: 600m 600m.
Remarks: Parking at castle. Parking at castle.

São Romão do Corgo 36C5

Quinta de Bourça, Lugar de Vila Nova. **GPS:** n41,44348 w7,9932.
free € 2,50 € 2,50. **Location:** Rural.
Distance: 11km.
Remarks: Portugal Tradicional.

São Salvador de Lordelo 36B6

R. da Igreja. **GPS:** n41,23472 w8,41139.

20 free Chfree. **Location:** Simple, quiet. **Surface:** gravel/sand.
01/01-31/12
Distance: 400m 400m 400m.

Silva 36B5

Lugar de Campelo. **GPS:** n41,96262 w8,66622.
39 € 6 € 3 Ch € 3 free. **Surface:** gravel.
Distance: 4km.

Torre de Moncorvo 36D6

GPS: n41,18083 w7,04167.
9 free Chfree. **Surface:** metalled. 01/01-31/12
Remarks: At sports park.

Valadares-SP do Sul 36B6

Cooperativa Mimos, Largo do Cruzeiro 1. **GPS:** n40,75704 w8,19997.

3 free. **Location:** Simple. **Surface:** grassy.
01/01-31/12
Distance: on the spot.
Remarks: Portugal Tradicional.

PT

ΔS Valpaços 36C5

Do Rabaçal, Rua Gago Coutinho. **GPS**: n41,63222 w7,24778.
Ch. 01/01-31/12

Viana do Castelo 36B5

Avenida Campo do Castelo. **GPS**: n41,69018 w8,83632.
free. **Location:** Urban. **Surface:** metalled. 01/01-31/12
Distance: centre 750m.

Viana do Castelo 36B5

Rua de Lima. **GPS**: n41,69534 w8,81875.
free. **Location:** Urban. **Surface:** unpaved.
Distance: centre 700m.
Remarks: Large parking along the Limia river.

ΔS Viana do Castelo 36B5

Cabedelo/Orbitur, Cabedelo - Darque. **GPS**: n41,67862 w8,82611.
€ 5,40 Ch.
16/01-15/11

Tourist information Viana do Castelo:
Posto de Turismo, Praça da Erva, www.cm-viana-castelo.pt.Bathing resort.
Campo do Costelo.Market. Fri.
Romaria da Nossa Senhora da Agonia.Procession with Gigantes (giants). 3rd week Aug.

ΔS Vila Chã 36B5

Sol de Vila Chã, Rua do Sol, Facho. **GPS**: n41,29825 w8,73263.
Ch. 01/01-31/12
Distance: 300m 10m on the spot 100m.

Vila do Conde 36B5

Av. Júlio Graça. **GPS**: n41,34476 w8,74541.

20 free. **Location:** Urban, simple, central, noisy. **Surface:** metalled.
01/01-31/12
Distance: 400m 150m 150m 200m 400m.
Remarks: Along the Este river.

Vila do Conde 36B5

Av. Marques de Sa Bandiera. **GPS**: n41,34270 w8,74587.

20 free. **Location:** Urban, simple, central. **Surface:** gravel/sand.
01/01-31/12
Distance: 500m on the spot 200m 400m.
Remarks: Parking to sea.

S Vila Nova de Cerveira 36B5

Av. dos Pescadores. **GPS**: n41,93823 w8,74685.
free Ch free. **Surface:** asphalted. 01/01-31/12
Distance: historical center 150m river-beach.
Remarks: Near Minho river and public pool park.

Vila Nova de Foz Côa 36C6

Rua Engenheiro Eugénio Nobre. **GPS**: n41,08028 w7,14806.
+50 free. **Location:** Rural. 01/01-31/12
Distance: 500m 500m.

S Vila Nova de Foz Côa 36C6

Autocross, N102. **GPS**: n41,06727 w7,15496.
Ch free.

ΔS Vila Nova de Gaia 36B6

Madalena, Rua de Cerro, Praia de Madalena. **GPS**: n41,10750 w8,65556.
Ch. 01/01-31/12
Remarks: Service only € 3,15-5,40.

Tourist information Vila Nova de Gaia:
City of the port wine, at the left bank of the river Douro, Port houses can be visited daily.
Caves A. A. Ferreira, Avenida Ramos Pinto, 70.The only real Portuguese company of port wine, Guided tour in english. 01/03-31/10 10-12.30h, 14-18h 01/11-28/02 Tue-Sa 10.30-12.30h, 14-18h. € 2,50.

ΔS Vila Real 36C6

Municipal de Vila Real, Rua Dr. Manuel Cardona, Quinta da Carreira. **GPS**: n41,30333 w7,73667.
Ch.
01/01-31/12

Tourist information Vila Real:
Solar de Mateus.Baroque country house, 18th century, known from label of the Matheus wine.

S Vinhais 36D5

GPS: n41,83409 e7,00306.
free Ch free. **Surface:** gravel. 01/01-31/12
Distance: 200m 100m.
Remarks: Nearby swimming pool.

Beira

S Aldeia da Ponte 38D1

Caminho do Freguil. **GPS**: n40,41092 w6,87159.

4 free Ch free. **Location:** Rural, simple. **Surface:** metalled.
01/01-31/12
Distance: 300m.
Remarks: Near old Roman bridge.

Almeida 36D6

GPS: n40,72295 w6,90489.

free. **Surface:** metalled. 01/01-31/12
Remarks: At fort-castle.

Anadia 38B1

Rua Seabras de Castro. **GPS**: n40,44056 w8,4375.

free. **Surface:** asphalted.
Distance: 100m 100m.
Remarks: At restaurants.

Aveiro 36B6

Parcue de S João, Canal São Roque. **GPS**: n40,64328 w8,65859.

10 free free. **Surface:** grasstiles. 01/01-31/12
Distance: 200m 25m 200m 200m.
Remarks: Parking at the Canal and A25.

Tourist information Aveiro:
Região de Turismo Rota da Luz, Rua João Mendonça, 8.
Ecomuseu da Troncalhada, Canal das Pirâmides.Salt-making. summer.
Museu de Aveiro, Av. Sta. Joana Princesa.Collection baroque art.
Tue-Su 10-17.30h.

Barril de Alva 38C1

EM517-1. **GPS**: n40,28611 w7,96167.

50 free Ch free. **Location:** Rural, simple, quiet. **Surface:** unpaved.
01/01-31/12
Distance: 500m river-beach on the spot.

Barriosa 38C1

Poço da Broca. **GPS**: n40,29366 w7,75376.

free. **Location:** Rural.
Distance: on the spot on the spot.
Remarks: Portugal Tradicional.

Belmonte 38C1

Parque de Santiago, N345. **GPS**: n40,27512 w7,35856.

4 free Ch WC free. **Surface:** metalled. 01/01-31/12
Distance: 500m on the spot 150m on the spot.

Castelo Bom 38D1

Avenida Santa Maria, N16. **GPS**: n40,61261 w6,83398.

3 free. **Location:** Rural, simple.
Surface: metalled.
01/01-31/12
Distance: on the spot.
Remarks: Typical village nearby spanish border.

Castelo Branco 38C1

Municipal de Castel Branco, N18. **GPS**: n39,85815 w7,49351.
Ch free. 01/05-31/10

Tourist information Castelo Branco:
Castelo.Ruins of castle of the Templars.
Alameda da Liberdade. Mo.

Castelo de Paiva 36B6

R. Emidio Navarro. **GPS**: n41,03955 w8,27406.

50 free Ch WC free. **Location:** Simple, central, quiet.
Surface: metalled. 01/01-31/12
Distance: on the spot on the spot on the spot.
Remarks: Market square.

Castelo Mendo 38C1

N16. **GPS**: n40,54894 w7,24083.

PT

3 free free. **Location:** Rural, simple. **Surface:** grassy/sand.
01/01-31/12
Distance: on the spot 6,8km.
Remarks: From Vilar Fornoso, P5, on entering the village.

Castelo Rodrigo — 36D6
GPS: n40,87778 w6,96611.

free. **Surface:** sand.
Remarks: At the entrance of fort.

Celorico da Beira — 36C6
GPS: n40,63389 w7,40472.

10 . **Location:** Isolated. **Surface:** metalled.
Distance: 2km.
Remarks: Parking sports complex.

PT

Cinfães — 36C6
GPS: n41,07167 w8,08719.

. **Surface:** metalled. 01/01-31/12
Distance: 100m 100m 100m.
Remarks: Parking on entering village.

Coimbra — 38B1
Av. Inês de Castro. **GPS**: n40,19970 w8,42905.

20 free Ch free. **Surface:** metalled. 01/01-31/12
Remarks: Max. 24h.

Tourist information Coimbra:
Posto de Turismo, Largo da Portagem.University town.
Portugal dos Pequeninos.Miniature Portugal. 9-19h.

Coimbrão — 38B1
Praia do Pedrógão. GPS: n39,91500 w8,95.
Chagainst payment . 16/02-15/12
Distance: 50m on the spot on the spot 10m.

Condeixa — 38B1
Av. Bombeiros Voluntarios de Condeixa. **GPS**: n40,11291 w8,49336.

6 free Chfree. **Surface:** asphalted. 01/01-31/12
Distance: 500m on the spot 300m.
Remarks: Max. 48h, market Fri-morning.

Condeixa — 38B1
Conímbriga, Praça da Repúbliça Condeixa. **GPS**: n40,09895 w8,4894.

5 free. **Location:** Simple. **Surface:** grassy/metalled. 01/01-31/12
Remarks: Parking next to archaeological site.

Covas do Monte-SP do Sul — 36C6
Covas do Monte. GPS: n40,88873 w8,09823.
free free.
Distance: 250m.
Remarks:
Portugal Tradicional.

Escalos de Baixo — 38C1
Hanmar, Estrada National 352. **GPS**: n39,89917 w7,40028.

20 € 8, May-Aug € 10 Ch WC included. **Surface:** grassy.
01/01-31/12
Distance: 1km 1km.

Estarreja — 36B6
R. Dr.Antonio Madureira. **GPS**: n40,75417 w8,56611.

6 € 2/24h Ch included. **Location:** Urban, simple, central. **Surface:** metalled. 01/01-31/12
Distance: on the spot on the spot on the spot.
Remarks: Max. 48h, check in Cafe Piscina, Ag. Seguros Rebelo, Tue market 100m.

S Estarreja 36B6

Ribeira do Maurão. **GPS**: n40,81328 w8,61588.

6 free Chfree. **Location:** Rural, simple, isolated, quiet. **Surface:** metalled. 01/01-31/12
Distance: on the spot on the spot.
Remarks: Nature reserve.

S Figueira da Foz 38B1

Av. de Espanha. **GPS**: n40,14856 w8,86791.

30 WC. **Surface:** asphalted. 01/01-31/12
Distance: on the spot on the spot 100m.

S Figueira da Foz 38B1

Gala/Orbitur, Matas Nacias, Gala. **GPS**: n40,11861 w8,85639.
Ch. 16/01-15/11
Remarks: Service only € 3,15-5,40.

S Figueira da Foz 38B1

Praia de Quiaios. **GPS**: n40,22083 w8,885.
Ch. 01/07-30/09
Distance: 500m on the spot on the spot 500m.
Remarks: Service only € 2,60-4,40.

Tourist information Figueira da Foz:
Posto de Turismo, Av. 25 de Abril.

S Fratel 38C2

Vila Velha de Ródão. **GPS**: n39,63250 w7,74694.

10 free Chfree. **Surface:** unpaved. 01/01-31/12
Distance: 200m 1km 300m 300m.

S Fundão 38C1

Quinta do Convento. GPS: n40,13276 w7,51205.
Ch WC . 01/01-31/12

S Furadouro 36B6

Praia do Furadouro. GPS: n40,87645 w8,67381.

30 free WC 50m. **Location:** Rural, simple, quiet. **Surface:** asphalted. 01/01-31/12
Distance: on the spot 300m 300m.
Remarks: Beach parking.

S Guarda 38C1

Parque Pólis, Rua da Direcção Geral de Viação. **GPS**: n40,54894 w7,24083.

20 free Chfree. **Location:** Simple. **Surface:** metalled. 01/01-31/12
Distance: historical centre 4km 2,4km 700m.
Remarks: Recreation park.

S Guarda 38C1

Rossio de Valhelhas. GPS: n40,40333 w7,40528.
Ch. 01/05-30/09
Distance: 50m 300m 150m 100m.

Tourist information Guarda:
Medieval city.

S Idanha-a-Nova 38C1

Municipal de Idanha-a-Nova, Albufeira da Barragem Marechel Carmona. **GPS**: n39,95056 w7,18722.
Ch. 01/01-31/12
Distance: 50m on the spot on the spot 8km.
Remarks: Service only € 2,60-4,40.

Idanha-a-Velha 38C1

N332. **GPS**: n39,99830 w7,1445.
.
Remarks: In village.

Tourist information Idanha-a-Velha:
Archeological tour.

PT

S Ilhavo 36B6

Av Ns.da Saude. **GPS**: n40,61417 w8,75222.

7 free Ch WC. **Surface:** metalled. 01/01-31/12

Distance: on the spot on the spot.

Remarks: Beach parking.

Ilhavo 36B6

Av. Infante Dom Henrique, Praia da Barra. **GPS**: n40,64375 w8,74456.

30 free. **Surface:** metalled. 01/01-31/12

Distance: 300m 300m.

Ilhavo 36B6

Costa Nova do Prado. **GPS**: n40,61222 w8,74917.

7 free. **Surface:** metalled. 01/01-31/12

Distance: on the spot on the spot on the spot on the spot.

Remarks: Beach parking.

Tourist information Ilhavo:

- Posto de Turismo de Ilhavo, Praça do Município.
- Museu Histórico da Vista Alegre, Fábrica de Porcelanas da Vista Alegre. Collection of porcelain. Tue-Fri 9-18h, Sa-Su 9-12.30h, 14-17h.
- Museu Marítimo de Ílhavo, Av. Dr. Rocha Madahil.Shipping museum. Tue-Fri 10-12.30h, 14.30-18h, Sa-Su 14.30-17.30h.

S Lorvão 38B1

Rua do Malhao. **GPS**: n40,25896 w8,31468.

10 free Ch free. **Surface:** metalled.

Luso 38B1

GPS: n40,38639 w8,38139.

10 free. **Surface:** metalled. 01/01-31/12

Remarks: Parking next to Hotel de Terme.

Tourist information Luso:

- Health resort.
- Mata Nacional do Buçaco.Nature reserve.

S Melo-Gouveia 38C1

Quinta das Cegonhas, Nabainhos. **GPS**: n40,52057 w7,54169.

50 € 14,50-18 Ch WC .

Remarks: N17 - the road between Celorico da Beira and Coimbra, milestone 114.

S Mira 36B6

Praia de Mira. **GPS**: n40,44472 w8,79806.

Ch. 16/01-15/11

Remarks: Service only € 3,15-5,40.

S Miranda do Corvo 38B1

Rua Porto Mourisco. **GPS**: n40,08803 w8,33232.

8 free Ch free. **Location:** Rural. **Surface:** asphalted.

01/01-31/12

Distance: 700m.

S Oleiros 38C1

R. Dr. Barata Relvas. **GPS**: n39,92056 w7,91389.

free Ch free. **Surface:** metalled. 01/01-31/12

S Pardilhó 36B6

Parque de Merendas, R. Joaquim Maria Resende. **GPS**: n40,80111 w8,63472.

15 € 2/48h Ch included. **Location:** Rural, comfortable, isolated, quiet. **Surface:** metalled. 01/01-31/12

Distance: 600m on the spot on the spot.

Remarks: Max. 48h.

S Penacova 38B1

Bairro de Carrazedos. **GPS**: n40,26722 w8,28306.

10 free Ch WC free. **Surface:** metalled. 01/01-31/12
Distance: 400m 3km 400m.

Penamacor — 38C1

Benquerença. **GPS:** n40,22938 w7,22136.

10 free Ch free. **Location:** Rural, simple, quiet. **Surface:** gravel/sand. 01/01-31/12
Distance: 2km on the spot.

Pinhel — 36C6

GPS: n40,77389 w7,06194.

.
Distance: on the spot on the spot.
Remarks: At town hall.

Praia de Mira — 36B6

Praia da Mira. **GPS:** n40,45800 w8,8025.

6 free. **Location:** Simple. **Surface:** metalled. 01/01-31/12
Distance: on the spot.
Remarks: Parking on beach.

Praia de Mira — 36B6

GPS: n40,44620 w8,80447.

20 free. **Surface:** sand.
Distance: 500m.
Remarks: Beach parking.

Praia de Quiaos — 38B1

Praia de Quiaos. **GPS:** n40,22034 w8,89116.

15 free. **Location:** Simple. **Surface:** metalled. 01/01-31/12
Remarks: Beach parking. Parking at beach north of village.

Sabugal — 38C1

Rua do Cemitério. **GPS:** n40,34843 w7,08653.

6 free Ch free. **Surface:** metalled. 01/01-31/12
Distance: 500m 400m.

Sangalhos — 36B6

R. do Mercado. **GPS:** n40,48639 w8,47528.

20 free Ch free. **Location:** Simple. **Surface:** metalled. 01/01-31/12
Remarks: At sports centre.

Santa Ovaia — 38C1

Ponte das Três Entradas, Avô. **GPS:** n40,30667 w7,87139.
€ 11 . **Surface:** grassy. 01/01-31/10
Distance: 10m on the spot on the spot on the spot 10m.

São João da Pesqueira — 36C6

Restaurant Carocha, N222. **GPS:** n41,15120 w7,42378.
50 free Ch free. 01/01-31/12
Distance: on the spot.
Remarks: Next to restaurant and Port wine cellar Cave Cadão.

PT

S Sao Joao de Areias 38C1

Terra de Iguanas, Estrada principal 76, Vila Dianteira. **GPS**: n40,39045 w8,08574.
4 € 7,50, 01/06,50-31/08 € 10 Ch included.
01/01-31/12
Remarks: Max. 3 nights, swimming pool incl.

São Lourenço do Bairro 38B1

Quinta do Encontro, N334. **GPS**: n40,44136 w8,49014.
free. 01/01-31/12
Remarks: Portugal Tradicional, vineyard/shop/restaurant, max. 24h.

S São Pedro do Sul 36C6

Termas São Pedro do Sul, N46. **GPS**: n40,74056 w8,08639.

6 free Chfree. **Location:** Simple. **Surface:** asphalted.
01/01-31/12
Distance: 1km.
Remarks: Max. 48h.

S Sertã 38B1

Palácio da Justiça, R. Baden Powell. **GPS**: n39,80028 w8,09944. .

free WC free. **Location:** Simple. **Surface:** metalled.
Distance: 100m 3km 50m 100m.

S Sertã 38B1

R. Amaro Vicente Martins. **GPS**: n39,79729 w8,09588.

4 free Ch free. **Location:** Simple. **Surface:** asphalted.
01/01-31/12
Distance: 500m 3km 50m.
Remarks: At sports park.

S Sertã 38B1

Albergue do Bonjardim, Nesperal, Sertã. **GPS**: n39,81306 w8,16278.

2 € 6 € 4 WC . **Location:** Luxurious, isolated. **Surface:** unpaved.
01/04-31/10
Distance: 200m 2,5km 1km 50m.
Remarks: Sauna, steam bath and covered pool € 7,50, breakfast € 7,50.

Tabua 38C1

Piscina. **GPS**: n40,36306 w8,03.

3 free. **Surface:** metalled.

Tabua 38C1

Rua Aurora Jesus Goncalves. **GPS**: n40,36306 w8,02278.

10 free. **Surface:** metalled.

Trancoso 36C6

Parque Sportivo. **GPS**: n40,77139 w7,36222.

3 free. **Surface:** metalled.

Trancoso 36C6

Av. Heróis de São Marcos. **GPS**: n40,77583 w7,35056.

PT

10 . **Surface:** metalled.
Distance: 50m.
Remarks: Note: Friday market day. Parking on entering the village.

S Vagos 36B6
Praia da Vagueira. **GPS**: n40,54944 w8,77056.
20 € 7,50, Oct-May € 5 Ch € 2. **Surface:** sand.
01/01-31/12
Remarks: Passerby € 2,50.

S Vagos 36B6
Vagueira, Gafanha da Boa Hora. **GPS**: n40,55806 w8,74528.
Ch . 01/01-31/12
Distance: 1km on the spot 1km 500m.
Remarks: Service only € 2,60-4,40.

Vagueira 36B6
Rua Arménio, Praia da Vagueira. **GPS**: n40,56506 w8,76697.

20 free. **Surface:** metalled.
Distance: 200m sandy beach 50m.
Remarks: Beach parking.

S Vila Nova de Oliveirinha 38C1
Quinta do Tapadinho, Rua da Quinta dos Brandões. **GPS**: n40,36520 w7,92195.

5 € 10 € 3 Ch € 3,50 WC included € 2,50.
Surface: grassy/sand. 01/01-31/12
Distance: 1km 6km 6km.

S Vila Pouca da Beira 38C1
Despinheiro, Avenida Principal. **GPS**: n40,30159 w7,9257.

4 € 8 WC € 1 € 4. **Location:** Rural, isolated, quiet.
Surface: grassy. 01/01-31/12
Distance: 500m 2km 2km 800m on the spot on the spot.

S Vilar Formoso 38D1
Zaza, Avenida das Tilia's, N332. **GPS**: n40,61528 w6,83833.

12 € 5/24h € 2 Ch included (12x)€ 1,50/day. **Location:** Simple.
Surface: asphalted/gravel. 01/01-31/12
Distance: 500m baker on site.

S Viseu 36C6
Av. Europa. **GPS**: n40,66533 w7,91681.
8 free Ch free.
Surface: asphalted.
01/01-31/12
Distance: on the spot 6km.
Tourist information Viseu:
Centre of Vinho do Dão.
Museu municipal, Castro Daire. Etnographical collection.

Portugal Central

S A-dos-Cunhados 38A2
R. Monsenhor José Fialho. **GPS**: n39,15222 w9,30083.

free Ch free. **Surface:** asphalted. 01/01-31/12
Distance: 100m 6km beach 7km 200m.

S Abrantes 38B2
Aquapolis, São Joao. **GPS**: n39,45489 w8,18977.

free Ch free. **Surface:** metalled. 01/01-31/12
Distance: 3km 4,7km 100m 6km.

Abrantes 38B2
Aquapolis, São Joao. **GPS**: n39,45333 w8,19056.

PT

10 free. **Surface:** metalled.
Distance: 3km 4,8km sandy beach.
Remarks: Along the Tagus river.

Abrantes 38B2

Largo do Pralvo. **GPS**: n39,44956 w8,18968.

10 free. **Surface:** metalled. 01/01-31/12
Distance: 1km 6,5km 1km 1km.
Remarks: Along the Tagus river.

Abrantes 38B2

Parque Urbano de São Lourenço, São Vincente. **GPS**: n39,47530 w8,21541.

10 free. **Surface:** grassy/gravel. 01/01-31/12
Distance: centre 2,4km 4,4km 50m 3,5km.
Remarks: Max. 48h.

Tourist information Abrantes:
Posto de Turismo, Esplanada 1º de Maio, www.cm-abrantes.pt.City with historical centre.

Alenquer 38A2

Alenquer camping, Casal das Pedras. **GPS**: n39,05917 w9,02833.
4 € 12,50 € 2,50 Ch. 01/01-31/12
Distance: on the spot on the spot.

Almourol 38B2

Castelo de Almourol, Praia do Ribatejo. **GPS**: n39,46295 w8,38297.

10 free. **Location:** Simple. **Surface:** metalled.
Distance: 2km 4km on the spot 2km.
Remarks: On the banks of the Tejo river, parking castle.

Arruda dos Vinhos 38A2

Casal da Pevide. GPS: n38,99861 w9,08417.

3 free Chfree. **Surface:** asphalted. 01/01-31/12
Distance: 2km on the spot on the spot.
Remarks: Parking Intermarché.

Baleal 38A2

Estrada do Baleal. **GPS**: n39,37240 w9,33702.

free. **Surface:** asphalted. 01/01-31/12
Distance: 2km sandy beach 50m on the spot 2km.
Remarks: Parking next to bar restaurant in village square, not recommended at the weekend.

Batalha 38B1

Parque Cónego M. Simões Inácio, Rua Cerca Conventual. **GPS**: n39,66134 w8,82516.

15 free Ch free. **Surface:** asphalted.
01/01-31/12 Mo.
Distance: 100m 250m on the spot.
Remarks: At football ground/tennis, max. 48h.

Cabo Espichel 38A3

P Cabo Espichel. GPS: n38,42031 w9,21353.
free. **Location:** Isolated. **Surface:** unpaved. 01/01-31/12
Distance: Sesimbra 13km At the sea.
Remarks: Beautiful view.

Cascais 38A2

Cap Raso. GPS: n38,71134 w9,48498.
free. **Surface:** sand. 01/01-31/12
Distance: 6km on the spot 6km.
Remarks: Parking near the cliffs Also possibility for overnight stay at restaurant Maremonte.

Cascais 38A2

Guincho, Areia, Guincho. **GPS**: n38,72167 w9,46639.
Ch. 01/01-31/12
Remarks: Service only € 3,15-5,40.

Tourist information Cascais:
www.cm-cascais.pt.Bathing resort.

PT

Constância 38B2

Estrada National. **GPS**: n39,47670 w8,34365.

20 free Chfree. **Location:** Comfortable. **Surface:** metalled.
01/01-31/12

Distance: 500m 2,3km on the spot 500m 300m.

Remarks: Along the Zêzere river.

Coruche 38B2

Area autocaravana, Rua 5 de Outubro. **GPS**: n38,96139 w8,51944.

100 free Chfree. **Surface:** metalled. 01/01-31/12 last Sa of the month.

Distance: on the spot on the spot.

Costa da Caparica 38A2

Caravanismo da Costa da Caparica, Santo António da Caparica. **GPS**: n38,65389 w9,23833.
Ch.
01/01-31/12

Distance: 500m on the spot on the spot 100m.

Remarks: Service only € 3,15-5,40.

Tourist information Costa da Caparica:

Popular bathing resort.

Dois Portos 38A2

GPS: n39,03689 w9,18098.

free. **Surface:** metalled. 01/01-31/12

Remarks: Village square.

Ericeira 38A2

Municipal de Mil Regos, N247, Casal do Moinho Velho. **GPS**: n38,97778 w9,41861.
Chfree. 01/01-31/12

Remarks: Service in front of campsite.

Tourist information Ericeira:

Seaside resort with fishing port.

Aldeia Museu de José Franco, Sobreiro.Miniature village.
9-19h. free.

Fátima 38B1

Rua de Sao Vicente de Paulo. **GPS**: n39,63389 w8,67111.

10 free WCfree. **Surface:** asphalted. 01/01-31/12

Distance: 1km 3,2km 100m 1km.

Remarks: May 12-13 festivities.

Foz do Arelho 38A2

Av. do Mar. **GPS**: n39,42888 w9,22201.

10 free WC. **Surface:** metalled. 01/01-31/12

Distance: 1km 50m on the spot 1,5km.

Remarks: Beach parking.

Lisbon 38A2

Av. de Brasilia. **GPS**: n38,69463 w9,19966.

50 free. **Surface:** asphalted.

Distance: city centre 6km 300m 500m 400m bus-tram.

Lisbon 38A2

Municipal de Lisboa-Monsanto, Monsanto, Estrada da Circunvalação. **GPS**: n38,72472 w9,20805.
Ch WC. 01/01-31/12

Distance: 3km on the spot on the spot 50m.

Tourist information Lisbon:

Lisboa Card.Card gives entrance to museums, public transport, available at: Rua Jardim do Regedor 50 (10-18), Mosteiros do Jeronimos, Museu dos Coches.
€ 18/24h, € 31/48h, € 38/72h.

Posto de Turismo, Rua do Arsenal, 15, www.atl-turismolisboa.pt.Capital of Portugal with a lot of curiosities.

Market. Tue, Sa.

32 Covered markets, most important market: Av. 24 de Julho.
6-14h Su.

Campo de Sta Clara.Flea market.

Rua de São Bento.Antiques market.

Arena near metro Campo Pequeno. 01/05-30/09 Thu.

Feira Popular.Fairground, opposite the Entrecampos metro. 01/05-30/09.

Oceanário, Parque das Nações.Aquarium. 10-19h.

Chiado.Elegant shopping district.
elevator 7-24h.

Mação 38B2

Campo de Feiras, Av. Vicente Mirrado. **GPS**: n39,55723 w7,99303.

PT

10 free Ch WC free. **Location:** Simple. **Surface:** metalled.
01/01-31/12
Distance: 500m 6km 500m 500m.
Remarks: Max. 48h.

S Mafra 38A2

Palacio Nacional. GPS: n38,93758 w9,33548.
free. 01/01-31/12

Tourist information Mafra:

Posto do turismo, Palácio Nacional de Mafra - Torreão Sul, Terreiro D. João V, www.cm-mafra.pt/turismo.

Parque Tapada Nacional, Portão do Codeçal.Safaripark. 10-19h.

Marinha Grande 38B1

São Pedro de Moel. **GPS:** n39,76974 w9,02752.

free. **Location:** Simple. **Surface:** metalled. 01/01-31/12
Distance: 10km 100m 50m.
Remarks: Beach parking.

S Marinha Grande 38B1

Parque de Campismo Orbitur, São Pedro de Moel. **GPS:** n39,75806 w9,02583.
Ch. 01/01-31/12
Remarks: Service only € 3,15-5,40.

Montijo 38A2

GPS: n38,70286 w8,97665.

50 free. **Surface:** metalled.
Distance: 800m 200m 100m 200m 2km.
Remarks: Parking at ferry-boat to Lisbon.

Nazaré 38B1

Avenue do Municipio. **GPS:** n39,59741 w9,0696.

7 free. **Surface:** asphalted. 01/01-31/12
Distance: 200m 250m 250m 750m.

S Nazaré 38B1

Valado, Mata do Valado. **GPS:** n39,59778 w9,05611.
Ch.
01/02-30/12
Remarks: Service only € 2,60-4,40.

Tourist information Nazaré:

Posto de Turismo, Avenida da República, www.cm-nazare.pt/nazare.htm. Bathing resort.

S Obidos 38A2

Rue do Ginasio. **GPS:** n39,35628 w9,15672.

20 € 6/24h Ch WC included. **Location:** Simple.
Surface: gravel/sand. 01/01-31/12
Distance: 500m 1km 500m 500m.

S Odivelas 38A2

Rolarlivre, Rua Alm. Gago Coutinho, Póvoa de Santo Adrião. **GPS:** n38,79605 w9,16384.
3 € 5 Ch included. **Surface:** metalled. 01/01-31/12
Distance: 700m 100m.
Remarks: Motorhome dealer, video surveillance, only service € 2,50.

S Outeiro da Cabeça 38A2

GPS: n39,19306 w9,1825.

free Ch free. **Surface:** gravel. 01/01-31/12
Distance: 300m 2,5km 300m 300m.

Palmela 38A3

GPS: n38,56664 w8,90032.

Remarks: Parking at castle.

Peniche 38A2

Av. Porto De Pesca. **GPS:** n39,35852 w9,37752.

PT

. **Location:** Simple. **Surface:** metalled. 01/01-31/12
Distance: 500m 900m 1km 500m 500m.
Remarks: At fire-station and marina.

Peniche 38A2
Farol do Cabo Cavoeiro, Caminho do Farol. **GPS:** n39,35989 w9,4082. .

. **Location:** Simple, isolated. **Surface:** metalled. 01/01-31/12
Distance: 5km 300m 1,5km 3km.
Remarks: At lighthouse.

Peniche 38A2
Praia de Consolação, Av. do Mar, Consolação. **GPS:** n39,32567 w9,35713. .

free. **Surface:** asphalted.
Distance: on the spot sandy beach.
Remarks: Beach parking.

Peniche 38A2
R. de Liberdade. **GPS:** n39,36577 w9,37417. .

. **Location:** Simple. **Surface:** sand. 01/01-31/12
Distance: 1,7km 50m 200m 200m.
Remarks: Nearby Intermarché.

S **Peniche** 38A2
Peniche Praia, Estrada Marginal Norte. **GPS:** n39,36959 w9,392. .

23 € 15,20, 2 pers.incl Ch WC included . **Surface:** grassy.
01/01-31/12
Distance: At the sea on the spot 1,5km 1,5km.

Tourist information Peniche:
Fortaleza de Peniche.Bathing resort.
Posto de Turismo, Rua Alexandre Herculano, www.cm-peniche.pt.Bathing resort.

S **Praia de Santa Cruz** 38A2
GPS: n39,14418 w9,37482.
free WC free. **Location:** Simple. **Surface:** asphalted.
01/01-31/12
Distance: 300m 20m on the spot 300m.
Remarks: Parking at the beach or near the cliffs.

Praia de Santa Cruz 38A2
GPS: n39,13640 w9,38006.
free. **Surface:** metalled.
Distance: on the spot 50m on the spot on the spot.

Ribamar 38A2
R. do Cacho Longo, São Lourençio. **GPS:** n39,01120 w9,42078.
free. **Location:** Simple, isolated. **Surface:** asphalted.
01/01-31/12
Distance: sandy beach on the spot 6km.

São Martinho do Porto 38A1
Av. Marigal. **GPS:** n39,50176 w9,14132. .

free. **Surface:** metalled. 01/01-31/12
Distance: 1,4km 5,5km sandy beach 50m 850m.

Sintra 38A2
R. Guilherme Gomes Fernandes. **GPS:** n38,79701 w9,38854.
4 free. **Location:** Simple. **Surface:** metalled.
Distance: 200m 200m 400m.

S **Tomar** 38B1
Av. Gen. Bernardo Faria. **GPS:** n39,59972 w8,41306.

free WC. **Location:** Simple. **Surface:** gravel.
01/01-31/12
Distance: 200m 200m 300m.
Remarks: Nearby railway station.

PT

Tourist information Tomar:
Sinagoga de Tomar, Museu Luso-Hebraico, Rua Dr. Joaquim Jacinto, 75.Synagogue and Jewish Portuguese history. free.
Convento de Cristo.Fortified monastery.
Festa dos Tabuleiros. Whitsuntide.
Barragem de Castelo de Bode.Artificial lake, 15km east of the city.

S Torres Vedras 38A2
Municipal da Praia de Santa Cruz. GPS: n39,13444 w9,37472.
Ch against payment. 01/01-31/12

S Vermoil 38B1
R. Vale de Fojo, Pombal. **GPS:** n39,85080 w8,66125.

5 free Ch free. **Surface:** gravel/sand. 01/01-31/12
Distance: 200m 300m 300m.
Remarks: At cemetery.

Alentejo

S Alcácer do Sal 38B3
Barragem Pego do Altar, Alcácer do Sal > N253 > Montemoro o Novo > N380. **GPS:** n38,42055 w8,39384.

15 free Ch WC free. **Location:** Rural. **Surface:** sand.
01/01-31/12
Distance: Alcácer do Sal 13km on the spot 100m.

Alcácer do Sal 38B3
Rua do Cabo da Vila. **GPS:** n38,36903 w8,50276.
free.
01/01-31/12
Distance: Old city 600m 5,6km 400m.
Remarks: Near arena.

Tourist information Alcácer do Sal:
Little town on the Rio Sado.

S Almograve 38A4
Avenida da Praia. **GPS:** n37,65276 w8,79305.

30 free free. **Location:** Simple. **Surface:** grasstiles.
01/01-31/12
Distance: on the spot.
Remarks: From village dir beach, in front of large square go to the left, sandy surface, rather remote parking.

Tourist information Almograve:
Bathing resort.

Alvito 38B3
Rua de Tapadinha. **GPS:** n38,25917 w7,99222.
free.
Remarks: At swimming pool.

S Avis 38B2
Municipal Albufeira do Maranhão, Barragam Albufeira do Maranhão. **GPS:** n39,05682 w7,91145.
Ch.
Distance: on the spot.
Remarks: Service only € 1,90.

Campo Maior 38C2
Barragem do Caia. GPS: n39,00308 w7,14219.

Tourist information Campo Maior:
Fortified town. 9-13h, 15-17h.

Castelo de Vide 38C2
GPS: n39,41583 w7,45778.

free.
Remarks: At the city walls.

Castelo de Vide 38C2
Estr. de São Vincente. **GPS:** n39,41028 w7,44917.
Remarks: At stadium.

Tourist information Castelo de Vide:
www.cm-castelo-vide.pt.Historical centre with medieval citadel.

S Cavaleiro 38A4
Cabo Sardano. GPS: n37,59810 w8,80608.

30 free. **Location:** Simple. **Surface:** sand. 01/01-31/12
Distance: on the spot.
Remarks: At lighthouse. From Cavaleiro dir of sea, at lighthouse to the left, sandy parking at football ground.

S Comporta 38A3
GPS: n38,38308 w8,78712.

PT

free. **Surface:** sand. 01/01-31/12
Distance: 250m 1km 300m 500m.
Remarks: Near the church.

Comporta 38A3
GPS: n38,37849 w8,78544.
. **Surface:** sand. 01/01-31/12
Remarks: Holiday centre of Banco do Espirito Santo.

S Elvas 38C3
Intermarché, Rue Paco Bandera. **GPS**: n38,87458 w7,18429.

15 free Chfree. **Surface:** asphalted. 01/01-31/12
Distance: historical centre 1,7km on the spot.
Remarks: At petrol station and supermarket, max. 48h.

Elvas 38C3
GPS: n38,87766 w7,17763.

. **Surface:** metalled.
Remarks: Parking aqueduct.

Tourist information Elvas:
Fortified city.

S Estremoz 38C3
GPS: n38,84252 w7,5858.

10 . **Surface:** metalled.
Distance: on the spot 50m 50m.
Remarks: Parking in the centre.

Tourist information Estremoz:
Market. Sa.

Evora 38B3
GPS: n38,57529 w7,90519.

free. **Surface:** gravel/metalled. 01/01-31/12
Remarks: Parking university, illuminated.

Evora 38B3
Ave Túlio Espanca, N114. **GPS**: n38,56655 w7,91541.

free. **Surface:** gravel/metalled. 01/01-31/12
Distance: 500m 800m 600m 1km.

Evora 38B3
Lago da Porta de Avis. **GPS**: n38,57672 w7,91096.

free.
Surface: gravel/metalled.
01/01-31/12
Remarks: Parking at aqueduct.

Tourist information Evora:
Posto de Turismo, Praça do Geraldo, www.cm-evora.pt.
City with historical centre.
Igreja de S. Francisco, Capela dos Ossos.Chapel of the bones.
8-18h 12-14h.
Tue.

S Ferreira do Alentejo 38B3
GPS: n38,05675 w8,11955.

PT

free . **Surface:** asphalted.
Distance: 500m 100m 1km 1,5km.
Remarks: Parking sports park.

S Grândola 38B3

Parque de Grândola. **GPS:** n38,18525 w8,564.

7 free Ch. **Location:** Simple. **Surface:** asphalted.
01/01-31/12
Distance: 1km 7,4km 600m 500m 1,4km.
Remarks: Next to sports fields.

S Lousal 38B3

Rua 25 Abril. **GPS:** n38,03591 w8,42908.

6 free Chfree. **Surface:** gravel.
01/01-31/12
Distance: 15km 250m 400m bakery on the spot.

S Luz 38C3

R. de Mourão. **GPS:** n38,34278 w7,37389.

4 free Chfree. **Surface:** metalled.

S Marvão 38C2

GPS: n39,39556 w7,37667.

12 free free. **Location:** Simple. **Surface:** metalled.
Distance: on the spot 500m.

Melides 38A3

Praia de Melides. GPS: n38,12897 w8,79262.

. **Surface:** metalled. 01/01-31/12
Distance: Melides 6,2km sandy beach on the spot.

Mértola 38B4

N122/IC27. **GPS:** n37,64250 w7,65833.

.
Distance: 200m 200m.

Mértola 38B4

Rua dos Bombeiros Voluntários. **GPS:** n37,64114 w7,66326.
10 free. **Surface:** gravel/sand.
Remarks: At fire-station.

Mértola 38B4

GPS: n37,64103 w7,6574.
.
Remarks: Along river.

Tourist information Mértola:
Convento São Francisco.Former convent, exposition room and atelier.
10-17h.

S Messejana 38B4

GPS: n37,83167 w8,24694.

50 €7 Ch. **Location:** Rural. 01/01-31/12
Distance: on the spot 10km.

Mina de São Domingos — 38C4

Praia Fluvial, R265. **GPS:** n37,67228 w7,50418.

20 free. **Location:** Simple. **Surface:** metalled/sand.
Distance: 50m.
Remarks: At recreation area, marked pitches.

S Mina de São Domingos — 38C4

GPS: n37,67052 w7,50194.
€2 Ch.

Monsaraz — 38C3

GPS: n38,44250 w7,38003.

±15 free. **Location:** Quiet. **Surface:** metalled. 01/01-31/12
Distance: 100m 100m.
Remarks: Near city wall, beautiful view.

S Monsaraz — 38C3

Rue da Fonte. **GPS:** n38,45317 w7,38117.

€3,50 Ch. Mo-Fr 8-21h, Sa-Su 8-12h
Remarks: Call for the key.

Tourist information Monsaraz:
www.monsaraz.com.pt/.Small medieval town.

A S Montargil — 38B2

Ponte de Sôr. **GPS:** n39,09972 w8,145.
Ch. 01/01-31/12
Remarks: Service only € 3-5.

S Montemor-o-Novo — 38B3

A6-IP7. **GPS:** n38,61791 w8,08014.
free free.
Surface: gravel/sand.
Remarks: Note: toll ticket is valid for 12 hours!. Parking motorway.

Odeceixe — 38A4

GPS: n37,43750 w8,79833.

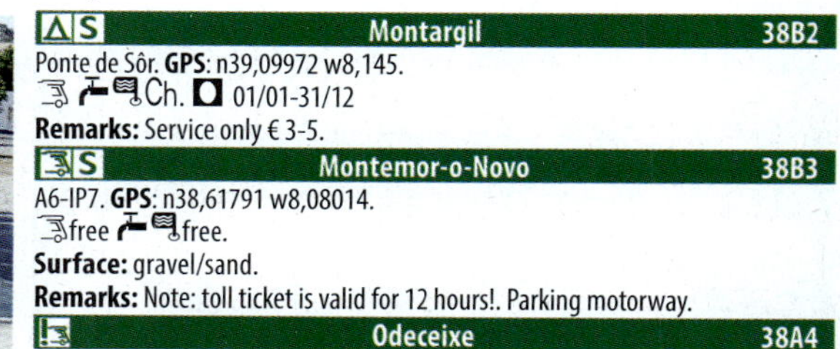

30 free. **Location:** Simple. **Surface:** sand. 01/01-31/12
Distance: 6km on the spot.
Remarks: Parking at beach, west of the village.

Odemira — 38A4

GPS: n37,59839 w8,64615.

free. **Surface:** asphalted. 01/01-31/12
Remarks: Parking beside river, northern part of village, after roundabout to the left.

S Pedrogão do Alentejo — 38B3

Alqueva Camping-Car Park, Estrada nacional 258, Km38,5. **GPS:** n38,11705 w7,63571.

25 first night € 7,50, € 6 each additional night Ch.
Location: Rural. **Surface:** gravel. 01/01-31/12
Distance: 1km 1km 1km 1km on the spot on the spot on the spot.

Ponte de Sôr — 38B2

Avenida da Liberdade. **GPS:** n39,24996 w8,00824.
free. **Surface:** asphalted. 01/01-31/12
Distance: 100m 100m.

S Porto Covo — 38A3

Rua Francisco Albino. **GPS:** n37,85225 w8,78874.
30 free Chfree. **Surface:** metalled. 01/01-31/12
Distance: centre 250m 750m.

Porto Covo — 38A3

Forte do Pessegueiro, Praia da Ilha. **GPS:** n37,49389 w8,47268.

PT

10. **Location:** Simple. **Surface:** sand. 01/01-31/12
Distance: 4km on the spot.
Remarks: Parking at castle, south.

Porto Covo — 38A3

Praia Grande, Rua do Mar. **GPS:** n37,85054 w8,79299.

15. **Location:** Simple. **Surface:** gravel.
Distance: 1km 100m 100m 1km.
Remarks: Parking to beach.

Reguengos de Monsaraz — 38C3

N255. **GPS:** n38,43077 w7,53315.

free. **Surface:** asphalted.
Remarks: Parking at swimming pool.

S Reguengos de Monsaraz — 38C3

Campo 25 de Abril. **GPS:** n38,42150 w7,53534.

€ 3,50 Ch.
Remarks: Next to fire station, dir Quimper.

Santa Clara-e-Velha — 38B4

Barragem de Santa Clara. GPS: n37,51303 w8,44024.

free. **Location:** Isolated. **Surface:** metalled/sand.
Distance: on the spot.
Remarks: Follow 'Pousada/Zona recreitiva balnear'.

S Santiago do Cacém — 38A2

Rua das Nogueiras. **GPS:** n38,80437 w9,22871.

7 free Chfree. **Surface:** grasstiles.
Distance: 600m 100m 600m.
Remarks: At swimming pool.

S Santo André — 38A3

Praia de Santo André, Lagoa de Santo Andre. **GPS:** n38,10067 w8,78943.

15 . **Location:** Simple. **Surface:** sand.
Distance: 5km on the spot on the spot bakery 1km.
Remarks: Beach parking.

S Santo André — 38A3

Lagoa de Santa André. GPS: n38,10972 w8,78722.
Ch . 17/01-14/11
Distance: 1km 500m on the spot 500m.
Remarks: Service only € 2,50.

S Santo António das Areias — 38C2

Camping Asseiceira, Asseiceira. **GPS:** n39,41012 w7,34062.
10 € 12-20 Ch WC . **Surface:** grassy. 01/01-31/12

São Martinho das Amoreiras — 38B4

N503. **GPS:** n37,56250 w8,34139.

free. **Surface:** metalled.
Remarks: At barrage.

PT

S Terrugem 38C3

Largo Joaquim Codero Vinaigre. **GPS**: n38,84556 w7,34861.

10 free Chfree. **Location:** Rural, simple, quiet.
Surface: asphalted.
Distance: 300m.

S Vendas Novas 38B3

GPS: n38,67795 w8,45609.
free. 01/01-31/12
Remarks: Parking at Caserma.

Vila Viçosa 38C3

Largo Gago Coutinho. **GPS**: n38,77661 w7,42034.

10 free. **Surface:** metalled.
Distance: 250m 25m 100m.

Algarve

S Albufeira 38B4

Parque da Galé, Rua do Barranco Vale Rabelho. **GPS**: n37,09347 w8,31125.

28 € 6,50 Ch (28x) included. **Location:** Comfortable. **Surface:** unpaved. 01/01-31/12
Distance: 600m 1,8km 200m 500m.

S Albufeira 38B4

Parque da Palmeira, Rua da Palmeira. **GPS**: n37,09829 w8,24339.

90 €7 Ch WC included. **Location:** Urban. **Surface:** gravel.
01/01-31/12
Distance: Old city 1,7km 7km 1,5km 800m Lidl bus terminal 300m.

Tourist information Albufeira:
Posto de Turismo, R. 5 de Outubro,, www.cm-albufeira.pt. 10-20h.
ZooMarine, N125.Attractions park, dolphinarium, aquarium. 10-20h.

S Alcoutim 38C4

Estrada da Pousada da Juventude. **GPS**: n37,47500 w7,47472.
free Chfree. **Surface:** sand.
01/01-31/12
Distance: 200m.
Remarks: Next to 'Centro de Saude'.

Tourist information Alcoutim:
Fortified city. 9-17.30h.

S Aljezur 38A4

Largo do Mercado. **GPS**: n37,31611 w8,80278.

10 free WCfree. **Location:** Simple. **Surface:** metalled.
01/01-31/12
Distance: 200m 500m.

Altura 38B4

Rua de Alagoa. **GPS**: n37,17138 w7,49952.

+10 free. **Surface:** sand.
Distance: 100m on the spot 100m.
Remarks: Beach parking.

S Alvor 38A4

Zona para autocaravanas, Praia de Alvor. **GPS**: n37,13107 w8,59373.

150 €4 Ch included. **Location:** Central. **Surface:** sand.
01/01-31/12
Distance: centre 400m 100m on the spot.

S Ameixial 38B4

Estacionamento de Autocaravannas. GPS: n37,36539 w7,97165.
10 free Chfree. **Location:** Rural, isolated, quiet. **Surface:** unpaved.
01/01-31/12

Cabo de São Vicente 38A4

N268. **GPS**: n37,02361 w8,995.

PT

8 free. **Surface:** metalled. 01/01-31/12
Distance: Sagres 6km.
Remarks: Parking at lighthouse.

S Caldas de Monchique 38A4

Parque Rural Autocaravanas Vale da Carrasqueira, Barracão 190. **GPS**: n37,27667 w8,54333.

14 € 12,50/24h Ch WC included . **Location:** Rural, comfortable. **Surface:** gravel. on the spot.

Carrapateira 38A4

Praia de Amado. GPS: n37,19623 w8,90156. .

30 free. **Location:** Simple. **Surface:** gravel.
Distance: Carrapateira 2km 100m on the spot.
Remarks: Beach parking.

Carrapateira 38A4

Praia de Bordeira. GPS: n37,19735 w8,90726. .

10 free. **Location:** Simple. **Surface:** metalled.
Distance: Carrapateira 2,5km.
Remarks: Parking near the cliffs, from the village dir of sea.

S Carvoeiro 38B4

Casa Long Yin, Sitio nas Travessadas. **GPS**: n37,11547 w8,47011.

5 € 10 Ch WC € 2,50 included.
Surface: grassy.
01/01-31/12
Distance: 1,5km 1,5km 300m 600m on the spot on the spot.
Remarks: Swimming pool incl.

Carvoeiro 38B4

Estr. do Farol. **GPS**: n37,08774 w8,44285.

8 . **Location:** Isolated. **Surface:** sand.
Distance: 500m on the spot.
Remarks: Parking at lighthouse.

Carvoeiro 38B4

Praia Marinha. GPS: n37,09026 w8,41254.

free. **Location:** Isolated. **Surface:** unpaved. 04/01-31/12
Distance: 4km on the spot.
Remarks: Beautiful view, beach parking.

S Castro Marim 38B4

Av. Dr. José Afonso Gomes. **GPS**: n37,21984 w7,44434.

± 20 free € 2 Ch. **Surface:** gravel.
01/01-31/12 2rd Sa of the month.
Distance: 1,3km 50m.
Remarks: Coins available at the shops.

Faro 38B5

Parking Largo de São Francisco. GPS: n37,01132 w7,93184.

PT

±6 free. **Surface:** metalled. 14-08h

Tourist information Faro:

Posto de Turismo, Rua da Misericórdia, 8-12.Capital of the Algarve with historical centre.

Ferragudo 38A4

Rue Aldeia Luis Francisco. **GPS**: n37,12264 w8,50359.
15 € 12,50 Ch WC included. **Surface:** unpaved. 01/01-31/12
Distance: 1km 7km 2,5km 1km.

Lagos 38A4

Area de servico, Junto ao Estadio Municipal de Lagos. **GPS**: n37,11563 w8,678.

20 € 3, from 4th night € 2,50 € 2/100 Ch WC free against payment.
Surface: gravel.
01/01-31/12
Distance: city centre 2km 7,3km 2,3km McDonalds 450m.
Remarks: Check in and pay at reception stadio, market 1st Sa each month.

Tourist information Lagos:

Posto de Turismo, Rua Vasco da Gama.
Lively port with historical centre.

Museu Municipal, Rua General Alberto da Silveira.
Regional museum.
9.30-12.30h, 14-17h holiday.

Luz de Tavira 38B5

Quinta do Xocolati, Sitio do Pinheiro 1077/E. **GPS**: n37,07311 w7,71814.
10 € 8-9 Ch (10x) WC included € 3,50 . 01/06-30/09
Distance: 4km 1km on the spot 200m 300m.

Manta Rota 38B4

Praia de Manta Rota, Quinta Manta Rota 15. **GPS**: n37,16513 w7,52096.

80 € 4 Ch 3h,€2/day included. **Surface:** metalled.
Distance: on the spot 6,5km 100m 100m 500m.

Moncarapacho 38B5

Far West Style Camp. GPS: n37,08344 w7,76608.
40 € 7 Ch WC included. **Location:** Rural, comfortable.
Surface: gravel/sand. 01/01-31/12
Distance: on the spot 3km.

Moncarapacho 38B5

Caravanas Algarve. GPS: n37,09502 w7,77427.

20 € 11 Ch . **Surface:** gravel. 01/01-31/12
Distance: 1km beach 6km 1km.

Odeleite 38B4

Almada D´Ouro Club-Algarve, M1063, Alcarias-Odeleite. **GPS**: n37,33187 w7,46865.

10 + 20 € 4,50 € 2,50 Ch € 2,50 € 5 included.
Location: Isolated, quiet. **Surface:** gravel. 01/01-31/12
Distance: Odeleite 2,3km on the spot.
Remarks: At hunting club, discount longer stays.

Pereiro 38B4

Parque de merendas do Pereiro, Pereiro. **GPS**: n37,44695 w7,5924.
16 free Ch free. **Surface:** unpaved. 01/01-31/12

Portimão 38A4

Praia da Rocha, Avenida Rio Arade,. **GPS**: n37,11898 w8,53837.

200 € 2,50 € 2/100liter Ch free. **Surface:** metalled/sand.
Distance: on the spot 100m on the spot 200m on the spot.

Portimão 38A4

Rue Très Castelos. **GPS**: n37,11969 w8,54723.

25 free. **Surface:** asphalted.
Distance: Praia da Rocha 700m sandy beach 250m 1km.

PT

Tourist information Portimão:
Posto de Turismo, Avenida de Zeca Afonso.
Port city.

S Quarteira 38B4

Estrada Fonte Santa, M527-2. **GPS**: n37,07322 w8,07716.

100 € 2/24h € 2 Ch € 2.
Surface: gravel.
01/01-31/12
Distance: 2km 6,8km sandy beach 2,5km 50m 150m Lidl on the spot.
Remarks: Tue 17h-Wed 17h adjacent parking because of Gypsy Market.

Tourist information Quarteira:
Bathing resort.

S Sagres 38A4

Rua Mareta. **GPS**: n37,00968 w8,93687.

10 free. **Location:** Simple. **Surface:** gravel/sand. 01/01-31/12
Distance: 400m on the spot.
Remarks: Service at the left-hand dir harbor. Parking behind tourist office.

Sagres 38A4

Fortaleze de Sagres. GPS: n37,00523 w8,94545.

50 free WC. **Surface:** asphalted. 01/01-31/12
Distance: 500m.
Remarks: At museum. Parking at fort.

Salema 38A4

Praia Boca do Rio. GPS: n37,06563 w8,82434.

20 free. **Location:** Simple. **Surface:** sand. 01/01-31/12
Distance: 2,2km 50m.
Remarks: Forbidden during Summer period.

S São Bartolomeu de Messines 38B4

Rua António Aleixo. **GPS**: n37,25514 w8,2847.

4 free Chfree. **Location:** Rural. **Surface:** gravel.
01/01-31/12
Distance: centre 150m 2,7km.
Remarks: Monday regional market.

S Silves 38B4

Club Autocaravana, N124. **GPS**: n37,21834 w8,36924.

15 € 5 Chincluded WC . **Location:** Rural, comfortable.
Surface: gravel/metalled. 01/01-31/12
Distance: 9km 100m.

S Silves 38B4

N124. **GPS**: n37,18528 w8,44222.

50 free free. **Surface:** asphalted/gravel. 01/01-31/12
Distance: 200m on the spot on the spot 200m on the spot.
Remarks: At swimming pool. Parking near the river and swimming pool.

Silves 38B4

Barregem do Arade, N124-3. **GPS**: n37,23960 w8,37699.

10 free. **Location:** Isolated. **Surface:** sand.
Distance: Silves 10km.

S Silves 38B4

Campismo Silves. GPS: n37,18452 e8,44223.

PT

13 € 5, peak season € 8,50 Ch WC € 3. **Surface:** grassy.
Distance: Silves 2km 300m 2km.
Remarks: Free fruits of the trees.

Tourist information Silves:
Museu Municipal de Arqueologia.Archeological findings.
Castello. 9-18h.
Festival da cerveja.Beer festival. July.

S Tavira 38B4
Parque de Autocaravanes. **GPS**: n37,13637 w7,64013.

20 € 9,90 Ch WC € 2 included. **Surface:** grassy/gravel. 15/09-15/06 summer.
Distance: 1km.
Remarks: Swimming pool.

Tourist information Tavira:
Castello. Mo-Fri 8-17.30h.

Vila do Bispo 38A4
N268. **GPS**: n37,08295 w8,90935.

10 free. **Location:** Simple. **Surface:** sand.
Distance: 500m on the spot.
Remarks: Beach parking. At football ground.

Vila do Bispo 38A4
Praia da Barriga, N1265. **GPS**: n37,09970 w8,94445.

free. **Surface:** asphalted.
Distance: Vila do Bispo 3,8km on the spot.

Remarks: Beach parking, from Vila do Bispo dir beaches Castelejo and Cordama, take most northern road at T-junction, 6km.

Vila do Bispo 38A4
Praia de Ingrina-Zavial. **GPS**: n37,04667 w8,88057.

4 free. **Location:** Simple. **Surface:** gravel/sand. 01/01-31/12
Distance: Vila do Bispo 6,7km 100m 200m on the spot.
Remarks: Beach parking.

S Vila do Bispo 38A4
Sagres, Cerro da Moita. **GPS**: n37,02278 w8,94583.
Ch 01/01-30/11
Distance: 2km on the spot on the spot 500m.

S Vila Real de Santo António 38C4
Avenida de República. **GPS**: n37,19955 w7,4153.

70 € 4 Ch included. **Surface:** metalled/sand.
Distance: 500m on the spot.

PT

DENMARK

Aalborg
Aahrus
Jutland
pages: 481-496
Odense
Funen
pages: 496-497
Copenhagen
Seeland, Lolland, Møn and Falster
pages: 497-499

DK

Capital: Copenhagen
Government: Constitutional monarchy
Official Language: Danish
Population: 5,605,000 (2013)
Area: 44,000m^2.

General information

Dialling code: 0045
General emergency: 112
Currency: Danish Krone (DKK), 1 DKK= 100 øre,
DKK 1 = € 0,13, € 1 = DKK 7,46,
DKK1 = £ 0,11, £ 1 = DKK 8,83 (October 2013)
Payments by credit card are accepted at almost every shop and restaurant.

Regulations for overnight stays/campsites

Overnight parking is allowed: for 1 night, if there is no local prohibition, but no "camping" activities are allowed.
Camping cards are obligatory when using Danish campsites: Camping Card International (CCI) or Camping Card Scandinavia is accepted. A card can be purchased at any campsite for DKK 100 (± € 13,40/ £11,30), valid for one year.

Additional public holidays 2014

May 16 Great Prayer Day
June 5 Danisch Constitution Day
June 23 Sankt Hans Eve

Denmark

Jutland

Aabybro 2B3

Birthe&Leif Brinkmann, Kanalvej 164. **GPS**: n57,11947 e9,73156.

3 DKK 50. **Location:** Simple, isolated. **Surface:** grassy.
01/01-31/12
Distance: 5km.

Aalborg 2B3

Aalborg, Skydebanevej 50. **GPS**: n57,05379 e9,87233.
DKK 105 Ch against payment. 01/01-31/12
Distance: on the spot.
Remarks: QuickStop: >20 - <10h.

Aalborg 2B3

Strandparken, Skydebanevej 20. **GPS**: n57,05502 e9,88499.
DKK 140 Ch against payment. 01/02-15/12
Remarks: QuickStop: >20 - <10h.

Tourist information Aalborg:
Aalborg Tourist & Convention Bureau, østeraagade 8, www.visitaalborg.com.
Søfarts - og Marinemuseum, Vestre Fjordvej 81.Maritime museum.
01/05-31/12.
Aalborg Zoo, Mølleparkvej 63.Zoo. 01/05-30/12.
Tivoliland, Karolinelundsvej 40.Amusement park. 12-19h.

Aalbæk 2B2

Aalbæk Havn, Sdr. Havnevej 65. **GPS**: n57,59306 e10,42686.

6 DKK 170 (6x) WC included. **Location:** Simple, quiet.
Surface: gravel.
01/01-31/12
Distance: 800m on the spot on the spot 800m 800m 250m.
Remarks: Pay at harbourmaster.

Aalbæk 2B2

Galleri & Selskabslokal Gyllegaard, Hirtshalsvej 48. **GPS**: n57,60619 e10,41757.

5 DKK 100. **Location:** Simple, isolated, quiet. **Surface:** grassy.
01/01-31/12
Distance: 4km 1km 4km 4km.

Aarhus 2B5

Aarhus centrum parkerinsplads, Kalkværksvej 2. **GPS**: n56,14815 e10,21015.

6 free free. **Location:** Urban, simple, central. **Surface:** asphalted.
01/01-31/12
Distance: 500m on the spot on the spot.
Remarks: Behind petrol station, max. 24h.

Aarhus 2B5

Aarhus Nord, Randersvej 400. **GPS**: n56,22672 e10,16335.
DKK 90 Ch against payment. 01/01-31/12
Remarks: QuickStop: >20 - <10h.

Åbenrå 2B6

Camperstop Aabenraa, Sønderskovvej 104. **GPS**: n55,02513 e9,41471.

34 € 14 Ch WC. **Surface:** grassy/gravel. 01/01-31/12
Distance: 2km 8km 400m.
Remarks: Chip-card available at campsite.

Åbenrå 2B6

Lystbådehavn, Kystvej 55. **GPS**: n55,03434 e9,42352.

48 DKK 125 Ch WC against payment. **Location:** Comfortable. **Surface:** gravel. 01/04-31/10
Distance: 1km on the spot on the spot on the spot 50m 200m on the spot on the spot.
Remarks: Harbour Åbenrå.

Tourist information Åbenrå:
ÅbenråTuristbureau, H. P. Hanssens Gade 5, www.visitaabenraa.dk.Old city with a lot of curiosities and restored city centre.
Den Gamle Smedie, Skibbrogade 13.Forge from 1845. Mo,Tue, Thu 9-12h. free.
Sønderjysk Spejdermuseum, Bjerggade 4 H.Scouting museum. Tue 10-15h. free.

Allingåbro 2C4

Dalgård, Nordkystvejen 65. **GPS**: n56,50895 e10,54593.
DKK 140 Ch against payment. 04/04-20/09
Remarks: QuickStop: >20 - <10h.

Aså 2B3

Asaa, Vodbindervej 13. **GPS**: n57,14635 e10,40249.

DK

DKK 125 Ch against payment. 04/04-28/09
Remarks: QuickStop: >20 - <10h.

S Augustenborg 2B6

Augustenborg Slot, Palævej. **GPS:** n54,94694 e9,85389.

70 DKK 100 Ch WC. **Location:** Rural, comfortable.
Surface: grassy. 01/01-31/12
Distance: 1,5km on the spot on the spot.

S Augustenborg 2B6

Hertugbyens, Ny Stavenbøl 1. **GPS:** n54,94639 e9,85951.
DKK 100 Ch against payment. 01/04-30/09
Remarks: QuickStop: >20 - <10h.

S Augustenborg 2B6

Yachthavn Peder Dahl, Langdel 6. **GPS:** n54,94074 e9,86942.

19 DKK 130 Ch DKK 25 WC. **Location:** Luxurious, central.
Surface: gravel. 01/04-15/10
Distance: 1km 1km on the spot.

S Bjert 2B6

Stensager Strand, Oluf Ravnsvej 16. **GPS:** n55,42076 e9,58785.
DKK 180 Ch against payment. 03/04-14/09
Remarks: QuickStop: >20 - <10h.

S Bredebro 2A6

Bredebro Kig-Nøj, Borgvej 13. **GPS:** n55,05247 e8,82554.
DKK 100 Ch against payment. 15/05-15/09
Remarks: QuickStop: >20 - <10h.

S Bredebro 2A6

Claus Cornelsen, Galgemark 9. **GPS:** n55,04853 e8,83270.

50 free Ch against payment. **Location:** Rural, simple, quiet.
Surface: gravel. 01/01-31/12
Distance: 1km.

S Brovst 2B3

Vilsbæk Rideskole ved Brovst, Kanalvej 34. **GPS:** n57,11895 e9,53640.

10 DKK 60 Ch WC included. **Location:** Rural, simple, isolated, quiet. **Surface:** grassy. 01/01-31/12
Distance: 2km.

S Brædstrup 2B5

Gudenå, Bolundvej 4. **GPS:** n55,93507 e9,65283.
DKK 125 Ch against payment. 04/04-27/09
Remarks: QuickStop: >20 - <10h.

S Brønderslev 2B3

Serritslev Fiskepark, Agårdsvej 35. **GPS:** n57,29750 e9,99597.

20 DKK 50 free WC. **Location:** Rural, simple, isolated, quiet.
Surface: grassy. 01/01-31/12
Distance: on the spot.

S Brørup 2A6

Foldingbro, Kongeåvej 110. **GPS:** n55,44113 e8,99978.
DKK 150 Ch against payment. 01/01-31/12
Remarks: QuickStop: >20 - <10h.

S Bylderup-Bov 2B6

Kristianshåb Autocamper Park, Kristianshåbvej 5. **GPS:** n54,96189 e9,06950.

50 DKK 100 incl. 2 pers Ch DKK 4/24h WC. **Location:** Rural, comfortable, isolated. **Surface:** grassy.
01/01-31/12
Distance: 6km 1km 5km.

S Bylderup-Bov 2B6

Boskov, Kvænholtvej 15. **GPS:** n54,94488 e9,06078.

10 DKK 60 Ch included. **Location:** Rural, simple, isolated.
Surface: grassy/gravel.
Distance: 200m.

S Bylderup-Bov 2B6

B&B Bredevad, Bredevadvej 5. **GPS**: n54,96885 e9,12138.

2 € 13, 2 pers.incl Ch WC included. **Location:** Rural.
Surface: .
Distance: 4km.

Tourist information Bylderup-Bov:
Schackenborg Slot, Schackenborg 2, Tønder.Visit the castle garden.
Sommerland Syd, Terkelsbøf, Tinglev.Amusement park. 01/05-30/06, 01/09-30/09 Sa-Su, 01/07-31/08 daily. DKK 150.

Bælum 2B4

Bakgaarden, Hælskovvej 2. **GPS**: n56,83815 e10,12007.

4 DKK 50 Ch included. **Surface:** grassy. 01/01-31/12
Distance: 1km 1km.

S Bønnerup 2C4

Bønnerup Lystbådehavn, Vestre Mole 2, Glesborg. **GPS**: n56,53139 e10,71139.

20 DKK 150 Ch (12x)included WC against payment.
Location: Rural, comfortable, quiet. **Surface:** gravel. 01/01-31/12
Distance: 500m on the spot on the spot 250m 400m.
Remarks: Parking at marina.

S Børkop 2B5

Brejning Lystbådehavn, Brejning Strand. **GPS**: n55,67431 e9,68920.

12 DKK 130 (12x) WC included. **Location:** Rural, simple, isolated, quiet. **Surface:** gravel/metalled. 01/01-31/12
Distance: Børkop 5km 4,1km 10m 10m.
Remarks: At marina, restaurant only in summer.

S Børkop 2B5

Mørkholt, Hagenvej 105 B. **GPS**: n55,65146 e9,72250.
DKK 140 Ch against payment. 01/01-31/12
Remarks: QuickStop: >20 - <10h.

Ebeltoft 2C5

Skøvgarde, Havmøllevej 5. **GPS**: n56,24475 e10,77902.

2 DKK 50. **Location:** Rural, simple, isolated, quiet. **Surface:** grassy.
01/01-31/12 on the spot.
Remarks: Pay at Havmøllevej 5 or 20.

S Ebeltoft 2C5

Blushøj, Elsegårdevej 53. **GPS**: n56,16795 e10,72943.
DKK 125 Ch against payment. 01/04-14/09
Remarks: QuickStop: >20 - <10h.

S Ebeltoft 2C5

Dråby Strand, Dråby Strandvej 13. **GPS**: n56,22172 e10,73778.
DKK 150 Ch against payment. 04/04-14/09
Remarks: QuickStop: >20 - <10h.

S Ebeltoft 2C5

Elsegårde, Kristoffenvejen 1. **GPS**: n56,16843 e10,72278.
DKK 140 Ch against payment. 01/01-31/12
Remarks: QuickStop: >20 - <10h.

S Ebeltoft 2C5

Krakær, Gl. Kærvej 18. **GPS**: n56,19730 e10,67426.
DKK 125 Ch against payment. 17/04-23/10
Remarks: QuickStop: >20 - <10h.

S Egå 2B5

Egå Marina, Egå Havvej 35. **GPS**: n56,21069 e10,28819.

7 DKK 145 Ch (7x) WC included. **Location:** Urban, comfortable. **Surface:** asphalted.
01/01-31/12
Distance: 2km 400m on the spot on the spot 600m 600m.
Remarks: Tallycard: service, electricity, sanitary building, caution DKK 50.

S Egtved 2B6

Egtved, Verstvej 9. **GPS**: n55,60680 e9,27870.
DKK 145 Ch against payment. 01/01-31/12
Remarks: QuickStop: >20 - <10h.

S Ejerslev 2A4

Ejerslev Havn, Utkærvej 5. **GPS**: n56,91855 e8,92096.

DK

10 DKK 110 Ch (10x) WC included. **Location:** Rural, isolated, quiet. **Surface:** gravel.
01/01-31/12
Distance: 4km on the spot 4km on the spot on the spot.
Remarks: Parking marina, bread service, bicycles available, last 2km gravel road.

S **Engesvan** 2B5

Pårup Autocamperplads, Silkeborgvej 8. **GPS**: n56,13694 e9,35028.
4 DKK 50 Ch included. **Location:** Urban, simple, central.
Surface: gravel. 01/04-01/11
Distance: on the spot.

Erslev 2A4

Inger-Marie og Knud Erik Nielsen, Bindeleddet 4. **GPS**: n56,83881 e8,68060.

4 DKK 40 . **Location:** Rural, simple, isolated, quiet. **Surface:** gravel.
01/01-31/12
Distance: 1km.

S **Esbjerg** 2A6

Nebelso, Vestervadsvej 17 Vester Nebel. **GPS**: n55,55000 e8,54361.

25 DKK 50 .
Location: Rural, simple, isolated, quiet.
Surface: grassy/gravel.
01/04-01/11
Distance: 15km on the spot.

S **Fanø** 2A6

Rødgard, Kirkevejen 13. **GPS**: n55,42501 e8,39100.
DKK 100 Ch against payment. 01/05-01/09
Remarks: QuickStop: >20 - <10h.

S **Fanø** 2A6

Rindby, Kirkevejen 18. **GPS**: n55,42560 e8,39097.
DKK 105 Ch against payment. 01/04-01/10
Remarks: QuickStop: >20 - <10h.

S **Fanø** 2A6

Fanø Fiskesø, Storetoft 30. **GPS**: n55,43401 e8,39294.
4 € 14 Ch WC against payment. **Surface:** gravel.
Distance: on the spot.
Remarks: At fish pond.

S **Fårvang** 2B4

Trust Camping, Sørkelvej 12. **GPS**: n56,28127 e9,66858.
DKK 285 Ch against payment. 14/03-31/12
Remarks: QuickStop: >20 - <10h.

Fjerritslev 2A3

Erna K Nielsen, Holmsøvej 31, Haverslev. **GPS**: n57,04102 e9,39252.

6 DKK 50 included. **Location:** Rural, simple, quiet. **Surface:** grassy. 01/01-31/12
Distance: Limfjord 1,7km.

Fjerritslev 2A3

Niels Balle, Hedegardsvej 19. **GPS**: n57,12505 e9,33422.

4 DKK 70 (1x)included. **Location:** Rural, simple, isolated. **Surface:** grassy. 01/01-31/12
Distance: 7km 4km.

S **Fjerritslev** 2A3

Jammerbugt, Thistedvej 546. **GPS**: n57,10869 e9,10194.
DKK 140 Ch against payment. 01/01-31/12
Remarks: QuickStop: >20 - <10h.

S **Flauenskjold** 2B3

Markedsplad, Agertoften 4, Dronninglund. **GPS**: n57,24854 e10,28477.

10 DKK 50 DKK 25 WC included. **Location:** Rural, simple, quiet.
Surface: grassy. 01/01-31/12
Distance: 5km.
Remarks: Money in envelope in mail box, festival and market place.

S **Fredericia** 2B6

Lystbådehavnen, Strandvejen 115/Sanddalbakke. **GPS**: n55,55246 e9,72805.

DK

8 DKK 100 Ch (8x) WC included. **Location:** Rural, simple, quiet. **Surface:** metalled.
01/01-31/12
Distance: 1km on the spot on the spot on the spot 1km 200m.
Remarks: Tallycard: service, electricity, sanitary building, caution DKK 50.

S Frederikshavn 2B3
Frederikshavn Marina, Søsportsvej 8. **GPS**: n57,42375 e10,52709.

20 DKK 150 Ch (10x) WC included. **Location:** Urban, comfortable, central, quiet. **Surface:** grassy/gravel. 01/01-31/12
Distance: 800m on the spot on the spot on the spot 700m.
Remarks: Pay at harbourmaster.

S Gistrup 2B4
Kirsten og Karl Age, Gunderupvej 164. **GPS**: n56,93476 e9,95844.

4 DKK 100 included. **Location:** Rural, simple, isolated.
Surface: gravel.

S Glesborg 2C4
Fjellerup Strands, Møllebækvej 6. **GPS**: n56,51677 e10,58855.
DKK 150 Ch against payment. 01/04-20/09
Remarks: QuickStop: >20 - <10h.

Grenaa 2C4
Fornæs Skibsophug, Folshøjvej. **GPS**: n56,41879 e10,91709.
10 free. **Surface:** grassy. 01/01-31/12

S Grenaa 2C4
Fornæs, Stensmarkvej 36. **GPS**: n56,45398 e10,94009.
DKK 150 Ch against payment. 04/04-21/09
Remarks: QuickStop: >20 - <10h.

Tourist information Grenaa:
Grenaa Turistbureau, Torvet 1.
Kattegat Centret.The underwater world and shark centre.
10-16/17h 13/12-26/12.

S Haderslev 2B6
Fam. Nowak, Felstrupvej 37. **GPS**: n55,25488 e9,52556.

2 free Service DKK 30. **Location:** Rural. **Surface:** gravel.
01/01-31/12
Distance: 3km 100m on the spot.
Remarks: Water and electricity € 4.

S Haderslev 2B6
Gammelbro, Gammelbrovej 70. **GPS**: n55,24888 e9,71244.
DKK 125 Ch against payment. 01/01-31/12
Remarks: QuickStop: >20 - <10h.

S Haderslev 2B6
Gåsevig Strand, Gåsevig 19. **GPS**: n55,14222 e9,49903.
DKK 109 Ch against payment. 01/04-19/10
Remarks: QuickStop: >20 - <10h.

S Haderslev 2B6
Halk, Brunbjerg 105. **GPS**: n55,18599 e9,65374.
DKK 110 Ch against payment. 03/04-28/09
Remarks: QuickStop: >20 - <10h.

Tourist information Haderslev:
Haderslev Turistbureau, Honnørkajen 1, www.haderslev-turist.dk.Well kept old centre.
Sillerup Mølle, Sillerup Møllevej 33.Mill, bake bread yourself.
15/06-15/09 Tue 10h.
Wachman's Tour.Excursion with the night watch in the old part of the city.
01/07-31/08 Thu 21h.

S Hadsund 2B4
Hvirvelkærgård, Kystvejen 202, Als. **GPS**: n56,76414 e10,28565.

10 DKK 90 DKK 30 WC included. **Location:** Rural, simple, quiet.
Surface: grassy. 01/01-31/12
Distance: 1km 1km.

Hadsund 2B4
Hadsund Havn, Skovvej 67. **GPS**: n56,70988 e10,10428.

10 DKK 130 WC included. **Location:** Rural, comfortable, quiet.
Surface: grassy. 01/01-31/12
Distance: 2km 2km 2km.

S Hadsund 2B4
Hadsund Camping, Stadionvej 33. **GPS**: n56,72110 e10,13377.
DKK 90 Ch against payment. 01/04-31/10

DK

Remarks: QuickStop: >20 - <10h.

Hadsund 2B4

østerHurup, Kystvejen 70. **GPS**: n56,79990 e10,27324.
DKK 120 Ch against payment. 02/04-23/10
Remarks: QuickStop: >20 - <10h.

Hadsund 2B4

Ingrid og Kristen Gade, Hobrovej 62. **GPS**: n56,70773 e10,07975.

4 DKK 100 (2x) WC included. **Location:** Rural, simple. **Surface:** grassy. 01/01-31/12

Tourist information Hadsund:
Hadsund Kommunes Turistbureau, Kystvejen 34.
Hadsund Egns Museum, Rosendals Allé 8.Local museum in old farm.
Mo-Fri 10-16h, Su 14-16.30h.

Hals 2B3

Hals, Vejdybet 2. **GPS**: n57,00163 e10,32343.
DKK 130 Ch against payment. 01/04-30/09
Remarks: QuickStop: >20 - <10h.

Hals 2B3

Lagunen, Lagunen 8. **GPS**: n57,04025 e10,36053.
DKK 130 Ch against payment. 04/04-13/09
Remarks: QuickStop: >20 - <10h.

Hanstholm 2A3

THy Minicamping (Rær Autocamperplads), Kærbakken 2. **GPS**: n57,08945 e8,67104.

20 DKK 100 Ch WC included. **Location:** Rural, comfortable. **Surface:** grassy. 01/01-31/12
Distance: Hanstholm 4km 5km.

Hanstholm 2A3

Hanstholm, Hamborgvej 95. **GPS**: n57,10909 e8,66724.
DKK 165 Ch against payment. 01/03-30/09
Remarks: QuickStop: >20 - <10h.

Tourist information Hanstholm:
Hanstholm Turistbureau, Bytorvet 9, www.hanstholmturist.dk.Biggest commercial fishing-port in Denmark.
Frøstrup mini-village, Søndergade 36, Frøstrup.Miniature village.
01/05-15/10 Wed-Thu 10-13h, 01/07-31/08 daily 13-16h.

Harboøre 2A4

Vesterhavs, Flyvholmvej 36. **GPS**: n56,62841 e8,15773.
DKK 115 Ch against payment. 04/04-16/09
Remarks: QuickStop: >20 - <10h.

Havndal 2B4

Udbyhøj Havn, Havnevej 62 Udbyhøj. **GPS**: n56,61111 e10,30583.

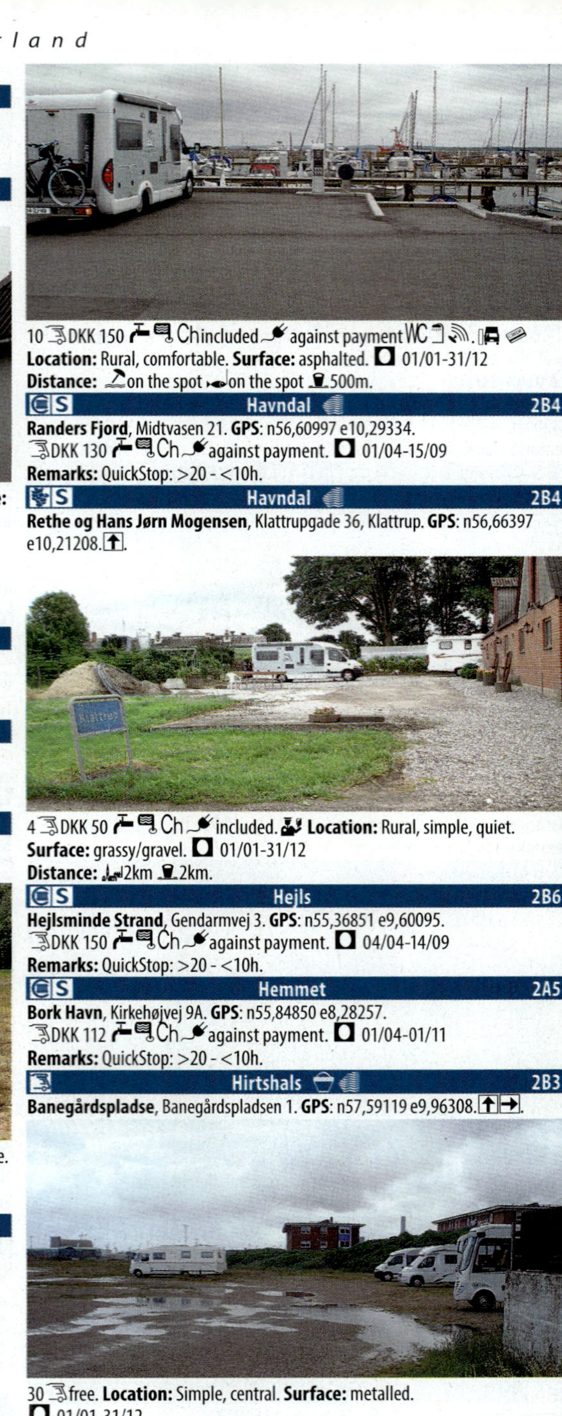

10 DKK 150 Ch included against payment WC .
Location: Rural, comfortable. **Surface:** asphalted. 01/01-31/12
Distance: on the spot on the spot 500m.

Havndal 2B4

Randers Fjord, Midtvasen 21. **GPS**: n56,60997 e10,29334.
DKK 130 Ch against payment. 01/04-15/09
Remarks: QuickStop: >20 - <10h.

Havndal 2B4

Rethe og Hans Jørn Mogensen, Klattrupgade 36, Klattrup. **GPS**: n56,66397 e10,21208.

4 DKK 50 Ch included. **Location:** Rural, simple, quiet. **Surface:** grassy/gravel. 01/01-31/12
Distance: 2km 2km.

Hejls 2B6

Hejlsminde Strand, Gendarmvej 3. **GPS**: n55,36851 e9,60095.
DKK 150 Ch against payment. 04/04-14/09
Remarks: QuickStop: >20 - <10h.

Hemmet 2A5

Bork Havn, Kirkehøjvej 9A. **GPS**: n55,84850 e8,28257.
DKK 112 Ch against payment. 01/04-01/11
Remarks: QuickStop: >20 - <10h.

Hirtshals 2B3

Banegårdspladse, Banegårdspladsen 1. **GPS**: n57,59119 e9,96308.

30 free. **Location:** Simple, central. **Surface:** metalled. 01/01-31/12
Distance: 600m 4,8km 600m on the spot.
Remarks: At station and ferry terminal.

Hirtshals 2B3

Willemoesvej. **GPS**: n57,59097 e9,98601.

DK

40 free. **Location:** Simple, quiet. **Surface:** unpaved.
01/01-31/12
Distance: 1km sandy beach 1km.
Remarks: Parking ferry to Norway.

Hirtshals 2B3

Tornby Strand, Strandvejen 13. **GPS**: n57,55540 e9,93264.
DKK 125 Ch against payment. 01/04-01/10
Remarks: QuickStop: >20 - <10h.

Tourist information Hirtshals:
Nordsømuseet, Willemoesvej 2.Oceanarium, large aquarium.
15/06-15/08 10-20h, 16/08-14/06 10-17h.

Hjallerup 2B3

Peter Bastholm Galleri Retro, Alborgvej 715. **GPS**: n57,17919 e10,15856.

5 DKK 100 . **Location:** Rural, isolated, quiet. **Surface:** gravel.
01/01-31/12
Distance: fish pond.

Hjørring 2B3

Thomas Lindrup, Tverstedvej 31. **GPS**: n57,57256 e10,12775.

6 DKK 120 (6x) WC included. **Location:** Rural, comfortable, isolated, quiet. **Surface:** grassy. 01/01-31/12

Hobro 2B4

Hobro Camping Gattenborg, Skivevej 35. **GPS**: n56,64015 e9,78265.
DKK 120 Ch against payment. 01/04-02/10
Remarks: QuickStop: >20 - <10h.

Holsted 2A6

Holsted Golfbanen, Bergardsvej 4, Vejen-Esberg. **GPS**: n55,52353 e8,93228.

15 € 10 WC. **Surface:** gravel. 01/04-30/10
Distance: 1km.

Horsens 2B5

Lystbådehavn, Jens Hjernøes Vej 32. **GPS**: n55,85764 e9,87417.

5 DKK 150 Ch WC included . **Location:** Rural, comfortable, quiet. **Surface:** gravel. 01/01-31/12
Distance: 3km on the spot on the spot on the spot.
Remarks: Harbour Horsen, special motorhome parking, Tallycard: service, electricity, sanitary building, caution DKK 50.

Horsens 2B5

Husodde, Husoddevej 85. **GPS**: n55,86035 e9,91537.
DKK 130 Ch against payment.
17/04-18/10
Remarks: QuickStop: >20 - <10h.

Tourist information Horsens:
Horsens Turistbureau, Søndergade 26, www.visitendelave.dk.
Dolmen "Jættestuen", åbjerg Skov.Dolmen. 01/01-31/12.
Danmarks Nimbus Tourings Motorcykle-Museum, Gasvej 21.Collection of motorcycles. 01/04-31/10 Sa-Su 11-16h.
Horsens Museum, Sundvej 1A.City museum. 01/09-30/06 Tue-Su 11-17h, 01/07-31/08 Mo-Su 10-16h.
Industrimuseet, Gasvej 17.Industry museum. 01/09-30/06 Tue-Su 11-16h, 01/07-31/08 Mo-Su 10-16h.

Hoven 2A5

Kvindehojskole, Bredgade 10, Tarm. **GPS**: n55,85065 e8,75938.

6 free WC free. **Location:** Urban, simple. **Surface:** gravel.
01/01-31/12
Distance: on the spot.
Remarks: Motorhome friendly town, parking and stay overnight possible at several places; Brugsen 2/3 campers; sport hall.

Hurup 2A4

Nordisk Folkecenter, Kammersgaardsvej 16. **GPS**: n56,69358 e8,41306.

DK

8 DKK 60 WC included. **Location:** Rural, simple, isolated, quiet.
Surface: gravel. 01/01-31/12
Distance: on the spot 4km.
Remarks: Check in at reception, access energy-park incl.

S Hvidbjerg 2A6

Hvidbjerg Strand Camping, Hvidjerg Strandvej. **GPS:** n55,54415 e8,13385.
4 DKK 95 Ch included. **Surface:** gravel. 01/04-31/10
Distance: 1,2km.

Hvide Sande 2A5

Autocamper P, Tungevej 6. **GPS:** n55,99722 e8,12222.

40 DKK 75. **Location:** Rural, simple, quiet.
Surface: gravel/metalled.
01/01-31/12
Distance: 200m on the spot 200m 300m on the spot.
Remarks: Beach parking, service Hvide Sande Camping, 1km, DKK 37,50.

S Hvide Sande 2A5

Bjerregaard, Sdr. Klitvej 185. **GPS:** n55,90620 e8,16565.
DKK 120 Ch against payment. 15/04-01/10
Remarks: QuickStop: >20 - <10h.

S Hvide Sande 2A5

Hvide Sande (Beltana), Karen Brands Vej 70. **GPS:** n55,98689 e8,13478.
DKK 110 Ch against payment. 03/04-26/10
Remarks: QuickStop: >20 - <10h.

S Højslev 2B4

Virksund, Sundvej 14. **GPS:** n56,60785 e9,28917.
DKK 220 Ch against payment. 04/04-20/09
Remarks: QuickStop: >20 - <10h.

S Ikast 2B5

Jens Jørgen Billo, Bangsvej 50, Tulstrup. **GPS:** n56,15480 e9,16197.

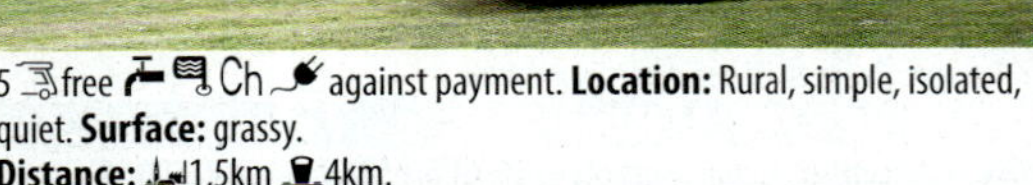

5 free Ch against payment. **Location:** Rural, simple, isolated, quiet. **Surface:** grassy.
Distance: 1,5km 4km.

S Juelsminde 2B5

Havn & Marina, Havnegade 15. **GPS:** n55,71457 e10,01509.

12 DKK 140 Ch (12x) WC included. **Location:** Rural, comfortable, central, quiet.
Surface: gravel.
01/05-30/09
Distance: 200m on the spot on the spot on the spot 200m.
Remarks: Tallycard: service, electricity, sanitary building, caution DKK 50.

S Karup 2A4

Hessellund Sø, Hesselundvej 12. **GPS:** n56,32308 e9,11501.
DKK 150 Ch against payment. 27/03-29/09
Remarks: QuickStop: >20 - <10h.

S Karup 2A4

2B Pack, Ulvedalsvej 43. **GPS:** n56,31528 e9,27361.
4 € 14 Ch . 23/03-29/10

S Kolding 2B6

Kolding Marina, Skamlingvejen 5. **GPS:** n55,48746 e9,50051.

15 DKK 110 Ch WC included. **Location:** Rural, comfortable, quiet. **Surface:** grassy/gravel. 01/05-01/10
Distance: 2,6km on the spot on the spot.
Remarks: At marina, Tallycard: service, electricity, sanitary building, caution DKK 50.

S Kvissel 2B3

Bondegård Hansen, Mejlingvej 65. **GPS:** n57,46753 e10,39556.

10 DKK 75 Ch WC included DKK 10. **Location:** Rural, comfortable, quiet. **Surface:** grassy. 01/01-31/12
Distance: 1km 5km.

S Langå 2B4

Langå, Skov Alle 16. **GPS:** n56,38780 e9,90439.
DKK 120 Ch against payment. 01/01-31/12
Remarks: QuickStop: >20 - <10h.

S Lemvig 2A4

Fjaltring Strand Høfte, Kjeldjergvej (Fjaltring). **GPS:** n56,47596 e8,12477.

DK

10 free WC. **Location:** Rural, simple, isolated, quiet. **Surface:** metalled.
Distance: 1km on the spot 1km.
Remarks: Beach parking.

Lemvig 2A4
Lemvig Havn, Toldbodgade. **GPS**: n56,55395 e8,30956.
10 free. **Surface:** gravel. 01/01-31/12
Distance: 250m 250m.
Remarks: Max. 12h.

Lemvig 2A4
Lemvig Strandcamping, Vinkelhagevej 6. **GPS**: n56,57061 e8,29054.
DKK 125 Ch against payment. 03/04-14/09
Remarks: QuickStop: >20 - <10h.

Tourist information Lemvig:
Lemvig Turistbureau, Toldbodgade 4, www.visitlemvig.dk.
Bovbjerg Fyr, Fyrvej 27.Lighthouse.

Løgstør 2B3
Løgstør Golfklub, Viborgvej 13, Ravnstrup. **GPS**: n56,94689 e9,25390.

10 DKK 110 (4x)included. **Location:** Simple, isolated, quiet.
Surface: gravel.
Distance: 2km 2km 2km.

Løgstør 2B3
Løgstør Lysbadehavn, Kanalvejen 19. **GPS**: n56,96728 e9,24528.

12 DKK 110 (12x) WC included. **Location:** Comfortable, central. **Surface:** grassy/metalled. 01/01-31/12
Distance: 200m on the spot on the spot on the spot 200m.

Løgstør 2B3
Løgstør, Skovbrynet 1. **GPS**: n56,96233 e9,24873.
DKK 100 Ch against payment. 01/01-31/12
Remarks: QuickStop: >20 - <10h.

Løgstør 2B3
Café Bondestuen, Over Aggersund 49. **GPS**: n57,00835 e9,28776.

6 free. **Location:** Rural, simple. **Surface:** gravel.
01/01-31/12

Løkken 2B3
Hugo Ottesen, Kettrupvej 80. **GPS**: n57,31135 e9,67861.

5 DKK 100 . **Location:** Rural, simple, isolated. **Surface:** grassy.
01/01-31/12

Løkken 2B3
Galleri Munkens Klit, Munkensvej 11. **GPS**: n57,33871 e9,70522.

10 DKK 100 DKK 5 WC included. **Location:** Rural, comfortable, isolated, quiet. **Surface:** grassy. 01/01-31/12
Distance: 3km.

Løkken 2B3
Gl.Klitgaard, Lyngbyvej 331. **GPS**: n57,41784 e9,76017.
DKK 148 Ch against payment. 15/04-23/10
Remarks: QuickStop: >20 - <10h.

Løkken 2B3
Grønhøj Strand, Kettrupvej 125. **GPS**: n57,32127 e9,67293.
DKK 100 Ch against payment. 15/04-18/09
Remarks: QuickStop: >20 - <10h.

Løkken 2B3
Løkken Strand, Furreby Kirkevej 97. **GPS**: n57,38533 e9,72571.
DKK 125 Ch against payment. 05/05-04/09
Remarks: QuickStop: >20 - <10h.

Løkken 2B3
Rolighed, Grønhoj Strandvej 35. **GPS**: n57,32143 e9,67818.
DKK 120 Ch against payment.
04/04-18/10
Remarks: QuickStop: >20 - <10h.

Tourist information Løkken:
Løkken Turistbureau, Harald Fischers Vej 8, www.loekken.dk.Bathing resort.
Kystfiskerimuseum, Løkkennordstrand.Fishery museum.
Vendsyssel historiske museum "Jens Thomsens Gård", Strandfogedgården i Rubjerg, Langelinie 2.Cultural past of the coast area. Hiking-trails.
16/06-15/09 Mo, Wed-Fri, Su 11-17h. free.
Familiy Farm Fun Park, Lyngbyvej 86, Vittrup.Animal park.
01/05-30/09.

DK

Malling 2B5

Ajstrup strand, Ajstrup Strandvej 81. **GPS**: n56,04131 e10,26472.
DKK 150 Ch against payment. 03/04-20/09
Remarks: QuickStop: >20 - <10h.

Mariager 2B4

Kongsdl Bådelaug, Kongsdal Havn 8. **GPS**: n56,68383 e10,07023.

24 DKK 120 Ch (24x) WC DKK 5/3minutes included.
Location: Rural, comfortable, isolated, quiet. **Surface:** gravel.
01/01-31/12
Distance: 7km on the spot on the spot.

Mariager 2B4

Mariager, Ny Havnevej 5A. **GPS**: n56,65399 e9,97640.
DKK 145 Ch against payment. 08/04-25/09
Remarks: QuickStop: >20 - <10h.

Nibe 2B3

Sølyst, Løgstørvej 2. **GPS**: n56,97248 e9,62460.
DKK 140 Ch against payment. 01/01-31/12
Remarks: QuickStop: >20 - <10h.

Nordborg 2B6

Lavensby Strand, Arnbjergvej 49. **GPS**: n55,07119 e9,79600.
DKK 109 Ch against payment. 27/03-31/10
Remarks: QuickStop: >20 - <10h.

Nordborg 2B6

Købingsmark, Købingsmarksvej 53. **GPS**: n55,07887 e9,72912.
DKK 120 Ch against payment. 01/04-25/10
Remarks: QuickStop: >20 - <10h.

Nordborg 2B6

Lone & Henning Carlsson, Kådnervej 7. **GPS**: n55,03194 e9,73111.

5 DKK 100 WC . **Location:** Rural, comfortable, quiet.
Surface: gravel. 01/01-31/12
Distance: 5km.
Remarks: Narrow entrance road.

Nykøbing Mors 2A4

Morsø Sejlklub & Marin, Jernbanevej 3A. **GPS**: n56,79282 e8,86370.

18 DKK 120 Ch WC included.
Location: Comfortable, quiet.

Surface: gravel. 01/01-31/12
Distance: 150m on the spot on the spot on the spot 200m.
Remarks: Tallycard: service, electricity, sanitary building, caution DKK 25.

Nørager 2B4

Stellplads E45 Autocamper, Fyrkildevej 39, Ladelund. **GPS**: n56,77505 e9,70986.

15 DKK 75 included . **Location:** Rural, simple, isolated, quiet.
Surface: grassy. 01/01-31/12
Distance: E45 5km.

Nørre Nebel 2A5

Nymindegab, Lyngtoften 12. **GPS**: n55,81368 e8,19992.
DKK 160 Ch against payment. 01/04-27/09
Remarks: QuickStop: >20 - <10h.

Odder 2B5

Jørgen Petersen, Aarhusvej 354. **GPS**: n56,01650 e10,18157.

3 DKK 75 Ch WC included. **Location:** Rural, luxurious, isolated, quiet. **Surface:** grassy/gravel. 01/01-31/12
Distance: 5km.

Odder 2B5

Odder strand Camping, Toldvejen 50. **GPS**: n55,93891 e10,25054.
DKK 110 Ch against payment. 01/04-21/09
Remarks: QuickStop: >20 - <10h.

Odder 2B5

Saksild Strand, Kystvejen 5. **GPS**: n55,98002 e10,24904.
DKK 160 Ch against payment. 01/04-18/10
Remarks: QuickStop: >20 - <10h.

Pandrup 2B3

Rødhus Klit, Rødhusmindevej 25. **GPS**: n57,20195 e9,58138.
DKK 110 Ch against payment. 01/04-25/09
Remarks: QuickStop: >20 - <10h.

Randers 2B4

Mellerup Bådelaug, Amtsvejen 153 Mellerup. **GPS**: n56,52431 e10,22213.

3 DKK 100 WC included. **Location:** Rural, simple, quiet.
Surface: gravel. 01/01-31/12
Distance: Mellerup 1,2km on the spot on the spot.
Remarks: Pay at harbourmaster.

DK

Randers 2B4

Randers havn, Toldbodgade 14. **GPS**: n56,46229 e10,05122.

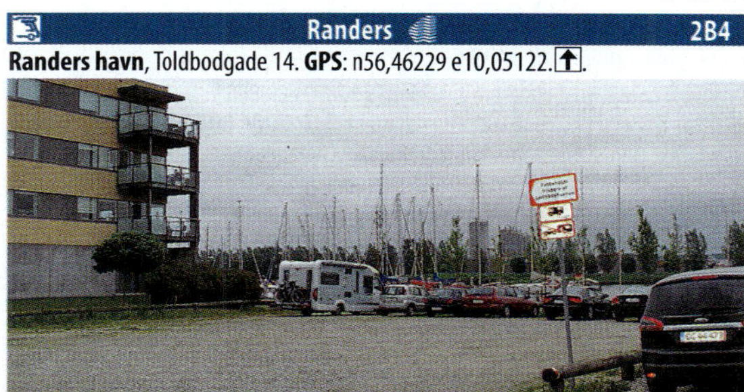

10 free. **Location:** Urban, simple. **Surface:** gravel.
01/01-31/12
Distance: 500m on the spot.
Remarks: Max. 24h.

Ribe 2A6

Fabelbo, Hølleskovvej 48. **GPS**: n55,24076 e8,86077.
free free. **Location:** Isolated, quiet. **Surface:** grassy.
01/01-31/12

Ribe 2A6

Stampemøllevej. **GPS**: n55,32480 e8,75740.

25 free WC free. **Location:** Urban, simple. **Surface:** asphalted.
01/01-31/12
Distance: 500m 100m 400m.
Remarks: Max. 48h, parking south of centre.

Ribe 2A6

Storkesøen, Haulundvej 164. **GPS**: n55,31703 e8,76022.

24 DKK 140 Ch included. **Location:** Rural, comfortable, quiet.
Surface: grassy. 01/01-31/12
Distance: 1km on the spot.
Remarks: At fish pond.

Ribe 2A6

Maglegaard, Toftlundvej 6. **GPS**: n55,31067 e8,79151.

3 DKK 100 DKK 20.

Location: Rural, simple, quiet.
Surface: grassy.
Distance: 3km.

Tourist information Ribe:
Ribe Tourism Office, Torvet 3, www.ribetourist.dk.Oldest city of Denmark to Ribeå River.
Vadehavscentret, Okholmvej 5.Wadden Sea centre.
10-16/17h 01/12-31/01.
Museet Ribes Vikinger, Odins Plads.Viking period in Denmark.
daily 10-16h, summer 10-18h 01/11-31/03 Mo.
Ribe Vikingecenter.Open air museum.
01/05-30/06, 01/09-15/10 Mo-Fri 10-15.30h, 01/07-31/08 daily 11-17h.
Weis Stue, Torvet 2.Oldest inn of Denmark with traditional Danish kitchen.

Ringkøbing 2A5

Lystbadenhavn, Fiskerstraede 60. **GPS**: n56,08611 e8,24056.

10 DKK 95 Ch (6x) WC included DKK 10/3minutes.
Location: Urban, comfortable, quiet. **Surface:** gravel. 01/01-31/12
Distance: on the spot on the spot on the spot 500m 500m.
Remarks: Parking at pier.

Ringkøbing 2A5

Autocamperplads, Vesterled 11. **GPS**: n56,09338 e8,23740.

20 DKK 70. **Location:** Urban, simple. **Surface:** gravel.
01/01-31/12
Distance: 700m 400m 400m 700m 700m.
Remarks: Pay with Danish coins.

Ringkøbing 2A5

Søndervig, Solvej 2. **GPS**: n56,11186 e8,11760.
DKK 115 Ch against payment. 04/04-25/10
Remarks: QuickStop: >20 - <10h.

Ringkøbing 2A5

æblehavens, Herningverj 105. **GPS**: n56,08699 e8,31642.
DKK 125 Ch against payment. 01/04-30/09
Remarks: QuickStop: >20 - <10h.

Tourist information Ringkøbing:
Ringkøbing Tourist Office, Vestergade 2, www.ringkobingfjord.dk.Bathing resort with old centre, several cycle and hiking trails available.
Fishing and Family Park West, Hovervej 56.Recreation park with swimming pool. 10h-sunset.

Roslev 2A4

Sundsøre Lystbådehavn, Sundsørevej. **GPS**: n56,70991 e9,17324.
DKK 120 WC included. **Location:** Isolated, quiet. **Surface:** grassy/gravel. 01/01-31/12
Distance: on the spot on the spot.
Remarks: At marina and ferry-boat.

Roslev 2A4

Glyngøre, Sundhøj 20A. **GPS**: n56,74401 e8,86259.

DK

DKK 125 Ch against payment. 01/04-12/10
Remarks: QuickStop: >20 - <10h.

S Roslev 2A4

Junget Strand, Jungetgårdvej 3. **GPS**: n56,76269 e9,10111.
DKK 120 Ch against payment. 01/04-01/10
Remarks: QuickStop: >20 - <10h.

S Ry 2B5

Birkhede, Lyngvej 14. **GPS**: n56,10428 e9,74089.
DKK 168 Ch against payment. 20/04-15/09
Remarks: QuickStop: >20 - <10h.

S Ry 2B5

Holmens, Klostervej 148. **GPS**: n56,07753 e9,76971.
DKK 130 Ch against payment. 04/04-27/09
Remarks: QuickStop: >20 - <10h.

Tourist information Ry:

Ry Turistbureau, Klostervej 3, www.visitry.com,.

Himmelbjergtårnet, Himmelbjergvej 20.Observation tower. 01/05-15/09 10-17h, 16/09-31/10 Sa-Su 10-16h. DKK 7,50.

Labyrinthia, Ryvej 2.Wooden labyrinth,. summer 10-18h.

S Rødding 2B6

Brændekilde, Haderslevvej 59. **GPS**: n55,35750 e9,18833.

10 free DKK 25 Ch DKK 25 WC. **Location:** Rural, simple, noisy.
Surface: metalled. 01/01-31/12
Distance: 1km.
Remarks: Max. 1 week.

Tourist information Rødding:

Midtsønderjyllands Turistbureau, Jels Møllegade 5, www.visitmidt.com.

S Rødekro 2B6

Rødekro Fiskepark, østermarkvej 3-7. **GPS**: n55,08806 e9,30889.

50 DKK 100 Ch DKK 2/kWh WC DKK 5 DKK 25. **Location:** Rural, simple, quiet. **Surface:** grassy. 01/01-31/12
Distance: 2km on the spot on the spot on the spot 100m.
Remarks: At fish lake.

Tourist information Rødekro:

Damgaard Mill, Foldingbrovej 6.Mill and agriculture museum. 01/05-30/09 Tue-Su 10-17h.

S Rømø 2A6

Lakolk, Lakolk 2. **GPS**: n55,14465 e8,49361.
DKK 124 Ch against payment. 15/04-18/10
Remarks: QuickStop: >20 - <10h.

S Saltum 2B3

Saltum Strand, Saltum Strandvej 141. **GPS**: n57,28560 e9,65228.
DKK 110 Ch against payment. 15/04-18/09
Remarks: QuickStop: >20 - <10h.

S Saltum 2B3

Guldager, Bondagervej 67. **GPS**: n57,29355 e9,65322.
DKK 122 Ch against payment. 05/04-25/09
Remarks: QuickStop: >20 - <10h.

S Sdr. Omme 2A5

Omme Å camping, Sønderbro 2. **GPS**: n55,83859 e8,88883.
DKK 130 Ch against payment. 01/04-30/09
Remarks: QuickStop: >20 - <10h.

S Silkeborg 2B5

Gudenåens, Vejlsøvej 7. **GPS**: n56,15414 e9,56004.
DKK 160 Ch against payment. 03/04-19/10
Remarks: QuickStop: >20 - <10h.

S Silkeborg 2B5

Sejs Bakker, Borgdalsvej 15-17. **GPS**: n56,14052 e9,62111.
DKK 125 Ch against payment. 08/04-11/09
Remarks: QuickStop: >20 - <10h.

S Silkeborg 2B5

Skyttehusets, Svejbækvej 3. **GPS**: n56,12050 e9,64440.
DKK 140 Ch against payment. 04/04-13/09
Remarks: QuickStop: >20 - <10h.

S Silkeborg 2B5

Sø-Camping, Århusvej 51. **GPS**: n56,16984 e9,57657.
DKK 170 Ch against payment.
15/04-18/10
Remarks: QuickStop: >20 - <10h.

Tourist information Silkeborg:

Silkeborg Turistbureau, åhavevej 2A, www.silkeborg.com.

AQUA, Vejlsøvej 55.Aquarium.
01/09-31/05 Mo-Fri 10-16h, Sa-Su 10-17h, 01/06-31/08 10-18h.

Hotel- og Restaurantmuseet "Ludvigslyst", Julsøvej 248.Original café/restaurant from 1906, demonstrations.
01/05-31/10 Tue-Su 10-22h. free.

KunstCentret Silkeborg Bad, Gjessøvej 40.Art museum.
01/10-30/04 Tue-Fri 12-16h, Sa-Su 11-17h, 01/05-30/09 Tue-Su 10-17h.

S Sindal 2B3

Sindal, Hjørringvej 125. **GPS**: n57,46849 e10,17945.
DKK 110 Ch against payment. 01/04-20/09
Remarks: QuickStop: >20 - <10h.

S Sjølund 2B6

Grønninghoved strand, Mosvigvej 21. **GPS**: n55,41105 e9,59220.
DKK 125 Ch against payment. 04/04-15/09
Remarks: QuickStop: >20 - <10h.

Skagen 2B2

P-plads på Grenen i Skagen, Akandevej. **GPS**: n57,73895 e10,63283.

20 DKK 150. **Location:** Rural, simple, isolated. **Surface:** asphalted.
01/01-31/12
Distance: 2km 100m 3km.

S Skagen 2B2

Råbjerg Mile, Kandestedvej 55. **GPS**: n57,65636 e10,45081.
DKK 110 Ch against payment. 17/04-23/10
Remarks: QuickStop: >20 - <10h.

S Skals 2B4

Ulbjerg, Skråhedevej 6. **GPS**: n56,64495 e9,33915.
DKK 125 Ch against payment. 01/01-31/12
Remarks: QuickStop: >20 - <10h.

S Skjern 2A5

Stauning Havn, Strandvejen, Stauning. **GPS**: n55,95488 e8,37352.
6, <10m DKK 75 Ch WC included. **Surface:** metalled.
01/01-31/12
Distance: Skjern 8km on the spot.

DK

Skjern 2A5

Skjern å Camping, Birkvej 37. **GPS**: n55,93316 e8,49291.
DKK 100 Ch against payment. 01/04-01/10
Remarks: QuickStop: >20 - <10h.

Skærbæk 2A6

Skærbæk, Ullerupvej 76. **GPS**: n55,16584 e8,77909.
DKK 120 Ch against payment. 01/01-31/12
Remarks: QuickStop: >20 - <10h.

Snedsted 2A4

Kaj Foget, Skyumvey 105. **GPS**: n56,84380 e8,59720.

6 DKK 50. **Location:** Rural, simple, isolated, quiet. **Surface:** grassy. 01/01-31/12

Spøttrup 2A4

Gyldendal hav, Vester Hærup Strandvej 34. **GPS**: n56,58107 e8,71066.

15 DKK 120 Ch (4x) WC included. **Location:** Rural, simple, quiet. **Surface:** gravel/sand. 01/01-31/12
Distance: sandy beach on the spot on the spot.

Storvorde 2B3

Egense Lystbådehavan, Kystvej 1. **GPS**: n56,98270 e10,30451.

6 DKK 110 (6x) WC . **Location:** Rural, simple, quiet. **Surface:** metalled. 01/01-31/12
Distance: on the spot on the spot 1km.
Remarks: Pay at harbourmaster.

Storvorde 2B3

Dokkedal, Kystvej 118. **GPS**: n56,93305 e10,26225.
DKK 110 Ch against payment. 01/01-31/12
Remarks: QuickStop: >20 - <10h.

Storvorde 2B3

Egense, Kystvej 6. **GPS**: n56,98071 e10,30086.
DKK 130 Ch against payment. 15/04-20/09
Remarks: QuickStop: >20 - <10h.

Stouby 2B5

Løgballe Autocamperplads, Løgballevej 12. **GPS**: n55,70765 e9,84359.

7 DKK 75 DKK 15 Ch (7x)DKK 30 WC. **Location:** Rural, simple, isolated, quiet. **Surface:** gravel. 01/04-01/10

Strandby 2B3

Strandby havn, Søndre Havnevej 27. **GPS**: n57,49249 e10,50245.

6 DKK 120 WC included. **Location:** Urban, simple. **Surface:** metalled. 01/01-31/12
Distance: on the spot on the spot on the spot on the spot on the spot.
Remarks: Pay at harbourmaster.

Struer 2A4

Holstebro-Struer Lystbådehavn, Fjordvejen. **GPS**: n56,49380 e8,59068.

4 DKK 124 WC Access sanitary building DKK 20 included.
Location: Urban, comfortable, quiet. **Surface:** gravel.
Distance: 100m 100m.
Remarks: At marina, Tallycard: service, electricity, sanitary building, caution DKK 50.

Struer 2A4

Toftum Brjerge, Gl. Landevej 4. **GPS**: n56,45530 e8,41190.
DKK 100 Ch against payment.
01/01-31/12
Remarks: QuickStop: >20 - <10h.

Tourist information Struer:

Gimsinghoved, Gimsinghoved 1.Former large Danish farm.

M Det gamle klubhus, V/Struer Lystbådehavn.Old Club building of the sailing club, mini museum. 01/04-15/11 10-22h. T free.

Sunds 2A5

Sunds Sø, Søgårdvej 2. **GPS**: n56,20846 e9,02335.
DKK 175 Ch against payment. 28/03-28/09
Remarks: QuickStop: >20 - <10h.

Sydals 5A1

Lysabildskov, Skovforten 4. **GPS**: n54,89159 e10,05268.
DKK 105 Ch against payment. 01/04-30/09
Remarks: QuickStop: >20 - <10h.

Tourist information Sydals:

i Sydals Turistbureau, Kegnæsvej 52, www.visitsydals.com.

Kegnæs Fyr, Nørre Landevej 7.Lighthouse. 01/06-30/09 Mo-Su 9-19h.

DK

DK

Sæby 2B3

Top Plads hos Ase en Helmer, Understedvej 65, Understed. **GPS**: n57,37249 e10,46447.

20 DKK 100 Ch WC . **Location:** Rural, comfortable, isolated, quiet. **Surface:** grassy. 01/01-31/12

Sæby 2B3

Lene en Knut Holdensgård, Holdenggårdvej 16, Sønder. **GPS**: n57,21616 e10,45253.

3 DKK 50 . **Location:** Rural, simple, isolated, quiet. **Surface:** grassy. 01/01-31/12

Sæby 2B3

Sæby Havn, Havnen 20. **GPS**: n57,33218 e10,53373.

20 DKK 150 (20x)included. **Location:** Urban, simple, central. **Surface:** asphalted. 01/01-31/12
Distance: 100m 100m 100m.

Sæby 2B3

Danbjerg, Hjørringvej 160. **GPS**: n57,32544 e10,36967.

6 DKK 50 . **Location:** Rural, simple, isolated, quiet. **Surface:** grassy/gravel. 01/01-31/12
Distance: 1km 1km.

Tourist information Sæby:

Sæby Turistbureau, Krystalgade 3, www.visitsaeby.dk.

Sæbygård Manor Museum, Sæbygaardvej 51.House from the Danish Renaissance. 01/06-31/08 10-17h.

Tarm 2A5

Par3Golf, Grimlundvej. **GPS**: n55,83819 e8,71321.
free. **Location:** Isolated, quiet. **Surface:** . 01/01-31/12
Distance: Tarm 19km.

Tarm 2A5

Skaven Strand, Skavenvej 32. **GPS**: n55,89181 e8,36780.
DKK 120 Ch against payment. 04/04-01/11
Remarks: QuickStop: >20 - <10h.

Tårs (Hjørring) 2B3

Vendelbo Vans Autocampere, Damhusvej 23. **GPS**: n57,38972 e10,11500.

8 DKK 50 Ch (8x) WC included. **Location:** Urban, comfortable, central, quiet. **Surface:** grassy/gravel. 01/01-31/12
Distance: 100m 500m 500m 300m 300m 200m.
Remarks: Motorhome dealer, max. 48h, use sanitary 9-17h.

Thisted 2A4

Vildsund, Parkvej 33A. **GPS**: n56,88017 e8,62477.
DKK 125 Ch against payment. 01/04-25/09
Remarks: QuickStop: >20 - <10h.

Thisted 2A4

Thisted, Iversensvej 3. **GPS**: n56,95309 e8,71249.
DKK 150 Ch against payment. 01/04-01/10
Remarks: QuickStop: >20 - <10h.

Tourist information Thisted:

Thisted Turistforening, Store Torv 6, www.thisted-turist.dk.Bathing resort.

Thisted Bryghus, Bryggerivej 10.Brewery, information at Turistbureau. summer Wed 11-13h. DKK 25.

Thorsager 2C4

Dagli Brugsen, Thorsgade 26. **GPS**: n56,34305 e10,46286.

4 free. **Location:** Urban, simple. **Surface:** gravel/metalled. 01/01-31/12
Distance: on the spot on the spot.
Remarks: Behind supermarket Brugsen.

Thyholm 2A4

Jegindø Havn, Havnegade. **GPS**: n56,65219 e8,63575.
DKK 110 WC included. **Surface:** gravel. 01/01-31/12
Remarks: At harbour.

Tim 2A5

Thorager, Søgårdvej 7. **GPS**: n56,20649 e8,25451.
DKK 90 Ch against payment. 01/04-30/09
Remarks: QuickStop: >20 - <10h.

S Tinglev 2B6

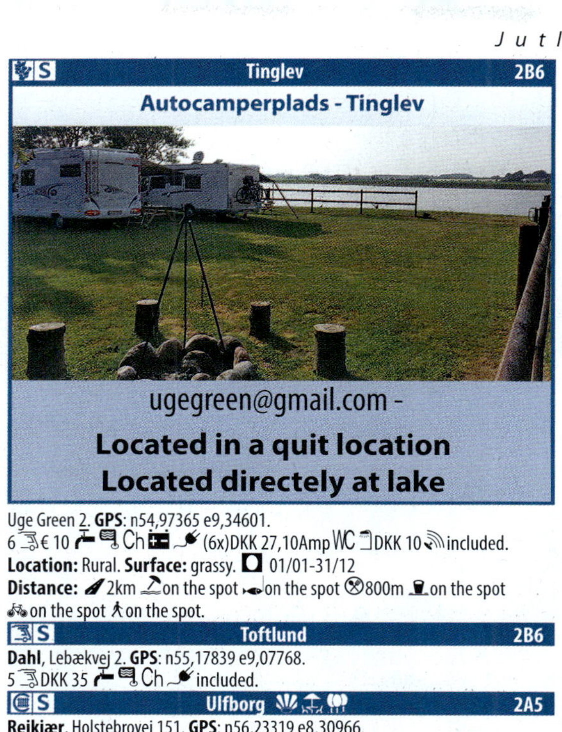

Uge Green 2. **GPS**: n54,97365 e9,34601.
6 € 10 Ch (6x)DKK 27,10Amp WC DKK 10 included.
Location: Rural. **Surface:** grassy. 01/01-31/12
Distance: 2km on the spot on the spot 800m on the spot on the spot on the spot.

S Toftlund 2B6

Dahl, Lebækvej 2. **GPS**: n55,17839 e9,07768.
5 DKK 35 Ch included.

S Ulfborg 2A5

Rejkjær, Holstebrovej 151. **GPS**: n56,23319 e8,30966.
DKK 98 Ch against payment. 03/04-18/10
Remarks: QuickStop: >20 - <10h.

S Ulfborg 2A5

Thorsminde, Klitrosevej 4. **GPS**: n56,25870 e8,13770.
DKK 150 Ch against payment. 03/04-18/10
Remarks: QuickStop: >20 - <10h.

S Ulfborg 2A5

Vedersø Klit, øhusevej 23. **GPS**: n56,25829 e8,14130.
DKK 150 Ch against payment. 04/04-18/10
Remarks: QuickStop: >20 - <10h.

Ulfborg 2A5

Tvind Skolecenter, Skorkærvej 8. **GPS**: n56,25636 e8,28110.

15 free. **Location:** Rural, simple, isolated. **Surface:** .
01/01-31/12
Distance: 8km 8km 8km.

Tourist information Ulfborg:
Ulfborg-Vemb Turistbureau, Bredgade 9, www.ulfborg-turist.dk.Situated between sea, heathland, forest and fjord.

Vandel 2B5

Dagli' Brugsen, Hans Thomsens Vej. **GPS**: n55,71285 e9,21800.
free. **Surface:** asphalted. 01/01-31/12
Remarks: At petrol station and supermarket, Legoland 6km.

S Vandel 2B5

Rastplads, Billundvej. **GPS**: n55,70687 e9,26709.
free WC free. **Surface:** forest soil. 01/01-31/12
Distance: on the spot 4km.
Remarks: Parking in the forest with place for campfire, Legoland 10km.

S Vejers Strand 2A6

Stjerne, Vejers Havvej 7. **GPS**: n55,61915 e8,14090.
DKK 110 Ch against payment. 01/01-31/12
Remarks: QuickStop: >20 - <10h.

S Vejers Strand 2A6

Vejers Familicamping, Vejers Havvej 15. **GPS**: n55,61950 e8,13594.
DKK 110 Ch against payment.
01/04-18/09
Remarks: QuickStop: >20 - <10h.

Tourist information Vejers Strand:
Vejers Turistinformation - Dan Turist, Vejers Havvej 81, www.bte.dk.Bathing resort, dunes and white beaches.
Tirpitz.German bunker.

S Vesløs 2A3

Amtoft Havn, Gårdbækvej 1. **GPS**: n57,00647 e8,94068.

10 DKK 100 Ch (10x) WC included free. **Location:** Rural, comfortable, quiet. **Surface:** grassy. 01/01-31/12
Distance: on the spot on the spot on the spot on the spot.

S Vesløs 2A3

Bygholm, Bygholmvej 27. **GPS**: n57,02603 e9,03733.
DKK 130 Ch against payment. 01/01-31/12
Remarks: QuickStop: >20 - <10h.

Vesløs 2A3

Vejlernes Grill & Kiosk, Aalborgvej 219B. **GPS**: n57,02518 e9,01585.

free. **Surface:** gravel. 01/01-31/12

S Vestervig 2A4

Krik-Vig, Krikvej 112. **GPS**: n56,77800 e8,26210.
DKK 100 Ch against payment. 04/04-27/09
Remarks: QuickStop: >20 - <10h.

S Vinderup 2A4

Vinderup, Sevelvej 75. **GPS**: n56,47488 e8,81184.
DKK 110 Ch against payment.
01/04-23/10
Remarks: QuickStop: >20 - <10h.

Tourist information Vinderup:
Hjerl Hedes Frilandsmuseum, Hjerl Hedevej 14.Open air museum.
01/04-31/10 10-17h.
Stubber Kloster, Stubbergård sø.Ruins of former Benedictine monastery.
01/01-31/12. free.

S Voerså 2B3

Parking Havn, Havstokken 11. **GPS**: n57,20389 e10,49389.

DK

20 DKK 120 Ch (20x) WC included. **Location:** Rural, comfortable, isolated. **Surface:** gravel. 01/04-31/10
Distance: 3km on the spot on the spot 3km 3km.
Remarks: DKK 120 in envelope in mail box.

AS Østbirk 2B5
Elite Camp Vestbirk, Møllehøjvej 4. **GPS:** n55,96840 e9,75000.
DKK 140 Ch against payment. 04/04-28/09
Remarks: QuickStop: >20 - <10h.

Funen

AS Asperup 2B6
Skovlund, Kystvejen 1. **GPS:** n55,50628 e9,89932.
DKK 140 Ch against payment. 08/04-20/09
Remarks: QuickStop: >20 - <10h.

AS Assens 2B6
Sandager Næs, Strandgårdsvej 12. **GPS:** n55,33399 e9,88964.
DKK 135 Ch against payment. 05/04-14/09
Remarks: QuickStop: >20 - <10h.

AS Assens 2B6
Willemoes, Næsvej 15. **GPS:** n55,26521 e9,88428.
DKK 140 Ch against payment. 09/04-14/09
Remarks: QuickStop: >20 - <10h.

Tourist information Assens:
Assens Turistbureau, Damgade 22, www.visit-vestfyn.dk.Historical city centre and harbour.
Ernst s Samlinger, østergade 57.Collection of art and antiques of the silversmith. 01/05-30/09 Sa 14h. DKK 50.
Vestfyns Hjemstavnsgård, Klaregade 23.,Gummerup, Glamsbjerg.Open air museum. 01/04-31/10 10-16h Mo.

Bagenkop 5B1
Koldkrigsmuseum Langelandsfor, Vognsbjergvej 4A. **GPS:** n54,75306 e10,71583.
DKK 85. **Surface:** metalled. 01/04-31/10
Remarks: Check in at museum.

Tourist information Bagenkop:
Koldkrigsmuseum Langelandsfort, Vognsbjergvej 4A.War museum. 1/4-30/10.

AS Ebberup 2B6
Aa Strand Camping, Aa Strandvej 61. **GPS:** n55,21698 e9,97442.
DKK 150 Ch against payment. 09/04-14/09
Remarks: QuickStop: >20 - <10h.

AS Ebberup 2B6
Helnæs, Strandbakken 21. **GPS:** n55,13326 e10,03869.
DKK 125 Ch against payment. 01/04-01/10
Remarks: QuickStop: >20 - <10h.

S Faaborg 2B6
Faaborg Havn, Kanalvej 19. **GPS:** n55,09368 e10,29524.
10 DKK 110 Ch included WC . **Surface:** asphalted. 01/01-31/12
Distance: 200m on the spot on the spot on the spot 500m 200m.
Remarks: Check in at harbourmaster.

AS Faaborg 2B6
Faaborg Camping, Odensevej 140. **GPS:** n55,11667 e10,24477.
DKK 140 Ch against payment. 01/01-31/12
Remarks: QuickStop: >20 - <10h.

S Gram 2A6
Anholm Fiskesø, Folevej 11. **GPS:** n55,30564 e8,99888.

15 € 6,75 Ch included. **Location:** Rural, simple, isolated, quiet. **Surface:** . 01/04-01/11
Distance: 5km on the spot 1km 5km.
Remarks: At fish pond.

S Gram 2A6
Annemettes, Ribelandevej 18. **GPS:** n55,28647 e9,00098. .

3 € 14 Ch . **Location:** Rural, simple, isolated, quiet. **Surface:** grassy/gravel.

AS Haarby 2B6
Løgismosestrand, Løgismoseskov 7. **GPS:** n55,18156 e10,07001.
DKK 120 Ch against payment. 08/04-19/10
Remarks: QuickStop: >20 - <10h.

AS Hesselager 2C6
Bøsøre strand, Bøsørevej 16. **GPS:** n55,19742 e10,80626.
DKK 150 Ch against payment. 04/04-18/10
Remarks: QuickStop: >20 - <10h.

AS Hesselager 2C6
Lundeborg Strand-Camping, Gl. Lundeborgvej 46. **GPS:** n55,14625 e10,78138.
DKK 120 Ch against payment. 09/04-14/09
Remarks: QuickStop: >20 - <10h.

CS Humble 5B1
Ristinge, Ristingevej 104. **GPS:** n54,81944 e10,63988.
DKK 140 Ch against payment. 09/04-06/09
Remarks: QuickStop: >20 - <10h.

AS Martofte 2C5
Fyns Hoved Camping, Fynshovedvej 748. **GPS:** n55,60764 e10,61905.
DKK 135 Ch against payment. 01/01-31/12
Remarks: QuickStop: >20 - <10h.

S Middelfart 2B6
Lystbådehavn, østre Hougvej 112. **GPS:** n55,49250 e9,73028.

12 DKK 125 Ch (12x) WC included. **Location:** Rural, luxurious, isolated, quiet. **Surface:** asphalted/metalled. 01/01-31/12
Distance: 2km on the spot on the spot on the spot on the spot.
Remarks: Harbour Middelfahrt, Tallycard: service, electricity, sanitary building, caution DKK 50.

DK

Middelfart 2B6

Vejlby Fed Camping, Rigelvej 1. **GPS:** n55,51949 e9,84975.
DKK 150 Ch against payment. 09/04-11/09
Remarks: QuickStop: >20 - <10h.

Middelfart 2B6

Røjle Klint Natur Camping, Røjle Klintvej 29. **GPS:** n55,55039 e9,81876.
DKK 120 Ch against payment. 01/01-31/12
Remarks: QuickStop: >20 - <10h.

Tourist information Middelfart:
Turistbureauet, Havnegade 21, middelfartturist.dk.

Nr. Åby 2B6

Ronæs strand, Ronæsvej 10. **GPS:** n55,43975 e9,82692.
DKK 110 Ch against payment. 01/04-13/09
Remarks: QuickStop: >20 - <10h.

Nyborg 2C6

GPS: n55,29734 e10,83963.
free Ch free. **Surface:** metalled.

Nyborg 2C6

Grønnehave strand, Rejstrupvej 83. **GPS:** n55,35646 e10,78767.
DKK 120 Ch against payment. 09/04-21/09
Remarks: QuickStop: >20 - <10h.

Nyborg 2C6

Nyborg strandcamping, Hjejlevej 99. **GPS:** n55,30543 e10,82236.
DKK 140 Ch against payment. 09/04-21/09
Remarks: QuickStop: >20 - <10h.

Tourist information Nyborg:
Nyborg Turistbureau, Torvet 9, www.nyborgturist.dk.Old reinforced city.
Mads Lerches Gård, Slotsgade 11.Local history. 01/04-31/10 10-15/17h.
Nyborg Fæstning, Slotsgade 1.Fortress.
Nyborg Slot / Danehofslottet, Slotsgade 34.Castle, end 12th century.
01/04-31/10 10-15/17h.

Odense 2C6

Tarup Campingcenter, Agerhatten 31. **GPS:** n55,36110 e10,46722.
20 free. **Surface:** grassy.
Distance: 6km 2km.

Otterup 2C6

Hasmark Strand, Strandvejen 205. **GPS:** n55,53692 e10,42248.
DKK 100 Ch against payment. 04/04-01/10
Remarks: QuickStop: >20 - <10h.

Rudkøbing 2C6

Billevænge, Spodsbjergvej 182. **GPS:** n54,92382 e10,81606.
DKK 125 Ch against payment. 04/04-18/10
Remarks: QuickStop: >20 - <10h.

Rudkøbing 2C6

Færgegårdens, Spodsbjergvej 335. **GPS:** n54,93219 e10,82945.
DKK 130 Ch against payment. 04/04-04/10
Remarks: QuickStop: >20 - <10h.

Skårup 2C6

Skårupøre, Skårupøre Strandvej 56 A. **GPS:** n55,06317 e10,69735.
DKK 100 Ch against payment. 01/05-01/09
Remarks: QuickStop: >20 - <10h.

Stenstrup 2C6

Tronbjerggård Strandhave, Rårudvej 8, Kirkeby. **GPS:** n55,11820 e10,57840.
2 DKK 50 WC.

Svendborg 2C6

Carlsberg, Sundbrovej 19. **GPS:** n55,03344 e10,61332.
DKK 115 Ch against payment. 04/04-28/09
Remarks: QuickStop: >20 - <10h.

Svendborg 2C6

Vindebyøre Camping, Vindbyørevej 52. **GPS:** n55,05416 e10,63019.
DKK 140 Ch against payment. 03/04-27/09
Remarks: QuickStop: >20 - <10h.

Svendborg 2C6

Idrætshallen, Ryttervej 70. **GPS:** n55,05668 e10,57613.
Ch.

Tourist information Svendborg:
Sydfyns Turistbureau, Centrumpladsen 4, www.visitsydfyn.dk.Old city centre, many bars and restaurants at the harbour.
Egeskov Slot, Kværndrup.Citadel with park and 6 museums.
Valdemars Slot, Slotsalléen 100, Troense, Tåsinge.Castle on the island Tåsinge, fully furnished. Easter, 01/04-30/04, 01/10-31/10 Sa-Su 10-17h, 01/05-30/09 10-17/18h.

Søby, ærø 2C6

Søby, Vitsø 10. **GPS:** n54,93628 e10,24358.
DKK 95 Ch against payment. 01/01-31/12
Remarks: QuickStop: >20 - <10h.

Tranekær 2C6

Lohals, Birkevej 11. **GPS:** n55,13390 e10,90501.
DKK 150 Ch against payment. 01/01-31/12
Remarks: QuickStop: >20 - <10h.

Varde 2A6

Fritidscenter, Lerpøtvej 55. **GPS:** n55,63294 e8,47447.
20 against payment against payment. **Surface:** grassy.
01/05-31/10
Remarks: At sports centre.

Varde 2A6

Jensen, Ringkøbingvej 143. **GPS:** n55,65762 e8,48942.
4 DKK 75 WC. **Location:** Rural, comfortable, isolated, quiet.
Surface: grassy/metalled.
Distance: 5km.

Varde 2A6

Joan & Preben Christensen, Ringkøbingvej 259, Hindsig. **GPS:** n55,72077 e8,49345.
5 DKK 50 Ch. **Location:** Rural, comfortable, quiet. **Surface:** grassy. 01/01-31/12
Distance: 12km 3km.

Seeland, Møn, Lolland and Falster

Boeslunde 2C6

Campinggaarden Boelunde, Rennebjergvej 110. **GPS:** n55,28463 e11,26837.
DKK 150 Ch against payment. 01/04-30/09
Remarks: QuickStop: >20 - <10h.

DK

Copenhagen 2D5

Copenhagen City Camp, Fisketorvet, Kalvebod Pladsvej. **GPS**: n55,65889 e12,55778.

100 DKK 35, DKK 75/pp Ch DKK 35. 01/06-31/08
Distance: within walking distance on the spot on the spot.
Remarks: Motorhome parking next to harbour and new shopping center Fisketorv.

Tourist information Copenhagen:

Copenhagen Card.Card gives free entrance to public transport, 60 museums and attractions. Available at Tourist Offices, hotels, camp-sites.

Tourist Information Center, Copenhagen Right Now, Vesterbrogade 4A, København V, www.visitcopenhagen.com.Capital of Denmark, design city, lot of curiosities and museums.

Dyrehavsbakken, Dyrehavevej 62, Klampenborg (ten n. van Kopenhagen). Popular amusement park, oldest park of Denmark, with among other things 100 attractions and 35 restaurants. free.

Tivoli, Vesterbrogade 3.Large amusement park in the centre of the city with among other things 32 restaurants, 26 attractions, shows, concerts etc. 11-21/1h.

Dannemare 5C1

Hummingen, Pumpehusvej 1. **GPS**: n54,71317 e11,24606.
DKK 140 Ch against payment. 04/04-17/10
Remarks: QuickStop: >20 - <10h.

Fakse 2D6

Feddet, Feddet 12. **GPS**: n55,17366 e12,10118.
DKK 126 Ch against payment. 01/01-31/12
Remarks: QuickStop: >20 - <10h.

Fakse 2D6

Vemmetofte, Ny Strandskov 1. **GPS**: n55,23919 e12,23994.
DKK 110 Chagainst payment. 01/01-31/12
Remarks: QuickStop: >20 - <10h.

Tourist information Fakse:

Faksekystens Turistinformation, Hovedgaden 29, Fakse Ladeplads, www.faksekysten.dk.The municipality Fakse has 30 kilometres coast-line, marked cycle and hiking routes.

Fortællerfestival, Fakse Lime Beach.Festival for story tellers. last weekend Jun.

Rivierafest, Fakse Ladeplads.Festival with free herring-table on Sunday. Thu-Su of week 29.

Farø 2D6

Farø, Grøsundvej. **GPS**: n54,94876 e11,98696.
20 free ChWCfree. **Surface:** asphalted.
Remarks: Exit 42 from E47.

Føllenslev 2C5

Vesterlyng, Ravnholtvej 3. **GPS**: n55,74278 e11,30883.
DKK 110 Ch against payment. 03/04-18/10
Remarks: QuickStop: >20 - <10h.

Guldborg 2D6

Guldborg, Guldborgvej 147. **GPS**: n54,85985 e11,73014.
DKK 110 Ch against payment. 01/04-01/10
Remarks: QuickStop: >20 - <10h.

Horbelev 5D1

Falster, Tværmosevej 2. **GPS**: n54,81358 e12,07409.
DKK 175 Ch against payment. 01/01-31/12
Remarks: QuickStop: >20 - <10h.

Hundested 2D5

Rosenholm, Torpmaglevejen 37. **GPS**: n55,96260 e11,86152.
DKK 90 Ch against payment. 01/01-31/12
Remarks: QuickStop: >20 - <10h.

Hundested 2D5

Sølager, Kulhusvej 2. **GPS**: n55,94669 e11,89909.
DKK 200 Ch against payment. 01/01-31/12
Remarks: QuickStop: >20 - <10h.

Hørve 2C5

Teglværksgårdens, Teglværksvej 9A. **GPS**: n55,75794 e11,36568.
DKK 120 Ch against payment. 01/01-31/12
Remarks: QuickStop: >20 - <10h.

Jyderup 2C5

Skarresø, Slagelsevej 40. **GPS**: n55,61179 e11,38698.
DKK 125 Ch against payment. 25/03-25/09
Remarks: QuickStop: >20 - <10h.

Karrebæksminde 2D6

De Hvide Svaner Camping, KarrebæKvej 741. **GPS**: n55,20160 e11,66371.
DKK 100 Ch against payment. 03/04-18/10
Remarks: QuickStop: >20 - <10h.

Korsør 2C6

Lystbådehavn, Sylowsvej 10. **GPS**: n55,32664 e11,13190.

DKK 120 WC against payment.

Korsør 2C6

Lystskov, Korsør Lystskov 2. **GPS**: n55,32219 e11,18505.
DKK 90 Ch against payment. 01/04-01/10
Remarks: QuickStop: >20 - <10h.

Korsør 2C6

Storebælt, Storebæltsvej 85. **GPS**: n55,34866 e11,10281.
DKK 140 Ch against payment. 01/01-31/12
Remarks: QuickStop: >20 - <10h.

Tourist information Korsør:

Korsør Tourist Information Office, Nygade 7, www.korsoer-turistbureau.dk.

The Great Belt Bridge and Nature Centre, Storebæltsvej 88.Exhibition about the construction of the bridge over the Grote Belt. 01/03-31/12 10-17/19h.

Korsør Fæstning, Korsør Coastal Battery, The Fortress, Søbatteriet 7.Fortress. 01/04-30/11 Tue-Su 11-16h.

Maribo 5C1

Skelstrupgåren Bed and Breakfas, Skelstupvej 3. **GPS**: n54,78774 e11,52095.
5 DKK 50 against payment. **Surface:** grassy.
Distance: 2,2km 4km.

Nakskov 5C1

Albuen Strand, Vesternæsvej 70. **GPS**: n54,78058 e10,99481.
DKK 100 Ch against payment. 05/04-20/09
Remarks: QuickStop: >20 - <10h.

Nykøbing 2D5

Nykøbing Havn, Korvetvej 10. **GPS**: n55,91610 e11,67287.
DKK 85 Ch WC. **Surface:** metalled.
Distance: on the spot.

Nykøbing F. 5D1

Falster City Camping, østre Allé 112. **GPS**: n54,76243 e11,89479.
DKK 120 Ch against payment. 01/04-01/12
Remarks: QuickStop: >20 - <10h.

Ringsted 2D6

Mogens Madsen, Vibevej 34. **GPS**: n55,44222 e11,80667.
3 free against payment. **Surface:** metalled. 01/01-31/12
Distance: 4 km 800m.

Rude 2D6

Bisserup, Skafterupvej 182. **GPS**: n55,21065 e11,49812.
DKK 140 Ch against payment. 01/04-18/10
Remarks: QuickStop: >20 - <10h.

DK

Rødby 5C1
Rødby Lystskov, Strandvej 3. **GPS**: n54,69850 e11,39163.
DKK 120 Ch against payment. 01/01-31/12
Remarks: QuickStop: >20 - <10h.

Rødvig 2D6
Rødvig Camping, Højstrupvej 2 A. **GPS**: n55,24346 e12,34999.
DKK 120. 01/04-28/09
Remarks: QuickStop: >20 - <10h.

Stege 2D6
Keldby Camping Møn, Pollerupvej 3. **GPS**: n54,99114 e12,35678.
DKK 130 Ch against payment. 01/01-18/10
Remarks: QuickStop: >20 - <10h.

Strøby 2D6
Stevns, Strandvejen 29. **GPS**: n55,40009 e12,29067.
DKK 115 Ch against payment. 01/01-31/12
Remarks: QuickStop: >20 - <10h.

Taastrup 2D5
Park Hotel, Brorsonsvej 3. **GPS**: n55,65389 e12,30000.
10 DKK 125 DKK 25 WC. **Surface:** metalled. 01/01-31/12
Distance: 300m 1,5km on the spot 300m.
Remarks: Breakfast buffet DKK 75.

Tårs (Harpelunde) 2C6
Fiskeri & lystbådehavn, Tårsvej. **GPS**: n54,87841 e11,02355.
DKK 85 WC.
Remarks: Harbour Tårs.

Torrig 2C6
Kragenæs Havn, Kragenæsvej 84. **GPS**: n54,91565 e11,35730.
DKK 125 Ch against payment. 03/04-27/09
Remarks: QuickStop: >20 - <10h.

Vallensbæk 2D5
Lystbådehavn, Vallensbæk Havnevej, Vallensbæk Strand. **GPS**: n55,62455 e12,38888.
15 DKK 100 Ch included.
Distance: 7km on the spot.
Remarks: Harbour Vallensbæk, nearby harbour office.

Vejby 2D5
Vejby Strand, Rågelejevej 37. **GPS**: n56,07538 e12,14100.
DKK 180 Ch against payment. 09/04-06/09
Remarks: QuickStop: >20 - <10h.

Vipperød 2D5
Tempelkrogens, Krogvejen 2. **GPS**: n55,66213 e11,76246.
DKK 100 Ch against payment. 01/01-31/12
Remarks: QuickStop: >20 - <10h.

GERMANY

Capital: Berlin
Government: Federal republic
Official Language: Germany
Population: 82.000.000.(2012)
Area: 356,970 km^2.

General information
Dialling code: 0049
General emergency: 112
Currency: Euro

Regulations for overnight stays
Overnight stays on the public highway are allowed, if there is no local prohibition, but no "camping" activities are allowed.

Additional public holidays 2014
January 6 Epiphany
April 18 Good Friday
April 21 Eastermonday
May 1 Labor Day
June 9 White Monday
June 19 Corpus Christi
August 15 Assumption of the Virgin Mary
October 3 Day of German Unity
November 1 All Saints' Day

Germany

Schleswig-Holstein

S Albersdorf 4D2

Freitzeitbad Albersdorf, Weg zur Badeanstalt 18. **GPS**: n54,15350 e9,28055.

6 € 15 swimming pool incl Ch (6x)included. **Location:** Rural, isolated, quiet. **Surface:** grassy. 01/05-31/08

Distance: 1km 100m 300m on the spot on the spot.

Remarks: Parking at swimming pool, max. 3 days.

S Altenhof 5A2

Wohnmobilpark Ostsee 'Grüner Jäger', Grünen Jäger. **GPS**: n54,44392 e9,90526.

80 € 8 Ch € 3/24h WC € 1. **Location:** Rural, simple, isolated, quiet. **Surface:** grassy. 01/01-31/12

Distance: Eckernförde 6km 2km on the spot 6km 200m busstop -> Kiel on the spot on the spot.

Remarks: Check in at restaurant Grüner, bread service.

S Aukrug 5A3

Zum Sportplatz 1. **GPS**: n54,07441 e9,79160.

8 € 8 Ch included. **Location:** Rural. **Surface:** grassy/metalled. 01/01-31/12

Distance: 1km 800m 1km on the spot on the spot.

Remarks: Check in and key service at pay-desk of swimming pool, max. 3 days.

S Aventoft 4C1

Bauernhof Clausen, Gotteskoogstrasse 5. **GPS**: n54,88250 e8,80722.

5 € 6 € 2 WC € 2. **Location:** Rural, simple, isolated, quiet.

Surface: grassy. 01/01-31/12

Distance: 5km 5km.

Remarks: <3000kg.

S Aventoft 4C1

Wohnmobillstellplatz Zu den Fuchswiesen, Revtoftweg 1. **GPS**: n54,87661 e8,84562.

15 € 5, dog € 1 Ch € 1,50. **Location:** Rural, simple, isolated, quiet. **Surface:** asphalted/grassy. 01/01-31/12

Distance: 3km 3km 3km on the spot.

Remarks: Bread-service.

Bad Bramstedt 5A3

Parkplatz P7, Am Bahnhof, König Christian Strasse. **GPS**: n53,92167 e9,88967.

5 free. **Location:** Urban, simple, central, noisy.

Surface: metalled.

01/01-31/12

Distance: centre 500m 500m 500m on the spot.

Remarks: At station, max. 1 night, service at camping Roland, Kielerstrasse.

Tourist information Bad Bramstedt:

Tourismusbüro Bad Bramstedt im Rathaus, Bleeck 17-19, www.bad-bramstedt.de.

S Bad Malente 5B2

Parkplatz Krützen, Sebastian Kneipp strasse. **GPS**: n54,17198 e10,54919.

8 € 2/pp € 1 € 1 Ch. **Location:** Rural, simple. **Surface:** metalled. 01/01-31/12

Distance: on the spot 500m 1km.

S Bad Oldesloe 5B3

Wohnmobilplatz Exer, Am Bürgerpark. **GPS**: n53,81101 e10,36915.

DE

8 free € 1/10minutes Ch (8x)€ 2/10h WC . **Location:** Urban, simple, quiet. **Surface:** metalled. 01/01-31/12
Distance: on the spot 3km on the spot 400m.

S Bad Segeberg 5B3

Kalkbergblick, Kastanienweg 1b. **GPS**: n53,93872 e10,31423.

25 € 8 Chincluded (15x)€ 3/night,6 Amp. **Location:** Rural, comfortable, quiet. **Surface:** gravel. 01/01-31/12
Distance: 500m A7 3km 600m Segerberger See 600m 500m 500m on the spot on the spot.
Remarks: Jun/Aug Karl May Spiele, open air theater.

S Barmstedt 5A3

Am Rantzauer See, Seestrasse 12. **GPS**: n53,78640 e9,76420.

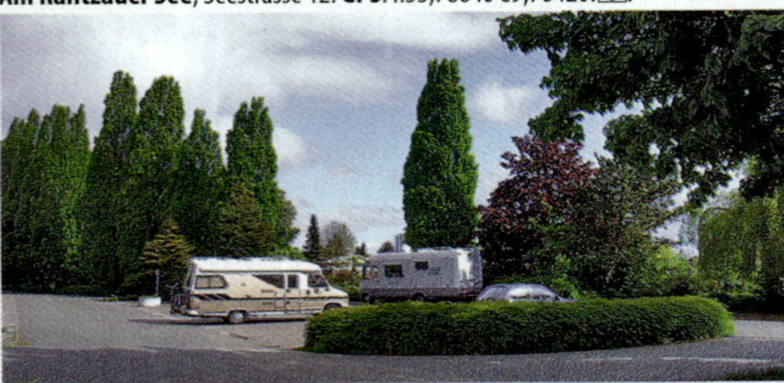

5 € 5 Ch WC included. **Surface:** metalled. 01/01-31/12
Distance: on the spot on the spot 500m.

S Behrensdorf 5B2

Campingpark Waldesruh, Neuland. **GPS**: n54,35754 e10,60216.

18 € 10-12 2 pers.incl, dog € 1,50 Ch € 1/24h WC .
Location: Rural, comfortable. **Surface:** grassy. 01/04-31/10
Distance: 2km on the spot on the spot on the spot on the spot.

S Bistensee 5A2

Ferienplatz bei Matz, Mühlenweg 1. **GPS**: n54,39538 e9,71386.

5 € 3 + € 3/pp included WC . **Location:** Rural, simple, isolated, quiet. **Surface:** grassy.
01/01-31/12
Distance: 500m 600m Bistensee on the spot 2km 1km on the spot on the spot.

Tourist information Bistensee:
www.bistensee.de.Village on lake of the same name.

S Blekendorf 5B2

Am Sehlendorfer Strand, Strandstrasse 24. **GPS**: n54,30571 e10,69358.

40 € 13,50 € 1 Ch included WC . **Location:** Rural, comfortable. **Surface:** grassy. 01/01-31/12
Distance: 1km on the spot on the spot on the spot 5km.

Bordesholm 5A2

Festplatz, Kielerstrasse. **GPS**: n54,18389 e10,02667.

6 free. **Location:** Rural, simple, quiet. **Surface:** grassy/sand.
01/01-31/12
Distance: 1,5km 4km.
Remarks: Max. 18h, service at petrol station.

S Bordesholm 5A2

Shell tankstelle, Bahnofstrasse 78. **GPS**: n54,17343 e10,03497.
Ch . 01/01-31/12

S Bosau 5B3

Dat Gröne Huus, Stadtbeker Strasse 97. **GPS**: n54,09198 e10,42886.

3 € 5, guests free € 3 . **Location:** Rural, simple, quiet.
Surface: gravel. 01/04-30/11

DE

Distance: 100m Großer Plöner See on the spot on the spot 1km.
Remarks: Bread-service.

Bösdorf 5B2

Wohnmobilcamp Augustfelde, Vierer See, Augustfelde. **GPS:** n54,12898 e10,45506.

16 € 11,50-13,50 Ch (16x) WC included € 0,75.
Surface: grassy. 01/04-25/10
Distance: on the spot on the spot on the spot on the spot.

Bösdorf 5B2

Campingpark Gut Ruhleben, Missionsweg 2, Ruhleben. **GPS:** n54,14308 e10,45021.

10 € 10,50-13,50 Ch included. **Location:** Rural, simple.
Surface: grassy/gravel. 01/04-30/09
Remarks: Max. 3 nights.

Bredstedt 4D1

Süderstraße. **GPS:** n54,61307 e8,97082.

5 free. **Location:** Rural. **Surface:** asphalted. 01/01-31/12
Distance: 900m Aldi 650m.
Remarks: Nearby swimming pool.

Brodersby 5A1

Camping Am Mussinder Fährhaus, Mussinder Fahrstrasse 33. **GPS:** n54,52500 e9,71583.

20 € 12 Ch WC. **Surface:** grassy. 01/04-31/10

Brodersby 5A1

Ferienhof Lassen, Grossbrodersbyer weg 5. **GPS:** n54,53829 e9,71443.

3 € 10 Ch included. **Location:** Rural, simple, quiet.
Surface: grassy.
Distance: 500m 2km 500m.

Brokdorf 4D3

Parkplatz, Dorfstrasse. **GPS:** n53,86417 e9,31667.

30 free € 1/5minutes € 1 Ch (30x)€ 0,50/kWh WC € 0,50.
Location: Rural, comfortable. **Surface:** metalled. 01/01-31/12
Distance: 800m 400m on the spot 500m on the spot on the spot.

Brunsbüttel 4D3

An der Braake, Am Freizeitbad. **GPS:** n53,89832 e9,13138.

12 free € 1 Ch. **Location:** Rural, comfortable, central, quiet.
Surface: grassy/metalled. 01/01-31/12
Distance: 500m 500m 500m on the spot.

Büdelsdorf 5A2

Hermann-Ehlers-Platz, Agnes Miegel Strasse. **GPS:** n54,31583 e9,69306.

10 free. **Location:** Simple, central. **Surface:** metalled.
01/01-31/12
Distance: on the spot 1km 1,5km.
Remarks: Max. 1 night.

Büsum 4D3

Wohnmobilstellplatz Nordsee, Dr. Martin Bahr Strasse. **GPS:** n54,12889 e8,86889.

DE

100 1/11-28/2 € 10, 1/3-31/10 € 13 € 0,50/50liter Ch WC € 0,50/day. **Location:** Rural, comfortable, isolated, quiet. **Surface:** grassy.
01/01-31/12
Distance: 1km 500m 300m.

P Büsum 4D3

Deichmuseum P2, Westereck 2. **GPS:** n54,14210 e8,84212.

50 free. **Location:** Simple, isolated, quiet.
Distance: 500m 500m.

S Dagebüll 4C1

Am Nordseedeich, Am Badedeich 15. **GPS:** n54,72666 e8,69527.

10 € 6 € 2. **Location:** Rural. **Surface:** grassy.
01/01-31/12
Distance: 5km 100m 100m on the spot bakery 300m.

S Damp 5A1

Wohnmobilpark Damp, Parkstrasse 2. **GPS:** n54,57750 e10,01667.

70 € 12 € 1/100liter Ch (60x)€ 0,60/kWh WC € 1/3minutes . **Location:** Rural, comfortable, quiet.
Surface: grassy/gravel. 01/01-31/12
Distance: on the spot on the spot on the spot 150m.

S Drelsdorf 4D1

Drelsdörper Krog, Dorfstrasse 23. **GPS:** n54,60555 e9,03555.

15 € 5, guests free € 2 WC. **Location:** Simple, central, noisy.
Surface: grassy. 01/01-31/12
Distance: 200m 2km.
Remarks: Along through road.

S Eckernförde 5A2

Parkplatz P1, Grüner Weg, B76. **GPS:** n54,46549 e9,83574.

46 € 1,60/h 10-20h, overnight stay free € 0,50/120liter € 0,50 Ch € 0,50 € 0,50/1kWh. **Location:** Urban, simple, central.
Surface: metalled. 01/01-31/12
Distance: 200m 250m 300m 300m 200m on the spot on the spot.
Remarks: Parking nearby centre and beach, along busy through road.

Tourist information Eckernförde:
Eckernförde Touristik GmbH, Am Exer 1, www.ostseebad-eckernfoerde.de.

S Elmshorn 5A3

Stellplatz Elmshorn, Nordufer. **GPS:** n53,75157 e9,65268.

6 free € 1/80liter Ch WC. **Location:** Urban, simple, central, quiet.
Surface: metalled. 01/01-31/12
Distance: 800m on the spot on the spot.
Remarks: Northern bank of the harbour, in front of centre.

Eutin 5B2

Elisabethstrasse. **GPS:** n54,13507 e10,60935.

5+3 free. **Location:** Urban. **Surface:** metalled. 01/01-31/12
Distance: on the spot.
Remarks: Parking at station.

DE

Eutin 5B2

Schloss-Parkplatz P11, Schlossstraße. **GPS**: n54,13828 e10,61990.
5 free. **Surface:** metalled. 01/01-31/12
Distance: Großer Eutiner See.

Fehmarn 5C2

Wohnmobilpark Wulfener Hals, Wulfener-Hals-Weg 16, Wulfen. **GPS**: n54,40687 e11,17489.

100 from € 11,80-27,40 Ch € 2,10 WC € 0,90.
Location: Rural, luxurious. **Surface:** grassy. 01/01-31/12
Distance: on the spot.

Fehmarn 5C2

Hintz-Heizungsbau, Landkirchenerweg 1b, Burg. **GPS**: n54,44228 e11,18967.

16 € 10 € 1 Ch (16x)€ 5. **Location:** Simple, quiet.
Surface: metalled. 01/01-31/12
Distance: on the spot.

Fehmarn 5C2

Kommunal- und Yachthafen Burgstaaken, Burgstaaken/am Binnensee, Burgstaaken. **GPS**: n54,42028 e11,19224.

15 € 10 21-08h. **Location:** Rural, simple. **Surface:** metalled.
01/01-31/12
Distance: 100m 100m.

Fehmarn 5C2

Parkplatz Ost, Osterstrasse, Burg. **GPS**: n54,43754 e11,19990.

30 € 8 (21-8h). **Location:** Urban, simple. **Surface:** metalled.
01/01-31/12
Distance: 100m.

Fehmarn 5C2

Camping Strukkamphuk, Strukkamp. **GPS**: n54,41239 e11,10223.

21 € 14,50-31 Ch WC included. **Location:** Rural.
Surface: grassy. 01/01-31/12
Distance: 10m.

Flensburg 4D1

Am Industriehafen, dir Flensburg Mürwick. **GPS**: n54,80444 e9,44388.

20 free. **Location:** Urban, simple, isolated, quiet.
Surface: gravel.
Distance: 1,5km on the spot on the spot.

Fockbek 5A2

Am Freibad, Grosse Rheie 17. **GPS**: n54,30190 e9,60331.

3 free Ch WC. **Location:** Rural, quiet. **Surface:** grassy/sand.
01/01-31/12
Distance: 800m 800m 800m on the spot on the spot.
Remarks: Parking swimming pool, max. 24h.

Friedrichskoog 4D3

P2, Nordseestrasse. **GPS**: n54,03272 e8,84833.

30 € 2, overnight stay free. **Location:** Rural, comfortable, isolated, quiet.
Surface: asphalted/grassy. 01/03-31/10
Distance: 1km 550m 800m.
Remarks: Bread-service.

Gelting 5A1

Hafen Wackerballig, Strandweg, Wackerballig. **GPS**: n54,75564 e9,87842.

DE

18 € 8 € 0,50/40liter Ch € 1,50/day WC € 0,50. **Location:** Rural, simple. **Surface:** grassy/gravel. 01/04-31/10

Distance: 1,5km on the spot 2km.

Remarks: Key sanitary building/waste dump at harbour master, caution € 20.

Glückstadt 4D3

Am Außenhafen, Am Hafen. **GPS**: n53,78560 e9,41088.

16 € 5. **Location:** Rural, comfortable. **Surface:** metalled.
01/01-31/12 high water.

Distance: 1km on the spot on the spot on the spot on the spot on the spot.

Remarks: Along the river Elbe.

Glückstadt 4D3

Park & Ride platz, Bahnhofstrasse. **GPS**: n53,78776 e9,43145.

10 free. **Location:** Urban, simple. **Surface:** asphalted.
01/01-31/12

Distance: 900m 200m on the spot on the spot.

Grödersby 5A1

WSG Arin/Grödersby, Friedenshöher Straße 21. **GPS**: n54,63444 e9,92944.

15 € 15 Ch WC € 3,dryer € 2 included. **Location:** Rural, simple, quiet. **Surface:** gravel/metalled. 01/05-30/09

Distance: 200m on the spot on the spot 200m on the spot.

Grömitz 5C2

Wohnmobilstellplatz am Lensterstrand, Blankwasserweg. **GPS**: n54,15650 e10,99134.

50 winter free, summer € 7,50 WC. **Location:** Rural. **Surface:** grassy.
01/01-31/12 water disconnected in winter.

Distance: on the spot on the spot.

Grömitz 5C2

Wohnmobilstellplatz, Gildestraße 14. **GPS**: n54,14490 e10,95262.

60 winter € 6, summer € 12 € 0,50 Ch (20x)€ 1/kWh.

Location: Rural, comfortable. **Surface:** metalled. 01/01-31/12

Distance: 200m on the spot 200m.

Großenbrode 5C2

Wassersportzentrum, Am Kai 29. **GPS**: n54,35583 e11,07798.

50 € 8-10 € 0,50/100liter Ch € 1/1kWh WC € 0,50 .

Location: Rural. **Surface:** grassy/metalled. 01/01-31/12

Distance: 300m on the spot 2km.

Großenbrode 5C2

Wohnmobilhafen Reise, Südstrand 1. **GPS**: n54,36170 e11,08567.

36 € 10-12 € 0,50 Ch WC € 0,50 € 5/24h. **Location:** Rural, comfortable. **Surface:** gravel. 01/01-31/12

Distance: on the spot 500m on the spot.

Grossenaspe 5A3

Wildpark Eekholt, Eekhol 1. **GPS**: n53,94819 e10,02916.

DE

10 free. **Location:** Rural, simple, isolated, quiet. **Surface:** grassy/sand. 01/01-31/12

Distance: 4km Grossenaspe Kiek ut Stuben, Game preserve > Wildpark.

S Großsolt 4D1

Stellplatz Mühlenbrück, Flensburger strasse, Mühlenbrück. **GPS**: n54,70853 e9,52243.

50 € 10 Ch (13x)€ 2/day WC € 0,50/3. **Location:** Rural, comfortable, quiet. **Surface:** gravel. 01/03--01/10

Distance: 200m.

S Hamburg 5A4

Wohnmobilhafen Hamburg, Grüner Deich 8, Hammerbrook. **GPS**: n53,54303 e10,02814.

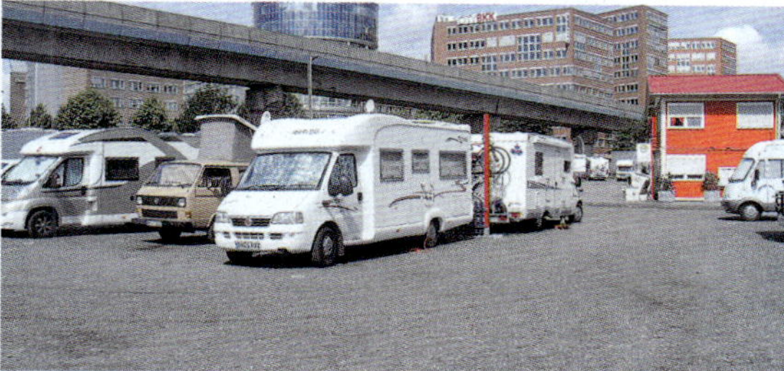

60 € 19 Ch WC . **Location:** Urban, simple, central, noisy. **Surface:** gravel. 01/01-31/12

Distance: 4km 200m.

S Hamburg 5A4

Wohnmobilplatz Hamburg Süd, Finkenrieker Hauptdeich 5. **GPS**: n53,47440 e10,00134.

80 € 12 € 1 € 1 Ch € 1 (10x)€ 1/2kWh WC € 1 . **Location:** Urban, simple, noisy. **Surface:** metalled. 01/01-31/12

Distance: 14km 100m 100m 5 min.

Hamburg 5A4

Am Strand Pauli, St. Pauli Hafenstraße. **GPS**: n53,54598 e9,96099.

20 € 8,50, weekend € 13. **Surface:** asphalted. 01/01-31/12

Distance: Hamburg Altstadt 2,4km on the spot many restaurant 100m 600m.

Tourist information Hamburg:

www.hamburg-tourismus.de.City-state on the mouth of the river Elbe, Hanseatic town and most important port city of Germany.

Hamburg-card.Card offers free entrance to public transport and museums, discounts on boat trips, zoo etc. Available at Tourist Information. T € 8 1 day, € 18/3 days, 1 adult max. 3 childeren.

Tourist Information am Hafen, St. Pauli Landungsbrücken, zwischen Brücke 4 und 5.

Tourist Information im Hauptbahnhof, Hauptausgang Kirchenallee.

Sankt Pauli.City district with well-known Reeperbahn.

Flohmarkt Barmbek, Hellbrookstrasse.Flea market. Fri 7-13h, Sa 7-16h.

Flohmarkt St. Pauli, Budapesterstrasse.Antiques and flea market. Sa 10-16h.

Flohschanze, Rinderschlachthalle St Pauli.Antiques and flea market. Sa 8-16h.

Tierpark Hagenbeck, Stellingen.Zoo. 01/01-31/12 9h.

Antikpassage, Klosterwall 9-21.Arcade with 39 antique stores. Tue-Fri 12-18h, Sa 10-16h.

S Hanerau-Hademarschen 4D3

Ferienhof Sievers, Wilhelmsburg. **GPS**: n54,12360 e9,38627.

6 € 10 Ch (6x) WC . **Location:** Rural, comfortable, isolated, quiet. **Surface:** grassy. 01/01-31/12

Distance: 2km.

S Harrislee 4D1

Skandic Camping, Am Oxer 17a. **GPS**: n54,79800 e9,36960.

5 € 5 Ch included WC € 1. **Location:** Urban, simple, isolated. **Surface:** metalled. 01/01-31/12

Distance: 6km.

Remarks: Motorhome dealer, accessory shop.

S Hasselberg 5A1

Camping Oehe-Draecht, Drecht. **GPS**: n54,71590 e9,99030.

10 €11 Ch € 3 WC included. **Location:** Rural, simple, quiet. **Surface:** grassy. 01/04-30/09

DE

Distance: 3km on the spot on the spot.

S **Heide** 4D2

Wohnmobilplatz Heide, Langvogt-Johannsen-strasse. **GPS**: n54,20181 e9,11319.

16 free € 1/100liter € 1 Ch € 1/2kWh. **Surface:** grasstiles/metalled.
01/01-31/12
Distance: 800m 5,5km 100m 300m.

S **Heiligenhafen** 5C2

Parkplatz Steinwarder, B207 Abfahrt Heiligenhafen. **GPS**: n54,37896 e10,97875.

90 € 7,50, peak season € 12/24h € 0,50 Ch (42x)€ 2 WC.
Surface: asphalted. 01/01-31/12
Distance: 400m on the spot on the spot.
Remarks: Direct access to the beach.

S **Heiligenhafen** 5C2

Reisemobilstellplatz Binnensee, Eichholzweg. **GPS**: n54,37721 e10,95548.

20 € 7,50-10 (21x)€ 2. **Location:** Urban.
Surface: metalled.
01/01-31/12
Distance: 1km on the spot.
Remarks: Max. 24h.

Tourist information Heiligenhafen:

Bicycle rental at Ostsee-Ferienpark.

Tourist-Information, Bergstrasse 43, www.heiligenhafen.de.Fishing-port and modern marina.

Hafenfest.Festival with events. July.

S **Hohenfelde** 5B2

Campingpark Ostseestrand, Strandstraße. **GPS**: n54,38588 e10,49152.

25 € 15 Ch WC included. **Location:** Rural, luxurious.
Surface: grassy. 01/04-15/10
Distance: 1km beach 150m 150m on the spot on the spot.

S **Hohenfelde** 5B2

Wohnmobilplatz Radeland, Strandstraße 18. **GPS**: n54,38278 e10,49295.

20 € 5 Ch € 0,60/kWh WC € 3/day. **Location:** Rural.
Surface: grassy/sand. 01/04-30/09
Distance: 300m.

S **Hohwacht** 5B2

Parkplatz Alt-Hohwacht, Strandstrasse. **GPS**: n54,31902 e10,67529.

20 € 10 € 1/80liter € 1 Ch (20x)€ 1/kWh. **Location:** Urban.
Surface: metalled. 01/01-31/12
Distance: on the spot on the spot.

S **Husum** 4D2

Loof's Wohnmobilhafen, Dockoogstrasse 7. **GPS**: n54,47451 e9,04249.

30 € 12 € 1 € 2 Ch € 2 (30x)€ 3 WC € 0,50. **Location:** Rural, simple, central, quiet. **Surface:** gravel.
01/01-31/12
Distance: 200m 200m 200m 200m 200m on the spot on the spot.

S **Husum** 4D2

Wohnmobilplatz Am Dockkoog, Dockoogstrasse 17. **GPS**: n54,47888 e9,01138.

DE

40 € 12 2 pers.incl, dog € 1 Ch WC included € 1. **Location:** Rural, simple, quiet. **Surface:** grassy. Easter-31/10
Distance: 500m 200m 200m on the spot on the spot on the spot.
Remarks: Max. 3 nights.

S **Itzehoe** 5A3
Malzmüllerwiesen, Schuhmacherallee. **GPS**: n53,91970 e9,51815.

5 free € 1/100liter € 1 Ch € 1. **Location:** Rural, simple, central, quiet. **Surface:** metalled/sand.
01/01-31/12 during event.
Distance: 600m 20m on the spot on the spot.

S **Jagel** 5A2
Wohnmobilhafen Jagel, Bundesstrasse 13. **GPS**: n54,45388 e9,53416.

31 € 10 Ch day WC . **Location:** Rural, comfortable, quiet. **Surface:** grassy. 01/01-31/12
Distance: 250m 4,5km.

S **Kaltenkirchen** 5A3
Reisemobilstellplatz Holstentherme, Norderstrasse 8. **GPS**: n53,84056 e9,94650.

20 free € 1/80liter € 1 Ch € 1 . **Location:** Quiet. **Surface:** grassy/gravel. 01/01-31/12
Distance: 1,5km 1km on the spot 1,5km on the spot.
Remarks: Coins available at pay-desk of theTherme.

S **Kappeln** 5A1
Anker Yachting, Am Hafen. **GPS**: n54,66715 e9,93718.

20 € 10-14 Ch € 0,50/kWh € 1. 01/01-31/12
Distance: 1km 1km 1km.
Remarks: At marina.

S **Kappeln** 5A1
Aral-Tankstelle, Eckernförder Strasse 9/B. **GPS**: n54,65688 e9,94480.

10 free Ch € 5/day. **Location:** Urban, simple. **Surface:** metalled.
01/01-31/12
Distance: 300m 2km on the spot.
Remarks: Caution key service € 25.

Tourist information Kappeln:
Port with museum boats.

S **Kellinghusen** 5A3
Am Freibad, Jacob-Fleischer-Strasse 6. **GPS**: n53,94715 e9,71035.

10 free € 0,50/100liter € 0,50 Ch (4x)€ 1/h WC use sanitary facilities at swimming pool. **Location:** Rural, quiet. **Surface:** gravel.
01/01-31/12
Distance: centre 500m 500m 500m.
Remarks: Check in at swimming pool.

S **Kiel** 5A2
Wohnmobilstellplatz Kiel, Förde und Kanalblick, Mecklenburgstrasse 58. Kiel-Wik. **GPS**: n54,36362 e10,14705.

33 € 11-13 Ch (33x)€ 3,50/24h WC € 1/5minutes € 3/time,dryer € 1. **Location:** Urban, simple, central, noisy. **Surface:** metalled. 01/01-31/12
Distance: 6,5km Imbiss on the spot 1,5km on the spot on the spot.
Remarks: Check in and pay at reception, bread service.

S **Kiel** 5A2
Olympiahafen Schilksee, Soling 26. **GPS**: n54,43033 e10,16634.

DE

20 € 10 € 0,50/3minutes € 1 Ch WC.
Surface: metalled.
01/01-31/12 last 2 weeks of Jun.
Distance: 13km 400m 400m.
Remarks: Check in and coins service at harbourmaster.

Tourist information Kiel:
Tourist Information Kiel e.V, Andreas-Gayk-Str. 31.
City on the mouth of fiord.
Schleswig-Holsteinisches Freilichtmuseum, Molfsee
.Open air museum.
01/04-31/10 daily 9-18h, 01/11-31/03 Su 11-16h.
€ 4,50, family card € 11.

Krempe 5A3

Am Schul- und Sportzentrum, Am Freibad. **GPS**: n53,83356 e9,49447.

3 free. **Location:** Rural, simple, quiet. **Surface:** gravel.
01/01-31/12
Distance: 200m.

Kremperheide 5A3

Heidekrug, Dorfstraße. **GPS**: n53,88006 e9,47967.
4 € 5, guests free. 01/01-31/12
Distance: on the spot.
Remarks: In front of restaurant.

Kropp 5A2

Hotel Wikingerhof, Tetenhusener Chaussee 1. **GPS**: n54,40638 e9,51055.

8 € 5, guests free WC. **Location:** Urban, simple, quiet.
Surface: metalled. 01/01-31/12
Distance: 300m on the spot 300m.

Kropp 5A2

Restaurant Rosengarten, Rheiderweg 7. **GPS**: n54,41388 e9,50138.

5 € 5 WC. **Location:** Urban, simple, quiet. **Surface:** metalled.
01/01-31/12
Distance: 200m on the spot 200m.

Kropp 5A2

Garage Audi-VW Thomsen, Werkstrasse 2. **GPS**: n54,41361 e9,52833.

5 € 5 Ch. **Location:** Urban, simple, noisy. **Surface:** metalled.
01/01-31/12
Distance: 300m 300m 300m.

Laboe 5B2

Ostseebad Laboe Ehrenmal, Steinerweg/Prof. Munzerring. **GPS**: n54,41029 e10,23289.

18 € 12 € 1/5minutes € 1 Ch. **Location:** Urban, simple.
Surface: metalled. 01/01-31/12
Distance: 1km 400m 400m on the spot 1km.

Ladelund 4D1

Am Naturbad, Stato. **GPS**: n54,84919 e9,03629.

4 € 5, € 10 swimming pool incl Ch WC included. **Location:** Rural, comfortable, isolated, quiet. **Surface:** grassy.
01/01-31/12
Distance: 1km on the spot.

Langballig 5A1

Campingplatz Langballigau, Strandweg 3, Langballigau. **GPS**: n54,82234 e9,65969.

DE

50 € 10, dog € 1 Ch € 2,50/night WC included € 1/time. **Location:** Rural, simple. **Surface:** grassy/gravel. 01/01-31/12
Distance: 100m on the spot.

S Langwedel 5A2

Caravanpark am Brahmsee, Mühlenstraße 30a. **GPS**: n54,21462 e9,91943.

20 € 10 € 1/80liter Ch € 2,50/24h,6 Amp WC sanitary at campsite. **Location:** Rural, comfortable, quiet. **Surface:** grassy/gravel. 01/01-31/12
Distance: 600m A7 3 km Brahmsee 500m 500m 7km.
Remarks: Check in at reception campsite, bread service.

S Lauenburg/Elbe 5B4

Marina Lauenburg/Yachthafen, Hafenstrasse 14. **GPS**: n53,37156 e10,56527.

10 € 7 € 1/100liter (8x)€ 1/kWh WC € 0,50 € 1 washing machine/dryer € 4. **Location:** Rural, comfortable. **Surface:** metalled. 01/01-31/12
Distance: 10 min walking on the spot 10 min walking.

S Lensahn 5C2

Reisemobilplatz Lensahn, Dr. Julius-Stinde strasse. **GPS**: n54,21446 e10,87745.

15 € 8 € 1/80liter Ch (4x)€ 2. **Location:** Rural, simple. **Surface:** grasstiles. 01/01-31/12
Distance: 1,5km on the spot 200m 2,5km.

S Lübeck 5B3

Wohnmobil Treff Lübeck, An der Hülshorst 11. **GPS**: n53,89510 e10,71088.

40 € 9/day Ch WC € 1/5minutes € 1,50. **Location:** Urban, luxurious, quiet. **Surface:** gravel. 02/01-31/10
Distance: 4,5km 5km on the spot 50m.

Lübeck 5B3

Wohnmobilstellplatz Lübeck Marienbrücke P4, Lastadie. **GPS**: n53,87147 e10,67904.

16 free, 18-10h. **Location:** Urban, simple. **Surface:** asphalted. 01/01-31/12
Distance: 500m 2km on the spot on the spot.
Remarks: Follow 'Media Docks'.

Tourist information Lübeck:

www.luebeck-tourismus.de.Old Hanseatic town, birth place of the Mann brothers.

Buddenbrookhaus, Mengstrasse 4.Literature museum with work of the Mann family.

01/04-31/10 10-18h, 01/11-31/03 10-17h.

€ 4,10, family card € 12,50.

Günter-Grass-Haus Kulturstiftung Hansestadt Lübeck, Glockengiesserstr. 21.Literature museum.

Museum Holstentor, Holstentorplatz.Historical museum.

10-16/17h. € 4 (incl. 3 children).

Niederegger Einkaufserlebnis, Café und Marzipan-Museum, Breite strasse 89.Marzipan, Lübecker speciality, museum, café and shop.

S Maasholm 5A1

Stellplatz am Yachthafen, Uleweg 31. **GPS**: n54,68334 e9,99436.

80 € 10 Ch € 2/day WC € 0,50 € 2. **Location:** Rural, comfortable, quiet. **Surface:** grassy/gravel. 01/01-31/12
Distance: 100m 5km on the spot on the spot 100m.
Remarks: Parking marina.

S Meldorf 4D3

Reisemobil-Stellplatz am Deich, Deichstraße 2. **GPS**: n54,09409 e8,95070.

DE

80 € 7, only overnight stay € 3,50 Ch (18x)€ 3 WC € 2.
Location: Rural, comfortable, isolated, quiet. **Surface:** grassy/metalled.
Easter-31/10
Distance: 7km on the spot Imbiss 10-18 uur on the spot on the spot.

Molfsee 5A2

Freilichtmuseum/Restaurant Drathenhof, Hamburger Landstrasse 99. **GPS:** n54,27411 e10,07571.

20 free, use of a meal desired WC at restaurant. **Location:** Central.
Surface: gravel. 01/01-31/12
Distance: on the spot on the spot on the spot on the spot on the spot.
Remarks: At open air museum.

DE

Mölln 5B4

Alt Möllner strasse. **GPS:** n53,62564 e10,68314.

20 € 7/24h (20x)included. **Location:** Rural. **Surface:** gravel.
01/01-31/12
Distance: 1km 250m 300m.
Remarks: Service: Vorkamp 19, GPS n53,62024, o10,67701.

Tourist information Mölln:
Small town to the old Salzstrasse, salt trail.

Neumünster 5A3

Bad am Stadtwald, Hansaring 177. **GPS:** n54,08078 e9,96064.

22 € 10 € 0,50/100liter € 0,50 Ch (22x)€ 0,50/1kWh WC €
0,50. **Location:** Rural, comfortable, central, quiet. **Surface:** grassy/gravel.
01/01-31/12
Distance: 2km A7 1 km on the spot 300m on the spot.
Remarks: Check in at swimming pool.

Neustadt in Holstein 5C2

Wohnmobilstellplatz Ostsee, Auf der Pelzer Wiese 45, Pelzerhaken. **GPS:** n54,08889 e10,87250.

90 € 12 + tourist tax (summer) € 1 € 1 Ch (90x)€ 1/2kWh WC
€ 2. **Location:** Rural, luxurious, noisy. **Surface:** grassy.
01/01-31/12
Distance: 900m 150m 900m 400m on the spot.

Neustadt in Holstein 5C2

P5, Am Binnenwasser. **GPS:** n54,11096 e10,81496.

10 Mo-Fr € 5/24h, Sa-Su free (2x)€ 0,50/kWh. **Location:** Urban, simple. **Surface:** metalled. 01/01-31/12
Distance: on the spot.

Niebüll 4C1

Parkplatz, Lornsenstrasse 19. **GPS:** n54,78901 e8,82546.

25 € 5 € 1 € 1 Ch (12x)€ 1. **Location:** Urban, simple, central, quiet.
Surface: grassy. 01/01-31/12
Distance: on the spot 200m.
Remarks: Parking swimming pool, max. 24h.

Nordstrand 4D2

Wohnmobilplatz Margarethenruh, Süderhafen 8. **GPS:** n54,46944 e8,91000.

21 € 14,80-17,50, 2 pers.incl. Ch € 2,60 WC € 3.

Location: Rural, comfortable, central, quiet. **Surface:** gravel.
01/01-31/12
Distance: 3km 300m 150m 3km.

S **Nordstrand** 4D2

Womoland, Norderquerweg 2. **GPS**: n54,51736 e8,93012.

38 € 7 + € 3,50/pp Ch € 2,50 WC . **Surface:** grassy/gravel. 01/01-31/12

S **Nordstrand** 4D2

Landgasthof Pohnshallig, Pohnshalligkoogstrasse 17. **GPS**: n54,49772 e8,92906.

4 € 5, guests free € 2,50. **Location:** Rural, simple. **Surface:** metalled.
01/07-31/10 Thu.
Distance: 3km on the spot 3km.
Remarks: Along through road.

Tourist information Nordstrand:
Former Wadden island.

S **Norgaardholz** 5A1

Campingplatz Nordstern, Nordstern 1. **GPS**: n54,78528 e9,79889.

10 € 6, dog € 1 Ch € 2/day WC Use sanitary € 4/night free.
Location: Rural, simple, quiet. **Surface:** gravel/metalled.
01/01-31/12
Distance: on the spot on the spot.

S **Ockholm** 4C1

Wohnmobilstellplätze Altes Pastorat Ockholm, Baderstrasse 5/6. **GPS**: n54,66517 e8,82940.

5 € 8 Ch (5x)€ 1,60 WC € 5,dryer € 5. **Location:** Rural, simple, isolated, quiet. **Surface:** grassy. 01/01-31/12
Remarks: Bread-service, along through road.

S **Oeversee** 4D1

Kranzbinderei Schnell, Frörupsand 2. **GPS**: n54,69134 e9,43602.

9 € 6 Ch € 1/night free. **Location:** Rural, simple, quiet.
Surface: grassy. 01/01-31/12
Distance: 500m.

S **Osterhever** 4C2

Stellplatz Norderheverkoog, Norderheverkoogstraße 12, Norderheverkoog. **GPS**: n54,39656 e8,76163.

10 € 6 € 1 Ch (10x)€ 3 WC € 1. **Location:** Rural. **Surface:** grassy. 01/04-31/10
Distance: 1km 2km 1km on the spot on the spot.
Remarks: Bread-service.

S **Pahlen** 4D2

Fischerstrasse 17. **GPS**: n54,27101 e9,30015.

12 € 6 + € 1/pp (12x) WC included. **Location:** Rural, comfortable, quiet. **Surface:** grassy. 01/01-31/12
Distance: 200m 50m 50m 200m 200m.

S **Plön** 5B2

Wohnmobilhafen Plön, Ascheberger straße 76. **GPS**: n54,14709 e10,39841.

14 € 15 Ch WC included. **Location:** Comfortable, noisy.
Surface: grassy/gravel. 01/04-15/12

DE

Distance: 1,5km on the spot.

S Plön 5B2

Womo-Stop Kleinen Plöner See, Hamburgerstrasse/Aschenberg strasse, B430. **GPS**: n54,15278 e10,40417.

16 € 5 € 0,50 € 0,50 Ch. **Location:** Simple. **Surface:** metalled.
01/01-31/12
Distance: on the spot.
Remarks: Max. 24h, in front of passage to beach. Driving ou village dir Neumünster.

Tourist information Plön:
Tourist Info Plön, Am Lübschen Tor 1, www.touristinfo-ploen.de.Small town around 17th century Schloss Plön. Many watersports.

S Pommerby 5A1

Campingplatz Seehof, Gammeldam 5. **GPS**: n54,76495 e9,96782.

5 € 3,75 + € 4,50/pp, child € 2, dog € 2 Ch € 2/day WC € 0,50/5 € 2,50/time. **Location:** Rural, simple, quiet. **Surface:** grassy/gravel.
01/04-31/10
Distance: on the spot on the spot.

S Preetz 5B2

Wohnmobilpark Kirchsee, Kahlbrook 25a. **GPS**: n54,22811 e10,28616.

10 € 5, 01/04-30/10 € 15 included WC . **Surface:** gravel.
01/01-31/12 service 01/11-31/03.
Distance: 10min on the spot on the spot.
Remarks: Bread-service, canoe and bicycle rental.

S Puttgarden 5C1

Wohnmobilplatz Johannisberg, Johannisbergstrasse. **GPS**: n54,50208 e11,18000.

50 € 6 + € 4/pp, dog € 2 € 2,50 Ch € 2,50 WC . **Location:** Rural, simple, quiet. **Surface:** grassy/metalled. 01/01-31/12
Distance: 2,5km 800m 800m on the spot.
Remarks: In nature reserve Am Grüner Brink, bread-service.

S Puttgarden 5C1

Bade- und Surfstrand Grüner Brink, Krögenweg. **GPS**: n54,51174 e11,18285.
30 € 8 € 2,50 Ch. **Surface:** gravel. 01/01-31/12
Distance: on the spot.

S Quickborn bei Burg 4D3

Am Helmschen-Bach, Hauptstraße 2. **GPS**: n54,01165 e9,21648.

6 € 5 . **Location:** Rural, comfortable, quiet. **Surface:** grassy.
01/04-30/09
Distance: 300m on the spot.

S Ratzeburg 5B3

Hallenbad Aqua Siwa, Fischerstrasse 43. **GPS**: n53,69567 e10,77598.

12 € 7 € 1/80liter Ch € 0,50/kWh. **Location:** Urban, simple, central, noisy. **Surface:** gravel. 01/01-31/12
Distance: 500m on the spot on the spot on the spot.
Remarks: On the island, at swimming pool.

S Reinfeld 5B3

Am Herrenteich, Klosterstraße. **GPS**: n53,83024 e10,48362.

5 free € 0,50/70liter € 0,50 Ch € 0,50/kWh. **Location:** Urban, simple, quiet. **Surface:** metalled. 01/01-31/12
Distance: 500m.

DE

S Rendsburg 5A2

Wohnmobil-Hafen Eiderblick, An der Untereider 9. **GPS**: n54,30406 e9,65610.

45 € 13 € 1/75liter Ch (45x)€ 0,50/1kWh WC € 0,50/7minutes against payment. **Location:** Urban, luxurious, central, quiet. **Surface:** gravel. 01/01-31/12

Distance: 800m on the spot 800m on the spot on the spot on the spot.

Remarks: Internetcafé, bread-service.

Tourist information Rendsburg:

Tourist-Information Nord-Ostsee-kanal, Altstädter Markt 1, www.rendsburg.de.Small town on canal.

Eiserne Lady.Train-bridge North Sea-Baltic Canal, 42m high.

Blue Line.City walk 3 km.

Hausbrauerei Niewarker, Paradeplatz.Guided tour and tastery.

S Reußenköge 4D1

Amsinck Haus, Sönke Nissenkoog 36a. **GPS**: n54,61666 e8,87027.

9 € 7 (6x)€ 2/day WC € 3. **Location:** Rural, comfortable, isolated, quiet. **Surface:** asphalted. 01/01-31/12

S Schacht-Audorf 5A2

WohnmobilPark Schacht-Audorf, K76. **GPS**: n54,30611 e9,71250.

38 € 10 € 0,50/100liter Ch (33x)€ 0,60/1kWh WC € 0,50/time € 1/time. **Location:** Rural, comfortable. **Surface:** gravel. 01/01-31/12

Distance: 700m A7 2km 800m 800m on the spot.

Remarks: Max. 3 nights.

S Scharbeutz 5B3

Reisemobilplatz Hamburger Ring, Hamburgerring/Trelleborg Strasse. **GPS**: n54,03028 e10,75222.

70 € 10/24h, 01/04-31/10 beach tax € 3,50 € 1/100liter Ch (2x)€ 1. **Location:** Rural. **Surface:** sand. 01/01-31/12

Distance: 300m 300m, dog friendly beach 1km 400m.

S Schashagen 5C2

Wohnmobilpark Ostseeblick, Biesdorf. **GPS**: n54,11934 e10,92108.

30 01/04-30/09 € 10-13, 2 pers.incl., dog € 1,50-2,50 Ch € 2,50 WC . **Location:** Rural, comfortable, quiet. **Surface:** grasstiles. 01/01-31/12 Service facilities.

Distance: 300m.

Remarks: If campsite is closed free, (6x) electricity € 1/5h.

S Schleswig 5A2

Am Stadthafen, Am Hafen 5. **GPS**: n54,51167 e9,56917.

45 € 14 Ch WC € 2,50/time included. **Location:** Urban, comfortable, central. **Surface:** gravel/metalled. 01/01-31/12

Distance: 150m 5km on the spot on the spot 50m 300m nearby 50m.

Remarks: Max 48h, check in at harbourmaster.

Tourist information Schleswig:

Tourist Information Schleswig, Plessenstrasse 7.Historical city, founded by the Vikings, Haithabu.

Schloß Gottorf.Regional museum, archeological museum and museum for art and culture.

Museum am Danewerk, Ochsenweg 5, Dannewerk.Fortifications, 650-1200. winter 10-16h, 01/04-31/10 Tue-Fri 9-17h, Sa-Su 10-18h.

Outsidermuseum, Stadweg 54.Creativity/art from psychiatry. Wed-Thu 14.30-17.30h.

Stadtmuseum, Friedrichstr 9.City museum. Tue-Su 10-17h.

Wikinger Museum Haithabu, Haddeby-Busdorf.All about the life of the Vikings. 01/04-31/10 9-17h, 01/11-31/03 Tue-Su 10-16h.

Tolk-Schau, Tolk.Family park. 01/04-30/09 10-18h.

DE

Schönberg/Ostsee 5B2

Brasilien, Seesternweg. **GPS**: n54,42408 e10,39116.

40 € 9, 15/05-15/09 € 11 Ch included. **Location:** Rural, simple. **Surface:** grassy. 01/01-31/12

Distance: 200m 200m.

Schönberg/Ostsee 5B2

Stellplatz Mittelstrand, Mittelstrand. **GPS**: n54,42233 e10,39573.

50 € 9, 15/05-15/09 € 11 Ch € 2 WC. **Location:** Rural.

Surface: grassy. 01/01-31/12

Distance: 200m 200m on the spot.

Remarks: Bread-service in summer period.

Seestermühe 5A4

Achtern Diek. **GPS**: n53,70333 e9,56232.

4 free. **Surface:** metalled. 01/01-31/12

Distance: 200m.

Sehestedt 5A2

Wohnmobilstellplatz Sehestedt, Fährstrasse 1. **GPS**: n54,36466 e9,81973.

13 € 7/24h € 0,50/80liter Ch. **Surface:** gravel.

01/01-31/12

Distance: 750m A7 13km on the spot 200m.

Remarks: Directly at North Sea-Baltic canal.

Sierksdorf 5B3

Wohnmobilstellplatz Hof Sierksdorf, Altonaer Straße. **GPS**: n54,06013 e10,75737.

15 € 11 € 1 € 1 Ch € 0,50/kWh WC . **Surface:** gravel.

01/04-15/10

Distance: beach 100m.

Simonsberg 4D2

Nordsee Camping Zum Seehund, Lundenbergweg 4. **GPS**: n54,45515 e8,96958.

30 € 15 Ch WC included € 5. **Location:** Rural, comfortable, isolated, quiet. **Surface:** gravel. Easter-31/10

Distance: 2km 500m on the spot on the spot.

Remarks: Use steam bath, sauna, fitness-studio incl.

Sörup 5A1

Südensee, Seeblick. **GPS**: n54,71216 e9,66611.

5 € 4 Ch € 2/night WC. **Location:** Rural, simple, quiet.

Surface: grassy. 01/01-31/12

Distance: on the spot on the spot kiosk.

Remarks: Parking at small lake.

St.Peter Ording 4C2

Reisemobilhafen St.Peter-Ording, Am Ketelskoog. **GPS**: n54,30881 e8,63522.

70 € 12 € 1/50liter Ch (70x)€ 0,60/kWh WC € 0,20 € 1 € 1.

Location: Rural, comfortable. **Surface:** gravel. 01/01-31/12

Distance: 300m 1km 300m 300m.

Remarks: Wed, market.

Tourist information St.Peter Ording:

www.st.peter-ording.de.Seaside resort on the Wadden coast.

Westküstenpark, Wohldweg 6.Animal park. summer 9.30-19h, winter 10.30h-sunset.

Süderlügum 4D1

Wohnmobilplatz Mehrzweckhalle, Jahnstrasse. **GPS**: n54,87472 e8,90306.

5 free. **Location:** Rural, central, quiet. **Surface:** metalled.

01/01-31/12

DE

Distance: 500m 300m.

S Timmendorfer Strand 5B3

Am Vogelpark, P4, Bäderrandstraße, B76. **GPS**: n53,99136 e10,81439.

50 € 7,50 + tourist tax € 0,50/120liter Ch . **Location:** Rural. **Surface:** grassy/sand. 01/01-31/12
Distance: 180m.
Remarks: Max. 1 night.

S Tönning 4D2

Wohnmobilplatz Eiderblick - Kapitänshaus, Am Strandweg. **GPS**: n54,30920 e8,93684.

33+15 € 11 2p incl., excl. tourist tax € 1/100liter Ch € 0,50/kWh included € 3,50,dryer € 3. **Location:** Rural, luxurious, isolated, quiet. **Surface:** grassy. 01/01-31/12
Distance: 500m on the spot on the spot on the spot.
Remarks: Along the Eider river.

S Travemünde 5C3

Wohnmobilparkplatz Kowitzberg, Kowitzberg. **GPS**: n53,97598 e10,87830.

49 15/5-14/9 € 10, 15/9-14/5 € 6 € 1/100liter Ch (48x)€ 1/5kWh.
Location: Urban. **Surface:** grassy. 01/01-31/12
Distance: 2,5km 800m 800m 300m 250m 50m.
Remarks: Near golfcourse and Brodtener Ufer.

S Travemünde 5C3

Parkplatz am Fischerreihafen, Auf dem Baggersand 15. **GPS**: n53,95556 e10,86139.

120 € 12-14 € 1/50liter Ch (5x)€ 3/kWh WC € 2. **Location:** Urban, simple. **Surface:** gravel. 01/01-31/12
Distance: beach 1,8km max. 250m express bus Altstadt Lubeck.
Remarks: Parking fishing port, no camping activities.

Tourist information Travemünde:
Lübeck und Travemünde Tourist-Service, Strandpromenade 1b, www.travemuende.de.

Uetersen 5A4

Am Stichhafen, Ziegelei. **GPS**: n53,67977 e9,66861.
4 free. **Surface:** metalled. 01/01-31/12
Distance: 400m 7,4km 300m.

S Wedel 5A4

Am Freibad. **GPS**: n53,57860 e9,69520.

20 € 6 € 1/10minutes Ch (14x)€ 1/8h WC . **Location:** Rural, simple, quiet. **Surface:** grassy/metalled.
01/01-31/12 during event.
Distance: 800m.
Remarks: Max. 3 days.

S Westerholz 5A1

Campingplatz Fördeblick, Kummle 1. **GPS**: n54,81998 e9,66686.
45 € 7 € 1 Ch € 2,50/night WC . **Location:** Rural, simple, quiet. **Surface:** grassy. 01/04-15/10
Distance: 150m.
Remarks: At Flensborg Fjord, max. 24h.

S Wilster 4D3

Colosseumplatz, Etatsrätin-doos-strasse 14-17. **GPS**: n53,92419 e9,37449.

15 free Ch € 0,50. **Location:** Urban, simple, central, quiet.
Surface: grassy/gravel. 01/01-31/12 fair.
Distance: 200m 100m on the spot.

Tourist information Wilster:
Wilstermarsch Service GmbH, Mühlenstrasse 13, www.wilstermarsch-service.de.

S Wischhafen 4D3

Hafenstrasse 6. **GPS**: n53,77278 e9,32278.

15 € 3 (6x)€ 1/kWh. **Location:** Rural, simple. **Surface:** grassy/gravel.
01/01-31/12

DE

Distance: ⊗500m 1km.

Wischhafen 4D3

Ziegelstraße, Gewerbegebiet Wischhafen. **GPS**: n53,76417 e9,32111.

8 €3 Chfree. **Location:** Rural, simple. **Surface:** gravel.
01/01-31/12
Distance: 1km 200m.

Wischhafen 4D3

Süder-Elbe, Glückstädter Straße. **GPS**: n53,78678 e9,34017.

15 €3. **Location:** Rural, simple, isolated. **Surface:** sand.
01/01-31/12
Distance: 3km ⊗150m.
Remarks: Parking at ferry-boat.

Wischhafen 4D3

Unterm Deich 7. **GPS**: n53,77528 e9,32111.

6 €3. **Location:** Rural, simple. **Surface:** grassy.
01/01-31/12
Distance: 300m ⊗on the spot 1km.

Tourist information Wischhafen:

M Kehdinger Küstenschifffahrtsmuseum, Unterm Deich 7.Shipping museum.
Easter-16/11. T €3.

Lower Saxony/Bremen

Adendorf 5B5

Freizeitzentrum, Scharnebecker Weg. **GPS**: n53,28925 e10,45398.

10 free (4x)€0,50/kWh. **Location:** Rural, simple, noisy.
01/01-31/12
Distance: 500m.
Remarks: Parking sports centre, max. 3 days, swimming pool and sauna on site.

Aerzen 9D2

Restaurant Waldquelle, Waldquelle 1. **GPS**: n52,05952 e9,26146.

3 €4 €1. **Surface:** metalled. 01/01-31/12 Tue.
Distance: 2km 1km 500m.

Ahlerstedt 5A4

Ahlerstedt Ottendorf, Rickstücken 2. **GPS**: n53,38908 e9,41017.

25 €8 Ch included. **Location:** Rural, simple.
Surface: metalled. 01/01-31/12
Distance: 3km 3km.

Alfeld/Leine 10A2

Bornstrasse. **GPS**: n51,98586 e9,82769.

4 free. **Surface:** metalled. 01/01-31/12
Distance: on the spot ⊗nearby 200m.
Remarks: Parking in city centre behind the evangelical church.

Altenau 10B2

Restaurant Alter Bahnhof, Rothenbergerstrasse 52. **GPS**: n51,79879 e10,43320.

20 €12, tourist tax incl €1 €1 Ch €3,50 WC. **Surface:** metalled.
01/01-31/12
Distance: 1km ⊗2km 1km on the spot on the spot 2km on the spot.

S Altenau 10B2

Kristall-Saunatherme Heißer Brocken, Karl-Reinecke-Weg 35. **GPS**: n51,79836 e10,44408.

20 € 10 excl. tourist tax Ch. **Surface:** metalled.

01/01-31/12

Distance: on the spot on the spot.

S Amelinghausen 5B5

Lopausee, Auf der Kalten Hude. **GPS**: n53,13324 e10,23441.

50 € 5, 1/9-1/7 € 3,50 Ch included. **Location:** Simple, isolated, quiet. **Surface:** gravel/sand.

01/01-31/12

Distance: 1km 100m 100m 1km 1km on the spot on the spot.

Remarks: Ticket at station, kiosk Lopausee, pay desk Waldbad and tourist office.

S Amelinghausen 5B5

Waldbad, Zum Lopautal. **GPS**: n53,12402 e10,23018.

40 € 8 Ch included. **Location:** Comfortable.

01/01-31/12

Distance: 1km 500m 1km 1km on the spot on the spot.

Remarks: Including access to swimming pool, bread-service.

Amelinghausen 5B5

Kronsbergheide, Hochseilgarten. **GPS**: n53,13500 e10,23389.

10 € 5, 1/9-1/7 € 3,50. **Location:** Rural, simple, isolated, quiet.

01/01-31/12

Distance: 1km 500m on the spot 1km 1km on the spot on the spot.

Remarks: Ticket at station, kiosk Lopausee, pay desk Waldbad and tourist office.

Amelinghausen 5B5

Schwindbeckerheide, Steinbeckerstrasse, Soderstorf. **GPS**: n53,12247 e10,09934.

15 € 5. **Location:** Rural, simple, isolated. **Surface:** metalled/sand.

01/01-31/12

Distance: 6km on the spot on the spot.

Remarks: Ticket at station, kiosk Lopausee, pay desk Waldbad and tourist office.

S Amelinghausen 5B5

Gasthaus Eichenkrug, Unter den Eichen 10, Dehnsen. **GPS**: n53,12804 e10,16817.

4 € 5 included. **Location:** Simple, isolated. **Surface:** metalled.

01/01-31/12

Distance: 4km on the spot 4km on the spot on the spot.

Remarks: Max. 3 nights.

S Amelinghausen 5B5

Gasthaus Schenck, Lüneburgerstrasse 48. **GPS**: n53,12568 e10,21426.

15 € 5 WC included. **Location:** Simple, central. **Surface:** metalled.

Distance: on the spot on the spot on the spot on the spot on the spot.

Tourist information Amelinghausen:

Touristikcenter Amelinghausen, Lüneburger strasse 55.Signposted cycle and hiking routes.

Oldendorfer Totenstatt.Hunnebed cineraria from the ice-age. guided tour 01/05-30/09.

Jachtmuseum Wulff, Hässelmühler WegOerrel. Wed-Sa 14-18h, Su 11-17h.

S Ankum 9B1

Ferienhof Buse-Glass, Tütingen 5. **GPS**: n52,51431 e7,86842.

DE

5 € 14 WC included. **Location:** Quiet. **Surface:** grassy.
01/01-31/12
Distance: 2,5km 500m 2,5km.

Apen 4B5

Am Freibad, Hauptstraße, Hengstforde. **GPS:** n53,21795 e7,78706.

10 free. **Location:** Rural, simple. **Surface:** metalled.
01/05-15/09
Distance: 5,8km 50 m.
Remarks: Swimming pool Hengstforde, along railwayline.

Apen 4B5

Viehmarktplatz, Hauptstraße. **GPS:** n53,21820 e7,80221.

10 free. **Location:** Simple. **Surface:** metalled. 01/01-31/12
Distance: 100m 5km.

Artlenburg 5B4

Am Sportboothafen, Am Deich 9. **GPS:** n53,37680 e10,48550.

40 € 10 Ch WC . **Location:** Comfortable, quiet.
Surface: grassy.
15/04-15/10
Distance: 500m on the spot on the spot 500m 500m 500m.
Remarks: Along the river Elbe.

Aurich 4B4

Alter Bahnhof, Emderstrasse. **GPS:** n53,47031 e7,47356.

12 free. **Surface:** metalled. 01/03-31/12
Distance: 200m on the spot.
Remarks: Max. 3 nights.

Aurich 4B4

An den Kiesgruben, Tannenhausen. **GPS:** n53,52173 e7,47834.

40 free. **Surface:** unpaved.
Distance: 10m on the spot.
Remarks: At the lake of Tannenhausen.

Aurich 4B4

Landgasthof Alte Post, Essenerstrasse. **GPS:** n53,54573 e7,60736.

6 € 6, guests € 3 € 1 Ch WC. **Surface:** metalled.
01/01-31/12
Distance: on the spot.
Remarks: Caution key service € 10.

Bad Bentheim 9A1

Am Mühlenberg, Mühlenberg. **GPS:** n52,29360 e7,10095.

10 € 7 € 1/80liter Ch € 0,50/kWh WC. **Location:** Rural. **Surface:** metalled. 01/01-31/12
Distance: 200m 50m on the spot on the spot.

Bad Bentheim 9A1

Am Schloßpark, Funkenstiege. **GPS:** n52,30328 e7,15448.

30 € 7 € 1/80liter Ch € 0,50/kWh WC. **Surface:** metalled.
01/01-31/12
Distance: 200m 100m.

Bad Bevensen 5B5

Reisemobilplatz, Am Waagekai. **GPS**: n53,07417 e10,60139.

30 € 10, 2 pers.incl Ch included € 1. **Location:** Rural, simple, quiet. **Surface:** gravel/sand. 01/01-31/12
Distance: 1km on the spot 1km 600m.

Bad Essen 9C1

Wohnmobilstellplatz Falkenburg, Falkenburg 3. **GPS**: n52,32352 e8,36384.

50 € 6, 3 pers.incl. € 1/100liter Ch € 2/4kWh WC € 0,50.
Location: Rural, comfortable, quiet. **Surface:** grassy/metalled.
01/03-30/10
Distance: 1,2km 900m 300m.
Remarks: Along the Mittelland canal, near marina.

Tourist information Bad Essen:
Tourist-Information Bad Essen, Lindenstr. 39, www.badessen.info.Small town with historical city centre.

Bad Gandersheim 10B2

Wohnmobil-Stellplatz Rio Gande, An der Wiek. **GPS**: n51,87191 e10,01881.

Photo

24 € 5/24h € 1/30liter Ch (14x)€ 0,50/kWh. **Surface:** gravel.
01/01-31/12
Distance: 400m 100m 200m.
Remarks: Bread-service in summer period. Follow 'P Stadtmitte' then 'Wohnmobilstellplatz'.

Tourist information Bad Gandersheim:
Tourist- Information, Stiftsfreiheit 12.Historical town with half-timbered houses.

Bad Lauterberg 10B3

Erlebnisbad Vitamar, Mast Tal 1. **GPS**: n51,63358 e10,48661.

5 free € 1 € 1 Ch. **Surface:** metalled. 01/01-31/12
Distance: 1,5km 1,5km 1,5km on the spot.

Bad Lauterberg 10B3

Wiesenbeker Teich. **GPS**: n51,61719 e10,49074.

4 € 13 Ch included. **Surface:** gravel. 01/01-31/12
Distance: on the spot.

Bad Lauterberg 10B3

Hotel-Restaurant Zur Post, Osterhagener Strasse 6. **GPS**: n51,59090 e10,48993.

3 guests free WC included. **Surface:** grassy/metalled.
01/01-31/12
Distance: on the spot on the spot 200m.

Bad Münder 10A1

Wermuthstrasse. **GPS**: n52,19837 e9,46067.

2 free. **Surface:** metalled. 01/01-31/12
Distance: 200m 200m on the spot on the spot.
Remarks: 19-9h.

Bad Münder 10A1

Rhomelbad, Lindenallee. **GPS**: n52,19305 e9,47111.

DE

10 free. **Surface:** metalled. 01/01-31/12
Distance: 400m on the spot 400m 200m.

Bad Nenndorf 10A1

Wohnmobilstellplatz am Schulzentrum, Bahnhofstrasse 77. **GPS**: n52,34294 e9,37666.
8 free € 2/45liter Ch (8x)€ 1/6h WC . **Surface:** metalled.
01/01-31/12
Distance: 700m 3,4km on the spot on the spot.

Bad Pyrmont 9D2

Reisemobilplatz am Gondelteich, Südstrasse/Milchweg. **GPS**: n51,98073 e9,24828.

22 € 7/24h 2 pers incl € 1/100liter € 1 Ch € 0,50/kWh.
Surface: asphalted.
01/01-31/12
Distance: 400m 500m 500m.
Remarks: To pay at swimming pool, free access Kurpark and palm tree garden, and several discounts.

Tourist information Bad Pyrmont:
Bad Pyrmont Tourismus GmbH, Europa-Platz 1, www.badpyrmont.de.Health resort.

Bad Sachsa 10C3

Wohnmobilplatz auf dem Schützenplatz, Im Osteral. **GPS**: n51,60361 e10,54939.

72 € 7 € 0,50 € 0,50 Ch € 0,50/kWh WC .
Surface: gravel.
01/01-31/12 3rd weekend July.
Distance: on the spot 800m.

Bad Sachsa 10C3

Gasthof Alter Grenzkrug, Nüxei 5. **GPS**: n51,56838 e10,52133.

20 € 5, guests free WC . **Surface:** asphalted/gravel.
01/01-31/12
Distance: 2km on the spot 2km.
Remarks: Arrival <21h.

Bad Sachsa 10C3

Zum Kachelofen, Schützenstrasse 13. **GPS**: n51,59778 e10,55056.

2 guests free. 01/01-31/12
Distance: on the spot on the spot 100m.
Remarks: Max. 2 days.

Bad Zwischenahn 4B5

Wohnmobilstellplatz Am Badepark, Am Badepark. **GPS**: n53,18722 e8,00021.

35 € 8,50 € 0,50/70liter Ch (35x)€ 1/2kWh WC € 3,(spa resort).
Location: Urban, simple. **Surface:** metalled.
01/01-31/12
Distance: on the spot 6,8km on the spot on the spot 100m 500m on the spot.

Balge 4D6

Blenhorster Bauernhof, Klünderberg 1. **GPS**: n52,71361 e9,13011.

20 € 5 included. **Surface:** grassy. 01/01-31/12
Distance: on the spot.

Balje 4D3

Naturkundemuseum Niederelbe, Neuenhof, Neuhaus. **GPS**: n53,81958 e9,03867.

DE

6 free. **Location:** Rural, simple, isolated.
01/01-31/12
Distance: 4km on the spot 4km 4km.

Barßel 4B5

Am Bootshafen, Deichstrasse. **GPS**: n53,16754 e7,73441.

14 + 20 € 6 Ch (34x)€ 2/24h WC included € 1. **Location:** Urban, simple. **Surface:** grasstiles. 01/01-31/12
Distance: 500m on the spot on the spot 500m.

Barsinghausen 10A1

Wohnmobilstellplatz am Besucherbergwerk Klosterstollen, Conrad-Bühreweg. **GPS**: n52,29858 e9,46943.

5 € 6,50 included. **Surface:** metalled. 01/01-31/12
Distance: 300m nearby 300m.
Remarks: Max. 3 days.

Berge 4B6

Stift Börstel, Börstel 5. **GPS**: n52,64957 e7,69438.
2 € 5, in envelope in mail box On demand. **Surface:** metalled.
01/01-31/12
Remarks: Near abbey, max. 2 nights.

Berge 4B6

Dorfteich Berge, Schienenweg 19. **GPS**: n52,62011 e7,75099.
2 free. 01/01-31/12

Bergen 5A6

Ziegeleiweg. **GPS**: n52,81273 e9,96457.

6 € 3,50 € 1 Ch . **Surface:** gravel. 01/01-31/12
Distance: nearby on the spot.
Remarks: Caution key € 20 at town hall.

Tourist information Bergen:
Wildpark Lüneburger Heide, Nindorf.Game preserve.
01/03-31/10 8-19h, 01/11-28/02 9-16.30h.

Berne 4C5

Fähranleger Motzen, Motzener Strasse. **GPS**: n53,17972 e8,55778.

4 free € 1 Ch (4x)€ 1. **Surface:** metalled. 01/01-31/12
Distance: 3,5km on the spot 1km 100m.
Remarks: Parking at ferry-boat at river Weser.

Bevern 10A2

Schwimm- und Freizeitzentrum, Jahnstrasse. **GPS**: n51,85750 e9,50805.

5 free. **Surface:** asphalted. 01/01-31/12
Distance: 1,2km 500m 500m.

Bienenbüttel 5B5

Wohnmobilstellplatz Ilmenauwiese, Niendorfer strasse, K42. **GPS**: n53,14514 e10,49051.

12 € 6 € 1/8minutes Ch (12x)€ 1/8h WC € 0,50. **Location:** Rural, comfortable, quiet. **Surface:** metalled. 01/01-31/12
Distance: 500m on the spot on the spot 500m 500m special sculpture route.
Remarks: Follow 'Ilmenauhalle'.

Bippen 9B1

Dorfteich, Hauptstrasse. **GPS**: n52,58209 e7,73887.
2 free. 01/01-31/12

Bippen 9B1

Ferienhof Neyenhuis, Hallweg. **GPS**: n52,59360 e7,73005.

DE

20 € 10 WC € 2. **Location:** Rural, simple, quiet.
Surface: grassy. 01/01-31/12
Distance: 1km.

Bippen 9B1

Gasthof Mol, Einigkeitsstraße 20, Lonnerbecke. **GPS:** n52,54337 e7,67118.
10 free Service € 7/day.
Distance: on the spot.

Bispingen 5A5

Parkplatz Oberhaverbeck, Oberhaverbeck. **GPS:** n53,14281 e9,91998.

100 € 3/day, € 6/night € 1/10minutes Ch (8x)€ 1/10h.
Location: Rural, simple, isolated. **Surface:** grassy/gravel.
01/01-31/12 Service: winter.
Distance: on the spot on the spot on the spot.
Remarks: In nature reserve the the Lüneburg Heide (heath).

Bispingen 5A5

Parking Rathaus, Borsteler Straße 4-6. **GPS:** n53,08499 e9,99789.

5 free. **Location:** Simple, central. **Surface:** metalled.
01/01-31/12
Distance: on the spot 1km 100m 100m on the spot on the spot.

Bispingen 5A5

Reiter- und Ferienhof Cohrs, Volkwardingen 1, Moorweg. **GPS:** n53,13409 e10,00047.

10 € 14 Ch included WC € 3. **Location:** Comfortable, isolated, quiet. **Surface:** grassy. 01/01-31/12

Distance: 3km 5,5km 500m 5km on the spot.
Remarks: Bread-service.

Bissendorf 9C1

Reisemobil-Center Veregge & Welz, Gewerbepark 14, A30 Abfahrt Bissendorf.
GPS: n52,24026 e8,13977.

5 free € 1/5minutes Ch (4x)€ 1/6h. **Location:** Urban, simple, quiet. **Surface:** metalled. 01/01-31/12
Distance: 1km 650m 800m 800m.

Bleckede 5C5

Campingpark Elbtalaue, Am Waldbad 23. **GPS:** n53,25948 e10,80526.

15 € 14, 2 pers incl € 1 Ch € 3,50/night,or € 0,50/0,8kWh WC included € 3,50,dryer € 3 € 4/day,€ 9/3 days.
Location: Rural, luxurious, isolated, quiet. **Surface:** grassy.
01/01-31/12
Distance: 2km 300m 800m 6km 50m.

Blomberg 4B4

Dorfplatz Blomberg, Hauptstrasse. **GPS:** n53,57718 e7,55815.

20 free Ch€ 1 € 0,50/30minutes WC. **Surface:** grassy/metalled.
01/01-31/12
Distance: on the spot 200m 200m 50m.

Bockenem 10B2

Am Freibad, In den Reesen. **GPS:** n52,00787 e10,13610.

5 free. **Surface:** grassy. 01/01-31/12
Distance: 800m 200m 300m.

DE

Bockenem 10B2

Hotel Sauer am Aral Autohof, Allensteiner strasse 7. **GPS**: n52,00224 e10,13379.

20 guests free € 1,50 Ch € 1,50 WC. **Surface:** metalled.
01/01-31/12
Distance: 300m on the spot 500m.

Bockhorn 4B5

Reisemobilplatz Germer, Am Geeschendamm 1. **GPS**: n53,38575 e8,00857.

30 € 6 € 1,50 Ch (30x)€ 1,50/24h WC € 2. **Location:** Comfortable. 01/01-31/12

Bockhorn 4B5

Erlebnisbad, Urwaldstrasse 35a. **GPS**: n53,39876 e7,99410.

5 free. **Location:** Rural. **Surface:** metalled.
01/01-31/12 on the spot.
Remarks: Parking swimming pool, max. 1 day.

Bockhorn 4B5

Gaststätte Altdeutsche Diele, Landesstrasse 11, Steinhausen. **GPS**: n53,41539 e8,03622.

3 free (3x)against payment. **Location:** Simple. **Surface:** metalled.
01/01-31/12

Bockhorn 4B5

Gaststätte Zum Sandkrug, Sandkrugsweg 21,Grabstede. **GPS**: n53,35893 e8,00186.

4 free. **Location:** Rural, simple, quiet. **Surface:** grassy.
01/01-31/12
Distance: on the spot.

Bodenwerder 10A2

Parkplatz Am Mühlentor. **GPS**: n51,98037 e9,51795.

15 € 6 € 1/10minutes € 1 Ch WC € 1. **Surface:** grassy/metalled.
01/01-31/12
Distance: 500m 500m 500m 500m.

Bohmte 9C1

Golfclub Arenshorst, Arenshorster Kirchweg 2. **GPS**: n52,35651 e8,28450.

3 guests free. **Location:** Rural, simple. **Surface:** grassy/metalled.
01/01-31/12
Distance: 3km on the spot 3km.

Bohmte 9C1

Landgasthaus Gieseke-Asshorn, Bremer strasse 55. **GPS**: n52,36674 e8,31261.

4 guests free free. **Location:** Urban, quiet. **Surface:** metalled.
01/01-31/12
Distance: on the spot on the spot 200m.

Bohmte 9C1

VARIOmobil Fahrzeugbau GmbH, Bremer strasse. **GPS**: n52,38623 e8,30761.

DE

2 free Ch free. **Location:** Rural, quiet. **Surface:** metalled.
01/01-31/12
Distance: 500m 1km 1km.
Remarks: Service only during opening hours.

Bomlitz 5A6

Am Weltvogelpark, Am Vogelpark. **GPS:** n52,88425 e9,59720.

50 free. **Location:** Rural, simple, central. **Surface:** grassy.
01/01-31/12
Distance: 2,5km on the spot 2,5km.
Remarks: Max. 1 night.

S Brake 4C5

Am Binnenhafen, Hafenstrasse. **GPS:** n53,32802 e8,48296.

4 free € 1 Ch € 1. **Surface:** metalled. 01/01-31/12
Distance: on the spot 100m 200m.

S Brake 4C5

City-Parkplatz, Breite Strasse. **GPS:** n53,32583 e8,47944.

2 free . **Surface:** metalled. 01/01-31/12
Distance: on the spot on the spot 100m.
Remarks: Key at touristoffice: An der Kaje ± 1km.

S Bramsche 9C1

Wohnmobilstellplatz Waldwinkel, Zum Dreschhaus 4. **GPS:** n52,39591 e8,10244.

60 € 6 € 1,50/70liter Ch (80x)€ 2 WC € 1. **Location:** Rural, comfortable, quiet. **Surface:** grassy. 01/01-31/12
Distance: 3,5km 100m 3,5km on the spot on the spot.
Remarks: Next to campsite Waldwinkel.

Bramsche 9C1

Hasebad, Malgartener strasse 49. **GPS:** n52,41493 e7,99423.

10 free. **Location:** Urban, simple, quiet. **Surface:** metalled.
01/01-31/12
Distance: 500m.

S Bramsche 9C1

Reisemobile Lewandowsky, Am Kanal 1b. **GPS:** n52,38524 e7,92958.

2 free Ch free € 2/day. **Location:** Rural, simple.
Surface: gravel.
01/01-31/12
Distance: 1km 1km 1km.
Remarks: Also repairs possible, walking and bicycle area.

Tourist information Bramsche:

- Stadtmarketing Bramsche GmbH, Maschstrasse 9, www.bramsche.de.
- Tuchmacher museum.History of the textile industry.
- Tue-Fri, Su 10-18h, Sa 14-18h. € 3.
- Varusschlacht im Osnabrücker Land.Battle of the Teutons against the Roman.
- 10-18h. € 5.

S Braunlage 10C2

Schützenplatz, Schützenstrasse 21. **GPS:** n51,71658 e10,60847.

85 € 9,50, tourist tax € 2,20/pp/day Ch WC included.

DE

01/01-31/12
Distance: Café Restaurant Hubertushöhe.
Remarks: Exit Braunlage-Mitte via Lauterberger Strasse and Bahnhofstrasse.

S Braunschweig 10B1

Theodor Heussstrasse. **GPS**: n52,24971 e10,52004.

15 free (16x)€ 1/h. **Surface:** asphalted. 01/01-31/12
Distance: 2km on the spot.
Remarks: Parking exhibition ground.

S Bremen 4D5

Wohnmobil Oase Bremen, Schoster born, via Emil von Behringstrasse. **GPS**: n53,06778 e8,86333.

10 € 13 € 2 Ch WC included,use luxurious bathroom € 5, sauna € 5 € 6. **Surface:** grasstiles. 01/01-31/12
Distance: 3km on the spot 50m Tram.

S Bremen 4D5

Am Kuhhirten, Kurhirtenweg. **GPS**: n53,06500 e8,81871.

30/45 € 10 € 1/100liter Ch (30x)€ 0,50/kWh WC Use sanitary € 1.
Surface: grasstiles.
Distance: Old city centre 1,3km 500m on the spot 800m Tram 700m.

S Bremen 4D5

Bremer Schweiz, Im Pohl, Lesum. **GPS**: n53,16765 e8,69560.

7 € 5/24h € 1/10minutes Ch (8x)€ 1.
Surface: gravel.

Tourist information Bremen:
Tourist Information, Obernstrasse en Hauptbahnhof, www.bremen-tourism.de.
Hanseatic city and second harbour of Germany.
Böttcherstrasse.Pedestrian passage.
Bremer Ratskeller.Winery, 650 German wines.
11-24h.
Antik- und Trödelmarkt, Weserpromenade Schlachte.Antiques and flea market.
Sa 8-14h.
Bremer Freimarkt, Marktplatz.Large folk festival.
15/10-31/10.

S Bremerhaven 4C4

Reisemobil-Parkplatz Doppelschleuse, An der Neuen Schleuse. **GPS**: n53,53230 e8,57607.

63 € 6,50 € 1 Ch € 0,50/kWh WC . **Surface:** asphalted.
01/01-31/12
Distance: 1,5km 1,5km 1,2km.
Remarks: Bread-service.

S Bremerhaven 4C4

Wohnmobil-Parkplatz Fischereihafen, Hoebelstrasse, Fischereihafen 1. **GPS**: n53,52664 e8,57586.

47 € 6,50 € 1/80liter Ch (36x)€ 0,50/kWh WC € 0,50.
Surface: asphalted/metalled. 01/01-31/12
Distance: 3km 500m 500m.
Remarks: Parking in harbour.

S Bremervörde 4D4

Wohnmobilstation - Bremervörde

touristik@bremervoerde.de - www.bremervoerde.de

Located directely at lake
Excellent location for city visit
Ideal base for walking and cycling

Wohnmobilstation Bremervörde, Kiebitzweg 1. **GPS**: n53,49453 e9,15576.

DE

40 € 9,50 Ch (21x)€ 3/day,10Amp WC included € 1.
Location: Rural, comfortable, quiet.
Surface: metalled. 01/01-31/12
Distance: 2km 100m 100m 300m 1km on the spot on the spot.

S Brietlingen 5B4

Reihersee, Grosse strabe. **GPS**: n53,34344 e10,45844.

50 € 8. **Location:** Rural, simple, isolated. **Surface:** grassy.
01/03-31/10
Distance: on the spot.

Brietlingen 5B4

Hotel Franck, Bundesstrasse 31b. **GPS**: n53,32951 e10,44491.

5 free (1x)€ 2/night.
Location: Rural, simple, quiet.
Distance: on the spot on the spot 500m.

S Bruchhausen-Vilsen 4D6

Reisemobilstellplatz Bruchhausen-Vilsen, Bollenstrasse. **GPS**: n52,82671 e8,99536.

20 € 6 € 1/100liter Ch (6x)included WC. **Surface:** gravel.
01/01-31/12
Distance: 200m 200m 200m.

S Bruchhausen-Vilsen 4D6

Forsthaus Heiligenberg, Heiligenberg 3. **GPS**: n52,80377 e8,99204.

2 guests free € 1/8h WC . **Surface:** gravel. 01/01-31/12
Distance: 4km on the spot 4km.

Remarks: Arrival <22h.

Tourist information Bruchhausen-Vilsen:
M Niedersächsisches Kleinbahn-Museum, Am Bahnhof 1.Railway museum.

S Buchholz/Nordheide 5A5

Buchholz/Nordheide, Weg zum Badeteich 20. **GPS**: n53,28202 e9,87495.

12 € 12-15 Ch (6x)€ 2 WC included . **Location:** Rural, comfortable. **Surface:** metalled/sand. 01/01-31/12
Distance: 200m on the spot on the spot 200m.

S Bückeburg 9D1

Neumarktplatz, Unterwallweg 5c. **GPS**: n52,26326 e9,05040.

15 € 1/80liter Ch (6x)€ 0,50/kWh. **Surface:** metalled.
01/01-31/12
Distance: 250m 250m 250m 250m.

S Bückeburg 9D1

Wohnmobilstellplatz am Schloss, Georgstrasse/Liebesallee. **GPS**: n52,25777 e9,04583.

30 € 5 € 1 Ch (24x)€ 1/12h . **Surface:** asphalted.
01/01-31/12
Distance: 500m 500m 500m 200m.

Büddenstedt 10C1

Am Sportplatz. **GPS**: n52,17567 e11,01843.

3 free. **Surface:** asphalted. 01/01-31/12
Distance: on the spot.
Remarks: Parking swimming pool.

DE

S Bunde (Nieder-Sachsen) 4A5

Am Friedhofsweg. **GPS**: n53,18500 e7,26639.

10 € 3 € 0,50 Ch € 1. **Surface:** grasstiles. 01/01-31/12
Distance: 100m 2,3km 350m 200m.
Remarks: At townhall, max. 3 days.

S Butjadingen 4C4

Henken's Stellplatz, Am Hafen 6, Fedderwardersiel. **GPS**: n53,59581 e8,35669.

100 free, Kurtaxe € 1,10/pp, € 2,20/pp (peak season) € 1 Ch € 1 € 2,50. **Surface:** grassy. 01/01-31/12
Distance: 1km on the spot on the spot on the spot on the spot.
Remarks: Bread-service.

S Butjadingen 4C4

Knaus Campingpark Burhave, Strand Allee, Burhave. **GPS**: n53,58306 e8,37000.

70 € 15, peak season € 17, Kurtaxe incl Ch . **Surface:** grassy.
15/04-15/10
Distance: 1km on the spot 200m 1km.
Remarks: Next to campsite.

S Butjadingen 4C4

Knaus Campingpark Eckwarderhörne, Butjadinger Strasse 116, Eckwarderhörne. **GPS**: n53,52107 e8,23670.

15 € 7, € 2,20/pp tourist tax Chincluded € 3,on camp site.
Surface: grassy. 01/01-31/12
Distance: 200m on the spot 200m 200m.

S Buxtehude 5A4

Pfingstmarktplatz, Cuxhavenerstrasse, Neukloster, B73. **GPS**: n53,47974 e9,63528.

40 free € 0,50/90liter Ch € 2. **Location:** Rural, simple. **Surface:** asphalted. 01/01-31/12 week before/after Whitsuntide.
Distance: 3km Imbiss bakery 200m.
Remarks: Key shower at Imbiss.

S Buxtehude 5A4

Schützenplatz, Genslerweg. **GPS**: n53,47139 e9,69528.

30 free € 1/90liter Ch (36x)€ 1/kWh. **Location:** Urban, central.
Surface: gravel. 01/01-31/12
Distance: nearby Old city centre 50m bakery 50m.

Tourist information Buxtehude:
City with historical half-timbered houses.
Das Fleth.Old inland-port.

S Cadenberge 4D3

Reisemobilvermietung Hennig, Alter Postweg 1. **GPS**: n53,76686 e9,05681.

4 € 5 € 0,50/100liter € 1,50/24h. **Location:** Rural, simple.
Surface: grassy. 01/01-31/12
Distance: on the spot on the spot 50m.

S Celle 5B6

Schützenplatz, Hafenstraße. **GPS**: n52,62794 e10,07348.

35 free € 1 Ch WC. **Surface:** grassy/metalled. 01/01-31/12
Distance: 150m 100m.

DE

Celle 5B6

Langensalzaplatz. **GPS**: n52,61842 e10,08052.

3 free. **Surface:** metalled. 01/01-31/12

Distance: on the spot.

Clenze 5C5

Regenbogen-Hof, Mützen. **GPS**: n52,94079 e10,93899.

5 € 5/pp Ch WC included. **Location:** Rural, simple, isolated, quiet. **Surface:** grassy. 01/01-31/12

Distance: 3km on the spot 3km on the spot.

Remarks: Arrival <22h.

Cloppenburg 4C6

Am Stadtpark, Hagenweg. **GPS**: n52,84649 e8,04687.

3 free € 0,50/80liter Ch. **Location:** Urban, simple. **Surface:** metalled. 01/01-31/12

Distance: 100m 2km.

Remarks: Max. 3 days.

Cloppenburg 4C6

Museumsdorf Cloppenburg, Bether Straße. **GPS**: n52,85197 e8,05335.

20 free. **Location:** Rural, simple. **Surface:** metalled. 01/01-31/12

Distance: 900m 1km.

Remarks: Parking in front of museum village, max. 24h.

Coppenbrügge 10A2

Parkplatz am Frei- und Hallenbad, Felsenkellerweg. **GPS**: n52,11562 e9,53579.

50 € 3,50 Ch included. **Surface:** metalled. 01/01-31/12

Distance: on the spot 500m 500m.

Remarks: Parking at swimming pool.

Cuxhaven 4C3

Duhner Allee, Duhnen. **GPS**: n53,88284 e8,64814.

60 € 10, 1/9-1/7 € 6 Ch € 2/day WC € 0,50 € 1. **Location:** Simple. **Surface:** asphalted. 01/01-31/12

Remarks: Beach parking, in front of campsite am Bäderring.

Cuxhaven 4C3

Elbe-Ferry, Am Fährhafen. **GPS**: n53,87508 e8,70315.

100 € 10-13, tourist tax incl Ch. **Location:** Urban, simple. **Surface:** asphalted. 01/01-31/12

Distance: 1km 500m.

Remarks: Bread-service. Harbour area, follow Fährhafen.

Cuxhaven 4C3

Privatparkplatz Kugelbake Halle, Nordfeldstraße. **GPS**: n53,89033 e8,67703.

80 € 8 Ch WC. **Location:** Urban, simple. **Surface:** metalled. 01/01-31/12

Distance: 200m 100m.

Cuxhaven 4C3

Campingplatz Finck, Am Sahlenburger Strand 25. **GPS**: n53,86039 e8,59167.

DE

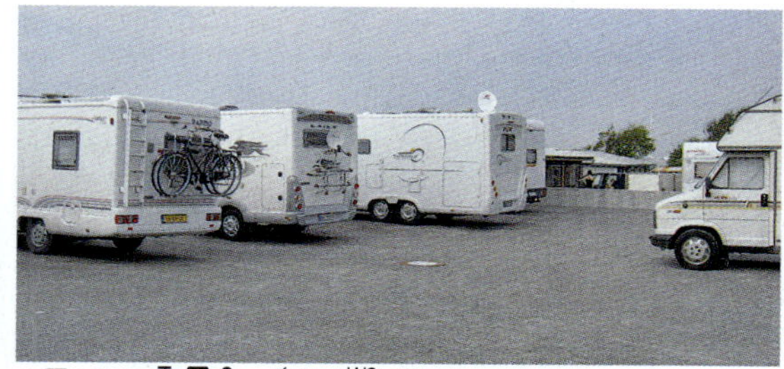

12 € 15,00 Ch (12x) WC. **Location:** Comfortable.
01/01-31/12
Distance: 3km on the spot on the spot on camp site 100m.

Tourist information Cuxhaven:

Nordseeheilbad Cuxhaven, Cuxhavener strasse 92, www.cuxhaven.de.Health resort in the Wadden region.

Neptuntaufe.Baptism of Neptune: beach of Duhne, Döse, Sahlenburg and Grimmershörn.
30/05-03/09.

S Damme 9C1

Am Flugplatz 8. **GPS**: n52,49055 e8,17925.

25 € 5 € 0,50/80liter Ch (12x)€ 0,50/kWh WC € 1. **Location:** Luxurious. **Surface:** grassy/gravel. 01/01-31/12
Distance: on the spot.
Remarks: Parking airport Damme.

S Damme 9C1

Olgahafen, Dümmerstrasse, Dümmerlohausen. **GPS**: n52,52917 e8,31098.

12 free € 1 Ch € 1. **Location:** Rural, simple, quiet. **Surface:** gravel.
01/01-31/12
Distance: 100m 100m on the spot bakery.
Remarks: At lake Dummen, max. 3 days.

Damme 9C1

Parkplatz Altes Amtsgericht, Große Straße. **GPS**: n52,52381 e8,19486.
5 free. **Surface:** metalled. 01/01-31/12
Distance: 300m.

S Delmenhorst 4C5

Reisemobilhafen Delmenhorst, An den Graften. **GPS**: n53,04722 e8,62278.

8 free Ch against payment. **Surface:** metalled.
01/01-31/12
Distance: on the spot 2,8km on the spot 200m.
Remarks: Max. 2 days.

S Detern 4B5

Reisemobilhafen Detern, Alte Heerstrasse 6, Stickhausen. **GPS**: n53,21560 e7,64743.

40 € 5 € 1/100liter Ch (44x)€ 2/24h WC € 1 € 0,50.
Location: Urban, luxurious. **Surface:** asphalted/gravel. 01/01-31/12
Distance: on the spot 6km on the spot on the spot on the spot on the spot on the spot.
Remarks: Behind Tourist-Info, bread-service.

S Diepenau 9D1

Am Bahnhof. **GPS**: n52,42470 e8,74106.

6 free € 1 Ch € 1/8h. **Surface:** metalled. 01/01-31/12
Distance: 500m 500m 500m.

S Diepholz 4C6

Parkplatz Am Heldenhain, Am Heldenhaim (B69). **GPS**: n52,61250 e8,37056.

12 free € 1 Ch (12x)€ 0,50/kWh. **Location:** Urban.
Surface: grassy. 01/01-31/12
Distance: 500m 500m 500m.

Ditzum 4A5

Reisemobil-platz Ditzum, Am Deich. **GPS**: n53,31555 e7,28666.

DE

20 € 5/night. **Surface:** metalled. 01/01-31/12
Distance: 100m 100m 100m 100m 300m.
Remarks: Waste dump € 1, shower € 1.

S **Ditzum** 4A5
Aktiv-Markt, Molkereistrasse. **GPS**: n53,31489 e7,27619.

4 € 5/24h € 1 Ch € 1/kWh. **Surface:** metalled.
01/01-31/12
Distance: 100m 300m 300m 100m on the spot.

S **Dollart** 4A5
Freizeitgelände, Denkmalstrasse 11, Ditzumerverlaat. **GPS**: n53,26028 e7,26861.

10 € 3/24h € 0,50 Ch (8x)€ 1/8h. **Surface:** metalled.
01/01-31/12 during event.
Distance: 250m on the spot on the spot 350m 250m.
Remarks: Max. 3 days.

S **Dornum** 4B4
P3, Schützenplatz. **GPS**: n53,64850 e7,42365.

15 € 9 Chincluded € 1/8h. **Surface:** grassy.
Distance: 300m 50m.
Remarks: Max. 1 night.

Dörpen 4A6
Festplatz, Veeneweg. **GPS**: n52,97115 e7,33425.

10 free. **Location:** Simple. **Surface:** grassy/metalled.
01/01-31/12 1st week in June: fair.
Distance: 500m on the spot 500m on the spot.

S **Dorum** 4C4
Wohnmobilhafen Wurster-Land, Am Neuen Deich 2a. **GPS**: n53,73838 e8,51966.

24 € 10 + € 1,50/pp tourist tax € 1/100liter Ch 24h WC
Location: Simple. **Surface:** metalled. 01/01-31/12
Distance: on the spot on the spot on the spot.
Remarks: Check in at Deichhotel.

S **Drage/Elbe** 5B4
Reisemobilplatz Stover Strand, Stover Strand 10. **GPS**: n53,42467 e10,29213.

100 € 12 € 1/80liter Ch (100x)€ 0,50/kWh WC € 0,50/4minutes washing machine/dryer € 4 € 2/h. **Location:** Comfortable.
Surface: grassy. 01/01-31/12
Distance: on the spot on the spot on the spot on the spot 500m on the spot on the spot.
Remarks: Next to campsite.

S **Drochtersen** 4D4
Krautsand, Deichverteitigungsweg. **GPS**: n53,75167 e9,39028.

12 € 10 (12x)included. **Location:** Rural, simple. **Surface:** metalled.
01/01-31/12
Distance: Elbestrand 300m.

DE

Drochtersen 4D4

Am Alten Hafen, Asseler Sand. **GPS**: n53,69418 e9,43928.

6 free. **Location:** Rural, simple. **Surface:** gravel.
01/01-31/12
Distance: 500m 1km.

Drochtersen 4D4

Hallenbad Drochtersen, Am Sportplatz. **GPS**: n53,70548 e9,38215.

6 free. **Location:** Simple. **Surface:** metalled. 01/01-31/12
Distance: 1km 1km.
Remarks: Parking at swimming pool.

Duderstadt 10B3

Parkplatz, Adenauerring. **GPS**: n51,51346 e10,27144.

free € 1 € 1 Ch against payment. **Surface:** gravel.
01/01-31/12
Distance: 800m 800m 200m 200m.
Remarks: Max. 1 night. East edge of the Altstadt.

Duderstadt 10B3

Eichsfeldhalle, August Werner Allee. **GPS**: n51,50662 e10,25890.

10 free. **Surface:** gravel. 01/01-31/12
Distance: 900m 900m 900m 700m.
Remarks: Max. 1 night.

Tourist information Duderstadt:
Gästeinformation der Stadt Duderstadt, Marktstrasse 66, www.duderstadt.de.Old part of town with half-timbered houses.

Edewecht 4B5

Rathhausstrasse. **GPS**: n53,12834 e7,98201.

20 free € 1/80liter Ch (8x)€ 1/6h. **Location:** Urban, simple.
Surface: grasstiles. 01/01-31/12
Distance: on the spot 400m Aldi 50m.

Egestorf 5A5

Naturerlebnisbad Acquadies, Ahornweg 5. **GPS**: n53,19796 e10,05455.

40 € 7 € 1 Ch (30x)€ 2/10h WC . **Location:** Simple, quiet.
Surface: gravel/metalled. 01/01-31/12
Distance: 1km 2,2km on the spot 700m 1km.
Remarks: At swimming pool.

Eggermühlen 9B1

Reiterhotel Vox, OT Bockraden 1. **GPS**: n52,57278 e7,79553.

8 € 25, clients € 7,50 Ch WC included. **Location:** Rural.
Surface: grassy. 01/01-31/12
Distance: 3km 3km.

Eggestedt 4C5

Eggestedt, Betonstrasse/Habichthorsterweg. **GPS**: n53,22819 e8,63902.

8 free. **Location:** Simple, isolated, noisy. **Surface:** metalled/sand.
01/01-31/12
Distance: 4km 400m.

Einbeck 10A2

Am Schwimmbad, Ochsenhofweg. **GPS**: n51,82433 e9,86464.

DE

30 free € 1/5minutes € 1 Ch. **Surface:** gravel. 01/01-31/12
Distance: 800m 500m 500m.
Remarks: Parking swimming pool, max. 1 night.

Tourist information Einbeck:
Tourist Information, Altes Rathaus, Marktplatz 6.Motorhome friendly beer town with half-timbered houses and city walls.
Blaudruckerei Wittram.350 years of printing fabrics. More info at Tourist Info.
Einbecker Bierdiplom.Guided tour and tastery, information at Tourist Information.
Alte Marktplatz. Wed + Sa morning.

S Elsfleth 4C5
Im Hafen, An der Kaje. **GPS**: n53,23771 e8,46545.

20 free € 1 Ch (8x)€ 1/8h. **Surface:** gravel.
01/01-31/12
Distance: on the spot on the spot on the spot on the spot on the spot.

S Emden 4A5
Am Hafentor, Am Eisenbahndock. **GPS**: n53,36306 e7,20778.

45 € 7 € 0,50/100liter € 0,50 Ch (36x)€ 0,50/kWh WC € 0,50 € 1 € 3. **Surface:** metalled. 01/01-31/12
Distance: 500m 500m 500m.
Remarks: Pay at harbourmaster.

Emden 4A5
Ostmole Ostufer, An der Nesserlander Schleuse. **GPS**: n53,36354 e7,20844.
free. **Surface:** metalled. 01/01-31/12
Distance: on the spot on the spot.

Emden 4A5
Wohnmobilstellplatz Knock, Jannes Ohling Strasse. **GPS**: n53,35559 e7,00367.

25 € 4,50. **Surface:** metalled. 01/01-31/12
Distance: 13km 500m on the spot 13km.
Remarks: Parking harbour.

Emmerthal 10A2
Gasthaus Zur Post, Grohnder Strasse 25. **GPS**: n52,02185 e9,41865.

20 guests free. **Surface:** asphalted. 01/01-31/12
Distance: 400m on the spot 500m.
Remarks: Arrival <17h.

S Emsbüren 9A1
Landgasthof Elberger Schlipse, Elbergen 1, Elbergen. **GPS**: n52,46825 e7,30103.

40 € 3 Ch (15x)€ 2,50/24h WC **Location:** Rural, quiet.
Surface: grassy. 01/01-31/12
Distance: 2km 100m 2km on the spot on the spot.

S Eschershausen 10A2
Reisemobil-Stellplatz am Angerplatz, Angerweg. **GPS**: n51,92965 e9,62806.
10 free Ch free. **Surface:** metalled. 01/01-31/12
Distance: 1km.

S Esens 4B4
Schützenplatz. **GPS**: n53,63921 e7,61077.

20 € 4 + tourist tax € 2,50/pp Ch included. **Surface:** grassy.
01/01-31/12
Distance: 50m 200m.

S Essel 5A6
Hotel Heide-Kröpke, Esseler Damm 1. **GPS**: n52,73240 e9,69419.

5 free. **Surface:** grassy. 01/01-31/12
Distance: on the spot 9km.
Remarks: Use of a meal desired, bird reserve Ostenholzer-Moor.

S Esterwegen 4B6

Am Erikasee. GPS: n52,99366 e7,66768.

6 free € 1/100liter Ch (6x)€ 1/2kWh WC. **Location:** Rural, simple, isolated. **Surface:** gravel/metalled. 01/01-31/12
Distance: 2km 100m Imbiss 80m.
Remarks: Walking and bicycle area.

Eystrup 4D6

Bahnhofstrasse 21. **GPS:** n52,78004 e9,21840.

5 free. **Surface:** grassy. 01/01-31/12
Remarks: Max. 5 days.

S Fassberg 5B6

Am Schützenplatz, Moorweg. **GPS:** n52,90518 e10,16991.

50 € 2 € 1 Ch WC. **Surface:** grassy. 01/01-31/12
Distance: 700m.

S Fassberg 5B6

Parkplatz Heidesee, Unterlüsserstrasse, L280, Müden. **GPS:** n52,87889 e10,12472.

20 € 2 € 1 Ch € 1. **Surface:** grassy.
01/01-31/12 end Sep.
Distance: 500m 1km.

Fassberg 5B6

Parkplatz am Wildpark, Willinghäuser Kirchweg, Müden. **GPS:** n52,87222 e10,10861.

20 € 2. **Surface:** grassy. 01/01-31/12
Distance: 1km 1km.

S Freiburg/Elbe 4D3

Am Bassin. **GPS:** n53,82285 e9,29305.

50 € 8 Ch WC included € 1. **Location:** Rural, simple.
Surface: metalled. 01/01-31/12
Distance: 200m 50m 300m 400m.
Remarks: Find more possibilities on the city plan.

S Friedeburg 4B4

Schützenplatz. GPS: n53,45488 e7,83349.

20 free Ch free (6x)€ 1/1. **Location:** Rural, simple.
Surface: grassy. 01/01-31/12
Distance: 15/05-15/09 400m.
Remarks: Max. 3 days.

S Fürstenau 9B1

Schlossinsel Fürstenau, Schlossplatz 1. **GPS:** n52,51638 e7,67333.

DE

2 free €3 Ch € 2/day. **Location:** Quiet. **Surface:** metalled.
01/01-31/12
Distance: 100m 100m 100m on the spot on the spot.
Remarks: Next to the castle.

Tourist information Fürstenau:
Touristisches Informationsbüro, im Alten Rathaus, Grosse strasse 27, www.fuerstenau.de.Small town around a medieval castle farm.

S Gartow 5D5
Imbiss am See, Springstraße 88. **GPS**: n53,02944 e11,44944.

20 € 5 WC. **Surface:** gravel/metalled. 01/04-30/10
Distance: 1km on the spot on the spot on the spot.
Remarks: Imbiss 11-21h.

Geeste 9A1
Am Speicherbecken, Biener Straße. **GPS**: n52,59407 e7,27417.

50 free. **Location:** Quiet. **Surface:** metalled. 01/01-31/12
Distance: 2km 100m.
Remarks: Max. 1 night.

Geeste 9A1
P Biotop/Ausblick, Osterbrocker Strasse. **GPS**: n52,59840 e7,29279.

4 free. **Surface:** metalled. 01/01-31/12
Distance: 1,5km 1,5km on the spot on the spot.
Remarks: Max. 1 night, hiking area.

S Gifhorn 10B1
Fischer Camping + Gas, Schmiedeweg 4. **GPS**: n52,50863 e10,48462.
8 free Ch . **Surface:** grassy. 01/01-31/12

Distance: 500m.
Remarks: Accessory shop.

S Gnarrenburg 4D4
Parkplatz Brillit, Alte Strasse, Brillit. **GPS**: n53,41390 e9,00007.

15 free Chfree. **Location:** Rural, simple. **Surface:** gravel.
01/01-31/12
Distance: 1km 3km 1km.
Remarks: At community centre.

S Gnarrenburg 4D4
Schulzentrum, Brilliterweg. **GPS**: n53,39000 e9,00028.

15 free Chfree. **Surface:** metalled. 01/01-31/12
Distance: 1km 500m.
Remarks: Sports centre.

S Gorleben 5C5
Am Sportboothafen, Ringstraße. **GPS**: n53,04972 e11,35111.

5 € 5 € 1/10minutes (4x)€ 1/10h WC . **Location:** Rural, comfortable, quiet. **Surface:** grasstiles. 01/01-31/12
Distance: on the spot on the spot 500m.
Remarks: Bakery 500m.

S Göttingen 10B3
Reisemobilhafen Eiswiese, Badeparadies Eiswiese, Windausweg 6. **GPS**: n51,52320 e9,92965.

28 € 9 € 1 Ch € 1 WC € 1/15h. **Surface:** gravel.
01/01-31/12
Distance: 500m 5,2km 100m 20-400m 100m 500m

100m.
Remarks: Follow Reisemobilplatz/Badeparadies Eiswiese/Stadion.

S Göttingen 10B3

VW-garage Südhannover, Kasseler-Landstrasse 53-69. **GPS**: n51,53053 e9,89780.

2 free Ch free. **Surface:** asphalted. 01/01-31/12
Distance: 2,5km 200m.

Tourist information Göttingen:

Gö-card.Card offers free access to public transport and discounts at museums, bathe etc. Available at Tourist Information. € 5/day.

Tourist-Information, Altes Rathaus, Markt 9, www.goettingen-tourismus.de.University town with old university buildings.

Bismarckhäuschen.Student appartment of the Reichskansler Otto von Bismarck. Tue 10-13h, Wed, Thu, Sa 13-17h.

S Grasberg 4D5

P&R, Wörpedorfer Straße. **GPS**: n53,18411 e8,98433.

10 free € 1 Ch (8x)€ 1/6h. **Location:** Simple. **Surface:** gravel. 01/01-31/12
Distance: on the spot on the spot on the spot > Bremen.

Gronau (Nieder-Sachsen) 10A2

Kuhmasch. **GPS**: n52,08265 e9,77034.

4 free. **Surface:** grassy. 01/01-31/12
Distance: 200m 300m 300m.

Großenkneten 4C6

Dorfplatz, Bahnhofstrasse, Huntlosen. **GPS**: n52,99139 e8,28611.

6 free. **Location:** Rural, simple. **Surface:** grasstiles. 01/01-31/12
Distance: on the spot 50m 1km.

Großenkneten 4C6

Wilhelm-Wellman-Platz, Ahlhorner Strasse. **GPS**: n52,94274 e8,25751.

15 free. **Location:** Rural, simple. **Surface:** grasstiles. 01/01-31/12
Distance: 200m 200m on the spot.

Großenwieden 9D1

Am Steinbrink. **GPS**: n52,17191 e9,18982.

5 free. **Location:** Rural. **Surface:** gravel.
Distance: on the spot Gasthaus/Biergarten 300m Weserradweg on the spot.

S Grossefehn 4B5

Ostfriesen-Bräu Bagband, Voerstad 8, Badband. **GPS**: n53,35034 e7,61060.

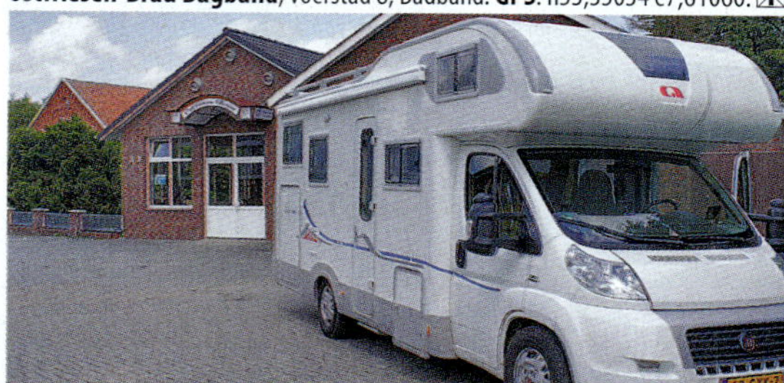

4 € 5,70, free with 3 beer included,16Amp WC. **Surface:** metalled. 01/01-31/12
Distance: 10km 4km on the spot 600m.

Grossheide 4A4

Kirchweg, Berumerfehn. **GPS**: n53,56040 e7,34713.

4 free. **Surface:** asphalted. 01/01-31/12
Distance: on the spot on the spot 2km.
Remarks: Max. 1 night.

S Hambergen 4D5

Festplatz, Kirchweg/Am Langenend. **GPS**: n53,31050 e8,82389.

DE

20 € 3,50 Ch . **Location:** Urban, simple. **Surface:** gravel/sand.
01/01-31/12
Distance: on the spot 50m 50m 1km on the spot
on the spot.
Remarks: Caution key service € 25.

S Hameln 10A2

Hannes Weserblick, Ruthenstrasse 14. **GPS**: n52,09623 e9,35853.

27 € 8/24h € 1/100liter Ch € 1/8h. **Surface:** metalled.
01/01-31/12
Distance: 1km 600m 600m 800m Weser-Radweg.

S Hankensbüttel 5B6

Parkplatz Am Boldhamm. **GPS**: n52,73111 e10,61417.

20 € 6 Ch WC included. **Surface:** grassy. 01/01-31/12
Remarks: Service: Mo/Fri 8 - 11h, Sa/Su 8-10h. Over railway passage, Emmerdorfstraße, Isenhagersee.

Tourist information Hankensbüttel:
Otter-Zentrum.Zoo.
15/03-31/10 9.30-18h, 01/11-14/03 9.30-17h 15/12-15/01.

S Hannoversch Münden 10A3

Parkplatz Tanzwerder. **GPS**: n51,42000 e9,64888.

30 € 5,10 € 1 Ch (8x)€ 1/8h. **Surface:** metalled. 01/01-31/12
Distance: 900m 100m.
Remarks: 01/11/- 31/03 no service. Follow centre.

Hannoversch Münden 10A3

Am Hochbad, Rattwerder. **GPS**: n51,40595 e9,64643.

15 free. **Surface:** asphalted. 01/01-31/12
Distance: 1,7km.

Hannoversch Münden 10A3

Am Werraweg. **GPS**: n51,41701 e9,66176.

5 free. **Surface:** metalled. 01/01-31/12
Distance: 1,5km.

S Hannoversch Münden 10A3

Camping Grüne Insel, Tanzwerder 1. **GPS**: n51,41694 e9,64751.

20 € 7 € 1 Ch € 0,50/kWh WC . **Surface:** grassy.
01/01-31/12
Distance: 100m 150m 150m.
Remarks: Max. 3t.

Tourist information Hannoversch Münden:
Touristik Naturpark Münden e.V, Rathaus, www.hann-muenden.net/spontan. Old city centre with 430 half-timbered houses.
Boat trip with steamer from Unterer Tanzwerder, close to the motorhome parking.
01/05-30/09 Tue-Su 10h-11.30h-13h-14.30h-16h, Wed 10-11.30h.

S Hardegsen 10A3

Wohnmobilhafen Steinbreite, Alte Uslarer Straße 1. **GPS**: n51,65093 e9,82267.

15 € 6 Ch WC . **Surface:** grasstiles. 01/01-31/12
Distance: 500m.

S Haren/Ems 4A6

Freizeitzentrum Schloss Danken, Rentmeisterstrasse. **GPS**: n52,79724 e7,20530.

DE

17 € 10/24h Ch (18x) WC € 1. **Location:** Rural, simple. **Surface:** grassy/gravel. 21/03-25/10
Distance: 1km 2,8km on the spot on the spot on the spot on the spot.

Haren/Ems 4A6

Schleusenstraße. **GPS:** n52,78873 e7,24705.
15 free. **Surface:** grasstiles. 01/01-31/12
Distance: 500m 550m.

Harsefeld 5A4

Klosterpark, Kirchenstrasse. **GPS:** n53,45384 e9,50344.

5 free. **Location:** Rural, simple. 01/01-31/12
Distance: 100m 100m 100m 100m on the spot on the spot.
Remarks: Parking park of monastery, max. 5 days.

Haselünne 4B6

Plesseparkplatz, Plessestrasse. **GPS:** n52,67210 e7,48865.

3 free € 2/10minutes Ch WC. **Location:** Urban, simple, noisy. **Surface:** metalled. 01/01-31/12
Distance: 400m 300m 300m.
Remarks: Parking behind town hall.

Haselünne 4B6

Lingener Strasse. **GPS:** n52,66778 e7,48222.

4 free. **Location:** Simple, quiet. **Surface:** metalled. 01/01-31/12
Distance: 400m 400m 400m 100m on the spot.
Remarks: Parking swimming pool.

Haselünne 4B6

Restaurant Esders-Ab der Hasebrücke, Lingenerstrasse 1. **GPS:** n52,66992 e7,48638.

10 € 10, guests free. **Location:** Urban. **Surface:** metalled.
Distance: 200m on the spot.

Helmstedt 10C1

Am Maschweg. **GPS:** n52,23535 e11,01128.

25 free. **Surface:** grassy.
Distance: 100m 50m.

Helmstedt 10C1

Brunnentheater, Brunnenweg 6A. **GPS:** n52,23676 e11,06411.

5 free. **Surface:** asphalted. 01/01-31/12

Helmstedt 10C1

Wallplatz. **GPS:** n52,22833 e11,01417.

3 free. **Surface:** asphalted. 01/01-31/12
Distance: on the spot on the spot.
Remarks: Parking in the centre.

Hermannsburg 5B6

Parkplatz Waldschwimmbad, Lotharstrasse 66. **GPS:** n52,82718 e10,10807.

DE

6 free € 0,50 Ch. **Surface:** metalled. 01/01-31/12
Distance: 500m.
Remarks: Parking at swimming pool.

Hermannsburg 5B6
Schützenplatz, Lotharstraße 75. **GPS**: n52,82787 e10,10963.

40 € 2 Ch. **Surface:** grassy. 01/01-31/12
Distance: 500m.
Remarks: Max. 1 night, service at Waldbad (50m).

Hermannsburg 5B6
Grillplatz Bonstorf, Schulstrasse. **GPS**: n52,86492 e10,05134.

4 free. **Surface:** grassy. 01/01-31/12
Distance: 5km.
Remarks: Parking sports park.

Hermannsburg 5B6
Parkplatz am Feuerwehrhaus, Weesenerstrasse, Weesen. **GPS**: n52,83645 e10,13692.

3 free. **Surface:** grassy. 01/01-31/12
Distance: 500m.
Remarks: Parking fire-station.

Hermannsburg 5B6
Parkplatz Örtzetal- Halle, Lutterweg. **GPS**: n52,83363 e10,09579.

5 free. **Surface:** metalled. 01/01-31/12
Distance: 100m.

Hermannsburg 5B6
Lutter Hof, Waldstrasse, Lutter. **GPS**: n52,84188 e10,09894.

5 € 5 included. **Surface:** grassy. 01/01-31/12

Herzlake 4B6
Hasetal, Im Mersch. **GPS**: n52,68211 e7,60780.

30 free Ch WC free. **Surface:** grassy. 01/03-30/11
Remarks: Parking sports centre.

Hesel 4B5
Marktplatz, Kirchstrasse. **GPS**: n53,30497 e7,59174.

12 € 4 € 1 Ch € 1/8h € 1,At swimming pool Hesel.
Surface: metalled. 01/01-31/12
Distance: on the spot 1km.

Hessisch Oldendorf 9D1
Südwall P1, Weserstrasse. **GPS**: n52,16693 e9,25049.

DE

10 free € 0,50/5minutes € 0,50Ch. **Surface:** metalled.
01/01-31/12
Distance: 650m 500m 500m.

S Hitzacker 5C5

Bleichwiesen, K36, Elbufferstrasse. **GPS:** n53,15074 e11,04941.

40 free € 1/70liter Ch (17x)€ 1/6h WC. **Location:** Rural, comfortable. **Surface:** metalled. 01/01-31/12
Distance: 200m 450m.
Remarks: Max. 2 nights.

S Hohne 5B6

Am Waldbad, Am Schwimmbad 23. **GPS:** n52,59340 e10,37398.
4 € 5 Ch WC included. **Surface:** gravel. 01/01-31/12
Distance: 1km.
Remarks: Use sanitary only during opening hours swimming pool.

S Hohnstorf/Elbe 5B4

Wohnmobilstellplatz Hohnstorf, Schulstraße 1. **GPS:** n53,36234 e10,56223.

8 € 8 Ch (3x)€ 1/10h. **Location:** Comfortable.
Surface: metalled. 01/01-31/12
Distance: on the spot 500m 500m.
Remarks: Along the river Elbe.

S Holdorf 9C1

Erholungszentrum Heidesee, Zum Heidesee 53. **GPS:** n52,57696 e8,11533.

60 € 4/pp Ch € 2. **Surface:** grasstiles. 01/03-15/10
Distance: 1,5km 3,4km sandy beach on the spot 1,5km.

Hollern 5A4

Am Deich, Twielenfleth. **GPS:** n53,60417 e9,55917.

15 € 5/0-24h. **Location:** Rural, simple. **Surface:** metalled.
01/01-31/12
Distance: 200m Imbiss 300m.
Remarks: Along the river Elbe.

S Holzminden 10A2

Mobilcamping, Stahler Ufer 16. **GPS:** n51,82681 e9,43909.

70 € 6,50 € 1/100liter Ch € 0,60/kWh WC € 0,50.
Surface: grassy. 01/01-31/12
Distance: 1,5km 100m 100m 200m.
Remarks: Bread-service.

S Hoya/Weser 4D6

Reisemobilstellplatz Weserblick, Stettiner Straße. **GPS:** n52,80106 e9,13987.

10 voluntary contribution € 1/150liter Ch. **Surface:** grassy/gravel.
01/01-31/12
Distance: 5 min walking 100m 5 min walking.

S Hude 4C5

Wohnmobilstellplatz Hude, Schützenstrasse. **GPS:** n53,10758 e8,45867.

10 free consumption. **Surface:** gravel.
01/01-31/12
Distance: on the spot on the spot 400m.
Remarks: Parking swimming pool.

Tourist information Hude:

DE

Zisterzienserkloster, Klosterhude.Monastery, 13th century.
Golf court; the 9 holes-court is accessible for everyone.

Hüde (49448) 9C1

Freizeitarena Dümmer See, Rohrdommelweg 33. **GPS**: n52,50176 e8,35425.

50 € 10 Ch € 2,50 WC. **Location:** Rural, quiet. **Surface:** grassy.
15/04-15/10
Distance: 150m on the spot.

Jade 4C5

Quittenweg, Süderschweiburg. **GPS**: n53,39139 e8,26639.

8 free € 1 Ch (8x)€ 1/8h. **Surface:** gravel.
Distance: on the spot 1km 800m.

Jade 4C5

Drei Eichen, Kreuzmoorstrasse 28. **GPS**: n53,31531 e8,23084.

10 € 10 Ch (3x) WC included against payment. **Location:** Rural, simple, quiet. **Surface:** grassy/gravel. 01/01-31/12
Distance: 4km.
Remarks: At manege.

Jade 4C5

Schützenhof, Am Schützenplatz, Vareler Strasse. **GPS**: n53,34111 e8,18667.

10 guests free (3x)On demand€ 2/night. **Location:** Simple. **Surface:** metalled. 01/01-31/12
Distance: on the spot on the spot on the spot.
Remarks: Parking of Shooting Club.

Jade 4C5

Jaderberg, Tiergartenstrasse 69, Jaderberg. **GPS**: n53,32679 e8,18521.

20 free. **Location:** Simple. **Surface:** gravel. 01/01-31/12
Distance: on the spot on the spot.
Remarks: Parking Jarderpark, zoo and adventure park.

Jever 4B4

Jahnstrasse, Jever-Nord. **GPS**: n53,57733 e7,89074.

20 € 7 Ch (20x)included. **Surface:** metalled. 01/01-31/12
Distance: 100m.
Remarks: Sports centre, max. 3 days, coins at petrol station Henn.

Tourist information Jever:
Jever Marketing und Tourismus GmbH, Alter Markt 18, www.stadt-jever.de.
Schloßmuseum.Castle, English gardens and museum. Tue-Su 10-18h, 01/07-31/08 Mo-Su 10-18h.
Frisiesches Brauhaus.Brewery with museum. Guided tour 2 hours, 2 drinks included.
Mo-Fri 9.30-16.30h, Sa 9.30-12.30h.

Jork 5A4

Am Yachthafen, Neuenschleuse. **GPS**: n53,55375 e9,66858.

18 free € 1/90liter Ch (18x)€ 0,50/kWh WC € 2. **Location:** Urban, simple. **Surface:** unpaved. 01/01-31/12
Distance: Jork 3km on the spot on the spot on the spot.
Remarks: Along the river Elbe.

Jork 5A4

Festplatz, Schützenhofstrasse/Festplatzweg. **GPS**: n53,53100 e9,68336.

80 free € 1/100liter Ch WC € 0,50. **Location:** Rural, simple. **Surface:** metalled. 01/01-31/12

DE

Distance: 200m 200m 200m.
Remarks: Parking event ground, max. 24h.

Jork 5A4

Stellplatz Lühe-Anleger, Fährstraße, Grünendeich. **GPS**: n53,57271 e9,63129.

10 € 10/24h. **Surface:** gravel. 01/01-31/12

Jork 5A4

Stubbe's Gasthaus, Lühe 46. **GPS**: n53,56861 e9,63333.

7 € 8 € 2. **Location:** Rural, comfortable. **Surface:** grasstiles.
01/01-31/12
Distance: on the spot.
Remarks: Picnic area Am Gartenteich, bread-service.

Kirchlinteln 4D6

Auf dem Kleberhof, Scharnhorster Weg 1. **GPS**: n52,95562 e9,30651.

7 € 10 (4x) WC included € 3. **Location:** Rural, comfortable, quiet. **Surface:** grassy. 01/01-31/12
Distance: 3,5km 6km 3,5km 3,5km.
Remarks: Bread-service.

Königslutter am Elm 10C1

P1 Niedernhof, Amtsgarten. **GPS**: n52,25009 e10,81996.
5 free free. **Surface:** grasstiles. 01/01-31/12

Krummendeich 4D3

Stellplatz Krummendeich, Schulweg 107. **GPS**: n53,83145 e9,20231.

5 free WC € 0,50 € 0,50. **Location:** Rural, simple. **Surface:** gravel.
01/01-31/12
Distance: 100m 300m.

Krummhörn 4A4

Parkplatz Greetsieler Zwillingsmühlen, Mühlenstrasse 3, Greetsiel. **GPS**: n53,49711 e7,10181.

50 € 10 € 2 Ch (40x) € 1/8h. **Surface:** gravel.
01/01-31/12
Distance: 250m.

Lamspringe 10B2

Am Bahnhof. **GPS**: n51,95404 e10,00656.

3 free. **Surface:** gravel. 01/01-31/12
Distance: 750m 400m 250m.

Lautenthal 10B2

Kaspar Bitter Strasse 7b. **GPS**: n51,87020 e10,28729.

25 € 4 + € 2 Kurtaxe € 1 Ch € 1 (10x) € 1/6h. **Surface:** gravel. 01/01-31/12
Distance: 300m 300m 500m 50m.

Leer 4B5

Am Hafen, Nessestrasse. **GPS**: n53,22527 e7,45472.

10 free WC € 0,50 € 1. **Location:** Urban, simple. **Surface:** asphalted/gravel.
01/01-31/12
Distance: 500m 300m 2km.
Remarks: Sanitary at offices Bruchbrücke, caution sanitary € 30.

Leer 4B5

P9, Grosse Bleiche. **GPS**: n53,22577 e7,44686.

DE

6 free € 1/100liter € 1 Ch (6x)€ 1/24h WC € 0,50 € 1. **Location:** Urban, simple. **Surface:** metalled. 01/01-31/12
Distance: 200m on the spot 2km.
Remarks: Sanitary at offices Bruchbrücke, caution sanitary € 30.

Leer 4B5

Hallen- und Freibad, Burfehnerweg 32. **GPS:** n53,23927 e7,44998.

10 free. **Location:** Urban, simple. **Surface:** metalled.
01/01-31/12
Distance: on the spot on the spot 1km.

Leer 4B5

Windmühlenhof Eiklenborg, Logabirumer Straße, Logabirum. **GPS:** n53,24745 e7,51582.
5 € 11 Ch WC € 2. **Surface:** grassy/metalled. 01/01-31/12
Remarks: Near old Dutch windmill.

Leese 9D1

Loccumer straße. **GPS:** n52,50272 e9,11733.

4 free. **Surface:** metalled. 01/01-31/12
Distance: 200m on the spot 200m.

Leese 9D1

Rasthaus Leeser Tanger, Bahlweg. **GPS:** n52,49372 e9,12055.

8 € 15, discount for clients included. **Surface:** metalled.
01/01-31/12
Distance: 800m on the spot.

Lembruch 9C1

Stellplatz Dümmer-See Lembruch, Seestraße. **GPS:** n52,52439 e8,36703.

20 free. **Location:** Rural. **Surface:** grassy. 01/01-31/12
Distance: 300m 100m.

Lembruch 9C1

Campingplatz Seeblick, Birkenallee. **GPS:** n52,52583 e8,36056.

20 € 9 Ch on camp site. **Location:** Rural. **Surface:** grassy.
01/01-31/12
Distance: 50m 50m.
Remarks: Max. 1 night.

Lemwerder 4C5

Reisemobilhafen Peter-Baxmann-Platz, Schulstrasse 44. **GPS:** n53,15784 e8,61783.

50 € 3 Ch (50x)free. **Surface:** gravel.
Distance: on the spot on the spot 500m.

Lemwerder 4C5

Vulkanparkplatz, Uferweg. **GPS:** n53,17000 e8,60028.

5 free. **Surface:** metalled. 01/01-31/12
Distance: 1km on the spot 1km 1km.

Lingen/Ems 9A1

Linus Bad, Teichstrasse. **GPS:** n52,51863 e7,30606.

16 free € 1 Ch (16x)€ 0,50/kWh. **Location:** Rural. **Surface:** gravel.
01/01-31/12
Distance: 1km on the spot on the spot.
Remarks: Max. 3 days.

Lüchow **5C5**

Parkstraße. **GPS**: n52,96983 e11,14594.

2 free. **Location:** Urban, simple. **Surface:** asphalted/metalled. 01/01-31/12
Distance: 900m 900m 1,7km.
Remarks: Max. 3 nights.

S Lüdersfeld **9D1**

Heinrichs'Reisemobil Stellplatz, Am Hülsebrink 10+11. **GPS**: n52,35972 e9,25512.
30+15 € 6 Ch . **Surface:** metalled.
Remarks: Bread-service.

S Lüneburg **5B5**

Am Sülzwiesen, Pieperweg. **GPS**: n53,24556 e10,39694.

50 € 8/24h € 1/10minutes Ch (40x)€ 1/8h,30/09-01/05 € 2/8h.
Location: Rural, comfortable, isolated, quiet. **Surface:** metalled. 01/01-31/12
Distance: 1km 300m.
Remarks: Max. 1 night.

S Mardorf **9D1**

Wohnmobilstellplatz Steinhuder Meer, Rote-Kreuz-Strasse 16. **GPS**: n52,48704 e9,30065.

60 € 6 € 1/100liter Ch (60x)€ 3. **Surface:** grassy.
01/01-31/12
Distance: 1km 300m 1km.
Remarks: Bread-service.

Melle **9C1**

Am Wellenbad 43. **GPS**: n52,20497 e8,32368.

10 free. **Location:** Simple, quiet. **Surface:** metalled.
01/01-31/12
Distance: on the spot 1,2km nearby 300m.
Remarks: Parking swimming pool.

S Meppen **4A6**

Reisemobilplatz am Hallenbad, An der Bleiche. **GPS**: n52,69107 e7,28399.

10 € 6 2 pers, swimming pool incl € 2/100liter Ch (4x)€ 1/12h.
Surface: metalled. 01/01-31/12
Distance: 200m on the spot 300m.
Remarks: Parking swimming pool, max. 2 nights.

Tourist information Meppen:
Tue-Sa morning.

Moormerland **4B5**

Am Rathausplatz, Theodor Heussstrasse 12, Warsingsfehn. **GPS**: n53,31062 e7,48618.

5 free. **Surface:** metalled. 01/01-31/12
Distance: 50m 250m 50m 50m.
Remarks: Parking townhall, max. 3 nights.

S Moormerland **4B5**

Bei Cassi, Deichlandstraße 10, Rorinchem. **GPS**: n53,32010 e7,35473.

DE

17 guests free Ch free. **Surface:** gravel.
01/01-31/12
Distance: on the spot.
Remarks: Restaurant is closed on Monday.

S Neuharlingersiel 4B4

Wohnmobilstellplatz am Ostanleger, Am Hafen Ost. **GPS**: n53,70173 e7,70741.

23 € 12 € 1 Ch included WC. **Location:** Rural, comfortable, quiet. **Surface:** metalled. 01/01-31/12
Distance: 500m 800m 1km.
Remarks: Max. 3 nights.

S Neuharlingersiel 4B4

Neuharlingersiel, Alt Addenhausen 4. **GPS**: n53,69580 e7,69021.

8 € 12, tourist tax incl € 1 Ch included WC on camp site on camp site. **Location:** Rural, simple. **Surface:** metalled.
01/01-31/12
Distance: 800m sandy beach 1km.
Remarks: Max. 1 night.

S Nienburg 4D6

Reisemobilstellplatz Nienburg/Weser, Oyler Straße. **GPS**: n52,64094 e9,20137.

18 € 5 € 1/120liter Ch (12x)€ 1/8h. **Surface:** gravel.
01/01-31/12
Distance: 10 min walking on the spot on the spot 300m 500m.
Remarks: Along the river Weser.

S Norddeich 4A4

Reisemobilhafen Ocean Wave, Itzendorferstrasse/Dörperweg. **GPS**: n53,61073 e7,15649.

50 € 13/24h, 2 pers., incl. 50% discount Erlebnisbad Ocean Wave Ch (47x) WC. **Surface:** metalled. 01/01-31/12
Distance: 100m 100m 100m 500m 100m.

S Norddeich 4A4

Womo Park Norddeich, Deichstraße 24. **GPS**: n53,60166 e7,13527.

48 € 9,50, tourist tax excl € 1/100liter Ch € 1/2kWh WC.
Surface: gravel. 01/01-31/12
Distance: 2km beach 1,5km, beach (dog allowed) 1km on the spot 500m 100m.
Remarks: Bread-service.

Tourist information Norddeich:
Tourist Information Norddeich, Dörper Weg 22, www.norddeich.de.

Norden 4A4

Am Hafen. **GPS**: n53,59055 e7,21176.

3 parking paid, free overnight stay. **Surface:** metalled. 01/01-31/12
Distance: 100m 100m 100m.

S Nordenham 4C4

Freizeitbad Störtebeker, Atenser Allee. **GPS**: n53,49472 e8,47444.

10 free Ch (8x)free € 2,at sauna. **Surface:** grasstiles.
Distance: on the spot on the spot on the spot.
Remarks: Bread-service.

DE

S Nordholz 4C4

Wuster Strasse 12, Spieka. **GPS**: n53,75772 e8,59409.

5 free € 1/100liter € 1 Ch (5x)€ 1/2kWh. **Location:** Rural, simple. **Surface:** metalled.
Distance: on the spot 100m.

S Nordhorn 9A1

Vechtesee, Heseperweg. **GPS**: n52,43683 e7,08190.

35 € 5 € 1/100liter Ch € 1/5h. **Location:** Rural. **Surface:** grassy. 01/01-31/12
Distance: 400m 300m 300m on the spot on the spot.

Northeim 10B3

In der Fluth. **GPS**: n51,70766 e10,00597.

20 free. **Surface:** gravel. 01/01-31/12
Distance: 300m.
Remarks: Max. 24h.

Northeim 10B3

Grosser Freizeitsee, Am Nordhafen. **GPS**: n51,72920 e9,96286.

30 free. **Surface:** gravel. 01/01-31/12
Distance: 5km on the spot 2km.

S Oberndorf/Oste 4D4

Wohnmobilplatz Bentwisch, Hoffmann-von-Fallersleben-Straße 10. **GPS**: n53,75398 e9,15054.

8 € 5 € 2/100liter Ch (6x)€ 2/8h WC € 0,50 € 0,50. **Location:** Rural, comfortable. **Surface:** grassy/gravel. 01/01-31/12
Distance: 2km 100m 100m on the spot.

Oldenburg 4C5

Am Küstenkanal, Westfalendamm. **GPS**: n53,12927 e8,21465.

3 free. **Location:** Rural, simple. **Surface:** gravel.
01/01-31/12
Distance: on the spot 1km on the spot 100m 400m.
Remarks: Alternative: in front of campsite Am Flötenteich, 53,166944 8,235, 2 pitches free.

Tourist information Oldenburg:

Oldenburg Tourismus und Marketing GmbH, Wallstrasse 14, www.oldenburg-tourist.de.Historical city centre.

Horst-Janssen-Museum.Modern museum concerning living and working Horst Janssen, 1929-1995, drawer and graphic artist.
Tue-Su 10-18h. € 3,50, family card € 7.

S Osnabrück 9C1

Schlosswallhalle, Heinrichstrasse. **GPS**: n52,27074 e8,03953.

8 € 5 € 1/100liter Ch. **Location:** Urban, simple. **Surface:** asphalted. 01/01-31/12
Distance: on the spot 300m 300m.

S Osnabrück 9C1

Wohnmobilplatz Netebad, Im Haseesch 6. **GPS**: n52,30470 e8,05413.

5 € 5 € 1/100liter Ch € 1/6h. **Location:** Urban, simple, quiet. **Surface:** grassy/metalled. 01/01-31/12

DE

Distance: on the spot.
Remarks: Max. 48h.

Osnabrück 9C1

Natruper Straße / Nobbenburger Straße. **GPS:** n52,28116 e8,03651.
€ 5. **Surface:** metalled. 01/01-31/12
Distance: 1,5km.

Tourist information Osnabrück:
Tourist Information, Bierstrasse 22-23, www.osnabrueck.de.

Osten 4D4

Festhalle, Altendorf 13. **GPS:** n53,69602 e9,18813.

5 € 5 Ch (2x)included. **Location:** Rural, simple. **Surface:** metalled. 01/01-31/12
Distance: on the spot on the spot 500m.
Remarks: Pay at Hotel Fährkrug.

Osterholz-Scharmbeck 4D5

August Schlüter Turnhalle, Lange Strasse. **GPS:** n53,22562 e8,79000.

4 free € 1 . **Location:** Urban, simple, central. **Surface:** metalled.
01/01-31/12

Osterode 10B3

Waldcampingplatz Eulenburg, Scheerenberger Straße 100. **GPS:** n51,72868 e10,28638.
13 € 8 Ch WC . 01/01-31/12
Distance: 2km.

Ostrhauderfehn 4B5

Reisemobilhafen Ostrhauderfehn, Hauptstrasse 115. **GPS:** n53,13872 e7,62318.

20 € 5 Ch (12x)€ 1/2kWh WC € 0,50 .
Surface: asphalted.
01/01-31/12 during fair in June.
Distance: 100m 100m 100m.
Remarks: Sanitary at bar, caution sanitary € 10.

Otterndorf 4D3

Parking Mitte, Jahnstrasse. **GPS:** n53,80861 e8,89444.

8 free. **Location:** Rural, simple. **Surface:** metalled.
01/01-31/12
Distance: on the spot 200m.

Otterndorf 4D3

Seglertreff, Schleuse 5. **GPS:** n53,82250 e8,89472.

12 free, 01/04-31/10 € 7,00 Ch € 2,50/24h WC .
Location: Rural, comfortable. **Surface:** metalled. 01/01-31/12
Distance: 2km 50m on the spot on the spot 2km on the spot on the spot.

Ottersberg 4D5

Am Sportzentrum, Fährwisch. **GPS:** n53,10721 e9,13558.

8 free € 1 Ch € 1/8h. **Location:** Simple. **Surface:** gravel/sand.
01/01-31/12
Distance: 500m 200m.

Ovelgönne 4C5

Burgdorf Ovelgönne, Am Sportplatz. **GPS:** n53,34333 e8,42750.

5 free Ch free. **Surface:** gravel. 01/01-31/12
Distance: 700m 700m 700m.

Oyten 4D5

KNAUS Reisemobilpark, Oyter See 1. **GPS:** n53,04645 e9,00396.

DE

20 € 12-15 € 2,20 Ch € 0,70/kWh WC included € 1 **Location:** Rural, comfortable. **Surface:** metalled. 01/04-01/11
Distance: 2,5km 3km Oyter See 150m.
Remarks: Caution key € 5.

Papenburg 4B5

Roten Kreuz, Rathausstraße. **GPS:** n53,07646 e7,39266.
30 free. **Surface:** gravel. 01/01-31/12
Distance: on the spot 300m.

Papenburg 4B5

Poggenpoel, Zum Poggenpoel. **GPS:** n53,06526 e7,42630.

20 € 8 € 3/100liter € 3 Ch (8x)€ 2/24h WC € 2 **Location:** Rural, simple. **Surface:** gravel. 01/01-31/12
Distance: 3,5km Badesee.
Remarks: At lake, max. 3 nights.

Rastede 4C5

Mühlenstraße. **GPS:** n53,24806 e8,20944.

4 free. **Location:** Urban, simple. **Surface:** metalled.
01/01-31/12
Distance: 1km 2,7km 1km 2km.

Rastede 4C5

Bauernmuseum, Raiffeisenstraße 60. **GPS:** n53,24627 e8,18579.

5 € 5 € 1 (5x)€ 1/24h. **Location:** Rural, simple, quiet.
Surface: grassy. 01/01-31/12
Distance: 1km 400m 100m.

Rehburg-Loccum 9D1

Wohnmobilstellplatz Rehburg, Auf der Bleiche. **GPS:** n52,47370 e9,23227.

8 € 5 € 1/12h. **Surface:** gravel. 01/01-31/12
Distance: 400m.

Tourist information Rehburg-Loccum:
Dinosaurierpark Münchehagen.Attractions park around the dinosaur.
28/02-30/11 10h, summers 9h.

Remels 4B5

Remelser Paddel- & Pedalstation, Raiffeisenstrasse/Uferstrasse. **GPS:** n53,30123 e7,75151.

5 € 5 Ch (4x)€ 2. **Surface:** metalled. 01/01-31/12
Distance: 500m 50m 500m.
Remarks: Max. 3 days, canoe and bicycle rental.

Remels 4B5

Schützenplatz, Schützenstraße. **GPS:** n53,30719 e7,74708.

10 € 5 Ch € 1/12h. **Surface:** grasstiles.
01/01-31/12 10/06-15/06.
Distance: 500m.
Remarks: Max. 3 nights.

Rhauderfehn 4B5

Paddel- und Pedalstation, Am Siel 8. **GPS:** n53,13878 e7,58689.

16 € 5 € 1/100liter Ch (16x)€ 1/8h WC € 2. **Location:** Rural, luxurious, quiet. **Surface:** grassy. 01/01-31/12
Distance: 500m on the spot on the spot 50m.

DE

Remarks: Caution sanitary € 10, canoe and bicycle rental.

Rhede/Ems 4A5

Emspark, Am Sportplatz 6. **GPS**: n53,05853 e7,27621.

5 free. **Location:** Simple. **Surface:** metalled. 01/01-31/12
Distance: 500m 500m 500m.
Remarks: Parking in front of sports park.

Rinteln 9D1

Reisemobilplatz am Weseranger, Dankerser strasse. **GPS**: n52,19226 e9,07842.

50 free € 2/100liter € 2 Ch € 2 (36x)€ 0,50/kWh. **Location:** Rural.
Surface: asphalted/gravel. 01/01-31/12
Distance: 1km on the spot on the spot 100m 400m 400m Weserradweg on the spot.

Rodewald 5A6

Am Freibad, Im Zentrum. **GPS**: n52,66369 e9,48020.

10 free (10x)€ 0,50/kWh. **Surface:** grasstiles. 01/01-31/12
Distance: 200m on the spot.

Rotenburg (Wümme) 5A5

Am Weichelsee, Bremer Straße. **GPS**: n53,11960 e9,38230.

20 € 5 € 2 Ch (20x)€ 2. **Location:** Rural, simple.
Surface: metalled. 01/01-31/12
Distance: 2km on the spot Strandhaus 2km on the spot.
Remarks: Check in at StrandHouse.

Salzgitter 10B1

Reisemobilstellplatz am Salzgittersee, Zum Salzgittersee. **GPS**: n52,15222 e10,31306.
12 free € 2/100liter Ch € 1/6h. **Surface:** grassy/metalled.
Distance: 1km on the spot nearby 200m.
Remarks: Max. 4 days.

Salzhausen 5B5

Am Waldbad, Schwienbrink. **GPS**: n53,22199 e10,17841.

6 free € 1/10minutes Ch free (4x)€ 1/8h. **Location:** Rural, simple.
Surface: gravel. 01/01-31/12
Distance: 1km 500m.

Salzhemmendorf 10A2

Naturerlebnisbad Lauenstein, Landstrasse, Hemmendorfer. **GPS**: n52,07952 e9,57124.
3 € 5. **Surface:** asphalted. 01/01-31/12
Distance: 500m.

Salzhemmendorf 10A2

Ith-Sole-Therme, In der Saale-Aue. **GPS**: n52,07093 e9,58564.

20 € 5 € 0,20/20liter € 1 Ch € 0,50/kWh. **Surface:** metalled.
01/01-31/12
Distance: 400m.

Salzhemmendorf 10A2

Rasti-land, Quanthofer strasse 9. **GPS**: n52,09706 e9,66451.

5 free. **Surface:** metalled.
Distance: 1km.
Remarks: Bus parking amusement park.

Tourist information Salzhemmendorf:
Rasti-Land, Quanthofer strasse 9.Amusement park. 01/04-31/10 10-17/18h, Apr, Sep: Mo, Sa, Su.

Sande (Nieder-Sachsen) 4B4

Am Markt. **GPS**: n53,50251 e8,01113.

DE

4 free. **Location:** Urban, simple. **Surface:** metalled.
01/01-31/12
Distance: 100m 100m 100m.

Sande (Nieder-Sachsen) 4B4

Sander See. GPS: n53,51162 e8,00206.

4 free. **Surface:** metalled. 01/01-31/12
Distance: 2km.

Sande (Nieder-Sachsen) 4B4

Fa. Freizeitmobile von der Kammer, Huntestraße 1. **GPS:** n53,49076 e8,02292.

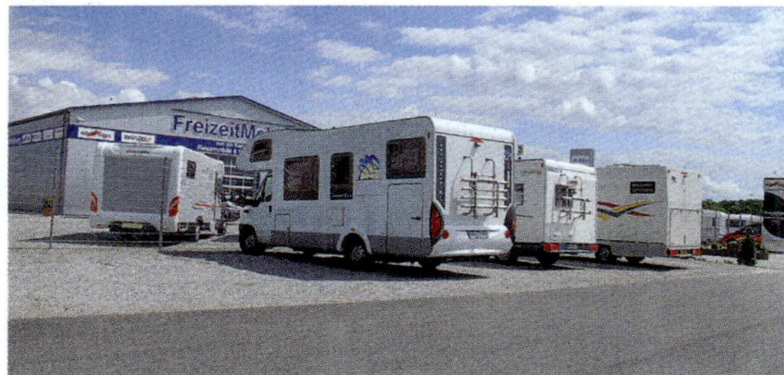

5 free Ch On demand. **Surface:** gravel.

Sandstedt 4C5

Wohnmobilstellplatz Sandstedt - Sandstedt

info@hagen-cux.de - www.hagen-cux.de

Beautiful view
Paved and flat motorhome pitches
Located near marina

Wohnmobilstellplatz Sandstedt, Am Radarturm 5. **GPS:** n53,36317 e8,51231.
10 free € 1/100liter € 1 Ch € 1 € 1.
Surface: metalled.
01/04-30/09
Distance: 500m 3km 100m 950m 100m.

Saterland 4B5

Reisemobilhafen am Maiglöckchensee, Am Sportplatz, Scharrel. **GPS:** n53,07060 e7,70116.

28+7 € 4 € 1/100liter € 1 Ch € 1 (28x)€ 2/24h WC € 0,50 € 2.
Location: Rural, luxurious, quiet. **Surface:** grassy. 01/01-31/12
Distance: 300m 50m 50m 1km 500m 500m.

Saterland 4B5

Reisemobilplatz Am Bootshafen, Hauptstrasse 640, Strücklingen. **GPS:** n53,12819 e7,66762.

15 € 3 € 1/100liter € 1 Ch € 1,50/24h WC € 1 € 0,50.
Location: Rural, simple. **Surface:** grassy/gravel. 01/01-31/12
Distance: 100m on the spot on the spot on the spot on the spot 100m.

Scharnebeck 5B5

Wohnmobilstellplatz Am Schiffshebewerk, Adendorfer Straße 40. **GPS:** n53,29196 e10,49320.

15 € 6/24h, park € 2 € 1/10minutes Ch (8x)€ 1/8h.
Location: Rural, comfortable, isolated, quiet. **Surface:** metalled.
01/01-31/12
Distance: 1km 200m Aldi 400m.
Remarks: Boat lift Scharnebeck, climbing wall 100m.

Schneverdingen 5A5

Am Quellenbad, Inseler Straße. **GPS:** n53,13110 e9,77280.

20 free € 2 Ch WC € 1. **Location:** Urban, simple. **Surface:** grassy.
01/01-31/12

DE

Distance: 2km on the spot on the spot on the spot.
Remarks: Use sanitary only during opening hours swimming pool.

S Schneverdingen 5A5

Wohnmobilhafen Lüneburger Heide, Badeweg 3, Heber. **GPS**: n53,07104 e9,86481.

38 € 12 € 1 Ch (38x)included WC Use sanitary € 2/pp.
Location: Rural, comfortable. **Surface:** grassy. 01/04-31/10
Distance: on camp site on the spot on the spot.
Remarks: Use sanitary facilities at campsite.

Schneverdingen 5A5

Parkplatz Festhalle, Im Osterwald. **GPS**: n53,11893 e9,80681.

4 free. **Location:** Simple. **Surface:** metalled. 01/01-31/12
Distance: 2km 2km.
Remarks: Entrance via Festhalle.

S Schneverdingen 5A5

Reisemobilhafen Lüneburgerheide, Badeweg 3, Heber. **GPS**: n53,07108 e9,86464.

5 € 12 Ch (5x) WC € 2,50. **Location:** Rural, luxurious, quiet. **Surface:** grasstiles/metalled. 01/04-31/10
Distance: 5km on camp site.
Remarks: Sanitary at campsite.

S Schneverdingen 5A5

Mariechens Hoff, Voßbarg 15, Reinsehlen. **GPS**: n53,17122 e9,83316.

8 € 8 Ch included (8x) € 0,40/kWh. **Location:** Rural, simple, isolated, quiet. **Surface:** grassy. 01/01-31/12

Distance: 7km 15km 3km 4 km on the spot on the spot.

Schöppenstedt 10C1

Elm-Asse-Platz, Schützenplatz am Berge. **GPS**: n52,14756 e10,77737.

15 free. **Surface:** asphalted. 01/01-31/12
Remarks: Parking next to sports ground and swimming pool.

Tourist information Schöppenstedt:

The region of Till Eulenspiegel. Tills-Tauf-Tour: cycle and hiking routesin the country of Jester Till, start at the Till Eulenspiegel museum.
Tue-Fri 14-17h, Sa-Su 11-17h.
M Till Eulenspiegelmuseum, Nordstrasse 4a.
Tue-Fri 14-17h, Sa-Su 11-17h Mo.

Schortens 4B4

Aqua-toll, Beethovenstrasse. **GPS**: n53,53961 e7,93780.

2 free. **Surface:** metalled. 01/01-31/12
Distance: 200m 25m.
Remarks: Parking swimming pool.

Schortens 4B4

Reisemobilstellplatz Fair-Cafe, Accumer Strasse 5. **GPS**: n53,55226 e7,97624.

3 guests free. **Surface:** unpaved. 01/01-31/12
Distance: 3km 100m.

S Schulenberg 10B2

Wiesenbergstrasse. **GPS**: n51,83535 e10,43464.

30 € 5 + € 1,20/pp € 1 Ch (6x) € 0,60/kWh WC. 01/01-31/12
Distance: on the spot.

DE

Remarks: Parking centre, view on Okerstausee.

S Schüttorf 9A1

Am Kuhmplatz, Graf-Egbert-Straße. **GPS**: n52,32123 e7,22642.

10 free Ch free. **Location:** Rural, simple. **Surface:** gravel. 01/01-31/12
Distance: 2,4km 100m.
Remarks: Parking swimming pool.

Schwanewede 4C5

Am Markt, Am Markt. **GPS**: n53,22412 e8,59644.

3 free. **Location:** Simple, central. **Surface:** metalled.
01/01-31/12
Distance: on the spot on the spot on the spot.

Schwanewede 4C5

Brücke zu Harriersand, Inselstraße. **GPS**: n53,26489 e8,49762.

5 free. **Location:** Rural, simple, isolated. **Surface:** grassy.
01/01-31/12
Distance: 7km.

Schwanewede 4C5

Löhnhorst, Hammersbeckerweg/Am Fosshall. **GPS**: n53,20355 e8,62453.

2 free. **Location:** Rural, simple, isolated, quiet. **Surface:** metalled.
01/01-31/12
Distance: 6km 6km 6km.

Schwanewede 4C5

Wohnmobilstellplatz, Klint, Neuenkirchen. **GPS**: n53,23670 e8,50919.

5 free. **Location:** Rural, simple, quiet. **Surface:** unpaved.
01/01-31/12
Distance: 500m.
Remarks: Dead end street.

S Selsingen 5A4

Wohnmobilstation, Im Sick. **GPS**: n53,42764 e9,50764.

25 free Ch free. **Location:** Rural, simple, quiet. **Surface:** metalled.
01/01-31/12
Distance: 500m 100m.

S Sittensen 5A5

Parkplatz, Mühlenstrasse. **GPS**: n53,27652 e9,50750.

5 free Ch WC free. **Location:** Simple, central. **Surface:** metalled.
01/01-31/12
Distance: centre 200m on the spot on the spot.

Soltau 5A5

Soltau Therme, Stubbendorffweg. **GPS**: n52,99301 e9,84443.

10 free. **Location:** Simple, central, quiet. **Surface:** metalled.
01/01-31/12
Distance: 1km on the spot on the spot on the spot.
Remarks: Max. 1 night.

Soltau 5A5

Heidepark. **GPS**: n53,02166 e9,87370.

DE

100 € 5. **Location:** Rural, simple, isolated. **Surface:** grasstiles.
01/01-31/12
Remarks: Parking amusement park.

Tourist information Soltau:
Small town at the border of the Lüneburg Heath.
Heidepark.Amusement park.
01/04-31/10 9-18h, 01/07-15/08 Sa 9-21h.

S Spieka-Neufeld 4C3

Wohnmobilhafen, Deichweg. **GPS**: n53,78899 e8,55060.

40 € 8 € 1/100liter Ch (18x)€ 1/2kWh. **Location:** Rural, simple.
Surface: gravel/metalled. 01/01-31/12
Distance: 300m on the spot on the spot 200m.
Remarks: Bread-service.

S St.Andreasberg 10B3

Panoramabad, Braunlagerstrasse. **GPS**: n51,71683 e10,52891.

20 € 8 Ch (20x) WC included. **Surface:** asphalted.
01/01-31/12
Distance: 750m 50m 750m 2km.

S St.Andreasberg 10B3

Silbererzgrube Samson, Am Samson 4. **GPS**: n51,71398 e10,51625.
20 € 10 Ch included. **Surface:** gravel. 01/01-31/12

S Stade 5A4

Wohnmobilstellplatz Am Schiffertor, Schiffertorsstrasse 21. **GPS**: n53,60278 e9,46667.

79 € 8,50/24h € 1/80liter Ch € 0,50/kWh. **Location:** Urban, central. **Surface:** gravel.
01/01-31/12
Distance: 500m 700m.

Tourist information Stade:
Tourist Information am Hafen, Hansestrasse 16.Renovated Hanseatic harbour.

S Stadland 4C4

Am Sportplatz, Hauptstrasse, Seefeld. **GPS**: n53,45639 e8,35778.

5 free € 1/10minutes (4x)€ 1/8h. **Surface:** asphalted.
01/01-31/12
Distance: on the spot on the spot on the spot.

S Stadland 4C4

Birkenweg, Kleinensiel. **GPS**: n53,44194 e8,47444.

4 free Ch free. **Surface:** metalled. 01/01-31/12
Distance: on the spot.
Remarks: At community centre.

S Stadland 4C4

Deichparkplatz, Fährstrasse, Kleinensiel. **GPS**: n53,44250 e8,47833.

5 free € 1 . **Surface:** gravel. 01/01-31/12
Distance: 200m Weserstrand.

S Stadland 4C4

Rathausplatz, Am Markt, Rodenkirchen. **GPS**: n53,39944 e8,45444.

10 free € 1/10minutes Ch (4x)€ 1/8h. **Surface:** metalled.
01/01-31/12 Thu 5-13h.
Distance: on the spot on the spot on the spot on the spot.

DE

Stadthagen 9D1

Reisemobilplatz am Tropicana, Jahnstraße 2. **GPS**: n52,32236 e9,18896.
free Ch WC against payment. **Surface:** metalled.
01/01-31/12

Stadtoldendorf 10A2

Mobilcamping unter den Homburg, Linnenkämper Strasse 33. **GPS**: n51,87777 e9,63500.

30 € 5/day € 1 . **Surface:** grassy. 01/01-31/12
Distance: 1km 50m 1km.

Steinfeld 9C1

Zur Schemder Bergmark, Dammer Strasse. **GPS**: n52,58308 e8,21476.

20 free € 1/100liter € 0,50 Ch € 0,50. **Location:** Rural, quiet.
Surface: metalled. 01/01-31/12
Distance: 500m 500m.
Remarks: Parking swimming pool.

Steinhude 10A1

Wohnmobilstellplatz Steinhude, Am Bruchdamm. **GPS**: n52,44874 e9,35478.

180 € 7,50 € 1 Ch (60x)€ 3/day WC € 1 washing machine/dryer € 2,50. **Surface:** grassy.
01/01-31/12
Distance: 500m 500m 500m 500m.
Remarks: Max. 3 nights, bread-service. Altenhagen > Steinude.

Tourist information Steinhude:
Marina on lake of the same name.

Steyerberg 4D6

Waldferienpark Steyerberg, Zum Ferienpark 37. **GPS**: n52,57395 e9,01096.

40 € 5 € 1 Ch € 2 WC € 2. **Surface:** metalled.
01/01-31/12
Distance: 1km 1km 1km.

Steyerberg 4D6

Gasthaus Zur Eiche, Sarninghausen 2. **GPS**: n52,56944 e8,99444.

15 guests free . **Surface:** grassy. 01/01-31/12

Stolzenau 9D1

Reisemobilstellplatz Stolzenau, Weserstrasse. **GPS**: n52,51021 e9,08104.

33 € 4 € 1 Ch (24x)€ 2/12h. **Surface:** grasstiles.
01/03-30/09
Distance: 250m on the spot on the spot 300m 300m.
Remarks: Along the Weser river.

Sulingen 4D6

Am Stadtsee, Kornstraße. **GPS**: n52,67653 e8,80127.

10 free € 1/5minutes € 1 Ch € 1. **Surface:** metalled.
01/01-31/12
Distance: 600m 300m.

Surwold 4B5

Erholungsgebiet Surwolds Wald, Waldstrasse. **GPS**: n52,96743 e7,51535.

DE

20 € 5 € 1/100liter Ch € 2 WC € 0,50. **Surface:** grassy.
01/01-31/12
Distance: 800m 250m.

Surwold 4B5

Privatplatz Klapper, Papenburgerstrasse 57. **GPS:** n53,01774 e7,48470.

10 € 10 Ch (4x)€ 1/24h WC € 2. **Location:** Rural, simple.
Surface: grassy. 01/01-31/12
Distance: 1km 1,5km 1km 1km.
Remarks: Swimming pool and picnic area available.

Tarmstedt 4D5

Landtechniek Grabau, Bahnhofstraße. **GPS:** n53,22421 e9,08728.

15 € 6 Ch included. **Location:** Simple. **Surface:** metalled.
01/01-31/12
Distance: on the spot 500m on the spot.

Thedinghausen 4D6

Reisemobilstellplatz Thedinghausen, Braunschweiger Straße. **GPS:** n52,96188 e9,03020.

8 free € 1 Ch € 1/6h WC. **Surface:** metalled.
01/01-31/12
Distance: 500m on the spot on the spot.

Twist 4A6

Am Hallenbad. **GPS:** n52,64719 e7,08918.

6 free € 1/100liter Ch (8x)€ 1/2kWh. **Surface:** metalled.
01/01-31/12
Distance: on the spot on the spot.
Remarks: Barefoot path.

Uchte 9D1

Balkenkamp. **GPS:** n52,49761 e8,90618.

3 free € 1 Ch. **Surface:** metalled. 01/01-31/12
Distance: 100m 500m 100m.

Uelsen 9A1

Festplatz, Hardinghauserstrasse. **GPS:** n52,49575 e6,88840.

10 free € 2 Ch WC. **Surface:** asphalted. 01/01-31/12

Uelzen 5B5

Im Sportboothafen, Riedweg 7. **GPS:** n52,95722 e10,59444.

8 € 8 + € 1/pp € 1/70liter € 1 Ch (8x)€ 1/6h WC included
washing machine/dryer € 2,50. **Location:** Rural, simple, quiet. **Surface:** metalled. 01/01-31/12
Distance: on the spot on the spot on the spot 1,9km on the spot on the spot.
Remarks: Playground, free bicycles available, max. 3 nights.

Undeloh 5A5

Am Naturschutzpark, Wilseder Straße. **GPS:** n53,19253 e9,97709.

DE

30 € 3/day, € 6/night. **Location:** Rural, simple. **Surface:** unpaved. 01/01-31/12
Distance: 500m 100m on the spot.
Remarks: In nature reserve the the Lüneburg Heide (heath).

S Uslar 10A3

Reisemobilpark am Badeland, Zur Schwarzen Erde. **GPS**: n51,66715 e9,62824.

20 € 6 + reduction swimming pool € 1/10minutes Ch € 1/8h WC . **Surface:** metalled. 01/01-31/12
Distance: 1km on the spot.

S Uslar 10A3

Am Lindenhof, Lindenhof 1. **GPS**: n51,67213 e9,62952.
5 first night € 8, € 2 each additional night Ch € 0,30/kWh.
01/01-31/12

Tourist information Uslar:
Touristik Information, Mühlentor 1,, www.uslarer-land.de.Historical little town with half-timbered houses.
Market, city centre. Fri 9-13h.
Alaris Schmetterlingspark.Butterfly park in tropical rain forest.
01/04-31/10 Tue-Su 9.30-17.30h.
Erlebniswald.Educational park, discovering nature.
01/01-31/12.
Uslarer Badeland.Swimming pool complex.
Sa/Su 10-18h, Tue-Fri 10-20h, Mo 10-13h.

Vechta 4C6

Am Hallenwellen- und Freibad, Dornbusch. **GPS**: n52,74000 e8,29639.

10 free. **Location:** Urban, simple. **Surface:** grassy/metalled.
01/01-31/12
Distance: 1km 1km 1km.
Remarks: Parking swimming pool, max. 3 days, service Bokenerddamm 40.

Vechta 4C6

Oldenburgerstraße. **GPS**: n52,73245 e8,28833.

5 free. **Location:** Urban, simple. **Surface:** metalled.
01/01-31/12
Distance: on the spot on the spot on the spot.

Visselhövede 5A5

Zu den Visselwiesen, Wüstenhof 1. **GPS**: n52,98530 e9,57772.

8 free. **Location:** Urban, simple. **Surface:** metalled.
01/01-31/12
Distance: 100m 200m.

S Walchum 4A6

Marinapark Emstal, Steinbilder Straße. **GPS**: n52,92680 e7,29624.

10 € 10 Ch (6x) WC € 1,50. **Location:** Rural.
Surface: grassy. 01/01-31/12
Distance: fishing permit obligatory 300m on the spot on the spot on the spot.

S Walsrode 5A6

Forellenhof, Hünzingen 3. **GPS**: n52,89855 e9,59122.

10 € 10 (2x). **Location:** Rural, simple, isolated, quiet.
Surface: grasstiles/grassy.
Distance: 3km on the spot 3km.
Remarks: Free with a meal.

Tourist information Walsrode:
Vogelpark Walsrode.Bird park and botanical garden. 01/03-31/10 8-19h.

S Wangerland 4B4

Am Yachthafen, Zum Hafen, Horumersiel. **GPS**: n53,68293 e8,02091.

DE

22 € 15,80 Ch WC included. **Surface:** concrete.
01/04-30/10
Distance: 600m on the spot.

S Wangerland 4B4

An der Ostdüne, Bäderstrasse, Hooksiel. **GPS:** n53,64103 e8,03514.

75 € 10 + € 2,90/pp Kurtaxe, dog € 3,10 Ch WC included.
Surface: gravel. 01/04-30/10
Distance: 1,7km beach ±250m.

S Wangerland 4B4

Nordsee-Camping-Schillig, Jadestraße, Schillig. **GPS:** n53,69986 e8,02338.

60+150 € 10 + € 2,90/pp Kurtaxe, dog € 3,10
Ch WC included. **Surface:** grassy. 01/04-31/10
Distance: 200m.

S Wardenburg 4C5

Keilstrasse, Astrup. **GPS:** n53,04770 e8,21197.

5 free (3x). **Location:** Urban, simple. **Surface:** gravel. 01/01-31/12
Distance: 2,5km.

Wardenburg 4C5

Marktplatz, Huntestraße. **GPS:** n53,06401 e8,19832.

3 free. **Location:** Urban, simple. **Surface:** metalled.
01/01-31/12
Distance: on the spot 3,6km.

S Weener 4B5

Am Alten Hafen, Panneborgstrasse. **GPS:** n53,16953 e7,36167.

45 € 7,50/24h € 1/100liter Ch (45x)€ 2,50/24h WC € 1.
Location: Urban, comfortable. **Surface:** asphalted. 01/01-31/12 during harbor festival 3rd week of June.
Distance: on the spot on the spot on the spot.
Remarks: Max. 3 days.

Weener 4B5

Am Yachthafen, Am Marina-Park. **GPS:** n53,16570 e7,36480.
24 € 7,50 € 2,50 € 2. **Surface:** metalled. 01/04-30/09
Distance: centre 1,2km 50m.

S Werlte 4B6

Kreutzmanns Mühle, Kirchstraße. **GPS:** n52,85463 e7,68155.

6 free € 1/100liter Ch (8x)€ 1/2kWh. **Location:** Urban, comfortable. **Surface:** metalled. 01/01-31/12
Distance: 200m 200m 200m.

S Westergellersen 5B5

Turniergelände Luhmühlen, Westergellerser Heide. **GPS:** n53,23306 e10,21623.

35 € 8 € 1 Ch (35x)€ 1/8h WC . **Location:** Rural, comfortable, isolated, quiet. **Surface:** grassy. 01/01-31/12
Distance: 4km 1,5km 4km 4km 2km.

DE

S Westerholt 4B4

Am Schul- und Sportzentrum, Ewigsweg. **GPS**: n53,59089 e7,44907.
5 free Ch free. **Surface:** metalled. 01/01-31/12
Distance: 500m 600m.

Westerstede 4B5

Albert-Post-Platz, Auf der Lohe. **GPS**: n53,25883 e7,92685.

5 free. **Location:** Urban, simple. **Surface:** metalled.
01/01-31/12
Distance: 100m 2km 250m.

Westerstede 4B5

Badesee Karlshof, Bekassinenweg. **GPS**: n53,18811 e7,86954.

5 free. **Location:** Rural, simple, isolated. **Surface:** gravel.
01/01-31/12
Distance: Badesee.
Remarks: Max. 3 days.

S Westerstede 4B5

Wohnmobilhafen Westerstede, Süderstraße 2. **GPS**: n53,24968 e7,93438.

50 € 5 Ch € 2/24h WC € 2/pppd Use sanitary € 2,50.
Location: Urban, comfortable, quiet. **Surface:** grassy/gravel.
01/01-31/12
Distance: 800m 1,4km McDonalds 200m.

S Westoverledingen 4B5

Rathausplatz, Bahnhofstrasse 18, Ihrhove. **GPS**: n53,16634 e7,45173.

3 free € 1/100liter Ch. **Location:** Urban, simple. **Surface:** grassy.
01/01-31/12 last week Jun.
Distance: on the spot 50m.
Remarks: At townhall.

S Westoverledingen 4B5

Reisemobilhafen zur Mühle, Mühlenstrasse 214, Steenfelderfehn. **GPS**: n53,12944 e7,44051.

30 € 5 Ch (18x)included. **Location:** Rural, simple.
Surface: grassy/metalled. 01/01-31/12
Distance: on the spot 1km.

S Westoverledingen 4B5

Schützenplatz Flachsmeer, Papenburger strasse 74, Flachsmeer. **GPS**: n53,12700 e7,46367.

10 € 5 (10x)included. **Location:** Rural, simple.
Surface: grassy. 01/01-31/12
Distance: on the spot 100m.

S Wiefelstede 4C5

Wohnmobilstellplatz am Bernsteinsee, Dorfstrasse 11, Conneforde. **GPS**: n53,32657 e8,06362.

25 € 6 € 0,50 € 2 Ch (25x)€ 0,50/kWh WC € 0,50 on camp site.
Location: Rural, comfortable. **Surface:** grassy. 01/01-31/12
Distance: on the spot on the spot.
Remarks: In front of campsite, caution sepkey € 5.

Wiefelstede 4C5

Freibad Wiefelstede, Alter Damm 11. **GPS**: n53,26146 e8,10713.

10 free. **Location:** Rural, simple, quiet. **Surface:** metalled.
01/01-31/12

DE

Distance: 500m on the spot 1,5km.

S Wiesmoor 4B4

Bootshafen Ottermeer, Am Stadion. **GPS**: n53,40951 e7,71841.

14 € 5,50 Ch included. **Surface:** grassy/metalled.
01/01-31/12
Distance: 1,5km.
Remarks: Key service at Gaststätte (12-19h).

S Wietzendorf 5A6

Übernachtungsoase Südsee Camp, Südsee camp 1. **GPS**: n52,93120 e9,96474.

40 € 12 € 1/100liter € 0,50/kWh WC € 0,50. **Surface:** metalled.
Distance: nearby on the spot.

S Wildeshausen 4C6

Am Krandel, Krandelstrasse. **GPS**: n52,90042 e8,42728.

16 € 5 € 1/80liter Ch (15x)included. **Location:** Rural, simple.
Surface: grassy/metalled. 01/01-31/12
Distance: 500m 4,4km 400m 700m.
Remarks: Parking at swimming pool.

S Wilhelmshaven 4C4

Wohnmobilhafen Nautimo, Friedenstrasse 99. **GPS**: n53,53546 e8,10104.

25 € 7 € 1 Ch (16x)€ 1/8h € 1. **Surface:** metalled.
01/01-31/12
Distance: 2km on the spot 800m.
Remarks: Max. 7 days.

S Wilhelmshaven 4C4

Wohnmobilstellplatz Schleuseninsel, Schleussenstrasse 37. **GPS**: n53,51478 e8,15218.

28 € 8, trailer € 5 € 0,50/50liter Ch (28x)€ 3/24h WC.
Surface: gravel. 01/01-31/12
Distance: 250m Jadebus.

S Wilhelmshaven 4C4

Am Freibad Nord, Möwenstraße 30. **GPS**: n53,57032 e8,10368.

6 € 3,50, free with use of swimming pool Ch € 1/6h WC.
Surface: gravel. 01/05-31/08
Distance: 1,5km.
Remarks: Use sanitary only during opening hours swimming pool.

S Wilhelmshaven 4C4

Reisemobilstellplatz Wilhelmshaven Südstadt, Banterweg 12. **GPS**: n53,51559 e8,09072.

15 € 8 Ch . **Surface:** gravel. 01/01-31/12

Wilhelmshaven 4C4

Fliegerdeich, Fliegerdeich. **GPS**: n53,50996 e8,12718.

40 € 6. **Location:** Rural. **Surface:** metalled. 01/01-31/12
Distance: 2,5km sea nearby.
Remarks: No camping activities.

Tourist information Wilhelmshaven:

Wilhelmshaven Touristik & Freizeit GmbH, Südstrand 108, www.whv-touristik.de.Large port city with the touristic centre Südstrand.

Aquarium Wilhelmshaven, Südstrand.Sea aquarium.

DE

10-18h.
Oceanis, Am Bontekai.Virtual under water station; museum and aquarium.
10-18h.
Deutsches Marinemuseum, Südstrand 125.
10-19h, 01/10-31/03 10-17h. € 7,50, family card € 18.
Piratenmuseum, Eberstrasse 88 A.History of the piracy.
01/04-31/10 11-17h.

Winsen/Luhe 5B4

Festplatz Bleiche, Tönnhäuserweg. **GPS**: n53,36452 e10,21228.

10 free. **Location:** Simple, central. **Surface:** asphalted.
01/01-31/12
Distance: 100m 100m 100m.

Winsen/Luhe 5B4

GreenEagle Golf, Radbrucher Straße 200. **GPS**: n53,32278 e10,22778.
15 free, playing golf obligatory. **Location:** Simple. **Surface:** gravel.
01/01-31/12
Distance: 6km 2,2km on the spot.

S **Winsen/Luhe** 5B4

Freizeit Center Albrecht, Porchestrasse 15, Gewerbegebiet Lühdorf. **GPS**: n53,33750 e10,21947.

11 free € 2 Ch (11x) WC. **Location:** Rural, simple.
Surface: metalled. 01/01-31/12
Distance: 4,5km on the spot.

S **Wittmund** 4B4

Hafen Harlesiel, Am Harlesiel. **GPS**: n53,70853 e7,80888.

54 € 10-13 + € 2 Kurtaxe Ch € 3 WC . **Surface:** metalled.
15/03-31/10
Distance: on the spot.
Remarks: Caution key electricity € 10.

Wittmund 4B4

Schützenplatz, Auricherstrasse. **GPS**: n53,55763 e7,69156.
30 free. **Surface:** grassy. 01/01-31/12
Distance: 800m bakery 200m.

S **Wolfsburg** 10C1

Autostadt, Berliner Brücke. **GPS**: n52,43436 e10,79947.
20 € 10 Ch included. **Surface:** asphalted. 01/01-31/12

Tourist information Wolfsburg:
Autostadt.Of the Volkswagen-concern; with pavilion of several car makes, car tower of 20 floors, test driving. 9-20h.

S **Zetel** 4B4

Johann Quathamer, Fuhrenkampstrasse 60. **GPS**: n53,40084 e7,91893.

15 € 7 € 1/100liter Ch (15x) WC included € 0,50.
Location: Rural, comfortable, quiet. **Surface:** grassy. 01/01-31/12
Distance: 4km.

S **Zetel** 4B4

Markthamm, Neuenburger Strasse. **GPS**: n53,41706 e7,97000.

40 free Ch free (6x) € 1/1kWh. **Location:** Urban, simple, central.
Surface: grasstiles. 01/01-31/12
Distance: on the spot Imbiss.
Remarks: Parking centre, max. 2 days, service Kläranlage open: Mo/Tue 11-23h, Thu/Sa 11-23h, Su 16-23h, max. 2 days.

Zetel 4B4

Driefeler Esch. **GPS**: n53,41835 e7,98445.

10 free. **Location:** Simple. **Surface:** gravel. 01/01-31/12
Remarks: Parking swimming pool, max. 48h.

Zetel 4B4

Schulmuseum Bohlenbergerfeld, Wehdestrasse. **GPS**: n53,41322 e7,92143.

25 free. **Location:** Rural, simple, isolated. **Surface:** grassy/gravel.
01/01-31/12
Distance: 2,5 km.

DE

Zetel 4B4

Urwald, Urwaldstrasse, Neuenburg. **GPS**: n53,39293 e7,96547.

20 free. **Location:** Rural, simple, quiet.
01/01-31/12
Remarks: Max. 1 day.

S Zetel 4B4

Kläranlage, Mohrstrasse. **GPS**: n53,42302 e7,97937.
Ch free. 01/01-31/12
Remarks: Mo/Thu 7-16h, Fri 7-13h, Sa/Su 9-9.30h.

Zeven 4D5

Viehmarkt, Meyerstrasse/Godenstedterstrasse. **GPS**: n53,29764 e9,27514.

4 free. **Location:** Simple. **Surface:** metalled. 01/01-31/12
Distance: 500m.

Mecklenburg-Western Pomerania

S Ahlbeck 6C2

Caravanplatz Am Wiesenrand, Gothenweg 5a. **GPS**: n53,94100 e14,17600.

24 € 10, peak season € 12,50 Ch € 2 WC € 1 € 3,dryer € 3.
Surface: grassy. 01/03-31/10
Distance: 10min 10min 500m 200m.
Remarks: Bread-service.

S Ahlbeck 6C2

Wohnmobilstellplatz Rauthe, Waldstrasse 7. **GPS**: n53,93660 e14,18660.

30 € 15 Ch WC € 2 € 4. **Surface:** grassy. 01/01-31/12
Distance: on the spot 5 min 200m 200m.

Ahlbeck 6C2

Parkplatz an der Grenze, Swinemüdestrasse. **GPS**: n53,92380 e14,21280.

30 € 5. **Surface:** metalled. 01/01-31/12
Distance: 3km.
Remarks: Max. 24h.

Ahrenshoop 6A2

Dorfstraße. **GPS**: n54,39155 e12,43914.

€ 7,50 day/€ 7,50 night. **Surface:** gravel. 01/01-31/12
Distance: 2km beach 50m.

S Alt Schwerin 6A4

Insel Camping Werder, Wendorf 8. **GPS**: n53,48696 e12,31833.

13 € 9,80 Ch € 2 washing machine/dryer € 3. **Surface:** grassy.
01/01-31/12
Distance: 4km on the spot on the spot on the spot.

S Altwarp 6D3

Hafen, Seestrasse. **GPS**: n53,73905 e14,27147.

40 € 11 Ch WC included. 01/01-31/12
Distance: on the spot 300m on the spot 300m 400m.

Anklam 6C3

Wasserwanderrastplatz, Demminer strasse. **GPS**: n53,85610 e13,67870.

5 € 5. **Surface:** metalled. 01/01-31/12
Distance: 500m on the spot.

Bansin 6C2

Waldparkplatz Bansin. **GPS**: n53,99800 e14,11260.

80 € 4/5 + € 2,50/pp Ch € 2 WC € 1. **Surface:** metalled.
01/05-30/09
Distance: 3km 400m 300m on the spot.

Bansin 6C2

Caravanstellplatz Jürgen Wille, Seestrasse 30. **GPS**: n53,96560 e14,13670.

9 € 9 + € 4/pp Ch € 0,40/kWh WC € 1 washing machine/dryer € 3 € 2,50/h. **Surface:** grassy. 01/01-31/12
Distance: 200m 800m.

Bansin 6C2

Udo Labahn, Seestrasse 35. **GPS**: n53,96520 e14,13510.

5 € 5 € 0,40/kWh. 01/01-31/12
Distance: 300m 300m.

Banzkow 5D4

Lewitz Mühle, An der Lewitzmühle 40. **GPS**: n53,52094 e11,50496.

10 € 20. **Surface:** asphalted. 01/01-31/12
Distance: on the spot 2km 5 min.

Bargeshagen 5D2

Firma Caravaning Nord, Rabenhorster Damm 3. **GPS**: n54,11198 e11,97174.

10 € 10 Ch included. **Surface:** grassy.
01/01-31/12
Distance: 3km 2km.
Remarks: Arrival < 18h, Sa < 13h.

Barth 6A2

Segelverein, Am Westhafen. **GPS**: n54,37130 e12,72510.

20 € 10 Ch € 2 WC € 1. **Surface:** grassy. 01/05-01/10
Distance: on the spot on the spot on the spot.

Barth 6A2

Wohnmobilparkplatz Barth, Am Osthafen. **GPS**: n54,36870 e12,77770.

30 € 7. **Surface:** metalled. 01/01-31/12
Distance: on the spot.

Beckerwitz 5C3

Ostseecamping Beckerwitzer Strand, Haus 2a. **GPS**: n53,94137 e11,31682.

DE

16 € 12, Jul-Aug € 16 Ch included. **Surface:** grassy.
01/04-15/10
Distance: on the spot.

S **Bergen/Rügen** 6B1

Wohnmobilstellplatz Rügen - Bergen auf Rügen

info@ruegen-mobile.de - www.wohnmobil-stellplatz-ruegen.de

Electricity at each pitch
Convenient for longer stays
Reservations possible

Wohnmobilstellplatz Rügen, Tilzower Weg 32A. **GPS**: n54,40757 e13,42949.
20 € 12 € 1/90liter Ch (16x),25Amp WC included € 2/6minutes € 4. **Surface:** metalled. 01/01-31/12
Distance: 1,5km 400m 500m 100m.
Remarks: Bread-service.

S **Binz** 6B1

Wohnmobil-Oase Rügen, Proraer Chaussee 60. **GPS**: n54,44819 e13,56181.

150 € 10, Jul/Aug € 13 € 1 € 1 Ch € 1/1kWh WC € 0,50 € 0,50 washing machine/dryer € 4. **Location:** Luxurious, isolated, quiet.
Surface: grassy/gravel. 01/04-31/10
Distance: Binz 5km 10 min 700m on the spot.
Remarks: Bread-service.

S **Binz** 6B1

Parkplatz Zentrum, Proraer Chaussee 8. **GPS**: n54,40278 e13,60194.

60 € 14/24h, € 3/2h € 1/50liter Ch included WC € 1.
Surface: grassy/metalled. 01/01-31/12
Distance: on the spot 50m on the spot.
Remarks: In the centre, parking next to Elf petrol station.

S **Bobitz** 5C3

Wohnmobilpark Rastplatz No. 6, Wismarsche strasse 6. **GPS**: n53,79451 e11,34458.

40 € 6, 2 pers.incl € 1 Ch € 2. **Surface:** grassy. 01/01-31/12
Distance: 2km 2km 2km.

S **Boiensdorf** 5D3

Am Strand, Werder. **GPS**: n54,02412 e11,54744.

€ 7 Ch WC € 0,30. **Surface:** grassy. 01/01-31/12
Distance: on the spot on the spot 50m.

S **Boltenhagen** 5C3

Krämer's Wohnmobilhafen, Ostsee-allee 58b. **GPS**: n53,98122 e11,21908.

45 Apr/Oct € 12 Nov/Mar € 10/2 pers incl. Ch € 2,50 WC.
01/01-31/12
Distance: 800m 200m 200m on the spot 700m on the spot.
Remarks: Bread-service in summer period.

S **Boltenhagen** 5C3

Wohnmobilpark Boltenhagen, Ostsee-allee 58. **GPS**: n53,98133 e11,21854.

DE

50 € 13 + € 2,10/pp Ch € 2 WC included € 1 . **Surface:** grassy. 01/01-31/12
Distance: 700m 200m 200m on the spot 700m.

Boltenhagen 5C3

Regenbogen Boltenhagen, Ostseeallee 54. **GPS**: n53,98196 e11,21714.

20 € 20 WC included. **Surface:** grassy/metalled.
01/01-31/12
Distance: 600m 200m 200m on the spot 700m on the spot.
Remarks: Max. 1 night.

Boltenhagen 5C3

Swin Golf Boltenhagen, Ausbau 15, Redewisch. **GPS**: n54,00851 e11,17180.

10 € 10 € 2. **Surface:** grassy. 01/04-31/10
Distance: on the spot.

Tourist information Boltenhagen:
Kurverwaltung, Ostseeallee 4, www.boltenhagen.de. Bathing resort in holiday region. Many biking possibilities.

Brenz 5D4

Landhaus Böttcher, Parchimer strasse 11. **GPS**: n53,38688 e11,67103.

5 € 10, guests free € 1,50 (4x)€ 2/day WC included. **Location:** Rural, simple. **Surface:** grassy/metalled. 01/01-31/12
Distance: on the spot 3km on the spot 5km 200m.

Broock 5D4

Hotel-Restaurant Am Worns-Berg, Am Worns-Berg 1. **GPS**: n53,46734 e12,10698.

6 € 5/pppn, guests free Ch € 2 WC € 1,50. **Surface:** gravel.
01/01-31/12
Distance: 5km 1,5km 1,5km on the spot 5km 500m.

Buchholz 6A4

Gasthof Zum Storchennest, Dorfstrasse 7. **GPS**: n53,27814 e12,64035.
15 € 10 Ch WC included. **Surface:** grassy. 01/01-31/12
Distance: 5km 300m 300m on the spot 10km.

Carpin 6B4

Landgasthof Am Schlesersee, Hauptstrasse 25. **GPS**: n53,35424 e13,24028.

10 € 5, guests free WC included. **Surface:** metalled.
01/01-31/12
Distance: 500m on the spot on the spot on the spot 4km.

Dabitz 6A2

Hafen Dabitz, Boddenstraße. **GPS**: n54,36217 e12,80610.

€ 6/night. **Surface:** gravel.
Distance: 500m on the spot.

Dalwitz 6A3

Ferien Gut Dalwitz, Dalwitz 46. **GPS**: n53,93484 e12,53830.

2 € 10 € 1 WC washing machine/dryer € 3 . **Surface:** grassy.
01/01-31/12
Distance: 15km on the spot on the spot.
Remarks: Parking estate.

Dassow 5C3

Reisemobilplatz Ostseestrand, Straße des Friedens 14, Rosenhagen. **GPS**: n53,96195 e10,93944.

DE

5 € 10 Ch € 3 WC € 3. **Location:** Rural, comfortable, quiet.
Surface: grassy. 01/01-31/12
Distance: 500m on the spot.
Remarks: At Café Strandgut.

S Dobbertin 5D4

Campingplatz Am Dobbertiner See, Am Zeltplatz 1. **GPS**: n53,61868 e12,06440.

10 € 10, 2 pers.incl Ch € 0,50/kWh. **Surface:** grassy.
01/04-31/10
Distance: 500m on the spot on the spot 500m 500m 500m.

S Dömitz 5C5

Campingpark Marina Dömitz, An der Schleuse 1. **GPS**: n53,14078 e11,25908.

26 € 10 Ch WC included. **Location:** Rural, comfortable, quiet.
Surface: grassy. 01/01-31/12
Distance: 400m 20m 20m 100m 800m.

S Dömitz 5C5

Dömitzer Hafen, Hafenplatz 3. **GPS**: n53,13724 e11,26034.

22 € 8 € 1/50liter Ch (10x)€ 2/day WC. **Location:** Rural, comfortable, quiet. **Surface:** grassy. 01/01-31/12
Distance: 1km 10m 10m 200m 800m 600m.

S Dranske/Bakenberg 6B1

Küstencamp, Nonnevitz 23. **GPS**: n54,66288 e13,26929.

18 € 15 Ch WC.
Distance: 400m 400m 100m 800m.
Remarks: Bread-service.

S Eldena 5D5

Bootshafen und Campingplatz Eldena, Am Bootshafen 1. **GPS**: n53,23163 e11,42422.

12 € 10,50 Ch WC included € 1,10 € 3,50,dryer € 3,50.
Location: Rural, comfortable, quiet. **Surface:** grassy. 01/04-31/10
Distance: 400m 10m 10m 50m 400m on the spot.

S Fresenbrügge 5D4

Womo & Caravan Stelplatz Eldekrug, Eldeufer 1. **GPS**: n53,26355 e11,54243.

20 € 10 € 1/100liter Ch € 0,50/kWh WC included € 1/pp.
Location: Rural, comfortable, isolated, quiet. **Surface:** grassy.
01/01-31/12
Distance: on the spot on the spot 2km 2km on the spot on the spot.

Graal-Müritz 5D2

Strandmitte, Buchenkampweg. **GPS**: n54,25663 e12,25005.

15 € 8. **Surface:** grassy/metalled. 01/01-31/12
Distance: 500m on the spot on the spot 500m 500m.

S Grabow 5D4

Stadthafen, Canalstrasse. **GPS**: n53,27738 e11,55949.

DE

18 free € 0,50/time Ch€ 0,50 WC€ 0,50 € 1.
Surface: metalled. 01/01-31/12, service: 8-9.30h and 18.30-20h
Distance: 200m 10m 10m 100m 50m.

S Greifswald 6B2

Caravanstellplatz Wöller, Chausseestraße 12. **GPS**: n54,07450 e13,35230.

40 € 10 Ch included WC Use sanitary € 5/day.
Surface: metalled. 01/01-31/12
Distance: 1km 800m 1km.

S Greifswald 6B2

Marktkauf, Dorfstrasse, Neuenkirchen. **GPS**: n54,11810 e13,36390.

10 free € 1 Ch (5x)€ 1. **Surface:** metalled. 01/01-31/12

S Greifswald 6B2

Am Museumhafen, Marienstraße 10. **GPS**: n54,09887 e13,38945.

20 € 11 € 2 Ch€ 2 € 1 WC .
Surface: metalled.
01/04-30/11
Distance: 8 min walking 300m.

Tourist information Greifswald:

Greifswald-Information, Rathausarkaden, Domstrasse, www.greifswald.de.Hanseatic city, with historical city centre.

Fischerdorf Greifswald-Wieck.
Fishermen's village worth seeing.

S Güstrow 6A3

Gleviner Platz. **GPS**: n53,79117 e12,18054.

3 free € 0,50 Ch WC. **Surface:** asphalted. 01/01-31/12
Distance: 400m 5km 5km 100m 100m.

S Güstrow 6A3

Am Tierpark, Verbindungschaussee 7. **GPS**: n53,79159 e12,21577.
30 € 15, 2 pers.incl Ch € 2,50. **Surface:** grassy.
01/01-31/12
Distance: 5km on the spot 5km.

S Gützkow 6B3

Rittergut Schloss Pentin, Zum Bollwerk 11. **GPS**: n53,91824 e13,46763.

40+10 € 8 € 0,50/80liter Ch € 0,50/kWh WC € 1. **Surface:** grassy/gravel. 01/01-31/12
Distance: 1km 400m.
Remarks: Bread-service.

Heiligendamm 5D2

Wohnmobilparkplatz, Kühlungsborner Strasse. **GPS**: n54,13927 e11,85281.

4 € 10. **Surface:** metalled. 01/01-31/12
Distance: 1,5km 1,5km.

S Heringsdorf 6C2

Pension Ariane, Bülowstrasse 13. **GPS**: n53,95240 e14,16600.

6 € 12 € 1/40liter Ch € 2 WC € 2. **Surface:** grassy.
01/04-30/09
Distance: on the spot 300m on the spot on the spot.

S Hornstorf 5D3

Gartencenter Offermann, Dorfstraße 1. **GPS**: n53,89473 e11,54159.

DE

20 € 10 Ch included. **Surface:** concrete. 01/01-31/12

Kägsdorf 5D2

Strandparkplatz Kägsdorf, Zum Strande. **GPS:** n54,14231 e11,66541.

20 € 15. **Surface:** grassy. 01/01-31/12
Distance: 20m 20m.

Kamminke 6C3

Stettinerhaff. **GPS:** n53,86750 e14,20480.

15 € 8. **Surface:** grassy. 01/01-31/12
Distance: on the spot on the spot.

Karenz 5C5

Reiterhof am Steinberg, Grebserstrasse 1. **GPS:** n53,23638 e11,34836.

3 € 10 € 1 Ch € 1,50 WC. **Location:** Rural, simple, isolated.
Surface: grassy. 01/01-31/12
Distance: 1km 1km 300m.
Remarks: Parking at manege. Karenz dir Eldena.

Kargow 6A4

Reisemobilstellplatz Ziegenwiese, Schwarzenhof 7. **GPS:** n53,46433 e12,79925.

10 € 7,50 € 3 Ch € 3. **Surface:** grassy. 01/01-31/12
Distance: 1km 1km 200m 4km.

Karnin 6C3

Hafen, Karnin 14a. **GPS:** n53,84450 e13,85860.

3 € 10 € 0,50/100liter Ch € 1 € 0,50/1kWh WC € 1.
Surface: metalled. 01/01-31/12
Distance: 500m.

Krassow 5D3

Caravan Krassow, Kastanienalle 56. **GPS:** n53,87379 e11,56618.

10 € 5 € 1 Ch € 2 WC. **Surface:** grassy/metalled.
01/01-31/12
Distance: 1,5km 1km 3km.

Kühlungsborn 5D2

Am Hafen, Hafenstrasse. **GPS:** n54,15063 e11,77150.

50 € 10/night. **Surface:** gravel. 01/01-31/12
Distance: 800m on the spot 600m.

Langen Brütz 5D3

Landhaus Bondzio, Hauptstrasse 21a. **GPS:** n53,65722 e11,55737.

DE

6 € 10 WC included € 2. **Surface:** asphalted/grassy. 01/01-31/12
Distance: 150m on the spot 50m.

Lassahn 5C4

Pension Seeblick, Dorfstrasse 59. **GPS**: n53,60271 e10,95342.

5 € 10, guests free included. **Surface:** grassy. 01/01-31/12

Lauterbach 6B1

Im-Jaich Wasserferienwelt, Am Yachthafen 1, Putbus. **GPS**: n54,34278 e13,50167.

20 € 7-8, € 1,20/pppd tourist tax WC included € 1 € 4,dryer € 3 . **Surface:** gravel. 01/01-31/12
Distance: 500m on the spot on the spot on the spot 800m.
Remarks: Seaview, bead kiosk.

Lenz über Malchow 6A4

Lenzer Hafen, Zum Hafen 1. **GPS**: n53,46793 e12,34929.

25 € 8,30- €12,40 Ch WC € 1,30 € 2. **Surface:** grassy.
01/03-31/10
Distance: 6km on the spot on the spot on the spot 6km.
Remarks: Parking eastern bank Plauersee.

Lohme 6B1

Knöpfle Dorfladen, Arkonastrasse 4. **GPS**: n54,58300 e13,61150.

14 € 12 € 1/90liter Ch WC € 0,50 € 2 . **Surface:** grassy/ metalled. 01/01-31/12
Distance: on the spot 200m on the spot on the spot on the spot.

Lohme 6B1

Königsstuhl P&R, Hagen. **GPS**: n54,56220 e13,62590.

60 € 8 € 2 Ch € 2 € 2,50/day WC € 1 . **Surface:** metalled.
01/01-31/12
Distance: on the spot 600m on the spot.

Tourist information Lohme:
Tourismusverein Gemeinde Lohme, Dorfstrasse 23.Holiday resort on the island Rügen, accessed by a bridge.

Ludwigslust 5D4

Am Schloss, Friedrich-Naumann-Allee. **GPS**: n53,32735 e11,49080. .

20 free € 1 € 1 Ch € 1 . **Location:** Rural, simple, quiet.
Surface: gravel/sand. 01/01-31/12
Distance: 600m 500m 600m.

Lütow 6C2

Yachtlieger Achterwasser, Netzelkow. **GPS**: n54,02690 e13,90950. .

22 € 1/meter + € 1/pp Ch € 2 WC € 2. **Surface:** grassy.
01/01-31/12
Distance: on the spot on the spot on the spot.
Remarks: Marina, peninsula Gormitz.

Malchin 6A3

Malchiner Kanu-club, Am Kanal 2. **GPS**: n53,74417 e12,76611.

DE

7 € 9 WC € 0,50 washing machine/dryer € 1. **Surface:** grassy. 01/01-31/12
Distance: 500m on the spot on the spot 500m 500m.

S Malchow 6A4

Marina Malchow, Ziegeleiweg 5. **GPS**: n53,46432 e12,42417.

20 € 10 Ch WC. **Surface:** grassy. 01/01-31/12
Distance: 2km on the spot on the spot 100m 4km 250m.

Malchow 6A4

Altstad Ost, Klosterstrasse. **GPS**: n53,47199 e12,43796.
15 free. **Surface:** asphalted. 01/01-31/12
Distance: 200m 200m 200m.

S Malchow 6A4

Wohnmobilstellplatz Am Plauer See, Zum Plauer See 1. **GPS**: n53,49192 e12,37268.

6 € 8-10, 2 pers.incl Ch € 1,50 WC € 1 € 5.
Surface: gravel. 01/01-31/12
Distance: 4km on the spot on the spot on the spot on the spot.

S Mistorf 5D3

Wohnmobilpark Mistorf, Dorfstraße 50. **GPS**: n53,88152 e12,14325.
10 € 8 Ch € 2,50 WC € 2,50. **Surface:** grassy.
01/01-31/10
Remarks: Check in at Imbiss, bread-service, grill and picknic area.

S Mönkebude 6C3

Stettinger Haff, Am Hafen. **GPS**: n53,77174 e13,96868.

25+15 € 8,50/ € 10 € 0,50/100liter Ch € 2/24h WC € 1 € 3,50, dryer € 3 € 1,50/h. **Surface:** grassy. 01/03-30/11
Distance: 50m nearby 50m.
Remarks: Excl. Tourist tax € 0,75, nov/apr service only on demand, peak season: sanitary installation.

Mönkebude 6C3

Gastätte Kregelin's Bistro, Hauptstrasse. **GPS**: n53,76663 e13,97614.

4 guests free. **Surface:** metalled.

S Muess 5D4

Awo Feriendorf Muess, Alte Crivitzer Landstrasse 6. **GPS**: n53,59995 e11,47940.

6 € 10 31/10-01/03, € 20 01/03-31/10 Ch WC included, winter fee no shower. **Surface:** grassy.
01/01-31/12
Distance: 100m 100m.
Remarks: At open air museum.

S Neu Kaliss 5C5

Find 's Hier, An der Elde 2. **GPS**: n53,17810 e11,29720.

13 € 8 € 1 Ch included € 2/night WC € 1. **Location:** Rural, simple, isolated, quiet. **Surface:** grassy. 01/01-31/12
Distance: on the spot on the spot on the spot 400m 400m.

S Neubrandenburg 6B4

Wassersportzentrum Tollensesee, Augustastrasse 7. **GPS**: n53,53861 e13,25665.

30 € 10 € 1 Ch € 0,50/kWh WC € 2/day. **Surface:** grassy/ metalled. 15/03-31/10

DE

Distance: 2km on the spot on the spot on the spot 1km.
Remarks: Water sports centre.

S Neuendorf 6A2

Wohnmobilstellplatz Saal Neuendorf, Am Hafen. **GPS**: n54,33516 e12,52812.

20 € 10 WC € 0,20 € 1. **Surface:** grassy. 01/04-31/10
Distance: on the spot Imbiss kiosk.

S Neuhof 6C2

Blasendorff, Labahnstrasse 10. **GPS**: n53,95940 e14,15680.

3 € 10 € 0,50/40liter € 1,70. **Surface:** grassy. 01/01-31/12
Distance: 10min 300m 300m.

S Neukloster 5D3

Wohnmobilpark Neuklostersee, Alte Gärtnerei 3. **GPS**: n53,86121 e11,69536.

69 16/3-15/10 € 9,50, 16/10-15/3 € 8 Ch € 1/2kWh WC € 1.
Surface: gravel. 01/01-31/12, toilets/showers 8-21h
Distance: 500m on the spot 50m 500m 1,2km 500m.

S Neustrelitz 6B4

Parkplatz Am Stadthafen, Zierker Nebenstrasse 6. **GPS**: n53,36568 e13,05551.

25 € 8 € 0,50/80liter € 1 Ch € 1 (25x)€ 0,50/kWh WC € 0,20 € 0,50 washing machine/dryer € 2. **Location:** Comfortable, quiet.
Surface: metalled.
Distance: on the spot 100m, swimming 1km 200m 100m 200m 200m on the spot on the spot.

Remarks: Coins available at harbourmaster (200m), historical centre.

S Niendorf 5C3

Poeler Forellenhof, Niendorf 13. **GPS**: n53,99454 e11,44714.

16 € 10 WC included. **Surface:** asphalted. 01/01-31/12
Distance: 1,5km on the spot on the spot on the spot 1,5km.
Remarks: Check in at restaurant.

S Nossentin 6A4

Am Fleesensee, Am Park 33. **GPS**: n53,51866 e12,46766.

4 € 8 WC included. **Surface:** grassy. 01/04-31/10
Distance: 5km 100m 100m on the spot 5km.

S Ostseebad Sellin/Rügen 6C1

Reisemobilhafen Sellin, Kiefernweg 4b. **GPS**: n54,37170 e13,70165.

50 € 12 € 0,50/50liter Ch € 1 € 0,50/kWh WC € 0,50 € 2/day.
Surface: grassy/metalled.
Distance: 300m 1km 1km 200m 300m 300m.

S Ostseebad Wustrow 6A2

Surfcenter Wustrow, An der Nebelstation 2. **GPS**: n54,34080 e12,38040.

30 € 8 + € 3/pp Ch € 2,50 WC . **Surface:** asphalted.
01/04-31/10
Distance: 1km 50m.

Ostseebad Wustrow 6A2

Hafenstraße. **GPS**: n54,34363 e12,40053.

DE

30 € 3/day, € 7/night. **Surface:** gravel.
Distance: 400m 1,5km on the spot.
Remarks: Max. 1 night.

S **Parchim** 5D4

Jachthafen, Am Fischerdamm. **GPS**: n53,42594 e11,84494.

8 € 5 € 0,50 Ch WC . **Surface:** asphalted. 01/01-31/12
Distance: 100m on the spot on the spot 100m 100m.

Passin 5D3

Hauptstrasse 20. **GPS**: n53,90274 e12,00091.

3 free. **Surface:** asphalted. 01/01-31/12
Remarks: Next to cemetery.

S **Pepelow** 5D3

Wohnmobilpark Pepelow, Strandweg 1. **GPS**: n54,03805 e11,58441.

12 € 10-12 Ch € 2,50 WC sanitary € 2/pp washing machine/dryer € 2,50. **Surface:** grassy. 01/01-31/12
Distance: 700m on the spot on the spot 200m 200m.

S **Petersdorf** 6A4

Hotel Haus Waldesruh, Lenzerstrasse 19. **GPS**: n53,45892 e12,36060.

10 € 7,50 € 1 Ch € 2 WC € 1,50 washing machine/dryer € 1,50.
Surface: grassy. 01/01-31/12
Distance: 7km 600m 600m on the spot 7km.

S **Poseritz** 6B2

Lindenkrug, Lindenstrasse 27+28. **GPS**: n54,30130 e13,27610.

4 guests free WC. **Surface:** metalled. 01/01-31/12
Distance: on the spot.

S **Priepert** 6B4

Wohnmobilpark Am Großen Priepertsee, An der Freiheit 8. **GPS**: n53,22043 e13,04201.

22 € 7 Ch € 2 WC € 1,50 washing machine/dryer € 5.
Surface: grassy. 01/01-31/12
Distance: 1,5km 1,5km.

Putgarten 6B1

Kaparkona Bahn, Am Sportplatz 2. **GPS**: n54,67190 e13,40800.

26 € 5. **Surface:** asphalted. 01/01-31/12
Remarks: Parking on entering the village.

Rerik 5D2

Dünenstrasse. **GPS**: n54,10520 e11,60843.

DE

10 € 10/08-18h. **Surface:** sand. 01/01-31/12
Distance: 500m on the spot on the spot 500m 500m.

S Röbel 6A4
Am Seglerhafen, Müritzpromenade 20. **GPS:** n53,38734 e12,61755.

45 € 12 Ch € 1 WC . **Surface:** grasstiles/metalled.
01/04-31/10
Distance: on the spot 300m.

S Roggendorf 5C3
Landhotel Hänsel, Kneeser strasse18. **GPS:** n53,69228 e11,01538.

8 € 6 Ch WC included. **Surface:** asphalted. 01/01-31/12
Distance: 200m on the spot 200m 200m.

Rostock 5D2
Parkplatz Stadtmitte, Am Bahnhof, Warnmünde. **GPS:** n54,17841 e12,09185.

100 € 6/3h, € 12/12h, € 16/24h. **Surface:** metalled.
01/01-31/12
Tourist information Rostock:
www.rostock.de.Hanseatic city with historical centre.

S Rüterberg 5C5
Wohmobilparkplatz Dorfrepublik Rüterberg, Ringstraße 2. **GPS:** n53,15294 e11,18511.

10 € 5/24h+ € 0,50/pp € 1/50liter € 1 Ch € 1 € 1/kWh WC € 1.
Location: Rural, simple, central, quiet. **Surface:** grassy.
01/01-31/12
Distance: 10m 50m.
Remarks: Bread-service.

S Schwerin 5C4
Am Hauptbahnhof, Wismarsche Straße. **GPS:** n53,63692 e11,40893.
4 € 8/24h € 1/80liter Ch (4x)€ 1/2kWh. **Location:** Simple, central. **Surface:** metalled.
Distance: on the spot.

S Schwerin 5C4
Marina-Nord Schwerin, Buchenweg 19. **GPS:** n53,64584 e11,43264.

20 € 10 + € 1/pp Ch (14x)€ 0,50/kWh WC € 1,50.
Surface: grassy. 15/04-15/10
Distance: 4km on the spot 1km.

Schwerin 5C4
Altstadt, Schliemannstraße-Werderstraße. **GPS:** n53,62978 e11,41975.
€ 8/24h. **Location:** Simple, central.
Surface: metalled.
Distance: on the spot.

Schwerin 5C4
Sport- und Kongresshalle, Wittenburgerstrasse 118. **GPS:** n53,62802 e11,39005.

50 free. **Surface:** grasstiles/metalled. 01/01-31/10
Distance: 500m 500m 100m.

S Seehof 5C3
Campingplatz Seehof, Am Zeltplatz 1. **GPS:** n53,69676 e11,43658.

DE

10 € 10 Ch WC included € 0,80. **Surface:** grassy.
01/01-31/10
Distance: 1,2km on the spot on the spot on the spot on the spot.

S Sehlen 6B1

Zur Kastanie, Dorfstrasse 24. **GPS:** n54,37820 e13,38870.

5 € 15 WC included. **Surface:** grassy/metalled.
01/04-31/10
Distance: on the spot on the spot.

S Sembzin 6A4

Rasthof Sembzin, Dorfstrasse 2. **GPS:** n53,46445 e12,60386.

16 € 8, guests free Ch WC € 1 € 2 € 2/24h.
Surface: grassy/gravel. 01/01-31/12
Distance: 5km on the spot.
Remarks: Swimming pool.

S Sievershagen 5D2

Ferienhof Dubberke, Alt Sievershagen 16. **GPS:** n54,11480 e12,03481.

5 € 10 Ch WC included. **Surface:** grassy. 01/01-31/10
Distance: 500m 800m.

S Sommersdorf 6B3

Wohnmobilpark Sommersdorf, Am Kummerower See. **GPS:** n53,79824 e12,87576.

23 € 8-10, 2 pers.incl € 3 Ch € 2,50/night WC € 2 € 2,50.
Surface: grassy. 01/01-31/12
Distance: on the spot on the spot on the spot.

S Sternberg 5D3

Sternberger, Maikamp 11. **GPS:** n53,71318 e11,81236.

15 € 12-€ 16 Ch € 2,70/day WC. **Surface:** grasstiles.
Easter-31/10
Distance: 1km on the spot on the spot on the spot 500m 500m.

S Stralsund 6B2

Caravan Center Dhanke, Werftstrasse 16. **GPS:** n54,30190 e13,10110.

60 € 12 € 1/5minutes Ch € 1. **Surface:** grassy/gravel.
01/01-31/12
Distance: 1,5km on the spot.

S Timmendorf 5C3

Strandparkplatz Timmendorf, Timmendorf Strand, Insel Poel. **GPS:** n53,99287 e11,38058.

60 € 4/day, € 3/night € 2,50 Ch € 1/2kWh € 1. **Surface:** grassy.
01/01-31/12
Distance: 150m 250m 200m 300m.

Ückeritz 6C2

Am Achterwasser, Mühlenstrasse. **GPS:** n54,01390 e14,04170.

DE

30 € 10. **Surface:** metalled. 01/01-31/12
Distance: 700m on the spot.

S Ueckermünde 6C3

An der Uecker, Ueckerstrasse 127. **GPS:** n53,73470 e14,04930.

13 € 7 included. **Surface:** grassy/metalled. 01/01-31/12
Distance: 200m 200m.

S Ueckermünde 6C3

Kron Bellin, Dorfstrasse 8b. **GPS:** n53,73760 e14,11400.

10 € 10, 2 pers.incl Ch € 2 WC . **Surface:** grassy.
01/04-31/10
Distance: on the spot on the spot on the spot.

S Usedom 6C3

Am Hafen Usedom, Peenestraße. **GPS:** n53,87099 e13,92679. .

20 € 5 Ch € 5 WC € 0,50 € 2. **Surface:** metalled.
01/01-31/12
Distance: 600m on the spot on the spot.
Remarks: At former fishing-port.

S Usedom 6C3

Gaststätte Haffschänke, Dorfstraße 19, Karnin. **GPS:** n53,84348 e13,86537.

20 € 7 Ch € 3 WC € 2,50. **Surface:** grassy. 01/01-31/12
Distance: on the spot on the spot on the spot.

S Vielank 5C5

Vielanker Brauhaus, Lindenplatz 1. **GPS:** n53,23443 e11,14023.

12 free € 3 WC. **Location:** Rural, simple, quiet. **Surface:** grassy.
01/01-31/12
Distance: 20m 20m.
Remarks: Check in at reception.

S Waren 6A4

Gärtnerei Steindorf-Sabath, Mecklenburgerstrasse. **GPS:** n53,51363 e12,69431.
.

50 € 8,50 Ch free € 0,50/kWh WC € 1. **Surface:** grassy/gravel.
01/01-31/12
Distance: 100m 1km 1km 1km 1km on the spot.

S Waren 6A4

Wohnmobilpark Waren, Zur stillen Bucht 3, Müritz. **GPS:** n53,51175 e12,65174.
.

49 € 8-14 Ch € 2,50 WC sanitary € 2/pp . **Surface:** grassy.
01/01-31/12
Distance: 3km on the spot on the spot on the spot on the spot
500m.

S Waren 6A4

Wohnmobilpark, Teterower Straße 35, Waren-Müritz. **GPS:** n53,52611 e12,67194.
.

DE

22 € 8/24h Ch € 2 WC € 1,50. **Surface:** grasstiles/grassy.
01/01-31/12
Distance: 4km 4km 4km 4km Edeka 10m.

S Waren 6A4

Womo-Stellplatz Waren, Strandstrasse 3b. **GPS:** n53,51194 e12,68583.

20 € 10 Ch included. **Surface:** metalled. 01/01-31/12
Distance: on the spot on the spot on the spot on the spot on the spot.

S Waren 6A4

Campingplatz Ecktannen, Fontanestraße 66. **GPS:** n53,49944 e12,66361.

16 € 16 Ch WC included washing machine/dryer € 2,60.
Surface: grasstiles/metalled. 01/01-31/12
Distance: 3,5km 500m 500m Bistro 3km on the spot.

S Wesenberg 6B4

Womo Stellplatz & Marina Wesenberg, Ahrensberger weg 11. **GPS:** n53,27666 e12,98694.

34 € 14, 2 pers.incl Ch WC included. **Surface:** grassy/gravel.
01/01-31/12
Distance: 1km on the spot on the spot on the spot 2,5km 1km.

S Wismar 5C3

Wohnmobilpark Westhafen Wismar, Schiffbauerdamm 12. **GPS:** n53,89430 e11,45151.

DE

50 € 7/12 uur € 9/24 uur € 1/100liter Ch € 1/8h WC € 1.
Surface: gravel.
01/01-31/12
Distance: 800m 300m, Burger King 400m 300m 800m 100m.

Tourist information Wismar:
Tourist Information, Am Markt 11.Hanseatic city a number of curiosities.

S Wittenbeck 5D2

Parkplatz, Bäderweg. **GPS:** n54,14513 e11,79277.

40 € 5 day/€ 5 night € 3 Ch WC. **Surface:** grassy. 01/01-31/12
Distance: 1,5km on the spot.

S Wittenbeck 5D2

Parkplatz, Bäderweg. **GPS:** n54,14437 e11,79268.

60 € 5 day/€ 5 night € 3 Ch WC. **Surface:** metalled.
01/01-31/12
Distance: 1,4km 1,4km.
Remarks: Follow signs Parkplatz.

Wittenburg 5C4

Snow parkfun, Zur Winterwelt 1. **GPS:** n53,51123 e11,08795.

50 free. **Surface:** metalled. 01/01-31/12 Mon, Tue.
Distance: 1,2km 1,3km on the spot.

S Wittenburg 5C4

Caravan Schiemann, Lehsener Chaussee 4. **GPS:** n53,50118 e11,07393.

Ch against payment.

S Zingst 6A1

Wohnmobilhafen Am Freesenbruch. GPS: n54,44060 e12,66058.
40 € 18-24, 2 pers.incl Ch € 2 WC included. 01/01-31/12

S Zingst 6A1

Straminke, Seestrasse. **GPS:** n54,44070 e12,70750.

40 € 15 WC. **Surface:** grassy. 01/01-31/12
Remarks: Parking beach passage 6, max. 1 day.

Tourist information Zingst:
Kur- und Tourismus GmbH, Seestrasse 56, www.zingst.de.Large bathing resort to the Baltic Sea.

Saxony Anhalt

S Ahlum 5C6

Fischreihütte Ahlumer See, Am Mühlenberg 63. **GPS:** n52,69541 e11,00583.

100 € 8 Ch € 0,50/kWh WC included. 01/01-31/12
Distance: on the spot on the spot.
Remarks: Bread-service.

S Aken/Elbe 11A2

Elbe Bootscenter, Am Russendamm. **GPS:** n51,85901 e12,03799.
10 € 10 + € 2/pp Ch € 2 WC. **Surface:** grassy.
01/04-31/10
Remarks: At marina.

S Allrode 10C3

Hotel Harzer Land, Teichstraße 28. **GPS:** n51,67774 e10,96478.

25 € 15,50 Ch WC included. **Surface:** grassy.
01/01-31/12
Distance: on the spot on the spot.

Altenbrak 10C2

Am Bielstein. **GPS:** n51,72569 e10,94196.

8 € 5, overnight stay free. **Location:** Rural, simple. **Surface:** metalled.
01/01-31/12
Distance: 100m on the spot 100m.

Altenbrak 10C2

Parkplatz Rappbodetalsperre, Hasselfelderstrasse, L96. **GPS:** n51,74298 e10,88770.

20 free. **Surface:** asphalted.

S Altenbrak 10C2

Hotel Zur Talsperre, Oberbecken 1. **GPS:** n51,73434 e10,90690.

50 € 10 Ch (20x)€ 0,40/kWh WC included. 01/01-31/12
Distance: on the spot.

S Arendsee 5D5

Im kleinen Elsebusch, Lüchower strasse 6a. **GPS:** n52,87656 e11,46121.

20 € 10 € 1 € 1 Ch. **Surface:** grassy. 01/01-31/12
Distance: 2,5km on the spot 2,5km.

S Bad Kösen 10D4

Am Saalebogen, Stendorfhaus 14. **GPS:** n51,11356 e11,69609.

DE

11 € 5 Ch € 2 WC sanitary € 1,50. **Surface:** grasstiles/metalled. 01/01-31/12
Distance: 3km 800m 800m.

S **Ballenstedt** 10D2
Verkehrslandeplatz Ballenstedt/Quedlinburg, Asmusstedt 13. **GPS:** n51,74190 e11,23427.

32 € 4/pppn Ch WC included. **Surface:** grasstiles/metalled. 01/01-31/12
Distance: 2km on the spot 2km 200m.

Berssel 10C2
Gasthof Zum Schloß, Am Schloß 1. **GPS:** n51,95266 e10,76027.
5 free. **Surface:** metalled.

S **Bertingen** 10D1
Freizeitgelände, Im Wald 2. **GPS:** n52,35994 e11,82264.

60 € 7,50 Ch included. **Surface:** grassy. 01/01-31/12
Distance: on the spot 5km.
Remarks: Bread-service.

S **Bitterfeld** 11A2
Woliday, Reudener Straße, Bitterfeld-Wolfen. **GPS:** n51,67102 e12,24842.

10 € 13 Ch WC included. **Surface:** grasstiles. 01/01-31/12
Remarks: Including access to swimming pool.

S **Blankenburg** 10C2
Am Schnappelberg, Schnappelberg 2. **GPS:** n51,78870 e10,96002.

15 € 4 € 1 Ch € 2 WC. **Surface:** metalled. 01/01-31/12
Distance: on the spot 300m on the spot.
Remarks: Waste dump € 0,50.

S **Brachwitz** 11A3
Marina Saale-Ufer, An der Fähre. **GPS:** n51,53441 e11,87083.

14 € 5 € 1 Ch (4x)€ 0,50/kWh WC. **Surface:** grassy. 01/01-31/12
Distance: 500m 500m 500m.

S **Burg bei Magdeburg** 10D1
Wassersportfreunde Burg, Am Kanal 20a. **GPS:** n52,28329 e11,84808.

6 € 10 € 1/100liter WC included. **Surface:** grassy. 01/05-30/09
Distance: on the spot.

S **Burg bei Magdeburg** 10D1
Eschenhof, Parchauer Chaussee 5. **GPS:** n52,28718 e11,86583.

15 € 10 Ch € 2 WC included. **Surface:** grassy. 01/01-31/12
Distance: on the spot on the spot 1km.

S **Darlingerode** 10C2
Wohnmobilpark Harzblick, Hinter den Gärten 11. **GPS:** n51,85278 e10,73667.

DE

15 € 8 Ch (12x)€ 0,50/kWh WC. **Surface:** grasstiles.
01/01-31/12
Distance: 500m 500m.

Elend 10C2

Waldbad Schenke, Am Waldbad 1. **GPS**: n51,74612 e10,69531.

15 € 5 (2x). **Surface:** grassy. 01/01-31/12

Haldensleben 10D1

Am Sportboothafen, Kronesruhe. **GPS**: n52,27933 e11,40240.

15 € 10 Chincluded € 0,50/kWh WC € 1. **Location:** Rural.
Surface: grassy. 15/04-31/10
Distance: 2km 14km on the spot on the spot 200m.
Remarks: Bread-service.

Haldensleben 10D1

Am Stendaler Turm, Bornsche Strasse. **GPS**: n52,29291 e11,41342.

10 free. **Surface:** concrete. 01/01-31/12
Distance: 200m 250m 150m Aldi.

Halle/Saale 11A3

Parkplatz, Fährstraße. **GPS**: n51,50256 e11,95245.

3 € 10/12h € 1 € 1/8h. **Surface:** metalled. 01/01-31/12
Distance: 2km 7km 200m 300m.

Harzgerode 10C3

Parkplatz Wallgarten, Wallstrasse. **GPS**: n51,64210 e11,14060.

5 free. **Surface:** metalled. 01/01-31/12
Distance: 100m 1km 3km 100m 100m 100m 1km.

Havelberg 6A6

Campinginsel. **GPS**: n52,82830 e12,06853.

€ 6 € 1 € 3 Ch (24x)€ 1/kWh. **Surface:** metalled.

Ilsenburg 10C2

Wohnmobilstellplatz Ilsetal, Ilsetal. **GPS**: n51,85386 e10,67013.

40 € 6, tourist tax € 1/pp € 2 Ch (24x)€ 2. **Surface:** metalled.
01/01-31/12
Distance: 700m 500m 2km 300m 800m 50m 15km
15km.

Kelbra 10C3

Seecamping Südharz, L1040. **GPS**: n51,42583 e11,00287.

DE

15 € 10-12 Ch included. **Location:** Rural. **Surface:** gravel.
01/01-31/12
Distance: 2,5km 100m 100m 100m.

Magdeburg 10D1

Stellplatz Petriförde, Petriförder 1. **GPS**: n52,13289 e11,64714.

50 € 5. **Surface:** metalled. 01/01-31/12
Distance: on the spot.
Remarks: Along the river Elbe.

S Naumburg(Saale) 11A4

Altstadtparkplatz Vogelwiese, Luisenstraße. **GPS**: n51,14861 e11,81391.

10 € 5/night € 0,50/80liter Ch € 0,50/kWh WC. **Surface:** metalled.
01/01-31/12
Distance: 500m 50m 500m 50m.
Remarks: Max. 3 days.

S Naumburg(Saale) 11A4

Caravan Rossol, Kroppentalstrasse 1. **GPS**: n51,15188 e11,82679.
10 € 5 € 3 € 3 € 3/night. **Surface:** grassy.
Distance: 1,2km.
Remarks: Waste dump € 1.

S Prettin 11B2

Bade- und Angelsee, Hinterfährstraße. **GPS**: n51,66485 e12,90551.

5 € 6 + € 2,80/pp Ch included € 0,30/kWh. **Surface:** gravel.
01/04-31/10
Distance: 1,2km.

S Quedlinburg 10C2

An den Fischteichen. **GPS**: n51,79308 e11,14863.

10 free € 1 € 1/6h. **Surface:** grasstiles/metalled.
01/01-31/12
Distance: 350m 300m 250m 150m.

S Quedlinburg 10C2

Marschlinger hof. **GPS**: n51,79138 e11,13965.

6 € 5/24h Ch (4x)€ 1/6h WC. **Surface:** metalled.
01/01-31/12
Distance: 100m 50m 400m 200m.
Remarks: Max. 7m.

S Quedlinburg 10C2

Schloßparkplatz, Schenkgasse. **GPS**: n51,78725 e11,13494.

6 € 3/24h Ch (4x)€ 1/6h. **Surface:** metalled.
01/01-31/12

S Salzwedel 5C6

Stellplatz der Hansestadt Salzwedel, Dämmchenweg 41. **GPS**: n52,85049 e11,13911.

6 € 3 Ch € 2 WC sanitary € 2. **Surface:** metalled.
01/01-31/12
Distance: historical centre 1km 100m.

Tourist information Salzwedel:
Former hanseatic city.

Sangerhausen 10D3

An der Walkmühle, Taubenberg. **GPS**: n51,49056 e11,31127.

50 free. **Surface:** sand. 01/01-31/12
Distance: 2km on the spot.

Sangerhausen 10D3

P7, An der Probstmühle. **GPS:** n51,47707 e11,30798.

20 free. **Surface:** sand. 01/01-31/12
Distance: 500m 200m 100m.

Sangerhausen 10D3

Rosarium, Sotterhäuser Weg. **GPS:** n51,47245 e11,31798.
€ 2 Ch. 15/04-15/10
Remarks: Check in at shop.

Seehausen 5D5

Stellplatz Seehausen, Schulstrasse 6. **GPS:** n52,89068 e11,75119.

50 € 5 Ch included. **Surface:** metalled. 01/01-31/12
Distance: 100m 200m.
Remarks: At tourist office.

Stendal 5D6

Nordwall-Schützenplatz. **GPS:** n52,61116 e11,86121.

20 free € 1/80liter € 1 Ch. **Surface:** grassy/metalled. 01/01-31/12
Distance: on the spot bakery 50m.

Tourist information Stendal:
Stendal Information, Kornmarkt 8.Hanseatic city with historical centre, city of the Brick Gothic.
Wickelmanmuseum.Founder of the modern archeology. Wed-Mo 10-17h.

Tangermünde 5D6

Tangerplatz, Klosterberg. **GPS:** n52,53774 e11,96803.

30 € 4 Ch included. **Surface:** metalled. 01/01-31/12

Wahrenberg 5D5

Stellplatz Storchenwiese, Eichenwinkel 34. **GPS:** n52,98342 e11,67362.

3 € 5 (3x)included. **Surface:** grassy. 01/01-31/12

Weddersleben 10C2

Lebenshilfe Harzkreis-Quedlinburg, Quedlinburgerstrasse 2. **GPS:** n51,76569 e11,09061.

12 € 15 Ch WC included against payment.
Surface: metalled. 01/01-31/12
Remarks: Commune for mentally disableds, special metalled part for motorhomes.

Weissenfels 11A4

Caravan- und Freizeitmarkt Gerth, Selauer Strasse. **GPS:** n51,19783 e11,99824.

7 free € 1/80liter Ch (4x)€ 0,50/kWh. **Surface:** asphalted.
01/01-31/12
Distance: on the spot on the spot.
Remarks: Industrial area Borau.

Wernigerode 10C2

Am Katzenteich. **GPS:** n51,83889 e10,78148.

DE

20 € 5 € 1/40liter Ch (20x)€ 1/kWh. **Surface:** grasstiles.
01/01-31/12
Distance: 500m.

S **Wernigerode** 10C2
Schlossparkplatz am Anger, Halberstädler strasse 1. **GPS**: n51,83807 e10,79535.

24 € 2,50, overnight stay free € 2 Ch. **Surface:** metalled.
01/01-31/12
Distance: 300m.

S **Wernigerode** 10C2
Gästehaus Familie Mann, Mühlental 76, B244. **GPS**: n51,81688 e10,81519.

5 € 10 Chincluded € 0,45/kWh € 0,50. **Surface:** gravel.
01/04-10/11
Distance: on the spot.
Remarks: Check in at restaurant, arrival before 22h.

S **Wörlitz** 11A2
Seeparke, Seespitze, K2376. **GPS**: n51,84820 e12,41277.

24 € 5 day/€ 5 night € 2WC Use sanitary € 0,50. **Surface:** asphalted.
01/01-31/12
Remarks: Parking at the edge the Wörlitzer park, max. 24h.

S **Wörlitz** 11A2
Hotel Coswiger Elbterrasse, Elbterrasse 1. **GPS**: n51,87750 e12,45097.

10 € 5 included. **Surface:** grassy.
01/01-31/12
Distance: on the spot.
Remarks: Free with a meal.

Tourist information Wörlitz:
Wörlitz-Information, Förstergasse 26, www.woerlitz-information.de.Park city; "Hier ists ietzt unendlich schön" according Goethe in 1778.

Brandenburg/Berlin

S **Abbendorf** 5D5
Gasthaus Dörpkrog an Diek, Am Deich 7. **GPS**: n52,89663 e11,90975.

6 € 5, guests free Ch WCincluded. 01/01-31/12
Remarks: Bread-service.

S **Alt-Zeschdorf** 6D6
Reiterhof Blumrich, Falkenhagerweg 11. **GPS**: n52,42649 e14,42328.

30 € 8,50 Ch included. **Surface:** grassy.
01/01-31/12 winter Mo.
Distance: 1,5km.
Remarks: At manege, bread-service.

S **Altdöbern** 11D2
Kfz Dienstleistungcenter, Senftenberger strasse 11. **GPS**: n51,64523 e14,03544.

20 € 10 WCincluded. **Surface:** metalled.
Distance: 500m on the spot 500m.

DE

Angermünde 6C5

NABU-Erlebniszentrum Blumberger Mühle. **GPS**: n53,03572 e13,96806.

10 free. **Surface:** metalled. 01/01-31/12

Bad Saarow 11D1

Parkplatz Strolin, Silberbergerstrasse. **GPS**: n52,28726 e14,03895.

4 free. **Surface:** metalled. 01/01-31/12
Distance: 100m 100m.

Bad Saarow 11D1

Ringstrasse. **GPS**: n52,29399 e14,06243.

6 free. **Surface:** metalled.
Distance: on the spot 300m 400m.

Bad Wilsnack 5D5

Zur gemütlichen Einkehr, Am Park 3. **GPS**: n52,95800 e11,95873.

15 € 5, free with a meal € 2,50 WC included. **Surface:** grassy.
01/01-31/12
Distance: on the spot on the spot 1km.

Bad Wilsnack 5D5

Kur- und Gradier-Therme Bad Wilsnack, Am Kähling. **GPS**: n52,96316 e11,95007.

18 € 10 + € 1 Kurtaxe pppd € 1/80liter Ch (8x)€ 1/kWh.
Surface: sand.
Distance: 500m 200m 500m.
Remarks: Check in at pay-desk of theTherme, bread-service.

Baumgarten 6B5

Märkischer Waidmann, Heidestrasse 33, OT Baumgarten Sonnenberg. **GPS**: n52,98028 e13,07444.

5 € 10 € 2 Ch (5x)€ 2/day WC € 0,50 . **Location:** Rural, comfortable. **Surface:** grassy/gravel. 01/01-31/12
Distance: 25km 600m 200m on the spot 6km 50m.
Remarks: € 10 reduction for guests, , fishing permit available at restaurant € 10/day.

Belzig 11B1

Springbach Mühle, Mühlenweg 2. **GPS**: n52,16523 e12,61078.

50 € 15 Ch . 01/01-31/12

Berlin 6B6

Historisches Fährhaus Berlin, Muggelbergallee 1, Berlin-Köpenick.
GPS: n52,41851 e13,58734.

15 01/03-01/11 € 18, 02/11-28/02 € 14 Ch included (15x)€ 2 WC € 1 € 5/stay. **Location:** Urban, luxurious, quiet. **Surface:** grassy/gravel. 01/01-31/12
Distance: on the spot 8km on the spot on the spot on the spot 100m, supermarket 750m 1km tram 100m.
Remarks: At old harbour.

Berlin 6B6

Wohnmobilpark Berlin, Waidmannsluster Damm 12-14. **GPS**: n52,59559 e13,28910.

DE

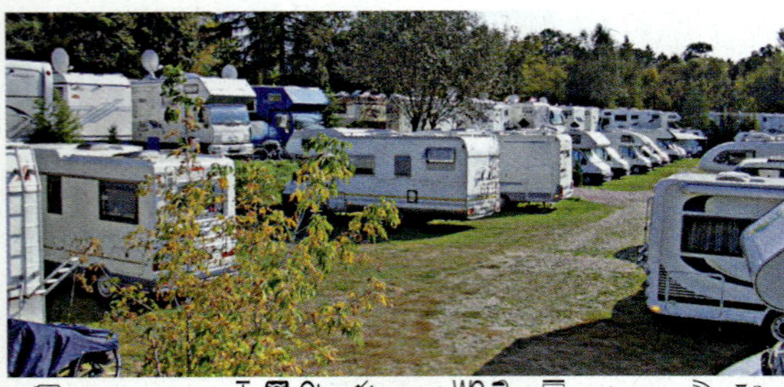

90 € 10-21, dog € 2 Ch € 3/24h WC € 1 € 3, dryer € 3.
Location: Central. **Surface:** grassy/metalled.
01/01-31/12
Distance: on the spot on the spot few minutes.
Remarks: Hotline-Nr.: 0176 – 99 55 25 00.

S Berlin 6B6

Reisemobilhafen Berlin Spandau, Askanierring 70. **GPS**: n52,55324 e13,20164.

130 € 15, 2 pers.incl € 1/100liter Ch included € 1 € 2/day.
Location: Central, noisy. 01/01-31/12
Distance: 100m 300m.
Remarks: Near approach route of airport, 23-5h quiet. In area of the former English barracks 'Alexander Barracks', A10 exit Berlin-Spandau, follow road till cross roads Heerstraße/Gatowerstraße, here to the left, at Flakenseerplatz straight on, Neuendorferstraße, before Hohenzollernring to the left.

S Berlin 6B6

Int. Reisemobilstation Berlin-Mitte, Chausseestrase 82. **GPS**: n52,53817 e13,37304.

45 € 18, > 9m € 20, summer € 20-22,50, incl. 2 pers Ch WC included. **Location:** Urban, comfortable, central, noisy.
Surface: grassy/metalled. 01/01-31/12
Distance: on the spot 500m 500m 200m.
Remarks: A100 exit Wedding/Seestrasse after ca. 2km to the right Mütterstrasse, this street becomes Chausseestrasse.

S Berlin 6B6

Köpenicker Hof, Stellingdamm 15, Berlin-Köpenick. **GPS**: n52,45929 e13,58532.

40 € 10, 2 pers.incl Ch included € 0,50/kWh WC € 1,50/night € 1,50/night. **Surface:** grassy/gravel. 01/01-31/12
Distance: Tram (centre 30min).
Remarks: Bread-service.

S Berlin 6B6

Marina Lanke Berlin, Scharfe Lanke 109-131. **GPS**: n52,50344 e13,18801.
15 € 7,50/5m, €12,50/7,5m + € 3,50/pp Ch WC included € 3, dryer € 2. **Location:** Urban.
Surface: metalled.
01/05-15/10
Distance: centre Berlin 16km on the spot on the spot 1km.
Remarks: Marina.

Tourist information Berlin:

Tourist Info, Europacenter, Eingang Budapester strasse 3; Brandenburgertor, Südflügel; Fernsehturm, Alexanderplatz, www.btm.de.Documentation available, via Internet.
Zeughaus.German historical museum.
Alexanderplatz.The old historical centre of Berlin.
Brandenburger Tor.Built in 1791 as a triumphal arch after the construction of the Berlin Wall the arch remained as a symbol of the German separation. free.
Fernsehturm.Television tower.
9-01h, 01/11-28/02 10-24h.
Haus am Checkpoint Charly, Friedrichstrasse 44.At the former border crossing. History of the Wall is told with photographs.
9-22h.
Holländische Viertel.Dutch district many cafés, luxurious boutiques and art galeries.
Reichstag, Platz der Republik.Old parliament building.
daily till 20h. free.
Funkturm en radiomuseum, Messedamm, Charlottenburg.Radio and television museum.
Tue-Su 10-23h.
Museum-Insel.Museum complex.
Schloß Charlottenburg, Luisenplatz.Summer residence of the Prussian kings.
Tue-Fri 9-17h, Sa-Su 10-17h.
Sloss Glienicke.Original country-house developed to castle.
15/05-15/10 Sa-Su 10-17h.
Antik- und Trödelmarkt, Ostbahnhof.
Sa 9-15h, Su 10-17h.
Kunst- und Flohmarkt, strasse des 17. Juni.Arts and fleamarket.
Sa-Su 11-17h.
Nollendorf rommelmarkt, Altes S-Bahnstation.
Wed-Mo 8-13h.
Trödelmarkt, Arkonaplatz.Flea market. Su 10-16h.
Türkische Markt, MaybachuferNeukölln.Turkish market.
Tue + Fri afternoon.
Zoologischer Garten, Hardenbergplatz 8.City-zoo.
01/04-30/09 9-18.30h, 01/10-31/10 9-18h, 01/11-28/02 9-17h.

S Brandenburg 11A1

Am Brandenburger Dom, Grillendamm. **GPS**: n52,41724 e12,56576.

60 € 10 € 1/100liter Ch € 1 WC € 1. 01/01-31/12
Distance: Neustadt 15min, Altstadt 15min.

Brandenburg 11A1

Wassersportzentrum Alte Feuerwache, Franz Zieglerstrasse 27. **GPS**: n52,40485 e12,54868.

25 € 8 Ch WC included € 1.
Surface: metalled.
01/01-31/12
Distance: 500m 500m.

Tourist information Brandenburg:
Tourist Information, Steinstrasse 66-67, www.stadt-brb.de.
Hanseatic city with historical centre.
Dom St. Peter und Paul.Cathedral.
Stadtmauer mit Tortürmen.
City wall and towers.

Brieske 11D3

Reimann, Brieske Dorf 27. **GPS**: n51,49203 e13,94743.

20 € 5 Ch WC included. **Surface:** grassy. 01/01-31/12
Distance: 200m 9,3km 2km.

Burg/Spreewald 11D2

Hagens Insel - Wasserwanderrastplatz, Weidenweg 4. **GPS**: n51,86138 e14,11527.

10 € 10 Ch WC included. **Surface:** grassy.

Burg/Spreewald 11D2

Hotel Kurhaus zum Spreewald, An der Hauptspree 1. **GPS**: n51,84388 e14,10972.

18 € 17/24h Ch included. **Surface:** grassy. 01/01-31/12

Burg/Spreewald 11D2

Landgasthof zur Wildbahn, Wildbahnweg 20. **GPS**: n51,85104 e14,09384.

9 € 13, 2 pers.incl, tourist tax € 1,50/pp, dog € 2 WC included.
Surface: metalled. 01/03-30/10

Dollenchen 11D2

Gasthaus Stuckatz, Hauptstrasse 29. **GPS**: n51,60745 e13,86226.

20 € 8 Ch WC included. **Surface:** grassy. 01/01-31/12
Distance: on the spot on the spot 3km.

Dreetz 6A6

Reiterhof Müller, Schulstrasse 61. **GPS**: n52,79322 e12,46698.

5 € 10 Ch WC included € 1. **Surface:** grassy. 01/04-31/10
Distance: 800m 300m 500m 500m.

Fürstenberg (Havel) 6B4

Marina Fürstenberg, Ravensbrücker Dorfstrasse 26. **GPS**: n53,19489 e13,14895.

DE

50 € 6 € 2 Ch € 3 WC € 1,50.
Surface: grassy.
01/01-31/12
Distance: 1km on the spot 1km.
Remarks: At marina, boat rental.

S Kienitz 6D6

Ferienhaus Marth, Kienitzeroderstrasse 20. **GPS**: n52,67616 e14,39890.

8 € 6 Ch € 1,50 WC € 1,50. **Surface:** grassy. 01/04-30/09
Distance: 3km 3km.

S Klein-Ossnig 11D2

Caravan-Krokor, Haupstrasse 12/a, B169. **GPS**: n51,69962 e14,27917.

8 € 6 Ch included. **Surface:** grassy. 01/01-31/12
Distance: on the spot 2km.
Remarks: Arrival only during opening hours: Mo-Fr 8-19, Sa 8-13.

S Kolkwitz 11D2

Papitzerstrasse 48. **GPS**: n51,76676 e14,22410.

3 € 10 Ch WC included. **Surface:** grassy. 01/01-31/12
Distance: 2,5km.

S Lübbenau 11D2

Autocamping im Spreewald, Chausseestrasse 17a, Lübbenau-Zerkwitz.
GPS: n51,86559 e13,93324.

6 € 13/24h, tourist tax € 1/pp, dog € 1 € 1,50 Ch WC included.
Surface: grasstiles. Easter-31/10
Distance: 2,5km 500m.

S Lübbenau 11D2

Am Bahnhof, Bahnhofstraße (B115). **GPS**: n51,86139 e13,96361.

10 € 10 € 1 Ch consumption. **Surface:** asphalted.
01/01-31/12
Distance: 800m 3,3km 350m 50m.
Remarks: Max. 48h.

Lübbenau 11D2

Kahnfährhafen Leipe, Dorfstrasse 34, Leipe. **GPS**: n51,85301 e14,05023.

4 € 5. **Surface:** metalled. 01/01-31/12
Distance: 11,6km.

S Lübbenau 11D2

Spreewaldhof Leipe, Leiper Dorfstraße 2, Leipe. **GPS**: n51,85161 e14,03912.

4 € 6 + € 1,50/pp tourist tax € 2/day WC included.
Surface: grassy.
Distance: on the spot.
Remarks: Bread-service.

S Luckenwalde 11B1

Restaurant Elsthal, Teichwiesenweg, Elsthal. **GPS**: n52,07428 e13,16744.
10 € 10 Ch included. **Surface:** sand. 01/01-31/12
Remarks: Max. <>2.35m.

DE

S Lychen 6B4

Marina-Yachthafen Lychensee, Schlüssstrasse 7. **GPS**: n53,21187 e13,29686.

6 € 1/meter Ch € 2 WC € 1. **Surface:** grassy. 15/04-15/10

Distance: 650m.

Remarks: Information at harbourmaster, boat rental.

S Nackel 6A5

Gaststätte Birkenhof, Segeletzerstrasse 2. **GPS**: n52,82503 e12,56528.

3 € 3 Ch € 3 WC. **Surface:** metalled.

Potsdam 6B6

Georg-Hermans Allee/Esplanade. **GPS**: n52,41946 e13,05130.

20 € 4/24h. **Surface:** asphalted. 01/01-31/12

Distance: 3km 500m 500m tram BUGA-Park.

Tourist information Potsdam:

Filmpark Babelsberg, August-Bebel-Str. 26-53.Attractions park concerning the film. 23/03-31/10 10-18h.

S Schmergow 6B6

Zum fröhlichen Landmann, Ziegeleiweg 17. **GPS**: n52,45416 e12,80553.

30 € 5, guests free € 2,50 Ch € 2,50. **Surface:** grassy. 01/01-31/12

S Schwedt-Oder 6D5

Wassersportzentrum Schwedt, Wasserplatz 4. **GPS**: n53,05759 e14,29861.

30 € 10 Ch WC included. **Surface:** grassy. 01/01-31/12

Distance: 1km on the spot on the spot 500m.

Remarks: Check in at harbourmaster or bar.

S Stolzenhagen 6D5

Am Kiez, Hohensaalenstrasse. **GPS**: n52,94916 e14,10833.

20 € 7,50 Ch € 2 WC Use sanitary € 2,50.

Distance: on the spot.

Remarks: Directly beside canal, bread-service.

S Templin 6C5

Alter Knehdenerstrasse. **GPS**: n53,12359 e13,49423.

40 free € 1 Ch. **Surface:** asphalted/metalled. 01/01-31/12

Distance: 300m 300m 300m.

S Tiefensee 6C6

Reisemobilplatz, Country Camping Tiefensee, Schmiedeweg 1. **GPS**: n52,68302 e13,84292.

30 € 12 Ch WC included € 0,50 01/01-31/12

Distance: on the spot on the spot on the spot on the spot on the spot on the spot.

S Weisen 5D5

Wohnmobilstellplatz Am Biotop, Heinrich-Heine-Strasse 4. **GPS**: n53,02062 e11,78086.

DE

5 free . **Surface:** gravel. 01/01-31/12

S Werder-Havel 11B1

An der Föhse. **GPS:** n52,37807 e12,93704.

20 € 5 Ch included (8x) € 2,50/day, (8x) € 0,50/kWh WC € 0,30.
Surface: gravel.
01/01-31/12
Distance: on the spot on the spot on the spot on the spot 100m.
Remarks: Check in at harbourmaster.

Saxony

Adorf 11A6

Waldbad, Waldbadstrasse 5. **GPS:** n50,30778 e12,25056.

free. **Surface:** metalled. 01/01-31/12
Distance: 1km 500m.
Remarks: Max. 24h.

S Amtsberg 11C5

Waldcamping Erzgebirge, B174, An der Dittersdorfer Höhe, Dittersdorf. **GPS:** n50,76583 e13,01444.

60 € 13-15 Ch € 2 WC included. **Surface:** grassy/metalled.
01/01-31/12

S Bad Düben 11B3

Im Kurgebiet, Parkstraße 1. **GPS:** n51,60122 e12,58278.

4 free, tourist tax € 1,20-1,50/pp € 1/80liter € 1 Ch € 1. **Location:** Rural.
Surface: metalled. 01/04-31/12
Distance: 750m 1,4km 1,4km.

S Bad Elster 11A6

Forsthausschänke, Heissenstein 19. **GPS:** n50,27194 e12,24639.

4 € 4 Ch included € 2. 01/01-31/12
Distance: 1,5km campsite 1,5km.

Tourist information Bad Elster:
Traditional health resort.

S Bad Lausick 11B4

Campingplatz Landidyll, Beuchaer Oberweg 7. **GPS:** n51,15200 e12,62663.
35 € 7,50 Ch WC included € 0,50. 01/01-31/12
Distance: on the spot on the spot 1km 2km.

Bad Lausick 11B4

Am Riff 3. **GPS:** n51,14321 e12,65383.
10 free. **Surface:** asphalted.
Remarks: At swimming pool.

S Bad Muskau 11D5

Am Fürst-Pückler-Park, Heideweg 2. **GPS:** n51,53365 e14,71727.
20 € 8 Ch € 2 WC included.
Distance: on the spot 4km 2km.

S Biehain 11D6

Erholungsgebiet Biehainer See'n, Am Waldsee. **GPS:** n51,28662 e14,92490.
10 € 5 Ch WC included.
Distance: 1km on the spot on the spot 2km.
Remarks: Max. 48h.

S Breitenbrunn 11B5

Sportpark Rabenberg, Rabenbergweg. **GPS:** n50,45556 e12,74417.

15 € 5 + € 5/pp Ch € 2/day WC € 0,50. **Surface:** metalled.
01/01-31/12
Distance: 5km 5km 5km.
Remarks: Arrival <22h, dog € 2/day.

S Crottendorf 11B5

Pension Kalkberg, Joachimsthaller strasse 294. **GPS:** n50,46378 e12,92238.
16 € 15 Ch included € 2. 01/01-31/12 Mo.
Distance: 4km on the spot 1,5km.

DE

Diesbar-Seusslitz 11C3

Restaurant Zum Rosengarten, S88, Meissnerstrasse 4, Nünchritz. **GPS**: n51,23333 e13,42667.

4 guests free Ch WC. **Surface:** metalled.
Distance: on the spot.
Remarks: Along the river Elbe.

Dresden 11D4

Parkplatz Grosse Meissner, Wiesentor Strasse. **GPS**: n51,05639 e13,74306.

30 € 14 <6,8m, € 16 6,8m-8m, € 20 > 8m € 2/100liter Ch€ 2 (14x)€ 4/day. **Location:** Urban. **Surface:** asphalted. 01/01-31/12
Distance: 100m.

Dresden 11D4

Sachsenplatz Dresden, Johannstadt Käthe-Kollwitz-Ufer 4, Johannstadt. **GPS**: n51,05700 e13,75990.
150 € 10 (25x)€ 3/24h. **Location:** Urban, central.
Distance: Altstadt 2,2km 300m Aldi 700m 500m.

Dresden 11D4

Werner Knopf, B6, Meissner Landstrasse. **GPS**: n51,08131 e13,65563.
16 € 5/6m + € 1/m € 2 € 2 € 1,50. **Location:** Urban.
Surface: grasstiles.
Distance: 6km 500m.
Remarks: Gate closes at 22h.

Dresden 11D4

Wohnmobilplatz Dresden, Kesselsdorfer Straße 153. **GPS**: n51,04004 e13,66963.
5 € 12 Ch € 2,50 € 2. **Location:** Urban.
Surface: gravel.
01/01-31/12
Distance: centre Dresden 4km 4km on the spot 800m 800m.
Remarks: At Wellnesshotel Landlust.

Dresden 11D4

Wohnmobilstellplatz am Blüherpark, Zinzendorfstraße 7. **GPS**: n51,04426 e13,74371.
50 € 14 € 1 € 1 € 3/night € 2. **Location:** Urban.
Surface: metalled. 01/01-31/12
Distance: 1km 5km 500m 450m.
Remarks: Check in at Cityherberge, Lingnerallee 3, 24/24.

Dresden 11D4

CaravaningPark Schaffer, Kötzschenbroderstrasse 125. **GPS**: n51,08639 e13,68222.

100 € 11 € 0,50/60liter € 0,50 Ch € 0,50 € 0,50/kWh WC € 0,50. **Location:** Urban, comfortable.
Surface: grassy.
01/01-31/12
Distance: Dresden 5km 2km 200m 500m 200m 500m.
Remarks: Repair possibilities motorhome, access <19h, bread service.

Tourist information Dresden:

Dresden-City-Card.
Card gives among other things for free public transport, entrance to many museums, discounts on boat trips, restaurants etc.
01/01-31/12. € 18/48h.
Tourist Information, Prager strasse; Schinkelwache/Theaterplatz, www.dresden.de.
Former residence city with many curiosities.
Frauenkiche.Protestant church.
Zwinger.Baroque complex in the old city center with important museums.
Tue-Su.
Albertinum Museum.Art collection.
Striezelmarkt, Altstadt.Christmas fair.
Dec.

Ebersbach/Sachsen 11D6

Fest- und Parkplatz am Freibad, Kottmarsdorfer Strasse. **GPS**: n51,00972 e14,59806.

7 € 5, € 10 service incl Ch . **Surface:** metalled.
01/04-30/10
Distance: 1km 500m 1km.

Eichigt 11A6

Landgasthof Süssebach, Hauptstrasse 9. **GPS**: n50,36278 e12,15583.

2 € 10 Ch WC included. 01/01-31/12
Distance: 3km.

Elsterheide 11D3

Wohnmobilstellplatz Lothar Meusel, Am Hochwald 27, Tätzschwitz. **GPS**: n51,48304 e14,10750.

DE

8 € 6,50-7,50 Ch WC included € 2,25. 01/04-31/10
Distance: 3km 8-10km.

S Freiberg 11C4

Messeplatz, Winklerstrasse. **GPS**: n50,92375 e13,34261.

3 free WC. **Surface:** grasstiles. 01/01-31/12
Distance: 300m 300m 300m 50m.

S Geierswalde 11D3

Ferien- und Freizeitpark Geierswalde See, Promenadeweg. **GPS**: n51,49547 e14,13146.
€ 6 € 2 Ch WC . **Surface:** grassy. 01/04-01/10
Distance: 500m Geierswaldesee 300m 5km.

S Grünhain 11B5

Freizeitpark, Auer Strasse 82, Haus des Gastes, Grünhain-Beierfeld. **GPS**: n50,58139 e12,79167.

6 € 5 € 1 € 1,customers free Ch € 1,50/day WC € 1.
Surface: metalled. 01/01-31/12
Distance: 1km on the spot 3km.

S Heidenau 11D4

Wohnmobilplatz Heidenau, Rudolf Breischeidstrasse 23. **GPS**: n50,98417 e13,85028.

20 € 9 € 1,50 Ch € 1,50 € 1,50. **Surface:** gravel. 01/04-31/10
Distance: Heidenau 4km 1,5km, Imbiss 50m 2km 1,5km.
Remarks: A17 exit Heidenau, dir Pirna (B172), in Heidenau follow signs.

S Hermsdorf 11D5

Ski- & Sporthotel SWF, Bahnhofstraße 7. **GPS**: n50,73241 e13,66400.
8 € 4, tourist tax € 0,50/pp € 2 € 2 Ch € 1/day. 01/01-31/12

S Hermsdorf 11D5

Autofhof Kanzfei, Kraftsdorferstrasse. **GPS**: n50,88902 e11,87206.
10 € 2,50 € 1/80liter Ch WC. **Surface:** metalled. 01/01-31/12
Distance: 2km 500m on the spot Shell-shop.

S Königsfeld-Stollsdorf 11B4

Spreer's Ferienhaus, Hauptstrasse 28. **GPS**: n51,04861 e12,74500.

4 € 8 Ch € 2. 01/01-31/12
Distance: 4km 4km.

S Königstein 11D4

Panoramhotel Lilienstein, Ebenheit 7. **GPS**: n50,92527 e14,07527.
10 € 10 .
Distance: on the spot.
Remarks: Bread-service and breakfast buffet.

S Leipzig 11A3

Campinghof Bartl, Bornaer Chaussee 36, Markkleeberg. **GPS**: n51,27000 e12,43194.

26 € 15 € 2 Ch € 2 WC . **Surface:** grassy/metalled.
01/01-31/12
Distance: Leipzig 5km 2km 1,5km.

S Leipzig 11A3

Querstraße 14. **GPS**: n51,34020 e12,38595.
20 € 10-15/24h € 3.
Distance: 8,5km.

Tourist information Leipzig:
Leipzig Information, Richard-Wagner-strasse 1, Leipzig, www.leipzig.de.

S Marienberg 11C5

Rätzteich, Gelobtland 27c. **GPS**: n50,62417 e13,17861.

3 € 3 € 1 € 1 Ch € 1 € 1. **Surface:** metalled. 01/01-31/12
Distance: 5km 500m 5km 3km.
Remarks: Recreation area.

S Oberschindmaas 11B5

Caravan Service Bressler, Zwickauerstrasse 78. **GPS**: n50,80889 e12,48667.

DE

3 € 4/night Ch free € 1. **Surface:** metalled. 01/01-31/12
Distance: 2,1km.

Oberwiesental 11C5

OTG Tennishalle, Vieren Strasse 1a. **GPS**: n50,42722 e12,96944.

20 € 11, 01/12-31/03 € 17 Ch WC included. **Surface:** metalled.
01/01-31/12
Distance: on the spot 250m.
Remarks: Parking tennishall, check in at reception tennishall < 22h, bread-service.

Rothersdorf 11B3

Zur-Tabak-Baude. **GPS**: n51,30647 e12,73830.

20 € 6, guests free. **Surface:** grassy. 01/01-31/12
Distance: 2km on the spot 1,5km.

Sebnitz 11D4

Touristik zentrum Sebnitz, Albert Kunzeweg 30-36. **GPS**: n50,96156 e14,27735.

30 € 6/pppd Ch WC included.
Surface: metalled.
01/04-31/10
Distance: 2km 1-2km 500m 2km Sebnitz.
Remarks: Swimming pool, tourist tax € 0,75/pppd.

Tourist information Sebnitz:

Touristinformation Sebnitz, Schillerstrasse 3.Silk flower city.

Thräna 11D6

Freizeitcamp, Zum Wildgehege, Hohendubrau. **GPS**: n51,23528 e14,69972.

10 € 5, campsite € 14,50 Ch € 0,45/kWh.
Surface: grassy/metalled. 01/05-30/09
Distance: Gaststätte 2,5km Gebelzig.

Zittau 11D6

Zittau Am Dreiländereck, Brückenstrasse 23. **GPS**: n50,89405 e14,82176.
40 € 7 € 1 Ch (16x)€ 1/8h WC . **Surface:** metalled.
01/01-31/12
Distance: 1,5km 200m.
Remarks: Three Countries' Corner Germany-Czech Republic-Poland.

Zwota 11B6

Alte Scheune Camping, Merkneukirchner Strasse 79. **GPS**: n50,35111 e12,38111.

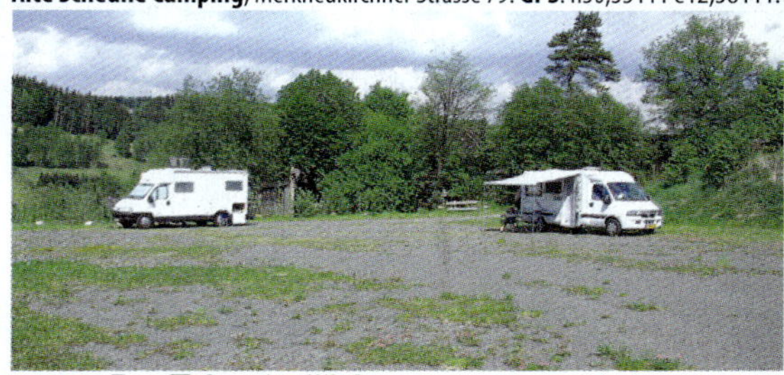

70 € 5 € 1 Ch € 2 WC € 1. **Surface:** metalled.
01/01-31/12
Distance: Klingenthal 6km 6km.

North Rhine Westphalia

Aachen 8D5

Aachen-Camping, Branderhofer Weg 11. **GPS**: n50,76111 e6,10306.

46 € 15/night Ch WC included € 1. **Location:** Urban, luxurious, central, quiet. **Surface:** metalled. 01/01-31/12
Distance: 1,7km 700m 700m 300m.
Remarks: Baker 8.30-09.00.

Aachen 8D5

Hotel-Restaurant-Café Sülte Mühle, Ölmühle 1, Lonnerbecke. **GPS**: n52,54972 e7,69594.
2 free € 2.

Tourist information Aachen:

Informationsbüro Elisenbrunnen, www.aachen.de.

Ahaus 9A2

Krimesplatz, Schlossstrasse. **GPS**: n52,07450 e7,00299.

DE

8 free € 0,50/80liter Ch (6x)€ 0,50/kWh WC. **Surface:** metalled. 01/01-31/12 during event.
Distance: on the spot.
Remarks: Parking in the centre, max. 3 nights.

S **Ahlen** 9B3

Freizeitbad Berliner Park, Dolbergerstrasse 66. **GPS**: n51,75559 e7,89694.

2 € 8/24h .
Distance: Nearby centre.
Remarks: Max. 3 nights.

S **Alpen** 8D3

An der Motte, Burgstrasse 66. **GPS**: n51,57985 e6,51846.

11 € 7,50 Ch included. **Location:** Rural, comfortable.
Surface: gravel. 01/01-31/12
Distance: 500m 2,5km 500m.

S **Altena** 9B4

Sauerlandhalle Pragpaul, Hermann Vossstrasse 14. **GPS**: n51,30861 e7,66056.

12 free € 0,50 € 0,50 Ch (6x)€ 0,50/1kWh. **Location:** Rural, simple, quiet. **Surface:** asphalted/gravel. 01/01-31/12
Distance: 2km 10km nearby 2km on the spot on the spot.

Altenbeken 9D3

Landhaus Friedenstal, Hüttenstrasse 42. **GPS**: n51,75992 e8,95111.

5 € 5 (5x)€ 2,50/24h WC On demand,at restaurant. **Location:** Simple, central. **Surface:** grassy/gravel. 01/01-31/12
Distance: 200m on the spot 200m.

S **Altenberge** 9B2

Sportpark Grosseberg, Bijlenweg. **GPS**: n52,05528 e7,47056.

20 free € 0,50 Ch. **Surface:** metalled. 01/01-31/12
Distance: on the spot nearby 1,5km.
Remarks: Parking sports centre.

Arnsberg 9C4

An der Schlacht/Ruhrstrasse. **GPS**: n51,40127 e8,06468.
4 free. **Location:** Simple. **Surface:** gravel.
Distance: 3,3km Lidl 50m.

S **Ascheberg** 9B2

Gasthaus Eickholt, Frieport 22, Davensberg. **GPS**: n51,82619 e7,59391.

6 guests free € 5 WC . **Surface:** grassy.
01/01-31/12 Wed.
Distance: 800m 5,5km on the spot 1km 800m.

S **Attendorn** 9C4

Haus Schnepper, Talstrasse 19. **GPS**: n51,10530 e7,95744.

15 guests free Ch free. **Surface:** metalled.
01/01-31/12
Distance: 1km on the spot 1km.

S **Attendorn** 9C4

Land-Hotel-Struck, Repetalstrasse 245, Niederhelden. **GPS**: n51,12073 e7,97284.

DE

6 guests free € 3,50 WC. 01/01-31/12
Distance: on the spot on the spot 2km on the spot on the spot.

S Bad Berleburg 9C4

Bismarckstraße. **GPS**: n51,04986 e8,39406.
3 free € 2/100liter Ch € 1/8h. **Surface:** metalled.
01/01-31/12
Distance: 500m 500m.

S Bad Berleburg 9C4

Pension-Bauernladen Schmelzhütte, K52 Hoheleye. **GPS**: n51,13874 e8,45742.

6 € 10 Ch € 2. **Surface:** asphalted. 01/01-31/12 Mo.
Distance: 1km on the spot 1km.
Remarks: Bread-service.

Bad Berleburg 9C4

Hotel-Restaurant Erholung - Laibach, Auf dem Laibach 1. **GPS**: n51,06776 e8,44527.

5 free with a meal (1x)€ 5/day WC. **Surface:** asphalted.
01/01-31/12
Distance: 5km on the spot 5km on the spot on the spot on the spot 1,5km.

S Bad Driburg 9D3

P Driburg Therme, Georg-Nave-Strasse 24. **GPS**: n51,74194 e9,02542.

10 € 5 + tourist tax (10x)€ 3/24h WC. **Location:** Rural, simple, quiet.
Surface: asphalted. 01/01-31/12
Distance: 1km on the spot 1km on the spot on the spot on the spot.

Remarks: Max. 7m, key electricity at pay-desk, caution € 10.

S Bad Laasphe 9C5

Mühlenstrasse. **GPS**: n50,92412 e8,41146.

7 € 6/day € 0,50/80liter Ch € 0,50/kWh. 01/01-31/12
Distance: 500m 500m 500m.
Remarks: Parking at town hall.

S Bad Laasphe 9C5

Hotel Jagdhof Glashütte, Glashütterstrasse 20, Volkholz. **GPS**: n50,92008 e8,28070.

6 € 13,80, free with a meal WC. **Location:** Rural. **Surface:** grassy. 01/01-31/12 23-24/12.
Distance: 4km on the spot on the spot 4km 1,5km.

S Bad Lippspringe 9D3

Arminiuspark, Burgstraße 10. **GPS**: n51,78124 e8,82447.

11 € 2,80/1p +1p € 2/pp Ch . **Location:** Urban, quiet. **Surface:** metalled. 01/01-31/12
Distance: 300m 350m on the spot on the spot.
Remarks: Pay at tourist office.

S Bad Münstereifel 9A6

Wohnmobilpark Eifel, Dr.Grevestraße 16. **GPS**: n50,54600 e6,76514.

30 € 7 + € 1/pp tourist tax € 1/100 € 1 Ch (30x)included WC € 1,80. **Location:** Rural, comfortable, quiet. **Surface:** grassy/metalled.
01/01-31/12
Distance: 350m on the spot 100m.
Remarks: Pay and coins at swimming pool, 20% discount pool.

DE

Bad Oeynhausen 9D1

Südbahnstraße/Detmolder Straße. **GPS**: n52,19680 e8,80038.

3 free. **Surface:** asphalted. 01/01-31/12

Remarks: Max. 2 days.

Bad Oeynhausen 9D1

Siekmeiers Hof, Volmerdingsener strasse 111. **GPS**: n52,24679 e8,78394.

10 guests free. **Location:** Urban, quiet. **Surface:** gravel. 01/01-31/12

Mon, Tue.

Distance: on the spot on the spot 1km.

Bad Salzuflen 9D2

Wohnmobil-Park Flachsheide, Forsthausweg. **GPS**: n52,09868 e8,74569.

25 € 7/day, tourist tax € 2,90/pp/day Ch WC included.

Location: Rural, quiet. 01/01-31/12

Distance: 1,5km 5,5km on the spot 500m 1,5km free.

Remarks: Follow 'Vitasol'.

Bad Sassendorf 9C3

Kurcamping Rumkerhof, Weslarnerstrasse 30. **GPS**: n51,59581 e8,17909.

93 € 8,50 Ch (93x)included. **Surface:** gravel. 01/01-31/12

Distance: 1,3km 1,3km.

Remarks: Bread-service, waste dump € 0,50.

Bad Waldliesborn 9C3

Wohnmobilstellplatz, Quellenstraße. **GPS**: n51,71759 e8,33587.

10 € 4,40, tourist tax € 2,10/pp € 2/10liter Ch (8x)€ 2/24h.

Location: Rural, quiet. **Surface:** gravel. 01/01-31/12

Distance: 400m 200m 400m 400m.

Remarks: Discount on access terme.

Bad Westernkotten 9C3

Wohnmobilplatz An den Sole-Thermen, Mühlenweg 1. **GPS**: n51,63126 e8,35195.

46 € 7, tourist tax € 2/pp € 1/100liter Ch € 0,50/kWh.

Surface: grassy. 01/01-31/12

Distance: bakery 300m.

Remarks: Bread-service.

Bad Wünnenberg 9D3

Wohnmobilhafen, In den Erlen. **GPS**: n51,52058 e8,70133.

12 € 4 € 1/100liter Ch (12x)€ 1/24h. **Location:** Urban, central.

Surface: gravel. 01/01-31/12

Distance: 100m 400m 100m 400m on the spot on the spot.

Balve 9B4

Am Hallenbad, In der Murmke 9. **GPS**: n51,32729 e7,86920.

3 free € 1/100liter € 1/kWh. **Location:** Urban, simple.

Surface: metalled. 01/01-31/12

Distance: 600m 600m 600m on the spot on the spot.

Barntrup 9D2

Badeanstaltsweg. **GPS**: n51,98790 e9,10990.

4 € 6 € 1/100liter Ch € 0,50/kWh. **Location:** Rural, simple.

Surface: asphalted. 01/01-31/12

Distance: 450m 450m 450m 450m.

Remarks: To be paid at campsite Teutoburger Wald.

DE

Barntrup 9D2

Ferienpark Teutoburger Wald, Badeanstaltsweg 4. **GPS**: n51,98768 e9,11027.

9 € 20,50 Ch (€ 5,Washing machine/dryer included.
Location: Rural, luxurious, quiet. **Surface:** grassy/metalled. 01/04-31/10
Distance: 450m 450m 450m 450m on the spot on the spot.

Beckum 9C3

Am Hallenbad, Paterweg 4. **GPS**: n51,75129 e8,03585.
3 free € 0,50/100liter Ch (2x)€ 0,50/1kWh. **Location:** Urban, simple. **Surface:** metalled. 01/01-31/12
Distance: 1km 1km 1km.

Bedburg-Hau 8D3

Womo-Moyland, Moyländer Allee 3a, Moyland. **GPS**: n51,75562 e6,24381.

50 € 5/24h, € 9/48h, € 12/72h € 0,50/100liter Ch € 2,50/24h.
Location: Rural, comfortable. **Surface:** grasstiles.
01/01-31/12
Distance: Kleve-zentrum 8km 300m.
Remarks: Schloss Moyland 300m, golf court 500m.

Bedburg-Hau 8D3

Landgasthaus Schwanenhof, Mühlenstraße 71, Ortsteil Schneppenbaum. **GPS**: n51,76096 e6,20404.

25 € 5 Ch (18x). **Location:** Rural, comfortable.
Surface: grassy. 01/01-31/12
Distance: 500m on the spot 1km.
Remarks: Bread-service.

Tourist information Bedburg-Hau:
Schloß Moyland, Am Schloss 4.Castle. Tue-Fri 11-18h, sa-su 10-18h, 1/4-31/3 tue-so 11-17h Mon.

Bergheim 9A5

Stellplatz Paffendorf, Königsstrasse/Kastanienallee. **GPS**: n50,96389 e6,61194.

8 free. **Location:** Rural, simple, quiet. **Surface:** asphalted.
01/01-31/12
Distance: Bergheim 2km 2,3km 300m 500m.
Remarks: Max. 2 days, castle Paffendorf 100m.

Bergkamen 9B3

Wohnmobilhafen Marina Rünthe, Hafenweg, Rünthe. **GPS**: n51,64106 e7,64309.
18 € 7/24h € 1/80liter Ch (12x)€ 0,50/kWh.
Surface: grassy/gravel. 01/01-31/12
Distance: 500m 3,8km.
Remarks: Only exact change, max. 3 days.

Bergkamen 9B3

Freizeitzentrum Im Häupen, Häupenweg 29. **GPS**: n51,61300 e7,63075.

5 free. **Surface:** metalled. 01/01-31/12
Distance: on the spot 3,4km on the spot on the spot.

Bestwig 9C4

Besucherbergwerk, Ziegelwiese, Ramsbeck. **GPS**: n51,31821 e8,40318.

6 free. **Location:** Simple. **Surface:** metalled. 01/01-31/12
Distance: 800m.

Bestwig 9C4

Ludwigstrasse. **GPS**: n51,36064 e8,40165.

4 free. **Location:** Simple, simple. **Surface:** metalled. 01/01-31/12
Distance: on the spot 300m 200m.

DE

Beverungen 10A3

Wohnmobilhafen Weser, Am Hakel. **GPS**: n51,66167 e9,37639.

12 free € 1/100liter Ch € 1 (12x)€ 1/6h. **Location:** Urban, simple. **Surface:** grassy/metalled. 01/01-31/12

Distance: on the spot on the spot on the spot on the spot on the spot.

Remarks: Next to Festplatz.

Bielefeld 9C2

Am Johannisberg, Dornbergerstrasse. **GPS**: n52,02270 e8,51155.

10 01/03-01/12 € 5/24h € 1/8 Ch (10x)€ 0,50/1kWh. **Location:** Rural, comfortable, quiet. **Surface:** metalled.

01/01-31/12

Distance: 2km Imbiss 2km 2km.

Billerbeck 9A2

Am Freibad, Osterwickerstrasse. **GPS**: n51,97928 e7,28190.

4 free Ch (4x)€ 1. **Surface:** gravel. 01/01-31/12

Distance: 500m 500m.

Remarks: At swimming pool, service Kläranlage.

Blankenheim 9A6

Weiherhalle, Koblenzerstrasse. **GPS**: n50,43499 e6,65439.

15 € 5/24h € 1/80liter Ch (12x)€ 2/10h. **Location:** Rural, simple. **Surface:** metalled. 01/01-31/12

Distance: 150m.

Bocholt 8D2

WoMo Park am Aasee, Uhlandstraße 39. **GPS**: n51,83496 e6,63146.

37 € 5 € 0,50/50liter Ch (20x)€ 0,50/kWh WC € 3,50,dryer € 2,50 . **Location:** Urban, central, noisy. **Surface:** metalled.

01/01-31/12

Distance: 300m 300m.

Bocholt 8D2

Inselbad Bahia, Hemdenerweg 169. **GPS**: n51,86265 e6,61002.

10 free Ch. **Location:** Rural, simple.

Surface: grasstiles.

01/01-31/12

Distance: 2,5km 450m 1km on the spot.

Remarks: Max. 48h, coins available at swimming pool.

Bocholt 8D2

Euregio-Gymnasium, Unter den Eichen, Blücherstrasse. **GPS**: n51,84884 e6,63700.

10 free. **Location:** Urban, simple. **Surface:** metalled.

01/01-31/12

Distance: 1km 700m on the spot.

Remarks: Parking 'Stadtswald', max. 3 nights.

Tourist information Bocholt:

Tourist-Info Bocholt, Europaplatz 26-28, www.bocholt.de.Motorhome friendly town, former center of textile industry, modern city centre.

Textilmuseum, Uhlandstrasse 50.Industry museum.

Tue-Su 10-18h.

Rathaus - Gasthausplatz.

Thu-evening.

Vier Räder und acht Rollen.Skating routes, available at Tourist-Info and on Internet.

Bonn 9A5

An der Rheinaue, Ludwig-Erhard-Allee. **GPS**: n50,70981 e7,13904.

18 free. **Surface:** asphalted. 01/01-31/12

Distance: centre 4km A565 4,6km 300m line 66 > Bonn centre.

Borken 9A2

Aquarius-Bad, Feldmark. **GPS**: n51,83644 e6,86479.

DE

20 free Chfree. **Location:** Rural, simple. **Surface:** grassy.
01/01-31/12
Distance: 1km 1km 1km.
Remarks: Parking swimming pool, max. 3 nights, service: Kläranlage Borken Mo-Thu 7-16h. Fri 7-11.30h.

Borken 9A2

Festplatz Weseke, Borkenwirther strasse, Weseke. **GPS**: n51,90529 e6,85210.

5 free. **Location:** Rural, simple. **Surface:** metalled.
01/01-31/12
Distance: 500m 500m 500m.
Remarks: Max. 3 nights.

Borken 9A2

Schlossklinik Pröbsting, Pröbstinger Allee. **GPS**: n51,83861 e6,80556.
10 free. **Surface:** metalled. 01/01-31/12
Distance: Badesee 150m.

Borken 9A2

Wasserburg Gemen, Coesfelderstrasse, Gemen. **GPS**: n51,86172 e6,86909.

5 free. **Location:** Rural, simple. **Surface:** metalled.
01/01-31/12
Distance: 1km 500m 500m 1km 1km.
Remarks: Parking sports park, max. 3 nights.

Borken 9A2

Camping Pröbstingersee, Dirkshof 11, Hoxfeld. **GPS**: n51,83237 e6,78764.

10 free Ch. **Surface:** metalled.
01/01-31/12

Distance: 6,5km 100m 100m.
Remarks: Max. 3 nights, service agains payment on campsite.

Borken 9A2

Gestüt Forellenhof Wolter, Zum Homborn 9. **GPS**: n51,86245 e6,89797.
15 € 11 Ch (7x)included. **Surface:** gravel. 01/01-31/12
Distance: Borken 3,5km fish pond on the spot.
Remarks: Check in at Gaststätte, € 5 euro discount coupon.

Tourist information Borken:
Tourist Info, Im Bahnhof, www.borken.de.

Bottrop 9A3

Warner Bros Movie World, Kirchhellen, Warner Allee 1. **GPS**: n51,62400 e6,97096.

100 free. **Surface:** asphalted. visiting hours park
Distance: 2,7km 100m 2,7km.

Tourist information Bottrop:
Alpincenter, Prosperstrasse.Indoor ski centre.
9-24h. day ticket € 25, <18h € 18.
Freizeitpark Schloß Beck.Amusement park.
01/03-31/10 9-18h.
Warner Bros Movie World, Kirchhellen.Attractions park concerning the film.
01/04-31/10 10-18h, summer, weekend 9-21/22h.

Brakel/Bellersen 9D2

Wohnmobilhafen Mühlengrund, Meinolfussstrasse 6. **GPS**: n51,77217 e9,18804.

23 € 8,50 € 0,50Ch (23x)included. **Location:** Rural, comfortable, isolated. **Surface:** grasstiles.
01/01-31/12
Distance: 800m 400m 800m 800m on the spot.

Tourist information Brakel/Bellersen:
www.bellersen.de.Health resort.

Bruchhausen 10A3

Bruchhäuserstrasse. **GPS**: n51,70714 e9,29192.

4 free. **Location:** Rural, simple. **Surface:** grassy/gravel. 01/01-31/12
Distance: 200m 200m 200m.

DE

S Brüggen 8D4

Freizeitplatz Brachter Wald, St.-Barbara-Straße 40–42, Bracht. **GPS**: n51,25713 e6,17022.
14 € 7,50, 2 pers.incl. Ch € 2/day WC € 1. **Surface:** grasstiles.
01/01-31/12
Distance: 2km on the spot on the spot.

S Brüggen 8D4

Wohnmobilhafen Brüggen, Bornerstraße 48. **GPS**: n51,24264 e6,18955.

30 € 4 Chincluded € 2. **Surface:** metalled. 01/01-31/12
Distance: 50m 100m 50m 50m.
Remarks: Behind Aldi-süd.

S Brühl 9A5

Phantasialand P1, Berggeiststrasse 31-41. **GPS**: n50,79919 e6,87875.

10 € 12,50/night WC. **Location:** Comfortable, quiet.
Surface: metalled.
04/04-31/10
Distance: 100m.

Tourist information Brühl:
Phantasialand.Large amusement park. 01/04-31/10 9-18h, winter changing visiting hours.

Bünde 9C1

Stadtgarten, Steinmeisterstrasse/Viktoriastrasse. **GPS**: n52,19869 e8,58986.

5 free. **Location:** Urban, simple. **Surface:** metalled.
01/01-31/12
Distance: 50m 50m 50m.
Remarks: Max. 72h.

Burbach 9C5

Hotel Zollhaus, Zollhaus 1, Lippe. **GPS**: n50,70417 e8,06730.

100 € 3. **Surface:** metalled. 01/01-31/12
Distance: on the spot.

S Büren 9C3

Parkplatz an der Afte, Fürstenberger Strasse. **GPS**: n51,54897 e8,56381.

8 free Ch. **Location:** Urban, simple.
01/01-31/12
Distance: on the spot 500m 200m.
Remarks: Parking nearby swimming pool.

S Coesfeld 9A2

Brauhaus Stephanus, Overhagenweg 1. **GPS**: n51,93719 e7,15617.
4 customers free. **Surface:** metalled. 01/01-31/12
Distance: on the spot.

S Dahlem 8D6

Flugplatz Dahlemer Binz, Dahlemer Binz. **GPS**: n50,40663 e6,53700.

3 free € 1 Ch. **Location:** Rural, simple. **Surface:** asphalted.
01/01-31/12
Distance: on the spot.
Remarks: Airport Dahlemer Binz.

S Dahlem 8D6

Wohnmobilstellplatz Kronenburger See, Seeuferstrasse 6. **GPS**: n50,35785 e6,46989.

16 € 8/24h € 1/120liter Ch (12x)included. **Location:** Rural, simple, quiet. **Surface:** grassy. 01/01-31/12
Remarks: At artificial lake.

DE

Delbrück 9C3

Landgasthaus Roseneck, Haselhorster Strasse 3. **GPS**: n51,75770 e8,43441.

10 € 5, free with a meal (10x)included. **Location:** Rural, simple. **Surface:** metalled. 01/01-31/12
Distance: 2km on the spot 2km.

Detmold 9D2

Detmolder City Camp, Bahnhofstrasse 8. **GPS**: n51,94055 e8,87123.

14 € 8 € 1/100liter Ch (14x)€ 2,16Amp WC . **Location:** Urban. **Surface:** asphalted. 01/01-31/12
Distance: 500m 500m 200m kiosk 50m.

Dinslaken 9A3

Am Rotbachsee, Am Freibad. **GPS**: n51,56707 e6,77807.

10 free. **Surface:** sand. 01/01-31/12
Distance: 100m 100m 100m.

Dormagen 9A4

Parkplatz Flügeldeich, Herrenweg, Feste Zons. **GPS**: n51,12553 e6,85001.

3 € 5. **Surface:** metalled. 01/01-31/12
Distance: 400m on the spot on the spot 100m 500m.
Remarks: Max. 3 days, near the Rhine river.

Dorsten 9A3

Reisemobilhafen An der Lippe, Zur Lippe. **GPS**: n51,66550 e6,96744.

38 € 5 Ch (34x)€ 1/8h. **Surface:** metalled/sand. 01/01-31/12
Distance: 300m 300m 300m.

Tourist information Dorsten:

Verkehrsverein Dorsten, Ursulastrasse 24.Former Hanseatic town on the Lippe.
Antikmarkt.Antiques market. 1st Su of the month.
Pferdemarkt.Horse market. 1st Su May.

Dortmund 9B3

Mobil-Camp Wischlingen, Wischlinger Weg 50-61, Wischlingen. **GPS**: n51,52001 e7,39868.

50 € 8, 2 pers.incl € 1/80liter Ch (30x)€ 0,50/kWh WC € 1.
Surface: asphalted. 01/01-31/12
Distance: 1km Rewe 1km 200m.
Remarks: Former tennis-court in recreation area. A45 exit DO-Marten, then follow signs.

Drensteinfurt 9B3

Am Erlbad, Im Erlfeld 2. **GPS**: n51,78972 e7,74778.
3 € 3 € 3 Ch WC . **Surface:** metalled. 01/05-01/10
Distance: 800m 9km.
Remarks: Check in at swimming pool, max. 8m.

Duisburg 9A3

Landschaftspark Duisburg-Nord, Emscherstraße 71, Meiderich. **GPS**: n51,48413 e6,78077.
5 free Ch. **Surface:** asphalted. 01/01-31/12
Distance: 1,6km.

Dülmen 9A2

Kapellenweg. **GPS**: n51,82331 e7,27945.

7 free free. **Surface:** metalled. 01/01-31/12
Distance: 500m.
Remarks: Parking sports centre south.

Dülmen 9A2

P6, Hüttendyk/Ecke Halterner Strasse. **GPS**: n51,82606 e7,27228.

DE

6 free € 1/80liter Ch € 1/8h. **Surface:** metalled.
01/01-31/12
Distance: 500m 50m 100m.
Remarks: Max. 1 night.

Dülmen 9A2

Reisemobilstellplatz Hausdulmen, Sandstrasse. **GPS:** n51,80707 e7,24746.

12 free. **Surface:** grassy. 01/01-31/12
Distance: 2,5km 500m 400m on the spot.

Düren 8D5

IG Reisemobilhafen Düren, Rurstrasse 188. **GPS:** n50,80861 e6,46556.

20 € 7 ,Passerby € 2 Chincluded (18x)€ 2. **Location:** Rural, simple, quiet. **Surface:** gravel.
Distance: 900m Bistro 100m Lidl 500m.

Düsseldorf 9A4

P Rheinterasse/Tonhalle, Joseph Bueys Ufer. **GPS:** n51,23710 e6,77029.

10 €12/day. **Surface:** metalled. 01/01-31/12
Distance: 3km 50m 1,3km.
Remarks: Parking at the Rhine River, follow city centre.

Düsseldorf 9A4

Wohnmobilstellplatz Düsseldorf/Erkrath, Heinrich-Hertz-Straße 18, Unterfeldhaus, Düsseldorf/Erkrath. **GPS:** n51,19825 e6,91679.

6 € 6 € 1/100liter Ch included. **Location:** Urban, simple, quiet. **Surface:** metalled. 01/01-31/12
Distance: 500m 5,5km 300m 50m.

Düsseldorf 9A4

Großmarkt/Daimler Chrysler, Ulmenstraße. **GPS:** n51,25920 e6,77854.

Chfree.

Tourist information Düsseldorf:

Tourist Info, Immermannstrasse, Gegenüber Station; Kö-Galerie/Finanzhaus, Berliner Alee; Burgplatz, Berliner Allee, www.duesseldorf-tourismus.de.Historical centre, important city of fashion, all large marks established in the Königsallee, Umweltzone: the green environmental badge is required.

During the Caravan Salon (by the end of August/beginning September) there is a large area for motorhomes available.
Free shuttlebus to the exhibition and Old city centre. Also several events on the exhibition grounds.

Eckenhagen 9B5

Rodener Festplatz, Rodener Platz. **GPS:** n50,98667 e7,69361.

20 free Chfree. **Location:** Urban, simple, quiet.
Surface: asphalted/gravel. 01/01-31/12
Distance: 200m 4km 300m 300m on the spot on the spot.

Emmerich 8D3

Yachthafen, Fackeldeystrasse 15-65. **GPS:** n51,83693 e6,21948.

75 € 8 € 0,50Ch (80x)€ 2,50WC € 0,50 € 1. **Location:** Rural, comfortable. **Surface:** grassy/metalled. 01/01-31/12
Distance: 2,5km on the spot on the spot on the spot on the spot

DE

on the spot.

Emmerich 8D3

Auf dem Eltenberg, Luitgardisstraße. **GPS**: n51,86559 e6,17265.

25 free. **Location:** Rural, simple. **Surface:** grasstiles.
01/01-31/12
Distance: 1km 1km on the spot.

Emmerich 8D3

P6, Kleiner Wall, Rheinpromenade. **GPS**: n51,83229 e6,23594.

6 free. **Location:** Urban, simple, noisy. **Surface:** unpaved.
01/01-31/12
Distance: on the spot.

Ennepetal 9B4

Firma Möller-Elektronic, Königstrasse 17, Oelkinghausen. **GPS**: n51,29086 e7,32050.

5 free €3 Ch . **Location:** Urban, simple, quiet. **Surface:** metalled.
01/01-31/12
Distance: 2km 11km 1km 200m on the spot on the spot.

Ennepetal 9B4

Am Platsch, Mittelstraße 108. **GPS**: n51,29295 e7,37668.

4 €3 included. **Surface:** gravel. 01/01-31/12
Distance: 10,8km 5km 5km on the spot on the spot Routes for nordic walking.
Remarks: Check in at pay-desk of swimming pool, on the spot: bistro, pool, sauna and golf court.

Ennigerloh 9C2

Am Freibad 3. **GPS**: n51,83304 e8,01629.
2 free €0,50/50liter Ch €0,50/kWh. **Surface:** metalled.
01/01-31/12
Distance: 600m.

Ennigerloh 9C2

Ferienhof Bettmann, Beesen 4. **GPS**: n51,84366 e7,99567.

4 €6/pp Ch WC .
Distance: 2km on the spot 3km.

Erftstadt 9A5

Mobilcamp am Ville-Express, Carl-Schurz-strasse 1a, Liblar. **GPS**: n50,81781 e6,81986.

11 €6 €1/80liter Ch (11x)€0,50/kWh. **Location:** Urban, comfortable. **Surface:** metalled. 01/01-31/12
Distance: 1km 4,4km 500m 200m 1km.

Erndtebrück 9C5

Pension Hofius, Hilchenbachterweg 2, Zinse. **GPS**: n51,00599 e8,21224.

3 €7/24h Ch WC . 01/01-31/12
Distance: 5km on the spot on the spot.

Everswinkel 9B2

Vitus-Bad, Alverkirchenerstrasse 29. **GPS**: n51,92309 e7,83776.

3 free Ch. **Surface:** metalled. 01/01-31/12
Distance: 500m on the spot on the spot.
Remarks: Parking swimming pool, Kläranlage Everswinkel, mo-thu 7.30-17 fr 7.30-12.15.

DE

Freudenberg 9B5

Lohmühle, P5. **GPS**: n50,89625 e7,87636.

5 free. **Surface:** metalled. 01/01-31/12
Distance: on the spot 100m 200m.
Remarks: Max. 3 days.

Gangelt 8D5

Rodebachtal, Am Freibad 13. **GPS**: n50,98583 e5,99806.

40 € 7, weekend € 10 Ch WC € 0,50/4minutes. **Location:** Rural, luxurious, quiet. **Surface:** metalled. 01/01-31/12
Distance: on the spot on the spot 1,5km.
Remarks: Caution key € 10.

Geldern 8D3

Am Holländer See, Am Holländer See 19. **GPS**: n51,51131 e6,32867.

50 € 5/24h, 3 days € 12 Ch € 0,50/kWh. **Surface:** grassy/metalled. 01/01-31/12
Distance: 1km 1km 1km.
Remarks: Parking in the centre.

Geldern 8D3

Reisemobilhafen Am Freibad, Am Freibad 6, Walbeck. **GPS**: n51,49461 e6,22666.

50 € 7/24h € 1/80liter Ch (36x)€ 0,50/kWh. **Surface:** grassy/sand. 01/01-31/12
Distance: city centre Walbeck 1km, city centre Geldern 6km 1km 1km.
Remarks: At swimming pool.

Geldern 8D3

Reisemobilstellplatz Am Sportplatz, Hülspassweg 20, Veert. **GPS**: n51,52960 e6,30347.

30 free. **Surface:** gravel. 01/01-31/12
Distance: city centre Veert 200m, city centre Geldern 2km 500m.
Remarks: Parking at sports park.

Geldern 8D3

Restaurant Zum Lüneböger, Venloerstrasse 120, Pont. **GPS**: n51,49021 e6,29822.

5 guests free. **Surface:** gravel. 01/01-31/12
Distance: on the spot on the spot.
Remarks: Only for guest.

Geldern 8D3

Freizeit-Store Diepers, Liebligstrasse 33. **GPS**: n51,52971 e6,35456.
€ 1 € 1Ch. 01/01-31/12
Remarks: Industrial area, north-east of the city.

Tourist information Geldern:

Internationaler Wettbewerb der strassenmaler und strassenmusikanten und -theatergruppen, Centrum.International street painting competition, street musicians and theater groups. beginning Sep.

Internationales Reisemobilfest.International festival for motorcaravanners with vast tourist program. Not necessary to book in advance,. last weekend April. free.

Gelsenkirchen 9A3

Revierpark Nienhausen, Feldmarkstraße 201. **GPS**: n51,50167 e7,06333.

20 € 7, 2 pers.incl. € 1/80liter Ch € 1/2kWh. **Surface:** metalled. 01/01-31/12
Distance: 2,8km 3,2km 100m 2km Tram 700m.
Remarks: Bread-service.

Gladbeck 9A3

Freitzeitstätte Witringer Wald, Bohmertstrasse 277. **GPS**: n51,55912 e6,98403.

DE

20 voluntary contribution Ch. **Surface:** grasstiles/grassy. 01/01-31/12
Distance: 2km 1km 200m 1km.
Remarks: Service at petrol station nearby.

S Goch 8D3

Friedensplatz, Thielenstrasse. **GPS**: n51,67556 e6,16639.

80 € 4/24h € 1/100liter Ch (60x)€ 0,50/kWh. **Surface:** grassy. 01/01-31/12
Distance: 700m on the spot 700m 700m 100m.
Remarks: Along the Niers river.

Goch 8D3

Freizeitbad GochNess, Kranenburger Strasse 20, Kessel. **GPS**: n51,70291 e6,08915.

6 free. **Surface:** grassy. 01/01-31/12
Distance: 1km 1km 1km.

Tourist information Goch:

KulTOURbühne Goch, Markt 15, www.goch.de.Motorhome friendly town on the Lower Rhine river.
Museum Goch, Kastellstrasse.Art and culture history.
Tue-Fri 10-17h, Sa-Su 11-17h.
Pilgrimage for motorhomes.
last weekend Jun.
Museumscafé Edison, Museum Goch.Collection of gramophones.
Su 15-17h.
Herrensitz-Route.Cycle route along the Meuse and the Niers, available at Kultourbühne Goch. € 5.

Grefrath 8D4

Eissportzentrum Grefrath, Stadionstrasse. **GPS**: n51,34889 e6,33972.
50 free. **Surface:** grasstiles.
Distance: 2km 300m 2km.
Remarks: Niederrheinisches Freilichtmuseum, Open air museum 650m.

Grefrath 8D4

Niers-Perle-Oedt, Mühlengasse 6. **GPS**: n51,32306 e6,37667.
7 free. **Surface:** asphalted.
Distance: 350m 450m 350m.

S Greven 9B2

Wohnmobilcamp Marina, Alten Fahrt Fuestrup,, Fuestruperstrasse 37, Fuestrup. **GPS**: n52,04449 e7,68328.

90 € 9 Ch € 1,50 WC € 0,50. 01/01-31/12
Distance: Restaurant/Biergarten 3km.
Remarks: Marina at canal.

S Gronau (Nordrhein-Westfalen) 9A1

Erholungsgebiet Dreiländersee, Brechter Weg. **GPS**: n52,23716 e7,08006.

90 free, 01/04-30/09 € 5/24h € 0,50/130liter Ch € 1/4h WC.
Surface: grassy/metalled. 01/01-31/12
Distance: 2km 100m on the spot 200m 50m (camping) on the spot.
Remarks: Parking nearby small lake.

S Haltern am See 9A3

Reisemobilstellplatz Silbersee II, Münsterstraße/Zum Vogelsberg. **GPS**: n51,79764 e7,21008.

15 € 10 € 1/80liter Ch € 1/8h. **Surface:** grassy. 01/04-31/10
Distance: Haltern 6km on the spot on the spot.
Remarks: At Silbersee.

S Haltern am See 9A3

Reisemobilstellplatz, Hullerner Straße/West, Lippspieker. **GPS**: n51,74278 e7,19525.

40 free € 1 Ch € 1/8h. **Surface:** metalled. 01/01-31/12

DE

Distance: Old city centre 1km 1km 100m.

Haltern am See 9A3

Reisemobilstellplatz Hellweg, RMS ReisemobileSpezialist, Hellweg 252.
GPS: n51,75589 e7,20127.

4 €6 €1 Ch €3,50. **Surface:** grassy/gravel. 01/01-31/12
Distance: Old city centre 1km 800m 800m.

Harsewinkel 9C2

Frei- und Hallenbad, Prozessionsweg 8. **GPS**: n51,96556 e8,21935.

15 free. **Surface:** grassy. 01/01-31/12
Distance: 200m 100m 200m.
Remarks: Parking next to swimming pool.

Hattingen 9A4

Wohnmobilstellplatz Ruhrtal, Ruhrdeich 24. **GPS**: n51,40839 e7,18091.

DE

15 €7 € 1/80liter Ch € 1/2kWh,12 free. **Location:** Rural, comfortable, quiet. **Surface:** gravel. 01/01-31/12
Distance: 2,5km 5km on the spot on the spot 500m 1km.
Remarks: Along ther Ruhr, next to midget golf, bread-service.

Hattingen 9A4

August-Bebel strasse. **GPS**: n51,39833 e7,18028.

2 €3. **Location:** Urban, simple, central, noisy. **Surface:** metalled.
01/01-31/12
Distance: on the spot 5km on the spot on the spot on the spot.
Remarks: At shopping centre Carré.

Hattingen 9A4

Roonstrasse. **GPS**: n51,40167 e7,18389.

2 free. **Location:** Urban, simple, quiet. **Surface:** asphalted/metalled.
01/01-31/12
Distance: 300m 5km 300m 300m.

Hattingen 9A4

Ruhrgasse, Bahnhofstrasse. **GPS**: n51,40127 e7,17700.

3 free. **Location:** Urban, simple, quiet. **Surface:** gravel.
01/01-31/12
Distance: 500m 5km 500m 500m.
Remarks: Parking behind the Amtshäusern, only on Sa and Su.

Hattingen 9A4

Wanderparkplatz, Isenbergstrasse. **GPS**: n51,38969 e7,15340.

3 free. **Location:** Rural, simple. **Surface:** gravel.
Mo-Fri, 01/01-31/12
Distance: 2km 5km 300m 1km on the spot on the spot on the spot.
Remarks: Parking along the Ruhr, max. 2 days.

Havixbeck 9B2

Freibad, Kardinal von Hartmann strasse. **GPS**: n51,97507 e7,42092.

4 free Ch On demand WC. **Surface:** metalled. 01/01-31/12
Remarks: Parking swimming pool, small pitches.

Havixbeck 9B2

Klute's Historischem Brauhaus, Poppenbeck 28. **GPS**: n51,98938 e7,39291.

15 free (8x)€ 5 . **Surface:** metalled. 01/01-31/12
Distance: 2km on the spot 2km.

Havixbeck 9B2

EDEKA, Blickallee 44. **GPS:** n51,97480 e7,41168.

4 free. **Surface:** metalled. 01/01-31/12
Distance: 100m 100m on the spot 100m.
Remarks: At supermarket, small pitches.

Heiligenhaus 9A4

Westfalenstrasse. **GPS:** n51,32853 e6,97327.
3 free. **Location:** Simple. **Surface:** metalled. 01/01-31/12
Distance: 200m 200m 200m.

S **Heimbach** 8D6

Womohafen Heimbach, An der Laag 4. **GPS:** n50,63683 e6,47265.

19 € 7,50/24h, tourist tax € 0,30/pp € 1/100liter Ch (20x)€ 0,50/kWh. **Location:** Rural, simple, noisy. **Surface:** gravel.
01/01-31/12
Distance: 200m 100m.
Remarks: Nearby Regioshuttle Rurtallbahn.

S **Heinsberg** 8D4

Heinsberg am Lago, Fritz-Bauer-Strasse 3. **GPS:** n51,07333 e6,09278.

44 P1 € 10/day, P2 € 10/2 days € 1/100liter Ch (31x)€ 0,50/kWh.
Location: Rural, luxurious, quiet. **Surface:** grasstiles.
Distance: 1km Bagger See on the spot 800m.

S **Hellenthal** 8D6

Grenzlandhalle Hellenthal, Aachenerstrasse. **GPS:** n50,49251 e6,43651.

15 free. **Location:** Rural, simple. **Surface:** grasstiles.
01/01-31/12
Distance: 500m 200m.
Remarks: Service on campsite.

S **Hellenthal** 8D6

Wohnmobilhafen Weißer Stein, Am Weissen Stein, Udenbreth, B265. **GPS:** n50,40896 e6,37220.

28 € 9 € 2 Ch (28x). **Location:** Rural, simple.
Surface: metalled. 01/01-31/12
Distance: on the spot on the spot.
Remarks: Winter sports area Hellenthal am Wald, service on campsite.

S **Hellenthal** 8D6

Breuerhof, Zum Wilsamtal 39, Udenbreth. **GPS:** n50,41081 e6,38992.

2 € 10 Ch (2x). **Location:** Rural, comfortable, quiet. **Surface:** metalled.
Distance: 2km on the spot.
Remarks: Check in at nr. 35.

Tourist information Hellenthal:

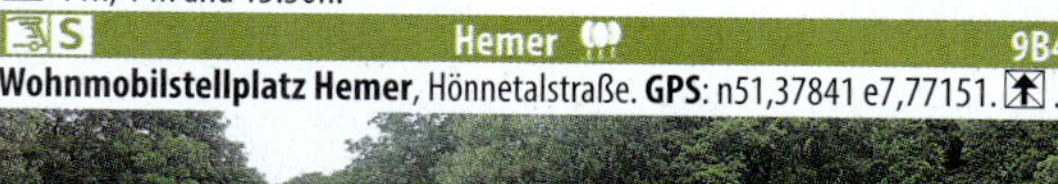

www.hellenthal.de.Small town the vulcany Eifel region.
Greifvogelstation.Predatory bird station.
01/11-31/03 9-17h, 01/04-31/10 9-18h.
Grube Wohlfahrt.Visit to the mine shaft and museum.
11h, 14h and 15.30h.

S **Hemer** 9B4

Wohnmobilstellplatz Hemer, Hönnetalstraße. **GPS:** n51,37841 e7,77151.

DE

20 € 2/8-20h € 1/100liter Ch€ 1 (12x)€ 0,50/kWh. **Location:** Urban, comfortable, quiet. **Surface:** asphalted/grassy. 01/01-31/12
Distance: 1km 6km 300m bakery 500m on the spot.

Herford 9D2

Am Stadion, Dennewitzstrasse 15. **GPS:** n52,10474 e8,68931.

3 free. **Location:** Rural, simple. 01/01-31/12
Distance: 2,5km 1,8km 100m 100m 2,5km 2,5km.

Herscheid 9B4

Am Warmwasserfreibad, Unterdorfstraße. **GPS:** n51,17567 e7,74368.

3 free € 1/10minutes Ch (4x)€ 1/8h. **Location:** Rural, comfortable, quiet. **Surface:** gravel. 01/01-31/12
Distance: 1,2km 10km 400m 650m on the spot.

Hilchenbach 9C5

Hallenbad Dahlbruch, Bernhard-Weiss-Platz, Dahlbruch. **GPS:** n50,97792 e8,05343.

3 free € 1/10minutes. **Surface:** asphalted/metalled.
Distance: 400m 400m.
Remarks: Parking behind swimming pool, max. 48h.

Hilchenbach 9C5

Bürgenhaus, Merklinghäuser weg, Müsen. **GPS:** n50,99267 e8,04497.

3 free. **Surface:** asphalted. 01/01-31/12
Remarks: Max. 48h.

Hilchenbach 9C5

Parkplatz P4, Rothenberger strasse, L728. **GPS:** n50,99702 e8,11103.

3 free. **Surface:** metalled. 01/01-31/12
Distance: 100m 200m 100m.
Remarks: Parking in front of shopping centre Gerberpark, max. 48h.

Hilchenbach 9C5

Landhotel Steubers Siebelnhof, Siebelnhoferstrasse, Vormwald. **GPS:** n50,98658 e8,13173.
4 € 20,50, use sanitary facilities/swimming pool sauna incl WC included.
01/01-31/12

Hille 9D1

Am Marktplatz, Sportplatzweg 31. **GPS:** n52,34205 e8,73017.

8 free € 1 Ch € 1. **Location:** Rural, quiet. **Surface:** gravel.
01/01-31/12
Distance: 1km 500m.

Hopsten 9B1

Dreifachturnhalle, Rüschendorfer strasse 4. **GPS:** n52,38900 e7,60230.

3 free Ch free. **Surface:** grassy. 01/01-31/12
Distance: 100m 100m 100m.
Remarks: Parking at gymnasium, max. 2 nights.

Horn 9D2

Wohnmobilhafen Mein Bad, Wällenweg, Bad Meinberg. **GPS:** n51,89818 e8,99249.

35 € 5 + € 2,60/pp tourist tax € 1/100liter Ch € 0,50/kWh.
Location: Rural, quiet. **Surface:** grassy/metalled. 01/01-31/12
Distance: 200m on the spot 200m 100m.
Remarks: Behind spa, discount at swimming pool.

DE

Hörstel 9B1

Wohnmobilhafen Riesenbeck, Postdamm-Lazarusbrücke. **GPS:** n52,25574 e7,63387.

13 free . 01/01-31/12

Distance: on the spot on the spot on the spot on the spot.

Remarks: Max. 3 nights.

Hövelhof 9D2

P Bahnhof, Westfalenstrasse. **GPS:** n51,82417 e8,66099.

6 free free (6x)€ 1/kWh. **Location:** Urban. **Surface:** gravel.
01/01-31/12

Distance: 500m 4,2km 500m 500m 50m on the spot on the spot.

Höxter 10A2

Freizeitanlage Godelheimer See, Godelheimer Strasse, Höxter-Godelheim. **GPS:** n51,75787 e9,37557.

50 € 6 Ch WC included. **Location:** Comfortable. **Surface:** grasstiles. 01/01-31/12 service: 01/10-01/04.

Distance: 2km on the spot river 500m on the spot 2km on the spot on the spot.

Remarks: Recreation area, bread-service + breakfast-service.

Höxter 10A2

Wohnmobilhafen Flossplatz, Milchweg. **GPS:** n51,77325 e9,38781.

50 € 6, only overnight stay € 4 € 1/100liter Ch (18x)€ 0,50/kWh. **Location:** Rural, comfortable, central, quiet. **Surface:** grassy/gravel.
01/01-31/12

Distance: 300m on the spot fishing permit available 100m 300m 500m on camp site 50m.

Remarks: Parking beside river Weser.

Hückelhoven 8D4

Hückelhovener Ruraue, Rheinstraße 4b. **GPS:** n51,05111 e6,21306.

6 € 4,50 € 0,50/100liter Ch € 0,50/kWh. **Location:** Rural, simple, isolated, quiet. **Surface:** metalled.
01/01-31/12 With snow.

Distance: 1,5km.

Hürtgenwald 8D5

Einmünding Kall-Rur, Zerkall. **GPS:** n50,69156 e6,45212.

10 free. **Location:** Rural, simple. **Surface:** gravel.
01/01-31/12

Distance: 100m on the spot on the spot 200m.

Remarks: Along the river Kall/Rur.

Hürtgenwald 8D5

Parkplatz Burgstrasse, Burgstrasse, Bergstein. **GPS:** n50,69582 e6,43848.

5 free. **Location:** Simple. **Surface:** metalled. 01/01-31/12

Hürtgenwald 8D5

Soldatenfriedhof, Höhenstrasse, Hürtgen. **GPS:** n50,70552 e6,36063.

9 free. **Location:** Rural, simple, noisy. **Surface:** asphalted.
01/01-31/12

Hürtgenwald 8D5

Simonskall 20, Kallweg. **GPS:** n50,66716 e6,35395.

DE

5 free. **Location:** Rural, comfortable, quiet. **Surface:** metalled.
01/01-31/12
Distance: 200m on the spot.

Hüsten 9C3

Parkplatz Große Wiese. **GPS**: n51,43151 e8,00475.
4 free. **Surface:** asphalted.
Distance: 2km.
Remarks: Next to the Sole-Bad.

Ibbenbüren 9B1

Aseebad, An der Umfluth 99. **GPS**: n52,26181 e7,73171.

20 € 3. **Surface:** grassy/metalled.
Distance: 2,3km.
Remarks: Parking next to swimming pool, max. 4 nights.

Ibbenbüren 9B1

Dorenthe, Hafenstrasse. **GPS**: n52,22056 e7,67944.
3 free. **Location:** Simple. 01/01-31/12
Distance: 7km on the spot.

Ibbenbüren 9B1

Sommerrodelbahn, Münsterstrasse 265. **GPS**: n52,24977 e7,70292.

10 free. **Surface:** metalled.
Distance: 1,2km.

Ibbenbüren 9B1

Gasthof Dickenberg, Rheinerstrasse 324. **GPS**: n52,31314 e7,66988.
20 free. **Surface:** metalled.
Distance: on the spot on the spot.

Tourist information Ibbenbüren:
Tourist-Information Ibbenbüren, Bachstrasse 14, www.ibbenbueren.de.
Ibbenbürener Bergbaumuseum.Mining museum.
01/05-30/09 2nd Sa of the month. free.
Motorrad-Museum, Lengericher strasse.Exhibition of motor cycles.
01/04-31/10 Sa 14-18, Su 10-18h.
Flea market.
1st Sa May, last Sa Oct.
Tollen Knollen, Neumarkt.Potato festival. weekend, beginning Oct.
Sommerrodelbahn, Münsterstrasse 265.Toboggan slide of 120 m.

Iserlohn 9B4

Parkplatz Seilerblick, Friesenstraße. **GPS**: n51,38456 e7,71128.

5 free € 1 Ch € 1 (4x)€ 0,50. **Location:** Urban, simple, noisy.
Surface: asphalted. 01/01-31/12
Distance: 2km 2,5km on the spot on the spot.
Remarks: Next to tennis-court.

Isselburg 8D3

Hotel Restaurant Brüggenhütte, Hahnerfeld 23, Anholt. **GPS**: n51,85301 e6,47187.

5 free. **Location:** Rural, simple. **Surface:** grassy.
01/01-31/12
Distance: 200m on the spot.
Remarks: Behind restaurant, along through road.

Isselburg 8D3

Parkplatz Zentrum, Münsterdeich. **GPS**: n51,83452 e6,46477.

3 free. **Location:** Simple. **Surface:** grassy. 01/01-31/12
Distance: on the spot on the spot 300m 100m.
Remarks: Parking centre, at the Issel, max. 72h.

Isselburg 8D3

Spargelhof Mäteling, Buchenallee 4, Anholt. **GPS**: n51,84120 e6,41597.

5 free. **Location:** Rural, simple. **Surface:** asphalted.
01/01-31/12
Distance: on the spot.
Remarks: Max. 72h.

DE

Isselburg 8D3

Bürgerhaus, Anholter strasse, Vehlingen. **GPS**: n51,83089 e6,42297.

3 free. **Location:** Rural, simple. **Surface:** gravel.
01/01-31/12 May.
Distance: on the spot.
Remarks: Max. 2 nights.

Isselburg 8D3

Ponyhof Leiting, Alte Bundesstrasse 3, Werth. **GPS**: n51,81332 e6,49258.

10 free. **Location:** Simple.
Surface: grassy.
01/01-31/12
Distance: on the spot.
Remarks: Max. 72h.

Tourist information Isselburg:
Isselburger Verkehrsverein e.V, Markt 9, www.isselburg-online.de.Motorhome friendly town.
Anholter Schweiz.Game preserve.
Wasserburg Anholt.Castle with English gardens.
01/05-30/09 Tue-Su 11-17h, 01/10-30/04 Su 13-17h.

Issum-Sevelen 8D3

Wohnmobilpark Hexenland-Sevelen, Koetherdyck 18. **GPS**: n51,49926 e6,43676.

20 € 8 Ch € 2/24h WC. **Surface:** gravel. 01/01-31/12
Distance: Sevelen 1km 200m 100m 1km.

Jülich 8D5

Brückenkopf-Park, Rurauenstrasse 11. **GPS**: n50,92345 e6,34029.

22 € 8,50 € 1/100liter Ch WC. **Location:** Simple, noisy.
Surface: grassy. 01/01-31/12 sanitary building: 1/11-31/3.
Remarks: Parking at bank of the Rur.

Tourist information Jülich:
Old fortress city.
Marktplatz. Tue, Thu, Sa 7-13h.

Kalkar 8D3

Reisemobilstellplatz Kalkar, Waysche strasse. **GPS**: n51,74008 e6,30101.

35-40 € 4/24h € 2/100liter Ch € 1/5kWh. **Location:** Rural, comfortable. **Surface:** grassy. 01/01-31/12
Distance: 500m 400m 700m.
Remarks: Max. 3 nights.

Tourist information Kalkar:
Touristik-Informationen Kalkar, Markt 20, www.kalkar.de.Attractive medieval centre.
KernWasser Wunderland.Amusement park.

Kall 8D6

Im Kallbachtal, Kapellenstrasse 25, Golbach. **GPS**: n50,52784 e6,53681.

6 € 6 € 1 Ch (8x)€ 0,50/kWh. **Location:** Rural, simple, quiet.
Surface: gravel. 01/01-31/12

Kamp-Lintfort 8D3

Pappelsee, Berthastraße 74. **GPS**: n51,50026 e6,53861.

20 free. **Surface:** asphalted. 01/01-31/12
Distance: 1,5km 1km 1,5km.

DE

Remarks: Caution € 2,50 to pay-desk of the park.

Tourist information Kamp-Lintfort:

Marktplatz, Eberstrasse. Thu, Sa.

Rathausplatz. Tue 7.30-13h.

Mittelalterlicher Markt, Abteiplatz.Medieval market.

3rd weekend Sep.

Kempen 8D4

Reisemobilpark Kempen am Aqua-sol, Berliner Allee. **GPS**: n51,36719 e6,40910.

29 € 7 € 1/80liter Ch € 0,50/kWh. **Surface:** metalled.

01/01-31/12

Distance: 1,5km on the spot 1,5km.

Kerken 8D4

Wohnmobilpark Aldekerker Platte, Kempener Straße 9, Aldekerk. **GPS**: n51,43551 e6,41902.

30 € 8 Ch € 2. **Surface:** grassy/gravel. 01/01-31/12

Distance: 600m 600m 600m.

Kevelaer 8D3

Den Heyberg, Im Auwelt 45, Twisteden. **GPS**: n51,56345 e6,19418.

150 € 8,50 Ch (150x)included. **Surface:** asphalted/metalled.

01/01-31/12

Distance: 2km 100m 2km 100m.

Remarks: Bread-service (weekend), barbecue place.

Kevelaer 8D3

Sporthotel Schravelsche Heide, Grotendonkerstrasse 54-58. **GPS**: n51,59556 e6,25306.

80 € 7,50 Ch WC included. **Surface:** grassy.

01/01-31/12

Distance: 1,5km 100m 1km.

Remarks: To pay at sanitary building tennis-courts.

Kevelaer 8D3

Europaplatz, Bahnhof/Geldernstrasse, B9. **GPS**: n51,57904 e6,25192.

3 free. **Surface:** asphalted.

Distance: 500m 500m on the spot.

Remarks: Follow 'Zweckplatz'.

Tourist information Kevelaer:

Traberpark Den Heyberg, Twisteden.Hippodrome.

Plantaria.Adventurepark with parrots, kangaroos, play garden etc.

10-18h.

Kirchhundem 9C4

Restaurant Rhein-Wester-Turm, Alfons Kleffmann, Rhein-Weser-Turm. **GPS**: n51,07109 e8,19791.

10 € 10 Ch included. 01/01-31/12

Distance: on the spot.

Kirchhundem 9C4

Panorama-Park, Rinsecker Straße 100. **GPS**: n51,06972 e8,17417.

10 free. 01/01-31/12

Kleve 8D3

Van-den-Bergh-Straße. **GPS**: n51,78917 e6,14836.

60 € 4 Ch (30x)€ 0,50/kWh. **Location:** Urban, simple.

Surface: metalled. 01/01-31/12

Distance: 500m.

Kleve 8D3

Reisemobilpark Kleve, Landwehr/Spyckstraße. **GPS**: n51,80083 e6,13222.

75 € 6,50, 2 pers.incl € 1 Ch (45x)€ 1,50 WC € 1.
Location: Comfortable. **Surface:** grassy/metalled. 01/01-31/12
Distance: Kleve-zentrum 1,5km 300m 400m.

Kleve 8D3

Parkplatz Bürgerhaus, Drususdeich, Rindern. **GPS**: n51,81212 e6,12884.

5 free. **Location:** Simple. **Surface:** asphalted. 01/01-31/12
Distance: Kleve-zentrum 2,3km 450m 400m.
Remarks: Behind church.

Kleve 8D3

Parkplatz Sporthalle Kleve-Kellen, Postdeich, Kellen. **GPS**: n51,80463 e6,16378.

20 free. **Location:** Rural, simple. **Surface:** metalled.
Distance: 2,5km Steakhaus 350m on the spot.

Kleve 8D3

Parkplatz Sportplatz Reichswalde, Dorfanger, Reichswalde. **GPS**: n51,75985 e6,10243.

10 free. **Location:** Urban, simple. **Surface:** metalled.
Distance: 5km 500m.

Kleve 8D3

Schenkenschanz. **GPS**: n51,83526 e6,11205.

5 free. **Location:** Simple. **Surface:** metalled. 01/01-31/12
Distance: 2,5km.

Kleve 8D3

Tiergarten, Tiergartenstrasse, B9 dir Nijmegen. **GPS**: n51,79784 e6,12059.

5 free. **Location:** Highway, simple. **Surface:** metalled.
01/01-31/12
Distance: 800m 250m.

Kleve 8D3

Wehrpöhl, Griethausen. **GPS**: n51,82476 e6,16448.

5 free. **Location:** Rural, simple. **Surface:** asphalted.
01/01-31/12
Distance: 2,5km 300m 300m.
Remarks: Access via Brienen.

Tourist information Kleve:

Kleve Marketing GmbH, Werftstraße 1, www.kleve.de.Area with many possibilities for hiking and biking.
Klever Stadtfest.City celebration. end Sep.
Tiergarten Kleve, Tiergartenstrasse.Animal park.

Köln 9A5

P+R-Terminals Haus Vorst, Emmy-Noether-Straße, Marsdorf, Cologne (Köln).
GPS: n50,91666 e6,84693.

21 free € 0,50/100liter Ch € 1/12h. **Location:** Urban, simple, noisy. **Surface:** metalled. 01/01-31/12
Distance: Old city centre 8km 450m 250m on the spot Tram centre 50m.

DE

Remarks: Max. 24h.

Köln 9A5

Reisemobilhafen Köln, An der Schanz, Cologne (Köln). **GPS**: n50,96265 e6,98254.

65 € 10/24h € 0,50 Ch (30x)€ 0,50/kWh. **Location:** Urban, comfortable, quiet. **Surface:** asphalted.
Distance: on the spot 5km metro 10 min walking.
Remarks: Along the Rhine river.

Königswinter 9A5

Hauptstrasse, Niederdollendorf. **GPS**: n50,69697 e7,17641.

30 free. **Location:** Urban, simple. **Surface:** asphalted/metalled.
01/01-31/12
Distance: 400m 9km 800m on the spot on the spot.

Kranenburg 8D3

Am Hallenbad, Großen Haag. **GPS**: n51,79242 e6,01033.

30 € 4 € 0,20/liter Ch (12x)€ 0,50/kWh. **Location:** Rural, simple. **Surface:** grassy. 01/01-31/12
Distance: 500m 1km 1km 500m 500m.
Remarks: Service 500m.

Kreuztal 9C5

Heugraben. **GPS**: n50,95778 e7,99167.

2 free € 1/100liter Ch € 1/2kWh. **Surface:** metalled.
Distance: 300m 7,5km 300m 300m station 100m.
Remarks: Max. 3 days.

Kürten 9B4

Wohnmobil Park - Kürten, Broch 8. **GPS**: n51,05586 e7,28943.

20 € 8 € 2 Ch included € 3. **Location:** Rural, simple, quiet.
Surface: gravel. 01/01-31/12
Distance: 2km 17km on the spot on the spot on the spot.
Remarks: Behind Sauna-/Badeland Splash.

Ladbergen 9B2

Rathauspark, Jahnstrasse. **GPS**: n52,13652 e7,74009.

10 free. **Surface:** grassy. 01/01-31/12
Distance: 200m 200m 200m.
Remarks: Parking behind town hall.

Ladbergen 9B2

Rest.-Cafe Zur Waldschänke, Erpenbecker Siedlung 63. **GPS**: n52,13474 e7,79422.
8 guests free WC. **Surface:** grassy.
Distance: 4km on the spot.

Lennestadt 9C4

Parkplatz P4, An der Sauerlandhalle. **GPS**: n51,10557 e8,08017.

4 free (4x)€ 0,50/4h. **Surface:** asphalted. 01/01-31/12
Distance: 700m 700m 100m.

Leverkusen 9A4

Camping-Caravaning Meier, Adolf-Kaschny-Straße 9, Küppersteg. **GPS**: n51,05211 e7,00003.

10 free € 0,50 Ch € 0,50. **Location:** Urban. **Surface:** gravel.
01/01-31/12

DE

Distance: 3,2km.
Remarks: Motorhome dealer, accessory shop, repairs.

S Lienen 9C2

Hallenfreibad, Holperdorperstrasse 37/39. **GPS:** n52,15575 e7,97392.

3 free Ch WC. **Surface:** metalled.
01/01-31/12
Distance: 1km.
Remarks: Parking next to swimming pool, max. 3 nights, to be paid at swimming pool.

Tourist information Lienen:
City centre with restored half-timbered houses.
Voss Hof, Baggerien 4.Biological dynamic farm products. Fri 15-18h, Sa 9-12h.

S Lindlar 9B5

Am Freizeitpark, Brionner Straße. **GPS:** n51,01550 e7,36645.
2 free € 1 Ch (4x)€ 1/6h. **Location:** Urban, simple. **Surface:** metalled. 01/01-31/12
Distance: 1km 16km 1km 1km on the spot on the spot.

S Lippstadt 9C3

Campingoase Lange, Dorfstraße 47, Benninghausen. **GPS:** n51,66103 e8,24435.

15 € 10, 2 pers.incl Ch included. **Location:** Rural, simple.
Surface: metalled. 01/01-31/12
Distance: 300m on the spot.

S Löhne 9D1

Reisemobilstellplatz, Albert-Schweitzer-strasse 12. **GPS:** n52,20399 e8,71892.

18 € 8 Chincluded (18x)€ 1/2kWh. **Location:** Rural, quiet.
Surface: metalled. 01/01-31/12
Distance: 500m 1km 100m 500m 500m.

S Lotte 9B1

Fam. Arendröwer, Am Nordberg 4. **GPS:** n52,26306 e7,89833.
4 € 8 Ch included. **Surface:** grassy/metalled. 01/03-01/10
Distance: 3km 500m 3km.

S Lotte 9B1

Tennishalle Lotte, Kornweg 3. **GPS:** n52,27192 e7,92275.
10 free Ch On demand. **Surface:** gravel. 01/01-31/12
Distance: 900m 3,5km 1km.

S Lübbecke 9C1

Stellplatz Lübbecke, Rahdener Straße. **GPS:** n52,31019 e8,61839.

4 € 6 service € 3 Ch service € 3. **Location:** Urban, central.
Surface: metalled. 01/01-31/12
Distance: 600m 500m.
Remarks: Max. 3 days.

S Lüdenscheid 9B4

Familienbad Nattenberg, Talstraße 59. **GPS:** n51,21042 e7,61803.

4 free € 1 Ch € 1/6h. **Location:** Urban, simple. **Surface:** metalled.
01/01-31/12
Distance: city centre 1,6km 4km Burger King 450m Aldi 900m on the spot.

S Lüdinghausen 9B3

Parkplatz Rosengarten, Am Rosengarten, Seppenrade. **GPS:** n51,76407 e7,39728.

2 free. **Surface:** asphalted. 01/01-31/12
Distance: 200m.

Lüdinghausen 9B3

Parkplatz Aqua-See, Rohrkamp 23. **GPS:** n51,77229 e7,42731.

2 free. **Surface:** metalled. 01/01-31/12
Distance: 1,5km on the spot.
Remarks: Parking swimming pool.

DE

S Marsberg 9D3

Wohnmobilhafen, Am Sportplatz. **GPS**: n51,45974 e8,84864.

4 € 5 Ch (4x)included. **Location:** Urban. **Surface:** asphalted. 01/01-31/12
Distance: 100m 200m 200m.
Remarks: Max. 5 days, caution key € 20 (pay-desk of theTherme).

S Mechernich 9A6

Parkplatz Essensgasse, Am Kirchberg, Kommern. **GPS**: n50,61376 e6,64479.

8 free. **Location:** Rural, simple, noisy. **Surface:** metalled. 01/01-31/12
Distance: historical centre 200m.
Remarks: Via B266.

Mechernich 9A6

Mühlental, Elisabethhütte, B477. **GPS**: n50,59686 e6,63207.

40 free. **Location:** Rural, simple, noisy. **Surface:** asphalted. 01/01-31/12
Distance: 500m.

S Meinerzhagen 9B4

An der Musikschule, Schulplatz. **GPS**: n51,10865 e7,64329.

3 free (4x)€ 0,50/kWh. **Location:** Urban, simple, quiet. **Surface:** asphalted. 01/01-31/12
Distance: 400m 3km 400m 400m on the spot on the spot.

S Meschede 9C4

Am Wofibad, Im Ohl 13, Freienohl. **GPS**: n51,37574 e8,17664.

3 free against payment. **Location:** Simple. **Surface:** metalled. 01/01-31/12

Meschede 9C4

P Hallenbad, Arnsberger Strasse. **GPS**: n51,34897 e8,27356.

3 free. **Location:** Simple. **Surface:** metalled. 18.30-9.30h
Distance: 500m on the spot on the spot 500m 500m.

S Meschede 9C4

Knaus Campingpark Hennesee, Mielinghausen 7. **GPS**: n51,29846 e8,26366.

16 € 8-10 € 1/60liter € 0,50 Ch € 0,50 (16x)€ 0,70/kWh WC sanitary € 2,30-3,50. **Surface:** grassy/metalled. 01/01-31/12
Distance: 5km 100m 100m on the spot on the spot on the spot on the spot.

S Mettingen 9B1

Hallenbad, Bahnhofstrasse 18-20. **GPS**: n52,31679 e7,78337.

3 free WC. **Surface:** metalled. 01/01-31/12
Distance: on the spot 200m 200m.
Remarks: Parking swimming pool, bicycle rent, service: Kläranlage, Neuenkirchenerstrasse 208.

S Minden 9D1

Reisemobilstellplatz Kanzlers Weide, Hausbergerstrasse. **GPS**: n52,28750 e8,92551.

DE

100 free € 1/120liter € 0,50Ch (18x)€ 0,50/kWh,6Amp. **Location:** Urban, simple, quiet. **Surface:** metalled. 01/01-31/12
Distance: 200m 50m 50m 200m 200m 200m.
Remarks: Max. 3 nights, not during large events.

Moers 8D3

Freizeitpark Schoßpark, Krefelder straße. **GPS**: n51,44659 e6,61642.

3 free. **Surface:** grasstiles. 01/01-31/12
Distance: 700m 700m 500m.

S Möhnesee 9C3

Freizeitanlage Möhnesee-Körbecke, Börnigeweg. **GPS**: n51,49160 e8,12555.

20 € 6/24h (8x)€ 2/24h. **Location:** Simple. **Surface:** metalled. 01/01-31/12
Distance: 1km on the spot on the spot 1km on the spot on the spot.
Remarks: Max. 24h.

S Möhnesee 9C3

Strandbad, Linkstraße 20, Delecke. **GPS**: n51,49177 e8,08255.
50 € 12 Ch (16x) WC included. **Location:** Rural, comfortable, quiet. **Surface:** gravel. 01/03-01/11
Distance: Möhnesee 3,5km 7,3km A44 Möhnesee.

Möhnesee 9C3

Völlinghausen, Kettelbötel. **GPS**: n51,47360 e8,19831.

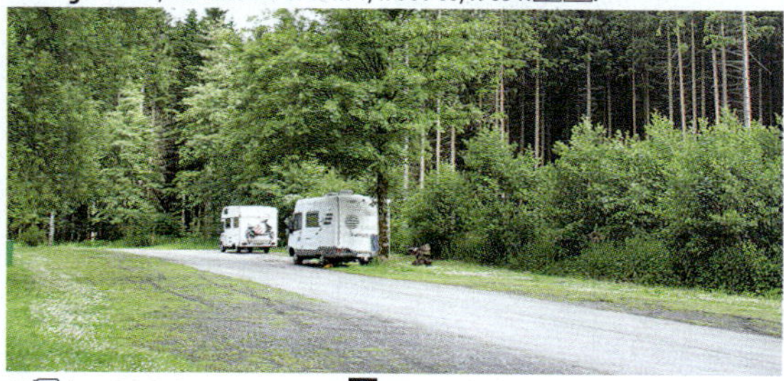

10 free. **Surface:** grassy/gravel. 01/01-31/12
Distance: 1,5km on the spot on the spot.

Mönchengladbach 8D4

Schloß Wickrath, Neukircherweg, Wickrath. **GPS**: n51,12889 e6,42258.

10 free. **Surface:** asphalted. 01/01-31/12
Distance: 2km 2km 500m.
Remarks: Parking behind castle (500m), max. 2 days. Follow 'P Schloß'.

S Mönchengladbach 8D4

Camping-Center Krings, Monschauerstrasse 12/32. **GPS**: n51,19454 e6,40884.

10 free Ch free. **Surface:** metalled. 01/01-31/12
Distance: 3km 1km 500m.
Remarks: Max. 2 nights, service during opening hours.

S Monschau 8D6

Biesweg, B258. **GPS**: n50,55389 e6,23194.

4 € 5/19-10h € 5/7minutes Ch (4x)€ 5/10h. **Location:** Simple, noisy. **Surface:** asphalted. 01/01-31/12
Distance: 600m 600m 600m.
Remarks: Max. 1 night.

Monschau 8D6

Haus Vennblick, Hauptstrasse 24, Höfen. **GPS**: n50,53934 e6,25292.

6 guests free. **Location:** Rural, simple, noisy.
Surface: gravel.
Distance: 300m on the spot 4km on the spot 4km.

Mülheim/Ruhr 9A4

Mintarder Straße 4. **GPS**: n51,41462 e6,86934.

DE

6 free. **Surface:** metalled. 01/01-31/12
Distance: 2,7km 50m 100m.
Remarks: Max. 72h.

S Mülheim/Ruhr 9A4

Hymer Zentrum, Kölner Strasse 35-37. **GPS**: n51,39985 e6,87700.
€ 0,50/80liter Ch.

S Münster 9B2

Campingplatz Münster, Laerer Werseufer. **GPS**: n51,94583 e7,69082.

24 € 15 Ch WC . 01/01-31/12
Distance: Münster 4,5km 100m on the spot 100m.

S Netphen 9C5

Freitzeitpark Netphen, P3, Brauersdorferstrasse. **GPS**: n50,91250 e8,12567.

3 € 3,50/day € 1/70liter Ch. **Surface:** metalled. 01/01-31/12
Distance: 2km 2km.
Remarks: Max. 48h, coins available at swimming pool.

S Nettersheim 9A6

Wohnmobilhafen Nettersheim, Urftstraße. **GPS**: n50,48591 e6,62597.

30 € 8/24h € 1 Ch included. **Location:** Rural, simple, quiet.
Surface: metalled. 01/01-31/12 on the spot on the spot.
Remarks: Bread-service.

Nettetal 8D4

Am Nettebruch, Flothender straße/Flothend. **GPS**: n51,30188 e6,26715.

3 free. **Surface:** grassy/gravel. 01/01-31/12
Distance: 1km on the spot on the spot 1km.

Nettetal 8D4

Am Krickenbeck See, Krickenbecker Allee 38. **GPS**: n51,34460 e6,25793.

50 € 8. **Surface:** asphalted. 01/01-31/12
Distance: 2km on the spot 2km.

Neuss 9A4

Allrounder Winterworld/Skihalle, An der Skihalle 1. **GPS**: n51,17316 e6,64862.

30 free. **Surface:** metalled. 01/01-31/12
Distance: on the spot indoor ski.
Remarks: A46, exit Neuss-Holzheim.

Nideggen 8D5

Parkplatz Danzley, Bahnhofstrasse. **GPS**: n50,69247 e6,47952.

14 free. **Location:** Rural, simple. **Surface:** metalled.
01/01-31/12
Distance: 500m 500m.

Nordkirchen 9B3

Hotel Plettenberger Hof, Schlossstrasse 28. **GPS**: n51,73659 e7,52819.

DE

2 guests free. **Surface:** asphalted. 01/01-31/12
Distance: 200m on the spot.

Nordkirchen 9B3

Minigolfpark, Am Schlosspark 5. **GPS**: n51,73553 e7,53494.

2 free. **Surface:** metalled. 01/03-31/10
Distance: 1km on the spot 100m.

Nottuln 9B2

Wellenfreibad/Hallenbad, Rudolf-Harbigstrasse. **GPS**: n51,92410 e7,34514.

5 free . **Surface:** metalled. 01/01-31/12
Distance: on the spot.
Remarks: Parking swimming pool, service during opening hours.

Oberhausen 9A3

Am Kaisergarten. **GPS**: n51,48690 e6,85551.

60 € 7 € 1 Ch € 0,50/3h. **Surface:** grassy.
01/01-31/12
Distance: Oberhausen City 30 min walking 1,6km 1,7km 1,7km.

Oberhausen 9A3

Parking 10 - CentrO, Arenastraße. **GPS**: n51,48930 e6,87063.

40 free. **Surface:** metalled. 01/01-31/12
Distance: 100m on the spot on the spot.
Remarks: At CentrO.

Tourist information Oberhausen:

CentrO Park, Promenade 10.Amusement park.
01/04-31/10 11-18/19h.
CentrO.Large shopping centre, 300 shops, 100 restaurants/bars and a market.
Mo-Thu 10-20h restaurant 10-22h, Fri-Sa 10-22h restaurant 10-24h.

Oedt 8D4

Wohnmobile-Stellplatz Niers-Perle-Oedt, Mühlengasse. **GPS**: n51,32327 e6,37650.

8 free. **Surface:** asphalted. 01/01-31/12
Distance: 800m 500m 500m.

Oelde 9C2

Pott's Brau und Backhaus, In der Geist 120. **GPS**: n51,81126 e8,13255.
6 € 5 € 1/60liter Ch included. **Location:** Simple.
Surface: grassy/metalled. 02/01-23/12
Distance: on the spot.

Olpe 9B4

Freizeitbad Olpe, Seeweg 5. **GPS**: n51,03242 e7,84163.

10 € 5 € 0,20/liter Ch (4x)€ 1/2kWh WC included,At swimming pool 7-22h. **Location:** Urban. **Surface:** asphalted. 01/01-31/12
Distance: 500m 2km 250m.
Remarks: Max. 3 days, on the banks of the Biggesee.

Ostbevern 9B2

Bever Bad, Am Hanfgarten 22. **GPS**: n52,03673 e7,84392.

DE

6 € 10 Ch WC. **Surface:** grassy. 01/01-31/12
Distance: 400m 300m 300m.
Remarks: Parking swimming pool, incl. entry swimming pool.

S Overhetfeld 8D4

Camp Graskamp, Graskamp 19. **GPS:** n51,22259 e6,13977.

5 € 10 Ch WC included. **Surface:** grassy. 01/01-31/12
Distance: 200m 200m on the spot.

S Paderborn 9D3

Maspernplatz, P4, Hathumarstrasse. **GPS:** n51,72278 e8,75417.

8 € 5/24h (4x)€ 0,50/h. **Location:** Urban, central, noisy.
Surface: metalled. 01/01-31/12
Distance: on the spot 4km 100m 500m on the spot.

Paderborn 9D3

Liboriberg, Liboriberg. **GPS:** n51,71543 e8,75529.

4 € 3,50/24h. **Location:** Urban, noisy.
01/01-31/12
Distance: on the spot on the spot on the spot on the spot.
Remarks: Small pitches.

Paderborn 9D3

Lippesee-Nordufer, Sennelagerstraße 58, Sande. **GPS:** n51,76087 e8,67756.

20 free. **Location:** Rural, simple. **Surface:** grassy.
01/01-31/12
Distance: 1km 150m 150m 1km 500m on the spot on the spot.
Remarks: North bank lake Lippe.

S Petershagen 9D1

Stellplatz Petershagen, Hohoffstrasse. **GPS:** n52,37532 e8,96875.

10 free € 1/90liter (8x)€ 1/kWh. **Location:** Urban, quiet.
Surface: metalled. 01/01-31/12
Distance: 100m 100m 100m.
Remarks: Nearby football ground, max. 3 days.

S Plettenberg 9B4

Aqua Magis, Albert Schweizerstrasse, Böddinghausen. **GPS:** n51,23220 e7,85308.

10 free € 1/40liter Ch (8x)€ 0,50. **Location:** Rural, comfortable, quiet. **Surface:** metalled. 01/01-31/12
Distance: on the spot 11km on the spot 200m on the spot on the spot.
Remarks: Max. 48h, at paradise pool.

S Raesfeld 9A3

Wohnmobilstellplatz Graf Alexander, Südring. **GPS:** n51,76523 e6,83035.
8 € 8 € 1 Ch € 1/12h WC. **Surface:** gravel.
01/01-31/12
Distance: 1km 150m.
Remarks: At historic moated castle, max. 2 nights.

S Recke 9B1

Yackthafen Marina Recke, Auf der Haar 23. **GPS:** n52,35082 e7,71174.

40 € 5 Ch (10x)€ 1,50 WC. **Surface:** grassy/metalled.
01/01-31/12
Distance: 1km, Recke 3,5km on the spot on the spot 900m 400m.
Remarks: Parking marina to Mittellland canal.

S Rees 8D3

Wohnmobilstellplatz, Ebentalstrasse. **GPS:** n51,76428 e6,38829.

31 € 6/day Ch included € 1. **Location:** Urban, comfortable.
Surface: grassy. 01/01-31/12
Distance: 400m.
Remarks: Behind swimming pool.

S Reken 9A2

Wohnmobilstellplatz Reken, Bergen 2a. **GPS:** n51,82864 e7,05895.

25 € 6 € 1/200liter Ch (10x)€ 0,50/kWh. **Surface:** grassy.
01/01-31/12
Distance: 1km 1km 1km.
Remarks: Max. 2 days.

Remscheid 9A4

Brückenpark Müngsten, Mügstener Brückenweg. **GPS:** n51,16833 e7,13750.

4 free. **Location:** Rural, simple, quiet. **Surface:** gravel.
01/01-31/12
Distance: 5km 4km 100m 100m on the spot.

Remscheid 9A4

Dörperhöhe, Bei Haus nr. 15, Lennep. **GPS:** n51,17986 e7,30205.
4 free. **Surface:** asphalted.

Remscheid 9A4

Jahnplatz, Am Stadion, Lennep. **GPS:** n51,19052 e7,26110.
4 free. **Surface:** asphalted. 01/01-31/12
Distance: historical centre of Lennep 300m.

S Remscheid 9A4

Garage Pauli GmbH, Lenneperstrasse 152 (Bundesstrasse 229). **GPS:** n51,18020 e7,22591.
Ch free. 01/01-31/12

S Rheda-Wiedenbrück 9C2

Am Werl, Gütersloherstrasse. **GPS:** n51,85456 e8,29768.

4 free Ch WC free. **Location:** Urban. **Surface:** metalled.
01/01-31/12
Distance: 300m 300m.
Remarks: Max. 3 days.

Rheda-Wiedenbrück 9C2

P Hallenbad, Ostring/Am Hallenbad, Wiederbrück. **GPS:** n51,83188 e8,32350.

4 free. **Location:** Urban, quiet. **Surface:** metalled. 01/01-31/12
Distance: 1km 200m bakery 200m on the spot on the spot.
Remarks: Parking swimming pool.

S Rhede 9A2

Reisemobilstellplatz Kettelerplatz, Kettelerstrasse 9. **GPS:** n51,83677 e6,69346.

15 free € 1/75liter Ch (6x)€ 1/2kWh. **Location:** Urban, simple.
Surface: grassy. 01/01-31/12
Distance: 750m 750m 500m.

Rhede 9A2

Hallen- und Freibad, Heideweg 59. **GPS:** n51,83164 e6,68635.

DE

2 free. **Location:** Urban, simple. **Surface:** metalled.
01/01-31/12
Distance: 1,5km.
Remarks: Parking swimming pool, max. 3 days.

Rheinbach 9A6

Parkplatz Freizeitpark/Erlebnisbad Monte Mare, Münstereifelerstraße 69. **GPS**: n50,61883 e6,93262.

4 free. **Location:** Rural, simple. **Surface:** metalled.
01/01-31/12
Distance: 1,5km 1,5km.
Remarks: Max. 3 days.

Rheine 9B1

Am Walshagenpark, Liobastrasse/Walshagenstrasse. **GPS**: n52,29562 e7,43580.
2 free. 01/01-31/12
Distance: 300m 300m 300m 300m.

Rheine 9B1

Im Stadtpark, Kopernikusstrasse. **GPS**: n52,28137 e7,45478.
2 free. **Surface:** metalled. 01/01-31/12

Rheine 9B1

Parkplatz Tennishalle, Gertrudenweg/Bentlager Weg, Bentlage. **GPS**: n52,29234 e7,42936.
3 free.
Distance: 350m.

Rheine 9B1

Parkplatz, Salinenstrasse, Bentlage. **GPS**: n52,29828 e7,41904.
3 free. **Surface:** metalled.

Rheine 9B1

Hotel Borchert, Russenweg 3. **GPS**: n52,29826 e7,48215.
3 free. **Surface:** metalled.
Remarks: Asphalted inner court.

Rheurdt 8D3

Wohnmobilhafen Ökodorf, St. Nikolausweg 15. **GPS**: n51,46382 e6,46780.

21 € 8 Ch € 2/24h WC. **Surface:** metalled. 01/01-31/12
Distance: 500m 500m 500m.

Rietberg 9C2

Jakobistrasse, Mastholte. **GPS**: n51,75667 e8,39111.

4 free € 0,50/80liter Ch. **Location:** Rural, central. **Surface:** asphalted.
01/01-31/12
Distance: 100m 100m 100m.

Rietberg 9C2

Am Heimathaus, Langenberger Strasse, Mastholte. **GPS**: n51,75765 e8,38945.

2 free. **Location:** Urban. **Surface:** asphalted. 01/01-31/12
Distance: 100m 100m 100m.

Rietberg 9C2

Schulzentrum, Torfweg. **GPS**: n51,80724 e8,43295.

2 free. **Location:** Urban, simple. **Surface:** metalled.
01/01-31/12
Distance: 200m 100m 200m 200m on the spot.

Roetgen 8D5

Am Bahnhof, Bahnhofstrasse. **GPS**: n50,64868 e6,18506.

10 free. **Location:** Rural, simple, noisy. **Surface:** gravel/metalled.
01/01-31/12
Distance: 300m 300m.

Rosendahl 9A2

Wohnmobilplatz Darfeld, Sudetenstrasse, Darfeld. **GPS**: n52,02696 e7,26501.

DE

20 free € 1/100liter Ch € 0,50/kWh. **Surface:** grassy/metalled.
01/01-31/12
Distance: 500m on the spot 500m.

Rüthen 9C3

Am Hachtor, Hachtorstrasse. **GPS:** n51,49405 e8,43119.

4 free. **Surface:** metalled. 01/01-31/12
Distance: 50m 50m 50m, Aldi 200m.

Saerbeck 9B2

Hotel-Rest. Stegemann, Westladbergen 71. **GPS:** n52,15169 e7,68343.
8 guests free. **Surface:** metalled. 01/01-31/12
Distance: 3km on the spot 3km.

Sassenberg 9C2

Parkplatz Feldmark, Feldmark. **GPS:** n52,00172 e8,06546.

3 free € 1/80liter Ch.
Distance: 4km on the spot on the spot.

Sassenberg 9C2

Freibad, Telgenkamp. **GPS:** n51,98378 e8,04981.

free.
Remarks: Parking swimming pool.

Schieder 9D2

Freizeitzentrum Schiedersee, Kronenbruch. **GPS:** n51,92073 e9,16471.

300 € 10 € 1/100liter Ch € 0,50/kWh WC € 0,50/time € 2 .
Location: Rural, comfortable, quiet. **Surface:** grassy/metalled.
01/01-31/12
Distance: 1,3km 50m 50m on the spot on the spot on the spot on the spot.

Schleiden 8D6

Wohnmobilhafen am Nationalpark-Eifel, Pfarrer-Kneipp-strasse, Gemünd.
GPS: n50,57855 e6,49107.

40 € 7 + € 1/pp tourist tax € 0,50/50liter Ch € 0,50/kWh 100m.
Location: Rural, comfortable, quiet. **Surface:** gravel/metalled.
01/01-31/12
Distance: within walking distance 500m 500m.
Remarks: Bread-service.

Schleiden 8D6

Am Freibad, Im Wiesengrund. **GPS:** n50,52993 e6,47022.

8 free. **Location:** Rural, simple, quiet. **Surface:** asphalted.

Schloss Holte/Stukenbrock 9D2

Reisemobilstellplatz Am Sennebach, Liemkerstrasse 27, Liemke. **GPS:** n51,86979 e8,61531.

20 € 5 € 2 Ch (18x)included. **Location:** Rural, isolated, quiet.
Surface: grasstiles. 01/01-31/12 service: sa/su.
Distance: 1km 1km.
Remarks: Behind Froli Kunstoffwerk Fromme.

Schmallenberg 9C4

Im Sorpetal, Winkhausen 21. **GPS:** n51,16083 e8,34056.

DE

12 € 9 € 0,50/80liter Ch (12x)€ 0,50/kWh. 01/01-31/12
Distance: on the spot 100m 2km 500m 1km on the spot.
Remarks: Trout pond, children's play garden, golf 500m.

S Schöppingen 9A2

Schulze Althoff, Heven 48. **GPS**: n52,07361 e7,22361.

30 € 12/night, 3p incl., +3p € 4/pp Ch WC included sanitary € 2/pp € 4. **Surface:** grassy.
Distance: 2,5km on the spot on the spot 2,5km on the spot.

S Senden 9B2

Sportpark Senden, Buldenerstrasse. **GPS**: n51,85419 e7,47433.

10 free Ch. **Surface:** grasstiles. 01/01-31/12
Distance: on the spot 200m 300m on the spot.
Remarks: Parking swimming pool.

S Senden 9B2

Ponyhof Steinhoff, Gettrup 37. **GPS**: n51,83305 e7,46878.

10 € 6 Ch € 0,50/kWh. **Surface:** grassy/metalled.
01/01-31/12
Distance: Senden 4km 2,5km 2,5km.

S Sendenhorst 9B2

Westor 31. **GPS**: n51,84286 e7,81849.

4 free € 0,50/40liter Ch € 0,50. **Surface:** metalled.
01/01-31/12
Distance: on the spot 300m 1km.

S Siegen 9C5

Am Hallenbad, Poststraße. **GPS**: n50,89463 e8,02405.

3 free € 1/10minutes Ch (2x)€ 1/8h. **Location:** Urban.
Surface: metalled. 01/01-31/12
Distance: 200m 200m 200m 250m on the spot on the spot.
Remarks: Max. 3 days.

S Siegen 9C5

An der Alche, Freudenbergerstraße 67. **GPS**: n50,88073 e8,00764.
4 free € 0,50/50liter Ch € 0,50/kWh. 01/01-31/12
Distance: 1km 5km 200m 1km.
Remarks: Max. 3 days.

S Simmerath 8D6

Wohnmobilhafen Rurseezentrum, Seeufer 1, Rurberg. **GPS**: n50,60658 e6,38177.

10 € 8/24h € 2 Ch. **Location:** Rural, comfortable.
Surface: grasstiles. 01/01-31/12
Distance: 100m 50m.

S Soest 9C3

City Motel, Altes Stellwerk 9. **GPS**: n51,57503 e8,11478.

14 € 8 Ch (14x) WC € 2/time € 3/time included. **Location:** Urban, comfortable, central, quiet. **Surface:** gravel.
01/01-31/12

DE

Distance: 200m 200m 200m 200m on the spot on the spot.

Solingen 9A4

Am Brandteich, Gräfrath. **GPS**: n51,21151 e7,07217.

10 free. **Location:** Urban, simple, quiet. **Surface:** concrete.
01/01-31/12
Distance: on the spot 2,7km on the spot 300m.
Remarks: Parking fire-station.

Stadtlohn 9A2

Freizeit- und Hallenbad, Uferstrasse 29. **GPS**: n51,99792 e6,93019.

4 against payment € 0,50/100liter Ch (4x)€ 1 WC.
Surface: metalled. 01/01-31/12
Distance: 800m.
Remarks: Parking swimming pool.

Steinfurt 9B2

Wohnmobilstellplatz Steinfurt, Liedekerkerstrasse 70, Burgsteinfurt. **GPS**: n52,14738 e7,34746.

25 voluntary contribution € 1/100liter Ch € 1/2kWh.
Surface: asphalted. 01/01-31/12
Distance: 300m 200m.
Remarks: Parking behind police station, max. 3 nights.

Steinhagen 9C2

Am Cronsbach. **GPS**: n51,99998 e8,42351.

2 free. **Location:** Urban, simple. **Surface:** metalled. 01/01-31/12
Distance: 100m 100m 100m.

Stemwede 9C1

Fest- und Schiesshalle, Schrottinghauserstrasse, Levern. **GPS**: n52,37217 e8,44552.

2 free. **Location:** Rural, simple, isolated. **Surface:** metalled.
01/01-31/12
Distance: 1,5km 1,5km 1,4km.

Stemwede 9C1

Park Stemwederberg, Stemwederbergstrasse/Freudeneck, Westrup. **GPS**: n52,43246 e8,43973.

8 free. **Location:** Rural, comfortable. **Surface:** grassy.
01/01-31/12
Distance: 2km 2km 2km on the spot.

Stemwede 9C1

Hotel-Gasthof Moorhof, Wagenfelderstrasse 34, Oppenwehe. **GPS**: n52,49979 e8,53507.

20 € 7, free with a meal included € 2,16Amp. **Location:** Rural, quiet. **Surface:** grassy. 01/01-31/12 Thu.
Distance: on the spot.

Stemwede 9C1

Rila Feinkost-Importe, Schröttinghauser Strasse/Hinterm Teich 3, Levern. **GPS**: n52,36783 e8,43833.

50 € 15 Ch WC included. **Location:** Rural, comfortable.
Surface: grassy/gravel. 01/01-31/12
Distance: on the spot.
Remarks: Incl. voucher € 6 for 'Rila erleben': restaurant, Tapas bar, food, garden,

DE

playground.

Straelen 8D1

Fitnessbad Wasserstraelen, Lingsforterstraße 100. **GPS**: n52,45201 e6,25708.

10 free € 0,50/80liter Ch (8x)€ 0,50/kWh. **Surface:** asphalted.
01/01-31/12
Distance: 1,2km 1km 1km.

Tourist information Straelen:
Verkehrsverein Straelen e.V, Rathausstrasse 1, www.straelen.de.City with historical center, cycle and skating routes.

Tecklenburg 9B1

Parkplatz Bismarckturm, Am Weingarten. **GPS**: n52,22129 e7,79905.

5 free. **Surface:** asphalted. 01/01-31/12
Distance: 800m.

Telgte 9B2

Am Dümmert, Emstor. **GPS**: n51,98497 e7,79151.
3 free € 1/100liter Ch € 1/1kWh. **Location:** Simple.
Surface: gravel. 01/01-31/12
Distance: 600m.

Telgte 9B2

Waldschwimmbad Klatenberge, Waldweg. **GPS**: n51,99459 e7,78328.

free Ch . **Surface:** asphalted. 01/01-31/12
Distance: 1km.
Remarks: Parking swimming pool, recreation area.

Telgte 9B2

Altes Gasthaus Lauheide, Lauheide 3, K17. **GPS**: n51,99862 e7,75319.

120 € 7,50 Ch included. **Surface:** grassy. 01/01-31/12
Distance: 4km on the spot.

Uedem 8D3

Reisemobilstellplatz Uedem, Bergstraße. **GPS**: n51,66173 e6,28734.

28 € 8 Ch (24x)€ 2/24h WC. **Surface:** grassy.
01/01-31/12
Distance: 1,5km.

Velbert 9A4

Unter der Saubrücke, Parkstraße, Velbert-Mitte. **GPS**: n51,34097 e7,03050.

8 € 3 € 1/100liter Ch € 0,50/kWh. **Location:** Urban, simple, quiet.
Surface: gravel. 01/01-31/12
Distance: 800m 1,6km 250m on the spot.

Velbert 9A4

Panoramabad Velbert-Neviges, Wiesenweg. **GPS**: n51,30582 e7,08546.

5 free € 1/80liter Ch. **Location:** Urban, simple, quiet.
Surface: concrete. 01/01-31/12
Distance: 800m nearby 500m.
Remarks: Parking swimming pool, max. 3 nights.

Velbert 9A4

Domparkplatz, Bernsaustrasse Schloss Hardenberg. **GPS**: n51,31565 e7,08724.

DE

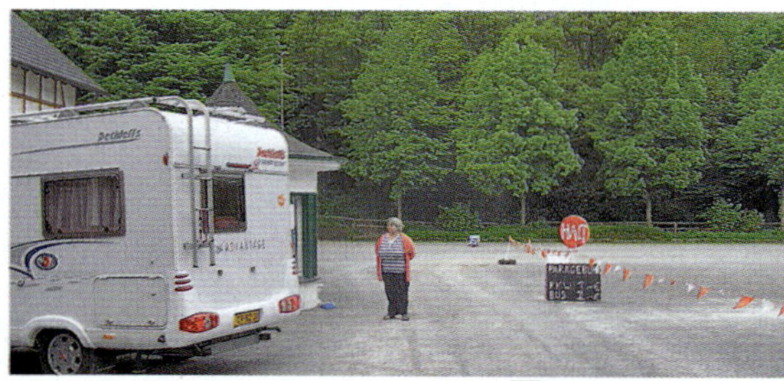

5 € 2. **Location:** Urban. **Surface:** gravel. 01/01-31/12
Distance: 600m on the spot.

Velbert 9A4

Nizzabad, Kalversiepen, Langenberg. **GPS:** n51,34362 e7,13766.

4 free. **Location:** Simple, quiet. **Surface:** gravel. 01/01-31/12
Distance: Langenberg 2,5km on the spot.

Velen 9A2

Erholungsgebiet Waldvelen, ven der Buss, Klyer Damm 8-10. **GPS:** n51,90167 e7,01167.

30 € 15, 2 pers.incl Ch (50x). **Location:** Rural, luxurious.
Surface: gravel. 01/01-31/12
Distance: 2km 8,5km.

Velen 9A2

Freibad Ramsdorf, Velener Straße, Ramsdorf. **GPS:** n51,88955 e6,92503.

5 free. **Surface:** asphalted. 01/01-31/12
Distance: Ramsdorf 300m.
Remarks: At swimming pool.

Viersen 8D4

Am Familienbad Ransberg, Heesstraße 80, Viersen-Dülken. **GPS:** n51,25083 e6,35291.

9 free € 0,50/100liter Ch (6x)€ 1/2kWh. **Surface:** metalled.
01/01-31/12
Distance: Dülken 400m, Viersen 3km 400m 2km 100m.
Remarks: Max. 3 days.

Vreden 9A2

Hotel Zum Möwenparadies, Zwillbrockstrasse 39. **GPS:** n52,05305 e6,70733.

10 € 10 Ch WC included. **Surface:** grassy. 01/01-31/12
Distance: on the spot on the spot on the spot 200m.

Vreden 9A2

Pension Ostendarp, Wüllenerstrasse 107. **GPS:** n52,03440 e6,84174.

5 free Ch WC. **Surface:** grassy. 01/01-31/12
Distance: 800m on the spot 300m.

Vreden 9A2

Wohnmobilpark Vreden, Ottensteiner Strasse 59. **GPS:** n52,03962 e6,84136.

30 € 8 Ch (20x)included WC € 2 € 3/h. **Surface:** grassy.
01/01-31/12
Distance: 500m on the spot.
Remarks: Guarded parking.

Wachtendonk 8D4

Bleiche P4, Achter de Stadt. **GPS:** n51,40601 e6,33170.

DE

18 €5 €0,50/80liter €0,50 Ch (12x)€0,50/kWh. **Surface:** gravel. 01/01-31/12

Distance: 400m 100m 400m.

Wadersloh 9C3

Im Klostergarten 18, Liesborn. **GPS**: n51,71414 e8,25960.

4 free €0,50/80liter Ch (4x)€0,50/12h. **Location:** Rural. **Surface:** metalled. 01/01-31/12

Distance: 400m 100m 400m on the spot on the spot.

Remarks: Behind gymnasium.

Waldbröl 9B5

Am Hallenbad, Vennstrassse. **GPS**: n50,87511 e7,60987.

5 free. **Location:** Rural, simple, quiet. **Surface:** metalled. 01/01-31/12

Distance: on the spot 18km on the spot on the spot.

Remarks: Max. 2 days.

Waldfeucht-Brüggelchen 8D4

Reisemobilstellplatz "Tilder Weg", Tilderweg. **GPS**: n51,07016 e5,99567.

18 €4 €0,50/80liter Ch (8x)€0,50/kWh. **Location:** Rural, simple, quiet. **Surface:** metalled. 01/01-31/12

Distance: 1km on the spot 500m.

Remarks: Max. 4 nights.

Waltrop 9B3

Restaurant Zur Lohburg, Lohburgerstrass 105, A2 Ausfahrt henreichenburg, Schiffshebewerk. **GPS**: n51,60613 e7,34882.

20 €5 €2. **Surface:** grassy. 01/01-31/12

Distance: 1km on the spot 1km.

Warburg 9D3

Schützenplatz, Paderborner Tor. **GPS**: n51,48993 e9,13810.

5 €5 Ch included. **Surface:** metalled.

Distance: 500m.

Warendorf 9C2

Beelener Strasse. **GPS**: n51,94975 e8,00127.

10 free.

Distance: 1,5km on the spot.

Remarks: Max. 24h.

Warendorf 9C2

Parkplatz Emssee, Sassenberger Strasse. **GPS**: n51,95514 e7,99797.

2 free. 01/01-31/12

Distance: 1km on the spot.

Remarks: Max. 24h.

Warendorf 9C2

Parkplatz Zwischen den Emsbrücken, Am Emswehr. **GPS**: n51,95426 e7,99164.

2 free. 01/01-31/12

Distance: 100m.

Remarks: Max. 24h.

Warstein 9C3

Camperpark zum Bayernstadl, Enkerbruch 12a. **GPS**: n51,43041 e8,37432.

18+22 € 8 € 1/100liter Ch (18x)€ 2/16,€ 1 summer, € 2 winter.
Surface: gravel. 01/01-31/12
Distance: 1,5km on the spot 1,5km 1,5km.
Remarks: Bread-service.

S Warstein 9C3

Vans in Paradise, Zu Hause im Waldpark. **GPS**: n51,42615 e8,35525.

60 € 15 Ch (76x),16Amp WC included € 2,dryer € 2. **Location:** Isolated, quiet. **Surface:** grassy/gravel. 01/01-31/12
Distance: 2km small menu 2km 2km.
Remarks: At Warstein brewery, bread-service + breakfast-service.

Warstein 9C3

Wohnmobilstellplatz, Dammweg. **GPS**: n51,45103 e8,34750.

5 free. **Location:** Simple. **Surface:** gravel/metalled.
01/01-31/12
Distance: 2km 500m 1km 1km.
Remarks: At sports park.

Tourist information Warstein:
Warsteiner Brauerei, Zu Hause im Waldpark.Guided tour 1.45h, 2 drinks included. daily 12-17, Su 13-15h.

S Wassenberg 8D4

Parkbad Wassenberg, Auf dem Taubenkamp 2. **GPS**: n51,09833 e6,14364.

12 € 5/day, € 20/week € 1/100 € 1 Ch € 0,50/kWh. **Location:** Rural, comfortable, quiet. **Surface:** metalled. 01/01-31/12
Distance: 1,5km.
Remarks: To pay at swimming pool.

S Weeze 8D3

Tierpark Fährsteg, L5 Fährsteg. **GPS**: n51,63047 e6,20130.

12 € 5 € 0,50/kWh. 01/01-31/12
Distance: 500m 500m.

S Weeze 8D3

Aral, Industriestraße. **GPS**: n51,62029 e6,20972.
€ 1 Ch.

S Wegberg 8D4

Wegberger Reisemobilstellplatz, Schul- und Sportzentrum, Maaseiker Strasse 67. **GPS**: n51,13389 e6,28266.

10 € 6 Ch included. **Surface:** gravel/sand.
01/01-31/12
Distance: 400m 400m 400m on the spot.
Remarks: Caution key € 20 at swimming pool.

S Werne 9B3

Natur Solebad, Am Hagen. **GPS**: n51,65910 e7,63414.

10 free € 1/80liter Ch € 0,50. **Surface:** metalled.
01/01-31/12
Distance: 400m 200m 400m.
Remarks: Parking swimming pool.

S Wiehl 9B5

Freizeitpark Wiehl, Brüchnerstrasse. **GPS**: n50,94716 e7,54585.

3 free € 1/80liter Ch. **Location:** Simple, central.
Surface: metalled.
Distance: 300m 5,4km 400m.

DE

Remarks: Parking next to recreation park and disco, max. 2 days.

Tourist information Wiehl:

www.wiehl.de.Small town in the green hills. 180 kilometres marked hiking routes.

Wiehler Dahlienschau.400 varieties of dahlias.

15/08-15/10 daily 8-18h. T free.

Wiehler Trofsteinhöhle.Caves Temperature is approx. 8°C.

15/03-31/10 9-17h, 01/11-14/03 Sa-Su 11-16h.

M Schloß Homburg/Museum des Oberbergisches Kreises, Nürnbrecht.

01/04-31/10 Tue-Sa 10-17h, Su 10-18h.

Bergische Postkutsche, Nümrecht Post.Ride by mail-coach between Wiehl and Nümbrecht. 01/05-30/09 Fri-Su 10-16h.

S **Wilnsdorf** 9C5

Wielandshof, Bauhofstraße 5. **GPS**: n50,80692 e8,10896.

5 €5 €0,50/60liter Ch (4x)€1/12h. **Surface:** gravel.

01/01-31/12

Distance: 900m 900m.

Remarks: Check in at farm.

Wilnsdorf 9C5

Gästehaus Wilgersdorf, Am Kalkhain 9-23, Wilgersdorf. **GPS**: n50,80751 e8,14782.

3 free. **Surface:** asphalted. 01/01-31/12

Distance: 500m on the spot 1km.

S **Windeck** 9B5

Am Sportplatz, Im Bungert, Herchen. **GPS**: n50,78025 e7,51308.

8 free (10x)€0,50/1kWh. **Location:** Rural, simple, quiet.

Surface: gravel. 01/01-31/12

Distance: 200m 8,5km 200m 200m on the spot on the spot.

Remarks: Parking sports park.

S **Windeck** 9B5

Hallenbad, Bergische strasse 21, Dattenfeld. **GPS**: n50,80754 e7,56105.

4 free €1,50 €1,50 Ch €1,50. **Location:** Rural, simple, quiet.

Surface: metalled. 01/01-31/12

Distance: 8,5km on the spot on the spot.

S **Windeck** 9B5

Museumsdorf Altwindeck, Im Thal Windeck 17, Alt-Windeck. **GPS**: n50,81276 e7,57554.

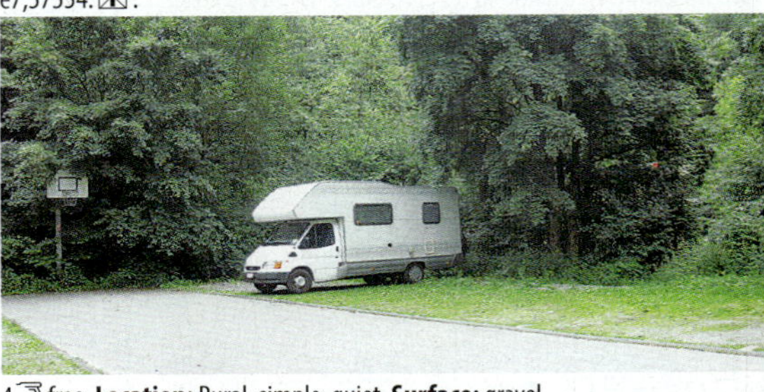

4 free. **Location:** Rural, simple, quiet. **Surface:** gravel.

01/01-31/12

Distance: 2km 8,5km on the spot 2km on the spot on the spot.

Remarks: Parking museum, max. 3 days.

Windeck 9B5

Auf dem Greent, Dattenfeld. **GPS**: n50,80697 e7,55495.

50 free. **Location:** Rural, simple, quiet. **Surface:** asphalted/grassy.

01/01-31/12

Distance: 500m 8,5km 500m 500m.

Remarks: Fair ground.

Windeck 9B5

Brunnenweg, Dattenfeld. **GPS**: n50,80486 e7,56087.

5 free. **Location:** Simple, quiet. **Surface:** grassy/gravel.

01/01-31/12

Distance: 200m 8km 200m 150m on the spot on the spot.

Remarks: Recreation park.

S **Winterberg** 9C4

Campingplatz Winterberg. **GPS**: n51,18632 e8,50445.

DE

€ 7,50-8 + € 5,50-6/pp, dog € 2 Ch (25x)€ 0,55/1kWh WC € 1/5minutes € 0,50/time. **Location:** Rural, luxurious. **Surface:** metalled.
Distance: 2km on the spot 2km 20m on the spot on the spot on the spot on the spot.
Remarks: Parking skiruns.

S Winterberg 9C4

Parkplatz Stadthalle, Schulstrasse. **GPS**: n51,19163 e8,53810.

20 € 8/24h € 0,50/50liter Ch (10x)€ 0,50/3h. **Surface:** metalled. 01/01-31/12
Distance: 1km 1km.

S Winterberg 9C4

Park Hochsauerland, Remmeswiese 10. **GPS**: n51,19869 e8,52524.

tariff camp site Ch WC. 01/01-31/12
Remarks: Parking skilift, reservation recommended in winter peak season: tel. 0049 2981 3249.

S Winterberg 9C4

Kirchmeier Sporthotel, Renauweg 54, Altastenberg. **GPS**: n51,19391 e8,46844.

10 € 26 + € 1,75/pp tourist tax (10x) WC.
Surface: asphalted. 01/01-31/12
Distance: Winterberg 5km on the spot on the spot 800m on the spot.
Remarks: Free entrance swimming pool, Dampfbad, sauna, shuttle-bus, cross-country skiing piste.

Winterberg 9C4

Bergrestaurant Bobhaus, Auf der Kappe 1. **GPS**: n51,18493 e8,50559.

8 € 12, free with a meal. **Location:** Rural.
Surface: asphalted.
Distance: 2km on the spot on the spot on the spot on the spot on the spot.
Remarks: Parking ski-lift, check in at restaurant.

S Witten 9B3

Reisemobil-Center, Pferdebachstrasse 150. **GPS**: n51,45411 e7,35246.

10 free € 1/80liter Ch. **Surface:** gravel. 01/01-31/12
Distance: 3km 3km 3km.

Wülfrath 9A4

Parkplatz, Mettmanner strasse 42. **GPS**: n51,28188 e7,02741.

10 free. **Location:** Urban, simple, quiet. **Surface:** concrete. 01/01-31/12
Distance: on the spot 500m 800m.

S Xanten 8D3

Womopark Xanten, Fürstenberg 6. **GPS**: n51,65413 e6,46389.

60+20 € 10 Ch included € 2 € 1. **Surface:** grassy. 01/01-31/12
Distance: 1,7km 300m 200m.

S Zülpich 9A5

Wohnmobilhafen am Zülpicher See, Am Wassersportsee. **GPS**: n50,67592 e6,65795.

DE

40 €5 €1 Ch (4x)€ 1. **Location:** Rural, simple, isolated.
Surface: grassy/metalled. 01/01-31/12
Distance: 100m.
Remarks: Service nearby tenniscourt 100m.

Rhineland-Palatinate/Saarland

S Alf 16D1

Freibad Arrastal, Junkergasse 1. **GPS:** n50,05273 e7,11326.

30 €6 Ch included. **Surface:** asphalted/grassy. 01/01-31/12
Distance: 800m.

Alken 9B6

P2, Grinschelheck. **GPS:** n50,24493 e7,44607.

6 free. **Surface:** metalled. 01/01-31/12
Distance: 500m on the spot 200m.

S Altdorf 17A3

Spelzenhof, Hauptstrasse 77. **GPS:** n49,28869 e8,22028.

6 €6 WC. **Surface:** grassy. 01/01-31/12
Distance: nearby on the spot nearby nearby.

S Altendiez 9C6

Restaurant Bimbes-Stubb, Lahnblick 4. **GPS:** n50,36612 e7,98041.

6 €5 €5. **Surface:** gravel. 01/01-31/12 Mo.
Distance: on the spot on the spot 500m.

S Altenglan 16D2

Draisine, Austrasse. **GPS:** n49,55001 e7,46465.

4 free € 1/80liter Ch (4x)€ 1/12h. **Surface:** gravel. 01/04-31/10
Distance: 100m 100m.

S Andernach 9B6

Wohnmobilstellplatz Andernach, Scheidsgasse/Uferstrasse. **GPS:** n50,44176 e7,40796.

70 €7 € 1/100liter Ch (40x). **Surface:** metalled.
01/01-31/12
Distance: on the spot 200m 400m.
Remarks: Max. 3 nights.

S Annweiler 17A3

Am Kurpark, Bindersbacherstrasse. **GPS:** n49,19624 e7,96817.

6 free €1 Ch WC. **Surface:** asphalted. 01/01-31/12
Distance: 1km 600m.

S Bacharach 17A1

Reisemobilplatz Bacharach, B9 Leinpfad. **GPS:** n50,05693 e7,77076.

DE

33 €7 €1 Ch (12x)€ 2,50/24h. **Surface:** gravel.
01/01-31/12 high water.
Distance: on the spot Rhine river 300m 300m.

S Bad Bergzabern 17A3

Schloßgärten, Weinbergstrasse. **GPS**: n49,10322 e7,99737.

5 €4 €1 €1 Ch €1. 01/01-31/12 water disconnected in winter.
Distance: on the spot on the spot 200m.

S Bad Bergzabern 17A3

Weingut Hitziger, Liebrauenbergweg 3. **GPS**: n49,10667 e7,99611.

€5 Ch €1. **Surface:** grassy. 01/01-31/12
Distance: 1km 2km 2km.

S Bad Dürkheim 17A2

In der Silz, Leistadterstrasse. **GPS**: n49,46944 e8,16722.

50 €6 €1/4minutes Ch €1/kWh. **Location:** Urban, simple.
Surface: grassy. 01/01-31/12
Distance: 300m 100m 300m 200m.
Remarks: Servicepoint at Knaus Park.

S Bad Dürkheim 17A2

Knaus park, In den Almen 3. **GPS**: n49,47472 e8,19167.

8 €7 €1/70liter Ch €0,50 €3/pp. **Surface:** gravel/metalled.
01/01-31/12

S Bad Ems 9B6

Yachthafen Kutscher's Marina, Nievernerstrasse 20. **GPS**: n50,33278 e7,70167.

12 €10 Ch €1/kWh WC €1. **Surface:** gravel.
01/03-15/11
Distance: on the spot 1km 300m.

S Bad Hönningen 9B6

Kristall Rheinpark-Therme, Allêe St. Pierre les Nemours 1. **GPS**: n50,51227 e7,30772.

15 €16 Ch WC €0,50 €2. **Surface:** grassy.
01/01-31/12
Distance: on the spot on the spot.

S Bad Kreuznach 17A1

Wohnmobilstellplatz Salinental, Karlshalle 2, Saline. **GPS**: n49,82778 e7,85001.

32 €11 €0,50/80liter Ch €2/night. **Surface:** gravel.
01/01-31/12
Distance: 2km on the spot on the spot 200m 2km on the spot.

S Bad Marienberg 9C5

Marienbad, Bismarckstrasse 65. **GPS**: n50,64466 e7,93528.

DE

10 € 10 € 1/100liter Ch (3x)€ 0,50/kWh. **Surface:** metalled.
01/01-31/12

S Bad Neuenahr 9A6

Reisemobilhafen, Kalvarienbergstrasse 1, Ahrweiler. **GPS**: n50,53891 e7,09600.

€ 7,50/24h Ch € 2 WC included € 1 € 2. **Surface:** grassy.
Distance: 200m.

S Bad Neuenahr 9A6

Am Schwimmbad. **GPS**: n50,53806 e7,10139.
14 € 6 Ch . **Surface:** metalled. 01/01-31/12
Distance: 600m 300m bakery 500m.
Remarks: Along the Ahr river.

DE

S Bad Neuenahr 9A6

Apolinaris-Stadion, Kreuzstrasse. **GPS**: n50,54456 e7,15132.

50 € 5/24h € 1/80liter Ch. **Surface:** asphalted. 01/01-31/12

Bad Neuenahr 9A6

St Piusstrasse. **GPS**: n50,53962 e7,10775.

10 € 5/24h. **Surface:** asphalted. 01/01-31/12
Remarks: Parking at the Ahr.

S Bad Sobernheim 17A2

Reisemobilstellplatz am Nohfels, Felkestraße. **GPS**: n49,77993 e7,65702.

39 € 7 € 1/80liter Ch (48x)€ 2/day . **Surface:** grassy/gravel.
01/01-31/12
Distance: 1km on the spot.
Remarks: Bread-service.

Baumholder 16D2

Freizeitzentrum Am Weiher, Ringstrasse. **GPS**: n49,61111 e7,33917.

3 free. **Surface:** asphalted. 01/01-31/12
Distance: 2km on the spot on the spot 250m.

S Becheln 9B6

Restaurant Zum Wolfsbusch, Emser strasse 1. **GPS**: n50,29609 e7,71503.

5 € 2, guests free € 2. **Surface:** gravel/metalled.
Distance: on the spot on the spot 300m.

S Beckingen 16C3

Brunnenstrasse, Düppenweiler. **GPS**: n49,41414 e6,76973.

10 € 2 € 1 Ch. **Surface:** metalled.

S Beckingen 16C3

Landgasthaus Wilscheider Hof, Zum Wilscheider Hof, Düppenweiler. **GPS**: n49,42585 e6,76431.

15 €5 € 1 WC . **Surface:** grassy. 01/01-31/12
Distance: 1,5km on the spot 1,5km.

S Bernkastel 16D1

Weingut Studert-Prüm im Maximin Hof, Hauptstrasse 150, Wehlen. **GPS:** n49,93771 e7,04811.

50 €9 Ch . **Surface:** grassy.
01/01-31/12
Distance: on the spot on the spot on the spot on the spot 500m.

PS Bernkastel 16D1

Nikolausufer. **GPS:** n49,91119 e7,06721.

40 10-18h Ch. **Location:** Urban. **Surface:** grasstiles. 01/01-31/12
Remarks: Max. 6h.

S Bexbach 16D3

Bexbacher Reisemobilhafen, Im Blumengarten. **GPS:** n49,34161 e7,25698.

35 € 6,50 € 1/80liter Ch (36x)€ 2,50/night WC. **Surface:** grassy.
01/01-31/12
Distance: 900m on the spot 500m 200m.
Remarks: Bread-service.

S Biebelnheim 17A2

Wohnmobilpark am Petersberg, Flonheimer Strasse 34. **GPS:** n49,79432 e8,16236.

20 €5 € 2 Ch € 2. **Surface:** metalled. 01/01-31/12
Distance: 1km 1,5km Bistro Am Petersberg 1km.
Remarks: Max. 2 nights.

S Bingen/Rhein 17A1

Wohnmobilpark Bingen, Mainzer Straße, Bingen/Kempten. **GPS:** n49,96860 e7,94417.

39 € 6,50/night Ch € 2/24h € 3,dryer € 3 € 2/h,€ 0,50/every next hour. **Surface:** grassy/metalled. 01/01-31/12
Distance: 1km 800m 2,7km.
Remarks: Bread-service.

S Birgel 9A6

Historische Wassermühle, Bahnhofstrasse 16. **GPS:** n50,31934 e6,61752.

10 € 15, free with a meal > € 15 Ch included. **Surface:** gravel.
01/01-31/12
Distance: 500m on the spot 1km.

S Blieskastel 16D3

Freizeitanlage Würzbacher Weiher, Marxstraße, Niederwürzbach. **GPS:** n49,24674 e7,19226.

10 € 4,50 Ch . **Surface:** grassy/gravel.
01/01-31/12
Distance: 500m on the spot on the spot 100m 600m 600m.
Remarks: At lake, Würzbacher Weiher.

S Blieskastel 16D3

Freizeitzentrum Blieskastel, Bliesaue 1, Webenheim. **GPS:** n49,23527 e7,26946.
5 free . **Surface:** metalled. 01/01-31/12

DE

Blieskastel 16D3

Hotel Restaurant Hubertushof, Kirschendell 32. **GPS**: n49,24456 e7,21573.

8 € 5, free with a meal . **Surface:** asphalted. 01/01-31/12
Distance: on the spot on the spot 1km.
Remarks: Max. 2 nights, arrival < 19h, bread-service.

Bobenthal/Bornich 17A3

Hotel-Restaurant St. Germanshof, Hauptstrasse 10. **GPS**: n49,04749 e7,89985.

4 guests free. **Surface:** metalled. 01/01-31/12 Mo.
Distance: 5km on the spot 7km.

Bockenheim 17C2

Weingut W. Kohl, Am Sonnenberg 3. **GPS**: n49,59902 e9,17925.

6 € 8/night WC included. **Surface:** metalled. 01/01-31/12
Distance: 500m 500m 3km.

Braubach 9B6

Braubacher Rheintreff, Rheinuferstrasse, B42. **GPS**: n50,26972 e7,64750.

30 € 7 Ch WC included € 3.
Surface: asphalted.
01/01-31/12
Distance: 300m on the spot on the spot 300m 300m 300m.

Brauneberg 16C1

Wohnmobilplatz Juffer, Moselweinstrasse. **GPS**: n49,90518 e6,97760.

15 € 7 Ch . **Surface:** metalled. 01/01-31/12
Distance: 100m on the spot 300m 300m 100m.

Bremm 16D1

Weingut Oster-Franzen, Calmontstrasse 96. **GPS**: n50,09593 e7,12383.

12 € 11, 2 pers.incl € 0,50/60liter Ch € 0,60/kWh WC € 1 washing machine/dryer € 3,50. **Surface:** gravel. 01/01-31/12

Briedern 16D1

Wohnmobilstellplatz Briedern, Birkenweg. **GPS**: n50,11165 e7,20867.

15 € 4. **Surface:** grassy.
Distance: 2km 300m 200m.

Burgen 16D1

Hotel Schmause Mühle, Baybachstrasse 50. **GPS**: n50,20859 e7,39365.

20 € 8 Ch € 2,50 WC € 1. 01/01-31/12
Distance: on the spot on the spot 300m.

Burrweiler 17A3

Wein- und Sektgut Hermann-Bruno Eberle, Böchingerstrasse 1a. **GPS**: n49,24649 e8,07989.

DE

3 € 6 WC. **Surface:** metalled. 01/01-31/12
Distance: 100m 200m.
Remarks: Arrival <21h.

S Burrweiler 17A3

Weingut Diether Bauer, Weinstrasse 52. **GPS:** n49,21982 e8,03059.
3 € 5 WC. **Surface:** metalled. 01/01-31/12
Distance: on the spot 300m.

S Burrweiler 17A3

Weingut Winzerhof, Am Schlossberg 3. **GPS:** n49,25147 e8,07902.

4 € 6 WC. **Surface:** metalled. 01/01-31/12
Distance: 1km 300m.

Cochem 16D1

Bergstrasse, K59. **GPS:** n50,15028 e7,17083.

€ 5 9-19h, overnight stay free.
Surface: grasstiles/metalled.
Distance: 300m 300m.

Cochem 16D1

Moselpromenade, B49. **GPS:** n50,14108 e7,16936.

12 € 1/h 8-19h, overnight stay free. **Surface:** metalled.

Cochem 16D1

Moselstrasse, B49. **GPS:** n50,15329 e7,16828.

16 € 1/h 8-19h, overnight stay free. **Surface:** metalled.
01/01-31/12
Distance: 700m 200m 200m on the spot.

S Dahn/Reichenbach 17A3

Altes Bahnhöf'l, An der Reichenbahn 6. **GPS:** n49,13890 e7,79908.

10 guests free WC. 01/01-31/12 Mo.
Distance: on the spot on the spot 500m.

S Dierbach 17A3

Jahnstrasse. **GPS:** n49,08177 e8,06201.
10 free Ch free. **Surface:** asphalted. 01/01-31/12

S Dierbach 17A3

Weingut-Weinstube Geiger, Hauptstrasse 1. **GPS:** n49,08344 e8,06673.

30 guests free WC. **Surface:** grassy. 01/01-31/12
Distance: on the spot 500m.

S Dohm 9A6

Am Heidberghof, Heidberghof 1, Dohm-Lammersdorf. **GPS:** n50,26696 e6,67366.

6 € 6-8 Ch (6x)€ 2 WC € 3,50. **Surface:** grassy/gravel.
Easter-01/11
Remarks: Incl. swimming pool (summer), bread-service.

S Dörrenbach 17A3

Übergasse. **GPS:** n49,08840 e7,96921.
10 € 5 Ch . **Surface:** unpaved. 01/01-31/12
Distance: 100m 700m.
Remarks: Next to sports fields.

DE

Eckersweiler 16D2

Am Sportplatz. GPS: n49,55646 e7,30577.
4 free. **Location:** Isolated. **Surface:** grassy. 01/01-31/12
Distance: 1,3km on the spot on the spot.

S Edenkoben 17A3

Wohnmobilstellplatz Kirchbergplatz, Bahnhofstraße. **GPS:** n49,28234 e8,13116.

40 € 5/24h € 0,50 Ch € 1. **Surface:** asphalted. 01/01-31/12
Distance: on the spot 300m Aldi 800m.

S Edenkoben 17A3

Obstgut & Brennerei Göring, Blücherstrasse 45. **GPS:** n49,27792 e8,13487.

5 € 5 € 3 Ch € 3. **Surface:** grassy. 01/01-31/12

Edenkoben 17A3

Gasthof Ziegelhütte, Luitpoldstrasse. **GPS:** n49,28539 e8,13872.

3 guests free. **Surface:** metalled. 01/01-31/12
Distance: on the spot on the spot on the spot.

S Edesheim 17A3

Weingut Boos, Ludwigstrasse 150. **GPS:** n49,25785 e8,11673.

3 € 5 . 01/01-31/12
Distance: 300m 1km.

S Edesheim 17A3

Weingut Erlenmühle, Erlenmühle 1. **GPS:** n49,26111 e8,11389.

3 € 6 . **Surface:** gravel. 01/01-31/12
Distance: 500m 1km.
Remarks: Arrival <22h.

S Edesheim 17A3

Weinstube Wolf, Ruprechtstrasse 20. **GPS:** n49,25976 e8,12935.
2 guests free included. 01/01-31/12
Distance: on the spot on the spot 200m.

S Ediger/Eller 16D1

Stellplatz Ediger, Moselweinstrasse. **GPS:** n50,09291 e7,16041.

15 € 4,50, 01/12-31/03 free € 1 Ch.
Surface: grassy/metalled.
01/01-31/12
Distance: 100m on the spot on the spot on the spot on the spot.
Remarks: Along the Moselle river in Ediger.

Ediger/Eller 16D1

Stellplatz Moselufer, Eller. **GPS:** n50,09915 e7,14370.

15 € 4,50, 01/12-31/03 free. **Surface:** metalled. 01/01-31/12
Distance: on the spot on the spot 200m.
Remarks: Along the Moselle river in Eller.

S Eisenschmitt 16C1

Hotel-Restaurant Molitors Mühle, Eichelhütte. **GPS:** n50,03681 e6,73766.

5 guests free WC. 01/01-31/12
Distance: 1km on the spot on the spot on the spot 1km 300m.
Remarks: Arrival <23h.

S Ellenz/Poltersdorf 16D1

Weingut Loosen, Im Goldbäumchen 4. **GPS**: n50,11389 e7,23528.

12 €8 WC. **Surface:** metalled. 01/01-31/12
Distance: on the spot 150m 500m 1km.

Tourist information Ellenz/Poltersdorf:
Wine- and holiday village on the Moselle river with half-timbered houses and winetasteries.
Strassenweinfest.Wine-growers and - houses open their doors, wine-tastery. end Sep.
Wein- und Heimatfeste.Traditional wine celebration. last weekend Jul, 1st weekend Aug.

S Elzweiler 16D2

Stellplatz Elzweiler, Hauptstraße. **GPS**: n49,58036 e7,51393.
2 free €1 Ch €1. **Surface:** metalled. 01/01-31/12
Distance: on the spot on the spot on the spot.

S Enkirch 16D1

Wohnmobilplatz an der Mosel, Moselvorgelände, B53. **GPS**: n49,98396 e7,12157.

200 €6 Ch €1,50/day WC €1. **Surface:** grassy.
Easter-31/10
Remarks: Along the Moselle river.

S Ensch 16C2

Reisemobilplatz An den Pappeln, Moselwiesen. **GPS**: n49,82917 e6,83389.

45 €5 €1/10minutes Ch €2. 01/04-31/10
Distance: 200m 300m 500m 100m.
Remarks: Bread-service.

Eppenbrunn 16D3

Im Sportzentrum. **GPS**: n49,11179 e7,56512.
6 free. **Surface:** metalled. 01/01-31/12
Distance: 500m on the spot 1km.
Remarks: Parking sports centre in nature reserve Pfälzer Wald.

S Ernst 16D1

Winzergenossenschaft der Kreises Cochem-Zell, Weingartenstrasse. **GPS**: n50,14339 e7,23237.

30 €8 Ch €5/10h. **Surface:** gravel. 01/01-31/12
Distance: 300m on the spot 200m 100m.

S Ernst 16D1

Mosella Restaurant, Weingatenstrasse. **GPS**: n50,14382 e7,23071.

18 €8 included. **Surface:** grassy.

S Eschbach 17A3

Weingut Wind, Weinstrasse 3-5. **GPS**: n49,17594 e8,02171.
3 €5, free for clients WC included. **Surface:** gravel.
01/01-31/12
Distance: on the spot on the spot 250m.

S Fischbach 16D2

Wohnmobilpark, Marktstraße 1. **GPS**: n49,74046 e7,40444.

50 €6,50/night Ch (40x)€2. **Surface:** grassy. 01/01-31/12
Distance: 800m on the spot 1,5km.
Remarks: Bread-service.

S Fischbach 16D2

Historisches Kupferbergwerk, Hosenbachstraße. **GPS**: n49,75398 e7,38287.
10 free. **Surface:** gravel. 01/01-31/12
Distance: 1,7km on the spot.
Remarks: Visitors' center former copper mine.

Föckelberg 16D2

Wildpark Potzberg, Auf dem Potzberg. **GPS**: n49,52240 e7,48079.
4 free. **Surface:** asphalted/sand. 01/01-31/12
Distance: 1km.

S Gau-Algesheim 17A1

Reimo Gau-Algesheim, Bingerstrasse 8. **GPS**: n49,96331 e8,01213.

DE

40 € 4/night Ch (40x)€ 2. **Surface:** metalled.
01/01-31/12
Distance: 800m 2,5km 500m 200m.

Gau-Odernheim 17A2

Petersberghalle, Mühlstraße. **GPS:** n49,78528 e8,19575.

3 free. **Surface:** metalled. 01/01-31/12
Distance: 200m 200m.

S Germersheim 17B3

Carnot'sche Mauer, Rüdolf von Habsburgstrasse. **GPS:** n49,22004 e8,37906.

8 € 3/24h € 1/100liter Ch € 1/kWh. **Surface:** grassy.
01/01-31/12

S Gerolstein 16C1

Wohnmobilplatz Gerolstein, Raderstrasse 22. **GPS:** n50,22147 e6,65501.

20 € 10/24h € 1/100liter Ch (12x)€ 1/day.
Surface: grassy/metalled. 01/01-31/12
Distance: nearby.

S Gillenfeld 16C1

Wohnmobilpark Pulvermaar, K14. **GPS:** n50,13294 e6,93218.

30 € 6 € 1/100liter Ch € 0,50/kWh. **Surface:** gravel.
01/01-31/12
Distance: on the spot on the spot 200m 200m 300m.

S Gillenfeld 16C1

Feriendorf Pulvermaar, Vulkanstrasse. **GPS:** n50,13000 e6,93194.

15 € 6, 2 pers.incl. Ch € 1,20/kWh WC . **Surface:** grassy.
01/03-30/11
Distance: 3km on the spot on the spot on the spot 3km.

Gimbsheim 17B2

Schwimbadstrasse. **GPS:** n49,77806 e8,38278.

8 € 4/night. **Surface:** asphalted/grassy. 15/05-15/09
Distance: 500m 300m.

S Gimbsheim 17B2

Weingut Falger-Baier, Alsheimerstrasse 25. **GPS:** n49,77733 e8,36959.
3 € 5 . 01/01-31/12
Distance: 3km Pizzeria 50m 500m.

S Glan-Münchweiler 16D2

Am Bahnhof, Bahnhofstraße. **GPS:** n49,46935 e7,44420.
3 free € 1 Ch € 1/2h. **Surface:** metalled. 01/01-31/12
Distance: 750m 150m on the spot.

S Graach/Mosel 16D1

Wohnmobilpark Sun-Park, Gestade 16a. **GPS:** n49,93267 e7,06035.

350 € 6/day € 1/100liter Ch € 0,60/kWh WC .
Surface: grasstiles.
Distance: 200m on the spot 200m 2km on the spot.

DE

Gundersheim 17A2

Huppert's Wohnmobile Wingert, Untere Grabenstraße 21. **GPS**: n49,69499 e8,20465.

12 € 5 € 2. **Surface:** gravel/sand. 01/01-31/12
Distance: on the spot 300m.
Remarks: Max. 3 nights.

Guntersblum 17B2

Am Sportanlage, Alsheimerstrasse 85. **GPS**: n49,78974 e8,34373.
12 € 5 € 1/80liter Ch € 0,50/kWh. **Surface:** gravel.
01/01-31/12
Distance: 500m 500m 500m.

Hachenburg 9B5

P4 - Burggarten, Alexanderring. **GPS**: n50,66250 e7,82694.

10 free € 1/70liter Ch € 1/6h WC. **Surface:** metalled.
01/01-31/12
Distance: on the spot on the spot 300m.

Hassloch 17B3

Holiday Park, Holiday Parkstrasse. **GPS**: n49,31667 e8,30528.

100 € 5,50 € 0,50 (12x). **Surface:** grassy. 01/04-01/11
Distance: 8km on the spot 8km.

Tourist information Hassloch:
Holiday Park.Attractions park with shows. 01/04-30/09 10h, summer 9h, Oct weekend. € 21.

Hauenstein 17A3

Stellplatz am Deutschen Schumuseum Hauenstein, Turnstrasse. **GPS**: n49,18896 e7,85669.

10 € 7 Ch. **Surface:** gravel. 01/01-31/12
Distance: on the spot 200m 300m.
Remarks: Pay at museum.

Heltersberg 17A3

Am Bergbad, Bergstrasse. **GPS**: n49,31654 e7,70380.
5 free. 01/01-31/12
Distance: 900m.
Remarks: Parking swimming pool.

Herrstein 16D2

Wohnmobilstellplatz Herrstein, Brühlstrasse. **GPS**: n49,77963 e7,33569.

3 free € 1/80liter € 0,50/kWh WC.
Surface: metalled.
01/01-31/12
Distance: 300m on the spot.
Remarks: Max. 48h.

Tourist information Herrstein:
Touristinformation Deutsche Edelsteinstraße, Brühlstrasse 16.Renovated mall half-timbered city.

Herxheim 17A3

Festhalle, Bonifatiusstraße. **GPS**: n49,14463 e8,21656.
8 free Ch. **Surface:** grasstiles. 01/01-31/12

Hillesheim 9A6

Markt- und Messeplatz, Am Viehmarkt. **GPS**: n50,28895 e6,67239.

6 € 4 Ch WC. **Surface:** gravel. 01/01-31/12
Distance: on the spot on the spot.

Hillesheim 9A6

Wohnmobilstellplatz Birkenhof, Birkenhof 1. **GPS**: n50,28639 e6,69083.

DE

4 €5 water and electricity € 2/night free. **Surface:** gravel.

Hillesheim 9A6

Wohnmobile Theres, Prümer Straße 20. **GPS**: n50,28957 e6,66310.

15 €5 Ch included. **Surface:** asphalted. 01/01/31/12

Distance: 750m 750m 750m.

Remarks: Motorhome dealer, accessory shop, repairs.

Hochspeyer 17A2

Am Schwimmbad, Mühlhofstraße. **GPS**: n49,44108 e7,89333.

6 €5 € 1/80liter Ch € 0,50/kWh. **Surface:** asphalted.

01/01-31/12 01/08-15/08.

Distance: 400m 400m bakery.

Hornbach 16D3

Wohnmobilpark Hornbach, Bahnhofstraße. **GPS**: n49,18419 e7,36601.

27 €6 € 1/60liter Ch (12x)€ 2/24h. **Surface:** gravel.

01/01-31/12

Distance: on the spot on the spot.

Idar/Oberstein 16D2

Edelsteinbörse, Hauptstrasse 100. **GPS**: n49,71932 e7,30313.

12 € 6/day, first 24h free € 1/70liter Ch WC. **Surface:** asphalted.

01/01-31/12

Distance: on the spot on the spot 300m.

Tourist information Idar/Oberstein:

Tourist Information, Georg-Maus-strasse 2, www.idar-oberstein.de.City of the gems.

Edelsteinminen des Steinkaulenberges.Gem mine. 15/03-15/11 9-17h.

Deutsches Edelsteinmuseum.Gem museum. 01/05-31/10 9-18h, 01/11-30/04 9-17h.

Jettenbach 16D2

Freizeitgelände Schwimmbad, Austrasse. **GPS**: n49,52919 e7,56453.

6 free Ch . **Surface:** asphalted. 01/01-31/12

Distance: 500m 800m.

Kamp-Bornhofen 16D1

Bistro Rheinufer, Rheinuferstrasse 66 A. **GPS**: n50,22305 e7,61888.

7 €7 € 1 € 1,50 WC. **Surface:** metalled.

01/01-31/12

Distance: on the spot on the spot 300m on the spot.

Remarks: Along the Rhine river, toilets only during opening hours restaurant.

Kandel 17A3

Adams Hof, Rheinzaberner Strasse 1. **GPS**: n49,08902 e8,22194.

30 € 2/night € 2 € 2/12h WC. **Surface:** grassy.

01/01-31/12

Distance: 1,5km on the spot on the spot 1,5km 1,5km.

Kempfeld 16D2

An der Wildenburg, Wildenburgstraße. **GPS**: n49,77588 e7,25423.

3 free. **Surface:** metalled. 01/01-31/12

Distance: 2km.

Kesten 16C1

Wohnmobilpark Kesten/Mosel, Urmetzgasse. **GPS**: n49,90306 e6,96232.

80 € 6/24h € 0,10/10liter Ch € 1,50/24h.

DE

Surface: grassy/metalled. 01/04-02/11
Distance: 300m 10m 300m 1km on the spot.
Remarks: Parking at the Moselle River, bread-service + breakfast-service.

S **Kinheim** 16D1

Am Moselufer, Moselweinstraße, B53. **GPS:** n49,97218 e7,05706.

40 € 6 Ch included. **Surface:** grassy. 01/01-31/12
Distance: 100m 150m.
Remarks: Parking at the Moselle River.

Tourist information Kinheim:
Tourist Information, Moselweinstrasse 14, www.kinheim.de.Wine village with half-timbered houses.
Tag den offenen Weinkeller.Open wine-cellars. 2nd Thu after Whitsuntide.
Wein- und Frülingsfest.Wine and spring celebration. Whitsuntide.
Winzerfest.Wine festival. 2nd weekend sep.

S **Kirchheimbolanden** 17A2

Messeplatz, Hitzfeldstrasse. **GPS**: n49,66667 e8,01501.

20 free € 1/70liter Ch € 0,50. **Surface:** metalled. 01/01-31/12
2nd weekend May-Aug-Oct.
Distance: 300m 300m on the spot.

S **Klüsserath** 16C2

Reisemobilpark Klüsserath, B53. **GPS:** n49,84316 e6,85437.

400 € 5,50 € 1/90liter Ch € 1,50. **Surface:** grassy.
Easter-31/10
Remarks: Along the Moselle river.

S **Kobern** 9B6

B416, Kobern-Gondorf. **GPS:** n50,30524 e7,46064.

30 € 5 € 1 Ch. **Surface:** metalled.

S **Köwerich** 16C2

Weingut Hans Klären-Maringer 'Off'm Herrach', Beethovenstrasse 40. **GPS:** n49,84169 e6,86242.

20 € 6 Ch € 0,50/kWh WC € 1. **Surface:** grassy.
01/01-31/12
Distance: 500m 500m 500m on the spot 2km 100m.
Remarks: Bread-service.

S **Kusel** 16D2

Parkplatz der Tuchfabriken, Trierer Straße 61. **GPS:** n49,54016 e7,39626.

3 free . **Surface:** asphalted. 01/04-31/10
Distance: 500m 300m.
Remarks: Max. 3 days, key service at Touristinformation (300m).

S **Landau** 17A3

Wellnessoase La Ola, Horstring 2. **GPS:** n49,20230 e8,14270.
5 € 10/24h € 4 Ch included. **Surface:** metalled.
01/01-31/12
Distance: 3km 500m.

S **Landstuhl** 16D3

Bahnstraße. **GPS:** n49,41595 e7,57092.
2 free Ch free. **Surface:** asphalted. 01/01-31/12
Distance: on the spot 1,3km 350m Aldi 100m.

S **Lauterecken** 16D2

Wohnmobilstellplatz Villa Toskana, Friedhofweg 3a. **GPS:** n49,65056 e7,58806.

DE

30 € 8 € 1/80liter Ch (18x)€ 1/8h. **Surface:** grassy/gravel.
01/01-31/12
Distance: 300m on the spot 100m.
Remarks: Bread-service.

Leimersheim 17B3

Sport- und Freizeithalle, Rheinstraße 42. **GPS**: n49,12534 e8,35457.
4 free. **Surface:** gravel. 01/01-31/12
Distance: 500m.

Leiwen 16C2

Moselblick, Flurgartenstrasse 2/ Weinallee. **GPS**: n49,82580 e6,88148.

15 € 7,50 Ch WC € 1 **Surface:** grassy.
Distance: on the spot on the spot 300m 500m.

Lemberg 17A3

Lemberger Weiher, Weiherstraße. **GPS**: n49,17284 e7,64731.
5 free. **Location:** Rural. **Surface:** grasstiles. 01/01-31/12
Distance: 600m on the spot on the spot.

Linz am Rhein 9B6

B42. **GPS**: n50,56291 e7,27982.

6 free. **Surface:** asphalted. 01/01-31/12
Distance: on the spot 50m.

Löf 9B6

SOG Dahmann, In der Mark 2. **GPS**: n50,23194 e7,43750.

9 free Ch (4x) WC. **Surface:** metalled. 01/01-31/12

Longuich/Mosel 16C2

Feiten, Rioler weg 2. **GPS**: n49,80288 e6,77894.

30 € 5 € 0,50/60liter Ch € 2 WC € 1. **Surface:** grassy.
01/01-31/12
Distance: 300m on the spot on the spot on the spot 1km.

Longuich/Mosel 16C2

WeinKulturgut Longen Schlöder, Kirchenweg 9. **GPS**: n49,81023 e6,76496.

8 € 5 € 1 (3x)€ 1,50 WC € 2. **Surface:** metalled. 01/01-31/12
Tue.
Distance: on the spot 500m.

Losheim am See 16C2

Reisemobilplatz am Stausee, Zum Stausee. **GPS**: n49,51999 e6,74123.

20 € 5 Ch WC included. **Surface:** asphalted/grassy.
01/01-31/12
Distance: 1km 100m 1km.
Remarks: Parking at lake, in front of Tourist-Information, incl. use sanitary and service on campsite 1km.

Lösnich 16D1

Stellplatz am Moselufer, Gestade. **GPS**: n49,97560 e7,04276.

96 € 6 Ch included € 1,50. **Surface:** grassy. 01/03-01/11
Distance: 3km.
Remarks: Along ther Moselle river, baker every morning.

Lutzerath 16C1

Trierer Strasse. **GPS**: n50,13015 e7,01002.

10 € 5/day € 0,50 Ch (6x)€ 0,50/kWh. **Surface:** asphalted.
01/01-31/12
Remarks: Check in at Hotel Restaurant Maas, Trierer Str. 30.

DE

Maikammer 17A3

Sporthalle Kalmit, Johannes Dammstrasse. **GPS**: n49,30307 e8,13219.

€ 4/day included. **Surface:** asphalted. 01/01-31/12

Distance: 100m nearby nearby.

Maikammer 17A3

Weingut Schädler, Dieterwiesenstraße. **GPS**: n49,30848 e8,12530.

3 € 7 WC included.

Distance: 500m 1km on the spot on the spot.

Maikammer 17A3

Weingut Hubert Müller, Raiffeisenstrasse 59. **GPS**: n49,30737 e8,13646.

3 € 10. **Surface:** gravel.

Distance: on the spot.

Manderscheid 16C1

Campingplatz Vulkaneifel, Herbstwiese. **GPS**: n50,09650 e6,80159.

8 € 6/pp, dog € 1,50 € 0,50/100liter Ch € 2,50 WC.

Surface: metalled. 15/03-31/10

Distance: 800m 800m 800m on camp site.

Manderscheid 16C1

Hotel Heidsmühle, Mosenbergstrasse 22. **GPS**: n50,08504 e6,80021.

20 free € 2,50. **Surface:** unpaved. 01/01-31/12

Mayen 9B6

Wohnmobilstellplatz am Viehmarkt, Polcherstrasse. **GPS**: n50,32194 e7,22806.

6 free € 1/80liter Ch WC. **Surface:** grassy. 01/01-31/12

Distance: 100m 100m 100m.

Mayschoss 9A6

Ahruferplatz, Am Bahnhof. **GPS**: n50,51736 e7,01948.

75 € 5,50 € 0,50/100liter Ch WC. **Surface:** metalled.

01/01-31/12

Distance: on the spot 100m on the spot 50m.

Remarks: Parking at station, along the Ahr.

Meckenheim 17A3

Wohnmobilstellplatz Meckenheim, Rödersheimerstraße. **GPS**: n49,41167 e8,24056.

6 free € 0,50/kWh. **Surface:** gravel.

Distance: 1km.

Mehring 16C2

Weingut Zellerhof, Zellerhof 1. **GPS**: n49,79395 e6,81987.

41 € 6 € 0,50/70liter Ch € 0,50/kWh WC € 1,50.

Surface: grassy/metalled. 01/01-31/12

Distance: 100m on the spot on the spot on the spot 100m.

Mehring 16C2

Wohnmobilstellplatz del Mosel, Moselweinstrasse 1. **GPS**: n49,79423 e6,81976.

60 € 5, 2 pers.incl € 0,50/100liter Ch € 2 WC € 1. **Surface:** grassy.

01/01-31/12

Distance: 100m on the spot 200m.

Meisenheim 17A2

Schwimmbad Meisenheim, In der Heimbach. **GPS**: n49,71472 e7,65750.

12 € 5 € 1/4minutes Ch (12x)€ 1/kWh. **Surface:** gravel.

01/01-31/12

DE

Distance: 1,6km on the spot 500m.

Mendig 9B6

Vulkanmuseum Lava-Dome, Brauerstraße 7–9. **GPS**: n50,37955 e7,28631.
20 free € 1 Ch (8x)€ 0,50/kWh. **Surface:** gravel.
01/01-31/12
Distance: Vulkanbrauhaus&Felsenkeller.

Merzig 16C3

Yachthafen Merzig, Saarwiesenring 10. **GPS**: n49,44205 e6,63566.

15 € 7 Ch € 0,50/kWh WC. **Surface:** metalled.
01/04-31/10
Distance: 1km on the spot 800m.

Merzig 16C3

Das Bad, Saarwiesenring 3. **GPS**: n49,44470 e6,62769.

12 € 6,50 € 1/100liter Ch € 1 included. **Surface:** grassy/gravel.
01/01-31/12
Distance: 2km on the spot 2km.
Remarks: Check in at swimming pool, caution key € 50.

Mettlach 16C2

Cloef-Atrium, An der Cloef, Mettlach-Orscholz. **GPS**: n49,50394 e6,53225.

€ 5 WC. **Surface:** gravel.
Remarks: Max. 24h.

Mettlach 16C2

Mettlacher Abtei-Bräu, Bahnhofstrasse 32. **GPS**: n49,49484 e6,59804.

€ 5 Chfree. **Surface:** gravel. 01/01-31/12
Distance: 500m on the spot.

Tourist information Mettlach:
Erlebniszentrum Villeroy&Boch. Mo-Fr: 9.30-19h, Sa 9.30-18h.
Villeroy&Boch Outletcenter, Freiherr-vom-Stein-Strasse 4-6. Mo-Fr: 9.30-19h, Sa 9.30-18h.

Minheim 16C1

Reisemobilpark Minheim. GPS: n49,86500 e6,94111.

88 € 6,50 € 1/100liter Ch € 1,50. **Surface:** grassy/gravel.
01/01-31/12
Remarks: Along the Moselle river, next to football ground.

Morbach 16D2

Reisemobilhafen Morbach, Zum Camping 15, Hoxel. **GPS**: n49,77855 e7,10695.

40 € 5/night € 1/80liter Ch (40x)€ 2/night. **Surface:** grassy.
16/03-15/11
Distance: 300m 300m.

Mülheim/Mosel 16C1

Weingut Mauch-Michels, Mühlenweg 4. **GPS**: n49,91058 e7,00640.
3 € 7,50 WC. **Surface:** metalled. 01/01-31/12
Distance: 2km on the spot 500m.

Neef 16D1

Wohnmobilstellplatz Zum Frauenberg. GPS: n50,09455 e7,13730.

50 € 6 Ch (42x)€ 2/24h,4Amp. **Surface:** grassy.
Easter-15/10
Remarks: Along the Moselle river, nearby sports fields.

Neuhäusel 9B6

Wohnmobilstellplatz Efferz, Im Feldchen. **GPS**: n50,38271 e7,70331.

DE

20 € 8 € 1 Ch (12x)€ 1/2kWh WC . **Surface:** metalled. 01/01-31/12
Distance: 250m 250m 250m 100m > Koblenz.
Remarks: Bread-service.

S Neumagen-Dhron 16C1

Yachthafen Neumagen, Moselstrasse 21. **GPS**: n49,85357 e6,89373.

30 <9m € 6, >9m € 8 + € 2,50/pp Ch € 0,60/kWh WC included € 3/24h. **Surface:** gravel. 01/01-31/12
Distance: 100m on the spot on the spot on the spot 1,3km.
Remarks: Check in at harbourmaster.

S Neumagen-Dhron 16C1

Gaststatte Beim Ketsch, Brückenstrasse 14/ In der Zeil. **GPS**: n49,86449 e6,90321.

100 € 5 € 1,50/3kWh WC € 2,50. 01/01-31/12
Distance: 200m on the spot 500m.
Remarks: Bread-service.

S Neunkirchen/Saar 16D3

Prießnitz, Zweibrücker Straße 148. **GPS**: n49,32766 e7,19375.

20 € 14 € 2,50 Ch WC included. **Surface:** grassy. 01/03-31/10
Distance: 3km 1,7km 1,4km.
Remarks: Next to campsite.

S Neustadt/Weinstrasse 17A3

Dammstrasse-Ost, Hambach. **GPS**: n49,33083 e8,13139.

20 free € 1 € 1 Ch. **Surface:** grassy. 01/01-31/12
Distance: nearby nearby nearby.

S Neustadt/Weinstrasse 17A3

Reisemobilstellpatz Stadtzentrum, Martin-Luther-Strasse. **GPS**: n49,35485 e8,15255.

30 € 4/24h Ch included (8x)€ 1/2kWh. **Surface:** asphalted. 01/01-31/12
Distance: 300m 250m Aldimarkt 50m.

Neustadt/Weinstrasse 17A3

Parkplatz am Rebenmeer, Am Falltor, Duttweiler. **GPS**: n49,30148 e8,21192.
10 free. **Surface:** metalled. 01/01-31/12

S Neustadt/Weinstrasse 17A3

Weingut Schäfer, Schiessmauer 56, Mussbach. **GPS**: n49,36335 e8,17111.

5 € 6 Ch € 4. 01/01-31/12
Remarks: Reservation recommended: 0 63 27 21 55.

Neustadt/Weinstrasse 17A3

Weingut Andres, Langensteinstrasse 22, Lachen-Speyersdorf. **GPS**: n49,33631 e8,20579.
3 free.

S Neustadt/Weinstrasse 17A3

Esso-Tankstelle, Martin-Luther-Strasse. **GPS**: n49,35948 e8,15160.
Ch free. 01/01-31/12

S Neuwied 9B6

Yachthafen Neuwied, Rheinstrasse 180. **GPS**: n50,43415 e7,47685.

30 € 7, 2 pers.incl. Ch € 0,50/kWh WC . **Surface:** metalled.

DE

01/01-31/12
Distance: 2km on the spot 2km.

S Niederkirchen bei Deidesheim 17A3

Wohnmobilstellplatz Niederkirchen, An de Sportanlage 1. **GPS**: n49,40891 e8,22141.
6 free € 1. **Surface:** gravel. 01/01-31/12
Distance: 1km.

Nohfelden 16D2

P3 Surferbasis, Gonnesweiler. **GPS**: n49,57010 e7,08410.

50 € 8. **Surface:** grassy. 01/01-31/12
Distance: 500m 3km.

S Nohfelden 16D2

Campingplatz Bostalsee, L325, Bosen. **GPS**: n49,56039 e7,06113.

10 € 8/24h € 0,50/50liter Ch € 1/2kWh. **Surface:** metalled.
01/01-31/12
Distance: 500m 200m on the spot 800m.

Nonnweiler 16C1

Stellplatz Am Hallenbad, Triererstrasse 2. **GPS**: n49,97225 e6,97186.

5 free. **Surface:** grassy/metalled. 01/01-31/12
Distance: on the spot on the spot 800m.
Remarks: Parking swimming pool, max. 48h.

S Ober-Hilbersheim 17A1

Napoleonshöhe, Sprendlingers Straße. **GPS**: n49,89785 e8,02421.

40 free Ch. **Surface:** grassy. 01/01-31/12
Distance: 300m.

S Ober-Olm 17A1

Wohnmobilplatz Mainz, Draiser Straße. **GPS**: n49,94298 e8,19237.
25 € 10 Ch included. **Surface:** grasstiles. 01/01-31/12
Distance: 3,8km 500m.

S Oberbrombach 16D2

Wohnmobilstellplatz Höhenblick, Sonnenberger Strasse. **GPS**: n49,69481 e7,25960.
30 € 7 Ch (20x)€ 2/24h. **Surface:** grassy/gravel.
01/01-31/12
Distance: 400m 600m.

S Oberwesel/Rhein 17A1

Camping Schönburgblick, Am Hafendamm / B9. **GPS**: n50,10294 e7,73663.

20 € 8,50/24h € 0,50/kWh WC € 2 € 2. **Surface:** grassy.
15/03-31/10
Distance: 800m on the spot on the spot on the spot 200m 400m.

S Oppenheim 17B1

Womoland Oppenheim, An der Festwiese. **GPS**: n49,85673 e8,36502.

20 € 7 € 1/50liter € 1 Ch € 3/24h. **Surface:** grassy.
01/01-31/12 week before/after Whitsuntide.
Distance: 500m 500m 500m.

S Osthofen 17B2

Festplatz Wonnegauhalle, Wonnegaustrasse. **GPS**: n49,69913 e8,32691.

50 free Chfree. **Surface:** gravel. 01/01-31/12
Distance: 500m 500m.

Osthofen 17B2

Sommerried Stadion, L439. **GPS**: n49,69222 e8,32805.

DE

10 free. **Surface:** grassy/sand. 01/01-31/12
Distance: 800m.
Remarks: Max. 48h.

S Osthofen 17B2
Weingut Borntaler Hof, Alter Westhofer Weg. **GPS**: n49,69985 e8,29860.

4 € 5 WC included. **Surface:** metalled. 01/01-31/12

S Ottweiler 16D3
Stellplatz Wingertsweiher, Am Wingertsweiher. **GPS**: n49,41250 e7,18083.

12 € 5/24h € 1/150liter € 1 Ch (6x)€ 3/8h. **Surface:** grassy/metalled. 01/01-31/12
Distance: 1,5km on the spot on the spot on the spot 1,5km 1km.
Remarks: Max. 7 days.

Tourist information Ottweiler:
Tourist-Information Ottweiler, Schloßhof 5, www.ottweiler.de.

S Palzem 16B2
Weingut E. Pauly, Obermoselstrasse 5. **GPS**: n49,56402 e6,37581.

5 € 7,50, free for clients WC. **Surface:** metalled.
01/01-31/12
Distance: 50m 4km.
Remarks: Not suitable for big motorhomes.

S Perl 16C2
Auf dem Sabel. **GPS**: n49,47906 e6,38508.

6 € 8, payment with SMS Ch € 2/8h. **Surface:** metalled.
01/01-31/12
Distance: 500m 3,5km 500m 500m.

S Piesport 16C1
Piesporter Goldtröpfchen, Moselstrasse. **GPS**: n49,87199 e6,92703.

30 € 6 € 1/80liter Ch € 1,50. **Surface:** gravel. 01/01-31/12
Distance: 100m on the spot on the spot on the spot 500m.
Remarks: Bread-service mo-sa.

S Piesport 16C1
Weingut Spang, Reisemobilplatz Rebengarten, In den Dur 11. **GPS**: n49,88282 e6,92669.

4 € 6/pp, guests free € 0,50/kWh WC . **Surface:** gravel.
01/01-31/12
Distance: on the spot 100m 100m 500m 500m.
Remarks: Bread-service.

S Piesport 16C1
Wohnmobilstellplatz Loreleyblick, Loreleyblick 20. **GPS**: n49,87380 e6,92535.

5 € 6 Ch (5x) € 1. **Surface:** gravel. 01/01-31/12
Distance: on the spot 1km 300m.

S Pirmasens 16D3
Am Messegelände, Zeppelinstraße. **GPS**: n49,20446 e7,60885.
8 € 5/24h € 1/100liter Ch € 1/6h. **Surface:** gravel.
01/01-31/12
Distance: 450m 6km 450m 450m.

DE

Polch 9B6

Niesmann&Bisschof, Clou-strasse 1. **GPS**: n50,30680 e7,30684.

25 free € 0,50/kWh. 01/01-31/12

Distance: on the spot on the spot.

Pronsfeld 16B1

Am Alten Bahnhof, Bahnhofstrasse. **GPS**: n50,16336 e6,33733.

50 € 5 € 0,50/60liter Ch € 0,50/kWh. **Surface:** gravel.
01/01-31/12

Distance: 600m 600m 700m 500m.

Pünderich 16D1

Wohnmobilstellplatz Pünderich. **GPS**: n50,04355 e7,12548.

40 € 6 Ch (12x)€ 1,50/24h. **Surface:** grassy.
01/04-31/10

Distance: on the spot on the spot on the spot 300m 500m.

Reil/Mosel 16D1

Am Moselufer, Moselstrasse. **GPS**: n50,02566 e7,11493.

70 € 6 Chfree (36x)€ 1,50. **Surface:** grassy. 01/03-31/10

Distance: 500m 450m.

Remarks: Along the Moselle river.

Reipoltskirchen 17A2

Wasserburg, Kegelbahnstrasse. **GPS**: n49,63448 e7,66373.

7 free € 1/4minutes Ch € 1/12h. **Surface:** metalled.
01/01-31/12

Distance: 150m on the spot bakery 100m.

Reipoltskirchen 17A2

Stellplatz Ausbacherhof, K42, Ausbacherhof. **GPS**: n49,61210 e7,65630.

4 free. **Surface:** gravel. 01/01-31/12

Remagen 9B6

Wohnmobilhafen Goldene Meile, Simrockweg 9–13. **GPS**: n50,57583 e7,25111.
15 € 12 € 1/90liter Ch € 1/6h. **Surface:** grassy.
01/01-31/12

Rheinbreitbach 9A6

Wohnmobilstellplatz Siebengebirgsblick, Rolandsecker Weg 8. **GPS**: n50,62193 e7,22812.
12 € 8 € 1 Ch € 1/2kWh. **Surface:** grassy/gravel.
01/01-31/12

Distance: 500m.

Rhodt unter Rietburg 17A3

Rhodt, Edesheimerstrasse, L506. **GPS**: n49,26926 e8,10974.

6 € 4. **Surface:** asphalted. 01/01-31/12

Distance: nearby nearby nearby.

Rhodt unter Rietburg 17A3

Fader Kastanienhof, L506. **GPS**: n49,26921 e8,10997.

12 € 10 Ch. **Surface:** gravel. 01/01-31/12

Distance: on the spot on the spot on the spot.

Remarks: Sep-Oct on reservation.

DE

S Rockenhausen 17A2

Reisemobilhafen Rockenhausen, Obermühle. **GPS**: n49,62136 e7,82146.
5 free € 1/80liter Ch € 1/6h. **Surface:** gravel.
01/01-31/12
Distance: 800m on the spot.
Remarks: At swimming pool.

S Saarbrücken 16C3

Reisemobilhafen Calypso, Deutschmühlental 7. **GPS**: n49,23027 e6,96222.

30 € 6 + reduction swimming pool Ch € 1/24h.
Surface: metalled. 01/01-31/12
Distance: on the spot on the spot 500m.
Remarks: To pay at swimming pool.

Tourist information Saarbrücken:
Tourist Information, Reichsstrasse 1 - Saar Galerie, www.die-region-saarbruecken.de.

S Saarburg 16C2

Reisemobilpark Saarburg, Am Saarufer. **GPS**: n49,60098 e6,55549.

72 € 8 € 1 Ch € 0,50/kWh WC € 10/week.
Distance: 850m 100m.
Remarks: Bread-service.

S Saarlouis 16C3

In den Fliesen, Sankt Nazairer Allee. **GPS**: n49,32146 e6,74267.
30 free Ch. **Surface:** metalled. 01/01-31/12
Remarks: At sports centre, bread-service.

S Sankt Aldegund 16D1

Am Moselstausee. **GPS**: n50,07899 e7,13119.

40 € 6 Ch included € 1,50. **Surface:** grassy/metalled.
01/04-01/12
Distance: 250m.

S Sankt Ingbert 16D3

Reisemobilplatz 'Das Blau', Spieser Landstraße. **GPS**: n49,28652 e7,13194.

8 free € 1/80liter Ch. **Surface:** grassy. 01/01-31/12
Distance: 1,5km 100m 1,7km.
Remarks: Next to parking swimming pool.

S Sankt Julian 16D2

An der Ölmühle, An der Lenschbach. **GPS**: n49,60758 e7,51480.
10 € 5 € 1 Ch € 1/kWh. 01/04-31/10
Distance: on the spot 300m.

Sankt Martin 17A3

Edenkoperstrasse. **GPS**: n49,29702 e8,10838.

19 € 6/day. **Surface:** asphalted. 01/01-31/12
Remarks: Max. 1 night.

Sankt Martin 17A3

Winzer Holger Schneider, Riedweg. **GPS**: n49,29814 e8,10824.

free for clients. **Surface:** gravel.

S Sankt Martin 17A3

Riedweg. **GPS**: n49,29814 e8,10824.
€ 1 Ch.

S Sankt Wendel 16D2

Am Wendelinuspark, Tholeyer Straße. **GPS**: n49,46907 e7,14267.

22 € 5 Ch free. **Surface:** metalled. 01/01-31/12
Distance: 1km on the spot 100m 20m.

S Schiersfeld 17A2

Sulzbachtal, Bismarkstraße. **GPS**: n49,69274 e7,76895.
8-12 free € 1 € 1/4kWh. **Surface:** gravel. 01/01-31/12
Distance: 500m bakery 500m Moscheltalradweg on the spot.

DE

S Schleich 16C2

Zum Moselufer, Kapellenstrasse 13. **GPS**: n49,81335 e6,84228.

6 € 5 Ch € 2 WC. **Surface:** grassy. 01/01-31/12
Distance: on the spot on the spot 200m.

S Schwabenheim/Selz 17A1

Reisemobilstellplatz Schwabenheim, Ingelheimer Straße. **GPS**: n49,93284 e8,09430.

10 free . **Surface:** gravel. 01/01-31/12
Distance: 200m 200m.
Remarks: Max. 72h.

S Schweich/Mosel bei Trier 16C2

Wohnmobilpark zum Fahrturm, Am Yachthafen. **GPS**: n49,81517 e6,75076.

40 < 6M € 11, 2 pers incl., + € 1/M Ch € 0,50/kWh,+ € 1.
Surface: grassy.
Distance: on the spot on the spot on the spot on the spot 50m.

S Simmern/Hunsrück 16D1

Wohnmobilstellplatz Simmern, Gemündener Straß. **GPS**: n49,98011 e7,52283.

3 free . **Surface:** metalled.
Distance: on the spot 250m 200m.

S Sinzig 9A6

Wohnmobilhafen Stellplatz 1 Sportpark, Bäderstrasse. **GPS**: n50,55142 e7,21746.

10 € 4/24h € 1 Ch. **Surface:** gravel. 01/01-31/12

Sinzig 9A6

Sinziger Schloß, Jahnstrasse. **GPS**: n50,54684 e7,24844.

20 free. **Surface:** metalled.
Distance: 100m.

S Sinzig 9A6

Wohnmobilhafen Stellplatz 2 Am Kurgarten, Bäderstrasse. **GPS**: n50,54912 e7,21749.

50 € 4/24h, electricity incl € 1 Ch . **Surface:** metalled.
01/01-31/12
Distance: 50m.

S Speyer 17B3

Techniek Museum Speyer, Geibstrasse. **GPS**: n49,31222 e8,45009.

€ 22 Ch WC included. **Surface:** grassy. 01/01-31/12
Remarks: Bread service, discount museum/theater.

S Speyer 17B3

An den Stadtwerken, Industriestraße 21. **GPS**: n49,30329 e8,44817.
€ 5 € 1 € 1 Ch € 1. **Surface:** asphalted.
Distance: 1,5km.

Tourist information Speyer:
M Technik Museum Speyer/Imax Filmtheater, Geibstrasse. Mo-Fr 9-18h, Sa-Su 9-17h.

S Spirkelbach 17A3

Grillplatz Spirkelbach. **GPS**: n49,19454 e7,88208.
4 € 7 Ch included. **Surface:** gravel. 01/01-31/12
Distance: 500m 500m on the spot on the spot.
Remarks: Nature reserve Pfalzer Wald.

S Sprendlingen 17A1

Wiesbach, Bachgasse/Bleichstrasse. **GPS**: n49,85424 e7,98538.

DE

30 free € 2/10minutes Ch € 2/day. **Surface:** asphalted.
01/01-31/12
Distance: 700m 3,4km 500m.
Remarks: Parking at swimming pool, entrance swimming pool € 2/day.

S Sprendlingen 17A1

Eura Mobil Stellplatz, Graf-von-Sponheimstrasse. **GPS**: n49,86297 e7,97612.

10 free € 1 Ch (10x)free. **Surface:** metalled.
01/01-31/12
Distance: 600m 4,4km 300m.
Remarks: Workdays from 9h guided tours (free).

S Stromberg 17A1

Reisemobilplatz Michels Land, Königsberger Straße. **GPS**: n49,94709 e7,78818.
6 € 5 Ch € 0,50/kWh. **Surface:** unpaved. 01/01-31/12
Distance: 500m 50m Lidl.

S Thalfang 16C2

Festplatz Thalfang, Talstrasse 2. **GPS**: n49,75028 e6,99944.

40 € 5 Ch (6x)free. **Surface:** gravel. 01/01-31/12
Distance: 200m on the spot 200m.
Remarks: Check in at swimming pool, max. 4 nights.

Thallichtenberg 16D2

Burg Lichtenberg, K23. **GPS**: n49,55716 e7,35975.

4 free. **Surface:** asphalted. 01/01-31/12
Distance: 300m 1km.
Remarks: Max. 3 days.

Tholey 16D2

Parkplatz Am Schaumburg, Am Schaumberg. **GPS**: n49,48965 e7,03804.

±20 free. **Surface:** metalled. 01/01-31/12
Distance: 100m.

S Traben-Trarbach 16D1

Rißbacher Straße. **GPS**: n49,96583 e7,10583.

45 € 10 Ch WC included. **Location:** Comfortable.
Surface: grassy. 01/10-31/12
Distance: 2km 1km.
Remarks: Along the Moselle river, entrance/exit between 8-22h.

S Trechtinghausen 17A1

Camping Marienort, Mainzer Straße. **GPS**: n50,00426 e7,85516.
20 € 7 Ch. **Surface:** grassy.
Distance: on the spot.

S Trier 16C2

Reisemobilpark Treviris, In den Moselauen. **GPS**: n49,74092 e6,62502.

120 € 0,10/h 10-18h, € 6/18-10h € 1/100liter Ch (30x)€ 0,50/kWh WC € 1. **Surface:** grasstiles.
01/01-31/12
Distance: on the spot.
Remarks: Along the river Moselle.

Tourist information Trier:

Tourist Information, An der Porta Nigra, www.trier.de.Old Roman city with the best kept and also largest Roman gate in Europe: Porta Nigra.

Triercard.Free city bus and discount at museums, boat trips, swimming pool etc. € 9 family card € 15 3 days.

S Trittenheim 16C2

Moselpromenade, Moselstrasse. **GPS**: n49,82436 e6,90295.

DE

50 €5 €0,50/100liter Ch (30x)€2,50/24h. **Surface:** metalled.
01/01-31/12
Distance: 500m on the spot on the spot 300m 400m.
Remarks: Bread-service.

S Unkel 9A6
P3, Parkplatz Hallenbad, Kamenerstrasse. **GPS:** n50,59776 e7,21962.

6 free €1/80liter Ch WC. **Surface:** asphalted. 01/01-31/12
Distance: 100m 100m 150m.

S Urmitz/Rhein 9B6
Wohnmobilhafen am Rhein, Kaltenengerser Straße 3. **GPS:** n50,41716 e7,52506.
15 €5 Ch . **Surface:** metalled. 01/01-31/12
Distance: on the spot 350m 300m.
Remarks: Along the Rhine river.

S Ürzig 16C1
Panorama-Mobilstellplatz Ürzig, Moselufer B53. **GPS:** n49,97870 e7,00768.

25 €8 Ch €1,50/day. **Surface:** grassy. 01/04-31/10
Distance: bakery 150m.
Remarks: Along the Moselle river.

S Vallendar 9B6
Rheinufer. **GPS:** n50,39749 e7,61277.
3 free Ch. **Surface:** metalled. 01/01-31/12
Distance: centre 500m 200m Aldi 200m.
Remarks: Along railwayline.

Valwig 16D1
Moselweinstrasse. **GPS:** n50,14271 e7,21292.

40 €5. **Surface:** grassy.
Distance: 100m on the spot 100m.

S Veldenz 16D1
Wohnmobilpark Veldenz, Hauptstrasse, K88. **GPS:** n49,89222 e7,01944.

40 €6 Ch (24x)included €2. **Surface:** grassy.
01/01-31/12
Distance: 300m 300m 300m 200m.

S Völklingen 16C3
Weltkulturerbe Völklinger Hütte, Rathausstraße. **GPS:** n49,24730 e6,84492.
5 free Ch . **Surface:** asphalted.
01/01-31/12
Distance: 1,1km 400m 850m.

S Wadern 16C2
An der Stadthalle. GPS: n49,54377 e6,89465.

10 free €1,50/day. **Surface:** metalled. 01/01-31/12
Distance: on the spot 3km on the spot 100m.
Remarks: Parking in centre.

Wadern 16C2
Noswendeler See, Noswendel. **GPS:** n49,53906 e6,88992.

5 free. 01/01-31/12
Distance: on the spot on the spot on the spot 3km.

Wadern 16C2
Zum Wiesental, Nunkirchen. **GPS:** n49,48905 e6,83679.

DE

5 free. 01/01-31/12
Distance: on the spot on the spot on the spot.

Wadern 16C2

Hotel Pension Steil, Schlossstrasse, Lockweiler. **GPS**: n49,52765 e6,90158.

4 guests free. **Surface:** metalled. 01/01-31/12
Distance: 1km on the spot 500m.

Wadern 16C2

Hotel Restaurant Reidelbacher Hof, Reidelbach 6, Reidelbach. **GPS**: n49,57694 e6,86056.
5 € 5, guests free. 01/01-31/12
Distance: 3km on the spot 3km.

Tourist information Wadern:

Tourist Information, Marktplatz 13, www.wadern.de.Nature reserve Saar Hunsrück, many signposted cycle and hiking routes.

Schloß Dagstuhl.

Weiherhof, Nunkirchen.Golf court, 9 holes. Sunday 10-12 Schnuppergolf, free try-out.

Waldalgesheim 17A1

An der Keltenhalle, Niedergasse. **GPS**: n49,95371 e7,83614.

25 € 4/night € 1 Ch € 2/6h. **Surface:** metalled.
01/01-31/12
Distance: 500m.

Waldfischbach-Burgalben 17A3

In den Bruchwiesen, Carentaner Platz. **GPS**: n49,28155 e7,64772.

6 free € 1/80liter Ch € 1/8h. **Surface:** asphalted.
01/01-31/12
Distance: 600m 100m.

Waldfischbach-Burgalben 17A3

Camping Clausensee. GPS: n49,27562 e7,72125.
10 € 15,50-19,50 Ch . **Surface:** grasstiles. 01/01-31/12
Distance: 8km on the spot on the spot.

Waxweiler 16B1

Wohnmobilplatz Waxweiler, Bahnhofstrasse. **GPS**: n50,09401 e6,35669.

20 € 5 € 1 Ch € 2. **Surface:** metalled. 01/01-31/12
Distance: on the spot 100m 500m.

Weiskirchen 16C2

Am Kurpark, Burgstrasse. **GPS**: n49,55868 e6,81810.

6 € 1,40/pp € 0,50 € 0,50 Ch € 0,50. **Surface:** metalled.
01/01-31/12
Distance: on the spot 500m 300m.
Remarks: Parking at the health resort, max. 2-3 days.

Westhofen 17A2

Parkplatz Nickelgarten, Am Nickelgarten. **GPS**: n49,70559 e8,24672.

15 free (12x)€ 1/8h. **Surface:** metalled. 01/01-31/12
Distance: 100m 4km 100m.
Remarks: Max. 3 days.

Westhofen 17A2

Weingut Dreihornmühle, An der Brennerei. **GPS**: n49,70375 e8,25288.

3 € 5, guests free € 1/day. **Surface:** grassy. 01/01-31/12
Distance: 600m 600m 150m.

DE

Westhofen 17A2

Tankstelle Raiffeisen. **GPS**: n49,70039 e8,24699.
Ch. 01/01-31/12
Remarks: Coins at petrol station.

Wintrich 16C1

Mosel Stellplatz Wintrich, Moselstrasse. **GPS**: n49,88417 e6,94833.

90 € 8 € 1/100liter Ch (90x)included WC € 1 free.
Surface: grassy/metalled. 01/01-31/12
Distance: 100m on the spot on the spot 100m bakery 300m.

Wintrich 16C1

Weingut Clemens, Kurfürstenstrasse 11. **GPS**: n49,89000 e6,95416.

10 € 5 € 2 Ch € 2. **Surface:** metalled. 01/01-31/12
Distance: on the spot on the spot 1km.

Wittlich 16C1

Zweibächen, Hasenmühlenweg. **GPS**: n49,99470 e6,87595.

30 € 5/24h € 1/80liter Ch. **Surface:** grassy. 01/01-31/12
Distance: 1km 1km 1km.
Remarks: Max. 3 days.

Worms 17B2

Wohnmobilhafen, Kastanienallee. **GPS**: n49,63458 e8,37513.

30 € 4/24h Ch .
Surface: gravel.
01/01-31/12
Distance: 15 min walking Rhine promenade 300m 500m
on the spot.

Remarks: Along river, service at Gaststätte Hagenbräu 300m from the parking.

Tourist information Worms:
Tourist Info, Neumarkt 14, www.worms.de.City with several curiosities, wine-city, Liebfrauenmilch.
Raschi-Haus, Hintere Judengasse 6.Jewish history, cemetery and synagogue.
Tue-Su 10-12.30h, 13.30-17/16.30h.
Gasthaus Brauerei Hagenbräu, Am Rhein 3.Restaurant with its own brewery.

Zell/Mosel 16D1

Wohnmobilstellplatz Römerquelle, Am Freizeitzentrum, Kaimt. **GPS**: n50,01632 e7,17662.

70 € 6 € 0,50/90liter Ch. **Surface:** grassy/metalled. 01/01-31/12
Distance: 1km on the spot on the spot 500m 1km.
Remarks: Along the Moselle river, bread-service.

Zell/Mosel 16D1

Am Fussgängerbrücke. **GPS**: n50,02729 e7,17811.

23 € 6 € 0,50/90liter Ch. **Surface:** asphalted. Easter-31/10
Distance: 300m on the spot on the spot 200m 300m.

Zweibrücken 16D3

Eitel's Wohnmobil-Stellplatz, Californiastraße. **GPS**: n49,26477 e7,36112.
25 € 7 € 0,50 Ch included. **Surface:** asphalted. 01/01-31/12
Distance: 100m.

Hesse

Aarbergen 9C6

Hauptstraße 58, Michelbach. **GPS**: n50,23093 e8,05926.
10 free. **Surface:** metalled.

Alsfeld 10A5

Erlenstadion, Fulder Weg. **GPS**: n50,74882 e9,27882.

10 free € 0,50 € 0,50 Ch. **Surface:** grasstiles.
Distance: 200m 1,8km.

Alsfeld 10A5

Hotel zum Schaferhof, A20 dir Eudorf. **GPS**: n50,76742 e9,29048.

DE

20 free. **Surface:** metalled. 01/01-31/12
Distance: on the spot on the spot.

S Alsfeld 10A5

Fina-tankstelle, Pfefferhöhe. **GPS:** n50,73366 e9,24128.

5 free € 0,50 € 0,50 WC € 2,50. **Surface:** metalled.
01/01-31/12
Distance: on the spot.

S Bad Arolsen 9D3

Reisemobilhafen Twistesee, Bericher Seeweg 1, Wetterburg. **GPS:** n51,38396 e9,06546.

100 € 8,50, tourist tax incl € 1/100liter Ch (100x)€ 1/2kWh WC € 1/5minutes. **Location:** Rural, comfortable, isolated.
Surface: grassy/gravel.
01/01-31/12
Distance: on the spot on the spot 1,5km on the spot on the spot.
Remarks: Directly at the lake, dogs beach, bread service.

S Bad Emstal 10A4

Erzeberg, Birkenstraße, Balhorn. **GPS:** n51,26927 e9,25147.
20 € 9, 4 pers incl., 1 pers + € 4 Ch € 0,50 included.
Surface: metalled. 01/01-31/12
Distance: 100m.
Remarks: Check in at swimming pool, use pool incl.

S Bad Emstal 10A4

Am Mineral-Thermalbad, Karlsbader Straße 4, Sand. **GPS:** n51,24858 e9,24952.

8 € 7, tourist tax incl € 1/100liter Ch (12x)€ 1/1kWh.
Location: Comfortable. **Surface:** gravel/metalled. 01/01-31/12
Distance: 1km on the spot on the spot on the spot.

S Bad Endbach 9C5

Kultur-, Sport- und Freizeitzentrum, Zur Kurmittelhaus. **GPS:** n50,75669 e8,47875.

18 € 5 Ch WC . 01/01-31/12
Distance: 1km on the spot 100m.
Remarks: Excl. tourist tax, service: Kläranlage, 2km, Mo/Thu 7-16h, Fri 7-12.30h, Sa/Su 8-10h.

S Bad Hersfeld 10A5

Acqua-fit, Kolpingstrasse 6. **GPS:** n50,86771 e9,72951.
20 € 3 Ch . **Surface:** metalled. 01/01-31/12
Distance: 2km.
Remarks: Swimming pool.

S Bad Hersfeld 10A5

Geistalbad, Am Schwimmbad. **GPS:** n50,87485 e9,70025.

20 € 5 € 1/80liter Ch (6x)€ 0,50/kWh. **Surface:** asphalted/metalled. 01/01-31/12
Distance: 50m 3,9km.
Remarks: Parking swimming pool.

Bad Hersfeld 10A5

Auf der Unteraue. **GPS:** n50,86231 e9,70340.

3 free. **Surface:** metalled. 01/01-31/12
Remarks: At tennis-court.

Bad Hersfeld 10A5

Waldhotel Glimmesmühle, Hombergerstrasse. **GPS:** n50,88420 e9,66984.

DE

10 free with a meal. **Surface:** metalled.
01/01-31/12
Distance: on the spot.

Tourist information Bad Hersfeld:
Tourist Information, Am Markt 1, www.bad-hersfeld.de/touristik.Medieval health resort and festival city on the Fulda river.
Lullusfest.Traditional folk festival for the honour of the founder of the city.
week 16/10.

S Bad Karlshafen 10A3

Am Rechten Weserufer, Am rechten Weserufer 2. **GPS**: n51,64508 e9,44953.

12 € 11 Ch (12x)€ 1/2kWh. **Location:** Central.
Surface: grasstiles/grassy. 01/01-31/12
Distance: on the spot on the spot on the spot on the spot on the spot on the spot.
Remarks: Max. 4 days.

Bad Nauheim 9D6

Usa-Wellenbad, Friedberger Strasse 16-20. **GPS**: n50,35352 e8,74305.

40 € 5. 01/01-31/12
Distance: 1km on the spot 300m on the spot.
Remarks: Check in at Wellenbad, 8-20h.

S Bad Orb 10A6

Am Busbahnhof, Austraße. **GPS**: n50,23014 e9,34659.
4 € 6 Ch . **Surface:** metalled. 01/01-31/12
Distance: 450m 300m.

S Bad Salzschlirf 10A5

Riedstrasse. **GPS**: n50,62090 e9,50304.

3 free € 1 Ch. **Surface:** asphalted.
01/01-31/12
Distance: 100m.

Tourist information Bad Salzschlirf:
Kur und Tourismus GmbH Bad Salzschlirf, Bahnhofstr. 22, www.bad-salzschlirf.de.Health resort.

S Bad Schwalbach 17A1

Am Kurpark, Reitallee 21. **GPS**: n50,13988 e8,06362.
4 free € 0,50/50liter Ch € 0,50/kWh. **Surface:** metalled. 01/01-31/12
Distance: 500m 400m.

S Bad Soden-Salmünster 10A6

Wohnmobilplatz am Kurpark, Parkstraße, Bad Soden. **GPS**: n50,28544 e9,35917.

30 € 5 € 1/70liter Ch € 1/2kWh. **Surface:** metalled.
01/01-31/12
Distance: on the spot on the spot on the spot.
Remarks: To pay at pay-desk of theTherme.

S Bad Sooden-Allendorf 10B4

Reisemobilhafen Franzrasen, Am Alten Festplatz, Allendorf. **GPS**: n51,27149 e9,97209.

100 € 5 Kurtaxe 1 pers. incl € 0,50/5minutes € 0,50 Ch (40x)€ 0,50/kWh,16Amp € 2,50/30minutes. **Location:** Rural, simple, isolated, quiet.
Surface: grassy/metalled. 01/01-31/12
Distance: 200m on the spot on the spot.

Tourist information Bad Sooden-Allendorf:
Tourist Information, Landgraf-Philipp-Platz 1-2, www.bad-sooden-allendorf.de.Health resort with many half-timbered houses.

S Bad Wildungen 9D4

Wohnmobilstellplatz Bad Wildungen, Bahnhofstrasse. **GPS**: n51,12008 e9,13631.

DE

16 free, voluntary contribution € 1/pppd € 1/45liter Ch (14x)€ 1/kWh. **Surface:** metalled. 01/01-31/12
Distance: 1,5km.
Remarks: Max. 7 days.

S Bad Zwesten 9D4

Hotel Altenburg, Hardtstrasse 1a. **GPS**: n51,05706 e9,17748.

3 € 10 WC included. **Surface:** metalled. 01/01-31/12
Distance: 400m on the spot 300m.

S Battenberg 9D4

Festhalle Battenberg, Festplatzweg. **GPS**: n51,00915 e8,63643.

3 free Ch. **Surface:** gravel/metalled. 01/01-31/12
Remarks: At community centre, service: Esso-station, Battenfelderstr. 6.

S Battenberg 9D4

Hallen- und Freibad, Senonchesstraße. **GPS**: n51,01233 e8,63532.

3 free Ch. **Surface:** asphalted. 01/01-31/12
Distance: on the spot 100m on the spot on the spot.
Remarks: Parking swimming pool, service: Esso-Station, Battenfelderstr. 6.

Tourist information Battenberg:

Tourist-Information Ederbergland Touristik e. V, Untermarkt 12, www.ederbergland-touristik.de.Small town high above the Eder valley.

Besucherbergwerk Burgbergstollen.150 years old mine shaft, can be reached from Marktplatz. 01/05-30/09 1st Su of the month 14-17h.

Stadtmuseum.Mining and hunting. Wed, Su 14-17h.

In winter cross-country trails on the Röhrberg.

S Baunatal 10A4

Parkstadion. **GPS**: n51,25865 e9,39956.

16 € 5/24h € 1/100liter Ch (16x)€ 0,50/kWh. **Location:** Rural, simple, quiet. **Surface:** gravel. 01/01-31/12
Distance: 500m 4km on the spot on the spot.
Remarks: Max. 3 days.

S Bebra 10A4

Natur- und Freizeitpark Fuldaue Breitenbachen Seen, Hersfelder Straße. **GPS**: n50,95899 e9,78764.

25 free € 1/100liter Ch (18x)€ 0,50/kWh. **Surface:** grassy. 01/01-31/12
Distance: 1km on the spot on the spot.

Bebra 10A4

Annastrasse 17. **GPS**: n50,97464 e9,79836.

4 free. **Surface:** asphalted. 01/01-31/12
Distance: 400m.
Remarks: Parking swimming pool.

Bebra 10A4

Mehrzweckparkplatz, Bei Laupfütze/Rathausstrasse. **GPS**: n50,97000 e9,79000.

5 free. **Surface:** metalled. 01/01-31/12
Distance: on the spot.

S Beerfelden 17C2

Parkplatz NordicCenter, Seeweg. **GPS**: n49,56034 e8,97557.

DE

4 free € 0,50/50liter Ch € 0,50/kWh. **Surface:** asphalted.
01/01-31/12
Distance: 1km.

Berkatal — 10B4

Am Sportplatz. **GPS**: n51,23763 e9,91504.

3 free. **Location:** Rural, simple, isolated, quiet. **Surface:** asphalted.
01/01-31/12
Distance: 800m 500m on the spot.

Biedenkopf — 9D5

Freizeitzentrum Sackpfeife, An der Berggaststätte. **GPS**: n50,94735 e8,53317.

6 € 5 . **Surface:** concrete. 01/01-31/12
Distance: on the spot on the spot.
Remarks: Max. 3 days.

Biedenkopf — 9D5

Parkplatz Stadtwerke, Mühlweg. **GPS**: n50,90925 e8,52687.

4 € 5/24h € 1/12h. **Surface:** metalled. 01/01-31/12
Distance: 200m.

Biedenkopf — 9D5

Parkhotel Bürgerhaus, Auf dem Radeköppel 2. **GPS**: n50,91183 e8,53515.

2 free with a meal. 01/01-31/12
Distance: on the spot on the spot 500m 12km 12km.

Tourist information Biedenkopf:

Tourist Information, Hainstr. 63, www.hessennet.de/biedenkopf.Old part of town with half-timbered houses.

Hinterlandmuseum Schloß Biedenkopf.Regional and cultural history.
01/04-15/11 10-18h Mo.
Freizeitzentrum Sackpfeife.

Braunfels — 9C6

Wohnmobilstation Schloss Braunfels, Jahnplatz. **GPS**: n50,51478 e8,38609.
4 € 5, € 7,50 service incl Ch .
Surface: metalled.
01/01-31/12
Distance: on the spot 350m.
Remarks: Pay and key service: Gasthof am Turm, Marktplatz 11, caution € 15.

Breuberg — 17C1

Bahnhofstraße 4, Neustadt. **GPS**: n49,81576 e9,04063.
4 free € 1/60liter € 1 Ch € 0,50/kWh. **Surface:** asphalted.
01/01-31/12
Distance: on the spot 300m 550m.

Burghaun — 10A5

Oberste Straße. **GPS**: n50,69179 e9,73203.
4 free € 1/100liter Ch € 0,50/kWh. **Surface:** asphalted.
01/01-31/12
Distance: 500m on the spot on the spot.

Calden — 10A3

Waldschwimmbad Calden, Zum Lindenrondell. **GPS**: n51,39420 e9,40064.

3 free. **Location:** Rural, simple, isolated. **Surface:** grassy.
01/01-31/12
Distance: 1km 1,5km 2km.

Diemelsee — 9D4

Terrassenparkplatz Hohes Rad, Hohes Rad 1. **GPS**: n51,33533 e8,75319.

20 € 5. **Surface:** metalled. 01/01-31/12

Dillenburg — 9C5

Aquarena-Bad, Stadionstrasse. **GPS**: n50,73994 e8,27815.

8 free € 1/90liter Ch (6x)€ 1/kWh. **Surface:** asphalted.
01/01-31/12
Distance: 300m.

Dillenburg — 9C5

Hotel Kanzelstein, Fasanenweg 2. **GPS**: n50,74538 e8,31473.
10 free with a meal. **Surface:** asphalted.

DE

4 free. **Surface:** metalled. 01/01-31/12
Distance: 800m 800m 700m 400m.

S Herbstein 10A6

An der VulkanTherme Herbstein, Zum Thermalbad 1. **GPS**: n50,56883 e9,34647.

11 € 5 + €0,80/pp tourist tax Ch . **Surface:** metalled.
01/01-31/12
Distance: 1,1km 800m.
Remarks: Coins available at pay-desk of theTherme.

S Hessisch Lichtenau 10A4

Sportcenter Fürstenhagen, Breslauer strasse 18. **GPS**: n51,20672 e9,69443.

10 € 5/24h € 1/80liter Ch € 0,50/kWh . **Location:** Rural, simple, quiet. **Surface:** metalled. 01/01-31/12
Distance: 3km 1km 2km.
Remarks: Check in at sport centre.

Hessisch Lichtenau 10A4

Alter Bahnhof/Western Rail Station, Bahnhofstrasse 5, Warlburg. **GPS**: n51,20055 e9,77833.

10 € 10. **Location:** Rural, isolated, quiet. **Surface:** asphalted.
01/01-31/12
Distance: 5km 700m 1km on the spot.

Hessisch Lichtenau 10A4

Hopfelderstrasse. **GPS**: n51,19417 e9,72389.

14 free. **Location:** Urban, simple, isolated, quiet. **Surface:** metalled.
01/01-31/12
Distance: 500m 400m 500m.

Hessisch Lichtenau 10A4

Wohnmobilstellplatz am Hallenbad, Freiherr vom Stein strasse 12. **GPS**: n51,20445 e9,72655.

6 free. **Location:** Rural, simple, isolated, quiet. **Surface:** metalled.
01/01-31/12
Distance: 600m.
Remarks: Parking swimming pool.

S Hessisch Lichtenau 10A4

Berggasthof Hohe Meissner, Hoher Meissner 1. **GPS**: n51,20376 e9,84852.

10 free WC. **Location:** Rural, simple, isolated, quiet.
Surface: metalled.
01/01-31/12
Distance: 10km on the spot on the spot on the spot on the spot.

Tourist information Hessisch Lichtenau:

Kultur- und Verkehrsamt, Rathaus, Zimmer 21, Landgrafenstrsse 52, www.hessisch-lichtenau.de.Characteristic 13th century small town, cycle and hiking routes available.

Hirzenhain 10A6

Festplatz Hirzenhain, Robert-Eichenauerweg. **GPS**: n50,39259 e9,13593.

6 free. **Surface:** metalled. 01/01-31/12
Distance: 100m.

S Hirzenhain 10A6

Müller-Mobil, Junkerwiese 2. **GPS**: n50,40004 e9,14744.

DE

5 free € 1/130liter . **Surface:** metalled. 01/01-31/12
Distance: 1,5km.

S Hofgeismar 10A3

Am Sälber Tor. **GPS**: n51,49521 e9,37547.

100 free € 1/80liter Ch (18x)€ 1/2kWh. **Location:** Rural, comfortable, central, quiet. **Surface:** gravel. 01/01-31/12
Distance: on the spot 300m on the spot on the spot.

Tourist information Hofgeismar:
Tourist-Info Märchenwald Reinhardswald, Markt 5, www.reinhardswald.de.

S Homberg/Efze 10A4

Wassmuthshäuserstrasse, Dresdener Alee. **GPS**: n51,02757 e9,41470.

6 free Ch free. **Surface:** metalled. 01/01-31/12
Distance: on the spot 1km 500m.

Tourist information Homberg/Efze:
Tourist Information, Obertorstrasse 4, www.homberg-efze.de.Medival city with some half-timbered houses.

S Hünfeld 10A5

Hessisches Kegelspiel, Zu den Unaben. **GPS**: n50,67626 e9,77622.

18 € 5 € 1/120liter Ch € 1/2kWh. 01/01-31/12
Distance: 500m 250m 500m.

S Hünfeld 10A5

Testplatz Haselgrund, Zum Haselsee. **GPS**: n50,67798 e9,77679.

50 free Ch WC. **Surface:** metalled.
Distance: 600m on the spot 600m.

S Kassel 10A4

Wohnmobilplatz Kassel, Am Sportzentrum/Giessenallee, Kassel-süd. **GPS**: n51,29250 e9,48750.

12 €12,50/day € 1/100liter € 0,50 Ch € 0,50 (8x)€ 0,50/kWh.
Location: Rural, simple, isolated, quiet.
01/01-31/12
Distance: 1,4km 500m 50m on the spot on the spot.
Remarks: Max. 3 nights, with parking ticket free public transport.

Tourist information Kassel:
Kassel Tourist, Obere Königsstrasse 15, www.kassel.de.
Capital of the German Märchenstrasse, fairy-tale trail.
Treppenstrasse, shopping promenade, modern architecture.

S Kaufungen 10A4

Festplatz, Am Steckkopf. **GPS**: n51,28525 e9,61956.

4 free € 2 Ch. **Location:** Rural, simple, quiet. **Surface:** metalled.
01/01-31/12
Distance: 800m Steinersee 300m 500m.
Remarks: 2013: during inspection service out of order.

S Kirchheim 10A5

Campingplatz Seepark, Brunnenstrasse 20. **GPS**: n50,81400 e9,52000.

25 € 10, dog € 2/day € 1 Ch € 2,50/day. **Surface:** metalled.
Distance: 5km 4,9km 20m on the spot 20m.

Lauterbach (Hessen) 10A5

Bleiche/Festplatz auf der grosse Bleiche, Bleichstrasse. **GPS**: n50,63849 e9,40444.

DE

20 free. 01/01-31/12
Distance: 100m on the spot.

Lauterbach (Hessen) 10A5

Freizeitzentrum, Am Sportfeld. **GPS**: n50,62758 e9,39288.

8 free. **Surface:** metalled. 01/01-31/12
Distance: 800m on the spot.

S Lauterbach (Hessen) 10A5

David-Eifertstrasse. **GPS**: n50,64288 e9,39393.
€ 1 Ch. 01/01-31/12
Distance: 300m.
Remarks: Industrial area Hopfengarten.

S Lindenfels 17B2

Parkplatz Kappstrasse, Kappstrasse. **GPS**: n49,68018 e8,78294.

18 free € 1/80liter Ch (4x)€ 0,50/6h WC. 01/01-31/12
Distance: on the spot on the spot.

Tourist information Lindenfels:
Health resort with historical centre.

S Lorsch 17B2

Karolingerplatz Lorsch, Klosterstraße. **GPS**: n49,65359 e8,57220.
15 free . **Surface:** gravel. 01/01-31/12

S Marburg 9D5

Jahnstraße. **GPS**: n50,80354 e8,77544.

8 € 7 € 1/100liter (4x)€ 1/4h. **Surface:** gravel. 01/01-31/12
Distance: 300m 500m.

S Michelstadt 17C2

Am Festplatz, Wiesenweg. **GPS**: n49,68038 e9,00143.

10 free € 1/70liter Ch € 1/2kWh. **Surface:** gravel.
Distance: 200m 200m 50m.

S Neukirchen 10A5

Birkenallee, Knüllgebirge. **GPS**: n50,86567 e9,34478.
5 free against payment. 01/01-31/12
Distance: 500m.

Tourist information Neukirchen:
Small health resort with half-timbered houses and city walls.

Oberaula 10A5

Am Golfplatz 1. **GPS**: n50,83590 e9,46211.

2 free. **Surface:** grassy. 01/01-31/12
Remarks: Parking golf court, max. 4 days.

Oberaula 10A5

Sportplatz, Schwimbadstrasse. **GPS**: n50,85421 e9,45908.

5 free. **Surface:** asphalted. 01/01-31/12

Oberaula 10A5

Teichstrasse. **GPS**: n50,85900 e9,47300.

10 free. **Surface:** metalled.
Remarks: Parking tennis-courts, max. 4 days.

S Ottrau 10A5

Am Schwimmbad 10. **GPS**: n50,80400 e9,38500.

DE

5 free. WC. **Surface:** asphalted. 01/01-31/12
Distance: on the spot.

S Poppenhausen 10B6

Sport- und Freizeitgelände Lüttergrund, Sebastian-Kneippweg, Wasserkuppe. **GPS:** n50,49012 e9,87689.

10 € 4 € 1 Ch € 1/6h. **Surface:** metalled. 01/01-31/12
Distance: 300m 300m 300m.

S Rasdorf 10B5

Sport- und Freizeitgelände, Setzelbacher Straße. **GPS:** n50,71422 e9,90306.
4 € 4 € 1/120liter Ch € 1/10h. **Surface:** metalled.
01/01-31/12
Distance: 850m 500m.
Remarks: Max. 3 days.

DE

S Reichelsheim/Odenwald 17B2

Reichenbergschule, Beerfurhterstrasse. **GPS:** n49,71507 e8,84234.

20 free € 1 Ch (8x)€ 0,50/kWh. **Surface:** asphalted. 01/01-31/12
Distance: 500m 100m.

Reinhardshagen 10A3

Freibad, Klinkersweg. **GPS:** n51,48694 e9,59194.

4 free. **Location:** Rural, simple, isolated. **Surface:** asphalted.
01/01-31/12
Distance: 2km on the spot 2km 2km on the spot on the spot on the spot.
Remarks: Parking swimming pool, OT Veckerhagen.

S Ringgau 10B4

Am Festplatz, In der Röste, Gandenborn. **GPS:** n51,08139 e10,04239.

20 free, service/electricity incl. € 7 Ch. **Location:** Rural, simple, quiet. **Surface:** gravel. 01/01-31/12
Distance: 100m 200m.

S Rotenburg a/d Fulda 10A4

Wohnmobilpark Am Wittlich, Braacher Straße 14. **GPS:** n51,00040 e9,71932.
40 € 4 € 1 Ch € 0,50/kWh. **Surface:** metalled. 01/01-31/12
Distance: Old city centre 650m.

Rotenburg a/d Fulda 10A4

Am Kuckucksmarktgelände, Braach. **GPS:** n51,00583 e9,69361.

15 free. 01/01-31/12
Distance: 200m on the spot 200m.

Rotenburg a/d Fulda 10A4

Im Heienbach. **GPS:** n51,00223 e9,74141.

10 free. 01/01-31/12
Remarks: Parking swimming pool.

S Rotenburg a/d Fulda 10A4

Biergarten Hof Hafermas, Rotenburgerstrasse 13, Braach. **GPS:** n51,00325 e9,69019.

3 free € 1 Ch. **Surface:** gravel. 01/01-31/12
Distance: on the spot on the spot.

Tourist information Rotenburg a/d Fulda:
Verkehrs- und Kulturamt, Weingasse 3.Motorhome friendly town, worth seeing, with historic old part and half-timbered houses, hiking and mountain

bike trails.

Kuckucksmarkt, Braach.Farmers market. 01/05-30/09 last weekend of the month10-18h.

S Schlitz 10A5

Damenweg. **GPS**: n50,66909 e9,56908.
3 free . **Surface:** gravel. 01/01-31/12
Remarks: At swimming pool.

S Schwalmstadt 10A5

Altstad Schwalmstadt-Treysa. **GPS**: n50,91447 e9,19327.

10 free Ch. 01/01-31/12
Distance: on the spot.
Remarks: Nearby, indicated on site.

S Schwalmstadt 10A5

Ziegenhain, Fünftenweg. **GPS**: n50,91753 e9,24633.

10 free Ch. 01/01-31/12
Distance: on the spot.
Remarks: Parking swimming pool, service indicated.

Tourist information Schwalmstadt:

Schwalm-Touristik e.V, Paradeplatz 7, www.schwalmstadt.de.

Museum der Schwalm, Ziegenhain.Collection of costumes. Tue-Fri en Su 10/11-12h, 15-17h, Sa 14-17h.

In-line skating.Signposted routes.

S Schwalmtal 10A5

Reisemobilplatz, Friedenstrasse, Schwalmtal-Storndorf. **GPS**: n50,65579 e9,26935.

8 free € 0,50/80liter Ch (6x)€ 0,50/kWh. **Surface:** asphalted.
01/01-31/12
Distance: 300m.
Remarks: Nearby sports park.

S Sontra 10B4

Langhelle/Jahnstrasse. **GPS**: n51,07227 e9,94673.

5 free € 0,50/80liter Ch € 1/12h WC. **Location:** Rural, simple, isolated, quiet. **Surface:** asphalted/metalled. 01/01-31/12
Distance: 600m on the spot.
Remarks: Parking behind swimming pool.

Sontra 10B4

Vimoutiersstrasse. **GPS**: n51,07139 e9,93306.
8 free. **Location:** Urban, simple. **Surface:** gravel/metalled.
01/01-31/12
Distance: 400m 300m 50m.

Steinau a/d Strasse 10A6

Am Steines. **GPS**: n50,31605 e9,46029.

3 free. **Surface:** asphalted. 01/01-31/12
Distance: 1km 150m.
Remarks: Parking next to bus stop, at sports centre.

S Tann/Rhön 10B5

Festplatz Tann, Am Unsbach. **GPS**: n50,64264 e10,01948.
10 € 5 € 1/120liter Ch € 1/2kWh. **Surface:** gravel.
01/01-31/12
Remarks: Max. 3 days.

S Ulrichstein 10A6

Reisemobilstellplatz Panoramablick, Erlenweg. **GPS**: n50,57588 e9,20619.

14 € 5 € 1/80liter Ch (6x)€ 0,50/kWh. **Surface:** asphalted.
01/01-31/12
Distance: 1km 1km 1km.
Remarks: Beautiful view.

Villmar 9C6

P3, König-Konrad-Straße. **GPS**: n50,39102 e8,18625.

DE

10 free. **Surface:** metalled.
Distance: on the spot.
Remarks: Parking at the river.

Vöhl 9D4

Camping-und Ferienpark Teichmann, Herzhausen. **GPS**: n51,17472 e8,89103.
3 € 10. **Surface:** metalled. 01/01-31/12
Distance: on the spot.
Remarks: Max. 1 night, >22h.

S Wahlsburg 10A3

Landhotel "Zum Anker", Weserstrasse 14. **GPS**: n51,62447 e9,55212.

60 € 8 € 0,50/50liter Ch (60x)€ 0,50/kWh WC . **Location:** Rural, comfortable, quiet. **Surface:** grassy. 01/01-31/12
Distance: 200m on the spot on the spot 500m on the spot on the spot.
Remarks: Bread-service.

S Waldeck 9D4

Seeblick Wohnmobil, Güldener Ort 12. **GPS**: n51,20309 e9,05004.
€ 10, 2 pers.incl Ch WC . **Surface:** grasstiles.
01/01-31/12
Distance: 50m on the spot.
Remarks: At Edersee.

S Waldkappel 10B4

Am Sportplatz. **GPS**: n51,14177 e9,87278.

4 free € 1/100liter. **Location:** Rural, simple, isolated, quiet.
Surface: gravel. 01/01-31/12
Distance: 400m 1km.
Remarks: At sports park.

S Wanfried 10B4

In der Weeraaue. **GPS**: n51,18722 e10,16528.

12 € 5 € 2/100liter Ch (12x)€ 1/24h. **Location:** Rural, simple, quiet. **Surface:** metalled. 01/01-31/12
Distance: 50m 50m on the spot on the spot.

S Weilburg 9C6

An der Hainallee. **GPS**: n50,48385 e8,25848.

20 € 7,50 Ch included. **Surface:** metalled. 01/01-31/12
Distance: on the spot on the spot.
Remarks: In front of Feuerwehrstützpunkt, caution key € 15.

S Weilmünster 9C6

Am Froschgraben, L3054. **GPS**: n50,43345 e8,37343.

20 free Ch free € 2/16h. 01/01-31/12
Distance: on the spot 100m 100m.

S Weilrod 9C6

Taunus Mobilcamp, Hochtaunusstrasse. **GPS**: n50,31138 e8,42581.

30 € 5 + € 1/pp, dog € 1 € 1/20liter Ch € 0,50/kWh WC .
Surface: metalled. 01/01-31/12
Distance: 300m 6km.

S Wetzlar 9C6

Lahninsel. **GPS**: n50,55506 e8,49794.
5 € 0,25/h, overnight stay free WC. **Surface:** asphalted.
01/01-31/12
Distance: 300m 1,5km 250m.

S Wiesbaden 17A1

Reisemobilhafen Wiesbaden, Wörther-See-Strasse/Saarstrasse. **GPS**: n50,05583 e8,20972.

32 € 12 € 1/80liter Ch (32x)€ 0,50/kWh. 01/01-31/12
Distance: 800m 800m.

Wiesbaden/Frauenstein 17A1

Alfred-Delp-Strasse/Frauenstein. **GPS**: n50,06755 e8,16526.

10 free. 01/01-31/12
Distance: 4km.
Remarks: Parking in front of sports park.

Willingen 9D4

Wohnmobilpark Willingen, Am Hagen. **GPS**: n51,29050 e8,61278.

55 € 12,50, 2 pers.incl € 1/100liter Ch € 1/8h WC € 1/10minutes.
Surface: metalled. 01/01-31/12
Distance: 1km 1km 1km 500m 500m.
Remarks: Discount at subtropical swimming pool and indoor skating rink.

Witzenhausen 10A4

Reisemobilplatz Diebesturm, Oberburgstrasse. **GPS**: n51,34110 e9,85435.

4 € 2,50 € 0,50/100liter Ch (4x)€ 0,50. **Location:** Urban, simple, central, noisy. **Surface:** gravel. 01/01-31/12
Distance: 500m on the spot 500m.

Witzenhausen 10A4

Reisemobilplatz Josef-Pott-Platz, Laubenweg. **GPS**: n51,34477 e9,85503.

10 € 5 € 1/100liter Ch (10x)€ 0,50/6h. **Location:** Rural, simple, quiet. **Surface:** metalled. 01/01-31/12
Distance: 800m 9km 800m Aldi 100m on the spot on the spot.

Witzenhausen 10A4

Haus des Gastes, Ringkopfstrasse, Dohrenbach. **GPS**: n51,31061 e9,83372.

8 € 4 Ch free€ 2/24h WC. **Location:** Rural, simple, isolated, quiet. **Surface:** metalled.
01/01-31/12
Distance: on the spot on the spot 300m on the spot.

Tourist information Witzenhausen:
Kesperkirmes. Village fair. beginning Jul.

Wolfhagen 9D4

Freizeitanlange Bruchwiesen, Siemensstrasse. **GPS**: n51,32944 e9,17083.

35 € 3 € 1/80liter Ch (12x)€ 1/8h. **Location:** Rural, simple, isolated, quiet. **Surface:** grassy/gravel. 01/01-31/12
Distance: on the spot 500m 200m on the spot on the spot.

Ziegenhagen 10A3

Erlebnispark Ziegenhagen, Ziegenberg 3. **GPS**: n51,37191 e9,76472.

30 € 5 € 1 Ch. **Location:** Simple, isolated, quiet. 01/03-31/10
Distance: 6km.

DE

Thuringia

Asbach/Sickenberg 10B4

Grenzmuseum Schifflersgrund, Sickenberger Straße 1. **GPS**: n51,28667 e10,01052.
6 free Ch. **Surface:** gravel.

Bad Berka 10D4

P2, Bleichstrasse. **GPS**: n50,89969 e11,28528.

3 free € 1/3minutes € 1 Ch (3x)€ 1/3h. **Surface:** asphalted.
01/01-31/12
Distance: 200m on the spot 200m 200m.
Remarks: 10/7/10 during inspection service out of order.

Bad Colberg/Heldburg 10C6

Rainbrünnlein. **GPS**: n50,27967 e10,73063.

10 free Ch free. **Surface:** metalled.
Distance: 100m 200m 200m.
Remarks: At sports park.

Bad Frankenhausen/Kyffhäuser 10C3

Bornstraße, B85. **GPS**: n51,35550 e11,10333.

6 € 12 included. **Location:** Rural. **Surface:** metalled.
01/01-31/12
Distance: 500m 200m 300m.
Remarks: Check in at pay-desk of the Therme.

Bad Klosterlausnitz 11A4

Kristall Sauna-Wellnesspark/Soletherme, Köstritzerstrasse 16. **GPS**: n50,91190 e11,87242.

15 € 10 + € 1,30/pp Kurtaxe € 1/80liter Ch € 1/2kWh WC.
Surface: gravel. 01/01-31/12
Distance: 800m 2,8km on the spot.

Bad Langensalza 10C4

Friederiken Therme, Böhmenstrasse. **GPS**: n51,11535 e10,64440.

8 € 2, tourist tax € 1,20/pp € 1 Ch (8x)€ 1/10h. **Surface:** metalled.
01/01-31/12
Distance: 1km 1km 200m.
Remarks: Parking spa resort.

Bad Liebenstein 10B5

Stadthalle, Ruhlaerstrasse 2. **GPS**: n50,81698 e10,34963.
5 overnight stay free. **Surface:** metalled.
Distance: 100m 100m 200m.

Bad Liebenstein 10B5

Villa Georg, Friedensallee 12. **GPS**: n50,81876 e10,35517.
€ 11 Ch WC included. **Surface:** gravel. 01/01-31/12
Distance: 500m on the spot 800m.

Bad Lobenstein 10D6

Ardesia Therme, Parkstrasse 8. **GPS**: n50,44981 e11,64294.

11 € 2,50, free with use of therme € 2 Ch € 0,50/kWh WC.
Surface: metalled. 01/01-31/12
Distance: 200m on the spot 200m on the spot.

Bad Salzungen 10B5

Werrastrasse. **GPS**: n50,81191 e10,23019.

15 free. **Surface:** gravel. 01/01-31/12

DE

Distance: 500m 250m 500m.
Remarks: At health resort next to the first German Keltenbad, max. 3 days, service Hersfelderstrasse 4.

S Bad Salzungen 10B5
Am Haad. **GPS**: n50,81867 e10,23376.

40 € 3/day € 2/day. **Surface:** grassy. 01/01-31/12
Distance: 2km 2km 2km.
Remarks: Max. 3 days.

S Bad Salzungen 10B5
Am Flössrasen, Flössrasen 1. **GPS**: n50,81541 e10,23748.

10 free (8x)€ 1/kWh. **Surface:** asphalted/grassy. 01/01-31/12
Distance: 500m 400m 400m.
Remarks: Max. 3 days.

S Bad Salzungen 10B5
Werrastrasse. **GPS**: n50.81521 e10,22558.
Ch.

Tourist information Bad Salzungen:
Tourist Information, Am Flössrasen 1.Health resort, several guided city walks available.

S Breitungen 10B5
Hotel Jagdhaus Seeblick, Seeblick. **GPS**: n50,74250 e10,32306.
30 € 5 WC. **Surface:** grassy. 01/01-31/12
Distance: 2km 1km on the spot 2km.

Dankmarshausen 10B5
Am Werraufer, Bootsanleger. **GPS**: n50,92695 e10,02092.
3 free.

S Dankmarshausen 10B5
Gaststätte Rhädenblick, Blumenweg 2. **GPS**: n50,92760 e10,01093.

10 customers free .
Distance: 500m on the spot 300m.

S Dankmarshausen 10B5
Hotel Waldschlösschen, Waldstrasse 31. **GPS**: n50,92573 e10,00726.
5 free with a meal . **Surface:** grasstiles.
Distance: 500m on the spot 300m.

Eisenach 10B4
Burg Wartburg. **GPS**: n50,96775 e10,30989.

10 € 5. **Surface:** metalled. 01/01-31/12
Remarks: Nearby castle Wartburg.

Eisenach 10B4
Karl Marxstrasse. **GPS**: n50,97861 e10,32083.

3 9-17h max. € 6, free overnight stay. **Surface:** gravel.
01/01-31/12
Distance: 500m 100m 100m.

S Eisenach 10B4
Wohnmobile A. Waldhelm, Ringstrasse 27. **GPS**: n51,00194 e10,32667.

6 € 6 € 2,50 Ch € 2,50/day. **Surface:** grasstiles.
01/01-31/12
Distance: 1km 1km 1km Shuttle bus.

Eisfeld 10C6
Weihbach. **GPS**: n50,42370 e10,90480.
3 free. **Surface:** asphalted. 01/01-31/12
Distance: on the spot on the spot.

S Eisfeld 10C6
Waldhotel Hubertus, Coburgerstrasse 501. **GPS**: n50,41649 e10,91312.
20 free, use of a meal desired € 2 € 2. **Surface:** asphalted/grassy.
01/01-31/12
Distance: 3km on the spot 2km on the spot.

S Erfurt 10C4
Domplatz, An den Graden. **GPS**: n50,97591 e11,02455.

4 € 8 (3x)€ 2. **Surface:** gravel. 01/01-31/12
Distance: on the spot on the spot on the spot on the spot.

DE

S Erfurt 10C4

Am Saunabad Trautmann, Paulinzellerweg 46, Melchendorf. **GPS**: n50,95404 e11,06654.
15 € 4,50,with electricity € 6 Ch WC € 1,50 washing machine/dryer € 3,50. **Surface:** gravel. 01/01-31/12
Distance: 300m.
Remarks: Discount on access sauna/wellness.

S Erfurt 10C4

P&R, Am Urbicher Kreuz. **GPS**: n50,94992 e11,09456.

15 free Ch. **Surface:** asphalted. 01/01-31/12
Distance: 7km Total-shop Tram till 24am.
Remarks: Service at petrol station Total. A4 > Erfurt Ost > L1052.

Erfurt 10C4

Eichenstrasse. **GPS**: n50,97327 e11,02737.

4 free. **Surface:** asphalted. 01/01-31/12
Distance: 200m 200m 300m on the spot.
Remarks: Max. 48h, parking, southern Altstadt.

Erfurt 10C4

Juri-Gagarin-Ring. **GPS**: n50,98111 e11,03472.

2 free. **Surface:** asphalted. 01/01-31/12
Distance: Old city centre 1km 500m 500m.
Remarks: Max. 48h, parking, eastern Altstadt.

Erfurt 10C4

P&R Parkplatz Messe, Gothaerstrasse. **GPS**: n50,95818 e10,98296.

4 free. **Surface:** asphalted. 01/01-31/12
Distance: centre 4km Bus <23.00h.
Remarks: Parking exhibition ground.

Erfurt 10C4

P&R Parkplatz Thüringerhalle, Werner-Seelenbinderstrasse. **GPS**: n50,95771 e11,03605.

10 free. **Surface:** gravel. 01/01-31/12
Distance: 2,6km Tram till 23am.
Remarks: Nearby B4, south edge of the city.

Tourist information Erfurt:

Erfurt-Card.Card gives for free entrance on among other things public transport and city museums, and discount on a lot of curiosities, guided tours, swimming pools, theater, souvernirs. € 14,90.

Tourist Information, Benediktsplatz 1, www.erfurt-tourist-info.de.Medieval centre with a lot of curiosities.

Stadtführung, Tourist Information, Benediktsplatz 1.Guided tour around the historic city center. 01/04-31/12 Mo-Fri 13h, Sa-Su 11h, 13h, 01/01-31/03 Sa-Su 11h, 13h. € 5,50.

S Friedrichroda 10C5

Wohnmobilstellplatz Ortlepp, Bahnhofstrasse 32a. **GPS**: n50,85981 e10,57631.

40 € 5,50, € 1,20/pp tourist tax Ch (6x)€ 0,50/kWh WC.
Surface: grassy. 01/01-31/12
Distance: 300m 200m on the spot.

Geschwenda 10C5

Kickelhanchen. **GPS**: n50,73051 e10,81395.
3 free. **Surface:** asphalted. 01/01-31/12
Distance: 1km on the spot 700m.
Remarks: Parking at sports park.

Geschwenda 10C5

Waldbad. **GPS**: n50,72395 e10,81752.
5 free. **Surface:** metalled. 01/01-31/12
Distance: 1,5km.

Geschwenda 10C5

Gasthof Diemelsee, Neue Sorge 38. **GPS**: n50,73138 e10,82000.
5 free with a meal. **Surface:** gravel. 01/01-31/12
Distance: on the spot 600m.

S Geschwenda 10C5

Lippert Reisemobile, Dieselstrasse. **GPS**: n50,72169 e10,82832.
3 free Ch free. **Surface:** asphalted.
Remarks: Motorhome dealer.

S Ichtershausen 10C5

Autohof, Thöreyerstrasse. **GPS**: n50,88824 e10,93478.

DE

20 € 6,50/24h, first hour free € 0,50 Ch€ 0,50 WC. **Surface:** asphalted. 01/01-31/12
Distance: 4km on the spot Esso-shop.
Remarks: A4 Ausfahrt 44.

S Ichtershausen 10C5
Freizeitfahrzeuge Mobilease, Feldstrasse 1. **GPS**: n50,86907 e10,96563.

5 € 5 Ch (4x)€ 2,50 WC during opening hours. **Surface:** gravel.
01/01-31/12
Distance: 3km 500m bakery 500m.

S Ilfeld 10C3
Gasthof Brauner Hirsch, Dorfstrasse 42, Sophienhof. **GPS**: n51,63467 e10,79223.

15 € 5 Ch (3x)€ 0,25/kWh WC € 2 . **Surface:** metalled. 01/01-31/12
Distance: on the spot 3km on the spot on the spot.

S Ilmenau 10C5
Festhalle, Naumannstrasse. **GPS**: n50,68139 e10,90472.

10 free € 1/80liter Ch. **Surface:** asphalted. 01/01-31/12
Distance: 500m 500m 500m.
Remarks: Max. 24h.

Lauscha 10D6
Parkplatz Am Pappenheimer Berg, Im Steinachgrund. **GPS**: n50,48721 e11,17246.

free. **Surface:** metalled. 01/01-31/12
Distance: 600m 500m 1km.
Remarks: Parking at ski-lift.

Lauscha 10D6
Parkplatz Obermühle. **GPS**: n50,48026 e11,16795.

10 free. **Surface:** asphalted. 01/01-31/12
Distance: 300m 100m 1km.

S Linda 11A5
Knappmühle, Ortsstraße. **GPS**: n50,68473 e11,78324.

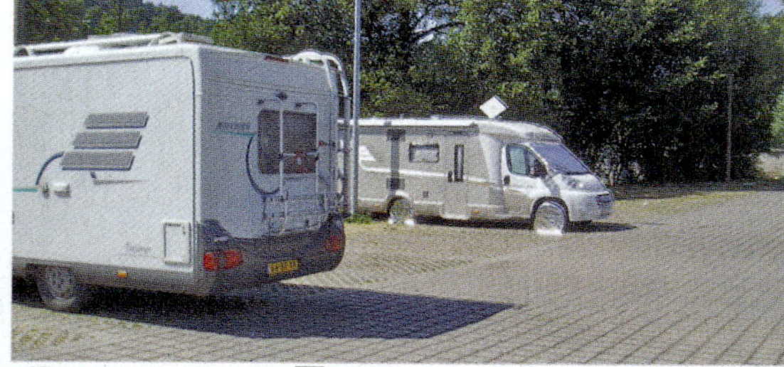

10 € 6 Ch (6x)€ 1/kWh. **Surface:** grassy/gravel.
01/03-31/10
Distance: 300m 5km 3km 5km.

Meiningen 10B5
Grossmutterwiesen, Werrastrasse. **GPS**: n50,56172 e10,41266.

5 free. **Surface:** concrete. 01/01-31/12
Distance: on the spot 200m 100m.
Remarks: Service possible at Kläranlage.

Meiningen 10B5
Volkshausplatz, Landsbergerstrasse. **GPS**: n50,57427 e10,41369.

DE

5 free. **Surface:** metalled. 01/01-31/12
Distance: 200m on the spot 200m 200m.
Remarks: Service possible at Kläranlage.

S Neustadt/Orla 11A5

Gaststätte & Pension Heinrichs-Ruhe, Heinrichsruhe 1, Rodaer Strasse. **GPS:** n50,75545 e11,75595.

10 free (6x)€ 0,50/kWh. **Surface:** grassy/gravel.
01/01-31/12 Restaurant: Mo.
Distance: 2,6km 12,2km on the spot 2,6km.

S Nimritz 10D5

Wohnmobilstellplatz Nimritz, Ortsstrasse 29. **GPS:** n50,70079 e11,64858.

10 voluntary contribution € 0,50 Ch (7x)€ 0,50/kWh. **Surface:** grasstiles.
Distance: 300m 300m.

S Nordhausen 10C3

Am Badehaus, Grimmelallee 40. **GPS:** n51,50450 e10,78508.

2 €5 €2 €1Ch€1 €1 €3. **Location:** Simple.
Surface: metalled.
Distance: 800m 500m 300m.

Nordhausen 10C3

Am Kuhberg, Parkallee. **GPS:** n51,51502 e10,78492.

10 free. **Surface:** asphalted. 01/01-31/12
Distance: 2km on the spot 500m.

S Oberhof 10C5

Wohnmobilstellplatz Winkler, Zeallerstrasse. **GPS:** n50,70278 e10,72694.
150 € 9/24h Ch € 2. **Surface:** asphalted. 01/01-31/12
Distance: on the spot 200m 500m on the spot.

Tourist information Oberhof:

Oberhof-Information, Crawinkler strasse 2, www.oberhof.de.Small winter sports resort, 150 days of snow per year. Snow-t elephone 036842 201 95.

Rennsteiggarten Oberhof.Botanical garden.
01/05-30/09 9-18, 01/10-31/10 9-17h.

Thüringer Wintersportausstellung, Crawinkler strasse 1 / Oberer Hof.Winter sport museum. 10-13h, 14-17h.

Rennsteig Thermen.Swimming pool complex.
daily 10-22h.

S Reichenbach 11A4

Heidlbergers Gastlichkeit und Freizeitsport, Rodaer Landstrasse. **GPS:** n50,86118 e11,87607.

50 € 7, guests free € 1 Ch (15x)€ 2/day WC € 2/pp. **Surface:** concrete. 01/01-31/12
Distance: 2km on the spot bakery 500m.

S Rudolstadt 10D5

Freizeit- und Erlebnisbad Saalemaxx, Hugo-Trinckler-Straße 6. **GPS:** n50,70635 e11,31659.
9 € 7/24h € 1/80liter € 1 Ch € 0,50/kWh. **Surface:** gravel.
01/01-31/12
Distance: 2km 100m.
Remarks: Discount at swimming pool.

Ruhla 10B5

Am Sportplatz, Burgstrasse. **GPS:** n50,91806 e10,39528.
€ 6/24h. **Surface:** metalled.
Distance: 300m 300m 400m.

Saalfeld 10D5

Reschwitzerstrasse, B281. **GPS:** n50,63720 e11,36751.

10 free. **Surface:** gravel. 01/01-31/12

DE

Distance: 2,8km.
Remarks: Parking at swimming pool.

S Saalfeld 10D5

Saalfelder Feengrotten, Feengrottenweg 2. **GPS:** n50,63468 e11,33982.

30 free € 3/5minutes € 3 Ch (6x)€ 0,50/kWh WC.
Surface: grassy. 01/01-31/12
Distance: 2,3km on the spot bakery 500m 500m.

S Schleiz 11A5

Spitzbergs Zollhaus, Burgkerstrasse 25. **GPS:** n50,55507 e11,73438.

5 € 5, free with a meal Ch (7x)€ 2/24h. **Surface:** gravel/metalled.
01/01-31/12 Mo.
Distance: 7km 5,4km on the spot 7km.

S Schleiz 11A5

HEM-Großtankstelle, Saalburgerstrasse. **GPS:** n50,55717 e11,78706.

8 € 2 € 1 € 1 Ch WC. **Surface:** asphalted.
01/01-31/12
Distance: 5km on the spot shop.
Remarks: Max. 24h, industrial area.

Sitzendorf 10D5

Sitzendorfer Porzellanmanufaktur, Hauptstrasse 26. **GPS:** n50,63174 e11,16788.
5 free. **Surface:** asphalted. 01/01-31/12
Distance: on the spot 200m 200m.

S Sondershausen 10C3

P7 zur Windleite, Hospitalstrasse. **GPS:** n51,37824 e10,86234.

5 free € 1 Ch (4x)€ 1/2h. **Surface:** metalled.
01/01-31/12
Distance: 2,5km 500m 100m.

Sondershausen 10C3

Freizeitpark Possen, Possen 1. **GPS:** n51,33800 e10,86265.

10 € 2/stay. **Surface:** metalled. 01/01-31/12
Distance: 5km on the spot.

S Stadtlengsfeld 10B5

Am Schwimmbad, Eisenacher Straße. **GPS:** n50,79065 e10,11373.
6 free . **Surface:** asphalted. 01/01-31/12
Distance: 1,5km.

S Tambach-Dietharz 10C5

Festplatz, Burgstallstraße. **GPS:** n50,78902 e10,60897.
4 free Ch . **Surface:** gravel. 01/01-31/12
Distance: on the spot on the spot.

S Tambach-Dietharz 10C5

Erlebnispark Lohmühle, Lohmühle 4. **GPS:** n50,81056 e10,62778.
40 € 6 + € 4/pp, dog € 2 € 2,50 Ch WC.
Surface: grassy.
Distance: on the spot 3km.
Remarks: Museum, Barefoot park.

S Themar 10C6

Am Hexenturm, Mauerstrasse. **GPS:** n50,50512 e10,61194.

5 free € 1/50liter Ch € 1/kWh. **Surface:** grasstiles.
01/01-31/12
Distance: 100m 300m 400m.
Remarks: Along the river Werra.

S Tiefenort 10B5

Krayenberg, Heerstatte. **GPS:** n50,83444 e10,16306.

5 free € 2/day. **Surface:** metalled. 01/03-31/10
Distance: on the spot on the spot 100m.

S Treffurt 10B4

Unter den Linden. **GPS:** n51,13398 e10,23659.

DE

20 free € 0,50/80liter Ch (8x)€ 0,50/kWh.
Location: Rural, simple, quiet.
Surface: grasstiles/grassy.
01/01-31/12 15/07-31/07.
Distance: 300m on the spot 50m 500m on the spot on the spot.
Remarks: Along the river, water closed during wintertime.

Tourist information Treffurt:
Small town with half-timbered houses and medival castle Normannstein.

Weimar 10D4
Hermann Brill-Platz. **GPS:** n50,98501 e11,31701.

20 € 4 (8-18h), overnight stay free. **Surface:** metalled. 01/01-31/12
Distance: Weimar centre 1,2km on the spot 500m.

Weimar 10D4
Saunabad Weimar, In der Buttergrube 11, Legefeld. **GPS:** n50,93573 e11,28678.

10 €5 (10x)included. **Surface:** metalled. 01/01-31/12
Distance: Weimar centre 6km.
Remarks: Use of sauna obligatory.

Zella-Mehlis 10C5
Toschis Station, An der Quelle 5. **GPS:** n50,64375 e10,68436.

20 €5 Ch (20x). **Surface:** grassy/gravel. 01/01-31/12
Distance: on the spot 300m.
Remarks: Check in at reception.

Zeulenroda 11A5
Badewelt Waikiki, Am Birkenwege 1. **GPS:** n50,66543 e11,99355.
6 free Ch water and electricity € 10/day. **Surface:** metalled.
01/01-31/12

Baden Württemberg

Aalen 18A4
Hirschbach, Hirschbachstrasse 68. **GPS:** n48,84524 e10,10712.

10 free € 1/80liter Ch. **Location:** Rural. **Surface:** asphalted. 01/01-31/12
Distance: 800m 100m 200m.
Remarks: At swimming pool, max. 3 days.

Aalen 18A4
Limes-Thermen, P1, Osterbucher Steige. **GPS:** n48,82047 e10,07918.

12 free. **Location:** Rural. **Surface:** grasstiles. 01/01-31/12
Distance: 100m.

Achern 17A5
Wohnmobilstellplatz Achern, Kapellenstrasse/Badstrasse. **GPS:** n48,62436 e8,07359.

12 € 4 € 1/100liter Ch (12x)€ 1/16h. **Location:** Urban, simple, quiet. **Surface:** gravel/metalled. 01/01-31/12
Distance: 500m 4,8km 650m on the spot on the spot.

Albstadt 17C5
Badkap. GPS: n48,21402 e8,97844.

25 free Chfree € 2,50/day. **Surface:** metalled.

DE

01/01-31/12
Distance: 1km 200m 500m.
Remarks: Parking swimming and sauna centre, max. 3 days.

Tourist information Albstadt:
Tourist Information, Marktstrasse 35, www.albstadt.de.
Mountain village with half-timbered houses, known for its textile industry.

Allensbach 24C1
Campingplatz Himmelreich, Strandweg 34. **GPS**: n47,71038 e9,08044.

6 € 12,50, tourist tax € 1,50 Ch (6x)€ 0,50/kWh WC € 0,90 € 2 . **Surface:** grasstiles/metalled. 15/03-15/10
Distance: 800m on the spot on the spot 800m 300m.

Allensbach 24C1
Gaststätte Zum Riesenberg, Professor-Schmider-strasse 10. **GPS**: n47,71544 e9,07629.

Allensbach 24C1
Landgasthaus Mindelsee, Gemeinmärk 7. **GPS**: n47,74279 e9,04411.

15 € 8. **Surface:** metalled. 01/01-31/12 Tue.
Distance: 5km on the spot.
Remarks: Max. 1 night.

Amtzell 24D1
Wohnmobilanlage Büchelweisen, Haus 3. **GPS**: n47,70871 e9,76684.

25 € 9 Ch (24x)€ 0,50/kWh WC € 3/day. **Surface:** grasstiles. 01/01-31/12
Distance: 1,5km 1km 1km on the spot 1,5km.
Remarks: Bread-service.

Aspach 17C3
Wanderparkplatz Fautenhau, Im Fautenhau, Hohrot. **GPS**: n48,97823 e9,39483.

5 free. **Location:** Rural. **Surface:** metalled. 01/01-31/12
Remarks: Parking p0, max. 1 night.

Aspach 17C3
Wanderparkplatz Heiligental, Heiligentalstrasse, Rietenau. **GPS**: n48,99158 e9,40519.

5 free. **Location:** Rural, quiet. **Surface:** asphalted/grassy. 01/01-31/12
Distance: on the spot.
Remarks: Max. 1 night.

Aspach 17C3
Wanderparkplatz Kelter, Kelterstrasse, Allmersbach. **GPS**: n48,99543 e9,39006.

5 free. **Location:** Rural, isolated. **Surface:** asphalted. 01/01-31/12
Distance: on the spot.
Remarks: Max. 1 night.

Aspach 17C3
Wanderparkplatz Lapidarium, Ortsstrasse, Kleinaspach. **GPS**: n48,99738 e9,35711.

2 free. **Location:** Simple. 01/01-31/12
Distance: on the spot 1km 1,5km on the spot.
Remarks: Max. 1 night.

Aulendorf 17D6
Schwaben-Therme, Ebisweilerstrasse 5. **GPS**: n47,95797 e9,63728.

DE

20 (P2-P3) free. **Location:** Rural. **Surface:** metalled.
01/01-31/12
Distance: 500m on the spot 500m.
Remarks: Parking swimming pool, max. 2 nights.

Backnang 17D4

Gartenstrasse. GPS: n48,95041 e9,45281.

4 free € 1/90liter Ch. **Location:** Rural, simple. **Surface:** gravel.
01/01-31/12
Distance: 1km 400m on the spot on the spot.

Bad Bellingen 24A1

Balinea Thermen, Badstrasse 14. **GPS:** n47,72963 e7,55233.

31 € 10 + € 1,45-2,25 tourist tax € 1/80liter Ch (24x)€ 1/kWh WC € 1,50. **Location:** Urban, noisy. **Surface:** asphalted/metalled.
01/01-31/12
Distance: 500m 5,5km on the spot on the spot.

Bad Buchau 17D6

Adelindis Therme, Am Kurpark. **GPS:** n48,06865 e9,60653.

21 € 9,50 XL-pitch € 11 € 1/80liter Ch € 0,50/kWh WC € 1.
Surface: metalled. 01/01-31/12
Distance: 500m.

Bad Buchau 17D6

Seegasse. GPS: n48,06801 e9,60977.

17 € 9,50 € 1/80liter Ch (17x)€ 0,50/kWh. **Surface:** metalled.
01/01-31/12
Distance: 500m.
Remarks: Adelindis Therme 300m.

Bad Buchau 17D6

Federseemuseum, Wellerstraße. **GPS:** n48,07051 e9,60949.

12 € 9 (12x)€ 0,50/kWh WC. **Location:** Rural. **Surface:** asphalted.
01/01-31/12
Distance: 800m.
Remarks: Adelindis Therme 500m.

Bad Buchau 17D6

Am Freibad, Friedhofstrasse. **GPS:** n48,06292 e9,61714.

10 € 9. **Surface:** asphalted. 01/01-31/12
Distance: 700m.

Bad Ditzenbach 17D4

Vinzenz Therme, Badstraße 20. **GPS:** n48,59003 e9,70553.

10 € 5, winter € 6 Ch. **Surface:** asphalted. 01/01-31/12

Bad Dürrheim 17B6

Reisemobilhafen Bad Dürrheim, Huberstraße 34/2. **GPS:** n48,01204 e8,53506.

300 € 9 € 1/100liter Ch € 2,50/night WC € 2.
Location: Rural, comfortable. **Surface:** gravel. 01/01-31/12
Distance: on the spot.
Remarks: Special health arrangement possible, bread service, pay at reception. Follow Solemar Parkplatz.

S Bad Herrenalb 17B4

Therme Siebentäler, Schweizer Wiese. **GPS**: n48,80334 e8,44067.

10 € 4,10 + € 2,50/pp € 1 € 1Ch € 1 (4x)€ 1. **Location:** Rural, simple. **Surface:** asphalted.
01/01-31/12
Distance: 500m 100m 200m 200m on the spot on the spot.
Remarks: Max. 2 nights, discount on access terme.

Tourist information Bad Herrenalb:
Tourismusbüro, Bahnhofsplatz 1, www.bad-herrenalb.de.Health resort.
Quellenerlebnispfad, Kurpark Herrenalb.Hiking trails past 60 fountains.

S Bad Krozingen 17A6

Vita Classica Therme, Thürachstraße. **GPS**: n47,91763 e7,68821.

75 € 10, from 7th night € 8,50 Chincluded € 2,50/4 Amp, € 3,50/16Amp WC € 3. **Location:** Rural, comfortable.
Surface: asphalted/metalled. 01/01-31/12
Distance: 500m 2km 50m 1km 1km 500m.
Remarks: Bread-service, trailer € 2,50.

S Bad Liebenzell 17B4

Campingpark Bad Liebenzell, Pforzheimer strasse 34. **GPS**: n48,77850 e8,73120.

16 € 8 + € 2/pp tourist tax Ch (16x) WC included € 3.
Location: Rural, simple, noisy. **Surface:** metalled/sand.
01/01-31/12
Distance: on the spot 17km 500m 100m on the spot on the spot on the spot.

S Bad Mergentheim 17D2

Festplatz beim Freibad, Erlenbachweg. **GPS**: n49,49194 e9,79167.

50 € 5 € 1/10minutes Ch (16x)€ 1/20h. **Surface:** metalled.
01/01-31/12
Distance: 1,5km 200m 2km 100m.
Remarks: Check in at restaurant tennispark.

S Bad Rappenau 17C3

Weinbrennerstrasse. **GPS**: n49,23517 e9,11396.

30 € 3/pp, child € 2 € 1/80liter Ch (16x)€ 1/4h. **Location:** Comfortable. **Surface:** metalled. 01/01-31/12
Distance: 1km 50m 1km.
Remarks: Therme 400m.

S Bad Rappenau 17C3

Autohof Bad Rappenau, A6, Wilhelm-Hauff-Straße 43, Fürfeld. **GPS**: n49,21043 e9,06927.
15 € 10, free for clients Ch. **Location:** Highway, simple.
Surface: metalled. 01/01-31/12
Distance: 300m on the spot on the spot.
Remarks: Breakfest-servic.

S Bad Säckingen 24A1

Reisemobilplatz Am Rheinufer, Ausstrasse. **GPS**: n47,54903 e7,94765.

DE

30 € 10/24h € 0,50/100liter € 0,20 Ch (39x) WC.
Location: Urban, comfortable, quiet.
Surface: gravel.
01/01-31/12 beginning Mar, end Oct.
Distance: 300m 6km 50m on the spot on the spot.
Remarks: Several offers, i.e. free public transport.

Tourist information Bad Säckingen:
Kurverwaltung GmbH, Waldshuter Stasse 20, www.bad-saeckingen.de.'Trumpet city' with colorfull centre, health resort.
TrompeterSchloß.Trumpeting museum. Tue, Thu, Su 14-17h.
Nachtwächterführungen.Evening tour guided by night watch in historical cloths and with lantern. Information and booking: Kurverwaltung. € 2.

S Bad Saulgau 17D6
GolfPark Bad Saulgau, Koppelweg 103. **GPS**: n47,97928 e9,48623.

30 € 10, golfers free € 1/100liter Ch € 1/6h. **Location:** Rural, quiet. **Surface:** metalled. 01/03-31/10
Distance: 4km on the spot 4km.

S Bad Saulgau 17D6
Wonhmobilstellplatz Sonnenhof-Therme, Am Schönen Moos. **GPS**: n48,01703 e9,48838.

53 € 11 + € 1,50/pp tourist tax stay Ch (69x)included.
Location: Rural. **Surface:** metalled. 01/01-31/12
Distance: on the spot on the spot on the spot.
Remarks: Discount on access terme, bread service.

S Bad Schönborn 17B3
Reisemobilhafen WellMobilPark, Kraichgaustraße 16. **GPS**: n49,21839 e8,67144.

90 € 8, >10m € 12 € 1/80liter Ch (112x)€ 0,50/kWh € 1,50. **Location:** Rural, luxurious. **Surface:** metalled. 01/01-31/12
Distance: 500m on the spot 1km 200m.
Remarks: Bread-service, swimming pool.

S Bad Schussenried 17D6
Am Zellersee, Zellerseeweg. **GPS**: n48,00160 e9,64724.

12 € 5 + € 1,20/pp tourist tax Ch. **Surface:** asphalted.
01/01-31/12
Distance: 900m on the spot on the spot.

S Bad Schussenried 17D6
Bierkrugmuseum, Wilhelm Schussenstrasse 12. **GPS**: n48,00325 e9,65902.

30 free Ch € 5,reduction for guests WC. **Location:** Quiet.
Surface: metalled.
01/01-31/12
Distance: on the spot 150m 250m.
Remarks: Brewery and brewery museum.

Tourist information Bad Schussenried:
Tourist Info, Klosterhof 5, www.bad-schussenried.de.Holiday resort and health resort.
Bierkrugmuseum.Collection of beer jugs. Tue-Su 10-17h.
Kloster Schussenried.History of the monastry. Easter-Oct 13.30-17.30h.

Bad Teinach 17B4
Zavelsteiner strasse. **GPS**: n48,68890 e8,69440.

20 free. **Location:** Rural, simple. **Surface:** asphalted.
01/01-31/12

DE

Distance: 50m ⊗100m 100m on the spot on the spot on the spot.
Remarks: Parking swimming pool, max. 24h.

S Bad Urach 17C5

Wohnmobilstellplatz Bad Urach, Bäderstrasse. **GPS:** n48,50060 e9,37713.

26 € 8 € 0,50 € 0,50 Ch included. **Surface:** asphalted. 01/01-31/12
Distance: on the spot 5km ⊗200m 800m 200m 10km 10km.

S Bad Waldsee 17D6

Bauernhof Lott, Mattenhaus 4. **GPS:** n47,95113 e9,75838.

10 € 10, 2 pers.incl, tourist tax € 2/pp Ch (10x)€ 0,50/kWh WC € 4. 01/03-30/11
Distance: 3,5km 3km 3km ⊗200m 3km.
Remarks: Bread-service. B3C, dir Ulm, ± 3 left, after Gasthof.

S Bad Waldsee 17D6

Waldsee-Therme, Unterurbacher weg. **GPS:** n47,91441 e9,76047.

40 € 5 + € 2/pp tourist tax € 1 € 1 Ch € 0,50/kWh.
Surface: metalled. 01/01-31/12
Distance: 1km 1km 1km ⊗500m 1km 500m.
Remarks: Bread-service.

S Bad Wildbad 17B4

Kernerstrasse. **GPS:** n48,74132 e8,54740.

16 € 5, tourist tax € 2,90/pp € 1/60liter Ch (16x)€ 2/8h.
Location: Rural, simple, noisy. **Surface:** asphalted.
01/01-31/12
Distance: 500m ⊗500m 300m on the spot on the spot on the spot.
Remarks: Max. 3 days.

Bad Wimpfen 17C3

Am alter Bahnhof, Carl Ulrichstrasse 1. **GPS:** n49,22942 e9,16745.

10 € 2, overnight stay free. **Location:** Urban, simple. **Surface:** gravel. 01/01-31/12
Distance: ⊗400m 400m 50m on the spot.

S Bad Wimpfen 17C3

An der Alten Saline 2. **GPS:** n49,23604 e9,15630.

8 € 8, tourist tax excl € 1/70liter Ch (8x)€ 1/12h WC. **Location:** Rural, comfortable, quiet. **Surface:** asphalted. 01/01-31/12
Distance: 800m.
Remarks: Parking at health resort.

S Bad Wurzach 17D6

Wohnmobilstellplatz Vitalium, Riedhalde. **GPS:** n47,91437 e9,90363.

17 € 5,50 + € 1,50/pp tourist tax € 0,50 € 0,50 Ch WC.
Location: Rural, quiet. **Surface:** asphalted. 01/01-31/12
Distance: 500m ⊗300m 500m.
Remarks: Check in at pay-desk of Vitalum.

S Baden-Baden 17B4

Wohnmobilparkplatz, Hubertusstraße 2, Badenscheuern. **GPS:** n48,78193 e8,20388.

28 € 12 € 1/100liter Ch (28x)€ 0,50/kWh. **Location:** Urban,

DE

comfortable, noisy. **Surface:** metalled. 01/01-31/12
Distance: Baden-Baden 4km 1km 100m 150m on the spot on the spot on the spot.
Remarks: Max. 4 days, terrain with video surveillance.

S Baiersbronn 17B5

Schelklewiesen, Neumühleweg/Lochweg. **GPS**: n48,51016 e8,37272.

15 € 6 € 1/80liter Ch (12x)€ 0,50/kWh. **Location:** Rural, simple, quiet. **Surface:** metalled. 01/01-31/12
Distance: 300m on the spot 100m 200m on the spot on the spot.

S Balingen 17C5

Wohnmobilstellplatz an der Eyach, Heinzlerstrasse. **GPS**: n48,27028 e8,85222.

10 free € 1 Ch (8x)€ 0,50/kWh. **Surface:** asphalted.
01/01-31/12
Distance: on the spot 500m 300m 300m.
Remarks: Max. 4 days.

Benningen am Neckar 17C4

Parkplatz Gemeindehalle, Max-Eyth Strasse. **GPS**: n48,94574 e9,23363.

4 free. **Location:** Rural, simple. **Surface:** metalled.
01/01-31/12
Distance: on the spot 50m 1km.

S Bernau im Schwarzwald 24A1

Sportzentrum Spitzenberg, Sportplatzstraße. **GPS**: n47,80614 e8,02803.

15 16/04-30/09 free, 01/10-15/04 € 3,50 + € 2,20/pp tourist tax €
1/100liter Ch € 1/8h WC . **Location:** Rural, simple, quiet. **Surface:** grassy/gravel. 01/01-31/12
Distance: 500m 1km 500m.
Remarks: Pay at tourist office.

S Besigheim 17C3

Wohnmobilstellplatz bei der Minigolfanlage, Auf dem Kies 32. **GPS**: n48,99771 e9,14863.

6 € 5 € 1/80liter Ch (6x)€ 0,50/kWh. **Location:** Rural, comfortable, quiet. **Surface:** metalled. 01/01-31/12
Distance: 500m 500m 200m 500m 200m on the spot on the spot.
Remarks: After 2 nights € 20/night.

Tourist information Besigheim:

Stadtverwaltung, Marktplatz 12, www.besigheim.de.

Beuron 17C6

Kloster Beuron, Abteistraße. **GPS**: n48,05306 e8,96704.

± 4 free. **Location:** Simple. **Surface:** gravel. 01/01-31/12
Remarks: Parking monastery.

S Beuron 17C6

Besi-Kanu-Sport, Bahnhofstrasse 29. **GPS**: n48,08597 e9,09559.

10 € 5 Ch WC included. **Surface:** gravel.
Distance: 1km 200m 5km.
Remarks: Canoe rental.

S Biberach/Riss 17D6

Rissstrasse. **GPS**: n48,10401 e9,79582.

DE

10 free, voluntary contribution Chfree. **Surface:** gravel.
01/01-31/12 service: 01/11-28/02.
Distance: 700m.
Remarks: Max. 3 days.

S Bietigheim-Bissingen 17C4

Wohnmobilstellplatz an der Enz, Mühlwiesenstrasse. **GPS**: n48,96110 e9,13329.

9 € 5 € 0,50/80liter Ch (8x)€ 0,50/kWh. **Location:** Urban. **Surface:** metalled. 01/01-31/12
Distance: 200m 1km 1km 100m 100m 100m.
Remarks: Max. 4 days, check in at Lama Bar.

Tourist information Bietigheim-Bissingen:
Tourist-Information, Marktplatz 10, www.bietigheim-bissingen.de.

S Blaubeuren 17D5

Parkplatz P6, Dodelweg. **GPS**: n48,41351 e9,79102.

20 € 5 € 1/5minutes Ch€ 1. **Surface:** metalled. 01/01-31/12
Distance: 1km 1km 1km 800m.
Remarks: Parking swimming pool, max. 2 days.

Blaustein 17D5

Freizeitbad Bad Blau, Boschstraße. **GPS**: n48,41757 e9,91630.
3 free. **Location:** Simple. **Surface:** gravel.
Distance: 6,5km 200m 500m.

S Blumberg 17B6

P1, Festplatz, Oberes Ried. **GPS**: n47,83943 e8,54226.

48 € 6,50-7,50 € 1/50liter Ch (36x)€ 1/24h. **Location:** Comfortable, quiet. **Surface:** gravel/metalled. 01/01-31/12
Distance: 800m 100m 80m.
Remarks: With payment: KONUS guest card with many advantages.

S Blumberg 17B6

P2, Parkplatz Bahnhof Zollhaus, Achdorf. **GPS**: n47,83767 e8,55777.

10 € 6,50-7,50 . **Location:** Urban, noisy. **Surface:** gravel.
01/01-31/12
Distance: 1,5km.

S Blumberg 17B6

P3, Achdorfer Tal. GPS: n47,83528 e8,49833.

10 € 6,50-7,50 € 1 Ch (12x)€ 1/night,winter € 1,50. **Location:** Rural, simple, isolated, quiet. **Surface:** gravel. 01/01-31/12
Distance: 4km.
Remarks: Caution key € 10 (connection electricity), service at Kläranlage 800m, with payment: KONUS guest card with many advantages.

S Böblingen 17C4

Parkplatz an der Sporthalle, Rudolf-Diesel-strasse/Stetner strasse. **GPS**: n48,67693 e9,01651.

3 free Chfree. **Surface:** metalled. 01/05-30/10
Distance: 1km 7km 500m 250m 100m.
Remarks: Max. 3 nights.

S Bodman-Ludwigshafen 17C6

Am Sportplatz. **GPS**: n47,82369 e9,05153.

20 € 8 Ch (4x)€ 2. **Location:** Simple. **Surface:** grassy/metalled.
01/01-31/12
Distance: 1km 3,2km 1,4km.

S Bonndorf 17B6

Wohnmobilstellplatz Holzschlag, Schulstrasse/Bonndorfer Strasse, Bonndorf-Holzschlag. **GPS**: n47,84970 e8,26784.

DE

€ 5 Ch included. **Location:** Simple, noisy.
Distance: 100m.

S Bönnigheim 17C3

Mineralfreibad Bönnigheim, Bachstrasse 40. **GPS:** n49,03910 e9,08439.

4 free . **Location:** Rural, simple. **Surface:** grasstiles/metalled.
01/01-31/12
Distance: 500m 500m 1km.
Remarks: Caution key water € 10.

S Bopfingen 18A4

Gasthof zum Bären, Nördlinger strasse 3. **GPS:** n48,85715 e10,35508.

€ 6 € 1 € 1 Ch € 1. **Surface:** asphalted. 01/01-31/12
Distance: on the spot 16km on the spot 100m.

S Boxberg 17D2

Gasthof Forellenhof Hagenmühle, Uiffinger strasse 74. **GPS:** n49,48710 e9,61299.

20 € 5 (8x)€ 2,50. **Surface:** grassy/gravel. 01/01-31/12
Distance: 2km on the spot 1km 200m.

S Brackenheim 17C3

Weingut und Besenwirtschaft 'Zum Alten Pflug', Seebergweg. **GPS:** n49,10261 e9,04994.

3 € 6, free for clients Ch (3x)€ 2 WC € 2. **Surface:** metalled.
01/01-31/12
Distance: 3km 3km.
Remarks: Sunday on demand.

S Brackenheim 17C3

Weingut Winkler, Stockheimer strasse 13. **GPS:** n49,08001 e9,06270.

5 € 5 included. **Location:** Rural, simple. **Surface:** grassy/metalled. 01/01-31/12
Distance: on the spot 10km 10km 300m 1km 300m.

S Breisach/Rhein 16D4

Wohnmobil-Parkplatz, Josef-Buebstrasse. **GPS:** n49,02944 e7,57576.

80 free 8-20h, € 6/night, 2 nights € 10, 3 nights € 13, winter free € 1/100liter € 1 Ch € 1. **Location:** Urban, simple. **Surface:** asphalted.
01/01-31/12 Other parking in case of festivities.
Distance: 300m on the spot on the spot 300m 1,5km.
Remarks: Ground of wine festival, bread-service.

Breisach/Rhein 16D4

Restaurant Am Rhein, Hafenstrasse 11. **GPS:** n49,04292 e7,57378.

5 free. **Location:** Simple. **Surface:** metalled. 01/01-31/12
Distance: 2km on the spot 500m.
Remarks: Guests only.

Tourist information Breisach/Rhein:
Tourist Information, Marktplatz 16, www.breisach.de.City wall and towers.
Tue-Su.

DE

Museum für Stadtgeschichte, Rheintor.Town history. free.
Weinfest Kaiserstuhl Tuniberg.Wine festivals. end Aug.

S Bretten 17B3

Reisemobil-Stellplatz Bretten, Willi-Hesselbacher-Weg. **GPS**: n49,02980 e8,71914.
4 free € 1/100liter € 1/10h. **Surface:** metalled.
Distance: city centre 1,5km.
Remarks: Max. 2 days.

Bruchsal 17B3

Giesgrabenweg. **GPS**: n49,13227 e8,58981.

2 free. **Location:** Urban, simple, central. **Surface:** metalled.
01/01-31/12
Distance: 1km 4km 100m 1km on the spot.
Remarks: At sports centre, max. 48h.

S Bruchsal 17B3

Autohaus Konrad, Murgstrasse 9-13, Gewerbegebiet Stegwiesen. **GPS**: n49,13700 e8,59437.

3 free € 1/80liter Ch (4x) WC . **Location:** Urban. **Surface:** metalled. 01/01-31/12
Distance: 2km 3km 2km 200m 300m.
Remarks: Max. 3 nights, service use during shop opening hours. Follow signs TÜV.

S Buchen (Odenwald) 17C2

Wohnmobilhafen Morretal, Mühltalstraße. **GPS**: n49,52888 e9,31020.
12 € 5/24h, 3 days € 20 € 1/100liter Ch € 1/kWh WC € 1/h.
Surface: metalled. 01/01-31/12
Remarks: Use sanitary only during opening hours swimming pool.

S Buchenbach 17A6

Wanglerhof, Vogtweg 1. **GPS**: n47,96820 e7,99269.

10 € 10 + € 1,20/pp tourist tax Ch included € 2/day.
Location: Rural, simple. **Surface:** grassy. 01/01-31/12
Distance: 1km 100m 1km.

S Bühl 17A4

Wohnmobilstellplatz am Schwarzwaldbad, Ludwig-Jahn-strasse 8. **GPS**: n48,68862 e8,12995.

50 € 5 € 2/100liter € 2 Ch . **Location:** Urban, simple, noisy.
Surface: metalled. 01/01-31/12
Distance: 1km 6km 500m 1km on the spot on the spot.
Remarks: Bread-service.

S Calw 17B4

Wohnmobilstellplatz Am Alten Bahnhof, Bahnhofstrasse. **GPS**: n48,70592 e8,73808.

6 free € 1/80liter € 1 Ch € 1 (4x)€ 0,50/kWh. **Location:** Rural, simple, noisy. **Surface:** asphalted. 01/01-31/12
Distance: 1km 100m 200m on the spot on the spot.

Cleebronn/Tripsdrill 17C3

Erlebnispark Tripsdrill. **GPS**: n49,03102 e9,05096.
100 free. **Location:** Rural, isolated, quiet.
Surface: grassy.
12/04/2014-02/11/2014
Distance: 1km on the spot 3km 400m.
Remarks: Max. 3 days.

Tourist information Cleebronn/Tripsdrill:
Erlebnispark Tripsdrill.Amusement park.
01/04-31/10 9-18h.

S Crailsheim 17D3

Autohof Euro Rastpark, Marco-Polo-Straße 1, Satteldorf. **GPS**: n49,18146 e10,06889.
10 € 5, free with a meal . **Surface:** metalled. 01/01-31/12
Distance: 600m on the spot.

S Dettenheim 17B3

Kartbahn Liedolsheim, Kartbahnring 1. **GPS**: n49,14326 e8,43118.

DE

20 free Ch (8x)€ 3 WC € 2,50. **Location:** Rural, simple, isolated. **Surface:** grassy/metalled. 01/01-31/12
Distance: 2km 2km 2km on the spot 5km.
Remarks: Parking at Karting.

S Donaueschingen 17B6

Prinz Fritz Allee. **GPS**: n47,94746 e8,51183.

10 free (14x)€ 1. **Location:** Rural, simple, quiet. **Surface:** grassy.
01/01-31/12
Distance: 1,5km Danube Bike Trail.
Remarks: Max. 2 days, service, 300m.

S Donaueschingen 17B6

Haberfeld. **GPS**: n47,94931 e8,52209.
€ 1/50liter Ch.
01/01-31/12
Remarks: Follow signs Kläranlage.

Tourist information Donaueschingen:

Tourismus- und Sportamt, Karlstrasse 58, www.donaueschingen.de.Horse city, named after the source of the River danube.
M Museum Karlsbau, Karlsplatz 7.Art collection Furstenberg.
Tue-Sa 10-13h, 14-17h, Su 10-17h. T € 5.
Der Donau Radweg.Signposted cycle route along the Donau.

S Durbach 17A5

Grol/Festplatz, Almstrasse. **GPS**: n48,49407 e8,01105.

15 € 6 (8x)€ 1/8h. **Location:** Simple. **Surface:** gravel.
01/01-31/12 festivities.
Distance: 500m 10km 50m.

S Durbach 17A5

Halle am Durbach, Wiesenstraße, Ebersweier. **GPS**: n48,50122 e7,98940.

6 € 6 € 1/80liter Ch (6x)4h. **Location:** Rural, simple. **Surface:** grasstiles. 01/01-31/12
Distance: 500m 10km 750m 200m.

S Eberbach 17C2

Wohnmobilstellplatz In der Au, In der Au. **GPS**: n49,46162 e8,97812.

7 free (6x)€ 1/2kWh WC. **Location:** Simple, isolated. **Surface:** gravel.
01/01-31/12 16/08-31/08.
Distance: 1km on the spot.
Remarks: Max. 2 nights.

Eberbach 17C2

Wohnmobilstellplatz Neckarlauer, B37, Uferstrasse. **GPS**: n49,46012 e8,98652.

10 free. **Location:** Central. **Surface:** metalled.
01/01-31/12 high water.
Distance: 300m 300m 500m.

S Eberbach 17C2

In der Au. **GPS**: n49,46217 e8,97351.
€ 1/80liter Ch.

Ebringen 17A6

An der Schönberghalle, Schulstraße 8. **GPS**: n47,95639 e7,77667.

3 free. **Location:** Simple. **Surface:** grasstiles. 01/01-31/12
Distance: 7,6km on the spot.
Remarks: Max. 6.5m, max. 2 days.

S Ehingen 17D5

Wohnmobilstellplatz, Am Stadion. **GPS**: n48,28053 e9,73571.

DE

10 free € 1/100liter Ch (4x)€ 1/4h. **Surface:** metalled.
01/01-31/12
Distance: 1km 1km on the spot 500m 10m Danube Bike Trail.

S Eichstetten 17A6

Weingut Köbelin, Altweg 131. **GPS**: n48,09472 e7,72083.

5 € 13 Ch included. **Location:** Rural, comfortable, isolated, quiet. **Surface:** gravel/sand.

S Eigeltingen 17C6

Landgasthof Mönchhof, Mönchhof. **GPS**: n47,88094 e8,95278.

4 guests free Ch . **Surface:** metalled. 01/01-31/12
Distance: 6km on the spot 4km.

S Eisenbach 17B6

Reisemobilpark Höchstberg. **GPS**: n47,94938 e8,25441.

20 € 8 + Kurtaxe € 1,60/pp € 1/100liter Ch (20x) included,Only in summer. **Location:** Rural, comfortable, quiet. **Surface:** grassy/gravel.
01/01-31/12
Distance: on the spot on the spot.
Remarks: At sports park, altitude 1033m.

S Ellwangen 18A3

Maxi-Autohof Ellwangen, Max-Eyth-Strasse 1. **GPS**: n48,95628 e10,18319.

15 € 5/night Ch WC against payment. **Location:** Highway.
Surface: asphalted. 01/01-31/12
Distance: 3km on the spot 1km.

S Emmendingen 17A6

Wohnmobilstellplatz am Sportfeld, Am Sportfeld. **GPS**: n48,11869 e7,84154.

20 free € 1/80liter Ch. **Location:** Urban, simple. **Surface:** asphalted.
01/01-31/12
Distance: 1km 400m 600m.
Remarks: Max. 3 days, in front of swimmingpool.

Endingen am Kaiserstuhl 17A6

P2 Stadthalle, Freiburger Weg. **GPS**: n48,13830 e7,70321.

20 free. **Location:** Urban, simple, central.
Surface: asphalted/metalled.
Distance: 200m 200m.

S Eppingen 17C3

Wohnmobilhalt am Parkweg, Am Altstadring. **GPS**: n49,13793 e8,91402.

4 free € 1/80liter € 1 Ch € 1 (4x)€ 1. **Location:** Rural, comfortable.
Surface: metalled. 01/01-31/12
Distance: 500m on the spot 500m on the spot on the spot.

Esslingen am Neckar 17C4

Äußerer Burgplatz, Mülbergerstraße. **GPS**: n48,74713 e9,31064.

DE

2 free. **Location:** Urban, simple. **Surface:** metalled.
01/01-31/12
Distance: 1km 1km on the spot 1km 300m.
Remarks: Max. 48h.

Tourist information Esslingen am Neckar:
Esslinger Stadtmarketing, Marktplatz 2, www.esslingen-tourist.de.

S Ettenheim 17A5

Ernst Caravan und Freizeit Center, Rudolf Hell Straße 32-44. **GPS**: n48,27431 e7,78161.

30 free € 1 € 1 Ch € 1 (12x)€ 0,50/kWh. **Location:** Highway, simple.
Surface: metalled. 01/01-31/12
Distance: 500m.
Remarks: Motorhome dealer, accessory shop, repairs.

S Ettlingen 17B4

Wohnmobilstellplatz Am Freibad, Schöllbronner strasse. **GPS**: n48,93561 e8,41747.

14 free € 1 Ch (8x)€ 1/kWh. **Location:** Urban, simple.
Surface: asphalted. 01/01-31/12
Distance: 100m 3,3km 100m 700m on the spot on the spot on the spot.
Remarks: Parking swimming pool, max. 48h.

S Filderstadt 17C4

Parkplatz P2, Tübinger Strasse 40. **GPS**: n48,67347 e9,21456.

8 € 5/24h € 1/80liter Ch (8x)€ 0,50/kWh,16Amp.
01/01-31/12

Distance: 500m 500m 500m 500m.
Remarks: Follow Filharmonie.

S Freiburg 17A6

Reisemobilplatz Freiburg, Bissierstrasse / Am Eschholzpark. **GPS**: n47,99915 e7,82643.

80 € 8, motorhome >7m + € 0,50/50cm € 1/100liter Ch (20x)€ 0,50/kWh free. **Location:** Urban, comfortable.
Surface: asphalted/gravel.
01/01-31/12
Distance: Old city centre 1,5km 4,3km 450m.
Remarks: Max. 3 days, green zone: environmental badge obligatory.

S Freiburg 17A6

WV-Südcaravan, Hanferstrasse 30, Hochdorf. **GPS**: n48,04146 e7,81473.

6 free € 1/80liter Ch. **Location:** Urban, simple.
Surface: asphalted/metalled.
01/01-31/12
Distance: Old city centre 10km 3km 300m 3km.
Remarks: During opening hours.

Tourist information Freiburg:
Freiburg Wirtschaft und Touristik GmbH & Co. KG, Rotteckring 14, www.freiburg.de.University town, city centre with many curiosities.
Augustinermuseum, Salzstrasse 32.Medieval ecclesiastical treasures.
Münster Unserer Lieben Frau, Münsterplatz.Built as a cemetery.
Tue-Su.
Bergwelt Schauinsland.

S Freudenberg 17C2

Hauptstrasse. **GPS**: n49,74001 e9,31938.

7 € 5/night € 1/15minutes Ch (6x)€ 1/8h,16Amp.
Surface: metalled. 01/01-31/12
Distance: 50m 20m 20m 300m 500m.

S Friedrichshafen 24D1

Neue Messe Friedrichshafen, Allmannsweilerstrasse. **GPS**: n47,67727 e9,51279.

€ 15 Ch (32x) WC. **Surface:** asphalted/metalled.
during fair
Distance: 3km on the spot.

DE

Friedrichshafen 24D1

Stellplatz Friedrichshafen, Lindauerstrasse 2. **GPS**: n47,65025 e9,49597.

20 € 10 € 1/80liter Ch WC. **Surface:** asphalted/metalled.
01/01-31/12
Distance: 200m 200m on the spot.
Remarks: Max. 3 nights. Follow signs campsite.

Gaildorf 17D3

Bleichgärten. **GPS**: n49,00224 e9,76587.

7 free Ch (4x)free,16Amp. **Location:** Simple. **Surface:** metalled.
01/01-31/12
Distance: 500m 400m 500m 500m.

Gammertingen 17C5

Reutlingerstrasse. **GPS**: n48,25611 e9,21056.

10 free. **Surface:** grassy/gravel. 01/01-31/12
Distance: 1km 1km 1km.

Geisingen 17B6

Reisemobilstellplatz Geisingen, Am Espen 8. **GPS**: n47,92016 e8,65153.
37 € 7 € 1/80liter Ch € 1/4kWh. **Surface:** unpaved.
01/01-31/12
Distance: 500m.

Gernsbach 17B4

Parkplatz Murginsel, Schlossstrasse/Klingelstrasse. **GPS**: n48,75934 e8,33900.

8 € 5 € 1/100liter Ch (8x)€ 1/12h WC. **Location:** Rural, simple.
Surface: asphalted. 01/01-31/12
Distance: 500m on the spot 500m 1km on the spot on the spot on the spot.
Remarks: Max. 7 days.

Gernsbach 17B4

Am Schwimmbad 1, Oberstrot. **GPS**: n48,74239 e8,34186.

5 free. **Location:** Rural, simple. **Surface:** grassy.
01/01-31/12
Distance: 200m 200m on the spot on the spot.
Remarks: At swimming pool.

Giengen 18A4

Reisemobilstation Charlottenhöhle, Lonetalstrasse 60, Hürben. **GPS**: n48,58412 e10,21203.

15 € 7 € 2 Ch (6x)€ 2/24h,16Amp WC € 2. **Location:** Rural, quiet.
Surface: gravel. 01/01-31/12
Remarks: At prehistoric cave, coins available at Hölenhaus.

Giengen 18A4

Am Schießberg, Auf dem Schießberg. **GPS**: n48,62975 e10,25159.

8 free. **Location:** Simple. **Surface:** gravel.
01/01-31/12
Distance: 1,5km 4,3km 1,5km 1,5km.

Tourist information Giengen:
Charlottenhöhle.Caves. 8.30-11.30h, 13.30-16.30h, Su 8.30-16.30h.
M Margarete Steiff Museum.Cuddling animals. Mo-Fri 13-16h, Sa 8.30-12h.
T free.

Göppingen 17D4

Hohen Staufenhalle, P1, Lorcherstrasse. **GPS**: n48,71176 e9,64816.

DE

10 free € 1/80liter Ch. **Location:** Urban. **Surface:** asphalted.
01/01-31/12
Distance: 1km 1km 1km.
Remarks: Max. 2 nights.

Grossbottwar 17C3

Parkplatz an der Wunnensteinhalle, In den Frauengärten. **GPS**: n49,00363 e9,28739.

3 free. **Surface:** metalled. 01/01-31/12
Distance: 400m 400m 200m.
Remarks: Max. 3 nights.

Gschwend 17D4

Naturbadesee, Frickenhofer Strasse. **GPS**: n48,93603 e9,75143.

3 free. **Location:** Rural. **Surface:** forest soil. 01/01-31/12
Distance: 1,5km.

Gschwend 17D4

Joosenhofer Sägmühle. **GPS**: n48,92312 e9,77393.

free € 1/80liter Ch. **Surface:** asphalted. 01/01-31/12

Güglingen 17C3

Oberes Tal. **GPS**: n49,06492 e8,99489.

6 free € 1 Ch. **Location:** Rural, simple. **Surface:** metalled.
01/01-31/12
Distance: 700m 500m Aldi-Lidl 500m on the spot on the spot.
Remarks: At swimming pool, max. 5 nights.

Haigerloch 17C5

Wohnmobilstellplatz Haigerloch, Weildorfer Kreuz 1. **GPS**: n48,36875 e8,79384.
10 free Ch . **Surface:** asphalted. 01/01-31/12
Distance: 300m.
Remarks: Max. 4 days.

Haslach/Kinzigtal 17A5

Klosterplatz, Ringstraße. **GPS**: n48,27572 e8,08509.

20 free. **Location:** Urban, simple. **Surface:** metalled.
01/01-31/12
Distance: 50m 150m 500m 100m.

Haslach/Kinzigtal 17A5

Parkplatz Eichenbach-sporthalle, Strickerweg. **GPS**: n48,27854 e8,07968.

10 free. **Location:** Simple. **Surface:** metalled. 01/01-31/12
Distance: 500m 300m.

Haslach/Kinzigtal 17A5

Waldseeparkplatz, Waldseeweg. **GPS**: n48,27161 e8,09148.

10 free. **Location:** Rural, simple. **Surface:** asphalted.
01/01-31/12
Distance: 1km 200m 1km.

DE

Hausach 17A5

Waldstadion, Waldstraße. **GPS**: n48,28058 e8,17829.

4 free WC. **Location:** Rural, simple, simple, quiet, noisy. **Surface:** gravel/sand. 01/01-31/12

Distance: 500m 100m.

Hausach 17A5

Badepark, Schanze 3. **GPS**: n48,28620 e8,16589.

6 free. **Location:** Simple. **Surface:** metalled. 01/01-31/12

Distance: on the spot 500m.

Remarks: Nearby swimming pool.

Hechingen 17C5

Weiher, Niederhechingerstrasse. **GPS**: n48,35797 e8,96093.

12 € 6 € 1 Ch € 0,50/kWh. **Surface:** metalled. 01/01-31/12

Remarks: Parking at sports park, adjacent walking and bicycle area.

Heidenheim 18A4

In den Seewiesen. **GPS**: n48,69455 e10,16410.

22 € 2/day € 1/70liter € 1 Ch (18x)€ 1/6h,16Amp. **Location:** Rural, simple. **Surface:** asphalted/gravel. 01/01-31/12

Distance: 5km 1km.

Heilbronn 17C3

Wertwiesenpark, Neckarhalde. **GPS**: n49,13047 e9,20469.

20 free € 1/100liter Ch (12x)€ 0,50/kWh. **Location:** Comfortable. **Surface:** metalled. 01/01-31/12

Distance: 2km 7km 100m 500m.

Heiligenberg 17C6

Sennerei Schläge, Betenbrunner strasse. **GPS**: n47,81892 e9,31445.

10 € 5/16-09h € 0,50 € 0,50 Ch. **Surface:** grassy/metalled. 01/01-31/12

Distance: 300m 300m 300m 200m bakery 200m.

Remarks: Max. 2 nights.

Herbrechtingen 18A4

P7 Eselstalparkplatz, Baumschulenweg. **GPS**: n48,61758 e10,17411.

15 € 7 € 2 Ch € 2/24h. **Location:** Rural, quiet. **Surface:** asphalted. 01/01-31/12

Remarks: Check in at Hölenhaus.

Hessigheim 17C3

Fasanenhof, Römerweg 1. **GPS**: n49,00939 e9,18877.

15 € 5 . **Location:** Rural, simple. 01/01-31/12

Distance: 3,5km on the spot shop with farm products on the spot on the spot.

Remarks: Farm/restaurant/Biergarten/shop.

Hessigheim 17C3

Felsengarten Kellerei Besigheim e.G., Am Felsengarten 1. **GPS**: n48,99612 e9,18068.

5 guests free . **Surface:** asphalted. 01/01-31/12

Distance: 1km on the spot 1km.

DE

Remarks: Max. 2 nights.

Heubach 17D4

Am Freibad, Mögglinger Strasse. **GPS**: n48,79802 e9,93831.

6 € 6 € 1/90liter Ch€ 0,50. **Surface:** grasstiles. 01/01-31/12
Distance: 200m Lidl 400m.

Höchenschwand 24B1

Natursportzentrum. **GPS**: n47,73652 e8,15990.

12 € 7 Ch (12x)€ 1/6h WC. **Location:** Rural, comfortable.
Surface: gravel. 01/01-31/12
Distance: 400m 100m 600m on the spot.

Holzmaden 17D4

Urwelt-Museum Hauff, Aichelbergerstrasse 75/90. **GPS**: n48,63482 e9,52771.
6 free. **Surface:** metalled. 01/01-31/12
Distance: 3km 2,2km.
Remarks: Max. 1 night.

Hornberg 17B6

Hotel Schöne Aussicht, Schöne Aussicht 1, Niederwasser. **GPS**: n48,19443 e8,18494.
4 € 8 included.
Distance: on the spot.

Hüfingen 17B6

Bräunlinger Straße. **GPS**: n47,92361 e8,48707.

22 € 5 € 1 Ch € 1. **Location:** Urban, comfortable, noisy.
Surface: grasstiles. 01/01-31/12
Distance: 300m 300m.
Remarks: Thu (market).

Hülben 17D5

Phönix-Wohnmobihafen, Kaltentalstrasse. **GPS**: n48,52620 e9,41227.

10 free € 0,50/80liter Ch (6x)€ 0,50/kWh. **Surface:** gravel.
01/01-31/12
Distance: 400m 400m 500m.
Remarks: Max. 5 days.

Ihringen 17A6

Kaiserstuhl Camping, Nachtwaid 5. **GPS**: n48,03083 e7,65778.

6 € 14,60 + tourist tax Ch € 1,80/3kWh WC included.
Location: Rural, comfortable. **Surface:** asphalted/metalled.
31/03-30/10
Distance: 600m 200m.

Ippesheim 18A2

Kempe's Autohof Gollhofen, Industriestraße 1. **GPS**: n49,58546 e10,17579.
25 € 5 WC. **Surface:** asphalted. 01/01-31/12
Distance: on the spot.

Isny 25A1

Parkplatz An der Untere Mühle, Seidenstrasse 43. **GPS**: n47,69457 e10,03780.

10 € 7,50 + € 1,50/pp tourist tax € 1/80liter Ch (8x)€ 0,50/kWh WC. **Location:** Urban. **Surface:** asphalted/gravel. 01/01-31/12
Distance: 300m 100m 300m 200m.
Remarks: Max. 2 nights.

Isny 25A1

Caravans Dethleffs, Rangenbergweg. **GPS**: n47,69938 e10,05490.

8 € 5 + € 1/pp tourist tax Ch included. **Surface:** metalled.
01/01-31/12

DE

Distance: 1km 1km 1km 1,4km 500m.
Remarks: Max. 3 nights.

Kaisersbach 17D4

Schwaben-Park, Hofwiesen 11, Gmeinweiler. **GPS**: n48,90304 e9,65484.

10 free. 01/04-31/10
Remarks: Inclining pitches.

Tourist information Kaisersbach:
Schwaben-Park.Amusement park. Easter-Oct 9-18h.

Kappelrodeck 17A5

Wohnmobileck am Heidenhof, Grüner Winkel. **GPS**: n48,58370 e8,12650.

18 € 5/day, 3 days € 10, 7 days € 20 € 1/100liter Ch (8x)€ 1/2kWh. **Location:** Rural, simple, quiet. **Surface:** gravel/metalled.
01/01-31/12
Distance: 800m 150m 500m on the spot on the spot.
Remarks: Max. 6 nights.

Karlsruhe 17B3

Am Yachthafen Maxau, Maxau am Rhein. **GPS**: n49,03720 e8,30583.

12 . 01/01-31/12
Distance: Karlsruhe 9km on the spot 2km.
Remarks: Along the Rhine river.

Karlsruhe 17B3

Ettlinger Allee. **GPS**: n48,98761 e8,40412.
5 free. **Surface:** asphalted. 01/01-31/12
Distance: centre 2,5km metro 400m.

Kehl 17A5

Reisemobilstellplatz Hurst, An den Sportanlagen 1, Kehl-Auenheim. **GPS**: n48,60653 e7,83146.

18 € 6 € 1 Ch (12x)€ 2/2kWh WC € 1. **Location:** Rural, simple, quiet. **Surface:** asphalted/grassy. 01/01-31/12
Distance: 500m on the spot 500m on the spot on the spot.
Remarks: Check in at cafe zum Ganz.

Kehl 17A5

Am Wasserturm, Schwimbadstrasse. **GPS**: n48,56381 e7,81498.

40 € 6 € 1/100liter Ch (16x)€ 0,50/kWh. **Location:** Urban, comfortable, quiet. **Surface:** grassy/metalled. 01/01-31/12
Distance: 100m 500m on the spot on the spot on the spot.
Remarks: Max. 3 days.

Kehl 17A5

Bürstner-Service-Centrum, Elsässer strasse 80, Kehl-Neumühl. **GPS**: n48,57010 e7,84042.

6 free € 1/100liter Ch (6x)€ 1/kWh WC . **Location:** Rural.
Surface: asphalted. 01/01-31/12
Distance: 1km 100m 600m on the spot on the spot.

Kenzingen 17A6

Ritter's Weingut, Rossleiteweg 1. **GPS**: n48,18739 e7,78343.

15 € 10/incl. 2 pers + € 2/pp € 2,50/day WC included.
Location: Comfortable. **Surface:** grassy/gravel. 01/01-31/12
Distance: 7,5km on the spot.

Kirchberg/Jagst 17D3

Wanderparkplatz Kirchberg-Tal, Hohen Loher Strasse. **GPS**: n49,20367 e9,98344.

DE

10 free. **Surface:** gravel. 01/01-31/12

Kisslegg 17D6

Strandbad Obersee, Strandbadweg. **GPS:** n47,79602 e9,87950.

10 free € 1/50liter Ch (5x)€ 1/3h WC. **Surface:** grassy/gravel. 01/01-31/12

Distance: 800m 100m 100m 100m 1km 400m.

Remarks: Max. 2 nights.

Kisslegg 17D6

Familiefreizeitgelände St Anna, Le Pouliguenstrasse. **GPS:** n47,79119 e9,87229.

3 free. **Surface:** grassy/metalled. 01/01-31/12

Distance: 800m 500m 500m.

Kisslegg 17D6

Seminarhotel Sonnenstrahl, Sebastian Kneipp strasse 1. **GPS:** n47,78421 e9,87973.

3 free. **Surface:** asphalted/metalled. 01/01-31/12

Distance: 800m on the spot 800m.

Remarks: Max. 2 nights.

Königschaffhausen 17A6

Wohnmobilgarten im Kirschenhof Schmidt, Königsweg 5. **GPS:** n48,14277 e7,66273.

16 € 11 + tourist tax € 1/pp Ch WC included € 1 in Caffl.

Location: Rural, comfortable. **Surface:** gravel/metalled. 01/01-31/12

Distance: 500m on the spot.

Remarks: Wifi in café.

Königsfeld 17B6

Reisemobilpark Bregnitzhof, Buchenberger Strasse 34. **GPS:** n48,14028 e8,40583.

21 € 8/night € 0,50 Ch € 1/8h. **Location:** Rural, luxurious, quiet. **Surface:** gravel. 01/01-31/12

Distance: 1km 10 min walking.

Remarks: Saunalandschaft Bregnitzhof, 18-holes golf course, check in between 14-19h.

Konstanz 24C1

Parkplatz Döbele, Döbeleplatz. **GPS:** n47,65794 e9,16933.

12 € 1/h, € 15/24h Ch WC included. **Surface:** asphalted/metalled. 01/01-31/12

Distance: 1km 800m 800m 200m 800m 500m.

Remarks: Max. 1 night.

Konstanz 24C1

Bauernhof Gebhardshof, Zum Hofgut 4, Wallhausen. **GPS:** n47,74321 e9,13702.

3 € 15 + tourist tax € 2/pp Ch WC € 0,50. **Surface:** grassy/metalled. 01/01-31/12

Distance: 1km 250m 250m 500m 500m Free bus.

Remarks: Call before arrival: 0049/01742048535.

Korb 17C4

Reisemobilstellplatz Unterm Korber Kopf, Brucknerstrasse 14. **GPS:** n48,84597 e9,35544.

6 € 3 € 0,50/80liter Ch (6x)€ 0,50/kWh. **Surface:** metalled.

01/01-31/12
Distance: 400m Gaststätte 300m 500m.

Kressbronn 24D1

Wohnmobilstellplatz Dorfkrug Tunau, Tunauerweg 4. **GPS:** n47,58999 e9,57512.

40 € 18 Ch (40x) WC € 1,50/pp . **Surface:** asphalted/grassy.
01/04-31/10
Distance: 1km 1km 1km on the spot 1km.

Kressbronn 24D1

Gohren am See. **GPS:** n47,58818 e9,56256.
11 € 12 Ch € 3/12h. 01/04-15/10

Külsheim 17D2

Am Schloss Külsheim, Kirchbergweg. **GPS:** n49,67123 e9,52255.

8 free € 0,50/80liter Ch (6x)€ 0,50/kWh. **Surface:** metalled.
01/01-31/12 10/09-25/09.
Distance: 300m.

Ladenburg 17B2

Wohnmobilstellplatz Ladenburg, Heidelberger Straße. **GPS:** n49,46596 e8,61460.

34 € 10 € 1/80liter Ch € 1/2kWh . **Location:** Urban, comfortable, central, quiet. **Surface:** grassy. 01/01-31/12
Distance: Altstadt 500m, Heidelberg 10km 3km 200m 200m.

Langenau 18A5

Karlstraße. **GPS:** n48,50193 e10,12203.
4 € 5 € 0,50/70liter € 0,50/1kWh. **Location:** Simple. **Surface:** metalled. 01/01-31/12
Distance: 500m 3,2km 300m 1,2km.

Langenbrettach 17C3

Freibad Langenbeutingen, Schwabbacker Strasse 24, Langenbeutingen. **GPS:** n49,21227 e9,40767.

3 free. **Location:** Rural. **Surface:** asphalted.
Remarks: Parking swimming pool.

Langenburg 17D3

Am Freibad, In der Strut 5. **GPS:** n49,24973 e9,86681.
3 free. **Surface:** gravel. 01/01-31/12
Distance: 1km.
Remarks: Not accessible coming from the west.

Lauchringen 24B1

An der Wutach, Badstrasse. **GPS:** n47,62556 e8,31361.

20 free, 01/04-01/11 € 5 Ch included (16x)€ 2/24h. **Location:** Rural, comfortable, quiet. **Surface:** gravel.
01/01-31/12 service: 01/11-01/04.
Distance: on the spot on the spot.
Remarks: Pay at town hall or swimming pool, key electricity at pool, caution € 20.

Lauda-Königshofen 17D2

Badstrasse, Lauda. **GPS:** n49,55886 e9,70099.

4 free. **Surface:** asphalted. 01/01-31/12
Distance: 1km.
Remarks: Parking at swimming pool.

Lauda-Königshofen 17D2

Gasthaus Zur Lamm, St. Josefstrasse 30-32, Marbach. **GPS:** n49,56568 e9,72834.

10 € 5/24h Ch (10x)included. **Surface:** asphalted. 01/01-31/12

DE

Distance: ⊗on the spot.

S Laufenburg 24A1

Laufenburg Baden P6, Andelsbachstraße. **GPS**: n47,56585 e8,06677.

6 €5 €2/5minutes Ch€2 (6x)€0,50/1kWh. **Location:** Urban, quiet. **Surface:** concrete. 01/01-31/12

Remarks: Along the Rhine river.

S Laupheim 17D5

Schloß Grosslaupheim, Klaus-Graf-Stauffenberg-Strasse. **GPS**: n48,23128 e9,88872.

7 €8 €0,50 €0,50 Ch€0,50 . **Location:** Rural. **Surface:** metalled.
01/01-31/12

Distance: on the spot.

Leonberg 17C4

Parkplatz Steinstrasse, Steinstrasse. **GPS**: n48,79705 e9,01751.

5 €1/night. **Surface:** metalled. 01/01-31/12 Sa 5-13h.

Distance: 400m ⊗150m 300m on the spot.

S Leutkirch im Allgäu 18A6

Wohnmobilstellplatz Leutkirch, Kemptener Straße. **GPS**: n47,82228 e10,03939.

14 €6 €1/100liter Ch €0,50/kWh. **Surface:** asphalted.
01/01-31/12

Distance: 1km ⊗300m.

S Löffingen 17B6

Waldbad Löffingen, Am Waldbad. **GPS**: n47,90017 e8,33287.

7 €8 + €2/pp tourist tax, 01/10-31/05 free (4x)included €0,50,At swimming pool. **Location:** Comfortable. **Surface:** concrete.
01/01-31/12 service 01/10-01/05.

Distance: Swimming pool ⊗on the spot.

Remarks: Check in at swimming pool.

Tourist information Löffingen:

Schwarzwaldpark.Game preserve and summer toboggan slide (€ 1.02 a time). Easter-Oct 9-18h.

S Malsch 17B4

Gast Caravanning, Daimlerstr. 20b. **GPS**: n48,89079 e8,30747.

6 free €1/80liter Ch. **Location:** Simple. **Surface:** asphalted/metalled.
01/01-31/12

Distance: 7,6km.

Remarks: Motorhome dealer, accessory shop.

S Mannheim/Friedrichsfeld 17B2

Güma Reisemobile, Steinzeugstrasse 21. **GPS**: n49,44570 e8,56780.

3 free Ch WC free. **Location:** Simple, noisy.
Surface: metalled.
01/01-31/12

Distance: 10km 1km 1km 300m.

Remarks: Max. 3 nights, sanitary use during shop opening hours.

S Marbach am Neckar 17C4

Parkplatz Bolzplatz, Poppenweiler/Weimarstrasse. **GPS**: n48,93389 e9,26278.

5 €5 Ch. **Location:** Rural, simple. **Surface:** metalled.

DE

01/01-31/12
Distance: 1km 6,2km 100m 600m 500m.
Remarks: Max. 2 nights, service: Gruppenklärwerk Häldenmühle, L1100.

Markelsheim 17D2

Engelsbergstrasse. **GPS:** n49,47537 e9,83474.

2 free. **Surface:** asphalted. 01/01-31/12 week of Whitsuntide.
Distance: 300m 300m.
Remarks: Max. 2 nights.

Meckenbeuren 24D1

Wohnmobilplatz Besenwirtschaft Georgshof, Pfingstweiderstrasse 10-12/1, Reute. **GPS:** n47,68022 e9,55308.

10 € 8 Ch (9x)€ 0,35/kWh € 1. **Surface:** grassy/gravel.
01/01-31/12
Distance: on the spot 200m 100m.

Meersburg/Bodensee 24C1

Ergeten, Allmendweg. **GPS:** n47,70160 e9,26898.

35+60 € 10/24h € 1/100liter € 1 Ch € 0,50/kWh WC.
Surface: metalled. 01/01-31/12
Distance: 1km 100m 50m shuttle to centre.
Remarks: At edge of city, + 2x parking Allmendweg P1 n47.70211, o 9.26983, P2 n47,70159, o 9,27172.

Tourist information Meersburg/Bodensee:
Gästeinformation, Kirchstrasse 4, www.meersburg.de.Tourist town with historical centre and promenade along Lake Constance.

Meißenheim 17A5

Wohnmobilpark Ortenau, Winkelstrasse 36. **GPS:** n48,41616 e7,77736.

24+24 € 5/day € 1/120liter (24x)€ 1/kWh. **Location:** Rural, comfortable. **Surface:** gravel/metalled. 01/01-31/12
Distance: 500m 800m.

Memmingen 18A6

Wohnmobilstellplatz Memmingen, Colmarer Straße/Hemmerlestraße. **GPS:** n47,99531 e10,18245.

20 € 1/2h, € 5/24h € 1/100liter Ch (18x)€ 0,50/kWh.
Location: Urban, simple. **Surface:** metalled. 01/01-31/12
Distance: 900m 2,2km 700m Lidl 600m.
Remarks: Max. 3 days.

Mengen 17C6

Südsee III, Uferweg 25. **GPS:** n48,03117 e9,28265.

20 € 7 € 1/80liter Ch (16x)€ 0,50/kWh. **Surface:** gravel.
01/01-31/12
Distance: 500m on the spot 500m.

Messkirch 17C6

Messplatz P2, Am Stachus. **GPS:** n47,99381 e9,11514.

5 free € 1/80liter Ch WC. **Surface:** metalled.
01/01-31/12, service 01/04-30/09
Distance: 500m 400m 200m 500m.

Metzingen 17C5

Reisemobilplatz Outletcity Metzingen, Stetterstrasse 4. **GPS:** n48,53241 e9,27574.

DE

20 € 10 Chincluded (6x)€ 2,16Amp. **Surface:** gravel.
01/01-31/12
Distance: 800m 800m 800m 800m shuttle every 15 min.

S Mosbach 17C3

Wasemweg. **GPS:** n49,36139 e9,14833.

10 free € 1/150liter Ch (10x)€ 1/12h. **Location:** Rural, comfortable, quiet. **Surface:** concrete. 01/01-31/12
Distance: 800m.

S Mössingen 17C5

Wohnmobilstellplatz Firstwald, Firstwaldstraße, Kernstadt. **GPS:** n48,41348 e9,06915.

10 free € 1 € 1 Ch (10x)€ 0,50/kWh,16Amp. **Surface:** grasstiles.
01/01-31/12
Distance: 1,5km 500m 1km 100m.

Muggensturm 17B4

Muggensturm, Vogesenstraße. **GPS:** n48,87946 e8,28721.

3 free. **Location:** Urban, simple. **Surface:** gravel.
01/01-31/12
Distance: 1,5km 4,4km beach 100m.

S Mühlberg 18A6

Ferienhof Musch, Unterer weg 7. **GPS:** n47,98534 e9,98697.

4 € 10, 2 pers.incl Ch (3x) WC € 3. **Surface:** grassy/metalled.
01/01-31/12
Distance: 10km 100m 100m 10km 10km.

Müllheim 24A1

Am Engelberg, Hügelheim. **GPS:** n47,83282 e7,62320.

2 free. **Location:** Rural, simple, isolated, quiet.
01/01-31/12
Distance: 500m 1,5km.

Müllheim 24A1

Am Nüsslegarten, Am Nüsslegarten, Britzingen. **GPS:** n47,82891 e7,67336.

2 free. **Location:** Rural, simple, quiet.
01/01-31/12

Müllheim 24A1

Freibad Müllheim, Ziegleweg 7. **GPS:** n47,80237 e7,63403.

3 free. **Location:** Urban, simple. **Surface:** asphalted.
01/01-31/12
Remarks: Next to swimming pool.

Müllheim 24A1

Parkplatz Nußbaumallee, Nußbaumallee. **GPS:** n47,80942 e7,62985.
3 free. **Location:** Urban, simple. **Surface:** asphalted.
01/01-31/12
Remarks: Max. 2 days.

S Müllheim 24A1

Markgräfler Kräuterhof, Im Käppeleacker 3, Hügelheim. **GPS:** n47,83237 e7,62045.

DE

4 free, free. **Location:** Urban, simple. **Surface:** grasstiles.
01/01-31/12
Distance: 500m 1km.
Remarks: Herbery, herb-Stube.

S Münsingen 17D5

Wiesentalstadion, Grafenecker Straße. **GPS:** n48,40939 e9,48580.
18 € 5/24h, 3 days € 12 € 1/100liter Ch € 1/6h. **Surface:** gravel.
01/01-31/12
Distance: 1km within walking distance on the spot.

S Murg 24A1

Am Freibad. **GPS:** n47,55196 e8,02403.

15 € 10 € 1/100liter € 0,50/1kWh. **Location:** Rural, comfortable, quiet. **Surface:** metalled. 01/01-31/12
Distance: 500m on the spot.

S Murrhardt 17D3

Parkplatz Festhalle, Kaiser-Ludwig-Straße 25. **GPS:** n48,97960 e9,57461.

3 free € 1/90liter Ch. **Location:** Rural, simple. **Surface:** asphalted.
01/01-31/12
Distance: 400m 100m.

S Nagold 17B5

Wohnmobilhafen, Am Glockenrain. **GPS:** n48,56389 e8,72306.

12 free € 1/80liter € 1 Ch € 1 (12x)€ 1/kWh. **Location:** Rural, simple, quiet. **Surface:** gravel/metalled. 01/01-31/12
Distance: 1km 25m 900m 400m on the spot on the spot.

Nagold 17B5

Am Bahnhof, Bahnhofstraße. **GPS:** n48,55791 e8,72748.

4 free. **Location:** Rural, simple, noisy. **Surface:** asphalted.
01/01-31/12
Distance: 700m 100m on the spot on the spot on the spot.
Remarks: Max. 4 nights.

S Nattheim 18A4

Ramensteinbad, Dieselstrasse 22. **GPS:** n48,70261 e10,23745.

4 free € 1/100liter Ch free € 1/2kWh. **Location:** Urban, quiet.
Surface: metalled. 01/01-31/12 25/04-07/05.
Distance: 500m 300m 200m Lidl.
Remarks: Parking swimming pool, max. 3 days.

S Neckarsulm 17C3

Aquatoll, Reisachmühlweg. **GPS:** n49,18802 e9,24302.

50 free € 2/60liter Ch. **Location:** Rural, simple.
Surface: asphalted/gravel. 01/01-31/12
Distance: 4km.
Remarks: Parking swimming pool, max. 24h.

S Neckarwestheim 17C3

Wohnmobilstellplätze Im Bühl, Liebensteiner Strasse. **GPS:** n49,04186 e9,18797.

2 free € 2 Ch (4x)€ 2/8h. **Surface:** metalled. 01/01-31/12
Distance: 500m 200m 500m.
Remarks: From 4th night € 25/night.

DE

S Neresheim 18A4

Stellplatz Alter Bahnhof, Dischinger Straße 11. **GPS**: n48,75102 e10,33957.

5 free € 1 Ch (4x)€ 1/4h. **Location:** Noisy. **Surface:** metalled.
01/01-31/12
Distance: on the spot 12km on the spot.
Remarks: Service during opening hours.

S Neuhausen ob Eck 17C6

Beim Friedhof. **GPS**: n47,97473 e8,92397.

8 voluntary contribution € 1 € 1 Ch (9x). **Surface:** metalled.
01/01-31/12
Distance: 300m 500m 1km 300m 2km 2km.
Remarks: Max. 3 nights.

DE

S Neunkirchen 17C3

Festplatz, Zwingenbergerstrasse. **GPS**: n49,38818 e9,01531.

8 free € 1/90liter Ch. **Location:** Simple, quiet. **Surface:** asphalted.
01/01-31/12
Distance: 300m.
Remarks: Service next to: Autohaus Weishaupt, Industriestrasse 3 (200m).

S Nordheim 17C3

Lauffener Straße. **GPS**: n49,10461 e9,13552.

2 € 5/3 days Ch included. **Location:** Simple. **Surface:** asphalted.
01/01-31/12 on the spot on the spot.
Remarks: Max. 3 days, in front of swimmingpool.

S Nordheim 17C3

Müllers Weingut unf Weinstube, Im Auerberg 3. **GPS**: n49,10236 e9,13810.

2 € 5,with electricity and water € 8 Ch.
Location: Rural.
Distance: 800m on the spot on the spot on the spot on the spot.

S Nordrach 17A5

Schwarzwald-Panorama Wohnmobilstellplatz, Im Dorf 29. **GPS**: n48,39873 e8,07927.

8 free € 1/10liter Ch (8x)6h. **Location:** Rural, simple, central.
Surface: metalled. 01/01-31/12
Distance: 100m 100m.

S Nürtingen 17C4

Reisemobilstellplatz, B313, Plätschwiesen, Oberensingen. **GPS**: n48,63645 e9,33051.

12 € 5/24h € 1 Ch (8x)€ 1. **Surface:** metalled.
Distance: 1km 500m.
Remarks: Max. 7 days.

S Oberkirch 17A5

Am Renchtalstadion, Renchallee. **GPS**: n48,52972 e8,07250.

21 € 5, € 7/2 days + €2 tourist tax € 1/80liter € 1 Ch (30x)€ 0,50/kWh. **Location:** Rural, simple, quiet. **Surface:** grassy/gravel. 01/01-31/12 week before and week after 1st weekend Sep.
Distance: 100m 100m 100m on the spot on the spot.

S Oberkirch 17A5

Waldparkplatz Schauenburg, Burgstraße 29. **GPS**: n48,53812 e8,09452.

4 €8 (4x)€2 . **Location:** Simple, isolated, quiet.
Surface: grassy/sand.
01/01-31/12
Distance: 500m.
Remarks: € 8 voucher, max 4 days.

Tourist information Oberkirch:
www.oberkirch.de.Wine city with historical centre. Many hiking routes.

S **Oberndorf/Neckar** 17B5

Neckarhalle, Austrasse 12. **GPS:** n48,28222 e8,58472.

8 free € 1/70liter Ch (4x)€ 1/kWh. **Location:** Rural, simple, noisy.
Surface: asphalted. 01/01-31/12
Distance: 2km 300m 200m 50m on the spot on the spot.

Oberstenfeld 17C3

Mineralfreibad, Beilsteiner Strasse 100. **GPS:** n49,03160 e9,31890.

4 free. **Surface:** asphalted. 01/01-31/12

S **Oberteuringen** 24D1

Ferienhof Kramer, St. Georg strasse 8. **GPS:** n47,73948 e9,47278.

8 €7 + €5,50/pp Ch (8x)€2 WC €4. **Surface:** gravel/metalled.
01/03-31/10
Distance: 2km on the spot 300m 300m.

S **Offenburg** 17A5

Strandbad Gifizsee, Platanenallee 15. **GPS:** n48,45785 e7,93663.
11 € 12 + € 3 /pp (peak season) € 1/80liter Ch (11x)€ 0,50/kWh WC . **Location:** Simple. **Surface:** grasstiles. 01/04-31/10
Distance: 2,5km 3,8km 100m on the spot 150m.
Remarks: Bread-service, dog € 1,50/night.

Offenburg 17A5

Bürgerpark, Stegermattstraße 26a. **GPS:** n48,46565 e7,94566.

2 free. **Location:** Urban, simple, quiet. **Surface:** asphalted/metalled.
01/01-31/12
Distance: 500m 300m.
Remarks: In front of swimmingpool.

S **Offenburg** 17A5

Camping Kuhn, Im Drachenacker 4. **GPS:** n48,48039 e7,92776.

10 free € 0,50/50liter Ch (8x)free. **Location:** Urban, simple.
Surface: metalled. 01/01-31/12
Distance: 2km 3,7km 500m.
Remarks: Service during opening hours.

Öhningen/Schienen 24C1

Landgasthof Schienerberg, Schienerbergstrasse 56. **GPS:** n47,69595 e8,90698.

6 free. **Surface:** gravel/metalled. 01/01-31/12 Tue.
Distance: 800m on the spot 800m.

S **Öhringen** 17D3

P Frei- und Hallenbad, Pfaffenmühlweg. **GPS:** n49,19771 e9,51137.

15 €8 Ch included. **Location:** Rural, simple. **Surface:** gravel.
01/01-31/12
Distance: 1km 100m.
Remarks: To pay at swimming pool, max. 3 days.

DE

Tourist information Öhringen:
Tourist Information, Markplatz 15, www.oehringen.de.Many signposted hiking routes.
RADius.Cycle route, 18km.

S Öllingen 18A5

Parking Rathaus, Hauptstrasse. **GPS**: n48,52816 e10,14813.

5 free € 4 Ch. **Surface:** grasstiles. 01/01-31/12

S Oppenau 17A5

Hauptstrasse. **GPS**: n48,47639 e8,16972.

6 free € 1/100liter Ch (6x)€ 1/8h. **Location:** Rural, simple, quiet.
Surface: gravel. 01/01-31/12
Distance: 300m 150m bakery 300m on the spot on the spot.

S Oppenweiler 17D3

Caravanstation, Murrwiesenstraße 15. **GPS**: n48,97999 e9,45898.

2 free € 1/80liter Ch. **Surface:** asphalted. 01/01-31/12
Distance: 600m.
Remarks: Max. 2 days.

S Ottenhöfen im Schwarzwald 17A5

Bauernhof Murhof, Murhof 1. **GPS**: n48,56005 e8,15350.

15 € 10, 2 pers.incl € 1/100liter Ch (15x)€ 0,50/kWh WC € 0,50.
Location: Rural, simple, quiet. **Surface:** grassy/metalled. 01/04-31/10
Distance: 1km 500m 500m on the spot.
Remarks: Swimming pool 200m.

S Pforzheim 17B4

Reisemobilplatz Oststadt am Enzauenpark, Wildersinnstraße. **GPS**: n48,89784 e8,72232.

15 free € 1/80liter (4x)€ 1/kWh. **Location:** Urban, simple, noisy.
Surface: metalled.
01/01-31/12
Distance: 1,5km 200m 100m on the spot on the spot on the spot.
Remarks: Max. 7 days, service 200m. In front of Ensauenpark, behind P&R.

Pforzheim 17B4

Parkplatz 2 Wildpark, Tiefenbronnerstraße. **GPS**: n48,87651 e8,71749.
€ 2-4/24h. **Location:** Urban.
Remarks: Max. 1 night.

S Pforzheim 17B4

Hohwiesenweg. **GPS**: n48,89750 e8,72674.
4 € 1/80liter € 1 Ch € 1 (2x)€ 1/kWh. **Location:** Simple, noisy.
Surface: metalled.
Distance: 1,5km 50m 100m on the spot on the spot on the spot.

S Pfullendorf 17C6

Seepark Linzgau, P-Ost, Bannholzerweg 18. **GPS**: n47,93097 e9,23728.
15 € 4/24h. **Surface:** unpaved. 01/01-31/12

S Pfullingen 17C5

Wohnmobilplatz Schönbergbad, Klosterstraße. **GPS**: n48,45537 e9,22812.
7 free € 1 Ch € 1/2kWh. **Surface:** grassy. 01/01-31/12
Distance: 1,5km nearby.
Remarks: Max. 4 days.

S Radolfzell 24C1

Stellplatz Hartplatz, Strandbadstrasse. **GPS**: n47,73784 e8,98007.

10 € 8/24h € 1/50liter Ch (6x)€ 0,50/kWh. **Surface:** asphalted.
01/01-31/12
Distance: 500m 700m 700m 500m 700m 100m.
Remarks: Max. 2 nights.

S Radolfzell 24C1

Stellplatz in den Herzen, Zeppelinstrasse. **GPS**: n47,73888 e8,95331.

15 € 8/24h € 1/80liter Ch (12x)€ 0,50/kWh. **Surface:** metalled.

DE

01/01-31/12
Distance: 1km 500m 1km.
Remarks: Max. 2 nights.

Radolfzell 24C1

Campingplatz Böhringer See, Hindenburgstrasse. **GPS**: n47,76176 e8,93488.

10 € 10 Ch (5x) WC € 1. **Surface:** metalled.
01/01-31/12
Distance: 1km on the spot 1km.

Rastatt 17A4

Leopoldring. **GPS**: n48,85409 e8,19970.

5 € 5 € 1/10minutes Ch (8x)€ 1/6h. **Location:** Simple.
Surface: metalled. 01/01-31/12
Distance: 500m 3,8km.
Remarks: Pay-desk of the swimming pool, Discount at swimming pool/sauna.

Ravensburg 17D6

Mühlbruckstrasse. **GPS**: n47,78196 e9,60001.

12 € 5 € 1/80liter Ch (6x)€ 0,50. **Surface:** metalled.
01/01-31/12
Distance: 2km 500m 200m 250m.
Remarks: Max. 3 nights.

Ravensburg 17D6

Carthago Reisemobilbau, Okatreut, Schmalegg. **GPS**: n47,79729 e9,54906.
6 free Chfree. **Surface:** gravel. 01/01-31/12

Tourist information Ravensburg:

Bodensee-Erlebniskarte.Card gives free access to all boats, telpher carriers, beaches etc. Around the Lake Constance in Germany, Switzerland and Austria.
€ 54/3 days.
Tourist Information, Kirchstrasse 16.City of the Tore und Turme, gates and towers.

Rechberghausen 17D4

Sportpark Lindach, Am Desenbach. **GPS**: n48,72405 e9,63594.

6 free € 0,50/80liter Ch (6x)€ 0,50/1kWh. **Location:** Rural, simple.
Surface: grassy. 01/04-01/10
Distance: 1km 500m 1km 1km 500m.

Reichenau 24C1

Zum Sandseele. **GPS**: n47,69887 e9,04711.

12 € 8 € 1/80liter Ch (8x)€ 1/2kWh. **Surface:** asphalted/metalled.
01/01-31/12
Distance: 1,5km on the spot on the spot 100m 2km.
Remarks: Max. 1 night. Follow signs campsite.

Reutlingen 17C5

Am Südbahnhof/Marktstrasse. **GPS**: n48,48280 e9,22982.

3 free Ch. **Surface:** gravel. 01/01-31/12
Distance: 3km on the spot on the spot.
Remarks: In front of motorhome dealer Berger.

Rheinau 17A5

Weberhaus World of Living, Am Erlenpark 1, Linx. **GPS**: n48,61944 e7,88709.

10 free Ch (4x)€ 1. **Location:** Rural, simple, quiet.
Surface: metalled. 01/01-31/12
Distance: 100m on the spot on the spot.
Remarks: Parc for building and living.

Rheinmünster 17A4

Freizeit Center Oberrhein, Am Campingpark 1. **GPS**: n48,77312 e8,04044.

DE

20 € 8 € 1/80liter Ch (20x)€ 0,50/kWh. **Location:** Rural, comfortable, quiet. **Surface:** grassy. 01/01-31/12
Distance: on the spot 200m on the spot on the spot.

S Riedlingen 17D6

Stadthalle, Hindenburgstraße. **GPS**: n48,15189 e9,47766.

3 free € 1/100liter Ch € 1/4h. **Location:** Urban.
Surface: asphalted. 01/01-31/12
Distance: 300m 200m 100m.

S Rottenburg/Neckar 17C5

Wohnmobilhafen am Neckarufer, Ulmenweg 4. **GPS**: n48,47213 e8,95010.

12 free € 1/80liter Ch € 0,50/kWh. **Surface:** asphalted.
01/01-31/12
Distance: 800m 800m 800m 800m.
Remarks: Max. 4 days.

Rottenburg/Neckar 17C5

Weggentalstrasse. **GPS**: n48,48072 e8,92769.

5 free. **Surface:** gravel. 01/01-31/12
Distance: 500m 500m 100m.
Remarks: Along the Neckar river.

S Rottweil 17B6

Parkplatz, Stadionstrasse. **GPS**: n48,15556 e8,62861.

€ 5 free € 1 Ch (16x)€ 1/8h. **Surface:** gravel.
01/01-31/12
Distance: 1km 1km 1km 500m.
Remarks: Parking stadium.

S Rust 17A5

Europapark Rust, Europa-Parkstrasse. **GPS**: n48,27189 e7,71745.

200 8-20h € 2/h (max. € 6), 20-8h € 2/h (max. € 22) € 1 Ch WC included. **Location:** Simple. **Surface:** asphalted.
03/04-07/11, 27/11-09/01 9-18
Distance: on the spot.

Tourist information Rust:
Europa-park, Europa-Park-Straße 2.Large amusement and theme park with Europe as theme.
03/04-07/11, 27/11-09/01 9-18h.

S Sankt Blasien 24A1

Rehbach in Menzenschwand, Rehbachweg, Sankt Blasien. **GPS**: n47,81306 e8,06933.

20 € 6 + tourist tax (16x)€ 3/24h. **Location:** Rural, simple, quiet.
Surface: gravel. 01/01-31/12
Distance: St Blasien 8km bakery 500m on the spot on the spot on the spot.
Remarks: At ski-lift Rehbach, during winter time not always easy to reach.

S Sasbachwalden 17A5

Wohnmobilstellplatz "Alde Gott", Talstraße 2. **GPS**: n48,61945 e8,12094.

DE

30 € 7 € 1/100liter Ch (20x)€ 2/24h. **Location:** Rural, comfortable, quiet. **Surface:** gravel/metalled. 01/01-31/12
Distance: centre 300m 9km 9km 100m 250m 250m 100m on the spot on the spot.
Remarks: Waterfall 1km, swimming pool 800m.

S Schiltach 17B5

P1, Lehewiese. **GPS**: n48,29111 e8,34250.

10 free (3x). **Location:** Simple, quiet. **Surface:** gravel. 01/01-31/12
Distance: 200m 50m 50m on the spot on the spot on the spot.
Remarks: Busy parking during the day.

S Schluchsee 24B1

P Aqua Fun, Faulenfürster Straße. **GPS**: n47,81569 e8,18113.

20 € 8 € 1/100liter € 1/8h. **Location:** Rural, comfortable, central, quiet. **Surface:** asphalted. 01/01-31/12
Distance: 200m.
Remarks: Max. 1 night.

S Schonach im Schwarzwald 17B6

Parkplatz Obertal, Schwimmbadweg. **GPS**: n48,14573 e8,18872.

10 € 7 € 1 € 0,50 Ch (8x)€ 1/8h. **Location:** Rural, comfortable. **Surface:** grasstiles. 01/01-31/12
Distance: 1km 650m on the spot on the spot.
Remarks: Free entrance swimming pool, ski-lift and public transport, max. 3 nights, coins at Tourist Info.

S Schorndorf 17D4

Gmünder Straße 84/1. **GPS**: n48,80539 e9,54187.

7 € 5 + € 4/pp € 2 Ch € 2 WC € 2 € 2 € 1. **Location:** Simple. **Surface:** metalled. 01/01-31/12
Distance: 10min.

S Schramberg 17B5

Bahnhofstraße, B462. **GPS**: n48,23017 e8,38323.

2 free € 1/80liter € 1 Ch € 1. **Location:** Rural, simple, noisy. **Surface:** metalled. 01/01-31/12
Distance: on the spot 100m 50m 10m on the spot on the spot.

S Schwäbisch Gmünd 17D4

Schiesstalplatz, Schiesstalstraße. **GPS**: n48,80543 e9,81308.

8 free € 1/50liter Ch (8x)€ 0,50/1kWh. **Location:** Rural, simple. **Surface:** gravel. 01/01-31/12
Distance: 1km 50m 500m.
Remarks: Motorhome < 7m, max. 5 days a month.

S Schwäbisch Hall 17D3

P5 Weilerwiese, Johanniterstrasse. **GPS**: n49,11666 e9,73269.

4 8-18h max. € 5, 18-8h max. € 2 (4x)€ 0,10/18minutes. **Location:** Urban, simple. **Surface:** asphalted. 01/01-31/12
Distance: 200m.
Remarks: Max. 24h. Follow P5.

S Schwaigern 17C3

Wohnmobilstellplatz Schaigern, Gemminger Straße 91. **GPS**: n49,14576 e9,04529.

DE

2 free € 1 Ch free. **Surface:** asphalted. 01/01-31/12
Distance: 1km 300m on the spot on the spot.

S Schwetzingen 17B3

Ketscher Landstrasse. **GPS:** n49,37803 e8,55820.

12 free € 3/80liter Ch. **Location:** Simple. **Surface:** grasstiles/metalled. 01/01-31/12
Distance: 500m on the spot on the spot on the spot on the spot.
Remarks: Max. 3 night, noisy place.

S Seelbach 17A5

Reisemobil-Wellness-Stellplatz Schwarzwälder Hof, Am Tretenbach. **GPS:** n48,30042 e7,94497.

16 € 18 € 1/90liter Ch (16x)1kWh WC . **Location:** Rural, comfortable. **Surface:** metalled. 01/01-31/12
Distance: 600m 100m.
Remarks: Including access to swimming pool, use sanitary facilities, entrance 1p wellness/sauna.

S Seewald 17B5

P4, L362. **GPS:** n48,55131 e8,49522.

17 free WC free. **Location:** Rural, simple, quiet. **Surface:** asphalted.
01/01-31/12 service 01/11-31/03.
Distance: 1,5km 25m 600m.

S Sigmaringen 17C6

Wohnmobilplatz Sigmaringen, Georg Zimmerer Straße 4. **GPS:** n48,08545 e9,21029.
20 € 5 Ch . **Surface:** metalled. 01/01-31/12

S Sindelfingen 17C4

RALL-Caravanning GmbH, Mahdentaltrasse 84. **GPS:** n48,70583 e9,02808.

3 free € 1/5minutes € 1 Ch € 1 (2x)free.
Surface: asphalted/metalled. 01/01-31/12
Distance: 1km.
Remarks: Max. 1 night.

S Singen 24C1

Schaffhauserstrasse. **GPS:** n47,75992 e8,82766.

20 free Ch (16x)€ 1/12h. **Surface:** grassy/gravel.
01/01-31/12, service 15/03-15/11
Distance: 1km on the spot 200m.
Remarks: Max. 72h.

Sinsheim 17C3

Schwimmbadweg 11b. **GPS:** n49,24778 e8,88667.

5 free. **Location:** Rural, comfortable, quiet. **Surface:** asphalted.
01/01-31/12
Distance: 1,5km 1,5km.
Remarks: Max. 48h.

S Stetten 24C1

Alte Brennerei, Riedetsweilerstrasse 5. **GPS:** n47,69326 e9,29788.

15 € 7 € 1 € 1 Ch (6x)€ 0,50/kWh. **Surface:** grassy/gravel.
01/01-31/12
Distance: 300m 2km 2km 300m 300m 300m.

DE

Stockach/Bodensee 17C6

Reisemobilhafen 'Papiermühle', Johann-Glatt-strasse 3. **GPS**: n47,84169 e8,99945.

85 € 10 € 0,50/50liter Ch (118x) WC. **Surface:** gravel/metalled.
01/01-31/12
Distance: 1,5km on the spot 700m.

Sulz am Neckar 17B5

Stellplatz Wöhrd, Ludwigstraße. **GPS**: n48,36427 e8,63681.

6 free € 1/80liter € 1 Ch (4x)€ 0,50/kWh. **Location:** Rural, simple, quiet. **Surface:** metalled. 01/01-31/12
Distance: 300m 100m 100m on the spot on the spot on the spot.

Sulzburg 17A6

Camping Sulzbachtal, Sonnmatt 4. **GPS**: n47,84773 e7,69868.

10 € 15 + tourist tax + Ecotaxe Ch (10x)€ 0,70/kWh WC included. **Location:** Comfortable. **Surface:** grassy/gravel. 01/01-31/12
Distance: 500m on the spot.

Tauberbischofsheim 17D2

P Freibad, Vittryallee. **GPS**: n49,62155 e9,66632.

3 free Ch WC free € 0,50,during opening hours. **Surface:** asphalted.
01/01-31/12
Distance: 500m 300m 300/600m 500m.
Remarks: Service: Kläranlage.

Tettnang 24D1

Loretostrasse. **GPS**: n47,66425 e9,59175.

14 € 5 € 1 € 1 Ch € 1 (8x)€ 1/8h. **Surface:** grassy/metalled.
01/01-31/12
Distance: 800m 200m 200m 200m.

Tettnang 24D1

Gutshof Camping Badhütten, Badhütten, Laimnau. **GPS**: n47,63370 e9,64668.

70 € 20 € 1 Ch € 1/3kWh WC € 1. **Surface:** grassy.
01/01-31/12

Titisee 17A6

Camping Bankenhof, Bruderhalde 31a. **GPS**: n47,88643 e8,13046.

8 € 13, 2 pers.incl Ch WC included € 2,60/time € 2/2h.
Location: Rural, comfortable, quiet. **Surface:** gravel/sand.
01/01-31/12
Distance: Titisee 600m.
Remarks: Pay at reception.

Todtmoos 24A1

Jägermatt, Vordertodtmoos. **GPS**: n47,73390 e8,00285.

30 € 5 Ch included. **Location:** Rural, simple, noisy.
Surface: gravel/metalled. 01/01-31/12
Distance: 1km 50m.

Triberg im Schwarzwald 17B6

Sommerauer Strasse, Nußberg. **GPS**: n48,13161 e8,25294.

DE

20 free. **Location:** Rural, simple. **Surface:** gravel.
01/01-31/12
Distance: 2km on the spot.

Trochtelfingen 17C5

Eberhard-von Werderberg-Halle, Siemensstrasse. **GPS:** n48,30811 e9,23546.

20 € 3 € 1/80liter Ch (4x)free,16Amp. **Surface:** gravel.
01/01-31/12
Distance: Old city centre 500m 500m.

Trochtelfingen 17C5

Kräuter- und Erlebnisgarten Alb-Gold Nudelfabrik, Grindel 1. **GPS:** n48,32838 e9,24001.

4 free. **Surface:** metalled. 01/01-31/12
Distance: 3km on the spot on the spot.
Remarks: Max. 2 nights.

Tourist information Trochtelfingen:
Historical little town with half-timbered houses.

Trossingen 17B6

Reisemobilplatz am Naturbad Troase, Steppach 5. **GPS:** n48,07703 e8,62192.

8 € 4 € 1/100liter Ch € 1/12h. **Surface:** gravel.
01/01-31/12

Tuttlingen 17C6

Stellplatz Donaupark, Stuttgarter strasse. **GPS:** n47,98490 e8,81316.

10 free € 1/5minutes € 1 Ch. **Surface:** metalled.
01/01-31/12
Distance: 500m 500m 500m 500m.
Remarks: Max. 3 nights.

Überlingen 24C1

Reisemobilhafen Überlingen, Kurt-Hahn-strasse. **GPS:** n47,77617 e9,15046.

20 € 6-10 € 0,50/70liter € 0,50 Ch (30x)€ 0,50/2kWh WC.
Surface: asphalted/gravel. 01/01-31/12
Distance: 1km 1km 1km 200m 1,5km 200m.
Remarks: Price incl. bus transport (max. 5 pers) to the city centre.

Uhldingen-Mühlhofen 24C1

Ehbachstrasse. **GPS:** n47,72535 e9,23649.

19 € 10 € 1 € 1 Ch WC. **Surface:** grasstiles/metalled.
01/01-31/12
Distance: 1km 2km 2km kiosk on the spot.
Remarks: Parking at edge of the village, max. 24h.

Tourist information Uhldingen-Mühlhofen:
Tourist Information, Schulstrasse 12, www.seeferien.com.Tourist town on the Lake Constance.
Pfalbaumuseum.Reconstruction village from 4000-850 before Christ.
01/04-31/10 daily 8-18/17h, 01/11-31/03 Sa-Su 9-16h.

Ulm 17D5

P+R Friedrichsau, Wielandstrasse. **GPS:** n48,40774 e10,00929.

50 free € 1 Ch. **Location:** Urban, simple, central. **Surface:** metalled.
01/01-31/12

DE

Distance: 175m on the spot.
Remarks: Max. 3 days, green zone: environmental badge obligatory.

Tourist information Ulm:
Ulm Touristik, Neue strasse 45, www.tourismus.ulm.de.

S Ummendorf 17D6

Bräuhaus Ummendorf, Bachstrasse 10. **GPS**: n48,06340 e9,83252.

5 free (5x)€ 3/day WC € 3. **Surface:** metalled.
01/01-31/12
Distance: 300m on the spot 800m 100m.
Remarks: 3 days free stay.

S Unterkirnach 17B6

Reisemobilhafen Am Rathaus, Rathausplatz. **GPS**: n48,07719 e8,36707.

16 € 9 Ch included. **Location:** Urban, luxurious, quiet.
Surface: gravel. 01/01-31/12
Distance: on the spot 400m 500m 200m 300m 200m 150m 400m.
Remarks: Pay at tourist office, alternative if full.

S Unterkirnach 17B6

Ackerloch-Grillschopf, Unteres Ackerloch 2. **GPS**: n48,08473 e8,36573.

20 € 4 + € 2,10/pp tourist tax Ch WC included. **Location:** Rural, simple. **Surface:** unpaved.
Distance: 1,5km on the spot on the spot on the spot on the spot.

Tourist information Unterkirnach:
Tourismusbüro Unterkirnach, Hauptstraße 5, www.unterkirnach.de.

S Untermünkheim 17D3

Wohnmobilpark Ostertag, Kupfer Straße 20, Übrigshausen. **GPS**: n49,17603 e9,71321.

10 € 8 Ch € 0,50 € 1. **Location:** Rural, comfortable.
Surface: grassy/gravel. 01/03-30/11
Distance: 50m.
Remarks: At manege.

S Villingen/Schwenningen 17B6

Messegelände VS-Schwenningen, Waldeckweg. **GPS**: n48,05028 e8,54056.

4 free € 1 Ch. **Location:** Urban, simple, noisy. **Surface:** asphalted.
01/01-31/12
Distance: 1km 500m.

Vogtsburg im Kaiserstuhl 17A6

Hauptstraße/L115, Oberrotweil. **GPS**: n48,09000 e7,64361.

8 free. **Location:** Rural, simple, isolated, quiet.
01/01-31/12
Distance: 800m.

S Waiblingen 17C4

Parkplatz Hallenbad, An der Talaue. **GPS**: n48,83029 e9,32540.

20 € 6/24h, 19-9h € 2 € 1/80liter Ch (6x)€ 1/1kWh WC. **Location:** Urban. **Surface:** gravel. 01/01-31/12
Distance: 500m 500m 50m 300m 600m.
Remarks: Parking swimming pool, during congresses special tariff, max. 3 nights.

S Waldkirch 17A6

Reisemobilstellplatz Am Stadtpark, Am Stadtrain. **GPS**: n48,09023 e7,95833.

DE

10 free € 1/80liter € 1 Ch € 1. **Location:** Urban, simple, central. **Surface:** asphalted. 01/01-31/12

Distance: 500m.

Remarks: Max. 2 days.

S Waldshut-Tiengen 24B1

Wohmobil-Park Waldshut-Tiengen, Jahnweg 22, Waldshut. **GPS**: n47,61121 e8,22513.

44 € 10 € 1/100liter Ch € 1/kWh € 0,50. **Location:** Urban, luxurious, quiet. **Surface:** metalled. 01/01-31/12

Distance: on the spot.

Remarks: Along the Rhine river, bread-service.

S Walldürn 17C2

Auerbergzentrum, Theodor-Heuss-Ring. **GPS**: n49,58506 e9,35421.

50 free € 1/80liter Ch (4x)€ 0,50/kWh,6Amp. **Surface:** metalled. 01/01-31/12

Distance: 800m on the spot 300m on the spot.

S Walldürn 17C2

Goldschmitt Technik-Center, Industrieparkstrasse. **GPS**: n49,58977 e9,39339.

30 free € 1/80liter Ch (12x)€ 0,50/kWh. **Surface:** asphalted. 01/01-31/12

Distance: 800m.

S Wangen im Allgäu 24D1

P17, Am Klösterle. **GPS**: n47,68160 e9,83401.

40 € 8 € 0,50/120liter Ch (28x) WC. **Surface:** metalled. 01/01-31/12

Distance: on the spot 500m 500m on the spot on the spot on the spot.

Remarks: Tourist tax € 1.

Tourist information Wangen im Allgäu:

Tourist Information, Parkplatz 1, Rathaus. Traditional small Bavarian town. Every Thursday city walk through historical city centre, 15.30-17. free. Wed.

S Wehr 24A1

Ludingarten. **GPS**: n47,62515 e7,90582.

10 € 10 € 1/100liter Ch (8x)€ 1/8h WC. **Location:** Simple, quiet. **Surface:** metalled. 01/01-31/12

Distance: nearby.

Remarks: Pay at tourist office, Hauptstr. 14 or Bistro Gleis 13, Bahnhofplatz.

Weikersheim 17D2

P HL-Wöhr, Heiliges Wöhr. **GPS**: n49,48197 e9,89708.

4 free. **Surface:** metalled. 01/01-31/12

Distance: 200m 300m.

Weikersheim 17D2

Parkplatz Tauberwiesen, August-Laukhuff-Straße 15. **GPS**: n49,48364 e9,89706.

30 free. **Surface:** gravel. 01/01-31/12

Distance: 300m 400m.

DE

Weikersheim 17D2

Campingplatz Schwabenmühle, Weikersheimer Strasse 21, Laudenbach. **GPS**: n49,45795 e9,92691.

10 € 7 Ch against payment. **Surface:** gravel.
01/01-31/12
Distance: 300m 200m.

Weil der Stadt 17C4

Festplatz, Jahnstrasse. **GPS**: n48,75268 e8,87453.

4 free € 1/80liter € 1 Ch € 1 (4x)€ 1/kWh. **Location:** Urban, simple, noisy. **Surface:** asphalted. 01/01-31/12
Distance: 300m 300m 250m on the spot on the spot.
Remarks: Max. 3 days.

Weingarten 17D6

Festplatz, Abt Hyller Strasse 55. **GPS**: n47,81009 e9,63041.
8 € 5 € 2 Ch € 2. **Surface:** metalled. 01/01-31/12
Distance: 1km.

Weinsberg 17C3

Eugen-Diez-Straße 2. **GPS**: n49,14846 e9,28464.
6 free € 1 Ch (6x)€ 0,50/kWh. **Location:** Rural, quiet. **Surface:** grasstiles. 01/01-31/12
Distance: 500m 2km on the spot on the spot.

Welzheim 17D4

Aichstruter Stausee, Seiboldsweiler, Aichstrut. **GPS**: n48,90020 e9,63719.

12 € 5 € 1/80liter Ch WC. **Surface:** gravel. 01/01-31/12
Distance: 5km on the spot on the spot on the spot.
Remarks: At artificial lake, max. 1 week.

Wertheim 17D1

Wohnmobilstellplatz An der Taubermündung, Linke Tauberstrasse. **GPS**: n49,76040 e9,51425.

54 € 5/24h € 1/90liter Ch. **Surface:** gravel.
01/01-31/12 2nd sa of the month + high water.
Distance: 500m.
Remarks: Along the Tauber river, max. 3 days.

Wertheim 17D1

Expocamp, Wertheim Caravaning & Freizeit, Hymerring 1. **GPS**: n49,77368 e9,58034.

90 free € 1/90liter Ch € 1/3h WC during opening hours.
Surface: asphalted. 01/01-31/12
Distance: 400m 3,7km.
Remarks: Bread-service mo-sa.

Tourist information Wertheim:
Tourist Information, Wenzelplatz 2, www.tourist-wertheim.de.Small tourist town with historical centre.
Glasmuseum, Mühlenstrasse 24. 01/04-31/10 Tue-Fri 10-12h, 14-17h, Sa-Su 14-17h.
Wertheim Village, Almosenberg.Outlet-shopping.

Wildberg 17B4

Wohnmobilstellplatz Wildberg. **GPS**: n48,62055 e8,74485.

4 + 10 free € 1/100liter Ch € 0,50/kWh. **Location:** Quiet.
Surface: grasstiles/grassy. 01/01-31/12 service 01/11-31/03.
Distance: historical centre 500m 700m 1km on the spot.
Remarks: Nearby monastery.

Wolfach 17B5

Trendcamping Schwarzwald, Schiltacher Straße 80, Halbmeil. **GPS**: n48,29053 e8,27763.

DE

6 € 15 + tourist tax Ch WC included € 3 € 2.
Location: Rural, simple, quiet. **Surface:** grassy/sand.
10/04-15/10
Distance: on the spot.

S Wolfach 17B5

Ferienhof Bartleshof, Ippichen 6, Ippichen. **GPS**: n48,30183 e8,26264.

5 € 15 Ch (4x) € 2 € 2. **Location:** Rural, simple, quiet.
Surface: grassy/gravel. 01/01-31/12
Distance: on the spot on the spot.
Remarks: € 10, reduction at restaurant.

Wolfegg/Allgäu 17D6

Gemeindehalle, Rötenbacher strasse 13. **GPS**: n47,81636 e9,79780.

4 free. **Surface:** metalled. 01/01-31/12
Distance: 200m 2km 2km 500m 500m 500m.
Remarks: Max. 3 nights.

Wolfegg/Allgäu 17D6

Hofgarten, Alttaner strasse. **GPS**: n47,82105 e9,79487.

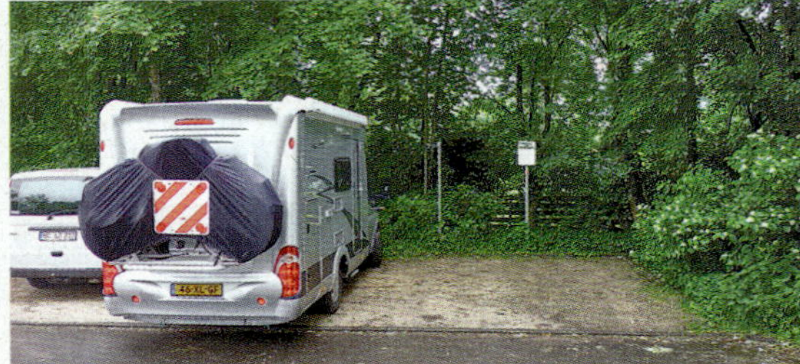

2 free. **Surface:** gravel/metalled. 01/01-31/12
Distance: on the spot.
Remarks: Max. 2 nights.

S Wolfegg/Allgäu 17D6

Gasthaus Adler, Eintürnerstrasse 38, Molpertshaus. **GPS**: n47,87029 e9,80622.

4 € 4 € 0,50 Ch € 0,50/kWh. **Surface:** gravel/metalled.
01/01-31/12
Distance: on the spot on the spot.

Wolfegg/Allgäu 17D6

Gasthof zum Bräuhaus, Rossberg 1. **GPS**: n47,86776 e9,78182.

3 free. **Surface:** metalled. 01/01-31/12
Distance: on the spot.

Wolfegg/Allgäu 17D6

Hotel-Gasthof zur Post, Rötenbacher strasse 5. **GPS**: n47,81978 e9,79339.

4 . 01/01-31/12
Distance: on the spot on the spot.

Wolfegg/Allgäu 17D6

Kurpark Wolfegg-Altann. **GPS**: n47,83861 e9,78750.
2 free.
Remarks: Max. 2 nights.

Tourist information Wolfegg/Allgäu:
Tourist Information, Rötenbacher strasse 13.
Health resort.
Automobilmuseum.200 oldtimers.
01/04-31/10 9.30-18h, 01/11-31/03 Su 10-17h.
Bauernhaus-museum.Open air museum.
01/04-31/10 Tue-Su 10-18/17h Mo Apr Oct.

S Wutöschingen 24B1

Wohnmobilplatz Degernau, Ofteringer Strasse 1, Degernau. **GPS**: n47,66639 e8,37917.

DE

17 € 6/day, 2 pers.incl € 1 € 1 Ch (12x)€ 0,50/kWh WC € 1 € 3 € 1/24h. **Location:** Rural, comfortable, quiet. **Surface:** grassy/gravel. 01/03-31/10
Distance: 10 min walking on the spot on the spot on the spot.
Remarks: Sauna, solarium.

S Zell am Harmersbach 17A5

Stellplatz am Schwimmbad, Nordracher Strasse. **GPS**: n48,35146 e8,05942.

14 € 3/20-12h € 1/10minutes Ch (8x)€ 1/10h. **Location:** Rural, simple, quiet. **Surface:** gravel. 01/01-31/12
Distance: 2km 2km.

Tourist information Zell am Harmersbach:
Tourist Info, Alte Kanzlei, www.zell.de.Old centre worth seeing.
Storchenturmmuseum.Town history. 01/04-31/10 14-17h. € 1,50.

Bavaria

S Absberg 18B3

Badehalbinsel Brombachsee, Gunzenhausen-Pleinfeld Ausfart Absberg. **GPS**: n49,13770 e10,87389.

150 € 8/24h € 0,20/60liter Ch (80x)€ 0,50/kWh WC € 0,50.
Location: Rural, comfortable, quiet. **Surface:** grassy.
01/04-01/10
Distance: 1km on the spot on the spot 1km on the spot on the spot.

Tourist information Absberg:
Health resort on the Kleiner Brombachsee and Igelsbachsee.

Adelsdorf 18B2

Neuhauser Hauptstrasse. **GPS**: n49,68500 e10,87556.

free. **Surface:** metalled.
Remarks: Next to sports fields.

S Adelsdorf 18B2

Gasthof Niebler, Neuhauser Hauptstrasse 30. **GPS**: n49,70017 e10,90221.

4 guests free . **Surface:** metalled.
Distance: on the spot on the spot.

Ahorn 10C6

Freizeitzentrum Wittman, Badstrasse 20, Eicha. **GPS**: n50,22537 e10,90252.

4 free. **Surface:** metalled. 01/01-31/12
Distance: on the spot 5km.

S Aichach 18B5

Reisemobilplatz, Franz-Beck-Strasse. **GPS**: n48,45889 e11,12611.

4 € 5 Ch free. **Location:** Urban, simple, quiet.
Surface: grassy/gravel. 01/01-31/12
Distance: 500m 500m 100m.

S Albertshofen 18A1

An der Fähre Mainstockheim-Albertshofen, Mainstraße. **GPS**: n49,77254 e10,15749.

10 € 5 Ch included. **Surface:** gravel. 01/01-31/12
Distance: on the spot on the spot 50m.
Remarks: Along Main river, closed when high water.

S Altmannstein 18C3

Gasthof Forster, Schulstrasse 9. **GPS**: n48,90125 e11,69559.

DE

20 guests free (4x)€ 2/night. **Surface:** asphalted.
01/01-31/12
Distance: on the spot on the spot 3km.
Remarks: Check in before 19h (Mo-Tue 16h), bread service.

S Altötting 19A5

Griesstraße. **GPS:** n48,22946 e12,67493.

8 free € 1/80liter Ch (8x)€ 1/4h WC. **Location:** Urban, simple, noisy. **Surface:** grasstiles. 01/01-31/12
Distance: 5 min on the spot on the spot.
Remarks: Max. 3 days.

S Altötting 19A5

P2 Dultplatz, Traunsteinerstrasse. **GPS:** n48,22287 e12,67921.

7 free € 1/10liter (8x)€ 1/4h. **Location:** Urban, simple, central.
Surface: gravel. 01/01-31/12
Distance: 700m.
Remarks: Max. 3 days.

Tourist information Altötting:
Verkehrsbüro Altötting im Rathaus, Kapellplatz 2a, www.altoetting-touristinfo.de.

S Altusried 18A6

Am Freibad, Im Tal 4. **GPS:** n47,79915 e10,21934.

10 € 5 € 1 Ch € 0,50/1kWh. **Location:** Rural, simple, quiet.
Surface: grassy/gravel. 01/01-31/12
Distance: 500m 700m.
Remarks: Parking at swimming pool.

S Alzenau 17C1

Wenzel's Weinscheune, Schlossbergstrasse 5. **GPS:** n50,07023 e9,07752.

10 guests free .
Distance: on the spot on the spot 1km.

S Amberg 18C2

Gasfabrikstraße. **GPS:** n49,44139 e11,86222.

10 free € 1/80liter Ch (12x)€ 1/12h. **Surface:** asphalted.
01/01-31/12
Distance: 500m 1km 1km.

Tourist information Amberg:
Tourist Information, Zeughausstrasse 1a, www.amberg.de. € 2.

S Ansbach 18A3

Freizeitbad Aquella, Am Stadion 2. **GPS:** n49,30459 e10,55852.

12 free € 0,50/50liter Ch (12x)€ 0,50/kWh. **Location:** Simple, central. **Surface:** metalled. 01/01-31/12
Distance: 1km 7,7km on the spot 1km on the spot.
Remarks: At swimming pool.

Ansbach 18A3

Autohof Ansbach, Vetterstrasse 1. **GPS:** n49,26295 e10,58381.
50 € 6, reduction for guests. **Surface:** asphalted. 01/01-31/12
Distance: 2km 700m on the spot on the spot.

S Arnbruck 19A3

Landhotel Rappenhof, Rappendorf 5. **GPS:** n49,13517 e12,95069.

5 € 10 Ch WC included. **Surface:** grassy. 01/01-31/12
Distance: 2km on the spot 2km 10km 8km.

DE

Remarks: Use of sauna against payment.

Arnstein 17D1

Badesee, Am Alten Schwimmbad. **GPS**: n49,97667 e9,95917.

3 free. **Surface:** grassy. 01/01-31/12

Distance: 100m snack 100m.

Remarks: At the old swimming pool.

Arnstein 17D1

Cancale Platz. **GPS**: n49,97625 e9,96564.

5 free. **Surface:** metalled. 01/01-31/12

Distance: 100m 100m 100m.

Arnstein 17D1

Caravaning Arnstein, Michael Wenzstrasse 9. **GPS**: n49,97361 e9,98444.

2 free Ch free. **Surface:** metalled. 01/01-31/12

Arzberg 11A6

Am Rathausplatz. **GPS**: n50,05528 e12,18870.

2 free. **Surface:** metalled. 01/01-31/12

Distance: 250m 300m 250m.

Aschaffenburg 17C1

Grossostheimerstrasse. **GPS**: n49,97139 e9,13722.

25 € 3/24h Ch (18x)€ 0,50/kWh. **Surface:** grassy/gravel.

01/01-31/12

Distance: historical centre 500m 8km.

Remarks: Parking along the Main, Altstadt, being indicated with with small signs, max. 3 days.

Tourist information Aschaffenburg:

Tourist Information, Schlossplatz 1, www.info-aschaffenburg.de.Historical centre.

Schloß Johannisburg.

Automuseum Rosso Bianco, Obernauer strasse 125.Collection of sports cars containing many makes including Porsche, Alfa Romeo, Ferrari, Lamborghini.

Su 10-18h 24/12-01/01. € 9, family card (5pers) € 23.

Stadtfest.City celebration. end Aug.

Voksfest, Volksfestplatz am Mainufer.Large folk festival.

2 week Jun.

Asschheim 18C5

Gasthof Zur Post, Ismaningerstrasse 11. **GPS**: n48,17433 e11,71490.

10 € 10. **Surface:** asphalted. 01/01-31/12

Distance: on the spot on the spot 300m.

Aufseß 18B1

Brauerei-Gasthof Reichold, Hochstahl 24. **GPS**: n49,88389 e11,26855.

38 € 5 € 1/90liter Ch (38x)€ 1 WC .

Surface: grassy/metalled. 01/01-31/12

Distance: on the spot.

Remarks: Bread-service, breakfast buffet € 6/pp.

Augsburg 18B5

Schillstraße 109, Lechhausen. **GPS**: n48,38914 e10,90435.

4 € 5 Ch € 1/2kWh WC . **Location:** Urban. **Surface:** gravel.

01/01-31/12

Distance: 3,2km Sportgaststätte 200m on the spot on the spot.

Remarks: At sports centre.

Augsburg 18B5

Wohnmobilstellplatz Wertach, Bürgemeister Ackermann strasse 1. **GPS**: n48,36944 e10,87750.

DE

12 € 8 € 1/90liter Ch € 1/6h. **Location:** Urban, simple.
Surface: gravel. 01/01-31/12
Distance: on the spot 4,5km on the spot on the spot 500m 500m.

Bad Abbach — 18D3

Kaiser-Therme, Kurallee 4. **GPS**: n48,92712 e12,04044.

34 € 8 + € 1,80/pp € 1/4minutes Ch (16x) WC.
Surface: grasstiles/grassy. 01/01-31/12
Distance: 2km.
Remarks: Check in at pay-desk of the Therme.

Bad Aibling — 18D6

Stellplatz an der Therme P13, Lindenstrasse/Heubergstrasse. **GPS**: n47,85639 e12,00583.

25 € 7 Ch € 0,50/kWh. **Location:** Comfortable.
Surface: grasstiles/metalled. 01/01-31/12
Distance: 500m 400m 500m 600m 100m.

Bad Bayersoien — 25B1

Wohnmobilstellplatz Bad Bayersoien, Am Bahnhof 6. **GPS**: n47,68798 e10,99820.

12 € 9/24h € 1/90liter Ch € 1/2kWh. **Location:** Rural, simple, quiet. **Surface:** gravel. 01/01-31/12
Distance: 400m 300m 300m 400m 400m.

Bad Birnbach — 19B4

Camping Arterhof, Hauptstraße 3, Lengham. **GPS**: n48,43512 e13,10939.

10 € 10 Ch WC included. **Location:** Rural, simple, quiet.
Surface: gravel. 01/01-31/12
Distance: on the spot.

Bad Bocklet — 10B6

Aschacherstrasse. **GPS**: n50,26490 e10,07486.

13 € 6 € 1/80liter Ch (13x)€ 0,50/kWh. **Surface:** metalled.
01/01-31/12
Distance: 500m Free bus to Bad Kissingen.

Bad Brückenau — 10B6

Schlosspark König Ludwig I, Schlüchterner Straße. **GPS**: n50,30556 e9,74861.

10 € 8 € 1/100liter Ch € 0,50/kWh. **Surface:** asphalted.
01/01-31/12
Distance: 4km 50m.

Bad Brückenau — 10B6

Sinnflut, Industriestrasse P5. **GPS**: n50,31212 e9,79607.

8 € 3 Ch (8x). **Surface:** gravel. 01/01-31/12
Distance: 250m 250m 250m.
Remarks: Parking swimming pool.

Bad Brückenau — 10B6

Stellplatz Bahnhofstrasse, Buchwaldstrasse. **GPS**: n50,30667 e9,78556.

DE

8 free € 0,50. **Surface:** metalled. 01/01-31/12
Distance: 50m on the spot on the spot on the spot.

Bad Brückenau 10B6

Pension Breitenbach, D286, Römershag. **GPS:** n50,31944 e9,82000.

3 free, use of a meal desired WC. **Surface:** asphalted/metalled.
01/01-31/12
Distance: 2km on the spot.

Bad Feilnbach 18D6

Gasthof Tiroler Hof, Aiblinger strasse 95. **GPS:** n47,76476 e12,03857.

3 guests free. **Location:** Simple, isolated. **Surface:** gravel.
01/01-31/12
Distance: on the spot on the spot 1km.

Bad Füssing 19B5

Campingplatz Holmerhof, Am Tennispark 10. **GPS:** n48,35798 e13,30658.

9 € 9,10 € 1/30liter Ch (9x)€ 2/kWh WC € 2. **Location:** Rural, simple. **Surface:** metalled. 01/01-31/12
Distance: 1km on the spot 1km.
Remarks: Max. 3 days, swimming pool available, use sanitary € 5/motorhome.

Bad Gögging 18C4

Limes-Therme, Am Brunnenforum 1. **GPS:** n48,81857 e11,78868.

+20 € 8, tourist tax excl € 1 Ch. **Surface:** asphalted. 01/01-31/12
Distance: 150m 150m 150m.
Remarks: Check in at pay-desk of the Therme.

Bad Griesbach 19B4

Mobilhafen Dreiquellenbad, Singham 40. **GPS:** n48,42023 e13,19261.

29 € 16,50, incl tourist tax € 1/80liter Ch (29x)€ 0,60/kWh included € 5. **Location:** Rural, simple, quiet. **Surface:** metalled.
01/01-31/12
Distance: 2km on the spot.
Remarks: Thermal-Vital-Oase incl., max. 3 days.

Bad Hindelang 25A1

Wiesengrund Wohnmobilpark, Parkplatz Wiesengrund 1. **GPS:** n47,49931 e10,37218.

30 € 8-10 + tourist tax € 2,10/pp, 7><16 € 1,60, <7 € 0,90 € 1/100liter Ch € 0,50/kWh WC € 1 . **Location:** Rural, luxurious, quiet. **Surface:** grassy/gravel. 01/01-31/12
Distance: on the spot 1km on the spot.

Bad Hindelang 25A1

Wohnmobilplatz Bergheimat, Passstraße 60, Oberjoch. **GPS:** n47,51791 e10,42142.

10 € 15, dog € 3,50 Ch WC € 1 . **Location:** Rural, simple, noisy. **Surface:** grassy/gravel. 01/01-31/12
Distance: on the spot on the spot.

Bad Kissingen 10B6

KissSalis Therme, Heiligenfelder Allee 16. **GPS:** n50,18861 e10,06139.

DE

18 € 4 + € 3,30/pp € 1/90liter Ch € 1/8h. **Surface:** asphalted.
01/01-31/12
Distance: 500m on the spot.

Bad Kohlgrub 25B1
Kur-Camping Waldruh, Sonnen 93. **GPS:** n47,65789 e11,04393.

16 € 10,40 + € 2,50/pp Ch € 0,40/kWh WC € 2,50.
Surface: gravel. 01/01-31/12
Distance: 1,5km 1,5km.

Bad Kohlgrub 25B1
Sanatorium Kurhaus Dr. Lauter, Kurhausstrasse 81. **GPS:** n47,66412 e11,04315.

4 € 12 . **Location:** Rural, simple, quiet. **Surface:** gravel.
01/01-31/12
Distance: 1,5km on the spot 1,5km 1km 1km.

Bad Königshofen 10C6
Frankentherme, Am Kurzentrum 1. **GPS:** n50,30003 e10,47503.

77 € 9 € 1 Ch € 0,50/kWh WC. **Surface:** grasstiles/metalled.
01/01-31/12
Remarks: Special health arrangements possible, washing-machine/dryer available, if full 2 alternatives will be given.

Tourist information Bad Königshofen:
Kurverwaltung Königshofen, Am Kurzentrum 1, www.bad-koenigshofen.de.Traditional small town with half-timbered houses, cycle and hiking routes in the surroundings.

Bad Kötzting 19A3
Kaitersbacher Hof, Kaitersbach 40. **GPS:** n49,15520 e12,89467.

10 € 5, free with a meal € 2,50. **Surface:** grassy/gravel.
01/12-31/10
Distance: 4km on the spot Aldi 2km 10km 8km.

Bad Neustadt 10B6
Parkplatz An der Saale. **GPS:** n50,31637 e10,22205.

60 € 8 € 1/50liter Ch . **Surface:** grasstiles. 01/01-31/12
Distance: 500m.

Bad Reichenhall 19A6
Wohnmobilpark Rupertus Therme, Hammerschmiedweg. **GPS:** n47,73466 e12,87536.

25 € 13, 2 pers.incl € 1/80liter Ch included. **Location:** Comfortable. **Surface:** gravel. 01/01-31/12
Distance: 500m on the spot.

Bad Rodach 10C6
Wohnmobilplatz Thermenaue, Thermalbadstrasse. **GPS:** n50,33452 e10,77499.

30 € 2,50 € 2 Ch € 2 WC. **Surface:** metalled.
Distance: on the spot on the spot 500m.

Bad Steben 10D6
An der Therme, P3, Steinbacher Straße. **GPS:** n50,36250 e11,63239.

DE

12 € 5 + €0,50/pp tourist tax € 0,50/80liter Ch € 0,50/kWh.
Surface: metalled. 01/01-31/12
Distance: 500m 200m 500m.

S Bad Tölz 18C6

Bürgermeister Stohlreiterpromenade. **GPS:** n47,76252 e11,55142.

30 € 8/24h € 1/50liter Ch. **Location:** Rural. **Surface:** asphalted.
01/01-31/12
Distance: 1km 500m 500m 500m.
Remarks: Max. 48h, Kurkarte incl.

Tourist information Bad Tölz:

Tourist Information, Max-Höfler-Platz 1.Health resort in the mountains of Upper Bavaria.

Alpamare.Large swimming pool complex with wave machine, Alpa, slides, sauna etc. Su-Thu 8-21h, Fri-Sa 8-22h, 24/12-01/01 8-16h.

Blombergbahn.Summer toboggan slide, 1226m. 01/04-30/09 9-18h. € 4.

40 km skiruns, 22 ski-lifts, ski schools.

S Bad Wiessee 18C6

Parkplatz am Strandbad Grieblinger, Am Strandbad. **GPS:** n47,72068 e11,72569.

6 € 5/12h, € 10/24h € 1/50liter Ch € 1/6h. **Location:** Rural, simple, quiet. **Surface:** gravel. 01/01-31/12
Distance: 1km on the spot 500m 300m.
Remarks: Max. 3 days.

S Bad Windsheim 18A2

Phoenix Reisemobilhafen, Bad Windsheimer Strasse 7. **GPS:** n49,51361 e10,41722.

100 € 10 € 1/100liter Ch (80x)€ 0,50/kWh WC € 1 washing machine/dryer € 2,50. **Surface:** gravel. 01/01-31/12
Distance: 1km 100m 500m.
Remarks: Bread-service.

Bad Windsheim 18A2

Fränkisches Freilandmuseum, Eisweiherweg. **GPS:** n49,49705 e10,41667.

20 € 5 + € 1/pp. **Surface:** grassy. 01/01-31/12
Distance: 1km 500m 500m.

S Bad Wörishofen 18B6

Therme Bad Wörishofen, Thermenallee 1. **GPS:** n48,02120 e10,59100.

25 € 9 € 1/100liter Ch included WC. **Location:** Urban, simple.
Surface: asphalted. 01/01-31/12
Distance: 1,5km 4,3km on the spot 500m on the spot.
Remarks: Check in at pay-desk of the Therme, <8m, max. 3 nights, bread-service.

S Balderschwang 25A1

Wohnmobilplatz Schwabenhof, Schwabenhof 23. **GPS:** n47,45745 e10,12963.

50 € 11-16 Ch € 3,50/day WC € 0,50. **Location:** Rural, comfortable, luxurious. **Surface:** grassy/gravel. 01/01-31/12
Distance: 3km on the spot 3km 100m 100m 100m.
Remarks: Bread-service.

S Bamberg 18B1

Wohnmobilplatz, Am Heinrichsdamm. **GPS:** n49,88583 e10,90221.

DE

25 € 12 € 1/100liter Ch € 0,50/kWh. **Surface:** gravel.
01/01-31/12
Distance: 10 min walking.
Remarks: Max. 24h.

Bärnau 18D1

Gasthof und Wald-Pension Blei, Altglashütte 4. **GPS:** n49,77222 e12,38880.

30 free Ch WC customers free. **Surface:** asphalted/grassy.
01/01-31/12
Distance: 6km on the spot 6km 100m.

Baunach 18B1

Sportplatz-Festplatz, Bahnhofstrasse 14-4. **GPS:** n49,98750 e10,85444.

5 free. **Surface:** grassy/metalled. 01/01-31/12
Remarks: Parking at the edge of nature reserve Haßberge, in the old part of the city, max. 2 nights.

Bayerbach 19B4

Wohnmobilhafen Vital, Huckenham 11. **GPS:** n48,41537 e13,13010. .

10 € 12,50 2 pers.incl, dog € 2,50 Ch (8x)€ 0,50/kWh WC included € 1. **Location:** Rural, simple, quiet. **Surface:** metalled.
01/01-31/12
Distance: 500m on the spot.
Remarks: Max. 3 nights, use sanitary facilities at campsite.

Bayreuth 18C1

Lohengrin Therme Bayreuth, Kurpormenade 5. **GPS:** n49,94319 e11,62861.

24 € 6 WC. **Surface:** metalled. 01/01-31/12
Distance: 1,5km 3,5km 500m 1km.
Remarks: Swimming pool available.

Bayrischzell 18D6

Wohnmobilstellplatz Bayrischzell, Seebergstraße. **GPS:** n47,67189 e12,01023.

20 € 10 € 0,50/80liter Ch (12x)€ 0,50/kWh. **Location:** Comfortable, central. **Surface:** gravel. 01/01-31/12
Distance: 400m 400m 400m 400m bus 5min on the spot.

Beilngries 18C3

An der Altmühl, An der Altmühl. **GPS:** n49,02655 e11,47121.

20 € 10 Ch WC included. **Location:** Urban, comfortable, central, quiet. **Surface:** grassy.
Remarks: Check in at reception.

Beilngries 18C3

Landgasthof Euringer, Dorfstrasse 23. **GPS:** n49,01054 e11,50261. .

6 guests free Ch . **Location:** Urban, simple, central.
Surface: metalled. 01/01-31/12
Distance: 4km on the spot 4km.

Benediktbeuern 18C6

Wohnmobilstellplatz Benediktbeuern, Schwimmbadstraße 37. **GPS:** n47,69920 e11,41556. .

DE

8 €7 Chincluded € 1/6h. **Location:** Rural, comfortable, quiet. **Surface:** asphalted. 15/03-01/11
Distance: 1km.
Remarks: Max. 3 nights, Alpenwarmbad 01/05-01/09 (swimming pool).

S Beratzhausen 18C3

Landgasthof Friesenmühle, Friesenmühle 1. **GPS:** n49,08534 e11,81176.

10 free, use of a meal desired (2x) WC. **Surface:** grassy/gravel. 01/01-31/12
Distance: 1km on the spot 1km.
Remarks: Apply< 22h.

S Berching 18C3

Stellplatz Schiffsanleger, Uferpromenade. **GPS:** n49,10972 e11,43910.
12 €5 €1 Ch € 1/8h. **Surface:** grasstiles/metalled. 01/01-31/12
Distance: 200m 50m on the spot 300m 100m.

S Berchtesgaden 19B6

Reisemobilplatz Rasp, Renothenweg 15, Oberau. **GPS:** n47,65172 e13,07038.

20 €8 + €2,10/pp tourist tax €2 Ch €2 WC. **Location:** Central, quiet. **Surface:** gravel. Easter-30/11
Distance: 500m 500m.

Bergen/Chiemgau 19A6

Parkplatz Hochfelln-Seilbahn, Maria-Eck-Straße 8. **GPS:** n47,79710 e12,59079.

10 €5. **Location:** Simple. **Surface:** metalled. 01/01-31/12
Distance: 1,2km on the spot on the spot.
Remarks: Parking ski-lift, max. 1 night.

S Bernried 19A3

Altes Gasthaus Artmeier, Innenstetten 45. **GPS:** n48,89675 e12,90262.

10 €5 € 1/100liter (4x)€ 1/day. **Location:** Rural, simple, quiet. **Surface:** gravel/sand.
Distance: 3km on the spot on the spot.

S Betzenstein 18C2

Ferienhotel Eibtaler Hof, Spies 8. **GPS:** n49,63551 e11,40437.

20 guests free €5 WC.
Distance: on the spot on the spot 5km 1km.

S Biesenhofen 18B6

Gasthof Stegmühle, Stegmühle 2. **GPS:** n47,82437 e10,64428.

4 €5, free with a meal Ch WC. **Location:** Simple. **Surface:** gravel/metalled. 01/01-31/12
Distance: 1km 1km on the spot 1km.

S Bischofsgrün 18C1

Rangenweg. **GPS:** n50,05407 e11,79292.

8 tourist tax € 1 to be paid at tourist office € 1 Ch (6x)€ 1. **Surface:** metalled. 01/01-31/12
Distance: 250m 500m nearby.

S Bischofsheim an der Rhön 10B6

Viehweg 1, Haselbach. **GPS:** n50,39506 e9,99593.

DE

12 € 5 € 1/80liter Ch. **Surface:** asphalted. 01/01-31/12
Distance: on the spot on the spot on the spot.
Remarks: Parking swimming pool in Haselbach.

Bischofswiesen 19A6

Götschen Alm, Kollertradte 21, Loipl. **GPS**: n47,64817 e12,93631.

20 guests free. **Surface:** gravel. 01/04-30/11
Distance: 2km on the spot 2km on the spot on the spot.

Blaichach 25A1

Alpen-Rundblick Mobil Camping, Am Eichbichl 1. **GPS**: n47,54615 e10,25917.

60 € 9,50/11,50 + € 1,20/pp € 1/80liter Ch (54x)€ 0,50/kWh WC € 1,50 € 2,50. **Location:** Luxurious. **Surface:** grassy/gravel.
01/01-31/12
Distance: 300m 3,3km on the spot on the spot 500m 500m 5km 1km.

Bodenmais 19A3

Concorde-Reisemobil-Stellplatz, Kötztinger Straße. **GPS**: n49,07147 e13,09273.

12 € 7 + tourist tax € 0,50/100liter Ch € 0,50/kWh.
Surface: asphalted.
01/01-31/12
Distance: 800m 200m 200m.
Remarks: Use swimming pool, sauna, fitness-studio incl.

Bodenmais 19A3

Kerzenwelt, Bahnhofstrasse. **GPS**: n49,06972 e13,09972.

5 € 8/20h. **Surface:** metalled. 01/01-01/11
Distance: nearby nearby nearby 500m nearby.

Bodenwöhr 18D2

Gasthof zum Troidlwirt, Bodenwöhrer strasse 6. **GPS**: n49,28305 e12,26272.

40 € 5/24h, guests free Ch (12x)€ 1 WC € 1.
Surface: grassy/gravel. 01/01-31/12
Distance: on the spot on the spot bakery 300m.

Bogen 19A3

Volksfestplatz, Kotaustraße 12. **GPS**: n48,90744 e12,68877.

5 € 10 € 2 Ch (5x)€ 2/8h. **Surface:** grassy/metalled.
01/01-31/12
Distance: 300m Edeka 100m.
Remarks: Check in at pay-desk of swiming pool.

Burgbernheim 18A2

Wohnmobilstellplatz im Gründlein, Freibadstrasse. **GPS**: n49,44627 e10,31869.

12 free € 1/100liter Ch € 0,50/kWh. **Surface:** grasstiles.
01/01-31/12
Distance: 500m 500m 500m 500m.

Burghaslach 18A2

Hotel-Restaurant Steigerwaldhaus, Oberrimbach 2. **GPS**: n49,72764 e10,53542.

DE

10 € 6, guests free. **Surface:** grassy. 01/01-31/12
Distance: 500m on the spot 5km.

S Burghausen 19A5

Waldpark Lindach, Berghamer Strasse 1. **GPS**: n48,15443 e12,80859.

16 € 5/24h € 1/80liter Ch (16x)€ 0,50/kWh WC . **Location:** Rural, comfortable, quiet. **Surface:** gravel.
01/01-31/12 sanitary 01/11-31/03.
Distance: 1,5km 500m 1,5km.
Remarks: Check in at Bürgerhaus Marktlerstr. 15a, caution key sanitary building € 20.

S Burgkirchen 19A5

Peterhof, Peterhof 24. **GPS**: n48,15096 e12,75025.

3 € 12,50, 2 pers.incl WC included . **Location:** Rural, simple, quiet. **Surface:** grassy. 01/01-31/12
Distance: 2km 2km 2km.

S Burgkunstadt 10D6

Alter Postweg. **GPS**: n50,13965 e11,25017.

4 free € 1 Ch. **Location:** Rural. **Surface:** gravel.
01/01-31/12
Distance: 100m 15km 100m 300m 300m on the spot on the spot.
Remarks: Max. 48h.

S Cadolzburg 18B2

Parkplatz Am Höhbuck, Am Höhbuck. **GPS**: n49,46123 e10,85188.
8 free Ch . **Surface:** metalled. 01/01-31/12
Distance: on the spot.

Chammünster 19A2

Berggasthaus Oedenturm, Am Oedenturm 11. **GPS**: n49,21056 e12,70444.

2 free, use of a meal desired. **Surface:** grassy/gravel.
01/01-31/12
Distance: 5km on the spot.

Coburg 10C6

Ketschenanger, Schutzenstrasse. **GPS**: n50,25306 e10,96417.

9 free. **Surface:** asphalted.
Distance: on the spot on the spot.
Remarks: Parking next to gymnasium, max. 48h.

S Coburg 10C6

Aral-station, Bambergerstrasse. **GPS**: n50,24833 e10,96639.

3 free € 1 Ch. **Surface:** metalled.
01/01-31/12
Distance: on the spot.

Tourist information Coburg:

Tourist Information, Herrngasse 4, www.coburg-tourist.de.Old residence city of the Sachsen-Coburg family. The Sachsen-Coburg family is related to several Eurpean Royal Houses.
Die Veste Coburg.Medieval fortress.
Coburger Puppenmuseum, Rückertstrasse 2/3, neben Schloss Ehrenburg.Doll museum.
9-17h.
Schloß Ehrenburg.
guided tour Tue-Su.

Deggendorf 19A3

Konstantin-Bader-Strasse, Konstantin-Bader-Straße. **GPS**: n48,82656 e12,96367.

DE

3 free. **Location:** Simple. **Surface:** asphalted. 01/01-31/12
Distance: centre 500m 250m.

S Deiningen 18A4

Cowabanga, Am Sportpark. **GPS:** n48,86292 e10,58042.

10 free € 2,50 WC. **Location:** Urban, simple. **Surface:** asphalted.
01/01-31/12
Distance: 2km on the spot.
Remarks: Parking sports centre.

S Denkendorf 18C3

Gasthof Lindenwirt, Hauptstrasse 43. **GPS:** n48,92806 e11,45568.

10 € 4 included. **Location:** Urban. **Surface:** gravel/sand.
01/01-31/12
Distance: on the spot 700m on the spot 200m on the spot on the spot.

S Dettelbach 18A1

Zur Mainfähre, Mainsondheimerstrasse. **GPS:** n49,80076 e10,16751.

35 € 5 € 1 Ch (24x)€ 0,50/kWh. **Surface:** grassy. 01/01-31/12
high water season.
Distance: 100m 100m 100m.

S Dießen 18B6

Seestraße. **GPS:** n47,95220 e11,10598.
12 € 8 € 1 Ch (12x)€ 4/8h. **Surface:** gravel. 01/01-31/12
Distance: 200m 200m 150m 150m.
Remarks: Max. 3 days.

S Dingolfing 19A4

Wohnmobilstellplatz Dingolfing, Wollanger/Prasserweg. **GPS:** n48,62827 e12,50206.

12 free € 1/80liter Ch (12x)€ 1/12h. **Location:** Rural, comfortable, quiet. **Surface:** gravel. 01/01-31/12
Distance: 400m 4,6km 250m.
Remarks: Nearby swimming pool.

S Dinkelsbühl 18A3

Park- & Campanlage, Dürrwanger Straße. **GPS:** n49,07812 e10,32906.

12 € 12 Ch included € 1,50. **Surface:** metalled.
01/01-31/12
Distance: 1,5km 100m 500m.
Remarks: To be paid at campsite (500m).

Dittelbrunn 18A1

Gasthaus Goldene Flasche, Strohgasse 1, Haubach. **GPS:** n50,09787 e10,20763.

3 € 1. **Surface:** metalled. 01/01-31/12
Distance: on the spot on the spot 200m.

S Donauwörth 18B4

Wohnmobilstellplatz am Festplatz, Neue Obermayerstrasse. **GPS:** n48,71490 e10,77874.

20 free € 1/80liter Ch € 1/8h. **Location:** Urban, simple.
Surface: asphalted. 01/01-31/12
Distance: on the spot on the spot 500m.
Remarks: Max. 1 night.

DE

Ebelsbach 18A1

Hotel-Gasthof Klosterbräu, Georg-Schäfer-Strasse 11. **GPS**: n49,98356 e10,67406.

7 € 7,50 Ch WC included. 01/01-31/12
Distance: 150m.
Remarks: Apply < 21h.

Ebermannstadt 18B1

P2, Oberes Tor. **GPS**: n49,78222 e11,18946.

10 free. **Surface:** metalled. 01/01-31/12
Distance: 750m 100m.

Ebermannstadt 18B1

P8, Bahnhofstrasse. **GPS**: n49,77750 e11,18722.

2 free. **Surface:** metalled. 01/01-31/12

Ebern 18A1

Wohnmobilhafen am Festplatz, Walk-Strasser-Anlage. **GPS**: n50,09312 e10,79496.

30 € 5 Ch € 2 WC included. **Surface:** metalled.
01/01-31/12
Distance: on the spot 1km 2km 100m 200m 100m.

Ebern 18A1

Dietz, Bahnhofstrasse. **GPS**: n50,10167 e10,78917.

4 free Ch WC. **Surface:** asphalted/grassy. 01/01-31/12

Tourist information Ebern:
Fremdenverkehrsamt, Rittergasse 3, www.tourismus-ebern.de.
Heimatmuseum am Grauturm, Marktplatz.History of the city. holidays Tue-Fri 14.30-17.30h, remaining Su 13.30-17.30h.

Ebrach 18A1

Naturbad, Schwimmbadweg. **GPS**: n49,84639 e10,48306.

5 free € 1 Ch WC. **Surface:** metalled. 01/01-31/12
Distance: 2km 2km 2km 500m.
Remarks: Parking swimming pool.

Eggenfelden 19A5

P2, Birkenallee. **GPS**: n48,40185 e12,77579.

5 free. **Location:** Simple, quiet. **Surface:** grassy/metalled.
01/01-31/12
Distance: 1km.
Remarks: Max. 3 days.

Eggenfelden 19A5

Tankstelle Breitner Shell, Tiefstadt 10. **GPS**: n48,39591 e12,76621.

€ 3 . **Location:** Simple. **Surface:** asphalted.
Remarks: Max. 1 night.

Eging am See 19B4

Bavaria Kur-Sport Camping Park, Grafenauer Str. 31. **GPS**: n48,72120 e13,26519.

DE

10 € 15 Ch (10x)included. **Location:** Rural, simple, quiet.
Surface: asphalted.
01/01-31/12
Remarks: Max. 2 days, check in at reception, use sanitary facilities at campsite.

S Eibelstadt 17D2

Wassersportclub Eibelstadt, Mainparkring. **GPS:** n49,73146 e9,98701.

35 € 10 € 1/5minutes Ch ,6Amp WC included € 1/time € 5.
Surface: grassy/gravel. 01/01-31/12
Distance: 2km 50m 50m 1km.
Remarks: Along the river Meno.

S Eichstätt 18B4

Schottenwiese/Volkfestplatz. **GPS:** n48,88400 e11,19816.

50 € 7 Ch (30x)€ 0,50/kWh WC € 0,50. **Location:** Urban, simple, central, quiet. **Surface:** metalled. 01/01-31/12 Eichstätter Volksfest.
Distance: 500m 500m on the spot on the spot.
Remarks: From Ingolstadt dir Volksfestplatz, follow Wohnmobil Stellplatz and P+R.

Tourist information Eichstätt:

Tourist Information, Domplatz 8, www.altmuehlnet.de.Baroque city in nature parc Altmühl, cycle and hiking routes.
Fossiliensuchen, Steinbruch.Searching for fossils. 01/04-31/10 8-20h.
Flohmarkt, Volksfestplatz.Flea market. 08/05, 19/06, 17/07, 18/09, 02/10.
Altstadtfest, Innenstad.City celebration. 01/07-03/07.
Eichstätter Volksfest, Volksfestplatz.Folk festival. 02/09-11/09.
Informationszentrum Naturpark Altmühltal, Notre Dame 1, voormalig klooster.Information centre nature reserve. 01/04-31/10 Mo-Sa 9-17h, Su 10-17h, 01/11-31/03 Mo-Thu 8-12h, 14-17h, Fri 8-12h. T free.

S Einsiedl 25C1

Wohnmobilstellplatz, B11. **GPS:** n47,57000 e11,30389.

80 € 5 € 1/70liter € 1/6h. **Location:** Rural, comfortable, quiet.
Surface: asphalted/gravel. 01/01-31/12
Distance: 500m on the spot on the spot 500m 3,5km 1,5km 1,5km.
Remarks: Max. 3 nights.

S Eisenheim 18A1

Weingut Herbert Schuler, An der Mainaue, Obereisenheim. **GPS:** n49,88883 e10,17942.

60 € 5 € 1/80liter Ch € 0,50. **Surface:** grassy/metalled.
01/01-31/12
Distance: on the spot on the spot on the spot.
Remarks: Along the river Meno.

Eltmann am Main 18A1

Parkplatz, Mainlände. **GPS:** n49,97306 e10,66250.

20 free. **Surface:** gravel. 01/01-31/12
Distance: 500m on the spot on the spot 100m 300m.

S Enderndorf 18B3

Wohnmobilstellplatz Panorama, Kreisstraße, Spalt-Enderndorf. **GPS:** n49,15028 e10,91083.

60 € 7,50 € 0,20/10liter Ch (60x)€ 0,60/kWh .
Surface: metalled. 01/04-31/10
Distance: 400m 400m 400m 400m 3km 150m.

S Enderndorf 18B3

Reisemobil-Stellplatz Enderndorf-West, Zum Hafen. **GPS:** n49,14777 e10,91126.

DE

25 € 8/24h € 0,20/100liter Ch € 0,50/kWh. **Location:** Rural, simple, isolated, quiet. **Surface:** grasstiles.
01/01-31/12
Distance: 200m 150m 200m 200m on the spot on the spot.

S Erbendorf 18C1

Am Stadtpark, Bahnhofstraße 21. **GPS**: n49,84144 e12,04769.

20 free € 1 Ch. **Surface:** gravel. 01/01-31/12
Distance: 100m 200m 200m.

S Erding 18D5

Wohnmobilpark Erding, Thermenallee. **GPS**: n48,29332 e11,88707.

55 € 10/day € 1/80liter Ch (55x)€ 1/2kWh.
Surface: grasstiles/metalled. 01/01-31/12
Distance: 2km 2km 2km 50m.

S Erding 18D5

Therme Erding, Thermenallee 1. **GPS**: n48,29332 e11,88707.

25 free WC. **Surface:** metalled. 01/01-31/12
Distance: 2km 2km 2km 50m.
Remarks: Max. 7 nights, swimming pool.

S Escherndorf 18A1

Campingplatz Escherndorf, An der Güß 9a. **GPS**: n49,85996 e10,17632.

22 € 8 Ch. **Surface:** grassy. 01/04-31/10
Distance: 300m 300m.

S Ettenbeuren 18A5

Wohnmobilpark Kammelaue, Zum Sportplatz 12. **GPS**: n48,37565 e10,36021.

40 € 7, € 13 service incl Ch WC. **Location:** Rural, comfortable, quiet. **Surface:** grasstiles/metalled. 01/04-31/10
Distance: 500m on the spot 500m on the spot on the spot.

S Feucht 18B2

Am Freibad Feuchtasia, Chormantelweg. **GPS**: n49,37848 e11,22495.

9 € 7 € 1/80liter Ch (8x)€ 1/2kWh. **Surface:** grasstiles.
01/01-31/12
Distance: 1km 900m.

Fichtelberg 18C1

Automobilmuseum, Eckert Naglerweg 9. **GPS**: n49,99760 e11,85820.

5 free. **Surface:** asphalted/metalled. 01/01-31/12
Distance: 100m.
Remarks: Parking museum.

S Fischen 25A1

Wohnmobil-Stellplatz Fischen, Mühlenstraße. **GPS**: n47,44950 e10,26946.

DE

12 € 8 + € 1,95/pp tourist tax € 1 € 1 Ch (12x)€ 1/12h.
Location: Rural, simple. **Surface:** asphalted.
Distance: 1,2km on the spot on the spot on the spot.
Remarks: Pay at Sportpark, Mühlenstraße 55.

S Forchheim 18B1

Auf der Sportinsel. **GPS:** n49,72120 e11,04939.

10 € 3 € 3 Ch WC . **Surface:** metalled. 01/01-31/12
Distance: 5 min walking on the spot on the spot.

S Frasdorf 18D6

Bauernhof Lederstube, Lederstube 3. **GPS:** n47,79521 e12,28774.

6 € 7 € 1,50 Ch € 3. **Location:** Rural, simple, isolated, quiet.
Surface: grassy/gravel. 01/03-30/09
Distance: 500m 800m 800m 800m.

Freilassing 19B6

Stellplatz Freilassing, Salzburgerstrasse. **GPS:** n47,84031 e12,98599.

5 free. **Surface:** asphalted. 01/01-31/12
Distance: 6km 100m.

Tourist information Freilassing:

Flea market.

S Freyung 19B3

Freizeitpark Solla, Solla. **GPS:** n48,80104 e13,54125.

12 € 5 € 1/80liter Ch (12x)€ 0,50/kWh. **Location:** Rural, simple, quiet. **Surface:** grasstiles. 01/01-31/12
Distance: 2km 500m on the spot on the spot.

Freyung 19B3

Parking Freibad, Zuppinger Straße. **GPS:** n48,80515 e13,54102.

10 free. **Location:** Urban, simple, quiet.
Surface: metalled.
01/01-31/12
Distance: 1km 1km 1km.

Tourist information Freyung:

www.freyungurlaub.de.Glass city, air health and winter sports resort.
Bergglashütte.Glass-blowing and exhibition of engraving.
Mo-Fri 9-18h, 01/05-30/09 Mo-Fri 9-18h, Su 10-12h, 14-16h.
Schloß Wolfstein.Hunting and fishery museum.
Tue-Su 10-17h 01/11-15/12.
Cross-country skiing in Freyung-Kreuzberg, 36 km trails.

Friedberg 18B5

Herrgottsruhstrasse. **GPS:** n48,35765 e10,99095.
4 free. **Surface:** gravel.
Distance: 600m 600m 600m.

Friedberg 18B5

Seestraße. **GPS:** n48,36540 e10,96529.

4 free. **Location:** Rural, simple, quiet. **Surface:** asphalted.
01/01-31/12
Distance: 1,8km 5km on the spot 400m on the spot on the spot.

S Friedberg 18B5

Marquardtstrasse 2/A. **GPS:** n48,34825 e10,99757.
Chfree.
Distance: on the spot.

S Friedenfels 18D1

Freibad, Badstrasse. **GPS:** n49,88639 e12,10417.

DE

15 € 3,50 . **Surface:** metalled. 01/01-31/12
Distance: 1,5km.
Remarks: Max. 3 days, service during opening hours.

Friedenfels 18D1
Steinwaldhalle Zentral, Am Hammerweiher. **GPS:** n49,88102 e12,10297.

15 € 3,50. **Surface:** metalled. 01/01-31/12
Distance: on the spot 25m.
Remarks: Max. 3 days, pay at tourist office, Café Am Steinwald, Gemmingenstr. 19.

Friedenfels 18D1
Stellplatz 'Ruhig', Weisteinerweg, Frauenreuth. **GPS:** n49,89278 e12,08556.

5 € 3,50. **Surface:** metalled. 01/01-31/12
Distance: 1,5km.
Remarks: Max. 3 days.

Tourist information Friedenfels:
Touristic region, signposted routes for Nordic Walking.

S **Füssen** 25B1
Camper's Stop, Abt Hafnerstrasse 9. **GPS:** n47,58186 e10,70080.

120 € 13, trailer € 5 € 0,50/150liter Ch € 1/1kWh WC € 0,50 € 2. **Location:** Urban, comfortable, noisy. **Surface:** gravel/metalled.
01/01-31/12
Distance: 1,5km 600m 600m terrace 50m 250m 4km 400m.

S **Füssen** 25B1
Wohnmobilstellplatz Füssen, Abt Hafnerstrasse 1. **GPS:** n47,58224 e10,70355.

30 € 13,50 Ch (6x)€ 2,50 WC € 0,50 € 2. **Location:** Noisy.
Surface: metalled.
01/01-31/12
Distance: 1,8km 1km 200m 300m 500m on the spot on the spot on the spot on the spot.

Tourist information Füssen:
Füssen Tourismus, Kaiser-Maximilian-Platz 1, www.stadt-fuessen.de.Located on the Forggen Lake in a spur of the Alpes.

S **Garmisch-Partenkirchen** 25B1
Alpencamp am Wank, Wankbahnstraße 2. **GPS:** n47,50573 e11,10802.

110 € 9, tourist tax > 16 € 2/pp, € 1 Umwelttaxe € 1/50liter Ch (110x)€ 1/1kWh WC € 1 . **Location:** Rural, comfortable.
Surface: asphalted. 01/01-31/12
Distance: 1km 2km 50m 700m 50m 2,5km 1,5km.

Tourist information Garmisch-Partenkirchen:
www.garmisch-partenkirchen.de.Famous winter sports resort on the Zugspitze.
Werdenfelsermuseum.Local museum. Tue-Fri 10-13h, 15-18h, Sa-Su 10-13h.
Ski school and ski rental, cross country trails, skating rink, swimming pools.

S **Gerolzhofen** 18A1
P3 Zur Volkach, Schallfelderstrasse. **GPS:** n49,89808 e10,35169.

2 €5 € 1 Ch (4x)€ 0,50/kWh. **Surface:** metalled.
01/01-31/12
Distance: on the spot.
Remarks: Max. 3 days.

Gerolzhofen 18A1
P1 Geomaris. GPS: n49,89980 e10,36035.

DE

6 free. **Surface:** asphalted. 01/01-31/12
Distance: 750m.
Remarks: Parking swimming pool.

Geslau 18A2

Bauernhof Mohrenhof, Lauterbach 3. **GPS:** n49,34630 e10,32500.

20 € 10-12 Ch € 0,50/kWh WC € 0,50 € 3 € 2,50/2h.
Surface: grassy. Easter-31/10
Distance: 500m on the spot.
Remarks: Bread-service.

Goldkronach 18C1

Schulstrasse. **GPS:** n50,01265 e11,68276.

4 free € 1/10minutes Ch (4x)€ 1/10h. **Surface:** gravel.
01/01-31/12
Distance: 500m 2km.

Grafenau 19B3

Grafenauer Kurpark, Freyunger Straße. **GPS:** n48,85605 e13,40456.

10 € 5 Kurtaxe incl € 1/80liter Ch included free. **Location:** Urban, simple, quiet. **Surface:** gravel.
01/01-31/12
Distance: 500m 600m 550m ReWe on the spot.
Remarks: Wifi in Touristinformation + 1/2h free internet in Stadtbücherei.

Gräfendorf 17D1

Roßmühle, Weickersgrüben. **GPS:** n50,10660 e9,78309.

4 free € 2/100liter Ch. **Surface:** metalled. 01/04-31/10
Distance: on the spot on the spot on the spot.
Remarks: Max. 24h, check in at shop.

Greding 18C3

Am Hallenbad. **GPS:** n49,04409 e11,35551.

20 free. **Location:** Urban. **Surface:** metalled.
01/01-31/12
Distance: Old city centre 300m 500m 250m 250m on the spot on the spot.
Remarks: Parking at city wall in front of swimming pool.

Tourist information Greding:
City wall and towers.
Christmas fair. Dec 13-19h.

Großheubach 17C2

Weingut Gasthaus "Zur Bretzel", Kirchstraße 1. **GPS:** n49,72620 e9,22083.
25 € 15 Ch WC included € 1. **Surface:** grassy/gravel.
Remarks: € 10, reduction.

Großweil 25C1

Aplengasthof Kreut-Alm, Kreut 1. **GPS:** n47,66184 e11,28286.

15 customers free . **Location:** Rural, simple, isolated, quiet.
Surface: asphalted. 01/03-31/10
Distance: 3,2km on the spot.

Großweil 25C1

Freilichtmuseum Glentleiten, An der Glentleiten 4. **GPS:** n47,66495 e11,28506.

DE

10 free. **Surface:** gravel.
Distance: 2km 3,5km Gaststätte - Biergarten 1km.
Remarks: Open air museum, only overnight stays.

S Günzburg 18A5

Waldbad, Heidenheimerstrasse. **GPS:** n48,46287 e10,26944.

24 € 5/24h € 1/100liter (24x)€ 0,50/kWh. **Location:** Simple.
Surface: gravel. 01/01-31/12 Danube Bike Trail.
Remarks: Parking swimming pool.

S Gunzenhausen 18B3

Surfzentrum Schlungenhof. GPS: n49,12790 e10,74559.

80 € 10/24h € 1 Ch included WC € 1 . **Location:** Rural, comfortable, quiet. **Surface:** grassy/gravel. 01/04-30/10
Distance: 100m on the spot 1,8km.

Gunzenhausen 18B3

Altmühlsee, Seezentrum Mühr. GPS: n49,13145 e10,73534.

40 € 3 day/€ 6 night. **Location:** Rural, comfortable, isolated, quiet.
Surface: grassy. 01/01-31/12
Distance: on the spot 200m on the spot on the spot.
Remarks: Max. 3 days.

S Hammelburg 17D1

Am Bleichrasen, P2, Am Weiher. **GPS:** n50,11390 e9,88820.

25 € 6/24h Ch € 0,50/kWh WC. **Surface:** asphalted.
01/01-31/12
Distance: 200m 200m 300m.

S Hammelburg 17D1

Schloß Saaleck, Am Schlossberg. **GPS:** n50,11194 e9,87778.

10 € 4 € 0,50/kWh WC. **Surface:** asphalted/metalled.
01/01-31/12
Distance: on the spot.

Hammelburg 17D1

Restaurant Nöth, Morlesauer Strasse 3. **GPS:** n50,11707 e9,80313.
5 . **Surface:** grassy.
Distance: on the spot.

S Hassfurt 18A1

Festplatz am Gries, Ringstrasse. **GPS:** n50,03068 e10,50094.

22 € 5/night € 1 Ch € 1 WC. **Surface:** asphalted. 01/01-31/12
Distance: 200m 10m 200m 200m.
Remarks: Parking along the Main, follow signs.

Herrieden 18A3

Volksfestplatz an der Altmühl, Staatsstrasse 2248. **GPS:** n49,23191 e10,49588.

10 free. **Surface:** asphalted. 01/01-31/12
Distance: 100m 200m 200m.
Remarks: Parking at the old mill bridge.

S Herrieden 18A3

ARAL-station, Am Eichelberg 2. **GPS:** n49,25820 e10,50239.

10 free € 1,50 Ch WC. **Surface:** asphalted. 01/01-31/12
Distance: 3km on the spot on the spot.

DE

Hersbruck 18C2

Fackelmanntherme Hersbruck, Badestraße. **GPS**: n49,51142 e11,44267.

6 € 6 € 1 Ch € 1/6h. **Surface:** gravel. 01/01-31/12
Distance: on the spot 200m 200m.
Remarks: Check in at pay-desk of the Therme.

Herzogenaurach 18B2

Freizeitbad Atlantis, Würzburger Straße 35. **GPS**: n49,57251 e10,86641.
12 € 6/24h Ch (12x). **Surface:** gravel. 01/01-31/12
Distance: on the spot.
Remarks: € 2 reduction swimming pool.

Hilpoltstein 18B3

Seezentrum Heuberg am Rothsee, Heuberg. **GPS**: n49,20954 e11,18595.

50 € 7,50 Ch. **Surface:** metalled.
01/01-31/12 Service: winter.
Distance: 200m 200m.

Hilpoltstein 18B3

Am Main-Donau Kanal. **GPS**: n49,20455 e11,18813.

30 € 6. **Surface:** grassy. 15/04-30/10
Distance: 1,9km Canal 1,9km 1km on the spot on the spot.

Tourist information Hilpoltstein:
Amt für Kultur und Tourismus, Maria-Dorothea-strasse 8, www.hilpoltstein.de.City on the Rothsee.
Burgfeste.Festival with events. beginning Aug.

Hof/Saale 11A6

Park Theresienstein, Ritter von Münch Strasse. **GPS**: n50,32956 e11,92041.

20 free. **Surface:** metalled. 01/01-31/12
Distance: 2,5km 1km.
Remarks: Max. 24h.

Hof/Saale 11A6

Utreusee, Wilhelm Löhe strasse. **GPS**: n50,28583 e11,91361.

20 free. **Surface:** asphalted/metalled. 01/01-31/12
Distance: 100m 50m 500m.
Remarks: Max. 24h.

Hof/Saale 11A6

Clean Park Buchta, Hofeckerstrasse/Ernst Reuterstrasse. **GPS**: n50,32641 e11,89248.

4 € 5 € 1 Ch .
Surface: metalled.
01/01-31/12
Distance: 2km 800m.
Remarks: Max. 72h.

Tourist information Hof/Saale:
Tourist-Information, am Rathaus, www.hof.de.Modern industrial town.
Bürgerpark Theresienstein.Landscape park according English example.
9-18h, winter 9-16h.
Untreusee.Lake with water sports.

Hofheim in Unterfranken 10C6

Wohnmobilplatz Hofheim, Johannisstraße 28. **GPS**: n50,14185 e10,51957.

30 € 7 € 1/80liter Ch € 0,50/kWh WC . **Surface:** grasstiles.
01/01-31/12
Distance: 750m 750m.
Remarks: Bread-service.

Hohenberg an der Eger 11A6

Wiesenfestplatz, Selberstrasse. **GPS**: n50,09762 e12,22085.

DE

10 free WC. **Surface:** metalled. 01/01-31/12
Distance: 200m 50m.
Remarks: Beautiful view.

Hohenburg 18C2
Sportplatz, Sportplatzweg 1. **GPS:** n49,29194 e11,80917.

6 € 7 € 2 WC. **Surface:** metalled. 01/01-31/12
Distance: 1km.
Remarks: Parking at sports park.

Huisheim 18B4
Waldparkplatz im Schwalbtal, Waldschenke 1, Gosheim. **GPS:** n48,84932 e10,71530.

10 € 5, guests free. **Location:** Rural, simple, quiet. **Surface:** asphalted. 01/01-31/12
Distance: on the spot.

Immenstadt 25A1
P 3 Viehmarktplatz, Badeweg. **GPS:** n47,56192 e10,20857.

6 free Ch WC. **Location:** Urban, simple, comfortable.
Surface: asphalted. 01/01-31/12
Distance: 700m.

Ingolstadt 18C4
Parkplatz Hallenbad, Jahnstrasse. **GPS:** n48,76025 e11,42038.

8 € 5 (9-17h), overnight stay free € 1/80liter Ch included.
Location: Urban, comfortable. **Surface:** metalled. 01/01-31/12
Distance: on the spot 1,6km on the spot on the spot on the spot on the spot.
Remarks: Parking sports park, max. 3 days.

Inzell 19A6
Camping Lindlbauer, Kreuzfeldstraße 44. **GPS:** n47,76717 e12,75417.

12 € 16 Ch WC included. **Location:** Rural.
Surface: metalled. 01/01-31/12
Distance: 1km.
Remarks: Max. 1 night, health resort 500m.

Iphofen 18A2
Einesheimer Tor. GPS: n49,70260 e10,26459.

8 free € 1 Ch WC. **Surface:** asphalted. 01/01-31/12
Distance: 200m.
Remarks: Parking at city wall.

Kastl/Oberpfalz 18C2
Wanderparkplatz Am Alten Bahnhof, Amberger Straße. **GPS:** n49,36657 e11,68388.

5 free Ch WC free. **Surface:** gravel. 01/01-31/12
Distance: 200m 200m 100m 50m.

Kaufbeuren 18B6
Wohnmobilplatz Kaufbeuren, Buronstraße. **GPS:** n47,89885 e10,61650.
8 free Ch free (6x)€ 0,50/2kWh. **Location:** Urban.
Surface: gravel.

DE

Distance: historical centre 3km.
Remarks: Max. 3 days.

S Kelheim 18C3

Volksfestplatz, Am Pflegerspitz. **GPS**: n48,91331 e11,87657.

50 € 6, 01/11-31/03 free Ch (18x)€ 1/2kWh WC.
Surface: metalled. 01/01-31/12 service 01/11-31/03.
Distance: 500m 500m.
Remarks: Hindmost part, max. 3 nights.

Tourist information Kelheim:

Tourist Information, Ludwigsplatz 14, www.kelheim.de.Historical little town on the Danube river.

Archäologisch Museum im Herzogkasten, Ledergasse 11.Archeological museum and history of the city. 01/04-31/10 Tue-Su 10-16h.

S Kemnath 18C1

Wohnmobilstellplatz Kemnath, Am Eisweier 8. **GPS**: n49,87219 e11,88774.

5 free € 1 Ch (6x)€ 1/6h WC. **Surface:** concrete.
01/01-31/12
Distance: 650m 650m 650m.

S Kempten 25A1

Illerstadion, Illerdamm/Jahnstrasse. **GPS**: n47,72915 e10,31940.

6 € 5 € 1 . **Location:** Urban, simple, noisy. **Surface:** metalled.
01/01-31/12
Distance: 500m 2,7km.

S Kiefersfelden 25D1

Hödenauer See, Wasserstrasse. **GPS**: n47,62881 e12,18949.

10 € 5 WC € 0,50. **Location:** Simple. **Surface:** gravel/sand.
01/01-31/12
Distance: 2km 3km on the spot 50m 300m.
Remarks: Max. 3 days.

Kiefersfelden 25D1

Rathausplatz. **GPS**: n47,61303 e12,18981.

20 € 10. **Location:** Simple. **Surface:** asphalted.
01/01-31/12
Distance: on the spot 2km 100m.
Remarks: Max. 3 days.

Tourist information Kiefersfelden:

Kur- und Verkehrsamt, Dorfstrasse 23, www.kiefersfelden.de.Mountain village in Oberbayern.

Blaahaus museum.Museum about daily living in ancient times.

01/05-31/10 Thu, Su 14-17h, 01/11-30/04 1st Su of the month 14-17h.

S Kirchenlamitz 11A6

REWE-Markt, Weißenstädter Straße. **GPS**: n50,14905 e11,94055.

12 free Ch free,voluntary contribution. **Location:** Comfortable.
Surface: asphalted. 01/01-31/12
Distance: 500m 10m.

S Kirchham 19B5

Erlebnispark Haslinger Hof, Ed 1. **GPS**: n48,34947 e13,29115.

25-30 Overnight stay € 17 (incl. € 9 voucher) Ch. **Location:** Rural, simple, quiet. **Surface:** gravel. 01/01-31/12
Distance: on the spot.

S Kitzingen 18A2

Wohnmobilpark Am Main, Bleichwasen, Etwashausen. **GPS**: n49,74274 e10,16491.

DE

30 € 5/24h € 1/80liter Ch € 0,50/kWh WC. **Surface:** asphalted.
01/01-31/12
Distance: 300m on the spot.
Remarks: Between Alter Mainbrücke and Nordbrücke.

Tourist information Kitzingen:
Tourist Information, Schrannenstraße 1.

S Klingenberg 16D2

Sonja's Wohnmobilhafen, Zur Einladung. **GPS**: n49,78370 e7,17805.

55 € 6,50 € 1 Ch (30x)€ 2. **Surface:** grassy. 01/01-31/12
Distance: 500m.

S Königsberg 18A1

Am Sportgelände, Buchweg. **GPS**: n50,08472 e10,57028.

6 free Ch. **Surface:** metalled. 01/01-31/12
Distance: 300m 300m 300m.
Remarks: Parking sports park.

S Königsbrunn 18B5

Königsallee. **GPS**: n48,27243 e10,88283.
12 € 6/24h € 1/100liter Ch (12x)€ 0,50. **Surface:** metalled.

S Kronach 10D6

Hammermühle, Am Sand. **GPS**: n50,23195 e11,32735.

10 € 2/24h Ch (4x)€ 0,50/kWh. **Surface:** asphalted.
01/01-31/12
Distance: 10min on the spot 200m on the spot.

S Kronach 10D6

Lucky Stable Ranch, Mostrach 1. **GPS**: n50,21840 e11,34012.
5 € 5, 2 pers.incl WC included € 1,50 € 1,50.
Surface: grassy/metalled. 01/01-31/12
Distance: 2km on the spot on the spot.
Remarks: At manege.

S Krün 25C1

Tennsee Reisemobilhafen, Am Tennsee 1. **GPS**: n47,49083 e11,25444.

37 € 12,50-18,50 + tourist tax € 1,50/pp, Umwelttaxe € 0,60/pp Ch € 0,70/kWh WC € 3 € 3/h. **Location:** Rural, comfortable, luxurious, quiet. **Surface:** grassy/gravel.
01/01-31/12 07/11-15/12.
Distance: 2,5km 800m 3km on the spot on the spot 100m on the spot on the spot 5km 300m.

S Kulmbach 10D6

Wohnmobilstellplatz Kulmbach, Am Schwedensteg. **GPS**: n50,11063 e11,45698.

25 € 3 € 1/100liter Ch (25x)€ 1/2kWh. **Surface:** gravel.
01/01-31/12 water disconnected in winter.
Distance: on the spot.

Kümmersbruck 18C2

Wohnmobilstellplatz Kümmersbruck, Am Butzenweg. **GPS**: n49,41978 e11,89651.

8 free. **Surface:** metalled. 01/01-31/12
Distance: 1km 1km.
Remarks: At sports centre.

S Lalling 19A3

Wohnmobilstellplatz Weber, Euschertsfurth 34. **GPS**: n48,83222 e13,14444.

DE

8 €8 Ch included (10x)€ 0,30/kWh € 1,50. **Location:** Rural, comfortable, quiet. **Surface:** grassy/metalled. 01/04-30/11
Distance: 1,5km 100m.
Remarks: Incl. swimming pool.

S Lalling 19A3
Lalling-Freizeitgelände, Waldstrasse. **GPS**: n48,84139 e13,13778.

2 free € 1/80liter Ch € 3/day. **Location:** Rural, simple, quiet.
Surface: metalled/sand. 01/01-31/12
Distance: 2km.
Remarks: At tennis-courts.

S Lalling 19A3
Familie Stelzer, Euschertsfurth 141. **GPS**: n48,83222 e13,13917.

4 €4 Service €1 . **Location:** Rural, simple, quiet.
Surface: asphalted/grassy.
Distance: 1km 1km.

S Lalling 19A3
Lallinger Hof, Hauptstrasse 23. **GPS**: n48,84560 e13,13851.

4-5 guests free against payment. **Location:** Rural, simple, quiet.
01/04-31/10
Distance: 250m 250m.
Remarks: Check in at restaurant.

S Lalling 19A3
Sieglinde, Obstgarten 13, Hunding. **GPS**: n48,84502 e13,14939.

3 €5 Ch included (2x)€ 2/day WC . **Location:** Rural, simple, quiet. **Surface:** grassy. 01/04-31/12
Distance: 700m.

Lalling 19A3
Gasthof zur Post, Pfarrweg. **GPS**: n48,84405 e13,14064.

15 free. **Location:** Rural, simple, quiet. **Surface:** metalled.
Distance: 200m 200m.

S Lalling 19A3
Erikas Wohlfühlplatz, Kleinfeld 6, Hunding. **GPS**: n48,84333 e13,17944.

10 €5 + €0,50/pp (10x)€ 1/day WC € 3. **Location:** Rural, simple, quiet. **Surface:** grassy/sand. 01/04-31/10
Distance: on the spot on the spot 3km 200m on the spot on the spot.
Remarks: Check in at Kleinfeld 6.

Lalling 19A3
Feng Shui Kurpark, Euschertsfurther Straße. **GPS**: n48,84137 e13,13952.

€ 1. **Surface:** gravel. 01/01-31/12
Remarks: Not indicated.

Tourist information Lalling:
Verhehrsamt Lallinger Winkel, Hauptstrasse 28, www.lalling.de.Holiday and fruit region Lallinger Winkel.
Töpferwerkstatt Pflugk, Pfarrweg 2, Lallinger Winkel.Pottery. Mo-Sa.
Fahrzeug- und kunstmuseum, Lalinger Winkel.Approx. 100 cars and 100 motorbikes. 01/03-31/10, 15/12-15/01 Fri-Su 13-17h.

DE

Landau/Isar 19A4

Am Festplatz, Harburger Straße 20/B20. **GPS**: n48,67712 e12,68323.

± 20 free € 1/100liter Ch (6x)€ 0,50/kWh. **Surface:** grassy/gravel.
01/01-31/12
Distance: 1,5km 2,3km McDonalds 200m bakery 200m.

Landsberg am Lech 18B6

Waitzinger Wiese, Gottesackerangerweg. **GPS**: n48,05534 e10,87371.

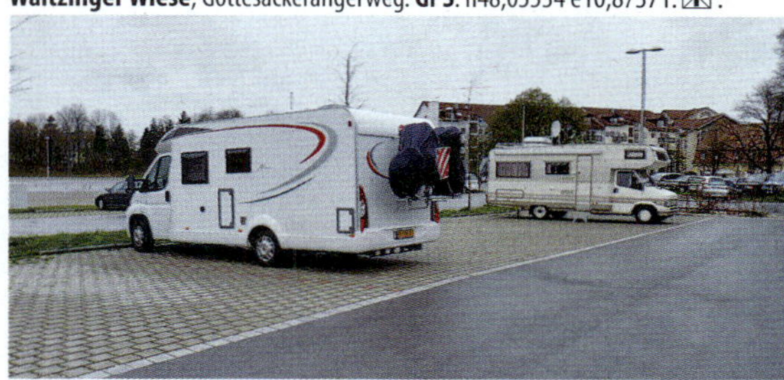

8 € 1/24h € 1/100liter Ch (8x)€ 0,50/6h WC € 0,50. **Location:** Urban, simple. **Surface:** metalled. 01/01-31/12
Distance: 400m 300m.

Lechbruck am See 25B1

Wohnmobilpark via Claudia, Via Claudia 6. **GPS**: n47,71556 e10,82139.

52 € 12,50-13,30 2 pers.incl, dog € 3-3,50 Ch WC € 1,50 € 2,50 . **Location:** Rural, comfortable, luxurious.
Surface: gravel. 01/01-31/12
Distance: 5km on the spot on the spot on the spot on the spot on the spot 10km on the spot.

Lenggries 25C1

Dürrachstrasse, Fall. **GPS**: n47,57039 e11,53380.

25 € 0,50/h, € 4/24h € 2 WC. **Location:** Isolated, quiet. **Surface:** metalled. 01/01-31/12
Distance: 250m 250m 150m 8km on the spot on the spot.
Remarks: Max. 7 days.

Lindau 24D1

Blauwiese, P1. GPS: n47,55869 e9,70130.

34 € 0,70/h € 0,50 € 0,50 Ch WC. **Surface:** metalled.
01/01-31/12
Distance: on the spot 1km 1km 500m 500m on the spot.

Lindau 24D1

Campingplatz Lindau am See, Frauenhoferstrasse, Lindau-Zech. **GPS**: n47,53764 e9,73148.

15 € 10/24h Ch WC included,on camp site. 15/03-31/10

Tourist information Lindau:

Tourist Information, Ludwigstrasse 68, www.lindau-tourismus.de.
Lindau Insel.Promenade along the lake with Mangturm, 700 years old lighthouse.
St Maria Kirche.Former monastery-church.
Haus zum Cavazzen, Marktplatz.Mechanical musical instruments, from musical boxes to jukeboxes. Tue-Su 10-12h, 14-17h.
Lindauer Hafen Konzerte, Promenade. summer Tue-Su.

Lohr/Main 17D1

Lohrer Mainlände, Osttangente. **GPS**: n49,99429 e9,58053.
20 € 5 € 1/100liter Ch € 1/4h. **Surface:** metalled.
01/04-31/10
Distance: 300m.
Remarks: Along Main river, max. 3 days.

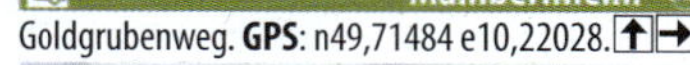

Mainbernheim 18A2

Goldgrubenweg. **GPS**: n49,71484 e10,22028.

10 free. **Surface:** metalled. 01/01-31/12
Distance: on the spot.

Mainstockheim 18A1

Wohnmobilhafen Mainstockheim, Albertshöfer strasse an de Fähre. **GPS**: n49,77173 e10,15595.

DE

30 €5 Ch . **Surface:** gravel. 01/01-31/12
Distance: on the spot on the spot 100m 100m.

S Manching 18C4
Am Braunweiher. GPS: n48,71078 e11,49602.

50 free € 1/80liter Ch. **Surface:** grasstiles/metalled.
01/01-31/12
Distance: 1,5km 1,3km Edeka 1km.

S Markt Wald 18A5
Wohnmobilpark Markt Wald, Bürgle 1a. **GPS:** n48,14602 e10,57517.

20 €7 € 1/100liter Ch € 0,50/kWh WC €2. **Location:** Rural, comfortable, quiet. **Surface:** grassy/gravel.
01/01-31/12
Distance: 1km on the spot on the spot on the spot 1km on the spot on the spot.
Remarks: At small lake, use sanitary facilities at campsite, bread-service.

Marktbreit 18A2
Am Kranen, Staatstraße. **GPS:** n49,66878 e10,14241.

3 free. **Surface:** metalled. 01/01-31/12
Distance: on the spot on the spot.
Remarks: Max. 1 day.

S Marktleuthen 11A6
Am Angerparkplatz. **GPS:** n50,12965 e11,99479.

10 free Ch free (10x)included € 0,50. **Surface:** metalled.
01/01-31/12
Distance: 250m 150m 200m.
Remarks: Bread-service.

S Marktredwitz 18D1
Wohnmobilstellplatz am Auenpark, Dörflaser Platz, Fabrikstraße. **GPS:** n49,99710 e12,08640.

20 free € 0,50 € 0,50 Ch (6x)€ 0,50/kWh. **Surface:** asphalted/gravel. 01/01-31/12
Distance: 300m 50m 150m.
Remarks: At park.

Marktredwitz 18D1
Angerplatz, Egerland-Kulturhaus, Fikentscherstrasse. **GPS:** n50,00379 e12,09506.

6 free. **Surface:** asphalted. 01/01-31/12
Distance: 1km 500m.

S Massing 19A5
Am Freilichtmuseum, Spirknerstraße. **GPS:** n48,39528 e12,60056.
10 free On demand. **Surface:** asphalted.
Distance: Museumstüberl.
Remarks: Parking open air museum, busy parking during the day.

Mehlmeisel 18C1
Parkplatz „Am Park". **GPS:** n49,97615 e11,85471.

free. **Surface:** metalled. 01/01-31/12
Distance: 250m 100m.

DE

Remarks: Max. 3 nights.

S Mellrichstadt 10B6

Malbachweg. **GPS:** n50,43139 e10,30972.

7 free € 1/80liter Ch € 0,50/kWh. **Surface:** asphalted.
01/01-31/12
Distance: 500m 750m 750m.

S Miltenberg 17C2

Jahnstrasse/Luitpoldstrasse. **GPS:** n49,70464 e9,25860.

20 free Ch WC.
Distance: 200m 200m.

Miltenberg 17C2

Am Yachthafen, Steingasserstrasse. **GPS:** n49,70446 e9,25435.

20 free. 01/01-31/12
Distance: 800m on the spot.
Remarks: Along the river Meno.

S Mistelgau 18B1

Therme Obernsees, An der Therme 1, Obernsees. **GPS:** n49,91630 e11,37831.

20 € 8 € 1/50liter Ch € 1/12h. **Surface:** grasstiles/metalled.
01/01-31/12
Distance: 1km Therme-Bistro.
Remarks: Discount on access terme.

S Mittenwald 25C1

Wohnmobil-Stellplatz Karwendel, Albert-Schott-Straße. **GPS:** n47,43792 e11,26411.

30 € 7/24h + € 4/pp tourist tax € 1/80liter Ch (30x)€ 0,80/kWh.
Location: Simple, noisy. **Surface:** asphalted/gravel. 01/01-31/12
Distance: 250m on the spot.
Remarks: Along railwayline.

Mitterteich 18D1

Am Freibad, Am Bad 1. **GPS:** n49,95060 e12,22468.

2 free. **Surface:** gravel. 01/01-31/12
Distance: 1km 1,2km.

S Mitterteich 18D1

Freizeithugl Großbüchlberg, Großbüchlberg 32. **GPS:** n49,97286 e12,22496.

15 € 12, 2 pers.incl Ch WC against payment.
01/01-31/12
Distance: 200m.
Remarks: Bread-service.

S Monheim 18B4

An der Stadthalle, Schulstraße. **GPS:** n48,84503 e10,85329.

7 free € 1 Ch € 1/10h. **Location:** Simple, central.
Surface: grasstiles. 01/01-31/12
Distance: 400m 500m 500m.

S Moosbach 18D2

Am Badeweiher Tröbes, Friedhofgasse. **GPS:** n49,59076 e12,41193.

6 € 5 Ch . **Surface:** gravel. 01/01-31/12
Distance: 250m 250m 250m.
Remarks: Check in at Gästeinformation.

S Mörnsheim 18B4

Wohnmobilstellplatz Hammermühle, Altendorf. **GPS:** n48,87455 e11,02948.

21 € 10, dog € 1 Chincluded € 0,60/kWh € 2. **Location:** Rural.
Surface: unpaved. 01/04-31/10
Distance: Altendorf 2km Imbiss, Biergarten on the spot on the spot.
Remarks: Nature reserve Altmühltal, bread service.

S München 18C5

Allianz-Arena Wohnmobilstellplätze, Werner-Heisenberg-Allee 25, Munich (München). **GPS:** n48,22089 e11,62505.

110 € 15 € 0,20/20liter (10x)€ 1/kWh. **Surface:** asphalted.
Distance: on the spot on the spot.

S München 18C5

Messe Riem, De-Gasperi-Bogen, MÜnchen-Riem, Munich (München). **GPS:** n48,13342 e11,70746.
1000 € 35/incl. 2 pers, € 15/pers Ch WC included. **Surface:** metalled. Oktoberfest
Distance: metro 300m.

S München 18C5

Wohnmobilstellplatz Oktoberfest, Siegenburger Straße 58, Laim, Munich (München). **GPS:** n48,12788 e11,52190.
250 € 18 + € 3/pp Ch WC included.
Surface: metalled.
Oktoberfest
Distance: 100m 500m.

Tourist information Munich (München):
Fremdenverkehrsamt München, Sendlinger Str. 1; Hauptbahnhof, Bahnhofstrasse 2, www.muenchen.de.
The capital of Bavaria. There are many beer gardens, old city with centre worth visiting.
München Welcome Card.Card gives for free entrance on among other things public transport and 50% discounts on curiosities.
€ 11/day 2 pers.
Agustinerbräu, Neuhauserstrasse 16.Brewery from 1644.
Schloß Nymphenburg.Former summer residence of the Witelbacher monarchs.
Tue-Su 9-12.30h, 13.30-17h.
Neumarkt.Ruins of citadel dominating the city.
Oktoberfest.Beer festival, special motorhome parking.

S Münnerstadt 10B6

Lache, P1, Seminarstrasse. **GPS:** n50,24957 e10,19086.

5 free € 1/90liter Ch € 0,50 WC . **Surface:** metalled.
01/01-31/12
Distance: 350m.

S Murnau am Staffelsee 25C1

Am Bahnhof Murnau, Am Bahnhof. **GPS:** n47,68005 e11,19447.

6 € 1/day € 1/100liter Ch € 1/2kWh. **Location:** Rural, comfortable, central, quiet. **Surface:** grasstiles/metalled.
01/01-31/12
Distance: 500m 10km 400m 300m on the spot.
Remarks: Max. 72h.

S Naila 11A6

Bahnhofstrasse. **GPS:** n50,33071 e11,71127.

2 free € 1 € 1 Ch€ 1. **Surface:** metalled. 01/01-31/12
Distance: 100m 300m.
Remarks: Parking left side of the station.

S Nesselwang 25A1

An der Riese, Altspitzbahn. **GPS:** n47,61995 e10,49830.

70 € 8 € 1 Ch (62x)€ 1/1kWh . **Location:** Rural, comfortable. **Surface:** gravel/metalled. 01/01-31/12
Distance: 500m 3,8km 1km 3km 200m 500m 500m on the spot 200m 200m.
Remarks: Baker every morning, code internet at tourist office. Follow parking P1.

Tourist information Nesselwang:
Tourist Information, Lindenstrasse 16, www.nesselwang.de.

S Neualbenreuth 18D1

Reisemobilhafen Sibyllenbad, Parkplatz P2, Kurallee. **GPS**: n49,98099 e12,42406.

21 € 8 + € 1/pp tourist tax Ch (20x)€ 0,50/kWh WC .
Surface: metalled. 01/01-31/12
Distance: 1,5km.
Remarks: Bread-service.

S Neuburg/Donau 18B4

Parkplatz P1, Schlösslwiese, Zur Ringmeierbucht. **GPS**: n48,74022 e11,18434.

30 free € 1 Ch. **Location:** Urban, simple, central, quiet.
Surface: gravel/sand. 01/01-31/12
Distance: 100m 400m on the spot on the spot.
Remarks: On the Danube river.

S Neuhaus/Inn 19B4

Rast & More, Straßfeld 7. **GPS**: n48,46228 e13,40720.

20 € 12 Ch (17x)€ 2/day WC . **Location:** Rural, comfortable, quiet. **Surface:** gravel. 01/02-30/11

Distance: 700m 5,2km 8km 500m 700m 700m.

Neumarkt/Oberpfalz 18C2

Woffenbacherstrasse. **GPS**: n49,28211 e11,44722.

30 free. **Surface:** grassy. 01/01-31/12
Remarks: At sports centre.

S Neumarkt/Oberpfalz 18C2

Fritz Berger, Fritz-Berger-Str. 1. **GPS**: n49,30500 e11,48444.

free Ch free. **Surface:** grassy. 01/01-31/12
Distance: 2km 2km.

Neusäß 18B5

Titania-Therme, Birkenallee 1. **GPS**: n48,40089 e10,82508.

5 free. **Location:** Urban, simple, central, quiet. **Surface:** metalled.
01/01-31/12
Distance: 1,2km 3km 1,2km on the spot on the spot.

S Neustadt/Aisch 18A2

Am Festplatz, Bei den Sommerkeller/Riedfelder Ortstrasse. **GPS**: n49,58187 e10,60271.

8 free € 1 Ch € 1. **Surface:** gravel. 01/01-31/12
Distance: 500m 500m 500m 500m on the spot.

Neustadt/Aisch 18A2

Am Waldwad, Eilersweg. **GPS**: n49,57462 e10,62993.

DE

6 free. **Surface:** grasstiles. 01/01-31/12
Distance: 3,5km 4km 4km 1km.

S Niederwern 17D1

Jahnstrasse. **GPS**: n50,06073 e10,17526.

30 free €3 Ch WC . **Surface:** asphalted. 01/01-31/12
Distance: on the spot on the spot.
Remarks: Max. 3 nights, near sports fields.

S Nordheim am Main 18A1

Zehnthofstrasse. **GPS**: n49,85952 e10,17909.

30 voluntary contribution Ch free. **Surface:** metalled.
01/01-31/12
Distance: 200m.
Remarks: Along the river Meno.

S Nördlingen 18A4

Kaiserwiese. **GPS**: n48,85488 e10,48445.

30 free €2 €2 Ch €2/kWh WC. **Location:** Urban, simple, quiet.
Surface: asphalted. 01/01-31/12
Distance: on the spot McDonalds.
Remarks: Max. 48h.

Nürnberg 18B2

Volkspark Dutzendteich, Munchener Strasse. **GPS**: n49,42403 e11,10586.

10 free. **Surface:** asphalted. 01/01-31/12
Distance: 4km 700m.
Remarks: Max. 3 nights.

Nürnberg 18B2

Volkspark Marienburg, Kilianstrasse. **GPS**: n49,47495 e11,09606.

8 free. **Surface:** grasstiles/metalled. 01/01-31/12
Distance: centre 4km 800m 800m on the spot.
Remarks: Max. 3 nights.

Nürnberg 18B2

Wöhrder See, Rechenberganlage, Dr Gustav Heinemannstrasse. **GPS**: n49,46041 e11,11548.

2 free. **Surface:** metalled. 01/01-31/12
Distance: 3km 500m.
Remarks: Max. 3 nights.

Tourist information Nürnberg:

City walk through old city centre, daily from Tourist Information, Hauptmarkt. 14.30h.

Königstrasse 93; Hauptmarkt, www.tourismus.nuernberg.de.Large living city with a long history and many curiosities.

Nürnberg Card.Card gives for free entrance on among other things public transport and museums, discounts on purchases, boat trips, city walks etc.

Albrecht Dürerhaus.The life and work of Albrecht Bürer. Su 10-17h, 01/07-30/09 Su, Mo 10-17h.

Spielzeugmuseum, Karlstrasse 13-15.Toy museum. Tue-Su 10-17h, Wed 10-21h.

Technisch Uhrenmuseum, Allerbergerstrasse 95.Watch collection of Karl Gebhardt. 8-20h. free.

Die Burg.Palace. 01/04-30/09 9-12h, 12.45-17h, 01/10-31/03 9.30-12h, 12.45-16h. € 3.

Tiergarten.Zoo.
01/04-30/09 8-19.30h, 01/10-31/03 9-17h.

S Oberammergau 25B1

Campingpark Oberammergau, Ettalerstrasse 56B. **GPS**: n47,59028 e11,06861.

DE

30 € 8 Ch WC against payment. **Location:** Simple. **Surface:** gravel. 01/01-31/12
Distance: 1,2km 400m 100m 1,2km 1km.
Remarks: Max. 24h.

S Oberaudorf 18D6

Pechler Hof, Tatzlwurmstrasse 5. **GPS**: n47,66132 e12,16890.

5 € 9 included. **Location:** Simple, central, quiet. **Surface:** grassy. 01/01-31/12
Distance: 1km 500m 200m 100m.

S Oberaudorf 18D6

Hotel Feuriger Tatzlwurm, Tatzlwurm, B307. **GPS**: n47,67223 e12,08448.

10 guests free . **Location:** Rural, simple. **Surface:** gravel/metalled. 01/01-31/12
Distance: on the spot on the spot.

S Oberelsbach 10B6

Wohnmobilstellplatz Oberelsbach, Gangolfstrasse. **GPS**: n50,44234 e10,11412.

6 € 5 € 1/80liter Ch (6x)€ 0,50/kWh. 01/01-31/12
Distance: 500m on the spot.
Remarks: Max. 3 days.

S Obermaiselstein 25A1

Wohnmobilplatz Allgäu, Am Goldbach 3, Niederdorf. **GPS**: n47,44422 e10,24288.

30 € 10 + € 1,30/pp Kurtaxe Ch (25x)€ 2/day WC € 1 .
Location: Rural, comfortable, luxurious. **Surface:** asphalted/gravel. 01/01-31/12
Distance: on the spot.

S Oberstdorf 25A1

Rubi-Camp, Rubinger Straße 34. **GPS**: n47,42340 e10,27772.

80 € 10 + € 2,60/pp Kurtaxe, dog € 3 Ch € 0,70/kWh WC . **Surface:** grassy. 01/01-31/12
Distance: 150m (skibus) on the spot on the spot.
Remarks: Bread-service.

S Oberstdorf 25A1

Wohnmobilstellplatz Oberstdorf, Enzenspergerweg 10. **GPS**: n47,40856 e10,28625.

150 € 12, tourist tax € 2,60/pp Ch € 2,50/24h WC .
Location: Rural, luxurious. **Surface:** grassy/metalled. 01/01-31/12
Distance: on the spot 250m 100m on the spot 500m 800m.

Tourist information Oberstdorf:
Tourist Information, Marktplatz 7, www.oberstdorf.de.Mountain village with many sporting possibilities in summer and winter.

S Oberthulba 10B6

Reisemobilstellplatz Thulbatal. **GPS**: n50,17419 e9,92499.

25 € 6,50, 2 pers.incl Ch € 2 WC € 0,80 € 2,30.
Surface: grasstiles. 15/03-15/11
Distance: 1km on the spot 150m.

DE

Oberviechtach 18D2

Am Freibad, Im Wiesengrund. **GPS**: n49,45296 e12,42458.

+5 free Ch (3x)free. **Surface:** asphalted. 01/01-31/12

Distance: 1km 600m.

Oettingen 18A3

Schießwasen. **GPS**: n48,95690 e10,60894.

4 free € 1/10minutes Ch (4x)€ 1/8h. **Location:** Simple, quiet. **Surface:** metalled.

01/01-31/12 last weekend Jul, 1st weekend Aug.

Distance: 10 min walking 500m.

Ostheim 10B6

Streuwiesenparkplatz, Nordheimer Straße/Alexander Straße. **GPS**: n50,45820 e10,22656.

6 € 3 € 1/80liter Ch € 0,50. **Surface:** metalled.

01/01-31/12

Distance: 300m 300m 300m.

Ottobeuren 18A6

Parking Sportwelt, Galgenberg 4. **GPS**: n47,94907 e10,29649.

10 free € 0,50/100liter Ch (6x)€ 0,50/kWh. **Location:** Urban, comfortable. **Surface:** metalled.

01/01-31/12

Distance: 1km.

Remarks: Coins available at Sportwelt (9-23h).

Parkstein 18D1

Basaltkegel von Parkstein, Basaltstrasse 16. **GPS**: n49,73179 e12,07127.

20 free. **Surface:** metalled. 01/01-31/12

Distance: 200m 50m.

Remarks: Nearbij Gasthof Bergstüberl, beautiful view.

Passau 19B4

Güterbahnhof, Regensburger strasse. **GPS**: n48,57406 e13,44495.

15 € 3/h, max. € 13/day Ch. **Location:** Urban, simple, noisy. **Surface:** metalled. 01/01-31/12

Distance: 500m 500m 500m 100m.

Remarks: Price incl. bus transport to the city centre.

Passau 19B4

Halser Straße. **GPS**: n48,57895 e13,47437.

13 € 1/h, max. € 8/day € 1/50liter Ch € 0,50/kWh. **Location:** Urban, comfortable, central. **Surface:** metalled.

01/01-31/12 high water.

Distance: centre 500m 500m 500m on the spot.

Remarks: Max. 24h.

Passau 19B4

Winterhafen, Regensburgerstrasse/Racklau. **GPS**: n48,57412 e13,42690.

60 free. **Surface:** gravel. 01/01-31/12 high water.

Distance: 2km On the Danube river on the spot 500m 500m 300m.

Pechbrunn 18D1

Ferien- und Reiterhof Timber Canyon, Silberrangen 1. **GPS**: n49,98393 e12,14844.

8 € 8/pp Ch WC included. 01/01-31/12

Distance: 2,5km.

Peiting 18B6

Ammergauer Strasse 22/A. **GPS**: n47,79317 e10,92227.
3 free. 01/01-31/12
Distance: 500m.
Remarks: Max. 48h, parking swimming pool.

S Petting 19A6

Stellplatz Schneiderhof, Seestrasse 11a. **GPS**: n47,91375 e12,81120.

4 € 14 incl. 2 pers., tourist tax incl Ch € 0,50/kWh WC included.
Surface: grassy.
Distance: 300m 1km 300m 300m 500m.

S Petting 19A6

Wolferstätte, Stubern 1. **GPS**: n47,88988 e12,78455.

3 € 12, 2 pers.incl € 2/100liter Ch WC . **Surface:** grassy.
01/05-30/10
Distance: 4km 5km 2km.
Remarks: Farm.

S Pfronten 25B1

Wohnmobilstellplatz Wohlfahrt, Am Wiesele 7, Weißbach. **GPS**: n47,59829 e10,55240.

45 € 10, 2 pers.incl € 0,50 Ch (48x) WC included € 0,50 € 3.
Surface: gravel. 01/01-31/12
Distance: Skibus 5km on the spot.

S Plattling 19A4

Freizeit- und Sportzentrum Plattling, Georg-Ecklstrasse. **GPS**: n48,77226 e12,87331.

20 free € 1/80liter Ch (4x)€ 0,50/kWh. **Location:** Rural, simple.
Surface: metalled. 01/01-31/12
Distance: 500m 500m.

Plech 18C2

Freizeitpark Fränkisches Wunderland, Zum Herrlesgrund 13. **GPS**: n49,65929 e11,46552.

10 free. **Surface:** gravel.
Distance: 1km 1km.

Tourist information Plech:
Freizeitpark Fränkisches Wunderland, Zum Herrlesgrund 13.Amusement park.
01/05-30/09. € 12,50.

S Pleystein 18D1

Reisemobilplatz Pleystein, Vohenstraußer Straße/Galgenbergweg. **GPS**: n49,64429 e12,40548.

10 free WC free. **Surface:** gravel. 01/01-31/12
Distance: 350m.

Poppenricht 18C2

Wohnmobilstellplatz an der Vils, Vilsstrasse. **GPS**: n49,48184 e11,83119.

20 free. **Surface:** gravel. 01/01-31/12
Distance: 1km on the spot 2km 1km.
Remarks: At sports centre, along the historic "Goldenen Straße" from Nürnberg to Prague.

S Pottenstein 18C1

Wohnmobilpark Pottenstein, Am langen Berg. **GPS**: n49,76294 e11,40826.

DE

25 € 7 € 1/100liter (6x)€ 1/kWh.
Surface: gravel.
01/01-31/12 Service: winter.
Distance: 1km Aldi 200m.

Tourist information Pottenstein:

Verkehrsbüro Pottenstein, Forchheimer strasse 1, www.pottenstein.de.City centre with half-timbered houses.

Teufelshöhle.Caves, constant temperature 9ºC and atmospheric humidity 98%. 01/04-31/10 9-17h.

Burg Pottenstein.1000 Jaar oude burcht. Tue-Su 10-17h.

Sommerrodelbahn.Toboggan slide 1km. 10-17h.

S Prichsenstadt 18A1

Wohnmobilstellplatz Schützengesellschaft 1752, Wiesentheider Straße 3. **GPS**: n49,81649 e10,34981.

5 € 5 € 1 € 2,50. **Surface:** gravel. 01/01-31/12
Distance: 300m on the spot.

S Prien am Chiemsee 18D6

Wohnmobilstellplatz Strandbad Schraml, Harrasser Strasse 39. **GPS**: n47,85400 e12,36679.

30 € 9/night, € 2,50/day Ch€ 3 WC. **Location:** Rural, simple, isolated. **Surface:** grassy/sand. 01/04-15/10
Distance: 1,5km 6km on the spot 500m on the spot.
Remarks: Steep ramp.

Tourist information Prien am Chiemsee:

Tourist Information, www.tourismus.prien.de.De Chiemsee is one of the biggest lakes of the Bavaria region, tourist area.

S Rain/Lech 18B4

Wohnmobilstellplatz Rain, Fasanenweg. **GPS**: n48,69195 e10,90699.

8 free € 1 Ch € 1/6h. **Surface:** metalled. 01/01-31/12
Distance: 1km on the spot on the spot.

S Ramsthal 17D1

Festplatz am Feuerwehrhaus, Hauptstrasse, K6-4. **GPS**: n50,13750 e10,06111.

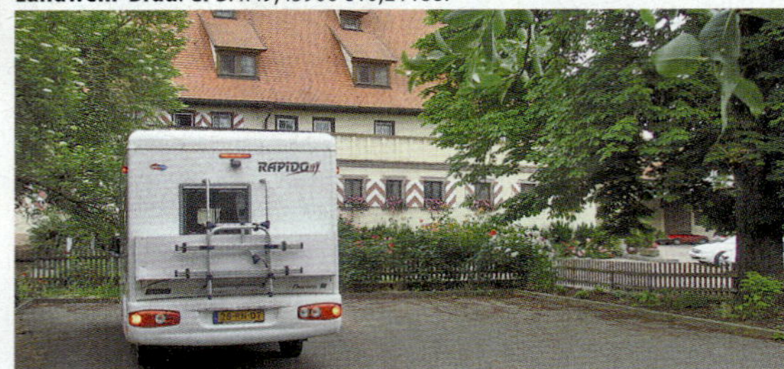

6 free € 1/100liter Ch WC € 1.
Surface: metalled.
01/01-31/12
Distance: on the spot Gasthof Wahler, Gaststätte zum Beck on the spot.

Reichelshofen 18A2

Landwehr-Bräu. **GPS**: n49,43906 e10,21188.

5 free. **Surface:** asphalted.
Remarks: Brewery.

S Reit im Winkl 19A6

Wohnmobilpark Reit im Winkl, Am Waldbahnhof 7, Groissenbach. **GPS**: n47,67013 e12,48358.

250 € 8-12 € 0,20/10liter Ch € 0,75/kWh WC . **Location:** Rural, quiet. **Surface:** grassy/metalled. 01/01-31/12
Distance: 1km 200m on the spot on the spot.
Remarks: Shuttle bus to ski-piste, use sanitary € 4,50-6/pppn.

S Reit im Winkl 19A6

Wohnmobilpark Seegatterl, Seegatterl 7. **GPS**: n47,65898 e12,54213.

DE

100 € 8-10, tourist tax excl € 0,20/10liter Ch € 0,75/kWh WC.
Location: Rural, quiet. **Surface:** grassy/gravel.
17/12-10/04, 01/06-15/10
Distance: 4km 1,5km 150m on the spot.

S Reit im Winkl 19A6

Gasthof Stoaner, Birnbacher Straße 34. **GPS**: n47,67900 e12,44930.
15 € 10, 2 pers.incl., winter € 12 Ch WC included. **Surface:** unpaved.
Remarks: At golf court.

S Riedenburg 18C3

Volksfestplatz, Austraße. **GPS**: n48,96446 e11,68181.

40 € 6 Ch € 1/8h. **Surface:** gravel/metalled.
01/01-31/12 last week of Aug.
Distance: 450m 300m 20m.
Remarks: At the Main-Danube Canal.

S Roßhaupten 25B1

Wohnmobilstellplatz Miller, Augsburger Strasse 23. **GPS**: n47,65889 e10,71944.

25 € 9, 4 pers.incl Ch (3x)€ 2 WC € 1. **Location:** Simple.
Surface: metalled. 01/01-31/12
Distance: 50m 1,2km 1,2km 200m 150m 150m 1km 500m.
Remarks: Next to Camping- und Freizeitmarkt, reparation work.

Röslau 11A6

Festplatz Geiersgarten, Eisnerstrasse. **GPS**: n50,08666 e11,97559.

3 free. **Surface:** grassy/gravel. 01/01-31/12
Distance: 1km 1km 1km.
Remarks: Max. 1 night.

S Rothenburg ob der Tauber 18A2

Parkplatz P2, Bensen Strasse. **GPS**: n49,37048 e10,18324.

25 € 10 € 1 Ch € 0,50/kWh WC. **Surface:** metalled.
01/01-31/12
Distance: within walking distance.

S Rothenburg ob der Tauber 18A2

Parkplatz P3, Weinsdorfer strasse. **GPS**: n49,38222 e10,18889.

30 € 10 € 1/100liter Ch WC. **Surface:** metalled.
01/01-31/12
Distance: on the spot.

Tourist information Rothenburg ob der Tauber:
Rothenburg Tourismus Service, Marktplatz, www.rothenburg.de.Small medieval town surround by ramparts.
Mittelalterliches Kriminalmuseum, Burggasse 3.History of 1000 years of jurisdiction.
01/04-31/10 9.30-18h, 01/11-28/02 14-16h, 01/12-31/12, 01/03-31/03 10-16h.
Schäfertanz.Traditional celebration.
27/03, 15/05, 04/09.

S Rothenkirchen 10D6

Waldschwimmbad. GPS: n50,37389 e11,31583.

40 € 5 € 0,50 Ch€ 1 (16x) WC included. **Surface:** metalled.
01/04-31/10
Distance: 1,5km.
Remarks: Parking swimming pool.

S Röthlein 18A1

Freizeit Reisch, Mühläckerstrasse 11. **GPS**: n49,98722 e10,22556.
1 € 0,50/50liter Ch € 0,50. **Surface:** asphalted. 01/01-31/12

Röthlein 18A1

Sportanlage TSV/Bundeskegelbahn, Friedhofstrasse. **GPS**: n49,98694 e10,21583.

DE

10 free. **Surface:** grassy.
Distance: on the spot.

S Röttingen 17D2

Wohnmobilplatz an der Tauber, Neubronner Straße. **GPS:** n49,50724 e9,96995.
20 € 5 € 1 Ch € 2/24h WC € 1,20. **Surface:** gravel. 01/04-31/10 last 2 weeks of August.
Distance: 300m 500m.
Remarks: Along the Tauber river.

S Ruhpolding 19A6

Campingplatz Ortnerhof, Ortsstraße 5. **GPS:** n47,74260 e12,66303.

16 € 9 Ch € 1,50 + € 0,60/kWh WC € 3 € 3/24h. **Location:** Rural. **Surface:** gravel. 01/01-31/12
Distance: 3km on the spot 2km on the spot.
Remarks: At golf court, max. 1 night.

S Scheidegg 24D1

Wohnmobilpark am Kurhaus, Am Hammerweiher 1. **GPS:** n47,57351 e9,84545.
20 € 6, € 1,70/pp tourist tax Ch included € 3 € 1,50.
Surface: gravel/metalled. 01/01-31/12
Distance: Minishop.
Remarks: Bread-service.

S Scheinfeld 18A2

Freibad Scheinfeld, Badstrasse 5. **GPS:** n49,67434 e10,46173.

2 € 6 Ch. **Surface:** gravel. 01/01-31/12
Remarks: At swimming pool.

S Schliersee 18D6

Am Spitzingsee, Spitzingstraße. **GPS:** n47,66648 e11,88851.

+10 summer € 12, winter € 9 (no service) Ch. **Location:** Rural, simple, isolated, quiet. **Surface:** gravel.
01/01-31/12 Service: winter.
Distance: 5,4km on the spot 500m on the spot on the spot on the spot.
Remarks: At lake, altitude 1085m.

S Schlüsselfeld 18A1

Bambergerstrasse. **GPS:** n49,75878 e10,62104.
5 free € 1/80liter. **Surface:** gravel. 01/01-31/12
Distance: on the spot.

S Schlüsselfeld 18A1

Concorde, Concorde-Straße 2–4. **GPS:** n49,76745 e10,56478.

20 free € 1/100liter Ch € 0,50/kWh. **Surface:** metalled.
01/01-31/12
Distance: 1km 1km 1km.
Remarks: At motohome manufacturer.

S Schnelldorf 18A3

BP-Truckstop Feuchtwangen, Rudolph Dieselstrasse 1. **GPS:** n49,17149 e10,24124.

20 € 6 € 1/80liter Ch (3x) WC € 2. **Surface:** metalled.
01/01-31/12
Distance: 300m on the spot on the spot.
Remarks: Reduction at restaurant € 5.

S Schöllkrippen 17C1

Naturerlebnisbad, Häfner-Ohnhaus-Straße. **GPS:** n50,08444 e9,25306.
35 € 5/24h € 1 Ch € 0,50/kWh. **Surface:** grassy.
01/01-31/12
Distance: 500m.

S Schongau 18B6

Festplatz, Lechuferstrasse. **GPS:** n47,80906 e10,89815.

DE

70 € 5 € 1/5liter Ch WC. **Location:** Urban, simple. **Surface:** asphalted.
service: 20/03-05/11 25/07-08/08.
Distance: 400m 100m 400m on the spot.
Remarks: Caution sanitary € 30, guests free.

Tourist information Schongau:
Tourist Information, Münzstrasse 1 - 3, www.schongau.de.City wall, towers and gates.

S Schonungen 18A1

Behr Reisemobile, An der Kemenate 6, Abersfeld, B303. **GPS**: n50,07352 e10,39366.

5 free Chfree. **Surface:** metalled. 01/01-31/12
Distance: 8km.
Remarks: Motorhome dealer, accessory shop.

Schrobenhausen 18C4

Am Klostergarten. GPS: n48,55835 e11,26234.

4 free. **Surface:** metalled. 01/01-31/12
Distance: 500m 500m 500m.

S Schrobenhausen 18C4

Kläranlage, Köningslachenerweg 12. **GPS**: n48,57420 e11,26930.
Ch.
Remarks: Mo-Thu 7-12h, 13-16h, Fr 7-12h.

S Schwandorf 18D2

Festplatz, Angerring, Krondorf. **GPS**: n49,33230 e12,10247.

30 free Chfree. **Surface:** asphalted/grassy.

01/01-31/12 week before/after Whitsuntide.
Distance: 500m 200m 500m.
Remarks: Along the Naab river.

S Schwangau 25B1

Wohnmobilpark Schwangau, Münchenerstrasse 151. **GPS**: n47,59167 e10,77250.

24 € 12,50-17,50, dog € 2 Ch (24x)€ 2,50WC
Location: Urban, comfortable. **Surface:** grassy/gravel. 01/01-31/12
Distance: 2km on the spot on the spot on the spot on the spot on the spot 1km on the spot.

Segnitz 18A2

Mainstraße. **GPS**: n49,67012 e10,14242.

4 free. **Surface:** metalled.
Distance: on the spot on the spot.
Remarks: Max. 1 day.

S Segnitz 18A2

Gasthaus zum Goldenen Anker, Mainstraße 8. **GPS**: n49,67063 e10,14344.

17 € 7,50 Ch. **Surface:** grassy/gravel.
01/01-31/12 Restaurant: Thu.
Distance: on the spot on the spot.
Remarks: Along the river Meno.

Selb 11A4

Wundsiedler Weiher. **GPS**: n51,15581 e12,13455.

20 free. **Surface:** gravel. 01/01-31/12
Distance: 2km 200m.

DE

Remarks: Hiking trails.

Selbitz 11A6

Autohof Bayers, Stegenwaldhauser Strasse. **GPS:** n50,32469 e11,78524.

free € 1/80liter Ch. **Surface:** asphalted. 01/01-31/12
Distance: 10m.
Remarks: Parking vans.

Siegsdorf 19A6

Gasthof Hörterer der Hammerwirt, Schmiedstrasse, B306, Hammer. **GPS:** n47,80096 e12,70392.

10 guests free WC. **Location:** Rural. **Surface:** metalled.
01/01-31/12 Wed.
Distance: on the spot 100m 100m 2,5km 300m.
Remarks: Max. 3 nights.

Sonthofen 25A1

Erlebnisbad Wonnemar, Stadionweg 5. **GPS:** n47,50344 e10,27883.

12 free. **Location:** Urban, simple. **Surface:** gravel.
01/01-31/12
Distance: 2,3km on the spot on the spot on the spot.
Remarks: Max. 1 night.

Steinach/Straubing 19A3

Firma Hubert Brandl Caravantastic, Gewerbering 11. **GPS:** n48,95639 e12,62250.

3 free € 1 . **Surface:** grassy. 01/01-31/12
Distance: 1,5km 2km 1km.
Remarks: Connection electricity < 18h.

Steinberg am See 18D2

Movin'G'round, Am Steinberger See. **GPS:** n49,28247 e12,17357.

10 free, use of a meal desired Ch . **Surface:** grassy.
Whitsuntide-30/09
Distance: 500m on the spot on the spot.

Steinhausen 17D6

Parkplatz, Am Reiterhof 1. **GPS:** n48,02746 e9,69476.

5 free. **Surface:** gravel. 01/01-31/12
Distance: 180m.

Suben 19B4

Raststätte Hotel Servus Europa Suben, Etzelshofen 125. **GPS:** n48,40078 e13,42593.
+10 € 10 Ch included. **Surface:** asphalted. 01/01-31/12
Distance: 50m 50m.

Sulzbach-Rosenberg 18C2

Großparkplatz, Bayreuther Straße. **GPS:** n49,50583 e11,74500.

4 free € 1/80liter Ch (4x)€ 0,50/kWh. **Surface:** metalled.
01/01-31/12
Distance: 300m 500m 500m.

Sulzemoos 18C5

Der Freistaat Caravaning, Ohmstrasse. **GPS:** n48,28267 e11,26084.

40 free € 1/80liter Ch (20x)€ 1/kWh WC. **Surface:** gravel.
01/01-31/12
Distance: 800m 800m McDonalds 800m 800m 600m.

DE

Tauberrettersheim 17D2

GPS: n49,49609 e9,93495.

6 free. **Surface:** grassy. 01/01-31/12
Distance: on the spot on the spot.
Remarks: Parking at the Tauber.

S Thierstein 11A6

Kaiserstein, Hirtweg. **GPS**: n50,10610 e12,10490.

10 € 4 Ch included voluntary contribution.
Surface: metalled. 01/01-31/12 01/10-31/03 water disconnected.
Distance: 500m 500m 500m.
Remarks: Max. 2 nights, beautiful view.

Tourist information Thierstein:
www.thierstein.de.Town in the Fichtel mountains, with ruins of a former fortress.

S Thüngersheim 17D1

Parkplatz Main-Aue, Am Schwimbad. **GPS**: n49,88084 e9,83717.
10 free . **Surface:** grassy. 01/04-31/10
Distance: 500m.
Remarks: Along the river Meno.

S Traunstein 19A6

Gasthaus Jobst, Balthasar Permoserstrasse 64, Rettenbach. **GPS**: n47,91188 e12,64899.

10 € 3, guests free € 2 Ch € 2,50. **Surface:** metalled. 01/01-31/12 Wed.

S Traunstein 19A6

Firma Grüaugl, Schmidhamerstrasse 31. **GPS**: n47,88227 e12,59941.

12 € 5 € 2 € 2 Ch € 0,50/kWh. **Location:** Isolated.
Surface: metalled. 01/01-31/12
Distance: on the spot.
Remarks: Camping equipment store.

S Treuchtlingen 18B3

Reisemobilstellplatz am Kurpark, Kästleinmühlenstrasse 20. **GPS**: n48,96028 e10,91778.

56 € 9,50 € 1/80liter Ch € 1/8h WC included. **Location:** Urban, comfortable, quiet. **Surface:** grasstiles. 01/01-31/12
Distance: 800m on the spot.
Remarks: Bread-service.

S Übersee/Chiemsee 19A6

Bauernhof Steiner, Almfischer 11, Stegen. **GPS**: n47,80963 e12,49136.

25 € 11, 2 pers.incl Ch € 0,40/kWh WC € 1,50. **Surface:** gravel. 01/01-31/12
Distance: Übersee 2km 4,6km Chiemsee 6km 1km.

S Übersee/Chiemsee 19A6

Wohmobilstellplatz Dusenhof, Stegen 4. **GPS**: n47,81237 e12,48843.

28 € 11, 2 pers.incl Ch € 0,50/kWh € 1. **Surface:** grassy/gravel. 01/01-31/12
Distance: Übersee 1km 4km Chiemsee 5km.
Remarks: Bread-service.

Viechtach 19A3

P1, Stadtmitte, Bierfeldstraße. **GPS**: n49,07876 e12,88235.

DE

6 free. **Surface:** metalled. 01/01-31/12
Distance: 400m 150m 50m.
Remarks: In front of supermarket Edeka, max. 3 nights.

Viechtach 19A3

P2, Stadthalle, Friedhofstrasse. **GPS:** n49,07722 e12,88528.

3 free. **Surface:** metalled. 01/01-31/12
Remarks: Max. 3 nights.

Viechtach 19A3

P5, TÜV, Karl-Gareis-Straße. **GPS:** n49,08222 e12,88306.

free. **Surface:** asphalted. 01/01-31/12
Distance: 500m 500m.
Remarks: Small pitches, max. 3 nights.

S **Viechtach** 19A3

Fam. Reisinger, Eging 1. **GPS:** n49,05417 e12,91333.

3 free. **Surface:** grassy. 01/01-31/12
Distance: Viechtach 4,5km.

S **Viechtach** 19A3

Johann Ebner, Lohmühlweg 2, Pirka. **GPS:** n49,10694 e12,87583.

3 € 8,50, electricity incl. **Surface:** grassy. 01/04-01/10
Distance: 8km.

S **Viechtach** 19A3

Landhotel Miethaner, Höllenstein 13. **GPS:** n49,12917 e12,87667.

4 free € 1/12h. **Surface:** asphalted. 01/01-31/12
Distance: 7km 1km on the spot on the spot 10km 2km.

Viechtach 19A3

Berghütte 'Zum Pröller', Hinterviechtach 3, Kollnburg. **GPS:** n49,02939 e12,83892.

3 free. **Surface:** gravel. 01/01-31/12
Distance: Viechtach 7km 20m.
Remarks: Parking at skipistes.

S **Viechtach** 19A3

Am Regenufer 1. **GPS:** n49,08303 e12,88824.
€1 €1 Ch. 01/01-31/12

Tourist information Viechtach:

Tourist Information, Spitalgasse 5, www.viechtach.de.Many hiking routes.
Agayrischen Gewölbe, Spitalgasse 5.Oldest building of the city. Discover the mysterious treasures of the past, the mysteries of the Pharaoh and the Tarot game. 01/04-31/10 Tue-Su 10-16h.
Kristallmuseum, Linprunstrasse 4.600 crystals, glass and gems.
9-18h, Sa-Su 10-16h.
Stadtplatz.Week market.
Wed 7-17h.

S **Vilshofen** 19B4

Yachthafen Vilshofen, Am Bootshafen. **GPS:** n48,63870 e13,18785.

DE

10 € 12 Ch (10x)€ 3/day WC € 1. **Location:** Comfortable, quiet. **Surface:** gravel. 01/04-30/11
Distance: 500m On the Danube river.

Vilshofen 19B4

Schiffanleger, Donaukade. **GPS**: n48,63833 e13,18000.

12 free. **Location:** Simple, noisy. **Surface:** asphalted. 01/01-31/12
Distance: 500m On the Danube river on the spot 500m 500m.
Remarks: Max. 1 night.

S **Vohenstrauss** 18D2

Stadthalle, Neuwirtshauser 11. **GPS**: n49,61872 e12,34523.

20 free WC. **Surface:** gravel. 01/01-31/12
Distance: 100m 800m 50m 100m.

Volkach 18A1

Mainschleife, Am Main. **GPS**: n49,86389 e10,22139.

40 € 5,50. **Surface:** gravel. 01/01-31/12
Distance: 500m on the spot on the spot 500m 500m.

S **Wackersberg** 18C6

Camping Demmelhof, Stallau 148. **GPS**: n47,75056 e11,49992.

12 € 15, 2 pers.incl Ch € 0,60/kWh WC € 0,50 € 3.
Surface: grassy. 01/01-31/12
Distance: 5km 500m 600m.

S **Wald** 25B1

Walder Badeweiher, Am Sportplatz. **GPS**: n47,72294 e10,56348.

10 € 5 Ch. **Location:** Rural, quiet. **Surface:** gravel. 01/01-31/12
Distance: 500m on the spot 250m on the spot on the spot.

S **Waldkirchen** 19B4

Karoli-Badepark, VDK Heimstrasse 1. **GPS**: n48,72222 e13,60278.

16 free € 1/50liter Ch (10x)€ 0,50/kWh WC. **Location:** Rural, simple, quiet. **Surface:** gravel. 01/01-31/12
Distance: 1km 25m 2km on the spot on the spot.
Remarks: Parking skating rink-swimming pool, use sanitary only during opening hours swimming pool, against payment.

S **Waldsassen** 18D1

P2 Schwanenwiese, Schwanengasse. **GPS**: n50,00526 e12,30739.

2x2 free € 2/10h. **Surface:** metalled. 01/01-31/12
Distance: 500m 500m 500m.
Remarks: Max. 3 days.

Waldsassen 18D1

Joseph-Wiesnetstrasse. **GPS**: n50,00250 e12,30361.

DE

2 free. **Surface:** metalled. 01/01-31/12
Distance: 100m 100m 100m.
Remarks: Max. 3 days.

S Wassertrüdingen 18A3

Parkplatz Entengraben. GPS: n49,03926 e10,59494.

12 voluntary contribution € 1/80liter Ch (6x)€ 1/8h. **Location:** Urban, simple, quiet. **Surface:** metalled. 01/01-31/12
Distance: on the spot on the spot on the spot 1km.

Weidenberg 18C1

Am Sportpark, In der Au. **GPS:** n49,93781 e11,73068.

10 free. **Surface:** gravel. 01/01-31/12
Distance: 750m Chinese restaurant 100m 1,5km.

S Weilheim in Oberbayern 18B6

Reisemobilplatz, Lohgasse. **GPS:** n47,84012 e11,13583.

8 € 4/24h € 0,50/50liter Ch € 0,50/kWh WC. **Location:** Urban, simple, central. **Surface:** asphalted. 01/01-31/12
Distance: Old city centre 500m 100m 200m.
Remarks: Along the Ammer river.

S Weismain 18B1

Kraus-Gelände, Burgkunstadterstrasse. **GPS:** n50,08639 e11,23872.

6 free € 0,50 Ch (6x)€ 0,50. **Surface:** asphalted.
01/01-31/12
Distance: on the spot.
Remarks: Parking in centre.

S Weissenburg 18B3

Kirchweihplatz, Limesbad, Badstrasse 5. **GPS:** n49,02476 e10,97180.

free € 1/80liter Ch. **Location:** Urban. **Surface:** metalled.
01/04-31/10
Distance: Old city centre 300m La Fattoria, Frauentorstrasse 11; Mai Tai, Bismarckanlage 16; Wittelsbacher Hof, Fr.Ebertstrasse 21 on the spot.

S Wertach 25A1

Camping Grüntensee, Grüntenseestraße 41. **GPS:** n47,61003 e10,44704.

12 € 15 + tourist tax € 1/pp Ch (12x)€ 0,50/kWh. **Location:** Rural, luxurious, quiet. **Surface:** gravel. 01/01-31/12
Distance: 2,5km 600m on the spot on the spot on the spot 1,5km 1,5km on the spot on the spot on the spot on the spot.

S Wertingen 18B4

Wohnmobilpark Wertingen, Am Bahnhof 4. **GPS:** n48,55948 e10,69065.

12 € 7 € 1 Ch € 2/day. **Location:** Urban, comfortable, central, quiet. **Surface:** grassy/gravel. 01/01-31/12
Distance: 800m 300m.

S Wiesenttal 18B1

Wohnmobilstellplatz Streitberg, Bahnhofstrasse, B470. **GPS:** n49,80782 e11,21636.

DE

7 € 2 Chfree. **Surface:** gravel. 01/01-31/12
Distance: 500m 500m 500m 500m 300m.

S Wolnzach 18C4

Schwimm- & Erlebnisbad Wolnzach, Hanslmühlweg 6. **GPS**: n48,59718 e11,62792.

4 free € 1/80liter Ch (4x)€ 0,50/kWh. **Surface:** metalled. 01/01-31/12
Distance: 600m 500m 600m.

Wonneberg 19A6

Gasthof Alpenblick, Traunsteiner Straße 21, Weibhausen. **GPS**: n47,89880 e12,69123.

5 free, use of a meal desired. **Location:** Simple. **Surface:** gravel.
Distance: on the spot.

S Wunsiedel 18C1

Ludwigstraße/Rot-Kreuz-Strasse. **GPS**: n50,03638 e11,99351.

6 € 5/24h Ch included. **Surface:** gravel. 01/01-31/12 water: Nov-March.
Distance: 600m 1km.
Remarks: Pay at tourist office.

Zeil am Main 18A1

Altstadtparkplatz, Mittelweg. **GPS**: n50,00667 e10,59583.

5 free. **Surface:** metalled. 01/01-31/12

Zeil am Main 18A1

Parkplatz Tuchanger, Oskar Winkler strasse. **GPS**: n50,01083 e10,59056.

20 free. **Surface:** metalled. 01/01-31/12
Distance: 1km 1km 1km.
Remarks: Parking gymnasium.

Tourist information Zeil am Main:

Tourist Information, www.zeil-am-main.de.Beer and wine region.
Brauereigasthof Göller "Zum alten Freyung".Brewery restaurant with regional specialities and Göller-beer. Mo-Su 9.30-01h.
Altstadt Weinfest.Wine festivals. 06/08-08/08.
Wein-Wander-Weg.Hiking trail through wine region.

S Zellingen 17D1

Am Freibad, Badstraße. **GPS**: n49,89621 e9,82665.
5 free Ch € 3. **Surface:** metalled. 01/01-31/12

Zirndorf 18B2

Playmobil Funpark, Brandstätterstrasse. **GPS**: n49,43087 e10,93935.
40 € 2. **Surface:** metalled.
Distance: on the spot.

DE

SWITZERLAND

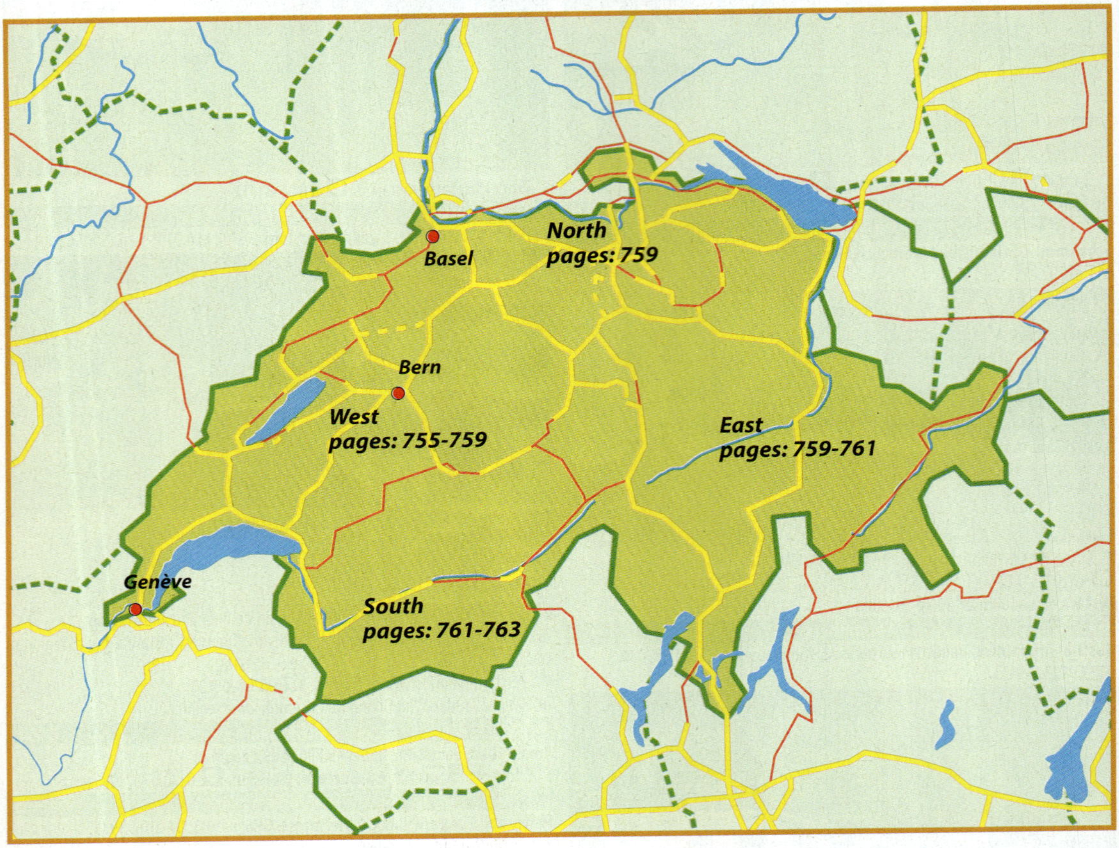

Basel

Bern

Genève

North
pages: 759

West
pages: 755-759

East
pages: 759-761

South
pages: 761-763

CH

Capital: Bern
Government: Direct democracy, Federal republic
Official Language: German, French, Italian, Romansh
Population: 7,996,000 (2013)
Area: 41,284 km^2.

General information
Dialling code: 0041.
General emergency: 112
Currency: Swiss franc (CHF), 1 CHF = € 0,81
1 CHF = £ 0,69 (October 2013)

Regulations for overnight stays
Overnight parking is allowed, max 15 hours.

Additional public holidays 2014
August 1National Day

Switzerland

Switzerland West

Aeschi 24A3
Panorama, Scheidgasse 272. **GPS**: n46,65399 e7,70070.
15/05-15/10

Avenches 23D3
Port-Plage. **GPS**: n46,90351 e7,04918.
01/04-01/10

Boltigen 23D4
Jaunpass. **GPS**: n46,59208 e7,33758.
01/01-31/12

Böningen 24A3
Seeblick, Campingstrasse 14. **GPS**: n46,68987 e7,89398.
Easter-01/10

Brienz 24A3
Aaregg. **GPS**: n46,74634 e8,04844.
01/04-01/11

Tourist information Brienz:
Alpen Region Brienz-Meiringen-Hasliberg, Bahnhofstrasse 22, Meiringen, www.alpenregion.ch.Village of wood-cutters.
during school hours 01/07-31/08.
Brienz Rothorn Bahn.Steam rack-railway.
01/06-31/10 8.45h. CHF 46.
Freilichtmuseum Ballenberg.Open air museum.
15/04-31/10 10-17h.

Bullet 23C3
Restaurant Les Cluds. **GPS**: n46,84248 e6,55991.

4 free CHF 10 Ch . **Surface:** asphalted.
Distance: on the spot.

Burgdorf 24A2
Waldegg, Waldeggweg. **GPS**: n47,05407 e7,62895.
01/04-31/10

Château-d'Oex 23D4
Le Berceau. **GPS**: n46,46673 e7,12529.
01/01-31/12

Cheyres 23C3
Route de Crevel. **GPS**: n46,81651 e6,78501.

free Chfree. **Surface:** asphalted. 01/01-31/12
Remarks: Parking at station.

Tourist information Cheyres:
Fête de vendanges.Wine festivals. beginning Oct.

Concise 23C3
Rue de Gare. **GPS**: n46,85057 e6,72218.

4 free CHF 3 Ch. **Surface:** gravel.
Remarks: At station and harbour.

Couvet 23C3
Sportzentrum Val de Travers. **GPS**: n46,92819 e6,64038.
free CHF 2 Ch.
Distance: nearby.

Tourist information Couvet:
12e Fête de l'Absinthe, Boveresse.

Cudrefin 23D3
Route de Neuchâtel. **GPS**: n46,96000 e7,02750.
Chfree.
Remarks: In front of camping Le Chablais.

Delémont 23D2
Route de Porrentruy. **GPS**: n47,36120 e7,33855.

5 free Ch free. **Surface:** grassy/metalled. 01/01-31/12
Distance: 200m.

Dürrenroth 24A2
Reisemobilstellplatz Blueberry Hill, Brunnen. **GPS**: n47,06563 e7,76553.

4 CHF 10 includedCHF 2. **Location:** Rural, comfortable, quiet.
Surface: gravel. 01/01-31/12
Distance: Dürrenroth 3,5km.
Remarks: Panoramic view.

Echallens 23C4
Chemin du Pont. **GPS**: n46,63945 e6,64096.

CH

5 free Ch free. **Surface:** asphalted. 01/01-31/12

Estavayer-le-Lac 23C3

Nouvelle-Plage. **GPS**: n46,85602 e6,84801.
. 01/04-01/10

Frutigen 24A4

Grassi. **GPS**: n46,58178 e7,64213.
. 01/01-31/12

Gampelen 23D3

Fanel, Seestraße. **GPS**: n47,00702 e7,05973.
. Easter-01/10

Grandson 23C3

Le Pécos, Rue du Pécos. **GPS**: n46,80371 e6,63575.
4 Ch. 01/04-01/10
Remarks: Next to campsite.

Grindelwald 24A4

Eigernordwand. **GPS**: n46,62135 e8,01683.
. 01/01-31/12

Tourist information Grindelwald:
Grindelwald Tourismus, www.grindelwald.com.Area of glaciers and permanent snow.
Jungfraubahn.Train journey to the highest train station of Europe.

Gryon 23D4

Place de la Barboleuse. **GPS**: n46,28222 e7,07028.

4 CHF 5 Ch. **Surface:** asphalted.
Distance: 200m.
Remarks: To be paid at office de tourisme.

Gstaad 23D4

Bellerive. **GPS**: n46,48106 e7,27328.
. 01/01-31/12

Gündlischwand 24A4

Säumertaverne, Am Chienbach 96. **GPS**: n46,63692 e7,92636.
guests free . **Location:** Rural, central.
Surface: asphalted.
Distance: 7km on the spot on the spot on the spot on the spot 6km on the spot.

Gwatt-Thun 24A3

Betllereiche. **GPS**: n46,72749 e7,62760.
. 01/04-01/10

Hinterkappelen 23D3

Kappelenbrucke, Wohlenstrasse 62. **GPS**: n46,96433 e7,38361.
. 01/01-31/12

Huttwil 24A2

Firma Flyer E-Bike, Luzernstrasse. **GPS**: n47,11527 e7,86795.

20 free Ch free. **Location:** Rural. **Surface:** gravel.
Distance: 500m.
Remarks: E-bike factory.

Interlaken 24A3

Hobby, Lehnweg 16. **GPS**: n46,68079 e7,82793.
. 01/04-01/10

Interlaken 24A3

Jungfraublick, Gsteigstraße 80. **GPS**: n46,67581 e7,86597.
. 01/05-01/10

Interlaken 24A3

Lazy-Rancho, Lehnweg 6. **GPS**: n46,68079 e7,82793.
. 01/04-01/10

Tourist information Interlaken:
Interlaken Tourismus, Höheweg 37, www.interlaken-tourism.ch.Jungfrau region, mountains and water.
Heimwehfluhbahn.Telpher carrier from 1906. 01/04-31/10.
Mistery Park.Attractions and themepark. 10-18h 25/12-01/01.

La Brévine 23C3

Les Varodes. **GPS**: n46,97195 e6,58860.

10 free Ch free. **Surface:** asphalted. 01/01-31/12
Distance: 3km on the spot.
Remarks: Parking at Lac des Tailleres.

La Chaux-de-Fonds 23C2

Bois du Couvent. **GPS**: n47,09334 e6,83593.
2 free Ch free. **Surface:** asphalted. 01/05-30-09
Remarks: In front of campsite du Bois du Couvent.

Tourist information La Chaux-de-Fonds:
Tourisme neuchâtelois - Montagnes, Espacité 1, Place Le Corbusier.Capital of the clock industry.
Musée International d'Horlogerie, Rue des Musée 29.Watch museum.
10-17h Mo, 25/12-01/01.
Musée paysan et artisanal, Rue des Crêtets 148.The farmers' life and old crafts industry.
01/04-31/10 14-17h, 01/11-28/02 Wed, Sa, Su 14-17h Mo, 01/03-31/03.

Langenthal 24A2

Lexa-Wohnmobile, Bern-Zürichstrasse 49b. **GPS**: n47,22461 e7,77944.

5 free Ch free. **Surface:** asphalted. 01/01-31/12
Distance: 2km.

Lausanne 23C4

GPS: n46,51734 e6,59777.

10 CHF 20 Ch WC.
Surface: grassy/metalled.
Distance: on the spot on the spot.
Remarks: Next to campsite the Vidy, free bus to centre.

Tourist information Lausanne:
Lausanne Tourisme, Avenue de Rhodanie 2, www.lausanne-tourisme.ch.Parking at the port, rack-railway to city centre.
Musée Olymique, Quai d'Ouchy 1.All about the Olympic games.
9-18h Mo, 01/10-30/04.

Lauterbrunnen 24A4
Jungfrau. **GPS**: n46,58834 e7,90882.
. 01/01-31/12

Lauterbrunnen 24A4
Schützenbach. **GPS**: n46,59047 e7,91194.
.
01/01-31/12

Tourist information Lauterbrunnen:
Lauterbrunnen Tourismus, Bahnhofplatz, www.wengen-muerren.ch/.Large winter sports area.
Jungfraubahn, Grindelwald.Train journey to the highest train station of Europe.
Klöppelstube, Altes Schulhaus.Making of bobbin lace.
Tue 14-17h. free.
Trümmelbachfälle, Lauterbrunnen dir Stechelberg.Underground waterfalls.
01/04-30/11 9-17h.

Le Landeron 23D3
Camp des Pêches. **GPS**: n47,05257 e7,06993.
. 01/04-15/10

Tourist information Le Landeron:
Restaurant Le Carnotzet, Rue de la Gare 22.Restaurant with regional specialities. Tue-Sa 11-14h, 17-23h Mo, Su.

Les Brenets 23C3
Champ de la Fontaine. **GPS**: n47,06588 e6,69898.

CHF 5 Ch. 01/01-31/12
Remarks: Nearby campsite Lac de Brenets.

Les-Ponts-de-Martel 23C3
Rue du Bugnon. **GPS**: n46,99644 e6,73065.

2 free Ch free. **Surface:** asphalted.
Remarks: At community centre.

Malvilliers 23C3
Hotel-Restaurant La Croisée, Route de Neuchâtel. **GPS**: n47,03200 e6,86779.
5 CHF5 Ch included. **Surface:** asphalted. 01/01-31/12

Meiringen 24B3
Alpencamping, Brüningstrasse 46. **GPS**: n46,73448 e8,17122.
8 CHF 31,90 Ch WC included. **Surface:** grassy.
Distance: 1km.

Morges 23C4
Le Petit Bois. **GPS**: n46,50446 e6,48894.
Ch against payment. 01/04-01/10
Remarks: Service at entrance campsite.

Moutier 23D2
Chemin de la Piscine. **GPS**: n47,27365 e7,37923.

5 free Ch free.
Remarks: At swimming pool.

Neuchâtel 23D3
Route des Falaises. **GPS**: n47,00145 e6,95735.

8 free Ch free.
Surface: grasstiles.
Distance: city centre 2km 300m 100m.
Remarks: Max. 24h.

Tourist information Neuchâtel:
Tourisme neuchâtelois, Hôtel des Postes.Medieval city on lake of same name.
Château de Boudry, Boudry.Wine museum.
Wed-Su 14-17h. CHF 10.
Château.Guided tour in French, German and English language.
01/04-30/09 each hour. free.
Le Creux-du-Van, Val-de-Travers.Nature reserve.
01/01-31/12.

Nyon 23B4
Piscine de Colovray, Route de la Piscine. **GPS**: n46,36989 e6,22842.

10 free Ch WC free.
Surface: asphalted.
Distance: 1km 1km 1km.

Tourist information Nyon:
Nyon Région Tourisme, www.nyon.ch.Old Roman city on the lake.
Musée du Léman, Quai Louis-Bonnard 8.Nature and culture of the lake.
01/04-31/10 10-12h, 14-18h, 01/11-31/03 14-18h Mo.
Fête de la Musique.Annual music festival. 3rd weekend Jun. free.

Oron-la-Ville 23C4
Chemin de Botollie. **GPS**: n46,57222 e6,81889.

CH

5 free. **Surface:** asphalted.

Payerne 23D3

Place de la Concorde. **GPS:** n46,81976 e6,93757.

2 free Chfree. **Surface:** asphalted. 01/01-31/12
Distance: on the spot on the spot.

Portalban 23D3

Route du Port. **GPS:** n46,92131 e6,95614.

17 CHF 20, 2 pers.incl Ch WC included. **Surface:** grasstiles.
01/01-31/12
Distance: on the spot on the spot on the spot.
Remarks: In port, nearby campsite.

Prêles 23D2

Prêles, Route de la Neuveville 61. **GPS:** n47,08404 e7,11262.
. 01/04-15/10

Rolle 23C4

Aux Vernes, Chemin des Vernes. **GPS:** n46,46152 e6,34457.
. 01/04-01/10

Romont 23D3

Rue de Château. **GPS:** n46,69535 e6,91877.

2 free Ch free. **Surface:** metalled.
Distance: on the spot on the spot on the spot.
Remarks: Near office de tourisme.

Tourist information Romont:
Office du Tourisme de Romont, Rue du Château 112, www.romont.ch.
Musée Suisse du Vitrail, Château.Glass painting art. 01/04-31/10 Tue-Su 10-13h, 14-18h, 01/11-31/03 Thu-Su 10-13h, 14-17h.
Pleureuses de Romont.Procession. Good Friday.

Saignelégier 23D2

Chemin de la Tuilerie. **GPS:** n47,25239 e7,00428.

free Ch against payment. **Surface:** metalled. 01/01-31/12
Distance: 700m.

Satigny 23B5

Bois de Bay, Route du Bois-de-Bay 19. **GPS:** n46,19856 e6,04724.
. 01/01-31/12

St.Aubin 23C3

Port de St-Aubin-Sauges. **GPS:** n46,89181 e6,77427.

10 CHF 20 Ch WC included. 01/01-31/12
Remarks: Parking port, nearby the capitainerie.

St.Blaise 23D3

Chemin des Pêcheurs. **GPS:** n47,01139 e6,98778.

12 CHF 8/24h Ch WC included. **Surface:** asphalted.
Distance: Neuchâtel 5km.

Ste.Croix 23C3

Grand-Rue, Auberson. **GPS:** n46,82019 e6,47230.

4 free Ch free. **Surface:** asphalted.
Distance: 2km on the spot.

Tourist information Ste.Croix:
Office du tourisme Sainte-Croix, Rue Neuve 6.

Vesenaz 23B5

Pointe a la Bise. **GPS**: n46,24517 e6,19331.
. 01/01-31/12

Zweisimmen 23D4

Vermeille, Eygässli 2. **GPS**: n46,56265 e7,37766.
. 01/01-31/12

Switzerland North

Bellerive 23D3

Hep, Route de Vallamand. **GPS**: n46,91813 e7,02063.

€ 7 Ch CHF 3 WC. **Surface:** grassy.

Brunnen 24B3

Hopfraeben. **GPS**: n46,99700 e8,59300.
. 01/05-01/10

Engelberg 24B3

Eienwäldli, Wasserfallstraße 108. **GPS**: n46,81009 e8,42243.

Frick 24A1

Hotel Engel, Hauptstraße 101. **GPS**: n47,50576 e8,02430.

20 free WC. **Surface:** gravel.
01/01-31/12
Distance: 300m 1,6km on the spot 50m 50m.
Remarks: Behind the hotel.

Tourist information Frick:
Tourismus Rheinfelden, Rheinfelden, www.rheinfelden.ch.
Sauriermuseum, Im Schulhaus, Schulstrasse 22. 1st, 3rd Su of the month.

Horw 24B3

Steinibachried. **GPS**: n47,01100 e8,31100.
. 01/04-01/10

Luzern 24B2

Lido, Lido Straße 19. **GPS**: n47,05097 e8,33694.
CHF 48. 15/03-15/11
Distance: on the spot.

Tourist information Luzern:
Tourist Information, Zentralstrasse 5.
Historical town centre with among other things die Kapelbrücke.
Gletchergarten, Denkmalstrasse 4.Nature monument.
01/04-31/10 9-18h, 01/11-31/03 10-17h.
Stadtbummel.Guided tour around the historic city center, 2 hours.
01/05-31/10 daily 9.45h, 01/11-30/04 Wed, Sa 9.45h.
CHF 18.

Reinach 24A1

Waldhort, Heideweg 16. **GPS**: n47,49923 e7,60296.
. 15/03-15/10

Sempach 24B2

Seeland. **GPS**: n47,12500 e8,18800.
. 01/04-01/10

Weggis 24B2

Bauernhof Gerberweid, Eichistrasse. **GPS**: n47,03616 e8,41213.

15 € 18 Ch included. **Surface:** grassy. 01/04-15/10
Distance: 2km 1km 1km 500m.

Willisau 24A2

Bisangmatt. **GPS**: n47,11937 e7,99829.

4 CHF 5 (4x)free. **Surface:** metalled. 01/01-31/12
Distance: 500m 500m 500m.
Remarks: At fire-station.

Zug 24B2

Zugersee, Chamer Fussweg 36. **GPS**: n47,17758 e8,49358.
. 01/04-01/10
Remarks: Max. ^3.17m.

Switzerland East

Andeer 24D3

Sut Baselgia. **GPS**: n46,60651 e9,42630.

Appenzell 24D2

Restaurant Eggli, Egglistrasse. **GPS**: n47,32104 e9,46565.
10 Ch guests free. **Surface:** asphalted. 01/01-31/12
Remarks: The most beautiful panorama of Appenzell.

Bivio 24D4

Wohnmobilplatz der Skilifte. **GPS**: n46,46304 e9,65597.

20 CHF 15/day Ch CHF 3,50. **Surface:** grasstiles.
01/01-31/12
Distance: nearby.
Remarks: Parking ski-lifts.

Tourist information Bivio:
Kur- und Verkehrsverein Bivio, www.bivio.ch/.Holiday village, 1769m, 260 inhabitants, winter sports destination with guaranteed snow.

Breil/Brigels 24C3

Bergbahnen BWA. **GPS**: n46,77104 e9,06770.

CH

20 CHF 5+ 2,90/pp CHF 2 Ch . **Surface:** metalled.
01/05-31/10
Distance: 600m on the spot Imbiss on the spot, restaurants 600m 600m nearby.

Tourist information Breil/Brigels:
Informationsbüro & Center Turistic Brigels-Dorf, Raiffeisenbank, www.brigels.ch.Summer: cycle and hiking routes, winter: cross-country skiing trails and 75km skiruns. Mo-Fri 9-12, 14-18, summer Mo-Fri 9-12, 14-18, Sa 14-16h.

Churwalden 24D3

Pradafenz, Girabodawag 34. **GPS**: n46,77636 e9,54178.
. 01/01-31/12

Davos 24D3

Rinerlodge Talstation, Rinerhornbahn, Davos Glaris. **GPS**: n46,74150 e9,77814.
10 CHF 29 Ch CHF 2. **Surface:** gravel.
Distance: 1km on the spot on the spot on the spot on the spot.
Remarks: Max. 24h.

Tourist information Davos:
Davos Tourismus, Promenade 67, Davos Platz, www.davos.ch.Spectacular summer and winter sports resort.
Davos Alpengarten.Botanical garden. 01/05-30/09 9-17h.
Berghaus Stafelalp, Frauenkirch.250 Year old inn where they still cook on a wood oven and shimmer paraffin lamps are lit.

Ennetbühl 24C2

CH

Stellplatz Gill, Schwägalpstrasse 1336. **GPS**: n47,24111 e9,21861.

15 CHF10 Ch (9x)CHF 0,40/kWh WC CHF 1 . **Surface:** metalled.
Distance: 400m on the spot 400m 400m.

Eschenz 24C1

Hüttenberg. GPS: n47,64480 e8,86003.
7 € 13 Ch WC included. 01/01-31/12
Remarks: In front of campsite.

Kreuzlingen 24C1

Fischerhaus, Promenadestraße 52. **GPS**: n47,64745 e9,19898.
. 01/04-01/11

Müstair 25B3

Clenga. GPS: n46,62900 e10,45400.
. 01/05-20/10

Neuhausen 24B1

Parkplatz Fischacker, Nohlstrasse. **GPS**: n47,67373 e8,60866.

50 € 7 Ch WC . **Surface:** grassy/metalled.
Distance: 200m on the spot 200m 1km.

Tourist information Neuhausen:
Der Rheinfall.Water falls.

Pontresina 25A4

Plauns. GPS: n46,46200 e9,93400.
. 01/06-15/10, 15/12-15/04

Samnaun 25A3

Wohnmobilplatz. GPS: n46,94906 e10,36705.

18 CHF 25-35/day, CHF 5,80/pp Ch WC . 01/01-31/12
Distance: on the spot.
Remarks: Possibility for reservation: www.samnaun.ch/de/forms/motorhome_form.cfm. Between Samnaun-Dorf and Samnaun Ravaisch.

Sankt Moritz 24D4

Olympiaschanze. GPS: n46,47800 e9,82600.
. 15/05-01/10

Tourist information Sankt Moritz:
Kur-& Verkehrsverein St. Moritz, Via Maistra 12, www.stmoritz.ch.Famous exclusive holiday resort.
Clean Energy Tour.Hiking trail, nature, energy, climate and weather adventure. Sign up at Kur- und Verkehrsverein St. Moritz. 15/06-01/10 Wed 13.45h duration 2,5 hours.

Savognin 24D3

Veia Sandeilas. **GPS**: n46,59660 e9,59226.
20 CHF 12 +CHF 6/pp Ch.
Remarks: Near the chair-lift, summer: parking at campsite Julia.

Splügen 24D4

Auf dem Sand. GPS: n46,54922 e9,31399.
. 01/01-31/12

Steckborn 24C1

Parkplatz P4, Schützengraben. **GPS**: n47,66684 e8,98474.

8 CHF 12/24h Ch (8x)included. **Surface:** metalled.
Distance: 400m 400m 400m 300m.

Vaduz/Liechtenstein 24D2

Rheinparkstadion, Rheindamm. **GPS**: n47,14022 e9,50945.

free Ch WC free. **Surface:** asphalted. 01/01-31/12
Distance: 1,8km.
Remarks: Parking near stadium, max. 24h.

Tourist information Vaduz/Liechtenstein:
Liechtenstein Tourismus, Städtle 37, www.vaduz.li.Monarchy on the Austrian-Swiss border.
Briefmarkenmuseum, Städtle 37.Postage stamp museum. 10-12h, 13-17h. free.
Kunstmuseum Lichtenstein, Städtle 32. Tue-Su 10-17h.
Skimuseum, Fabrikstrasse 5.100 years ski history. Mo-Fri 14-18h.
Erlebniswelt Neuguthof, Neugutweg 30.Maize labyrinth with wild-west city. 15/06-30/09 Wed 13-18h, Sa-Su 10-20h, holidays Mo-Fri 10-20h, Sa-Su 10-22h.

S Vals 24C3
Bergbahnen Vals. **GPS**: n46,60891 e9,17438.

10 CHF 10 + 2,20/pp free. **Surface:** metalled. summer
Distance: 300m on the spot 300m 300m on the spot.
Remarks: Parking funicular railway.

Zürich 24B2
Seeburcht, Seestrasse 559. **GPS**: n47,33641 e8,53960.
. 01/05-01/10

Tourist information Zürich:
Zürich Tourismus, Im Hauptbahnhof, www.zuerich.com.Historical city with large pedestrian area.
Scot & Scotch, Wohllebgasse 7, Schipfe.Wiskey-shop in the old city, 750 diferent kinds, also tastery.
Tue-Fri 12-18.30h, Sa 12-17h.
Sechseläuten.Traditional spring celebration. 3rd Mo Ap.
Zoo Zürich, Zürichbergstrasse 221.Zoo.
01/03-31/10 9-18h, 01/11-28/02 9-17h.

Switzerland South

Agno 24C5
Eurocampo, Via di Molinnazzo. **GPS**: n45,99547 e8,90063.
. 01/04-01/10

Avegno 24C5
Piccolo Paradiso. **GPS**: n46,20100 e8,74300.
. 01/03-01/11

S Bellinzona 24C5
Centro Sportivo, Viale Giuseppe Motta. **GPS**: n46,20116 e9,01729.

7 CHF 10 Chagainst payment. **Surface:** asphalted. 01/01-31/12
Distance: 1,5km 4km.
Remarks: Max. 48h.

Tourist information Bellinzona:
Bellinzona Tourismus, Viale Stazione 18, www.bellizonaturismo.ch.Turrita, city of the towers, walls and castles.
Castelgrande. 01/01-31/12 10-18h.
Castello di Montebello. 01/03-30/11 10-18h.
Castello di Sasso Corbaro. 01/03-30/11 10-18h.
Palestra di Roccia San Paolo, Palazo Civico.Climbing garden for beginners and experienced, 30.000^{2}m, 23 climbing trails.

Bouveret 23C4
Rive Bleue. **GPS**: n46,38645 e6,86041.
. 01/04-30/09
Remarks: Autoroute Leman, exit Villeneuve-Evian.

Brig 24A4
Brigerbad. **GPS**: n46,29995 e7,93617.
.

S Champéry 23C5
Route de la Fin. **GPS**: n46,17478 e6,87022.

6 CHF 18 Ch included. **Surface:** asphalted. 01/01-31/12
Distance: on the spot.
Remarks: Parking supermarket, nearby the télépherique.

Evolène 24A5
Evolène. **GPS**: n46,11075 e7,49654.
. 01/01-31/12

Gordevio 24C4
Bella Riva. **GPS**: n46,22293 e8,74313.
. 01/04-01/10

S Grimentz 24A5
Aire camping-car l'Ilôt Bosquet, Route de Moiry. **GPS**: n46,17432 e7,57271.

20 CHF 5 + CHF 2,50/pp tourist tax Ch CHF 3. **Surface:** gravel. 01/01-31/12
Distance: on the spot on the spot on the spot on the spot nearby nearby.
Remarks: Pay and coins at tourist office, free entrance swimming pool

CH

(summer), public transport.

Tourist information Grimentz:

Grimentz/St.Jean Tourisme, www.grimentz.ch.Many signposted cycle and hiking routes.

La Maison bourgeoisiale.Life of the citizens of Grimentz. guided tour Mo. free.

Grimselpas 24B4

Hotel Grimselblick, Totensee. **GPS**: n46,56115 e8,33673.
20 free . **Surface:** asphalted.
Distance: on the spot.
Remarks: Service at hotel.

La Fouly 23D5

Les Glaciers. **GPS**: n45,93351 e7,09361.
. 15/05-30/09

Les Haudères 24A5

Molignon. **GPS**: n46,09061 e7,50776.
. 01/01-31/12

Leukerbad 24A4

Winterstellplatz, Parkplatz Fischweiher. **GPS**: n46,37907 e7,63004.
CHF 8/day. 01/11-15/04

Locarno 24C5

Parco della Pace, Via Gioacchino Respini. **GPS**: n46,16011 e8,80255.

50 € 10/24h. **Surface:** gravel.
Distance: 900m 100m 100m.
Remarks: Max. 24h.

Tourist information Locarno:

Ente Turistico Lago Maggiore, Via B. Luini 3, www.maggiore.ch.City with the mildest climate of Switzerland.

Rasa.Touristic car-free miniature village, can be reached by first taking the Centrovall-track, till Verdasio, then the small telpher carrier to Rasa.

Tenero-Locarno-Tenero.Free boat service.
31/05-30/09.

Martigny 23D5

Place de la Fondation Gianadda. **GPS**: n46,09585 e7,07143.

5 free. **Surface:** asphalted.

Martigny 23D5

Les Neuvilles, Rue du Levant 68. **GPS**: n46,09787 e7,07930.
. 01/02-31/12

Tourist information Martigny:

Office de Tourisme de Martigny, Place Centrale 9, www.martignytourism.ch.Gallo-Roman city with many archeological curiosities.

Fondation Pierre Gianadda, Rue du Forum.Art and culture museum with archeological museum.
01/06-30/11 9-19h, 01/12-31/05 10-18h.

Gorges du Durnand.Hiking trail through the gorge of the river Durnand.

Meride 24C5

Parco al Sole. **GPS**: n45,88806 e8,94944.
. 01/05-01/10

Molinazzo di Montegio 24C5

Tresiana. **GPS**: n45,98990 e8,81576.
. Easter-01/11

Muzzano-Lugano 24C5

Piodella di Agnuzzo. **GPS**: n45,99463 e8,90857.
. 01/01-31/12

Raron 24A4

Santa Monica, Kantonstrasse 56. **GPS**: n46,30007 e7,82374.
. 01/01-31/12

Reckingen 24B4

Ellbogen. **GPS**: n46,45790 e8,25355.
. 01/05-01/11

Saas Fee 24A5

Parkplatz P4. **GPS**: n46,11090 e7,93208.

100 CHF 26/24h Chincluded CHF 2 WC.
01/01-31/12 service in winter.

Saillon 23D5

Relais de Sarvaz. **GPS**: n46,15951 e7,16542.

5 free CHF 5 Ch.

Tourist information Saillon:

Office du tourisme, Bains de Saillon.Small medieval town.

La fausse monnaie au grand jour.Museum of counterfeit money.
Wed-Su 14-17h.

Bains de Saillon.Thermal centre.
8-21h.

Sentier des Vitraux.Hiking trail, 45 minutes, through wine region.

Sierre 24A4

Bois de Finges. **GPS**: n46,29362 e7,55777.
. 01/05-01/10

Sierre 24A4

Auberge de la Promenade, Sous-Géronde 41. **GPS**: n46,28476 e7,53683.
10 Chagainst payment.

Tourist information Sierre:

Office du Tourisme de Sierre, Salgesch et environs, Place de la Gare 10, www.sierre-anniviers.ch.Cité du Soleil, city of the sun, wine region.

Musée Valaisan de la Vigne et du Vin, Château de Villa, Rue Sainte-Catherine 4.2 museums connected by wineroute.
01/04-30/11, Tue-Su 14-17h. CHF 5, family CHF 12.

Marche des Cépages.March of the vine, information: sierre@sierre-anniviers.ch.

Happyland New, Route Foulon, Granges.Amusement park. 01/03-31/10 11-18h.

Simplon 24A4

Col du Simplon. **GPS**: n46,24944 e8,03056.
free Chfree.

Sion 23D5

Botza, Route du Camping 1, Vétroz. **GPS**: n46,20585 e7,27855.
. 01/01-31/12

Tourist information Sion:

Restaurant Cave de Tous Vents, Rue des Châteaux 16.Restaurant in the arched cellars of the city. 17-24h.

St.Léonard 23D5

Place du Lac Souterrain. **GPS**: n46,25564 e7,42600..

5 CHF 20/night Ch WC included. **Surface:** asphalted/grassy.
Distance: 5,5km.
Remarks: To pay at Bar Domino.

Tenero 24C5

Campofelice, Via Alle Brere 7. **GPS**: n46,17353 e8,85401.
. 01/04-27/10

Tenero 24C5

Lido Mappo, Via Mappo. **GPS**: n46,17850 e8,84519.
. 15/03-01/11

Tenero 24C5

Tamaro, Via Mappo 32. **GPS**: n46,17525 e8,84779.
. 15/03-01/11

Tourist information Tenero:

Ente turistico di Tenero, Via ai Giardini, www.tenero-tourism.ch.Holiday village on Lake Maggiore.
Grotto Scalinata, Via Contra.Restaurant with regional products.
Verzascadal.Walking route of arts, information at VVV.

Trient 23D5

GPS: n46,04645 e6,99499.
CHF 4 .

Vétroz 23D5

Restaurant L'As de Pique. **GPS**: n46,20556 e7,27833.
Ch CHF 15, guests free.

Tourist information Vétroz:

Office du Tourisme, Rue Lombarde 24, Le Bourg, Conthey.
Relais du Valais Ancienne Abbay, Rte de l'Abbaye 35.Restaurant in former abbey.

AUSTRIA

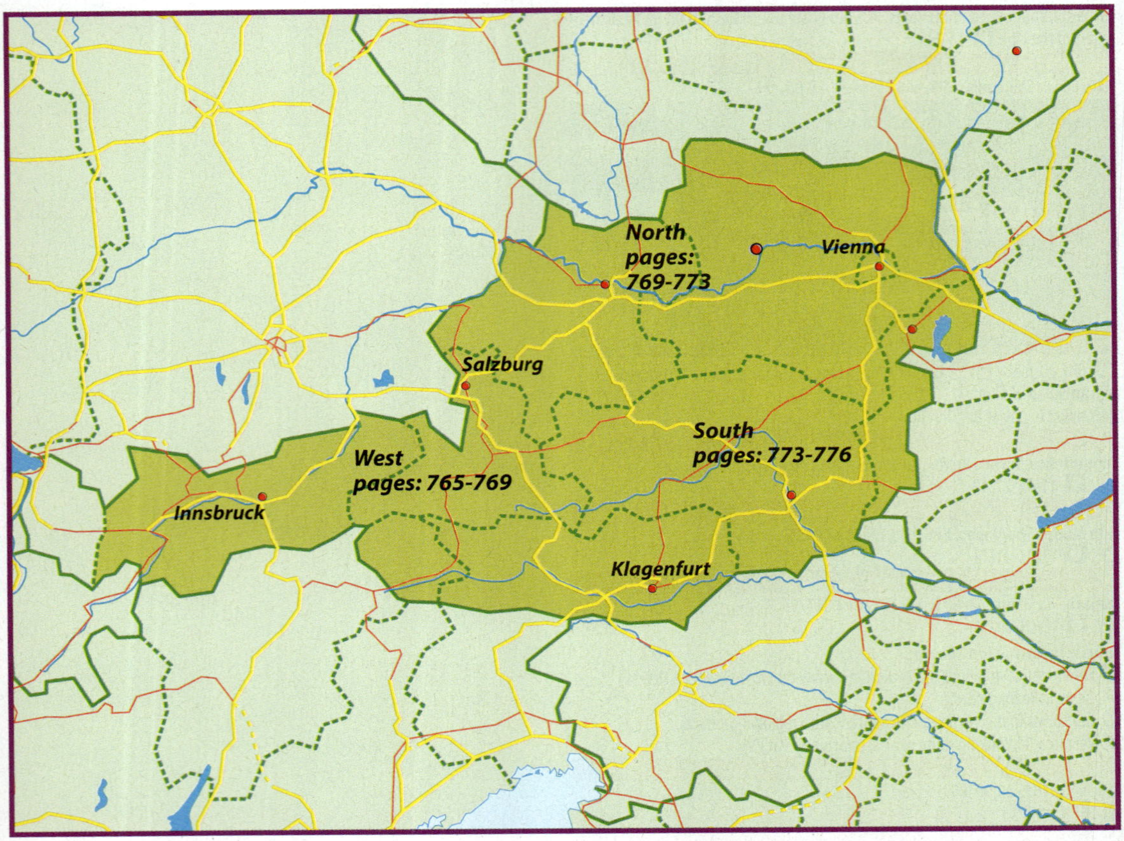

Salzburg
Vienna
Innsbruck
Klagenfurt
North pages: 769-773
West pages: 765-769
South pages: 773-776

AT

Capital: Vienna
Government: federal, parliamentarian, democratic republic
Official Language: German
Population: 8,300,000 (2012)
Area: 83,857 km^2

General information

Dialling code: 0043
General emergency: 112
Currency: Euro.

Regulations for overnight stays

In general overnight parking is allowed, except: Tyrol, Vienna, nature reserves and in areas where locally prohibited. No "camping" activities allowed and disposal wastewater must be at official places.

Additional public holidays 2014

January 6 Epiphany
May 1 Labor Day
June 19 Corpus Christi
August 15 Assumption of the Virgin Mary
October 26 National Holiday
November 1 All Saints' Day
December 8 Immaculate Conception

Austria

Austria West

Achenkirch 25C1

Camping Achensee, Achenkirch 17. **GPS**: n47,49947 e11,70655.
8 from € 13 2 pers incl Ch WC included. **Surface:** gravel.
01/01-31/12
Distance: on the spot on the spot.
Remarks: Extra pers € 7, electricity winter € 0,70/kWh, dog € 4,50.

Altenmarkt im Pongau 26B1

Bauernhof Kellerbauer, Kellerdörfl Palfen 7. **GPS**: n47,37015 e13,42923.
10 € 12 Ch . 01/01-31/12

Aschau im Zillertal 25D1

Aufenfeld, Distelberg 1. **GPS**: n47,26318 e11,90063.
€ 19-€ 32,70 Ch WC .

Biberwier 25B1

Marienbergstrasse 15. **GPS**: n47,37528 e10,88944.

15 € 10 Ch € 1 € 2. **Surface:** grassy. 01/01-31/12
Distance: on the spot 2km on the spot on the spot.
Remarks: Nearby campsite Alpencamp Marienberg.

Bichlbach 25B1

Almkopfbahn. **GPS**: n47,42367 e10,78116.

15 . 01/01-31/12
Distance: 5km on the spot on the spot on the spot.
Remarks: Parking next to valley station.

Tourist information Bichlbach:
Tourismusbüro, Kirchhof 22.

Bregenz 24D1

Parkplatz Talstation Pfänderbahn. **GPS**: n47,50538 e9,75308.
€ 9/day, overnight stay free.

Tourist information Bregenz:
Bregenz Tourismus & Stadtmarketing, Bahnhofstraße 14, www.tiscover.at/bregenz.Historical city on the Lake Constance.
Altes Rathaus, Oberstadt.Half-timbered house 1661.
Pfänderbahn.Panorama gondola to station Pfänder 1064.
9-19h 08/11-19/11.
Vorarlberger Landesmuseum, Kornmarktplatz 1.Culture and art history.
Tue-Su 9-12h, 14-17h. € 1,45.
Kloster Mehrerau, Mehrerauerstrasße 66.Abbey, 1097, with neo-Roman church.

Breitenwang 25B1

Seespitze. **GPS**: n47,47417 e10,78472.
. 01/05-15/10

Breitenwang 25B1

Sennalpe. **GPS**: n47,48639 e10,83972.
. 15/12-15/10

Bruck an der Großglocknerstraße 26A1

Woferlgut. **GPS**: n47,28361 e12,81667.
. 01/01-31/12

Tourist information Bruck an der Großglocknerstraße:
Wild- und Freizeitpark Ferleiten, Großglocknerstrasse.Zoo and amusement park. 01/05-30/11 8h-sunset.

Ehrwald 25B1

Tiroler Zugspitze, Obermoos. **GPS**: n47,42731 e10,94096.
10 € 15/17.00-10.00h against payment. 01/01-31/12
Remarks: Parking in front of campsite.

Faschina 25A2

Sportcafé Domig, Haus nr 92. **GPS**: n47,27263 e9,90717.
5 € 11 Ch included. 01/01-31/12
Remarks: At B193.

Feichten/Kaunertal 25B2

Kaunertal. **GPS**: n47,05333 e10,75056.
. 01/05-30/09

Fieberbrunn 26A1

Tirol-camp. **GPS**: n47,46833 e12,55389.
. 01/01-31/12

Fügen 25D1

Zillertal Hell. **GPS**: n47,35934 e11,85198.
10 against payment Ch against payment. **Surface:** metalled.
01/01-31/12

Galtür 25A2

Silvretta-Bundesstraße, B188, Wirl. **GPS**: n46,96570 e10,16390.

€ 15 Ch. **Surface:** metalled. winter
Distance: 100m on the spot on the spot on the spot.
Remarks: Free skibus to Ischgl.

Gerlos 25D2

Bauernhof Schönachhof, Schönachtal 242. **GPS**: n47,22639 e12,05476.

10 € 12 Ch WC . 01/01-31/12

Tourist information Gerlos:
Tourismusverband Gerlos, Haus Nr. 141.Mountain village.
Activ Wellness.Free wellness program. 01/07-30/09.

Gries am Brenner 25C2

Alpengasthof, Nößlach 483. **GPS**: n47,04229 e11,47455.
50 WC free.
Remarks: Brenner highway exit Nößlach.

Haiming 25B2

Center-Oberland, Bundeßtraße 9a. **GPS**: n47,24147 e10,87755.
Ch . 01/01-31/12

Hall in Tirol 25C2

Wohnmobilpark, Scheidensteinstraße 24. **GPS**: n47,28444 e11,49665.

AT

10 € 15 Ch included. 01/05-30/09
Distance: 400m 200m Gastätte 300m.

Tourist information Hall in Tirol:
Tourismusverband, Wallpachgasse 5, www.tiscover.at/hall.Historical little town.

S Hochfilzen 26A1
Schulgasse. **GPS**: n47,47000 e12,62250.

5 free Chfree. **Surface:** gravel.
Distance: on the spot.
Remarks: Behind fire-station, max. 3 nights.

S Hütten 26A1
Parkplatz Asitzbahn, Sportarena Leogang, B164. **GPS**: n47,43963 e12,72040.
50 € 5 + tourist tax Ch (9x) WC € 2.
Distance: 3,5km.

S Hüttschlag 26B2
Bauernhof Stockham-Camping. GPS: n47,14775 e13,28947.
5 € 10 Ch . 01/01-31/12
Distance: 6km 150m 6km.

S Ischgl 25A2
Mathoner Straße 5, Ischgl-Mathon. **GPS**: n46,98967 e10,24751.
15 € 15 Ch . **Surface:** metalled. 01/01-31/12
Distance: 1km.
Remarks: Free skibus to Ischgl and Galtür.

Itter 25D1
Schloßberg. GPS: n47,46641 e12,13975.
. 01/01-31/12

Jenbach 25D1
Gasthof Rieder, Fischl 3. **GPS**: n47,40131 e11,77500.

5 against payment.
Remarks: Only for guest of the restaurant.

Kitzbühel 26A1
Schwarzsee. GPS: n47,45924 e12,36209.
. 01/01-31/12

Kössen 19A6
Wilder Kaiser. GPS: n47,65369 e12,41560.
. 01/01-31/12

Kramsach 25D1
Seeblick Toni. GPS: n47,46175 e11,90664.
. 01/01-31/12

Krimml 25D2
P2. GPS: n47,21805 e12,17519.

free.

S Krimml 25D2
Hotel Krimmlerfälle, Wasserfallstraße 42. **GPS**: n47,21617 e12,17185.

10 € 11 Ch . 15/05-25/10

Kufstein 25D1
Kufstein. GPS: n47,57576 e12,15910.
. 01/05-01/11

Landeck 25B2
Riffler. GPS: n47,14250 e10,56139.
. 01/06-30/04

Tourist information Landeck:
See.Farmer village and winter sports resort.
Tourismusverband TirolWest.Holiday resort in the mountains. Many ski areas in surroundings.
Schloss Landeck, Schlossweg.Renovated castle. 01/05-30/09 Tue-Su 10-17h, 1/10-26/10 Tue-Su 14-17h.

Längenfeld 25B2
Ötztal. GPS: n47,07228 e10,96434.
. 01/01-31/12

Leutasch 25C1
Holiday-Camping. GPS: n47,39861 e11,17936.
. 10/12-31/10

Lienz 26A2
Seewiese, Tristachersee. **GPS**: n46,80655 e12,80313.

. 15/05-30/09

Tourist information Lienz:
Tourismusverband Lienzer Dolomiten, Europaplatz 1, www.tiscover.com/ Lienz.Capital East Tyrol.
Schloß Bruck, Schloßberg 1.Regional museum. 01/06-15/09 10-18h, 16/09-31/10 Tue-Su 10-17h. € 6, family card € 12.

AT

Maria Alm 26A1

Stegerbauer, Schattberg 11. **GPS**: n47,39767 e12,90355.
6 € 8, tourist tax excl Ch € 2,50. 01/01-31/12
Distance: 1km 500m 1km 1km 1km.

Matrei 26A2

Matreier Tauernhaus. **GPS**: n47,11833 e12,49778.
100 € 4. 01/05-30/11

Maurach am Achensee 25D1

Rofan Seilbahn P2, Bundesstrasse. **GPS**: n47,42445 e11,75224.

5 Ch. 01/04-30/11
Distance: 400m.

Maurach am Achensee 25D1

Wimmer, Buchau 8. **GPS**: n47,43319 e11,73456.
. 01/01-31/12

Nassereith 25B2

Roßbach, Roßbach 325. **GPS**: n47,31153 e10,85270.

€ 16 Ch included. **Surface:** grassy. 01/01-31/12
Distance: 500m.

Natters 25C2

Natterer See. **GPS**: n47,23749 e11,34195.
. 15/04-15/10

Nenzing 24D2

Alpencamping Nenzing. **GPS**: n47,18258 e9,68216.
. 01/01-31/12

Tourist information Nenzing:
Tourismusbüro Nenzing, Landstraße 1.

Neukirchen 25D2

Panoramastellplatz, Scheffau 96. **GPS**: n47,23862 e12,24083.

9 € 6,50, guests free Ch . **Surface:** gravel.
01/01-31/12
Distance: 4km on the spot on the spot on the spot.
Remarks: Bread-service.

Neustift 25C2

Edelweiss, Volderau. **GPS**: n47,06801 e11,25295.
€ 16, 2 pers.incl Ch included. 01/01-31/12

Neustift 25C2

Stubai. **GPS**: n47,11021 e11,30895.
. 01/01-31/12

Tourist information Neustift:
Fulpmes.Health resort and winter sports centre.
Tourismusverband Neustift, www.tourismus-tirol.com/neustift.
Stubaier Gletsjerpfad.Trail (45min) from Station Eisgrat.

Nüziders 24D2

Sonnenberg. **GPS**: n47,16939 e9,80722.
. 01/05-01/10

Tourist information Nüziders:
Ms Brigitte Burtscher, Sonnenbergstr. 21 a.Tourist information.
Tourismus & Freizeit Bludenz, Werdenbergerstr. 42, Bludenz.Alps city.

Oberndorf in Tirol 26A1

Gasthof zum Schnitzel Profi, Paß Thurnstraße 10. **GPS**: n47,47709 e12,38391.
6 guests free .
Remarks: Max. 1 night.

Obsteig 25B2

Gasthof zum Lenz, Gschwent 282. **GPS**: n47,30930 e10,94482.

18 € 15 Ch included. 01/01-31/12
Distance: on the spot.

Pfunds 25B2

Wohnmobilplatz Via Claudiasee, Rauth 714. **GPS**: n46,95429 e10,51171.
€ 7 + tourist tax € 1,50/pp Ch WC .
Surface: grassy/metalled.
Distance: 2km 200m.
Remarks: Bread-service.

Radstadt 26B1

Tauerncamping Lerchenhof. **GPS**: n47,38728 e13,46107.
. 01/01-31/12

Ried im Oberinntal 25B2

Dreiländereck. **GPS**: n47,05594 e10,65638.

. 01/01-31/12

Tourist information Ried im Oberinntal:
Serfaus.High car-free mountain village, large ski area.

Schwaz 25C1

Swarovskistraße. **GPS**: n47,34655 e11,70436.

AT

10 €4 €2 Ch €2.
01/01-31/12
Distance: 500m.

Tourist information Schwaz:
Tourismusverband Silberregion Karwendel, Franz-Josef-Straße 2, www.silberregion-karwendel.at.
Schwazer Silberbergwerk. 01/05-31/10.

Seefeld in Tirol 25C1
Alpin Seefeld. GPS: n47,33731 e11,17861.
. 01/01-31/12

Sölden 25B2
Sölden. GPS: n46,95782 e11,01200.
. 15/06-01/05

Söll 25D1
Franzlhof. GPS: n47,50772 e12,18975.
. 01/01-31/12

St.Johann im Pongau 26B1
Kastenhof. GPS: n47,34185 e13,19751.
. 01/01-31/12

St.Johann im Tirol 26A1
Michelnhof. GPS: n47,51056 e12,40893.
. 01/01-31/12

St.Martin bei Lofer 26A1
Park Grubhof. GPS: n47,57510 e12,70834.
. 01/05-01/10

Stams 25B2
Eichenwald-Stams. GPS: n47,27506 e10,98645.
. 01/01-31/12

Steinach am Brenner 25C2
Gasthaus Wolf, Brennerstraße 36. **GPS**: n47,06704 e11,48574.
5 guests free .
Remarks: At the old Brennerstraße.

Stumm 25D1
Gasthof Rißbacher Hof, Ahrnbachstraße 37. **GPS**: n47,27951 e11,89347.

3 €8.

Tweng 26C1
Landhotel Postgut, Tweng 2. **GPS**: n47,19058 e13,60210.

5 €8. **Surface:** metalled. 01/01-31/12
Distance: on the spot on the spot.

Waidring 26A1
Steinplatte. GPS: n47,58344 e12,58286.
. 01/01-31/12

Walchsee 18D6
Seespitz. GPS: n47,64863 e12,31436.
. 01/01-31/12

Wenns/Piller 25B2
Gasthof Sonne, Piller 41. **GPS**: n47,13581 e10,69390.

3 €5 .
Remarks: Altitude 1350m.

Werfen 26B1
Vierthaler. GPS: n47,44567 e13,21223.
. 15/04-30/09

Tourist information Werfen:
Village with citadel Hohenwerfen. Easter-Oct 9-17h.
Eisriesenwelt.Largest ice caves in the world. Route to the caves is rather steep, caves can also be reached by telpher carrier. 01/05-31/10 9-15.30h.

Wiesing 25D1
Inntal. GPS: n47,40585 e11,80536.

. 01/01-31/12

Zell am See 26A1
Seecamp. GPS: n47,33973 e12,80907.
. 01/01-31/12

Tourist information Zell am See:
Zell am See Information, Brucker Bundesstrasse 1a, www.zellamsee.com. Tourist town, summer and winter.
Gletscherskigebiet Kitzsteinhorn, Kaprun.Large winter sports area. Summer skiing on glacier.

Zell am Ziller 25D2
Hofer. GPS: n47,22818 e11,88585.
. 01/01-31/12

Tourist information Zell am Ziller:
www.zell.at.Former mining village, place of finding gold.

AT

Zillertalbahn.Steam train Zell-Jenbach.
Gauderfest.Traditional folk festival. 1st weekend May.

Austria North

Aggsbach Markt 27A1

Badestrand. GPS: n48,29814 e15,40497.

16 € 3,20, € 1,90/pp Ch € 1.
Distance: 500m 50m Donaustüberl 500m.
Remarks: Parking at the Danube river.

Alland 27B1

ÖMV-tankstelle Groschner&KarrerOHG, Gewerbestraße 550. **GPS:** n48,06734 e16,06364.

20 free Chagainst payment. **Surface:** asphalted. 01/01-31/12
Remarks: Parking motorway.

Tourist information Alland:
Ehemalig Jagdschloss, Mayerling. summer 9-12.30h, 13.30-18h, winter 9-12.30h, 13.30-17h 05/04-06/04.
Tropfsteinhöhle.Caves. 01/04-30/09 Sa, Su 9-17h, 01/07-31/08 Mo-Fri 15-16.30h Sa-Su 9-17h 01/11-31/03. € 1,90/3.

Altenmarkt an der Triesting 27B1

Gasthof Zum Kleinen Semmering, Hafnerberg 15. **GPS:** n48,01762 e16,01383.

10 free WC. **Surface:** metalled.
Distance: 2,3km 2,3km.

Altlengbach 27B1

Latra Wohnwagen, Reitermühlstraße 16. **GPS:** n48,15481 e15,91520.
Ch.
Remarks: A1 exit Altlengbach, 40 km west of Vienna.

Arbesbach 27A1

Am Ganser. **GPS:** n48,49123 e14,95683.
15 free . 01/01-31/12
Distance: 500m 500m 500m 500m.
Remarks: Check in at town hall.

Armschlag 27A1

Mohndorf. **GPS:** n48,45222 e15,21944.
5 € 3 Ch . **Surface:** asphalted. 01/01-31/12
Distance: 2km.

Aschbach Markt 27A1

Fam. Edtbauer, Auckental 1 u. 2. **GPS:** n48,10682 e14,69988.
8 € 2. 15/04-30/10
Distance: 7km 3km 7km.

Bad Großpertholz 27A1

Busparkplatz Naturpark Nordwald, Scheiben. **GPS:** n48,61765 e14,81548.
.

Bernhardsthal 27B1

Schulstrasse. **GPS:** n48,69402 e16,87481.

5 free. **Surface:** grassy.
01/01-31/12
Distance: 500m on the spot on the spot weekends only.

Deutsch Jahrndorf 27B1

Söldnergasse 19. **GPS:** n48,00777 e17,11073.

17 voluntary contribution Ch. **Surface:** grassy. 01/01-31/12
Distance: 500m 500m on the spot.
Remarks: Max. 3 nights.

Ebensee 19C6

Busparkplatz am Traunsee, Trauneck. **GPS:** n47,81283 e13,77730.
.

Eferding 19C4

Parkplatz direkt an der Donau, Brandstatt, Pupping. **GPS:** n48,33503 e14,02698.
.

Eggenburg 27B1

tourismusinfo@eggenburg.at - www.eggenburg.at
Medieval town
Pleasant tourist resort
Convenient for longer stays

Stellplatz an der Stadtmauer, Erzherzog-Karl-Ring 19.
GPS: n48,64513 e15,81745.
8 € 4 € 1/10minutes Ch (8x)€ 1/6h. **Surface:** metalled.
01/04-31/10

AT

Distance: on the spot 4km creek 300m 200m 500m on the spot 300m.

Erlauf 27A1

Gasthof Plaika Wirt, Plaika 1. **GPS**: n48,16866 e15,16436.
10 guests free .
Remarks: A1, between exit Ibbs and Pöchlarn.

Gallneukirchen 19D4

Freizeitcentrum, Veitsdorfer Weg 10. **GPS**: n48,36045 e14,40797.
5 free. 01/01-31/12
Distance: 1km 1km.

Gaming 27A2

Kartause. **GPS**: n47,92463 e15,08223.

Gars am Kamp 27A1

Gföhler Strasse/Strandgasse, Thunau am Kamp. **GPS**: n48,59300 e15,65723.

5 free. **Surface:** gravel. 01/01-31/12
Distance: 200m on the spot 200m.
Remarks: Nearby swimming pool.

Geboltskirchen 19C5

Parkplatz Badesee Geboltskirchen, Leithen. **GPS**: n48,16472 e13,66235.

Gmünden 19C6

Gasthof Egger, Ohlsdorferstr. 1. **GPS**: n47,92807 e13,79623.
5 € 5 Ch. 01/01-31/12
Distance: 2km 3km 1km.

Gosau 19B6

Hotel Gosauschmied, Gosau 57. **GPS**: n47,55072 e13,51607.
10 € 10 Ch On demand. **Surface:** asphalted. 01/01-31/12
Distance: 3km on the spot 3km on the spot 500m on the spot.

Gumpoldskirchen 27B1

Neustiftgasse. **GPS**: n48,04423 e16,27552.
Ch.

Hainburg/Donau 27B1

Parkplatz an der Donau, Parkweg. **GPS**: n48,15110 e16,94440.

Surface: asphalted. 01/01-31/12
Distance: 500m on the spot.

Haslach 19C4

Gasthof Furtmühle, Schwackerreith 20, St.Oswald. **GPS**: n48,60497 e14,01967.
15 against payment. 01/01-31/12
Remarks: 5km north of Haslach.

Hohenau/March 27B1

Freizeitzentrum, Kindergartenstrasse. **GPS**: n48,61095 e16,91010.

free. **Surface:** asphalted. 01/01-31/12
Remarks: Swimming pool 200m.

Hollenstein/Ybbs 27A2

Gasthof Staudach, Walcherbauer 5. **GPS**: n47,80703 e14,76687.
4 € 14, 4 pers.incl Ch .
Distance: 200m 10m 200m.

Kefermarkt 27A1

Schloßbrauerei Weinberg, Weinberg 2. **GPS**: n48,44856 e14,53957.
5 guests free.

Klosterneuburg 27B1

Euromobil Campers, Bahnhofplatz 16, Kritzendorf. **GPS**: n48,33582 e16,29863.

4 € 4 Ch. 01/01-31/12
Distance: 12,5km nearby nearby.
Remarks: Lock-up parking, guarded. Motorhome parking at S-Bahnstation.

Klosterneuburg 27B1

Donaupark. **GPS**: n48,31055 e16,32710.
. 01/03-01/12

Tourist information Klosterneuburg:
Tourismusverein Klosterneuburg, Niedermarkt 4, www.klosterneuburg.net.
Stift Klosterneuburg, Stiftsplatz 1.Monastery.

Königswiesen 27A1

Freibad, Badgasse 4. **GPS**: n48,40450 e14,84080.
3 € 1 + € 1/pp + tourist tax Ch WC. 01/01-31/12
Distance: 500m 10m Freibadbuffet 300m.
Remarks: Parking swimming pool, service at water purification plant.

Kremsmünster 19C5

Parkplatz Benediktiner Stift, Fuxjägerstraße. **GPS**: n48,05407 e14,12607.

Laimbach am Ostrong 27A1

Bauernhof Stoiber, Wagmühle 34. **GPS**: n48,31711 e15,11636.
5 € 12 Ch .
Distance: 300m 300m 300m.

Langschlag-Mitterschlag 27A1

Freizeitanlage Frauenwieserteich, Böhmerwald-Bundesstraße. **GPS**: n48,58038 e14,83507.
10 free. 01/01-31/12
Distance: 5km 5km.

Marchtrenk 19C5

Imbiß Koutek, Eichenstraße 2. **GPS**: n48,19055 e14,11893.
10 . 01/01-31/12
Distance: 1km 2,3km on the spot 50m.

Mondsee 19B6

Geflügelhof Schweighofer, Schwand 10. **GPS**: n47,88186 e13,31105.
5 € 10 Ch . 01/01-31/12
Remarks: A1, exit Mondsee, after <Gasthof Kasten>to the left, second farm.

Tourist information Mondsee:
Tourismusverband Mondseeland, Dr. Franz Müller Straße 3,

AT

www.mondsee.at.Holiday region.
M Heimat- und Pfahlbaumuseum, Marschall-Wrede-Platz 1.Historical museum. 01/05-31/10 10-17h.
M Rauchhaus, Hilfbergstraße 5.Farm museum. 10-18h, Sa-Su 10-17h.

S Naarn 27A1

Bauernhof Mostschenke, Dirnwagram 1. **GPS**: n48,21750 e14,61972.
5 € 5, free with a meal Ch WC.
Remarks: Max. 4 days, arrival till 19.30. Naarn dir Mitterkirchen, at garage to the right, then first farm at the right.

Nußdorf am Attersee 19B6

Seecamping Gruber. **GPS**: n47,87965 e13,52444.
. 15/04-15/10

Orth/Donau 27B1

P2, Am Rosenhügel. **GPS**: n48,14523 e16,70383.

free. **Surface:** metalled. 01/01-31/12
Distance: on the spot.

S Ottenschlag 27A1

Florianigasse. **GPS**: n48,42361 e15,22750.

8-10 € 5 € 1/10minutes Ch € 1/8h. **Surface:** metalled.
Distance: 500m Gaststätte 500m.

S Pillichsdorf 27B1

Am Tennisclub, Bahnstraße 8A. **GPS**: n48,36167 e16,53750.

8 free, use facilities clubhouse € 10 Ch WC .
01/01-31/12
Distance: 500m, Vienna 15km 300m 500m on the spot.
Remarks: Use facilities clubhouse possible.

S Pulkau 27B1

Rat-Cumfe Straße. **GPS**: n48,70430 e15,86637.

8 € 5 € 1/10minutes Ch € 1/6h. **Surface:** gravel.
01/01-31/12
Distance: 500m 300m on the spot on the spot.

Purgstall an der Erlauf 27A1

Purgstall. **GPS**: n48,05625 e15,12973.
. 01/01-31/12

S Ranshofen 19A5

Vereinslokal, Scheuhub 2. **GPS**: n48,23228 e12,99893.
10 free . 01/01-31/12
Distance: 2km 2km 2km.

Reichenau/Rax 27B2

Kaiserbrunn, Bundesstraße Höllental 27. **GPS**: n47,73480 e15,79188.

free. **Surface:** metalled.

S Reichenau/Rax 27B2

Gasthof Flackl Wirt, Hinterleiten 12. **GPS**: n47,69056 e15,82778.

5 € 11,50 breakfest incl included WC at restaurant.
Distance: 1,5km on the spot.
Remarks: From B27 follow Gasthof.

Retz 27B1

Stellplatz Retz, Jahnstraße. **GPS**: n48,75382 e15,95105.

5 free. **Surface:** asphalted.
Distance: 500m 500m.

Tourist information Retz:
Tourismusbüro, Hauptplatz 30, www.weinerlebnis-retz.at.

AT

Rossatzbach 27A1

Aggsteiner-Bundesstraße. **GPS**: n48,38750 e15,51722.

12 € 10 Ch (12x) WC included. 01/01-31/12

Distance: 300m on the spot 1,5km.

Remarks: Vinotheek 300m.

Rust 27B2

Reisebus-Parkplatz, Amhafen. **GPS**: n47,80405 e16,67873.

Ch.

Scharnstein 19C5

Camping Schatzlmühle, Viechtwang 1A. **GPS**: n47,91578 e13,97353.

5 € 8, tourist tax excl. 01/01-31/12

Distance: 2km on the spot 600m on the spot on the spot on the spot.

Schönberg 27A1

Freizeitzentrum, Badgasse. **GPS**: n48,52063 e15,69377.

5 € 5, first night free (1x) WC included € 1. **Surface:** asphalted.

01/01-31/12, service Easter-01/11

Distance: 200m on the spot on the spot 200m.

Remarks: Shower during opening hours. Along river.

Schremms 27A1

Parkplatz Stadthalle. **GPS**: n48,79142 e15,07113.

. 01/01-31/12

Distance: 500m.

Remarks: Max. 1 night.

St.Martin am Ybbsfelde 27A1

Gemeindeparkplatz. **GPS**: n48,16465 e15,01995.

. 01/01-31/12

St.Pankraz 19C6

Parkplatz Klauser Stausee, Klaus an der Pyhmbahn. **GPS**: n47,82733 e14,15703.

.

St.Wolfgang 19B6

Appesbach. **GPS**: n47,73231 e13,46374.

. 01/04-01/11

Stockerau 27B1

Hallenbad Wellness Oase, Pestalozzigasse. **GPS**: n48,39385 e16,21912.

7 free € 2 Ch WC sanitary in swimming pool. **Surface:** gravel.

01/01-31/12

Distance: 1,5km.

Traisen 27A1

Traisen. **GPS**: n48,04216 e15,60294.

. 15/02-15/11

Tulln an der Donau 27B1

Donaupark Tulln. **GPS**: n48,33324 e16,07151.

. 01/05-01/10

Unterach am Attersee 19B6

Inselcamping. **GPS**: n47,80096 e13,48251.

. 15/05-15/09

Tourist information Unterach am Attersee:

Ferienregion Attersee Infobüro Unterach, Hauptstraße 9, www.oberoesterreich.at/unterach.Holiday resort at Lake Atter.

Naturlehrpfad Edelkastanienwald.Hiking trail through nature reserve.

Waldhausen im Strudengau 27A1

Badesee, Schloßberg. **GPS**: n48,28420 e14,95883.

6 free € 1/10minutes Ch. 01/01-31/12

Distance: 2km on the spot on the spot 2km 2km.

Weistrach 27A1

Parkplatz Sportplatz. **GPS**: n48,05475 e14,58167.

10 free. 01/01-31/12

Distance: 200m 200m.

Wien 27B1

Kurpark Oberlaa, Filmteichstrasse 5, Vienna (Wien). **GPS**: n48,15211 e16,39767.

.

Wien 27B1

Neue Donau, Am Kleehäufel, Vienna (Wien). **GPS**: n48,20836 e16,44602.

. Easter-30/09

Remarks: East of Vienna.

Wien 27B1

Wien Süd, Breitenfursterstraße, Vienna (Wien). **GPS**: n48,14969 e16,30030.

. 01/05-30/09

Wien 27B1

Weingut Heuriger Schilling, Langenzersdorferstraße 54, Wien-Strebersdorf, Vienna (Wien). **GPS**: n48,29856 e16,38421.

2 € 5, guests free Ch WC. **Surface:** gravel.

Feb, Apr, Jun. Aug, Oct other months.

Distance: Vienna 15km on the spot.

Remarks: Max. 3 days. A22, exit Strebersdorf.

Wien 27B1

Waldrebengasse 3. **GPS**: n48,22552 e16,46271.

Ch. Mo-Fri 7-16.30

Tourist information Vienna (Wien):

Overnight parking prohibited.

Tourist-Info, Albertinaplatz 1, info.wien.at/.Imperial city, many curiosities,

capital of the classic music.
Wien-Karte.Card gives entrance to public transport and discounts on museums, curiosities. Available at Tourist-Info and hotels. € 16,90.
Spanische Hofreitschule, Michaelerplatz 1.Spanish Riding School, morning-training can be visited without reservation. 9.40-12.30h.
Kunsthistorisches Museum, Maria Theresien-Platz.Important painting collection. Tue-Su 10-18h, Thu 10-21h. € 10, family card € 20.
Wurstelprater.Amusement park. 15/03-15/10 10-24h.

Wiener Neustadt 27B2

Parkplatz Stadion, Stadionstrasse. **GPS**: n47,82156 e16,25629.

20. 01/01-31/12
Distance: 500m on the spot.

Wilfersdorf 27B1

Schloss Wilfersdorf, Parkplatz am Schloss. **GPS**: n48,58600 e16,64514.

3 € 4 WC. 01/01-31/12
Distance: 100m 300m on the spot.
Remarks: Check in at Schloss, 10-16h tue/su.

Zwettl 27A1

Wirtshaus zur Minidampfbahn, 47, Teichhäuser bei Zwettl. **GPS**: n48,66278 e15,15444.

6-10 free free Ch € 2,50 € 2. **Surface:** grassy/metalled.
01/01-31/12
Distance: 2km 200m on the spot 2,5km.

Austria South

Andau 27B2

Puszasee. **GPS**: n47,77536 e17,03265.
€ 11 Ch € 1,85. 15/04-15/10

Annenheim 26C3

Ossiachersee. **GPS**: n46,65631 e13,89168.
€ 20,8- € 26,4 Ch WC included. 01/05-15/09

Tourist information Annenheim:
Treffen.Former residence of the counts of Treffen.

Bad Gams 27A3

Freizeitzentrums GamsBad, Bad Gams 2. **GPS**: n46,86730 e15,22743.

6 € 5 Ch. **Surface:** grasstiles/metalled. 01/01-31/12
Distance: 200m on the spot 200m 100m 200m.
Remarks: Check in at Gamsbad.

Bad Sankt Leonhard 27A3

Bachwegbrücke. **GPS**: n46,96037 e14,79358.

8 free. 01/01-31/12
Remarks: Parking behind Spar-supermarket.

Bleiburg 27A3

Grabenstraße. **GPS**: n46,59130 e14,79550.

4 free. **Surface:** grasstiles. 01/01-31/12
Distance: on the spot 100m on the spot 200m.

Deutschlandsberg 27A3

Koralmhalle, Höhe Frauentalerstraße 51. **GPS**: n46,81783 e15,22248.

2 free. **Surface:** asphalted. 01/01-31/12
Distance: 200m on the spot 100m on the spot.

Döbriach 26C2

Brunner am See. **GPS**: n46,76778 e13,64806.
. 01/01-31/12

Döbriach 26C2

Mössler. **GPS**: n46,77444 e13,65556.
. 01/04-01/11

Tourist information Döbriach:
Tourismusbüro Millstatt, Marktplatz 8, Millstatt.Tourist town and health resort to the Millstättersee.

AT

Drobollach 26C3

Marhof. **GPS**: n46,59031 e13,91340.
. 01/05-01/10

Tourist information Drobollach:

Terra Medica, Bad Bleiberg.Cave with beneficial effect. T € 16 1h therapy.
Terra Mystica, Bad Bleiberg.Miners cave. 01/05-31/10 10-15h, 01/07-31/08 9.30-16.30h.

Eberndorf 27A3

Gösseldorfersee. **GPS**: n46,57532 e14,62319.
. 01/05-01/10

Eberndorf 27A3

Rutar Lido. **GPS**: n46,58455 e14,62615.
. 01/01-31/12

Faak/See 26C3

Gruber. **GPS**: n46,57254 e13,93242.
. 01/05-01/10

Faak/See 26C3

Poglitsch. **GPS**: n46,56972 e13,90694.
. Easter-15/10

S **Ferlach** 27A3

Messeparkplatz Schloß Ferlach. **GPS**: n46,52633 e14,29750.

30 € 4 € 1/10minutes Ch € 1. **Surface:** metalled.
01/01-31/12
Distance: 500m on the spot 300m 300m 300m.
Remarks: Max. 3 days.

S **Gamlitz** 27B3

Schloßweingut Melcher, Eckberger Weinstraße. **GPS**: n46,72054 e15,55409.

10 WC free with a meal. 8-23h
Distance: on the spot on the spot 150m.
Remarks: After restaurant, go up to the right.

Gleinstätten 27B3

Gleinstätten. **GPS**: n46,75167 e15,36111.
. 01/04-01/10

S **Hermagor** 26C3

Schluga. **GPS**: n46,63147 e13,39532.
6 € 12, dog € 3,90. **Surface:** grassy. 01/01-31/12
Distance: winter free shuttle to piste.

Hermagor 26C3

Max Presseggersee. **GPS**: n46,63022 e13,45423.
. 01/05-01/10

Tourist information Hermagor:

Presseggersee.Nature reserve, no motor boats allowed.

S **Horitschon** 27B2

Weingut Duschanek, Hauptstraße 104. **GPS**: n47,59162 e16,53493.

6 € 3, guests free Ch € 2 WC. **Surface:** metalled.
01/01-31/12
Distance: 600m on the spot 600m on the spot.

S **Jagerberg** 27B3

GPS: n46,85692 e15,74292.

5 free € 0,50/60liter Ch. **Surface:** gravel. 01/01-31/12
Distance: 200m 200m 200m 200m.
Remarks: Follow 'Sportanlage'.

Jennersdorf 27B2

Jennersdorf. **GPS**: n46,94558 e16,13372.
. 01/04-01/11

S **Judenburg** 27A2

Erlebnisbad, Fichtenhainstraße. **GPS**: n47,16407 e14,65308.

5 € 5 Ch WC free. **Surface:** gravel. 01/01-31/12
Distance: 500m 200m 200m.

S **Kötschach-Mauthen** 26B3

Gasthof Gailberghöhe, Gailberg 3. **GPS**: n46,71525 e12,96753.
70 € 14,50, 2 pers.incl. Ch WC included.
Surface: asphalted/gravel. 01/05-15/11, 15/12-15/03
Distance: 7km on the spot 7km 2km 7km.

Ledenitzen 26C3

Ferien am Walde. **GPS**: n46,57046 e13,95161.
. 01/05-01/10

S **Liezen** 27A2

Sportzentrum, Friedau. **GPS**: n47,56500 e14,23333.

AT

3 free € 1. **Surface:** gravel. 01/01-31/12
Distance: 1km 300m 1km on the spot.

Malta 26C2

Maltatal. GPS: n46,94958 e13,50975.
. 01/04-01/11

Tourist information Malta:
Gmünd.Small fortified medieval town.
Porsche Museum, Gmünd.Former place of residence of Ferdinand Porsche, 1944-1950. 15/05-15/10 9-18h, 16/10-14/5 10-16h.

Mörbisch/Neusiedlersee 27B2

Seefestspiele, P3, Seestrasse. **GPS**: n47,75470 e16,69592.

30 € 3,50. **Surface:** grassy. 01/01-31/12
Distance: 2km on the spot.
Remarks: Parking at marina.

Mörtschach 26B2

Gasthof Suntiger, Mörtschach 35. **GPS**: n46,92287 e12,91348.

4 guests free . **Surface:** grassy.

Mühlen 27A2

Am Badesee. GPS: n47,03719 e14,48780.
. 01/05-30/09

Murfeld 27B3

Gasthof Dorfheuriger Rom Thomas, Dorfstrasse 1, Unterschwarza. **GPS**: n46,71612 e15,67612.

50 € 5 Ch WC . **Surface:** grassy. 01/01-31/12
Distance: 200m on the spot.
Remarks: Bread-service.

Oberrakitsch 27B3

Ölmühle Sixt, Oberrakitsch 115. **GPS**: n46,73863 e15,74605.

10 € 12 Ch WC. **Surface:** gravel. 01/01-31/12
Distance: 1km on the spot 1km 3km 4km.

Obervellach 26B2

Sport Erlebnis. GPS: n46,92658 e13,20195.
.

Oberwölz 26D1

Schloß Rothenfels. GPS: n47,20697 e14,28051.
€ 18,50, 2 pers.incl Ch WC included. 01/04-01/11

Tourist information Oberwölz:
Urlaubsregion Murau, Am Bahnhof, St. Lorenzen/Murau.Oldest small town of Styria.
Blasmusikmuseum.Music museum. 10-15h. € 3.

Ossiach 26D3

Kalkgruber. GPS: n46,68730 e14,01941.
. 01/05-01/10

Ossiach 26D3

Kölbl. GPS: n46,66200 e13,97267.
. 01/04-01/11

Ossiach 26D3

Lampele. GPS: n46,68267 e13,99865.
. 01/05-01/10

Ossiach 26D3

Ossiach. GPS: n46,66367 e13,97452.
. 01/05-01/10

Ossiach 26D3

Parth. GPS: n46,66517 e13,97697.
. 01/01-31/12

Tourist information Ossiach:
www.ossiach.at/.Tourist town.

Pölfing-Brunn 27A3

Kipferlbad, Badstraße 13. **GPS**: n46,72422 e15,29268.

10 free. **Surface:** grassy. 01/01-31/12
Distance: 1km on the spot on the spot 1km 1km.

Schiefling am See 26D3

Weißes Rössl. GPS: n46,61810 e14,10428.
. 01/05-01/10

Schladming 26C1

Talstation Planai-West. GPS: n47,39005 e13,67638.
30 € 17 excl. tourist tax Ch . winter
Distance: 25m on the spot.
Remarks: Valley station ski-lift.

Schwanberg 27A3

Freibad, Badgasse. **GPS**: n46,76361 e15,20639.

AT

4 free 15/09-15/05, € 6 16/05-14/09 On demand WC.
Surface: gravel. 01/01-31/12
Distance: 500m on the spot on the spot 500m 500m.

Soboth 27A3

Parkplatz Soboth-Stausee. GPS: n46,68142 e15,03805.

free. **Surface:** asphalted.
Distance: 5km.
Remarks: Parking at artificial lake.

St Stefan im Rosental 27B2

Schichenauerstraße 6. **GPS**: n46,90634 e15,71431.
6 free € 1/100liter Ch (6x)€ 0,60/kWh. **Surface:** gravel.
01/01-31/12
Distance: 200m 200m 200m.

St.Andrä 27B2

Zicksee. GPS: n47,79205 e16,91428.
. 01/04-01/10

St.Primus 27A3

Turnersee. GPS: n46,58588 e14,56568.
. 01/05-01/10

Stainz 27A3

Parkplatz 3, Ettendorfer Straße. **GPS**: n46,89377 e15,26823.

3 free. **Surface:** metalled. **Distance:** 100m 100m 100m.

Tourist information Stainz:
Region Süd-Weststeiermark, Hauptplatz 34, www.stainz.at.Das Land des Schilcher, country of the Austrian rosé wine.
Der Stainzer Flascherlzug.Narrow-gauge steam train.
01/05-31/10 Sa-Su 15h.
Ren(nt)t a Traktor, Anton Nettwall, Sommereben 95, St. Stefan ob Stainz.With a tractor through Schilcherland. € 50 1/2 day.

Unterlamm 27B2

Stefan's Heuriger Sieglhof, Magland 44. **GPS**: n46,98152 e16,09172.

15 € 1/pp Ch. 01/01-31/12
Distance: 4km on the spot on the spot on the spot.

Veitsch 27A2

Marktgemeindeamt. GPS: n47,57896 e15,48961.

3 free. **Surface:** asphalted. 01/01-31/12
Distance: 300m 100m 100m 100m.

Villach 26C3

Berghof. GPS: n46,65290 e13,93307.
. 01/04-15/10

Tourist information Villach:
Villach Tourismus, Rathausplatz 1, www.villach.at.Tourist town.
Mo-Fri 10-17h.
Therme Warmbad, Kadischenallee 25-27.Thermal bath and health centre.

Vordernberg 27A2

Hauptplatz 2. **GPS**: n47,48617 e14,99202.

6 € 1/10minutes Ch € 1/8h. **Surface:** gravel. 01/01-31/12
Distance: 500m 500m 500m on the spot.

AT

ITALY

Trentino Alto Adige pages: 792-798
Friuli Venezia Giulia pages: 813-815
Aosta Valley pages: 778-779
Lombardy pages: 798-806
Veneto pages: 806-812
Milaan
Piemonte pages: 779-792
Emilia-Romagna pages: 815-826
Liguria pages: 826-828
Florence
San Marino pages: 844
Marche pages: 844-854
Tuscany pages: 828-844
Umbria pages: 859-862
Abruzzo pages: 862-865
Rome
Molise pages: 865
Lazio pages: 854-859
Campania pages: 869-870
Puglia pages: 865-869
Basilicata pages: 870
Sardinia pages: 872-873
Calabria pages: 870-872
Palermo
Sicily pages: 873-878

Capital: Rome
Government: parliamentarian republic
Official Language: Italian
Population: 60,700,000 (2012)
Area: 301,318 km^2

General information

Dialling code: 0039
General emergency: 112
Currency: Euro
Credit cards are accepted almost everywhere.

Regulations for overnight stays

Wild camping is allowed with permission of municipality, police or property owner when no problems occur.

Additional public holidays 2014

January 6 Epiphany
April 25 Liberation Day
May 1 Labor Day
June 2 Festa della Republica, National Holiday
August 15 Assumption of the Virgin Mary
November 1 All Saints' Day
November 2 Armistice Day
December 8 Immaculate Conception

Italy

Aosta Valley

Antey-Saint-André 24A6

Località Filey, SR46. **GPS**: n45,81246 e7,58898.
15 free Ch. **Surface:** metalled. 01/01-31/12
Distance: 850m.

Aosta 23D6

Via Cadutti del Lavoro. **GPS**: n45,73600 e7,33035.

30 € 12/24h € 1/100liter € 2 Ch € 1/kWh. **Location:** Urban, noisy. **Surface:** asphalted. 01/01-31/12 Thu-morning closed because of market.
Distance: on the spot 4,5km 200m.
Remarks: Parking closes at 22h.

Tourist information Aosta:
U.I.A.T. (Ufficio Informazioni e di Accoglienza Turistica), Piazza Chanoux, 8, www.regione.vda.it/turismo.Historical city. 9.30-12h, 14-17.30h, summer 9-19h.

Aymavilles 23D6

Strada Comunale del Moulins. **GPS**: n45,70125 e7,23960.
20 € 8/24h . **Surface:** metalled. 01/05-31/10
Distance: on the spot 2km.

Bionaz 23D5

Area Attrezzata Bosco di Lexert. **GPS**: n45,87458 e7,42381.
€ 10/night Ch.
Remarks: Picnic area at small lake.

Brusson 24A6

Foyer du Ski, Rue Vollon. **GPS**: n45,76617 e7,71117.

50 € 10/24h Ch included. **Surface:** grassy/metalled. 01/01-31/12
Distance: on the spot.
Remarks: At lake. On the road dir Campoluc.

Cervinia/Breuil 24A5

GPS: n45,92614 e7,62026.

50 € 7/24h Ch. **Surface:** asphalted. 01/01-31/12
Distance: 1km Lago Blu 400m on the spot.
Remarks: Shuttle to centre. 1km before entering the village, nearby cross roads with Cieloalto.

Champorcher 24A6

Area pic-nic, Loc. Chardonney. **GPS**: n45,62153 e7,60654.
free free. **Surface:** grassy/metalled.
Remarks: Nearby parking funicular railway.

Chatillon 24A6

Area Camper attrezzata Chatillon, Località Chopine. **GPS**: n45,74889 e7,62388.
€ 6/12h Ch . **Surface:** metalled. 01/01-31/12
Distance: historical centre 500m.

Cogne 23D6

Fraz. Lillaz. **GPS**: n45,59602 e7,38815.

38 € 8, 1/7-31/8 + 24/12-6/1 € 10 Ch. **Surface:** asphalted. 01/01-31/12
Distance: 100m on the spot 100m 100m.

Cogne 23D6

Fraz. Revettaz. **GPS**: n45,60840 e7,35830.

120 € 8, 1/7-31/8 + 24/12-6/1 € 10 Ch € 2. **Surface:** asphalted. 01/01-31/12 water disconnected in winter.

Tourist information Cogne:
Parco Nacionale Gran Paradiso, Vall d'Aosta.Nature reserve, information centres: Dégioz, Rhêmes-Notre-Dame and Cogne.

Courmayeur 23D6

Funivia Val Veny. **GPS**: n45,81428 e6,95612.
free . **Surface:** metalled. 01/01-31/12
Distance: 3km on the spot.

Gressoney 24A5

P Weissmatten, Via Bildschocke, Saint Jean. **GPS**: n45,76028 e7,83556.

15/12-31/03 - 01/07-31/08 € 10/24h . **Surface:** asphalted. 01/01-31/12
Remarks: Parking funicular railway.

Gressoney 24A5

Tschaval, La Trinité. **GPS**: n45,85657 e7,81362.

IT

36 € 12/24h, May-Oct € 10 Ch € 3 WC. **Surface:** metalled.
01/01-31/12, 24/24h
Distance: 2 restaurants 300m on the spot on the spot on the spot 200m.

Hône 24A6

Via Raffort. **GPS**: n45,61169 e7,73262.
10 € 8 Ch included. **Surface:** metalled. 01/01-31/12
Distance: 350m 7km.
Remarks: Max. 48h.

La Thuile 23D6

Area Azzura. GPS: n45,70823 e6,95335.

75 € 12/24h Ch (45x)€ 3. **Surface:** metalled.
01/01-31/12
Distance: 500m 500m 100m.

Pont-Saint-Martin 24A6

Piazzale Palazzetto dello Sport. GPS: n45,60025 e7,79338.
free. **Surface:** asphalted.
Distance: 1km.

Rhemes Notre Dame 23D6

Loc. Chanavey. **GPS**: n45,57960 e7,12392.
€ 5 included. **Surface:** metalled.
Distance: on the spot.

Rhemes Notre Dame 23D6

Frazione Bruil. **GPS**: n45,57148 e7,11848.
20 free. **Surface:** asphalted.

Saint-Denis 24A6

Strada Regionale del Col Saint Pantaléon, Loc. Plaù. **GPS**: n45,77129 e7,56092.
10 free Ch free. **Surface:** grasstiles/grassy.
Distance: 16km.

Saint-Oyen 23D6

Rue de Flassin. **GPS**: n45,82133 e7,20822.
€ 12/24h Ch WC included € 1. 01/01-31/12
Distance: 22km on the spot on the spot.

Torgnon 24A6

Plan Prorion. **GPS**: n45,80397 e7,55490.
25 € 8/24h Ch. **Surface:** asphalted. 01/01-31/12
Distance: 50m.

Valgrisenche 23D6

Frazione Bonne. **GPS**: n45,61931 e7,05930.

20 € 10/24h Ch € 3. **Surface:** grassy/sand.
Remarks: At weir.

Valsavarenche 23D6

GPS: n45,59229 e7,20839.
€ 5/12h Ch. **Surface:** grasstiles. 01/01-31/12
Distance: 100m.
Remarks: Check in at town hall Tabaccheria or Bar Lo Fourquin, with registration number motorhome.

Verrès 24A6

Via Stazione. **GPS**: n45,66214 e7,69356.

6 € 5 free. **Surface:** asphalted.
Distance: 1,5km.

Piedmont

Acqui Terme 31B2

Area comunale, SS456, Viale Einaudi. **GPS**: n44,66533 e8,47228.

150 € 5 Ch (16x)included WC. **Location:** Urban, comfortable, central, noisy. **Surface:** grasstiles/metalled.
01/01-31/12
Distance: 1,5km 25km 50m 250m.

Alba 31A2

Alba Village, Corso Piave 219, loc. San Cassiano. **GPS**: n44,68537 e8,01019.

20 € 8 + € 0,50/pp tourist tax € 0,50/30liter Ch free. **Location:** Urban, comfortable, central. **Surface:** grassy.
01/01-31/12

IT

Distance: 2,5km 1km on the spot 100m on the spot.
Remarks: Nearby Hotel&Camping Alba Village, max. 48h, guarded parking, check in at reception.

S Alessandria 31B1

Area comunale, Viale Teresa Michel. **GPS**: n44,92075 e8,62722.
25 free Ch. **Location:** Urban, simple. **Surface:** asphalted.
01/01-31/12
Distance: 2km 2km on the spot 500m on the spot.

S Asti 31B2

Piazza Campo del Palio. **GPS**: n44,89712 e8,21057.
>50 free . **Location:** Urban, simple, central, noisy. **Surface:** asphalted.
01/01-31/12 Wed-Sa.
Distance: on the spot on the spot on the spot.

S Avigliana 30D1

Piazzale Grande Torino, Via Pontetto. **GPS**: n45,07342 e7,39075.

free Ch free. **Surface:** asphalted.
Distance: 1km 4,6km.
Remarks: Nearby sports complex.

Tourist information Avigliana:
Ufficio Informazioni e di Accoglienza Turistica, Piazza del Popolo,2.Historical city.
Thu.

S Bairo 31A1

SP 41, Via Cornaletto. **GPS**: n45,38681 e7,75796.

free Ch free. **Surface:** gravel. 01/01-31/12
Remarks: Max. 3 days.

S Barge 30D2

Via Fiorita. **GPS**: n44,72684 e7,32028.

5 free Ch free. **Surface:** asphalted.
Distance: 800m on the spot.

S Baveno 24B5

Area Comunale, Piazza Umberto Giordano. **GPS**: n45,91139 e8,50056.

40 € 12/24h Ch WC included.
Surface: metalled.
01/01-31/12
Distance: 500m 2,8km Lago Maggiore 300m 300m.
Remarks: Max. 72h, no camping activities.

S Biella 24B6

Area Comunale, Piazzale Sandro Pertini. **GPS**: n45,55559 e8,06760.

30 free free. **Location:** Urban. **Surface:** asphalted.
01/01-31/12
Distance: on the spot 100m station 100m.
Remarks: Square next to station F.S San Paolo.

Tourist information Biella:
A.T.L. (Agenzia Turistica Locale), Piazza V. Veneto, 3.

S Bielmonte 24B6

Piazzale 2, SS232. **GPS**: n45,66250 e8,08472.
8 € 3,50 Ch included € 3,50.
Remarks: Follow Panoramica Zegna, funicular railway 500m.

S Borgo San Dalmazzo 31A3

P Area Camper, Strada Communale Del Cimitero. **GPS**: n44,32889 e7,49167.

free Ch free. **Surface:** asphalted.
Distance: 100m.
Remarks: At sports park.

S Borgosesia 24B6

Piazza Valentino milanaccio, Via Varallo. **GPS**: n45,72005 e8,27408.

IT

8 free Chfree. **Location:** Urban. **Surface:** asphalted.
01/01-31/12 Jun.
Distance: 300m.
Remarks: Sa market.

S Candelo 24B6

Area Comunale, Via C. Pavese/Via F. Bianco. **GPS**: n45,54244 e8,11524.

10 free Chfree. **Location:** Urban, quiet. **Surface:** gravel.
01/01-31/12
Distance: 400m 400m 100m.
Remarks: Nearby sports center.

S Candelo 24B6

Area Ricetto, Via Mulino. **GPS**: n45,54624 e8,11573.

25 free Ch free. **Location:** Comfortable. **Surface:** metalled.
01/01-31/12
Distance: 400m 400m.

S Canelli 31B2

Piazza Unione Europea. **GPS**: n44,72039 e8,29369.

15 free Chfree. **Location:** Urban, simple, noisy. **Surface:** asphalted.
01/01-31/12
Distance: 500m on the spot on the spot on the spot.

S Cannobio 24C5

Area Comunale, Via Al Fiume / Via San Rocco. **GPS**: n46,06179 e8,69242.

20 € 15/24h Ch WCfree. **Location:** Rural. **Surface:** grasstiles.
01/01-31/12
Distance: 500m on the spot 500m 300m.

Remarks: Along river, max. 3 days.

Tourist information Cannobio:
U.I.A.T. (Ufficio Informazioni e di Accoglienza Turistica), Viale V. Veneto, 4.Historical little town with palace and Renaissance church.
Su.

S Carcoforo 24B5

Le Giare, SP11, Loc. Tetto Minocco. **GPS**: n45,90769 e8,05130.

100 € 10/day, € 15/weekend, € 40/week Chfree (16x)€ 1,50 WC € 1. **Surface:** grassy. 01/03-30/09
Distance: on the spot 50m 300m.
Remarks: Along the Egua river.

S Casale Monferrato 31B1

Palazzetto dello Sport Paolo Ferraris, Via Visconti. **GPS**: n45,12556 e8,46194.

15 free in shopping centre. **Location:** Rural. **Surface:** asphalted.
01/01-31/12
Distance: 1,5km 3,6km 200m 200m.
Remarks: At sports centre.

Casale Monferrato 31B1

Parcheggio Castello, Piazza Castello. **GPS**: n45,13722 e8,44806.

>10 free. **Location:** Urban, simple, central, noisy.
Surface: asphalted.
Distance: 200m 4km 100m 250m on the spot on the spot.

S Casaleggio Boiro 31B2

Via Castello. **GPS**: n44,63354 e8,73254.

IT

8 free Chfree (6x)included. **Location:** Rural, comfortable, quiet.
Surface: gravel. 01/01-31/12
Distance: 250m 10km 150m 250m.

S Castelletto Stura 31A2

Via Cuneo. **GPS**: n44,44194 e7,63444.

free free. **Surface:** gravel.
Remarks: Nearby sports park.

Castiglione Falletto 31A2

Area comunale, Piazzale Muntelier. **GPS**: n44,62379 e7,97486.

10 free Chfree . **Location:** Rural, comfortable, quiet.
Surface: metalled. 01/01-31/12
Distance: 100m 100m 100m.

S Castiglione Tinella 31B2

Camperstop Ai Ciuvin, Agriturismo, Strada Manzotti 3. **GPS**: n44,73357 e8,18140.

12 € 20 Ch WC. **Location:** Rural, comfortable, isolated, quiet.
Surface: grassy. 01/01-31/12
Distance: 15km 20km on the spot 15km.
Remarks: Max. 48h.

S Cavour 30D2

Via Giacomo Puccini. **GPS**: n44,78861 e7,37667.

18 free Chfree. **Surface:** metalled.
Distance: 400m 100m.
Remarks: Nearby SP152.

S Ceresole Reale 30D1

Borgata Chiapili Inferiore, SP50. **GPS**: n45,45142 e7,18587.
€ 8 € 4 Ch € 3. **Surface:** unpaved.
Distance: 4km Ristorante Lo Sciatore 2km.
Remarks: Along the Orco river, National Park 'Gran Paradiso'.

S Ceresole Reale 30D1

Borgota Villa, SP50. **GPS**: n45,44053 e7,21066.

40 free WC free. **Surface:** grassy/gravel.
Distance: Ceresole Reale 2km on the spot 200m.
Remarks: Altitude 1350m, National Park 'Gran Paradiso'.

S Cesana Torinese 30D2

Area Sosta Camper Casa Cesana, Viale Sen. Bouvier. **GPS**: n44,94782 e6,79516.

12 € 10/24h Chincluded (12x)€ 3/day,6Amp. **Surface:** asphalted.
01/01-31/12
Distance: 300m 50m.

S Cherasco 31A2

Parking Area Camper, Piazza Giovanni Paolo II. **GPS**: n44,64946 e7,85529.

8 free Ch (8x)free WC. **Location:** Rural, simple, quiet.
Surface: asphalted. 01/01-31/12
Distance: 400m 3,7km 200m 300m.
Remarks: Max. 48h.

S Chieri 31A1

Piazza Quarini, via Bernardo Vittone. **GPS**: n45,00488 e7,82724.

12 free Chfree. **Surface:** asphalted.

IT

Distance: on the spot.
Remarks: Behind Barracks.

S Chivasso 31A1

Piazza Libertini. **GPS**: n45,18514 e7,89296.

free € 2. **Surface:** asphalted.
Distance: 300m.
Remarks: Parking swimming pool.

S Chivasso 31A1

Via Ceresa. **GPS**: n45,19470 e7,88955.

free € 2. **Surface:** asphalted.
Distance: 300m.

Tourist information Chivasso:
Ufficio Informazioni, Palazzo del Lavoro Lungo Piazza D'Armi.Tourist information.

S Collegno 31A1

Collegno Area Sosta Camper, Corso Pastrengo. **GPS**: n45,08070 e7,58313.

30 free € 0,50 Ch € 0,50. **Surface:** asphalted.
Distance: 4km on the spot.
Remarks: Terrain with video surveillance, coins available at Autolavaggio Il Draghetto.

S Cravagliana 24B5

Pian delle Fate, Loc. Brugarolo, SP di Valle Mastallone. **GPS**: n45,85223 e8,22473.

30 € 14/24h Ch (4x) WC included. **Surface:** grassy.
15/03-15/10

Distance: on the spot on the spot.

S Cuceglio 31A1

Area Camper Erbaluce, Via Porta Pia 69/71. **GPS**: n45,34724 e7,81168.
free . **Surface:** metalled.

S Cuneo 31A3

Via Discesa Bellavista. **GPS**: n44,39495 e7,54878.

free Ch free. **Surface:** asphalted.
Distance: 250m.
Remarks: Dir Torino/Saluzzo, before the old bridge over the Stura river.

Tourist information Cuneo:
U.I.A.T. (Ufficio Informazioni e di Accoglienza Turistica), Piazza Bovens, www.cuneoholiday.com.Historical city.
Piazza Galimberti. Tue.

Demonte 30D3

Via G. Nicolai. **GPS**: n44,31551 e7,29495.
. **Surface:** asphalted.
Remarks: Market square.

S Donato 24A6

Area Camper Fabrizio de André, Via S. Pertini, SP405. **GPS**: n45,52774 e7,90944.

6 € 3/night WC free. **Location:** Rural. **Surface:** grasstiles.
01/01-31/12
Distance: 300m 300m.
Remarks: Pay at Tabaccheria in the village.

S Entracque 31A3

Parcheggio Camper Real Park, Ponterosso. **GPS**: n44,26111 e7,37750.

66 € 6 included. **Surface:** grassy.
Distance: 3km on the spot on the spot 6km.
Remarks: Max. 2 days, recreation park.

S Entracque 31A3

Centro Sci Nordico Gelas. GPS: n44,22852 e7,38927.
20 € 10/24h, € 15/48h . **Surface:** grassy/sand.
Distance: on the spot 20m.

S Entracque 31A3

Via del Mulino. **GPS**: n44,23389 e7,39723.
65 € 10/24h, € 15/48h included.

IT

Distance: 300m.

Fenestrelle 30D1

Le Casermette. **GPS**: n45,03671 e7,05090.
25 € 10 Ch € 3. **Surface:** unpaved.

Fenestrelle 30D1

GPS: n45,03889 e7,04583.

9 free. **Surface:** grassy.
Remarks: Next to cemetery.

Frabosa Soprana 31A3

Grotta di Bossea, Loc.Bossea 10. **GPS**: n44,24077 e7,83939.
5 free Ch free WC. **Location:** Rural, simple, isolated.
Surface: asphalted. 01/01-31/12
Distance: 12km on the spot on the spot 12km on the spot.
Remarks: Parking at the caves.

Garessio 31A3

Area Comunale, Str.Provinciale del Colle di San Bernardo (P582). **GPS**: n44,19927 e8,02587.

30 free Ch free. **Location:** Rural, simple. **Surface:** asphalted.
01/01-31/12
Distance: 1km 22km 1km 1km.

Genola 31A2

Grosso Vacanze, Via Divisione Alpina Cuneense 2, SS20. **GPS**: n44,59751 e7,65982.
free Ch . **Surface:** metalled. 01/01-31/12
Remarks: Motorhome dealer, accessory shop.

Giaveno 30D1

GPS: n45,04137 e7,36135.

free free. **Surface:** metalled.
Distance: 100m.
Remarks: SP187 Roundabout dir Torino.

Grinzane Cavour 31A2

Piazza Ugo Genta, Via Bricco. **GPS**: n44,65515 e7,98936.

3 free Ch free. **Location:** Rural, simple, isolated, noisy.
Surface: asphalted. 01/01-31/12
Distance: 500m 500m 2km on the spot.

Ivrea 24A6

La Dora d'Ivrea, Via Dora Baltea. **GPS**: n45,46334 e7,87621.

8 € 5 € 3 Ch. **Surface:** asphalted. 01/01-31/12
Distance: 500m 4,5km Ipermercato 800m 350m.
Remarks: Along the river side.

Tourist information Ivrea:
I.A.T. (Ufficio Informazioni e di Accoglienza Turistica), Corso Vercelli, 1.

Locana 31A1

Via Nusiglie. **GPS**: n45,41361 e7,46278.
€ 5/24h € 3/24h WC.

Macugnaga 24A5

Pecetto, Di Iacchine Pierluigi Loc. Pecetto. **GPS**: n45,97015 e7,95352.

28 € 10, 2 nights € 15 Ch WC free. **Location:** Rural, simple, quiet.
Surface: concrete. 01/05-30/11
Distance: 1km 100m 500m 100m on the spot.
Remarks: At ski-lift.

Madonna del Sasso 24B6

Area Comunale, Via Santuario, Fraz. Boleto. **GPS**: n45,78974 e8,37222.

8 free Ch free. **Surface:** grasstiles. 01/01-31/12
Distance: 200m Lago d'Orta 700m 100m 50m.
Remarks: Narrow entrance, view at Lago d'Orta.

IT

Maglione 31A1

SP78, Via Cigliano. **GPS**: n45,34338 e8,01456.

20 free. **Surface:** grassy.
Distance: on the spot 50m.
Remarks: Art city. Nearby SS44, dir Borgo d'Ale.

S Marsaglia 31A2

Via della Stazione, SP115. **GPS**: n44,45228 e7,97929.
18 € 13 Ch WC. **Surface:** asphalted/grassy. 01/01-31/12
Distance: on the spot.
Remarks: Inspection june 2013: closed because of renovation.

S Mirabello Monferrato 31B1

SS31. **GPS**: n45,03016 e8,52946.

8 free €2 Ch€1. **Location:** Simple, isolated, quiet. **Surface:** asphalted. 01/01-31/12
Distance: 900m 10km 800m 50m 50m.

S Mombaruzzo 31B2

Club Agrisportivo Mombaruzzo, SP4. **GPS**: n44,77993 e8,45061.
€ 10 Ch €2 WC. 01/01-31/12
Distance: 1,5km.

S Mondovì 31A3

Piazza le Giardini. **GPS**: n44,39430 e7,82370.
free Chfree. **Location:** Simple, noisy. **Surface:** asphalted.
01/01-31/12
Distance: 500m.
Remarks: Parking under railway bridge.

S Mondovì 31A3

Piazza Repubblica. **GPS**: n44,38964 e7,81930.
free. **Location:** Urban, simple, central. **Surface:** asphalted.
01/01-31/12
Distance: 400m 5km 50m 100m on the spot.
Remarks: Nearby the old station.

S Mondovì 31A3

Mondovicino Outlet Center. GPS: n44,41889 e7,84966.
free Ch. **Location:** Simple. **Surface:** asphalted.
Distance: 4km 1,2km on the spot.
Remarks: Parking at Outlet Center and Centro Commercial.

S Mongrando 24A6

Area Comunale, Via dei Giovanni. **GPS**: n45,52543 e8,00595.

15 € 4/24h Ch included. **Location:** Urban, quiet.
Surface: grasstiles. 01/01-31/12
Distance: 900m.
Remarks: At sports centre.

S Montalto Dora 24A6

La vecchia stazione. GPS: n45,49067 e7,85903.
€ 7/24h Ch. **Surface:** asphalted. 01/01-31/12
Distance: 10km 100m 200m.

S Montiglio Monferrato 31A1

Via Padre Carpignano. **GPS**: n45,06261 e8,10045.
25 free.

S Niella Tanaro 31A2

Agriturismo i Fornelli, Via Fornello 1. **GPS**: n44,41418 e7,90988.

3 €5 €3,50 Ch €2,50/24h WC. **Location:** Rural, simple, isolated, quiet. **Surface:** grassy/gravel. 01/01-31/12
Distance: 4km 2km 1km 10km.
Remarks: Farm products.

S Nizza Monferrato 31B2

Parking Camper Piazzale S.Pertini, Piazzale Sandro Pertini. **GPS**: n44,77140 e8,35346.

14 €5 Ch Service, electricity incl. € 3. **Location:** Urban, comfortable, central, quiet. **Surface:** grassy.
01/01-31/12
Distance: 200m 20km 500m 500m.
Remarks: Gate closed, first call Motorhome Club Nicese between 9-20h.

S Novi Ligure 31B2

Viale Pinan Cichero, zona stadio comunale. **GPS**: n44,77006 e8,78200.

IT

25 free free. **Location:** Urban, simple, noisy. **Surface:** asphalted.
01/01-31/12
Distance: 1,5km 2km on the spot 600m.
Remarks: Parking gymnasium.

S Occimiano 31B1
Via Circonvallazione. **GPS:** n45,05834 e8,50940.

5 € 5 Ch included. **Location:** Rural, comfortable.
Surface: asphalted. 01/01-31/12
Distance: 250m 15km 250m 400m.
Remarks: To be paid at bar Concordia.

S Oggebbio 24C5
Fiesta, Via Martiri Oggebbiesi 6. **GPS:** n45,99680 e8,65304.

20 € 18/24h Ch WC included € 1 € 5,/24h.
Location: Luxurious. **Surface:** gravel.
01/06-31/12
Distance: on the spot 700m.
Remarks: Attention: narrow road, view on Lago Maggiore.

S Omegna 24B5
Lido di Omegna, Via Caduti di Bologna. **GPS:** n45,86340 e8,39840.

25 € 8-15 Ch € 3. **Surface:** metalled. 01/01-31/12
Distance: 1,8km beach.
Remarks: Caution key electricity € 30.

S Ormea 31A3
Via Orti della Rana. **GPS:** n44,14532 e7,90751.

10 € 10 Ch. **Location:** Rural, comfortable, quiet. **Surface:** grasstiles.
01/01-31/12
Distance: 1km 500m 1km.

S Oropa 24A6
Area di Santuari, Via Santuario di Oropa. **GPS:** n45,62864 e7,97530.

31 € 10, 01/05-30/09 € 15, 01/07-31/08 € 21 Ch WC .
Location: Rural. **Surface:** metalled. 01/01-31/12 snow.
Distance: 500m.

S Orta San Giulio 24B6
Via Panoramica. **GPS:** n45,79729 e8,41527.

20 € 10/24h Ch. **Surface:** asphalted. 01/01-31/12
Distance: 500m Lago d'Orta 500m 100m.

Orta San Giulio 24B6
Parco del Sacro Monte, Via Sacro Monte. **GPS:** n45,79732 e8,41204.

8 free. **Surface:** gravel. 01/01-31/12
Distance: 900m 400m.
Remarks: Max. 48h.

S Ovada 31B2
Via Gramsci. **GPS:** n44,64084 e8,64920.

IT

25 free free. **Location:** Simple, central. **Surface:** metalled.
01/01-31/12
Distance: 300m 3km 100m 500m.

Paesana 30D2

Via Roma. **GPS**: n44,68139 e7,27639.

free. **Surface:** grassy.
Distance: on the spot.
Remarks: To provincial route along the left bank of the Po river.

S Piatto 24B6

Area Comunale, Fraz. Malina. **GPS**: n45,58908 e8,13630.

10 free Ch. **Location:** Urban. **Surface:** asphalted.
01/01-31/12
Remarks: At sports park.

S Pietraporzio 30D3

Via Nazionale, SS21. **GPS**: n44,34868 e7,01831.
10 € 5/24h Ch . **Surface:** asphalted. 01/01-31/12

S Pinerolo 30D2

Parco Olimpico, Piazza Carlo Alberto Dalla Chiesa. **GPS**: n44,88917 e7,35111.

10 free Ch (10x)against payment. **Surface:** metalled.
Distance: 300m 300m 200m.
Remarks: Nearby sports park.

S Pollone 24A6

Burcina di Pollone, Via Felice Piacenza. **GPS**: n45,58548 e8,00521.

20 € 10/24h Ch WC included € 2. **Location:** Rural, comfortable. **Surface:** grasstiles. 01/01-31/12
Distance: 600m on the spot.
Remarks: At parco Naturale Burcina.

S Pombia 24C6

Safari Park, SS 32 km 23,4. **GPS**: n45,64167 e8,61740.
free WC. **Surface:** asphalted.

S Ponderano 24B6

Area Comunale, Strada Vicinale al Cimitero. **GPS**: n45,53683 e8,04949.

10 free free. **Location:** Urban, simple. **Surface:** gravel.
01/01-31/12
Distance: 400m.
Remarks: Nearby sports park.

S Pont Canavese 31A1

Via Roma. **GPS**: n45,42153 e7,60020.
12 € 7 € 2 Ch € 2. **Surface:** grassy. 01/01-31/12
Distance: on the spot.
Remarks: Max. 48h.

S Pontechianale 30D2

Area Camper, Fraz Maddalena. **GPS**: n44,62158 e7,02776.
€ 8/24h . **Surface:** grassy.

S Pragelato 30D1

Fraz. Pattemouche, Valtroncea. **GPS**: n44,98736 e6,92090.

€ 8/24h Ch . **Surface:** unpaved. 01/01-31/12
Distance: on the spot.
Remarks: Former camsite, service only during winter period.

S Prali 30D2

Fraz.Ghigo. **GPS**: n44,89150 e7,04982.

IT

free free. **Surface:** grassy.
Distance: 300m on the spot.
Remarks: Nearby SP169, along the river.

S Prato Nevoso 31A3

Area Stalle Lunghe, Via Corona Boreale. **GPS:** n44,25200 e7,78192.

€ 15-20 Ch . **Surface:** asphalted. 01/01-31/12
Distance: on the spot A6 33km on the spot 50m on the spot.

Prato Nevoso 31A3

Piazza G. Dodero. **GPS:** n44,25200 e7,78192.

10 free. **Location:** Rural, simple, central. **Surface:** asphalted. 01/01-31/12
Distance: on the spot on the spot on the spot on the spot.

S Rimasco 24B5

Il Laghetto, Strada del Lago. **GPS:** n45,86109 e8,06450.

20 € 10/24h Ch € 2/day WC included. **Surface:** grassy.
01/05-30/09 Restaurant: Tue.
Distance: on the spot on the spot.

S Riva Valdobbia 24A6

Area Lo Chalet, Fraz Gabbio. **GPS:** n45,83467 e7,95469.

48 € 13/24h Ch € 3 WC included. **Surface:** grassy/metalled.
01/04-31/10
Distance: on the spot on the spot.
Remarks: Along river.

S Rivoli 31A1

Campo sportivo, Via Isonzo. **GPS:** n45,08147 e7,51037.

free free. **Surface:** asphalted.
Distance: 1,5km.
Remarks: Parking sports park.

Rivoli 31A1

Piazzale Mafalda di Savoia. **GPS:** n45,06994 e7,51097.
free. **Surface:** asphalted.
Distance: 500m 2,5km.
Remarks: Parking castle.

S Romano Canavese 31A1

Piazza Bachelet, via Montalenghe, SP82. **GPS:** n45,38782 e7,86396.

8 free (2x). **Surface:** grassy/metalled. 01/01-31/12
Distance: 2,2km.

S Rosta 31A1

Via Buttigliera Alta 2, Via Piave. **GPS:** n45,07106 e7,46333.
free € 2 Ch € 2. **Surface:** asphalted. 01/01-31/12
Distance: on the spot train > Turin 19min.

S Saluzzo 31A2

Distributore AGIP, Via Torino. **GPS:** n44,65609 e7,49798.
free free.
Remarks: At petrol station.

S San Damiano d'Asti 31A2

Via Monsignor Franco. **GPS:** n44,82659 e8,05921.

IT

50 free Ch. **Location:** Rural, simple. **Surface:** gravel.
01/01-31/12
Distance: 1km 1km 1km.
Remarks: At cemetery.

S San Damiano d'Asti 31A2

Azienda Agricola Cascina Piana, Fraz S.Grato. **GPS:** n44,85136 e8,07417.

25 € 8-10 Ch (8x) WC included. **Location:** Rural, comfortable, isolated, quiet. **Surface:** grassy. 01/01-31/12
Distance: 1,5km 1,5km 500m.
Remarks: Farm products.

S Sanfront 30D2

Via Montebracco, SP26. **GPS:** n44,64944 e7,32056.

free Chfree. **Surface:** gravel.
Remarks: At sports park, max. 24h.

S Santa Maria Maggiore 24B5

Area Verde Attrezzata, Via Alfredo Belcastro/via Pineta. **GPS:** n46,13219 e8,45500.

32 € 15/24h Ch . **Location:** Rural.
Surface: gravel.
01/01-31/12
Distance: 200m on the spot.
Remarks: Max. 48h. Follow 'Centro del Fondo'.

S Santa Maria Maggiore 24B5

Agriturismo Al Piano delle Lutte, Via Domodossola 57. **GPS:** n46,13569 e8,44753.

3 € 10/24h Ch consumption WC . **Location:** Rural, simple.
Surface: grassy/gravel. 01/01-31/12
Distance: on the spot.

S Sant'Antonino di Susa 30D1

Area Sosta Il Sentiero Dei Franchi, Borgo Cresto 16/1. **GPS:** n45,09973 e7,27754.
20 € 10/24h Ch . **Surface:** gravel. 01/01-31/12
Distance: on the spot.

S Sant'Antonino di Susa 30D1

Area Sosta Il Sentiero Dei Franchi, Borgo Cresto 16/1. **GPS:** n45,09973 e7,27754.
20 € 10 Ch € 2. **Surface:** grassy/gravel. 01/01-31/12
Distance: on the spot.

S Sestriere 30D1

Lago Losetta, Strada Azzurri d'Italia. **GPS:** n44,96465 e6,88141.
120 € 10/24h Ch . **Surface:** gravel. 01/01-31/12
Distance: 800m Shuttle bus to ski-piste.

S Sommariva Perno 31A2

Area comunale, Loc.Piano, SP0. **GPS:** n44,75126 e7,89667.

10 free Chfree. **Location:** Rural, simple, noisy. **Surface:** gravel.
01/01-31/12
Distance: 500m 13km 250m 250m.

S Susa 30D1

Piazza Repubblica. **GPS:** n45,13861 e7,05389.

12 free Ch free. **Surface:** asphalted. 01/01-31/12
Distance: 300m.

S Tagliolo Monferrato 31B2

Str. del Varo. **GPS:** n44,63760 e8,67029.
21 € 5/24h Ch. **Location:** Rural, simple, quiet.
Surface: grassy/gravel.
01/01-31/12
Distance: 250m 2km 200m 400m.
Remarks: Max. 72 uur, keycard barrier at Bar/Tabac, caution € 10.

S Torino 31A1

Piazza d'Armi, Corso Monte Lungo, Turin (Torino). **GPS:** n45,04848 e7,65651.
25 free Chfree. **Surface:** grassy/metalled.

IT

Distance: city centre 3km on the spot.
Remarks: In opposite of police station.

S Torino 31A1

Corso Casale 327. **GPS**: n45,08084 e7,72993.

free free. **Surface:** asphalted.
Distance: 800m nearby.

S Torino 31A1

Parco Ruffini, Corso Lione/Corso Carlo Piaggia, Turin (Torino). **GPS**: n45,05686 e7,63166.

free free. **Surface:** asphalted.

S Torino 31A1

Strada Castello di Mirafiori/via Artom, zona sud. **GPS**: n45,00900 e7,64873.
free Ch free. **Surface:** asphalted.

Tourist information Turin (Torino):
U.I.A.T. (Ufficio Informazioni e di Accoglienza Turistica), Piazza Castello, 161. Important industrial city with a lot of monuments and museums. Olympic Winter Games 2006.
Mole Antonelliana.National Film museum.
Museo Nazionale dell'Automobile, Corso Unità d'Italia 40.Museum of motor-cars. Tue-Sa, 10-18.30h, Su 10-20.30h Mo.
Palazzo Madame.Historical art.
Palazzo Reale.Royal palace.
Cathedral, 1498.
Basilica di Superga.Baroque basilica.

S Usseaux 30D1

Fraz. Fraisse-Pourrieres, SR23. **GPS**: n45,04170 e6,98518.
€ 15 Ch WC. **Surface:** grassy.

S Usseaux 30D1

Lago del Laux, Via Lago 7. **GPS**: n45,04166 e7,02222.
100 € 10 Ch included € 2. **Surface:** grassy. 01/06-31/10
Distance: 500m 200m 5km.

S Valdieri 30D3

Centro Alpino S.Anna, Loc. S. Anna. **GPS**: n44,24513 e7,32548.

40 € 12 Ch included. **Surface:** grassy/gravel.
Distance: 100m on the spot 100m.
Remarks: Narrow entrance (bridge).

S Valdieri 30D3

Parco Alpi Marittime, Terme di Valdieri. **GPS**: n44,20546 e7,26840.
€ 6 Ch. **Surface:** metalled. 01/01-31/12

S Valle Mosso 24B6

Piazza Alpini d'Italia. **GPS**: n45,63316 e8,14629.

3 free Ch free. **Location:** Urban. **Surface:** asphalted.
01/01-31/12
Distance: on the spot Conad 20m 50m.

S Varallo 24B6

Area Comunale, Via Sant'Antonio. **GPS**: n45,81797 e8,24857.

8 € 10/24h Ch included. **Location:** Urban, quiet. **Surface:** gravel/sand. 01/01-31/12
Distance: 500m 500m.
Remarks: To be paid at town hall.

S Venaria Reale 31A1

Relax and Go, Via Scodeggio 15. **GPS**: n45,14108 e7,62404.
15 € 15 Ch. **Surface:** grassy.
Distance: 650m bus GTT, tram 11>Turin.

S Venasca 31A2

SP8, Via Provinciale. **GPS**: n44,56620 e7,39328.

20 free free. **Surface:** sand.
Distance: 600m.

S Verbania 24B5

Area Comunale, Viale Sant´Anna. **GPS**: n45,92896 e8,56468.

6 free free. **Location:** Urban, simple. **Surface:** asphalted.

IT

01/01-31/12
Distance: on the spot 100m 200m.

S Verbania 24B5

Area Zone Arena, Via San Bernardino. **GPS**: n45,93143 e8,57106.
13 € 10/24h included. **Location:** Simple. **Surface:** asphalted.
01/01-31/12
Distance: 600m 50m 100m 250m.

S Vercelli 31B1

Via Trento, c/o piazzale Pala-hockey. **GPS**: n45,33417 e8,41861.

10 free free. **Location:** Urban, simple. **Surface:** asphalted.
01/01-31/12
Distance: 1,5km 6km 50m 1,5km on the spot.

Tourist information Vercelli:
U.I.A.T. (Ufficio Informazioni e di Accoglienza Turistica), www.turismovalsesiavercelli.it.
Basilica di Sant'Andrea.Basilica, part of abbey.

S Vialfrè 31A1

Via Luigi Emanuel, SP55. **GPS**: n45,38298 e7,81754.

free free. **Surface:** metalled.
Distance: 6km 300m 300m.

S Vidracco 31A1

Damanhur Crea, Via Baldissero 21. **GPS**: n45,42884 e7,75327.

€ 8/24h Ch (24x) WC included. **Surface:** asphalted.
Distance: cafetaria on the spot.

Tourist information Vidracco:
Damanhur Crea, Via Baldissero 21.Extraordinary Italian artistic and spritual community.

S Villar Focchiardo 30D1

Area Camper Villar Focchiardo, Via Fratta, SS24. **GPS**: n45,11336 e7,22408.

52 € 5, weekend € 8 Chfree. **Surface:** grassy.
01/01-31/12 camper service: 01/11-31/03.
Distance: 4,5km.

Tourist information Villar Focchiardo:
Susa.Small medieval mountain village.

S Villar Pellice 30D2

Parco Flissia, Via Cave del Fin. **GPS**: n44,80472 e7,15083.

€ 6 free. **Surface:** grassy.
Distance: on the spot on the spot fishing permit obligatory agriturismo.
Remarks: Nearby SP161.

S Vinadio 30D3

Area di Sosta Communale, Bagni di Vinadio, Fraz. Strapesi. **GPS**: n44,28747 e7,07534.

30 € 11/24h Ch free. **Surface:** gravel.
Distance: 300m on the spot on the spot.
Remarks: Parking at the spa resort of Strapeis, altitude 1350m.

S Vinadio 30D3

Piazza d'Armi, SS21. **GPS**: n44,30667 e7,17083.

1/6-31/8 € 5 Chfree. **Surface:** asphalted.
Distance: 400m.

S Volpedo 31C2

Lungo Curone Matteotti. **GPS**: n44,88512 e8,98707.

IT

6 free Chfree. **Surface:** grassy/gravel.
Distance: 600m.
Remarks: At sports park.

S Zubiena 24A6
Prà Gros Agriturismo, SS338, Casale Montino. **GPS:** n45,49812 e7,98934.

6 . **Location:** Rural. **Surface:** gravel/metalled.
Distance: on the spot.

Trentino South Tyrol

S Andalo 25C4
Via Rindole, 6, Loc. Rindole. **GPS:** n46,16113 e11,00647.

80 € 15 Ch € 5. **Surface:** asphalted. summer
Distance: 200m on the spot.
Remarks: Beautiful view, service only € 5.

Arco 25B5
Piazzale Carmellini, Viale Paolina Caproni. **GPS:** n45,92232 e10,89032.

13 € 1/4h, max. € 10/24h. **Surface:** asphalted. 01/01-31/12
Distance: 200m 200m.

S Arco 25B5
Viale Rovereto. **GPS:** n45,91820 e10,89225.
Chfree.

S Barbiano 25C3
Kollmann Stop, Frazione Colma, SS12. **GPS:** n46,58728 e11,52401.

15 € 10, in envelope in mail box Ch included. **Location:** Simple, noisy. **Surface:** gravel. 01/01-31/12
Distance: 300m 9km 300m 300m on the spot on the spot.
Remarks: Max. 48h, along the through road.

S Bolzano/Bozen 25C4
Parking Fiera Messe, Via Bruno Buozzi. **GPS:** n46,47417 e11,32617.

30 free Chfree. **Location:** Urban, simple, noisy. **Surface:** asphalted. 01/01-31/12
Distance: centre 4km 1,1km on the spot 4km on the spot.
Remarks: Along railwayline.

S Bolzano/Bozen 25C4
Via Maso della Pieve. **GPS:** n46,47327 e11,33693.

8 € 0,70/h mo-fr 8-19h, sa 8-13, overnight stay free Ch. **Location:** Urban, simple, noisy. **Surface:** asphalted. 01/01-31/12
Distance: city centre 3km 100m on the spot.

S Borgo Valsugana 25C5
Via Tommaso Temanza. **GPS:** n46,05444 e11,46361.

18 € 10/24h Ch included. **Surface:** metalled.
Distance: 100m 20m 20m 100m 100m.
Remarks: Max. 48h, service only € 5.

Braies 25D3
P2, Lago di Braies, Fraz. San Vito. **GPS:** n46,70265 e12,08520.

IT

25 € 5-15 € 0,50. **Location:** Rural, simple, quiet. **Surface:** gravel. 30/05-31/10
Distance: Braies 5km Lago di Braies 250m 250m 5km on the spot on the spot.

Brentonico 25C5

Via al Dosset. **GPS**: n45,81540 e10,95581.

11 € 7 € 2 Ch € 3. **Surface:** asphalted. 01/01-31/12
Distance: 400m 10km 250m 300m.

Brunico/Bruneck 25D3

P2, Piazza Mercato di Stegona. **GPS**: n46,79558 e11,93006.

>25 free. **Location:** Urban, simple, noisy. **Surface:** gravel. 01/01-31/12
Distance: 800m 500m 500m on the spot on the spot on the spot.

Tourist information Brunico/Bruneck:

Associazione Turistica, Via Europa,24.Fortified city, 14th century.
Regional museum.
Annual fair. last week Oct.

Caldes 25B4

Rafting Val di Sole, Loc. Contrè. **GPS**: n46,36139 e10,94528.

30 € 10, Jul € 13, Aug € 15 € 6. **Surface:** asphalted. 01/04-30/09
Distance: 2km 200m 2km.

Caldonazzo 25C5

Via al Lago. **GPS**: n46,00501 e11,26307.

20 € 6/21-9h (1/6-30/9). **Surface:** grassy/sand. 01/01-31/12
Distance: 500m 300m.

Cavalese 25C4

P Fondovalle, SP232. **GPS**: n46,28438 e11,47256.

50 € 10 . **Location:** Simple. **Surface:** grasstiles/metalled. 01/01-31/12

Chiusa 25C3

Gamp, Via Gries 10. **GPS**: n46,64128 e11,57244.

20 € 14/24h 2 pers. + 2 children incl, dog € 2 Ch included.
Location: Rural, simple. **Surface:** grassy. 01/01-31/12
Distance: 300m 800m on the spot mini market 100m on the spot on the spot.

Corvara in Badia 25D3

P Corvara, Strada Planac SS244. **GPS**: n46,54105 e11,88388.

10 free. **Location:** Rural, simple, isolated. **Surface:** gravel. 01/01-31/12
Distance: 3,5km 3,5km.

Dimaro 25B4

Camper Solander, Loc. Rovina. **GPS**: n46,32488 e10,86215.

IT

10 € 20/24h, € 10/night Ch WC included. **Surface:** gravel. 01/01-31/12
Distance: on the spot.
Remarks: Near campsite Dolomiti.

Dimaro 25B4

Hotel Belvedere, SS239. **GPS:** n46,29734 e10,86765.
€ 15/24h Ch included. **Surface:** asphalted. 01/01-31/12

Folgaria 25C5

Parcheggio, Via Andrea Maffei, SS350, Fraz. Costa. **GPS:** n45,91688 e11,18656.

20 free. **Surface:** gravel. 01/01-31/12
Distance: on the spot 100m 100m on the spot on the spot.

Gargazzone 25C3

Weisshof-Törgelle-Keller, Landstrasse 65 SS38. **GPS:** n46,58500 e11,20528.

10 € 10 Ch € 2/24h WC € 1. **Location:** Rural, simple, quiet.
Surface: grassy/gravel.
01/01-31/12
Distance: 2km 1,5km 500m 2km on the spot on the spot on the spot.
Remarks: Reservation for Christmas holidays, tel.: +39 (0)473 292448.

Tourist information Gargazzone:
Consorzio Turistico, Via Maria Trost, 5, Merano, www.meranerland.com.Place with medicinal sources.
Castel Tirolo, 4km N. de Merano.Regional museum. 01/03-31/12.
Merano. Tue, Fri.
Festa della Città, Merano. 1st weekend Aug.

Glorenza 25B3

Glurms Camping im Park, > SS41. **GPS:** n46,67067 e10,54520.

40 € 10/12 Ch € 2 WC . **Surface:** grassy.
Distance: 500m on the spot.
Remarks: Along the Adige river.

La Villa in Badia 25D3

Odlina, Strada Ninz, 49. **GPS:** n46,58889 e11,90028.

45 summer € 20, winter € 30 Ch WC included € 5 € 3.
Location: Rural, luxurious, quiet. **Surface:** metalled. 01/01-31/12
Distance: 400m 150m 150m on the spot on the spot on the spot 300m.
Remarks: Use of sauna against payment, reservation for Christmas holidays: info@odina.it.

Lago 25C4

Via Tresselume. **GPS:** n46,28291 e11,52557.

30 free € 1 € 2 Ch € 1 (12x) € 2/8h. **Location:** Rural, simple.
Surface: metalled. 01/01-31/12
Distance: 200m 200m.

Lavarone 25C5

Prà Grando, Via Padova. **GPS:** n45,93602 e11,27099.

40 € 14 May/June/July, € 15 Aug, € 18 Dec-April Ch included.
Surface: grassy/gravel. 01/05-30/09, 01/12-31/03
Distance: 300m 32km Lago di Lavarone 1km 1km 300m 300m 300m 1km 1km.

Lavarone 25C5

SS 349, Loc Moar. **GPS:** n45,94575 e11,26397.

10 € 0,40/h € 0,50 Ch. Location: **Location:** Simple.
Surface: metalled.
Distance: 800m Lago di Lavarone 1,9km 500m.

S Levico Terme 25C5

Lago di Levico, Loc Pleina. **GPS**: n46,00655 e11,28793.

35 € 15 Ch WC. **Surface:** grassy. 01/01-31/12
Distance: 1,3km 200m, Lido di Levico 1,1km 50m 50m on the spot.

S Levico Terme 25C5

Bici Grill, Via Antonio Tararotti. **GPS**: n46,00099 e11,24571.

6 guests free Ch.

S Moena 25D4

Bar Il Giardino, SS 48 Forno di Moena. **GPS**: n46,35238 e11,63149.

50 € 10-12 Ch included € 4/24h. **Location:** Rural, comfortable, central. **Surface:** grassy/metalled. 01/01-31/12
Distance: 3,5km 500m 2km 300m on the spot on the spot on the spot.
Remarks: Max. 48h, skibus comes at parking.

S Molveno 25B4

Area attrezzata per camper Lago di Molveno, Via Lungolago, 25, Loc. Ischia. **GPS**: n46,14018 e10,96011.

50 € 12, € 18 (24/12-9/1, 23/4-24/6, 4/9-1/10), € 26 (25/6-3/9) Ch included. **Surface:** metalled. 01/01-31/12
Distance: 800m 200m 200m 100m.

S Molveno 25B4

Via Lungolago,Loc. Ischia. **GPS**: n46,14165 e10,95727.

20 € 9, € 14 (24/12-9/1, 23/4-24/6, 4/9-1/10), € 22 (25/6-3/9) Ch included. **Surface:** metalled. 01/01-31/12
Distance: 1km 400m 200m 100m.

S Pergine Valsugana 25C5

Soleando Camperparking, Via al lago 23/A. **GPS**: n46,05184 e11,22494.

10 €12/day Ch.
Surface: gravel.
Distance: 600m lake 1km 300m 300m 100m.
Remarks: Dir 'Lago di Caldenazzo'.

Tourist information Pergine Valsugana:
I www.apt.trento.it.City at the foot of the Dolomites with historical centre.
M Palazzo Pretorio, Trento.Ecclesiastical museum.

S Predazzo 25D4

Latemar 2200, SS48, dir Moena. **GPS**: n46,32582 e11,59970.

50 free, peak season € 7-10/24h Ch included. **Location:** Rural, simple, noisy. **Surface:** asphalted/gravel. 01/01-31/12
Distance: 2,5km 2,5km on the spot on the spot on the spot on the spot on the spot.
Remarks: Parking ski-lifts.

IT

Rabbi — 25B4

Area camper Plan, Loc. Plan, Bagni di Rabbi. **GPS**: n46,40619 e10,82629.

105 € 14-21, 2 pers.incl. Ch WC included against payment.
Surface: metalled. 01/06-30/09
Distance: 600m.
Remarks: Former campsite, max. 48h.

Racines — 25C3

Sportzone Ratschings, Belprato, Stanghe. **GPS**: n46,88254 e11,38383.

20 free. **Location:** Rural, simple. **Surface:** gravel.
01/01-31/12
Distance: 400m 5km 400m 400m 400m
Gilfenklammroute.

IT

Riva del Garda — 25B5

Via Monte Brione. **GPS**: n45,87986 e10,85872.

41 € 8/day Ch included. **Surface:** grasstiles.
Distance: 1,5km 200m.
Remarks: Max. 48h.

Tourist information Riva del Garda:
A.P.T. (Azienda di Promozione Turistica), Giardini di Porta Orientale 8, www.gardatrentino.de.Tourist town at Lake Garda.
Museo Civico, Piazza Battisti.

Rovereto — 25C5

Stadio Quercia, Via Palestrina. **GPS**: n45,90232 e11,03704.

8 free Ch free. **Surface:** asphalted. 01/01-31/12
Distance: 1,5km 2km.

Tourist information Rovereto:
A.P.T. (Azienda di Promozione Turistica), Via Dante, 63, www.apt.rovereto.tn.it.
Castello di Rovereto.War museum. Tue-Su 01/01-28/02.
Castel Beseno. Tue-Su.

San Candido — 26A3

Area di Sosta Camper, Via Prato alla Drava, 1/A. **GPS**: n46,73924 e12,36559.

90 € 15 Ch WC included € 2.
Location: Rural, comfortable, quiet. **Surface:** gravel.
01/01 - 31/12
Distance: 6km on the spot 500m on the spot on the spot on the spot 2km 500m.
Remarks: Bicycle rental. Nearby the frontier station.

San Guiseppe al Lago — 25C4

Posteggio Camper Lago di Caldero, San Guiseppe 18. **GPS**: n46,39038 e11,25663.

35 € 15/night Ch WC . **Location:** Rural, comfortable, quiet.
Surface: gravel. 13/03-15/11
Distance: 5km Caldero Private beach 50m Nearby campsite.
Remarks: Max. 4 days.

San Martino di Castrozza — 25D4

Area camper Tognola, Loc.Tognola. **GPS**: n46,25373 e11,80158.

80 € 12 included Ch € 1/80minutes. **Location:** Rural, comfortable, quiet. **Surface:** gravel. 01/01-31/12
Distance: 1,5km 500m on the spot on the spot on the spot.
Remarks: Next to ski-lift, free shuttle bus.

San Vigilio di Marebbe — 25D3

Restaurant Pizzeria Rittenkeller, Ras-Costa 2. **GPS**: n46,70630 e11,92920.

120 01/04-30/11 € 20, 01/12-31/03 € 25 Ch included.
Location: Rural, simple, quiet. **Surface:** gravel.
01/01-31/12
Distance: 600m 500m on the spot 600m 600m on the spot 600m.
Remarks: Next to ski-lift, reservation for Christmas holidays: info@ritterkeller.it.

Santa Cristina Valgardena 25D3

P1 Monte Pana, Strada Pana. **GPS**: n46,55174 e11,71624.

50 free, peak season € 4/day. **Location:** Simple, isolated, quiet.
Surface: gravel. 01/01-31/12
Distance: 2,5km 2,5km.
Remarks: Max. 7 days, narrow entrance road, altitude 1650m.

Selva di Val Gardena 25D3

Piz Sella, Strada Plan de Gralba. **GPS**: n46,53204 e11,77230.

15 free, Winter € 6/day, € 6 night. **Location:** Rural, simple. **Surface:** gravel.
01/01-31/12
Distance: 4km 150m on the spot on the spot.
Remarks: Inclining pitches.

Sesto/Sexten 26A3

Caravanpark Sexten, SS52 St Josefstrasse 54. **GPS**: n46,66741 e12,39996.

36 € 23-29 Ch WC included € 4 € 2. **Location:** Rural, luxurious, quiet. **Surface:** grasstiles. 01/01-31/12
Distance: 3km on the spot on the spot on the spot on the spot on the spot 900m on the spot.
Remarks: Sauna and spa.

Silandro 25B3

Via Ospedale, Silandro/. **GPS**: n46,62721 e10,78185.

free. **Surface:** grasstiles.
Distance: 500m 500m.

Siusi 25C3

Seiseralm, Via Rosegarten. **GPS**: n46,54048 e11,56600.

>25 free WC. **Location:** Rural, simple, quiet. **Surface:** gravel.
Distance: 500m on the spot 500m on the spot on the spot on the spot.
Remarks: Parking at Seiseralm-lift.

Smarano 25C4

Area Sosta Ostaria del Filò, Viale Merlonga 48/a. **GPS**: n46,34962 e11,10956.

43 € 10-13-15 Ch WC . **Surface:** grassy. 01/01-31/12
Distance: 1km on the spot.
Remarks: Check in at restaurant.

Solda 25B4

GPS: n46,51448 e10,59578.
25 free. **Location:** Simple. **Surface:** gravel. 01/01-31/12
Distance: 1km 100m on the spot on the spot.

Tirolo 25C3

Via principale. **GPS**: n46,68636 e11,15904.

15 € 10,50/night WC. **Location:** Rural, simple, quiet.
Surface: asphalted. 01/01-31/12
Distance: 200m 50m 200m 50m on the spot on the spot.

IT

Tirolo 25C3

Schneeburghof, Monte Benedetto 26. **GPS**: n46,67789 e11,16495.

20 € 23 Ch included. **Location:** Comfortable. **Surface:** grassy.
Distance: on the spot.

Tonadico 25D4

Lanterna Verde, Via Zocchet 10. **GPS**: n46,18216 e11,84318.

45 € 15 Ch included WC. **Location:** Rural, comfortable, quiet.
Surface: grasstiles. 01/01-31/12
Distance: 1km 100m 1km on the spot on the spot on the spot 15km 15km.
Remarks: Max. 48h, check in at restaurant.

Trento 25C5

P Zuffo, Loc. Vela. **GPS**: n46,07650 e11,11050.

20 € 5 € 1 Ch. **Surface:** asphalted. 01/01-31/12
Distance: 1,8km 150m 200m.
Remarks: A22, slip-road Trento Centro.

Trento 25C5

Parking Trentino, Via Santi Cosma e Damiano 64. **GPS**: n46,07674 e11,10411.

20 € 15 Ch included. **Surface:** grassy. 01/01-31/12
Distance: 1,8km 300m 300m.
Remarks: Call for entrance code: 3389004343 Mr. Pisetta.

Trento 25C5

P3 Giardino Botanico Fondo Viote, SP85. **GPS**: n46,02445 e11,03973.

100 free. **Location:** Rural, simple, isolated, quiet. **Surface:** asphalted.
01/01-31/12
Distance: 18km Trento 150m.
Remarks: Max. 48h.

Tourist information Trento:

I.A.T. (Ufficio Informazioni e di Accoglienza Turistica), Via Romagnosi, 3.

Tres 25C4

A Monte del Paese, SP della Predaia. **GPS**: n46,32040 e11,10202.

15 € 10/24h Ch WC included. **Surface:** gravel.
01/01-31/12
Distance: 800m.

Lombardy

Alzano Lombardo 24D6

Via Europa. **GPS**: n45,73690 e9,72007.

3 . **Surface:** asphalted.
Remarks: At sports park.

Biassono 24D6

Via al Parco/Via della Sciavatera. **GPS**: n45,63102 e9,28865.

free Ch free. **Surface:** asphalted. 01/01-31/12
Distance: 500m Centro Commerciale Vilasanta 4km train > Milan 500m.

Borgofranco sul Po 32A1

Via Filipo Turati. **GPS**: n45,04775 e11,20524.

IT

free Chfree. **Surface:** grassy.
01/01-31/12 water: frost.
Distance: 600m 200m.

S Bormio 25A4

Bormio 2000, Via Battaglion Morbegno. **GPS**: n46,46260 e10,37190.

€ 8/24h Chincluded. **Surface:** sand. 01/01-31/12
Distance: 500m 500m on the spot.
Remarks: Parking funicular railway, service only € 5.

Tourist information Bormio:

Ufficio Informazioni e di Accoglienza Turistica, Via Roma, 131/b.Alps city, large winter sport area, also summer skiing.

Parco Nazionale dello Stelvio.Region with 50 glacier lakes and high mountain peaks. Access around Bormio.

S Campione 25B5

Area Camper Campione del Garda, Via Verdi. **GPS**: n45,75651 e10,74985.

30 € 10/24h . **Surface:** unpaved. 01/04-31/10
Distance: 500m on the spot 200m.

S Capo di Ponte 25A5

Concarena, Via Santo Stefano. **GPS**: n46,02447 e10,34325.

12 € 8/24h, 1/10-28/2 free Ch WC included.
Surface: asphalted. 01/01-31/12
Distance: 300m 300m 300m.

S Certosa di Pavia 31C1

Parking Certosa, Via di Vittorio, SP27. **GPS**: n45,25702 e9,14152.

€ 4/night, € 4/day Chfree. **Surface:** gravel.
01/01-31/12 water disconnected in winter.
Distance: 200m.
Remarks: Monastery Certosa di Pavia 450m.

S Certosa di Pavia 31C1

Località Certosa Monumento. **GPS**: n45,25574 e9,14632.

€ 4/night, € 4/day Ch WCfree. **Surface:** sand.
01/01-31/12
Distance: 500m.
Remarks: Monastery Certosa di Pavia 80m.

S Chiavenna 24D4

Piazzale Leonardo da Vinci, Via A. Moro, SS36. **GPS**: n46,31424 e9,39631.

free Chfree. **Surface:** asphalted.
Distance: 800m 200m.

Tourist information Chiavenna:

U.I.A.T.(Ufficio Informazioni e Accoglienza Turistica), Via Vittorio Emanuele II, 2.

S Chiesa in Valmalenco 25A4

Loc. Vassalini. **GPS**: n46,27020 e9,85670.

free € 3. **Surface:** gravel.
Distance: 1km 200m.

S Clusone 25A5

Busgarina, Via Vago 6, loc Fiorine. **GPS**: n45,87312 e9,91642.

IT

80 € 13 Ch (33x)€ 2 € 1/7minutes. 01/01-31/12
Distance: on the spot.

S Clusone 25A5

Viale Vittorio Veneto. **GPS**: n45,88926 e9,95812.

5 free Chfree. **Surface:** asphalted.
Distance: Nearby centre on the spot.
Remarks: Max. 48h.

S Colico 24D5

L'Ontano, Via Montecchio Nord. **GPS**: n46,14213 e9,37452.

25 € 15/24h Ch WC € 1/3minutes. **Surface:** metalled. 01/02-31/12
Distance: 500m on the spot on the spot.
Remarks: View on Lake Como.

S Cremona 31D1

Piazzale della Croce Rossa, Via Mantova. **GPS**: n45,13744 e10,03464.

free Chfree. **Surface:** asphalted. 01/01-31/12
Distance: on the spot 3km on the spot 200m on the spot.
Remarks: Nearby stadium.

S Desenzano del Garda 25B6

Pit-Stop La Spiaggia, Via Valtenesi, 19. **GPS**: n45,48783 e10,52468.

70 € 10/24h Chincluded. **Surface:** gravel. 01/01-31/12
Distance: 200m Pizzeria Stella Del Garda 10m.

S Esine 25A5

Parco e Ristorante Le Fontanelle, Via Toroselle 12, SS42. **GPS**: n45,90302 e10,21820.

15 Ch. **Surface:** grassy. 01/01-31/12
Distance: 4km on the spot.

S Gandino 25A5

Via Giovanni Pascoli. **GPS**: n45,81286 e9,90538.

2 free Chfree. **Surface:** metalled. 01/01-31/12
Distance: historical centre 250m.
Remarks: Max. 48h.

S Gavirate 24C5

Via Cavour. **GPS**: n45,83913 e8,72105.

30 € 8/day Ch € 1/12h. **Surface:** grassy/metalled. 01/01-31/12
Distance: 200m 10m.

S Germignaga 24C5

Via A. Bodmer. **GPS**: n45,99630 e8,72421.

IT

6 € 15/24h € 2 Ch € 2. **Surface:** asphalted. 01/01-31/12
Distance: 500m on the spot 500m.

Iseo 25A6

Via Gorzoni. **GPS**: n45,65360 e10,04379.

free. **Surface:** unpaved. 01/01-31/12
Distance: 1km 250m 600m.

Tourist information Iseo:
I.A.T. (Ufficio Informazioni e di Accoglienza Turistica), Lungolago Marconi, 2.Old fishermen's village.
Week market. Fri.

Lecco 24D5

Via Arturo Toscanini, Loc. Bione di Lecco. **GPS**: n45,83136 e9,40779.

12 free Chfree. **Surface:** asphalted.
Distance: 2,8km.
Remarks: At lake Garlate, cycle routes.

Livigno 25A4

Stella Alpina, Via Palipert 570. **GPS**: n46,50515 e10,11958.

28 € 15 Ch € 3 WC . **Surface:** gravel. 01/01-31/12
Distance: 400m Free bus.

Livigno 25A4

Trepalle, SS301. **GPS**: n46,52655 e10,17578.

50 € 10 Chfree. **Surface:** asphalted.
Distance: Livigno 6,6km 200m bus to Livigno every 40 minutes on the spot.

Tourist information Livigno:
U.A.I.T.(Ufficio Informazioni e Accoglienza Turistica), Via Saroch.
Latteria di Livigno, Via Pemonte 911.Discover the secrets of dairy products from Livigno. On Wednesday the possibility of preparing meals, costs € 7, from 14h. summer Mo-Fr 8-20h.

Lodrino 25A6

Via Kennedy, Localité Dade. **GPS**: n45,71450 e10,28107.

3 free Ch free. **Surface:** asphalted. 01/01-31/12
Distance: 500m.

Luino 24C5

Via Gorizia. **GPS**: n45,97406 e8,75019.

16 € 9 € 3. **Surface:** asphalted/grassy. 01/01-31/12
Distance: 3km on the spot.
Remarks: Next to sports fields.

Magnacavallo 32A1

Via Salvador Allende. **GPS**: n45,00587 e11,17906.

free Chfree. **Surface:** asphalted. 01/01-31/12
Distance: 200m.
Remarks: At sports park.

Mandello del Lario 24D5

Area Cima, Via Giulio Cesare. **GPS**: n45,91830 e9,31589.

IT

12 free Ch. **Surface:** asphalted. 01/01-31/12
Distance: 800m Lago di Lecco 400m.

Mantova 32A1

Parco Paganini, Via Fiera 11, Grazie di Curtatone, Curtatone. **GPS:** n45,15333 e10,69111.

108 € 10 € 3 Ch € 3 WC included. **Surface:** asphalted/grassy.
01/03-13/11
Distance: 300m, Mantova 6km 300m 4km, bakery 300m.

Mantova 32A1

Sparafucile, Via Legnago 1/a. **GPS:** n45,16336 e10,81244.
54 € 10/12-12h, € 15/24h Ch included WC . **Location:** Luxurious. **Surface:** grassy/metalled. 01/01-31/12
Distance: 1km 4km.

Mantova 32A1

Anconetta. **GPS:** n45,15322 e10,79864.

free. **Surface:** asphalted. 01/01-31/12
Distance: on the spot.
Remarks: Marina.

Tourist information Mantova:
I.A.T. (Ufficio Informazioni e di Accoglienza Turistica), Piazza Mantegna, 6, www.mantova.it.

Merate 24D6

Via Papa Giovanni Paolo I, loc. Sartirana. **GPS:** n45,71326 e9,41865.

7 € 5,50 Ch . **Surface:** grasstiles.

Milano 31C1

Ripamonti SNC, Via Ripamonti 481, Milan (Milano). **GPS:** n45,40914 e9,20937.

30 € 20/24h Ch € 5 WC included. **Surface:** asphalted.
Distance: on the spot Milan 40min.
Remarks: Monitored parking.

Tourist information Milan (Milano):
U.I.A.T. (Ufficio Informazioni e di Accoglienza Turistica), Via Marcon, 1, www.milanoinfotourist.it.Large city and economic heart of the country.
Castello Sforzesco.
Palazzo Reale.Contemporary art.
Duomo.History of Gothic architecture. Tue-Su.
Via Fauché. Tue, Sa.
Mercatone del Naviglio Grande, Naviglio Grande.Antiques market, 400 stalls. last Su of the month.
Galleria.

Moglia 32A1

Via Tazio Nuvolari. **GPS:** n44,93639 e10,91582.

14 free Ch free. **Surface:** asphalted. 01/01-31/12
Distance: 300m A22 7km 300m.
Remarks: At swimming pool.

Monte Marenzo 24D6

Via Papa Gionvanni. **GPS:** n45,77639 e9,45222.

6 free free. **Surface:** gravel. 01/01-31/12
Distance: 300m.

Monzambano 25B6

Area attrezzata camper Comunale di Monzambano, Via Degli Alpini n. 9. **GPS:** n45,38916 e10,69277.

IT

140 € 12/24h (24x) included € 1/12h. **Surface:** gravel.
01/01-31/12
Distance: 100m 300m, bakery 100m.
Remarks: Max. 48h.

Tourist information Monzambano:
I.A.T. (Ufficio Informazioni e di Accoglienza Turistica), Piazza Tito Zaniboni, 2.

Morbegno 24D5

Area Sosta Camper Morbegno, Via del Foss. **GPS:** n46,14419 e9,57500.
22 € 10 Ch included. **Location:** Rural. **Surface:** grasstiles.
01/01-31/12
Distance: historical centre 500m 100m Skibus on the spot.

Niardo 25A5

Area di sosta Mr. Sanders, Località Crist. **GPS:** n45,97690 e10,31959.

20 € 10 Ch € 2 WC . **Surface:** metalled. 01/01-31/12
Distance: Niardo 1,3km on the spot on the spot.
Remarks: Bread-service.

Nova Milanese 24D6

Via G. Brodolini. **GPS:** n45,58298 e9,19668.

4 free free. **Surface:** asphalted. 01/01-31/12
Distance: 500m 1,6km 200m.

Novate Mezzola 24D4

Via al Lido. **GPS:** n46,21083 e9,45000.

25 free. **Surface:** grassy/gravel.
Distance: 800m 40m 800m.
Remarks: At lake Novate, signposted cycle route.

Olginate 24D6

Via Cesare Cantù. **GPS:** n45,79523 e9,41610.

46 € 8/12h Ch . **Surface:** metalled.
01/01-31/12 Thu>16h-Fri<16h (market).
Distance: 200m on the spot.
Remarks: At Olginate lake.

Pizzighettone 31D1

Via De Gasperi. **GPS:** n45,18538 e9,79402.

4 free Chfree. **Surface:** gravel. 01/01-31/12
Distance: 400m Lidl 100m.

Rovetta 25A5

Campo sportivo, Via Papa Giovanni XIII. **GPS:** n45,88892 e9,98224.

free Ch. **Surface:** asphalted.
Remarks: Parking at gymnasium.

Ruino 31C1

Agriturismo Adriana Tarantani, Loc. Tre Venti. **GPS:** n44,92833 e9,26311.

6 free with a meal Ch . **Surface:** grassy/gravel.
01/01-31/12
Distance: 1km on the spot.

Sabbioneta 32A1

Via Piccola Atene. **GPS:** n44,99459 e10,48849.

IT

15 free free. **Surface:** metalled. 01/01-31/12
Distance: 200m 400m.

S Santa Caterina Valfurva 25B4

Baita de Naségn, Via Forni, loc. Nassegno. **GPS:** n46,40917 e10,50833.

€ 12 Ch € 3. **Surface:** grassy.
Distance: on the spot on the spot.

Tourist information Santa Caterina Valfurva:
I.A.T. (Ufficio Informazioni e di Accoglienza Turistica), Piazza Magliavaca.

S Saronno 24C6

Via E.H.Griegh. **GPS:** n45,61265 e9,04274.

free € 1/100liter Ch. **Surface:** asphalted. 01/01-31/12
Distance: 1,5km 3,5km 500m 200m.

Saronno 24C6

Via Dalmazia 11. **GPS:** n45,62446 e9,02469.

2 free. **Surface:** concrete. 01/01-31/12
Remarks: Max. 24h.

S Sartirana Lomellina 31B1

Via Cavour. **GPS:** n45,11337 e8,66936.

3 free Chfree. **Surface:** asphalted.
01/01-31/12 Sa-morning market.
Distance: 100m 200m 100m on the spot.

S Seriate 24D6

Corso Europa. **GPS:** n45,67920 e9,72897.

free Chfree. **Surface:** asphalted.
Distance: 700m 50m.
Remarks: In front of supermarket UNES.

S Sirmione 25B6

Camper Park Sirmione, Via Cantarane. **GPS:** n45,46083 e10,63333.

150 € 20/24h, € 11/20.30-9.30h Ch € 3 included.
Surface: gravel. 15/03-31/10
Distance: 1,5km Lake Garda 100m 1km 100m.

S Sirmione 25B6

Piazzale Montebaldo. **GPS:** n45,48694 e10,61028.

21 from € 2,50 1/2h till-€ 21/24h Ch WC. **Surface:** asphalted. 01/01-31/12
Distance: 200m on the spot 50m 200m.
Remarks: Parking on entering the village, in opposite of castle.

Tourist information Sirmione:
I.A.T. (Ufficio Informazioni e di Accoglienza Turistica), Viale Marconi, 2.City around medieval castle.

S Sondrio 25A5

Area Sportiva, Via Vanoni. **GPS:** n46,16064 e9,86957.

6 free Ch free. **Surface:** asphalted.
Distance: 600m.
Remarks: Parking sports park.

S Sorico 24D5

La Punta, Boschetto III Traversa. **GPS**: n46,16386 e9,38158.

53 € 18/day € 2/kWh WC € 1. **Surface:** metalled.
01/01-31/12
Distance: 400m on the spot on the spot.
Remarks: View on Lake Como.

S Stezzano 24D6

Via Pietro Mascagni. **GPS**: n45,65594 e9,65301.

free Ch free. **Surface:** asphalted.

S Sulzano 25A6

Parking Gerolo, Via Tassano 14. **GPS**: n45,63546 e10,07665.

25 € 13/24h, € 15/24h (1/3-30/9), € 10/night Ch WC.
Surface: grassy. 01/01-31/12
Distance: 300m 400m 300m.

S Ternate 24C6

Via Roma. **GPS**: n45,78006 e8,69780.

8 free Ch (2x)free. **Surface:** unpaved. 01/01-31/12
Distance: on the spot 100m on the spot on the spot.
Remarks: At Comabbio lake.

S Tirano 25A4

Area Camper Tirano, Via Polveriera/Via Sala Piero. **GPS**: n46,21361 e10,15722.

20 € 10/24h Ch included. **Location:** Comfortable. **Surface:** metalled.
Distance: 1km station 800m.

Tourist information Tirano:

Bernina Express.The highest-altitude trans-Alpine line in Europe, with one of the steepest gradients in the world between Tirano (It) and Chur (Ch). UNESCO's List of World Heritage. ± € 100/pp return ticket (Tirano-Chur), ± € 45/pp return ticket (Tirano-Pontresina).

S Torbole 25B5

Tr@ns.it, Via Al Cor. **GPS**: n45,87264 e10,87260.

120 € 30/24h, € 48/48h Ch WC included. **Surface:** grassy.
01/01-31/12
Distance: on the spot on the spot on the spot on the spot.
Remarks: Along Lake Garda, max. 48h.

S Toscolano Maderno 25B6

Area Sosta Maderno, Via Promontorio. **GPS**: n45,63487 e10,61103.

25 € 25 Ch WC included. **Surface:** grassy. 01/01-31/12
Distance: 500m.

IT

Treviglio 24D6

Via al Malgari. **GPS**: n45,53142 e9,59710.

4 free Chfree. **Surface:** metalled. 01/01-31/12

Distance: 700m 400m.

Remarks: At sports park.

Varzi 31C2

Strada Circonvallazione. **GPS**: n44,82172 e9,19727.

30 free, summer € 10 Chfree. **Surface:** asphalted/metalled.
01/01-31/12

Distance: 200m on the spot.

Remarks: Along the Staffora river.

Veneto

Arquà Polesine 32B1

Ostello Canalbianco, SS 16, n15. **GPS**: n44,99665 e11,76243.

12 € 10 .

Distance: on the spot.

Asiago 25C5

P Verdi Mosele, SS349, Via Giuseppe Verdi. **GPS**: n45,87129 e11,50026.

20 € 1/h, € 4/day. **Surface:** asphalted. 01/01-31/12

Distance: 300m 500m.

Asolo 25D5

Area Camper Communale, Via Forestuzzo. **GPS**: n45,79637 e11,91283.

12 € 7 Ch (14x)included. **Surface:** grassy/sand.
01/01-31/12

Distance: 400m 400m 400m.

Remarks: Access 8-19.30h, barbecue place, picnic area.

Auronzo di Cadore 26A3

Taiarezze, SR48, Via Reaneloc. **GPS**: n46,56217 e12,41640.

30 € 8, 20/07-31/08 and 24/12-06/01 € 12 Chincluded. **Location:** Rural, simple, quiet. **Surface:** asphalted. 01/01-31/12

Distance: 1,5km on the spot on the spot on the spot on the spot on the spot on the spot 1,6km 1,6km.

Remarks: Max. 48h, payment only with coins.

Barbarano Vicentino 25D6

Viale Vittorio Veneto 66. **GPS**: n45,40725 e11,54654.

3 free free. **Surface:** asphalted. 01/01-31/12

Distance: 200m 200m 200m.

Remarks: In village.

Bardolino 25B6

P Prandini, Piazzale Prandini. **GPS**: n45,55083 e10,72341.

10 € 15/24h .

Remarks: Along the through road.

Tourist information Bardolino:

I.A.T. (Ufficio Informazioni e di Accoglienza Turistica), Piazzale Aldo Moro.

Bassano del Grappa 25D5

Parcheggio Gerosa, Via Kolbe. **GPS**: n45,75831 e11,73091.

20 € 10 Ch included. **Surface:** asphalted. 01/01-31/12

Distance: 300m 300m 300m on the spot.

Remarks: Max. 48h.

Bassano del Grappa 25D5

Prato Santo Caterina, Via Chini 6. **GPS**: n45,76009 e11,73413.
free.
Distance: on the spot.

Tourist information Bassano del Grappa:
I.A.T. (Ufficio Informazioni e di Accoglienza Turistica), Largo Corona D'Italia, 35.

Belluno 26A4

Rio Cavalli, Via Sagrogna 74. **GPS**: n46,15646 e12,26136.

20 € 10, electricity included € 15 € 5.
Location: Comfortable, central, quiet. **Surface:** grassy/sand.
01/01-31/12
Distance: 3km 6km on the spot on the spot 3km on the spot.

Belluno 26A4

Viale dei Dendrofori, loc. Lambioi. **GPS**: n46,13712 e12,21371.

12 8-18 € 0,80/h, overnight stay free Ch free. **Location:** Simple, central, noisy. **Surface:** grasstiles/metalled. 01/01-31/12
Distance: 100m 100m 100m.
Remarks: Nearby swimming pool and skating rink.

Bibione 26B5

Strada Brussa. **GPS**: n45,62458 e12,95866.

100 € 7/day, overnight stay free WC. **Location:** Rural, simple, isolated, quiet. **Surface:** grassy. 25/04-30/09
Distance: sandy beach 250m.
Remarks: Dog permitted on the beach, guarded during the day.

Borghetto di Valeggio sul Mincio 25B6

Camper parking Visconteo, Strada provinciale 55. **GPS**: n45,35537 e10,72017.

60 € 10/24h € 3 Ch € 1/12h. **Location:** Rural, comfortable.
Surface: gravel.
Distance: on the spot Lake Garda 13km 250m on the spot on the spot.
Remarks: Borghetto 200m.

Caorle 26B5

Area di sosta Ai Parchi, Via Traghete. **GPS**: n45,60490 e12,88500.

65 € 11-16/24h Ch (60x)€ 4/kWh WC € 1/3minutes.
Location: Comfortable, isolated, noisy.
Surface: gravel.
01/01-31/12
Distance: historical centre 1,1km 500m 300m 300m 350m 150m.
Remarks: Max. 72h, guarded parking, Luna Park 150m, Parco Acquatico 150m.

Cavallino-Treporti 26A6

Spiaggia di Cà Ballarin, Via Gabrielle Berton. **GPS**: n45,45998 e12,51659.

4 free. **Location:** Simple, central, quiet. **Surface:** sand.
01/05-31/10
Distance: 1km on the spot on the spot on the spot 1km 300m.
Remarks: Beach parking.

Tourist information Cavallino-Treporti:
I.A.T. (Ufficio Informazioni e di Accoglienza Turistica), Via Ramo II Delle Saline, 23.
Week market. Tue-Thu morning.

Chioggia 32C1

2 Palme, Lungomare Adriatica. **GPS**: n45,22122 e12,29624.

100 € 12, peak season € 20, Su/holidays € 15 Ch (100x) WC included € 0,50. **Location:** Urban, simple, central.
Surface: grassy/gravel. 01/01-31/12
Distance: centre 1,8km 200m.
Remarks: Chioggia: little Venice.

Conegliano 26A5

Area de Sosta Campeggio Club Conegliano, Via Don Bosco, SS13. **GPS**: n45,87799 e12,30111.

IT

30 € 12/24h Ch (16x)included WC . **Location:** Simple, central, quiet. **Surface:** grassy. 01/01-31/12
Distance: 2km nearby on the spot.

S Cortina d'Ampezzo 25D3

Fiames, SS51. **GPS**: n46,57504 e12,11650.

>100 free, peak season € 12-15 Ch. **Location:** Rural, simple, comfortable, quiet. **Surface:** grassy/metalled. 01/01-31/12
Distance: 5km on the spot 5km 200m on the spot on the spot 5km 5km.
Remarks: Max. 48h.

Tourist information Cortina d'Ampezzo:
Ufficio Informazioni, Piazzetta S.Francesco, 8.Famous winter sports resort.

S Domegge di Cadore Belluno 26A3

Camping Cologna, Vallesella di Cadore. **GPS**: n46,44605 e12,40658.

30 € 10 Ch. **Location:** Rural, simple, quiet. **Surface:** grassy. 01/05-20/10
Distance: 1km At the lake on the spot on the spot 1km 1km on the spot on the spot.
Remarks: Max. 24h, narrow entrance road.

S Feltre 25D5

Piazale Pra del Vescovo, Viale A. Gaggia. **GPS**: n46,02013 e11,90792.

15 free Chfree. **Surface:** metalled. 01/01-31/12
Distance: 500m 500m 500m 500m.
Remarks: Max. 48h.

S Ferrara di Monte Baldo 25B6

Via Chiesa. **GPS**: n45,67794 e10,85491.

16 free Ch (16x). **Location:** Rural, simple, isolated, quiet. **Surface:** gravel. 01/01-31/12
Distance: 300m 300m 300m on the spot on the spot.

S Garda 25B6

P Centro, SS249. **GPS**: n45,57501 e10,71019.

20 € 13/24h WC. **Surface:** metalled. 01/01-31/12
Distance: 200m on the spot on the spot.

S Garda 25B6

Via Preite. **GPS**: n45,57620 e10,71404.
30 free, easter-31/10 € 12 Ch. **Surface:** metalled. service: Easter-31/10
Distance: 300m Lake Garda 300m.

Tourist information Garda:
I.A.T. (Ufficio Informazioni e di Accoglienza Turistica), Piazza Donatori di Sangue, 1.

Lazise 25B6

Parking Lazise Dardo, Via San Martino, SP31. **GPS**: n45,50623 e10,73584.

15 € 17/24h. **Surface:** asphalted. 01/01-31/12
Distance: 200m 5,8km 200m 200m 200m.

S Lido di Jesolo 26B6

Area camping Albatros, Via Correr 102/A. **GPS**: n45,52477 e12,68995.

131 € 9-17 Ch WC included. **Location:** Comfortable, isolated, quiet. **Surface:** grassy. 01/03-31/10

Distance: 500m 700m 100m 100m 100m 100m.

S Lido di Jesolo 26B6

Boscopineta, Via Vettor Pisani. **GPS**: n45,52278 e12,69178.

250 € 10-20 Ch WC. **Location:** Comfortable, central.
Surface: grassy. 01/01-31/12
Distance: 400m.

S Lido di Jesolo 26B6

Camping Park dei Dogi, Viale Oriente. **GPS**: n45,52146 e12,68828.

200 € 14-26, 4 pers.incl. Ch WC included € 0,50.
Location: Comfortable, central, quiet. **Surface:** grassy. 01/01-31/12
Distance: 200m sandy beach 200m 40m 40m 20m.

S Lido di Jesolo 26B6

Jesolo Camper Don Bosco, Via Oriente/via G.Don Bosco. **GPS**: n45,52188 e12,68943.

250 € 10-20 Ch € 3/1kWh WC € 1 € 5. **Surface:** grassy/gravel.
01/01-31/12
Distance: within walking distance 100m on the spot 100m on the spot. **Remarks:** Bus to Venice stops in front of motorhome parking.

S Lido di Jesolo 26B6

Parcheggio Mare d'Oriente, Viale Oriente, Lido di Jesolo est. **GPS**: n45,52083 e12,68556.

€ 10/24h, € 13/Sunday, Aug Ch included. **Location:** Simple, central, quiet. **Surface:** grassy. summer
Distance: 100m 100m on the spot on the spot on the spot.
Remarks: Servicepoint at Don Bosco, incl.

S Livinallongo del Col di Lana 25D3

Sportbar del Ghiaccio, Via Piagn,6 Arabba. **GPS**: n46,49678 e11,87692.

50 € 10/24h, Jul-Aug-Dec € 14 Ch (17x)€ 3/24h WC € 3.
Location: Rural, comfortable, quiet. **Surface:** grassy/gravel.
01/01-31/12
Distance: on the spot on the spot 200m 200m on the spot on the spot 200m.
Remarks: At the skating rink, check in at bar.

S Malcesine 25B5

Camping Lombardi, Via Navene, loc. Campagnola. **GPS**: n45,78429 e10,82187.

20 € 17/24h, 28/06-01/09 € 20/24h € 1 Ch WC € 1.
Surface: unpaved. 01/04-31/10
Distance: 3km Lake Garda 500m.
Remarks: Max. 48h.

P Marghera 26A6

Parcheggio Terminal Service, Via dei Petroli 1/3 angolo via della Libertà. **GPS**: n45,46806 e12,26589.

€ 10/24h. **Location:** Simple, central, quiet.
01/01-31/12
Distance: > Venice.
Remarks: Monitored parking.

S Mirano 26A6

Camper Club Mirano, Via viasana, 4. **GPS**: n45,49322 e12,08968.

€ 12/24h Ch. **Location:** Comfortable.

IT

Surface: grasstiles.
Distance: historical centre 1,5km 8km 300m Padua-Venice.
Remarks: For entrance email: camperclubmirano@libero.it of phone 3479831010.

S Misurina 26A3
Piazzale Loita, Via Monte Piana. **GPS**: n46,58839 e12,25737.

50 € 8, 20/07-31/08 - 24/12-06/01 € 12 Ch included. **Location:** Rural, simple, simple, central, noisy. **Surface:** gravel.
01/01-31/12
Distance: 300m 500m 50m 300m on the spot on the spot on the spot 3km.

Misurina 26A3
P camper Rifugio Auronzo, Rifugio Auronzo. **GPS**: n46,61267 e12,29342.

40 € 33 toll road incl., extra night € 15. **Location:** Rural, simple, isolated. **Surface:** gravel. 01/05-30/10
Distance: Misurina 12km on the spot 12km on the spot Tre Cime di Lavadero 15km.
Remarks: Beautiful view.

S Montagnana 32B1
Via Circonvallazione. **GPS**: n45,23528 e11,46639.

20 free Ch WC free. **Surface:** asphalted. 01/01-31/12
Distance: 200m 200m 200m.
Remarks: At sports centre.

S Padova 25D6
P1, Piazza della Pace Ytzhak Rabbin, Via cinquantottesimo Fanteria, Padua (Padova). **GPS**: n45,39686 e11,87673.
8-20h € 10, 20-8h € 10, 18-10h € 20 Ch. **Surface:** asphalted. 01/01-31/12
Distance: on the spot 6km on the spot on the spot on the spot.

Tourist information Padua (Padova):
U.I.A.T. (Ufficio Informazioni e di Accoglienza Turistica, Galleria Pedrocchi, www.turismopadova.it.Old university city.
Caffe Pedrocchi, Via Oberdan.Café, meeting point for students.
Capella degli Scrovegni.Chapel.

S Peschiera del Garda 25B6
P4, Via Milano 67. **GPS**: n45,44179 e10,67768.

33 € 15/24h Ch free. **Surface:** asphalted. 01/01-31/12
Distance: 5km Lake Garda 300m 100m nearby.
Remarks: Parking nearby campsite Bella Italia.

Tourist information Peschiera del Garda:
Tourist town at Lake Garda.
Mo-morning.

Porto Tolle 32C1
Via strada del Mare, loc. Barricata, SP38. **GPS**: n44,84997 e12,46342.

50 € 3,50. **Location:** Rural, quiet. **Surface:** grassy/sand.
Distance: 50m.
Remarks: Beach parking.

S Punta Sabbioni 26A6
Parking Dante Alighieri, Dante Alighieri 26. **GPS**: n45,44132 e12,42131.

36 € 17-20 + € 3/pp Ch € 3 WC € 3. **Location:** Simple, central, quiet. **Surface:** grassy.
01/01-31/12
Distance: on the spot 1,5km 700m free shuttle to beach.
Remarks: Monitored parking, arrival <22h, ferry boat to Venice 500m.

S Punta Sabbioni 26A6
Agricamping da Scarpa, Via Pealto 17. **GPS**: n45,44279 e12,44055.

15 € 14-16 + € 5/pp Ch WC included. **Surface:** grassy.
01/01-31/12
Distance: 500m on the spot 500m ferry Venice 1,5km.

S Recoaro Terme 25C6
Area Communale, Via Della Restistenza. **GPS**: n45,70469 e11,22874.

IT

16 € 5/24h € 0,10/10liter Ch (16x)€ 0,50/2h,6Amp.
01/01-31/12
Distance: on the spot on the spot on the spot on the spot on the spot.

S Santo Stefano di Cadore 26A3

Albergo Gasperina, Loc. Cima Canale, Val Visdende. **GPS**: n46,60835 e12,63053.

49 € 11/24h, Aug € 12 Ch (49x)€ 3/day WC included € 2.
Surface: gravel.
25/04-01/10
Distance: 12km 300m on the spot 6km on the spot on the spot.
Remarks: Check in at restaurant, bread-service.

S Sappada 26A3

Area Camper, Borgata Palù. **GPS**: n46,56254 e12,67991.

60 € 10/24h Ch (24x)included. **Location:** Rural, simple, quiet.
Surface: gravel. 01/01-31/12
Distance: 1,1km 500m 1km on the spot on the spot 100m.
Remarks: Keycard at townhall, caution key € 5.

S Schio 25C5

Parking Palasport, Viale dell'Industria. **GPS**: n45,71389 e11,37599.

4 free Ch free. **Surface:** asphalted. 01/01-31/12
Distance: 1km 1km 1km on the spot on the spot.

S Sernaglia della Battaglia 26A5

Area attrezzata Le Grave, Via Passo Barca, Falzè di Piave. **GPS**: n45,85676 e12,16566.

26 € 5/12h, € 8/24h Ch included € 2/24h. **Location:** Simple.
Surface: grassy. 01/01-31/12
Distance: 150m on the spot 100m 150m 300m.

S Soave 25C6

Via Invalidi del Lavoro. **GPS**: n45,42340 e11,24541.

8 free Ch (8x)free,16Amp. 01/01-31/12
Distance: 200m 3km on the spot 200m 200m 300m.

S Torre di Mosto 26B5

Agriturismo La Via Antiga, Via S. Martino 13. **GPS**: n45,64389 e12,67056.

8 € 15/day Ch (5x)included. **Location:** Simple, isolated, quiet.
Surface: grassy/gravel. 01/03-30/09
Distance: 7km.

S Treviso 26A5

Parking ex Foro Boario, Via Castello d'Amore. **GPS**: n45,67014 e12,25733.

13 free Ch free. **Surface:** metalled. 01/01-31/12
Distance: 500m 11,5km 500m 500m 200m.
Remarks: Max. 48h.

S Treviso 26A5

Via Giovanni Boccaccio. **GPS**: n45,66769 e12,26361.

IT

40 free Chfree. **Location:** Simple, central, noisy. **Surface:** asphalted.
01/01-31/12
Distance: 1km 500m 500m 300m.
Remarks: Along railwayline.

Tourist information Treviso:
U.I.A.T. (Ufficio Informazioni e di Accoglienza Turistica), Piazza Monte di Pieta, 8.Fortified small town with canals.
Sile.Fish-market on island.

S Venezia 26A6
Parcheggio Al Tronchetto, Venice (Venezia) . **GPS**: n45,44146 e12,30514.

€ 21/0-12h, 12-24h € 16 Ch .
Location: Urban, simple, central, quiet. **Surface:** asphalted.
01/01-31/12
Distance: 2km on the spot ferry Venice.

S Venezia 26A6
Parco di San Giuliano, Via San Giuliano, Venice (Venezia). **GPS**: n45,46742 e12,27916.

100 € 10/24h € 3 Ch WC . **Location:** Simple, central, quiet.
Surface: grassy. 01/01-31/12
Distance: ferry Venice 100m.

Tourist information Venice (Venezia):
A.P.T. (Azienda di Promozione Turistica), www.turismovenezia.it.Historical city consits of 117 islands, 150 canals and 400 bridges.
Murano.Famous for its glass industry, museum.

S Verona 25C6
Area sosta camper Porta Palio, Via dalla Bona. **GPS**: n45,43354 e10,97879.

37 € 5/4h, € 10/24h Chincluded. **Surface:** asphalted.
01/01-31/12
Distance: 500m Pizza (ordering service) bus 62 > centre.

S Verona 25C6
Agricamping Corte Finiletto, Strada Bresciana, 41. **GPS**: n45,44651 e10,91917.

€ 18, 2 pers.incl Ch € 2 WC . **Surface:** grassy/gravel.

Tourist information Verona:
U.I.A.T. (Ufficio Informazioni e di Accoglienza Turistica), Piazza XXV Aprile-c/o stazione "Porta Nuova".Historical city with palaces and squares.
Arena.Large anfiteatro, in July/August opera performances.
Via Capella.Known for the love drama of Romeo and Juliet.
Piazza dellen Erbe. daily.

S Vicenza 25D6
Park Interscambio CentroBus, Via Bassano, Zona sud-est. **GPS**: n45,54321 e11,55886.

40 € 8,40/24h WCincluded. **Surface:** asphalted. 01/01-31/12
during event.
Distance: 2km on the spot Free bus to centre, every 15 min.
Remarks: At stadium.

S Vicenza 25D6
Park Interscambio CentroBus, Viale Cricoli, Zona nord. **GPS**: n45,56418 e11,54903.

18 € 8,40/24h Ch WCincluded. **Surface:** asphalted.
01/01-31/12

Distance: 1,6km on the spot on the spot Free bus to centre.
Remarks: Ring-road dir Bassano.

Tourist information Vicenza:
U.I.A.T. (Ufficio Informazioni e di Accoglienza Turistica), Piazza Matteotti, 12, www.vicenzae.org.City with many palaces, former residence of 16th century architect.
La Rotonda.Famous villa designed by Palladio. summer: Wed.
Quartiere delle Barche.District with palaces in Venetian style.

Friuli Venezia Giulia

S Andreis 26A4

SP20. **GPS**: n46,19880 e12,61157.

€ 5/day . **Location:** Simple. **Surface:** grassy/gravel.
Distance: little stream.

S Barcis 26A4

Loc. Portuz, SS251. **GPS**: n46,19055 e12,56507.

20 € 12/24h Ch . **Location:** Comfortable, isolated, quiet.
Surface: grasstiles/metalled. 01/01-31/12
Distance: 400m on the spot 500m 500m.
Remarks: At the lake of Barcis.

S Corno di Rosazzo 26C4

Via dei Pini. **GPS**: n45,98955 e13,43917.

8 free . **Location:** Rural, simple, quiet. **Surface:** asphalted.
01/01-31/12
Distance: 300m.

S Dolegna del Collio 26C4

Frazione Vencò. **GPS**: n46,00370 e13,47700.

free Ch . **Surface:** asphalted.
Distance: Dolegna del Collio 4km.
Remarks: Picnic area, 50m from border with Slovenia.

S Forni di Sopra 26A3

Santa Viela, SS52. **GPS**: n46,42500 e12,57036.

20 € 7-9 Chfree. **Location:** Rural, simple, noisy.
Surface: asphalted. 01/01-31/12
Distance: 800m on the spot 800m 400m on the spot on the spot on the spot on the spot.
Remarks: No camping activity. Parking outside the village, dir Lorenzago di Cadore.

S Gemona del Friuli 26B4

Piazzale Mons. Battista Monai. **GPS**: n46,27585 e13,13728.
free Chfree. **Location:** Simple, central, noisy.
Surface: asphalted.
Distance: on the spot 3,3km.

S Gorizia 26C4

Viale Antonio Oriani. **GPS**: n45,94554 e13,61603.

30 free Chfree. **Location:** Simple, quiet. **Surface:** asphalted.
01/01-31/12
Distance: centre 500m.

S Gradisca d'Isonzo 26C5

Viale Trieste. **GPS**: n45,88577 e13,49582.

3 free Chfree. **Location:** Central. **Surface:** asphalted.
Distance: on the spot 2,3km on the spot on the spot.

IT

Remarks: Max. 48h.

S Grado 26C5

Viala Italia. **GPS:** n45,68218 e13,41230.

40 € 12 Ch included. **Location:** Simple. **Surface:** asphalted.
01/01-31/12
Distance: 1km 24km 600m.

S Montereale Valcellina 26A4

Via dell'Omo. **GPS:** n46,15168 e12,66122.

15 free Ch. **Location:** Urban. **Surface:** asphalted.
01/01-31/12
Distance: 500m 300m.

S Pordenone 26A5

Agip, SS13, Pordenone. **GPS:** n45,97236 e12,64332.

8 € 3/24h Ch. **Location:** Urban, simple, isolated, quiet.
Surface: asphalted. 01/01-31/12
Distance: 1km 3km 200m 200m.
Remarks: To be paid at petrol station.

Tourist information Pordenone:
Infopoint Turismo, Via Damiani 2c.

S San Daniele del Friuli 26B4

Via Udine, SP16. **GPS:** n46,15610 e13,01368.

20 free Ch free. **Location:** Comfortable, central, quiet.
Surface: grasstiles. 01/01-31/12
Distance: 300m on the spot 300m 200m.
Remarks: Parking sports park.

S San Vito al Tagliamento 26B5

Area di sosta San Vito al Tagliamento, Via Pulet. **GPS:** n45,91224 e12,86590.

12 € 5/12h, € 8/24h, € 15/48h € 1 Ch . **Location:** Rural, simple, isolated, quiet. **Surface:** asphalted. 01/01-31/12
Distance: 500m 15km 500m 500m 500m.
Remarks: Open the gate manually.

S Sauris 26A3

Prosciuttificio Wolf Sauris, Sauris di Sotto 88. **GPS:** n46,46756 e12,70833.
10 free free WC. **Location:** Rural, simple, quiet. **Surface:** asphalted.
Distance: on the spot 150m on the spot.

S Tarcento 26B4

Plein-air Torre, Via Sotto Colle Verzan. **GPS:** n46,21496 e13,22503.

10 free Ch free. **Location:** Simple, quiet.
Surface: grasstiles.
Distance: 200m 200m 200m.
Remarks: Nearby sports center, no camping activity, max. 72h.

S Tarvisio 26C3

Parcheggio P3, Via Armando Diaz. **GPS:** n46,50426 e13,57157.

25 € 0,60/h Ch. **Location:** Urban, simple, central.
Surface: metalled.
Distance: on the spot 100m 100m.

S Trieste 26C5

Via Von Bruck, Torre del Lloyd. **GPS:** n45,63710 e13,76990.

IT

50 € 4 Chfree. **Location:** Highway, simple, noisy. **Surface:** asphalted.
01/01-31/12
Distance: 3km shuttle to centre.
Remarks: Pitches under motorway, max. 72h.

Trieste 26C5

Piazzale 11 settembre 2001, Viale Miramare. **GPS**: n45,68250 e13,75138.

20 free. **Location:** Urban, simple, quiet. **Surface:** metalled.
Distance: on the spot.
Remarks: In front of porticciolo di Barcola, quiet at night.

Trieste 26C5

Via Ottaviano Augusto. **GPS**: n45,64599 e13,75654.

free. **Location:** Urban. **Surface:** asphalted. 01/01-31/12
Distance: centre 500m 100m on the spot.
Remarks: In opposite of Piazza Unitá d'Italia.

Tourist information Trieste:
A.I.A.T (Agenzia di Informazione e di Accoglienza Turistica), Via San Nicolo, 20, www.triestetourism.it.Large port city with many place of interest.
Grotta del Giganta.Caves. Tue-Su, 01/07-31/08 Mo-Su.

S Zoppola 26B5

Via Manteghe. **GPS**: n45,96502 e12,78019.

2 free Chfree. **Location:** Rural, isolated, quiet. **Surface:** metalled.
01/01-31/12
Distance: centre 800m.
Remarks: At gymnasium.

Emilia-Romagna

S Anita 32C2

Agriturismo Prato Pozzo, Via Rotta Martinella 34/a. **GPS**: n44,54892 e12,13322.

20 € 5 + € 5/pp, guests free Ch (12x)€ 2,50/day WC included .
Location: Rural, comfortable, isolated, quiet. **Surface:** grassy/metalled.
01/01-31/12
Distance: 1km 500m 500m on the spot 1km 1km.

S Argenta 32B2

Via Galassi. **GPS**: n44,61345 e11,83983.

10 free free. **Surface:** metalled. 01/01-31/12
Distance: 200m 200m 200m 200m.
Remarks: At tennis-courts.

Tourist information Argenta:
U.I.A.T.(Ufficio Informazzioni e di Accoglienza Turistica), Piazza Marconi, 1.

S Bagnacavallo 32C2

Parcheggio bocciodromo, Via Stradello. **GPS**: n44,42191 e11,97390.

free free. **Surface:** asphalted. 01/01-31/12
Distance: 700m 2,5km 700m 200m.

Bagno di Romagna 32C3

Via Lungo Savio 1. **GPS**: n43,84108 e11,96532.

10 free. **Surface:** metalled. 01/01-31/12
Distance: 500m 1km 500m 500m.
Remarks: Parking swimming pool.

Tourist information Bagno di Romagna:
U.I.A.T.(Ufficio Informazzioni e di Accoglienza Turistica), Via Fiorentina, 38.
Week market. Fri 7.30-12.30h.

IT

S Bellaria-Igea Marina 32C3

Parking delle Robinie, Via Pinzon 258, Igea Marina, Zona sud. **GPS**: n44,12783 e12,48873.

106 € 10-12, Apr-Sept € 14,00-16,50 Ch € 2,50/day € 1/time.
Location: Rural, comfortable, central, quiet. **Surface:** grassy/gravel.
15/03-05/10, 08-23h
Distance: 10m 200m 100m 50m.

S Bellaria-Igea Marina 32C3

Mare d'Inverno, Via Murri, 13. **GPS**: n44,11639 e12,49972.

45 € 8, peak season € 10, holidays + € 2 Ch € 2,50/day € 1/time.
Location: Rural, comfortable, quiet. **Surface:** grassy.
Easter-30/09
Distance: 800m 200m 800m 1,5km, bakery 800m 100m.

S Bellaria-Igea Marina 32C3

Area di sosta Rio Pircio, Via Benivieni 4, Igea Marina. **GPS**: n44,12688 e12,48849.

68 € 10-18/24h Ch € 2/day WC € 1/time hot shower € 1.
Location: Rural, comfortable, central, quiet. **Surface:** grassy.
01/01-31/12
Distance: 100m 200m 250m.

S Bellaria-Igea Marina 32C3

L'Adriatico Parking, Via Benivieni, 12. **GPS**: n44,12644 e12,48740.

60 € 10-16/24h Ch € 2,50/day € 1/time against payment € 1/24h,€ 5/week. **Location:** Rural, comfortable, quiet. **Surface:** grassy.
Easter-Oct
Distance: 250m.

Tourist information Bellaria-Igea Marina:
U.I.A.T.(Ufficio Informazzioni e di Accoglienza Turistica), Via Leonardo da Vinci, 2.

S Berceto 31D2

Via P. Salas. **GPS**: n44,51123 e9,98589.

20 € 7 Ch WC included. **Surface:** asphalted.
01/01-31/12
Distance: 200m 4km 200m 200m on the spot on the spot.
Remarks: Key at kiosk in front of restaurant Rina, caution key € 20.

S Bertinoro 32C3

Via Superga, SP 83, fraz Fratta Terme. **GPS**: n44,13788 e12,10355.

free Ch free. **Surface:** asphalted. 01/01-31/12
Distance: 1km 1km 1km 300m.
Remarks: Near spa resort and sports centre.

S Bertinoro 32C3

Azienda agricola Achille Budellacci, Via Palmeggiana 516, loc. Capocolle. **GPS**: n44,15214 e12,16325.
2 € 5, free for clients € 1/100liter Ch WC included.
01/01-31/12
Distance: 5km 5km 5km.

S Bomporto 32A2

Piazza dello Sport, Via Verdi. **GPS**: n44,72886 e11,03585.

10 free free. **Location:** Urban, simple.
Surface: metalled.
Distance: 500m 500m.
Remarks: Parking at sports park.

Borello 32C3

Via Fiera. **GPS**: n44,05315 e12,17847.

IT

5 free. **Surface:** asphalted. 01/01-31/12
Distance: 100m 1,2km 500m 100m 100m.
Remarks: Near post office.

S Brisighella 32B2

Piazzale Donatori di Sangue. **GPS:** n44,22168 e11,77883.

18 free Chfree. **Surface:** asphalted. 01/01-31/12
Distance: 1km 1km 1km 500m.

S Brisighella 32B2

Agriturismo Torre del Marino, Via Torre del Marino 45. **GPS:** n44,25447 e11,75867.

4 free Ch (3x) WC. **Surface:** asphalted. 01/01-31/12
Distance: 8km on the spot.
Remarks: Restaurant is closed on Monday.

S Carpi 32A2

Piazzale delle Piscine. **GPS:** n44,78444 e10,86817.

free Chfree. **Surface:** metalled.
Distance: 300m 50m on the spot.
Remarks: Parking swimming pool.

S Casal Borsetti 32C2

Area Sosta Camper Mare e Parco, Via Ortolani. **GPS:** n44,55000 e12,27997.

238 € 9, 01/06-01/09 € 11 Chincluded € 3/24h WC . **Location:** Rural, comfortable, central, quiet. **Surface:** grassy/metalled.
01/01-31/12
Distance: 150m 150m.

S Casola Valsenio 32B3

Viale Domenico Neri. **GPS:** n44,22483 e11,62392.
4 free free. **Surface:** asphalted. 01/01-31/12
Distance: 100m 500m 100m.

Casola Valsenio 32B3

Via don Milani/Via Antonio Gramsci. **GPS:** n44,22597 e11,62953.

3 free. **Surface:** asphalted. 01/01-31/12
Distance: 300m 500m 500m.
Remarks: At old city centre.

Tourist information Casola Valsenio:

I.A.T.(Ufficio Informazzioni Turistica), Via Roma, 48/a.

S Castel Bolognese 32B2

Via Donati, SS 9. **GPS:** n44,31611 e11,79280.

50 free Chfree.
Distance: 300m.
Remarks: At sports park.

S Castel San Pietro Terme 32B2

Via Oriani. **GPS:** n44,39725 e11,59197.

100 free € 1 Ch WC € 0,20. **Surface:** asphalted. 01/01-31/12
Distance: 300m 4,2km 200m 250m 250m 250m.
Remarks: Nearby hospital.

IT

S Castellarano 32A2

Parco Don Reverberi, Via Don Reverberi. **GPS**: n44,50777 e10,73419.

5 free Ch free. **Location:** Rural, simple. **Surface:** asphalted. 01/01-31/12

Distance: 500m 500m 500m 500m 500m.

S Castelnovo ne' Monti 32A2

Impianti Sportivi, Zona PEP, Via Fratelli Cervi, SS63. **GPS**: n44,43277 e10,41133.

4 free Ch free. **Location:** Simple, quiet. **Surface:** asphalted. 01/01-31/12

Distance: 500m on the spot.

Remarks: On entering the village from Reggio Emilia.

S Cervia 32C2

Via Aldo Ascione, Cervia-nord. **GPS**: n44,28151 e12,32459.

50 free Ch free. **Location:** Simple, isolated, noisy. **Surface:** asphalted. 01/01-31/12

Distance: 3km 3km 1,3km.

S Cervia 32C2

Viale Tritone, Fraz. Pinarella. **GPS**: n44,23984 e12,35883.

40 free Ch free. **Location:** Urban, simple, noisy. **Surface:** asphalted/metalled. 01/01-31/12

Distance: 750m 900m on the spot.

S Cervia 32C2

Terme di Cervia, Viale C. Forlanini, Cervia-nord. **GPS**: n44,27335 e12,32964.

50 € 8/24h € 2. **Location:** Rural, quiet. **Surface:** grassy/gravel. 01/04-30/11

Distance: 3km 3km 50m.

Remarks: Parking spa resort.

Tourist information Cervia:

U.I.A.T.(Ufficio Informazzioni e di Accoglienza Turistica), Vale Matteotti, 39-41, www.turismo.comunecervia.it.

Week market. Thu.

S Cesena 32C3

Agriturismo Macin, Via San Mauro 5280. **GPS**: n44,13592 e12,16953.

2 € 5, free for clients Ch WC included. **Surface:** grassy/metalled. 01/01-31/12

Distance: 5km 8,4km 5km 5km.

S Cesenatico 32C2

Piazzale della Rocca. **GPS**: n44,19855 e12,39086.

35 free Ch free. **Location:** Simple. **Surface:** metalled. 01/01-31/12

Distance: 500m 2km 200m 500m 200m.

Remarks: 2nd parking.

S Cesenatico 32C2

Via Mazzini, zona Ponente. **GPS**: n44,21408 e12,38008.

21 € 12/24h Ch included. **Location:** Rural, simple. **Surface:** grassy/gravel. 01/01-31/12

Distance: centre 3,5km 800m.

Remarks: At entrance campsite Cesenatico, max. 48h.

IT

Civitella di Romagna 32C3

Agriturismo Acero Rosseo, Via Seggio. **GPS**: n44,00200 e11,97539.

20 guests free free. **Surface:** grassy. 01/01-31/12

Distance: 5km on the spot 5km.

Collecchio 31D2

Via Spezia. **GPS**: n44,75178 e10,22265.

8 free Ch. **Location:** Simple. **Surface:** asphalted.
01/01-31/12

Distance: 500m.

Comacchio 32C2

Area di sosta Cavallari, Via Villaggio San Carlo 9. **GPS**: n44,70297 e12,16862.

90 € 13 Ch Service € 4 included WC € 2/time. **Location:** Rural, luxurious, quiet. **Surface:** grassy. 01/01-31/12

Distance: 1km.

Comacchio 32C2

Via Fattibello. **GPS**: n44,69095 e12,18447.

13 free. **Location:** Rural, central, quiet. **Surface:** asphalted.
01/01-31/12

Distance: 300m.

Conselice 32B2

Agriturismo Massari, Via Coronella 110, Chiesanuova di Conselice. **GPS**: n44,53167 e11,81856.

10 € 9/pp, guests free Ch WC included.

Surface: metalled. 01/01-31/12

Distance: 1,5km 200m on the spot 1,5km.

Cusercoli 32C3

Agriturismo Ca'Bionda, Via San Giovanni 41. **GPS**: n44,04153 e11,97544.

20 free Ch free WC. **Surface:** metalled.

Distance: 3,5km on the spot 3,5km.

Remarks: Last 3km narrow road, swimming pool.

Faenza 32B2

Via Proventa. **GPS**: n44,31272 e11,89289.

2 free Ch free. **Surface:** asphalted. 01/01-31/12

Distance: 4km 2km.

Remarks: Industrial area, A14 exit Faenza, SP8 dir centre.

Faenza 32B2

Agriturismo Trerè, Via Casale 19. **GPS**: n44,29968 e11,80368.

5 € 8 + € 5/pp, guests free Ch € 2 WC. **Surface:** metalled.
01/01-31/12

Distance: 7km on the spot 200m on the spot.

Remarks: Dog € 1, swimming pool € 5. Follow Agriturismo Trerè.

Faenza 32B2

Agriturismo Il Laghetto del Sole, Via Pittora 37. **GPS**: n44,25128 e11,88717.

IT

20 € 5 Ch (4x) WC . **Surface:** metalled. 01/02-31/10
Distance: 4,5km 200m 200m on the spot 4km.

S Faenza 32B2

Centro vendita Faenza Caravan, Via Emilia Ponent 76/c. **GPS**: n44,30353 e11,84294.

free Chfree. **Surface:** metalled. 01/01-31/12
Distance: 3km 350m.
Remarks: Service during opening hours.

Tourist information Faenza:
I.A.T.(Ufficio Informazioni e di Accoglienza Turistica), VOLTONE DELLA MOLINELLA, 2.

S Ferrara 32B1

Via Darsena 40/Corso Isonzo. **GPS**: n44,83468 e11,60795.

30 € 6/24h € 1/100liter € 2 Ch€ 1. **Surface:** metalled.
01/01-31/12
Distance: 800m 6,5km 250m 500m 50m.

Tourist information Ferrara:
U.I.A.T. (Ufficio Informazioni e di Accoglienza Turistica), Castello Estense. Historical city.
Museo della Cattedrale. gift.
Castello Estence.
Palazzo Scifanoia.
Mo, Fri.

S Fontanellato 31D1

Via Caduti di Cefalonia. **GPS**: n44,88195 e10,17762.

30 free free. **Location:** Simple, quiet. **Surface:** asphalted.
01/01-31/12
Distance: centre 500m 5,4km 500m.
Remarks: At cemetery.

S Fontanellato 31D1

Via Nazionale Emilia. **GPS**: n44,87797 e10,16987.

20 free Ch (16x) WCfree. **Surface:** asphalted.
01/01-31/12
Distance: 300m 6km 200m 500m.

Forlimpopoli 32C3

Via De Gasperi. **GPS**: n44,19044 e12,12608.

free. **Surface:** asphalted. 01/01-31/12
Distance: 100m 100m 100m 100m.
Remarks: Nearby railway station.

S Forlimpopoli 32C3

Palazzetto dello Sport, Via del Tulipano. **GPS**: n44,18432 e12,11843.
Chfree.
Remarks: In front of gymnasium.

S Gropparello 31D2

Via D. Aligieri. **GPS**: n44,83521 e9,73051.

€ 10 free. **Location:** Rural, simple, quiet. **Surface:** asphalted.
01/01-31/12
Distance: 100m 500m.
Remarks: Castello di Gropparello 300m.

S Guastalla 32A1

Piazzale Ugo Foscolo. **GPS**: n44,92364 e10,65148.

free free (6x)€ 3. **Surface:** asphalted. 01/01-31/12

Distance: historical centre 300m 1,5km 600m 100m.

Remarks: Cycle route along the Po river.

S Imola 32B2

Via 1° Maggio, Via Salvador Allende. **GPS**: n44,37083 e11,72093.

free free. **Surface:** asphalted. 01/01-31/12

Distance: 1,5km 2,7km trattoria Ca' del Pozzo 500m 100m.

Remarks: Industrial area.

S Imola 32B2

Via Pirandello. **GPS**: n44,34628 e11,70922.

30 free free. **Surface:** grassy/sand. 01/01-31/12

Distance: 700m 50m 80m 50m supermercato Famila.

Remarks: In front of the Ferrari Circuit. Follow signs autodromo.

Tourist information Imola:

I.A.T.(Ufficio Informazioni e di Accoglienza Turistica), Via Emilia, 135.

Piazza Gramsci. Mo-Thu, Sa 8-12.30h.

S Lagosanto 32C1

Ristorante Il Varano, Via Valle Oppio 6, Marozzo di Lagosanto. **GPS**: n44,78167 e12,12533.

36 € 15, guests free Ch (36x) WC. **Location:** Rural, comfortable, quiet. **Surface:** gravel. 01/01-31/12

Distance: 3km 12km on the spot 500m.

S Langhirano 31D2

Salumificio La Perla, Quinzano. **GPS**: n44,58748 e10,23783.

50 free. **Location:** Rural, simple, quiet. **Surface:** gravel. 01/01-31/12

Distance: 3km on the spot 3km on the spot.

Remarks: Producer Parma ham.

S Langhirano 31D2

La Fazenda, Cascinapiano di Langhirano. **GPS**: n44,63322 e10,27410.

50 € 10, guests € 5 WC included. **Location:** Simple, quiet. **Surface:** grassy/gravel. 01/01-31/12

Distance: 1km on the spot on the spot 500m.

S Maranello 32A2

Area Camper Maranello, Via Fondo Val Tiepido 77, Torre Maina. **GPS**: n44,50008 e10,87384.

10 € 5 Ch WC. **Location:** Rural, comfortable, quiet. **Surface:** unpaved. 01/01-31/12

Distance: on the spot shuttle Bologna-Modena on the spot.

Remarks: Entrance code available at bar.

S Marzaglia 32A2

Area di sosta Marzaglia, Strada Pomposiana 305. **GPS**: n44,63514 e10,80733.

30 € 5/pppd Ch € 1,50/day WC. **Location:** Rural, comfortable, quiet. **Surface:** gravel. 01/01-31/12

Distance: Modena 10km 7km.

IT

Mesola 32C1

Oasi Park II, Via Cristina 84, SP27, Bosco Mesola. **GPS**: n44,86822 e12,24898.

130 € 8-15 Ch (100x)€ 2/day WC against payment included. **Location:** Rural, comfortable, quiet. **Surface:** grassy.
01/03-01/11
Distance: 400m 1km. **Remarks:** Borrow cycles for free.

Mesola 32C1

Via Beatrice d'Este. **GPS**: n44,92331 e12,23469.

6 free Ch free. **Location:** Rural, simple. **Surface:** asphalted.
01/01-31/12
Distance: 400m 400m 150m.
Remarks: Parking sports park.

Mesola 32C1

Agriturismo Ca'Laura, SP 27, Bosco Mesola. **GPS**: n44,87122 e12,24444.

6 € 15 Ch WC. **Location:** Luxurious, quiet. **Surface:** metalled.
01/01-31/12
Distance: 10km on the spot 1km 1km.
Remarks: Swimming pool, training golf course.

Mirandola 32A1

Via Luigi Galvani. **GPS**: n44,89812 e11,06199.
10 free Ch free. **Location:** Simple, quiet. **Surface:** gravel.
Distance: 500m 1km 1km 500m.
Remarks: At cemetery.

Misano Adriatico 32D3

Centro Caravan Misano, Via Taveleto 53. **GPS**: n43,96694 e12,67306.

12 € 18 Ch (12x)€ 2,6Amp WC € 0,50 included.
Location: Luxurious, quiet. **Surface:** grassy. 01/01-31/12
Distance: 500m 5km 2km 500m 500m.
Remarks: Video surveillance, caution key service € 10.

Modena 32A2

Camper Club Mutina, Strada Collegarola 76/A, zona Vaciglio. **GPS**: n44,61361 e10,94444.

32 € 15/24h Ch WC included. **Location:** Rural, comfortable, luxurious, quiet. **Surface:** asphalted. 01/01-31/12
Distance: 600m 3km 600m on the spot.

Modena 32A2

Ristorante Pizzeria Taverna Napoleone, Via San Lorenzo 44. **GPS**: n44,57567 e10,96415.

10 free free. **Location:** Rural. **Surface:** metalled.
01/01-31/12
Distance: 5km 2,8km pizzeria 5km.
Remarks: 10% discount at restaurant. A1 exit Modena-sud.

Tourist information Modena:

U.I..A.T. (Ufficio Informazioni e di Accoglienza Turistica), Piazza Grande, 17, www.comune.modena.it/infoturismo/guidaturismo.City with factories of Ferrari and Masserati.

Galleria Ferrari, Via Dino Ferrari 43, Maranello.Museum of motor-cars.

Monticelli d'Ongina 31D1

Piazza Resistenza. **GPS**: n45,09050 e9,93537.

10 free Ch free. **Location:** Simple, quiet. **Surface:** asphalted.
01/01-31/12
Distance: centre 300m 6,2km 300m 300m.

Parma 31D2

Area Camper Parma, Largo XXIV Agosto 1942, n° 21/a. **GPS**: n44,80931 e10,28495.

IT

30 € 1/8-22h, € 8/night Ch WC € 1.
Surface: grasstiles.
01/01-31/12
Distance: centre 3,5km 7km Lidl 100m 100m.
Remarks: Monitored parking, motorhome washing place 50m.

Tourist information Parma:
U.I.A.T. (Ufficio Informazioni e di Accoglienza Turistica), Via Melloni,1, turismo.comune.parma.it/turismo.
Palazzo Pilotta. morning.
Via Verdi.Week market. Wed-Sa 7-14h.

S Pavullo nel Frignano 32A2

Via Degli Abeti. **GPS**: n44,34294 e10,83309.

12 free Chfree. **Location:** Comfortable, quiet.
Surface: gravel/sand.
Distance: 700m 600m 600m 600m.
Remarks: Picnic area.

S Porto Corsini 32C2

Pro Loco, Via G. Guizzetti. **GPS**: n44,49620 e12,27950.

155 01/04-30/09 € 9, 01/06-30/09 € 11 Ch € 3/day WC.
Location: Rural, comfortable, quiet. **Surface:** grassy. 01/04-30/09
Distance: 500m 200m 300m 300m 300m.

S Portomaggiore 32B2

Via Giuseppe Mazzini. **GPS**: n44,69584 e11,81389.

10 free free. **Surface:** asphalted. 01/01-31/12
Distance: 500m 500m 500m.

Remarks: Nearby cemetery.

Tourist information Portomaggiore:
Valli di Comacchio.Nature reserve, in winter whereabouts birds.

Premilcuore 32B3

Parcheggio Fluviale, Loc. Fontanalba. **GPS**: n43,97618 e11,77615.

free, 15/05-15/09 € 5. **Surface:** metalled. 01/01-31/12
Distance: 500m 20m 500m 50m.
Remarks: Along river.

S Ravenna 32C2

Parking Bus-Camper, Via E.Ferrari. Loc.Classe. **GPS**: n44,37849 e12,23461.

30 free free. **Location:** Urban, simple. **Surface:** grasstiles.
01/01-31/12
Distance: Ravenna centre 6km.
Remarks: Nearby basilica.

S Ravenna 32C2

Piazza della Resistenza. **GPS**: n44,41433 e12,18852.

10 € 0,50/h, € 2,50/24h Chfree. **Location:** Urban, simple, central.
Surface: grasstiles. 01/01-31/12
Distance: historical centre 500m 5km 150m 500m 50m.
Remarks: Max. 24h.

S Ravenna 32C2

Via Pomposa. **GPS**: n44,43002 e12,20827.

10 free Chfree. **Surface:** asphalted. 01/01-31/12
Distance: city centre 2km 100m on the spot.

IT

Ravenna 32C2

Via Teodorico. **GPS**: n44,42317 e12,20981.

10 free Chfree. **Location:** Urban, simple, quiet. **Surface:** asphalted.
01/01-31/12
Distance: 500m on the spot.
Remarks: In front of the Mausoleum.

Ravenna 32C2

Via Brancaleone/circonvallazione S. Gaetanino. **GPS**: n44,42339 e12,20478.

25 free. **Location:** Urban, simple, noisy. **Surface:** metalled.
01/01-31/12
Distance: 200m 5km 100m 200m 200m 10m.
Remarks: Next to Rocca Brancaleone.

Ravenna 32C2

Area Camper Atrezzata, Eurolandia, SS16. **GPS**: n44,33533 e12,26949.

68 € 10/day, € 15/2 days Chincluded. **Location:** Rural, simple.
Surface: gravel. 01/01-31/12

Ravenna 32C2

Parco Divertimenti Mirabilandia, SS16, via Romea Sud 463. **GPS**: n44,33290 e12,26966.

400 € 15 free. **Location:** Rural, simple, noisy.
Surface: gravel.
Distance: Ravenna centre 10km McDonalds.
Remarks: Max. 48h.

Tourist information Ravenna:
U.I.A.T. (Ufficio Informazioni e di Accoglienza Turistica), Via Salara, 8/12, www.turismo.ravenna.it.City of the mosaics, historical city with many curiosities.
Piazza Garibaldi.Antiques market.
3rd weekend of the month.
Parco Divertimenti Mirabilandia, SS16, via Romea Sud 463.Amusement park.
01/04-15/09.

Reggio nell'Emilia 32A2

Parking Ex Foro Boario, Via XX Settembre. **GPS**: n44,70941 e10,62463.

200 free Chfree. **Location:** Urban, simple. **Surface:** grasstiles.
01/01-31/12
Distance: 1km 3,7km 100m 500m Free bus to centre.

Riccione 32D3

Piazza 1° Maggio. **GPS**: n44,00392 e12,65115.

10 free € 4 Ch. **Location:** Urban, simple, central, quiet.
Surface: asphalted. 01/01-31/12 Service: winter.
Distance: 100m 500m 500m 100m 50m.

Rimini 32C3

Park Settebello, Viale Roma 86. **GPS**: n44,06068 e12,57572.

300 € 10/24h € 2 € 2 (80x)€ 3/day. **Location:** Urban, simple, central, noisy. **Surface:** metalled. 01/01-31/12
Distance: 200m 500m.
Remarks: Next to cinema Settebello.

Rimini 32C3

Sostaverde La Valletta, Via Della Lama 47, SS 16. **GPS**: n44,09889 e12,49867.

150 € 10/24h € 3 WC included. **Location:** Rural, noisy.

Surface: grassy/gravel. 01/04-30/09
Distance: Rimini 11km 3,8km 2km 800m 800m.
Remarks: Beachshuttle.

Rimini 32C3

P30 Chiabrera, Via Chiabrera. **GPS:** n44,04803 e12,59548.
01/05-30/09 € 12,10. **Location:** Urban, simple, central, noisy.
Surface: asphalted.

Tourist information Rimini:
U.I.A.T. (Ufficio Informazioni e di Accoglienza Turistica), Piazzale Frederico Fellini, 3, www.riminiturismo.it/.Popular bathing resort.
Casa Zanni, Via Casale, 205, Villa Verucchio.Restaurant with authentic Italian cuisine.

Ro 32B1

Mulino sul Po. GPS: n44,95498 e11,75668.

4 free (4x)free. **Location:** Rural, simple.
Surface: metalled.
Distance: 1km on the spot on the spot.
Remarks: Along the Po river.

Rocca San Casciano 32B3

GPS: n44,06173 e11,84604.
4 free € 1/100liter Ch € 1/4h. **Location:** Rural. **Surface:** metalled.
01/01-31/12
Distance: 300m 100m.

Rubiera 32A2

Via della Chiusa. **GPS:** n44,64229 e10,77765.

free Ch. **Location:** Simple, quiet. **Surface:** asphalted.
01/01-31/12
Remarks: At sports park.

Sala Baganza 31D2

Via Vittorio Emanuele, 42. **GPS:** n44,70856 e10,23070.

2 free Ch (4x)free. **Location:** Rural, simple, quiet.
Surface: asphalted. 01/01-31/12
Distance: 500m 15km 500m.

Salsomaggiore Terme 31D2

Via Antonio Gramsci. **GPS:** n44,82005 e9,98981.

20 free free. **Location:** Urban, simple, quiet. **Surface:** gravel.
01/01-31/12
Distance: 800m.
Remarks: Parking next to station.

San Piero in Bagno 32C3

Via G.Mazzini. **GPS:** n43,86353 e11,97692.

5 free. **Surface:** asphalted. 01/01-31/12
Distance: 500m 1km 500m 500m 200m.

Santa Sofia 32C3

Piazzale K. Marx. **GPS:** n43,94165 e11,90930.

free Ch. **Surface:** asphalted. 01/01-31/12
Distance: 200m.

Tourist information Santa Sofia:
Foreste Casentinesi.National nature reserve.

Serramazzoni 32A2

Piazza Olimpico. **GPS:** n44,42223 e10,79402.

20 free Chfree. **Location:** Urban. **Surface:** asphalted.
01/01-31/12
Distance: 300m 100m 300m 300m 300m 800m.

Serramazzoni 32A2

Via Giardini Nord, Montagnana di Serramazzoni. **GPS:** n44,47250 e10,82005.

IT

15 free. **Location:** Rural, simple, quiet. **Surface:** gravel.
01/01-31/12
Distance: 8km Maranello 8km.
Remarks: Maranello: Ferrari factory and museum.

Tourist information Serramazzoni:
Ufficio Turistico, Piazzo Tasso,7.

S Soragna 31D1

Via Matteotti / via Gramsci. **GPS**: n44,92988 e10,12566.

10 free Chfree. **Location:** Urban, simple, quiet. **Surface:** asphalted.
01/01-31/12
Distance: 120m 200m 200m.

Suviana 32A3

Via Lungo Lago. **GPS**: n44,12039 e11,04592.

60 Free, hollidays € 9. **Location:** Rural, simple, quiet.
Surface: asphalted.
Distance: on the spot on the spot on the spot.
Remarks: At lake Suviana.

S Terenzo 31D2

Loc. Bardone. **GPS**: n44,62528 e10,10083.

10 € 13 Ch WC included. **Location:** Rural, comfortable, quiet. **Surface:** metalled. 01/01-31/12
Distance: 200m 12km 12km on the spot.

S Tredozio 32B3

Via Salvo D'Acquisto. **GPS**: n44,07431 e11,73228.

10 € 5 Ch. **Surface:** metalled. 01/01-31/12
Distance: 1,5km 200m camping 1,5km.
Remarks: Next to campsite Le Volte, max. 48h, reductions at restaurant/ swimming-pool.

S Tresigallo 32B1

Fraz. Finale di Rero. **GPS**: n44,81643 e11,90050.
free.
Remarks: Nearby sports park.

S Vergato 32A2

SS 64, Bologna-Pistoia. **GPS**: n44,28952 e11,11270.

25 free Chfree. **Location:** Rural, simple. **Surface:** asphalted.
01/01-31/12
Distance: 400m 400m 500m 500m.
Remarks: On entering de village from Bologna.

Liguria

S Borghetto Santo Spirito 31B3

Via Tevere. **GPS**: n44,11548 e8,23758.

150 € 10 Ch (50x)€ 3/day,16Amp. **Surface:** gravel.
Distance: 1,1km 2,5km 400m.
Remarks: Along the river Varatella.

S Castelnuovo Magra 31D3

Agriturismo Cascina dei Peri, Via Montefrancio 71. **GPS**: n44,10355 e10,00734.

6 € 8,50/pp, children free Ch € 3 WC included € 5.

Surface: grassy/gravel. 01/01-31/12
Distance: 2,4km.
Remarks: Dinner € 20/pp wine incl. (to order <16h), selling of wine and olive oil, swimming pool from june.

S Cengio 31B2
Area Attrezzata Cengio Isole, Via Isole. **GPS:** n44,39083 e8,20194.

free Chfree. **Surface:** asphalted.
Distance: 600m on the spot on the spot.
Remarks: Nearby sports park.

S Cervo 31A3
Via Steria. **GPS:** n43,92833 e8,10527.

130 € 8-12/day Ch € 3/24h. **Surface:** gravel.
01/01-31/12
Distance: 2,5km.

S Diano Marina 31A3
Oasi Park, Via Sori 5. **GPS:** n43,90667 e8,07083.

300 € 5-15/day Ch € 2 WC . **Surface:** grassy/gravel.
01/01-31/12
Distance: 600m 6,8km 700m 600m 600m 600m.
Remarks: Beachshuttle.

S Diano Marina 31A3
Il bowling di Diano, Via Diano S. Pietro, 71 - Diano Castello. **GPS:** n43,91683 e8,07576.

€ 5-10-15/day Ch . **Surface:** unpaved.
Distance: 500m 5,5km 500m on the spot 50m.

Remarks: Swimming pool, bar, bowling.

S Diano Marina 31A3
Al Roseto, Via Case Parse, San siro, Diano Castello. **GPS:** n43,91983 e8,07733.

€ 12, free for clients Ch WC € 2 . 01/01-31/12
Distance: 5,5km.
Remarks: At Floriculturist, shuttle to beach.

Tourist information Diano Marina:
I.A.T. (Ufficio Informazioni e di Accoglienza Turistica), Corso Garibaldi, 60.

S Finale Ligure 31B3
Loc. Caprazoppa. **GPS:** n44,16549 e8,33750.
100 € 8/12h, € 15/24h Chagainst payment.
Distance: 4km on the spot.

S La Spezia 31D3
Viale San Bartolomeo. **GPS:** n44,10417 e9,85917.

100 voluntary contribution free. **Surface:** grassy.
8-20h 12.30-13.30h.
Distance: 4km.
Remarks: Monitored parking.

Tourist information La Spezia:
Lerici.Former fishing village, nowadays holiday resort.
Cinque Terre.Protected coast area.
Castello di Lerici, Lerici. 01/04-31/10.
Lerici. Sa-morning.

S Levanto 31C3
SP556, Loc. Moltedi. **GPS:** n44,17476 e9,61836.

16 € 12/12h, € 15/24h, € 20/36h Chfree. 01/01-31/12
Distance: 500m 1km train 100m.
Remarks: Behind railway station, good location for visiting the Cinque Terre by train.

S Loano 31B3
Camper Park, Via Silvio Amico, via delle Fornaci.. **GPS:** n44,13111 e8,24111.

44 € 10/24h Ch 6Amp WC included. **Surface:** gravel.
Distance: 1,4km 7km 1,5km 200m.
Remarks: Max. 48h.

Tourist information Loano:
U.I.A.T. (Ufficio Informazioni e di Accoglienza Turistica), Toirano, www.italianriviera.com.Small medieval town.
Grotta di Santa Lucia, Toirano.Stalactites and stalagmites.
Grotta della Basura, Toirano.Man and beast from the stone age.

S Pietra Ligure 31B3

Area Camper, Via Crispi 43. **GPS**: n44,15484 e8,28397.

53 € 13/24h, 01/06-30/09 € 16/24h Ch (53x)included WC € 0,70. **Surface:** gravel.
Distance: 200m.

S Portovenere 31D3

Via Olivo, Loc. Cavo. **GPS**: n44,05961 e9,84843.

20 € 1,85/h 8-20h, overnight stay free Ch. **Surface:** metalled.
01/01-31/12
Distance: 2km 750m 600m 50m.

S San Bartolomeo al Mare 31A3

Via Manzoni. **GPS**: n43,92432 e8,10489.
10 € 8/24h free. **Surface:** gravel.
Distance: 2,5km.
Remarks: Along the river Stera, max. 48h.

San Rocco 31C3

Viale Franco Molfino/Camogli. **GPS**: n44,33472 e9,16084.

9 € 9/8-20h. **Surface:** asphalted.
Distance: on the spot.
Remarks: Marked hiking trails in Parco di Portofino (45min-2h).

S Santo Stefano al Mare 31A4

Camper Village, Strada Porsani. **GPS**: n43,84378 e7,90824.

60 € 12-20/24h Ch € 3 WC. **Surface:** gravel.
Distance: 10km 800m on the spot.
Remarks: Free shuttle.

S Torriglia 31C2

GPS: n44,51667 e9,16000.

10 free Chfree. **Surface:** grasstiles.
Distance: 200m.
Remarks: Municipal parking.

Tuscany

S Alberese 32B6

Parco Naturale della Maremma, Via del Bersagliere. **GPS**: n42,66944 e11,10416.

50 € 9/day, € 6/½day Chfree. **Surface:** sand.
01/04-30/09
Distance: 100m 7km on the spot.

S Anghiari 32C4

Via Campo della Fiera. **GPS**: n43,53904 e12,05291.

8 free Chfree. **Surface:** asphalted.
Distance: on the spot on the spot on the spot.

IT

Anghiari 32C4

Agriturismo Val della Pieve, Via della Fossa 8. **GPS**: n43,53657 e12,05131.

10 € 12 Ch € 3 WC . **Surface:** gravel.
01/01-31/12
Distance: 300m 300m 300m 300m.
Remarks: Swimming pool € 3/pppd.

Anghiari 32C4

Agriturismo La Taverna dei Sorci, San Lorenzo. **GPS**: n43,51467 e12,07799.

20 free . **Surface:** metalled. 01/01-31/12
Distance: on the spot.

Arcidosso 32B5

Parco Faunistico Monte Amiata, Località Poderi. **GPS**: n42,83740 e11,52922.

15 free Ch. **Location:** Rural, simple, central, quiet. **Surface:** grassy.
01/01-31/12
Distance: 10km.
Remarks: Nature reserve.

Arezzo 32C4

Via Da Palestrina/via Tarlati (centro-nord). **GPS**: n43,47213 e11,88773.

30 € 8 Ch free. **Surface:** asphalted.
Distance: historical centre 1km.

Arezzo 32C4

P Tarlati, Via Guido Tarlati. **GPS**: n43,47237 e11,88362.

50 free. **Location:** Urban, central. **Surface:** grasstiles.
01/01-31/12
Distance: city centre 1km 500m 300m.

Tourist information Arezzo:
Informazioni Turistiche, Piazza della Repubblica, 28.
Week market.

Barberino di Mugello 32B3

SS65, Fraz. Monte di Fó. **GPS**: n44,07613 e11,28062.

30 free Ch free. **Surface:** metalled.
Distance: 4km 150m (camping) 150m (camping).
Remarks: In front of campsite Il Sergente.

Barga 32A3

Area San Cristoforo, Via Hayange. **GPS**: n44,07234 e10,48131.

€ 10/24h Ch (10x) WC 200m.
Distance: centro storico within walking distance.

Bibbiena 32C3

Agricola Casentinese, Loc. Casanova 63. **GPS**: n43,71669 e11,85173.

€ 12, Apr, May, Oct € 15, Jun-Sep € 18, 2 pers.incl Ch WC included € 5,ironing services € 5. **Surface:** gravel.
15/03-01/11, Christmas
Distance: 4km on the spot on the spot.
Remarks: Swimming pool € 5/pp (free with a meal).

Borghetto 32C4

GPS: n43,18415 e12,02372.

IT

4 free free. **Surface:** asphalted. 01/01-31/12
Distance: 150m 100m.

Borgo a Mozzano — S — 32A3

Via I° Maggio, SP2. **GPS:** n43,97612 e10,54113.

4 free Ch (4x)free. **Surface:** gravel.
Distance: 200m Serchio river.
Remarks: At tourist office.

Buonconvento — 32B5

Viale della Liberta. **GPS:** n43,13854 e11,48109.

free. **Location:** Simple. **Surface:** unpaved.
Distance: 50m 50m.
Remarks: SS2 exit centre, in opposite of the city walls.

Buonconvento — S — 32B5

Viale Ferruccio Parri. **GPS:** n43,13065 e11,48349.

€ 1 Ch. 01/01-31/12

Calci — S — 32A4

Via Brogiotti. **GPS:** n43,72769 e10,51722.

6 € 8/24h Ch included. **Surface:** asphalted. 01/01-31/12
Distance: 100m 200m.
Remarks: At sports park, payment only with coins.

Campiglia Marittima — S — 32A5

Parcheggio La Pieve, Via di Venturina. **GPS:** n43,05672 e10,61439.

4 free Chfree. **Location:** Rural. **Surface:** asphalted.
Distance: 350m 450m 500m.
Remarks: Near gymnasium, in opposite of cemetery.

Capraia e Limite — S — 32A3

Via delle Ginestre, zona industriale, loc. Capraia Fiorentina. **GPS:** n43,73660 e11,00442.

free Chfree. **Surface:** metalled.

Casola in Lunigiana — S — 31D3

GPS: n44,19916 e10,17333.

20 € 7 + € 5/pp Ch WC included. **Surface:** grassy. 01/01-31/12
Distance: on the spot.
Remarks: At little stream with swimming area.

Castagneto Carducci — S — 32A5

Camperesort, Via Aurelia 373/B. **GPS:** n43,15630 e10,56097.

50 € 10 + € 7/pp, 16/09-14/06 € 5/pp Ch WC € 0,50 € 3 included. **Location:** Luxurious. **Surface:** grassy/gravel. 01/01-31/12
Distance: 1,2km on the spot.
Remarks: Swimming pool incl.

IT

Castagneto Carducci 32A5

Via del Seggio, Marina di Castagneto. **GPS**: n43,18401 e10,54841.

30 € 10/24h Chfree. **Surface:** unpaved.
Distance: 2km 500m 2,5km 2,5km.

Castagneto Carducci 32A5

Viale delle Palme, Marina di Castagneto. **GPS**: n43,19323 e10,54152.

20 € 10/24h Ch. **Surface:** unpaved.
Distance: 100m.
Remarks: Max. 48h, also dog beach.

Castel del Piano 32B5

Via Po. **GPS**: n42,88872 e11,53733.

30 free Chfree. **Location:** Rural, simple. **Surface:** asphalted.
01/01-31/12
Distance: 500m.
Remarks: Follow 'P long stay'.

Castelfiorentino 32A4

Ara Comunale, Via Che Guevara, circonvallazione Ovest. **GPS**: n43,60885 e10,96365.

5 free free. **Location:** Simple, isolated. **Surface:** asphalted.
Distance: 1,5km 1,5km 1,5km.

Castellina in Chianti 32B4

La Strada del Chianti, SR222. **GPS**: n43,47330 e11,28760.

15 € 10/24h, 01/11-31/03 free € 0,20/10liter Ch (8x)included WC € 0,50. **Location:** Rural, comfortable. **Surface:** asphalted.
01/01-31/12
Distance: 200m.

Tourist information Castellina in Chianti:
Uffici Informazione Turistica, Via Ferruccio 40.
Via IV Novembre.Week market. Sa-morning.

Castelnuovo di Garfagnana 32A3

Via Valmaira. **GPS**: n44,11447 e10,40304.

free Chfree. **Surface:** metalled. 01/01-31/12
Distance: 1km.
Remarks: At sports park.

Castelnuovo di Val de Cecina 32A5

Via della Fonte, Sasso Pisano. **GPS**: n43,16748 e10,86586.

10 free € 2 Ch € 3/12h. **Location:** Rural. **Surface:** metalled.
01/01-31/12
Distance: 100m 200m.

Castiglion Fiorentino 32C4

Piazza Garibaldi, viale Marconi. **GPS**: n43,34465 e11,92278.

20 free Chfree WC. **Location:** Rural, simple. **Surface:** asphalted.
01/01-31/12 Fri-morning market.
Distance: on the spot on the spot.

Castiglione della Pescaia 32A5

Rocchette Serignano, Via Rio Palma, Rocchette. **GPS**: n42,77970 e10,79955.

IT

± 50 € 20/day Ch (18x)included € 1. **Surface:** unpaved.
01/04-30/09
Distance: Castiglione della Pescaia 7km 200m 200m.
Remarks: Beach parking, unguarded.

S Castiglione della Pescaia 32A5

Viale Kennedy, SS158. **GPS**: n42,77447 e10,84395.

40 Apr-Jun, Sep € 12, Jul/Aug € 15 Ch. **Surface:** asphalted.
01/04-30/09
Distance: 4km 500m 4km 4km.

S Castiglione d'Orcia 32B5

Area Pro Loco, Viale Marconi. **GPS**: n43,00292 e11,61552.

5 free free. **Location:** Rural, simple. **Surface:** gravel/sand. 01/01-31/12
Distance: 200m on the spot.

Tourist information Castiglione d'Orcia:
Rocco d'Orcia.Medieval citadel.

S Certaldo 32A4

Area Comunale, Piazza dei Macelli. **GPS**: n43,54629 e11,04611.

10 free Chfree. **Location:** Rural. **Surface:** metalled.
01/01-31/12
Distance: medieval centre 150m (elevator) 150m 250m.

S Chiusdino 32B5

Abbazia San Galgano, SS441. **GPS**: n43,15283 e11,15137.

15 € 1,50/h, € 10/8-20h, overnight stay free (9x)free. **Location:** Rural, isolated, quiet. **Surface:** grasstiles. 01/01-31/12
Distance: 12km 300m.
Remarks: Abbey of San Galgano 300m.

S Chiusi 32C5

Via Torri del Fornello. **GPS**: n43,01461 e11,94972.

5 free free. **Surface:** asphalted.
Distance: 100m 4,5km.
Remarks: Next to school.

S Cutigliano 32A3

Via di Risorgimento/Sp37. **GPS**: n44,09877 e10,75450.
14 € 1,50/h, € 15/24h Ch.
Remarks: Max. 24h.

S Dicomano 32B3

Via Ciro Fabbroni. **GPS**: n43,88965 e11,52150.

16 free Chfree. **Surface:** asphalted. 01/01-31/12
Distance: 500m 500m 500m.

S Equi Terme 31D3

Via della Stazione. **GPS**: n44,17009 e10,15513.

40 € 10/night Ch included. **Surface:** gravel.
Distance: 100m.
Remarks: Near spa resort (100m), caves (500m) and marble quarry.

S Firenze 32B3

FiPark, Viale Europa, Fraz. Bagno a Ripoli, Florence (Firenze). **GPS**: n43,75554 e11,30609.

40 7-19h € 1,50/h, 19-7h € 1/h, € 15/24jh Ch. **Surface:** metalled. 01/01-31/12
Distance: bus 23/33 > centre.

S Firenze 32B3

Area sociale 'Flog', Via M Mercati 24/b, zona Careggi, Florence (Firenze). **GPS**: n43,79491 e11,24835.

€ 15/24h € 3 Ch. **Surface:** gravel. 01/01-31/12
Distance: city centre 2km Pizzeria centre : bus 4, 6-24h.

S Firenze 32B3

Florence Park Scandicci, Via di Scandicci 241, Florence (Firenze). **GPS**: n43,76267 e11,20875.

25 € 15 Ch included. **Location:** Urban, comfortable, central.
Surface: metalled. 01/01-31/12
Distance: 4km 5km 150m.
Remarks: Terrain with video surveillance.

S Firenze 32B3

Gelsomino SCAF, Via del Gelsomino 11, Florence (Firenze). **GPS**: n43,75173 e11,24388.
€ 15/24h Ch included. **Surface:** asphalted. 01/01-31/12
Distance: 2km on the spot.

Tourist information Florence (Firenze):
U.I.A.T. (Ufficio Informazioni e di Accoglienza Turistica), Piazza Stazione, 4, www.firenze.turismo.toscana.it.Renaissance city with many curiosities.
Ponte Vechio.Famous bridge with jeweller's shops.
Cappella Brancacci, Santa Maria del Carmine.Renovated frescoes.
The Mall, le griffe, Via Europa 8, Leccio Reggello.Factory outlet.

Firenzuola 32B3

Area Picnic, Loc. Badia a Moscheta. **GPS**: n44,07586 e11,42064.

10 free. **Surface:** gravel. 01/01-31/12
Distance: Firenzuola 8km 500m agriturismo Badia di Moscheta.

Firenzuola 32B3

Loc. Pieve di Camaggiore. **GPS**: n44,14594 e11,45361.

20 free. **Surface:** grasstiles. 01/01-31/12
Distance: Firenzuola 10km river 100m.
Remarks: Playground.

S Fivizzano 31D3

Agriturismo Ristorante Al Vecchio Tino, Loc. Germalla 1, Monte dei Bianchi. **GPS**: n44,17155 e10,13325.
6 € 12 Ch included. **Surface:** grassy. 01/01-31/12

Foiano della Chiana 32C4

Outlet Village Valdichiana, Via Enzo Ferrari 5, loc. Farniole. **GPS**: n43,22489 e11,80291.

10 free. **Location:** Simple. **Surface:** asphalted. 01/01-31/12
Distance: on the spot on the spot.
Remarks: Motorhome parking at Outlet.

S Follonica 32A5

Eucalyptus Camper Park, Via Sanzio. **GPS**: n42,92804 e10,77569.

40 € 10 € 4 Ch included € 1.
Distance: beach 1,8km 1km 1km.

S Gaiole in Chianti 32B4

Via Michelangelo Buonarroti. **GPS**: n43,46434 e11,43440.

IT

free Chfree. **Location:** Rural, simple. **Surface:** metalled.
01/01-31/12
Remarks: Nearby football ground.

S Gallicano 32A3
Via dei Cipressi. **GPS:** n44,05827 e10,44565.

4 free Ch (2x)free. **Surface:** metalled. 01/01-31/12
Distance: 500m.
Remarks: Grotta del Vento.

S Greve in Chianti 32B4
Monte S. Michele, Via Montebeni. **GPS:** n43,59066 e11,31355.

17 free free. **Location:** Rural, comfortable, quiet. **Surface:** metalled.
01/01-31/12
Distance: 500m 500m.

Tourist information Greve in Chianti:
Ufficio Informazioni, Via Luca Cini, 1.
Sa-morning.

S Isola dElba 32A5
San Bennato, Cavo. **GPS:** n42,85459 e10,42267.
50 € 18/24h Ch € 2 € 1. **Surface:** gravel.
01/06-30/09
Distance: 600m 400m.

S Isola dElba 32A5
Loc. Bocchetto, Porto Azzurro. **GPS:** n42,77114 e10,39985.
60 € 15/24h .
Remarks: Nearby cemetery.

S Isola dElba 32A5
Sighello, area La Pila, Marina di Campo. **GPS:** n42,75905 e10,23645.
20 € 10/15 Ch € 3. **Surface:** unpaved. 01/05-30/09
Distance: 1,5km.
Remarks: At sports park.

S Larciano 32A3
Residence Poggetto, Via Stradella 1489. **GPS:** n43,83319 e10,88042.

15 € 10/24h, free with a meal Ch . **Surface:** grassy/gravel.
01/01-31/12
Distance: 1km 1km.

S Livorno 32A4
Il Cavalluccio, Via G. Pascoli 12, Fraz Quercianella. **GPS:** n43,46027 e10,36222.

44 € 18/night Ch WC included. **Surface:** unpaved.
Distance: sea 50m.

Livorno 32A4
Piazza Ordoardo Borrani, Viale d'Antignano. **GPS:** n43,50465 e10,32144.

50 free. **Location:** Rural. **Surface:** asphalted.
Distance: 400m Antignano 100m 300m.

Tourist information Livorno:
Ufficio Informazioni, Piazza del Municipio.Medieval port city.

S Lucca 32A3
Il Serchio, Via del Tiro a Segno 704, loc. Sant'Anna. **GPS:** n43,85000 e10,48583.

66 € 20/24h Ch (66x),4 WC € 4,50 included.
Surface: grasstiles. 01/03-31/01
Distance: 1km 2km 500m on the spot 2km on the spot.
Remarks: Swimming pool € 5/pp.

S Lucca 32A3
P-Caravana, Viale Gaetano Luporini. **GPS:** n43,84028 e10,48878.

IT

65 € 10/24h, € 3/h Ch included. **Surface:** asphalted.
Distance: 5 min walking 2km.

Tourist information Lucca:
A.P.T. (Azienda di Promozione Turistica), Piazza Guidiccioni, 2.Historical city with ramparts.
Casa di Puccini, Via di Poggio.Birth place of the composer. Tue-Su.
Wed, Sa, 3rd Su of the month antiques market.

S Lucignano 32B4

SP19. **GPS:** n43,27664 e11,74512.

20 free Ch (9x)free. **Location:** Rural, simple. **Surface:** grassy.
01/01-31/12
Distance: 500m.
Remarks: At the edge of village.

S Marina di Cecina 32A4

Parcheggio Aqua Park, Marina di Cecina. **GPS:** n43,30070 e10,49948.

100 01/03-15/11 € 8 Ch. **Location:** Rural. **Surface:** metalled.
01/01-31/12
Distance: 2km 1km 200m 200m.

S Marina di Cecina 32A4

Via della Cecinella. **GPS:** n43,29278 e10,50785.

30 1/3-15/11 € 8/24h Ch. **Location:** Rural, simple, quiet.
Surface: asphalted. 01/01-31/12
Distance: 2km 300m 2km 2km.

S Marina di Grosseto 32B5

Oasi di Maremma, SP158 delle Collacchie Km 34,4. **GPS:** n42,72611 e10,99055.

100 € 15, peak season € 18, 4 pers.incl Ch (100x)€ 2 WC € 1
€ 3. **Surface:** grassy. 01/04-30/09
Distance: 1km 1km 1km 1km on the spot.
Remarks: Water at each pitch, shuttle € 1,50/pp.

S Marina di Grosseto 32B5

Area di sosta l'Oasi, S332 > dir San Vincenzo d'Elba. **GPS:** n42,73466 e10,97483.

50 Jun € 14, Jul/Aug € 18, Sep € 12, 4 pers.incl Ch € 2 WC € 2
. **Surface:** grassy. Easter-30/09
Distance: Marina 1,5km 1,1km 400m nearby.

Marina di Grosseto 32B5

Via Costiera, SP158. **GPS:** n42,73722 e10,96388.

50 free. **Surface:** gravel. 01/01-31/12
Distance: 2km 400m.

Tourist information Marina di Grosseto:
Parco Naturale della Maremma.Nature reserve.
Wed, Sa, Su 9h 01/06-30/09 guided walk 7h, 16h.

S Marina di Pisa 31D4

Parcheggio Camper Pisamo, Viale Gabriela d'Annunzio. **GPS:** n43,67908 e10,27830.
130 € 15/24h Ch . **Surface:** sand. 01/01-31/12
Distance: sea 1km.

S Marradi 32B3

Area Attrezzata, Via San Benedetto. **GPS:** n44,07347 e11,61166.

IT

30 free Ch € 5. Surface: asphalted. 01/01-31/12
Distance: 50m.
Remarks: Caution key service € 7.

S Massa Marittima 32A5

Viale del Risorgimento. GPS: n43,04530 e10,89050.

7 free Chfree. Surface: asphalted. 01/01-31/12
Distance: historical centre 650m 600m 500m on the spot.

S Minucciano 31D3

Agriturismo Da Pasquino, Perdetola. GPS: n44,16644 e10,21514.
50 free with a meal Ch .

S Montalcino 32B5

Geen, Via Osticcio. GPS: n43,04913 e11,48749.

30 € 5/24h Chfree. Location: Rural, comfortable, quiet. Surface: asphalted/metalled. 01/01-31/12
Distance: 700m 700m 700m.

S Monte San Savino 32B4

Via del Casalino. GPS: n43,33177 e11,72204.

20 free Chfree. Location: Rural, simple. Surface: gravel. 01/01-31/12
Distance: on the spot 4,2km 200m.
Remarks: Steep path.

Montecatini Terme 32A3

Piazza Pietro Leopoldo, SS 436. GPS: n43,88286 e10,76386.
40 free. Surface: asphalted. 01/01-31/12 Thu (market).
Distance: 3km 500m 500m.

Remarks: In front of stadium.

S Montemignaio 32B3

Via Molino. GPS: n43,73989 e11,62024.
free free. Surface: gravel. 01/01-31/12
Distance: 150m.

S Montepulciano 32C5

P5, Piazza Pietro Nenni. GPS: n43,09577 e11,78684.

32 € 10/24h free. Location: Rural, simple. Surface: asphalted.
01/01-31/12 Thu-morning closed because of market.
Distance: 200m 100m 400m.

Monteriggioni 32B4

Strada di Monteriggioni. GPS: n43,38801 e11,22511.

12 € 1/h 8-20h, max. € 5, overnight stay free. Location: Rural, comfortable. Surface: gravel. 01/01-31/12
Distance: 300m 1,4km 300m on the spot.

S Monteroni d'Arbia 32B4

Via San Giusto. GPS: n43,23048 e11,42371.

free Chfree. Location: Rural, simple. Surface: sand.
01/01-31/12
Distance: 50m.
Remarks: P centre.

S Montespertoli 32B4

Molino del Ponte, Via Volterrana Nord. GPS: n43,65606 e11,08445.

5 free € 1/100liter € 2Ch. Location: Rural. Surface: metalled.
01/01-31/12

Distance: Montespertoli 2,3km on the spot 400m.

S Montevarchi 32B4

Via B. Latini. **GPS**: n43,53052 e11,56784.

free free. **Location:** Urban, simple. **Surface:** asphalted.
Distance: 7km Coop.
Remarks: Nearby stadium.

S Montopoli in Val d'Arno 32A4

Piazza Amerigo Vespucci, Via di Masoria. **GPS**: n43,67333 e10,75222.

31 free Ch free. **Surface:** metalled. 01/01-31/12
Distance: within walking distance.

S Orbetello 32B6

Lanino Parco Sosta, Loc. Santa Liberata. **GPS**: n42,43346 e11,15959.

50 € 10/motorhome, € 8/pp, € 5/child Ch (40x)included WC.
Surface: grassy/gravel. 01/01-31/12
Distance: Orbetello 5km 50m 200m alimentari.
Remarks: Max. 72h.

S Palazzuolo sul Senio 32B3

Parcheggio Casone, Via Casone. **GPS**: n44,11073 e11,54968.

100 free Ch free. **Surface:** asphalted. 01/01-31/12
Distance: 100m 100m 100m.

Palazzuolo sul Senio 32B3

Via Francesco Pagliazzi. **GPS**: n44,11551 e11,54984.

6 free. **Surface:** metalled. 01/01-31/12
Distance: on the spot.
Remarks: Next to cemetery, upper part of the parking.

S Peccioli 32A4

Parco Preistorico, Via Cappuccini. **GPS**: n43,55694 e10,71889.

15 free, after 2 days € 5/day WC. **Location:** Rural, simple.
Surface: gravel. 01/01-31/12
Distance: 500m 500m 2km.
Remarks: Playground, picknic area.

Tourist information Peccioli:

Parco Preistorico, Via Cappuccini. 01/01-31/12.

S Pienza 32B5

Via Mencattelli e Foro Boario. **GPS**: n43,07799 e11,68087.

8-20h: € 1,50/1h, € 5/4h, € 10/8h, overnight stay free Ch included WC. **Location:** Rural, simple. **Surface:** asphalted.
01/01-31/12 Fri-morning market.
Distance: 100m.

S Pieve Santo Stefano 32C3

Grey camper, Via della Verna. **GPS**: n43,67000 e12,03750.

15 € 10 Ch WC included. **Surface:** metalled.
01/01-31/12
Distance: on the spot 1,7km.
Remarks: Nearby viaduct E45.

S Piombino 32A5

Camperoasi, Loc. Mortelliccio, Riotorto. **GPS**: n42,95416 e10,66638.

IT

93 € 20, Apr-Jun, Sep € 30, Jul/Aug € 40 Ch WC included € 0,50 **Location:** Comfortable. **Surface:** grasstiles/grassy. 01/01-31/12 01/10-31/03 Mo-Thu.
Distance: 200m 50m 50m.
Remarks: Water/drainage at each pitch, reception open: 9.30-12.30 14-19.30, 10% discount on presentation of the guide 2012.

S Piombino 32A5

Carbonifera 1, Loc. Torre Mozza. **GPS:** n42,94750 e10,69277.

± 75 € 2/h, € 18/24h Chincluded. **Surface:** grassy/gravel.
Distance: 50m.
Remarks: Beach parking, no camping activity.

S Piombino 32A5

Parcheggio Caldanelle, Loc. Caldanelle. **GPS:** n43,00216 e10,52816.

150 € 2/h, € 17/8-20h, overnight stay free Ch.
Location: Isolated, quiet. **Surface:** grassy.
01/01-31/12
Distance: Piombino 9km 1,5km.
Remarks: Beach parking, shuttle, no camping activity.

S Piombino 32A5

Perelli 1-3, Loc. Perelli. **GPS:** n42,95527 e10,61944.

50 € 2/h, € 16/8-20h, overnight stay free Chfree. **Location:** Quiet.
Surface: grassy/sand. 01/06-30/09
Distance: sandy beach Perelli 1.
Remarks: Beach parking, no camping activity, dog beach, service: Perelli 3.

S Piombino 32A5

Via della Pace. **GPS:** n42,93777 e10,52194.

15 free € 0,10/10liter Ch. **Location:** Urban, noisy. **Surface:** metalled.
01/01-31/12
Distance: 500m 1km 700m 800m.

S Pisa 32A4

Parcheggio camper, Via di Pratale 78. **GPS:** n43,72106 e10,42066.

100 € 12/night, € 1/h, € 5/6h € 3 Ch . **Location:** Quiet.
Surface: asphalted.
Distance: 800m 7km on the spot.
Remarks: Monitored parking. A12, exit 12 Pisa north.

Tourist information Pisa:

Agenzia per il turismo di Pisa, Via S. Pellico n° 6; Piazza Vittorio Emanuale; Piazza Arcivescovado, 8.

S Pistoia 32A3

Via Marino Marini/via della Quiete. **GPS:** n43,94389 e10,91556.
50 free . **Surface:** asphalted.
Distance: city centre 1km 6km on the spot.
Remarks: At sports park.

S Pistoia 32A3

Agricamper Podere Campofossato. **GPS:** n43,99503 e10,89520.
8 € 20 Ch included.
Distance: 50m.
Remarks: Regional products.

S Poggibonsi 32B4

Via Fortezza Medicea, loc. Vallone. **GPS:** n43,46203 e11,14593.

± 15 free € 0,10/10liter Ch (6x)€ 1/12h. **Location:** Rural.
Surface: gravel. 01/01-31/12
Distance: centre 500m 400m 500m.

Tourist information Poggibonsi:

Monteriggioni.Walled small town.

S Pontassieve 32B3

Viale Hanoi/viale Lisbona. **GPS:** n43,77370 e11,42764.
free Chfree. **Surface:** asphalted.

S Poppi 32B3

La Crocina, Viale dei Pini. **GPS:** n43,71982 e11,76529.

12 free Ch free € 3/5h. **Surface:** asphalted.
01/01-31/12
Distance: historical centre 500m 300m.

Porto Ercole 32B6

Le Miniere, SP di Porto Ercole. **GPS**: n42,41749 e11,20386.

130 € 23/24h, Aug € 25, Sep € 20 Ch WC included € 0,50 € 5. **Surface:** grassy.
Easter-30/09
Distance: Porto Ercole 2km 800m 800m.
Remarks: Free shuttle to beach, bread-service, borrow cycles for free.

Porto Ercole 32B6

Parking Da Renzo, SC della Feniglia. **GPS**: n42,41527 e11,20777.

150 € 18 € 7 Ch € 3. **Surface:** grassy.
Easter-01/10
Distance: Porto Ercole 3km beach 1km 800m.
Remarks: Beach shuttle, no camping activity.

Pratovecchio 32B3

Via Uffenheim. **GPS**: n43,78680 e11,71932.

12 free Ch free. **Surface:** asphalted. 01/01-31/12
Distance: 50m 100m 100m.
Remarks: Along the river, follow signs instead of GPS.

Radda in Chianti 32B4

Viale 20 Settembre. **GPS**: n43,48643 e11,37543.

6 € 12/24h WC free. **Location:** Rural, simple. **Surface:** metalled.
01/01-31/12
Distance: 200m (stairs).

Radicofani 32C5

Via della Mossa. **GPS**: n42,89427 e11,77598.

5 free Ch free. **Location:** Rural, simple. **Surface:** grassy/gravel.
01/01-31/12
Distance: 400m.

Radicondoli 32B4

Il Pianetto. **GPS**: n43,25888 e11,04250.

€ 1/1h, >1 hour € 0,50/h Ch (16x). **Surface:** unpaved.
01/01-31/12
Distance: medieval centre 300m 300m 2km.

Rapolano Terme 32B4

Villa dei Boschi, Loc. Villa dei Boschi 50, Fraz San Gimignanello, SP10. **GPS**: n43,22829 e11,65429.

20 € 15, free with a meal WC included. **Location:** Rural, simple.
Surface: grassy. 01/01-31/12
Distance: on the spot.

Rapolano Terme 32B4

Area di sosta Le Terme, Via Trieste. **GPS**: n43,29243 e11,60752.

IT

64 € 5/6h, € 8/12h, € 12/24h Ch WC included € 2.
Location: Rural, comfortable. **Surface:** gravel/metalled. 01/01-31/12
Distance: 500m 50m 200m.

Remarks: Terme Antica Querciolaia 50m.

S Rosignano Marittimo 32A4
Molino a Fuoco, Via dei Cavalleggeri Antica, Vada. **GPS**: n43,32816 e10,46005.

70 1/4-15/9 € 10 Ch. **Surface:** grassy/gravel.
Distance: 400m 500m 400m 400m.
Remarks: Max. 72h.

S Rosignano Marittimo 32A4
Il Fortullino, Loc. Castiglioncello. **GPS**: n43,42889 e10,39750.

150 € 15/night, Jul-Aug € 20 Ch included. **Surface:** unpaved.
01/04-30/09
Distance: Castiglioncello 4km, Livorno 20km, Pisa 40km 150m Pizzeria 100m 5km.
Remarks: 4Km north from Castiglioncello.

S Rosignano Marittimo 32A4
SP39, Via Aurelia, Loc Caletta. **GPS**: n43,39900 e10,42807.

18 € 8 free. **Surface:** metalled.
Distance: on the spot 300m 100m.
Remarks: Along busy through road, max. 48h.

Rosignano Marittimo 32A4
Parcheggio del Lillatro, Via Fratelli Gigli, loc Lillatro. **GPS**: n43,38380 e10,43206.

40 € 9. **Location:** Simple, isolated, quiet. **Surface:** sand.
Easter-31/10
Distance: 50m 50m.

Rosignano Marittimo 32A4
Sportiva Vada, Via Mare Mediterraneo, Vada. **GPS**: n43,35208 e10,45183.

75 € 10/day. **Location:** Rural, quiet. **Surface:** unpaved.
01/04-01/10
Distance: 400m 200m 200m 400m.

San Casciano dei Bagni 32C5
Via Della Pineta. **GPS**: n42,86530 e11,87383.

15 free. **Location:** Rural, simple. **Surface:** gravel/sand.
01/01-31/12
Distance: 500m.

S San Casciano dei Bagni 32C5
Piazzale del Ponte. **GPS**: n42,87024 e11,87742.

15 € 5/12h, € 10/24h Ch. **Surface:** asphalted. 01/01-31/12
Distance: 100m.
Remarks: Near spa resort.

S San Casciano in Val di Pesa 32B4
Parco Il Poggione. **GPS**: n43,65395 e11,18768.

IT

5 free free.

San Gimignano 32A4

Area di Sosta Santa Chiara, Via di Castel San Gimignano, Loc. Fprmace. **GPS**: n43,45572 e11,03476.

30 € 22/24h € 2 Ch WC included. **Location:** Rural, luxurious. **Surface:** gravel. 01/01-31/12

Distance: 3km osteria/bar 1,5km shuttle.

Remarks: Free shuttle bus to San Gimignano, tennis.

San Gimignano 32A4

Park Santa Lucia, Loc. Santa Lucia. **GPS**: n43,45205 e11,05586.

± 30 € 1/h, € 15/24h Ch (14x)included. **Location:** Rural, simple. **Surface:** gravel.

Distance: 3km Citybus Linea 1.

Remarks: Next to swimming pool, 24/24 video surveillance, shuttle to city centre.

San Miniato Basso 32A4

Piazza G. Impastato, Via Pestalozzi/Via G. Pizzigoni, zona industriale. **GPS**: n43,69417 e10,83638.

free free. **Surface:** asphalted.

San Miniato Basso 32A4

Rimessaggio/Area Camper Il Salice, Via Pier delle Vigne 28/A, loc. La Catena. **GPS**: n43,68434 e10,82224.

39 € 15/24h Ch WC . **Surface:** gravel. 01/01-31/12

Distance: 1km on the spot.

Remarks: Shuttle to centre, max. 3 days.

San Piero a Sieve 32B3

GPS: n43,96260 e11,32732.

free € 2 Ch. **Surface:** metalled.

Distance: 500m 250m.

San Quirico d'Orcia 32B5

Via delle Scuole. **GPS**: n43,05607 e11,60682.

30 € 10/24h free. **Location:** Rural, simple. **Surface:** asphalted.
01/01-31/12

Distance: 200m.

Remarks: Picnic area, children's play garden.

San Quirico d'Orcia 32B5

Strada di Bagno Vignoni, Bagno Vignoni. **GPS**: n43,02904 e11,62450.

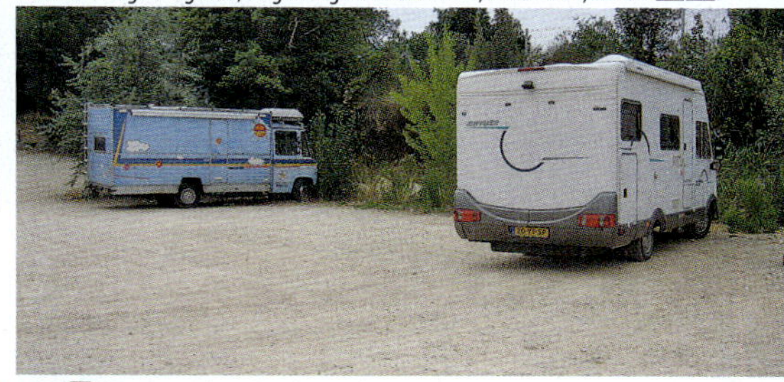

± 20 free. **Location:** Rural, simple, quiet.
Surface: unpaved.
01/01-31/12

Distance: 350m.

Remarks: Parco dei Mulini: natural hot springs, free entrance, 400m.

San Romano in Garfagnana 31D3

Via Campo Sportivo/via Prà di Lago. **GPS**: n44,17243 e10,34199.

15 free Chfree. **Surface:** grassy. 01/01-31/12

Remarks: At sports park, Parco Avventura Selva del Buffardello 100m.

IT

S San Vincenzo 32A5

Via Biserno. **GPS**: n43,08790 e10,54134.

90 € 10/24h free. **Surface:** sand. 01/01-31/12

Distance: 1km beach 200m 50m 50m.

Remarks: Beach parking, no camping activity.

S Sansepolcro 32C4

Viale Alessandro Volta. **GPS**: n43,56976 e12,13727.

20 free Chfree. **Location:** Urban, simple. **Surface:** asphalted. 01/01-31/12

Distance: 200m.

S Sansepolcro 32C4

Podere Violino, Loc. Gricigmano. **GPS**: n43,55539 e12,12312.

8 € 6 + € 5/pp Ch WC included.

Surface: grassy.

Distance: 2km river on the spot 500m.

Remarks: Swimming pool available, restaurant closed on Sunday.

S Santa Fiora 32B5

Strada di San Rocco. **GPS**: n42,83531 e11,58397.

20 free Chfree (6x)€ 1/2h. **Location:** Rural, simple. **Surface:** gravel/sand. 01/01-31/12

Distance: 450m.

S Saturnia 32B5

L'Alveare dei Pinzi, Strada della Peschiera, Saturnia. **GPS**: n42,65597 e11,50368.

400 € 14/24h Ch (120x)€ 2 WC included € 0,50 € 6.

Surface: metalled. 01/01-31/12

Distance: Saturnia 3km 1,5km on the spot.

Remarks: Panoramic view, free shuttle to spa resort and Saturnia, termen en Saturnia, Terme di Saturnia (sulfur baths) 1km, Cascate del Mulino (water fall, free entry) 1,5km, bread-service, bar/snack/fruit.

S Saturnia 32B5

La Quercia, Via Aurina 15. **GPS**: n42,66667 e11,50457.

30 € 15/24h Ch WC € 0,50. **Surface:** gravel. 01/01-31/12

Distance: 200m 100m 100m.

Remarks: Shuttle bus, Terme di Saturnia (sulfur baths) 1,7km, Cascate del Mulino (water fall, free entry) 2,5km.

S Scarperia 32B3

Ranch Ricavo, Via di Galliano 21. **GPS**: n44,01189 e11,30681.

20 € 10 Ch included. **Surface:** grassy. 01/01-31/12

Distance: 5km on the spot 5km.

S Sestino 32C3

Via Travicello. **GPS**: n43,71223 e12,30356.

12 free free. **Surface:** grasstiles.

Distance: 2km.

Remarks: Nearby sports park.

S Sesto Fiorentino 32B3

Area Antica Etruria, Via Ferruccio Parri. **GPS**: n43,84150 e11,17667.

50 € 16/24h Ch WC included. **Surface:** asphalted. 01/01-31/12

Distance: 1,5km 30m > Florence.
Remarks: Monitored motorhome stopover.

S Sesto Fiorentino 32B3
Viale Ariosto. **GPS**: n43,83238 e11,18997.

15 free Ch free. **Surface:** asphalted. 01/01-31/12
Distance: 3km on the spot train 100m.
Remarks: In front of Lidl supermarket, 20 mins to Florence by train.

S Siena 32B4
P1, Palasport, Via Achille Sclavo. **GPS**: n43,33323 e11,31739.

75 € 20/motorhome (8.00-20.00h) Ch WC free. **Location:** Urban, simple. **Surface:** metalled. 01/01-31/12
Distance: on the spot.

S Siena 32B4
P2, Il Fagiolone, Via di Pescaia. **GPS**: n43,31456 e11,31760.

€ 20/motorhome (8-20h), overnight stay free WC free. **Location:** Urban, simple, noisy. **Surface:** metalled. 01/01-31/12
Distance: on the spot.
Remarks: Along busy through road.

Siena 32B4
Acqua Calda, Via Fausto Coppi. **GPS**: n43,33627 e11,29695.

free. **Location:** Urban, simple. **Surface:** asphalted. 01/01-31/12
Distance: 650m bus 10 centre Siena.

Siena 32B4
Via delle Province/via Napoli. **GPS**: n43,34168 e11,30512.

free. **Location:** Urban, simple, noisy. **Surface:** asphalted.
01/01-31/12
Distance: 200m McDonalds on the spot.

Tourist information Siena:
A.T. (Ufficio Informazioni e di Accoglienza Turistica), Piazza del Campo, 56, www.siena.turismo.toscana.it.Historical city.
Palazzo Publico.Gothic town hall from 1342.
Torre del Mangia.Bell tower. daily.
Duomo.Romanesque Gothic cathedral.
La Lizza.Week market. Wed morning.
Palio, Piazza del Campo.Famous historical horse race.
02/07, 16/08.

S Stia 32B3
Parco comunale del Canto della Rana, Via Londa, SP556. **GPS**: n43,80407 e11,70282.

18 free Ch free. **Surface:** gravel. 01/01-31/12
Distance: 500m.

S Suvereto 32A5
Via dei Forni. **GPS**: n43,07572 e10,67802.

12 free free. **Location:** Rural, simple, quiet. **Surface:** grassy.
01/01-31/12
Distance: medieval centre 200m 300m 300m.

S Torrita di Siena 32C4
Via di Ciliano. **GPS**: n43,16475 e11,77173.

6 free Ch free. **Location:** Rural, comfortable, quiet.

IT

Surface: grasstiles/metalled. 01/01-31/12
Distance: 400m 200m.

S Venturina 32A5

Parco Termale Calidario, Via del Bottaccio. **GPS**: n43,03666 e10,60000.

20 free € 0,10/10liter Ch. **Location:** Quiet. **Surface:** metalled.
01/01-31/12
Distance: 800m 50m 800m.
Remarks: Thermal centre 50m.

S Viareggio 31D3

Via Martiri di Belfiore. **GPS**: n43,88120 e10,25080.

44 € 15/24h Ch included. **Surface:** asphalted.
01/01-31/12
Distance: 1km 2,5km.
Remarks: Check in at All Events Festival Puccini Viareggio, Viale Regina Margherita 1, 43,8673339 10,2431529, terrain with video surveillance.

IT

S Vinci 32A3

Via Girolamo Calvi. **GPS**: n43,78080 e10,92830.
12 free Chfree. **Surface:** metalled. 01/01-31/12
Distance: 300m.
Remarks: At sports park.

S Volterra 32A4

Parking P3, Fonti Docciola, Viale Dei Filosofi. **GPS**: n43,40306 e10,86417.

15 € 8/24h Chfree. **Location:** Urban. **Surface:** gravel.
Distance: historical center 100m 200m 300m.

San Marino

S San Marino 32C3

P13, Baldasserona, Borgo Maggiore. **GPS**: n43,94054 e12,44289.

50 free Ch. **Surface:** asphalted.

S San Marino 32C3

Strada Genghe di Atto, Acquaviva. **GPS**: n43,94491 e12,42963.

5 free Ch WC free. **Surface:** asphalted.

San Marino 32C3

P10, Via Napoleone Boneparte. **GPS**: n43,93567 e12,44362.

20 € 8/24h. **Surface:** asphalted.
Remarks: Elevator to centre 50m.

Tourist information San Marino:

Palazzo de Turismo, Contrada Omagnano, 20, www.visitsanmarino.com. Tourist office.
Borgo Maggiore.Week market. Thu.

Marche

S Abbadia di Fiastra 32B3

Parcheggio, Via Ettore Pinzani. **GPS**: n43,89368 e11,53703.

10 free Ch WC free. **Surface:** asphalted. 01/01-31/12
Distance: 500m 500m 500m 10m.

S Acqualagna 32D3

Parco Le Querce, Via Pianacce 1, Loc Furlo. **GPS**: n43,63681 e12,69968.

90 € 15/night Ch WC included against payment.
Surface: grassy. 26/03-30/09
Distance: Acqualagna 5km 700m.

Tourist information Acqualagna:
Week market. Thu.

Acquasanta Terme 33C2

Fra. Cagnano. **GPS**: n42,77096 e13,41388.

15 free. **Surface:** asphalted.
Distance: 200m Ristorante Laterna.
Remarks: At sports park.

Amandola 33B2

Piazzale Sandro Pertini. **GPS**: n42,97085 e13,35488.
€ 8,50 Ch WC included. **Surface:** asphalted. 01/01-31/12
Distance: 850m.

Ancona 27A6

Via Sanzio Blasi, Loc. Posatore. **GPS**: n43,59964 e13,48530.

30 € 12-13 Ch (24x)included. **Location:** Simple. **Surface:** asphalted/grassy. 01/01-31/12
Distance: 4,5km 10m.
Remarks: Max. 72, entrance between 8-22h.

Ancona 27A6

Centro Commerciale Auchan, Via Scataglini, Zona Industriale Baraccola, SS16, Ancona-sud. **GPS**: n43,55133 e13,51506.

25 free free. **Location:** Simple.
Surface: grasstiles.
01/01-31/12
Distance: 8km 3,6km.
Remarks: A14 exit Ancona south >Pesaro.

Tourist information Ancona:
Riviera del Conera.Touristic peninsula with beaches and several bathing resorts.
U.I.A.T. (Ufficio Informazioni e di Accoglienza Turistica), Stazione Maritiema. Old port city.

Apecchio 32C4

Via Isidoro Pazzaglia. **GPS**: n43,55938 e12,41969.
10 free Ch (6x)free. **Surface:** metalled. 01/01-31/12
Distance: 100m 50m.

Tourist information Apecchio:
Week market. Fri-morning.

Ascoli Piceno 33C2

Ex Seminario, Viale Alcide Gasperi. **GPS**: n42,85222 e13,58222.

20 € 4. **Surface:** asphalted.
Distance: city centre 100m 200m 200m.
Remarks: Guarded parking.

Ascoli Piceno 33C2

Bed & Breakfast Chartaria, Via Adriatico. **GPS**: n42,84792 e13,57306.
7 € 15 € 3. **Surface:** grassy.

Tourist information Ascoli Piceno:
City with many monumental bldg.
Wed, Sa.

Borgo Pace 32C3

Fraz. Lamoli, Loc Ripa, SS73bis km 25+500. **GPS**: n43,66284 e12,29509.

15 free. **Surface:** grassy. 01/01-31/12
Distance: 100m, Borgo Pace 5km 100m 100m.

Camerino 33B2

Via Macario Muzio. **GPS**: n43,13677 e13,06718.

8 free Ch free € 1/4h WC. **Location:** Rural. **Surface:** asphalted.
01/01-31/12
Distance: centre 500m 350m.
Remarks: Escalator to city centre, beautiful view.

IT

Carpegna 32C3

Via Aldo Moro. **GPS**: n43,78083 e12,34040.

10 free € 1 Ch € 0,60/h. **Surface:** concrete. 01/01-31/12
Distance: 300m 300m.

Castelfidardo 33C1

Croce Verde, Via Lumumba/via Donato Bramonte. **GPS**: n43,46603 e13,55563.

3 free free. **Location:** Simple. **Surface:** asphalted.
01/01-31/12
Distance: 200m.
Remarks: Max. 48h.

Cerreto D'Esi 33B1

Via Dante Alighieri. **GPS**: n43,32714 e12,99114.

10 free . **Location:** Simple. **Surface:** metalled.
01/01-31/12
Distance: 500m.

Colmurano 33B2

Via Piero della Francesca, Contrada Peschiera. **GPS**: n43,16260 e13,35828.

8 free Ch WC free. **Surface:** asphalted. 01/01-31/12
Distance: 400m.
Remarks: Near sports park and historical centre.

Corinaldo 32D3

Viale Dante. **GPS**: n43,64703 e13,04910.

8 free Ch free. **Location:** Simple. **Surface:** asphalted.
01/01-31/12
Distance: 400m 50m.

Corinaldo 32D3

Ristorante Camping Colverde, Via per Montalboddo 52. **GPS**: n43,63504 e13,09743.

10 € 13, guests € 10 Ch WC ,on camp site included,on camp site.
Location: Rural, simple.
Surface: grassy.
01/01-31/12
Distance: 5km on the spot.

Tourist information Corinaldo:

I.A.T. (Ufficio Informazioni e di Accoglienza Turistica), Via del Corso ex Convento Agostiniani.Medieval mountain village in the wine area of Verdicchio.

Cossignano 33C2

Via Gallo. **GPS**: n42,98050 e13,69213.

6 € 6 € 3 Ch included. **Location:** Simple. **Surface:** metalled.
01/01-31/12
Distance: 500m.

Cupramontana 33B1

Verdicchio, SP 11. **GPS**: n43,43934 e13,11837.

10 free free Ch (10x). **Location:** Simple, noisy. **Surface:** metalled.
01/01-31/12
Distance: 100m 500m.
Remarks: Beautiful view of Monte San Vicino.

Fabriano 33B1

Fraz. Poggio San Romualdo. **GPS**: n43,36473 e13,02534.

IT

35 free free. **Location:** Rural, simple, quiet. **Surface:** grassy.
01/01-31/12
Distance: 3,5km on the spot.

Fabriano 33B1

Via Bruno Buozzi. **GPS**: n43,34650 e12,91645.

18 free € 0,20/10liter Ch (6x)€ 3/12h. **Location:** Simple.
Surface: grassy. 01/01-31/12
Distance: 3km.
Remarks: Next to sports centre.

Falerone 33C2

Ex-stazione FS di Piane di Falerone, Via Togliatti. **GPS**: n43,09944 e13,49944.

15 free Ch free. **Surface:** metalled.
Distance: 100m 200m.
Remarks: Nearby the old station and theatre Romano.

Fano 32D3

Lungomare Sassonia, Via Ruggeri. **GPS**: n43,84238 e13,03197.

60 € 7-8,50 included (20x)€ 2/day WC € 0,50/day.
Surface: grassy/gravel. 01/01-31/12
Distance: 1km 2km 50m 50m 600m.

Fano 32D3

Area di Sosta Adriatico, SS16, Torrette di Fano. **GPS**: n43,80789 e13,08198.

30 € 13-20, Camperstop 18-9h€ 8-10 Ch (12x) WC included€ 0,50 € 3/time. **Location:** Comfortable. **Surface:** grassy/gravel.
24/04-15/09
Distance: 4km 9km 200m 50m 500m.
Remarks: Service only € 5.

Fano 32D3

Viale Kennedy. **GPS**: n43,84557 e13,01133.

16-20 free Ch free. **Location:** Simple. **Surface:** asphalted.
01/01-31/12
Distance: 200m 2,7km 800m.
Remarks: Nearby cemetery.

Fano 32D3

Campo Nunzia, SS Adriactica Sud-Loc. Torrette di Fano. **GPS**: n43,80444 e13,08472.

28 € 10-15 Ch € 3/24h WC € 3. **Location:** Comfortable.
Surface: grassy/gravel. 24/04-01/09
Distance: 7km 10km 150m.

Fano 32D3

BarRistorante La Tratta, Via Fratelli Zuccari 37. **GPS**: n43,83589 e13,04182.

14 € 6. **Location:** Simple, quiet. **Surface:** grassy. 01/04-01/10
Distance: 2,5km 50m on the spot on the spot.
Remarks: P camper.

Tourist information Fano:
U.I.A.T. (Ufficio Informazioni e di Accoglienza Turistica), Via Cesare Battisti, 10.Seaside resort with historical centre.

IT

Wed, Sa.

S Fermo 33C1

Area Camper 2004, Via della Filosofia/Via delle Arti. **GPS**: n43,15085 e13,81382.

100 € 9,with electricity € 11, weekend € 16, with electricity € 20 Ch (32x)included hot shower against payment. **Surface:** grassy.
01/04-15/09
Distance: 2,5km on the spot.

S Fermo 33C1

Baia dei Gabbiani, Viale A. de Gasperi, Lido S. Tomasso. **GPS**: n43,22158 e13,78113.

50 € 13-15, Aug € 20 Ch € 0,50. **Surface:** grassy/gravel.
01/04-30/09
Distance: 6,6km Private beach.

S Fermo 33C1

Onda Verde, Via Usodimare, Lido di Fermo. **GPS**: n43,20289 e13,78825.

100 € 10-€ 18 (Aug) Ch 2Amp WC included. **Surface:** grassy.
01/04-30/09
Distance: Fermo 10km 5,4km 10m 10-500m 200m.

S Fossombrone 32D3

Via Oberdan. **GPS**: n43,69301 e12,81835.

8 free Ch. **Surface:** asphalted. 01/01-31/12
Distance: 500m 1,4km.

Tourist information Fossombrone:

I.A.T. (Ufficio Informazioni e di Accoglienza Turistica), Via Roma, 23.

Week market. Mo.

S Genga 33B1

Frasassi, Fraz San Vittore. **GPS**: n43,40321 e12,97597.

50 free WC free. **Location:** Simple, quiet. **Surface:** gravel.
01/01-31/12
Distance: 7km on the spot.
Remarks: Nearby pay-desk Gole di Frasassi, free shuttle.

S Gradara 32D3

Parking P1, Piazza Paolo e Francesca. **GPS**: n43,94083 e12,77083.

14 € 10/24h Ch WC free. **Location:** Simple, central.
Surface: asphalted. 01/01-31/12
Distance: historical center 100m 7,3km on the spot 400m.
Remarks: Parking in the centre.

S Grottammare 33C2

Via Carlo Alberto dalla Chiesa. **GPS**: n42,96673 e13,87694.

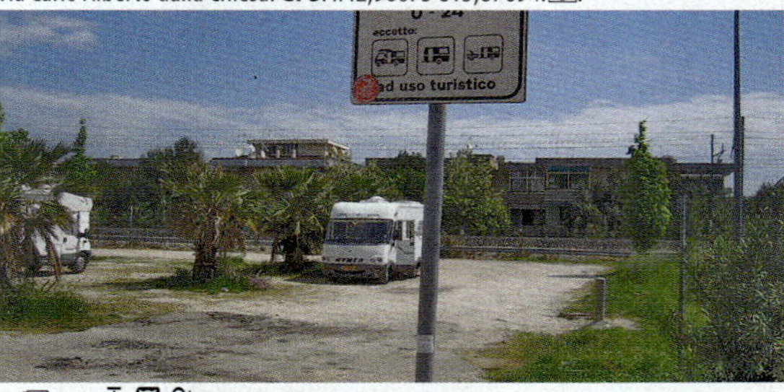

30 free Ch free. **Surface:** gravel/sand.
Distance: 2,7km 500m 500m on the spot.
Remarks: Behind centro commerciale Cityper, along railwayline.

S Grottammare 33C2

Briciola di Sole, Contr. Granaro 19. **GPS**: n42,98278 e13,84000.

14 € 15, guests free Ch included. **Surface:** gravel/metalled.
01/04-31/10
Distance: 2,5km sea 5km on the spot 2km.
Remarks: Located on estate, restaurant with traditional kitchen.

IT

Jesi 33B1

Via Zannoni. **GPS**: n43,51882 e13,24180.

10 free free. **Location:** Simple, quiet. **Surface:** asphalted.
01/01-31/12
Distance: 500m centro storico.

Tourist information Jesi:
Area with many vineyards.
Grotte di Frasassi.Caves.

Loreto 33C1

Area Camper Pro Loco, Via Maccari. **GPS**: n43,44125 e13,61491.

65 € 12/24h Ch included (20x)€ 3/day WC € 1/time.
Location: Comfortable. **Surface:** grasstiles. 01/01-31/12
Distance: 150m 15km.
Remarks: Max. 48h.

Loreto 33C1

Parking P1, Via Benedetto XXV. **GPS**: n43,44129 e13,60756.

6 € 6/day, overnight stay free WC. **Surface:** asphalted.
Distance: 300m 50m.
Remarks: Parking at city wall.

Macerata 33B1

Stadio Helvia Recina, Via dei Velini. **GPS**: n43,30701 e13,43722.

20 free € 1/15minutes free. **Location:** Urban, simple.
Surface: asphalted. 01/01-31/12
Distance: 3,5km.

Macerata Feltria 32C3

Loc. San Gasparre. **GPS**: n43,80098 e12,42886.

4 free Ch WC free. **Surface:** metalled. 01/01-31/12
Distance: 1km on the spot Pizzeria.
Remarks: Along Aspa river.

Tourist information Macerata Feltria:
Week market. Tue.

Marina di Montemarciano 33B1

Lungomare Alfredo Cappellini. **GPS**: n43,65936 e13,32780.

40 € 0,70/h Ch (32x)€ 2. **Location:** Simple, noisy.
Surface: gravel. 15/05-15/09
Distance: 4km 9km pebbled beach 60m 100m.
Remarks: To coast road and railwayline.

Marotta 32D3

Area di Sosta Marotta, Lungomare Colombo 157, Mondolfo. **GPS**: n43,76067 e13,15312.

80 € 8-11 Ch (80x)€ 2/24h WC included,cold. **Location:** Simple. **Surface:** grassy. 01/04-30/09
Distance: 500m 1,5km 50m on the spot.
Remarks: Between coast road and railwayline.

Matelica 33B1

Porte Capamante, Via Circonvallazione. **GPS**: n43,25917 e13,01083.

6-8 free free. **Location:** Simple. **Surface:** asphalted. 01/01-31/12
Distance: 200m 200m 200m.

IT

Matelica 33B1

Country House Salomone, Località Salomone 437. **GPS**: n43,29635 e13,00031.

20 €7, free with a meal (16x)included WC at restaurant.
Location: Rural, simple. **Surface:** grassy/gravel. 01/01-31/12
Distance: on the spot.

Mercatello sul Metauro 32C4

Agricampeggio Cá Montioni, Via Guinza 23. **GPS**: n43,62930 e12,30502.

11 €15 Ch WC. **Surface:** metalled. 01/01-31/12
Distance: 3km 200m.
Remarks: Farm products.

Mergo 33B1

Area Sosta Comunale, Via Colli. **GPS**: n43,47394 e13,03598.

10 free Ch free (8x). **Location:** Simple. **Surface:** concrete. 01/01-31/12
Distance: 300m.
Remarks: Nearby sports park.

Mondavio 32D3

Borgo Gramsci. **GPS**: n43,67487 e12,96700.

5 free WC free,50m. **Location:** Simple. **Surface:** metalled. 01/01-31/12
Distance: historical center 100m 100m 200m.
Remarks: Nearby old town and medieval citadel Roveresca.

Tourist information Mondavio:
Week market. Mo.

Montalto delle Marche 33C2

Via Cupremse. **GPS**: n42,98726 e13,60870.

6 free free. **Surface:** metalled. 01/01-31/12
Distance: 100m.

Monte San Giusto 33C1

Campo Sportivo, Via Magellano, Villa San Filippo. **GPS**: n43,26343 e13,60070.

20 free Ch free. **Surface:** asphalted.
Distance: 1km.

Monte Vidon Corrado 33C2

Viale Trento e Trieste. **GPS**: n43,12182 e13,48501.

4 free Ch free. **Surface:** metalled. 01/01-31/12
Distance: 200m 200m.

Montefiore dell'Aso 33C2

Piazza Pietro Nenni. **GPS**: n43,04992 e13,75021.

10 free Ch free. **Surface:** sand. 01/01-31/12
Distance: 200m.
Remarks: Follow parco communale.

Montefiore dell'Aso 33C2

Agricamper Il Poggio del Belvedere, Contrada Aso no. 11. **GPS**: n43,04611 e13,72500.

IT

6 € 8/pp Ch WC included. **Surface:** metalled.
01/01-31/12

S Montelupone 33C1

Loc. San Firmano. **GPS:** n43,36383 e13,54950.

20 free free. **Location:** Simple. **Surface:** asphalted.
Distance: 500m.
Remarks: Parking sports park.

S Montelupone 33C1

Via Allesandro Manzoni. **GPS:** n43,34300 e13,57080.

10 free free. **Location:** Simple. **Surface:** asphalted.
01/01-31/12
Remarks: Parking city park.

S Morro d'Alba 33B1

Area Comunale, Via degli Orti. **GPS:** n43,60198 e13,21263.

10 free free. **Location:** Simple, quiet.
Surface: asphalted.
01/01-31/12
Distance: 500m.
Remarks: Access with electronic card, Bar Pro Loco or town hall.

S Offida 33C2

Via Tommaso Castelli. **GPS:** n42,93689 e13,69180.

10 free free. 01/01-31/12
Remarks: At the city walls.

Pedaso 33C2

Via Martiri della Libertà. **GPS:** n43,09985 e13,84272.
free. **Surface:** asphalted. 01/01-31/12
Distance: on the spot on the spot 150m.
Remarks: Parking at the beach..

S Pesaro 32D3

Via dell Aquedotto. **GPS:** n43,90842 e12,90097.

12 free Chfree (12x)€ 1. **Surface:** asphalted.
Distance: 7,5km.

Tourist information Pesaro:
I.A.T. (Ufficio Informazioni e di Accoglienza Turistica), Viale Trieste, 164.
Week market. Tue.

S Petritoli 33C2

Impianti Sportivi. GPS: n43,07306 e13,65139.

free Chfree. **Surface:** sand. 01/01-31/12
Distance: 1km.
Remarks: Sports park.

S Piandimeleto 32C3

Via Giacomo Leopardi. **GPS:** n43,72541 e12,41328.

9 free Chfree. **Surface:** grassy. 01/01-31/12
Distance: 100m.

IT

S Pietrarubbia 32C3

Vulcangas, Via Montefeltresca 107, Ponte Cappuccini. **GPS**: n43,80278 e12,36667.

2 free WC free. **Surface:** metalled. 01/01-31/12

Distance: 200m.

S Pievebovigliana 33B2

Via Rancia. **GPS**: n43,06583 e13,08526.

10 free Ch. **Surface:** asphalted. 01/01-31/12

Distance: 300m.

S Pioraco 33B2

Loc. Buchetto, SS361 km77. **GPS**: n43,18010 e12,97422.

18 (+20) € 13 (16x) WC included. **Location:** Rural, comfortable, quiet. **Surface:** gravel. 01/01-31/12

Distance: 700m on the spot summer on the spot.

S Pollenza 33B1

Contrada Morazzano. **GPS**: n43,26482 e13,34614.

8 free free. **Location:** Simple. **Surface:** asphalted. 01/01-31/12

Distance: 500m.

Remarks: Max. 48h, nearby elevator to centre.

S Porto Recanati 27A6

Karting Club Pista del Conero, Viale Scarfiotti, loc. Scossicci. **GPS**: n43,47067 e13,64246.

80 € 15/24h Ch (80x) WC included € 1 free.

Location: Simple, noisy. **Surface:** gravel. 01/04-30/09

Distance: 100m 200m.

S Porto Recanati 27A6

Pro Loco, Viale Scarfiotti, loc. Scossicci. **GPS**: n43,44605 e13,65639.

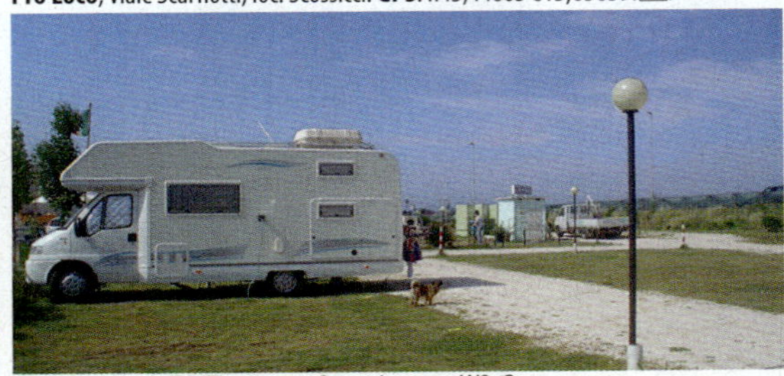

40 € 10/24h included Ch (8x) € 2 WC € 1. **Location:** Simple. **Surface:** grassy. 01/04-30/09

Distance: 500m 3km 50m 200m 1km.

Remarks: Max. 72h. Along coast road in northern dir.

S Porto San Giorgio 33C1

La Perla Adriatico, Via San Martino 13. **GPS**: n43,16400 e13,80836.

75 € 12/18 Ch WC . **Surface:** unpaved. 01/01-31/12

Distance: beach 200m 300m.

Remarks: Shuttle bus.

S Potenza Picena 33C1

Via Togliatti, Porto Potenza Picena. **GPS**: n43,36167 e13,69306.

free Ch (3x). **Surface:** asphalted. 01/01-31/12

Distance: 200m 200m 200m.

S Recanati 33C1

Camperclub Recanati, Viale Giovanni XXIII. **GPS**: n43,40245 e13,55777.

30 free (22x) free. **Location:** Urban, simple. **Surface:** asphalted. 01/01-31/12

Distance: 500m.

IT

S San Benedetto del Tronto 33C2

Viale dello Sport. **GPS**: n42,92312 e13,89527.↑.

20 free Ch free. **Surface:** asphalted.
Distance: 4,3km 500m.
Remarks: Along railwayline, under viaduct.

S San Leo 32C3

Via Michele Rosa. **GPS**: n43,89871 e12,34950.↑→.

20 free Ch free. **Surface:** asphalted. 01/01-31/12
Distance: 500m on the spot.

S San Severino Marche 33B1

P7, Viale Mazzini. **GPS**: n43,22757 e13,18836.↑→.

12 free free (12x)€ 0,50/4h. **Location:** Simple, quiet.
Surface: asphalted. 01/01-31/12
Distance: 800m.
Remarks: Parking sports park.

S Sant'Agata Feltria 32C3

Piazzale Europa. **GPS**: n43,86386 e12,20549.↑→.

40 € 8/24h (6x)free. **Surface:** asphalted.
Distance: 100m.

S Sarnano 33B2

Via Corridoni. **GPS**: n43,03444 e13,29972.↑.

15 free Ch WC free. **Surface:** asphalted.
Distance: 100m 100m 100m.

S Sassocorvaro 32C3

Via dell'Industria, loc. Marcatale. **GPS**: n43,79341 e12,49379.
Ch.
Remarks: In front of cemetery, overnight stay: 43.7911 12.4925.

S Sassoferrato 33B1

Via Raffaello Sanzio. **GPS**: n43,43122 e12,85471.↑.

7 free free (6x)€ 1/day. **Location:** Simple. **Surface:** asphalted.
01/01-31/12
Distance: 500m.

S Senigallia 32D3

Via F. Podesti 234, SS16, Senigallia-sud. **GPS**: n43,70483 e13,23764.↑.

14 free free. **Location:** Simple, noisy. **Surface:** asphalted.
01/01-31/12
Distance: 3km 3,3km 150m.
Remarks: Max. 48h, along busy road, next to petrol station.

S Tolentino 33B1

GPS: n43,20773 e13,28784.

3 free free. **Surface:** asphalted. 01/01-31/12
Distance: 200m 200m.

S Urbania 32C3

GPS: n43,67916 e12,51277.↑→.
free Ch free.

IT

Distance: 1km.
Remarks: Behind former summer residence of dukes of Urbania, biking trail.

S Urbania 32C3

Piazzale Fosso del Maltempo, Viale Michelangelo. **GPS:** n43,66482 e12,52191.

7 free Ch free. **Surface:** asphalted. 01/01-31/12
Distance: 500m.

Tourist information Urbania:
I.A.T. (Ufficio Informazioni e di Accoglienza Turistica), Corso Vittorio Emanuele, 21.Old city named after Pope Urbanus VII.
Week market. Thu.

S Urbino 32D3

Via Pablo Neruda. **GPS:** n43,73333 e12,62722.

10 free Chfree. **Surface:** metalled. 01/01-31/12
Distance: historical centre 2,5km.

Tourist information Urbino:
I.A.T. (Ufficio Informazioni e di Accoglienza Turistica), Piazza del Rinascimento, 1.Small medieval town with famous Palazzo Ducale.
01/06-31/10 9-19h, Su 9-13h, Mo 9-14h.
Week market. Sa.

S Urbisaglia 33B1

Abbadia di Fiastra, P4. **GPS:** n43,22111 e13,40722.

20 free Ch free. **Surface:** metalled.
01/01-31/12
Distance: 4km 50m.
Remarks: Parking monastery, archaeological park Urbs Salvia 3km, hiking area.

S Visso 33B2

Largo Gregorio XIII. **GPS:** n42,93139 e13,09141.

15 free Chfree € 0,80/h. **Surface:** asphalted.
Distance: 800m.

Lazio

S Acquapendente 32C5

Agriturismo Buonomore, SS2 via Cassia km 130. **GPS:** n42,73367 e11,88361.

8 € 15, Aug € 30 Ch WC included.
01/01-31/12
Distance: 3km on the spot.

S Acquapendente 32C5

Via Campo Boario. **GPS:** n42,74130 e11,86280.

free Chfree. **Surface:** asphalted/metalled.
Distance: 250m 250m.

S Albano Laziale 33B4

Piazza Guerucci. **GPS:** n41,73206 e12,65213.
Ch. **Surface:** asphalted.
Remarks: Next to post office and sports park.

S Amatrice 33B3

AgriCamper Amatrice, Località Retrosi. **GPS:** n42,62349 e13,31788.
20 € 13 Ch. **Surface:** gravel.
Remarks: Located in national nature reserve Gran Sasso.

S Bolsena 32C5

Guadetto, Via della Chiusa. **GPS:** n42,63604 e11,98695.

30 € 14/24h Ch included. **Surface:** grassy/sand.
01/01-31/12

Distance: 500m 10m.

Bolsena 32C5

Via Santa Maria. **GPS**: n42,63898 e11,98562.

50 € 5/12h, € 10/24h. **Surface:** asphalted. 01/01-31/12

Distance: 800m 100m on the spot 400m 400m 100m.

Tourist information Bolsena:

Citadel and ramparts.

Bracciano 33A4

Le Mimose, Via del Lago 25. **GPS**: n42,10856 e12,17893.

50 € 14/24h Ch € 3. **Surface:** gravel. 01/01-31/12

Distance: 800m Lago di Bracciano 250m 150m.

Capodimonte 32C6

Temporanea. GPS: n42,55979 e11,88714.

50 € 10/24h Ch. **Surface:** grassy. 01/01-31/12

Distance: 2km on the spot.

Remarks: At lake Bolsena, check in at bar.

Cassino 33C5

Parking Europa, Via Agnone 5. **GPS**: n41,48289 e13,83750.

€ 13 Ch against payment.

Distance: 800m.

Tourist information Cassino:

I.A.T. (Ufficio Informazioni e di Accoglienza Turistica), Via G. Di Biasio, 54.

Castel di Tora 33B3

Via Turano, SP34. **GPS**: n42,21362 e12,96888.

15 € 5/24h Ch . **Surface:** gravel. 01/01-31/12

Distance: 1km on the spot.

Remarks: At Turano lake.

Castel Gandolfo 33B4

Parcheggio Bus Lago Albano, Via Spiaggia del Lago. **GPS**: n41,75797 e12,65359.

€ 10/24h. **Surface:** asphalted. 01/01-31/12

Distance: on the spot on the spot 800m > Rome.

Remarks: At lake Albano.

Castel Gandolfo 33B4

Ristorante I Quadri 2000, Via dei Pescatori 21. **GPS**: n41,74930 e12,65384.

10 € 15/24h Ch . **Surface:** sand. 01/01-31/12

Distance: on the spot on the spot.

Remarks: Private beach at Lago di Albano.

Castro dei Volsci 33C5

Via Fosso 35. **GPS**: n41,51282 e13,39010.

Remarks: Nearby restaurant Le Rocco.

Civita Castellana 33A3

Via Terni. **GPS**: n42,29905 e12,41520.

300 free free. **Surface:** asphalted. 01/01-31/12

Distance: 50m. **Remarks:** At cemetery.

Tourist information Civita Castellana:

Palazzo Farnese, Caprarola.Pentagonal country house, accessed by winding staircase.

Colle di Tora 33B3

Via Maria Letizia Giuliani. **GPS**: n42,20898 e12,94915.

15 € 5/24h Ch. **Surface:** gravel. 01/01-31/12

Distance: on the spot on the spot on the spot.

Remarks: At Turano lake.

Colleferro 33B4

Viale Europa. **GPS**: n41,72540 e13,00989.

Distance: 5km.

Remarks: Next to swimming pool.

Tourist information Colleferro:

Anagni.Region with number of old settlements.

Farfa in Sabina 33B3

Abbazia di Santa Maria, SP41A. **GPS**: n42,22166 e12,71603.

free Chfree. **Surface:** gravel. 01/01-31/12

Distance: 4,7km.

Gaeta 33C5

Playa Colorada, Torre S.Agostino, SS 213, Sperlonga>Gaeta. **GPS**: n41,22583 e13,50502.

30 € 28-30, 2 pers.incl Ch WCincluded € 1.

Surface: grassy/gravel. 01/04-30/09

Distance: on the spot bar/restaurant on the spot.

Gradoli 32C6

Parcheggio camper San Magno, Strada di Gradoli, SP114 km 6+137. **GPS**: n42,59925 e11,86547.

IT

50 € 10 Ch . **Surface:** grassy. 01/01-31/12
Distance: 7km on the spot 500m.
Remarks: At lake Bolsena.

S Ladispoli 33A4

Area Sosta Torre Flavia, Via Roma. **GPS**: n41,95954 e12,05282.

300 8-20h € 6, 20-8h € 6 € 3 Ch € 3 WC € 0,50.
Surface: grassy/sand. 01/01-31/12
Distance: 1,2km on the spot on the spot 2km.
Remarks: At the beach.

S Ladispoli 33A4

Area Sosta Lady Beach, Via Roma. **GPS**: n41,95829 e12,05585.
30 € 10/24h Ch WC € 0,50. **Surface:** grassy/sand.
Distance: 800m on the spot.

S Latina 33B5

Area Camper Alte Marea, Strada Lungomare 3253, SP39, Loc. Foce Verde. **GPS**: n41,41043 e12,86008.

100 € 10-15 Ch included. **Surface:** grassy.
Easter-30/09
Distance: on the spot 50m on the spot.

Latina 33B5

Strada Provinciale Lungomare, Pontino. **GPS**: n41,38482 e12,91657.

free. **Surface:** gravel.
Distance: on the spot on the spot.

S Leonessa 33B3

GPS: n42,56436 e12,96172.

50 free . **Surface:** asphalted.
Distance: 500m 500m 500m 300m.

S Lubriano 32C5

Parco Paime, Piazza Palme. **GPS**: n42,63500 e12,10512.

17 € 6/24h (36x).
Surface: grasstiles.
01/01-31/12
Distance: 1km on the spot.

S Lunghezza 33B4

Camper Club Mira Lago Roma Est, Via Lunghezzina 75. **GPS**: n41,93159 e12,67642.
€ 18/24h Ch € 2 WC . **Surface:** grassy.
Distance: 700m on the spot.
Remarks: At 2 small lakes.

S Montalto di Castro 32B6

Via Arbea, Marina di Montalto di Castro. **GPS**: n42,32981 e11,57699.

50 € 10/24h, € 5 01/10-31/12 Ch free. **Location:** Rural. **Surface:** grassy/gravel. 01/01-31/12
Distance: 250m 200m 200m 200m.

S Montalto di Castro 32B6

Via Torre Marina, Marina di Montalto di Castro. **GPS**: n42,32137 e11,59015.

64 € 5, 15/05-15/09 € 10 Ch included. **Surface:** sand.
01/01-31/12
Distance: 500m 200m 400m 300m.

S Montefiascone 32C6

Cantina di Montefiascone, Via Grilli 2. **GPS**: n42,53346 e12,04293.

30 free Ch . **Surface:** metalled. 01/01-31/12
Distance: 1km.

S Montefiascone 32C6

Agricamper Bella Cima, Strada Limitone. **GPS**: n42,52241 e12,00767.

18 € 15/24h Ch included. **Surface:** gravel.
01/01-31/12
Distance: 4km 4km 4km.
Remarks: Swimming pool.

S Nettuno 33B5

Area Sosta L'Ippocampo, Via Palestrina 9. **GPS**: n41,47354 e12,68916.
50 € 10 Ch . **Surface:** gravel. 01/01-31/12
Distance: 3km.

S Oriolo Romano 33A4

Via degli Artigiani. **GPS**: n42,16699 e12,13902.
free free. **Surface:** asphalted. 01/01-31/12
Distance: 850m on the spot station 600m Roma-Viterbo.

S Pescia Romana 32B6

Area La Pineta, Loc. Marina di Pescia Romana. **GPS**: n42,36367 e11,49738.

50 € 10-18 Ch € 3 € 1. **Surface:** grassy. Easter-30/09
Distance: Pescia Romana 7km 100m 100m.

S Pescia Romana 32B6

Campeggio Club degli Amici. GPS: n42,36717 e11,48828.
20 € 6/10 + € 6/10,50/pp Ch WC included € 4.
Surface: sand. 01/05-3rd Su Sep
Distance: lava beach 100m on the spot.

S Rieti 33B3

Via Fonte Cottorella. **GPS**: n42,39548 e12,86463.

10 free . **Surface:** asphalted. 01/01-31/12
Distance: historical center 100m.

S Roma 33B4

Area Attrezzata LGP Roma, Via Casilina 700, Rome (Roma). **GPS**: n41,87595 e12,55515.

200 € 15/<8m, € 22/8><10m, € 30/10><15m Ch included .
Surface: grassy. 01/01-31/12
Distance: 100m 100m bus service to city centre day and night.
Remarks: Accessory shop, repairs, trailer/additonal car € 15 on separate parking € 7. Exit 18 ring road (G.R.A.), follow Roma centro, ± 4km dir centre, company is on the left side of the road, turning after 2nd lights.

S Roma 33B4

Oasi del Camper, Via dell'Ippodromo di Tor di Valle 1, Rome (Roma). **GPS**: n41,82021 e12,43545.

€ 20 Ch included. **Surface:** gravel.
01/01-31/12, 24/24h
Distance: city centre 10km 150m Arbino metro 150m.
Remarks: Terrain with video surveillance. Exit 28 ring road (G.R.A.), follow Roma centro, keep right Roma Ostiense, further indicated.

S Roma 33B4

Prato Smeraldo, Via Ardeatina/Via di Tor Pagnotta 424, Rome (Roma). **GPS**: n41,80970 e12,52857.
€ 16 Ch included.
01/01-31/12, 24/24h
Distance: on the spot on the spot on the spot.
Remarks: Exit 25 ring road (G.R.A.), second light to the right, Via di Tor Pagnotta.

S Roma 33B4

Le Terrazze, Via di Fioranello 170, Rome (Roma). **GPS**: n41,79250 e12,54083.
300 € 20, max. 4 pers.incl € 2 Ch (40x)included.
Surface: metalled.
01/01-31/12
Remarks: Excursions. Exit 25 ring road (G.R.A.), dir Santuario Divino Amore.

S Roma 33B4

Parcheggio IAT, Air terminal Ostiense, Piazza G. da Verrazzano 9, Zone Mercati Generali, Rome (Roma). **GPS**: n41,86931 e12,48944.
€ 1,50, at least € 6 Ch included.

IT

Surface: asphalted.
Distance: metro 1km.

Tourist information Rome (Roma):

Città del Vaticano.Domicile of the pope. Independent state since 1929.

A.P.T. (Azienda di Promozione Turistica), Via Parigi, 11, www.romaturismo.it.Capital of the country, a lot of curiosities in the old town centre. Roma Archeologica Card: 7-days ticket € 20, free entrance to Roman National Museum, Colosseum, Palatine, Baths of Caracalla, Tomb of Cecilia Metella and Villa of the Quintili.

Piazza del Campidoglio.

Palatino, Via di S. Gregorio, 30.Archeological site.

9h-sunset. € 8, incl. Colosseum.

Subiaco.

Musei Vaticani, Città del Vaticano.Paintings and art objects.

Basilica di San Pietro.Basilica with Sistine Chapel.

Colosseo, Piazza del Colosseo.Colosseum, anfiteatro, the most important monument of ancient Rome. 9h-sunset. € 8.

Foro Romane, Via dei Fori Imperiali.Novel Forum, the political, economic, and religious centre of ancient Rome.

9h-sunset. free.

Pantheon, Piazza della Rotonda.Church of Santa Maria ad Martyres.

8.30-19.30h, Su 9-18h, Mass Sa 17, Su 10.30h, 16.30h. free.

Città del Vaticano.Pope blesses the mob for the window of the library.

Su 12h.

Piazza di Spagna.

S San Felice Circeo 33B5

Circeo Camper Da Paolo, Viale Europa 1. **GPS**: n41,24095 e13,10426.

60 € 20-26 Ch WC included. **Surface:** grassy.
01/01-31/12
Distance: 100m 10m 100m 100m 100m.

S San Felice Circeo 33B5

Area Camper La Rosa dei Venti, Viale Europa 9A. **GPS**: n41,24387 e13,10819.

50 € 24/12-12h € 3 Ch . **Surface:** gravel. 01/01-31/12
Distance: 500m 10m on the spot 600m 600m.

Tourist information San Felice Circeo:

Tue-morning.

S Sperlonga 33C5

Aree di Sosta Oasi, SS 213, Sperlonga>Gaeta. **GPS**: n41,23596 e13,49069.

30 € 20 Ch WC included € 1. **Surface:** gravel.
Distance: 50m 50m.
Remarks: Monitored parking.

S Sperlonga 33C5

Sosta Camper Internationale, SS 213, Sperlonga>Gaeta. **GPS**: n41,23598 e13,49045.

30 € 20-25 Ch WC included € 1. **Surface:** gravel.
Distance: on the spot on the spot.
Remarks: Monitored parking.

Tarquinia 32C6

Largo Barriera San Giusto. **GPS**: n42,25307 e11,75410.

5 free. **Surface:** asphalted. 01/01-31/12
Distance: 100m 100m 100m.
Remarks: Archeological site 1km.

Tarquinia 32C6

Viale Andrea Doria/via Odisseo, Lido di Tarquinia. **GPS**: n42,22516 e11,70897.

Distance: sandy beach 450m.

S Tivoli 33B4

Via Aquaregna. **GPS**: n41,95841 e12,80465.
30 free Ch. **Surface:** asphalted.
01/01-31/12 Wed, market.
Distance: 400m.
Remarks: Along the Aniene river.

Tourist information Tivoli:

Villa d'Este.Country house with gardens and fountains, 16th century.

Villa Adriana.Roman villa.

S Tuscania 32C6

Via Nazario Sauro. **GPS**: n42,42432 e11,87542.

IT

12 free free. **Surface:** asphalted. 01/01-31/12
Distance: 250m 250m 250m.
Remarks: At cemetery.

S Villa San Giovanni in Tuscia 32C6
Via P.M. Liberati. **GPS:** n42,28160 e12,05282.
free Ch. **Surface:** asphalted. 01/01-31/12
Distance: 200m.

S Viterbo 32C6
Piazza Mariano Romiti, loc. Belcolle. **GPS:** n42,40897 e12,11049.
50 free free. **Surface:** asphalted. 01/01-31/12
Distance: Lazise centre 300m on the spot.

S Viterbo 32C6
Bed&breakfast Axia, Strada Procoio 2/C. **GPS:** n42,41157 e12,05061.

30 € 12 Ch € 3. **Surface:** grassy. 01/01-31/12
Distance: Viterbo 4km.
Remarks: 10% discount at entrance Terme dei Papi (900m).

Viterbo 32C6
Agriturismo Monteparadiso, Loc. Monterazzano. **GPS:** n42,43192 e12,03004.

5 guests free. **Surface:** gravel.
Distance: 7km.
Remarks: Near Termale Bullicame and Terme dei Papi.

Viterbo 32C6
Terme dei Papi, Strada Montarone. **GPS:** n42,41487 e12,06351.

100 free. **Surface:** grassy/gravel. 01/01-31/12

Distance: 3km.
Remarks: At Terme dei Papi.

Vitorchiano 32C6
SP23 Via della Teverina. **GPS:** n42,47152 e12,17212.

10 free. **Surface:** asphalted. 01/01-31/12
Distance: 500m.

Umbria

S Amelia 32D6
Piazzale del Mercato, Via Rimembranze. **GPS:** n42,55200 e12,41880.
10 free Chfree. **Surface:** asphalted.
Distance: 50m 50m 50m.

S Assisi 33A2
Via Giosuè Borsi, loc. Santa Maria degli Angeli. **GPS:** n43,05972 e12,58747.

€ 16/24h, € 1,60/h Ch . **Surface:** asphalted.
01/01-31/12
Distance: 2km bus >Assisi 20min (retour € 1,80).

Assisi 33A2
Area San Vetturino, SS147. **GPS:** n43,07710 e12,59957.

30 € 14/24h, € 2/h. **Surface:** asphalted. 01/01-31/12
Distance: 500m.
Remarks: Convento di San Francesco 1km.

Assisi 33A2
Viale Vittorio Emanuele II/SS147. **GPS:** n43,06864 e12,61420.

10 € 20/24h. **Surface:** gravel. 01/01-31/12

IT

Distance: city centre 100m.

Bevagna — 33A2

Via Madonna del Cuore. **GPS:** n42,93417 e12,60639.

50 free Ch WC free. **Surface:** gravel.
Distance: 100m 100m 100m.

Cannara — 33A2

Via Giaime Pintor, Loc. Casone. **GPS:** n42,99272 e12,57840.

20 free Ch free. **Surface:** asphalted.
Distance: 300m 300m.
Remarks: At sports park XXV Aprile, cycle routes.

Tourist information Cannara:
U.I.A.T. (Ufficio Informazioni e di Accoglienza Turistica), Piazza del Commune, Assisi.Medieval pilgrimage city.
Assisi.Historical city.

Cascia — 33B2

Piazzale Papa Leone XIII, Via della Molinella. **GPS:** n42,71968 e13,01605.

50 € 8/day, overnight stay free Ch free. **Surface:** asphalted.
01/01-31/12
Distance: 300m 300m 300m 100m 100m.
Remarks: Escalator to city centre, service closed during wintertime.

Cascia — 33B2

Strada Statale Discascia. **GPS:** n42,72139 e13,01778.
20 € 7/24h included. **Surface:** gravel. 01/01-31/12
Distance: 1km.

Castelluccio di Norcia — 33B2

Pian Grande. GPS: n42,80045 e13,18947.
free. **Surface:** grassy. 01/01-31/12
Distance: Castelluccio 5km.
Remarks: Parco Nazionale dei Monti Sibilini.

Castiglione del Lago — 32C5

Viale Divisione Partigiani Garibaldi. **GPS:** n43,12389 e12,05054.

free. **Surface:** asphalted/sand.
Distance: 800m on the spot.
Remarks: At lake Trasimeno.

Città di Castello — 32C4

Piazzale E. Fermi. **GPS:** n43,45892 e12,23465.
free Ch free. **Surface:** gravel.
Distance: 300m 1,5km.

Città di Castello — 32C4

La Fontana del Boschetto, Via Aretina 38. **GPS:** n43,45737 e12,22882.
€ 12 Ch .
Distance: 2km on the spot.
Remarks: Free shuttle.

Ferentillo — 33B3

SS Valnerina, loc. Precetto. **GPS:** n42,61915 e12,78483.
10 free . **Surface:** asphalted.
Distance: 200m.

Ficulle — 32C5

Parco Cittadino, Via Orvieto SR 71. **GPS:** n42,83044 e12,06828.

25 free Ch free. **Surface:** gravel.
Distance: 500m 10km 1km 500m.

Gualdo Tadino — 33B1

Piazza Federico II di Svevia. **GPS:** n43,23143 e12,78062.
free Ch free. **Surface:** asphalted.

Gualdo Tadino — 33B1

Via Perugia. **GPS:** n43,23756 e12,77235.
100 free free.
Distance: 400m 20m.
Remarks: Nearby stadium.

Gubbio — 32D4

Camperclub Gubbio, Via del Bottegone. **GPS:** n43,35000 e12,56389.

80 free, 20-8h € 5 Ch free (8x)€ 1/2h.
Surface: asphalted.
Distance: historical centre, 10 min walking 100m 200m.

Monte Castello di Vibio — 32C5

Via Bartolomeo Jacopo della Rovere. **GPS:** n42,84185 e12,35076.

10 free Chfree. **Surface:** gravel. 01/01-31/12
Distance: 350m 50m.

Montefalco 33A2

Viale delle Vittoria. **GPS:** n42,89230 e12,64791.

15 free Ch € 1/1h WC. **Surface:** grasstiles.

Montone 32C4

Via Aldo Bologni. **GPS:** n43,36346 e12,32499.
€ 10/24h Ch. **Surface:** asphalted. 01/01-31/12
Distance: 200m 250m.
Remarks: At sports park.

Orvieto 32C5

Area Sosta Camper Orvieto, Strada della Direttissima, Piazza delle Pace. **GPS:** n42,72562 e12,12736.

36 € 18/day Ch WC included. **Surface:** metalled.
01/01-31/12
Distance: funicular (retour € 1,60) 5 min 2,4km 50m pizzeria.

Tourist information Orvieto:
U.I.A.T. (Ufficio Informazioni e di Accoglienza Turistica), Piazza Duomo, 24.City on volcanic plateau.
Del Crocifisso del Tufo.Ruins of Etruscan city.

Panicale 32C5

Area Camper, Viale della Repubblica. **GPS:** n43,02806 e12,10222.

8 € 8/24h € 0,50 Ch € 0,50/kWh. **Surface:** grasstiles.
01/01-31/12
Distance: 100m 100m 50m.

Passignano sul Trasimeno 32C4

Via Europa, SS75bis, km 35,8. **GPS:** n43,18509 e12,14348.

4 € 12/24h € 0,30/100liter Ch € 0,30/h WC. **Surface:** asphalted.
01/01-31/12
Distance: 400m 100m.
Remarks: At lake Trasimeno.

Perugia 32C5

Piazzale del Bove, Via Giovanni Ruggia. **GPS:** n43,09810 e12,38386.

50 free Chfree. **Surface:** asphalted.
Distance: 1,5km on the spot.
Remarks: Parking police station.

Tourist information Perugia:
A.T. (Ufficio Informazioni e di Accoglienza Turistica), Via Mazinni, 6, www.umbria.turismo.it.
Palazzo dei Priori.
Tue.

San Gemini 33A3

Via della Libertà. **GPS:** n42,61200 e12,54372.
16 Ch WC. **Surface:** metalled. 01/01-31/12
Distance: 300m 100m.

Scheggia e Pascelupo 32D4

Camper Scheggia, Via Campo Sportivo. **GPS:** n43,40007 e12,66674.
€ 12/24h Ch included. **Surface:** gravel. 01/01-31/12
Distance: 450m 500m.

Spello 33B2

Via Centrale Umbra. **GPS:** n42,99371 e12,66730.

70 € 6/24h Ch. **Surface:** asphalted.
Distance: 500m 1,1km 500m 500m.
Remarks: Parking sports park.

Spoleto 33B2

Parcheggio Ponciano, Via del Tiro a Segno. **GPS:** n42,73687 e12,74212.

IT

20 € 5/24h. **Surface:** gravel. 01/01-31/12
Distance: 500m 500m 500m.
Remarks: Escalator to city centre.

S Spoleto 33B2

Via dei Filosofi. **GPS:** n42,74619 e12,73214.

free free. **Surface:** gravel.
Distance: 800m.

Tourist information Spoleto:
U.I.A.T. (Ufficio Informazioni e di Accoglienza Turistica), Piazza del Liberta, 7.
Montefalco.Village worth seeing, parking outside village, narrow streets.
Ponte delle Torri.Aqueduct, 14th century.
Tue, Fri.
Art festival. 01/06-31/07.

S Terni 33B3

Via Lombardo Radice. **GPS:** n42,56634 e12,63577.

€ 4/48h € 0,50 Ch included. **Surface:** asphalted.
Distance: 50m 50m.
Remarks: Exit Raccordo Roma-Perugia, near cemetery.

Terni 33B3

Piazzale Felice Fatati, SR209. **GPS:** n42,55690 e12,72006.

free. **Surface:** unpaved.
Distance: Terni 7km on the spot.
Remarks: Nearby waterfalls, along river.

S Todi 32C5

Area Porta Orvietana, Viale di Montesanto. **GPS:** n42,78120 e12,40168.

16 € 14/24h, € 3/h Ch. **Surface:** asphalted.
Remarks: Elevator (free) to centre.

S Torgiano 32C5

Via Perugia. **GPS:** n43,02917 e12,43833.

10 free Chfree. **Surface:** asphalted. 01/01-31/12
Distance: 200m 3,5km 200m 300m.

S Trevi 33B2

Via Costa San Paolo. **GPS:** n42,87829 e12,75221.

50 free Chfree. **Surface:** grasstiles. 01/01-31/12
Distance: 500m 5,1km.
Remarks: At the swimming pool.

Abruzzo

S Anversa degli Abruzzi 33C4

Bioagriturismo La Porta dei Parchi, Piazza Roma 3. **GPS:** n42,00014 e13,79899.

4 € 10, free with a meal Ch WC included.
Surface: metalled. 01/01-31/12
Distance: on the spot.

S Campotosto 33C3

Via Lago, SR557. **GPS:** n42,56208 e13,34805.
€ 5 . **Surface:** grassy. 01/01-31/12
Distance: Campotosto 3km on the spot.
Remarks: At lake Campotosto.

S Cansano 33D4

Agriturismo Pietro Ruscitti, Via Vecchia Della Stazione. **GPS**: n42,00253 e14,01132.
10 against payment Ch against payment.

S Casalbordino 33D3

Portobello, SS16, km 503, Lido di Casalbordino. **GPS**: n42,17070 e14,63928.

8 against payment Ch (8x). **Surface:** asphalted. 01/01-31/12
Distance: 1,5km 3km.
Remarks: Check in at bar.

S Fossacesia 33D3

Area Camper, Via Lungomare 16b. **GPS**: n42,24067 e14,52988.

24 € 6,50 Ch included. **Surface:** gravel/sand.
01/05-30/09
Distance: 6,5km on the spot.
Remarks: Pebbled beach.

S Isola del Gran Sasso 33C3

S.Gabriele dell Addolorata. **GPS**: n42,51712 e13,65634.

free Ch. **Surface:** gravel/sand.
Distance: on the spot 4km on the spot on the spot.
Remarks: Nearby basilica.

S Lanciano 33D3

Area Attrezzata, Strada provinciale Lanciano-Frisa, Lancianovecchia. **GPS**: n42,23385 e14,39106.

50 free Ch WC free. **Surface:** asphalted.
Distance: 300m (stairs and elevator).
Remarks: At city walls, upper part of the parking.

Tourist information Lanciano:
Historical city with medieval Jewish district, Ripa Sacca.

S L'Aquila 33C3

Via Strinella. **GPS**: n42,35323 e13,40708.
10 free Ch free. **Surface:** asphalted.
Distance: 500m.
Remarks: In front of Hotel Federico II, adjacent Parco del Castello.

Tourist information L'Aquila:
U.I.A.T. (Ufficio Informazioni e di Accoglienza Turistica), Piazza S. Maria di Paganinca, 5.Capital of the province on the foot of the Gran Sasso.

S Notaresco 33C2

Via Martiri della Libertà. **GPS**: n42,65527 e13,89578.
10 free Ch free against payment. **Surface:** asphalted.
Distance: on the spot.
Remarks: At tennis-courts.

S Penne 33C3

Agriturismo Il Portico, Contrada Colle Serangelo 26. **GPS**: n42,45592 e13,95165.

15 € 10, free with a meal Ch (7x)€ 3 WC included. **Surface:** grassy.

S Pescasseroli 33C4

Area Camper S.Andrea, Loc. Sant'Andrea. **GPS**: n41,79888 e13,79222.

€ 15, 2 pers.incl Ch WC included. 8-13h, 14.30-20h
Remarks: Free shuttle to centre.

Tourist information Pescasseroli:
I.A.T. (Ufficio Informazioni e di Accoglienza Turistica), Viale Principe di Napoli.
Parco Nazionale d'Abruzzo.Nature reserve.

Pineto 33C2

Ristorante Aria e Sole, Borgo Santa Maria. **GPS**: n42,60891 e14,04341.

Distance: 200m.
Remarks: Nearby exit highway A14.

S Roccaraso 33D4

Hotel Park Il Poggio, SS17, C.da Poggio, 1 , Loc Il Poggio. **GPS**: n41,82638 e14,10111.

IT

18 € 20 Ch (18x)included.
Distance: on the spot.
Remarks: Shuttle to piste.

S Roseto degli Abruzzi 33C2

Area di Sosta Camper Romeo, Via degli Orti 13, loc. Cologna Spiaggia. **GPS**: n42,72287 e13,98076.

40 € 20/24h Ch (40x) WC included € 1. **Surface:** grassy.
01/01-31/12
Distance: 200m 750m on the spot 100m.

S Roseto degli Abruzzi 33C2

Area di sosta Isola del Sole, Piana degli Ulivi. **GPS**: n42,66902 e14,01189.

11 € 20 Ch (11x)€ 2 WC included. **Surface:** metalled. 01/01-31/12
Distance: 3km 3km.
Remarks: Swimming pool (summer).

S Roseto degli Abruzzi 33C2

Palazzo dello Sport. **GPS**: n42,66012 e14,02382.

free Ch free. **Surface:** asphalted.

Roseto degli Abruzzi 33C2

Lungomare Trieste/via Danubio. **GPS**: n42,66187 e14,03059.

50 free. **Surface:** unpaved.
Distance: on the spot.
Remarks: Max. 72h. 500m before campsite Arcobaleno.

S San Demetrio nei Vestini 33C3

La Grotta di Stiffe, Fraz. Stiffe. **GPS**: n42,25567 e13,54811.

free € 2,50 Ch € 2,50. **Surface:** metalled/sand.
Distance: l'Aquila 18km.

S San Salvo Marina 34A1

Parking on the Beach, Via Amerigo Vespucci 20. **GPS**: n42,07233 e14,76945.

35 € 15/30 Ch (30x)€ 3 WC included € 8. **Surface:** asphalted.
01/01-31/12
Distance: 2km 50m sandy beach 50m Centro Commerciale 2km.

S San Salvo Marina 34A1

Area Sosta Communale per Autocaravan. **GPS**: n42,07195 e14,76289.

30 € 15/24h, € 20/48h, € 30/72h Ch WC included cold shower.
Surface: grassy. 01/06-31/08
Distance: 300m 2,2km 300m.

Santo Stefano di Sessanio 33C3

GPS: n42,34706 e13,64545.
free. 01/01-31/12

S Santo Stefano di Sessanio 33C3

Ostello del Cavaliere, Piazza Della Giudea. **GPS**: n42,34429 e13,64314.
5 guests free . **Surface:** metalled.
Distance: 300m.

S Sant'Egidio alla Vibrata 33C2

Zona industriale. **GPS**: n42,81937 e13,69915.

free Ch free. **Surface:** asphalted.

S Torino di Sangro 33D3

Area camper Vitale, Lido le Morgie. **GPS**: n42,20403 e14,60349.

100 € 10 Ch € 2 WC € 0,50. **Surface:** grassy/sand.
Distance: 8km beach 70m.

S Tortoreto Lido 33C2

Via Napoli. **GPS**: n42,78552 e13,95013.
30 € 12/24h Ch WC . **Surface:** asphalted.
01/01-31/12
Distance: beach 200m.

S Villalago 33C4

SP82b. **GPS**: n41,92255 e13,85621.

13 free Chfree. **Surface:** asphalted.
Distance: on the spot.
Remarks: At lake Scanno.

Molise

S Campobasso 34A2

Area di sosta Dominick Ferrante, Contrada Calvario 1. **GPS**: n41,56886 e14,65118.

20 € 10/24h, € 15/48h Ch included. **Surface:** gravel.
Distance: 800m.
Remarks: Nearby SP41 dir Roccaspromonte.

S Monteroduni 33D4

Oasi San Nazzaro. GPS: n41,53448 e14,15924.

40 € 10, free with a meal Ch (6x)included. **Surface:** grassy.
01/01-31/12
Distance: Fish lake on the spot.

S Petacciato Marina 34A1

SS16 Adriatica km535,5, Termoli ri Vasto. **GPS**: n42,02432 e14,88739.

60 € 15 Ch (50x)included WC . **Surface:** gravel/sand.
01/06-30/09
Distance: on the spot on the spot on the spot.
Remarks: Access via gate next to tower ruins.

S Petacciato Marina 34A1

Parking spiaggia, Via del Mare, SS16. **GPS**: n42,03543 e14,85337.

40 € 6, 8-20h against payment. **Surface:** asphalted.
Distance: 9,5km 50m.
Remarks: Reserved place for motorhomes.

S Termoli 34A1

Centro Commerciale Sannicola, SS 87 Sannitica, km216-256. **GPS**: n41,93880 e14,98754.

20 free Chfree. **Surface:** asphalted. 01/01-31/12

Puglia

S Alberobello 34C1

Parcheggio Nel Verde, Via Cadore. **GPS**: n40,78266 e17,23418.

60 € 15/24h, € 10/12h, € 8/6h Chincluded € 3.
Surface: grassy/gravel. 01/01-31/12
Distance: Trulli-centre 50m 50m 100m.

Tourist information Alberobello:

Centre of the Trulli-region. Trulli houses are curious houses built without motar.

Thu-morning.

IT

S Bari 34C1

Gran Parcheggio Alberotanza, Via Alberotaza, 43A. **GPS**: n41,09520 e16,87868.

250 € 15 € 0,50/30liter € 2,50Ch € 0,50/kWh.
Surface: asphalted. 01/01-31/12
Distance: 7,8km 500m 500m.
Remarks: Monitored parking.

Tourist information Bari:
A.P.T. (Azienda di Promozione Turistica), Piazza Moro, 33, www.regione.puglia.it.Important port city.

S Brindisi 34D1

Area Attrezzata, Strada Minnuta 6. **GPS**: n40,63517 e17,91824.

€ 10 Ch WC included. **Surface:** asphalted. 01/01-31/12
Remarks: 24/24 surveillance.

Tourist information Brindisi:
A.P.T. (Azienda di Promozione Turistica), Via C. Colombo, 88, www.pugliaturismo.com.Important port city.

Castellana Grotte 34C1

Le Grotte di Castellana. **GPS**: n40,87543 e17,14900.

€ 5. **Surface:** grassy/gravel. 01/01-31/12
Remarks: Parking at the caves of Castellana, overnight stay permitted.

S Gallipoli 34D2

GPS: n40,06000 e18,03939.
€ 13 Ch € 5.
Distance: 5km.

S Lecce 34D1

Camperpark Fuori Le Mura, Via S.Oronzo Fuori Le Mura, 20. **GPS**: n40,39340 e18,16581.

21 € 15/24h Ch WC. 01/01-31/12
Distance: city centre 3km 300m.
Remarks: Shuttle to centre.

S Lesina 34A1

Oasi, Via Ludovica Ariosto. **GPS**: n41,86472 e15,35806.

15 € 12, Sept-Mar-Apr € 15, May/Aug € 18 Ch WC included.
Surface: asphalted. 01/01-31/12
Distance: 300m on the spot 500m.

S Lucera 34A1

Via Montello. **GPS**: n41,49987 e15,33223.

100 free . **Surface:** asphalted. 01/01-31/12
Remarks: At station.

Tourist information Lucera:
Art city with castle from 13th century and religious history.

S Margherita di Savoia 34B1

Lido Baywatch, Via Barletta. **GPS**: n41,36222 e16,17361.

12 € 15, Aug € 20 Ch WC included. **Surface:** gravel/sand.
01/01-31/12
Distance: 2km on the spot on the spot.

S Massafra 34C1

Area di Sosta La Stella, SS7, SS Appia km 633, Le Forche. **GPS**: n40,59201 e17,09904.

IT

20 € 10/16.00-12.00, € 20/24h Ch (18x) WC included € 1.
Surface: grassy. 01/01-31/12
Distance: 1km 500-700m 1km.
Remarks: Beachshuttle € 2.

S Mattinata 34B1
Punta Grugno, SS89dirB. **GPS:** n41,69797 e16,06236.

80 € 11, Jun € 13, Jul € 16, Aug € 20 Ch € 2,50 WC € 0,80.
Surface: grassy/sand. 01/04-01/10
Distance: Mattinata 2km pebbled beach on the spot 2km.

S Mattinata 34B1
Eden Park, Porto di Mattinata, SP53. **GPS:** n41,70667 e16,06556.

25 € 10, Jul/Aug € 20 Ch WC included € 0,50. **Surface:** grassy/sand.
01/06-31/08
Distance: 1km pebbled beach on the spot 1km 1km.

S Melendugno 34D1
Area attrezzata SantAndrea - Salento, SP366 km 20.5, Sant'Andrea. **GPS:** n40,25550 e18,43748.
15 € 25/24h Ch WC.
Distance: 500m on the spot.
Remarks: Beachshuttle.

S Melendugno 34D1
Camper club 'Campo Carleo', Az. Agr.la di De Pascalis Antonio S., Strada provinciale Lecce-Melendugno-San Foca, km.18. **GPS:** n40,27724 e18,40510.
40 € 10-15, 20/07-31/08 € 30 Ch € 5 WC. **Surface:** unpaved.
01/01-31/12
Distance: 1,5km.
Remarks: Free shuttle.

S Monopoli 34C1
Area du Sosta Camper Lido Millennium, SP90, Loc. Capitolo, SS16 km850 Uscita Capitolo. **GPS:** n40,90374 e17,35261.

100 € 12-15-18 Ch 6Amp WC included. **Surface:** gravel.
Easter-30/09
Distance: 500m 50m 50m 50m.
Remarks: Private beach.

S Otranto 34D1
Area Camper Fontanelle, Sp366, km28. **GPS:** n40,19159 e18,45494.

€ 15/24h Ch WC against payment.
Distance: Otranto 5km beach 200m.
Remarks: Shuttle bus to Otranto.

S Otranto 34D1
Oasy Park, Via Renis. **GPS:** n40,14029 e18,48621.

50 € 20 3 pers.incl Ch (70x),16Amp WC included € 1 € 4.
Surface: grassy/gravel. 01/01-31/12
Distance: 400m 700m 400m 400m.

Tourist information Otranto:
I.A.T. (Ufficio Informazioni e di Accoglienza Turistica), Piazza Castello, 8.

S Peschici 34A1
Camper Marina Picola, Loc. Pantanello, Baia di Peschici. **GPS:** n41,94528 e16,00528.

45 Apr € 12, May € 13, Jun/Sep € 15, Jul € 20, Aug € 25
Ch WC included € 0,50. **Surface:** grassy/sand. 01/04-30/09
Distance: 2,5km, walking 800m (stairs) sandy beach 50m.

S Peschici 34A1
AgriCamper Pane e Vino, SS89 km 2,6. **GPS:** n41,92372 e16,01534.
20 € 10 Ch WC. **Surface:** sand.

IT

Distance: 3,5km on the spot.

Peschici 34A1

Area attrezzata per camper Dattoli, Via Spiaggia, SS89. **GPS**: n41,94522 e16,01138.
14 € 15 Ch WC included € 0,50. **Surface:** unpaved.
Distance: Old city 300m (stairs) 100m 100m.

Tourist information Peschici:
I.A.T. (Ufficio Informazioni e di Accoglienza Turistica), Via Magenta, 3.

Putignano 34C1

Grotte di Putignano, SS172. **GPS**: n40,85706 e17,10944.
free. 01/01-31/12

Rodi Garganico 34A1

Area sosta camper Isola Bella, Via delle More. **GPS**: n41,92444 e15,84166.

30 € 15-20, Aug € 25 Ch WC included. **Surface:** grassy/sand.
01/06-15/09
Distance: Lido del Sole 1,5km, Rodi Garganico 3,8km sandy beach 10m on the spot 100m 1,5km.

San Giovanni Rotondo 34A1

Coppa Cicuta, Strada Comunale Pozzocavo-Tre Carrini. **GPS**: n41,69599 e15,70423.

30 € 10, park € 5 Ch (30x)€ 1,50/night WC included € 10.
Surface: gravel. 01/01-31/12
Distance: 3km on the spot.
Remarks: Shuttle € 2/pp.

San Giovanni Rotondo 34A1

Di Cerbo, Circonvallazione Sud, SP45bis. **GPS**: n41,69725 e15,73097.
20 € 13 Ch WC € 0,50 € 1. **Surface:** asphalted. 01/01-31/12
Distance: 1km on the spot on the spot on the spot.
Remarks: Shuttle bus.

San Giovanni Rotondo 34A1

Viale Padre Pio. **GPS**: n41,70902 e15,70379.
150 € 2,50, overnight stay free. **Surface:** asphalted.
Remarks: Shrine Padre Pio 200m.

Sannicola 34D2

Campo delle Bandiere, Loc. Padula Bianca. **GPS**: n40,09681 e18,01297.
€ 20 Ch WC . **Surface:** sand. 01/06-01/09
Distance: sandy beach.

Santa Maria al Bagno 34D1

Area Camper Mondonuovo, Via Torre Mozza. **GPS**: n40,13494 e18,00166.
30 € 15 Ch . **Surface:** grassy. 01/01-31/12
Distance: beach 500m.

Torre Canne di Fasano 34C1

Lido Tavernese, SS379, uscita Torre Canne Sud. **GPS**: n40,82023 e17,49875.

200 € 13, Aug € 15 Ch (80x)€ 2 WC included € 1.
Surface: grassy.
Distance: 3,5km on the spot 01/07-31/08.

Torre Canne di Fasano 34C1

Il Privilegio Camper Service, Via Appia, SP90 > Savelletri. **GPS**: n40,84363 e17,46359.
Ch . **Surface:** gravel.
Remarks: Beach club.

Troia 34A1

Via Sant'Antonio. **GPS**: n41,36158 e15,30616.

12 free Ch . **Surface:** asphalted. 01/01-31/12
Distance: 200m.
Remarks: Near the cathedral.

Uggiano la Chiesa 34D1

Agriturismo Mulino a Vento, Via Badisco 59. **GPS**: n40,09694 e18,46006.
40 € 30, 2 pers.incl Ch .
Distance: beach 4km on the spot.
Remarks: Swimming pool.

Vico del Gargano 34A1

Lido Azzurro. **GPS**: n41,94208 e15,98303.

80 Oct-Apr € 10, May-June € 15, Jul/Aug € 25 Ch € 3,(Aug) WC included € 1. **Surface:** sand. 01/01-31/12
Distance: Valazzo 4km sandy beach 1km (camping).

Vieste 34B1

Fusilo Rosina, Contrada S.Lucia. **GPS**: n41,91028 e16,12944.

IT

70 Jun-Sep € 15, Jul € 20, Aug € 27,50 Ch (70x)included WC € 0,50. **Surface:** grassy. 01/06-15/09
Distance: 4km 300m 50m 100m 50m.

S Vieste 34B1
Residence Euro 92, Enrico Mattei 119. **GPS:** n41,85639 e16,17417.

50 € 15 (3p incl.), peak season € 20-27 (2p incl.) Ch WC included. **Surface:** grassy. 01/04-31/10
Distance: on the spot 200m 100m.

S Vieste 34B1
Area Eden Blu, Lungomare Enrico Mattei. **GPS:** n41,85985 e16,17396.
40 € 20 Ch WC. **Surface:** unpaved. 01/04-31/10
Distance: on the spot.

Vieste 34B1
Bagno Lido Azzurro, Loc. Lido di Portonuovo. **GPS:** n41,84942 e16,17755.
. **Surface:** sand. 01/01-31/12
Distance: on the spot on the spot.

Tourist information Vieste:
I.A.T. (Ufficio Informazioni e di Accoglienza Turistica), Piazza Kennedy.
Mo.

S Zapponeta 34B1
Zapponeta Beach, Via del Mare. **GPS:** n41,45694 e15,96083.

30 € 10, 1/7-15/7, 15/8-31/8 €12, 15/7-15/8 € 15/2 pers incl Ch € 2 WC included € 0,50. **Surface:** grassy/metalled. 01/04-30/09
Distance: 250m on the spot on the spot 500m 500m.
Remarks: Narrow entrance.

Campania

S Bacoli 33D6
Sea Oasi Village, Via Strada Romana, loc. Fusaro. **GPS:** n40,82194 e14,04791.
± 100 € 15/20/24h, 4 pers.incl Ch € 5 WC € 1. **Surface:** grassy/sand.
Distance: on the spot.
Remarks: At the beach.

S Bacoli 33D6
Parco Naturale Agriturismo Fondi di Baia, Via Fondi di Baia. **GPS:** n40,81132 e14,07518.

20 € 10 Ch included. **Surface:** asphalted. 01/01-31/12
Distance: 3km Baia 700m 100m.

S Benevento 34A2
Tennis Airola, Via Domenico Mustilli. **GPS:** n41,13141 e14,78960.
€ 5. 01/01-31/12
Distance: 500m 1,8km.

Tourist information Benevento:
U.I.A.T. (Ufficio Informazioni e di Accoglienza Turistica), Piazza Roma, 11, www.eptbenevento.it.City with historical monuments.
Piazza Risorgimento en Piazza Santa Maria. Wed, Sa 8-13h.

Casalbore 34A2
Agriturismo Le Mainarde. **GPS:** n41,24516 e15,00242.
30 € 15. 01/01-31/12
Distance: on the spot.

S Cava de' Tirreni 34A2
Via Ido Longo, loc. Sant'Arcangelo. **GPS:** n40,69984 e14,69553.
free Ch free.
Distance: 2,3km.

Tourist information Cava de' Tirreni:
Salerno.City with medieval centre.
A.A.C.S.T.(Azienda Autonoma di Cura Soggiorno e Turismo), Corso Roma, 19, Amalfi.Popular bathing resort.
Museo Civico, Amalfi.Museum with Tavole Amalfitane, the old Law of the Sea. 8-14h, Sa 8-12h holiday.

S Contursi Terme 34B2
Agriturismo Il Giardino, Loc. Prato. **GPS:** n40,64891 e15,23002.
€ 10 Ch.
Distance: 4,4km on the spot.
Remarks: Le Terme Vulpacchio 50m.

S Marina di Camerota 34B3
Parcheggio Europa, Loc. Sirene. **GPS:** n40,00302 e15,36493.
€ 18. Easter-30/09
Distance: on the spot.

S Napoli 33D6
Parking IPM, Via Colli Aminei 27, Naples (Napoli). **GPS:** n40,87038 e14,24616.

7-21h € 10 21-8h €10 Ch included € 2. **Surface:** asphalted.
01/01-31/12
Distance: 1,2km bus R4 centre Napoli 30m.
Remarks: Monitored parking.

Tourist information Naples (Napoli):
A.A.C.S.T.(Azienda Autonoma di Cura Soggiorno e Turismo), Palazzo Reale, www.regione.campania.it.Capital of the province with many monuments and cultural treasures.
Vesuvio.Volcano, observatorium on western edge of the crater. Visit with guide possible.
Mergellina.Small peninsula with fishing-port and marina.
Teatro San Carlo.Opera building.
Museo Nazionale Archeologico di Napoli, Piazza Museo Nazionale 19.Antique hellenic-roman civilisation. Tue-Su 9-14h.
Palazzo Reale.Royal palace. 9-13.30h Mo.
Duomo San Gennaro.Cathedral with original interior.
Ercolano/Herculaneum.Ancient city buried together with Pompeii. 9-14.45h, holidays 9-18.15h.
Mercato Corso Malta. Mo, Fri.

S Paestum 34B3
Camper Village Maremirtilli, Via Linora di Paestum, SP278. **GPS:** n40,37607 e15,00119.
70 € 13-25 Ch WC.

IT

Paestum 34B3

Hotel Mandetta, Via Torre di Mare, 2. **GPS**: n40,41529 e14,99093.
20 € 15-20 Ch.
Distance: 500m on the spot on the spot.

Tourist information Paestum:
A.A.C.S.T.(Azienda Autonoma di Cura Soggiorno e Turismo), Via Magna Grecia, 151.Old city, founded by the Greeks. In the surroundings many vestiges from that time. 9h-sunset.

Palinuro 34B3

Via Palorcio. **GPS**: n40,03722 e15,30944.
€15 Ch WC.
Distance: 700m.

Pompei 33D6

Parking Plinio, Via Plinio 98. **GPS**: n40,74710 e14,48756.

30 8-20h € 10, 8-8h € 19, 20-8h € 12. **Surface:** asphalted.
01/01-31/12
Distance: Archeological site Pompei 250m 300m.
Remarks: Monitored parking.

Pompei 33D6

Camping Pompei, Via Plinio 113. **GPS**: n40,74675 e14,48496.
€ 15,50-20, 2 pers.incl Ch WC included.
Location: Urban. **Surface:** grassy.
01/01-31/12
Remarks: Entrance acient city 150m.

Tourist information Pompei:
Ancient city at the foot of Vesuvius.
9h-sunset holiday.

Pozzuoli 33D6

Castagnaro Parking - Pozzuoli - Napoli

info@castagnaroparking.it - www.castagnaroparking.it

Open all year
Paved and flat motorhome pitches
Excursions

Castagnaro Park, Via del Castagnaro 1. **GPS**: n40,86942 e14,12165.
85 € 15 Ch (85x)€ 3/24h WC included € 2.
Surface: grassy/gravel. 01/01-31/12
Distance: 300m 4km 400m 500m 300m.
Remarks: Guarded parking, reservation during Christmas period.

Tourist information Pozzuoli:
Cuma.Archeological site.
9-14.45h, summer 18h.

Sala Consilina 34B2

Via Santa Maria della Misericordia. **GPS**: n40,41376 e15,56397.
20 € 5/night Ch included. **Surface:** metalled. 01/01-31/12
Distance: 1,5km 500m 2,5km 1,5km 15km 15km.
Remarks: Nearby hotel Vallis Dea, 300m>A3.

San Gregorio Matese 33D5

Cooperative Falode, Loc. Acqua di Santa Maria Castello. **GPS**: n41,40547 e14,42756.
40 Ch against payment.

Tramonti 34A2

Agriturismo Costiera Amalfitana - Tramonti

info@costieraamalfitana.it - www.costieraamalfitana.it

Open all year
Bar-restaurant
Picnic area

Agriturismo Costiera Amalfitana, Via Falcone, 12 - Frazione Pietre.
GPS: n40,69929 e14,61811.
10 01/09-14/06 € 22, 15/06-31/08 - 23/12-06/01 € 30 Ch WC included. **Location:** Rural, comfortable.
Surface: grassy/gravel. 01/01-31/12
Distance: 50m 15km 6km on the spot 30m 500m on the spot.
Remarks: Amalfi Coast.

Basilicata

Grumento Nova 34B2

Agriturismo Al Parco Verde, Contrada Spineto, Moliterno-Grumento. **GPS**: n40,28110 e15,90563.
20 € 20 Ch WC included. **Surface:** grassy. 01/06-01/10
Distance: 8km 2km 5km on the spot 2km 1km.
Remarks: Archeological site 200m.

Metaponto 34C2

Camper parking Nettuno, Viale Magna Grecia, Metaponto Lido. **GPS**: n40,35693 e16,83221.

50 € 10/24h, € 15/01/07-31/08 Ch WC included € 1.
Surface: grassy/gravel. 01/01-31/12
Distance: 50m on the spot 300m.

Tourist information Metaponto:
Archeological site. 9h-sunset.

Calabria

Amantea 34C3

Garden Park Caterina, SS. 18, loc Coreca. **GPS**: n39,09383 e16,08508.
10 € 8-12 € 3,50 Ch € 1,50. **Surface:** grassy. 15/06-15/09
Distance: on the spot on the spot on the spot nearby.

Bova Marina 34D5

Mafalda's Camper Park, Via Sotto Ferrovia, loc. San Pasquale. **GPS**: n37,92422 e15,94800.
20 € 10-20 Ch included. **Surface:** gravel/sand.
Distance: 3km on the spot on the spot 200m 500m.
Remarks: Acces via unmetalled road along the beach.

Catanzaro Marina 34D3

Il Chioschetto, Via Carlo Pisacane 24. **GPS**: n38,83321 e16,64862.

10 free. **Location:** Simple. **Surface:** sand.
Distance: sandy beach.

Cirella 34C3

Area Camper Ulisse, SS 18 km 270, Diamante. **GPS**: n39,72500 e15,80930.

130 € 8-15 Ch WC included. **Surface:** grassy/sand.
01/04-31/10
Distance: 800m on the spot on the spot on the spot on the spot on the spot.

Cirella 34C3

Lido Alexander, SS 18, Diamante. **GPS**: n39,72168 e15,81097.

50 € 6 to € 20 peak season Ch € 3 WC included € 1 € 3.
Surface: grassy/gravel. 01/01-31/12
Distance: 1,5km on the spot on the spot on the spot on the spot.

Cirella 34C3

Lido delle Sirene, SS 18, Contr. Riviere. **GPS**: n39,71822 e15,81137.

100 € 11 Ch WC. **Surface:** grassy. 01/06-20/09
Distance: 1km on the spot on the spot on the spot 1km.

Cirella 34C3

Lido Tropical, Viale Glauco, 9, Diamante. **GPS**: n39,69222 e15,81556.

200 € 8-18, Aug € 25 Ch WC. **Surface:** grassy/sand.
01/01-31/12
Distance: 1,5km on the spot on the spot 200m 200m shuttle to town.

Cirò Marina 28D3

Via Maddalena. **GPS**: n39,35998 e17,12910.
25 € 6, 01/06-31/08 € 12. **Surface:** unpaved. 01/01-31/12
Distance: 1,2km 50m.

Condofuri Marina 34D5

Agriturismo Antonino Gemelli, Via Salinella 37. **GPS**: n37,92372 e15,85150.
20 € 15-20 Ch WC. **Surface:** gravel/sand.
01/01-31/12
Distance: 500m 100m.

Corigliano Calabro 34C3

B&B Club Tepee, Contrada Sant'Agata 42, SS106bis > Cantinella. **GPS**: n39,64140 e16,38617.
€ 10 Ch.
Distance: Corigliano 14km.

Cropani Marina 34D3

Sena Park, Viale Venezia 34. **GPS**: n38,91143 e16,80963.
25 € 15 Ch WC € 0,50. **Surface:** grassy/sand.
01/01-31/12
Distance: 500m 400m 400m ristorante/pizzeria 500m.
Remarks: Washing motorhome € 20.

Crotone 34D3

Coda Campione, Hera Lacinia Mare, Via Per Capo Colonna. **GPS**: n39,04193 e17,15297.
10 € 25 Ch. **Surface:** gravel/metalled.
Distance: on the spot on the spot on the spot 100m 200m.
Remarks: Next to campsite.

Morano Calabro 34C3

Via Gaetano Scorza. **GPS**: n39,84098 e16,13731.

40 free. **Surface:** asphalted. 01/01-31/12
Distance: 200m 7km 200m 200m.
Remarks: Next to church of San Bernardino, panoramic view.

Palmi 34C4

Sosta Camper Prajola, Lungomare Donna Canfora. **GPS**: n38,39333 e15,86277.

IT

25 € 15/24h Ch WC included. **Location:** Simple.
Surface: gravel. 01/01-31/12
Distance: on the spot.

S Praia a Mare 34B3

Nuova Playa, Contr. Fiucci. **GPS**: n39,86885 e15,78943.

15 € 15, peak season € 25 Ch included. **Surface:** grassy.
01/01-31/12
Distance: 2km on the spot on the spot 100m 2km.
Remarks: In front of Dino island, black sandy beach.

S Praia a Mare 34B3

Punto Mare, Loc. Fiuzzi. **GPS**: n39,87633 e15,78727.

30 € 6 Ch € 5. **Surface:** grassy. 01/06-30/09
Distance: 800m 600m 600m 500m 500m.

S Rossano 34D4

Sosta Camper Il Faro, C. da Foresta Faro Campo Trionto. **GPS**: n39,62148 e16,75146.

12 € 13-25 Ch WC included. **Location:** Comfortable, isolated.
Surface: grassy. 01/01-31/12
Distance: 2km, Rossano 12km sandy beach on the spot.

S Scalea 34B3

Dolce Vita, Via Fiume Lao 7. **GPS**: n39,79667 e15,79265.

100 € 7, Jul € 10, Aug € 13 Ch € 5 WC.
Surface: grassy.
01/05-30/09
Distance: on the spot on the spot on the spot on the spot 800m.

S Scalea 34B3

Lido Zio Tom, Corso Mediterraneo km 261,7. **GPS**: n39,81306 e15,78917.

140 € 8, July € 11, Aug € 14 Ch € 2,4Amp WC hot shower against payment. **Surface:** grassy/gravel. 15/04-15/10
Distance: on the spot 300m 1km 1,5km.

Sardinia

S Aglientu 31C4

Oasi Gallura, Localita' Vignola Mare 19, SP 90 km 53. **GPS**: n41,12556 e9,06167.
70 € 13-19 Ch € 2,50 WC hot shower € 1 € 5.
Distance: 50m on the spot on the spot.

S Alghero 31B5

Camperpark I Platani, Ss 291 Km 32,5 S.Maria la Palma - Fertilia. **GPS**: n40,60693 e8,27522.

€ 16, Jul €18, Aug € 20 Ch WC included € 5.
Distance: Alghero 7km 1,5km.
Remarks: Monitored parking 24/24, shuttle bus to beach, swimming pool.

S Alghero 31B5

Paradise Park, Loc. Le Bombarde. **GPS**: n40,59180 e8,25610.

100 ± € 18 Ch WC included.
Distance: 350m 350m on the spot on the spot 50m.

IT

S Bosa 31C5
S'Abba Drucche Spiagge, SP49 Alghero-Bosa km 38+800. **GPS**: n40,31671 e8,47368.
€ 15-20 Ch WC € 1 € 7. **Surface:** unpaved.
01/06-30/09
Distance: on the spot on the spot.

S Buggerru 31C6
Area Terrazze. GPS: n39,40317 e8,40250.

50 € 20/24h Ch € 5. **Surface:** sand.
Distance: 200m on the spot.
Remarks: Beach parking.

S Buggerru 31C6
Loc. Cala Domestica. **GPS**: n39,41757 e8,41147.
50 € 10 cold shower. **Surface:** sand.
Distance: 4km on the spot.
Remarks: Beach parking.

Tourist information Buggerru:
I.A.T. (Ufficio Informazioni e di Accoglienza Turistica), Strada Provinciale.

S Domus de Maria 31C6
Loc. Spartivento, Chia. **GPS**: n38,88962 e8,86437.
€ 15/24h Ch cold shower. **Surface:** sand.
Easter-30/09
Distance: on the spot on the spot on the spot.
Remarks: In front of Hotel Su Giudeu.

S Ghilarza 31C5
SS131 km 6. **GPS**: n40,12604 e8,83942.
free € 0,50 .

S Nuoro 31C5
P.le Anfiteatro cittadino, Piazza Veneto. **GPS**: n40,31652 e9,32587.
30 free Chfree.

S Oristano 31C5
Stadio Tharros, Via Dorando Petri. **GPS**: n39,89710 e8,58927.
free Chfree.
Distance: 500m Porta Nuova 650m.

S Oristano 31C5
Zona sportiva Sa Rodia, Viale Repubblica. **GPS**: n39,90605 e8,57878.
free Chfree.
Distance: historical centre.
Remarks: Parking in front of swimming pool.

San Teodoro 31C4
Via Donat Cattin. **GPS**: n40,76658 e9,66884.
30 € 20.

San Teodoro 31C4
Via Marconi, Loc.La Cinta. **GPS**: n40,77243 e9,66990.
€ 5.
Distance: on the spot.
Remarks: Beach parking.

S Santa Maria Navarrese 31C5
Area di sosta Costa Orientale, Loc.Tancau. **GPS**: n39,98770 e9,68750.
€ 12-16 Ch WC .
Distance: 15 min walking.

S Sorso 31C4
Camp Site, Via degli Oleandri, SP 81 km 13, Platamona Lido. **GPS**: n40,81565 e8,46462.
50 € 12-18 Ch WC . 01/01-31/12
Distance: 300m nearby on the spot.

S Stintino 31B4
La Pineta, Loc. Pozzo S.Nicola, SP34. **GPS**: n40,86843 e8,23610.
€ 19, Aug € 21 Ch WCincluded hot shower € 1. **Surface:** grassy/sand.
Distance: 3,5km on the spot.
Remarks: Free shuttle to beach.

S Tonara 31C5
Ostello delle Gioventù, Via Muggianeddu, 2. **GPS**: n40,02855 e9,17542.
€ 10 Ch . 01/01-31/12
Distance: on the spot.

S Valledoria 31C4
Punto Maragnani, Via Cristoforo Colombo, Loc. Maragnani. **GPS**: n40,92470 e8,79548.
€ 18/24h Ch WC included.
Distance: 50m 200m.

S Villaputzu 31C6
Area di sosta camper Torimar, via Nazionale 236, SS125. **GPS**: n39,46017 e9,60290.
€ 8-16 Ch WC against payment.
Distance: Villaputzu 6km 50m.

S Villasimius 31C6
Gli Aranci, Viale dei Carrubi, loc. Pranu Zinnigas. **GPS**: n39,14997 e9,51292.
100 € 20 Ch WC included. 01/05-30/09
Distance: 2km 3km.
Remarks: Beachshuttle.

Sicily

S Augusta 34C6
Area Attrezzata Camper Nelly, SS114 - Km 118,5, Contrada Agnone Bagni. **GPS**: n37,31148 e15,09260.
€ 13, July € 14, Aug € 15/day Ch WC included.
01/01-31/12. **Distance:** 6km.

Caltagirone 34C6
Loc. San Giovanni. **GPS**: n37,23808 e14,50781.
.

S Caltanissetta 34B6
Via Guastaferro. **GPS**: n37,48959 e14,04515.
Chfree.

S Castellammare del Golfo 34A6
Playtime, Viale Leonardo da Vinci, SS187. **GPS**: n38,02494 e12,89086.
€ 15/24h Ch WC . **Surface:** grassy.
Distance: 200m 1km.

S Castelluzzo 34A6
Parcheggio Trinacria, Via Calazza. **GPS**: n38,10694 e12,72861.

± 40 against payment . **Surface:** gravel. summer
Distance: 400m 500m 500m.
Remarks: Beach parking.

Castelluzzo 34A6
Parking Macari, SP16. **GPS**: n38,13564 e12,73638.

free. **Surface:** sand.

IT

Castelluzzo 34A6

SP16. **GPS**: n38,12166 e12,72666.

free. **Surface:** gravel.
Distance: on the spot.
Remarks: Beach parking.

Enna 34C6

Ennacamper, C/da S.Giuseppe, Pergusa. **GPS**: n37,52277 e14,29000.
€ 10/24h Ch Service € 5 € 2. **Surface:** sand.
Remarks: Free shuttle, cleaning motorhome € 5.

Enna 34C6

Castello di Lombardia, Via Nino Savarrese. **GPS**: n37,56764 e14,28724.
free.
Distance: on the spot.
Remarks: Parking at castle.

Francavilla di Sicilia 34C5

Maremonti, Via Cappuccini. **GPS**: n37,90855 e15,14347.

±50 gift. **Surface:** unpaved. 01/01-31/12
Distance: 400m Riverbed.
Remarks: Gole dell'Alcantara 6km.

Furnari 34C5

Tonnarella, Corso Palermo 6. **GPS**: n38,13218 e15,12469.

44 € 15, Jun € 16, Jul € 18, Aug € 20 Ch WC included € 0,50.
Surface: gravel. 01/01-31/12
Distance: on the spot on the spot 150m 250m.
Remarks: Excursion to the Eolie-islands.

Gela 34C6

Meridiana Park, Via Torre di Manfria, Contrada Piano Marina. **GPS**: n37,11166 e14,12444.
80 € 15/day Ch WC. **Surface:** grassy.
Distance: Gela 14km 1,2km.
Remarks: Swimming pool, sandy beach.

Giardini Naxos 34C5

Parking Lagani, Via Stralcina 22, zona Recanati. **GPS**: n37,82092 e15,26753.

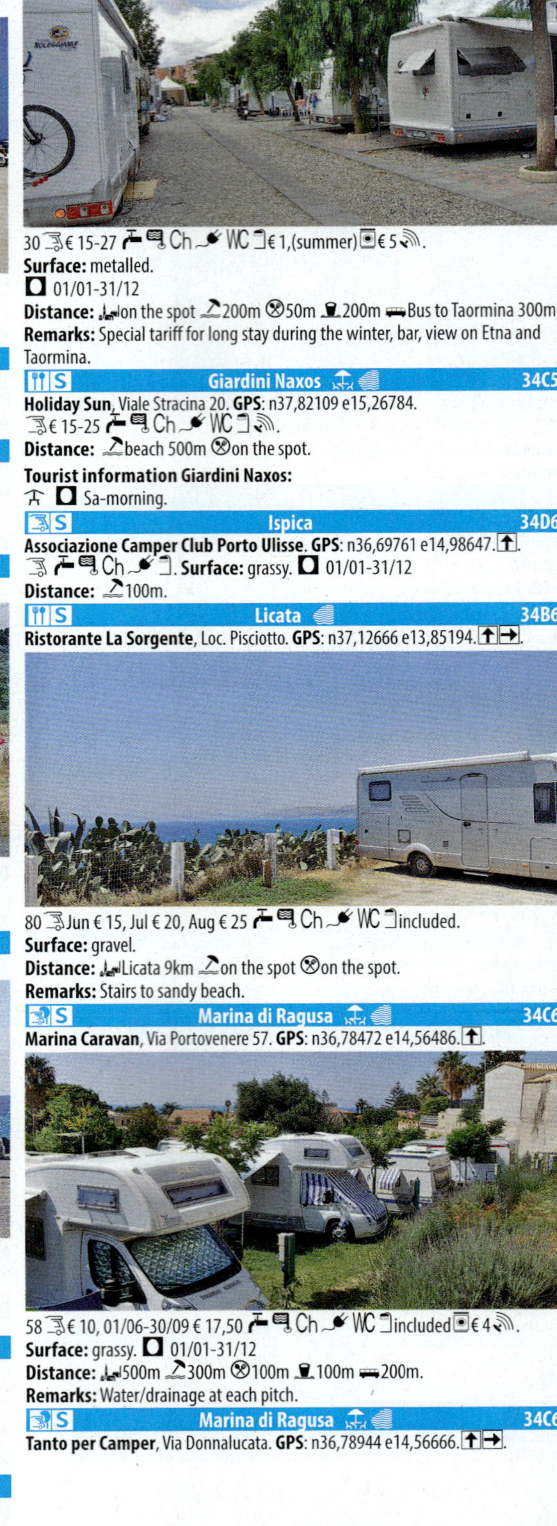

30 € 15-27 Ch WC € 1,(summer) € 5.
Surface: metalled.
01/01-31/12
Distance: on the spot 200m 50m 200m Bus to Taormina 300m.
Remarks: Special tariff for long stay during the winter, bar, view on Etna and Taormina.

Giardini Naxos 34C5

Holiday Sun, Viale Stracina 20. **GPS**: n37,82109 e15,26784.
€ 15-25 Ch WC.
Distance: beach 500m on the spot.

Tourist information Giardini Naxos:
Sa-morning.

Ispica 34D6

Associazione Camper Club Porto Ulisse. **GPS**: n36,69761 e14,98647.
Ch. **Surface:** grassy. 01/01-31/12
Distance: 100m.

Licata 34B6

Ristorante La Sorgente, Loc. Pisciotto. **GPS**: n37,12666 e13,85194.

80 Jun € 15, Jul € 20, Aug € 25 Ch WC included.
Surface: gravel.
Distance: Licata 9km on the spot on the spot.
Remarks: Stairs to sandy beach.

Marina di Ragusa 34C6

Marina Caravan, Via Portovenere 57. **GPS**: n36,78472 e14,56486.

58 € 10, 01/06-30/09 € 17,50 Ch WC included € 4.
Surface: grassy. 01/01-31/12
Distance: 500m 300m 100m 100m 200m.
Remarks: Water/drainage at each pitch.

Marina di Ragusa 34C6

Tanto per Camper, Via Donnalucata. **GPS**: n36,78944 e14,56666.

IT

40 15/9-14/6 € 10, 15/6-26/7 € 12, 27/7-30/8 € 15,, 2 pers.incl Ch WC included € 0,50 € 4. **Surface:** grassy/gravel. 01/01-31/12
Distance: 800m 1,5km 100m 800m.
Remarks: Beachshuttle € 0,50.

S Marsala 34A6
Beach Sibiliana, Contrada Fossarunza 205/z 14. **GPS:** n37,73520 e12,47497.
50 € 17 Ch WC.
Distance: 50m.

S Marsala 34A6
Nautisub Club S. Teodoro, Contrada Birgi. **GPS:** n37,91046 e12,46178.

± 50 € 15/20 Ch. **Surface:** grassy. 01/05-30/09
Distance: 5km on the spot on the spot.
Remarks: Sandy beach.

S Marsala 34A6
Via Colonnello Maltese. **GPS:** n37,79621 e12,43164.
Ch.
Distance: on the spot on the spot.

Tourist information Marsala:
I.A.T. (Ufficio Informazioni e di Accoglienza Turistica), Via XI Maggio, 100.
Cassaro Marsala, old city centre.

S Montallegro 34B6
Agriturismo Torre Salsa, Bove Marina. **GPS:** n37,37583 e13,32222.

20 € 15-22 € 4 Ch consumption WC € 1 € 6 € 1,50/h.
Surface: grassy. 01/01-31/12
Distance: 700m.
Remarks: Pitches on the beach without service, estate 300 acres, hiking and mountain bike trails.

S Montevago 34A6
Agricamper Mastragostino - Villa dei Pini. **GPS:** n37,70083 e12,98000.
€ 15 Ch included. 01/01-31/12
Distance: 200m.

S Montevago 34A6
Centro Terme Acqua Pia, Loc. Acque Calde. **GPS:** n37,70602 e12,98092.
20 against payment. 01/04-31/10

S Motta Camastra 34C5
S185, fraz. Ficarazzi. **GPS:** n37,87876 e15,17615.

10 € 10, Jul/Aug € 15 Ch WC included. **Surface:** grassy/gravel.
Distance: 300m 1km.
Remarks: In front of entrance of Gole dell'Alcantara.

S Mussomeli 34B6
Piazzale Mongibello. **GPS:** n37,58343 e13,74956.
free Ch.
Distance: historical centre.

S Noto 34D6
Airone, Via San Corrado, Lido di Noto. **GPS:** n36,85916 e15,11555.

50 Jun/Sep € 10, Jul/Aug € 15 Ch € 2 WC hot shower € 0,50.
Surface: grassy/sand. 01/06-15/09
Distance: 100m 100m 750m Bus to Noto 100m.

S Noto 34D6
Il Canneto, Viale Lido di Noto, Lido di Noto. **GPS:** n36,86083 e15,11944.

55 Jun € 12, Jul/Aug € 15 incl. 4 pers Ch € 2 WC.
Surface: grassy/sand.
Distance: on the spot 1,2km.
Remarks: Bread-service and meals, direct access to the beach.

S Noto 34D6
NotoParking, Contrada Faldino, Noto. **GPS:** n36,88353 e15,08595.

40 € 13-15 Ch € 3 WC € 1. **Surface:** grassy/gravel.
01/01-31/12
Distance: 1km 3km 200m 200m.
Remarks: Free shuttle bus to Noto, organised excursions in the surroundings.

IT

Noto 34D6

Parcheggio Calamosche, Oasi di Vendicari. **GPS**: n36,81611 e15,09888.

40-50 € 12 WC included. **Surface:** grassy. 01/01-31/12
Distance: Noto 10km 20 min walking bar/restaurant.

Oliveri 34C5

Azimut Sosta Camper, Corso Cristoforo Colombo. **GPS**: n38,12840 e15,05833.
100 € 12-15-20-22 Ch (100x),6Amp WC included.
Surface: grassy/gravel. 01/03-31/10
Distance: 500m, Tindari 1,2km 2,5km beach 50m 50m 50m 200m 10m 100m 100m 200m.

Pachino 34D6

Dragomar, Strada Marzamemi Portopalo di Capo Passero, Marzamemi. **GPS**: n36,72732 e15,12083.

30 € 10-15 Ch WC. **Surface:** gravel. 01/01-31/12
Distance: on the spot 400m 600m.
Remarks: Seaview, no beach.

Pachino 34D6

La Cabana Service, Viale le Aloha, Contrada Granelli. **GPS**: n36,70562 e15,00689.

200 € 15, Jul/Aug € 20 Ch WC included hot shower € 1.
Surface: grassy/sand. 01/01-31/12
Distance: Pachino 7km on the spot on the spot.
Remarks: Sandy beach, bar.

Palermo 34B6

Green Park, Via Quarto dei Mille 11b. **GPS**: n38,11016 e13,34307.
€ 20/24h Ch included. **Surface:** asphalted.
Distance: piazza Indipendenza 300m.

Palermo 34B6

Parking Ospedale Cervello, Via Trabucco. **GPS**: n38,15619 e13,31354.

Remarks: Nearby hospital.

Palermo 34B6

Via Uditore 17. **GPS**: n38,13140 e13,32515.
Ch WC. **Surface:** asphalted.
Remarks: Shuttle to centre.

Palermo 34B6

Piazza Alcide De Gasperi. **GPS**: n38,15170 e13,33944.
free. **Surface:** asphalted.
Distance: on the spot.
Remarks: Nearby stadium.

Palermo 34B6

Freesbee Parking, Via Imperatore Federico 116. **GPS**: n38,14722 e13,35277.
100 € 20 Ch WC € 1. **Surface:** asphalted.
Distance: Cathedral Palermo 400m 150m.
Remarks: Motorhome dealer Idea Vacanze, 24/24 surveillance.

Tourist information Palermo:

U.I.A.T. (Ufficio Informazioni e di Accoglienza Turistica), Piazza Castelnuovo, 34, www.regione.sicilia.it/turismo.Capital of Sicilly, port and economical heart of the Island.

San Giovanni degli Eremiti.

Santa Catarina.

Vucciria, Via Cassari-Argenteria.Palermo's most famous, picturesque and historic market.

Piazza Armerina 34C6

Agriturismo Agricasale, Contrada Ciavarina. **GPS**: n37,34032 e14,38840.
€ 15 Ch included.
Distance: 2km bar/restaurant.
Remarks: Swimming pool € 3/pppd.

Piazza Armerina 34C6

Agriturismo Gigliotto, SS 117bis km60. **GPS**: n37,37298 e14,35592.
4.
Remarks: Large swimming pool.

Piazza Armerina 34C6

SP90. **GPS**: n37,36674 e14,33426.
against payment Ch against payment.
Distance: on the spot.
Remarks: Villa del Casale Romano 400m.

Porto Empedocle 34B6

Punta Piccola Park, Scala dei Turchi, SP68. **GPS**: n37,28916 e13,49250.

IT

99 May € 18, Jun € 20, 1-15 Jul € 23 15 Jul-31 Aug € 23 Ch (65x) WC € 1. **Surface:** gravel. 25/04-30/09
Distance: 2,5km on the spot 200m 1km.
Remarks: Direct access to sandy beach. SS115 km 178.70 SP68 dir Zona Lidi di Porto Empedocle.

Tourist information Porto Empedocle:
A.A.P.I.T.(Azienda Autonoma Provinciale per l'Incremento Turistico), Vialle della Vittoria, 255, Agrigento.
Valle dei Templi, Agrigento.The Valley of The Temples, archeology.

S Portopalo di Capo Passero 34D6
Cicogna. **GPS**: n36,68333 e15,13638.
20 Jun/Sep € 10, Jul/Aug € 15 Ch (20x)included . **Surface:** gravel.
Distance: 50m sandy beach 300m.

S Pozzallo 34C6
Il Giardino di Epicuro, SP67. **GPS**: n36,73128 e14,86240.

50 € 8, Jun € 10, Jul/Aug € 13 Ch (22x)€ 2 cold shower.
Surface: grassy/sand. 01/05-30/09
Distance: 500m on the spot 50m 300m.
Remarks: Sandy beach.

S Pozzallo 34C6
Salvamar, Zona Porto di Pozzallo. **GPS**: n36,71541 e14,82240.

30 € 10-€ 20 (Aug) Ch € 3 € 1. **Surface:** grassy.
01/01-31/12
Distance: 200m 500m 1km.

S Realmonte 34B6
Sosta camper Zanzibar, C/o Capo Rossello. **GPS**: n37,29495 e13,45438.

100 € 12-22, 01/10-30/03 € 10 Ch WC included hot shower € 1.
Surface: gravel. 01/01-31/12
Distance: sandy beach on the spot 150m.
Remarks: Bus to Valle dei Templi (€ 7/pp, min. 4 pers).

S Reitano 34B5
Via Lungomare Colonna. **GPS**: n38,01407 e14,33081.
€10 Ch € 0,50.
Distance: on the spot.

S Ribera 34B6
Kamemi, SS115, Secca Grande. **GPS**: n37,43840 e13,24469.
Camperstop € 8 Ch. 01/01-31/12 01/07-31/08 No Camperstop.

S Roccalumera 34C5
Park Jonio, Via Collegio, SS114 Roccalumera > Nizza di Sicilia. **GPS**: n37,97943 e15,39752.

60 € 13/24h, Jul/Aug € 15 Ch (60x) . **Surface:** gravel.
Distance: within walking distance 250m Bar/snack on the spot.
Remarks: In front of Centro Sportivo.

San Giovanni La Punta 34C5
Entertainmentcity Isivillage, Via Fisichelli 63. **GPS**: n37,58929 e15,08612.
guests free. **Surface:** asphalted.

S San Vito Lo Capo 34A6
Via Faro 36. **GPS**: n38,18472 e12,73277.

30 Jun € 15, Jul € 20, Aug € 25 Ch included hot shower € 1.
Surface: asphalted/grassy.
Distance: 1km on the spot 300m 1km.
Remarks: Terrace on the sea, no beach, sandy beach 400m.

S San Vito Lo Capo 34A6
Via Savoia 13. **GPS**: n38,16222 e12,73666.

IT

90 € 10, Jun € 12, Jul € 15, Aug € 18 Ch (90x) WC € 0,50 € 5.
Surface: gravel. 01/01-31/12
Distance: 300m 1,4km 1km 1km.
Remarks: Free shuttle to beach.

San Vito Lo Capo 34A6
Via la Piana. **GPS**: n38,16886 e12,74307.

free. **Surface:** unpaved.
Distance: 800m 800m.
Remarks: Free shuttle to centre.

S Sciacca 34B6
La Playa, C. da S. Giorgio 153. **GPS**: n37,49472 e13,16000.

30 Jun/Sep € 18, Jul € 21, Aug € 25 Ch WC included.
Surface: gravel. 01/06-30/09
Distance: Sciacca 13km 100m 100m 10km.
Remarks: Beach parking, bread service.

S Scicli 34C6
Club Piccadilly, Via Mare Adriatico, Donnalucata. **GPS**: n36,74750 e14,66306.
€ 15-30 Ch WC . 01/01-31/12
Distance: 3km sandy beach 100m.

S Scopello 34A6
Azienda agricola Plaia Antonella, Fraz. Scopello. **GPS**: n38,06777 e12,81777.

50 € 17/24h Ch included. **Surface:** gravel.
01/05-30/09

Distance: historical centre 200m 1,5km 100m 400m.
Remarks: Shuttle to beach and Riserva dello Zingaro € 2,50/pp, farm products.

S Siracusa 34D6
Parcheggio Von Platen, Via Augusto Von Platen 38. **GPS**: n37,07692 e15,28738.
€ 15/day Ch WC .
Remarks: Near archeological site and museum.

S Siracusa 34D6
Via Procione 6, zona Golfetto, Fontane Bianche. **GPS**: n36,96361 e15,22027.
€ 20 Ch WC . **Surface:** unpaved.
Distance: Siracusa 15km on the spot.
Remarks: Bus to Siracusa, natural swimming pool in sea.

S Sutera 34B6
Piazza Rettore Carruba. **GPS**: n37,52450 e13,72960.
free Ch. **Surface:** asphalted.
Distance: on the spot on the spot.

S Taormina 34C5

Sosta Camper Pier Giovanni - Taormina

yek@tiscali.it - www.facebook.com/SostaCamperPiergiovanni

Located in a quit location
Open all year
Washing-machine

Sosta Camper Pier Giovanni, Trappitello, Via Spagnuolo.
GPS: n37,82196 e15,24502.
15 € 10-15 Ch WC included. **Surface:** grassy/metalled.
01/01-31/12
Distance: 500m 4km 300m 300m.

S Terme Vigliatore 34C5
Area Trinacria, Via Lungomare Marchesana. **GPS**: n38,14018 e15,14596.

120 € 12, peak season € 18 Ch included. **Surface:** grassy.
01/01-31/12
Distance: 50m pizzeria 200m 200m.
Remarks: Excursion to the Eolie-islands.

S Trapani 34A6
Hotel Le Saline, SP21 km4, contrada Nubia-Paceco. **GPS**: n37,98304 e12,53106.
20 € 15-20 Ch . **Surface:** metalled.

SLOVENIA

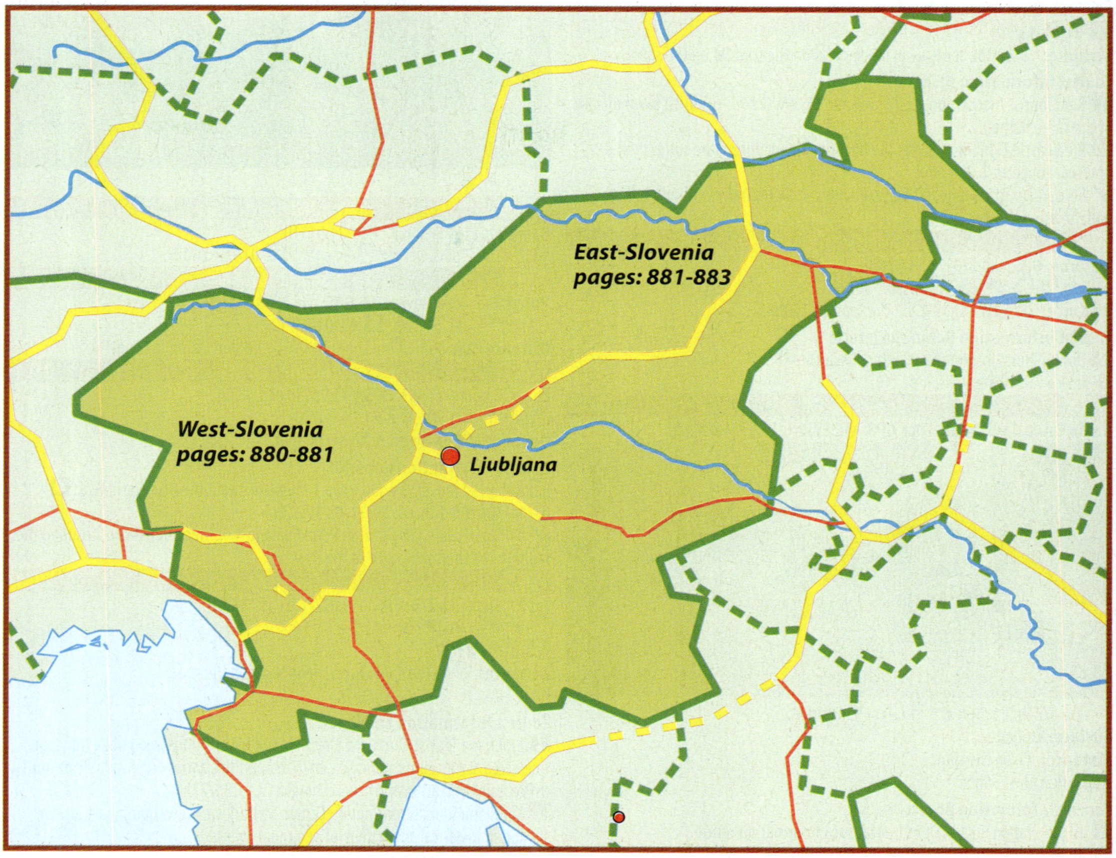

East-Slovenia
pages: 881-883

West-Slovenia
pages: 880-881

Ljubljana

Capital: Ljubljana
Government: parliamentarian republic
Official Language: Slovenian
Population: 2.055,000 (2012)
Area: 20,273 km^2.

General information

Dialling code: 00386
General emergency: 112
Currency: Euro
Credit card are accepted almost everywhere.

Regulations for overnight stays

There is no regulation against overnight camping, but it is not yet generally accepted. In the National Park Triglav wild camping is forbidden.

Additional public holidays 2014

February 8 Prešern Day - Slovenian cultural festival
April 27 Uprising against the Occupation Day
May 1 Labour Day
June 25 National Holiday
August 15 Assumption of the Virgin Mary
October 31 Reformation Day
November 1 All Saints' Day
December 26 Independence Day

Slovenia

Slovenia West

Bled 26D3

Bled, Kidriceva 10c. **GPS**: n46,36162 e14,08221.
€ 16-€ 25 Ch .
01/04-15/10
Distance: on the spot on the spot on the spot on the spot.

Tourist information Bled:
Bled Tourist Association, Cesta svobode 15, www.bled.si.Tourist town on lake of the same name.
Bled Castle.Exhibition about the history of Bled, during the summer also open-air concerts. 8-17h.
Soteska Vintgar Gorge, TD Gorje, Podhom 0, Gorje.Trail over bridges and galleries along a river.

Bohinjsko jezero 26C4

Zlatorog. **GPS**: n46,27917 e13,83611.
Ch . 01/05-30/09
Distance: on the spot on the spot 150m.

Tourist information Bohinjsko jezero:
Bohinj Tourst Information Center, Ribčev laz 48.
Savica Falls.Water falls.

Bovec 26C4

Kanin Cable Car Station, Dvor. **GPS**: n46,33306 e13,53944.

15 € 6/24h, € 8/36h Ch included.
Surface: asphalted.
Distance: on the spot.
Remarks: Max. 36h.

Tourist information Bovec:
Triglav National Park, Dom Trenta, Soča.Information centre.
Kluže Fortress, Trg golobarskih žrtev 8.Fort above gorge.
Oltimers Gathering, Kanin.Gathering of skiers in traditional ski equipment.
Easter Mo.
Soča Trail, Soča.Hiking trail along the Soca river.

DovjeMojstrana 26D3

Kamne. **GPS**: n46,46444 e13,95778.
Ch . 01/01-31/12
Distance: 1km 1km.

Izola 26C6

Cankarjev Drevored. **GPS**: n45,53806 e13,66444.

5 € 15 Ch (4x)free. **Surface:** asphalted.
Distance: 500m.

Jerzersko 26D3

Oranic tourist farm Makek, Zg. Jezersko 77. **GPS**: n46,38978 e14,50835.

€ 8 WC.

Kamniška Bistrica 27A3

Kamp Alpe. **GPS**: n46,30510 e14,61110.
10 € 14, 2 pers.incl Ch . 01/05-01/10

Kobarid 26C4

Koren, Drezneske Ravne 333. **GPS**: n46,25083 e13,58667.
Ch . 01/01-31/12
Distance: 500m on the spot on the spot on the spot.

Kobarid 26C4

Lazar, Gregorciceva 63. **GPS**: n46,25530 e13,58720.
Ch . 01/04-31/10
Distance: on the spot on the spot.

Tourist information Kobarid:
Kobariski muzej, Gregorciceva 1.Museum about the first World War. 01/04-30/09 9-18h, 01/10-31/03 10-17h.
Tolmin Chutes, LTO Sotočje, Petra Skalarja 4, Tolmin.Touristic route along the rapid to the thermal source of the river.

Ljubljana 27A3

Ježica, Dunajska 270. **GPS**: n46,09778 e14,51889.
Ch .
01/01-31/12
Distance: on the spot on the spot on the spot.

Tourist information Ljubljana:
Ljubljana Tourist Card.Card offers among other things free public transport, free acces at museums and discount in restaurants, shops etc. Available at Tourist Office, railway station and several hotels. T € 35/72h.
Ljubljana Tourist Information Center, Stritarjeva, www.ljubljana-tourism.si.Capital, historical city with a lot of annual events.
National museum, Muzjeska 1.Archeological and historical museum. 10-18h, Thu 10-20h Mo.
Plecnik museum, Kurunova 4.Architectonic museum in the house of Joze Plecnik. Tue, Thu 10-14h.
Slovene Natural History Museum, Muzjeska 1.Zoological and botanic museum. daily 10-18h, Thu 10-20h Mo.
Ljubljana Castle.Medieval fortress, tourist train at town centre. 01/10-30/04 10-21h, 01/05-30/09 9-22h.
Markt, Vodnikov trg. daily, summer 6-18h, winter 6-16h.
Zoo Ljubljana.Zoo. summer 9-19h, winter 9-16h.

Locatec 26D4

A1. **GPS**: n45,89854 e14,25570.

6 free WC free.
Distance: 100m.
Remarks: Guarded parking petrol station LOM II, on both sides of the highway PO-LJ.

SL

Luče 27A3

Camp Smica, Luče 4. **GPS**: n46,35644 e14,74290.
Ch . 01/05-30/10
Distance: on the spot on the spot 900m.

Lukovica 27A3

OMV Istrabenz. **GPS**: n46,16690 e14,69380.
2 free.
Remarks: Parking petrol station OMV Istrabenz.

Portorož 26C6

Strunjan, Strunjan 23. **GPS**: n45,52570 e13,61087.
Ch . 01/01-31/12
Distance: on the spot on the spot 100m.

Tourist information Portorož:
Tourist Information Portorož, Obala 16.Lively bathing resort.
Turistična organizacija Koper, Verdijeva 10, Koper.City with a Venetian past and a lot of curiosities.
Pomorski muzej Sergej Mašera, Cankarjevo nabrežje 3, Piran.Maritime museum. 9-12h, 15-18h, 01/07-31/08 9-12h, 18-21h Mo.

Postojna 26D5

Veliki Otok. **GPS**: n45,78028 e14,20333.

30 € 18 Ch included.
Surface: concrete.
01/05-30/09
Distance: 1km 3km.
Remarks: Postojna caves 300m.

Tourist information Postojna:
Križna jama, Bloška polica 7, Grahovo.Largest water caves of Slovenia.
Perdjama Grad.Castle, 16th century and caves. 01/05-30/09 9-18, 01/10-30/04 10-16h.
Postojnska Jama, Jamska cesta 30.Postojna caves.
01/05-30/09 9-18, 01/10-30/04 10-16h.

Smlednik 26D4

Hotel Kanu, Valburga 7. **GPS**: n46,16785 e14,43046.
Ch . 01/01-31/12
Remarks: 5km from motorway.

Tolmin 26C4

Kamp Siber, Klanec 8. **GPS**: n46,18082 e13,73792.

50 Ch WC included. **Location:** Rural. **Surface:** grassy/gravel.
01/01-31/12
Distance: 1km on the spot on the spot 1km.

Zalošce 26C5

Saksida Winery. **GPS**: n45,89039 e13,74732.
10 Ch WC .
Distance: 4,6km.

Slovenia East

Celje 27B3

Parking Glazija, Ljubljanska cesta 20. **GPS**: n46,23059 e15,26010.
4 € 10 included.
Surface: metalled.

Tourist information Celje:
Celje Tourist Information Center, Trg celjskih knezov 9.
Jama Pekel, Šempeter.Caves.
Stari Grad Castle.Remainders of castle.
Rimska Nekropola, Šempeter.Roman Necropolis, archeological parc.

Dolenjske Toplice 27B4

Kamp Polje. **GPS**: n45,76739 e15,05151.

25 € 8/24h Ch. **Location:** Rural, comfortable. **Surface:** unpaved.
01/03-15/11
Distance: 800m on the spot on the spot 800m 800m on the spot on the spot.
Remarks: Along the Krka river, Terme Dolenjske Toplice 800m.

Ivanjkovci 27B3

Vinoteka Svetinjska Klet, Svetinje 5. **GPS**: n46,46220 e16,16990.

2 free . **Surface:** metalled.

Kamnica 27B3

Gostilna Koblarjev Zaliv, Na otok 20. **GPS**: n46,56560 e15,61908.

20 free, use of a meal desired.
Surface: grassy. 01/01-31/12
Distance: Maribor 2km on the spot on the spot on the spot 2km 300m.
Remarks: Walking and bicycle area along the Drava river to Maribor centre.

Laško 27B3

Zdraviliške Laško, Zdraviliška 4. **GPS**: n46,15944 e15,23143.

SL

6 € 10/day.
Distance: on the spot on the spot on the spot on the spot.

Tourist information Laško:
Laško Tourist Information Center, Trg svobode 8.

Lendava 27B3

Terme Lendava. GPS: n46,55396 e16,45813.
€ 24, 2 pers.incl Ch € 4. 01/01-31/12
Remarks: Including access spa resort.

Ljutomer 27B3

Grostilna Tmek. GPS: n46,55516 e16,21929.

25 free. **Surface:** grassy. 01/01-31/12
Distance: on the spot on the spot on the spot.

Moravske Toplice 27B3

Kamp Moravske Toplice, Kranjčeva ulica 12 . **GPS**: n46,68298 e16,21953.
€ 32, 2 pers.incl Ch € 4. 01/01-31/12
Distance: 100m 200m.
Remarks: Including access spa resort 3000.

Tourist information Moravske Toplice:
Goričko Regional Park, Ulica ob igrišču 3, www.park-goricko.org.Information centre.

Obrežje Jug 27B3

OMV Istrabenz. GPS: n45,85517 e15,68513.
2 free.
Remarks: Parking petrol station OMV Istrabenz.

Podčetrtek 27B3

Terme Olimia Kamp Natura, Zdravilška cesta 24. **GPS**: n46,15619 e15,60792.
15 € 16,60, 2 pers.incl Ch € 3,20. 21/04-30/09
Distance: on the spot on the spot.
Remarks: Including access spa resort € 30,80.

Tourist information Podčetrtek:
Sedovška Homestead, Aškercev trg 24, Šmarje pri Jelšah.Traditional farmstead.
M Rogatec Open-air Museum, Ptujska cesta 23, Rogatec.Open air museum, 18-20th century.
Božjepotna Marijina cerkev, Sladka Gora, Šmarje pri Jelšah.Pilgrimage church.
Olimje Monastery and Pharmacy, Olimje 82.Monastery and one of the oldest pharmacies in the world.

Podsmreka 27A3

A2. **GPS**: n45,94805 e14,77065.
5 free free.
Distance: 100m.
Remarks: Guarded parking petrol station Petrol Podsmereka, highway Novo Mesto-Ljubljana.

Prebold 27B3

Dolina, Dolenja Vas 147. **GPS**: n46,24018 e15,09268.
Ch. 01/01-31/12
Distance: 200m 200m.

Ptuj 27B3

Avtokamp Terme Ptuj, Pot v toplice 9. **GPS**: n46,42109 e15,85548.

€ 28, 2 pers.incl, including access spa resort Ch € 4.
01/01-31/12
Remarks: Only overnight stays € 13 >18h <10h.

Tourist information Ptuj:
Maribor Tourist Board, Partizanska 47, Maribor, www.maribor-tourism.si.Old city with historical centre.
Tourist Information Center, Slovenski Trg 14, www.ptuj-turism.si.
M Mariborski Grad, Maribor.Castle, 15th century, regional museum. 01/04-31/12 Tue-Sa 9-17h, Su 9-14h Mo.
M Ptujski Grad.Castle, 11th century with regional museum. 01/05-31/10 9-18h.

Rečica ob Savinji 27A3

Menina. GPS: n46,31167 e14,90917.
Ch. 01/01-31/12
Distance: on the spot on the spot 300m.

Tourist information Rečica ob Savinji:
Mozirski gaj, Hribernikova 1, Mozirje.Botanical garden. 01/04-31/10.
M Musej Premogovništva, Stari jašek - Koroška cesta, Velenje.Coalmine museum.

Rogla 27B3

Climate Resort and Walking Centre. GPS: n46,45347 e15,33423.

4 € 10/motorhome included.
Remarks: Altitude 1517m, tourist tax € 1 pp, 20% discount on swimming pool of the hotel.

Solcava 27A3

Park Logarska Dolina, Logarska Dolina 9. **GPS**: n46,39870 e14,63100.
€ 10.

Tepanje 27B3

GPS: n46,34776 e15,48695.
5 free free.
Remarks: Guarded parking petrol station Petrol Tepanje I, on both sides of the highway Maribor-Ljubljana.

Visnja Gora 27A4

Kopaliska Ulica 25. **GPS**: n45,95258 e14,75210.

20 Ch WC . **Location:** Rural. **Surface:** grassy/sand.
01/01-31/12
Distance: on the spot 1,7km on the spot.

Zrece 27B3

Thermal Spa. GPS: n46,37096 e15,39021.

4 € 10/motorhome included.
Remarks: Tourist tax € 1 pp, 20% discount on swimming pool of the hotel.

SL

CROATIA

Inland pages: 891-892
Zagreb
Rijeka
Istria/KvarnerBay pages: 885-887
Pula
Dalmatia pages: 888-891
Zadar
Dalmatia pages: 888-891
Split
Dubrovnik

HR

Capital: Zagreb
Government: parliamentarian democracy
Official Language: Croatian
Population: 4,500,000 (2012)
Area: 56,594 km^2.

General information

Dialling code: 00385
General emergency: 112
Currency: Kuna, kn, 1 kuna = 100 lipa, 1kn = € 0,13
1kn= £0,11 (October 2013)
Credit card are accepted almost everywhere.

Regulations for overnight stays

Wild camping is forbidden.

Additional public holidays 2014

January 6 Epiphany
May 1 Labor Day
June 19 Corpus Christi
June 22 Dan antifasisticke borbe, Anti-Fascist Resistance Day
June 25 Dan drzavnosti, National Holiday
August 5 Victorie Day and National Thanksgiving
August 15 Assumption of the Virgin Mary
October 8 Independence Day

Croatia

Istria/Kvarner Bay

S — Baderna — 26C6

Farm Pino, Olives & Oil, Katun 1. **GPS**: n45,21913 e13,72903.
24 € 10 + € 3/pp € 4 Ch. **Surface:** metalled/sand.

Bašanija — 26C6

Svjetionicarska ulica. **GPS**: n45,49064 e13,49190.
15 € 8-16. **Location:** Rural. **Surface:** grassy/gravel.
01/01-31/12
Distance: on the spot on the spot 500m.

S — Cres/Cres — 27A4

Kovačine, Melin I, 20. **GPS**: n44,96278 e14,39694.
from € 14,80 Ch WC included.
15/04-15/10
Distance: on the spot.

Tourist information Cres/Cres:
Turisticka zajednica, Riva Creskih Kapetana, www.tzg-cres.hr.Island can be reached with ferry service from Brestova, south of Rijeka and Valbiska, west Krk.

S — Cres/Martinšćica — 27A5

Slatina. **GPS**: n44,82091 e14,34238.
from € 15 Ch WC . 15/04-31/10

S — Cres/Nerezine — 27A5

Baldarin, Punta Križa. **GPS**: n44,61680 e14,50834.
from € 13,35 Ch WC included. 15/04-01/10
Distance: 3,5km on the spot.
Lopari, Nerezine. **GPS**: n44,68253 e14,39846. . 15/04-30/09
Preko Mosta, Osor 76, Nerezine. . 01/05-30/09
Rapoća, Rapoća, Nerezine. **GPS**: n44,66357 e14,39756. . 01/05-30/09

Cres/Osor — 27A5

Bijar. **GPS**: n44,69428 e14,39550. . 01/05-30/09

Cres/Valun — 27A5

Zdovice, Kastanija bb. **GPS**: n44,90598 e14,35900. . 15/01-01/10

Crikvenica — 27A4

Kacjak, Kacjak BB. **GPS**: n45,16703 e14,70511. . 15/05-15/09

Tourist information Crikvenica:
Turisticka zajednica, Trg Stepana Radica 1.

Fažana — 27A5

Bi Village, Dragonja 115. **GPS**: n44,91750 e13,81111. .
01/04-15/11

Tourist information Fažana:
Nationaal Park Brijuni, Brijuni.Nature reserve, boat connection from Fažana.
daily.

Ičići — 26C6

Opatija. **GPS**: n45,31083 e14,28472. . 01/04-01/10

Klenovica — 27A4

Klenovica, Zidinice BB. **GPS**: n45,09667 e14,84556. . 01/05-30/09
Distance: on the spot on the spot.

S — Koromačno — 27A4

Tunarica. **GPS**: n44,96917 e14,09889.
from € 16 Ch WC included. 20/05-05/09

Kraljevica — 27A4

Ostro. **GPS**: n45,27109 e14,56402. . 01/05-30/09

Krk/Baška — 27A4

Zablace, Emila Geitslicha 34, Baška. **GPS**: n44,96694 e14,74528. .
01/05-01/10

Tourist information Krk/Baška:
Tourist Information, Kralja Zvonimira 114, www.tz-baska.hr.Largest bathing resort on the island with beautiful beaches.

Krk/Klimno — 27A4

Kampiralište, U. Soline, Klimno Br. 8. . **Remarks:** Mini-camp.
Klimno, Uvala Soline. **GPS**: n45,15036 e14,60886. .
Remarks: Mini-camp.

S — Krk/Krk — 27A4

Srecko Krajacic, Narodnog preporoda 51. **GPS**: n45,02900 e14,58100.

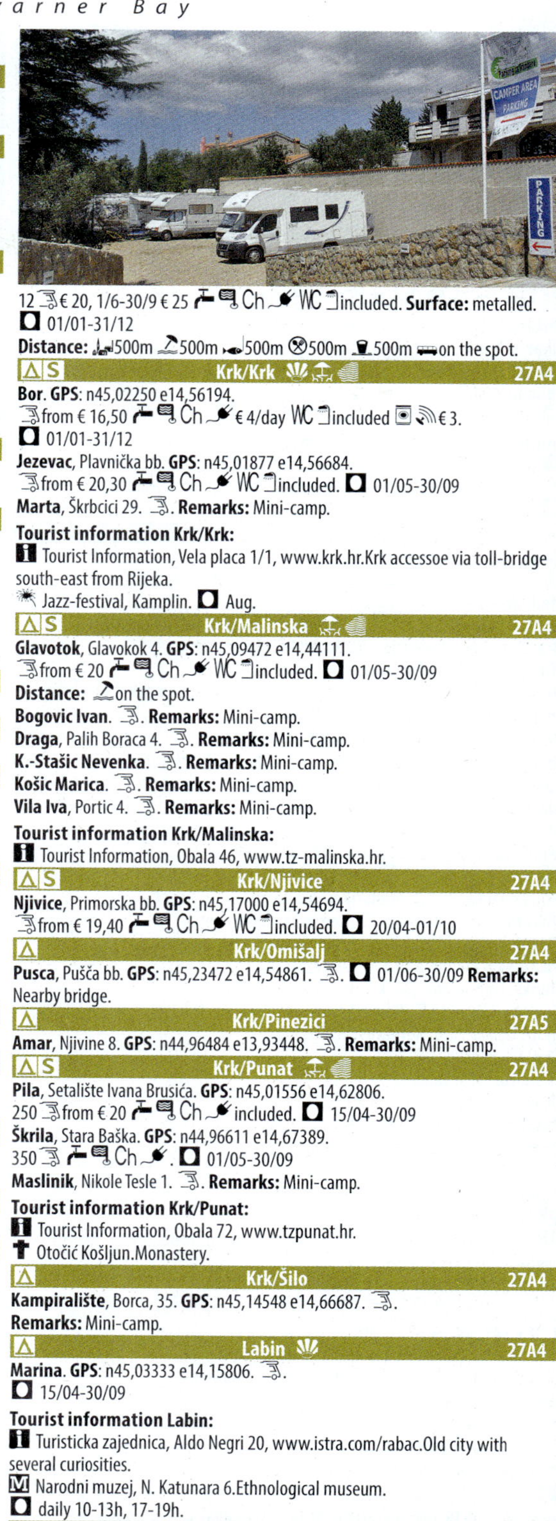

12 € 20, 1/6-30/9 € 25 Ch WC included. **Surface:** metalled.
01/01-31/12
Distance: 500m 500m 500m 500m 500m on the spot.

S — Krk/Krk — 27A4

Bor. **GPS**: n45,02250 e14,56194.
from € 16,50 Ch € 4/day WC included € 3.
01/01-31/12
Jezevac, Plavnička bb. **GPS**: n45,01877 e14,56684.
from € 20,30 Ch WC included. 01/05-30/09
Marta, Škrbcici 29. . **Remarks:** Mini-camp.

Tourist information Krk/Krk:
Tourist Information, Vela placa 1/1, www.krk.hr.Krk accessoe via toll-bridge south-east from Rijeka.
Jazz-festival, Kamplin. Aug.

S — Krk/Malinska — 27A4

Glavotok, Glavokok 4. **GPS**: n45,09472 e14,44111.
from € 20 Ch WC included. 01/05-30/09
Distance: on the spot.
Bogovic Ivan. . **Remarks:** Mini-camp.
Draga, Palih Boraca 4. . **Remarks:** Mini-camp.
K.-Stašic Nevenka. . **Remarks:** Mini-camp.
Košic Marica. . **Remarks:** Mini-camp.
Vila Iva, Portic 4. . **Remarks:** Mini-camp.

Tourist information Krk/Malinska:
Tourist Information, Obala 46, www.tz-malinska.hr.

S — Krk/Njivice — 27A4

Njivice, Primorska bb. **GPS**: n45,17000 e14,54694.
from € 19,40 Ch WC included. 20/04-01/10

Krk/Omišalj — 27A4

Pusca, Pušča bb. **GPS**: n45,23472 e14,54861. . 01/06-30/09 **Remarks:** Nearby bridge.

Krk/Pinezici — 27A5

Amar, Njivine 8. **GPS**: n44,96484 e13,93448. . **Remarks:** Mini-camp.

S — Krk/Punat — 27A4

Pila, Setalište Ivana Brusića. **GPS**: n45,01556 e14,62806.
250 from € 20 Ch included. 15/04-30/09
Škrila, Stara Baška. **GPS**: n44,96611 e14,67389.
350 Ch . 01/05-30/09
Maslinik, Nikole Tesle 1. . **Remarks:** Mini-camp.

Tourist information Krk/Punat:
Tourist Information, Obala 72, www.tzpunat.hr.
Otočić Košljun.Monastery.

Krk/Šilo — 27A4

Kampiralište, Borca, 35. **GPS**: n45,14548 e14,66687. .
Remarks: Mini-camp.

Labin — 27A4

Marina. **GPS**: n45,03333 e14,15806. .
15/04-30/09

Tourist information Labin:
Turisticka zajednica, Aldo Negri 20, www.istra.com/rabac.Old city with several curiosities.
Narodni muzej, N. Katunara 6.Ethnological museum.
daily 10-13h, 17-19h.

S — Lošinj/Mali Lošinj — 27A5

Kredo. **GPS**: n44,53444 e14,44751.

HR

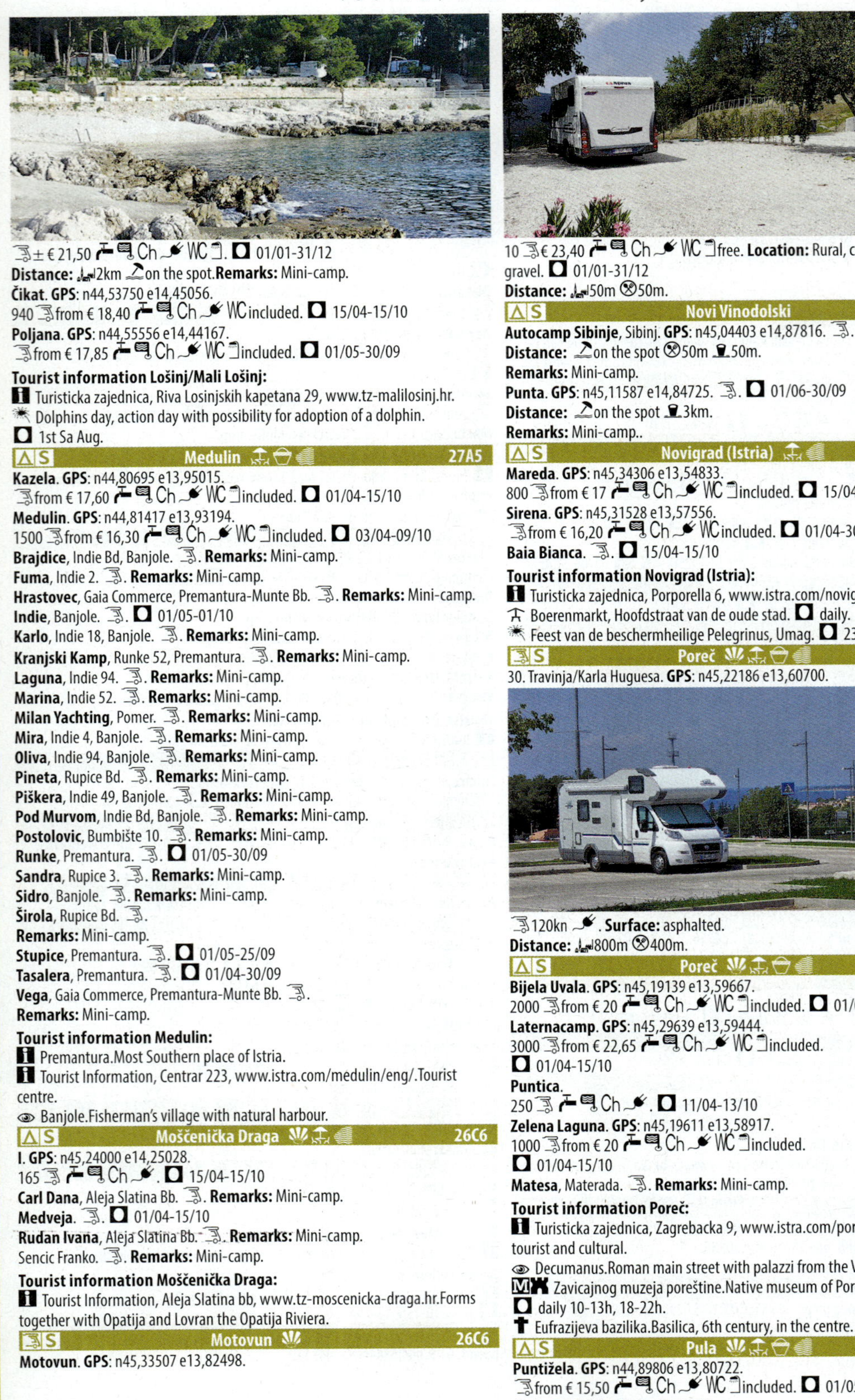

± € 21,50 Ch WC . 01/01-31/12
Distance: 2km on the spot.**Remarks:** Mini-camp.
Čikat. GPS: n44,53750 e14,45056.
940 from € 18,40 Ch WC included. 15/04-15/10
Poljana. GPS: n44,55556 e14,44167.
from € 17,85 Ch WC included. 01/05-30/09

Tourist information Lošinj/Mali Lošinj:
Turisticka zajednica, Riva Losinjskih kapetana 29, www.tz-malilosinj.hr.
Dolphins day, action day with possibility for adoption of a dolphin.
1st Sa Aug.

Medulin 27A5
Kazela. GPS: n44,80695 e13,95015.
from € 17,60 Ch WC included. 01/04-15/10
Medulin. GPS: n44,81417 e13,93194.
1500 from € 16,30 Ch WC included. 03/04-09/10
Brajdice, Indie Bd, Banjole. . **Remarks:** Mini-camp.
Fuma, Indie 2. . **Remarks:** Mini-camp.
Hrastovec, Gaia Commerce, Premantura-Munte Bb. . **Remarks:** Mini-camp.
Indie, Banjole. . 01/05-01/10
Karlo, Indie 18, Banjole. . **Remarks:** Mini-camp.
Kranjski Kamp, Runke 52, Premantura. . **Remarks:** Mini-camp.
Laguna, Indie 94. . **Remarks:** Mini-camp.
Marina, Indie 52. . **Remarks:** Mini-camp.
Milan Yachting, Pomer. . **Remarks:** Mini-camp.
Mira, Indie 4, Banjole. . **Remarks:** Mini-camp.
Oliva, Indie 94, Banjole. . **Remarks:** Mini-camp.
Pineta, Rupice Bd. . **Remarks:** Mini-camp.
Piškera, Indie 49, Banjole. . **Remarks:** Mini-camp.
Pod Murvom, Indie Bd, Banjole. . **Remarks:** Mini-camp.
Postolovic, Bumbište 10. . **Remarks:** Mini-camp.
Runke, Premantura. . 01/05-30/09
Sandra, Rupice 3. . **Remarks:** Mini-camp.
Sidro, Banjole. . **Remarks:** Mini-camp.
Širola, Rupice Bd. .
Remarks: Mini-camp.
Stupice, Premantura. . 01/05-25/09
Tasalera, Premantura. . 01/04-30/09
Vega, Gaia Commerce, Premantura-Munte Bb. .
Remarks: Mini-camp.

Tourist information Medulin:
Premantura.Most Southern place of Istria.
Tourist Information, Centrar 223, www.istra.com/medulin/eng/.Tourist centre.
Banjole.Fisherman's village with natural harbour.

Moščenička Draga 26C6
I. GPS: n45,24000 e14,25028.
165 Ch . 15/04-15/10
Carl Dana, Aleja Slatina Bb. . **Remarks:** Mini-camp.
Medveja. . 01/04-15/10
Rudan Ivana, Aleja Slatina Bb. . **Remarks:** Mini-camp.
Sencic Franko. . **Remarks:** Mini-camp.

Tourist information Moščenička Draga:
Tourist Information, Aleja Slatina bb, www.tz-moscenicka-draga.hr.Forms together with Opatija and Lovran the Opatija Riviera.

Motovun 26C6
Motovun. GPS: n45,33507 e13,82498.

10 € 23,40 Ch WC free. **Location:** Rural, comfortable. **Surface:** gravel. 01/01-31/12
Distance: 50m 50m.

Novi Vinodolski 27B4
Autocamp Sibinje, Sibinj. **GPS**: n45,04403 e14,87816. .
Distance: on the spot 50m 50m.
Remarks: Mini-camp.
Punta. GPS: n45,11587 e14,84725. . 01/06-30/09
Distance: on the spot 3km.
Remarks: Mini-camp..

Novigrad (Istria) 26C6
Mareda. GPS: n45,34306 e13,54833.
800 from € 17 Ch WC included. 15/04-30/09
Sirena. GPS: n45,31528 e13,57556.
from € 16,20 Ch WC included. 01/04-30/09
Baia Bianca. . 15/04-15/10

Tourist information Novigrad (Istria):
Turisticka zajednica, Porporella 6, www.istra.com/novigrad.
Boerenmarkt, Hoofdstraat van de oude stad. daily.
Feest van de beschermheilige Pelegrinus, Umag. 23/05.

Poreč 26C6
30. Travinja/Karla Huguesa. **GPS**: n45,22186 e13,60700.

120kn . **Surface:** asphalted.
Distance: 800m 400m.

Poreč 26C6
Bijela Uvala. GPS: n45,19139 e13,59667.
2000 from € 20 Ch WC included. 01/04-15/10
Laternacamp. GPS: n45,29639 e13,59444.
3000 from € 22,65 Ch WC included.
01/04-15/10
Puntica.
250 Ch . 11/04-13/10
Zelena Laguna. GPS: n45,19611 e13,58917.
1000 from € 20 Ch WC included.
01/04-15/10
Matesa, Materada. . **Remarks:** Mini-camp.

Tourist information Poreč:
Turisticka zajednica, Zagrebacka 9, www.istra.com/porec.Old city, centre tourist and cultural.
Decumanus.Roman main street with palazzi from the Venetian time.
Zavicajnog muzeja poreštine.Native museum of Porec.
daily 10-13h, 18-22h.
Eufrazijeva bazilika.Basilica, 6th century, in the centre. daily 7-19h.

Pula 27A5
Puntižela. GPS: n44,89806 e13,80722.
from € 15,50 Ch WC included. 01/05-31/10
Stoja. GPS: n44,86000 e13,81472.

750 from € 17,40 Ch WC included. 03/04-02/11
Colona, Bale/Valle. . **Remarks:** Mini-camp.
Kažun, Family-Turist, Pavicini 5a, Marcana. . **Remarks:** Mini-camp.
Luka Krnica, Krnica. . **Remarks:** Mini-camp.
San Pol, Bale/Valle. . **Remarks:** Mini-camp.
Youth Hostel, Valsaline 4. .
Remarks: Mini-camp.

Tourist information Pula:
Turisticka zajednica, Forum 3, www.istra.com/pula.
Arheoloski Muzej Istre, Carrarina 3.Archeological museum.
winter Mo-Fri 9-14h, summer Mo-Sa 9-19h.
Amfiteatar.Large anfiteatro from Roman time. daily 8-21h.
Ljetni klasicni Festival, Amfitheatar.Opera festival. Aug.

Rab 27A5

Mel, Kampor 319. **GPS**: n44,79390 e14,70302. . **Remarks:** Mini-camp.
Planka, Kampor 326. . **Remarks:** Mini-camp.

Tourist information Rab:
Tourist Information, Mali Palit bb.

Rabac 27A4

Oliva. **GPS**: n45,07960 e14,14777.
300 Ch WC . 15/03-30/09
Distance: on the spot.

Tourist information Rabac:
Tourist Information, Aldo Negri 20, Labin, www.rabac.hr.Former Fishing village now bathing resort.

Rijeka 26C6

Preluk Katalinic, Preluk 1. **GPS**: n45,35595 e14,32691. .
Remarks: Mini-camp.

Tourist information Rijeka:
Turisticka zajednica, Uzarska 14, www.grad-rijeka.hr/.
Tourist Information, Kastav 47, Kastav.Walled city with rich history.
Pomorski i povijesni muzej, Muzejski trg 1.Navy museum. Mo-Fri 10-13h, 18-21h.
Velika trznica.Market opposite to Modello palace.
Bella Nedeja, Kastav.Traditional wine celebration.
1st weekend Oct.
Carnaval van Rijeka. Feb.

Rovinj 27A4

Camping Polari. **GPS**: n45,06300 e13,67480.

87kn-174kn, Fr-Sa + 20% Ch . **Surface:** grassy. 22/03-02/10
Distance: on the spot.
Remarks: Camperstop max. 48h.
Mon Paradiso, Uvala Veštar. **GPS**: n45,04947 e13,69000.
40 from € 17,20 Ch . 01/06-30/09 **Remarks:** Mini-camp.
Polari. **GPS**: n45,06258 e13,67477.
2150 from € 22,50 Ch WC included. 01/04-30/09
Porton Biondi. **GPS**: n45,09410 e13,64232.
from € 16,95 Ch WC included. 01/04-30/09
Valdaliso. **GPS**: n45,10389 e13,62500.
400 from € 16 Ch WC included. 20/04-15/10
Vestar. **GPS**: n45,05389 e13,68639.
800 from € 23,10 Ch WC included. 15/04-30/09
Savinjska Dolina, Špandiga Bb. . **Remarks:** Mini-camp.
Špandiga, Špandiga Bb. . **Remarks:** Mini-camp.
Ulika, Polari Bd. **GPS**: n45,06528 e13,67583.
€ 15-28 2 pers incl. 01/04-01/10 **Remarks:** Mini-camp.

Rovinj 27A4

Pizza-Grill Babilon.

20 130kn WC included. 01/01-31/12 **Remarks:** 2,5km before Rovinj at the right-side of the road.

Tourist information Rovinj:
Turisticka zajednica, Budicin 12, www.istra.com/rovinj.City has been a cultural monument since 1963.
Aquarium, Obala G. Paliage 5. daily 9-21h.
Palazzo Califfi, Trg Marsala Tita 11. Tue-Su 10.30-14h, summer 18-20h.
Market.
Grisia, Grisia.Art festival. 2nd week Aug.

Savudrija 26C6

Pineta. **GPS**: n45,48667 e13,49250.
from € 16,50 Ch WC included. 15/04-30/09
Veli Jože, Borozija. **GPS**: n45,49556 e13,50444.
from € 14,70 Ch WC included. 01/04-30/09
Koncar. . **Remarks:** Mini-camp.
Koncar, Ravna Dolina. . 01/05-30/09

Tourist information Savudrija:
Tourist Information, Istarska 2.

Selce 27A4

Selce. **GPS**: n45,15175 e14,72267. . 01/04-31/10
Uvala Slana. **GPS**: n45,15250 e14,71972. . 01/05-30/09

Tourist information Selce:
Tourist Information, Setaliste Ivana Jelicica 1 .
Finida. **GPS**: n45,39278 e13,54194.
from € 15,20 Ch WC included. 15/04-30/09

Umag 26C6

Ladin Gaj.
1800 Ch . 15/04-30/09
Stella Maris. **GPS**: n45,45056 e13,52278.
400 from € 17 Ch WC included. 15/04-15/10
Bencic. . **Remarks:** Mini-camp.

Tourist information Umag:
Tourist Information, Obala J.B.Tita 3/II.

Vrsar 27A4

Camping Valkanela. **GPS**: n45,16509 e13,60871.

€ 10, Jun € 14,50, Jul-Aug € 20 + tourist tax Ch included.
Surface: grassy. 23/04-23/09
Distance: on the spot.
Remarks: Camperstop max. 48h, use camp-site facilities incl.

Vrsar 27A4

Porto Sole. **GPS**: n45,14139 e13,60222.
800 from € 19 Ch WC included. 15/04-30/09

Tourist information Vrsar:
Tourist Information, Rade koncara 46, www.istra.com/vrsar/.

HR

Dalmatia

Babino Polje 27D6

Marina, Ropa 11. **GPS**: n42,73543 e17,54650. . **Remarks:** Mini-camp.
Mungos. . **Remarks:** Mini-camp.

Baška Voda 27C6

Basko Polje. **GPS**: n43,34878 e16,96478. . 15/05-30/09
Niko. . **Remarks:** Mini-camp.

Tourist information Baška Voda:
Turisticka zajednica, Obala Kralja Tomislava 16, Makarska, www.baskavoda.hr.
Gradski Muzej, Obala Kralja Tomislava 17/I, Makarska.City museum.
daily 7-15h.
Malakoloski Muzej, Franjevacki Put 1, Makarska.Mollusc museum.
daily 11-12h.

Bibinje 27B5

Božidar. . **Remarks:** Mini-camp.
Dido, Punta. . **Remarks:** Mini-camp.
Ivan Sikiric, Bibinje 152. . **Remarks:** Mini-camp.
Maslina, Punta. . **Remarks:** Mini-camp.
Maslinovi Dvori, Punta. **GPS**: n44,06222 e15,29306. .
Remarks: Mini-camp.
Mladen. . **Remarks:** Mini-camp.
Niko. . **Remarks:** Mini-camp.
Punta, Rajko Kero. . **Remarks:** Mini-camp.
Punta, Z.Sikirica 10. . **Remarks:** Mini-camp.
Puntica, Bibinje 41. . **Remarks:** Mini-camp.

Tourist information Bibinje:
Tourist Information, Bibinje bb.

Biograd na Moru 27B5

Bošana, Šetalište Bošana Bb. . **Remarks:** Mini-camp.
Crvena Luka. . 01/06-30/09
Crvena Luka.
250 . 01/06-30/09
Dijana & Josip, Put Solina 26. **GPS**: n43,93422 e15,44828. . **Remarks:** Mini-camp.
Mia, Rajic Turizam. . **Remarks:** Mini-camp.
Soline. . 01/05-30/09

Tourist information Biograd na Moru:
Tourist Information, Trg hrvatskih velikana 2, www.biograd.org.Old city with historical centre, lively bathing resort.

Bol 27C6

Kito. **GPS**: n43,26389 e16,64806. . 01/05-31/10

Drace-Pelješac 27D6

Plaža, Janjina. **GPS**: n42,92477 e17,43079. . **Remarks:** Mini-camp.

Dubrovnik 27D6

Autokamp Kate, Tupina 1- Milini. **GPS**: n42,62472 e18,20806. .
10/04-01/11
Porto, Srebreno. . 01/05-01/10
Rudine, Orašac. .
01/06-30/09

Tourist information Dubrovnik:
Turisticka zajednica, Cvijete Zuzoric 1/2, www.dubrovnik-online.hr.City with a rich cultural history.
Aquarium, D. Jude 2. Mo-Sa 9-13h.
City Walls, Gundulićeva poljana 2.City wall surround the entire Old City. 10-15h, 01/04-31/10 9-18.30h.
Place Stradun.Main street with Onofrio-fountain and Sveti Frane monastery.
Dubrovacki Muzej, Pred Dvorom 3.History of the city. Mo-Sa 9-14h.
Pomorski Muzej, Sveti Ivan.Shipping museum. Tue-Sa 9-13h.
Rector's Palace, Pred dvorom 1.Bogisic-collection.
Mo-Sa 9.30-13h.
Zomerfestival. 10/07-25/08.

Dugi Rat 27C6

Ante, Duce Rogac. . **Remarks:** Mini-camp.
B, Duce Rogac. . **Remarks:** Mini-camp.
Darko, Duce Rogac. . **Remarks:** Mini-camp.
Dijana, Duce Rogac. . **Remarks:** Mini-camp.
Duce, Duce Rogac. . **Remarks:** Mini-camp.
Ivan, Duce Rogac. . **Remarks:** Mini-camp.
Ivo. . **Remarks:** Mini-camp.
Ivo, Duce Rogac. **GPS**: n43,44111 e16,65778. . **Remarks:** Mini-camp.
Ljubica, Duce Rogac. . **Remarks:** Mini-camp.
Luka, Duce Rogac. . **Remarks:** Mini-camp.
Mira, Duce Rogac. . **Remarks:** Mini-camp.
Miroslav, Duce Rogac. . **Remarks:** Mini-camp.
More, Duce Rogac. . **Remarks:** Mini-camp.
Oru, Orij, Duce Rogac. . **Remarks:** Mini-camp.
Raj, Duce Rogac. . **Remarks:** Mini-camp.
Studenac, Duce Rogac. . **Remarks:** Mini-camp.

Tourist information Dugi Rat:
Tourist Information, Poljicka cesta 133.

Grebaštica 27B6

Ante&Toni, Brodarica. **GPS**: n43,63833 e15,95833. . 01/05-01/10
Distance: 100m on the spot.
Remarks: Mini-camp..
Tomas, D8. **GPS**: n43,62986 e15,95443. .
Distance: on the spot.
Remarks: Mini-camp..

Kaštel Kambelovac 27C6

U Dragama, A. Starcevica 39. **GPS**: n43,55045 e16,38269. . **Remarks:** Mini-camp.

Kaštel Štafilic 27C6

Koludrovac, Resnik Bb. **GPS**: n43,54985 e16,32873. . **Remarks:** Mini-camp.
Adria. **GPS**: n43,55143 e16,35349. . **Remarks:** Mini-camp.

Kaštel Stari 27C6

Kamp- Biluš Josip. .
Remarks: Mini-camp.

Kolan 27B5

Sveti Duh. **GPS**: n44,51654 e14,95175. . **Remarks:** Mini-camp.

Korčula 27C6

Kalac. **GPS**: n42,95056 e17,14500. from € 11. 01/06-01/10
Mala Glavica, Lumbarda. . **Remarks:** Mini-camp.
Mala Gršcica, Mala Gršcica, Korcula, Tonka Boglic, Blato. . **Remarks:** Mini-camp.
Mini Camp, Lumbarda Br. 8. . **Remarks:** Mini-camp.
Oskorušica, Oskorušica 27/ VI, Racišce. . **Remarks:** Mini-camp.
Potirina, Ružica Šeparovic, Burcina, Blato. . **Remarks:** Mini-camp.
Ravno, Blato. . **Remarks:** Mini-camp.
Relax, Racišce. . **Remarks:** Mini-camp.
Solitudo, Sv. Anton, Lumbarajska Cesta. . **Remarks:** Mini-camp.
Uvala Racišce, Lumbarda 83. . **Remarks:** Mini-camp.
Vela Postrana, Lumbardra 142. . **Remarks:** Mini-camp.

Tourist information Korčula:
Turisticka zajednica, Obala Tudmana, www.korcula.net.City with historical centre, birth-place Marco Polo.
Gradski Muzej, Palaca Gabrielli.City museum. 9-13h, 01/07-31/08 9-13h, 17-19h.
Zbirka Ikona, Trg Svih Sveti.Icon museum. 01/07-31/08 10-12h, 17-19h.
Marco Polo fest. 09/07-11/07.
Zwaarddansfestival. daily 04/07-23/08.

Korenica 27B5

Bistro Marina. **GPS**: n44,74702 e15,70464.
10 . **Location:** Urban. **Surface:** metalled.
Distance: 100m.
Remarks: Free with a meal.

Kornati/Murter 27B5

Slanica. **GPS**: n43,82056 e15,57472.
from € 14,30 WC included. 01/05-15/10
Jazina, Tisno. . 01/05-30/09
Jezera-Lovišča, Jezera. . 15/04-15/10
Kosirina, Betina. . 01/05-30/09
Plitka Vala, Betina. . 01/05-30/09

Tourist information Kornati/Murter:
Tourist Information, Rudina 3, www.tzo-murter.hr.Village where old crafts industry are carried out.

Kucište 27C6

Palme. **GPS**: n42,97639 e17,12917.
€ 16,50-23 2 pers incl. 01/06-01/10
Lovor, Viganj-Dol. . **Remarks:** Mini-camp.

HR

Mimoza, Viganj. **Remarks:** Mini-camp.
Plaža, Viganj 4, Od Gaja. **Remarks:** Mini-camp.
Ponta, Viganj 5. **Remarks:** Mini-camp.
Vocnjak, Viganj 6. **Remarks:** Mini-camp.

Lokva Rogoznica 27C6

Artina. **Remarks:** Mini-camp.
Linda. **GPS**: n43,40934 e16,76415. **Remarks:** Mini-camp.

Lovište 27C6

Lupiš. **GPS**: n43,02675 e17,03171. **Remarks:** Mini-camp.

Lukoran 27B5

Novi Kamp, Punta 28. **GPS**: n44,10538 e15,15518. **Remarks:** Mini-camp.

Mlini 27D6

Kate, Tupina 1. **GPS**: n42,62472 e18,20806. **Remarks:** Mini-camp.
Laguna, Za Gospom, Plat. **Remarks:** Mini-camp.
Matkovica, Srebreno 8. **Remarks:** Mini-camp.
Paradiso, Plat. **Remarks:** Mini-camp.
Porto, Srebreno. **Remarks:** Mini-camp.
Tigar, Kneza Branimira 41, 020-488-980. **Remarks:** Mini-camp.

Mljet 27D6

Marina, Marina Matana,Ropa 11. **GPS**: n42,75260 e17,46000. **Remarks:** Mini-camp.

Tourist information Mljet:
Tourist Information, Zabrezje 2.

Mokalo 27C6

Adriatic. **GPS**: n42,97694 e17,22500. 01/04-31/10

Molunat 29D6

Adriatic II. **Remarks:** Mini-camp.
Adriatic I, Višnjici 4, Đurinici. **Remarks:** Mini-camp.
Marinero, Molunat 40. **Remarks:** Mini-camp.

Nin 27B5

Dišpet, Ždrijac. **Remarks:** Mini-camp.
Nick, Ždrijac. **Remarks:** Mini-camp.
Nin, Nin 33. **Remarks:** Mini-camp.
Ninska Laguna. **GPS**: n44,24639 e15,17389. **Remarks:** Mini-camp.

Tourist information Nin:
Tourist Information, Trg Hrvatskih branitelja 1, www.nin.hr.
Arheološka zbirka Nin, Trg Kraljevac 8.Archeological museum. 01/10-31/5 8-14h, 01/06-30/09 8-22h.

Novigrad (Dalmatia) 27B5

Adria-Sol Mulic. **GPS**: n44,18472 e15,54944. **Remarks:** Mini-camp.

Omiš 27C6

Lisicina. **GPS**: n43,44407 e16,69216. **Remarks:** Mini-camp.
Ribnjak. 01/06-30/09

Opuzen 27D6

Rio, Put Zlatinovca 23. **GPS**: n43,01730 e17,56156. 01/05-01/10

Orašac 27D6

Pod Maslinom, Put prema moru b.b.. **GPS**: n42,69907 e18,00592.
€ 11,50-15, 2 pers.incl Ch WC. 01/05-30/09 **Remarks:** Mini-camp.
Peca, Na Pržini 38. **Remarks:** Mini-camp.

Pag 27B5

Dinjiška 1. **Remarks:** Mini-camp.
Košljun. **Remarks:** Mini-camp.
Košljun, Košljun B.B.. **Remarks:** Mini-camp.
Milka, Dinjiška Bb, Dinjiška. **Remarks:** Mini-camp.
Simuni. **GPS**: n44,43766 e15,05408. 04/04-01/10

Tourist information Pag:
Tourist Information, Ulica od Spitala bb, www.pag-tourism.hr.

Pakoštane 27B5

Kozarica. **GPS**: n43,91833 e15,51028.
from € 15,70 Ch WC included. 15/04-15/10
Adriatik. **Remarks:** Mini-camp.
Blaž. **Remarks:** Mini-camp.
Cuka, Brune Bušića 62. **Remarks:** Mini-camp.
Dalmacija. **Remarks:** Mini-camp.
Delfin, Uvala Dugovaca 13, Drage. **Remarks:** Mini-camp.
Dugovaca, Drage. **Remarks:** Mini-camp.
Dujo, Put Malenice, Drage. **Remarks:** Mini-camp.
Karaba, B. Bušica Bb. **Remarks:** Mini-camp.
Kico, Drage. **Remarks:** Mini-camp.
Marela, Kralja Tomislava 26, Drage. **Remarks:** Mini-camp.
Mario, Drage. **Remarks:** Mini-camp.
Nirvana. **GPS**: n43,90989 e15,50767. **Remarks:** Mini-camp.
Nordsee. 01/04-03/10
Pakoštane. **Remarks:** Mini-camp.
Srecko. **Remarks:** Mini-camp.
Strana. **Remarks:** Mini-camp.

Tourist information Pakoštane:
Tourist Information, Trg Kraljice Jelene 78, pakostane.tripod.com.Seaside resort between the sea and the lake of Vrana, Vransko Jezero.

Pelješac/Orebić 27C6

Glavna Plaža. **GPS**: n42,97583 e17,18917.
from € 15 Ch WC included.
15/05-01/10
Trstenica, Šetalište Kneza Domagoja 50. **GPS**: n42,98095 e17,19435.
from € 18,70 Ch WC included. **Remarks:** Mini-camp.
Bor. **Remarks:** Mini-camp.
Cico, J.B. Jelacica 5. **Remarks:** Mini-camp.
Orebic. **Remarks:** Mini-camp.
Paradiso. **GPS**: n42,97475 e17,23497. **Remarks:** Mini-camp.
Paradiso, Obala Pomoraca 30 A. **Remarks:** Mini-camp.
Perna. 01/05-30/09
Ponta. **Remarks:** Mini-camp.
Radic. **Remarks:** Mini-camp.
Videla, Put Ruskovica 25. **Remarks:** Mini-camp.
Vocnjak. **Remarks:** Mini-camp.

Tourist information Pelješac/Orebić:
Tourist Information, Trg Mimbeli bb, www.peljesac.info/orebic.Tourist town on the island Pelješac.

Pelješac/Trpanj 27C6

Divna. **GPS**: n43,00944 e17,26806. **Remarks:** Mini-camp.
Vrila. **GPS**: n43,00360 e17,28467. 20/05-10/10

Tourist information Pelješac/Trpanj:
Tourist Information, Zalo 7, www.peljesac.info/trpanj.

Petrcane 27B5

Maestral, Put X. **Remarks:** Mini-camp.
Pineta, Punta Radman 21. **GPS**: n44,18362 e15,16291. **Remarks:** Mini-camp.
Punta Radman. **Remarks:** Mini-camp.
Šime, Petrcane 6. **Remarks:** Mini-camp.

Podgora 27C6

Sutikla. **GPS**: n43,23451 e17,07741. 01/05-30/09

Podstrana 27C6

Car, Sv. Martin 180. **GPS**: n43,48446 e16,55274. **Remarks:** Mini-camp.
Tamaris, Sv.Martin 114. **GPS**: n43,47551 e16,56383.
50 from € 16,50. 01/01-31/12
Distance: on the spot. **Remarks:** Mini-camp..

Tourist information Podstrana:
Sinjska alka, Sinj.Knight celebration. 05/08.

Posedarje 27B5

Bristi. **Remarks:** Mini-camp.
Kristina. **GPS**: n44,21239 e15,46858. **Remarks:** Mini-camp.
Staro Selo, Brace Dežmalj. **Remarks:** Mini-camp.

Povijana 27B5

Mali Dubrovnik, Kralja P. Svacica 1. **Remarks:** Mini-camp.
Tomi, Ante Starcevica Bb. **GPS**: n44,34624 e15,11292. **Remarks:** Mini-camp.

Primošten 27B6

Adriatic. **GPS**: n43,60645 e15,92193.
from € 24 Ch WC included. 01/05-15/10

Privlaka 27B5

Maritim. **GPS**: n44,27391 e15,13178.
from € 15 Ch included. 01/05-15/10
Darinka. **Remarks:** Mini-camp.

Ražanac 27B5

Planik. **GPS**: n44,27778 e15,34472.
€ 4,75-7,30 + € 2,95-4,50/pp. 15/05-30/09 **Remarks:** Mini-camp.
Puntica. **GPS**: n44,28389 e15,34306.

HR

€ 11 - € 19. **Remarks:** Mini-camp.

Rovanjska 27B5

Tamaris. **GPS**: n44,25003 e15,53806. . **Remarks:** Mini-camp.

Senj 27B4

Skver. **GPS**: n44,99389 e14,89978.
40 Ch WC. **Location:** Comfortable. **Surface:** gravel/metalled.
01/04-01/10
Distance: 500m on the spot on the spot 150m.
Bunica, Bunica 33. **GPS**: n45,02607 e14,88630. . **Remarks:** Mini-camp.
Ujca, M. Cihlar Nehajeva, 4. **GPS**: n44,96833 e14,92167.
from € 16,20. 01/05-01/10
Distance: on the spot. **Remarks:** Mini-camp.

Tourist information Senj:
Turistièka zajednica grada Senja i informativni centar, Stara cesta 2.

Šibenik 27B5

Krka. **GPS**: n43,79463 e15,68120.

free. 01/01-31/12
Remarks: 1km from Krka waterfalls.

Šibenik 27B5

Solaris.
Ch. 15/03-30/11
Solaris-Zablaće. . 01/05-30/09

Tourist information Šibenik:
Turisticka zajednica, Ulica Fausta Vrancica 18, www.summernet.hr.
Internationaal kinderfestival. 22/06-06/07.
Nacionalni Park Krka, Krka.Nature reserve.

Slano 27D6

Bambo. **GPS**: n42,78588 e17,89234.
10 from € 13 Ch WC included. **Remarks:** Mini-camp.
Auto Kamp, Osredina 5, Majkovi. . **Remarks:** Mini-camp.
Banici, Vedrana Limov, Banici. . **Remarks:** Mini-camp.
Banja, Put Od Banje. . **Remarks:** Mini-camp.
Budina, Banici. . **Remarks:** Mini-camp.
Maslina, Grguici. . **Remarks:** Mini-camp.
Milic, Sladenovici. .
Remarks: Mini-camp.
Rogac, Grgurici.
€ 4-5 + € 2-2,50/pp. 01/04-31/10 **Remarks:** Mini-camp.
Sladenovici, Sladenovici 9. .
Remarks: Mini-camp.

Slatine 27C6

Domic, Put Porta 71, Ciove. **GPS**: n43,50014 e16,32985. .
Remarks: Mini-camp.

Split 27C6

Stobreč. **GPS**: n43,50401 e16,52644.

from € 20 Ch WC included € 0,30. **Location:** Urban.
01/01-31/12
Distance: centre ±7km on the spot.

Tourist information Split:
Turisticka zajednica, Trg Republike 2/1, www.visitsplit.com.
Arheoloski Muzej, Zrinjsko-Frankopanska 25.Findings from Roman time and Middle Ages. Tue-Fri 9-14h, Sa-Su 9-13h, 01/06-30/09 Tue-Fri 9-12, 13-20h, Sa-Su 9-13h.
Etnografski Muzej, Narodni Trg 1.Clothing and jewellery. Tue-Fri 10-13h, 18-21h, Sa-Su 10-13h.
Galerija Ivana Mestrovica, Setaliste I. Mestrovica 46.Gallery. Mo-Sa 10-18h, Su 10-14h.
Muzej Grada, Papaliveca 1.City museum. Mo-Sa 9-13h.
Muzej Hrvatskih Arheoloskih Spomenika, S. Gunjace bb.Archeological findings. Mo-Sa 9-20h.
Dioklecijanova palača.Roman palace.

Starigrad/Paklenica 27B5

Camp National Park, Paklenica.
30-38kn, 20-25kn/pp Ch. 01/04-31/10 **Remarks:** Mini-camp.
Adria, Punta Bb, Paklenica. . **Remarks:** Mini-camp.
Anica Kuk, Paklenickal7, Paklenica. . **Remarks:** Mini-camp.
Igor, Seline 124, Seline, Paklenica. . **Remarks:** Mini-camp.
Jaz, Seline, 17, Seline, Paklenica. . **Remarks:** Mini-camp.
Katic, Joze Dokoze 1, Paklenica. . **Remarks:** Mini-camp.
Marin, Put Stanova, 32, Paklenica. . **Remarks:** Mini-camp.
Marin, Seline, Joko, Paklenica. . **Remarks:** Mini-camp.
Marko, Paklenicka 7, Paklenica. . **Remarks:** Mini-camp.
Matija, Paklenica. . **Remarks:** Mini-camp.
Michael, Put Plantaže Bb, Paklenica. . **Remarks:** Mini-camp.
Palklenica. . 01/05-01/10
Paron Šime, Seline 12, Paklenica. . **Remarks:** Mini-camp.
Peko, Paklenica. . **Remarks:** Mini-camp.
Pinus, Ive Senjanina 5, Paklenica. . **Remarks:** Mini-camp.
Pisak, Paklenica. . **Remarks:** Mini-camp.
Plantaža, Put Plantaže 2, Paklenica. **GPS**: n44,29417 e15,44000. . **Remarks:** Mini-camp.
Popo, Kod Abulante, Paklinica. . **Remarks:** Mini-camp.
Senjski Porat, Joze Dokoza 17, Paklenica. . **Remarks:** Mini-camp.
Vesna, Paklenicka 103, Paklenica. . **Remarks:** Mini-camp.
Vrša, Seline, Jazic, Paklenica. . **Remarks:** Mini-camp.
Zrakoplovac, Selina, Paklenica. .
Remarks: Mini-camp.

Tourist information Starigrad/Paklenica:
Nacionalni park "Paklenica".Nature reserve, 150 km biking ad hiking trails, bird observation, tunnels and caves. T 30kn/day.

Ston 27D6

Ficovic, Hodilje. . **Remarks:** Mini-camp.
Prapratna. **GPS**: n42,81778 e17,67611. . 01/06-30/09
Vrela, Pelješac. . **Remarks:** Mini-camp.

Sukošan 27B5

Brajde. . **Remarks:** Mini-camp.
Brajde. . **Remarks:** Mini-camp.
Fontana. **GPS**: n44,04643 e15,31436. . **Remarks:** Mini-camp.
Ivana, Mala Makarska 120. . **Remarks:** Mini-camp.
Jadran. . **Remarks:** Mini-camp.
Jaz. . **Remarks:** Mini-camp.
Kaj. . **Remarks:** Mini-camp.
Malenica, Mala Makarska. . **Remarks:** Mini-camp.
Mira. . **Remarks:** Mini-camp.
Mrkva. . **Remarks:** Mini-camp.
Oliva. . **Remarks:** Mini-camp.
Podvare. . **Remarks:** Mini-camp.
Porto Dl Oro. . **Remarks:** Mini-camp.
Punta. . **Remarks:** Mini-camp.
Seka. . **Remarks:** Mini-camp.
Školjka. . **Remarks:** Mini-camp.
Stela. . **Remarks:** Mini-camp.
Zlošane. . **Remarks:** Mini-camp.

Supetar 27C6

Supetar. **GPS**: n43,38050 e16,56082. . 01/06-30/09

HR

Sutivan 27C6

Mlin, Brac. **GPS**: n43,38316 e16,47795. . **Remarks:** Mini-camp.

Sv. Filip I Jakov 27B5

Djardin. **GPS**: n43,96139 e15,42750.
from € 18 Ch included. 01/05-30/09

Filip. **GPS**: n43,96055 **e15,42910**.
from € 15,20 Ch included. **Remarks:** Mini-camp.

Ante, Turanj. . **Remarks:** Mini-camp.

Barbarossa. . **Remarks:** Mini-camp.

Bepo, Turanj. . **Remarks:** Mini-camp.

Bozo 23207 Sv. Filip I Jakov, Sv. Petar, Bozo Colic, Sv. Petar. . **Remarks:** Mini-camp.

Frane Mladi, A. Starcevica 8 D, Turanj. . **Remarks:** Mini-camp.

Ivan, Medine, Turanj. . **Remarks:** Mini-camp.

Ivan, Sv. Petar 155. . **Remarks:** Mini-camp.

Ivan, Turanj 233. . **Remarks:** Mini-camp.

Ivo, Sv. Petar. . **Remarks:** Mini-camp.

J & A, Turanj. . **Remarks:** Mini-camp.

Jakov. . **Remarks:** Mini-camp.

Jugo, Turanj. . **Remarks:** Mini-camp.

Krca, Turanj. . **Remarks:** Mini-camp.

Livada. . **Remarks:** Mini-camp.

Lovre, Turanj. . **Remarks:** Mini-camp.

Maestral, Turanj 448. . **Remarks:** Mini-camp.

Maja, Vukovarska 54, Sv. Petar. . **Remarks:** Mini-camp.

Mara, Turanj. . **Remarks:** Mini-camp.

Marko, Sv. Petar. . **Remarks:** Mini-camp.

Martin, Sv. Petar 240. . **Remarks:** Mini-camp.

Medine. . **Remarks:** Mini-camp.

Mile, Sv. Petar. . **Remarks:** Mini-camp.

Mladen, Turanj 233. . **Remarks:** Mini-camp.

Moce. . **Remarks:** Mini-camp.

Njive, Turanj. . **Remarks:** Mini-camp.

Punta, Sv. Petar. . **Remarks:** Mini-camp.

Rio. **GPS**: n43,95583 e15,43500. . **Remarks:** Mini-camp.

Roko, Turanj. . **Remarks:** Mini-camp.

Šime. . **Remarks:** Mini-camp.

Tina. .
Remarks: Mini-camp.

Tourist information Sv. Filip I Jakov:
Tourist Information, Kuntrata bb, www.sv-filipjakov.hr/.

Tkon 27B5

Adriana. **GPS**: n43,91753 e15,42601. . **Remarks:** Mini-camp.

Brist. . **Remarks:** Mini-camp.

Dužica. . **Remarks:** Mini-camp.

Tribanj 27B5

Ante, Kruščica. . **Remarks:** Mini-camp.

C.T.T., Kopovine. . **Remarks:** Mini-camp.

Mate, Kruščica. **GPS**: n44,34983 e15,31575. . **Remarks:** Mini-camp.

Punta Šibuljina, Šibuljina. . **Remarks:** Mini-camp.

Venus, Šibuljina. . **Remarks:** Mini-camp.

Trogir 27C6

Seget, Seget Donji. **GPS**: n43,51904 e16,22430.
50 from € 21. 01/03-31/10
Distance: 800m on the spot.
Remarks: Mini-camp..

Trogir 27C6

Vranjica Belvedere, Seget Vranjica. **GPS**: n43,51196 e16,19159.
from € 20 Ch WC . 15/04-15/10

Tourist information Trogir:
Tourist Information, Ivana Pavla II Square, www.trogir-online.com.City with rich culture from Greek, Roman and Venetian time.
Town Museum, Fanfogna palace, Garagnin.History of the city. 16/09-14/06 by request-14h, 15/06-15/09 9-21h.
Zbirka Kairos.Ecclesiastical art collection. 15/6-15/9 8-13, 15-19h.
Fort Kamerlengo. 15/6-15/9 9-20h.
Katedrala St. Lawrence.Bell-tower of Cathedral of St. Lawrence, 47m. 15/6-15/9 9-12, 16-19h. 5kn.

Vela Luka 27C6

Mindel, Stani 193. **GPS**: n42,98389 e16,67083. . 01/01-31/12

Viganj 27C6

Antony Boy. **GPS**: n42,97917 e17,10750. . 01/01-31/12

Vinjerac 27B5

Niko, Stara Cesta 1. **GPS**: n44,25571 e15,46251. . **Remarks:** Mini-camp.

Vir 27B5

Luka. . **Remarks:** Mini-camp.

Matea. . 01/06-01/10

Slatina. . **Remarks:** Mini-camp.

Vir. **GPS**: n44,29174 e15,11996. . **Remarks:** Mini-camp.

Vodice 27B6

Imperial. **GPS**: n43,75278 e15,79000.
from € 22 Ch . 01/05-15/10

Rutke, Udovicic A. Kule, 13. . **Remarks:** Mini-camp.

Vransko Jezero 27B5

Crkvine. **GPS**: n43,93035 e15,51012. . 15/04-15/10

Vrsi 27B5

Bor, Mulo. . **Remarks:** Mini-camp.

Mulic, Mulo. **GPS**: n44,26085 e15,23323. . **Remarks:** Mini-camp.

Perkovic, Augusta Šenoe 7. . **Remarks:** Mini-camp.

Punta, Mulo. . **Remarks:** Mini-camp.

Zaboric 27B6

Jasenovo. **GPS**: n43,65116 e15,95025.
50 from € 13 Ch WC . 01/05-01/10
Distance: on the spot.
Remarks: Mini-camp..

Zadar 27B5

Rosmari, Emanuela Vidovica 2. **GPS**: n44,13250 e15,20861.
20 Ch WC .
Distance: on the spot on the spot.
Remarks: Mini-camp.

Borik. **GPS**: n44,13528 e15,21528. . 01/05-30/09

Tourist information Zadar:
Turisticka zajednica, I. Smiljanica bb, www.zadar.hr.
Trg Pet Bunara.Square of the five fountains.
Arheoloski Muzej, Simuna Kozicica Benje bb.Archeological findings. Mo-Sa 9-13h, 18-20h.
Muziekavonden in de St. Donatius van Zadar. 01/07-15/08.

Zaostrog 27C6

Uvala Borova. **GPS**: n43,13181 e17,28742. . 01/05-30/09

Zaton 27B5

Zaton. **GPS**: n44,23385 e15,16671. . 01/05/30/09

Tourist information Zaton:
Tourist Information, Hrvatskih branitelja 2, www.zaton.hr.

Ždrelac 27B5

Ruža. **GPS**: n44,00925 e15,28067. . **Remarks:** Mini-camp.

Ublog, Dobropoljana. . **Remarks:** Mini-camp.

Živogošće 27C6

Dole. **GPS**: n43,18910 e17,15622. . 01/05-30/09

Žrnovo 27C6

Palma. . **Remarks:** Mini-camp.

Žrnovo 27C6

Tri Žala, Uvala Tri Žala 808. **GPS**: n42,95724 e17,11215. .
Remarks: Mini-camp.

Vrbovica, Uvala Vrbovica. . **Remarks:** Mini-camp.

Žuljana 27D6

Maslina, Brijezi 2. . **Remarks:** Mini-camp.

Sunce, Kraj 29. . **Remarks:** Mini-camp.

Vucina I. . **Remarks:** Mini-camp.

Vucina II, Kraj 93. . **Remarks:** Mini-camp.

Žuljana, Kraj 71. **GPS**: n42,89359 e17,45479. . **Remarks:** Mini-camp.

Inland

Lipovac 27D4

Spacva. **GPS**: n45,04593 e18,99682. . 01/05-01/10

Plitviča 27B4

Bear, Seliste Dreznicko 52. **GPS**: n44,94804 e15,63639.

HR

15 € 20 Ch WC included. **Surface:** grassy. 01/04-01/11
Remarks: Water falls Plitvica 5km, baker every morning.

S Plitviča 27B4

Cvetkovic, Jezerce 28. **GPS**: n44,86338 e15,63967.

20 € 20 Ch WC included free. **Surface:** grassy/gravel.
Remarks: Water falls Plitvica 2km.

Plitviča 27B4

Korana. GPS: n44,99260 e15,64916.
€ 6 + € 5/pp.

Tourist information Plitviča:

Nacionalni Park Plitviča Jezera, www.np-plitvicka-jezera.hr.National park Plitvice lakes. 9-17h.

HR

Racovica 27B4

Turist. GPS: n44,97222 e15,64750.

GREECE

North
pages: 902

Central Greece
pages: 894-896

Igoumentisa

Athens

Patras

Peloponnisos/Attica
pages: 896-902

Capital: Athens
Government: Parliamentary democracy
Official Language: Greek
Population: 11.300.000 (2012)
Area: 131,990 km^2.

General information
Dialling code: 0030
General emergency: 112
Currency: Euro

Regulations for overnight stays
Wild camping and overnight parking is not officially allowed. Overnight parking places mentioned here are not official motorhome stopovers but tolerated areas.

Additional public holidays 2014
January 6 Epiphany
March10 Ash Monday, 41 days before Easter
March 25 Independence Day
May 1 Labor Day
August 15 Assumption of the Virgin Mary
October 28 National Holiday, Ochi day

Greece

Central Greece

Agios Nikolaos 35B4

GPS: n38,34959 e22,15661.
. 01/01-31/12
Remarks: Parking at harbour.

S Ammoudia 35A4

GPS: n39,23989 e20,48116.

. **Surface:** sand.
Distance: on the spot on the spot on the spot 200m 50m.
Remarks: Beach parking.

S Ammoudia 35A4

GPS: n39,23636 e20,48073.

. **Surface:** gravel/sand.
Distance: on the spot 50m on the spot 100m 250m.
Remarks: Parking in harbour.

Arahova 35C4

GPS: n38,47948 e22,58164.
. 01/01-31/12
Remarks: Parking in village.

S Boukka 35B4

GPS: n38,93125 e21,14200.

. **Surface:** sand.
Distance: on the spot.
Remarks: Parking beach, next to sports fields.

S Corfu 35A4

Dionysus, Dassia. **GPS**: n39,66472 e19,84440.
Ch . 15/04-15/10

S Corfu 35A4

Dolphin Camping, Sidari. **GPS**: n39,78890 e19,72354.
Ch. 15/04-31/10
Remarks: Corfu-town dir Sidari/Roda, after that dir Sidari.

S Corfu 35A4

Karda Beach, Dassia. **GPS**: n39,68611 e19,83861.
Ch. 01/04-15/10
Distance: on the spot.

Tourist information Corfu:
Kerkyra (Corfu).Capital of the island.
Esplanada, Kerkyra (Corfu).Meeting point for inhabitants and tourists.
Kerkyra (Corfu).
Frurion, Kerkyra (Corfu).Citadel, 1550.
Aqualand, Corfu Water Park, Ag.Ioannis.
Leisure pool park.

S Delphi 35C4

Apollon. GPS: n38,48388 e22,47550.
23 Ch. 01/01-31/12

S Delphi 35C4

Delphi Camping. GPS: n38,47833 e22,47450.
Ch. 20/03-30/11

Delphi 35C4

Chrissa. GPS: n38,47267 e22,46206.
. 01/01-31/12

Tourist information Delphi:
Site of Delphi.Archeological site. 7.30-17.30h holiday. € 6.

Eratini 35B4

N48/E65 km 47. **GPS**: n38,33838 e22,19385.

. **Surface:** grassy/sand.
Distance: on the spot on the spot.
Remarks: < 3,5t. Beach parking.

S Erétria 35C4

Milos Camping. GPS: n38,39139 e23,77556.
Ch. **Remarks:** From Chalkis dir Eretria, 1 km in before the village on the right-hand of the road.

Tourist information Erétria:
Seaside resort and archological site Antique Eretria.

S Gliki 35A4

Taverne Panorama. GPS: n39,32726 e20,61568.

guests free WC . **Surface:** grassy.
Distance: 500m 500m.
Remarks: Along Acheron river.

S Hiliadou 35B4

GPS: n38,39321 e21,92023.

. **Surface:** gravel.
Distance: Nafpaktos 7km on the spot.
Remarks: Beach parking.

Igoumenítsa 35A4
GPS: n39,51278 e20,25741.
.
Distance: on the spot 600m on the spot.
Remarks: Parking supermarket at the ring-road 6, dir Ioánnina.

Tourist information Igoumenítsa:
Important port city.
Goumani (titani).Archeological site.

Ioánnina 35A3
Sta Papagou 7. **GPS**: n39,67319 e20,85476.
30 € 8. **Surface:** metalled. 01/01-31/12
Distance: 100m 100m 100m.
Remarks: Monitored parking.

Ioánnina 35A3
Limnopoula. **GPS**: n39,67770 e20,84280.
.
01/04-15/10

Tourist information Ioánnina:
Capital of Epirus, important city in the Turkish time.
Perama.Caves.
daily.
Nisi.Island with museum (Turkish time).

Itea 35C4
Ayannis, Kirra. **GPS**: n38,42440 e22,45880.
.

Itea 35C4
Kaparelis, Kirra. **GPS**: n38,43273 e22,45099.
. 01/01-31/12

Tourist information Itea:
Nautical Museum, Mouseio, 4, Galaxídi.

Krioneri 35B4
GPS: n38,34397 e21,58823.
. **Surface:** gravel. 01/01-31/12
Distance: on the spot on the spot 300m.
Remarks: Parking at the beach.

Levkas 35A4
Vlycho. **GPS**: n38,68318 e20,69819.
.
Distance: on the spot.
Remarks: Parking on the quay.

Levkas 35A4
Dessimi Beach, Vlicho, Lefkada (Levkas). **GPS**: n38,67250 e20,71100.
. 01/04-30/11

Levkas 35A4
Poros Beach, Poros, Lefkada (Levkas). **GPS**: n39,64095 e20,69700.
. 01/05-30/09

Mesolóngi 35B4
GPS: n38,36313 e21,41763.
. 01/01-31/12
Remarks: Parking harbour.

Tourist information Mesolóngi:
Tourist Information, Spyridonos Trikoupi 29.Fishing town.

Metéora 35B4
Meteora Garden, Kalambaka. **GPS**: n39,70869 e21,60915.
Ch. 01/01-31/12
Remarks: 1 km after Kalambaka dir Ioannina at the right-hand of the way.

Metéora 35B4
Rizos International, Kalambaka. **GPS**: n39,69010 e21,64564.
Ch. 01/01-31/12

Metéora 35B4
Vrachos Kastraki, Kastraki. **GPS**: n39,71338 e21,61588.
Ch. 01/01-31/12
Remarks: Kalambaka dir Kastraki after 1 km from beginning village on the left-hand of the road.

Metéora 35B4
Taverna Arsenis, East Street, Kalambaka. **GPS**: n38,69923 e21,64109.
8 guests free WC . 01/01-31/12

Tourist information Metéora:
Important cultural inheritance, 24 monasteries built on enormous sandstone peaks, of which 6 can be visited.
9-13h, 15-17h. against payment.

Métsovo 35A3
GPS: n39,76898 e21,17749.
.
Remarks: Parking dir village after leaving the main road, also parking in village.

Tourist information Métsovo:
Traditional mountain village.
Archotiko Tositsa.Restored 18th century mansion, museum or folk art.
8.30-13h, 16-18h. € 2.

Nafpaktos 35B4
Xiliadou, N48/E65 km 80,5. **GPS**: n38,38139 e21,81661.
. **Surface:** gravel/sand.
Distance: on the spot on the spot nearby.
Remarks: Parking at the beach.

Nafpaktos 35B4
Platanitis Beach. **GPS**: n38,36824 e21,78007.
Ch. 15/05-31/10
Remarks: From Antirron dir Nafpaktos, ±5km before Nafpaktos on the right-hand of the road.

Nafpaktos 35B4
Dounis Beach. **GPS**: n38,34288 e21,77013.
.
01/05-31/10

Tourist information Nafpaktos:
Old city with Venetian
Castle and circular walled harbor.

Paralia Agias Annas 35C4
Agia Anna. **GPS**: n38,85976 e23,44418.
. 01/05-30/09

Parga 35A4
Enjoy Lichnos. **GPS**: n39,28358 e20,43340.
Ch. 01/05-15/10
Remarks: Igoumenitsa dir Parga ± 4 km before Parga.

Parga 35A4
Valtos Camping.
GPS: n39,28556 e20,38972.
.
01/05-30/09

Tourist information Parga:
Lively bathing resort.
Necromanteion of Ephyra.
Oracle of death.

Pilion 35C3
Hellas, Kato Gatzea. **GPS**: n39,31110 e23,10916.
Ch. 01/04-31/10
Remarks: Places directly at sandy beach. Volos dir Argalagti, 16 km after Volos.

Pilion 35C3
Olizon, Milina. **GPS**: n39,16472 e23,21666.
Ch. 01/05-15/10

GR

Remarks: Volos centre to Argalasti, then dir Horton-Milina.

Pilion — 35C3

Sikia Fig Tree, Kato Gatzea. **GPS:** n39,30770 e2,11030.

Ch. 01/04-15/10

Remarks: Volos dir Agria-Tsangarada - 18 km from Volos.

Tourist information Pilion:

Mythological peninsula, beautiful nature, authentic mountain villages and fishing towns.

Agios Ioánnis.Holiday resort with lively beaches.

Tourist Information, Plateia Riga Feraiou, Vólos.The fastest growing industrial area of the country.

Makrinitsa.Village worth seeing, car-free.

Miliés.Folk museum. 01/04-31/10 Tue-Su, 01/11-31/03 Wed-Su.

Archeological Museum, Athanasáki 1, Vólos. Tue-Su holiday.

Plataria — 35A4

GPS: n39,44606 e20,27409.

. **Surface:** grassy/sand. 01/01-31/12

Distance: 500m on the spot on the spot 200m 250m.

Remarks: Parking at the beach.

Plataria — 35A4

Nautilos. GPS: n39,44389 e20,25806.

Ch. 01/04-20/10

Remarks: Igoumenitsa dir Parga, exit Sivota, 15 km after Plataria.

Plataria — 35A4

Kalami Beach. GPS: n39,47361 e20,24083.

. 20/03-15/10

Préveza — 35A4

Mitikas. GPS: n39,01719 e20,71555.

. **Surface:** asphalted/gravel.

Distance: Preveza 7km on the spot on the spot 500m.

Remarks: Parking at the beach.

Préveza — 35A4

GPS: n38,95008 e20,75498.

.

Remarks: Parking on the quay.

Tourist information Préveza:

Port city with interesting neighborhoods.

Kassópi, Kassópi.Archeological site.

Nikopolis.Old Roman city.

Stilada — 35C4

Interstation. GPS: n38,89701 e22,65573.

Ch. 01/01-31/12

Remarks: Highway Lamia-Thessaloniki, 3 km after Stylidia on the right-hand of the road.

Vagia — 35C4

Restaurant Ynaiopio, Palaia Ethniki Odos Athinon-Lamias. **GPS:** n38,34322 e23,19412.

free with a meal.

Vonitsa — 35A4

Agio Sotiriou. GPS: n38,93188 e20,91802.

. **Surface:** grassy.

Distance: Vonitsa 3km lake on the spot taverne 3km.

Remarks: N42, from Vonitsa exit left after km34, follow road 1km.

Peloponnisos/Attica

Agia Kyriaki — 35C6

GPS: n36,71883 e23,02305.

.

Remarks: At the beach.

Agios Andreas — 35C5

GPS: n37,37120 e22,78262.

WC free. **Surface:** gravel.

Distance: 3km on the spot on the spot on the spot.

Remarks: Parking in harbour.

Agios Andreas — 35C5

Camping Agios Andreas. GPS: n36,86664 e21,92087.

. 20/04-30/09

Distance: on the spot.

Agios Fokas — 35C6

GPS: n36,59722 e23,05917.

. **Surface:** sand.

Distance: Monemvasia 13km.

Remarks: Parking at pier.

Agios Kiriaki — 35B5

GPS: n37,11963 e21,57611.

. 01/01-31/12

Remarks: Road number 9 exit Filiatra, at the beach.

Alepochori — 35B5

Poseidon. GPS: n37,98419 e21,79712.

.

Assini — 35C5

Ancient Assini Beach. GPS: n37,53139 e22,88306.

. 01/04-31/10

GR

Assini 35C5
Kastraki. **GPS**: n37,52861 e22,87556.
. 01/04-01/10
Remarks: South of Nafplio.

Athens 35C4
GPS: n37,96987 e23,72263.
. 01/01-31/12
Remarks: Parking of the Acropolis, guarding after authorization Probably only outside the main season.

Athens 35C4
Athens camping, Leoforis Athinon. **GPS**: n38,00889 e23,67222.
€ 25, 2 pers.incl Ch included.
01/01-31/12

Tourist information Athens:
Capital of the country, city with a lot of curiosities, new city is a modern one.
Monasteraki.
Old district with Athenian flea market.
Su 8-14h.
Panathenaic Stadium.Stadium of the first Olympic Games in 1896.
Plaka.Old district around the Acropolis.
Tomb of the Unknown Soldier, Plateía Syntágmatos.Sunday 11h changing of the guard.
Acropolis.Archeological site.
01/05-31/10 Mo-Fri 8-18.30h, Sa-Su 8.30-14.30h, 01/11-30/04 8.30-16.30h
01/05, 28/10, holiday.

Diakofto 35B4
GPS: n38,19747 e22,20167.

. **Surface:** asphalted.
01/01-31/12
Distance: on the spot on the spot on the spot 500m.
Remarks: A8/E65 Patras/Korinthos, 50km south east of Patras, at harbour.

Tourist information Diakofto:
Rack railway, Kalavryta.Train journey with rack-railway.

Dimitsána 35B5
Kefalari tou Ai-Yanni. **GPS**: n37,59058 e22,04286.
4.
Remarks: Parking watermuseum, 2km south of Dimitsána.

Tourist information Dimitsána:
Loúsios-kloof.5km long and 300m deep, marked trails.

Elefsina 35C4
GPS: n38,04235 e23,53942.
. 01/01-31/12
Remarks: Athens dir Korinthos, parking in front of the ruins in the city center.

Eleonas Diakofto Achaia 35B4
Eleon Beach. **GPS**: n38,19938 e22,17201.
.

Epidaurus 35C5
GPS: n37,59675 e23,07444.

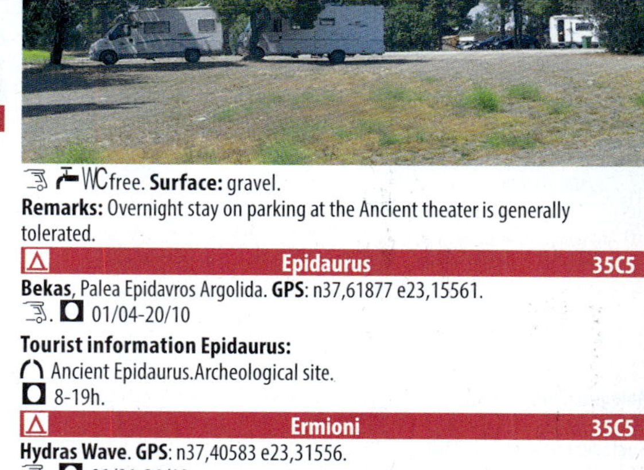

WC free. **Surface:** gravel.
Remarks: Overnight stay on parking at the Ancient theater is generally tolerated.

Epidaurus 35C5
Bekas, Palea Epidavros Argolida. **GPS**: n37,61877 e23,15561.
. 01/04-20/10

Tourist information Epidaurus:
Ancient Epidaurus.Archeological site.
8-19h.

Ermioni 35C5
Hydras Wave. **GPS**: n37,40583 e23,31556.
. 01/01-31/12

Galatas 35C5
GPS: n37,49591 e23,45101.
.
Remarks: Exit south, at the quay.

Gerolimenas 35C6
GPS: n36,48230 e22,39969.

. **Surface:** asphalted/grassy.
Distance: on the spot on the spot 50m on the spot.
Remarks: Parking at the beach.

Gialova Pylou 35B6
Navarino Beach. **GPS**: n36,94770 e21,70620.
Ch. 01/04-31/10

Glifa Kyllini 35B5
Ionion. **GPS**: n37,83640 e21,13340.
Ch. 01/01-31/12

Gythion 35C6
GPS: n36,78883 e22,58225.
.
Remarks: Tolerated place. At the beach, ± 5km from Gythion dir Skala.

Gythion 35C6
Gythion Bay. **GPS**: n36,72920 e22,55243.
Ch. 01/01-31/12

Kakovatos 35B5
GPS: n37,45721 e21,63869.
. **Surface:** asphalted.
Remarks: Parking areas along the beach.

GR

Kalogria 35B5

Kalogria Camper Stop, Kalogria Peloponnes. **GPS**: n38,15986 e21,37162.
40 € 10, 16/07-31/08 € 12 Ch (20x)€ 3/day WC included.
Surface: unpaved. 01/05-31/10
Distance: 5km 11km 250m 300m 50m on the spot on the spot on the spot on the spot.

Tourist information Kalogria:
Kotychi, Lapas.Visitors centre, swamp area.

Kamares 35C6

GPS: n36,68253 e22,52187.

. **Surface:** sand.
Distance: on the spot on the spot 350m.
Remarks: At the beach.

Kameras Irion 35C6

Poseidon. **GPS**: n36,68826 e22,51753.
.

Kastro 35B5

Loutra Kilinis. **GPS**: n37,86533 e21,10903.
WC free.
Remarks: Parking at the beach.

Kastro 35B5

Killinis Beach. **GPS**: n37,87413 e21,10748.

. **Surface:** grassy/sand.
Distance: 2km on the spot on the spot Beach taverne.

Tourist information Kastro:
Chlemoutsi.Medieval castle.

Kato Alissos 35B5

Kato Allissos. **GPS**: n38,14986 e21,57740.
€ 19 Ch . 01/04-20/10

Remarks: Plenty of shade from olive trees, lemon trees and poplars. Patras dir Pyrgos, take the Old National Road at first occasion, after 20 km to the right, dir campsite.

Kifisiá 35C4

Dionissiotis. **GPS**: n38,10535 e23,81355.
ChWC. 01/01-31/12
Remarks: 18km north of Athens, route Athens dir Lamia.

Tourist information Kifisiá:
Holiday resort of the Athenian since the Roman time.
Gouländris, Levidou 13.History of nature.

Kilada Ermionidos 35C5

Relax. **GPS**: n37,40974 e23,12691.
. 01/04-15/10

Killini 35B5

GPS: n37,93460 e21,14664.

. **Surface:** asphalted/sand.
Distance: on the spot on the spot on the spot 200m on the spot.
Remarks: Parking in harbour.

Korfos 35C5

GPS: n37,76361 e23,13302.

. **Surface:** gravel.
Remarks: At fishing port.

Korinthos 35C5

Afrodites Waters, Ancient Corinth. **GPS**: n37,91139 e22,87861.

30 € 10 Ch WC . 01/01-31/12
Distance: 350m 350m 350m.

Korinthos 35C5

GPS: n37,88983 e22,86761.
.
Remarks: Parking Akrokorinth.

Korinthos 35C5

Ancient Korinthos. **GPS**: n37,90750 e22,87806.

.

Korinthos 35C5

Blue Dolphin, Lecheon. **GPS**: n37,93460 e22,86490.
Ch. 01/04-15/10
Remarks: Some kilometres west of Korinthos.

Korinthos 35C5

Isthmia Beach, Isthmia. **GPS**: n37,88950 e23,00530.
. 15/04-15/10

Tourist information Korinthos:
Important trade centre.
Korinth Canal.Canal, 23m wide.
Acrocorinth.Fortress.
8-19h. free.
Ancient Korinthos.Archeological site.
01/04-31/10 8-19h, 01/11-31/03 8-17h
25/12-26/12, 01/01, 25/03, Easter, 01/05.

Koroni 35B6

GPS: n36,79729 e21,96002.

.
Remarks: Parking at harbour.

Koroni 35B6

Camping Koroni. **GPS**: n36,81168 e21,93303.
.
Distance: 600m on the spot.

Koroni 35B6

Memi Beach. **GPS**: n36,99270 e21,50200.
. 01/05-30/09
Remarks: At harbour, narrow access.

Tourist information Koroni:
Port city with Venetian castle, 1206.

Kotronas 35C6

GPS: n36,61899 e22,49367.

free. **Surface:** concrete.
Distance: on the spot on the spot 50m.
Remarks: Parking at pier.

Kyparissia 35B5

Kyparissia. **GPS**: n37,25830 e21,67170.
. 04/04-30/09

Lambiri 35B4

Tsolis, Old National Road. **GPS**: n38,32083 e21,97194.
. 15/04-30/09

Legrena 35D5

GPS: n37,66206 e23,99772.
. 01/01-31/12
Remarks: The most southern point, south of Athens, at sandy beach.

Marathon 35D4

Ramnous. **GPS**: n38,13139 e24,00722.
.
01/04-31/10

Tourist information Marathon:
www.marathon.gr.
The name marathon, course of 41 km, comes from this town.

Mayroyouni/Gythion 35C6

Meltemi. **GPS**: n36,72986 e22,55360.
.

Tourist information Mayroyouni/Gythion:
Tourist Information Areópoli, Vasiléos Pávlou 21, Máni.
Peninsula.
Pýrgos Diroú, Máni.Caves.

Monemvasía 35C6

GPS: n36,68875 e23,05076.
. **Surface:** asphalted.
Distance: on the spot on the spot shuttle to old town.
Remarks: May cause problems during peak season. Parking on both sides before the bridge to the island.

Monemvasía 35C6

GPS: n36,68240 e23,03821.
.
Remarks: Parking in harbour.

Tourist information Monemvasía:
Fortified city, lower town have been restored.
Agía Sofia.Church 13th century.

Mycenae 35C5

Atreus. **GPS**: n37,71911 e22,74114.
. 01/01-31/12

Tourist information Mycenae:
Archeological Museum, Argos.
Archeological site. 1/4-31/10 8-19h, 1/11-31/3 8-17h holiday.
Agora Argos, Argos.Archeological site. summer 8.30-15h.

Nafplio 35C5

GPS: n37,76860 e22,99850.
2.
Remarks: Parking new train station.

Nafplio 35C5

GPS: n37,56823 e22,80170.

. **Surface:** asphalted.

GR

Distance: 500m ⊗300m.
Remarks: Parking marina.

Tourist information Nafplio:
Tourist information, Ikostispémtis Martiou 2.First Greek capital.
Archeological Museum. Tue-Su 8.30-15h Mo.
Palamídi.Citadel 18th century.

Nea Makri 35D4
Nea Makri, Marathonos Ave 156. **GPS**: n38,09285 e23,97379.
. 01/01-31/12

Neo Itylo 35C6
GPS: n36,69246 e22,38969.

. **Surface:** asphalted.
Distance: on the spot on the spot ⊗50m.
Remarks: Not in front of hotel. At the beach.

Olympia 35B5
Alphios. **GPS**: n37,64360 e21,61930.
. 01/04-31/10

Olympia 35B5
Olympia. **GPS**: n37,65090 e21,62460.
. 01/01-31/12
Remarks: 500m before Olympia.

Tourist information Olympia:
Archeological Museum.Important Greek archeological museum.
Mo 11-19h, Tue-Su 8-19h.

Paralia Astros 35C5
GPS: n37,44475 e22,74800.

. **Surface:** gravel.
Distance: on the spot on the spot ⊗200m.
Remarks: At the beach, 12km north from Paralia Astros.

Paralia Platanou 35B4
GPS: n38,17104 e22,26828.

. **Surface:** gravel.
Distance: on the spot.
Remarks: At the beach.

Paralia Rizomilos 35B4
GPS: n38,21898 e22,14745.

free. **Surface:** gravel.
Distance: on the spot on the spot ⊗on the spot mini market (summer).
Remarks: Not in front of hotel. At the beach.

Pátra 35B5
Golden Sunset, Old national Road km 19. **GPS**: n38,14389 e21,58778.
. 01/04-15/10

Tourist information Pátra:
Tourist Information, Filepimonos 26.Big city and important harbour.
Archaïa Klauss.First commercial producer of wine of Greece.

Perahóra 35C4
GPS: n38,01520 e22,91564.
.
Distance: ⊗on the spot.
Remarks: Parking at the beach.

Petalidi 35B6
GPS: n36,95850 e21,93450.
. **Surface:** asphalted.
Remarks: Nearby marina and football ground.

Petalidi 35B6
GPS: n36,95915 e21,92870.

. **Surface:** asphalted.
Distance: ⊗on the spot.
Remarks: Parking in village, near the sea.

Plaka 35C5
GPS: n37,14824 e22,89222.

20 € 5/24h WC included. **Surface:** asphalted.
Distance: on the spot on the spot ⊗50m 50m on the spot.
Remarks: Motorhome parking at the beach, can be reached by narrow road.

Porto Kagio 35C6
Taverna Porto. **GPS**: n36,42811 e22,48697.
max. 3 guests free. **Surface:** grassy.
Distance: on the spot on the spot ⊗on the spot mini market.

Pylos 35B6

GPS: n36,91633 e21,69524.

. **Surface:** concrete.
Distance: 100m 100m.
Remarks: Parking at pier.

Rafina 35D4

GPS: n38,01835 e24,01227.
.
01/01-31/12
Remarks: Exit harbour.

Tourist information Rafina:
Lively fishing port, Mati: stylish holiday village.

Salandi 35C5

GPS: n37,44748 e23,12474.

. **Surface:** gravel.
Distance: Didyma 5km on the spot on the spot.
Remarks: At the beach.

Savalia 35B5

Savalia Beach. **GPS**: n37,79685 e21,25578.

. **Surface:** asphalted.
Distance: on the spot on the spot.

Skoutari 35C6

GPS: n36,65984 e22,49762.

max. 3 . **Surface:** concrete.
Distance: on the spot on the spot within walking distance.

Remarks: At fishing port.

Sounion 35D5

Camping Bacchus. **GPS**: n37,67694 e24,04750.
. 01/01-31/12
Remarks: 60km S of Athens.

Tourist information Sounion:
Mineralogical Museum, Lavrió.
Old mine shaft of the silvermines.
Wed, Sa-Su.
Archeological site.

Tolo 35C5

GPS: n37,51469 e22,85662.

WC. **Surface:** asphalted.
Distance: 500m 100m on the spot 200m.
Remarks: Tolerated place. At fishing port.

Tyrchu 35C5

Taverne Ostria. **GPS**: n37,31414 e22,82054.

3 guests free. **Surface:** gravel. 15/05-30/09
Distance: Tyros 10km on the spot on the spot on the spot.
Remarks: At the beach, via steep path.

Zacharo 35B5

Wohnmobil-Stellplatz. **GPS**: n37,47994 e21,62237.

50 € 12 Ch WC included € 2. **Surface:** grassy/gravel.
01/01-31/12
Distance: 2km on the spot on the spot 300m 2km.
Remarks: Motorhome parking at the beach.

Zacharo 35B5

GPS: n37,51917 e21,60248.

GR

Distance: on the spot.
Remarks: North of lake, follow Thermal Springs of Kaifa.

Zacharo 35B5

Tholo Beach. GPS: n37,41160 e21,66830.
01/04-31/10

Greece North

Ag.Mamas Moudania 35C3

Ouzoni Beach. GPS: n40,21611 e23,31833.
01/05-30/09

Akt Armenistis Sithonia 35C3

Armenistis. GPS: n40,15222 e23,91361.
01/05-15/09

Alexandroúpoli 35D2

GPS: n40,84364 e25,87693.

Remarks: Parking harbour.

Alexandroúpoli 35D2

Apollonias. **GPS:** n40,84342 e25,86477.

Remarks: Parking near stadium.

GR

Tourist information Alexandroúpoli:
Tourist Information, Mákris.Large holiday resort, beautiful beach.

Gerakani 35C2

Kouyoni. GPS: n40,26464 e23,46347.
01/05-30/09

S Kastoriá 35A3

GPS: n40,50441 e21,27992.
against payment.
Remarks: Voluntary contribution. Parking near monastery.

Lithóchoro 35B3

Olympios Zeus. GPS: n40,09333 e22,56472.

Tourist information Lithóchoro:
Tourist Information, Evangelou Karavákou 20.Hiking cards for sale detailing excursions in the National Park of Mount Olympus.
Ancient Díon.Archeological findings.
daily holiday.

Metamorphosi 35C3

Sunny Bay. GPS: n40,22694 e23,58944.
01/05-31/10

S Moustheni 35C2

Moystheni Station. GPS: n40,84085 e24,11623.
free Ch.
Surface: asphalted.
Distance: 10m on the spot mini market.
Remarks: Special part for motor homes, shop, restaurant, station 24/24.

S Neos Marmaras 35C3

Areti. GPS: n40,02389 e23,81722.
Ch. 01/05-15/10

Nikiti Akti Koytloumousi 35C3

Lacara. GPS: n40,17229 e23,85272.
01/05-30/09

Ouranoupoli 35C2

Ouranoupoli. GPS: n40,33944 e23,97056.

S Porto Lagos 35D2

GPS: n41,00633 e25,12028.

5 free. **Surface:** asphalted.
Distance: on the spot.
Remarks: Parking at pier.

Sithonia 35C3

Kalamitsi. GPS: n39,98750 e23,98694.

Sithonia 35C3

Sithon. GPS: n40,23472 e23,56472.
01/05-30/09

INDEX

INDEX

INDEX